October 24–28, 2011
Glasgow, Scotland, UK

Association for Computing Machinery

Advancing Computing as a Science & Profession

CIKM 2011 GLASGOW

CIKM'11

Proceedings of the 2011 ACM International Conference on Information and Knowledge Management

Sponsored by:

ACM SIGIR & ACM SIGWEB

Association for
Computing Machinery

Advancing Computing as a Science & Profession

The Association for Computing Machinery
2 Penn Plaza, Suite 701
New York, New York 10121-0701

ISBN: 978-1-4503-0717-8 (Digital)

ISBN: 978-1-4503-1353-7 (Print)

Additional copies may be ordered prepaid from:

ACM Order Department
PO Box 30777
New York, NY 10087-0777, USA

Phone: 1-800-342-6626 (USA and Canada)
+1-212-626-0500 (Global)
Fax: +1-212-944-1318
E-mail: acmhelp@acm.org
Hours of Operation: 8:30 am – 4:30 pm ET

ACM Order Number: 605110

Printed in the USA

CIKM 2011 Chairs' Welcome

On behalf of the organizing committee, it is our great pleasure to welcome you to the *20th ACM Conference on Information and Knowledge Management* in Glasgow!

Since its inception, the CIKM conference has provided a unique international forum for the presentation, discussion and dissemination of research findings in data management, information retrieval and knowledge management. The purpose of the conference is to identify challenging problems facing the development of future knowledge and information systems and to shape future research directions through the publication of high quality, applied and theoretical research findings. The conference has been a leading forum in which experts from academic, industry and the public sector gather to exchange ideas, research achievements and technical developments in multidisciplinary research areas.

CIKM is one of the world's most recognized conferences in the field. This year CIKM received 918 full paper submissions, 220 poster submissions, and 56 demonstration submissions. This is a great demonstration of the lively research areas that contribute to the CIKM area. In addition, CIKM 2011 will host 10 tutorials from leading researchers, 15 workshops on cutting-edge areas of research, a panel session on Social and Collaborative Search and a dedicated Industry Day featuring leading industrial practitioners. We are grateful to all authors who chose to submit their research to CIKM 2011 and are very excited by the final program.

CIKM values interdisciplinary research and we are proud to present three keynote speakers, Professor Justin Zobel, Professor Maurizio Lenzerini and Professor David Karger, all of whom will give presentations that cross discipline boundaries.

The program of CIKM 2011 represents a huge amount of effort on behalf of many people. The contributions to the technical program were selected by a large program committee headed by our three program chairs, Arjen de Vries, Bettina Berendt and Wenfei Fan. We are grateful to them for all their hard work in managing such a complex reviewing task and to their senior program committee members, program committee members and additional reviewers who freely gave their time, effort and intelligence to the difficult task of selecting which contributions would form the program. We are also very grateful to Fidel Cacheda, Matt Lease and Sara Hawkins, who monitored and managed the process of editing the proceedings to meet very tight production schedules.

We are also grateful to Gianni Amati who ran CIKM's first dedicated poster submission route; Omar Alonso who managed the demonstrations track and introduced demo boaster sessions into the program; Craig Macdonald who handled the very difficult job of organizing the workshop program; Jaap Kamps and Fabrizio Silvestri who solicited a great range of tutorials; Donald Metzler who was a great publicity chair; Leif Azzopardi for handling the student award scheme and student volunteers; Ryen White and Marius Pasca who were very active sponsorship chairs and whose hard work allowed us to award grants to several student attendees; Daniel Tunkelang and Tony Russell-Rose for organizing such an interesting Industry program; Jeremy Pickens for organizing an exciting panel session; David Carmel for organizing the Best Paper Awards committee. The local arrangements team has been superbly managed by Jon Richie, our local arrangements chair who has made a huge effort into every aspect of the conference. Finally, we value the efforts of Richard McCreadie (invitation letters) and Rodrygo Santos (website & social media).

We would like to express our appreciation to all our sponsors: EMC^2, Microsoft Research, Google, Yahoo! Research, SAP, Yandex, IBM Research, eBay Research Labs, Cambridge University Press, Springer, Taylor & Francis and CrossRef. Google generously provided travel support for East European attendees and Springer kindly sponsored the Best Paper Awards. All their generous sponsorship and support made this conference successful and possible. We would also like to thank the sponsoring SIGs, SIGIR and SIGWEB, and their respective chairs, James Allan (SIGIR), Ethan Munson and Simon Harper (SIGWEB) for their advice and support.

It is a great pleasure to be able to welcome you to CIKM 2011 in Glasgow. We hope that attendees find the technical program of CIKM 2011 to be interesting and productive and you enjoy CIKM 2011 and your stay in Glasgow.

Iadh Ounis
CIKM 2011 General Co-Chair
University of Glasgow

Ian Ruthven
CIKM 2011 General Co-Chair
University of Strathclyde

Message from the Program Committee Chairs

Welcome to the 20th ACM Conference on Information and Knowledge Management. Since 1992, CIKM has been successfully bringing together leading researchers from the database, information retrieval, and knowledge management communities. The purpose of the conference is to identify challenging problems facing the development of future knowledge and information systems, and to shape future research directions through the publication of high-quality research findings, both theoretical and applied. In CIKM 2011, we continued the tradition of promoting collaboration among the general areas of databases, information retrieval, and knowledge management. This year's call for papers attracted 918 submissions from Africa, the Americas, Asia, Australia, Europe, and the Middle East. The program committee accepted 134 submissions as full papers for oral presentation (15%), an additional 93 as short papers for oral presentation and 98 as poster presentations (a cumulative acceptance rate of 35%). We also accepted 21 demonstrations, 10 tutorials and 15 workshops. CIKM 2011 also organized the first direct call for poster submissions, resulting in 220 submissions and 66 poster acceptances.

We'd like to acknowledge everyone who made this technical program possible. First, we would like to thank the authors for providing the contents of the program: the conference would not be possible without your contributions. Our gratitude goes out to the program committee and external reviewers, who worked extremely hard in providing feedback on the submissions. The senior program committees deserve much recognition for shepherding the review process and for helping along the way. A very big "thank you" goes out to all the countless others who have contributed to making CIKM 2011 a success. Finally, we would like to thank all our corporate sponsors for their generous support.

We hope that you will find this program interesting and thought-provoking. Please enjoy the conference and the opportunity to network with friends and colleagues from around the world.

Bettina Berendt
CIKM 2011 KM Chair
Katholieke Universiteit Leuven, Belgium

Arjen de Vries
CIKM 2011 IR Chair
Centrum Wiskunde & Informatica, The Netherlands

Wenfei Fan
CIKM 2011 DB Chair
University of Edinburgh, UK

Table of Contents

Session 5: Type and Structure

Session Chair: Leif Azzopardi *(University of Glasgow)*

Session 6: Machine Learning for Information Retrieval

Session Chair: Stephen Robertson *(Microsoft Research Cambridge)*

Session 7: Information Retrieval Implementation Techniques

Session Chair: Justin Zobel *(The University of Melbourne)*

Session 8: Language Technology and Information Retrieval

Session Chair: Jussi Karlgen *(Swedish Institute of Computer Science)*

Session 9: Results in Context

Session Chair: Noriko Kando *(NII)*

Session 10: Algorithms

Session Chair: Felix Naumann *(Hasso-Plattner-Institute)*

Session 11: Image Retrieval

Session Chair: Yi Chang *(Yahoo! Labs)*

Session 14: Evaluation and Analysis

Session Chair: Jaap Kamps *(University of Amsterdam)*

Session 15: Classification and Evaluation

Session Chair: Nicolas Garcia Pedrajas *(University of Córdoba)*

Session 16: Information Filtering

Session Chair: Yan Zhang *(Vermont Information Processing)*

Session 17: Topics and Events

Session Chair: Ram Akella *(Stanford University & University of California)*

Session 18: Temporal, Stream and Spatial Information

Session Chair: Massimo Ruffolo *(ICAR-CNR)*

Session 19: Text Mining

Session Chair: Yunyao Li *(IBM Research)*

Session 25: Link Prediction

Session Chair: B. Barla Cambazoglu *(Yahoo! Research)*

Session 26: Link, Graph and Relation Mining

Session Chair: Roi Blanco *(Yahoo! Research)*

Session 27: Science, the Past, and the Future

Session Chair: Giorgio Orsi *(University of Oxford)*

Session 28: Information Extraction and Entities

Session Chair: Xiaofeng Yu *(The Chinese University of Hong Kong)*

Session 29: Queries, Questions and Tags Mining

Session Chair: Jian-Tao Sun *(Microsoft Research Asia)*

Session 30: Preparing, Mining and Evaluating with and for Different Views

Session Chair: Hwanjo Yu *(POSTECH)*

Session 31: Information Extraction and Semantic Techniques

Session 32: Data on the Web

Session 33: Query Processing and Optimization

Session 34: Semantic Web and Information Retrieval

Session Chair: Alfredo Cuzzocrea *(University of Calabria)*

Session 35: Query Answering and Social Search

Session Chair: Yuqing Wu *(Indiana University)*

Session 36: Distributed Data Management and Data Integration

Session Chair: Philip Bohannon *(Yahoo! Research)*

VOLUME 3

Poster Session: Information Retrieval

Poster Session: Knowledge Management

Poster Session: Databases

Demonstration Session 1

Demonstration Session 2

Demonstration Session 3

Co-located Tutorial Summaries

Co-located Workshop Summaries

Panel

CIKM 2011 Conference Organization

General Conference Chairs: Iadh Ounis *(University of Glasgow, UK)*
Ian Ruthven *(University of Strathclyde, UK)*

Chair-at-Large: Craig Macdonald *(University of Glasgow, UK)*

DB Track Program Chair: Wenfei Fan *(University of Edinburgh, UK)*

IR Track Program Chair: Arjen de Vries *(Centrum Wiskunde & Informatica, The Netherlands)*

KM Track Program Chair: Bettina Berendt *(Katholieke Universiteit Leuven, Belgium)*

Workshops Chair: Craig Macdonald *(University of Glasgow, UK)*

Posters Chair: Gianni Amati *(FUB, Italy)*

Tutorials Chairs: Jaap Kamps *(University of Amsterdam, The Netherlands)*
Fabrizio Silvestri *(ISTI-CNR, Italy)*

Industry Event Chairs: Daniel Tunkelang *(LinkedIn, US)*
Tony Russell-Rose *(UXLabs and City University London, UK)*

Demonstrations Chair: Omar Alonso *(Microsoft, US)*

Panel Chair: Jeremy Pickens *(Catalyst Repository Systems, US)*

Proceedings Chairs: Fidel Cacheda *(University of A Coruña, Spain)*
Matt Lease *(University of Texas at Austin, US)*

Local Arrangements Chair: Jon Ritchie *(University of Glasgow, UK)*

Travel Award Chair: Leif Azzopardi *(University of Glasgow, UK)*

Publicity Chair: Donald Metzler *(University of Southern California ,US)*

Sponsorship Chairs: Marius Pasca *(Google, US)*
Ryen White *(Microsoft Research, US)*

Awards Chair: David Carmel *(IBM Research Lab, Israel)*

Registration Chair: Richard McCreadie *(University of Glasgow, UK)*,

Steering Committee Chair: E.K. Park *(City University of New York, US)*

Steering Committee:

Charles Clarke *(University of Waterloo, Canada)*
Ophir Frieder *(Georgetown University, US)*
David Grossman *(Illinois Institute of Technology, US)*
Alberto Leander *(Federal University of Minas Gerais, Brazil)*
Charles Nicholas *(University of Maryland Baltimore County, US)*
Calton Pu *(Georgia Tech, US)*
Il Yeol Song *(Drexel Uinversity, US)*
Philip S. Yu *(University of Illinois at Chicago, US)*

CIKM 2011 DB Track Program Committees

Senior Program Committee:

Marcelo Arenas (*Pontificia Universidad Católica de Chile, Chile)*
Pablo Barcelo (*Universidad de Chile, Chile)*
Philip Bohannon (*Yahoo! Research, US)*
Diego Calvanese (*Free University of Bozen-Bolzano, Italy)*
Chee-Yong Chan (*National University of Singapore, Singapore)*
Lei Chen (*Hong Kong University of Science and Technology, Hong Kong)*
Giuseppe De Giacomo (*University of Rome La Sapienza, Italy)*
Xin (Luna) Dong (*ATT Labs-Research, US)*
Alan Fekete (*University of Sydney, Australia)*
Floris Geerts (*University of Edinburgh, UK)*
Torsten Grust (*Universität Tübingen, Germany)*
Anastasios Kementsietsidis (*IBM T.J. Watson Research Center, US)*
Frank McSherry (*Microsoft Research Silicon Valley, US)*
Divesh Srivastava (*AT&T Labs, US)*
Yufei Tao (*Chinese University of Hong Kong, Hong Kong)*
Jeffrey Yu (*Chinese University of Hong Kong, Hong Kong)*

Program Committee:

Ashraf Aboulnaga (*University of Waterloo, Canada)*
Yanif Ahmad (*Johns Hopkins University, US)*
Denilson Barbosa (*University of Alberta, Canada)*
Zohra Bellahsene (*Université Montpellier, France)*
Michael Benedikt (*Oxford University, UK)*
Leopoldo Bertossi (*Carleton University, Canada)*
Mikolaj Bojanczyk (*Warsaw University, Poland)*
Angela Bonifati (*CNR, Italy)*
Michael Cafarella (*University of Michigan, US)*
Zhipeng Cai (*Mississippi State University, US)*
Kevin C. Chang (*University of Illinois, US)*
Haiming Chen (*Chinese Academy of Sciences, China)*
Wenguang Chen (*Peking University, China)*
Rada Chirkova (*North Carolina State University, US)*
Gao Cong (*NTU, Singapore)*
Richard Connor (*University of Strathclyde, UK)*
Alfredo Cuzzocrea (*University of Calabria, Italy)*
Anish Das Sarma (*Google Research, US)*
Ting Deng (*Beihang University, China)*
Jens Dittrich (*Saarland University, Germany)*
Guozhu Dong (*Wright State University, US)*
Songyun Duan (*IBM T.J. Watson Research Center, US)*
Irini Fundulaki (*Foundation for Research and Technology - Hellas, Greece)*
Avigdor Gal (*Technion - Israel Institute of Technology, Israel)*

Program Committee (continued):

Minos Garofalakis (*Technical University of Crete, Greece)*
Tingjian Ge (*University of Kentucky, US)*
Lukasz Golab (*AT&T Labs Research, US)*
Wook-Shin Han (*Kyungpook National University, Korea)*
Sven Helmer (*Birkbeck, University of London, UK)*
Kien Hua (*University of Central Florida, US)*
Ela Hunt (*ETH Zurich, Switzerland)*
Seung-won Hwang (*POSTECH, Korea)*
Zack Ives (*University of Pennsylvania, US)*
Gao Jun (*Peking University, China)*
Jaewoo Kang (*Korea University, Korea)*
Carl-Christian Kanne (*IBM Almaden Research Center, US)*
Raghav Kaushik (*Microsoft Research, US)*
Eamonn Keogh (*University of California Riverside, US)*
Benny Kimelfeld (*IBM, US)*
Masaru Kitsuregawa (*University of Tokyo, Japan)*
Solmaz Kolahi (*University of British Columbia, Canada)*
Hank Korth (*Lehigh University, Bethlehem, US)*
Maurizio Lenzerini (*Università di Roma La Sapienza, Italy)*
Feifei Li (*Florida State University, US)*
Yingshu Li (*Georgia State University, US)*
Jianzhong Li (*Harbin Institute of Technology, China)*
Xiang Lian (*HKUST, Hong Kong)*
Xuemin Lin (*University of New South Wales, Australia)*
Shuai Ma (*Beihang University, China)*
Jayant Madhavan (*Google, US)*
Ioana Manolescu (*INRIA, France)*
Wim Martens (*Technische Universität Dortmund, Germany)*
Maarten Marx (*University of Amsterdam, The Netherlands)*
Weiyi Meng (*SUNY Binghamton, US)*
Bongki Moon (*University of Arizona, US)*
Filip Murlak (*University of Warsaw, Poland)*
Muthu Muthukrishnan (*Rutgers University, US)*
Rimma Nehme (*Microsoft, US)*
Wolfgang Nejdl (*University of Hannover, Germany)*
Joachim Niehren (*INRIA Lille, France)*
Werner Nutt (*Free University of Bozen-Bolzano, Italy)*
Dan Olteanu (*Oxford University, UK)*
Dimitris Papadias (*HKUST, Hong Kong)*
Mary-Angela Papalaskari (*Villanova University, US)*
Alexandra Poulovassilis (*Birkbeck, University of London, UK)*
Sunil Prabhakar (*Purdue University, US)*
Lu Qin (*CUHK, China)*
Christopher Re (*University of Wisconsin-Madison, US)*
Dimitris Sacharidis (*IMIS "Athena" Research Centre , Greece)*
Arnaud Sahuguet (*Google, US)*
Marc H Scholl (*Universitaet Konstanz, Germany)*
Thomas Schwentick (*TU Dortmund, Germany)*
Jianhua Shao (*Cardiff University, UK)*
Mohamed Sharaf (*University of Queensland, Australia)*
Kian Lee Tan (*National University of Singapore, Singapore)*
Nan Tang (*University of Edinburgh, UK)*
Val Tannen (*University of Pennsylvania, US)*
Evimaria Terzi (*Boston University, US)*
Jens Teubner (*ETH Zurich, Switzerland)*

Program Committee (continued):

Alex Thomo (*University of Victoria, Canada)*
Marcos Vaz Salles (*Cornell University, US)*
Dirk Van Gucht (*Indiana University, US)*
Millist Vincent (*University of South Australia, Australia)*
Wei Wang (*University of North Carolina, US)*
Hongzhi Wang (*Harbin Institute of Technology, China)*
Jianmin Wang (*Tsinghua University, China)*
Junhu Wang (*Griffith University, Australia)*
Wei Wang (*Fudan University, China)*
Haixun Wang (*Microsoft Research Asia, China)*
Jianyong Wang (*Tsinghua University, China)*
Jef Wijsen (*University of Mons, Belgium)*
Ouri E. Wolfson (*University of Illinois at Chicago, US)*
Limsoon Wong (*National University of Singapore, Singapore)*
Peter Wood (*Birkbeck, University of London, UK)*
Yuqing Wu (*Indiana University, US)*
Ming Xiong (*Google, US)*
Fei Xu (*Microsoft, US)*
Ke Yi (*Hong Kong University of Science and Technology, Hong Kong)*
Ken Yocum (*UC San Diego, US)*
Clement Yu (*University of Illinois at Chicago, US)*
Xiaohui Yu (*York University, Canada)*

CIKM 2011 IR Track Program Committees

Senior Program Committee:

James Allan (*University of Massachusetts Amherst, US)*
Javed Aslam (*Northeastern University, US)*
Leif Azzopardi (*University of Glasgow, UK)*
Nicholas Belkin (*Rutgers University, US)*
Paul Bennett (*Microsoft Research, US)*
Wray Buntine (*National ICT Australia Limited, NICTA), Australia)*
Yi Chang (*Yahoo! Labs, US)*
Paul Clough (*University of Sheffield, UK)*
Fabio Crestani (*University of Lugano, Switzerland)*
Maarten de Rijke (*University of Amsterdam, The Netherlands)*
Patrick Gallinari (*University Pierre & Marie Curie, France)*
Bin Gao (*Microsoft Research Asia, China)*
Cathal Gurrin (*Dublin City University, Ireland)*
Djoerd Hiemstra (*University of Twente, The Netherlands)*
Winston Hsu (*National Taiwan University, Taiwan)*
Panos Ipeirotis (*New York University, US)*
Gareth Jones (*Dublin City University, Ireland)*
Jaap Kamps (*University of Amsterdam, The Netherlands)*
Noriko Kando (*NII, Japan)*
Jaana Kekäläinen (*University of Tampere, Finland)*
Oren Kurland (*Technion, Israel)*
Elizabeth Liddy (*Syracuse University, US)*
Mounia Lalmas (*Yahoo! Research, Spain)*
Paul McNamee (*Johns Hopkins University, US)*
Peter Mika (*Yahoo! Research Barcelona, Spain)*
Wolfgang Nejdl (*L3S Research Center, Germany)*
Omar Alonso (*Microsoft Research, US)*
Tetsuya Sakai (*Microsoft Research Asia, China)*
Fabrizio Silvestri (*ISTI - CNR, Italy)*
Torsten Suel (*NYU Poly, US)*
Andrew Trotman (*University of Otago, New Zealand)*
Ellen Voorhees (*National Institute of Standards and Technology, US)*
Jun Wang (*University College London, UK)*
Ji-Rong Wen (*Microsoft Research Asia, China)*
Ryen White (*Microsoft Research, US)*
Emine Yilmaz (*Microsoft Research Cambridge, UK)*
ChengXiang Zhai (*University of Illinois at Urbana-Champaign, US)*
Min Zhang (*Tsinghua University, China)*

Program Committee: Maristella Agosti (*University of Padua, Italy)*
Robin Aly (*University of Twente, The Netherlands)*
Giambattista Amati (*Fondazione Ugo Bordoni, Italy)*
Marcos Andre Goncalves (*Universidade Federal de Minas Gerais, Brazil)*
Avi Arampatzis (*Democritus University of Thrace, Greece)*
Jaime Arguello (*Carnegie Mellon University, US)*
Hany Azzam (*Queen Mary, University of London, UK)*
Jing Bai (*Microsoft Corporation, US)*
Niranjan Balasubramanian (*University of Massachusetts Amherst, US)*
Krisztian Balog (*Norwegian University of Science and Technolog, Norway)*
Alejandro Bellogín Kouki (*Universidad Autónoma de Madrid, Spain)*
Michael Bendersky (*University of Massachusetts, Amherst, US)*
Paul Bennett (*Microsoft Research, US)*
Pushpak Bhattacharyya (*IIT Bombay, India)*
Jiang Bian (*Yahoo! Labs, US)*
Cui Bin (*Beijing University, China)*
Roi Blanco (*Yahoo! Research Barcelona, Spain)*
Toine Bogers (*RSLIS, Denmark)*
Gloria Bordogna (*CNR IDPA, Italy)*
Corrado Boscarino (*Centrum Wiskunde & Informatica, The Netherlands)*
Mohand Boughanem (*Universite Paul Sabatier, France)*
Sam Brody (*Rutgers, US)*
Wray Buntine (*National ICT Australia Limited, Australia)*
Fidel Cacheda (*University of Coruña, Spain)*
Pavel Calado (*Technical Univ. of Lisbon, Portugal)*
Gilberto Camara (*INPE - National Institute for Space Research, Brazil)*
Guihong Cao (*Microsoft, US)*
Ben Carterette (*University of Delaware, US)*
Marc-Allen Cartright (*University of Massachusetts Amherst, US)*
Pablo Castells (*Universidad Autonoma de Madrid, Spain)*
Carlos Castillo (*Yahoo! Research, Spain)*
Zheng Chen (*Microsoft Research Asia, China)*
Xueqi Cheng (*Institute of Computing Technology, CAS, China)*
Gordon Cormack (*University of Waterloo, Canada)*
Ricardo da Silva Torres (*University of Campinas, Brazil)*
Franciska de Jong (*University of Twente, The Netherlands)*
Gianluca Demartini (*Université de Fribourg, Switzerland)*
Ludovic Denoyer (*LIP6, France)*
Giorgio Maria Di Nunzio (*University of Padova, Italy)*
Fernando Diaz (*Yahoo! Research, US)*
Lan Du (*ANU & NICTA, Australia)*
Carsten Eickhoff (*Delft University of Technology, The Netherlands)*
Li Fan (*Yahoo, US)*
Hui Fang (*University of Delaware, US)*
Ayman Farahat (*Yahoo, US)*
Henry Feild (*University of Massachusetts Amherst, US)*
Juanma Fernández-Luna (*University of Granada, Spain)*
Nicola Ferro (*University of Padova, Italy)*

Program Committee (continued):

Dennis Fetterly (*Microsoft Research, US)*
Boudin Florian (*Université d'Avignon, France)*
Colum Foley (*Dublin City University, Ireland)*
Ingo Frommholz (*University of Bedfordshire, UK)*
Susan Gauch (*University of Arkansas, US)*
Eric Gaussier (*Laboratoire d'Informatique de Grenoble, France)*
Shlomo Geva (*Queensland University of Technology, Australia)*
Fredric Gey (*University of California, Berkeley, US)*
Ayse Goker (*City University London, UK)*
Gregory Grefenstette (*EXALEAD, France)*
Nils Grimsmo (*NTNU, Norway)*
Maxim Gurevich (*Yahoo! Research, US)*
Karl Gyllstrom (*Katholieke Universiteit Leuven, Belgium)*
Harry Halpin (*University of Edinburgh, UK)*
Claudia Hauff (*Delft University of Technology, The Netherlands)*
David Hawking (*Funnelback Ltd and Australian National University, Australia)*
Daqing He (*University of Pittsburgh, US)*
Jiyin He (*Centrum Wiskunde & Informatica, The Netherlands)*
Ben He (*Graduate University of CAS, China)*
Andreas Henrich (*University of Bamberg, Germany)*
Eduard Hoenkamp (*Queensland University of Technology, Australia)*
Katja Hofmann (*University of Amsterdam, The Netherlands)*
Laura Hollink (*Delft University of Technology, The Netherlands)*
Vera Hollink (*Centrum Wiskunde & Informatica, The Netherlands)*
Vivian Hu (*York University, Canada)*
Xuanjing Huang (*Fudan University, China), China)*
Gilles Hubert (*IRIT, University of Toulouse, France)*
Tereza Iofciu (*L3S Research Center, Germany)*
Daxin Jiang (*Microsoft Research Asia, China)*
Hideo Joho (*University of Tsukuba, Japan)*
Joemon Jose (*University of Glasgow, UK)*
Vanja Josifovski (*Yahoo! Research, US)*
Marko Junkkari (*University of Tampere, FI)*
Changsung Kang (*Yahoo! Labs, US)*
Gabriella Kazai (*Microsoft Research, UK)*
Heikki Keskustalo (*University of Tampere, FI)*
Jinyoung Kim (*University of Massachusetts, Amherst, US)*
Sang-Wook Kim (*Hanyang University, Korea)*
Irwin King (*The Chinese University Hong Kong, Hong Kong)*
Marijn Koolen (*University of Amsterdam, The Netherlands)*
Veit Koeppen (*Otto-von-Guericke-Universität Magdeburg, Germany)*
Donald Kraft (*Colorado Technical University, US)*
Raghu Krishnapuram (*IBM India Research Lab, India)*
Jérôme Kunegis (*University of Koblenz-Landau, Germany)*
Monica Landoni (*University of Lugano, Switzerland)*
Birger Larsen (*Royal School of LIS, Denmark)*
Martha Larson (*Delft University of Technology, The Netherlands)*
Hady Lauw (*Institute for Infocomm Research, Singapore)*
Victor Lavrenko (*University of Edinburgh, UK)*
Fotis Lazarinis (*University of Teesside, UK)*
Ronny Lempel (*Yahoo! Labs, Israel)*
Johannes Leveling (*CNGL, Dublin City University, Ireland)*

Program Committee (continued):

Qing Li (*City University of Hong Kong, Hong Kong)*
Huajing Li (*Facebook, US)*
Wen Li (*Delft University of Technology, The Netherlands)*
Xiaoming Li (*Peking University, China)*
Zhoujun Li (*Beihang University, China)*
Xia Lin (*Drexel University, US)*
Chin-Yew Lin (*Microsoft Research Asia, China)*
Hongfei Lin (*Dalian University of Technology, China)*
Yang Liu (*Shandong University, China)*
Alexander Löser (*TU Berlin, Germany)*
Claudio Lucchese (*ISTI-CNR Pisa, Italy)*
Yuanhua Lv (*University of Illinois Urbana-Champaign, US)*
Craig Macdonald (*University of Glasgow, UK)*
Walid Magdy (*Dublin City University, Ireland)*
Marco Maggini (*University of Siena, Italy)*
Yosi Mass (*IBM Research Lab at Haifa, Israel)*
James Mayfield (*Johns Hopkins University, US)*
Richard Mccreadie (*University of Glasgow, UK)*
Edgar Meij (*University of Amsterdam, The Netherlands)*
Dalila Mekhaldi (*University of Wolverhampton, UK)*
Donald Metzler (*University of Southern California, US)*
Jun Miao (*York University, Canada)*
Natasa Milic-Frayling (*Microsoft Research, UK)*
Vibhu Mittal (*Root-1, US)*
Dunja Mladenic (*Jozef Stefan Institute, Slovenia)*
Marie-Francine Moens (*Katholieke Universiteit Leuven, Belgium)*
Josiane Mothe (*Université de Toulouse, France)*
Vanessa Murdock (*Yahoo! Research, Spain)*
Arlindo L. Oliveira (*Instituto Superior Tecnico / INESC-ID, Portugal)*
Sandeep Pandey (*Yahoo Research, US)*
Gabriella Pasi (*Università degli Studi di Milano Bicocca, Italy)*
Raffaele Perego (*ISTI-CNR, Italy)*
Nils Pharo (*Oslo University College, Norway)*
Karen Pinel-Sauvagnat (*IRIT, University of Toulouse, France)*
Benjamin Piwowarski (*University of Glasgow, UK)*
Vassilis Plachouras (*Presans, France)*
Barbara Poblete (*Yahoo! Research, CL)*
Tamara Polajnar (*University of Glasgow, UK)*
Jeffrey Pound (*University of Waterloo, Canada)*
Kunal Punera (*Yahoo! Research, US)*
Tao Qin (*Microsoft Research Asia, China)*
Novi Quadrianto (*ANU & NICTA, Australia)*
Filip Radlinski (*Microsoft, Canada)*
Davood Rafiei (*University of Alberta, Canada)*
Georgina Ramirez (*Universitat Pompeu Fabra, Spain)*
Jan Ramon (*Katholieke Universiteit Leuven, Belgium)*
Edie Rasmussen (*University of British Columbia, Canada)*
Andreas Rauber (*Vienna University of Technology, Austria)*
Stephen Robertson (*Microsoft Research Cambridge, UK)*
Monica Rogati (*LinkedIn, US)*
Stevan Rudinac (*Delft University of Technology, The Netherlands)*
Scott Sanner (*NICTA & ANU, Australia)*

Program Committee (continued):

Rodrygo Santos (*University of Glasgow, UK)*
Ralf Schenkel (*Max-Planck-Institut Informatik, Germany, Germany)*
Falk Scholer (*RMIT University, Australia)*
Pavel Serdyukov (*Yandex, RU)*
James G Shanahan (*Church and Duncan Group, US)*
Milad Shokouhi (*Microsoft Research, UK)*
Wolf Siberski (*L3S Research Center, University of Hannover, Germany)*
Mark Smucker (*University of Waterloo, Canada)*
Cees Snoek (*University of Amsterdam, The Netherlands)*
Dawei Song (*Robert Gordon University, UK)*
Benno Stein (*Bauhaus-Universität Weimar, Germany)*
Venkata Subramaniam (*IBM Research India, India)*
Krysta M. Svore (*Microsoft Research, US)*
Lynda Tamine (*IRIT- Paul Sabatier University, France)*
Paul Thompson (*Dartmouth Medical School, US)*
Nicola Tonellotto (*CNR, Italy)*
Thanh D. Tran (*Institute AIFB, KIT, Germany)*
Dolf Trieschnigg (*University of Twente, The Netherlands)*
Ming-Feng Tsai (*National Chengchi University, Taiwan)*
Theodora Tsikrika (*University of Applied Sciences Western Switzerland, Switzerland)*
David Vallet (*Universidad Autonoma de Madrid, Spain)*
Arthur van Bunningen (*Teezir, The Netherlands)*
Theo P. van der Weide (*Radboud University, The Netherlands)*
Olga Vechtomova (*University of Waterloo, Canada)*
Suzan Verberne (*Radboud University Nijmegen, The Netherlands)*
Jesus Vilares (*University of A Coruña, Spain)*
Robert Villa (*University of Sheffield, UK)*
Vishwa Vinay (*Microsoft Research, UK)*
Stefanos Vrochidis (*CERTH-ITI, Greece)*
Xiaojun Wan (*Peking University, China)*
Bin Wang (*Institute of Computing Technology, CAS, China)*
Christian Wartena (*Novay, The Netherlands)*
Takashi Washio (*ISIR - Osaka University, Japan)*
William Webber (*University of Melbourne, Australia)*
Wouter Weerkamp (*University of Amsterdam, The Netherlands)*
Thijs Westerveld (*Teezir, The Netherlands)*
Yuchen Wu (*Google, US)*
Wensi Xi (*Google, US)*
Christopher C. Yang (*Drexel University, US)*
Shuang-Hong Yang (*Georgia Institute of Technology, US)*
Zheng Ye (*York University, Canada)*
Wai Gen Yee (*Orbitz, LLC, US)*
Xing Yi (*University of Massachusetts, Amherst, US)*
Hwan-Seung Yong (*Ewha Womans University, KR)*
Shichao Zhang (*Guangxi Normal University, China)*
Jun Zhao (*National Laboratory of Pattern Recognition, China)*
Zhaohui Zheng (*Yahoo! Inc, US)*
Ding Zhou (*Facebook, US)*
Nivio Ziviani (*UFMG, Brazil)*

CIKM 2011 KM Track Program Committees

Senior Program Committee:

Sarabjot Anand (*University of Warwick, UK)*
Francesco Bonchi (*Yahoo! Research, Spain)*
Ulrik Brandes (*University of Konstanz, Germany)*
Ronen Feldman (*Hebrew University of Jerusalem, Israel)*
Fosca Giannotti (*CNR, Italy)*
Dunja Mladenic (*Jozef Stefan Institute, Slovenia)*
Bamshad Mobasher (*DePaul University, US)*
Siegfried Nijssen (*Katholieke Universiteit Leuven*, Belgium)
Sanjay Ranka (*University of Florida, US)*
Yucel Saygin (*Sabanci University, Turkey)*
Myra Spiliopoulou (*University of Magdeburg, Germany)*
Xindong Wu (*University of Vermont, US)*
Qiang Yang (*Hong Kong University of Science and Technology, Hong Kong)*
Xingquan Zhu (*University of Technology Sydney, Australia)*

Program Committee: Ram Akella (Stanford University & University of California)
Rocio Alaiz-Rodriguez (*University of Leon, Spain)*
Reda Alhajj (*University of Calgary, Canada)*
Aijun An (*York University, Canada)*
Shin Ando (*Gunma University, Japan)*
Marie-Aude Aufaure (*Ecole Centrale Paris, France)*
Rina Azoulay (*Jerusalem College of Technology, Israel)*
James Bailey (*University of Melbourne, Australia)*
Farokh Bastani (*University of Texas at Dallas, US)*
Michele Berlingerio (*ISTI-CNR Pisa, Italy)*
Sam Brody (*Rutgers University, US)*
Gilberto Camara (*INPE - National Institute for Space Research, Brazil)*
B. Barla Cambazoglu (*Yahoo! Research, Spain)*
K. Selcuk Candan (*Arizona State University, US)*
James Caverlee (*Texas A&M University, US)*
Chia-Hui Chang (*National Central University, Taiwan)*
Philip Chan (*Florida Institute of Technology, US)*
Sharma Chakravarthy (*University of Texas at Arlington, US)*
Narayanan Chatapuramkrishnan (*Washington State University, US)*
Cindy Chen (*University of Massachusetts Lowell, US)*
Li Chen (*Hong Kong Baptist University, Hong Kong)*
Ming-Syan Chen (*Research Center for Information Technology, Taiwan)*
Shu-Ching Chen (*Florida International University, US)*
Weizhu Chen (*Microsoft Research Asia, China)*
Xue-wen Chen (*Unversity of Kansas, US)*
Hong Cheng (*Chinese University of Hong Kong, Hong Kong)*
Kun-Ta Chuang (*National Cheng Kung University, Taiwan)*
Luísa Coheur (*Instituto Superior Técnico / L2F - INESC-ID, Portugal)*
Carlo Combi (*University of Verona, Italy)*
Manuel Contero (*Universidad Politécnica de Valencia, Spain)*
Francisco Couto (*Universidade de Lisboa, Portugal)*
Alfredo Cuzzocrea (*University of Calabria, Italy)*
Martine De Cock (*Ghent University, Belgium)*
Pablo de la Fuente (*Universidad de Valladolid, Spain)*
Pasquale De Meo (*Università di Messina, Italy)*
Tommaso Di Noia (*Politecnico di Bari, Italy)*
Wei Ding (*University of Massachusetts Boston, US)*
Juergen Dix (*Clausthal University of Technology, Germany)*
Debora Donato (*Yahoo! Labs, US)*
Dejing Dou (*University of Oregon, US)*
Brian Eoff (*Texas A&M University, US)*
Wei Fan (*IBM T.J.Watson, US)*
Olivier Ferret (*CEA LIST, France)*
Blaz Fortuna (*Jozef Stefan Institute, Slovenia)*
Johannes Fuernkranz (*TU Darmstadt, Germany)*

Program Committee (continued):

Tim Furche (*Oxford University, UK)*
Jose Gamez (*University of Castilla-La Mancha, Spain)*
Matjaz Gams (*Jozef Stefan Institute, Slovenia)*
Nicolas Garcia-Pedrajas (*University of Córdoba, Spain)*
Minos Garofalakis (*Technical University of Crete, Greece)*
Bugra Gedik (*IBM Research, US)*
Michael Gertz (*University of Heidelberg, Germany)*
Rayid Ghani (*Accenture Technology Labs, US)*
S.K. Ghosh (*Indian Institute of Technology, Kharagpur, IN)*
Bart Goethals (*University of Antwerp, Belgium)*
Jesus Gonzalez (*National Institute Astrophysics, Optics and Electronics, Mexico)*
Sergio Greco (*University of Calabria, Italy)*
Le Gruenwald (*University of Oklahoma, US)*
Christian Gütl (*Curtin University of Technology, Austria)*
Ido Guy (*IBM Research Haifa, Israel)*
Peng Han (*Chongqing Academy of Science & Technology, China)*
Dan He (*University of California, Los Angeles, US)*
Andreas Hotho (*University of Würzburg, Germany)*
Vagelis Hristidis (*Florida International University, US)*
Kien Hua (*University of Central Florida, US)*
Luke Huan (*University of Kansas, US)*
Jimmy Huang (*York University, Canada)*
Eyke Huellermeier (*Marburg University, Germany)*
Jing Jiang (*Singapore Management University, Singapore)*
Wei Jiang (*Missouri University of Science and Technology, US)*
Ruoming Jin (*Kent state University, US)*
Zhi Jin (*Peking University, China)*
Murat Kantarcioglu (*University of Texas at Dallas, US)*
Hung-Yu Kao (*National Cheng Kung University, Taiwan)*
Shiva Kasiviswanathan (*IBM T.J. Watson Research Center, US)*
Chan Keith (*Hong Kong Polytechnic University, Hong Kong)*
Eamonn Keogh (*University of California Riverside, US)*
Vlado Keselj (*Dalhousie University, Canada)*
Latifur Khan (*University of Texas at Dallas, US)*
Deepak Khemani (*IIT Madras, India)*
Hyerin Kim (*Korea Advanced Institute of Technology, Korea)*
Frank Klawonn (*Ostfalia University of Applied Sciences, Germany)*
Alek Kolcz (*Microsoft Live Labs, US)*
Patty Kostkova (*City eHealth Research Centre, UK)*
Wai Lam (*Chinese University of Hong Kong, Hong Kong)*
Won Suk Lee (*Yonsei University Korea, Korea)*
Young-Koo Lee (*Kyung Hee University, Korea)*
Carson K. Leung (*University of Manitoba, Canada)*
Bin Li (*University of Technology, Sydney, Australia)*

Program Committee (continued):

Jianzhong Li (*Harbin Institute of Technology, China)*
Tao Li (*Florida International University, US)*
Althea Liang (*HP Cloud and Security Lab, Singapore)*
Giuseppe Liotta (*Università di Perugia, Italy)*
Huan Liu (*Arizona State University, US)*
Nathan Liu (*Hong Kong University of Science and Technology, Hong Kong)*
Yan Liu (*IBM Research, US)*
Yang Liu (*Shandong University, China)*
Ying Liu (*KAIST, South Korea)*
Dmitri Loguinov (*Texas A&M University, US)*
Chang-Tien Lu (*Virginia Tech, US)*
Ping Luo (*Hewlett Packard Labs China, China)*
Mondher Maddouri (*URPAH, Tunisia)*
Hiroshi Mamitsuka (*Kyoto University, Japan)*
Bruno Martins (*Instituto Superior Técnico / INESC-ID, Portugal)*
Sergio Mascetti (*Università degli Studi di Milano, Italy)*
Stan Matwin (*University of Ottawa, Canada)*
Guy Melancon (*Université Bordeaux I, France)*
Gabor Melli (*PredictionWorks Inc., Canada)*
Ernestina Menasalvas (*Universidad Politecnica de Madrid, Spain)*
Ralf Moeller (*Hamburg University of Technology, Germany)*
Yang-Sae Moon (*Kangwon National University, Korea)*
Roser Morante (*University of Antwerp, Belgium)*
Ion Muslea (*Language Weaver, US)*
Mirco Nanni (*CNR, Italy)*
Olfa Nasraoui (*University of Louisville, US)*
Roberto Navigli (*Sapienza University of Rome, Italy)*
Tim Oates (*University of Maryland Baltimore County, US)*
Daniel O'Leary (*University of Southern California, US)*
Jonice Oliveira (*Federal University of Rio de Janeiro, Brazil)*
Weike Pan (*HKUST, China)*
Youngja Park (*IBM Research, US)*
Nikos Pelekis (*University of Piraeus, Greece)*
Kumaraguru Ponnurangam (*Indraprastha Institute of Information Technology, India)*
Vikram Pudi (*IIIT Hyderabad, India)*
Naren Ramakrishnan (*Virginia Tech, US)*
Vikas Raykar (*Siemens Healthcare, US)*
Daniele Riboni (*Universita degli Studi di Milano, Italy)*
Rong Pan (*Sun Yat-sen University, China)*
Massimo Ruffolo (*ICAR-CNR, Italy)*
Giovanni Maria Sacco (*Universita di Torino, Italy)*
Kazuhiro Seki (*Kobe University, Japan)*
Yi-dong Shen (*Chinese Academy of Science, China)*
Kyuseok Shim (*Seoul National University, Korea)*
Andrzej Skowron (*University of Warsaw, Poland)*
Dominik Slezak (*University of Warsaw, Poland)*

Program Committee (continued):

Manas Somaiya (*Ebay Inc., US)*
Bingjun Sun (*eBay/Shopping.com, US)*
Xiaoping Sun (*Chinese Academy of Science, China)*
Einoshin Suzuki (*Kyushu University, Japan)*
Keishi Tajima (*Kyoto University, Japan)*
Pang-Ning Tan (*Michigan State University, US)*
Lei Tang (*Yahoo! Labs, US)*
Maguelonne Teisseire (*TETIS, France)*
Konstantinos Tserpes (*National Technical University of Athens, Greece)*
Christopher Thomas (*Kno.e.sis Center, US)*
Agma Traina (*University of Sao Paulo at Sao Carlos, Brazil)*
Celine Vens (*Katholieke Universiteit Leuven, Belgium)*
Maria Virvou (*University of Piraeus, Greece)*
Xiaojun Wan (*Peking University, China)*
Haixun Wang (*Microsoft Research Asia, China)*
Jason Wang (*New Jersey Institute of Technology, US)*
Wei Wang (*University of North Carolina, US)*
Wei Wei (*Norwegian University of Science and Technology, Norway)*
Albert Weichselbraun (*Vienna University of Economics and Busines, Austria)*
Dwi Widyantoro (*STEI - Bandung Institute of Technology, Indonesia)*
Tak-Lam Wong (*The Hong Kong Institute of Education, Hong Kong)*
Bin Wu (*Beijing University of Posts and Telecom, China)*
Hui Xiong (*Rutgers University, US)*
Li Xiong (*Emory University, US)*
Jeonghee Yi (*Yahoo!, US)*
Jin Soung Yoo (*Indiana University - Purdue University, US)*
Hwanjo Yu (*POSTECH, Korea)*
Philip Yu (*University of Illinois at Chicago, US)*
Shipeng Yu (*Siemens Medical Solutions, US)*
Xiaofeng YU (*Chinese University of Hong Kong, China)*
Li Yunyao (*IBM Research, US)*
Markus Zanker (*Alpen-Adria-Universitaet Klagenfurt, Austria)*
Yi Zeng (*Beijing University of Technology China, China)*
Chengqi Zhang (*University of Technology Sydney, Australia)*
Dongsong Zhang (*University of Maryland Baltimore County, US)*
Yan Zhang (*Vermont Information Processing, US)*
Jessie Zhao (*York University, Canada)*
Lina Zhou (*University of Maryland Baltimore County, US)*
Geraldo Zimbrao (*Federal University of Rio de Janeiro, Brazil)*
Albrecht Zimmermann (*Katholieke Universiteit Leuven, Belgium)*

CIKM 2011 Industry Track, Workshop, Tutorial and Demonstration Committees

Industry Track Program Committee:

Steve Beitzel (*Telcordia Technologies, US)*
Jidong Chen (*EMC Research China, China)*
Nikesh Garera (*Kosmix, US)*
David Grossman (*Illinois Institute of Technology, US)*
Yoshinori Hara (*Kyoto University, Japan)*
Arvind Hulgeri (*Persistent Systems, India)*
Mizuho Iwaihara (*Waseda University, Japan)*
Giridhar Kumaran (*Microsoft Corporation, US)*
Ni Lao (*Carnegie Mellon University, US)*
Jonathan Ledlie (*Nokia Research, US)*
Wookey Lee (*Inha University, Korea)*
Wen-Syan Li (*Directorial MTS, China)*
Einat Minkov (*University of Haifa, Israel)*
Fuchun Peng (*Microsoft, US)*
Diego Puppin (*Google, US)*
Prasan Roy (*IBM Research, India)*
Robert Warren (*University of Waterloo, Canada)*

Tutorial Program Committee:

Daniel J. Abadi (*Yale University, US)*
Philip A. Bernstein (*Microsoft, US)*
Albert Bifet (*University of Waikato, New Zealand)*
Francesco Bonchi (*Yahoo!, Spain)*
Gianluca Demartini (*University of Fribourg, Switzerland)*
Thore Graepel (*Microsoft, UK)*
Antonio Gulli (*Microsoft, UK)*
Djoerd Hiemstra (*University of Twente, The Netherlands)*
Rosie Jones (*Akamai, US)*
Jaap Kamps (*University of Amsterdam, The Netherlands)*
Ray R. Larson (*UC Berkeley, US)*
Leonid Libkin (*University of Edinburgh, UK)*
Claudio Lucchese (*ISTI-CNR, Italy)*
Paul Ogilvie (*LinkedIn, US)*
Fabrizio Silvestri (*ISTI-CNR, Italy)*
Trevor Strohman (*Google, US)*
Daniel Tunkelang (*LinkedIn, US)*
Arjen P. de Vries (*CWI & Technical University of Delft, The Netherlands)*
Daniel J. Abadi (*Yale University, US)*
Philip A. Bernstein (*Microsoft, US)*

Demonstration Program Committee:

Enrique Alfonseca (*Google, Switzerland)*
Klaus Berberich (*Max-Planck Institute, Germany)*
Joaquin Delgado (*Yahoo, US)*
Alex Dow (*Microsoft, US)*
Conny Junghans (*University of Heidelberg, Germany)*
Vasilis Kandylas (*Microsoft, US)*
Jussi Karlgren (*SICS, Sweden)*
Dmitry Lenkov (*Oracle, US)*
David Losada (*University of Santiago de Compostela, Spain)*
Bertram Ludaescher (*University of California, Davis, US)*
Gerard de Melo (*Max-Planck Institute, Germany)*
Ullas Nambiar (*IBM Research, India)*
Alexandros Ntoulas (*Zynga, US)*
Ximena Olivares (*eBay, US)*
Cristobal Pedregal-Martin (*Oracle, US)*
Alvaro Pereira (*Federal University of Ouro Preto, Brazil)*
Igor Perisic (*LinkedIn, US)*
Jorge Quiane-Ruiz (*Saarland University, Germany)*
Mandar Rahurkar (*Yahoo!, US)*
Martin Theobald (*Max-Planck, Germany)*

Workshop Program Committee:

Karl Aberer (*EPFL, Switzerland)*
James Allan (*University of Massachusetts, Amherst, US)*
Roi Blanco (*Yahoo! Research, Spain)*
Pia Borlund (*Royal School of Library and Information Science, Denmark)*
Wray Buntine (*NICTA, Australia)*
Marcos Goncalves (*Universidade Federal de Minas Gerais, Brazil)*
Alasdair Gray (*University of Manchester, UK)*
Donna Harman (*NIST, US)*
Bill Hersh (*Oregon Health & Science University, US)*
Noriko Kando (*National Institute of Informatics, Japan)*
Anastasios Kementsietsidis (*IBM Research, US)*
Elizabeth Liddy (*Syracuse University, US)*
Hervé Martin (*Joseph Fourier University (France)*
Mirjam Minor (*University Trier, Germany)*
Pavel Serdyukov (*Yandex LLC, Russia)*
Nicola Tonellotto (*CNR, Italy)*
Rosina Weber (*Drexel University, US)*
Emine Yilmaz (*Microsoft, UK)*
Shichao Zhang (*University of Technology Sydney, Australia)*

Poster Program Committee:

Alberto Abello (*Universitat Politecnica de Catalunya, Spain)*
Omar Alonso (*Microsoft, US)*
Miguel Alonso (*University of A Coruña, Spain)*
Robin Aly (*University of Twente, Netherlands)*
Giuseppe Amodeo (*University of L'Aquila, Italy)*
Shin Ando (*Gunma University, Japan)*
Avi Arampatzis (*Democritus University of Thrace, Greece)*
M. Eduardo Ares (*University of A Coruña, Spain)*
Álvaro Barreiro (*University of A Coruña, Spain)*
Steve Beitzel (*Telcordia Technologies, US)*
Pushpak Bhattacharyya (*IIT Bombay, India)*
Jiang Bian (*Yahoo! Labs, US)*
Marco Bianchi (*Fondazione Ugo Bordoni, Italy)*
Cui Bin (*Beijing University, China)*
Roi Blanco (*Yahoo! Research, Spain)*
Angela Bonifati (*CNR, Italy)*
Gloria Bordogna (*CNR IDPA, Italy)*
Mohand Boughanem (*Universite Paul Sabatier, France)*
Panagiotis Bouros (*National Technical University of Athens, Greece)*
Peter Bruza (*Queensland University of Technology, Australia)*
Fidel Cacheda (*University of A Coruña, Spain)*
Zhipeng Cai (*Mississippi State University, US)*
Pavel Calado (*Technical Univ. of Lisbon, Portugal)*
Fazli Can (*Bilkent Univeristy, Turkey)*
Ivan Cantador (*Universidad Autonoma de Madrid, Spain)*
Longbing Cao (*University of Technology Sydney, Australia)*
Mark Carman (*Monash University, Australia)*
Claudio Carpineto (*Fondazione Ugo Bordoni, Italy)*
Yi Chang (*Yahoo Labs, US)*
Narayanan Chatapuramkrishnan (*Washington State University, US)*
Francine Chen (*FXPAL, US)*
Shu-Ching Chen (*Florida International University, US)*
Haiming Chen (*Chinese Academy of Sciences, China)*
Wenguang Chen (*Peking University, China)*
Rada Chirkova (*North Carolina State University, US)*
Stephane Clinchant (*Xerox Research Centre Europe, France)*
Richard Connor (*University of Strathclyde, UK)*
Francisco Couto (*Universidade de Lisboa, Portugal)*
Ricardo da Silva Torres (*University of Campinas, Brazil)*
Jing Dai (*IBM T.J. Watson Research Center, US)*
Atish Das Sarma (*Google Research, US)*
Martine De Cock (*Ghent University, Belgium)*
Pablo de la Fuente (*Universidad de Valladolid, Spain)*
Giorgio Maria Di Nunzio (*University of Padova, Italy)*
Wei Ding (*University of Massachusetts, Boston, US)*
Fabien Duchateau (*Norwegian University of Science and Technology, Norway)*

Poster Program Committee (continued):

Bill Eberle (*Tennessee Tech University, US)*
Hui Fang (*University of Delaware, US)*
Nicola Ferro (*University of Padova, Italy)*
Boudin Florian (*Université d'Avignon, France)*
Giorgio Gambosi (*University of Rome "Tor Vergata", Italy)*
Giorgos Giannopoulos (*NTU Athens, Greece)*
Jesus Gonzalez (*National Institute of Astrophysics, Optics and Electronics, Mexico)*
Sergio Greco (*University of Calabria, Italy)*
Gregory Grefenstette (*EXALEAD, France)*
Cathal Gurrin (*Dublin City University, Ireland)*
Ido Guy (*IBM Research Haifa, Israel)*
Claudia Hauff (*Delft University of Technology, Netherlands)*
Ben He (*Graduate University of Chinese Academy of Sciences, China)*
Andreas Henrich (*University of Bamberg, Germany)*
Vivian Hu (*York University, Canada)*
Qiang Huang (*University of East Anglia, UK)*
Rong Huang (*NC State University, US)*
Xiaojiang Huang (*Peking University, China)*
Gilles Hubert (*IRIT, University of Toulouse, France)*
Kai Hui (*Graduate University of Chinese Academy of Sciences, China)*
Arvind Hulgeri (*Persistent Systems, India)*
Ela Hunt (*ETH Zurich, Switzerland)*
Seung-won Hwang (*POSTECH, Korea)*
Giacomo Inches (*University of Lugano, Switzerland)*
Jing Jiang (*Singapore Management University, Singapore)*
Hideo Joho (*University of Tsukuba, Japan)*
Gao Jun (*Peking University, China)*
Mouna Kacimi (*Free University of Bozen-Bolzano, Italy)*
Toshihiro Kamishima (*AIST, Japan)*
Jaewoo Kang (*Korea University, Korea)*
Abhijith Kashyap (*Florida International University, US)*
Gabriella Kazai (*Microsoft Research, UK)*
Chan Keith (*The Hong Kong Polytechnic University, Hong Kong)*
Anastasios Kementsietsidis (*IBM T.J. Watson Research Center, US)*
Eamonn Keogh (*University of California Riverside, US)*
Sang-Wook Kim (*Hanyang University, Korea)*
Benny Kimelfeld (*IBM, US)*
Iraklis Klampanos (*University of Glasgow, UK)*
Solmaz Kolahi (*University of British Columbia, Canada)*
Donald Kraft (*Colorado Technical University, US)*
Giridhar Kumaran (*Microsoft Corporation, US)*
Wai Lam (*The Chinese University of Hong Kong, Hong Kong)*
Monica Landoni (*University of Lugano, Switzerland)*
Ni Lao (*Carnegie Mellon University, US)*
Birger Larsen (*Royal School of LIS, Denmark)*
Martha Larson (*Delft University of Technology, Netherlands)*
Hady Lauw (*Institute for Infocomm Research, Singapore)*
Won Suk Lee (*Yonsei University Korea, Korea)*
Maurizio Lenzerini (*Università di Roma La Sapienza, Italy)*
Johannes Leveling (*CNGL, Dublin City University, Ireland)*
Bin Li (*University of Technology, Sydney, Australia)*

Poster Program Committee (continued):

Wei Li (*IBM Silicon Valley Lab, US)*
Huiying Li (*Peking University, China)*
Hongfei Lin (*Dalian Univ. of Technology, China)*
Christina Lioma (*University of Stuttgart, Germany)*
Giuseppe Liotta (*Università di Perugia, Italy)*
Yang Liu (*Shandong University, China)*
David Losada (*University of Santiago de Compostela, Spain)*
Robert Luk (*The Hong Kong Polytechnic University, Hong Kong)*
Ping Luo (*Hewlett Packard Labs China, China)*
Shuai Ma (*Beihang University, China)*
Craig Macdonald (*University of Glasgow, UK)*
Andrew MacFarlane (*City University London, UK)*
Ioana Manolescu (*INRIA, France)*
Maarten Marx (*University of Amsterdam, Netherlands)*
Richard McCreadie (*University of Glasgow, UK)*
Gabor Melli (*PredictionWorks, Canada)*
Umar Minhas (*University of Waterloo, Canada)*
Einat Minkov (*University of Haifa, Israel)*
Vibhu Mittal (*Root-1, US)*
Dunja Mladenic (*Jozef Stefan Institute, Slovenia)*
Marie-Francine Moens (*Katholieke Universiteit Leuven, Belgium)*
Yang-Sae Moon (*Kangwon National University, Korea)*
Alessandro Moschitti (*DISI, University of Trento, Italy)*
Miyuki Nakano (*University of Tokyo, Japan)*
Mirco Nanni (*ISTI-CNR, Italy)*
Dan Olteanu (*Oxford University, UK)*
Iadh Ounis (*University of Glasgow, UK)*
Dimitris Papadias (*HKUST, Hong Kong)*
Mary-Angela Papalaskari (*Villanova University, US)*
Javier Parapar (*University of A Coruña, Spain)*
Pawel Parys (*University of Warsaw, Poland)*
Nikos Pelekis (*University of Piraeus, Greece)*
Benjamin Piwowarski (*University of Glasgow, UK)*
Vassilis Plachouras (*PRESANS, France)*
Barbara Poblete (*Yahoo! Research, Chile)*
Edie Rasmussen (*University of British Columbia, Canada)*
Francisco J. Ribadas-Pena (*University of Vigo, Spain)*
Pan Rong (*Sun Yat-sen University, China)*
Prasan Roy (*IBM Research, India)*
Stefan Rüger (*The Open University, UK)*
Keun Ho Ryu (*Chungbuk National University, Korea)*
Giovanni Maria Sacco (*Università di Torino, Italy)*
Dimitris Sacharidis (*IMIS "Athena" Research Centre , Greece)*

Poster Program Committee (continued):

Rodrygo Santos (*University of Glasgow, UK)*
Ulrike Sattler (*University of Manchester, UK)*
Jacques Savoy (*University of Neuchatel, Switzerland)*
Maximilian Schich (*CCNR, Northeastern University, US)*
Falk Scholer (*RMIT University, Australia)*
Giovanni Semeraro (*University of Bari, Italy)*
Pavel Serdyukov (*Yandex, Russia)*
Yue Shi (*Delft University of Technology, Netherlands)*
Kyuseok Shim (*Seoul National University, Korea)*
Milad Shokouhi (*Microsoft Research, UK)*
Mário J. Silva (*Instituto Superior Técnico/INESC-ID, Portugal)*
Andrzej Skowron (*University of Warsaw, Poland)*
Amanda Spink (*Loughborough University, UK)*
Venkata Subramaniam (*IBM Research India, IN)*
Xiaoping Sun (*ICT, CanadaS, China)*
Bingjun Sun (*eBay/Shopping.com, US)*
Xuning Tang (*Drexel University, US)*
David Taniar (*Monash University, Australia)*
Dacheng Tao (*University Technology Sydney, Australia)*
Jens Teubner (*ETH Zurich, CH)*
Paul Thomas (*CSIRO, Australia)*
Alex Thomo (*University of Victoria, Canada)*
Paul Thompson (*Dartmouth Medical School, US)*
Anastasios Tombros (*Queen Mary University of London, UK)*
Ming-Feng Tsai (*National Chengchi University, Taiwan)*
Ivor Wai-Hung Tsang (*Nanyang Technological University, Singapore)*
David Vallet (*Universidad Autonoma de Madrid, Spain)*
Theo van der Weide (*Radboud University Nijmegen, Netherlands)*
Thanasis Vergoulis (*National Technical University of Athens, Greece)*
Jesus Vilares (*University of A Coruna, Spain)*
Manuel Vilares (*University of Vigo, Spain)*
Vishwa Vinay (*Microsoft Research, UK)*
Xiaojun Wan (*Peking University, China)*
Jianyong Wang (*Tsinghua University, China)*
Hongzhi Wang (*Harbin Institute of Technology, China)*
William Webber (*Computer Science and Software Engineering, Australia)*
Jef Wijsen (*University of Mons, Belgium)*
Peter Wood (*Birkbeck, University of London, UK)*
Yuqing Wu (*Indiana University, Bloomington, US)*
Lei Xie (*NorthWestern Polytechnical University, China)*
Hui Xiong (*Rutgers University, US)*
Hongbo Xu (*Chinese Academy of Sciences Beijing, China)*
Grace Hui Yang (*Institute of Computing Technology, Chinese Academy of Sciences, China)*

Poster Program Committee (continued):

Zheng Ye (*York University, Canada)*
Wai Gen Yee (*Orbitz Worldwide, US)*
Jeonghee Yi (*Yahoo! Inc, US)*
Emine Yilmaz (*Microsoft Research Cambridge, UK)*
Ken Yocum (*University of California, San Diego, US)*
Xiaohui Yu (*York University, Canada)*
Markus Zanker (*Alpen-Adria-Universitaet Klagenfurt, Austria)*
Yi Zeng (*Beijing University Of Technology, China)*
Yan Zhang (*Vermont Information Processing, US)*
Peng Zhang (*The Robert Gordon University, UK)*
Peng Zhang (*Texas State University - San Marcos, US)*
Wei Zhang (*Amazon.com Inc., US)*
Jessie Zhao (*York University, Canada)*
Zhi-Hua Zhou (*Nanjing University, China)*
Dong Zhou (*Trinity College Dublin, Ireland)*
Jianhan Zhu (*University College London, UK)*
Xingquan Zhu (*University of Technology, Australia)*
Guido Zuccon (*University of Glasgow, UK)*

CIKM 2011 Additional Reviewers

Additional reviewers:

Jaafar Ben Abdallah
Joel Barajas
Letizia Bertolaja
Romaric Besançon
Karla Caballero
Weiwei Cheng
Krzysztof Dembczynski
Nurcan Durak
Liyue Fan
Stefan Gindl
Jonatan Gomez
Slawomir Goryczka
Basheer Hawwash
Christian Kop
Elizabeth Leon
Thomas Lukasiewicz
Ana Cristina Mendes
Roberto Mirizzi
Thomas Peetz
Arthur Pitman
Esin Saka
Sofiane Sellah
Christian Sengstock
Jannik Strötgen
Ilija Subasic
Abhradeep Guha Thakurata
Jasna Tusek
Mathias Verbeke
Carmen Ruiz Vicente
Willem Waegeman
Chunye Wang
Xufei Wang
Albert Weichselbraun
Evan Wei Xiang
Yonghui Xiao
Lili Zhao
Erheng Zhong

CIKM 2011 Sponsors & Supporters

Sponsors: SIGIR Special Interest Group on Information Retrieval; sigweb

Platinum Supporter: EMC²

Gold Supporters: Google™; Microsoft Research

Silver Supporter: SAP®

Bronze Supporters: eBay® Research Labs; YAHOO! LABS; Yandex

Supporters: crossref; IBM Research

Exhibitors: Cambridge University Press; Taylor & Francis Group an informa business; Springer the language of science

Organisations: Glasgow: Scotland with style; University of Glasgow; University of Strathclyde Glasgow

Search Result Diversification for Enterprise Data

Wei Zheng, Hui Fang
Dept. of Electrical and Computer Engineering
University of Delaware
Newark, DE USA
{zwei,hfang}@udel.edu

Conglei Yao, Min Wang
HP Labs China
Haidian District
Beijing, China
{conglei.yao, min.wang6}@hp.com

ABSTRACT

Search result diversification aims to return a list of diversified relevant documents in order to satisfy different user information needs. Most of the efforts focused on Web Search, and few studies have considered another important search domain, i.e., enterprise search. Unlike Web search, enterprise search deals with both unstructured and structured data. In this paper, we propose to integrate the structured and unstructured data to discover meaningful query subtopics in search result diversification. Experimental results show that integrating structured and unstructured information allows us to discover high quality query, which are effective in diversifying the retrieval results.

Categories and Subject Descriptors

H.3.3 [**Information Search and Retrieval**]: Retrieval Models

General Terms

Algorithm

Keywords

enterprise search, diversification, query subtopics

1. INTRODUCTION

Traditional search engines rank documents mainly based on their relevance scores. As a result, top ranked results often contain relevant yet redundant information and may not be able to satisfy different user information needs. To overcome this limitation, it is necessary to diversify search results so that the returned documents would cover different pieces of relevant information, i.e. query subtopics. One of the key challenges is to identify meaningful query subtopics [16]. Almost all the existing studies on search result diversification focus on Web search, and the query subtopics are often extracted from the unstructured text and query logs [2, 6, 13]. However, less attention has been paid to solving the problem in enterprise search. Enterprise search is important because poor search results within enterprises could cause significant loss of productivities [8]. Unlike Web, enterprise data is more heterogeneous and integrated, and contain both unstructured and structured information.

In this paper, we study the problem of result diversification for enterprise search with the focus on extracting high-quality query subtopics from the integrated enterprise data. We first describe how to extract query subtopics from either the structured databases or the unstructured documents. We find that the subtopics extracted from *structured* data contain high-quality terms but have vocabulary gap with the retrieved documents while the subtopics extracted from *unstructured* data can better represent the document content but may contain a lot of noisy terms. Thus, we propose a method to integrate the subtopics extracted from *structured* data with the ones from *unstructured* data.

To evaluate the proposed query subtopic identification methods, we use the results as query subtopics and then diversify search results using a state of the art subtopic-based diversification method [13]. Experimental results over a real-world enterprise data collection demonstrate that the integrated information of enterprise data can provide high-quality query subtopics which lead to better diversification results.

2. RELATED WORK

Search result diversification has attracted a lot of attention recently [4]. Subtopic-based diversification methods aim to maximize the coverage of query subtopics in the retrieved documents [1, 13], and they are shown to perform better than redundancy-based methods on TREC collections [4].

One of the key challenges of the subtopic-based diversification methods is to extract the subtopics for a given query. Some studies tried to extract query subtopics from the retrieved documents using either document clustering [2] or topic modeling methods such as PLSA [12]. However, this type of methods cannot perform well because the generated subtopics often contain lots of noisy terms. To generate subtopics of better quality, a few studies utilized taxonomy such as Open Directory Project (ODP [1]) to extract subtopics [10, 14]. Although taxonomy-based methods provide high-quality subtopics, there is often a vocabulary gap between the taxonomy and the retrieved documents which could limit the effectiveness of the subtopics.

[1]http://www.dmoz.org/

Another way of generating subtopics of better quality is to use query suggestions from Web search engines [13]. However, query suggestion methods cannot generate collection-dependent subtopics which may hinder the diversification performance. Dou et al. [6] extracted subtopics from different sources and diversify documents based on their coverage on different categories of subtopics. However, their method does not generate more meaningful subtopics using the unique features of different categories of subtopics.

Unlike previous studies on result diversification, this work focuses on solving the problem in the context of enterprise search, which has received much less attention despite its importance [8]. Our main contributions include: (1) we propose a novel query subtopic identification method for search result diversification, which can generate collection-dependent and high-quality subtopics; and (2) this is the first study that looked into how to better leverage the integrated information in enterprise data to improve the performance of search result diversification system.

3. SUBTOPIC EXTRACTION AND INTEGRATION

The enterprise data contain not only *unstructured* documents but also *structured* databases which often contain high-quality and domain-dependent information. In this section, we first describe how to extract subtopics from the documents and databases. We then propose the method to integrate these subtopics and generate the high-quality subtopics that are effective in result diversification.

3.1 Subtopic Extraction from Structured Data

We now study the problem of extracting subtopics from the structured data, i.e., the relational database. A unique characteristic of structured data such as the databases is the use of schema, which provides the meaning of the data as well as the domain knowledge. The schema information such as relations among different tables makes it possible to construct a multi-level concept hierarchy of the data in the databases. The goal is to select K subtopics that cover different relevant information of the query. Some existing studies [3, 5] diversify results using the information in the database schema, but they ignore the concept hierarchy indicated by the relations among schemas. Intuitively, a node contains more relevant information if not only the node itself is relevant to the query but also most of its descendants are relevant [9]. We therefore compute the relevance score of a node s_i based on the average similarity between the nodes in the sub-tree rooted at s_i and the query.

$$rel(s_i, q) = \frac{\sum_{s \in T_{s_i}} sim(s, q)}{|T_{s_i}|} \quad (1)$$

where s_i is the ith node in the database structure, i.e., a subtopic candidate, T_{s_i} is the sub-tree rooted at s_i and q is the query. $sim(s, q)$ is the semantic similarity between s and the query. We compute it based on the term co-occurrence information.

$$sim(s, q) = \frac{\sum_{t \in s} sim(t, q)}{|s|} \quad (2)$$

where t is a term in s and $sim(t, q)$ is the semantic similarity between the term and the query based on term co-occurrence information in the document set [7].

We iteratively select K nodes having the highest scores as the subtopics. In order to avoid different subtopics covering redundant information, we only select the node that is neither the ancestor nor the descendant of any previously selected nodes. These subtopics selected from the database often contain high-quality and domain-dependent information about the query. For example, the subtopics of the query "*printer*" cover the relevant information of printer types, accessories and customer service.

3.2 Subtopic Extraction from Unstructured Data

We can apply PLSA [11] method to mine the subtopic information from the unstructured data, i.e., original retrieved documents of the query. In order to avoid the overlapping information in different subtopics, the system assigns each term to the cluster where it has the highest score in the PLSA result.

$$s'(t) = \arg\max_{s' \in S'} score(t, s') \quad (3)$$

where S' is the set of subtopics, i.e., PLSA clusters, t is a term and $s'(t)$ is the subtopic that t is assigned to.

Each PLSA cluster is a subtopic. These subtopics are extracted from the clusters of documents and are therefore effective in distinguish documents covering different information of the query.

3.3 Subtopic Integration

The subtopics extracted from the databases contain high-quality information of the query and the subtopics extracted from retrieved documents contain the terms that can distinguish documents covering different subtopics of the query. Therefore, we propose to integrate the subtopics extracted from these two sources.

The task of subtopic integration in this section is that, given the K subtopics extracted from the databases and K subtopics extracted from documents, we combine them into K integrated subtopics where each subtopic contains M terms. Since the final goal of search result diversification is to diversify documents, we propose to use the subtopics extracted from database, containing high-quality information, to guide selection of integrated subtopic terms from subtopics extracted from documents. Specifically, in each query, we first propose to connect each subtopic of databases with a subtopic of documents based on their semantic similarity:

$$s_i = \arg\max_{s \in S} sim(s, s'_i) \quad (4)$$

where S is the set of subtopics extracted from the database, s'_i is the ith subtopic extracted from the documents, $sim(s, s'_i)$ is the semantic similarity between the subtopic of database and the subtopic of documents, and s_i is the subtopic of database assigned to s'_i. We assume the connection between these subtopics is 1 to 1, in order to simplify the problem. We leave other methods of connection for our future work.

For each subtopic extracted from the documents, we then select terms based on their semantic similarity to the connected subtopic of database [7]. The selected terms from each subtopic would form a new integrated subtopic that utilizes the information from both databases and documents. These integrated subtopics are generated by the guidance of subtopics extracted from database, so they often contain the information of higher quality. Moreover, their terms are extracted from the clusters of documents, so they could solve the problem of vocabulary mismatch and are more effective in diversifying documents.

Algorithm 1 Subtopic Integration

Input: a query q, a set of K document subtopics S', a set of K database subtopics S, semantic similarity between subtopics $sim(s, s')$, semantic similarity between the term and subtopic $sim(t, s)$, number of subtopic terms M
Output: integrated subtopic set S^* where $|S^*| = K$

1: /*Assigning database subtopics to document subtopics*/
2: **for** $s'_i \in S'$ **do**
3: $\quad s_i = \arg\max_{s \in S} sim(s, s'_i)$
4: $\quad S = S \setminus \{s_i\}$
5: **end for**
6: /*Selecting terms from each document subtopic*/
7: $S^* = \emptyset$
8: **for** $s'_i \in S'$ **do**
9: $\quad s^* = \emptyset$ /*select M terms from each subtopic*/
10: $\quad$ **while** $|s^*| < M$ *and* $|s^*| < |s'_i|$ **do**
11: $\qquad t^* = \arg\max_{t \in s'_i \setminus s^*} sim(t, s_i)$
12: $\qquad s^* = s^* \cup t^*$
13: $\quad$ **end while**
14: $\quad S^* = S^* \cup \{s^*\}$
15: **end for**
16: **return** S^*

We now describe the details of our method in Algorithm 1. The first step is to connect a subtopic extracted from databases with a subtopic extracted from retrieved documents. For each subtopic extracted from documents, we find the most similar subtopic extracted from databases based on the term semantic similarity [7], i.e., lines 2-5 in Algorithm 1. The second step is to select M terms from each subtopic of documents as the terms in an intergraded subtopic. The term selection criteria is that we select the terms that have the highest semantic similarity with the connected database subtopic, as described in lines 7-15.

4. EXPERIMENTS

4.1 Enterprise Data Set

We evaluate the proposed subtopic extraction and integration methods over the collection of HP company. The data set includes both *unstructured data*, which consists of 477,800 web pages crawled from the web site of a computer company, and *structured data*, which includes 25 relational databases of the company.

To evaluate the performance of result diversification methods, we construct a query set and corresponding judgments following the procedure used in the diversity task of TREC Web track [4]. We construct the query set by selecting 50 popular queries from a query log during July 1st, 2010 and July 7th, 2010 of the same company. The average number of terms per query for the query set is 2.2. The 50 queries are selected from the query log in the following steps: (1) rank all the terms based on their frequencies in the query log; (2) manually select 100 meaningful terms from the top-ranked terms; (3) rank all the queries in the query log based on the number of selected terms contained in the queries; and (4) manually select 50 queries from the top-ranked queries to cover different product information in the database. The judgments are created by seven human judgers. The judgment file includes subtopics in each query and the documents relevant to each subtopic. The average number of subtopics per query is 4.12, which is close to the number from TREC diversity collections, i.e., 4.61.

We now discuss how to construct the concept hierarchy based on the structured information, i.e., relational databases. These tables are related to each other based on the foreign/primary keys. We only use the tables related to the products because most of the queries in the query log are related to the products. However, the proposed methods can be applied on any other enterprise databases and collections. We use the data in five tables containing the most important information of the products to build the concept hierarchy. These tables and their data form a concept hierarchy based on the relations among their foreign and primary keys. The levels in the hierarchy, from up to down, in the hierarchy are *product type* containing 8 nodes, *product marketing category* with 54 nodes, *product marketing subcategory* with 134 nodes, *product series* with 983 nodes and *product name* with 3,238 nodes. Each node in a level is the information of the product related to that level. One node in a lower level belongs to a ancestor node in the higher level and one node in the higher level has one or more descendants in the lower level.

4.2 Experiment Design

We first use the Dirichlet smoothing language model retrieval function [15] to retrieve documents for each query from the document collection, and then extract the subtopics using different methods. With these extracted subtopics, the retrieved results are then diversified using a state of the art diversification method, i.e., *xQuAD* [13]. xQuAD [13] computes the score of the document based on the similarity between the document and the query, the importance of the subtopics and the similarity between the document and subtopics. It iteratively selects the documents that are not only similar to the query but also similar to the subtopics that have not been well covered by previously selected documents.

The diversification results are evaluated using α-nDCG on three depths, 5, 10 and 20 top-ranked documents, which are the official evaluation measures applied in the TREC diversity task [4]. α is the parameter to adjust the contribution of the document covering a relevant while novel subtopic. We set it to be 0.5 which is the default value used in TREC.

We implemented three baseline systems: (1) *NoDiverse* which is the original retrieval results of Dirichlet function without diversification; (2) *FixedLevel* which manually sets the levels of subtopics in the hierarchy of the database and selects nodes in those levels that are relevant to the query as subtopics [10]. We use the highest two levels in the hierarchy of enterprise database since the number of nodes on the highest level is too small, i.e., 8; and (3) *QuerySugg* that submits each query to a web search engine and uses the suggested queries from the web search engine as subtopics. We use *DB*, *PLSA* and *Combine* to denote the methods of extracting subtopics from the database, the documents and integrated information, respectively, as described in Section 3. Each subtopic in *PLSA* is the cluster with the top-ranked M terms in that cluster.

Table 1: Optimal Performance Comparison of Subtopic Extraction/Integration Methods

Methods	α-nDCG@5	α-nDCG@10	α-nDCG@20
Nodiverse	0.279	0.330	0.374
FixedLevel	0.256	0.305	0.340
QuerySugg	0.280	0.322	0.374
DB	0.220	0.274	0.310
PLSA	0.298	0.352	0.404
Combine	**0.331**	**0.375**	**0.418**

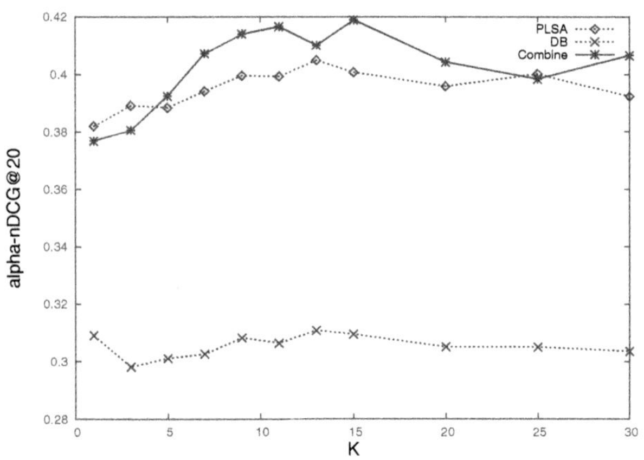

Figure 1: Impact of Number of Subtopics K on the Diversification Performances

4.3 Effectiveness of Subtopic Extraction and Integration Methods

We compare the effectiveness of different subtopic extraction methods and report the results in Table 1. We can make the following interesting observations.

First, *Combine* outperforms other methods. *Combine* can integrate the high-quality information in DB subtopics with the information in $PLSA$ that is effective in distinguishing documents covering different subtopics. Therefore, it can outperform both DB and $PLSA$. However, its improvement over $PLSA$, especially on α-nDCG@20, is not significant. Therefore, we further analyze the results of these two methods in every query. We find that *Combine* outperforms $PLSA$ in more queries, where *Combine* performs better in 21 queries and $PLSA$ performs better in 16 queries. What's more, *Combine* is more effective in queries where the diversity performances of the original retrieval results are better. The average α-nDCG@20 value of original retrieval results in queries where *Combine* performs better is 0.463 while the value in queries where $PLSA$ performs better is 0.351. It shows that we may apply different methods according to the diversity quality of the original retrieval result of the query. We leave this for our future work.

Second, DB performs worse than $PLSA$. This is due to the vocabulary gap between the database and retrieved web pages. Therefore, the subtopics in DB are not effective in diversifying the documents although they contain high-quality information relevant to the query.

Figure 1 shows the diversification performances with different number of subtopics K. The number of subtopic terms M is set to be the optimum value on each point. The optimum numbers of subtopics in $PLSA$ and *Combine* are 13 and 15, representatively. *Combine* outperforms $PLSA$ in most values of K. The performance of DB does not change significantly with the values of K because the vocabulary gap between the subtopics of DB and original retrieved documents makes these subtopics ineffective in diversifying documents.

5. CONCLUSIONS AND FUTURE WORK

In this paper, we propose the method of integrating the structured and unstructured data to extract subtopics for search result diversification. The experimental result shows that the integrated subtopics can cover different information of the query and are effective in diversifying the documents. In the future, we plan to study how to diversify search results by utilizing the hierarchical structure of the databases.

6. ACKNOWLEDGEMENTS

This material is based upon work supported by the National Science Foundation under Grant Number IIS-1017026 and HP Labs Innovation Research Program. We thank the anonymous CIKM reviewers for their useful comments.

7. REFERENCES

[1] R. Agrawal, S. Gollapudi, A. Halverson, and S. Ieong. Diversifying Search Results. In *WSDM*, 2009.

[2] B. Carterette and P. Chandar. Probabilistic Models of Novel Document Rankings for Faceted Topic Retrieval. In *CIKM*, 2009.

[3] Z. Chen and T. Li. Addressing diverse user preferences in sql-query-result navigation. In *Proceedings of SIGMOD'07*, 2007.

[4] C. L. A. Clarke, N. Craswell, and I. Soboroff. Overview of the TREC 2009 Web Track. In *Proceedings of TREC'09*, 2009.

[5] E. Demidova, P. Fankhauser, X. Zhou, and W. Nejdl. Divq: Diversification for keyword search over structured databases. In *Proceedings of SIGIR'10*, 2010.

[6] Z. Dou, S. Hu, K. Chen, R. Song, and J. R. Wen. Multi-dimensional search result diversification. In *Proceedings of WSDM'11*, 2011.

[7] H. Fang and C. Zhai. Semantic Term Matching in Axiomatic Approaches to Information Retrieval. In *SIGIR*, 2006.

[8] S. Feldman and C. Sherman. The High Cost of Not Finding Information. In *Technical Report No. 29127, IDC*, 2003.

[9] S. Geva. Gpx - gardens point xml ir at inex 2006. In *Proceedings of INEX'06*, 2006.

[10] C. Hauff and D. Hiemstra. University of Twente @ TREC 2009: Indexing half a billion web pages. In *Proceedings of TREC'09*, 2009.

[11] T. Hofmann. Probabilistic latent semantic analysis. In *Proceedings of UAI'99*, 1999.

[12] P. Lubell-Doughtie and K. Hofmann. Improving result diversity using probabilistic latent semantic analysis. In *Proceedings of DIR'11*, 2011.

[13] R. L. T. Santos, C. Macdonald, and I. Ounis. Exploiting Query Reformulations for Web Search Result Diversification. In *WWW*, 2010.

[14] R. L. T. Santos, C. Macdonald, and I. Ounis. Selectively Diversifying Web Search Results. In *CIKM*, 2010.

[15] C. Zhai and J. Lafferty. A study of smoothing methods for language models applied to ad hoc information retrieval. In *Proceedings of SIGIR'01*, 2001.

[16] W. Zheng, X. Wang, H. Fang, and H. Cheng. An exploration of pattern-based subtopic modeling for search result diversification. In *Proceedings of JCDL'11*, 2011.

Diversification for Multi-domain Result Sets *

Alessandro Bozzon, Marco Brambilla, Piero Fraternali, Marco Tagliasacchi
Politecnico di Milano, Dipartimento di Elettronica e Informazione
P.zza Leorardo Da Vinci 32, 20133 - Milano - Italy
{name.surname}@polimi.it

ABSTRACT

Multi-domain search answers to queries spanning multiple entities, like "Find an affordable house in a city with low criminality index, good schools and medical services", by producing ranked sets of entity combinations that maximize relevance, measured by a function expressing the user's preferences. Due to the combinatorial nature of results, good entity instances (e.g., inexpensive houses) tend to appear repeatedly in top-ranked combinations. To improve the quality of the result set, it is important to balance relevance (i.e., high values of the ranking function) with diversity, which promotes different, yet almost equally relevant, entities in the top-k combinations. This paper explores two different notions of diversity for multi-domain result sets, compares experimentally alternative algorithms for the trade-off between relevance and diversity, and performs a user study for evaluating the utility of diversification in multi-domain queries.

Categories and Subject Descriptors

H.3.3 [**Information Search and Retrieval**]: Search Process; H.3.4 [**System and Software**]: Performance Evaluation (efficiency and effectiveness); H.3.5 [**On-line Information Services**]: Web-based services

General Terms

Theory, Experimentation, Performance

Keywords

Result diversification, multi-domain search

*The research leading to these results has received funding from the European Research Council under the 2008 Call for "IDEAS Advanced Grants" as part of the Search Computing (SeCo) project. We wish to thank A. Vaccarella and M. Follo for their contribution to the implementation of the query analysis framework.

CIKM'11, October 24–28, 2011, Glasgow, Scotland, UK.

1. INTRODUCTION

Multi-domain search tries to respond to queries that involve multiple correlated concepts [2, 4]. Formally, multi-domain queries can be represented as rank-join queries over a set of relations, representing the wrapped data sources [10]. Each item in the result set is a combination of objects that satisfy the join and selection conditions, and the result set is ranked according to a scoring function. Due to the combinatorial nature of multi-domain search, the number of combinations in the result set is normally very high, and strongly relevant objects tend to combine repeatedly with many other concepts, requiring the user to scroll down the list of results deeply to see alternative, maybe only slightly less relevant,objects. Improving the diversity of the result set is the aim of *diversification*, which can be defined in the context of multi-domain search as the selection of K elements out of a universe of N combinations, so to maximize a quality criterion that combines the *relevance* and the *diversity* of the objects of distinct types seen by the user.

The contributions of the paper includes: **(1)** the formalization of the diversification problem in the context of multi-domain search; following the approach in [9], we propose two criteria for comparing combinations (*categorical* and *quantitative* diversity); **(2)** a study of the behavior of three known greedy algorithms, testing the hypothesis that the diversification algorithms improve the quality of the result set with respect to a baseline constituted by the selection of the most relevant K combinations; **(3)** an evaluation of the perception and utility of diversification in multi-domain search with a user study based on selection tasks involving combinations of correlated objects.

The paper is organized as follows: Section 2 presents the formalization of the problem and introduces different diversity measures for combinations; Section 3 illustrates the results of the experimental activity; Section 4 discusses previous work; Section 5 concludes and discusses future work.

2. MULTI-DOMAIN DIVERSIFICATION

Consider a set of relations $R_1, R_2, \ldots, R_n$, where each R_i denotes the result set returned by invoking a search service σ_i over a Web data source. Each tuple $t_i \in R_i =< a_i^1, a_i^2, \ldots, a_i^{m_i} >$ has schema $R_i(\mathtt{A}_i^1 : \mathtt{D}_i^1, \ldots, \mathtt{A}_i^{m_i} : \mathtt{D}_i^{m_i})$, where $\mathtt{A}_i^{m_i}$ is an attribute of relation R_i and $\mathtt{D}_i^{m_i}$ is the associated domain. As usual in measurement theory, we distinguish the domains $\mathtt{D}_i^k$ into *categorical*, when values admit only equality test, and *quantitative*, when values can be organized in vectors embedded in a metric space.

A multi-domain query over the search services $\sigma_1, \ldots \sigma_n$ is defined as a join query $q = R_1 \bowtie \ldots \bowtie R_n$ over the relations $R_1, \ldots, R_n$, where the join predicate can be arbitrary. We call *combination* an element of the join $\tau = t_1 \bowtie \cdots \bowtie t_n =< a_1^1, a_1^2, \ldots, a_1^{m_1}, \ldots, a_n^1, a_n^2, \ldots, a_n^{m_n} >$, and *result set* $\mathcal{R}$ the set of combinations satisfying the query q.

2.1 Relevance

The goal of multi-domain search is to support the user in selecting one or more combinations from the result set of a multi-domain query, so to maximize the satisfaction of his information seeking task. To this end, combinations can be presented in order of relevance, according to a user-defined *relevance score function* $S(\tau, q)$, which can be assumed to be normalized in the $[0, 1]$ range, where 1 indicates the highest relevance. When the result set $\mathcal{R}$ is sorted, e.g. in descending order of relevance, τ_k indicates the k-th combination of $\mathcal{R}$. For instance, given the relations *Hotel*(`HName`, `HLoc`, `HRating`, `HPrice`), *Restaurant*(`RName`, `RLoc`, `RRating`, `RPrice`), and *Museum*(`MName`, `MLoc`, `MRating`, `MPrice`), consider a function *city()*, which returns the city where the geographical coordinates of a location belong to, and the multi-domain query q = select * from *Hotel*, *Restaurant*, *Museum* where $city(\texttt{HLoc}) = \texttt{Milan} \wedge city(\texttt{RLoc}) = city(\texttt{HLoc}) \wedge city(\texttt{MLoc}) = city(\texttt{HLoc})$. The overall price of the combination $S(\tau, q) = sum(\texttt{HPrice}[t_h], \texttt{RPrice}[t_r], \texttt{MPrice}[t_m])$ could be used to rank hotel, restaurant and museum triples.

Note that S is a simple linear (thus monotone) functions based solely on a subset of the attribute values of the constituent tuples, but more complex functions, not necessarily monotone, that might incorporate external knowledge (e.g. road maps) are allowed.

2.2 Diversity

We consider two different criteria to express the similarity (or symmetrically, the diversity) of combinations: **(1)** *Categorical diversity*: two combinations are compared based on the equality of the values of one or more categorical attributes of the tuples that constitute them. As a special case, categorical diversity can be based on the key attributes: this means evaluating if an object (or sub-combination of objects) is repeated in the two combinations. **(2)** *Quantitative diversity*: the diversity of two combinations is defined as their distance, expressed by some metric function.

In both cases, for each pair of combinations τ_u and τ_v, it is possible to define a diversity measure $\delta : \mathcal{R} \times \mathcal{R} \to [0, 1]$, normalized in the $[0, 1]$ interval, where 0 indicates maximum similarity.

DEFINITION 2.1. *Let $\mathtt{A}_i^{j_{i,1}}, \ldots, \mathtt{A}_i^{j_{i,d_i}}$ be a subset of d_i attributes of relation R_i and $\mathbf{v}_i(\tau) = [a_i^{j_{i,1}}, \ldots, a_i^{j_{i,d_i}}]^T$ the projection of a combination τ on such attributes. Categorical diversity is defined as $\delta(\tau_u, \tau_v) = 1 - \frac{1}{n}\sum_{i=1}^{n} \mathbb{1}_{\mathbf{v}_i(\tau_u) = \mathbf{v}_i(\tau_v)}$, where n is the number of relations R_i and $\mathbb{1}$ is the indicator function, returning one when the predicate is satisfied.*

Intuitively, categorical diversity is the percentage of tuples in two combinations that do not coincide on the attributes $\mathtt{A}_i^{j_{i,1}}, \ldots, \mathtt{A}_i^{j_{i,d_i}}$. When these attributes are the key, categorical diversity can be interpreted as the percentage of objects that appear only in one of the two combinations.

DEFINITION 2.2. *Let $\mathbf{v}_i(\tau)$ be as in Definition 2.1. Let $\mathbf{v}(\tau) = [\mathbf{v}_1(\tau), \ldots, \mathbf{v}_n(\tau)]^T = [v_1(\tau), \ldots, v_d(\tau)]^T$ denote the concatenation of length $d = d_1 + \ldots + d_n$ of such vectors. Given d user-defined weights $w_1 \ldots, w_d$ and a normalization constant δ_{max}, quantitative diversity is defined as $\delta(\tau_u, \tau_v) = \frac{1}{\delta_{max}} \sqrt[p]{\sum_{l=1}^{d} w_l |v_l(\tau_u) - v_l(\tau_v)|^p}$*

Quantitative diversity between combinations τ_u, τ_v is formalized as the (weighted) l_p-norm of the difference between the vectors $\mathbf{v}(\tau_u)$ and $\mathbf{v}(\tau_v)$. The normalization constant can be chosen, e.g., as the maximum distance value between pairs of combinations in the result set.

2.3 Computing Relevant and Diverse Combinations

Let $N = |\mathcal{R}|$ denote the number of combinations in the result set and $\mathcal{R}_K \subseteq \mathcal{R}$ the subset of combinations that are presented to the user, where $K = |\mathcal{R}_K|$. We are interested in identifying a subset $\mathcal{R}_K$ which is both *relevant* and *diverse*. Fixing the relevance score $S(\cdot, q)$, the dissimilarity function $\delta(\cdot, \cdot)$, and a given integer K, we aim at selecting a set $\mathcal{R}_K \subseteq \mathcal{R}$ of combinations, which is the solution of the following optimization problem [9]: $\mathcal{R}_K^* = \underset{\mathcal{R}_K \subseteq \mathcal{R}, |\mathcal{R}_K| = K}{\operatorname{argmax}} F(\mathcal{R}_K, S(\cdot, q), \delta(\cdot, \cdot))$, where $F(\cdot)$ is an objective function that takes into account both relevance and diversity.

Two commonly used objective functions are `MaxSum` and `MaxMin`, as defined in [9]. Solving the problem for such functions is NP-hard, as it can be reduced to the minimum k-center problem. Nevertheless, greedy algorithms exist [9], which give a 2-approximation solution in polynomial time. The underlying idea for those algorithm is to create an auxiliary function $\delta'(\cdot, \cdot)$ and iteratively construct the solution by incrementally adding combinations in such a way as to locally maximize the given objective function. A $\lambda > 0$ parameter specifies the trade-off between relevance and diversity. Another objective function, closely related to the aforementioned ones, is *Maximal Marginal Relevance* (`MMR`), initially proposed in [3]. Indeed, `MMR` implicitly maximizes an hybrid objective function whereby relevance scores are summed together, while the minimum distance between pairs of objects is controlled.

3. EXPERIMENTS

We conducted quantitative experiments and a subjective user study to understand how the considered diversification algorithms perform with respect to each other and to the non-diversified baseline. The experiments address both *categorical* and *quantitative* diversity measures. All the algorithms were evaluated using a $\lambda = 1$, thus giving equal importance to both diversity and ranking.

3.1 Evaluation measures

The evaluation of diversity in multi-domain result sets must assess the ability of a given algorithm to retrieve useful and diverse tuples within the first K results in the query answer. We therefore adapted the *α-Discounted Cumulative Gain* (α-DCG_K) [5] to measure the usefulness (gain) of a tuple $t_i \in R_i$ – where $R_1, \ldots, R_n$ are the relations involved in a multi-domain query – based on its position in the result list and its novelty w.r.t. the previous results in the ranking. Therefore, we define α-DCG_K as $\alpha\text{-}DCG_K = \sum_{k=1}^{K} \frac{\sum_{i=1}^{n} J(\tau_k, t_i)(1-\alpha)^{r_{t_i,k-1}}}{\log_2(1+j)}$, where $J(\tau_k, t_i)$

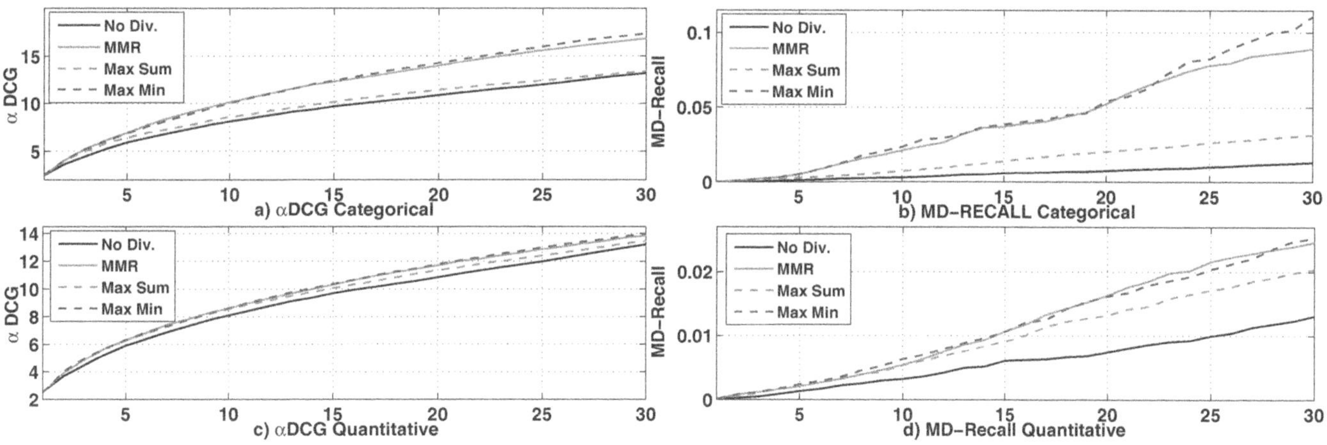

Figure 1: Experimental results for α-DCG_K (a,c) and MD-$Recall_K$ (b,d) measures.

returns 1 when tuple t_i appears in a combination τ_k at position k in the result set and 0 otherwise. J is defined as $J(\tau_k, t_i) = \mathbb{1}_{\pi_{R_i}(\tau_k)=t_i}$, where π_{R_i} denotes the projection over the attributes of R_i, and $r_{t_i,k-1} = \sum_{j=1}^{k-1} J(\tau_j, t_i)$ quantifies the number of combinations up to position $k-1$ that contain the tuple t_i. In our experiments, α is set to 0.5 to evaluate novelty and relevance equally.

Sub-topic recall at rank K (S-$Recall_K$) [12] is a recall measure often applied to evaluate diversification algorithms. In multi-domain search, a tuple in a combination can be assimilated to a subtopic in a document. Therefore, multi-domain recall at rank K – MD-$Recall_K = \prod_{i=1}^{n} \frac{|\cup_{k=1}^{K} R_i^k|}{|R_i|}$, measures, for each relation R_i involved in a query (with $i = 1 \dots n$) and for all rank positions k from 1 to K, the set of *distinct* tuples ($R_i^k = \{t_i \in R_i | \exists j \leq k. \pi_{R_i}(\tau_j) = t_i\}$) retrieved in the result set, with respect to the entire population of the relation ($|R_i|$).

3.2 Datasets

Experiment has been performed on two usage scenarios. In the first scenario – Night Out *(NO)* – a user looks for a museum, a restaurant, and a hotel in Milan. We created a dataset consisting of the *Hotel* (50 tuples), *Restaurant* (50 tuples), and *Museum* (50 tuples) relations, computing the mutual location distances, and defining three quantitative relevance scores – the combination cost, the total walking distance, and the average ratings.

In the Study Abroad *(SA)* scenario, a user looks for a U.S. university, considering the rating of the university, the quality of life in the area, and the overall cost, including accommodation. The supporting dataset consists of three relations *University* (60 US universities with their academic quality score[1], walkability score of the surroundings[2], and average tuition fee), *State* (including their crime rate), and *Flat* (1200 flats). Joins were performed on the *state* attribute. We defined three relevance scores: the overall yearly expenditure, a "quality" index [3], and the distance between the university and the flat.

[1]Source: http://archive.ics.uci.edu/ml/machine-learning-databases/university/

[2]WalkScore - http://www.walkscore.com/

[3]A function of the academic quality score, the walkability index of a university and the crime rate in a state

3.3 Quantitative Evaluation

Figure 1 shows the average results for multiple execution of 20 queries on both datasets; each query applies one of the score functions described in Section 3.2, and diversification according to categorical and quantitative distance. Each data point of the X-axis represents the k-th element in the result-set.

Using the categorical diversity function, `MMR` and `MaxMin` always outperform the un-diversified baseline, while `MaxSum` does not provide significant improvements. One can also notice that `MMR` and `MaxMin` offer similar performance: this is not surprising, as the greedy algorithms for the two objective functions are also very similar.

Using the quantitative distance, all algorithms provide similar performance; `MMR` and `MaxMin` degrade their performance w.r.t. categorical distance, and behave only slightly better than the baseline. This may also be influenced by the chosen quality measures (α-DCG_K and MD-$Recall_K$), that are based on diversity of extracted objects and therefore are more suited to evaluate categorical diversification. Overall, these results support the hypothesis that diversification algorithms can improve the quality of multi-domain result sets.

3.4 User Study

The goal of the user study was to assess the benefits in terms of user experience of adopting diversification algorithms. We considered only categorical distance, as it provided better performance in the quantitative analysis. We also excluded `MaxMin` from the evaluation, as provided performance comparable to `MMR`.

The experiment was designed as a controlled *between-subject* study, where 66 users[4] were required to perform the *Study Abroad* task. A common user interface has been created, showing the combinations of one result set to let the user choose *three* preferred combinations. The interface presented combinations in a paginated list (10 combinations per page), and a shopping cart widget let users save their favorite results. Each participant was assigned to one of the three experiments in a round-robin fashion. For each experiment we collected the total task completion time and the

[4]Bachelor and Master students; 95% male; age range from 20 to 28 years old.

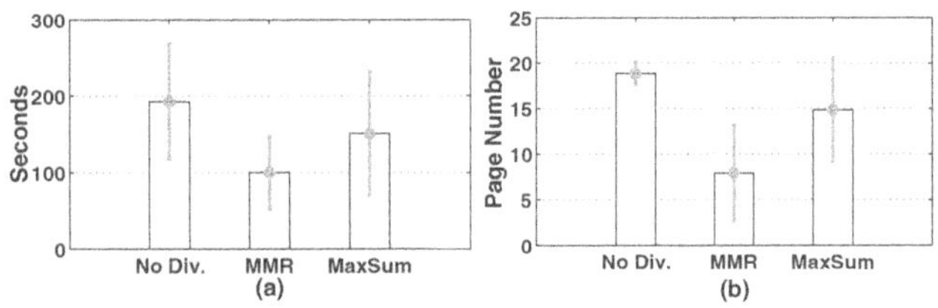

Figure 2: Average user completion time for the task (a) and average number of result pages explored (b).

number of visited result pages. Each participant took an average of 8 minutes to complete the task. Figure 2 shows the average and standard deviation of the completion time and the number of explored pages. We observe that `MMR` and `MaxSum` lead, on average, to 45% and 13% reduction in terms of task completion time, and 60% and 16% reduction in terms of number of explored pages, w.r.t. the baseline. A Kruskal-Wallis one-way, non parametric ANOVA test, provided evidence of the fact that, for each measure, the average values are different at significance level $\alpha = 0.01$.

4. RELATED WORK

Result diversification is a well-investigated topic: recent works overview and classify the existing approaches [8] and provide a systematic axiomatization of the problem [9]. A broad distinction can be done between the contributions that focus on diversifying search results for document collections [1, 7] and those that concentrate instead on structured data sets [6, 11]. Our work is mostly related to diversification applied to structured data. The work in [11] examines the diversification considering an attribute-based notion of similarity. Multi-domain diversification, as discussed in this paper, is a broader problem; it could be partially reduced to prefix-based diversification only in the case of categorical diversity. Keyword search in structured databases is addressed in [6], where diversification is applied to query interpretations, which are assumed to be available from the knowledge of the database content and query logs. Our work assumes, for simplicity, unambiguous queries and thus a fixed interpretation, but could reuse the interpretation diversification approach of [6] to cope for multi-domain searches with more than one possible interpretation.

5. CONCLUSIONS

This work discusses how the diversification techniques well studied in the context of IR can be extended to support multi-domain search applications. We experimentally tested three diversification algorithms, showing that they can introduce a significant degree of diversification in the result set; we also conducted a user study, which demonstrated a positive perception of the utility of diversification by users. In the future, we plan to extend this work by characterizing the interplay between the score function and the similarity measure, to better understand the circumstances when relevance alone is sufficient to diversify; the goal is to end up with a clear methodology for application developers to choose the most promising scoring and diversity functions, based on the available statistics on data distribution, and user preferences.

6. REFERENCES

[1] R. Agrawal, S. Gollapudi, A. Halverson, and S. Ieong. Diversifying search results. In *WSDM '09: Proceedings of the Second ACM International Conference on Web Search and Data Mining*, pages 5–14, New York, NY, USA, 2009. ACM.

[2] A. Bozzon, M. Brambilla, S. Ceri, and P. Fraternali. Liquid query: multi-domain exploratory search on the web. In *WWW '10: Proceedings of the 19th international conference on World wide web*, pages 161–170, New York, NY, USA, 2010. ACM.

[3] J. Carbonell and J. Goldstein. The use of mmr, diversity-based reranking for reordering documents and producing summaries. In *SIGIR '98: Proceedings of the 21st annual international ACM SIGIR conference on Research and development in information retrieval*, pages 335–336, New York, NY, USA, 1998. ACM.

[4] S. Ceri and M. Brambilla, editors. *Search Computing Trends and Developments*, volume 6585. Springer, Mar. 2011.

[5] C. L. Clarke, M. Kolla, G. V. Cormack, O. Vechtomova, A. Ashkan, S. Büttcher, and I. MacKinnon. Novelty and diversity in information retrieval evaluation. In *SIGIR '08: Proceedings of the 31st annual international ACM SIGIR conference on Research and development in information retrieval*, pages 659–666, New York, NY, USA, 2008. ACM.

[6] E. Demidova, P. Fankhauser, X. Zhou, and W. Nejdl. Divq: diversification for keyword search over structured databases. In *SIGIR '10: Proceeding of the 33rd international ACM SIGIR conference on Research and development in information retrieval*, pages 331–338, New York, NY, USA, 2010. ACM.

[7] Z. Dou et al. Multi-dimensional search result diversification. In *Proceedings of the fourth ACM international conference on Web search and data mining*, WSDM '11, pages 475–484, New York, NY, USA, 2011. ACM.

[8] M. Drosou and E. Pitoura. Search result diversification. *ACM SIGMOD Record*, 39:41–47, September 2010.

[9] S. Gollapudi and A. Sharma. An axiomatic approach for result diversification. In *WWW '09: Proceedings of the 18th international conference on World wide web*, pages 381–390, New York, NY, USA, 2009. ACM.

[10] D. Martinenghi and M. Tagliasacchi. Proximity rank join. *Proceedings of the VLDB Endowment*, 3:352–363, September 2010.

[11] E. Vee, U. Srivastava, J. Shanmugasundaram, P. Bhat, and S. A. Yahia. Efficient computation of diverse query results. In *ICDE '08: Proceedings of the 2008 IEEE 24th International Conference on Data Engineering*, pages 228–236, Washington, DC, USA, 2008. IEEE Computer Society.

[12] C. X. Zhai, W. W. Cohen, and J. Lafferty. Beyond independent relevance: methods and evaluation metrics for subtopic retrieval. In *SIGIR '03: Proceedings of the 26th annual international ACM SIGIR conference on Research and development in informaion retrieval*, pages 10–17, New York, NY, USA, 2003. ACM.

A Peer's-Eye View: Network Term Clouds in a Peer-to-Peer System

Raynor Vliegendhart
R.Vliegendhart@tudelft.nl

Martha Larson
M.A.Larson@tudelft.nl

Christoph Kofler
C.Kofler@tudelft.nl

Johan Pouwelse
J.A.Pouwelse@tudelft.nl

Delft University of Technology, Mekelweg 4, 2628 CD Delft, The Netherlands

ABSTRACT

We investigate term clouds that represent the content available in a peer-to-peer (P2P) network. Such network term clouds are non-trivial to generate in distributed settings. Our term cloud generator was implemented and released in Tribler—a widely-used, server-free P2P system—to support users in understanding the sorts of content available. Our evaluation and analysis focuses on three aspects of the clouds: *coverage*, *usefulness* and *accumulation speed*. A live experiment demonstrates that individual peers accumulate substantial network-level information, indicating good coverage of the overall content of the system. The results of a user study carried out on a crowdsourcing platform confirm the usefulness of clouds, showing that they succeed in conveying to users information on the type of content available in the network. An analysis of five example peers reveals that accumulation speeds of terms at new peers can support the development of a semantically diverse term set quickly after a cold start. This work represents the first investigation of term clouds in a live, 100% server-free P2P setting.

Categories and Subject Descriptors: H.3 [Information Storage and Retrieval]: H.3.3 Information Search and Retrieval—*Search process*; H.3.4 Systems and Software—*Distributed systems*

General Terms: Performance, Experimentation

Keywords: P2P, term cloud, gossip protocol, user study

1. INTRODUCTION

New users encountering a search system can search more effectively if they have appropriate expectations of the sort of content that can be found in the system. Tribler is a real-world peer-to-peer (P2P) file-sharing system (downloadable from http://www.tribler.org) that offers a search functionality [7]. We developed and implemented a term cloud generator in order to promote successful searches by providing users with an impression of the types of content available in the system. Informal observation of user interaction patterns suggests that users having more experience with the Tribler system formulate a greater number of successful queries. The term clouds are intended to provide a quicker substitute for system interaction experience. If the clouds support users in understanding which information needs Tribler can fulfill, it can be expected that their queries better match the content of the system, leading, in the long term, to higher satisfaction and better user retention rates.

The term clouds are generated using the frequency counts of terms extracted from the names of files within the network that are accumulated at an individual peer by way of the underlying process used to exchange information among peers. This paper investigates the question of whether effective term clouds reflecting overall network content can be created in a distributed environment. We focus on three aspects: *coverage*, *usefulness* and *accumulation speed*. Note that this focus excludes investigation of cloud animation. Here, we simply state that animation switches cloud views at regular intervals to give the user the impression of the scope and dynamic development of the content of the system. Analysis of use pattern statistics and long-term impact on the uptake of Tribler are also left for future work.

In a completely distributed environment such as Tribler, building a network term cloud is non-trivial. Within the network, content is stored not on a central server with a 'bird's-eye' view, but rather at the individual peers. An individual peer can receive information about content at other peers only by communicating with its direct neighbors. In other words, in an environment that is 100% server free, the only view of the content collection that is available is a 'peer's-eye' view. In order for term clouds to be useful, the communication between peers must provide fast and high-coverage information about the content in the network. The key contribution of this paper is to demonstrate that a server-free architecture does not prevent peers from generating clouds that provide a global overview and are helpful for users.

After presenting background and related work, we report results of a live discovery experiment investigating cloud *coverage*, i.e., how well 'peer's-eye' clouds reflect network-level content. Then, we investigate the *usefulness* of the clouds, i.e., their ability to convey an impression of the content of the network to users, with a user study. Finally, we examine the *accumulation speed* of the clouds with a qualitative analysis of the cold start phase of example peers that reflects the experience of new users entering the network. We finish with our conclusion and outlook.

CIKM'11, October 24–28, 2011, Glasgow, Scotland, UK.

2. BACKGROUND AND RELATED WORK

The basic motivation for using term clouds to communicate the content of the system to users derives from work on tag clouds, which shows that clouds support browsing and discovery [8]. Our term clouds contain mixed uni- and bigram terms. This design choice is based on studies showing user preference for bigram or mixed clouds [4], which suggest that longer terms are easier for users to interpret. Since our aim is to investigate the viability of peer's-eye clouds in a P2P setting, we do not focus on the specific benefits derived from individual design characteristics of clouds, e.g., the use of terms vs. tags or the benefits of mixing terms in clouds.

Understanding our network term cloud requires careful distinction between 100% server free P2P systems and solutions with central dependencies. The presence of a central component in the design of a P2P system allows a significant simplification of the search set up, e.g., search in Napster using a central file index. In such a system, generation of term clouds is trivial. However, in a fully decentralized, i.e., 100% server free, P2P system such as Tribler, there is no central point that can, e.g., aggregate term frequencies and peers are required to propagate or search for information throughout the network. Depending on its network topology, a P2P system can use different communication protocols based on, e.g., flooding [5]. Gossip-based algorithms [2] provide the relative advantage of scalability and Tribler uses its own specific gossip protocol called Buddycast [6]. Through the exchange of periodic Buddycast messages, a peer discovers other peers and new content. Each message contains a list of live peers (divided into peers similar to the sending peer and peers that have been selected randomly), a download profile of the sending peer and a list of selected content hashes known by the sending peer. When a peer finds a peer with a similar download profile or an unknown content hash, it can connect to that peer or request the metadata of the file corresponding to that hash. Note that although the similarity relationship between connected peers is a distinguishing characteristic of Tribler, here, we exclude it from consideration in order to ensure our results achieve better generalization beyond Tribler to server-free P2P in general. If a peer downloads a file, it retrieves the file's content using the BitTorrent protocol [1].

Work closely related to our own is limited, and arguably effectively restricted to a single research effort, [3]. This work proposes an architecture for aggregation and representation of information resources that enables tagging in a P2P network with a Distributed Hash Table (DHT) topology. A DHT is a structured P2P network in which nodes and values are assigned a key through a hashing function and can be found using key-based routing. The basic challenge, that of information aggregation in a distributed environment, faced in [3] is shared with our work. However, our work differs in that Tribler is an unstructured P2P network, with greater flexibility and lower security risk. Further, here, we focus on term discovery, while [3] investigates maintaining frequency approximations of previously-known tags.

3. NETWORK TERM CLOUDS

Network term clouds are created by extracting terms from the filenames and accumulating raw counts. Peers acquire filenames from neighbors through torrent files and in turn pass these torrent files along again. The collecting of torrent files is driven by the Buddycast protocol, which allows peers to discover new content as described in the previous section. A torrent file contains metadata required for the BitTorrent protocol to download an actual file [1]. The metadata includes the filename, size and integrity hashes. From a filename both unigram and bigram terms are extracted. The unigram terms are obtained by tokenizing the filename using non-alphanumeric characters as delimiters. English stopwords and unigrams shorter than three characters are ignored. Bigram terms are constructed by joining the first two unigrams extracted from a filename, based on the assumption that the most important unigrams are at the beginning of a filename. The extracted unigram and bigram terms are displayed together in a single mixed cloud.

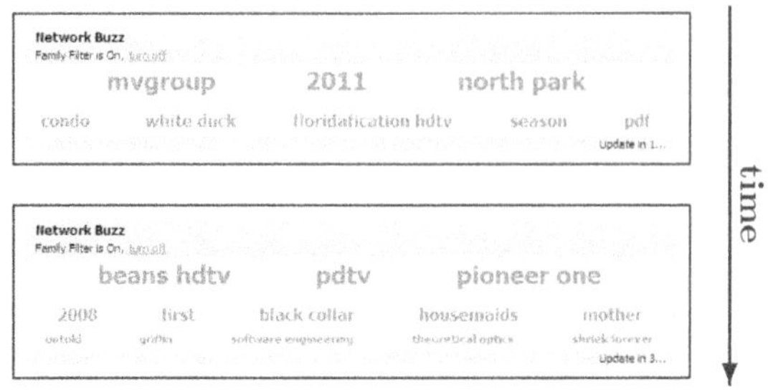

Figure 1: Network term cloud: peer's-eye view (two snapshots of the animated cloud in Tribler)

The network term cloud in Tribler is illustrated in Figure 1, which pictures two frames of the cloud, which is animated. Each frame of the animated term cloud shows for five seconds a random sample of 13 terms from high, medium and low frequency levels represented on three different tiers. The design decision to include three levels of frequency enhances the user's impression of the network content as evolving, since new terms are low frequency and would be completely excluded from the cloud, had frequency been the sole criterion for inclusion in the cloud. We restrict ourselves here mentioning the tiers, but do not investigate them further in the current work. The network term cloud can be observed live by downloading and installing Tribler; as an alternative we provide a demonstration video: http://youtu.be/hZeQlf5V8tA.

4. LIVE TERM DISCOVERY EXPERIMENT

The first aspect of the network term cloud we investigate is *coverage*. We carry out a live experiment within the Tribler network whose aim is to discover whether peer's-eye views of the network are mutually exclusive or whether the coverage of terms accumulated at a peer is substantial enough to support the generation of a cloud representing the overall content of the network. We acquired filenames at each of a pool of 30 peers under our control during their normal operation within the P2P system over an extended period of time (ca. 671 hours) and extracted terms from them. The 30 peers were started in succession on a single machine, joined the network, and only executed Buddycast to discover new peers and new content. Our peers did not initiate any downloads and did not build up a download profile. In this way, we ensured that they only connected to random and not semantically similar peers, as mentioned above. During the whole experiment they did not leave the system.

In Figure 2, discovery of terms from filenames is illustrated over time for the first four hours of the experiment.

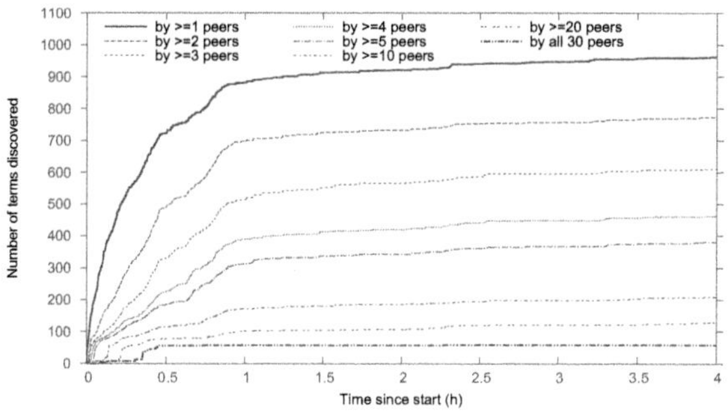

Figure 2: Peer-level discovery of terms over time

Each line represents the intersection of the number of terms discovered by a given number of peers, with the bottom line showing terms discovered by all peers. This figure yields several important insights. First, peers are far from discovering mutually exclusive term sets in the network, but rather a large overlap can be seen between the term sets that accumulate at the individual peers. Recall, that it is not possible to collect a complete global view of network content and that we approximate this view using the pool of peers under our control. In particular, we assume that terms discovered by at least one of the peers are representative of the overall content of the system. Figure 2 shows that peers in our pool discover a substantial proportion of the global term set. Second, the system does not reach a steady state, but rather the number of terms discovered by a single peer keeps growing and the other peers never converge with respect to the composition of their term sets. The growth reflects the constant entry of new content into the system. Although only the first four hours are pictured in Figure 2, the parallel growth trend is displayed during the entire collection interval of ca. 671 hours. Note that the flatness of the lowest lines in Figure 2 before ca. 0.4 hours can be attributed to the sequential startup of the peers. In order to get better insight on the early startup phase of peers, we will return later to investigate term accumulation immediately after the cold start of a peer.

We carried out an additional analysis to investigate the nature of those terms that are discovered by some peers, and thus assumed to belong to the global view, but not by others. In particular, we are interested in determining whether individual peers are likely to miss high frequency terms, under the assumption that such terms are the most important for characterizing the network-level collection. Figure 3 plots the probability that a term will fail to be discovered by one of the peers in our pool against the global frequency of that term estimated using the peer pool at two time-points in the life of a peer: a relatively immature (4 hours) and a mature (24 hours) stage. The exact times were chosen according to Tribler-specific considerations: four hours is the smallest resolution with which we can observe peers entering and leaving the network and 24 hours is the point at which Tribler considers the startup phase to have ended and switches messaging to a lower rate. We use Figure 3 to draw important general conclusions. First, it can be seen that the terms the most likely to be missed are in general low frequency terms. For high frequency terms, the miss probability approaches zero. Second, although the mature peer has fewer terms with high miss probabilities, the difference with the immature peer is not staggering, suggesting that the discovery process is already effective early in the life of a peer. In sum, the 'peer's-eye' view does not vary radically from peer to peer and does well in approximating the 'bird's-eye' view, generally missing a relatively restricted set of lower frequency terms.

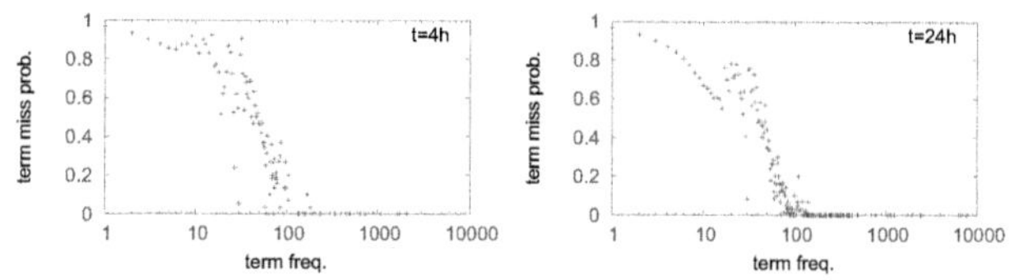

Figure 3: Term discovery failure vs. term frequency

5. USER STUDY

The second aspect of the network term cloud we investigate is *usefulness*. We performed a user study to investigate the question of whether term clouds can act as a surrogate for user experience with Tribler. We measure understanding of the collection in terms of the ability of a user to classify a file as either available or not available in Tribler. Informal observation of user interaction patterns provides evidence that a preponderance of Tribler queries correspond to known item search needs. We assume that the ability of a user to predict the availability of a file in Tribler reflects the ability to formulate successful searches.

We carried out experiments using Amazon Mechanical Turk (http://www.mturk.com), a crowdsourcing platform providing access to a pool of workers. Details of the study design and set up, including the crowdsourcing quality control mechanism to ensure serious user study participants, are described in [9]. The study investigates two conditions: `no-cloud`, in which the subject is presented with a mockup and a basic description of the system, and `with-cloud`, in which the subject is additionally presented with a series of five term clouds, such as they would be viewed (in animated sequence) in the system. The clouds were selected randomly using the set of terms that had been discovered after four hours by a typical peer chosen from our peer pool.

The file list we ask the subjects of the user study to classify consists of 100 filenames, half drawn from the Tribler system and half fake. The fake filenames were generated to represent types of content that were chosen by a panel of 'expert' users with extensive Tribler experience. They correspond to five categories clearly not represented in the Tribler system: 'home videos', 'news' and 'how-to videos', 'commercials' and 'sports'. The real filenames represented types of potentially findable content: 'TV', 'movies', 'music', 'software' and 'books'. The basis of the fake filenames were titles of existing videos from popular websites and titles of news items. The titles were modified to resemble the filenames of the real files, such that the difference between the two was disguised. This was done by adding plausible group names, format extensions and format specifications to the title.

In total, 184 workers took part in the user study, making a total of 4000 classification decisions divided over the 100 filenames. Subjects were first offered the `no-cloud` and then the `with-cloud` condition; they could participate in one or both conditions—offering this option effectively gave us access to more subjects. The filenames in each condition were mutually exclusive, but chosen to be comparable.

Table 1: User filename prediction (%correct)

	no-cloud	with-cloud
real	57.0%	63.1%
TV	66.3%	63.8%
movies	59.5%	69.5%†
music	59.5%	65.5%
software	50.5%	63.5%†
books	45.0%	55.0%†
fake	51.9%	52.1%
home videos	53.5%	49.5%
news	61.5%	61.5%
how-to	55.5%	61.0%
commercials	51.7%	42.5%
sports	33.8%	45.5%†
all	54.5%	57.6%†

† *Statistically significant improvement, Pearson's χ^2 test ($\alpha = 0.05$)*

Accuracy in the `no-cloud` condition was 54.5% and rose to 57.6% in the `with-cloud` condition (Table 1), a significant improvement according to Pearson's χ^2 test ($\alpha = 0.05$). The above-random performance in the `no-cloud` condition reflects assumptions that the users make about the content of the system from their prior file-sharing experience and the short description of the task. Out of 92 workers, 28 explicitly referred to the cloud when they were asked to justify one of their classification decisions, confirming that the clouds were consulted. Statistically significant improvements of the `with-cloud` over the `no-cloud` condition were observed in four categories: 'movies', 'software', 'books' and 'sports'. These results suggest that users do indeed gain an impression of the system content via the term cloud. The effect measured here is subtle, however, combined with aspects not yet studied here (e.g., use of cloud to support browsing, volume of user clicks) has a potential to increase user satisfaction with the system. Gains in specific categories less conventionally associated with file sharing (e.g., books) make term clouds particularly valuable for our P2P system.

6. COLD START ANALYSIS

The final aspect of the network term cloud we investigate is *accumulation speed*. We examine the cold start phase of five example peers from our pool with the aim of gaining an impression of the potential of very young clouds to be helpful to users, an issue assumed to be important for retention of new Tribler users. Our analysis procedure is based on the insight that it is not necessary for two clouds to be exactly identical in order to be equally useful to the user. For this reason, we concentrate not on the identities of cloud terms, but rather on their semantic diversity. We take diversity to reflect the ability of the clouds to convey an impression of the variety and scope of the content available in the network. We assume that certain terms in the cloud trigger users to infer the presence of certain types of content in the system. In particular, we focus on the categories of content known to exist in the system and used in the user study. For each of the terms in example clouds from our five peers, we make a best guess on which category it might reflect. In the case of TV vs. movies, it is often difficult to make a single best guess and in this case we label the term with a combined TV/movie category. Figure 4 shows the distribution of the terms over the categories in the clouds at four points along the life of the peer (2min, 10min, 4h and 24h). Between 2min and 10min clouds become mature enough to contain a full set of 13 terms. Although not all categories are present in the youngest (2min) clouds, the diversity is still good. Further, clouds at peers older than 10min are not radically more diverse, suggesting that very young clouds can be just as effective as mature clouds.

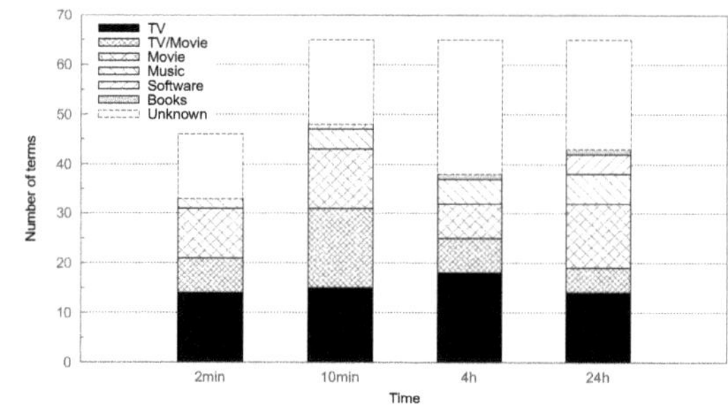

Figure 4: Semantic diversity of term clouds

7. CONCLUSION AND OUTLOOK

We have demonstrated that information aggregated at a single peer within a distributed system is adequate to support generation of term clouds that provide a user with useful information about the content of the system. Since the Tribler client attracts heavy use—it has been downloaded more than 800,000 times within the last five years—even a small or modest improvement in users' understanding of the system has the potential to lead to a large impact in terms of improved query success and better user experience. Further, communication of an impression of the global content of a P2P network to users is critical as P2P moves into new domains, since it helps users to quickly shake outdated assumptions about the nature of the items being shared by file sharing. Future work will involve analysis of the click behavior of users interacting with the term cloud and will shed light on the details of cloud use, particularly on the ability of clouds to support browsing and discovery and to improve the retention of new users of the system.

8. ACKNOWLEDGMENTS

The research leading to these results has received funding from the European Commission's 7th Framework Programme under grant agreement N° 216444 (PetaMedia).

9. REFERENCES

[1] B. Cohen. Incentives build robustness in BitTorrent. In *Workshop on Economics of Peer-to-Peer systems*, 2003.

[2] P. Costa et al. Exploring the interdisciplinary connections of gossip-based systems. *ACM SIGOPS Operating Systems Review*, 41(5):51–60, 2007.

[3] O. Görlitz, S. Sizov, and S. Staab. PINTS: Peer-to-Peer Infrastructure for Tagging Systems. In *International Conference on Peer-to-Peer Systems*. USENIX, 2008.

[4] R. Kaptein, D. Hiemstra, and J. Kamps. How different are language models and word clouds? In *ECIR 2010*, volume 5993 of *LNCS*, pages 556–568, Berlin, March 2010.

[5] E. K. Lua et al. A survey and comparison of peer-to-peer overlay network schemes. *Communications Surveys & Tutorials, IEEE*, 7(2), 2005.

[6] J. Pouwelse et al. Buddycast: an operational peer-to-peer epidemic protocol stack. In *ASCI 2008*.

[7] J. Pouwelse et al. Tribler: A social-based peer-to-peer system. *Concurrency and Computation: Practice and Experience*, 20(2), 2008.

[8] J. Sinclair and M. Cardew-Hall. The folksonomy tag cloud: when is it useful? *J Inf Sci*, 34(1), 2008.

[9] R. Vliegendhart, M. Larson, C. Kofler, C. Eickhoff, and J. Pouwelse. Investigating Factors Influencing Crowdsourcing Tasks with High Imaginative Load. In *WSDM'11 Workshop on Crowdsourcing for Search and Data Mining*, February 2011.

RerankEverything: A Reranking Interface for Exploring Search Results

Takehiro Yamamoto Satoshi Nakamura Katsumi Tanaka

Department of Social Informatics, Graduate School of Informatics, Kyoto University
Yoshida-Honmachi, Sakyo, Kyoto 606-8501, Japan
+81-75-753-5969
{tyamamot, nakamura, tanaka}@dl.kuis.kyoto-u.ac.jp

ABSTRACT

This paper proposes a system called "RerankEverything", which enables users to rerank search results in any search service, such as a Web search engine, an e-commerce site, a hotel reservation site, and so on. This system helps users explore diverse search results. In conventional search services, interactions between users and systems are quite limited and complicated. By using RerankEverything, users can interactively explore search results in accordance with their interests by reranking search results from various viewpoints. Experimental results show that our system potentially help users search more proactively. When using our system, users were more likely to click search results that were initially low ranked. Users also browsed through more diverse search results by reranking search results after giving various types of feedback with our system.

Categories and Subject Descriptors

H.5.2 **[Information Interfaces and Presentation]**: User Interfaces – *Graphical user interfaces, Interaction styles.*

General Terms: Design, Human Factors.

Keywords: Search user interfaces, information retrieval, reranking interaction.

1. INTRODUCTION

People access the World Wide Web for various purposes, such as acquiring knowledge, purchasing something, making travel plans, reserving hotels, or just watching interesting videos. To find the desired information, people use many kinds of search services such as Web search engines, e-commerce sites, hotel reservation sites, video sharing sites, and so on. When using a search service, users usually issue a query to it. The service then selects contents from its index, ranks them in accordance with its own criteria, and finally displays them as search results. These search services have become important information resources for many people.

However, it is not always easy for users to obtain satisfactory information from search results because of the following problems:

- It is difficult for users to come up with appropriate queries that clearly describe their information needs. Since users' information needs are often not clearly defined, their queries are often too short and ambiguous. Therefore, it is difficult for search services to estimate users' information needs from only the received queries and rank results in ways that will satisfy all users.
- Some services provide advanced search functions such as filtering or sorting, so that users can refine search results in accordance with their needs. However, such functions are provided only by the *service-side*: a user cannot filter or sort search results from a certain viewpoint if a service does not provide such a function. Moreover, advanced search functions are not easy for most users to use because these interfaces are often complicated. In addition, the interfaces differ depending on the services.

Consequently, interactions between users and services are limited and complicated. This fundamental problem limits users to browsing search results passively. When the user's information needs are not well defined, it is especially important for the user to iteratively search and browse information [2]. If users were able to flexibly refine search results on the basis of their own criteria, they could obtain more useful content in accordance with their interests. Our goal is to realize such a *user-side* interactive search system.

In this paper, we propose a system called *RerankEverything*, which enables users to rerank search results in any search service. In the system, users can intuitively rerank results by simply selecting an interesting term, or a numeric value of a search result. Our system provides users not only the reranking interface, but also a tag cloud to encourage users to explore search results from various viewpoints, and a simple interface to specify an html element that contains a search result to recognize structures of the search results page.

2. SYSTEM ARCHITECTURE

We implemented our system (*http://rerank.jp/rerankeverything.xpi*) as an extension to the Mozilla Firefox Web browser. Our system mainly consists of three components.

2.1 Reranking Interface

In our system, users can give both term-based feedback and numerical feedback by using the same interaction style, simply selecting an interesting part of a search result (Figure 1). When a user selects a certain term and presses the promote/demote button, the system then reranks the results by promoting/demoting results that contain the selected term. Similarly, a user can sort search results according to a selected numerical attribute.

Figure 2 illustrates how the user reranks search results on a search results page of Google Scholar, a search engine specializing in academic publications. First, the user issues the query "pseudo relevance feedback". Then, the user starts browsing search results

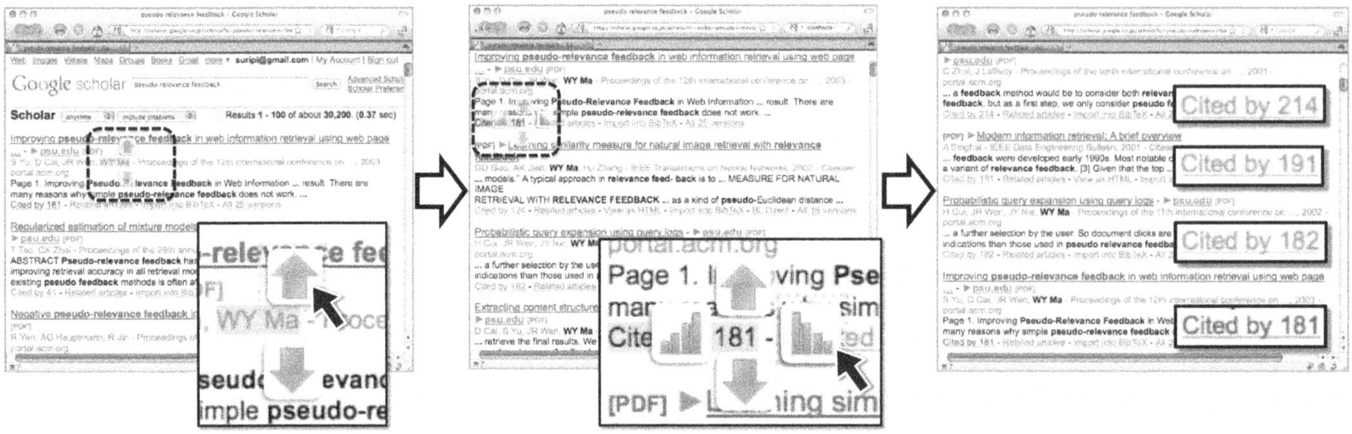

Figure 2. Reranking publication results with both term-based and numerical feedback in publication search. Users can give both term-based and numerical feedback to system and rerank search results by simply selecting area of interest and clicking appropriate button.

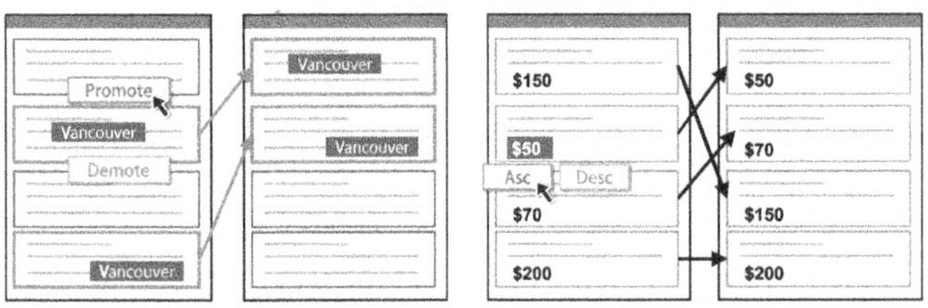

Figure 1. Reranking search results using direct interaction.

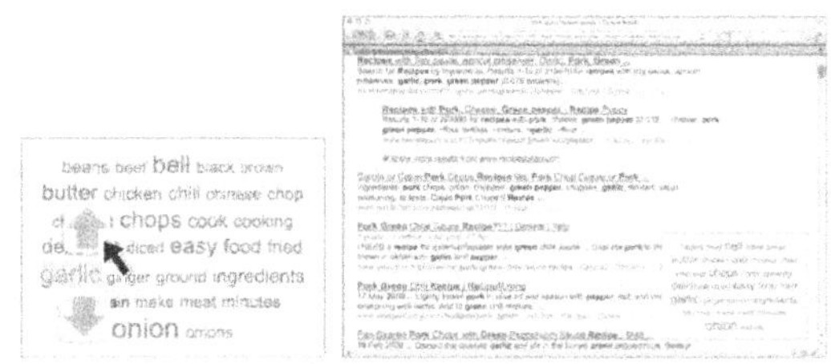

Figure 3. Example *TermCloud* for Web search results of query "pork green pepper recipes".

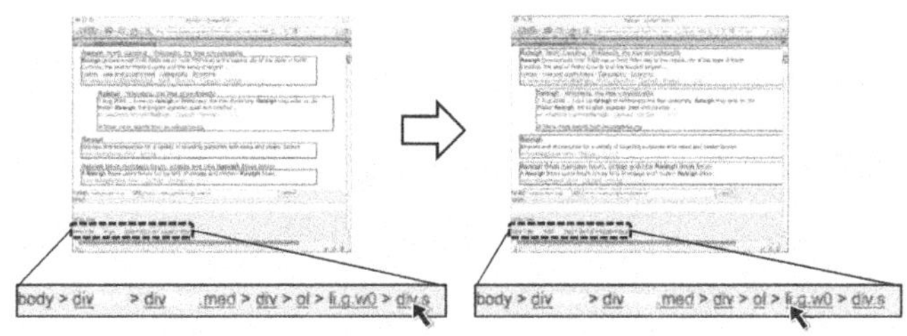

Figure 4. Wrapper generation interface.

and takes an interested in papers authored by Wei-Ying Ma. The user selects "WY Ma" and presses the promote button to promote search results containing "WY Ma". If the user wants to browse papers in descending order of the citation counts, the user selects "Cited by 181" (in this case, the user can select just "181" to sort results) in the search results, and the system then displays four buttons with which to rerank them. After the user clicks the descending button, the system sorts the search results in accordance with the number of citations, as shown on the right-hand image in Figure 2.

In this way, users can interactively rerank search results in accordance with their interests. Google Scholar does not provide search functions to sort results in accordance with the citation counts, although it does display these counts in the search results. Our system thus enables users to sort using this attribute even when the service does not provide such a sorting function.

2.2 TermCloud

To encourage users to explore search results from various viewpoints, our system displays *TermCloud*, which are generated from terms that frequently appear in search results. Users can give term-based feedback and rerank search results by simply clicking a term in a *TermCloud*. Figure 3 shows an example of a *TermCloud* of Web search results for the query "pork green pepper recipes." In that case, the system displays some terms that are related to cooking like "garlic", "onion", "Chinese", "easy" and so on. Because a *TermCloud* might bring interesting and various terms in search results to the attention of users, we expect users will be more likely to find valuable and diverse search results.

2.3 Wrapper Generation Interface

The number of existing search services is huge and the structures of search results vary according to the services. To detect a structure of search results in an HTML source of a target page, we need to prepare wrappers for each service. Our system provides an interface to generate wrappers based on simple user interactions. The interface also works interactively inside a Web browser and requires no special knowledge of DOM, JavaScript, XPath, etc.

Our idea is to visualize nodes that the system currently recognizes as search results while a user moves the mouse cursor. Figure 4 illustrates how a user would generate a wrapper that works on the Google Web search engine. As the user moves the mouse cursor, the system displays visual feedback by forms of rectangle indicating which nodes the system recognizes as search results.

3. USER STUDY

To investigate how our system affects users' search behavior, we conducted two user studies. The first evaluated the usefulness of our system compared with the conventional search service in the specific search task. The second investigated how users use our system in their daily browsing.

3.1 Task-based Study

To evaluate how our reranking interaction supports users seeking information, we conducted a user study. We think our reranking interaction become important when the user's information needs are not well defined and the user needs to browse search results from diverse viewpoints. Therefore, we prepared such search tasks and compared the effectiveness of performing the tasks between our system and conventional search services.

We recruited eight students from our university as participants: four graduate students, and four undergraduate students. All were male. The subjects did our experiment individually. In the study, we first asked the subjects to watch a three-minute-long instruction video (*http://rerank.jp/everything/demo.mp4*) that explained how to rerank search results. After they watched the video, we asked the subjects to visit a Web search engine and spend five minutes learning how to use our system. Then we asked the subjects to perform the following tasks:

- You are seeking recipes for tomorrow's dinner. Use the Web search engine with our system and find as many interesting recipes that contain pork and green pepper as possible in five minutes.
- After that, use the Web search engine without using our system and find as many interesting recipes that contain beef and onion as possible in five minutes.

During the task, when the subjects found a search result that contained information about an interesting recipe, they were asked to double-click it, which changed its background color. In the experiment, if necessary, the subjects were allowed to perform all kinds of interactions that the Web search engine provided, such as following links from search results, modifying their queries, using advanced search options, clicking suggested queries, and so on, regardless of whether they were using our system or not. The wrapper for the Web search engine was prepared in our system in advance so the subjects did not need to create any wrappers.

To prevent the order effect, we divided eight subjects into four groups and changed the order of queries ("pork and green pepper" and "beef and onion") and interfaces for searching for the information ("using our system" and "without using our system".)

3.1.1 Results

From the study, we can see that the numbers of selected search results highly depended on the subjects. For example, one user chose many results (67 results) using our system and another user chose much fewer results (4 results) using our system. Average numbers of search results that subjects selected when using our system were not significantly different from those without using our system t_{14}=0.37, p>.05). However, we can see that 6 out of 8 subjects can find more results when they used our system. These results show that our system could support users in finding more interesting results than conventional search engines alone. In the conventional search engines, the ways for users to state their interests are limited to query modification or advanced search options. On the other hand, in addition to these functions, users can state their interests by selecting or clicking terms in the search results and TermCloud by using our system. Thus, users could easily collect search results that contain interesting terms like ingredients and adjectives by performing reranking operations.

When the subjects used only the Web search engine, the average number of query modifications during the task was 0.625 (five query modifications within the whole subjects.) Four modifications were the modifications that the subjective adds some keywords to the previous queries. One modification was the modification that the subject replaces some keywords in the previous query to another keyword. This result indicates that users tend to *narrow down* the information space when they use the Web search engine alone. On the other hand, the average number of reranking operations was 6.25 when they used our system. These results indicate that our system helps users to *explore* search results from diverse viewpoints. Figures 5 and 6 respectively show the distributions of initial ranks of search results that the subjects judged to be interesting with and without using our system. The initial rank of a search result means the rank of the search result before the subjects performed any reranking operation. Comparing the results in Figures 5 and 6, we found that the subjects were more likely to find originally low-ranked search results by using our system. These low-ranked search results are usually hard to find by using only conventional search engines. This result indicates that when using our system, users are more likely to browse different search results by reranking search results, even if they issue the same query. Although the tasks in this study were limited and the number of subjects was small, the results of this study indicate that our system can potentially enable users to search more proactively. In the future, we plan to conduct this kind of study with more diverse search tasks and more diverse subjects.

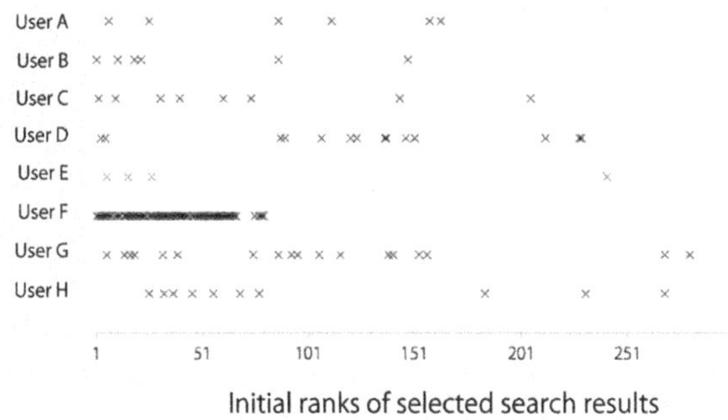

Figure 5. Distributions of initial ranks of selected search results (using our system).

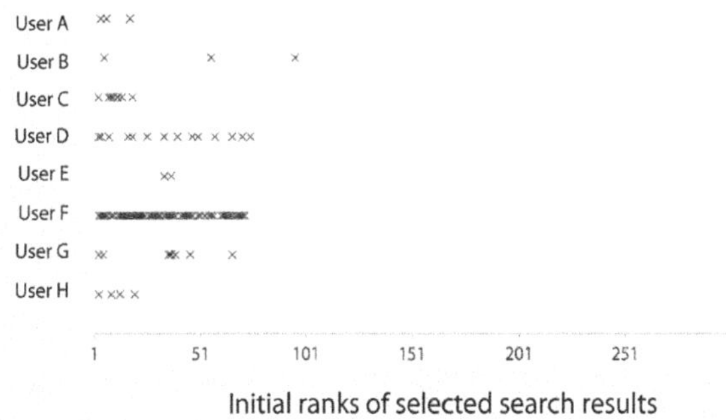

Figure 6. Distributions of initial ranks of selected search results (without using our system).

3.2 Longitudinal use of Our System

Second, to evaluate how our system would affect users' daily search behavior, we conducted a user study. The purpose of this study was to investigate how users interacted with various search results in our system.

Seven subjects participated in this study. Two subjects had participated in the experiments discussed in the previous user study. Of the remaining five subjects, four were graduate students and one was a faculty member of the university. All subjects were active Web researchers and reported using Firefox as their default Web browser.

In the study, we first asked the subjects to watch the instruction video described above. After they watched the video, we asked them to install our prototype system on their Firefox browser for the user study. The system already contained several wrappers for major search services such as Google, Yahoo!, Bing, Amazon, and so on. The subjects were allowed to use our system for seven days. In the study, we did not impose any specific search tasks on the subjects. We asked the subjects to freely use our system since we wanted to investigate how our system would affect users' daily search behavior.

3.2.1 Results

During the test period, we collected 408 reranking operations from the subjects. The distribution of the types of reranking operation and the areas where users performed reranking operations are shown in Table 1. From the results, we can observe that about 70% of the reranking operations were promotion operations. One subject performed promotion operations eight times on one search results page. On the other hand, demotion operations were rarely used. As much literature has explained [1], it was difficult for users to give negative feedback. The total queries issued to search engines were 452, and 17.7% queries were reranked. We think this percentage is not small since most queries that were not reranked were navigational query and users did not need to rerank search results.

Half of the term-based feedback was done in the TermCloud area. This indicates the TermCloud was effective in suggesting terms for reranking search results. When the subjects used Web search engines, 62% (94/151) of term-feedbacks were performed in TermCloud. On the other hand, when the subjects used other search services, such as publication search service and e-commerce sites, only 32% (51/150) of term-feedbacks were performed in TermCloud. Web search results consisted of more unstructured text such as titles and snippets, so the subjects might have had difficulty in finding interesting terms from the search results. Therefore, for Web searching, the subjects selected terms in TermCloud rather than in search results. Moreover, such unstructured text contains various terms, so TermClouds generated from Web search results could display unexpected and interesting terms to the subjects.

Numerical feedback was used for various services such as e-commerce sites, publication sites, video sharing sites, and so on. For example, the number of views and the uploaded dates were used on video sharing sites to sort video search results. The citation count and the publication year were often used on publication search services. For Web searching, some subjects tried to sort search results using numerical feedback. For example, one subject issued the query "iPod" and sorted search results by selecting "64GB" in a search result. Thus the search results containing "160GB" were reranked higher. In this way, our dynamic attribute extraction method allowed the subjects to utilize Web search results as ad hoc structured resources. Overall, however, the subjects rarely used numerical feedback in Web searching (only 22 times). We think this was because sorting Web search results was an unfamiliar task for the subjects and it was not easy for them to find appropriate numerical attributes from unstructured Web search results. Moreover, our extraction method is simple, so it often fails to extract correct attributes from Web search engines. To address these problems, we plan to develop some kinds of TermCloud-like suggestion systems that will suggest numerical attributes for sorting search results and a more sophisticated extraction method using surrounding text of the selected text.

Table 1. Distributions of reranking operations.

	Reranking operation types				
	Term-based		Numerical		
Reranked Area	Pro mote	De mote	Asc	Desc	Total
Search results	138	18	15	92	263
TermCloud	131	14	-	-	145
Total	269	32	15	92	408

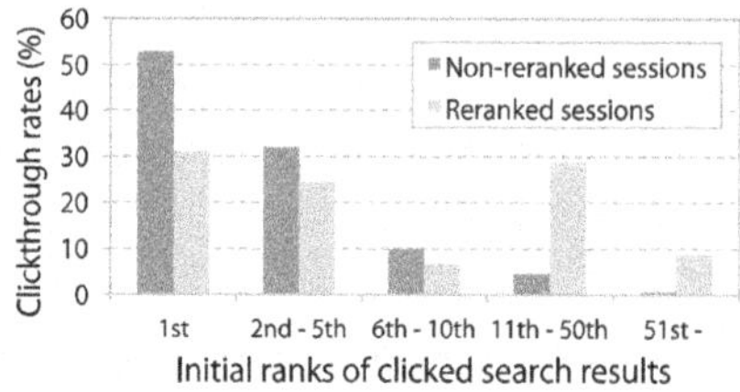

Figure 7. Comparison of clickthrough rates.

Finally, to investigate what kind of search results the subjects clicked, we measured the clickthrough rates in our system. To evaluate the effectiveness of reranking, we divided all sessions into two groups: non-reranked sessions and reranked sessions. To detect a session unit, when a subject visited a search result page, our system automatically assigned a session ID to the page. Non-reranked sessions represent sessions in which the subjects did not perform any reranking. Reranked sessions represent sessions in which the subjects performed at least one reranking. Figure 7 shows the clickthrough rates obtained from these two groups. We found the results to be similar to those from the previous study.

4. CONCLUSION

We have developed and evaluated a system called "RerankEverything", which provides unified and simple interaction techniques to enable users to rerank search results. Our experimental results showed that our system enables users to browse and explore search results more proactively. From system logs of the user study, we found that users reranked search results from various viewpoints and that they were more likely to click initially low-ranked search results when using our system. These kinds of search activities can potentially help users find more diverse information.

5. ACKNOWLEDGMENTS

This work was supported in part by Grant-in-Aid for JSPS Fellows (#09J55302), Grant-in-Aid for challenging Exploratory Research (#22650018), Grant-in-Aid for Young Scientists (A) (#23680006), and by "Informatics Education and Research Center for Knowledge-Circulating Society" (Project Leader: Katsumi Tanaka, MEXT Global COE Program, Kyoto University).

6. REFERENCES

[1] N.J. Belkin, C. Cool, D. Kelly, S.J. Lin, S.Y Park, J. Perez-Carballo and C. Sikora. Iterative exploration, design and evaluation of support for query reformulation in interactive information retrieval. *Information Processing and Management*, 37(3), pp. 404–434, 2001.

[2] R.W. White and R. Roth. Exploratory search: beyond the query-response paradigm. *Synthesis Lectures on Information Concepts, Retrieval, and Services*, 1(1), pp. 1–98, 2009.

HealthTrust: Trust-based Retrieval of YouTube's Diabetes Channels

Luis Fernandez-Luque
Northern Research Institute & Computer Science Department, University of Tromsø
Tromsø, Norway
luis.luque@norut.no

Randi Karlsen
Computer Science Department, University of Tromsø & Northern Research Institute
Tromsø, Norway
randi@cs.uit.no

Genevieve B Melton
Institute for Health Informatics
University of Minnesota
Minneapolis, USA
gmelton@umn.edu

ABSTRACT

The Internet has become one of the main sources of consumer health information. Health consumers have access to ever-growing health information resources, especially since the rise of the Social Media. For example, over 20.000 videos have been uploaded by American hospitals on to YouTube. To find health videos is challenging because of factors like tags spamming and misleading information. Previous studies have found difficulties when searching for good health videos in YouTube, including false information (e.g., herbal cures for diabetes or cancer).

Our objective was to extract information about the trustworthiness of the diabetes YouTube's channels using link analysis of the diabetes online community by developing an algorithm, called HealthTrust, based on Hyperlink-Induced Topic Search (HITS) for ranking the most authoritative diabetes channels. The ranked list of channels from HealthTrust was compared with the list of the most relevant diabetes channels from YouTube. Two healthcare professionals made a blinded classification of channels based on whether they would recommend the channel to a patient. HealthTrust performed better for retrieving channels recommended by the professional reviewers. HealthTrust performed several times better than YouTube for filtering out the worst channels (i.e., those not recommended by any expert reviewer).

Categories and Subject Descriptors

J.3 [**Life and Medical Sciences**]: Health; H.3.3 [**Information Search and Retrieval**]: Content Analysis and Indexing

General Terms

Algorithms

Keywords

Health, Videos, YouTube, Information Retrieval, Diabetes, Social Media, Health Informatics

1. INTRODUCTION

The main source of health information for people in many countries is the Internet [1, 2]. Many health authorities, hospitals and patients are publishing online health information. Increasingly, health information content is being disseminated through social media platforms (e.g., blogs, YouTube, Twitter) [3]. For example, there are hundreds of American hospitals that have uploaded over 20,000 videos on YouTube.

Despite the vast amount of health videos in YouTube, finding relevant online health videos is not an easy task. One of the main problems of health information content on the Internet is finding trustworthy sources that do not contain misleading or bogus information. Sadly, misleading information such as herbal cures for cancer is very common [4, 5, 6] . In one extreme example, it can be easier to find videos or websites promoting anorexia as a lifestyle than reliable content about this devastating disease[5]. Therefore, there is a need for robust information retrieval approaches that filter out this type of misleading content or spam.

Over the past several years, many different approaches have been applied to assist health consumers in finding online health resources [7, 8]. Many different projects and studies are highlighting difficulties in retrieving good health information[7, 8, 9, 10]. A very common approach is the creation of quality labels for trustworthy websites. These websites are largely manually evaluated and, in a few cases, incorporated with automatic approaches, which extract metadata about content quality [7, 8]. In most cases, the "quality" of health information has been focused on the accuracy of the information and not other parameters such as likeability.

Manual or semi-automatic approaches face problems of scalability in the current environment of expanding online content and information overload. To our knowledge, link analysis has not been explored to retrieve online health information for health consumers. However, several new European projects (i.e., Meco [11] and Khresmoi [12]) are exploring new information retrieval techniques for online medical content.

In the area of web information retrieval several techniques have been developed based on link analysis (e.g., Hyperlink-Induced Topic Search (HITS) [13] and PageRank [14]) and more recently trust-based approaches (e.g., TrustRank [15]).

Those approaches are not adapted to the particularities of health information retrieval. For example, it is common that when searching health information, very popular content (e.g., content featuring a celebrity) is highly ranked but it is not relevant from a health point of view.

Additionally, many information retrieval algorithms are designed to avoid the problem of the "Tightly Knit Community Effect" (TKCE) [16]. In many cases, it has been believed that the links within those communities may decrease the quality of search algorithms. We hypothesize that in the health domain the situation may be the opposite and the TKCE effect is not negative. In fact, online communities of patients can be very effective in filtering misleading information [17]. Our main research question is whether trust-based metrics, such as HITS' authoritativeness, within a health community can improve information retrieval. We designed a search algorithm, HealthTrust, that is an adaptation of HITS to increase the effect of the TKCE of health communities.

This paper is structured as follows. In the "Related Work" section we provide an overview of health information retrieval and web information retrieval. In the next sections, we present our approach and the evaluation of "HealthTrust" for finding relevant health channels from the online community of diabetes in YouTube.

2. RELATED WORK

Search engines are widely used by Internet users. Currently most search engines leverage the graph structure of the web, using link analysis as the main source of information about reputable sites. Most of those techniques are inspired by mathematical graph theory and social network analysis where web sites are part of an interlinked graph.

One of the earliest successes in search engines was the algorithm PageRank [14]. In PageRank, a score is given to all Internet nodes based on their prestige, measured by the number of links pointing at the node. The main advantage of PageRank is that it can be calculated prior to query time. Another popular algorithm for web search is HITS [13]. With HITS, nodes are given two scores: "authorities" and "hubs". In HITS, values of incoming links are not the same for all nodes; if the link comes from an authority it will have more value than a link from a less prestigious node. HITS needs to be calculated at query time and therefore it is not the best solution for large data sets.

Many other approaches have been tested since the introduction of HITS and PageRank, especially to address new challenges of the web (e.g., spamming). Some of those are exploring the trust of the nodes in order to make the rankings, such as TrustRank [15]. TrustRank is based on a white list of websites that have been evaluated by experts, so it is not a fully automatic approach.

Health information retrieval is not an easy domain for most web search engines. Reputation based on incoming links can lead to inadvertently highly ranking of harmful content. Polemic content (e.g., anti vaccination, bogus cures for cancer) tends to be highly ranked [4, 5, 6] since this content can have many incoming links for reasons other than having useful health information.

A traditional approach in the health domain is to rely on expert evaluation. Certified websites can get "quality labels" after a manual review process. One problem of manual approaches is how to cope with the current information overload situation and expansion of the Internet, requiring a scalable solution. A few projects are addressing the automatic extraction of different quality features about health websites for information retrieval purposes [11, 7, 8, 12, 9], but to our knowledge none of them have focused on social media and link analysis.

Outside the health domain, there have been several studies of online communities and reputation in YouTube. Yo-Sub et al. analyzed the reputation of end users in YouTube [18]. Siersdorsfer et al. evaluated an approach to predict the ratings of YouTube comments [19]. Dadvison et al recently published a detailed description of how videos are recommended within YouTube [20]. However, there are no publications about how is implemented the search engine in YouTube.

3. HEALTHTRUST

Although it has been suggested that "Tightly Knit Community Effect" is negative when seeking relevant resources, we believe that in the health domain, the effect can be the opposite. Relevant health videos in YouTube can be "buried" under highly popular videos that are not health related at all. For example, a video about a singer who has diabetes will be highly ranked. Our algorithm HealthTrust is aiming at ranking the search results based on the popularity of the content within a health-related "tightly knit" community. In this study we are exploring the use case of diabetes channels within YouTube.

3.1 Implementation

We tested different link analysis algorithms and configurations before designing our algorithm. Of those HITS had the most promising results and therefore we based our algorithm on an adaptation of HITS. The main reason to avoid testing multiple algorithms in this study is the difficulty to engage healthcare professionals to evaluate the retrieved results.

HealthTrust is an adaptation of the search algorithm HITS. In the HITS, "authoritative" values are calculated at query time and used to rank the search results. In HealthTrust, we calculate the HITS for all the members of a predefined health community. Later, the HITS authoritative scores, which we call HealthTrust, can be used for any query at indexing time.

In HealthTrust, authoritative values will represent the trust on that source within its health community. Our approach in searching content using HealthTrust has several steps. First, "trust" scores are calculated for all content (i.e., videos) and content providers (i.e., video channels) within the community of interest, in our case the diabetes community in YouTube. These scores are then used to rank search results of content.

The starting point for the algorithm HealthTrust is a data set with information about an online community (here the diabetes community in YouTube). In this study we extracted all the channels about diabetes using YouTube Search API. To model the diabetes social network, the channels are considered nodes and their edges are the links between channels (e.g., favorite videos, subscriptions, friendships). Then, we calculate the HITS authority value for all the users on the community. This value that we call HealthTrust is related to the trust of the health community to that channel source. There were several particularities of YouTube videos that were taken into account. For example,

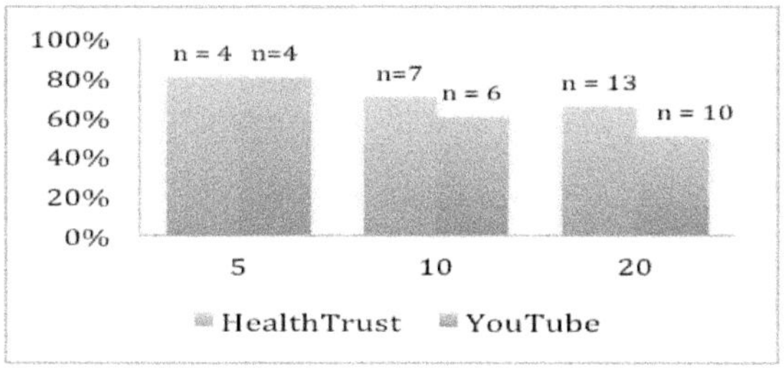

Figure 1: Precision at K (%): channels recommended by both reviewers.

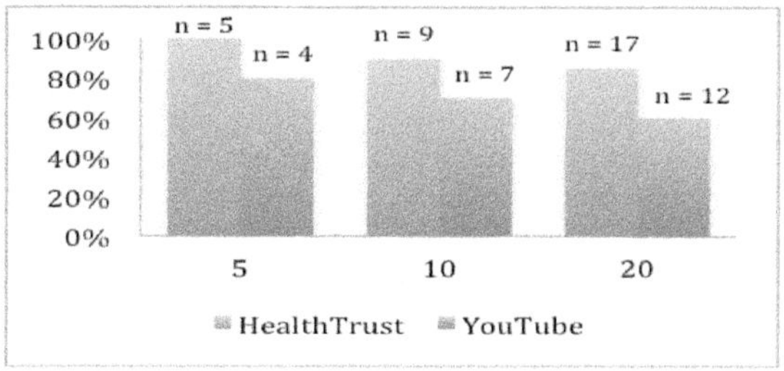

Figure 2: Precision at K (%) for channels recommended by at least one reviewer

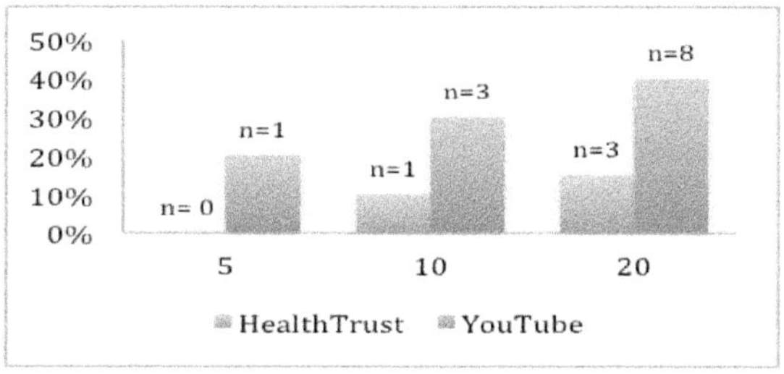

Figure 3: Spam channels (%) for different lists sizes. Channels are not recommended by any of the reviewers.

some channels do not share their favorites or subscriptions or have limited comments in their videos.

HealthTrust scores for videos can also be calculated in a similar approach. In this case, videos are considered also nodes. Favorites and uploads will be edges between channels and videos. Finally, the HealthTrust score of a video will be a combination between the HealthTrust value of the video and its channel. That video HealthTrust score can be used for ranking search results. That possibility is not addressed in this paper, but is part of our future work. As explained in the following section, in this study we are evaluating the correlation between the HealthTrust score of a channel and its likeness of being recommended by a healthcare professional.

4. EVALUATION

In this study, we evaluated our hypothesis that HealthTrust scores for diabetes channels would be a better indicator of relevance compared to diabetes channel rankings in YouTube.

In May 2010, using the YouTube API, we searched all channels with the query diabetes. In total we extracted 219 channels, 182 favorite links, 247 friendships, 106 subscriptions and 5,133 videos from those channels. These channels about diabetes form a community where members are linked by "favorite", "subscriptions", "friendships" and "comments". Using this data set, we calculated HITS scores of channels using the Java Jung API. Edges between channels were subscriptions, favorites and friendships. We discarded as an edge channels favoring their own videos. We define the intra-community HITS authority score as HealthTrust since it reflects trust of the community in that content provider.

We created a data set with the top20 most relevant diabetes channels from YouTube search and the top20 channels with highest HealthTrust. These channels were alphabetically ordered and evaluated by two healthcare professionals. The experts evaluated whether they would recommend the channels to a patient with diabetes or not. Two channels were deleted from YouTube by their account owners before the second reviewer analyzed them, so for those two channels we only took into account scores from the first reviewer.

The lists of top20 channels from YouTube and HealthTrust contained 34 channels. 18 channels were recommended by all reviewers, 6 by half of them and 10 by none of them. The Kappa Cohen value of the reviewers was estimated as 0.61 with a lower and upper boundary of 0.34 and of 0.89 respectively. A Kappa value of 0.61 is considered good agreement.

4.1 Results

We studied the Precision at K (k= 5, 10 and 20) considering that a relevant channel has to be recommended by both professionals. Those channels represent the most relevant channels. As shown in Figure 1, HealthTrust performed better than YouTube channel search. HealthTrust also performed better when considering relevant channels recommended by at least one professional, Figure 2. In most cases, the disagreement between the professionals occurred in channels where authors were patients and not healthcare professionals.

Retrieving spam content with misleading information has a very bad impact in the perceived quality of the retrieved results. Therefore, we compared how many channels were not recommended by any of the experts, Figure 3. In this case, HealthTrust performed much better than YouTube. We observed that many spam channels were selling cures for diabetes or were not health related (e.g., Dance remix). Some of those channels were using many tags and different techniques to get higher ranked in YouTube. For example, the tag "Jonas" (e.g., a famous singer with diabetes) was used in many videos that had nothing to do with the singer. In contrast, high quality videos from health authorities used very few tags.

5. DISCUSSION

There are significant limitations in our study. First of all, we have a very limited data set of evaluated channels so our results are weak from a statistical point of view. In addition, more research is needed to determine if HealthTrust would perform better based on other algorithms such as PageRank. As part of the future work, we will evaluate our approach with more content and patients. That evaluation will address aspects such as efficacy of HealthTrust for retrieving relevant health videos with a larger dataset.

The results of our study show that there is a significant amount of channels highly ranked by YouTube of very low quality (i.e., not recommended by either reviewer) where our

HealthTrust approach performed well for filtering channels with the lowest quality. This finding is coherent with our observations that videos with polemic (e.g., alternative herbal medicine) or funny content (e.g., famous singers videos) are highly popular in the YouTube but not inside the diabetes community. YouTube search, as most information retrieval systems, appears to highly popular content for average users rather than popular content within the tightly knit community (e.g. diabetes community). Therefore, our preliminary results suggest that Tightly Knit Community Effect may help filter out the worst quality content from a health point of view.

We were surprised by the low HealthTrust rank of authoritative channels such as the CDC (Centers for Diseases Control and Prevention). There are many factors involved in this problem. These channels do not promote social interactions (e.g., subscriptions, friendship) as many other channels do. Another reason is that those channels are closer to a more general health-related community than diabetes community. To combine trust analysis from different health-related communities and sub-communities can be an area of future research. Moreover, it remains to be seen if our approach will work in health domain where there is not a large engaged community of users linking each other's content. Another problematic scenario will be a sub-domains where there is a big community of users promoting misleading information. For example, communities promoting anorexia as a lifestyle [5].

6. ACKNOWLEDGMENTS

This project belongs to the Tromsø Telemedicine Laboratory co-funded by the Research Council of Norway, project 174934. The authors would like to thank Prof. Joseph A. Konstan and MD Ignacio Basagoiti for their help.

7. REFERENCES

[1] Fox S. Online health search 2006. Technical report, Pew Internet American Life Project, Washington, DC, October 2006.

[2] Per Egil Kummervold, Catherine E Chronaki, Berthold Lausen, Hans-Ulrich Prokosch, Janne Rasmussen, Silvina Santana, Andrzej Staniszewski, and Silje Camilla Wangberg. ehealth trends in europe 2005-2007: a population-based survey. *J Med Internet Res*, 10(4):e42, 2008.

[3] Jones S Fox S. The social life of health information. Technical report, Pew Internet American Life Project, 2009.

[4] Ambarish Pandey, Nivedita Patni, Mansher Singh, Akshay Sood, and Gayatri Singh. Youtube as a source of information on the h1n1 influenza pandemic. *Am J Prev Med*, 38(3):e1–3, Mar 2010.

[5] Mark L Norris, Katherine M Boydell, Leora Pinhas, and Debra K Katzman. Ana and the internet: a review of pro-anorexia websites. *Int J Eat Disord*, 39(6):443–7, Sep 2006.

[6] Kevin A Ache and Lorraine S Wallace. Human papillomavirus vaccination coverage on youtube. *Am J Prev Med*, 35(4):389–92, Oct 2008.

[7] Miquel Angel Mayer, Vangelis Karkaletsis, Kostas Stamatakis, Angela Leis, Dagmar Villarroel, Christian Thomeczek, Martin Labský, Fernando López-Ostenero, and Timo Honkela. Medieq-quality labelling of medical web content using multilingual information extraction. *Stud Health Technol Inform*, 121:183–90, 2006.

[8] M A Mayer, S J Darmoni, M Fiene, C Köhler, Thomas R Roth-Berghofer, and G Eysenbach. Medcircle: collaboration for internet rating, certification, labelling and evaluation of health information on the world-wide-web. *Stud Health Technol Inform*, 95:667–72, 2003.

[9] Liza Greenberg, Guy D'Andrea, and Dan Lorence. Setting the public agenda for online health search: a white paper and action agenda. *J Med Internet Res*, 6(2):e18, Jun 2004.

[10] Elmer V Bernstam, Muhammad F Walji, Smitha Sagaram, Deepak Sagaram, Craig W Johnson, and Funda Meric-Bernstam. Commonly cited website quality criteria are not effective at identifying inaccurate online information about breast cancer. *Cancer*, 112(6):1206–13, Mar 2008.

[11] Meco project http://meco-project.eu.

[12] Khresmoi project http://www.khresmoi.eu.

[13] Jon M. Kleinberg. Authoritative sources in a hyperlinked environment. *J. ACM*, 46:604–632, September 1999.

[14] Lawrence Page, Sergey Brin, Rajeev Motwani, and Terry Winograd. The pagerank citation ranking: Bringing order to the web. Technical Report 1999-66, Stanford InfoLab, November 1999. Previous number = SIDL-WP-1999-0120.

[15] Zoltán Gyöngyi, Hector Garcia-Molina, and Jan Pedersen. Combating web spam with trustrank. In *Proceedings of the Thirtieth international conference on Very large data bases - Volume 30*, VLDB '04, pages 576–587. VLDB Endowment, 2004.

[16] R. Lempel and S. Moran. The stochastic approach for link-structure analysis (salsa) and the tkc effect. *Comput. Netw.*, 33:387–401, June 2000.

[17] Adol Esquivel, Funda Meric-Bernstam, and Elmer V Bernstam. Accuracy and self correction of information received from an internet breast cancer list: content analysis. *BMJ*, 332(7547):939–42, Apr 2006.

[18] Yo-Sub Han, Laehyun Kim, and Jeong-Won Cha. Evaluation of user reputation on youtube. In *Proceedings of the 3d International Conference on Online Communities and Social Computing: Held as Part of HCI International 2009*, OCSC '09, pages 346–353, Berlin, Heidelberg, 2009. Springer-Verlag.

[19] Stefan Siersdorfer, Sergiu Chelaru, Wolfgang Nejdl, and Jose San Pedro. How useful are your comments?: analyzing and predicting youtube comments and comment ratings. In *Proceedings of the 19th international conference on World wide web*, WWW '10, pages 891–900, New York, NY, USA, 2010. ACM.

[20] James Davidson, Benjamin Liebald, Junning Liu, Palash Nandy, Taylor Van Vleet, Ullas Gargi, Sujoy Gupta, Yu He, Mike Lambert, Blake Livingston, and Dasarathi Sampath. The youtube video recommendation system. In *Proceedings of the fourth ACM conference on Recommender systems*, RecSys '10, pages 293–296, New York, NY, USA, 2010. ACM.

Item Categorization in the e-Commerce Domain

Dan Shen
eBay Research Labs
No. 88 KeYuan Rd
Shanghai, China
dashen@ebay.com

Jean-David Ruvini
eBay Research Labs
2005 E Hamilton Ave
San Jose, CA 95125
jruvini@ebay.com

Manas Somaiya
eBay Research Labs
2005 E Hamilton Ave
San Jose, CA 95125
msomaiya@ebay.com

Neel Sundaresan
eBay Research Labs
2005 E Hamilton Ave
San Jose, CA 95125
nsundaresan@ebay.com

ABSTRACT

Hierarchical classification is a challenging problem yet bears a broad application in real-world tasks. Item categorization in the ecommerce domain is such an example. In a large-scale industrial setting such as eBay, a vast amount of items need to be categorized into a large number of leaf categories, on top of which a complex topic hierarchy is defined. Other than the scale challenges, item data is extremely sparse and skewed distributed over categories, and exhibits heterogeneous characteristics across categories. A common strategy for hierarchical classification is the "gates-and-experts" methods, where a high-level classification is made first (the gates), followed by a low-level distinction (the experts). In this paper, we propose to leverage domain-specific feature generation and modeling techniques to greatly enhance the classification accuracy of the experts. In particular, we innovatively derive features to encode various rich domain knowledge and linguistic hints, and then adapt a SVM-based model to distinguish several very confusing category groups appeared as the performance bottleneck of a currently deployed live system at eBay. We use illustrative examples and empirical results to demonstrate the effectiveness of our approach, particularly the merit of smartly designed domain-specific features.

Categories and Subject Descriptors

H.4 [**Information Systems Applications**]: Miscellaneous

General Terms

Algorithms

Keywords

Product, Accessory, Classification, Catalog

CIKM'11, October 24–28, 2011, Glasgow, Scotland, UK.

1. INTRODUCTION

Online commerce has gained popularity since the past decade. eBay, one of the largest online C2C marketplaces, features a very large and long-tail inventory with millions of items entered into the marketplace everyday. To manage items effectively and help buyers find them easily, eBay organizes items into fine-grained categories structured as a topic hierarchy. Item categorization is fundamental to many aspects during an item life cycle, including assigning relevant specifics, inspecting listing violation, charging insertion and final value fees, surfacing the item to users through either searching or browsing, and finally converting item to purchase. The task of item categorization can be formulated as a text classification problem intuitively. However, it is more challenging compared with traditional text classification tasks due to the peculiarities arise from a real large-scale e-Commerce environment, as described in [7]. We especially desire a model capable of: (1) processing huge volume of training and testing data, and large number of classes; (2) handling effectively data sparseness and unbalanced distribution, and (3) making real-time prediction of item categories.

In real-world text categorization applications, categories are typically organized into concept hierarchies or taxonomies. Extensive researches have shown the value of hierarchical information [5, 8, 3, 1, 10, 2]. Comparing with the conventional flatten classification approach which treats leaf categories separately regardless of the hierarchical structure on top of them and distinguishes a category from all others in one run, hierarchical classification [5, 8, 3] uses a "gates-and-experts" strategy with the top-level distinctions serving as "gate" to the lower level "experts". The core idea is to decompose a large-scale classification problem into a simple model to make coarse-grained classification, followed by a sophisticated model to make fine-grained distinction. The coarse-grained classification deals with a very large number of examples while maintaining satisfactory classification accuracy; and the fine-grained distinction is learned only within a subtree under each top level category thus can afford more complex feature generation and classification algorithms. Shen et al. [7] further generated a problem-specific latent hierarchy rather than employing the existing human-defined topic structure for the hierarchical classification. They proposed a graph-based clustering method to group highly-confusing categories and applied more sophisticated learning algorithm to distinguish the categories within each group.

Based on the hierarchical classification framework [7], this paper further explores how to design fine-grained models to distinguish those highly-confusing categories at the second level of classification. It is observed that there are 15.7% groups of confusing categories belonging to the Electronic domain on eBay site, hence we will use this domain for illustration onwards. The electronics domain consists of four meta categories including Cameras & Photo, Cell Phones & PDAs, Computers & Networking and Consumer Electronics. The major challenge of categorization in this domain is to differentiate among the categories of *product*, *product accessory*, *accessory bundles* and *whole sale*, for examples:

(i) Cell Phones & PDAs → Cell Phones & Smartphones

(ii) Cell Phones & PDAs → Cell Phone & PDA Accessories → Screen Protectors

(iii) Cell Phones & PDAs → Cell Phone & PDA Accessories → Batteries

(iv) Cell Phones & PDAs → Cell Phone & PDA Accessories → Cases, Covers & Skins

(v) Cell Phones & PDAs → Cell Phone & PDA Accessories → Faceplates, Decals & Stickers

(vi) Cell Phones & PDAs → Cell Phone & PDA Accessories → Chargers & Cradles

(vii) Cell Phones & PDAs → Cell Phone & PDA Accessories → Accessory Bundles

(viii) Cell Phones & PDAs → Wholesale Lots → Cell Phones

In order to effectively differentiate among most confusing categories, it is necessary to incorporate domain specific knowledge into the second-level classification model. In this paper, we innovatively encode various domain knowledge into smartly designed features, including morphological features, quantity features and pattern features, under a SVM framework. Our goal is to effectively classify *product*, *product accessory*, *accessory bundles* and *whole sale* categories. Experimental results on real-world large-scale e-commence data show that the problem-specific model significantly outperforms the existing model on the site which only uses unigram words of item titles as features.

The model will be applied to determine the most proper category automatically or to recommend categories for sellers' listings. Also, the work can be utilized to detect outlier items within each category to assist in fraud detection. It is observed that vicious sellers generally like to put *product accessory* items into *product* category, which will compromise user experiences, for instance, the buyers see many cheap "*iphone case*" or "*screen protector*" in the first page when they search "*iphone 4*" or click into the "*Cell Phones & PDAs → Cell Phones & Smartphones*" category.

The remainder of this paper is structured as follows. We first introduce the SVM-based item categorization briefly. Next, we describe the features designed for the item categorization in Electronics domain. Finally we show and discuss experimental results with real-world ecommerce data. We conclude the paper with future works.

2. SVM-BASED ITEM CATEGORIZATION

Support Vector Machines (SVM) [9] has strong theoretical motivation in statistical learning theory. Extensive empirical comparisons on text classification [11, 6] have shown that among the methods available today, SVM achieves superb generalization performance and therefore is considered as the state-of-the-art in text classification.

SVM constructs a binary classifier that predicts whether an instance $\vec{x}$ is positive or negative, where the instance is represented as a feature vector. In the case of linearly separable instances, the decision $f(x) = sgn(\vec{w} \cdot \vec{x} + b)$ is made based on a separating hyperplane $\vec{w} \cdot \vec{x} + b = 0$ ($\vec{w} \in \mathcal{R}^n, b \in \mathcal{R}$). SVM is to find the optimal hyperplane that separates the positive and negative training instances with a maximal margin, by solving a dual quadratic programming problem. In the case of linearly non-separable, SVM projects the instances from the original space $\mathcal{R}^n$ to a higher dimensional space $\mathcal{R}^N$ based on a kernel function $K(\vec{x_1}, \vec{x_2}) = \Phi(\vec{x_1}) \cdot \Phi(\vec{x_2})$. By this means, a linear separation will be made in the new space. We employed a highly efficient implementation of SVM with linear kernel, LibLinear [4] for the item categorization. This package also supports multi-class classification using one-versus-the-rest strategy.

3. FEATURE SET

When a seller lists an item on eBay, he or she is asked to write a title to briefly describe the item. Once the title is entered, the site suggests proper categories for the seller to choose. So the item categorization is only based on the information from item title. Title of an item on eBay site usually contains 10 words.

In data preprocessing step, item titles are first tokenized, and then punctuations are eliminated. A small stopword list is used to omit the most common words. Furthermore, we observe that (1) numbers are indicative to distinguish between *single sale* and *whole sale* categories, and (2) prepositions, such as *with* and *for*, are useful to judge *product* and *accessory* categories. Therefore, contrary to conventional text classification tasks, we keep numbers and prepositions in titles. The existing model uses the unigrams of title words as features. For certain domains, however, we observe that unigrams of words are not capable of differentiating between *product* and *accessory* categories. For example, the items "*Apple iphone 3G Black (16GB)+External Case Cover*" and "*FOR Apple iphone 3G leather case cover black*" belong to different categories while they share a large portion of words. Therefore, it is necessary to explore more domain-specific predictive features. In addition to unigram words, we propose three feature sets including morphological features, quantity features and pattern features for the item categorization in Electronics domain.

Morphological Features These features are to capture the special words which mix alphabets and digits, such as *w755*, *i325*, *XV6175*, *SPH-M520* and *3G*. These words are represented as the features *AlphaDigit*, *Alpha-AlphaDigit* and *DigitAlpha*, which usually indicate model names of electronic products.

Quantity Features We collect the evidence from item title to indicate quantity of an item. The most frequent words which occur adjacent to a digit expression in the "*Wholesale Lots*", "*Accessory Bundles*" and "*Multi-Packs*" categories are extracted. The words, along with the adjacent digit slot, will be regarded as a multiple-quantity pattern, such as *<digit> pcs*, *<digit>x*, *<digit> pk*, *<digit> pack*, *<digit> in1*. In addition, the phrases, such as *"lots of"* and *"wholesale"* in titles are very indicative of *"Wholesale Lots"* categories. The pattern *"<phrase> + <phrase>"* are useful for *"Accessory Bundles"* categories, such as *"Car+Home charger+Case cover pouch for at&t ZTE F160"*. The evidence of titles starting with digit expression are also helpful to detect the multiple quantity items.

Pattern Features There are two steps to generate pattern features: key phrase extraction and key phrase relation identification. For each group of categories, we first extract bi-grams of words from training data, rank them by frequency and select the ones which cover at least 10% training instances in one category. Some examples in different groups are shown in Table 1. We found that these words are usually the main nouns or noun phrases of some compound phrases and are essential for the semantics of the phrases. Next, we identify how the key phrases are connected in titles, including the relation between key phrases, and the relation between key phrase and preposition, such as *"for"* and *"with"*. For examples, the pattern *"case cover for"* frequently occurs in the category *"Cell Phones & PDAs → Cell Phone & PDA Accessories → Cases, Covers & Skins"*, while the pattern *"apple iphone with"* indicates the category *"Cell Phones & PDAs → Cell Phones & Smartphones"*.

4. EXPERIMENTS

The eBay category structure is a six-level topic hierarchy, where there are 39 top-level nodes called meta categories, and more than 20,000 bottom-level nodes called leaf categories. The hierarchy was designed and maintained by human experts. The item categorization is to classify items into leaf categories. A labeled training dataset is collected from all of the sold items on eBay site over 20 days. The trained model is then evaluated on the sold items in the 3 days after the training period. There are totally 11,855,161 items for training and 2,399,460 for testing.

In the hierarchical framework, as described by [7], the KNN-based model (the first-level classifier) classifies items into latent groups, then a SVM-based model (the second-level classifier) further differentiates the categories within a group. The groups are generated based on the confusing score between leaf categories, as proposed in [7]. In our empirical evaluation, we focus on the second-level classification for the category groups in the Electronics domain. The system is evaluated on the largest 5 groups in this domain containing 85,794 items in the test set, as shown in Table 2.

We use the categories assigned by sellers as the proxy of ground-truth labels, under the assumption that items successfully sold have been placed into appropriate categories by sellers. Although the assumption does not always hold, it avoids the otherwise very expensive human labeling, and serves as a good approximation. We observed an error rate of 15% on sold items by seller labeling against editorial validation. This error rate in label approximation can give a loose upper bound of actual prediction error, based on observed experimental results.

We compare the domain-specific SVM-based classification model (*SVM_DS*) with the existing SVM model which employs only bag of title words as features (*SVM_BOW*). The model is evaluated on the top 5 groups individually with the precision measure.

Table 3: Overall Performance on the Top 5 groups

Group	#Cat.	#Test data	SVM_BOW	SVM_DS
G1	11	49354	94.5%	96.2%
G2	7	15492	92.0%	93.6%
G3	2	7617	94.2%	95.7%
G4	2	7137	84.2%	85.5%
G5	2	6194	92.9%	95.8%

Table 3 shows the number of categories, the number of items for testing and the overall precisions of *SVM_BOW* and *SVM_DS* for each group. At all of the groups, *SVM_DS* consistently outperforms *SVM_BOW*. It is important to note that 1-2% of precision lift is considered to be significant, since the base number of items to be categorized is in the order of hundreds of millions and one percent error rate may impact millions of users' experiences. The results clearly show that various rich domain knowledge and linguistic patterns are predictive signals for distinguishing subtle categories.

5. CONCLUSION

We have demonstrated the value of carefully designed domain-specific features, in the context of hierarchical classification. We argue that with the "gates-and-experts" strategy for hierarchical classification, many predictive signals are quite localized, thus motivating a closer attention for these domain-specific features. In traditional text classification literature, local features are generally not recommended, that is also why a simple frequency-based feature selection works near optimal in many tasks. However, in a real-world environment where data heterogeneity and sparseness become predominant, a serious study of local pattern will pay off. We have demonstrated our approach with intriguing examples, and proposed several innovative ways to derive features based on rich domain knowledge and linguistic hints.

6. ACKNOWLEDGMENTS

The authors greatly appreciate catalog product development team (Rajyashree Mukherjee, Suresh Raman and Niraj Kothari) and catalog product manager (Chelly Yan) for the valuable discussion and effective collaboration in the successful product deployment.

7. REFERENCES

[1] L. Cai and T. Hofmann. Hierarchical document categorization with support vector machines. In *Proc. of the 13th ACM International Conference on Information and Knowledge Management(CIKM)*, pages 78–87, 2004.

[2] O. Dekel, J. Keshet, and Y. Singer. Large margin hierarchical classification. In *Proc. of the 21st International Conference on Machine Learning(ICML)*, pages 27–34, 2004.

[3] S. T. Dumais and H. Chen. Hierarchical classification of web content. In *Proc. of the ACM SIGIR Conference on Research and Development in Information Retrieval*, pages 256–263, 2000.

[4] R. E. Fan, K. W. Chang, C. J. Hsieh, X. R. Wang, and C. J. Lin. Liblinear: A library for large linear

Table 1: Examples of key phrases in the different category groups

Group	Category	Key Phrase
Cell Phone	Cell Phone & Smartphones Cell Phone Accessories Accessory Bundles Wholesale Lots	apple iphone, cell phone, blackberry curve, hard case, screen protector, case cover, usb cable, lcd display, wall charger, phone battery, battery charger
Computer Networking	Computer Components PC Desktops PC Laptops & Notebooks Computer Accessories	compaq presario, power adapter, lcd screen hp pavilion, desktop computer, hp compaq, laptop motherboard, dell optiplex, dell latitude, apple macbook, laptop battery, toshiba satellite
Cameras & Photo	Camcorders Digital Cameras	digital camcorder, video camera, camcorder dv, nikon coolpix, kodak easyshare, canon eos, sony cyber

Table 2: The top 5 groups with most confusing categories

Group	Categories
G1	Electronics → iPod & MP3 Accessories → Armbands Electronics → iPod & MP3 Accessories → Cases Cell Phones & PDAs → Cell Phones & Smartphones Cell Phones & PDAs → Cell Phone & PDA Accessories → Accessory Bundles Cell Phones & PDAs → Replacement Parts & Tools Cell Phones & PDAs → Cell Phone & PDA Accessories → Screen Protectors Cell Phones & PDAs → Cell Phone & PDA Accessories → Batteries Cell Phones & PDAs → Wholesale Lots → Cell Phones Cell Phones & PDAs → Cell Phone & PDA Accessories → Cases, Covers & Skins Cell Phones & PDAs → Cell Phone & PDA Accessories → Faceplates, Decals & Stickers Cell Phones & PDAs → Cell Phone & PDA Accessories → Chargers & Cradles
G2	Computers & Networking → Computer Components → Desktops & Laptops for Repair Computers & Networking → Computer Components → Motherboards Computers & Networking → Computer Accessories → Laptop Adapters & Chargers > Standard, AC Computers & Networking → PC Desktops Computers & Networking → PC Laptops & Netbooks Computers & Networking → Computer Accessories → Laptop Batteries Computers & Networking → Computer Components → Laptop Screens & LCD Panels
G3	Cameras & Photo → Camcorders Cameras & Photo → Digital Cameras
G4	Cameras & Photo → Film Photography → Film Cameras Cameras & Photo → Lenses & Filters → Lenses
G5	Computers & Networking → iPads & Tablets Computers & Networking → iPad & Tablet Accessories

classification. *Journal of Machine Learning Research*, pages 1871–1874, 2008.

[5] D. Koller and M. Sahami. Hierarchically classifying docuemnts using very few words. In *Proc. of the 14th International Conference on Machine Learning(ICML)*, pages 171–178, 1997.

[6] F. Sebastiani. Machine learning in automated text categorization. *ACM Computing Surveys (CSUR)*, 34:1–47, 2002.

[7] D. Shen, M. Somaiya, J. D. Ruvini, and N. Sundaresan. Large-scale hierarchical item categorization for e-commerce. *eBay Research Labs Technical Report*, 2011.

[8] A. S.Weigend, E. D.Wiener, and J. O. Pedersen. Exploiting hierarchy in text categorization. *Information Retrieval*, pages 193–216, 1999.

[9] V. N. Vapnik. *Statistical learning theory*, 1998.

[10] K. Weinberger and O. Chapelle. Large margin taxonomy embedding with an application to document categorization. *Advances in Neural Information Processing Systems*, pages 1737–1744, 2008.

[11] Y. Yang and X. Liu. A re-examination of text categorization methods. In *Proc. of the ACM SIGIR Conference on Research and Development in Information Retrieval*, pages 42–49, 1999.

An Efficient Method for Using Machine Translation Technologies in Cross-Language Patent Search

Walid Magdy and Gareth J. F. Jones
Centre for Next Generation Localization
School of Computing, Dublin City University, Dublin 9, Ireland
{wmagdy, gjones}@computing.dcu.ie

ABSTRACT
Topics in prior-art patent search are typically full patent applications and relevant items are patents often taken from sources in different languages. Cross language patent retrieval (CLPR) technologies support searching for relevant patents across multiple languages. As such, CLPR requires a translation process between topic and document languages. The most popular method for crossing the language barrier in cross language information retrieval (CLIR) in general is machine translation (MT). High quality MT systems are becoming widely available for many language pairs and generally have higher effectiveness for CLIR than dictionary based methods. However for patent search, using MT for translation of the very long search queries requires significant time and computational resources. We present a novel MT approach specifically designed for CLIR in general and CLPR in particular. In this method information retrieval (IR) text pre-processing in the form of stop word removal and stemming are applied to the MT training corpus prior to the training phase of the MT system. Applying this step leads to a significant decrease in the MT computational and resource requirements in both the training and translation phases. Experiments on the CLEF-IP 2010 CLPR task show the new technique to be 5 to 23 times faster than standard MT for query translation, while maintaining statistically indistinguishable IR effectiveness. Furthermore the new method is significantly better than standard MT when only limited translation training resources are available.

Categories and Subject Descriptors
H.3 [**Information Storage and Retrieval**]: H.3.3 Information Search and Retrieval

General Terms
Algorithms, Performance, Experimentation.

Keywords
Patent Retrieval; Cross-Language Information Retrieval; Machine Translation.

1. INTRODUCTION
Interest in patent retrieval research has shown considerable growth in recent years. The focus of most of this research has mainly been on exploring methods for monolingual patent search tasks, where the emphasis has been on indexing techniques for patents and query formulation for topics. However, an important and largely overlooked topic in patent retrieval is international and hence multilingual patent search. Patents on the same topic may be published in different countries in different languages, and it is important for patent examiners to be able to locate relevant existing patents whatever language they are published in. Hence an important topic in patent retrieval is cross-language information retrieval (CLIR), where the topic is a patent application in one language and the objective is to find relevant prior-art patents in other languages [2, 6]. In recent years machine translation (MT) has become established as the dominant technique for translation in CLIR. This has largely come about due to the increased availability of high quality MT systems, which usually achieve better CLIR effectiveness than dictionary-based translation methods. Standard MT systems focus on generating proper translations that are morphologically and syntactically correct. Development of effective MT systems requires large training resources and high computational power for training and translation. This is an important issue for patent CLIR where queries are typically very long, sometimes taking the form of a full patent application; meaning that query translation using MT systems can be very slow and computationally demanding. However, in contrast to MT, the focus for information retrieval (IR) is on the conceptual meaning of the search words regardless of their surface form. Thus much of the complexity of the standard MT process is not required for effective CLIR. The significant time and resources required for translation of patent topics in cross language patent retrieval (CLPR) has not received much attention to date. In addition, some language pairs have limited suitable training data available, meaning that it is not possible to train an effective MT system for these language pairs leading to low CLPR effectiveness.

In this paper, a novel adaptation of MT for CLIR is presented which addresses the high computational cost and resource requirements of MT for CLPR. The is demonstrated to be up to 23 times faster than standard MT in both the training and decoding phases for the CLEF-IP 2010 patent search task. Retrieval effectiveness using the new approach is shown to be statistically indistinguishable from that obtained using standard MT. Furthermore, it is found to be statistically significantly better than standard MT when only a small amount of data is used to train the system.

2. PATENT SEARCH
In recent years, several IR evaluation campaign have included tracks exploring recall-orientated tasks. Two of these are the NTCIR [2] and CLEF [6] patent search tracks, which have examined ad-hoc search, invalidity search, and prior-art search.

In this paper, we focus on the prior-art patent search task, which is concerned with finding all relevant patents that can invalidate the novelty of a patent application or at least that have common parts to that patent [6]. The full patent application submitted to the patent office is considered as the topic, and patent citations that are identified by the patent office are taken as the relevant documents, therefore the objective in prior-art patent search is to find these citations of patents automatically.

CLPR has featured as a task at both NTCIR and CLEF. The typical procedure adopted for CLPR has been to translate the query into the target collection language using one of the available free MT systems, and then to perform search in the document language. Thus this research has treated the translation stage as a black box without any control over the translation process. In addition, little attention has been directed toward the time taken for the translation process.

3. ADAPTING MT FOR CLIR

3.1 Basic Concept

The basic idea of the new approach is to train an MT system for translation of topics or documents in CLIR using training data pre-processed for IR. The pre-processing uses the standard stages performed by most IR systems. specifically case folding, stop word removal, and stemming. These operations aim to improve retrieval efficiency and improve effectiveness by matching different surface forms of words. While these are standard processes in IR, for standard MT applying these operations would be destructive to the quality of the translated output. For example, the translated sentence "*he are an great idea to applied stem by information retrieving*" instead of "*It is a great idea to apply stemming in information retrieval*" would be considered a very bad translation from an MT perspective. However, from an IR perspective this output is fine since it contains all the information needed for the retrieval process, since both are the same after IR pre-processing: "*great idea appli stem informat retriev*".

Our hypothesis is that training an MT system using corpora pre-processed for IR can lead to similar or improved translated text from the IR perspective, which consequently can lead to better retrieval effectiveness. In addition, the training of the MT system is expected to be much faster and more efficient, since a large proportion of the training text represented by the stop words will be removed, and the rest will be normalized creating a smaller vocabulary. Further this reduced vocabulary should mean that a smaller training corpus will be found to be as effective as a larger unprocessed one for translation in CLIR.

3.2 MT Training and Decoding

Figure 1 presents the workflow of the proposed CLIR system. The upper part represents the MT training which produces the translation model used for the translation step in the CLIR. The new "Text Processing" step introduced for both languages in the parallel corpus works by applying the standard IR pre-processing steps. The resulting translation model is in the "Processed" form, where words are in their stemmed form and no stop words are present. For consistency, the terms "Processed" and "Text Processing" in the remainder of the paper refer to "case folding", "stop word removal" and "stemming".

For query translation in CLIR when using MT, a query in source "S" language is translated into target "T" language; the translated query is then processed in language "T" for search. Actually, when using MT for CLIR, longer queries are preferable since they tend to be more grammatical, therefore better translation can be achieved using an MT system taking context into account, leading to better retrieval effectiveness. The novel translation approach introduced here is shown in the lower part of Figure 1. It can be seen that the "Text Processing" step has been moved to be a step prior to translation instead of a posterior step in the standard CLIR workflow. Therefore, the processing is applied to the source language query which produces a much shorter input with a reduced vocabulary to be translated using the processed MT model. The output from the translation process is in the processed form, and therefore no additional processing of the query is required. This query is used directly to search the index of documents and produce a list of retrieved results.

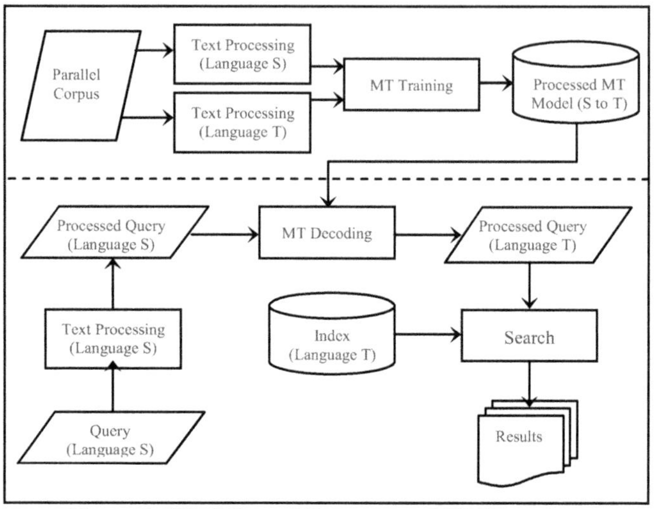

Figure 1: Workflow of the proposed CLIR system

4. EXPERIMENTAL INVESTIGATION

The experimental investigation examines three main dimensions of the proposed approach. The first is to explores the effect of processing the words before the MT step. The second investigates the efficiency of the proposed translation process according to the computational requirements for the MT training and decoding phases when compared to translation using standard MT. However, more emphasis is given to the decoding time for query translation since it is the online processing time for translating the query which is generally more significant to the user. The third dimension considers the effect of using a limited amount of training data on the retrieval effectiveness.

Retrieval effectiveness in this investigation is measured using MAP and the recently introduced patent retrieval evaluation score (PRES) [3]. PRES is an evaluation score designed for recall-oriented tasks where the objective is to find all possible relevant documents at the highest possible ranks. PRES emphasises the quality of the system in retrieving a large portion of the relevant documents at relatively high rank based on a user specific cut-off (N_{max}). In our analysis, we focus on PRES since it is specifically designed for measuring retrieval effectiveness in patent search, where it combines recall and quality of ranking in one score. Moreover, it is used in CLEF-IP track since 2010 to evaluate the performance of the submitted runs. Significance is tested using a Wilcoxon test with p-value 0.05. In addition, the times for training the MT systems and for decoding (translating) the topics are calculated for both methods.

4.1 Test Data

The cross language search task in CLEF-IP 2010 is used for our experiments. The main objective is to find relevant patents in a multilingual collection that are related to patent applications filed in French and German languages. The patent collection consists of 1.35M patents from the European Patent Office (EPO) with 69%

of them in English and 31% in German and French. The German and French patents are provided with many sections manually pre-translated into English, including the patent title, abstract and claims. The English text of all patents in the collection was indexed to create an index of documents in English only. The CLEF-IP track provided two sets of topics; 300 training topics of which 89 are German, 15 are French, and the remainder are English; and 2000 test topics of which 520 are German, 134 are French, and the rest are English. Both sets of topics are patent applications filed after those in the patent collection and do not contain translations. For the CLPR experiments, the 89 German training topics and the 134 French test topics were selected to have a similar number of topics for each query language.

Since the patent collection comes from the EPO, most of the patents in the collection have the title and claims sections translated into three languages (English, French, and German). For the MT experiments, more than 8M (~8.1M) parallel sentences in English, German, and French were extracted from the collection for use as the MT training set. The average length of the English sentences in the corpus is 28 words.

4.2 Baseline Construction

Query formulation from the patent topic is one of the main challenges in patent search [2, 6]. To construct a baseline retrieval run, we tested a number of query formulation approaches based on the best runs submitted to the CLEF-IP 2010 [6]. Based on these existing runs, our query formulation used the title, abstract, description, claims, and classification sections. We followed the our query formulation originally presented in [4], where the query is constructed using terms in the topic after translation that appeared more than two times across the sections when combined and all bigram terms that appeared more than three times, with the term frequency acting as weight for these terms. The Indri search toolkit[1] was used for indexing and search, Porter stemmer was applied for the queries and documents, and a list of 684 stop words from patent domain used in [4] was filtered out from text.

Two baseline runs were prepared for each query language: the first baseline used Google translate to translate the German and French topics into English, as was done by most of the participants in CLEF-IP 2010 [6]. For the second and main baseline, we used the MaTrEx MT system[2] [7]. The 8M extracted sentences were used to train the MaTrEx MT system to create two translation models: (French→English) and (German→English). The default configuration and training parameters of the MaTrEx system were used to generate the translation model, which was then used to translate the German and French test topics into English. Table 1 shows the MAP and PRES values for each of the baselines for the French and German topics. From these results it can be seen that, for the French topics the Google and MaTrEx MT systems achieved similar retrieval effectiveness. However for German topics Google translate achieved lower performance with respect to both MAP and PRES, this can be attributed to the many unusual compounds found in the text that require a training corpus in a similar domain in order to be translated effectively. For the translation time using MaTrEx, it was found that the average translation time was 31 mins for the French patent topic (which contain 7,058 words on average) and 12 mins for the German patent topic (which contain 3,571 words on average) on a server machine (Intel Xeon quad-core processor, 2.83GHz, 12MB cache, and 32GB RAM). However, the average search time using all the translated text as a query was 42 secs for French topics and 14 secs German topics on a desktop machine (Intel Core2Due, 3GHz, 6MB cache, 3GB RAM). This highlights the importance of developing faster translation techniques for patent topics.

Table 1: Baseline runs for the German and French topics

	French		German	
	MAP	PRES	MAP	PRES
Google	0.087	0.413	0.067	0.466
MaTrEx	0.085	0.413	0.075	0.487

5. EXPERIMENTS WITH THE NEW CLIR MT APPROACH

The same training dataset of parallel sentences was used to train the MaTrEx MT system again, but after pre-processing the data ("processed MT"). This was then compared to the standard MT system without pre-processing the data ("ordinary MT"). In addition, several portions of the training data were selected and used to train alternative MT systems to explore the performance of both MT systems when less training examples are available. For these experiments subsets 800k, 80k, 8k and 2k sentences were extracted at random from the full 8M training set and used to train the additional MT systems.

5.1 Results

Table 2 shows the retrieval effectiveness measured by MAP and PRES, the out-of-vocabulary (OOV) rates when decoding the topics, and decoding time for French and German topics compared when using ordinary MT vs. processed MT for the cross language patent search task.

For the retrieval effectiveness measured by MAP and PRES, it can be seen that the difference in the retrieval effectiveness using both translation methods is not significant compared to each other for almost all training sizes. However, with smaller training sets (2k), it is found that the processed MT achieved significantly better retrieval effectiveness than the ordinary MT for both query languages when compared using PRES. For the French topics when using processed MT, results remain statistically indistinguishable from Google translate for training sizes 8M, 800k, and 80k. However, for ordinary MT, the 80k training set translation led to retrieval that is statistically worse than Google translate when compared using PRES. These results show that the new approach has higher effectiveness when limited amounts of training data are available.

To analyse the reason behind these results, the OOV percentage while translating the patent topics is also reported in Table 2. It can be seen that the stemming performed in the "Text Processing" step in the processed MT system reduces the number of OOV terms, leading to the presence of a translation. In particular, it can be seen that for small size training sets, the standard translation approach suffers from a large percentage of OOVs, while the processed MT system overcomes part of this problem. The German topics suffer from higher OOV than the French ones due to the presence of productive compounds in German.

The second main benefit of the new approach to translation is shown clearly in the last row of Table 2, which compares the average decoding time required to translate a patent topic into English using both approaches. It can be seen that the processed MT system is at least 5 times faster than the ordinary MT system

[1] http://www.lemurproject.org/indri/

[2] http://www.openmatrex.org/

Table 2: Retrieval effectiveness, OOV, and decoding time for French and German topics compared when using ordinary MT vs. processed MT for the cross language patent search task. Underlined values indicate that the result is indistinguishable from Google translate, and '*' indicates that processed MT is statistically better than ordinary MT

		French						German					
		Google	2k	8K	80K	800K	8M	Google	2k	8K	80K	800K	8M
MAP	Processed MT	0.087	0.069	0.067	0.079	0.085	0.084	0.067	0.039	0.050	0.050	0.071	0.079
	Ordinary MT		0.062	0.069	0.079	0.086	0.085		0.034	0.057	0.050	0.070	0.075
PRES	Processed MT	0.413	0.343*	0.369	0.399	0.414	0.419	0.466	0.332*	0.405	0.455	0.471	0.483
	Ordinary MT		0.323	0.360	0.396	0.412	0.413		0.260	0.394	0.445	0.484	0.487
OOV (%)	Processed MT	NA	20.7%	11.6%	5.0%	2.6%	1.6%	NA	40.7%	28.3%	13.6%	7.0%	4.2%
	Ordinary MT		28.6%	16.8%	7.3%	3.0%	1.6%		49.8%	35.8%	18.0%	8.9%	4.2%
Decoding time (*mm:ss*)	Processed MT	NA	00:19	01:05	03:06	04:44	06:03	NA	00:07	00:17	01:01	01:58	02:49
	Ordinary MT		06:43	09:30	15:09	21:31	30:35		02:33	03:46	05:47	07:58	11:24

when using the same training parallel corpus. In addition, with smaller sized training data sets, the speed of decoding using the new MT system reaches up to 23 times faster than the ordinary MT system. Furthermore, the decoding time needed for the processed MT system when it is trained with 8M parallel sentence is comparable to the decoding time required for the ordinary system when it is trained with only 2k examples.

Similar results to those shown in Table 2 were obtained for the training time, where the training time for the processed MT system was 5 to 13 times faster than the ordinary MT system.

5.2 Discussion

Comparing the retrieval effectiveness of the processed vs. the ordinary MT systems when a very small training corpus was used (only 2k) performance was statistically indistinguishable when compared by MAP, but statistically better for processed MT when compared by PRES. This result means that while the systems cannot be distinguished when compared with respect to finding relevant documents at very high ranks, the processed MT is noticeably better when compared to standard MT for finding a greater number of relevant documents at higher ranks. For a recall-oriented search task such as patent retrieval, PRES is a more a meaningful score, since the average number of documents to be examined for this task is often large, sometimes reaching hundreds of documents [1].

The large difference in the average translation time for a French patent compared to that of a German patent stems from the length of the patents, where the French patents are nearly double the length of the German patents on average due to word compounding in the German patents. In addition, the high percentage of the OOV terms in the German patents speeds up the translation since no translation is examined for OOV words.

Removing the stop words from the text reduces the amount of text to be translated by nearly half. However, the gain in speed is much more than the double (5 to 23 times). The reason for this comes from the nature of stop words, where the MT takes a longer time to translate them in order to select the proper translation in the proper position. Additionally, stemming reduces the vocabulary in the MT model leading to less choices of translation for terms, which leads to higher translation speed.

6. CONCLUSION

This paper has presented a novel technique for adapting MT systems for the purpose of CLIR. Although the technique mainly comprises a re-ordering of the workflow of the steps in CLIR, the impact was shown to be significantly more efficient in the resource and computational requirements of the MT process. The new technique was tested on the patent search task that usually requires a large amount of training data and for which the query translation time that can reach more than 50 times the search time. Experimental results show that processing the text by stop word removal and stemming before MT training and decoding leads to speeding up the translation process by up to 23 times. In addition, this technique proved to be much more effective when a limited amount of data is available.

For future work, the approach should be tested for different types of CLIR tasks including ad hoc and web search, especially for languages where limited MT training resources are available.

7. ACKNOWLEDGEMENT

This research is supported by the Science Foundation Ireland (Grant 07/CE/I1142) as part of the Centre for Next Generation Localisation (CNGL) project.

8. REFERENCES

1 Azzopardi L., H. Joho and W. Vanderbauwhede. A Survey on Patent Users Search Behavior, Search Functionality and System Requirements. *IRF Report* 2010-0001, (2010)

2 Fujii A., M. Iwayama, and N. Kando. Overview of patent retrieval task at NTCIR-4. In *Proceedings of NTCIR-4*, (2004)

3 Magdy W. and G. J. F. Jones. PRES: a Score Metric for Evaluating Recall-Oriented Information Retrieval Applications. In *Proceedings of SIGIR'10*, (2010)

4 Magdy W. and G. J. F. Jones. Applying the KISS Principle for the CLEF-IP 2010 Prior Art Candidate Patent Search Task. In *Proceedings of CLEF-2010,* (2010)

5 Oard, D. W. and Diekema, A. R. Cross-Language Information Retrieval. In: *WILLIAMS, M. (ed.) Annual Review of Information Science ARIST*, (1998)

6 Piroi F. CLEF-IP 2010: Retrieval Experiments in the Intellectual Property Domain. In *Proceedings of CLEF-2010,* (2010)

7 Stroppa, N. and A. Way. 2006. MaTrEx: DCU Machine Translation System for IWSLT 2006. In *Proceedings of IWSLT*, (2006)

8 Wang J., D. W. Oard. Combining Bidirectional Translation and Synonymy for Cross-Language Information Retrieval. In *Proceedings of SIGIR'06*, (2006)

Understanding the Types of Information Humans Associate with Geographic Objects

Ahmet Aker
University of Sheffield
a.aker@dcs.shef.ac.uk

Robert Gaizauskas
University of Sheffield
r.gaizauskas@sheffield.ac.uk

ABSTRACT

In this paper we investigate what sorts of information humans request about geographical objects of the same type. For example, *Edinburgh Castle* and the *Bodiam Castle* are two objects of the same type – *castle*. The question is whether specific information is requested for the object type *castle* and how this information differs for objects of other types, e.g. *church*, *museum* or *lake*. We aim to answer this question using an online survey. In the survey we showed 184 participants 200 images pertaining to urban and rural objects and asked them to write questions for which they would like to know the answers when seeing those objects. Our analysis of 7644 questions collected in the survey shows that humans have shared ideas of what to ask about geographical objects. When the object types resemble each other (e.g. *church, temple*) the requested information is similar for the objects of these types. Otherwise, the information is specific to an object type. Our results can guide tasks involving automatic generation of templates for image descriptions, and their assessment, as well as image indexing and organization.

Categories and Subject Descriptors

IR [**Language technologies for IR**]: [NLP, IE, Summarization, QA]; IR [**Evaluation, Test collections, Crowdsourcing for IR**]: [Mechanical Turk]

General Terms

NLP, Summarization, Image Description Generation

Keywords

Geographical object description

1. INTRODUCTION

In every day life we see and categorize things in our built or natural environment. For instance, if we look at different churches, we see that each of them has different style, different look, different size, some of them are newer than the others, etc., but still we are able to categorize all of them as churches. For categorization purposes visual attributes such as the style and the size of a church might be enough; however, to report about each church separately we need more attributes whose values make each church distinguishable from others.

Knowing what sets of attributes people use to describe geographical objects has several applications. Text summarization employed to automatically generate descriptions of geographical objects can be improved by incorporating human preferences into the output summaries. Template based summarization methods, for example, have been used successfully for news event summarization [2, 3]. The same strategy can be applied to the task of generation of descriptions for geographical objects, e.g. for purposes of generating descriptions for images of these objects. Templates can be derived from the set of attributes relevant to humans to bias the summarization system towards the text units containing the values for these attributes. Furthermore, the attributes could be used in a guided summarization task as organized by the Document Understanding Conferences (DUC)[1] and the Text Analysis Conference (TAC).[2] Additionally, the attributes can be used to evaluate the output of an automatic summarization system by testing whether highly relevant attributes are covered in the output summary. Furthermore, the attributes supply a guide for what to index for images pertaining to locations. If information highly relevant for humans is used for indexing, this could lead to better retrieval and organization of those images.

For such applications it is relevant to know whether there is a general set of attributes that people use to describe any geographical object. Or, given that humans categorize objects into types (e.g. church, museum, etc.), are the sets of attributes specific to single object types, or perhaps shared between types that are subtypes of a common higher level type (e.g. church and temple are both religious buildings)?

In this paper we aim to address these questions. Specifically, we ask: For what attributes related to geographic objects would people like to know the values when seeing such an object? And: Is this set of attributes specific to a particular object type (e.g. church) or shared between different object types?

We aim to answer these questions using an online survey conducted on Mechanical Turk. In the experiment we show the participants different images of objects from around the world. Our set of images contains only images of static fea-

CIKM'11, October 24–28, 2011, Glasgow, Scotland, UK.

[1] http://duc.nist.gov/
[2] http://www.nist.gov/tac/

Table 1: Objects types used in the experiment.

Urban types	Rural types
abbey, aquarium, avenue, basilica, boulevard, building, cathedral, cemetery, church, gallery, house, monument, museum, opera house, palace, parliament, prison, railway, railway station, residence, square, stadium, temple, tower, university, zoo	beach, canal, cave, garden, glacier, island, lake, mountain, park, peak, river, ski resort, village, volcano

Table 2: Example attributes with related questions.

location	where is garwood glacier?, where exactly is edmonton?, where it's located?
foundationyear	when was it build?, which year was this zoo opened?, when it was established?

tures of the built or natural landscape, i.e. objects with persistent geo-coordinates, such as buildings and mountains, and not images of objects which move about in such landscapes, e.g. people, cars, etc. We ask the participants to write questions for which they would like to know the answers when seeing each image. We collected 7644 questions from 184 participants. The results of our analysis reveal that people share ideas as to what to ask about geographical objects in general. When the object types resemble each other, the requested information is similar. Otherwise, this information is specific to a specific type.

In this paper we first present the experimental setting of our survey and outline the preprocessing process of the data (Section 2). In Section 3 we present our analysis and report and discuss the results. We conclude the paper in Section 4.

2. EXPERIMENTAL SETTING

2.1 Experiment

In the experiment we showed the participants an image pertaining to a particular object or place. We also presented the participants with the name of the place (e.g. *Eiffel Tower*) and its object type (e.g. *tower*). The participants were asked to take the role of a tourist and provide ten questions for which they would like to know the answers when they see the place shown in the image. We showed images picturing places of 40 different object types randomly chosen from our entire set of 107 object types. From these 40 object types 25 are urban and 15 rural types (see Table 1). For each object type five different places were shown. For example, for the object type *tower* the images of *Eiffel Tower, Flag Tower of Hanoi, BT Tower, Munttoren, Bettisons Folly* were shown. These places (towers) were manually selected from Wikipedia. Each image was shown to five different participants. We ran the experiment for four weeks. In total we collected 7644 questions for 187 different places. The questions came from 184 different participants. The expected number of questions was 10.000 (40 types $\times$ 5 objects $\times$ 5 participants $\times$ 10 questions). However, there are some objects for which we only have questions from two or three workers. Most objects have 40 questions. The number of questions for the urban types is 4815 and for the rural ones 2829. We used Mechanical Turk for our experiment.

2.2 Question Preprocessing

We manually analyzed all questions in order to assess quality. Approximately 2% of the questions were empty because not all the workers wrote 10 questions for each object. Moreover, some questions are only related to the image itself rather than to the place shown in the image (e.g. *"when the picture is taken?", "how many flowers you found in the image?", "is there a bus in the picture?"*). In addition to these, some questions present non-resolved references so it is impossible to know what object they refer to (e.g. *"what language do **they** speak?"*). Finally, there are questions which bear no relation at all with the object in the image (e.g. *"how is the manager?"*). These questions do not address the task, which is to ask questions about the *object* shown in the image, not about the image itself or related information. Therefore, we categorized all these questions as noise which makes up 19% (1479 out of 7644) of the entire question set.

We categorized the remaining 81% of the questions (6169 out of 7644) by the *attribute* the worker was seeking the value for with his/her question. An attribute is an abstract grouping of similar questions. We regard two or more questions as similar if their answers refer to the same information type. For instance, we regard the questions *"where is garwood glacier?* and *"where exactly is edmonton?"* as similar because both aim for answers related to the information type *location*. We name the attribute according to the information type it refers to (e.g. *location*). Table 2 shows examples attributes with questions.

In total we identified 146 attributes, however, 95 of them contain less than five questions, so we ignore these attributes in further analysis. We analyse the remaining set of 51 attributes (see Table 3), each of which has at least five questions related to.

3. ANALYSIS

3.1 Is there a set of attributes that people generally associate with geographic objects?

In Table 3 the 51 attributes are given. The left column of the table shows the very frequent addressed attributes (*top ten*). More than 65% of the questions can be categorized by these ten attributes. This means that people do share ideas as to what types of information are required about a place, and the set of *top ten* attributes captures the majority of these information types. However, although these attributes occur for many object types, their *popularity* is not the same for all the object types with which they are associated.

We define the popularity of an attribute for an object type as the number of questions categorized under this attribute for that particular object type. Attribute popularity indicates how important the type of information represented by the attribute is for the particular object type.

For instance, the attribute *visiting* is the most popular attribute (has the maximum number of 52 questions) in the object type *museum* (see Table 4). This indicates that it is most important for people to know how much the entry to the museum costs or when the museum opens. This information is more relevant than, e.g. knowing when the museum was built. However, if we look at the object type *house*, we can see that the same attribute *visiting* is not the most popular one. It occurs at position five with only 11 questions. For this object type people seem to be interested most in knowing the *design* of the house and less in information related to visiting.

The remaining 35% of the questions are spread over the remaining *41* attributes as shown in the right column (*below top ten*) of Table 3. From this list we can observe that there

Table 3: **Attributes used to categorize the questions.**

Top Ten	Below Top Ten
visiting, location, foundationyear, surrounding, features, history, size, design, mostattraction, naming	purpose, istouristattraction, height, visitors, founder, owner, events, type, status, habitants, designer, constructioninfo, temperature, length, eruptioninfo, comparison, capacity, depth, maintainance, arts, studentsinfo, subjectsofferred, gravesinfo, preacher, firstdiscovery, parkinginfo, religioninfo, destination, origin, workers, width, travellers, travelcost, waterinfo, travelling, firstclimber, tributaries, prayertime, personinmonument, snowinformation, firstfounder

Table 4: **List of attributes (eight most frequent) for example object types. The numbers within the brackets attached to each attribute indicate how many questions were categorized by that attribute.**

Object Type	Attributes
cathedral	location(30), visiting(23), foundationyear(16), history(12), founder(9), size(8), design(8), preacher(6)
house	design(27), location(22), foundationyear(16), owner(13), visiting(11), history(10), istouristattraction(9), founder(9)
museum	visiting(52), location(22), foundationyear(22), mostattraction(10), features(9), history(8), arts(5), owner(5)
opera house	visiting(33), foundationyear(20), location(17), events(17), mostattraction(10), surrounding(10), designer(9), owner(8)
volcano	erruptioninfo(42), visiting(26), location(21), surrounding(20), height(15), status(14), foundationyear(7), naming(6)
zoo	visiting(41), features(34), location(19), foundationyear(14), size(10), mostattraction(8), surrounding(5), owner(5)

are some specific attributes which are likely to be present only in a specific object type or in very few object types. For instance, as shown in Table 4 the attribute *erruptioninfo* is associated only with the object type *volcano*. This attribute contains questions related to the eruption of different volcanos. From Table 4 we can see that this attribute is also the most popular for the *volcano* object type, while information related to *visiting*, *location*, etc., which is generally most frequently asked for, comes after *erruptioninfo*. From this we can conclude that even though object types share the *top ten* attributes, the differences in attribute popularity indicate that these are not equally important for all object types. Therefore, the question arises as to whether each object type has an associated specific set of attributes, or whether the attributes relevant to it are shared between several object types. This is our second research question.

3.2 Is each set of attributes specific to a particular object type or shared between several object types?

To address this question we compare different object types and investigate the degree of similarity between them. We assume, if two object types are similar, then they will not only share a set of attributes, but the attributes within this set will also have similar popularity ranking.

We use Kendall's Tau rank correlation coefficient as a metric which indicates similarity between object types, while considering the attribute popularity ranking in their attribute sets. Kendall's Tau correlation coefficient is equal or close to 1 if two events are highly correlated in rankings and close to 0 if there exists little or no correlation between the ranks of the two events.

The attributes are ranked according to their popularity, i.e. the number of questions contained under each attribute. If attributes of two different object types have similar rankings, this is an indication that these attributes are of similar importance for both object types. Kendall's Tau for these object types will return a high correlation for the pair, and we will refer to such object types as similar. A difference in attribute rankings between different object types indicates that these attribute sets are more specific to the one object type and not shared by the other(s). In this case Kendall's Tau will return a low correlation, and we will refer to such object types as dissimilar.

In our analysis we report comparisons based on three different sets of attributes:*all*, *top ten* and *below top ten*. *All* is the entire set of attributes shown in Table 3 (attributes from columns *top ten* and *below top ten*). The *top ten* attributes include the top ten attributes which are shared between most of the object types and thus more likely to render similarity. The *below top ten* set contains all remaining attributes which are as we assume above rather object type specific.

3.2.1 Results

If *all* attributes are taken, there is in general a correlation between object types in both urban and rural categories. On average the urban object types correlate with *0.55* (median *0.57*) and the rural types with *0.53* (median *0.53*). The mean and median correlation coefficient lie close to each other, which indicates that the distribution of highly correlating object types is similar to that of object types with low correlation. To analyse this result further, we aim to identify the object types whose correlation coefficient is higher than the mean correlation and those which are correlated with a coefficient lower than the mean. We also aim to understand whether there are object types which are only highly correlated when top ten most frequent attributes are considered and whose correlation potentially drops for the remaining set of attributes.

Table 5 shows three groups of object type pairs in rural and urban areas. In the first column the object type pairs whose correlation coefficient is higher than the mean for *all* attributes are shown. The second column shows the object type pairs whose correlation is higher than the mean in the *top ten* attributes, but drops below the mean for the *below top ten* attributes. Finally, in the third column the pairs which are correlated with the coefficient lower than the mean for *all* attributes are presented.

From Table 5 we can see that high correlation in attributes is always present when the object types have e.g., the same look, design or the same purpose. For the urban areas we have object types such as *church*, *basilica*, *abbey*, *cathedral*

Table 5: Change of correlation between object types when different sets of attributes are taken for comparison.

Always High Correlation	High Correlation in Top Ten and Low Correlation in Below Top Ten Attributes	Always low correlation
church;temple, abbey;temple, building;tower, building;residence, abbey;basilica, house;residence, abbey;church, basilica;temple, basilica;cathedral, museum;operahouse, house;palace, gallery;museum	house;prison, museum;railway, basilica;railway, monument;prison, university;cathedral, prison;palace, prison;cathedral, cemetery;aquarium, railwaystation;cathedral, cemetery;parliament	prison;aquarium, monument;railway, railway;cathedral, university;railway, museum;prison, temple;railway, railway;operahouse, parliament;railway, abbey;railway, tower;railway
mountain;volcano, mountain;skiresort, mountain;peak, peak;volcano, peak;glacier, mountain;glacier, glacier;skiresort, park;garden, lake;canal, canal;river	village;river, lake;island, canal;volcano, island;river, mountain;river, peak;lake, island;garden, canal;glacier, skiresort;garden, mountain;canal	lake;volcano, canal;island, lake;glacier, glacier;river, canal;village, lake;garden, village;garden, glacier;village, island;glacier, park;cave

and *temple* which correlate with a coefficient higher than the mean of *0.55* when *all* attributes are considered. A similar picture can be drawn for other urban object types such as *house-residence*, *building-residence* or *museum-operahouse*. In rural areas, object types related to mountainous areas (e.g. *glacier, mountain, peak, volcano, ski resort* etc.) are correlated above the mean of *0.53*. The same is valid for water bodies like *canal, lake, river*, etc.

All these object types clearly share features like look, design, purpose, etc. The correlation coefficient is always low for object types which do not share these aspects such as the ones shown in the third column of Table 5. This indicates that aspects used for categorizing objects into object types also play a role in deciding which object types are similar for purposes of describing them.

However, the second column of the tables also highlights the importance of shared ideas of what information is relevant for describing geographic objects for object type similarity (Section 3.1). The object types shown in the second column of the tables are correlated above the mean for *top ten* attributes and their correlation drops below the mean when *below top ten* attributes are used.

3.3 Discussion

Our analyses have shown that people taking the role of a tourist do share ideas as to what information is relevant for describing geographic objects, and we identified a set of information types that reflects these ideas. However, although we could say that there are clearly several information types which people like to know when seeing any geographic object, it was also clear that not every type of information is equally relevant for each object type. These findings prompted the question, whether each object type has a specific set of information associated with it, or whether object types can be grouped according to how they are described by people.

We found that some object types are similar and not only share the information types associated with them, but also the importance ranking of these types. Such similar objects were mostly objects of similar purpose, look or design (e.g. churches and temples, rivers and lakes, etc.). This indicates that sets of features which people use to categorize objects also plays a role in deciding which information should be used to describe these objects. However, some object types which do not share these features are still similar in terms of which information is required to describe them. In these cases people will refer to the shared set of frequently requested attributes we identified.

4. CONCLUSION

In this paper we investigated which information types (attributes) humans associate with geographic objects from urban and rural landscapes. We identified a set of attributes which were relevant for any geographic object type, but also found that an appreciable proportion of attributes is object type specific. Even in the set of shared information types, not all information types were equally important for each object type. Based on the importance ranking of information types for each object type, we were able to identify similar object types.

In our earlier work we extracted the information types which humans associate with geographic objects from existing text resources describing locations around the world and used them to automatically generate image descriptions [1]. One of our future works will be to compare the information types we identified in this paper with the ones extracted from these existing text resources. If these correlate with the set of attributes obtained through our user survey, we could regard the text descriptions containing these attributes as conceptual models of geographic objects of the same type.

5. REFERENCES

[1] A. Aker and R. Gaizauskas. Generating image descriptions using dependency relational patterns. In *Proceedings of the 48th Annual Meeting of the Association for Computational Linguistics*, pages 1250–1258. Association for Computational Linguistics, 2010.

[2] K. McKeown and D. Radev. Generating summaries of multiple news articles. *Proc. of the 18th annual international ACM SIGIR conference on Research and development in information retrieval*, pages 74–82, 1995.

[3] D. Radev and K. McKeown. Generating natural language summaries from multiple on-line sources. *Computational Linguistics*, 24(3):470–500, 1998.

Google, Bing and a New Perspective on Ranking Similarity

Bruno Cardoso and João Magalhães
Departamento de Informática, Centro de Informática e Tecnologias da Informação
Faculdade de Ciências e Tecnologia, Universidade Nova de Lisboa
2829-516 Caparica, Portugal
b.m.pinto.cardoso@gmail.com, jmag@di.fct.unl.pt

ABSTRACT

In this paper, we propose a framework to characterize and compare two search engine results. Typical user-queries are ambiguous and, consequentially, each search engine will compute ranks in different manners, attempting to answer them in the best possible way. Thus, each search engine will have its own bias. Given the importance of the first page results in Web Search Engines, in this paper we propose a framework to assess the information presented in the first page by measuring the information entropy and the correlations between two ranks. Employing the recently proposed Rank-Biased Overlap measure [2] we compare to which extent do Bing and Google rankings in fact differ. We also extend this measure and propose a measure for comparing the information entropy present in two ranks. The proposed measure is based on the correlation of two ranks and the application of Jensen-Shannon's divergence among two document sets. Our methodology starts with 40,000 user queries and crawls the search results for these queries on both search engines. The results allow us to determine the search engines correlations, crawling coverage, information overlap, and information entropy.

Categories and Subject Descriptors

H.3.5 [**On-line Information Services**].

General Terms

Measurement, Experimentation.

Keywords

Search engines comparison, Rank-biased Overlap, Jensen-Shannon divergence, Content Aware Rank Similarity.

1. INTRODUCTION

Nowadays, Web users depend upon Web Search Engines (WSE) to find the information they need. In fact, given the uncontrolled organization of the Web, about 85% of the users use WSEs to ease the task of locating information [5]. The short textual length of the queries traditionally used in these engines, added to the myriad of all possible user intentions and information needs, account for leveraging their ambiguity [4]. As a countermeasure, instead of responding to user queries with single documents, WSEs attempt to do so by returning lists of diverse documents to cover some of the different senses of the query. Thus, when querying different WSEs with the same query, their returned ranks won't necessarily be the same, even though they index the same data – the Web. One of the most immediate comparisons relates to search results usefulness, i.e., how relevant are the sets of items returned by the search engines as responses to submitted queries. This type of evaluation is directly linked to human relevance judgments [1] and there is, at least, one extended study that compares WSEs through the perspective of result usefulness [7], relying upon relevance judgments for 1,000 queries. Yet, another question would be: given the same queries, and without relevance judgments, will Bing and Google produce the same ranks, with similar contents, or will their returned ranks tendentially diverge? There are a number of proposals that attempt to establish ranking similarity evaluations, although, to the extent of our knowledge, they usually make specific evaluations addressing the problem by comparing the differences on the lists' ordering.

In the present work, we do not use relevance judgments and assume ranks as an intermediary step that takes users to their real interest: the information contained in the documents pointed by the ranked URLs. To encompass this conception, we've developed a new measure, *Content Aware Ranking Similarity*, to assess not only the divergence of the returned rankings but also the diversity of the retrieved information. The proposed measure is based on the correlation of two ranks and the application of Jensen-Shannon's divergence among two set of documents. Our methodology starts with 40,000 user queries (obtained from TREC Web Track) and crawls the search results for these queries on both search engines. We present results for comparing two search engines in terms of (i) indexed domains, (ii) rank correlation, (iii) mutual diversity, and (iv) joint analysis of rank correlation and mutual diversity.

CIKM'11, October 24–28, 2011, Glasgow, Scotland, UK.

2. RELATED WORK

2.1 Rank-biased Overlap

To address the problem of measuring ranking similarity, there are several popular statistical measures that could be used right out of the box, such as Kendall's τ. However, given the scale of their search domain (the Web), WSEs do not enjoy the same properties as domain-specific search engines, such as a complete rank of the entire set of documents and full access to the same set of documents. In fact, WSE's first page results are obtained through the truncation of larger, ordered by relevance, URL listings and this truncation may occur at any depth; furthermore, the retrieved rankings are usually non-conjoint, since the items returned by two different search engines may not be the same; finally, when browsing through rankings, users expect to find their answers amongst the first ranked results. These are all aspects that are not fully dealt by these traditional measures. In fact, when comparing two rankings, Kendall's τ would require them to be conjoint, would not consider the increased importance of top documents and the computed τ values are heavily related to a rank's depth. As such, this measure is not the most adequate [2] to evaluate WSE rankings. On the other hand, *Rank-Biased Overlap* (RBO) is a measure proposed by Webber et al. [1] to evaluate the similarity of rankings with particular characteristics, namely: *incompleteness*, not listing all elements in the search domain; *top-weightiness*, as the top of the list is more important than the tail and *indefiniteness*, as the decision to truncate the ranking at any depth is arbitrary. Even though the authors did acknowledge the existence of some metrics that account for top-weighted and non-conjoint rankings, their work revealed that none of them handled the arbitrary cutoff depth and do not maintain monotonicity as it varies. Moreover, there is a point to RBO that adds to its interest even further: it models – to a degree – a very human-like characteristic, and one that is especially present when browsing through WSE's results - the user's decreasing patience. Indeed, RBO considers list entry matching closer to the top as having more influence on ranking similarity than matching occurrences further down the ranking - much like a web surfer's fading patience would take him to consider, if asked to compare two long rankings. Rank-biased Overlap metric computes the correlations of non-conjoint ranks, i.e., $RBO \in [0,1]$, where uncorrelated ranks correspond to 0 and completely correlated ranks correspond to 1.

2.2 Divergence Measures

Divergence measures provide a numeric value to assess the difference between two statistical distributions. Kullback-Leibler divergence is the usual choice for assessing the divergence among two statistical distributions:

$$KL(p \parallel q) = \sum p_i \log\left(p_i/q_i\right)$$

In our case, we've opted for Jensen-Shannon divergence since it has some important properties, such as symmetry and its value is always finite. See [6] for details.

3. AN EVALUATION METHODOLOGY

In the present work, we used a set of 40,000 distinct queries from the TREC Web Track. This query collection is representative of the heterogeneity of the universe of user queries. Each query was submitted to Bing and Google's online search API through simple HTTP requests and their returned rankings were stored in a local database. Each list of retrieved results was truncated to a maximum of 16 results per query, resulting in 639,004 retrieved documents for Google and 639,846 for Bing. Since the research we've conducted required analysis for each of the retrieved documents' contents and given their sheer number, we've only considered pure HTML documents or, at least, documents containing HTML formatted information.

3.1 Crawler Coverage

The aforementioned process provided a perspective on the way that each search engine crawling coverage of the Web, yielding 95,354 common domains, 114,583 domains exclusively crawled by Bing and 121,877 domains exclusive to Google. From here, it follows that Google has a broader view of the Web, having retrieved more 7,294 domains than Bing, in our tests.

3.2 Non-conjoint Rank Correlation

To provide a better response to the challenge of comparing Bing and Google, we've delved into the task of measuring the correlation between the URLs of the two ranks. Due to the previously presented reasons, we've found RBO to be the most adequate measure to assess WSE's ranks. So, we've applied RBO to the rank pairs returned by Google and Bing when responding to the submitted queries. We summarize our RBO findings in the histogram below.

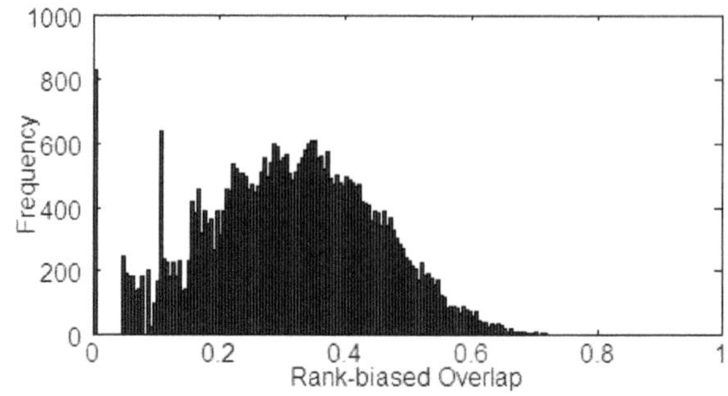

Figure 1. RBO measurements (200 bins)

From the histogram, we can observe that the rankings computed by each of the engines were, for the most part, dissimilar. In fact, the RBO score distribution has a mean of 0.314, with a standard deviation of 0.138. Moreover, only 8.64% (approx.) of the queries returned rankings having RBO similarity above 0.5. This fact, added by the large amount of queries scoring RBOs near 0, is enough to let us conclude that there are significant differences to be found on the two WSE's ranking algorithms.

3.3 Mutual Diversity

3.3.1 Motivation

So far, we've compared two search engines through their indexed domains and the correlation of their retrieved URLs. However, since the most likely reason that takes a user to perform a query on a WSE is a real need for information, it makes sense to extend ranking similarity evaluation beyond the URL listing. For instance, consider the case of two different engines that returned totally disjoint rankings, but where each of the featured URL points to documents with the same content. Although RBO – as well as any rank similarity measure that only considers rank positions – would promptly evaluate the ranks as completely uncorrelated, it is expectable that a user would deem them as having the same information value: in essence, these two rankings would be very similar indeed. From this perspective, we argue that evaluating correlation solely through ranked URLs is an incomplete way of assessing the similarity between two ranks. Consequentially, we've extended our research to compare the contents of the retrieved documents. In this section we will address the human perception of information similarity and measure the information contained in the two ranks to assess the information content of each rank.

In contrast to more traditional Information Retrieval systems, queries used on WSE are usually very short descriptions of a user's information need (on the average, composed by 2.21 terms) [3]. Not surprisingly, such concise descriptions may be subject to high degrees of ambiguity and this is further aggravated by the daunting heterogeneity of the universe of users. Since the answers to queries are returned as sets of ranked lists, it is possible to include documents for more than one interpretation, so, perfect query disambiguation is not a requirement. If we consider a WSE return results as a whole, i.e. an amount of documents/information aiming at answering a particular query, it makes sense to ponder the use of measures such *diversity*. Indeed, after querying a search engine, it is expectable for all of the retrieved documents to have different contents - although all of them should be related to, at least, one plausible interpretation of the submitted query.

3.3.2 *Internal Diversity of a Rank*

The measure we've chosen to evaluate a ranking diversity was the Jensen-Shannon divergence, JS_{div}. This divergence is, by definition, a measure of similarity between two probability distributions. To use it, we computed a histogram of word occurrences out of a given document textual contents – a *bag-of-words* representation –, and obtained a simple probability distributions that can be directly used in the divergence's calculus[1]. For the particular case of two documents, Jensen-Shannon's divergence provides an evaluation about the extent to which they are similar to one another. However, since this work is about comparing two search engine rankings rather than two single documents, we've adapted the divergence's application context in the following way: for a given rank, we define its *internal diversity*, D_i as the sum of the Shannon-Jensen divergences found between the documents of each possible combination of two. For a hypothetical ranking *r*, we formalize:

$$D_{int}(r) = \sum JS_{div}\left(C_2^r\right), \qquad (1)$$

where C_2^r is a combination of two documents of rank *r*. Since Jensen-Shannon diversity's image set is $\Re_0^+$, it follows immediately that the sum of any arbitrary number of diversity values are also mapped to the same range, i.e. $D_i \rightarrow \Re_0^+$. Equation (1) will return a value for the diversity of a single ranking, which will be higher for more dissimilar documents.

If this same metric is used to directly compare documents of two ranks, the results may be somewhat misleading. In fact, although equation (1) is computed out of document textual content, it does not encompass any relevance judgments and, as a consequence, there is a possibility for even two fully distinct rankings to yield the same internal diversity score. For instance, the ambiguous query "light" may be reasonably interpreted as concerning the electromagnetic radiation or the absence of weight (other interpretations being possible). Of course, if two engines followed divergent interpretations, it's fair to expect each returned set of documents to be essentially different. However, to obtain the same internal diversity values, it's enough for them to share the same amount of word diversity.

3.3.3 *Information Divergence of Two Rankings*

To address the issue above, we extend the internal diversity definition and create a new measure that establishes a direct relation between two ranks, the *relative diversity* D_r. Then, for two different rankings r_1 and r_2, we propose the diversity of r_1 relative to r_2, to be the sum of the diversities computed between each possible combination of two documents, with one of them being present on r_1 and r_2 and the other being exclusive to r_1. This can be expressed as the Cartesian product of the set of common documents and the set of r_1's exclusive documents. Formalizing for the aforementioned rankings:

$$D_r\left(r_1, r_2\right) = \sum\left(JS_{div}(d_1, d_2)\right), \qquad \begin{cases} d_1 \in r_1 \cap r_2, \\ d_2 \in r_1, \end{cases} \qquad (2)$$

[1] To increase cross-document matches, we've removed all HTML tags, *stopwords*, and stemmed the resulting words.

with $D_r \rightarrow \Re_0^+$. Since the explained procedure explicitly depends upon the existence of a subset of documents that exclusively belong to r_1, there is a possibility for $D_r\left(r_1, r_2\right)$ to be different from $D_r\left(r_2, r_1\right)$. That way, in order to perform conclusive comparisons between the rankings, both values must be calculated. After accomplishing the described steps, we have two relative diversity values: one for the diversity of r_1 relative to r_2 and another for the diversity of r_2 relative to r_1. Finally, we can obtain an indicative measure out of these values by simply calculating their difference. To this end we propose a new definition, the *mutual diversity*,

$$D_m\left(r_1, r_2\right) = D_r\left(r_1, r_2\right) - D_r\left(r_2, r_1\right), \qquad (3)$$

where $D_m \rightarrow \Re$. As a consequence a special case occurs when two ranks have no documents in common. Following from the constraints of equation (2), the resulting value will implicitly be zero. Thus, when lacking shared documents to compute a meaningful D_m value, we replace the relative diversities in (2) by the values of each ranking's internal divergence (1). Then, for this particular case, we assume the mutual diversity to be:

$$D_m\left(r_1, r_2\right) = D_i\left(r_1\right) - D_i\left(r_2\right) \qquad (4)$$

Thus, for two rankings r_1 and r_2, D_m will be 0 when both have the same diversity; D_m will tend to negative infinity as r_2 gets more diverse than r_1, and to positive infinity as r_1 gets more diverse than r_2.

Due to time constraints, we have performed the diversity evaluations on the returned rankings for the first 33,500 queries, out of the 40,000 that compose the original set. Our mutual diversity findings are summarized in the following histogram (when Google's rankings are more diverse than Bing's, the values fall in the range $\left]0, +\infty\right[$ and in $\left]-\infty, 0\right[$, otherwise):

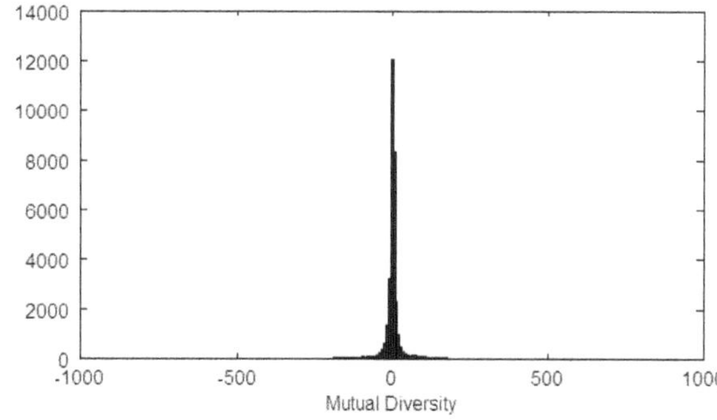

Figure 2. Mutual Diversity measurements (200 bins).

As depicted in the graph, the Mutual Diversity approximately follows a normal distribution around the mean value of -4.0697, with a standard deviation value of 68.204. Moreover, only 1.3% of the queries yielded rankings with Mutual Diversities outside the interval $\left[-200, 200\right]$. These measurements hint that the differences at the document information level may not be as obvious as the ranking related ones, as measured by RBO. In fact, the narrowness of the curve in (Figure 2) tells us that the retrieved information, for the majority of the queries, is not very divergent and this allows us to infer that the query interpretation also does not drastically differ greatly between engines. Nevertheless, the Mutual Diversity mean value of -4.0697 also indicates that Bing tends to answer queries in more diverse ways than Google and this can happen as a result of particular differences in query interpretation, (perhaps intentionally) weaker query disambiguation strategies, or due to the ranking of longer, more entropic, less concise documents.

3.4 Aligning RBO and Mutual Diversity

So far, we have presented two disjoint perspectives on ranking similarity evaluation: one, RBO, which assumes ranks as ordered lists of URLs; and another, the Mutual Diversity, that sees ranks as document sets whose significance lies solely on their textual contents. Even though they produce expressive ranking similarity evaluations all by themselves, each one evaluates specific properties of search results. It would be more convenient to combine both measures into a single one – especially one that does not jeopardizes their individual expressiveness. To this end, we now propose a new, conjoint, similarity definition, the *Content Aware Rank Similarity* (CARS). Then, for a pair of rankings, r_1 and r_2, we assume a two dimensional vector, having the first and second components set to be their Mutual Diversity and RBO evaluations, respectively. If we normalize all of the Mutual Diversity's values so that $D_m \to [0,1]$ (for instance, by computing the absolute value of their division by the maximum registered value of D_m), we obtain similarity vectors mapped onto the space bounded by (0,0) and (1,1). It follows immediately that, in this space, the vector (0,1) stands for total similarity between two ranks, both in terms of Mutual Diversity and RBO. We say that CARS is the distance between the ranking pair similarity vector and the total similarity vector. The normalized expression of CARS is,

$$CARS(r_1,r_2) = \frac{\left\|\left(D_m(r_1,r_2), RBO(r_1,r_2)\right) - (0,1)\right\|_2}{\left\|(1,1)\right\|} = \frac{\left\|\left(D_m(r_1,r_2), RBO(r_1,r_2) - 1\right)\right\|_2}{\left\|(1,1)\right\|}, \quad (5)$$

resulting in values in the interval $[0,1]$, with 0 standing for equal ranks and 1 for completely different ranks.

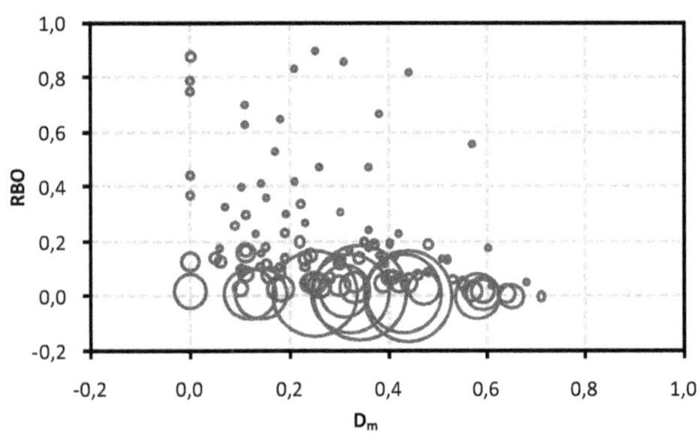

Figure 3. Density of the CARS similarity vectors.

We represent our CARS's similarity findings in Figure 3 (the circle's diameters represent the density of vectors in the center of the circle). The chart shows that, despite the obvious differences on the rankings as plain, relevance ordered, URL lists (significant vector density near RBO=0), the differences at the level of the conveyed information are more subtle. In fact, it now appears that RBO is too quick to dismiss the ranking pairs as dissimilar, since, after evaluating the information contained on the documents, the rankings are no longer considered so dissimilar (they're close to the point (0,1)).

To further support the comprehensiveness of the proposed measure, CARS, it is interesting to note how most of the ranks for the same queries are highly uncorrelated (RBO=0), but share some information as measured by the Mutual Divergence of those ranks (most of the ranks fall in the $D_m = 0.5$ zone)

4. CONCLUSIONS

In the present work, we have measured the differences in Google and Bing's search results for the same set of queries. We've conducted an evaluation from two distinct points of view: a more classic one, based on RBO, that assumes returned ranks as relevance ordered URL lists and, afterwards, we've proposed a new one, the Mutual Diversity, that sees rankings as sets of documents conveying information. Lastly, we've proposed a way of joining these two disjoint evaluations into another, CARS, that provides a simple but more profound evaluation on ranking similarity. Since it forces a second, content based, iteration when evaluating ranking similarity, it was a positive result to see that CARS had a direct impact on pure RBO evaluations.

Since we've attempted to extend the concept of ranking similarity to the level of the information conveyed by the retrieved documents, and given the n-grams potentially increased linguistic expressivity when compared to that of single words, we would consider them as an important future work.

Finally, it is important to observe that CARS is not, like RBO, a ranking similarity evaluator but is rather a pair-wise comparison of two search engine results.

Acknowledgments. This work has been funded by the Portuguese Foundation for Science and Technology under project references PTDC/EIA-EIA/111518/2009 and PEst-OE/EEI/UI0527/2011, Centro de Informática e Tecnologias da Informação (CITI/ FCT/ UNL) - 2011-2012.

5. REFERENCES

[1] J. Bar-Ilan. 2005. Comparing rankings of search results on the web. *Inf. Process. Manage.* 41, 6,December 2005.

[2] W. Webber, A. Moffat, and J. Zobel. A similarity measure for indefinite rankings. *ACM Trans. Inf. Syst.* 28, 4, 2010.

[3] B. J. Jansen, A. Spink, and T. Saracevic. 2000. Real life, real users, and real needs: a study and analysis of user queries on the web. *Inf. Process. Manage.* 36, 2 2000.

[4] B. J. Jansen, D. L. Booth, and A. Spink. Determining the user intent of web search engine queries. *Int'l conference on World Wide Web*. ACM, NY, USA, April 2007.

[5] S. Lawrence and C. Lee Giles. Accessibility of information on the Web. *Intelligence* 11, 1, April 2000.

[6] T. M. Cover and J. A. Thomas, *Elements of information theory*: John Wiley & Sons, 1991.

[7] H. Zaragoza, B. Cambazoglu, and R. Baeza-Yates. Web search solved?: all result rankings the same?. *ACM Int'l Conf. on Inf. and Knowledge Management*, NY, USA.

Effectiveness Beyond the First Crawl Tier

Rodrygo L. T. Santos
rodrygo@dcs.gla.ac.uk

Craig Macdonald
craigm@dcs.gla.ac.uk

Iadh Ounis
ounis@dcs.gla.ac.uk

School of Computing Science
University of Glasgow
G12 8QQ Glasgow, UK

ABSTRACT

Modern Web crawlers seek to visit quality documents first, and re-visit them more frequently than other documents. As a result, the first-tier crawl of a Web corpus is typically of higher quality compared to subsequent crawls. In this paper, we investigate the impact of first-tier documents on adhoc retrieval performance. In particular, we analyse the retrieval performance of runs submitted to the adhoc task of the TREC 2009 Web track in terms of how they rank first-tier documents and how these documents contribute to the performance of each run. Our results show that the performance of these runs is heavily dependent on their ability to rank first-tier documents. Moreover, we show that, different from leading Web search engines, their attempt to go beyond the first tier almost always results in decreased performance. Finally, we show that selectively removing spam from different tiers can be a direction for fully exploiting documents beyond the first tier.

Categories & Subject Descriptors: H.3.3 [Information Storage & Retrieval]: Information Search & Retrieval

General Terms: Performance, Experimentation

Keywords: Crawl Tiers, Effectiveness

1. INTRODUCTION

As the bandwidth, storage, and processing resources of any search engine to crawl and index the Web are limited, crawlers are guided by policies which focus on pages that are more likely to be relevant to user queries [6]. For instance, while breadth-first crawling finds high-value pages early [6], the OPIC (online page importance computation) measure is more often used in creating prioritisation policies [1].

The ClueWeb09 Web corpus[1] of 1.2 billion documents has provided the research community with a large sample of the Web, crawled in a language-specific manner. Figure 1 shows a schematic view of this corpus. For the purposes of the Text REtrieval Conference (TREC), the 500-million-document English subset of ClueWeb09 was designated 'category A'. Of this subset, a smaller subset with 50 million documents was designated 'category B'. The category B subset is reported to reflect the highest crawl priority, including a large number of high quality seed documents, as well as a snapshot of Wikipedia. As such, this subset roughly represents the first tier of a commercial search engine index.

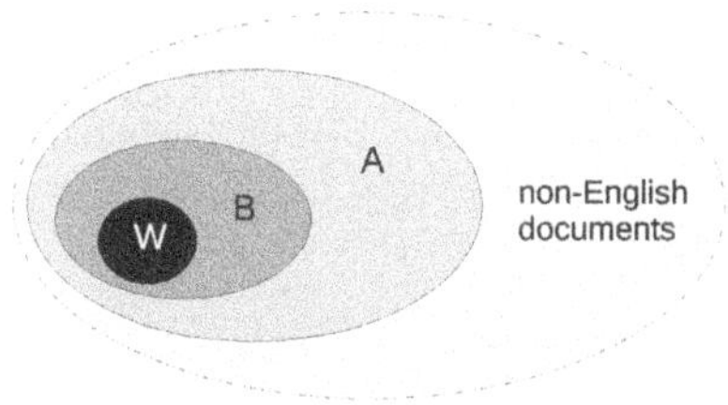

Figure 1: Schematic view of ClueWeb09, highlighting categories A and B, as well as Wikipedia (W).

For the adhoc task of the TREC 2009 and 2010 Web tracks, participants were encouraged to submit runs using both the category A and category B subsets of ClueWeb09. In this paper, we examine the effectiveness of the TREC 2009 category A adhoc runs,[2] particularly in light of the presence of first-tier documents from the category B subset. Our analysis reveals that B documents contribute substantially to the early performance of the A runs, while the impact of Wikipedia documents is less pronounced. On the other hand, going beyond the first tier can prove extremely rewarding, provided that spam is handled adequately.

In the remainder of this paper, Section 2 analyses the relevance assessments for the TREC 2009 Web track. Section 3 analyses the bias towards first-tier documents in the TREC submitted runs and two commercial search engines. Section 4 investigates the impact of the different tiers on the retrieval performance of these runs, as well as the impact of spam on each tier. Our conclusions follow in Section 5.

2. RELEVANCE ASSESSMENTS ANALYSIS

The adhoc task of the TREC 2009 Web track accepted both category A and B runs, which were pooled separately [3]. In this work, we focus on the category A runs and relevance assessments. In particular, these runs directly permit an assessment of the impact of first-tier documents (category B) on the effectiveness of rankings produced out of a larger crawl (category A). Table 1 reports the statistics of the category A, category B, and Wikipedia (denoted 'W') subsets of ClueWeb09, as well as the relevance assessments for the submitted category A adhoc runs to the TREC 2009 Web track. Besides absolute figures, we also show percent figures

[1] `http://boston.lti.cs.cmu.edu/clueweb09/`

[2] The runs submitted by the TREC 2010 participating groups were not publicly available at the time of writing.

CIKM'11, October 24–28, 2011, Glasgow, Scotland, UK.
ACM 978-1-4503-0717-8/11/10.

denoting the fraction of B documents in A, as well as of W documents in B. Assuming that the order of the crawl was not correlated with relevance, we would expect 10% of the relevant documents to come from category B, as it represents 10% of the size of the category A subset. Likewise, we would expect 11.9% of relevant B documents to come from W. However, from the statistics in Table 1, there is a clear bias towards category B documents, as well as towards Wikipedia documents, both in terms of the documents assessed for relevance, and those judged relevant.

	number of documents		
set	crawled	judged	relevant
A	503,903,810	18,666	5,684
B ⊂ A	50,220,423 (10.0%)	8,183 (43.8%)	2,828 (49.8%)
W ⊂ B	5,957,529 (11.9%)	1,755 (21.4%)	669 (23.7%)

Table 1: Statistics of the relevance assessments for the TREC 2009 Web track category A adhoc runs.

3. RUNS ANALYSIS

To investigate the effect of first-tier documents on retrieval effectiveness, we firstly analyse their impact on the submitted A runs of the participating groups in the adhoc task of the TREC 2009 Web track. Since these runs were pooled to depth 12, we measure retrieval effectiveness at rank 10, which is also suitable in a Web search context [5]. Additionally, to enable the appropriate evaluation of unofficial TREC runs (i.e., runs that did not contribute to the TREC assessment pooling), all effectiveness measures are reported in terms of estimated precision at rank 10 (estP@10), as calculated using the Minimal Test Collections (MTC) method [2]. Besides the officially submitted category A TREC runs, we also analyse the performance of runs produced by two leading Web search engines (WSEs). In particular, for each of the TREC 2009 Web track queries, we obtain up to 1000 results from these WSEs using their public APIs.[3] The URLs retrieved by each WSE are then normalised and matched against those in the ClueWeb09 corpus. While this procedure is necessary to enable the reuse of the TREC Web track relevance assessments, the obtained rankings should be seen as a 'lower bound' of what these WSEs could have produced if they constrained themselves to the ClueWeb09 corpus. For each of the 37 submitted category A runs and the two WSEs runs, we measure the fraction of category B documents among the top 10, which we denote B@10. Figure 2(a) shows a scatter plot of estP@10 vs. B@10. Analogously, we measure the fraction of Wikipedia documents in the top 10, denoted W@10. The scatter plot estP@10 vs. W@10 is shown in Figure 2(b).

From Figure 2(a), we observe a wide spread of B@10 values, with a concentration around 0.1. This ratio is akin to the expected number of category B documents, which amounts to one tenth of all category A in ClueWeb09. However, this is markedly low in contrast to the aforementioned ratio of relevant documents from category B (i.e., 49.8% from Table 1). Moreover, we note that both WSEs (denoted with a • in the figure) exhibit B@10 around 0.5, which is much closer to the relevance expectation of 49.8%. Furthermore, from Figure 2(a), it appears that estP@10 is correlated with B@10. In particular, many of the runs with poor retrieval performance lowly rank category B documents. Conversely, other runs with higher B@10 are more likely to have higher performance. Indeed, the Spearman's ρ correlation coefficient between B@10 and estP@10 is 0.76, which attests the strength of this observation.

From Figure 2(b), we note that W@10 is concentrated around two separate regions: the first one (around 0.05) comprises runs that did not seem to deploy any special treatment for Wikipedia documents, while the second one (from 0.8 onwards) includes runs that apparently specifically targeted Wikipedia (indeed, one of the runs has W@10 equal to 1). Compared to B@10, W@10 shows a lower correlation with respect to the runs' attained estP@10 (Spearman's $\rho = 0.49$), which suggests that the impact of Wikipedia documents on the retrieval performance is less pronounced than that of first-tier documents in general (i.e., the B subset).

To illustrate these observations, Figures 3(a) and (b) show a breakdown of the top 10 retrieved documents and the relevant documents among these, respectively, averaged across all TREC 2009 Web track queries for each run. In both figures, the officially submitted runs and the two WSEs runs are ordered by estP@10, from worst to best, with the WSEs being the overall best. From Figure 3(a), we first observe that more effective runs indeed favour category B documents, with some of these runs also highly favouring Wikipedia documents. Nonetheless, the best runs (i.e., those by the considered WSEs) appear to deploy a retrieval strategy that better resembles the distribution of relevant documents in Table 1, with a balance between A and B documents. However, from Figure 3(b), we note that, of all retrieved documents, those from Wikipedia are the most likely to be relevant. Other category B documents (i.e., B-W) are the next 'safest' documents, while only the best performing runs are able to identify a substantial amount of relevant documents from the remaining A (i.e., A-B) subset.

In addition to the relevance bias discussed in Section 2, this observation leads to an interesting finding: while being potentially very rewarding (nearly half of all relevant documents are not in category B), going beyond the first-tier of ClueWeb09 is also more challenging. In the next section, we investigate whether doing so is necessary for an effective performance, and what one could do towards this direction.

4. BEYOND THE FIRST TIER

Given the high prevalence of first-tier category B documents in the best performing A adhoc runs, we now assess how the presence of *non*-first-tier documents affected these runs. In particular, by contrasting these runs' ability to rank A and B documents, we can evaluate how well they perform beyond the first tier. To this end, Figure 4(a) shows a scatter plot contrasting the estP@10 of the A runs to the estP@10 of the same runs once all documents not in category B have been removed. Points above the $y = x$ line represent runs that are improved by the removal of the non-first-tier documents, while points under the line represent otherwise.

From Figure 4(a), we can see that almost all of the submitted A runs are improved by removing non-first-tier documents (i.e., documents in category A, but not in category B). Indeed, some runs with around 0.15 estP@10 are increased to 0.50, and only four runs are unaffected by the removal of non-first-tier documents. In contrast, we note that the runs by commercial search engines (denoted with

[3]Requests were sent anonymously to the US version of the WSEs, so as to isolate any customisation or localisation effects. All results were retrieved on February 7th, 2011.

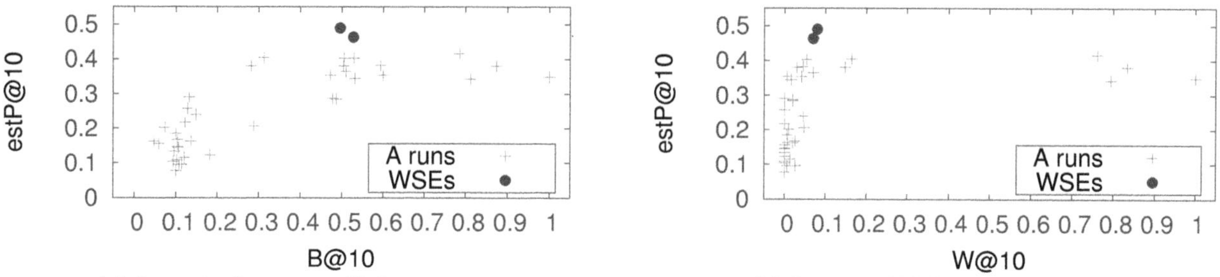

(a) Impact of category B documents (b) Impact of Wikipedia documents

Figure 2: Retrieval performance for various amounts of (a) category B and (b) Wikipedia documents for the 37 TREC 2009 A adhoc runs (+) and two commercial search engines (•).

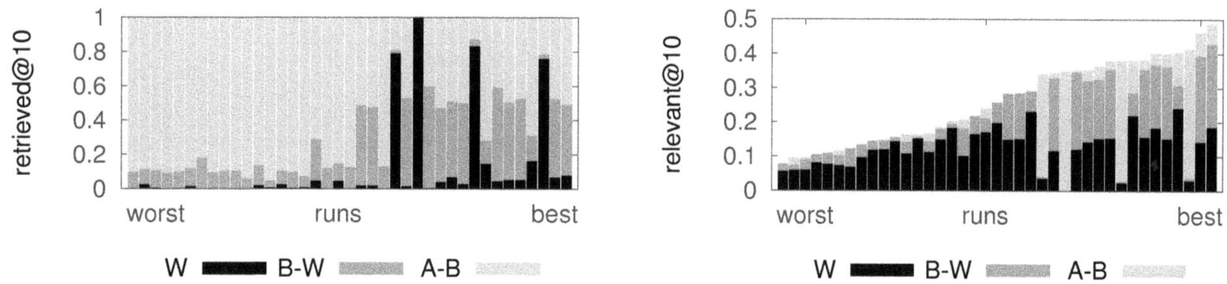

(a) Composition of documents retrieved (b) Composition of relevants retrieved

Figure 3: Composition of the top 10 documents (a) retrieved and (b) relevant across all runs. Runs are ordered by estP@10, from worst to best. The two best runs (the rightmost) are from Web search engines.

•) are both under the $y = x$ line, and as such, have been degraded by the removal of the non-first-tier documents. It seems that, in contrast to the TREC submitted runs, the commercial search engines are able to identify and competently rank relevant documents beyond the first tier.

Figure 4(b) shows the results of a similar experiment. This time, however, we analyse the importance of Wikipedia documents within the first tier. To this end, Figure 4(b) contrasts the subset of B documents in each of the considered runs to their subset of Wikipedia documents. Analogously to Figure 4(a), points above the $y = x$ line denote runs that benefit from ranking only Wikipedia documents, while points below the line denote runs that perform better when ranking all B documents. From Figure 4(b), roughly half of the runs fall on each side of the $y = x$. As a noticeable distinction, the markedly degraded performance of the two considered Web search engines when restricted to only ranking Wikipedia documents is due to their low coverage of these documents for the TREC 2009 Web track queries.

The results in Figure 4(a) show that the submitted TREC runs performed generally poorly at ranking non-first-tier documents. Analogously, from Figure 4(b), it is apparent that some runs cannot even effectively handle first-tier documents outwith Wikipedia. Cormack et al. [4] have shown that ClueWeb09 is severely affected by spam documents. To verify whether the results in Figures 4(a) and (b) are a mere reflection of the considered runs' inability to effectively handle spam, we repeat the same experiments after spam is filtered out. To this end, following Cormack et al. [4], we remove the 70% 'spammiest' documents from ClueWeb09 using their provided 'fusion' scores. The results of this investigation are shown in Figures 5(a) and (b).

From Figure 5(a), we observe that, although removing spam reduces the harm of going beyond the first tier, most runs still lie above the $y = x$ line, and are hence improved by restricting themselves to B documents. From Figure 5(b), we observe a different scenario, with most runs now lying under the $y = x$ line, meaning that going beyond Wikipedia and reaching out to the entire B subset is safer after spam removal. The different behaviours observed in Figures 5(a) and (b) suggest that spam removal, although overall beneficial, has a different impact on the different tiers.

To analyse whether this is the case, Figure 6 shows the impact of different spam removal configurations (averaged across all runs analysed in this paper) on the different strata of ClueWeb09: Wikipedia (W), non-Wikipedia category B (i.e., B-W), and non-category B (i.e., A-B). From the figure, as expected, spam removal can only hurt when applied to the W stratum, as Wikipedia is a spam-free corpus. When the B-W stratum is considered, only marginal improvements are observed for individual runs, with a decreased performance on average as spam is removed. Finally, substantial improvements are observed when the A-B stratum is considered. This result complements the findings of Cormack et al. [4], by showing that ClueWeb09 A indeed benefits from spam removal, but mostly from outside its first tier. As a result, a natural direction for improving retrieval performance on this collection is to selectively remove spam on the different strata (e.g., with a lenient spam removal threshold on the first tier, and a more aggressive threshold on the rest).

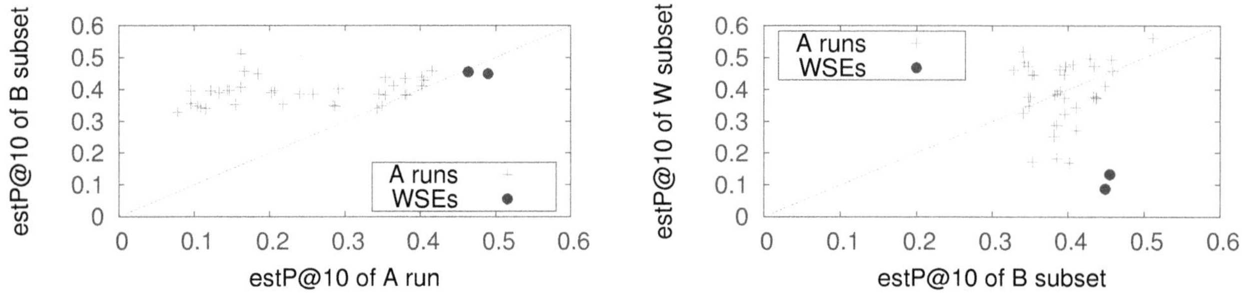

(a) Performance of category B documents

(b) Performance of Wikipedia documents

Figure 4: Retrieval performance of (a) category B vs. category A documents, as well as of (b) Wikipedia vs. category B documents, for the TREC runs (+) and Web search engines (•).

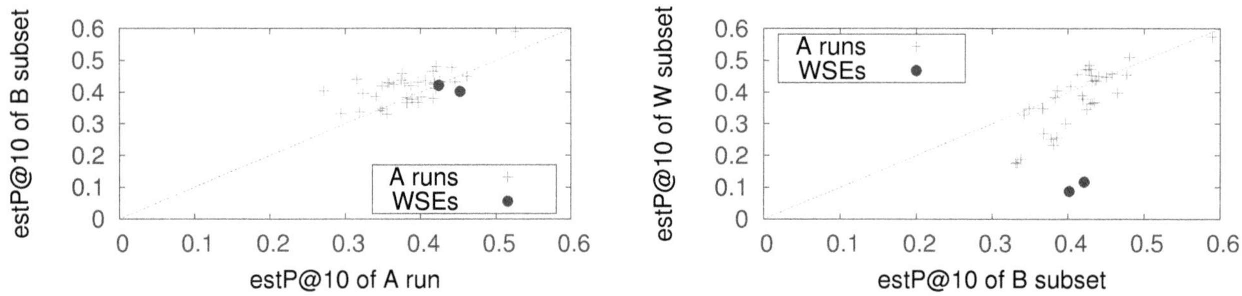

(a) Performance of category B documents

(b) Performance of Wikipedia documents

Figure 5: Retrieval performance of (a) category B vs. category A documents, as well as of (b) Wikipedia vs. category B documents, for the TREC runs (+) and Web search engines (•) after spam removal (70%).

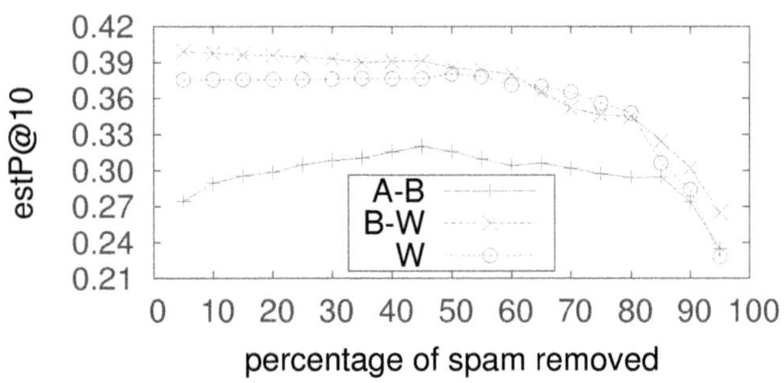

Figure 6: Per-subset average retrieval performance across all runs analysed in this paper as documents automatically classified as spam are removed.

5. CONCLUSIONS AND DISCUSSION

While it is well known that crawling order brings high-value documents early, the extent to which these documents are influential in the retrieval process requires further study. In this paper, we analysed the impact of the first-tier of the ClueWeb09 collection on the effectiveness of the submitted A runs to the TREC 2009 Web track adhoc task. Our experiments found that the official TREC runs that retrieved more first-tier documents were more likely to have higher effectiveness ($\rho = 0.76$). Moreover, by taking the extreme case of removing all non first-tier documents from these runs, we found that the effectiveness of almost all TREC runs was markedly enhanced. In contrast, when evaluating commercial Web search engines for the same queries, the removal of non first-tier documents was detrimental to effectiveness, suggesting that these commercial search engines are better at identifying relevant documents beyond the first crawl tier than the TREC systems. Finally, we have shown that the difference between the various tiers cannot be fully explained by the higher frequency of spam on the lower tiers. As a result, a possible direction for attaining an effective retrieval performance beyond the first tier is to apply different spam removal strategies on different tiers.

6. REFERENCES

[1] R. Baeza-Yates, C. Castillo, M. Marin, and A. Rodriguez. Crawling a country: better strategies than breadth-first for web page ordering. In *Proc. of WWW*, pages 864–872, 2005.

[2] B. Carterette, J. Allan, and R. Sitaraman. Minimal test collections for retrieval evaluation. In *Proc. of SIGIR*, pages 268–275.

[3] C. L. A. Clarke, N. Craswell, and I. Soboroff. Overview of the TREC 2009 Web track. In *Proc. of TREC*, 2009.

[4] G. V. Cormack, M. D. Smucker, and C. L. A. Clarke. Efficient and effective spam filtering and re-ranking for large Web datasets. *Inf. Retr.*, 2011.

[5] B. J. Jansen, A. Spink, J. Bateman, and T. Saracevic. Real life information retrieval: a study of user queries on the Web. *SIGIR Forum*, 32(1):5–17, 1998.

[6] M. Najork and J. L. Wiener. Breadth-first crawling yields high-quality pages. In *Proc. of WWW*, pages 114–118, 2001.

Worker Types and Personality Traits in Crowdsourcing Relevance Labels

Gabriella Kazai
Microsoft Research
Cambridge, UK
v-gabkaz@microsoft.com

Jaap Kamps
University of Amsterdam
The Netherlands
kamps@uva.nl

Natasa Milic-Frayling
Microsoft Research
Cambridge, UK
natasamf@microsoft.com

ABSTRACT

Crowdsourcing platforms offer unprecedented opportunities for creating evaluation benchmarks, but suffer from varied output quality from crowd workers who possess different levels of competence and aspiration. This raises new challenges for quality control and requires an in-depth understanding of how workers' characteristics relate to the quality of their work. In this paper, we use behavioral observations (HIT completion time, fraction of useful labels, label accuracy) to define five worker types: Spammer, Sloppy, Incompetent, Competent, Diligent. Using data collected from workers engaged in the crowdsourced evaluation of the INEX 2010 Book Track *Prove It* task, we relate the worker types to label accuracy and personality trait information along the 'Big Five' personality dimensions. We expect that these new insights about the types of crowd workers and the quality of their work will inform how to design HITs to attract the best workers to a task and explain why certain HIT designs are more effective than others.

Categories and Subject Descriptors: H.3.4 [**Information Storage and Retrieval**]: Systems and Software—*performance evaluation (efficiency and effectiveness)*

General Terms: Design, Experimentation, Human Factors

Keywords: Crowdsourcing relevance labels, BFI test, worker typology

1. INTRODUCTION

Crowdsourcing [7] is emerging as an economically viable approach to scaling up efforts that require large-scale human input. In particular, it has been considered as a feasible alternative to employing editorial judges to collect relevance labels for evaluation of search engines [1, 2, 6, 11, 12]. With the convenience of crowdsourcing platforms, such as CrowdFlower or Amazon's Mechanical Turk (AMT), such labels can now be collected with ease from an almost unlimited global workforce. However, this comes at a price. Crowd workers come from different socio-economic backgrounds, with different skills and motivations, and complete tasks with varying levels of success [18]. As a result, crowdsourcing can suffer from low quality output due to dishonest, random, and sloppy workers' behavior, e.g., [4, 11, 16, 21]. Thus, various methods have been proposed to detect unethical and sloppy workers, e.g., by analyzing patterns in the worker's output and time spent on a task [4, 14, 19, 21], or by observing agreement levels among the workers and with a 'gold standard' set of trusted labels [1, 6, 11, 12].

More recently, increasing attention is being paid to studying characteristics of the workers themselves and how these relate to the quality of their work. For example, [3] experiment with a range of hypothetical assessor archetypes and examine the effects of associated assessor errors on the evaluation of IR systems. They differentiate between unenthusiastic, optimistic, pessimistic, topic-disgruntled, lazy, fatigued and 'Markovian' assessor models and use these models to simulate assessors going through the process of making judgments in the TREC Million Query track test collections. The work of [20] presents a classification of crowd workers, differentiating between two types of ethical workers (sloppy and proper), and two types of unethical workers (random spammers and uniform spammers). A total of 850 votes obtained from 33 crowd workers for 10 topics from the TREC 2010 Web Track ad-hoc task are used to confirm this classification. Related works in the broader area of online behavior have studied Internet users' personality traits, which are relatively stable, enduring properties of people and are also key in influencing behavior [10]. Personality traits have been shown to relate to user behavior in the context of e-commerce, e.g., [8], social media, e.g., [5] and web browsing and searching behavior, e.g., [15].

In this paper, we conduct a study of the crowd workers characteristics and propose a typology that reflects their observable behavior with the crowdsourcing platform, e.g., average time a worker spent on a task or the number of useful labels they contributed. Specifically, we analyze the data collected from the workers engaged in a relevance labelling task over 2100 topic-document pairs from the INEX 2010 Book Track's test collection. We classify the workers according to our typology and examine the personality traits that characterize the different groups of workers. Our analysis aims to answer the following research questions:

- Are behavior and personality traits related to label accuracy?
- What can analysis by worker types reveal about groups of workers?

In the next section we detail our experimental methodology and define the worker typology comprising five categories: spammers, sloppy, incompetent, competent, and diligent workers. Section 3 studies the behavior and personality of workers in relation to their accuracy, and Section 4 analyzes the worker types. We conclude in Section 5.

2. STUDY SETUP AND TYPOLOGY

In this section we discuss the setup of our crowdsourcing experiment on AMT and define a typology of crowd workers.

CIKM'11, October 24–28, 2011, Glasgow, Scotland, UK.

Table 1: BFI test (1=Disagree strongly, ..., 5=Agree strongly)

I see myself as someone who ...	
1. ... is reserved	(1)(2)(3)(4)(5)
2. ... is generally trusting	(1)(2)(3)(4)(5)
3. ... tends to be lazy	(1)(2)(3)(4)(5)
4. ... is relaxed, handles stress well	(1)(2)(3)(4)(5)
5. ... has few artistic interests	(1)(2)(3)(4)(5)
6. ... is outgoing, sociable	(1)(2)(3)(4)(5)
7. ... tends to find fault with others	(1)(2)(3)(4)(5)
8. ... does a thorough job	(1)(2)(3)(4)(5)
9. ... gets nervous easily	(1)(2)(3)(4)(5)
10. ... has an active imagination	(1)(2)(3)(4)(5)

Scoring the BFI-10 scales (averages of two rows): Extraversion: 1R, 6; Agreeableness: 2, 7R; Conscientiousness: 3R, 8; Neuroticism: 4R, 9; Openness: 5R; 10 (R = item is reversed-scored). Reproduced from [17].

2.1 Labeling Task and Data

For our crowdsourcing experiments, we use a relevance labeling task and ask workers on AMT to label pages of digitized books from the INEX Book Track's test collection [13]. We use 21 topics and 3,557 page level relevance judgments collected from the INEX participants as our gold set (GS).

For each topic, we create 10 HITs, each containing 10 book pages of which on average 4.5 are GS pages with known labels of which roughly half, 2.2, are known relevant pages. This results in a total of 210 HITs where each HIT is assigned to 3 workers, resulting in 630 HIT assignments. We payed $0.25 per HIT assignment, costing a total of $173.25, including commission fees. This HIT design is that of the Simple Design (SD) in [12].

2.2 Personality Traits Survey

As part of the HIT design, we included a questionnaire to collect personality traits information on the workers. We used a standard 10 question test [17] used to measure the five personality dimensions by Goldberg [10], aka the 'Big Five' (BFI), see Table 1: *Openness* is the tendency to be imaginative, independent, and interested in variety (high score) vs. practical, conforming, and interested in routine (low score). *Conscientiousness* is the tendency to show self-discipline, act dutifully, be organized, careful, and disciplined (high score) vs. disorganized, careless, and impulsive (low score). *Extraversion* is the tendency to be sociable, fun-loving, and affectionate (high score) vs. retiring, somber, and reserved (low score). *Agreeableness* is the tendency to be compassionate and cooperative, trusting, and helpful (high score) vs. self-interested, suspicious, antagonistic and uncooperative (low score). *Neuroticism* is the tendency to be calm, secure, and self-satisfied (low score) vs. anxious, insecure, emotional instable and self-pitying (high score).

2.3 Behavioral Observations

We calculate the following measures that characterizes workers' behavior based on observations on the collected data: the number of HITs completed by a worker (#HITs), the average amount of time a worker spent on a HIT (AvgTime), the percentage of useful labels (i.e., relevant/non-relevant vs. missing labels or labels like 'cannot judge') contributed (%Rel), and the ratio of correct labels based on agreement with the gold set (Accuracy).

2.4 Data Analysis Methods

In all our analysis, we calculate statistics per worker and aggregate these to groups of workers sharing a characteristic. For survey style questions, we take the most frequent response over the different HITs per worker. For quantitative measures, e.g., time spent per HIT, we take the arithmetic mean.

2.5 Worker Typology

Since a key challenge in crowdsourcing is to attract workers with desirable characteristics and behavior and deter those with undesired behavior, we define a simple typology of workers based on combination of the observable variables:

- *Diligent workers* take care in completing their HITs and may thus be characterized by a high ratio of useful labels, longer average time spent per HIT, and a high label accuracy.
- *Competent workers* may be skilled workers who provide many useful labels and obtain a high accuracy, but work fast, making them very efficient and effective workers.
- *Sloppy workers* care little about the quality of their work. They may still provide a high fraction of useful labels, but they work as fast as possible, spending relative little time per HIT. As a result, their Accuracy is expected to be low.
- *Incompetent workers* may also provide many useful labels, but despite spending considerable time per HIT only obtain a low accuracy, plausibly due to lacking skills or competencies such as a poor understanding of the task.
- *Spammers* may come in different shapes and forms, but those workers that deliver very few useful labels are an obvious case of malicious workers.

We attach no particular importance to the exact label of an individual worker, rather, we view these types as approximations of groups of workers, useful for analysis and for making sense of the inherently noisy crowdsourcing data. For example, another typology may class subsets of sloppy or incompetent workers as spammers.

3. ANALYSIS OF CROWD WORKERS

In this section we analyze the behavior, the personality traits and accuracy of the crowd workers who took part in our experiment.

3.1 Behavioral Observations

A total of 155 workers completed 630 HITs, yielding an average of 4.1 HIT per worker, but with median of 1 and maximum of 86 HITs per worker, see Figure 1a. Similarly to other studies, e.g., [1, 9], HIT uptake follows a power law like distribution—over 54% of the workers is only observed during a single HIT. The average HIT completion time has a mean of 560 seconds but with a large standard deviation of 390 seconds, shown in Figure 1a. Figure 1b shows relatively high ratio of useful relevance labels (%Rel), with a mean of 0.76 and standard deviation (std.) of 0.27, and much lower and varied levels of label accuracy measured on the gold set (Accuracy), with a mean of 0.53 and std. 0.32.

Looking at the average label accuracy achieved by a worker, we find no significant relation between the number of HITs completed by a worker and their accuracy. This is not surprising given that most workers complete only a single HIT. The average time per HIT is, however, significantly related to accuracy (Pearson correlation r of 0.22, $p < 0.01$), see Figure 1d. Moreover, we find that the fraction of useful labels obtained is strongly correlated to accuracy, the relation is highly significant (Pearson $r = 0.66$, $p < 0.001$), shown in Figure 1e.

3.2 Personality Traits

Figure 1c shows the distribution of responses to the BFI questionnaire. For *Openness* we observe a mean score of 3.44 (std. 0.71, median 3.0) suggesting a tendency toward artistic interests and active imagination. The mean score of *Conscientiousness* is higher with 3.80 (std. 0.82, median 4) suggesting that workers do a thorough job. *Extraversion* has a mean 3.14 (std. 0.98, median 3)

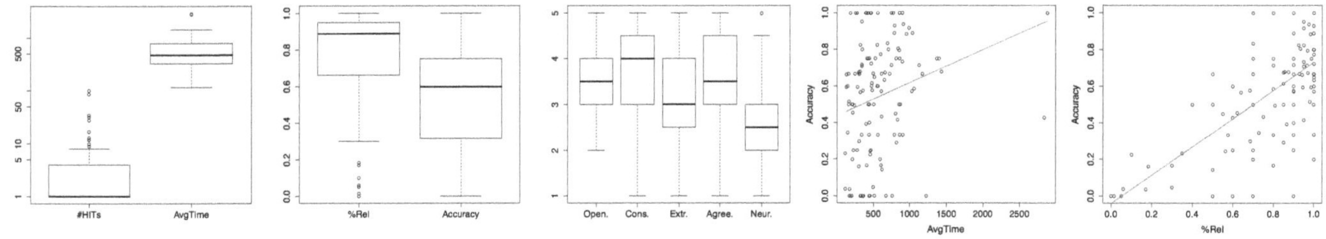

Figure 1: Behavioral observations and personality traits per worker: (a) the number of HITs (#HITs) and average time per HIT (AvgTime), (b) ratio of useful labels (%Rel) and label accuracy (Accuracy), (c) average scores on BFI personality traits, (d) correlation between AvgTime and Accuracy, and (e) correlation between %Rel and Accuracy.

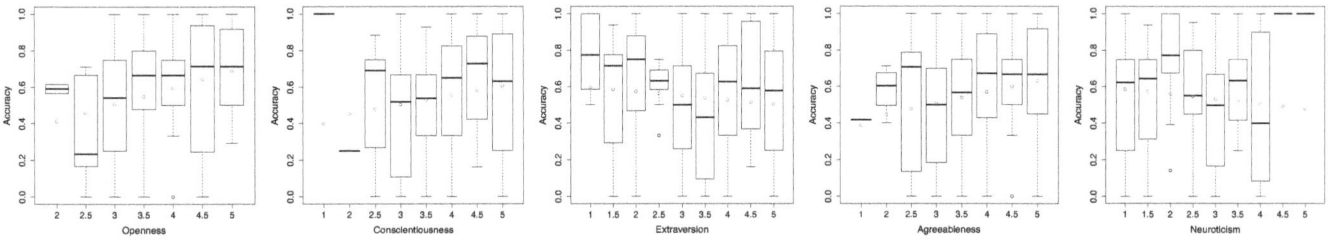

Figure 2: Accuracy over personality traits

exhibiting no particular disposition on this trait. We observe again a high score for *Agreeableness* with a mean of 3.58 (std. 0.83, median 3.5), suggesting that worker are generally trusting and helpful. Finally, we find a low mean score for *Neuroticism*, 2.56 (std. 0.90, median 2.5) which suggests a relaxed nature of the workers.

Among the personality traits, we find that *Openness* significantly relates to accuracy (Spearman $r = 0.19$, $p < 0.05$), see Figure 2. *Conscientiousness* and *Agreeableness* also have a positive relation to accuracy ($r = 0.10$, not significant and $r = 0.16$, not significant, resp.). *Extraversion* and *Neuroticism* exhibit a negative relation ($r = -0.11$, not significant and $r = -0.08$, not significant, resp.). In general, the results suggest that for high label accuracy, one should attract workers that score high on openness, conscientiousness, and agreeableness, and score low on extraversion and neuroticism.

So far, we related behavioral observations and personality traits to accuracy and found strong relations with %Rel and AvgTime, but mostly weak relations with personality traits. This suggests that the behavioral observations are more effective at distinguishing low quality work for the job at hand, but the personality characteristics, which reflect the person rather than the precise task performance, can be useful to distinguish between good and better workers.

4. ANALYSIS BY WORKER TYPES

In this section we use the typology of workers introduced in Section 2.5 with a 60% threshold for %Rel and Accuracy, and the median time of 468 seconds as threshold for AvgTime, see Table 2.

4.1 Behavior by Worker Type

Our segmentation resulted in a strong correlation between workers types and accuracy (ANOVA, $p < 0.001$). Figure 3a shows the mean accuracy of workers fitting a particular type. Spammers are clearly differentiated from the rest of the workers with very low accuracy while diligent workers obtain the highest label accuracy against the gold set. Although we used label accuracy to define competent and diligent workers relative to incompetent and sloppy workers, it is interesting to note the differences within these two groups. Competent workers underperform diligent ones on average, and show higher performance variation. Among the competent workers, those who work more diligently and spend longer on the task achieve higher label accuracy (Pearson correlation r of 0.40, $p < 0.05$). This suggests that a more granular definition of worker types may be useful in the analysis, e.g., differentiating 'diligent and competent' workers. On the other hand, among diligent workers, AvgTime is only weakly correlated with Accuracy ($r=0.15$, not significant), suggesting that this group of workers is more consistent in their behavior. Interestingly, the relation between AvgTime and Accuracy is much weaker among incompetent workers ($r=0.03$, not significant) and spammers ($r=0.21$, not significant), and negative for sloppy workers ($r=-0.30$, not significant). This suggests that time is less useful for detecting these types of workers.

Table 2: Distribution of workers over types

	Spammer	Sloppy	Incompetent	Competent	Diligent
%Rel	Low	High	High	High	High
AvgTime	–	Low	High	Low	High
Accuracy	–	Low	Low	High	High
Workers	37	29	22	25	42

Earlier we saw that the number of HITs completed by a worker was unhelpful in characterizing workers' performance in the entire crowd sample. However, when we break the sample down by worker types, see Figure 3b, we find that surprisingly, accuracy decreases with a higher number of completed HITs, not only for spammers ($r=-0.14$, not significant), but also for competent ($r=-0.26$, not significant) and diligent workers ($r=-0.37$, $p<0.05$). This may signal fatigue or insufficient ratio of pay verse effort, thus the more serious, but possibly digruntled, workers leaving the task. At the same time, we also see evidence of some competent and diligent workers being 'hooked' on the task, completing as many as 35 HITs (competent, max 24 HITs per diligent worker). The distribution of number of HITs completed is particularly marked for incompetent workers, most of whom do not return after (a not so successful) first try. Sloppy workers have the highest 'return-rate', where the performance of workers decreases with the more HITs they complete ($r=0.37$, $p=0.05$). Again, this suggests that in a refined typology such workers may be labelled as 'sloppy spammers'.

4.2 Personality Traits

Figure 4 shows the personality traits over worker types. For *Openness*, we see marked differences across worker types (ANOVA,

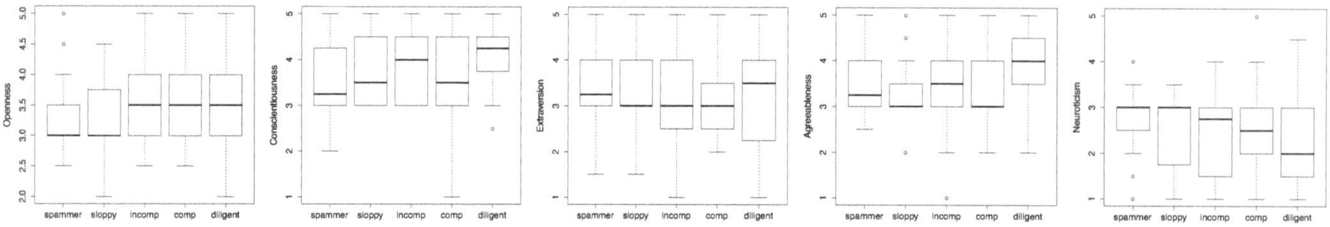

Figure 4: Personality traits over worker types: Openness, Conscientiousness, Extraversion, Agreeableness and Neuroticism

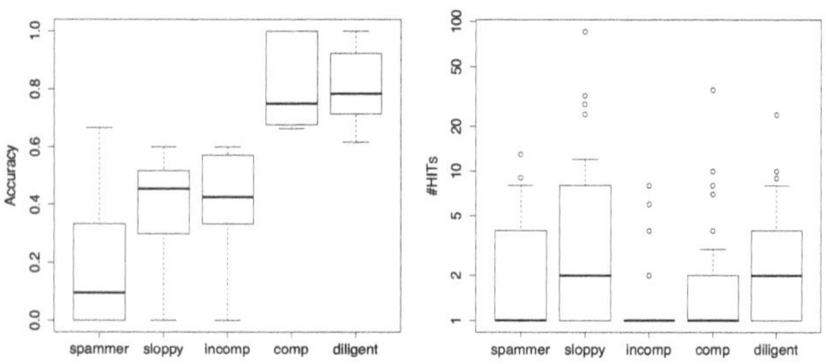

Figure 3: Accuracy and number of HITs by worker types

not significant), with diligent, competent, but also incompetent workers (who try but fail) having higher levels of openness. In terms of *Conscientiousness*, we see higher levels for the competent and diligent types, but the difference is not significant across types. Interestingly, among competent workers there is a relatively large difference between highly conscientiousness workers (with a score of >3.5), who achieve an average accuracy of 92% vs less conscientiousness workers who obtain an average of 74% accuracy. We find no correlation between *Extraversion* and worker types; this trait is not useful for distinguishing between desirable and undesirable workers. In terms of *Agreeableness* we see that faster workers (i.e., sloppy and competent) have noticeably lower scores than the others on this personality trait. Finally, for *Neuroticism*, we see lower levels for the competent and especially for the diligent workers, but the difference is not significant across types. We note that the distribution of BFI scores for spammers is markedly different from other types, with high peaks around the score of 3 for all five traits.

5. CONCLUSIONS

The main focus of this paper is the study of the crowd workers' characteristics, performed on the workers engaged in the crowdsourced evaluation of the INEX 2010 Book TrackâĂŹs *Prove It* task. We observed workers' behavioral patterns (number of HITs completed, average HIT completion time, fraction of useful labels contributed by a worker) and their personality profiles, based on the Big Five personality traits. We related these characteristics to the accuracy of the labels provided by the workers and found a strong correlation with HIT completion time, fraction of useful labels, and the Openness trait. Based on the behavioral patterns we defined five worker types (Spammer, Sloppy, Incompetent, Competent, Diligent) and demonstrated the benefits of such a segmentation for further analysis of the workers' data. By combining such behavioral typologies with the workers' personality traits, we can potentially identify the best workers for a given job and develop methods to attract them. Indeed, in our specific case, we showed that several workers' characteristics strongly correlate with the label quality. Such findings are useful not only for segmenting and analyzing the collected data but explaining how different HIT designs lead to different output quality by attracting different crowds.

REFERENCES

[1] O. Alonso and R. A. Baeza-Yates. Design and implementation of relevance assessments using crowdsourcing. In *Proc. ECIR'11*, pages 153–164, 2011.

[2] O. Alonso, D. E. Rose, and B. Stewart. Crowdsourcing for relevance evaluation. *SIGIR Forum*, 42:9–15, November 2008.

[3] B. Carterette and I. Soboroff. The effect of assessor error on ir system evaluation. In *Proc. SIGIR'10*, pages 539–546. ACM, 2010.

[4] J. S. Downs, M. B. Holbrook, S. Sheng, and L. F. Cranor. Are your participants gaming the system?: screening Mechanical Turk workers. In *Proc. CHI'10*, pages 2399–2402, 2010.

[5] S. D. Gosling, S. Gaddis, and S. Vazire. Personality impressions based on Facebook profiles. *Psychology*, pages 1–4, 2007.

[6] C. Grady and M. Lease. Crowdsourcing document relevance assessment with Mechanical Turk. In *Proc. CSLDAMT'10*, pages 172–179, 2010.

[7] J. Howe. *Crowdsourcing: Why the Power of the Crowd Is Driving the Future of Business*. Crown Publishing Group, 2008.

[8] J.-H. Huang and Y.-C. Yang. The relationship between personality traits and online shopping motivations. *Social Behavior and Personality*, 38:673–680, 2010.

[9] P. G. Ipeirotis. Analyzing the Amazon Mechanical Turk marketplace. *XRDS*, 17:16–21, 2010.

[10] O. P. John, L. P. Naumann, and C. J. Soto. Paradigm shift to the integrative big-five trait taxonomy. In *Handbook of personality*, chapter 4, pages 114–212. Guilford Press, New York NY, 2008.

[11] G. Kazai. In search of quality in crowdsourcing for search engine evaluation. In *Proc. ECIR'11*, pages 165–176, 2011.

[12] G. Kazai, J. Kamps, M. Koolen, and N. Milic-Frayling. Crowdsourcing for book search evaluation: impact of HIT design on comparative system ranking. In *Proc. SIGIR'11*, pages 205–214, 2011.

[13] G. Kazai, M. Koolen, J. Kamps, A. Doucet, and M. Landoni. Overview of the INEX 2010 book track: Scaling up the evaluation using crowdsourcing. In *Proc. INEX'10*, pages 101–120, 2011.

[14] A. Kittur, E. H. Chi, and B. Suh. Crowdsourcing user studies with Mechanical Turk. In *Proc. CHI'08*, CHI '08, pages 453–456, 2008.

[15] M. Kosinski, F. Radlinski, and P. Kohli. Personality and online behavior. In *Proc. CIKM'11*, 2011. ACM.

[16] J. Le, A. Edmonds, V. Hester, and L. Biewald. Ensuring quality in crowdsourced search relevance evaluation: The effects of training question distribution. In *Proc. CSE'10*, pages 21–26, 2010.

[17] B. Rammstedt and O. P. John. Measuring personality in one minute or less: A 10-item short version of the Big Five Inventory in English and German. *Journal of Research in Personality*, 41:203–212, 2007.

[18] J. Ross, L. Irani, M. S. Silberman, A. Zaldivar, and B. Tomlinson. Who are the crowdworkers?: shifting demographics in Mechanical Turk. In *Proc. CHI 2010*, pages 2863–2872. ACM, 2010.

[19] R. Snow, B. O'Connor, D. Jurafsky, and A. Y. Ng. Cheap and fast—but is it good?: evaluating non-expert annotations for natural language tasks. In *Proc. EMNLP'08*, pages 254–263, 2008.

[20] J. Vuurens, A. P. de Vries, and C. Eickhoff. How much spam can you take? an analysis of crowdsourcing results to increase accuracy. In *Proc. ACM SIGIR Workshop on Crowdsourcing for Information Retrieval (CIR'11)*, pages 21–26, 2011. ACM.

[21] D. Zhu and B. Carterette. An analysis of assessor behavior in crowdsourced preference judgments. In *Proc. CSE'10*, pages 17–20, 2010.

A Nugget-based Test Collection Construction Paradigm

Shahzad Rajput Virgil Pavlu Peter B. Golbus Javed A. Aslam

College of Computer and Information Science
Northeastern University
360 Huntington Ave, #202 WVH
Boston, MA 02115, USA
{rajput, vip, pgolbus, jaa}@ccs.neu.edu

ABSTRACT

The problem of building test collections is central to the development of information retrieval systems such as search engines. Starting with a few relevant "nuggets" of information manually extracted from existing TREC corpora, we implement and test a methodology that finds and correctly assesses the vast majority of relevant documents found by TREC assessors—as well as up to four times more additional relevant documents. Our methodology produces highly accurate test collections that hold the promise of addressing the issues of scalability, reusability, and applicability.

Categories and Subject Descriptors

H.3 [**Information Systems**]: Information Storage and Retrieval; H.3.4 [**Systems and Software**]: Performance Evaluation

General Terms

Measurement, Performance

1. INTRODUCTION

The key limitation of the Cranfield paradigm is that *the information relevant to a topic is encoded by documents.* Thus, assessing the performance of an information retrieval system requires effectively complete relevance judgments.

For large collections of documents and/or topics, it is impractical to assess the relevance of each document to each topic. Instead, a small subset of the documents is chosen. A number of IR systems are used to find documents believed to be relevant to the topics. A "pool" of these documents is selected to be judged; only the relevance of these documents is assessed.

This gives rise to the following problems:

1. **Scalability:** The Cranfield paradigm and its variants cannot scale to large collections and/or topic sets. For example, the query "Barack Obama" yields about 233 million results on Google as of August 2011; it would be impossible to judge any meaningful sample of these documents at a reasonable cost or in a reasonable amount of time.

2. **Reusability:** For static collections, novel systems will retrieve unjudged but relevant documents, and the assessments of these systems will be inaccurate. For dynamic collections (such as the World Wide Web), new documents will be added and old documents removed, rendering even statically constructed "effectively complete" relevance assessments incomplete over time.

3. **Applicability:** It can be difficult to apply a test collection designed for one retrieval task to another retrieval task. The current methodologies used to address the issues of scale and reusability can exacerbate this problem.

Various attempts to address the issues described above have been proposed. Sampling techniques such as statAP [6], the Minimal Test Collection methodology [5] and their variants have been used extensively in various TREC tracks. A carefully chosen sample of documents is drawn from the pool, these documents are judged, and a *statistical estimate* of the true value of a performance measure over that pool is derived. Given that accurate estimates can be derived using samples as small as roughly 5% of the entire pool, these methods permit the use of pools 20 times the size of standard fully-judged pools. However, this is only a stop-gap measure. These methods cannot scale to collections the size of the web and do not address the issue of dynamic collections. Furthermore, they reduce applicability in that the samples drawn and estimates obtained are typically tailored to specific evaluation measures, *e.g.* average precision.

Crowd-sourcing relevance judgments, via, for example, Mechanical Turk, has also been proposed [1]. However, this too is only a stop-gap measure, allowing us to use collections larger in roughly direct proportion to the relative ease (in time or cost) of crowd-sourced judgments vs. assessor judgments: if 10 to 100 crowd-sourced judgments can be obtained in the same time or at the same cost as 1 assessor judgment, then pools one to two orders of magnitude larger than standard pools can be contemplated. But this still does not scale to the web, or address the issue of dynamic collections. The use of click-through data has also been proposed [8], but this is only applicable to the web, and only for those topics and documents with sufficient "clicks".

In order to address the inherent limitations of the Cranfield paradigm, we propose a test collection construction

CIKM'11, October 24–28, 2011, Glasgow, Scotland, UK.

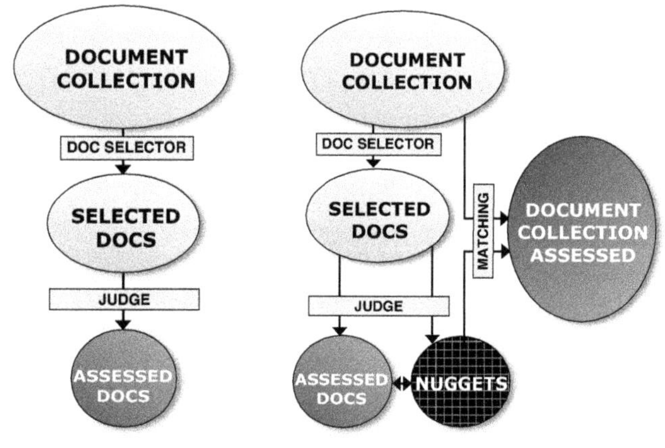

Figure 1: For a given query, selected documents are evaluated as "relevant/nonrelevant". Left: Traditional TREC strategy for relevance. Right: Proposed nuggets methodology.

methodology based on *information nuggets*. We refer to minimal, atomic units of relevant information as "nuggets". Nuggets can range from simple answers, such as people's names, to full sentences or paragraphs. In this model, assessors mark the information that is relevant contained within a document, rather than mark the documents containing relevant information. This relevant *information* is used to automatically assign relevance judgments to documents.

2. METHODOLOGY

The Cranfield paradigm and its variants encode the information relevant to a topic by *documents*. Our hypothesis is that while the number of *documents* potentially relevant to a topic can be enormous, the amount of *information* relevant to a topic, the nuggets, is far, far smaller. Thus, collecting and encoding the relatively small set of nuggets, as opposed to the dynamically changing and effectively infinite set of *documents*, relevant to a topic will enable us to address the issues of scalability, reusability, and applicability.

Figure 1 graphically illustrates the differences between the traditional Cranfield-style methodology (left) and the nugget-based methodology proposed (right). The nuggets themselves are the relevant and useful pieces of information for a given topic—the information that the user seeks. As a set, they yield a natural encoding of the information relevant to a topic. In principle, if this set is complete, we can use the nuggets to infer the relevance of any document.

To build our test collection, we ask assessors to view documents as before. However, rather than providing binary or graded relevance judgments, we instead ask the assessor to extract nuggets. These nuggets, the information relevant to a topic, are used to automatically infer the relevance of arbitrary documents in the collection.

3. PILOT IMPLEMENTATION

Building a test collection in our framework consists of three distinct tasks (the rectangular boxes in Figure 1, right): (1) selecting documents from which to extract nuggets, (2) extracting nuggets from those documents, and (3) using the extracted nuggets to algorithmically create relevance judgments for any desired subset of the corpus. Each of these tasks could be performed in various ways; in this section, we document the decisions we made in implementing our methodology.

Document Selection. Any human assessment of documents must use a procedure to select the documents to be judged. Generally, documents retrieved by many systems and/or at higher ranks are preferred to documents retrieved by fewer systems and/or at lower ranks. We used the statAP selection mechanism because it has been shown to be an effective document selection procedure in previous TREC ad hoc tracks for system evaluation [6].

Nugget Extraction. Nugget extraction was performed by our internal assessors (primarily graduate students engaged in IR research). For each *relevant* document in the sample, the assessor was asked to extract the relevant nuggets (see Figure 2 for the nugget extraction interface). They were instructed to find the smallest piece of text that constitutes relevant information in and of itself. However, assessors were not restricted to text as it appears in the document; slight modifications of the text, *e.g.* co-reference disambiguation, deleting contextual stopwords, etc. were encouraged. In the end, the vast majority of nuggets collected were relevant information extracts encoded in the form of actual text contained in relevant documents.

Assessors were also given the option of adding topic keywords, which would be used later as a retrieval filter. If a topic has keywords associated with it, a document must contain at least one keyword to be considered relevant for that topic. For example, consider the topic "`JFK assassination`". An assessor might add the keyword "`Kennedy`". If a document does not contain this term, it will not be considered relevant.

Inferred Relevance Judgements. To test our methodology, we implemented a text-based matching algorithm that automatically infers the relevance of documents given the nuggets extracted. According to the typical TREC definition of relevance for ad hoc retrieval, a document is considered relevant if it contains a single relevant piece of information. Thus, if a document contains a piece of text sufficiently similar to a known relevant information nugget, then the document must necessarily be relevant. Therefore, each document was given a relevance score based on whether it matched any nugget.

The matching algorithm is based on a variant of *shingle matching*, which is often used in near-duplicate detection [4]. A shingle is a sequence of k consecutive words in a piece of text. For example, after stopwording, the nugget `"John Kennedy was elected president in 1960"` has the following shingles for $k = 3$: (`John Kennedy elected`), (`Kennedy elected president`), and (`elected president 1960`).

Given the set of nuggets, we computed a relevance score for each document by (1) computing a score for each shingle, (2) combining these shingle scores to obtain a score for each nugget, and (3) combining these nugget scores to obtain a score for the document:

- **Shingle score:** For any nugget and each shingle of size k, let S be the minimum *span* of words in the document that contains all shingle words in any order. A shingle matches well if it is contained in a small span. We used the algorithm presented in [7] to find

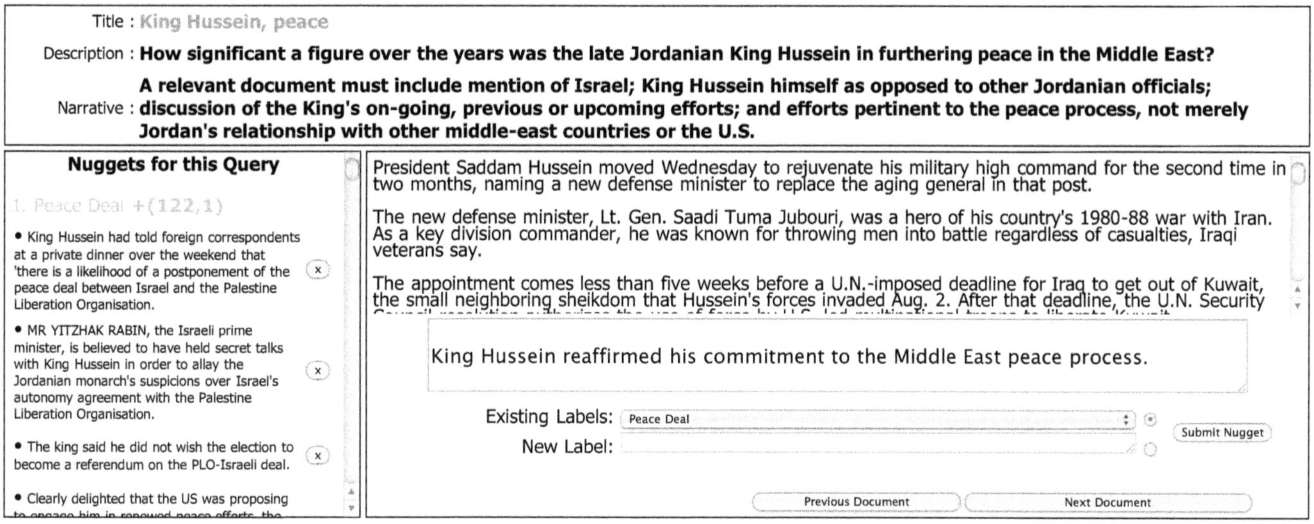

Figure 2: Nugget extraction interface.

the shortest span of shingle words in a text document in linear time. We define the shingle score as follows:

$$shingleScore = \lambda^{(S-k)/k},$$

where λ is a fixed decay parameter. We found $\lambda = 0.95$ to be an effective value. Note that in contrast to standard shingle matching, we do not require all shingle words to be present in the matching document in the same order or contiguously; by our definition, such a shingle would have a "perfect" shingle score of 1.

- **Nugget score:** To obtain a score for each nugget, we average the scores of each of its shingles:

$$nuggetScore = \frac{1}{\#shingles} \sum_{s \in shingles} shingleScore(s).$$

- **Document score:** Since we wish to know if the document matched at least one nugget, the relevance score of each document is defined to be the maximum nugget score of the document:

$$docScore = \max_{n \in nuggets} nuggetScore(n).$$

- **Inferred relevance judgment:** We convert a document relevance score to an inferred relevance judgment by simple thresholding. The threshold $\theta = 0.8$ is held constant across all experiments.

4. VALIDATION

In order to show that our methodology produces useful test collections and addresses the issues of scalability, reusability, and applicability, we must show that our inferred relevance judgments are correct and that our system can return far more relevant documents than traditional methods. To this end, we constructed two separate test collections based on well-studied collections produced by previous TREC tracks.

The first experiment uses ad hoc retrieval data from the TREC 8 ad hoc task: a collection built around a corpus of about 500,000 clean text newswire articles. It is considered to have effectively complete assessments, with an average of about 1,736 assessed documents for each of 50 queries. We refer to this data collectively (documents, judgments, queries, systems) as "ad hoc".

The second experiment is based on data from the TREC09 web track diversity task, which uses the ClueWeb09 html collection of about one billion documents. It contains an average of only about 528 documents assessed per query. This data is referred to as "web".

Using statAP sampling, we selected 200 documents for each query from each collection. Of these documents, we extracted nuggets from only those that had been judged *relevant* by TREC assessors. The TREC 8 ad hoc collection sample, denoted "SampleAdHoc", consists of approximately 11% of the documents assessed by TREC. The TREC09 web sample, denoted "SampleWeb", consists of approximately 38% of the documents assessed by TREC. On average, about 87 nuggets were extracted per query for the ad hoc sample, and about 62 nuggets were extracted per query for the web sample. (See table below.)

Sample	Relevant Documents	Nuggets
SampleAdHoc	34.02	86.98
SampleWeb	25.18	61.82

Given the nuggets extracted, we employ the matching algorithm to infer binary relevance for all documents not contained in our sample. The relevance judgments produced are referred to by the sample of documents from which nuggets were extracted, *e.g.* "SampleAdHoc+InfRel(Nuggets)" refers to the judgments by TREC assessors of documents in the ad hoc sample, plus the judgments inferred for the remaining documents.

We demonstrate the correctness of our inferred judgments in two ways: by comparing our judgments to those provided by TREC, and by verifying the inferred relevance of documents that were not assessed by TREC with independent human assessors. However, we must bear in mind that the notion of correctness of relevance judgments is somewhat problematic. Inter-assessor disagreement [3, 9] is a well known phenomenon, as the question of relevance is ambiguous for many documents. Even if our inferences were perfect, we would still expect to see disagreement with our inferences and any other judgments.

After thresholding, we can compare our inferred judgments against the published TREC qrel, measuring precision, recall, F1, etc. (See table below.)

Truncated Result List	MAP	Precision	Recall	F1
SampleAdHoc	0.48	0.18	0.47	0.26
SampleAdHoc+InfRel	0.76	0.88	0.65	0.75
SampleWeb	0.24	0.23	0.25	0.24
SampleWeb+InfRel	0.75	0.88	0.60	0.71

For comparison, a previously published comparison of inferred relevance judgments to existing qrels [2] cites an F1 of 0.68 (compared with our F1=0.75). From this we conclude that the relevance judgments produced by our methodology are very similar to those produced by the TREC assessors.

To test the hypothesis that our method finds many additional relevant documents, as well as to further test the correctness of our inferred relevance judgments, we also validated the correctness of our relevance judgments for documents from the web corpus not assessed by TREC. Our matching algorithm marked an average of about 400 additional documents as relevant per query. We selected a uniform random sample of about 80 per query and performed a validation of these inferred relevance assessments using Amazon's Mechanical Turk service.[1] (See table below.) Note that the "outside qrel" numbers given below are maximum likelihood estimates of the number of documents in each category given the random sample that was judged.

	Within qrel	Outside qrel	Total
Judged Rel	2,969	14,624	17,593
Judged NonRel	411	5,329	5,740
Total	3,380	19,953	23,333
Agreement	87.84%	73.29%	75.40%

This experiment resulted in an agreement of 73.29% between the Mechanical Turk judges and our inferred assessments. Given the overall sample size of about 4000 documents, there is a 99.9% statistical confidence that the number of relevant documents outside the TREC qrel is at least 14,049.

Overall, even with nuggets extracted from a small sample of assessed documents, we were able to correctly infer relevance for a large number of relevant documents, with limited false positive mistakes and within the realm of inter-assessor disagreement.

5. CONCLUSION AND FUTURE WORK

Our methodology produces reliable relevance judgments at a substantially reduced cost. Based on reasonable assumptions,[2] we were able to construct SampleAdHoc in one-sixth the time and SampleWeb in half the time that TREC required to create the underlying collections.

Preliminary results with our nugget-based test collections indicate that the relevance judgments inferred from nuggets are also accurate enough to perform reliable and reusable system evaluations; in our pilot study, we obtained system orderings with Kendall's τ at or above 0.9 as compared to ground truth TREC assessments.

In future work, we intend to explore the application of nuggets to areas such as learning-to-rank, novelty and diversity, and so-called "knowledge engines" such as Wolfram|Alpha. We also hope to develop new performance metrics that uses nugget matching to directly measure the information content of the documents in a ranked list, rather than simply measuring the ranks at which relevant documents appear.

Acknowledgment: This material is based upon work supported by the National Science Foundation under Grant No. IIS-1017903. Any opinions, findings and conclusions or recommendations expressed in this material are those of the author(s) and do not necessarily reflect the views of the National Science Foundation (NSF).

[1]mturk.com. Each Mechanical Turk job was verified for quality: each job consisted of 30 documents, out of which 10 were verification documents with known TREC assessments. Turkers were required to correctly assess 70% of these 10 documents; otherwise, the job was not accepted. Furthermore, some jobs were performed by multiple judges. If a document had multiple assessments for a given query, the majority vote was used. In case of a tie, the document was discarded from measurement.

[2]Private communication with a TREC organizer.

6. REFERENCES

[1] *33rd ACM SIGIR Workshop on Crowdsourcing for Search Evaluation*, Geneva, Switzerland, 2010.

[2] Javed A. Aslam and Emine Yilmaz. Inferring document relevance via average precision. In Susan Dumais, Efthimis N. Efthimiadis, David Hawking, and Kalervo Jarvelin, editors, *Proceedings of the 29th Annual International ACM SIGIR Conference on Research and Development in Information Retrieval*, pages 601–602. ACM Press, August 2006.

[3] Peter Bailey, Nick Craswell, Ian Soboroff, Paul Thomas, Arjen P. de Vries, and Emine Yilmaz. Relevance assessment: Are judges exchangeable and does it matter? In *Proceedings of the 31st annual international ACM SIGIR conference on Research and development in information retrieval*, SIGIR '08, pages 667–674, New York, NY, USA, 2008. ACM.

[4] Andrei Z. Broder. Identifying and filtering near-duplicate documents. In *Proceedings of the 11th Annual Symposium on Combinatorial Pattern Matching*, COM '00, pages 1–10, London, UK, 2000. Springer-Verlag.

[5] Ben Carterette, James Allan, and Ramesh K. Sitaraman. Minimal test collections for retrieval evaluation. In *Proceedings of SIGIR*, pages 268–275, 2006.

[6] Ben Carterette, Virgil Pavlu, Evangelos Kanoulas, Javed A. Aslam, and James Allan. Evaluation over thousands of queries. In Sung-Hyon Myaeng, Douglas W. Oard, Fabrizio Sebastiani, Tat-Seng Chua, and Mun-Kew Leong, editors, *Proceedings of the 31st Annual International ACM SIGIR Conference on Research and Development in Information Retrieval*, pages 651–658. ACM Press, July 2008.

[7] Steve Krenzel. Finding blurbs. Website. http://www.stevekrenzel.com/articles/blurbs.

[8] Filip Radlinski, Madhu Kurup, and Thorsten Joachims. How does clickthrough data reflect retrieval quality? In *Proceeding of the 17th ACM conference on Information and knowledge management*, CIKM '08, pages 43–52, New York, NY, USA, 2008. ACM.

[9] Ellen M. Voorhees. Variations in relevance judgments and the measurement of retrieval effectiveness. *Inf. Process. Manage.*, 36:697–716, September 2000.

Recency Ranking by Diversification of Result Set

Andrey Styskin, Fedor Romanenko, Fedor Vorobyev, Pavel Serdyukov
Search Quality Group, Yandex
119021, Leo Tolstoy 16
Moscow, Russia
{styskin, fedor, melton, pavser}@yandex-team.ru

ABSTRACT

In this paper, we propose a web search retrieval approach which automatically detects recency sensitive queries and increases the freshness of the ordinary document ranking by a degree proportional to the probability of the need in recent content. We propose to solve the recency ranking problem by using result diversification principles and deal with the query's non-topical ambiguity appearing when the need in recent content can be detected only with uncertainty. Our offline and online experiments with millions of queries from real search engine users demonstrate the significant increase in satisfaction of users presented with a search result generated by our approach.

Categories and Subject Descriptors:
H.3 [Information Storage and Retrieval]: H.3.3 Information Search and Retrieval.

General Terms:
Algorithms, Measurement, Performance, Experimentation.

Keywords:
Recency ranking, diversity, web search.

1. INTRODUCTION

Modern web search engines face the need to consider different non-topical facets of relevance when ranking web documents in response to user queries. While the need in a certain document feature, besides the topical relevance, might be expressed only implicitly in the query, it is still important to recognize its presence in order to adequately satisfy the underlying information need. However, the quality of such recognition cannot be perfect in all cases. Consequently, it brings a certain level of non-topical ambiguity to the queries, which must be taken into account when generating a search result.

One of the most popular non-topical facets of relevance is document freshness. In this paper, we demonstrate how to deal with query ambiguity surrounding the need for recent information. Such ambiguity typically appears during short periods of time, when users become increasingly interested in one newsworthy aspect, typically an event, related to a well-known entity: a person (e.g. [Michael Jackson]) or a location (e.g. [Japan]). For example, consider the query [michael jackson]. There has been constant and continuing interest in the biography and discography of Michael Jackson, which can be satisfied even by non-fresh documents, but users issuing the query [michael jackson] on (June 25, 2009) were often looking for the freshest news related to the Michael Jackson's death. But both intents (news and discography) continued even during this period.

Recently, a number of techniques for search result diversification has been proposed in order to compensate for topical ambiguity of queries and increase the chance to satisfy the user. We propose to follow the same principles to deal with recency sensitive queries and their non-topical ambiguity. Our approach aims to maximize the probability that the average user finds some useful information among the search results on recency sensitive queries by blending necessary amount of recent results into the result set. To the best of our knowledge, our paper describes the first attempt to tackle the problem of non-topical query ambiguity with a result set diversification technique.

The main contributions of this paper include: 1) the approach to recency ranking by means of search result set diversification, 2) a thorough offline and online evaluation of the proposed approach in terms of a search result quality metric and the overall user satisfaction.

The remainder of the paper is organized as follows. We first review the related work in Section 2. Section 3 describes our machine learning based approach to obtaining a smooth probability of the need in recent content for a query. Section 4 explains how we utilize that probability to diversify ordinary document rankings with fresh documents. Section 5 presents the results of evaluation and Section 6 concludes the paper and outlines the research questions left for future work.

2. RELATED WORK

There are only a few papers focused exclusively on recency ranking. The pioneering work in this area proposed to learn a ranking function which is trained using a subset of features that help to infer the recency of page content [3]. The follow-up work extended that subset to include features extracted from the micro-blogging data stream [4]. Our approach differs in a number of aspects. For one, we try to deal with temporal ambiguity of queries and balance the number of fresh and ordinary relevant documents in the

CIKM'11, October 24–28, 2011, Glasgow, Scotland, UK.

result set, based on the smooth probability of the need in recent content. As a result, while the aforementioned works focus entirely on improving the ranking for one specific case (breaking news queries, 1-2% of search engine's traffic), we aim to affect the ordinary ranking by explicitly increasing its freshness for any query with non-zero probability of the need in recent content. The inference of query's recency sensitivity plays an important role in recency ranking. The aforementioned works detected only highly recency sensitive queries using a linear combination of a few features. In a similar way, Arguello et. al. [5] used a number of features to find verticals relevant for a query, including the News vertical. While those methods focused on binary classification of a query, our work is rather based on regression to obtain and utilize the precise estimate of the probability of the need in recent content.

Our work is also largely based on the principles of search result diversification. In [2], a framework for evaluation that systematically rewards diversity was proposed. In [1], a systematic approach to diversifying results that aims to minimize the risk of dissatisfaction of the average user was presented. A number of follow-up papers were published recently which we do not cover here due to space constraints. Our work complements the research in this area by demonstrating that diversification principles and algorithms are also helpful to increase the chance to satisfy the user in the presence of non-topical query ambiguity.

3. RECENCY SENSITIVE QUERY CLASSIFICATION

In order to quantify the ambiguity of a recency sensitive query, we learned a regression model which predicted the level of interest in recent documents for a particular query and a particular time slot. We used around 30 different features (including their minor modifications) previously described in the papers dealing with similar problems (see Section 2). We do not provide a thorough analysis of feature importance due to space constraints. The most valuable features were the probabilities of queries to be generated by language models of recent content from different sources, including the query, social and news data streams, as well as the probability of a click on a news item.

To train the regression model we asked annotators to provide labels of recency sensitivity for a set of queries. In order to preselect a list of candidate queries for assessment, we defined a small threshold on each feature used to learn our regression function and filtered out all queries that did not have at least one feature value exceeding the corresponding threshold. As a result, we collected judgments for a set of 4000 unique queries issued to Yandex (www.yandex.ru) web search engine (the major russian search engine) over the period of three weeks. On each day during this period, judges were presented with the queries submitted by search engine users on that particular day and were asked to determine whether these queries express an interest in upcoming or ongoing events for which web search users would prefer recent content. Labeling queries basically represented the manual assignment of the probabilities that a particular query is recency sensitive. So, if a query was strictly about a recent event it received the probability of 0.95 (e.g. [flood in thailand] on the day of the event). If a query's primary interest was related to a recent event, but many users would also like to see just topically relevant results, it was labeled with 0.75 (e.g. the query [oscar] on the day of the ceremony). If the query's primary interest was not likely to be focused on a particular event, but there was some chance that users issuing such a query would look for some fresh content, assessors assigned the probability of 0.25 (e.g. it always makes sense to present users with some recent content in response to the query [britney spears]). Otherwise, a query was assigned zero probability to be recency sensitive. Each query was labeled by 3 assessors. Average Cohen's kappa coefficient between all pairs of assessors was 0.76, which is considered a substantial agreement.

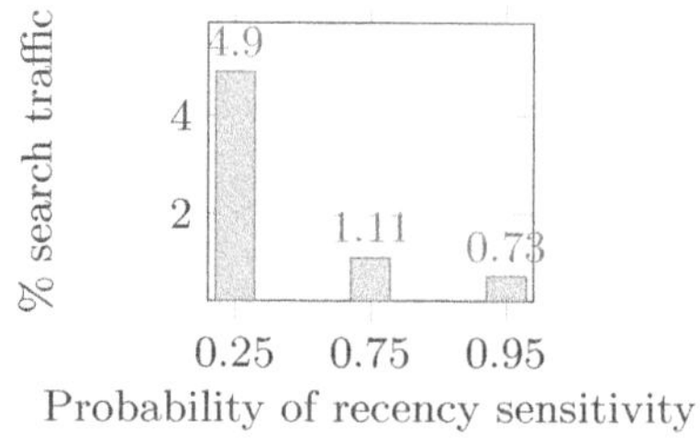

Figure 1: Recency sensitive queries traffic coverage

We learned the regression model to assign smooth probability of the need in fresh content to any query using Gradient Boosted Regression Trees (GDBT) [8]. Recency sensitive queries traffic coverage by these types based on 4000 human made judgments is illustrated on Figure 1.

4. DIVERSIFICATION OF THE SEARCH RESULT WITH FRESH DOCUMENTS

4.1 Diversification method

To produce a search result for recency sensitive queries we follow the search result set diversification principles. Namely, we aim to maximize the utility of the diversified search result expressed in terms of the Expected Reciprocal Rank measure, which we extended to include an abandonment probability and to handle multiple query intents. Both extensions are proposed by Chapelle et. al. [9] and we combine both of them in this work. We call this metric Intent Aware Expected Reciprocal Rank with Abandonment (ERR-IAA) and regard as the objective we aim to maximize:

$$\text{ERR-IAA} = \sum_{i=1}^{r} pBreak^{r} * \sum_{t} P(t|q) * \prod_{i=1}^{r-1} (1 - R_i^t) * R_r^t, \quad (1)$$

where $P(t|q)$ is taken from the distribution over two classes of information needs t (the need in fresh topically relevant documents and the need in any topically relevant documents) for the given query q. Each document is assigned the probability R_r^t to satisfy the information need of type t at position r. We take into account the probability that the documents at the previous $r-1$ positions have not satisfied that need. We also assume that any user always may stop (abandon the search result) at rank r with the abandonment probability $pBreak^r$ due to accumulated frustration ($pBreak$ is empirically set to 0.85 in our experiments).

We assume that the optimal search result page is the one which maximizes the ERR-IAA measure. In order to maxi-

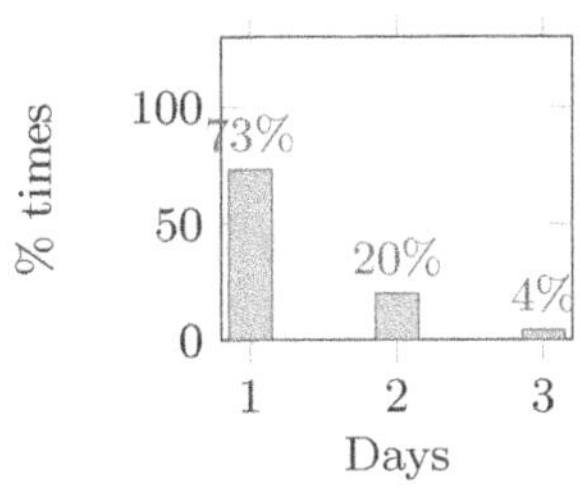

Figure 2: Cumulative share of query instances submitted since the day of the first query

mize it, we follow the greedy approach described by Agrawal et. al. [1] and select the document, whose selection leads to the maximum increase of the objective at each step of the selection process.

4.2 Aggregation of ordinary and fresh results

We also assume that any web document is fresh only for 3 days since the time of its creation or the last update. We use a proprietary algorithm to extract the correct and the most relevant timestamp from document content. Our choice of the number of days is motivated by the following observations. First, according to the studies by Dong et. al. [3], assessors, who judged the freshness of a set of documents, found out that the 1–4 days old documents are the ones most likely containing fresh content. Second, the peak of interest in new events lasts for three days in average according to our analysis of 100,000 spiky and long-tail (so, previously unseen) queries submitted by users of Yandex search engine in January, 2011. Figure 2 shows average share of total query volume for each such a query per for each day since the 1st day they become first known to the search engine until the 3rd day when their popularity falls off almost completely.

Guided by our definition of a fresh document, we produce the ranking of fresh topically relevant documents by simply removing the outdated documents from the initial ranking. As a result, we have two document rankings which we use to maximize the ERR-IAA measure, described by Equation 1: the one containing any topically relevant documents and the one containing only fresh topically relevant documents.

However, in order to proceed with maximization of our objective, we still needed to determine the probabilities of relevance R_i^t. In order to be independent of specific retrieval scores, which may significantly vary over queries and bear a relative, rather than absolute meaning, we turn document ranks into their probabilities of relevance using the internal search engine's statistics about the probability to encounter a relevant document at the specific position. So, since we fixed the probabilities of document relevance for each of two aggregated rankings, the final ordering of documents depended only on the probabilistic output of our classifier of query's recency sensitivity.

5. EXPERIMENTS

5.1 Offline results

The research questions we aim to answer in this subsection are how our search quality objective (ERR-IAA) changes while we aggregate two result sets: ordinary and fresh, and how the quality of our classifier of query's recency sensitivity affects the quality of such aggregation.

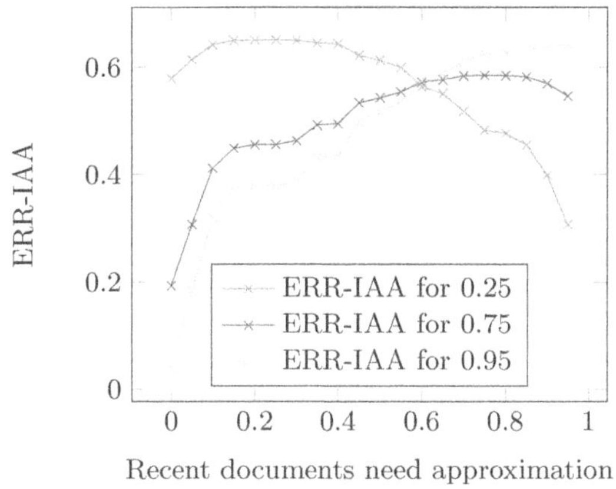

Figure 3: ERR-IAA for queries with different "true" probabilities of need in fresh content

Figure 3 demonstrates how ERR-IAA changes as the estimation of the probability of the need in recent documents deviates from its true value for the three different true values assigned by our assessors: 0.25, 0.75 and 0.95. As we see, while minor errors in the probability estimation do not significantly affect the quality of the aggregated ranking, it is evidently important to keep the errors low as the ranking quality drops quite rapidly with their increase.

Further, we analyze the quality of the aggregation for the recency sensitivity classifier that we use in this work (Figure 4). We split our queries judged by their recency sensitivity (see Section 3) into two parts (training and test, 2000 queries each) and conduct the evaluation via two-fold cross-validation. We train our classifier on the training set of queries and evaluate how its accuracy affects the quality of the aggregation on the test set. Note, that in a real setting that we simulate in this experiment, the initial ranking naturally contains some number of fresh documents. As a result, ERR-IAA measured on the ordinary ranking starts to grow as the recency need probability approaches 1.0, since the queries with such high probability of the need in recent content are typically the queries that are unambiguous: highly descriptive and possessing enough discriminating power to retrieve very relevant content. For example, for the query [europe alert icelandic ash cloud], both the ordinary result set and the fresh result set are quite similar on the day of the infamous volcano eruption. The major gain from applying the diversification comes for the queries with probabilities of the need in recent content from 0.3 to 0.8. This is to be expected, as our approach to recency ranking focuses on the cases of temporal query ambiguity, in contrast to the previous approaches, which aim to maximize the quality of ranking for the queries with no temporal ambiguity (see [3, 4] for more details).

5.2 Online results

In order to test our approach in terms of web search engine metrics measuring user satisfaction, we conducted an A/B test [7]. Some users of Yandex search engine were always presented with ordinary search results (control bucket), which were never diversified with fresh documents, and some

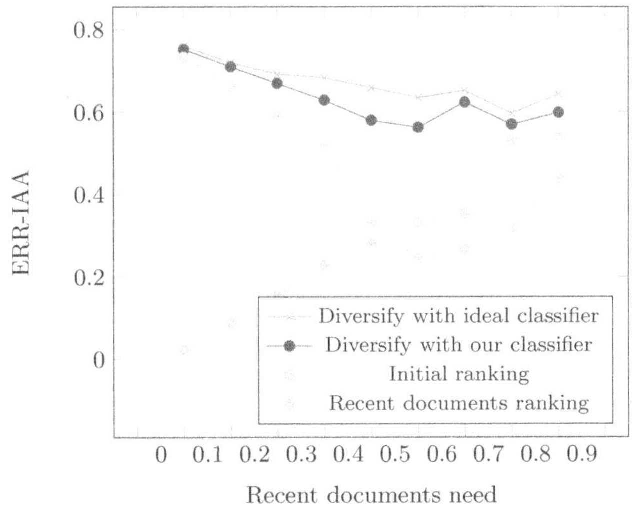

Figure 4: ERR-IAA for queries with different level of ambiguity, diversified and non-diversified rankings

users were presented with diversified search results (treatment bucket). We ran the experiment for 13 days in March 2011 and that involved about 10 million queries in each bucket (issued by real users as we filtered out bots and spammers). We measured user satisfaction using metrics suggested by Radlinski et. al. [10], as they are known to correlate with search result quality. Final results for the control and the treatment are listed in Table 1.

Table 1: User behavior metrics for the control and the treatment buckets

Metric	Meaning	Contr	Treat
Abandonment Rate	% of queries with no results clicked	33.65	32.77
Time to first click	Time to first click on any result (in sec)	10.95	10.76
1st Position CTR	% of queries with 1st position clicked	44.22	45.31
2nd Position CTR	% of queries with 2nd position clicked	14.88	14.92
First Click Position	Position of first click	1.91	1.87

All metrics in the treatment are significantly different from metrics in the control (Mann-Whitney U test, $\alpha = 0.01$) and all these differences indicate the increase of search result quality after diversification. In other words, the decrease of abandonment rate means less cases when users could not find any relevant result, the decrease of the mean first click position indicates that top results became more relevant, the decrease of the mean time to first click also indicates that relevant results received higher ranks and hence could be spotted faster, and the increase of CTRs of the URLs at the first two positions also indicates their increased relevance.

6. CONCLUSIONS AND FUTURE WORK

In this paper, we present an approach to improve recency ranking, while preserving the overall relevance of the ordinary search result. We developed a multi-grade recency sensitive queries classifier that predicts the degree of the need in recent documents. We further demonstrated how to diversify the ordinary search result with fresh documents by maximizing the search quality measure which takes the query's temporal ambiguity into account. We demonstrated the behavior of our diversification model in different cases using a set of judged queries. We finally confirmed the intuitions behind our approaches by a large-scale online experiment involving millions of queries from real users.

While we consider a fixed time window to determine if documents are fresh, it definitely makes more sense to determine time window which takes the essence of the information need expressed in the query into account. We also need to more systematically handle the challenge of score normalization to obtain the probabilities of document relevance generated according to each possible definition of relevance. In this regard, we look forward to exploit the techniques of results merging developed in the area of Distributed Information Retrieval [6].

The diversification based approach to recency ranking can be also useful to aggregate documents from a set of relevant verticals (videos, images or shopping items). However, the danger of over-diversification is not well studied yet. It is not clear if users would prefer too many results of different kinds blended into one search result page. Our long term goal is to develop a unified approach to deal with several kinds of query ambiguities: topical and non-topical.

7. REFERENCES

[1] Rakesh Agrawal, Sreenivas Gollapudi, Alan Halverson, Samuel Ieong. Diversifying Search Results. In *WSDM'09*

[2] Charles L. A. Clarke, Maheedhar Kolla, Gordon V. Cormack, Olga Vechtomova, Azin Ashkan, Stefan Buttcher, Ian MacKinnon. Novelty and Diversity in Information Retrieval Evaluation In *SIGIR'09*, 2009.

[3] Anlei Dong, Yi Chang, Zhaohui Zheng, Gilad Mishne, Jing Bai, Ruiqiang Zhang, Karolina Buchner, Ciya Liao, Fernando Diaz. Towards Recency Ranking in Web Search In *WSDM'10*, 2010.

[4] Anlei Dong, Ruiqiang Zhang, Pranam Kolari, Jing Bai, Fernando Diaz, Yi Chang, Zhaohui Zheng. Time is of the Essence: Improving Recency Ranking Using Twitter Data In *WWW'10*, 2010.

[5] Jaime Arguello, Fernando Diaz, Jamie Callan, Jean-Francois Crespo. Sources of Evidence for Vertical Selection. In *SIGIR'09*, 2009.

[6] J. Callan. Distributed information retrieval. In W. B. Croft, editor, Advances in Information Retrieval.

[7] Ron Kohavi, Randy Henne, and Dan Sommerfield Practical Guide to Controlled Experiments on the Web: Listen to Your Customers not to the HiPPO. In *KDD '07*, pages 959–967, 2007.

[8] Jerome H. Friedman. Greedy function approximation: A gradient boosting machine In *Annals of Statistics, 29*, pages 1189–1232, 2001.

[9] O. Chapelle, D. Metlzer, Y. Zhang, and P. Grinspan. Expected reciprocal rank for graded relevance. In *Proceedings of the 18th ACM conference on Information and knowledge management*, pages 621–630, 2009.

[10] Filip Radlinski, Madhu Kurup, Thorsten Joachims How Does Clickthrough Data Reflect Retrieval Quality? In *CIKM'08*, pages 26–30, 2008.

Patent Query Reduction using Pseudo-Relevance Feedback

Debasis Ganguly Johannes Leveling Walid Magdy Gareth J. F. Jones
School of Computing, Centre for Next Generation Localisation
Dublin City University, Dublin 9, Ireland
{dganguly, jleveling, wmagdy, gjones}@computing.dcu.ie

ABSTRACT

Queries in patent prior art search are full patent applications and much longer than standard ad hoc search and web search topics. Standard information retrieval (IR) techniques are not entirely effective for patent prior art search because of ambiguous terms in these massive queries. Reducing patent queries by extracting key terms has been shown to be ineffective mainly because it is not clear what the focus of the query is. An optimal query reduction algorithm must thus seek to retain the useful terms for retrieval favouring recall of relevant patents, but remove terms which impair IR effectiveness. We propose a new query reduction technique decomposing a patent application into constituent text segments and computing the Language Modeling (LM) similarities by calculating the probability of generating each segment from the top ranked documents. We reduce a patent query by removing the least similar segments from the query, hypothesising that removal of these segments can increase the precision of retrieval, while still retaining the useful context to achieve high recall. Experiments on the patent prior art search collection CLEF-IP 2010 show that the proposed method outperforms standard pseudo-relevance feedback (PRF) and a naive method of query reduction based on removal of unit frequency terms (UFTs).

Categories and Subject Descriptors

H.3.3 [**INFORMATION STORAGE AND RETRIEVAL**]: Information Search and Retrieval—*Query formulation, Relevance Feedback*

General Terms

Experimentation, Performance, Measurement

Keywords

Query Reduction, Patent Search, Pseudo-Relevance Feedback

1. INTRODUCTION

Patent prior art search involves ad hoc search for already filed patents which may invalidate or at least describe prior art work in a patent application, (henceforth referred to as query patent in this paper). The primary objective and challenges of patent prior art search are different from those of standard ad hoc text and web search. These differences can be summarised as follows: a) the queries are full patent applications comprising of hundreds of words on average in contrast to ad hoc search and web search where the queries typically constitute of two or three words; and b) patent prior art search is a recall oriented task where the primary focus is to retrieve all relevant documents at early ranks in contrast to ad hoc and web search, which is precision oriented.

Another challenge in patent prior art search is the vocabulary mismatch between the existing filed patents and the query patent which arises often due to the obscure style of writing a patent (patentese). Long patent queries comprising of several hundreds of terms fail to represent a focused information need required for high precision retrieval. In addition to this, vocabulary mismatch can be aggravated if naive key word extraction methods are applied in an attempt to form a reduced query, thus in effect leading to a degradation of recall. A balance between precision and recall can be achieved by a careful trade-off between what to remove from the query patent and a reduced query applied to the patent retrieval system. This paper attempts to achieve an effective trade-off in reducing query patents for prior art patent search by utilizing pseudo-relevance information from top ranked retrieved documents.

When applied in standard ad hoc search tasks, pseudo-relevance feedback (PRF) expands the initial query by adding terms which occur most frequently in the assumed relevant top ranked documents from an initial retrieval step in attempt to retrieve relevant documents at higher ranks. However, the massive length of patent queries is not conducive to the query expansion step in PRF because precision at top ranks is low, focus is not clear and added terms are noisy, which in effect introduce further ambiguity to the query. Instead, a more intuitive process is to apply PRF in a reverse process of query reduction. In contrast to ad hoc IR, where query expansion is used to move the initial query representation closer to that of the pseudo-relevant documents, we use pseudo-relevance information to make the feedback query more similar to the pseudo-relevant documents by reducing the original query.

The remainder of this paper is organized as follows: Section 2 surveys related work on patent prior art search, Section 3 describes our proposed method of query reduction in detail, Section 4 describes the experiments and discusses the results, and finally Section 5 concludes the paper with directions for future work.

2. RELATED WORK

The real life working principle undertaken by patent examiners to manually formulate queries for invalidating claims, involves selecting high frequency terms from the text of query-patent claim.

CIKM'11, October 24–28, 2011, Glasgow, Scotland, UK.

Some early work on keyword extraction to form a reduced query, modelled on this real-life methodology of patent examiners includes that of [11, 4]. More recent work by Xue and Croft [17] advocates the use of full patent text as the query to reduce the burden on patent examiners and concludes with the observation that usage of the whole patent text with raw term frequencies gives the best mean average precision (MAP). Recent work in the CLEF-IP [1] task has shown that best retrieval results are obtained when terms are used from all the fields of the query patents [14]. Fujii [2] showed that retrieval effectiveness can be improved by merging IR methods with citation extraction. Magdy et al. [9] show that the best performing run of CLEF-IP 2010 uses citations extracted by training a Conditional Random Field (CRF), whereas the second best run uses a list of citations extracted from the patent numbers within the description field of some patent queries. They also show that a simple IR approach of using terms from all fields of a patent-query with a frequency of at least two, merged with extracted citations achieves a statistically indistinguishable performance compared to the best run which employs sophisticated methods of retrieval using two complementary indices, one constructed by extracting terms from the patent collection and the other built from terminological resources such as the Wikipedia. As the baseline run for this paper we follow the simpler approach of the second ranked participating group and show that our method of query reduction produces better results without using citations.

Magdy and Jones [7] report that MAP can be a misleading metric for patent prior art search because of its inherent characteristic of favouring precision more than recall, and proposed the PRES (Patent Retrieval Evaluation Score) metric which measures the system recall and quality of ranking in one score. Our experiments report an improvement in both MAP and PRES over the baseline.

Ad hoc IR on news and web data has been shown to improve both in MAP and average recall measures by the use of PRF, due to the fact that additional terms from pseudo-relevant documents bridge the vocabulary gap between the query and the documents relevant to it in the collection [16, 15]. However, query expansion is associated with the risk of additional terms contributing to a drift in the original information need followed by a degradation of retrieval effectiveness in the feedback step [13]. Unfortunately all existing work on PRF coupled with query expansion for patent prior art search tasks report a degradation in MAP [5, 12, 8].

3. QUERY REDUCTION

3.1 Motivation

The important observations to be made from existing work as discussed in Section 2 are that patent prior art search achieves best retrieval performance when: i) information from all the fields of the query patents are used; ii) unit frequency terms (UFTs), i.e. terms which occur only once in the patent query are eliminated; and iii) no PRF is applied. This provides the motivation to devise a more intelligent technique of reducing queries in comparison to a naive frequency based cut-off and to develop techniques of exploiting the potential benefits of PRF. The work presented in this paper hence tries to reduce queries intelligently by utilizing pseudo-relevance. The main idea behind the approach is that since patent queries are long, retrieval performance can suffer because of a strong likelihood of presence of ambiguous terms which tend to boost the scores of non-relevant documents. However it is not always reasonable to assume that low frequency terms are the harmful ones. Instead, retrieved pseudo-relevant documents can give us an estimation of the distribution of useful terms.

[1]`http://www.ir-facility.org/clef-ip`

Algorithm 1 `QueryReduction`$(q, R, \tau, wsize, window)$

1: q : The original patent query.
2: R : Set of pseudo-relevant documents retrieved after an initial run.
3: τ : Fraction of segments to retain in the query. The remaining (i.e. $(1-\tau)$) fraction of segments are removed from the query.
4: $wsize$: Number of words in each window.
5: $window$: A boolean flag set to 0 for decomposing into sentences.
6: $S \leftarrow$ `DecomposeQuery`$(q, wsize, window)$
7: **for** $i = 1$ to $|R|$ **do**
8:   {Compute and aggregate the LM similarities}
9:   **for** $j = 1$ to $length[S]$ **do**
10:     $S[j].sim \leftarrow S[j].sim + \texttt{LMSim}(S[j], R_i)$
11:   **end for**
12: **end for**
13: Sort the set S such that $S_\alpha.sim \geq S_\beta.sim \quad \forall \alpha < \beta$
14: **for** $i = 0$ to $\tau \cdot length[S]$ **do**
15:   $RQ \leftarrow RQ \cup S_i$
16: **end for**
17: **return** RQ

3.2 Term Context

Term proximity plays a key-role in IR. Local Context Analysis (LCA) hypothesises that good expansion concepts tend to co-occur with query terms in the top ranked documents [16]. LCA decomposes the document text into fixed length passages and ranks candidate expansion terms by computing co-occurrences weighted by the *idf* (inverse document frequency) of query terms, the assumption being that co-occurrence of a term with a rare query term carries more weight. Relevance Based Language Model (RLM) theoretically establishes the LCA principle, where it is assumed that the expansion terms are generated from an underlying relevance model, which generates both the relevant documents and the query terms [6]. The probability of generating an expansion term from the relevance model is estimated by the co-occurrence of that term with the query terms.

In our method, we utilize the context of terms in a slightly different way. In one of the variants, we investigate the constituent sentences and in the other, we decompose the query into fixed length non-overlapping word windows. Our query reduction method works by removing the subset of segments (*sentences* or *word windows*), least similar to the top ranked documents from the query.

3.3 Query Reduction Algorithm

Algorithm 1 outlines the working steps of our proposed query reduction method. Line 6 calls the procedure `DecomposeQuery` which either breaks up the query text into component sentences or fixed length non-overlapping windows of $wsize$ words. The parameter $wsize$ thus controls the amount of contextual information that is used for computing the Language Model (LM) similarities. Line 10 aggregates the LM similarities of a query segment q_s with each $|R|$ top ranked document. The LM similarity equation that we use involves Jelinek-Mercer smoothing as described in [3] and is shown in Equation 1.

$$\log P(q_s|d) = \sum_{t \in q_s} n(t) \log(1 + \frac{\lambda_i P(t|d)}{(1-\lambda_i)P(t)}) \qquad (1)$$

$$\log P(q_s|R) = \sum_{d \in R} \log P(q_s|d) \qquad (2)$$

We show the log-transformed equation of the multinomial term generation model, $n(t)$ being the term frequency of t in query seg-

Table 1: Choosing the strongest baseline

Run description	Parameters R	Parameters T	Avg. query length	Metrics MAP	Metrics PRES
BL_1: Using all terms	-	-	628.21	0.0785	0.3903
BL_2: Removing UFTs	-	-	381.90	**0.1278**	**0.4604**
BL_3: BL_2 and PRF	5	50	678.21	0.0719	0.2649

ment q_s. The accumulated score as shown in Equation 2 computes the combined probability of generating a query segment q_s from each pseudo-relevant document. The idea is that a query segment q_s with a low probability of generation from the pseudo-relevant document language model is likely to be *out-of-context* with respect to the actual information need of the query patent.

In Line 13 we sort the query segments by the accumulated LM scores and retain the top τ fraction of the segments in the reduced query. The parameter τ can thus be used to control the amount of reduction. A higher value of τ would remove less segments and a lower value would remove more. Another parameter that is used to control the amount of proximity information is the window size $wsize$. When $wsize$ is set to 1, each window is comprised of an individual term and the method reduces to pure term deletion without any contextual evidence. A value of $wsize$ which is too small may miss the desired proximity information, whereas a value which is too high may run the risk of removing useful information from the query. Therefore this parameter has to be tuned carefully. A simple way to avoid tuning the parameter $wsize$ is to rely on the implicit semantic context represented by natural sentence boundaries instead of working with word windows.

4. EXPERIMENTS

4.1 Description and Parameter Settings

To evaluate our approach, we use the patent collection CLEF-IP 2010, which is comprised of 2.68 million patents from the European Patent Office (EPO). We restrict our retrieval experiments only to the English subset of the collection which constitutes 68% of the collection. Relevance assessments are provided for 1348 topics which are patent applications having *title*, *abstract*, *claims* and *description* fields. In addition to using a standard list of stopwordswe also removed formulas, numeric references, chemical symbols and patent jargons such as *method*, *system*, *device*. A Porter stemmer [10] was used to stem the words. SMART[2] with LM (Equation 1), was used for retrieval, with λ set to 0.4.

4.2 Choosing the Baseline

In order to choose the strongest possible baseline to compare our method against, we attempted naive query reduction and PRF using RLM [6]. We start with a retrieval run by using all terms from all fields of a patent query and then generate another retrieval run with a shorter query obtained by removing the UFTs. We see that this naive query reduction method results in 62.8% improvement of MAP as compared to the run which uses all terms. PRF was attempted on this improved run with different settings for the number of pseudo-relevant documents to use (R), and the number of query expansion terms (T). All the PRF runs show a degradation in MAP. Table 1 summarises the results and shows the best feedback run that we obtained. We choose the best configuration, i.e. the second run of Table 1 as the baseline for the query reduction experiments.

[2] `ftp://ftp.cs.cornell.edu/pub/smart/`

4.3 Sentence Removal

The following parameters were varied in our experiments: i) the number of pseudo-relevant documents to use in computing the probabilities of generating every query sentence; and ii) the fraction of sentences to retain in the query. To find the optimal range of the parameters, we varied τ in $[0.1, 0.9]$ in steps of 2 for 5, 10, 20 and 50 pseudo-relevant documents. Figure 1 shows that the best results are obtained when τ is set to 0.9. Retrieval results with too few or too much pseudo-relevance are unstable, as seen from the sharp drop of the line $R = 10$ from 0.7 to 0.9, sharp peak of $R = 5$ line from 0.7 to 0.9, and low IR effectiveness for the line $R = 50$ in $[0.1, 0.5]$. An important observation to be made here is that using a very small number of pseudo-relevant documents may result in an unpredictable retrieval performance because the estimated probabilities of generating query segments from too few a documents may not be accurate.

4.4 Word Window Removal

In this section, we investigate the effect of varying the window size $wsize$ on retrieval. We take the best settings as found in Section 4.3, i.e. we use $R = 20$ and $\tau = 0.9$ and use discrete valued window sizes of 5, 20, 50 and 100. The right graph of Figure 1 shows that optimal results are obtained by employing windows of 20 words. The figure also portrays a degradation of retrieval performance for windows which are too short, as seen from the left-most point of the graph. This can be attributed to the fact that very short windows imply a higher chance of a match of all the constituent words within a pseudo-relevant document. For example, the probability of generating a one-term window from a document d is $P(t_1|d)$, whereas for a two-term window, the probability is $P(t_1|d)P(t_2|d) \leq P(t_1|d)$. Thus, the accumulated LM scores being comparatively higher are not very reliable for very short windows. On the other hand, windows which are too long may result in too much information being removed from the queries resulting in a degradation of MAP. The window version of the query reduction mechanism outperforms the sentence based one. This again can be attributed to the length variation of sentences, some being too short and the others too long. Too short ones suffer from unreliable estimates of generation probabilities from the pseudo-relevant documents, whereas too long ones contribute to removal of too much of information. Word windows of fixed lengths can overcome this length variation problem.

4.5 Discussion

Table 2 shows the results of segment based query reduction. An interesting observation is that the average number of unique query terms for the best performing segment removal runs, both for sentence and window, are higher than the baseline, which shows that even UFTs can play an important role in retrieval. We find that the average number of query terms for the window based removal is higher, thus contributing to a higher recall as evident from the higher value of PRES without compromising average precision, as evident from the higher value of MAP. The new method is able to outperform the strongest baseline BL_2 by 7.28%. Although the improvement is not statistically significant, as evaluated by Wilcoxon test on per-topic average precisions, the percentage gain is non-trivial, keeping in mind the fact that all standard PRF methods fail on the patent prior art search leading to a degradation in IR effectiveness. In fact we see that window based query reduction significantly outperforms the best PRF by a 90.68% increase in MAP. The improvements in PRES are very small for both variants of the reduction algorithm.

Figure 1: Effect of varying the number of pseudo-relevant documents (R) and the fraction of sentences to retain (τ) on MAP (left). Effect of window size ($wsize$) variation with the best settings of sentence reduction, i.e. $R = 20$ and $\tau = 0.9$ (right).

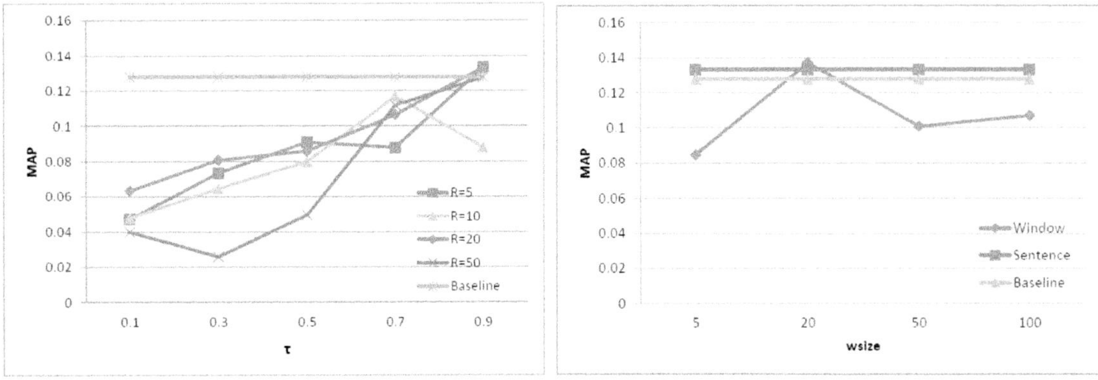

Table 2: Query Reduction performance on CLEF-IP 2010 topic set.

Run Description	Parameters			Avg. # of	MAP Relative gains over baseline				PRES Relative gains over baseline			
	R	τ	$wsize$	query terms	Absolute	BL_1	BL_2	BL_3	Absolute	BL_1	BL_2	BL_3
Sentence removal	20	0.9	-	474.99	0.1333	69.80%	4.30%	85.39%	0.4615	18.24%	0.23%	74.21%
Word window removal	20	0.9	20	547.59	**0.1371**	74.65%	7.28%	90.68%	**0.4674**	19.75%	1.52%	76.44%

5. CONCLUSION

The main contribution of the paper is the adaptation of pseudo-relevance for query reduction, instead of using it for query expansion. This is particularly useful in the domain of patent search because queries in patent prior art search are full patents and very much longer than ad hoc search queries. The method has been demonstrated to work well on the CLEF-IP 2010 patent prior art search task. Our work is a step ahead towards using PRF to improve MAP in patent prior art search, where all the previous PRF approaches have been reported to fail to improve retrieval effectiveness over initial retrieval.

There are several possible avenues along which our work can be extended in future, including a) devising a method for predicting whether query reduction would improve retrieval effectiveness for a query analogous to selective query expansion [1]; and b) exploring pseudo-relevance based summarisation techniques to reduce the length of a query analogous to the method of query based multi-document summarisation.

Acknowledgments

This research is supported by the Science Foundation Ireland (Grant 07/CE/I1142) as part of the Centre for Next Generation Localisation (CNGL) project.

6. REFERENCES

[1] S. Cronen-Townsend, Y. Zhou, and W. B. Croft. A framework for selective query expansion. In *CIKM 2004*, pages 236–237. ACM, 2004.

[2] A. Fujii. Enhancing patent retrieval by citation analysis. In *SIGIR*, pages 793–794. ACM, 2007.

[3] D. Hiemstra. *Using Language Models for Information Retrieval*. PhD thesis, Center of Telematics and Information Technology, AE Enschede, 2000.

[4] H. Itoh, H. Mano, and Y. Ogawa. Term distillation in patent retrieval. In *Proceedings of the ACL-2003 workshop on Patent corpus processing - Volume 20*, pages 41–45, Stroudsburg, PA, USA, 2003.

[5] K. Kishida. Experiment on pseudo relevance feedback method using taylor formula at NTCIR-3 patent retrieval task. In *NTCIR-3*, 2003.

[6] V. Lavrenko and B. W. Croft. Relevance based language models. In *SIGIR 2001*, pages 120–127. ACM, 2001.

[7] W. Magdy and G. J. Jones. PRES: a score metric for evaluating recall-oriented information retrieval applications. In *SIGIR 2010*, pages 611–618, 2010.

[8] W. Magdy, J. Leveling, and G. J. F. Jones. Exploring structured documents and query formulation techniques for patent retrieval. In *CLEF-2009*, pages 410–417, 2010.

[9] W. Magdy, P. Lopez, and G. J. F. Jones. Simple vs. sophisticated approaches for patent prior-art search. In *ECIR*, pages 725–728, 2011.

[10] M. F. Porter. An algorithm for suffix stripping. *Program*, 14(3):130–137, 1980.

[11] T. Takaki. Query terms extraction from patent document for invalidity search. In *NTCIR-5*, 2005.

[12] H. Takuechi, N. Uramoto, and K. Takeda. Experiments on patent retrieval at NTCIR-5 workshop. In *NTCIR-5*, 2005.

[13] E. L. Terra and R. Warren. Poison pills: harmful relevant documents in feedback. In *CIKM 2005*, pages 319–320. ACM, 2005.

[14] M. Z. Wanagiri and M. Adriani. Prior art retrieval using various patent document fields contents. In *CLEF-2010 (Notebook Papers/LABs/Workshops)*, 2010.

[15] R. H. Warren and T. Liu. A review of relevance feedback experiments at the 2003 Reliable Information Access (RIA) workshop. In *SIGIR 2004*, pages 570–571. ACM, 2004.

[16] J. Xu and W. B. Croft. Improving the effectiveness of informational retrieval with Local Context Analysis. *ACM Transactions on information systems*, 18:79–112, 2000.

[17] X. Xue and W. B. Croft. Transforming patents into prior-art queries. In *SIGIR*, pages 808–809, 2009.

Relevance Feedback Exploiting Query-Specific Document Manifolds

Chang Wang[*], Emine Yilmaz[†,‡], Martin Szummer[‡]

wangchan@us.ibm.com, eminey@microsoft.com eyilmaz@ku.edu.tr ,szummer@microsoft.com

[*] IBM T. J. Watson Research Lab, New York, USA
[†] Koc University, Istanbul, Turkey
[‡] Microsoft Research, Cambridge, UK

ABSTRACT

We incorporate relevance feedback into a learning to rank framework by exploiting query-specific document similarities. Given a few judged feedback documents and many retrieved but unjudged documents for a query, we learn a function that adjusts the initial ranking score of each document. Scores are fit so that documents with similar term content get similar scores, and scores of judged documents are close to their labels. By such smoothing along the manifold of retrieved documents, we avoid overfitting, and can therefore learn a detailed query-specific scoring function with several dozen term weights.

Categories and Subject Descriptors: H.3.3 [Information Storage and Retrieval]: Information Search and Retrieval

General Terms: Algorithms

Keywords: Relevance Feedback, Manifold Learning

1. INTRODUCTION

Relevance feedback has been shown to be an effective way of improving accuracy in interactive information retrieval. Hence, many different algorithms that can use explicit or implicit feedback have been proposed in the literature.

Relevance feedback for probabilistic retrieval models works by changing the estimation of model parameters using the information provided by the relevant documents [10]. In the case of language modeling, on the other hand, feedback documents are used to alter the estimate of the query language model [7] or the relevance model [8]. Rocchio's algorithm incorporates relevance feedback information into the vector space model [11]. It is based on constructing a centroid vector from the feedback documents and moving the original query vector towards this centroid vector.

Recently, several machine learning techniques have been proposed to solve relevance feedback problems. Among them, global ranking using continuous conditional random fields (C-CRF) [9] is the closest to our work. C-CRF [9] exploits a ranking model defined as a function on all the judged documents with respect to the query. To infer the parameters of the ranking models, C-CRF also considers similarity between documents based on the contents. There are two main differences between C-CRF and our work. First, C-CRF does not make use of unjudged documents in learning. This could lead to overfitting problems, since the number of the judged documents in the case of relevance feedback is typically small. Second, C-CRF uses raw document contents to compute similarity between documents, while we are using query-specific content from each document for similarity computation.

During the past few years, there has been significant change in retrieval systems. Most modern search engines are now based on the learning to rank approach, which involves calculating a rich and diverse set of features that capture some aspect of relevance of the submitted query and a document. They then learn a combination of these features based on training data [3, 4]. Most relevance feedback algorithms are based on expanding the query by adding weighted terms from the feedback documents [11]. Even though learning to rank approaches are now popular for ranking, few relevance feedback algorithms follow that paradigm [6].

The challenge in applying the learning to rank paradigm stems from the fact that the number of given (judged) relevance feedback documents is very small, typically ten or less. At the same time the number of possible expansion terms is very large, on the order of vocabulary size, yielding a very large space of potential expansions to be considered. This unfavorable proportion of a small number of judged relevance feedback documents to the huge expansion space makes the problem difficult. An attempt at applying learning to rank methods involves taking an initial base ranker and adapting it by training it with the relevance feedback documents for the query; however, when this is done naively, it leads to overfitting (to the labelled documents).

In this paper, we incorporate relevance feedback into a learning to rank framework by exploiting query-specific document similarities. Given a few judged feedback documents and many retrieved but unjudged documents for a query, we learn a function that adjusts the initial ranking score of each document. Scores are regularized so that documents with similar term contents get similar scores, and scores of judged

CIKM'11, October 24–28, 2011, Glasgow, Scotland, UK.

documents are close to their labels. By such smoothing along the manifold of retrieved documents, we avoid overfitting, and can therefore learn a detailed query-specific scoring function. Using data from TREC and OHSUMED collections, we show that our algorithm produces significantly better results than relevance feedback methods trained only on judged feedback documents.

2. THE ALGORITHM

For each query: $A = \{a_1, \cdots, a_m\}$ represents the set of retrieved documents, where a_i is the original representation (using features like BM25, tf-idf, etc) of document i. $B = \{b_1, \cdots, b_l\}$, represents the judgement, where b_i is a_i's label ($l << m$). For example, we can use '+1' to represent "relevant", '-1' to represent "non-relevant". B is a $1 \times l$ matrix. The initial ranking model F_0 provides a ranking score for each document. $X = \{x_1, \cdots, x_m\}$ is a $t \times m$ matrix, where x_i is the new representation of document i. The desired adjustment $Y = \{y_1, \cdots, y_l\} = \{b_1 - F_0(a_1), \cdots, b_l - F_0(a_l)\}$, Y is a $1 \times l$ matrix.

The problem is formalized as follows: given a document set $X = \{x_1, \cdots, x_m\}$ represented over words, and the desired adjustment $Y = \{y_1, \cdots, y_l\}$ for the judged documents $\{x_1, \cdots, x_l\}$, where $l << m$, we want to construct a mapping function f to project any document x_i to a new space, where $f^T x_i$ matches x_i's desired adjustment y_i. In addition, we also want f to preserve the document manifold topology, such that similar documents get similar adjustments.

2.1 Notation

Notations used in the algorithm are as follows: W is a weight matrix, where $W_{i,j} = e^{-\|x_i - x_j\|^2}$ models the similarity of x_i and x_j. $\|x_i - x_j\|$ stands for the Euclidean distance between x_i and x_j in the vector space. D is a diagonal matrix: $D_{i,i} = \sum_j W_{i,j}$. $\mathcal{L} = D^{-0.5}(D - W)D^{-0.5}$ is the normalized graph Laplacian matrix corresponding to W. I is an $l \times l$ identity matrix. $U = \begin{pmatrix} I & 0 \\ 0 & 0 \end{pmatrix}$ is an $m \times m$ matrix. μ is a weight scalar. "Gap" vector $V = [y_1, \cdots y_l, 0, \cdots, 0]$ is a $1 \times m$ matrix. $()^+$ represents pseudo inverse.

2.2 The Cost Function

Solution to the problem is given by the mapping function f to minimize the following cost function:

$$\begin{aligned} & C(f) \\ = & \sum_{i \le l} (f^T x_i - (b_i - F_0(a_i)))^2 + \mu \sum_{i,j} (f^T x_i - f^T x_j)^2 W_{i,j}. \\ = & \sum_{i \le l} (f^T x_i - y_i)^2 + \mu \sum_{i,j} (f^T x_i - f^T x_j)^2 W_{i,j}. \end{aligned}$$

The first term of $C(f)$ is based on judged documents, and penalizes the difference between the mapped result of x_i and its desired adjustment y_i. The second term does not take label information into account. It guarantees that the neighborhood relationship (defined by document contents) within X will be preserved in the mapping. When x_i and x_j are similar, the corresponding $W_{i,j}$ is big. If f maps x_i and x_j to different positions, f will be penalized. The second term is useful to bound the mapping function f and prevents overfitting from happening. Here μ is the weight of the second term. When $\mu = 0$, the model disregards the unlabelled data, and data manifold topology is not respected.

This formulation is similar to score regularization [6], except that (i) we learn a parametric function of x rather than a nonparametric set of regularized scores, and (ii) the function represents an adjustment (an error) between the judgements and the initial ranking model F_0, instead of a function that directly approximates the judgements. The latter appears to be more difficult, and did not work as well in initial testing.

2.3 Dictionary Construction

Our algorithm makes use of query specific document similarities. The similarities are computed using a separate dictionary that depends on the contents of the feedback documents for each query. When we construct query specific dictionaries, we follow an idea that is commonly used in query expansion. In the first step, we retrieve all non-stop words from relevant judged documents. For each word, we sum up its term frequencies in all relevant judged documents resulting in $score^+$ and its term frequencies in all non-relevant judged documents resulting in $score^-$. We sort the terms using $score^+ - score^-$ following descending order. The top t words will be used in our query specific dictionary. We also add the query words to the dictionary if they are not already there.

2.4 The Main Algorithm and its Explanation

The main algorithm to re-rank documents for each query is given in Figure 1. For each judged document, our query-level re-ranker provides an adjustment for the initial ranking model to close the gap between the true label and the initial ranking score. The adjustment has to be learned from the judged documents. However, given the fact that the number of the judged documents is always small, the adjustment could overfit to the judged documents. To solve this problem, we add a regularizer that guarantees that documents (including both labeled and unlabeled documents) with similar contents get similar adjustments.

A question that naturally arises is how to define the query-specific similarity of documents. We know that the documents are represented by features like BM25, tf-idf in the initial ranking model. Such features only describe the relationship between query and document. They are not good to compute similarity between documents. A more reasonable way to compute document similarity is to use document contents. In this scenario, similarity between documents also depends on the given query as the similarities are computed only using the words in the query specific dictionaries. For different queries, the contributions of the same word could be quite different. Our query-level re-ranker uses the contents of the judged documents to create a dictionary that only has useful words for that query. When we compute similarity using document contents, we only consider the words in that dictionary.

2.5 Advantages

Our algorithm offers the following advantages:

(1) The algorithm exploits unlabeled data in the form of document contents. This allows it to learn a more complex retrieval function that weights individual terms. Overfitting is controlled by using the unlabeled data for manifold regularization.

(2) The algorithm relies on manifold learning, a rich model that does not rely on any strong distributional assumptions

1. **Represent each document using query-specific document contents: $X = \{x_1, \cdots, x_m\}$, where x_i is defined by t features, where the jth component is the term frequency of the jth word in the query specific dictionary in document i.**
2. **Construct graph Laplacian matrix $\mathcal{L}$ modeling the document manifold.**
3. **Construct the difference vector $V = [y_1, \cdots y_l, 0, \cdots, 0]$: For $i \in \{1, \cdots l\}$, compute the difference y_i between the base ranking score $F_0(a_i)$ and label b_i.**
4. **New ranking model $f = (X(U + \mu\mathcal{L})X^T)^{+}XUV^T$.**
5. **Ranking score for document i is $F_0(a_i) + f^T x_i$.**

Figure 1: Relevance feedback ranker algorithm.

about the data. In contrast, other algorithms make more limiting assumptions about the data, such as Gaussianity.

(3) Only two parameters need to be manually set: μ controls how much we like to focus on manifold topology preservation. For simplicity, we use the same value for μ in all experiments. t is the maximum size of the query specific dictionary. We set it to 200 in all the tests.

(4) Closed form solution: unlike most approaches in this area, our algorithm (like [6]) provides a closed form solution of the result. The solution is global optimal regarding the cost function $C(f)$.

3. JUSTIFICATION

Our main algorithm is based on manifold regularization framework [2], which goes beyond regular regression models in that it applies constraints to those coefficients, such that the topology of the given data manifold will also be respected. A manifold is a mathematical space that on a small enough scale resembles the Euclidean space, but the global structure of a manifold may be more complicated. Manifold topology represents how instances (including both labeled and unlabeld instances) in the space is connected. Preserving manifold topology can be understood as a constraint that neighbors in the manifold space will be modulated in a similar way. Computing the optimal weights in a regression model and preserving manifold topology are conflicting objectives, manifold regularization provides a way to ideally balance the two goals.

Theorem 1: $f = (X(U + \mu\mathcal{L})X^T)^{+}XUV^T$ minimizes the cost function $C(f)$.

Proof:

Given the input X, we want to find the optimal mapping function f such that $C(f)$ is minimized:

$$f = \arg\min_f C(f).$$

It is easy to verify that

$$\sum_{i \le l}(f^T x_i - y_i)^2 = f^T XUX^T f - 2f^T XUV^T + VUV^T.$$

We can also verify that

$$\mu \sum_{i,j}(f^T x_i - f^T x_j)^2 W_{i,j} = \mu f^T X\mathcal{L}X^T f.$$

$$C(f) = (f^T XUX^T f - 2f^T XUV^T + VUV^T) + \mu f^T X\mathcal{L}X^T f.$$

Using the Lagrange multiplier trick, we have

$$XUX^T f + \mu X\mathcal{L}X^T f = XUV^T.$$

This implies that

$$X(U + \mu\mathcal{L})X^T f = XUV^T.$$

So $f = (X(U + \mu\mathcal{L})X^T)^{+}XUV^T$. □

Interestingly, the solution to f includes $\mathcal{L}$, the normalized graph Laplacian matrix [5], which models data manifold topology. Recently, spectral graph theory combined with classical differential geometry and global analysis on manifolds forms the theoretical basis for "Laplacian" techniques for function approximation and learning on graphs and manifolds, using the eigenfunctions of a Laplace operator naturally defined on the data manifold to reveal hidden structure.

4. EXPERIMENTAL RESULTS

In our experiments, we use data from two different collections: OHSUMED and TREC 6–8 ad-hoc. The OHSUMED collection contains 106 queries in total, and each query contains about 150 judged documents on average, with an average 20% of them being relevant. The TREC collection employs a subset of Letor 3 features, as in [1]. This dataset contains 150 queries, roughly 1,500 documents are retrieved for each query, and roughly 7% of them are relevant. Both datasets are split into 5 folds, where each fold contains training, validation and testing sets. In all the experiments through this paper, we set $\mu = 100$.

In a standard relevance feedback task, there is an initial base ranking, which is shown to a user and the user gives feedback on some documents in this initial ranking. Our base ranker is a linear regression model. One way of using relevance feedback information is to use the labels of the feedback documents for a query to train a separate ranking model for that query that fits the difference from the base ranker. We call this approach the Query-level Greedy feedback Ranker (QGR). Another way is Positive-Negative feedback Ranker (PNR), which is an active relevance feedback approach [12]. The PNR model was shown to outperform standard relevance feedback algorithms such as Rocchio and language modelling based relevance feedback. Hence, we mainly compare our algorithm only with the PNR model.

For each of the 5 folds in the datasets, we run our base ranking algorithm on the queries on these sets. We then assume that the feedback documents are the top k documents retrieved by the base ranker (we tried $k = 5$ and 10 in this paper). We employ average precision (AP) to compare the quality of the manifold model with the base ranking model, the QGR model, and the PNR model. Our approach consistently outperforms the other methods, and the differences are statistically significant using a sign-rank test (Figure 2). For the TREC dataset, the results of the query greedy ranker are not included in the plot as the performance of the algorithm is much worse than the other three algorithms. Compared to PNR, which is implemented in the same algorithmic framework except using non-query-specific document contents to compute document similarity, manifold model achieves better results in all experiment settings. This is a strong indicator to show that the query-specific

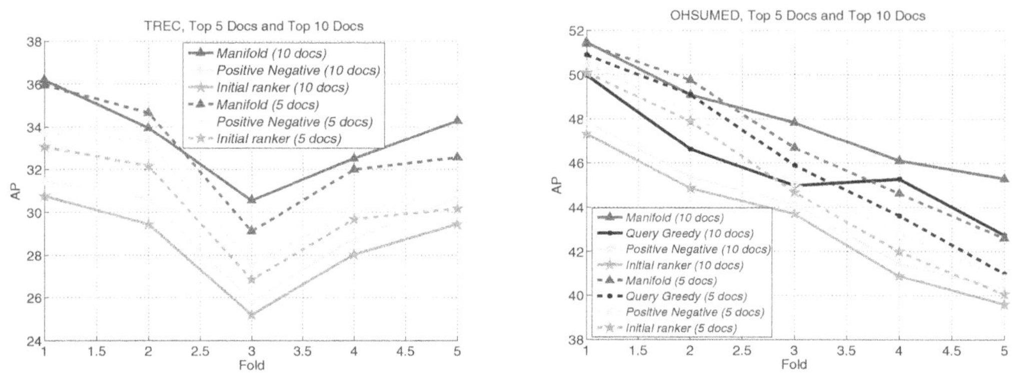

Figure 2: Improvements over the 5 folds for (left) TREC and (right) OHSUMED datasets when the feedback documents are the top 5 and 10 documents in the base ranking. Performances of two initial rankers ($k = 5, 10$) are different, because we throw away queries with no relevant (positive) feedback documents.

Table 1: An example to illustrate the behaviors of manifold model and query-level greedy model

Doc ID	1	2	3	4	5	6	7	8	9	10
Label	1	1	1	-1	1	-1	-1	-1	-1	1
Judged? 1:Yes 0:No	1	1	1	1	1	0	0	0	0	0
Initial Ranking Score	-0.6338	-0.2916	0.2835	-0.2635	0.1482	-1.0036	-1.0369	-0.9072	-0.7359	-0.3886
Greedy Re-ranking Score	1	1	1	-1	1	**-9.6383**	-1.5661	**164.2987**	-0.2086	-0.9875
Manifold Re-ranking Score	0.993	0.223	0.8615	0.2423	0.6801	-0.5156	-0.5491	-0.4094	-0.2456	0.1498

document contents can provide extra valuable information to query-level feedback rankers. The QGR model can be thought as a special case of a manifold model, where manifold topology is not respected. In these experiments, the greedy feedback ranker does not return satisfying results. The reason for this is that the greedy model can easily overfit for the feedback data.

In Table 1, we compare greedy model and manifold model in a real example. When initial ranking scores, judgements of 5 documents and a large amount of unjudged documents (only 5 are shown) are given, both models make adjustment to the original ranking scores. The greedy approach does not respect the manifold topology, so it assigns perfect reranking scores to the judged documents. But the ranking scores of the unjudged documents (documents with label -1) could be dramatically changed (see the big changes in the table). We carried out another experiment (not included in the figure) of query-level feedback ranker without using the base ranker; this yielded poor results. The reason is that the number of judged documents for each query is too small to construct a good feedback ranker (without a base ranker) even when manifold topology is respected. Base rankers are valuable, since they provide prior knowledge to help the feedback rankers when the feedback is limited.

5. CONCLUSIONS

We present a novel algorithm to incorporate relevance feedback into a learning to rank framework by exploiting query-specific document contents. Given a few judged feedback documents and many retrieved but unjudged documents for a query, our algorithm provides an optimal solution to adjust the base ranking score of each document, such that scores of judged documents are close to their labels and documents with similar term contents get similar adjustments.

6. REFERENCES

[1] J. A. Aslam, E. Kanoulas, V. Pavlu, S. Savev, and E. Yilmaz. Document selection methodologies for efficient and effective learning-to-rank. In *SIGIR*, 2009.

[2] M. Belkin, P. Niyogi, and V. Sindhwani. Manifold regularization: a geometric framework for learning from labeled and unlabeled examples. 2006.

[3] C. Burges, T. Shaked, E. Renshaw, A. Lazier, M. Deeds, N. Hamilton, and G. Hullender. Learning to rank using gradient descent. In *Proceedings of the 22nd international conference on Machine learning*, pages 89–96, New York, NY, USA, 2005. ACM.

[4] C. J. C. Burges, R. Ragno, and Q. V. Le. Learning to rank with nonsmooth cost functions. In *NIPS*, pages 193–200, 2006.

[5] F. Chung. *Spectral graph theory*. 1997.

[6] F. D. Diaz. Improving relevance feedback in language modeling with score regularization. In *SIGIR*, 2008.

[7] J. Lafferty and C. Zhai. Document language models, query models, and risk minimization for information retrieval. In *Proceedings of the 24th ACM SIGIR conference on Research and development in information retrieval*, pages 111–119, New York, NY, USA, 2001. ACM.

[8] V. Lavrenko and W. B. Croft. Relevance based language models. In *Proceedings of the 24th ACM SIGIR conference on Research and development in information retrieval*, pages 120–127, New York, NY, USA, 2001. ACM.

[9] T. Qin, T. Liu, X. Zhang, D. Wang, and H. Li. Global ranking using continuous conditional random fields. In *NIPS*, 2008.

[10] S. E. Robertson and K. Sparck Jones. Relevance weighting of search terms. pages 143–160, 1988.

[11] J. Rocchio. *Relevance Feedback in Information Retrieval*, pages 313–323. 1971.

[12] Z. Xu and R. Akella. A bayesian logistic regression model for active relevance feedback. In *SIGIR*, 2008.

Insights into Explicit Semantic Analysis

Thomas Gottron
University of Koblenz-Landau
56070 Koblenz, Germany
gottron@uni-koblenz.de

Maik Anderka
Bauhaus-Universität Weimar
99421 Weimar, Germany
maik.anderka@uni-weimar.de

Benno Stein
Bauhaus-Universität Weimar
99421 Weimar, Germany
benno.stein@uni-weimar.de

ABSTRACT

Since its debut the *Explicit Semantic Analysis* (ESA) has received much attention in the IR community. ESA has been proven to perform surprisingly well in several tasks and in different contexts. However, given the conceptual motivation for ESA, recent work has observed unexpected behavior. In this paper we look at the foundations of ESA from a theoretical point of view and employ a general probabilistic model for term weights which reveals how ESA actually works. Based on this model we explain some of the phenomena that have been observed in previous work and support our findings with new experiments. Moreover, we provide a theoretical grounding on how the size and the composition of the index collection affect the ESA-based computation of similarity values for texts.

Categories and Subject Descriptors: H.3.3 [Information Storage and Retrieval]: Information Search and Retrieval—*Retrieval models*; H.1.1 [Models and Principles]: Systems and Information Theory— *General systems theory*

General Terms: Experimentation, Standardization, Theory

1. INTRODUCTION

Gabrilovich and Markovitch introduced the concept of Explicit Semantic Analysis (ESA) in 2007 [4]. The idea underlying ESA is to represent and compare texts (from single terms to entire documents) as vectors in a high dimensional *concept space*. Each dimension in this space corresponds to an explicit semantic concept, where the concepts are considered to be "thematically (or topically) orthogonal". The entries in the concept vector of a given text quantify the associations between the text and the respective concepts. In order to compute such association values, each concept is represented by an index document. Gabrilovich and Markovitch use Wikipedia articles as index documents since Wikipedia covers a wide range of topics, while each article is focused on one topic. This topical focus is needed for the orthogonality property of the concepts and is referred to as *concept hypothesis*.

Since its introduction the ESA model has been adopted quickly in the IR community, which might be attributed to the following facts: the basic idea is pretty simple, Wikipedia is freely available, and the concept representation of documents is easy to interpret.

CIKM'11, October 24–28, 2011, Glasgow, Scotland, UK.

Table 1: Correlation of ESA-based similarities with human assessments, depending on index collection, number of index documents, and weighting scheme (reproduced from [1]).

Index collection	Number of index documents					
	1,000	10,000	50,000	100,000	150,000	200,000
VSM (baseline)	0.717	0.717	0.717	0.717	0.717	0.717
Wikipedia, tf-idf	0.742	0.784	0.782	0.782	0.781	0.781
Merged topics, tf-idf	0.738	0.767	0.768	0.769	0.769	0.777
Reuters, tf-idf	0.767	0.795	0.802	0.800	0.800	0.800
Random Gaussian, tf	0.703	0.716	0.717	0.717	0.717	0.717

However, recent work reveals that the central concept hypothesis is not required [1]. It has been shown experimentally that instead of the conceptually orthogonal Wikipedia articles, using documents from the Reuters corpus as well as randomly concatenated Wikipedia articles lead to a comparable performance. Even when using random term weights to construct the vectors representing concepts, ESA still achieves quite good performance values. These unexpected results cannot be aligned with the common explanation of ESA and motivate a deeper analysis of how ESA actually works.

The paper in hand takes a theoretical look at ESA and proposes a probabilistic term weight model to describe the computed similarity values. Our contributions are threefold: (1) we show which information of an index collection is actually exploited by ESA, (2) we investigate the impact of certain features of an index collection (such as size and composition), and (3) we explain the surprisingly good performance of ESA when using index vectors with random term weights. Altogether, the paper gives further evidence that ESA is a variation of the generalized vector space model (GVSM) [8].

2. RELATED WORK

ESA was introduced as an approach to compute the semantic relatedness of terms or short phrases [4]—we explain the technical details in Section 2.2. Meanwhile, ESA has been adopted successfully in many applications. In [3] ESA contributes directly to the estimation of the relevance of documents for a given query. In other settings ESA is used to compute the semantic relatedness of terms [5], which are then used as parameters in other retrieval models (e.g., an extension of BM-25). A cross-lingual extension (CL-ESA) that exploits interlanguage links of Wikipedia articles is covered in [6] and [7]. In [2] it is shown that CL-ESA is superior to other retrieval models which are based on implicit semantics.

Anderka and Stein revisited ESA in [1] and found syntactic parallels to the GVSM—a brief introduction of the GVSM is given in Section 2.1. They also present some initial analysis targeting the impact of the index collection on the performance of ESA, see Table 1. Two findings are quite interesting: First, employing Wikipedia as index collection does not perform best; e.g., using the Reuters corpus results in a better performance, even though the concept hypothesis is not satisfied in this case. Second, using index vectors with random term weights (Random Gaussian) performs nearly as good as using Wikipedia articles. This eventually led the authors to the conclusion, that the initial concept hypothesis in ESA does not hold.

2.1 GVSM in a Nutshell

Under the traditional vector space model (VSM) a document x is represented as a vector $\mathbf{x}$ based on a weighted combination of n-dimensional term vectors $\mathbf{t}_j$:

$$\mathbf{x} = \sum_{j=1}^{m} w(t_j, x) \cdot \mathbf{t}_j \tag{1}$$

where $w(t_j, x)$ is the weight of term t_j in document x. The similarity between two documents x and y is measured via the inner product of the respective vectors $\mathbf{x}$ and $\mathbf{y}$:

$$sim_{\text{VSM}}(x, y) = \langle \mathbf{x}, \mathbf{y} \rangle \tag{2}$$

$$= \left\langle \sum_{j=1}^{m} w(t_j, x) \cdot \mathbf{t}_j, \sum_{k=1}^{m} w(t_k, y) \cdot \mathbf{t}_k \right\rangle \tag{3}$$

$$= \sum_{j=1}^{m} \sum_{k=1}^{m} w(t_j, x) \cdot w(t_k, y) \cdot \langle \mathbf{t}_j, \mathbf{t}_k \rangle \tag{4}$$

In the classical VSM, the term vectors $\mathbf{t}_j$ have only a single non-zero entry, are orthogonal and of unit length. This allows to represent documents as term weight vectors and the above product becomes $\langle \mathbf{x}, \mathbf{y} \rangle = \sum_{j=1}^{m} w(t_j, x) \cdot w(t_j, y)$. This simplification also renders the VSM incapable of capturing interdependence of terms.

The generalized vector space model (GVSM) [8] considers term correlations. Based on term co-occurrence information, the values for $\langle \mathbf{t}_j, \mathbf{t}_k \rangle$ are estimated and stored as entries g_{jk} in a matrix G. This allows for maintaining the document representation as weight vectors and formulating the similarity of two documents x and y as follows:

$$sim_{\text{GVSM}}(x, y) = \mathbf{x}^T \cdot G \cdot \mathbf{y} \tag{5}$$

2.2 ESA in a Nutshell

Let D be an index collection of n documents, each of which describing a single concept. Further, let V be a vocabulary with m different terms that occur in D. In the original publication [4] the index collection is build from Wikipedia articles in order to cover a wide range of different concepts. Under the ESA model, a document x is represented as a concept vector $\mathbf{u}$, where each entry in $\mathbf{u}$ corresponds to the inner product of $\mathbf{x}$ and $\mathbf{d}_i$, with $d_i \in D$:

$$\mathbf{u}^T = (\langle \mathbf{d}_1, \mathbf{x} \rangle, \langle \mathbf{d}_2, \mathbf{x} \rangle, \ldots, \langle \mathbf{d}_n, \mathbf{x} \rangle), \tag{6}$$

where $\mathbf{x}$ and $\mathbf{d}_i$ are the VSM representations of x and d_i, which are m-dimensional vectors containing a weight for each term in V. Here, the original publication suggests to use a standard tf-idf weighing scheme. The inner product $\langle \mathbf{d}_i, \mathbf{x} \rangle$ corresponds to the similarity of x and d_i under the VSM; it quantifies the association between x and the concept which is defined by d_i.

Under the ESA model, the similarity between two documents x and y is defined by the cosine measure that is applied to the respective concept vectors $\mathbf{u}$ and $\mathbf{v}$:

$$sim_{\text{ESA}}(x, y) = \cos(\mathbf{u}, \mathbf{v}) = \frac{\langle \mathbf{u}, \mathbf{v} \rangle}{|\mathbf{u}| \cdot |\mathbf{v}|} \tag{7}$$

3. THEORETICAL ANALYSIS OF ESA

The findings in [1] motivate a deeper analysis of ESA and the need to understand what actually happens when comparing vectors in the concept space. We start with a reformulation of sim_{ESA} (see Equation 7) using the definitions of the concept vector entries:

$$sim_{\text{ESA}}(x, y) = \frac{1}{|\mathbf{u}| \cdot |\mathbf{v}|} \sum_{i=1}^{n} \langle \mathbf{d}_i, \mathbf{x} \rangle \cdot \langle \mathbf{d}_i, \mathbf{y} \rangle \tag{8}$$

$$= \frac{1}{|\mathbf{u}| \cdot |\mathbf{v}|} \sum_{j=1}^{m} \sum_{k=1}^{m} w(t_j, x) \cdot w(t_k, y) \cdot g_{jk} \tag{9}$$

where $g_{jk} = \sum_{i=1}^{n} w(t_j, d_i) \cdot w(t_k, d_i)$. Essentially this leads to a structural reformulation of ESA as GVSM, which is also observed in [1]. The g_{jk} are of particular interest as they contribute the entries in matrix G, see Equation 5. In Section 3.1 we will take a closer look at how these values evolve.

First we note that the g_{jk} also appear in the length normalization:

$$|\mathbf{u}| = \sqrt{\sum_{i=1}^{n} (\langle \mathbf{d}_i, \mathbf{x} \rangle)^2} \tag{10}$$

$$= \sqrt{\sum_{i=1}^{n} \left[\sum_{j=1}^{m} w(t_j, d_i) \cdot w(t_j, x) \right]^2} \tag{11}$$

$$= \sqrt{\sum_{j=1}^{m} \sum_{k=1}^{m} w(t_j, x) \cdot w(t_k, x) \cdot g_{jk}} \tag{12}$$

The recurrence of the g_{jk} is of interest because it allows us to scale G with a factor $a > 0$ without affecting the similarity measure. This can be seen by extending each g_{jk} into $a \cdot \frac{1}{a} \cdot g_{jk}$ and factoring $\frac{1}{a}$ out of the sum:

$$sim_{\text{ESA}}(x, y) = \underbrace{\frac{\frac{1}{a}}{|\mathbf{u}| \cdot |\mathbf{v}|}}_{*} \cdot \sum_{j=1}^{m} \sum_{k=1}^{m} w(t_j, x) \cdot w(t_k, y) \cdot (a \cdot g_{jk})$$

The same can be done in the calculations of the vector lengths for $\mathbf{u}$ and $\mathbf{v}$ in the denominator of the fraction marked with the asterisk ($*$). The resulting $\sqrt{\frac{1}{a}} \cdot \sqrt{\frac{1}{a}}$ can be canceled against the $\frac{1}{a}$ in the numerator. I.e., we can scale the g_{jk} without changing the values of the similarity measure. We will use a scale of $\frac{1}{n}$ to counterbalance the increasing values in the entries of the matrix for growing n. Altogether, we will work with a scaled version G' of the matrix with the entries:

$$g'_{jk} = \frac{1}{n} \sum_{i=1}^{n} w(t_j, d_i) \cdot w(t_k, d_i) \tag{13}$$

Based on G', the ESA similarity measure can be formulated in analogy to the GVSM:

$$sim_{\text{ESA}}(x, y) = \frac{1}{|\mathbf{u}| \cdot |\mathbf{v}|} \cdot \mathbf{x}^T \cdot G' \cdot \mathbf{y}, \tag{14}$$

where the only difference to Equation 5 is the length normalization factor;[1] $|\mathbf{u}|$ can be represented in the form $\sqrt{\mathbf{x}^T \cdot G' \cdot \mathbf{x}}$.

[1]In the original GVSM this factor is omitted since the weight vectors are considered to be normalized.

3.1 Probabilistic Model of Term Weights

In order to derive conclusions about the values of the g'_{jk}, we model the term weights $w(t_j, d_i)$ for the documents $d_i \in D$ as random variables. Typically, term weights are based on features such as term frequency, document frequency, or document length. In many (probabilistic) IR models, these features are modeled as random variables themselves. So, the idea to assume the term weights to be random variables is not far fetched.

The representation of a document d_i is assumed to be a tuple of random variables $(W_{1i}, W_{2i}, \ldots, W_{mi})$, where W_{ji} models the weight of term t_j. For each term t_j we consider all W_{ji} to be i.i.d. over the documents. This implies two assumptions: (1) the term weights in a particular document do not depend on weights in other documents, and (2) the joint distribution of all weights is the same for each document.

Both assumptions can be derived directly from our document model. We consider a document as the realization of the terms occurring in it; i.e., terms form a document—and not the other way around. Of course, there will be latent influences in a document (author, topic, intended auditorium, language style, etc.) which influence the choice and joint distribution of the words. These can be captured by the interdependence of the W_{ji} within a document, about which we explicitly make no assumption. Based on this document model, the g'_{ik} represent the mean over products of random variables W_{ji}:

$$g'_{jk} = \frac{1}{n} \sum_{i=1}^{n} W_{ji} \cdot W_{ki} \tag{15}$$

Since the W_{ji} are i.i.d. with respect to the documents, the law of large numbers provides the almost sure convergence for $n \to \infty$:

$$g'_{jk} \xrightarrow{a.s.} E(W_{ji} \cdot W_{ki}) = Cov(W_{ji}, W_{ki}) + E(W_{ji}) \cdot E(W_{ki}) \tag{16}$$

I.e., in general the entries g'_{jk} converge to a representation that captures the covariance of the term weights. This suits the concept of the matrix G in the GVSM, where the entries are supposed to represent the correlation of term vectors; however, the approach to determine the correlation values is different.[2] A second interesting observation is that a single g'_{jk} determines the measure of semantic relatedness for the terms t_j and t_k. So, ESA considers the common distribution of the weights of those two terms in the index collection to measure semantic relatedness. The covariance denotes the deviation from a random and uncorrelated co-occurrence of terms. Hence, rather than exploiting orthogonal concepts, ESA actually benefits from redundant usage of terms in documents. This reveals that there is no substantive evidence for the benefit of the concept hypothesis.

4. EXPERIMENTS

The ESA formulation of the previous section will help us to investigate properties of the index collection. In particular, we investigate the document number and the topic composition, and we explain the fact that ESA still works with random weight vectors. Beyond explaining observations from previous work, we extend the results reported in [1] to empirically support our theoretical findings.

[2]The details of how the entries in the matrix G are calculated in the original GVSM approach go beyond the scope of this paper and can be found in [8].

4.1 Index Collection Size

From a practical point of view the index collection size affects the runtime of ESA, since a given document needs to be compared against all index documents. Given this constraint, a small index collection is favorable. However, given the convergence in Equation 16, a large index collection is favorable since it reduces the variance of the g'_{jk} entries. A small variance is desired because it eliminates random fluctuations, which might be caused by outlier documents in the index collection.

This hypothesis is supported by the experiment results shown in Table 1: With increasing number of index documents the performance of ESA becomes more stable. Only if randomly concatenated Wikipedia articles are used as index documents (merged topics), the performance shows a significant increase at $200,000$ documents. Within the merged topics collection each index documents is generated by concatenating 10 randomly drawn Wikipedia articles with at least 1,000 words. However, given the size of the index collection several articles must have been reused; i.e., the assumption of the W_{ji} to be independent across the documents cannot hold, which might explain this artifact in the data.[3]

4.2 Topic Composition

Equation 16 and the reformulation of ESA as a special case of the GVSM in Equation 14 show that the index collection essentially provides term correlation information. Moreover, ESA operates on the overlap of the vocabulary defined by the documents x and y, as well as the vocabulary defined by the index documents. The summands in Equation 9 contain the term $w(t_j, x) \cdot w(t_k, y) \cdot g_{jk}$, which contributes to the similarity score if and only if $w(t_j, x)$, $w(t_k, y)$, and g_{jk} are nonzero. I.e., one will benefit from the correlation information of two terms only if they occur in different documents x, y, as well as in the index collection. One hence might argue that an index collection that covers the same topic domain like the compared documents will be more beneficial than a collection about a different topic, just because of the vocabulary overlap. Again, this hypothesis is supported by the experimental results in Table 1. Note that using the Reuters corpus as index collection entails a better performance than using Wikipedia articles. A similar observation was also made by Müller and Gurevich in [5]. The results in Table 1 are based on a test corpus of news documents from the Australian Broadcasting Corporation's news mail service, which focus on international politics; see [1] for further details.

It is important to note that the wide topic range in Wikipedia can also be a disadvantage: even if the vocabulary overlap is large, homonyms from different topics will introduce noise and distortions in the correlation information. For instance, the term "capital" has several meanings (capital city, financial capital, capital letters or top part of a column). At a semantic level the meanings of this term are individually correlated with different other terms. At a syntactical level the semantic differences are lost and the correlations of all meanings with, for instance, the term "government", get blurred. In a narrow domain corpus such as Reuters it is likely that the number of different meanings of a term is low. By contrast, Wikipedia contains most—if not all—different meanings and thus introduces much more noise in the correlation weights of G'. I.e., the original motivation of using Wikipedia because of its topic range can be counterproductive when addressing a particular topic domain.

[3]In January 2010 Wikipedia contained less than 2,000,000 articles with 1,000 words. http://stats.wikimedia.org/EN/TablesWikipediaEN.htm

Table 2: Correlation of ESA-based similarities with human similarity assessments, depending on index collection and number of index documents. As weighing scheme tf-idf is used.

Index collection	Number of index documents			
	1,000	10,000	50,000	100,000
VSM (baseline)	0.717	0.717	0.717	0.717
DMOZ - sport	0.700	0.748	0.752	0.752
DMOZ - science	0.703	0.736	0.743	0.743
DMOZ - news	0.754	0.784	0.788	-
Wikipedia - arts	0.709	0.757	0.760	0.759
Wikipedia - science	0.726	0.776	0.780	0.779
Wikipedia - politics	0.776	0.798	0.798	0.798

To substantiate this hypothesis we conduct a focused crawl of documents from both the open directory project (DMOZ) and Wikipedia. We create different index collections of up to 100,000 documents with a topical focus on sports, science and news for DMOZ, as well as on arts, science and politics for Wikipedia.[4] For each index collection we apply the same evaluation procedure as in [1], using the test corpus of news documents from the Australian Broadcasting Corporation's news mail service. The results are shown in Table 2. The best results are achieved with index collections based on news documents and politics documents, which shows that ESA benefits from an index collection about the same topic domain like the documents that are to be compared.

4.3 Random Weight Vectors

The authors of [1] report that an index collection with term weights created by a random process yield good results as well. The term weights were chosen to be independently $N(0, 1)$ distributed. We can directly use these parameter settings here in order to obtain $Var(W_j) = 1$, $E(W_j) = 0$ and $Cov(W_j, W_j) = 0$ for $j \neq k$. Using this in the Equation 16 results for $j \neq k$ in:

$$g'_{jk} \xrightarrow{a.s.} Cov(W_{ji}, W_{ki}) + E(W_{ji}) \cdot E(W_{ki}) = 0 \quad (17)$$

The elements g'_{jj} on the main diagonal are treated differently:

$$g'_{jj} \xrightarrow{a.s.} Cov(W_{ji}, W_{ji}) + E(W_{ji}) \cdot E(W_{ji}) = 1 \quad (18)$$

For $n \to \infty$ we observe that G' becomes a $m \times m$ unit matrix I. A unit matrix in the GVSM corresponds to the classical VSM with orthonormal term vectors. Also this theoretical finding is reflected by the results shown in Table 1. With increasing size of the randomly generated index collection (Random Gaussian) the performance converges towards a value of 0.717, which is the same value one obtains with the classical VSM baseline.

5. CONCLUSIONS

As main contribution we develop a view of ESA that shows its conceptual equivalence with the GVSM, independent of the choice of term weights for the index documents. On the basis of this reformulation and by employing a probabilistic model for term weights, we show that ESA essentially captures term correlation information from the index collection. This correlation information is exploited to match different terms in compared documents, which also shows that the concept hypothesis has no (obvious) mathematical basis.

In addition, we develop a deeper understanding of the influence of the index collection: (1) Increasing the number of index documents causes the correlation values for terms to converge, and hence, larger index collections provide more reliable correlation information. (2) The application of ESA in a specific domain benefits from taking an index collection from the same topic domain while, on the other hand, a "general topic corpus" such as Wikipedia introduces noise. Finally, our model is able to explain the behavior of ESA when using random term weights in index documents: with increasing document number the ESA-based similarities converge to the classical VSM using the cosine measure.

Our theoretical findings are supported by empirical results presented in related work. We also support our findings by new empirical analysis using different topically focused index collections. The paper also explains the behavior of ESA that seemed to be contradictory to the assumptions previously made on how ESA works.

Given these insights into ESA, future work will deal with the analysis and development of measures that can support the choice of a suitable index collection for a given task and context. Vocabulary overlap or a comparison of the distribution of term weights are first candidates to be considered. A second step is the composition within the index collection. Given the impact on runtime performance, it is of interest to reduce the size of the index collection while maintaining the effectiveness. Finally, also the impact of the findings presented here on CL-ESA should be explored.

[4]The DMOZ category *news* comprises only 67,809 documents.

6. REFERENCES

[1] M. Anderka and B. Stein. The ESA retrieval model revisited. In *Proceedings of the 32nd International ACM SIGIR Conference on Research and Development in Information Retrieval (SIGIR 09)*, pages 670–671. ACM, 2009.

[2] P. Cimiano, A. Schultz, S. Sizov, P. Sorg, and S. Staab. Explicit versus latent concept models for cross-language information retrieval. In *Proceedings of the 21st International Joint Conference on Artificial Intelligence (IJCAI 09)*, pages 1513–1518. Morgan Kaufmann Publishers Inc., 2009.

[3] O. Egozi, E. Gabrilovich, and S. Markovitch. Concept-based feature generation and selection for information retrieval. In *Proceedings of the 23rd National Conference on Artificial Intelligence (AAAI 08)*, pages 1132–1137. AAAI Press, 2008.

[4] E. Gabrilovich and S. Markovitch. Computing semantic relatedness using Wikipedia-based explicit semantic analysis. In *Proceedings of the 20th International Joint Conference on Artificial Intelligence (IJCAI 07)*, pages 1606–1611. Morgan Kaufmann Publishers Inc., 2007.

[5] C. Müller and I. Gurevych. Semantically enhanced term frequency. In *Advances in Information Retrieval: Proceedings of the 32nd European Conference on IR Research (ECIR 10)*, volume 5993 of *Lecture Notes in Computer Science*, pages 598–601. Springer, 2010.

[6] M. Potthast, B. Stein, and M. Anderka. A Wikipedia-based multilingual retrieval model. In *Advances in Information Retrieval: Proceedings of the 30th European Conference on IR Research (ECIR 08)*, volume 4956 of *Lecture Notes in Computer Science*, pages 522–530. Springer, 2008.

[7] P. Sorg and P. Cimiano. Cross-lingual information retrieval with explicit semantic analysis. In *Working Notes for the CLEF 2008 Workshop (CLEF 08)*, 2008.

[8] S. K. M. Wong, W. Ziarko, and P. C. N. Wong. Generalized vector spaces model in information retrieval. In *Proceedings of the 8th International ACM SIGIR Conference on Research and Development in Information Retrieval (SIGIR 85)*, pages 18–25. ACM, 1985.

On Bias Problem in Relevance Feedback

Qianli Xing*
State Key Lab of Intelligent Tech. & Sys.
Tsinghua National Lab for
Information Science & Technology
Dept. of Computer Science & Technology
Tsinghua University, Beijing 100084, China
xingqianli@gmail.com

Yi Zhang, Lanbo Zhang
School of Engineering
University of California, Santa Cruz
Santa Cruz, CA 95064, USA
{yiz,lanbo}@soe.ucsc.edu

ABSTRACT

Relevance feedback is an effective approach to improve retrieval quality over the initial query. Typical relevance feedback methods usually select top-ranked documents for relevance judgments, then query expansion or model updating are carried out based on the feedback documents. However, the number of feedback documents is usually limited due to expensive human labeling. Thus relevant documents in the feedback set are hardly representative of all relevant documents and the feedback set is actually biased. As a result, the performance of relevance feedback will get hurt. In this paper, we first show how and where the bias problem exists through experiments. Then we study how the bias can be reduced by utilizing the unlabeled documents. After analyzing the usefulness of a document to relevance feedback, we propose an approach that extends the feedback set with carefully selected unlabeled documents by heuristics. Our experiment results show that the extended feedback set has less bias than the original feedback set and better performance can be achieved when the extended feedback set is used for relevance feedback.

Categories and Subject Descriptors: H.3.3 [Information Search and Retrieval]: Relevance feedback, Retrieval models

General Terms: Experimentation, Algorithms.

Keywords: Relevance feedback, bias, novelty, heuristic.

1. INTRODUCTION

In typical relevance feedback methods, feedback documents are usually the top documents retrieved against the initial query. The number of feedback documents is limited due to the expensive user efforts of making relevance judgments. On one hand, the insufficient relevant documents will make the feedback set less representative, namely biased, and thus the performance of relevance feedback will be limited. On the other hand, the redundant information among feedback documents will aggravate the bias of feedback set. For these reasons, the feedback set of top-ranked documents are very likely to be biased because of both insufficient quantity and the similarity among documents.

To recall as many relevant documents as possible, an effective way is to include diverse information in the feedback set. Some previous work studied how to actively select documents which are both relevant and novel for true relevance feedback[5, 6] and pseudo relevance feedback[1]. However in the problem setting that a set of feedback documents is given, which is more likely to happen in reality, these active methods are not available.

In reality, the feedback set is usually a set of top-retrieved documents. Given the feedback set consisting of relevant/irrelevant documents, how to reduce the bias of the feedback set before carrying out relevance feedback is still an open problem. As far as we are concerned, there's little work studying the bias problem of the feedback set. In this paper, we focus on the properties of the feedback set and study how bias is caused. Then an approach that selects unlabeled documents to extend the feedback set is proposed. The documents to select are supposed to be helpful to reduce the bias of feedback set so several heuristics are used for the document selection.

2. BIAS OF FEEDBACK SET

As a feedback set consisting of top-ranked documents tends to be biased, the result of relevance feedback will probably be worse than using a feedback set that contains the same number of relevant documents with better representativeness. In this section, we first show the bias of the feedback set generally exists regardless of retrieval method and feedback method by a control experiment, then we study which feedback sets suffer most from the bias problem.

2.1 Experiment Setting

We conduct our experiments on two standard TREC data sets : the AQUAINT data set used in TREC 2005 HARD track and the RCV1 (Reuters Corpus Volume 1) data set used in TREC 2002 filtering track. There are 50 topics for each data set and only titles are used for retrieval. BM25 and KL-Divergence Language Model are used as our retrieval models. Rocchio algorithm[3] and Collection Mixture Model[7] are the feedback methods for the two retrieval models respectively. We implement the retrieval system and the models using Lemur toolkits with default parameters. Porter stemming and stop words removal are adopted be-

*This work was done when the author was a visiting student at UC Santa Cruz

CIKM'11, October 24–28, 2011, Glasgow, Scotland, UK.

Table 1: Performance of relevance feedback. A star (*) and two stars (**) indicate the improvement over Top K is significant according to t-test with p-value threshold of 0.1 and 0.05 respectively.

BM25	No RF	Top 10	Random
AQUAINT	0.183	0.290	0.310*
RCV1	0.269	0.425	0.515**
Language Model	No RF	Top 10	Random
AQUAINT	0.149	0.241	0.243
RCV1	0.286	0.345	0.372**

Table 2: Features of feedback set S_r

Feature	Calculation
RelDocNum	$\lvert S_r \rvert$
InnerSimAvg	$\frac{\lvert S_r\rvert(\lvert S_r\rvert-1)}{2}\sum_{d_i,d_j\in S_r;i<j} Sim(d_i,d_j)$
InnerSimMin	$\min_{d_i,d_j\in S_r;i<j} Sim(d_i,d_j)$
InnerSimMax	$\max_{d_i,d_j\in S_r;i<j} Sim(d_i,d_j)$
InterSimAvg	$\frac{1}{\lvert S_r\rvert\lvert S_{res}\rvert}\sum_{d_i\in S_r}\sum_{d_j\in S_{res}} Sim(d_i,d_j)$
InterSimMin	$\min_{d_i\in S_r,d_j\in S_{res}} Sim(d_i,d_j)$
InterSimMax	$\max_{d_i\in S_r,d_j\in S_{res}} Sim(d_i,d_j)$

fore building index. As earlier study has shown that relevant documents are more valuable than irrelevant documents[4], only relevant documents are used by the feedback methods. The relevance judgments are provided by TREC assessors and the recall-based metric MAP (Mean Average Precision) is used for evaluation.

2.2 How the Bias Exists?

In order to show the bias of feedback set using top-ranked documents, we conduct experiments on two feedback sets, which are described as:

Top k: Select the relevant documents from top k retrieved documents as feedback set.

Random: Select the same number of relevant documents as Top from the set of all relevant documents to the query.

Random can be viewed as an approximation of unbiased feedback set because of the random sampling among all relevant documents. The results of relevance feedback are shown in Table 1. As we can see, *Random* consistently performs better than Top on different data sets and retrieval methods. It indicates that feedback set used in Top is biased. The performance gap between Top and *Random* can be viewed as the degree of the bias.

2.3 Where the Bias Exists?

As bias generally exists in feedback sets, which feedback sets suffer most from the bias problem? To answer the question, we investigate the relationship between bias and some of the features of the feedback set. The features are listed in Table 2 and related notations are: S_r is the feedback set of relevant documents; S_{nr} is the feedback set of irrelevant documents; S_{res} is the residual set of relevant documents with respect to S_r in the space of all relevant documents. Here $Sim(d_i, d_j)$ is calculated by cosine similarity.

The ground truth of the degree of bias is defined as the performance gap between Top and *Random* mentioned in previous section. Correlation coefficients are then calculated between the bias and each feature over two data sets with BM25 retrieval model and Rocchio feedback. Experiment results show that $InterSimAvg$ and $InnerSimMin$ are two most correlated features. It indicates that the bias tends to be serious when 1) the similarity between S_r and S_{res} is small; 2) the documents in S_r are similar to each other ($InnerSimMin$ is large).

3. EXTENDING FEEDBACK SET

Since bias exists in feedback set due to lack of diversity, one way to reduce it is to extend the feedback set by adding additional documents. The additional documents are supposed to be both relevant and novel so that novel information could be introduced into the feedback set. In this sections, we study which documents to use for the extension.

3.1 Usefulness of Unlabeled Documents

As we want to select documents that are useful to reduce the bias of the feedback set and thus boost the performance of relevance feedback, we define the ground-truth of usefulness of document d_i as the MAP improvement achieved by adding d_i to S_r for relevance feedback. In order to find such documents, we extract some features of document in Table 3, then we evaluate how these features are correlated with usefulness. Here the similarity score $Sim(d_i, d_j)$ is calculated in the similarity space of the retrieval method used.

As is shown in Table 4, we notice that over the set of all documents, usefulness is not strongly correlated with any of these features. However, the correlations are much stronger over the set of relevant documents. It implies the importance of relevance. Without the precondition of relevance, it's hard to tell whether an unlabeled document is useful or not by using these features directly.

To identify the relevance, we find that $AvgSimPos$ and $MaxSimPos$ are both good features over the set of all documents. However, it's interesting to notice that over the set of relevant documents, $AvgSimPos$ and $MaxSimPos$ become negatively correlated with usefulness but $Novelty$ becomes a good feature. These facts indicate that when relevance is guaranteed, documents with novelty are more useful to reduce the bias.

3.2 Heuristics for Document Selection

According to the analysis of usefulness of documents, we propose several heuristics to select useful unlabeled documents for the extension of feedback set.

3.2.1 H1:Single-link

Typical centroid-based relevance feedback algorithms prefer to recall documents that are close to the centroid of the feedback documents, while some relevant documents that are only similar to some of the relevant documents will be missed. As $MaxSimPos$ and $MaxSimNeg$ are shown to be well correlated with relevance in Table 4, we utilize these two features to find relevant candidates. The idea is if a document is close to any document in S_r and far away from each relevant in S_{nr}, we believe the document tends to be relevant. Because the relevance is measured by two individual documents in S_r and S_{nr} respectively, we call this heuristic 'Single-link'. On the other hand, novelty is the key factor of usefulness for relevant documents, so we also introduce the novelty component into this heuristic. For a document d,

Table 3: Features of document d

Feature	Description	Calculation
DocLength	the number of words in the document.	$\|d\|$
QuerySim	the similarity with the initial query q	$Sim(q,d)$
AvgSimPos	the average similarity with each document in S_r	$\frac{1}{\|S_r\|}\sum_{d_i \in S_r} Sim(d,d_i)$
AvgSimNeg	the average similarity with each document in S_{nr}	$\frac{1}{\|S_{nr}\|}\sum_{d_i \in S_{nr}} Sim(d,d_i)$
MaxSimPos	the largest similarity with the document in S_r	$\max_{d_i \in S_r} Sim(d,d_i)$
MaxSimNeg	the smallest similarity with the document in S_{nr}	$\max_{d_i \in S_{nr}} Sim(d,d_i)$
Novelty	the portion of new appearing words with respect to S_r	$\left\|W_d \cap \overline{\bigcup_{d_i \in S_r} W_{d_i}}\right\| / \|W_d\|$

Table 4: The correlation between the features and the relevance/usefulness over the set of all/relevant documents

	Relevance	Usefulness	
	all docs	all docs	rel docs
DocLength	0.027	0.011	0.004
QuerySim	0.116	-0.033	-0.119
AvgSimPos	0.299	0.004	-0.254
AvgSimNeg	-0.036	0.066	-0.245
MaxSimPos	0.394	-0.099	-0.197
MaxSimNeg	-0.133	-0.168	-0.142
Novelty	-0.339	-0.182	0.251

the heuristic of usefulness is calculated as:

$$H_1(d) = \begin{array}{l}(MaxSimPos(d) - MaxSimNeg(d)) \\ \times Novelty(d)\end{array} \quad (1)$$

3.2.2 H2:Stretch-out

Compared to Single-link, we also propose a more conservative heuristic called 'Stretch-out'. As we have found that the density, namely the average similarity between any two documents in the feedback set, is an important factor that causes the bias. This heuristic targets to select documents which will dilute the density while maintaining relevance. The selected documents should be as novel as possible but still in the range of S_r. In other words, the radius of the S_r in similarity space should not be increased after the extension. Radius of a feedback set is measured by $InnerSimMin$ (in Table 2). The heuristic is denoted as:

$$H_2(d) = \begin{cases} -density(S_r \cup \{d\}) & , \quad r(S_r \cup \{d\}) \leq r(S_r) \\ 0 & , \quad r(S_r \cup \{d\}) > r(S_r) \end{cases} \quad (2)$$

A non-zero high score for this heuristic means the selected document d is in the acceptable range of relevance and will dilute the density of the feedback set after d is added.

3.2.3 H3:Centroid-locate

As shown before, the distance to the center of relevant documents is a good indicator of relevance and representativeness[2]. Many typical feedback methods are also centroid-based, such as Rocchio algorithm. So for this heuristic, we naturally select documents that are close to the center of the feedback set for extension. The heuristic is simply calculated as:

$$H_3(d) = \frac{1}{|S_r|} \sum_{d_i \in S_r} Sim(d, d_i) \quad (3)$$

Note that in fact this heuristic works in the similar way as the centroid-based feedback methods such as Rocchio, so the relevance feedback on the extended feedback set can also be viewed as a 2-round relevance feedback.

4. EXPERIMENTAL RESULTS

In our experiments, we assume the relevance judgments of top 10 documents are given. Then the proposed heuristics are used to select unlabeled documents to extend the feedback set. In the extended feedback set, documents with explicit relevance judgments are given weight 1.0 while documents selected by heuristics are given a reduced weight λ (set to 0.5) in relevance feedback. Figure 1 shows the performance of relevance feedback (measured by MAP) and the percentage of relevant documents found by the heuristics when using different number of documents for extension.

The first row of Figure 1 shows MAP values, while the second row reflects the proportion of relevant documents in all documents found by the heuristics. According to these results, we have the following observations and analysis:

1)*Relevance is a necessity*: The baseline method (Pseudo) is always among the worst improving the performance of relevance feedback. The simple explanation is that it doesn't consider relevance when selecting documents so consequently it's among the worst in finding relevant documents. H2 also fails to locate relevant documents accurately at the beginning when k is small, so it doesn't help the overall performance as well. We can imagine when many irrelevant documents are used as relevant documents in relevance feedback, the performance drops anyway.

2)*Average similarity is not the best choice*: Usually given a set of relevant documents, we tend to believe that a document that is close to all relevant documents is relevant. H3 is the heuristic that follows this idea. But in fact, this assumption may not hold in different similarity spaces. Figure 1 shows that H3 does well in selecting relevant documents in BM25 model but fails in Language Model (even fails the baseline on RCV1 data set). On the contrary, H1 is always among the best in selecting relevant documents even with the novelty component that is negatively correlated to relevance (shown in Table 4). It indicates that the relevance component of H1 is quite effective. The reason why H1 is consistently good is the Single-link strategy we use, in which a document is believed to be relevant if it's close to any relevant document, instead of all relevant documents. In some similarity space, a document that has a large average similarity doesn't mean it's similar enough to any relevant document so that we can judge it as relevant. Instead, the Single-link assumption is much more robust in different similarity spaces according to this result.

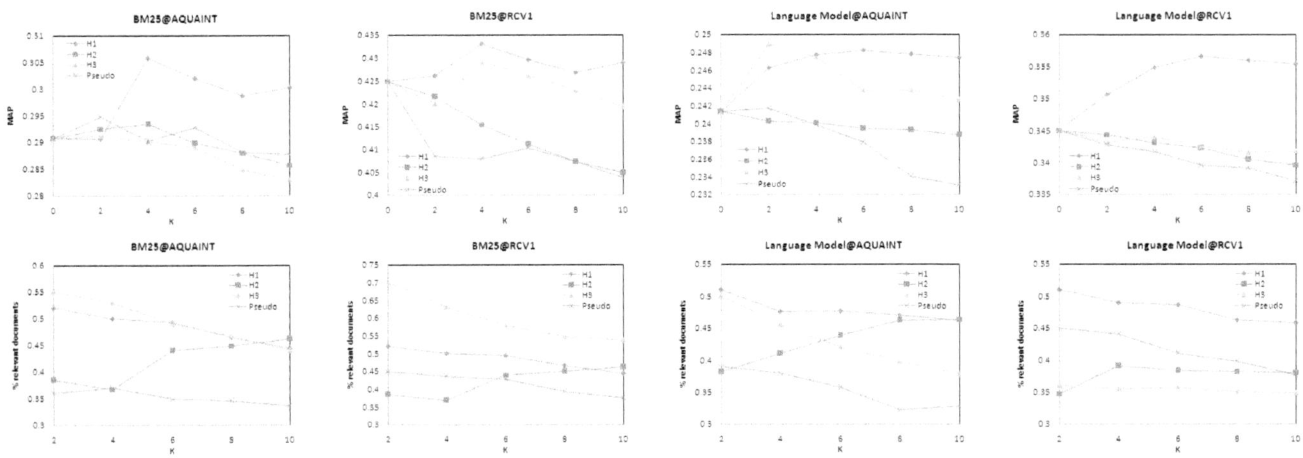

Figure 1: The performance of relevance feedback using the extended feedback set based on top 10 documents. K is the number of unlabeled documents added to the feedback set. $K = 0$ means the original feedback set is used. Pseudo is a baseline in which unlabeled documents are selected by the order of the original ranking.

3)*Novelty plays key role*: With respect to the performance after relevance feedback, H1 consistently works well on every combination of retrieval method and data set. It even has a trend of getting better when the percentage of relevant documents found begins to drop as more unlabeled documents are used. One of the reasons for the good performance is that H1 finds relevant documents well, which we described before. However, we notice that even sometimes with fewer relevant documents, H1 is still be able to outperform the other heuristics on the overall performance of relevance feedback. This fact implies the number of relevant documents is not the only reason that H1 improves the relevance feedback. Another important reason is the novelty. Without consideration of novelty, we see H3 is much less effective than H1 even with more relevant documents. BM25@AQUAINT in Figure 1 shows a very good example of the importance of novelty, in which H1 and H3 both find relevant documents very well. However as a result, H1 performs best for relevance feedback whereas H3 even loses the baseline. The reason why the documents found by H3 are so useless to relevance feedback is the lack of novelty. Redundant relevant documents won't help recall new relevant documents in relevance feedback.

Overall, introducing novelty is the key to reduce the bias of the feedback set. However, we should note that novelty is helpful only when it has the support from relevance. For example, H2 is designed to find documents that increase the diversity of feedback set. But as relevance part fails, the documents selected by H2 hurt the relevance feedback instead of doing any good.

5. CONCLUSION AND FUTURE WORK

This paper studied the bias problem in relevance feedback. We first showed the typical feedback set using top documents is biased by revealing the performance gap compared to a random sampling method. Then we found that feedback sets with high inner-similarity are more likely to be biased. Given a feedback set, we further studied how to reduce the bias by selecting unlabeled documents to extend the feedback set. Several heuristics are proposed for document selection, in which H1 is most effective. Although the improvement on MAP is not dramatic, our work still suggests that selectively using unlabeled documents can reduce the bias of a given feedback set and improve the performance of relevance feedback consequently. For the future work, we would consider developing a learning algorithm for document selection instead of using heuristics. We are also interested in adopting other intent-aware metrics for further evaluation.

6. ACKNOWLEDGMENTS

This research was supported by China Scholarship Council, Natural Science Foundation of China (60736044, 60903107) and Research Fund for the Doctoral Program of Higher Education of China (20090002120005).

7. REFERENCES

[1] K. S. Lee, W. B. Croft, and J. Allan. A cluster-based resampling method for pseudo-relevance feedback. In *Proceedings of the 31st ACM SIGIR*, SIGIR '08.

[2] F. Raiber and O. Kurland. On identifying representative relevant documents. In *Proceedings of the 19th ACM international conference on Information and knowledge management*, CIKM '10.

[3] J. Rocchio. Relevance feedback in information retrieval. In *The SMART Retrieval System*, pages 313–323. PrenticeHall Inc., 1971.

[4] G. Salton and M. J. McGill. *Introduction to Modern Information Retrieval*. McGraw-Hill, Inc., 1986.

[5] X. Shen and C. Zhai. Active feedback in ad hoc information retrieval. In *Proceedings of the 28th ACM SIGIR*, SIGIR '05.

[6] Z. Xu, R. Akella, and Y. Zhang. Incorporating diversity and density in active learning for relevance feedback. In *Proceedings of the 29th European conference on IR research*, ECIR'07.

[7] C. Zhai and J. Lafferty. Model-based feedback in the language modeling approach to information retrieval. In *Proceedings of the tenth international conference on Information and knowledge management*, CIKM '01.

Selecting Related Terms in Query-logs using Two-Stage SimRank

Yunlong Ma, Hongfei Lin, Yuan Lin
Information Retrieval Laboratory
School of Computer Science and Technology
Dalian University of Technology
Dalian 116023, China
kevinma@mail.dlut.edu.cn, hflin@dlut.edu.cn, yuanlin@mail.dlut.edu.cn

ABSTRACT

It is commonly believed that query logs from Web search are a gold mine for search business, because they reflect users' preference over Web pages presented by search engines, so a lot of studies based on query logs have been carried out in the last few years. In this study, we assume that two queries are relevant to each other when they have same clicked page in their result lists, and we also consider the queries' topics of user's need. Thus, we propose a Two-Stage SimRank (called TSS in this paper) algorithm based on SimRank and some clustering algorithms to compute the similarity among queries, and then use it to discover relevant terms for query expansion, considering the information of topics and the global relationships of queries concurrently, with a query log collected by a practical search engine.

Experimental results on two TREC test collections show that our approach can discover qualified terms effectively and improve retrieval performance.

Categories and Subject Descriptors: H.3.3 [Information Storage and Retrieval]: Query Reformulation

General Terms: Algorithms, Experimentation.

Keywords: Search Engine, Query Expansion, Query Logs.

1. INTRODUCTION

In general, most web search engines discover relevant documents for a query. Unfortunately, queries which are submitted to search engines always contain very few keywords or phrases, and people often use different words to describe concepts in their queries from which is used to describe the same concepts in documents by authors. To solve this problem, query expansion (QE) approaches [7, 10, 8] have been widely used, which focus on generating new queries by adding words to the original query.

In this paper, we focus on query expansion (QE) based on the recent history of data in query logs, and present a novel approach to select good terms for it. In general, we look into association and similar patterns at the level of terms through analyzing the relations of terms inside a query log in a real search engine, and treat them as candidate terms. We try to generate a historical query-click graph which records the clicks generated by URLs when a user input a query. The query-click graph is a weighted bi-partite graph [4], with queries on one side and URLs on the other one. Then, a term-relationship graph which is obtained by several transformations from the query-click graph could reflect the direct connections of the terms in query logs. Our term selecting approach is based on the notion of SimRank [6], which can compute similarity between any two terms in the term-relationship graph. However, in our case, we need to extend SimRank to take into account the weights of the edges in graphs [3]. In addition, queries in query log are clustered by the similarity scores, and we propose a Two-Stage SimRank (TSS) algorithm by considering the information of categories and the global relationships of queries concurrently. Finally, term pairs have the higher TSS similarity scores are thought to be more useful for QE.

In next section, we discuss how we construct the query-click graph and term-relationship graph from query logs. Section 3 describes our Two-Stage SimRank algorithm and the candidate terms selecting process of our query expansion strategy. Section 4 contains the experimental results, as well as a discussion of those results and the last section is a conclusion.

2. QUERY ANALYSIS

2.1 Query-Click Graph Building

Query-click graph (also known as query-document graph) is introduced by [3], which is a weighted bi-partite graph. The nodes in the one set represent queries and the nodes in the other set represent URLs which appear in query logs. An edge appears between a query q and a URL u if a user has issued the query and clicked on the URL in the list of results. Let $G_{QC} = \{V_{QC}, E_{QC}\}$ be a bi-partite graph such that $V_{QC} = \{v_q, u_v\} = Q \cup U$ and $E_{QC} = \{v_{qu}\} = Q \times U$, where Q is a set of all queries in query logs and U is a set of URLs clicked for those queries. Let $\omega(e_{qu})$ be a weighting function for an edge $e_{qu} \in E_{QC}$, for this instance, it is the number of clicks for a query q on a URL u. Specifically, the query-click graph is constructed by the process which Figure 1 shows.

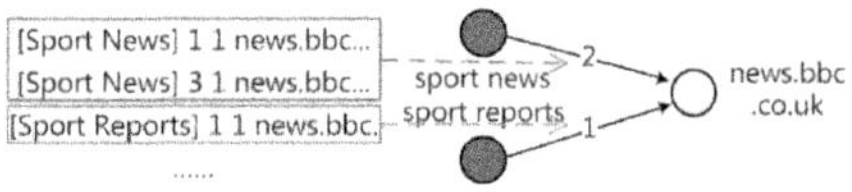

Figure 1: Query-Click Graph Construction

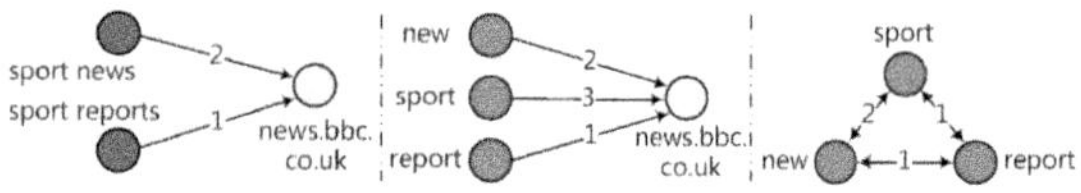

Figure 2: Term-Relationship Graph Construction

2.2 Term-Relationship Graph Building

Although the query-click graph can reflect all queries, URLs and the connections between them in query logs, then we can discover knowledge at the level of queries.

But in this paper, we propose to use query logs for query expansion at the level of terms through analyzing the relations inside queries. Thus we need a term-level graph which we called term-relationship graph, is a weighted and directed graph. We model terms and relationships as a graph $G_T = \{V_T, E_T\}$, where nodes in $V_T = \{v_t\}$ represent terms inside query logs and edges in $E_T = \{e_t\}$ represent relationships between terms. The weight of edge $\omega(e_{ij})$ which is the number of co-occurrence represents association degree between two terms i and j.

The term-relationship graph can be obtained by two transformations from the query-click graph (See Figure 2): (1) Query nodes substitution. (2) URL nodes elimination. Specifically, in the elimination process, for every term node pair (v_{t_1}, v_{t_2}) and every URL node v_u, if there are two edges from v_{t_1} to v_u and from v_{t_2} to v_u concurrently, then add the weight of edge $e_{t_1 t_2}$ in G_T to $c(v_{t_1}, v_{t_2}, v_u)$.

$$c(v_{t_1}, v_{t_2}, v_u) = \min(\omega(v_{t_1} \to v_u), \omega(v_{t_2} \to v_u)) \quad (1)$$

3. TWO-STAGE SIMRANK EXPANSION

3.1 Normalized Weight SimRank

SimRank [4] is a method for computing object similarities, applicable in any domain with object-to-object relationships, that measures similarity of the structural context in which objects occur, based on their relationships with other objects. Unfortunately, because of the weight on graph edges, the naive SimRank fails to properly identify term similarities in our application, so we need to extend SimRank to take into account the weights of the edges in graphs.

In general, in order to utilize the edge weights in the computation of similarity scores. We first normalize the in-edge weights for every node v_t in the term-relationship graph by following the next equation:

$$\sum_{i}^{|I(v_t)|} \omega(I_i(v_t) \to v_t) = 1 \quad (2)$$

And then, we can incorporate the normalized weight into the SimRank equations as Equation 3 and 4, which named Normalized Weight SimRank (NWS)[9].

Table 1: Data statistics of Robust-04 and Gov-2

Corpus	Docs	Queries
Robust-04	528,155	No.301-450
Gov-2	25,205,179	No.701-850

$$NWS(v_a, v_b) = \sum_{i}^{|I(v_a)|} \sum_{j}^{|I(v_b)|} NWST(I_i(v_a), I_j(v_b)) \quad (3)$$

$$\begin{aligned} &NWST(I_i(v_a), I_j(v_b)) \\ &= \omega(I_i(v_a) \to v_a)\omega(I_j(v_b) \to v_b) NWS(I_i(v_a), I_j(v_b)) \end{aligned} \quad (4)$$

3.2 Two-Stage SimRank

Query Clustering

Obviously, there is a common assumption that in most case the original queries users submitted always have one or more topics of users' need, so we consider that a global term mining in whole query log set may cause noise and topic drift. Therefore, we compute the similarly scores for each query pair in the full query-click graph (Section 3.1), and then cluster all queries in K topic groups. Specifically, the clustering algorithm and the value of K may have many strategies in practice, and the strategy we choose will be show in detail in Section 4.3.

After clustering, we can obtain one full query-click graph and several sub graph of query-click. After several transformations have been described in Subsection 2.2, the main and sub term-relationship graphs are obtained finally.

Interpolation of Similarity

Finally, considering the topics, for any term t in query q, we can find a group which describes the same main topic with q, and then mining several related terms to t by NWS algorithm. Unfortunately, because of the scale of the sub graph, the term t maybe haven't appeared in it, so we do not neglect the global similarly and combine group and global similarly as the follow:

$$\begin{aligned} TTS(v_a, v_b) = \; & \alpha \cdot NWS_{group}(v_a, v_b) \\ & + (1 - \alpha) \cdot NWS_{globle}(v_a, v_b) \end{aligned} \quad (5)$$

where α is a constant between 0 and 1, gives the weight of group similarly in the final similarly, and its setting will be showed in detail in Section 4.4.

3.3 Query Expansion

For any given query $q = w_1 ... w_{i-1} w_i w_{i+1} ... w_n$, our approach will iterate through all terms w_i and try to find similar terms in the query log for each of them. For each w_i, the approach selects candidate terms and do query expansion by following four steps: (1) We classify query q into several group, and obtain the sub term-relationship graphs. (2) If there is a node of t_i in the global term-relationship graph, then consider every terms t_j with $TSS(v_i, v_j) \neq 0$ as a candidate term. (3) Remain only the top M expansion candidate terms t_j sorted by their $TSS(v_i, v_j)$. (4) Join all remaining candidate terms in the original query, and then retrieval using the new query. In the follow sections, the method above is called TSSE (Two-Stage SimRank based Expansion).

4. EVALUATION

4.1 Experimental Dataset

Our experiments are based on the query log distributed by AOL, containing 36,389,567 records, 10,154,742 distinct queries and 657,426 users. Most of them are in English and sampled during three month, including an anonymous user-id, a query, a timestamp, and the clicked results (for each result, the position on the result page is also provided).

The evaluation is done using two standard TREC collections: Robust-04 and Gov-2, with the details in Table 1. In particular, we treat all topic titles as queries and neglect their description.

4.2 Baseline

In order to evaluate the effectiveness of our method, we use three methods as the baselines for comparison.

(1) The Language Model was implemented by the Indri toolkit [1], in which the Dirichlet smoothing prior μ was set to 1500 empirically [5], and this method is denoted by LM-Dir.

(2) A Relevance-Based Language Model was also implemented by the Indri, which is one of the PRF expansion approaches, based on the method by Lavrenko and Croft [7] and denoted by RM.

(3) The expansion method only based on Normalized Weight SimRank is denoted by NWSE (details in Subsection 3.1). The parameter d_m (the maximum number of in-edges) is set to 500 empirically [9].

4.3 Query Expansion with TSSE

For creating the term-relationship graph, we creat the query-click graph first, which contains approximately 4 million query nodes and 2 million clicked URL nodes.

Before the term-relationships' construction, let's discuss how to cluster the queries by the query-click graph. We comput queries' similarity scores by NWS (details in subsection 3.1) first, and then use the K-means clustering algorithm with these scores to cluster all the queries into K groups. The intent of query clustering is to group them according to the topics which just meet the users' need, so we investigate the Open Directory Project (ODP) which is the largest, most comprehensive human-edited directory of the Web [2], and set K to 15 (the number of top-level topics in ODP). Finally, we train a SVM model according to the K groups, therefore, for each new query, it can be divided into one of the fifteen groups and we will use this information to compute the TSS scores.

Now we have obtained one full query-click graph and several sub graphs of query-click, after several transformations have been described in Subsection 2.2, the full and sub term-relationship graphs are also obtained finally, containing 413, 013 term nodes.

According to the description in Subsection 3.3, we can discover candidate terms with importance degrees (TSS scores) for every new query, and expand the original query. The candidate terms and the original query terms are combined using "*#weight*" operator and "*#combine*" operator

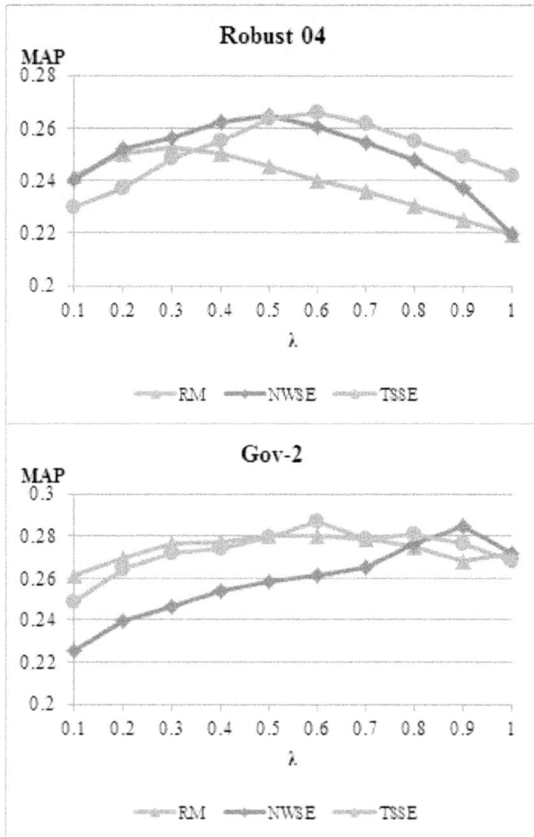

Figure 3: MAP performance of all query expansion approach when M=30

implemented by the Indri [1], and Equation 6 is implemented by creating an Indri-query of the form:

$$\#weight(\lambda(Q_{ori}) \quad (1.0-\lambda)(Q_{exp})) \tag{6}$$

where Q_{ori} is the original query and λ is free parameter which determines the weight given to the original query. For now, we work out a complete strategy for selecting expansion terms and creating the final query. In the following passages, the expansion approach above will be named TSSE, and we will focus on its performance in ad-hoc retrieval.

4.4 Results

Before doing some detail testing, Figure 3 shows the results of assigning different λ on two TREC collections, when M (the number of candidate terms remained) is set to 30 and α (in Equation 5) is set to 0.5 empirically. As it can be seen in Figure 3, the RM method perform well when the value of λ is set to 0.3 for Robust-04 and 0.6 for Gov-2. On the other hand, the TSSE method performs the best on MAP indicator when λ is set to 0.6 for both two TREC collection. Finally, we set the parameter to optimal values above for each of methods.

Similarly, let's discuss the parameter α for interpolation in the TSS algorithm now. Figure 4 shows that how the α influences the retrieval performance, when M is also set to 30 and λ is set to 0.6. We find clearly that the queries work best when parameter α is equal to 0.4 for Robust-04 and

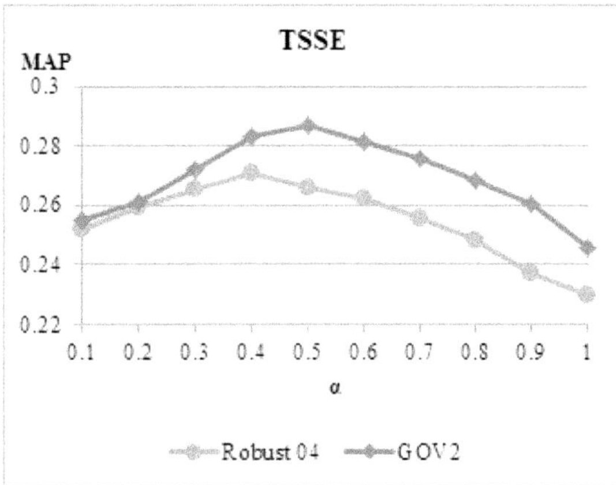

Figure 4: MAP performance of TSSE approach when λ=0.6

Table 2: MAP scores of various methods

Meth.	**MAP**					
	Robust-04					
LM	0.220	0.220	0.220	0.220	0.220	0.220
RM	0.241	0.249	0.253	0.254	0.2534	**0.253**
NWSE	0.262	0.269	0.265	0.265	0.256	0.243
TSSE	**0.268**	**0.273**	**0.271**	**0.266**	**0.261**	0.249
	Gov-2					
LM	0.272	0.272	0.272	0.272	0.272	0.272
RM	0.270	0.277	0.280	0.281	0.281	**0.282**
NWSE	0.282	0.285	0.284	0.285	**0.282**	0.273
TSSE	**0.283**	**0.286**	**0.286**	**0.285**	0.281	0.276
M	**10**	**20**	**30**	**40**	**50**	**60**

0.5 for Gov-2 respectively, so the value is fixed in the detail testing.

We propose to use MAP and precision at top 10 (P@10) to measure retrieval effectiveness for all experiments. Finally, after several ad-hoc retrieval testing on two TREC standard collections, we list Table 2 and Table 3 to show the results.

5. CONCLUSION

In this paper, we have explored the AOL query log as a resource for query expansion. We generated a weighted bi-partite query-click graph, with queries on one side and URLs on the other, and then, clustered queries in several sub graphs. After that we obtained term-relationship graphs by several transformations from the full and sub query-click graphs respectively. Finally, a new method have been proposed for mining quality expansion terms from query log. Our algorithm named Two-Stage SimRank was based on a revised SimRank algorithm, and we measured the importance of expansion terms according to their TSS scores with the terms in the original queries. In the last section, our experiments showed that the expansion terms extracted from AOL query log were better than those extracted from the feedback documents, using a relevance-based language modeling method, on the two different TREC collections.

6. ACKNOWLEDGMENTS

This work is supported by grant from the Natural Science Foundation of China (No.60673039 and 60973068), the National High Tech Research and Development Plan of China (No.2006AA01Z151), National Social Science Foundation of China (No.08BTQ025), the Project Sponsored by the Scientific Research Foundation for the Returned Overseas Chinese Scholars, State Education Ministry and The Research Fund for the Doctoral Program of Higher Education (No.20090041110002).

Table 3: P@10 scores of various methods

Meth.	**Precision@10**					
	Robust-04					
LM	0.407	0.407	0.407	0.407	0.407	0.407
RM	0.410	0.414	0.412	0.415	0.410	0.408
NWSE	**0.432**	0.437	0.432	0.433	0.427	0.418
TSSE	0.431	**0.444**	**0.440**	**0.440**	**0.434**	**0.421**
	Gov-2					
LM	0.466	0.466	0.466	0.466	0.466	0.466
RM	0.462	0.470	0.472	0.478	0.480	0.478
NWSE	0.488	**0.502**	0.492	0.488	**0.492**	0.482
TSSE	**0.492**	**0.502**	**0.505**	**0.493**	**0.492**	**0.484**
M	**10**	**20**	**30**	**40**	**50**	**60**

7. REFERENCES

[1] Indri toolkit. http://www.lemurproject.org/indri.php.

[2] Open directory project (odp). http://www.dmoz.org/.

[3] I. Antonellis, H. G. Molina, and C. C. Chang. Simrank++: Query rewriting through link analysis of the click graph. In *Proceedings of VLDB 2008*, pages 408–421, August 2008.

[4] P. Boldi, F. Bonchi, and C. Castillo. Query suggestions using query-flow graphs. In *Proceedings of WSCD 2009*, pages 51–58. ACM, February 2009.

[5] B. Croft, D. Metzler, and T. Strohman. *Search Engines: Information Retrieval in Practice.* Addison-Wesley Publishing Company, Reading, Massachusetts, 2009.

[6] G. Jeh and J. Widom. Simrank: A measure of structural-context similarity. In *Proceedings of SIGKDD 2002*, pages 538–543. ACM, July 2002.

[7] V. Lavrenko and W. B. Croft. Relevance-based language models. In *SIGIR 2001: Proceedings of the 24th annual international ACM SIGIR conference on Research and development in information retrieval*, pages 120–127. ACM, September 2001.

[8] K. S. Lee, W. B. Croft, and J. Allan. A cluster-based resampling method for pseudo-relevance feedback. In *SIGIR 2008: Proceedings of the 31st annual international ACM SIGIR conference on Research and development in information retrieval*, pages 235–242. ACM, July 2008.

[9] Y. L. Ma, H. F. Lin, and S. Jin. A revised simrank approach for query expansion. In *Proceedings of AIRS 2010*, pages 564–575. Springer, December 2010.

[10] T. Tao and C. X. Zhai. Regularized estimation of mixture models for robust pseudo-relevance feedback. In *SIGIR 2006: Proceedings of the 29th annual international ACM SIGIR conference on Research and development in information retrieval*, pages 162–169. ACM, August 2006.

On Relevance, Time and Query Expansion

Giuseppe Amodeo
IASI-CNR, Univ. of L'Aquila
Rome, Italy
gamodeo@fub.it

Giambattista Amati
Fondazione Ugo Bordoni
Rome, Italy
gba@fub.it

Giorgio Gambosi
"Tor Vergata" University
Rome, Italy
gambosi@mat.uniroma2.it

Abstract

We present the results of our exploratory analysis on the relationship that exists between relevance and time. We observe how the amount of documents published in a given interval of time is related to the probability of relevance, and, using the time series analysis, we show the existence of a correlation between time and relevance. As an initial application of this analysis, we study query expansion exploiting the detection of publication time peaks over the Blog06 collection. We finally propose an effective approach for the query expansion in the blog search domain. Our approach is based on the documents publication trend being so completely independent of any external resource.

Categories and Subject Descriptors

H.3.0 [**Information Storage and Retrieval**]: General; H.3.1 [**Information Storage and Retrieval**]: Content Analysis and Indexing; H.3.3 [**Information Storage and Retrieval**]: Information Search and Retrieval

General Terms

Theory, Experimentation

Keywords

time series, query expansion, relevance distribution

1. INTRODUCTION

Nowadays, social networks, blogs, forums are attracting an increasing number of users, and information needs change quickly: freshness of the retrieved information is becoming central.

Taking into account the temporal evolution of data becomes thus mandatory. In the most recent editions of the TREC Blog track, the top news stories identification task was a hot one ([11]) and it is still central in the real-time search task[1]. Moreover, commercial applications such as RecordedFuture[2], Google Trends[3] and Yahoo!'s TimeExplorer[4] [12] are examples of the application of time analysis in a commercial framework .

In all these examples, there is an underlying belief that taking into account the time of a document (e.g. the publication date), or of a query (e.g. the submission time) can improve effectiveness.

For example, in queries like "olympics" or "September 11", the publication date of some news related to the query can be useful to boost the prediction of relevance with the topic, as in the Time-based language models [8]. Conversely, queries like "whole foods" or "stock options" seem to be less related to particular events. Starting from these observations, we classify queries in two categories: "*events driven*" or "*events free*".

In this paper we study the relationship between the publication date of a document and its relevance with respect to a query. We thus want to answer such questions as: does a boost in the number of document publications correspond to an increasing probability of relevance? Can time be used to refine relevance prediction of documents with respect to a query?

To achieve our aims we first analyze how relevance changes over time using time series. We derive time series from the result sets of documents and, in parallel, from the set of relevant documents, we then compare these two time series. Notice that this approach depends on the collection only, without the need of logging query traffic or other user dependent information.

We further propose a modification of Rocchio's query expansion algorithm that takes into account the time dimension in order to improve the effectiveness of the retrieval.

Our analyses show that the amount of document published in a time slice is deeply related to the probability of relevance, at least in the Blog06 collection. The effectiveness of deriving QE algorithm proposed, also shows that information related to the distribution of documents over time can be successfully used to define new QE models.

2. RELATED WORK

The information retrieval community has shown an increasing interest in online news and blogs domains in the latest years. Temporal information is often analysed in order

[1]http://sites.google.com/site/trecmicroblogtrack/
[2]http://www.recordedfuture.com
[3]http://www.google.com/trends
[4]http://fbmya01.barcelonamedia.org:8080/future/

CIKM'11, October 24–28, 2011, Glasgow, Scotland, UK.

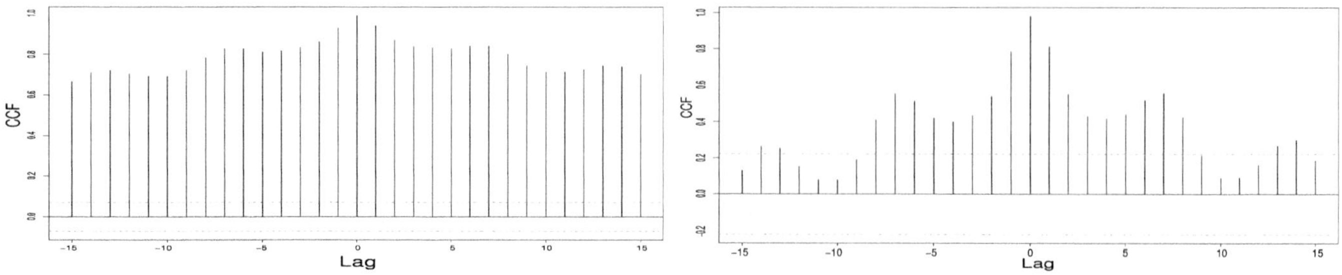

Figure 1: Cross Correlation Function for time series of relevant and retrieved documents with $0 \leq \tau \leq 15$. The images are related to the whole collection of documents (on the left) and the crawling time only (on the right).

to provide new perspective or representation of documents collection [1, 5, 12]. Furthermore, the time dimension has been explored to discover relationships among terms to support forecasting in [20].

Other works apply time series to the analysis of temporal evolution of information ([2, 13]). Time series analysis has also been adopted in other papers where the discovery of existing relationship among queries starting from the query logs is considered ([21, 7, 14]).

Finally, in [15, 4] it is shown how time-stamps of documents can be used to increase the precision of search. The assumption that time and relevance can be analysed in order to define effective retrieval models has been exploited in timed language models ([8, 19, 3]).

The application of time analysis on the blog search problem is instead quite new. Many and various works aim to increase the retrieval performance in blog domain using external resources [17] but not so with the time dimension.

3. TIME DIMENSION

The results set of a search engine is typically shown to the final user as a flat list of documents sorted by some relevance scores. How to improve the effectiveness of the retrieval phase is one of the main challenge in IR. Starting from the results set, a common approach is to analyse how relevance is related to scores or ranks. Learning to Rank is the most famous and effective application of this approach. The connections existing between relevance and score (or rank) are the starting point of this kind of approaches. We try to apply similar analyses to other sources of informations that related to documents in the collection.

Increasingly, new collections of documents contain further data besides text. This is the case of newspapers, blogs, tweets where each "document unit" is enriched with extra information: timestamps of publication, author's details, cross references and so on. Our aim is to propose an analysis of the relationship between relevance and time.

In collections where the freshness of information is a critical aspect, the time dimension has a central role. In this case, the interest for a specific topic often corresponds to a burst in published documents related to it. Let us consider, for example, a newspaper with main focus on political or current events. When a news story arises, an increasing trend in publishing news on that story happens. After a period during which the story remains hot, the space that the newspaper assigns to it decreases and vanishes. In a such case, we say that the topic is "*event driven*", i.e. there is something that happens and generate the interest for that topic in the collection. Of course there are also topics that are not related to a specific event, like the "weather forecasting". For these kind of topics, events that happen and are related to the topic, can just influence the trend in publication, but does not cause a real change of interest. In this case we say that the topic is "*events free*".

Our assumption is that a spike in the publication of document related to a topic is related to an increasing interest for the topic. Thus, given a relevance assessment for documents related to a given topic we can build a time series of relevance. The relevance is somehow related to the amount of documents published. We aim to discover which kind of connection exists between the two.

We do not analyse the whole set of documents in the collection for this analysis, but we focus only on the result set of a query. We consider the result set as a cluster of documents that *could be* relevant to the query. Hence, starting from a result set of (pseudo-relevant) documents, we build the time series for their publication dates. We then compare this time series with the one built from the publication time of (true) relevant documents. Comparing these time series, we can bring out some clues on how related are time and relevance between the sets of relevant and retrieved documents.

Packing the time in bins with a given granularity, we then compute the probability of relevance for each time unit. We can so derive considerations on how the relevance changes according to the spikes in publication of pseudo-relevance document.

For our experimentation we used the Blog06Collection ([9]) with the evaluations related to Blog TREC competition of 2006, 2007 and 2008 ([10, 18, 16]). The dataset includes 150 topics for 3.2 million of blogposts. The crawling was performed between 06/12/2005 and 21/02/2006 but the publication dates of gathered documents cover a period of more than 2 years. Of course, the amount of documents published is large in the crawling time interval but tends quickly to zero outside. For this reason we repeated our analysis considering first the whole collection time (from January 1st, 2004 to February 21st, 2006) and then the crawling period.

3.1 Construction of Time Series

In order to build a time series $Y = y_1, \ldots, y_n$ starting from a set of documents, we group all documents published at the same time t:

	Full Time				Crawling Time			
	Min.	Max.	μ	σ^2	Min.	Max.	μ	σ^2
BL1	0.1216	0.9916	0.7459	0.0364	0.0635	0.9889	0.6122	0.0745
BL2	0.1688	0.9960	0.7145	0.0343	0.0087	0.9957	0.5363	0.0854
BL3	0.1313	0.9943	0.7204	0.0412	0.0586	0.9942	0.5805	0.0832
BL4	0.1577	0.9923	0.7496	0.0368	0.0471	0.9916	0.6043	0.0769
BL5	0.0914	0.9881	0.7094	0.0480	0.1461	0.9917	0.5935	0.0824
	0.1342	0.9925	0.7280	0.0393	0.0648	0.9924	0.5854	0.0805

Table 1: Min, Max, Mean and Variance values of crosscorrelation function at lag 0 for each baselines. Values are average over all the 150 topics.

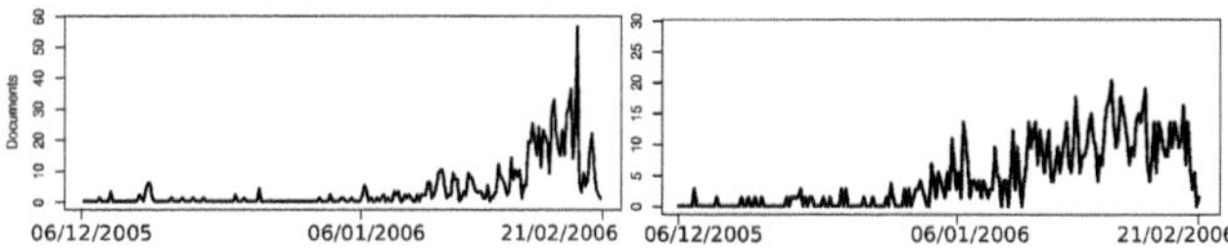

Figure 2: On the left an example of *event driven* query ("olympics") and on the right an example of *event free* query ("whole food").

$$y_t = \sum_{d \in \mathcal{D}} f_t(d); \quad (1)$$

where $\mathcal{D}$ is the set of documents and

$$f_t(d) = \begin{cases} 1 \text{ if } d \text{ is published at time } t \\ 0 \text{ otherwise} \end{cases} \quad (2)$$

We can choose t as a time interval: a day, a week or a month. In this way we can provide a binning of documents in time units. In our experimentation we choose t equal to a single day, so obtaining a daily binning of documents.

We apply this approach to both results set and relevant documents.

3.2 Relevance distribution over time

We tried to analyse how retrieved and relevant documents are distributed over time and how much they are related each other. We built the time series X for relevant documents using the assessment provided by TREC for blog competitions from 2006 to 2008, where evaluations for 150 queries are provided. Furthermore, 5 vanilla baselines are provided by NIST for the TREC 2008 competition ([18]). We built a time series Y for retrieved documents using these baselines. We then evaluated the correlation between these two time series by applying the Cross Correlation Function (CCF) ρ of two univariate time series, defined as

$$\rho_{xy}(\tau) = \frac{E[(x_t - \mu_x)(y_{t+\tau} - \mu_y)]}{\sigma_x \sigma_y} \quad (3)$$

where μ_x and μ_y are the mean values of time series X_t and Y_t respectively, and σ_x, σ_y are the corresponding standard deviations.

We computed the values of CCF for each query separately with $0 \leq \tau \leq 15$. In figure 1 we report the mean CCF function values for all 150 queries on all the baselines.

We used as indicator of correlation, the mean value of CCF for all the queries in a baseline when $\tau = 0$. Thus, we obtain a measure of how the time series are related without any lag. Table 1 shows the mean, variance, min and max values for each baseline as well as their average. The resulting mean value of the cross correlation over all the baselines is 0.7280 with a variance of 0.0393. We can conclude that there is a strong correlation between the two series. This observation suggests that the models used to retrieve documents are able to collect documents that are published according to a trend similar to the one followed by the relevant document.

Giving a deeper look to the shape of time series, we infer that, in general, there are two kind of queries. Those that have spikes in publications around a specific date (*events driven queries*) and those that show no specific correlation with a particular date (*events free queries*). Figure 2 shows two examples of these kind of queries.

3.3 Timed Query Expansion

We now try to more deeply analyse the correlation existing between relevance and the time dimension. We know that bursts in the time series of relevant documents are related to spikes in the time series of retrieved documents. Thus, we assume that pseudo-relevant documents in a peak are more suitable to be relevant with respect to the topic.

We applied Rocchio's algorithm in order to evaluate the correlation existing between peaks and relevance. In queries that are driven by events, we assume that the highest peaks are coupled to the events causing the interest for the topic. Thus, we restrict the query expansion to documents belonging to time bursts in order to improve the retrieval effectiveness with respect to the standard blind query expansion. More in details, we select top ranked documents in the highest peaks as "pseudo relevant", while documents outside peaks are considered as not relevant. We can then apply Rocchio's algorithm for relevance feedback:

$$q_m = \alpha q_0 + \beta \frac{1}{|D_r|} \sum_{d_j \in D_r} d_j - \gamma \frac{1}{|D_{nr}|} \sum_{d_j \in D_{nr}} d_j \quad (4)$$

3.4 Results on Timed Query Expansion

We used Dfreel as retrieval model, but we notice that the model is not important in our analysis. The blind relevance feedback baseline achieves a MAP equal to 0.3067, while our timed Rocchio's algorithm achieves MAP equal to 0.3126 with $\alpha = 1$, $\beta = 0.9$ and $\gamma = 0.1$. Finally, we obtained a statistically significant MAP of 0.3298 with $\alpha = \beta = 1$ and $\gamma = 0$, that is using only publication date peaks. All the query expansions were performed using 10 documents and 10 terms for the expansion. These improvements suggets the effectiveness of temporal query expansion approach.

Note that the Blog06 is a collection in which the query expansion algorithms usually fail [6, 18]. The fact that we can improve the effectiveness of a standard retrieval, seems in this case a remarkable result.

4. CONCLUSIONS AND FUTURE WORKS

We analysed the relationship between time and relevance on the Blog06 collection. We showed how the trends of the publication dates of the set of relevant documents and of the set of the retrieved documents are very close to each other. That is, the time series based on the publication dates of the set of retrieved documents is correlated to the trend of the set of relevant documents. This correlation is exploited to increase the effectiveness of search by applying a time-based query expansion algorithm based on a Rocchio-like query expansion. Our result is a first step to a deeper study of the correlation between time and relevance, and future work will focus more on the correlation in the case of event driven queries rather than for event free queries. We can so deal with the query periodicity so analysing the relationship existing among temporal query dynamics and their effects on relevance.

We also notice that query expansion hardly improves the effectiveness of retrieval on the Blog06 collection, without using any external resource. To further test the effectiveness of our approach, we'll perform a deeper analysis on timed QE comparing it with others QE techniques based on external evidences.

We will also make a similar study to other Web collections and refine our preliminary model of timed query expansion.

5. REFERENCES

[1] O. Alonso, M. Gertz, and R. Baeza-Yates. Clustering and exploring search results using timeline constructions. In *CIKM '09: Proceeding of the 18th ACM conference on Information and knowledge management*, pages 97–106, New York, NY, USA, 2009. ACM.

[2] K. Balog and M. de Rijke. Decomposing bloggers' moods - towards a time series analysis of moods in the blogosphere, 2006.

[3] K. Berberich, S. Bedathur, O. Alonso, and G. Weikum. *Advances in Information Retrieval*, volume 5993/2010 of *Lecture Notes in Computer Science*, chapter A Language Modeling Approach for Temporal Information Needs. Springer, 2010.

[4] K. Berberich, S. J. Bedathur, T. Neumann, and G. Weikum. A time machine for text search. In *Proceedings of SIGIR*, 2007.

[5] R. Catizone, A. Dalli, and Y. Wilks. Evaluating automatically generated timelines from the web. In *Proceedings of LREC 2006*, 2006.

[6] Jonathan L. Elsas, Jaime Arguello, Jamie Callan, and Jaime G. Carbonell. Retrieval and feedback models for blog feed search. In *Proceedings of the 31st annual international ACM SIGIR conference on Research and development in information retrieval*, SIGIR '08, pages 347–354, New York, NY, USA, 2008. ACM.

[7] A. Kulkarni, J. Teevan, K.M. Svore, and S.T. Dumais. Understanding temporal query dynamics. In *WSDM*, 2011.

[8] X. Li and W. B. Croft. Time-based language models. In *CIKM '03: Proceedings of the twelfth international conference on Information and knowledge management*, pages 469–475, New York, NY, USA, 2003. ACM.

[9] C. Macdonald and I. Ounis. The trec blogs06 collection : Creating and analysing a blog test collection. *DCS Technical Report Series*, 2006.

[10] C. Macdonald, I. Ounis, and I. Soboroff. Overview of the trec-2007 blog track. In *Proc. of the 16th Text Retrieval Conference (TREC)*, 2007.

[11] C. Macdonald and I. Soboroff. Overview of the trec-2009 blog track. In *Proc. of the 18th Text Retrieval Conference (TREC)*, 2009.

[12] M. Matthews, P. Tolchinsky, R. Blanco, J. Atserias, P. Mika, and H. Zaragoza. Searching through time in the new york times. In *In procedings of Fourth Workshop on Human Computer Interaction and Information Retrieval*, 2010.

[13] G. Mishne, K. Balog, M. de Rijke, and B. Ernsting. Moodviews: Tracking and searching mood-annotated blog posts. In *Int. Conf. on Weblogs and Social Media*, 2007.

[14] M. Murata, H. Toda, Y. Matsuura, R. Kataoka, and T. Mochizuki. Detecting periodic changes in search intentions in a search engine. In *CIKM*, 2010.

[15] K. Norvag. Supporting temporal text-containment queries in temporal document databases. *Journal of Data and Knowledge Engineering*, 49(1):105–125, 2004.

[16] I. Ounis, M. de Rijke, C. Macdonald, G. A. Mishne, and I. Soboroff. Overview of the trec-2006 blog track. In *TREC 2006 Working Notes*, 2006.

[17] I. Ounis, C. Macdonald, and I. Soboroff. On the trec blog track. In *Proc. of the 2nd International Conference on Weblogs and Social Media (ICWSM)*, 2008.

[18] I. Ounis, C. Macdonald, and I. Soboroff. Overview of the trec-2008 blog track. In *Proc. of the 17th Text Retrieval Conference (TREC)*, 2008.

[19] J. M. Ponte and W. B. Croft. A language modeling approach to information retrieval. In *SIGIR '98: Proceedings of the 21st annual international ACM SIGIR conference on Research and development in information retrieval*, pages 275–281, New York, NY, USA, 1998. ACM.

[20] K. Radinsky, S. Davidovich, and S. Markovitch. Predicting the news of tomorrow using patterns in web search queries. In *ICWI*, 2008.

[21] Y. Zhang, B.J. Jansen, and A. Spink. Time series analysis of a web search engine transaction log. *Inf. Processing. Manage.*, 2008.

Diverse Retrieval via Greedy Optimization of Expected 1-call@k in a Latent Subtopic Relevance Model

Scott Sanner
NICTA & the ANU
Canberra, Australia
first.last@nicta.com.au

Shengbo Guo
Xerox Research Centre Europe
Grenoble, France
first.last@xrce.xerox.com

Thore Graepel
Microsoft Research
Cambridge, UK
thoreg@microsoft.com

Sadegh Kharazmi
RMIT & NICTA
Melbourne, Australia
first.last@rmit.edu.au

Sarvnaz Karimi
NICTA & The University of Melbourne, Dept. CSSE
first.last@nicta.com.au

ABSTRACT

It has been previously observed that optimization of the 1-call@k relevance objective (i.e., a set-based objective that is 1 if at least one document is relevant, otherwise 0) empirically correlates with diverse retrieval. In this paper, we proceed one step further and show theoretically that greedily optimizing expected 1-call@k w.r.t. a latent subtopic model of binary relevance leads to a diverse retrieval algorithm sharing many features of existing diversification approaches. This new result is complementary to a variety of diverse retrieval algorithms derived from alternate rank-based relevance criteria such as average precision and reciprocal rank. As such, the derivation presented here for expected 1-call@k provides a novel theoretical perspective on the *emergence of diversity via a latent subtopic model of relevance* — an idea underlying both ambiguous and faceted subtopic retrieval that have been used to motivate diverse retrieval.

Categories and Subject Descriptors

H.3.3 [**Information Search and Retrieval**]: Retrieval Models

General Terms

Algorithms

Keywords

diversity, set-level relevance, maximal marginal relevance

1. DIVERSE RETRIEVAL AND SUBTOPICS

One of the basic tenets of set-based information retrieval is to minimize redundancy, hence maximize diversity, in the result set to increase the chance that the results will contain items relevant to the user's query [9]. Hence, *diverse retrieval* can be defined as a *set-level* retrieval objective that takes into account inter-document relevance dependences when producing a result set relevant to a query.

Subtopic retrieval — "the task of finding documents that cover as many *different* subtopics of a general topic as possible" [19] — has often been noted as a motivating case for diverse retrieval. That is, if a query has multiple facets that should be covered by a result set, or a query has multiple ambiguous interpretations, then a retrieval algorithm should try to "cover" all of these subtopics in its result set. It is this subtopic-based motivation for diverse retrieval — a motivation which also underlies the TREC 6-8 Interactive tracks[1] and TREC 2009-2010 Diversity subset of the Web tracks[2] — that we draw on for the latent subtopic binary relevance model presented in this paper.

If one wants to optimize a result set to cover all possible query subtopics, the question naturally arises as to what set-level relevance objective should be optimized? Wang and Zhu [17] have shown that natural forms of diversification arise via the optimization of *average precision* [3] and *reciprocal rank* [15]. While these results directly motivate diverse retrieval via *rank-based* (ordered set) relevance criteria, they do not use the subtopic motivation for diversity. We use this alternate subtopic motivation in this paper, where we define binary relevance via a *latent subtopic model*. With this definition of relevance, we then optimize the expectation of the *n-call@k set-based* relevance criteria (specifically for $n = 1$) that takes the value 1 if at least n of k documents in a result set are relevant and 0 otherwise [6]. We conjecture that an optimal result set w.r.t. this objective and relevance model will attempt to cover all subtopics in order to ensure that at least one document is relevant, hence yielding diversity.

One may ask why we focus on the n-call@k metric with $n = 1$ rather than $n > 1$ for diverse retrieval? In [16] (Figure 2c), Wang and Zhu observed that optimizing 1-call@k correlates *most strongly* with diverse retrieval, while as $n \to k$, retrieval becomes less diverse. The reasons for this are simple: as $n \to k$, a higher proportion of documents are required to be relevant; if the top-ranked document is deemed most relevant, similar documents are also likely to be relevant, discouraging diversity. At the other extreme, $n = 1$ encourages diversity since only one relevant document is needed.

CIKM'11, October 24–28, 2011, Glasgow, Scotland, UK.

[1] `http://www-nlpir.nist.gov/projects/t8i/t8i.html`
[2] `http://trec.nist.gov/data/web09.html` (also `web10`)

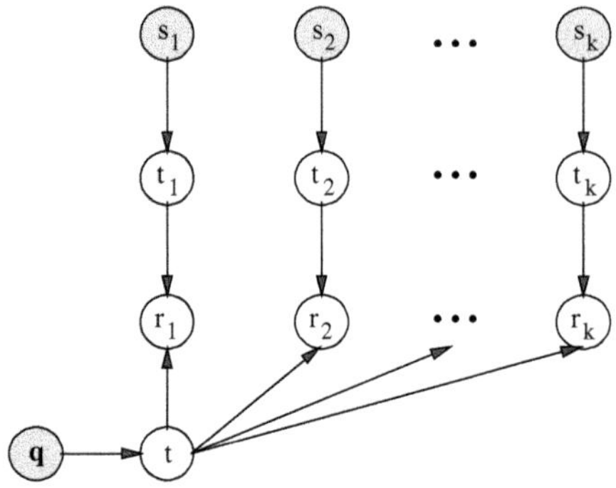

Figure 1: Latent subtopic binary relevance model.

In the rest of this paper, we derive a diverse retrieval algorithm via greedy optimization of *expected 1-call@k in a latent subtopic binary relevance model* and compare it to a variety of existing diversification approaches.

2. OPTIMIZING EXPECTED 1-CALL@K

Given an *item set* D (e.g., a set of documents) where retrieved items are denoted as $s_i \in D$, we aim to select an optimal subset of items $S_k^* \subset D$ (where $|S_k^*| = k$ and $k < |D|$) relevant to a given query $\mathbf{q}$ (e.g., query terms). For computational efficiency, we will build S_k^* in a greedy manner by choosing the next optimal selection s_k^* given the previous set of optimal selections $S_{k-1}^* = \{s_1^*, \ldots, s_{k-1}^*\}$ and recursively defining $S_k^* = S_{k-1}^* \cup \{s_k^*\}$ with $S_0^* = \emptyset$.

One of the most popular result set diversification methods is Maximal Marginal Relevance (MMR) [4] that chooses s_k^* greedily according to the following criteria:

$$s_k^* = \underset{s_k \in D \setminus S_{k-1}^*}{\arg\max} [\lambda(\mathrm{Sim}_1(\mathbf{q}, s_k)) - (1-\lambda) \max_{s_i \in S_{k-1}^*} \mathrm{Sim}_2(s_i, s_k)]. \quad (1)$$

Here, similarity metric Sim_1 measures query-item relevance, metric Sim_2 measures the similarity between two items, and the parameter $\lambda \in [0, 1]$ trades off relevance and diversity. In the case of s_1^*, the maximization term is vacuous (=0). We take special note of this form for MMR optimization since the results we derive next will bear a close resemblance.

To begin the derivation, we provide a directed graphical model in Figure 1 to formalize the independence assumptions in a probabilistic subtopic model of binary relevance. Shaded nodes represent observed variables while unshaded nodes are latent. The observed variables are the vector of query terms $\mathbf{q}$ and selected items s_i (where for $1 \le i \le k$, $s_i \in D$). For the subtopic variables, let T be a discrete subtopic set. Then variables $t_i \in T$ represent subtopics for respective s_i and $t \in T$ represents a subtopic for query $\mathbf{q}$. The r_i are binary variables indicating whether the respective selected items s_i are relevant (1) or not (0).

The conditional probability tables (CPTs) are as follows: $P(t_i|s_i)$ and $P(t|\mathbf{q})$ respectively represent the subtopic distribution for item s_i and query $\mathbf{q}$. The remaining CPTs are for relevance variables r_i, where item s_i is deemed *relevant* ($r_i = 1$) *iff its subtopic* t_i *matches query subtopic* t:

$$P(r_i = 1|t, t_i) = \mathbb{I}[t_i = t]$$

Here, $\mathbb{I}[\cdot]$ is 1 when its argument is true and 0 otherwise.

We now formally define the *expected 1-call@k* objective:

$$\text{Exp-1-Call@}k(S_k, \mathbf{q}) = \mathbb{E}\left[\bigvee_{i=1}^{k} r_i = 1 \,\middle|\, s_1, \ldots, s_k, \mathbf{q}\right] \quad (2)$$

Since jointly optimizing Exp-1-Call@$k(S_k, \mathbf{q})$ is NP-hard, we take a greedy approach similar to MMR where we choose the best s_k^* assuming that S_{k-1}^* is given. Then following [6], we can greedily optimize this objective as follows:[3]

$$\begin{aligned}
s_k^* &= \underset{s_k}{\arg\max}\ \text{Exp-1-Call@}k(S_{k-1}^* \cup \{s_k\}, \mathbf{q}) \\
&= \underset{s_k}{\arg\max}\, \mathbb{E}\left[\bigvee_{i=1}^{k} r_i = 1 \,\middle|\, S_{k-1}^*, s_k, \mathbf{q}\right] \\
&= \underset{s_k}{\arg\max}\, \mathbb{E}\Bigg[(r_1 = 1) \vee (r_2 = 1 \wedge r_1 = 0) \vee \cdots \vee \\
&\qquad \left(r_k = 1 \wedge \bigwedge_{i=1}^{k-1} r_i = 0\right) \Bigg|\, S_{k-1}^*, s_k, \mathbf{q}\Bigg] \\
&= \underset{s_k}{\arg\max} \sum_{i=1}^{k} P(r_i = 1, \{r_j = 0\}_{j<i} \,|\, \{s_j^*\}_{j \le i, j<k}, \{s_k\}_{k=i}, \mathbf{q}) \\
&= \underset{s_k}{\arg\max} \sum_{i=1}^{k} P(r_i = 1 \,|\, \{r_j = 0\}_{j<i}, \{s_j^*\}_{j \le i, j<k}, \{s_k\}_{k=i}, \mathbf{q}) \\
&\qquad P(\{r_j = 0\}_{j<i} \,|\, \{s_j^*\}_{j<i}, \mathbf{q}) \\
&= \underset{s_k}{\arg\max}\, P(r_k = 1 \,|\, \{r_j = 0\}_{j<k}, S_{k-1}^*, s_k, \mathbf{q}) \qquad (3)
\end{aligned}$$

Here, we applied a logical equivalence, exploited additivity of exclusive events, rewrote the expectation of a binary event as its probability, exploited d-separation to remove irrelevant conditions, factorized each joint into a conditional and prior, and removed terms and factors independent of s_k. Thus, we need only maximize s_k's probability of relevance conditioned on the query and previous selections (assumed irrelevant).

Next we evaluate the final query from (3) w.r.t. our graphical model of subtopic relevance from Figure 1:

$$\begin{aligned}
s_k^* &= \underset{s_k}{\arg\max}\, P(r_k = 1 \,|\, \{r_j = 0\}_{j<k}, S_{k-1}^*, s_k, \mathbf{q}) \\
&= \underset{s_k}{\arg\max} \sum_{t_1, \cdots, t_k, t} P(t|\mathbf{q}) P(t_k|s_k) \mathbb{I}[t_k = t] \prod_{i=1}^{k-1} P(t_i|s_i^*) \mathbb{I}[t_i \ne t] \\
&= \underset{s_k}{\arg\max} \sum_{t} P(t|\mathbf{q}) \sum_{t_k} P(t_k|s_k) \mathbb{I}[t_k = t] \prod_{i=1}^{k-1} \sum_{t_i} P(t_i|s_i^*) \mathbb{I}[t_i \ne t] \\
&= \underset{s_k}{\arg\max} \sum_{t} P(t|\mathbf{q}) P(t_k = t|s_k) \boxed{\prod_{i=1}^{k-1} (1 - P(t_i = t|s_i^*))}
\end{aligned}$$

Defining $\tilde{P}(t|S_{k-1}^*) = 1 - \square = 1 - \prod_{i=1}^{k-1}(1 - P(t_i = t|s_i^*))$, this is the probability that set S_{k-1}^* already *covers* topic t w.r.t. a *noisy-or* interpretation. Substituting $(1 - \tilde{P}(t|S_{k-1}^*))$ for $\square$ since $(1 - \tilde{P}(t|S_{k-1}^*)) = 1 - (1 - \square) = \square$, we obtain

$$\begin{aligned}
s_k^* &= \underset{s_k}{\arg\max} \sum_{t} P(t|\mathbf{q}) P(t_k = t|s_k) \left(1 - \tilde{P}(t|S_{k-1}^*)\right) \\
&= \underset{s_k}{\arg\max} \sum_{t} \underbrace{P(t|\mathbf{q}) P(t_k = t|s_k)}_{\text{query similarity}} \\
&\qquad - \sum_{t} \underbrace{P(t|\mathbf{q}) P(t_k = t|s_k) \tilde{P}(t|S_{k-1}^*)}_{\text{query-reweighted diversity}}. \qquad (4)
\end{aligned}$$

This final result in (4) has a clear interpretation as a diverse information retrieval algorithm where D consists of

[3]The notation $\{\cdot\}_C$ refers to a (possibly empty) set of variables (or variable assignments) $\cdot$ that meet constraints C.

Table 1: MMR vs Exp-1-call@k on various ranking measures of diversity.

Testbed	Algorithm	ERR-IA@5	ERR-IA@10	ERR-IA@20	α-nDCG@5	α-nDCG@10	α-nDCG@20	MAP-IA
TREC6-8	MMR ($\lambda = .5$)	0.0433	0.0548	0.0607	0.2310	0.2590	0.2728	0.0361
	Exp-1-call@k	0.0456	0.0561	0.0621	0.2332	0.2602	0.2750	0.0365
ClueWeb 2009	MMR ($\lambda = .5$)	0.0984	0.1085	0.1174	0.1500	0.1696	0.2045	0.0095
	Exp-1-call@k	0.0972	0.1084	0.1158	0.1435	0.1698	0.1997	0.0123
ClueWeb 2010	MMR ($\lambda = .5$)	0.1198	0.1422	0.1503	0.1516	0.2066	0.2339	0.0085
	Exp-1-call@k	0.1211	0.1408	0.1550	0.1527	0.1984	0.2476	0.0093

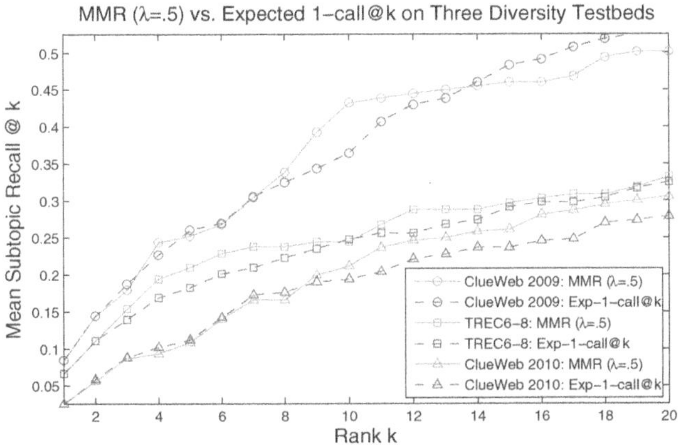

Figure 2: MMR vs Exp-1-call@k on subtopic recall.

documents: at each step, s_k is chosen so as to maximize a similarity function while minimizing a diversity penalty that increases as S^*_{k-1}'s coverage of *query-relevant* subtopics in document s_k increases. Thus we have achieved our goal of *deriving* a diverse retrieval algorithm via optimization of Exp-1-call@k in a latent subtopic model of binary relevance.

3. RELATED WORK

3.1 MMR

The result in (4) is strikingly similar to MMR — it contains two terms, one for query similarity and the other for result set diversification, where each term represents a similarity kernel — more specifically a *probability product kernel* (PPK) [11] that is an inner product of probability vectors (or more generally, functions). More formally, let $\mathbf{T}'$, $\mathbf{T}_k$, and $\mathbf{T}_{S^*_{k-1}}$ be respective topic probability vectors $P(t' = t|\mathbf{q})$, $P(t_k = t|s_k)$ and $\tilde{P}(t_k = t|S^*_{k-1})$ with vector indices for each topic $t \in T$. Then the similarity and diversity terms from (4) can be respectively written as

$$\sum_{t \in T} P(t' = t|\mathbf{q})P(t_k = t|s_k) = \langle \mathbf{T}', \mathbf{T}_k \rangle \text{ and} \quad (5)$$

$$\sum_{t \in T} P(t|\mathbf{q})P(t_k = t|s_k)\tilde{P}(t|S^*_{k-1}) = \langle \mathbf{T}_k, \mathbf{T}_{S^*_{k-1}} \rangle_{\mathbf{T}'}. \quad (6)$$

Here, we let $\langle \cdot, \cdot \rangle$ denote an inner product of two vectors and $\langle \cdot, \cdot \rangle_{\mathbf{v}}$ a $\mathbf{v}$-*reweighted* inner product, defined as in (6).

While having similarity and diversity terms similar to MMR, Exp-1-call@k in (4) clearly differs from MMR:

1. While MMR's definition allows for any similarity function, not just PPKs, we note that *equating words to subtopics*, popular kernels like TF and TFIDF [13] can be viewed directly as PPKs if the TF and TFIDF vectors are L_1 normalized to represent probability vectors.
2. MMR uses a maximization term for diversity, whereas optimization of Exp-1-call@k instead calls for a product (noisy-or) diversity term $\tilde{P}(t|S^*_{k-1})$. We note that a noisy-or reduces to a max when the subtopic probabilities are deterministic (0 or 1).
3. While MMR proposes a λ term to explicitly trade off the similarity and diversity terms, the greedy optimization of Exp-1-call@k in (4) yields no such trade-off term (or alternately, an implicit $\lambda = .5$). Although it seems a tunable λ is not needed for maximizing Exp-1-call@k, it may be desirable when maximizing surrogate retrieval objectives (e.g., ranking objectives).
4. Optimizing Exp-1-call@k introduces query-specific relevance into the diversification term as shown by the query topic ($\mathbf{T}'$) reweighted diversity function in (6).

To verify whether the differences between MMR and Exp-1-call@k matter empirically, we compare the two algorithms across a number of metrics on three diversity testbeds: the TREC 6-8 Interactive Track[1] (17 queries) and 2009 and 2010 ClueWeb Diversity tasks of the TREC Web Track[2] (50 queries each). On these testbeds, we evaluate *mean subtopic recall@k* [19] (fraction of total annotated aspects/subtopics covered by a result set at rank k, averaged over queries), which is an appropriate loss function for the *set-level* metric (2) [6]. We also evaluate a variety of more recent *rank-based* diversity evaluation metrics such as intent-aware expected reciprocal rank (ERR-IA@k) [5], α-nDCG@k [7], and intent-aware mean average precision (MAP-IA) [1].

We use MMR with $\lambda = 0.5$ to match the equal weighting of similarity and diversity in Exp-1-call@k. An LDA [2] topic model is trained on the top-100 OKAPI BM25 [12] results for each query (on its respective collection) and these subtopic distributions are used for the similarity and diversity kernels in both algorithms: for MMR we choose Sim_1 and Sim_2 kernels as in (5) — effectively LDA variants of latent semantic indexing (LSI) [8] kernels; for Exp-1-call@k, we use the similarity and diversity kernels respectively defined in (5) and (6). Both MMR and Exp-1-call@k are used to rank the top-20 documents from the top-100 OKAPI BM25 results.

Results in Table 1 and Figure 2 show the performances of MMR and Exp-1-call@k on the three diversity testbeds across various diversity measures; although there are minor performance differences, we note that these differences are not statistically significant w.r.t. 95% confidence intervals. Nonetheless, the results appear to indicate that the structural similarities in the use of MMR and the optimization of Exp-1-call@k outweigh the differences in this evaluation.

3.2 Other Diversification Approaches

Recent years have seen numerous proposals for diversification approaches and here we summarize the relationship between optimization of Exp-1-call@k and representatives of these alternative approaches:

Portfolio Theory: [16] motivates diversification in set-based information retrieval by a risk-minimizing portfolio selection approach. Viewing a result set as an investment portfolio with the objective to maximize return while minimizing risk, the derived result of [16] mimics both MMR and Exp-1-call@k in that the similarity term may be viewed as *expected portfolio payoff* (relevance) and the diversity term may be viewed as *expected portfolio risk*, which increases as the correlations between documents in the result set increase. One major difference in this framework is that rather than computing the diversity term via a max (MMR) or product (Exp-1-call@k) the portfolio theory derivation uses a summation — we examine the implications of this next.

Set Covering: Yue and Joachims [18] propose a set covering approach for training SVMs to predict diverse result sets for information retrieval. In their work, they equate subtopics with words and build a loss function for SVM training that penalizes result sets according to the sum of weights of query-relevant words *not* covered by the result set. While their approach provides a "hard" set-covering view of diversity, we note that an expansion of $\tilde{P}(t|S^*_{k-1})$ used in the diversity term of (4) provides a "soft" latent set-covering interpretation; that is, s_k is chosen so as to best cover (in a probabilistic sense) the latent topic space not already covered by $\{s^*_1, \ldots, s^*_{k-1}\}$. Formally, expanding the product in $\tilde{P}(t|S^*_{k-1}) = \prod_{i=1}^{k-1}(1 - P(t_i = t|s^*_i))$, collecting terms and writing it as a series, we arrive at a form that reflects the inclusion-exclusion principle applied to the calculation of probability that topic t is covered by $\{s^*_1, \ldots, s^*_{k-1}\}$:

$$\prod_{i=1}^{k-1}(1 - P(t_i = t|s^*_i))$$
$$= 1 - \left[\sum_{i=1}^{k-1} P(t_i = t|s^*_i) - \sum_{i=1}^{k-1}\sum_{j=1}^{k-1} P(t_i = t|s^*_i)P(t_j = t|s^*_j) + \cdots - (-1)^{k-1}\prod_{i=1}^{k-1} P(t_i = t|s^*_i)\right] \quad (7)$$

This result has a natural interpretation: the first summation term determines the coverage of topic t by each document s_i $(1 \leq i \leq k-1)$ currently in the result set, the second double summation term corrects the first term by removing the joint probability mass from all pairs of documents that was double counted, and so on according to the principle of inclusion-exclusion. (7) not only provides a probabilistic set covering view of Exp-1-call@k, but it also suggests that a portfolio approach to diversity using only the first summation would overcount each document's contribution to the diversity metric according to this set covering perspective.

Subtopic Relevance Models: We use a subtopic relevance model that is a simplified version of the model in [10] with fewer dependence assumptions. In other work, Zhai *et al* [19] present an empirical risk minimization view of dependent document retrieval from a subtopic perspective, where they derive a formalization of the *greedy* selection step that is similar to MMR and to a lesser extent, Exp-1-call@k.

Set-based Relevance Objectives: Chen and Karger [6], whose derivation we extended, directly optimize 1-call@k, but their intention is not to formalize MMR and instead use naïve Bayes to directly evaluate (3). Agrawal et al [1] and Santos et al (xQuad) [14] both specify set-based diversity metrics *very* similar to Exp-1-call@k but do not provide formal derivations as we have done in this work.

Ranking Based Objectives: Finally, returning to our introductory motivation, Wang and Zhu [17] have shown that natural forms of result set diversification arise via the optimization of average precision [3] and reciprocal rank [15]. Both of these methods share the view of directly optimizing a *ranking-based* objective, whereas this paper proposes a novel derivation from the alternate view of optimizing a *set-based* objective w.r.t. a subtopic model of relevance. However, even though Exp-1-call@k is a set-based objective, an indirect consequence of (and motivation for) greedily optimizing it is that documents added earlier yield a greater increase in objective than those added later; this yields a natural rank ordering on the greedy Exp-1-call@k result set.

4. CONCLUSION

This paper presented a new derivation of diverse retrieval by directly optimizing the expected 1-call@k set-based retrieval objective w.r.t. a latent subtopic model of binary relevance. This result both motivates and contrasts with various related diversification approaches, providing a new theoretical basis for the investigation of diverse retrieval.

Acknowledgements

NICTA is funded by the Australian Government as represented by the Department of Broadband, Communications and the Digital Economy and the Australian Research Council through the ICT Centre of Excellence program.

5. REFERENCES

[1] R. Agrawal, S. Gollapudi, A. Halverson, and S. Ieong. Diversifying search results. In *WSDM-09*, 5–14, ACM, 2009.

[2] D. M. Blei, A. Y. Ng, and M. I. Jordan. Latent Dirichlet allocation. *Journal of Machine Learning Research (JLMR)*, 3:993–1022, 2003.

[3] C. Buckley and E. M. Voorhees. Evaluating evaluation measure stability. In *SIGIR-00*, 33–40, ACM, 2000.

[4] J. Carbonell and J. Goldstein. The use of MMR, diversity-based reranking for reording documents and producing summaries. In *SIGIR-98*, 335–336, ACM, 1998.

[5] O. Chapelle, D. Metzler, Y. Zhang, and P. Grinspan. Expected reciprocal rank for graded relevance. In *CIKM-09*, 621–630, ACM, 2009.

[6] H. Chen and D. R. Karger. Less is more: Probabilistic models for retrieving fewer relevant documents. In *SIGIR-06*, 429–436, ACM, 2006.

[7] C. Clarke, M. Kolla, G. Cormack, O. Vechtomova, A. Ashkan, S. Büttcher, and I. MacKinnon. Novelty and diversity in information retrieval evaluation. In *SIGIR-08*, 659–666, ACM, 2008.

[8] S. Deerwester, S. T. Dumaisand, G. W. Furnas, T. K. Landauer, and R. Harshman. Indexing by latent semantic analysis. *Journal of the American Society for Information Science*, 41(6):391–407, 1990.

[9] W. Goffman. On relevance as a measure. *Information Storage and Retrieval*, 2(3):201–203, 1964.

[10] S. Guo and S. Sanner. Probabilistic latent maximal marginal relevance. In *SIGIR-10*, 833–834, ACM, 2010.

[11] T. Jebara, R. Kondor, and A. Howard. Probability product kernels. *Journal of Machine Learning Research (JLMR)*, 5:819–844, 2004.

[12] S. Robertson and S. Walker. Some simple approximations to the 2-poisson model for probabilistic weighted retrieval. In *SIGIR-94*, 345–354, ACM, 1994.

[13] G. Salton and M. McGill. *Introduction to modern information retrieval*. McGraw-Hill, 1983.

[14] R. L. Santos, C. Macdonald, and I. Ounis. Exploiting query reformulations for web search result diversification. In *WWW-10*, 881–890, ACM, 2010.

[15] E. M. Voorhees. TREC-8 question answering track report. In *Proceedings of the 8th Text Retrieval Conference*, pages 77–82, 1999.

[16] J. Wang and J. Zhu. Portfolio theory of information retrieval. In *SIGIR-09*, 115–122. ACM, 2009.

[17] J. Wang and J. Zhu. On statistical analysis and optimization of information retrieval effectiveness metrics. In *SIGIR-10*, 226–233, ACM, 2010.

[18] Y. Yue and T. Joachims. Predicting diverse subsets using structural SVMs. In *ICML-08*, 1224–1231, ACM, 2008.

[19] C. Zhai, W. W. Cohen, and J. Lafferty. Beyond independent relevance: Methods and evaluation metrics for subtopic retrieval. In *SIGIR-03*, pages 10–17. ACM, 2003.

Hybrid Models for Future Event Prediction

Giuseppe Amodeo*
IASI-CNR, Univ. of L'Aquila
Rome, Italy
gamodeo@fub.it

Roi Blanco
Yahoo! Research
Barcelona, Spain
roi@yahoo-inc.com

Ulf Brefeld
Yahoo! Research
Barcelona, Spain
brefeld@yahoo-inc.com

Abstract

We present a hybrid method to turn off-the-shelf information retrieval (IR) systems into future event predictors. Given a query, a time series model is trained on the publication dates of the retrieved documents to capture trends and periodicity of the associated events. The periodicity of historic data is used to estimate a probabilistic model to predict future bursts. Finally, a hybrid model is obtained by intertwining the probabilistic and the time-series model. Our empirical results on the New York Times corpus show that autocorrelation functions of time-series suffice to classify queries accurately and that our hybrid models lead to more accurate future event predictions than baseline competitors.

Categories and Subject Descriptors

H.3.0 [**Information Storage and Retrieval**]: General; H.3.1 [**Information Storage and Retrieval**]: Content Analysis and Indexing; H.3.3 [**Information Storage and Retrieval**]: Information Search and Retrieval

General Terms

Theory, Experimentation

Keywords

Future prediction, information retrieval, event prediction, time series, ARMA, ARIMA, SARIMA, web search

1. INTRODUCTION

Predicting the future is one of the oldest goals of mankind. While early approaches were assembled from heuristics and introspection, modern data repositories and information retrieval systems provide means for data-driven model generation and their quantitative analysis.

*This work was performed during an internship at Yahoo! Research and is partially supported by the EU Large Scale Integrated Project LivingKnowledge (contract no. 231126).

CIKM'11, October 24–28, 2011, Glasgow, Scotland, UK.

In contrast to previously published query volume based approaches [9, 7, 8], we study content-based models of time. We focus on time series that consist of user generated content retrieved according to a user query. That is, we are not only able to predict *when* a topic will be important in the future but also contribute to *why* this will be the case by analyzing the retrieved content. Additionally, our approach is independent of external resources and can be deployed to any document collection without the need of logging huge amounts of query traffic to perform predictions.

A natural way to deal with time series are the autoregressive moving average (ARMA) models and their derivatives that capture *periodicity* and *trend* of the data. The two criteria are fundamental for our analysis: periodicity determines whether predicting future events is an appropriate means for the actual time series as non-periodic or even random events such as natural disasters are not predictable by definition. The trend of a time series plays an important role as a continuously increasing amount of publications does not automatically imply the dawn of an upcoming event but could also be the result of a growing public interest, as for instance the query *global warming.*

The future event prediction consists of 3 stages. Each time series is classified using state-of-the-art machine learning techniques into four categories *periodic, partially-periodic, trend-based,* and *random* solely on the basis of its autocorrelation function. For periodic and partially-periodic time series, we adapt a probabilistic model to the periodicity of the autocorrelation function. A hybrid model is then computed by intertwining the probabilistic model with the original time series model for future event prediction.

We empirically evaluate all steps carefully using the New York Times corpus. Our results show that the classification of the time series can be accomplished with high accuracy and that the probabilistic model captures the regularities of periodic and partially-periodic time series very well. We further observe that the future time series predicted by the hybrid model are close to the ground-truth.

The remainder of our paper is structured as follows. Section 2 reviews related work. We present the hybrid model in Section 3 and report on empirical results in Section 4. Section 5 concludes the paper.

2. RELATED WORK

Goel et al. [7, 8] track unemployment levels and home sales by examining the number of times related queries have been submitted to a search engine and Choi and Varian [9] study the effects of query volume on future automobile, home, and retail sales, as well as travel behavior. Chien et al. [5] study semantically related queries based on their temporal correlation. Gamon et al. [6] study the relationship and information flow between news platforms and Radinsky et al. [12] study term co-occurrences to predict upcoming trends. Recent work by Alonso et al. [2] and Catizone et al. [4] suggests that the time dimension can be further exploited by automatically creating time-lines from temporal information extracted from documents. In fact, some applications already make use of the temporal aspect to enhance search result presentation.

Time-series analysis has been adopted also to discover existing relationship among queries starting from the query logs. Zhang et al. [14] present a survey on the use of time series analysis for query logs. Kulkarni et al. [10] extract features for classifying queries according to their popularity and over time and Murata et al. [11] focus on temporal changes in search behavior. Finally, Adar et al. [1] analyzed the correlation of user behavior and external events. Contrarily to these approaches, we solely rely on the contents of the documents to generate the time series.

3. HYBRID MODELS FOR PREDICTING FUTURE EVENTS

In this section, we present our hybrid approach to future event prediction where we define an event as *an external and not directly observable incident, influencing the common interest in a topic.* Indicators of events are therefore bursts in the time series or, in other words, peaks. That is, from a practical point, peak prediction and event prediction are identical. Nevertheless, we keep the distinction because events act like latent variables that alter the time series at certain points in time which we then observe as peaks in the data.

Our approach comprises the following steps: Given an indexed document collection, we retrieve a set of documents related to a user query and translate the retrieved content into a time series. The resulting time series is classified to determine whether event prediction is an appropriate means for processing the query. If the time series is not rejected, a peak detection is performed and a probabilistic model is trained to predict future bursts that match our definition of events. Finally, we compute a hybrid model that combines the predicted events with the time series.

3.1 From Queries to Time Series

Given an input query, we retrieve the set of sentences that contain mentions of the query terms. Sentences are ranked using BM25 [13]. Finally, we bin the retrieved sentences using their publication dates. The size of the bins depends on the granularity of the data and could for instance be day-wise, week-wise or month-wise. The resulting histogram is our time series $y = y_1, y_2, \dots, y_T$ that consists of counts of the retrieved documents in the respective time-bins.

3.2 Time Series Classification

Obviously, not all queries are suitable for event prediction. To decide whether predicting events is useful for a given time series y, we classify y into four categories: (i) *periodic* time series exhibit a general, repetitive pattern, (ii) *partially periodic* time series possess some repetitive regularities which are however not as striking as in the previous case, (iii) *trend-based* time series follow a general increasing or decreasing trend (e.g., 'global warming') which is also the main characteristic, and finally (iv) *random* time series do not exhibit any regularities or structure that could be exploited. If a query is classified as periodic or partially-periodic it is further processed, otherwise discarded.

3.3 Historic Peak Detection

The previous section showed that we can derive high-level information from the time series. For event prediction, however, we need to be able to detect bursts of interest. Such information needs are reflected by peaks in the time series. A peak can be defined as follows:

DEFINITION 1 (PEAK). *Let y be a time series and g a function of y. An element y_t is called a peak with respect to g, if (a) and (b) hold:*
(a) y_t is a local maximum.
(b) $y_t \geq g(y)$.

The function g realizes a thresholding and guarantees that only popular and isolated peaks are returned. Possible choices are for instance the mean, the median, or a quartile function.

3.4 Future Peak Prediction

The periodicity of a time series is determined by the distance (i.e., the number of lags) between maximal values of the autocorrelation function. This is equivalent to measuring the distance between two sign changes. The periodicity is then simply given by the average distance across all sign changes. Nevertheless, in the presence of noise it might happen that some peaks are not detected in the first place and the above described strategy is prone to fail. In the following, we present a robust method to predict peaks in the presence of noise.

We compute the probability of y_t being a peak as follows: Let b be the number of detected peaks and a be the average periodicity, we shift the actual time slice t across the time series by multiples of periodicity a and count the number of encountered peaks,

$$c(y_t) = \sum_{j=0}^{b-1} I[j \cdot a + t], \tag{1}$$

where $I[z]$ is the indicator function returning 1 if y_z is a peak according to Definition 1 and 0 otherwise. After normalization we obtain

$$P(y_t = \text{peak}) := \frac{c(y_t)}{\max_j c(y_j)}. \tag{2}$$

The measure P can be interpreted as a Bernoulli variable for each y_t. Whether a time slice y_t is finally treated as a peak is determined by a drawing $x_t \sim Uniform(0, 1)$ for each time t and accepting y_t as a peak if $P(y_t) \geq x_t$ and rejecting it otherwise. Note that we obtain at least one peak with probability 1 because of the division by the maximum.

3.5 Hybrid Models for Event Prediction

The predicted peaks of the previous section are a collection of time-stamps where we expect peaks. We now combine the baseline time series model with the set of predicted peaks.

We devise a simple but effective combination method. Let $Q = \{q_1, \dots, q_j\}$ be the set of detected peaks in the historical

Table 1: **Query classification results.**

Features	SVM	BNet	CART	J48	RF	Log
TS	34.18	53.64	57.55	49.82	31.68	52.64
NTS	54.45	44.36	32.45	36.91	34.26	40.64
ACF	78.91	76.09	76.00	71.27	**84.26**	78.73

Table 2: Results for the peak detection.

	Prec	Rec	F1
Mean	67.6	92.2	78.0
Median	45.9	93.4	61.5
1st Quartile	77.6	80.6	79.1

data, $P = \{p_1, \ldots, p_k\}$ be the set of predicted peaks, and $y = y_1, \ldots, y_T$ the future part of the time series model. The hybrid method simply substitutes the value of y_t by the average of the detected peaks in the historical data for all $t \in P$. That is, the prediction $\hat{y} = \hat{y}_1, \ldots, \hat{y}_T$ of the hybrid model is given by

$$\hat{y}_t = \begin{cases} \frac{1}{|Q|} \sum_{q \in Q} y_q & : \ t \in P \\ y_t + k \cdot (\bar{y} - y_t) & : \ \text{otherwise} \end{cases} \tag{3}$$

for all $t = 1, \ldots, T$, where $\bar{y}$ is the mean of the historical data. The constant k compresses the time series model around the mean to exclude interferences between predicted peaks and large values of y_t that are not peaks and thus acts like a normalization factor. Throughout the paper we use the value $k = 0.4$ that performed well in tests with a small subset of time series.

4. EMPIRICAL EVALUATION

In this section we report on our empirical results. We use the New York Times corpus and apply a 3-fold cross validation together with the AIC criterion [3] for model selection in all our experiments. SARIMA models [3] are observed to consistently outperform ARMA and ARIMA models and we discard the latter two from the presentation and refer to SARIMA as the baseline time series model in the remainder.

The New York Times corpus is a publicly available collection of over 1.8 million New York Times articles annotated with rich metadata. It spans between January 1, 1987 and July 19, 2007. We collect queries from past TREC competitions and added a couple of own queries. The final set consists of 108 queries related to events (e.g., "super bowl"), accidents (e.g., "railway accidents"), tv series (e.g., "the simpsons"), and new technologies (e.g., "blackberry"), as well as time-related queries (e.g., "summer"). Using monthly binning for the content, our data comprises 25 periodic, 15 partially periodic, 31 trend-based, and 37 random time series. We use a monthly binning for the New York Times corpus.

4.1 Evaluation of Time Series Classification

We translate the queries into time series according to Section 3.1 and classify them manually into the four categories *periodic*, *partially periodic*, *trend-based*, and *random* for evaluation. We compare the predictive performance of Support Vector Machines with RBF kernel (SVM), Bayesian Nets (BNet), logistic regression (Log), and decision trees SCART (CART), random forests (RF), and J48 C4.5 (J48). We use three different sets of features: The time series itself (TS), a normalized variant thereof (NTS), and the autocorrelation function (ACF).

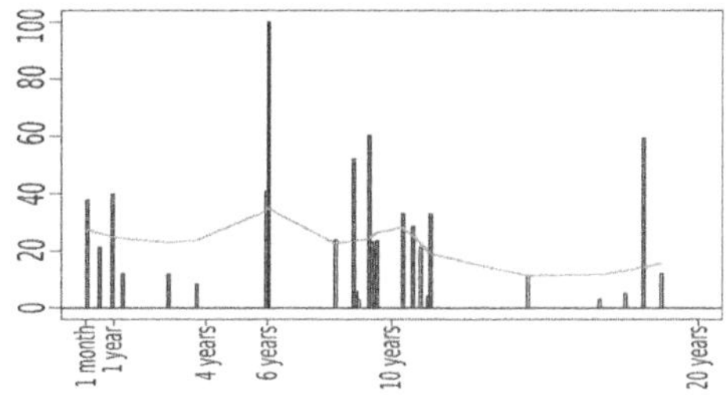

Figure 1: Feature importance for NYT.

The results are shown in Table 1. All methods perform best using the autocorrelation function which captures the nature of the problem reasonably well. The best result is attained by random forests with an accuracy of 84% which is significantly better than the performance of its competitors.

Figure 1 shows the most important features of the random forest which correspond to lags of the autocorrelation function. Unsurprisingly, periodicity is captured on a monthly and yearly basis by the classifier. Furthermore, multiples thereof are used for detecting reoccurring events. This is for instance the case for the most important feature which captures correlations of 6 years. While there is no event in the data that is repeated every 6th year, the period is ideal for capturing reoccurring annual, biennial, and triennial events.

4.2 Evaluation of Historical Peak Detection

For evaluating our peak detection strategy, we label all peaks in the time series manually. Our algorithm for automatic peak detection is a straight forward implementation of Definition 1. To allow for reusing the results for the peak prediction in the next section, we use only the first half of each time series for detecting the peaks and leave the remainder untouched.

Table 2 shows the results for periodic and partially periodic queries using mean, median, and first quartile as underlying function g (see Definition 1). The left part of the table shows the outcome for all queries. The results can be characterized by an excellent recall and a reasonable prediction, which however not accurate enough by itself.

4.3 Future Peak Prediction

We now apply the obtained results to peak and event prediction on the remaining half of the time series. Before we report the results, we need to define some evaluation criteria that are suitable for comparing two sets of peaks.

Besides standard Precision and Recall, we consider weighted variants thereof to take the severeness of erroneous peaks into account. For instance, consider a time series with only a single peak and two predictions, one is very close but not in the same time-stamp as the true peak and other one is far away. Both predictions would realize a precision and recall of zero with respect to the standard definitions. The weighted counterparts w-Precision and w-Recall weight the error by the number of months between the true peak and the prediction to capture the difference in the predictions. Finally, we denote by MPD the mean distance of the predicted peak and the ground-truth.

We compare our approach denoted as *Pred* detailed in Section 3.4 with three baselines. The first is simply predict-

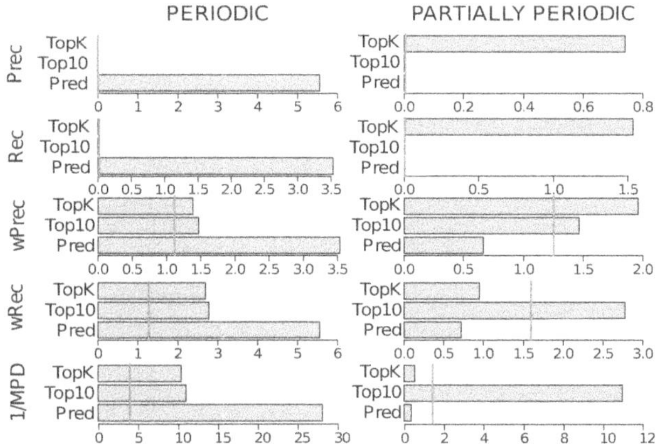

Figure 2: Results for peak prediction.

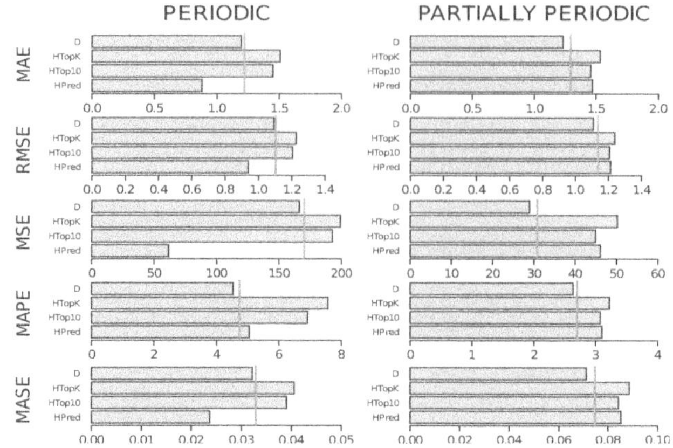

Figure 3: Evaluation of the hybrid model.

ing the publication dates of the top-10 retrieved documents as peaks, denoted by *Top-10*. The second baseline called *Top-k* is identical to top-10 but instead of 10 documents, we take k, where k is the number of previously detected peaks in the peak detection. The third one is the SARIMA model which is also used to compute the periodicity. Peaks are predicted using the peak detection strategy with a 1st quartile function.

Figure 2 shows the results. The rows are the five evaluation measures and the columns correspond to the four categories. Note that we inverted MPD so that higher values are always better. The SARIMA baseline is indicated by red bars. Our method indicated by *Pred* improves all evaluation metrics for periodic time series significantly. For the partially-periodic category, this is surprisingly not the case. Here, Top-10 and Top-k work significantly better.

4.4 Evaluation of the Predicted Time Series

In contrast to the peak prediction of the previous section, the hybrid model outputs a time series, hence we can compute its autocorrelation function, plot correlograms, and apply well-known distance-based performance metrics such as Mean Absolute Error (MAE), Root Mean Square Error (RMSE), Mean Squared Error (MSE), Mean Absolute Percentage Error (MAPE), and Mean Absolute Scaled Error (MASE).

We compare the hybrid model with the true continuation (the right half) of the time series. We deploy the three different peak prediction methods of the previous section in combination with the hybrid approach (see Equation 3): hybrid+top10 (HTop10), hybrid+top-k (HTopK), as well as hybrid+Pred (HPred). To better understand the difference between peak prediction (case 1 in Equation 3) and smoothing (case 2 in Equation 3), we deploy another baseline, denoted as D, that simply smoothes all values of the SARIMA forecasting by applying $\hat{y}_t = y_t + k(\bar{y} - y_t)$ to all time slices. Additionally, the vanilla SARIMA model is included (red bars).

The figure shows the evaluation metrics row-wise and the columns depict the four categories. The SARIMA models compute a conservative prediction with respect to the mean that is, in general, improved using smoothing for periodic trends. Unsurprisingly, simply smoothing the time series around its mean (method D) does not change its predictive performance. However, using the hybrid method (HPred) significantly reduces the prediction error of the SARIMA model for periodic queries and performs best in our study.

5. CONCLUSIONS

In this paper we studied content-based future event prediction. For a given query, we translated the retrieved documents into a time series so that events become (indirectly) observable in the time series by bursts and peaks. Our approach is twofold: Firstly, time series are classified into four categories to determine whether event prediction can reasonably be applied. We experimented with several classifiers and features derived from the autocorrelation function. The best result was obtained using a random forest together with the autocorrelation function of the time series, yielding an accuracy of 84%.

Secondly, we extracted the periodicity of time series using again the autocorrelation function and estimated a probabilistic model to predict future peaks which are then intertwined with the baseline SARIMA model to produce a more competitive prediction model. The hybrid method is shown to significantly improve future event prediction compared to baseline methods including the original SARIMA model.

6. REFERENCES

[1] E. Adar, D.S. Weld, B.N. Bershad, and S.S. Gribble. Why we search: visualizing and predicting user behavior. In *WWW*, 2007.

[2] O. Alonso, M. Gertz, and R. Baeza-Yates. Clustering and exploring search results using timeline constructions. In *CIKM*, 2009.

[3] George E. P. Box, Gwilym M. Jenkins, and Gregory C. Reinsel. *Time Series Analysis: Forecasting and Control.* Wiley Series in Probability and Statistics, 4th edition, 2008.

[4] R. Catizone, A. Dalli, and Y. Wilks. Evaluating automatically generated timelines from the web. In *LREC*, 2006.

[5] S. Chien and N. Immorlica. Semantic similarity between search engine queries using temporal correlation. In *WWW*, 2005.

[6] M. Gamon, S. Basu, D. Belenko, D. Fisher, M. Hurst, and A. önig. Blews: Using blogs to provide context for news articles. In *ICWSM*, 2008.

[7] S. Goel, J.M. Hofman, S. Lahaie, D.M. Pennock, and D.J. Watts. Predicting consumer behavior with web search. *National Academy of Sciences*, 2010.

[8] S. Goel, D. M. Reeves, D.J. Watts, and D.M. Pennock. Prediction without markets. In *EC*, 2010.

[9] H. Varian H. Choi. Predicting the present with google trends. Technical report, 2009.

[10] A. Kulkarni, J. Teevan, K.M. Svore, and S.T. Dumais. Understanding temporal query dynamics. In *WSDM*, 2011.

[11] M. Murata, H. Toda, Y. Matsuura, R. Kataoka, and T. Mochizuki. Detecting periodic changes in search intentions in a search engine. In *CIKM*, 2010.

[12] K. Radinsky, S. Davidovich, and S. Markovitch. Predicting the news of tomorrow using patterns in web search queries. In *ICWI*, 2008.

[13] S. E. Robertson and S. Walker. Some simple effective approximations to the 2-poisson model for probabilistic weighted retrieval. In *SIGIR*, 1994.

[14] Y. Zhang, B.J. Jansen, and A. Spink. Time series analysis of a web search engine transaction log. *Inf. Processing. Manage.*, 2008.

Adaptive Term Frequency Normalization for BM25

Yuanhua Lv
Department of Computer Science
University of Illinois at Urbana-Champaign
Urbana, IL 61801
ylv2@uiuc.edu

ChengXiang Zhai
Department of Computer Science
University of Illinois at Urbana-Champaign
Urbana, IL 61801
czhai@cs.uiuc.edu

ABSTRACT

A key component of BM25 contributing to its success is its sub-linear term frequency (TF) normalization formula. The scale and shape of this TF normalization component is controlled by a parameter k_1, which is generally set to a *term-independent* constant. We hypothesize and show empirically that in order to optimize retrieval performance, this parameter should be set in a *term-specific* way. Following this intuition, we propose an information gain measure to directly estimate the contributions of repeated term occurrences, which is then exploited to fit the BM25 function to predict a *term-specific* k_1. Our experiment results show that the proposed approach, *without needing any training data*, can efficiently and automatically estimate a term-specific k_1, and is more effective and robust than the standard BM25.

Categories and Subject Descriptors

H.3.3 [**Information Search and Retrieval**]: Retrieval models

General Terms

Algorithms

Keywords

BM25, Term frequency, adaptation, information gain

1. INTRODUCTION

The Okapi BM25 retrieval function [9, 11] has been the state-of-the-art for nearly two decades. The BM25 formula, as presented in [3], scores a document D with respect to query Q as follows:

$$\sum_{q \in Q \cap D} \frac{(k_3+1) \cdot c(q,Q)}{k_3 + c(q,Q)} \cdot dtf(q,D) \cdot \log \frac{N+1}{df(q)+0.5} \quad (1)$$

where $c(q,Q)$ is the count of term q in Q, N is the total number of documents, $df(q)$ is the document frequency of q, and k_3 is a parameter.

CIKM'11, October 24–28, 2011, Glasgow, Scotland, UK.

A key component of BM25 contributing to its success is its sub-linear term frequency (TF) normalization formula:

$$dtf(q,D) = \frac{(k_1+1) \cdot c(q,D)}{k_1\left(1 - b + b\frac{|D|}{avdl}\right) + c(q,D)} = \frac{(k_1+1) \cdot c'(q,D)}{k_1 + c'(q,D)} \quad (2)$$

where

$$c'(q,D) = \frac{c(q,D)}{1 - b + b\frac{|D|}{avdl}} \quad (3)$$

is the pivoted normalization method [12] for document length normalization. Here $b \in [0,1]$ is the slope parameter, $|D|$ represents document length, $avdl$ stands for average document length, and $c(q,D)$ is the raw TF of q in D.

The scale and shape of this TF normalization component is controlled by a parameter k_1, which is generally set to a *term-independent* constant [9, 6, 3]. Although many studies have attempted to improve BM25 from various perspectives, e.g., [10, 4, 8, 7], in all these studies, the sub-linear TF normalization formula with a fixed and term-independent parameter setting remained the same as the original BM25 [11], and no work has attempted to improve the TF normalization of BM25 through adaptively normalizing TF for individual terms. In this paper, we propose to automatically set k_1 in a per-term basis.

Our work is motivated by the observation that k_1 is intuitively related to the rate of increase in score contribution from matching an additional occurrence of a term. We notice that the optimal rate of score increase for a term generally should depend on the global tendency of the term to be repeated. Specifically, the increase of score from occurrences t to occurrences $t+1$ is related to how many of those documents with at least t occurrences of the term in the collection actually have at least $t+1$ occurrences of the term. Intuitively, if almost all documents containing at least t occurrences of the term actually contain at least $t+1$ occurrences, the score increase should be smaller, whereas if very few of those documents actually contain at least $t+1$ occurrences (i.e., they mostly contain exactly t occurrences), the score increase from t to $t+1$ should be larger. Our intuition that k_1 should be set in a per-term basis is also confirmed in the empirical plots in Figure 1.

Following this intuition, we develop an unsupervised approach to *adaptively* predict the optimal k_1 value for each term based on the counts of documents containing different levels of TF for a query term. Specifically, we propose to measure the contribution of the occurrences of a query term using the information gain of "observing one more token of the same query term", which can be estimated directly based

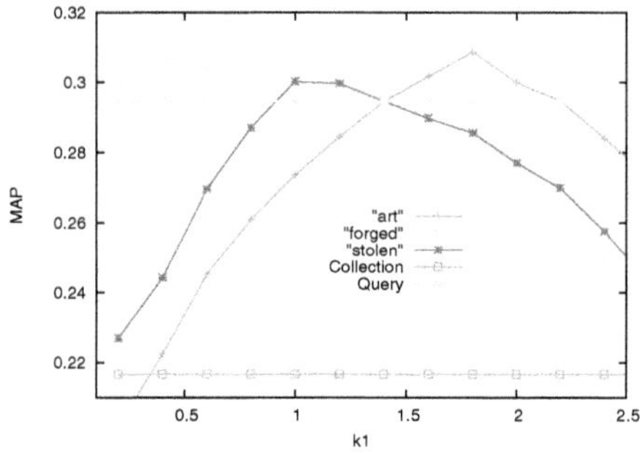

Figure 1: Comparison of different strategies for optimizing k_1 for TREC query topic 422, where we optimize k_1 for the whole collection ("Collection"), for this particular query ("Query"), and for each individual term (while we use the setting of "Query" for the other two terms), respectively.

on term statistics, and then we can fit the BM25 function with these contribution scores to solve a k_1 for each term.

Our experiment results on multiple test collections show that the proposed approach can effectively and efficiently estimate a term-specific k_1, and that it not only achieves better retrieval performance than a well-tuned BM25, but also is more robust than the standard BM25.

2. ADAPTIVE TF NORMALIZATION

We propose to measure the contribution of the observed t occurrences of a query term q in document D using the information gain (denoted as IG_q^t) of "encountering one more occurrence of q" in the current document D. Following the divergence from randomness (DFR) framework [1], we also assume that the probability that the observed term contributions to select a relevant document is high, if the probability of encountering one more token of the same term in a relevant document is similarly high, i.e., if D really talks about q, q would be likely to appear again. The probability of a further success in encountering a term is thus a conditional probability that gradually increases as t increases. However, on the other hand, if successes were brought about by pure chance, then the conditional probability would be constant no matter how t changes, but this constant could still be very large. Considering these intuitions and analysis, we hypothesize that the *information gain* of "encountering one more token of the same term" should be an appropriate measure of the contribution of the observed t term occurrences:

$$\frac{(k_1+1)\cdot t}{k_1+t}\cdot idf(q) \propto IG_q^t \tag{4}$$

Next, we introduce how to compute the information gain IG_q^t and how to estimate k_1.

2.1 Information Gain Measuring Term Contributions

The probability of a further success in encountering a term q conditioned on the current observed t occurrences is denoted as $p(t+1|t,q)$ in our paper. The use of this probability is not entirely novel: the Laplace's law of succession was used to estimate a similar probability in [1]. However, their methods do not consider the characteristics of q and are *term-independent*. In order to estimate a term-specific probability, we exploit term statistics of q. Specifically, we approximate $p(t+1|t,q)$ with the probability of randomly picking a document that will contain at least $t+1$ occurrences of q from a document set of which each document contains at least t occurrences of q, formally,

$$p(t+1|t,q) = \frac{df_{t+1}(q)+0.5}{df_t(q)+1} \tag{5}$$

where 0.5 and 1 are used to smooth the probability to avoid zero probabilities (can be interpreted as hyperparameters of a beta prior distribution). Similarly, we have an "initial occurrence" probability $p(1|0,q)$, which is the probability of randomly picking a document that contains q:

$$p(1|0,q) = \frac{df(q)+0.5}{N+1} \tag{6}$$

Hence, the information gain of "encountering one more token" is the change of *information content* from an initial state to the current state of observing t occurrences:

$$IG_q^t = -\log_2\left(\frac{df(q)+0.5}{N+1}\right) + \log_2\left(\frac{df_{t+1}(q)+0.5}{df_t(q)+1}\right) \tag{7}$$

where the definition of informative content as $-\log_2 P$ was given in semantic information theory [5].

However, it is well-known that longer documents tend to have higher TF. Following BM25, we also choose the pivoted normalization method [12], as shown in Equation 3, to obtain the normalized version of TF as $t = c'(q,D)$. Yet there is another problem after document length normalization: $t = c'(q,D)$ is usually no longer an integer, and thus it may not make sense to talk about the probability of encountering "one" more token conditioned on $c'(q,D)$. Our solution is to simply calculate a list of IG_q^t values only for *integers* $t \in \{0,1,2,\cdots\}$, and then use a few sample IG_q^t values to fit BM25. To estimate the information gain for an integer t, we define $df_t(q)$ in a more formal way.

$$df_t(q) = \begin{cases} |\{D|c'(q,D) \geq t-0.5\}| & \text{if } t \in \{2,3,\cdots\} \\ df(q) & \text{if } t = 1 \\ N & \text{if } t = 0 \end{cases} \tag{8}$$

Here we use the rounding technique, which intuitively makes sense. For example, it is not reasonable to exclude a document D from $df_2(q)$ if $c'(q,D) = 1.99$. Empirical analysis also shows that this rounding technique works very well.

It is observed that, when t becomes very large, the estimated information gain values are often noisy due to document sparseness (i.e., $df_t(q)$ may be too small). To address this problem, we only calculate IG_q^t for $t \in \{0,1,\cdots,T\}$, where T is chosen heuristically as the smallest integer that breaks up the word burstiness rule [2], i.e., $IG_q^T > IG_q^{T+1}$.

It is interesting to see that, besides document length normalization, the information gain measure also achieves both an IDF effect and a term-specific TF normalization effect. Note that $\left(-\log_2 \frac{df(q)+0.5}{N+1}\right)$ in Formula 7 is essentially the traditional IDF formula. And according to the word burstiness phenomenon [2], as t increases and becomes large, the second component of IG_q^t generally would also increase, and the increasing rate should be *term-dependent*.

2.2 Fitting BM25 with Information Gains

Empirical evidence shows that it is beneficial to set k_1 in a per-term basis. However, how can we achieve this goal?

Intuitively, k_1 is related to the "score gain" of matching a term t times, so we can try to measure "information gain" and connect k_1 with the proposed IG_q^t, i.e., we can now estimate k_1 by relating the BM25 TF component to IG_q^t.

Specifically, in Formula 4, we assume that the score distribution of the information gain measure is proportional to the score distribution of BM25. Now we align the two distributions at a special point, $t = 1$. We know that when $t = 1$, the left side and the right side of the Formula 4 appear to be $idf(q)$ and IG_q^1 respectively. So we can align two distributions by normalizing both sides of Formula 4 to make their score be 1.0 when $t = 1$, formally,

$$\frac{IG_q^t}{IG_q^1} = \frac{(k_1 + 1) \cdot t}{k_1 + t} \tag{9}$$

Because we have already obtained values $\{IG_q^0, IG_q^1, \cdots, IG_q^T\}$, we can estimate the optimal value of $k_1(q)$, i.e., the q-specific k_1, using a curve-fitting technique and the least square method:

$$\hat{k_1}(q) = \arg\min_{k_1} \sum_{i=0}^{T} \left(\frac{IG_q^t}{IG_q^1} - \frac{(k_1 + 1) \cdot t}{k_1 + t} \right)^2 \tag{10}$$

The estimation of $\hat{k_1}(q)$ only relies on a few IG_q^t values which can be calculated very quickly given the inverted index. So the estimation process is very efficient. Moreover, because $\hat{k_1}$ and IG_q^1 are generally not affected by online factors, they can also be pre-computed offline.

Now we can solve IG_q^t by substituting Equation 10 into 9, and then use IG_q^t to replace the left side of Formula 4, which leads to a BM25-like retrieval function, called BM25-adpt,

$$\sum_{q \in Q \cap D} qtf(q, Q) \cdot \frac{c'(q, D)(\hat{k_1}(q) + 1)}{\hat{k_1}(q) + c'(q, D)} \cdot IG_q^1 \tag{11}$$

It is clear that BM25-adpt has fewer parameters than the standard BM25, since a term specific parameter $\hat{k_1}(q)$ can be estimated automatically using Formula 10.

Moreover, comparing BM25-adpt with the standard BM25, there is also another interesting difference in the implementation of IDF: BM25-adpt uses a novel IDF formula, IG_q^1. From the definition of IG_q^t in Formula 7, we can see that IG_q^1 is essentially a *second-order* IDF, which not only considers the discrimination power of a term (i.e., $-\log_2 \frac{df(q)+0.5}{N+1}$), but also captures *randomness* of the repeated occurrences (i.e., $\log_2 \frac{df_2(q)+0.5}{df_1(q)+1}$). Our experiments have also shown that IG_q^1 works as effectively as the traditional IDF.

3. EXPERIMENTS

We used several standard TREC collections in our study: TREC8, Robust04, WT2G and WT10G. Queries were taken from the title field of the TREC topics. The preprocessing of documents and queries included Porter stemming and stopword removing using a total of 418 standard stopwords.

We used two variations of the standard BM25 function as our baselines, "BM25-basic" and "BM25". They differ from each other only in the parameter setting. Specifically, in "BM25-basic", k_1 was fixed to 1.2 as suggested in [6], while b was well tuned; this tuning strategy has been frequently used in many studies, e.g., [3], in order to reduce the effort of parameter tuning. In "BM25", both b and k_1 were optimized; "BM25" represents the upper bound of the standard BM25 function, which, however, requires significantly more tuning effort than "BM25-basic". In the proposed method, which is labeled as "BM25-adpt", we only tuned parameter b since k_1 was eliminated, so it requires the same amout of effort as "BM25-basic" for parameter tuning. In all runs, $k_3 = 1000$.

Collection	BM25-basic	BM25	BM25-adpt
TREC8	0.2459	0.2557	**0.2595**$^+$
Robust04	0.2507	0.2543	**0.2571**$^+$
WT2G	0.3191	0.3198	**0.3215**$^+$
WT10G	0.2065	0.2099	**0.2122**

Table 1: Optimal performance comparison.

Collection	BM25-basic	BM25	BM25-adpt
Robust04	0.2507	0.2536	**0.2571**$^+$
WT10G	0.2034	0.2056	**0.2091**$^+$

Table 2: Performance comparison using cross validation.

In our experiments, the top-ranked 1000 documents for each run were compared in terms of their mean average precisions (MAP). Note that the superscripts + and $*$ indicate that the MAP improvements of BM25-adpt over BM25-basic and BM25 are statistically significant respectively.

3.1 Performance Comparison

We compare the optimal performance of different methods in Table 1. It is observed that "BM25-adpt" works effectively: its improvements over "BM25-basic" are statistically significant in most cases, and it even outperforms "BM25" consistently. It suggests that our way of automatically setting a term-specific $k_1(q)$, needing significantly less effort for parameter tuning, outperforms the standard way of manually tuning a term-independent parameter.

Comparison of optimal performance alone may raise some concern of over-fitting. So we further use a 5-fold cross-validation method to verify our observations on Robust04 and WT10G. The results are reported in Table 2. Overall, the comparison results are consistent with our previous observations.

In practice, we may not have appropriate training data in the same domain for all queries. So we are also interested in the robustness of a retrieval algorithm when the training and test sets are from different domains. In this experiment, we simulate such a scenario: TREC, WT10G, and WT2G collections are used as the training sets respectively to train the retrieval functions, which are then evaluated on Robust04. The results are presented in Table 3. It shows clearly that the proposed method "BM25-adpt" is more robust, and it significantly outperforms both "BM25-basic" and "BM25". This suggests that our algorithms, although with less parameters, perform more robustly.

3.2 Parameter Analysis

Parameter b in BM25 controls the influence of document length in TF normalization. So we are interested in how the setting of b affects the retrieval performance of our method. We set $k_1 = 1.2$ [6] in the standard BM25 algorithm so as to focus on the sensitivity of parameter b. Note that b is the only parameter that we need to tune in the proposed algorithm "BM25-adpt". The sensitivity curves are drawn in Figure 2 (left). We can see that the setting of b affects the retrieval performance of both methods significantly. However, our method appears consistently more effective and robust

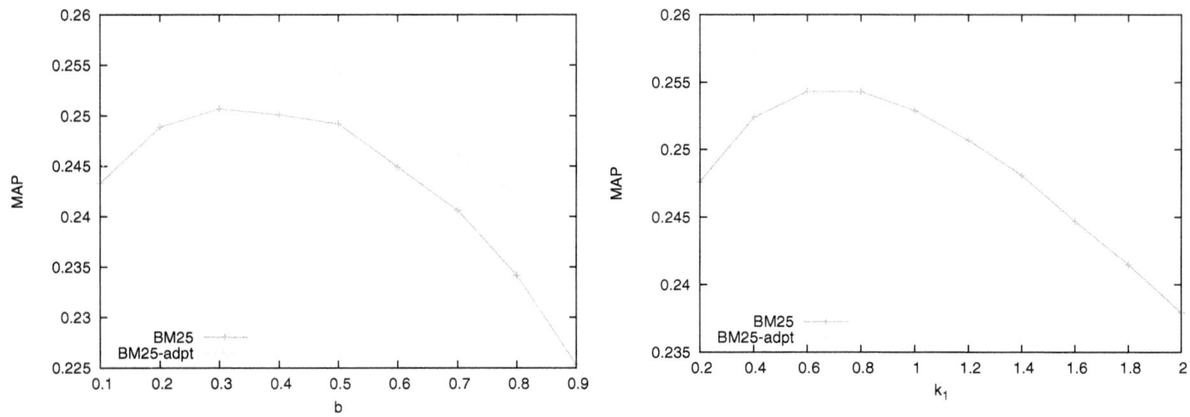

Figure 2: Sensitivity of MAP to parameter b (left) and k_1 (right) on collection Robust04.

Training	BM25-basic	BM25	BM25-adpt
TREC8	0.2507	0.2524	**0.2571**$^{+*}$
WT10G	0.2501	0.2538	**0.2571**$^{+*}$
WT2G	0.2489	0.2527	**0.2556**$^{+*}$

Table 3: Performance comparison on Robust04 using other collections for parameter training.

than the standard BM25 when we vary b. We also see that when b deviates from its optimal setting, the MAP of the standard BM25 often drops more quickly than our method; one possible explanation is that our method can be able to adjust k_1 adaptively for each b.

In the above analysis, we set $k_1 = 1.2$ in the standard BM25. Since a better-tuned k_1 can often lead to better performance as we have shown in Figure 1, so we want to know how critical this k_1 is and how likely a standard BM25 with manually tuned k_1 can achieve performance similar to our method. We thus set the parameter b in each method to its corresponding optimal value, and then vary $k1$ from 0.2 to 2.0 to examine the sensitivity of k_1, which is shown in Figure 2 (right). We can see that the standard BM25 is quite sensitive to k_1, and even with the optimal setting for k_1, its performance is still lower than "BM25-adpt".

4. CONCLUSIONS AND FUTURE WORK

BM25 has been a state-of-the-art retrieval function for a long time. The important parameter k_1 has so far been manually set to a term-independent constant based on a training data set. In this paper, we proposed a novel unsupervised approaches to *automatically* and *adaptively* set parameter k_1 in BM25 for each term and each collection. Specifically, we developed an information gain measure to directly estimate the contributions of repeated term occurrences, which was explored to fit the BM25 function to solve a term-specific k_1 without needing any training data. Our experiment results on multiple test collections show that the proposed approach works more effectively and robustly than the standard BM25 with a manually tuned k_1. As a "by product" of the derived formulas, we effectively eliminated the k_1 parameter from BM25. Thus with the proposed adaptive BM25 formula, we only need to tune parameter b, which can reduce significantly the effort for parameter tuning.

There are many interesting problems for future research. For example, how to also adaptively set another important parameter in BM25, i.e., b? how to adaptively set k_1 at the query level instead of term-level, since terms in the same query should interact with each other in TF normalization?

5. ACKNOWLEDGMENTS

We thank the anonymous reviewers for their useful comments. This material is based upon work supported by the National Science Foundation under Grant Numbers IIS-0713581, CNS-0834709, and CNS-1028381, a Sloan Research Fellowship, and a Yahoo! Key Scientific Challenge Award.

6. REFERENCES

[1] Gianni Amati and Cornelis Joost Van Rijsbergen. Probabilistic models of information retrieval based on measuring the divergence from randomness. *ACM Trans. Inf. Syst.*, 20:357–389, October 2002.

[2] Kenneth W. Church and William A. Gale. Poisson mixtures. *Natural Language Engineering*, 1:163–190, 1995.

[3] Hui Fang, Tao Tao, and ChengXiang Zhai. A formal study of information retrieval heuristics. In *SIGIR '04*, pages 49–56, 2004.

[4] Ben He and Iadh Ounis. On setting the hyper-parameters of term frequency normalization for information retrieval. *ACM Trans. Inf. Syst.*, 25, July 2007.

[5] Jaakko Hintikka. On Semantic Information. In J. Hintikka and P. Suppes, editors, *Information and Inference*, pages 3–27. D. Reidel Pub., 1970.

[6] K. Sparck Jones, S. Walker, and S. E. Robertson. A probabilistic model of information retrieval: development and comparative experiments. In *Information Processing and Management*, pages 779–840, 2000.

[7] Yuanhua Lv and ChengXiang Zhai. Lower-bounding term frequency normalization. In *CIKM '11*, 2011.

[8] Yuanhua Lv and ChengXiang Zhai. When documents are very long, bm25 fails! In *SIGIR '11*, pages 1103–1104, 2011.

[9] S. E. Robertson and S. Walker. Some simple effective approximations to the 2-poisson model for probabilistic weighted retrieval. In *SIGIR '94*, pages 232–241, 1994.

[10] Stephen Robertson, Hugo Zaragoza, and Michael Taylor. Simple bm25 extension to multiple weighted fields. In *CIKM '04*, pages 42–49, 2004.

[11] Stephen E. Robertson, Steve Walker, Susan Jones, Micheline Hancock-Beaulieu, and Mike Gatford. Okapi at trec-3. In *TREC '94*, pages 109–126, 1994.

[12] Amit Singhal, Chris Buckley, and Mandar Mitra. Pivoted document length normalization. In *SIGIR '96*, pages 21–29, 1996.

An Unsupervised Ranking Method Based on a Technical Difficulty Terrain*

Shoaib Jameel, Wai Lam
Systems Engineering and Engineering Management,
The Chinese University of Hong Kong
{msjameel,wlam}@se.cuhk.edu.hk

Ching-man Au Yeung†
ASTRI,
3/F Bio-informatics Centre, 2 Science Park West Avenue,
Hong Kong
albertauyeung@astri.org

Sheaujiun Chyan
Systems Engineering and Engineering Management,
The Chinese University of Hong Kong
chyan.sheaujiun@gmail.com

ABSTRACT

Users look for information that can suit their level of expertise, but it often takes a mammoth effort to trace such information. One has to sift through multiple pages to look for one that fits the appropriate technical background. In this paper, a query-independent ranking system is proposed for technical web pages. The pages returned by the system are sorted by their relative technical difficulty in either ascending or descending order specified by the user. The technical difficulty of a document i.e. terms in sequence, is first computed by the combination of each individual term's geometry in the low-dimensional latent semantic indexing (LSI) space, which can be visualized as a conceptual terrain. Then the pages are ranked based on the expected cost to get over the terrain. Results indicate that our terrain based method outperforms traditional readability measures.

Categories and Subject Descriptors

H.3.3 [**Information Search and Retrieval**]: Information filtering, Retrieval models, Search process, Selection process; H.3.7 [**Digital libraries**]

General Terms

Algorithms, Experimentation

*The work is supported by grants from the Research Grant Council of the Hong Kong Special Administrative Region, China (Project Codes: CUHK4128/07 and CUHK413510). This work is also affiliated with the Microsoft-CUHK Joint Laboratory for Human-centric Computing and Interface Technologies.

†Au Yeung contributed to this paper while he was at the NTT Communication Science Laboratories, Kyoto, Japan.

CIKM'11, October 24–28, 2011, Glasgow, Scotland, UK.

Keywords

Conceptual Hop Model, LSI, Technical Expertise

1. INTRODUCTION

Readers can find it difficult to comprehend technical articles outside their domain of specialization because they are not acquainted with the jargon or technical concepts of that domain. A computer scientist looking for introductory information about "fever" will probably want to visit a web page meant for general public. A medical research student would probably want to go to websites meant for medical researchers in order to know the current trends in pharmaceutical research. Search engines currently return a mix of introductory and advanced documents [8], which means that a person has to carefully read the web pages one by one in order to stumble upon the one that can fit her background knowledge and technical understanding. We propose a ranking system that can sort web pages based on technical difficulty for any domain. We evaluate the model on the medical domain.

Domain expertise relates to the knowledge of the subject of a particular domain [15]. In our work, technicality of each term is computed based on the observation in the LSI space. Then, we apply this formulation towards web page ranking where the "Conceptual Hop Model" (CHM) follows term order in the web page and "hops" from one term to another in succession which incurs certain "cost". In the end, an expected cost is computed. If the expected cost is high, the web page is more technical. To make text comprehensibility easy for the learner, the path that the learner has to face during reading process should be as easy as possible [12].

The main contributions of this work are: a new method to find the technicality of every term in the web page in the low dimensional latent semantic space and a new method which computes the "cost" involved when hopping from one term to another in the terrain.

2. RELATED WORKS

Traditional readability formulae have been used extensively in determining the grade level of articles. Flesch-Kincaid [7], Dale-Chall[1] and Lexile^{TM}[14] etc. are some of the commonly used readability measurement techniques. Wolfe et al. [16] describe the use of latent semantic analysis (LSA) in matching readers and texts. Textual coherence

Table 1: **A TDM built by selecting terms from PubMed and Yahoo! Health documents.**

	P1	P2	P3	P4	Y1	Y2	Y3	Y4	Y5
acne	1	0	0	0	1	0	0	0	0
insulinotropic	1	0	0	0	0	0	0	0	0
postrandial	1	0	0	0	0	0	0	0	0
abnormal	0	1	0	0	0	0	1	0	0
ichthyosis	0	1	1	1	0	0	0	0	0
mitotic	0	1	1	0	0	0	0	0	0
mutation	0	0	1	1	0	0	0	0	0
found	0	0	0	1	0	1	0	0	0
human	0	0	0	1	0	1	0	0	0
follicle	0	0	0	0	1	0	0	0	0
later	0	0	0	0	1	1	0	0	1
body	0	0	0	0	0	1	0	0	0
death	0	0	0	0	0	1	0	0	1
oncogenes	0	0	0	0	0	1	1	2	0
result	0	0	0	0	0	0	1	1	0
transformed	0	0	0	0	0	0	1	0	1
cancer	0	0	0	0	0	0	0	1	1

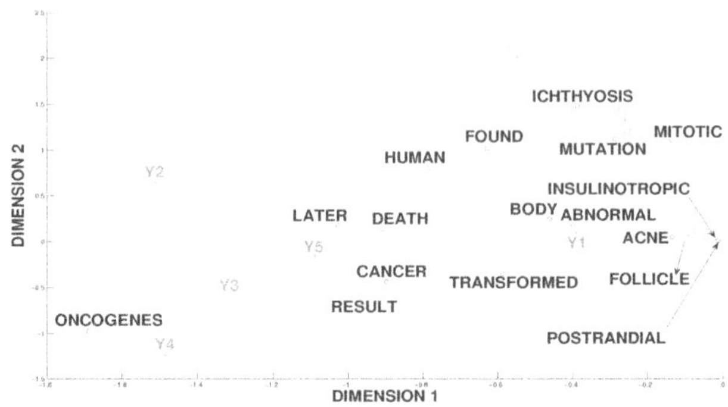

Figure 1: A two-dimensional plot showing the position of terms (circular markers) and documents (plus shaped markers) in the latent semantic space.

is another related concept that uses statistical or natural language processing techniques to determine the text comprehensibility [5, 4].

In [8], the authors begin with the definition of the *introductory* and *advanced* documents. They have used a supervised learning method to build a classifier (FAMCLASS) to predict web pages as introductory or advanced. In [2], the authors build a smoothed unigram model to predict the grade level of the text. The authors have stated that traditional readability measures perform poorly on web pages because they are short, contain lots of noise (like irrelevant strings due to pre-processing), presence of tables, images etc.

Nakatani et al. [13], describe a method for re-ranking search results of a web search engine (Easiest-First Search) in descending order of their comprehensibility using the Japanese Wikipedia. The work of Yan et al. [17] has similar objective as in this paper. The authors state that document scope and document cohesion are important parameters in finding simple texts. The authors have used a controlled vocabulary thesaurus termed as Medical Subject Headings (MeSH). However, the applicability of such methods in the other domains will always be a concern as one requires similar kind of controlled vocabulary. In our model, CHM, distance between consecutive terms is a measure of the "conceptual cohesion" between terms and "hops" between terms gauge the difficulty in conquering that bigram.

3. OBSERVATIONS IN THE LATENT SEMANTIC SPACE

Latent Semantic Indexing [3] makes use of the Term Document Matrix (TDM) on which a matrix decomposition method "Singular Value Decomposition" (SVD) is applied. The most noticeable observation is that terms which are unique or central to a document remain close to the document vectors. Terms which are used frequently, e.g. the general English language words like *"result"*, *"human"*, *"body"* etc., are usually far away from the highly technical document vectors. Only few technical terms move far away from their document vectors.

We construct a small document collection by selecting sentences from Yahoo! Health (document IDs beginning with alphabet Y) and PubMed (document IDs beginning with alphabet P) for illustrating our idea. These terms have been taken from sentences present in different documents from our real test collection, for example one such sentence from PubMed corpus is - *"**Mitotic** recombination in patients with **ichthyosis** causes reversion of dominant **mutations** in KRT10."*, where the terms in bold have been considered in the TDM. The choice of terms in the TDM is based on the property of the corpus itself. For instance, PubMed articles are more technical than Yahoo! Health, therefore more technical terms have been chosen from PubMed than Yahoo! Health. SVD is then applied on the TDM to get the term and the document co-ordinates in two dimensions. A similar small example can be found in [10]. Figure 1 is a reconstruction of the original vector space after reducing the dimensions to two by applying SVD to the TDM in Table 1.

From Figure 1 it is evident that PubMed and Yahoo! Health articles form two separate clusters in the latent space. Technical terms like *"follicle"*, *"postrandial"* etc., are very close to their own document vectors. General terms like *"body"*, *"found"*, *"transformed"*, *"human"*, *"result"* etc., can be seen far from their document vectors. $Y1$ and $P1$ describe about the same theme *"acne"*, hence are close to each other. But $P1$ being more technical, has many technical terms in close proximity. Technical terms are closer to $P1$ than $Y1$, suggesting $P1$ is more technical than $Y1$.

3.1 The Notion of Term Technicality

Similarity between a document and a term in the latent semantic space is inversely proportional to the distance between them [9]. Based on the concept of similarity, "technicality" is the amount of technical tinge a term gives to the document and is based on the closeness to the document vector in the low dimensional latent semantic space.

Mathematically, the technicality F_t^d of a term t in document d can be written as:

$$F_t^d = \frac{idf_t}{(r_t^d + \epsilon)} \tag{1}$$

where, r_t^d is the semantic distance (Euclidean) between the term and document vectors in the latent semantic space. ϵ is a small constant added to avoid the case when $r_t^d = 0$. idf_t is the Inverse Document Frequency of term t.

Consider the term *"later"* in Figure 1. This is a general term but is located close to the document vector $Y5$ in the latent space. In a large document collection, the global importance of this term will be less. Hence, idf_t ensures that technicality of a general term remains low. *"oncogenes"* is

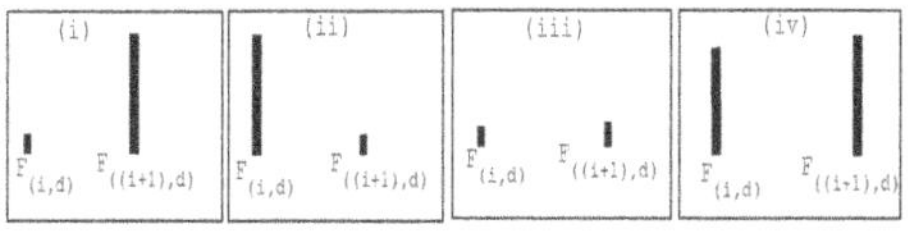

Figure 2: Four important scenarios when transiting from one term to another in the terrain.

shared among three documents. It is a technical term and hence the global importance will be high. It can be clearly seen from the TDM (Table 1) that $Y2$ has more general terms than $Y4$. Hence, $Y4$ is more technical than $Y2$ (and also $Y3$). Therefore, *"oncogenes"* is more central to $Y4$. Technical term like *"follicle"* is closer to the document vector and its $idf_{(follicle)}$ will be high, hence technicality will be high. General terms like *"found"*, *"human"* etc. will have low technicality as their idf_t will be low and their distance from the document vectors will be large in which they occur.

4. THE CONCEPTUAL HOP MODEL (CHM)

4.1 Formulation

Hops in CHM occur by taking two consecutive terms at positions i and $(i+1)$ i.e. a bi-gram in the document d. In doing so, some cost $C^d_{i,i+1}$ is incurred. Let $s^d_{i,i+1}$ denote the "Euclidean distance" between terms in the bi-gram in the latent semantic space. Let $n^d_{i,i+1}$ be the number of "same bigram" that have been encountered previously in the web page d until the current position $(i+1)$.

The cost $C^d_{i,i+1}$ incurred when hopping from term i to term $(i+1)$, which are characterized by technicalities F^d_i and F^d_{i+1} respectively in document d, separated by a distance $s^d_{i,i+1}$ is given as:

$$C^d_{i,i+1} = \frac{(F^d_i + F^d_{i+1}) \times [s^d_{i,i+1}]^{sgn(s^d_{i,i+1}-1)\times F^d_{i+1}}}{n^d_{i,i+1}+1} \quad (2)$$

where $sgn(...)$ is defined as the signum function that extracts the sign of a real number.

4.2 Analysis

Figure 2 shows four important cases in hopping, and will be used as a graphical depiction in order to justify the expressions in Equation 2. The distance $s^d_{i,i+1}$ has been kept constant in all the cases for better understanding.

$(F^d_i + F^d_{i+1})$ measures the combined technicality of the bigram. The limitation of this expression is that it fails to distinguish cases in Figure 2(i) and 2(ii). Cohesion property in the conceptual terrain is handled by $[s^d_{i,i+1}]^{sgn(s^d_{i,i+1}-1)\times F^d_{i+1}}$. If the terms at positions i and $(i+1)$ come from completely different concept spaces, difficulty in understanding them will be high as the reader encounters a "big conceptual leap" in order to relate two completely different concepts. There might be cases where the Euclidean distance between the term pairs may be $0 < s^d_{i,i+1} < 1$ which will affect the monotonicity of the function. Thus the expression $sgn(s^d_{i,i+1} - 1)$ is introduced. A document contains more number of non-domain concepts than domain specific concepts. Consequently, the cost values for such documents will be much skewed. In order to make the cost computation more sensitive to different technicalities, F^d_{i+1} has been chosen as an exponent to compensate for the skewness. If a reader has already encountered the same bigram before; then the ease with which a reader will cross the same bigram in the next encounter will be relatively more than that in the previous encounters. Division by the number of same bigrams, $n^d_{i,i+1}$ seen so far ensures that there is a constant reduction in cost in every same encounter.

5. THE RANKING FUNCTION

If the terrain is highly rugged or the document is too technical; then the reader will face immense difficulties in comprehending it. The ranking function considers the expected cost in order to complete the terrain. The expected cost E^d for document d can be written as:

$$E^d = \frac{\sum_{i=1}^{W_d-1} C^d_{i,i+1}}{W^d - 1} \quad (3)$$

where $C^d_{i,i+1}$ is defined in Equation 2 and W^d is the number of terms in document d.

6. EXPERIMENTS AND RESULTS

6.1 Data Set - Medical Corpus

Medical documents contain a high distribution of technical concepts. We crawled web pages from two different sources, Yahoo! Health (2976 documents with 20109 unique terms) and PubMed (3087 documents with 145016 unique terms). Yahoo! Health articles are written for general public who have little or no understanding of medical concepts. PubMed documents are research papers written by health professionals.

6.2 Comparison with the Baselines

Most of the procedures for experimentation were followed from [2]. Hence, major details about the baselines (the baselines are Models: M3 and M4 in Table 2) described there are being omitted here. One change that is made relates to the number of words used, where in [2] the authors have used 100 token passages but we use full length passages and then normalize by the total number of words in the document. CHM's semantic components are "technicality" and "conceptual cohesion" with no syntactic component.

Flesch-Kincaid readability metric with both semantic and syntactic components is considered in our experiments. SMOG [11] with its semantic and syntactic components is another baseline. To compute these measures "style"[1] package was used. We add all the technicalities for a web page (computed in Section 3.1) and take its mean (Model $M7$). Hence, term order is lost in this baseline. Model $M6$ is another baseline where we remove the technicalities from the CHM and use the $tf \times idf$ values instead.

6.3 Human Ratings for top-k Pool

Normalized Cumulative Discounted Gain (nDCG) [6] was chosen as the performance measure, and is calculated as:

$$W(i) = \frac{1}{Z_n} \sum_{i=1}^{n} \frac{2^{r(i)} - 1}{\log(1+i)} \quad (4)$$

where Z_n is the normalization constant such that a perfect list gets a score of 1, $r(i)$ denotes the rank label of the ith document in the ranked list, n is length of the ranked list.

[1] *http://www.gnu.org/software/diction/diction.html*

Table 2: nDCG@k for Medical corpus.

Reference Numbers	Models	nDCG@10	nDCG@50	nDCG@100	nDCG@150	nDCG@200
M1	CHM without stop words	1.0	1.0	1.0	0.997	0.997
M2	CHM with stop words	1.0	1.0	1.0	1.0	1.0
M3	MLF	0.066	0.066	0.075	0.077	0.075
M4	Flesch-Kincaid	0.292	0.376	0.410	0.424	0.430
M5	SMOG	0.215	0.299	0.348	0.371	0.388
M6	CHM-$tf \times idf$ with stopwords	1.0	1.0	1.0	0.988	0.965
M7	Using the technicality mean	1.0	0.984	0.963	0.958	0.962

"depth-k" pooling was adopted where "top-k" documents from all models were accumulated and the rest were assumed irrelevant. In the "top-k" pool where $k = 200$, the number of unique documents were 1249. Annotations from three people were used (mode of the scores was considered) who gave the relevance rating values. Two of them had basic knowledge of medical science while one was a medical student.

Relevance rating is in the range of "0 and 4". "0" means that the document is completely advanced at that position. "1" indicates that the document contains rich use of jargon or technical terms without explaining them. Relevance rating of "2" means that the text requires some background knowledge of the topic because some technical terms are not explained. "3" means that the author has used technical terms and has defined them. Relevance rating of "4" means that the document is technically simple without the use of any jargon and the text can be easily comprehended by a beginner looking for technically introductory articles.

Table 2 shows the results when the documents are ordered from technically introductory to advanced. CHM with stop words (Model $M2$) has fared well as compared to the other models as it ranked technically introductory web pages at the top of the results containing no jargon. Model $M1$ ranked some of PubMed's case study articles which contained jargon. Other models ($M3$, $M4$ and $M5$) mainly tap readability features but CHM is able to capture technical difficulty i.e. technical concepts and the cohesion between concepts. These models ($M3$, $M4$, $M5$ and also $M6$, $M7$) ranked few medical news and quiz web pages at the top of the results, which indeed were not meant for a beginner who wanted to read technically simpler articles.

7. CONCLUSIONS AND FUTURE WORK

In this paper, we presented the problem of determining the technical difficulty of a web page in domain specific information retrieval. Ranking documents based on technical expertise can help in learning and also development of reader's expertise [15]. Different readability formulae are not directly applicable even though their syntactic and semantic components are used. CHM is able to capture word level technical difficulty, concept level cohesion, and the intricacy experienced when hopping from one term to another in the concept terrain. In future, importance of hyperlinks would be studied, which act as an "added help" given by the author to the reader. If a technical term has been hyperlinked to another web page, the author expects the reader to go to that web page, get acquainted with the definition of the term and come back to the original web page.

8. ACKNOWLEDGMENTS

The authors would like to thank Wei Gao, Bo Chen, Binyang Li and Haiqin Yang for their comments in the paper.

9. REFERENCES

[1] J. S. Chall and E. Dale. Readability revisited: the new dale-chall readability formula. 1995.

[2] K. Collins-Thompson and J. Callan. Predicting reading difficulty with statistical language models. *J. Am. Soc. Inf. Sci. Technol.*, 56:1448–1462, November 2005.

[3] S. Deerwester, S. T. Dumais, G. W. Furnas, T. K. Landauer, and R. Harshman. Indexing by latent semantic analysis. *Journal of the American Society for Information Science*, 41:391–407, 1990.

[4] C. R. Fletcher, S. T. Chrysler, P. van den Broek, J. A. Deaton, and C. P. Bloom. The role of co-occurrence, co-reference, and causality in the coherence of conjoined sentences. In *R. F. Lorch, and E. J. O'Brien (Eds.), Sources of coherence in reading*, pages 203–218, 1995.

[5] P. W. Foltz, W. Kintsch, and T. K. Landauer. The measurement of textual coherence with latent semantic analysis. *Discourse Process*, 15:285–307, 1998.

[6] K. Järvelin and J. Kekäläinen. Ir evaluation methods for retrieving highly relevant documents. In *Proceedings of SIGIR*, pages 41–48, 2000.

[7] J. P. Kincaid, R. P. Fishburne, R. L. Rogers, and B. S. Chissom. Derivation of New Readability Formulas (Automated Readability Index, Fog Count and Flesch Reading Ease Formula) for Navy Enlisted Personnel. Technical report, Feb. 1975.

[8] G. Kumaran, R. Jones, and O. Madani. Biasing web search results for topic familiarity. In *Proceedings of CIKM*, pages 271–272, 2005.

[9] T. Landauer and S. Dumais. A solution to plato's problem: The latent semantic analysis theory of acquisition, induction, and representation of knowledge. *Psychological Review*, 104(2):211–240, 1997.

[10] T. K. Landauer, P. W. Foltz, and D. Laham. An Introduction to Latent Semantic Analysis. *Discourse Processes*, (25):259–284, 1998.

[11] G. H. M. Laughlin. Smog grading-a new readability formula. *Journal of Reading*, 12(8):pp. 639–646, 1969.

[12] D. S. McNamara, E. Kintsch, N. B. Songer, and W. Kintsch. Are good texts always better? interactions of text coherence, background knowledge, and levels of understanding in learning from text. *Cognition and Instruction*, 14(1):pp. 1–43, 1996.

[13] M. Nakatani, A. Jatowt, and K. Tanaka. Easiest-first search: towards comprehension-based web search. In *Proceeding of CIKM*, pages 2057–2060, 2009.

[14] A. Stenner, I. Horabin, D. Smith, and M. Smith. The lexile framework. 1988.

[15] R. W. White, S. T. Dumais, and J. Teevan. Characterizing the influence of domain expertise on web search behavior. In *Proceedings of the WSDM*, pages 132–141, 2009.

[16] M. B. W. Wolfe, M. E. Schreiner, B. Rehder, D. Laham, P. W. Foltz, W. Kintsch, and T. K. Landauer. Learning from text: Matching readers and texts by latent semantic analysis. *Discourse Processes*, 25(2/3):309–336, 1998.

[17] X. Yan, D. Song, and X. Li. Concept-based document readability in domain specific information retrieval. In *Proceedings of CIKM*, pages 540–549, 2006.

When Close Enough Is Good Enough: Approximate Positional Indexes for Efficient Ranked Retrieval

Tamer Elsayed
King Abdullah University of Science and Technology
Thuwal, Saudi Arabia
tamer.elsayedaly@kaust.edu.sa

Jimmy Lin
The iSchool
University of Maryland
College Park, MD
jimmylin@umd.edu

Donald Metzler
Information Sciences Institute
Univ. of Southern California
Marina del Rey, CA
metzler@isi.edu

ABSTRACT

Previous research has shown that features based on term proximity are important for effective retrieval. However, they incur substantial costs in terms of larger inverted indexes and slower query execution times as compared to term-based features. This paper explores whether term proximity features based on *approximate* term positions are as effective as those based on *exact* term positions. We introduce the novel notion of *approximate positional indexes* based on dividing documents into coarse-grained *buckets* and recording term positions with respect to those buckets. We propose different approaches to defining the buckets and compactly encoding bucket ids. In the context of linear ranking functions, experimental results show that features based on approximate term positions are able to achieve effectiveness comparable to exact term positions, but with smaller indexes and faster query evaluation.

Categories and Subject Descriptors: H.3.3 [Information Storage and Retrieval]: Information Search and Retrieval

General Terms: Algorithms, Performance

Keywords: term proximity, efficiency, learning to rank

1. INTRODUCTION

In information retrieval, efficiency (speed) and effectiveness (quality) are often in tension, since good relevance signals are frequently expensive to compute during ranking. For example, term proximity features are good predictors of relevance but are costly to compute compared to term-based features. This paper proposes to reduce the cost of computing term proximity features by introducing *approximate positional indexes*, a novel method of encoding term positions in the payload of postings lists.

There are two aspects of cost associated with term proximity features. The first is index size: in order for a ranking model to support term proximity features, term positions must be encoded in postings payloads. The second is the speed of computing term proximity features at retrieval time. For example, to determine if two query terms occur within w terms of each other during ranking, term positions must be decoded and checked. This is computationally expensive compared to term-based features.

The central hypothesis explored in this paper is the following: are term proximity features based on approximate term positions as effective as those based on exact term positions? The answer turns out to be yes, in that a fuzzy notion of term proximity yields ranking functions, trained in a learning to rank framework, that are comparable in effectiveness to similar models that use exact term proximity features. The basic insight is that instead of recording exact term positions, we divide documents into coarse-grained buckets and record in which bucket the term occurs. We explore different approaches to defining and compressing the buckets. Our best variant algorithm yields substantial reductions in both index size and query evaluation time.

CIKM'11, October 24–28, 2011, Glasgow, Scotland, UK.

2. RELATED WORK

It is widely recognized that term proximity features contribute to improvements in retrieval effectiveness over term-based features (i.e., "bag of words") alone. Early studies date back to the 1980s [4], and there has been no shortage of studies on the topic since then [3, 9, 1]. More recently, Markov random fields [7] provide a theoretically-motivated framework for understanding and reasoning about term dependencies using undirected graphical models.

Of course, to support term proximity features, it is necessary to store term position information in the postings. Existing compression techniques for encoding positional information [10] can be considered lossless, and they achieve different tradeoffs between compression rate and decoding speed. Our work tackles an orthogonal issue related to *representing* term positions, where we can take advantage of previous work on compression.

One common approach to faster query evaluation is index pruning [2]. Experiments have shown that it is possible to discard postings that are unlikely to contribute much to a document's score, thus yielding a smaller index—translating into faster ranking. Index pruning differs from our work in that we retain all postings, but encode positional information in a more compact (but lossy) manner.

3. RETRIEVAL MODEL

Our work uses linear feature-based ranking functions [7] of the form $S(Q, D) = \sum_j \lambda_j f_j(Q, D)$, where Q is a query, D is a document, $f_j(Q, D)$ is a feature function, and λ_j is the weight assigned to feature j. More specifically, this work uses a particular instantiation of the Markov random field model known as the *sequential dependence* (SD) model [7]:

$$
\begin{aligned}
S(Q, D) \quad = \quad & \lambda_T \sum_{q \in Q} f_T(q, D) + \\
& \lambda_U \sum_{q_j, q_{j+1} \in Q} f_O(q_j, q_{j+1}, D) + \\
& \lambda_O \sum_{q_j, q_{j+1} \in Q} f_U(q_j, q_{j+1}, D)
\end{aligned}
$$

where f_T is defined over query unigrams, and f_O and f_U are defined over query bigrams. The latter two are term proximity features: f_O corresponds to phrase matches and f_U corresponds to query term co-occurrence within a particular span. The λ's are parameters that need to be learned. The original formulation of the SD model defines features in terms of language modeling query likelihoods with Dirichlet smoothing [7]. Here, we adopt an alternative formulation based on BM25 scores [8]. In practice, we have discovered that BM25 scores are slightly more effective, but the differences are not statistically significant in most cases.

3.1 Approximate Positions

The central hypothesis we explore in this paper is whether term proximity features based on approximate term positions are as effective as those based on exact term positions. Our basic idea is that instead of storing exact term positions in the index, we divide each document into coarser-grained *buckets* and record the id (i.e., the sequential number) of the bucket in which the term occurs.

We explored two different approaches to defining buckets:

Variable-Width Buckets. We can divide each document into a fixed number of buckets b, where each bucket represents a span of term positions within that document. Under this scheme, buckets in different documents will have different widths, which means that long documents receive a coarser-grained treatment than short documents.

Fixed-Width Buckets. As an alternative, we can fix the bucket size w and let the number of buckets in a document vary with the document length. This in effect selects a single level of granularity at which to model term positions in the entire collection.

We explored two different approaches for coding bucket ids:

Integer Coding. We treat bucket ids as an array of integers and use standard gap-based compression techniques to code them (using γ codes [10]).

Bit-Array Coding. Bucket positions are coded in a bit-array. That is, the kth bit of the bit-array is set to one if the kth bucket contains the term, or zero otherwise. This scheme works well if the number of buckets is equal to a machine word in the variable-width bucket scheme. Furthermore, as an optimization, checking for term proximity (e.g., if two terms are found in the same bucket) translates into efficient bitwise operations.

Note that in both cases, we only code the presence or absence of terms in a bucket, but not the number of terms that occur in that bucket. In other words, the approximate positions do not capture term frequency.

3.2 Proximity Features

To parallel the f_O and f_U term proximity features in the sequential dependence model, we introduce the three following approximate proximity operators. Each operator is defined over an adjacent pair of query terms (i.e., a query bigram), just as the original features are:

- SAMEBUCKET(q_j, q_{j+1}, D) matches any positional bucket that contains both q_j and q_{j+1}.
- ORDADJBUCKETS(q_j, q_{j+1}, D) matches if q_j occurs in a bucket at position i and q_{j+1} occurs in a bucket at position $i + 1$. That is, the two terms must appear in order across adjacent bins.
- UNORDADJBUCKETS(q_j, q_{j+1}, D) matches if q_j occurs in a bucket at position i and q_{j+1} occurs in the bucket at position $i - 1$ or $i + 1$, i.e., adjacent buckets. Unlike the previous operator, which requires the two terms to appear in the correct order, this operator allows for unordered matches.

These features share the same functional form (i.e., weighted using BM25) as their exact positional counterparts. To estimate the parameters of our linear models, we employ greedy feature selection—a simple but effective learning to rank approach that directly optimizes for the retrieval metric of interest (e.g., MAP) described by Metzler [6].

4. EXPERIMENTAL EVALUATION

We implemented the approximate positional indexes described above with Ivory [5]. Inverted indexes adopt a standard compression scheme: document id gaps are compressed with Golomb codes and term frequencies are coded with γ codes. For baselines, we created an index with no positional information and an index with exact term positional information. In the latter index, term positions are converted into gap differences and compressed with γ codes.

Indexes were constructed using Hadoop, and retrieval experiments were performed on a server with dual Intel Xeon quad-core processors (E5620 2.4GHz), 64GB RAM, and six 2TB 7.2K RPM SATA drives in RAID-6 configuration (running Red Hat Linux). All experiments used a single thread and performed retrieval on a single, monolithic index (i.e., no document partitioning), returning 1000 hits per query.

For evaluation, we used two TREC web collections: Gov2 (topics 701–850) and the first English segment of ClueWeb09 (topics 1–50). In each case, queries were split sequentially into training and test sets of equal size. All parameters were estimated on the training set and all results reported on the test sets. Retrieval effectiveness is measured in terms of mean average precision (MAP) and precision at 10 (P@10). A one-side paired t-test (with $p = 0.05$) was used to determine the statistical significance of differences in the metrics.

4.1 Baselines and Approximate Models

We used the following baselines as points of comparison: classic **BM25**; **BM25-*sd***, the basic sequential dependence model with BM25 scores and default parameters; and **BM25-*sd-t***, a variant of BM25-*sd* for which the model parameters were trained on a per-collection basis. This allowed the model to adapt to collection-specific characteristics, rather than using the same default parameters for all collections as is done with BM25-*sd*. Our BM25 runs used

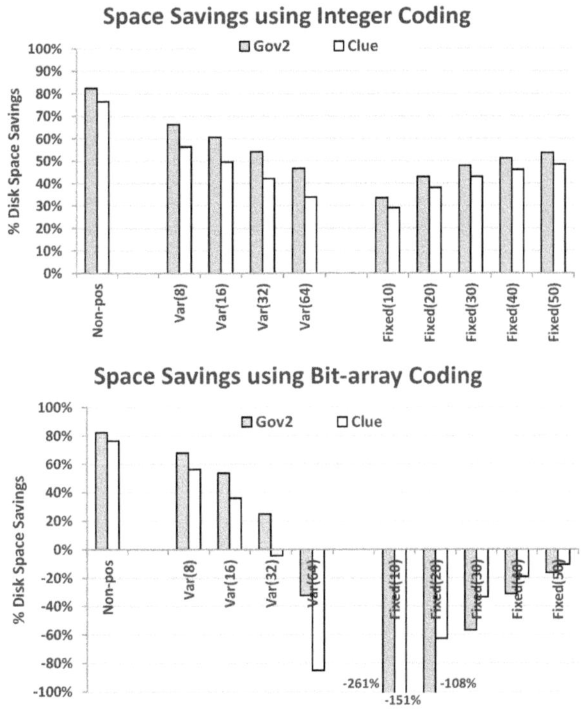

Figure 1: Percentage reduction in index size with respect to exact positional indexes. Non-positional indexes (left-most bars) provide upper bounds.

the non-positional indexes since they do not require any positional information for ranking documents, while the other two baselines used the exact positional indexes, which were needed to compute the exact term proximity features.

In our experiments, we used nine variants of approximate positional indexes that have different bucket types: variable-width buckets with number of buckets $b = 8, 16, 32, 64$—each denoted as Var(b)—and fixed-width buckets with bucket size $w = 10, 20, 30, 40, 50$—each denoted as Fixed(w).

4.2 Results

We now describe our experimental analysis of approximate positional indexes and proximity features in terms of index size, retrieval effectiveness, and query evaluation speed.

4.2.1 Index Size

Figure 1 compares the sizes of the approximate positional indexes with respect to exact positional indexes. Bars plot space savings, so higher is better. For reference, the left-most bars show the space savings of non-positional indexes (i.e., discarding positional information altogether), which ranges between 76% to 82%. This serves as an upper bound.

The two collections exhibit similar patterns. As expected, we notice that as the number of buckets per document (b) increases in the variable-width models or as the bucket size (w) deceases in the fixed-width models, the index size increases (and thus the space savings decrease). In some cases, the bit-array coding indexes are actually bigger than exact positional indexes.

The figures also show a clear advantage to the integer coding scheme in terms of index size (space savings range from 29% to 66%) compared with the bit-array scheme.

	MAP		P@10	
	Gov2	Clue	Gov2	Clue
Baselines				
BM25	0.3162	0.2251	0.5787	0.3800
BM25-*sd*	**0.3505**	0.2312	0.5920	0.3800
BM25-*sd-t*	**0.3447**	0.2340	**0.6107**	0.3840
Variable width				
$b = 8$	**0.3223**	<u>0.2252*</u>	0.5813	<u>0.3800*</u>
$b = 16$	**0.3229**	0.1933	0.5813*	0.2560
$b = 32$	**0.3234**	<u>0.2250*</u>	0.5813*	<u>0.3800*</u>
$b = 64$	**0.3220**	0.2067	<u>0.5880*</u>	0.3080
Fixed width				
$w = 10$	<u>**0.3376**</u>	<u>0.2256*</u>	<u>0.5920*</u>	<u>0.3760*</u>
$w = 20$	<u>**0.3426***</u>	<u>0.2261*</u>	0.5787*	<u>0.3800*</u>
$w = 30$	<u>**0.3385**</u>	0.2247*	<u>0.5933*</u>	<u>0.3760*</u>
$w = 40$	<u>**0.3382**</u>	0.2250*	0.5867*	<u>0.3800*</u>
$w = 50$	<u>**0.3346**</u>	0.2243*	0.5853*	<u>0.3800*</u>

Table 1: Retrieval effectiveness. Bold values indicate stat. sig. over BM25; star-annotated and underlined values indicate *n.s.* compared to BM25-*sd* and BM25-*sd-t*, respectively.

4.2.2 Retrieval Effectiveness

Table 1 presents retrieval effectiveness in terms of MAP and P@10 for the test collections. We annotated the effectiveness values to indicate results of significance testing between the approximate positional models and the baselines: bold values indicate statistically-significant improvements over BM25, and star-annotated and underlined values indicate *no* statistically-significant difference compared with BM25-*sd* and BM25-*sd-t*, respectively.

MAP results reported in the table indicate that, in the Gov2 collection, all approximate positional models exhibit significant improvements over BM25. Moreover, all of the fixed-width models have no statistically-significant differences with BM25-*sd-t*. While the MAP results are generally in favor of our approximate models for Gov2, the Clue results are more mixed. The table shows that the baselines aren't very different from each other, and this might explain the lack of significant improvement of our approximate models over BM25.

Although the P@10 results indicate that our approximate models are not significantly better than BM25, the models are also not statistically different from the other baselines either. This suggests that term proximity features are better at enhancing precision at lower ranks, since they consistently improve MAP.

Considering the absolute MAP and P@10 scores in addition to the results of the statistical significance tests, we see that the fixed-width models are consistently better than the variable-width models. We hypothesize that variable-width models introduce a great deal of variance (or noise) into the proximity features (such as SameBucket) because window sizes vary greatly depending on the document length (i.e., very short for short documents, very long for long documents)—or more accurately, on the *variance* of document lengths within a collection. If all documents have the same length (i.e., zero variance), then Var(b) would behave exactly the same as Fixed($avgdl/w$). However, as the variance increases, the definition of proximity features becomes less "consistent", which ultimately yields noisy feature values and thus less effective results.

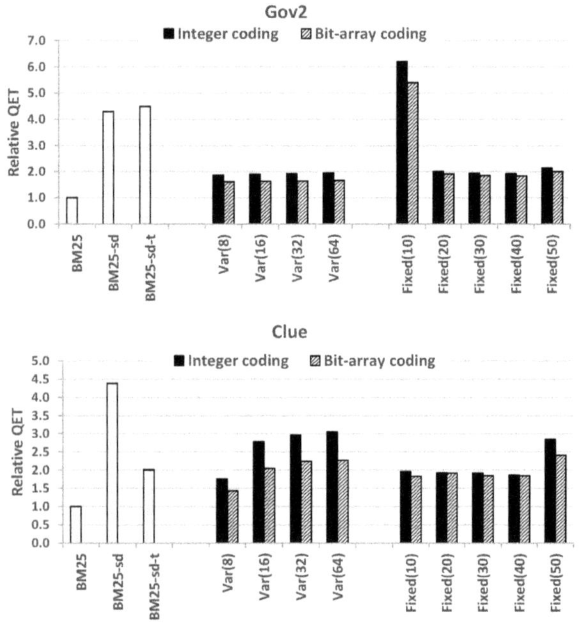

Figure 2: Average normalized query execution time of baselines and different approximations.

The results of the fixed-width models show that, as the width of the bucket decreases, the effectiveness improves. This is expected since smaller buckets yield more accurate approximate positional information. Overall, the fixed-width models Fixed(10) and Fixed(20) are the best among all the approximate positional models.

4.2.3 Retrieval Efficiency

Figure 2 shows the average (over three trials) query execution time (QET) for each collection across a variety of approximate positional indexing strategies. The QET figures are normalized with respect to baseline BM25, which uses the non-positional indexes, and thus the bars show how much slower (in relative terms) the other conditions are.

Comparing integer and bit-array coding, we notice that the latter is generally faster but not substantially. BM25-*sd-t* is comparable to BM25-*sd* on Gov2. For Clue, the learned BM25-*sd-t* model uses fewer features than BM25-*sd*, simply as an artifact of the greedy feature selection algorithm, and as a result it is substantially slower.

Rather than exhaustively explain all the results, we focus on the Fixed(10) and Fixed(20) models, which yielded consistently strong effectiveness (from the previous section). For Gov2, we observe a substantial reduction in QET with the Fixed(20) model (−57%) compared to both variants of the *sd* models. In the Fixed(10) model, the greedy feature selection algorithm uses more features, and thus is substantially slower. The results for Clue show that both Fixed(10) and Fixed(20) are significantly faster (−57%) than BM25-*sd* and exhibit comparable efficiency (−5%) to BM25-*sd-t*.

Overall, the Fixed(20) model not only exhibits effectiveness that is comparable to the BM25-*sd* model, but also strong efficiency characteristics—a substantial reduction in index size and query execution time. This particular setting nicely balances a small index footprint, good effectiveness, and fast query execution.

5. CONCLUSIONS

Term proximity features are useful for a variety of search tasks, especially those that deal with large collections such as web search. However, full positional indexes can consume a large amount of space and positionally-aware retrieval models that utilize such indexes are considerably slower than their non-positional counterparts. To help minimize the time and space costs of positional indexes, we proposed a novel indexing strategy called approximate positional indexes and a corresponding retrieval model. These indexes break documents into fixed or variable width buckets and encode which buckets a term occurs in, either using integer or bit-array coding.

Our experimental results, carried out over two TREC web collections, show that our proposed methods are able to achieve comparable effectiveness to term-proximity models based on full positional indexes, but with smaller indexes and faster query execution times. Therefore, the proposed methodology provides system designers with a viable "middle ground" in the efficiency-effectiveness tradeoff space to better balance quality, time, and space.

6. ACKNOWLEDGMENTS

This work has been supported by NSF awards IIS-0836560, IIS-0916043, and CCF-1018625. Any opinions expressed are the authors'. The second author is grateful to Esther and Kiri for their loving support and dedicates this work to Joshua and Jacob.

7. REFERENCES

[1] S. Büttcher, C. Clarke, and B. Lushman. Term proximity scoring for ad-hoc retrieval on very large text collections. In *SIGIR*, 2006.

[2] D. Carmel, D. Cohen, R. Fagin, E. Farchi, M. Herscovici, Y. Maarek, and A. Soffer. Static index pruning for information retrieval systems. In *SIGIR*, 2001.

[3] W. Croft, H. Turtle, and D. Lewis. The use of phrases and structured queries in information retrieval. In *SIGIR*, 1991.

[4] J. Fagan. Experiments in automatic phrase indexing for document retrieval: A comparison of syntactic and non-syntactic methods. Technical report, Cornell University, 1987.

[5] J. Lin, D. Metzler, T. Elsayed, and L. Wang. Of Ivory and Smurfs: Loxodontan MapReduce experiments for web search. In *TREC*, 2009.

[6] D. Metzler. Automatic feature selection in the Markov random field model for information retrieval. In *CIKM*, 2007.

[7] D. Metzler and W. Croft. A Markov random field model for term dependencies. In *SIGIR*, 2005.

[8] S. Robertson, S. Walker, M. Hancock-Beaulieu, M. Gatford, and A. Payne. Okapi at TREC-4. In *TREC*, 1995.

[9] M. Srikanth and R. Srihari. Biterm language models for document retrieval. In *SIGIR*, 2002.

[10] I. Witten, A. Moffat, and T. Bell. *Managing Gigabytes: Compressing and Indexing Documents and Images.* Morgan Kaufmann, 1999.

Index Tuning for Query-log based On-line Index Maintenance

Sairam Gurajada*
Max-Planck-Institut für Informatik
Saarbrücken, Germany
gurajada@mpi-inf.mpg.de

Sreenivasa Kumar P.
Indian Institute of Technology Madras
Chennai, India
psk@cse.iitm.ac.in

ABSTRACT

The existing query-log based on-line index maintenance approaches rely on frequency distribution of terms in the static query-log. Though these approaches are proved to be efficient, but in real world, the frequency distribution of the terms changes over a period of time. This negatively affects the efficiency of the static query-log based approaches. To overcome this problem, we propose an index tuning strategy for reorganizing the indexes according to the latest frequency distribution of the terms captured from query-logs. Experimental results show that the proposed tuning strategy improves the performance of static query-log based approaches.

Categories and Subject Descriptors: H.3.1 [Information Storage and Retrieval]: Content Analysis and Indexing—*Indexing Methods*; H.3.2 [Information Storage and Retrieval]: Information Storage—*File Organization*; H.3.3 [Information Storage and Retrieval]: Information Search and Retrieval—*Search Process*

General Terms: Algorithms, Performance

Keywords: Inverted File, Inverted Index, Search Engine, Query Log

1. INTRODUCTION

Inverted indexes are an important and widely used data structure for index maintenance in Information Retrieval (IR) systems. They comprise of *dictionary* (for storing terms) and *postings lists* (for storing postings of individual terms) [12]. Postings represent the information about a document for a particular term. Based on the requirement, the postings store information as little as document ID to as large as positional information of term in documents, term frequencies etc. A query to an IR system is a list of terms along with constraints. The result is a list of documents obtained by applying the constraints in the query, which is then ordered by a ranking method.

Based on the temporal characteristics of the document collections, an inverted index is built either in off-line mode or on-line mode. In off-line mode, it is assumed that the entire document collection is known and remains static during index construction. The final index is a single large inverted index. Though we get high query performance, this approach is not applicable to the dynamic corpus of documents. On-line indexing on the other hand is designed for such dynamic scenarios. They provide flexibility of querying the index and alter the document collection during index construction. This type of indexing is needed for the cases where queries should be processed readily after a document is indexed, eg., news search.

Many algorithms [1, 11, 5, 10, 8, 2, 3, 4, 6] were proposed in the recent past to perform indexing dynamic document collections. Recently, Gurajada et al. [7] proposed a new selective merge-based on-line index maintenance approach based on frequency distribution of query-logs. They maintain separate indexes for frequent and infrequent terms and adopt different merge strategies. Terms are classified into frequent and infrequent a priori using a static query-log. The use of static query-logs has performance limits when the frequency distribution of existing terms is altered. In addition, any new terms appearing in the new logs are treated as infrequent and do not benefit from the index organization. For example, the query *Barrack Obama* which was rarely appearing before 2008 has later became highly frequent. The query, for instance *Twitter*, which is not present few years back is now frequently queried. Such cases are inefficiently handled by static query-log based approaches. To handle this problem, we propose an index tuning strategy for these approaches to address dynamic query-logs.

The central idea of the index tuning is to consider frequency distribution of new query-log and identify the misplaced terms. The misplaced terms (called as *diff-terms*) along with their postings list form a *diff-term index*. The diff-term index is then handled like an other auxiliary index and added to the existing index by query-log based approaches.

The contributions of this paper are:

- We present an *index tuning* strategy to improve the index maintenance performance for dynamic query-logs.
- We provide a performance study of our strategy applied on existing query-log based on-line indexing approaches.

*The work was carried out when the author was at Indian Institute of Technology Madras, India

CIKM'11, October 24–28, 2011, Glasgow, Scotland, UK.

2. BACKGROUND

Here, we discuss a brief overview of the query-log based approaches on which index tuning is applied, and the AOL query-log analysis which forms the basis for our proposed index tuning strategy.

2.1 Query-log based on-line indexing

In [7], authors proposed a merge based on-line indexing approach using the frequency distribution of terms in the query-log. The pivotal idea of query-log based approaches is to partition the index into two: frequent-term index and infrequent-term index, and adopt a different merge policy for each. For partitioning the index, they proposed a *horizontal partitioning* technique in addition to the vertical partitioning approach. Horizontal partitioning splits the index using a *split-point* (threshold) calculated by applying *pareto* principle (80-20) on frequency distribution of terms in the query-log. Frequent terms (>*split-point*) along with their postings lists form frequent-term index and the rest form infrequent-term index.

Based on the horizontal partitioning, three query-log based approaches are proposed in [7] - Single-split Immediate Merge, Single-split Multi-partition, and Multi-split Indexing approach. These three approaches follow a general paradigm used for on-line indexing. An auxiliary index is maintained in the main memory and continuously updated with new documents. Once the auxiliary index size reaches the allowed quota, it is either merged with an on-disk index (with cascading merges) or moved as a new partition. Query-log based approaches are multi-partition approaches, i.e. they result in more than one on-disk index to exist simultaneously. These approaches generalize the idea of Logarithmic merge and Geometric partitioning approaches and use horizontal partitioning for splitting the indexes. A brief overview of the query-log based approaches is given below:

i. Single-split Immediate Merge

In Single-split Immediate Merge, the auxiliary index, when it is required to be moved to disk, is merged with the index at Partition 0. Based on user defined value of r (maximum no. of merges allowed), the index at Partition 0 is split into frequent-term and infrequent-term index using horizontal partitioning. The frequent-term index is maintained using immediate merge policy and infrequent-term index by a lazy merge policy (a generalized logarithmic merge). This indexing scheme provides a high degree of query performance since frequent-term index is a large single partitioned index. However, the index maintenance costs are expensive but better than naïve immediate merge approach.

ii. Single-split Multi-Partition

In Single-split Immediate Merge, the advantages of using lazy merge policy for the large infrequent-term index are shadowed by the use of very expensive immediate merge policy for frequent-term index. This limits the Single-split immediate merge policy from providing better trade-off between index maintenance costs and query performance. Single-split Multi-partition overcomes this problem by adopting an incremental multi-partition active merge policy (a generalized geometric partitioning) for maintaining frequent-term index. This indexing approach achieves a much better trade-off than the one offered by Single-split immediate merge.

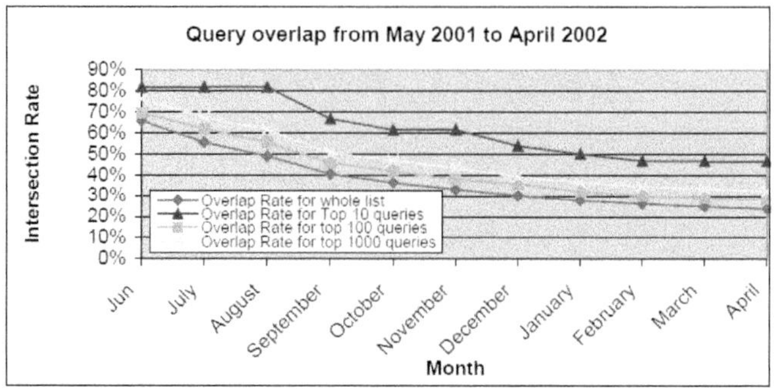

Figure 1: Graph representing overlap rate of AOL query-log from May 2001 to April 2002[1]

iii. Multi-split Indexing

Although Single-split multi-partition provides a better trade-off and performs better than Geometric partitioning, there are some short comings with this approach. For instance, terms those fall below the split-point are treated identically to the terms that rarely appear in query-log. Similarly, terms that just crossed the split-point enjoy an expensive merge policy. This impacts the performance of single-split multi-partition both in index maintenance via first instance and query performance through second instance. To overcome this, multi-split indexing leverages the power law distribution of term frequencies and recursively defines multiple split-points. Multi-split on-disk indexes are the result of applying recursive horizontal partitioning better represented by an *index tree*. This approach achieves a better trade-off than Single-split multi-partition approach.

2.2 AOL query-log analysis

G Pass et al. [9] performed analysis over AOL query-log and presented some temporal characteristics of queries. They used two measures *Overlap rate* and *Correlation Coefficient* to analyse the query-logs from May 2001 to April 2002. Their findings[1] in Figure 1 shows that the percentage overlap of queries in two different query-logs decreases with time. The overlap rate on average for consecutive months is 0.905, consecutive quarters is 0.833, consecutive semi-yearly is 0.795. For the whole year only $20 - 30$ % of all unique queries survive, and the longer a query survives the more likely it survives in future logs. This suggests that the use of static query-log for index maintenance is inefficient and index tuning is essential to make query-log based approaches efficient.

3. INDEX TUNING

Index Tuning refers to transformation of the existing index into a new index. The new index incorporates the changes to the term frequencies observed in the new query-log. Index tuning is a three step process: 1) Identifying the *diff-terms*, terms whose frequency is changed, 2) Building a *diff-terms index* for diff-terms, and 3) Merging the diff-terms index with the existing on-disk index.

Identifying the diff-terms: The first step in the index tuning process is to identify diff-terms. We define a *diff-log*, which comprises of the terms whose frequencies had changed

[1]Query-Log Analysis, www.ir.iit.edu/~abdur/publications /QueryResearch.pdf

Algorithm 1: IndexTuning(onDiskIndexroot, diffLog)

```
begin
    for each term in diffLog do
        pList ← extractPostings(onDiskIndexroot,term);
        addList(diffTermIndex,pList);
    InsBlock(onDiskIndexroot, diffTermIndex) ;
end
```

from old query-log to the new query-log. Since over a time span, a large number of terms have frequency changes, it is inefficient to consider all of them to be recorded into diff-log for index tuning. Instead, we record only the terms which are mis-classified according to new log, i.e we take the new query-log and compute the new thresholds based on 80-20 principle. Mis-classified terms (or diff-terms) are the terms which are infrequent in old query-log and frequent in new query-log or vice-versa.

Building diff-term index: After the diff-terms are identified, the next step is to build a diff-term index. During the diff-term index construction, the postings list of the terms are extracted from the existing on-disk index and grouped together to form the diff-term index. Extracting the postings list for a term is similar to querying the term, this involves traversing through all the indexes for collecting its postings. Every time a postings list for a term is extracted from an index, the postings are not deleted immediately, but they are copied and marked as delete for efficiency purpose. The final postings list for a term is the concatenation of all the identified postings. This list is added to the diff-term index.

Merging the diff-terms index with on-disk index: The final step involved is to merge the diff-term index with the existing on-disk index. The merging step is similar to the merging of an auxiliary index with the on-disk index. The diff-term index is first merged with the on-disk index at partition 0, which can trigger cascading merges. Before invoking the merging process, the split-points (threshold) are updated to the new split-points that are obtained from the new query-log using the 80-20 % split principle.

Algorithm 1 describes the general index tuning approach. For each term in the computed diff-log, first its postings are extracted from the on-disk index and the term along with its postings are added to the diff-term index. After processing all the terms in diff-log, the final diff-term index is merged with existing on-disk index (by the InsBlock() described in [7]). Since the three query-log based approaches follow different merging schemes, they result in different costs for index tuning mainly influenced by the extraction process costs.

Extraction in Single-split approaches

Algorithm 2 describes the process of extracting the postings for a given term `term`. First the `term`'s frequency is obtained from old query-log and compared with the split-point. If the `term` is frequent, all the frequent-term indexes are queried, otherwise infrequent-term indexes are queried for extracting postings. For efficiency reasons, extracting postings list operation does not delete the postings but marks them as deleted in the partitions which contain the term. Subsequently during the merge phase, the postings are deleted in those partitions which participate in merging.

Algorithm 2: extractPostings(onDiskIndexroot, `term`)

```
begin
    // For Single-split approaches;
    node ← onDiskIndexroot;
    if frequent(term) then
        // For SSIM, sizeOf(frequentIndexesList) is 1;
        for each index in frequentIndexesList do
            pList ← extract(frequentIndex, term);
    else
        for each index in inFrequentIndexesList do
            pList ← extract(index, term);
    return pList;
end
```

Algorithm 3: extractPostings(onDiskIndexroot, `term`)

```
begin
    // For Multi-split approach;
    node ← onDiskIndexroot;
    if node is NULL then
        return NULL;
    pList ← extract(node,term);
    if frequent(term) > nodeThreshold then
        pList ← concat(pList,extractPostings(node→right);
    else
        pList ← concat(pList,extractPostings(node→left);
end
return pList;
```

Extraction in Multi-split approaches

Multi-partition approaches maintain the indexes that are represented by an index tree. Extraction, similar to querying, is a recursive binary search over the index tree. After extracting the postings list at a node, if the term's frequency is greater than node's split-point value the extraction continues over right sub-tree otherwise left sub-tree partitions are considered. Since the average query times for multi-split approaches are slightly expensive compared to Single-split multi-partition approaches, the index tuning costs also follow the same pattern. The algorithm for extracting postings list for a term is presented in Algorithm 3.

4. PERFORMANCE STUDY

Datasets: For our performance study of index tuning strategy applied over the three query-log based on-line indexing approaches, we used Wikipedia[2] collection of 85GB containing 7 million documents. The average size of the document in the collection is around 12KB. For evaluating the query performance, we used AOL query-log containing 1.2 million terms. For the performance study of index tuning approaches, we generated a synthetic query-log from AOL query-log. The synthetic query-log is generated by taking all the queries from the original query-log and changing their frequency of occurrence. For our test purpose, we made 20% of random queries change from frequent to infrequent or vice-versa. From the synthetic log, we computed the diff-log, that contains only the terms which are frequent in old query-log and infrequent in new query-log or the terms which are infrequent in old query-log and frequent in new log.

We performed the evaluation of index tuning over three on line indexing approaches: 1) Single-split Immediate merge

[2]http://static.wikipedia.org

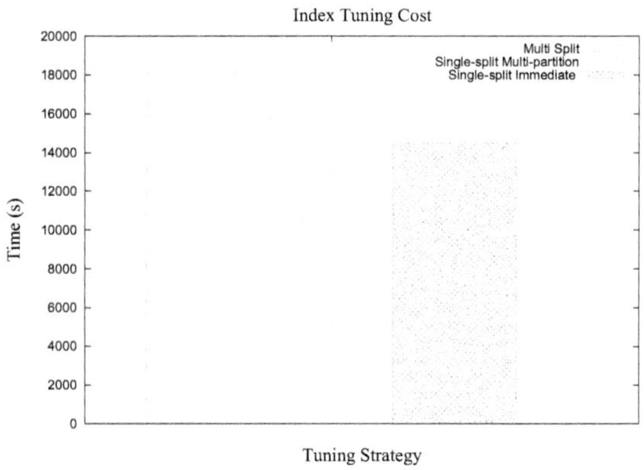

Figure 2: Index tuning costs for three on-line indexing approaches

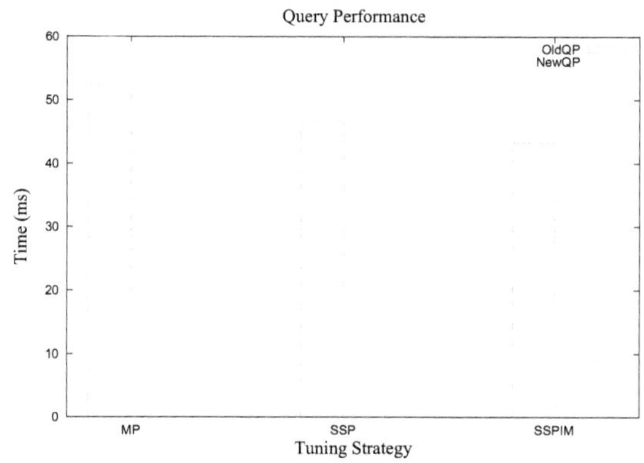

Figure 3: Query performance after index tuning

2) Single-split Multiple Partition approach and 3) Multi-partition approach. In the performance study, we evaluated the time taken for tuning the existing on-line index into a new one which is based on the new query-log, and also compared the average time taken for each query in old index and new index.

Figure 2 shows the evaluation of the index tuning costs for the three approaches. Here, one can observe that the index tuning costs for Single-split Immediate merge index is lower compared to the other approaches. This is because, the extraction of postings from an index for a term is proportional to the querying time taken for that term. For our test case, we observed that index tuning cost for Single-split Immediate Merge is **7%** less of the Single-split Multiple Partition approach and **25%** less of the Multi-split Indexing approach.

The evaluation query times after the index tuning for the three approaches is shown in Figure 3. Here, we can observe that the new query times are almost same for all the three approaches. This is because, we have taken only the diff-log queries for evaluation. Since all the diff-log terms form a single index after index tuning and merged with the existing on-disk index, we have the same query time for diff-terms with respect to all the approaches. But this will change once the usage of on-line indexing is resumed. From our experimental study, we observed a significant improvement in query performance. For Single-split Immediate merge (SSIM) the query performance is improved by **58%**, for Single-split Multiple Partition approach (SSMP) the improvement is by **61%**, and for Multi-split approach the improvement is by **64%**.

5. CONCLUSIONS

In this paper, we propose an index tuning approach for query-log based on-line index strategies. The proposed approach overcomes the problems faced by query-log based approaches with dynamic query-logs. We exploit the frequency distribution of query-logs to compare and identify the terms that are inefficiently handled in the existing index and use a tuning approach to reorganize the existing index. Index tuning cost for a query-log based approach is directly proportional to its query costs. As index tuning reorganizes the existing index, it substantially improves the query performance for the terms which are inefficiently handled before by query-log based approaches. Thus, the use of index tuning helps in improving the performance of query-log based approaches and make them viable to dynamic changes in query-logs.

6. ACKNOWLEDGEMENTS

We would like to thank Max-Planck-Institut für Informatik, Saarbrücken, Germany for their generous support.

7. REFERENCES

[1] E. W. Brown, J. P. Callan, and W. B. Croft. Fast incremental indexing for full-text information retrieval. In *VLDB '94*, pages 192–202, San Francisco, CA, USA, 1994. Morgan Kaufmann Publishers Inc.

[2] S. Büttcher and C. L. A. Clarke. Indexing time vs. query time: trade-offs in dynamic information retrieval systems. In *CIKM '05: Proceedings of the 14th ACM CIKM*, pages 317–318, New York, NY, USA, 2005. ACM.

[3] S. Büttcher, C. L. A. Clarke, and B. Lushman. Hybrid index maintenance for growing text collections. In *In SIGIR 2006: Proceedings of the 29th annual international ACM SIGIR*, pages 356–363, 2006.

[4] T. Chiueh and L. Huang. Efficient real-time index updates in text retrieval systems. Technical report, Experimental Computer Systems Lab, Department of Computer Science, State University of New, 1998.

[5] D. Cutting and J. Pedersen. Optimization for dynamic inverted index maintenance. In *SIGIR '90: Proceedings of the 13th annual international ACM SIGIR*, pages 405–411, New York, NY, USA, 1990. ACM.

[6] R. Guo, X. Cheng, H. Xu, and B. Wang. Efficient on-line index maintenance for dynamic text collections by using dynamic balancing tree. In *CIKM '07: Proceedings of the sixteenth ACM CIKM*, pages 751–760, New York, NY, USA, 2007. ACM.

[7] S. Gurajada and S. K. P. On-line index maintenance using horizontal partitioning. In *Proceeding of the 18th ACM CIKM*, CIKM '09, pages 435–444, New York, NY, USA, 2009. ACM.

[8] N. Lester, A. Moffat, and J. Zobel. Fast on-line index construction by geometric partitioning. In *CIKM '05: Proceedings of the 14th ACM CIKM*, pages 776–783, New York, NY, USA, 2005. ACM.

[9] G. Pass, A. Chowdhury, and C. Torgeson. A picture of search. In *InfoScale '06: Proceedings of the 1st international conference on Scalable information systems*, page 1, New York, NY, USA, 2006. ACM.

[10] I. M. Strategies, N. Lester, J. Zobel, and H. E. Williams. In-place versus re-build versus re-merge:. In *In Proceedings of the 27th Conference on ACS*, pages 15–23. Society, Inc, 2004.

[11] A. Tomasic, H. García-Molina, and K. Shoens. Incremental updates of inverted lists for text document retrieval. In *SIGMOD '94: Proceedings of the 1994 ACM SIGMOD*, pages 289–300, New York, NY, USA, 1994. ACM.

[12] I. H. Witten, A. Moffat, and T. C. Bell. *Managing gigabytes (2nd ed.): compressing and indexing documents and images.* Morgan Kaufmann Publishers Inc., San Francisco, CA, USA, 1999.

Efficient Phrase Querying with Flat Position Index

Dongdong Shan, Wayne Xin Zhao, Jing He, Rui Yan, Hongfei Yan and Xiaoming Li
School of Electronics Engineering and Computer Science, Peking University, China
{shandd2008, batmanfly, peaceful.he, yhf1029}@gmail.com,{ r.yan, lxm}@pku.edu.cn

ABSTRACT

A large proportion of search engine queries contain phrases, namely a sequence of adjacent words. In this paper, we propose to use flat position index (a.k.a schema-independent index) for phrase query evaluation. In the flat position index, the entire document collection is viewed as a huge sequence of tokens. Each token is represented by one flat position, which is a unique position offset from the beginning of the collection. Each indexed term is associated with a list of the flat positions about that term in the sequence. To recover *DocID* from flat positions efficiently, we propose a novel cache sensitive look-up table (CSLT), which is much faster than existing search algorithms. Experiments on TREC GOV2 data collection show that flat position index can reduce the index size and speed up phrase querying substantially, compared with traditional word-level index.

Categories and Subject Descriptors

H.3.3 [**Information Search and Retrieval**]: [Search process, efficiency]

General Terms

Algorithms, Performance, Experimentation

Keywords

Flat position index, Phrase query evaluation

1. INTRODUCTION

With the explosive growth of Web data, how to seek information efficiently and effectively has been a very important problem to both research community and industry. Search engines have become the most commonly used tools for Web information retrieval, and it is necessary to process thousands of queries per second. A significant fraction of the submitted queries contain phrases, namely a sequence of adjacent words. Users can submit explicit phrase queries to search engines typically by enclosing them in quotation marks. [3] reported that there were 8.3% of explicit phrase queries in excite log during 1997-1999. In addition, users can also submit implicit phrase queries. [7] analyzed a large amount of AltaVista's query logs, finding that many queries without explicit phrase operator were actually implicit phrase searches. Recently, [9]analyzed Twitter search log and found that about 15.22% percent of the queries are celebrity names, which are possibe phrase queries. It indicates that phrase querying is very important for social network websites, too.

Usually, search engine employs a two-step approach for evaluating phrase queries based on the traditional word-level index [2]. In the traditional word-level index, each indexed term is associated with a posting list, and each posting is a triplet, namely a document identifier (*DocID*), an in-document term frequency (*TF*), and a list of term offsets in that document. With the traditional word-level index, search engines first intersect *DocID* sets to get a list of candidate documents that possibly contain the phrase, and then checks whether the query terms are adjacent or not in the candidate documents. However, as suggested in [3], the traditional word-level index is not efficient since the cost for processing common term's posting list is very high. To solve this problem, one crude method is to remove stop words in queries, which may result in incorrect query evaluation. Other methods [3, 10] add auxiliary structures (e.g. N-gram, partial next word index, phrase index, etc) to speed up phrase query evaluation. One shortcoming of these methods is that not all the candidate documents retrieved in the first step contain the target phrase, which adds un-necessary overloads and slows down the overall processing.

To seek one more efficient way for phrase search, in this paper, we propose to use the flat position index for phrase query evaluation. Flat position index (a.k.a *schema-independent index*) was first proposed by [5] to process queries on structured text, and [6] presented an overall description of its structure. In the flat position index, it views the whole document collection as a single sequence of tokens. Thus, each token can be represented by a unique position offset from the beginning of the collection. For each indexed term, the posting list is composed by a list of position offsets. Flat position index has many potential advantages over the traditional word-level index due to the simple structure. First, *DocID* and *TF* information need not be stored, which results in smaller index. Second, the flat position structure is able to support the queries with position constraints very flexibly, e.g. proximity search and phrase search.

Though the structure of flat position index is very simple and elegant, few studies have presented the implementation details of one real retrieval system with it, and none reported the real performance of it in public literature. It is challenging to deploy flat position index into real systems at least in three aspects:

- How to effectively represent all the flat positions when the document collection is extremely large, i.e. the number of

CIKM'11, October 24–28, 2011, Glasgow, Scotland, UK.

tokens exceeds the maximum range a 32-bit number can represent.

- Since *DocID* is not contained in flat posting lists, how to efficiently recover the original *DocID* from the flat position.
- How to apply existing state-of-art index techniques in flat position index, e.g. compression algorithms.

In this paper, we build a real retrieval system with the flat position index, and we empirically examine the performance of phrase query evaluation based on that. To the best of our knowledge, it's the first study to explore the flat position index for evaluating phrase queries. To solve the first challenge, we divide the whole collection space into several subspaces. Each subspace is a subset of the whole document collection, and each token in that can be represented as a 32-bit integer identifier. To recover *DocID* efficiently, we propose and implement a novel cache sensitive look-up table(CSLT) to map the flat position into corresponding DocID efficiently. The algorithmic complexity for each mapping operation is $O(1)$. The experiments show that it is three times faster than CSS (cache sensitive search) tree [4].

We construct extensive experiments based on *TREC GOV2* collection and compare our results with the traditional word-level index for phrase evaluation. Without nextword structures, flat position index can reduce the index size by 6.3% and speed up phrase evaluation by 31.3%, compared with traditional word-level index. With nextword structures, flat position index can reduce the index size by 7.3% and speed up phrase evaluation by 33.5%, compared with traditional word-level index. We also examine how auxiliary structures affect the performance of phrase querying for flat position index.

2. FLAT POSITION INDEX

In the traditional word-level index [2], each posting of a term t is represented by a triplet, formally we have

$$(d, f_{d,t}, [o_{d,1}, ..., o_{d,f_{d,t}}]), \quad (1)$$

where d is the document identifier, $f_{d,t}$ is the number of occurrences of t in the document (*TF*) and the $o_{d,(\cdot)}$ are the increasingly ordered offsets of t occuring in the document d. With this structure, traditional phrase querying is a two-step approach: perform *DocID* set intersection to get a list of candidate documents, and then check whether candidate documents contain the target phrase query. However, not all the documents retrieved in the first step are the final results. To address this problem, in this section, we introduce flat position index and discuss how to use it for phrase querying.

2.1 Structure of Flat Position Index

Flat position index [5, 6] views the whole document collection as a single sequence of tokens, and each token in the collection has one global and unique identifier (i.e. one flat position). Flat position index is composed by three main components: dictionary, inverted index file and a document boundary array. Similar to that in traditional word-level index, the dictionary contains various statistics information such as document frequency (*DF*) and collection frequency (*CF*) for the terms in the collection. Posting lists of indexed terms are stored in the inverted index file. The posting list is composed by a list of flat positions, i.e. global offset values. The document boundary array stores all boundaries of documents in the collection, which is used to map a flat position into corresponding *DocID*. We present one example in Figure 1 to illustrate the structure of the flat position index. In this example, the whole document collection consists of five documents. The first occurrence of term

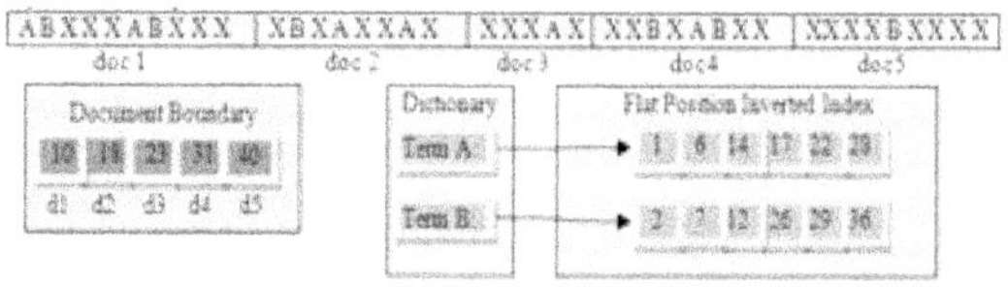

Figure 1: An example for the structure of flat position index.

A is the first token in this collection, so its flat position is 1. Similarly, the flat positions for the first and the third occurrences of term B are respectively 2 and 12. Interestingly, we can see that flat position index doesn't store *DocID* and *TF* information.

When the size of collection is very large, the maximum flat position in the collection may not be represented by a 32-bit integer, e.g., GOV2 collection has 23 billion tokens. One naïve method is to use a 64-bit integer to represent a flat position. However, it has two limitations: 1) more space is needed to store a position in memory; 2) some state-of-the-art compression algorithms can't work for 64-bit integers [1]. To address those problems, we propose to use the *subspace dividing* method, which divides the whole collection into several subspaces. In each subspace, flat positions can be represented by a 32-bit integer, and each subspace is indexed by an subspace identifier. After subspace dividing, each flat position is represented by two 32-bit integers: the subspace identifier and the offset in that subspace. In practice, flat positions in one block usually have the same subspace identifier, so we can just store one subspace identifier for one block to reduce the space.

2.2 Flat Position Mapping

Since there's no explicit *DocID* information in the flat position index, we have to recover the *DocID* from flat positions in query evaluation. The problem of recovering *DocID* can be formulated in a more general problem: given an integer m and an ordered array $\{T_i\}_{i=0}^{n-1}$, find out an index number k ($0 \leq k \leq n-1$) so that $T_k < m$ and $T_{k+1} \geq m$.

A couple of methods can be used to solve this problem: binary search, m-array search trees, CSS-tree (cache sensitive search tree) and CPSS-tree (cache/page sensitive search tree) [4] . Though CSS-tree and CPSS-tree are cache conscious data structures, the time complexity is still $O(\log_m(n))$, which is not efficient enough for an extremely large arrays.

To speed up the position mapping, we propose a novel cache sensitive look-up table (CSLT). The idea is to reduce the number of cache misses by making most of searching operations in a cache line [4].

Let the size of cache line be 2^a bytes , the average document length be l and each element in document boundary array cost 2^b bytes. We assume that the lengths of documents in the collection do not vary too much. The number of documents in a cache line is nearly 2^{a-b}, and a cache line can cover $l * 2^{a-b}$ positions on average. The position space that a cache line cover is called as a cache line position space (CLPS), which is a sub-range of flat positions in the whole collection. The whole position space can be divided into several CLPSs. If the biggest position value in the collection is L, then the number of CLPS is $\lfloor \frac{L}{l*2^{a-b}} \rfloor + 1$. We use a two-layer structure to implement CSLT. The first layer is a *index array* to record the offsets where each CLPS starts; the second layer is the document boundary array. The index array can be built very efficiently as follows: linear scan the document boundary array, assign each boundary value in it to the corresponding CLPS and set the i-th entry in the index array with the offset of the smallest document boundary value in the i-th CLPS.

The time complexity of building the index array is $O(n)$, n is the number of documents in collection. For recovering *DocID* from

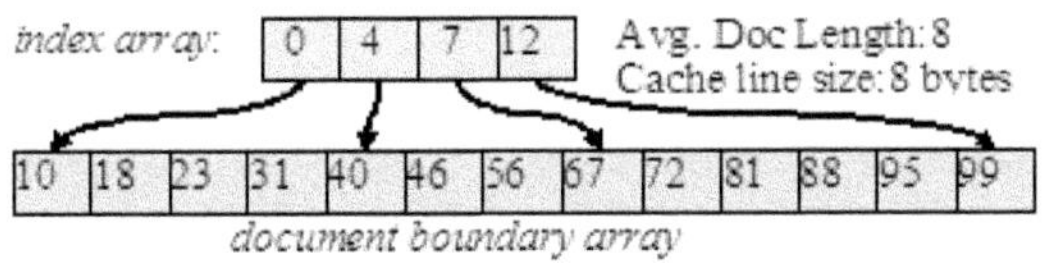

Figure 2: An example for the structure of CSLT.

one flat position, it includes two steps: 1) Compute the offset in the index array by dividing the position by the size of CLPS. Read the value S in corresponding entry of the *index array*. 2) Linear scan the document boundary array from S, and stop when the value of current entry is bigger than the searching position. Return the boundary offset in document boundary array.

Figure 2 illustrates the structure of CSLT. In this example, we have $a = 3$, $b = 1$ and $l = 8$, so a cache line can cover 32 positions and there are totally four CLPS. Then we show how to set the entries of the index array. For example, the second CLPS ranges from 32 to 63, and the fifth entry of the document boundary array is the first boundary value belonging to this CLPS. So we set second entry of the index array to the corresponding offset, i.e. 4. For recovering *DocID* from one flat position 45, we first derive that this position belongs to the second CLPS (45 divided by 32), then we load the second entry of index array to get 4. Second we begin to scan the document boundary array from the fifth element. We skip the first entry 40 since it's smaller than 45. We stop at the second entry 46 (bigger than the searched number 45). The offset of this entry in the document boundary array is 5. So we know that the flat position 45 is mapped to *DocID* 5.

The time complexity of CSLT is O(1). The expected number of cache miss for mapping a position to *DocID* is 2 on average: one in the index array and the other in the document boundary array.

2.3 Auxiliary Structures

For flat position index, we consider two kinds of auxiliary structures common used in traditional word-level index, namely skip lists and nextword structure [10]. Skip lists can reduce the amount of data for decoding while nextword can speed up phrase querying. Both of them can be easily adaptive to flat position index since flat position index is also one variation of word-level inverted index. See Section 3.1 for details.

3. EXPERIMENTS AND RESULTS

3.1 Experiment Setup

Dataset: We use the TREC GOV2 collection, which consists of 25.2 million web pages crawled from the .gov Internet domain. We use two different sets of queries in our experiments. One query set was used in TREC06 efficiency task of Terabyte track. The other query set is sampled from the MSN Search Spring 2006 Query logs. The detailed statistics are shown in Table 1. We run all the experiments on the server with two Quad-Core Intel Xeon 5310(1.66GHz) processors (we only use one core for our experiments) and 8GB of RAM. For each query evaluation, we first load all the necessary posting lists into the main memory.

Query processing: There are two main approaches to process queries [2], either using *DAAT(document-at-a-time)* or using *TAAT(term-at-a-time)* for the standard word-level inverted index. These two approaches can be employed in flat position index, too. In our experiments, we empirically find that *DAAT* is more efficient for phrase querying for both flat position index and the traditional word-level inverted index, so in the following sections, all our experiments are based on *DAAT*.

Compression algorithms: We test four state-of-art compressions algorithms in both the standard word-level inverted index and flat position index, including PForDelta, Group Varint [6], Rice and VarByte. In our experiments, we find that PForDelta and Rice results in smaller index size than the others, and PForDelta is much faster than Rice (about 6 times) in decoding data. To make a tradeoff between decoding speed and index size, we select PForDelta as the major compression algorithm for both the standard word-level inverted index and flat position index in the following experiments. When the length of one posting list is less than 128, we use VarByte algorithm.

Table 1: Statistics of two query sets.

	TREC query set	MSN query set
#queries	100K	61K
average query length	3.1	2.5

Table 2: Skip distance for different posting list lengths.

Posting list length	Flat position index	Word-level index
$x > 10^7$	384	128
$10^5 < x < 10^7$	64	32
$10^3 < x < 10^5$	32	32
Otherwise	0	0

Skip lists: Skip list has been commonly used to speed up processing queries. When adding skip list to an index, it's very important to set a reasonable skip distance. Here we follow [8]'s approach to set list-length-dependent skip lengths. We show our setting of skip lengths for different posting lists in Table 2. After adding skip list, the index size increased by about 1%. Skip lists affect the index size very little but speed up the query evaluation substantially. In the following experiments, all indexes are added with skip lists by default if not particularly mentioned.

Nextword index: Nextword index [10] is proposed to speed up phrase querying. To see how it affects the performance of phrase query evaluation, we add top-5 partial nextword index to both the traditional word-level index and the flat position index. For comparisons, we also keep the original indexes without nextword index.

3.2 Results

Performance of *DocID* mapping: We first evaluate the performance of CSLT for *DocID* mapping. We compare four search algorithms, namely linear search, binary search, CSS tree, and our proposed CSLT. We collect the posting lists of $5K$ query terms as our test data. We use a $25M$ document boundary array, which is sampled from GOV2 test collection. In Figure 3 , we can see that 1) our CSLT performs much better than all the others when the length of posting list is smaller than 5×10^6, the major reason is that the number of expected cache misses for CSLT is smaller than the others; 2) while for very long posting lists (e.g. posting lists of stopwords), linear search performs best since we need to perform *DocID* mapping for most of documents in the collection. Based on the analysis above, we use the linear search algorithm when the length of boundary array is bigger than $\frac{N}{4}$, where N is the document number in collection; otherwise, we use the proposed CSLT.

Index size: We examine the index sizes with/without top 5 partial nextword in both traditional word-level index and flat position index. As shown in Table 3, we find that flat position index reduces the index size substantially. The major reason is that it doesn't store *DocID* and *TF*.

Performance of phrase querying: Generally, the overall phrase query evaluation into four steps: 1) loading data; 2) decoding data;

Table 3: Index size with/without nextword structure.

	Flat	Trad.	Flat+NW	Trad.+NW
Index size(GB)	29.6(-6.3%)	31.6	34.1(-7.3%)	36.6

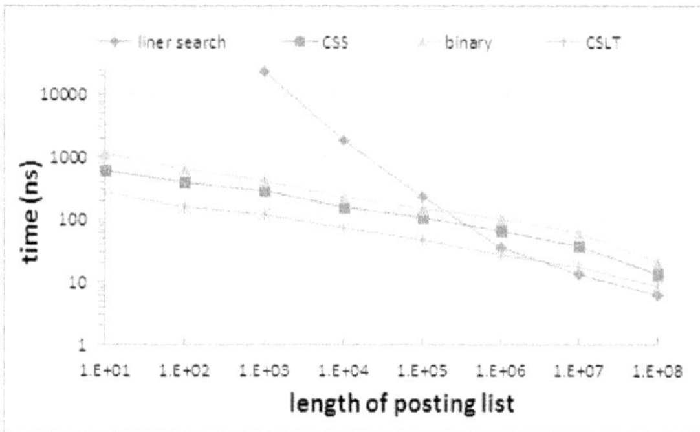

Figure 3: Results of recovering *DocID* for different algorithms.

Table 4: Performance of phrase querying in TREC query set.

	Inverted		Inverted+NW	
	Flat	Trad.	Flat	Trad.
Decoding	0.0556	0.0998	0.0418	0.0758
Finding phrase	0.0711	0.0848	0.0479	0.0590
Total time	0.1267	0.1846	0.0897	0.1348

3) finding phrase; 4) scoring documents. To see why flat position index is more effective in phrase querying, we further examine time costs in each individual step. The time for loading data is not considered since we've loaded all the necessary data into main memory before each query evaluation. We also ignore the fourth step since it is the same for traditional word-level inverted index and flat position index. We further consider two kinds of index structures: a) inverted index without nextword (denoted as *Inverted*); b) inverted index with top 5 nextword structure (denoted as *Inverted+NW*). The results on TREC and MSN query sets are shown respectively in Table 4 and 5. We can see that 1) flat position index is more efficient for query evaluation with/without nextword; 2) flat position index reduces decoding time significantly; 3) nextword can improve query evaluation for both traditional word-level index and flat position index.

Examine the effect of different auxiliary structures: In our experiments, we consider two kinds of auxiliary structures for flat position index, skip list and nextword index. We examine how these auxiliary structures affect the performance of phrase querying for flat position index. We consider four kinds of index as comparisons: raw index, raw index with only skip list, raw index with only top 5 nextwords index, raw index with both skip list and top 5 nextwords index. Fig 4 presents the average processing time of different query lengths using flat position index with different auxiliary structures. The major findings are 1) both skip list and nextword index improve the performance of phrase querying for flat position index, and skip list is more helpful than nextword; 2) skip list together with nextword gives the best performance; 3) when the length of phrase query is long, auxiliary structures is very necessary to improve the performance of phrase querying. We also performed these comparison experiment in traditional word-level index, and we got the similar findings.

4. DISCUSSION AND CONCLUSIONS

In this paper, we propose to use flat position index for efficient phrase querying. We construct extensive experiments based on TREC GOV2 collection. We find that flat position index is very efficient for phrase evaluation. In the future, we plan to do more exploration on how to apply flat position index to general query evaluation. One possible way is to explicitly store *DocID* and *TF* information in flat position index; since flat position index is very efficient to deal with proximity information, another promising way is to transform non-phrase queries into equivalent or approximate queries with proximity constraints. Flat position index can be also used as an auxiliary structure to support efficient proximity related queries.

Table 5: Performance of phrase querying in MSN query set.

	Inverted		Inverted+NW	
	Flat	Trad.	Flat	Trad.
Decoding	0.0602	0.1066	0.0487	0.0860
Finding phrase	0.0685	0.0756	0.0558	0.0618
Total time	0.1287	0.1822	0.1045	0.1478

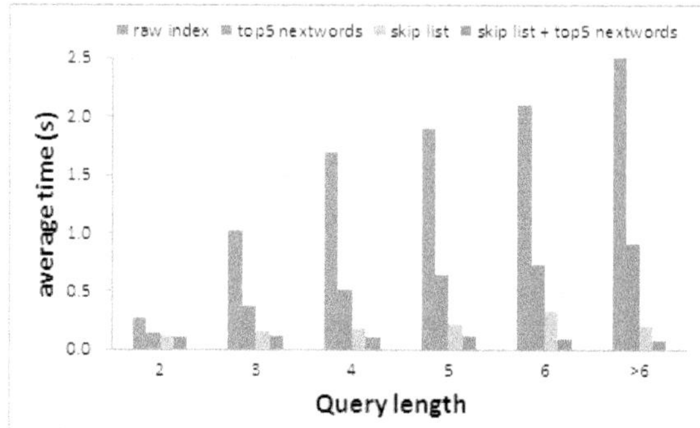

Figure 4: Average processing time of different query lengths using flat position index with different auxiliary structures.

Acknowledgments

This work has been partially supported by HGJ 2010 Grant 2011ZX01042-001-001 and NSFC with Grant No.61073082, 60933004.

5. REFERENCES

[1] V. N. Anh and A. Moffat. Inverted index compression using word-aligned binary codes. *Inf. Retr.*, 2005.

[2] V. N. Anh and A. Moffat. Structured index organizations for high-throughput text querying. In *SPIRE*, 2006.

[3] D. Bahle, H. E. Williams, and J. Zobel. Efficient phrase querying with an auxiliary index. In *SIGIR*, 2002.

[4] S. Büttcher and C. L. A. Clarke. Index compression is good, especially for random access. In *CIKM*, pages 761–770, New York, NY, USA, 2007. ACM.

[5] C. L. Clarke, G. V. Cormack, and F. J. Burkowski. An Algebra for Structured Text Search and A Framework for its Implementation. *The Computer Journal*, 1995.

[6] J. Dean. Invited talk: Challenges in building large-scale information retrieval systems. In *WSDM*, 2009.

[7] C. Silverstein, H. Marais, M. Henzinger, and M. Moricz. Analysis of a very large web search engine query log. *SIGIR Forum*, 1999.

[8] T. Strohman and W. B. Croft. Efficient document retrieval in main memory. In *SIGIR*, 2007.

[9] J. Teevan, D. Ramage, and M. R. Morris. #twittersearch: a comparison of microblog search and web search. In *WSDM*, 2011.

[10] H. E. Williams, J. Zobel, and D. Bahle. Fast phrase querying with combined indexes. *ACM Trans. Inf. Syst.*, 2004.

Trained Trigger Language Model for Sentence Retrieval in QA: Bridging the Vocabulary Gap

Saeedeh Momtazi*, Dietrich Klakow
Spoken Language Systems
Saarland University, Saarbrücken, Germany
{saeedeh.momtazi,dietrich.klakow}@lsv.uni-saarland.de

ABSTRACT

We propose a novel language model for sentence retrieval in Question Answering (QA) systems called *trained trigger language model*. This model addresses the word mismatch problem in information retrieval. The proposed model captures pairs of trigger and target words while training on a large corpus. The word pairs are extracted based on both unsupervised and supervised approaches while different notions of triggering are used. In addition, we study the impact of corpus size and domain for a supervised model. All notions of the trained trigger model are finally used in a language model-based sentence retrieval framework. Our experiments on TREC QA collection verify that the proposed model significantly improves the sentence retrieval performance compared to the state-of-the-art translation model and class model which address the same problem.

Categories and Subject Descriptors: H.3.3 [Information Storage and Retrieval]:Information Search and Retrieval

General Terms: Theory, Algorithm, Experimentation

Keywords: sentence retrieval, language modeling, triggering, question answering

1. INTRODUCTION

Sentence retrieval plays an important role in QA systems. It aims to find small segments of text that contain an exact answer to the users' questions. The brevity of sentences compared to documents exacerbates the usual term mismatch problem which should taken into consideration while designing a sentence retrieval engine.

The word unigram model is the most common approach used in the majority of information retrieval literature. When estimating word unigrams, the model only considers the exact literal words present in the query. Since no relationship between words is considered by this model, it will fail to retrieve other relevant information. Different techniques such as translation model [1] and class model [7] proposed to overcome the term mismatch problem. In this paper, we introduce a new model called *trained trigger language model* which uses another approach to this aim. In the proposed model, we assume that by training a language model on a large corpus, we can find pairs of trigger and target words; so that in the retrieval step, if the trigger word appears in an input question and the target word appears in a sentence, then we can say there is a relation between the question and the sentence even though they share no or few terms.

The structure of the paper is as follows. Section 2 introduces the proposed trained trigger language model. Different notions of triggering are described in Section 3. In Section 4, we show how the proposed model can be integrated with the exact matching method to improve the system performance. In Section 5, the experimental results are presented. Finally, Section 6 concludes the paper.

2. THE TRIGGER MODEL

In the word unigram model, the probability of generating the query Q given the observation of the sentence model S is estimated by:

$$P(Q|S) = \prod_{i=1}^{M} P(q_i|S) \qquad (1)$$

In this model, for each sentence in the search space a separate language model is trained to estimate parameters; and then using the maximum likelihood estimation, $P(q_i|S)$ is calculated:

$$P_{\text{word}}(q_i|S) = \frac{f_S(q_i)}{\sum_w f_S(w)} \qquad (2)$$

where $f_S(q_i)$ is the number of times the query term q_i appears in the sentence S and w denotes vocabulary words. As a result, based on the maximum likelihood estimation, $P(Q|S)$ for word unigram is defined as:

$$P_{\text{word}}(Q|S) = \prod_{i=1}^{M} \frac{f_S(q_i)}{\sum_w f_S(w)} \qquad (3)$$

In contrast, in the trained trigger language model, a single model is trained on a large corpus first. Then, the trained model is being used for all of the sentences to be retrieved. The trained model is represented by $f(w, w')$, where $f(w, w')$ is the number of times the word w triggers the target w'. There are different notions of triggering that can be used to find pairs of trigger and target words. The notions of triggering used in our experiments are discussed in Section 3. Having a trained model based on trigger and target words, for each word in the query and each word in

*Saeedeh Momtazi's present affiliation is Hasso-Plattner-Institut, Potsdam, Germany

CIKM'11, October 24–28, 2011, Glasgow, Scotland, UK.

the sentence, the probability of generating the query term given the sentence term is calculated as follows:

$$P_{\text{trigger}}(q_i|s_j) = \frac{f_C(q_i, s_j)}{\sum_{q_i} f_C(q_i, s_j)} \quad (4)$$

where s_j is the jth term in the sentence and $f_C(q_i, s_j)$ is the number of times the query term q_i triggers the sentence word s_j based on the training corpus C. Using the proposed triggering method for calculating $P(q_i|s_j)$, the likelihood of generating query term q_i given the sentence S is defined as:

$$P_{\text{trigger}}(q_i|S) = \frac{1}{N}\sum_{j=1}^{N} P_{\text{trigger}}(q_i|s_j) \quad (5)$$

where N is the sentence length. As a result, $P(Q|S)$ based on the trained trigger language model is defined as follows:

$$P_{\text{trigger}}(Q|S) = (\frac{1}{N})^M \prod_{i=1}^{M}\sum_{j=1}^{N} \frac{f_C(q_i, s_j)}{\sum_{q_i} f_C(q_i, s_j)} \quad (6)$$

Similar to the basic word unigram model, a smoothing technique is required to deal with zero probabilities of unseen words. Any of the smoothing methods proposed for the word unigram model can also be applied to this model.

Comparing the time complexity of the proposed model with the normal unigram model. For each input query, the word unigram model is running in $O(KM)$ time, where K is the number of sentences in the search space and M is the query length. In the trained trigger language model, we have an additional factor which is the number of words in the sentence to be retrieved. As a result, the running time of the trigger model is $O(KMN)$. Although the time complexity of our model is higher than the word unigram model, it is still identical to the translation model.

3. TYPES OF TRIGGERING

3.1 Inside Sentence Triggering

This model assumes that there is a relation between the words which appear in the same sentences. To use *inside sentence triggering*, the model should be trained on a large unannotated corpus while considering that each word in a sentence triggers all other words in the same sentence.

Using this model, we can retrieve sentences which do not share many terms with the query, but their terms frequently co-occur with the query terms in the same sentences of the training corpus. To be more precise, consider the sample sentences in Figure 1 and the following question and the answer sentence:

Q: *"Who invented the automobile?"*

A: *"Nicolas Joseph Cugnot invented the first self propelled mechanical vehicle."*

Using the question as a query in word unigram, we only have one common term *"invent"* between the query and the sentence which is not enough to rank this correct sentence highly, since there are many sentences in the search space which contain the word *"invent"*, such as:

– *"Edison invented the first commercially practical light."*

– *"Alexander Graham Bell of Scotland is the inventor of the first practical telephone."*

Inside sentence triggering, however, gives a higher score to the correct sentence; because it knows the word *"automobile"* triggers the target word *"vehicle"*, since they frequently co-occur in the same sentences of the training corpus.

S:	*"The word automobile means a vehicle that moves itself."*
S:	*"An automobile includes at least two seats located one behind the other and attachable to a vehicle floor."*

Figure 1: Inside sentence triggering samples

S1:	*"Wembley Stadium was built by Australian company Brookfield Multiplex."*
S2:	*"The stadium was scheduled to open in 2006."*
S1:	*"The structure of Eiffel Tower was built between 1887 and 1889."*
S2:	*"The tower was inaugurated on 31 March 1889, and opened on 6 May."*

Figure 2: Across sentence triggering samples

3.2 Across Sentence Triggering

Across sentence triggering uses a wider context than inside sentence triggering: it considers that each word in a sentence triggers all words in the next sentence of the training corpus. Because two adjacent sentences normally talk about the same topic and it is very likely that different words with the same concept are used in two consecutive sentences.

As an example, consider a corpus which contains the adjacent sentences presented in Figure 2. Using such a training corpus, we can find that the word *"build"* triggers the word *"open"* which is in the next sentence. As a result, this trained trigger model can retrieve the correct answer for the following question:

Q: *"Where was the first McDonald's built?"*

A: *"Two brothers from Manchester, Dick and Mac McDonald, open the first McDonald's in California."*

It is clear that word unigram is not able to rank the correct sentence highly; because there are many sentences in the search space talking about *"first McDonald's"*, but non-relevant to the question, such as:

– *"The site of the first McDonald's to be franchised by Ray Kroc is now a museum in Des Plaines, Illinois."*

– *"The first McDonald's TV commercial was a pretty low-budget affair."*

3.3 Question and Answer Pair Triggering

Another notion of triggering derives from using more supervision when training the model. This notion of triggering requires a set of question and answer pairs as a training corpus. In *question and answer pair triggering*, each word in the question triggers all words which appear in the answer sentence. Again this model can retrieve sentences which share no or few words with the question but their terms frequently co-occur with question terms in question and answer pairs that are used to train the model.

As an example, consider the following question and its correct answer sentence.

Q: *"How high is Everest?"*

A: *"Everest is 29,029 feet."*

Similar to the previous examples, the above question and answer share a very limited number of terms, in this case only the term *"Everest"*. As a result, it is very unlikely that the word unigram model ranks the correct answer highly. Because there are many non-relevant sentences in the search space which contain the word *"Everest"*, such as:

– *"Everest is located in Nepal."*

Q:	*"How high is Mount Hood?"*	
A:	*"Mount Hood is in the Cascade Mountain range and is 11,245 feet."*	
Q:	*"How high is Pikes peak?"*	
A:	*"Pikes peak, Colorado At 14,110 feet, altitude sickness is a consideration when driving up this mountain."*	

Figure 3: QA pair triggering samples

– *"Everest has two main climbing routes."*
However, the question and answer pair triggering model gives a higher score to the correct sentence because the model knows that in a large portion of questions that contain the word *"high"*, the term *"feet"* appears in the answer, as shown in Figure 3. As a result, in the trained model, the word *"high"* triggers the target word *"feet"*.

4. THE INTERPOLATION MODEL

As mentioned, the proposed trained trigger language model aims to capture relationships between words and use these relations in the retrieval step. As a result, the model is able to find more relevant sentences and increase system recall reasonably. This method may decrease the system precision, however, by retrieving more non-relevant sentences. To avoid this problem, it is essential to use word unigram in combination with the other notions of triggering. To this end, we use the linear interpolation [3] of our proposed triggering model and the baseline exact matching model, thereby benefiting from the advantages of both models and avoiding their disadvantages.

To use the interpolation of word unigram and triggering, the probability of generating q_i is computed from Equation 2 and 5 and interpolated by weighting parameter λ which is tuned using the held-out data:

$$P(Q|S) = \prod_{i=1}^{M}[\lambda\ P_{\text{trigger}}(q_i|S) + (1-\lambda)\ P_{\text{word}}(q_i|S)] \quad (7)$$

5. EXPERIMENTAL RESULTS

5.1 The Dataset

To evaluate our methods, we used the set of factoid questions from TREC[1] 2005 and 2006 QA track. The set of questions from 2006 was used as test data, while the 2005 question set was used as held-out data to study the smoothing parameters and interpolation weights. The TREC QA 2006 contains 75 question-series that each of them focuses on a target. The series contained a total of 403 factoid questions. For sentence-level relevance judgments, we used the *Question Answer Sentence Pair (QASP)* corpus [4].

For each of the proposed notions of triggering, we need to estimate the corresponding parameters during a training phase using a training corpus. For a part of experiments which applies inside or across sentence triggering, a large unannotated corpus is required to train the models in an unsupervised fashion. For this purpose, we used *AQUAINT1* corpus[2]. For the other part of experiments, which uses question and answer pair triggering, we need to train our models in a supervised fashion in which a corpus of question and answer sentence pairs is required. As for the supervised

Table 1: Performance of the trained trigger language model with different notions of triggering interpolated with word unigram. (TTLM stands for Trained Trigger Language Model)

Model	MAP	MRR
Word Unigram	0.3701	0.5047
Unigram + Inside Sentence TTLM	0.4351	0.5572
Unigram + Across Sentence TTLM	0.4381	0.5631
Unigram + QA Pair TTLM (QASP)	0.4208	0.5492
Unigram + QA Pair TTLM (Yahoo)	0.4371	0.5654

model, we used the QASP corpus[3] and the *Yahoo! Answers Comprehensive Questions and Answers* corpus[4]. Since the questions of TREC QA 2005 and 2006 of the QASP corpus are used as held-out and test data respectively, we only used the questions of 2002-2004 of the corpus for training, so that there is no overlap between the train and evaluation sets.

5.2 Results and Discussion

To evaluate different notions of triggering we interpolated them with the word unigram model which consider the exact matching between query terms and sentence terms. As we mentioned in Section 4, the proposed triggering types only consider contextual information and they do not give a priority to the sentences that contain the query words. As a result, each of the triggering types are interpolated with word unigram as baseline. Table 1 presents the results of our experiments, interpolating different notions of triggering with word unigram. For all experiments, we used Bayesian smoothing with Dirichlet prior. The results show that using any of the contextual information in addition to the exact matching model significantly improves sentence retrieval performance compared to the word unigram model in which all the improvements are highly statistically significant ($p < 0.01$) according to the 2-tailed paired t-test.

The results verify that both exact matching and triggering models play important roles in retrieving answer sentences. When the exact matching model avoids returning non-relevant sentences, it fails to find most of the relevant sentences which share few words with the question. The triggering model, on the other hand, is able to capture more relevant sentences and enhance retrieval performance when it is integrated with the exact matching model. In addition to the above observation, comparing different notions of triggering, the following points should be highlighted:

- Comparing the results of the unsupervised notions triggering, we can see that inside sentence triggering and across sentence triggering perform close to each other. It might be due to the similar word relationship that they capture.
- Comparing the results of question and answer triggering based on different corpora, we can see that the model trained on the Yahoo! Answers corpus outperforms the model trained on the QASP corpus. This observation indicates that even though the Yahoo! Answers corpus is from a different and much broader domain than the QASP corpus and it includes more noisier data than QASP, it significantly improves the system performance due to sheer size. In addition, this result shows that although automatic QA systems are

[1]`http://trec.nist.gov`
[2]See catalog number LDC2002T31 at `http://www.ldc.upenn.edu/Catalog`

[3]`http://homepages.inf.ed.ac.uk/s0570760/data`
[4]`http://webscope.sandbox.yahoo.com`

Table 2: Comparing the results of trained trigger model with the translation model and class model. Significant differences with the translation model and class model are marked by t and c respectively.

Model	Estimation	MAP	MRR
Unigram	-	0.3701	0.5047
Translation	Mutual Information	0.3927	0.5348
Class-based	Word Bigram	0.4174	0.5527
Trigger	Inside Sentence	0.4351^{**t}_{**c}	0.5572
Trigger	Across Sentence	0.4381^{**t}_{**c}	0.5631^{*t}

considered a different topic from community QA forums, the later ones can be a great help to improve the performance of the former ones.

- Overall, the question and answer pair triggering based on the Yahoo! Answers corpus, which achieved the best performance in supervised training, performs similar to the unsupervised notions of triggering. This observation shows that even without using an annotated corpus we can achieve significant improvements that are comparable with the supervised methods.

As we saw, using the trained trigger language model significantly improves sentence retrieval performance compared to the standard word unigram model which does not consider such contextual information. In another step of our experiments, we compared our proposed trained trigger model with the state-of-the-art language modeling techniques which address the same problem of information retrieval. To this aim, we implemented the translation model [1] in which mutual information is used for estimating the translation probability [5]. As shown by Karimzadehgan and Zhai [5], normalized mutual information between word pairs is the best estimation of the statistical translation model and outperforms the original translation model [1] which is estimated based on synthetic queries. Following Karimzadehgan and Zhai [5], we estimated translation models using normalized mutual information between word pairs and regularized the models by self-translation probabilities. To have a reasonable comparison between the translation model and our trained trigger model, we used the AQUAINT1 corpus for calculating mutual information.

In addition to the translation model, we also implemented the class-based model using cluster of words [7]. The class-based model is also aims to relax the exact matching assumption made by the word unigram model. As shown by Momtazi et al. [6] using bigram statistics of terms in a corpus is the best estimation for word clustering. Following Momtazi and Klakow [7], we used Brown word clustering algorithm [2] while using word bigram statistics to cluster lexical items. To estimate word bigrams, we again used the AQUAINT1 corpus. Therefore, we have an identical corpus for all three models. Table 2 presents the results of the translation and the class-based models. To have the models being comparable, we repeated parts of our results from Table 1. We only represented the triggering models which use the same corpus (AQUAINT1) for training. Results are marked as significant* ($p < 0.05$), or highly significant** ($p < 0.01$), or neither according to 2-tailed paired t-test.

As shown by the tabulated results, the proposed trained trigger language model significantly outperforms the translation and the class models. Although these two models also address the word mismatch problem and outperform the standard word unigram model, both of them underperform our trained trigger language model. These results verify the superiority of the trained trigger language model in capturing word relationships compared to the translation and the class models.

6. CONCLUDING REMARKS

In this paper, we proposed a new language model for sentence-level retrieval which is able to capture term relationships by finding pairs of trigger and target words based on their co-occurrence. AQUAINT1 as a large corpus of raw text is used to train our trigger language model in an unsupervised fashion while two different types of triggering have been considered: inside sentence triggering which uses the information of co-occurring words in the same sentences, and across sentence triggering which crosses sentence boundaries and finds relation between terms that appear in two consecutive sentences. The QASP corpus from TREC QA track and the Yahoo! Answers corpus from Yahoo QA forum are used to train our model in a supervised fashion called question and answer pair triggering.

The results indicated that our trained trigger language model outperforms the state-of-the-art translation model and class model. The proposed model achieved 2.63% *absolute* improvement in MAP compared to the class model based on Brown word clustering algorithm [7]. The model also achieved 5.10% *absolute* improvement compared to the translation model based on mutual information [5].

7. ACKNOWLEDGMENTS

The authors would like to thank Yahoo! Labs Webscope for their Yahoo! Answers Comprehensive Questions and Answers corpus. Saeedeh Momtazi is funded by the German research foundation DFG through the International Research Training Group (IRTG 715).

8. REFERENCES

[1] A. Berger and J. Lafferty. Information Retrieval as Statistical Translation. In *ACM SIGIR*, pages 222–229. ACM, 1999.

[2] P. Brown, V. Pietra, P. Souza, J. Lai, and R. Mercer. Class-based N-gram Models of Natural Language. *Computational Linguistics*, 18(4):467–479, 1992.

[3] F. Jelinek and R. Mercer. Interpolated Estimation of Markov Source Parameters from Sparse Data. In *Proceedings of an International Workshop on Pattern Recognition in Practice*, 1989.

[4] M. Kaisser and J. Lowe. Creating a Research Collection of Question Answer Sentence Pairs with Amazon's Mechanical Turk. In *LREC*, 2008.

[5] M. Karimzadehgan and C. Zhai. Estimation of Statistical Translation Models based on Mutual Information for Ad-hoc Information Retrieval. In *ACM SIGIR*, pages 323–330. ACM, 2010.

[6] S. Momtazi, S. Khudanpur, and D. Klakow. A Comparative Study of Word Co-occurrence for Term Clustering in Language Model-based Sentence Retrieval. In *NAACL-HLT*. Association for Computational Linguistics, 2010.

[7] S. Momtazi and D. Klakow. A Word Clustering Approach for Language Model-based Sentence Retrieval in Question Answering Systems. In *ACM CIKM*, pages 1911–1914. ACM, 2009.

Topic Modeling for Named Entity Queries

Xiaobing Xue
Center for Intelligent Information Retrieval
Computer Science Department
University of Massachusetts, Amherst, MA, 01003, USA
xuexb@cs.umass.edu

Xiaoxin Yin
Microsoft Research
One Microsoft Way
Redmond, WA 98052
xyin@microsoft.com

ABSTRACT

Named entities are observed in a large portion of web search queries (named entity queries), where each entity can be associated with many different query terms that refer to various aspects of this entity. Organizing these query terms into topics helps understand major search intents about entities and the discovered topics are useful for applications such as query suggestion. Furthermore, we notice that named entities can often be organized into categories and those from the same category share many generic topics. Therefore, working on a category of named entities instead of individual ones helps avoid the problems caused by the sparsity and noise in the data. In this paper, Named Entity Topic Model (NETM) is proposed to discover generic topics for a category of named entities, where the quality of the generic topics is improved through the model design and the parameter initialization. Experiments based on query log data show that NETM discovers high-quality topics and outperforms the state-of-the-art techniques by 12.8% based on F1 measure.

Categories and Subject Descriptors

H.3.3 [Information Storage and Retrieval]: Information Search and Retrieval

General Terms

Algorithms, Experimentation, Performance

Keywords

Verbose Query, Query Distribution, Query Reformulation

1. INTRODUCTION

Named entities have been widely observed in web search queries. It is reported in [7] that about 71% of queries in the search traffic contain named entities. The *named entity* or simply *entity* discussed here is defined as any proper name, such as names of film actors/actresses, names of car models and names of cities. We study *named entity queries*, which consist of two parts: *the named entity* and *the topic term*. For example, considering two named entity queries "Britney Spears biography" and "Seattle things to do", "Britney Spears" and "Seattle" are named entities and "biography" and "things to do" are the corresponding topic terms. Note that a topic term could be either a word or a phrase.

CIKM'11, October 24–28, 2011, Glasgow, Scotland, UK.

Table 1: The topic terms observed for the named entity "Seattle"

restaurants, things to do in, events, apartments, attractions, airport shuttle, dining, transportation, vacation rentals, houses for rent in, brunch, subway			
Topic 1	**Topic 2**	**Topic 3**	**Topic 4**
things to do in events attractions	airport shuttle transportation subway	restaurants dining brunch	apartments vacation rentals houses for rent in

Many different topic terms are usually observed for a named entity, where each of them refers to some topic about this named entity. Some examples of the topic terms observed for the named entity "Seattle" are displayed in the upper part of Table 1 (ranked by their query frequencies). Organizing these topic terms according to their underlying topics helps search engines understand major search intents about "Seattle". An approach proposed in this paper[1] is able to group these terms into four major topics (as shown in the lower part of Table 1).

Motivated by the above example, we study how to automatically discover topics for named entities from their associated topic terms. The discovered topics and their associated topic terms can be used in applications such as query suggestion. For instance, when the user searches for the query "Seattle tourism", it is useful to suggest the alternative queries from the same topic (Topic 1) such as "Seattle things to do" and "Seattle attractions". It is also useful to allow the user to explore other topics about "Seattle" such as its transportation (Topic 2) and restaurants (Topic 3).

Furthermore, we notice that named entities can be organized by categories. The named entities from the same category share many generic topics. For example, "Boston", "Chicago", "San Francisco" and "Seattle" all belong to the US City category and the topics discovered for "Seattle" above are also applicable to the other three cities. Therefore, instead of detecting topics for individual named entity, we consider to discover *generic topics* for a category of named entities, which avoids the problems caused by the sparsity and noise in the topic terms of individual named entity, especially for those unpopular ones.

Topic modeling for documents [8, 2] has been widely studied in the literature. Similar ideas are applied here to named entity queries. Specifically, we transform the query click

[1]The details will be described in the following parts.

data into a collection of pseudo documents, where each pseudo document consists of topic terms related to a certain named entity. In this paper, we propose a novel topic modeling approach, i.e. Named Entity Topic Model (NETM), which detects the generic topics for a category of named entities. Two strategies are used by NETM to improve the quality of the generic topics. First, the *entity-specific topic* is introduced in the model to include the topic terms that are specific to a certain or a small number of named entities and cannot be classified into any generic topic. For example, the topic terms "Mandalay Bay" and "Caesars Palace" are both famous hotels of "Las Vegas" and they are less likely to appear with other entities. An analysis based on sampled named entity queries shows that 35% queries contain the topic terms applied to only one named entity, thus, without the entity-specific topics, these terms would have to be assigned to some generic topics. Second, a parameter initialization strategy based on the seed term selection guides the model to focus on the generic topics. Experiments based on query log data show that NETM discovers high-quality topics and outperforms the state-of-the-art techniques by 12.8% based on F1 measure.

2. RELATED WORK

This paper studies how to organize topic terms according to their underlying topics, which is somehow similar to previous work on query suggestion that groups semantically related queries together. Different techniques have been proposed including using temporal behavior [11, 5], considering session context [6, 4], building query flow graphs[3] and combining click data and session data [10]. In general, these techniques work on individual queries and thus cannot work well for unpopular queries. In this paper, the generic topics are discovered for a category of named entities, which can be reasonably applied to those unpopular named entities.

Wang et al [12] used query reformulation data extracted from search session to mine broad latent query aspects. They detected common query aspects applicable to most queries. However, a large portion of important topics are category specific and thus can not be detected by their approach.

Paşca and Durme [9] studied how to extract open-domain classes and class attributes from web documents and query logs. However, they did not consider how to organize these class attributes into different topics.

Balasubramanian and Cucerzan [1] studied to generate topic pages of living people. Their aspect model for each person is simply a collection of cooccurrence words with that person. These words are also not organized into topics.

Recently, Yin and Shah [13] considered to build taxonomy of search intents for named entity queries. Our work, independently developed during the same period as their work, shares several related insights. Despite the high level similarities, the approaches used are significantly different.

Topic model has been studied for a long time in information retrieval and natural language processing. The classic models include PLSA [8] and LDA [2]. Recently, this approach has been applied to a lot of novel applications.

3. NOTATIONS AND PROBLEM DEFINITION

We have a category of entities[2] $E = \{e_1, e_2, ..., e_{|E|}\}$, where $|E|$ denotes the size of E. It is usually easy to get such categories of entities. For example, Wikipedia provides a category for almost any reasonable category of entities.

A vocabulary $V = \{t_1, t_2, ..., t_{|V|}\}$ consists of all possible topic terms about entities in E. A topic term is the part of a query excluding the entity. Note that a topic term can be either a single word or a phrase.

The query click data consists of a set of named entity queries, a set of URLs, and the number of clicks of each query on each URL. The named entity queries are denoted as $Q = \{q|q = (e,t), e \in E, t \in V\}$, where e denotes the entity and t denotes the topic term. The URLs are denoted as $L = \{l_1, l_2, ..., l_{|L|}\}$. The click relations are denoted as $R = \{(q,l) : f(q,l)\}$, where $f(q,l)$ denotes the number of times l is clicked for query q.

A topic T is defined as a multinomial distribution over the vocabulary V of topic terms, where $\sum_{t \in V} P(t|T) = 1$. Here, $P(t|T)$ is the parameters of the topic T. Given a category of entities E, we want to learn k generic topics $GT = \{T_1, T_2, ..., T_k\}$ shared by most entities of this category. In order to improve the quality of GT, we introduce an entity-specific topic for each entity, which is $ET = \{T_{e_1}, T_{e_2}, ..., T_{e_{|E|}}\}$ for all entities. For example, "reviews" is a generic topic learned for the category "car model", where terms like "reviews", "road test" and "ratings" receive high probabilities. For entity "Dodge Charger", its entity-specific topic assigns high probabilities to terms like "police car", "Daytona" and "Super Bee".

4. PSEUDO DOCUMENT CONSTRUCTION

Here, we describe how to transform query click data into a collection of pseudo documents. A pseudo document d is the set of topic terms that appear together with a particular entity e in queries with clicks on a certain URL l. It is defined for each pair of entity and URL (e, l), where d consists of topic terms t that have been used with e as queries (e, t). In addition, l must receive some clicks after posing (e, t). Formally, $d_{e,l} = \{t : c(d,t)\}$. $c(d,t)$ denotes the frequency of t in d, which is equal to $f((e,t),l)$, i.e. the click count on l for query (e,t). The topic terms associated with the same entity and URL pair are likely to talk about the same topic, since a URL (the corresponding web page) usually provides information for one or a few related aspects of an entity. Thus, the above construction process satisfies the assumption of topic models [8, 2], where words co-occurring frequently in documents should belong to the same topic.

For example, the topic terms "2009 accessories", "coupe accessaries" and "accessories" appear with the entity-URL pair (Honda Accord, `http://automobiles.honda.com/...`), thus a pseudo document is constructed for this entity-URL pair that contains all these three terms.

A collection of pseudo documents is defined as $C = \{d_{e,l}|e \in E, l \in L\}$. Our task is to learn generic topics GT from C. We will use "document" for "pseudo document" unless indicated otherwise.

5. TOPIC MODELING FOR NAMED ENTITY QUERIES

5.1 Named Entity Topic Model

In Named Entity Topic Model, we assume each term of a document $d_{e,l}$ is selected either from k generic topics $GT = \{T_1, T_2, ..., T_k\}$, or from the corresponding entity-specific topic

[2]We use "entity" and "named entity" exchangeably.

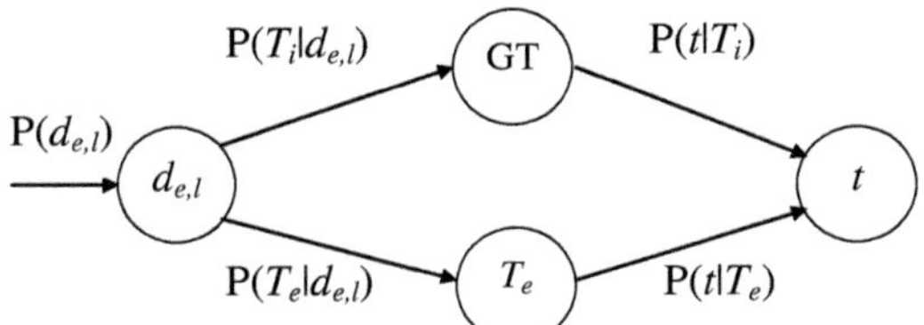

Figure 1: Generation process of NETM.

T_e. The generic topics are used to model topic terms applicable to most entities. The entity-specific topic is used to model topic terms specific to a certain entity. The log likelihood of generating the collection $C = \{d_{e,l}|e \in E, l \in L\}$ is given as follows:

$$Log(C) = \sum_{t \in V, d_{e,l} \in C} c(d_{e,l}, t) \log P(d_{e,l}, t) \quad (1)$$

$$P(d_{e,l}, t) = P(d_{e,l})[\sum_{i=1}^{k} P(T_i|d_{e,l})P(t|T_i) + P(T_e|d_{e,l})P(t|T_e)] \quad (2)$$

Eq. 1 shows that the log likelihood of generating the collection is calculated based on each document and topic term pair $(d_{e,l}, t)$. Eq. 2 calculates the probability of generating such pair, i.e. $P(d_{e,l}, t)$, where $P(T_i|d_{e,l})$ is the probability of selecting a generic topic T_i and $P(T_e|d_{e,l})$ is the probability of selecting the entity-specific topic. After selecting any topic, a topic term t can be generated with the probability $P(t|T_i)$ and $P(t|T_e)$ correspondingly. $P(t|T_i)$ is the parameters of the generic topics and $P(t|T_e)$ is the parameters of the entity-specific topic. The generation process of NETM is further illustrated in Fig. 1. Note that among all entity-specific topics in ET, only T_e that corresponds to the entity e in the subscript of $d_{e,l}$ is used to generate $(d_{e,l}, t)$. The parameters are estimated through Expectation Maximization (EM). The details are omitted due to space limitation.

5.2 Generic Topics Initialization

Here we discuss how to improve the quality of the generic topics through appropriate initialization of its parameters. First, we rank all topic terms t based on the number of entities $NE(t)$ that t has been associated with. Second, we recover the underlying language model of a term t using Zhai and Lafferty's method [14]. Here, the underlying language model LM_t of t is a multinomial distribution, where high probabilities are assigned to not only t but also its semantically related terms. Third, given the top ranked seed terms and their associated underlying language models LM_t, we can easily pick the top k seed terms and use their LM_t to initialize k generic topics. LM_t also helps avoid picking very similar terms, since the similarities between two seed terms can be measured by the KL-divergence between their underlying language models.

6. EXPERIMENTS

6.1 Configuration

We test our approaches on a diverse set of categories of entities, which are chosen to cover different types of entities frequently appearing in user queries. They are shown in Table 2 with number of entities in each category. We remove all entities with an disambiguation page on Wikipedia. The query click data is extracted from the query log of a commercial search engine from 2008/01/01 to 2008/12/31.

Table 2: Categories of named entities

category	#entity	category	#entity
car models	873	universities	7286
clothing stores	114	us cities	236
film actors	19442	us presidents	47
musicians	22846	us retail companies	186
restaurants	735		

The baselines are PLSA [8] and LDA [2], the state-of-the-art topic modeling approaches. PLSA and LDA are applied to the collection of pseudo documents generated. For a fair comparison, different approaches generate the same number of generic topics, i.e. 20 topics. How to dynamically decide the number of topics is beyond the scope of this paper. We implement PLSA by ourselves according to [8]. An existing package LDA-C is used for LDA[3].

6.2 Examples

We display some examples of the generic topics learned by PLSA, LDA and NETM. Table 3 shows two generic topics learned for "universities" and "cars models". The top terms are displayed for each topic[4]. In Table 3, PLSA and LDA mix the terms about different topics together. For example, for the topic "car parts", terms about car parts, terms about car sale like "used" and "for sale", terms about car review like "road test" and terms about car repair like "transmission problems" are also mixed together. In contrast, the quality of the topics generated by NETM is much better. For the topic "universities alumni", NETM also discovers important terms such as "alumni directory" and "class rings".

6.3 Evaluation

In this part, we quantitatively compare the quality of the generic topics generated by different approaches. For each category in Table 2, we sample 100 named entity queries from the query log data based on query frequencies to form the test set (in total 100×9=900 queries). For each topic modeling approach TM (i.e. PLSA, LDA and NETM), given a test query (e, t), where e is the entity and t is the topic term, TM will return a generic topic T_i with the highest probability $P(t|T_i)$ among all generic topics. The returned topic T_i is displayed to the annotator[5]. Then, the annotator (from Amazon Mechanical Turk[6]) is asked to provide a relevance judgment (yes or no) according to whether the topic term in the query is well covered by the returned topic. For each pair of query and topic, three different annotators are asked to provide judgments. The standard F1 measure is used here to measure performance.

First, we compare PLSA, LDA and NETM in Table 4. LDA fails to run on four categories (film actors, musicians, US cities and US retail companies), since the size of the collection is too large, which causes the memory problem for LDA-C.

Table 4 shows that NETM consistently outperforms PLSA and LDA on most categories. On average, NETM significantly improves LDA by 13.8% on categories where LDA can run and NETM significantly improves PLSA by 12.8% on all categories.

[3]http://www.cs.princeton.edu/~blei/lda-c/
[4]The name of the topic is constructed by combining the name of categories and the top one term of this topic.
[5]Since annotators are usually not patient to read too much information, only top ranked terms of a topic are displayed.
[6]http://mturk.amazon.com

Table 3: Examples of generic topics learned for categories "universities" and "car model".

PLSA	LDA	NETM	PLSA	LDA	NETM
"car parts"			"universities alumni"		
parts	parts	parts	alumni	alumni	alumni
used	used	accessories	ranking	ranking	alumni association
for sale	for sale	body parts	law school	law school	homecoming
problems	recalls	accesories	school of law	school of law	homecoming 2008
sale	problems	afermaket parts	review	rankings	alumni directory
auto parts	recall	auto parts	rankings	alumni association	class rings
road test	transmission	used parts	alumni association	school of medicine	graduates
transmission problems	sale	oem parts	school of medicine	homecoming	class ring

Table 4: Comparisons of different approaches. The best performance (F1) of each category is bolded.

category	PLSA	LDA	NETM	vs. PLSA	vs. LDA
car model	0.478	0.422	**0.596**	24.7%	41.2%
clothing store	0.589	0.578	**0.676**	14.8%	17.1%
restaurants	0.579	0.585	**0.595**	2.7%	1.7%
universities	0.475	0.508	**0.538**	13.5%	5.9%
US president	0.581	0.519	**0.592**	1.9%	13.9%
average above	0.536	0.514	**0.585**	9.0%	13.8%
film actors	0.575	n/a	**0.615**	7.1%	n/a
musician	**0.553**	n/a	0.514	-7.1%	n/a
US cities	0.304	n/a	**0.625**	105.7%	n/a
US retail	0.718	n/a	**0.731**	1.8%	n/a
average all	0.534	n/a	**0.603**	12.8%	n/a

Table 5: Comparisons with PLSA(LM_t). The best performance (F1) of each category is bolded.

category	PLSA	PLSA(LM_t)	NETM
car model	0.478	0.567	**0.596**
clothing store	0.589	0.599	**0.676**
restaurants	0.579	0.561	**0.595**
universities	0.475	**0.565**	0.538
US president	0.581	0.588	**0.592**
film actors	0.575	**0.684**	0.615
musician	**0.553**	0.536	0.514
US cities	0.304	0.604	**0.625**
Us retail	0.718	0.635	**0.731**
average	0.534	0.568	**0.603**

Second, we make further analysis to understand where the advantages of NETM come. Aforementioned, two strategies are used by NETM to improve the quality of generic topics: the modeling of entity-specific topics and the initialization method. In order to separate their effects, we consider a new approach PLSA(LM_t), that uses the same initialization method as NETM for PLSA, but not modeling the entity-specific topics. The comparisons of each approach are displayed in Table 5.

Table 5 shows that PLSA(LM_t) is better than PLSA, but it is still worse than NETM. Therefore, the advantages of NETM come from both strategies.

Some example is provided to show the effect of the initialization method used by NETM. For the "car model" category, PLSA discovers two generic topics (pictures/wallpaper/ebay...) and (photos/forums/video...)that should have been merged into the same topic. In contrast, NETM successfully avoids this problem by discovering a generic topic (pictures/wallpaper/photos), since NETM recovers the language model of "pictures" for initialization, which not only assigns high probability to "pictures" but also to "photos".

Another example is provided to show the effect of modeling the entity-specific topics. NETM puts the term "watergate" into the entity-specific topic of "Richard Nixon" from the "US president" category. Without any special design for this type of terms, PLSA "randomly" organizes "watergate" into a topic (family tree/ house/descendants of/...) and the probability assigned is as high as 0.014, which deceases the quality of generic topics.

7. CONCLUSION

Named entity queries consist of a big portion of web query traffic. Discovering topics underlying named entity queries are useful for various search applications. A novel topic modeling approach NETM is proposed in this paper to discover generic topics for a category of named entities. Experiments show that NETM detects high-quality topics and significantly outperforms the state-of-the-art techniques.

8. REFERENCES

[1] N. Balasubramanian and S. Cucerzan. Automatic generation of topic pages using query-based aspect models. In *CIKM09*, pages 2049–2052.

[2] D. M. Blei, A. Y. Ng, and M. I. Jordan. Latent dirichlet allocation. *Journal of Machine Learning Research*, 3:993–1022, 2003.

[3] P. Boldi, F. Bonchi, C. Castillo, D. Donato, A. Gionis, and S. Vigna. The query flow graph: model and applications. In *CIKM08*, pages 609–618.

[4] H. Cao, D. Jiang, J. Pei, Q. He, Z. Liao, E. Chen, and H. Li. Context-aware query suggestion by mining click-through and session data. In *KDD08*, pages 875–883.

[5] S. Chien and N. Immorlica. Semantic similarity between search engine queries using temporal correlation. In *WWW05*, pages 2–11.

[6] S. Cucerzan and E. Brill. Extracting semantically related queries by exploiting user session information. In *research.microsoft.com/en-us/people/silviu/np-www06.pdf*, 2006.

[7] J. Guo, G. Xu, X. Cheng, and H. Li. Named entity recognition in query. In *SIGIR09*, pages 267–274.

[8] T. Hofmann. Probabilistic latent semantic analysis. In *UAI99*, pages 289–296.

[9] M. Paşca and B. V. Durme. Weakly-supervised acquisition of open-domain classes and class attributes from web documents and query logs. In *ACL-HLT08*, pages 19–27.

[10] E. Sadikov, J. Madhavan, L. Wang, and A. Halevy. Clustering query refinements by user intent. In *WWW10*, pages 841–850.

[11] M. Vlachos, C. Meek, Z. Vagena, and D. Gunopulos. Identifying similarities, periodicities and bursts for online search queries. In *SIGMOD04*, pages 131–142.

[12] X. Wang, D. Chakrabarti, and K. Punera. Mining broad latent query aspects from search sessions. In *KDD09*, pages 867–876.

[13] X. Yin and S. Shah. Building taxonomy of web search intents for name entity queries. In *WWW10*, pages 1001–1010.

[14] C. Zhai and J. Lafferty. Model-based feedback in the language modeling approach to information retrieval. In *CIKM01*, pages 403–410.

Semantic Convolution Kernels Over Dependency Trees

Danilo Croce
DII
University of Tor Vergata
00133 Roma, Italy
croce@info.uniroma2.it

Alessandro Moschitti
DISI
University of Trento
38123 Povo (TN), Italy
moschitti@disi.unitn.it

Roberto Basili
DII
University of Tor Vergata
00133 Roma, Italy
basili@info.uniroma2.it

ABSTRACT

In recent years, natural language processing techniques have been used more and more in IR. Among other syntactic and semantic parsing are effective methods for the design of complex applications like for example question answering and sentiment analysis. Unfortunately, extracting feature representations suitable for machine learning algorithms from linguistic structures is typically difficult. In this paper, we describe one of the most advanced piece of technology for automatic engineering of syntactic and semantic patterns. This method merges together convolution dependency tree kernels with lexical similarities. It can efficiently and effectively measure the similarity between dependency structures, whose lexical nodes are in part or completely different. Its use in powerful algorithm such as Support Vector Machines (SVMs) allows for fast design of accurate automatic systems. We report some experiments on question classification, which show an unprecedented result, e.g., 41% of error reduction of the former state-of-the-art, along with the analysis of the nice properties of the approach.

Categories and Subject Descriptors: H.3.3 [**Information Systems**]: Information Search and Retrieval - *Selection process; Retrieval models; Information filtering.*

General Terms: Algorithms.

Keywords: Kernel Methods, Natural Language Processing, Question Answering, Support Vector Machines, Syntactic Semantic Structures.

1. INTRODUCTION

Recent years have shown that syntactic and semantic structures are becoming essential for solving complex IR tasks, e.g., in question answering [17, 15, 2, 16] and opinion mining [9, 10, 11].

Tree kernels are a valid approach to avoid the difficulty of manually designing effective features from linguistic structures [14]. Indeed, they can directly define a similarity between data points in terms of all possible substructures in an implicit vector space. However, when the availability of training data is scarce, lexical data in the structures above should be generalized to obtain more general structural patterns.

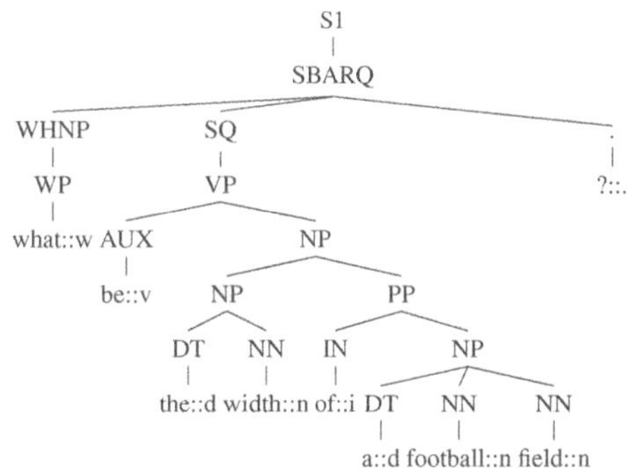

Figure 1: The Constituent Tree (CT) of a question.

In this perspective, one interesting approach, proposed in [3, 4], encoded lexical similarity in tree kernels. The model is essentially the Syntactic Tree Kernel (STK) proposed in [6], in which syntactic fragments from constituency trees can be matched even if they differ in the leaf nodes (i.e., they are constituted by related words with different surface forms). This kernel uses matching scores between fragments (i.e., features) lower than one, depending on the semantic similarity of the corresponding leaves in the syntactic fragments.

Although, such idea is promising and interesting, shows clear limitations: (i) rather limited possibility to exploit semantic smoothing, e.g., trivially the syntactic structure associated with *the big beautiful apple* will only match *apple/orange* when compared to *a nice large orange*; and (ii) STK cannot be effectively applied to dependency structures, e.g., see experiments and motivation in [14]. To overcome such issues, in [7], we augmented the tree kernel in [14], namely the Partial Tree Kernel (PTK), which generalizes STK, with node similarity, e.g. between the lexical nodes. This allows for using any tree and any similarity between nodes in any position of the tree (not just on the leaves as in [4]). In other words, the new Smoothed PTK (SPTK) can automatically provide the learning algorithm, e.g., Support Vector Machines (SVMs), with a huge set of generalized structural patterns by simply applying it to the structural representation of instances of the target task.

In this paper, we analyze SPTK in terms of accuracy, efficiency and error analysis by also comparing it with previous kernels. The extensive experimentation on the question classification (QC) dataset shows that SPTK outperforms any previous kernels achieving an unprecedented result of 41% of error reduction with respect to the former state-of-the-art and it is rather efficient and can be thus applied to a large class of machine learning tasks.

CIKM'11, October 24–28, 2011, Glasgow, Scotland, UK.

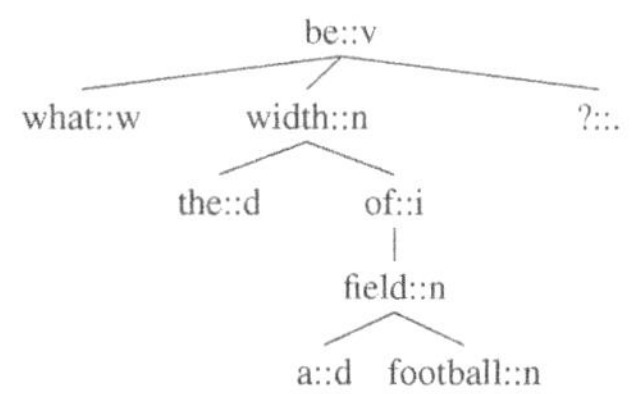

Figure 2: Lexical Only Centered Tree (LOCT).

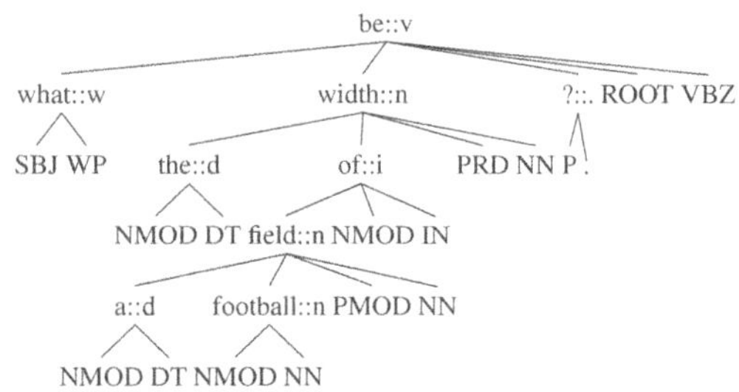

Figure 3: Lexical Centered Tree (LCT).

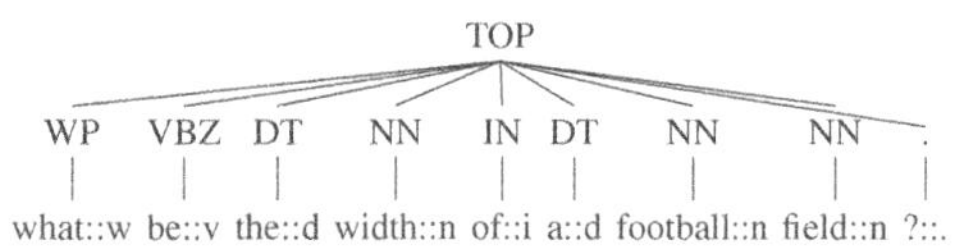

Figure 4: Lexical and PoS-Tag Sequences Tree (LPST).

It should be also noted that the most important property of SPTK is its generalization ability, which of course is extremely useful in scarce training data condition.

In the reminder of this paper, Section 2 illustrates our representation of questions by means of syntactic structures. Section 3 presents the experimental evaluation for QC and Section 4 derives the conclusions.

2. COMPUTATIONAL STRUCTURES FOR QUESTION CLASSIFICATION

Thanks to structural kernel similarity, a question classification (QC) task can be easily modeled by representing questions, i.e., the classification objects, with their parse trees. Several syntactic representations exist, we report the most interesting and effective structures that we proposed in [7]. Given the following sentence:

(s1) *What is the width of a football field?*

the representation tree according to a phrase structure paradigm, i.e. constituency tree (CT), is in Fig. 1. We apply lemmatization to the lexicals to improve generalization and, at the same time, we add a generalized PoS-tag, i.e. noun (n::), verb (v::), adjective (::a), determiner (::d) and so on, to them. This is useful to measure similarity between lexicals belonging to the same grammatical category.

Our conversion of dependency structures in dependency trees is done in two steps:

- we generate the tree that includes only lexicals, where the edges encode their dependencies. We call it the Lexical Only Centered Tree (LOCT), e.g. see Fig. 2.
- To each lexical node, we add two leftmost children, which encode the grammatical function and POS-Tag, i.e., node features. We call this structure the Lexical Centered Tree (LCT), e.g. see Fig. 3.

	STK	PTK	SPTK (LSA)
CT	91.20%	90.80%	91.00%
LOCT	-	89.20%	93.20%
LCT	-	90.80%	**94.80%**
LPST	-	89.40%	89.60%
BOW		88.80%	

Table 1: Accuracy of structural kernels applied to different structures on QC

Additionally, for comparative purposes, we define a flat structure, the Lexical and PoS-tag Sequences Tree (LPST), e.g. see Fig. 4, which ignores the syntactic structure of the sentence being a simple sequence of PoS-tag nodes, where lexicals are simply added as children.

3. EXPERIMENTS

The aim of the experiments is to analyze the role of lexical similarity embedded in syntactic structures. For this purpose, we present results on QC and the related error analysis.

3.1 Setup

Our referring corpus is the UIUC dataset [13]. It is composed by a training set of 5,452 questions and a test set of 500 questions[1]. The latter are organized in six coarse-grained classes, i.e., ABBREVIATION, ENTITY, DESCRIPTION, HUMAN, LOCATION and NUMBER.

For learning our models, we extended the SVM-LightTK software[2] [14, 15] (which includes structural kernels, i.e., STK and PTK in SVMLight [8]) with the smooth match between tree nodes, i.e. the SPTK defined in [7].

For generating constituency trees, we used Charniak's parser [5] whereas we applied LTH syntactic parser (described in [12]) to generate dependency trees.

The lexical similarity was designed with LSA applied to ukWak [1], which is a large scale document collection made by 2 billion tokens (see [7] for more details). We implemented multi-classification using *one-vs-all* scheme and selecting the category associated with the maximum SVM margin.

3.2 Classification Results

The F1 of SVMs using (i) STK applied to CT and (ii) PTK and SPTK applied to the several structures for QC is reported in Table 1. The first column shows the different structures described in Section 2. The first row lists the tree kernel models. The last row reports the accuracy of bag-of-words (BOW), which is a linear kernel applied to vectors of words.

It is worth nothing that:

- BOW produces high accuracy, i.e. 88.8% but it is improved by STK, current state-of-the-art[3] in QC [18, 14, 17];
- PTK applied to the same tree of STK (i.e. CT) produces a slightly lower value (non-statistically significant difference); and
- PTK applied to LCT, which contains structures but also grammatical functions and PoS-tags, achieves higher accuracy than

[1]http://cogcomp.cs.illinois.edu/Data/QA/QC/
[2]http://disi.unitn.it/moschitti/Tree-Kernel.htm
[3]Note that higher accuracy values for smoothed STK are shown in [4] but the one optimizing a validation set is not shown.

when applied to LOCT (no grammatical/syntactic features) or to LPST (no structure).

Most importantly, SPTK (using LSA similarity):

- improves PTK on all the syntactic-based structures;
- gets the lowest improvement when applied to CT; and
- achieves the impressive result of 94.80% with LCT, i.e, more than 41% of relative reduction of the BOW error.

This suggests that patterns formed by sequences of similar lexicals need to be selected according to their syntactic structures to produce accurate results. Indeed, when syntax is missing such as for the unstructured lexical sequences of LPST, the accuracy does not highly improve.

To better understand the role of lexical similarity in syntactic structures, in the next section, we will outline the advantages of SPTK over the other models by analyzing classification errors.

3.3 Error Analysis

Table 2 shows four questions of the test set (labelled form 1 to 4) along with: the flags +/- asserting the presence or not of an error, the classification model, the true label of the question and the one given by the classifiers.

The first question is not correctly classified by BOW, which assigned ENTITY category. Indeed, from a bag-of-words perspective ENTITY and LOCATION are equally probable for Question 1, e.g., the question *What is the French cognac produced in province?* uses the same words but asks for an entity. However, it is enough to add some syntactic cues to solve the above ambiguity. For example, the previous question would generate a dependency between *What* and *is* whereas Question 1 generates a dependency between *What* and *French province*. These syntactic features are contained in both tree representation paradigms. As a consequence, all the syntactic-based models correctly classify this example.

The second question is mistaken by all models but SPTK. The explanation is that without knowing that *ruler* is a person, it is not possible to infer the expected category of the answer. Indeed, if *ruler* had been a synonym of *army* or *region* the expected answer type would have been ENTITY. SPTK can disambiguate between ENTITY and HUMAN by exploiting the similarity with the training question *What Mexican leader was shot dead in 1923 ?*. This shows some structural similarity, which is reinforced by the lexical similarity between *French* and *Mexican*, between *ruler* and *leader*, and between *defeat* and *shot*.

A similar rationale applies to the third question: without knowing that *peninsula* indicates a geographic location the most probable category could be ENTITY. In contrast, SPTK can provide the correct answer by measuring the structural similarity of Question 3 with the training question: *What island group is Guadalcanal a part of ?* along with the lexical similarity between *peninsula* and *island* and between *Spain* and *Guadalcanal*.

The last question is correctly classified only using the dependency structure. The BOW model is too influenced by words such as *least*, *amount* and *per*. The costituency structure fails as well, probably because it does not contain structures encoding lexical trigrams like *what-state-have*, which instead are subtrees of LCT.

Finally, the errors of SPTK refer to questions like *What did Jesse Jackson organize?*, where the classifier selected ENTITY instead of HUMAN category, or *What is the melting point of copper ?* where ENTITY is selected instead of the correct NUMBER. These are clear examples where specific background knowledge is needed to provide the correct answer.

What French province is cognac produced in? (1)			
-	BOW	LOC	ENTY
+	CT-STK		LOC
+	LCT-PTK		LOC
+	LCT-SPTK		LOC
What French ruler was defeated at the battle of Waterloo? (2)			
-	BOW	HUM	ENTY
-	CT-STK		ENTY
-	LCT-PTK		ENTY
+	LCT-SPTK		HUM
What peninsula is Spain part of? (3)			
-	BOW	LOC	ENTY
-	CT-STK		ENTY
-	LCT-PTK		ENTY
+	LCT-SPTK		LOC
What state has the least amount of rain per year? (4)			
-	BOW	LOC	NUM
-	CT-STK		NUM
+	LCT-PTK		LOC
+	LCT-SPTK		LOC

Table 2: Some interesting question classification case

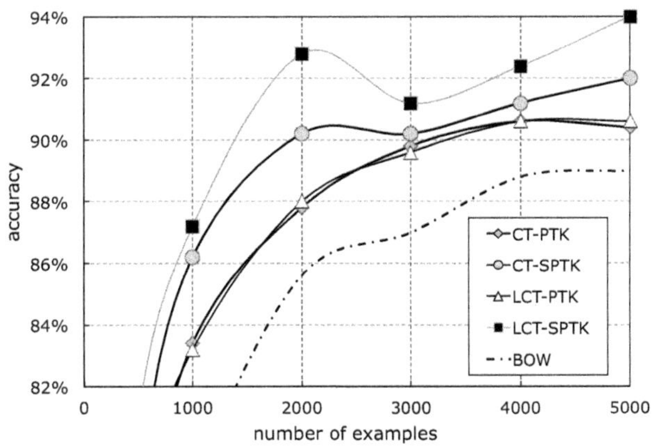

Figure 5: Learning curves: comparison with no similarity

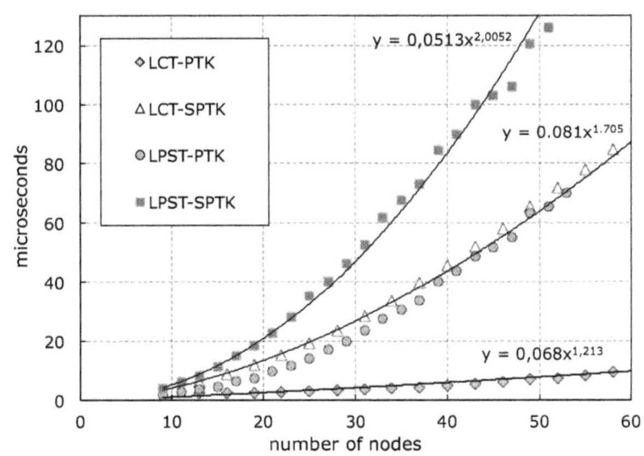

Figure 6: Micro-seconds for each kernel computation

3.4 Kernel generalization and efficiency

To understand the role of syntactic/semantic kernels, it is interesting to study their impact on the SVM generalization. For this purpose, Fig. 5 reports the learning curve of BOW, of STK and PTK applied to CT and of PTK and SPTK applied to LCT. We note that:

- BOW learning curve is clearly below those of syntactic-based models;
- LCT and CT (dependency and constituency paradigms) show very similar curves, suggesting that the two syntactic representations are equivalent; and
- when SPTK is used (i.e., CT-SPTK and LCT-SPTK) the generalization of SVMs meaningful increases.
- SPTK applied to LCT shows the steepest curve, achieving with just 1/5 of the available data the same accuracy of BOW on all data.

The benefits in terms of accuracy of SPTK are clear thus it is important to demonstrate that it can be efficiently applied to large datasets. For this purpose, we plotted the average running time of each computation of PTK and SPTK applied to the different structures. We divided the examples from QC based on the number of nodes in each example. Fig. 6 shows the elapsed time in function of the number of nodes for different tree representations. We note that: (i) LCT-PTK is very fast as we used the fast algorithm designed in [14]; (ii) LCT-SPTK is also very fast as it uses the same algorithm of PTK but, as it tends to match many more tree fragments, its complexity increases. However, the equation of the curve fit, shown in the figure, suggests that the trend is sub-quadratic, i.e., $x^{1.7}$. This efficiency is due to the tree structure, which imposes hierarchical matching of subtrees. (iii) Only when SPTK is applied to LPST, which has no structure, it matches all possible similar subsequences of nodes. This increases its computational complexity, which results in an order higher than 2.

4. CONCLUSIONS

This paper has investigated the properties of a novel tree kernel, namely SPTK, which can encode generalized syntactic patterns from dependency or constituency structures. The main characteristic of SPTK is its ability to measure the similarity between syntactic structures, which are partially similar and whose lexical nodes can be different but related, e.g., Mexican and Spain. This allows SVMs to exploit large feature spaces, automatically generated from dependency substructures.

We have tested SPTK on the question classification (QC) task by also comparing with previous state-of-the-art models. The results show that SPTK with SVMs achieves an unprecedented result for QC, i.e., 94.8% of accuracy.

The error analysis has revealed that syntactic structures are needed to disambiguate the lexical semantics of questions. However, they may be either too general if lexicals are not part of them or too sparse if they are based on several lexicals. Therefore, SPTK, generalizing the latter, provides a compromise that improves accuracy and generalization ability of SVMs.

Finally, we have also investigated the computational complexity of SPTK by empirically showing that it can easily scale to large datasets. Such result enables many promising future research directions: the most important being the use of SPTK for many IR tasks with many different similarities. It is also interesting to note that SPTK can be applied to trees completely different from syntactic parses, e.g., XML trees, on which a general semantic similarity can be defined between nodes.

Acknowledgements

This work has been partially supported by the EC project FP247758: Trustworthy Eternal Systems via Evolving Software, Data and Knowledge (EternalS).

5. REFERENCES

[1] M. Baroni, S. Bernardini, A. Ferraresi, and E. Zanchetta. The wacky wide web: a collection of very large linguistically processed web-crawled corpora. *Language Resources and Evaluation*, 43(3):209–226, 2009.

[2] M. W. Bilotti, J. L. Elsas, J. Carbonell, and E. Nyberg. Rank learning for factoid question answering with linguistic and semantic constraints. In *Proceedings of ACM CIKM*, 2010.

[3] S. Bloehdorn and A. Moschitti. Combined syntactic and semantic kernels for text classification. In *Proceedings of ECIR 2007, Rome, Italy*, 2007.

[4] S. Bloehdorn and A. Moschitti. Structure and semantics for expressive text kernels. In *Proceedings of CIKM*, 2007.

[5] E. Charniak. A maximum-entropy-inspired parser. In *Proceedings of NAACL'00*, 2000.

[6] M. Collins and N. Duffy. New Ranking Algorithms for Parsing and Tagging: Kernels over Discrete Structures, and the Voted Perceptron. In *Proceedings of ACL'02*, 2002.

[7] D. Croce, A. Moschitti, and R. Basili. Structured lexical similarity via convolution kernels on dependency trees. In *Proceedings of EMNLP*, Edinburgh, Scotland, UK., 2011.

[8] T. Joachims. Estimating the generalization performance of a SVM efficiently. In *Proceedings of ICML'00*, 2000.

[9] R. Johansson and A. Moschitti. Reranking models in fine-grained opinion analysis. In *Proceedings of Coling 2010*, pages 519–527, Beijing, China, 2010.

[10] R. Johansson and A. Moschitti. Syntactic and semantic structure for opinion expression detection. In *Proceedings of CoNLL*, pages 67–76, Uppsala, Sweden, 2010.

[11] R. Johansson and A. Moschitti. Extracting opinion expressions and their polarities – exploration of pipelines and joint models. In *Proceedings of ACL-HLT*, Portland, Oregon, USA, 2011.

[12] R. Johansson and P. Nugues. Dependency-based syntactic–semantic analysis with PropBank and NomBank. In *Proceedings of CoNLL*, Manchester, United Kingdom, 2008.

[13] X. Li and D. Roth. Learning question classifiers. In *Proceedings of ACL'02*, 2002.

[14] A. Moschitti. Efficient convolution kernels for dependency and constituent syntactic trees. In *Proceedings of ECML'06*, pages 318–329, 2006.

[15] A. Moschitti. Kernel methods, syntax and semantics for relational text categorization. In *Proceeding of CIKM '08*, NY, USA, 2008.

[16] A. Moschitti, J. Chu-carroll, S. Patwardhan, J. Fan, and G. Riccardi. Using syntactic and semantic structural kernels for classifying definition questions in jeopardy! In *Proceedings of EMNLP*, Edinburgh, Scotland, UK., 2011.

[17] A. Moschitti, S. Quarteroni, R. Basili, and S. Manandhar. Exploiting syntactic and shallow semantic kernels for question/answer classification. In *Proceedings of ACL'07*, 2007.

[18] D. Zhang and W. S. Lee. Question classification using support vector machines. In *Proceedings of ACM SIGIR*. ACM Press, 2003.

Recommending Citations with Translation Model

Yang Lu, Jing He, Dongdong Shan, Hongfei Yan
Department of Computer Science and Technology, Peking University, China
{luyang,hj,sdd,yhf}@net.pku.edu.cn

ABSTRACT

Citation Recommendation is useful for an author to find out the papers or books that can support the materials she is writing about. It is a challengeable problem since the vocabulary used in the content of papers and in the citation contexts are usually quite different. To address this problem, we propose to use translation model, which can bridge the gap between two heterogeneous languages. We conduct an experiment and find the translation model can provide much better candidates of citations than the state-of-the-art methods.

Categories and Subject Descriptors

H.3.3 [**Information Systems**]: Information Search and Retrieval

General Terms

Algorithms, Experimentation

Keywords

Citation Recommendation, Translation Model

1. INTRODUCTION

The citation recommendation system is very useful for an author who is writing a paper or a book. It is a general case that the author forgets the specific paper containing some material when she wrote about it. The material may be a method, some statistic data or the conclusion from other researchers. If the author misses the detailed citation for these materials, the reviewers or editors may ask the author to add. Figure 1 shows a wikipedia example, in which the editor labels "citation needed" at the location where a citation is needed. (Such location is usually called *citation placeholder*). For the authors or the editors, it would be easier if the citation recommendation system can provide some candidate papers containing the required information about the used material.

CIKM'11, October 24–28, 2011, Glasgow, Scotland, UK.

For *x,y* on *S*, certain functions *K*(*x,y*) can be expressed as an inner product (in usually a different space). *K* is often referred to as a *kernel* or a *kernel function*. The word *kernel* is used in different ways throughout mathematics. The kernel of linear algebra (meaning set of solutions) is close in meaning but not exactly the same.[citation needed]

If one is lucky or insightful regarding a particular machine learning problem, one may manually construct \varphi: S \to V such that

Figure 1: A Citation Needed Example on Wikipedia

A quick solution is to take the context of the *citation placeholder* as a query, and search the papers' content with some state-of-the-art IR methods. Unfortunately, this kind of method cannot work very well. The main reason is that the vocabulary used in the citation context is not same as that used in the paper's content. For example, the abstract usually only contains very brief information about a paper, but the full text may contain too much noise. In some other cases, the jargon may be different for different research fields or/and for different periods.

Instead of the paper's own content, some researchers leverage the paper's cited context to represent the paper [3]. The assumption of this method is that the cited contexts of one paper may be similar to each other. However, one difficulty for this method is that the cited context of one paper is usually sparse due to the long tail phenomenon. For some recent paper, they may even have no citation yet. Therefore, it is very challengeable to find out the papers with very few citations.

In this paper, we address the citation recommendation problem with the translation model. The translation model is originally used in translation text in one language to another, and it is also applied in retrieving the document whose content is heterogeneous to the queries (e.g., cross-language retrieval). In the citation recommendation problem, the citation contexts and the content of papers are actually quite different in nature, and the translation model can bridge the gap between them. We conduct an experiment on a paper collection, and find the translation model can perform better than the state-of-art method.

The contribution of this paper is as follows:

1. We propose translation model for the citation recommendation problem

2. We deploys an experiment to verify that the translation model works better than two baseline methods

3. We compare the performance of translation models on

different fields of the paper content, finding the abstract based model can perform better

2. RELATED WORK

In this section, we will introduce the related in citation recommendation and translation model.

2.1 Citation Recommendation

Citation recommendation is a research problem of recommending citation candidate for a manuscript or a *citation placeholder* in a manuscript. Shaparenko et al. [8] proposed to employ language model to compare the citation context and the source paper content, but it usually leads to low recall due to the mismatching vocabulary used. He et al. [3] employed other citation contexts to represent one paper. In addition, they also consider other citation contexts in the same manuscript of the query *citation placeholder*. Some researchers [10, 6] proposed to use topic models to predict whether there should be a link (citation relation) between two documents.

Besides the text information, some researchers also make use of the citation information for this task. They generally require the manuscript has already contained some other citations. McNee et al. [5] employed the collaborative filtering technique to make use of the existing citation information. They assumed the documents that are usually co-cited with the existing citations are likely cited by the current manuscript. Zhou et al. [13] proposed a semisupervised learning method to spread the citation relation in multiple graphs (e.g., paper-paper citation graph, paper-author writing graph, etc.). Some researchers [9, 11] combined the text information and partial citation information to recommend citations. In this paper, we focus on modeling the text information for citation recommendation, and our method can potentially be combined with the existing citation based methods.

2.2 Translation Model

Translation Model was introduced to be used for information retrieval by Berger et al. [1]. The main idea is that it can translate the words in the documents to the query terms, so it can bridge the vocabulary gap between the query and the document. Because of its translation manner, it can be naturally applied in the cross-language retrieval [7, 4] and other applications where queries and documents use different vocabularies. Xue et al. [12] employed it to find the relevant QA pair for the question in natural language. Gao et al. [2] used it to bridge the vocabulary gap between the Web search query and the page title. There is also vocabulary gap between the paper content and the citation context, so it is appropriate to use translation model to address the citation recommendation problem.

3. TRANSLATION MODEL FOR CITATION RECOMMENDATION

In this section, we first introduce the method for estimating the translation model, and then apply the translation model for ranking the papers.

3.1 Translation Model Estimation

Translation model defines the probability of translating one word in one language into a word in another language. For the citation recommendation, we assume the languages used in the citation contexts and in the papers' content (document) are different, so we need to bridge these two languages by translating one word in the document (w_d) to one word in the citation context (w_c).

To estimate the translation model for the citation recommendation problem, we need a training data including a set of citation context and document pair $T = \{(c, d)\}$, in which the citation context c references the document d. The translation model can be estimated by maximizing the likelihood of citations contexts with their corresponding documents:

$$t^* = \arg\max_t = \prod_{(c,d)\in T} P(c|d, t) \quad (1)$$

The translation model with this formula can be estimated by the EM algorithm. In the practice, the translation model is usually heuristically approximated by a simpler version, which can compute much more efficiently [2]:

$$P(w_c|w_d) = \frac{count(w_c, w_d)}{count(w_d)} \quad (2)$$

where $count(w_c, w_d)$ is the count of (c, d) pairs in the training data T, in which document d contains the word w_d, and the context c contains word w_c, and $count(w_d)$ is the count of (c, d) pairs in which the document d contains word w_d.

The translation model usually cannot work very well due to the small self translation probability $P(w|w)$. In the citation recommendation problem, the small self translation probability may lead to underestimate the score of the document containing the words in the citation context. Xue et al. [12] proposed a method to boost the self translation probability and showed improvement in retrieval performance:

$$P_{self}(w_c|w_d) = \beta \cdot 1(w_c = w_d) + (1 - \beta) \cdot P(w_c|w_d) \quad (3)$$

where $1(w_c = w_d)$ is a signal function which outputs 1 when the word w_c is same as the word w_d, and $P(w_c|w_d)$ is the pure translation probability calculated by Eq 2. We can find the model without self translation boosting is a special case of Eq. 3 when $\beta = 0$.

One concern of using translation model is that it would be very expensive, both in word-to-word translation probability matrix storage and the online retrieval processing. One heuristic method is to store only top K translated words for each word, so that the storage and processing complexity would be drastically reduced. We would test the sensitiveness of parameter K in our experiment.

3.2 Documents Ranking

In this section, we will utilize the translation model derived in the previous section for ranking the documents. Denote the citation context containing m words as $c = \{c_1, \ldots, c_m\}$, and the source content containing n words as $d = \{d_1, \ldots, d_n\}$. Taking the citation context as the query, one document d can be scored by the query likelihood model:

$$P(c|d) = \prod_{c_i\in c} P(c_i|d) \quad (4)$$

where $P(c_i|d)$ is the likelihood of word c_i of the document language model of d.

In the practice, the query likelihood is generally calculated by smoothing the maximum likelihood estimation of the document with the collection language model.

$$P(c_i|d) = \alpha \cdot P_{ml}(c_i|C) + (1 - \alpha) \cdot P_{ml}(c_i|d) \quad (5)$$

where $P_{ml}(w|C)$ and $P_{ml}(w|d)$ the maximum likelihood estimation of a word in the collection and a document d respectively.

Since the vocabulary used in the citation contexts and the documents are usually different, it may not perform very well by deriving the word c_i in the context from the document d's language model directly, and the translation model can bridge the gap as follows:

$$P(c_i|d) = \alpha \cdot P_{ml}(c_i|C) + (1-\alpha) \cdot \sum_{d_j \in d} P(c_i|d_j) P_{ml}(d_j|d) \quad (6)$$

where $P(c_i|d_j)$ is the translation probability from word d_j to word c_i calculated by Eq. 3. This model takes into account both document generative probability and the translation probability.

4. EXPERIMENTS AND RESULTS

In this section, we describe our experiment setup and report the results.

4.1 Experiment Setup

Dataset

The dataset is a collection of 5,183 papers from 1988 to 2010, mainly in the information retrieval and text mining direction. For each paper, we extract all *citations placeholders* and the corresponding *citation contexts* (three surrouding sentences). In the collection, we find that 1,499 papers have been cited by the other papers, and 6,166 citation contexts reference the papers in the collection. In the experiment, all papers in the collection composed the document collection, and a randomly selected set of 200 citation contexts are used as queries.

Evaluation Metric

For each *citation placeholder*, we search the papers that may be referenced at this citation placeholder. Each retrieval model would return a ranked list of papers. Since there may be one or more references for one citation context, we use Mean Average Precision (MAP) as the evaluation metric:

$$\mathrm{MAP}(d_1, \ldots, d_N) = \frac{\sum_i \frac{R(d_i)}{i} \sum_{j \le i} R(d_j)}{\sum_i R(d_i)} \quad (7)$$

where $R(d_i)$ is a binary function indicating whether document d_i is relevant or not . For our problem, the papers really cited at the citation placeholder are judged as the relevant documents.

Compared Methods

We use two baselines: query likelihood language model and the context-aware relevance model [3]. For both the query likelihood language model and our translation model, it can consider the abstract or the full text as the document content, so we have two versions for these two models. For the translation model, we use the self translation boosting method described in section 3.1, so we still need to test the effect of the self translation boosting in our experiment. The compared methods are described in Table 1.

4.2 Results

Table 2 shows the best result for each compared method on our dataset. The parameter tuning results would be presented in Section 4.3. The first row shows the methods, and the second row shows the average MAP scores across the test queries. We find the difference between each pair of methods is significant with p-value 0.05 by paired t-test.

Table 1: Citation Recommendation Methods

Name	Description
LM_a	query likelihood language model on abstract
LM_f	query likelihood language model on full text
CRM	context-aware relevance model by He et al.[3]
TM_a	translation model on abstract
TM_f	translation model on full text
TM_{sa}	translation model with self boosting on abstract
TM_{sf}	translation model with self boosting on full text

Table 2: Performance of the Citation Recommending Methods

LM_a	LM_f	CRM	TM_a	TM_f	TM_{sa}	TM_{sf}
0.122	0.211	0.238	0.519	0.494	0.571	0.535

There are some interesting findings from the results: First, the translation models perform much better than the language model and the context-aware relevance model. It indicates the effectiveness of using translation models for the citation recommendation problem.

Second, the translation models on both abstract and full text are better than the corresponding query likelihood language models. It reminds that the vocabulary between the citation context and the source content are different, so the such kind of "translation" is needed.

Third, for the translation model (with or without self translation boosting), it performs better on the abstract than on the full text. On the contrary, the language model performs better on the full text than on the abstract. The abstract may miss some information of a paper, and the citation context may talk about the missing information. For the language model, it cannot generate the missing information from the abstract, but for the translation model, it is still possible to generate such information from translation. The full text contains all information that can help to generate the citation context, so it benefits the language model, but it may harm the translation model due to too much noise introduced to the translation matrix.

Finally, we validate that the context-aware relevance model outperforms the language model, but it is still not as good at the translation model.

4.3 Parameter Tuning

In this section, we report the results of parameter tuning. There are three parameters used in our translation model: $\alpha \in (0, 1]$ controls the mixture weight of the global collection model, $\beta \in [0, 1]$ controls how much the self translation boosting is, and the parameter K controls the number of translated words for each word. We iterate all the ranges for these three parameters (for K, we iterate between $(0, 1000]$), and we report the results for each parameter tuning when the other parameters are set as the optimal values.

In the experiment, we find the performance would increase when α value becomes smaller, and it keeps stable when the value is quite small, so we just set α to be a very small value (10^{-5} in our experiment) to prevent the zero probability in some cases. It indicates that the collection model smooth is almost useless in this scenario. One possible explanation is that the word probability has been implicitly smoothed by the translation model.

We tune the β value in the range from 0 to 1, finding the best performance can be acquired when the value is between 0 and 0.2. Figure 2 presents the results for β in the range between 0 and 0.2. From the results, we can find the it needs larger self translation boosting for the language on abstract. The words in the abstract are generally more important than those in the full text, so abstract words should be more translated to themselves. On the contrary, the full text words contain more noise, so they are better represented in their translated forms.

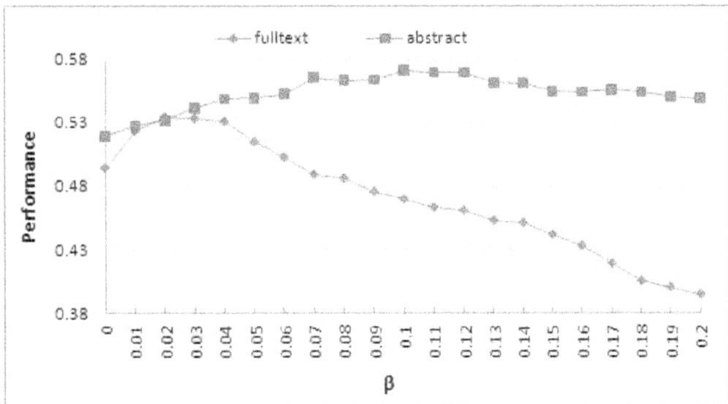

Figure 2: Parameter Tuning on Self Translation Probability Boosting

Figure 3 presents the results for different translated word numbers. We note that the translated word number K can also affect the efficiency of the model, the model with larger K value will process more slowly. The optimal K value is 400 for the full text translation model and 800 for the abstract translation model. The abstract of a paper is usually short and brief, thus it needs to translate to more words that possibly appear in the citation context. From the result, we can find the performance is quite robust to the K value selection.

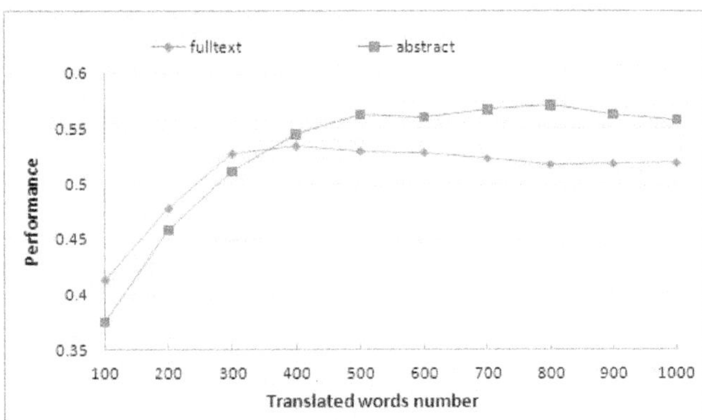

Figure 3: Parameter Tuning on Translated Word Number

5. CONCLUSION AND FUTURE WORK

We propose to use the translation retrieval model for the citation recommendation problem. The citation recommendation problem is challengeable due to the vocabulary gap between the citation context and the paper's content, and translation model can well bridge this gap. In the future, we can extend to consider more features such as other citations in the paper and the paper's global content for better citation recommendation.

Acknowledgement

This work has been partially supported by HGJ 2010 Grant 2011ZX01042-001-001 and NSFC with Grant No.61073082, 60933004.

6. REFERENCES

[1] Berger, A., and Lafferty, J. Information retrieval as statistical translation. In *Proceedings of SIGIR '99* (1999), pp. 222–229.

[2] Gao, J., He, X., and Nie, J.-Y. Clickthrough-based translation models for web search: from word models to phrase models. In *Proceedings of CIKM '10* (2010), pp. 1139–1148.

[3] He, Q., Pei, J., Kifer, D., Mitra, P., and Giles, L. Context-aware citation recommendation. In *Proceedings of WWW'10* (2010), pp. 421–430.

[4] Lavrenko, V., Choquette, M., and Croft, W. B. Cross-lingual relevance models. In *Proceedings of SIGIR '02* (2002), pp. 175–182.

[5] McNee, S. M., Albert, I., Cosley, D., Gopalkrishnan, P., Lam, S. K., Rashid, A. M., Konstan, J. A., and Riedl, J. On the recommending of citations for research papers. In *Proceedings of CSCW '02* (2002), pp. 116–125.

[6] Nallapati, R. M., Ahmed, A., Xing, E. P., and Cohen, W. W. Joint latent topic models for text and citations. In *Proceeding of KDD '08* (2008), pp. 542–550.

[7] Nie, J.-Y., Simard, M., Isabelle, P., and Durand, R. Cross-language information retrieval based on parallel texts and automatic mining of parallel texts from the web. In *Proceedings SIGIR'99* (1999), pp. 74–81.

[8] Shaparenko, B., and Joachims, T. Identifying the original contribution of a document via language modeling. In *Proceedings of SIGIR '09* (2009), pp. 696–697.

[9] Strohman, T., and Croft, W. B. Efficient document retrieval in main memory. In *Proceedings of SIGIR '07* (2007), pp. 175–182.

[10] Tang, J., and Zhang, J. A discriminative approach to topic-based citation recommendation. In *Proceedings of PAKDD '09* (2009), pp. 572–579.

[11] Torres, R., McNee, S. M., Abel, M., Konstan, J. A., and Riedl, J. Enhancing digital libraries with techlens+. In *Proceedings of JCDL '04* (2004), pp. 228–236.

[12] Xue, X., Jeon, J., and Croft, W. B. Retrieval models for question and answer archives. In *Proceeding of SIGIR '08* (2008), pp. 475–482.

[13] Zhou, D., Zhu, S., Yu, K., Song, X., Tseng, B. L., Zha, H., and Giles, C. L. Learning multiple graphs for document recommendations. In *Proceeding of WWW '08* (2008), pp. 141–150.

Extracting Adjective Facets from Community Q&A Corpus

Takehiro Yamamoto, Satoshi Nakamura, Katsumi Tanaka
Department of Social Informatics, Graduate School of Informatics
Kyoto University
Yoshida-Honmachi, Sakyo, Kyoto 606-8501, Japan
{tyamamot, nakamura, tanaka}@dl.kuis.kyoto-u.ac.jp

ABSTRACT

In this paper, we propose a method for helping users explore information via Web searches by using a question and answer (Q&A) corpus archived in a community Q&A site. When users do not have clear information needs and have little knowledge about the task domain, it is difficult for them to create queries that adequately reflect their information needs. We focused on terms like "famous temples," "historical townscapes," and "delicious sweets," which we call *adjective facets*, and developed a method of extracting these facets from question and answer archives at a community Q&A site. We evaluated the effectiveness of our adjective facets by comparing them with several baselines.

Categories and Subject Descriptors

H.3.3 [**Information Systems**]: Information Search and Retrieval

General Terms

Design, Human Factors

Keywords

Information retrieval, community Q&A, exploratory search.

1. INTRODUCTION

Recent advancements in Web search engines have enabled users to quickly obtain the information they require by issuing a single appropriate query. For example, when users want to know tomorrow's weather in Kyoto, they issue the query "Kyoto weather" to a search engine and visit the highest-ranked search results to obtain the information they require.

With some search tasks, however, users need to generate multiple queries from different aspects and perform searches iteratively. For example, if users who have never been to Kyoto want to make travel plans to visit there, they need to gather information about various aspects of Kyoto. Users

CIKM'11, October 24–28, 2011, Glasgow, Scotland, UK.

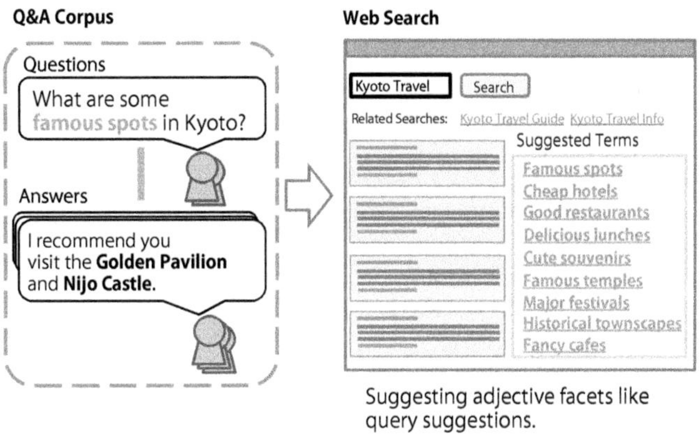

Figure 1: The concept behind our approach. We use a Q&A corpus to enhance Web searches.

searching for sightseeing spots in Kyoto might be interested in information about famous temples, places where they can enjoy leaves changing color, minor shrines, or historical castles. They also might be interested in information about famous local foods in Kyoto, restaurants that serve local foods, or authentic Japanese-sweets. Since content on the Web is constantly increasing and the information needs of people who are searching for it have become increasingly complex, the importance of exploratory Web searches has become paramount [5].

However, conventional Web search engines are not sufficiently supporting users doing exploratory Web searches. The basic problem is that it is not easy for users to create queries that adequately reflect their information needs. Query suggestion [2] is a widely used technique in commercial Web search engines to assist users with generating queries. However, since query suggestion is based on the query logs of people searching the Web, it often provides excessively popular queries like "Kyoto travel guide" or "Kyoto travel information," which are not specific enough to elicit users' interests or to encourage them to browse for more information. We need to provide more appealing terms that can attract users to interests they might not have been aware of and encourage them to browse for more search results.

When users ask their friends for some information, there are various interactions between them, which is in stark contrast to using an electronic search system. In addition, there are no constraints that concern search systems. For example, when users ask one of their friends for information about traveling to Kyoto, they might ask, "I want to visit some famous temples in Kyoto. Which ones should I visit."

Then, their friends might answer, "I recommend visiting the Golden Pavilion and Nijo Castle." If we can adapt such human-human interactions to Web searches, those searching the Web can interactively explore information according to their interests and find more information than they can with conventional search systems.

In this work, we focus on community question and answer (Q&A) sites, where people post questions and answers to support users' exploratory Web searches. The Q&A corpora that are archived in Q&A sites are caches of human-human dialogues. The key idea of our research is to use Q&A corpora to enhance Web searches, especially exploratory Web searches (Figure 1). If we can extract questioners' interests (like "famous temples"), such knowledge can easily be applied to Web searches.

We focused on terms like *famous temples* or *delicious Japanese-sweets*, which we call the *adjective facets* of a given query, and developed a method of extracting adjective facets from questions in a Q&A corpus. The method first takes into consideration relationships between questions that contain the adjective facets and answers that contain *entities* (like "Golden Pavilion") and then constructs a facet-entity bipartite graph, which represents the question-answer co-occurrence of adjective facets and entities. The method then applies the HITS algorithm to the bipartite graph to rank possible adjective facets. We evaluated the effectiveness of our adjective facets by comparing them with several baselines.

2. EXTRACTING ADJECTIVE FACETS

The popularity of community Q&A sites such as Yahoo! Answers and Baidu Zhidao, where people directly use natural language to post questions and answers, has recently been rapidly increasing. We will first describe and define the *adjective facets* used in our work. We will then present the core algorithms used in our method.

2.1 Adjective Facets

From our preliminary experiment, we found that people on a Q&A site are more likely to use "adjectives" than those on the Web. We focused on adjectives and extracted user's adjective-based interests from a Q&A corpus and used them to support exploratory Web searches. However, suggesting adjectives on their own, such as "famous" or "cheap," to Web searchers are not so useful since their meaning are quite ambiguous. In contrast, adjective-noun combinations like "famous temples" or "cheap hotels" are both more meaningful and more interesting for users. Thus, we define an *adjective facet* as a nominal phrase that matches the lexical syntactic pattern of <*adjective*> <*noun*>. The objective of this work is to extract good adjective facets that attract users' interests from a Q&A corpus in order to supporting exploratory Web searches, like Figure 1. Our adjective facets have two characteristics in terms of supporting Web searches.

One is *unexpectedness* of terms. One important aspect of suggesting terms is to help users think up new approaches to searches. If all the terms that are suggested to users are easily generated for them, this does not effectively help them to explore information from various aspects. It is common for people to issue only nouns as queries when using Web search engines. Therefore, adjective facets, simply because they contain adjectives, are difficult for users to generate as queries and, thus, unexpected to users.

Second is *generality* of terms. For example, it is not so useful for the system to suggest term "Futaba" to users for the query "Kyoto travel" if they have little knowledge about Kyoto, since they cannot understand the meaning of the suggested term and cannot make judgments on its relevance to the query. However, it is easy for all users to understand the meaning of terms like "famous Japanese-sweets shop". It is important to suggest terms to users that are not specific within in a certain domain in this way, especially when they do not have enough knowledge about the target domain.

2.2 Approach to Ranking Adjective Facets

We consider the question-answer co-occurrence between adjective facets and *entities* to rank adjective facets. For example, if a question is related to "famous temples" in Kyoto, the possible answers to this would intuitively contain the specific names of temples, such as "the Golden Pavilion" or "Kiyomizu temple," that are related to the adjective facet. We called specific terms, such as the names of places, restaurants, events, people, books and so on, *entities*. Since entities can be important information that meets the questioners' interests, the adjective facets that lead to the entities might attract Web searchers' interests.

In this work, we made the following two assumptions:

- If important entities appear in an answer, adjective facets that appear in the question of the answer are important.
- If important adjective facets appear in a question, entities that appear in the related answers are important.

These assumptions are quite similar to those in the HITS algorithm [4], which calculates the importance of Web pages using a bipartite graph. Therefore, we consider the relationship between adjectives facets and entities as a bipartite graph and apply the HITS algorithm to the graph to rank important adjective facets.

2.3 Overview

Our method works in accordance with the following flows.

1. The method accepts query $\mathbf{q}$ made by a user.
2. The method retrieves question-answer pairs that contain query $\mathbf{q}$ in their question part. C denotes the set of retrieved question-answer pairs, $C = \{(q_1, a_1), \ldots, (q_n, a_m)\}$, Q denotes the set of all questions in C, $Q = \{q_1, \ldots, q_n\}$, and A denotes the set of all answers in C, $A = \{a_1, \ldots, a_m\}$, and $n \leq m$.
3. The method then extracts all adjective facets $F = \{f_1, \ldots, f_{|F|}\}$ that appear in Q using a morphological analyzer. The method also extracts all entities $E = \{e_1, \ldots, e_{|E|}\}$ that appear in A. To extract entities, we used a Japanese named entity recognition module[1] and regarded the named entities that were tagged as <ORGANIZATION>, <LOCATION> and <ARTIFACT> as entities in this work.
4. After extracting adjective facets F and entities E, the method constructs a facet-entity bipartite graph G.
5. The method ranks possible adjective facets using graph G and outputs the top k ranked adjective facets. Our system then displays the obtained adjective facets to the user.

[1]http://chasen.org/~ taku/software/cabocha/

2.4 Facet-Entity Bipartite Graph

We first construct a facet-entity bipartite graph $G = (F \cup E, \mathcal{E})$, where F and E denote the node set and $\mathcal{E}$ represents the edge set between facets F and entities E. If adjective facet $f_i \in F$ and entity $e_j \in E$ co-occur in the same question-answer pair, there is an edge between f_i and e_j.

After constructing the graph, we calculate a weight for each edge $(f_i, e_i) \in \mathcal{E}$. Let $c(f_i, e_j)$ be a weight of edge (f_i, e_j). We define $c(f_i, e_j)$ as the number of question-answer pairs in C that contain f_i in their question part and e_j in their answer part.

Let w_{ij}^{fe} be the transition probability from adjective facet f_i to entity e_j. w_{ij}^{fe} is defined as $w_{ij}^{fe} = \frac{c(f_i,e_j)}{\sum_{e_l \in E} c(f_i,e_l)}$. Similarly, the transition probability w_{ji}^{ef} from entity e_j to adjective facet f_i is defined as $w_{ji}^{ef} = \frac{c(f_i,e_j)}{\sum_{f_k \in F} c(f_k,e_j)}$.

2.5 Ranking Adjective Facets using HITS

To apply the HITS algorithm to the facet-entity bipartite graph G, we used the Co-HITS [3] framework proposed by Deng et al. Co-HITS is a general algorithm to stochastically calculate the importance of the nodes in a bipartite graph, and it contains HITS as a special case.

Let the score of adjective facet f_i be x_i and the score of entity e_j be y_j. x_i and y_j can be calculated by iterating the following two formulae:

$$x_i = \sum_{e_j \in E} w_{ji}^{ef} y_j, \quad y_j = \sum_{f_i \in F} w_{ij}^{fe} x_i \qquad (1)$$

We can obtain important adjective facets on the basis of score x_i by solving Equation (1).

2.6 Query Association

Calculating Equation (1) enables us to obtain important adjective facets. However, if we simply apply Equation (1) to the bipartite graph, some irrelevant adjective facets (like "good advice") also obtain high scores. These irrelevant adjective facets frequently appear in questions but are not related to query $\mathbf{q}$. Therefore, we incorporate the bipartite graph G with the association between query $\mathbf{q}$ and adjective facets F to remove irrelevant adjective facets.

By using the Co-HITS algorithm, we can consider the initial importance of each node in the bipartite graph. If x_i^0 is an initial importance of adjective facet f_i, Equation (1) can be modified to

$$x_i = (1 - \lambda_f)x_i^0 + \lambda_f \sum_{e_j \in E} w_{ji}^{ef} y_j$$
$$y_j = \sum_{f_k \in F} w_{ij}^{fe} x_i, \qquad (2)$$

where $\lambda_f \in [0, 1]$ are the parameter that balances the initial scores x_i^0. If λ_f is set to 1, this equation is equal to Equation (1).

To calculate the association between adjective facet f_i and query $\mathbf{q}$, we calculate the term co-occurrence within a Q&A corpus. We used *expected pointwise mutual information* [1]. For given query $\mathbf{q}$ and adjective facet f_i, expected pointwise mutual information $\text{epmi}(\mathbf{q}, f_i)$ is defined as

$$\text{epmi}(\mathbf{q}, f_i) = P(\mathbf{q}, f_i) \cdot \log \frac{P(\mathbf{q}, f_i)}{P(\mathbf{q})P(f_i)} \qquad (3)$$

Table 1: Categories and example queries used in the experiment.

Category	Example Query
Sports	World Cup
Science & Academics	study Mathematics
Politics & News	earthquake countermeasures
Travel	Kyoto travel
PC & Electronics	smartphone
Health	Meniere's disease
Business & Finance	investment trust
Relationships & Life	wedding party
Education & Parenting	children discipline
Home & Food	potato recipes

To estimate probabilities $P(\mathbf{q})$, $P(f_i)$, and $P(\mathbf{q}, f_i)$, we use simple normalized frequencies: $P(\mathbf{q}) = \frac{n_{\mathbf{q}}}{N}$, $P(f_i) = \frac{n_{f_i}}{N}$ and $P(\mathbf{q}, f_i) = \frac{n_{\mathbf{q} \wedge f_i}}{N}$. Here, $n_{\mathbf{q}}$ and n_{f_i} denote the number of questions in the Q&A corpus that contain $\mathbf{q}$ and f_i, respectively. $n_{\mathbf{q} \wedge f_i}$ denotes the number of questions that contain both $\mathbf{q}$ and f_i. N denotes the total number of questions in the Q&A corpus. We set $N = 30,000,000$, which nearly equals the number of questions posted on Yahoo! Japan Chiebukuro. If the two terms frequently co-occur in the same question, the score takes a high value.

By using $\text{epmi}(\mathbf{q}, f_i)$, the initial importance of adjective facet f_i can be computed as $x_i^0 = \frac{\text{epmi}(\mathbf{q},f_i)}{\sum_{f_k \in F} \text{epmi}(\mathbf{q},f_k)}$. Given the initial relevance x_i^0, x_i and y_j can be calculated by iterating the Equation (2).

3. EXPERIMENTS

3.1 Experimental Settings

To determine the effectiveness of our proposed approach, we prepared four methods.

- Frequent adjective facets in Web search results (**WEB**): This method first obtains 1,000 Web search results for given query $\mathbf{q}$ using the Yahoo! Japan Web search API. It then extracts adjective facets appear in the search results and outputs the 15 most frequent ones.
- Query suggestions (**QS**): This method first obtains query suggestions of given query $\mathbf{q}$ by using the Yahoo! Japan Related words API. The method then outputs the top 15 query suggestions while removing the terms contained in $\mathbf{q}$.
- Our method using HITS ($\mathbf{QA}_{hits}$): This method outputs the top 15 adjective facets that are ranked highest by Equation (1). We used Yahoo! Japan Chiebukuro's API and obtained 1,000 questions and related answers.
- Our method using HITS and query association ($\mathbf{QA}_{h+q}$): This method outputs the top 15 adjective facets that are ranked highest by Equation (2). We set parameter $\lambda_f = 0.5$.

3.2 Method

To evaluate the effectiveness of our method with diverse topics, we prepared 10 categories and six queries for each category (60 queries in total). The categories and example queries used in the experiment are listed in Table 1.

Table 2: Average scores (AVG) and MAP@k for the four methods (highest values in bold).

	AVG	MAP@5	MAP@10	MAP@15
QS	2.699	0.561	0.502	0.478
WEB	2.612	0.532	0.498	0.483
QA$_{hits}$	2.508	0.507	0.489	0.469
QA$_{h+q}$	**2.701**	**0.592**	**0.566**	**0.536**

We asked six volunteers to participate in the experiment. We divided the 60 queries into two groups and each participant evaluated 30 queries (10 categories × 3 queries.) The order of the queries showed to each volunteers were balanced. The experiment proceeded as follows.

- We first gave short descriptions of the required information (e.g., "You are planning to travel to Kyoto" or "You are planning to purchase a new smartphone").
- Next, we showed the participants 60 terms, which had been extracted from the four methods described in Section 3.1. The 60 terms were randomly placed.
- For each term, participants were asked to judge how much they wanted to check the information suggested for it in a five-point Likert scale (1 = *not interested at all* and 5 = *strongly interested*).

3.3 Results

Table 2 shows the results for average score (AVG) and mean average precision at cutoff $k = 5, 10$ and 15 (MAP@k) of the four methods. Terms that scored 4 and 5 were deemed relevant and terms that scored 1, 2, and 3 were deemed irrelevant to measure mean average precision. From the results in Table 2, we can see that our proposed method **QA**$_{h+q}$ outperformed **WEB** and **QA**$_{hits}$ in terms of all measures. We also found that the average scores of **QS** and **QA**$_{h+q}$ were the almost same. simply considering the relationships between adjective facets and co-occurring entities. This results indicate that adjective facets extracted from Q&A corpus can attract users' interests and that a Q&A corpus can be a valuable resource to support exploratory Web searches.

We further analyzed the experimental results in terms of the categories used in the experiment. Table 3 shows the average scores of the four methods for each category. We can see that the effectiveness of our method depended on the category. For example, **QA**$_{h+q}$ got over 3.00 average score in the "Sports", "Travel", and "Home & Food" categories. On the other hand, it got much lower average score in the "Science & Academic" and "Politics & News" categories. From this result, we can estimate that the importance of adjectives depend on the types of knowledge that users are required. When users are searching for information related to a topic that requires highly technical or specialized knowledge of them, objective opinions or technical terms might be more important to inform their information needs of a Web search engine than adjectives. With such topics, like politics or science, adjective facets might not preferred by users since those topics require advanced knowledge of users. On the other hand, in the topics related to the "Sports" and "Travel", "Home & Food" categories, subjective opinions or viewpoints might be important to find information, thus, adjective facets were preferred by the participants.

Table 4 shows example adjective facets that our method **QA**$_{h+q}$ suggested to the participants. Since these terms are seldom suggested by conventional query suggestions, our method has the potential of complementing the conventional query suggestions.

Table 3: Average scores for each category (highest values in bold).

Category	QS	WEB	QA$_{hits}$	QA$_{h+q}$
Sports	2.492	2.210	2.813	**3.163**
Science&Academics	**2.472**	2.167	2.032	2.290
Politics&News	**2.421**	2.393	2.194	2.349
Travel	2.881	2.849	**3.536**	3.440
PC&Electronics	**3.032**	2.530	2.478	2.534
Health	**2.992**	2.810	2.571	2.639
Business&Finance	**3.004**	2.905	2.429	2.627
Relationship&Life	2.758	**3.024**	2.262	2.488
Education&Parenting	2.397	2.437	2.159	**2.452**
Home&Food	2.544	2.802	2.603	**3.028**

Table 4: Example adjective facets.

Query	Examples	
Japanese	great hitters	favorite teams
	young players	cool players
Kyoto travel	famous temples	minor places
	beautiful spots	cheap hotels
Influenza	severe headache	accurate knowledge
	cold chill	correct hand-washing

4. CONCLUSIONS

Our experimental results showed that our approach could suggest more terms that users judged interesting than other baselines in several topics. We plan to further analyze the relationships between the topics and effectiveness of adjective facets. Moreover, we plan to develop a ranking algorithm for queries that contain adjective facets and conduct experiments to evaluate the effectiveness our adjective facets in actual search scenarios.

5. ACKNOWLEDGMENTS

This work was supported in part by Grant-in-Aid for JSPS Fellows (#09J55302), Grant-in-Aid for challenging Exploratory Research (#22650018), Grant-in-Aid for Young Scientists (A) (#23680006), and by "Informatics Education and Research Center for Knowledge-Circulating Society" (Project Leader: Katsumi Tanaka, MEXT Global COE Program, Kyoto University).

6. REFERENCES

[1] B. Croft, D. Metzler, and T. Strohman. *Search Engines: Information Retrieval in Practice.* Addison-Wesley Publishing Company, USA, 2009.

[2] H. Cui, J. Wen, J. Nie, and W. Ma. Probabilistic Query Expansion Using Query Logs. In *Proceedings of the 11th International Conference on World Wide Web*, pages 325–332, 2002.

[3] H. Deng, M. R. Lyu, and I. King. A Generalized Co-HITS Algorithm and its Application to Bipartite Graphs. In *Proceedings of the 15th ACM SIGKDD international conference on Knowledge discovery and data mining*, pages 239–248, 2009.

[4] J. M. Kleinberg. Authoritative Sources in a Hyperlinked Environment. *J. ACM*, 46:604–632, 1999.

[5] R. White and R. Roth. Exploratory Search: Beyond the Query-Response Paradigm. *Synthesis Lectures on Information Concepts, Retrieval, and Services*, 1(1):1–98, 2009.

A Novel Framework of Training Hidden Markov Support Vector Machines from Lightly-Annotated Data

Deyu Zhou
School of Computer Science and Engineering
Southeast University, Nanjing, China
d.zhou@seu.edu.cn

Yulan He
Knowledge Media Institute
Open University, UK
y.he@open.ac.uk

ABSTRACT

Natural language understanding (NLU) aims to map sentences to their semantic mean representations. Statistical approaches to NLU normally require fully-annotated training data where each sentence is paired with its word-level semantic annotations. In this paper, we propose a novel learning framework which trains the Hidden Markov Support Vector Machines without the use of expensive fully-annotated data. In particular, our learning approach takes as input a training set of sentences labeled with abstract semantic annotations encoding underlying embedded structural relations and automatically induces derivation rules that map sentences to their semantic meaning representations. The proposed approach has been tested on the DARPA Communicator Data and achieved 93.18% in F-measure, which outperforms the previously proposed approaches of training the hidden vector state model or conditional random fields from unaligned data, with a relative error reduction rate of 43.3% and 10.6% being achieved.

Categories and Subject Descriptors

I.2.7 [**Artificial Intelligence**]: Natural Language Processing—*Text analysis*

General Terms

Algorithms, Experimentation

Keywords

Hidden Markov support vector machines (HM-SVMs), Natural language understanding, Semantic parsing

1. INTRODUCTION

The natural language understanding problem can be considered as a mapping problem where the aim is to map a sentence to its semantic meaning representation (or abstract semantic annotation) such as the one shown below.

CIKM'11, October 24–28, 2011, Glasgow, UK.

I want to return to Dallas on Thursday.
`RETURN(TOLOC(CITY(Dallas)) ON(DATE(Thursday)))`

This is a *structured classification* task which predicts output labels (semantic tag or concept sequences) C from input sentences S where the output labels have rich internal structures. It is a highly challenging problem because the derivation from each sentence to its abstract semantic annotation is not annotated in the training data and is considered hidden. Although a hierarchical hidden state structure could be used to model embedded structural context in sentences, such as the Hidden Vector State (HVS) model [4], which learns a probabilistic push-down automaton, it cannot include a large number of correlated lexical or syntactic features in input sentences, and it cannot handle any arbitrary embedded relations since it only supports right-branching semantic structures. Other approaches learn semantic parsers that map natural language sentences into a formal meaning representation such as lambda calculus or first-order logic [6, 2]. However these systems either require a hand-built, ambiguous combinatory categorial grammar template to learn a probabilistic semantic parser [6], or assume the existence of an unambiguous, context-free grammar of the target meaning representations [2].

Conditional Random Fields (CRFs) have been extensively studied for sequence labeling. Most applications require the availability of fully annotated data, i.e., an explicit alignment of sentence and word-level labels. Mann and McCallum [5] use labeled features instead of fully labeled instances to train linear-chain CRFs. Generalized expectation criteria are used to express a preference for parameter settings in which the model's distribution on unlabeled data matches a target distribution. They tested their approach on the classified advertisements data set (CLASSIFIED) [3] and achieved 68.3% accuracy with only labeled features. Zhou and He [7] proposed an iterative learning approach based on expectation maximization (EM) to train the CRFs from abstract semantic annotations. They achieved 92% in F-measure on the DARPA Communicator Data.

In this paper, we propose a novel learning approach to train the HM-SVMs from unaligned data. It first computes expectations using initial model parameters. Parsing results are then filtered based on a measure describing the level of agreement with the sentence abstract semantic annotations and fed into model learning using the cutting-plane algorithm. With the re-estimated parameters, the learning of HM-SVMs goes to the next iteration until no more improvements could be achieved. The rest of this paper is organized as follows. Section 2 introduces HM-SVMs. The proposed learning procedure to train HM-SVMs from abstract semantic annotations is presented in Section 3. Experimental setup and results are discussed in Section 4. Finally, Section 5 concludes the paper.

2. HIDDEN MARKOV SUPPORT VECTOR MACHINES (HM-SVMS)

Given a set of training data $(S_i, C_i), i = 1, \ldots N$, to learn a function that assigns to a sequence of words $S = (s^1 \cdots s^T), s^i \in \mathbf{s}, i = 1, \ldots T$, a sequence of semantic concepts or tags $C = (c^1 c^2 \ldots c^T), c^i \in \mathbf{c}, i = 1, \ldots T$, a common approach is to find a discriminant function $F : \mathcal{S} \times \mathcal{C} \rightarrow \mathbb{R}$ that assigns a score to every input $S \in \mathcal{S}$ and every semantic tag sequence $C \in \mathcal{C}$. In order to obtain a prediction $f(S) \in \mathcal{C}$, the function is maximized with respect to $f(S) = \underset{C \in \mathcal{C}}{\operatorname{argmax}} F(S, C)$.

In particular, the function $F(S, C)$ is assumed to be linear in some combined feature representation of S and C in HM-SVMs [1], $F(S, C) := \langle w, \Phi(S, C) \rangle$. The parameters w are adjusted so that the true semantic tag sequence C_i scores higher than all other tag sequences $C \in \mathcal{C}_i := \mathcal{C} \backslash C_i$ with a large margin. To achieve the goal, the following optimization problem is solved instead:

$$\min_{\xi_i \in \mathbb{R}, w \in \mathcal{F}} \quad Cons \sum_i \xi_i + \frac{1}{2} \|w\|^2 \tag{1}$$
$$\text{s.t.} \quad \langle w, \Phi(S, C_i) \rangle - \langle w, \Phi(S, C) \rangle \geq 1 - \xi_i,$$
$$\forall i = 1, \ldots N \text{ and } C \in \mathcal{C} \backslash C_i$$

where ξ_i is non-negative slack variables allowing one to increase the global margin by paying a local penalty on some outlying examples, and $Cons$ dictates the desired trade off between margin size and outliers. To solve Equation 1, the dual of the equation is solved instead. The solution $\hat{w}$ can be written as

$$\hat{w} = \sum_{i=1}^{N} \sum_{C \in \mathcal{C}} \alpha_i(C) \Phi(S_i, C), \tag{2}$$

where $\alpha_i(C)$ is the Lagrange multiplier of the constraint associated with example i and C_i.

3. TRAINING HM-SVMS FROM ABSTRACT SEMANTIC ANNOTATIONS

To train HM-SVMs from abstract semantic annotations, we extended the use of expectation maximization (EM) algorithm to estimate model parameters. The EM algorithm is an efficient iterative procedure to compute the maximum likelihood (ML) estimate in the presence of missing or hidden data. The EM algorithm is divided into two steps. In the E-step, the missing data are estimated given the observed data and current estimate of model parameters. In the M-step, the likelihood function is maximized under the assumption that the missing data are known. We summarize the procedure of learning HM-SVMs from abstract semantic annotations in Figure 3. The details of each step are given in the subsequent sections.

3.1 Initialization

Given a sentence labeled with an abstract semantic annotation as shown in Table 1, we first expand the annotation to the flattened semantic tag sequence as in Table 1(a). In order to cater for irrelevant input words, a DUMMY tag is introduced in the preterminal position. Hence, the flattened semantic tag sequence is finally expanded to the semantic tag sequence as in Table 1(b).

Input: A set of sentences $\mathbf{S} = \{S_i, i = 1, \ldots, N\}$ and their corresponding semantic annotations $\mathbf{A} = \{A_i, i = 1, \ldots, N\}$
Output: The trained HM-SVMs with parameters Θ
Procedure:

1. **Initialization**:
   For each A_i, expand the annotation to the flattened semantic tag sequence C_i.
   Estimate the initial model parameters Θ_0 using $\mathbf{S}$ and the flattened semantic tag sequences $\mathbf{C} = \{C_i, i = 1, \ldots, N\}$.
   Set $\Theta = \Theta_0$.
2. **Expectation**:
   For each S_i, generate the semantic tag sequence $\hat{C}_i$ using the HM-SVMs with the current model parameters Θ.
3. **Filtering**:
   For the generated semantic tag sequences $\hat{\mathbf{C}} = \{\hat{C}_i, i = 1, \ldots, N\}$, filter $\hat{\mathbf{C}}$ based on a score function which measures the agreement of the generated semantic tag sequences with the actual flattened semantic tag sequences $\mathbf{C}$.
4. **Maximization**:
   Re-estimate model parameters Θ' using the filtered $\hat{\mathbf{C}}$ and set $\Theta = \Theta'$.
5. If converged, Output Θ.
   Else go to Step 2.

Figure 1: Procedure of learning HM-SVMs from abstract semantic annotations.

Table 1: Abstract semantic annotation and its flattened semantic tag sequence.

Sentence: I want to return to Dallas on Thursday.
Annotation: `RETURN(TOLOC(CITY(Dallas)) ON(DATE(Thursday)))`

(a) Flattened semantic tag list:
`RETURN RETURN+TOLOC RETURN+TOLOC+CITY(Dallas)`
`RETURN+ON RETURN+ON+DATE(Thursday)`

(b) Expanded semantic tag list:
`RETURN RETURN+DUMMY RETURN+TOLOC RETURN+TOLOC+DUMMY`
`RETURN+TOLOC+CITY(Dallas)`
`RETURN+TOLOC+CITY(Dallas)+DUMMY`
`RETURN+ON RETURN+ON+DUMMY RETURN+ON+DATE(Thursday)`
`RETURN+ON+DATE(Thursday)+DUMMY`

3.2 Expectation

We first need to calculate the most likely semantic tag sequence $\hat{C}$ for each sentence $S = (s^1 \cdots s^T)$, $\hat{C} = \underset{C \in \mathcal{C}}{\operatorname{argmax}} F(S, C)$ where $F : \mathcal{S} \times \mathcal{C} \rightarrow \mathbb{R}$ is a discriminant function and can be decomposed into two components, $F(S, C) = F_1(S, C) +$

$F_2(S, C)$, where

$$F_1(S,C) = \sum_{\sigma\in\mathbf{c},\tau\in\mathbf{c}} \delta(\sigma,\tau) \sum_{l=1}^{T} [[c^{l-1} = \sigma \wedge c^l = \tau]] \quad (3)$$

$$F_2(S,C) = \sum_{\sigma\in\mathbf{c}} \sum_{l=1}^{T} \gamma(s^l,\sigma)[[c^l = \sigma]] \quad (4)$$

Here, $\delta(\sigma, \tau)$ is considered as the co-efficient for the transition from state (or semantic tag) σ to state τ while $\gamma(s^l, \sigma)$ can be treated as the co-efficient for the emission of word s^l from state σ. They are defined as follows,

$$\delta(\sigma,\tau) = \sum_{i,\overline{C}} \alpha_i(\overline{C}) \sum_{m=1}^{|\overline{C}|} [[\overline{c}^{m-1} = \sigma \wedge \overline{c}^m = \tau]] \quad (5)$$

$$\gamma(s^l,\sigma) = \sum_{i,m} \sum_{C} [[c^m = \sigma]] \alpha_i(C) k(s^l, s_i^m) \quad (6)$$

where $k(s^l, s_i^m) = \langle \Psi(s^l), \Psi(s_i^m) \rangle$ describes the similarity of the input patterns Ψ between word s^l and word s_i^m, the mth word in the training example i, $\alpha_i(C)$ is a set of dual parameters or Lagrange multiplier of the constraint associated with example i and semantic tag sequence C as in Equation 2. Using the results derived in Equations 5 and 6, Viterbi decoding can be performed to generate the best semantic tag sequence.

To incorporate the constraints as defined in the abstract semantic annotations, the values of $\delta(\sigma, \tau)$ and $\gamma(s^l, \sigma)$ are modified for each sentence,

$$\delta(\sigma,\tau) = \begin{cases} 0, \text{ when } g(\sigma,\tau) = 1 \\ \sum_{i,\overline{C}} \alpha_i(\overline{C}) \sum_m [[\overline{c}^{m-1} = \sigma \wedge \overline{c}^m = \tau]], \text{otherwise} \end{cases}$$

$$\gamma(s^l,\sigma) = \begin{cases} 0, \text{ when } h(\sigma, s^l) = 1 \\ \sum_{i,m} \sum_C [[c^m = \sigma]] \alpha_i(C) k(s^l, s_i^m), \text{otherwise} \end{cases}$$

where $g(\sigma, \tau)$ and $h(\sigma, s^l)$ are defined as follows,

$$g(\sigma,\tau) = \begin{cases} 1, & \tau \text{ is not in the allowable semantic tag list} \\ 0, & \text{otherwise} \end{cases}$$

$$h(\sigma,s^l) = \begin{cases} 1, & \sigma \text{ is not of class type and } s^l \text{ is of class type} \\ 0, & \text{otherwise} \end{cases}$$

$g(\sigma, \tau)$ and $h(\sigma, s^l)$ in fact encodes the two constraints implied from abstract annotations. Firstly, state transitions are only allowed if both incoming and outgoing states are listed in the semantic annotation defined for the sentence. Secondly, if there is a lexical item attached to a preterminal tag of a flattened semantic tag, that semantic tag must appear bound to that lexical item in the training annotation. For example, in the annotation shown in Table 1, 'Dallas' belongs to a lexical class 'CITY'. Hence, it can only be tagged with semantic tags containing a preterminal tag 'CITY'.

3.3 Filtering

For each sentence, the semantic tag sequences generated in the *Expectation* step are further processed based on a measure on the agreement of the semantic tag sequence $T = \{t_1, t_2, ..., t_n\}$ with its corresponding abstract semantic annotation A. The score of T is defined as

$$Score(T) = 2 * \frac{S_{recall} * S_{precision}}{S_{recall} + S_{precision}}, \quad (7)$$

where $S_{precision} = N_r/n, S_{Recall} = N_r/p$. Here, N_r is the number of the semantic tags in T which also occur in A, n is the number of semantic tags in T, and p is the number of semantic tags in the flattened semantic tag sequence for A. The score is similar to the F-measure which is the harmonic mean of precision and recall. It essentially measures the agreement of the generated semantic tag sequence with the abstract semantic annotation. We filter out sentences with their score below certain predefined threshold and the remaining sentences together with their generated semantic tag sequences are fed into the next *Maximization* step. In our experiments, we empirically set the threshold to 0.1.

3.4 Maximization

Given the filtered training examples from the *Filtering* step, the parameters w are adjusted so that the true semantic tag sequence C_i scores higher than all the other tag sequences $C \in \mathcal{C}_i := \mathcal{C} \backslash C_i$ with a large margin. To achieve the goal, the optimization problem as stated in Equation 1 is solved using an online learning approach as described in [1]. In short, it works as follows, a pattern sequence S_i is presented and the optimal semantic tag sequence $\hat{C}_i = f(S_i)$ is computed by employing Viterbi decoding. If $\hat{C}_i$ is correct, no update is performed. Otherwise, the weight vector w is updated based on the difference from the true semantic tag sequence $\Delta\Phi = \Phi(S_i, \hat{C}_i) - \Phi(S_i, C_i)$.

4. EXPERIMENTS

Experiments have been conducted on the DARPA Communicator data[1] which were collected in 461 days. From these, 46 days were randomly selected for use as test set data and the remainder were used for training. After cleaning up the data, the training set consist of 12702 utterances while the test set contains 1178 utterances.

The abstract semantic annotations used for training only list a set of valid semantic tags and the dominance relationships between them without considering the actual realized semantic tag sequence or attempting to identify explicit word/concept pairs. Thus, it avoids the need for expensive tree-bank style annotations. For example, for the sentence "Show me flights from Boston to New York", the abstract annotation would be
`FLIGHT(FROMLOC(CITY) TOLOC(CITY))`.

To evaluate the performance of the model, a reference frame structure was derived for every test set sentence consisting of slot/value pairs. An example of a reference frame is:

Show me flights from Boston to New York.	
Frame:	FLIGHT
Slots:	FROMLOC.CITY = Boston
	TOLOC.CITY = New York

Performance was then measured in terms of F-measure on slot/value pairs, which combines the precision (P) and recall (R) values with equal weight and is defined as $F = (P + R)/2PR$. We modified the open source SVM^{hmm2} to train and test the HM-SVMs on abstract annotations.

[1] `http://www.bltek.com/spoken-dialog-systems/cu-communicator.html`

[2] `http://www.cs.cornell.edu/people/tj/svm_light/svm_hmm.html`

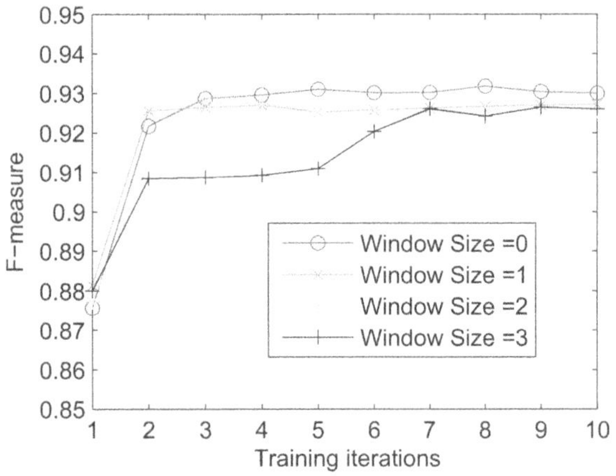

Figure 2: Comparison of performance on models learned with feature sets chosen based on different window sizes.

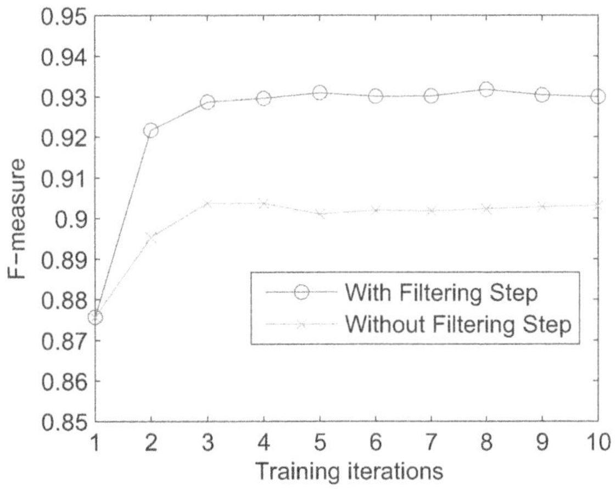

Figure 3: Comparisons of performance with or without the *Filtering* stage.

We employed word features (such as current word, previous word, and next word, etc) and part-of-speech (POS) features (such as current POS tag, previous one, and next one, etc) for training. To explore the impact of the choices of features, we explored with feature sets comprising of words or POS tags occurring before or after the current word within some predefined window size. Figure 2 shows the performance of our proposed approach with the window size varying between 0 and 3. Surprisingly, the model learned with feature set chosen by setting window size 0 gives the best overall performance. Varying window size between 1 and 3 only impacts the convergence rate and does not lead to any performance difference at the end of the learning procedure.

In a second set of experiments, we compare the performance with or without the *Filtering* step as discussed in Section 3.3. Figure 3 shows that the *Filtering* step is indeed crucial as it boosted the performance by nearly 3%.

We compare the performance of HM-SVMs with HVS and CRFs, all trained on abstract semantic annotations. The HVS model [4] was previously proposed based on the hypothesis that a suitably constrained hierarchical model may be trainable without treebank data whilst simultaneously retaining sufficient ability to capture the hierarchical structure need to robustly extract task domain semantics. Such a constrained hierarchical model can be conveniently implemented using the HVS model which extends the HMM model by expanding each state to encode the stack of a push-down automaton. While it is hard to incorporate arbitrary input features to HVS learning, both HM-SVMs and CRFs have the capability to deal with overlapping features. A learning approach of training CRFs from abstract annotations was previously proposed in [7]. Table 2 shows that HM-SVMs outperforms both HVS and CRFs with a relative error reduction of 43.3% and 10.6% being achieved respectively. The superior performance of HM-SVMs over CRFs shows the advantage of HM-SVMs on learning non-linear discriminant functions via kernel functions.

Table 2: Overall comparison with other models.

Measurement	HVS	CRFs	HM-SVMs
Recall (%)	87.81	92.27	92.04
Precision (%)	88.13	92.48	94.36
F-measure (%)	87.97	92.37	93.18

5. CONCLUSIONS

In this paper, we proposed an effective learning approach which can train HM-SVMs without the expensive annotated data. It takes as input a training set of sentences labeled with abstract semantic annotations encoding underlying embedded structural relations and automatically induces derivation rules that map sentences to semantic meaning representation. We evaluated the performance of our proposed learning approach on the DARPA Communicator Data and showed that it outperforms two other models, HVS and CRFs, also trained on abstract annotations.

6. REFERENCES

[1] Y. Altun, I. Tsochantaridis, and T. Hofmann. Hidden Markov Support Vector Machines. In *ICML*, pages 3–10, 2003.

[2] R. Ge and R. Mooney. Learning a Compositional Semantic Parser using an Existing Syntactic Parser. In *ACL*, pages 611–619, 2009.

[3] T. Grenager, D. Klein, and C. D. Manning. Unsupervised learning of field segmentation models for information extraction. In *ACL*, pages 371–378, 2005.

[4] Y. He and S. Young. Semantic processing using the hidden vector state model. *Computer Speech and Language*, 19(1):85–106, 2005.

[5] G. S. Mann and A. Mccallum. Generalized expectation criteria for semi-supervised learning of conditional random fields. In *ACL*, pages 870–878, 2008.

[6] L. Zettlemoyer and M. Collins. Learning to map sentences to logical form: Structured classification with probabilistic categorial grammars. In *UAI*, 2005.

[7] D. Zhou and Y. He. Learning conditional random fields from unaligned data for natural language understanding. In *ECIR*, pages 283–288, 2011.

Learning to Recommend Questions Based on Public Interest *

Jun Wang
State Key Laboratory of Software Development Environment
Beihang University, Beijing 100191
junwangbuaa@gmail.com

Xia Hu
Department of Computer Science and Engineering
Arizona State University, Tempe 85281
xiahu@asu.edu

Zhoujun Li
State Key Laboratory of Software Development Environment
Beihang University,Beijing 100191
lizj@buaa.edu.cn

Wenhan Chao
Beihang University
Beijing 100191
chanwenhan@buaa.edu.cn

Biyun Hu
Beihang University
Beijing 100191
byhu8210@gmail.com

ABSTRACT

This paper is concerned with the problem of question recommendation in the setting of Community Question Answering (CQA). Given a question as query, our goal is to rank all of the retrieved questions according to their likelihood of being good recommendations for the query. In this paper, we propose a notion of public interest, and show how public interest can boost the performance of question recommendation. In particular, to model public interest in question recommendation, we build a language model to combine relevance score to the query and popularity score regarding question popularity. Experimental results on Yahoo!Answers dataset demonstrate the performance of question recommendation can be greatly improved with considering the public interest.

Categories and Subject Descriptors

H.3.3 [**Information Storage and Retrieval**]: Information Search and Retrieval—*information filtering, selection precess*

General Terms

Algorithms, Experimentation

Keywords

Public Interest, Question Recommendation, CQA

*This work is supported by State Key Laboratory of Software Development Environment(SKLSDE-2011ZX-03).

CIKM'11, October 24–28, 2011, Glasgow, Scotland, UK.

1. INTRODUCTION

Community Question Answering (CQA), in which users answer questions posted by others, is gaining a large number of audiences in recent years, and has accumulated millions of questions and answers over time. These CQA portals provide an alternative channel for obtaining information on the web: rather than browsing results of search engines, users present detailed information needs and get direct response authored by humans [1].

With the exponential growth in data volume, the problem in CQA portals is how to answer users' questions efficiently. It was observed that in Yahoo!Answers[1] only 17.6% of questions received satisfied answers within 48 hours and nearly 20% of unresolved questions received no response [4], which showed that the popular CQA portal performs poorly in solving users' questions directly. This problem gives rise to question recommendation techniques that help users locate interesting questions. To date, most previous work [4] [6] have been done to solve this problem by analyzing users' information, such as the users' interests, whether she is an expert or is available to provide an answer. Unfortunately, the fact is that users usually are reluctant to provide their personal information when they browse or search question. Thus, it is relatively hard to predict whether a question is interesting to a specific user when the profile information of the user is not available [6].

In the setting of CQA, many users share the same or similar interests. Usually, "the wisdom of the crowds" for information needs are expressed by some frequently asked questions. If these popular questions can be identified and be used for recommending, we believe it can save much time for most users either in crafting successful questions or obtaining satisfied answers. Based on this observation, in this paper, we attempt to employ public interest to boost question recommendation performance. We try to model the question popularity to measure the public interest. Two perspectives are considered in the popularity measurement — possibility of question repeated by other people and users' response to this question. To the best of our knowledge, this is the first attempt of learning to recommend questions from

[1]http://answers.yahoo.com/

this aspect. In the question recommendation framework, we first use the question popularity to model the public interest. Then we build a language model for question recommendation, which combines relevance score to the query and popularity score regarding question popularity.

2. QUESTION RECOMMENDATION BASED ON PUBLIC INTEREST

An ideal question that should be recommended to a query should have 1) a high relevance score to the query; 2) a high question popularity score among related questions. As the question popularity score is independent to the query, it can be calculated offline. In this section, we first present our method on the question popularity measurement. Then we build a language model for question recommendation, which naturally combines the popularity score and relevance score.

2.1 Question Popularity

We drive the popularity of a question from two observations — the probability that the question would be repeated by other people and the people's response to this question. The method is based on two assumptions:

Assumption 1: The higher possibility would be a question repeated by other people, the more popularity the question is.

Assumption 2: The more responses does a question receive, the more popularity the question is.

2.1.1 Question Popularity Based on Question Repeated Possibility

If a topic is very interesting to people, there can be many lexically similar questions related to the topic in the question collection. Among those similar questions, the most central questions with the highest repeated possibility can be regarded as the most popular ones regarding the topic. To measure the question repeated possibility, we use the LexRank Method [3]. The LexRank estimates the centrality(repeated possibility) of a question in a manner similar to the PageRank [2].

First, we construct an undirected graph of questions based on similarities between each two questions. As the question in CQA is usually a short sentence, it may occur sparseness problem when using cosine method to measure the similarity between questions. Since the answers in CQA systems are manually crafted by users, they are usually more comprehensive which can provide more context information than questions. Intuitively, two questions should be semantically similar if their corresponding answers are similar, even though there is little word overlap between the two questions. Based on this observation, we use the answers similarity to improve the question similarity measurement.

Let i and j be two questions, $ans(i)$ and $ans(j)$ be the answer of i and j respectively. The similarity between i and j is defined as:

$$S(i,j) = \frac{sim(i,j) + sim(ans(i), ans(j))}{2} \tag{1}$$

The function $sim(\cdot)$ determines the lexically similarity between two sentences. Clearly, there are many possible selections for the similarity method, we choose cosine here and leave other methods for future work.

An undirected graph is constructed based on the similarities between questions. In the graph, each node represents a question and two nodes are connected if the similarity between them exceeds a certain threshold value. In our work, we set the threshold to be 0.5. If the normalized similarity exceed 0.5, then there is an edge between the two questions.

Second, for a question u, the repeated possibility $p(u)$ is calculated with the following weighting scheme:

$$p(u) = \frac{d}{N} + (1-d) \sum_{v \in adj[u]} \frac{S(u,v)}{\sum_{z \in adj[v]} S(z,v)} p(v) \tag{2}$$

where N is the total number of nodes in the graph, d is a "damping factor", which is typically chosen in the interval [0.1, 0.2] [2], and $adj[u]$ is the set of questions that adjacent to u. $S(u,v)$ is defined in eq.1. Erkan and Radev presented an algorithm for the eq.2. For more details, please see [3].

2.1.2 Question Popularity Based on Response Information

According to Assumption 2, the more responses does a question receive, the more popularity the question is. In this paper, we explore the answers statistic features to estimate the response information and leave other features such as user ratings or comments for future work. For a question q, the impact of response information $w(q)$ on q's popularity is defined as :

$$w(q) = f(q, an_q) / \sum_{p \in C} f(p, an_p) \tag{3}$$

where C denotes the collection of questions, an_q is the number of answers of q, and $f(p, an_p)$ is defined as:

$$f(q, an_q) = \begin{cases} an_q & \text{if } an_q < cutN \\ cutN & \text{otherwise} \end{cases} \tag{4}$$

where $cutN$ is an integer which is supposed to be the largest number of answers of a question in a specific collection. According to the statistic information of the question collection in our dataset, we set $cutN$ to be 30.

Considering both impacts of question repeated possibility and responses information, the final function of question popularity is defined as:

$$Pop(q) = d \cdot w(q) + (1-d) \sum_{q' \in adj[q]} \frac{S(q,q')}{\sum_{u \in adj[q']} S(u,q')} Pop(q') \tag{5}$$

where $w(q)$ is defined in eq.3

2.2 Question Recommendation

Given a question as a query q', the recommendation model is defined as the probabilistic of generating query q' from the question language model q as follows:

$$P(q|q') = \frac{P(q'|q)P(q)}{P(q')} \tag{6}$$

As the likelihood $P(q')$ of q' does not affect the ranking of questions so it can be ignored by the rank preserving the principle.

The generation probability $P(q'|q)$ can be decomposed into a unigram model:

In eq.6, $P(q)$ is the prior probability of question q, reflecting a static rank of the question, independent on query q'. As the question popularity $Pop(q)$ defined in section 2.1 is the likelihood of a question and independent on a specific query, we can use the question popularity $Pop(q)$ as the prior probability of question q. So the probability of question q should be recommended to query q' is defined as:

$$R(q|q') \propto \alpha logPop(q) + \sum_{q \in q'} logP(t|q') \quad (7)$$

where α is a constant factor to indicate the importance of question popularity, which will be discussed in experiments. The unigram probability P(t|q') is defined as eq.8:

$$P(t|q') = \lambda P_{mle}(t|q') + (1 - \lambda) P_{mle}(t|C) \quad (8)$$

where

$$P_{mle}(t|q') = \frac{\#(t,q')}{|q'|}, P_{mle}(t|C) = \frac{\#(t,C)}{|C|}$$

and $\#(t,q')$ denotes the time that term t appeared in q', $|q'|$ denotes the length of q', C denotes the question collection, λ is a smoothing parameter and set to 0.2 in our experiments, the same as [7][5].

3. EXPERIMENTS

3.1 Data Set and Experiment Setup

We collected 17,680 questions in "diet & fitness" category from Yahoo!Answers as the experiment dataset. We randomly select 50 questions as query questions and use different methods to recommend questions to the query. Top 10 results of each query were judged by human. First, we employ different method to recommend questions to each query. For each method, we collect the top 10 results of each query. Then we combined different results together by query. Then an assessor is asked to label it with 'relevant' or 'irrelevant'. If a returned result is considered as a good recommendation for the queried question, the assessor will label it 'relevant'; otherwise, the assessor will label it 'irrelevant'. A good recommendation of a query means that the recommended question should not only be relevant to the query but also be representative among the related questions.

We want to investigate the effectiveness of question popularity to the performance of question recommendation. Thus we compare the performance of the following methods.

- **Rec_NoP**: Each question has equal question popularity score.
- **Rec_QP1**: Question popularity is estimated by question repeated possibility based on Assumption 1 and question similarity is measured by cosine method on questions.
- **Rec_QR2**: Question popularity is estimated by question repeated possibility based on Assumption 1 and question similarity is measured by improved question similarity measurement (eq.1). The question popularity is calculated with eq.2;
- **Rec_AP**: Question popularity is estimated based on Assumption 2 with eq.3. The recommendation function becomes:

$$R(q|q') \propto \alpha logw(q) + \sum_{t \in q'} logP(t|q')$$

- **Rec_QAP**: Question popularity is estimated based on both Assumption 1 and Assumption 2 with eq.5. Eq.7 is used as the recommendation function.

We use MAP (Mean Average of Precision), MRR (Mean Reciprocal Rank), and Precision@10 as metric to evaluate the performance of each method.

MAP calculates the mean of average precisions over a set of queries. MAP is calculated as:

$$MAP = \frac{1}{|Q_r|} \sum_{q \in Q_r} \frac{\sum_{r=1}^{n} P(r) rel(r)}{|R_q|} \quad (9)$$

where Q_r is a set of test queries, R_q is the set of relevant questions for q, r is the rank, n is the number of returned results, here $n = 10$, $rel(\cdot)$ is a binary function on the relevance of a given function, and $P(\cdot)$ is precision at a given cut-off rank.

MRR is calculated as :

$$MRR = \frac{1}{|Q_r|} \sum_{q \in Q_r} \frac{1}{r_q} \quad (10)$$

where Q_r is a set of test queries, r_q is the rank of the first relevant question for q. Precison@n is the fraction of the top n questions recommend that are relevant, it is calculated as:

$$Precision@n = \frac{\sum_{i=1}^{n} rel(i)}{n} \quad (11)$$

where $rel(\cdot)$ is a binary function on the relevance of a given rank, and here $n = 10$.

3.2 Impact of Question Popularity

In order to evaluate the effect of question popularity, controlled by the value of λ , for question recommendation, we tested different settings of λ with different question popularity estimation methods. Figure 1 gives the performance of Rec_QP1, Rec_QP2, Rec_AP and Rec_QAP with different settings of. From Figure 1 (a) and (b) we find that when is setting around 0.1, Rec_QP1 performs best, around 0.3, Rec_QP2 performs best, around 0.4, Rec_AP and Rec_QAP performs best.

3.3 Experiment Results

Table 1 reports each method's performance measured by MAP, MRR and Precison@10. Each row reports the results of a method and the improvement compared with other methods.

- **Rec_QP1** vs.**Rec_QP2**
  Both of the two methods are based on Assumption 1 when calculating the question popularity. Rec_Q1 employs Song et al[4] method to measure the similarity between questions while Rec_QP2 employs our improvement question similarity measurement. The results in table 1 show that Rec_QP2 out performs Rec_QP1 in terms of MAP and MRR but performs poorly in Precison@10. This result indicates that our proposed method on question similarity measurement can partially improve recommendation performance.
- **Rec_AP** vs.**Rec_NoP**
  Rec_AP is based on Assumption 2 when calculating the question popularity. The results in table 1 show that Rec_AP performs little better than Rec_NoP in MAP but worse in MRR and Precision@10. This result indicates that just using the number of answers of a question to estimate question popularity improve question recommendation performance hardly. Thus,

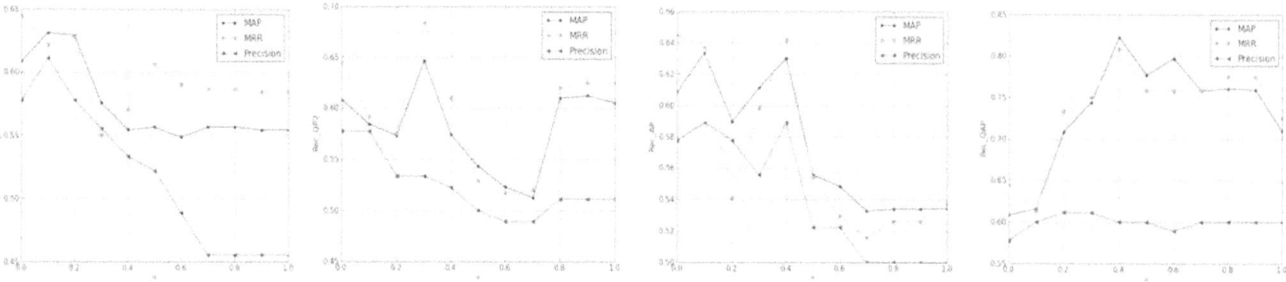

(a) Rec_QP1 (b) Rec_QP2 (c) Rec_AP (d) Rec_QAP

Figure 1: The effect of question popularity with different methods. (a) Rec_QP1: question popularity is estimated by question repeated possibility and question similarity is measured by cosine method on questions (b) Rec_QP2: Question popularity is estimated from question repeated possibility with improved question similarity measurement. (c) Rec_AP: question popularity is estimated from the responses to questions (d) Rec_QAP: the combination of method (b) and (c)

Table 1: Question recommendation performance on Yahoo! Answers dataset

Methods	*MAP*	*MRR*	*Precision@10*
Rec_NoP	0.608571	0.6444444	0.5777778
Rec_QP1	0.631433	0.6217857	0.6111111
imp.Rec_NoP	3.76%	-3.52%	5.77%
Rec_QP2	0.646389	0.6833333	0.5333333
imp.Rec_NoP	6.21%	6.03%	-7.69%
imp.Rec_QP1	2.37%	9.90%	-12.73%
Rec_AP	0.63345	0.6366667	0.5888889
imp.Rec_NoP	4.09%	-1.21%	1.92%
imp.Rec_QP1	0.32%	-2.39%	-3.64%
Rec_QAP	0.822738	0.808333	0.6
imp.Rec_Nop	35.19%	25.43%	3.85%
imp.Rec_QP1	30.30%	30.00%	-1.82%
imp.Rec_QP2	27.28%	18.29%	12.50%
imp.Rec_AP	29.88%	26.96%	1.88%

in our experiments, we use the combination of question repeated possibility and number of answers information for further improvement of question popularity estimation.

- **Rec_QAP** vs.**Rec_NoP**
  Compared with the baseline method Rec_NoP, our method Rec_QAP consistently shows better performance in terms of all the evaluation measures. It can support our hypothesis that question popularity driven from both question repeated possibility and number of answers can improve question recommendation performance significantly.

4. CONCLUSIONS

In this paper, we propose to employ public interest to boost the performance of question recommendation. The question popularity is used to measure the public interest on a question. Two factors, named question repeated possibility and questions' responses information, are examined in assessing question popularity. Experimental results on Yahoo!Answers dataset demonstrate that leveraging public interest can significantly improve the performance of question recommendation. In addition, utilizing similarity between answers and questions can provide more accurate questions popularity estimation and thus give a better question recommendation performance. Furthermore, questions' responses information can also boost the performance of question recommendation. Experiments demonstrate that the combination of question repeated possibility and questions' responses information gives a better estimation on question popularity and greatly boosts the performance of question recommendation. However, our experiments have conducted with one domain. Additional experiments on larger and heterogeneous collections are essentially required for deep analysis of our proposed method. It will be our future work.

5. REFERENCES

[1] E. Agichtein, C. Castillo, and D. Donato. Finding high-quality content in social media. In *WSDM'09*, pages 183–193, 2009.

[2] S. Brin and L. Page. The anatomy of a large-scale hypertextual web search engine. *Computer Networks and ISDN Systems*, 30(1-7):107–117, 1998.

[3] G. Erkan and D. R. Radev. Graph-based lexical centrality as salience in text summarization. *Journal of Artificial Intelligence Research*, 22:457–479, 2004.

[4] B. Li and I. King. Routing questions to appropriate answerers in community question answering services. In *CIKM'10*, pages 1585–1588, 2010.

[5] A. S. M A Suryanto, Ee-Peng Lim and et al. Quality-aware collaborative question answering methods and evaluation. In *WSDM'09*, pages 142–152, 2009.

[6] K. Sun, Y. Cao, X. Song, and et al. Learning to recommend questions based on user ratings. In *CIKM'09*, pages 751–758, 2009.

[7] C. Zhai and J. Lafferty. A study of smoothing methods for language models applied to ad hoc information retrieval. In *SIGIR'01*, pages 334–342, 2001.

CQC : Classifying Questions in CQA Websites

Amit Singh
IBM Research, India
amising3@in.ibm.com

Karthik Visweswariah
IBM Research, India
v-karthik@in.ibm.com

ABSTRACT

Community Question Answering portals like Yahoo! Answers have recently become a popular method for seeking information online. Users express their information need as questions for which other users generate potential answers. These questions are organized into pre-defined hierarchical categories to facilitate effective answering, hence Question Classification is an important aspect of these systems. In this paper we propose a novel system, CQC, for automatically classifying new questions into one of the hierarchical categories. Experiments conducted on large scale real data from Yahoo Answers! show that the proposed techniques are effective and outperform existing methods significantly.

Categories and Subject Descriptors

H.3.3 [**Information storage and retrieval**]: Information search and retrieval

General Terms

Algorithms, Design, Experimentation, Management

Keywords

Question Classification, Nearest Neighbour, Translation Model

1. INTRODUCTION

Over the past few years community-based question answering (CQA) portals like Naver (www.naver.com), Yahoo! Answers (answers.yahoo.com), Baidu Zhidao (zhidao.baidu.com) and WikiAnswers (wiki.answers.com) have gained a lot of popularity. These portals allow users to both submit questions to be answered and answer questions asked by other user. Due to the open collaborative model of these services, over time a tremendous number of question and answer pairs have been collected, that serves as a valuable source of information.

Most CQA portals organize questions by a predefined set of categories. When submitting a new question, users are required to assign a category label to it. Assigning a correct category label (Question Classification(QC)) plays a very important role in enabling other users to find and answer questions in their area of expertise. These category tags also enhance the future usefulness of the Q&A repository by allowing users to systematically navigate to information of interest. While important, assigning correct category tags is an onerous activity for the user. This is because finding the correct category requires knowledge of the category hierarchy which users might not have. In the following example taken from Yahoo! Answers, the onus is on the user to find the existence and relevance of a category for his question, as all of the listed categories have questions related to important aspects of the question i.e. tattoos, skin, allergy.

Q: How will it effect me if I get a tattoo even though my skin is allergic to alcohol ?
1: [Beauty & Style]→[Skin & Body]→[Tattoos]
2: [Health]→[Diseases & Conditions]→[Skin Conditions]
3: [Health]→[Diseases & Conditions]→[Allergies]
4: [Beauty & Style]→[Skin & Bod]→[Other-Skin & Body]
5: [Arts & Humanities]→[Visual Arts]→[Drawing & Illustration]

Yahoo! Answers has a 3 level category structure with roughly 26 top-level and 1065 leaf level categories. These categories span a variety of topics such as *Internet*, *Health*, *Politics* and *Science*. Each question in Yahoo! Answers is associated with one leaf category. Moreover, some categories like *[Style]→[Skin & Body]→[Tattoos]* are topical where any subset of questions generally show a high degree of similarity to any other subset. On the other hand categories like *[Beauty & Style]→[Skin & Bod]→[Other-Skin & Body]* (hence forth referred to as a general class *Others*) are quite general and clearly created for sake of completeness. In addition to being hierarchical, category structure of a CQA portal is fairly static. On the contrary, topics discussed by users evolve over time. This results in existing categories becoming less coherent (more generic) in terms of the topics discussed. This is an important challenge that any QC system has to deal with. CQA portals try to handle this using special categories, *Others*, meant for classifying questions that don't fit in the hierarchy. But this causes a new problem where the *Others* category is incorrectly used by users for categorizing questions that would normally fit in an existing more specific category. In Yahoo! Answers we found that > 17% of the top categories in terms of the number of question asked,

CIKM'11, October 24–28, 2011, Glasgow, Scotland, UK.

were of type *Others*, while they are only 10% of the overall leaf level category count.

At a high level, QC is a text classification task [5]. However, the fact that questions are short makes the task particularly challenging. Existing QC approaches mainly deal with the task of classifying TREC style factual questions into a small number of semantic categories. For example [3] classified questions in to two level hierarchy containing 6 coarse classes (ABBREVIATION, ENTITY, DESCRIPTION, HUMAN, LOCATION and NUMERIC VALUE) and 50 fine classes. Here, the answer type of the question *"What's the best metro-accessible bar in DC for a first date?"* might be *[Location]→[Others]*. In contrast we are interested in classifying questions into a large number of topical classes (>1000), we might, for example, classify the question above into the category *[Dining Out]→[United States]→[Washington, D.C.]*.

2. OUR APPROACH

The QC task is to assign a category tag t_{user} to a new user question q_{user}. For the QC task, we use a nearest neighbor approach to find a subset of most relevant questions (Q_{k-sim}) and hence related categories for q_{user}. We then predict t_{user} using Q_{k-sim}. Since classification of q_{user} is an online task, the classification model learnt from Q_{k-sim} should be computationally efficient to train. Motivation for our neighborhood based approach is 2 fold. Firstly, several studies of human perception [4] have argued that representating categories by similarity to prototypes is better than defining them as lists of features in presence of large number of categories describing potentially related objects. Also as compared to a small set of categories, classification on a large-scale hierarchy is known to be very expensive and not up to the mark for many target categories, especially the ones that are related to each other.

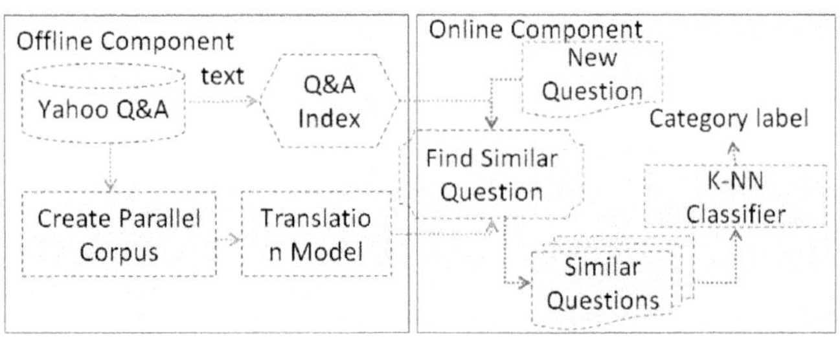

Figure 1: CQC Architecture

2.1 System Architecture

Figure 1 outlines the architecture of CQC. It comprises of an offline component and an online component. The offline component processes the CQA archive and creates models to retrieve k questions (Q_{k-sim}) that are most similar to q_{user}. Prior work [6] has shown that translation based retrieval models work well for finding Q_{k-sim}. So our CQC system uses them to calculate $sim(q, q_{user})$[1]. The online component employs a nearest neighbor classifier based on Q_{k-sim} and returns the category t_{user} corresponding to q_{user} as described below.

[1] $sim_{ret}(q, q_{user})$ is $sim(q, q_{user})$, as calculated by retrieval models

2.2 Classification Model

We use the class labels of the k most similar neighbors (Q_{k-sim}) according to a similarity function ($sim(q, q_{user})$) to predict the class of a user question q_{user}. The classes of these neighbors $q \in Q_{k-sim}$ are weighted using a similarity function $sim(q, q_{user})$ that captures the similarity of a neighbor q to q_{user} and a function $CatRel(q, t)$ that captures relationship of the neighbor q to the category tag t being scored. Thus, our scoring function is:

$$score(q_{user}, t) = \omega(t) * \left\{ \sum_{q \in Q_{k-sim}} sim(q, q_{user}) * CatRel(q, t) \right\} \quad (1)$$

and our decision function is:

$$t_{user} = \arg\max_t (score(q_{user}, t)). \quad (2)$$

Equation 1 indicates that contribution of a neighbor q_i towards a category t would be high if it is highly similar to q_{user} and also strongly coherent with t. This tackles the coherency related problem mentioned in Section 1. To alleviate effect of inductive bias, $\omega(.)$ weighs each category t by its size relative to the overall size of the collection C as defined by Equation 3. Here parameter γ controls the effect of category size on the overall score.

$$\omega(t) = \left\{ \frac{|t|}{|C|} \right\}^{-\gamma} \quad (3)$$

Based on how we define $sim(q, q_{user})$ we can have several configurations of Equation 2. We propose UNIFORM and RET-SCORE as two possible ways to define $sim(q, q_{user})$.

$$sim(q, q_{user}) = \begin{cases} 1 & \text{if } q \in Q_{k-sim} \\ 0 & \text{otherwise} \end{cases} \quad (4)$$

UNIFORM weighs each neighbor equally while in RET-SCORE neighbors are weighted by the same similarity score [$sim_{ret}(q, q_{user})$] used to retrieve the top k questions Q_{k-sim}. Formal definitions are given in Equation 4 and Equation 5, respectively.

$$sim(q, q_{user}) = \begin{cases} sim_{ret}(q, q_{user}) & \text{if } q \in Q_{k-sim} \\ 0 & \text{otherwise} \end{cases} \quad (5)$$

Similarly based on definition of $CatRel(q, t_i)$ in Equation 6 and Equation 7 henceforth referred to as INDICATOR, CAT-WEIGHTED we have two more configurations of Equation 2.

$$CatRel(q, t) = \begin{cases} 1 & \text{if } t \text{ is category of q} \\ 0 & \text{otherwise} \end{cases} \quad (6)$$

$$CatRel(q, t) = P(t|q) \quad (7)$$

In INDICATOR configuration, each neighbor q contributes to the score of only one category based on its category tag in our archive. This makes the standard assumption that each question can belong to only one category and is correctly tagged in our archive. This is not true for many questions in Yahoo! Answers. In fact, as mentioned earlier, categories like *Others* contain lots of questions that can easily be assigned to other categories. CAT-WEIGHTED handles these issues by weighing each neighbor by the posterior probability $P(t|q)$ using a Naive-Bayes model. $P(t|q)$ can be computed

Retrieval Models	MAP	%chg	MRR	%chg	R-Prec	%chg	Prec@5	%chg
VSM	0.251		0.452		0.242		0.230	
OKAPI	0.352	40.23	0.551	21.90	0.320	32.23	0.290	26.08
TRLM	0.440	75.29	0.645	42.69	0.410	69.42	0.343	49.13

Table 1: Retrieval results with VSM used as the baseline evaluation system

as given in Equation 8, where d_j is term frequency of word w_j in question q and N is the vocabulary size.

$$P(t|q) \quad \propto \quad P(t) \prod_{j=1}^{N} P(w_j|t)^{d_j} \tag{8}$$

$P(w|t)$ can be estimated offline from our CQA archive using Equation 9. $P_{ml}(w|C)$ is the probability that the term w is generated from the collection C.

$$P(w|t) = (1-\theta)P_{ml}(w|t) + \theta P_{ml}(w|C) \tag{9}$$

In using a K-NN classifier, the main challenge is in coming up with a suitable similarity function $sim_{ret}(q, q_{user})$ to retrieve Q_{k-sim}, the set of k most similar questions. In particular, bridging lexical gaps between q_{user} and other questions in the Q&A archives has been a major challenge. We use translation models (TRLM)[6] to solve this problem.

3. EVALUATION

We crawled a dataset of ~6 million questions and answers from Yahoo! Answers spanning all the leaf level categories. This was the master repository used for all our experiments. Questions in the repository spanned 26 categories at the top level and > 1065 categories at the leaf level. On an average we had ~6000 questions per category. A large percentage (~ 40%) of the categories in the Yahoo! Answers dataset had fewer than 6000 questions available.

Table 1 shows empirical evaluation results of our retrieval system for finding Q_{k-sim}. TRLM outperforms other models in all the measures. In our retrieval experiments we used 228 queries. For each query q_{user} we considered the top 25 results and human annotators were asked to mark if the retrieved questions Q_{20-sim} were relevant to q_{user}.

3.1 Classification Evaluation

In this section, we discuss results of our CQC system described earlier in Section 2.2. For the purpose of training the baseline SVM models, we sampled around 1 million examples spanning all the classes. For a fair comparison, all the models listed in Table 1 used this sampled data as their base corpus (C) for retrieval. In addition to this, we selected around 0.1 million questions covering all the categories as our test data. Category tags for the sampled question were used as the ground truth.

3.1.1 Baselines for Classification

We use a flat multi-class classification(F-SVM) and a hierarchical classification(H-SVM) [1] using SVM as our baseline methods. For both the baselines, we have used a linear kernel and linear SVM [2], one v/s rest setting. For evaluating QC performance we use the standard evaluations metrics i.e. macro-averaged F_1 (*macro-F_1*) and micro-averaged F_1 (*micro-F_1*)

3.1.2 CQC configurations

Of the four possible configurations, following are the 2 basic configurations of our CQC system in which all the neighbors are weighed equally independent of their similarity to q_{user}.

UNIFORM + INDICATOR $[U+I]$: Each neighbor gives a unit contribution towards its category.

UNIFORM + CAT-WEIGHTED $[U+C]$: Each neighbor gives a contribution proportional to its relation to the category t, given by $CatRel(q, t)$.

In the remaining 2 configurations, each neighbor q, is weighed proportional to $sim(q, q_{user})$.

RET-SCORE + INDICATOR $[R+I]$: Each neighbor contributes a score proportaional to $sim(q, q_{user})$ towards its category.

RET-SCORE + CAT-WEIGHTED $[R+C]$: Each neighbor gives a contribution proportional to $CatRel(q, t)$ and $sim(q, q_{user})$.

One instance of each of the above configurations (henceforth denoted with subscript "Base"[2]) where VSM is used to retrieve top-k similar questions, is the simplest configuration of our system. These configurations are directly comparable to the two SVM baselines as all of them operate in the same feature space (words in a question).

3.1.3 Parameters Selection (k, γ and θ)

We use cross validation to estimate a good value of k (number of neighbors i.e $|Q_{k-sim}|$). Here we experiment with various k values and the value achieving the highest *macro-F_1* is selected as the optimal value. We found that choosing k in the range of $10 < k < 15$ was good for all configuration of our CQC system. Similarly θ used in Equation 9 was set to 0.15 and $[0.4, 0.65]$ serves as a good range for γ.

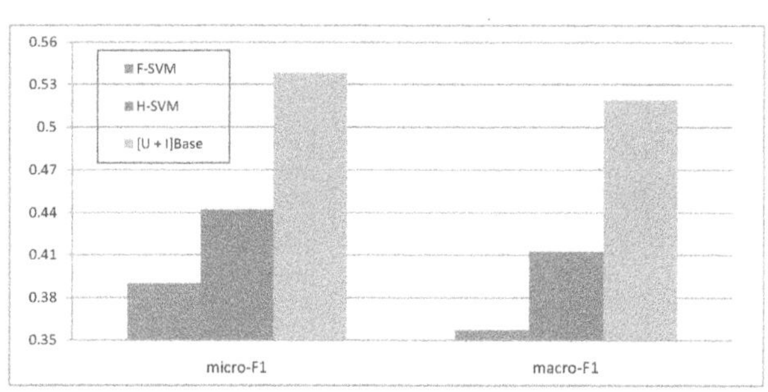

Figure 2: Comparison of basic CQC configurations ($k = 10$) with SVM baselines.

[2]e.g. $[U+I]_{Base}$

3.1.4 Result Analysis

Figure 2 compares the performance of SVM baselines against $[U+I]_{Base}$. Parameter values used for $[U+I]_{Base}$ are $\gamma = 0.6$ and $k = 10$. We see that our basic CQC configuration outperforms F-SVM by 38% and H-SVM by 21% in *micro*-F_1. Similar behaviour is also observed for *macro*-F_1. This validates our basic hypothesis that neighborhood based classification strategy helps in the presence of large category hierarchy with several related classes. Next, we compare the remaining 3 basic configurations to $[U+I]_{Base}$ for different values of k. As shown in Figure 3, all 3 of them perform better than $[U+I]_{Base}$. $[R+C]_{Base}$ outperforms $[U+I]_{Base}$ in both the measures by ~7%. Similar relative performance is observed for *macro*-F_1. All the configurations give the best performance for $k = 10$. Performance gradually drops after that due to the introduction of questions from topically incoherent categories. Until now we only looked at

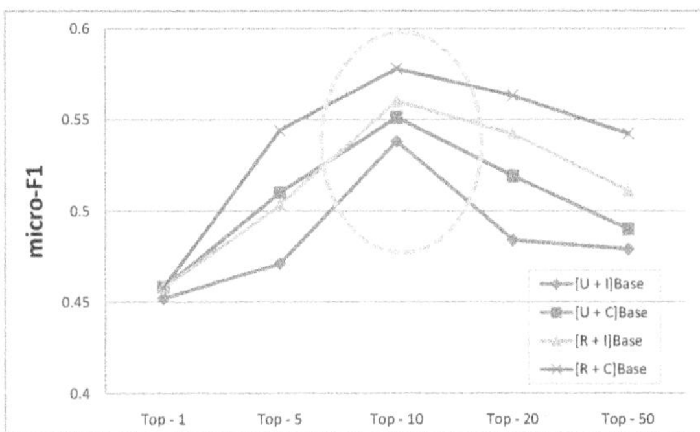

Figure 3: *micro*-F_1 comparison of CQC configurations for different values of k.

CQC performance using a VSM model (only questions) for retrieval. Figure 4 outlines *micro*-F_1 performance of CQC configurations using retrieval models presented in Table 1. Among the CQC configuration classes, $[R+C]$ outperforms others for all values of k. $[R+C]$ with R=(TRLM) is the best overall configuration and performs ~12.25% better than $[U+I]_{Base}$ and ~36.65% better than H-SVM.

The key pattern observed across all the results is that improvements in retrieval performance results in improved classification performance of our CQC system. We did statistical significance tests (t-Test) for comparing the performance (already reported in this section) of important configurations like F-SVM v/s H-SVM, H-SVM v/s $[U+I]_{Base}$, $[U+I]_{Base}$ v/s $[R+C]_{Base}$ and $[R+C]_{Base}$ v/s $[R+C]$ with R=(VSM|OKAPI|TRLM). All these differences are significant with P-value < 0.001%.

CatRel(q,t) / RET-SCORE	INDICATOR	% Δ	CAT-WEIGHTED	% Δ
VSM	0.56	4.09	0.578	7.43
OKAPI	0.58	7.81	0.591	9.85
TRLM	0.59	9.67	0.604	12.3

Figure 4: *micro*-F_1 comparison of CQC configurations with $[U+I]_{Base}$ having value of 0.538 as baseline.

As mentioned earlier, since classification of q_{user} is an online task, it is highly desirable that the classification model learnt from Q_{k-sim} take minimal training time. Hence classifiers like SVM are not recommended as its training time

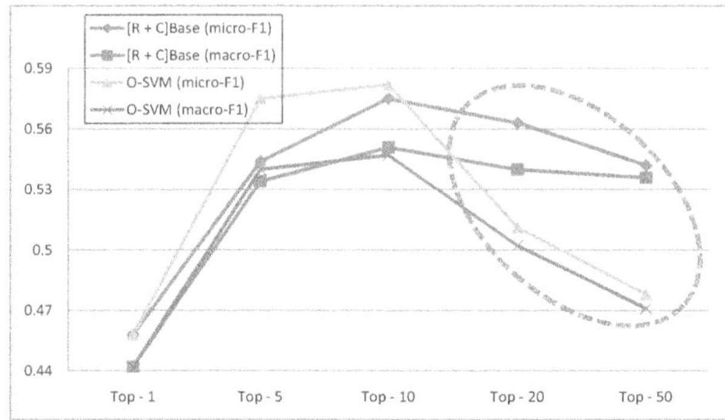

Figure 5: Comparison of $[R+C]_{Base}$ with O-SVM for different values of k.

may prevent us from recommending predicted category labels back to user in a timely manner. For the sake of completeness of analysis, we also compare flat multiclass SVM classifier (O-SVM) trained on categories (t_{k-sim}) covered by Q_{k-sim} with our $[R+C]_{Base}$ configuration. As shown in Figure 5, for small values of k it performs similar to $[R+C]_{Base}$. As the value of k increases, beyond a point it becomes much worse due to the increase in size of t_{k-sim}.

4. CONCLUSION AND FUTURE WORK

In this paper, we propose a novel QC system to classify a new question into one of the hierarchical categories of a CQA portal. We used translation based models to retrieve lexically and semantically similar questions. We use a neighborhood based classifier on the retrieved questions to classify new questions. CQC configuration of $[R+C]$ with R=[TRLM] is the best overall configuration and performs ~48% better than hierarchical SVM based baseline system.

5. REFERENCES

[1] S. Dumais and H. Chen. Hierarchical classification of web content. In *Proceedings of the 23rd annual international ACM SIGIR conference on Research and development in information retrieval*, SIGIR '00, pages 256–263, New York, NY, USA, 2000. ACM.

[2] T. Joachims. Training linear svms in linear time. In *Proceedings of the 12th ACM SIGKDD international conference on Knowledge discovery and data mining*, KDD '06, pages 217–226, New York, NY, USA, 2006. ACM.

[3] X. Li and D. Roth. Learning question classifiers. In *Proceedings of the 19th international conference on Computational linguistics - Volume 1*, COLING '02, pages 1–7, Stroudsburg, PA, USA, 2002. Association for Computational Linguistics.

[4] E. H. Rosch. Natural categories. *Cognitive Psychology*, 4:328–350, 1973.

[5] F. Sebastiani. Machine learning in automated text categorization. *ACM Comput. Surv.*, 34:1–47, March 2002.

[6] X. Xue, J. Jeon, and W. B. Croft. Retrieval models for question and answer archives. In *SIGIR '08: Proceedings of the 31st annual international ACM SIGIR conference on Research and development in information retrieval*, pages 475–482, New York, NY, USA, 2008. ACM.

Automatic Query Reformulation with Syntactic Operators to Alleviate Search Difficulty

Huizhong Duan
University of Illinois at Urbana-Champaign
201 N Goodwin Ave
Urbana, IL 61801 USA
duan9@illinois.edu

Rui Li
University of Illinois at Urbana-Champaign
201 N Goodwin Ave
Urbana, IL 61801 USA
ruili1@illinois.edu

ChengXiang Zhai
University of Illinois at Urbana-Champaign
201 N Goodwin Ave
Urbana, IL 61801 USA
czhai@cs.uiuc.edu

ABSTRACT

Modern search engines usually provide a query language with a set of advanced syntactic operators (e.g., plus sign to require a term's appearance, or quotation marks to require a phrase's appearance) which if used appropriately, can significantly improve the effectiveness of a plain keyword query. However, they are rarely used by ordinary users due to the intrinsic difficulties and users' lack of corpora statistics. In this paper, we propose to automatically reformulate queries that do not work well by selectively adding syntactic operators. Particularly, we propose to perform syntactic operator-based query reformulation when a retrieval system detects users encounter difficulty in search as indicated by users' behaviors such as scanning over top *k* documents without click-through. We frame the problem of automatic reformulation with syntactic operators as a supervised learning problem, and propose a set of effective features to represent queries with syntactic operators. Experiment results verify the effectiveness of the proposed method and its applicability as a query suggestion mechanism for search engines. As a negative feedback strategy, syntactic operator-based query reformulation also shows promising results in improving search results for difficult queries as compared with existing methods.

Categories and Subject Descriptors

H.3.3 [**INFORMATION STORAGE AND RETRIEVAL**]: Information Search and Retrieval – *query formulation*

General Terms

Algorithms, Performance, Experimentation

Keywords

Query reformulation, syntactic operator, search difficulty.

1. INTRODUCTION

Query languages of modern search engines usually include a set of advanced syntactic operators to supplement traditional keyword query [1, 2]. For instance, a necessity operator (plus sign) preceding a query term requires the term to be present in each relevant document; a phrase operator (a pair of quotation marks) imposes that relevant documents must contain the phrase consisting of the quoted terms. To distinguish from keyword query, we refer to a query with syntactic operators as a *syntax query*. For example, Figure 1a shows a keyword query, while Figure 1b and Figure 1c show two *syntax queries* which have the same set of terms as the keyword query shown in Figure 1a. For convenience of discussion, we further denote this type of syntactic operator-based reformulation as *syntactic reformulation*.

If used appropriately, syntactic reformulation can be very effective for improving retrieval accuracy, turning an otherwise ineffective query to an effective one. Figure 1 shows an example of using syntactic reformulation to improve the top ranked results with a major US search engine[1]. As we can see from Figure 1a, none of the top ranked documents is relevant to the query. In contrast, in Figure 1b, by using the syntactic query with the necessity constraint on term "unix", we are able to find two (2nd and 3rd) relevant documents out of the top three. This is because the search engine overlooked the term "unix" in the original query, which is typically due to the coarse estimation of term importance. By imposing the necessity constraint, the query emphasizes the importance of the term and re-ranks the results according to whether it is contained in each document. In Figure 1c, with an even more complicated syntactic reformulation, we further impose a phrase constraint on "default java". This effectively eliminates the possible ambiguities of the query caused by matching terms separately. As a result, all the top three ranked documents are relevant documents. The proper use of syntactic operators not only clarifies user's information need, but also gives clues to the retrieval system on how to optimize the search results.

However, very few users make use of the syntactic operators in their daily search activities. Statistics[2] from a search engine query log show that only less than 0.5% queries used syntactic operators. This is either because users are unfamiliar with the semantics of the operator, or because they lack the appropriate knowledge and statistics to formulate working syntax queries.

In this paper, we propose to help users take advantage of the rich query syntax by automatically formulating potentially effective syntax queries based on keyword queries. Particularly, we propose to automatically perform the query reformulation with syntactic operators when users encounter difficulty in search. Such

[1] http://www.google.com

[2] Based on a sample of MSN query log in 2006.

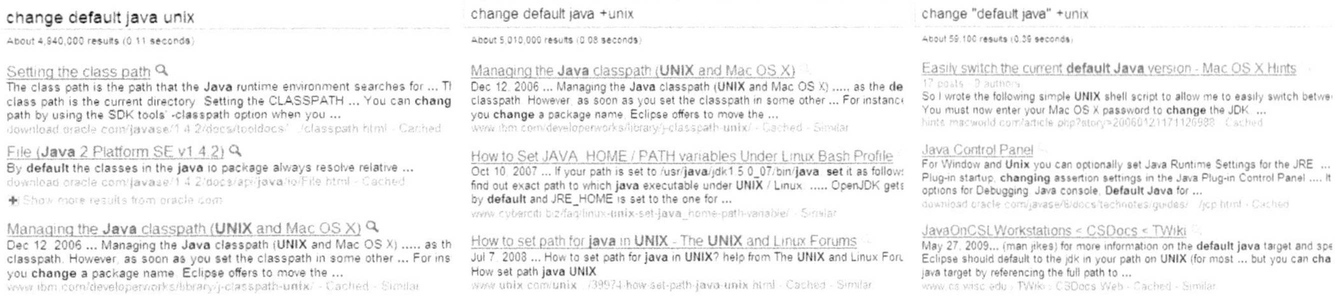

a b c

Figure 1. Example of Using Syntactic Operators for Improving Search Result.

difficulty could be detected through monitoring users' behaviors. For instance, one possible indicator could be when a user skipped a page of top ranked results to the next page. Our assumption is that if a user can find relevant documents in the top ranked results, she is likely satisfied with the original ranking and thus there is no much need for syntactic reformulation. We thus focus on studying how to exploit query syntax reformulation to help users when it is evident that the user cannot find any relevant document in the top k results. This scenario is similar to the case of negative relevance feedback [11, 12] in the sense that there is a common goal of re-ranking the unseen results based on a small number of negative examples already encountered by the user. However, while existing negative feedback techniques primarily rely on word frequency analysis in the negative examples to improve the query representation [11], we study how to leverage query syntax operators to improve the syntax of a query, which is a different and complementary strategy and has two advantages over the existing methods for negative feedback: first, it has better interpretability to users. i.e., the suggested reformulated query can be more easily verified by a user if deployed in an interactive feedback system; second, while most negative feedback methods "blindly" treat a whole document as non-relevant, our method would attempt to "diagnose" the cause of poor results and correct any missing semantic constraint via appropriate syntactic operator.

To perform automatic syntactic reformulation, we adopt a supervised learning framework. Particularly, we cast the problem as to predict the potential benefit of each candidate syntax query in improving the performance of a given keyword query. If we are confident on the potential improvement, we can suggest the reformulation to the user or use it directly to refine the search result. One problem in training the prediction model is that syntactic reformulations of different keyword queries may not have comparable performances. To circumvent this problem, we make use of the learning to rank techniques.

We propose and study three types of features to represent the characteristics of a syntax query. Query difficulty measures the intrinsic difficulty of syntax query. Distinguishability computes the amount of changes a syntax query brings to the original result. Negativity measures the similarity between the candidate query and the negative relevance feedback. The three types of features are all generalized features that can be computed for any filtering-based operators. Experiments demonstrate their effectiveness in formulating highly beneficial syntax queries.

2. RELATED WORK

Query reformulation/refinement is a broad topic on using modified versions of queries to improve search results. Our work is naturally subsumed by this topic. Under this broad topic, query expansion, query contraction, spelling correction have been extensively studied. Guo et al. [5] proposed a modified CRF model for simultaneously performing spelling correction and query segmentation. Yet it is unclear whether the proposed method is applicable to different types of operators, especially in alleviating search difficulty. In this paper, we conduct systematic study on query reformulation with syntactic operators to alleviate search difficulty. Besides explicit reformulation of query, there are also studies on implicit refinement of queries, such as term proximity [8, 9] and term necessity [13] refinement. This type of refinement is usually transparent to users and makes more subtle changes to original results. Compared with these work, the explicit use of syntactic operator has the advantage of being more interpretable and easy to implement, especially across different retrieval systems.

Our research is also strongly related to the work on negative feedback. Wang et al. used EM algorithm to estimate language models for negative feedback and use them to re-rank the rest of the results [11, 12]. Our method also uses the negative feedback information to assist search difficulty, but it distinguishes itself by making use of syntactic operators to introduce additional semantics to the query. Compared with existing methods, this is a novel complementary approach and potentially provides better usage of the negative feedback.

3. AUTOMATIC REFORMULATION WITH SYNTACTIC OPERATORS

We formulate the automatic syntactic reformulation of keyword queries as a supervised learning problem. Particularly, we cast the problem as to predict the potential performance improvement from each candidate syntax query over a given keyword query.

Formally, given a keyword query q, a syntactic operator op and a target performance metric M, our goal is to find a list of syntactic reformulations of q through the use of op, denoted as $S_{op}(q) = \{q_1, q_2, \dots, q_n\}$, which is ranked according to M in descending order: $M(q_1) > M(q_2) > \cdots > M(q_n)$. When it is required to output top m suggestions, the system will respond with a list consisting of $q_1, q_2, \dots q_m$. When a syntactic reformulation is required to directly refine the search results, the system will output the top ranked query q_1 if $M'(q_1) = M(q_1) - M(q) > 0$, or otherwise the original query q. The training process is to learn a function f, which takes a set of features of a syntax query q_i and predict the performance improvement $M'(q_i)$.

Since there are an exponential number of possible syntax queries for each syntactic operator, we limit the system to consider single appearance of each operator. Although we only explore the limited scope of use of these operators, the proposed methodology is general and can be potentially applicable to other filtering-based operators and multiple uses of each operator.

To solve the learning problem, a natural way is to use a regression model. In this method, a model will be learned to predict the performance for any possible syntax query. One problem with this method is that the performances of syntax queries reformulated based on different keyword queries are usually not directly comparable. To circumvent the problem, we adopt the learning to rank framework. In this setting, syntax queries generated from each keyword query are considered as a group; the loss function is defined on the ranking order of members in each group instead of on the absolute value of the performance. This loss function is more natural in our problem setting and avoids the issue of incomparability. We then use the learned model to predict the potential benefit in performance for each candidate in syntactic reformulation. Particularly, we adopt Ranking SVM [7] as our learning method.

3.1 Features

We propose three types of features, namely *difficulty*, *distinguishability* and *negativity*. All three types of features are defined in a general way so that they can be computed for any type of filtering-based operators. As used in previous discussions, we denote q as the keyword query, op as the target operator and q_x as a syntactic reformulation of q with operator op.

3.1.1 Difficulty

The difficulty feature aims to measure the intrinsic difficulty of a syntax query. Query difficulty prediction has been widely studied in recent years [4, 6]. We modify the clarity feature [4] slightly to make it applicable to syntax queries:

$$\begin{aligned} Clarity(q_x) &= KL(\theta_m || \theta_C) \\ &= \sum_{w \in V} p(w|\theta_m) log \frac{p(w|\theta_m)}{p(w|\theta_C)} \end{aligned} \quad (1)$$

where θ_m is the language model estimated from the set of matched documents S_m of q_x, θ_C is the language model estimated from the entire collection. Queries with high clarity are more likely to work well.

In addition to clarity, we propose another difficulty feature, which is inspired by the inverse document frequency (IDF). We generalize this concept to compute the specificity of a syntax query:

$$GIDF(q_x) = \log(\frac{N_c - N_{S_m} + 0.5}{N_{S_m} + 0.5}) \quad (2)$$

where N_c and N_{S_m} are the number of documents in the entire collection and matched set, respectively. Intuitively, a query matching fewer documents is more specific and meaningful.

3.1.2 Distinguishability

The idea of the distinguishability feature is to quantify the changes a syntax query brings to the original query. For this purpose, we define cross clarity between θ_m and θ_q, the language model estimated from the search results of q:

$$CrossClarity(q_x, q) = KL(\theta_m || \theta_q) \quad (3)$$

This feature measures the change in the topical formation of the syntax query q_x and the original query q.

Besides measuring content changes, we use another feature to measure the change in the ranking of documents. Particularly, we measure the correlation between the document rankings of q and q_x:

$$Cor(q_x, q) = \frac{\#concord(q_x, q) - \#discord(q_x, q)}{\frac{1}{2} N_q (N_q - 1)} \quad (4)$$

where $concord(q_x, q)$ and $discord(q_x, q)$ are the sets of concordant pairs and discordant pairs between the two ranking lists of search results of q_x and q. The correlation feature quantifies the changes q_x brings to the original ranking of q.

3.1.3 Negativity

The negativity feature measures the similarity between the syntax query q_x and the negative documents. A query less similar to the negative documents naturally has higher chances of working well.

Again, we define the content based negativity feature as the cross clarity between the language model estimated from the matched documents S_m and the language model estimated from the negative feedback documents S_n.

In addition, we define another negative feature as the generalized inverse negative frequency (GINF):

$$GINF(S_m, S_n) = \log(\frac{N_{S_n} + 0.5}{N_{S_m \cap S_n} + 0.5}) \quad (5)$$

In effect, this feature indicates the necessity of requiring a particular operator in the original keyword query.

By computing negativity features with different operators, we are actually "diagnosing" why the original query does not work well.

3.2 Combining Operators in Prediction

Our proposed algorithm not only works for predicting each operator separately, but can also be applied to predict different operators jointly, as filters can be applied additively. We refer to this joint prediction method as *Operator-Combination*.

An alternative method is *Result-Combination*, in which we predict each operator separately and select the reformulation with the best predicted performance. In practice we find this method not only more effective but also more efficient than the Operator-Combination, as it considers much fewer candidates in prediction.

4. EXPERIMENTS

4.1 Experiment Setup

We use TREC 2004 Robust track [10] as our experiment dataset. The title field and description field of the queries are used to represent (relatively) short query and (relatively) long query, respectively. Not all the queries are difficult queries. To simulate the scenario of search difficulty, we adopt the minimum deletion method proposed in [11]. We use BM25 [3] as our baseline. In addition, we also implement *MultiNeg*, a state-of-the-art method for using negative feedback [11]. It is worth noting that our method does not conflict with existing methods for using negative feedback. Instead, we use negative feedback in a different manner, which could potentially bring complementary factor to the existing methods. To test this idea, we further combine the use of syntactic reformulation with the MultiNeg method.

We evaluate automatic syntactic reformulation with necessity and phrase operator by using them to directly refine search result by re-ranking unseen documents. NDCG@10 is used as the primary metric. All the reported results are based on 5-fold cross validation. Statistical significance is indicated by * (p-value<0.05).

4.2 Experiment Results

Table 1 and Table 2 show the performances on long queries (description) and short queries (title) respectively. We see that for long queries, reformulation with necessity operator achieves higher performances than with phrase operator. However, for short queries, phrase operator tends to work better. Long queries are much more verbose and noisy, and thus more likely have the central topic missed in returned documents. Reformulation with necessity operator is more useful here as it discovers the important but underrepresented topical term and ensures it to be matched. A short query has fewer keywords and therefore less noise. However, the connection between keywords is usually lost as a cost of being succinct. Reformulation with phrase operator alleviates the problem by imposing the phrase constraint strongly connected terms. We also see the Result-Combination strategy always outperforms Operator-Combination. Result-Combination usually brings further improvement to the performance. More importantly, it provides a more robust solution compared with reformulation with single type of operator.

Table 1. Automatic Syntactic Reformulation to Directly Refine Search Results for Long Queries (Description)

Run Name	NDCG@10	P@1	MAP
Baseline	0.065	0.157	0.089
Necessity	0.077*	0.205*	0.104*
Phrase	0.069	0.161	0.093
Operator-Combination	0.065	0.161	0.088
Result-Combination	0.079*	0.209*	0.114*
MultiNeg	0.074*	0.216*	0.093
RC+MultiNeg	0.081*	0.221*	0.115*

Table 2. Automatic Syntactic Reformulation to Directly Refine Search Results for Short Queries (Title)

Run Name	NDCG@10	P@1	MAP
Baseline	0.078	0.217	0.111
Necessity	0.081	0.229	0.115
Phrase	0.083	0.221	0.119*
Operator-Combination	0.076	0.201	0.108
Result-Combination	0.082	0.225	0.119*
MultiNeg	0.078	0.216	0.111
RC+MultiNeg	0.084*	0.225	0.119*

Result-Combination outperforms MultiNeg. MultiNeg method takes the entire content of a negative document as non-relevant. In our method, we try to find the commonly missing semantics among negative examples. Compared with MultiNeg, this is a more precise way of using negative feedback and is therefore more effective. The performance could be further improved by combining syntactic reformulation with MultiNeg (RC-MultiNeg). Since our method does not directly use the negative information to refine scores of documents, it is complementary with the existing methods that work in this way.

We see that it is generally more difficult to improve the search results for short queries. Short queries are typically more succinct. As a result, there is less room for applying syntactic operators.

5. CONCLUSION AND FUTURE WORK

The ability to help users reformulate effective queries when their original queries don't work well is a crucial criterion for a good retrieval system. In this paper we propose and study a novel way of automatic query reformulation through the use of query syntax operators. With appropriate use of syntactic operators, we are able to detect the "missing semantics" in the original query and amend it in the reformulated query.

We formulate automatic syntactic reformulation as a supervised learning problem under the framework of learning to rank. We propose a set of effective features to represent the characteristics of syntax queries. The proposed approach is general; it can be applied to syntactic reformulation with any filtering-based operators, and can be directly incorporated into an existing search engine to improve user's experience with difficult queries.

Extensive experiments are conducted to test the effectiveness of the proposed methods. For the task of directly refining future search results with the reformulated query, we observe promising results in improving the performance. It is demonstrated that with proper strategy, we could combine the reformulations with different operators to achieve a robust solution. Our method is also complementary with existing methods for using negative relevance feedback as further performance improvements are observed when they are combined in use.

In future, we plan to explore the use of more useful syntactic operators for query reformulation to alleviate search difficulty.

6. REFERENCES

[1] http://www.google.com/support/websearch/bin/answer.py?hl=en&answer=136861

[2] http://msdn.microsoft.com/en-us/library/ff795620.aspx

[3] http://en.wikipedia.org/wiki/Okapi_BM25

[4] Steve Cronen-Townsend, Yun Zhou, and W. Bruce Croft. Predicting query performance. In *SIGIR '02*, 2002.

[5] Jiafeng Guo, Gu Xu, Hang Li, and Xueqi Cheng. A unified and discriminative model for query refinement. In *SIGIR '08*, 2008.

[6] Claudia Hauff, Djoerd Hiemstra, and Franciska de Jong. A survey of pre-retrieval query performance predictors. In *CIKM '08*, 2008.

[7] Thorsten Joachims. Optimizing search engines using clickthrough data. In *KDD '02*, 2002.

[8] Yves Rasolofo and Jacques Savoy. 2003. Term proximity scoring for keyword-based retrieval systems. In *ECIR'03*, 2003.

[9] Tao Tao and ChengXiang Zhai. An exploration of proximity measures in information retrieval. In *SIGIR '07*, 2007.

[10] Ellen M. Voorhees. Overview of the trec 2004 robust retrieval track. In *TREC '04*, 2004.

[11] Xuanhui Wang, Hui Fang, and ChengXiang Zhai. A study of methods for negative relevance feedback. In *SIGIR '08*, 2008.

[12] Xuanhui Wang, Hui Fang, and ChengXiang Zhai. Improve retrieval accuracy for difficult queries using negative feedback. In *CIKM '07*, 2007.

[13] Le Zhao and Jamie Callan. Term necessity prediction. In *CIKM '10*, 2010.

Question Routing in Community Question Answering: Putting Category in Its Place

Baichuan Li
The Chinese University of Hong Kong, Hong Kong
bcli@cse.cuhk.edu.hk

Irwin King*
AT&T Labs Research, USA & The Chinese University of Hong Kong, Hong Kong
irwin@research.att.com
king@cse.cuhk.edu.hk

Michael R. Lyu
The Chinese University of Hong Kong, Hong Kong
lyu@cse.cuhk.edu.hk

ABSTRACT

This paper investigates a ground-breaking incorporation of question category to Question Routing (QR) in Community Question Answering (CQA) services. The incorporation of question category was designed to estimate answerer expertise for routing questions to potential answerers. Two category-sensitive Language Models (LMs) were developed with large-scale real world data sets being experimented. Results demonstrated that higher accuracies of routing questions with lower computational costs were achieved, relative to traditional Query Likelihood LM (QLLM), state-of-the-art Cluster-Based LM (CBLM) and the mixture of Latent Dirichlet Allocation and QLLM (LDALM).

Categories and Subject Descriptors

H.3.3 [**Information Storage and Retrieval**]: Information Search and Retrieval—*information filtering, selection process*

General Terms

Algorithms, Experimentation, Performance

Keywords

question routing, community question answering, question category, category-sensitive language model

1. INTRODUCTION

Since the inception of forums for asking and answering questions, Community Question Answering (CQA) services have been providing users with web platforms to obtain useful information, for example, the development of Yahoo! Answers[1] and Quora[2]. In recent years, the efficiency of CQA services, however, is challenged by a sharp increase of questions raised in the communities. Such increasing amount of questions have thus influenced access of answerers to their appropriate questions, with the process of question answering being hindered in CQA services [2]. To facilitate answerer access to proper questions, an approach of Question Routing (QR) has been initiated and developed in CQA services [2, 4, 6, 3, 7].

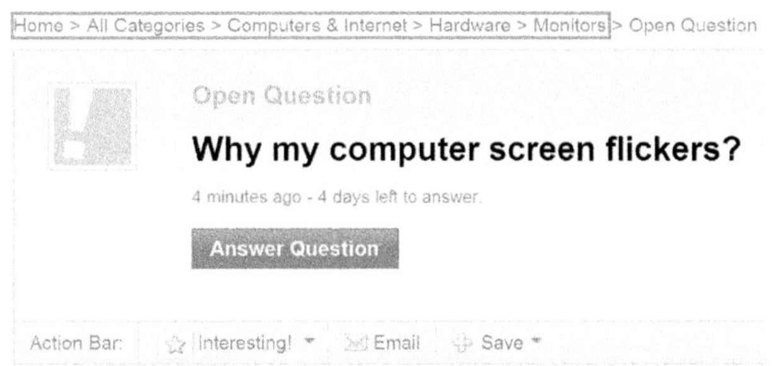

Figure 1: An example of question category in CQA services (captured from Yahoo! Answers on January 20, 2011)

The concept of QR refers to routing newly posted questions to potential answerers; the appropriateness of potential answerers (expertise estimation, hereafter) is estimated based on archives of their previously answered questions. Volumes of studies have been conducted regarding expertise estimation, including Query Likelihood Language Model (QLLM) [5], Cluster-Based Language Model (CBLM) [7], mixture of Latent Dirichlet Allocation (LDA) and QLLM [4]. However, as for *an answerer*, a complete set of questions the answerer has answered is utilized in the models, although certain amount of answered questions might be irrelevant to questions to be routed. To solve this problem, question category will be utilized to sifted out irrelevant questions in profile of *an answerer* for expertise estimation. In CQA services, askers have to choose a category for the question they asked. As shown in Fig. 1, each question is classified into a particular category. The categories of new questions would allow much latitude in screening irrelevant questions of *an answerer* to enhance the efficiency of expertise estimation. To date, few attempts have been made regarding category

*Irwin King is currently on leave from CUHK to be with AT&T Labs.

[1]http://answers.yahoo.com
[2]http://www.quora.com

CIKM'11, October 24–28, 2011, Glasgow, Scotland, UK.

information in studies of QR. This study was thus designed to fill the gap.

The paper is organized as follows. Related work is first reviewed in Section 2. Category-sensitive LMs are developed in Section 3. Experimental setup as well as results are then reported in Section 4 and 5. In the end, a conclusion is drawn in Section 6.

2. RELATED WORK

Expertise estimation, as mentioned, has been of paramount importance to assess potential of answerers for solving questions to be routed [2, 4, 6, 3, 7]. In studies of expertise estimation, two families of models have been widely employed: Language Models [3, 7] and Topic Models [2, 6]. Cao et al. [1] leveraged question category to enhance question retrieval in CQA and the experimental results ensured this approach's effectiveness on various of retrieval models. To our knowledge, no previous work, however, estimates answerer expertise using question category for QR.

3. QUESTION CATEGORY FOR ROUTING QUESTIONS

Let $C = \{c_1, c_2, c_3, ..., c_n\}$ represents all leaf categories, the basic category-sensitive LM (**BCS-LM**) is defined as follows:

$$E(u_i, q_r, c_j) \equiv P_{bcs}(u_i|q_r, c_j), \quad (1)$$

$$P_{bcs}(u_i|q_r, c_j) \propto P_{bcs}(q_r, c_j|u_i)P(u_i), \quad (2)$$

$$P_{bcs}(q_r, c_j|u_i) = P_{bcs}(q_r|c_j, u_i)P(c_j|u_i), \quad (3)$$

$$P_{bcs}(q_r|c_j, u_i) = P_{bcs}(q_r|c_j, q_{u_i}) = \prod_{\omega \in q_r} P(\omega|q_{u_{ij}}), \quad (4)$$

and

$$P(\omega|q_{u_{ij}}) = (1-\lambda)P_{ml}(\omega|q_{u_{ij}}) + \lambda P_{ml}(\omega|Coll), \quad (5)$$

where c_j is q_r's category, $P(c_j|u_i)$ denotes the probability of answering questions in c_j for u_i, and $q_{u_{ij}}$ represents the question texts of all previously answered questions in c_j for u_i.

It is noted that **BCS-LM** is based on the *same-leaf-category* assumption, with potential answerers under *similar* leaf categories being omitted. As shown in Fig. 2, CQA portals like Yahoo! Answers set refined category hierarchy. Under one main category, there exist similar leaf categories. For example, the leaf categories of "*Programming & Design*" and "*Software*" in Fig. 2. Answerers with expertise in "*Programming & Design*" may also be an expert on questions asked in "*Software*". To supply such omissions, we have come up with a transferred category-sensitive QLLM (**TCS-LM**) as follows:

$$P_{tcs}(q_r, c_j|u_i) = \frac{\beta P_{bcs}(q_r, c_j|u_i) + \sum_{c_k \in Tran(c_j)} T(c_k \rightarrow c_j)P_{bcs}(q_r, c_k|u_i)}{\beta + \sum_{c_k \in Tran(c_j)} T(c_k \rightarrow c_j)}, \quad (6)$$

where β adjusts the weight between the original leaf category and other similar leaf categories, the lower β, more weights are given to similar categories. $Tran(c_j)$ denotes the set of categories which are transferable from (similar to) c_j and $T(c_k \rightarrow c_j)$ represents the probability of transferring from category c_k to c_j.

We define

$$c_k \in Tran(c_j) \ if \ T(c_k \rightarrow c_j) \geq \delta, \quad (7)$$

where δ is a threshold between 0 and 1.

We use an answerer-based approach to estimate the transferring probability between two categories, which assumes that if there are many same answerers posting answers in two categories, these two categories should be similar with each other. To be specific, we construct a category-answerer matrix E from resolved questions, each row of E represents one (leaf) category and each column represents one answerer. In addition, the value of e_{ji} denotes the number of answers u_i provided in category c_j. Let $\mathbf{e}_j$ and $\mathbf{e}_k$ denote two row vectors of c_j and c_k, we apply the cosine similarity to estimate the transferring probability ($T_{ans}(\cdot)$) between two categories:

$$T_{ans}(c_j \rightarrow c_k) = T_{ans}(c_k \rightarrow c_j) = \frac{\mathbf{e}_j \cdot \mathbf{e}_k}{|\mathbf{e}_j||\mathbf{e}_k|}. \quad (8)$$

4. EXPERIMENTAL SETUP

4.1 Data Collection

The data comprised over 400, 000 resolved questions (June to October 2010) from *Computers & Internet* and *Entertainment & Music* categories of Yahoo! Answers through provided API[3]. The two categories included 20 and 25 leaf categories respectively[4]. Table 1 reports the statistics of datasets. As for all selected questions, the information regarding *affiliated category*, *texts* and *answerer IDs* was available. Those questions were further classified into Set A (Test data, questions posted after 6 May: 382,695 questions, 1,335,892 answers and 243,167 answerers) and Set B (Archive data, remaining questions: 50,377 questions, 174,639 answers and 49,466 answerers). In addition, answerers in Set A were used as ground truth.

Table 1: Description of the Yahoo! Answers data set (after stop words removing and stemming)

Number of questions	433,072
Number of answers	1,510,531
Average number of answers for one question	3.49
Maximum number of answers for one question	50
Mean first reply duration (in minutes)	197.32
Average question length in words (both subject and content)	43.87
Average answer length in words	30.08
Number of askers	240,277
Number of answerers	270,043
Number of both askers and answerers	68,551
Number of askers only	171,726
Number of answerers only	201,492

4.2 Methods Compared

Cluster-based language model (CBLM) [7] and mixture of LDA and QLLM (LDALM) [4] were selected to be compared

[3]http://developer.yahoo.com/answers/

[4]The leaf category *Polls & Surveys* was excluded since this leaf category was used to elicit public opinion. The dataset was thus composed of 44 leaf categories.

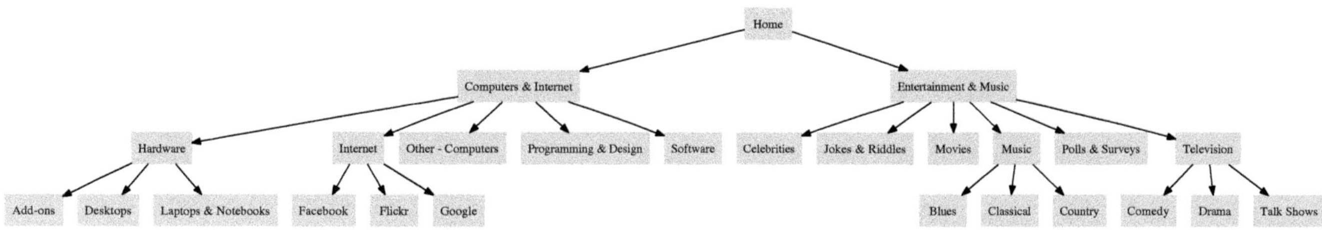

Figure 2: Part of category hierarchy in Yahoo! Answers

with category-sensitive LMs for expertise estimation based on the following two considerations:

1. In CBLM [7], similar questions under same topic are clustered and answerer expertise is estimated through calculating answerer's contribution to each cluster and the similarity between the routed question and each cluster. In CQA portals, each leaf category could be treated as a cluster and thus CBLM could be employed. Therefore, we applied CBLM to explore whether such "category-sensitive" setting was comparable with our category-sensitive LMs.

2. Experimental results in [4] showed that utilizing latent topics boosted the performance of QLLM for expertise estimation. Therefore, we intended to compare the effectiveness of latent topics and explicit categories as they both consider semantic in expertise estimation.

In addition, the original QLLM was included in comparisons as the baseline method. We used the tool GibbsLDA++[5] to estimate the posterior probabilities of LDA (say, θ of each answerer and ϕ of each topic). The default setting was adopted and the number of latent topics was set as 100 empirically.

4.3 Evaluation Metrics

We adopted *Precision at K*, *Mean Average Precision* and *Mean Reciprocal Rank* as evaluation metrics for the ranking lists generated by various LMs in expertise estimation. Furthermore, we employed the mean QR time (MQRT) which calculates the average time spent on routing one question (including expertise estimation and ranking) as the metric of time efficiency for all methods.

We set $\beta = 3.5$ for TCS-LM in the experiments empirically as this setting yields the best performance. As it is time-consuming to test all questions in Set A (Test set), we sampled 440 questions randomly from Set A (10 questions from each leaf category) as testing data. All algorithms ran in a PC with two 2.4GHz CPUs and 3G main memory.

5. EXPERIMENTAL RESULTS

5.1 Category-Sensitive LMs

Table 2 reports $Prec@K$ for all algorithms with different Ks from 1 to 100, and Table 3 presents the MRR and MAP of all methods. Table 4 gives the time-efficiency of each method in QR based on MQRT.

[5]http://gibbslda.sourceforge.net/

5.1.1 Higher Accuracies

From Table 2 we observe that, for various of Ks, both BCS-LM and TCS-LM outperform QLLM significantly on $Prec@K$. For instance, when routing questions to the top 1 answerers, on average QLLM gives less than 8 successful routings per 100; BCS-LM and TCS-LM make more than 11 and 12 successful routings, which improve QLLM by 40.13% and 54.34% respectively. For other Ks, category sensitive LMs also perform better than QLLM.

The MRR of BCS-LM and TCS-LM increase that of QLLM by 29.66% and 34.59%. From the definition of MRR, each new question will be answered by at least one answerer in the top 5 answerers using BCS-LM or TCS-LM. However, with QLLM on average we have to route the question to almost top 7 answerers to get an answer.

As to MAP, BCS-LM and TCS-LM improve QLLM by 33.08% and 37.29% respectively and it shows that category sensitive LMs give more accurate rankings on the whole.

To sum up, the above results have assured the effectiveness of utilizing category information in expertise estimation.

5.1.2 Lower Costs

Now let's turn to the time costs of QLLM and category-sensitive LMs. Table 4 gives the average time of routing a question for each model. We find that BCS-LM saves 47.16% of time while TCS-LM costs 13.80% less time than QLLM, which demonstrates that category-sensitive LMs are more time-efficient than QLLM in expertise estimation and thus make QR faster. The lower costs of BCS-LM lie in only relevant profiles are utilized in expertise estimation, which reduces the computational cost. TCS-LM spends more time than BCS-LM because of employing profiles in relevant categories for expertise estimation. Although TCS-LM is more time-consuming than BCS-LM, it is possible to reduce the time through parallel computing since the expertise estimation with different categories' profiles is independent with each other.

5.1.3 BCS-LM vs. TCS-LM

Looking at Table 2, we find that similar categories improve accuracies of expertise estimation when K is small. In particular, the $Prec@1$ of TCS-LM is 10.14% higher than those of BCS-LM. In addition, the $Prec@10$ of TCS-LM is 2.04% more accurate than that of BCS-LM. Although when K becomes large (say, high than 40), TCS-LM improves fewer or even a little worse than BCS-LM, the former one is still a better choice as a QR system has to route a question to minimum number of potential answerers in practice. The MRR and MAP of TCS-LM are also better than those of BCS-LM from Table 3. TCS-LM utilizes similar categories' profiles

Table 2: Different methods' *Prec@K* in QR versus various *K*s (best results in bold)

K	QLLM	BCS-LM	TCS-LM	LDALM	CBLM
1	0.0795	0.1114 (↑40.13%)	**0.1227** (↑54.34%)	0.0989 (↑24.40%)	0.0000
3	0.1659	**0.2364** (↑42.50%)	0.2340 (↑41.05%)	0.1950 (↑17.54%)	0.0000
5	0.2091	**0.2727** (↑30.42%)	0.2705 (↑29.36%)	0.2455 (↑17.41%)	0.0000
10	0.2705	0.3386 (↑25.18%)	**0.3455** (↑27.73%)	0.3102 (↑14.68%)	0.0000
20	0.3386	0.3909 (↑15.45%)	**0.3932** (↑16.13%)	0.3710 (↑9.57%)	0.0091
40	0.4136	0.4523 (↑9.36%)	**0.4591** (↑11.00%)	0.4392 (↑6.19%)	0.0273
60	0.4477	**0.4818** (↑7.62%)	0.4795 (↑7.10%)	0.4649 (↑3.84%)	0.0545
80	0.4727	**0.4955** (↑4.82%)	0.4909 (↑3.85%)	0.4867 (↑2.96%)	0.0727
100	0.4909	**0.5159** (↑5.09%)	0.5114 (↑4.18%)	0.4979 (↑1.43%)	0.0795

Table 3: MRR and MAP of various models (best results in bold)

Method	MRR	MAP
QLLM	0.1460	0.1070
BCS-QLLM	0.1893 (↑29.66%)	0.1424 (↑33.08%)
TCS-QLLM	**0.1965** (↑34.59%)	**0.1469** (↑37.29%)
LDALM	0.1695 (↑16.10%)	0.1281 (↑19.72%)
CBLM	0.0031	0.0024

Table 4: Various methods' MQRT in QR (in seconds)

QLLM	BCS-QLLM	TCS-QLLM	LDALM	CBLM
10.4271	5.5098	8.9884	16.7689	4.2488

and assign weights to these profiles according to the degree of similarities. Therefore, they give more precise expertise estimation and thus improve QR's performance.

5.1.4 Category Sensitive LMs vs. CBLM vs. LDALM

Across these four methods, CBLM performs the worst. The probable reason is that a great amount of answerers only answered in one cluster (leaf category), as such their contributions to this cluster are 1. Under this circumstance, these answerers' expertise is actually measured by those clusters' "expertise", which will cause many answerers to own the same expertise and thus make the ranking meaningless. LDALM increases *Prec@K* of QLLM, which shows the impact of utilizing latent topics, but explicit question category provides more help than latent topics as category-sensitive LMs outperform LDALM at various *K*s. MRR and MAP of these four methods report the similar results and detail will not be provided here.

When turning to MQRT, we find that CBLM works the best, followed by BCS-LM and TCS-LM, while LDALM costs much more time in inference. CBLM estimates answerer expertise through combining answerer's contribution to each cluster (which is pre-computed) and the probability of generating the routed question from each cluster (which is efficient to calculate), thus it makes the fastest estimation. However, the estimation made by CBLM is most inaccurate, as stated above. On the whole, category-sensitive LMs are time-efficient among the four methods.

In summary, category-sensitive LMs give more accurate expertise estimation than CBLM and LDALM and at the same time keep high time-efficiency.

6. CONCLUSION

This paper reported here is an investigation of applying question category to QR in CQA services. The question category was adopted to the development of category-sensitive LMs for estimating answerer expertise. Experiments on large-scale real world data revealed that category-sensitive LMs obtained more accuracies of expertise estimation, relative to QLLM and state-of-the-art algorithms including CBLM and LDALM. Results of experiments have proven that higher accuracies with lower costs are achieved due to the inclusion of question category in routing questions, which have therefore provided empirical evidence to validate the incorporation of question category in QR for CQA services. In future work, effects of question category on the content quality of answers and questions in CQA services can be further detected.

ACKNOWLEDGEMENT

This work is supported by two grants from the Research Grants Council of the Hong Kong SAR, China (Project No. CUHK 413210 and Project No. CUHK 415410) and a grant supported by a research funding from Google Focused Grant Project "Mobile 2014".

7. REFERENCES

[1] X. Cao, G. Cong, B. Cui, C. S. Jensen, and C. Zhang. The use of categorization information in language models for question retrieval. In *Proc. of CIKM*, 2009.

[2] J. Guo, S. Xu, S. Bao, and Y. Yu. Tapping on the potential of Q&A community by recommending answer providers. In *Proc. of CIKM*, 2008.

[3] B. Li and I. King. Routing questions to appropriate answerers in community question answering services. In *Proc. of CIKM*, 2010.

[4] M. Liu, Y. Liu, and Q. Yang. Predicting best answerers for new questions in community question answering. In *Proc. of WAIM*, 2010.

[5] X. Liu, W. B. Croft, and M. Koll. Finding experts in community-based question-answering services. In *Proc. of CIKM*, 2005.

[6] M. Qu, G. Qiu, X. He, C. Zhang, H. Wu, J. Bu, and C. Chen. Probabilistic question recommendation for question answering communities. In *Proc. of WWW*, 2009.

[7] Y. Zhou, G. Cong, B. Cui, C. S. Jensen, and J. Yao. Routing questions to the right users in online communities. In *Proc. of ICDE*, 2009.

Fact-Based Question Decomposition for Candidate Answer Re-Ranking

Aditya Kalyanpur Siddharth Patwardhan Branimir Boguraev
Adam Lally Jennifer Chu-Carroll
IBM T.J.Watson Research Center, P.O. Box 218, Yorktown Heights, NY 10598
{adityakal,siddharth,bran,alally,jencc}@us.ibm.com

ABSTRACT

Factoid questions often contain one or more assertions (facts) about their answers. However, existing question-answering (QA) systems have not investigated how the multiple facts may be leveraged to enhance system performance. We argue that decomposing complex factoid questions can benefit QA, as an answer candidate is more likely to be correct if multiple independent facts support it. We categorize decomposable questions as parallel or nested, depending on processing strategy required. We present a novel decomposition framework—for parallel *and* nested questions—which can be overlaid on top of traditional QA systems. It contains decomposition rules for identifying fact sub-questions, a question-rewriting component and a candidate re-ranker. In a particularly challenging domain for our baseline QA system, our framework shows a statistically significant improvement in end-to-end QA performance.

Categories and Subject Descriptors

I.2.7 [**Artificial Intelligence**]: Natural Language Processing—*text analysis, language parsing and understanding*

General Terms

Algorithms, Design

Keywords

Question Answering, Question Decomposition

1. INTRODUCTION

We look at complex factoid questions, specifically ones which contain multiple facts related to the correct answer, as in e.g. *Which company with origins dating back to 1876 became the first U.S. company to have 1 million stockholders in 1951?*. Two facts of relevance here are the time-frame of the company's origins, and it becoming the first to reach a particular landmark. We use the decomposed facts to garner independent, but potentially mutually-reinforcing, support for the correct answer from independent sources of evidence.

Recent approaches to QA acknowledge that some questions need decomposing, to tease out information beyond what "single-shot" QA systems generally assume. They tend to defer to discourse and/or semantics of the question, and use complex processes like textual entailment [4], question refocusing [2, 3], or temporal/spatial analysis [6, 2]. Decomposition work has mostly looked at "beyond factoid" questions. In contrast, we develop decomposition to improve quality of QA for a broad set of *factoids*. The questions we use (from the popular TV quiz show Jeopardy!) cover numerous topics, and make for an excellent test bed for open-domain QA.[1]

Our definition of "decomposable" questions—containing independent support for the correct answer—leads to categorizing such questions into *parallel* and *nested*. The example above, and an example from our data—*This country singer who did time in San Quentin was pardoned by Governor Ronald Reagan*—are parallel decomposable: subquestions can be evaluated independently of one another. In contrast, nested questions require sequential processing, with the answer to an 'inner' sub-question plugged into the 'outer': *It was named for Britain's last Stuart monarch, who gave the city its charter in 1708*. In this work we develop a uniform framework for handling decomposable questions of both types, and demonstrate that it is capable of improving the end-to-end performance of a state-of-the-art QA system.

2. FACT-BASED DECOMPOSITION

A single-shot QA system may find answers whose supporting evidence satisfies only some of the question's facts, and ignores the remainder of the question. At the same time, looking at all question terms as a whole, instead of separate meaningful facts, may distract the search for candidate answers. For nested decomposable questions, the missing piece of information implied by the 'inner' fact is often a facilitator to obtaining the correct answer. We would like to be able to enhance such single-shot systems so they can decompose questions (when appropriate) and identify parts thereof to be further processed, in parallel or in sequence.

Figure 1 shows the high-level architecture of such an adaptation. Ours is a "meta" framework overlaid on top of an existing QA system. It can be conceptualized around four main components.

[1]In this data, questions are posed in a declarative format, with highly stylized marking of question focus. This should not detract from referring to them as 'questions'.

CIKM'11, October 24–28, 2011, Glasgow, Scotland, UK.

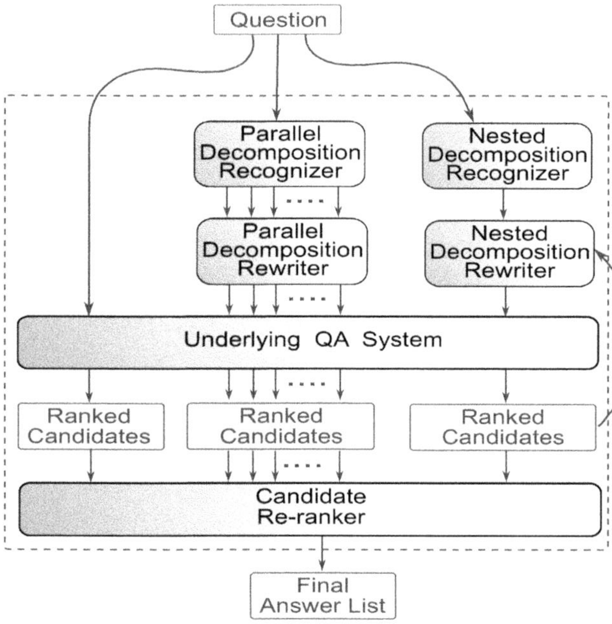

Figure 1: Fact-Based Decomposition Framework

Decomposition Recognizers analyze the question and identify decomposable parts (facts) using largely lexico-syntactic cues (Section 3). *Question Rewriters* reformulate the facts as sub-questions, adding key contextual information (Section 4.1). *Underlying QA System* generates, for any factoid question, a ranked list of answer candidates, each with a *confidence* corresponding to the probability of the answer being correct [1]. *Candidate Re-rankers* combine ranked answers to the original question with solutions for the decomposed facts (sub-questions) and generate a uniformly ranked answer list. Candidate answer confidences are used either by a machine learning-based approach or by a heuristic selection strategy to do the final ranking (Section 4.2).

We use the QA system described in [1]. However, our meta-framework will host any system that satisfies two criteria: it can solve factoid questions by providing answers with confidences reflecting their probability of being correct; it can separate the question's topic information from its main content by weighing the former less than the latter.

The figure highlights the distinction between parallel and nested processing: the parallel decomposition components produce multiple (two or more) sub-questions, submitted to the underlying QA system; the nested components generate inner-outer sub-question pairs, processed via a feedback loop re-invoking the underlying QA capability.

3. DECOMPOSITION RECOGNIZERS

Finding the question segments representative of independent facts about the correct answer is not trivial: multiple facts can be 'weaved' into a single complex question in a variety of ways: modifiers to the focus[2], subordinate clauses, attached prepositional phrases, may all be expressing facts. From a fact-checking perspective, we consider facts to be expressions of relations between the focus and one or more entities (named entities, dates or quotations) as these tend to be more substantial or meaningful. This, coupled with a set of syntactic cues we have found to be reliable indicators for decomposition, allows us to generalize recognition rules for question decomposition.

[2]The *focus* is the part of the question referring to the answer.

3.1 Decomposition Rules

Our rules exploit fine-grained lexico-syntactic information, and fall within three major categories: *independent subtrees*, *composable units* and *segments with qualifiers*. The rules in each rule set target both parallel and nested configurations. Details of rule sets fall outside of the scope of this paper; below we outline some highlights, as representative examples.

Independent Subtrees: Intuitively, potentially independent facts—capturing unique information about the answer—would be in clauses distinct from the rest of the question: e.g. relative or subordinate constructions. In the absence of more focused contextual information (see below), such configurations are indicative of parallel decomposition. The syntactic labels connecting such subtrees to the focus are generally good indicators for "breaking away" a subtree from the question as a decomposable fact. Thus in *The name of this character, first introduced in 1894, comes from the Hindi for "bear"*, an independent fact about the answer is "*this character, introduced in 1894*" (note that "*this character*" is the focus). This category also triggers on conjunctions as decomposition points, as in *Its original name meant "bitter water" and it was made palatable to Europeans after the Spaniards added sugar.*

Configurational information, reinforced by lexical cues, is used to determine the question's decomposition profile, parallel or nested. The syntactic contour of the first example in this section shows that both the main and subordinate clauses characterize the (same) focus entity: a clear indicator that the sub-questions are parallel. Conversely, *A controversial 1979 war film was based on a 1902 work by this author* exhibits a very different set of configurational properties. The focus is just one of several underspecified entities which do not 'share' their facts (e.g. via a common head). This is indicative of nestedness, with the inner sub-question around an unspecified, non-focus element (*"a controversial 1979 war film"*), and the outer taken from the complement of the original question (*"[film] was based on a 1902 work by this author"*). Nested decomposition returns a pair of sub-questions; but there may be more than one way to decompose into an inner-outer.

Composable Units: An alternate strategy for identifying facts is to "compose" them by combining elements from the question. In contrast to "breaking off" independent subtrees, rules in this set combine different parts of the tree into a sub-question. For instance, the focus with its pre- and post-modifiers (if they are sufficiently specific) can be interpreted as separate, parallel, fact(s). Alternatively, finding the focus itself in a modifier position may be a signal of nestedness: in *To honor his work, this man's daughter took the name Maria Celeste when she became a nun in 1616*, the focus is dominated by an underspecified node, *"daughter"*. Traversing such a tree without descending to focus level "carves out" an inner sub-question, itself focused on the dominating (linking) node: *"To honor his work, [this] daughter took the name Maria Celeste ..."*.

Segments with Qualifiers: This group of rules detects focus modifiers which are relative qualifiers: *"the first"*, *"only"*, *"the westernmost"*. Such qualifiers need to be "completed" by information from elsewhere: *"the third man"* is meaningless without a supporting clause, e.g. *"the third man ... to climb Mt. Everest"*. The rules here combine characteristics of the other two rule sets, to manipulate independent subtrees and compose them with modifiers to the focus.

3.2 Decomposition Filters

Several heuristic filters reduce over-generation; primarily, they discard facts that do not contain a named entity, a quoted string, or a temporal (time or date) expression—this is in line with our definition of fact, earlier in this section.

We also discard facts with significant overlap with the entire question, or with other facts from previously applied rules. This is based on a (partial order) prioritization of rules, reflecting intuitions (borne by inspecting rule results) of how informative the facts generated by the rule are.

4. USING DECOMPOSITION

4.1 Sub-question Rewriting

Submitting a decomposed sub-question, as-is, to the underlying QA system meets serious problems: sub-questions are often much shorter than the original, and tend to not have a unique answer. Moreover, some of the information from the full question that was dropped in the sub-question may offer relevant contextual cues crucial for coming up with the correct answer. In extreme cases, loss of context may lead to recall failures—thus defeating the whole purpose of decomposing in the first place.

Sub-question rewriting provides such crucial contextual information. For a sub-question Q_i, we first obtain the set of all named entities and nouns (minus stopwords) in the original question text that are not present in Q_i. We then insert these keywords into the topic of the original question.[3] Finally, the underlying QA system is given the enriched topic/sub-question pair; recall that our decomposition framework (Section 2) expects to be able to take advantage of the differential weighting of information in a question's topic and content. Sub-question rewriting thus ensures that the larger context of the original question is still taken into account when evaluating a sub-question, although with less weight.

4.2 Candidate Re-ranking

The different decomposition regimes require different strategies for using the sets of candidate answers, with confidences. In the parallel case, a final set of uniformly ranked answers needs to be composed from the set of ranked answer lists produced by independently solving the sub-questions. In the nested case, a subset of the answer list to the inner sub-question needs to be selected for substitution into the outer.

Parallel Decomposition A simple approach to assigning a final score for each candidate answer is to multiply scores for each of the sub-questions—given the assumption that they are independent. However, sub-question rewriting breaks this assumption. Also, different decomposition rules have different precision and recall: thus sub-questions ought not to be weighed equally. In the extreme case of rules producing bad decompositions, it makes sense to fall back to the original question: therefore the confidence of the 'single-shot' pass (Figure 1) should also inform the final decision. Consequently, we train a machine learning model to combine information across sub-question answer confidences.

To capture this range of information, the model uses the following features: whether a candidate was a top answer to the full (non-decomposed) question; confidence value for a candidate answer to full question; number of sub-questions with candidate answer in top 10; and a feature for every (parallel) rule set, whose value is the confidence of the candidate answer for a fact derived by this rule set.

If a candidate answer is not in the answer list of the full question or any of the decomposed sub-questions, the corresponding feature value is set to *missing*. If a rule produces multiple sub-question, the corresponding (rule) feature value for the candidate answer is set to the sum of the confidences obtained for that answer across all the sub-questions. For the machine-learning algorithm, we use the Weka implementation [7] of logistic regression with instance weighting (weights are tuned over the development set).

Nested Decomposition Each candidate answer from the inner sub-question's answer list, if substituted into the outer sub-question, has ramifications on end-to-end accuracy: incorrect answers from the inner lead to incorrect final answers. We rely on the ability of the underlying QA system to produce meaningful confidences for its answers. Thus only the top answer to the inner sub-question is considered for substitution in the outer—if its confidence exceeds some threshold (obtained by tuning over the development set).

With an answer to the inner sub-question, we are now in a position to rewrite the outer. Similar to the case for parallel sub-questions, we also adhere to the policy of providing additional relevant contextual information to the system (cf. Section 4.1).

A simple heuristic strategy appeals to joint probability of the inner-outer pair to perform candidate re-ranking: the confidence of the top answer to the outer sub-question is multiplied with that of the top answer to the inner question; the product is compared with the top-ranking confidence for the full question; the answer with the higher confidence is selected as final.

5. EVALUATION

5.1 Data

Our data set—with ground truth for both training a system and evaluating its performance—is a collection of Jeopardy! question-answer pairs (from `www.j-archive.com`). Given our focus on question decomposition, only Final Jeopardy! (FJ) questions are in our test set: they tend to be complex, with multiple constraints, and typically much harder to answer (for humans and the underlying QA system alike). Approximately 3000 FJ questions are split into 1138 for training, 517 for development and 1269 for testing (blind data).

5.2 Experiments

The parallel decomposition rules were defined and tuned on the development set of 517 questions. The final re-ranking model (with features as in Section 4.2) was built over our FJ training set (Section 5.1). It was trained for logistic regression with instance re-weighting, setting the negative instance weight 0.25 times lower (based on analysis over the develop-

[3] Jeopardy! questions topics are confined to a *category* field.

QA System	End-to-End Accuracy	Decomposable Q Accuracy
PB	635/1269 (50.05%)	339/598 (56.68%)
PD-QR	634/1269 (49.96%)	338/598 (56.52%)
PD+QR	**643/1269 (50.66%)**	**347/598 (58.02%)**
NB	635/1269 (50.05%)	129/255 (50.58%)
ND+QR	**640/1269 (50.43%)**	**134/255 (52.54%)**

Table 1: Evaluating Decomposition

ment set, and motivated by the underlying QA system's tendency to generate many more negative answers than positive ones). To determine the impact of our context-preserving sub-question rewriting strategy (Section 4.1), we modified the algorithm to issue the sub-question as-is, using the original category (topic). The results of applying the parallel decomposition rules followed by the re-ranking model to the 1269 test questions are shown in Table 1.

In the table, PB refers to Parallel Baseline (the performance of the underlying QA system with decomposition disabled), NB refers to Nested Baseline (same configuration as PB but separately run on nested decomposable questions), PD and ND refer to Parallel and Nested Decomposition systems respectively, and QR refers to Question Rewriting.

Nested decomposition strategy (Section 4.2) was similarly evaluated, comparing the (nested) baseline to a heuristic re-ranking approach (whose parameter thresholds were tuned on the development set). Results are also in Table 1.

5.3 Discussion of Results

Table 1 shows the parallel decomposition rules applying to a large fraction of the test set (598 out of 1269 questions). Interestingly, the performance of the baseline QA system on the decomposable set is 56.6%, i.e. 6% higher than the overall performance. One reason for this is that parallel-decomposable questions typically contain more information (more than one fact/constraint to be satisfied by the answer) and the system can, in some cases, exploit this redundancy (e.g. when a fact is strongly associated with the correct answer and there is evidence in the sources supporting this).

Decomposition without sub-question rewriting does not show much impact over the baseline: question context is clearly crucial for QA. With rewriting to maintain context, our parallel decomposition algorithm achieves an improvement of 1.4% (10 gains/2 losses) on the decomposable question set, which translated to an end-to-end gain of 0.6%.

The nested decomposition rules fired on roughly a fourth of the test set (255 out of 1269 questions); the performance of the baseline QA system on the nested decomposable set was roughly the same as the overall performance (and much lower than the parallel decomposable cases). The likely explanation is that nested questions are harder to solve than parallel: correct solution to the inner is crucial for finding the answer to the outer, whereas parallel sub-questions are, by definition, independent. Our nested decomposition algorithm using the heuristic re-ranking approach achieves an improvement of 2% (6 gains/1 loss) on the decomposable question set, which translated to an end-to-end gain of 0.4%.

The impact of using both parallel and nested decomposition is a 1.5% gain in accuracy on the decomposable set, and a 1% gain on end-to-end system accuracy (our rules for finding parallel and nested decompositions are disjoint so a given question cannot fall in both classes).

A key point concerning these results is that the baseline QA system represents state-of-the-art in solving Jeopardy! questions. Moreover, our FJ evaluation data is known to be harder than regular Jeopardy! questions. We estimate qualified Jeopardy! players' accuracy on FJ to be 48% (based on player performance statistics from `j-archive`). A gain of 1% end-to-end on such questions is, therefore, a strong improvement. McNemar's test with Yates' correction for continuity [5] found the results to be statistically significant, where significance is assessed for $p < .05$.

6. CONCLUSION

We argue that a question decomposition capability can enhance the quality of factoid QA. We have developed a general-purpose decomposition framework for complex factoid questions, which distinguishes between parallel (independent) and nested (sequential) question types, and accommodates appropriate strategies for solving both. The framework can be overlayed on any QA system that provides answers with confidences, and that considers the topic of the question separate from its main content.

In addition to the typology of decomposable question types (and associated detection rules), we propose a novel question rewriting approach to mitigate the loss-of-context problem when dealing with shorter (non unique) facts, and a re-ranking strategy that suitably combines results of the decomposition analysis with information from the single-shot QA approach.

This decomposition capability brings an improvement to the performance of a state-of-the-art factoid answering QA system—in the domain of Final Jeopardy!, which even qualified human players find difficult—by 1.5% on decomposable questions: a statistically significant gain.

7. REFERENCES

[1] D. Ferrucci, E. Brown, J. Chu-Carroll, J. Fan, D. Gondek, A. Kalyanpur, A. Lally, J. W. Murdock, E. Nyberg, J. Prager, and N. Schlaefer. Building Watson: An overview of the DeepQA project. *AI Magazine*, 2010.

[2] S. Hartrumpf. Semantic Decomposition for Question Answering. In *Proceedings of ECAI-18*, Greece, 2008.

[3] B. Katz, G. Borchardt, and S. Felshin. Syntactic and Semantic Decomposition Strategies for Question Answering from Multiple Sources. In *Proceedings of the AAAI Workshop on Inference for Textual Question Answering*, pages 35–41, Pittsburgh, PA, July 2005.

[4] F. Lacatusu, A. Hickl, and S. Harabagiu. The Impact of Question Decomposition on the Quality of Answer Summaries. In *Proceedings of LREC-5*, Italy, 2006.

[5] Q. McNemar. Note on the Sampling Error of the Difference Between Correlated Proportions or Percentages. *Psychometrika*, 12(2):153–157, 1947.

[6] E. Saquete, P. Martínez-Barco, R. Muñoz, and J. Vicedo. Splitting Complex Temporal Questions for Question Answering Systems. In *Proceedings of the 42nd ACL*, Spain, July 2004.

[7] I. Witten and E. Frank. *Data Mining—Practical Machine Learning Tools and Techniques.* Morgan–Kaufmann, San Francisco, CA, 2000.

CoDet: Sentence-based Containment Detection in News Corpora

Emre Varol, Fazli Can, Cevdet Aykanat, Oguz Kaya
Computer Engineering Department, Bilkent University
Ankara, Turkey
{ evarol, canf, aykanat } @cs.bilkent.edu.tr, oguzkaya87@gmail.com

ABSTRACT

We study a generalized version of the near-duplicate detection problem which concerns whether a document is a subset of another document. In text-based applications, document containment can be observed in exact-duplicates, near-duplicates, or containments, where the first two are special cases of the third. We introduce a novel method, called CoDet, which focuses particularly on this problem, and compare its performance with four well-known near-duplicate detection methods (DSC, full fingerprinting, I-Match, and SimHash) that are adapted to containment detection. Our method is expandable to different domains, and especially suitable for streaming news. Experimental results show that CoDet effectively and efficiently produces remarkable results in detecting containments.

Categories and Subject Descriptors

H.3.7 [**Digital Libraries**]: Collection, System Issues.

General Terms: Algorithms, Experimentation, Performance, Reliability

Keywords: Corpus Tree, Document Containment, Duplicate Detection, Similarity, Test Collection Preparation.

1. INTRODUCTION

Near-duplicate detection is an important task in various web applications. Due to reasons such as mirroring, plagiarism, and versioning such documents are common in many web applications [17]. For example, Internet news sources generally disseminate slightly different versions of news stories coming from syndicated agencies by making small changes in the news articles. Identifying such documents increases the efficiency and effectiveness of search engines.

We consider a generalized version of the near-duplicate detection problem and investigate whether a document is a subset of another document [2]. In text-based applications, document containment can be observed in near-duplicates and containments. We refer to identifying such document pairs as the document containment detection problem. We study this problem within the context of news corpora that involve streaming news articles.

If a document d_C possesses all the information that document d_A has, then d_C is said to contain d_A, which is denoted as $d_C \supseteq d_A$, and this relation is called *containment*. Moreover, if two documents contain roughly the same content, they are *near-duplicates* [6]. Although near-duplicate condition is a special case of containment, these two cases are not usually distinguished from each other [15]. Similar to the "conditional equivalence" concept defined by Zobel and Bernstein [17], if $d_C \supseteq d_A$, then a news-consumer who have already read d_C would have no need to read d_A. Of course, $d_C \supseteq d_A$ does not necessarily imply $d_A \supseteq d_C$, i.e. containment relation is asymmetric. By detecting $d_C \supseteq d_A$, news consumers that have already seen d_C can be informed to skip reading d_A.

In related studies, containment problem is addressed by near-duplicate detection algorithms. Therefore, we compare performance of CoDet with well-known near-duplicate detection approaches.

Contributions of this study are the following. We introduce a sentence-based containment detection method adaptable to different text-based problem domains, and especially suitable for streaming news; show that our approach outperforms commonly known near-duplicate detection methods; and construct a test collection using a novel pooling technique, which enables us to make reliable judgments for the relative effectiveness of algorithms using limited human assessments.

2. RELATED WORK

In near-duplicate detection similarity measurement plays an important role [11]. By using similarity, two documents are defined as duplicates if their similarity or resemblance [3] exceeds a certain threshold value. Such approaches are applied to identify roughly the same documents, which have the same content except for slight modifications [1]. In comparisons, factors other than similarity may also play a role. Conrad and Schriber [7] after consulting librarians deem that two documents are duplicates if they have 80% overlap and 20 variations in length.

Similarity measures may use all words in documents in calculation. Instead of using each word, a sequence of them, shingles, may be used. In shingling approaches, if two documents have significant number of shingles in common, then they are considered as similar (near-duplicate). Well-known shingling techniques include for example COPS [1] and DSC (Digital Syntactic Clustering) [3]. COPS uses the sentences (or small units) to generate hash codes and stores these in a table to see if a document contains a sentence. Wang and Chang propose using the sequence of sentence lengths for near-duplicate detection and they evaluated different configurations of sentence-level and word-level algorithms [14].

Shingling and similarity approaches suffer from efficiency issues. As a result a new strategy emerged which is based on hashing of the whole document. I-Match [6] is a commonly known approach that uses this strategy. It filters terms based on collection statistics (*idf* values). Charikar's [5] Simhash method is based on the idea of creating a hash by using document features (words, bigram, trigrams, etc.). It compares bit differences of these signatures to decide if two documents are near-duplicate or not. Yang and Callan [15] use clustering concepts for efficiency. While clustering documents they use additional information

CIKM'11, October 24–28, 2011, Glasgow, Scotland, UK.

extracted from documents and structural relationships among document pairs.

Hajishirzi et al. [9] propose an adaptable method for near duplicate detection by representing documents as real valued sparse k-gram vectors, where weights are learnt to optimize a similarity function. Zhang et al. [18] address the partial-duplicate detection problem by doing sentence level near-duplicate detection and sequence matching. Their algorithm generates a signature for each sentence and sentences that have the same signature are considered as near-duplicates. Theobald et al. [13] propose SpotSigs algorithm that combines stopword antecedents with short chains of adjacent content terms to create signatures.

3. CODET ALGORITHM

3.1 Containment Similarity Concept

CoDet is a novel sentence-based containment detection algorithm. It employs a new similarity measure called containment similarity (CS). It measures to what extent a document d_A is contained by another document d_C, which is defined as

$$CS(d_C, d_A) = \sum_{s_i \in S_C} \sum_{s_j \in S_A} cs(s_i, s_j) \quad (1)$$

where S_A and S_C denote the set of sentences in d_A and d_C, respectively. The function $cs(s_i, s_j)$ indicates containment similarity between sentences s_i and s_j, which is calculated as

$$cs(s_i, s_j) = \sum_{k=1}^{len_{f(s_i,\, s_j)}} k \times idf\left(w_{f(s_i,s_j),k}\right) \quad (2)$$

where $f(s_i, s_j)$ denotes the word sequence representing the longest word prefix match of the sentences s_i and s_j, len_t is the length of the word sequence t, and $w_{t,k}$ stands for the kth word in the word sequence t. For example, let s_1 be "John is happy." and s_2 be "John is sad." then $f(s_1, s_2)$ is a word sequence (John, is), $len_{f(s_1,s_2)}$ is 2 and $w_{f(s1,\,s2),1}$ is *John*.

As can be seen in Formula 2, containment similarity between two sentences grows significantly as their word prefix match gets longer. The containment similarity of a document to itself is referred to as self-containment similarity (SCS).

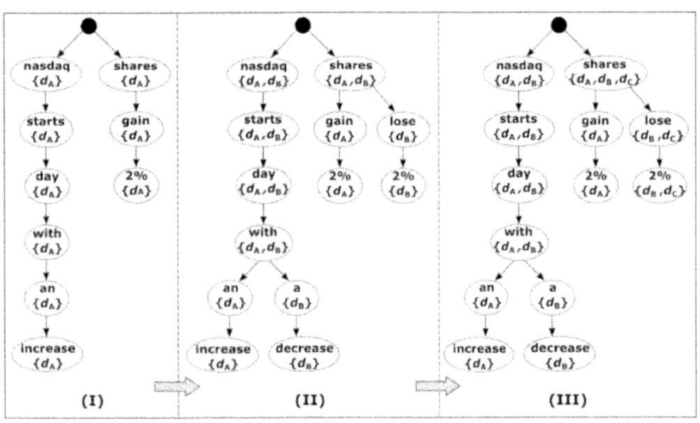

Fig. 1. Insertion of three documents d_A: "NASDAQ starts day with an increase. Shares gain 2%.", d_B: "NASDAQ starts the day with a decrease. Shares lose 2%.", and d_C: "Shares lose 2%.". For the sake of clarity, words of sentences are not sorted according to their *idf* values.

3.2 Containment Similarity Calculation

For efficient calculation of containment similarities, we utilize a data structure called *corpus tree*. The corpus tree begins with a virtual root node which contains a pointer list storing the locations of the children nodes in the next level. In addition to pointer list, nodes other than the root contain a label and a document list. The label represents the node's term and the document list contains visiting document ids.

Let d_A denote a document with a set of sentences $S_A = \{s_1, s_2 \ldots s_n\}$. Processing of d_A involves processing all of its sentences. Insertion of s_i ($1 \leq i \leq n$) to the corpus tree is performed as follows: First, words of s_i are sorted according to their *idf* values in descending order. Let $<w_1, w_2 \ldots w_m>$ denote the sequence of words in s_i after sorting. These words are inserted into the corpus tree starting from the virtual root node. If the root has a child ch_{w_1} with label w_1, then similarity values of d_A with all documents in ch_{w_1}'s document list are increased according to Formula 2. Otherwise, a new child node ch_{w_1} with label w_1 is created and added to the root's pointer list. In the next step, we treat ch_{w_1} as we did the root, and insert the following word w_2 of s_i similarly. The insertion of s_i finishes after all of its words are processed. The remaining sentences of d_A are handled in the same manner. The same is done for the remaining sentences of d_A.

Fig. 1. shows how the corpus tree grows with sentence insertions. In Fig. 1-I, d_A's sentences "NASDAQ starts day with an increase." and "Shares gain 2%." are inserted to the corpus tree starting from the virtual root, which is shown by a dark circle. Since the tree is initially empty, while inserting the first sentence all the nodes with labels $<$*nasdaq*, *starts*, *day*, *with*, *an*, *increase*$>$ are created. Similarly, insertion of the second sentence creates nodes with labels $<$*shares*, *gain*, *2%*$>$. In Fig. 1-II, during the insertion of the sentence "NASDAQ starts day with a decrease." previously created nodes with labels $<$*nasdaq*, *starts*, *day*, *with*$>$ are visited and updated. Also, two nodes with labels $<$*a*, *decrease*$>$ are created. Insertion of the sentence "Shares lose 2%." visits the node with label *shares* and creates two nodes with labels $<$*lose*, *2%*$>$. Thus, similarity value of d_A and d_B is increased by summation of each revisited node's impact values, which is calculated by multiplication of node's depth and *idf* value of its label. For example, contribution of the node with label starts is $(2 \times (\log(3/2) + 1))$ because its depth is 2 and word starts appears in 2 of 3 documents (in the experiments, the *idf* values are obtained from a large reference collection). The final structure of the corpus tree after the insertion of d_C is shown in Fig. 1-III.

To decide whether a document d_A is contained by another document d_C, CoDet uses $CS(d_A, d_C)$ as well as $SCS(d_A)$ values. If $(CS(d_A, d_C) / SCS(d_A))$ exceeds the equivalency threshold level (ETL), d_C is said to contain d_A. In the experiments, different ETL values are tested.

3.3 Complexity Analysis

For each scenario, let n denote the number of documents and let c denote the average number of words per document, which is treated as constant.

First Scenario (One Content, n Documents): In this case, each document has the same content; therefore, *corpus tree* contains c nodes. Each node contains n integers in its document list. As a result, the memory requirement of the corpus tree is O(n) but due to pairwise containment similarity increase operations the algorithm takes $O(n^2)$ time.

Second Scenario (n Different Contents, n Documents): In this case, each document has totally different content. Thus, corpus tree contains nc nodes (one node for each word). Each node contains only one document id in its document list. Therefore, asymptotically the memory requirement of the corpus tree is O(n) and the algorithm takes O(n) time.

The first scenario is the worst case for CoDet, where the algorithm performs nonlinearly. The second one is the best case for CoDet and the algorithm runs in linear time. In practice the algorithm behaves as if it is linear because average number of near-duplicate per document is significantly smaller than n. Also CoDet is especially suitable for streaming news since with a time window concept, which makes older documents to be removed from the corpus tree, the corpus tree does not grow too much.

4. EXPERIMENTAL SETUP

We used four algorithms to compare their effectiveness and efficiency with CoDet. These algorithms are:

DSC: Every *three* overlapping substrings of size *four* in the documents are hashed. If a document d_C contains *60%* of d_A's hash values, we say $d_C \supseteq d_A$ [3].

Full Fingerprinting (FFP): For each document, all substrings of size *four* are hashed. If document d_C contains *60%* of d_A's hash values, then, $d_C \supseteq d_A$.

I-Match: First *two* words with the highest *idf* values are ignored. After that, *ten* words with the highest *idf* values are used to create a fingerprint for each document. When a pair of documents has the same fingerprint, the pair is marked as containment [6].

SimHash: First *two* words with the highest *idf* values are ignored. Then, each unique term of a document is hashed. We use a vector v, whose size is equal to the hash value bit size, to determine the final SimHash [5] value. For each term t, i^{th} element of the vector v is updated as follows: If i^{th} bit of the hash value of t is *zero*, then it is decreased by *idf* of w. It is increased by the *idf* otherwise. Finally, if i^{th} element of v is positive, i^{th} bit of the SimHash value is set to *one*; otherwise it is set to *zero*. When a pair of documents' SimHash values has a Hamming distance less than *three*, the pair is considered as containment.

For hashing, SHA1 [6] algorithm is used in all methods. Stopword elimination and a word truncation-based stemming (first-5) are performed before the detection process. I-Match, SimHash and CoDet requires *idf* values. These values are obtained from a large reference collection (defined in the next section). In order to do a fair evaluation, each algorithm's parameters are optimized to give the best results for efficiency.

We performed the experimentation on a machine with quad 2.1Ghz six-core AMD Opteron processors with six 128 KB L1, 512 KB L2, and one 6MB L3 cache. It has 128 GB memory and operating system Debian Linux v5.0.5.

4.1 Test Collection Preparation

There is no gold-standard test collection for containment detection in news corpora; therefore, we prepared a test dataset from the Turkish TDT (Topic Detection and Tracking) news collection *(BilCol-2005)* [4] which contains 209,305 streaming (time-ordered) news articles obtained from five different Turkish web news sources.

For efficiency measurement, we used all documents of *BilCol-2005*. For effectiveness measurement, we used the first 5,000 documents of *BilCol-2005*. It is practically impossible to provide human assessment for each document pair in this sub-collection. Our approach to human assessments is similar to the pooling method used in TREC for the evaluation of IR systems [16]. For the creation of the dataset, we obtained a number of possible containments by running all five methods (including CoDet) with permissive parameters. In this way, methods nominate all pairs that would normally be chosen with their selective parameters, together with several additional pairs as containment candidates. Since the methods are executed with permissive parameters, we expect that most of the real containments will be added to the test collection. All pairs of documents, which are marked as containments by any of the methods, are brought to the attention of human assessors to determine whether they actually are containments. Note that in order to measure the effectiveness of a new algorithm with this test dataset, adding human assessments only for containment candidates that are nominated solely by this new algorithm to our dataset is sufficient.

By this approach, our dataset includes only true positive (TP) and false positive (FP) document pairs returned by any of our permissive algorithms. excluding true negative and false negative pairs do not change the relative effectiveness rankings of selective algorithms during the test phase; because, if a permissive algorithm marks a pair as negative (non-containment), then its selective counterpart should also marks that pair as negative. Therefore, including TN and FN pairs of permissive algorithms in our dataset would not contribute to the number of positive pairs (TP's and FP's) returned by any selective algorithm during the test phase. Hence, using our pruned dataset, precision[1] values of the selective algorithms remain unchanged with respect to precision values they would obtain in a full dataset having annotations for all possible document pairs. Similarly, recall values of the selective algorithms decrease proportionally (with the same ratio of total number of containments in the pruned dataset to the total number of containments in the full dataset, for all algorithms) with respect to recall values they would obtain in the full dataset.

Our pooling process generated 4,727 document pairs nominations. We performed a human-based annotation to obtain a ground truth. The pooled document pairs are divided into 20 groups containing about the same number of nominations. Each document pair is annotated by two assessors. The assessors are asked if the nominated document pairs are actually containments. The assessors identified 2,875 containment cases. The size of our dataset is comparable with the annotated test collections reported in related studies [13].

In information retrieval, human assessors may have different opinions about the relevance of a document to a query. A similar situation arises in our assessments. For example, for the document pair d_C = "XYZ shares increase 10% from 100 to 110." and d_A = "XYZ shares increase from 100 to 110.", some assessors may say that d_C and d_A are near-duplicates, while some others may claim d_C contains d_A, but the d_A does not contain d_C. In such cases we expect disagreements among human assessors. In order to validate the reliability of the assessments, we measured the agreements of the judgments by using the Cohen's Kappa measure, and obtained an average agreement rate of 0.73. This indicates almost a substantial agreement [10], which is an important evidence for the reliability of our test dataset. Furthermore, such conflicts are resolved by an additional assessor.

5. EXPERIMENTAL RESULTS

In this section, we first investigate the impacts of the following parameters on the performance of CoDet: Processed Suffix Count (PSC), Depth Threshold (DT), and Word Sorting (WS). This discussion is followed by efficiency and effectiveness performance of CoDet with those of four well-known near-duplicate detection algorithms. Effectiveness measurement is done by precision, recall and F_1 values. Impacts of parameters and effectiveness experiments are done on prepared test collection. Efficiency experiment is performed with the whole *BilCol-2005*.

5.1 Impacts of Parameters

Processed Suffix Count (PSC): It determines how many suffixes of each sentence are inserted to the corpus tree. If the PSC is 3, the processed suffixes for "NASDAQ starts day with an increase." are the sentence itself, <starts, day, with, an, increase> and <day, with, an, increase> Increasing PSC increases space requirement

[1] Precision (P) = |TP| / (|TP| + |FP|). where |S| is the cardinality of the set S. Recall (R) = |TP| / (|TP| + |FN|). F_1 = 2PR / (P + R).

but do not change effectiveness considerably as shown in Fig. 2: Different PSC values result in close F_1 scores.

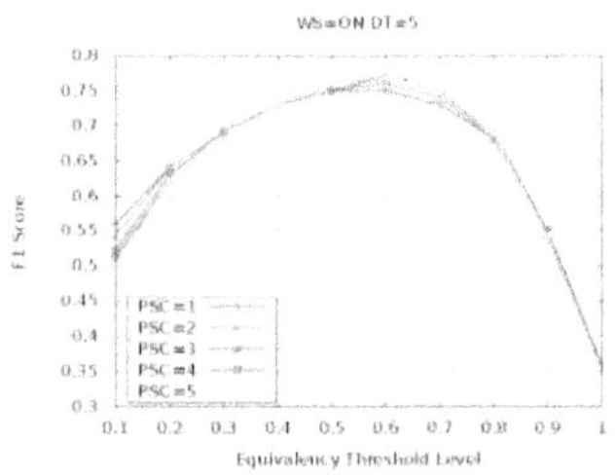

Fig. 2. Effect of Processed Suffix Count (PSC).

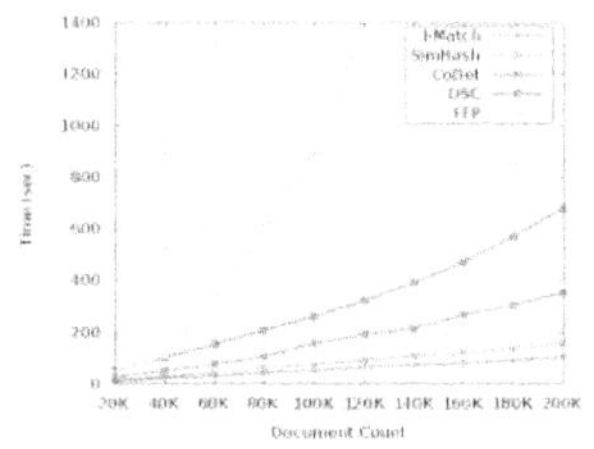

Fig. 3. Efficiency Comparison: Execution Time vs. Document Count.

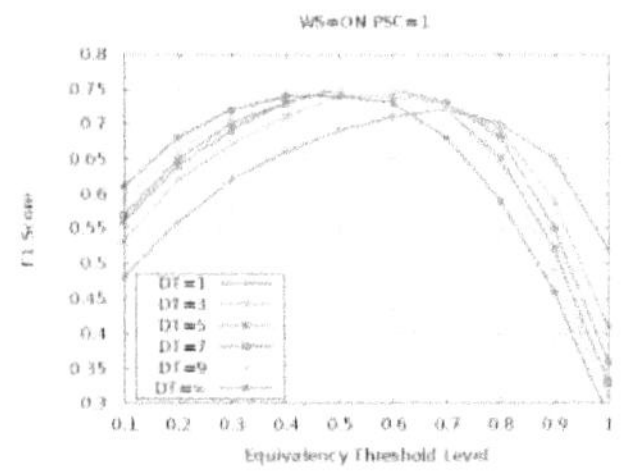

Fig. 4. Effect of Depth Threshold (DT): Word Sorting (WS) is on.

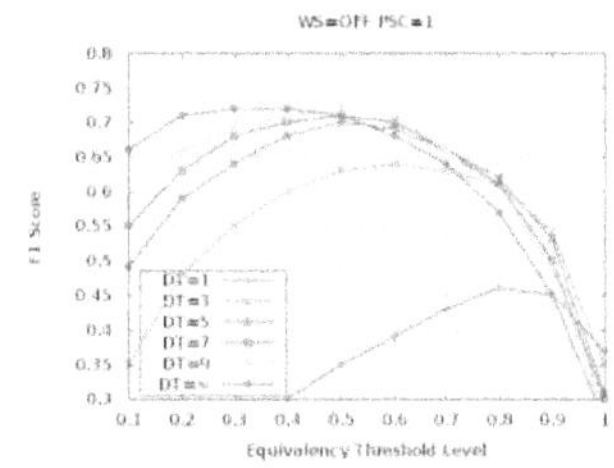

Fig. 5. Effect of Depth Threshold (DT): Word Sorting (WS) is off.

Depth Threshold (DT): It determines how many words of a sentence are processed. If the DT is 3, the processed words "NASDAQ starts day with an increase." are <*nasdaq, starts, day*>. Fig. 4 and 5 show the effect of DT on F_1 score. Sorting words of a sentence by *idf* values places representative words close to the virtual root. Thus, results are better for small DT values when word sorting is enabled. It avoids the noise effect of insignificant words in similarity calculations. In the experiments, DT value of 5 gives the best result; also smaller DT values yield a similar performance. Thus, instead of having the corpus tree structure, an algorithm that considers only a few most significant words from each sentence can improve efficiency without sacrificing effectiveness significantly.

Word Sorting (WS): Sorting words in sentences by *idf* values causes important words to be located close to the virtual root. Since most sentences start with common words, by using word sorting, we avoid many redundant similarity calculations. In the experiments, enabling word sorting decreases average number of calculated similarity values per document from 341 to 3.53.

5.2 Comparing with Other Algorithms

The efficiency results are given in Fig. 3. As the number of documents increase, execution time of full fingerprinting increases non-linearly. It calculates similarity values for each document pair that has at least one substring in common. Hence, it is not feasible for large collections. CoDet performs as the third best algorithm in time efficiency; the corpus tree accesses impose many random memory accesses, which disturb cache coherency. Our results show that I-Match, SimHash and CoDet are scalable to large collections.

Table 1 shows the effectiveness results. The best performance with a value of 0.85 F_1 score is observed with FFP since it calculates text overlaps between document pairs having a common substring. Therefore, without making any semantic analysis, it is difficult to outperform FFP in terms of effectiveness with a time-linear algorithm. CoDet finds text overlaps by only using important words of sentences and is the second best in terms of effectiveness with an F_1 score of 0.76. I-Match, SimHash, and DSC perform poorly with respective F_1 scores of 0.45, 0.39, and 0.30. FFP is not feasible for large collections; thus, CoDet is the most suitable algorithm for containment detection in news corpora.

Table 1. Effectiveness Comparison

Algorithm	Precision	Recall	F_1 Measure
FFP	0.82	0.88	0.85
CoDet	0.75	0.76	0.76
I-Match	0.72	0.33	0.45
SimHash	0.53	0.30	0.39
DSC	0.22	0.45	0.30

6. CONCLUSIONS

In this work we investigate containment detection problem, which is a more generalized version of the near-duplicate detection problem. We introduce a new approach, and compare its performance with four other well-known methods. As the experimental results demonstrate CoDet is preferable to all these methods; since it produces considerably better results in a feasible time. It also has desirable features such as time-linear efficiency and scalability, which enriches its practical value. Our method is versatile, can be improved, and can be extended to different problem domains.

7. REFERENCES

[1] Brin, S., Davis, J., Garcia-Molina, H.: Copy detection mechanisms for digital documents. ACM SIGMOD Conf. (1995) 398-409.

[2] Broder, A.: On the resemblance and containment of documents. Proc. of Compression and Complexity of Sequences (1997) p.21.

[3] Broder, A. Z., Glassman, S. C., Manasse, M. S., Zweig, G.: Syntactic clustering of the web. Computer Networks and ISDN Systems, 29(8-13) (1997) 1157-1166.

[4] Can, F., Kocberber, S., Baglioglu, O., Kardas, S., Ocalan, H. C., Uyar, E.: New event detection and topic tracking in Turkish. *JASIST* 61(4) (2010) 802-819.

[5] Charikar, M.: Similarity estimation techniques from rounding algorithms. ACM STOC (2002) 380-388.

[6] Chowdury, A., Frieder, O., Grossman, D., McCabe, M. C.: Collection statistics for fast duplicate document detection. ACM TOIS, 20(2) (2002) 171-191.

[7] Conrad, J. G., Schriber, C. P.: Managing déjà vu: Collection building for the identification of duplicate documents. *JASIST*, 57(7) (2006) 921-923.

[8] Deng, F., Rafiei, D.: Approximately detecting duplicates for streaming data using stable Bloom filters. ACM SIGMOD Conf. (2006) 25-36.

[9] Hajishirzi H., Yih W., Kolcz A.: Adaptive near-duplicate detection via similarity learning. ACM SIGIR Conf. (2010): 419-426.

[10] Landis, J. R., Koch, G. G.: The measurement of observer agreement for categorical data. *Biometrics*, 33(1) (1977) 159–174.

[11] Manku, G. S., Jain, A., Sarma, A. D.: Detecting near-duplicates for web crawling. ACM WWW Conf. (2007) 141-150.

[12] Monostori, K., Zaslavsky, A. B., Schmidt, H. W.: Efficiency of data structures for detecting overlaps in digital documents. ACSC (2001) 140-147.

[13] Theobald, M., Siddharth, J., Paepcke, A.: SpotSigs: robust and efficient near duplicate detection in large web collections. ACM SIGIR '08 Conf. 563-570.

[14] Wang, J. H., Chang, H. C.: Exploiting sentence-level features for near-duplicate document detection. AIRS Conf. (2009) 205–217

[15] Yang, H., Callan, J. P.: Near-duplicate detection by instance-level constrained clustering. ACM SIGIR Conf. (2006) 421-428.

[16] Zobel, J.: How reliable are the results of large-scale information retrieval experiments? ACM SIGIR Conf. (1998) 307-314.

[17] Zobel, J., Bernstein, Y.:. The case of the duplicate documents measurement, search, and science. *LNCS*, Vol. 3841. (2006) 26-39.

[18] Zhang, Q., Zhang, Y., Yu, H., Huang, X.: Efficient partial-duplicate detection based on sequence matching. ACM SIGIR Conf. (2010) 675-682.

Smoothing NDCG Metrics Using Tied Scores

Andrey Kustarev, Ilya Segalovich, Evgeniy Grechnikov,
Yury Logachev, Pavel Serdyukov, Yury Ustinovskiy
Yandex
Leo Tolstoy st. 8, Moscow, Russia
kustarev@yandex-team.ru, iseg@yandex-team.ru, grechnik@yandex-team.ru,
ylogachev@yandex-team.ru, pavser@yandex-team.ru, yuraust@yandex-team.ru

ABSTRACT

One of the promising directions in research on learning to rank concerns the problem of appropriate choice of the objective function to maximize by means of machine learning algorithms. We describe a novel technique of smoothing an arbitrary ranking metric and demonstrate how to utilize it to maximize the retrieval quality in terms of the $NDCG$ metric. The idea behind our listwise ranking model called TieRank is the artificial probabilistic tying of predicted relevance scores at each iteration of the learning process, which defines a distribution on the set of all permutations of retrieved documents. Such distribution provides us with a desired smoothed version of the target retrieval quality metric, which is possible to maximize using a gradient descent method. Experiments on LETOR collections show that TieRank outperforms most of the existing learning to rank algorithms.

Categories and Subject Descriptions: H.3.3 [Information Storage and Retrieval]: Information Search and Retrieval

General Terms: Algorithm, Experimentation, Performance

Keywords: learning to rank, ranking function, information retrieval measures

1. INTRODUCTION

Learning to rank is one of the most challenging problems in the field of Information Retrieval. A general learning to rank problem is usually defined as the problem of constructing a ranking function given a set of query-document pairs with their relevance labels and extracted features. Such a function assigns retrieval scores to documents, so that they could be sorted by their actual relevance to the given query using these scores. This set-up does not allow to apply standard gradient descent methods directly to the retrieval quality measures, since those measures are typically discontinuous functions of predicted retrieval scores. One class of approaches proposed to cope with this problem suggests to optimize not the quality measure itself, but its smooth modification, what still leads to the optimization in terms of the initial measure.

A number of proposed smooth modifications of retrieval quality metrics corresponds to certain distributions on the set S_m of all permutations of m retrieved documents. One of the first methods based on this idea is ListNet algorithm [2] which aims to minimize the cross-entropy between two Luce-Plackett probability distributions: one based on relevance labels and another one based on retrieval scores. Computational complexity of ListNet is considerably high, so authors focus on inferring the probability of retrieving a document at top positions only. SoftRank method [5] is based on the corrupting of the predicted scores s_j with Gaussian noise with standard deviation σ. This randomization produces a smooth probability distribution on S_m. However, in general case, this distribution is infeasible to compute, so authors implement a smoothed metric using a pairwise approach to estimate the distribution. Another distribution over permutations, motivated by Boltzmann distribution was studied in the scope of BoltzRank algorithm [4]. This distribution was used to better handle the estimation of the target distribution in SoftRank. SmoothRank algorithm, which is very similar to SoftRank, relies on a simplified version of Gaussian noise function [3] and focuses on making an appropriate choice of the smoothing parameter σ. To be more precise, this method heuristically defines probabilities $h_{i,j}$ of ranking the i-th document at j-th position after corrupting the ranking function with noise.

In this paper, we introduce a learning to rank method which is somewhat close in spirit to the above-mentioned methods, as it optimizes a smoothed variant of the $NDCG$-metric. We assume that each predicted score s_j is a Bernoulli random variable with two integer values $\lfloor s_j \rfloor$ and $\lceil s_j \rceil$ and a parameter that depends on s_j. Each possible combination of these variables results into a ranking function producing tied scores. A ranking produced by such a function, which we call a *partial ordering*, is the core element of our approach. After we define a distribution on the set of partial orderings, we consider the expectation of $NDCG@k$ as the smooth objective function. In order to calculate the $NDCG@k$ metric on a partial ordering, we use the method proposed by McSherry and Najork [6]. By applying gradient boosting tree-based algorithm [1] to the problem of objective function maximization, we learn a ranking function. Since our algorithm is based on artificial tying of retrieval scores, we call it TieRank.

CIKM'11, October 24–28, 2011, Glasgow, Scotland, UK.

The crucial point in such methods is the choice of the appropriate distribution, so we list the major advances of the distribution introduced in our TieRank algorithm.

- The objective function of TieRank is a smooth function of the predicted scores s_j even at the points with tie in the ranking, as opposed to SmoothRank. The authors of SmoothRank insist that non-differentiability of the objective function at particular points does not cause any problem to a gradient descent method and confirm this observation with the results on LETOR collections. However, our experiments demonstrate that in some cases, the employment of continuous, but not everywhere differentiable objective functions, leads to a considerable degradation of a learning to rank algorithm's performance.

- The distribution used in TieRank is rather simple, and it can be used directly for the explicit calculation of the objective function. On the contrary, the distributions introduced in the above-mentioned methods are used implicitly either to estimate the required intermediate probabilities (as in SoftRank and BoltzRank algorithms) or, as a motivation to define heuristically the same probabilities (as in SmoothRank).

The remainder of this paper is organized as follows. The next section describes our approach in details. First, Section 2.1 provides a high-level description of our method. Then we proceed with the definition of tied $NDCG@k$ metric in Section 2.2. In Section 2.3 we provide a detailed introduction into the distribution implemented in TieRank and define a smooth objective function. Section 3 contains the experimental results. Conclusions and possible ways to extend the presented work are discussed in the final section.

2. METHOD

2.1 General Framework

Let $D^i = \{d^i_1, \ldots, d^i_m\}$ be the set of documents retrieved for the query q^i and $\{rel^i(1), \ldots, rel^i(m)\}$ be their relevance labels. Each query-document pair is represented by a vector of features and our goal is to rank the documents in D^i according to their relevance to the query q^i. Given the training data consisting of above-described queries and document sets, we learn a function f of query-document features, which assigns a score $f(q^i, d^i_j) = s^i_j$ to each pair (q^i, d^i_j), and then we sort the set of documents D^i according to these scores (from now on, we omit i indices).

To measure the effectiveness of the ranking model usually $Precision$, AP, DCG, $NDCG$ metrics are used. We focus on optimizing the NDCG metric in this work. The value of the $DCG@k$ metric (discount cumulative gain at the position k) of the ordering $\sigma = \{v_1, \ldots, v_m\}$ is:

$$DCG@k(\sigma) = \sum_{j=1}^{k} G(rel(v_j))D(j),$$

where v_j is the identifier of the document retrieved at the position j, $G(rel(v_j))$ is its gain and $D(j)$ is the discount function. Typically $G(r) = 2^r - 1$ and $D(j) = 1/\log(1+j)$. The $NDCG@k$ metric (normalized discount cumulative gain at the position k) is $NDCG@k(\sigma) = DCG@k(\sigma)/DCG@k_p$, where $DCG@k_p$ is a discount cumulative gain of the perfect ordering according to true relevance labels $rel(i)$.

All of the mentioned metrics depend only on the final ordering of the set of documents and human relevance labels and cannot be optimized directly by the gradient descent, since objective quality measure is locally constant discontinuous function of the predicted scores s_j.

Now we explicitly describe the class of the smoothed IR metrics, mentioned in the introduction, which are used in most of the listwise approaches, and, in particular, in SoftRank and SmoothRank algorithms. Let M be any ranking metric considered as a function on the set of all permutations S_m of the documents retrieved for a given query, $M\colon S_m \to \mathbb{R}$. Let's fix any family of probability distributions P on the set S_m, parameterized by scores $\{s_j\}$, such that for any exact ordering $\sigma \in S_m$ the probability $P(\sigma; s_1, \ldots, s_m)$ is a smooth function of s_j. The new ranking metric M_s is the expectation value of the random variable M:

$$M_s(s_1, \ldots, s_m) := E(M) = \sum_{\sigma \in S_m} M(\sigma)P(\sigma; s_1, \ldots, s_m).$$

Since $M(\sigma)$ are constants and $P(\sigma; s_1, \ldots, s_m)$ are smooth functions of s_j, the proposed metric is a smooth variant of the initial metric M and thus it can be directly maximized by a standard gradient boosting method.

In the next section we explain how to generalize the $NDCG@k$ metric to the ranking functions with tied scores.

2.2 Tied Scores

The problem of tied scores in performance evaluation was considered in [6]. We want to compute retrieval quality metrics not only for exact orderings $\sigma \in S_m$, but also for partial orderings as well. Under *partial ordering* τ we assume a partition of the set of all documents $D = \{d_1 \ldots, d_m\}$ into an ordered set of relevance groups of the sizes $n_1, \ldots, n_l$, $n_1 + \cdots + n_l = m$. We say that the exact ordering σ is obtained from the partial ordering τ, if there exists a permutation of documents in every group such that the overall ordering is σ.

It is essential to define the value of the metric M for the partial ordering τ as an average of $n_1! \cdot n_2! \cdot \ldots \cdot n_l!$ M-values of all exact orderings σ obtained from the τ. In general, the corresponding sum is very computationally expensive. However, for many IR metrics the naive expression of the averaged metric, which contains $n_1! \cdot n_2! \cdot \ldots \cdot n_l!$ summands can be reduced to a very simple one and computed directly. Below is the equation for the averaged DCG, which was introduced by McSherry and Najork [6]. Its $NDCG$ analogue will be used further in our method. Let t_i be the end of i-th group of the partial ordering τ, i.e. $t_i = n_1 + \cdots + n_i$, then the value of the $DCG@k$ metric for the partial ordering $\tau = (v_1, \ldots, v_{t_1}) \succ \cdots \succ (v_{t_{l-1}+1}, \ldots, v_{t_l})$ is (see [6] for details):

$$DCG@k(\tau) = \sum_{i=1}^{l} \left(\left(\frac{1}{n_i} \sum_{j=t_i+1}^{t_{i+1}} G(rel(v_j)) \right) \sum_{j=t_i+1}^{\min(t_{i+1},k)} D(j) \right)$$

where $G(r) = 2^r - 1$ and $D(j) = 1/\log(1+j)$.

Further we explain how we arrive from the predicted scores s_j to the distribution on the set of partial orderings and to compute the expectation of the $NDCG@k$ metric using the above-mentioned equation.

2.3 A Rounding-Based Distribution Over Partial Orderings

The key idea of our approach is to define the distribution $P(\tau; s_1, \ldots, s_m)$ on the set of partial orderings and compute the corresponding expectation value of the tied $NDCG$-metric introduced in the previous section. Roughly speaking, we round each of the predicted scores s_j up or down with some probability.

Let's assume that at a new iteration of the learning process we obtain scores $s_1, \ldots, s_m$. We replace each s_j with a Bernoulli random variable $\beta(q, d_j)$ with two values $\lfloor s_j \rfloor$ and $\lceil s_j \rceil$ and a parameter $p = \varphi(s_j - \lfloor s_j \rfloor)$:

$$p_0(s_j) := P(\beta(q, d_j)) = \lfloor s_j \rfloor) = \varphi(s_j - \lfloor s_j \rfloor)$$

$$p_1(s_j) := P(\beta(q, d_j)) = \lceil s_j \rceil) = \varphi(\lceil s_j \rceil - s_j)$$

where $\varphi(x)$ is the monotone decreasing function on $[0; 1]$ satisfying the following conditions:

$$\varphi(0) = 1; \quad \varphi(x) \geq 0; \quad \varphi(x) + \varphi(1 - x) = 1; \quad \varphi'(0) = 0.$$

This set of m random variables defines the distribution on the set of 2^m predicted score lists with ties and thus on partial orderings of the set of all documents retrieved for the query q. The corresponding objective function is

$$M_s(s_1, \ldots, s_m) = \\ = \sum_{(\alpha_1, \ldots, \alpha_m) \in \{0,1\}^m} M(\tau) p_{\alpha_1}(s_1) \cdots p_{\alpha_m}(s_m)$$

where α_j is 0 if $\beta(q, d_j) = \lfloor s_j \rfloor$ and 1 if $\beta(q, d_j) = \lceil s_j \rceil$ and $\tau = \tau(\alpha_1, \ldots, \alpha_m)$ is a partial ordering, which corresponds to the particular outcome of m Bernoulli trials $\beta(q, d_j), j = 1, \ldots, m$.

Let us discuss in detail the conditions on the function $\varphi(x)$. First of them, $\varphi(0) = 1$, just means that we do not round s_j, if it is already integer. The following two conditions ensure that $P(\beta(q, d_j))$ is a true probability function. The latter condition guarantees the smoothness of the objective function M_s at integer points, as could be seen from the next equation for the gradient of M_s. We have evaluated two possible functions φ: the linear function $\varphi_l(x) = 1 - x$ and the spline function $\varphi_s(x) = 2x^3 - 3x^2 + 1$. The first one does not satisfy the last condition, but it still defines a reasonable distribution on the set of all partial orderings. The second one is a simple polynomial function which meets all four conditions. It is important to note, that the performance of the spline function has turned out to be far better. This observation indicates that in some cases continuous, but not everywhere differentiable functions of s_j, cannot be effectively optimized by gradient descent algorithms.

The gradient of M_s is defined as:

$$\frac{\partial M_s(s_1, \ldots, s_m)}{\partial s_j} = \\ = \sum_{(\alpha_1, \ldots, \alpha_m) \in \{0,1\}^m} M(\tau) p_{\alpha_1}(s_1) \cdots p'_{\alpha_j}(s_j) \cdots p_{\alpha_m}(s_m),$$

where $p'_{\alpha_j}(s_j)$ is $\varphi'(s_j - \lfloor s_j \rfloor)$ if $\alpha_j = 0$ and $-\varphi'(s_j - \lfloor s_j \rfloor)$ if $\alpha_j = 1$.

The computation of the gradient of the objective function for a query q requires $O(m2^m)$ operations, so its complexity is considerably high. However, as long as we define the initial performance metric as $M = NDCG@k$, $k \leq 10$, or if the number of retrieved documents per query is not high, the algorithm runs in a reasonable time. In our learning process we take randomly up to d documents per query from each of the relevance groups. Such a way of sampling is similar to the sampling used in SoftRank algorithm. In a manner similar to the authors of SoftRank, we also do not use any cut-off after this sampling and compute the smoothed $NDCG@m$, where m is the number of selected documents for the given query. This is not a very strong restriction since most search engines display only 10 results per page and users often look only at a few top ranked documents. Thus, it is reasonable to optimize the objective function relying on a relatively small subset of retrieved documents. The results on LETOR collection reported further in this paper confirm our intuitions.

In order to illustrate our method with a simple example, we describe how TieRank solves the following ranking problem. Let's assume that at some iteration for the given query q we have two documents d_1 and d_2 with relevance labels $rel(1) = 2$, $rel(2) = 1$ and predicted scores $s_1 = 0.3$, $s_2 = 0.6$. We further consider that each of the scores s_1, s_2 is a random variable and obtain 4 possible outcomes with probabilities:

$$P(\beta(q, d_1) = \beta(q, d_2) = 0) = \varphi(0.3)\varphi(0.6)$$

$$P(\beta(q, d_1) = 1, \beta(q, d_2) = 0) = \varphi(0.7)\varphi(0.6)$$

$$P(\beta(q, d_1) = 0, \beta(q, d_2) = 1) = \varphi(0.3)\varphi(0.4)$$

$$P(\beta(q, d_1) = \beta(q, d_2) = 1) = \varphi(0.7)\varphi(0.4)$$

The $NDCG@2$ scores of the corresponding rankings are $M(\tau_1) = M(\tau_4) = 0.9$, $M(\tau_2) = 1$, $M(\tau_3) = 0.8$ therefore in the case $s_1, s_2 \in [0; 1]$, the smoothed metric is:

$$M_s(s_1, s_2) = 0.9\varphi(s_1)\varphi(s_2) + \varphi(1 - s_1)\varphi(s_2) + \\ + 0.8\varphi(s_1)\varphi(1 - s_2) + 0.9\varphi(1 - s_1)\varphi(1 - s_2)$$

According to the equation of the derivative of M_s we have (here $\varphi(x) = 2x^3 - 3x^2 + 1$):

$$\frac{\partial M_s}{\partial s_1}(0.3, 0.6) = 0.126 \quad \frac{\partial M_s}{\partial s_2}(0.3, 0.6) = -0.144$$

Predictably, at a new iteration we should increase the score of d_1 and decrease the score of d_2.

Now we briefly describe the gradient boosting method [1] used for the optimization of the smooth function of predicted scores. Parameters of the algorithm are the depth of each tree, the number I of iterations in the learning process, the number d of documents for sampling and the regularization multiplier ε. At each iteration, the algorithm learns a tree model that best approximates the gradient of the objective function and adds it to the current ranking function $f(q, d)$. The following algorithm describes the learning process:

1. Initialize predicted scores $s_j = 0.5$
2. For $i = 1$ to I do

- Sample d documents per query per relevance group
- Compute gradient $\frac{\partial M_s}{\partial s_j}$
- Find regression tree $t(q, d)$ which approximates the gradient of M_s

Table 1: Performance on the MQ2007 collection.

Method	NDCG@k									
	1	2	3	4	5	6	7	8	9	10
RankBoost	41.34	40.94	40.72	41.22	41.83	42.27	42.67	43.23	43.92	44.64
AdaRank-NDGG	38.76	39.67	40.44	40.67	41.02	41.56	42.03	42.58	43.19	43.69
ListNet	40.02	40.63	40.91	41.44	41.70	42.29	42.75	43.28	43.81	44.40
TieRank	**42.32**	**42.37**	**42.08**	**42.14**	**42.26**	**42.57**	**43.06**	**43.67**	**44.16**	**44.70**

Table 2: Performance on the TD2004 collection.

Method	NDCG@k									
	1	2	3	4	5	6	7	8	9	10
RankBoost	50.67	43.33	42.95	40.53	**38.78**	**37.65**	36.39	**35.94**	**35.27**	**35.04**
AdaRank-NDGG	42.67	38.00	36.88	35.24	35.14	33.76	32.97	32.84	32.12	31.63
ListNet	36.00	34.67	35.73	34.69	33.25	32.70	32.51	32.06	31.88	31.75
SmoothRank	49.33	40.67	38.75	35.81	36.29	35.49	34.74	33.92	33.34	33.31
TieRank	**52.00**	**52.00**	**45.29**	**40.64**	38.33	37.12	**36.54**	35.44	35.16	34.95

- Update current ranking function $f(q,d) = f(q,d) + \varepsilon t(q,d)$

3. EVALUATION

We have evaluated TieRank on two LETOR collections: TD2004 from LETOR3 and MQ2007 from LETOR4. Training data in these collections consists of 5 pre-folded sets for cross-validation. TD2004 web collection, also known as TREC-2004, consists of 75 queries and 74146 documents with binary relevance labels for query-document pairs. MQ2007 collection consists of 784 queries and 15211 documents with 3 types of relevance labels for query-document pairs. In Tables 1 and 2 we report the performance of TieRank on these collections in comparison with the baseline methods. Due to paper space constraints, we compare our performance only with the most competitive baselines. In general, the less is regularization multiplier ε and the more documents we sample, the better model we learn, however, as long as we are restricted by the computational complexity of our model, we had to fix the regularization multiplier $\varepsilon = 0.001$ and the set sample count $d = 6$. So, we sample $m \leq 18$ documents per query for experiments with MQ2007 collection and $m \leq 12$ documents per query for experiments with TD2004. We optimized the number I of trees in our model (the parameter, which controls overfitting) and the depth of trees relying on the ordinary $NDCG@5$ metric on the validation folds. Then we evaluated our models on the test sets and measured their average performance in terms of the $NDCG@K$ metric. It turns out that during the learning process on these collections all predicted scores lie in the segment $[0;1]$, thus typically we obtain 2 groups in the corresponding partial orderings.

The results on MQ2007 show that TieRank outperforms all other methods for all truncation levels, including tree-based method RankBoost. On TD2004 collection TieRank outperforms the best baseline RankBoost only for small truncation levels. This is not surprising, since TD2004 collection has binary relevance labels (so optimization of $NDCG@k$ metrics is less appropriate) and contains ~1000 documents per query vs. ~20 documents in MQ2007 (so sampling is not as reasonable in this case). Comparison of TieRank with closely related SmoothRank method on TD2004 shows that our method performs better for all truncation levels.

4. CONCLUSIONS

In this paper, we have introduced a novel smoothing technique, and applied it to the $NDCG@k$ ranking metric. Our method is based on a new distribution on the set of partial orderings. The advantages of our approach are the smoothness of the objective function, its direct dependence on the initial performance metric and the possibility of its exact computation. We applied a gradient boosting learning algorithm to optimization of the proposed smoothed metric and learned rankers on several open collections. The evaluation on MQ2007 and TD2004 LETOR collections demonstrated that TieRank outperforms the most competitive baseline learning to rank approaches. We believe that principles embodied in the proposed smoothing technique have the potential to advance the research on learning to rank.

Since one of the main disadvantages of our algorithm is its computational complexity, we plan to implement some analogue of the averaging technique from [6] to simplify the calculation of the gradient of the objective function. We are also going to study in detail the influence of document sampling on the quality of a ranking model. Also it is interesting to investigate TieRank application to optimization of other retrieval quality measures (i.e. cascade metrics, such as ERR).

5. REFERENCES

[1] J. Friedman. Greedy Function Approximation: A Gradient Boosting Machine. Annals of Statistics, 29(5), 1189-1232, 2001.

[2] Z. Cao, T. Qin, T.-Y. Liu, M.-F. Tsai, H. Li. Learning to rank: from pairwise approach to listwise approach. In *Proc. of ICML* , 129-136, 2007.

[3] Chapelle, O., Wu, M.: Gradient descent optimization of smoothed information retrieval metrics. Inf. Retr. 216-235, 2010

[4] M. Volkovs, R. Zemel. Boltzrank: learning to maximize expected ranking gain. In *Proc. of ICML*, 1089-1096, 2009.

[5] M. Taylor, J. Guiver, S. Robertson, T. Minka. Softrank: optimizing non-smooth rank metrics. In *Proc. of WSDM*, 77-86, 2008.

[6] F. McSherry, M. Najork. Computing Information Retrieval Performance Measures Efficiently in the Presence of Tied Scores. In *Proc. of ECIR*, 414-421, 2008.

Learning to Rank with Cross Entropy

Yuan Lin, Hongfei Lin, Jiajin Wu, Kan Xu
School of Computer Science and Technology, Dalian University of Technology
No.2 LingGong Road GanJingZi district Dalian, China
{yuanlin, wujiajin}@mail.dlut.edu.cn {hflin, xukan} @dlut.edu.cn

ABSTRACT

Learning to rank algorithms are usually grouped into three types: the point wise approach, the pairwise approach, and the listwise approach, according to the input spaces. Much of the prior work is based on the three approaches to learn the ranking model to predict the relevance of a document to a query. In this paper, we focus on the problem of constructing new input space based on groups of documents with the same relevance judgment. A novel approach is proposed based on cross entropy to improve the existing ranking method. The experimental results show that our approach leads to significant improvements in retrieval effectiveness.

Categories and Subject Descriptors

H.3.3 [**Information Search and Retrieval**]: Search and Retrieval—*Retrieval models*

General Terms

Algorithms, Experimentation, Performance

Keywords

Learning to Rank, Groups, Relevance Judgment, Cross Entropy

1. INTRODUCTION

Learning to rank [3] has become an important research issue for information retrieval. The basic premise for learning to rank approaches is that there are three types of input spaces: pointwise, pairwise, and listwise samples. There is nearly no approaches based on other samples. Among the three approaches, the listwise approaches have achieved the best ranking performance on Letor data set [4]. However, the existing listwsie approaches are still not effective enough to rank the documents by relevance. Some techniques [2, 5] have been devised to improve this kind of approaches for better performance. One of such novel ideas is to construct new samples to improve the ranking accuracy [2].

CIKM'11, October 24–28, 2011, Glasgow, Scotland, UK.
Copyright 2011 ACM 978-1-4503-0717-8/11/10 ...$10.00.

Although the top-k framework [5] and the group-wise approaches [2] can generate some good performance for ranking, the loss function of the approaches are all based on likelihood loss, which does not reveal the extendibility of the approaches.

In this paper, we show that we can effectively rank the list of documents with respect to a query based on group-wise approach. By using the listwise based ListNet [1] loss function, Cross Entropy Loss, our method can lead to significant improvements in retrieval effectiveness.

2. CROSS ENTROPY LOSS BASED RANKING METHOD

2.1 ListNet

ListNet [1] is a robust and effective listwise approach that has achieved good performance in most data sets. It is a feature-based ranking algorithm that minimizes a probabilistic listwise loss function which is the cross entropy loss based on Luce model.The cross entropy loss function is calculated as:

$$L(y_n, z_n(f_\omega)) = -\sum_{\forall\pi\in\Pi} P_{y_x}(\pi)log(P_{z_x(f_\omega)}(\pi)) \quad (1)$$

The ranking function is denoted as f_w that is defined based on the neural network model. Given a feature vector x_d with respect to q_n, $f_w(x_d)$ assigns a score to it. Given a query q_n , the ranking function f_w can generate a score list $z_n(f_w) = (f_w(x_1), f_w(x_2), ..., f_w(x_k))$. y_x is the ground truth for the document list. Π is the set of all possible permutations of k documents, $P_s(\pi)$ is permutation probability of π according to s, which is based on Luce model as follows:

$$P_s(\pi) = \prod_{j=1}^{n} \frac{\exp(s_{\pi(j)})}{\sum_{k=j}^{n} \exp(s_{\pi(k)})} \quad (2)$$

where $s_{\pi(j)}$ denotes the score of object at position j of permutation π.

ListNet introduces the cross entropy loss into the listwise method for the first time.This approach almost achieves the best ranking performance on most of the measure metrics on the Letor dataset [4], so the improvement to ListNet is quite meaningful.

2.2 Top-k Framework based Cross Entropy

Top-k framework [5] aims to improve the top-k ranking performance by reforming the likelihood loss in order to make top-k subgroup order sensitive. The cross entropy loss function for Top-k Framework can be defined as:

$$L(f(x), y) = D(P(\pi|x;\psi_y) \parallel P(\pi|x;f)) \quad (3)$$

where D is cross entropy loss. $P(\pi|x;\psi_y)$ and $P(\pi|x;f)$ are Luce model based permutation probabilities. The score vector of the ground truth permutation is produced by a mapping function $\psi_y() : R_d \rightarrow R$, which retains the order in a permutation, i.e., if m>n, then $\psi_y(m)>\psi_y(n)$. In order to optimize the top-k ranking accuracy, it lets the mapping function retain the order of documents within the top k positions of the ground truth permutation and assigns to all the remaining positions a small value ϵ (which is smaller than the score of any object ranked at the top-k positions), i.e.$\psi_y(x_{y(1)}) > \cdots > \psi_y(x_{y(k)}) > \psi_y(x_{y(k+1)}) = \cdots = \psi_y(x_{y(n)}) = 0$. It can be proved that after the modification, the cosine loss becomes top-k subgroup order sensitive [5]. However there are still some problems with the framework. Suppose we have a hypothesis list for the ground truth of six documents, i.e. 2, 2, 2, 1, 0, 0 (2 defined as very relevant, 1 defined as relevant and 0 defined as irrelevant). If k=2, then after processing by mapping function ψ_y, the new ground truth of six documents may be 2, 2, -1, -1, -1, -1. Although the loss function may be sensitive to the top-2 ranking positions, which may tend to improve the top-k ranking accuracy. it may make a mistake to the document at position 3, which is very relevant to the query, is treated as the documents at position 5 and 6, which is not relevant to the given query, and so is the document at position 4, which is the relevant document. The error caused by mapping function to the training samples can also decrease the performance of the ranking model.

For the cross entropy loss function top-k framework just proposes the method to change the mapping function, but no experimental results for validating the effectiveness of the method. For reforming the cross entropy loss function, it makes the mapping function retain the order for the top k positions in a permutation and map all the remaining positions to a small value ϵ, which is smaller than the score of any object ranked at the top-k positions.

In this paper we will experiment to validate whether the method works. First, we implement the top-k ListNet. The results on Letor data set is shown in Figure 1 evaluated by NDCG@3. We tried different values of k (i.e., k=1, 3, 10, and the exact length of the ranked list). Obviously the last case corresponds to the original cross entropy loss in ListNet. From Figure 1 we can see that the top-3 ranking accuracies of ListNet cannot be significantly improved with the modifications. There is no one single method that can always achieve best performance on the three collection, and the performance is even descending on TD2004. That may be caused by the selection of the value of k, which is chosen arbitrarily as a fixed value for each query. It may result in that for the two documents with similar feature vectors and same label, which can be annotated by different values based on mapping function. It can cause the label confusion, which can affect the loss function in the process of training, and ultimately reduce the performance of the ranking function. It seems that the cross entropy loss based top-k framework can not improve the ranking performance effectively because the mapping function is easy to make the label confusion for the training documents.

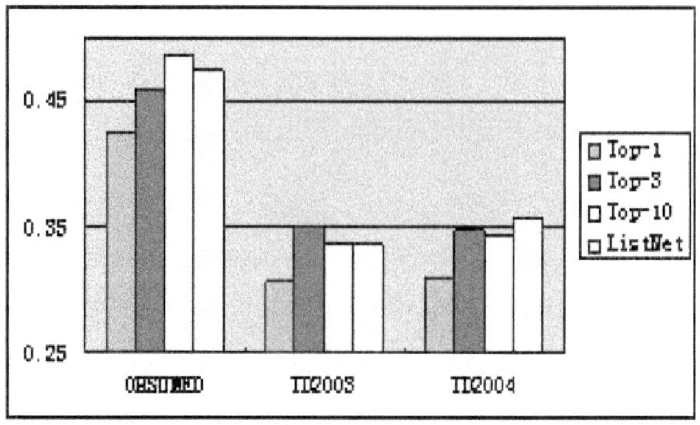

Figure 1: Effectiveness of different values of k

3. GROUP RANKING FRAMEWORK

In fact, the top-k ranking loss function is based on the documents on the top-k positions. As the true loss only depends on top-k documents, the selection of k is very important to the final ranking results. In order to avert the label confusion it is natural to set the value of k equal to the number of relevant documents so that the top-k framework is sensitive to the relevant document. However, the relevance of document is not just only relevant or irrelevant. There may be multiple relevance judgments as 2 (definitely relevant), 1 (possibly relevant), 0 (irrelevant) used in the OHSUMED collection of Letor data set [4]. And the loss function can not consider the relevant documents with the different relevance judgement as the same ones. It may affect the performance of ranking model. In this paper, we use the idea of grouping to solve the problem.

3.1 Group-group Sample

Each query $q^{(i)}$is associated with a list of documents$D^{(i)} = \{D_1^{(i)}, D_2^{(i)}, \cdots, D_n^{(i)}\}$. $D_j^{(i)}$ denotes the group of documents with the same relevance judgement j. n is the number of relevance degree for the documents. Furthermore, each list of documents $D^{(i)}$ is associated with a list of judgments (scores) $Y^{(i)} = \{Y_1^{(i)}, Y_2^{(i)}, \cdots, Y_n^{(i)}\}$ where $Y_j^{(i)}$ denotes the judgment on the group document $D_j^{(i)}$ with respect to query $q^{(i)}$. i.e. $j = 2$, then the relevance degree of the group of $D_2^{(i)}$ is 2. The documents with respect to a given query in training set can be divided into several groups in which the documents with same labels are gathered together. The groups are the basis of group-group samples. We make the pair of groups as the pairwise method. The pattern is constructed of a group with higher level label and a group with lower level label, For the query $q^{(i)}$ with the relevance degree n=3 (0, 1, 2), we can construct the training sample like this: $D_g^{(i)} = \{D_{2,1}^{(i)}, D_{2,0}^{(i)}, D_{1,0}^{(i)}\}$ which is called group-group sample. The group sample $D_{2,1}^{(i)}$ includes all the documents in the group $D_1^{(i)}$ and $D_2^{(i)}$. Furthermore, each list of group sample documents is associated with a list of judgments (scores) $Y_g^{(i)} = \{Y_{2,1}^{(i)}, Y_{2,0}^{(i)}, Y_{1,0}^{(i)}\}$. We then create a ranking function f ; for each feature vector $x^{(i)}$ (corresponding to document $d^{(i)}$ in the group sample), it outputs a score $f(x)$. For the list of feature vectors x in the group sample we obtain a list of $Z_g^{(i)} = \{f(x_1^{(i)}), f(x_2^{(i)}), \cdots, f(x_m^{(i)})\}$, m is the length of the list of documents in the group sample. The goal of learning is formalized as minimization of the total losses with respect to the training group-group sample.

$$\sum_{i=1}^{l} L_g(Y_g^{(i)}, Z_g^{(i)}) \tag{4}$$

where L_g is a group sample loss function. m is the number of the group samples in the training data. After defining the group-group sample, we can optimize the top-k framework for the further ranking performance.

3.2 Group Sample based Cross Entropy Loss

Group ranking framework is similar to the top-k ranking framework [5]. However, the samples of the two methods are different, and the meaning of k is different. The true loss of group ranking is defined as:

$$l_r(f(x), y) = \begin{cases} 0, if\ \hat{y}(i) = y(i)\ \forall i \in \{1, \ldots, r\}, \hat{y} = f(x) \\ 1,\ otherwise; \end{cases} \tag{5}$$

where the r is decided by the number of documents with the higher label in the group ranking samples, and the expected risk of group ranking loss becomes

$$L_g(f) = \int_{X \times Y} l_r(f(x), y) dP(x, y) \tag{6}$$

where X is the input space whose elements are the group samples to be ranked, Y is the output space whose elements are permutations of groups. and the optimal ranking function with respect to the group ranking true loss is:

$$f(x) = argmax_{G_r(j_1, j_2, \ldots, j_r) \in G_r} P(G_r(j_1, j_2, \ldots, j_r)|x) \tag{7}$$

where $G_r(j_1, j_2, \ldots, j_r)$ $=\{y \in Y | y(t) = j_t, \forall t = 1, 2, \ldots, r\}$ denotes a group sample in which all the permutations have the top-r,which is decided by the number of documents with higher relevance label, true loss. In this paper, the surrogate loss function is based on cross entropy for the group-group samples, which is described as follows:

$$L_g(\psi_g(y_g), z_g(f_\omega)) = -\sum_{\forall g \in G} P_{\psi_g(y_g(x))}(g) log(P_{z_x(f_\omega)}(g)) \tag{8}$$

$z_g(f_w)$ is the score list for the group sample generated by ranking function f_w. y_x is the ground truth for the document list of the sample. G is the set of all possible permutations of the documents in the group sample, $P_s(g)$ is the permutation probability of g according to s. By introducing the group-group sample into the cross entropy loss, we can deal with the relevant label confusion easily for the top-k framework. For the mapping function ψ_g, we set the value of the k to be the length of the list of the documents with higher relevant label in the group sample, which can still retain the order in a permutation. For the group sample we propose the mapping function ψ_g as follows. Let the mapping function retain the value of the label of the group with the higher relevant label, but for the lower relevant label, the label will be set to a smaller value ϵ in order to make the loss function more sensitive to the documents with the higher relevant label in the new samples. Algorithm 1 shows the learning algorithm of group ranking, which is similar to ListNet [1]. This paper adopts the neural network framework for training and optimization.

Algorithm1 Group ranking algorithm
Input: a set of listwise examples
$\{(X, Y)|(x(1), y(1)), (x(2), y(2)), \ldots, (x(m), y(m))\}$
Iteration T, learning rate η
Constructing group samples from listwise samples:
$\{(X_g, Y_g)|(x_1, y_1), (x_2, y_2), \ldots, (x_n, y_n)\}$
Initialize parameter ω
For t=1 to T do
Compute gradient $\Delta\omega$:
$\Delta\omega = \frac{\partial L_g}{\partial \omega}$
Update $\omega = \omega - \eta \cdot \Delta\omega$
End For
Output: parameter vector of the ranking function: ω.

Table 1: Ranking accuracies of ranking methods on OHSUMED, $*$ and $\dagger$ indicate significant improvement to ListNet and Top-10 of our approach GroupCE ($p \leqslant 0.05$)

Methods	MAP	N@1	N@3	N@10
ListNet	0.4457	0.5326	0.4732	0.4410
Top-10	0.4465	0.5126	0.4859	0.4411
GroupCE	0.4564	0.5628*†	0.5007*†	0.4583*†

Group sample can be taken as a ranked list with respect to a virtual given query. Therefore, the theory analysis of the top-k ranking framework [5] also works for the group ranking framework.

4. EXPERIMENTS

4.1 Experiment Settings

We evaluate our methods on the Letor3.0 data set released by Microsoft Research Asia. This data set contains two collections: the OHSUMED collection and the .Gov collection. The collections we use to evaluate our experiment are OHSUMED, TD2003 and TD2004 which are the subsets from .Gov collection. We adopt NDCG@n and MAP to evaluate the performance of ranking functions.

4.2 Experiment Results

First we compare our method with the existing methods based on cross entropy. We take Top-10 ranking method and original cross entropy loss based approach ListNet as baseline methods to make comparison with our cross entropy loss based group ranking method GroupCE. The results are listed in Table 1-3.

From Table 1-3, We can see that although Top-10 methods on the letor data sets aims to improve the ListNet, in fact

Table 2: Ranking accuracies of ranking methods on TD2003

Methods	MAP	N@1	N@3	N@10
ListNet	0.2753	0.4000	0.3365	0.3484
Top-10	0.2458	0.2667	0.3462	0.3371
GroupCE	0.2818†	0.3867†	0.3582*†	0.3650*†

Table 3: Ranking accuracies of ranking methods on TD2004

Methods	MAP	N@1	N@3	N@10
ListNet	0.2231	0.3600	0.3573	0.3175
Top-10	0.2275	0.4400	0.3427	0.3157
GroupCE	$0.2485^{*\dagger}$	$0.4933^{*\dagger}$	$0.4024^{*\dagger}$	$0.3377^{*\dagger}$

Table 4: Ranking accuracies on OHSUMED collection

Methods	MAP	N@1	N@3	N@10
Regression	0.4220	0.4456	0.4426	0.4110
RankSVM	0.4334	0.4958	0.4207	0.4140
FRank	0.4439	0.5300	0.4812	0.4433
SVMMAP	0.4453	0.5229	0.4663	0.4319
GroupMLE	0.4517	0.5589	0.4888	0.4572
GroupCE	**0.4564**	**0.5628**	**0.5007**	**0.4583**

the improvement is too marginal, and some evaluations even show Top-10 is no better than ListNet. It may be caused by relevance label confusion as we discuss in the Section 2.2. However, GroupCE achieves the best performance among all the methods on the OHSUMED and TD2004 datasets in terms of almost all of the measures. It also performs fairly well as compared to the other methods on the TD2003 dataset. Especially for MAP and NDCG@10, it outperforms all the other methods on all the datasets. The performance of GroupCE is also better than Top-10 ListNet. We also conduct the significant experiments to evaluate the improvement of our approach, the results reveal that our approach can indeed improve the original cross entropy based methods significantly. The main reason is that the loss function method is relevant documents sensitive and also secures the label classification clarity. The group ranking framework can deal with the label confusion easily, because it annotates the document in the same group by the same value. From the above experimental results, we can come to the conclusion that it is better to use the modified group loss functions than the original surrogate loss functions.

We also examine the performance of our methods compared with the existing methods. We select several representative ranking algorithms compared with our cross entropy based group ranking method. The ranking algorithms include pointwise approach: Regression, pairwise approach: RankSVM and FRank and also Listwise approach method: SVMMAP. Especially we compare our method with group ranking method based on likelihood loss [2] (GroupMLE for short). The results are listed in Table 4-5.

We also choose OHSUMED, TD2003 and TD2004 collection as the test collections. The results on the test collections show that method of group ranking are useful in enhancing performance of IR systems comparing with existing methods. The GroupCE method almost boosts the ranking accuracies in the terms of all measures. Compared with GroupMLE, our method also achieve better performance on ranking accuracies. It shows that cross entropy loss is more appropriate than likelihood loss to construct the loss function based on group ranking framework.

Table 5: Ranking accuracies on TD2003

Methods	MAP	N@1	N@3	N@10
Regression	0.2409	0.3200	0.3071	0.3263
RankSVM	0.2628	0.3200	0.3441	0.3461
FRank	0.2031	0.3000	0.2671	0.2690
SVMMAP	0.2445	0.3200	0.3199	0.3282
GroupMLE	0.2811	0.3267	**0.3587**	0.3568
GroupCE	**0.2818**	**0.3867**	0.3582	**0.3650**

Table 6: Ranking accuracies on TD2004

Methods	MAP	N@1	N@3	N@10
Regression	0.2078	0.3600	0.3352	0.3031
RankSVM	0.2237	0.4133	0.3467	0.3078
FRank	0.2388	0.4933	0.3875	0.3331
SVMMAP	0.2049	0.2933	0.3035	0.2907
GroupMLE	0.2386	0.4267	0.3424	0.3175
GroupCE	**0.2485**	**0.4933**	**0.4024**	**0.3377**

5. CONCLUSION

In this paper, we have proposed a novel group ranking approach based on cross entropy loss to improve the ranking performance. In the new framework, the true loss is defined on the relevant documents, and our experiments have shown that GroupCE can significantly outperform its original versions based on cross entropy. For future work, we will continue to study the theory basis of the group ranking framework to examine whether the ranking performance can be improved further.

6. ACKNOWLEDGMENTS

This work is supported by grant from the Natural Science Foundation of China (No.60673039 and 60973068), the National High Tech Research and Development Plan of China (No.2006AA01Z151), National Social Science Foundation of China (No.08BTQ025), the Project Sponsored by the Scientific Research Foundation for the Returned Overseas Chinese Scholars, State Education Ministry and The Research Fund for the Doctoral Program of Higher Education (No.20090041 110002), Science Foundation for Youth Scholars of Dalian University of Technology.

7. REFERENCES

[1] Z. Cao, T. Qin, T. Y. Liu, M. F. Tsai, and H. Li. Learning to rank: From pairwise approach to listwise approach. In *Proceedings of the ICML*, pages 129–136, 2007.

[2] Y. Lin, H. Lin, Z. Ye, S. Jin, and X. L. Sun. Learning to rank with groups. In *Proceedings of CIKM*, pages 1589–1592, 2010.

[3] T. Y. Liu. Learning to rank for information retrieval. *Foundations and Trends in Information Retrieval*, 3(3):225–331, 2009.

[4] T. Y. Liu, J. Xu, T. Qin, W. Xiong, and H. Li. Letor: Benchmark dataset for research on learning to rank for information retrieval. In *Proceedings of the Learning to Rank workshop in SIGIR*, pages 3–10, 2007.

[5] F. Xia, T. Y. Liu, and H. Li. Statistical consistency of top-k ranking. In *Proceedings of NIPS*, pages 2098–2106, 2009.

Predicting Document Effectiveness in Pseudo Relevance Feedback

Mostafa Keikha*, Jangwon Seo‡, W. Bruce Croft‡, Fabio Crestani*
* University of Lugano, Lugano, Switzerland
‡ CIIR, University of Massachusetts Amherst, Amherst, MA
mostafa.keikha@usi.ch, jangwon@cs.umass.edu
croft@cs.umass.edu, fabio.crestani@usi.ch

ABSTRACT

Pseudo relevance feedback (PRF) is one of effective practices in Information Retrieval. In particular, PRF via the relevance model (RM) has been widely used due to the theoretical soundness and effectiveness. In a PRF scenario, an underlying relevance model is inferred by combining language models of the top retrieved documents where the contribution of each document is assumed to be proportional to its score for the initial query. However, it is not clear that selecting the top retrieved documents only by the initial retrieval scores is actually the optimal way for query expansion.

We show that the initial score of a document is not a good indicator of its effectiveness in query expansion. Our experiments show that if we can estimate the true effectiveness of the top retrieved documents, we can obtain almost 50% improvement over RM. Based on this observation, we introduce various document features that can be used to estimate the effectiveness of documents. Our experiments on the TREC Robust collection show that the proposed features make good predictors, and PRF using the effectiveness predictors can achieve statistically significant improvements over RM.

Categories and Subject Descriptors

H.3.3 [**Information Storage and Retrieval**]: Information Search and Retrieval

General Terms

Algorithms, Experimentation

Keywords

Pseudo Relevance Feedback, Relevance Model

1. INTRODUCTION

Pseudo relevance feedback (PRF) is a well-studied technique for improving the performance of a retrieval system in Information Retrieval. Among a variety of instances of PRF, the relevance model is one of the widely used techniques because not only does it fit well in language modeling frameworks but also it has been shown to be effective for many tasks.

The relevance model (RM) is used to select the most appropriate terms (feedback terms) from the top retrieved documents by the initial search (feedback documents) to expand the original query [4]. Feedback terms for query expansion are selected based on their relevance to the initial query:

$$P(w|\theta_Q) \propto \sum_{D \in \mathbb{D}} P(w|D)P(Q|D) \quad (1)$$

where $\mathbb{D}$ is a set of feedback documents for the initial query Q.

One of the major issues in PRF is selecting the most appropriate feedback documents to be used in the expansion phase. Implementations of RM usually use the top retrieved documents based on their retrieval scores for the initial query. However, since not all the top retrieved documents are relevant, there is a high chance that we use non-relevant documents for expansion.

In order to investigate relations between the initial retrieval score of a document and its effectiveness as a source of query expansion, we conducted the following pilot study on the TREC Robust collection (see Section 3 for more details about the collection). First, we selected the top 100 documents based on the Dirichlet-smoothed language model scores for each topic. We then generated an expanded query based on each retrieved document. Note that the algorithm used for query expansion is RM where only one feedback document exists. This expanded query was submitted as a new query to the same query evaluation system. That is, we obtained 100 different expanded queries and their ranked lists. Average Precision (AP) of each expanded query is presumably the real effectiveness of the corresponding document for query expansion.

The Pearson correlation coefficient between the initial scores of the documents and the AP scores of their corresponding expanded queries tells us how good the initial scores of the documents are as effectiveness estimators. In our pilot study with 250 of the TREC Robust04 topics, the correlation coefficient is -0.32. This indicates a strong negative correlation meaning that the initial scores are poor indicators for selecting documents. Therefore, the initial scores need to be replaced by better estimators for better PRF.

In this work, we address the problem of finding better weighting of feedback documents for RM. Although good

CIKM'11, October 24–28, 2011, Glasgow, Scotland, UK.

document weighting for PRF is critical in RM, there has been relatively little work that addresses this issue. For example, Seo and Croft [7] changed the weighting scheme for combining multiple documents for RM. Other studies have exploited resampling methods to select better documents [1, 5]. However, they did not attempt to find better weights for documents. In this paper, we propose a novel discriminative technique estimating the effectiveness of documents for PRF. More specifically, we introduce various features for documents and a learning approach. By incorporating our estimated effectiveness values into the relevance model formulation as document weights, we demonstrate that our proposed technique can achieve significant improvements over the generic RM.

2. DOCUMENT SELECTION FOR QUERY EXPANSION

2.1 Importance of Document Effectiveness

Before trying to estimate the effectiveness of each document, it is important to know how good the PRF results would be if feedback documents are selected according to the real effectiveness values. To this end, we use the average precision score by each expanded query as the effectiveness value of the document used for generating that expanded query and analyze them.

In order to analyze the effect of using the real effectiveness, we must decide how to use it. For example, RM aggregates the document models of feedback documents by the weighted average and generates a single model that is assumed to represent the relevance probability of each term for the original query. Similarly, we can use the effectiveness of each document as its weight and estimate a single relevance model as follows:

$$P(w|Q) \propto \sum_{D \in \mathbb{D}} P(w|D) \mathit{Effectiveness}(D, Q) \qquad (2)$$

where $\mathbb{D}$ is a set of the top 10 documents with the highest effectiveness values among the top 100 documents retrieved by the initial query Q. *Effectiveness(D,Q)* is the effectiveness of document D for query expansion via RM and in the ideal case will be the average precision score of the expanded query by the relevance model estimated from D. Note that in the original RM formulation as shown in (1), the query-likelihood of the original query is used instead of the effectiveness. We call this method **ORACLE**$_S$.

Another approach would be to generate multiple ranked lists based on different expanded queries and aggregate the ranked lists to produce a single ranked list afterward. The intuition behind this approach is that there can be some useful terms in some good documents which do not appear in other documents. That is, when generating a single relevance model, these useful terms might be discarded in the final expanded query. To avoid these pitfalls, we try to combine different ranked lists, weighted by the effectiveness of its corresponding document:

$$\mathit{Score}(D', Q) = \sum_{D \in \mathbb{D}} \mathit{Score}(D', Q_D) \mathit{Effectiveness}(D, Q) \qquad (3)$$

where Q_D is an expanded query by document D and $\mathit{Score}(D', Q_D)$ is the query evaluation score of document D' for the expanded query. We call this method **ORACLE**$_M$.

Table 1: Evaluation results using the true document effectiveness

Model	MAP	P@10	Bpref
LM	0.2794	0.4434	0.2687
RM	0.3085	0.4505	0.2853
ORACLE$_M$	**0.4582**	**0.6303**	**0.4459**
ORACLE$_S$	0.4284	0.5909	0.4020

We conducted experiments using the true effectiveness values over the TREC Robust04 queries. Throughout this paper, we fixed the number of feedback terms and the number of feedback documents to 10. These values were selected since they showed the best performance for RM and we did not separately tune them for other methods.

Table 1 shows the performance of the methods using the real effectiveness of documents in comparison to two baselines, i.e., **LM** (the Dirichlet-smoothed language model) and **RM** (the traditional relevance model). As we see, if we know the true effectiveness of documents, we can achieve significant improvements over **RM**. The improvements by the *Oracle_Multiple* are greater and can be up to 50%. These results give us a good motivation for estimating the document effectiveness for query expansion.

2.2 Predicting the Document Effectiveness

In order to detect the most useful documents for query expansion, we extract a set of features that can help us predict the effectiveness of each document. These features are mainly based on the content of each document and its relation with other top retrieved documents. Table 2 summarizes features that we use.

Type1 features (f1-f3) are query independent features that capture some properties of a document and its relation with the collection.

Type2 features (f4-f6) are based on the initial retrieval score of the document and its similarity to the traditional relevance model of the query.

Type3 features (f7-f13) are based on similarity of the document with other top retrieved documents. For example, f7 is the average similarity of the document with other top retrieved documents. Since f7 can be biased toward a few highly similar documents, we define f8 as the number of the documents with higher similarity than a threshold. We set the threshold to be the average similarity between all pairs of the top retrieved documents.

For a term t, we define $Com(t, \mathbb{D})$ which shows how common t is in the top retrieved documents:

$$Com(t, \mathbb{D}) = \frac{\sum_{D \in \mathbb{D}} I(t \in D)}{|\mathbb{D}|} \qquad (4)$$

Based on this function, we can define a set of new features for each document. The arithmetic mean, geometric mean and the minimum of the $Com(t, \mathbb{D})$ over all the terms in a document are three of the features that we use (f9-f11).

We assume that an effective document for query expansion has most of its terms in common with other top retrieved documents and so has high arithmetic mean of $Com(t, \mathbb{D})$ values. At the same time, the document would have few terms that are not very popular and accordingly has a low minimum or geometric mean values (those non-popular terms

Table 2: Features used in the regression model for document D

Type	Feature	Description
Type1	f1	Size of D
	f2	Kullback-Leibler (KL) divergence between $p(w\|D)$ and collection model $p(w\|C)$
	f3	Entropy of multinomial distribution $p(w\|D)$
Type2	f4	Querylikelihood score $p(q\|D)$
	f5	KL divergence between $p(w\|D)$ and relevance model $p(w\|\theta_Q)$
	f6	Number of common terms between D and feedback terms selected by $p(w\|\theta_Q)$
Type3	f7	$1/\|\mathbb{D}\| \sum_{D' \in \mathbb{D}} similarity(D, D')$
	f8	$\|\{D' \in \mathbb{D} \| similarity(D', D) > threshold\}\|$
	f9	Arithmetic mean of $Com(t, \mathbb{D})$ over terms t's in D
	f10	Geometric mean of $Com(t, \mathbb{D})$ over terms t's in D
	f11	Minimum of $Com(t, \mathbb{D})$ over terms t's in D
	f12	f9 / f10
	f13	f9 / f11

are the reason that query expansion based on the single best document works better than the traditional RM). Based on this assumption, we define new features by dividing the arithmetic mean of the $Com(t, \mathbb{D})$ by its minimum or geometric mean. We expect these features to have high values for the effective documents.

To learn a document effectiveness prediction model using these features, we consider the following regression problem.

$$\arg\min_{\Phi} \sum_{Q \in T} \sum_{D \in \mathbb{D}_Q} ||\Phi(F(D)) - Effectiveness(D)||^2 \quad (5)$$

where T is a set of training topics, $\mathbb{D}_Q$ is a set of the top 100 retrieved documents for query Q, and F is a mapping from documents to feature spaces. The effectiveness to be learned is the average precision score of each document.

We solve this problem using the Stochastic Gradient Boosting Tree algorithm by Friedman [2]. Then, Φ is an additive model of multiple decision trees. Since some of our features showed non-linear relations with the AP scores in our preliminary experiments, non-linear models based on decision trees such as the Stochastic Gradient Boosting Tree are an appropriate choice.

The learned model on a training set is used to predict the effectiveness of documents on a test set. We select the top 10 documents based on their predicted values. These documents are used for query expansion according to techniques of Equation (2) and (3). Single or multiple expanded queries generated using these methods are called $\textbf{PREDICT}_S$ and $\textbf{PREDICT}_M$ respectively.

3. EXPERIMENTS

We evaluated our proposed methods on the TREC Robust04 collection which consists of newswire articles. The collection includes more than 500,000 documents and 250 queries. We used 150 queries for training (topic 301-450) and 100 queries for testing (topic 600-700). We used titles of the topics as queries.

We used the Terrier system[1] to index the collection with the default stemming and stopwords removal. The language modeling approach using the Dirichlet smoothing was used to retrieve and score the top documents for query expansion.

In our experiments, the estimated relevance model is interpolated with the original query model as follows:

$$P(w|\theta'_Q) = (1 - \alpha)P(w|\theta_Q) + \alpha P(w|Q) \quad (6)$$

α is a parameter and in our experiments is set to be 0.5 which has been shown to be effective in previous studies [6]. This interpolation approach is often used to improve retrieval performance.

To estimate language model $P(w|D)$ of the top retrieved documents in the feedback phase, we employ the parsimonious language model and filter out the collection model from the document model using the Expectation Maximization algorithm in order to obtain the most informative terms for each document [3].

For the Stochastic Gradient Boosting Tree (SGBT), we used the `gbm`[2] package implemented in `R`. The bagging option was turned on and the bagging portion parameter was set to 0.5. The number of decision trees and the depth of decision trees were set to 2000 and 7, respectively.

Table 3: Evaluation results using the estimated document effectiveness. † and ‡ indicate statistically significant improvements on two baselines, i.e., LM and RM respectively (paired t-test with p-value < 0.05).

Model	MAP		P@10	Bpref	
LM	0.2794		0.4434	0.2687	
RM	0.3085	†	0.4505	0.2853	†
$\textbf{PREDICT}_M$	0.3296	†‡	0.4586	**0.3130**	†‡
$\textbf{PREDICT}_S$	**0.3317**	†‡	**0.4626**	0.3095	†‡

Table 4: The top five influential features

Feature	Relative Influence
f4	0.35
f9	0.21
f2	0.13
f1	0.09
f6	0.07

Table 3 shows the performance of the predicted values using the proposed methods. We can see that both $\textbf{PREDICT}_S$ and $\textbf{PREDICT}_M$ outperform LM and RM. Interestingly, as opposed to the oracle experiments, $\textbf{PREDICT}_S$ demonstrates better performance than $\textbf{PREDICT}_M$. This is mainly due to the sensitivity of $\textbf{PREDICT}_M$ to the regression er-

[1] `http://ir.dcs.gla.ac.uk/terrier/`

[2] `http://cran.r-project.org/web/packages/gbm/`

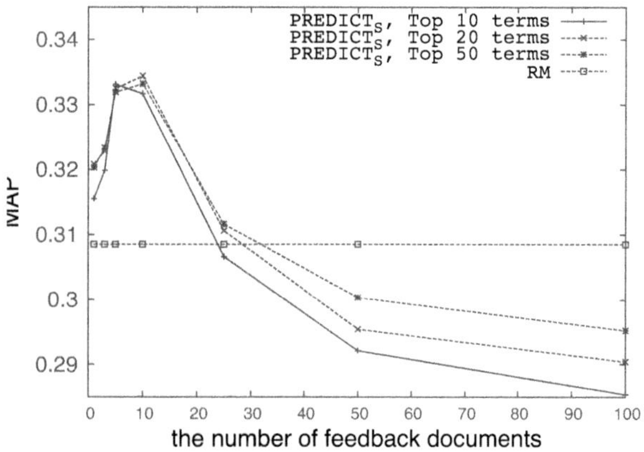

Figure 1: Sensitivity of PREDICT$_S$ to the number of feedback documents.

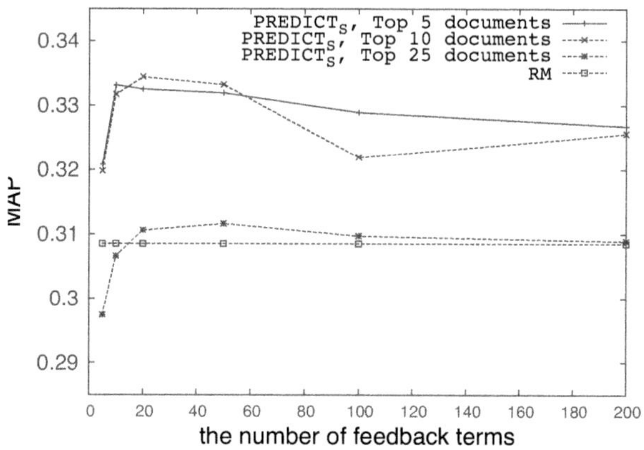

Figure 2: Sensitivity of PREDICT$_S$ to the number of feedback terms.

ror. Since **PREDICT**$_S$ combines multiple document models, it is less likely that a bad document has a high influence over the final term distribution.

We can calculate the relative influence of each feature from the learned SGBT according to [2]. Table 4 shows the top five influential features. Interestingly, while the initial score is not a good indicator by itself, it has the highest influence. Another noteworthy observation is that each of the three types of features (Type1, Type2 and Type3) have a representative in the top three influential features. This shows that all the three types of features need to be considered.

The Pearson correlation coefficient between the predicted values and the true values of effectiveness is +0.53, which indicates a strong correlation. However, there is still considerable room for improvement.

As mentioned before, the reported results are obtained using the top 10 terms extracted from the top 10 documents. In order to investigate the effect of these numbers, we run **PREDICT**$_S$, varying the numbers of feedback documents and feedback terms. Figure 1 and 2 show the effect of these parameters on the performance of the system. The performance appears more sensitive to the number of feedback documents than the number of feedback terms. In Figure 1, when selecting more than 25 documents, regardless of the number of feedback terms, the performance significantly drops. On the other hand, in Figure 2, with a proper choice of the number of feedback documents, e.g., 5 or 10, the effect of the number of feedback terms is minimized. Nevertheless, the best performance is achieved when the number of feedback terms is around 20.

4. CONCLUSION AND FUTURE WORK

In this paper, we investigated the effectiveness of the initial retrieved documents in terms of the performance of pseudo relevance feedback. We showed that the the initial score of a document is not a good indicator for its effectiveness. Based on this observation, we proposed various features that help us predict the effectiveness of documents. The predicted effectiveness values were used as weights of feedback documents for the proposed pseudo relevance feedback techniques. Our experiments showed that the proposed techniques using the predicted effectiveness can achieve statistically significant improvements over the relevance model.

Despite the significant improvements, the results are still far short of the ideal (oracle) situation yet. One direction for future work would be to define better features so that the effectiveness of documents can be more accurately predicted.

Also, in this work, a simple aggregation method is used for some proposed algorithms (e.g., **PREDICT**$_M$) requiring the aggregation of multiple ranked lists. Accordingly, another interesting extension of this work would be leveraging advanced aggregation techniques that have been well-studied in federated search.

5. ACKNOWLEDGEMENT

This work was supported by Swiss National Science Foundation (SNSF) for the "Temporal Analysis of User Generated Data" project as a grant for "Prospective Researcher" to visit CIIR at University of Massachusetts Amherst.

6. REFERENCES

[1] K. Collins-Thompson and J. Callan. Estimation and use of uncertainty in pseudo-relevance feedback. In *Proceedings of SIGIR 2007*, pages 303–310, 2007.

[2] J. H. Friedman. Stochastic gradient boosting. *Computational Statistics and Data Analysis*, 38:367–378, 1999.

[3] D. Hiemstra, S. Robertson, and H. Zaragoza. Parsimonious language models for information retrieval. In *Proceedings of SIGIR 2004*, pages 178–185, 2004.

[4] V. Lavrenko and W. B. Croft. Relevance-based language models. In *Proceedings of SIGIR 2001*, pages 120–127, 2001.

[5] K. S. Lee, W. B. Croft, and J. Allan. A cluster-based resampling method for pseudo-relevance feedback. In *Proceedings of SIGIR 2008*, pages 235–242, 2008.

[6] Y. Lv and C. Zhai. Positional relevance model for pseudo-relevance feedback. In *Proceedings of SIGIR 2010*, pages 579–586, 2010.

[7] J. Seo and W. B. Croft. Geometric representations for multiple documents. In *Proceeding of SIGIR 2010*, pages 251–258, 2010.

Learning to Rank Categories for Web Queries

Prashant Ullegaddi*
Language Technologies Research Centre
International Institute of Information Technology
Hyderabad 500 032
prashant.ullegaddi@research.iiit.ac.in

Vasudeva Varma
Language Technologies Research Centre
International Institute of Information Technology
Hyderabad 500 032
vv@iiit.ac.in

ABSTRACT

In web search, understanding the user intent plays an important role in improving search experience of the end users. Such an intent can be represented by the categories which the user query belongs to. In this work, we propose an information retrieval based approach to query categorization with an emphasis on learning category rankings. To carry out categorization we first represent a category by web documents (from Open Directory Project) that describe the semantics of the category. Then, we learn the category rankings for the queries using 'learning to rank' techniques. To show that the results obtained are consistent and do not vary across datasets, we evaluate our approach on two datasets including the publicly available KDD Cup dataset. We report an overall improvement of 20% on all evaluation metrics (*precision*, *recall* and $F - measure$) over two baselines: a text categorization baseline and an unsupervised IR baseline.

Categories and Subject Descriptors

H.3.3 [**Information Systems**]: Information Storage and Retrieval—*Information Search and Retrieval*

General Terms

Algorithms, Experimentation

Keywords

Query categorization, query classification, learning to rank

1. INTRODUCTION

In this work, we address Query Categorization (QC), which involves classifying a given query into one or more pre-defined categories which the query can belong to; thus effectively providing a means to understand the user intent of the query. Such a topical categorization of queries into pre-defined categories can have many applications. The need for QC originated from a federated search paradigm where the task is to search simultaneously various multiple online databases and web resources. In a federated search scenario, knowing the categories of a query beforehand can help in determining the sources of evidence for vertical selection [1]. Secondly, QC can also be used in categorical organization of the search results [7]; thus helping the user easily navigate through the results. Advertisements relevant to the user query can be placed on the search results page, thus enriching the users' search experience [2].

Most of the existing approaches [5, 6] treat QC as a text categorization problem, and solve the problem accordingly. Text categorization [3] has been a well studied problem. Though query categorization can be viewed as a text categorization problem as approached in [5, 6], QC is complicated by the presence of very short text (short queries). On the other hand, we propose an information retrieval based approach (Section 3) with an attempt to learn category rankings for a query. Here, we try to learn the rankings which capture query-to-category relationships using an already categorized document corpus such as Open Directory Project[1] (ODP). We evaluate the performance of our system on two different datasets (Section 4) including the publicly available KDD Cup 2005[2] dataset.

This work aims at answering the following research questions relevant to QC: 1) can we solve query categorization by treating it *purely* as an Information Retrieval (IR) problem?, 2) can we utilize already categorized documents to perform query categorization?, 3) can we learn to rank the categories for a given query?

2. PROBLEM DEFINITION

QC is formally defined in Definition 1.

DEFINITION 1. *Suppose there exists a set of* L *categories* $\mathcal{C} = \{c_1, c_2, \cdots, c_L\}$. *Assume that we are given a set of* n *queries* $Q_{train} = \{Q_1, Q_2, \cdots, Q_n\}$ *and for each query* Q *in* Q_{train} *a set of relevant categories* $\mathcal{C}^{(Q)} \in \mathcal{C}$ *is given. Now the goal is to learn a ranking model* $h(\cdot)$ *such that for any query* $Q^{(i)}$, *the learnt model* h *can find a subset* $\mathcal{C}^{(i)}(= h(\mathcal{C}))$ *of the set* $\mathcal{C}$:

$$\mathcal{C}^{(i)} = \{c_1^{(i)}, c_2^{(i)}, \cdots, c_M^{(i)}\},$$

such that, $rel(c_j^{(i)}) \geq rel(c_{j+1}^{(i)})$ *where* $1 \leq j < M$, *with* $M \leq L$, *and where* $rel(c_j^{(i)})$ *indicates the relevance of a category* $c_j^{(i)}$ *for the given query* $Q^{(i)}$

*Part of the work described herein was conducted while the first author was an intern at Yahoo! Labs India.

[1] http://www.dmoz.org/

[2] http://www.sigkdd.org/kdd2005/kddcup.html

CIKM'11, October 24–28, 2011, Glasgow, Scotland, UK.

Here, L can vary over time, but it is safe to assume that L will be fixed over a reasonable amount of time. $rel(\cdot)$ is relevance function that returns relevance score of a category for a given query. Categories are usually hierarchically organized.

3. APPROACH

We present an IR based approach to query categorization with an attempt to learn category rankings for a given web query. However at the same time, application of IR techniques to solve QC is not a straightforward task since the category names for queries may not contain sufficient context which is required to retrieve and rank categories in order to solve QC with an IR approach. To address this problem, we first represent the categories by a set of documents that better describe the semantics of the categories. We follow it up by discussing query representation for this approach which is required to retrieve documents that are topically similar to the query. Then, we present 'learning to rank' for categorizing queries along with a discussion on ranking features used.

3.1 Category Representation

Solving QC as an IR problem requires category representation since category names themselves do not contain enough context. We chose to use the categories of Open Directory Project (ODP) as the set of pre-defined intermediate categories ($\mathcal{C}^{(I)}$) since it has categories that cover most of the web and for each category, there are web pages grouped under that category. The web pages associated with a category describe its semantics. At the time of documenting this work, ODP had over 4.5 million web pages, organized into approximately 590K categories. Ignoring non-English web pages and categories, we ended up with 2.4 million web pages, organized into approximately 380K categories. We can safely assume that the documents in a category contain the concepts that describe the semantics of the category and hence the documents represent the category.

Now, we have a set of pre-defined categories and a corpus of documents describing the semantics of those categories. These data are needed to perform QC task in our approach since these data enable us to treat QC as an IR problem. Notations $\mathcal{C}^{(I)}$ and $\mathcal{D}$[3] now represent the categories in ODP and corpus of web pages in ODP, respectively. For each document $d \in \mathcal{D}$, we have a set of categories $\mathcal{C}^d \in \mathcal{C}^{(I)}$ associated with the document. Or conversely, for each category $c \in \mathcal{C}^{(I)}$, there is a set of documents $\mathcal{D}^c \in \mathcal{D}$ that define the semantics of the category. Now that we have a document corpus representing the semantics of set of pre-defined categories, we proceed to represent the query so that concepts defining the query are covered.

3.2 Query Representation

Usually, users express their information need through a short query, often containing a few words. Hence, we need a way to represent a query such that the newly formed query is able to identify the most relevant documents which are topically identical to the query since our task is to carry out topical categorization of a query. We emphasize here that retrieved documents need not be highly relevant to a query, those documents which are topically similar to the query are good enough to carry out the categorization process. In fact, even a document that is not relevant to the query but topically similar to the query would assist the system in query categorization. For example, assume that the query is "rafael nadal". In this case, the documents that are not related to concept "rafael nadal" but are related to concepts like "tennis", "sports" are good enough to aid QC. That is, even a document talking about "roger federer" would help in categorizing the query "rafael nadal" since the document is topically similar to the query. Hence, we claim that our system can even benefit from the topically similar irrelevant documents as well.

Also, this step is indeed needed, since our corpus $\mathcal{D}$ may not contain the exact query. As an example, assume that the query "serena williams" does not have an exact match in the corpus. However, when the query is represented with key concepts like "tennis", "wta", "wimbledon", there is a high probability that the expanded query, now, identifies some related documents from $\mathcal{D}$ which are topically similar to the query "serena williams". Each of these retrieved documents is associated with a category, in turn associating the query with these categories. We want to learn such associations (query-to-category) through a 'learning to rank' framework.

Thus, we claim that even in the absence of an exact query match, the documents that match the query-related topics/concepts/terms are good enough to carry out the query categorization. One of the advantages of applying IR to QC over applying IR to document retrieval is that QC does not require that the retrieved documents to be relevant to the query but instead it requires the documents to be categorically similar to the query. This fact is leveraged in our information retrieval approach to QC and forms the basis of our work. Once the documents which are topically related to query are retrieved, we attempt to 'learn to rank' these documents for a query effectively resulting in query categorization.

To expand a query for concepts, we submit the query to a web search engine and we collect the title, and a snippet of top N hits. Unlike other systems which work with the whole text content of top hits for a query, we chose to work with only title and snippet of the top hits, since most of the times context of the query is clear through the title and snippet of the top hits.

Once the text in title and snippet of top N hits is obtained through the use of a web search engine, we stem each term in the text and rank the stemmed terms by document frequency metric (in the process we filter out stop words since they do not any add useful information to determine query topics. We use a static list of commonly occurring words as stop words.). Document frequency (df) is chosen with the intuition that terms that occur in most of the top N hits, for a query, are most likely concepts that can represent the query. Each stemmed term t in the text of title and snippet of top N hits is weighted by:

$$df(t) = \sum_{d \in D_q^N} 1(t \in d), \quad (1)$$

where D_q^N represents the set of (title, snippet) pairs of the top N hits, obtained for a query q and $1(p)$ indicates truth

[3] Henceforth, we refer to the ODP web pages collected for, defining and representing categories, by the corpus $\mathcal{D}$. Unless explicitly stated, by $\mathcal{D}$, we mean the ODP documents corpus and by $\mathcal{C}^{(I)}$, we mean the categories in ODP space.

value of the proposition p and is given by:

$$1(p) = \begin{cases} 1 & \text{if } p \text{ is true} \\ 0 & \text{otherwise} \end{cases} .$$

We use the top n stemmed terms to represent the query.

3.3 Category Mapper

Before introducing learning to rank approach, we discuss the category mapper (which maps ODP categories to the target ones) since our target categories are different from that of ODP categories. We map an intermediate category to a target category by matching stemmed keywords between them. An intermediate category $c^{(I)}$ gets mapped to one of the target categories as follows:

$$t = \underset{t \in \mathcal{C}^{(T)}}{\text{argmin}} \quad f(t, c^{(I)})$$

where $f(t, c^{(I)}) = \frac{1}{1+level(t,c^{(I)})}$. Here $level(t, c^{(I)})$ gives the level at which the target category t occurs in the intermediate category $c^{(I)}$ which needs to be mapped. $level(t, c^{(I)})$ returns zero if target category does not occur. In the intermediate category 'Sports/Resources/News_and_Media', target category 'Sports' is occurring at level 1 and 'News' is occurring at level 3.

Given a set of intermediate categories $\mathcal{C}^{(q)}$ for a query, the categories in target space to which most of the categories in $\mathcal{C}^{(q)}$ are getting mapped to are ranked higher, and top categories in target space are returned as the probable categories of the query.

3.4 Learning to Rank Based Categorization

Having described both category and query representation which enable us to treat query categorization as an IR problem, we now proceed to discuss how an attempt is made at applying 'learning to rank' techniques to solve QC. A detailled study of 'learning to rank' can be found in the book [4]. First we represent each category by a set of documents that describe the semantics of the category as described earlier. At the end of this representation we have a resulting corpus $\mathcal{D}$ where each document belongs to at least one category as described earlier. Now we construct training data ($\mathcal{X}$) from labeled query dataset along with relevance judgments so that the resulting data is in a form that can be consumed by a 'learning to rank' algorithm. That is, each (query, document) pair is represented by a set of ranking features (to be discussed in the following section). Then, we apply learning to rank techniques such as Ranking SVM to learn the ranking model $L^{(T)}$ from the training data ($\mathcal{X}$).

Now given any query q_t, we use this model ($L^{(T)}$) to rank the categories. First we retrieve the documents from the corpus $\mathcal{D}$ and rank them using the learnt model. Then, categories of these documents are mapped to the subject categories under consideration using the category mapper discussed earlier.

3.5 Ranking Features

The features used for learning category rankings are similar to the ones used by 'learning to rank' community. We included features such as relevance scores on different fields of the document: "title", "body", "category" and "whole document". We considered IR models such as TF*IDF, Okapi BM25, and language modeling for IR to compute features. We considered three smoothing techniques with Language Modelling, namely, Dirichlet, Jelinek-Mercer and two stage smoothing. In all, we had 20 features describing each (query, document) pair. We used Lemur[4] toolkit to compute these features.

4. EVALUATION

We evaluate our QC system for applications such as federated search. Federated search requires high precision prediction of categories for a query since the cost of selecting a wrong vertical is very high. A wrong vertical search result would also affect the search experience of the end users. Hence, in this evaluation, we will weight the precision much higher than recall while measuring the performance of the systems.

We conducted a thorough evaluation of our approach on two datasets: classified 7K US queries sampled from Yahoo! Search and the publicly available KDD Cup 2005 dataset. For all experiments in the section, we set the value of N, number of top hits used to represent the query, to 40 for performance reasons. To avoid noise, we pick only top 10 stemmed terms to represent the query according to Equation 1. Since we want our application to be precise in predicting categories, we pick top 50 documents after ranking. Again this parameter is application dependent and less interesting in the context of the paper. In both the evaluations, we use our system as a binary categorizer.

4.1 Evaluation Measures

We use the evaluation measures defined by KDD Cup 2005 competition. This evaluation is similar to the one used by text categorization community. The evaluation measures—precision, recall, and F_β—are defined, respectively, as follows:

$$Precision = \frac{\sum_i \#\{\text{Queries correctly tagged as category } C_i\}}{\sum_i \#\{\text{Queries tagged as category } C_i\}}$$

$$Recall = \frac{\sum_i \#\{\text{Queries correctly tagged as category } C_i\}}{\sum_i \#\{\text{Queries tagged as } C_i \text{ by human labelers}\}}$$

$$F_\beta = \frac{(1+\beta^2) \times Precision \times Recall}{\beta^2 \times Precision + Recall}$$

4.2 Editorial Evaluation

Most of the existing works are evaluated either on a smaller dataset or on an older dataset and hence it is not clear about the practical application of such systems. In reality, a web search engine is expected to deal with billions of queries a day. Thus we evaluate our system on a larger and recent dataset. In this section, we brief on the details of our editorial dataset and also present the results obtained on this dataset compared against an unsupervised baseline and a supervised text categorization baseline.

4.2.1 Dataset

This editorial dataset consists of queries sampled from search query logs of Yahoo! Search over 13 weeks from January to March 2010. All duplicate queries were removed from this sampled set resulting in about 7k queries. Professional editors were provided with a taxonomy containing

[4] `http://www.lemurproject.org/`

21 categories: Autos, Finance, Food, Games, Health, Image/Video, Jobs, Local/Regional, Movies, Music, TV, Media, News, People Search, Product/Shopping, Real Estate, Reference, Social Networking, Sports, Technology, Travel; targeting different verticals for federated search. They manually classified each query into at least one category.

4.2.2 *Results*

We compare our system against two baselines: a supervised text categorization based baseline and an unsupervised baseline constructed on an IR approach. Our text categorizer baseline consists of a supervised text categorization based categorizer. We chose text categorization method as one of the baselines since most of the existing approaches treat QC as a text categorization problem and solve accordingly. We train an SVM using only word features of the queries to categorize queries since SVMs are the best text categorizers known to date [3].

Our second baseline, IR based approach, was constructed as follows: all ODP documents were indexed with stemming. All 7k queries after stemming were searched against this index to retrieve the relevant documents. Once the query relevant documents are retrieved they are mapped to the target taxonomy using the category mapper discussed earlier. In this way categories for every query is predicted. We chose to predict at most one category for each query since predicting more than one category for a query would require a thresholding strategy to avoid false positives which might affect applications such as federated search.

Approach	Precision	Recall	$F_{0.5}$
Text Categorizer (B_1)	39.56%	30.82%	37.03%
IR baseline (B_2)	40.09%	31.65%	38.06%
Our System	48.14%	37.92%	45.68%
Improvement over B_1	21.68%	23.03%	23.33%
Improvement over B_2	20.09%	19.81%	20.02%

Table 1: Relevancy measures on 7k classified queries sampled from search query logs of Yahoo! Search for the year 2010.

We report the relevancy metrics precision, recall and $F_{0.5}$ scores of our system and baseline in Table 1. For our system and text categorizer baseline, we report the five fold cross validation results on those 7k queries. The results indicate that our system has an overall improvement of around 20% over both the baselines on all measures. The results obtained for our system have significant improvement over the two baselines, indicating that learning to rank could be the key in improving precision of QC systems.

4.3 KDD Cup Evaluation

4.3.1 *Dataset*

The importance of query categorization was highlighted in KDD Cup 2005. The task was to classify 800K web queries into one or more of 67 pre-defined categories. Each query had to be classified into a ranked list of at most 5 categories. The categories were organized into two levels, with 7 nodes at top level. After the competition, a set of 800 queries, labeled independently by three labelers was also released for evaluation. Each query was labeled into at most 5 categories by each labeler. We omitted categories of the type "Others" from the evaluation, since finding the mapping was not easy.

4.3.2 *Results*

As three labelers labeled the evaluation set of 800 queries, the results reported in this section are averaged over the values evaluated on each of them.

Approach	Precision	F1
State of the art [5]	41.40%	44.40%
Best today [6]	46.50%	46.10%
Our System	59.50%	33.10%

Table 2: Precision and F1 values on evaluation set of KDD Cup 2005 data set.

We use our system as an off-the-shelf query categorizer without tuning the system in anyway for evaluation on KDD Cup dataset. That is we do not retrain the model on KDD dataset, but instead we directly use the 'learning to rank' model learnt from the editorial evaluation (Section 4.2). We compare our system against the existing systems in Table 2. We believe that the results obtained so far complement our goal of improving precision for applications such as federated search.

5. CONCLUSION

We attempted to solve QC by applying 'learning to rank' technique to learn rankings of categories for a query. This required us to represent a category by set of documents which better describe the semantics of that category. This setting was required so that we could apply IR techniques and subsequently 'learning to rank' algorithm to perform QC eventually. As future work, it will be interesting to see if categories can be better represented by other semi-structured data such as Wikipedia. Advantage with Wikpedia data is that, it has its own category taxonomy and every Wikipedia article is well structured with well defined topics.

6. ACKNOWLEDGEMENTS

We are thankful to Yahoo! Labs, Bangalore for granting access to the classified query dataset.

7. REFERENCES

[1] J. Arguello, F. Diaz, J. Callan, and J.-F. Crespo. Sources of evidence for vertical selection. In *SIGIR '09*, pages 315–322.

[2] A. Z. Broder, P. Ciccolo, M. Fontoura, E. Gabrilovich, V. Josifovski, and L. Riedel. Search advertising using web relevance feedback. In *CIKM '08*, pages 1013–1022.

[3] T. Joachims. Text categorization with suport vector machines: Learning with many relevant features. In *ECML '98*, pages 137–142. Springer-Verlag.

[4] T.-Y. Liu. Learning to rank for information retrieval. 3(3):225–331, 2009.

[5] D. Shen, R. Pan, J.-T. Sun, J. J. Pan, K. Wu, J. Yin, and Q. Yang. Q2c@ust: our winning solution to query classification in kddcup 2005. *SIGKDD Explor. Newsl.*, 7(2):100–110, 2005.

[6] D. Shen, J.-T. Sun, Q. Yang, and Z. Chen. Building bridges for web query classification. In *SIGIR '06*.

[7] X. Wang and C. Zhai. Learn from web search logs to organize search results. In *SIGIR '07*, pages 87–94.

Supervised Language Modeling for Temporal Resolution of Texts

Abhimanu Kumar
Dept. of Computer Science
University of Texas at Austin
abhimanu@cs.utexas.edu

Matthew Lease
School of Information
University of Texas at Austin
ml@ischool.utexas.edu

Jason Baldridge
Department of Linguistics
University of Texas at Austin
jbaldrid@mail.utexas.edu

ABSTRACT

We investigate *temporal resolution* of documents, such as determining the date of publication of a story based on its text. We describe and evaluate a model that build histograms encoding the probability of different temporal periods for a document. We construct histograms based on the Kullback-Leibler Divergence between the language model for a test document and supervised language models for each interval. Initial results indicate this language modeling approach is effective for predicting the dates of publication of short stories, which contain few explicit mentions of years.

Categories and Subject Descriptors

H.3.1 [**Content Analysis and Indexing**]

General Terms

Algorithms, Design, Experimentation, Performance

Keywords

time, temporal information, text mining, document dating

1. INTRODUCTION

There is a long tradition of work on temporal analysis of texts. In computational linguistics, the primary focus has been on the fine-grained level of temporal ordering of individual events necessary for deep natural language understanding [1, 24]. In Information Retrieval (IR), research has investigated time-sensitivity document ranking [9, 17], time-based organization and presentation of search results [2], how queries and documents change over time [16], etc.

This paper describes temporal analysis of documents using methods rooted in both computational linguistics and IR. While accurate extraction and resolution of explicit mentions of time (absolute or relative) is clearly important [2], our primary focus here is the challenge of learning implicit temporal distributions over natural language use at-large. As a concrete example, consider the word *wireless*. Introduced in the early 20th century to refer to radios, it fell into disuse and then its meaning shifted later that century to describe any form of communication without cables (e.g. internet access). As such, the word *wireless* embodies implicit time cues, a notion we might generalize by inferring its complete temporal distribution as well as that of all other words. By harnessing many such implicit cues in combination across a document, we might further infer a unique temporal distribution for the overall document.

As in prior document dating studies, we partition the timeline (and document collection) to infer an unique language model (LM) underlying each time period [10, 14]. While prior work considered texts from the past 10-20 years, our work is more historically-oriented, predicting publication dates for historical works of fiction.

After estimating a similar LM underlying each document [20], we measure similarity between each document's LM and each time period's LM, yielding a distribution over the timeline for each document [10, 14]. In addition to document dating applications, this distribution has potential to inform work in computational humanities, specifically scholars' understandings of how a work was influenced by or reflects different time periods.

We predict publication dates of short stories from the Gutenberg project[1] published between 1798 to 2008. Gutenberg stories are labeled by publication year. Our inference task is then to predict the publication year given the story's text. These short works of fiction typically use relatively few explicit temporal expressions or mentions of real-life named entities. We refer to the stories as *documents*, with Gutenberg defining a document *collection c* consisting of N documents: $c = d_{1:N}$. Our best model achieves a median error of 23 years from the true publication dates.

2. RELATED WORK

Annotation and corpora. Recent years have brought increased interest in creating new, richly annotated corpora for training and evaluating time-sensitive models. TimeBank [21] and Wikiwars [19] are great exemplars of such work. They have been used for tasks like modeling event structure (e.g. work of [7] on TimeBank).

Document dating. Prior work on LM-based document dating [10, 14] partitioned the timeline (and document collection) to infer a unique LM underlying each time period. A LM underlying each document [20] was also estimated and used to measure similarity vs. each time period's LM, yielding a distribution over the timeline for each document. However, while prior work focused on the past 10-20 years, our work is more historically-oriented, modeling the timeline from the present day back to the 18th century.

Foundational work by de Jong et al. [10] considered Dutch newspaper articles from 1999-2005 and compared language models using the normalised log-likelihood ratio measure (NLLR), a variant of KL-divergence. Linear and Dirichlet smoothing were ap-

[1]`http://www.gutenberg.org`

CIKM'11, October 24–28, 2011, Glasgow, Scotland, UK.

plied, apparently to the partition LMs but not the document LMs. They also distinguish between output granularity of time (to be predicted) and the granularity of time modeled. Kanhabua et al. [14] extended de Jong et al.'s model with notions of temporal entropy, use of search term trends from Google Zeitgeist, and semantic preprocessing. Temporal entropy weights terms differently based on how well a term distinguishes between time partitions and how important a term is to a specific partition. Semantic techniques included part-of-speech tagging, collocation extraction, word sense disambiguation, and concept extraction. They created a time-labeled document collection by downloading web pages from the Internet Archive spanning an eight year period. In follow-on work inferring temporal properties of queries [15], they used the New York Times annotated corpus, with articles spanning 1987-2007.

IR Applications. IR research has investigated time-sensitivity query interpretation and document ranking [17, 9], time-based organization and presentation of search results [2], how queries and documents change over time [16], etc. One of the first LM-based temporal approaches by Li and Croft [17] used explicit document dates to estimate a more informative document prior. More recent work by Dakka et al. [9] automatically identify important time intervals likely to be of interest for a query and similarly integrate knowledge of document publication date into the ranking function. The most relevant work to ours is that by Alonso et al. [2], who provide valuable background on motivation, overview and discussion of temporal analysis in IR. Using explicit temporal metadata and expressions, they create *temporal document profiles* to cluster documents and create timelines for exploring search results.

Time-sensitive topic modeling. There has been a variety of work on time based topic-analysis in texts in recent years, such as Dynamic Topic Models [6]. Subsequent work [5] proposes probabilistic time series models to analyze the time evolution of topics in a large document collection. They take a sequential collection of documents of a particular area e.g. news articles and determine how topics evolve over time - topics appearing and disappearing, new topics emerging and older ones fading away. [25] provide a model to evaluate variations in the occurrence of topics in large corpora over a period of time. There have been other interesting contributions such as work by [18] which studies the history of ideas in a research field using topic models, by [8] which provides the temporal analysis of blogs and by [27] which gives models for mining cluster evaluation from time varying text corpora.

Geolocation. Temporal resolution can be seen as a natural pairing with geolocation: both are ways of connecting texts to simple, but tremendously intuitive and useful, models of aspects of the real world. There has been a long-standing interest in finding ways to connect documents to specific places on the earth, especially for geographic information retrieval [12, 3]. Of particular relevance to our paper is Wing and Baldridge's LM based method of measuring similarity of documents with language models for discrete geodesic cells on the earth's surface [26].

Authorship attribution. A final relevant work is the LM-based authorship attribution work by Zhao et al. [28]. They similarly partition the corpus by author, build partition-specific LMs, and infer authorship based on model similarity computed with KL-divergence and Dirichlet smoothing. They also consider English literature from the Gutenberg Project. Unlike us, they train directly on this corpus instead of applying LMs from another domain.

3. MODELING AND ESTIMATION

Following aforementioned prior work [2, 10, 14], we quantize continuous time into discrete units. Our terminology and formalization most closely follow that of Alonso et al. [2]. The smallest temporal granularity we consider in this work is a single year, though the methods we describe can in principle be used with units of finer granularity such as days, weeks, months, etc.

A *chronon* is an atomic interval x upon which a discrete timeline is constructed [2]. In this paper, a chronon consists of δ years, where δ is a tunable parameter. Given δ, the timeline T_δ is decomposed into a sequence of n contiguous, non-overlapping chronons $\mathbf{x} = x_{1:n}$, where $n = \frac{\Delta}{\delta}$.

We model the affinity between each chronon x and a document d by estimating the discrete distribution $P(x|d)$, a document-specific normalized histogram over the timeline of chronons $x_{1:n}$. In the next section, we use $P(x|d)$ to infer affinity between d and different chronons as well as longer granules. We describe an LM-based approach for inferring affinity between chronon x and document d as a function of model divergence between latent unigram distributions $P(w|d)$ and $P(w|x)$ (similar to [10, 14]).

We model the likelihood of each chronon x for a given document d. By forming a unique "pseudo-document" d^x associated with each chronon x, we estimate Θ^x from d^x and estimate $P(x|d)$ by comparing the similarity of Θ^d and Θ^x [10, 14]. Whereas prior work measured similarity via NLLR (§2), we compute the unnormalized likelihood of some x given d via standard (inverse) KL-divergence $\mathcal{D}(\Theta^d||\Theta^x)^{-1}$ and normalize in straight-forward fashion over all chronons $x_{1:n}$:

$$P_{wa}(x|d) = \frac{\mathcal{D}(\Theta^d||\Theta^x)^{-1}}{\sum_x \mathcal{D}(\Theta^d||\Theta^x)^{-1}} \tag{1}$$

We generate the "pseudo-document" d^x for each chronon x by including all training documents whose labeled span overlaps x.

As in prior work [10, 14, 28], we adopt Dirichlet smoothing to regularlize partition LMs. However, rather than adopt a single fixed prior for all documents and chronons, we instead define document-chronon specific priors. Let $|V_{d^x} \cup V_d|$ denote the document-chronon specific vocabulary for some collection document d_i and pseudo-document d^x. For each document-chronon pair, we define the prior to be a uniform distribution over this specific vocabulary: $\frac{1}{|V_{d^x} \cup V_{d_i}|}$. For any collection document or pseudo-document d, we perform Dirichlet smoothing of form:

$$\hat{\theta^d_w} = \eta \frac{f^d_w}{|d|} + (1-\eta)\frac{1}{|V_{d^x} \cup V_d|}\ , \ \eta = \frac{|d|}{|d| + \mu} \tag{2}$$

Rather than specify the hyper-parameter μ directly, however, we introduce another hyper-parameter λ, where $\mu = \frac{\lambda}{|V_{d^x} \cup V_{d_i}|}$.

The intuition for this smoothing is that mass is provided only for the words that are present in the collection document or the chronon's pseudo-document, ignoring other words. Thus, the divergence calculation is done only with respect to either the document or the chronon we have evidence for. There are many chronons for which we have little textual evidence; if these are smoothed with respect to all words in the collection, then those terms dominate the divergence calculation. When a short document is evaluated against a low-evidence chronon, smoothing over all words leads to many terms (few of which actually occur in the document or the chronon) having similar probabilities, leading to low divergence.

To infer a representative chronon x^d for each document, **MAXCHRONON** simply selects the most-likely chronon under $P(x|d)$:

$$\mathbf{x^d_{mc}} = \arg\max_{x \in \mathbf{x}} P(x|d) \tag{3}$$

We use MAXCHRONON to predict a chronon for the document and then select the first year in that chronon as the predicted year.

4. EVALUATION

Data. We use 678 Gutenberg short stories, split into development and test sets of 333 and 345 each, respectively. Strictly speaking, this split is not actually necessary for our reported experiments since we tune out-of-domain on a separate corpus (see below). Nonetheless, we also plan to tune in-domain in our future work, so we have gone ahead and used the division now for direct comparison to later results. The average, minimum and maximum word count of these stories are 14k, 11k and 100k respectively. All numeric tokens and standard stopwords are removed.

Wikipedia Biographies. We tune parameters using an external corpus of biographies from the September 4, 2010 dump of English Wikipedia[2] (our use of Wikipedia here is motivated by other preliminary work on it to be further developed in our future work). We consider individuals whose complete lives occurred within the year range 3800 B.C. to 2010 A.D. We extract the lifetime of each individual via each article's *Infobox* `birth_date` and `death_date` fields. We exclude biographies which do not specify both fields or which fall outside the year range considered. Given the lifetime of each individual, we take the midpoint of individual's lifetime as the gold standard year to match for the biography. We note that as is often typical of Wikipedia coverage, the distribution of biographies is quite skewed toward recent times.

As examples of the kinds of distributions we obtain for Wikipedia biographies, Figure 1 shows graphs of $P(x|d)$ for (a) Plato and (b) Abraham Lincoln. Recall that these are based on no explicit temporal expressions. For Plato, there is a clear spike around the time he was alive, along with another rising bump toward the current day, reflecting modern interest in him. For Lincoln, there is a single peak at 1835—very close to the 1837 midpoint of his life.

Parameters and Estimation. We set WORDAFFINITY's smoothing parameter $\lambda = 1$ without any tuning (left for future work). The chronon size δ was tuned through experimentation to optimize performance on the Wikipedia biography collection. Two salient points of note are: (a) the task will be more challenging since we have a tune/test corpus mismatch between Wikipedia vs. Gutenberg, and (b) a particular challenge of this is differences in vocabulary selection between recently written Wikipedia articles and historical fiction in the Gutenberg stories.

As in prior work [10, 14], we smooth chronon pseudo-document language models but not document models. While smoothing both may potentially help, smoothing the former is strictly necessary to prevent division by zero in the KL-divergence calculation.

Year Prediction. The gold standard to match for each document is a labeled year (publication year for Gutenberg, lifetime midpoint for Wikipedia). Given document d, we predict the year to be the first year from x^d_{mc}, the most-likely chronon for d over the timeline.

When predicting a single year for a document, a natural error measure between the predicted year $\hat{y}$ and the actual year y^* is the difference $|\hat{y} - y^*|$. We compute this difference for each document, then compute and report the mean and median of differences across documents. Similar distance error measures have also been used with document geolocation [13, 26].

Baseline. As a simple baseline, we consider a fixed prediction of the year 1903 for all stories: the midpoint of publication date range (1798-2008) in the collection. This assumes that one knows a rough range of possible publication dates, which might be reasonable in many cases and provide a useful starting point for comparison.

Development Set Tuning and Results. Using the Wikipedia biographies, we tune $\delta \in \{1, 2, \ldots, 100\}$ and examine mean error

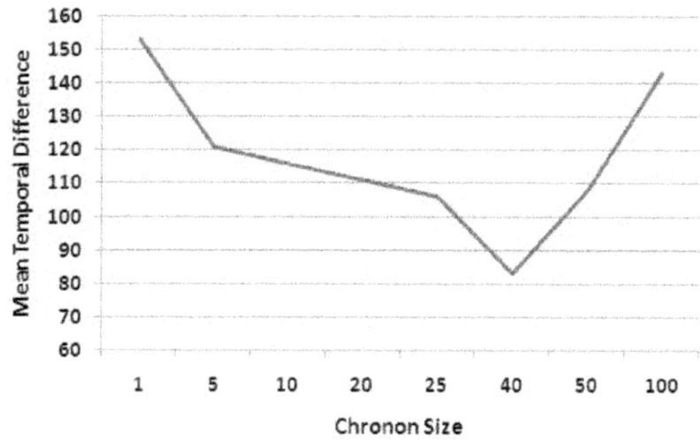

Figure 2: Chronon size δ vs. resultant mean error of year predictions for lifespan midpoints in Wikipedia biographies.

in predicted year. Error roughly varies between 85-155, with $\delta = 40$ seen to yield optimal mean year prediction error (see Figure 2). Next, we use $\delta = 40$ on the Gutenberg collection. In comparison to the 1903 baseline, mean prediction error is reduced from 36 to 28 years, with median prediction error cut from 50 to 32 years.

Test Set Results. While results show only a modest reduction of mean error in year predictions for the model vs. the 1903 baseline (37 to 34), median error is more than halved, dropping from 50 to 23. This provides a promising validation of our initial work that words which are not temporal expressions still convey important temporal information that can be exploited for historical document dating, even when (a) the model was trained on a different domain and (b) there is only a range of 210 years under consideration and the baseline represents the exact midpoint.

5. CONCLUSION

We have shown that it is possible to perform accurate temporal resolution of texts by combining evidence from both explicit temporal expressions and the implicit temporal properties of general words. We create a partitioned timeline with language models in each partition; these are used to determine a probability over the timeline for new test documents. The models are effective enough that they can predict publication dates on out-of-domain stories from a 210 year period to within 32 years on average.

There are a number of ways to improve the present approach. For example, we might smooth LMs for the chronons themselves such that we infer similar temporal distributions proportional to proximity between chronons. Similar intuition has appeared in LM-based IR work in various forms: similar queries should have similar LMs, similar documents should have similar LMs [23], and similar documents should receive similar scores when compared to to some other fixed model [11].

Another, obvious idea is to consider n-grams rather than unigrams: e.g., *civil war* has different temporal properties from *civil* and *war* on their own. Ultimately, one of our interests in this general line of inquiry is to create models of word meaning that are *grounded*. In most computational models of word meaning, a word is characterized in terms of other words—a circular (though useful) model. However, there is recent interest in models that connect words to properties of the real world, such as conceptual representations [4] and models of space [22] and time. A relevant task for this idea is word sense disambiguation. For example, the word *apple* could be a reference to the fruit (general over time), the record company formed by the Beatles (1960-1970s, primarily), or Apple Inc. (1976-present). Identifying the temporal properties of the

[2] `http://download.wikimedia.org/enwiki/20100904/enwiki-20100904-pages-articles.xml.bz2`

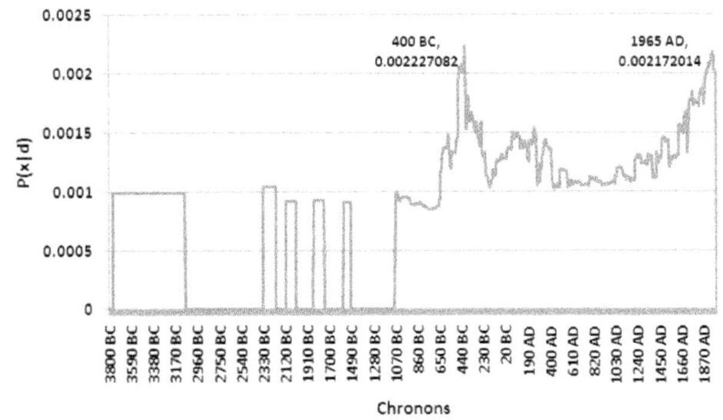

(a)

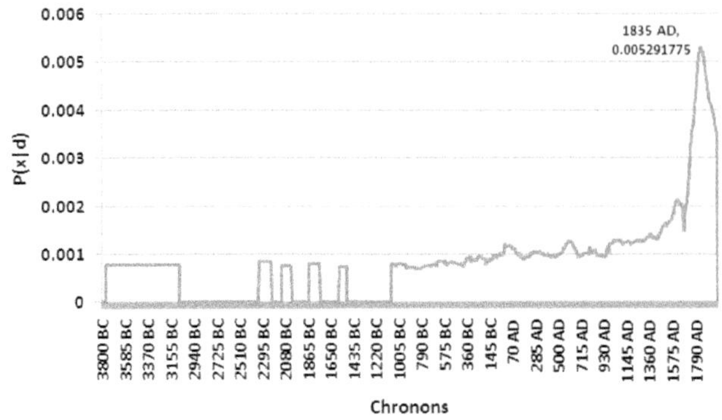

(b)

Figure 1: Example $P(x|d)$ distributions for the biographies of (a) Plato (428-348 B.C.) and (b) Abraham Lincoln (1809-1965).

text can be part of disambiguating such terms and help us keep a computer or record company from falling on Isaac Newton's head.

Acknowledgments

We thank the anonymous reviewers for their valuable feedback and suggestions. This work was partially supported by a John P. Commons Fellowship for Matthew Lease and by a grant from the Morris Memorial Trust Fund of the New York Community Trust.

6. REFERENCES

[1] J. F. Allen. Maintaining knowledge about temporal intervals. In *Communications of the ACM, Volume 26 Issue 11*, 1983.

[2] O. Alonso, M. Gertz, and R. Baeza-Yates. Clustering and exploring search results using timeline constructions. In *Proceeding of the 18th ACM Conference on Information and Knowledge Management (CIKM)*, pages 97–106, 2009.

[3] G. Andogah. *Geographically Constrained Information Retrieval.* PhD thesis, University of Groningen, Netherlands, May 2010.

[4] M. Baroni, B. Murphy, E. Barbu, and M. Poesio. Strudel: A corpus-based semantic model based on properties and types. *Cognitive Science*, 34(2):222–254, 2010.

[5] D. Blei, C. Wang, and D. Heckerman. Continuous time dynamic topic models. In *Intl. Conference on Machine Learning (ICML)*, 2008.

[6] D. M. Blei and J. D. Lafferty. Dynamic topic models. In *23rd Intl. Conference on Machine Learning (ICML)*, 2006.

[7] N. Chambers and D. Jurafsky. Jointly combining implicit constraints improves temporal ordering. In *EMNLP*, 2008.

[8] Y. Chi, S. Zhu, X. Song, J. Tatemura, and B. L. Tseng. Structural and temporal analysis of the blogosphere through community factorization. In *Proc. of 13th SIGKDD*, 2007.

[9] W. Dakka, L. Gravano, and P. Ipeirotis. Answering general time-sensitive queries. *Knowledge and Data Engineering, IEEE Transactions on*, (99), 2010. Pre-print.

[10] F. de de Jong, H. Rode, and D. Hiemstra. Temporal language models for the disclosure of historical text. In *XVIth International Conference of the Association for History and Computing (AHC)*, pages 161–168, 2005.

[11] F. Diaz. Regularizing query-based retrieval scores. *Information Retrieval*, 10(6):531–562, 2007.

[12] J. Ding, L. Gravano, and N. Shivakumar. Computing geographical scopes of web resources. In *Proc. of the 26th Intl. Conference on Very Large Data Bases (VLDB)*, pages 545–556, 2000.

[13] J. Eisenstein, B. O'Connor, N. A. Smith, and E. P. Xing. A latent variable model for geographic lexical variation. In *Proceedings of the 2010 Conference on Empirical Methods in Natural Language Processing*, pages 1277–1287, 2010.

[14] N. Kanhabua and K. Nørvåg. Improving temporal language models for determining time of non-timestamped documents. In *12th European conf. Research and Advanced Technology for Digital Libraries (ECDL)*, pages 358–370, 2008.

[15] N. Kanhabua and K. Nørvåg. Determining time of queries for re-ranking search results. In *14th European conference on Research and Advanced Technology for Digital Libraries (ECDL)*, pages 261–272, 2010.

[16] A. Kulkarni, J. Teevan, K. Svore, and S. Dumais. Understanding temporal query dynamics. In *Proceedings of the 4th ACM International conference on Web Search and Data Mining (WSDM)*, pages 167–176, 2011.

[17] X. Li and W. Croft. Time-based language models. In *12th International Conference on Information and Knowledge Management (CIKM)*, pages 469–475, 2003.

[18] C. D. Manning, D. Hall, and D. Jurafsky. Studying the history of ideas using topic models. In *ACL*, 2008.

[19] P. Mazur and R. Dale. Wikiwars: A new corpus for research on temporal expressions. In *EMNLP*, Massachusetts, 2010.

[20] J. M. Ponte and W. B. Croft. A language modeling approach to information retrieval. In *SIGIR*, pages 275–281, 1998.

[21] J. Pustejovsky, P. Hanks, R. Sauri, A. See, D. Day, L. Ferro, R. Gaizauskas, M. Lazo, A. Setzer, and B. Sundheim. The TimeBank corpus. *Corpus Linguistics*, pages 647–656, 2003.

[22] M. Speriosu, T. Brown, T. Moon, J. Baldridge, and K. Erk. Connecting language and geography with region-topic models. In *1st Workshop on Computational Models of Spatial Language Interpretation*, 2010.

[23] T. Tao, X. Wang, Q. Mei, and C. Zhai. Language model information retrieval with document expansion. In *Human Language Technology Conference of the North American Chapter of the Association of Computational Linguistics (HLT-NAACL)*, pages 407–414, 2006.

[24] M. B. Vilain and B. Beranek. A system for reasoning about time. In *Proceedings of the Second National Conference on Artificial Intelligence (AAAI)*, Pittsburgh, 1982.

[25] X. Wang and A. McCallum. Topics over time: A non-markov continuous-time model of topical trends. In *Knowledge Discovery and Data-mining (KDD)*, 2006.

[26] B. Wing and J. Baldridge. Simple supervised document geolocation with geodesic grids. In *ACL-HLT*, 2011.

[27] J. Zhang, Y. Song, and C. Zhang. Evolutionary hierarchical dirichlet processes for multiple correlated time-varying corpora. In *Proceedings of the 16th ACM SIGKDD*, 2010.

[28] Y. Zhao, J. Zobel, and P. Vines. Using relative entropy for authorship attribution. *Third Asia Information Retrieval Symposium (AIRS)*, pages 92–105, 2006.

Context-Aware Query Recommendation by Learning High-Order Relation in Query Logs

Xiaohui Yan, Jiafeng Guo, Xueqi Cheng
Institute of Computing Technology, CAS
Beijing, China 100190
{yanxiaohui, guojiafeng}@software.ict.ac.cn, cxq@ict.ac.cn

ABSTRACT

Query recommendation has been widely used in modern search engines. Recently, several context-aware methods have been proposed to improve the accuracy of recommendation by mining query sequence patterns from query sessions. However, the existing methods usually do not address the ambiguity of queries explicitly and often suffer from the sparsity of the training data. In this paper, we propose a novel context-aware query recommendation approach by modeling the high-order relation between queries and clicks in query log, which captures users' latent search intents. Empirical experiment results demonstrate that our approach outperforms the baseline methods in providing high quality recommendations for ambiguous queries.

Categories and Subject Descriptors

H.3.3 [**Information Storage and Retrieval**]: Information Search and Retrieval—*Query formulation*

General Terms

Algorithms, Experimentation, Theory

Keywords

Context-Aware, High-Order Model, Search Intent

1. INTRODUCTION

Tradition query recommendation approaches often find similar queries to suggest for each other[2, 1]. However, since queries are usually very short and ambiguous[6], a same query may convey totally different search intents in different cases. For example, the query "saturn" may either refer to a planet name or a car manufacturer. To only suggest similar queries based on the current query may not work well in such cases.

Recently, some context-aware approaches have been proposed to address the problem of recommendation for ambiguous queries[5, 3]. The basic idea of these methods is to leverage the query sequence patterns from query sessions [1]. That is, if a user queried "solar system" recently, it would be naturally recommend "planet saturn" or "uranus" to him when he is searching "saturn".

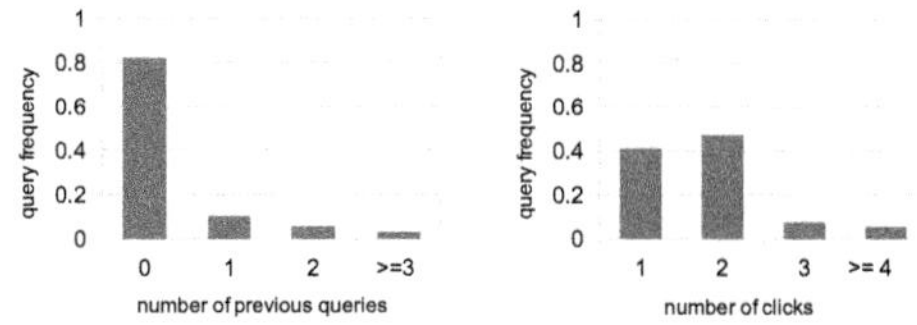

Figure 1: Query frequency with (a) different number of previous queries in the same session, (b) different number of clicks in query logs

However, these context-aware methods based on query sequence patterns matching have two major weaknesses. Firstly, they do not address the ambiguity of queries explicitly. Queries are usually viewed as the basic units in previous approaches without modeling their underlying search intents. Secondly, they mainly rely on the query sequence patterns existing in query logs, hence may suffer from the sparsity of data. We examined one month query logs from a commercial search engine. As Figure 1(a) shows, the number of query sequence patterns drops dramatically as their length increasing. Even worse, about 80% queries come from single-query sessions which means no previous queries existed.

On the contrary, we find that the click-through from a query often provides rich information that can clarify user's search intent for ambiguous queries. For example, when a user submits a query "saturn" , the search engine may return pages about both the Saturn planet and Saturn cars. Once the user clicking a URL in result pages about planet, it's clear that he cares about Saturn planet. Compared to the previous queries, the click-through from the current query always plays more direct effect on user's next search behavior Besides, we also find the click-through information is often more abundant than query sequence patterns in query logs, as Figure 1(b) shows, more than half of queries has one or more clicks, which may alleviate the sparsity problem.

Motivated by the above observations, we propose a probabilistic context-aware query recommendation approach by modeling the high-order relations between the current query, its click and the next query for recommendation. In our model, the ambiguity of queries can be resolved by intro-

[1] A query session is regard as a sequence of queries and clicks, performed by a user within a short period of time (e.g. 30 minutes) in a search process

CIKM'11, October 24–28, 2011, Glasgow, Scotland, UK.

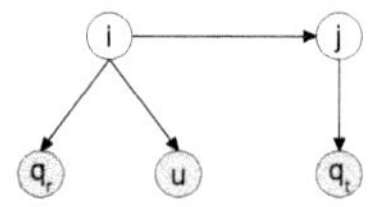

Figure 2: Graphical structure for a RUT triple $\langle q_r, u, q_t \rangle$.

ducing the latent factors over queries and their clicks. Once we have learned the fine-grained search intents underlying a query and its click-through, we can generate more accurate context-aware recommendation.

2. PROBLEM SETTING

To facilitate the discussion, we will first define some terminologies, and then give a formulation of our problem.

Definition 1. if a query q_t closely follows q_r in a query session, we denote q_r as a *refer query* (of q_t), and q_t as a *target query* (of q_r). All of the refer queries in query logs form the *refer query set* Q_r. Correspondingly, we define the *target query set* Q_t as the set of all target queries in query logs.

Definition 2. if a query q_t closely follows q_r in a query session, and a URL u is a click-through with q_r in this session, we call the triple $\langle q_r, u, q_t \rangle$ a *RUT* triple.

From a probabilistic view, the query recommendation task is to find top ranked q_ts with respect to the probability $P(q_t|q_r, u)$ for recommendation, given the contextual information $\langle q_r, u \rangle$. Because $P(q_r, u)$ is fixed when $\langle q_r, u \rangle$ is given, the condition probabilty is proportional to the joint one $P(q_r, u, q_t)$. Therefore, the remaining problem is how to estimate the joint probability $P(q_r, u, q_t)$. Now we summarize the objective of our model as follows:

Problem Statement 1. Given a set of RUT triples and their frequencies, the objective is to learn the probability $P(q_r, u, q_t)$, for $q_r \in Q_r$, $q_t \in Q_t$ and $u \in U$, where U is the URLs set in query logs.

3. OUR APPROACH

3.1 The High-Order Model

To estimate the probability $P(q_r, u, q_t)$, we propose a generative model which captures the high-order relations between user's current query, click and the next query. The graphical structure of our model is shown in Figure 2. It explains a query refinement process as follows. At first, a user has search intent i with probability $P(i)$. He submits query q_r with probability $P(q_r|i)$, and then clicks a URL in result pages with probability $P(u|i)$. Depending on his last search intent, he derives another related search intent j with probability $P(j|i)$, and formulate the next query q_t with probability $P(q_t|j)$. Here we name search intent i as *refer intent* (of search intent j), and search intent j as *target intent* (of search intent i) for convenience.

Based on the above generative model, we can write the joint distribution as

$$P(q_r, u, q_t) = \sum_{i,j} P(q_r|i)P(u|i)P(i,j)P(q_t|j). \qquad (1)$$

Furthermore, we assume all the RUT triples follow an identical independent distribution. The likelihood of all the observed data then can be written as

$$l = \prod_{q_r,u,q_t} \left[\sum_{i,j} P(q_r|i)P(u|i)P(i,j)P(q_t|j) \right]^{n(q_r,u,q_t)}, \qquad (2)$$

with parameters $\Theta = \{P(q_r|i), P(u|i), P(i,j), P(q_t|j)\}$.

3.2 Parameters Estimation

The parameters Θ can be learned by the Expectation Maximization (EM) algorithm[4]. By standard calculates one arrives at the following E-step and M-step, which will be repeated alternatively until convergence.

E-step:

$$P(i,j|q_r,u,q_t) = \frac{P(i,j)P(q_r|i)P(u|i)P(q_t|j)}{\sum_{i',j'} P(i,j)P(q_r|i')P(u|i')P(q_t|j')}, \qquad (3)$$

M-step:

$$P(i,j) = \frac{\sum_{q_r,u,q_t} n(q_r,u,q_t)P(i,j|q_r,u,q_t)}{\sum_{q'_r,u',q'_t} n(q'_r,u',q'_t)}, \qquad (4)$$

$$P(q_r|i) = \frac{\sum_{u,q_t,j} n(q_r,u,q_t)P(i,j|q_r,u,q_t)}{\sum_{q'_r,u',q'_t,j'} n(q'_r,u',q'_t)P(i,j'|q'_r,u',q'_t)}, \qquad (5)$$

$$P(u|i) = \frac{\sum_{q_r,q_t,j} n(q_r,u,q_t)P(i,j|q_r,u,q_t)}{\sum_{q'_r,u',q'_t,j'} n(q'_r,u',q'_t)P(i,j'|q'_r,u',q'_t)}, \qquad (6)$$

$$P(q_t|j) = \frac{\sum_{q_r,u,i} n(p_r,u,p_t)P(i,j|q_r,u,q_t)}{\sum_{q'_r,u',q'_t,i'} n(q'_r,u',q'_t)P(i',j|q'_r,u',q'_t)}. \qquad (7)$$

3.3 Model Reduction

However, the EM algorithm in this problem may not be very efficient because of the extremely high dimensions of queries and URLs. In fact, we may not necessarily rely on the specific clicked URL u to identify the refer intent. We can leverage the topic or semantic category of the clicked URL u for the same purpose. Therefore, we map the URLs to their semantic categories c, whose dimensions are much lower than the URLs.

Here we use the Open Directory Project[2] data for the URL-category mapping. In ODP, a URL might be assigned to more than one categories. Hence, a URL u corresponds to a vector $\vec{c}$ in the category space as follows

$$u \rightarrow \vec{c} = (w_{u,c_1}, w_{u,c_2}, ..., w_{u,c_n}),$$

where $w_{u,c}$ is the weight of each category for u defined by:

$$w_{u,c_i} = \begin{cases} 0 & \text{if u not belong to the ist category } c_i \\ 1/k & k \text{ is the number of non-zero elements in } \vec{c} \end{cases}.$$

Finally, we transform each RUT triple to *RCT* triples (Refer query, Category, Target query) as

$$\langle q_1, u, q_2 \rangle \rightarrow \begin{cases} \langle q_1, c_1, q_2 \rangle \\ ... \\ \langle q_1, c_n, q_2 \rangle \end{cases}.$$

The frequency of a RCT triple, denoted by $n(\cdot)$, can be calculated as the product of the weight and the frequency of

[2]http://www.dmoz.org/

the corresponding RUT triple

$$n(q_1, c, q_2) = n(q_1, u, q_2) \times w_{u,c}. \quad (8)$$

We can then obtain a similar high-order model over the RCT triples and estimate the corresponding parameters with a much lower cost.

3.4 Query Recommendation Generation

With the above learned models, we now describe how to generate recommendations for a given context pair $\langle q_r, u\rangle$. Our approach is based on the assumption that the URL is conditionally independent on queries given the categories of a URL. In this way, $P(q_t|q, u)$ can be calculated as:

$$P(q_t|q_r, u) = \frac{\sum_{c \in C} P(u|c)P(q_r, c, q_t)}{P(q_r, u)} \quad (9)$$

By considering

$$P(u) = \frac{n(u)}{\sum_{u \in U} n(u)}, \quad (10)$$

$$P(c|u) = w_{u,c}, \quad (11)$$

we have

$$P(u, c) = P(c|u)P(u) = \frac{n(u)w_{u,c}}{\sum_{u' \in U} n(u)}, \quad (12)$$

$$P(u|c) = \frac{P(u,c)}{\sum_u P(u,c)} = \frac{n(u)w_{u,c}}{\sum_{u' \in U} n(u')w_{u,c}}, \quad (13)$$

if q_r and u are given, we combine (9) and (13) and result in

$$P(q_t|q_r, u) \propto g(q_t; q_r, u) = \sum_{c \in C} \frac{n(u)w_{u,c}P(q_r, c, q_t)}{\sum_{u' \in U} n(u')w_{u',c}} \quad (14)$$

Therefore, we can use $g(q_t; q_r, u)$ as a score function of $q_t \in Q_t$ for recommendation.

3.5 Model Training

In practice, the performance of the EM algorithm is highly related to two factors: the number of latent factors and initialized parameters. We propose a special clustering method to tackle these two problems together, so that we can further improve both the efficiency and effectiveness of the learning process.

Hidden Dimension Selection by clustering. We introduce this clustering method by taking clustering over q_ts as an example. Firstly, since the feature space $\{\langle q_r, c\rangle\}$ of q_t is sparse, we assume that if two target query q_{t_1} and q_{t_2} co-occurred with the same $\langle q_r, c\rangle$, they tend to have the same target intent. We extract all the q_t's from RCT triples as an initial cluster for each $\langle q_r, c\rangle$. The weight of each q_t for an initial cluster is set as the frequency $n(q_r, c, q_t)$ of the triple $\langle q_r, c, q_t\rangle$ in the query log.

Secondly, since many $\langle q_r, c\rangle$ pairs may have similar latent search intent, we utilize traditional clustering methods (e.g. hierarchical clustering) to merge the initial clusters based some similarity measure (e.g. cosine similarity). Instead of specifying the clusters number, a minimal similarity threshold min_s is used to control the merging steps. Once two clusters are merged, the weights of each q_t are accumulated.

We also clustering q_r's in the same way, by considering $\langle c, q_t\rangle$ as a single target intent as an initial cluster.

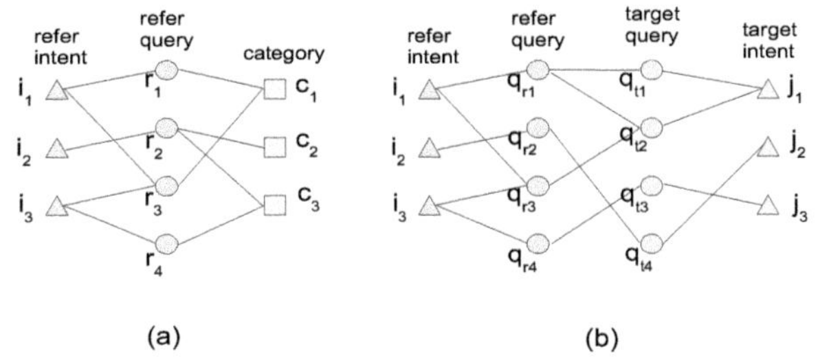

Figure 3: Example of (a) a $\langle i, q_r, c\rangle$ tripartite graph, (b) a $\langle i, q_r, q_t, j\rangle$ multipartite graph

Parameters Initialization. By utilizing the clustering results to initialize the parameters, we can significantly reduce the number of parameters.

$P(q_r|i)$ and $P(q_t|j)$ can be initialized directly from clustering results by normalizing the weights of queries in each cluster. However, $P(c|i)$ and $P(i, j)$ are not so easy to initialized from the clustering result. However, given all $P(q_r|i)$'s, $P(q_t|j)$'s and $n(q_r, c, q_t)$'s, we can grasp some instructive relation between c and i, and between intent i and intent j by putting them in multipartite graphs showing in Figure 3. Figure 3(a) is constructed by connecting a refer intent node i_k to a refer query node q_{r_k} if $P(q_{r_k}|i_k) > 0$, and connecting q_{r_k} to a category node c_k if $n(q_{r_k}, c_k) > 0$ in the training RCT triples. The idea is that we only need to initialize such $P(c|i)$s that there exists a path from c to i in the tripartite graph. For other $P(c|i)$s, even if we assign them non-zero values, the EM iterations will reduce them to zero at last. The proof is not difficult and we skip it due to the space limitation. After extracting all such kind of $P(c|i)$s, we randomly initialize them and then perform normalization for each intent i. The $P(i, j)$ initialization is almost the same, with a different multipartite graph showing in Figure 3(b). In which, q_{r_k} connect to q_{t_l} if $n(q_{r_k}, q_{t_l}) > 0$, and q_{t_k} if $P(q_{t_k}|j_k) > 0$.

4. EXPERIMENTAL RESULTS

4.1 Dataset and Baselines

Our experiments are based on the "Spring 2006 Data Asset" distributed by Microsoft Research[3]. We compared our result with three baselines: Co-occurrence (Co-occ), which recommends queries occurring after (may not adjacent) test query q most often in training query sessions; N-gram, which recommends queries closely following the query sequence most often; Context-Aware and Concept-Based method (CACB) [3]. The only difference of CACB from N-gram is that CACB clusters queries to "concepts" by their clicks, and then transform query sequences into concept sequences. To generate recommendation, a concept is represented by the most frequent query in it.

We compared these methods based on a collection of ambiguous queries. Here, we take a simple approach to extract possible ambiguous queries. By exploiting the URL-category data we extracted from ODP, we find queries with clicked URLs from multiple different categories are more likely to be ambiguous. We thus randomly extract 1000 query sessions, whose last query's clicked URL belongs to different

[3]http://research.microsoft.com/users/nickcr/wscd09/

Table 1: **Examples for refer intents and target intents involve the query "saturn", but with two different means. The second row is top 5 queries in the intent, and the third row is categories corresponding to refer intent**

i_{1935}	i_{19645}	j_{34564}	j_{29915}
gmc vehicles **saturn** volvo suv honda chevrolet	**saturn** neptune uranus planet mercury venus	**saturn** mustang ford nissan hyundai	solar system planet mercury earth planets in order **saturn**
Automotive	Astronomy		

Table 2: Query recommendation examples with different context

context: saturn → nineplanets.org			
Co-occ	N-gram	CACB	High-order
solar system uranus diameter uranus saturn cars saturn roadster	pontiac solar system saturn cars scion kia	toyota mitsubish honda hyundai solar system	uranus uranus diameter solar system earth astrology
context:honda ⇒ saturn → satrun.com			
Co-occ	N-gram	CACB	High-order
solar system uranus diameter uranus saturn cars saturn roadster	pontiac saturn cars toyota	toyota pontiac scion gm com	saturn sky saturn roadster saturn cars pontiac mazda

categories, as our test data. Recommendation is conduct on the last query of each session. Finally, the recommendation results are manually assessed by three judges to decide whether the recommendation is meaningful or not.

Precision and recall are used to evaluate the quality of the results of these methods quantitatively. Here, precision is defined as the average ratio of meaningful ones over the all recommendations generated by a method for a test query. While recall is defined as the average ratio of meaningful recommendations found by a method over all meaningful ones in the training data. Nevertheless, it's impossible to collect all the meaningful recommendations in such a large scale data. Instead, we use the TREC pooling method to construct a pool of meaningful recommendations collecting from the top 5 recommendations of all these methods. Recall metric of each method is then calculated base on this pool.

4.2 Experiments Results

Qualitative Evaluations. In Table 1, we show two refer intents and two target intents learned by the high-order model. It's clear that i_{1935} and j_{34564} talk about cars, which is consistent with the ODP category "Automotive", while i_{19645} and j_{29915} are about planet. Furthermore, Table 2 shows recommendations of all the methods under different contexts, we can see that the High-order model can provide more accurate results than others in these cases.

Quantitative Evaluations. Figure 4 shows the precision and recall across the top 5 positions for each method. In precision, the High-order method outperforms N-gram and CACB. All of the three methods can outperform the Co-occ method significantly. It shows that for ambiguous queries, the context-aware manner can capture users' search intent more accurately than the context-free ones. In recall, our High-order method significantly outperforms the other methods. The sequence pattern based methods performs

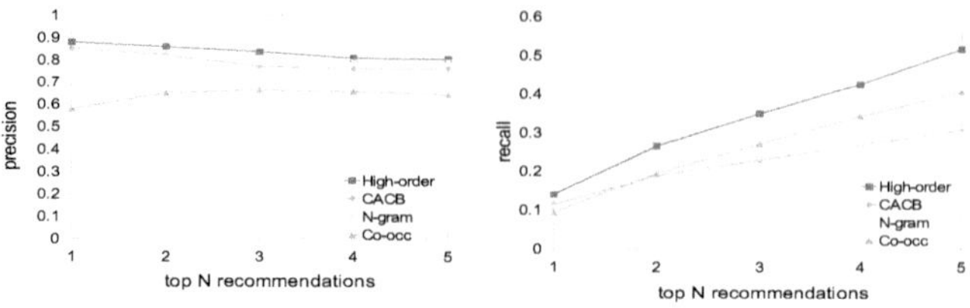

Figure 4: (a) Precision and (b) Recall of query recommendation across the top 5 positions over different methods

worst, due to the sparsity of the sequence patterns in query logs. While our approach can clearly benefit from the rich click-through information.

5. CONCLUSIONS

We address the problem of context-aware query recommendation. Unlike the existing approaches which leverage query sequence patterns in query sessions, we use the click-through of the given query as the major clue of users' search intents to provide context-aware recommendation. We proposed a probabilistic model by learning the High-order relations between the current query, its click-though and the next query. Compared with existing methods, our approach achieves both better precision and recall on recommendations for ambiguous queries.

6. ACKNOWLEDGMENTS

This research work was funded by the National High-tech R&D Program of China under grant No. 2010AA012500, and the National Natural Science Foundation of China under Grant No. 61003166 and Grant No. 60933005.

7. REFERENCES

[1] R. Baeza-Yates, C. Hurtado, and M. Mendoza. Query recommendation using query logs in search engines. In W. Lindner, M. Mesiti, C. Türker, Y. Tzitzikas, and A. Vakali, editors, *Current Trends in Database Technology - EDBT 2004 Workshops*, volume 3268 of *Lecture Notes in Computer Science*, pages 395–397. Springer Berlin / Heidelberg, 2005.

[2] D. Beeferman and A. Berger. Agglomerative clustering of a search engine query log. In *Proceedings of the sixth ACM SIGKDD international conference on Knowledge discovery and data mining*, KDD '00, pages 407–416, New York, NY, USA, 2000. ACM.

[3] H. Cao, D. Jiang, J. Pei, Q. He, Z. Liao, E. Chen, and H. Li. Context-aware query suggestion by mining click-through and session data. In *Proceeding of the 14th ACM SIGKDD international conference on Knowledge discovery and data mining*, KDD '08, pages 875–883, New York, NY, USA, 2008. ACM.

[4] A. P. Dempster, N. M. Laird, and D. B. Rubin. Maximum likelihood from incomplete data via the em algorithm. *JOURNAL OF THE ROYAL STATISTICAL SOCIETY, SERIES B*, 39(1):1–38, 1977.

[5] B. M. Fonseca, P. B. Golgher, E. S. de Moura, and N. Ziviani. Using association rules to discover search engines related queries. In *Proceedings of the First Conference on Latin American Web Congress*, pages 66–, Washington, DC, USA, 2003. IEEE Computer Society.

[6] J.-R. Wen, J.-Y. Nie, and H.-J. Zhang. Clustering user queries of a search engine. In *Proceedings of the 10th international conference on World Wide Web*, WWW '01, pages 162–168, New York, NY, USA, 2001. ACM.

Efficient l_p-Norm Multiple Feature Metric Learning for Image Categorization

Shuhui Wang[1] Qingming Huang[1, 2] Shuqiang Jiang[1] Qi Tian[3]

[1]Key Lab of Intell. Info. Process., Inst. of Comput. Tech., CAS, Beijing, 100190, China {shwang,sqjiang}@jdl.ac.cn

[2]Graduate University, Chinese Academy of Sciences, Beijing, 100049, China qmhuang@jdl.ac.cn

[3]Dept. of Computer Science, Univ. of Texas at San Antonio, TX78249, U.S.A. qitian@cs.utsa.edu

ABSTRACT

Previous metric learning approaches are only able to learn the metric based on single concatenated multivariate feature representation. However, for many real world problems with multiple feature representation such as image categorization, the model trained by previous approaches will degrade because of sparsity brought by significant dimension growth and uncontrolled influence from each feature channel. In this paper, we propose an efficient distance metric learning model which adapts Distance Metric Learning on multiple feature representations. The aim is to learn the *Mahalanobis* matrices for each independent feature and their non-sparse l_p-norm weight coefficients simultaneously by maximizing the margin of the overall learned distance metric among the pairs from the same class and the distance of pairs from different classes. We further extend this method to nonlinear kernel learning and category specific metric learning, which demonstrate the applicability of using many existing kernels for image data and exploring the hierarchical semantic structures for large scale image datasets. Experiments on various datasets demonstrate the promising power of our method.

Categories and Subject Descriptors

I.5.2 [**Pattern Recognition**]: Design Methodology—*Classifier design and evaluation*

General Terms: Algorithms, Performance, Experimentation

1. INTRODUCTION

A good distance metric stands in the core for many learning methods, for example, the kernel methods and nearest neighbor method. A commonly used distance metric is the *Euclidean* distance, a choice which has both the advantages of simplicity and generality. Despite of these advantages, for many real world classification tasks, the *Euclidean* distance is not well adapted. Metric learning is an emerging area of statistical learning in which the goal is to learn a more powerful distance metric from a set of labeled samples or weakly labeled samples. With a learned distance metric, even the simplest lazy learning method such as k-NN can achieve good generalization power. In fact, significant improvements have been observed within several distinguished solutions for this problem, such as neighborhood components analysis [6], large margin k-NN classification [15], and information theoretic metric learning [3].

For many real world applications, there will be multiple descriptions for a single data item. For example, Web image can be represented by shape feature, texture feature, color feature and textual feature extracted from the surrounding text. These features may have heterogeneous statistical characteristics. Previously, to make use of multiple features, a common way is concatenating all the features into one single feature vector. Then a classification model is obtained based on this concatenated representation. However, this will lead to explosive dimension increases, and the contribution of each original feature channel cannot be controlled. Moreover, the correlation among features usually contains noisy information that may lead to unpredictable risk of model degradation and over-fitting. For metric learning, the *Mahalanobis* matrix usually have $O(k^2)$ coefficients compared with $O(k)$ for linear SVM, where k denotes the average dimension of each feature representation. Therefore, the significant increase of computation as well as over-fitting brought by metric learning with concatenated feature are two major intrinsic weaknesses for applying previous metric learning approaches to application with multiple feature representation.

Recently, Multiple Kernel Learning [1][10][11][12] has been proposed to solve the problem of learning with multiple features and kernel representations. The aim is to maximize the margin on the training data and approximately find sparse weights to calculate the similarity using several features and kernels. Kloft *et al.* [8] and Vishwanathan *et al.* [14] proposed l_p-MKL, which imposes arbitrary non-sparse l_p norm on the kernel weight coefficients. Promising results and good generalization power have been reported by their studies. In this paper, borrowing the idea from l_p-MKL [14], we try to learn an overall combined distance metric by simultaneously optimizing a set of distance metrics on each independent feature channel. Our model requires only $O(Mk^2)$ coefficients to optimize instead of $O(M^2k^2)$ for metric learning with concatenated features, so the *curse-of-dimensionality* problem will be alleviated. We formulated our problem into the max-margin framework. The *Frobenius* norm and l_p squared norm are imposed on each *Mahalanobis* matrix and the weight coefficients of feature channels respectively.

By considering the cluttered distribution in feature space of the image data, we make two extensions of our method so that it is capable of real world image categorization. Firstly, the model can be easily kernelized as the inner product of each feature channel is preserved. Therefore, the existing image kernels are applicable to the specific features, such as spatial pyramid kernel and χ^2 kernel for visual bag-of-word feature. Secondly, we adapt our method to learn categorical specific metrics. In this paper, we

CIKM'11, October 24–28, 2011, Glasgow, Scotland, UK.

study the capability of our localized metric learning method so as to provide a guidance to reach a good balance of computational complexity and performance for large scale image applications.

In this paper, we propose an efficient multiple feature distance metric learning method by considering all the mentioned issues. We will introduce our work as follows: We describe our distance metric model in Section 2. Experiments are conducted and discussed in Section 3. In Section 4 we summarize the paper.

2. METHOD

2.1 Multiple Feature Metric Learning

Suppose we are given a set of N training samples with class labels, denoted by $\{(\mathbf{x}_i, c_i) \mid i = 1,...,N\}$, where $\mathbf{x}_i$ represents a training sample and c_i denotes its class label. For each $\mathbf{x}_i$, we calculate M different types of features, denoted by $x_i^{(m)}, m = 1,...,M$. For each data pair $(\mathbf{x}_i, \mathbf{x}_j)$, their original distance and learned distance metric with respect to different features are represented by $\overline{d}_{i,l}^{(m)}$ and $\widetilde{d}_{i,j}^{(m)}$. In this paper, we define the overall distance metric and similarity between any data pairs as:

$$\begin{aligned} \widetilde{d}_{i,j} &= \sum_{m=1}^{M} \widetilde{d}_{i,j}^{(m)}, \quad \widetilde{d}_{i,j}^{(m)} = (x_i^{(m)} - x_j^{(m)})^t A^{(m)} (x_i^{(m)} - x_j^{(m)}) \\ \widetilde{K}_{i,j} &= \sum_{m=1}^{M} \widetilde{K}_{i,j}^{(m)}, \quad \widetilde{K}_{i,j}^{(m)} = (x_i^{(m)})^t A^{(m)} x_j^{(m)} \end{aligned} \tag{1}$$

Where $A^{(m)}$ denotes the *Mahalanobis* matrix for the mth each feature. The training data is represented by a set of triplets as:

$$P^3 : (i, j, l), \ s.t. \ c(i) = c(j), \ c(i) \neq c(l) \tag{2}$$

We introduce a non-negative weight coefficient b_m on each feature representation as well as a set of initial *Mahalanobis* matrices $A_0^{(1)},...,A_0^{(M)}$. Borrowing the ideas from structural risk minimization and [14], we introduce the following convex objective function as:

$$\begin{aligned} &\min_{\mathbf{b},\mathbf{A}} \frac{1}{2}\sum_{m=1}^{M} \frac{1}{b_m} \| A^{(m)} - A_0^{(m)} \|_{Fro}^2 + C\sum_{ijl} \xi_{ijl} + \frac{\eta}{2} \| \mathbf{b} \|_p^2 \\ &s.t. \ \ \widetilde{d}_{i,l} - \widetilde{d}_{i,j} \geq 1 - \xi_{ijl}, \ \xi_{ijl} \geq 0, b_m \geq 0, p > 1, \ A^{(m)} \succeq 0 \end{aligned} \tag{3}$$

Where the original *Mahalanobis* matrices $A_0^{(1)},...,A_0^{(M)}$ can be a set of identity matrix, or it can be any *Mahalanobis* matrices learned on some other dataset. Following the similar derivation of [14], we obtain the dual problem as:

$$\min_{\boldsymbol{\alpha}} R(\boldsymbol{\alpha}) = \frac{1}{8\eta}\left(\sum_{m=1}^{M} \left(\boldsymbol{\alpha}^t \mathbf{Q}^{(m)} \boldsymbol{\alpha} \right)^q \right)^{2/q} - (\mathbf{1} - \mathbf{s})^t \boldsymbol{\alpha}, \ s.t. \ 0 \leq \alpha_{ijl} \leq C \tag{4}$$

Where $1/p + 1/q = 1$, $\mathbf{1}$ denotes a vector with all ones, and:

$$\begin{aligned} s_{ijl} &= \overline{d}_{i,l} - \overline{d}_{i,j} = \sum_{m=1}^{M} \left(\overline{d}_{i,l}^{(m)} - \overline{d}_{i,j}^{(m)} \right), \ Q_{ijl,i'j'l'}^{(m)} = tr\left(\left(\hat{x}_{ijl}^{(m)} \right)^t * \hat{x}_{i'j'l'}^{(m)} \right) \\ \hat{x}_{ijl}^{(m)} &= \left(x_j^{(m)} - x_l^{(m)} \right)\left(x_i^{(m)} \right)^T + x_l^{(m)} \left(x_l^{(m)} \right)^T \\ &\quad + x_i^{(m)} \left(x_j^{(m)} - x_l^{(m)} \right)^T - x_j^{(m)} \left(x_j^{(m)} \right)^T \end{aligned}$$

For $p>1$, b_m has the following form:

$$b_m = \frac{1}{2\eta} o_m^{q-1} \left(\sum_{m'=1}^{M} \left(o_{m'} \right)^q \right)^{2/q-1}, o_m = \boldsymbol{\alpha}^t \mathbf{Q}^{(m)} \boldsymbol{\alpha} \tag{5}$$

In this paper, $A^{(m)}$ is not guaranteed to be positive semi-definite. Although in most case we observe that there is no negative eigenvalues for $A^{(m)}$, one can set the negative eigenvalues to be 0 to make $A^{(m)}$ to be positive semi-definite. In future study, we will investigate the positive semi-definiteness of the learned metric.

2.2 Metric Learning with Kernel

The previous description can be easily kernelized by replacing all $\mathbf{x}$ by $\phi(x)$, where ϕ is the feature map corresponding to any given kernel. We denote the original kernel for each feature channel as $K^{(m)}$, then the learned kernel is given by:

$$\begin{aligned} &\widetilde{K}(x_a, x_b) = \sum_{m=1}^{M} K^{(m)}(x_a, x_b) + \sum_{m=1}^{M}\sum_{t'=1}^{T} \rho_{ij} b^{(m)} \bullet \\ &\left(K^{(m)}(x_a, x_i) - K^{(m)}(x_a, x_j) \right)\left(K^{(m)}(x_b, x_i) - K^{(m)}(x_b, x_j) \right) \end{aligned} \tag{6}$$

Where ρ_{ij} is calculated by reorganizing the support vector representation into the weighted combination of training pairs.

2.3 Category Specific Metric Learning

Since a single metric is not robust to deal with real world image categorization with hundreds to thousands of classes, a better way is to learn multiple metrics where a subset of classes share a single metric. We use an automatic hierarchical grouping method according to the overall average similarity on multiple feature representations among different classes. We calculate the average multiple feature representations on the images from each class, so that each semantic class will have an average image feature on the concatenated feature representation. We conduct hierarchical clustering on these feature representations. Then a hierarchical visual semantic structure can be obtained. We use different level of the hierarchical structure from this hierarchy so that each metric corresponds to different category structures and different average number of classes.

2.4 Solver

Since the dual problem (4) is differentiable with respect to $\boldsymbol{\alpha}$, there are many possible solutions that can be used to solve this problem. We propose a special purpose solver based on the recent proposed coordinate gradient descent method [7], which applies Newton-Raphson method to solve a one-variable sub-problem each time until convergence. Moreover, we implement two acceleration schemes proposed by [7], namely, random permutation of sub-problems and shrinking with gradient thresholding. Due to limited space, we omit the details of the optimization process. Readers may refer to our technical report.

2.5 Training Triplet Generation

Our method requires that the data should be organized as pairs, it leads to $O(N^2)$ scale in terms of training data size. However, as has been discussed in literatures such as [6], the neighborhood of each data is most influential to the model. Thus using this heuristic reduces the training data size to $O(N)$ scale. For the linear case in our method, we adopt Locality Sensitive Hashing [4] for approximated nearest neighbor search. For the kernel version, we adopt the KLSH [9]. We build KLSH for each feature channel, and the overall hash code for each image is the concatenation of the hash code vector from all feature channels.

3. EXPERIMENTS

We conduct experiments on 3 different image dataset, the Yale Face B face recognition dataset, the NUS-WIDE-OBJ [2] and the ImageNet-250 dataset [16] which is composed of 250 classes of images covering many common visual concepts including various kinds of categories. Each image category in ImageNet-250 contains more than 500 images. For Yale Face B, We extract 4 types of image features on this dataset, the original gray level feature, the LBP feature on the original image, the Gabor feature from 40 filters with different scales and orientations, and the Gabor LBP feature. For NUS-WIDE-OBJ, five image features are provided by [2] including color features (CM, CH, CORR), edge histogram (EDH) and wavelet features (WT). We calculate 9 types of features and image kernels for ImageNet-250. Note that in linear cases, we reduce the dimensionality on each single feature with dimensionality higher than 300 by using PCA. The ratios of random training/testing split for the three datasets are 0.7/0.3, *default* and 0.6/0.4, respectively. We conduct evaluation on 10 different random splits for each dataset, and all the reported results are the averaging of all the data splits as done in [15].

We denote our linear and kernelized multiple feature metric learning method as MFDML-L and MFDML-K. We compare our methods with 6 baseline approaches using concatenated feature representation on the three datasets: (1) EUC: the Euclidean metric on the concatenated feature. (2) EUC-PCA: the Euclidean metric on the concatenated feature representation after dimensional reduction using PCA. (3) ITML [3]. (4) LFDA [13]: localized FDA. (5) LMNN: Large Margin Nearest Neighbor method [15]. (6) NCA [6]. We implement our code using Matlab. The computing devices include a desktop computer with Intel i5 760 CPU and 4G RAM and another desktop with Intel Core2 E7500 and 4G RAM.

Another important issue is the setting of model parameters. Although the optimal setting can be found by cross validation, we notice that the performance is not very sensitive to different settings. For all the experiments, we set $A_0^{(m)} = I$, C=5, and $\eta = 1$. We heuristically set p=2 for all the experiments as [14] shows that this setting provides good solution

3.1 Evaluation Criteria

We adopt *Mean Accuracy* (*MA*) which records the average percent of correct predictions among all the classes. We use k-NN as the learning and predicting model. Suppose the number of returned nearest neighbors for each query is N_R, we denote the number of images from each category in the retrieved nearest neighbors as a vector $[N_1,...,N_C]$ and $N_R = \sum N_q$. Since multiple category specific metrics are learned for different subset of classes, we denote the task of learning each metric as $\mathbf{T}_t$. The decision output of query $\boldsymbol{x}$ is calculated as follows:

$$Q = \arg\max_q \frac{1}{|N_q|} \sum_{j=1}^{|N_q|} \widetilde{K}_t(\mathbf{x}, \mathbf{x}_t^j)|_{j\in q,\ q\in\mathbf{T}_t} \quad q \in [1, C] \tag{7}$$

Where $\widetilde{K}_t(\mathbf{x}, \mathbf{x}_j)|_{j\in q,\ q\in\mathbf{T}_t}$ denotes the learned similarities between $\boldsymbol{x}$ and the qth class samples $\mathbf{x}_j$. Because class q belongs to the tth task, we use the task specific similarity $\widetilde{K}_t$.

3.2 Yale Face Data B

In this part, we conduct single metric MFDML-L and MFDML-K since there is no semantic structure existing in the face data. The results of the performance on test data using with different number of nearest neighbors are demonstrated in Figure 1. We observe that for almost all the best recognition rate was achieved when the number of nearest neighbors is set to be 3. When the nearest number increases, the performance will degrades possibly because the training data only contains less than 2K training images. A slightly different result is observed in our approach MFDML-L, where the highest recognition rate is achieved when the neighborhood size is 7. The best performance of our method MFDML-K slightly outperforms the state-of-the-art LMNN. Another observation for Figure 1 is that the performance of our method decreases much slowly compared with other approaches, which demonstrates the robustness of our method on the setting of nearest neighbors. Finally, the highest performance for the baselines is 98.6% by LMNN, which outperforms the recognition rate 95.95% reported in [15] which uses the pixel values as the feature. The highest performance for our method MFDML-K reaches 98.98%. The results strongly support the claim that distance metric learning with multiple features usually achieves better generalization than single feature for image classification.

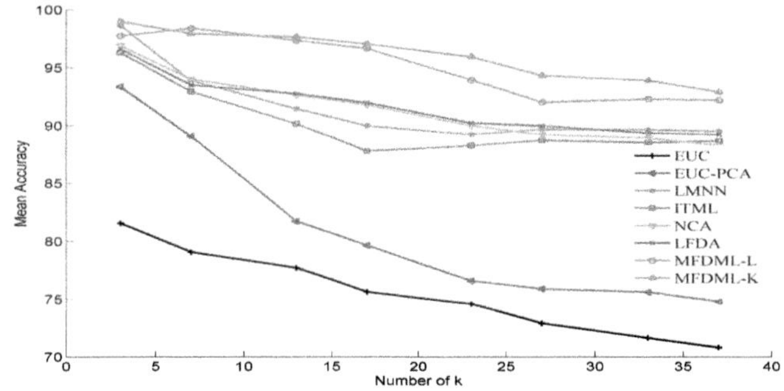

Figure 1: The recognition accuracies on Yale Face B dataset with respect to different numbers of nearest neighbors.

3.3 Number of Metrics and Kernels

We study how our multiple metrics improves the performances with different number of kernels. To this end, we conduct experiment on ImageNet-250 datasets. We test MFDML-K for this experiment. We use the data driven hierarchical clustering method as introduced in Section 2.4 to form multi-level category group structures. The performance with different number of metrics and kernels are shown in Table 1. We demonstrate the results using different number of metrics (row) and number of features (column). We see that when using more features, the performance is improved. This observation is consistent with many previous MKL studies. For the semantic categorization on ImageNet-250 dataset, when the number of metrics increases, the performance is improved. When the number of metrics is small, increasing the number of metrics will lead to significant improvements. When the number of metrics is more than 62, increasing the number of metrics lead to slight improvement. In fact, for large scale image applications, one can seek a better tradeoff between performance and efficiency by using different number of metrics.

Table 1: The performance of MFDML-K with different number of metrics and features on ImageNet-250

	2	4	6	9
1	0.334	0.354	0.361	0.372
4	0.365	0.368	0.387	0.410
16	0.378	0.381	0.410	0.433
62	0.384	0.398	0.431	0.453
250	0.387	0.412	0.441	0.464

3.4 NUS-WIDE-OBJ

In this experiment, the recognition rates of the best single feature (wavelet feature) and using all the features are shown in Table 3. We observe an interesting phenomenon that for some feature such as EDH, the distance metric learned by LMNN or ITML underperform the simplest Euclidean metric. The model trained by LMNN and ITML on the concatenated feature representation even underperform the model trained by wavelet feature (WT), which shows the inflexibility of previous DML approaches on learning with heterogeneous feature. However, our method achieves remarkable improvement at almost all the situations except that when the neighborhood size is 3, LMNN achieves the highest performance by using WT. This result proves the effectiveness of our distance metric learning when facing with multiple features, especially on the classification problems on Web image. When the number of nearest neighbors k increases, the performance is likely to be enhanced in the experiment because of the complicated neighborhood structure. We observe a decrease in the improvement rate for larger neighborhood size. Therefore, there will be a neighborhood size k_0 around 20 that our methods and other baseline approaches achieve the best results.

3.5 ImageNet-250

In this section, we conduct experiments to compare our methods with several state-of-the-art similarity learning and distance metric learning approaches mentioned in previous sections on visual semantic categorization. We denote learning category specific metrics for each class using LMNN by st-LMNN, and learning one unified metric using LMNN as u-LMNN. We conduct our category specific linear metric learning and kernel learning method for each visual category, which corresponds to 250 learned metrics. The results are shown in Table 2. We see that MFDML-K achieves the highest performance by using all the features. We see from both the performance of st-LMNN and our approaches that multiple metrics are indeed helpful for enhancing the performance. MFDML-L does not significantly outperform st-LMNN because we conduct PCA to avoid dimension explosion, which is an important pre-processing technique required by many existing linear distance metric learning method. In general, our methods achieve promising results on real world image semantic categorization, especially when using image kernels.

Table 2: The accuracy on ImageNet-250 data

EUC	EUC-PCA	st-LMNN	u-LMNN	NCA
0.192	0.264	0.367	0.324	0.315
ITML	LFDA	MFDML-L	MFDML-K	
0.298	0.305	0.373	**0.464**	

4. CONCLUSION

In this paper, we address the problem of metric learning with multiple features. We propose a new distance metric learning method which learns an overall distance metric by optimizing a set of *Mahalanobis* matrix for several feature representations at one time. We made two extensions to facilitate our method with learning with real world image data. The first is kernelizing the model so that it can take advantage of many existing image kernels, and the second is to learn multiple metrics according to a pre-computed semantic structure. The experiments on three image datasets show remarkable performance on the effectiveness and efficiency of our method compared with several state-of-the-art DML approaches. For future study, we will study how to combine our method with the existing LSH technique for efficient metric learning and the applications of retrieval.

5. ACKNOWLEDGEMENT

This work was supported in part by National Natural Science Foundation of China: 61025011, 60833006 and 61070108, in part by Beijing Natural Science Foundation: 4092042 and 4111003, and in part by NSF IIS 1052851, Google Faculty Research Award, gift grants from FXPAL, and NEC Labs of America, Cupertino, CA, to Dr. Qi Tian, respectively.

6. REFERENCES

[1] F. Bach, G. Lanckriet, and M. Jordan. Multiple Kernel Learning, Conic Duality, and the SMO Algorithm. *ICML*, 2004.

[2] T.-S. Chua, J. Tang, R. Hong, H. Li, Z. Luo, and Y.-T. Zheng. "NUS-WIDE: A Real-World Web Image Database from National University of Singapore", *ACM International Conference on Image and Video Retrieval*. Greece. Jul. 8-10, 2009

[3] J. V. Davis, B. Kulis, P. Jain, S. Sra, and I. S. Dhillon. Information-theoretic metric learning. *ICML*, 2007.

[4] M. Charikar. Similarity Estimation Techniques from Rounding Algorithms. In *ACM Symposium on Theory of Computing*, 2002.

[5] A. Globerson, S. Roweis. Metric learning by collapsing classes. *NIPS*, 2006.

[6] J. Goldberger, S. Roweis, G. Hinton, R. Salakhutdinov. Neighborhood Component Analysis. *NIPS*, 2005.

[7] C.-J. Hsieh, K.-W. Chang, C.-J. Lin, S. S. Keerthi and S. Sundararajan. A dual coordinate descent method for large scale linear SVM. *ICML*, 2008.

[8] M. Kloft, U. Brefeld, S. Sonnenburg, P. Laskov, K. R. Muller, A. Zien. Efficient and Accurate l_p norm Multiple Kernel Learning. *NIPS*, 2009.

[9] B. Kulis, and K. Grauman. Kernelized Locality Sensitive Hashing for Scalable Image Search. *ICCV*, 2009.

[10] G. Lanckriet, N. Cristianini, P. Bartlett, L. Ghaoui and M. Jordan. Learning the Kernel Matrix with Semi-definite Programming. *JMLR*, 5:27–72, 2004.

[11] A. Rakotomamonjy, F. Bach, S. Canu, and Y. Grandvalet. SimpleMKL. *JMLR*, 9:2491–2521, 2008.

[12] S. Sonnenburg, G. Ratsch, C. Schafer, and B. Scholkopf. Large Scale Multiple Kernel Learning. *JMLR*, 7:1531-1565, 2006.

[13] M. Sugiyama. Dimensionality Reduction of Multimodal Labeled Data by Local Fisher Discriminant Analysis. *JMLR*, 8, pp.1027-1061, 2007.

[14] S. V. N. Vishwanathan, Z. Sun, N. Theera-Ampornpunt, M. Varma. Multiple Kernel Learning and the SMO Algorithm. *NIPS*, 2010.

[15] K. Q. Weinberger, L. K. Saul. Distance metric learning for large margin nearest neighbor classification. *JMLR*, 10: 207-244, 2009.

[16] http://www.image-net.org.

Table 3: The recognition accuracy (%) with different k using the best single feature and combined features

WT	3	5	7	9	11	13	15	17	19
EUC-PCA	20.9	23.42	24.85	25.49	26.41	26.9	27.1	27.65	27.76
LMNN	**21.56**	24.31	25.47	26.61	27.12	27.56	28.05	28.09	28.55
ITML	20.56	23.44	25.46	26.41	26.94	27.45	27.92	28.24	28.32

Combined	3	5	7	9	11	13	15	17	19
EUC-PCA	20.26	22.53	23.67	24.20	24.69	25.13	25.47	25.67	25.78
ITML	19.82	22.87	24.11	25.04	25.98	26.17	26.64	26.88	27.51
LMNN	14.12	15.97	16.76	17.33	18.04	18.23	18.70	18.96	19.17
MFDML-L	19.54	26.31	28.03	29.36	30.10	30.92	31.34	31.59	31.76
MFDML-K	21.31	**28.79**	**31.94**	**33.57**	**34.68**	**35.03**	**35.82**	**36.05**	**36.19**

Re-ranking by Local Re-Scoring for Video Indexing and Retrieval

Bahjat Safadi
UJF-Grenoble 1 / UPMF-Grenoble 2 / Grenoble INP / CNRS, LIG UMR 5217, Grenoble, F-38041, France
Bahjat.Safadi@imag.fr

Georges Quénot
UJF-Grenoble 1 / UPMF-Grenoble 2 / Grenoble INP / CNRS, LIG UMR 5217, Grenoble, F-38041, France
Georges.Quenot@imag.fr

ABSTRACT

Video retrieval can be done by ranking the samples according to their probability scores that were predicted by classifiers. It is often possible to improve the retrieval performance by re-ranking the samples. In this paper, we proposed a re-ranking method that improves the performance of semantic video indexing and retrieval, by re-evaluating the scores of the shots by the homogeneity and the nature of the video they belong to. Compared to previous works, the proposed method provides a framework for the re-ranking via the homogeneous distribution of video shots content in a temporal sequence. The experimental results showed that the proposed re-ranking method was able to improve the system performance by about 18% in average on the TRECVID 2010 semantic indexing task, videos collection with homogeneous contents. For TRECVID 2008, in the case of collections of videos with non-homogeneous contents, the system performance was improved by about 11-13%.

Categories and Subject Descriptors

H.3.1 [**Information Storage and Retrieval**]: Content Analysis and Indexing—*Abstracting methods, Indexing methods*; I.2.6 [**Artificial Intelligence**]: Learning—*Concept learning*

General Terms

Algorithms, Experimentation

Keywords

Video Indexing and Retrieval, Re-ranking

1. INTRODUCTION

Semantic indexing and retrieval for video databases has been a very active research field over the past few years. The global goal is to automatically describe the videos, then to index them by their contents. Nevertheless, retrieving relevant samples and easily navigating within large collection, are still very difficult tasks.

Generally, semantic indexing is achieved by supervised learning approaches, in which it is based on training classifier on positive and negative samples of a target concept (the development set). This classifier will generate a model, which will be used to predict the likeliness of new samples (the test set) to contain the target concept. The likeliness is often computed homogeneously to a probability for each data sample to contain the concept. Retrieval can then be done by ranking the samples according to their probability scores. Such ranking is initially done with a score independently for each sample using only information from the development set. It is often possible to improve the indexing or retrieval performance by re-ranking the samples, considering the results of the initial ranking on the whole test collection. Thus, re-ranking may lead to retrieve more relevant samples at the top of the ranked list. Recently, several methods have been proposed and developed for re-ranking. We review below some of these methods.

In context fusion [3, 5], the results of different searching models (concept-based search model, text-based search model and query by example) are used to re-rank the ranked lists. In fact, the focus here is on fusing output scores of different models. This method needs to train new classifiers on new descriptors. Since we also use, in our work, the fusion of output scores obtained by multiple models, we took this as a baseline approach.

Classification-based re-ranking [4], where the initial results of a baseline system are used to discover the co-occurrence patterns between the target semantics and extracted features. This is very similar to *"learning to rank"*[2], which is based on training a ranking model which can precisely predict the ranking lists in the dataset. In [4], the authors used the top-ranked and low-ranked samples respectively, as pseudo-positive and pseudo-negative examples to train a new classification model for ranking, and the classification margin for a target concept is regarded as its (new) reranked. The use of SVM as the classification model, leads to the method called *RankSVM*[2]. Ordinal re-ranking as it was proposed in [8], where the author re-ranks an initial results by using the co-occurrence patterns via the ranking functions. The final score is the weighting combination of the original score and the re-ranked scores. They adopted a training method to train the Re-ranking algorithm on some concepts, and the re-ranking algorithm was applied to rerank the remaining concepts.

In the case of video collections: the retrieval units are often some video shots, rather than the whole videos themselves. Our contribution in this paper is to re-rank the video shots according to their initial scores, which were obtained from initial classifiers, and according to the video knowledge and nature. Compared with the work in [7], where the authors re-ranked the initial results of shots using the video knowledge score, which was estimated by calculating the arithmetic mean on the initial scores of all shots within the same video. This paper goes further: the generalized mean rule was adopted to calculate global score for each shot, depending on the knowledge obtained from the scores of its neighbors within the video, and it has been proved to be more efficient. Moreover, we studied the effectiveness of the re-ranking when applied on homogeneous and non homogeneous databases. Two windowing functions, the Rectangular and the Gaussian, were used on the neighbors of each shot to calculate its global score.

The paper is organized as follows: Our re-ranking method is presented in section 2, section 3 describes the experimental results and section 4 presents our concluding remarks.

2. RE-RANKING METHOD

In multimedia systems based video retrieval, we need to rank the video shots according to an estimation of their relevance to what the user is likely to want to see. This estimation can be the prediction score obtained by the trained model, as the likeliness of a shot to contain a target concept. Usually the order of the samples in the ranked lists contains some irrelevant samples, where in this case we can use a re-scoring method in order to minimize the error within these ranked lists.

The method we proposed here, considers the hypothesis that videos have rather homogeneous contents, and that the presence of a given concept in a video depends a lot on the nature of the video itself, and that the estimated scores are computed independently for all video shots in the corpus. The proposed re-ranking method is done by re-scoring the video shots, and this is done in two steps: First, for each shot, we compute global score z, this is calculated through the initial scores of its predefined neighbors within the same video. Then this global score will be used to re-evaluate the initial score of each shot. Let the test collection consists of a set of videos $V = (v_1, v_2, \dots, v_m)$, m being the number of videos in the collection. Each video v_i composed of a sequence of shots $v_i = (s_{i1}, s_{i2}, \dots, s_{in_i})$, n_i being the number of shots of v_i. For each shot s_{ij}, an initial classification score x_{ij} is computed from supervised learning on the development set.

Many options –including *(arithmetic mean, min, max, geometric mean, harmonic mean and root mean square)*– are possible for the computation of a global score z_{ij} for the shot x_{ik} in video v_i, from its neighbor shots. We considered the formula of a generalization mean rule, equation 1, to be the method to calculate the global scores of each shot in the video, since all the above methods can be inherited from this rule, by evaluating different parameters of α.

$$z_{ij} = \left(\frac{\sum_k f_\theta(j,k)(x_{ik})^\alpha}{\sum_k f_\theta(j,k)} \right)^{1/\alpha} \quad (1)$$

where x_{ik} indicates the score of shot k in video i, and α defines the used function, and it has to be tuned by cross-validation. Hence, different values of α leads to different functions, such as:($\alpha = -\infty$: Min; $\alpha = \infty$: Max; $\alpha = 0$: Geometric Mean; $\alpha = 1$: Arithmetic Mean; $\alpha = -1$: Harmonic Mean and $\alpha = 2$: Root Mean Square). $f_\theta(j,k)$ works as a window around the current shot j, to its neighbor shots in the $video_i$. In this paper, two kinds of windowing functions are considered: the rectangular ("hard") and the Gaussian ("soft"). In both cases, the size of the window is defined by a parameter θ. For the rectangular window, the number of neighbors of each shot in video i is given by $2\theta + 1$.For the Gaussian window, we have applied $\sigma = \sqrt{\theta(\theta+1)/3}$ so that both windowing functions have the same variance for the same value of θ. This θ parameters has also to be tuned within the training (or development set). $\theta = 0$ gives the baseline, it correspond to the initial ranking and $\theta = \infty$ uses a global score of the video itself which is calculated from all the shots belonging to it, in other words ($z_{ij} = z_i$).

After these global scores z_{ij} are calculated, the score of each shot is updated according to its previous score and its global score obtained from the video (its neighbors) knowledge. Again, many options were possible and we chose a weighted multiplicative fusion:

$$x'_{ij} = x_{ij}^{1-\gamma} \times z_{ij}^{\gamma}, \quad (2)$$

where γ is a parameter that controls the "strength" of the re-ranking method. This parameter also has to be tuned by cross-validation within the development collection.

3. EXPERIMENTS

In this section, we present our experiments in which we have evaluated the proposed re-ranking method on semantic indexing task. The experiments were conducted on TRECVID 2008 and 2010 databases. Each database consists of two large sets; the development and the test set. Table. 1 shows general information about these two databases. The TRECVID 2010 development set (2010d) consists of 119685 shots of 3173 videos with average of 37 shots per video, and the test set (2010t) consists of 146788 shots of 8467 videos with average of 17 shots per video, which might tells that videos in this database are homogeneous. The TRECVID 2008 development set (2008d) consists of 43616 shots of 219 videos with average of 199 shots per video, and the test set (2008t) consists of 42461 shots of 219 videos with average of 193 shots per video, videos are not homogeneous.

Table 1: databases' sizes.

Collection		Concepts	Shots/Videos	Min/Mean/Max
2010	dev	130	119685/3173	1/37/1381
	test	30	146788/8467	1/17/1423
2008	dev	20	43616/219	19/199/1003
	test	20	42461/219	14/193/1029

3.1 Re-ranking on semantic indexing task TRECVID 2010

This experiment was conducted on TRECVID 2010, which provided 130 concepts with ground truth labels in a training set. The evaluation was done by calculating the Mean Average Precision (MAP) on only 30 concepts that were chosen by NIST. We have evaluated the re-ranking method on four different initial classification results, which have been submitted to TRECVID 2010, including different fusion strategies such as weighted and direct optimized weighted fusion *(Fusion_MAP and Fusion_OPT)*, also the combination of these two fusion types with the genetic fusion *(Fusion_GA_-MAP and Fusion_GA_OPT)*. These fusion strategies were applied on score vectors obtained by training different systems on 45 different descriptors including audio and visual descriptors, which have been produced by the partners of the IRIM project of the GDR-ISIS [1]. Each of these fusion ways -of the classification results- can be considered as the context fusion method, which we took as the baseline method to our re-ranking algorithm.

3.1.1 Parameters' optimization

The tuning of α, θ and γ parameters (Eq. 1 and Eq. 2 in section 2), was conducted using the aforementioned initial classification results, which are calculated on the TRECVID 2010 development set. The aim of this tuning is to get the best values of α, θ and γ that gives the best performance of our system.

Figure 1 shows the results of tuning α and γ, in which we report the performance of the system in function with γ. We used the MAP on the 130 concepts as evaluation metric. Each plot, in the (top) sub-figure, is related to different value of α, and it shows the MAP with different values of γ (including $\gamma = 0$ and $\gamma = \inf$). For each video, we have set θ to be the number of all shots related to it, and we have used the initial scores of *Fusion_MAP* for evaluation. From the plots, as we can see, $\alpha = 1$ and $\alpha = 2$ are performing better that the others, and the best result can be obtained with $\alpha = 2$ (Root Mean Square) and $\gamma = 0.4$. Moreover, in Figure 1 (bottom), we show the performance of the system, on the same collection, using the four used initial scores with $\alpha = 2$. As we can see, the highest performance, on each of the initial scores, was achieved when applying the re-ranking method with $\gamma = 0.4$.

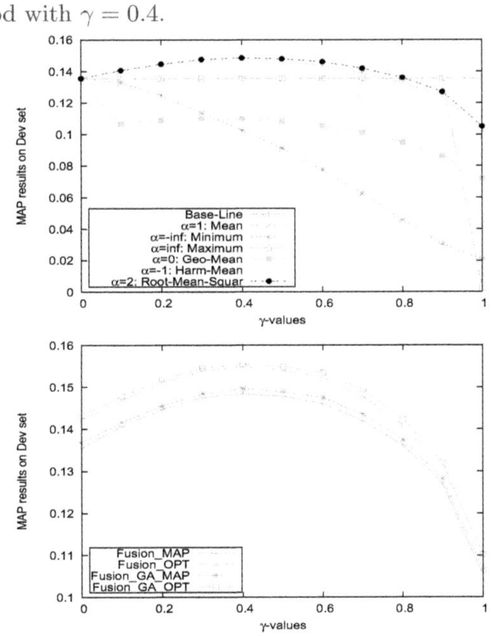

Figure 1: Tuning α (top) and γ (bottom) parameters on TRECVID 2010 development set.

Let's consider now the θ parameter in Equation 1. As mentioned before, this parameter controls the range on which we expect the video to have homogeneous content. The optimal value for this range is likely to depend upon the collection contents. We rerun the previous evaluations with different values of θ, including the baseline $\theta = 0$ and $\theta = \infty$ which means that the global score of each video is assigned to all the shots belonging to it ($z_{ij} = z_i$). Figure 2 shows the MAP calculated on the 130 concepts on the *Fusion_GA_OPT* run, which we consider as the best run as shown in figure 1 (bottom). The evaluations were done using the Rectangular and Gaussian windows with different θ-equivalent parameters for the re-ranking method. We have applied a sliding window of size $2\theta + 1$, as the neighbors of shot j using rectangular function, and $\sigma = \sqrt{\theta(\theta+1)/3}$ using Gaussian window. Thus, the two windowing functions have the same variance for the same value of θ. As we can see, the best result was obtained when $\theta = \infty$ for the two window functions. This is due to the fact that videos in the TRECVID 2010 collection are quite short (a few minutes in average), and they have homogeneous contents. Thus, local re-scoring does not perform better than global re-scoring.

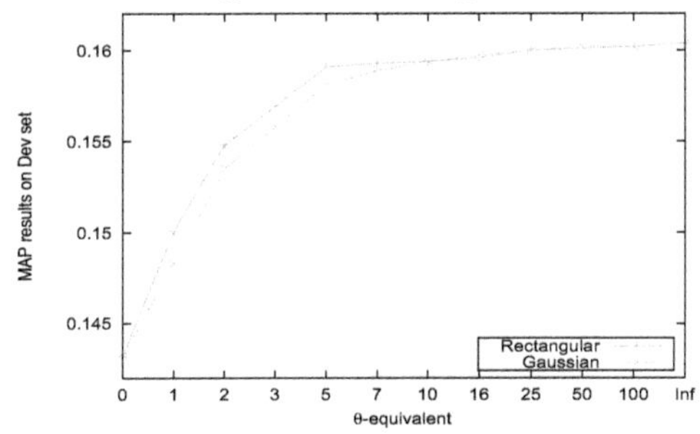

Figure 2: Tuning θ-equivalent parameters on TRECVID 2010 development set, using *Fusion_GA_OPT* run.

3.1.2 Evaluation on the test set

We have applied the proposed method on the TRECVID 2010 test set; with the best parameters obtained by the cross-validation, $\alpha = 2$, $\gamma = 0.4$ and $\theta = \infty$ with the two windowing functions (Rectangular and Gaussian. We have compared the new results –obtained after re-ranking– with the results of the initial scoring methods obtained using the best run; the *Fusion_GA_OPT* run.

We report, in table 2, the results (MAP on the 30 concepts) of the evaluation of the re-ranking method on TRECVID 2010 test set. As we can see, our proposed method has significantly improved the performance of the initial scoring methods; on this collection the proposed re-ranking method, with the fully homogeneity $\theta = \infty$, was able to improve the system performance with about 18% in average. The absolute MAP values are significantly different than in cross-validation (on the development set); this is mostly due to the fact that the set of concepts is different (30 only out of 130).

Table 2: Results of the re-ranking method on the test set of TRECVID 2010.

	θ/σ	MAP
Baseline	0	0.0480
ALL	∞	0.0568 (+18%)
Rectangular	$\theta = \infty$	0.0568 (+18%)
Gaussian	$\sigma = \infty$	0.0568 (+18%)

3.2 Re-ranking on HLF task TRECVID 2008

We have conducted the second experiment on TRECVID 2008 High-Level Feature Extraction task (HLF). Considering the Mean Average Precision (MAP) on these 20 concepts to be the performance metric. The evaluation of the re-ranking method has been conducted using the simple late fusion of four types of image descriptors taken from IRIM GDR-ISIS partners [1], (including a combination of color histogram and Gabor transform, texture patterns, quaternionic wavelets and bag of SIFTs). The Multiple-SVM classifiers with RBF kernel was used as classification system, and it was implemented as in [6]. Since, TRECVID 2008 sets are not as homogeneous as TRECVID 2010 sets (see table. 1), we have fixed the optimal parameters $\alpha = 2$ and $\gamma = 0.4$, taken from section 3.1.1. The goal was to find the best value of θ for the re-ranking method, when dealing with non-homogeneous videos .

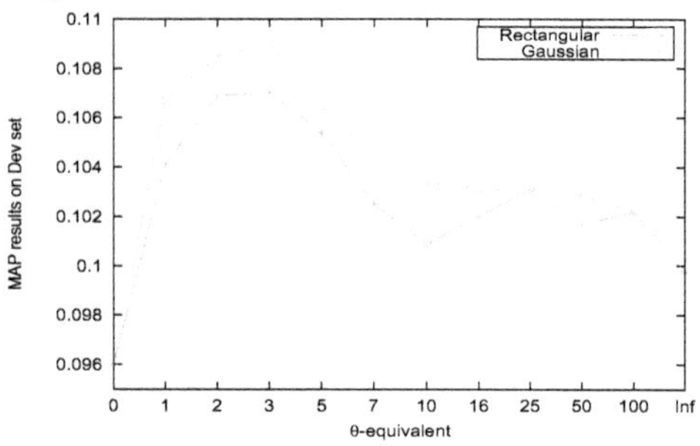

Figure 3: Tuning θ-equivalent parameter on TRECVID 2008, using the fusion of four descriptors.

We have evaluated our method on TRECVID 2008 development set using the late fusion of the four aforementioned descriptors, with different values of θ-equivalent parameter, within the same conditions as in section 3.1.1. We present the performance of the systems in Figure 3, which shows the MAP (calculated on the 20 concepts) with different values of θ-equivalent in both functions, the rectangular and Gaussian. As we can see, the Gaussian performance better than the rectangular function, and the performance using the two windowing functions was significantly enhanced when θ-equivalent is small and the best result was given when $\theta = 3$. In the Gaussian function when $\theta = 3 \rightarrow \sigma = \sqrt{3(3+1)/3} = 2$.

Furthermore, we have evaluated the re-ranking method with the optimal values $\alpha = 2, \gamma = 0.4$ and $\theta = 3$, on TRECVID 2008. It was evaluated using the two windowing functions. We report the final results in Table 3, in which we show the performance using deferent values of θ: $\theta = 0$ is the baseline, $\theta = \infty$ corresponds to applying the re-ranking on the whole videos, and the optimal θ-equivalent values(θ/σ) which defines respectively the rectangular and Gaussian functions. As we can see, the re-ranking with the optimal θ can significantly enhance the performance of the retrieval system. As expected, this collection is not homogeneous and there is not much enhancement when re-ranking by a global score on the whole video. When applying the re-ranking with ($\alpha = 0.4, \gamma = 0.4, \theta = 3$), the performance of the system was enhanced in average by about 11-13% on the late fusion of the used descriptors with both the Gaussian and the rectangular windows.

Table 3: Results of the re-ranking method on the Test set of TRECVID 2008.

	θ/σ	MAP
Baseline	0	0.099
ALL	∞	0.101 (+2%)
Rectangular	$\theta = 3$	0.112 (+13%)
Gaussian	$\sigma = 2$	0.109 (+11%)

4. CONCLUSIONS

Video retrieval can be done by ranking the samples according to their probability scores that were predicted by classifiers. It is often possible to improve the retrieval performance by re-ranking the samples. In this paper, we proposed a re-ranking method that improves the performance of semantic video indexing and retrieval, by re-evaluating the scores of the shots using the homogeneity and the nature of the video they belong to.

The experimental results showed that the proposed re-ranking method was able to improve the system performance by about 18% in average on the TRECVID 2010 semantic indexing task, videos collection with homogeneous contents. For TRECVID 2008, in the case of collections of videos with non-homogeneous contents, the system performance was improved by about 11-13%.

Acknowledgements

This work was partly realized as part of the Quaero Program funded by OSEO, French State agency for innovation.

5. REFERENCES

[1] D. Gorisse, F. Precioso, P. Gosselin, L. Granjon, D. Pellerin, M. Rombaut, H. Bredin, L. Koenig, H. Lachambre, E. El Khoury, R. Vieux, B. Mansencal, Y. Zhou, J. Benois-Pineau, H. Jégou, S. Ayache, B. Safadi, Y. Tong, F. Thollard, G. Quénot, A. Benoit, and P. Lambert. IRIM at TRECVID 2010: High Level Feature Extraction and Instance Search. In *TREC Video Retrieval Evaluation workshop*, Gaithersburg, MD USA, nov 2010. NIST.

[2] R. Herbrich, T. Graepel, and K. Obermayer. Support vector learning for ordinal regression. In *Ninth Intl. Conf. on Artificial Neural Networks*, pages 97–102, 1999.

[3] W. Jiang, S.-F. Chang, and A. C. Loui. Context-based concept fusion with boosted conditional random fields. In *ICASSP (1)*, pages 949–952, 2007.

[4] L. S. Kennedy and S.-F. Chang. A reranking approach for context-based concept fusion in video indexing and retrieval. In *Proceedings of the 6th ACM international conference on Image and video retrieval*, CIVR '07, pages 333–340, New York, NY, USA, 2007. ACM.

[5] J. Liu, W. Lai, X.-S. Hua, Y. Huang, and S. Li. Video search re-ranking via multi-graph propagation. In *Proceedings of the 15th international conference on Multimedia*, MULTIMEDIA '07, pages 208–217, New York, NY, USA, 2007. ACM.

[6] B. Safadi and G. Quénot. Active learning with multiple classifiers for multimedia indexing. Grenoble, France, June 2010. CBMI.

[7] F. Wang and B. Merialdo. Eurecom at trecvid 2009 high-level feature extraction. In *TREC2009 notebook*, 16-17 Nov 2009.

[8] Y.-H. Yang and W. H. Hsu. Video search reranking via online ordinal reranking. In *ICME*, pages 285–288, 2008.

Tightly Coupling Visual and Linguistic Features for Enriching Audio-Based Web Browsing Experience

Muhammad Asiful Islam, Faisal Ahmed, Yevgen Borodin, I.V. Ramakrishnan
Computer Science, Stony Brook University
Stony Brook, NY 11794, USA
{maislam, faiahmed, borodin, ram}@cs.sunysb.edu

ABSTRACT

People who are blind use screen readers for browsing web pages. Since screen readers read out content serially, a naive readout tends to mix irrelevant and relevant content thereby disrupting the coherency of the material being read out and confusing the listener. To address this problem we can partition web pages into coherent segments and narrate each such piece separately. Extant methods to do segmentation use visual and structural cues without taking the semantics into account and consequently create segments containing irrelevant material. In this paper, we describe a new technique for creating coherent segments by tightly coupling visual, structural, and linguistic features present in the content. A notable aspect of the technique is that it produces segments with little irrelevant content. Preliminary experiments indicate that the technique is effective in creating highly coherent segments and the experiences of an early adopter who is blind suggest that it enriches the overall browsing experience.

Categories and Subject Descriptors

H.5.2 [**Information interfaces and presentation**]: User Interfaces; H.3.3 [**Information storage and retrieval**]: Search and Retrieval

General Terms

Algorithms, Design, Human Factors

Keywords

Singular Value Decomposition, Clustering, Segmentation, Screen Reader, Blind

1. INTRODUCTION

Blind people listen to digital content by having it read out aloud by screen readers. This read out is an inherently serial process. So a naive read out of a web page, especially multi-themed content-rich web pages such as on-line news and e-commerce web sites, will mix relevant content with irrelevant items during the serial read out. This kind of intermixed read outs can confuse and disorient the listener.

Let's suppose that the web page fragment shown in Figure 1 has been organized into four segments labeled S1 through S4. Each segment represents one dominant theme: taxonomy dominates S1; the dominant theme in S2 is a narrative about gadgetry; S3's theme is referrals to some popular topics; S4 is advertisement.

Observe that S2 consists of content pieces labeled 1 through 4. Screen readers such as JAWS [6] and Apple's VoiceOver [1] will narrate S2's content by reading out the leaf nodes of its corresponding DOM (sub)tree in left-to-right order which is: piece labeled 1 followed by 2, 3, 4. Pieces labeled 1 and 4 are consecutive paragraphs making up the dominant theme in S2, namely, a narrative of "using gadgetry". The other pieces 2 and 3 in S2 are irrelevant to this main narrative. Thus the read out of a segment such as S2 that consists of several irrelevant content items disrupts the flow of the main narrative in several places causing confusion and difficulty in following it.

Segments such as S1 through S4 can be identified using web page segmentation methods. Many such methods have appeared in the literature (e.g., [3, 5, 4]). Segmentation technology is beginning to be embraced in commercial products. In fact the segments S1 through S4 in Figure 1 were produced by Apple's auto web spot in VoiceOver.

By and large the reported segmentation methods (including auto web spot) exploit the idea that content elements making up a segment exhibit consistency in presentation style (captured by *visual* cues) and spatial locality (captured by *structural* cues). The problem of relying solely on such visual and structural clues for segmenting is that the resulting segments consist of content elements that are coherent in a "presentational" but not necessarily in a semantic sense. For example, observe in S2 that although pieces 1 through 4 exhibit presentation consistency and spatial locality to be included in the same segment, pieces 2 and 3 bear no semantic similarity to the pieces 1 and 4 that constitute the main narrative.

Eliminating such extraneous items is an interesting problem that is addressed in this paper. The idea is to exploit linguistic, visual and structural features in the segmentation process. The effect of such a tight coupling will create segments whose elements are spatially local, as well as linguistically and presentationally similar. Applying this idea will further refine S2 into 3 smaller segments as shown in

CIKM'11, October 24–28, 2011, Glasgow, Scotland, UK.

Figure 1: An example of a segmented web page

Figure 1. The para pieces 1 and 4 get into one segment since they are all semantically similar whereas each of the remaining non-para pieces - 2 and 3 - form a separate segment by themselves since they bear no semantic similarity to any other piece.

Overview of our Approach

We adapt Latent Semantic Analysis (LSA) [8] for this problem. LSA is a technique that computes the linguistic similarity of text documents. It will, for instance, compute a high degree of similarity for the para pieces in S2 and a low similarity value for the others. However, LSA relies only on words as features for computing linguistic similarity. On the other hand, we also want to utilize visual and structural similarities. So we expand the feature sets used in LSA to include both visual features, as well as words as features. LSA with this expanded feature computes a *composite* similarity score among the web elements based on their visual/structural/linguistic features combined. This adaptation of LSA is a fully automatic online process with no a priori training. Following the LSA step we utilize the composite score to automatically cluster the web elements bottom-up into coherent thematic segments.

The paper is organized as follows: Section 2 gives a brief overview our algorithm; experimental results and preliminary user experience with an early adopter (who is blind) are presented in Sections 3; Section 4 discusses related works; Conclusions appear in Section 5.

2. TECHNICAL APPROACH

2.1 Latent Semantic Analysis

Latent Semantic Analysis (LSA) [8] is a powerful technique for analyzing relationships in a set of text documents based on the terms (i.e., words) present in those documents. Let W be a $m \times n$ term-document matrix in which cell (i, j) is associated with the occurrence of term i in document j.

$$W = \begin{bmatrix} w_{1,1} & \dots & w_{1,n} \\ \vdots & \ddots & \vdots \\ w_{m,1} & \dots & w_{m,n} \end{bmatrix} \tag{1}$$

LSA uses Singular Value Decomposition (SVD) [8] to project terms onto a reduced vector space. SVD of W is defined as:

$$W = U \Sigma V^T \tag{2}$$

where U and V denote the left and right singular matrices respectively and Σ is the diagonal matrix whose diagonal elements are singular values arranged in descending order. Note that each singular value represents the importance of each dimension. By setting less important dimensions to zero LSA retains only the important information and gets rid of irrelevant details. Suppose we keep only the k ($\leq min(m, n)$) largest singular values and set others to zero. Then the rank-k approximation to W is:

$$W_k = U \Sigma_k V^T \tag{3}$$

This reduced LSA is a relatively more compact representation of similarity and maps synonyms to the same dimension in the reduced vector space.

2.1.1 *Extending LSA with Presentational Features*

Traditionally LSA has been primarily used for analyzing text documents based on linguistic features in the context of NLP and IR applications. For the problem of identifying coherent segments that is addressed in this paper, we propose extending LSA with visual and structural features of web elements. In our formulation each web element is considered as a document and each term represents either a visual, structural or linguistic attribute of a web element. For our problem the matrix W is a $m \times n$ attribute-web element matrix; $w_{i,j}$ is 1(0) whenever attribute i is present(absent) in web element j. Each column vector (e_j) represents a web element and each row vector (a_i) represents an attribute.

$$e_j = \begin{bmatrix} w_{1,j} \\ \vdots \\ w_{m,j} \end{bmatrix} \tag{4}$$

$$a_i^T = \begin{bmatrix} w_{i,1} & \dots & w_{i,n} \end{bmatrix} \tag{5}$$

The idea behind using visual, structural and linguistic attributes together is to identify more coherent segments with very little irrelevant material.

2.2 Coherency in Segmentation

Algorithm *CoherentSeg* is a high-level algorithmic sketch of our ideas for identifying segments with high degree of coherency. Given a web page P it first computes a matrix M representing the similarity among the web elements of P based on visual/structural/linguistic features. The computation of the matrix is based on LSA with the extended feature set. Following this step the similarity information in matrix M is utilized to cluster the web elements into assorted coherent segments. We point out that Algorithm *CoherentSeg* operates on web pages in real-time.

Algorithm *CoherentSeg*
Input: P: A web page
Output: S: A set of coherent segments of P
1. $M \leftarrow ComputeSimilarityMatrix(P)$.
2. $S \leftarrow ClusterSegments(M)$.

2.2.1 Similarity Matrix Computation

Given a web page P we compute a matrix M consisting of similarity values between every pair of web elements. What follows is a description of the steps of similarity matrix computation.

Feature Extraction: We traverse the DOM tree of the web page to collect attribute value data of the web elements in the page. The attribute data of a web page element includes *text-attributes, x-position, y-position, width, height, bgcolor, font, parent-id, div-id, table-id, form-id, p-tag-id, UL-id, LI-id.*

Now we construct an attribute-element matrix W where columns represent web page elements and rows represent attributes. As mentioned earlier $w_{i,j}$ is 1 if the ith attribute is present in the jth element, otherwise it is 0.

Singular Value Decomposition: In this step we decompose the original matrix W into three components: the term/attribute matrix U, the document/web element matrix V and the singular matrix Σ. Each singular value in Σ represents the importance of a dimension. Unimportant dimensions are characterized by singular values which are close to zero. These are set to 0 and we get the matrix Σ_k. The product of these three matrices W_k gives a low rank approximation to W.

Similarity Matrix Construction: W_k is used to compute the element-element similarity matrix M. The (i,j) entry in M denotes the similarity between elements i and j. Note that, column vectors of W_k correspond to the web elements. Given two column vectors e_i, e_j in W_k we compute the cosine similarity between elements i and j. M will now be used to cluster the web page elements into coherent segments.

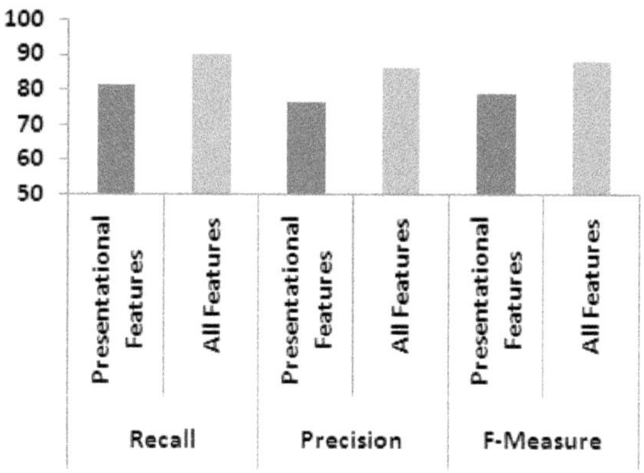

Figure 2: Accuracy of the segmentation algorithm

2.2.2 Clustering Segments

We iteratively cluster the web elements bottom-up into larger coherent segments based on similarity matrix M. Initially each web element is a separate segment by itself. Two maximally similar segments are merged together to get a new segment. This process continues until the clustering quality is less than a threshold value. The threshold is set to the average of all the similarity values in matrix M. Our empirical study suggests that this approach gives high accuracy across different web sites.

Matrix M also comes into play in the computation of intra and inter cluster similarities of segments. *Intra-cluster similarity* is the measure of similarity of the elements in a cluster or segment whereas *Inter-cluster similarity* is the measure of similarity between two clusters or segments.

We compute intra and inter-cluster similarity and clustering quality using [10]. We determine the pair of segments (S_i, S_j) which has the highest inter-cluster similarity. All the web page elements of this segment pair are merged together to construct a new segment. The algorithm iterates as long as the quality of clustering after replacing S_i, S_j with their merged segment is above the threshold. Otherwise it terminates declaring the current segments as the final output.

It is worthwhile mentioning that by restricting the feature set to include only the visual and structural attributes of web elements Algorithm *CoherentSeg* will identify segments that are spatially local and have presentational consistency (such as segments S_1 to S_4 in Figure 1) akin to the algorithms in [3, 1].

3. EVALUATION

To evaluate our algorithm's performance, we collected a dataset of 300 web pages from different domains (e.g., news, shopping, education, email, encyclopedia, weather forecast, etc.). A total of 5,478 segments were identified and labeled manually in those web pages. We then ran our segmentation algorithm on the dataset. Since the algorithm did not require any training, the entire dataset was used for testing purposes.

We tested our segmentation algorithm, first, considering only visual and structural features of web elements. We then repeated the experiment using visual, structural, and linguistic features. Figure 2 illustrates the average recall,

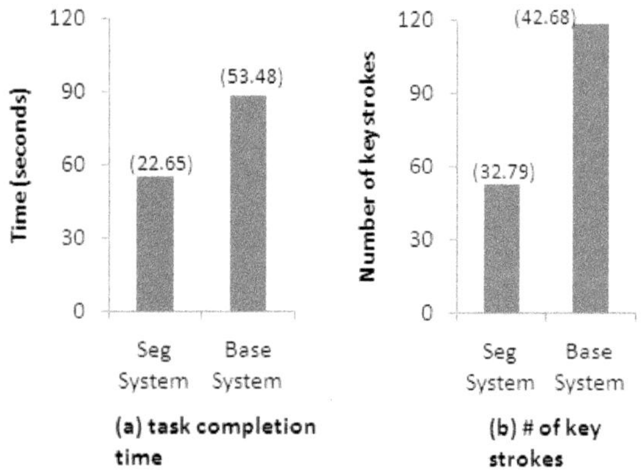

Figure 3: Mean and st. dev. of task completion time and keyboard shortcuts

precision, and F-measure for the two experiments. As expected, using the combination of linguistic, visual and structural features, we were able to achieve higher (by 10%) overall accuracy with more coherent segments.

To get a sense of the user experience we conducted another experiment with a early adopter who is blind. We used the HearSay [2] aural web browser which provides standard screen-reading functionalities similar to JAWS [6]. For the study, we extended HearSay with an interface for navigating segments. The interface shortcuts allowed users to navigate back and forward among the coherent segments produced by *CoherentSeg*. We will refer to this extended version as the segmentation system.

We asked the blind user to perform various browsing tasks using both systems. The tasks included finding specific information in news articles, Wiki, weather reports, shopping sites, emails, etc. During the study we measured the time and the number of shortcuts used to complete each task. Figure 3 presents the summary of the results. On the average the user was able to complete the tasks 1.61 times faster with segmentation system compared to the base system, and pressed fewer shortcuts. The ability to quickly navigate among the identified segments helped the subject to skip irrelevant information. The user agreed that the segmentation system enhanced the browsing experience.

4. RELATED WORK

VoiceOver(VO) [1] is a screen reader with a number of useful features for web navigation. Its "auto web spot" does web-segmentation based on visual and structural information of the web page. The key advantage of using this feature is that users can jump from one web spot to another using shortcuts. However, as VO primarily considers presentational features of web elements, it is frequently unable to identify coherent segments.

The Readability [9] tool converts any web page into a clean reading view. Given an online article page, readability extracts the main article, ignoring all the irrelevant parts (e.g., advertisements, menus, headers, footers, etc.). However it is not able to handle web pages with more than one article. Note that, the segmentation approach proposed in this paper is also able to extract main content.

VIPS [3] employs rules to analyze structural information to segment web pages. Consequently it does not work well on web content where linguistic attributes are important.

Guo et. al. [5] describe a general-purpose approach to partitioning web pages. Instead of using any domain-specific knowledge they use visual layout information and presentation style similarity to determine the spatial locality of the web elements. The idea of contextual browsing is introduced in [7] where visual and structural information was used for web page segmentation.

5. CONCLUSIONS

In this paper, we described an algorithm for generating clutter-free thematic segments from web pages by adapting LSA, a technique pioneered for IR and NLP applications. The segments generated by our algorithm are amenable for distraction-free narration by TTS engines. This is very important to Web users who are blind because now they can listen to web content without becoming confused and disoriented.

A novel aspect of our algorithm is the incorporation of visual and structural features of web elements in addition to the "words as features," traditionally used in LSA. This facilitates the generation of segments that are spatially local as well as thematic in "form and content". Another interesting aspect is that our algorithm operates in real-time and neither uses prior training data nor does it do any parameter learning.

Quantitative evaluation showed that our algorithm has high recall and precision. The results of a preliminary user study with a blind individual have been encouraging.

Acknowledgements: This work was supported in part by NSF grants CNS-0751083 and IIS-0808678.

6. REFERENCES

[1] Apple. Voiceover, screen reader from apple (http://www.apple.com/accessibility/voiceover). 2010.

[2] Y. Borodin, F. Ahmed, M. A. Islam, Y. Puzis, V. Melnyk, S. Feng, I. V. Ramakrishnan, and G. Dausch. Hearsay: a new generation context-driven multi-modal assistive web browser. In *WWW*, 2010.

[3] D. Cai, S. Yu, J.-R. Wen, and W.-Y. Ma. VIPS: a vision-based page segmentation algorithm. *Microsoft Technical Report*, (MSR-TR-2003-79), 2003.

[4] D. Chakrabarti, R. Kumar, and K. Punera. A graph-theoretic approach to webpage segmentation. In *WWW*, pages 377–386, 2008.

[5] H.-F. Guo, J. Mahmud, Y. Borodin, A. Stent, and I. V. Ramakrishnan. A general approach for partitioning web page content based on geometric and style information. In *ICDAR*, pages 929–933, 2007.

[6] JAWS. (http://www.freedomscientific.com). 2010.

[7] J. Mahmud, Y. Borodin, and I. V. Ramakrishnan. Csurf: a context-driven non-visual web-browser. In *WWW*, pages 31–40, 2007.

[8] C. D. Manning, P. Raghavan, and H. Schütze. Introduction to information retrieval. *Cambridge University Press*, 2008.

[9] Readability. (https://www.readability.com). 2010.

[10] A. Strehl. Relationship-based clustering and cluster ensembles for high-dimensional data mining. *PhD thesis, UT Austin*, May 2002.

Robust Video Fingerprinting based on Hierarchical Symmetric Difference Feature

Jungho Lee, Seungjae Lee, Yongseok Seo, Wonyoung Yoo
Electronics and Telecommunications Research Institute
218 Gajeong-ro, Yuseong-gu
Daejeon, South Korea
+82-42-860-1735
{junglee, seungjlee, yongseok, zero2}@etri.re.kr

ABSTRACT
The piracy of copyrighted digital content over the Internet infringes copyrights and damages the digital content industry. Accordingly, identifying and monitoring technology on the online content service like fingerprinting is getting valuable through the explosion of digital content sharing. This paper proposes a robust video fingerprinting feature to identify a modified video clip from a large scale database. Hierarchical symmetric difference feature is proposed in order to offer efficient video fingerprinting. The feature is robust and pairwise independent against various video modifications such as compression, resizing, or cropping. Moreover, videos undergoing a transformation such as flipping or mirroring can be identified by simply disordering the bit pattern of fingerprints. The performance of the proposed feature is extensively experimented on 6,482 hours of database and the experimental results show that the proposed fingerprinting is efficient and robust against various modifications.

Categories and Subject Descriptors
H.3.3 [**Information Storage and Retrieval**]: Information Search and Retrieval

General Terms
Algorithms, Experimentation

Keywords
Video Fingerprinting, Video Filtering, Video Identification, Content-based Filtering

1. INTRODUCTION
In recent years, information on the Internet has been flooded by popularized digital devices and online media services such as smart phones, mp3 players, mobile video players, video-on-demand, and music-on-demand. Thus, searching and managing technologies are required to handle massive information. In the meantime, copyright violations such as file sharing without permission are becoming a social problem. The piracy of copyrighted content over the Internet infringes copyrights and damages the digital content industry. There have been many researches on protecting illegal file sharing and managing massive amounts of digital content. Video fingerprinting provides a fast and reliable identification method of video content and is used to identify, monitor, and block copyright-violating digital video. The method uses perceptual features extracted from video content that have discriminating characteristics.

Researches on video fingerprinting have been focused on the spatial, temporal, color, and transform domains of a video. Bhat and Nayar proposed an ordinal measure that divides a video frame into sub-blocks and orders the sub-blocks by their mean value of pixel intensities [1]. Some other studies used an ordinal measure along with a resampled frame, temporal trail of the ranking value, and motion direction and color histograms [2]-[4]. These methods have slightly different facets but commonly show a good performance for global modifications such as brightness changes, blurring and compression. However, its discriminating performance is not sufficient for locally modified video that has been cropped or undergone logo or caption insertion because sub-block ranking is mixed up by local intensity changes. Oostveen *et al.* proposes a binary video feature that employs the differential value between neighboring sub-blocks through a temporal FIR filter and abstracts its result [5]. The feature is simple and has compact size but, could lose its discriminating characteristic when the difference between neighboring sub-blocks is insufficiently small for reliable abstraction. Lee and Yoo use condensed edge distribution in divided sub-blocks, named centroids, of gradient orientation, which shows robust performance for global variations such as brightness, contrast, and color changes [6]. Iwamoto *et al.* also use edge information as a fingerprint, and their method is robust to caption superimposition [7]. Shivakumar proposes shot-based fingerprinting that detects the temporal locations of a shot change in a video and estimates the duration between shots [8]. However, this fingerprinting is not sufficient when used solitarily because shot detection is inaccurate in many cases.

In this paper, we propose hierarchical symmetric difference (HSD) video fingerprinting feature against the unintentional modification of video, including brightness, blurring, cropping, compression, frame-rate modification, resolution modification, screen flipping and screen mirroring, to search and protect copyrighted digital video content, and an efficient matching method for large-scale databases. The proposed feature is compact, precise, and efficient as compared to centroids of gradients method and has been verified for a large-scale video database experimentally.

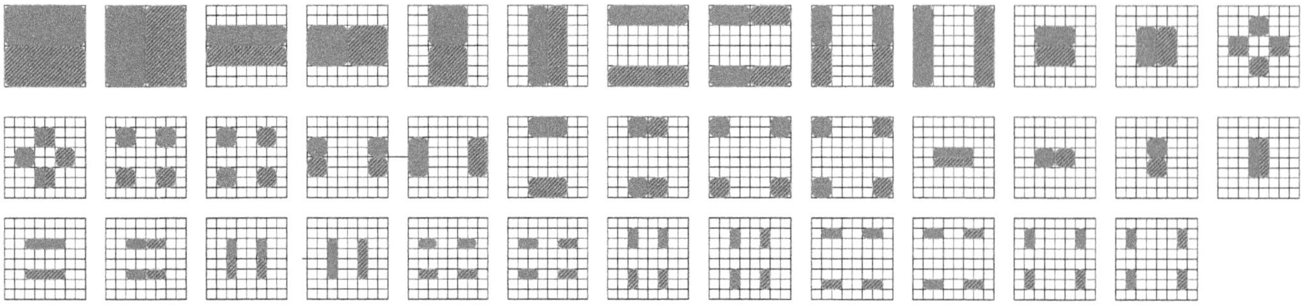

Figure 1: 38 Hierarchical Symmetric Difference Video Fingerprinting Features

2. Hierarchical Symmetric Difference Feature

Mass storage is required when we build a video fingerprinting database even when the fingerprint has a small feature size because a video is composed of a large amount of frames. It is even worse for copyrighted video filtering when the database contains thousands of videos. Thus, the compactness and structure for rapid matching are mandatory in video fingerprinting. In this paper, a hierarchical symmetric difference, which represents the essential feature of frames with a compact feature size, is used for precise matching. To extract proposed feature, a video input is resampled in the temporal direction to reduce the number of frames to be processed, and then normalized into a fixed resolution of 320*240. A normalized frame is grayscaled then a frame is divided into *m*n* sub-blocks, and its *p*th local mean value of luminance *ML(p)* is calculated as described in (1) before extract HSD. Then, HSD of the *p*th block means *DBM(p)* is obtained by subtracting the symmetrically distributed sub-blocks as in (2). We build 38 pairs of a symmetric structure from 8*8 sub-blocks. As shown in Figure 1, the former part of the symmetrical sub-block pair is occupy the wide area of a frame, and the organizing area is reduced by going back to the latter pair. In the figure, plane-red blocks represent *Region A* and striped-blue blocks are *Region B*.

The order of HSD is hierarchically organized, so the former structure includes features from the latter structures. This organization of structure is useful when searching from a large scaled database. Former features could be used for fingerprint indexing to retrieve the database quickly by excluding dissimilar fingerprints, and latter features are used for calculating precise distance from the candidates.

$$ML(p) = \frac{1}{(i+j)} \sum_{x=0,y=0}^{x=i,y=j} I(x,y) \quad (1)$$

$$DBM(p) = ML_A(p) - ML_B(p) \quad (2)$$

We compress the HSD through binarization in order to reduce fingerprint size as described in (3), and use 38 structural pairs to guarantee the performance. If the feature is extracted at a rate of 5 frames per second, the fingerprint size of one hour of video is 84kbytes. Also, it takes an advantage of computation because of its simplicity of calculation especially when a database is organized with a massive number of videos.

$$HSD(p) = \begin{cases} 1, & DBM(p) > 0 \\ 0, & else. \end{cases} \quad (3)$$

3. MATCHING AND DISTANCE MEASURE

Efficiency is the most important factor in identifying a video in a large-scaled database, especially for commercial applications. Usually, a linear search shows the best performance in data matching, but it is not applicable for a massive database due to the searching time. The proposed method uses former 8 features out of 38 in Figure 1 as an index to reduce the matching time. These former features occupy larger regions in the feature domain.

We use hamming distance as in (4) to compare the query clip's fingerprint $\bar{f}_1$ with candidate $\bar{f}_2$. A matched fingerprint is decided based on the bit error rate (BER). For example, *L*38*bit pairs are compared when a query is composed of *L* frames, and the BER is calculated in *L-1* summation and *L*XOR* operations.

$$D(\bar{f}_1, \bar{f}_2) = \sum_{bits} XOR(\bar{f}_1[n], \bar{f}_2[n]) \quad (4)$$

The BER distribution of fingerprint pairs of a perceptually different clip and modified clip are experimentally obtained for 10 and 20 sec videos by the experiments as shown as Figure 2(a) and (b). Modification1 is lossy compression (LC), Modification2 is brightness change (BR), Modification3 is resizing (SZ), Modification4 is frame rate change (FR) before lossy compression, and Modification5 is an aggregation of all modifications. We present a false rejection ratio for BER=0.2 in Table 1, and it is certain that the longer fingerprint length (*L*) reduces the error rate. The false alarm ratio for BER=0.2 is zero in both 10 and 20sec.

To analyze fales alram probability, we use binomial distirution *B(n,p)* with *p=0.5* because of Hamming distance is used for a distance measure in the proposed method, and the probability *p* is determined by experiments. A binomial distribution is regarded as normal distribution *N(np, npq)* when *n* is large enough, so P_{FA} could be adjusted as in (5). However, each bit of a fingerprint is not identically independently distributed, and the variance of is supposed to increase in multiples of *k* as in (6) by Haitsma in [9].

Table 1: Probability of a false rejection (P_{FR}) for perceptually different videos with BER=0.2

Modification	P_{FR} (10sec)	P_{FR} (20sec)
LC	0	0
LC+BR	0.000159769	0
LC+SZ	0	0
LC+FR	0	0
LC+BR+SZ+FR	0.000243457	0

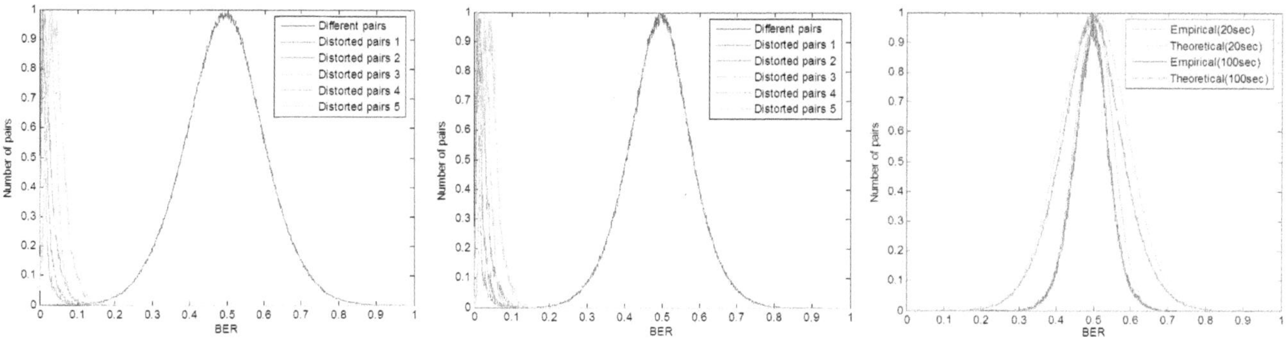

(a) **(b)** **(c)**

Figure 2: (a) Distributions of perceptually different and modified fingerprint pairs for 10 sec (b) Distributions of perceptually different and modified fingerprint pairs for 20 sec (c) Comparison of empirical and theoretical distributions of different fingerprint pairs with 20sec (k=124) and 100sec (k=190)

$$N(\mu,\sigma^2) = N(np, npq) = \frac{1}{\sqrt{2\pi npq}} e^{-\frac{(x-np)^2}{2npq}} \quad (5)$$

$$N(np, knpq) \quad (6)$$

$$P_{FA} = \int_{-\infty}^{t} \frac{1}{\sqrt{2\pi knpq}} e^{-\frac{(x-np)^2}{2knpq}} dx \quad (7)$$

Figure 2(c) shows the empirical distribution of 7,611,579 different fingerprint pairs. The length n of HSD is 3,800 for a 20sec clip when the video is normalized as 5fps, and (np, $knpq$) becomes (1900, k*950). For a 100sec clips, n is 19,000 and (np, $knpq$) becomes (9500, 4750). Thus, the value of k for a 20sec clip is estimated as 124.1 compared to empirical distribution (1874.3, 117900), and k=190 for 100sec clips compared to the empirical value (9373.4, 904290). The probability of a false alarm for 20sec clips with BER=0.2 is 5.8664e-004 theoretically by (7), and it is not so far from the empirical value of 9.14e-004. If 100 sec length clips are used, a false alarm in the proposed method is approximately expected as 2.22e-009 for BER=0.2. The false alarm is estimated as 0.01 for 20sec clips and 5.515e-005 for 100sec clips, respectively, when BER=0.3.

4. EXPERIMENTS AND RESULTS

The performance of the proposed video fingerprinting is evaluated using 230,160 pairs of video clips for robustness comparison, and 6,482 hours of videos are used for overall performance evaluation. Experiments were performed on a Pentium dual core (2.8GHz CPU, 6MB cache, and 4GB RAM). HSD features of 38 dimensions are extracted from normalized video, 320*240 spatially and 5fps temporally. The performance of the proposed system is evaluated by its success ratio and searching time. In the success rate, we allow time line margin of error in original video within 1sec and use 0.1 of BER for the matching threshold.

We compare the proposed fingerprint with the centroids of gradients [6] in a receiver operating characteristics (ROC) curve that plots the false rejection rate (P_{FR}) versus false alarm rate (P_{FA}) in order to evaluate the performance of the features. Sixteen former features and 16 latter features of the proposed fingerprint are evaluated separately to have an equal feature vector dimension with the centroid of gradients. Hamming distance is employed to compare the coded fingerprints extracted from 10 sec video lengths at 10fps and 320*240 resolution. A total of 230,160 pairs of original and modified videos are experimented on to obtain a false rejection ratio, and 15,223,158 video clips that are perceptually different from a query clip are experimented on to obtain a false alarm ratio. ROC curves are displayed in Figure 3. For a fixed false alarm ratio, the 16 latter features have a smaller false rejection ratio in most of the steps shown in Figure 3. This is induced by the difference of area in forming the feature, and this means that the former features are robust against severely modified video, and that the latter features are appropriate for finding an exactly matched clip. Thus, HSD features can be organized differently based on the goal of the identification system. The performance of centroids of gradients is in the middle of the 16 former and latter features, but it is slightly better than the two curves in the extremely low false alarm ratio.

41,000 video clips are experimented on using 6,482 hours of database to evaluate the performance for a large-scale database. Three kinds of modifications are added to query video in the reflection of file sharing circumstances.

ModificationA - Add Gaussian blur (GB) and increase the brightness (BR) 20% before re-compressing the query video.

ModificationB - Insert a subtitle (ST), which possesses 12% of the frame area, and resize (SZ) to 320*240 before re-compression.

ModificationC- Crop (CR) the frame 15% before re-compressing (LC) the clip by 500kbps.

A total of 123,000 modified clips overall are queried to evaluate the robustness, and 95.49% of the clips are successfully identified, where the average search time is 1.53sec as shown in Table 2. In the result, the success rate for *ModificationC* is lower than *ModificationA* and *ModificationB*. The relatively low success rate

Table 2: False alarm and false rejection ratio of the proposed method for 6,482hours of a video database

Modification	Success Rate	P_{FA} (%)	P_{FR} (%)	Time(sec)
A(GB+BR)	96.946	0	3.054	1.53
B(ST+SZ)	96.122	0	3.878	1.42
C(CR+LC)	93.393	0	6.607	1.50
Overall	95.487	0	4.513	1.49
Unlisted	0	0	0	1.21

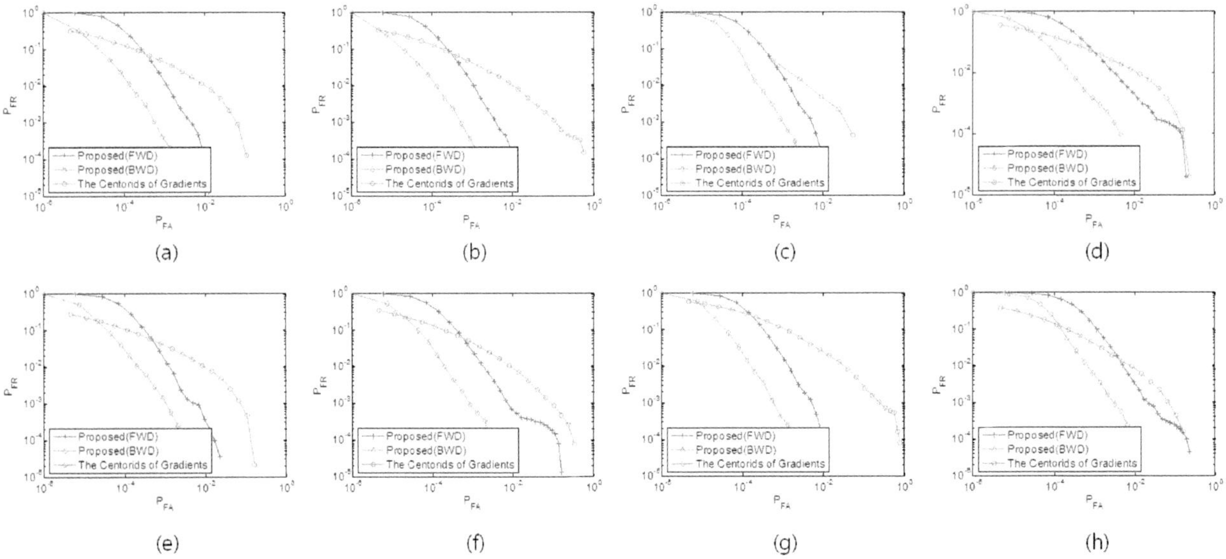

Figure 3: ROCs for various modifications: (a) Lossy compression (Divx @ 250kbps), (b) Lossy compression (Divx @ 250kbps)+blurring (Gaussian with *r*=2), (c) Lossy compression (Divx @ 250kbps)+Resizing(to CIF), (d) Lossy compression (Divx @ 250kbps)+brightness(+25%), (e) Lossy compression (Divx @ 250kbps)+frame rate change(29.97fps to 24fps), (f) Lossy compression (Divx @ 250kbps)+contrast(+20%), (g) Lossy compression (Divx @ 250kbps)+rotation(+1 degree), and (h) Lossy compression (Divx @ 250kbps)+brightness(+25%)+Resizing (to CIF)+frame rate change (29.97fps to 24fps).

of *ModificationC* is expected because changed HSD values by cropping the frame affect the success rate. However, this weakness is acceptable because the cropping is done around the outside of the frame and does not severely interrupt the center area in usual situations. We also experimented on 31,600 unlisted video clips that are not included in the database to verify the pairwise independence, and its result is a 0% success rate as listed in Table 2.

5. CONCLUSION AND FUTURE WORK

In this paper, a video fingerprinting based on hierarchical symmetric difference is proposed. The proposed video fingerprint is superior in pairwise independence for a large-scale database and is robust against usual video modifications, in addition to its sufficiently high speed identification performance, which is required for commercial applications. The variables that control the identification performance are theoretically estimated and experimentally verified. Further research will focus on the candidate search method such as scene duration detection to minimize the searching speed. Concisely selected features of HSD could be a solution for robust candidate searching by categorizing the database.

6. ACKNOWLEDGEMENTS

This work was supported by the IT R&D program of MSCT/KEIT. [10035229, Development of content protection and distribution technology on DRM-free environments]

7. REFERENCES

[1] Dinkar N. Bhat and Shree K. Nayar. 1998. Ordinal Measures for Image Correspondence. *IEEE Trans. on Pattern Analysis and Machine Intelligence*. 20, 4 (Apr. 1998), 415-423.

[2] A. Hampapur, K.H. Hyun, and R. Bolle. 2002. Comparison of Sequence Matching Techniques for Video Copy Detection. In *Proceedings of Storage and Retrieval for Media Databases* (San Jose, USA, Jan. 20-25, 2002). 194-201.

[3] X. Hua, X. Chen, and H. Zhang. 2004. Robust Video Signature based on Ordinal Measure. In *Proceedings of IEEE International Conference on Image Processing* (Singapore, Oct. 24-27, 2004). 685-688.

[4] C. Kim and B. Vasudev. 2005. Spatiotemporal Sequence Matching for Efficient Video Copy Detection. *IEEE Trans. on Circuits and Systems for Video Technology*. 15, 1 (Jan. 2005), 127-132.

[5] J. Oostveen, T. Kalker and J. Haitsma. 2002. Feature Extraction and a Database Strategy for Video Fingerprinting. In *Proceedings of 5th International Conference on Recent Advances in Visual Information Systems*(Hsin Chu, Taiwan, Mar. 11-13, 2002). 117-128.

[6] S.I. Lee and C.D. Yoo. 2008. Robust Video Fingerprinting for Content-Based Video Identification. *IEEE Trans. on Circults and Systems for Video Technology*. 18, 7 (July 2008), 983-988.

[7] K. Iwamoto, E. Kasutani and A. Yamada. 2006. Image Signature Robust to Caption Superimposition for Video Sequence Identification. In *Proceedings of IEEE International Conference on Image Processing*(Atlanta, USA, Oct. 8-11, 2006). 3185-3188.

[8] N. Shivakumar. 1999. *Detecting Digital Copyright Violation on the Internet*. Doctoral Thesis. Stanford University.

[9] J. Haitsma and T. Kalker. 2002. A Highly Robust Audio Fingerprinting System. In *Proceedings of 3rd International Society for Music Information Retrieval*(Paris, France, Oct. 13-17, 2002). 107-115.

Image Clustering Fusion Technique Based on BFS

Luca Costantini
Fondazione Ugo Bordoni
Viale del Policlinico, 147
00161 Roma, Italy
+39 06 5480 3801
lcostantini@fub.it

Raffaele Nicolussi
Fondazione Ugo Bordoni
Viale del Policlinico, 147
00161 Roma, Italy
+39 06 5480 3323
rnicolussi@fub.it

ABSTRACT

With the increasing in number and size of databases dedicated to the storage of visual content, the need for effective retrieval systems has become crucial. The proposed method makes a significant contribution to meet this need through a technique in which sets of clusters are fused together to create an unique and more significant set of clusters. The images are represented by some features and then are grouped by these features, that are considered one by one. A probability matrix is then built and explored by the breadth first search algorithm with the aim of select an unique set of clusters. Experimental results, obtained using two different datasets, show the effectiveness of the proposed technique. Furthermore, the proposed approach overcomes the drawback of tuning a set of parameters that fuse the similarity measurement obtained by each feature to get an overall similarity between two images.

Categories and Subject Descriptors

I.5.3 [**Pattern Recognition**]: Clustering—*algorithms*

General Terms

Algorithms, Performance, Experimentation.

Keywords

Image clustering, BFS, CBIR, clustering fusion.

1. INTRODUCTION

Due to the huge amount of digital informations the methods to retrieve information are become very important and this has increased the research efforts in this area. Nowadays, the digital information is not only textual (*e.g.*, documents) but it can be also visual (*e.g.*, images, videos), both of them have the same importance from the users point of view. In this scenario, the methods to compute the similarity between two images and to retrieve visual informations in a database are needed. In content-based image retrieval (CBIR) systems the query by example strategy is often employed. Furthermore, due to the size of the database, the users has often the need to groups in clusters the images that the systems consider similar to the query image. There are several ways to achieve this result but the main problem, faced by all these methods, is how to compare two images [2, 10, 8, 6]. Actually, the most effort is to understand the image semantic content [4, 7, 11] and compare the images using their content. Otherwise, the similarity between two images can be obtained by using the low level features, such as color, textures, edges, object shape and so on. Since these features are heterogeneous, they could be represented and compared in different ways, to get an overall similarity measure between two images is not a trivial task. Indeed, the importance given to each feature is tuned by coefficients that normally are found empirically. Obviously this technique shows an high cost in terms of time machine and therefore has a further room for improvement. On the other hand, machine learning techniques could be used to find the optimal value of the coefficients. Instead, the proposed method has the advantage that it does not need any coefficients to get an overall metric. Roughly speaking, the system processes the query image extracting its low level features and producing a ranking for each feature. The first images of these rankings are considering relevant with respect to the query and are put in a set. Considering the feature one by one, these images are grouped in sets of clusters. Obviously, the number of the sets of clusters is equal to the number of features. These sets of clusters are fused by building the probability matrix and it is thresholded to obtain a binary matrix that can be seen as the representation of a graph. The final set of clusters, that is shown to the users, is determined through the research of connected sub-graphs in this matrix via the well-known breadth first search (BFS) algorithm. The proposed approach is scalable to the number of considered features. Indeed, it is possible to increase easily the number of features used and hopefully improving the performances of the system. The results show a significant improvement compared with the technique used in [2]. Due to the fact that this is a very novel approach no other comparisons are allowed, indeed at the best of our knowledge, the problem is not exhaustively addressed in literature.

The paper is organized as follows. In section 2 the used method to represent an image is explained. The clustering algorithm and the clustering fusion technique are described in section 3. The experimental results are shown in section 4. Finally, the conclusions are drawn in section 5.

CIKM'11, October 24–28, 2011, Glasgow, Scotland, UK.

2. IMAGE REPRESENTATION

Any image is represented by using the low level features vectors. In particular the features used are the textures, the color and the edges.

2.1 Textures

The textures are analyzed using the Laguerre Gauss functions [3]. These functions belong to the class of Circular Harmonic Functions (CHFs). The functions identified by the indexes $n = 1$ and $k = 0$, and $n = 3$ and $k = 0$, at three different resolutions are used. Since the Laguerre Gauss functions are complex, the marginal density of the real part and the imaginary part are separately approximated by using the Generalized Gaussian Density (GGD). The GGD can be completely described by two parameters: α, β. Then, the textures are represented by a vector made up of 24 elements. The similarity between two textures vectors are computed by using the Kullback-Leibler distance [5, 3], as follows

$$D_T = \sum_{i=1}^{12} \log\left(\frac{\beta_i^f \alpha_i^g \Gamma\left(\frac{1}{\beta_i^g}\right)}{\beta_i^g \alpha_i^f \Gamma\left(\frac{1}{\beta_i^f}\right)}\right) + \\ + \left(\frac{\alpha_i^f}{\alpha_i^g}\right)^{\beta_i^g} \frac{\Gamma\left(\frac{\beta_i^g+1}{\beta_i^f}\right)}{\Gamma\left(\frac{1}{\beta_i^f}\right)} - \frac{1}{\beta_i^f} \quad (1)$$

where g and f denote two different images and i denotes the ith GGD. The described textures analysis is separately performed on the R, G, B, and Y components. Then, for each component, we have a vector made up of 24 elements.

2.2 Color

The representation of the color feature is performed by using the chromatic components of the YUV color space, [9]. The U e V components are represented by the mean value, the second and the third centered moment, obtaining a vector made up of 6 elements. The similarity measurement between two color vectors is computed by the Euclidean Distance, as follows

$$D_C = \sqrt{\sum_{i=1}^{6} \left(CV_i^f - CV_i^g\right)^2} \quad (2)$$

where CV_i^f denotes the ith element of the color vector computed on the image f.

2.3 Edges

The edges feature is represented by using the phase histogram of the edge points. The first operation is the selection of the most important edge points. These edge points are selected combining two maps by the AND operator. The first map is computed by using the Laplace operator, the second one by using the Laguerre Gauss function $n = 1$ and $k = 0$, at the high resolution. Once the most important edge points are selected, their phase is estimated by computing the phase of the Laguerre Gauss coefficients. The phase histogram is computed considering the range $[0, \pi]$ quantized in 36 steps of 5 degrees each one. As for the color vectors, the similarity measurement is computed by the Euclidean Distance, as follows

$$D_E = \sqrt{\sum_{i=1}^{36} \left(PH_i^f - PH_i^g\right)^2} \quad (3)$$

where PH_i^f is the ith element of the phase histogram computed on the image f.

2.4 Overall similarity

Each image is then represented by six vectors that have different meaning and different methods to perform the comparison. Generally, the overall similarity between two images is computed as follows

$$D_{tot} = \sum_{i=1}^{I} \delta_i D_i \quad (4)$$

where D_i denotes the similarity computed by using the ith feature, δ_i is a weight that tunes the importance given to the ith feature and I is the number of the features. In the classical approach it is necessary to find the correct values of δ_i to get the best performances, and this is a not trivial task. For this reason in the next section we propose a novel approach to fuse the results obtained by the use of the features in independent way.

3. PROPOSED APPROACH

3.1 Main idea

The content-based image retrieval systems are typically based on a query image, and the images in the dataset are ranked according to the similarity with it. The final ranking provided to the users depend on the query, on the similarity measurement and on the dataset. Indeed, when the query is not properly chosen to represent what the users are looking for, they are not satisfy by the ranking. Since the query is only an example, it could happen that the images not ranked in the first positions may be important from the users point of view, especially when the dataset is very large and heterogeneous. Finally, the similarity measurement is important to define if two images are similar or not. In this scenario a clustering algorithm, that groups relevant images into clusters, allows a better analysis of the results provided by the systems. The aim of this work is to fuse the results obtained by the clustering algorithm in which the similarity between two images is measured by using independently each feature. In [2] an overall metric were defined as shown in equation 4. As said in the previous section, this approach need to find the correct value of the weights δ_i. These values depend on the metric used for each feature and on the images belonging to the dataset. To overcame this drawback we first apply the clustering algorithm considering the feature one by one, and then we fuse the results to obtain the final set of clusters.

3.2 Clustering algorithm

In this work we use the clustering algorithm proposed in [2]. The algorithm can be summarized in three steps:

1. The images in the dataset are ranked according to the similarity with the query image. The first N images make up a set s_i. The value of the similarity between the query image and the Nth image is used to set the threshold th_1 in the next steps. This step is performed

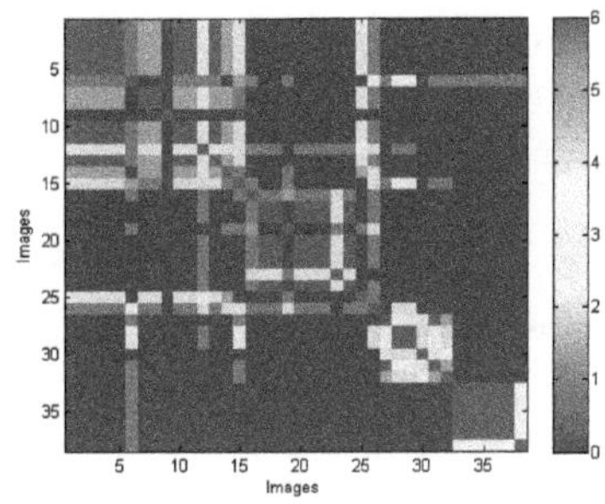

Figure 1: Example of probability matrix.

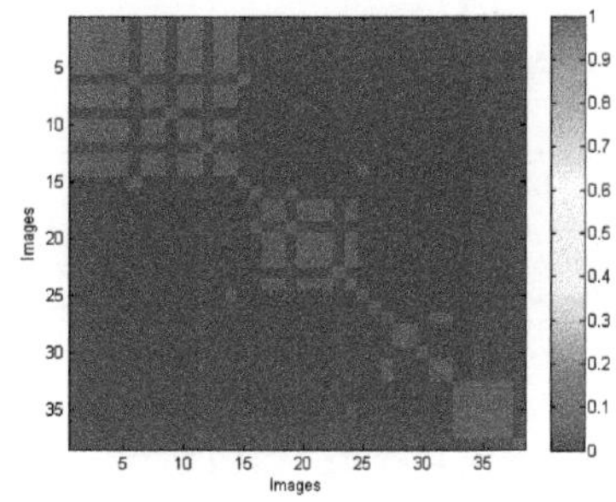

Figure 2: Thresholded version of the probability matrix shown in figure 1.

for each feature, at the end of this step the sets s_i are joint to get the set S.

2. The images belonging to the set S are ranked according to the last image of the set, and the most similar are grouped together. The images are considered similar if the similarity measure, computed by using the features one by one, is lower than the threshold th_1. This step is iterated until each image in S belong to a cluster. Furthermore, each cluster is represented with the features vectors computed by averaging the vectors of the images that belong to it.

3. The operations performed in the previous step are repeated to the clusters created at the end of the second step. The threshold th_1 is increased if no new cluster is created. This step ends when the number of clusters is higher than a value chosen by the users.

Since the second and the third steps are performed for each feature, we get six sets of clusters (*i.e.*, six is the number of the features) that need to be fused to create an unique set of clusters to show to the users.

3.3 Clustering Fusion based on BFS

The aim of the clustering fusion is to create an unique set of clusters from the six sets of clusters, obtained as it is explained in the previous section. The clustering fusion technique proposed in this work is made up of two steps. In the first step the results obtained by the clustering algorithm are analyzed and the probability matrix is built. Let $p(r, c)$ be the generic value of the probability matrix $\boldsymbol{P}$ in the position r, c. The generic element $p(r, c)$ of the matrix represents the probability that the rth image is put with the cth image. The six sets of clusters are analyzed one by one and the matrix $\boldsymbol{P}$ is updated. Indeed, the value of $p(r, c)$ is increased each time that the rth image and the cth image belong to the same cluster, [10]. If $p(r, c) = k$, where k denotes the number of the used features, the rth image and the cth image are put in the same cluster by considering every feature. An example of the probability matrix is shown in figure 1. By doing so we fuse the results obtained by considering the features one by one without using the equation 4, then avoiding to find the optimal values of δ_i. Once the probability matrix is built, it is thresholded to get a binary matrix, as shown in figure 2. This matrix can be seen as the representation of a graph and then can be analyzed by using the breadth first search algorithm. In this context the images with an high probability (*i.e.*, higher than the chosen value of minimum probability $p_{\min}$) to be put in the same cluster are linked. The BFS algorithm is used to find the connected images that are the final clusters. Indeed, starting from the first image the BFS algorithm explores the matrix to find all the images connected with it. These images make up the first final cluster and the connections related to these images are removed. This operations are repeated until all the connections on the matrix are removed.

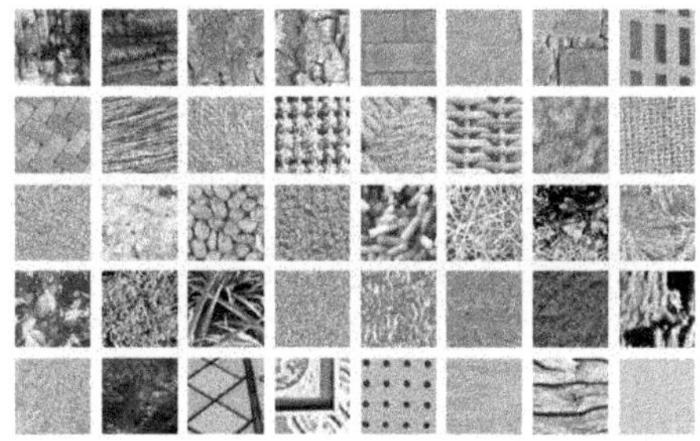

Figure 3: Examples of the images in the Vision Texture dataset.

4. EXPERIMENTAL RESULTS

The performances of the proposed technique are evaluated by using two different datasets. The first one is the Vision Texture [1] that is made up of 640 images divided in 40 classes, see figure 3. This dataset is used to allow a comparison with the results shown in [2]. The performances of the system are evaluated also by using a more complex dataset that was not used in [2]. It is a subset of the Corel dataset, made up of 9 classes with 16 elements each one, see figure 4. The experimental results are shown in table 1 and table 2. It is important to define that an impure cluster is a cluster containing at least one outsider, and an outsider is an image put in a wrong cluster. In table 1 the results obtained by the proposed method are compared with the results shown in [2] that use an overall metric to compare the images, see equation 4. In our method we have to set only the value of $p_{\min}$ used to obtain a binary matrix from the probability matrix $\boldsymbol{P}$. Since the features used are six, we set $p_{\min}$ equal to 5 and 6. Comparing the first and the second column of table 1 we can see that the average number of the outsiders in each cluster decreases in our method. Furthermore, we get the same average percentage of impure clusters but with an higher average number of clusters created, always very similar to the true average number of clusters (*i.e.*, the number

Figure 4: Examples of the classes belonging to the subset of Corel dataset used.

Table 1: Experimental results obtained by using the dataset shown in figure 3.

	Results of [2]	Our method ($p_{min} = 5$)	Our method ($p_{min} = 6$)
Average percentage of impure clusters	6.17%	6.14%	1.16%
Average outsiders in in each cluster	3.54	1.95	1.10
Average number of clusters created	5.74	8.22	9.34
True average number of clusters	4.63	7.07	5.96

of classes that are represented at least by one image in the set S). In the third column the performances improve but the ratio between the number of created clusters and the true number of cluster increases. Finally, the performances of the method are evaluated by using the dataset shown in figure 4, see table 2. Although, the dataset is more complicated the performances are quite good. It is important to notice that using our method no parameter need to be tuned.

5. CONCLUSIONS

In this work a novel technique to fuse clusters of images based on the BFS is presented. A set of relevant images is selected and its elements are grouped in clusters using the features one by one. These sets of clusters are fused together to obtain the final set of clusters. This leads to a completely unsupervised system that does not require the tuning of any parameter. The experimental results obtained are good for both of the used datasets. Indeed, the number of outsiders is always less than 2 for each cluster and the percentage of impure clusters created decreases as the number of features used increases. Furthermore, it is easily possible to add or to remove heterogeneous features (e.g., GPS data and textual annotation if available, EXIF data and so on) used to represent the images.

6. REFERENCES

[1] Mit, vision and modeling group. vision texture. In *http://vismod.media.mit.edu/pub/VisTex.*

[2] L. Costantini, L. Capodiferro, M. Carli, and A. Neri. A fair ranking method for image database retrieval. In *The first International Workshop on Living Web: Making Web Diversity a true asset*, 2009.

[3] L. Costantini, P. Sità, L. Capodiferro, and A. Neri. Laguerre gauss analysis for image retrieval based on color texture. In *IS&T SPIE Electronic Imaging Science and Technology*, 2010.

[4] I. J. Cox, M. Miller, T. P. Minka, T. Papathoman, and P. Yianilos. The bayesian image retrieval system: Pichunter theory, implementation and psychological experiments. *IEEE Transactions on Image Processing*, 9(1):20–37, 2000.

[5] M. N. Do and M. Vetterli. Wavelet-based texture retrieval using generalized gaussian density and kullback-leibler distance. *IEEE Transactions on Image Processing*, 11(2), 2002.

[6] H. Flickner, W. Sawhney, J. Niblack, Q. Ashley, Q. Huang, B. Dom, M. Gorkani, J. Hafner, D. Lee, D. Pettovic, D. Steele, and P. Anker. Querying by image and video content: The qbic system. *IEEE Transactions on Computers*, 28:23–32, 1995.

[7] Y. Herdiyeni, S. Nurdiati, and I. Daud. Image semantic extraction using latent semantic indexing on image retrieval automatic-annotation. In *Soft Computing and Pattern Recognition*, 2009.

[8] S. Wei, Y. Zhao, Z. Zhu, and N. Liu. Multimodal fusion for video search reranking. *IEEE Transactions on Knowledge and Data Engineering*, 22(8), August 2010.

[9] A. Yanagawa, W. Hsu, and S.-F. Chang. Brief descriptions of visual features for baseline trecvid concept detectors. In *ADVENT Technical Report 219-2006-5 Columbia University*, 2006.

[10] J. Zhang, J. Gao, M. Zhou, and J. Wang. Improving the effectiveness of information retrieval with clustering and fusion. *Computational Linguistics and Chinese Language Processing*, 6(1):109–125, February 2001.

[11] T. Zhang and Y. Fu. An image semantic retrieval system design and realization. In *International Conference on Machine Learning and Cybernetics*, 2005.

Table 2: Experimental results obtained by using the dataset shown in figure 4.

	$p_{min} = 5$	$p_{min} = 6$
Average percentage of impure clusters	20.32%	2.64%
Average outsiders in in each cluster	1.86	1.00
Average number of clusters created	6.41	4.94
True average number of clusters	4.19	3.17

Efficient Retrieval of 3D Building Models Using Embeddings of Attributed Subgraphs

Raoul Wessel
Computer Graphics Group,
University of Bonn, Germany
wesselr@cs.uni-bonn.de

Sebastian Ochmann
Computer Graphics Group,
University of Bonn, Germany
ochmann@cs.uni-bonn.de

Richard Vock
Computer Graphics Group,
University of Bonn, Germany
vock@cs.uni-bonn.de

Ina Blümel
TIB Hannover, Germany
ina.bluemel@tib.uni-hannover.de

Reinhard Klein
Computer Graphics Group,
University of Bonn, Germany
rk@cs.uni-bonn.de

ABSTRACT

We present a novel method for retrieval and classification of 3D building models that is tailored to the specific requirements of architects. In contrast to common approaches our algorithm relies on the interior spatial arrangement of rooms instead of exterior geometric shape. We first represent the internal topological building structure by a Room Connectivity Graph (RCG). To enable fast and efficient retrieval and classification with RCGs, we transform the structured graph representation into a vector-based one by introducing a new concept of subgraph embeddings. We provide comprehensive experiments showing that the introduced subgraph embeddings yield superior performance compared to state-of-the-art graph retrieval approaches.

Categories and Subject Descriptors: H.3.1 Information Storage and Retrieval: Content Analysis and Indexing; H.3.3 Information Storage and RetrievalInformation Search and Retrieval; I.3.m Computer GraphicsMiscellaneous; I.5.m Pattern RecognitionMiscellaneous

General Terms: Algorithms, Experimentation, Performance.

Keywords: Graph-based Retrieval, Bag-of-Features, 3D Object Retrieval.

1. INTRODUCTION

3D modeling has become a crucial ingredient of today's architectural design process. Despite numerous tools, creation of building models still remains a time consuming and expensive task, rendering reuse of existing models either for inspirational purposes or for integration into own drafts indispensable.To facilitate reutilization, efficient retrieval and classification strategies for building models are essential.

An important aspect in building retrieval is the interior building topology. We depict an early part of the planning process in Figure 1. Starting the preliminary design of a building with a given schedule of spaces (1a), architects arrange rooms and their connections in graphs representing topological structures (1b). These topologies strongly characterize buildings and express their internal organization [8]. In the next step, these abstract graphs are used as templates to develop concrete 2D floor plans, see Figure 1c (here overlaid with the 3D building models). Note that different floor plans can be generated out of the same schedule of spaces through early decisions concerning the topology and outer parameters like global building form. Rooms, their properties and groupings plus the chosen connections in between constitute certain structural patterns (see Section 3.2). Those patterns refer to building zones (e.g. private or public) and to building types [7].

Dwelling, 140 m^2			
Living room	up to 60 m^2	Kitchen	10 – 14 m^2
Room(s)	12 – 14 m^2	Eating	12 – 18 m^2
Bathroom	7 – 10 m^2	Storage/Utility	6 m^2
WC	3 m^2	Corridor	as required

(a)

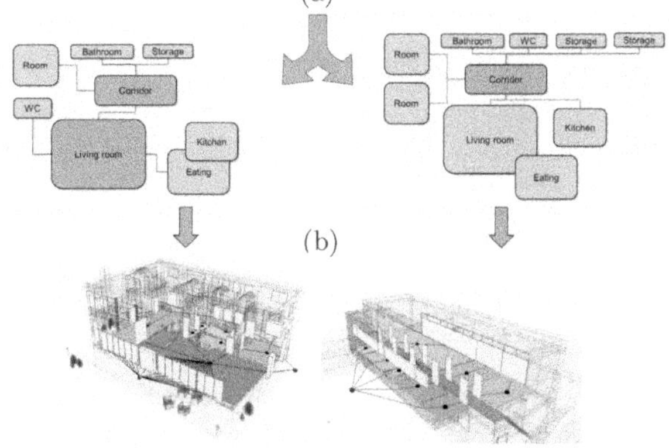

(b)

(c)

Figure 1: **Architectural design chain.** a) Schedule of spaces. b) Two possible arrangements of spaces. c) Resulting buildings with floor plans.

To enable efficient retrieval and classification of building models according to their internal structure, we use recently introduced Room Connectivity Graphs [14] as descriptors and suggest a new efficient retrieval method. It uses derived high-level room type attributes that closely resemble an architect's understanding of floor plans and a new vector-based representation of RCGs that is based on embeddings of attributed subgraphs. We compare the retrieval performance of our method to that achieved by human architecture experts. Results show that our approach using subgraph embeddings and high-level attributes is superior to other methods in terms of retrieval and classification performance with respect to our suggested classification scheme. Note that in this paper we focus on the presentation of achieved retrieval and classification results. For a thorough introduction to our newly introduced subgraph embeddings we refer to [15].

2. RELATED WORK

In the following we briefly summarize three important methods for attributed graph similarity computation.

Edit Distances The basic idea behind graph edit distances is to define graph dissimilarity by the minimum amount of deformation that is necessary to transform one graph into another [12]. Since determining the edit path is NP-hard [16], Riesen et al. [10] propose efficient approximate graph edit distances which are also an ingredient of our approach.

Graph Kernels Graph kernels [5] transfer techniques originating from statistical learning theory that are defined in terms of inner products to structured data. A common strategy in graph kernel design is to incorporate similarity of substructures like random walks, subtrees, cyclic patterns, or shortest paths [2, 4].

Graph Embeddings Graph embeddings transform structural graph data into a vector-based representation. A graph is thereby defined in terms of its similarity to a codebook of graphs. Riesen et al. [11] compute *Lipschitz embeddings* using approximate edit distance [10]. Approaches based on embeddings of subgraphs instead of complete graphs are presented in [1] and [9].

3. ROOM CONNECTIVITY GRAPHS

Following the description in [14], a RCG $G = (V, E)$ characterizes a single storey or a whole building according to the topology of the underlying floor plans. Attributed nodes $v_i \in V$ represent rooms. Interesting and useful room properties range from low-level geometric attributes like e.g. area, height, perimeter, to high-level semantic attributes like room type (corridor, distributor, balcony, etc.). Edges $e_j \in E$ represent connections between rooms. They can be assigned low-level attributes like width, height, or high-level attributes like connection type (door, staircase, etc.).

For our approach, we use the algorithm by Wessel et al. [14] for automatic extraction of RCGs and low-level geometric attributes from unstructured 3D polygon soups.

3.1 Low-level Attributes

Node Attributes For each room node $v \in V$, we represent the following room properties in a feature vector $a_{prop}(v)$: $Conn(v)$ denotes the relative number of doors in this room with respect to the total number of doors in the storey. It represents how much the room contributes to the connectivity of the storey. $A_{global}(v)$ globally characterizes the area of the room with respect to the area of the whole story, while $A_{local}(v)$ describes the area with respect to that of the surrounding rooms. The $has\_window(v)$ property is an indicator for the amenity value of the room, e.g. living rooms always contain windows while corridors or lumber-rooms are often windowless. The perimeter-to-area ratio $P2AR(v)$ is used to identify corridor-like rooms. In many cases, corridors serving as distributors in a storey are stretched relatively long but are not very wide. In contrast, rooms with high amenity value tend to be more square-shaped.

Edge Attributes As in this work we concentrate on single storeys, we only need to consider edges representing doors. It would be possible to additionally characterize doors by their properties in a similar way as the room property vector. However, as our data mostly consist of residential buildings, the diversity of doors is relatively small, which is why we do not represent them more detailed.

3.2 High-level Node Attributes

We introduce five classes of floor types that are of great importance to architectural planning processes because they notably comprehend the crucial question of room access and zoning of floors in interactive and private spaces. They follow common guidelines of this field, see e.g. [13].

Floor Types The `corridor type` (Figure 2a) is characterized by a corridor which is the dominant path through the storey. The corridor's only purpose is to connect rooms, it has no amenity value. The `distributor type` (2b) is similar to the corridor type. However, a large room instead of a corridor serves as the connecting element. This room is often the biggest one of the storey, with amenity values itself. In a `loft type` floor (2c), the whole storey mainly consists of one large room which can contain several adjustable zones with different functions. In a `hierarchical` floor (2d), there exists a separation between a dominant area which leads to further areas, where a second distribution is conducted. This second distribution can be either the previously defined corridor or distributor type. `Chain type` (2e) floors are characterized by *access rooms* that are arranged like a chain, so that the connection only exists between one space and the next.

Like Schneider [13] accurately described with the statement "After all, the truly exciting solutions often lie on the line between two or more of these categories[...]", it has to be taken into account that some of the floors cannot be assigned to a category with absolute certainty, neither by machine nor human classifiers.

Predicting Room Types The introduced floor classes can be easily described using architectural terms that characterize room types like corridor, access room, or distributor with amenity value. Our idea is to transform low-level geometric room attributes into high-level room types to better reflect an architect's understanding of floor plans and thereby to improve retrieval and classification performance. We identify corridors (C), distributors (D), access rooms (AR), and one-door spaces ($1S$) as high-level room types that are crucial for floor charaterization. To automatically derive the high-level room type from the extracted low-level attributes we use supervised learning. Let $\mathcal{L} = \{C, D, AR, 1S\}$ denote the set of room types. Suppose we have a training set of low-level room attributes with assigned labels $l(a_{prop}(v_i)) \in \mathcal{L}$. We then use a support vector machine (SVM) to learn a discriminant function that maps geometric room attributes to room type classes. For increased robustness, we assign the rooms in the testing set a vector a_{label} representing the predicted distribution over the room type labels rather than only the most likely one.

Ground Truth Generation For our learning approach we need ground truth, i.e. a set of low-level training attributes with assigned labels $l(a_{prop}(v_i))$ must be available.

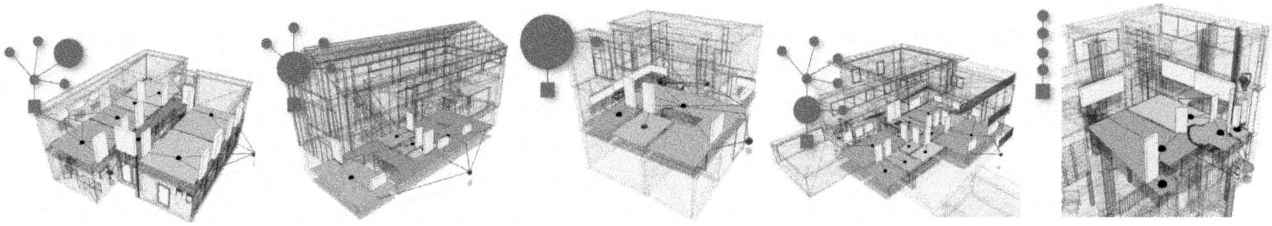

(a) corridor type (b) distributor type (c) loft type (d) hierarchical type (e) chain type

Figure 2: **Floor types.** Rooms serving as corridor or distributor are depicted in blue, all other rooms in green. Doors are visualized in yellow, windows in light blue. The pictograms in dark blue show ideal examples of the different room types.

A possible way would be to assign the labels manually. However, a training set of 100 RCGs can easily contain several thousand rooms, rendering this method cumbersome. We instead generate ground truth for a large number of rooms automatically. All graphs in the training set have been assigned to one of the classes described above. By that, we can infer the assignment of single nodes to room types: Rooms in the `corridor` class with high connectivity (more than two doors) are likely to be corridors; rooms in the `distributor` class with high connectivity (more than two doors) are likely to be distributors; rooms with exactly one door not belonging to the `loft` class are one-door spaces; rooms with exactly two doors not belonging to the `loft` class are access rooms.

Note that we do not assign labels to all rooms because of ambiguities. E.g., highly connected rooms in the `hierarchical` floor class might be either corridors or distributors, and the central room of a loft could be regarded as any of the above defined room types depending on its connectivity. Our assumptions are of course simplifications and only apply to RCGs that are perfectly and uniquely assignable to a single class, which is not the case for all of our data.

4. SUBGRAPH EMBEDDINGS

In the following we introduce the two building blocks for subgraph embedding, decomposition into subgraphs and codebook generation. We finally describe how to construct the vector-based RCG representation

Subgraph Mining Following the results on efficient subgraph mining presented in [6], we use two different sampling strategies, *Forest Fire (FF)* and *Random Walk (RW).* FF sampling patterns look similar to those of a spreading fire. RWs on the other hand rather reflect chain-like structures similar to those generated by depth-first search.

Codebook Generation We split the set of RCGs into a *training set* used for codebook generation and a *test set* used for evaluation. Note that all RCGs originating from different storeys of the same building are always included in either of the sets to avoid overfitting. We then sample a certain number of subgraphs from the samples in the training set and apply a k-medoid clustering using approximate edit distances [10] to generate the codebook graphs.

Subgraph Embeddings Consider a single RCG from the testing set. We first sample a number of n subgraphs in the above described way.We compute the approximate graph edit distance between each sampled subgraph and each codebook graph. Rather than characterizing subgraphs by their closest codebook graph, we describe them by a Gibbs distribution over the codebook for increased robustness leading to a Bag-of-Features representation.

5. EVALUATION

We evaluate our approach based on subgraph embeddings against three other strategies regarding retrieval performance. For *approximate graph edit distances*, we compute the distance between two RCGs based on the algorithm described in [10]. For *Lipschitz embeddings*, we split the set of graphs into a training set constituting the codebook and a test set.We compute the distance of all graphs in the test set to all codebook graphs using approximate edit distances, resulting in a vector of fixed length for each graph. The dissimilarity of two graphs is measured using the L_2 distance of the embeddings. We additionally evaluate the performance of *exponential random walk kernels* [2]. For our *subgraph embeddings*, we follow the description in Section 4 to compute a vector-based Bag-of-Features description for RCGs. Comparison of two RCGs is based on the L_2 distance of the embeddings. For more details on parameters for subgraph mining, codebook size and cross-validation we refer to [15].

Influence of Attributes For each method we evaluate low-level geometric attributes, high-level room types and the complete absence of room attributes. We additionally examine the influence of neglecting edges when evaluating approximate graph edit distances, such that only room similarity is considered during matching. Note however that low-level and high-level room attributes contain implicit knowledge about adjacent edges.

5.1 Results

Retrieval We first evaluate the retrieval performance of each method separately regarding the influence of attributes and topology, see precision-recall plots 3a-d. Note that for graph kernels (Figure 3c) we do not evaluate neglecting edges because construction of the adjacency matrix would not be possible. Using high-level room types instead of low-level attributes boosts the retrieval performance. We attribute this to the learned room types that are much closer to an architect's understanding of floor plans than its geometric properties alone. Incorporation of edges during the matching in general improves results to a performance that cannot not be achieved using nodes alone.

In 3e we compare all four methods using the individually best setting with high-level room types and edges. Taking into account that floors cannot be assigned to a category absolutely certain, we additionally provide the averaged retrieval performance achieved by three human classifiers all having an educational background in architecture. Approximate edit distances perform better than Lipschitz embeddings for small recall values, for larger recall this tendency is inverted, which is consistent with the results described in

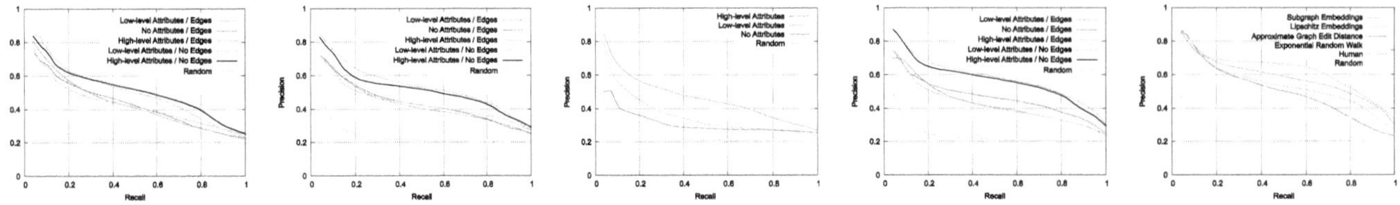

(a) Aproximate graph edit distances (b) Lipschitz embeddings (c) Exponential random walk kernels (d) Subgraph embeddings **(our method)** (e) Comparison of best performing strategies

Figure 3: **Retrieval results.** State-of-the-art methods (a-c), our own method (d), and comparison between all methods including human classifier preformance (e).

<table>
<tr><th></th><th>Lipschitz embeddings</th><th>Subgraph embeddings</th></tr>
<tr><td>Low-level attributes | no egdes</td><td>56.9 ± 2.4</td><td>61.1 ± 2.1</td></tr>
<tr><td>No attributes | edges</td><td>63.3 ± 3.7</td><td>63.4 ± 3.5</td></tr>
<tr><td>Low-level attributes | edges</td><td>64.9 ± 3.0</td><td>65.0 ± 3.6</td></tr>
<tr><td>High-level attributes | no edges</td><td>75.9 ± 2.9</td><td>78.0 ± 3.2</td></tr>
<tr><td>High-level attributes | edges</td><td>77.0 ± 3.9</td><td>79.5 ± 2.6</td></tr>
<tr><td>Human classifier</td><td colspan="2">79.1 ± 3.4</td></tr>
</table>

Table 1: **Classification results.** The table shows floor classification rates using graph embeddings and subgraph embeddings.

[11]. The exponential random walk kernel perform worst, except for quite large recall values it is superior to approximate edit distances. Our method using subgraph embeddings performs better than the three other methods, especially for increasing recall. The human classifiers' average retrieval performance is slightly worse than the automatic methods for small recall values but unambigously superior for recall values larger than 0.2. Human classifiers are always superior if no room types are learned.

Classification We additionally evaluate the classification performance of vector-based subgraph and Lipschitz embeddings using standard C-SVM with RBF kernel [3], see Table 1. For every feature setting, subgraph embeddings perform better than Lipschitz embeddings. Using predictions of room types based on geometric room attributes boosts the performance. Additionally, combining topology and predicted room types leads to better results than using only topology or only room attributes or their derived floor types.

6. CONCLUSION

We introduced a new approach for retrieval and classification of building models based on their internal structure that is represented by RCGs. The method adopts the Bag-of-Features paradigm and transfers it to structured data described by attributed subgraphs. We additionally proposed a method to substitute low-level geometric room attributes by high-level room type predictions. Our evaluation showed that our method using subgraph embeddings and high-level attributes results in improved retrieval and classification performance compared to three other methods.

Future work should investigate the extension from RCGs representing single storeys to graphs representing complete buildings. Analogously, the classification scheme should be extended to floor plan classes covering several storeys (e.g. maisonette, split-level). Additionally, the influence of further geometric attributes should be examined.

Acknowledgements This work was partially supported by the German Research Foundation (DFG) under grants KL 1142/8-2 and INST 1647/14-1 (`www.probado.de`).

7. REFERENCES

[1] E. Barbu, P. Héroux, S. Adam, and É. Trupin. Using bags of symbols for automatic indexing of graphical document image databases. In *Graphics Recognition (GREC)*, pages 195–205, 2005.

[2] K. M. Borgwardt. *Graph Kernels.* PhD thesis, Ludwig-Maximilians-University Munich, 2007.

[3] C.-C. Chang and C.-J. Lin. *LIBSVM: a library for support vector machines*, 2001. Software available at `http://www.csie.ntu.edu.tw/~cjlin/libsvm`.

[4] T. Gärtner. *Kernels for Structured Data.* PhD thesis, Universität Bonn, 2005.

[5] D. Haussler. Convolution kernels on discrete structures. Technical Report UCS-CRL-99-10, University of California at Santa Cruz, 1999.

[6] J. Leskovec and C. Faloutsos. Sampling from large graphs. In *Proceedings of the 12th ACM SIGKDD*, pages 631–636, New York, NY, USA, 2006. ACM.

[7] W. Meyer-Bohe. *Grundrisse öffentlicher Gebäude. Synoptische Gebäudetypologie.* Ernst & Sohn, 1997.

[8] W. J. Mitchell. *The Logic of Architecture: Design, Computation, and Cognition.* MIT Press, Cambridge, MA, USA, 1st edition, 1990.

[9] B. Özdemir and S. Aksoy. Image classification using subgraph histogram representation. In *Proceedings of ICPR '10*, pages 1112–1115, 2010.

[10] K. Riesen and H. Bunke. Approximate graph edit distance computation by means of bipartite graph matching. *Img. and Vis. Comp.*, 27(7):950–959, 2009.

[11] K. Riesen and H. Bunke. Graph classification by means of lipschitz embedding. *IEEE SMC Part B*, 39:1472–1483, December 2009.

[12] A. Sanfeliu and K. Fu. A distance measure between attributed relational graphs for pattern recognition. *IEEE SMC*, 13:353–362, 1983.

[13] F. Schneider. *Floor Plan Manual Housing.* Birkhäuser, third edition, April 2004.

[14] R. Wessel, I. Blümel, and R. Klein. The room connectivity graph. In *Proceedings of WSCG 2008*, Feb. 2008.

[15] R. Wessel, S. Ochmann, R. Vock, I. Blümel, and R. Klein. Efficient retrieval of 3d building models using embeddings of attributed subgraphs. Technical Report CG-2011-2, University of Bonn, Aug. 2011.

[16] Z. Zeng, A. K. H. Tung, J. Wang, J. Feng, and L. Zhou. Comparing stars. *Proceedings of the VLDB Endowment*, 2:25–36, August 2009.

Constructing Seminal Paper Genealogy

Duck-Ho Bae
Hanyang University
Seoul, Korea
dhbae@agape.hanyang.ac.kr

Se-Mi Hwang
Hanyang University
Seoul, Korea
semi@agape.hanyang.ac.kr

Sang-Wook Kim
Hanyang University
Seoul, Korea
wook@hanyang.ac.kr

Christos Faloutsos
Carnegie Mellon University
Pittsburgh, PA, USA
christos@cs.cmu.edu

ABSTRACT

When a researcher starts with a new topic, it would be very useful if seminal papers in the topic and their relationships are provided in advance. We propose an approach to construct seminal paper genealogy and show the effectiveness and efficiency of our approach.

Categories and Subject Descriptors

H.4 [**Information Systems Applications**]: Miscellaneous

General Terms

Algorithms, Measurement, Design

Keywords

Seminal Paper Finding, Paper Genealogy Construction

1. INTRODUCTION

When a researcher starts with a new topic, she or he faces the problem of literature survey for the topic. This requires her or him to spend a considerable amount of time for searching for *high-quality* and *relevant* papers from conferences, journals, or scholar search engines. For doing literature survey, it is also important to understand a *research trend* which gives us insight on the topic. If one grasps the research trend in the topic by thorough literature survey, she or he will predict the future research direction well, and thus will perform successful researches. However, during the literature survey, it is extremely difficult to catch such a trend because the coverage of survey could be limited and/or the understanding of the topic could be insufficient.

Therefore, it is crucial to identify seminal papers in a research topic in question and the relationships among them. The construction of *seminal paper genealogy* will reduce the efforts of literature survey greatly and will enable to easily catch the trend of the research domain. More specifically, in this paper, we address two problems: (1) finding the seminal papers and (2) constructing their genealogy automatically from a set of papers belonging to the same topic. We first suggest the four goals for seminal paper finding and propose a novel method that makes them satisfied (Section 2). Second, we identify two requirements of an influence measure for paper genealogy and examine the characteristics of candidates for being used as our influence measure and their applicability to our seminal paper genealogy (Section 3). Finally, we verify the effectiveness and efficiency of our proposed approach through extensive experiments (Section 4).

CIKM'11, October 24–28, 2011, Glasgow, Scotland, UK.

2. SEMINAL PAPER FINDING

2.1 Goals for Finding Seminal Papers

A seminal paper could be an old paper that is highly original and thus is cited by a lot of papers for a long time. On the other hand, it also could be a root of a recent trend and recognized as a rising star. The following is our list of goals in those finding seminal papers.

- *Goal 1: Find such papers cited by many papers and/or highly cited papers.* If a paper p is cited by a number of papers and/or highly cited papers, it means that p is a high-quality paper and thus has a great impact on the topic.
- *Goal 2: Find such papers cited a lot by relevant papers in the same topic.* The papers in the same topic published after a paper p have responsibility to cite p if p is authoritative and relevant to them. If they did not cite p, it means that the quality or importance of p in the topic is not that significant.
- *Goal 3: Find such papers cited by the papers that are published much later.* Authors do not want to miss *recent* papers in the reference section of their papers if it is authoritative and relevant to their papers. In this situation, if authors cite an old paper at the time of their writing, this indicates that the old paper is regarded very important. Therefore, a paper is considered seminal if it is cited by many relevant papers that were published much later.
- *Goal 4: Include young seminal papers even though they do not get a lot of citations from other papers.* Normally, recent papers have a chance to get citations much less than old papers because only a small number of papers are published after them. So, they are unlikely to be included as seminal papers if a simple citation-based method is employed[7][9]. However, the inclusion of such recent papers in a set of seminal papers enables users to understand a recent research trend.

2.2 Seminality Score

A *seminality score* of a paper is a score that measures the degree of how much the paper satisfies the four goals mentioned in Section 2.1. We have a citation graph, where nodes represent papers belonging to a given topic and edges do citations among them: i.e., if a paper p_1 cites another paper p_2, a directed edge from p_1 to p_2 appears in the graph. By analyzing the graph, we get seminality scores of all the papers. Because we want interpretable results and thus prefer a probabilistic framework, our method is based on the *Random Walk with Restart* (RWR)[7].

RWR successfully determines the authority of a paper in the citation graph. Therefore, this RWR-based computation for the seminality score makes Goal 1 of seminal paper finding satisfied.

Equation 1 shows the concept of RWR[7].

$$\vec{r} = (1-c)W\vec{r} + c\vec{e} \tag{1}$$

where W is an $n \times n$ row-normalized citation matrix, $\vec{e}$ is an $n \times 1$ restart vector with $e_i = 1/n$, c is a restart probability, and $\vec{r}$ is an $n \times 1$ seminality score vector.

In order to achieve Goal 2, we propose two solutions. First, we introduce a new notion of *customized RWR* (cRWR), which is a method of computing a seminality score for a *single* paper i. We change restart vector $\vec{e}^{(i)}$ in cRWR to be sensitive to the similarity of other papers to paper i instead of uniform distribution that is employed in the original RWR. Namely, for paper i, we employ a customized $\vec{e}^{(i)}$ in RWR-based computation. Here,

$$e_j^{(i)} = sim(i,j)/Z \tag{2}$$

where $sim(i,j)$ is a similarity between paper i and paper j, and Z ($= \sum_{k \in N} sim(i,k)$, *where N is a set of all the papers in the topic*) is a normalization factor.

As a result, owing to customized $\vec{e}^{(i)}$, cRWR accumulates a more seminality score (i.e., more honored) for paper i when it is cited by *relevant* papers rather than by non-relevant papers.

Second, we change citation matrix W based on the similarity between citing and cited papers as follows:

$$W_{i,j} = sim(i,j) \;/ \sum_{k \in CitedBy(i)} sim(i,k) \tag{3}$$

where $CitedBy(i)$ is a set of all the papers cited by paper i. With this modification, when a paper distributes its score to its citing papers, it gives a larger score to a more relevant paper. Thus, paper i gets a high score when it receives citations from many relevant papers. As a result, the two solutions make Goal 2 satisfied.

To achieve Goal 3, we reflect the difference of publication years between two papers in restart vector $\vec{e}^{(i)}$. We adopt an exponential growth function to give some incentive to a pair of papers of a large difference in publication years. The modified restart vector is as follows:

$$e_j^{(i)} = \left\{ sim(i,j) * e^{|yr(i)-yr(j)|/t} \right\}/Z \tag{4}$$

where $yr(i)$ is the publication year of paper i, and t is a scaling parameter that needs to be tuned to get a suitable value.

By using the exponential growth function, $\vec{e}_j^{(i)}$ becomes higher when the difference of publication years between papers i and j gets larger. Thus, paper i gets a high seminality score when it receives many citations from the papers having long temporal-distance from it, which implies Goal 3 is satisfied.

Finally, to find young seminal papers (Goal 4), we modify restart vector $\vec{e}^{(i)}$ in such a way that the restart probabilities of the papers published before paper i are set to 0 as in Equation 5. This makes all the papers take part in a fair competition regardless of their ages: (1) Old papers have a lot of following papers that are published after them and thus can cite them. Therefore, the customized restart vector $\vec{e}^{(i)}$ of old paper i has a lot of small probability values. As a result, old paper i cannot get a high seminality score unless it is cited by most papers published after it. (2) Recent papers, on the other hand, have a few papers published after them and can get a high seminality score if they are cited by a few papers published after them relatively. Thus, a seminality score of paper i is greatly affected by the *ratio* of the papers that are able to cite paper i to the papers that actually cite paper i instead of the *absolute number* of papers that cite paper i. Therefore, Goal 4 can be satisfied.

$$\begin{aligned} e_j^{(i)} &= \left\{ sim(i,j) * e^{|yr(i)-yr(j)|/t} \right\}/Z \quad \text{if } yr(i) \le yr(j) \\ e_j^{(i)} &= 0 \quad \text{otherwise} \end{aligned} \tag{5}$$

3. CONSTRUCTING GENEALOGY

3.1 Overview

A paper is influenced by some papers that have been previously published, which is represented in the form of its citations. However, the degrees of influence of the cited papers on a citing paper are different[1]. In this paper, we model the influence relationship of two papers as a *parent-child relationship*: A parent paper p has a great influence on a child paper c. A *genealogy* is defined as a set of all parent-child relationships among seminal papers in a topic.

We adopt the *Markovian assumption* which is employed in [1]. The authors are sure to cite the papers having a significant influence on their paper. Therefore, in finding the parent-child relationship, it is sufficient to consider those pairs of papers having a citation relationship only, rather than all the possible pairs of papers.

The procedure of constructing genealogy is sketched as follows: For every paper c, we do Step 1 through Step 3.

- **Step 1.** For a paper c, we measure an influence score from every paper p cited by paper c. The paper p is considered as a candidate parent paper.
- **Step 2.** Among candidate parent papers, we select the top m papers having the largest influence scores as the final parent papers of child paper c.
- **Step 3.** we draw directed links from the parent papers to child paper c.

3.2 Influence Score

The *influence score* of a parent paper p to a child paper c indicates the degree of paper c is influenced by paper p. The influence score can be measured in diverse ways. However, to understand the influence between citing and cited papers, the influence measure should satisfy the following requirements.

- *Requirement 1: It should reflect the strength of the influence correctly.* If a cited paper has a great influence on a citing paper, the score between the two papers should appear to be high. On the contrary, it should be low if the two papers are unrelated or not influenced by each other.
- *Requirement 2: It should consider the temporal-distance between citing and cited papers.* If the difference of their publication years is large, the degree of influence between the two papers should be small because there are other more influencial papers published during the time window between the two years. So, it is desirable to penalize the influence score when the difference of publication years is large.

We decided to use text-based[2] or link-based[3][8][10] similarity as our candidate influence measure. The reasoning behind this decision is that if a child paper c was influenced by a parent paper p, then their texts and/or citations should be similar to each other to some degree.

Here, we discuss which of them is appropriate for being used as our influence score. The degree of influence between two papers is well evaluated in all the similarity measures. If a paper c was influenced by another paper p, these two papers are meant to deal with the same issue. So, their texts have a number of common terms. Similarly, they also have common citations. Therefore, Requirement 1 is satisfied with all the similarity measures.

In Requirement 2, text-based similarity measures do not take the temporal-distance between papers into account at all, and thus cannot satisfy Requirement 2. On the other hand, link-based similarity measures consider the temporal-distance. Because authors tend to cite recent quality papers in a topic, old and young papers have different sets of citations even though they deal with the same issue. The similarity between two papers becomes small in this case. Thus, link-based similarity measures satisfy Requirement 2.

4. EXPERIMENTS

4.1 Environment for Experiments

For experiments, we used 1,071,973 papers in DBLP dataset[5] downloaded on March, 2009 and extracted their citation information from Libra[1]. We first found seminal papers and then constructed their genealogy on three well-known topics of clustering, association rules, and graph mining. The ground truth for seminal papers was extracted from the reference section of each topic in a well-known data mining textbook[2].

4.2 Finding Seminal Papers

We measured the *Mean Average Precision* (MAP) of three different paper ranking methods, RWR[7], PopRank[6], and our Seminal Paper Finding (SPF). We conducted 3-fold cross validation for parameter tuning of previous ranking methods. As a result, the parameter c was set to 0.5 for previous ranking methods which was shown to provide the best performance. The parameters for our SPF method were set to $c = 0.5$ and $t = 2.6$.

The results are shown in Table 1. Our proposed method performs better than any other methods. This is because SPF method performs much better in finding recent seminal papers (Table 2 clearly shows this result).

Table 1: MAP scores of three different methods

	RWR	PopRank	SPF
MAP	0.589	0.627	0.670

We also measured the recall at top 30 to evaluate the performance of each method in finding recent papers. Table 2 shows the results. Our SPF method finds both old and recent seminal papers very well and its recall is higher than those of any other methods. Although the recall of SPF in old papers is slightly lower than those of RWR, it boosts recall levels a lot in recent papers.

We did qualitative evaluation for our SPF method. We present only the result of the SPF method on a clustering topic due to the limited space. Table 3 shows the list of the top 20 seminal papers sorted by the publication year. Our method found not only old seminal papers such as CLARANS (#1), DBSCAN (#3), and BIRCH (#4), but also relatively recently-published papers such as Chameleon (#13), LOF (#16), and Data Streams (#19 and #20).

[1]http://academic.research.microsoft.com/

Table 2: Recall scores of three different methods

	RWR	PopRank	SPF
Old	0.726	0.660	0.711
Recent	0.239	0.336	0.435
Average	0.483	0.498	0.573

4.3 Constructing Paper Genealogy

Due to the space limitations, we show only the genealogy on the clustering topic. First, we found 20 seminal papers, shown in Table 3, and then constructed genealogy using Inter-Connection[10], the state-of-the-art link-based similarity method for scientific literature, with the most significant parent-child relationship only as shown in Figure 1.

Figure 1(a) shows the genealogy using Inter-Connection, which satisfies all our requirements. The genealogy of the clustering topic originates from Paper #1 in our database. As time goes by, the topic was developed into several sub-topics such as density-based clustering (#3 and #11), hierarchical clustering (#4, #8, and #18), high dimensional clustering (#7 and #12), outlier detection (#9 and #16), and data stream clustering (#14, #20, #18, and #19).

Because Inter-Connection can reflect the temporal-distance, two papers could be in parent-child relationship when their publication years are close to each other. This contributes to producing a nice genealogy. Even when the temporal-distance between two papers is large, however, Inter-Connection could connect them by a parent-child relationship if they have a strong influence relationship. The connection between Papers #3 and #11 (both address density-based clustering) shows this example.

Figure 1(b) shows the genealogy using Cosine similarity[2]. Different from the genealogy using Inter-Connection, the genealogy originated from two papers (#1 and #2). Because Cosine similarity does not consider the temporal-distance between two papers, it directly connects Paper #11 to Paper #1 (the origin) instead of Paper #3 that has a great influence on Paper #11 and was published later than Paper #1.

In summary, Inter-Connection (link-based similarity method) performs better than Cosine similarity (text-based similarity method) in constructing seminal paper genealogy. On the other two topics, we performed the same experiments and obtained similar results.

5. RELATED WORK

Ranking Ranking is one of the most important issues in the scientific literature domain. Unlike the ranking algorithms for web pages such as PageRank[7] and HITS[4] that only use hyperlinks, ranking algorithms for academic and scientific literature try to use information such as authors and publication venues in addition to the citation information in order to measure the authority of a paper more accurately. Browsing-based model[9] and PopRank[6] utilize the author-paper relationships in ranking in addition to the citation relationships. Furthermore, PopRank considers additional publication venue-paper relationships.

Similarity measure The similarity measures can be classified into two categories: (1) text-based measures that consider the terms contained in the title, abstract, keywords, and body of a paper as features of the paper in similarity computation[2], and (2) link-based measures that consider the papers commonly *cited by* or *citing* a pair of papers in computing similarity of the two papers[3][8][10]

Table 3: Top 20 seminal papers found on the clustering topic

No.	Title	Publisher	Year
1	Efficient and Effective Clustering Methods for Spatial Data Mining	VLDB	1994
2	A Database Interface for Clustering in Large Spatial Databases	KDD	1995
3	A Density-Based Algorithm for Discovering Clusters in Large Spatial Databases with Noise	KDD	1996
4	BIRCH: An Efficient Data Clustering Method for Very Large Databases	SIGMOD	1996
5	STING: A Statistical Information Grid Approach to Spatial Data Mining	VLDB	1997
6	Scaling Clustering Algorithms to Large Databases	KDD	1998
7	Automatic Subspace Clustering of High Dimensional Data for Data Mining Applications	SIGMOD	1998
8	CURE: An Efficient Clustering Algorithm for Large Databases	SIGMOD	1998
9	Algorithms for Mining Distance-Based Outliers in Large Datasets	VLDB	1998
10	Extensions to the k-Means Algorithm for Clustering Large Data Sets with Categorical Values	DMKD	1998
11	OPTICS: Ordering Points To Identify the Clustering Structure	SIGMOD	1999
12	Fast Algorithms for Projected Clustering	SIGMOD	1999
13	Chameleon: Hierarchical Clustering using Dynamic Modeling	IEEE Computer	1999
14	Clustering Data Streams: Theory and Practice	IEEE TKDE	2000
15	Biclustering of Expression Data	ISMD	2000
16	LOF: Identifying Density-Based Local Outliers	SIGMOD	2000
17	NiagaraCQ: A Scalable Continuous Query System for Internet Databases	SIGMOD	2000
18	ROCK: A Robust Clustering Algorithm for Categorical Attributes	Inf. Syst.	2000
19	Models and Issues in Data Stream Systems	PODS	2002
20	A Framework for Clustering Evolving Data Streams	VLDB	2003

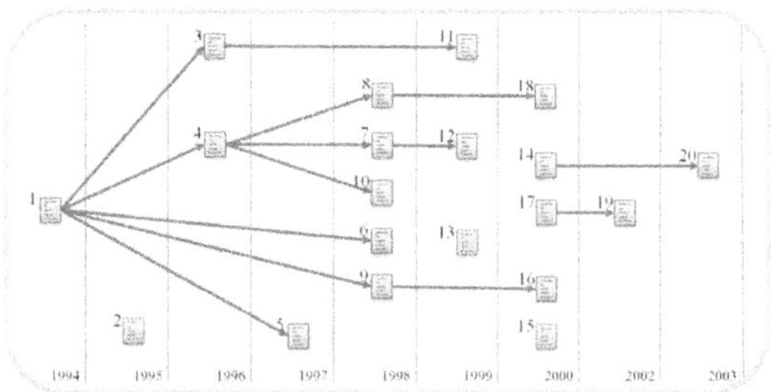

(a) Inter-Connection.

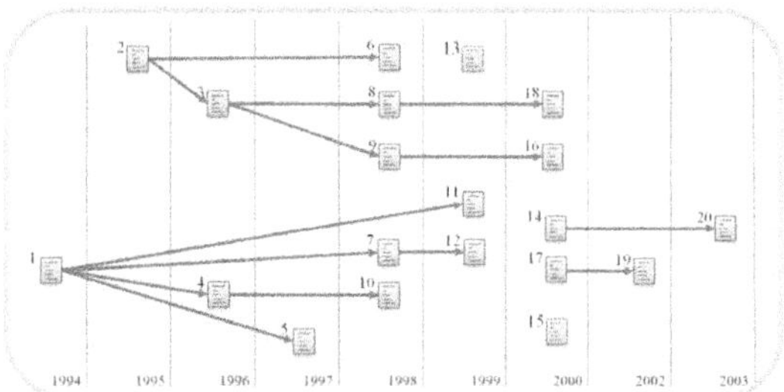

(b) Cosine similarity.

Figure 1: Seminal paper genealogy on the clustering topic.

6. CONCLUSIONS

In this paper, we proposed effective and efficient solutions to the problem of constructing seminal paper genealogy: (1) We formulated the problem of constructing seminal paper genealogy. (2) We proposed a novel algorithm for finding seminal papers in the framework of RWR. (3) We addressed influence scores among papers and proposed a method for genealogy construction by using them. (4) We verified the effectiveness and efficiency of the proposed methods by conducting extensive experiments.

7. ACKNOWLEDGE

This research was supported by the MKE(The Ministry of Knowledge Economy), Korea, under the Convergence-ITRC(Convergence Information Technology Research Center) support program (NIPA-2011-C6150-1101-0001) supervised by the NIPA(National IT Industry Promotion Agency), the National Research Foundation of Korea(NRF) grant funded by the Korea government(MEST) (No. 2008-0061006), and NHN Corp. Any opinions, findings, and conclusions or recommendations expressed in this material are the authors' and do not necessarily reflect those of the sponsors.

8. REFERENCES

[1] L. Dietz, S. Bickel, and T. Scheffer, "Unsupervised Prediction of Citation Influences," In *Proc. Int'l Conf. on Machine Learning*, ICML, pp. 233-244, 2007.

[2] J. Han and M. Kamber, *Data Mining: Concepts and Techniques(2nd Edition)*, Morgan Kaufmann, 2006.

[3] M. Kessler, "Bibliographic Coupling between Scientific Papers," *Journal of the American Documentation*, Vol. 14, No. 1, pp. 10-25, 1963.

[4] J. Kleinberg, "Authoritative Sources in a Hyperlinked Environment," *Journal of the ACM*, Vol. 46, No. 5, pp. 604-632, 1999.

[5] M. Ley, "DBLP: Some Lessons Learned," In *Proc. Int'l Conf. on Very Large DataBases*, VLDB, pp. 1493-1500, 2009.

[6] Z. Nie et al., "Object-Level Ranking: Bringing Order to Web Objects," In *Proc. Int'l Conf. of World Wide Web*, WWW, pp. 567-574, 2005.

[7] L. Page et al., The PageRank Citation Ranking: Bringing Order to the Web, *Technical Report*, Standford University, 1999.

[8] H. Small, "Co-citation in the Scientific Literature: A New Measure of the Relationship between Two Documents," *Journal of the American Society for Information Science*, Vol. 24, No. 4, pp. 265-269, 1973.

[9] S. Yan and D. Lee, "Toward Alternative Measures for Ranking Venues: a Case of Database Research Community," In *Proc. Int'l Conf. on Digital Libraries*, JCDL, 2007.

[10] S. Yoon, S. Kim, and S. Park, "A Link-based Similarity Measure for Scientific Literature," In *Proc. Int'l Conf. of World Wide Web*, WWW, pp. 1213-1214, 2010.

Leveraging Wikipedia Concept and Category Information to Enhance Contextual Advertising

Zongda Wu
Wenzhou University, China
zongda1983@163.com

Guandong Xu
Victoria University, Australia
guandong.xu@vu.edu.au

Rong Pan
Aalborg University, Denmark
rpan@cs.aau.dk

Yanchun Zhang
Victoria University, Australia
yanchun.zhang@vu.edu.au

Zhiwen Hu
Wenzhou University, China
sunneyhu@gmail.com

Jianfeng Lu
Zhejiang Normal University
lujianfeng@zjnu.cn

ABSTRACT

As a prevalent type of Web advertising, contextual advertising refers to the placement of the most relevant ads into a Web page, so as to increase the number of ad-clicks. However, some problems of homonymy and polysemy, low intersection of keywords etc., can lead to the selection of irrelevant ads for a page. In this paper, we present a new contextual advertising approach to overcome the problems, which uses Wikipedia concept and category information to enrich the content representation of an ad (or a page). First, we map each ad and page into a keyword vector, a concept vector and a category vector. Next, we select the relevant ads for a given page based on a similarity metric that combines the above three feature vectors together. Last, we evaluate our approach by using real ads, pages, as well as a great number of concepts and categories of Wikipedia. Experimental results show that our approach can improve the precision of ads-selection effectively.

Categories and Subject Descriptors

H.3.3 [**Information Storage and Retrieval**]: Information Search and Retrieval

General Terms

Algorithms, Experimentation, Theory

1. INTRODUCTION

PwC[1] predicts that Web advertising will become the 2nd largest advertising medium in America after television within the next 4 years, and its spending will increase from 24.2 billion dollars in 2009 to 34.4 billion dollars in 2014. As an important type of Web advertising, contextual advertising aims to embed the most relevant ads into a page, so as to increase the number of ad-clicks. Most contextual advertising approaches were based on the keyword matching, which estimated the ad relevance based on the co-occurrence of the same keywords between pages and ads [1, 2]. However, as pointed out in [3, 4], the keyword matching may lead to the problems such as homonymy and polysemy, low intersection of keywords, and context mismatch, consequently, degrading its effectiveness.

To solve these problems, in the area of text classification, a new approach called Wikipedia matching was proposed in [5, 6, 7], which uses Wikipedia, the largest knowledge base, as a reference model to enrich the content representation of text documents, so as to improve the accuracy of similarity computation among documents. It was then applied into contextual advertising in [4], and has been proved its effectiveness on solving the problems encountered in the keyword matching. However, this approach may lead to the following problems that decrease its effectiveness in practical contextual advertising. (1) Its limited coverage over semantic concepts. To enhance performance, it only chooses a small part of articles from Wikipedia as a reference model. As a result, for many pages not properly characterized by the reference articles, it is impossible to find out the articles that share the same topics with the pages, thus, leading to the returning of irrelevant ads for the pages. (2) Its time-consuming performance. To solve the limited coverage over semantics, a very straightforward way is to choose a sufficient number of reference articles from Wikipedia. However, this will result in a seriously decreased performance, because the time spending of fulltext matching between all the reference articles and the ads (or pages) is very high.

In order to better balance effectiveness and efficiency, we in this paper present a new contextual advertising approach by combining Wikipedia knowledge with the keyword matching, which considers two aspects of similarity between ads and pages, where the keyword-based similarity captures the textual commonness, while the Wikipedia-based similarity measures the relatedness from the semantic perspectives of concepts and categories. Its process consists of the following three steps. First, we choose a sufficient number of articles from Wikipedia, to cover as many concepts as possible. Next, we map each ad (as well as each page) into a keyword

[1]PricewaterhouseCoopers - http://www.pwc.com

CIKM'11, October 24–28, 2011, Glasgow, Scotland, UK.

vector, a concept vector and a category vector. Last, combining the three feature vectors together, we make the top-N ads selection. The experimental results show that our approach can improve the accuracy of ads selection effectively. And, due to avoiding time-consuming fulltext matching between all the reference articles and the pages (or ads), our approach also obtains a good running performance.

2. RELATED WORK

The keyword matching approach estimated the ad relevance by analyzing the co-occurrence of the same keywords within ads and within pages. One of the recent results on applying the keyword matching into contextual advertising was presented in [2], whose main idea was to use a technique called "Impedance Coupling Strategy" to augment a page with additional keywords from other similar pages, so as to overcome the problem of low intersection of keywords between pages and ads. Under the assumption that an ad can be seen as a noisy translation of a page, it was proposed in [8] to select the ads that provide the best translation for a page. In [9], it was proposed to leverage sentiment detection to improve contextual advertising. In [10], the authors proposed to use lexical graphs created from web corpora as a means of computing improved content similarity metrics between ads and pages. However, as pointed out in [4, 5, 6], the main drawback of the keyword matching approach is that it may lead to the problems of homonymy and polysemy etc., resulting in degrading the relevance of selected ads to their pages.

For solving the problems of homonymy and polysemy etc., the Wikipedia matching was proposed, whose main idea is to leverage the Wikipedia as an intermediate reference model to enhance the semantic representation of text documents and thus improve the precision of similarity measure among documents. In [4], a solution to contextual advertising was proposed by using the Wikipedia matching. In this solution, a group of reference articles is first chosen from Wikipedia. Next, through using the articles as the intermediate reference model on which the ads and the page is re-expressed as feature vectors, the ads that exhibit more relevance to a targeted page are determined, and a ranking function to select the most relevant ads to the page is constructed. In [5, 6, 7], a similar method was proposed aiming to textual document clustering. It was proposed in [11] to use Wikipedia to understand a user's query intent, without the need to collect large quantities of examples to train an intent classifier. However, the main drawback of the traditional Wikipedia matching is due to the problems that we have mentioned in Section 1 (i.e., the problems of limited coverage of semantic concepts and time-consuming performance) can dramatically degrade the relevance of selected ads with their pages.

3. METHODOLOGY

Figure 1 shows the framework of our approach to improving contextual advertising using the Wikipedia knowledge, where each ad or page is mapped into a keyword vector, a concept vector and a category vector, and then the three vectors are combined together to measure the similarity between a page and an ad. This process is similar to that used in [6] for clustering, but has a different way for constructing concept vector and category vector. We below introduce how to construct such two types of feature vectors.

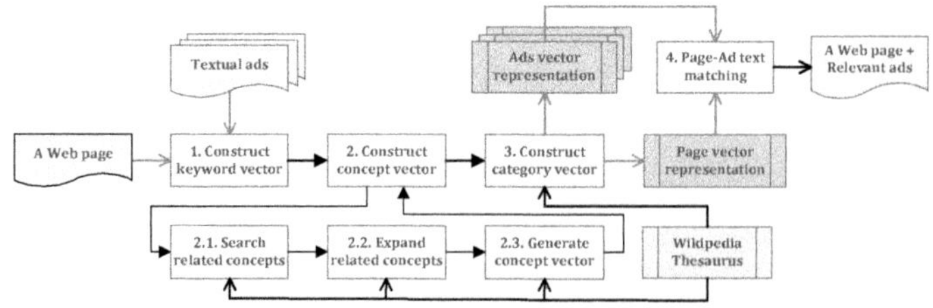

Figure 1: Contextual advertising framework

3.1 Constructing Concept Vector

As shown in Figure 1, the process of generating a concept vector includes the following three steps: (1) search related concepts appearing in an ad (or a page); (2) add concepts semantically related to the previous ones; and (3) generate a concept vector based on the frequency values of the concepts that are semantically related to the ad. We below introduce these steps, respectively.

(1) Searching Related Concepts. This step aims to determine a set of related concepts for an ad (or a page) and to count their frequency values in the ad. First, we scan a given ad to find all the Wikipedia titles that appear in the ad. Such titles are called related titles, and the concepts associated with them are called related concepts. We search related titles using a similar method mentioned in [7]. Once we determine a set of titles related to an ad, actually, we determine a set of concepts related to the ad. Next, we compute the frequency of each related concept to the ad. Let $\mathbf{count}(\boldsymbol{t}, \boldsymbol{a})$ be the frequency of a related title $\boldsymbol{t}$ appearing in a page $\boldsymbol{a}$, which is determined above. Let $\mathbf{cots}(\boldsymbol{t})$ be a set of concepts associated with the title $\boldsymbol{t}$, i.e., each of which satisfying that at least one of its titles is identical to $\boldsymbol{t}$. Then, the frequency of occurrences of any concept $\boldsymbol{c}$ related to $\boldsymbol{t}$ in $\boldsymbol{a}$ is computed as follows: if $\boldsymbol{t}$ is not a title of the concept $\boldsymbol{c}$, then $\mathbf{count}(\boldsymbol{c}, \boldsymbol{t}, \boldsymbol{a}) = 0$; and otherwise,

$$\mathbf{count}(\boldsymbol{c}, \boldsymbol{t}, \boldsymbol{a}) = \left(\frac{\mathbf{sim^k}(\boldsymbol{c}, \boldsymbol{a})}{\sum_{c' \in \mathbf{cots}(\boldsymbol{t})} \mathbf{sim^k}(c', \boldsymbol{a})} \right) \cdot \mathbf{count}(\boldsymbol{t}, \boldsymbol{a})$$

where $\mathbf{sim^k}(\boldsymbol{c}, \boldsymbol{a})$ denotes the similarity between $\boldsymbol{a}$ and $\boldsymbol{c}$ computed using the traditional keyword matching.

In Wikipedia, a concept may have several titles [11], and thus to count the actual frequency of occurrences of a concept in a given ad, we need to sum up the frequency value of the concept related to each one of its titles appearing in the ad. Let $\mathbf{titles}(\boldsymbol{a})$ be all the titles appearing in an ad $\boldsymbol{a}$ (i.e., the related titles of $\boldsymbol{a}$). Then, the frequency of any concept $\boldsymbol{c}$ appearing in $\boldsymbol{a}$ is computed as follows:

$$\mathbf{count}(\boldsymbol{c}, \boldsymbol{a}) = \sum\nolimits_{\boldsymbol{t} \in \mathbf{titles}(\boldsymbol{a})} \mathbf{count}(\boldsymbol{c}, \boldsymbol{t}, \boldsymbol{a})$$

Now, we determine a set $\mathbf{C}(\boldsymbol{a}) = \{\mathbf{count}(\boldsymbol{c}_j, \boldsymbol{a})\}_{j=1}^{N_a^c}$, consisting of frequency of each related concept in an ad $\boldsymbol{a}$, where N_a^c is the number of related concepts in $\boldsymbol{a}$. Similarly, we determine a set $\mathbf{C}(\boldsymbol{p}) = \{\mathbf{count}(\boldsymbol{c}_j, \boldsymbol{p})\}_{j=1}^{N_p^c}$ for a page $\boldsymbol{p}$.

(2) Expanding Related Concepts. There are fewer keywords in an ad $\boldsymbol{a}$ than a generic document, due to its limited size, so $\mathbf{C}(\boldsymbol{a})$ is of a smaller size, resulting in the decreased precision of similarity computation between pages and ads. However, two Wikipedia concepts are hyperlinked to each other, generally, denoting that the two concepts are semantically related to each other [11]. So, this step aims to expand and enrich $\mathbf{C}(\boldsymbol{a})$, based on the hyperlinks within concepts. Actually, the expansion is a process of breadth-first graph traversal that starts from the concepts associated with $\mathbf{C}(\boldsymbol{a})$. First, for each concept $\boldsymbol{c}$ in $\mathbf{C}(\boldsymbol{a})$, we obtain all the concepts hyperlinking to $\boldsymbol{c}$, noted as $\mathbf{cots}(\boldsymbol{c})$. Second, we calculate the frequency value of each concept $\boldsymbol{e}$ in $\mathbf{cots}(\boldsymbol{c})$:

$$\mathbf{count}(\boldsymbol{e},\boldsymbol{a}) = \left(\frac{\mathbf{num}^{\mathbf{k}}(\boldsymbol{e},\boldsymbol{c})}{\sum\limits_{e' \in \mathbf{cots}(c)} \mathbf{num}^{\mathbf{k}}(e',\boldsymbol{c})}\right) \cdot \mathbf{count}(\boldsymbol{c},\boldsymbol{a})$$

where $\mathbf{num}^{\mathbf{k}}(\boldsymbol{e},\boldsymbol{c})$ denotes the number of hyperlinks between the concepts $\boldsymbol{e}$ and $\boldsymbol{c}$.

Third, if $\mathbf{count}(\boldsymbol{e},\boldsymbol{a})$ is greater a given parameter μ that is assigned by users to control the depth of graph traversal, then $\mathbf{count}(\boldsymbol{e},\boldsymbol{a})$ would be added into $\mathbf{C}(\boldsymbol{a})$. Such a process is kept on until all the concepts (including the new added ones) associated with $\mathbf{C}(\boldsymbol{a})$ are traversed. Similarly, we can expand $\mathbf{C}(\boldsymbol{p})$ for a page $\boldsymbol{p}$.

(3) Generating Concept Vector. After the above step, $\mathbf{C}(\boldsymbol{a})$ would be expanded with more concepts that are all semantically related to the ad $\boldsymbol{a}$, i.e., obtaining a set of frequency values of concepts for $\boldsymbol{a}$. Similarly to the traditional keyword matching, based on $\mathbf{C}(\boldsymbol{a})$, we can generate a concept vector for $\boldsymbol{a}$, which consists of the *tf-idf* values [12] of all the concepts in $\mathbf{C}(\boldsymbol{a})$. We also generate a concept vector for a page $\boldsymbol{p}$. Last, we compute the concept-based semantic similarity $\mathbf{sim}^{\mathbf{c}}(\boldsymbol{a},\boldsymbol{p})$ between $\boldsymbol{p}$ and $\boldsymbol{a}$, by using the two concept vectors.

3.2 Category Vector Construction

In this subsection, by combining concept vector and the hierarchical relation between concepts and categories or within categories, we describe how to generate a category vector for an ad (or a page), and leverage it further to enrich the semantic representation for pages and ads.

Let $\mathbf{cots}(\boldsymbol{d})$ be all the concepts that belong to a category $\boldsymbol{d}$, and $\mathbf{cats}(\boldsymbol{d})$ all the immediate subcategories that belong to $\boldsymbol{d}$ (i.e., there is a hyperlink from each category in $\mathbf{cats}(\boldsymbol{d})$ to $\boldsymbol{d}$). $\mathbf{cots}(\boldsymbol{d})$ and $\mathbf{cats}(\boldsymbol{d})$ are determined by the hierarchical categorization system in Wikipedia. Then, we define the related frequency of any category $\boldsymbol{d}$ appearing in an ad (or a page) $\boldsymbol{a}$ as follows:

$$\mathbf{count}(\boldsymbol{d},\boldsymbol{a}) = \sum_{c \in \mathbf{cots}(\boldsymbol{d})} \frac{\mathbf{count}(c,\boldsymbol{a})}{\alpha_1} + \sum_{d' \in \mathbf{cats}(\boldsymbol{d})} \frac{\mathbf{count}(d',\boldsymbol{p})}{\alpha_2}$$

where α_1 and α_2 are two attenuation coefficients, used to balance importance of frequency values of categories in different depths.

Now, we determine a set $\mathbf{D}(\boldsymbol{a}) = \{\mathbf{count}(\boldsymbol{d}_j,\boldsymbol{a})\}_{j=1}^{N_a^d}$, consisting of frequency of each category related to an ad $\boldsymbol{a}$, where N_a^d is the number of related categories in $\boldsymbol{a}$. The generation of $\mathbf{D}(\boldsymbol{a})$ for an ad $\boldsymbol{a}$ is also a process of breadth-first graph traversal starting from the concepts associated with $\mathbf{C}(\boldsymbol{a})$. However, the traversed graph consists of (1) nodes, concepts and categories, and (2) edges, the hyperlinks within concepts and categories, as well as the hyperlinks within categories. Furthermore, based on $\mathbf{D}(\boldsymbol{a})$, we can generate a category vector for the ad $\boldsymbol{a}$, which consists of the *tf-idf* values of all the categories in $\mathbf{D}(\boldsymbol{a})$. Similarly, we also generate a category vector for a page $\boldsymbol{p}$. Last, we can compute the category-based semantic similarity $\mathbf{sim}^{\mathbf{d}}(\boldsymbol{a},\boldsymbol{p})$ between $\boldsymbol{p}$ and $\boldsymbol{a}$, by using the two category vectors.

Item	Number
General pages in dataset	50
Ambiguous pages in dataset	27
Textual ads in dataset	10,244
Wikipedia articles (Wikipedia concepts)	260,000
Wikipedia categories	12,000

Table 1: Dataset characteristics

Item	Explanation
K	solely based on keyword vectors
C	solely based on concept vector
D	solely based on category vector
KC	based on keyword vector and concept vector
KD	based on keyword vector and category vector
CD	based on concept vector and category vector
KCD	based on keyword vector, concept vector and category vector

Table 2: 7 contextual advertising strategies based on different combinations of feature vectors

3.3 Similarity Computation

Now, each ad (or page) has been represented as three feature vectors: a keyword vector, a concept vector and a category vector. So, when measuring similarity between an ad and a page, we combine the similarity values calculated using the three feature vectors. For a given page $\boldsymbol{p}$ and an ad $\boldsymbol{a}$, the similarity between $\boldsymbol{p}$ and $\boldsymbol{a}$ can be computed as follows:

$$\mathbf{sim}(\boldsymbol{a},\boldsymbol{p}) = \alpha \cdot \mathbf{sim}^{\mathbf{k}}(\boldsymbol{a},\boldsymbol{p}) + \eta \cdot \mathbf{sim}^{\mathbf{c}}(\boldsymbol{a},\boldsymbol{p}) + \zeta \cdot \mathbf{sim}^{\mathbf{d}}(\boldsymbol{a},\boldsymbol{p})$$

where the coefficients α, η and ζ indicate the importance of concept vector and category vector in measuring the semantic similarity between the page and the ad, which also can be used to balance the keyword matching and the Wikipedia matching. And $\alpha + \eta + \zeta = 1$.

4. EXPERIMENTS

We evaluated experimentally our approach using a dataset that contains 50 generic pages, 27 ambiguous pages and 10, 224 ads, more detailed characteristics of which are shown as Table 1. For each page, we collected human judgment scores that describe the relevance of ads selected by each of the candidate strategies (see Table 2). The human judgment

Strategy	K	C	D	KC	KD	CD	KCD
Time (ms)	45	290	765	293	775	758	780

Table 3: Running performance for the 7 strategies

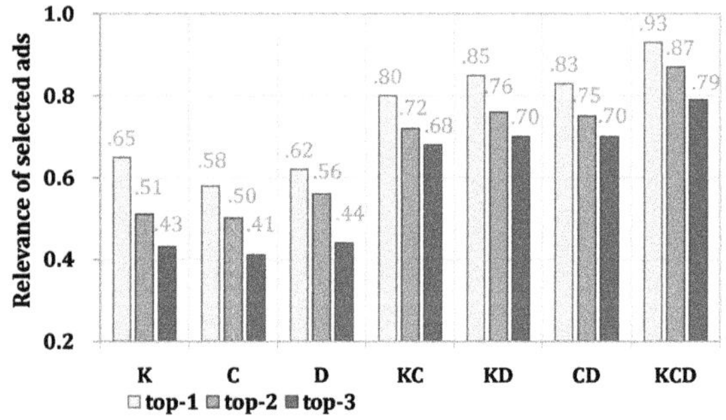

Figure 2: Average relevance for the ads selected by the 7 candidate strategies for general pages

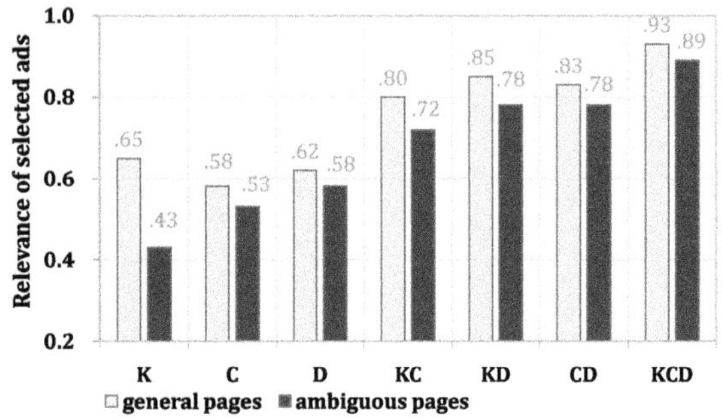

Figure 3: Average relevance for the ads selected by the 7 strategies for general or ambiguous pages

scores for the relevance of embedded ads to a page were determined by using a similar method in [5, 6], and were completed by at least two human assessors in a scale between 0.0 to 1.0.

The first group of experiments aimed to evaluate the execution time of selecting relevant ads for pages. Here, the work of generating feature vectors for all the ads, has been completed in advance (i.e., completed offline). In each ads-selection for a page, we only concern the execution time consumed by (1) generating the feature vectors for the page, and (2) computing the similarity between the page and each ad to choose the most relevant ads. The results are presented in Table 3. The second group of experiments aimed to evaluate the relevance scores of embedded ads to their pages. In our experiments, we invited evaluation assessors to mark score for each ad based on the relevance of the ad to its page, and then averaged the relevance scores given by the evaluation assessors. The results are shown in Figure 2. In the third group of experiments, we have chosen a special dataset that consists of 27 ambiguous pages. In the pages, there are many ambiguous keywords, such as Puma (company versus lion), Rock (person versus music), Driver (software versus car), Game (software versus sports), Window (OS versus glass) and so on. The experimental results of running the seven candidate strategies over the ambiguous pages are shown in Figure 3.

5. CONCLUSIONS

In order to improve contextual advertising, we in this paper presented a new approach by incorporating the Wikipedia concept and category information into the traditional keyword matching to enrich the content representation of pages and ads. We described how to map each ad (or page) into a keyword vector, a concept vector and a category vector, as well as how to combine the three feature vectors together for making the top-N ads selection.

From the experimental results in Section 4, we have the following conclusions. (1) Our approach obtains a satisfactory running performance (the time spending of ads-selection for a page is less than 1000 ms). This is due to avoiding to conduct the time-consuming fulltext matching operation between pages and all the referenced articles, which is used in the previously published Wikipedia contextual advertising approach. (2) Our approach obtains a better effectiveness, i.e., it can well improve the accuracy of ads-selection (the relevance score of embedded ads to their pages is generally greater than 0.8). This is due to that we use the Wikipedia knowledge to enrich the semantic representation of pages and ads, and use them to measure the semantic similarity between pages and ads; while, compared to the surface text information contained in pages and ads, the semantic information has a better stability, i.e., it can reflect out the similarity between pages and ads more accurately.

Funding: This work is supported by the National Science Foundation of the Zhejiang Province of China, under grant Y1100137, the Education Research Program of the Zhejiang Province of China, under grant Y201016197, the Science and Technology Program of the Wenzhou City of China, under grant 2009G0339 and grant S20100055.

6. REFERENCES

[1] A. Lacerda, M. Cristo, M. G. Andre et al. Learning to advertise. In *SIGIR*, 2006.

[2] B. Ribeiro-Neto, M. Cristo, P. B. Golgher et al. Impedance coupling in content-targeted advertising. In *SIGIR*, 2005.

[3] A. Anagnostopoulos, A. Broder, E. Gabrilovich et al. Just-in-time contextual advertising. In *CIKM*, 2007.

[4] A. N. Pak, and C.-W. Chung. A Wikipedia matching approach to contextual advertising. *WWWJ*, 13: 251-274, 2010.

[5] J. Hu, L. J. Fang, Y. Cao, H.-J. Zeng et al. Enhancing text clustering by leveraging Wikipedia semantics. In *SIGIR*, 2008.

[6] X. H. Hu, X. D. Zhang, C. M. Lu et al. Exploiting Wikipedia as external knowledge for document clustering. In *SIGKDD*, 2009.

[7] P. Wang, J. Hu, H.-J. Zeng et al. Using Wikipedia knowledge to improve text classification. *KAIS*, 19: 265-281, 2009.

[8] V. Murdock, M. Ciaramita and V. Plachouras. A noisy-channel approach to contextual advertising. In *SIGKDD* workshops 2007.

[9] T.-K. Fan and C.-H. Chang, "Sentiment-oriented contextual advertising". *KAIS*, 23:321-344, 2010.

[10] S. Papadopoulos, F. Menemenis, Y. Kompatsiaris et al. Lexical graphs for improved contextual ad recommendation. In *ECIR*, 2009.

[11] J. Hu, G. Wang, F. Lochovsky et al. Understanding user's query intent with Wikipedia. In *WWW*, 2009.

[12] H. C. Wu, R. W. P. Luk, K. F. Wong et al. Interpreting TF-IDF term weights as making relevance decisions. ACM TOIS 26, 2008.

Beyond Relevance in Marketplace Search

Nish Parikh Neel Sundaresan
eBay Research Labs
2065 Hamilton Ave,
San Jose, CA, 95125, USA.
{nparikh, nsundaresan}@ebay.com

ABSTRACT
In this paper we study diversity and its relations to search relevance in the context of an online marketplace. We conduct a large-scale log-based study using click-stream data from a leading eCommerce site. We introduce 3 main metrics – selection (diversity), trust, and value. In our analysis we also show how these interact with relevance in different ways. We study the benefits of diversity and also show why guaranteeing diversity is important.

Categories and Subject Descriptors
H.3.3 [**Information Storage and Retrieval**]: Information Search and Retrieval – *information filtering.*

General Terms
Economics, Experimentation, Measurement.

Keywords
eCommerce, search, diversity, relevance, trust, value, selection

1. MOTIVATION AND BACKGROUND
Relevance in ranking for keyword search has been extensively studied. Since search queries are likely to have different interpretations for different users, showing diverse set of results is necessary. For instance, for a generic query like "mp3 players" different kinds of mp3 players should be returned. Ideally, the result set should properly account for the interest of the overall user population.

Diversity in information retrieval and web search has also been well studied [2]. [4] describes Maximal Marginal Relevance (MMR) criterion to reduce redundancy while maintaining query relevance in re-ranking retrieved documents. Each document in the ranked list is selected according to a combined criterion of query relevance and novelty of information.

[1] shows efficient query processing techniques that guarantee diversity. Although some attributes of a narrow section of inventory (automobiles) that impact diversity are discussed in, it does not provide enough insight into what dimensions impact user satisfaction and diversity in eCommerce search. Our work focuses on bridging this gap. As little work has been done around diversity in eCommerce search, we study and describe the role of relevance and diversity in eCommerce search by using large-scale retrospective datasets from a leading eCommerce site which has at any point in time millions of items for sale in different categories by different sellers.

In section 2 we describe various dimensions that affect search results. In section 3 we describe experiments to discover the interactions between these dimensions and also show why guaranteeing diversity in product search is essential. Finally, we note our conclusions and plan for future work in section 4.

CIKM'11, October 24 - 28, 2011, Glasgow, Scotland, UK.

2. ECOMMERCE SEARCH DIMENSIONS
For online marketplaces supporting C2C and B2C transactions sellers pay to list their inventory, however, the engine has to sort items based upon what the buyer is likely to buy and also provide a good buying experience. Various factors which influence buyer satisfaction, marketplace reputation and sell-through of items for sale come into play. Some of these factors which need to be considered in building the item result set are discussed below.

2.1 Trust
For online retailers like Wal-Mart and Target the trust or reputation associated with the products is that of the online retailer itself as they control and manage the entire inventory sold on their site. However, in a multi-buyer to multi-seller marketplace, as there are many sellers selling different items, the trust factor associated with every item is different. If the same product is being sold for the same price by two different sellers with different reputations, buyers would surely want to buy it from the seller with a better reputation. The trust associated with an item is based on the reputation of the seller who is selling the item. The reputation score for a seller could again be influenced by various factors like feedback from former buyers, return policy for items sold by the seller, shipping options offered by the seller and other factors. Total trust associated with a result set which we refer to as τ would be dependent on the collection of trust values of every individual item in the result set. For our experiments we use seller data and feedback from former buyers to compute the trust value of every item. τ determines the long term health of the marketplace.

2.2 Value
In today's online world, buyers have a lot of choice. A compelling value proposition is something that many buyers look for, before completing their purchase. Given two exactly same items with the same trust score, buyers are more likely to buy the

one with a lower price. Thus, value proposition provided by an item to the buyer is a function of the price of the item. If the price of an item is less than the typical selling prices of similar items then the value proposition for the item is high and vice versa. The total value aspect associated with a result set would be dependent on the average value provided by all the items that the result set comprises of and we refer to it as V.

2.3 Selection

Diversity of an item set is an indicator of the variety of items found in the result set. On eCommerce sites, the different factors determining diversity of result set could be types of sellers, auctions vs. fixed price items, shipping options, payment options and also factors like what product types or categories the surfaced inventory belongs to (For e.g., if a user issues a vague or ambiguous query like "peru" the items in the corresponding result set could belong to different categories like "Stamps", "Coins and Paper Money", "Postcards", "Art" and many others).

If relevance is not impacted, then providing a wider selection to buyers is good in general. We calculate diversity of a result set based on 3 different factors; the diversity of sellers whose items are present in the set, the diversity of the items based on format of the item and the diversity measured in terms of the amount of people whose interests would be satisfied by the result set.

We calculate the seller diversity using this Simpson's index metric.

$S_d = 1 - \frac{\sum_n n(n-1)}{N(N-1)}$, where S_d is the seller diversity, N is the total number of items in the result set, and n is the total number of items in the result set from one particular seller.

Format diversity F_d is calculated in a similar way. For our work, we have considered two formats: fixed price items and auction items.

We use data from a leading eCommerce site which has individual items for sale, and where many of the long-tail items are not necessarily grouped by product ids, or UPC/EAN/ISBN numbers.

As most users don't look beyond the first couple of pages of the result, the goal is to be able to show all kinds of desirable items for sale on the first page of results. Although two individuals might issue the same query, their intents could be different. We look at past history of user activity to associate desirable items with a given query. As described in [3] we mine the user click-through, buying and bidding behavior to find out a mapping from queries to features. For example, if users in the past issued a search for "roger federer" and then ended up buying "t-shirts", "collectibles", and "rackets", then we will have a mapping from the query "roger federer" to the features ("t-shirts", "collectibles", "rackets") with some weights (w_1, w_2, w_3). This query to feature mapping is based on a desirability metric. So if lot of "roger federer posters" were available on sale but none of them got bought on site after querying for "roger federer", then the vector for the query "roger federer" would have the feature "poster" with a negative weight. Given a result set R for a query Q, we look at the feature vector V for query Q and try to see how many of the positive features for Q are found in R, which gives a measure of desired item diversity I_d. The feature set of R is the collection of terms found in the titles of any of the items found in R. So if for the query "roger federer" t-shirts, collectibles and rackets were found in the result set, the item diversity score I_d would be 1.0, else it would be some number between 0 and 1.0 depending on which features for the query "roger federer" were found in the result set R and the weights for those features.

We combine these individual diversities to get a composite selection score, $S = \phi(S_d, F_d, I_d)$. Our approach to learning the function ϕ is similar to the approach used in computing Maximal Marginal Relevance (MMR) [4]. We use a linear combination function to express total selection score S as a linear combination of individual diversities S_d, F_d and I_d.

$$S = \alpha S_d + \beta F_d + (1 - (\alpha + \beta)) I_d, \text{ where}$$

$$0 \le \alpha \le 1 \; and \; 0 \le \beta \le 1 \; and \; 0 \le (1 - (\alpha + \beta)) \le 1.$$

We learn the weights α and β through human judgments and use a function ϕ which linearly combines S_d, F_d and I_d in proportions 0.2, 0.4 and 0.4 respectively.

2.4 Relevance

As a simple measure of relevance, we see how every individual item in the set is relevant to the query. The total relevance of the item set for the query is then an average of the relevance of individual items for the query.

The relevance of an item I for a query Q is again calculated using the feature vector V for the query Q which was described in section 2.3. The vector V for query Q is comprised of different features with positive and negative weights. An item I can be represented as a vector $V_i = (t_1, t_2, \ldots, t_n)$ where t_i are the terms in the title of the item. The relevance value of item I for query Q is, $r_i = \left(\frac{\sum_{i=1}^{n} w_i}{\sum_{i=1}^{n} |w_i|} \right)$, Where w_i is the weight for the term t_i in the feature vector V for query Q. If a term t_i is not present in the feature vector for query Q then $w_i = 0$.

Thus $-1 \le r_i \le 1$. The average of the relevance values r_i for all the items in the result set gives the relevance ρ ($-1 \le \rho \le 1$) for the result set.

Most eCommerce sites provide an option for users to sort the retrieved item set using deterministic sort factors like "Price: Low to High" or "Best-selling" or "Time: Newly Listed" or "Distance: nearest first" etc. If the search engine is Boolean and ranks the items based on some factors like price of item or auction ending time, there is a higher probability that irrelevant items will show up in the result set. This is true in case of queries like "ipod nano" where the intent of most buyers is to buy an mp3 player but a Boolean search with *TimeRank* sort might show only "skins", "chargers" and "batteries" depending on the available inventory for each of these kinds of items.

2.5 Perturbation

As discussed in sections 2.3 and 2.4, we use historical click-through and user activity information to map a query to features, and this information is used to calculate selection (S) and relevance (ρ). Thus, it becomes important that in construction of the ideal result set, room be left for a perturbation factor P , so that new items (not indicated in the query to feature mapping), also have some non-zero probability of making it to the ideal result set. Some queries to feature mappings remain stable over time while others do not. For example, we extracted some historical data to see how the top feature related to the query "poster" changes with time. It changes rapidly and dynamically as new movies or celebrities get popular. Similar changes in features for the query "harry potter" were observed as new books and movies were released. Identical effects are observed when newer models of electronic products get released as well.

3. EXPERIMENTS

Our experiments consisted of running queries against the search engine, obtaining the item set from the first page of search results, and calculating various measures for those item sets. For our experiments we used 3 different sets of queries. The first set consists of 50 most frequent queries on the site which cover close to 2% of total volume of traffic because of the power-law nature of search traffic and we refer to it as *TopQueriesSet*. We also looked at top 1000 queries and randomly picked 100 queries out of those 1000. This forms our second set which we refer to as the *RandomQueriesSet*. We mined user sessions to find the sessions in which users issue a query and then exit the site i.e. they don't do any other viewing, bidding or buying activity after issuing the search. We collected such queries and these queries comprise our third set which we refer to as *ExitQueriesSet*.

For our experiments we have used two different ranking options. The first option is ranking by time (*TimeRank*), where the items that are about to expire show up first. The second option is ranking by RelevanceMatch (*RelevanceMatchRank*) which is provided by the site to sort items by some multi-dimensional relevance function. We calculated the trust, value, selection and relevance scores for item sets returned by queries from *TopQueriesSet* and *RandomQueriesSet*. We performed the experiments using both *TimeRank* and *RelevanceMatchRank* and analyzed various dimensions.

The trust scores are better for *TopQueriesSet* as compared to *RandomQueriesSet* irrespective of the ranking used. This shows that popular and in-demand items (head inventory) are usually available to be bought from reputable sellers. However, the not so popular items in the long tail may not always be available from reputed sellers. We also observed that with either set, the values of τ (trust) and ρ (relevance) are higher with *RelevanceMatchRank* as compared to *TimeRank* as the conditional ranking algorithm in *RelevanceMatchRank* uses some of the features that we use to measure τ and ρ of the retrieved item set. For *TimeRank,* values of ρ are low for many queries irrespective of the query set being *TopQueriesSet* or *RandomQueriesSet.* Selection S is not dependent on the query set (*TopQueriesSet* or *RandomQueriesSet*), neither is it dependent on the ranking. S is different for different queries (varied from 0.35 to 0.78) and it is observed that S is a function of how vague, ambiguous or generalized the query is. ν is high and stable irrespective of the ranking algorithm applied or the query set used, implying that generally the result item sets do offer a high value proposition.

In order to understand and observe the importance of diverse result sets, we experiment to observe the correlation between the diversity of the result set and the exit rate of users from site.

There are many users who search for items and then exit without performing any other on-site activity. These search terms are available in *ExitQueriesSet*. We see that some users exit because no items are returned for their query or few items are returned for their query and those items don't pique their interest.

However, there is another section of users, who issue queries, and who also see a full page of item results, but they still quit the site, without even clicking on the items. This could happen if the items were irrelevant, so relevance does impact exit rates. However, there are user sessions where exits happened after search for which items were shown with a reasonably high value of the relevance factor. We try to observe if this has any correlation with diversity. An item set with reduced diversity although relevant, may not be able to account for the interests of the overall user population.

Some queries for which S was low but ρ was high and led to users exiting from site are shown below in Table 1.

Table 1 Values of S for some queries from *ExitQueriesSet* which had a high value of ρ . Note that only items that are available for sale, tagged as desirable based on historical query mappings but still were not found in the result set are discussed. Only a couple of representative items are discussed for every query.

Query (S)	Some observations from Result Set
Oeuf (0.20)	Did not find armbands and measuring cups. Did find some form of Tupperware.
Johnsons (0.30)	Found vintage items but did not find matchboxes and fishing lures.
Alfa 75 (0.37)	Found lights for alfa 75 but did not find alternator.
Albert (0.38)	Found jerseys and vintage items but did not find diamond pendants and green wood tree salad plates.
Game board (0.40)	Found backgammon, wooden and vintage game boards but did not find game boards for Parcheesi and checkers.

It can be seen that many queries in Table 1 are generic. It is difficult to know which game board a user is looking for when a user searches for "game board". However, for users who are specifically looking for something but using generic queries; not finding what they want is frustrating and those users might just walk away. As seen from column 2 of Table 1, items shown for these queries were relevant, but as there were lot of items that could be reasonably relevant (based on historical click-through data) to these vague queries, probably items that the user was looking for were missing from the result set and the user just exited the site after the search.

As the queries get more specific usually the desirable diversity found in result set also goes up because more specific the query, less the number of different desired items matching the query and higher the chance that most of those themes get captured by the item set. For example, the query "game board" has a low S of 0.40 but the query "monopoly game board" has a selection score S of 0.65.

3.1 Correlation between S and ρ

In order to see if diversity S and relevance ρ are correlated we calculated those scores for different queries. A high value of selection S did not necessarily mean that the result set had a good relevance ρ and vice versa.

The queries with high values of S as well as ρ lead to a good buyer experience. The queries with low values of both S and ρ lead to a poor buyer experience. However, both values would be low with a *RelevanceMatchRank* sort only if appropriate inventory is not available on the site, and is more of an inventory availability problem than a search or ranking problem.

Queries leading to result sets with high S and low ρ usually have good variety of items but are missing variety within popular items. To please most users with optimal satisfaction a good balance of S and ρ is needed.

Queries leading to result sets with high ρ and low S are of interest to our study. As described in section 3 , such result sets cause some users to walk away as they don't see any items matching their interest. The average selection score for queries that led to exit is 0.61. As a comparison the average selection score of top queries was 0.72. Table 2 shows values of S for some popular ipod related queries leading to high user satisfaction. The higher satisfaction was measured in terms of number of sales in user sessions in which those queries were issued. It can be seen that queries that lead to higher satisfaction have higher selection (S) scores for corresponding result sets.

Table 2 Table indicating Selection (S) values for popular ipod related queries which led to a satisfying buyer experience. The S values for these queries are much higher than those seen for *ExitQueriesSet*

Query	(S)	Query	(S)
ipod touch 8gb	0.85	iphone 3g	0.84
ipod touch	0.87	unlocked cell phones	0.80
apple ipod touch 32 gb	0.82	ipod nano 4th generation 8gb	0.82

3.2 Do S , ρ relate to User Satisfaction?

In order to precisely measure and quantify the impact of diversity on satisfaction of users, we looked at a large sample of click-stream logs (More than 1M queries conducted by users). We looked at all search impressions, for which the relevance ρ of item set shown was above a threshold $t_r = 0.4$ determined empirically. We term these impressions as data points with $\rho = high$. We looked at all impressions which led to user satisfaction and user dissatisfaction. User satisfaction was defined as a click on one of the items shown to the user. User dissatisfaction was defined as exit from the site. For all these search impressions we also measured the selection score S . Selection score $S \le 0.3$ was referred to as $S = low$ and selection score $S > 0.3$ was referred to as $S = high$. We observed that

$\left(\frac{P(exit / S = high, \rho = high)}{P(exit \mid S = low, \rho = high)}\right) = 0.62$. This ratio is statistically significant based on the large number of samples from the data we used. This shows that on pages with relevant item sets, the probability of a user being dissatisfied is significantly increased if the diversity of the item sets on the page is lowered. Thus, it is essential to guarantee diversity and proper selection to be able to satisfy most users from the population. None of these factors are highly correlated and in order to satisfy majority of buyer population the result set needs to be optimized based on τ (Trust), υ (Value Proposition), S (Selection / Diversity), ρ (Relevance) and P (Perturbation).

4. CONCLUSIONS AND FUTURE WORK

We described factors that need to be optimized in eCommerce search in order to minimize the risk of dissatisfaction of the average user. We conducted a large-scale empirical study to find out the interplay between these factors – trust, value, selection, relevance and perturbation. We also showed through log analysis that lack of diversity is correlated with metrics like exits of users from site and that a lack of diversity could have a detrimental impact on an online marketplace.

An advanced search interface like the one we describe in [5] gives more control to the user but also requires more inputs from the user, due to which we believe its utility is limited to experts. As part of future work we would like to build a ranking function that can optimize search results based on the above mentioned factors to be able to help the non-expert average users.

5. REFERENCES

[1] Vee, E., Srivastava, U., Shanmugasundaram, J., Bhat, P., Yahia, S.A. Efficient Computation of Diverse Query Results. ICDE (2008), 228-236.

[2] Agarwal, R., Gollapudi S., Halverson A., Ieong S. Diversifying Search Results. WSDM (2009). 5-14.

[3] Parikh N., Sundaresan N. Inferring Semantic Query Relations from Collective User Behavior. CIKM (2008), 349-358.

[4] Carbonell J., Goldstein J. The use of MMR, Diversity-Based Re-ranking for Reordering Documents and Producing Summaries. SIGIR (1998), 335-336.

[5] Parikh N., Sundaresan N. A User-Tunable Approach to Marketplace Search. WWW (Companion Volume) 2011. 245-248.

Relative Effect of Spam and Irrelevant Documents on User Interaction with Search Engines

Timothy Jones
Australian National University
Canberra, Australia
tim.jones@anu.edu.au

David Hawking
Funnelback Pty Ltd & Australian National Univ.
Canberra, Australia
david.hawking@acm.org

Paul Thomas
CSIRO
Canberra, Australia
paul.thomas@csiro.au

Ramesh Sankaranarayana
Australian National University
Canberra, Australia
ramesh@cs.anu.edu.au

ABSTRACT

Meaningful evaluation of web search must take account of spam. Here we conduct a user experiment to investigate whether satisfaction with search engine result pages as a whole is harmed more by spam or by irrelevant documents.

On some measures, search result pages are differentially harmed by the insertion of spam and irrelevant documents. Additionally we find that when users are given two documents of equal utility, the one with the lower spam score will be preferred; a result page without any spam documents will be preferred to one with spam; and an irrelevant document high in a result list is surprisingly more damaging to user satisfaction than a spam document. We conclude that web ranking and evaluation should consider both utility (relevance) and "spamminess" of documents.

Categories and Subject Descriptors

H.3.3 [**Information Storage and Retrieval**]: Information Search and Retrieval—*Search process*

General Terms

Measurement, Human Factors

Keywords

Web Search, Web Spam, Adversarial Information Retrieval

1. INTRODUCTION

Web spam documents—documents designed to achieve an unfairly high rank for some page or pages—are a problem in web search. The topic of web spam dectection has received much recent attention. However, relatively little attention has been paid to the problem of spam nullification—understanding how to correctly deal with spam documents once detected [3]. In order to understand how to appropriately nullify spam documents, it is important to investigate the relationship between spam and relevance. Understanding this relationship is also valuable when evaluating spam nullification. For example, if users see spam as equivalent to irrelevant documents, then the effectiveness of spam removal can be measured using traditional evaluation methods.

In this paper we examine the relationship between spam and relevance, to determine whether spam labels are required when measuring spam nullification. We present the first study we are aware of which compares user reaction to spam documents to user reaction on other low value documents (in this case irrelevant documents). We find that not only do users prefer spam results to irrelevant results, but surprisingly a click on a spam document can sometimes increase the user's satisfaction with a result set.

2. PREVIOUS WORK

Users behave differently when faced with spam and non-spam documents. Spam documents receive nearly all of their visits from search engines, whereas non-spam documents are also visited via a variety of other means (direct links, bookmarks, etc.) [6]. Similarly, when a user views a document from a spam site, they are unlikely to navigate to many other documents within that site.

This user browsing behaviour can be exploited to detect spam. In [7] and [9], the user browsing graph is used to detect spam. This exploits the property that users are unlikely to navigate to spam pages from other pages in the web graph. A similar approach is to use the view and click graphs obtainable from query logs [2].

Here we also consider non-spam, irrelevant, documents and ask: do spam and irrelevant documents induce similar user behaviour, or do users react differently to the two?

3. EXPERIMENT DESIGN

Participants in our investigation were assigned information gathering tasks and asked to complete them using our search engine. Unknown to users, each task was completed using a different search engine: either a high quality engine, or one of six degraded engines. Task order was controlled in order to avoid carry-over effects.

Including a practice task, users completed eight tasks using seven different engines. After each task, users reported

CIKM'11, October 24–28, 2011, Glasgow, Scotland, UK.

their success in completing the task. Users were told they could end the task if they had been searching fruitlessly for several minutes.

3.1 Controlling for engine quality

In this experiment, live web search performance was degraded by a predetermined amount. To do this, we inserted low value documents into the results provided by the high quality search engine (Yahoo!'s "BOSS" API, `developer.yahoo.com/search/boss/`). Our model for estimating the degredation to NDCG@10 scores caused by various patterns of inserted documents is described in more detail in [8].

From this model, and assuming that both spam and irrelevant documents provide zero gain to the user, we test three expected degradations to NDCG@10 score: 0.2, 0.4 and 0.8. The pattern to achieve a degradation of 0.2 is insertion at ranks 2 and 3; that is, after inserting zero-value documents at ranks 2 and 3, we expect the NDCG@10 score to drop by 0.2. For 0.4 we insert at ranks 1, 3, 8, and 9, and for 0.8 we insert at ranks 1, 2, 4, 5, 6, 7, 9, and 10.

Insertions. Three irrelevant engines were constructed by inserting irrelevant documents into result pages from the high quality engine. We denote the least degraded engine *(i:2,3)*, indicating that *i*rrelevant documents were inserted at positions 2 and 3. The other engines were *(i:1,3,8,9)* and *(i:1,2,4,5,6,7,8,9,10)*.

In order to provide a comparison with the irrelevant documents, spam engines were also created. These engines were identical to the irrelevant engines, except spam documents were inserted instead. These engines were *(s:2,3)*, indicating that *s*pam documents were inserted at positions 2 and 3, *(s:1,3,8,9)* and *(s:1,2,4,5,6,7,8,9,10)*.

Sourcing spam and irrelevant documents. Selecting spam documents using a commercial search engine is difficult, as we can expect the commercial engine to be taking steps to remove spam from the results. However, the ClueWeb'09 collection is a recent collection that has spam labels provided [4]. We retrieve spam documents for insertion by submitting users' queries to a spam-only index of ClueWeb'09 Category B. Because we use their real queries, the spam documents will appear to be answers to a user's search. Documents selected in this manner appear to be low quality, clearly spam, and will have some overlap with the query.

Selecting irrelevant documents is more complex. Several methods were considered, but we found the best results were achieved by adding low meaning terms (such as buzzwords) to the query. We selected a joke buzzword generator available online (`www.1728.com/buzzword.htm`), and used the output to add terms to the user's query. This approach works surprisingly well when using a commercial search engine. Results appear targetted to the query, are non-spam but are of little use.

3.2 Logging

Logging was performed using JavaScript served along with the results page. Several features were logged, including query text, depth of result page, clicks on search results, scrolls on search pages, the index of visible results after scrolls and focus switches away and back to the search result page (which occur when the user switches tabs or uses the browser back and forward navigation buttons).

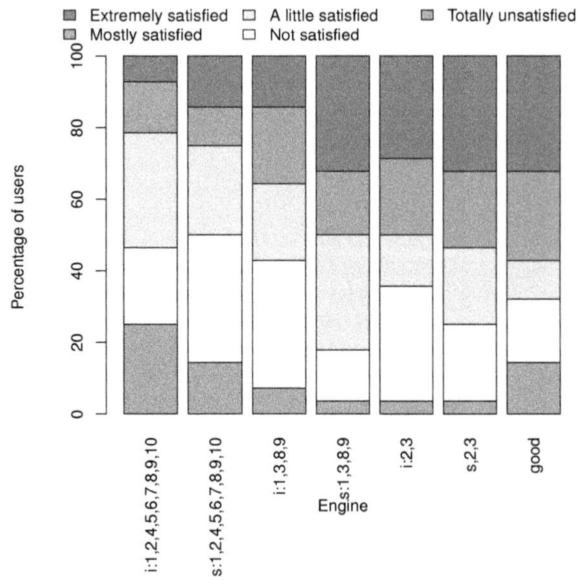

Figure 1: User reported satisfaction (lowest value used for each user).

As already discussed, upon task completion, users self-reported task success on a three point scale, which we report as *success*, *partial success* or *failure*.

We also obtained user judgements on the result set quality. To prevent these judgements from affecting user behaviour, explicit ratings were only solicited after all tasks were completed. After all tasks were completed, users were shown previous queries from each task, and asked to rate their satisfaction with the first result page on a five point scale. Up to five queries were randomly selected from each task, for a maximum total of 40 queries rated per user. This total was less if a user had submitted less than 5 queries for any task.

3.3 Tasks used

Participants were given eight information gathering tasks, each of which required several searches to complete. Three of the tasks were created for students in Canberra, three were chosen from the 2002 TREC interactive track, and the remaining two from other work [5].

4. RESULTS

Ignoring the practice task, the 28 users submitted a total of 525 queries over 7 tasks. We did not see significant differences in the number of queries submitted to each engine.

During the experiment, users clicked on a total of 459 search results. Of the 525 queries, a total of 144 (33 %) queries did not have any clicks.

4.1 Overall success and satisfaction

Users appear to have been uniformly successful across all engines—users were successful around 80% of the time, and a χ^2 test indicated that the engine used caused no significant effect on reported user success. This continued success, even with degraded engines, is consistent with previous work.

A manual examination of the ratings revealed that users tended to rate queries highly after they were successful in a task. In order to prevent this affecting results, we examine the lowest reported satisfaction per user per task or engine. This gives us a lower bound on the user's satisfaction during the completion use of a given engine.

Figure 4 shows the lower bound on user reported satisfaction on each engine. Engines that we expect to be of higher quality tend to be associated with queries leading to higher reported satisfaction. Using a χ^2 test to compare the degraded engine to an expected distribution of ratings (actually the observed distribution on the good engine) we find *(i:1,2,4,5,6,7,8,9,10)*, *(s:1,2,4,5,6,7,8,9,10)*, *(i:1,3,8,9)* and *(s:1,3,8,9)* to differ significantly from the good engine with $p < 0.05$, while the other two engines showed no significant differences.

4.2 Satisfaction on spam vs irrelevance

In total, there were 173 queries with irrelevant documents inserted, and 197 queries with spam documents inserted. We label queries with at least one spam document inserted *spam*; queries with at least one irrelevant document inserted *irrelevant*; and queries with no insertions—i.e. those directly from the search engine—are labelled *live*.

Figure 2(a) shows the distribution of ratings between the different type of queries. The ratings differ significantly across the three types of query (χ^2 tests, $p < 0.05$). As can be seen in the figure, live result sets are twice as likely to be marked highly satisfactory, whereas a higher proportion of irrelevant or spam result sets are given lower ratings.

To see how early in the result set this preference emerges, we examine satisfaction based on the type of the result at rank one. Interestingly, the trend is not the same as when the type of the whole set was considered (Figure 2(b)). There is no statistical difference between the distributions of ratings when the first document is a live search result and when the first document is an inserted spam document. However, there is a significant difference between having the first document as a spam or live result and having the first document as an irrelevant result. Having a spam document at rank one does not affect the rating of the query, but an irrelevant document at the same position is likely to be associated with a lower rating.

4.3 Clicks on inserted documents

During the course of the experiment, 459 search results were clicked. However, there were proportionally fewer clicks than impressions on spam and irrelevant results, while there were proportionally more clicks on the live results (χ^2 test, $p \ll 0.005$)—unsurprisingly, users were less interested in spam and irrelevant documents than in live search results.

There is a significant difference between the distributions of ratings of queries in which users clicked a spam document, and the queries in which users clicked an irrelevant document. Figure 3 shows that users rated the queries in which they had clicked on a spam document higher than those in which they had clicked on an irrelevant document.

Where irrelevant documents were inserted, there is no significant difference in ratings whether or not irrelevant documents were clicked, which indicates that the click on the irrelevant document does not affect user satisfaction.

However, where spam was inserted there is a significant difference between the distribution of ratings for queries where the spam was or was not clicked. Contrary to expectation, it appears that queries in which spam documents were clicked are actually rated higher than queries in which spam documents are shown but only live search results are clicked (t-test, $p = 0.05$), although the difference is small. This implies that reading a spam document is sometimes useful, although the presence of spam documents in the list is usually a bad thing.

4.4 Time cost of inserted documents

Low value documents may introduce other costs to the user, such as extra reading time. To model reading time, we calculated the duration of each query, defined as the time between subsequent query submissions (or between the final query in a session and an answer for the task). We found queries with spam or irrelevant documents inserted took significantly longer (mean 10 seconds) to complete than queries without insertions. However, there was no significant difference between the mean time taken on queries with spam and on queries with irrelevant documents.

We also calculated the mean time per click on each query, defined here as the duration of each query divided by (1 + the number of clicks). This mean time per click showed the same properties as the mean duration. The same is true again for the mean duration of queries with clicks on spam, irrelevant, or live results. We conclude that the insertion of spam or irrelevant documents causes the query duration to lengthen equally.

An alternative way to model reading time is to measure the time to first click on each query. Again, queries with no insertions require significantly less reading time (in this case around 2 seconds), and there was no significant difference between the spam and irrelevant queries.

5. DISCUSSION AND CONCLUSIONS

Queries with no inserted documents achieve nearly twice the proportion of "extremely satisfactory" ratings as those with spam, and nearly three times that of those with irrelevant documents (Figure 2(a)). Interestingly, queries with spam documents inserted are generally rated as more satisfactory than queries with irrelevant documents inserted, and this is especially pronounced at rank one. This implies that live results are usually preferred to spam documents, and that both are always preferred to irrelevant documents. The result that both spam and live results at rank one receive the same overall satisfaction rating may imply that users have trouble telling the difference between spam and non-spam documents.

Both spam and irrelevant documents slow down users by around 10 seconds per query on average. Increased user effort—measured by time per query—has been shown to decrease user satisfaction scores [1], so this may explain some of the decrease in satisfaction caused by spam and irrelevant documents. However, because the time per query was increased identically between spam and irrelevant insertions, but satisfaction was lower when irrelevant documents were shown, it is unlikely that increased user effort is the only factor impacting on user satisfaction in this case.

It is especially interesting that while a click on an irrelevant document has no effect on user satisfaction, a click on a spam document does not make things worse and sometimes actually increases user satisfaction. This implies that many spam documents are actually useful, or at least attractive.

These observations suggest general principles. First, we should not rank simply by relevance, ignoring spam labels: given two documents of equal utility, the non-spam docu-

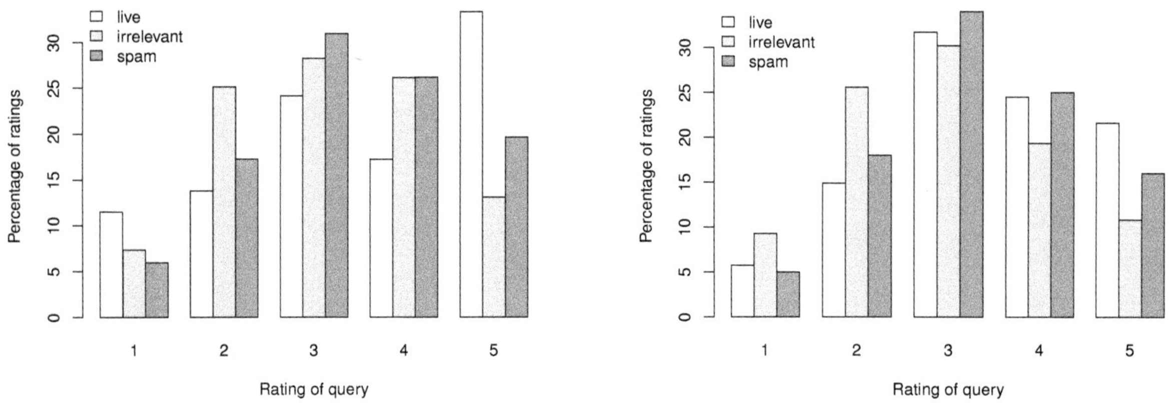

(a) Based on the type of document inserted

(b) Based on the type of document at rank 1

Figure 2: Ratings of queries based on the type of document inserted. 5 is high rating, 1 is low.

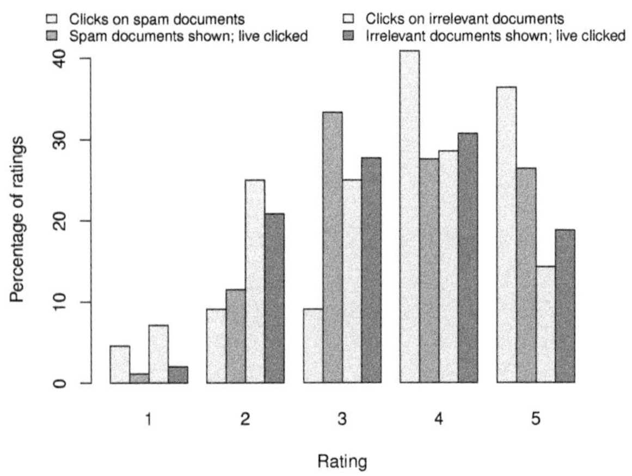

Figure 3: Ratings of queries in which spam or irrelevant documents received clicks.

ment should be preferred. On the other hand, nor can we discard all spam: spam documents might be relevant, and in many cases including spam doesn't hurt users' opinion overall. Ranking should consider both attributes.

One simple way to do this, especially if relevance and spam scores are quantised, might be to sort by relevance and break ties by spam scores. If estimated relevance and spam scores are used, this could provide a ranking for search engines; if documents are labelled for relevance and spam, this could provide a ranking against which to evaluate. Other more sophisticated ranking methods are of course possible. Regardless of the details, we argue that two scores, not just one, are needed for each document: both relevance and spamminess.

We summarise our observations of ranking and spam thus: The insertion of either irrelevant or spam documents into a result set increases the time a user takes to process the set, and by approximately the same amount; given two documents of equal utility, but differing spam scores, the document with the least spam should be preferred (live > spam); a result list without spam documents is more satisfactory than a result list with spam documents, assuming equal utility between the two lists; and an irrelevant document high in the result list is more damaging to user satisfaction than a spam document high in the result list (spam > irrelevant).

Relevant non-spam documents are better than spam; spam is better than irrelevance. Clearly, the design of a ranker or a metric to satisfy the above observations is a complex topic for future research, but at a minimum rankers should counsider both relevance and spamminess as separate attributes.

6. REFERENCES

[1] A. Al-Maskari and M. Sanderson. A review of factors influencing user satisfaction in information retrieval. *JASIST*, 61(5):859–868, 2010.

[2] C. Castillo, C. Corsi, D. Donato, P. Ferragina, and A. Gionis. Query log mining for detecting polysemy and spam. In *Proc. WebKDD*. Springer, 2008.

[3] C. Castillo and B. D. Davison. Adversarial web search. *Foundations and Trends in Information Retrieval*, 4:377–486.

[4] G. V. Cormack, M. D. Smucker, and C. L. A. Clarke. Efficient and effective spam filtering and re-ranking for large web datasets. *CoRR*, abs/1004.5168, 2010.

[5] C. Liu, J. Gwizdka, and J. Liu. Helping identify when users find useful documents: examination of query reformulation intervals. In *Proc. IIiX*, 2010.

[6] Y. Liu, R. Cen, M. Zhang, S. Ma, and L. Ru. Identifying web spam with user behavior analysis. In *Proc. AIRWeb*, 2008.

[7] Y. Liu, M. Zhang, S. Ma, and L. Ru. User browsing graph: structure, evolution and application. In *WSDM (Late Breaking-Results)*, 2009.

[8] P. Thomas, T. Jones, and D. Hawking. What deliberately degrading search quality tells us about discount functions. In *Proc. SIGIR*, 2011.

[9] H. Yu, Y. Liu, M. Zhang, L. Ru, and S. Ma. Web spam identification with user browsing graph. In *Proc. AIRS*, 2009.

Inferring Query Aspects from Reformulations Using Clustering

Van Dang, Xiaobing Xue and W. Bruce Croft
Center for Intelligent Information Retrieval
Department of Computer Science
University of Massachusetts
Amherst, MA 01003
{vdang, xuexb, croft}@cs.umass.edu

ABSTRACT

When the information need is not clear from the user query, a good strategy would be to return documents that cover as many aspects of the query as possible. To do this, the possible aspects of the query need to be automatically identified. In this paper, we propose to do this by clustering reformulated queries generated from publicly available resources and using each cluster to represent an aspect of the query. Our results show that the automatically generated reformulations for the TREC Web Track queries match up quite well with actual sub-topics of these queries identified by TREC experts. Moreover, agglomerative clustering using query-to-query similarity based on co-occurrence in text passages can provide clusters of high quality that potentially can be used to identify aspects.

Categories and Subject Descriptors

H.3.3 [**Information Search and Retrieval**]: Query Formulation

General Terms

Algorithms, Measurement, Performance, Experimentation.

Keywords

Query diversity, query reformulation, clustering, anchor text.

1. INTRODUCTION

User queries do not always clearly represent the actual information need. They can be ambiguous or underspecified. Ambiguous queries are those that have different interpretations such as "TREC", which might refer to the home page of Texas Real Estate Commission or Text Retrieval Conference. Underspecified queries are queries with a known interpretation that have different aspects or sub-topics that may be relevant. For example, the user submitting the query "apple inc." might be looking for general information about the company or products of the company.

In order to deal with these queries, retrieval systems should retrieve documents that are relevant to different aspects of the query rather than a single, dominating aspect. Conventional information retrieval (IR) systems can do little for these types of queries since they rank documents without regard to possible meanings the query might have.

Dealing with these types of queries is the motivation for introducing diversity into search results, to make the set of returned documents cover as many aspects of the queries as possible. Existing work in this area generally relies on an intial retrieval and then selecting documents from the retrieved set according to some criteria. These methods can be categorized as *implicit* and *explicit*. The implicit approach [2, 13] chooses documents different to those that have been previously selected without modeling the actual sub-topics of the query. The explicit approach, on the other hand, explicitly models aspects of a query using a taxonomy [1], relevant documents [3] or reformulations [10, 12]. Many of the explicit models, however, assume the availablility of the optimal aspect representation for a query, leaving their effectiveness with automatically generated aspects unclear.

In this paper, we propose a simple method to generate reformulations that represent possible aspects of a query from anchor text and the Microsoft Web N-Gram Services [1], both of which are publicly available. We first generate reformulations by using these resources, and then cluster them using different clustering algorithms with different similarity measures. Our experiments show that many of the reformulations we generate for TREC queries in fact correspond well with their sub-topics as identified by TREC experts.

2. GENERATING REFORMULATIONS

Even though many techniques have been proposed for query reformulation, most of them aim to generate queries that are more effective than the original query [7, 5]. Their effectiveness for providing reformulations that cover different intents is thus unclear. Therefore, instead of using these models, we use a rather simple technique to generate reformulations from publicly available resources including anchor text extracted from a web collection and the Microsoft N-gram Services.

[1] http://research.microsoft.com/en-us/collaboration/focus/cs/web-ngram.aspx

2.1 Anchor Text

Anchor text is known to be an effective feature for web search [9]. Previous researchers have observed the similarity between anchor text and queries [6, 5]. Therefore, in this paper, we treat each anchor text as a reformulation that can potentially represent one aspect of a query.

The web collection from which we extract the anchor text is the English portion of the ClueWeb-09 category A [2]. It contains 500 million pages in English that were crawled from the web during early 2009. We extracted all pairs of anchor text and associated urls from the web pages in this collection.

Web pages are connected to one another via links, each of which is associated with some anchor text. A link is called *internal* if two connected pages are from the same domain and *external* if they come from different domains. Since most of the internal links are for navigation purposes, their associated anchor text is not very helpful. Typical examples of such anchor text are "home" and "index". As a result, we only consider *external* links.

In order to reduce noise, we discarded anchors that contain non-English words and those that contain navigation-triggered words such as "click", "download" and "subscribe". We also removed anchors that contain only numbers and stop words. Among the resulting anchors, we keep only those with frequency greater than 1 and are connected to at least *two* urls. The resulting anchor text collection contains 8, 215, 751 unique anchors.

For any given query, we use the top-M most frequent anchor texts that contain all of its terms as its reformulations.

2.2 Microsoft Web N-gram Services

The Microsoft Web N-gram Services provide smoothed n-gram models built from document body, document title, anchor text and queries in the Bing query log separately. Each model gives the probability of seeing an unigram u coming after an n-gram n, or $P(u|n)$.

For each query q, we obtain the top-M unigrams u with largest $P(u|q)$. Each reformulation is formed by adding u to q.

We put all reformulations generated from the two sources above into a list L. Since we aim to use each reformulation as a query aspect, we keep only those with reasonably high frequency. Ideally, we can obtain this frequency from query logs. Because we rely only on publicly available resources, we approximate this frequency by the number of times the query appears in a web collection. Finally, we order the reformulations in L by their frequency and keep only the top-M, which will be the candidates for clustering.

3. CLUSTERING

The list of reformulated queries generated above are then clustered into groups, each of which is considered a coarse representation of a query aspect. The clustering is based on a measure of query similarity.

3.1 Similarity Measures

3.1.1 Relevance Models

Since the queries are short, computing their similarity based only on the query words is not likely to be effective. Instead, we expand a query with documents that are likely to be relevant to it. Specifically, we represent each query q by the relevance model $P_q(w|R)$ [8] estimated from the top-10 documents returned by the query likelihood retrieval model for q.

The similarity of two reformulations r_1 and r_2 is then the KL-divergence between their relevance models $P_{r_1}(w|R)$ and $P_{r_2}(w|R)$. We also try the cosine similarity measure as an alternative to KL-divergence.

3.1.2 Co-occurrence At Passage Level

Since estimating relevance models for every reformulation is computationally expensive, we also examine a more efficient method based on passage analysis. The idea is that two queries are more similar if they co-occur often in the same text passages. Therefore, for every pair of reformulations r_i and r_j, we compute N_i and N_j – the number of passages in which each of them occurs, and N – the number of passages in which they co-occur. The similarity between r_i and r_j is given by the Jaccard score:

$$sim(r_i, r_j) = \frac{N}{N_i + N_j - N}$$

3.2 Clustering Algorithms

We applied two standard clustering algorithms: K-Means and Agglomerative Clustering.

3.2.1 K-Means Clustering

The algorithm initializes each of the K clusters with a random reformulation. It then iteratively partitions all reformulations into K clusters in which each reformulation is assigned to the cluster that is most similar to it. The similarity between a query and a cluster is the average similarity between this query and all the other queries in the cluster. The algorithm terminates when the cluster assignment for reformulations does not change.

3.2.2 Agglomerative Clustering

Agglomerative clustering has an advantage over K-Means in that we do not have to specify the number of clusters beforehand. The standard algorithm treats each reformulation as a singleton cluster. It sucessively merges pairs of clusters that are most similar to each other until some creteria is achieved. In our experiments, the algorithm stops when the intra-cluster similarity drops below a certain threshold τ. We use complete-link to compute the similarity between two clusters, which is the minimum pair-wise similarity between the two clusters.

This procedure generally produces a deep binary tree, which is unnessary in our case since we are not interested in the tree structure. Therefore, we collapse all leave nodes, which correspond to our generated reformulations, starting from the third level (excluding the root node) to their parent and use these parent nodes as our resulting clusters.

4. EXPERIMENTS

In our experiments, we use queries from TREC Web Track 2009 and 2010. This query set contain 100 queries. Each query comes with associated sub-topics identified by TREC experts. On average, there are 4.6 subtopics per query.

For each query, we generate reformulations as described in Section 2. We evaluate the quality of these reformulations

[2]http://boston.lti.cs.cmu.edu/Data/clueweb09/

by judging how many of them correspond to the actual sub-topics identified by TREC experts. Then, we evaluate the clusters provided by different combinations of clustering algorithms and similarity measures.

4.1 Data Preparation and Parameter Settings

We used ClueWeb-09 category B as the web collection both for estimating the frequency of reformulations and estimating the co-occurrence statistics. For frequency estimation, we found it too strict to require the exact query to appear in the document. Therefore, we relaxed this by counting the number of times all of the query's terms co-occur within a windows of size 10 and used this as its frequency. For passage analysis, two reformulations are considered co-occurring in the same text passage if all of their terms co-occur within a window of size 20.

We set the number of reformulations $M = 100$ in all of our experiments. As for K-Means, we empirically set $K = 10$.

4.2 Quality of Reformulations

As mentioned in Section 2, we put all reformulations generated from different sources together for each query and keep only top-100 most frequent ones. Among these reformulations, 15% is exclusively from the anchor text, 76% is exclusively from the Web N-gram service and 9% is from both sources.

In this experiment, two graduate students independently judge each of those 100 reformulations to see if it corresponds to any actual sub-topics of the query. A reformulation is then labeled by the corresponding sub-topic, or "none" if it does not match with any of the sub-topics. The inter-agreement between our two judges is 94%.

An actual sub-topic of the query is considered covered if at least one of the reformulations corresponds to it. Fig. 1 shows the percentage of subtopics (averaged across all queries) covered by the top-N of the 100 reformulations with N varying from 10 to 100. In general, the reformulations covers on average about 60% of the actual sub-topics, which is promising considering these reformulations are acquired in a very simple way. This suggests that publicly available resources are very useful at identifying aspects of queries.

It is worth noting that the reformulations that do not correspond to any of the aspects are not necessarily bad. In fact, many of them represent valid intents that were not identified by TREC experts. We leave the evaluation of these reformulations for future work.

4.3 Quality of Clustering

In this section, we tried different combinations of clustering algorithms and similarity measures to cluster all reformulations we have generated. We expect the techniques to be able to put reformulations with the same label into the same cluster.

To evaluate the quality of the generated clusters, we use the Rand index (RI), a well-known cluster quality measure. It computes the percentage of decisions that are correct and is calculated as follows:

$$RI = \frac{TP + TN}{TP + FP + FN + TN}$$

where TP (true positive) is the number of pairs of reformulations with the same labels that are put into the same cluster, TN (true negative) is the number of pairs with different labels that are put into the same cluster, FN (false negative) is the number of pairs with the same labels that are put into different clusters, and FP (false positive) is the number of pairs with different labels that are put into the same clusters. Reformulations with the label "none" are ignored in this computation since "none" is not a topic. Table 1 shows the RI score that different combinations achieve.

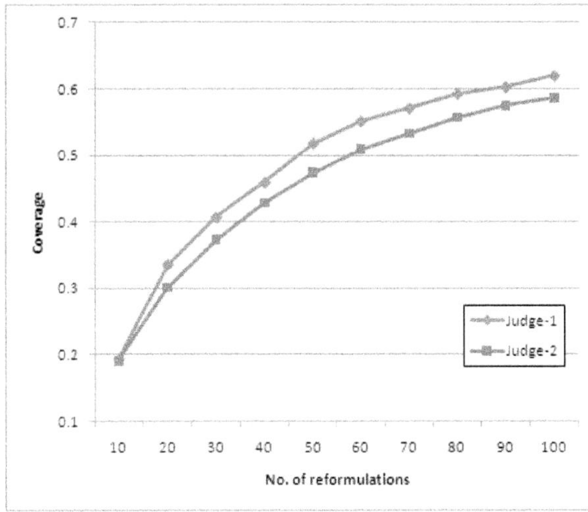

Figure 1: Quality of the generated reformulations in terms of how many of the actual sub-topics of the queries they cover.

Table 1: Quality of the automatically generated reformulations.

		RM+Cos.	RM+KL	PS+JAC
Judge-1	Agglo.	0.64	0.67	**0.76**
	K-Means	0.5	0.55	0.59
Judge-2	Agglo.	0.63	0.7	**0.73**
	K-Means	0.48	0.55	0.57

The first thing we observe from Table 1 is that agglomerative clustering consistently outperforms K-Means. The reason seems to be due to the fact that K-Means forces every reformulations to be in some cluster. This can result in unrelated reformulations being put into the same cluster. Once clusters are filled with unrelated reformulations, the centroids of those clusters are not very different from each other, making the cluster assignment in the next iteration unreliable. Agglomerative clustering only merges two clusters if they are very similar to each other, and has a lower chance of putting reformulations into unrelated clusters.

Secondly, Table 1 shows that the similarity measure based on co-occurrence is consistently better than those based on relevance models. It should be noted that most of the reformulations, especially those generated from the Microsoft N-Gram Services, are different to each other by only one word. The longer the original query, the less impact the augmented word has on the relevance model. As a result, the relevance models for these reformulations are more similar than they should be. The similarity measure based on co-occurence, on the other hand, is not affected as much by the length of the original query. Two reformulations are similar as long as their augmented words co-occur with each other and with

Table 2: **Example of clusters generated by agglomerative clustering for the query "satellite"**

{satellite tv; satellite tv vs cable; satellite network}
{satellite radio; sirius satellite radio; xm satellite radio}
{satellite image; google maps satellite}
{satellite internet}
{weather satellite; satellite climate}
{satellite technology; satellite development}
{satellite broadband}

the original query. This gives the co-occurrence-based measure superiority over the other two.

Tables 2 presents an example of clusters generated by agglomerative clustering with the co-occurrence similarity measure for the query "satellite".

5. RELATED WORK

Existing work in query diversity focuses mainly on selecting a diverse subset of documents returned by an initial retrieval. Maximal Marginal Relevance (MMR) [2] is a well-known example of this approach. It sequentially selects documents that are most different to those previously selected. Probabilistic versions of MMR have also been investigated [13, 4]. While these approaches only aim to select documents that cover different topics, others model the query's aspects explicitly [3, 1, 12].

Our approach is different to this existing research in that it works on the query side. It aims to generate clusters of reformulations, each of which represents one aspect of the query. In this preliminary study, even though we have not explicity diversified the set of reformulations, the clustering has this effect. Since clustering aims to put similar reformulations together, reformulations representing different aspects should be put in different clusters.

Query-side diversification has been investigated by Radlinski and Dumais [10]. However they use a proprietary query log whereas we examine the usefulness of publicly available resources. The most similar work to ours is that done by Radlinski et al. [11] in which they also infer queries' intents. However, they also rely on proprietary query logs.

Our approach does have a relationship to document-side diversification. The aspects our method generates for queries can be used by models such as [1, 12]. In addition, these models search for candidates from a set of documents retrieved for the original query. Our aspects are reformulations of the original query, and can be combined with the query to retrieve more potential documents for document-side models to work with.

6. CONCLUSIONS

In this paper, we have shown that reformulations for queries obtained from publicly available resources such as anchor text and Microsoft Web N-Gram Services match up well with the actual sub-topics of the queries. We then tested whether clusters of reformulations represent aspects, using different clustering algorithms and query similarity measures. We found that agglomerative clustering consistently outperforms K-Means and the similarity measure based on co-occurence is not only more effecient but also works better than similarity based on relevance models.

We observe that many of the clusters we obtained have very high intra-cluster consistency. We plan to build aspect representation from each cluster and use these in retrieval experiments.

Since clustering puts similar reformulations together, it has the effect of diversification because diverse reformulations should go to different clusters. Therefore, it would be interesting to see how clustering performs compared to applying existing techniques such as MMR on the set of reformulations.

As noted earlier, our method identified many interesting aspects that were not present in the TREC judgment. In the future, we will evaluate these reformulations, and identify how many of them represent valid aspects.

7. ACKNOWLEDGMENTS

This work was supported in part by the Center for Intelligent Information Retrieval and in part by ARRA NSF IIS-9014442. Any opinions, findings and conclusions or recommendations expressed in this material are the authors' and do not necessarily reflect those of the sponsor.

8. REFERENCES

[1] R. Agrawal, S. Gollapudi, A. Halverson and S. Leong. Diversifying Search Results. In *Proceedings of WSDM*, 2009.

[2] J. Carbonell and J. Goldstein. The Use of MMR, Diversity-based Reranking for Reordering Documents and Producing Summaries. In *Proceedings of SIGIR*, 1998.

[3] B. Carterette and P. Chandar. Probabilistic Models of Novel Document Rankings for Faceted Topic Retrieval In *Proceedings of CIKM*, 2009.

[4] H. Chen and D.R. Karger. Less is More: Probabilistic Models for Retrieving Fewer Relevant Documents In *Proceedings of SIGIR*, 2006.

[5] V. Dang and W.B. Croft. Query Reformulation Using Anchor Text. In *Proceedings of WSDM*, 2010.

[6] N. Eiron and K.S. McCurley. Analysis of Anchor Text for Web Search. In *Proceedings of SIGIR*, 2003.

[7] R. Jones, B. Rey and O. Madani. Generating Query Substitutions. In *Proceedings of WWW*, 2006.

[8] V. Lavrenko and W.B. Croft. Relevance-based Language Models. In *Proceedings of SIGIR*, 2001.

[9] D. Metzler, J. Novak, H. Cui, and S. Reddy. Building Enriched Document Representations Using Aggregated Anchor Text. In *Proceedings of SIGIR*, 2009.

[10] F. Radlinski and S. Dumais. Improving Personalized Web Search Using Result Diversification. In *Proceedings of SIGIR*, 2006.

[11] F. Radlinski, M. Szummer, and N. Craswell. Inferring Query Intent from Reformulations and Clicks. In *Proceedings of WWW*, 2010.

[12] R. Santos, C. Macdonald and I. Ounis. Exploiting Query Reformulation for Web Search Result Diversification In *Proceedings of WWW*, 2010.

[13] C. Zhai, W. Cohen and J. Lafferty. Beyond Independent Relevance: Methods and Evaluation Metrics for Subtopic Retrieval. In *Proceedings of SIGIR*, 2003.

Advertiser-Centric Approach to Understand User Click Behavior in Sponsored Search

Sungchul Kim*
POSTECH
Pohang, South Korea
subright@postech.ac.kr

Tao Qin, Tie-Yan Liu
Microsoft Research Asia
Beijing, China
{taoqin,tyliu}@microsoft.com

Hwanjo Yu
POSTECH
Pohang, South Korea
hwanjoyu@postech.ac.kr

ABSTRACT

Sponsored search is the major business model of commercial search engines. The number of clicks on ads is a key indicator of success for both advertisers and search engines, and increasing ad clicks is a goal of both of them. Many existing works stand on the view of search engines concerning how to help search engines to earn more revenue by accurately predicting ad clicks. Unlike the existing works, this paper aims at understanding user clicks on ads from "the view of advertisers", in order to help advertisers to improve their ad quality and therefore advertising effectiveness. To do this, a factor graph model is proposed, which considers two advertiser-controllable factors to understand user click behaviors: the relevance between a query and an ad, which has been well studied in previous literatures, and the "attractiveness" of the ad, which is a newly-proposed concept. The proposed model can be used to predict user clicks and also to mine a set of attractive words that could be leveraged to improve the quality of the ads. We have verified the effectiveness of the proposed approach using real-world datasets, through quantitative evaluations and informative case studies.

Categories and Subject Descriptors: H.3.5[INFORMATION STORAGE AND RETRIEVAL]: On-line Information Services

General Terms: Algorithms, Experimentation.

Keywords: Search advertising, Attractiveness model, Click behavior

1. INTRODUCTION

Sponsored search is the prevalent revenue source of major search engines, and search engines and advertisers would like to see more clicks on ads. To obtain more clicks, the first step is to understand why users click on ads or understand user click behaviors. Existing works investigates user click behaviors on ads from the view of search engines [4, 11]. However, the analyses on user click behaviors do not directly help advertisers improve their ads, since many factors used in click prediction cannot be accessible and controlled by advertisers. Unlike the existing works, we look at the problem from the perspective of advertisers. In particular, we want to find the factors that explain user click behaviors, which can be exploited by the advertisers to improve their ads and attract more clicks.

*The work was performed when the first author was intern at Microsoft Research Asia.

CIKM'11, October 24–28, 2011, Glasgow, Scotland, UK.

Buy arcade games
Bring the fun of the arcade home. classic games like pac-man & more.
www.nextag.com/arcade-games

Free arcade game
Play pac-man for free! download now & get free unlimited play
www.populardownloads.com/pacman

Figure 1: Comparison of two ads for query "arcade games"

It has been widely accepted that the relevance between a query and an ad is an important factor to explain user click behaviors. However, there are some cases that relevance might not be able to explain what we have observed. For example, Fig. 1 shows two ads for query "arcade games". The first ad is more relevant to the query than the second ad, as it contains query terms in both the title and the description. However, the logs show that the second ad has much more clicks than the first one although the second ad is relatively less relevant to the query. Through a user study, we find that people tend to click on the second ad because they think some words in it are attractive, such as "free" and "unlimited". We call this factor "**attractiveness**", which refers to how likely an ad (or a word in the ad) attract users' attention and trigger them to click.

To understand how relevance and ad attractiveness affect user clicks, we model user clicks using a factor graph model [5]. In the graph, (1) the attractiveness of a word in an ad depends on a set of attractiveness features extracted for the word; (2) the attractiveness of an ad depends on the attractiveness of all the words in it; (3) the relevance between an ad and a query depends on a set of relevance features; and (4) user clicks depend on both relevance and attractiveness of the ad. The model can be used to predict clicks, compute relevance scores, and infer the attractiveness score of a given word or ad. In particular, the inferred attractiveness scores of words can also be used as references for advertisers to effectively improve their ads and attract more clicks.

We have conducted experiments on real-world data, i.e., sponsored search logs obtained from a commercial search engine. According to our experiment results, show that advertisers should pay attention to the attractiveness of their ads.

This paper is organized as follows. Section 2 introduces two factors of user click behaviors from advertisers' view. Section 3 describes our factor graph model. Section 4 presents experimental results and demonstrates several examples of attractive words and ads. Section 5 concludes our study.

2. RELEVANCE AND ATTRACTIVENESS

Relevance between a query and an ad is an important factor to explain user click behaviors in sponsored search [10, 8]. However, some ads matching the query well still have relatively low click rates while other ads not exactly matching the query in their descriptions obtain many clicks [2, 9]. These observations imply the existence of other important factors beyond relevance which influence user click behaviors.

We conducted a user study to better understand this situation by asking users for the reason why they choose ads less relavant than other ads. Twenty users participated in the study, and their feedback shows that user click behaviors are easily affected by special words in the ad, which are very attractractive to the users. Examples of such words include "free", "great", and "save". Therefore, we propose the concept of "attractiveness", which means how attractive an ad or a word in the ad is to a user and how likely the ad will attract user's click. In other words, if two ads have similar degree of relevance, it is more likely that a user will notice the one with a larger attractiveness score and click on it.

The idea of attractiveness is somehow similar to that of "call-to-action" in marketing[1]. There are some differences between attractiveness and call-to-action: 1) The latter is binary: a word/phrase is either a call-to-action word/phrase or not; while the former measures the degree that a word (or an ad) attracts users' attention. 2) Call-to-action words are mostly verbs; while attractive words can be with different POS tags, as will be demonstrated in the experiment section.

Given that both relevance and attractiveness are important to explain user click behaviors, we consider both of them to obtain in-depth understanding of user clicks. Note that both relevance (e.g., inserting query words into ad title/description) and attractiveness (e.g., using attractive words to compose an ad) are controllable factors for advertisers.

3. USER CLICK BEHAVIOR MODEL

We propose a factor graph model (Fig. 2) to understand user click behaviors. In this graph, the node c represents whether an ad is clicked (c=1) or not (c=0), and we define the click probability using a logistic function:

$$p(c = 1|s) = \frac{1}{1 + e^{-s}} \quad (1)$$

where s is the click score: a larger click score means that the ad is more likely clicked by users.

The score s depends on the relevance score r and the attractiveness score a of the ad, and we define the probability $p(s|r, a, w_c)$ using a Gaussian distribution:

$$p(s|r, a, w_c) \sim N(w_{c,1}r + w_{c,2}a, \beta_c), \quad (2)$$

where w_c is the weight vector and β_c is a hyper parameter controlling the precision, and we assume that the weight vector w_c has a Gaussian prior, $w_c \sim N(\mu_c, \sigma_c)$.

Given r and a, we can estimate the click probability as follows.

$$p(c|r, a) = \int\int p(c|s)p(s|r, a, w_c)p(w_c)dw_c ds \quad (3)$$

[1]http://lyrishq.lyris.com/index.php/Email-Marketing/8-Tips-for-a-Stronger-Call-to-Action.html

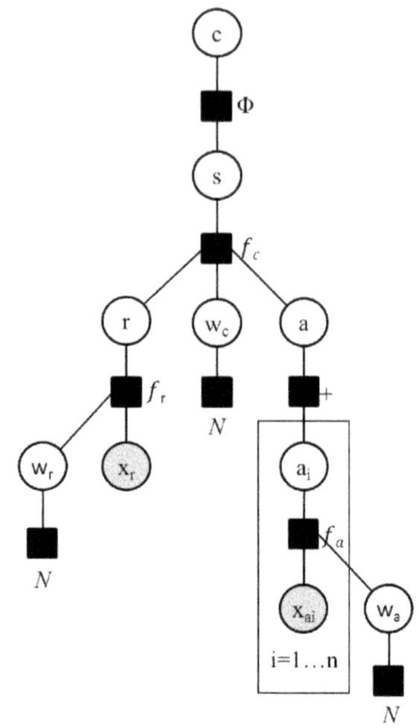

Figure 2: A factor graph of the user click behavior model

3.1 Relevance

Relevance score r between an ad and a query is estimated for each ad-query pair. r is a Gaussian random variable that takes the linear combination of the relevance features, x_r with w_r as its mean, and hyper parameter β_r as its variance.. We extract the widely used relevance features x_r using the query words and the ad [7, 9, 12].

Given relevance features x_r, we compute the joint probability of r, w_r as follows,

$$p(r, w_r|x_r) = p(r|w_r, x_r)p(w_r) \quad (4)$$

where $p(r|w_r, x_r)$ is $N(\langle w_r, x_r\rangle, \beta_r)$.

If the prior of w_r is known, we can estimate the probability of the relevance score for a query-ad pair as follows.

$$p(r|x_r) = \int p(r, w_r|x_r)dw_r \quad (5)$$

3.2 Attractiveness

To estimate the attractiveness score, we introduce two latent variables a_i for word-level attractiveness and a for the ad-level attractiveness model.

3.2.1 *Word-Level Attractiveness*

The node a_i indicates the attractiveness score of a word i, which takes the linear combination of the attractiveness features x_{a_i} with w_a as its mean and β_{a_i} as its variance.

We extract two kinds of attractiveness features: 1) features to represent words' visible and textual features [9] such as their position in ads, length, POS tag [3], and so on and 2) features based on previous impressions and clicks which are historical evidences about users' preferences on ads and words including entropy to penalize those words that are too general or too rare.

With the features, we compute the joint probability of a_i, w_a given attractiveness features x_{a_i} as follows.

$$p(a_i, w_a|x_{a_i}) = p(a_i|w_a, x_{a_i})p(w_a) \quad (6)$$

where $p(a_i|w_a, x_{a_i})$ is $N(<w_a, x_{a_i}>, \beta_{a_i})$.

If the prior of weight vector w_a is known, we can estimate the probability of the attractiveness score for a word as follows.

$$p(a_i|x_{a_i}) = \int p(a_i, w_a|x_{a_i})dw_a \quad (7)$$

3.2.2 *Ad-Level Attractiveness*

We assume that the attractiveness score of an ad is a Gaussian random variable, and takes the sum of each word's attractiveness as its mean: $a|\{a_i\}_{i=1}^n \sim N(\sum_{i=1}^n a_i, \beta_a)$, where a is the attractiveness score of an ad, a_i is the attractiveness score of the i-th word in the ad, and β_a is a hyperparameter.

Combining with the word-level attractiveness model, according to the factor graph, we have

$$p(a, \{a_i\}_{i=1}^n, w_a|x_a) = p(a|\{a_i\}_{i=1}^n)(\prod_i p(a_i|w_a, x_{a_i}))p(w_a) \quad (8)$$

where $x_a = \{x_{a_i}\}_{i=1}^n$, and n is the number of words in the ad. By marginalizing $\{a_i\}_{i=1}^n$ and w_a, the probability of the attractiveness score of an ad can be computed as below.

$$p(a|x_a) = \int\int p(a, \{a_i\}_{i=1}^n, w_a|x_a)dw_a d\{a_i\}_{i=1}^n \quad (9)$$

3.3 Learning and Inference

The probability of a click given the relevance features x_r and the word-level attractiveness features x_a can be written as below.

$$p(c|x_r, x_a) = \int\int p(c|r, a)p(r|x_r)p(a|x_a)drda, \quad (10)$$

In this model, the parameters, $\mu_r, \sigma_r, \mu_a, \sigma_a, \mu_c, \sigma_c$, are learned from training data [5]. We use Infer.Net [6] to learn the parameters by likelihood maximization.

After learning the parameters, we can infer the most likely attractiveness score of a new word or a new ad as follows:

$$a_i^* = \arg\max_{a_i} p(a_i|x_{a_i}), \quad (11)$$

where $p(a_i|x_{a_i})$ is defined in Eqn (7), and

$$a^* = \arg\max_{a} p(a|x_a), \quad (12)$$

where $p(a|x_a)$ is defined in Eqn (9).

4. EXPERIMENTS

We conduct experiments on the sponsored search log obtained from a commercial search engine to evaluate the proposed method. We used two-weeks sponsored search logs, with the first week for training and the second week for test. In our experiments, we consider six categories of queries: computers, games, health, society, recreation, and sports. For each sample query randomly selected from each category, we only consider the ads that have been shown in search result pages since the ads that have not been shown in search result pages cannot affect user click behavior.

4.1 Results

With the learned model, we can infer the click probability for each ad-query pair using its relevance features and word-level attractiveness features. Then we use this probability to rank all the ads related to a query in the test set. We use Precision-recall (P-R) curves to measure the accuracy of the method [1, 9]. For comparison, we also trained a model using only the relevance features. We call R-model for the model considering only relevance, and RA-model for the model considering both or relevance and attractiveness.

Fig. 3 shows that P-R curve of R-model is lower than the RA-model in most categories (Fig. 3), indicating that although relevance is an important factor for search engine to select and display ads, combination of relevance and attractiveness explains user click behaviors on ads in a much better way.

Table 1: General attractive words list

free, online, find, official, save, shop, great, site, instant, deal, qualified, faster, address, affordable, price, low, instantly, guaranteed, local, fundamental, professional, compare, today

(a) R:6 RA:5 CTR:13

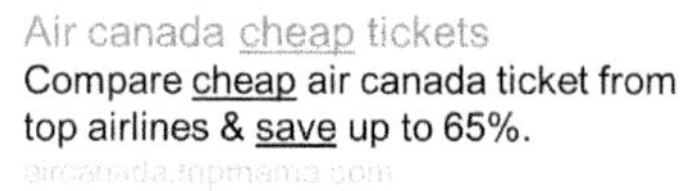

(b) R:6 RA:2 CTR:2

Figure 4: Comparison of two ads where R and RA is rank of c estimated by only r, and both of r and a, respectively. CTR is actual rank.

4.2 Case Study: Attractive Words and Ads

Table 1 shows a list of attractive words independent of categories. Advertisers may want to use them regardless of ads categories. Fig. 4 compares two real ads – one matching the query well and the other containing the attractive words. Data shows that the second ad gets larger click-through rate for the query. This example shows that for the ads with similar relevance scores, people will tend to click those with larger attractiveness scores. According to our experiments, our RA-model produces more accurate ranking than the R-model on the example as shown in Fig. 4.

Note that the attractive words and attractive ads can serve as a good reference for advertisers to improve their ads quality so as to attract more clicks on them. For example, they can replace a less attractive word by its more attractive synonym. Considering the strong relationship between attractiveness and clicks, advertisers can expect much more clicks after making such changes to their ads.

4.3 Discussions

All advertisers may want to use the attractive words identified by our model in order to make their ads more attractive. However, if a word is contained in every ad, users will not be attracted by the word any more. Therefore, the attractiveness of a word will change over time, and we may need to re-train our model periodically to reflect the change of users' click behaviors.

Another important issue is that clicks are not the final goal of advertisers. By making ads more attractive advertisers can earn more clicks, but they will also spend more money. To get better Return On Investment (ROI), advertisers should also pay attention to improving the quality of their landing pages. If the landing pages are of bad quality, users will not make any transactions in their websites.

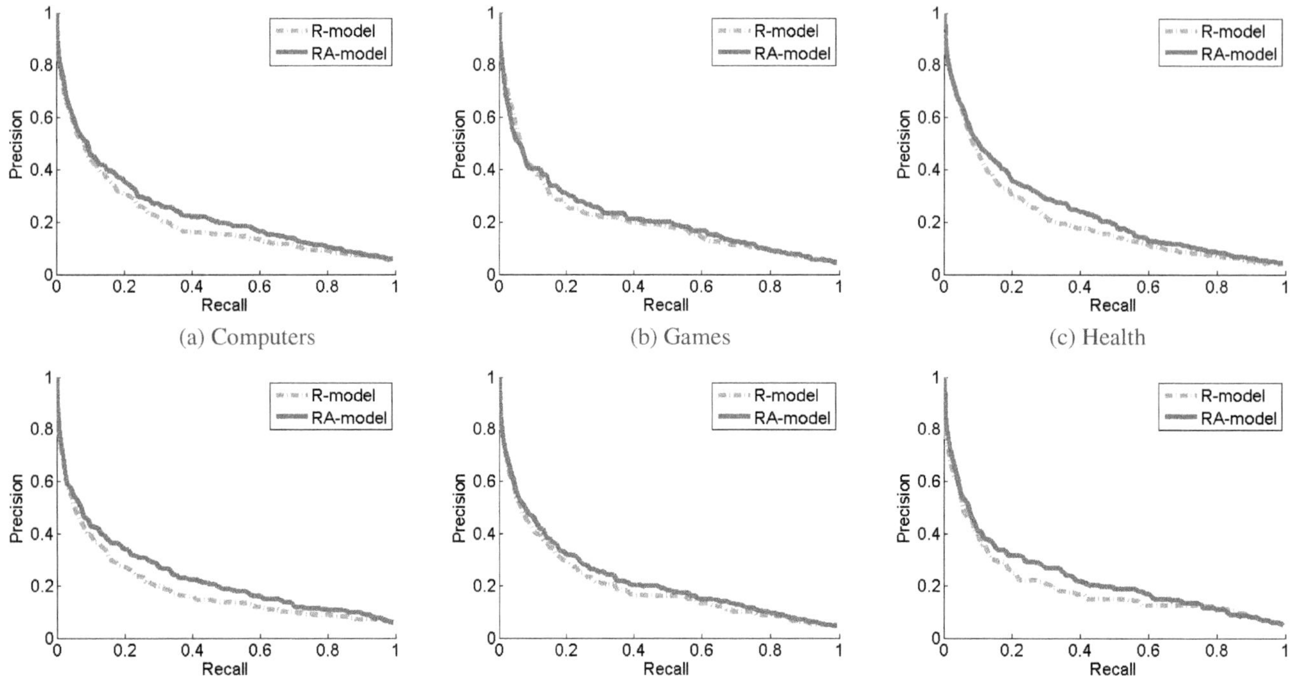

(a) Computers (b) Games (c) Health
(d) Society (e) Recreation (f) Sports

Figure 3: Comparison using precision-recall curve.

5. CONCLUSIONS AND FUTURE WORK

In this paper, we analyze user click behaviors in sponsored search from advertisers' view. We propose a factor graph model to discover how relevance and attractiveness affect user clicks. Our study shows that attractiveness can enhance relevance to explain user click behaviors. Furthermore, our model can estimate the attractiveness score of each word and each ad, which can serve as a useful reference for advertisers to improve their ads so as to attract more clicks.

There are several aspects to further investigate in the future. First, we will enhance the accuracy of our model by using more advanced features. Second, we plan to investigate more novel way to help advertisers based on the concept of attractiveness. i.e., how to automatically help advertisers optimize their ads, which is clearly more useful for advertisers.

6. REFERENCES

[1] J. Attenberg, S. Pandey, and T. Suel. Modeling and predicting user behavior in sponsored search. KDD, pages 1067–1076, 2009.

[2] G. Buscher, S. T. Dumais, and E. Cutrell. The good, the bad, and the random: an eye-tracking study of ad quality in web search. SIGIR, pages 42–49, 2010.

[3] C. Fellbaum, editor. *WordNet Electronic Lexical Database*. Cambridge, MA ; London, 1998.

[4] T. Graepel, J. Q. Candela, T. Borchert, and R. Herbrich. Web-scale Bayesian click-through rate prediction for sponsored search advertising in Microsoft's Bing search engine. ICML, pages 13–20, 2010.

[5] F. R. Kschischang, B. J. Frey, and H. A. Loeliger. Factor graphs and the sum-product algorithm. *IEEE Transactions on Information Theory*, 47, 2001.

[6] T. Minka, J. Winn, J. Guiver, and D. Knowles. Infer.NET 2.4, 2010. Microsoft Research Cambridge. http://research.microsoft.com/infernet.

[7] T. Qin, T. Liu, J. Xu, and H. Li. LETOR: A benchmark collection for research on learning to rank for information retrieval. *Information Retrieval*, pages 1–29, 2010.

[8] B. A. Ribeiro-Neto, M. Cristo, P. B. Golgher, and E. S. de Moura. Impedance coupling in content-targeted advertising. SIGIR, pages 496–503, 2005.

[9] M. Richardson, E. Dominowska, and R. Ragno. Predicting clicks: estimating the click-through rate for new ads. WWW, pages 521–530, 2007.

[10] C. Wang, P. Zhang, R. Choi, and M. D'Eredita. Understanding consumers attitude toward advertising. Eighth Americas Conference on Information Systems., pages 1143–1148, 2002.

[11] W. Xu, E. Manavoglu, and E. Cantu-Paz. Temporal click model for sponsored search. SIGIR, pages 106–113. ACM, 2010.

[12] Y. Zhu, G. Wang, J. Yang, D. Wang, J. Yan, J. Hu, and Z. Chen. Optimizing search engine revenue in sponsored search. SIGIR, pages 588–595, 2009.

Supervised Matching of Comments with News Article Segments

Dyut Kumar Sil
Dept CSA, IISc, Bangalore
dyutkumar@csa.iisc.ernet.in

Srinivasan H Sengamedu
Yahoo! Labs, Bangalore
shs@yahoo-inc.com

Chiranjib Bhattacharyya
Dept CSA, IISc, Bangalore
chiru@csa.iisc.ernet.in

ABSTRACT

Comments constitute an important part of Web 2.0. In this paper, we consider comments on news articles. To simplify the task of relating the comment content to the article content the comments are about, we propose the idea of showing comments alongside article segments and explore automatic mapping of comments to article segments. This task is challenging because of the vocabulary mismatch between the articles and the comments. We present supervised and unsupervised techniques for aligning comments to segments the of article the comments are about. More specifically, we provide a novel formulation of supervised alignment problem using the framework of structured classification. Our experimental results show that structured classification model performs better than unsupervised matching and binary classification model.

Categories and Subject Descriptors

H.3.1 [**Information Systems**]: Information Storage and Retrieval

General Terms

Algorithms

Keywords

Comments, Structured Classification, Enrichment, ESA

1. INTRODUCTION

User generated content is the central theme of Web 2.0. While there are several forms of user generated content like blogs, photo/video uploads, reviews, etc., comments are the primary form of user interaction in several sites. Comments form a light-weight mechanism for user participation as they are primarily reactive. Recently [3] proposed mapping comments to article segments to simplify readers' task of relating comment content to article content.

CIKM'11, October 24–28, 2011, Glasgow, Scotland, UK.

In this paper we consider a variation of the problem proposed in [3]. More specifically, while [3] addressed the unsupervised matching problem, we consider supervised matching. We state the problem formally as follows.

Problem Statement: Let an article A be characterized by the set of segments $S(A) = \{s_1, \ldots, s_{n_s}\}$, where a segment s_k could be a paragraph, sentence, etc. and they form a partition of the article A. The comments associated with article A are denoted $C(A) = \{c_1, \cdots, c_{n_c}\}$. Given a set of matching (comment, segment) pairs, the goal is to design a learning machine which, when presented with a article A and its associated comments, $C(A)$, correctly identifies for each comment, $c \in C(A)$, the related segment or segments in $S(A)$. □

Technical Contributions.

Our technical contributions directly address the above challenges and are two fold. In a machine learning scenario, the key elements are the features as well as the classification technique. We address and contribute on both fronts.

Supervised Classification: We provide two different formulations for the supervised comment alignment problem – the well-known binary classification as well as the less familiar structured classification. We show that structured classification outperforms binary classification.

Enriched Topic Features: Extending the ideas of enrichment presented in [3], we propose the use of Explicit Semantic Analysis [1] for the comment alignment task.

The problem of retrieving article segments for comments has the distinct flavor of traditional information retrieval where segments can be considered documents and the comments can be considered queries. We show through our experiments that the proposed techniques outperform two traditional IR representatives, viz., Lucene and Indri. We also show that the notion of enrichment complements traditional IR features.

The paper is organized as follows. Section 2 discusses the main contribution that of possible supervised approaches to match comments and segments. Section 3 proposes two novel feature representations: *enriched* representation using ESA [1] and coreference features. Section 4 contains the experimental results. The paper closes with conclusions and a discussion.

2. MATCHING COMMENTS WITH SEGMENTS

There is no readymade solution strategy for the problem statement given before. To this end we investigate both supervised and unsupervised strategies. To begin the discussion, we assume that we are given a dataset $\mathcal{D}$ defined on a collection of articles $\{A_1, \dots, A_n\}$ where

$$\begin{aligned} \mathcal{D} &= \{ (c_{ij}, S_{ij}) \mid c_{ij} \in C(A_i), \quad (1) \\ & \quad S_{ij} = \{s | s \in S(A_i) \wedge c_{ij} \text{ is about } s\}, \; i = 1, \dots n\} \end{aligned}$$

2.1 Supervised Approach for Matching comments with Segments

In this section we formulate the supervised learning problem in two ways, namely the structured learning approach and the binary classification approach.

2.1.1 Structured Learning for locating segments

In the structured learning setup [4], one considers the problem of assigning labels $y \in \mathcal{Y}$, one of many labels, to an observation $x \in \mathcal{X}$. Structured classification proceeds by assuming that, given an x and w, the following function

$$f(x) = \arg\max_{y \in \mathcal{Y}} \mathbf{w}^\top \psi(x, y)$$

is tractable where $\psi(x, y) : \mathcal{X} \times \mathcal{Y} \to \mathbb{R}^d$ is a suitably defined feature function.

In this paper, we discuss relevant details of structured learning as applied to the problem at hand. For a detailed review of structured learning see [4].

In the structured learning setup we make an assumption that in (1), each c_{ij} is mapped to *only one* segment, in other words $|S_{ij}| = 1$, where the cardinality of S_{ij} is denoted by $|S_{ij}|$. The resultant dataset is written as $\mathcal{D} = \{(c_{ij}, s_{ij})\}$, where s_{ij} denotes the segment correspond to c_{ij}. We wish to explore structured learning framework for this dataset.

We begin by assuming that $\psi(c, s) : C(A) \times S(A) \to \mathbb{R}^d$ is a given feature function. For more description of ψ, see Section 3.3. Given a $\mathbf{w} \in \mathbb{R}^d$, we wish to infer the segment associated with a comment c in a particular article A

$$f(c) = \arg\max_{s \in S(A)} \mathbf{w}^\top \psi(c, s) \quad (2)$$

which can be computed by straightforward enumeration as $|S(A)|$ is low.

The learning of $\mathbf{w}$ on a training set depends on the specific loss function. For the problem at hand we use

$$\Delta(s, f(c_{ij})) = \mathbf{1}_{s_{ij} \neq f(c_{ij})} \quad (3)$$

where $\mathbf{1}$ is the indicator function. The idea is to choose $\mathbf{w}$ such that for each comment $c_{ij} \in C(A_i)$, the score of the correct segment s_{ij} will be highest among all the other segments. This can be ensured by requiring that $\mathbf{w}^\top \psi(c_{ij}, s_{ij}) \geq \mathbf{w}^\top \psi(c, s), \quad \forall s \in S(A) - s_{ij}$. This immediately motivates the following optimization problem.

$$\min_{\mathbf{w}, \xi \geq 0} \frac{1}{2} \|\mathbf{w}\|^2 + \frac{C}{N} \sum_{i=1}^{n} \sum_{j=1}^{|C(A_i)|} \xi_{ij}$$

subject to

$$\begin{aligned} \mathbf{w}^T \psi(c_{ij}, s_{ij}) &\geq \mathbf{w}^\top \psi(c_{ij}, s) + 1 - \xi_{ij}, \\ & \quad \forall s \in S(A_i) - s_{ij}, \; c_{ij} \in C(A_i), \text{ and} \\ \xi_{ij} &\geq 0 \end{aligned}$$

Lemma: *At optimality,*

$$\sum_{i=1}^{n} \sum_{j=1}^{|C(A_i)|} \xi_{ij} \geq \Delta(s_{ij}, f(c_{ij}))$$

where Δ *is defined in* (3) *and* f *is defined in* (2).

Proof:
Let $s = f(c_{ij}) \neq s_{ij}$ be the segment identified by (2). Then see that

$$\xi_{ij} \geq 1 - \left(w^\top \psi(c_{ij}, s_{ij}) - w^\top \psi(c_{ij}, s)\right)$$

By definition of s the difference of scores

$$\mathbf{w}^\top \delta_{ij} \psi(s) = \left(\mathbf{w}^\top \psi(c_{ij}, s_{ij}) - \mathbf{w}^\top \psi(c_{ij}, s)\right) \leq 0 \quad (4)$$

which implies that $\xi_{ij} \geq 1$. The claim holds whenever the assignment implemented by (2) disagrees with the correct segment s_{ij}. Noting that ξ_{ij} is lower-bounded by 0, the claim is proved. □

The optimization problem pertaining to the learning problem is a Quadratic Program (QP) involving d variables and $\sum_{i=1}^{n} |C(A_i)|(|S(A_i)| - 1)$ constraints. The values of $|C(A_i)|$ are around 10 and that of $|S(A_i)|$ are often $10-15$ depending on the segmentation. The number of constraints is linear in the number of articles. In general solving such problems is hard as there could be large number of constraints. See [4] for the general case. Fortunately, we can solve the original problem directly by using a Convex QP as the number of constraints is small.

2.1.2 Binary Classification

In the previous section we discussed a strategy based on structured learning. But as noted the setting applies when dataset (1) is restricted to have only one segment assigned to each comment. We use the same $\psi(c, s)$ and define a classification problem. We assign a label $Y : C(A) \times S(A) \to \{\pm 1\}$ to all (comment, segment) pairs as follows: $Y(c_{ij}, s) = 1, \; \forall s \in S_{ij}$. Using this one could immediately rewrite (1) as a dataset $D = \{(\phi(c_{ij}, s), Y(c_{ij}, s)\}$, which is essentially a binary classification problem. This immediately motivates a SVM-like approach

$$\min_{\mathbf{w}, \xi \geq 0} \frac{1}{2} \|\mathbf{w}\|^2 + \frac{C}{N} \sum_{i=1}^{n} \sum_{j=1}^{|C(A_i)|} \sum_{k=1}^{|S(A_i)|} \xi_{ijk}$$

subject to

$$\begin{aligned} Y(c_{ij}, s_{ik}) \mathbf{w}^\top \psi(c_{ij}, s_{ik}) &\geq 1 - \xi_{ijk}, \\ & \quad \forall c_{ij} \in C(A_i), s_{ik} \in S(A_i), \text{ and} \\ \xi_{ijk} &\geq 0 \end{aligned}$$

Again we use a generic SVM solver for this purpose.

2.2 Unsupervised Matching

One could choose to ignore the segments and instead choose to learn a similarity function by exploratory analysis. The key idea is to design a similarity function $sim(c, s) : C(A) \times S(A) \to \mathbb{R}$ such that for a fixed c it will enable us to evaluate how similar a comment c is to a particular segment s. To this end we consider that a comment or segment is represented by a vector as represented by $\phi(\cdot)$. Given such a representation, we define the the cosine similarity

$$sim(c, s) = \frac{\phi(c)^\top \phi(s)}{\|\phi(c)\| \|\phi(s)\|} \quad \text{(COSINE)}$$

The vectors $\phi(c)$ and $\phi(s)$ are obtained from various feature functions discussed in Section 3.

3. REPRESENTATION

In our previous work [3] we have experimented with several feature representations for comment alignment namely bag of words (BOW), semi-supervised PLSA, and Latent Dirichlet Allocation (LDA). However because of extremely short length of comments and segments they are not very useful to capture the *semantics*. To address this issue we propose to leverage external corpus to have a more *enriched* representation. To this end we propose Explicit Semantic Analysis and coreference features.

3.1 Explicit Semantic Analysis

Unlike the above latent space approaches like LDA and SS-PLSA described above, explicit semantic analysis (ESA) uses a rich external corpus for representation [1]. Wikipedia is usually the corpus of choice. Let a be a Wikipedia article. For a term t, let $k_{t,a}$ denote the strength of association of t to a. Since Wikipedia has pages for most of the important concepts (people, places, events, organizations, etc.), we can consider $k_{t,a}$ as the affinity of t to the concept a and the vector $\mathbf{k}_t$ of all such weights as a representation of t in the concept space represented by Wikipedia.

Given a document d, the feature vector for d is given by

$$\phi(d) = \sum_{t \in d} w_{t,d}\mathbf{k}_t$$

In our case the document d could be a segment or a comment.

3.2 Coreference features

In addition to bag of words features, we also add a class of lexical and semantic features we call *coreference features* because of their widespread use in coreference resolution.

These features are listed below.

1. Number: Singular, Plural
2. Gender: Male, Female, Neuter, Unknown
3. Semantic class: Person, Location, Organization, Date, Time, Money, Percent, Object
4. Animacy: Human, Animal

These features are calculated using dictionaries, Stanford NER and Wordnet. Using this, we associate a 16-dimensional binary feature with each token t.

As mentioned before, these features are very popular in coreference resolution literature [2]. We can think of comment mapping as more complex form of reference resolution where we want to identify whether a comment directly or indirectly refers to an article segment. While these features are defined at token level for references in the coreference literature, we define them at segment or comment level. More formally, let f_t be the binary feature vector associated with a token t. The feature vector for a segment/comment s is given by

$$\sum_{t \in s} f_t$$

3.3 Cumulative Feature Vector

Given a comment c and a segment s, we can calculate features: BOW, LDA topics, SS-PLSA topics, Coreference features, and ESA for both c and s. For each of these features, we then calculate the cosine similarity. The final feature vector consists of BOW cosine similarity, Lucene score, Indri Score, LDA topic similarity, SS-PLSA similarity, Coreference feature similarity, and ESA similarity.

4. EXPERIMENTAL RESULTS

In this section we investigate several key questions related to the models proposed before. Broadly there are three questions one would like to explore.
(**a**) The effectiveness of the feature representations. We investigate empirically the effect of *enrichment*.
(**b**) Does supervision increase performance?
(**c**) Comparison between structured approach vis-a-vis binary classification.
In this section we explore these issues.

4.1 Experimental Setup

Datasets.

We created a dataset D by collecting 208 news articles along with ≈ 10 comments for each of the articles from `http://news.yahoo.com`. There were a total of 1079 comments in the corpus. We also created another dataset $D_{enriched}$ with same articles and comments as of D but with each of the articles enriched with additional (4–8) related articles. The related articles for an original article have been found by Google news search (`http://news.google.com`) with title of the original article as the search query.

The articles have an average length of 383.9 words (after stemming and stop word removal), 19.3 segments and 5.3 comments. The average length of comments is 24.6 words. In $D_{enriched}$, an average of 1316.2 words and 56.2 segments were added per article.

We created ground truth for for all the comments of all articles in the dataset. We have experimented with both the datasets D and $D_{enriched}$ with different methods discussed in Section 3.

Evaluation Metrics.

Let S_{ij} be the set of true related article-segments (found by human inspection) for comment c_{ij} as in (1).

If $|S_{ij}| > 1$, then c_{ij} has multiple related article-segments or if $|S_{ij}| = 0$, c_{ij} has no related article-segment.

Let r_{ij} be the retrieved result for comment c_{ij}. We consider this to be correct if $r_{ij} \in S_{ij}$.

The *Retrieval Index* is defined as:

$$RI = \frac{|\bigcup_{i=1}^{M}\{c_{ij} \in C(A_i) : r_{ij} \in S_{ij}\}|}{|\bigcup_{i=1}^{M} C(A_i)|}$$

i.e., RI is the ratio of number of correctly matched comments and total number of comments. Even if a comment is associated with multiple segments, we use only one segment from the classifier. It can be seen that most of the comments are short and are usually about one specific topic discussed in the article. Hence the above formulation of using only one retrieved segment is reasonable.

All the numbers reported here are the results of 10-fold cross validation.

Technique	RI
Unsupervised	58.9%
Binary SVM	62.6%
SVMStruct	**63.5%**

Table 1: RI for unsupervised and supevised matching techniques.

Features for supervised classification: To provide a rich feature space for the classification models, we use a binned representation of each feature. Let s be the value of a feature S (e.g., BOW similarity score). We choose a set T_S of thresholds for S. Then the binned representation of s is

$$< \mathbf{1}_{[s>t]} : \forall t \in T_S >$$

We thus convert each underlying feature to a T_S-dimensional feature capturing $T_S + 1$ bins. For example, if $s = 0.35$ and $T_S = \{0.1, 0.5, 0.9\}$, then the binned feature representation of s is $< 1\ 0\ 0 >$. In our experiments, $|T_S| = 10$ worked well.

4.2 Performance Comparison

Effectiveness of supervised techniques.

In the first experiment, for each comments and the segments of the article it corresponds to, we calculate the following seven features: BOW, LDA (or enriched LDA, denoted eLDA), SS-LDA, ESA, Coreference features, Lucene, and Indri. The features were binned as discussed above. The best results for SVMStruct were obtained with binned representation while that for binary SVM were obtained with non-binned representation. Since the number of matching segments for a comment is much smaller than the number of non-matching comments, the training data is unbalanced. We randomly sampled a subset of negative examples. The best C obtained using parameter sweeps for StructSVM is 0.5 while that for binary SVM is 1.1.

Table 1 shows RI for unsupervised matching as well as binary and structured SVM classifiers.

1. Supervised approaches have higher RI compared to the unsupervised approach. Binary SVM has a RI gain of 6.3% and structured SVM has a gain of 7.8% compared to unsupervised matching.

2. Structured classification performs better than binary classification by 1.4%.

Effectiveness of Enrichment.

The best performance using unsupervised matching is achieved by combining eLDA with BOW on enriched corpus – 57.8% of the comments are matched correctly (Table 2(b)). eLDA+BOW improves LDA by 124% and BOW by 3.4%.

It should be noted that all feature bring down the effectiveness of BOW when combined with it except eLDA. This shows that enriched topics provide a representation that is complementary to BOW.

It can also be seen that while ESA outperforms eLDA (by 14%), eLDA+BOW is more effective compared to ESA+BOW (by 8%).

Note: In Table 2, only eLDA features are computed on the enriched dataset as other features like BOW, PLSA, etc. cannot exploit the enriched dataset.

Feature	RI
BOW	55.9%
Lucene	57.2%
Indri	56.1%
SS-PLSA	51.4%
SS-PLSA+BOW	54.1%
ESA	41.0%
ESA + BOW	53.8%
LDA	25.8%
LDA+BOW	53.6%
Coreference	28.5%
Coreference + BOW	51.7%
Random	7.2%

(a) Performance on the Comment Dataset (D).

Feature	RI
eLDA	36.0%
eLDA+BOW	**57.8%**

(b) Performance on the Enriched Dataset ($D_{enriched}$).

Table 2: Effectiveness of enrichment using unsupervised matching. The table show RI scores for different features on two datasets – D and $\mathbf{D}_{enriched}$.

5. CONCLUSIONS AND DISCUSSION

In this paper, we have proposed new approaches to the problem of aligning comments to relevant parts of the article to reduce the readers' cognitive burden. We first pose this problem as a structured classification problem as well as a binary classification problem. We show that structured classification outperforms binary classification. We then explore two additional features for this task: Explicit Semantic Analysis and coreference features. Explicit Semantic Representation using Wikipedia does not perform well. This implies corpus-specific enrichments are more effective compared to generic enrichment schemes. In future work, we plan to explore increasing the effectiveness of corpus-specific enrichment schemes. For enrichment, the source and selection of documents, number of documents needed, etc. are very important and we plan to come up with systematic guidelines for these.

6. REFERENCES

[1] E. Gabrilovich and S. Markovitch. Computing semantic relatedness using Wikipedia-based Explicit Semantic Analysis. In *IJCAI*, 2007.

[2] A. Rahman and V. Ng. Narrowing the modeling gap: A cluster-ranking approach to coreference resolution. *JAIR*, 2011.

[3] D. K. Sil, S. H. Sengamedu, and C. Bhattacharyya. ReadAlong: Reading articles and comments together. In *WWW*, 2011.

[4] I. Tsochantaridis, T. Joachims, T. Hofmann, and Y. Altun. Support vector learning for interdependent and structured output spaces. *JMLR*, 2005.

User Action Interpretation for Personalized Content Optimization in Recommender Systems

Anlei Dong
Yahoo! Labs
701 First Avenue
Sunnyvale, CA 94089
anlei@yahoo-inc.com

Jiang Bian
Yahoo! Labs
701 First Avenue
Sunnyvale, CA 94089
jbian@yahoo-inc.com

Xiaofeng He
Microsoft Search Technology Center Asia
Microsoft China Lt.
xihe@microsoft.com

Srihari Reddy
Yahoo! Labs
701 First Avenue
Sunnyvale, CA 94089
sriharir@yahoo-inc.com

Yi Chang
Yahoo! Labs
701 First Avenue
Sunnyvale, CA 94089
yichang@yahoo-inc.com

ABSTRACT

User interaction plays a vital role in recommender systems. Previous studies on algorithmic recommender systems have mainly focused on modeling techniques and feature development. Traditionally, implicit user feedback or explicit user ratings on the recommended items form the basis for designing and training of recommendation algorithms. But user interactions in real-world Web applications (e.g., a portal website with different recommendation modules in the interface) are unlikely to be as ideal as those assumed by previously proposed models. To address this problem, we build an online learning framework for personalized recommendation. We argue that appropriate user action interpretation is critical for a recommender system. The main contribution in this paper is an approach of interpreting users' actions for the online learning to achieve better item relevance estimation. Our experiments on the large-scale data from a commercial Web recommender system demonstrate significant improvement in terms of a precision metric over the baseline model that does not incorporate user action interpretation. The efficacy of this new algorithm is also proved by the online test results on real user traffic.

Categories and Subject Descriptors

H.3.3 [**Information Storage and Retrieval**]: Information Search and Retrieval

General Terms

Algorithms, Experiments

Keywords

action interpretation, content optimization,personalization

CIKM'11, October 24–28, 2011, Glasgow, Scotland, UK.

1. INTRODUCTION

Digital content publishers, including portal websites, such as MSN and Yahoo!, have started providing Web users with a wide range of modules of Web content in a timely fashion. As shown in Figure 1, the portal Yahoo! presents today's emerging events, news of various aspects, and trending queries from a search engine to Web users. However, Web users usually have short attention spans while facing the explosion of Web content, referred as *information overload*. Therefore, it is necessary for those Web publishers to optimize their content by identifying the most relevant content to attract and retain users to their site on an ongoing basis.

An effective automatic recommendation system becomes indispensable for serving the users who visit portal websites, and personalization is also a desirable feature since it can further tailor content presentation to suit individual's interests rather than take the traditional "one-size-fits-all" approach.

In this paper, we propose a *parallel-serving-buckets* online learning framework which can instantaneously model the user actions, i.e. browse and click, in the recommender system so as to better serve the users. We use a dedicated model to estimate the relevance score for each candidate content item, which is specified as estimating the click-through rate (CTR) in our online learning framework. To achieve personalization, we employ a divide-and-conquer strategy which categorizes users into diverse groups based on their interests as modeled by user action information.

Our main contribution is: an approach of interpreting users' actions for the online learning to achieve better item relevance estimation, by taking into consideration the factor of user engagement.

The rest of this paper is organized as follows. In Section 2, we propose our online learning framework for recommendation and point out the critical challenge for achieving personalization and reaching better performance. Section 3 proposes appropriate user action interpretation to refine our online learning approach which can result in better performance recommendation. A large-scale evaluation and discussion based on the data from a commercial portal website are presented in Section 4, including testing the models on real user traffic. We conclude the paper in Section 5.

2. PERSONALIZED RECOMMENDATION

In this section, we introduce our recommender system framework and its components, which can achieve effective personalization through online learning. Furthermore, we point out the critical

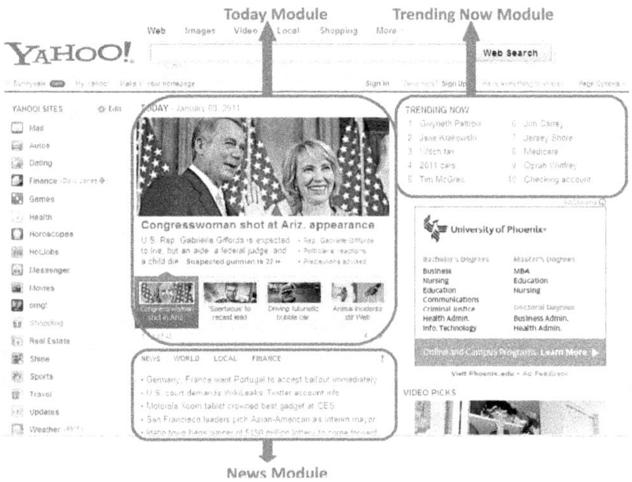

Figure 1: A snapshot of Yahoo! front page. The page contains multiple recommendation modules such as *Today module*, *Trending Now module* and *News module*.

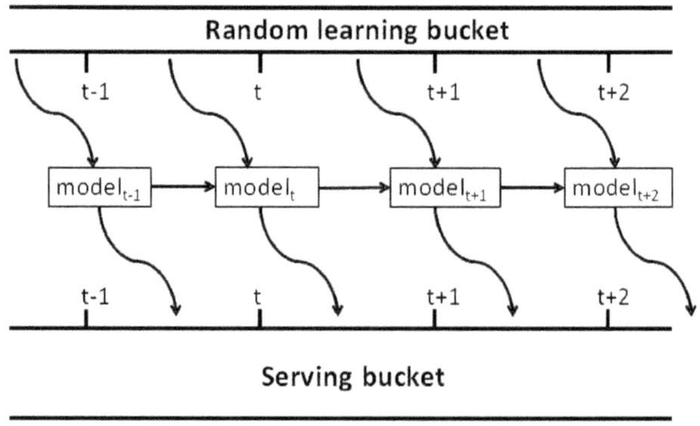

Figure 2: Online learning flowchart. A Random learning bucket is used for exploration purpose. At the end of each time interval, the model for each candidate item is updated based on the users' clicks and views in random learning bucket during this time interval. In the next time interval, the updated model is applied to the corresponding candidate item in the serving bucket. In this way, all the candidate items are displayed by ranking scores (computed by their corresponding updated models) in the serving bucket.

challenges for building such a system, which will be addressed in detail in the next section.

2.1 Problem formulation

We target recommendation applications of web portal frontpages. Our goal is to optimize content recommendation such that a certain user engagement metric, such as overall click-through rate (CTR), is maximized. For a pool of candidate items, human editors can be employed to manually rank the candidate items according to content attractiveness and users' interests and then recommend top ranked items to users. However, it requires expensive human effort and cannot guarantee that the most attractive and relevant items are recommended to users due to the interest gap between editors and Web users. Therefore, we attempt to design a recommender system that achieves content recommendation by automatically estimating candidate items' attractiveness and relevance to users' interests. Such a recommender system has three critical characteristics:

1. *Online learning.* To attract more users to browse and click content displayed on the portal frontpage, an online learning methodology is necessary because it enable us to model users' behaviors (i.e. clicks and views) on the frontpage as implicit feedback and adapt the recommendation model in real time (or almost real time) to user feedback, so as to serve more relevant content to users and provide better recommendation optimization. Figure 2 illustrates the flowchart of this online learning approach. To achieve better recommendation, it becomes essential to employ an effective method for updating per-item models. In this paper, we employ an *Estimated Most Popular* (EMP) model ([1]) to estimate CTR.

2. *Per-item model.* For each candidate item in the recommender system, we use a dedicated model to estimate its attractiveness/relevance score. We then rank all items by their respective scores in the descending order and display the top ranked ones to users. Under the scenario of online learning where real-time user feedbacks are available, the ranking score of an item can be estimated by its click-through rate (CTR), which represents a strong signal of attractiveness of this item to users. In the rest of this paper, we will apply the per-item model by default without explicit declaration.

3. *Personalization.* We use a personalization approach to provide users with a personalized experience of highly attractive and relevant content, so as to enhance user engagement, conversions, and long-term loyalty. A *divide-and-conquer* strategy is employed to achieve personalization: we divide users into a few different groups based on user profiles; for each group of users, the recommender system serves them with the models which are updated using only the feedback information created by the users belonging to the same group. This approach is called *user segmentation*.

2.2 Challenge

In this section, we have presented the online learning approach for our recommender system which implements personalization based on user segmentation. However, there is a critical challenge for implementing this recommender system:

Within each group, how to best utilize user feedback information to achieve effective online learning? The learning samples provided for online learning are characterized based on user feedback actions (i.e., clicks and views). However, after conducting user segmentation, learning samples in each user segment are not as ample as using all samples, therefore, correct understanding of user actions becomes more critical for obtaining effective recommendation models.

3. USER ACTION INTERPRETATION

We argue that good understanding and exploitation of user actions, including clicks and views, can effectively benefit the modeling by better understanding users' general interests and the items' attractiveness to users.

As shown in Figure 1, there is usually more than one content recommendation module on portal website. Different content modules are likely to compete with each other on a densely packed interface such as the frontpage of the portal website. Therefore, one user visit on the portal website may not necessarily mean the user is really engaged in all the content modules displayed to the user. Here, engagement means that the user examined or at least partly examined recommended content. For example, when a user visits the

Yahoo! frontpage as shown in Figure 1, it is possible she totally ignores the displayed Trending Now module contents as she may be attracted by the contents of other modules such as Today module, or she directly goes for other services such as search and e-mail.

For a recommendation module, accurate CTR estimation should be based on the events where users were really engaged in this module, instead of all the events where the contents of this module were merely displayed to the users. In our work, we identify three categories of events regarding user engagement:

1. **Click event**: *click event* is an event where the user clicked one or more items in the module after she opened the web page. In a click event, the user is engaged in the module under study because she must have examined at least some of items recommended by the module. Obviously, click events is useful for CTR estimation.

2. **Click-other event**: *click-other event* contains at least one action on other application/modules in the interface (such as clicking items displayed by other modules, doing search in search box, etc). Obviously, click-other events should be excluded from being used for CTR estimation.

3. **Non-click event**: besides click events and clicks-other events, there are also *non-click events* in which users had no action such as click or search after they opened the web page. For a non-click event, unlike click event or click-other event, it is not straightforward to determine whether or not the user actually examined the module under study as usually the system cannot track user's eyes. However, based on user's historic behaviors, it is still possible to deduce if the user intends to examine the module or not. Intuitively, if a user often clicked the module under study in the past, it implies this user is interested in this module so that it is likely she actually examined the module in the latest event. For a user, we can check the number of clicks on the module during a specified length of past period and use such click number to present the prior probability that this user actually examined the module in the event.

4. EXPERIMENTS

4.1 Setup

4.1.1 Data Set

To validate our proposed approaches, we conduct experiments on the data from a real-world content recommendation module, i.e. the Trending Now module on the Yahoo! frontpage (as shown in Figure 1). We collected events in terms of *views* and *clicks* from a *random learning bucket* of the Trending Now module during ten days from November 30th, 2010 to December 9th, 2010. The pool of candidate items may change multiple times during each day. To protect privacy, all the users are anonymized in this dataset.

In the *random learning bucket*, candidate queries are randomly selected and displayed to users at all of positions with equal chances. An event records a user's action on the served content items (i.e. trending queries) on the Trending Now module, which is either "*view*" or "*click*". More specifically, we represent each event e as a set of tuples:

$$e = \langle u, t, p, q_p, a \rangle, \; p = 1, 2, \ldots, 10$$

where u denotes the user, t represents the time stamp for this event, q is the served query, p denotes the position at which the trending query q is displayed (there are ten positions on the Trending Now module), a represents the action which is either *view* or *click*. Note that one logged *view* event e only means that the query q was displayed to the user u, who did not necessarily examine the query. In the whole dataset, there are totally hundreds of millions of events with multiple millions of unique users.

Table 1: An illustrative example for evaluation metric (precision) computation. For an actual event in the random learning bucket, Item 1 was ranked at Position 1 and clicked by the user. For Model 1: $precision_1$ **= 1,** $precision_2$ **= 1,** $precision_3$ **= 1, and so on. For Model 2:** $precision_1$ **= 0,** $precision_2$ **= 0,** $precision_3$ **= 1, and so on. Model 1 is regarded as a better model as the clicked item is ranked higher by Model 1.**

actual ranking	predicted ranking by Model 1	predicted ranking by Model 2
1 (clicked)	**1**	2
2	5	3
3	4	**1**
4	3	5
5	2	4

4.1.2 Evaluation Metrics

Before we apply a new model to the production system with real user traffic, we need to evaluate different candidate models by some offline experiments. In our offline experiments, we simulate the online learning procedure as illustrated in Figure 2: all per-item models at time t are updated based on the click/view samples during the latest 5-minute interval $[t-1, t]$ in the *random learning bucket*; the updated models are then applied to the candidate items during the next time interval $[t, t+1]$ so that we use the item ranking predicted by the updated models. For the clicks that actually happened during $[t, t+1]$ in the *random learning bucket*, the evaluation metric is computed by comparing these actual clicks with the predicted ranking. Intuitively, a good modeling approach should lead to high correlation between the actual clicks and the predicted ranking.

More specifically, for those clicks that actually happened at Position 1 in the *random learning bucket*, we define $precision_i$ as the number of the clicked items that are ranked at Position from 1 to i by the model prediction. Table 1 illustrates two examples for such precision computation. Note that the reason we only use the clicks at Position 1 for evaluation is that the clicks on other positions should be counted with more weight due to position bias, so it is more straightforward to use clicks at Position 1 for evaluation. To protect business-sensitive information, we report only relative precision, instead of precision itself.

In the following experiments, we evaluate different methods for obtaining the per-item models on the Trend Now dataset described in Section 4.1.1. By following the online learning simulation procedure during the 10-day period, the overall precision values are computed by aggregating the precision of recommendation in each of the 5-minute time intervals.

4.2 Effects of user engagement

We now explore effects of different types of user engagement on our online learning approach. As shown above, we have evaluated the recommendation performance if using only *click events* for model learning. In this section, we will first analyze the effects of *click-other events* by measuring the performance of the recommendation model which excludes all *click-other events* for model learning. Table 2 demonstrates the relative precision gains when

Table 2: Relative precision gain when training without *click-other event* over training on the original whole dataset.

Model	$prec_1$	$prec_2$	$prec_3$	$prec_4$	$prec_{10}$
EMP-kmeans	11.11%	7.05%	8.22%	7.70%	5.46%

training without *click-other events* over training on original whole

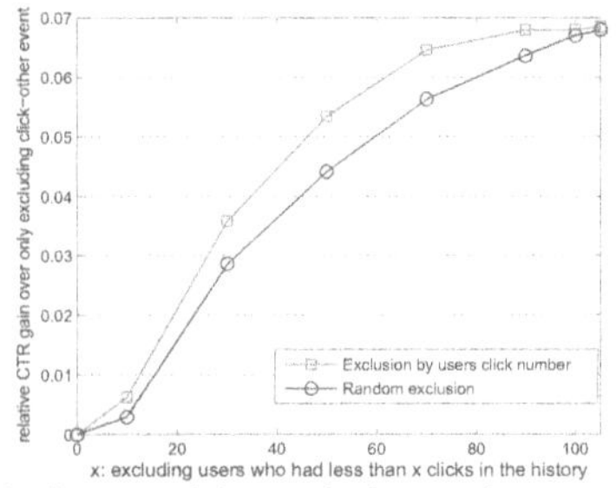

Figure 3: Relative precision gain by various user segmentation methods over the baseline, conducted on the original dataset.

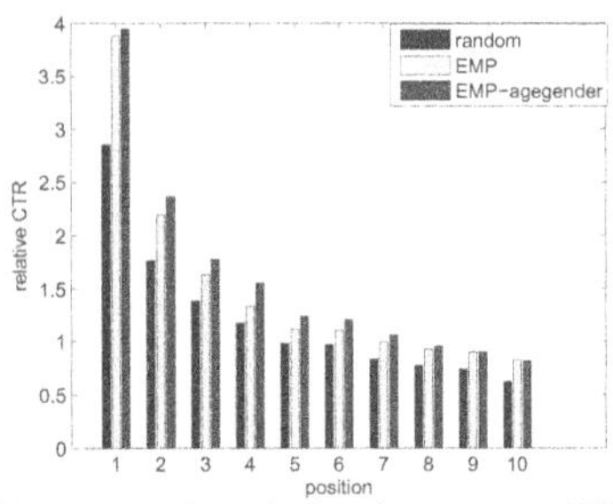

Figure 4: CTR comparison in bucket test at different positions.

dataset. This table clearly shows that excluding *click-other events* can improve CTR estimation.

As discussed in Section 3, besides *click events* and *click-other events*, there are also *non-click events* in which users had no action after they opened the Yahoo! frontpage. Unlike *click events* or *click-other events*, it is not straightforward to determine whether *non-click events* are useful for CTR estimating. We hypothesize that the utility of such event highly depends on the corresponding user's previous engagement on the module. The intuition is that if a user previously had higher *click* engagement on a content module, it is more likely she will examine the module in a future event.

To validate our hypothesis, we evaluate the performance of **EMP-kmeans** by gradually excluding the *non-click events* based on the number of clicks the corresponding user generated during a specified length of time. Figure 3 illustrates the precision values at Position 1, compared with another **EMP-kmeans** method which randomly excludes the same number of users. Note that, in this experiment, we have pre-processed the training data by removing all *click-other events*, and we will never exclude any user who has ever engaged in a *click events*. From this figure, we can find that gradually excluding *non-click events* based on users' previous number of clicks performs better than random exclusion, which indicates that the history of users' previous engagement is a good signal to judge the users' potential engagement in future events.

4.3 Bucket test results

Based on the simulation results we previously presented, we also online-test two models on real users. The two models are the **EMP** model (baseline) and the **EMP-agegender** model. Regarding learning samples for model update, **EMP** model uses all events while **EMP-agegender** model uses only click events. Now we will compare them by bucket test. We divide users into 3 different buckets. The first bucket is our random learning bucket, which only occupies a small amount of user traffic. The other two buckets are serving buckets, which rank queries by the **EMP** model and the **EMP-agegender** model respectively, and display the queries to the users within the corresponding buckets. These two serving buckets

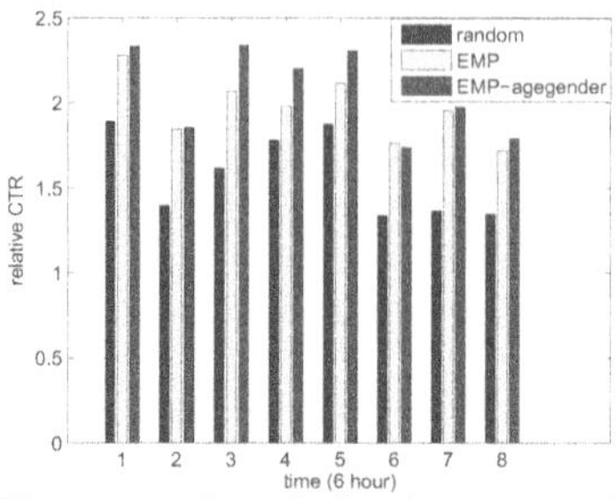

Figure 5: CTR comparison in bucket test at 8 consecutive 6-hour time slots during 2 days.

have similar amounts of user traffic. We run the bucket test over two days, and we compare the CTRs of the two buckets. Overall, the CTR in the **EMP-agegender** model bucket is 6.01% higher than the **EMP** model bucket.

We also compare CTRs at different positions and different times, as shown in Figure 4 and Figure 5 respectively. To protect confidential information, we do not show absolute CTRs; instead, we do scaling on all CTRs by a constant scaling factor. Therefore, we can observe the relative CTRs in different buckets. In Figure 4 and Figure 5, we first observe that the random learning bucket always has lowest CTRs. This is not surprising since the purpose of this bucket is only for exploration.

In terms of the CTR improvement of the **EMP-agegender** model over the **EMP** model, Figure 4 shows that the most significant improvement comes from the top positions while the improvement is less at lower positions. This trend verifies that compared with the **EMP** model, the **EMP-agegender** model presents queries at top positions which are more relevant to the users.

For the two days' test period, we divide the 48 hours into 8 consecutive 6-hour time slots. In Figure 5, we compare the CTRs of different buckets within each of these time slots. We observe that at different time slots, the improvements by the **EMP-agegender** model are different. The reason is that the content pool is changing over time. During some time slots, there are very popular items that are attractive to all users. In this case, the personalization model the **EMP-agegender** is not so effective. During other time slots, the candidate items are more appropriate for personalization so that the **EMP-agegender** model is more effective.

5. CONCLUSION

In this paper, we have studied a few important topics towards user action interpretation in recommender systems. We build a personalized content optimization system using *parallel-serving-buckets* framework. In this framework, we introduce action interpretation for improving online learning. We explore the effect of user engagement in the online learning procedure. Large-scale evaluations demonstrate that we can significantly improve the performance of the recommender system by integrating these user action interpretation factors.

6. REFERENCES

[1] D. Agarwal and B.-C. Chen and P. Elango, Spatio-Temporal models for estimating click-through rate. In *Proc. of the 18th International World Wide Web Conference (WWW)*, 2009.

A Personalized Recommendation System on Scholarly Publications

Maria Soledad Pera
Computer Science Department
Brigham Young University
Provo, Utah 84602, U.S.A.
soledadpera@gmail.com

Yiu-Kai Ng
Computer Science Department
Brigham Young University
Provo, Utah 84602, U.S.A.
ng@compsci.byu.edu

ABSTRACT

Researchers, as well as ordinary users who seek information in diverse academic fields, turn to the web to search for publications of interest. Even though scholarly publication recommenders have been developed to facilitate the task of discovering literature pertinent to their users, they (i) are not *personalized* enough to meet users' expectations, since they provide the same suggestions to users sharing similar profiles/preferences, (ii) generate recommendations pertaining to each user's general interests as opposed to the specific need of the user, and (iii) fail to take full advantages of valuable user-generated data at social websites that can enhance their performance. To address these problems, we propose *PubRec*, a recommender that suggests closely-related references to a particular publication P tailored to a specific user U, which minimizes the time and efforts imposed on U in browsing through general recommended publications. Empirical studies conducted using data extracted from CiteULike (i) verify the efficiency of the *recommendation* and *ranking* strategies adopted by *PubRec* and (ii) show that *PubRec* significantly outperforms other baseline recommenders.

Categories and Subject Descriptors

H.3.3 [**Information Storage and Retrieval**]: Information Search and Retrieval—*Information Filtering*

General Terms

Algorithms

1. INTRODUCTION

Researchers, as well as ordinary users, who seek materials in diverse academic fields, can turn to customized search engines, such as Google Scholar or ACM Portal, to locate publications of interest. These tools, however, are designed to retrieve articles matching the information need specified by a user in a keyword query and are inadequate for performing personalized and contextual searches [11]. Scholarly publication recommenders [4] are context-dependent and thus infer users' interest to suggest articles that potentially match the preferences of a user. Although these recommenders have been thoroughly studied over the past decade, a shortcoming of their design methodology is the "one-size-fits-all" premise. Due to their assumption on group preference, which leads to the suggestion of same publications to users sharing similar profiles regardless of the individual interest of the users, their recommendations are not *personalized* enough [7]. In addition, these recommenders provide suggestions pertaining to the users' general interests, which unlikely match the instant need of an individual user and yield extraneous recommendations the user is required to browse through.

With the increasing popularity of social websites, such as Delicious(.com) and CiteULike(.org), which archive user-generated data (i.e., social connections and tags), a new era of research on advancing the design of recommender systems is emerging [10]. Even though recently-developed recommenders consider the rich resource of information available on social websites, to the best of our knowledge, none of them generate *personalized* recommendations on *scholarly publications*. For this reason, we introduce *PubRec*, a personalized recommender that addresses the shortcomings of traditional recommenders and takes advantage of users' data archived on CiteULike to enhance the quality of its recommendations on scholarly publications. The proposed recommender facilitates the process of discovering academic citations related to a particular publication to provide relevant references to its users, a common inquire conducted very frequently within the academic setting. While existing recommenders suggest publications for a user U based on the (contents of) publications included in U's profile/personal library, *PubRec* recommends articles tailored to the specific information need of U captured on a particular publication P. Based on the premise that U treasures recommendations made by people with whom (s)he has an explicit connection, *PubRec* recommends articles among the publications bookmarked by U's connections on CiteULike that are *relevant* (in content) to P to a certain degree.

2. OUR PROPOSED RECOMMENDER

PubRec extracts data from CiteULike to generate personalized recommendations of scientific references, i.e., scholarly publications or simply publications, for CiteULike users. Given a CiteULike user *Cusr* and a publication P (that *Cusr* is interested in), *PubRec* first identifies *Cusr*'s *connections*. Hereafter, using word-correlation factors, *PubRec*

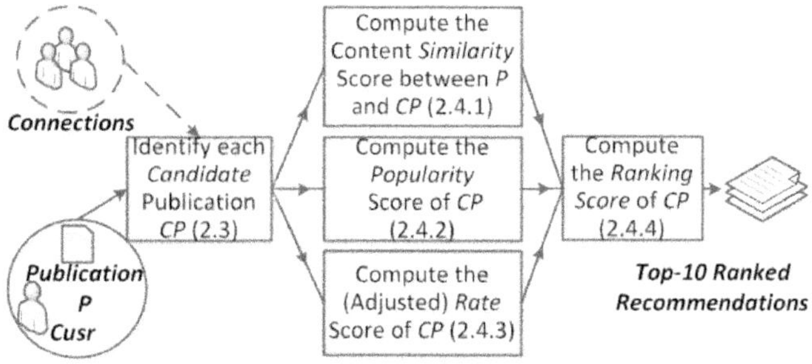

Figure 1: The architecture of *PubRec*

determines the set of publications, denoted *CandidateP*, among the ones included in the personal libraries of *Cusr*'s connections that are similar in content to *P* to a certain degree. *PubRec* computes a ranking score for each publication in *CandidateP* and recommends the Top-10 publications with the highest ranking scores to *Cusr*. The process of *PubRec* is illustrated in Figure 1.

2.1 CiteULike

CiteULike, which is one of the leading social web systems developed for managing and sharing bibliographic references, includes 5,237,158 indexed articles (as of May 24, 2011) and allows its users to search, organize, and share publications. A CiteULike user's *personal library* includes a number of bibliographic references that the user has bookmarked. Besides bookmarking publications and maintaining their metadata, abstracts, and links to the publishers' websites, CiteULike users can add *personal comments* and *tags* to publications in their personal libraries [4]. Each publication *P* indexed in CiteULike is associated with a list of tags that are provided by the CiteULike users who have bookmarked *P*. The list is used by *PubRec* to infer the tag cloud of *P*, i.e., a global visual representation of the *tags* and their *frequencies* assigned to *P*. CiteULike users can also assign a *reading priority* to a publication using a 5-star rating scale. In this rating system, one star (five stars, respectively) is associated with the label "I don't really want to read it" ("Top priority!", respectively), which indicates that the user is not eager to read (very interested in reading, respectively) the corresponding publication.

Serving as a social website, CiteULike offers its users an infrastructure to establish *explicit* communication channels with other CiteULike users. Explicitly-connected users, called *connections* in CiteULike, can exchange private messages and share bibliographic references of interest with one another. (To find out all the social features offered by CiteULike, see wiki.citeulike.org/index.php/Social_Features.)

2.2 Word Correlation Factors

PubRec relies on the pre-computed word-correlation factors in the word-correlation matrix [8] to determine the *similarity* between any two tags assigned to their respective publications, which capture and represent their contents.

Each correlation factor, which was calculated using a set of approximately 880,000 Wikipedia(.org) documents, indicates the degree of similarity of the two corresponding words[1] based on their (i) *frequency of co-occurrence* and (ii) *relative distances* in each Wikipedia document.

2.3 Selecting Candidate Publications

As the number of publications bookmarked by *Cusr*'s connections can be large, it is inefficient to compare each publication with *P*, a publication of interest to *Cusr*, to identify the ones similar to *P* to be recommended to *Cusr*, since the comparisons significantly prolong the processing time of *PubRec*. To minimize the number of comparisons and thus reduce the processing time required in generating recommendations, *PubRec* applies a *filtering* strategy on articles included in the personal libraries of *Cusr*'s connections to generate a subset of articles, denoted *CandidateP*, to be considered for recommendation. Each publication in *CandidateP* contains at least one tag *exactly matching* or *highly similar* to one of the tags of *P* assigned by *Cusr*. As publications in *CandidateP* and *P* share same (or analogous) tags, *PubRec* expects they are similar (to a degree) in content and address the *same* or *similar* topic.

To identify highly similar tags, *PubRec* employs a reduced version of the word-correlation matrix (introduced in Section 2.2) which contains 13% of the most frequently-occurring words (based on their frequencies of occurrence in the Wikipedia documents), and for the remaining 87% of the less-frequently-occurring words only the exact-matched correlation factor, i.e., 1.0, is used.

2.4 Ranking of Scholarly Publications

PubRec ranks each publication *CP* in *CandidateP* to prioritize them for recommendation using (i) the *degree of similarity* between *P* and *CP*, (ii) the *number of connections* who include *CP* in their personal libraries, and (iii) the adjusted *rating* (or simply *rate*) score given to *CP* by each connection of *Cusr* who has bookmarked *CP*.

2.4.1 Content Similarity of P and CP

To determine the degree of *similarity* between *P* and *CP*, *PubRec* adds the word-correlation factors between each tag in the tag cloud of *P* and *CP* in CiteULike, respectively. We consider the tags in the tag cloud of *P* (*CP*, respectively), since these tags provide a more comprehensive description of (the content of) *P* (*CP*, respectively), as opposed to the personal tags assigned to *P* (*CP*, respectively), which only reflect the personal opinion of and vocabulary used by *Cusr* (one of *Cusr*'s connections, respectively) in describing (the content of) *P* (*CP*, respectively).

2.4.2 Popularity of Scholarly Publications

Besides computing the (content) similarity between *P* and *CP*, *PubRec* considers the *popularity* of *CP*, which denotes the number of *Cusr*'s connections who include *CP* in their personal libraries.

Publications that have attracted the attention of a number of *Cusr*'s connections are more likely bookmarked in the personal libraries of *Cusr*'s connections. *PubRec* weights the fact that publications frequently-bookmarked by *Cusr*'s connections may also be of interest to *Cusr*, since *Cusr* and his/her connections share common interests to a certain degree. While solely relying on the popularity of an item in performing the recommendations task (which does not ap-

[1]Words in the Wikipedia documents were *stemmed* after all the *stopwords*, such as articles and prepositions, which do not play a significant role in representing the content of a document, were removed. From now on, unless stated otherwise, (key)words/tags refer to non-stop, stemmed (key)words/tags.

ply to *PubRec*) can lead to less diverse, i.e., less personalized, recommendations, Adomavicius and Kwon [1] claim that the accuracy of the recommendations can be enhanced by considering the popularity of an item during the recommendation process.

2.4.3 Rate of Publications

PubRec considers the number of stars given by *Cusr*'s connections to each publication in *CandidateP* and assign *higher weight* to those given *high ratings* by the connections, since users tend to favor highly-rated items more than the ones assigned lower ratings [5].

A connection, who includes in his/her library a significant number of articles on the same (or similar to the) topic T of P, is interested in T, which can be interpreted as the connection is likely more knowledgeable on or familiar with T and thus is more *reliable* in rating articles on T. Based on this premise, if the rating R of a candidate publication CP is assigned by the connection who is familiar with the topic of P, which is the same or similar to the topic of CP, then R should be perceived as more trustworthy than the rating assigned to CP by a connection who is less interested in or familiar with the topic of P. *PubRec* adjusts the *rating* provided by each *Cusr*'s connection, denoted *Ccon*, on CP based on the *reliability* of *Ccon* in assigning ratings to publications on the topic related to the one addressed in P.

2.4.4 Rank Aggregation

Having determined the (i) degree of *similarity* between P and each CP in *CandidateP*, (ii) the *popularity* score of CP, and (iii) the adjusted *rating* score assigned to CP by each *Cusr*'s connection, *PubRec* computes the *ranking* score of CP by adopting CombMNZ [9], a popular *linear combination strategy*. CombMNZ combines multiple existing lists of rankings on an item into a *joint ranking*, a task known as *rank aggregation* or *data fusion* [9].

The rank aggregation strategy adopted by *PubRec* accounts for the fact that *not* all of the publications are assigned a non-zero score in each (input) ranked list of publications. By adopting CombMNZ, *PubRec* considers the *strength* of each evidence, i.e., scores in each of the ranked lists, as opposed to simply positioning higher in the ranking publications with a non-zero score in all of the ranked lists of publications, regardless of the values of the corresponding scores in each list. As a result, *PubRec* can position higher in the ranking of generated recommendations a candidate publication CP that is more closely related (in content) to P, highly-popular among *Cusr*'s connections, and without a rating score than a publication that is less similar to P, less popular, and poorly-rated.

3. EXPERIMENTAL RESULTS

In this section, we introduce the dataset, evaluation protocol, and metrics (in Sections 3.1, 3.2, and 3.3, respectively) which are used for assessing the performance of *PubRec*. We detail the empirical study conducted for evaluating the effectiveness of *PubRec* and compare its performance with existing baseline recommenders (in Section 3.4).

3.1 Dataset

We constructed a dataset with data extracted from CiteULike. We first identified users who have recently bookmarked articles on CiteULike and randomly selected a set of fifty of them[2], denoted "active users." For each active user U we extracted U's connections. Thereafter, we retrieved the personal tags and ratings of each article in U's personal library (posted under the personal libraries of U's connections, respectively). The dataset also includes the set of tags (along with their frequencies of occurrence) in the (inferred) tag cloud of each scholarly publication bookmarked by either an active user or one of his/her connections. The resultant dataset includes 183 distinct users (fifty of which are active users and the remaining ones are their connections), 103,723 distinct scholarly publications, and 35,034 distinct tags. Since, as previously stated, *PubRec* generates personalized recommendations for an active user on a particular publication, we evaluate *PubRec* based on the recommendations generated for each of the 21,867 user-publication pairs, called *Test_Pairs*, in the constructed dataset.

3.2 Evaluation Protocol

We measure the overall performance of *PubRec*, using the metrics to be introduced in Section 3.3, on the recommendations generated for each user(U)-publication(P) pair in *Test_Pairs*. As a *ground truth*, i.e., the (non-)relevance of a recommendation R generated by *PubRec* for a U-P pair, we rely on the publications bookmarked by U on CiteULike. R is *relevant* if it is included in U's personal library (excluding P) and is *non-relevant*, otherwise, a commonly-employed protocol for assessing recommendation systems [3, 4].

3.3 Metrics

We treat *PubRec* as a content retrieval system that recommends to its users a list of ten publications relevant to a submitted query, a publication in our case, which is a commonly-adopted evaluation strategy [3, 4], and apply *Precision@K*, *Mean Reciprocal Rank*, and *Normalized Discounted Cumulative Gain* [6] to evaluate the recommendation accuracy of *PubRec*, in addition to its ranking strategy.

3.4 Performance Evaluation

To demonstrate and verify the effectiveness of our proposed recommender, we compare the performance of *PubRec* with two well-known, widely-adopted baseline recommender systems: *SocialRecommender* (*SR*) [3] and *TagVectorSimilarity* (*TVS*) [2]. While the former adopts a collaborative filtering strategy, the later is a content-based recommender.

Given that *PubRec* and *SR* recommend publications included in the personal libraries of active users' connections to make recommendations, we restricted the publications to be considered for recommendations by *TVS* to those bookmarked by active users' connections and thus conduct a fair, i.e., comparable, assessment among the recommenders.

Prior to comparing the aforementioned recommenders, we determined the *relevance* of each publication recommended by *SR* (*TVS*, respectively) for each user-publication pair in *Test_Pairs* according to the evaluation protocol detailed in Section 3.2 and the metrics introduced in Section 3.3. Note that since only publications existing in a user's library are considered relevant, it is not possible to account for potentially relevant publications that the user has not bookmarked. Thus, the computed precision scores are underestimated, a well-known limitation of the protocol introduced in Section 3.2. As this limitation affects *PubRec*, *SR*, and

[2]CiteULike users lacking explicit connections were excluded.

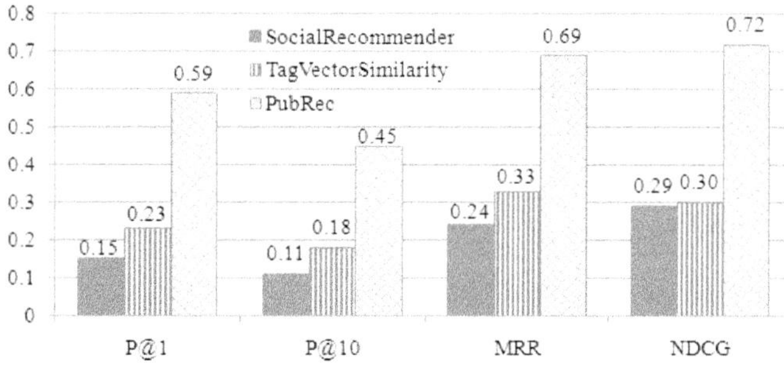

Figure 2: The $P@1$, $P@10$, MRR, and $NDCG$ scores of SR, TVS, and $PubRec$, respectively

TVS, the precision values are consistent for comparative purposes [3].

As shown in Figure 2, the $P@1$ scores achieved by SR and TVS are 0.15 and 0.23, respectively, which are at least 36% lower than the $P@1$ score of *PubRec*. Also shown in Figure 2 are the $P@10$ scores of SR, TVS, and *PubRec*, which are 0.11, 0.18, and 0.45 respectively. The $P@1$ scores indicate that more than $\frac{1}{2}$ (close to $\frac{1}{7}$ and $\frac{1}{4}$, respectively) of the time, the first publication recommended by *PubRec* (SR and TVS, respectively) is relevant. In addition, the $P@10$ values show that close to half of the scholarly publications recommended by *PubRec* are relevant, as opposed to the approximately one-tenth (one-fifth, respectively) recommended by SR (TVS, respectively).

Figure 2 also shows the MRR scores of SR, TVS, and *PubRec*. These scores reflect that while on the average *PubRec* users are required to browse through less than *two* ($\cong \frac{1}{0.69} = 1.44 < 2$) recommended publications before locating one that is related to a scholarly publication that (s)he is interested in, users relying on SR and TVS are required to scan through at least *four* ($\cong \frac{1}{0.24} = 4.16$) and *three* ($\cong \frac{1}{0.33} = 3.03$) recommended publications, respectively before locating one that is of interest.

The $NDCG$ scores calculated for the evaluated recommenders are also shown in Figure 2. The $NDCG$ score of *PubRec*, which is 0.72, is over 40% higher than the $NDCG$ scores computed for SR or TVS, which are 0.29 and 0.30, respectively. A significantly higher $NDCG$ value indicates that *PubRec* is notably more effective than SR and TVS in ranking higher in the list of recommendations scholarly publications that are relevant.

4. CONCLUSIONS

We have introduced a personalized publication recommender, denoted *PubRec*, which is simple and requires neither supervision nor domain-specific information in generating recommendations. *PubRec* is based on the premise that a user U values recommendations made by people with whom U has an explicit connection, a design methodology that differs from existing recommenders which suggest recommended items inferred from users unknown to U. Recommendations suggested by *PubRec* are *personalized*, since it considers the personal preference of U to make suggestions, instead of providing the *same* recommendations to users who share the same or similar profile information/common interests. Furthermore, while existing *user-centric* recommenders provide recommendations pertaining to U's general interests, *PubRec* recommends articles relevant to a particular publication P given U. The unique design methodologies employed by *PubRec* facilitate the process of identifying academic publications relevant to an article A of interest to an individual user who conducts a search of references for A, a task performed in the academic setting on a regular basis.

To assess the performance of *PubRec* and existing baseline recommenders, we have conducted an empirical study using data extracted from CiteULike. The study has demonstrated (i) the effectiveness of the *recommendation* and *ranking* strategies adopted by *PubRec* and (ii) the superiority of *PubRec* over baseline recommenders. The results of the conducted experiments verify that by considering (i) collaborative annotations, i.e., tags and ratings, extracted from a social website, along with (ii) *connections* established among the users in a social environment we can enhance the quality of recommendations on publications.

While *PubRec* is currently applied for recommending scholarly publications, we intent to further enhance our proposed recommender so that it can simultaneously suggest any number of multimedia items, i.e., songs or movies, provided that *collaborative data* describing items of interest and *explicit connections* among users can be extracted from a social networking environment.

5. REFERENCES

[1] G. Adomavicius and Y. Kwon. Improving Aggregate Recommendation Diversity Using Ranking-Based Techniques. IEEE TKDE - In Press, 2011.

[2] C. Basu, H. Hirsh, W. Cohen, and C. Nevill-Manning. Technical Paper Recommendation: A Study in Combining Multiple Information Sources. *JAIR*, 1:231–252, 2001.

[3] A. Bellogin, I. Cantador, and P. Castells. A Study of Heterogeneity in Recommendations for a Social Music Service. In *ACM HetRec*, pages 1–8, 2010.

[4] T. Bogers and A. van den Bosch. Recommending Scientific Articles Using CiteULike. In *ACM RecSys*, pages 287–290, 2008.

[5] P. Cremonesi, Y. Koren, and R. Turrin. Performance of Recommender Algorithms on Top-N Recommendation Tasks. In *ACM RecSys*, pages 39–46, 2010.

[6] W. Croft, D. Metzler, and T. Strohman. *Search Engines: Information Retrieval in Practice*. Addison Wesley, 2010.

[7] J. Jung, K. Kim, H. Lee, and S. Park. Are You Satisfied with Your Recommendation Service?: Discovering Social Networks for Personalized Mobile Services. In *KES-AMSTA*, pages 567–573, 2008.

[8] J. Koberstein and Y.-K. Ng. Using Word Clusters to Detect Similar Web Documents. In *KSEM*, pages 215–228, 2006.

[9] J. Lee. Analyses of Multiple Evidence Combination. In *ACM SIGIR*, pages 267–276, 1997.

[10] H. Ma, D. Zhou, C. Liu, M. Lyu, and I. King. Recommender Systems with Social Regularization. In *ACM WSDM*, pages 287–296, 2011.

[11] R.White, P. Bailey, and L. Chen. Predicting User Interests from Contextual Information. In *ACM SIGIR*, pages 363–370, 2009.

Collaborative Exploratory Search in Real-World Context

Naoki Tani
Danushka Bollegala
Shuhei Iitsuka
Yutaka Matsuo
The University of Tokyo,
Hongo 7-3-1, Tokyo
113-8656, Japan
tani@mi.ci.i.u-tokyo.ac.jp
danushka@iba.t.u-tokyo.ac.jp
(iitsuka|matsuo)@biz-model.t.u-tokyo.ac.jp

Naiwala Chandrasiri,
Kazunari Nawa
Toyota InfoTechnology Center
Aksasaka 6-6-20, Tokyo
107-0052, Japan
(np-chandrasiri|nawa)@jp.toyota-itc.com

Keisuke Okamoto
Toyota Motor Corp.
3-3-25 Higashi Ikebukuro
Tokyo, 170-8405, Japan
keisuke@okamoto.tec.toyota.co.jp

ABSTRACT

We propose *Collaborative Exploratory Search (CES)*, which is an integration of dialog analysis and web search that involves multiparty collaboration to accomplish an exploratory information retrieval goal. Given a real-time dialog between users on a single topic; we define CES as the task of automatically detecting the topic of the dialog and retrieving task-relevant web pages to support the dialog. To recognize the task of the dialog, we apply the *Author–Topic* model as a topic model. Then, *attribute extraction* is applied to the dialog to obtain the attributes of the tasks. Finally, a specific search query is generated to identify the task-relevant information. We implement and evaluate the CES system for a commercial in-vehicle conversation. We also develop an iPad application that listens to conversations among users and continuously retrieves relevant web pages. Our experimental results reveal that the proposed method outperforms existing methods, which demonstrates the potential usefulness of collaborative exploratory search with practically usable accuracy levels.

Categories and Subject Descriptors

H.3.3 [**Information Systems**]: Information Search and Retrieval

General Terms

Algorithms

Keywords

Personalized and Collaborative Search, Information Extraction

1. INTRODUCTION

During the last decade, web searching has become commonplace in our everyday lives. Currently, most search engines supply query-based searching that is designed to navigate a user to those web pages that are most relevant to the user's query. The use of web searching has become very common in our lives. Therefore, many new scenarios of searching arise.

For example, as cars become smarter, a driver might want to search web pages while driving a car to obtain information related to destination or nearby events. Although current navigation systems cannot not usually access the web, some car manufacturers, such as Toyota, already provide a premium service for customers to search information from the web assisted by a dedicated telephone operator. The following conversation illustrates such a situation.

> *Driver: "Hello. I want to eat something special in Kyoto this evening."*
> *Operator: "OK. What kind of cuisine would you like?"*
> *Driver: "Well..., traditional Japanese."*
> *Operator: "OK, sir. Let me search for traditional Japanese restaurants in Kyoto."*
> *(Operator searches the web.)*
> *Operator: "There is a good restaurant named Kitcho in Kyoto near your location."*
> *Driver: "Is it good?"*
> *(Operator searches the web.)*
> *Operator: "I can not guarantee the taste, but it's been awarded three stars by Michelin."*
> *Driver: "OK. Could you set the location into the GPS?"*
> *Operator: "Certainly. I sent that information to your car."*

In this scenario, the driver has an information need and the operator makes a search, the search is conducted during a dialog, keywords are extracted from the dialog and fed into the search engine, and the search results are provided promptly and help the task in the dialog. In this paper, we specifically address such a situation: multiple persons collaboratively search the web during the conversation. Our system automatically analyzes the discourse, makes a customized query, and shows the results promptly.

As described in this paper, we propose *Collaborative Exploratory Search (CES)*. CES can be considered as the combination of multi-domain exploratory search and collaborative search. It is an integration of dialog analysis and web search that involves multiparty collaboration to accomplish an exploratory information retrieval goal. The goal of CES is to support users' collaboration in searching. Given a real-time dialog between users on a single topic, CES extracts topic and attribute–value pairs of a dialog and seeks relevant web pages automatically. Using real-time dialog as input data, it enables unconscious search and does not block collaboration.

The outline of the proposed method is shown in Figure 1. As shown in Figure 1, we break down the CES into three parts: (i)

CIKM'11, October 24–28, 2011, Glasgow, Scotland, UK.

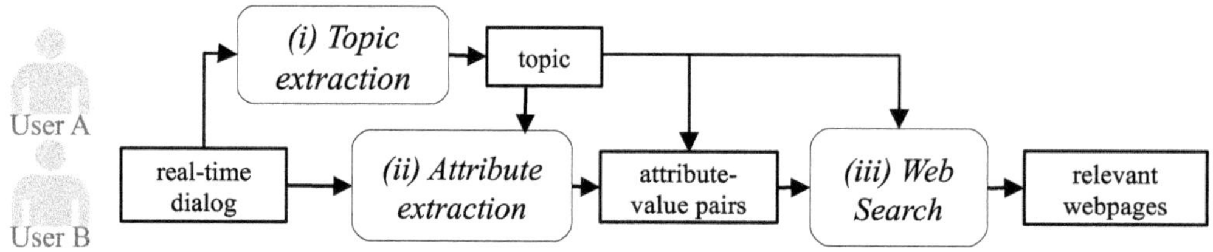

Figure 1: Outline of the proposed system.

topic extraction, (ii) attribute extraction, and (iii) web search. For topic extraction, we apply the *Author–Topic (AT)* model, an unsupervised topic detection algorithm to detect the topic of a dialog between users. For attribute extraction, we apply a two-stage method to obtain attribute–value pairs. Then the customized query is generated and the search results are shown in part (iii). We evaluate our CES approach using an actual dialog dataset by drivers and operators in Toyota. The results show that we can detect the task in a conversation with 50% accuracy in unsupervised topic extraction, and attain a 0.67 F-measure in attribute extraction.

2. RELATED WORK

Exploratory search is defined as the situation in which the user starts from a not-so-well-defined information need and progressively discovers more on his need and on the information available to address it [6]. Kotov et al. [4] proposed a questionguided search, in which a retrieval system would generate potentially interesting questions to the users automatically. The question-guided search system returns "Who is John Kennedy?" or "When was Kennedy sworn as the President of the United States?" if users entered query "john kennedy". Rajaraman [10] produced Kosmix web service[1]: Kosmix is a generalpurpose topic discovery engine, which responds to keyword search using a topic page that summarizes the most relevant information related to the subject associated to the search. Bozzon et al. [3] proposed Liquid Query, a paradigm that exploits the power of underlying search services and provides the user with a multi-domain exploratory search environment (e.g., travels, music, shows, food, movies, and so on). Recent studies have revealed that most people want to search with other people [5, 12]. A survey [7] of 204 people revealed that 53.4% of participants do some collaborative search tasks: travel planning, shopping, literature search, technical information, and so on. For example, TeamSearch [9] is a tabletop application that enables small, co-located groups to search for digital photographs from a metadata-tagged repository. S3 [8] allows users to share useful sites found during a web search asynchronously by representing search results in a persistent file format that can be sent to and augmented by several people. Amershi et al. introduced CoSearch [1], a system that is intended to improve the experience of co-located collaborative web search by leveraging readily available devices such as mobile phones and extra mice.

3. PROBLEM DEFINITION

Let us consider the situation where two agents, A and B, are having a dialog D about a particular topic T. Dialog D includes some attributes V. D can be represented as a vector (hereinafter designated as a dialog vector)

$$d = (a_i, b_j, ...)^T$$

where a_i and b_j are sequences of words (may or may not be complete sentences) uttered respectively by A and B. Elements in d are sorted in the order they are uttered by A and B. Only relative ordering of utterances is considered, thereby ignoring the absolute time information. Given a dialog vector d, we define collaborative exploratory search (CES) as the problem of retrieving a set of web documents L, that is relevant to the topic T and attributes V discussed in the dialog D. To develop a CES system we must perform three tasks: (a) extract the topic being discussed by the speakers in the dialog (Section 4), (b) extract attributes and their values regarding the main topic discussed in the dialog (Section 5), and (c) form queries using the extracted attributes and their values to domain-specific search engines to retrieve information to support the conversation (Section 6).

[1]http://www.kosmix.com/

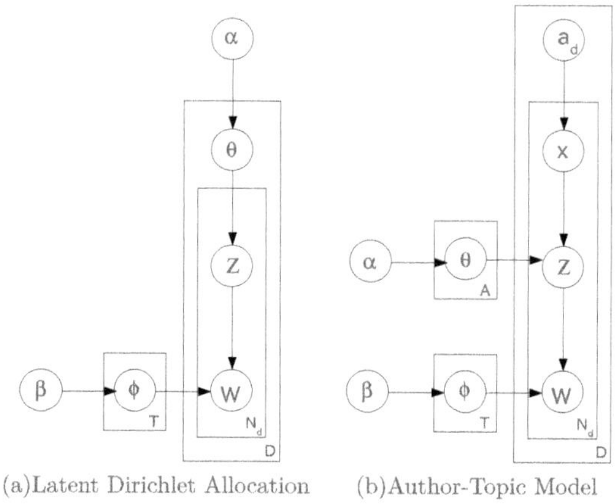

(a)Latent Dirichlet Allocation (b)Author-Topic Model

Figure 2: Topic models: LDA and AT.

4. TOPIC EXTRACTION

We briefly review the Latent Dirichlet Allocation (LDA) model and Author–Topic (AT) model, which we use in our system. LDA is a Bayesian network that generates a document using a mixture of topics [2]. In its generative process, for each document d, a multinomial distribution θ_d over topics is randomly sampled from a Dirichlet distribution with parameter α; then, to generate each word, a topic z_{di} is chosen from this topic distribution, and a word, w_{di}, is generated by random sampling from a topic-specific multinomial distribution $\phi_{z_{di}}$. Figure 2 (a) shows the graphical model for LDA.

Despite its simplicity and numerous applications, LDA cannot capture the authorship of documents. For example, multiple authors might contribute to a particular document and we might want to extract topics considering both word distribution as well the authors who wrote those words in a document. The Author–Topic (AT) model [11] extends LDA by incorporating author information for topic extraction. Figure 2 (b) shows an AT model. Specifically, each author is associated with a multinomial distribution over topics, represented by θ. Each topic is associated with a multinomial distribution over words, represented by ϕ. The multinomial distributions θ and ϕ have a symmetric Dirichlet prior with hyperparameters α and β. For each word in a document, we sample an author x uniformly from a_d, then sample a topic z from the multinomial distribution θ associated with author x and sample a word w from a multinomial topic distribution ϕ associated with topic z. This sampling process is repeated N_d times to generate a document d (here, N_d is the total number of words in document d). The AT model has two sets of unknown parameters – A author-topic distributions θ, and T topic distributions ϕ – as well as the latent variables corresponding to the assignments of individual words to topics z and authors x. It has been shown that parameter estimation via Expectation-Maximization (EM) algorithm engenders local maxima and is computationally inefficient in topic models. Consequently, Gibbs sampling has been used to estimate the parameters in AT models. Once we have estimated the parameters θ and ϕ, we can use those values to compute the posterior probability of $p(t|D)$, to assign a topic to a given document D. We model a multi-party dialog using AT model as follows. Each author in the AT model is replaced by a speaker who participates in a dialog. A document in the AT model is replaced by a single dialog. Moreover, the words that comprise a document are replaced by the utterances in the corresponding dialog. By modeling a multi-party dialog as an AT model, we leverage on existing work on topic models to solve the collaborative explorative search problem.

5. ATTRIBUTE EXTRACTION

Once we have identified the topic of the conversation, we must extract keywords related to that topic to retrieve information to support the conversation from a Web search engine. We extract attributes and values for the main topic as keywords. For example, if the topic is about a hotel reservation, then we extract attribute values such as the location of the hotel, the number of people staying, the check-in date, the check-out date, desired price range, Extracting attributes from texts has received much attention lately as a result of the increasing demand in information extraction systems. Watanabe et al. proposed a two-stage attribute extraction method [13], which we use in our CES system. First, given a dialog D, we mark all occurrences that are likely to be values of some attributes. We designate such occurrences as *candidates*. The candidate identification is done using a named entity recognizing tool and a gazetteer. Entity types such as personal names, locations, and organizations are selected as candidate attributes. In addition, we create lists of awards, universities, nationalities, etc. and use those lists in a gazetteer to mark candidate attributes. Having input from both the named entity recognition tool as well as the gazetteer enables an attribute extraction system to recognize a large number of attributes in texts. In the second stage, from the set of identified candidates we select the ones that are likely to be attributes relevant to the topic of the dialog. For this purpose we employ a distance-based heuristic. Specifically, given a list of candidate attributes and their occurrences in a text, we compute the distance between each attribute and the topic of the document. Candidates that are in close proximity to the topic of the document are selected as attributes for that document.

6. MULTI-DOMAIN SEARCH

After identifying the topic in a dialog and extracting appropriate keywords for that topic, we retrieve information relevant to the topic using domain specific search engines. Here, the input is the topic and attribute-value pairs extracted from the target dialog, and the output is a list of web pages which is most relevant to the task, which satisfies the requirement of attribute-value pairs. We obtain relevant information from not only surface web but also from the deep web using many web service APIs. We can thereby obtain the largest range of information and can mutually compare the results obtained using several web services. For example, the system gets HOTEL dialog among users and extracts attribute–value pairs such as (place, "Tokyo"), (heads, 2), (price, $100). In this case, the system searches for a hotel in Tokyo with a twin-bed room for $100 or less. In order for a user to compare results, web pages are selected widely from various perspectives. For instance, if users are searching for a restaurant, then we show the most popular restaurant and high-class restaurants. Users can choose from them depending on their tastes.

Table 1: Basic statistics for each task in Toyota dialog dataset.

task	#dialogs	duration	#of turns	#of utterances
HOTEL	30	158 s	110	611
NAVIGATION	53	154 s	67	354
RESTAURANT	73	148 s	91	500
SHOP	20	143 s	71	381
PARKING	18	131 s	69	397
CALL	17	156 s	87	502

7. EXPERIMENTS

We evaluate the performance of CES in this section. As shown in Figure 1, CES are decomposed into three tasks: topic extraction, attribute extraction, and web search. We conduct two sets of experiments to evaluate our CES system. First, we measure the performance of topic extraction. Then we evaluate the attribute extraction method and show how many attributes are correctly chosen.

We use a dialog dataset provided by Toyota Motor Corp. The dataset includes records of conversations between a driver and an operator: A call center operator provides a concierge service to drivers and provides information services such as recommendation and reservation of restaurants, hotels, or shops, and providing a phone number or the location of landmarks and so on. The data include a speaker, utterances obtained by speech recognition plus manual fixing, and time. For privacy reasons, the names of drivers and operators are anonymized. We target Japanese real-time dialog, although our method does not depend on any specific language. The Toyota dialog dataset includes 604 dialogs and 47,322 utterances, consisting of 356,618 words. We extract attribute-value pairs and divide dialogs into six tasks as shown in Table 1. The RESTAURANT and NAVIGATION tasks are the most numerous. Drivers often want to know the locations of places, or want to search for restaurants. Although the durations of the dialogs are not so varied among tasks, the average number of turns presents some tendencies: HOTEL and RESTAURANT needs more turns than others. Drivers must clarify their preferences and a higher degree of interaction might be necessary.

We first measure the performance of topic extraction. The task is to classify the dialog into one of the six task types. We devide 604 dialogs into 404 training data and 200 test data. We annotated the task type of each dialog manually. We use pLDA[2] as a baseline with the number of topics T=10. LDA parameters are set to $\alpha = 0.1$ and $\beta = 0.01$. Table 3 presents the performance of AT model, used in our CES system, and a baseline. Overall, the precision and recall of AT are higher than those of LDA. Table 2 portrays a confusion matrix of classification. The upper part is the result of LDA; the lower part is the result of AT model. Apparently, LDA classifies dialog mostly to NAVIGATION and RESTAURANT, whereas AT model classifies into all tasks properly. From the AT result, we can find that HOTEL and RESTAURANT tasks are confusing because both

[2]http://code.google.com/p/plda/

Table 2: Confusion matrix of the topic extraction. Legend: H (HOTEL), N (NAVIGATION), R (RESTAURANT), S (SHOP), P (PARKING), C (CALL).

(a) LDA: Baseline

true label	H	N	R	S	P	C	Recall
	predicted label						
H	**0**	21	2	3	1	0	0.00
N	0	**43**	1	2	5	0	0.84
R	0	43	**14**	7	6	0	0.20
S	0	12	3	**3**	0	0	0.17
P	0	2	3	2	**2**	0	0.22
C	0	5	0	0	0	**0**	0.00
Precision	0.00	0.34	0.60	0.18	0.14	0.00	

(b) AT model: Proposed method

true label	H	N	R	S	P	C	Recall
	predicted label						
S	**16**	3	4	2	0	3	0.57
N	3	**23**	9	9	0	8	0.44
R	18	6	**25**	11	0	6	0.38
S	2	1	4	**9**	0	1	0.53
P	0	1	4	2	**2**	4	0.15
C	2	1	3	0	0	**4**	0.40
Precision	0.39	0.66	0.51	0.27	1.00	0.15	

Table 3: Performance of the proposed method and baselines.

Method	Precision	Recall	F-score
LDA	0.21	0.24	0.22
AT (proposed)	**0.50**	**0.41**	**0.45**

include conversations about the location, number of people, prices, and reservation. Next, we evaluate attribute extraction after obtaining the task of each dialog. We use 200 labeled dialogs as test data. We compare five methods: AE-clueword, AE-clueword-driver, AE-clueword-operator, AE-driver, and AE-operator. The AE-clueword is the proposed method, which extracts attribute values based on clue words. The AE-clueword-driver extracts information only from the utterances from a driver, and AE-clueword-operator extracts information only from those of an operator. The AE-driver and AE-operator extract attribute values using candidates of attribute values. Each chooses randomly one candidate value from either the driver's utterances or from the operator's utterances.

Table 4 presents results of the experiment. The proposed clue word methods score high. In dialog, an attribute and an attribute value often appear as an adjacency pair, so clue words to represent attributes are efficient to find attribute values for each task. Consequently, the AE-clueword-driver and AE-driver outperform AE-clueword-operator and AE-operator. It is apparent that a user's utterances are likely to include attribute values rather than an operator's because CES in this context is mainly intended to fulfill the drivers information needs. Overall, the proposed methods on topic extraction and attribute extraction outperform the baseline methods, demonstrating the effectiveness of our approach. Experimental results show that the CES model performs better than LDA in terms of both precision and recall on the topic extraction task. In the Toyota dialog dataset, there are two parties: an operator and a driver. Modeling those two speakers in the AT model enables us to detect the topic of the dialog accurately. Although there exist standard benchmark test collections such as TREC evaluation benchmark for Web information retrieval systems and standard evaluation measures such as average precision or normalized discounted cumulative gain (NDCG), evaluating a collaborative search system

Table 4: Performance of the proposed method and baselines in the attribute extraction task.

Method	Precision	Recall	F-score
AE-clueword (proposed)	**0.65**	**0.73**	**0.68**
AE-clueword-driver	0.63	0.71	0.67
AE-clueword-operator	0.58	0.65	0.61
AE-driver	0.52	0.59	0.55
AE-operator	0.50	0.56	0.53

is a challenging task because of the lack of any gold standard for the collaborative search task or evaluation measures that take into account the collaborative nature of the task. Developing test collections and evaluation measures are important future research directions in this field. To underscore the effectiveness of the CES model, we developed a prototypical CES application for use on iPad.

8. CONCLUSION

We proposed collaborative exploratory search (CES), which involves multiparty collaboration to accomplish an exploratory information retrieval goal. Experimental results from a topic extraction and attributes extraction task showed that the proposed method outperforms baselines.

9. REFERENCES

[1] S. Amershi and M. R. Morris. Cosearch: A system for co-located collaborative web search. *CHI'08*, April 2008.

[2] D. M. Blei, A. Y. Ng, and M. I. Jordan. Latent dirichlet allocation. *Journal of Machine Learning Research*, pages 993–1022, 2003.

[3] A. Bozzon, M. Brambilla, S. Ceri, and P. Fraternali. Liquid query: Multi-domain exploratory search on the web. *WWW'10*, pages 161–170, April 2010.

[4] A. Kotov and C. Zhai. Towards natural question-guided search. *WWW'10*, pages 26–30, April 2010.

[5] A. Large, J. Beheshti, and T. Rahman. Gender differences in collaborative web searching behavior: an elementary school study. *Information Processing and Management*, 38:427–443, 2002.

[6] G. Marchionini. Exploratory search: from finding to understanding. *Communications ACM*, 49(4):41–46, 2006.

[7] M. R. Morris. A survey of collaborative web search practices. *In proc. of CHI*, pages 1657–1660, April 2008.

[8] M. R. Morris and E. Horvitz. S3: Storable, shareable search. *Interact*, pages 120–123, 2007.

[9] M. R. Morris, A. Paepcke, and T. Winograd. Teamsearch: Comparing techniques for co-present collaborative search of digital media. *TABLETOP' 06*, pages 97–104, 2006.

[10] A. Rajaraman. Kosmix: Highperformance topic exploration using the deep web. *VLDB'09*, August 2009.

[11] M. Rosen-Zvi, T. Griffths, M. Steyvers, and P. Smyth. The author-topic model for authors and documents. *UAI'04*, 2004.

[12] M. B. Twidale, D. M. Nichols, and C. D. Paice. Browsing in a collaborative process. *Information Processing and Management*, 33(6):761–783, 1997.

[13] K. Watanabe, D. Bollegala, Y. Matsuo, and M. Ishizuka. A two-step approach to extracting atrtibutes for people on the web. In *Proc. Second Web People Search Task (WePS2) Workshop*, 2009.

Beyond Precision@10: Clustering the Long Tail of Web Search Results

Benno Stein Tim Gollub Dennis Hoppe

Bauhaus-Universität Weimar
99421 Weimar, Germany
<first name>.<last name>@uni-weimar.de

ABSTRACT

The paper addresses the missing user acceptance of web search result clustering. We report on selected analyses and propose new concepts to improve existing result clustering approaches. Our findings in a nutshell are: (1) *Don't compete with a search engine's top hits.* In response to a query we presume search engines to return an optimal result list in the sense of the probabilistic ranking principle: documents that are expected by the majority of users are placed on top and form the result list head. We argue that, with respect to the top results, it is not beneficial to replace this established form of result presentation. (2) *Improve document access in the result list tail.* Documents that address the information need of "minorities" appear at some position in the result list tail. Especially for ambiguous and multi-faceted queries we expect this tail to be long, with many users appreciating different documents. In this situation web search result clustering can improve user satisfaction by reorganizing the long tail into topic-specific clusters. (3) *Avoid shadowing when constructing cluster labels.* We show that most of the cluster labels that are generated by current clustering technology occur within the snippets of the result list head—an effect which we call *shadowing*. The value of such labels for topic organization and navigating within a clustering of the entire result list is limited. We propose and analyze a filtering approach to significantly alleviate the label shadowing effect.

Categories and Subject Descriptors: H.3.3 [Information Storage and Retrieval]: Information Search and Retrieval—*Clustering* H.3.3 [Information Storage and Retrieval]: Information Search and Retrieval—*Search process*
General Terms: Algorithms, Experimentation, Measurement
Keywords: search result clustering, cluster labeling

1. INTRODUCTION

Web search is the task of finding a document in the World Wide Web in order to satisfy a user's information need that is specified as a query. Deriving the "true" information need from a query is a challenge, and search engines often retrieve millions of documents from which only a fraction is relevant for the user. To reduce the negative impact of irrelevant documents, search engines apply a result presentation strategy, which can be characterized as either *relevance-based* or *diversity-based.*

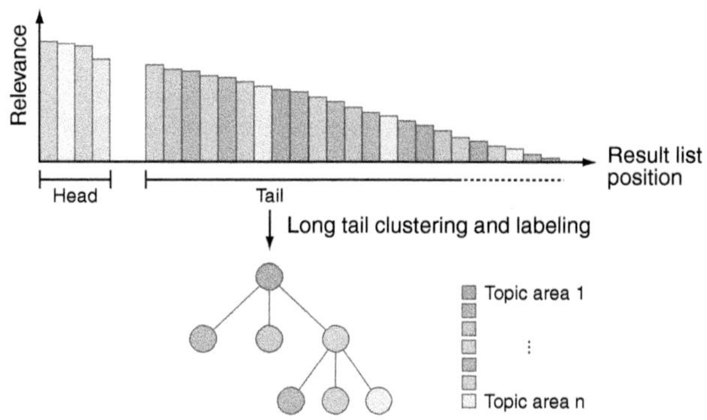

Figure 1: Result presentation by competence partitioning: combine the ranked result list head with a clustering of the result list tail.

The objective of the relevance-based strategy, which is the predominant strategy at this time, is to serve those information needs that are most likely associated with the query. The results are organized as a ranked list. The relevance-based strategy is extremely effective if a user can spot a desired document among the top ranks. If not, the user has to resort to a sequential search in the result list tail, which is ineffective since no topic-specific structuring is provided. Two recent user studies complement these observations impressively: A study from 2010 reviews the top five results of 1 000 queries sampled from the query log of a major search engine and reports that more than 90% of these queries are served excellent by all major search engines [28]. A study from 2008 reveals that only 8% of the users are willing to skim through more than three result pages, which corresponds to less than 30 search results [13].

On the other hand, the objective of the diversity-based strategy is to serve multiple information needs "in parallel". A well-known representative of this strategy is web search result clustering [4]. Search engines that implement this strategy group similar documents into clusters and try to construct descriptive cluster labels to guide users during their search. If the clustering is effective and the labeling is expressive, diversity-based search engines can serve a multitude of information needs associated with a query equally well. Users with uncommon information needs or multi-faceted informational queries especially benefit from the structured information access provided by the clustering.

In this paper we propose to exploit both result presentation strategies by combining the head of a ranked result list with a clustering of those documents found in the tail and not covered by the head. Figure 1 illustrates the paradigm. Notice that this *competence partitioning* strategy is fundamentally different from the current practice of web search result clustering engines: by resorting to the result

This work is supported in part by the German Science Foundation under grants STE1019/2-1 and FU205/22-1.

list head, we exploit the "wisdom" of the search engine developers. By clustering a filtered result list tail, we prevent a user from sifting through many result pages.

The remainder of this paper is organized as follows. Section 2 gives a focused overview of the state of the art, while Section 3 contributes analytical insights and methodological elements of our approach. (1) A critical analysis of the role that result clustering can play for web search, (2) a quantification of the label shadowing effect, and (3) a filtering approach to exploit the idea of long tail clustering. Compared to existing result clustering approaches we report on less shadowing in the discovered clusters.

2. RELATED WORK

Web search result clustering is a heterogeneous research field, overlapping with and influenced by cluster analysis, cluster labeling, web snippet clustering, subtopic retrieval, search result classification, query type identification, query diversification, and faceted search. This mixture of related fields is not without reason: until this day web search result clustering is not properly solved. A fact which is rooted in the difficulty of the task itself but also in a misunderstanding of the very problem and, last but not least, in the ever changing user expectations and requirements:

- Most web search result clustering systems exploit only the text of the search result snippets, and clustering short texts is difficult [19].
- Is clustering the problem or labeling? Meanwhile, most researchers lean towards the latter [21].
- A user with a known item finding problem has different expectations than a user who wants to overview a new field. A user who experienced the monothetic characteristic of a faceted search application expects the same topical orthogonality from search result clustering [12].

The existing systems for web search result clustering can be distinguished along three dimensions [4]: data-centric, description-centric, and description-aware. *Data-centric systems* give top priority to clustering, while the formation of cluster labels has no effect on the partitioning of the snippets. The labels are usually derived from a cluster's mathematical representation, e.g., a centroid or a medoid under a bag-of-words model, and hence the generated labels form a sequence of probably unrelated words, often lacking understandability. Examples for such systems are WebCat [11] and AIsearch [21]. *Description-centric systems*, by contrast, employ cluster analysis solely for the purpose of discovering topics within a collection. Snippet partitioning is achieved by monothetic clustering, where each feature is used in an isolated manner to partition a collection into (overlapping) clusters. This approach leads to an improved understandability, which is bought with a possibly acceptable decrease in the clustering quality. Examples for such systems are Lingo [18], DisCover [15] and KeySRC [3]. *Description-aware systems*, finally, interweave the processes of clustering and labeling. In the existing systems of this type, such as Grouper [27] or SnakeT [9], labeling affects a polythetic cluster analysis. Although monothetic clustering is preferred, Carpineto et al. [4] note that none of the three system types is per definition superior to the others. The acceptance and usability of a system for web search result clustering depends on the quality of its components. We provide entry points and recent results from the respective fields for those who are interested in background technology:

Cluster Labeling. The salient properties of good cluster labels are comprehensibility, descriptiveness, and discriminative power [21]. Phrases are the basic building blocks of labels, whereas noun phrases [20], named entities [23], and title phrases [10] are recently discussed alternatives to improve comprehensibility. Descriptiveness means that a label should speak for each document in a cluster [25], while discriminative power means that the semantic overlap of a label between two clusters should be minimal.

Table 1: Comparison of ranked result lists (RRL), query diversification (QD), web search result clustering (WSRC), and faceted search (FS).

	RRL	QD	WSRC	FS
Complexity	low	high	high	very high
Navigational queries	+	+	–	–
Informational queries	–	+	++	++
Common information need	+	+	–	–
Uncommon information need	–	–	+	+
Exploratory search	–	–	+	++
Disambiguation	–	+	++	++
Optimization criterion	relevance	relevance, diversity	diversity	diversity

Subtopic Retrieval. Subtopic retrieval is related to web search result clustering, since one is interested in grouping different aspects of an undirected, informational query. In this regard Bernardini et al. [3] employ keyphrase filtering, while Carpineto and Romano [6] combine the results from various result clustering systems.

Result Classification. At first sight, classifying snippets into a predefined taxonomy (e.g. from the Open Directory Project) sounds perfect in order to group search results into human-understandable categories [16]. However, web directories cannot deal with the dynamics of the web, and the limited number of available categories cannot suit arbitrary queries [17].

Query Diversification. Diversification is a rather new approach to deal with ambiguous queries by re-ranking relevance-based result lists [1, 22, 26]. The objective is to make the head of a result list both maximally relevant and diverse. Query diversification helps users to find relevant information if they are searching only for a specific source; if users are interested in retrieving a set of relevant snippets for a given query, result clustering is superior. In addition, query diversification is limited, because the result list head is short.

Faceted Search. Faceted search can be considered as a "controlled, monothetic cluster analysis". Without doubt, facets excel in satisfying the three label properties mentioned above. The automatic and ad-hoc generation of facets is an active research field, but currently this problem must be considered as unsolved [24]. Table 1 overviews and completes the outlined pros and cons of the result presentation strategies discussed.

3. LONG TAIL CLUSTERING

In the following we discuss the competence partitioning strategy as illustrated in Figure 1 and introduce a tailored clustering approach, which we refer to as *LongTailClustering*.

3.1 Towards Better Search Result Clustering

Relevance-based search engines answer navigational as well as the popular non-navigational queries almost perfectly. For such kinds of information needs, web search result clustering and related technology cannot compete. Aside from the navigational overhead (selecting, focusing, and browsing a cluster) the current clustering approaches struggle with the labeling problem as well as with runtime issues [4]. One might argue that providing a comprehensive cluster containing all relevant results is always appreciated. But experience shows that often a fraction of the documents is sufficient to satisfy an information need. Once a relevant result is at the user's disposal, alternative and more robust techniques exist to retrieve additional relevant documents: (1) search engines allow for searching

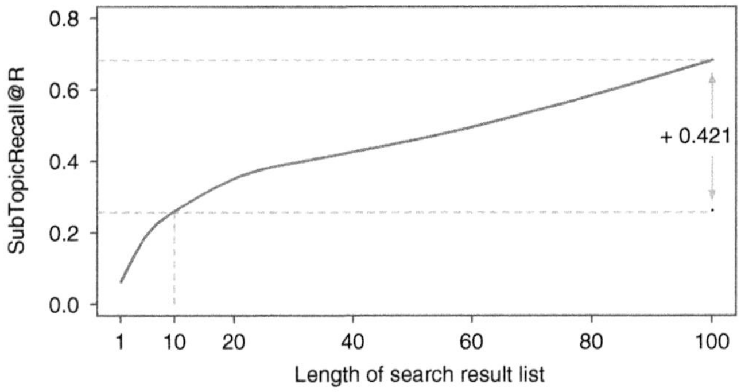

Figure 2: Average subtopic recall for the topics of the AMBIENT dataset. For each topic, we retrieve $N = 100$ search results from eTools (http://www.etools.ch).

similar documents given a particular result, (2) rephrasing the original query inspired by a relevant result became an accepted search strategy [14], and (3) the web itself as a hyperlinked document collection is a great resource for a guided search.

Given the impressive performance of relevance-based search engines, the outlined picture might raise the question whether web search result clustering is of any use. In Section 1, we identified the accessibility of the result list tail as the major weakness of ranked result lists. If we show that the result list tail is valuable and covers further query aspects, a perspective towards better search result clustering emerges.

In order to quantify the potential of the result list tail, we study two datasets: TREC Web Track 2009/2010 [7, 8] and AMBIENT [5]. Each dataset consists of a set T of search topics, with 100 and 44 elements, respectively. For each topic $t \in T$ a number of subtopics is provided. TREC features on average 4.6 subtopics, whereas AMBIENT provides 18 subtopics on average. Every subtopic focuses on a different aspect of t. We form the set S_t as the union of t's subtopics, where we only consider the noun phrases of each subtopic description. Topic terms as well as stopwords present in the noun phrases are discarded. E.g., the topic t="fahrenheit" of the AMBIENT dataset comprises subtopics such as "scale temperature", "michael moore movie", and "band". A standard search engine is queried with each topic $t \in T$ in order to obtain a ranked list $D_t = d_1, \ldots, d_N$ of the top N results, where each $d \in D_t$ denotes a result snippet. A subtopic of t is said to be *covered* by a snippet d, if at least two of its terms occur in d. In the special case of a single term subtopic, the single term has to appear in d. The set of all subtopics of t that are covered by a snippet d is denoted as $\text{coverage}(d, S_t)$. We are interested in the subtopic recall for a result list D_t at rank R, which is defined as the fraction of subtopics covered by the first R results [29]:

$$\text{SubTopicRecall@R} = \frac{|\cup_{i=1}^{R} \text{coverage}(d_i, S_t)|}{|S_t|}, \qquad (1)$$

with $d_i \in D_t$. Figure 2 illustrates the average subtopic recall for all topics in T of the AMBIENT dataset. The TREC Web Track dataset reveals equivalent characteristics. The diagram shows that on average the first N=100 results for a topic cover 66.6% of all subtopics. If we define the result list head to comprise the first ten results, it covers 24.5% of all subtopics; additional 42.1% of the subtopics are covered by the result list tail, rendering the tail a valuable information source. In summary, if web search result clustering can be tailored to organize just the remaining subtopics, it will perfectly complement the result list head and enable a more efficient and effective result analysis. The key to such a complementing behavior lies in the alleviation of the shadowing effect.

3.2 The Shadowing Effect

To generate a clustering that complements the head of a result list, the topics of documents that are to be clustered must differ from the topics already covered by the result list head. We refer to the effect of undesired topic repetition as *shadowing*. To quantify the shadowing effect, we perform state-of-the-art result clustering with Lingo on three different kinds of result lists: (a) the unmodified result list D_t to resemble the standard scenario of existing clustering search engines such as Yippy and Carrot Search[1], (b) the tail of D_t, as a naive application of our idea, and (c) a subset of the tail of D_t, which is filtered with respect to the topics of the head. In the following we set the number of generated clusters per clustering (= per topic t) to ten; the respective cluster labels for a clustering are denoted as L_t. Cluster labels $l \in L_t$ are phrases such as "Fahrenheit 9/11" or "Wellington based Web Design Collective". Then, the shadowing at rank R can be expressed by replacing in Equation (1) the set of subtopics S_t with the set of cluster labels L_t:

$$\text{Shadowing@R} = \frac{|\cup_{i=1}^{R} \text{coverage}(d_i, L_t)|}{|L_t|},$$

with $d_i \in D_t$. Figure 3 illustrates the result of this analysis. The shadowing effect when clustering result list (a) is obvious: the Shadowing@10 is 0.417, i.e., about four cluster labels occur in the snippets of the head of the result lists. One might expect that clustering just the tail gives a reasonable smaller shadowing, which is not the case as can be seen in the results for result list (b). The reason for this behavior is that the topics from the head reappear throughout the entire result list. For our two datasets, up to 18% of the search result snippets in the tail cover the subtopics from the head. Finally, the filtered result list (c) reduces the shadowing effect by 31.6%, entailing a Shadowing@10 of only 0.1. Thus, nine out of ten cluster refer to subtopics present only in the tail.

3.3 Long Tail Filtering of Search Results

We now present a basic procedure to filter the result list tail. The aim of the filtering is to exclusively eliminate all results which cover topics from the head. We expect to satisfy the following two demands: (1) a reduction of the shadowing effect, and (2) a stable or increased subtopic recall after the filtering. Our procedure is detailed below.

```
LongTailClustering
Input:        query
Parameters:   headSize, n
Output:       tailClustering
1. ANALYZEHEAD(query)
      resultList = SEARCH(query)
      headTopics = ANALYZE(resultList, headSize)
2. CLUSTERTAIL(query, headTopics)
      augmentedQuery = query ∧ ¬headTopics
      filteredTail = SEARCH(augmentedQuery)
      tailClustering = CLUSTER(filteredTail, n)
return tailClustering
```

LongTailClustering, as presented, is a generic procedure, and the choices of the search engine `SEARCH`, the topic analyzer `ANALYZE`, and the clustering algorithm `CLUSTER` are user-specific. We experimented with a variety of configurations and see further research opportunities for this task. At present, the best overall results are achieved with the following setup: First, given a query, we receive from the meta-search engine eTools a result list of size $N = 200$.

[1]`http://www.yippy.com, http://www.carrotsearch.com`

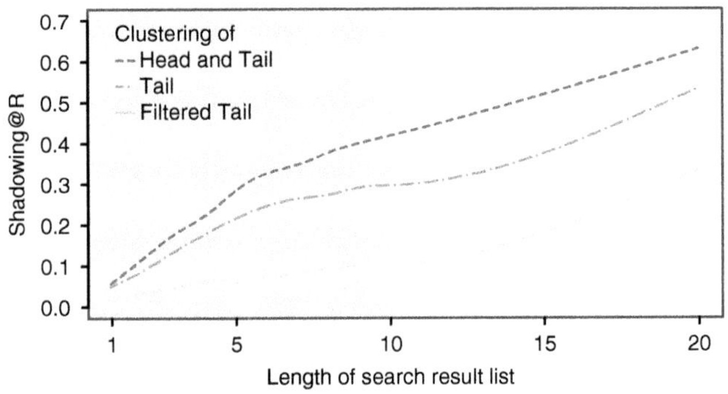

Figure 3: Average shadowing for the topics of the AMBIENT dataset. Three different result sets are considered for the cluster analysis.

In the context of our evaluation, this search engine turned out to provide a higher snippet quality than did Bing or Yahoo. The quality of the snippets is of high importance, since we are interested in finding topics in short texts. For this topic analysis, we extract all noun phrases [2] of maximum length four from the first ten results of the list. Each extracted noun phrase is treated as a topic that has to be filtered from the result list tail in the second step. For this purpose an augmented query is formed, which combines the original query with all noun phrases prefixed by the NOT operator. For instance, the augmented query for "fahrenheit" starts with "fahrenheit -"scale temperature" -"taiwanese boy band" -"video game"". An augmented query can either be used to filter the original result list directly or to send a new request to the search engine. In the latter case, the wisdom of the search engine developers is exploited again. For our experiments with the TREC Web Track and AMBIENT topics, better results are achieved with the former method. For the final clustering, we apply Lingo to the first 90 results of the filtered result list. As already noted and illustrated in Figure 3, the applied *LongTailClustering* procedure reduces the shadowing effect significantly.

In a final experiment, we investigate whether our filtering procedure retains the subtopics that do not appear in the head. For that, we substitute the original result list tail by its filtered version and measure the subtopic recall at rank 100. We find, that although 53.8% of the search results are eliminated in the course of *LongTailClustering*, the filtered result list still reaches a subtopic recall at 100 of 0.64, i.e., contains 96.4% of the subtopics from the original result list (cf. Figure 2). Hence, our procedure successfully implements our idea of moving the focus of web search result clustering to the subtopics that appear exclusively in the result list tail.

4. CONCLUSIONS

A main achievement of our research is that we release web search result clustering from being considered direct competitor to ranked result lists. Instead, we see cluster analysis as a complementary presentation tool to improve the accessibility of relevant documents in the long tail of result lists. This way, web search result clustering goes in line with other advanced search tools such as related search, query suggestions, or the Google Wonderwheel. We have provided the measures SubTopicRecall@R and Shadowing@R to quantify our considerations, and we give empirical evidence for the claimed effects. With *LongTailClustering* we present a procedure that is tailored to the characteristics of our view: *LongTailClustering* is able to cope with the shadowing effect and to increase the density of subtopics that are exclusive for the result list tail. Our current research further analyzes the potential of long tail result clustering and the adaptation of existing clustering technology for this purpose.

5. REFERENCES

[1] R. Agrawal, S. Gollapudi, A. Halverson, and S. Ieong. Diversifying Search Results. In *Proceedings of WSDM 2009*, pages 5–14.

[2] K. Barker and N. Cornacchia. Using Noun Phrase Heads to Extract Document Keyphrases. In *Proceedings of AI 2000*, pages 40–52.

[3] A. Bernardini, C. Carpineto, and M. D'Amico. Full-Subtopic Retrieval with Keyphrase-Based Search Results Clustering. In *Proceedings of WI-IAT 2009*, pages 206–213.

[4] C. Carpineto, S. Osiński, G. Romano, D. Weiss. A Survey of Web Clustering Engines. *ACM Comp. Surveys*, 41(3):Article 17, 2009.

[5] C. Carpineto and G. Romano. AMBIENT dataset. `http://credo.fub.it/ambient`, 2008.

[6] C. Carpineto and G. Romano. Optimal Meta Search Results Clustering. In *Proceedings of SIGIR 2010*, pages 170–177.

[7] C.L.A. Clarke, N. Craswell, and I. Soboroff. Overview of the TREC 2009 Web Track. `http://plg.uwaterloo.ca/~trecweb/2009.html`, 2009.

[8] C.L.A. Clarke, N. Craswell, I. Soboroff, and G.V. Cormack. Overview of the TREC 2010 Web Track. `http://plg.uwaterloo.ca/~trecweb/2010.html`, 2010.

[9] P. Ferragina and A. Gullì. A Personalized Search Engine Based on Web-Snippet Hierarchical Clustering. In *Proceedings of WWW 2005*, pages 801–810.

[10] F. Geraci, M. Pellegrini, M. Maggini, and F. Sebastiani. Cluster Generation and Cluster Labelling for Web Snippets: A Fast and Accurate Hierarchical Solution. In *Proceedings of SPIRE 2006*, pages 25–36.

[11] F. Giannotti, M. Nanni, D. Predreschi, and F. Samaritani. WebCat: Automatic Categorization of Web Search Results. In *Proceedings of SEBD 2003*, pages 507–518.

[12] M.A. Hearst. Clustering versus Faceted Categories for Information Exploration. *Commun. ACM*, 49(4): pages 59–61, 2006.

[13] iProspect.com, Inc. iProspect Blended Search Results Study. `http://www.iprospect.com`, 2008.

[14] R. Jones and K.L. Klinkner. Beyond the Session Timeout: Automatic Hierarchical Segmentation of Search Topics in Query Logs. In *Proceedings of CIKM 2008*, pages 699–708.

[15] K. Kummamuru, R. Lotlikar, S. Roy, K. Singal, R. Krishnapuram. A Hierarchical Monothetic Document Clustering Algorithm for Summarization and Browsing Search Results. In *Proceedings of WWW 2004*, pages 658–665.

[16] Z.-Y. Ming, K. Wang, and T.-S. Chua. Prototype Hierarchy Based Clustering for the Categorization and Navigation of Web Collections. In *Proceedings of SIGIR 2010*, pages 2–9.

[17] R. Navigli and G. Crisafulli. Inducing Word Senses to improve Web Search Result Clustering. In *Proc. of EMNLP 2010*, pages 116–126.

[18] S. Osiński, J. Stefanowski, and D. Weiss. Lingo: Search Results Clustering Algorithm Based on Singular Value Decomposition. In *Proceedings of IIPWM 2004*, pages 359–368.

[19] D. Pinto, J.-M. Benedí, and P. Rosso. Clustering Narrow-Domain Short Texts by Using the Kullback-Leibler Distance. In *Proceedings of CICling 2007*, pages 611–622.

[20] J. Stefanowski and D. Weiss. Comprehensible and Accurate Cluster Labels in Text Clustering. In *Proceedings of RIAO 2007*.

[21] B. Stein and S. Meyer zu Eißen. Topic Identification: Framework and Application. In *Proceedings of i-KNOW 2004*, pages 353–360.

[22] A. Swaminathan, C.V. Mathew, and D. Kirovski. Essential Pages. In *Proceedings of WI-IAT 2009*, pages 173–182.

[23] H. Toda and R. Kataoka. A Clustering Method for News Articles Retrieval System. In *Proceedings of WWW 2005*, pages 988–989.

[24] D. Tunkelang. Faceted Search. Morgan & Claypool Publishers, 2009.

[25] D. Weiss. Descriptive Clustering as a Method for Exploring Text Collections. Ph.D. diss., Poznań Univ. of Technology, Poland, 2006.

[26] M.J. Welch, J. Cho, and C. Olston. Search Result Diversity for Informational Queries. In *Proceedings of WWW 2011*, pages 237–246.

[27] O. Zamir and O. Etzioni. Grouper: A dynamic Clustering Interface to Web Search Results. In *Proceedings of WWW 1999*, pages 1361–1374.

[28] H. Zaragoza, B. B. Cambazoglu, and R. Baeza-Yates. Web Search Solved? All Result Rankings the Same?. In *Proceedings of CIKM 2010*, pages 529–538.

[29] C. Zhai, W. W. Cohen, and J. Lafferty. Beyond Independent Relevance: Methods and Evaluation Metrics for Subtopic Retrieval. In *Proceedings of SIGIR 2003*, pages 10–17.

Spectral Analysis of a Blogosphere

Sang-Wook Kim
Hanyang University
Seoul, 133-791, Korea
wook@hanyang.ac.kr

Ki-Nam Kim
Hanyang University
Seoul, 133-791, Korea
kinam83@gmail.com

Christos Faloutsos
Carnegie Mellon University
Pittsburgh, PA 15237, USA
christos@cs.cmu.edu

Joon-Ho Lee
NHN Corp.
Seongnam 266-1, Korea
joonho@nhn.com

ABSTRACT

A blogosphere is a representative example of online social networks. In this paper, we address spectral analysis of a blogosphere. We model a real-world blogosphere as a matrix and a tensor, and then analyze it by using the SVD and PARAFAC decomposition. According to the results, the SVD successfully identified communities, each of which focuses on a specific topic, and also found hub blogs and authoritative posts within each community. The PARAFAC decomposition also succeeded in extracting more communities of finer granules than the SVD. Also, the PARAFAC decomposition could identify the dominant keywords in addition to the hub blogs and authoritative posts honored in each community.

Categories and Subject Descriptors
H.2.8 [Database Applications] Data mining
G.1.3 [Numerical Analysis] Numerical Linear Algebra-*Singular value decomposition*

General Terms: Experimentation, Human Factors

Keywords: Blogosphere, matrix factorization, tensor factorization, SVD, PARAFAC decomposition

1. INTRODUCTION

A *social network* is a way of expressing a group of people within some society and the relationships among them as a network [5][8][9][10]. With the development of the Internet, social networks have appeared online. A *blogosphere* is a representative example of online social networks [12][13]. A blog is a personal website where a blogger can write his or her thoughts in posts online [4]. A blogger can perform reproductive actions on a post in someone else's blog: typically, trackbacks and scraps. *Trackback* is writing a new post A related to an existing post B and putting a link to B within A; Unique to blog sites in Korea, *scrap* is copying an existing post in someone else's blog as a new post in one's own blog [6][7]. These two actions are reliable (compared to comments) and thus can be used for understanding activities occurring in the blogosphere. The blogosphere has continued to expand its influence, so analyzing its characteristics is important to grasp the dynamics of the real world.

The most challenging issues in business applications related to a blogosphere include (1) identifying communities, (2) finding authoritative contents in each community, and (3) finding hub blogs in each community. In this paper, we are going to touch these three issues in a unified mathematical framework.

A blogosphere can be modeled as a *matrix* and a *tensor* whose dimensions correspond to blogs, posts, and keywords contained in posts. In this paper, we perform spectral analysis on a real-life blogosphere by using the singular value decomposition (SVD) [1][3] and the PARAFAC decomposition [2], which are representative matrix and tensor factorization techniques, respectively. According to the experimental results, the two techniques are shown to be quite useful in identifying communities of different granularities and also in finding *hub blogs*, *authoritative posts*, and *dominant keywords* in each community.

To the best of the authors' knowledge, this is the first contribution that applies the SVD and the PARAFAC decomposition to a huge volume of real-world blog data and provides meaningful implications on the three important issues above.

This paper is organized as follows. Section 2 briefly surveys the SVD and PARAFAC decomposition, our mathematical tools for analyzing the blogosphere. Sections 3 and 4 present our results analyzed by using the SVD and PARAFAC decomposition, respectively. Finally, Section 5 summarizes and concludes the paper.

2. TOOLS FOR ANALYSIS

2.1 SVD

Using the SVD, an $N \times M$ matrix A is expressed as follows [1][4].

$$A = \sum_{r=1}^{rank(A)} (\lambda_r u_r \circ v_r) \qquad (1)$$

where $rank(A)$ is the *rank* of matrix A, λ_r is the singular value, u_r is the left singular vector, and v_r is the right singular vector. The notation '$\circ$' denotes the outer product of the

CIKM'11, October 24–28, 2011, Glasgow, Scotland, UK.

two vectors. Also, for space and time efficiency reasons, it is often approximated by only using R ($\ll rank(A)$) singular values as follows.

$$A \approx \sum_{r=1}^{R} (\lambda_r u_r \circ v_r) \quad (2)$$

where λ_r ($\lambda_1 \geqq \lambda_2 \geqq ... \geqq \lambda_R > 0$) is one of the largest R singular values.

By using the SVD, we can uncover R most important concepts hidden in the relationships among N row objects and M column objects in matrix A [1]. Also, u_r can be thought of as the degrees of *row objects* in relevance to concept r. Similarly, v_r is those of *column objects* in relevance to concept r.

2.2 PARAFAC decomposition

A *tensor* is a multidimensional array, a generalized version of a two-dimensional matrix [2]. Also, the PARAFAC decomposition can be considered as a higher-order generalization of the matrix SVD. Using the PARAFAC decomposition, an $N \times M \times K$ three-way *tensor* is expressed by

$$B \approx \sum_{r=1}^{R} \lambda_r u_r \circ v_r \circ w_r \quad (3)$$

where $u_r \circ v_r \circ w_r$ indicates a three-way outer product.

Similar to the SVD, u_r can be thought of as the strength of *the first dimension objects* in relevance to concept r, v_r is that of *the second dimension objects* in relevance to concept r, and finally, w_r is that of *the third dimension objects* in relevance to concept r [11]. The choice of R, the number of concepts, is done manually in the PARAFAC decomposition.

3. SVD-BASED ANALYSIS

For the analysis, we used anonymized real-world blog data which was collected from *blog.naver.com*, the largest blogosphere in Korea. From the title of every post, we extracted the non-trivial terms as its *keywords*. As a result, we could have information on blogs, posts, keywords, and actions as features of the blogosphere. To keep noisy keywords from being included, we eliminated *stop words* such as *the* and *a*. As a result, the total numbers of posts, blogs, and keywords were 1,614,242, 995,048, and 51,785, respectively. We converted the blog data as an $N \times M$ matrix A where N is the number of blogs and M is the number of posts. A_{ij} is 1 if blog i has performed an action on post j, and 0 otherwise. By using the SVD, matrix A is expressed as in Equation (2).

By applying the SVD to matrix A, we obtained following results. R, rank of A, is six; The first six singular values in λ_r have all the energy (= sum of λ_r's) and their energy levels appear as in Figure 1. So, R indicates there are six large communities in the blogosphere. Singular vectors u_r and v_r give the degrees of relevance of blogs and posts to community r. By using u_r and v_r, we could identify the blogs of good hub and posts of good authority in community r.

We analyzed each of six communities in more detail. First, we examined the most frequently appearing terms in all the posts belonging to each community r. By this analysis, we also could identify the main topic dealt with in each community. The first column of Table 1 shows the main topics, and the second column does four terms most frequently occurring in posts.

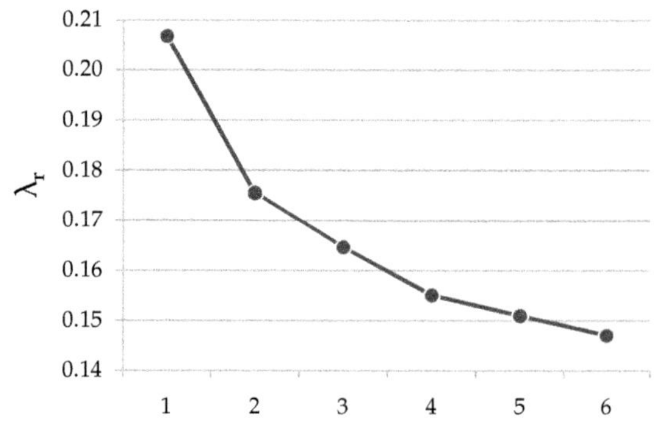

Figure 1: Energy levels in the SVD.

Table 1: Most frequent terms in six communities

Topic	Most frequent terms
Food recipes	food, fried food, taste, cheese
D.I.Y	reform, apple box, fabrication, material
Entertainment	stars, photos, movies, entertainment
Interior	interior, labels, reform, collections
Pop music	love, Super Junior, OST, idol stars
Classic music	movement, sonata, concerto, Bach

Table 2: Top five authoritative posts in the first and second communities

Post title (C1)	Score	Actions
Korean rice cakes: a recipe	0.154	857
Let's enjoy a dish of noodles!	0.151	808
Home-made pizza	0.151	948
Best food in the thanks-giving day	0.150	604
Fantastic Korean-styled pizza	0.149	671
Post title (C2)	Score	Actions
Making a paper frame with A4	0.422	3098
Fabricating a natural furniture	0.291	1647
Reforming a medicine cabinet	0.239	1246
Arrangement box for accessories	0.229	1383
Information of DIY, reforming..	0.229	1512

Table 2 shows the title, the score in v_r, and the number of received actions of the top five *authoritative posts* belonging to the first and second communities (r = 1, 2). Via this detailed analysis, we confirmed the two things in each community. First, the posts of high scores in v_r have quality contents highly related to the topic of r, and they also have been scraped and trackbacked by many other blogs in r. This indicates they are playing a role of authoritative posts in r.

Table 3 shows, for each of the top five *hub blogs* in the first and second communities, the most frequently occurring terms, the respective score in u_r, and the number of actions taken. Second, the blogs of high scores in u_r have scraped or tackbacked a number of posts whose contents are of good quality and also highly relevant to the topic in r. This implies that these blogs are hubs in r.

Table 3: Top five hub blogs in the first and second communities

Most frequent terms in a blog (C1)	Score	Actions
fried food, roast food, sauce, food	0.110	444
fried food, food, sauce, taste	0.100	315
potato, taste, boiled food, sandwich	0.095	378
flavor, Kimchi, taste, fried food	0.082	99
food, fried food, Kimchi, healthy food	0.081	142
Most frequent terms in a blog (C2)	**Score**	**Actions**
reform, box, case, space	0.081	125
bag, chair, fabracition, reform	0.069	542
reform, furniture, wood, box	0.067	154
reform, apple box, DIY, fabrication	0.062	119
fabrication, reform, shelf, box	0.062	99

We observe that the authoritative posts and hub blogs within the first community *C1* have the titles and keywords relevant to 'food recipes', which coincides with its main topic as shown in Table 1. Similarly, we also see that the authoritative posts and hub blogs within the second community *C2* are highly related to 'Shaping' that is a main topic of the second community. In summary, the SVD successfully extracted six communities, and also found good hub blogs and good authoritative posts in each community.

4. PARAFAC-BASED ANALYSIS

We converted the blog data to an $N \times M \times K$ three-way tensor B where N is the number of blogs, M is the number of posts, and K is the number of keywords. B_{ijk} is 1 if blog i has performed an action on post j that has keyword k inside, and 0 otherwise. By using the PARAFAC decomposition, tensor B is expressed as in Equation (3).

Vectors u_r, v_r, and w_r provide the degree of the relevance of blogs, posts, and keywords to community r. So, the blogs, posts, and keywords having high scores in u_r, v_r, and w_r are all considered inter-related to one another in community r. We set R as 10 to 50 in step of 10 in applying the PARAFAC decomposition to tensor B. Figure 2 shows the energy levels of 50 PARAFAC decomposition factors for tensor B.

Table 4 shows different sets of communities depending on the choice of parameter R, the number of factors in the PARAFAC decomposition, 10 through 50. Each *row* represents a set of communities obtained by using a specific R. An *entry* in a row is represented by *topic(i)* that implies a topic and i communities related to the topic. For example, *English(2)* in the first row, we know that there are two communities whose members are interested in *English*. The

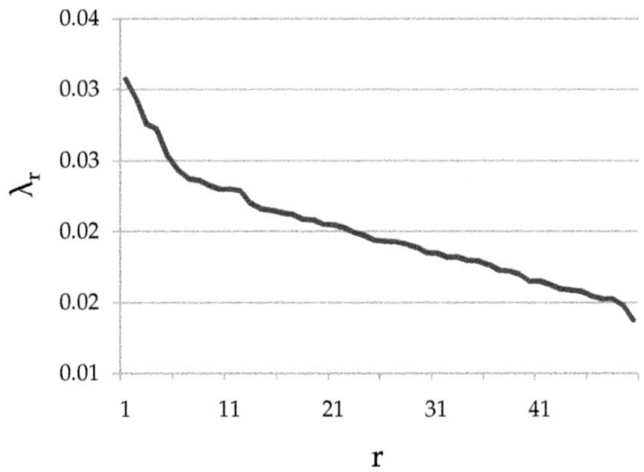

Figure 2: Energy levels in the PARAFAC decomposition.

larger R, the more communities extracted. When the value of R increases, we could find new communities. The boldface entry in a row indicates the community that is not found in previous stages with smaller R. For instance, the community related to 'movies' appears first in the PARAFAC decomposition with $R = 40$.

Table 4: Communities extracted with different R

R	Communities extracted
10	Reform(2), Papers(2), Japanese(1), English(2), Accessories(1), Habits(1), Functionality(1)
20	Reform(1), Papers(2), Japanese(2), English(5), Accessories(1), Habits(2), Functionality(1), **Blood types(1), Character(1), Entertainer(1), Food(3)**
30	Reform(3), Papers(5), Japanese(2), English(9), Accessories(2), Habits(1), Functionality(1), Blood types(1), Character(1), Food(4), **Proverb(1)**
40	Reform(6), Papers(7), Japanese(1), English(7), Accessories(2), Habits(3), Functionality(1), Blood types(1), Character(2), Entertainer(1), Food(5), Proverbrb(1), **Good ideas(1), Movies(2)**
50	Reform(7), Papers(7), Japanese(2), English(13), Accessories(1), Habits(4), Functionality(1), Blood types(1), Character(2), Food(5), Proverb(1), Good ideas(1), Movies(1), Diary(1), **Constellation(1), Advertisement(1), TOEIC(1)**

Table 5 exemplifies three communities. For each community, we show (1) the most dominant four keywords, (2) the most frequent four terms in a blog, and (3) the title of the top four authoritative posts. We see that the keywords, titles, and the most frequent terms are in accordance with one another in each community.

In summary, the PARAFAC decomposition successfully identifies communities, and also extracts a set of dominant keywords, a set of posts of good authority, and a set of blogs

Table 5: Dominant keywords, top authoritative posts, and top hub blogs in three communities

Keywords (C1)	Most frequent terms in a blog (C1)
english, rules, US, pronunciation	english, life, description, conversation
	US, pronunciation, rules, english
	US, pronunciation, rules, english
	US, life, fried food, cheese
	Top post title (C1)
	rules for difficult pronunciation
	english expressions for phone calls
	english pronunciation
	useful English expressions
Keywords (C2)	**Most frequent terms in a blog (C2)**
mufflers, needles, fingers, knitwork	mufflers, needles, figers, school
	mufflers, needles, figers, knitwork
	making, mufflers, figers, socks
	finger, knitwork, design, mufflers
	Top post title (C2)
	making a muffler within 30 minutes
	knitting for neckcloth with fingers
	hand-knitting school
	hand-knitted mufflers
Keywords (C3)	**Most frequent terms in a blog (C3)**
habits, values, you, language	habits, language, life, happiness
	values, reason, habits, you
	values, sensation, habits, language
	ruiner, habits, man, success
	Top post title (C3)
	language habits for your value
	decisive habits to success
	ways to build good relationships
	habitual ways for successful studies

of good hub in each community. We found some communities deal with the identical (or at least very similar) topic. Compared to the case with the SVD, we could find more communities of finer granules with the PARAFAC decomposition by setting R to a large value.

5. CONCLUSIONS

In this paper, we have addressed the analysis of a blogosphere by using the SVD and PARAFAC decomposition. The SVD identified six communities from the blogosphere, and also found the blogs, posts, and keywords that are interrelated in each community. The PARAFAC decomposition worked similarly but found more communities of finer granules. Possible applications of these results could be extracting related sub-communities, finding power blogs, and ranking popular posts under a given topic.

6. ACKNOWLEDGMENTS

This work was supported by the National Research Foundation of Korea(NRF) grant funded by the Korea government(MEST) (Grant No. 2008-0061006) and NHN Corp. Any opinions, findings, and conclusions or recommendations expressed in this material are the authors' and do not necessarily reflect those of the sponsors.

7. REFERENCES

[1] F. Korn, H. Jagadish, and C. Faloutsos, "Efficiently Supporting Ad-Hoc Queries in Large Datasets of Time Sequences," In *Proc. of ACM Int'l. Conf. on Management of Data*, ACM SIGMOD, pp. 289-300, 1997.

[2] T. Kolda and B. Bader, "Tensor Decompositions and Applications," *Journal of SIAM Review*, Vol. 51, No. 3, pp. 455-500, 2009.

[3] I. Jolliffe, *Principal Component Analysis*, Springer Verlag, 2002.

[4] J. Leskovec et al., "Cascading Behavior in Large Blog Graphs," *SIAM Int'l. Conf. on Data Mining*, SDM, 2007.

[5] J. Leskovec, J. Kleinberg, and C. Faloutsos, "Graph Evolution: Densification and Shrinking Diameters," *ACM Trans. on Knowledge Discovery from Data*, ACM TKDD, Vol. 1, No. 1, 2007.

[6] S. H. Yoon, J. H. Shin, S. W. Kim, and S. J. Park, "Extraction of a Latent Blog Community Based on Subject," In *Proc. of ACM Int'l. Conf. on Information and Knowledge Management*, ACM CIKM, pp. 1529-1532, 2009.

[7] Y. S. Kwon, S. W. Kim, and S. J. Park, "An Analysis of Information Diffusion in the Blog World," In *Proc. ACM CIKM Workshop on Complex Networks in Information & Knowledge Management*, ACM CNIKM, pp. 27-30, 2009.

[8] S. C. Baek, S. W. Kang, H. Noh, and S. W. Kim, "Contents-Based Analysis of Community Formation and Evolution in Blogspace," In *Proc. IEEE ICDE Workshop on Modeling, Managing, and Mining of Evolving Social Networks*, IEEE M3SN, pp. 1607-1610, 2009.

[9] S. H. Lim, S. W. Kim, S. J. Park, and J. H. Lee, "Determining Content Power Users in a Blog Network," In *Proc. of ACM KDD Workshop on Social Network Mining and Analysis*, ACM SNA-KDD, 2009.

[10] Y. S. Kwon, S. W. Kim, S. J. Park, S. H. Lim, and J. B. Lee, "The Information Diffusion Model in the Blog World," In *Proc. of ACM KDD Workshop on Social Network Mining and Analysis*, ACM SNA-KDD, 2009.

[11] B. Bader and T. Kolda, MATLAB Tensor Toolbox Version 2.3, http://csmr.ca.sandia.gov/~tgkolda/TensorToolbox/, July 2009.

[12] M. Goetz et al., "Modeling Blog Dynamics," *Int'l. Conf. on Weblogs and Social Media*, pp. 26-33, 2009.

[13] M. McGlohon et al., "Finding Patterns in Blog Shapes and Blog Evolution," *Int'l. Conf. on Weblogs and Social Media*, 2007.

Citation Chain Aggregation: An Interaction Model to Support Citation Cycling

Timothy Cribbin
People and Interactivity Research Centre
Brunel University
Uxbridge, UK
timothy.cribbin@brunel.ac.uk

ABSTRACT

Citation chaining is a powerful means of exploring the academic literature. Starting from just one or two known relevant items, a naïve researcher can cycle backwards and forwards through the citation graph to generate a rich overview of key works, authors and journals relating to their topic. Whilst online citation indexes greatly facilitate this process, the size and complexity of the search space can rapidly escalate. In this paper, we propose a novel interaction model called citation chain aggregation (CCA). CCA employs a simple three-list view which highlights the overlaps that occur between the first-generation relations of known relevant items. As more relevant articles are identified, differences in the frequencies of citations made by or to unseen articles provide strong relevance feedback cues. The benefits of this technique are illustrated using a simple case study.

Categories and Subject Descriptors

H.3.3 [**Information Storage and Retrieval**]: Information Search and Retrieval–*Retrieval models, Relevance feedback, Search process*; H.3.7 [**Information Storage and Retrieval**]: Digital Libraries–*User issues.*

General Terms

Design, Human Factors

Keywords

Citation index, chaining, polyrepresentation, digital library, search user interface

1. INTRODUCTION

Chaining is a search mode that exploits the networks of relationships that emerge as a result of citation behavior. Backward chaining [4] or footnote chasing [1] involves looking up articles that are cited by a known seed article. In contrast, forward chaining [4] or citation searching [1] involves going forwards in time to find relevant articles that cite a known article. Cawkell [3] describes the method of *citation cycling*, in which backward and forward chaining are used in combination to build an overview of an unfamiliar field. The researcher begins by noting the most useful citations in some initial seed article. They then forward chain to the articles that cite these articles, note their citations and forward chain from these. As the cycle continues, key articles, authors and journals gradually become apparent.

Backward chaining is commonly applied by most academic disciplines, given the established practices of citation and referencing. In contrast, forward chaining has only recently been made feasible through the introduction of citation indexes. Since the 1990s these indexes have been accessible online through hypertext interfaces [3]. Services like Thomson-Reuter's Web of Science (WOS), ACM's Digital Library and the open-source CiteSeerX greatly facilitate locomotion through citation graphs by providing hyperlinks alongside each article record to cited and citing article records. Online citation indexes also enable other useful functionality such as the *related records* search, which ranks records according to the degree of bibliographic coupling with a seed article. Whilst there is little doubt that these visual interfaces have greatly facilitated the practice of citation cycling, two key problems still face the user engaged in citation cycling.

The first problem is one of managing the *size of the search space*. Even a single iteration of citation cycling can result in a large, heterogeneous search space, particularly on the forward chain side. A single influential article might cite perhaps a dozen or so well chosen works, but in turn be cited hundreds or even thousands of times, for a diversity of reasons. Without judicious filtering, the number of articles to follow-up can become unwieldy after just one or two iterations [3].

Deciding which articles to follow-up is a difficult task because authors' reasons for citation can vary widely in both purpose and salience [4]. Judging citations made by a known article is relatively simple because they reflect the intentions of a single project and are contextualized by their location within the text. However, the motivations for citations made to an article, reflecting the work of various authors over many years, may be quite diverse and not always immediately apparent from reading article surrogates [1]. Ranking search results by citation count alone is not always helpful if, for example, the researcher's interest does not relate to the primary impact of the seed. Citation counts also favor older articles over more recent publications. Related record searching provides a convenient proxy for citation cycling i.e. finding articles that cite some or all of the same articles as the seed. Whilst this can alleviate the latter issue, effective cycling still depends on the judicious selection of citations in order to control both the quality and quantity of accumulated articles [3, 6]. At the current time, none of the citation indexes provides an option to refine a related search to only take selected citations into account.

The second problem can be best described as the *focus and context problem*. The objective of citation cycling is to build a coherent picture or overview of the literature relating to some topic [3]. Current hypertext interfaces employ a simple paging model, in which the user navigates the citation graph in a step-wise fashion from one node of interest to another. Typically the user begins by viewing an article summary before scrolling down or clicking through to a list of cited or citing articles, from which they can then select and navigate through to a new article summary, and so on. As they move from one node to the next they will tend to follow many interweaving paths within the citation graph. Yet the user's view is always narrowly focused on either the current article, its citations or citing articles. As such, the user's awareness of the developing context – the relative salience of relevant articles and their inter-relationships – is dependent upon their ability to assimilate these many local views into a coherent a mental model of the space.

In this paper, we propose a new interaction model for citation cycling which addresses these and other limitations of associated with current citation index interfaces. The model employs a three-list view to represent the aggregated sets of first-order citations (one generation back and forth) associated with the set of one or more known relevant articles. Known, relevant article records are displayed in the central 'pearl' list, whilst the left- and the right-hand lists display all unique articles that are cited by and cite the pearl articles. Following the cognitive overlap hypothesis [5, 6], articles that relate to more known articles are deemed more salient. As more articles are added to the pearl list, clear differences emerge in terms of the number of relational 'hits' they make with the pearl, providing valuable relevance feedback to the user. We call this interaction model Citation Chain Aggregation (CCA).

2. RELATED WORK

Given the focus and context problem, the idea of visualizing relevant sub-graphs of the citation index has been explored by several studies (e.g. Butterfly: [7]; Circleview: [2]; CAVis: [9] and [11]). Perhaps the earliest and best known example is the Butterfly visualizer [7]. The body of each butterfly object is used to display metadata about a specific article record, whilst the wings display annotated links to cited (left) and citing (right) articles. Clicking on a link creates a new butterfly instance focusing on that article. Citation chains are conveyed by folding-away the wings and placing butterfly objects side by side, again with the cited articles to the left of citing items.

The idea of representing a single generation citation chain in *cited-focus-citing* order (see also [11]) is a natural mapping that has been translated into the CCA prototype design. However, a pervasive issue associated with all approaches to visualizing citation graphs is one of controlling visual clutter. The local citation graph surrounding just a few related articles can be large and complex. Representing such a graph neatly and usably in iconic format is problematic enough, but effective navigational support also requires details in context. Finding the balance between overview and sufficient detail typically restricts the size of the visible context to just one current focus article and one or two generations of ancestors and descendants [2, 11]. Also, when the cardinality is high, less salient citation links must be either hidden (e.g. [2, 7]) or suppressed in some way [e.g. 11].

We contend that a solution to the clutter problem may be to forgo the convention of visualizing the graph *per se* and to focus instead on a more abstract representation of the evolving context. The interaction model proposed here draws inspiration from work in the area of information retrieval, specifically Ingwersen's principle of polyrepresentation [5] and related work by Larsen [6]. Studies by McCain [8] and Pao [10] have shown that the overlap in results sets retrieved from multiple, cognitively distinct queries tend to identify the most relevant articles. For instance, Pao [10] found that the overlap between documents retrieved from both a keyword search on MEDLINE and a citation search increased precision by some six to eight times.

More recently, Larsen [6] demonstrated how the "boomerang" effect can improve search precision, by combining keyword and citation search without the need to provide expert-defined seed articles. Larsen proposed a three step method. In step one, multiple queries are made to separate indexes (e.g. title, keywords and abstract). Each search will tend to produce different results. However the *cognitive overlap hypothesis* predicts that citations common to multiple sets will tend to be the most important. As such, in step two, only citations made by articles in two or more of the step one sets are retained. In step three, a forward citation search is performed for all of the retained citations. Finally, these citing articles are ranked by the number of step two sub-sets they relate to. Using this method, Larsen found that rated precision tended to increase significantly inline with the degree of overlap.

3. CITATION CHAIN AGGREGATION

Larsen's method represents an effective proxy for citation cycling. However, CCA improves upon this approach by being more interactive and open-ended. Larsen's aim was to reduce inconsistency resulting from the need to select appropriate 'seed' documents [8]. In contrast, we see the task of 'pearl growing' from a one or two seed articles as a natural and likely scenario [1, 4]. As such, in the CCA model, the user has complete control over which articles participate in the cycling process. For example, the user can begin with a single article, select just a handful of key citations, simultaneously forward chain from all of these articles and immediately see the resulting overlaps in terms of both citing and cited articles. The user is then free to select whichever articles they wish, from either side, to continue the cycling process. Note that the model is also flexible enough to emulate the boomerang strategy in some form, although this isn't currently implemented in the prototype.

The fundamental concept in CCA is the *citation chain*. We define a citation chain as the sub-graph describing an article and all of its immediate ancestors (cited articles) and descendents (citing articles). In the conventional hypertext model, the user can only view one citation chain (or part-thereof) at a time. CCA, on the other hand, aggregates multiple citation chains into a single three-list view (Figure 1).

A citation cycling episode begins with the researcher adding one or more relevant articles to the pearl list. This can be achieved by entering a unique identifier or by importing results from a search (or any other list of references). When an article is added, the system sends a query to the citation index web service to retrieve all its cited and citing articles. The results are then displayed in the requisite peripheral lists. If an article is not already in its target list then a new item is added, otherwise the item's counter is incremented to reflect another instance of overlap or 'hit' between citation chains. Note, therefore, that any article can be a member of any number of lists.

Figure 1 shows the result after just two related articles have been added to the pearl list. The seed article was added first (upper black circle), followed by one of its citations, selected from the resulting items in the cited list. The Venn diagram shows that many of the citations, both to and from the two pearl articles, are shared. The sketch below shows how the results are displayed in the list views. Each list item comprises various fields. In addition to bibliographic data (author, date etc) the left hand field in each view shows an overlap counter. We can see that half of the articles in the citing list cite both pearl articles (count of two), whilst half of the cited items are cited by both articles. Following the cognitive overlap hypothesis, list items can be sorted from high to low by this 'hit' counter to provide relevance feedback. As more items are added to the pearl list, so the differentiation between unseen articles increases. Within the pearl list, an item's counter field represents the number of pearl items that cite it. In this case, the second article is attributed a count of one. Gradually as more articles are added, the differentiation that emerges here provides a measure of salience within the pearl list.

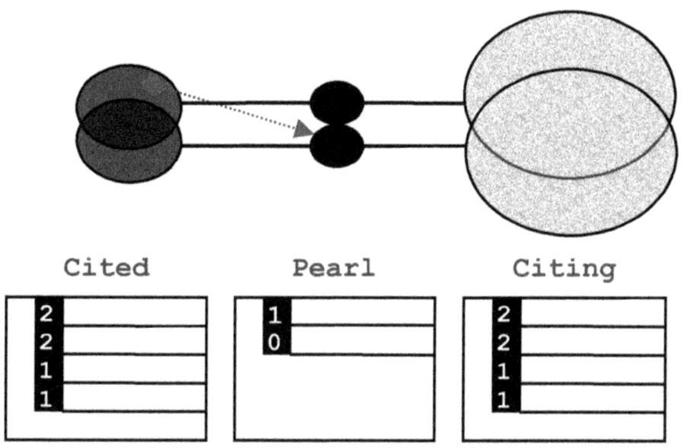

Figure 1. Citation chain aggregation of two articles.

4. PROTOTYPE

The prototype required direct and reliable access to a comprehensive online citation index. The first prototype utilized the open REST API of CiteSeerX (http://citeseerx.ist.psu.edu). The open nature of the API was convenient for an initial proof-of-concept, but the database lacked the coverage required for field testing, being mainly focused on the CS literature. Permission was therefore obtained from Thomson-Reuters to use their WOS SOAP API, which enabled a more widely useful prototype to be developed. Both versions have almost identical interfaces and functionality, sharing much of the same code in terms of presentation and interaction routines. The key differences lie in the implementation of search requests and handling of the responses.

The screenshot shown in Figure 2 is from the WOS version. The three lists are situated at the top of the interface. By default, lists are sorted from high to low by the overlap counter field (first column). Lists can be re-sorted by any field by clicking on the column header. The user can click on any list item to view the article record, which is displayed underneath in a text box. Where available, the user can link directly to the publisher's web-site to view the full text article. Tight coupling is employed to convey relationships. Clicking on a cited/citing item causes related records in the pearl list to be highlighted in bold. Likewise, clicking on a pearl item highlights related records in the peripheral lists. Occurrences of pearl members in the peripheral lists are de-emphasized in grey. Seed articles can be located by executing a WOS search. Search results can be viewed and directly transferred to the pearl list from within the interface. Currently topic, title, author and date search fields are supported.

Internally, all article records are stored within a single array defined by a custom type. This type is composed of fields describing the article's bibliographic data and set membership (cited, pearl and citing). Note that a record can belong to any number of sets. Cited and citing status fields are, in turn, defined by a sub-type that maintains a count and index of any relationships with pearl articles.

Server response times are the only bottleneck when it comes to performance, particularly when requesting citing articles, which must be retrieved in batches of 100 records. However, most updates complete within just a few seconds. Updates that do not involve server requests remain near-instant even when the array contains thousands of items.

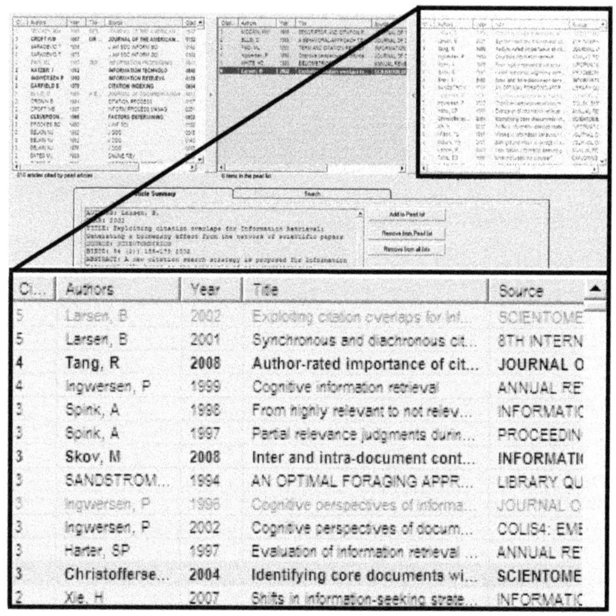

Figure 2. Prototype system interface (top) with close-up view of citing articles list (bottom).

5. WALKTHROUGH

We have yet to complete the first round of formal user testing. However, the utility of CCA can be demonstrated informally by walking through a single citation cycling iteration.

A convenient example is to use Larsen's [6] paper on the 'boomerang effect' as a seed. This cites 31 articles in total, but we begin by selecting just a handful of citations that seem most pertinent to our interests. First Ellis [4], as the seminal paper about citation chaining, is transferred to the pearl. Next, Ingwersen's [5] paper on polyrepresentation, which evidently forms the theoretical basis for Larsen's retrieval model, is added. We back this up with McCain [8] and Pao [10] which provide empirical evidence in support of the cognitive overlap hypothesis. Finally, we identify a fifth citation, White and McCain [12], a seminal paper on co-citation analysis, in the hope of picking up other work that has investigated the relationship between co-citation and search.

The result is a total of 611 cited articles and 616 citing articles. Clearly too many to browse through exhaustively! However, the sorted citing list reveals that only a handful (<10%) of items cite more than one pearl article. In fact just 12 (2%) cite three or more of the six pearl articles (see Table 1), with a further 47 (7.7%) citing two.

WOS related records (top-ten only) and citing articles (total of six) searches were requested for the seed article. Table 1 compares the results with the CCA rankings. The top CCA rank is, predictably, the seed itself. The next article, also with an overlap score of five, is a conference paper on the boomerang effect co-authored by Larsen and Ingwersen, which predates the seed but was not cited by it. This is followed by Tang and then Ingwersen, each with scores of four. Tang is particularly interesting as it was ranked lowest amongst the related records (10th) and was only the third highest cited (two cites) amongst those citing the seed.

Table 1: Articles citing three or more pearl articles

Citing List	Overlap	Related to seed	Cites Seed
Larsen (2002) Sciento.	5		
Larsen (2001) ISSI-2001	5	✓	
Tang (2008) J. Doc	4	✓	✓
Ingwersen (1999) ARIST	4	✓	
Spink (1998) IP&M	3		
Spink (1997) Proc. ASIS	3		
Skov (2008) IP&M	3		✓
Sandstrom (1994) Lib. Quart.	3		
Ingwersen (1996) J. Doc	3	✓	
Ingwersen (2002) COLIS 4	3		
Harter (1997) ARIST	3	✓	
Christoffersen (2004) Sciento.	3	✓	✓

More generally, it is interesting to see how some items are promoted whilst others are demoted. Six out of the top-ten related items remain highly ranked after CCA. The dropped items were all science mapping, rather than information retrieval studies, and so were indeed less relevant. Finally, a further four articles are new entries that were not picked up by either of the comparison searches.

Bear in mind that this example is the result after just a single iteration. The CCA model allows for an open-ended interaction with the citation index. The user can therefore engage in a game of 'citation tennis', cycling backwards and forwards, until they are satisfied with the contents of their pearl list.

6. CONCLUSIONS AND FUTURE WORK

This paper has proposed a new interaction model to support citation cycling. CCA resolves key issues associated with existing hypertext- and visualization-based interfaces. The most notable advantages are its simplicity and scalability, both in terms of system requirements and the user experience. We have demonstrated informally how just a single backward-forward chaining cycle can provides clear and useful relevance feedback on unseen articles. This analysis needs to be followed-up with formal empirical studies. Work is in progress to evaluate the benefits to researchers as they use the system both in the laboratory and over extended periods in the field.

Future work will also explore ways of improving the prototype with additional functionality. There are many possible enhancements that can be made to support interaction within larger citation graphs, including content similarity ranking, visualization and dynamic filtering.

Finally, CCA is a flexible model that may be adapted and optimized for a variety of different information tasks, ranging from exploration through to checking the completeness of referencing during editing and review. Moreover, its use is not limited only to academic literature search, but potentially any information space that can be represented as a directed graph. Obvious domains for future evaluation include legal search, patent analysis (prior-art search) and web search.

7. REFERENCES

[1] Bates, M. 1989. The design of browsing and berrypicking techniques for the online search interface. *Online Review,* 13, 5, 407-431.

[2] Bergström, P. and Whitehead, E.J. 2006. CircleView: scalable visualization and navigation of citation networks. In *Proceedings of 2006 Symposium on Interactive Visual Information Collections and Activity* (College Station, TX).

[3] Cawkell, A.E. 1998. Checking research progress on 'image retrieval by shape-matching' using the Web of Science. *Aslib Proceedings*, 50, 2, 27-31.

[4] Ellis, D. 1989. A behavioural approach to information retrieval system design. *Journal of Documentation*, 45, 3, 171-212.

[5] Ingwersen, P. 1996. Cognitive perspectives of information retrieval interaction: elements of a cognitive IR theory. *Journal of Documentation*, 52, 1, 3-50.

[6] Larsen, B. 2002. Exploiting citation overlaps for information retrieval: generating a boomerang effect from the network of scientific papers. *Scientometrics*, 54, 2. 155-178.

[7] Mackinlay, J.D., Rao, R. and Card, S.K. 1995. An organic user interface for searching citation links. In *Proceedings of SIGCHI Conference on Human Factors in Computing Systems* (Denver, CO). 67-73.

[8] McCain, K.W. 1989. Descriptor and citation retrieval in the medical behavioral sciences literature: Retrieval overlaps and novelty distribution. *Journal of the American Society for Information Science*, 40, 2, 110-114.

[9] Nguyen, Q.V., Huang, M.L. and Simo, S. 2007. Visualization of relational structure among scientific articles. In *Proceedings of the 9th International Conference on Visual Information Systems* (Shanghai, China). 415-425.

[10] Pao, M.L. 1993. Term and citation retrieval - a field-study. *Information Processing & Management*, 29, 1. 95-112.

[11] Schäfer, U. and Kasterka, U. 2010. Scientific authoring support: a tool to navigate in typed citation graphs. In *Proceedings of NAACL HLT 2010 Workshop on Computational Linguistics and Writing* (Los Angeles, CA). 7-14.

[12] White, H. and McCain, K. 1998. Visualizing a discipline: an author co-citation analysis of information science, 1972–1995. *Journal of the American Society for Information Science*, 49, 4. 327-355.

Collaborative Blacklist Generation via Searches-and-Clicks

Lung-Hao Lee and Hsin-Hsi Chen
Department of Computer Science and Information Engineering
National Taiwan University
Taipei, Taiwan
{d98922011, hhchen}@ntu.edu.tw

ABSTRACT
This paper presents an intent conformity model to collaboratively generate blacklists for cyberporn filtering. A novel porn detection framework via searches-and-clicks is proposed to explore collective intelligence embedded in query logs. Firstly, the clicked pages are represented in terms of the weighted queries to reflect the degrees related to pornography. Consequently, these weighted queries are regarded as discriminative features to calculate the pornography indicator by an inverse chi-square method for candidate determination. Finally, a candidate whose URL contains at least one pornographic keyword is included in our collaborative blacklists. The experiments on a MSN porn data set indicate that the generated blacklist achieves a high precision, while maintaining a favorably low false positive rate. In addition, real-life filtering simulations reveal that our blacklist is more effective than some publicly released blacklists.

Categories and Subject Descriptors
H.3.3 [**Information Search and Retrieval**]: *Information filtering*

General Terms
Experimentation, Human Factors.

Keywords
Collaborative cyberporn filtering, search intents, user behaviors

1. INTRODUCTION
Filtering the wide spreading objectionable web content, e.g., pornography, violence, drug and gambling, has attracted intensive attention for protecting children or anyone else from inappropriate materials [11]. The URL blocking approach rejects any requests to URLs on a blacklist, while accepting requests to URLs that are not blacklisted [7, 12]. The dynamics of the web requires such a blacklist to be constantly updated for sustainable blocking performance. Traditionally, the URLs in blacklists are manually listed or automatically generated by intelligent content analysis.

Different form the previous work, we generate blacklists with collective intelligence embedded in search query logs, but without web page content. Submitting queries to search engines and clicking search results are two common operations in daily life. These actions provide implicit taggings on web pages, which are useful feedbacks to search engines for filtering inappropriate materials in necessary situations.

CIKM'11, October 24-28, 2011, Glasgow, Scotland, UK.

How to follow the changing trails of objectionable web sites and maintain a steady and satisfactory filtering performance is a major challenging issue. In this paper, we explore the variability of objectionable one, which was successfully accessed in search query logs, to approximately keep up with the changing trails. Query log analysis showed that the top three categories in terms of popularity are pornography, entertainment and music [1]. About 25% of the highest used query terms apparently dealt with sexual topic [3]. We take the pornography, a category of top popularity, as a target to demonstrate the filtering effectiveness.

This paper proposes an intent conformity model for collaborative blacklist generation via searches-and-clicks. Firstly, the clicked pages are represented in terms of the queries that retrieve them. After weighting the issued queries with the degrees related to pornography, the pornography indicator of a web page is calculated by an inverse chi-square method. A clicked page is regarded as a candidate if its pornography indicator is larger than a threshold. Finally, we further check the corresponding URLs of the candidates with the help of their host name and path information. Candidate URLs are included in a blacklist if their URLs contain pornographic keywords.

2. RELATED WORK
Pornography is usually named differently. The socially accepted variants contain adult material, explicit sexuality, and nudity in related work. Traditional filtering techniques regard this problem as categorization with statically crawled data sets. The intelligent content analysis approach attempts to understand the context in which the discriminative features appear and make classification decision. Several numerical algorithms, including neural networks [8], statistical text analysis [7], and pattern recognition techniques [5] were used to train the classifier for pornography filtering. Features from skin pixels were usually adopted for pornographic image recognition [13]. Motion information was combined with image features in detecting pornographic video content [4]. In addition to content features, analysis of linking structure through hyperlinks was also used to filter internet pornography [2]. The URL-based features were empirically shown as an effective approach for correctly identifying pornographic websites [12]. Moreover, query-URL click pairs were also exploited for clustering the similar pornographic images [10]. The strength of intelligent content analysis lies in its superior accuracy achieved by analyzing texts and images on web pages. However, comparatively more training time and human intervention are needed for the claimed performance.

Different from the previous work which focuses on intelligent content analysis by web content and structure mining, we only exploit users' searches-and-clicks from query logs for web usage mining. In this study, we analyze query logs to reflect implicitly collective intelligence from users' perspectives to collaboratively generate pornographic blacklists for cyberporn filtering.

3. INTENT CONFORMITY MODEL

Our intent conformity model includes two steps, i.e., indicator calculation and category recognition. The details are described in the following subsections.

3.1 Indicator Calculation

A user intent may be transformed to a query with many-to-many relationships. The same intent may be in terms of the same or different queries issued by users at different time. Beitzel et al. [1] employed manually defined domain-specific keywords to determine the categories of the issued queries. The study of web sexual queries also indicated sexual query terms are constrained in range and variance [9]. In our model, suspected query terms are identified with an automatically constructed lexicon. Firstly, we select terms from the catalog of pornographic web sites as seed queries. Empirical observations show that the catalog of pornographic web sites usually implicitly reflects porn-seeking information needs. Consequently, we use any five queries of seeds as combination for expanding related query terms by Google Sets. Google Sets automatically creates sets of related terms from the given seeds. For example, given three terms "sex", "naked" and "porn", Google Sets will predict at most 50 related items such as "nude", "xxx" and "f-word". All automatically expanded terms and seeds are put in our constructed lexicon for suspected query identification. In total, there are 410 expanded terms and seeds in the lexicon.

How to weight the issued queries with the degrees of domain-specific tendency is challenging. A query term is identified as a suspected term if it is contained in our automatically constructed pornographic lexicon. Equation (1) shows the porn tendency weight of an issued query q, denoted as w_q, where st_q and t_q are the number of suspected query terms and the number of query terms in q, respectively. Queries are weighted in the range of 0 to 1 in such a way that the values above (or below) 0,5 are considered positive (or negative) to pornography-seeking intents.

$$w_q = \frac{st_q}{t_q} \tag{1}$$

Clicked web pages are represented in terms of the queries retrieving them. Assume a clicked URL u is retrieved by n queries, $q_1, q_2, \ldots, q_n$, in search query logs. The pornography indicator of u is determined by an inverse chi-square method defined in Equations (2)-(4). This indicator value of pornography is calculated using two p-values derived from inverse chi-square distribution, assuming the null hypothesis H_0 is that the clicked web page is a random collection of issued queries, each independent of the others, is true; the alternative hypothesis H_1 indicates the null hypothesis is not true. In Equation (2), $\prod_{i=1}^{n} w_{q_i}$ denotes a maximum likelihood estimator; $-2*\ln\prod_{i=1}^{n} w_{q_i}$ is an asymptotical chi-square distribution with $2n$ degrees of freedom; $C^{-1}()$ denotes an inverse chi-square function to derive the p-value from a chi-square distributed random variable. The p-value derived from $C^{-1}()$ in Equation (2) is named as P (Positive). In Equation (3), we replace w_q with $(1-w_q)$, which denotes the non-porn tendency of an individual issued query, and N (Negative) stands for the p-value derived in this hypothesis testing. The indicator value of pornography, denoted as I, specifying the difference between the values of P and N, is normalized to be in the range of 0~1 by Equation (4).

$$P = C^{-1}(-2*\ln\prod_{i=1}^{n} w_{q_i}, 2n) \tag{2}$$

$$N = C^{-1}(-2*\ln\prod_{i=1}^{n} (1-w_{q_i}), 2n) \tag{3}$$

$$I = \frac{1+P-N}{2} \tag{4}$$

A clicked page can be in terms of the related queries with similar intents in search query logs. For example, the clicked pages retrieved by the query term "sex" are very likely to be also retrieved by the term "naked". This nonrandom tendency produces results of small p-value (either P or N) to reject the null hypothesis. A pornographic web page has a much smaller value of N than that of P, so that the indicator value is close to 1. By contrast, a non-pornographic web page has a much smaller value of P than that of N. Therefore, the indicator value is close to 0. We regard a clicked page as a candidate if its I-value is larger than a threshold.

In a related work, Lee and Luh [7] employed an inverse chi-square method to mine content features from web pages for blacklist generation. Different from their supervised learning approach, we use weighted queries as discriminative features to represent clicked pages for pornography indicator calculation. Unsupervised learning with query logs relieves the extra human efforts to label data for training a classifier. In addition, classifying a URL with our model is a cost-effective operation compared to crawl web pages and extract their content features.

In our statistics, the clicked web pages are represented in terms of 40.2 weighted queries on average. The number of weighted queries and the threshold are two factors in the inverse chi-square method. In the later experiments, we use at most 150 queries of the higher weight w_q to represent a clicked page and the threshold is empirically set to 0.65, as suggested by the related study [7].

3.2 Category Recognition

In the past, URL-based features were empirically shown as an effective approach for correctly identifying pornographic websites [12]. A categorical keyword set is formulated automatically for category recognition as follows. We first employ the blacklist released publicly in URLBlacklist.com to collect categorical keywords common used in URLs of pornographic web pages, then remove "http://" and "/" from URLs, further segment the remaining part of host name and path into all possible n-grams, and finally compose a 172-categorical-keyword set by consulting a pornographic dictionary, which is available online at theporndictionary.com. A candidate whose URL contains at least one categorical keyword will be included in our pornographic blacklist for collaborative cyberporn filtering.

4. EXPERIMENTS

4.1 Data Sets

The data set comes from the MSN 2006 RFP data. It consists of an MSN search query log excerpt with 15 million queries from US users during May 2006. Data made available include the issued queries, the clicked URLs and the time-stamps. We randomly selected 1% of MSN search query logs and removed those queries issued only once because no collective intelligence was involved in them. After sampling, we manually labeled the pages as ground truth by examining their contents. Those pages which could not be accessed successfully at the labeling time were ignored. The number of queries in our testing data set is 1,631,961, of which 43,198 queries are unique. Total 5,821 and 10,135 unique URLs are annotated in porn and non-porn categories, respectively.

4.2 Blacklist Generation Performance

For performance evaluation, we use three metrics: precision, recall and false positive rate. False positive rate is the proportion of non-pornographic web pages that are incorrectly classified as pornographic ones. From filtering point of view, incorrect blocking will cause unfair penalties. In addition to achieving high filtering performance, reducing false positive errors is also important.

Four query logs based models shown as follows are compared to demonstrate their performance differences in blacklist generation.

(1) *User Intent* model

This model exploited implicit collective intelligence from query logs for pornographic blacklist generation [6]. Firstly, suspected queries are identified along with their clicked URLs by an automatically constructed lexicon. A candidate URL is determined if the number of clicks satisfies some majority voting rules. Finally, a candidate whose URL contains at least one categorical keyword will be included in a blacklist.

(2) Inverse chi-square with query features (*InChi2-Query*) model

This model only considers the first step of our proposed intent conformity model, i.e., the method specified in Section 3.1. If the indicator value of a clicked page is larger than a pre-defined threshold, the corresponding URL is included in a blacklist.

(3) *URL Checking* model

The category of a clicked page is determined by its corresponding URL. This model only considers the second step of our intent conformity model specified in Section 3.2.

(4) *Intent Conformity* model

This model considers the two steps proposed in Sections 3.1 and 3.2 together for collaborative blacklist generation.

Figure 1 shows experimental results of these four models on the MSN porn data set. *URL Checking* model achieves the best recall, but the worst false positive rate. It reveals that URL contains categorical keywords does not always represent the category of web pages. Error analysis shows that most of non-pornographic pages, e.g., those describing sex education, nude art, and adult dating, with categorical n-grams in their host names or paths for clear category recognition usually lead to false positive cases.

User Intent and *InChi2-Query* models achieve promising precision and false positive rate, but relatively worse of recall. For *User Intent* model, we further analyze the reason of lower recall, and find that the number of clicks is distributed among different URLs of the same pornographic content. In such a case, the clicks cannot satisfy any majority voting rules. Because pornographic content is the major target for objectionable web content filtering, the pornographic content providers create more hosts and redirections to avoid being found and filtered. For *InChi2-Query* model, the issued queries are usually short and the suspected query terms cannot be completely identified, especially the names of web sites for navigational query to particular porn sites or the names of pornographic actress, which leads to incorrect query weighting with pornography tendency.

The *Intent Conformity* model achieves the best precision 0.8242, while maintaining the lowest false positive rate 0.0413 of all the models. It naturally reveals that exploiting searches-and-clicks in query logs is an effective approach for collaborative blacklist generation with collective intelligence.

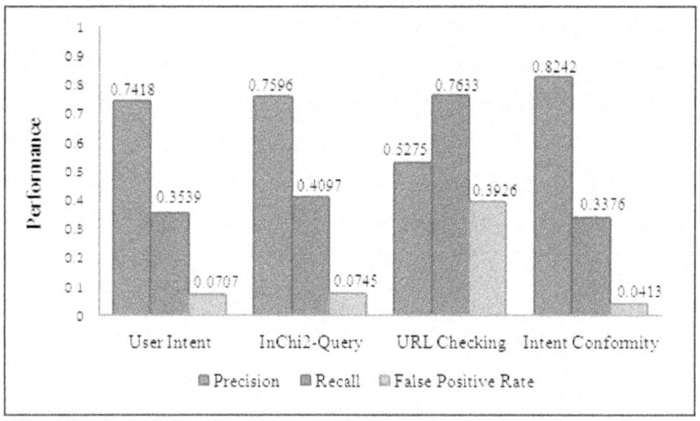

Figure 1. Performance of various methods on testing data set.

4.3 Filtering Effect Comparisons

We also conduct experiments for comparing filtering effects among different blacklists. The data set in Section 4.1 is divided into two parts: the first half of query logs, i.e., from May 1st to May 15th, for generating blacklists and the second half of query logs, i.e., from May 16th to May 31st, for verifying filtering effects. Totally, 4,742 and 7,988 unique URLs are regarded as porn and non-porn for investigating real-life filtering effects.

Of the five blacklists to be compared, two blacklists are generated using the *User Intent* model [6] and our *Intent Conformity* model, respectively. There are near 1 thousand URLs in these two query log based blacklists. The three others are publicly released pornographic blacklists from *SquidGuard* (http://www.squidguard.org/), *Shalla Secure Services* (http://www.shallalist.de/) and *URLBlacklist.com*. They consist of about 51 thousands, 55 thousands, and 171 thousands URLs, respectively.

For filtering evaluation, the number of blocking cases, denoting as #Block, illustrates total pornographic URLs that have correctly included in the blacklists. The number of over-blocking cases, denoting as #Over-Block, shows how many non-pornographic URLs are incorrectly listed in the blacklists.

Table 1 shows the filtering effects among blacklists. We can find that the three public blacklists cover very few blocking cases, even over-blocking normal accesses, although the number of URLs in the lists is much larger than that of the lists generated by query log based models. It reveals that the coverage of pornographic blacklist is a very important issue. If a blacklist does not reflect real user web surfing behaviors, its filtering effect will be very limited. The blacklists generated by *User Intent* and *Intent Conformity* models are much closer to the real-world situation of user accesses, due to searches-and-clicks in query logs reflect collective intelligence during web surfing.

Table 1. Comparison of filtering effects among blacklists

Blacklist	#Block	#Over-Block
SquidGuard	0	1
Shalla Secure Services	2	3
URLBlacklist.com	9	0
User Intent	1,256	436
Intent Conformity	924	149

Comparing the *User Intent* and the *Intent Conformity* models, the former can block slightly more pornographic URLs, and the latter can decrease about two-third of over-blocking cases of normal accesses. Obviously, *Intent Conformity* model is more proper to incorporate implicit user intents and collective intelligence to search engines to mask the search results before users click them.

5. DISCUSSION

Query ambiguity is a challenging issue for intent conformity approach. For example, the information need for query "breast" may be related to "breast cancer". A query term with different intents results in many different pages to be clicked.

The same query issued independently by the same or different users with similar intents may have different search results at different time. That will affect the clicking behaviors of users. Capturing the refreshing relationship between search engines and blacklist generation may have some effects on filtering performance.

6. CONCLUSIONS AND FUTURE WORK

This paper proposes an effective intent conformity method for collaborative blacklist generation and its application on cyberporn filtering. It only exploits searches-and-clicks in query logs, but without crawling the content of a URL and manually labeling training data for machine learning. The experiments on a MSN porn data set indicate that the generated blacklist achieves a high precision, while maintaining a favorably low false positive rate. In addition, real-life filtering simulations reveal that our user-centric blacklists are more effective than some publicly released blacklists for cyberporn filtering. Obviously, our intent conformity method is much closer to real-world users' surfing behaviors to reflect real-life situation.

We will extend this method to other objectionable domains such as gambling, drugs, violence, and suicide. A more aggressive query weighting scheme will be investigated in the future to represent clicked pages for achieving more satisfactory filtering performance.

7. ACKNOWLEDGEMENTS

This research was partially supported by National Science Council, Taiwan under grant NSC99-2221-E-002-167-MY3. We are also grateful to Microsoft Research Asia for the support of MSN Search Query Log excerpt.

8. REFERENCES

[1] Beitzel, S. M., Jensen, E. C., Chowdhury, A., Grossman, D., and Frieder, O. 2004. Hourly analysis of a very large topically categorized web query log. In *Proceedings of the 27th Annual International ACM SIGIR Conference on Research and Development in information retrieval*, 321-328.

[2] Hammami, M., Chahir, Y., and Chen, L. 2006. WebGuard: a web filtering engine combining textual, structural, and visual content-based analysis. *IEEE Transactions on Knowledge and Data Engineering*, 18(2), 272-284.

[3] Jansen, B. J., Spink, A., and Tefko, S. 2000. Real life, real users, and real needs: a study and analysis of user queries on the web. *Information Processing and Management,* 36(2), 207-227.

[4] Jansohn, C., Ulges, A., and Breuel, T. M. 2009. Detecting pornographic video content by combing image features with motion information. In *Proceedings of the 17th ACM International Conference on Multimedia*, 601-604.

[5] Lee, J.-S., Kuo, Y.-M., Chung, P.-C., and Chen, E.-L. 2007. Naked image detection based on adaptive and extensible skin color model. *Pattern Recognition,* 40(8), 2261-2270.

[6] Lee, L.-H., and Chen, H.-H. 2011. Collaborative cyberporn filtering with collective intelligence. In *Proceedings of the 34th Annual International ACM SIGIR Conference on Research and Development in Information Retrieval.* 1153-1154.

[7] Lee, L.-H., and Luh, C.-J. 2008. Generation of pornographic blacklist and its incremental update using an inverse chi-square based method. *Information Processing and Management*, 44(5), 1698-1706.

[8] Lee, P. Y., Hui, S. C., and Fong, A. C. M. 2005. An intelligent categorization engine for bilingual web content filtering. *IEEE Transaction on Multimedia*, 7(6), 1183-1190.

[9] Spink, A., Ozmutlu, H. C., and Lorence, D. P. 2004. Web searching for sexual information: an exploratory study. *Information Processing and Management*, 40(1), 113-123.

[10] Szummer, M. and Craswell, N. 2008. Behavioral classification on the click graph. In *Proceedings of the 17th International World Wide Web Conference*, 1241-1242.

[11] Weitzner, D. J. 2007. Free speech and child protection on the web. *IEEE Internet Computing,* 11(3), 86-89.

[12] Zhang, J., Qin, J., and Yan, Q. 2006. The role of URLs in objectionable web content categorization. In *Proceedings of the IEEE/WIC/ACM International Conference on Web Intelligence*, 277-283.

[13] Zuo, H., Hu, W., and Wu, O. 2010. Patch-based skin color detection and its application to pornography image filtering. In *Proceedings of the 19th International World Wide Web Conference*, 1227-1228.

Attention Prediction on Social Media Brand Pages

Himabindu Lakkaraju
IBM Research - India
Bangalore, India
klakkara@in.ibm.com

Jitendra Ajmera
IBM Research - India
New Delhi, India
jajmera1@in.ibm.com

ABSTRACT

In this paper, we deal with the problem of predicting how much attention a newly submitted post would receive from fellow community members of closed communities in social networking sites. Though the concept of attention is subjective, the number of comments received by a post serves as a very good indicator of the same. Unlike previous work which primarily made use of either content features or the network features (friendship links on the network), we exploit both the content features and community level features (for instance, what time of the day is the community more active) for tackling this problem. Further, we focus on dedicated pages of corporate brands on social media websites and accordingly extract important features from the content and community activity of such brand pages. The attention prediction task finds direct application in the listening, monitoring and engaging activities of the businesses that have such brand-pages. In this paper, we formulate the problem of attention prediction on social media brand pages. We further propose *Attention Prediction* (AP) framework which integrates the various features that influence the attention received by a post using classification and regression based approaches. Experimental results on real world data extracted from some highly active brand pages on Facebook demonstrate the efficacy of the proposed framework.

Categories and Subject Descriptors

H.3.3 [**Information Storage and Retrieval**]: Information Search and Retrieval

General Terms

Algorithms, Experimentation

Keywords

Social Media Analysis, Brand Pages, Popularity Prediction

1. INTRODUCTION

The ever growing amount of user generated content and active participation over social media have recently attracted considerable public and scientific interest. A number of different studies estimate that the time spent on social networking websites is 20-25% of the total time spent on the internet. A significant portion of this social media usage is critial for businesses to listen, monitor and respond. There exist many forums, blogs, news-sites and message-boards where customers express their opinions, complaints, questions, suggestions etc. regarding products and services.

Businesses are increasingly becoming aware of this trend and devising strategies to best make use of this social media channel. It is now common to see 'pages' of various businesses on commonly used social networking websites[1]. These pages are used by companies to make announcements and get feedback from customers about their products or services. Customers themselves use these brand pages for availing discounts, read reviews, access information, submit opinion etc. In some cases, companies (customers) are also using these pages for providing (accessing) customer service. Since the nature of brand page usage varies across 'authors' of user generated content, it is desirable for businesses to be able to prioritize the content for listening and responding. While the exact prioritization schema may depend on an application requirement, we focus on prioritizing the posts based on their popularity. Although this prediction may not entirely solve the problem of prioritization, it can serve as an important feature in the overall prioritization schema. Such prediction may be helpful for both the corporate brands as well as their customers. Companies can use this for targeted advertising, filtering, monitoring and prioritized responding while the customers can access relevant filtered content.

Our main contributions through this paper are :

- We formulate the problem of predicting the popularity of a particular post on a brand page on a social networking site.
- We present a detailed study of the features which would aid us in solving the problem. Further, we present a classification / regression based approach to solve the problem at hand.
- We carry out extensive experimentation on some of the most active brand pages on Facebook thereby demonstrating the effectiveness of the proposed framework.

2. RELATED WORK

Predicting the popularity of newly submitted online content has been of great interest to the research community

[1]We refer to such pages as brand pages through out this paper

recently. Although popularity itself is a subjective concept, some of the standard metrics like the number of comments a particular item of content receives serve as indicators of the content's popularity.

Several approaches have been proposed to deal with the problem of predicting the content popularity across diverse domains tackling various applications. Survival analysis framework was used in [3] to predict the overall number of comments by observing a thread for 2-3 days. This is based on the earlier finding by Szabo and Huberman [9] that correlates long time popularity of content with its early measured popularity. Lerman and Hogg [4] developed a stochastic model of user behavior that allowed prediction of popularity based on early user reaction to new content. Their model considers the complex interaction among content quality, web site design and influence among users. Their study uses the social dynamics of Digg website framework where different users can vote for an article and change the way and location where it is presented on the website. It is argued in the paper that the inherent story 'quality' or 'interestingness' cannot be directly measured from the data and should be estimated from the early reaction to the story. The approaches described use early reaction of users to content in order to predict the content's overall popularity. This may not be desirable in the brand-page analysis scenario presented in this paper where the early reaction itself is the most important part for the businesses to make use of. The current study therefore utilizes factors which are available since the time the story is submitted.

Yano et al. [10] studied a related problem of predicting whether a user would comment on a given blog post. They proposed the usage of latent Drichlet association (LDA) probabilistic model [1] for generation of blog posts and comments jointly. They used the information from the previous posts that a user has commented on in order to predict future responses of the user. Although related to our work, it is not easy to apply this kind of approach to social media brand pages, the reason being that it is impossible to check if each user would be interested in commenting on a particular post due to the sheer volume of the users in the community.

Several Twitter specific scientific studies have also studied a related problem of predicting whether a tweet will be re-tweeted. Most of these studies [8, 5, 11] concluded that the social features (number of followers, friends, lists etc.) have the maximum effect on retweetability. A collaborative filtering approach was used in [11] to study the retweet behaviour persistent among pairs of users. They used author information, number of the followers and number of words in the tweet for this study. A passive-aggressive algorithm was used in [5] to predict the retweetability. Although it was found in [5] that while the social features alone perform very well, there is substantial gain in also using content specific features. These content specific features comprised of novelty, trending words, and other meta information of the tweet (whether the tweet is a reply to some other tweet etc.).

As discussed above, though most of the previous work tackled the problem of predicting the content popularity, it is not straightforward to apply these existing techniques in the context of social networking sites. Thus we propose an *Attention Prediction* framework for dealing with this problem. This framework combines social and content specific features in order to facilitate the prediction of content popularity in online social networking sites.

3. ATTENTION PREDICTION FRAMEWORK

In this section, we first outline the problem definition and then describe in detail the approach we employ to solve the post popularity prediction problem in the context of social networking sites.

Post Popularity Prediction Problem : Given a brand page **B** on a social networking site comprising of a set of posts **P** of cardinality N with the associated popularity measure **C**, predict the popularity c_{N+1} of a new incoming post p_{N+1}.

Our Approach : We make use of a combination of content specific, temporal and author specific features that would enable better capture of the underlying patterns of the data, thus, facilitating better predictions.

- **Content Specific Features:** Post content plays a very important role in terms of defining what would be interesting to a community. Our *Attention Prediction* framework makes use of the following content based features:

  Presence of Characteristic Keywords: Bulk of the posts on brand pages pertain to querying information about the products/services associated with the brand. Further, people also express their opinions about various products and services. The presence of products and services in a particular post itself serves as a valuable input. However, capturing the presence of such interesting entities is a very challenging problem. In order to do this, we adopt an approach loosely based on the approach outlined in [7]. This approach primarily makes use of the principle that those words which are occurring frequently in the discussions on the brand page, but are not frequent enough in any general post (for instance, that posted by some user on his own wall) qualify as characteristic keywords. To instantiate this, let us consider the word 'Pontiac', it is easy to see that this word would typically appear relatively frequently on brand pages of car manufacturers but is less frequent in normal discussions or posts on any other page. Hence this would qualify as a potential keyword.

  Presence of Sentiments: Positive and negative sentiment expressions usually act as very good indicators of attention prediction. Whenever someone expresses a negative sentiment about a particular product/service, supporters (or refuters) of that statement tend to comment on the post. In our framework, we employ sentiwordnet [2] to identify some of the explicit sentiment words. However, since we are dealing with microtext, where people usually tend to write short hand notations for most of the words, we also employ a loose spelling and context based approach to extract more sentiment words. According to this approach, we first identify the actual sentiment words using sentiwordnet. We further take the appropriate context words of these words into account and identify the words which co-occur with them, these are likely to be other sentiment expressions. Finally, in order to obtain the polarity of the sentiment expression, we do a phonetic spelling based comparison with the words which have been gathered from sentiwordnet and find the nearest neighbor in each case.

Presence of Additional Metadata: Additional metadata like presence of links/videos/pictures etc. is also used as a feature. During our analysis, we observed that presence of some of such metadata boosts the attention that would be garnered by a particular post.

Post Classification: Identifying if a given post is spam, query, opinion expression forms another crucial content based feature. Note that a post may actually belong to both query and opinion expression classes. On the other hand, a class like spam is exclusive. If a given post belongs to a query class or not is determined by rule based methods which involve detecting the presence of words like 'can', 'will' etc. at the beginning of a particular sentence and also the presence of question marks. Opinion expressions are detected using the method discussed above. Any post which does not fall into one of these two categories is put into the 'non-technical' category which may involve informal greetings or spam which we do not try to predict the popularity for as it is highly unlikely that they impact the brand in anyway.

- **Author Specific Features:** In most of the online discussion forums, brand pages being no exception, the identity of the author is very crucial in estimating the popularity of a post. For example, if there is an announcement from the brand page, then it is likely to garner a lot of attention. Further, if a highly influential user in the community points out a flaw in a product/service, it is highly likely that the post would become popular with a lot of people agreeing/disagreeing with the same. For our purpose, we keep track of the average number of comments a post from a particular user would receive and use this as one of the features.

- **Temporal Activity in the Community:** Finally, we turn our attention to one of the most important factors, the temporal activity in the community. This factor is very important because during certain peak times like when there is a new product being launched by a brand, there is typically a lot more activity in the forum. In order to capture this as one of the features, we make use of the average number of comments that the forum received in the preceding time interval 't' (We have experimented with various values of t ranging from an hour to two days and found that a period of 6 hours was best suited).

On obtaining all the features discussed above, we learn SVM based classification and regression models[2].

4. EXPERIMENTATION

In this section, we briefly discuss the experimentation that we carried out to demonstrate the effectiveness of our *Attention Prediction* framework. In order to evaluate the task of popularity prediction, we consider the number of comments that a post receives as an indicator of popularity. So, we pose the task of attention prediction of a particular post as predicting the number of comments that a post would garner in particular temporal and contextual environment. Further, we report the performance of our framework over -

- Classification : In order to pose the task of attention prediction as a classification problem, we consider 5 different classes for the number of comments - Very less attention, Less attention, Mediocre attention, High Attention, Very High attention.
- Regression : In order to identify how much our prediction is off by the actual number of comments, we evaluate the attention prediction problem from a regression perspective.

We also train the classification/regression mechanisms to evaluate how well they perform in predicting the attention for different time periods i.e how effective is our approach to answer questions like how much of attention is this post going to receive within the first hour of it being posted.

Datasets: In order to validate our approach, we collected the posts and comments from three different highly active brand pages on Facebook for a period of about one week. We collected a total of 35,809 posts and their associated comments. A detailed description of the dataset is given in Table 1. For all our experiments, we have used the last 25% of the posts on each brand page as the test set. The initial 75% of the set was used for training the models.

Table 1: Details of the Dataset - Data Collected for one week

Brand Page	# of users	# of posts	# of active users	# of comments
General Motors	256941	7022	4056	18975
Bestbuy	3055096	10142	7986	35876
Nokia	3520071	18645	8092	63032

Baselines: To compare the performance of our approach with the state-of-the-art, we implemented an user-centric approach as proposed in [6] and [10]. For each user, we determine if the user would be interested in commenting on a given post or not, based upon the user's topics of interest. These topics of interest are identified using Latent Dirichlet Allocation [1] for each user.

4.1 Attention Prediction as Classification Problem

As explained above, we posed the problem at hand as a classification problem with 4 different classes each corresponding to the number of comments - Very less attention (<10% of the maximum of comments garnered) Less attention (<25% of the maximum of comments garnered), Mediocre attention (<50% of the maximum of comments garnered), High Attention (<75% of the maximum of comments garnered), Very High attention (>75% of the maximum of comments garnered).

Experimentation: After tagging the posts in the dataset with the appropriate classes (based on the number of comments received), we run the SVM classification training module using the initial 75% of the posts from each brand page as our training set. This aided us in learning the weights for each of the individual features corresponding to content, author and temporal activity. We tested the performance of our framework on the remaining 25% of the data for each brand page. We simulated the process of comments pouring in according to the time and appropriately updated the training set with the same every one hour. Also, we compare

[2]http://svmlight.joachims.org/

Table 2: Performance of Attention Prediction and Baseline - Classification

	Attention Prediction		Baseline	
	Precision	Recall	Precision	Recall
1 hour	0.68	0.72	0.53	0.61
3 hours	0.71	0.67	0.57	0.56
8 hours	0.71	0.66	0.59	0.52
1 day	0.76	0.68	0.62	0.55
2 days	0.77	0.68	0.63	0.56

Table 3: Performance of Attention Prediction and Baseline - Regression

	Attention Prediction	Baseline
	Predictive R^2	Predictive R^2
1 hour	0.321	0.08
3 hours	0.324	0.10
8 hours	0.418	0.123
1 day	0.432	0.187
2 days	0.541	0.246

the predictions of our approach in terms of the number of the comments received by each post in the test set at intervals of 1 hour, 3 hours, 8 hours, 1 day, 2 days. We present the results for the same in Table 2.

Discussion: As can be seen from Table 2, our attention prediction framework outperforms the baseline in predicting the popularity of the posts at different time intervals since the time they are first posted. Analysis of this kind of behavior revealed that this problem of predicting the post popularity cannot be tackled well using user centric techniques highlighted in [6] and [10]. These user centric techniques primarily make use of individual user interests in order to predict if the user is likely to comment on a post or not. However, more often than not, whether a particular user would comment on a post or not is governed not just by the topics of interest, but also by various other external issues like time the user logs in and checks his social networking profile, how active the user is in the current period of time etc. Bearing these issues in mind, dynamic behavior of users is not always predictive of the post popularity, hence our experiments also reveal the need for aggregate techniques as opposed to user specific ones for attention prediction.

4.2 Attention Prediction as Regression Problem

In this subsection, we discuss the results of posing attention prediction problem as a regression problem. We again present our results in terms of predicting the number of comments at different time intervals for each post.

Experimentation: We make use of support vector regression model for the training phase. As earlier, we make use of 75% of the data from each brand page for training and the remaining for testing. We use the predictive-R^2 statistic to evaluate the performance. We present the results for the same in Table 3.

Discussion: As can be seen, our framework outperforms the baseline even in this case of regression. As in the previous case, the best performance is achieved in the case of both AP framework and the baseline when predicting the number of comments at the end of 2 days. During our analysis, we found that the task of predicting comments a post will receive at initial time intervals is much more noisy compared to the stable state prediction of popularity for each post. The same is reflected in the results in Tables 2 and 3.

5. CONCLUSIONS AND FUTURE WORK

In this work, we have formulated the problem of predicting a post's popularity on brand pages in social networking sites. We further presented a detailed analysis of the features that would aid us in doing the same. We posed this as classification and regression problem and tried to study the performance in terms of accurately predicting the number of comments a post would receive. Further, we have tried to keep our approach generic enough to be extended to most communities or discussion forums, however, on typical discussion forums, user specific interests on commenting are likely to play a bigger role. An interesting direction to this work would be to gauge how a combination of user specific interests when coupled with the aggregate analysis would perform on the task of attention prediction on social media brand pages.

6. REFERENCES

[1] D. Blei., A. Ng, and M. Jordan. Latent drichlet allocation. *Journal of machine learning research*, 3, 2003.

[2] K. Denecke. Using sentiwordnet for multilingual sentiment analysis. *International conference on Data Engineering (ICDE)*, pages 507–512, 2008.

[3] J. G. Lee, S. Moon, and K. Salamatian. An approach to model and predict the popularity of online contents with explanatory factors. *International Conference on Web Intelligence and Intelligent Agent Technology (WI-IAT), 2010*, pages 623–630, 2010.

[4] K. Lerman and T. Hogg. Using a model of social dynamics to predict popularity of news. *World Wide Web Conference (WWW)*, pages 621–630, 2010.

[5] S. Petrovic, M. Osborne, and V. Lavrenko. Rt to win! predicting message propagation in twitter. *ICWSM*, 2011.

[6] H. Purohit, Y. Ruan, A. Joshi, S. Parthasarathy, and A. Sheth. Understanding user-community engagement by multi-faceted features: A case study on twitter. *Social Media Analytics Workshop at World Wide Web (WWW) Conference*, 2011.

[7] C. Scaffidi, K. Bierhoff, E. Chang, M.Felker, H.Ng, and C.Jin. Red opal : product-feature scoring from reviews. *Proceedings of the 8th ACM conference on Electronic commerce*, 2008.

[8] B. Suh, L. Hong, P. Pirolli, and E. H. Chi. Want to be retweeted? large scale analytics on factors impacting retweet in twitter network. *IEEE International Conference on Social Computing*, pages 177–184, 2010.

[9] G. Szabo and B. A. Huberman. Predicting the popularity of online content. *Social Science Research Network Working Paper Series*, 2008.

[10] T. Yano, W. W. Cohen, and N. A. Smith. Predicting response to political blog posts with topic models. *Proceedings of NAACL-HLT*, pages 477–485, 2009.

[11] T. R. Zaman, R. Herbrich, J. van Gael, and D. Stern. Predicting information spreading in twitter. *In Workshop on Computational Social Science and the Wisdom of Crowds, NIPS*, 2010.

Do They Belong to the Same Class? Active Learning by Querying Pairwise Label Homogeneity

Yifan Fu, Bin Li, Xingquan Zhu, Chengqi Zhang
Centre for Quantum Computation & Intelligent Systems, Faculty of Eng. & Info. Technology
University of Technology, Sydney, NSW 2007, Australia
{Yifan.Fu@student, Bin.Li-1@,xqzhu@it,chengqi@it}.uts.edu.au

ABSTRACT

Traditional active learning methods request experts to provide ground truths to the queried instances, which can be expensive in practice. An alternative solution is to ask nonexpert labelers to do such labeling work, which can not tell the definite class labels. In this paper, we propose a new active learning paradigm, in which a nonexpert labeler is only asked "whether a pair of instances belong to the same class". To instantiate the proposed paradigm, we adopt the MinCut algorithm as the base classifier. We first construct a graph based on the pairwise distance of all the labeled and unlabeled instances and then repeatedly update the unlabeled edge weights on the max-flow paths in the graph. Finally, we select an unlabeled subset of nodes with the highest prediction confidence as the labeled data, which are included into the labeled data set to learn a new classifier for the next round of active learning. The experimental results and comparisons, with state-of-the-art methods, demonstrate that our active learning paradigm can result in good performance with nonexpert labelers.

Categories and Subject Descriptors

H.2.8 [**Database Management**]: Database applications—*Data mining*

General Terms

Algorithms, Design, Performance

Keywords

Active Learning, Weak Labeling, Label Homogeneity

1. INTRODUCTION

In many real-world applications, manually labeling massive data collections is expensive and unpractical. Active learning [2, 6] intends to address this issue by selecting a subset of most critical instances for labeling. An active learner aims to achieve high accuracy using as few labeled instances as possible, thereby minimizing the cost of obtaining labeled instances [7]. In most traditional active learning methods, an expert is required to provide ground truths to the queried instances and the model will be learned based on the labeled data. The learned model is applied to the unlabeled data again and another subset of unlabeled data is selected to ask for the expert's labeling. This procedure is iterated many rounds until some criteria are met.

Although active learning only requires a subset of instances to be labeled, it is still not a simple task for that the selected data set is still large and the active learning iterations can last for quite long time. Moreover, since the model will be learned only based on a subset of the entire data set, the labeling quality for the selected instances is extremely crucial for the model's performance. Thus, the labeling task in active learning is still expensive in many cases.

Recently, researchers resort to committees of nonexpert labelers, who are cheaper but can only provide weak and noisy labels, for data labeling. Some works based on this idea have been proposed, such as [8, 5], which only consider the labeling issue in supervised learning scenarios. However, such weak and noisy labels may not be helpful in active learning scenarios for two reasons: (1) Since only a small subset of critical instances are selected for labeling, the labeling quality in active learning is more sensitive to the model's performance than that in plain supervised learning. (2) Since active learning is consisted of multiple learning iterations, the errors induced in each round will be passed onto the following rounds and will be amplified. Thus, asking nonexpert labelers to directly provide noisy class labels may not be appropriate in active learning.

In this paper, we propose a new active learning paradigm, in which a nonexpert labeler is only asked "whether a pair of instances belong to the same class". The proposed paradigm is based on the following assumption: **For a nonexpert labeler, it is difficult to tell the definite class label of an instance by linking its content to a conceptual label (which needs domain knowledge), while, it is easier to directly compare the content of two instances and tell their label homogeneity (which only needs intuition).** Based on this assumption, the underlying queries for active learning is to generate pairwise constraints between labels, which will be incorporated into the learning procedure. Figure 1 illustrates the difference between the traditional active learning paradigm and the proposed one. Compared to a specific label in the traditional strategy, our strategy only acquires a pairwise label homogeneity information ("yes/no") in each query, which is much easier/cheaper to implement for a labeler.

CIKM'11, October 24–28, 2011, Glasgow, Scotland, UK.

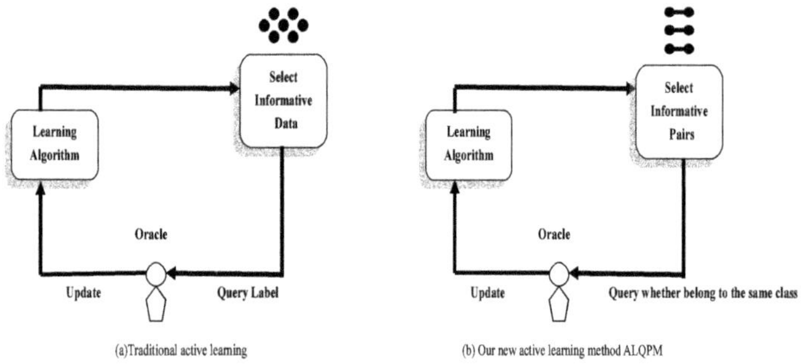

Figure 1: Traditional active learning paradigm versus our new active learning paradigm.

We instantiate the proposed active learning paradigm by adopting the MinCut [1] as the base classifier, which naturally rests on a pairwise similarity graph for nodes bipartition (data binary classification) by minimizing the sum of the edge weights between two partitions (one for positive and the other one for negative instances). Our algorithm is inspired by [1] that generates a set of MinCut classifiers by adding randomness to the graph structure and makes prediction on unlabeled data according to the majority votes among the classifiers. We incorporate the MinCut algorithm into our active learning paradigm to build an effective active learner. Some features of the proposed active learning method are highlighted as follows:

- We query pairwise label homogeneity rather than a specific label. When a MinCut classifier is built, we query the unlabeled edges on the max-flow paths.
- Instead of randomize updating edge weights in a given graph, we dynamically adjust edges weights on the max-flow paths according to query results.
- We use a confidence based data selection criterion to choose data with high prediction confidence among the MinCut classifiers to extend the training set.

The remainder of the paper is organized as follows. We introduce related work in Section 2. The problem formulation and the proposed solutions are discussed in Sections 3 and 4, respectively. Experiments are reported in Section 5, and we conclude the paper in Section 6.

2. RELATED WORK

Most traditional active learning methods pose queries on instance labels in each round of active learning iterations (please refer to a survey on active learning [6] for details). However, labeling each queried instance is still a time-consuming task. In recent years, a variety of query strategies have been proposed to select most informative instances for labeling to reduce the labeling cost.

In [3], the authors proposed a feature based query method in active learning, which utilizes a simple feature for labeling instances.a generalized query is included in [4] to label instances in groups. However, they do not take into account real data distribution. Moreover, [4] utilizes a randomly generated synthetic data set to reflect real data distribution, which may lead to adding noise.

To reduce expensive labeling cost, researchers resort to committees of nonexpert labelers to provide weak and noisy labels in supervised learning [8, 5]. However, since the labeling quality is much more sensitive to the model's performance in active learning than that in plain supervised learning due to a limited number of labeled data. Asking nonexpert labelers to directly provide noisy class labels may not be appropriate in active learning. Otherwise, the errors induced in each query round will be passed onto the following rounds and will be amplified.

In contrast to the above methods, the proposed active learning paradigm employs nonexpert labelers to perform labeling in each round of active learning iterations, but only request them to provide pairwise label homogeneity information (answer "yes/no"). Compared to specifying class labels, answering "whether two instances belong to the same class" is much simpler for nonexpert labelers and the queried results are more reliable for training prediction models.

3. PROBLEM FORMULATION

3.1 Notations

Given a data set $\mathcal{D}$, which comprises a labeled subset $\mathcal{D}^L$, an unlabeled subset $\mathcal{D}^U$, and a test set $\mathcal{D}^T$. At first, $\mathcal{D}^L \bigcup \mathcal{D}^U$ is casted into a graph $\mathcal{G} = (\mathcal{V}, \mathcal{E})$ based on some similarity measures, where $\mathcal{V} = \mathcal{D}^L \bigcup \mathcal{D}^U$, and $\mathcal{E} \subseteq \mathcal{V} \times \mathcal{V}$. Each edge e has a weight $w(e)$. Each node v_i is denoted by $v_i = \{v_{i,1}, \cdots, v_{i,m}; y_i\}$, where $v_{i,j}$ denotes the jth attribute value of the node and y_i denotes v_i's class label. If v_i is unlabeled, we denote it by $v_i = \{v_{i,1}, \cdots, v_{i,m}; ?\}$. All labeled nodes form an labeled vertices subset $\mathcal{V}^L$ and the remaining unlabeled nodes in $\mathcal{G}$ form an unlabeled vertices subset $\mathcal{V}^U$, with $\mathcal{V} = \mathcal{V}^L \cup \mathcal{V}^U$ and $\mathcal{V}^L \cap \mathcal{V}^U = \emptyset$.

Assume a nonexpert labeler exists to answer queries on whether a pair of samples (v_i, v_j) belong to the same class or not, our **aim** is to query the labeler for a number of times, through which we can infer labels for a batch (*i.e.* a subset Δ) of instances from $\mathcal{V}^U$ (*i.e.*, $\mathcal{V}^U = \mathcal{V}^U \setminus \Delta$ and $\mathcal{V}^L = \mathcal{V}^L \cup \Delta$), such that when the requested number of nodes are labeled, a classifier trained on $\mathcal{V}^L$ has the maximum prediction accuracy in classifying test set $\mathcal{D}^T$.

3.2 Method Overview

In order to train a classifier on $\mathcal{V}^L$ with maximum prediction accuracy, a commonly employed principle for active learning is to label a batch of most informative data. Following this principle, we employ MinCut algorithm to infer the unlabeled data memberships. We then query all the unlabeled edges in the max-flow paths with a pairwise label homogeneity question. According to the query results, our algorithm updates the weights of edges whose two vertices are queried pairs. This process iterates k times, with k MinCut classifiers generated. All the unlabeled nodes can be resorted according to the prediction confidence on the k MinCut classifiers. Therefore, our goal is to select an optimal subset with the highest confidence values. The overall algorithm procedure is described in Algorithm 1.

4. THE PROPOSED METHOD

4.1 Graph Construction

Given a binary classification task with a set of labeled data $\mathcal{D}^L$ and a set of unlabeled data $\mathcal{D}^U$, we use $\mathcal{L}_p$ to indicate the set of positive data in $\mathcal{D}^L$, and $\mathcal{L}_n$ to denote the set of negative data in $\mathcal{D}^L$. The graph construction is as follows.

Algorithm 1 Active Learning by Querying Pairwise Label Homogeneity

```
while update times <k do
    construct a MinCut classifier with graph G;
    predict memebership of unlabeled vertices V^U;
    query class homogeneity on unlabeled pairs(v^i_M, v^j_M) in MaxFlow paths M;
    update edge weights of queried pairs;
end while
calculate unlabeled vertices V^U confidence;
resort V^U and labeling first top budgetΔ nodes with maximal probable class;
V^U ⟵ V^U \ Δ;
V^L ⟵ V^L ∪ Δ;
```

- **Add *Classification* Vertices**. Since we use MinCut algorithm, we need to set a source vertex and a sink vertex. Therefore we add two binary classification vertices v_p and v_n, which are treated as source and sink separately. Thus, we build a weighted graph $\mathcal{G} =< \mathcal{V}, \mathcal{E} >$, where $\mathcal{V} = \mathcal{L}_p \bigcup \mathcal{L}_n \bigcup \{v_p, v_n\}$,and $\mathcal{E} \subseteq \mathcal{V} \times \mathcal{V}$. Each edge e associates with a weight $w(e)$. All the other vertices except two *Classification vertices* called *Data vertices* .
- **Set Edge Weights containing Classification Vertices** For classification vertices,they are only connected with labeled vertices having the same class membership, the edge weight between two vertices is a specific large value $\Re$. Exactly, $w(v, v_p) = \Re$ for all $v \in \mathcal{V}^L$ and $w(v, v_n) = \Re$ for all $v \in \mathcal{V}^U$.
- **Set Edge Weights containing Data Vertices** In order to reduce graph size, capturing the major relationship between vertices, we use K-nearest neighbors algorithms to generate the edges for each *data vertex*. The edge weights between *data vertices* represent the similarity between them. Specifically, the weight function used in the paper is:

$$w(v_i, v_j) = E^{-d(v_i, v_j)} \tag{1}$$

where $d(v_i, v_j)$ denotes the distance on attributes between two vertices. For categorical attribute, we use *Hamming* distance measure, and for numerical attribute, we use *Euclidean* distance measure.

4.2 Weight Adjustment in MinCuts

4.2.1 MaxFlow MinCut Theorem

The max-flow min-cut theorem states that given a flow network, the maximum flow passing from source node to sink node equals the minimum cut for all the possible cuts in the network. Given a directed weighted graph $\mathcal{G} = (\mathcal{V}, \mathcal{E})$ with s and t being the source and the sink, respectively. The capacity of an edge $e(u, v)$, denoted by $w(u, v)$, is its weight. It represents the maximum flow that can pass through an edge.

A flow from the edge $e(u, v)$ denoted by $f(u, v)$, is subject to the following two constraints:

Capacity Constraint $$f(u, v) \leq w(u, v) \tag{2}$$

Conservation Constraint $$\sum_{(q,u)\in\mathcal{E}} f(q, u) = \sum_{(u,b)\in\mathcal{E}} f(u, b) \tag{3}$$

where $u \in \mathcal{E} \backslash \{s, t\}$. Therefore the flow from source to sink is denoted by

$$f_{s\to t} = \sum_{(s,v)\in\mathcal{E}} f(s, v) \tag{4}$$

where s is source vertex. The maximum flow problem is to maximize $f_{s\to t}$ with as much flow from s to t as possible.

The maximum flow through a series of paths relies on the smallest flow of the edge on each path, which is also the bottleneck of each path. That means if such bottleneck edges are removed from the network, it leads to no flow can pass from the source to the sink. As a result, we can determine a minimum cut using maximum flow algorithm.

4.2.2 Weight Adjustment using Label Homogeneity Query

In general, a graph may have many mimimum cuts, whereas max-flow algorithm exits when a minimum cut is found. This may generate an extremely imbalanced cut, that is, a small cluster associated with a big one. Furthermore, an initial small amount of labeled subset could not generate a cut closed to the genuine distributions of the underlying data. To this end, we employ active learning to obtain extra information by querying unlabeled pairs on maximal flow paths. Here we just query "whether the pair belong to the same class". According to the query results,we adjust weight of the edges formed by queried pairs. This weight updating scheme is defined as follows:

$$w(u, v) = \begin{cases} w(u, v) \times (1 + \partial), & \text{if y(u)=y(v)} \quad (5) \\ w(u, v) \times (1 - \partial), & \text{if y(u)} \neq \text{y(v)} \quad (6) \end{cases}$$

where ∂ is an adjustment factor, which determines weight updating scale($0 <\partial< 1$). When the pair has the same class label, the corresponding edge weight increases by ∂, otherwise, the relevant edge weight decreases by ∂. We iteratively use MinCut algorithm to update edges weights, avoiding imbalanced cut issue and refining decision boundary.

4.3 Confidence based Data Selection

When a MinCut algorithm is instantiated, the class labels of all the unlabeled vertices are inferred by the cut.During weight updating circle, a community of MinCut classifiers is generated.We report the prediction on each classifier for each unlabeled vertex in the graph, such that an ouput distribution can be calculated for each unlabeled vertex. We treat the maximal probability output value as the final prediction result, and the value is considered as the *confidence* of each unlabeled vertex. We sort the unlabeled vertices based on their *confidence* values. The top budget vertices formed an optimal labeling set Δ, with the final prediction as their labels. We add Δ into labeled training set to train a model and make prediction on the test set $\mathcal{D}^\mathcal{T}$.

5. EXPERIMENTS

We implement the proposed method and a number of baseline methods using Java and WEKA data mining tools. For fair comparisons, all experiments are based on 10 times 10-fold cross validation, with all methods compared using the same training and test data sets (the initial randomly labeled samples are also the same for all methods). For performance analysis, we compare our method with supervised learning methods and semi-supervised methods. If our algorithm's accuracy is higher than the other two kinds of

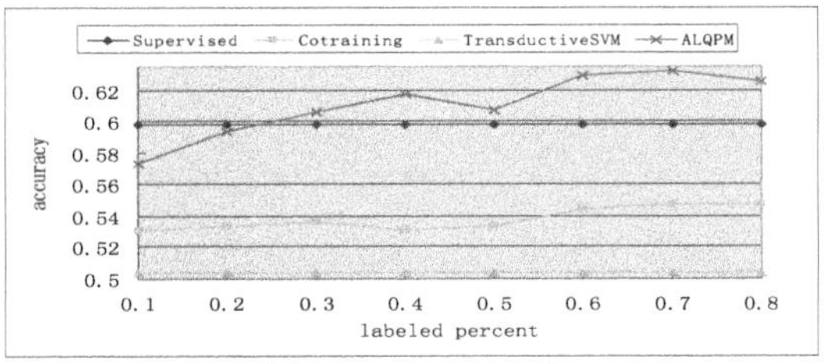

(a) Liver Dataset)

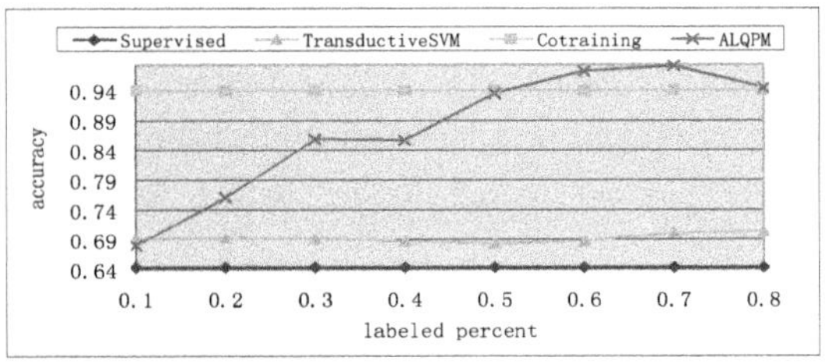

(b) Monks1 Dataset

Figure 2: Accuracy comparisons with different portions of labeled samples, the batch size is fixed to 0.1

algorithms, we conclude that the new approach has a better active learning performance than its peers.

5.1 Baseline Methods

For the experimental comparisons, we also use a number of mainstream supervised and semi-supervised methods.

- **Supervised learning** a classifier is trained with initial labeled data only.
- **Co-training Algorithm** a semi-supervised learning technique that selects data with the same predictions on two classifiers built with two randomly selected features subspaces (without overlapping).
- **Transductive SVM Algorithm** which utilizes unlabeled data to train a semi-supervised SVM learning model.

5.2 Experimental Results

In experiments, we use initially labeled subset to train a ***supervised*** classifier, and the union of the labeled and unlabeled set is used to train a ***transductiveSVM*** classifier. For ***cotraining*** algorithm and our new algorithms ***ALQPM***, we compare the performances with respect to different percentages of labeled samples, which vary from 10% to 80% as indexed by x-axis and y-axis shows the accuracies of the classifiers trained from the corresponding labeled samples. For all the experiments, we fix the batch size to 0.1. In the paper, we report experimental results for Liver and Monks1 datasets on the above four algorithms.

In Figure2(a), supervised classifier performs much better than cotraining and TransductiveSVM. Cotraining is always superior to TransductiveSVM, with slightly increase on accuracies. When labeling 20% or more samples, the proposed new method, ALQPM, outperforms supervised method. As more samples being labeled by the proposed approach, we also observe continuous accuracy gain. Our observations conclude that our new sample selection strategy can achieve good accuracy with a small amount of labeled data, which, in turn, reduces the sample labeling cost.

The results in Figure2(b) show that cotraining algorithm is superior to supervised method and TransductiveSVM. This is mainly because by employing a data selection scheme, important samples can be selected to help improve the underlying learning model. Our results also show that TransductiveSVM outperforms supervised method for all percentages of selected samples, which asserts that incorporating unlabeled sample to the learning process can provide additional information to benefit the model training.

Comparing Figures 2(a) and 2(b), it is clear that the performance of ALQPM will continuously improve with more samples to be labeled, whereas the performance of cotraining algorithm remains relatively stable most of times. This asserts that using multiple independent views to label samples, like Co-Training does, has very limited contributions, compared to the proposed pair-wise homogeneity query strategy.

6. CONCLUSIONS

In this paper, we formulated a new active learning paradigm, in which a nonexpert labeler is asked to answer the label homogeneity of a pair of instances instead of a specific label for an individual instance. To solve the problem, we proposed to incorporate queried results into a MinCut based active learner by updating unlabeled pair weights on the max-flow paths in the graph. Then we select an optimal unlabeled subset of nodes according to their prediction confidence to extend the labeled data set for model training. Experiment results demonstrated that our new active learning paradigm can achieve good performance compared to various state-of-the-art methods.

Acknowledgements

This work is supported by Australian Research Council's Future Fellowship under project number FT100100971 and Centre for Quantum Computation & Intelligent Systems.

7. REFERENCES

[1] A. Blum, J. Lafferty, M. R. Rwebangira, and R. Reddy. Seim-supervise learinng using randomized mincuts. In *Proceedings of ICML*, 2004.

[2] D. Cohn, Z. Ghahramani, and M. Jordan. Active learning with statistical models. *Journal of Artificial Intelligence Research*, pages 129–145, 1996.

[3] G. Druck, G. Mann, and A. McCallum. Learning from labeled features using generalized expectation criteria. In *Proceedings of SIGIR*, pages 595–602, 2008.

[4] J. Du and C. C. Ling. Asking generalized queries to domain experts to improve learning. *IEEE TKDE*, pages 812–825, 2010.

[5] V. C. Raykar, S. Yu, L. Zhao, A. Jerebko, C. Florin, G. Hermosillo-Valadez, L. Bogoni, and L. Moy. Supervised learning from multiple experts: Whom to trust when everyone lies a bit. In *Proc. of ICML*, 2009.

[6] B. Settles. Active learning literature survey. *Technical Report 1648*, 2009.

[7] B. Settles and M. Craven. An analysis of active learning strategies for sequence labeling tasks. In *Proceedings of EMNLP*, pages 1070–1079, 2008.

[8] V. S. Sheng, F. Provost, and P. G. Ipeirotis. Get another label? improving data quality and data mining using multiple, noisy labelers. In *Proc. of KDD*, 2008.

Structured Data Classification by means of Matrix Factorization

Paolo Garza
Dipartimento di Elettronica e Informazione
Politecnico di Milano
Milano, Italy
garza@elet.polimi.it

ABSTRACT

Singular Value Decomposition (SVD) has been extensively used in the classification context as a preprocessing step aiming to reduce the number of features of the input space. Traditional classification algorithms are then applied on the new space to generate accurate models. In this paper, we propose a different use of SVD. In our approach SVD is the building block of a new classification algorithm, called CMF, and not that of a feature reduction algorithm. In particular, we propose a new classification algorithm where the classification model corresponds to the k largest right singular vectors of the factorization of the training dataset obtained by applying SVD. The selected singular vectors allows representing the main "characteristics" of the training data and can be used to provide accurate predictions.

The experiments performed on 15 structured UCI datasets show that CMF is efficient and, despite its simplicity, it is more accurate than many state of the art classification algorithms.

Categories and Subject Descriptors

H.4 [**Information Systems Applications**]: Miscellaneous

General Terms

Algorithms, Experimentation

Keywords

Classification, Singular Value Decomposition

1. INTRODUCTION

The classification problem consists in generating an abstract model of a set of classes, called classifier, which is built from a set of labeled training data. The classifier is then used to assign an appropriate class label to new test data for which the class label is unknown. Many approaches have been proposed to generate accurate classification models [1, 4, 5, 8, 11] in the context of structured (relational) datasets. In this paper, we propose a new classification algorithm based on Singular Value Decomposition (SVD). SVD has been extensively used in the classification context, and in other contexts, as a preprocessing step in order to reduce the dimensionality (i.e., number of features) of the analyzed data. Data are mapped from the original space into a more compact space on top of which traditional classification algorithms are applied. In this paper, inspired by the use of SVD and matrix factorization as predictive algorithms in recommender systems [10], we propose a new classifier where the model is based on the matrix factorization of the training dataset. The new classifier is called CMF (**C**lassification by means of **M**atrix **F**actorization). CMF exploits SVD to perform a matrix factorization of the training dataset and then selects the k largest singular values and the related right singular vectors to identify the k most important "characteristics" of the training data. The selected singular vectors represent our classification model. An interesting property of the selected k singular vectors [13] is that they can be used to compute the optimal rank-k approximation of D, denote as $\widetilde{D_k}$ (i.e., the best approximation of D based on the first k components). Given a data $d \in D$, singular vectors can be exploited to compute its approximation $\widetilde{d} \in \widetilde{D_k}$ (the difference between $\widetilde{d}$ and d is approximately zero if enough singular vectors are used). We argue that the singular vectors extracted from the training data are representative also of the test data, because test data and training data are characterized by a similar behavior. Hence, given an arbitrary test data t, for which the class label is unknown, we can use the singular vectors obtained by factorizing the training data to compute the approximation $\widetilde{t}$ of t. Also for the test data, the difference between $\widetilde{t}$ and t should be close to zero. We exploit this assumption to select the most appropriate class label for new data. The new data t is labeled with the class label c_i that allows obtaining the approximation $\widetilde{t}$ more close to t. The idea is that the class label that allows minimizing the difference between t and $\widetilde{t}$ is also the one that allows obtaining a tuple more similar to those included in the training dataset. The approach is simple, but the initial set of experiments performed on 15 UCI datasets show that CMF is both efficient and accurate.

Different from the majority of the state of the art classification algorithms, CMF is characterized by only one parameter (k). Moreover, this parameter can be easily estimated by analyzing the accuracy achieved by CMF on the training

CIKM'11, October 24–28, 2011, Glasgow, Scotland, UK.

data. This is an interesting property because usually the parameter tuning operation is a tough task.

2. THE CMF ALGORITHM

In the first part of this section the needed background knowledge is introduced (Section 2.1). Then the proposed algorithm is described.

2.1 Background

Given a $n \times f$ matrix D, its singular value decomposition (SVD) is a factorization of the form

$$D = U\Sigma V^T \tag{1}$$

where U is a $n \times n$ unitary matrix, Σ is a $n \times f$ diagonal matrix, and V is a $f \times f$ unitary matrix. With V^T we denote the transpose matrix of V. The diagonal entries $\sigma_i = \Sigma(i,i)$ of Σ are called singular values of D, while the columns of U and the columns of V are called the left singular vectors of D and the right singular vectors of D, respectively.

It is well known [13] that the optimal rank-k approximation of D, denoted as $\widetilde{D_k}$ in the following, can be generated by selecting the k largest singular values and the associated singular vectors. In particular, $\widetilde{D_k}$ is computed as follows.

$$\widetilde{D_k} = U_k \Sigma_k V_k^T \tag{2}$$

where U_k is a $n \times k$ matrix composed of the k left singular vectors associated with the k largest singular values, Σ_k is a $k \times k$ diagonal matrix with the k largest singular values of Σ on the diagonal, and V_k is a $f \times k$ matrix composed of the k right singular vectors associated with the k largest singular values.

To generate the model exploited by CMF, we need to express $\widetilde{D_k}$ as a function of the original (training data) matrix D and the matrixes composing its factorization. Since V is a unitary matrix, it follows that V^TV is equal to the identity matrix I. Hence, Equation 3 trivially follows from Equation 1.

$$DV = U\Sigma V^T V = U\Sigma I = U\Sigma \tag{3}$$

Equation 4 also follows.

$$DV_k = U_k \Sigma_k \tag{4}$$

We can exploit Equation 4 to rewrite Equation 2 as follows.

$$\widetilde{D_k} = U_k \Sigma_k V_k^T = DV_k V_k^T \tag{5}$$

Hence, given an arbitrary data $d \in D$, the approximation of d, denoted as $\widetilde{d}$, can be computable as follows.

$$\widetilde{d} = dV_k V_k^T \tag{6}$$

If k is set properly only the minor components, which are usually given by noise, are pruned and the obtained matrix $\widetilde{D_k}$ is a good approximation of D. Hence, $\widetilde{d} - d \approx 0$ for all $d \in D$.

In Section 2.3, we will show how Equation 6 can be used to compute the approximation of an arbitrary new test data t and how the obtained result can be exploited to label the new data.

2.2 Model generation

Given a $n \times f$ matrix D (the training dataset), where n is the number of training data and f the number of attributes (including the class attribute), the training model is generated by applying SVD on D and by selecting the value of k (the number of singular vectors). The training model of CMF is equal to the matrix V_k obtained by performing the training data factorization (see Equation 2).

Since SVD can be computed only on numerical matrixes, before applying CMF all the categorical attributes (including the class label) are transformed in numerical attributes by mapping their values to consecutive positive integers.

As discussed in [13], the complexity of the SVD computation of a $n \times f$ matrix D is $O(nf^2)$. Hence, also the complexity of the training step of CMF is $O(nf^2)$.

2.3 New data classification

Equation 6 can be exploited to compute an approximation of any data characterized by the schema of D (i.e., the same set of attributes). Hence, given an arbitrary test data t compatible with the schema of D, its approximation, denoted as $\widetilde{t}$, can be computed as

$$\widetilde{t} = tV_k V_k^T \tag{7}$$

Since t is a test data, its class label is unknown (i.e., the class attribute is set to null). Before applying Formula 7 a valid value must be assigned to the class attribute of t. We argue that the most appropriate value for the class attribute is the class label c_i that minimizes the difference between t and its approximation $\widetilde{t}$. The idea is that the main characteristics of t are similar to those of the training data and hence the factorization computed on the training dataset D fits well also on the test data t. Hence, the class label c_i that allows minimizing the difference between t and its approximation $\widetilde{t}$ is the one that must be selected.

More formally, the classification of an arbitrary new data t is performed as follows. We denote as t_{c_i} the data obtained by labeling t with the class label c_i (i.e., the value of the class attribute of t is set to c_i). For each generated data t_{c_i} its approximation $\widetilde{t_{c_i}}$ is computed as $\widetilde{t_{c_i}} = t_{c_i} V_k V_k^T$. Then, for each pair $(t_{c_i}, \widetilde{t_{c_i}})$ the difference between t_{c_i} and $\widetilde{t_{c_i}}$ is computed as

$$\Delta_{t_{c_i}} = \sum_{\forall A_j \in schema(D)} |\widetilde{t_{c_i}}.A_j - t_{c_i}.A_j| \tag{8}$$

where A_j is the j-th attribute of the considered data. CMF labels the test data t with the class label c_i^* that allows obtaining the minimum difference. c_i^* is computed by applying Formula 9.

$$c_i^* = \underset{c_i \in C}{\operatorname{argmin}}(\Delta_{t_{c_i}}) \tag{9}$$

3. EXPERIMENTAL RESULTS

We performed a set of experiments on 15 UCI datasets [7] to analyze the accuracy achieved by CMF and its execution time. The main characteristics of the 15 UCI datasets are reported in the first 4 columns of Table 1. We compared CMF with six classification algorithms: a nearest neighbor classifier (K-NN [1]), Support Vector Machines (SVMs [4]), decision trees (C4.5 [12]), a rule based classifier (Ripper [5]), a bayesian classifier (Bayesian network [8]), and an associative classifier (L^3 [2]). We used the available Weka [9] implementations of the six algorithms to compute the accuracy of the selected algorithms on the 15 UCI datasets. The CMF algorithm was implemented in Octave [6].

Table 1: Accuracy comparison

Dataset	Records	Attributes	Classes	Accuracy%							
				CMF		K-NN (K=3)	SVMs	C4.5	Ripper	Bayesian network	L^3
				k							
Australian	690	15	2	14	85.36	83.76	55.79	85.07	84.20	85.21	**85.94**
Breast	699	11	2	2	93.99	96.70	66.09	93.99	95.70	**97.13**	95.85
Ecoli	336	8	8	6	83.04	**85.71**	75.89	82.73	82.14	81.25	82.73
German	1000	25	2	9	74.40	71.40	72.00	**74.70**	72.60	73.70	73.40
Harberman	306	4	2	3	**74.18**	68.95	72.54	70.26	71.56	71.56	69.28
Heart	270	14	2	9	**83.33**	77.40	55.92	77.03	75.92	82.22	82.22
Hepatitis	255	20	2	7	61.29	59.35	57.41	59.35	63.87	61.93	**66.45**
Horse	300	28	2	24	85.00	76.33	68.33	83.33	86.33	**88.66**	88.00
Iono	351	35	2	15	88.60	85.47	**92.30**	90.02	90.31	90.31	91.45
Iris	150	5	3	4	**98.67**	96.00	97.33	95.33	94.66	94.00	93.33
Labor	40	27	2	11	87.50	87.50	**95.00**	92.50	80.00	90.00	92.50
Pima	768	9	2	8	74.35	73.82	65.10	73.43	74.08	75.26	**77.08**
Transfusion	748	5	2	3	77.41	75.66	75.93	**77.80**	77.54	74.86	65.37
Wine	178	14	3	7	96.07	97.19	45.50	93.25	92.69	**98.87**	98.31
Yeast	1484	9	10	8	55.46	54.38	43.26	55.32	**58.15**	57.47	55.05
Average					81.24	79.31	69.23	80.27	79.98	81.50	81.13

Table 2: CMF vs the other classification algorithms. Win/Draw/Loss are the datasets where CMF has higher/equal/lower accuracy than the classifier in column

Win/Draw/Loss	K-NN (K=3)	SVMs	C4.5	Ripper	Bayesian network	L^3
CMF	11/1/3	13/0/2	10/1/4	9/0/6	7/0/8	7/0/8

All the experiments were performed on a laptop with a 2.2-GHz AMD Turion Dual-Core RM-75 processor and 4.0 Gbytes of main memory, running Kubuntu 10.04.

3.1 Accuracy

The accuracy measure is used to analyze the ability of the classifier to correctly classify unlabeled data. In particular, it is the ratio of the number of correctly classified data over the total number of given test data. The experiments on the accuracy measure have been performed by using a 10 fold cross validation test. For all the considered classification algorithms we set the parameters to their standard values, according to the setting reported in the related papers. CMF is characterized by the k parameter (i.e., the number of selected singular values). For each dataset, the appropriate value of k has been obtained by selecting the value of k that achieves the best accuracy value on the training data. Hence, the value of k has been automatically set. This is an interesting property of our algorithm. The selection of the best parameter setting for the other classification algorithms is usually a tough task because they are usually characterized by many parameters and the best setting for the training set is usually not a good setting for the test set. Differently, we have empirically checked that the best value of k, for CMF, is usually the same on both the training and the test set.

The obtained results are reported in Table 1. For each dataset the accuracy of the classifier that achieves the highest accuracy value is reported in boldface. Based on Table 1, Table 2 summarizes the accuracy comparisons of CMF with respect to the other classification algorithms. For each comparison, Win/Draw/Loss are the number of datasets where the accuracy of CMF is higher/equal/lower than the compared classifier.

The results reported in Table 1 highlight that CMF is, on the average, more accurate than five of the considered algorithms (+1.93% against K-NN, +12.01% against SVMs, +0.97% against C4.5, +1.26% against Ripper, and +0.11% against L^3). Only the Bayesian network classifier is, on the average, slightly more accurate than CMF (+0.26% with respect to CMF). Hence, despite its simplicity, CMF allows obtaining interesting results. The summary reported in Table 2 confirms the good results achieved by CMF. Except for Bayesian network and L^3, the reported results show that CMF wins on the majority of the considered datasets with respect to the other algorithms.

3.2 Execution time

We analyzed both the model generation time and the classification time of CMF on the 15 UCI datasets. The obtained model generation time for each dataset is reported in Table 3. We do not report the model generation time of the other algorithms because they are implemented in java, while CMF is implemented in Octave. Hence, execution time comparison will be unfair. The training time of CMF is at most 0.33s for the considered datasets and the average training time is 0.27s. The model generation time of CMF could be further reduced by exploiting ad-hoc SVD libraries such as SVDPACK [3].

As expected the execution time is related to the number of records and attributes. Since the complexity of the singular value decomposition is $O(\text{num. of records}*\text{num. of attributes}^2)$, the dataset with the highest training time is also the one

Table 3: Model generation time of CMF

Dataset	Records	Attributes	Records × Attributes^2	Training time (s)
Australian	690	15	1.55E+005	0.29
Breast	699	11	8.46E+004	0.27
Ecoli	336	8	2.15E+004	0.25
German	1000	25	6.25E+005	0.33
Harberman	306	4	4.90E+003	0.26
Heart	270	14	5.29E+004	0.25
hepatitis	255	20	1.02E+005	0.25
Horse	300	28	2.35E+005	0.29
Iono	351	35	4.30E+005	0.29
Iris	150	5	3.75E+003	0.24
Labor	40	27	2.92E+004	0.25
Pima	768	9	6.22E+004	0.26
Transfusion	748	5	1.87E+004	0.25
Wine	178	14	3.49E+004	0.26
Yeast	1484	9	1.20E+005	0.30

with the highest value of numb. of records*num. of attributes^2 (see Column (4) of Table 3).

We also measured the average classification time per data. The average classification time per data on the 15 UCI datasets is 0.73ms. The classification step of CMF is very efficient because it is based on the computation of the products between the vectors t_{c_i} and the matrix V.

3.2.1 Scalability

We performed a set of experiments to analyze in detail the model generation time of CMF with respect to the characteristics of the training dataset. We generated a set of synthetic datasets by means of the IBM data generator[1] with classification function 2. Figure 1 shows the model generation time when varying the number of records from 10,000 to 100,000 on datasets with ten attributes. Figure 2 reports the execution time with respect to the number of attributes (from 5 to 30 attributes). As expected the execution time increases not linearly with respect to the number of attributes (Figure 2), while, differently from the expected theoretical results, the execution time increases not linearly also with respect to the number of records (Figure 1). This result is probably related to the SVD implementation available in Octave. A linear execution time, with respect to the number of records, could be obtained by using the approach described in [13].

All the performed experiments need at most 110s. Hence, CMF efficiently handles structured datasets characterized by a large set of training data (up to 100,000 records) and attributes (up to 30 attributes).

4. CONCLUSIONS

In this paper, we proposed a simple but efficient and accurate classifier based on SVD. The performed experiments show that CMF achieves interesting results on structured datasets. We are working on the application of the proposed approach to textual classification. However, CMF cannot be straightforwardly applied to textual data because the number of features is significantly larger.

[1]http://www.almaden.ibm.com/software/quest/Resources/datasets

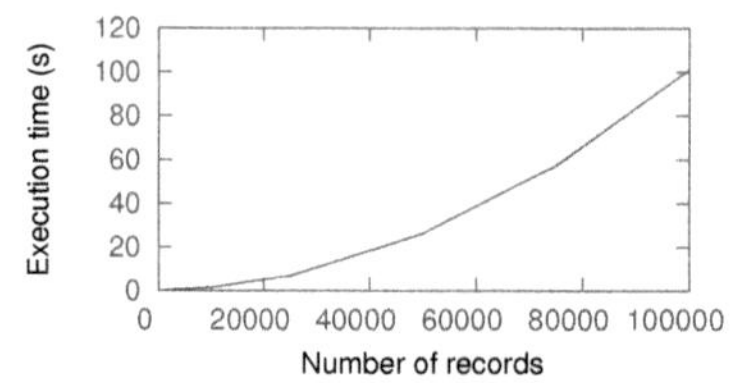

Figure 1: Scalability with respect to the number of records. 10 attributes for each dataset.

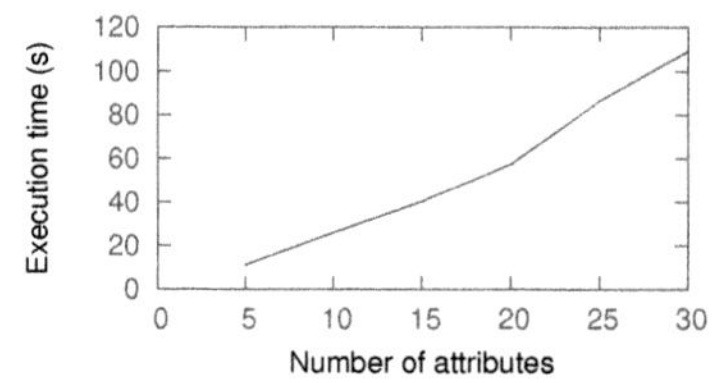

Figure 2: Scalability with respect to the number of attributes. 50,000 records for each dataset.

5. REFERENCES

[1] D. Aha and D. Kibler. Instance-based learning algorithms. *Machine Learning*, 6(1):37–66, 1991.

[2] E. Baralis, S. Chiusano, and P. Garza. A lazy approach to associative classification. *IEEE Transactions on Knowledge and Data Engineering*, 20(2):156–171, 2008.

[3] M. Berry. Large scale singular value computations. *International Journal of Supercomputer Applications*, 6(1):13–49, 1992.

[4] C.-C. Chang and C.-J. Lin. LIBSVM: A library for support vector machines. *ACM Transactions on Intelligent Systems and Technology*, 2(3):1–27, 2011.

[5] W. W. Cohen. Fast effective rule induction. In *Proceedings of the twelfth International Conference on Machine Learning*, pages 115–123, 1995.

[6] J. W. Eaton, D. Bateman, and S. Hauberg. *Gnu Octave Manual Version 3*. Network Theory, 2008.

[7] A. Frank and A. Asuncion. UCI machine learning repository, 2010.

[8] N. Friedman, D. Geiger, and M. Goldszmidt. Bayesian network classifiers. *Machine Learning*, 29(2-3):131–163, 1997.

[9] M. Hall, E. Frank, G. Holmes, B. Pfahringer, P. Reutemann, and I. H. Witten. The weka data mining software: an update. *SIGKDD Explor. Newsl.*, 11(1):10–18, 2009.

[10] Y. Koren, R. Bell, and C. Volinsky. Matrix factorization techniques for recommender systems. *Computer*, 42(8):30–37, 2009.

[11] B. Liu, W. Hsu, and Y. Ma. Integrating classification and association rule mining. In *Proceedings of the 4th International Conference on Knowledge Discovery and Data Mining*, pages 80–86, 1998.

[12] R. Quinlan. *C4.5: Programs for Machine Learning*. Morgan Kaufmann Publishers, San Mateo, CA, 1993.

[13] L. N. Trefethen and D. Bau. *Numerical linear algebra*. SIAM, 1997.

Transfer Active Learning

Zhenfeng Zhu
School of Info. and Eng.,
Zhengzhou University
100 Kexue Road
Zhengzhou, P.R. China
iezfzhu@zzu.edu.cn

Xingquan Zhu
QCIS Centre, Faculty of Eng.
and Info. Technology
Univ. of Technology, Sydney
NSW 2007, Australia
xqzhu@it.uts.edu.au

Yangdong Ye*
School of Info. and Eng.,
Zhengzhou University
100 Kexue Road
Zhengzhou, P.R. China
ieydye@zzu.edu.cn

Yue-Fei Guo
School of Computer Science
Fudan University
Shanghai 200433, P.R. China
yfguo@fudan.edu.cn

Xiangyang Xue
School of Computer Science
Fudan University
Shanghai 200433, P.R. China
xyxue@fudan.edu.cn

ABSTRACT

Active learning traditionally assumes that labeled and unlabeled samples are subject to the same distributions and the goal of an active learner is to label the most informative unlabeled samples. In reality, situations may exist that we may not have unlabeled samples from the same domain as the labeled samples (*i.e.* target domain), whereas samples from auxiliary domains might be available. Under such situations, an interesting question is whether an active learner can actively label samples from auxiliary domains to benefit the target domain. In this paper, we propose a transfer active learning method, namely Transfer Active SVM (TrAcSVM), which uses a limited number of target instances to iteratively discover and label informative auxiliary instances. TrAcSVM employs an extended sigmoid function as instance weight updating approach to adjust the models for prediction of (newly arrived) target data. Experimental results on real-world data sets demonstrate that TrAcSVM obtains better efficiency and prediction accuracy than its peers.

Categories and Subject Descriptors

I.5.4 [**Pattern Recognition**]: Applications—*computer vision, text processing*

General Terms

Algorithms

Keywords

Transfer learning, active learning, classification

*Corresponding author.

CIKM'11, October 24–28, 2011, Glasgow, Scotland, UK.

1. INTRODUCTION

Active learning methods traditionally assume that a rich set of unlabeled samples, which are subject to the same distribution as labeled samples, are provided for an active learner to label the most informative ones to improve the classifiers built from the labeled set. In many applications, one may find that samples for target domains are very difficult to collect, whereas plenty of unlabeled samples from auxiliary domains may exist. Under such situations, an immediate question is whether an active learner can selectively label samples from auxiliary domains to improve the learning for the target domain.

Indeed, given two sets of labeled samples S and D, where S is identified as the target domain and samples in D are from similar but not identical distributions as S, transfer learning [1, 6, 7] and cross-domain learning [8] have shown to be very successful in transferring knowledge from auxiliary domains D to improve the learning for the target domain S. Accordingly, if unlabeled samples from auxiliary domains are suitably labeled, existing transfer learning methods have the capacity to utilize their knowledge to benefit the learning for the target domain. As a result, the problem becomes that which of the unlabeled samples in the auxiliary domains should be labeled such that they can help improve the learning for the target domain.

In this paper, we formulate the above problem as *transfer active learning*, and propose a transfer active learning model, TrAcSVM, to solve the problem. The proposed method uses several labeled target data to iteratively project auxiliary data to low dimensional spaces and label informative auxiliary data, by employing an instance weighting mechanism. Experimental comparisons with some baseline methods, demonstrate that TrAcSVM is efficient for obtaining better prediction accuracies and faster convergence speed by actively labeling auxiliary data.

2. TRANSFER ACTIVE LEARNING

2.1 Problem Definition

Denote $S = [s_1, s_2, \cdots, s_t] \in \mathbb{R}^{m\times t}$ the *same-distribution* (**target**) data matrix consisting of t instances in m-dimensional spaces and the column vector $L_S = [l_1, l_2, \cdots, l_t]^T$ is used to assign a class label $+1$ or -1 for each instance in S. Similar to S, symbol $D = [d_1, d_2, \cdots, d_n] \in \mathbb{R}^{m \times n}$ (t is a small integer and $t \ll n$) is the *different-distribution* (**auxiliary**) data matrix consisting of n instances in m-dimensional spaces. In addition, the symbol Z denotes the labeled training data.

For traditional active learning, both labeled and unlabeled data are assumed to share the same distributions. To build prediction models, one can actively select and label informative samples from S. For some applications, the number of same-distribution data t might be too small to produce strong training model, or it is difficult/expensive or time-consuming to label the same-distribution instances. As a result, it may be difficult to obtain a rich set of same-distribution labeled data, whereas finding a large number of different-distribution samples from auxiliary domain might be easily achieved. Accordingly, the problem described above can be regarded as discovering and labeling auxiliary data, such that their knowledge can be properly transferred to the target domain and help build a classifier with maximum prediction accuracy.

2.2 Solution for the Defined Problem

To integrate transfer learning into active learning, two fundamental challenges include (1) how to determine and select informative auxiliary data for labeling, and (2) how to transfer knowledge in the labeled auxiliary data to the target data. In this paper, the former is solved by using a small number of labeled target data to find useful auxiliary data. For the latter, we use an instance-level weighting mechanism to achieve transfer learning. More specifically, when initializing the prediction model by employing proximal support vector machine (PSVM) method [3], the training set Z consists of target set S with only t instances. In each iteration, we utilize the initial model to project auxiliary data to low-dimensional spaces and actively select an informative auxiliary instance $d \in D$ for labeling and adjust weight values of all labeled instances in Z. Accordingly, the training model is improved gradually.

In the following sections, we first introduce PSVM method as a basic classifier. Based on this approach, we further describe the method for finding informative auxiliary instances, followed by detailed procedures on sample weight updating for transfer active learning.

2.3 Proximal Support Vector Machine

Proximal Support Vector Machine (PSVM) method is a simplified SVM classifier [3]. Assume the instance matrix X is equal to $[x_1, x_2, ..., x_{n'}] \in \mathbb{R}^{m \times n'}$, the label vector $L \in \mathbb{R}^{n' \times 1}$ is used to assign a class label $+1$ or -1 for each instance, and $e \in \mathbb{R}^{n' \times 1}$ is a column vector of ones in n'-dimensional space. The classifier based on PSVM can be simplified as follows,

$$\omega = (\delta I + ZZ^T)^{-1} ZL = (\delta I + A)^{-1} ZL = \hat{A}^{-1} ZL, \quad (1)$$

where $Z = [X; -e] (z = [x^T, -1]^T \in Z)$, δ is the regularization parameter, and ω determines a decision boundary, *i.e.* a classifier, which can be used for prediction.

2.4 Informative Instance Searching

Intuitively, for transfer learning, informative auxiliary instances should be those which are similar to the target data, so we can use several target instances to determine whether an auxiliary data is worth of labeling. Accordingly, when using ± 1 as class labels and considering the model parameter ω as projection matrix, we believe that informative instances in the one dimensional projection space should be those which are near to the zero value. In fact, one only needs to make the projection P equal to $D\omega$. To this end, we can maximize Eq. (2) to discover this type of instances.

$$f(D, \omega) = e^{-(D\omega)^2}. \quad (2)$$

2.5 Instance Weight Updating

Using labeled target set $Z \leftarrow S$, we can easily train an initial projection model. Once a useful auxiliary instance is labeled and included in the training set Z, we recalculate the weight values for the target data and newly included auxiliary data by left multiplying a weight matrix λ to be updated on Z^T and L. The weight matrix λ, with the initial values is given as follows.

$$\lambda = I, \Lambda = \lambda^T \lambda = I, \quad (3)$$

where I is the unit matrix and Λ is used to conveniently adjust the model parameter ω like Eq. (4).

$$\omega = g(Z, \Lambda, L) = (\delta I + Z\Lambda Z^T)^{-1} Z\Lambda L. \quad (4)$$

During the weight updating process, Λ is adjusted by using the feedback mechanism based on the prediction errors on matrix Z, which includes target and auxiliary data.

For the weight updating method in TrAdaBoost [2], in each iteration, the instance weight for auxiliary data decreases by multiplying a value which is less or equal to 1, and the weight value for target data increases by multiplying a value witch is greater than or equal to 1. As a result, the weight values for auxiliary data and target data fall into the range (0, 1] and [1, Max), respectively, where Max may be much larger than 1. Because the weight values are not bounded in a certain range, the weight updating of the target instance might result in over-fitting. To solve the problem, we employ and reconstruct a sigmoid function as follows.

$$\Lambda_{jj} = \begin{cases} 1 + \frac{1}{1+e^{P(z_j)l_j}} & 1 \le j \le t, \\ \frac{1}{1+e^{-P(z_j)l_j}} & t+1 \le j \le t+i, \end{cases} \quad (5)$$

where $P(z_j)$ is the predicted label of the instance $z_j \in Z = [S, d_1, d_2, \cdots, d_i]$, with the label set denoted by $\{+1, -1\}$.

For binary classification problem using ± 1 as labels, if the label is correctly predicted, the multiplication $P(z_j)l_j$ is a positive value. Otherwise, it is a negative one. Accordingly, for target data, the value $1 + \frac{1}{1+e^x}$ falls into the range (1, 2), and for auxiliary data, the value $\frac{1}{1+e^{-x}}$ falls into the range (0, 1). As a result, Eq. (5) explicitly limits the weight of auxiliary and target instances into different bounded ranges.

3. TRACSVM ALGORITHM

Algorithm 1 lists detailed procedures of TrAcSVM, which contains two main steps including finding informative auxiliary instances (Step 6) and adjusting model parameter ω (Step 12).

In Algorithm 1, the target data S which only include several instances, are provided in a batch format to initialize the model parameters (as show on Step 4), whereas the auxiliary data D are incrementally included into the learning process. Once the first active auxiliary instance $d_i \in D$ is acquired (Step 6), TrAcSVM uses Eq. (5) to update Λ on Step 11, followed by the updating of ω on Step 12. The **For** loop between Steps 5 and 13 repeats until all n instances in the auxiliary set D are processed. The final model parameter ω is used to predict test samples.

Algorithm 1 Pseudocode of TrAcSVM algorithm

Input: Target data $< S, L_S >$, auxiliary data $< D >$, regularization parameter δ, iteration number n.
Output: The prediction model ω.

```
[t, m] = size(S); /* m: dimension, t: target instance.*/
Z = S and L = L_S; /* Initialize Z and L.*/
Λ = I^{t×t} for Z; /* Initialize instance weight.*/
Initialize ω using Eq. (4);
for i = 1 to n do
    Find the i^{th} auxiliary instance d with maximal value of e^{-(Dω)^2};
    Annotate the label l of d by Oracle;
    Delete d from D;
    Extend Z and L to include d and l, respectively;
    Extend Λ such that Λ(t + i, t + i) = 1;
    Update Λ using Eq. (5);
    Update ω using Eq. (4).
end for
```

4. EXPERIMENTAL RESULTS

Benchmark Methods: Presumably, a simple transfer active learning method is to apply a random labeling module to an existing transfer learning method, such as TrAdaBoost [2]. In each iteration, we randomly label one auxiliary instance and adjust weight values of all labeled instances by using TrAdaBoost algorithm. Then, we can use Eq. (4) to generate new prediction result. We call this benchmark method RTrSVM, namely random sampling transfer SVM.

The proposed method TrAcSVM is compared with RTrSVM and a boosting-based transfer learning algorithm TrAdaBoost [2]. For fairness of the comparisons, we use PSVM [3] as the basic classifier for all methods. In the paper, we mainly report learning efficiency and prediction accuracy with respect to different benchmark data sets.

4.1 Benchmark Data Sets

Our test bed consists of two real-world data sets: 20 News Group (20NG) [4] and USPS image data [5].

Table 1: Data Sets from 20NG.

Data Sets	Subcategories	
comp	comp.sys.ibm.pc.hardware (comp1), comp.sys.mac.hardware (comp2)	
rec	rec.sport.baseball (rec1), rec.sport.hockey (rec2)	
	Auxiliary Data	Target Data
20NG_1 (+&-)	comp1&rec1	comp2&rec2

20NG data sets have a hierarchical structure. To simulate transfer learning reality, we reassign the hierarchical structure like that in [2].

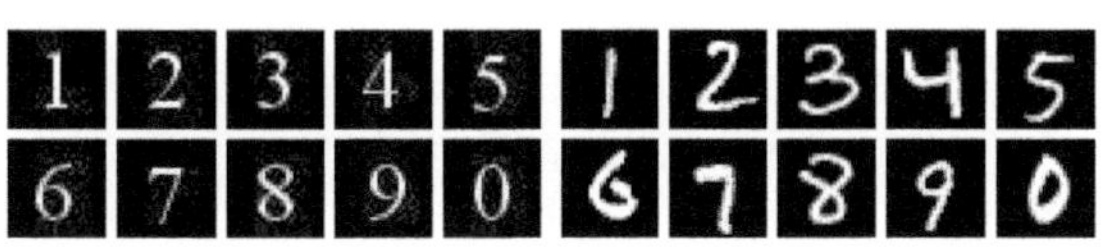

Figure 1: Samples for printed (1st-5th columns) and hand-written digits (6th-10th columns)

USPS Digit data sets are collected from the US Postal Service (USPS) database which consists of hand-written images (digits). To enable active learning, we treat hand-written digit recognition as the learning task and use printed digits to enhance the prediction on the hand-written images. Fig.1 demonstrates some image samples. Because digit pairs 3 and 8 are visually similar, we select them to demonstrate the algorithm performance.

In our experiments, the auxiliary and target data are similar to each other. Therefore, their roles can be switched. In the paper, we also report the reverse (from target data to auxiliary ones) transfer active learning results.

4.2 Experimental Settings

To compare the performance of the three methods (RTrSVM, TrAcSVM, and TrAdaBoost), we use PSVM as the base learner for all methods and report their average performance over ten time repetitions for each data set. In each repetition, the number of labeled instances for the target set is fixed to 10 instances and the remaining instances in the target set are used as test samples. The transfer active learning modules are applied to label auxiliary data set which contains 200 instances and generate prediction models.

4.3 Comparisons of Experimental Results

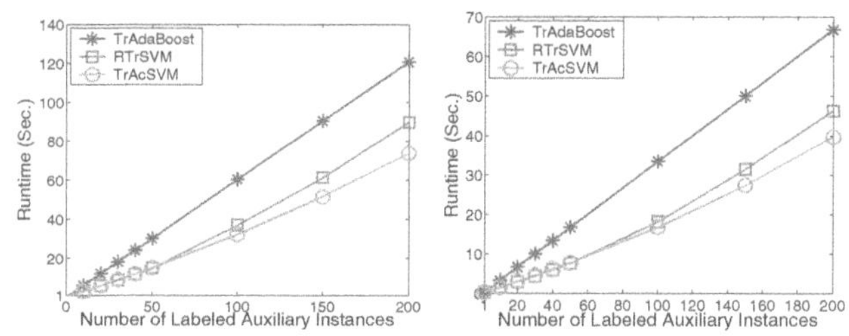

(a) Runtime comparison on 20NG_1 (b) Runtime comparison on 3&8 pair

Figure 2: Average runtime on 20NG_1 and 3&8, respectively.

In Fig.2, we report the system runtime comparison on two data sets. As we have explained in the experimental settings, in each experiment, the training set consists of 210 training instances. For RTrSVM and TrAcSVM, they incrementally label and include one auxiliary instance into the training process and record the system runtime once the processing for one auxiliary instance is done. For TrAdaBoost, we use all 200 randomly selected auxiliary instances in each iteration to train a weak classifiers with the number of iterations equal to that of different-distribution training instances used by RTrSVM and TrAcSVM. As a result, we can obtain a curve for each method to report the system runtime *w.r.t.* the increase of the auxiliary instances.

The results in Fig.2 show that all methods linearly scale up to the increasing size of the auxiliary instances. In each iteration, TrAdaBoost must adjust the weight and model parameter on all labeled training data, therefore, the runtime of TrAdaBoost is linearly increasing with respect to the number of iterations. For RTrSVM and TrAcSVM, the number of training instances gradually increases and approaches to that of TrAdaBoost. As a result, their runtime is a little less than that of TrAdaBoost and also linearly increases with respect to the number of auxiliary instances n.

In Fig.3 we report the algorithm performance for transfer active learning, including forward transfer learning and reverse transfer learning (from target data to auxiliary data).

From the results showing in the figures, it is clear that

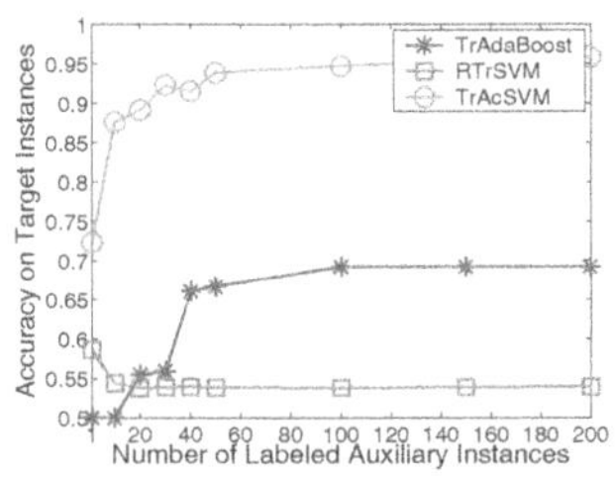

(a) Transfer learning for 20NG_1

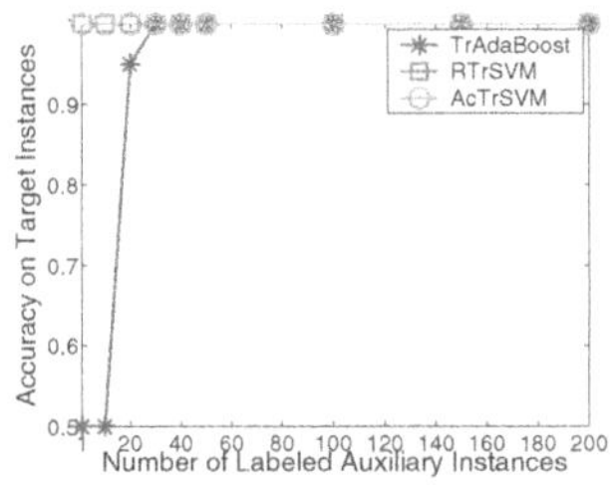

(b) Transfer learning for 3&8 pair

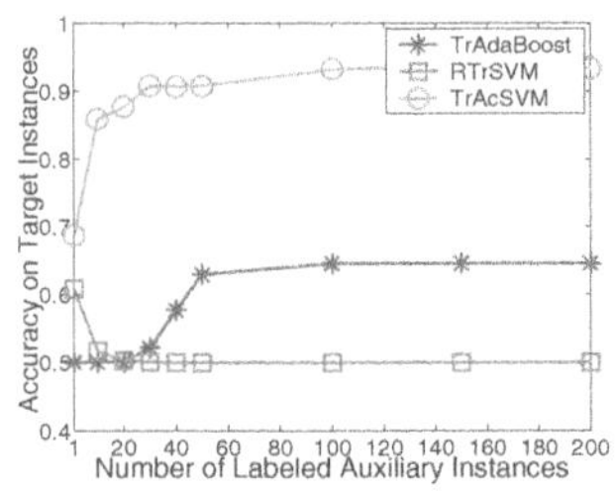

(c) R. Transfer learning for 20NG_1

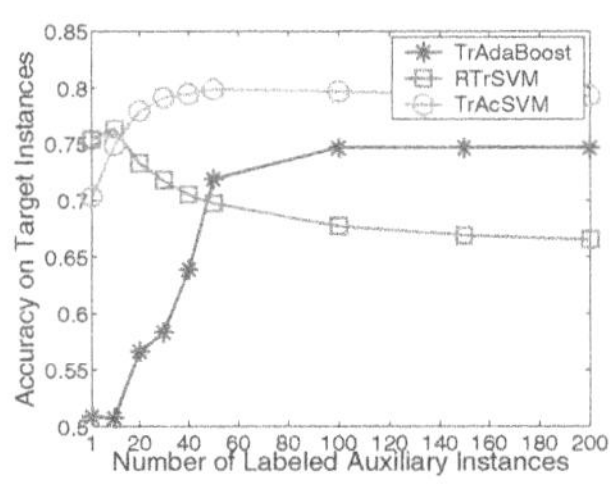

(d) R. Transfer learning for 3&8 pair

Figure 3: Average prediction accuracies on 20NG_1 and 3&8 pair. Transfer active learning from auxiliary to target data (a) 20NG_1, (b) 3&8, as well as the reverse learning from target to auxiliary data (c) 20NG_1 and (d) 3&8.

the prediction accuracies of TrAcSVM are constantly better than others, and its accuracy gain is particularly significant when only a very limited number of auxiliary instances are labeled for training. For most data sets in our experiments, the results of TrAdaBoost are relatively poor at the beginning. After a sufficient number of iterations, the results of TrAdaBoost can pick up and eventually become comparable to others. For RTrSVM, in most situations, the increase of labeled auxiliary data is not useful for improving the prediction performance, which asserts that randomly labeling auxiliary samples, like RTrSVM does, is ineffective for boosting the learner performance for target data.

In Figs.3(c) and (d), we also report the reverse transfer active learning results where the target and the auxiliary sets switch their roles and the objective is to learn a prediction model for the auxiliary data by transferring knowledge from the target data. Our results indicate that knowledge transfer between target and auxiliary data is largely bidirectional, as long as the two tasks are relevant to each other.

When comparing results across Figs.3(a), (b), (c) and (d) for different target set sizes, it is clear that the smaller the size of the labeled auxiliary set, the better the transfer active learning can help improve the learning on the target set. Note that Fig.3(b) shows slightly different trends from others. This is mainly because the target data (hand-written digits) have more generalization performance than auxiliary samples (printed digits). For RTrSVM and TrAcSVM, when the initial labeled target data already produces a strong model (the prediction accuracy is 100%), labeling more auxiliary data does not bring additional improvement. For TrAdaBoost, all labeled auxiliary data and target data are used together to train initial classifiers. Because the number of labeled auxiliary data is much more than that of target instances, the initial classifiers are strongly dominated by the auxiliary data. As a result, the prediction accuracy of TrAdaBoost is low at the beginning of the iteration. With more iterations and more classifiers combined together, the instance weighting mechanisms of TrAdaBoost can help adjust the weight values for auxiliary instances, and improve TrAdaBoost's prediction accuracy.

In summary, by actively selecting informative auxiliary data and employing the proposed instance level weighting mechanism, TrAcSVM achieves much better prediction accuracies and faster convergence speed than its opponents, the non-active methods.

5. CONCLUSIONS

In this paper, we proposed a transfer active learning method TrAcSVM. We argued that traditional active learning merely focuses on labeling samples which are from the same distributions as the target data but does not have mechanisms to actively select samples from auxiliary domains to improve the learning for target data. To solve the problem, we proposed TrAcSVM which combines transfer learning and active learning in an effective way. TrAcSVM uses a small number of target data to obtain labeling information for auxiliary instances, such that labeled auxiliary instances can help build accurate prediction models for the target data. Experimental results on text and image data demonstrated that TrAcSVM can obtain better runtime performance, faster convergence speed and higher prediction accuracy than its peers.

Acknowledgments

This work was partially supported under Australian Research Council's Future Fellowship funding scheme (project number FT100100971), and by National 973 Program (No. 2010CB327906), NSF of China under Grant (No.60773048, No. 60873178, No. 60875003, and No. 60674109), the State Key Laboratory Program under Grant(No. RCS2009K003), the National High Technology Research and Development Program of China (No. 2009AA01A346).

6. REFERENCES

[1] R. Caruana. Multitask learning. *Mach. Learn.*, 28:41–75, 1997.

[2] W. Dai, Q. Yang, G.-R. Xue, and Y. Yu. Boosting for transfer learning. In *Proc. 24th Int. Conf. Mach. Learn.*, pages 193–200, 2007.

[3] G. Fung and O. L. Mangasarian. Proximal support vector machine classifiers. pages 77–86. Proc. 7th ACM SIGKDD, 2001.

[4] K. Lang. Newsweeder: Learning to filter netnews. In *Proc. of ICML*, pages 331–339, 1995.

[5] Y. LeCun, Y. B. L. Bottou, and P. Haffner. Gradient-based learning applied to document recognition. *Proc. IEEE*, 86(11):2278–2324, 1998.

[6] S. J. Pan and Q. Yang. A survey on transfer learning. *IEEE TKDE*, 22(10):1345–1359, 2010.

[7] S. Thrun. Is learning the n-th thing any easier than learning the first? In *Adv. Neural Inform. Process. Syst.*, pages 640–646, 1996.

[8] X. Zhu. Cross-domain semi-supervised learning using feature formulation. *IEEE Trans. on Systems Man and Cyber. (B)*, DOI:10.1109/TSMCB.2011.2157999, 2011.

A Probabilistic Approach to Nearest-Neighbor Classification: Naive Hubness Bayesian *k*NN

Nenad Tomašev
Institute Jožef Stefan
Jamova 39
Ljubljana, Slovenia
nenad.tomasev@ijs.si

Miloš Radovanović
Department of Mathematics and Informatics
Trg D. Obradovića 4
Novi Sad, Serbia
radacha@dmi.uns.ac.rs

Dunja Mladenić
Institute Jožef Stefan
Jamova 39
Ljubljana, Slovenia
dunja.mladenic@ijs.si

Mirjana Ivanović
Department of Mathematics and Informatics
Trg D. Obradovića 4
Novi Sad, Serbia
mira@dmi.uns.ac.rs

ABSTRACT

Most machine-learning tasks, including classification, involve dealing with high-dimensional data. It was recently shown that the phenomenon of hubness, inherent to high-dimensional data, can be exploited to improve methods based on nearest neighbors (NNs). Hubness refers to the emergence of points (hubs) that appear among the k NNs of many other points in the data, and constitute influential points for kNN classification. In this paper, we present a new probabilistic approach to kNN classification, naive hubness Bayesian k-nearest neighbor (NHBNN), which employs hubness for computing class likelihood estimates. Experiments show that NHBNN compares favorably to different variants of the kNN classifier, including probabilistic kNN (PNN) which is often used as an underlying probabilistic framework for NN classification, signifying that NHBNN is a promising alternative framework for developing probabilistic NN algorithms.

Categories and Subject Descriptors

I.2.6 [**Artificial Intelligence**]: Learning; I.5.1 [**Pattern Recognition**]: Models

General Terms

Algorithms, Experimentation, Theory

1. INTRODUCTION

High dimensionality is known to pose certain limitations on the effectiveness of many machine-learning algorithms. Nowadays, the majority of data one has to deal with is, unfortunately, high-dimensional. This includes text, images, video, medical records, data streams etc. All such data is sparse, since data size requirements for proper density estimates rise exponentially with the number of dimensions. Furthermore, there exists the phenomenon of distance concentration, which has been thoroughly explored in the past [4]. In high-dimensional spaces, distances between points drawn from the same distribution tend to become relatively similar to one another, so some doubts have been raised about the usefulness of the notion of nearest neighbors in high-dimensional settings [3]. Nevertheless, the k-nearest neighbor (kNN) classifier is a widely used classification method that operates by a majority vote on a k-nearest-neighbor set [1].

Hubness is a phenomenon related specifically to nearest-neighbor methods. Let $N_k(x)$ denote the number of k-occurrences of point x, i.e., the number of times x occurs in k-nearest-neighbor lists of other data points. When the (intrinsic) dimensionality of data is high, significant skew in the distribution of $N_k(x)$ can be observed. This leads to the emergence of *hubs*, data points which are included in many more neighbor lists than other points. The number of k-occurrences of point x, $N_k(x)$, will be referred to as the hubness score of x. A hubness-based weighted voting scheme for kNN, proposed in [8], was shown to often lead to improvement when working with high-dimensional data.

Our goal is to examine if it is possible to incorporate hubness information for Bayesian class prediction. Hubness is interpreted as prior information about occurrences of elements in k-neighbor sets and is used to set up a Bayesian k-nearest neighbor model. The proposed approach is fundamentally different from related methods, from which a representative selection is reviewed in Section 2. Section 3 presents our probabilistic framework for using hubness, and proposes the naive hubness Bayesian k-nearest neighbor classification algorithm (NHBNN). Experimental comparison of NHBNN with related approaches is performed in Section 4, while the last section gives concluding remarks and an outline for future work.

2. RELATED WORK

Introducing weights to votes in kNN is not all that uncommon. Defining vote weights $w_k(x_i)$ based on hubness

CIKM'11, October 24–28, 2011, Glasgow, Scotland, UK.
Copyright 2011 ACM 978-1-4503-0717-8/11/10 ...$10.00.

was introduced in [8]. The hubness of each point can be decomposed into two parts, which will be referred to as *good hubness* and *bad hubness*, respectively: $N_k(x_i) = GN_k(x_i) + BN_k(x_i)$. Good hubness represents those k-occurrences of x_i where labels match, i.e., the label of x_i and the label of the data point which has x_i in its neighbor set are the same. Bad hubness, on the other hand, originates from label mismatches. In high-dimensional spaces, hubs become increasingly influential, since they are found in many k-neighbor sets. We can distinguish between good hubs and bad hubs based on how often label mismatches occur. Bad hubs exhibit a distinctively detrimental influence. Hubness-weighted kNN [8] aims to reduce the influence of bad hubs, which is how it improves on the basic kNN classifier. The approach is as follows. Standardized bad hubness is computed as: $h_b(x_i, k) = (BN_k(x_i) - \mu_{BN_k})/\sigma_{BN_k}$, where μ_{BN_k} is mean bad hubness and σ_{BN_k} the standard deviation. The weight associated with x_i is then $w_k(x_i) = e^{-h_b(x_i,k)}$.

One of the disadvantages of the standard kNN classifier is that it does not output meaningful probabilities associated with class prediction. Performing a count of the number of votes given to each class and making the class probabilities somehow proportional to those counts is, admittedly, simple enough – but is not a really good measure of confidence, especially for lower k values. A Bayesian solution to this problem was proposed in [6] and is known as probabilistic k-nearest neighbor (PNN). It has been shown that PNN does not offer an improvement in accuracy over the basic kNN [7]. Extensions of PNN have been proposed which improve its overall performance [2, 5].

3. BAYESIAN VIEW ON HUBNESS

In our approach, we wanted to exploit the information provided by *reverse* nearest neighbors, while being aware of hubs in high dimensions. The way in which hubness had previously been exploited in hubness-weighted kNN is somewhat rigid, so we decided to extend it. In multi-class scenarios, all label mismatches in k-occurrences of point x were collapsed to a single quantity – *bad hubness*. Our idea was to observe class-specific label mismatches. This led us to define *class hubness*.

Thereby, the total number of k-occurrences is decomposed in the following manner: $N_k(x_i) = \sum_{c=1}^{C} N_{k,c}(x_i)$. $N_{k,c}(x_i)$ signifies the number of k-occurrences of point x_i in neighborhoods of elements of class c. Let $D_k(x)$ denote the k-neighbor set of x. We interpret the k-occurrence of x_i in $D_k(x)$ as an event which carries information that gives certain evidence to class affiliation of x.

Before we continue, we should first emphasize the main difficulty of such reverse nearest neighbor reasoning. Some points may never appear in kNN sets and therefore have – no reverse nearest neighbors. In high-dimensional data this happens more often, due to the hubness phenomenon. Such points which appear either never or rarely as nearest neighbors we will refer to as *anti-hubs*.

On the other hand, in hubs there is a lot of occurrence information to infer from. Suppose that x_h is one such hub and c_h its label. In some cases, the labels of the majority of reverse neighbors of x_h might be different from c_h. In such cases, when we observe $x_h \in D_k(x)$, this should not be considered as strong evidence in favor of class c_h. This is why we feel that taking class hubness into consideration may prove quite beneficial.

Let $D = (X, Y)$ be the data set, so that $y_i \in Y$ is the label of $x_i \in X$. We would like to estimate $p(y = c|D_k(x))$. We view $D_k(x)$ as being the result of k random draws from D where each x_i has probability $p_t(x_i|D_t(x), x)$ of being drawn at time t, where $t \in \{1, 2, \ldots, k\}$. Since the concepts of t-neighbor and $(t+1)$-neighbor are quite similar, we disregard the exact position of x_i in the list, which endows us with more information to work with.

Let $x_i \in X$ and x_{it}, for $t \in \{1, 2, \ldots, k\}$, be the k nearest neighbors of x_i. We focus on a naive Bayesian estimate which takes the form shown in Eq. 1:

$$p(y_i = c|D_k(x_i)) \propto p(y_i = c) \prod_{t=1}^{k} p(x_{it} \in D_k(x_i)|y_i = c). \quad (1)$$

The independence assumption obviously does not hold in most cases. However, it was shown in the past that this is not necessary for the naive Bayesian approach to work [9].

The main problem lies in estimating the probabilities on the right-hand side of Eq. 1, especially for anti-hubs, which will be treated as a special case. Also, each point was included to its own neighbor set at the 0th position, ensuring that each $N_k(x_i) \geq 1$.

For clarity we shorten the notation by denoting $p(x_{it} \in D_k(x_i)|y_i = c)$ as $p_{x_i,c,k}(x_{it})$, and by n_c the number of elements of class c. Also, let $N_{k,c_1}(c_2)$ be the total number of k-occurrences of elements from class c_2 in neighborhoods of elements belonging to c_1.

Let (x, y) be an element from the neighborhood of x_i. Also, let $(x_g, y_g) \in \bigcup_{x_j : y_j = c} D_k(x_j)$. The derivation of the probability estimate is given in Eq. 2:

$$\begin{aligned} & p_{x_i,c,k}(x_{it}) & (2) \\ &= p_{x_i,k}(y = y_{it}|y_i = c) \cdot p_{x_i,k}(x = x_{it}|y = y_{it}) \\ &\approx p_{c,k}(y_g = y_{it}) \cdot p_{c,k}(x_g = x_{it}|y_g = y_{it}) \\ &= \frac{N_{k,c}(y_{it})}{n_c \cdot (k+1)} \cdot \frac{N_{k,c}(x_{it})}{\sum_{j:y_j = y_{it}} N_{k,c}(x_j)} = \frac{N_{k,c}(x_{it})}{n_c \cdot (k+1)} \\ &\approx \frac{N_{k,c}(x_{it}) + \lambda}{n_c \cdot (k+1) + \lambda|D|} = \bar{p}_{x_i,c,k}(x_{it}), \end{aligned}$$

where λ is the Laplace estimator, ensuring non-zero probabilities. When dealing with anti-hubs, however, the outlined approximation can not be expected to yield reliable probability estimates. This is why for anti-hubs we partly infer the probability from what is known about the typical points from the same class and their hubness, as shown in Eq. 3.

$$p_{x_i,c,k}(x_{it}) \approx \begin{cases} \bar{p}_{x_i,c,k}(x_{it}), & \text{if } N_k(x_{it}) > \theta, \\ u_{x_i,c,k}(x_{it}), & \text{if } N_k(x_{it}) \leq \theta. \end{cases}$$

$$u_{x_i,c,k}(x_{it}) = \alpha_h \cdot \bar{p}_{x_i,c,k}(x_{it}) + (1 - \alpha_h) \cdot \acute{p}_{x_i,c,k}(x_{it}). \quad (3)$$

We propose two approaches to defining $\acute{p}_{x_i,c,k}(x_{it})$. Both are based on the approximation given in Eq. 4:

$$N_{k,c}(x_{it}) \approx N_{k,c}(y_{it})/n_{y_{it}}. \quad (4)$$

We will refer to using this estimate as the *global approximative approach*. We could also take local information into account by inferring $N_{k,c}(y_{it})$ from some k_{est}-neighborhood of x_{it} instead, as given in Eq. 5. We will refer to this estimate as the *local approximative approach*. In our experiments we invariably used $k_{\text{est}} = 20$.

$$N_{k,c}(x_{it}) \approx \frac{N_{x_i,k_{est},k,c}(y_{it})}{n_{k_{est},y_{it}}} = \frac{\sum_{j \in D_{k_{est}}(x_{it}):y_j=y_{it}} N_{k,c}(x_j)}{|x \in D_{k_{est}}(x_{it}) : y = y_{it}|}. \quad (5)$$

In the end we obtain $\acute{p}_{x_i,c,k}(x_{it})$ from Eq. 3 by plugging either the local or the global class hubness estimate instead of the original $N_{k,c}(x_{it})$ into $\bar{p}_{x_i,c,k}(x_{it})$. In other words:

$$\acute{p}_{x_i,c,k}(x_{it}) = \begin{cases} \frac{N_{k,c}(y_{it})+\lambda}{n_c \cdot n_{y_{it}} \cdot (k+1)+\lambda C}, & \text{if global,} \\ \frac{N_{k_{est},k,c}(y_{it})+\lambda}{n_c \cdot n_{k_{est},y_{it}} \cdot (k+1)+\lambda C}, & \text{if local.} \end{cases}$$

Class affiliation of x is determined as $y = \arg\max_c p(y = c|D_k(x))$. In case of an unlikely tie we assign according to the prior class probabilities, i.e., the majority class. We name the algorithm which performs this classification, based on approximations given in Eqs. 1, 2, 3, 4, and 5, the *naive hubness Bayesian k-nearest neighbor* (**NHBNN**). Several parameters are required for the algorithm to work, but they can also be inferred from the training set by leave-one-out cross-validation.

Algorithm 1 NHBNN: Training

```
Input: (X,Y,k,k_est,θ,α_h)
training set T = (X,Y) ⊂ R^{d×1}
number of neighbors k ∈ {1,2...n−1}
local estimate width k_est ∈ {1,2...n−1}
hubness score threshold θ ∈ [0, max_{x_i∈T} N_k(x_i))
hubness prevalence α_h ∈ [0,1]
Train:
calculateClassPriors()
kNeighbors = findNeighborSets(T, k)
kEstNeighbors = findNeighborSets(T, k_est)
for all (x_i, y_i) ∈ (X,Y) do
  for all c = 1...C do
    count N_{k,c}(x_i)
    N_{k,c}(y_i) += N_{k,c}(x_i)
    for all c̄ = 1...C do
      count N_{x_i,k_est,k,c}(c̄)
    end for
  end for
  N_k(x_i) = Σ_{c=1}^{C} N_{k,c}(x_i)
end for{only after the global estimates are calculated}
{we finish by calculating the probabilities}
for all (x_i, y_i) ∈ (X,Y) do
  calculate p̄_{x_i,c,k}(x_it) by Eq. 3
end for
```

4. EXPERIMENTAL EVALUATION

The data sets used for evaluation are summarized in Table 1. Eighteen data sets of various dimensionalities originate from the University of California, Irvine (UCI) Machine Learning Repository, two high-dimensional gene expression microarray data sets (colonTumor, ovarian) are from the Kent Ridge (KR) Bio-Medical Data Set Repository, and five data sets represent subsets of images taken from the ImageNet repository. We extracted SIFT features from all images, formed quantized 400-dimensional representations [11], and then appended 16-bin color distribution information to obtain the final 416-dimensional feature vectors. More details on these five image data sets are given in [10].

All data sets are summarized in Table 1, whose columns respectively denote data-set name, size, dimensionality (d), number of classes (C), and the observed skewness of the distribution of N_5 (S_{N_5}) [8]. Euclidean distance was used as a dissimilarity measure for the first 20 data sets from the table and Manhattan distance for the last five image data sets. We see that the hubness phenomenon is much more pronounced in image data.

Table 1: Summary of data sets.

Data set	size	d	C	S_{N_5}
arcene	100	10000	2	0.25
colonTumor	62	2000	2	0.76
dexter	300	20000	2	3.35
diabetes	768	8	2	0.34
ecoli	336	7	8	0.43
glass	214	9	6	0.13
ionosphere	351	34	2	1.48
iris	150	4	3	0.25
mfeat-factors	2000	216	10	0.79
mfeat-fourier	2000	76	10	0.87
ovarian	253	15154	2	0.66
page-blocks	5473	10	5	0.25
parkinsons	195	22	2	−0.04
segment	2310	19	7	0.32
sonar	208	60	2	1.41
spectrometer	531	100	10	0.42
yeast	1484	8	10	0.40
vehicle	846	18	4	0.71
wdbc	569	30	2	0.09
wine	178	13	3	0.04
ImgNet-s3	2731	416	3	8.38
ImgNet-s4	6054	416	4	7.69
ImgNet-s5	6555	416	5	14.73
ImgNet-s6	6010	416	6	8.42
ImgNet-s7	10544	416	7	7.66

Experiments were performed in three different setups. The first two setups used only the first 20 listed data sets. The image data sets were considered separately, for reasons that will be explained later.

In the first round of experiments we examined how NHB-NN performs for a fixed k value and some fixed parameter configuration over all data sets. The conclusion from the results from this round (omitted due to space considerations) is that global and local versions of NHBNN exhibit similar performance, and are both superior to kNN and hw-kNN.

In the second round of experiments our aim was to compare the algorithms when automatically searching for proper parameters (as well as estimation schemes) on each fold of 10 times 10-fold cross validation, with the recorded accuracies compared using the corrected resampled t-test. Here, we also included PNN in the comparison with NHBNN. For kNN, hw-kNN and NHBNN we used $k \in \{1, 2 \ldots, 10\}$. For PNN we allowed a larger maximum neighborhood size, this being the way it was used in the original article [6]. The maximum k for PNN was set to $\min(500, \lfloor n/4 \rfloor)$, where n is the data-set size. We set PNN to use 1500 evaluation points. The results are shown in Table 2.

In both experimental settings, NHBNN performs quite well. Significant improvements over kNN were observed, with 5-1 and 4-0 in statistically significant wins in the two observed experimental setups, respectively. NHBNN compares favorably to PNN, since it achieves 7-0 in statistically significant wins.

In the first two experimental setups no significant difference between hw-kNN and NHBNN was observed. This is not all that surprising, since most UCI data sets are binary classification problems, low-to-medium (intrinsically) dimensional with small skewness in the distribution of k-occurrences, as seen in Table 1. Furthermore, many of the

Table 2: Comparison of NHBNN with several other classifiers, featuring automatic search for best parameters and approaches on each cross-validation fold. The symbols ∘/• denote statistically significant better/worse performance with respect to NHBNN, at significance level $p < 0.01$.

Data set	kNN	hw-kNN	PNN	NHBNN
arcene	70.5±14.6	73.5±14.3	74.9±14.0	74.9±14.2
colonTumor	64.9±19.9	73.3±19.2	72.6±18.8	74.5±18.1
dexter	60.2±19.1	69.7± 9.3	65.3±13.3	66.9± 7.8
diabetes	76.6± 5.2	72.0± 4.6	73.5± 5.1	74.1± 4.6
ecoli	85.4± 5.9	85.1± 5.9	82.8± 6.9	83.9± 6.4
glass	71.3±10.2	68.8± 9.6	63.3± 9.3	68.1±10.9
ionosphere	89.9± 4.8	87.0± 5.9	78.0± 8.4 •	91.7± 5.0
iris	96.9± 4.0	95.3± 4.8	95.4± 4.8	95.3± 5.8
mfeat-factors	92.9± 1.8 •	95.4± 1.4	89.8± 4.5 •	95.8± 1.4
mfeat-fourier	77.4± 3.0 •	80.3± 2.6	75.2± 5.0 •	81.2± 2.7
ovarian	92.8± 5.1	93.9± 5.0	89.2± 6.9	92.1± 5.6
page-blocks	93.5± 1.0 •	96.0± 0.8	92.1± 1.5 •	95.4± 1.3
parkinsons	82.4± 7.4 •	92.2± 5.7	86.7± 8.5	91.6± 6.9
segment	89.9± 2.1	91.2± 1.7	71.2± 7.5 •	90.7± 1.7
sonar	83.0± 8.1	85.1± 6.9	72.6±11.0 •	84.0± 7.8
spectrometer	77.7± 5.2	81.3± 4.9	81.6± 5.1	81.7± 5.4
vehicle	60.7± 4.5	66.4± 5.0	55.7± 7.1 •	64.0± 5
wdbc	95.4± 3.1	96.4± 2.3	95.1± 3.2	95.8± 3.8
wine	98.4± 2.8	95.3± 4.8	95.9± 4.8	95.4± 4.8
yeast	58.9± 4.0	52.9± 4.0	54.9± 4.9	54.9± 3.8
Average	80.94	82.56	78.29	82.60

UCI data are small, rendering statistical comparisons more difficult. This is why we decided to run a separate comparison on the five ImageNet data sets. They are multi-class classification problems and also exhibit a very high skew in the distribution of $N_k(x)$.

The three algorithms – kNN, hw-kNN and NHBNN were compared on five ImageNet subsets and the results are given in Table 3. The comparisons were performed for a fixed neighborhood of $k = 5$. The threshold θ in NHBNN was set to zero so that neither local or global estimate is used, only what information is available from the point label and hubness. We opted for such a configuration to show that, even though the local and global approach described in the paper provide greater flexibility in dealing with anti-hubs, they are by no means necessary for the basic idea to function.

The results from this third experimental setup differ greatly from the previous two, showing an even more convincing difference between NHBNN and kNN on high-dimensional data, as well as enabling us to differentiate between hw-kNN and NHBNN. On these data sets, we see that using class-specific hubness does, indeed, lead to better results. The improvement is usually modest, but this is due to the fact that both algorithms exploit the same phenomenon – hubness. However, NHBNN is to be preferred in cases when dealing with intrinsically high-dimensional multi-class data.

5. CONCLUSIONS AND FUTURE WORK

We presented a novel algorithm for probabilistic NN classification, naive hubness Bayesian k-NN (NHBNN). Hubness is a phenomenon inherent to high-dimensional data which has only recently been taken into serious consideration and has never before been used in a Bayesian framework. We have shown in this paper that taking point hubness into account may be beneficial to nearest-neighbor methods and that it should be more thoroughly investigated. The proposed algorithm differs in its conception greatly from the probabilistic k-nearest neighbor (PNN) and related methods, therefore representing an alternative approach that is open for further improvements.

Table 3: Comparison of NHBNN with kNN and hw-kNN on ImageNet data for $k = 5$. The symbols ∘/• denote statistically significant better/worse performance with respect to NHBNN for $p < 0.01$ and $*$ denotes those cases when NHBNN is deemed better at significance level $0.01 \leq p < 0.05$.

Data set	kNN	hw-kNN	NHBNN
ImgNet-s3	72.0±2.7 •	80.8±2.3	81.8±2.3
ImgNet-s4	56.2±2.0 •	63.3±1.9 *	64.6±1.9
ImgNet-s5	46.6±2.0 •	56.3±1.7 •	61.8±1.9
ImgNet-s6	60.1±2.2 •	68.1±1.6 *	69.4±1.7
ImgNet-s7	43.4±1.7 •	55.1±1.5 •	58.2±1.5
Average	55.66	64.72	67.16

Acknowledgments. This work was supported by bilateral project between Slovenia and Serbia "Correlating Images and Words: Enhancing Image Analysis Through Machine Learning and Semantic Technologies," the Slovenian Research Agency, the Serbian Ministry of Education and Science through project no. OI174023, "Intelligent Techniques and Their Integration into Wide-Spectrum Decision Support," and the ICT Programme of the EC under PASCAL2 (ICT-NoE-216886) and PlanetData (ICT-NoE-257641).

6. REFERENCES

[1] T. Cover and P. Hart. Nearest neighbor pattern classification. *IEEE T Inform Theory*, 13:21–27, 1967.

[2] L. Cucala, J. M. Marin, C. P. Robert, and D. M. Titterington. A Bayesian reassessment of nearest-neighbor classification. *J Am Stat Assoc*, 104:263–273, 2009.

[3] R. J. Durrant and A. Kabán. When is 'nearest neighbour' meaningful: A converse theorem and implications. *J Complexity*, 25(4):385–397, 2009.

[4] D. François, V. Wertz, and M. Verleysen. The concentration of fractional distances. *IEEE T Knowl Data En*, 19:873–886, 2007.

[5] R. Guo and S. Chakraborty. Bayesian adaptive nearest neighbor. *Stat Anal Data Min*, 3:92–105, 2010.

[6] C. C. Holmes and N. M. Adams. A probabilistic nearest neighbor method for statistical pattern recognition. *J R Stat Soc B*, 64:295–306, 2002.

[7] S. Manocha and M. A. Girolami. An empirical analysis of the probabilistic k-nearest neighbour classifier. *Pattern Recogn Lett*, 28:1818–1824, 2007.

[8] M. Radovanović, A. Nanopoulos, and M. Ivanović. Hubs in space: Popular nearest neighbors in high-dimensional data. *J Mach Learn Res*, 11:2487–2531, 2010.

[9] I. Rish. An empirical study of the naive Bayes classifier. In *Proc. IJCAI Workshop on Empirical Methods in Artificial Intelligence*, 2001.

[10] N. Tomašev, M. Radovanović, M. Ivanović, and D. Mladenić. Hubness-based fuzzy measures for high-dimensional k-nearest neighbor classification. In *Proc. 7th Int. Conf. on Machine Learning and Data Mining (MLDM)*, 2011.

[11] Z. Zhang and R. Zhang. *Multimedia Data Mining: a Systematic Introduction to Concepts and Theory*. Chapman and Hall, 2008.

Representing Document as Dependency Graph for Document Clustering

Yujing Wang[1]*, Xiaochuan Ni[2], Jian-Tao Sun[2], Yunhai Tong[1], Zheng Chen[2]

[1]Key Laboratory of Machine Perception
Peking University
Beijing 100871, P. R. China
{wangyj, tongyh}@cis.pku.edu.cn

[2]Microsoft Research Asia
No.5 Danling Street, Haidian District
Beijing 100080, P. R. China
{xini, jtsun, zhengc}@microsoft.com

ABSTRACT

In traditional clustering methods, a document is often represented as "bag of words" (in BOW model) or n-grams (in suffix tree document model) without considering the natural language relationships between the words. In this paper, we propose a novel approach DGDC (Dependency Graph-based Document Clustering algorithm) to address this issue. In our algorithm, each document is represented as a dependency graph where the nodes correspond to words which can be seen as meta-descriptions of the document; whereas the edges stand for the relations between pairs of words. A new similarity measure is proposed to compute the pairwise similarity of documents based on their corresponding dependency graphs. By applying the new similarity measure in the *Group-average* Agglomerative Hierarchial Clustering (GAHC) algorithm, the final clusters of documents can be obtained. The experiments were carried out on five public document datasets. The empirical results have indicated that the DGDC algorithm can achieve better performance in document clustering tasks compared with other approaches based on the BOW model and suffix tree document model.

Categories and Subject Descriptors

I.5.3 [**Pattern Recognition**]: Clustering - *algorithms, similarity measures*; H.3.1 [**Content Analysis and Indexing**]: Linguistic processing; I.2.7 [**Artificial Intelligence**]: Natural Language Processing - *text analysis*

General Terms

Algorithms, Experimentation

*This work is done when the first author is visiting Microsoft Research Asia.

CIKM'11, October 24–28, 2011, Glasgow, Scotland, UK.

Keywords

Document Clustering, Dependency Graph, Document Representation Model, Similarity Measure

1. INTRODUCTION

Document clustering techniques usually rely on four modules: document representation model, similarity measure, clustering model and the clustering algorithm which generates clusters based on the document representation model [5]. Among all these modules, the document representation model is very fundamental and crucial for the clustering results.

The most basic model for document representation is the Vector Space Document (VSD) model. In this model, the document is regarded as "bag of words" (BOW), without considering the relationships between the words. In order to achieve better clustering results, many efforts have been made to seek more informative document representation models. The n-gram model [12] is one of those efforts, which can be viewed as an extension of BOW model but includes all ordered sequences of less than n words in the feature vector. The suffix tree document model [14] considers a document to be a set of suffix substrings and constructs a suffix tree using substrings of all documents in the corpus. It provides a flexible n-gram approach by identifying all overlapping phrases among documents as Longest Common Prefixes (LCPs) [9]. Some research works [7, 6, 13] also leveraged ontologies to enrich the representation of documents. WordNet [6], Mesh [13] and Wikipedia [7] have been adopted and improvements were achieved in document clustering tasks. However, the pairwise relationships of words which are suggested in the natural language sentences are still ignored in these document representation models.

In this paper, we propose a more informative document representation model, namely the Dependency Graph-based Document (DGD) model. In this model, each document is represented as a dependency graph where each node corresponds to a word which can be seen as a meta-description of the document. The edges between nodes are used to catch the semantic relations between word pairs. A novel similarity measure is also proposed for calculating the similarity of documents based on their corresponding dependency graphs. The Dependency Graph-based Document Clustering (DGDC) algorithm is conducted in the following steps: (1) Construct a dependency graph for each document. (2) Calculate the similarity of each pair of documents based on the novel similarity measure. (3) Generate the final clusters of documents by the *Group-average* Agglomerative Hierarchical Clustering (GAHC) algorithm [14]. The experiments were carried out on five public document datasets. The empirical results have indicated that the DGDC algorithm can achieve better performance in document clustering tasks compared with other approaches based on the BOW model and the suffix tree document model.

2. DEPENDENCY GRAPH-BASED DOCUMENT CLUSTERING ALGORITHM

2.1 Dependency Graph-based Document Model

Suppose d is a document with a vocabulary set $W = \{w_1, w_2, ..., w_n\}$, where w_i stands for a word which appears in d and $w_i \neq w_j$ for $\forall i \neq j$. Since stopwords (e.g., the, is) count little for the meaning of the whole document, we exclude them from the vocabulary set. The dependency graph G corresponding to document d is denoted as $G = (V, E)$. $V = \{v_1, v_2, ..., v_n\}$ is the set of vertices in the graph, where each vertex v_i corresponds to w_i in the vocabulary set. $E = \{e_1, e_2, ..., e_m\}$ is the collection of edges, where each edge e_j is associated to a pair of vertices, which indicates that there is some relationship between them.

Consider a document A, which has the content "Beijing is a big city. The city is very beautiful". Figure 1 shows the dependency graph corresponding to the document. Assume that we have two documents A and B. A is "Beijing is a big city. The city is very beautiful". B is "Beijing is a very beautiful city which is big". These two documents have the same semantic meaning so that they should have high similarity between each other. However, as they are literally organized by different word sequences, the similarity is much lower than expected according to the n-gram model and the suffix tree document model. In our model, document A and B correspond to the same dependency graph which correctly indicates that they are semantically equal with each other.

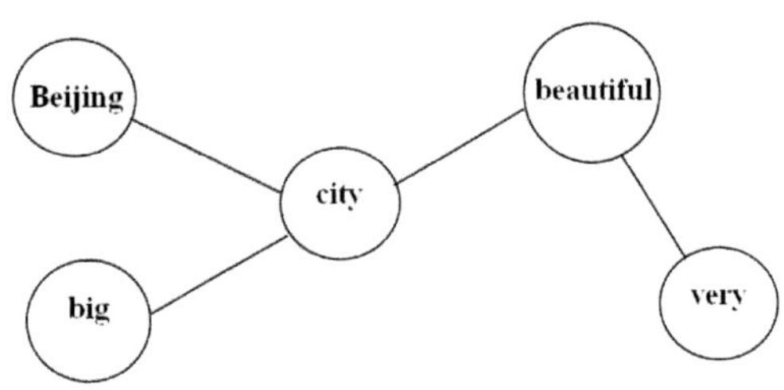

Figure 1: The dependency graph generated for "Beijing is a big city. The city is very beautiful."

In practice, a dependency parser (e.g. the Stanford parser [2]) is needed to obtain word relations from the original sentences. Using the parser, the dependency graph can be constructed in the following steps. Initially, there are no vertices and edges in the graph. Then the vertices and edges are added by processing each sentence in the document sequentially. For each sentence, we parse it using the dependency parser, which outputs a set of words and the identified pairwise relations between them. The non-stopwords are then added to the vertex set if they are not contained in the graph before. Thus, each non-stopword in the output is associated with one vertex in the graph. Finally, for each pairwise relation suggested by the parser, a new edge will be generated between the corresponding vertices if it does not exist in the graph.

2.2 Similarity Measure

Given a dependency graph $G = (V, E)$, suppose the vertex is denoted by v_i and w_i is the word corresponding to v_i. The weight of vertex v_i associated to document d can be calculated by the traditional *tf-idf* measure.

After representing the documents as weighted dependency graphs, the similarity of two documents can be calculated based on their corresponding graphs. Suppose there are two documents d_1 and d_2 in the global corpus D, whose corresponding graphs are $G_1 = (V_1, E_1)$ and $G_2 = (V_2, E_2)$ respectively. $V_1 \bigcup V_2$ is the collection of nodes contained in G_1 and G_2, where the nodes corresponding to the same word are considered the same. The feature weight matrix R_1 for document d_1 is defined as $R_1 = \{r_{ij} | 0 \leq i, j < |V_1 \bigcup V_2|\}$. When $i = j$, r_{ij} is actually the weight of single word feature denoted by node v_i. When $i \neq j$, r_{ij} measures the importance of the relation between v_i and v_j.

Mathematically, r_{ij} is defined as:

$$r_{ij} = \begin{cases} c(v_i, d_1) \cdot \beta & \text{if } i = j \\ \sqrt{c(v_i, d_1) \cdot c(v_j, d_1)} \cdot f_{G_1}(v_i, v_j) & \text{otherwise} \end{cases} \quad (1)$$

where $c(v_i, d_1)$ is the weight of vertex v_i associated to document d_1. β is a constant coefficient to balance single word features (when $i = j$) and relation features (when $i \neq j$). $f_{G_1}(v_i, v_j)$ is a penalty function which depicts how tightly the vertex v_i and v_j are connected with each other in G_1. It can be calculated by:

$$f_{G_1}(v_i, v_j) = \begin{cases} 0 & \text{if } v_i \notin V_1 \text{ or } v_j \notin V_1 \\ \left(\frac{1}{dist_{G_1}(v_i, v_j)}\right)^{\alpha} & \text{otherwise} \end{cases} \quad (2)$$

where $dist_{G_1}(v_i, v_j)$ is the distance (length of the shortest path) between v_i and v_j in G_1, α is a penalty coefficient. The lengths of all the edges in the graph are set to 1.

Let $R_1 = \{r_1(i,j)\}$ and $R_2 = \{r_2(i,j)\}$, The similarity of these two feature weight matrixes is computed by

$$Sim(R_1, R_2) = \sum_{i \leq j} r_1(i,j) \cdot r_2(i,j) \quad (3)$$

Consequently, the similarity of two documents d_1 and d_2 is defined as:

$$Sim(d_1, d_2) = \frac{Sim(R_1, R_2)}{\sqrt{Sim(R_1, R_1) \cdot Sim(R_2, R_2)}} \quad (4)$$

such that $Sim(d_1, d_2) \in [0, 1]$.

2.3 Clustering Algorithm

The *Group-average* Agglomerative Hierarchical Clustering (GAHC) algorithm is adopted in the cluster generating procedure. The algorithm considers each document as a unique cluster initially and selects a pair of clusters to merge repeatedly in the merging procedure. In each turn, the pair of most similar clusters are selected to be merged. The similarity of two clusters is calculated by the *group-average* measure.

One important issue for hierarchical clustering is to determine which step to terminate in the merging procedure [11]. One way to solve this problem is using a pre-defined number of clusters or setting a constant threshold of similarity for termination. However, neither of the strategies are practical for various kinds of corpus in applications. Motivated by [11], we leverage the R^2 criterion to determine the terminating point in the merging procedure.

The R^2 value represents the proportion of variance accounted for by the clusters, which is estimated by:

$$R^2 = 1 - \frac{\sum_k \sum_{d_i,d_j \in C_k} Dist(d_i, d_j)}{\sum_{d_i,d_j \in D} Dist(d_i, d_j)} \quad (5)$$

where C_k stands for the kth cluster, $Dist(d_i, d_j) \in [0, 1]$ estimates the distance between document d_i and d_j. We define:

$$Dist(d_i, d_j) = 1 - Sim(d_i, d_j) \quad (6)$$

We can plot R^2 with respect to the number of remaining clusters in each step. The place where the curve levels off is selected to be the terminating point.

3. EXPERIMENTS

3.1 Experimental Setup

We select five public document datasets: *CSTR*, *Reuters3*, *News-diff3*, *News-sim3* and *News-mod6*, which are commonly used to evaluate document clustering and categorization methods. *CSTR*[1] consists of abstracts for technical reports. *Reuters3* is generated from the *Reuters-21578*[2] corpus. We choose three popular topics (grain, trade, and crude) and randomly select 100 documents for each topic. *News-diff3*, *News-sim3* and *News-mod6* datasets [1] are derived from the *20-Newsgroups* corpus[3]. The *News-diff3* dataset consists of three different newsgroups (alt.atheism, rec.sport.baseball, and sci.space) and the *News-sim3* dataset contains three similar newsgroups (comp.graphics, comp.os.ms-windows.misc, and comp.windows.x). The *News-mod6* dataset consists of 600 documents from 6 newsgroups (rec.sport.baseball, sci.space, alt.atheism, talk.politics.guns, comp.windows.x, and soc.religion.christian). In the *News-mod6* dataset, some topics are similar while others are different from each other. Table 1 summarizes the characteristics of these five datasets.

Table 1: Summary of datasets

Dataset	Number of document	Number of class	Average document length (by word)
CSTR	635	4	149.4
Reuters3	300	3	463.0
news-diff3	300	3	363.9
news-sim3	300	3	397.9
news-mod6	600	6	649.8

[1] *http://www.cs.rochester.edu/trs*

[2] *http://www.daviddlewis.com/resources/testcollections/*

[3] http://people.csail.mit.edu/jrennie/20Newsgroups/

Three metrics are adopted in our experiments to evaluate the performance of document clustering: *normalized mutual information (NMI)* [4], *F-measure* [3] and *purity* [15].

In our experiments, the Stanford parser[4] [8] is used to obtain word dependencies. The Porter stemming algorithm [10] is utilized to stem the words in original documents. Instead of using a standard stopword list, we determine the stopwords by calculating the document frequency *df* of each word, similar to that in [3]. A word w_i is considered to be stopword if $\frac{df(w_i)}{|D|} > 0.5$, where $df(w_i)$ is the number of documents containing w_i in the global corpus and $|D|$ is the size of global corpus. The parameters in the similarity measure are set as $\alpha = 0.5$ and $\beta = 0.5$ experimentally.

The baseline approach utilizes the "bag of words" (BOW) model for document representation and weights each word in the feature vector by *tf-idf* measure. We also compare our algorithm with NSTC [3] method, which represents the documents as a suffix tree and performs clustering based on a suffix tree similarity measure. According to [3], the maximum length of Longest Common Prefixes (LCPs) in the suffix tree is set to be 5. To obtain a fair comparison between the DGDC algorithm and other approaches, we adopt the same way of word stemming and stopword recognition. Moreover, the *Group-average* Agglomerative Hierarchical Clustering algorithm is utilized to generate clusters in all the three approaches and the R^2 criterion is adopted to determine the cluster number.

3.2 Results

Firstly, we demonstrate the feasibility of using R^2 criterion to determine the actual stop point in the *Group-average* Agglomerative Hierarchical Clustering (GAHC) algorithm. An example is illustrated by applying the DGDC algorithm on *news-diff3* dataset. Figure 2 plots the R^2 value with respect to the number of remaining clusters in each step. It can be noticed that the curve levels off at point A (the number of clusters is 9 and the value of R^2 is 0.851) in the figure, so that the merging procedure will be terminated when the number of remaining clusters equals to 9. As shown in Figure 3, it is exactly the point where the best performance can be achieved. Therefore, the R^2 criterion provides an appropriate and practical way to determine the point of termination in the merging procedure.

Secondly, we compare our algorithm with other approaches. The clustering results of different algorithms on five datasets are shown in Table 2, measured by *NMI*, *F-measure* and *purity* respectively. The number of remaining clusters is also listed to indicate the place of termination. As shown in Table 2, the DGDC algorithm outperforms other approaches on all the five datasets.

4. CONCLUSION AND DISCUSSION

In this paper, we propose a novel document representation model. A new similarity measure for documents is also proposed, which calculates the similarity based on dependency graphs. The similarity measure is applied to the *Group-average* Agglomerative Hierarchical Clustering (GAHC) algorithm and promising results are obtained in the document clustering experiments.

[4] The parser is available for download as open source at: http://nlp.stanford.edu/downloads/lex-parser.shtml

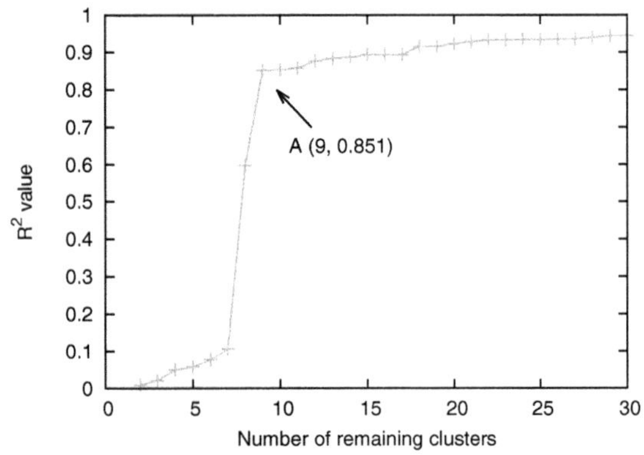

Figure 2: The plot of R^2 value with respect to the number of remaining clusters

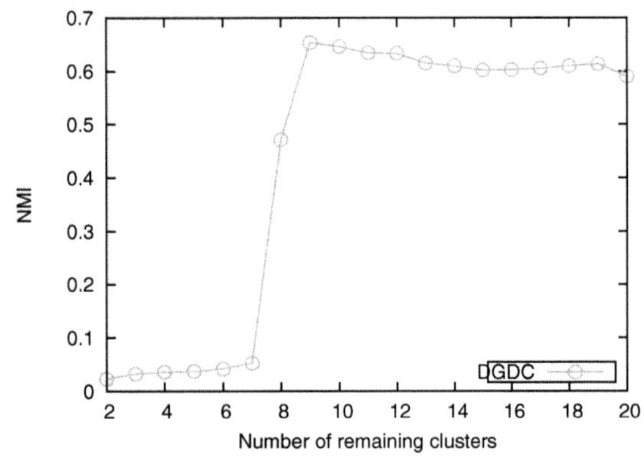

Figure 3: The plot of *NMI* value by DGDC algorithm on *news-diff3* dataset

Although good results have been achieved, we have to point out the limitation of the algorithm. Firstly, it takes $O(Nm^2 \log m + N^2m^2)$ to calculate all the pairwise similarities of documents, where N stands for the number of documents in the corpus and m represents the average word length of the documents. This high time complexity will make the algorithm computationally prohibitive for clustering tasks that deal with large corpus. Moreover, the R^2 criterion used in this approach for cluster number estimation is not fully automatic and sometimes needs manual efforts to help.

Table 2: Clustering results on five datasets

Algorithm	NMI	F-measure	Purity	Number of clusters
CSTR				
DGDC	**0.654**	**0.862**	**0.872**	10
NSTC	0.593	0.797	0.775	11
BOW	0.597	0.769	0.820	18
Reuters3				
DGDC	**0.592**	**0.778**	**0.897**	13
NSTC	0.468	0.671	0.850	10
BOW	0.532	0.706	0.887	13
News-diff3				
DGDC	**0.657**	**0.893**	0.903	10
NSTC	0.648	0.888	**0.913**	8
BOW	0.505	0.790	0.863	17
News-mod6				
DGDC	**0.767**	**0.834**	**0.810**	15
NSTC	0.738	0.819	0.795	16
BOW	0.734	0.814	0.807	20
News-sim3				
DGDC	**0.251**	**0.471**	**0.713**	16
NSTC	0.221	0.444	0.663	20
BOW	0.210	0.464	0.637	20

5. REFERENCES

[1] A. Banerjee, I. Dhillon, J. Ghosh, and S. Sra. Generative model-based clustering of directional data. In *Proceedings of KDD'03*, pages 19–28.

[2] D. Cer, M.-C. de Marneffe, D. Jurafsky, and C. Manning. Parsing to stanford dependencies: Trade-offs between speed and accuracy. In *Proceedings of LREC'2010*, pages 1628–1632.

[3] H. Chim and X. Deng. A new suffix tree similarity measure for document clustering. In *Proceedings of WWW'07*, pages 218–225.

[4] B. E. Dom. An information-theoretic external cluster-validity measure. *Research Report RJ 10219, IBM*, 2001.

[5] K. M. Hammouda and M. S. Kamel. Efficient phrase-based document indexing for web document clustering. *IEEE Transactions on Knowledge and Data Engineering*, 16(10):1279–1296, 2004.

[6] A. Hotho, S. Staab, and G. Stumme. Wordnet improves text document clustering. In *Proceedings of Semantic Web Workshop, SIGIR'03.*

[7] X. Hu, X. Zhang, C. Lu, E. K. Park, and X. Zhou. Exploiting wikipedia as external knowledge for document clustering. In *Proceedings of KDD'09*, pages 389–396.

[8] D. Klein and C. Manning. Accurate unlexicalized parsing. In *Proceedings of the 41st Annual Meeting of the Association for Computational Linguistics*, 2003.

[9] U. manber and G. Myers. Suffix arrays: a new method for on-line string searches. *SIAM Journal on Computing*, 22(5):935–948, 1993.

[10] M. Porter. New models in probabilistic information retrieval. *British Library Research and development Report No.5587*, 1980.

[11] W. S. Sarle. Cubic clustering criterion. *SAS Technical Report A-108*, Cary, NC: SAS Institute Inc. 1980.

[12] A. Tomovic, P. Janicic, and V. KeŽelj. N-gram-based classification and unsupervised hierarchical clustering of genome sequences. *Computer Methods and Programs in Biomedicine*, 81(2):137–153, 2006.

[13] I. Yoo, X. Hu, and I.-Y. Song. Integration of semantic-based bipartite graph representation and mutual refinement strategy for biomedical literature clustering. In *Proceedings of KDD'06*, pages 791–796.

[14] O. zamir and O. Etzioni. Web document clustering: A feasibility demonstration. In *Proceedings of SIGIR'98.*

[15] Y. Zhao and G. Karypis. Criterion functions for document clustering: Experiments and analysis. *Technical Report, Department of Computer Science, University of Minnesota*, 2002.

Finding Redundant and Complementary Communities in Multidimensional Networks

Michele Berlingerio
KDDLab ISTI-CNR
Via G. Moruzzi, 1, 56124
Pisa, Italy
michele.berlingerio@isti.cnr.it

Michele Coscia
KDDLab University of Pisa
Largo B. Pontecorvo, 3, 56127
Pisa, Italy
coscia@di.unipi.it

Fosca Giannotti
KDDLab ISTI-CNR
Via G. Moruzzi, 1, 56124
Pisa, Italy
fosca.giannotti@isti.cnr.it

ABSTRACT

Community Discovery in networks is the problem of detecting, for each node, its membership to one of more groups of nodes, the *communities*, that are densely connected, or highly interactive. We define this problem for multidimensional networks, i.e. where more than one connection may reside between any two nodes. We introduce two measures able to characterize the communities found. Our experiments on real world data support the methodology proposed, and open the way for a new class of algorithms, aimed at capturing the multifaceted complexity of connections among nodes in a network.

Categories and Subject Descriptors: G.2.2 [Graph Theory]: Graph Algorithms; H.2.8 [Database Applications]: Data Mining

General Terms: Algorithms, Theory

Keywords: Multidimensional Network Analysis, Community Discovery

1. INTRODUCTION

Inspired by real-world scenarios such as social networks, technology networks, the Web, and so on, in the last years, wide and multidisciplinary research has been devoted to the extraction of non trivial knowledge from such networks. One crucial task in network analysis is Community Discovery, i.e., the discovery of group of nodes densely connected, or highly related. There exist many techniques able to identify communities in networks [2], allowing to detect hierarchical connections, influential nodes in communities, or just group of nodes that share some properties or behaviors. Among the most popular approaches, we recall: the prolific modularity-oriented class [1]; a label propagation approach [5]; and a community discovery algorithm based on random walks [4]. Most of the existing approaches are limited to monodimensional networks, i.e. networks where there can be only one interaction between any two nodes. We deal with *multidimensional networks*, where multiple connections may exist between a pair of nodes, reflecting various interactions (i.e., dimensions) between them. Multidimensionality in real networks may be expressed by either different types of connections (two persons may be connected because they are friends, colleagues, and so on), or different quantitative values of one specific relation (co-authorship between two authors may occur in several different years, for example). In this scenario, we introduce the problem of *Multidimensional Community Discovery*. An example of multidimensional community discovery algorithm exists in literature. In [3] the authors extend the definition of modularity to fit to the multidimensional case, which they call "multislice". However, in this work authors do not consider any definition of "multidimensional community", neither they characterize and analyze the communities found.Instead, we define a concept of multidimensional community, and we introduce two new measures aimed at analyzing the multidimensional properties of the communities discovered. We then show the results obtained by applying our framework on real-world networks, giving a few examples of interesting multidimensional communities found in a movie collaboration network.

CIKM'11, October 24–28, 2011, Glasgow, Scotland, UK.

2. FINDING AND CHARACTERIZING MULTIDIMENSIONAL COMMUNITIES

We use a *multigraph* to model a multidimensional network and its properties. For the sake of simplicity, in our model we only consider undirected multigraphs and since we do not consider node labels, hereafter we use *edge-labeled undirected multigraphs*, denoted by a triple $\mathcal{G} = (V, E, D)$ where: V is a set of nodes; D is a set of labels; E is a set of labeled edges, i.e. the set of triples (u, v, d) where $u, v \in V$ are nodes and $d \in D$ is a label. Also, we use the term *dimension* to indicate *label*, and we say that a node *belongs to* or *appears in* a given dimension d if there is at least one edge labeled with d adjacent to it. We assume that given a pair of nodes $u, v \in V$ and a label $d \in D$ only one edge (u, v, d) may exist. Thus, each pair of nodes in $\mathcal{G}$ can be connected by at most $|D|$ possible edges.

2.1 Multidimensional Community

Adding multidimensionality to the problem of community discovery leads to an opinable concept of multidimensional community. We start with a high-level possible definition, then we add more semantic to it.

Definition 1 (Multidimensional Community). *A* multidimensional community *is a set of nodes densely connected in a multidimensional network.*

While in a monodimensional network the density of a com-

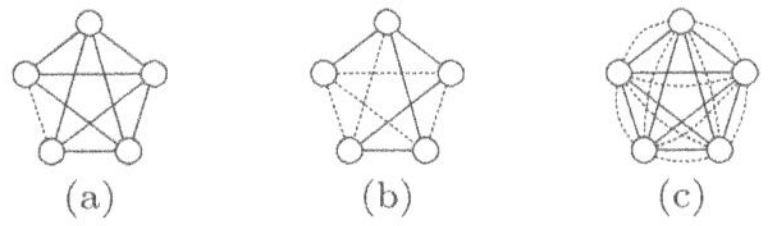

Figure 1: Multidimensional communities

munity refers unambiguously to the ratio between the number of edges among the nodes and the number of all possible edges, the multidimensional setting offers an additional degree of freedom. Consider Figure 1: in (a) we have a community whose density mostly depends by the connectivity provided by one dimension; in (b) we have a different situation, as both the dimensions are contributing to the density of the community. Should the two be considered equivalent or can we discern among them? In order to answer this question, we define two measures, γ and ρ, aimed at capturing two different phenomena that can be detected in a community. Hereafter, we use this notation: c is a multidimensional community; d is a dimension in D; D_c is the subset of D appearing in c; P is set of pairs (u, v) connected by at least one dimension in the network; $\overline{P} \subseteq P$ is the set of pairs (u, v) connected exclusively by one dimension; $\overline{\overline{P}} = P \setminus \overline{P}$ is the set of pairs connected by at least two dimensions; P_c is the subset of P appearing in c; $P_{c,d}$ is the set of pairs (u, v) in c connected at least in d and $\overline{P_{c,d}} \subseteq P_{c,d}$ is the set of pairs (u, v) in c connected exclusively in d; $\overline{\overline{P_c}} \subseteq \overline{\overline{P}}$ is the subset of $\overline{\overline{P}}$ containing only pairs in c.

2.2 Complementarity γ

The first measure, γ, that we call *complementarity*, is the conjunction of three concepts: **variety** $\mathcal{V}_c$, i.e. how many different dimensions are detectable among the community c; **exclusivity** $\mathcal{E}_c$, i.e. how many pairs of nodes are connected by just one dimension within c; **homogeneity** $\mathcal{H}_c$, i.e. how uniform is the distribution of the number of edges per dimension in c. We want this measure to be higher when each of the above is high. A natural way to achieve this is to aggregate them by their product:

$$\gamma_c = \mathcal{V}_c \times \mathcal{E}_c \times \mathcal{H}_c \tag{1}$$

We now have to define the three concepts. Variety can be computed by

$$\mathcal{V}_c = \frac{|D_c| - 1}{|D| - 1} \tag{2}$$

as the number of dimensions expressed with the community c over the total number of dimensions within the network. The two negative terms serve as corrections to make Variety take values in $[0, 1]$. Note that Variety defined as above would be undefined when $|D| = 1$, but this would mean having a monodimensional network, where the use of γ would be meaningless.

Exclusivity can be computed as the ratio between the number of exclusive connections within the community and the total number of connected pairs in c:

$$\mathcal{E}_c = \frac{\sum_{d \in D} |\overline{P_{c,d}}|}{|P_c|} \tag{3}$$

This term is equal to zero when there are no exclusive connections, i.e. every pair of nodes in c is connected by at least two dimensions, while it is equal to one when every pair in c is connected by only one dimension. The formula is not defined for $|P_c| = 0$, which happens only for communities of only one node, for which it has no sense to compute γ.

Finally, we have to define Homogeneity. We want this term to be equal to one when the edges within the community are uniformly distributed among the dimensions represented in c. The simplest way to measure this is to look at the standard deviation of the distribution of the edges in c on the dimensions. We define:

$$\sigma_c = \sqrt{\frac{\sum_{d \in D} (|P_{c,d}| - avg_c)^2}{|D|}} \tag{4}$$

where avg_c is the mean of the distribution, as the standard deviation of the number of edges per dimension in c, and:

$$\sigma_c^{max} = \sqrt{\frac{(max(|P_{c,d}|) - 1)^2}{2}} \tag{5}$$

where $max(|P_{c,d}|)$ is the number of edges belonging to the dimension more represented in c, as the maximum theoretic standard deviation. Then, we can define Homogeneity as:

$$\mathcal{H}_c = 1 - \frac{\sigma_c}{\sigma_c^{max}} \tag{6}$$

where we subtract the right term to one, in order to make $\mathcal{H}_c$ equal to one when the right term is zero, i.e. when the edges are uniformly distributed among the different dimensions.

If we could have the complete set of communities of a network, we could make a more precise estimation of σ_c^{max}:

$$\sigma_c^{max} = \sqrt{\frac{(max(|P_{c,d}|) - min(|P_{c,d}|))^2}{2}} \tag{7}$$

where $min(|P_{c,d}|)$ is the number of edges belonging to the dimension having the lowest number of edges among all the communities.

In the exceptional case in which all the communities would see all the dimensions represented with the same number of edges, the two normalization coefficients σ_c^{max} would be equal to zero, making the right term of Equation 3 undefined. In this case, being the denominator an upper bound, also the numerator would be equal to zero. But this is the ideal topology of a network where the Homogeneity is maximum since all the edges are uniformly distributed, and then we can handle this case, without lack of generality, by defining $\mathcal{H}_c$ as:

$$\mathcal{H}_c = \begin{cases} 1 & \text{if } \sigma_c = 0 \\ 1 - \frac{\sigma_c}{\sigma_c^{max}} & \text{otherwise} \end{cases} \tag{8}$$

EXAMPLE 1 (MULTIDIMENSIONAL COMMUNITIES AND γ). *Consider Figure 1. We see three different multidimensional communities, each of them with different multidimensional structures: in (a), the standard deviation of the number of edges per dimension is the maximum possible, hence $\mathcal{H}_c = 0$, thus $\gamma = 0$; in (b), every term of the complementarity is equal to one, thus $\gamma = 1$; in (c), the exclusivity is zero, as every pair is connected by two dimensions, hence $\gamma = 0$.*

2.3 Redundancy ρ

The second measure we define is the *redundancy*, capturing the phenomenon for which a set of nodes that constitute a community in a dimension, constitute a community also in other dimensions. We can see this measure as a simple indicator of the redundancy of the connections: the more dimensions connect each pair of nodes within a community, the higher the redundancy will be. We can then define ρ by counting how many pairs have redundant connections, normalizing by the theoretical maximum:

$$\rho_c = \sum_{(u,v) \in \overline{\overline{P_c}}} \frac{|\{d : \exists (u, v, d) \in E\}|}{|D| \times |P_c|} \tag{9}$$

With the help of Figure 1 we see how ρ takes values in $[0, 1]$: in 1(b), each pair of nodes is connected in only one dimension, then $|\overline{\overline{P_c}}| = 0$ and the numerator is equal to zero; in 1(c), all the node pairs are connected in all the dimensions of D, which is equivalent to the number of connected pairs $|P_c|$ multiplied by the number of network dimensions $|D|$ (the denominator), making $\rho = 1$. We see that ρ is undefined for communities formed by one single node, where $|P_c| = 0$ and then the denominator is equal to zero. For this type of communities, however, the redundancy measure is not meaningful, thus we can ignore this case.

2.4 Problem definition

We can now formulate the problem under investigation:

PROBLEM 1 ($\mathcal{MCD}$). *Given a multidimensional network $\mathcal{G}$, find the complete set of multidimensional communities $\mathcal{C}$, and characterize each $c \in \mathcal{C}$ according to γ and ρ.*

3. A FRAMEWORK FOR $\mathcal{MCD}$

A complete solution for our problem would require to design an algorithm for extracting multidimensional communities, driven by the multidimensional density of the connections among nodes. However, it is difficult to define multidimensional density as universal, which is exactly what makes γ and ρ both meaningful. In addition, we believe that trivial design choices may lead to an algorithm producing communities with distributions of γ and ρ possibly unfairly unbalanced by the decisions taken. Moreover, we believe that the main contributions of this paper are the problem definition and the characterization of the communities by the introduction of γ and ρ. For all these reasons, here we propose a different solution based on existing, monodimensional, algorithms.

In order to be able to apply existing solutions to multidimensional network, and to be able to extract multidimensional communities, we have to introduce a mapping function ϕ able to transform a multidimensional network in a monodimensional one, trying to keep as much information as possible, and a function ϕ' which recovers multidimensional information from monodimensional communities. The logical workflow to solve $\mathcal{MCD}$ is then:

$$\mathcal{G} \xrightarrow{\phi} G \xrightarrow{CD} C \xrightarrow{\phi'} \mathcal{C} \rightarrow \gamma, \rho\ (c \in \mathcal{C}) \quad (10)$$

where ϕ is a function that converts a multidimensional network $\mathcal{G}$ to a monodimensional network G, CD is any algorithm for community discovery on monodimensional networks, ϕ' is a function that, for each monodimensional community c, restores the multidimensional connections originally residing among the nodes of c in $\mathcal{G}$, thus returning a set of multidimensional communities $\mathcal{C}$, on which we are then able to compute our evaluating functions γ and ρ.

3.1 Three possible ϕ mappings

There can be several different definitions for ϕ, leading to different monodimensional networks built from $\mathcal{G}$. One possible class of them can be designed by simply *flattening* multidimensional edges to monodimensional ones, possibly weighting the monodimensional edges by some functions of the original multidimensional structure. In the following we assume to use a weight-based class of ϕ functions, and we define three different weighting strategies ϕ.

The first we define is μ and requires to weight the (u, v) edge in G with 1 if there exists at least one dimension connecting u and v in $\mathcal{G}$, or, in formula:

$$\mu_{u,v} = \begin{cases} 1 & \text{if } \{\exists\, d : (u, v, d) \in E\} \\ 0 & \text{otherwise} \end{cases} \quad (11)$$

In the remainder of the paper, we refer is as ϕ_μ. This flattening clearly looses most of the multidimensional information residing in $\mathcal{G}$, except the neighborhood: any two nodes connected in $\mathcal{G}$ are also connected in G. One small improvement would be counting the number of dimensions connecting any two nodes u and v and using this as weight for the monodimensional edge added. We call this weight ν, which can be defined as:

$$\nu_{u,v} = |\{d : (u, v, d) \in E\}| \quad (12)$$

and we refer to the ϕ built upon ν as ϕ_ν.

We now consider a slight modification of ν that, instead of taking into account only the connection between u and v, also looks at their neighborhood, motivated by the intuition that common neighbors will likely be in the same community of u and v. We refer to this weight as η and define it as:

$$\eta_{u,v} = 1 + \frac{|N_{u,l} \cap N_{v,l}|}{|N_{u,l} \cup N_{v,l}| - 2} \quad (13)$$

where $N_{\cdot,l}$ is the set of neighbors in dimension d for a node. This is actually a multidimensional version of the clustering coefficient, and, according to the intuition behind it, should be able to better reflect the strength of the ties. We call ϕ_η the weight based on η. Note that there could be many other possible weighting strategy, as well as other different class of ϕ relying on different principles.However, to keep complexity low, and for sake of simplicity, in this paper we only examine the results obtained by using the three ϕ defined above.

3.2 The choice for CD

Any algorithm for community discovery can be used in our workflow, with one *caveat*: it should be able to handle edge weights. In our experiments, we present the results obtained by using an algorithm based on random walk [4], one based on label propagation [5] and one based of the fast greedy optimization of the modularity [1] as choices for possible monodimensional community discoverer. In our analysis we show how the choice among these three does not significantly affect the resulting distribution of γ and ρ.

3.3 Returning multidimensional communities

To get back restoring the original multidimensional information for each connected pair we only have to restore its original multidimensional connectivity in $\mathcal{G}$.

4. EXPERIMENTS

Our network was extracted from the Internet Movie Database (http://www.imdb.com). It is a collaboration network of years 2000-2009, where each node represents a person involved in a movie, and two persons are connected if they where involved in the same movie. We considered each year as a dimension of the network. Basic statistics of these networks are reported in Table 1. The framework, available for download[1], was implemented using R and igraph.

For the CD step, we chose three different algorithms: on based on random walk [4] (WT), one based on label propagation [5] (LP) and one based of the fast greedy optimization of the modularity [1] (FGM). WT and FGM returns the complete dendrograms of the communities, thus chose to take the cut maximizing the modularity as the best cut.

[1]http://kdd.isti.cnr.it/MCDF

Network	$\|V\|$	$\|E\|$	$\|P\|$	$\|D\|$	k	N	#cc	%GC	%SE
IMDb	28042	1291625	1131951	10	92.12	80.73	28	99.77	79.13

Table 1: Basic statistics: k is the average degree, N the average num. of neighbors, $\#cc$ the num. of connected components, $\%GC$ the ratio of nodes in the giant component, $\%SE$ is computed as $|\overline{P}|/|E|$

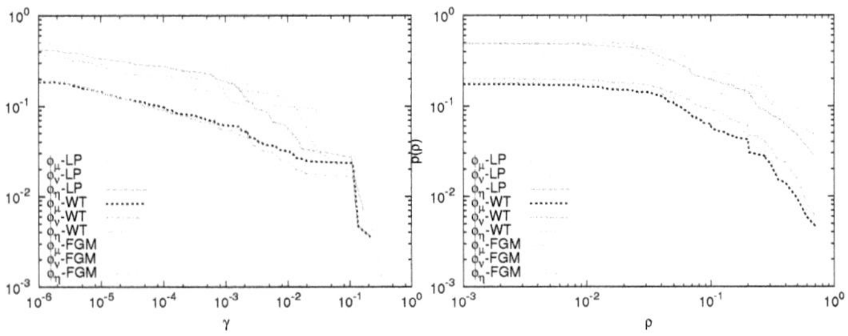

Figure 2: The cumulative distributions for γ and ρ in IMDb (color image).

Network	ϕ	LP		WT		FGM	
		$\|\mathcal{C}\|$	Q	$\|\mathcal{C}\|$	Q	$\|\mathcal{C}\|$	Q
IMDb	ϕ_μ	87	0.415	860	0.494	64	0.442
	ϕ_ν	124	**0.483**	847	**0.541**	66	**0.536**
	ϕ_η	148	0.460	823	0.507	63	0.530

Table 2: Communities ($|\mathcal{C}|$) and modularity (Q)

4.1 Quantitative Evaluation

Purpose of this section is to give a quantitative analysis of the results obtained driven by the following questions: **Q1** Can we evaluate the performances of the different choices of ϕ and CD? **Q2** How does the choice of ϕ and CD affect the distribution of γ and ρ over the communities? **Q3** What is the best choice of ϕ and CD parameters? In order to answer Q1, we looked at the values of the modularity measure (as defined in [1]), computed on the resulting set of communities C. This measure gives a value between -1 and 1, indicating how "good" nodes where partitioned into groups. The higher the value of modularity, the higher the partitioning reflects the division in the community of the graph that maximizes intra-community edges and minimizes inter-community edges. In Table 2 we report the modularity values, highlighting in bold, for each algorithm, which ϕ produced the highest value. We are interested in seeing whether a specific combination of ϕ and CD tends to produce higher scores. We notice that according best preprocessor was ϕ_ν , as it produces the best partition with each algorithm. In order to answer Q2, we analyzed the distribution of γ and ρ for the output of each ϕ-algorithm combination. These distributions are depicted in Figure 2. The distributions are generally overlapping and there is not a universally dominant combination. This confirms that our workflow does not significantly affect the distribution of the two measures. In addition, the information in Figure 2 may be used in conjunction with modularity in order to achieve richer knowledge about the results. Modularity, in fact, indicates how well the network is partitioned, and γ and/or ρ distributions characterize the multidimensional structure of the partitioning. One last consideration can be done looking at Table 2: there is no strong prevalence of one choice of parameters over the others. The same happens also for the distributions of γ and ρ. This suggest that the best answer for Q3 really depends on the final analysis of the network: the application scenario, the semantic of the dimensions and the time budget for running the experiments should drive

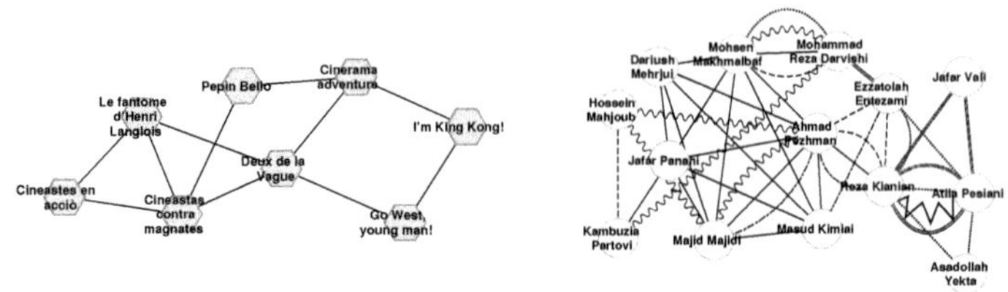

(a) high γ (0.005) in IMDb (b) high ρ (0.05) in IMDb

Figure 3: A few interesting communities found, with their γ or ρ.

the analyst towards the proper choice of the two parameters for our framework.

4.2 Analysis of Interesting Communities

We extracted two examples of communities with a relatively high (among the top 10%) score of γ and one with a relatively high ρ. We found one community with high complementarity, which was too large to be easily represented (more than 150 nodes). In Figure 3(a) we give a representation of it: each node is a clique within the community. Each group was found to represent a different documentary (titles provided as node labels) dedicated to a few important persons related to the cinema. The community has high complementarity because the personalities in a single documentary (such as Alfred Hitchcock or Jean-Luc Godard) are connected only by the year of release of the documentary itself, because they were not in activity in our sample of years, therefore not bound together by their own works. The connections between the documentaries are due to some movie stars present in both films. Redundancy in IMDb is able to identify large teams with continuous collaborations along many years. One group following this rule is composed by some masters of the Iranian cinema (Figure 3(b)), like Makhmalbaf and Panahi, both prominent directors in the Cannes and Venice Festivals.

5. CONCLUSIONS AND FUTURE WORK

We have addressed the problem of finding and characterizing communities in multidimensinal networks. We have given a possible definition of multidimensional community and then provided two different measures aimed at quantify and disambiguate the *density* of the community found, and devised a framework for our problem. Our results obtained on real world networks are encouraging, and provided a basis for future research on this direction. We plan to investigate the possibility of creating a multidimensional community discovery algorithm driven by γ and ρ scores.

6. REFERENCES

[1] Aaron Clauset, M. E. J. Newman, and Cristopher Moore. Finding community structure in very large networks. *Physical Review E*, 70:066111, 2004.

[2] Santo Fortunato. Community detection in graphs. *Physics Reports*, 486(3-5):75 – 174, 2010.

[3] P. J. Mucha, T. Richardson, K. Macon, M. A. Porter, and J.-P. Onnela. Community structure in time-dependent, multiscale, and multiplex networks. *Science 328, 876*, 2010.

[4] Pascal Pons and Matthieu Latapy. Computing communities in large networks using random walks. In *ISCIS 2005*, volume 3733, chapter 31, pages 284–293. Springer, Berlin, Heidelberg, 2005.

[5] Usha Nandini Raghavan, Reka Albert, and Soundar Kumara. Near linear time algorithm to detect community structures in large-scale networks. *Physical Review E*, 76:036106, 2007.

Promotional Subspace Mining with EProbe Framework

Yan Zhang
Vermont Information Processing
402 Watertower Circle
Colchester, Vermont 05446, U.S.A.
zxlm80@gmail.com

Yiyu Jia
Vermont Information Processing
402 Watertower Circle
Colchester, Vermont 05446, U.S.A.
yiyu.jia@gmail.com

Wei Jin
258 IACC Building A9
Dept. of Computer Science, North Dakota State Univ.
Fargo, North Dakota, 58108-6050, U.S.A.
wei.jin@ndsu.edu

ABSTRACT

In multidimensional data, Promotional Subspace Mining (PSM) aims to find out outstanding subspaces for a given object, and to discover meaningful rules from them. In PSM, one major research issue is to produce top subspaces efficiently given a predefined subspace ranking measure. A common approach is to achieve an exact solution, which searches through the entire subspace search space and evaluate the target object's rank in every subspace, assisted with possible pruning strategies. In this paper, we propose EProbe, an **E**fficient Subspace **Prob**ing framework. This novel framework strives to initialize the idea of "early stop" of the top subspace search process. The essential goal is to provide a scalable, cost-effective, and flexible solution where its accuracy can be traded with the efficiency using adjustable parameters. This framework is especially useful when the computation resources are insufficient and only a limited number of candidate subspaces can be evaluated. As a first attempt to seek solutions under EProbe framework, we propose two novel algorithms SRatio and SlidingCluster. In our experiments, we illustrate that these two algorithms could produce a more effective subspace traversal order. Being effective, the top-k subspaces included in the final results are shown to be evaluated in the early stage of the subspace traversal process.

Categories and Subject Descriptors
I.0 [Computing Methodologies]: GENERAL
General Terms: Algorithms
Keywords: promotional subspace mining, top subspaces, early stop

1. INTRODUCTION

In many real-world applications, objects are given ranks based on a predefined score measurement. Whether for a single person or a merchandize product, they can be ranked because there exist comparable objects in the same category. For examples, an athlete has other athletes as competitors in terms of the performance score; and a product has other similar products as competitors in terms of the sales revenue. It is worth noting that, for multi-dimensional data, a target object's rank may vary in different subspaces. To find out the potential top subspaces, in many areas, can be very useful.

CIKM'11, October 24–28, 2011, Glasgow, Scotland, UK.

One motivating application area is to promote the target object from the subspaces where it ranks high. For example, when promoting a notebook computer, the information "ranked the 3rd in terms of battery life" can be more informative than the information "ranked the 15th in an overall feature evaluation" for a potential buyer.

The problem then becomes, how to pinpoint these top subspaces? In [1], the authors proposed Promotion Query, a database query function with the functionality of returning top ranked subspaces with a multidimensional data set as the input. The authors propose two categories of methods: (1) evaluating through the entire subspace search space, assisted with some pruning techniques; and (2) constructing data cubes to make some calculations off-line, so as to achieve fast querying operations in OLAP applications. However, the major challenges that pose on these methods include the scalability issue, and the complexity of the data cubes' design & maintenance issue.

By considering these important research issues, we suggest a completely different approach for the problem of producing top subspaces in multi-dimensional data. We propose EProbe – an **E**fficient Subspace **Prob**ing framework. As opposed to commonly adopted strategies that produce an exact solution, this novel framework aims at generating a flexible solution where its accuracy can be traded with efficiency using adjustable parameters. The ideal situation is, when the computation resources suffice for the task, an exact solution will be produced; otherwise, the accuracy of the result can be sacrificed with the return of the computational speed-up.

As a first effort to implement this EProbe framework, we propose two heuristics, which lead to two novel algorithms SRatio and SlidingCluster. The former applies score ratio (SR) based subspace sorting to obtain a sorted subspace set. The latter further includes the design of subspace sampling from sliding subspace clusters. Both algorithms strive to achieve an "early stop" of the subspace search, when a certain number of top subspaces have been probed and evaluated. By using two evaluation metrics: AVG TraceIndex and Coverage, we compare SRatio and SlidingCluster with a baseline algorithm DFP (**D**epth **F**irst **P**arent Subspace Pruning). We show an remarkable superiority of algorithm SRatio (SlidingCluster with $w = 1$) over DFP; and a consistent and significant improvement of algorithm SlidingCluster over SRatio, when only a limited number of candidate subspaces can be evaluated.

The remaining of this article is organized as follows. In Section 2, we define relevant concepts and introduce necessary notations. In Section 3, we present the EProbe framework and the heuristics that generate algorithms SRatio and SlidingCluster. In Section 4, we describe our data and present the experimental results. We finally conclude this work and discuss our future work in Section 5.

2. PROBLEM STATEMENT

We first introduce the preliminaries and definitions in Section 2.1, then we formulate our problem in Section 2.2.

2.1 Preliminaries and Definitions

Assuming we are given a data set D, which consists of a set of n instances. Also assuming that D has d categorical attributes $A = \{A_1, A_2, \ldots, A_d\}$, an object attribute A_{obj} denoting object IDs, and a score attribute A_{score} denoting the non-negative score of the corresponding object in a specific subspace. We denote the domain in which a variable X takes value from as $\mathsf{dom}(X)$. Specifically, we denote the complete set of competitive objects by $O = \mathsf{dom}(A_{obj})$, in which the target object ID $t_a \in O$ is given by the user. We also have $\mathsf{dom}(A_{score}) = \mathbb{R}^+$. A subspace is represented as $S = \{A_1 = a_{11}, A_2 = a_{21}, \cdots, A_d = a_{d1}\}$, where $a_{i1} \in \mathsf{dom}(A_i)$ or $a_{i1} = *$. The value "*" refers to "any", which indicates any value in the corresponding attribute is included. S induces a projection of the data set $D_S(\subseteq D)$ and a subspace of objects $O_S(\subseteq O)$. We represent the full attribute space $S_* = \{A_1 = *, A_2 = *, \cdots, A_d = *\}$, a short form of which is $S_* = \{*\}$. We denote N_0 as the number of candidate spaces in the entire subspace search space.

Due to the space limit, please refer to [1] for the definitions of concepts "Parent-Child Subspace", "Seen-Unseen Subspace", "Rank of an object", "Significance Sig", and "Promotiveness P".

Definition 1: (SR: Score Ratio of an Object) If the score of target object A in subspace S is denoted as $\mathsf{SUM}^S(t_a)$, and the score of all the objects in S is denoted as $\sum_{t \in O_S} \mathsf{SUM}^S(t)$, the score ratio SR of t_a in S is defined as the ratio of these two measures, as shown in Eq. (1).

$$\mathsf{SR}_S(t_a) = \frac{\mathsf{SUM}^S(t_a)}{\sum_{t \in O_S} \mathsf{SUM}^S(t)} \tag{1}$$

Definition 2: (TraceIndex of a Subspace) The TraceIndex of subspace S, $\mathsf{TraceIndex}(S)$ is defined as the ordinal position, at which S is being evaluated. $\mathsf{TraceIndex}(S) \in [1, N_0]$.

Definition 3: (Distance: Distance between Two Subspaces) Given subspace $S_1 = \{A_1 = a_{11}, A_2 = a_{21}, \cdots, A_d = a_{d1}\}$, and subspace $S_2 = \{A_1 = a_{12}, A_2 = a_{22}, \cdots, A_d = a_{d2}\}$, the distance between S_1 and S_2 is defined as the Hamming Distance between S_1 and S_2, i.e. the number of positions at which the corresponding attribute values are different [2]. $\mathsf{Distance}(S_1, S_2)$ can be calculated as shown in Eq. (2).

$$\mathsf{Distance}(S_1, S_2) = \sum_{i=1}^{d} \mathcal{I}(a_{i1} \neq a_{i2}) \tag{2}$$

In Eq. (2), $\mathcal{I}$ denotes an indicator function, which returns 1 when the values on the corresponding attribute does not equal and 0 otherwise. If S_1 is a parent subspace of S_2, $\mathsf{Distance}(S_1, S_2) = \mathsf{Distance}(S_2, S_1) = 1$.

2.2 Problem Formulation

Based on the notations and definitions specified in Section 2.1, we present the target problem as follows. Assuming we are given multi-dimensional data set D, target object A, and subspace ranking measure P. Assuming I_k is the subspace set that contains the subspaces with k largest P, and r ($r \leq N_0$) is the number of subspaces that can be evaluated.

For a given r, the proposed problem is to find a subspace set I_r ($|I_r| = r$), in which k_r of these r subspaces belong to I_k, such that k_r ($k_r \leq k$) is maximized.

3. EPROBE FRAMEWORK

EProbe is an efficient subspace probing framework that aims at providing a scalable, cost-effective, and flexible solution for producing top-k subspaces in multidimensional data. The essential concept of EProbe is the development of an accuracy-efficiency tradable solution along with the limited computation resources. Following this framework, we propose the idea of "early stop" of the subspace search, when a certain number of top subspaces have been probed and evaluated. To be specific, we intend to find a special subspace traversal order, such that the subspaces being evaluated earlier have higher probability to be included in the final top-k subspace result set. The ideal situation is, when the computation resources suffice for the task, an exact solution will be produced; otherwise, the accuracy of the result can be sacrificed with the return of the computational speed-up.

The question is, how feasible it is to design an "early stop" criterion? Obviously, it is impossible to define an exact measure that positively correlates P while maintains a time complexity at the same level as or a lower level than P, because the target object's Rank is non-monotonic over any parent-child subspaces, and the subspace ranking measure P is a monotonic function of Rank.

However, when considering the attributes of the real-world data, it is still feasible to produce a more efficient subspace traversal order. For a candidate subspace and a given target object, the ranking measure P value is closely related to two factors: internal and external factors, respectively. First, it is positively correlated with the score of the target object itself. Second, it is negatively correlated with the combined score effects of other competitive objects. In other words, both a higher core of the target object, and a lower score of competitive objects will contribute to a higher P. Motivated from the observation that the score distribution of all the competitive objects in the data partly reflects their comparative position, we develop following heuristic.

Heuristic 1: Given target object A, a subspace' score ratio SR tends to be positively correlated with the measure P.

Based on this heuristic, we propose algorithm SRatio, in which the subspace traversal order is formed based on the score ratio SR. In other words, the SR of every candidate subspace is calculated first, and their P values will be evaluated with a descending order of their corresponding SR.

Although the score ratio SR is a good indicator of the comparative position of the target object among its peers, it still cannot serve as a precise metric to correlate the P value. This is because the impact coming from the external factor – the score fluctuation

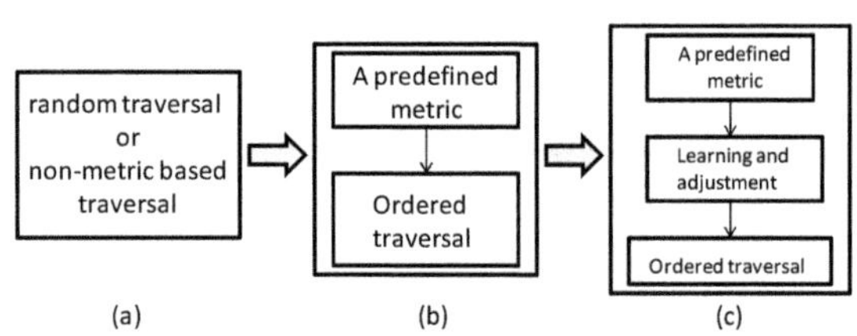

Figure 1: Algorithm Design under EProbe Framework

Figure 1 shows the three improving algorithm designs, of which design (a) shows a random or non-metric based subspace traversal order; design (b) shows a metric based subspace traversal order; and design (c) shows a metric based and learning/adjustment enhanced traversal order. The algorithms DFP, SRatio, and SlidingCluster are representatives of these three designs, respectively. We compare these three methods in Section 4.

of other competitive objects also play an important role. As shown in Figure 1 (c), it will be more effective if a learning and/or adjustment module that considers this external factor can be appropriately designed. Therefore, we come up with following heuristic, based on which the algorithm SlidingCluster is proposed.

Heuristic 2: Subspaces with close SR and close genealogy relationship tend to share similar value of measure P.

The genealogy relationship between subspaces S_1 and S_2 can be measured by the Distance measure, as shown in Eq. (2). When $\text{Distance}(S_1, S_2) = 1$, S_1 and S_2 are regarded having the closest genealogy relationship. This heuristic is formed based on the following observations. An object's score in a subspace S is accumulated by a set of child subspaces of S. Assuming the object A shows high score in a parent subspace compared to other objects, it is very likely, if not guaranteed, that object A excels in one or more child subspaces as well. Therefore, there exist many situations in which parent-child subspaces may share very close value of measure P.

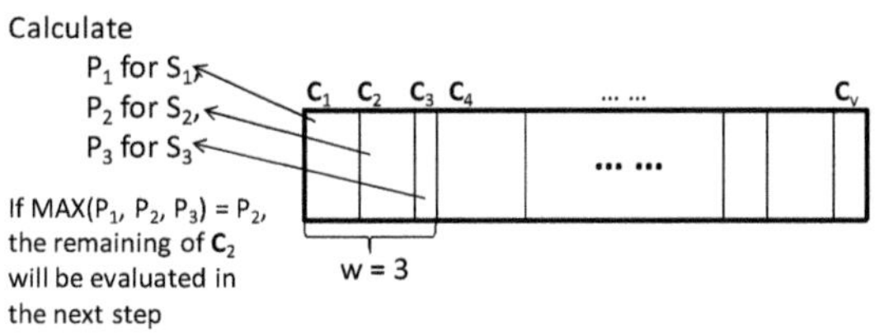

Figure 2: An Illustration of Algorithm SlidingCluster

In Figure 2, we illustrate the idea of algorithm SlidingCluster. At first, the same as algorithm SRatio, the candidate subspaces are ordered based on the score ratio SR. Then the ordered sequence of candidate subspaces will be split into neighboring clusters based on **Heuristic 2**. By specifying a window size w, one candidate subspace will be sampled from each of the top w clusters. After calculating the measure P of these sampled subspaces, the subspace with the largest P is selected, and the corresponding cluster will be selected as well. The remaining subspaces in this cluster then will be evaluated. Following that, the next subspace cluster is included into the current cluster window. And again, a subspace will be sampled, evaluated, and compared from this cluster. This procedure continues until all the subspace clusters are evaluated.

4. EXPERIMENTAL RESULTS

In Section 3, we have proposed two new design components: SR based subspace sorting, and sliding cluster subspace sampling, which are distinguished from any random or non-metric based subspace exploration methods. We develop algorithm SRatio by considering the first component, and algorithm SlidingCluster by considering both components. The essential purpose of our experiments is to explore whether these two algorithms can produce a more effective subspace traversal order. Being effective, the top-k subspaces to be included in the final results are to be evaluated in the early stage of the subspace traversal process. For comparison purpose, we use a baseline method DFP, which applies a depth first subspace evaluation order from the root subspace ($S_* = \{*\}$) to leaf subspaces (dimension attribute with non-star values). In the remaining of this section, we first introduce the experiment settings and evaluation measures in Section 4.1, then we report and analyze the experimental results in Section 4.2.

Table 1: Product_Sales Data Description

Obj ID	Global Rank	$N(S_i)$	Cluster Size
A	50	692	132
B	28	2197	315
C	27	4183	502
D	23	6994	962
E	18	12191	1243
F	22	20200	1065

Objects can be ranked by their aggregated score. We use 6 different objects A, B, C, D, E, F, as the target objects to perform the experiments. These objects are ranked 50, 28, 27, 23, 18, and 22 respectively, among 89 objects, in the full attribute spaces. $N(S_i)$ denotes the number of candidate subspaces in the corresponding subspace search space. The "Cluster Size" column shows the number of subspace clusters being produced based on **Heuristic 2**.

4.1 Experiment Settings

We perform our experiments on a machine with an Intel Core i5 2.27GHz processor, and 3.5GB of memory. We implement algorithms DFP, SRatio, and SlidingCluster using JDK 1.6 on Linux kernel 2.6.34 OS. When we evaluate the comparative experimental results on these three algorithms, we develop the AVG TraceIndex and the Coverage as the major evaluation measures, where these two measures can be calculated based on Eq. (3) and Eq. (4) respectively. We report the results with two varying variables: the window size w, and different target objects with varying number of candidate subspaces $N(S_i)$. We set the distance $d = 1$ and the threshold minsup = 100.

$$\text{AVG TraceIndex} = \frac{\sum_{i=1}^{k} \text{TraceIndex}(S_i)}{k} \quad (3)$$

As defined in **Definition 2**, the TraceIndex of a subspace denotes the ordinal position on which this subspace is being evaluated. For the top-k subspaces that are eventually produced, the objective is to rather evaluate them on earlier ordinal positions. Therefore, the average TraceIndex of the top-k subspaces, as shown in Eq. (3), qualifies a good indicator of the performance.

$$\text{Coverage} = \frac{\sum_{i=1}^{k} \mathcal{I}(\text{TraceIndex}(S_i) \leq r)}{k} \times 100\% \quad (4)$$

In this study, the proposed problem is to obtain top subspaces when only a limited number of subspaces can be evaluated. It indicates that when the subspace evaluation is terminated in an intermediate spot without finishing traversing the search space N_O, it is hoped that a significant portion of the top-k subspaces have been evaluated. The measure Coverage, as defined in Eq. (4), indicates the percentage of the subspaces that are in the final top-k result when the first r subspaces are evaluated. $\mathcal{I}$ denotes an indicator function, which returns 1 when the condition is true and 0 otherwise. $\mathcal{I}$ enforces that only those subspaces with TraceIndex not greater than r will count.

4.2 Product_Sales Data

In this experiment, we use Product_Sales data. Product_Sales data contains 66,801 record tuples, and each record has six categorical subspace attributes, the cardinalities of which are 6, 305, 8, 25, 3, 30 and 4, respectively; and one non-negative numerical attribute Score. The theme of this data set is about the sales revenue of different product brands. In Table 1, we show the characteristics of the target objects we experiment with. We choose these six specific target objects mainly because we intend to investigate how it affects the performance of algorithms when the number of candidate subspaces increase. We do not disclose the detailed theme of the data for privacy reasons.

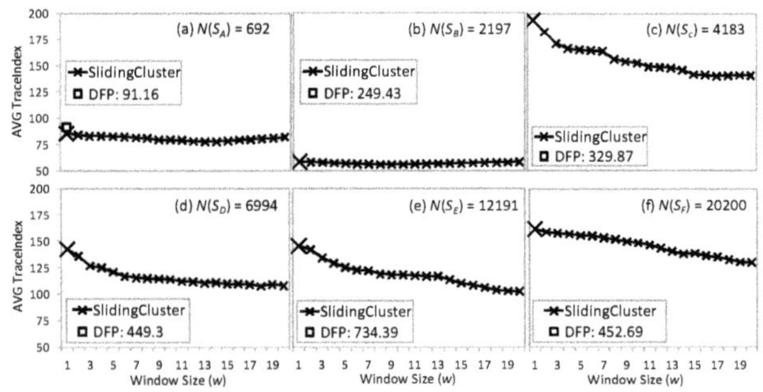

Figure 3: Average TraceIndex Comparison

Figures 3 (a)-(f) show the average TraceIndex of top-k subspaces when the window size w increases for target objects with different number of candidate subspaces. The x-axis represents the window size w, where $w \in \{1, 2, \cdots, 19, 20\}$; and the y-axis represents the AVG TraceIndex of the top-k subspaces. $N(S_i)(i \in \{A, B, C, D, E, F\})$ denotes the number of candidate subspaces in the corresponding subspace search space. The big sized "X" represents the data point of algorithm SRatio.

Varying w. w represents the window size of subspace clusters applied in the subspace sampling procedure in algorithm SlidingCluster. Figure 3 and 4 respectively show the comparison result on measures AVG TraceIndex and Coverage of the three algorithms: DFP, SRatio, and SlidingCluster, along with the varying window size w, where $w \in \{1, 2, \cdots, 19, 20\}$, and $k = r = 100$. The experiment trial with low AVG TraceIndex and high Coverage indicates a promising result. When the window size $w = 1$, algorithm SlidingCluster degrades to SRatio, we therefore use a big sized "X" to represent the corresponding data point. For algorithm DFP, only Figure 3 (a) shows the corresponding data point. It is because the data points are all positioned out of the plot area for other experiment trials, when comparing the results with the same scale. As a remedy, we record AVG TraceIndex of DFP algorithm on the corresponding legend. Because the subspace traversal order of algorithm DFP is not manipulated, its average TraceIndex of the top-k subspaces is significantly higher than those produced by SRatio and SlidingCluster. Meanwhile, when the window size w enlarges, the average TraceIndex further decreases consistently. These evidences clearly indicate that, the average ordinal order of the top subspaces being evaluated has been brought forward effectively when using our proposed methods. As a result, SRatio and SlidingCluster have higher chance than DFP to produce the most important subspaces when the computation resources are limited and only the first r of N_0 candidate subspaces can be evaluated.

We are able to draw the same conclusion by examining Figure 4 as well. This figure shows the percentage of the top subspaces that are actually catched when the first r subspaces have been evaluated. Generally speaking, our experiments show an remarkable advance of algorithm SRatio over algorithm DFP; and a significant improvement of algorithm SlidingCluster over algorithm SRatio. When the window size w enlarges, the Coverage of SlidingCluster consistently improves. Taking Figure 4 (b) as an example, we suppose the computation resources are only sufficient to finish evaluating the first $r = 100$ subspaces. For algorithm DFP, only 9% subspaces in the final top $k = 100$ subspaces will have been evaluated by the time of algorithm terminating at $r = 100$. However, 80% and 87% top subspaces will have been evaluated for SRatio and SlidingCluster with $w = 20$.

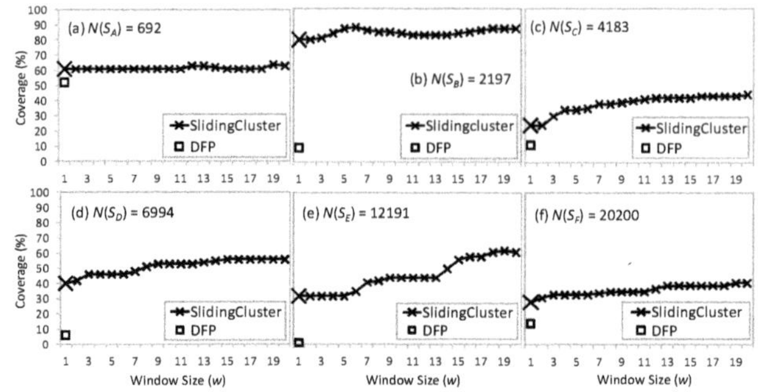

Figure 4: Subspace Coverage Comparison with Varying w

Figures 4 (a)-(f) show the top-k subspace coverage when the window size w increases for target objects with different number of candidate subspaces. The x-axis represents the window size w, where $w \in \{1, 2, \cdots, 19, 20\}$; and the y-axis represents the Coverage of the top-k subspaces. $N(S_i)(i \in \{A, B, C, D, E, F\})$ denotes the number of candidate subspaces in the corresponding subspace search space. The big sized "X" represents the data point of algorithm SRatio.

5. CONCLUSION AND FUTURE WORK

In multi-dimensional data, the problem of promotional subspace mining (PSM) aims to find out outstanding subspaces for promoting a given object among a group of competitive objects. One major research problem is how to produce the top subspaces efficiently given a predefined subspace ranking measure. In this paper, we proposed a novel EProbe framework to address the scalability issue of this problem under the assumption that limited computation resources are enforced. We initialized the "early stop" idea by designing the algorithms SRatio and SlidingCluster, and showed very promising results in our experiments. We plan on our future work in two directions. Firstly, we will perform extensive experiments on data sets with different concepts and distribution, on different target objects within the same data set, and on relatively small or large k top subspaces. We will design and develop statistical models that consider the window size w, the number of subspaces r that should be evaluated, and the expected Coverage to achieve. Secondly, we have plan to refine the learning/adjustment module of the EProbe framework. In algorithm SlidingCluster, we had assumed that the values of measure P within the same subspace cluster were close. However, this assumption may be violated if the ranks of the competitive objects change violently. We will design a self-adaptive machine learning unit, which updates the window size w and the distance d according to the values of measure P of already evaluated subspaces. We will also investigate more sophisticated partition clustering methods [3, 4].

6. REFERENCES

[1] Tianyi Wu, Tong Xin, Qiaozhu Mei, and Jiawei Han. Promotion analysis in multidimensional space. In *VLDB 2009*, pages 109–120, Lyon, France, 2009.

[2] R. W. Hamming. Error detecting and error correcting codes. *Bell System Tech Journal*, 9:147–160, 1950.

[3] Ian Davidson, Kiri L. Wagstaff, and Sugato Basu. Measuring constraint-set utility for partitional clustering algorithms. In *PKDD 2006*, pages 115–126, Berlin, Germany, 2006.

[4] Omar Alonso, Michael Gertz, and Ricardo Baeza-Yates. Clustering and exploring search results using timeline constructions. In *ACM CIKM 2009*, pages 97–106, Hong Kong, China, 2009.

A Partitioning Method for Symbolic Interval Data Based on Kernelized Metric

Bruno A. Pimentel
Centro de Informática, Universidade Federal de Pernambuco, Av. Jornalista Anibal Fernandes s/n, 50740-560, Recife, PE, Brazil
bap@cin.ufpe.br

Anderson F.B.F. da Costa
Centro de Informática, Universidade Federal de Pernambuco, Av. Jornalista Anibal Fernandes s/n, 50740-560, Recife, PE, Brazil
afbfc@cin.ufpe.br

Renata M.C.R. de Souza
Centro de Informática, Universidade Federal de Pernambuco, Av. Jornalista Anibal Fernandes s/n, 50740-560, Recife, PE, Brazil
rmcrs@cin.ufpe.br

ABSTRACT

To solve the problem of situations with nonlinearly separable clusters, kernel clustering methods have been proposed. Symbolic Data Analysis (SDA) has emerged to deal with variables that can have intervals, histograms, and even functions as values, in order to consider the variability and/or uncertainty innate to the data. In this paper, we present a K-means clustering method based in kernelized squared L_2 distance for symbolic interval-type data. Experiments with real and syntectic symbolic interval-type data sets are considered.

Categories and Subject Descriptors

I.5.3 [**Pattern Recognition**]: Clustering

General Terms

Theory

Keywords

Kernel, partitioning method, kernelized metric, interval data.

1. INTRODUCTION

Currently, with the explosive growth in the use of databases and the huge volume of data stored, the clustering has become a subject of great interest and the cluster analysis has been used in many application domains like pattern recognition, machine learning, data mining and computer vision [7] [3]. The objective of the cluster analysis is to group a set of elements into clusters such that elements within a cluster have a high degree of similarity, while elements belonging to different clusters have a high degree of dissimilarity.

One of the most popular partitioning method is K-Means. However, this algorithm present a serious limitation: it can only find linearly separable clusters. To solve the problem of situations with nonlinearly separable clusters, kernel clustering methods have been proposed. These methods are able to produce nonlinear separating hyper surfaces among clusters [4]. The Kernel Fuzzy c-Means was proposed [9] aiming to replace a kernel-induced distance metric for the original Euclidean distance of the fuzzy partitioning method FCM. The methodology of kernelized metrics is described in [4] and [9]. Methods based on kernelization of the metric compute the cluster center and the distance between centers and patterns using kernel functions.

Research has shown that data sets involving numeric data only are not as rich in information for the complexity of the data found in real problems, such as databases used by the company. Therefore, Symbolic Data Analysis (SDA) has emerged to deal with variables in order to consider the variability and/or uncertainty innate to the data [2]. The main goal of SDA is to use statistical techniques for representation of information that is made using symbolic data associated with rules, probability distributions or intervals and extend classical data analysis techniques, such as, clustering, factorial techniques, decision trees and another. Thus, the techniques SDA become a powerful tool when used in clustering methods, which causes a constant growth in research to improve these techniques.

In this paper, we present a K-means clustering method based in kernelized squared L_2 distance for symbolic interval-type data. This method is an hard version of the fuzzy K-Means cluster algorithm based on methodology of kernelized metrics presented in [4] to treat symbolic interval data. The paper is organized as follows. In order to compare the proposed method in this paper with a hard clustering method for interval data, Section 2 presents a K-Means clustering method introduced in [1]. In Section 3, we introduce K-Means clustering method based on kernelized metric for symbolic interval data. To validate this new method, Section 4 presents experiments with real and syntectic symbolic interval-type data sets. The evaluation of the clustering results furnished by the methods is based on the computation of an external cluster validity index and the global error rate of classification. In Section 5, the concluding remarks are given.

CIKM'11, October 24–28, 2011, Glasgow, Scotland, UK.

2. A K-MEANS METHOD FOR INTERVAL DATA

Let Ω be a set of n objects indexed by i and described by p symbolic interval-valued variables indexed by j. Each object i is represented by a vector of intervals $\mathbf{x}_i = ([a_i^1, b_i^1], \ldots, [a_i^p, b_i^p])^T$. Similar to the object, the prototype of a cluster $C_k (k = 1, \ldots, K)$ is also represented as a vector of intervals $\mathbf{y}_k = ([\alpha_i^1, \beta_i^1], \ldots, [\alpha_i^p, \beta_i^p])^T$. Thus, the partition $P = (C_1, \ldots, C_K)$ from Ω in K clusters where each cluster has a prototype described by the vector $\mathbf{y}_k$.

The problem of clustering concerns to find a partition P of Ω into K disjoint clusters $C_1, \ldots, C_K$ and a set of prototypes $\{\mathbf{y}_1, \ldots, \mathbf{y}_K\}$ such that minimizes a clustering criterion defined as:

$$J = \sum_{k=1}^{K} \sum_{i \in C_k} \|\mathbf{x}_i - \mathbf{y}_k\|^2. \quad (1)$$

where

$$\|\mathbf{x}_i - \mathbf{y}_k\|^2 = \sum_{j=1}^{p} \left[\left(a_i^j - \alpha_k^j\right)^2 + \left(b_i^j - \beta_k^j\right)^2 \right]. \quad (2)$$

The prototype minimizing the criterion is an interval vector given by:

$$\mathbf{y}_k = \frac{1}{|C_k|} \sum_{i \in C_k} \mathbf{x}_i \quad (3)$$

SCHEMA OF THE KM-IV ALGORITHM

1. **Initialization**
   Choose (randomly) a partition $\{C_1 \ldots, C_K\}$ of Ω or choose (randomly) K distinct objects $\mathbf{y}_1, \ldots, \mathbf{y}_K$, belonging to Ω and assign each object i to the closest object $\mathbf{y}_{k*}$ $(k* = argmin_{k=1,\ldots,K} \sum_{j=1}^{p}[(a_i^j - \alpha_k^j)^2 + (b_i^j - \beta_k^j)^2]$ to construct the initial partition $\{C_1, \ldots, C_K\}$.
2. **Representation step: definition of the best prototypes** For $k = 1, \ldots, K$ compute the prototype $\mathbf{y}_k = ([\alpha_k^1, \beta_k^1] \ldots, [\alpha_k^p, \beta_k^p])$ where α_k^j is the average of the values of the set $\{a_i^j : i \in C_k\}$ and β_k^j is the the average of the values of the set $\{b_i^j : i \in C_k\}$ $(j = 1, \ldots, p)$.
3. **Allocation step: definition of the best partition**
   $test \leftarrow 0$

   for $i = 1$ to n do
   define the winning cluster C_{k*} such that

   $$k* = arg \min_{k=1,\ldots,K} \|\mathbf{x}_i - \mathbf{y}_k\|^2$$

   if $i \in C_k$ and $k* \neq k$
   $test \leftarrow 1$
   $C_{k*} \leftarrow C_{k*} \cup \{i\}$
   $C_k \leftarrow C_k \setminus \{i\}$

4. **Stopping criterion**
   If $test = 0$ then STOP, otherwise go to step 2.

3. A K-MEANS METHOD FOR INTERVAL DATA USING KERNELIZED METRIC

This section introduces k-means method for interval data with kernelized metric (here called KKM-IV). Let a nonlinear function ϕ that performs the mapping from the input space to an high dimensional interval feature space as $\Im : \mathbf{x}_i \rightarrow \phi(\mathbf{x}_i)$. Consider a set of K centers in high interval feature space $\{\phi(\mathbf{y}_1), \ldots, \phi(\mathbf{y}_k)\}$.

The problem of clustering concerns to find a partition of Ω into K disjoint clusters $P = \{C_1, \ldots, C_K\}$ such that minimizes a criterion function defined as

$$J^{\Im} = \sum_{k=1}^{K} \sum_{i \in C_k} \|\phi(\mathbf{x}_i) - \phi(\mathbf{y}_k)\|^2. \quad (4)$$

The function ϕ is not explicit and it is not possible to compute the Equation (4). Nevertheless, it is possible to calculate the distances between patterns and clusters centers by using a kernel trick for interval data called K. In this work, the kernel trick is defined by boundaries of the intervals separately and it given by

$$K(\mathbf{x}_i, \mathbf{x}_l) = \phi(\mathbf{x}_i) \cdot \phi(\mathbf{x}_l) = \zeta(\mathbf{x}_{iL}) \cdot \zeta(\mathbf{x}_{lL}) + \zeta(\mathbf{x}_{iU}) \cdot \zeta(\mathbf{x}_{lU}). \quad (5)$$

where $\mathbf{x}_{iL} = (a_i^1, \ldots, a_i^p)^T$ and $\mathbf{x}_{iU} = (b_i^1, \ldots, b_i^p)^T$ represent the lower and upper bounds of the intervals of the $i - th$ object of Ω, respectively and ζ a nonlinear function that performs the mapping from a point input space to an high dimensional feature space.

The $k - th$ cluster center is an interval vector given by:

$$\mathbf{y}_k = \frac{\sum_{i \in C_k} K(\mathbf{x}_i, \mathbf{y}_k)\mathbf{x}_i}{\sum_{i \in C_k} K(\mathbf{x}_i, \mathbf{y}_k)}. \quad (6)$$

Expanding the Equation (4) and using the kernel trick, the criterion function $J^{\Im}$ can be rewrite as:

$$J^{\Im} = \sum_{k=1}^{K} \sum_{i \in C_k} K(\mathbf{x}_i, \mathbf{x}_i) - 2K(\mathbf{x}_i, \mathbf{y}_k) + K(\mathbf{y}_k, \mathbf{y}_k). \quad (7)$$

Some kernel function examples for interval data are given as:

Table 1: Examples of Kernel Functions

RBF kernel	$K(\mathbf{x}_i, \mathbf{x}_l) =$	$exp(-\|\mathbf{x}_{iL} - \mathbf{x}_{lL}\|^2)/2\sigma^2 +$ $exp(-\|\mathbf{x}_{iU} - \mathbf{x}_{lU}\|^2)/2\sigma^2$
Polynomial kernel	$K(\mathbf{x}_i, \mathbf{x}_l) =$	$(\mathbf{x}_{iL}.\mathbf{x}_{lL} + 1)^d + (\mathbf{x}_{iU}.\mathbf{x}_{lU} + 1)^d$
Sigmoidal kernel	$K(\mathbf{x}_i, \mathbf{x}_l) =$	$tanh(a(\mathbf{x}_{iL}.\mathbf{x}_{lL}) + b) +$ $tanh(a(\mathbf{x}_{iU}.\mathbf{x}_{lU}) + b)$

where

$$\|\mathbf{x}_{iL} - \mathbf{x}_{lL}\|^2 = \sum_{j=1}^{p}(a_i^j - a_l^j)^2, \|\mathbf{x}_{iU} - \mathbf{x}_{lU}\|^2 = \sum_{j=1}^{p}(b_i^j - b_l^j)^2 \quad (8)$$

The algorithm sets a $n \times n$ kernel matrix $\mathbf{K} = \{K(\mathbf{x}_i, \mathbf{x}_l)\}$ and initial partition and performs iteratively the reassigning of the individual to closest cluster until the criterion $J^{\Im}$ reaches a stationary value representing a local minimum.

SCHEMA OF THE KKM-IV ALGORITHM

1. **Pre-processing step: compute new feature space**
   Compute the Kernel matrix $\boldsymbol{K}$ using the RBF kernel for interval data.
2. **Initialization step: obtaining an initial partition**
   Randomly choose a partition of Ω into K clusters.
3. **Allocation step: updating the partition**
   $test \leftarrow 0$
   for $k = 1$ to K compute $\mathbf{v}_k$ according to Equation 6.

   for $i = 1$ to n do
   define the winning cluster C_{k*} such that

   $$k = arg\ \min_{h=1,\dots,K} \|\phi(\mathbf{x}_i) - \phi(\mathbf{y}_k)\|^2.$$

   if $i \in C_k$ and $k \neq h$
   $test \leftarrow 1$
   $C_k \leftarrow C_k \cup \{i\}$
   $C_h \leftarrow C_h \setminus \{i\}$
4. **Stopping criterion**
   If $test = 0$ then STOP, otherwise go to step 3.

4. EXPERIMENTAL RESULTS AND COMPARISON

In order to validate the efficiency of the proposed method, this section presents the clustering results considering real and synthetic interval data sets . Here, our aim is to achieve a comparison of the kernelized K-means method with the K-means method for interval data. Regarding the kernelized K-means method, it was used the RBF kernel function with $\sigma = 1$. To measure the clustering quality provided by KM-IV and KKM-IV methods, we used the corrected Rand index (CR) [6] and the overall error rate of classification (OERC).

4.1 Monte Carlo experiments

In order to build interval data sets from quantitative data sets, each point (s_1, s_2) of these quantitative data sets is considered as the 'seed' of a rectangle. Each rectangle is therefore a vector of two intervals defined by $([s_1 - \gamma_1/2, s_1 + \gamma_1/2], [s_2 - \gamma_2/2, s_2 + \gamma_2/2])$. The parameters $\gamma 1$ and γ_2 are the width and the height of the rectangle. They are drawn randomly within a given range of values.

The interval data set 1 is formed by two rings, each representing a class. The first ring has radius equal to 12 and 100 individuals. The second ring has radius equal to 5 and 50 individuals. Figure 1 represents this data set with two rings using the predefined interval $[1, 2]$.

The interval data set 2 describes a spiral whose each arm is defined in polar coordinates (r, θ) by the equation $r = a + b\theta$, where a and b are real numbers and θ in angular measurements. The parameter a controls the initial radius of the each arm of the spiral, while b is related with distance between successive turns. This data set has 90 individuals scattered among four classes contained 15, 20, 25 and 30, respectively. The total angle $\theta = 120$ degrees with $a = 10$ and $b = 5$. Figure 2 displays the interval data set 2 using the predefined interval $[1, 5]$.

In the framework of a Monte Carlo experiment, 100 replications are considered for each interval data set, as well as

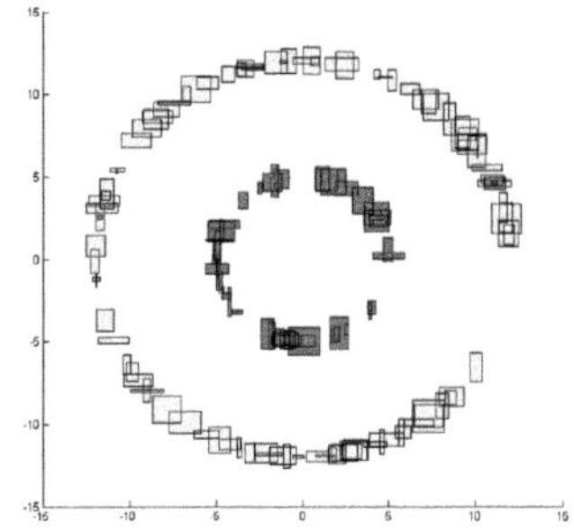

Figure 1: Symbolic interval data set 1: two rings

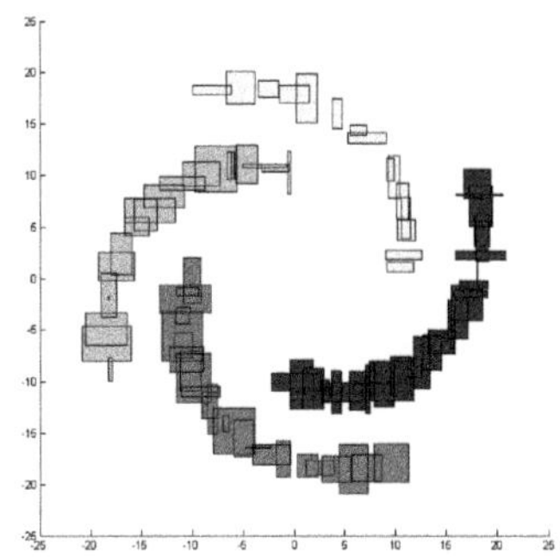

Figure 2: Symbolic interval data set 2: spiral with four arms

for each of the following intervals: $[1, 2], [1, 5], [1, 10], [1, 15]$ and $[1, 20]$. The average of the corrected Rand index as well as average of the overall error rate of classification are calculated. In each replication a clustering method is run (until the convergence to a stationary value of the adequacy criterion J or $J^{\Im}$) 200 times and the best result, according to the criterion J or $J^{\Im}$, is selected.

Table 2 shows the CR index and the OERC metric for the KM-IV and KKM-IV methods for the interval data set 1. As expected for this data configuration with two nonlinear clusters, the performance of the KKM-IV method is superior to that of the KM-IV one.

Table 2: Comparison of the clustering methods for interval data set 1

Predefined Interval	KM-IV		KKM-IV	
	CR index	OERC	CR index	OERC
[1,2]	-0.0706 (0.0931)	0.2890 (0.0401)	0.4335 (0.0678)	0.1396 (0.0164)
[1,5]	-0.0615 (0.0740)	0.2836 (0.0333)	0.4376 (0.0697)	0.1386 (0.0169)
[1,10]	-0.0544 (0.0812)	0.2830 (0.0348)	0.4433 (0.0586)	0.1372 (0.0142)
[1,15]	-0.0602 (0.0903)	0.2865 (0.0391)	0.4502 (0.0600)	0.1356 (0.0146)
[1,20]	-0.0695 (0.0855)	0.2881 (0.0385)	0.4371 (0.0756)	0.1387 (0.0184)

Table 3 shows the results of the CR index and OERC metric for interval data set 2. Again, the KKM-IV method outperforms the KM-IV one.

Table 3: **Comparison of the clustering methods for interval data set 2**

Predefined Interval	KM-IV CR index	KM-IV OERC	KKM-IV CR index	KKM-IV OERC
[1,2]	0.1046 (0.0278)	0.4368 (0.0548)	0.2316 (0.0343)	0.3443 (0.0814)
[1,5]	0.1029 (0.0283)	0.4307 (0.0456)	0.2242 (0.0332)	0.3500 (0.0816)
[1,10]	0.1062 (0.0282)	0.4242 (0.0393)	0.2518 (0.0311)	0.3310 (0.0777)
[1,15]	0.1054 (0.0280)	0.4241 (0.0349)	0.2557 (0.0339)	0.3306 (0.0809)
[1,20]	0.1256 (0.0323)	0.4165 (0.0445)	0.2450 (0.0291)	0.3418 (0.0854)

4.2 City-temperature interval data set

This interval data set [5] concerns 37 cities, each city is described by 12 interval variables which are minimum and the maximum temperatures of 12 months in degree centigrade. Table 4 shows part of this data set.

Table 4: Minimum and the maximum temperatures of cities in degree centigrade

Cities	Jan	Feb	...	Nov	Dec
Amsterdan	[−4, 4]	[−5, 3]	...	[1, 10]	[−1, 4]
Athens	[6, 12]	[6, 12]	...	[11, 18]	[8, 14]
Bahrain	[13, 19]	[14, 19]	...	[20, 26]	[15, 21]
Bombay	[19, 28]	[19, 28]	...	[14, 26]	[10, 20]
Calcutta	[13, 27]	[16, 29]	...	[18, 29]	[13, 26]
Colombo	[22, 30]	[22, 30]	...	[23, 29]	[22, 30]
⋮	⋮	⋮	⋮	⋮	⋮
Toronto	[−8, −1]	[−8, −1]	...	[−1, 17]	[−5, 1]
Vienna	[−2, 1]	[−1, 3]	...	[2, 7]	[1, 3]
Zurich	[−11, 9]	[−8, 15]	...	[0, 19]	[−11, 8]

The CR indices obtained from the comparison between the a priori partition and the partitions given by the KKM-IV and KM-IV methods are, respectively, 0.629 and 0.610 and the OERC for methods are, respectively, 0.189 and 0.270. Therefore, the performance of the KKM-IV method is better than to that of the KM-IV one for this application data set.

4.3 Agaricus interval data set

This data set was extracted from [8] and contains information on species of fungi. Agaricus is a genus of mostly medium to large gilled mushrooms. Well known members of the genus Agaricus are the bisporus, the "button mushroom" common in supermarkets and the campestris, the "meadow mushroom", a popular edible mushroom which is common in pastures and grasslands in many temperate areas of the world. This data set consists of 24 mushrooms, each mushroom described by 5 interval variables: width of the pileus, width of the stipe, thickness of the stipe, height and width of spores. Table 5 shows part of this data set. It is composed of two classes: edible (E) and inedible (I).

For this application, the CR indices calculated for the KM-IV and KKM-IV methods are, respectively, −0.599 and 0.314, respectively. The OERC metrics for the KM-IV and KKM-IV methods are, respectively, 0.500 and 0.167. Again, the KKM-IV is best option for this real interval data set.

Table 5: Information about Agaricus species known to occur in California

Species	pileus's width	stipe's width	stipe's thickness	spores's height	spores's width
Albolutescens	[6, 12]	[2, 7]	[1.5, 3]	[6, 7.5]	[4, 5]
Arvensis	[6, 21]	[4, 14]	[1, 3.5]	[6.5, 9]	[4.5, 6]
Benesii	[4, 8]	[5, 11]	[1, 2]	[5, 6]	[3, 4]
Bernardii	[7, 16]	[4, 7]	[3, 4.5]	[5.5, 7]	[5.5, 6.5]
Bisporus	[5, 12]	[2, 5]	[1.5, 2.5]	[6, 8.5]	[4.5, 6]
⋮	⋮	⋮	⋮	⋮	⋮
Subrutilescens	[6, 14]	[6, 12]	[1, 2]	[4, 6]	[3.5, 4.5]
Subrufescens	[6, 13]	[6, 12]	[1.5, 2.5]	[5.5, 6.5]	[4, 4.5]
Xanthodermus	[5, 17]	[4, 14]	[1, 3.5]	[5, 6]	[4, 5.5]

5. CONCLUSIONS

In this paper, we have presented a new clustering method for symbolic interval data based kernelized metric. This method is an K-Means for symbolic interval data using kernel functions to compute distances between clusters and prototypes. The evaluation of this method in comparison with a K-Means clustering method for interval data having adequacy criterion based on single Euclidean distance was carried out. The accuracy of the results provided by these clustering methods were assessed by the corrected Rand index and overall error rate considering synthetic and real data sets. Concerning the CR index and the overall error rate for these synthetic and real interval data sets, the proposed method in this paper outperformed the K-Means clustering method.

6. ACKNOWLEDGMENTS

The authors would like to thank CNPq, CAPES and FACEPE (Brazilian Agencies) for their financial support.

7. REFERENCES

[1] F. D. Carvalho, P. Brito, and H. Bock. Dynamic clustering for interval data based on l2 distance. *Computational Statistics*, 21(2):231–250, 2006.

[2] E. Diday and M. Noirhomme-Fraiture. *Symbolic Data Analysis And The Sodas Software*. Wiley-Interscience Publishers, 2008.

[3] R. O. Duda, P. E. Hart, and D. G. Stork. *Pattern Classification*. John Wiely and Sons, 2001.

[4] M. Filippone, F. Camastra, F.Masulli, and S. Rovetta. A survey of kernel and spectral methods for clustering. *Pattern Recognition*, 41:176–190, 2008.

[5] D. Guru, B. Kiranagi, and P. Nagabhushan. Multivalued type dissimilarity measure and concept of mutual dissimilarity value for clustering symbolic patterns. *Pattern Recognition*, pages 1203–1213, 2004.

[6] L. Hubert and A. P. Comparing partitions. *Journal of Classification*, 2:193–218, 1985.

[7] A. K. Jain, M. N. Murty, and P. J. Flynn. Data clustering: a review. *ACM Computing Surveys*, 31(3):264–323, 1999.

[8] M. Wood and F. Stevens. Agaricus. http://www.mykoweb.com/CAF/genera/Agaricus.html, July 2010.

[9] D. Q. Zhang and S. C. Chen. Kernel-based fuzzy and possibilistic c-means clustering. *In Proceedings of the International Conference Artificial Neural Network*, pages 122–125, 2003.

Hierarchy Evolution for Improved Classification

Xiaoguang Qi Brian D. Davison
Department of Computer Science & Engineering, Lehigh University
Bethlehem, PA 18015 USA
{xiq204,davison}@cse.lehigh.edu

ABSTRACT

Hierarchical classification has been shown to have superior performance than flat classification. It is typically performed on hierarchies created by and for humans rather than for classification performance. As a result, classification based on such hierarchies often yields suboptimal results. In this paper, we propose a novel genetic algorithm-based method on hierarchy adaptation for improved classification. Our approach customizes the typical GA to optimize classification hierarchies. In several text classification tasks, our approach produced hierarchies that significantly improved upon the accuracy of the original hierarchy as well as hierarchies generated by state-of-the-art methods.

Categories and Subject Descriptors

I.5.2 [**Pattern Recognition**]: Design Methodology—*Classifier design and evaluation*; H.3.3 [**Information Storage and Retrieval**]: Information Search and Retrieval—*Information filtering*

General Terms

Algorithms, Performance

Keywords

Topical categorization, Hierarchical classification, SVM

1. INTRODUCTION

Classification can be performed based on a flat set of categories, or on categories organized as a hierarchy. In flat classification, a single classifier learns to classify instances into one of the target categories. In hierarchical classification, a separate classifier is trained for each non-leaf node in the hierarchy. During training, each classifier is trained to categorize the instances that belong to any of the descendants of the current node into its direct subcategories. When deployed, an instance is first classified by the root classifier, and then passed to one of the first level categories with the highest probability. This process is repeated iteratively from top to bottom, invoking one classifier at each level, until reaching a leaf node. Prior work has shown that hierarchical classification has performance superior to that of flat classification (e.g., [3, 5, 1]).

Hierarchical classification is typically performed utilizing human-defined hierarchies, reflecting a human view of the domain. However, these hierarchies are usually created without consideration for automated classification. As a result, hierarchical classification based on such hierarchies is unlikely to yield optimal performance.

In this paper, we propose a new method based on genetic algorithms to create hierarchies better suited for automatic classification. In our approach, each hierarchy is considered to be an individual. Starting from a group of randomly generated seed hierarchies, genetic operators are randomly applied to each hierarchy to slightly reorganize the categories. The newly generated hierarchies are evaluated and a subset that are better fitted for classification are kept, eliminating hierarchies with poor classification performance from the population. This process is repeated until no significant progress can be made. In our experiments on several text classification tasks, our algorithm significantly improved the classification accuracy compared to the original hierarchy and also outperformed state-of-the-art adaptation approaches. Our contributions include:

- a new approach to improved classification by hierarchy adaptation; and,
- adaptation of genetic operators on hierarchies and an analysis of their utility.

The basic idea of generating/adapting hierarchies for better classification is not new. Li et al. [4] proposed a method of using linear discriminant projection to generate hierarchies. In this approach, all the documents within the hierarchy are first projected onto a lower dimensional space. Then, the leaf categories are clustered using hierarchical agglomerative clustering to generate the hierarchy. Tang et al. [8] proposed a method for hierarchy adaptation by iteratively checking each node in the hierarchy, and making slight modifications locally. This approach can also be used to model dynamic change of taxonomies [7]. Additional related work may be found in our full report [6].

There are at least two main differences that separate our approach from previous work:

- After each iteration, we keep a comparatively large number of best performing hierarchies rather than only keep the best one and discard the rest; we will show later that the best hierarchy does not always come from an adaptation of the previous best hierarchy.
- Unlike previous approaches that gradually adapt a hierarchy by making a slight change at a step, the crossover operators we customize for hierarchy evolution allow a new hierarchy

CIKM'11, October 24–28, 2011, Glasgow, Scotland, UK.

to inherit characteristics from both parents, so that it is significantly different from either parent. This will take previous approaches many more iterations to achieve, or perhaps unachievable at all because of greedy search strategies.

2. APPROACH

As introduced previously, hierarchical classification can often perform better than flat classification. However, this is not always true.It depends on the choice of hierarchy. In order to further motivate this work using real-world data, we randomly selected 7 leaf categories containing 227 documents from LSHTC dataset (see Section 3.1 for details), exhaustively generated all the possible hierarchies based on the selected categories, and tested the classification performance for every hierarchy. In total, 39,208 hierarchies were generated, out of which 48.2% perform worse than flat classification in terms of accuracy. This verifies our intuition that improving hierarchical classification needs a well-chosen hierarchy. In the following, we will describe how to adapt genetic algorithms to search for a better hierarchy.

2.1 Overview

A genetic algorithm (GA) is a search/optimization method that resembles the evolution process of organisms in nature. Like any other search method, it searches through the solution space of a problem, looking for an optimal solution. In our problem, we consider each possible hierarchy to be a solution (or an individual in GA, specifically). As illustrated by the small example above, our solution space is often too large to perform an exhaustive search except for very small datasets.

A typical GA usually starts with an initial population of individuals, then iteratively repeats the following search procedure until the stopping criterion is satisfied. In each iteration, a subset of individuals is selected for reproduction by applying mutation and crossover operations on them. Then the fitness of each new individual is evaluated, and low-fitness individuals are dropped, leaving a better fitted population as the start of next iteration. In our approach, we will leave the high level procedure of GAs as described above unchanged, while adapting representation method and reproduction operators to make them fit the hierarchical classification problem. We chose a GA instead of other generic search methods for at least two reasons. First, it intrinsically supports large populations rather than greedy, single path optimization. Second, we can adapt its reproduction operators to allow significant changes to the solutions without changing the high level search procedure.

2.2 Hierarchy representation

In our work, each hierarchy is represented as a sequence of numeric IDs and parentheses, in which each ID corresponds to a leaf category, and each pair of parentheses represents a more generic category consisting of the categories in between them. Multiple levels in the hierarchy are reflected using nested parentheses.

More formally, we represent a hierarchy using the following rules:

1. Each leaf node is represented by its numeric id;
2. Each non-leaf node is represented by a list of all its children nodes enclosed in a pair of parentheses;
3. The hierarchy is represented recursively using Rule 1 and 2.
4. The outermost pair of parentheses is omitted.

Figure 1 illustrates a small example, which will be represented as (1 2 5) ((3 6) 4).

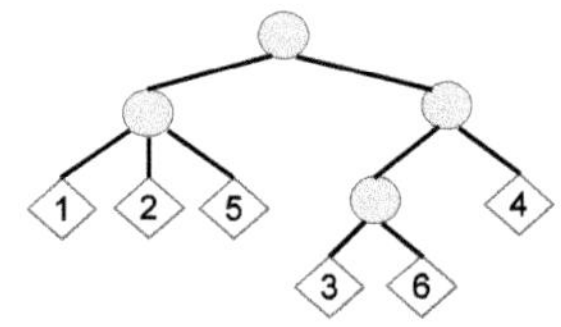

Figure 1: A small hierarchy example.

The hierarchy representation method above serializes a hierarchical tree into a sequence of tokens. However, different representations may correspond to the same hierarchy. For example, (1 2 5) ((3 6) 4) and (2 1 5) ((6 3) 4) define the same hierarchy. We detect duplicate hierarchies using a two-step canonicalization. We first remove unnecessary parentheses, then sort siblings according to the minimal class id in its subtree (refer to our report [6] for details).

2.3 Reproduction

2.3.1 Mutation

In typical GA, mutation is performed by switching a random bit in the chromosome string. However, this operation is not as straightforward in the hierarchical setting. We design three mutation methods that are suitable for hierarchy evolution: promotion, grouping, and switching.

The *promotion* operator randomly selects a node n (which can be either a leaf or non-leaf node), and promote n as a child of its grandparent, i.e., n becomes a sibling of its parent node. The *grouping* operator randomly selects two sibling nodes and groups them together. If a non-leaf node n has k children, $C = \{c_i | i = 1..k\}$, where $k \geq 2$. We randomly select two nodes c_x and c_y from c_1 through c_k, and remove them from C. Then we add a new node c_z into C so that c_z becomes a child node of n. Finally, we make c_x and c_y children of c_z. The *switching* operator randomly selects two nodes m and n (and the subtrees rooted at those locations) in the whole hierarchy, and switches their positions.

2.3.2 Crossover

In a typical GA, crossover is performed by swapping segments of the chromosome string between the parents. In the hierarchical setting, however, directly swapping parts of the hierarchy representation will generate invalid hierarchies. Therefore, we need crossover methods customized for hierarchy evolution.

We used two types of methods: swap crossover and structural crossover. The two parents are noted as h_{p1} and h_{p2}, the children h_{c1} and h_{c2}. In *swap crossover*, a child h_{c1} is generated using the following steps. First a split point p is randomly chosen in h_{p1}. We note the the part starting from the beginning of the representation string to the split point p as h'_{p1}. We remove the segment after p from h_{p1} and only consider h'_{p1}. Then right parentheses are added at the end to balance with the existing left parentheses. Suppose S is the set of leaf nodes that appear in h'_{p1}; we go through h_{p2} and remove all the nodes n if $n \in S$. This removal transforms h_{p2} into h'_{p2}. Finally, h'_{p1} and h'_{p2} are concatenated to form h_{c1}. The other child h_{c2} is generated by switching h_{p1} and h_{p2} before applying the above procedure. Figure 2 illustrates the process of swap crossover.

For our second approach, we note that a hierarchy can be seen as an integration of two independent characteristics: the tree structure and the placement of leaf nodes. At a high level, *structural crossover* aims to "mix and match" these two factors. A child hierarchy inherits the structural information from one parent, and

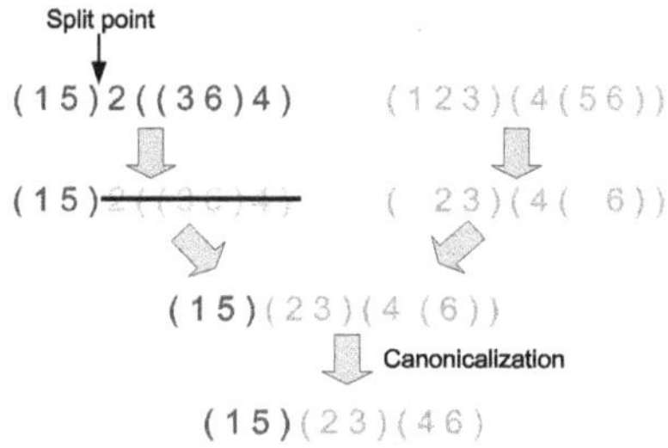

Figure 2: An example of swap crossover.

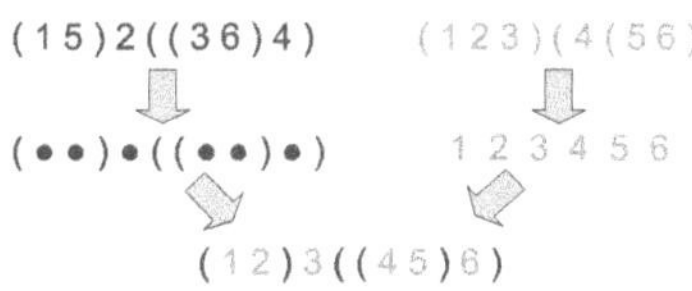

Figure 3: An example of structural crossover.

placement of leaf nodes from the other. In our implementation, h_{c1} is generated using the following method. First, every leaf node in h_{p1}'s representation is replaced with a blank space. Then these blank spaces are filled with the leaf nodes in h_{p2} using the order that they appear in h_{p2}. h_{c2} is generated by switching h_{p1} and h_{p2}. Figure 3 illustrates the process of structural crossover.

A GA requires a fitness function for evaluating new individuals. We define the fitness of a hierarchy as the classification accuracy using this hierarchy evaluated on validation data. A GA also needs a stopping criterion to terminate the iterative evolution process. In our algorithm, we keep a watch list of the top N_{watch} best hierarchies. If the performance of the top hierarchies does not change between two consecutive iterations, the algorithm terminates. In the following experiments, we set N_{watch} to 5.

3. EXPERIMENTS

3.1 Experimental setup

We used three public datasets to test our algorithm. The first two datasets are from the first Large Scale Hierarchical Text Classification (LSHTC) challenge[1] held in 2009. We selected a toy dataset from Task 1 with 36 leaf categories and 333 documents, which will be referred to as LSHTC-a. We also used the dry-run dataset from Task 1, which has 1,139 leaf categories and 8,181 documents. We will refer to this dataset as LSHTC-b. Both datasets are partitioned into three subsets: a training set used to train classifiers during the training process, a validation set used to estimate the fitness score of each generated hierarchy, and a test set to evaluate the final output hierarchy. The third dataset is WebKB[2], containing 7 leaf categories and 8,282 documents. We performed four-fold cross-validation on WebKB. LibSVM [2] is used as the base classifier to implement the standard hierarchical SVM. We used all the default settings in LibSVM, including the radial basis function kernel as it yields better performance than the linear kernel on the datasets we used. In our algorithm, we set the population size to 100 on LSHTC-a and WebKB, 500 on LSHTC-b.

We compared our approach (Evolution) with two existing state-of-the-art approaches: a hierarchy adaptation approach called Hierarchy Adjusting Algorithm (HAA) [8], and a hierarchy generation approach called Linear Projection (LP) [4]. We implemented HAA according to the algorithm outlined in Figure 12 and 13 of [8]. All three search methods were implemented. In our implementation of HAA, we set the stopping criterion to 0.001. That is, when the improvement between two consecutive iterations is less than 0.001, the algorithm terminates. We also compared our algorithm with Linear Projection on WebKB dataset. Instead of re-implementing the LP algorithm, we directly used the automatically generated hierarchy on WebKB reported in the Linear Projection paper, and performed the four-fold cross-validation based on that hierarchy.

[1] http://lshtc.iit.demokritos.gr/node/1

[2] http://www.cs.cmu.edu/afs/cs/project/theo-20/www/data/

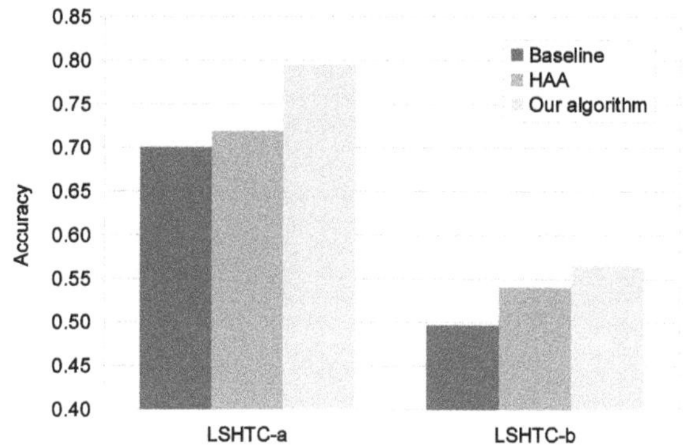

Figure 4: Accuracy on LSHTC datasets compared across different methods.

3.2 Experimental results

On LSHTC-a, our algorithm converged after seven iterations, improving the performance on the test set from 70% to 79.5% (averaged across three runs using different random seeds). HAA converged after two iterations with the accuracy improved to 71.9%. On LSHTC-b, it took 49 iterations for our algorithm to converge, and 18 iterations for HAA. HAA improved upon the baseline's accuracy of 49.6% to 54.0% , while our algorithm's final output hierarchies have an average accuracy of 56.5% across three runs using different random seeds. The results are shown in Figure 4.

On WebKB, we compared our algorithm with flat classification, HAA, and Linear Projection. The flat classification has an accuracy of 70.3% averaged across the four folds. Linear Projection and HAA improve the accuracy to 74.6% and 75.4%, respectively. Our algorithm further improves to 76.4%, a 21% reduction in error rate compared with flat classification. Figure 5 shows the average performance and standard deviation for each method. Two-tailed t-tests showed the improvement of our algorithm over other algorithms is statistically significant.

3.3 Analysis

As we pointed out previously, our approach differs from existing hierarchy adaptation approaches from at least two aspects: making significant changes to hierarchies and a larger population size to maintain population variety. Now we analyze quantitatively whether these differences make our approach outperform existing methods. The following analysis is performed on LSHTC-b.

In order to evaluate the effectiveness of the genetic operators, we calculate the improvement that each type of operator brings to a hierarchy. Figure 6 shows the average improvement in terms of accuracy. On average, all the five operators have a negative impact on the accuracy. For example, the "swap crossover" even decreases accuracy by 0.018 when averaged across all evolution

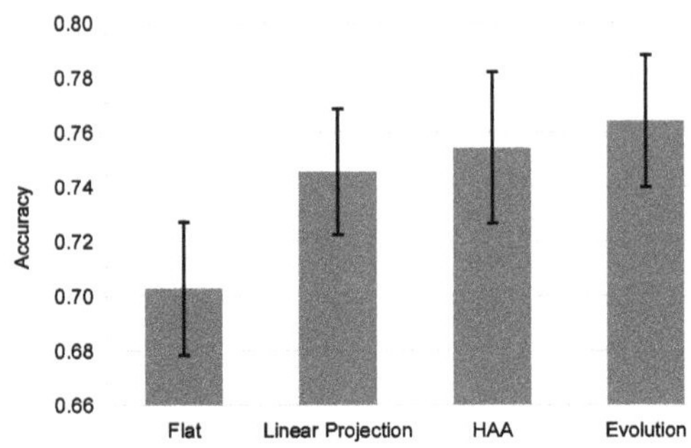

Figure 5: Accuracy on WebKB dataset compared across different methods.

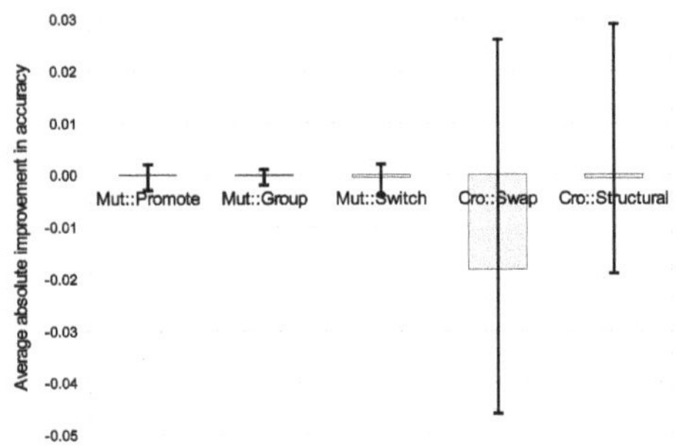

Figure 6: Improvement compared across different genetic operators.

operations. That is, on average, every time a "swap crossover" is applied on a hierarchy, the newly generated hierarchy has an accuracy lowered by 0.018. Fortunately, the genetic algorithm only keeps the best hierarchies in the population, and discards the rest. Therefore, the degradation is counter-balanced by such a selection process, making an overall increasing trend (as we showed previously in experimental results). We also calculated the standard deviation of the improvement, as well as minimal and maximal improvement. The error bars in Figure 6 show the minimal and maximal improvement. The standard deviation of the operators are 0.0004, 0.0005, 0.0009, 0.0100, 0.0028, respectively. This indicates that the mutation operators only have slight impact on the accuracy while changes made by crossover are more significant. In the best case, "swap crossover" improved accuracy by 0.026, "structural crossover" improved 0.029, while all the mutation operators can only improve no more than 0.002 at their best. These statistics match our intuition that more significant changes can potentially bring better improvements than local modifications.

Unlike previous approaches that only carry the best hierarchy into the next iteration, we keep hundreds of hierarchies in the population. This raises a reasonable concern about our approach: is the large population necessary? To answer this question, we first identified the top-N hierarchies at each iteration, then back-traced their parents from the previous iteration, and finally found out the ranks for their parents. The results are plotted in Figure 7. The x-axis shows the range of the parents' ranking. For example, range 1 corresponds to rank 1 through 50. Range 10 corresponds to rank 451 through 500. We can see that most parents rank above 300, while still leaving a significant portion between 300 and 500. From another point of view, if we were to keep only 50 hierarchies, we would have lost approximately 88% of the top 1 hierarchies at each iteration, 84% of the top 5 and top 10. Although we could probably

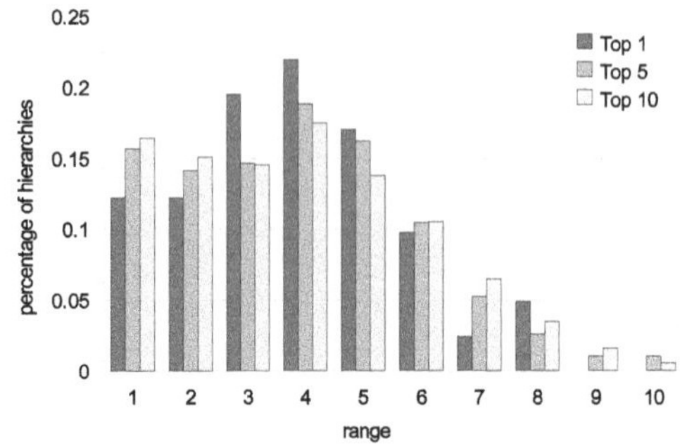

Figure 7: Parent rankings of top hierarchies.

shrink the population size by 20% without significant degradation in accuracy, this supports the idea that the comparatively large population is necessary.

4. CONCLUSION

In this paper, we proposed a hierarchy adaptation approach using the standard mechanisms of a genetic algorithm along with special genetic operators customized for hierarchies. Unlike previous approaches which only keep the best hierarchy in the search process and modify the hierarchy locally at each step, our approach maintains population variety by allowing simultaneous evolution of a much larger population, and enables significant changes during evolution. Experiments on multiple classification tasks showed that the proposed algorithm can significantly improve automatic classification, outperforming existing state-of-the-art approaches. Our analysis showed that the variety in population and customized reproduction operators are important to improvement in classification.

Acknowledgments

We thank Dr. Hector Munoz-Avila for discussions that inspired the use of genetic algorithms, and Liangjie Hong and Na Dai for helpful discussions. This material is based upon work supported by the National Science Foundation under Grant Number IIS-0545875.

5. REFERENCES

[1] P. N. Bennett and N. Nguyen. Refined experts: Improving classification in large taxonomies. In *Proc. 32nd Annual Int'l ACM SIGIR Conf. on Research and Dev. in Info. Retr.*, pages 11–18, 2009.

[2] C.-C. Chang and C.-J. Lin. *LIBSVM: a library for support vector machines*, 2001. Software available at http://www.csie.ntu.edu.tw/~cjlin/libsvm.

[3] S. Dumais and H. Chen. Hierarchical classification of web content. In *Proc. 23rd Annual Int'l ACM SIGIR Conf. on Research and Dev. in Information Retr.*, pages 256–263, 2000.

[4] T. Li, S. Zhu, and M. Ogihara. Hierarchical document classification using automatically generated hierarchy. *J. Intell. Inf. Syst.*, 29:211–230, October 2007.

[5] T.-Y. Liu, Y. Yang, H. Wan, H.-J. Zeng, Z. Chen, and W.-Y. Ma. Support vector machines classification with a very large-scale taxonomy. *SIGKDD Explorations Newsletter*, 7(1):36–43, 2005.

[6] X. Qi and B. D. Davison. Optimizing hierarchical classification through tree evolution. Technical Report LU-CSE-11-002, Dept. of Computer Science and Engineering, Lehigh University, 2011.

[7] L. Tang, H. Liu, J. Zhang, N. Agarwal, and J. J. Salerno. Topic taxonomy adaptation for group profiling. *ACM Trans. Knowl. Discov. Data*, 1:1:1–1:28, February 2008.

[8] L. Tang, J. Zhang, and H. Liu. Acclimatizing taxonomic semantics for hierarchical content classification. In *Proc. of the 12th ACM SIGKDD Int'l Conf. on Knowledge Discovery and Data Mining*, pages 384–393, 2006.

Using Random Walks for Multi-label Classification

Chaokun Wang[1,3,4], Wei Zheng[1], Zhang Liu[1,2], Yiyuan Bai[1,2], Jianmin Wang[1,3,4]
[1] School of Software, Tsinghua University, Beijing 100084, China
[2] Department of Computer Science and Technology, Tsinghua University
[3] Tsinghua National Laboratory for Information Science and Technology
[4] Key Laboratory for Information System Security, Ministry of Education
{chaokun,jimwang}@tsinghua.edu.cn,{zhengw04,liuzhang08,byy06}@mails.thu.edu.cn

ABSTRACT

The Multi-Label Classification (MLC) problem has aroused wide concern in these years since the multi-labeled data appears in many applications, such as page categorization, tag recommendation, mining of semantic web data, social network analysis, and so forth. In this paper, we propose a novel MLC solution based on the random walk model, called MLRW. MLRW maps the multi-labeled instances to graphs, on which the random walk is applied. When an unlabeled data is fed, MLRW transforms the original multi-label problem to some single-label subproblems. Experimental results on several real-world data sets demonstrate that MLRW is a better solution to the MLC problems than many other existing multi-label classification methods.

Categories and Subject Descriptors

H.3.2 [**Information Storage**]: Record classification; I.5.2 [**Design Methodology**]: Classifier design and evaluation; H.2.8 [**Database Applications**]: Data mining

General Terms

Algorithm, Design, Experimentation, Measurement

Keywords

multi-label classification, multi-label random walk graph, multi-label random walk graph collection, multi-label random walk model

1. INTRODUCTION

The data classification problem aims to assign each data point to a set of categories. It is widely applied in many fields, such as web information retrieval, management and mining of web data, social system analysis, etc. In traditional data classification problems, each data point is assigned to only one category/class. It is expected to make a decision on whether each unclassified data point belongs to a given category or not. This kind of problems is also called the *Single-Label Classification* (SLC) problems.

In many situations, however, a data point may belong to more than one category simultaneously. For example, in *ACM Computing Classification System*, there are a total of 11 first-level and 81 second-level categories and subject descriptors. An article may be assigned to more than one category by the author(s), and thus can be retrieved from different categories in the ACM digital library as well. This kind of classification problems is called the *Multi-Label Classification* (MLC) problems. The relevance and co-occurrence between different labels make the MLC problems quite different from traditional SLC problems. Thus, traditional SLC methods cannot be directly applied to the MLC problems [5].

Recent MLC solutions can be summarized into two categories, i.e., the *Problem Transformation* (PT) methods and the *Algorithm Adaptation* (AA) methods. The former aims at transforming an MLC problem to a set of SLC problems, to which the traditional SLC methods can be applied; the latter aims to adapt existing SLC algorithms as MLC solutions.

In this paper, we propose a novel Multi-Label classification method based on the Random Walk model, called *MLRW*. MLRW is a kind of PT method. In MLRW, the random walk model is extended as a reasonable representation of the multi-label data. Therefore, the original multi-label input space is mapped to a *multi-label random walk graph*. The connectivity between vertices in this graph indicates the relationship between different data points which share one or more same labels.

The main contributions of this paper are as follows.

- The concept of multi-label random walk graph is proposed. The multi-label training instances are mapped to a multi-label random walk graph.
- MLRW, a novel multi-label classification method based on the random walk model, is proposed. It maps the multi-labeled instances and an unlabeled instance to a collection of multi-label random walk graphs. On these graphs, the random walk model is applied and the output vectors are utilized to build a binary classifier for each label. Therefore, MLRW transforms the original multi-label classification problem to some binary classification subproblems, which can be resolved by traditional classification methods.
- We make extensive comparison experiments between MLRW and many other state-of-the-art multi-label classification methods. Experimental results on the real data sets demonstrate that MLRW provides a better solution than these methods.

This work was partially supported by the National Natural Science Foundation of China (No. 60803016,No. 61170064), Tsinghua National Laboratory for Information Science and Technology (TNLIST) Cross-discipline Foundation, and the National HeGaoJi Key Project (No. 2010ZX01042-002-002-01).

CIKM'11, October 24–28, 2011, Glasgow, Scotland, UK.

2. PROBLEM DEFINITION

Given a d-dimensional space R^d and a finite label set $\mathcal{Y} = \{\lambda_1, \lambda_2, \ldots, \lambda_q\}$, the training set D is

$$D = \{(x_i, L^*(x_i)) \mid x_i \in \mathrm{R}^d, L^*(x_i) \subseteq \mathcal{Y}, 1 \le i \le m\}, \quad (1)$$

where x_i is a training instance in R^d, $L^*(x_i)$ the *actual label set* of x_i and m the number of training instances in D. Similarly, the testing set H consisting of n instances is

$$H = \{(t_j, L^*(t_j)) \mid t_j \in \mathrm{R}^d, L^*(t_j) \subseteq \mathcal{Y}, 1 \le j \le n\}. \quad (2)$$

Definition 1 (Multi-Label Classification, MLC). *Given a multi-label classification function $f : \mathrm{R}^d \to 2^{\mathcal{Y}}$, when a test instance $t \in \mathrm{R}^d$ arrives, the* predicted label set *of t is obtained by applying $f(t)$, denoted as $L(t)$ ($L(t) \subseteq \mathcal{Y}$). It is aimed to learn the function f on the training set D, such that for all instances $(t_j, L^*(t_j))$ in H, the average difference between $L(t_j)$ and $L^*(t_j)$ is as small as possible.*

3. THE MLRW METHOD

In this section, the overview of the MLRW method is introduced first. The rest subsections give a detailed description of the method step by step.

3.1 Overview

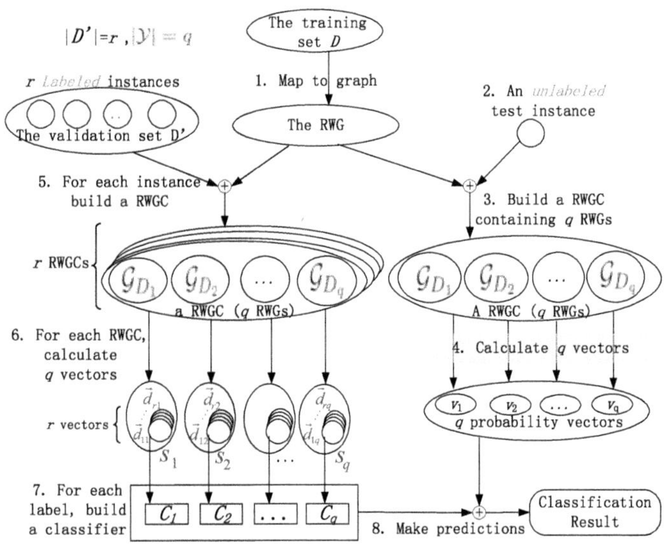

Figure 1: The workflow of MLRW

As shown in Fig. 1, MLRW takes the following steps to deal with the MLC problems.

(1) **Step 1: Map the multi-labeled instances to multi-label random walk graphs.** MLRW maps the multi-label training instances to a multi-label *Random Walk Graph* (RWG), denoted as G (See Section 3.2 for details).

(2) **Step 2–4: Random walks.** When an unlabeled instance t arrives, a multi-label *Random Walk Graph Collection* (RWGC) consisting of q RWGs is built on t and G. And then, the random walk is carried out on each RWG of the RWGC to get the output vectors (See Section 3.3 for details).

(3) **Step 5–7: Transform to single-label problems.** The output vectors mentioned above are utilized to build a classifier for each label. As a result, MLRW transforms the original multi-label problem to some single-label problems with the help of validation set D' (See Section 3.4 for details). Some traditional machine learning methods, such as SVM, Bayes and Decision Tree, can be utilized to build the classifiers.

(4) **Step 8: Make final predictions.** The binary classifiers built in *Step 5–7* are utilized to make the final prediction.

3.2 Multi-label Random Walk Graph

In MLRW, the multi-label training instances are mapped to a multi-label random walk graph (RWG) first. The operations in this subsection correspond to *Step 1* in Fig. 1.

Definition 2 (Multi-label Random Walk Graph). *Let D be a training set. The multi-label random walk graph of D is an undirected graph $\mathcal{G}_D = (V, E)$, where $V = \{x_i | (x_i, L^*(x_i)) \in D\}$, $E = \{(x_i, x_j) | \forall (x_i, L^*(x_i)), (x_j, L^*(x_j)) \in D, L^*(x_i) \cap L^*(x_j) \neq \emptyset\}$.*

In $\mathcal{G}_D$, each training instance is mapped to a vertex. The vertices carrying one or more same labels are connected.

At each vertex in $\mathcal{G}_D$, the walker has two choices, traveling to one of its neighbor vertices, or randomly teleporting to some vertex in the RWG. The probability of teleporting within the graph is called the *teleporting probability*, denoted as α, and the probability of traveling to one of its neighbors is denoted as $1 - \alpha$. It can be proved that the walk processing in the MLRW method is ergodic, therefore the walk processing tends to be convergent, from which we obtain a stable output vector.

Furthermore, the weight of each edge in $\mathcal{G}_D$ is calculated. The weight matrix is denoted as W_D, in which the element

$$[W_D]_{ij} = [W_D]_{ji} = \begin{cases} \infty, & x_i \neq x_j, (x_i, x_j) \notin E \\ 0, & x_i = x_j \\ ||x_i - x_j||, & x_i \neq x_j, (x_i, x_j) \in E \end{cases} \quad (3)$$

Similar to [1], the *Euclidean Distance* is utilized.

Without loss of generality, we assume that $\mathcal{G}_D$ is a connected graph. If not, we can split $\mathcal{G}_D$ into a series of *connected components*. Each connected component corresponds to a subset of $\mathcal{Y}$, and the subsets are disjoint from each other. Meanwhile, this situation indicates the existence of irrelevant label subsets in $\mathcal{Y}$. As a result, the original MLC problem can be broken up into several independent MLC subproblems so that the MLRW method can be applied to each subproblem.

3.3 Multi-Label Random Walk Model

The operations in this subsection correspond to *Step 2–4* in Fig. 1. When an unlabeled instance t is fed (*Step 2*), the following two operations, which correspond to *Step 3* and *Step 4*, will be carried out, respectively. (1) For each label $\lambda_l \in \mathcal{Y}$, we connect t with all the vertices carrying λ_l, i.e. $\lambda_l \in L^*(x_i)$, to form a new RWG. We denote this event as $t \lhd \lambda_l$. Since there are q labels in $\mathcal{Y}$, we get q RWGs to form a random walk graph collection (RWGC). (2) On each RWG in the RWGC, the random walk is carried out and a vector is obtained. In this paper, this vector is utilized to describe the similarity between t and each label in the label set. And then, the conditional probability vector is calculated. Since there are q RWGs in the RWGC, we get q conditional probability vectors, denoted as $\vec{d_{tl}} (l = 1, 2, \ldots, q)$.

3.3.1 Multi-label Random Walk Graph Collection

We build a multi-label random walk graph collection (R-WGC) on the aforementioned RWG $\mathcal{G}_D$ and the unlabeled instance t (*Step 3*).

Definition 3 (Random Walk Graph Collection). *Let D be a training set, $\mathcal{Y}$ the label set, R^d the d-dimensional* *input space, an instance $t \in \mathrm{R}^d$. The multi-label random walk graph collection (RWGC) of D and t is*

$$\mathbb{G}_{D,t} = \{\mathcal{G}_{D_i} | D_i = D \bigcup \{(t, \{\lambda_i\})\}, 1 \leq i \leq |\mathcal{Y}|\}, \quad (4)$$

where $\mathcal{G}_{D_i}$ is the RWG built on $D \bigcup \{(t, \{\lambda_i\})\}$.

After that, the random walk is carried out on each RWG in the RWGC.

3.3.2 Random Walks

Random walks are assumed to be Markov processes [3]. The random walk is carried out on each RWG, where at each step the walker travels to its neighbor vertices or randomly teleports to some vertex in the RWG according to a probability distribution. In our random walk model, at each vertex the walker prefers to go to its nearer points. The less the distance is, the higher probability it travels to. We cannot say about the exact position of the walker after some steps. The position is random, but we can calculate the distribution. In this paper, this distribution is utilized to describe the similarity between an unlabeled instance t and each label in $\mathcal{Y}$.

In random walks, four input parameters are needed. They are the adjacency matrix M, the initial value of the vector $\vec{s_u}$, i.e. $\vec{s_0}$, the teleporting vector $\vec{d}$ and the teleporting probability α.

The initial vector $\vec{s_0}$ represents how the walk starts. Each random walk consists of a number of iterations. At each iteration, the vector $\vec{s_u}$ is updated as follows.

$$\vec{s_{u+1}} = (1 - \alpha) \cdot M^T \cdot \vec{s_u} + \alpha \cdot \vec{d} \ (u = 0, 1, 2, \ldots) \quad (5)$$

The Equ. (5) is applied iteratively until $\vec{s_u} = \vec{s_{u+1}}$. In this situation, we say the random walk is convergent and denote the vector of $\vec{s_u}$ as $\vec{\pi}$, such that

$$\vec{\pi} = (1 - \alpha) \cdot M^T \cdot \vec{\pi} + \alpha \cdot \vec{d}. \quad (6)$$

In actual applications, if $||\vec{s_{u+1}} - \vec{s_u}|| < \epsilon$ (ϵ is a predefined threshold), let $\vec{\pi} = \vec{s_u}$. In our experiments, the value of ϵ is set to 10^{-6}.

Suppose the random walk is carried out on the RWG $\mathcal{G}_{D_l}$ of $\mathbb{G}_{D,t}$. The vector $\vec{\pi}$ is a $(|\mathrm{D}|+1)$-dimensional vector and its first element $\vec{\pi}[1]$ corresponds the situation that the walker remains at the starting position of t. We define the *Similarity Score* between the instance t and the training instance $x_i \in D$ to be the $(i+1)^{\mathrm{th}}$ element of the vector $\vec{\pi}$, such as

$$\mathrm{Similarity}(t, x_i) = \vec{\pi}[i+1] \ \ (1 \leq i \leq |D|) \quad (7)$$

For each label λ_k, the training instances carrying label λ_k are selected and their similarity scores are averaged as the similarity score between t and the label λ_k, such as

$$\mathrm{Similarity}(t, \lambda_k) = \mathrm{avg}\{\mathrm{Similarity}(t, x_i) | x_i \in D, \lambda_k \in L^*(x_i)\}. \quad (8)$$

And then, the conditional probability vector $P(\lambda_k \in L(t) | t \lhd \lambda_l)$ will be

$$\vec{d_{tl}}[k] = P(\lambda_k \in L(t) | t \lhd \lambda_l) = \frac{\mathrm{Similarity}(t, \lambda_k)}{\sum_{i=1}^{q} \mathrm{Similarity}(t, \lambda_i)}, \quad (9)$$

where $k = 1, 2, \ldots, q$ and $\vec{d_{i\,l}}[k]$ is the kth element of $\vec{d_{i\,l}}$. $\vec{d_{i\,l}}[k]$ indicates the conditional probability that the predicted label set of t_i includes λ_k when $t_i \lhd \lambda_l$.

3.4 Problem Transformation

We make use of a *validation set* to transform the original MLC problem to some SLC subproblems. The validation set, denoted as D', is a *labeled* data set which is similar to the training set, but the two data sets have no common instance. It will be utilized to build a classifier for each label in $\mathcal{Y}$.

For each instance $z_i \in D'$, *Step 5–6* are taken, which are similar to *Step 3–4*. After that, we get a series of vectors as Equ. (9), denoted as $\vec{d_{i\,1}}, \vec{d_{i\,2}}, \ldots, \vec{d_{i\,q}}$ as follows.

$$\vec{d_{i\,l}}[k] = P(\lambda_k \in L(z_i) | z_i \lhd \lambda_l), \ \ (k = 1, 2, \ldots, q), \quad (10)$$

After that, we make use of these vectors to build a new training set for each label (*Step 7*).

Suppose S_l is the new training set for the label λ_l. S_l is generated on the vectors of $\{\vec{d_{il}} | z_i \in D'\}$. The vector $\vec{d_{il}}$ is marked as a positive training instance for the label λ_l if the actual label set of z_i contains λ_l, i.e., $\lambda_l \in L^*(z_i)$. Otherwise, $\vec{d_{il}}$ is marked as a negative training instance for λ_l. Formally,

$$S_l = \{T_l, F_l\}, \quad (11)$$

$$T_l = \{(\vec{d_{il}}, +1) | \lambda_l \in L^*(z_i), z_i \in D'\}, \quad (12)$$

$$F_l = \{(\vec{d_{il}}, -1) | \lambda_l \notin L^*(z_i), z_i \in D'\}. \quad (13)$$

When an unlabeled instance arrives, after *Step 1–4* is taken, the q output vectors will be applied as the inputs of the q classifiers respectively to get the final prediction result (*Step 8*). The comparison of different classifiers is presented in Section 4.2, in which some popular classification models, such as SVM, ID3 decision tree, kNN, AdaBoost, Naïve Bayes, are involved.

4. EXPERIMENTS

MLRW provides much more accurate predictions than many other MLC methods. Experimental results and related theoretical analysis will be involved in this section.

4.1 Experimental Setup

There are two types of measures for MLC methods, i.e. the ranking based measures and the classification based ones [5]. For a testing set H denoted as Equ. (2), the *multi-label average precision*, *one-error*, *coverage* are utilized as the ranking based measurements. The traditional single-label measurements of *precision*, *recall* and *F-measure* have also been adapted as classification based multi-label measurements.

In this paper, the experiments were carried out on the *yeast* and *scene* data sets (all publicly available), which stood for the biology and image data[1].

We implemented MLRW based on *MuLan*[2], which is an open source Java library for multi-label learning tasks. Based on *Weka*[3], MuLan implements many state-of-the-art multi-label classification algorithms. All the experiments were carried out on a PC with an Intel® Core™ 2.33 GHz CPU, 2GB memory and 1.0TB hard disk. The OS of the PC was Ubuntu Server 9.10 and the version of JDK was 1.6.0.

4.2 The Effectiveness of MLRW

The multi-label learning methods of *binary relevance* (BR) [6], *label powerset* (LP) [4], *calibrated label ranking* (CLR) [2], *random-k label set* (RA*k*EL) [7], *include labels* (IL) [6] and *multi-label k-nearest neighbor* (ML*k*NN) [8] were involved in the comparison experiments. The base classifier of BR, LP, CLR and IL was the frequently used support vector machine

[1]http://mulan.sourceforge.net/datasets.html
[2]http://mulan.sourceforge.net/
[3]http://www.cs.waikato.ac.nz/~ml/weka/

Table 1: Parameter settings

Algorithm	Parameter	Value
SVM	*kernel*	linear/polynomial/RBF/sigmoid
LP	*accept threshold*	0.5
MLkNN	k	2–10
RAkEL	k	3
	n	$2q$
	accept threshold	0.5
MLRW	α	0.15

Table 2: Multi-label evaluations on *Yeast*

Algorithm	One-Error	Coverage	Avg-Precision	Precision	Recall	F-measure
BR	0.2551	10.8364	0.5500	0.7009	0.5605	0.6222
LP	0.2551	9.8441	0.6415	0.5850	0.5504	0.5617
CLR	0.2597	7.7971	0.7097	0.6386	0.5917	0.6140
IL	0.5038	8.2468	0.4123	0.5920	0.5857	0.5883
RAkEL	0.2911	7.6543	0.7096	0.6200	0.6032	0.6115
MLkNN	0.2844	7.4143	**0.7284**	**0.7356**	0.5432	0.6249
MLRW	**0.2451**	**7.4100**	0.7069	0.6617	**0.7168**	**0.6879**

(SVM). As an implementation of the SVM model, the "libSVM" library was utilized[4]. As shown in Table 1, for each SVM in our experiments we had examined 4 most used kernel functions, i.e. the linear, polynomial, RBF(Gaussian) and sigmoid kernels. The one conducts the best result (F-measure) was selected. In MLkNN, we changed the value of k from 2 to 10 and selected the one making best result (F-measure), e.g. k was set to 3 for *yeast*. For RAkEL, k was set to the recommended value, i.e. $k = 3, n = 2q$.

Before each experiment, we mixed the original training and testing data sets. The experiments were then carried out with a 5-fold cross validation. The ratio between the training and the validation set was 4 to 1. Noticed that the training, validation and testing sets were disjoint from each other. Each experiment was repeated for 10 times with a random sampling and permutation as a preprocess. Table 2 and 3 showed the average results over these 50 runs of the experiment.

Taking the *yeast* data set for example, experimental results showed that the *one-error* and *coverage* of MLRW were the best of all methods. Also, MLRW achieved a good output on the evaluation of *average-precision*. The best value of *coverage* indicates the smallest cost to find out all proper labels. The best *one-error* result implicates the top ranked output of MLRW is usually a credible result. In many applications, such as web search, advertisement recommendation, personalized customization, the top ranked result(s) usually attracts more attention. MLRW will be an applicable solution in these situations. On the aforementioned multi-label measurements of multi-label precision, recall and F-measure, the BR, LP, CLR, IL, RAkEL and MLkNN methods were also utilized to make comparisons. For MLRW, AdaBoost.M1 was utilized to build the classifiers in *Step 7* Similarly, they were the average results of 10 runs of each approach with 5-fold cross validation. Among all MLC methods in the experiment, MLRW provided the most accurate outputs. In detail, on F-measure MLRW achieved a 10.08% improvement compared to MLkNN, which took the second place. In BR, the prediction of each label was considered as an independent task and the label relationships were completely ignored. MLRW achieved a 10.50% improvement than BR. As another kind of MLC method, LP encoded each multi-label combination into a new label. It thus significantly increased the total number of labels and made the prediction much more complicated. In this experiment, MLRW achieved a 22.46% improvement than LP.

[4]http://www.csie.ntu.edu.tw/~cjlin/libsvm/

Table 3: Multi-label evaluations on *Scene*

Algorithm	One-Error	Coverage	Avg-Precision	Precision	Recall	F-measure
BR	0.5762	1.8473	0.5986	0.7621	0.4330	0.5522
LP	0.2800	0.9190	0.7995	0.7200	0.6605	0.6889
CLR	0.2400	**0.5140**	0.8553	0.7409	0.6559	0.6958
IL	0.4260	1.2844	0.7121	0.6133	0.6055	0.6093
RAkEL	0.3178	0.9930	0.7858	**0.9145**	0.3633	0.5200
MLkNN	0.2912	0.6650	0.8526	0.7823	0.6472	0.7083
MLRW	**0.2260**	0.8271	**0.8710**	0.8014	**0.6755**	**0.7330**

MLkNN, which made use of the statistical information to carry out predictions, did better than other MLC methods except MLRW. But there were two shortcomings in the MLkNN method. One was that the value of the parameter k should be decided manually and it might rely on the actual data set. Another defect of MLkNN was that k nearest neighbor(s) of each data point was (were) found directly in the original input space. As the dimension of the input space grew, no matter which distance function was utilized (Euclidean distance, Manhattan distance, or others), the distances between any two data points tended to be similar. The phenomenon was the well-known curse of dimensionality. Both of the two aspects delivered negative effects on the prediction results. MLRW made use of the distance between two data points to build the random walk graph, but it just connected those data points sharing same label(s), leaving other points unconnected, i.e. the distances were infinite. Additionally, MLRW transformed the original input space into a q-dimensional one, making MLRW more applicable to high-dimensional data than MLkNN. In conclusion, MLRW is a more effective solution to the MLC problems than MLkNN and other MLC methods.

5. CONCLUSIONS

In this paper, we proposed a novel multi-label classification method based on the random walk model, called MLRW. It maps the multi-label data to graphs, on which the random walk model is applied. And then, the original multi-label classification problem is transformed to some binary classification subproblems, which can be resolved by traditional classification methods. Experimental results on real data sets show that MLRW is an effective solution to the multi-label classification problems. In future works, we will focus on the reduction of time consumption of MLRW to further improve its performance.

6. REFERENCES

[1] W. Chen, J. Yan, B. Zhang, Z. Chen, and Q. Yang. Document transformation for multi-label feature selection in text categorization. *ICDM*, pages 451–456, 2007.

[2] J. Fürnkranz, E. Hüllermeier, E. Loza Mencía, and K. Brinker. Multilabel classification via calibrated label ranking. *Machine Learning*, 73(2):133–153, 2008.

[3] L. Lovász. Random walks on graphs: A survey. *Combinatorics, Paul Erdos is Eighty*, 2(1):1–46, 1993.

[4] J. Read, B. Pfahringer, and G. Holmes. Multi-label classification using ensembles of pruned sets. *ICDM*, pages 995–1000, 2009.

[5] G. Tsoumakas and I. Katakis. Multi-label classification: An overview. *International Journal of Data Warehousing and Mining*, 3(3):1–13, 2007.

[6] G. Tsoumakas, I. Katakis, and I. Vlahavas. Mining multi-label data. In O. Maimon and L. Rokach, editors, *Data Mining and Knowledge Discovery Handbook*, pages 667–685. Springer, 2010.

[7] G. Tsoumakas and I. Vlahavas. Random k-labelsets: An ensemble method for multilabel classification. *ECML*, pages 406–417, 2007.

[8] M.-L. Zhang and Z.-H. Zhou. Ml-knn: A lazy learning approach to multi-label learning. *Pattern Recogn.*, 40(7):2038–2048, 2007.

Latent Feature Encoding using Dyadic and Relational Data

Shin Ando
Dept. of Computer Science
Gunma University, Japan
shin.ando@acm.org

ABSTRACT

Learning from dyadic and relational data is a fundamental problem for IR and KDD applications in web and social media domain. Basic behaviors and characteristics of users and documents are typically described by a collection of dyads, i.e., pairs of entities. Discriminative features extracted from such data are essential in exploratory and discriminatory analyses. Relational properties of the entities reflect pair-wise similarities and their collective community structure which are also valuable for discriminative learning. A challenging aspect of learning from the relational data in many domains, is that the generative process of relational links appears noisy and is not well described by a stochastic model. In this paper, we present a principled approach for learning discriminative features from heterogeneous sources of dyadic and relational data. We propose an information-theoretic framework called Latent Feature Encoding (LFE) which projects the entities and the links to a latent feature space in the analogy of *lossy*-encoding. Projection is formalized as a maximization of the mutual information preserved in the latent features, regularized by the compression rate of encoding. The regularization is emphasized over more probable links to account for the noisiness of the observation. An empirical evaluation of the proposed method using text and social media datasets is presented. Performances in supervised and unsupervised learning tasks are compared with those of conventional latent feature extraction methods.

Categories and Subject Descriptors

G.3 [Mathematics of Computing]: Probability and Statistics - Statistical Computing; H.3.3 [Information Search and Retrieval]: Information Search and Retrieval - Clustering; I.2.7 [Natural Language Processing]: Text analysis

General Terms

Algorithms, Theory, Experimentation

Keywords

dimensionality reduction, latent topic analysis, topic-link analysis, document clustering, text categorization

1. INTRODUCTION

Learning from dyadic and relational data is a fundamental problem for information retrieval and knowledge discovery from web and social media data, such as hyper-linked text and social networks. In many domains, the basic characteristics and behaviors are described by a collection of dyads, or pairs of entities, e.g., document-term co-occurrences and sales/purchase events for consumer-product pairs. Discriminative features extracted from the dyadic data provides the basis for exploratory and discriminatory analyses. In text mining, popular algorithms such as pLSI and LDA project documents to a topic-model parameter feature space, in which text categorization and clustering are effectively performed [3, 9].

Relational properties such as friendship-links and cross-citations are also valuable for discriminative learning as they reflect pair-wise similarities or correlations and the collective community structure of entities. Recent studies suggest that the connectivity of the relational links is relevant to the *manifold* structure of the data. Many high-dimensional, real-world data such as text and images are shown to be distributed over low-dimensional *manifold* [7] and can be projected to a low-dimensional feature space while preserving the intrinsic structure. In text mining, carefully selected relations, such as nearest-neighbor links, can help generate low-dimensional topic features that improve classification and clustering performances [4]. Auxiliary hyper-links such as cross-reference and co-authorship can also be leveraged to infer low-perplexity topic-models [6].

A challenging aspect of learning from relational data, meanwhile, is the *noisiness* of the observed links. In a social network, a connection may be associated with various types of interactions between the entities. However, such variety is usually not reflected by the attributes of the links. The generative process can appear *noisy* as a result, and is difficult to describe using a stochastic model. In within-network classification problems, the precision is known to decrease when latent features extracted from noisy relational links [?]. In text domain, modeling the link generation process is a challenging problem, and a practical precision for link prediction is yet to be achieved using typical models such as topology-based or node-similarity-based models [6, 8].

The motivation of our work is to develop a principled approach for learning latent features from heterogeneous sources of dyadic and relational data and also to effectively exploit noisy observations of the relational links. In this paper, we propose Latent Feature Encoding (LFE) framework, which formalizes the projection of entities to a latent-feature space in the analogy of *lossy*-encoding. The quality of *lossy*-encoding is measured in two-fold: 1) the rate, i.e., the average number of bits required to express the encoded data, and 2) the loss of reproducibility of the original data. We associate the latter measure with an entropic quantity of predictive information preserved in the latent features. The projection is formalized as a maximization of the predictive information with regularization using the rate of encoding. Regularization of LFE framework penalizes the dissimilarities between the linked entities in the latent-feature space so that its neighborhood structure reflects the relational properties. The regularization integrates a stochastic model of the link generation among entities. The penalty is emphasized on links that are probable with regards to the generative model to account for the noisiness of observed links.

2. LATENT FEATURE ENCODING

2.1 Review of Latent Topic Encoding

This section reviews the formalization of the information-theoretic framework [1] for latent topic analysis. Let D denote a variable representing the documents $\mathcal{D} = \{d_i\}_{i=1}^{\eta}$ and Z the latent variable representing the unobserved topics taking a value from $\mathcal{Z} = \{z_i\}_{i=1}^{\kappa}$. In the analogy of *lossy*-encoding, Z is viewed as an encoding of the source signal D. The measure of quality in *lossy*-encoding is two-fold: the rate $\mathcal{R}$ and the distortion $\mathcal{T}$. The rate of encoding is the average number of bits required to send the encoded signal, which is upper-bound by the mutual information between the source and the encoded signal, i.e., $\mathcal{R} = I(Z; D)$. The distortion is a user-defined function to measure the loss of reproducibility of the source signal. For the purpose of topic analysis, we associate distortion $\mathcal{T}$ with the mutual information shared between the documents and the topics, $\mathcal{T} = -I(V; Z)$. We denote by a variable V the vector representation of documents based on the occurrence/frequency of the vocabulary terms $\mathcal{W} = \{w_i\}_{i=1}^{\tau}$.

Minimizing the compression rate and the average distortion at a given trade-off is a central problem for lossy-compression. Given a coefficient β, the rate-distortion function $\mathcal{L}$ is defined

$$\mathcal{L} = \mathcal{R} + \beta\mathcal{T} = I(Z; D) - \beta I(V; Z) \tag{1}$$

$\mathcal{L}$ is a functional of $p(Z|D)$, $p(Z)$, and $p(V|Z)$. Using a variational approach, $\mathcal{L}$ is minimized with respect to each parameter [1].

The output $p(Z|d)$ represents how strong the respective topics are reflected in d. It is also an encoding the document and serves as a κ-dimensional feature vector for discriminative learning. In the following, we refer to this framework as Latent Topic Encoding (LTE).

2.2 Formalization

In this section, we extend the LTE framework for linked documents viewing Z as an encoding of the co-occurrences of links and documents. Let $\mathcal{Y} = \{y_h\}_{h=1}^{\psi}$ denote the set of observed links. We denote the documents linked by y_h as $\varepsilon(y_h) = \{d, d'\}$. The generative process of a relational link y is modeled via the conditional probability with regards to a document d, $p(y|d)$. Generative models used in link prediction problems are generally categorized as either node-information-based or topological-information-based. We employ a logistic model based on the similarity of topic-parameter vectors, which is of the former category and used commonly for topic discovery [6, 8].

The probability function for two documents to be connected by a link is denoted by ϕ. ϕ is defined by a sigmoid function σ and document feature-vectors $\mathbf{q}(d) = p(Z|d)$ as follows

$$\phi(\{d, d'\}) = \sigma(\nu^T(\mathbf{q}_d \circ \mathbf{q}_{d'} + \pi)) \tag{2}$$

where $\circ$ is the Hadamard product and ν, π parametrizes σ.

$p(y|d)$ is defined from ϕ as follows

$$p(y|d) = \begin{cases} \phi(\varepsilon(y)) & \text{if } z \in \varepsilon(y) \\ 0 & \text{otherwise} \end{cases} \tag{3}$$

Let Y denote the variable representing the values of y. The average rate for Z encoding the co-occurrence of links and the documents is upper-bound by

$$\mathcal{R}' = I(Z; (D, Y)) = I(Z; D) + I(Z; Y|D) \tag{4}$$

The first term in (4) is the rate of encoding the documents equivalent to $\mathcal{R}$. The second term represents the rate for encoding the links given the documents and is rewritten as

$$I(Z; Y|D) = \sum_{z,y,d} p(z|y, d)p(y|d)p(d) \log \frac{p(z|y, d)}{p(z|d)} \tag{5}$$

Intuitively, (5) is interpreted as the expected KL divergence of the topic distributions $p(Z|d)$ between documents sharing an existing link y, i.e., $\{d : p(y|d) \neq 0\}$. Note that from the Bayes' rule,

$$p(z|d) = \sum_{y} p(z|y, d)p(y|d) \tag{6}$$

Latent Feature Encoding (LFE), is formalized as a minimization problem using $\mathcal{R}'$ as the regularization term. From above discussions, reducing $\mathcal{R}'$ induces the homogeneity of $p(Z|d)$ among linked documents. Also note that in (5), the contribution of each link to $\mathcal{R}'$ is weighted by $p(y|d)$. Thus, a stronger emphasis is placed on the homogeneity over links with a higher conditional probability.

The loss function for LFE is defined as

$$\mathcal{L}' = \mathcal{R}' + \beta\mathcal{T} \tag{7}$$

A variational approach for solving the minimization of the functional $\mathcal{L}'$ is described in the next section.

2.3 Parameter Estimation

From the definitions of mutual and conditional mutual information, $\mathcal{L}'$ is a functional of $p(Z|Y, D)$, $p(Z)$, and $p(V|Z)$.

In the following, we outline the variational approach for addressing the minimization problem

$$\arg \min_{p(Z|Y,D)} \mathcal{L}'$$

The detail of the derivation is omitted.

From (7), we define a variational problem

$$\frac{\partial \mathcal{L}'}{\partial p(z|y, d)} = \frac{\partial \mathcal{R}'}{\partial p(z|y, d)} + \frac{\partial \mathcal{T}}{\partial p(z|y, d)} = 0 \tag{8}$$

The partial derivatives of $\mathcal{R}' = I(Z;(D,Y))$ and $\mathcal{T} = -I(V;Z)$ are given as follows.

$$\frac{\partial \mathcal{R}'}{\partial p(z|y,d)} = p(y,d)\log\frac{p(z|y,d)}{p(z)} \quad (9)$$

$$\frac{\partial \mathcal{T}}{\partial p(z|y,d)} = p(y,d)\left\{-\sum_{v} p(v|d)\log\frac{p(v|z)}{p(v)}\right\} \quad (10)$$

Substituting the derivatives to (8) and introducing Lagrange multipliers, we solve for $p(z|y,d)$

$$p(z|y,d) = \frac{p(z)}{\zeta(y,d)} e^{\left(-\beta\sum_{v} p(v|d)\log\frac{p(v|d)}{p(v|z)}\right)} \quad (11)$$

where $\zeta(y,d)$ denotes the normalizer.

From (6), $p(z|d)$ can be written as the weighed average of $p(z|y,d)$ over the documents sharing a link with d

$$p(z|d) = \frac{1}{\#\varrho(d)}\sum_{y\in\varrho(d)} p(y|d)\frac{p(z)}{\zeta(y,d)} e^{(-\mathrm{KL}[p(v|z)|p(v|d)])} \quad (12)$$

where $\varrho(d)$ denotes the set of links stemming from d.

Given $p(z|d)$, $p(z)$ is determined from the Bayes rule (??). Since $I(Z;(Y,D))$ is independent of $p(\mathbf{v}|z)$, $p(\mathbf{v}|z)$ is estimated to maximize $I(V;Z)$ and thereby to minimize $\mathcal{L}'$ given fixed $p(z|d)$ and $p(z)$. Let $p(\mathbf{v}|z;\theta_z)$ denote the probability function parametrized by an instance θ_z in a parametric space Θ. $I(V;Z)$ is maximized with the maximum likelihood estimate $\hat{\theta}_z$ [1].

$$\hat{\theta}_z = \arg\max_{\theta\in\Theta}\sum_{\mathbf{v},z}\log p(\mathbf{v}|z;\theta) \quad (13)$$

In this work, $p(\mathbf{v}|z;\theta)$ is modeled by a multinomial distribution. Let $\theta = (\vartheta_1,\ldots,\vartheta_\tau)$ denote an instance in the τ-nomial model parameter space. The likelihood of $\mathbf{v} = (v_1,\ldots,v_\tau)$ given θ is

$$p(\mathbf{v};\theta) = S!\prod_{j=1}^{\tau}\frac{\vartheta_j^{v_j}}{v_j!} \quad (14)$$

where S is the sum of all word occurrences.

We parametrize $p(\mathbf{v}|z)$ with a multinomial parameter θ_z, i.e., $p(\mathbf{v}|z) = p(\mathbf{v};\theta_z)$. From a set of documents $\mathcal{D}$ and $p(Z|D)$, the maximum likelihood estimate $\hat{\theta}_z = (\hat{\vartheta}_{z1},\ldots,\hat{\vartheta}_{z\tau})$ is given as follows.

$$\hat{\vartheta}_{zj} = \frac{\sum_{d\in\mathcal{D}} p(z|d)v_j}{\sum_j\sum_{d\in\mathcal{D}} p(z|d)v_j} \quad (15)$$

From $p(z)$ and $p(v|z)$, $p(z|y,d)$ can be updated by (11). A local minimum of $\mathcal{L}'$ is obtained by iteratively updating the three sets of parameters by (11), (??), and (13).

A key difference of LFE framework from LTE is exhibited in the updating equation for $p(Z|D)$. (12) shows that in LFE, $p(z|d)$ is updated with regards to other documents linked to d. The update propagates the latent feature $p(Z|d)$ between the linked documents, thereby transferring the relational properties to a Euclidean neighborhood structure in the model-parameter space.

3. EMPIRICAL EVALUATION

We present an empirical evaluation of LFE algorithm using text and social media datasets.

3.1 Text Classification

3.1.1 *Data Description*

Two datasets are taken from well-known benchmarks: Reuters-21578 and 20Newsgroups corpora.

From Reuters-21578, we selected topics with at least 50 articles which totals to 37 categories and 6896 documents. For 20Newsgroups, we selected eight subcategories belonging to the major categories of science and recreation. The selected subcategories are: sci.crypt, sci.electronics, sci.med, sci.space, rec.autos, rec.motorcycles, rec.sport.baseball, and rec.sport.hockey. The vocabulary consists of $\tau = 2000$ terms with largest values of $I(w;D) = \sum_d p(w,d)\log\frac{p(w|d)}{p(w)}$. We refer to these datasets as R37 and NG2.4, respectively.

The relational properties of R37 and NG2.4 were generated by linking q-nearest neighbors from each document. [4, 5] have shown that the nearest-neighbor graph of documents can provide information about the local data structure that are valuable for topic discovery. Neighbors are selected based on the cosine distance between their word-frequency vector representations. Since the results were robust for $q = 4, 8, 12$, we only show the results for $q = 8$.

3.1.2 *Setup*

We train SVM classifiers on the output $p(Z|d)$ of LFE and evaluate the accuracy on the test set. The accuracy of the classifiers can indicate the amount of discriminative information preserved in the representation [3]. The classifiers are trained and evaluated using baseline methods in the same manner. The following methods are employed as baselines: LTE, pLSA, Non-negative Matrix Factorization (NMF), and Locally-consistent Topic Modeling (LTM) [5]. NMF yields feature vectors from a non-negative factorization of the term-document co-occurrence matrix. LTM is a variant of pLSA which employs a graph-Laplacian function to regularize parameter estimation.

For NG2.4, we predict the major category of the documents. For R37, we predict whether the label of the document is *acq*, *earn*, or *other*, which includes the rest of the document altogether. The proportion of the respective labels approximates to 6:10:17. The experiment is carried out with different numbers of topics κ, which is a common parameter among all methods. LFE is executed with $\beta = 10$. We tested various β in the interval of $[5:50]$ and found the performance to be robust among those values.

3.1.3 *Results*

We compared the classification accuracy of respective methods on R37, with κ ranging from 10 to 40. The classification accuracy on NG2.4, is compared with κ ranging from 2 to 20. Two methods incorporating the link structures, LFE and LTM, yielded best accuracies. The tendencies of other methods differ slightly between smaller and larger values of κ. The performances of LTE and LTM similarly converge at $\kappa = 20$ and $\kappa = 15$ for R37 and NG2.4 respectively. LFE performed better in comparison for larger κ.

3.2 Text Clustering

3.3 Setup

The estimated topic model parameters $p(Z|d)$ is used as features for clustering documents with k-means algorithm. The same methods from previous sections are used for the baseline. LFE and the baseline methods are applied to R37 dataset with κ ranging from 10 to 40.

3.3.1 Evaluation

To measure the quality of clustering, we define Conditional Entropy Ratio (CER), the ratio of conditional entropy of the true topics C after learning the prediction $\tilde{C}$.

$$\mathrm{CER}(C, \tilde{C}) = \frac{H(C|\tilde{C})}{H(C)} \quad (16)$$

Note that CER ≥ 0 and the equality stands when two partitioning are identical.

CER can be written in relation to the Normalized Mutual Information (NMI) as follows

$$\mathrm{CER}(C, \tilde{C}) = 1 - \mathrm{NMI}(C, \tilde{C}) \quad (17)$$

provided that $p(C|\tilde{C})$ is a hard-mapping and $H(C) > H(\tilde{C})$. CER is comparable between different trials from using a fixed denominator as shown in (16).

For NMF, we calculate CER from NMI by (17). For the rest of the baselines and the proposed methods, $p(C|\tilde{C})$ is computed from $p(\tilde{C}|D)$ as follows

$$p(c|\tilde{c}) = \sum p(c|d) \frac{p(\tilde{c}|d)}{\sum_{\tilde{c}} p(\tilde{c}|d)} \quad (18)$$

3.3.2 Results

Comparison the CER for R37 dataset, LFE outperformed the baseline methods significantly for each value of κ. LFE also performs consistently over different values of κ. This is a practical advantage as overestimated value for κ may be used in practice.

3.4 Topic Discovery

3.4.1 Data Description

For the next experiment, another dataset is taken from bibliographical records of Digital Bibliography and Library Project (DBLP). Publications from four conferences: ECML, ICDM, ICDE, and VLDB, during 1998-2004 were extracted, and all titles by each unique author were concatenated. The graph edges were generated between authors with at least one co-authored paper. The graph includes 3111 vertices (texts) and 6674 edges. $\tau = 2000$ vocabulary terms are selected based on $I(w; D)$. We refer to this dataset as DBLP4.

3.4.2 Setup

For topic discovery task, we evaluate a list of terms with the largest probabilities in θ_z for each z. The terms reflect the content of the topic, and the consistency of the terms and known semantics is a key measure for topic discovery. We make intuitive comparison of the terms extracted from DBLP4 using LFE, pLSA, and LTM. The initial $p(Z|D)$ and the number of topics to $\kappa = 4$, corresponding to the number of conferences, is replicated for all methods.

3.4.3 Results

Twelve terms with the largest probability values among topics z_1-z_4 of pLSA, LTM, and LFE, were examined manually. The topic z_4 of pLSA is recognizable as database-related terms. In the rest of the topics, biology/machine learning/data engineering related terms are inter-mixed. In comparison, the representative terms for LTM and LFE are semantically more distinctive. Topics z_1, z_3, and z_4 for LFE are recognizable as machine learning, data engineering, and database-related terms respectively, with few biological terms dispersed among z_2, z_3, and z_4. The topic z_2 of LTM includes both data mining and machine learning terms. Terms related to data engineering appear mostly in topic z_3 but also in z_4. z_1 consists of distinct machine leaning terms but are different from that of LFE. Overall, the terms extracted from LFE capture the topics of four conferences and makes better distinction compared to baselines.

4. CONCLUSION

In this paper, we presented a general framework called LFE for learning discriminative features from dyadic and relational data based on the principles of *lossy*-encoding. LFE formalizes a projection of linked entities to a latent feature space with a regularization framework to preserve the relational structure of the entities as the neighborhood structure in the projected space. The performance in text categorization tasks indicate that the proposed method preserve more discriminative information in the projected parameter space by exploiting the link structure. Empirical comparison of the topic-representative terms in the topic discovery task showed that the proposed method can extract terms that are more in agreement with intuitive categories of the text.

5. REFERENCES

[1] S. Ando. Clustering needles in a haystack: An information theoretic analysis of minority and outlier detection. In ICDM '07: Procs. of the 2007 Seventh IEEE Intl. Conf. on Data Mining, pages 13–22, 2007.

[2] S. Ando and E. Suzuki. Detection of unique temporal segments by information theoretic meta-clustering. In KDD '09: Procs. of the 15th ACM SIGKDD Intl. Conf. on Knowledge discovery and data mining, pages 59–68, 2009.

[3] D. Blei, A. Ng, and M. Jordan. Latent dirichlet allocation. J. Mach. Learn. Res., 3:993–1022, 2003.

[4] D. Cai, Q. Mei, J. Han, and C. Zhai. Modeling hidden topics on document manifold. In CIKM '08: Proceeding of the 17th ACM Conf. on Information and knowledge management, pages 911–920, 2008.

[5] D. Cai, X. Wang, and X. He. Probabilistic dyadic data analysis with local and global consistency. In ICML '09: Procs. of the 26th Annual Intl. Conf. on Machine Learning, pages 105–112, 2009.

[6] J. Chang and D. Blei. Relational topic models for document networks. In Procs. of the Twelfth Intl. Conf. on Artificial Intelligence and Statistics, volume 5, pages 81–88, 2009.

[7] X. He and P. Niyogi. Locality preserving projections. In Advances in Neural Information Processing Systems 16. 2004.

[8] Y. Liu, A. Niculescu-Mizil, and W. Gryc. Topic-link LDA: joint models of topic and author community. In ICML '09: Procs. of the 26th Annual Intl. Conf. on Machine Learning, pages 665–672, 2009.

[9] W. Xu, X. Liu, and Y. Gong. Document clustering based on non-negative matrix factorization. In SIGIR '03: Procs. of the 26th annual Intl. ACM SIGIR Conf. on Research and development in informaion retrieval, pages 267–273, 2003.

Learning Kernels with Upper Bounds of Leave-One-Out Error

Yong Liu
yongliu@tju.edu.cn

Shizhong Liao
szliao@tju.edu.cn

Yuexian Hou
yxhou@tju.edu.cn

School of Computer Science and Technology
Tianjin University, Tianjin 300072, P. R. China

ABSTRACT

We propose a new leaning method for Multiple Kernel Learning (MKL) based on the upper bounds of the leave-one-out error that is an almost unbiased estimate of the expected generalization error. Specifically, we first present two new formulations for MKL by minimizing the upper bounds of the leave-one-out error. Then, we compute the derivatives of these bounds and design an efficient iterative algorithm for solving these formulations. Experimental results show that the proposed method gives better accuracy results than that of both SVM with the uniform combination of basis kernels and other state-of-art kernel learning approaches.

Categories and Subject Descriptors

I.2.6 [**Artificial Intelligence**]: Learning—*Parameter Learning*; H.2.8 [**Database Management**]: Database Applications—*Data Mining*; I.5.2 [**Pattern Recognition**]: Design Methodology—*Classifier Design and Evaluation*

General Terms

Algorithms, Theory, Experimentation

Keywords

Multiple Kernel Learning (MKL), Support Vector Machine, Leave-One-Out Error, Generalization Error Bound

1. INTRODUCTION

Kernel methods, such as support vector machines (SVM), have been widely used in pattern recognition and machine learning. A good kernel function, which implicitly characterizes a suitable transformation of input data, can greatly benefit the accuracy of the predictor. However, when there are many available kernels, it is difficult for the user to pick out a suitable one.

Instead of using a single kernel, recent applications have shown that using multiple kernels can enhance the interpretability of the decision function and improve performance. In such cases, a convenient approach is to consider the kernel as a convex combination of the basis kernels. Within this framework, the problem of learning the kernel is transformed to the problem of deciding the combination coefficients. Lanckriet et al. [7] formulate this problem as a semidefinite programming problem which allows to learn the combination coefficients and SVM classifier together, which is usually called multiple kernel learning (MKL). To enhance the computational efficiency, different approaches for solving this MKL problem have been proposed, semi-infinite linear program [9], second-order cone program [6], gradient-based methods [8], and second-order optimization [2].

For SVM, it is well known that the estimation error, which denotes the gap between the expected error and the empirical error, is bounded by $\sqrt{O(R^2\gamma^{-2})/\ell}$, where R is the radius of the minimum enclosing ball of training data in the feature space endowed with the kernel used, γ is the margin of SVM classifier, and ℓ is the number of training data. However, most existing MKL approaches decide the value of combination coefficients only by maximizing the margin γ^2. In this way, although γ^2 is the maximum, the R^2 may be very large too, so the estimation error bound may be too loose to guarantee good generalization performance of SVM.

To address the above problem, we directly minimize the upper bounds of expected error to decide the combination coefficients. Specifically, we first present two minimization formulations for MKL based on upper bounds of leave-one-out error. Using the derivatives of these bounds with respect to combination coefficients, we then propose a gradient descent algorithm to address these minimization formulations. Experiments show that our method gives significant performance improvements both over SVM with the uniform combination of basis kernels and over other state-of-art kernel learning methods.

2. MULTIPLE KERNEL LEARNING

We consider the classification learning problem from training data $D = \{(\boldsymbol{x}_1, y_1), \ldots, (\boldsymbol{x}_\ell, y_\ell)\}$ where $\boldsymbol{x}_i$ belongs to some input space $\mathcal{X}$ and $y_i \in \{+1, -1\}$ denoting the class label of examples $\boldsymbol{x}_i$. In the Support Vector Machines (SVM) methodology, we map these input points to a feature space using a kernel function $K(\boldsymbol{x}_i, \boldsymbol{x}_j)$ that defines an inner product in this feature space, that is, $K(\boldsymbol{x}_i, \boldsymbol{x}_j) = \Phi(\boldsymbol{x}_i) \cdot \Phi(\boldsymbol{x}_j)$, where $\Phi(\boldsymbol{x})$ is a mapping of $\boldsymbol{x}$ to a reproducing kernel Hilbert space $\mathcal{H}$ induced by K.

Here, we consider the kernel $K_{\boldsymbol{\theta}}$ depending on a set of parameters $\boldsymbol{\theta}$. The classifier given by the SVM is $f(\boldsymbol{x}) = \mathrm{sign}(\sum_{i=1}^{\ell} \alpha_i^0 y_i K_{\boldsymbol{\theta}}(\boldsymbol{x}_i, \boldsymbol{x}) + b)$, where the coefficients $\boldsymbol{\alpha}^0$ are the solution of the following optimization problem:

$$\begin{aligned}\max_{\boldsymbol{\alpha}} \ & \sum_{i=1}^{\ell} \alpha_i - \frac{1}{2}\sum_{i,j=1}^{\ell} \alpha_i\alpha_j K_{\boldsymbol{\theta}}(\boldsymbol{x}_i,\boldsymbol{x}_j) \\ \text{s.t.} \ & \sum_{i=1}^{\ell} \alpha_i y_i = 0, \ \alpha_i \geq 0, \ i = 1,\ldots,\ell.\end{aligned} \tag{1}$$

This formulation of the SVM optimization problem is called the *hard margin* formulation since no training errors are allowed. For the non-separable case, one needs to allow training errors which results in the so called *soft margin* SVM algorithm. It can be shown that *soft margin* SVM with quadratic penalization of errors can be considered as a special case of the *hard margin* version with the modified kernel (see [5]). So in the rest paper, we only focus on the *hard margin* SVM.

The used kernel we consider is a linear convex combination of multiple basis kernels, as

$$K_{\boldsymbol{\theta}} = \sum_{i=1}^{m} \theta_i K_i, \quad \text{with } \theta_i \geq 0, \ \sum_{i=1}^{m} \theta_i = 1,$$

where $K_i, i = 1\ldots,m$ are the basic kernels and m is the total number of basic kernels. Within this framework, the problem of learning the kernel is transformed to the problem of deciding the combination coefficients $\boldsymbol{\theta} = (\theta_1,\ldots,\theta_m)^{\mathrm{T}}$.

2.1 Estimating the Performance of SVM

Ideally we would like to choose the value of the combination coefficients $\boldsymbol{\theta}$ that minimize the true risk of the SVM classifier. Unfortunately, since this quantity is not accessible, one has to build estimates or bounds for it.

Leave-One-Out Error.

The leave-one-out procedure consists of removing one element from the training data, constructing the decision rule on the basis of the remaining training data and then testing on the removed element.

Let us denote the number of errors in the leave-one-out procedure by $\mathcal{L}((\boldsymbol{x}_1,y_1),\ldots,(\boldsymbol{x}_\ell,y_\ell))$ and by f^i the classifier obtained with an SVM when the training data $(\boldsymbol{x}_i,y_i)$ removed, so we can write that $\mathcal{L}((\boldsymbol{x}_1,y_1),\ldots,(\boldsymbol{x}_\ell,y_\ell)) = \sum_{p=1}^{\ell}\phi(-y_p f^p(\boldsymbol{x}_p))$, where ϕ is a step function: $\phi(t) = 1$ when $t > 0$ and $\phi(t) = 0$ otherwise. It is known that the leave-one-out procedure gives an almost unbiased estimate of the expected generalization error.

Although the leave-one-out estimator is a good choice when estimating the generalization error, it is very costly to actually compute since it requires running the training algorithm ℓ times. The strategy is thus to upper bound or approximate this estimator by an easy to compute quantity T having.

Radius-Margin Bound.

For *hard margin* SVM without threshold (b=0), Vapnik [10] proposes the following upper bound of leave-one-out procedure:

$$\mathcal{L}((\boldsymbol{x}_1,y_1),\ldots,(\boldsymbol{x}_\ell,y_\ell)) \leq \frac{R^2_{K_{\boldsymbol{\theta}}}}{\gamma^2_{K_{\boldsymbol{\theta}}}} =: T_{\text{RM}},$$

where $R_{K_{\boldsymbol{\theta}}}$ is the radius of the smallest sphere enclosing the training points in the feature space and $\gamma_{K_{\boldsymbol{\theta}}}$ is the margin of the SVM classifier with $K_{\boldsymbol{\theta}}$.

Span Bound.

Vapnik & Chapelle [3] derive an estimate using the concept of span of support vectors. Under the assumption that the set of support vectors remains the same during the leave-one-out procedure,

$$\mathcal{L}((\boldsymbol{x}_1,y_1),\ldots,(\boldsymbol{x}_\ell,y_\ell)) \leq \sum_{p=1}^{\ell} \phi\left(\alpha_p^0 S_p^2 - 1\right) =: T_{\text{Span}},$$

S_p is the distance between the point $\Phi_{K_{\boldsymbol{\theta}}}(\boldsymbol{x}_p)$ and the set Γ_p, where $\Gamma_p = \left\{\sum_{i\neq p,\alpha_i^0>0}\lambda_i\Phi_{K_{\boldsymbol{\theta}}}(\boldsymbol{x}_i) \,\middle|\, \sum_{i\neq p}\lambda_i = 1\right\}$.

2.2 Multiple Kernel Learning Formulations

To guarantee good generalization performance of SVM, we consider to minimize the upper bounds of leave-one-out error. Two minimization formulations for Multiple Kernel Learning are proposed:
With the radius-margin bound.

$$\min_{\boldsymbol{\theta}} T_{\text{RM}} := \frac{R^2_{K_{\boldsymbol{\theta}}}}{\gamma^2_{K_{\boldsymbol{\theta}}}}, \quad \text{s.t. } \theta_i \geq 0, \ \sum_{i=1}^{m}\theta_i = 1. \tag{2}$$

With the span bound:

$$\min_{\boldsymbol{\theta}} T_{\text{Span}} := \sum_{p=1}^{\ell}\phi\left(\alpha_p^0 S_p^2 - 1\right), \ \text{s.t.}\theta_i \geq 0, \ \sum_{i=1}^{m}\theta_i = 1. \tag{3}$$

3. SOLVING THE MKL PROBLEM

In order to solve the optimization problems (2) and (3), the projected gradient algorithm is adopted, which requires the computation of the derivatives of T_{RM} and T_{Span}.

3.1 Computing Derivative of Radius-Margin

According to [4], we know that the radius of the minimum enclosing ball $R^2_{K_{\boldsymbol{\theta}}}$ can be obtained by:

$$\begin{aligned}R^2_{K_{\boldsymbol{\theta}}} = \max_{\boldsymbol{\beta}} \ & \sum_{i=1}^{\ell}\beta_i K_{\boldsymbol{\theta}}(\boldsymbol{x}_i,\boldsymbol{x}_i) - \sum_{i,j=1}^{\ell}\beta_i\beta_j K_{\boldsymbol{\theta}}(\boldsymbol{x}_i,\boldsymbol{x}_j) \\ \text{s.t.} \ & \sum_{i=1}^{\ell}\beta_i = 1, \beta_i \geq 0.\end{aligned} \tag{4}$$

The derivative of T_{RM} with respect to θ_k is given in the following theorem:

THEOREM 1. *Let the parameters* $\boldsymbol{\alpha}^0 = (\alpha_1^0,\ldots,\alpha_\ell^0)^{\mathrm{T}}$ *and* $\boldsymbol{\beta}^0 = (\beta_1^0,\ldots,\beta_\ell^0)^{\mathrm{T}}$ *are the solutions of optimization problem (1) and (4) respectively. Denote vectors* $\boldsymbol{\mu} = (K_k(\boldsymbol{x}_1,\boldsymbol{x}_1),\ldots,K_k(\boldsymbol{x}_\ell,\boldsymbol{x}_\ell))^{\mathrm{T}}$ *and* $\boldsymbol{\nu} = (K_{\boldsymbol{\theta}}(\boldsymbol{x}_1,\boldsymbol{x}_1),\ldots,K_{\boldsymbol{\theta}}(\boldsymbol{x}_\ell,\boldsymbol{x}_\ell))^{\mathrm{T}}$. *Then, the derivative of* T_{RM} *with respect to* θ_k *can be written as*

$$\frac{\partial T_{\text{RM}}}{\partial\theta_k} = -\mathbf{1}^{\mathrm{T}}\boldsymbol{\alpha}^0(\boldsymbol{\mu}^{\mathrm{T}}\boldsymbol{\beta}^0 - \boldsymbol{\beta}^{0\mathrm{T}}\boldsymbol{K}_k\boldsymbol{\beta}^0) + Z(\boldsymbol{\alpha}^{0\mathrm{T}}\boldsymbol{K}_k\boldsymbol{\alpha}^0)/2,$$

where $Z = \boldsymbol{\nu}^{\mathrm{T}}\boldsymbol{\beta}^0 - \boldsymbol{\beta}^{0\mathrm{T}}\boldsymbol{K}_{\boldsymbol{\theta}}\boldsymbol{\beta}^0$, $\boldsymbol{K}_k$ *and* $\boldsymbol{K}_{\boldsymbol{\theta}}$ *are the kernel matrices corresponding to kernel* K_k *and* $K_{\boldsymbol{\theta}}$ *respectively.*

PROOF. Note that $\frac{\partial T_{\text{RM}}}{\partial\theta_k} = \|\frac{1}{\gamma^2_{K_{\boldsymbol{\theta}}}}\|_2^2\frac{\partial R^2_{K_{\boldsymbol{\theta}}}}{\partial\theta_k} + R^2_{K_{\boldsymbol{\theta}}}\frac{\partial\|1/\gamma^2_{K_{\boldsymbol{\theta}}}\|_2^2}{\partial\theta_k}$.
According to [4], $\frac{\partial\|1/\gamma^2_{K_{\boldsymbol{\theta}}}\|_2^2}{\partial\theta_k} = -\frac{1}{2}\sum_{i,j=1}^{\ell}\alpha_i^0\alpha_j^0 y_i y_j\frac{\partial K_{\boldsymbol{\theta}}(\boldsymbol{x}_i,\boldsymbol{x}_j)}{\partial\theta_k}$

and $\frac{\partial R^2_{K_{\boldsymbol{\theta}}}}{\partial \theta_k} = \sum_{i=1}^{\ell} \beta_i^0 \frac{\partial K_{\boldsymbol{\theta}}(\boldsymbol{x}_i,\boldsymbol{x}_i)}{\partial \theta_k} - \sum_{i,j=1}^{\ell} \beta_i^0 \beta_j^0 \frac{\partial K_{\boldsymbol{\theta}}(\boldsymbol{x}_i,\boldsymbol{x}_j)}{\partial \theta_k}$. Since $K_{\boldsymbol{\theta}} = \sum_{i=1}^{m} \theta_i K_i$, thus $\frac{\partial K_{\boldsymbol{\theta}}(\boldsymbol{x}_i,\boldsymbol{x}_j)}{\partial \theta_k} = K_k(\boldsymbol{x}_i,\boldsymbol{x}_j)$. It is shown in [10] that $1/\gamma^2_{K_{\boldsymbol{\theta}}} = \sum_{i=1}^{\ell} \alpha_i^0$. Thus the theorem is proven. □

3.2 Computing the Derivative of Span Bound

The estimate of the performance of SVM through the span bound (3) requires the use of the step function ϕ which is not differentiable. However, we would like to use the projected gradient method to minimize this estimate of the test error. So we must smooth this step function. Similar to [4], we consider to use a contracting function : $\phi(\boldsymbol{x}) = (1+\exp(-c\boldsymbol{x}+d))^{-1}$, where c, d are non-negative constants. In our experiment, we took $c = 5$ and $d = 0$ which is the same as in [4].

Let sv denote the set of support vectors, $\text{sv} = \{\boldsymbol{x}_i | \alpha_i^0 > 0, i = 1, \ldots, \ell\}$, $\boldsymbol{K}_{\boldsymbol{\theta}_{\text{sv}}}$ are the kernel matrix corresponding to sv, $\tilde{\boldsymbol{K}}_{\boldsymbol{\theta}_{\text{sv}}} = \begin{pmatrix} \boldsymbol{K}_{\boldsymbol{\theta}_{\text{sv}}} & \mathbf{1} \\ \mathbf{1}^{\text{T}} & 0 \end{pmatrix}$ and $\boldsymbol{K}^0_{k_{\text{sv}}} = \begin{pmatrix} \boldsymbol{K}_{k_{\text{sv}}} & \mathbf{0} \\ \mathbf{0}^{\text{T}} & 0 \end{pmatrix}$, where $\mathbf{1}$ is all-ones vector and $\mathbf{0}$ is all-zeros vector.

THEOREM 2. *The derivative of the span S_p^2 with respect to the parameter θ_k can be written as*

$$\frac{\partial S_p^2}{\partial \theta_k} = S_p^4 \left(\tilde{\boldsymbol{K}}^{-1}_{\boldsymbol{\theta}_{\text{sv}}} \boldsymbol{K}^0_{k_{\text{sv}}} \tilde{\boldsymbol{K}}^{-1}_{\boldsymbol{\theta}_{\text{sv}}} \right)_{pp}. \tag{5}$$

PROOF. Note that $\frac{\partial \tilde{\boldsymbol{K}}_{\boldsymbol{\theta}_{\text{sv}}}}{\partial \theta_k} = \boldsymbol{K}^0_{k_{\text{sv}}}$. According to [4], we know that $S_p^2 = 1/\left(\tilde{\boldsymbol{K}}^{-1}_{\boldsymbol{\theta}_{\text{sv}}}\right)_{pp}$. Thus, it is easy to verify that $\frac{\partial S_p^2}{\partial \theta_k} = S_p^4 \left(\tilde{\boldsymbol{K}}^{-1}_{\boldsymbol{\theta}_{\text{sv}}} \frac{\partial \tilde{\boldsymbol{K}}_{\boldsymbol{\theta}_{\text{sv}}}}{\partial \theta_k} \tilde{\boldsymbol{K}}^{-1}_{\boldsymbol{\theta}_{\text{sv}}} \right)_{pp} = S_p^4 \left(\tilde{\boldsymbol{K}}^{-1}_{\boldsymbol{\theta}_{\text{sv}}} \boldsymbol{K}^0_{k_{\text{sv}}} \tilde{\boldsymbol{K}}^{-1}_{\boldsymbol{\theta}_{\text{sv}}} \right)_{pp}$, the theorem is proven. □

There is however a problem in this approach: the value given by the span is not continuous. Inspired by the Chapelle et al. [4], we replace the constraint by a regularization term in the computation of the span to smooth the span value,

$$\bar{S}_p^2 = \min_{\boldsymbol{\lambda}, \sum \lambda_i = 1} \left\| \Phi_{K_{\boldsymbol{\theta}}}(\boldsymbol{x}_p) - \sum_{i \neq p}^{\ell} \lambda_i \Phi_{K_{\boldsymbol{\theta}}}(\boldsymbol{x}_i) \right\| + \eta \sum_{i \neq p}^{\ell} \frac{1}{\alpha_i^0} \lambda_i^2.$$

With this new definition of the span, the $\bar{S}_p^2$ can be written as $\bar{S}_p^2 = 1/(\tilde{\boldsymbol{K}}_{\boldsymbol{\theta}_{\text{sv}}} + \boldsymbol{Q})^{-1}_{pp} - \boldsymbol{Q}_{pp}$, where $\boldsymbol{Q}$ is a diagonal matrix with elements $[\boldsymbol{Q}]_{ii} = \eta/\alpha_i^0$, $[\boldsymbol{Q}]_{n_{\text{sv}}+1, n_{\text{sv}}+1} = 0$ and n_{sv} is the number of support vectors.

THEOREM 3. *Assuming that $\boldsymbol{G}$ is a diagonal matrix with the elements $[\boldsymbol{G}]_{ii} = -\eta/(\alpha^0_{\text{sv}_i})^2$ and $[\boldsymbol{G}]_{n_{\text{sv}}+1, n_{\text{sv}}+1} = 0$. $\bar{\boldsymbol{A}}$ is the inverse of $\tilde{\boldsymbol{K}}_{\boldsymbol{\theta}_{\text{sv}}}$ with the last row and last column removed. Then*

$$\frac{\partial \bar{S}_p^2}{\partial \theta_k} = \left(1/\boldsymbol{B}^{-1}_{pp}\right)^2 \left(\boldsymbol{B}^{-1}(\boldsymbol{K}^0_{k_{\text{sv}}} + \boldsymbol{G}\boldsymbol{F})\boldsymbol{B}^{-1}\right)_{pp} - (\boldsymbol{G}\boldsymbol{F})_{pp},$$

where $\boldsymbol{B} = \tilde{\boldsymbol{K}}_{\boldsymbol{\theta}_{\text{sv}}} + \boldsymbol{Q}$, $\boldsymbol{Y}_{\text{sv}} = diag((y_{\text{sv}_1}, \ldots, y_{\text{sv}_{n_{\text{sv}}}})^{\text{T}})$ and $\boldsymbol{F} = diag(\boldsymbol{Y}_{\text{sv}} \bar{\boldsymbol{A}} \boldsymbol{K}_{k_{\text{sv}}} \boldsymbol{Y}_{\text{sv}} \boldsymbol{\alpha}^0_{\text{sv}}; 0)$.

PROOF. Recall that $\bar{S}_p^2 = 1/(\tilde{\boldsymbol{K}}_{\boldsymbol{\theta}_{\text{sv}}} + \boldsymbol{Q})^{-1}_{pp} - \boldsymbol{Q}_{pp}$, Thus $\frac{\partial \bar{S}_p^2}{\partial \theta_k} = \left(1/\boldsymbol{B}^{-1}_{pp}\right)^2 \left(\boldsymbol{B}^{-1}\left(\frac{\partial \tilde{\boldsymbol{K}}_{\boldsymbol{\theta}_{\text{sv}}}}{\partial \theta_k} + \frac{\partial \boldsymbol{Q}}{\partial \theta_k}\right)\boldsymbol{B}^{-1}\right)_{pp} - \left(\frac{\partial \boldsymbol{Q}}{\partial \theta_k}\right)_{pp}$. According to [2], we know that $\frac{\partial \boldsymbol{\alpha}^0_{\text{sv}}}{\partial \theta_k} = -\boldsymbol{Y}_{\text{sv}} \bar{\boldsymbol{A}} \boldsymbol{K}_{k_{\text{sv}}} \boldsymbol{Y}_{\text{sv}} \boldsymbol{\alpha}^0_{\text{sv}}$. Thus it is easy to verify that $\frac{\partial \boldsymbol{Q}}{\partial \theta_k} = \boldsymbol{G}\boldsymbol{F}$. In addition, since $\frac{\partial \tilde{\boldsymbol{K}}_{\boldsymbol{\theta}_{\text{sv}}}}{\partial \theta_k} = \boldsymbol{K}^0_{k_{\text{sv}}}$, the theorem is proven. □

4. ALGORITHM

For convenience, we use $T_{\boldsymbol{\theta}}$ to denote T_{RM} or T_{Span}. With the derivative of $T_{\boldsymbol{\theta}}$ with respect to the combination coefficients, we use the standard gradient projection approach with the Armijo rule [1] for selecting step sizes to address optimization problems (2) and (3). The overall algorithm is described in Algorithm 1 and Algorithm 2 which show that the above described steps are performed until a stopping criterion is met. This stopping criterion can be either based on a duality gap, or more simply, on a maximal number of iterations, or on the variation of $\boldsymbol{\theta}$ between two consecutive steps.

Algorithm 1: Adaptive Radius-Margin Multiple Kernel Learning Algorithm (RMMKL)

```
set θ_i^1 = 1/m for i = 1, ..., m
for t = 1, 2, ... do
    solve the classical SVM problem with
      K_θ = Σ_{i=1}^m θ_i^t K_i;
    solve the optimization problem (4);
    compute ∂T_RM/∂θ_k for k = 1, 2, ..., m;
    compute descent direction D_t and optimal step γ_t;
    θ_k^{t+1} ← θ_k^t + γ_t D_{t,k};
    if stopping criterion then
        break
    end if
end for
```

Algorithm 2: Adaptive Span Multiple Kernel Learning Algorithm (SPMKL)

```
set θ_i^1 = 1/m for i = 1, ..., m
for t = 1, 2, ... do
    solve the classical SVM problem with
      K_θ = Σ_{i=1}^m θ_i^t K_i;
    compute the inverse of the matrices K̃_θsv and B;
    compute ∂T_Span/∂θ_k for k = 1, 2, ..., m;
    compute descent direction D_t and optimal step γ_t;
    θ_k^{t+1} ← θ_k^t + γ_t D_{t,k};
    if stopping criterion then
        break
    end if
end for
```

5. EXPERIMENTS

In this section, we illustrate the performances of our presented RMMKL and SPMKL approachs, in comparison with SVM with the uniform combination of basis kernels (Unif) where $K_{\boldsymbol{\theta}} = \sum_{i=1}^{m} \frac{1}{m} K_i$, the kernel learning approach (KL) [4] which only learns a single kernel, and the margin-based MKL method (MKL) [8].

The evaluation is made on eleven public available data sets from UCI repository [1] and LIBSVM Data[2] (see Table 1). For a fair comparison, we have selected the same termination criterion for the iterative algorithms (KL, MKL, RMMKL and SPMKL): iteration terminates when $\|\boldsymbol{\theta}^{t+1} - \boldsymbol{\theta}^t\|_2 / \|\boldsymbol{\theta}^t\|_2 \leq 0.01$ or the maximal number of iteration (500)

[1] http://www.ics.uci.edu/~mlearn/MLRepository.html.
[2] http://www.csie.ntu.edu.tw/~cjlin/libsvm.

Table 1: The testing accuracies (Acc) with standard deviations, and the average numbers of selected basis kernels (Nk). We set the numbers of our method to be bold if our method outperforms both Unif and other two kernel learning approaches.

Index	1		2		3		4		5	
Method	Unif		KL		MKL		RMMKL		SPMKL	
Data sets	Acc	Nk	Acc	Nk	Acc	Nk	Acc	Nk	Acc	Nk
Ionosphere	94.1 ± 1.2	20	84.5 ± 1.8	1	92.9 ± 1.6	3.8	**95.7** ± 1.0	2.8	**96.9** ± 0.8	2.6
Splice	52.7 ± 0.1	20	74.2 ± 2.5	1	79.8 ± 1.6	1.0	**88.0** ± 2.4	3.2	**88.2** ± 2.4	2.2
Live	58.0 ± 0.0	20	64.2 ± 3.9	1	59.1 ± 1.4	4.2	64.1 ± 4.2	3.6	**64.4** ± 4.2	4.0
Fourclass	81.2 ± 1.9	20	94.4 ± 1.4	1	97.8 ± 1.4	7.8	**100** ± 0.0	1.0	**100** ± 0.0	1.6
Heart	83.9 ± 2.1	20	83.4 ± 5.2	1	84.1 ± 5.7	7.4	**84.2** ± 5.4	5.2	84.0 ± 5.9	5.8
Germannum	70.0 ± 0.0	20	71.6 ± 1.8	1	70.0 ± 0.0	6.2	**73.7** ± 1.6	5.4	**74.1** ± 1.2	5.0
Musk1	62.4 ± 2.4	20	62.9 ± 3.1	1	85.5 ± 3.1	2.0	**93.3** ± 2.3	3.0	**93.5** ± 2.2	3.8
Mdbc	94.6 ± 1.7	20	97.5 ± 1.8	1	97.0 ± 1.8	1.2	97.4 ± 1.6	5.2	**98.4** ± 2.9	6.0
Mpbc	76.3 ± 2.7	20	58.0 ± 6.5	1	76.4 ± 2.9	7.2	**76.5** ± 1.6	2.8	**77.5** ± 2.9	3.2
Sonar	77.5 ± 1.8	20	80.2 ± 5.7	1	81.0 ± 5.2	2.6	**86.0** ± 2.6	2.8	**86.6** ± 2.6	2.6
Coloncancer	67.2 ± 11	20	78.4 ± 3.6	1	82.6 ± 8.5	13	**85.2** ± 4.2	7.2	**86.8** ± 5.6	5.6

has been reached. We use gaussian kernels $K_{\text{Gauss}}(\boldsymbol{x}, \boldsymbol{x}') = \exp\left(-\|\boldsymbol{x} - \boldsymbol{x}'\|_2^2/2\sigma^2\right)$ and polynomial kernels $K_{\text{Ploy}}(\boldsymbol{x}, \boldsymbol{x}') = \left(1 + \boldsymbol{x} \cdot \boldsymbol{x}'\right)^d$ as our basis kernels: 10 gaussian kernels with bandwidths $\sigma \in \{0.5, 1, 2, 5, 7, 10, 12, 15, 17, 20\}$ and 10 polynomial kernels of degree d from 1 to 10.

The experimental setting of the KL is the same as the one used in [4]. The code of MKL is from SimpleMKL [8]. The initial $\boldsymbol{\theta}$ is set to be $\frac{1}{20}\mathbf{1}$. The trade-off coefficients C in SVM, KL, MKL, RMMKL and SPMKL are automatically determined by 4-fold cross-validations on training sets. In all methods, C is selected from the set $\{0.01, 0.1, 1, 10, 100\}$. For each data set, we have run all the algorithms 50 times with different training and test splits (50% of all the examples for training and testing).

The average accuracies with standard deviations and average numbers of selected basis kernels are reported in Table 1. The results in Table 1 can be summarized as follows: Our methods (Index 4,5) give the best results on most data sets. RMMKL outperforms all other methods (Index 1, 2, 3) on 9 out of 11 sets, and also give results closing to the best ones of other methods on the remaining 2 sets. In particular, RMMKL gains 5 or more percents of accuracies on Splice, Liver, Musk1 and Sonar over MKL, and gains more than 10 percents on Ionosphere, Splice, Musk1, Mpbc over KL. On the set Musk1, RMMKL even gains 20.4 percents over KL. For SPMKL (Index 5) the results are similar to RMMKL: SPMKL outperforms other methods (Index 1, 2, 3) on 10 out of 11 sets, with only 1 inverse result. So it implicates that learning based on the kernel expect error bound can guarantee good generalization performance of the SVM.

6. CONCLUSIONS

Based on the upper bounds of the leave-one-out error, we present an accurate and efficient MKL method. we first establish two optimization formulations, and then propose the efficient gradient-based algorithms, called RMMKL and SPMKL, for computing the formulations. Experimental results validate that our approach outperforms both SVM with the uniform combination of basic kernels and other state-of-art kernel learning methods.

Future work aims at improving both speed and sparsity in kernels of the algorithm and extending this method to other SVM algorithm such as the one-class SVM or the SVR. We also plan to explore a new criterion based on the spectral of the integral operators to measure the kernel or kernel matrix for MKL.

Acknowledgments

The work is supported in part by the FP7 Marie Curie International Research Staff Exchange Scheme (IRSES) under grant No. 247590, the National Natural Science Foundation of China under grant No. 61070044, and the Natural Science Foundation of Tianjin under grant No. 11JCYBJC00700.

7. REFERENCES

[1] D. P. Bertsekas. *Nonlinear programming*. Athena Scientific Belmont, MA, 1999.

[2] O. Chapelle and A. Rakotomamonjy. Second order optimization of kernel parameters. In *Proceedings of the NIPS Workshop on Kernel Learning: Automatic Selection of Optimal Kernels*. Cambridge, MA: MIT Press, 2008.

[3] O. Chapelle and V. Vapnik. Model selection for support vector machines. In *Advances in Neural Information Processing Systems 12*. Cambridge, MA: MIT Press, 1999.

[4] O. Chapelle, V. Vapnik, O. Bousquet, and S. Mukherjee. Choosing multiple parameters for support vector machines. *Machine Learning*, 46(1):131–159, 2002.

[5] C. Cortes and V. Vapnik. Support-vector networks. *Machine learning*, 20(3):273–297, 1995.

[6] L. Jia, S. Liao, and L. Ding. Learning with uncertain kernel matrix set. *Journal of Computer Science and Technology*, 25(4):709–727, 2010.

[7] G. R. Lanckriet, N. Cristianini, P. Bartlett, L. E. Ghaoui, and M. I. Jordan. Learning the kernel matrix with semidefinite programming. *The Journal of Machine Learning Research*, 5:27–72, 2004.

[8] A. Rakotomamonjy, F. Bach, S. Canu, and Y. Grandvalet. Simplemkl. *Journal of Machine Learning Research*, 9:2491–2521, 2008.

[9] S. Sonnenburg, G. Rätsch, and C. Schäfer. A general and efficient multiple kernel learning algorithm. In *Advances in Neural Information Processing Systems 18*. Cambridge, MA: MIT Press, 2006.

[10] V. Vapnik. *Statistical learning theory*. Wiley-Interscience, New York, 1998.

KLEAP: An Efficient Cleaning Method to Remove Cross-reads in RFID Streams

Guoqiong Liao
School of Info. Tech.
Jiangxi Univ. of Finan. & Eco.
Nanchang, China
liaoguoqiong@163.com

Jing Li
School of Info. Tech.
Jiangxi Univ. of Finan. & Eco.
Nanchang, China
xicheng218@163.com

Lei Chen
Dept. of CSE
Hong Kong Univ. of Sci.&Tech.
Hong Kong, China
leichen@cse.ust.hk

Changxuan Wan
School of Info. Tech.
Jiangxi Univ. of Finan. & Eco.
Nanchang, China
wanchangxuan@263.net

ABSTRACT

Recently, the RFID technology has been widely used in many kinds of applications. However, because of the interference from environmental factors and limitations of the radio frequency technology, the data streams collected by the RFID readers are usually contain a lot of cross-reads. To address this issue, we propose a KerneL dEnsity-bAsed Probability cleaning method (KLEAP) to remove cross-reads within a sliding window. The method estimates the density of each tag using a kernel-based function. The reader corresponding to the micro-cluster with the largest density will be regarded as the position that the tagged object should locate in current window, and the readings derived from other readers will be treated as the cross-reads. Experiments verify the effectiveness and efficiency of the proposed method.

Categories and Subject Descriptors

H2.8 [**Data Mining**]: Database Application – *data mining*

General Terms

Algorithms; Performance; Design; Experimentation

Keywords

Cross-reads, Kernel density estimator, RFID data cleaning, RFID data streams

1. INTRODUCTION

Recently, the radio frequency identification (RFID) technology has been used in many kinds of applications such as retail supermarkets and supply chain, but the issue of false reads on RFID tags is critical to apply it widely for monitoring and tracing the tagged items [1].

*This research has been funded in part by National Natural Science Foundation of China (No.60863016), Natural Science Foundation of Jiangxi of China (No.2008GQS0019), Science Foundation of Jiangxi Provincial Department of Education of China (GJJ10694)

CIKM'11, October 24-28, 2011, Glasgow, Scotland, UK.

Basically, the false reads in RFID streams can be classified into two categories [2]:

1) Missing-Reads. Though a RFID tag indeed locates in the range of a reader, it might not be read at all, thus, leading to a false belief that the tag is not present. This may be caused by the weakness of RF signal, shortage of power, shield of signal between the tag and the reader, and the collision between tags. This type of errors is also referred as false negatives.

2) Cross-Reads. When a RFID tag locates outside the range of a reader, but it might be captured by this reader which leads another false belief that the object is present in the scope of this reader. Cross-reads may be arisen by the reflection of metal items, the abrupt strengthen of RF, and the change of antenna directions. This type of errors is also called false positives.

The presences of missing-reads and cross-reads in the RFID streams collected by RFID readers can result in the location uncertainty of tags. For example, when a tagged object is not detected by a reader at some time, we are not sure whether the tag doesn't locate in the region of the reader. Similarly, when a tagged object is captured by a reader, we are also not sure whether the tag indeed locates in the region of the reader. Therefore, the existence of missing-reads and cross-reads make the tasks such as real-time monitoring and tracing difficult.

People have already noticed the negative effects brought by the false reads, and some works have been conducted to eliminate the defects. Among these works, most focus on reducing the number of missing-reads, such as using a smooth filter to interpolate the missing reads within a window[3], applying a sample-based approach to recovery the missing-reads[4], using Bayesian inference to clean RFID raw data[5].

We know in an application of real-time monitoring and tracking, the presence of missing-reads only losses the locations of the tagged objects temporarily, which can be resolved by repeatable readings[3]. However, cross-reads often result in providing wrong information, and the existence of cross-reads will limit the wide usage of RFID technology. However, due to the dynamic and massive properties of RFID streams, it is not trivial to remove cross-reads due to the unique characteristics:

1) The uncertainty of the reading. Generally, an item in a store or a library will be assigned on a static shelf, but customers or readers sometimes might move it to another shelf. Therefore, when a tag is captured by a reader, due to the uncertainty of position information about the tag and the randomness about the generation of cross-reads, we cannot accurately determine whether the reading about the tag is caused by moving the tag into the detection range or by the cross-reads.

2) The process of real-time stream. As we know, a RFID reader keeps on sending RF signals to tags and receives the reflected signals. Therefore, the captured RFID data by a reader is often presented in the form of stream, which requires the real-time processing, that is, the process speed for the RFID data steam must be as fast as the data arriving speed. Otherwise, the useful data will get lost.

SMURF [5] can adapt the size of window to reduce false positives, but it can not eliminate the cross-reads generated by physical factors. Wang et al. [6] removed the cross-reads using a simple counting method based on the hypothesis that cross-reads generally have a low occurrence rate compared to normal true readings. However, the effectiveness of the method is directly related to the counting threshold, which is hard to set if the users do not have much domain knowledge. Furthermore, if the number of the cross-reads is more than that of the normal true readings, the approach may produce wrong filter results.

Motivated by the necessity to remove cross-reads, in this paper, we design an effective KerneL dEnsity-bAsed Probability cleaning method (KLEAP) to remove cross-reads over a RFID data stream. The rest of the paper is arranged as follows. Section 2 gives the problem definition. In Section 3, we describe a kernel-based cleaning method through estimate computing kernel density We discuss experiments results in Section 4. Finally, the paper is concluded.

2. PROBLEM DEFINITION

A RFID stream can be segmented into a sequence of disjoint time windows, and in each window, it is assumed the probability that a tagged item moves from a site to another (i.e., the position change) is very low. Because a window may contain multiple read cycles in the real RFID application environment, it may produce multiple readings about a tag in a window. In a time window, a tag may be reported appearing within the detection ranges of multiples different readers. In order to determine the real position of the tags, we need to get a position distribution of the tag in a window. The reason that we want to get the distribution of each tag is that the reader near the tag will have more readings and receive stronger signals than the reader far from the tag.

1) The reader whose detection range covers T will produce more observations than the reader whose detected range does not cover T.

2) For the observations on T, the average signal strength of the observations produced by the reader whose detection range covers T will be higher than that of the observations produced by the reader whose detection range does not cover T.

We can represent an observation on a tagged object T_i collected by reader R_j in window W_k as a V_{ij}^k :

$$V_{ij}^k =< T_i, R_j, \tau_k, SS > \quad (1)$$

Where τ_k is the logic timestamp of observations produced in W_k, and SS represents the receiving signal strength. The greater the value of SS is, the stronger the signal strength is. We can group the observations of tags based on their IDs in each window when a new observation arrives. The grouping results on each tag can be represented as a stream. For example, all of observations on T_i collected in window W_k form a data stream as follows.

$$DS_i = V_{i1}^k, V_{i1}^k, V_{i1}^k, V_{i2}^k, V_{i2}^k, V_{i3}^k \cdots \quad (2)$$

Thus, we can get a data stream for each tag to record all readings of the tag produced by different readers in each window. In order to save the memory space and reduce the cost of computation, we group all of observations V_{ij}^k about T_i collected by R_j in W_k into a micro-cluster C_{ij}^k , which can be defined as following:

$$\overline{C}_{ij}^k =< T_i, R_j, \tau_k, \overline{SS}, D_{ij}^k, p_{ij}^k > \quad (3)$$

where $\overline{SS}$ is the average signal strength of T_i captured by R_j within W_k; D_{ij}^k is total number of observations that R_j detects T_i in W_k; P_{ij}^k represents the probability that T_i locates in the reading range of R_j when it is detected by R_j.

By now, the problem of detecting cross-reads can be transferred into deriving the true location of T_i from all micro-clusters of T_i.

3. KERNEL DENSITY-BASED PROBABILITY CLEANING METHOD

The difficulty for filtering cross-reads is how to identify cross-reads. In this work, we consider cross-reads as *outliers*, thus, the determination of cross-reads is transformed into the issue of detecting outliers on data streams. The density-based methods often perform well than the distance-based one [7], so we apply the density-based methods to detect cross-reads.

3.1 Overview of Our Solutions

To obtain the location, we exploit the method of kernel density estimator to compute the density of C_{ij}^k . Based on the densities of all micro-clusters of T_i, we can infer that T_i is in the detection range of the reader corresponding to the micro-cluster who has the largest density. For example, as shown in Figure 1, C_{i1}^{k-1} has the largest density at $W_{k-1,}$ and C_{i1}^k has also the largest density at W_k, both indicate that tag T_i should locate within the detection range of R_1. Note that, when more than two micro-clusters have the same density, we will choose the reader which has the largest probability that a tag should locate.

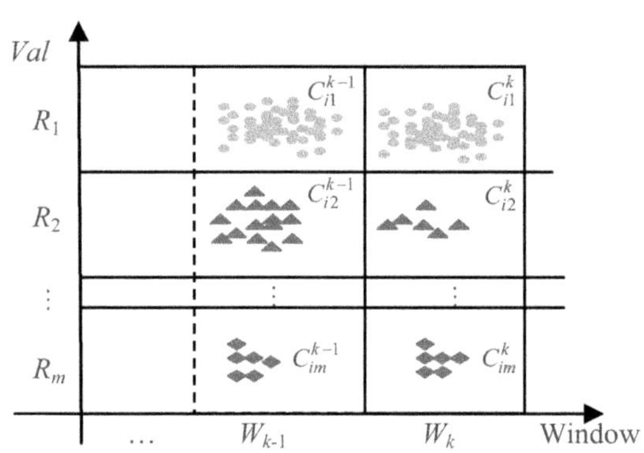

- the observation produced by reader R_1 in different windows
- ▲ the observation produced by reader R_2 in different windows
- ◆ the observation produced by reader R_m in different windows

Figure 1. Micro-clusters in window W_{k-1} and W_k

3.2 Cleaning Methods Based on Kernel Density Estimator

In our study, in order to acquire enough sample observations, the time of actual observation is characterized by the window. It is assumed the cross-reads are irrelevance in different windows. According to the method of kernel density estimator, the kernel density of all observed sample points is defined as follows.

Definition 1. Let $X_1, X_2, \ldots, X_n$ be the sample points of independent random variables with the same distribution in space R^d, then the kernel density estimator of a sample point X can be calculated as following:

$$\hat{f}_h(X) = \frac{1}{n}\sum_{i=1}^{n} K_{d,h}(X_i - X) \quad (4)$$

where K is a kernel function, h is a smoothing parameter(i.e., bandwidth), d is the number of the space dimension, and n is the number of sample points.

In this paper, we use a standard Gaussian function as K, which mean is zero and variance is 1. Thus the variance is controlled indirectly through the parameter h.

$$K_{d,h}(X_i - X) = \frac{1}{(\sqrt{2\pi}h)^d}\prod_{i=1}^{d} e^{-\frac{(x_i-x)^2}{2h^2}} = \frac{1}{(\sqrt{2\pi}h)^d} e^{-\frac{\sum_i (x_i-x)^2}{2h^2}} \quad (5)$$

Generally, the read cycle of a reader is very small (about 0.5ms). If a window size is 1s, the reader will produce about 2000 observation readings for one tag without including the cross-reads. If the number of tags is large, it is very time-consuming to estimate the kernel density due to the huge volume of data.

In order to extend the method to the situation with large scale of tags, we borrow the idea of micro-clusters in clustering algorithms to compress the data set.

Firstly, a centroid is chosen for each tag to maintain a micro-cluster based on reader IDs.

Then, when a new data arrives, it will be assigned to the corresponding centroid of the micro-cluster that it should belong to. Thus, the centroid of a micro-cluster can be used to represent all data points of a tag within the cluster, to compress the volume of data and reduce largely the overhead to compute kernel density.

In the end, each micro-cluster is regarded as a pseudo-point. At this time, we only need to compute the contribution of each centroid in the micro-cluster to other data points.

Now, we can define the density estimator as the sum of weights of the kernel functions, where each weight equals the number of observations that the tag is detected by the reader in different micro-clusters (i.e., D_{ij}^k).

Therefore, if micro-clusters $C_{i1}^k \ldots C_{im}^k$ contain all the data points of T_i, the density estimator is defined as follows:

$$\hat{f}_{i,h}^k(X) = \frac{1}{\sum_{j=1}^{m} D_{ij}^k}\sum_{j=1}^{m} D_{ij}^k \cdot K_{d,h}(\overline{C}_{ij}^k - X) \quad (6)$$

where

$$K_{d,h}(\overline{C}_{ij}^k - X) = \frac{1}{(\sqrt{2\pi}h)^d}\prod_{j=1}^{d} e^{-\frac{(c_j-x)^2}{2h^2}} = \frac{1}{(\sqrt{2\pi}h)^d} e^{-\frac{\sum_j (c_j-x)^2}{2h^2}} \quad (7)$$

and $\overline{C}_{ij}^k - X$ represents the distance between X and the centriod of $\overline{C}_{ij}^k$. This distance is calculated on the attributions $< R_s, \overline{SS} >$ by Formula (8):

$$d(X,Y) = \sum_{i=p+1}^{n} \delta(x_i, y_j) . \sum_{i=1}^{p} d(x_i, y_i)^2 \quad (8)$$

In Formula (6), because only R_j and SS bar is used to calculate the kernel function, so the value of d is 2. The parameter h only affects the smoothness of kernel density estimator. For it is not a key factor in our algorithm, we didn't discuss the details about it in the paper. In the experiments discussed in Section 4, the value of h is set as 0.3.

It is assumed that X and Y have n attributions $A_1^N, A_2^N, \cdots, A_p^N, A_{p+1}^C, \cdots, A_n^C$, of which, $A_1^N, A_2^N, \cdots, A_p^N$ are numeric attributions (e.g., the signal strength), and $A_{p+1}^C, A_{p+2}^C, \cdots, A_n^C$ are categorical attributions (e.g., the IDs of readers). $d(X,Y)$ is a float number made up of two parts: the integer part is the sum of Hamming distances $\sum_{i=p+1}^{n} \delta(x_i, y_i)$, which can be computed according to Formula (9), and the decimal part is $\sum_{i=1}^{p} d(x_i, y_i)^2$, which is a sum of the Euclidean distances between the corresponding attributions.

$$\delta(x_i, y_i) = \begin{cases} 0 & (x_i = y_i) \\ 1 & (x_i \neq y_i) \end{cases} \quad (9)$$

After we calculate the distributed densities of all the sample points, we can query the micro-cluster which has the largest sum of the sample densities. As a consequence, the reader corresponding to the micro-cluster with largest density is the position that the tagged object should locate in the current window. The readings derived from other readers will be treated as cross-reads.

Because we have m readers, the computation cost of Formula (6) is $O(m)$. In addition, we should compute the density for each tag through formula (6), and there are n tags. Then, the computational complexity of kernel density estimator is $O(m*n)$.

4. PERFORMANCE TESTING AND ANALYSIS

In the paper, we focus on cleaning cross-reads from the uncertain RFID data stream caused by physical factors, e.g., the reflection of metal items. Throughput and precision ratio are selected as the metrics to measure the performance.

Throughput = Total number of observation events processed/Total processing time;

Precision=The number of detected cross-reads/The number of actual cross-reads.

We developed a simulator for a retail store scenario that produces synthetic RFID streams. Under this scenario, we can control various factors, such as the distance between tags and readers, antenna direction, signal reflection strength, etc. Table 1 lists main experimental parameters.

Table 1. Experimental parameters

Parameter	Description	Value
SF	Sampling frequency	20 events/sec.
M	Number of tags	50~500
WS	Window size	10~10000sec.
W_k	Number of windows	10~50
SS	Signal strength	0~100

Experiment 1. Test the precision if tags move using KLEAP and Naïve methods.

In order to show the advantage of the KDE-based method, an experiment is designed to test the precision comparing with two naïve methods. The first naïve method (Naïve1) is a simple and intuitive method which only counts the number of times a tag is captured by a reader to determine tags' position[6]. For a tag, the reader with the largest observed number is the reader that the tag should locate. The second naïve method (Naïve2) only compares the average signal strength which a tag is captured by each reader within one window to determine the position of tags. For a tag, the reader with the largest average signal strength is the reader that the tag should belong to.

The precision results of the three methods are shown in Figure 2, which show the precision of KLEAP method is much higher than those of the naïve approaches. The reason is that the two naïve approaches cannot map data point into a multiple dimension space.

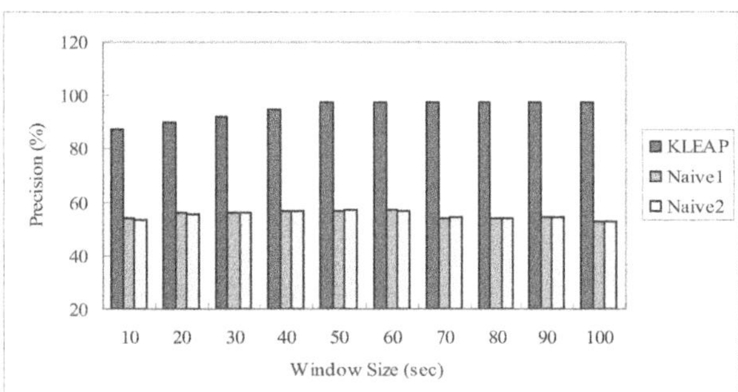

Figure 2. Precision of KLEAP and the naïve methods

Experiment 2. Test the scalability in the case of multiple tags

This experiment is designed to test the scalability of KLEAP method in the situation with multiple tags. Assumed there are *M* tags are evenly spread in three detected range of readers. When *M* is varying from 50 to 500 and W_k=50, *WS*=30s, the throughput and precision of the method are shown in Figures 3 and 4.

We can see from Figure 3, the throughput will decrease with the increase of tag number. This is because the volume of steam data in the windows will increase as the number of tags increases. However, the precision changed little (See Figure 4), which shows that KLEAP can apply into the situation with large volume of tags.

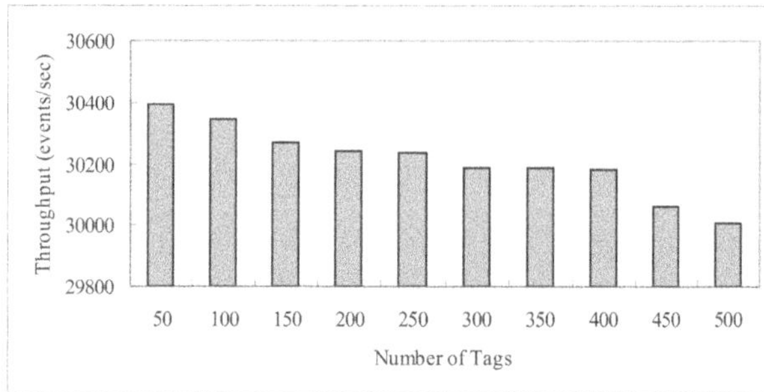

Figure 3. Throughput of KLEAP with multiple tags

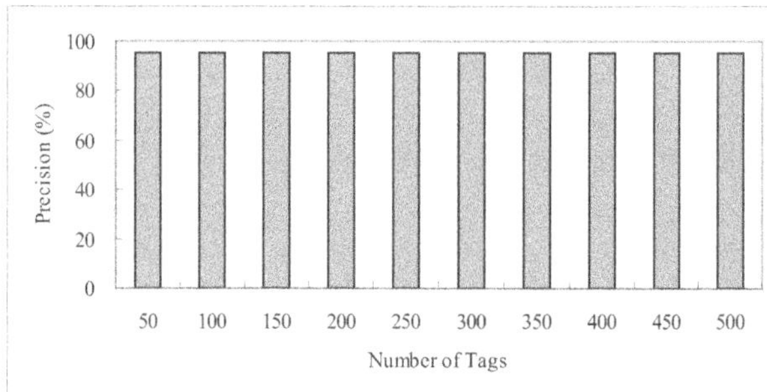

Figure 4. Precision of KLEAP with multiple tags

5. CONCLUSIONS

Due to the existence of cross-reads in RFID streams, in this paper, we propose an efficient kernel density-based probability cleaning method, called KLEAP, to filter the cross-reads in RFID data streams. KLEAP detects the exact positions of tags over the RFID data streams through examining the kernel densities of each tag captured by multiple readers. The computational complexity of kernel density estimator is $O(m*n)$.

In the future, we will enhance KLEAP performance further in two aspects: use probability information to implement increment computation and adjust window size adaptively.

6. REFERENCES

[1] S. S. Chawathe, V. Krishnamurthy, S. Ramachandran, et al. Managing RFID data. In *Proc. of VLDB (*Toronto, Canada. August 29-September 3, 2004). VLDB'04,1189-1195.

[2] C.Floerkmeier. A probabilistic approach to address uncertainty of RFID. Auto-ID Labs Research Workshop, Zurich, Switzerland, 2004.

[3] S. R. Jeffery, M. Garofalakis, and M. J. Franklin. Adaptive Cleaning for RFID Data Streams. In *Proc. of VLDB* (Seoul, Korea, September 12-15, 2006). VLDB'06, 163-174.

[4] J. Xie, J. Yang, Y. Chen, et al. A Sampling-Based Approach to Information Recovery. In *Proc. of ICDE* (Cancún, México, April 7-12, 2008). ICDE'08, 476-485.

[5] Haiquan Chen and Wei-Shinn Ku and Haixun Wang. Leveraging Spatio-Temporal Redundancy for RFID Data Cleansing. In *Proc. of SIGMOD* (Indianapolis, Indiana, USA, June 6-11,2010). SIGMOD'10, 51-62.

[6] Y. Bai, F. Wang, and P. Liu. Efficiently Filtering RFID Data Streams. In *Proc. VLDB Workshop on Clean Databases*(Seoul, Korea, September 12-15, 2006), 50-57.

A Diversity Measure Leveraging Domain Specific Auxiliary Information

Narayan Bhamidipati
Yahoo! Labs
Bangalore, India
narayanb@yahoo-inc.com

Nagaraj Kota
Yahoo! Labs
Bangalore, India
nagarajk@yahoo-inc.com

ABSTRACT

This article deals with the notion of reduction in uncertainty when the probability mass is distributed over similar values than dissimilar values. Shannon's entropy is a frequently used information theoretic measure of the uncertainty associated with random variables, but it depends solely on the set of values the probability mass function assumes, and does not take into consideration whether the mass is distributed among extreme values or not. A similarity structure, possibly obtained through domain knowledge, on the values assumed by the random variable may reduce the associated uncertainty. More the similarity, less the uncertainty. A novel measure named Similarity Adjusted Entropy (or Sim-adjusted Entropy for short), that generalizes Shannon's entropy, is then proposed to capture the effects of this similarity structure. Sim-adjusted entropy provides a mechanism for incorporating the domain expertise into an entropy based framework for solving various data mining tasks. Applications highlighted in this manuscript include clustering of categorical data and measuring audience diversity. Experiments performed on Yahoo! Answers data set demonstrate the ability of the proposed method to obtain more cohesive clusters. Another set of experiments confirm the utility of the proposed measure for measuring audience diversity.

Categories and Subject Descriptors

H.1.1 [**Systems and Information Theory**]: Information Theory

General Terms

Entropy, Similarity, Audience Diversity, Categorical Clustering, Information Theory

1. INTRODUCTION

The present article introduces the notion of measuring uncertainty based on not just the probabilities involved but also on the states to which those probabilities were assigned. Additional information, referred to as similarity between the various states, is integrated into the standard definitions of uncertainty measures. This proposed measure would take into consideration given information like "Rain" and "Drizzle" are more similar than "Rain" and "Sunny", and suggest that the case of "equally likely to Rain or Drizzle" involves less uncertainty than the case of "equally likely to Rain or be Sunny". This novel measure, named Similarity Adjusted Entropy (or Sim-adjusted Entropy), provides a mechanism for measuring uncertainty in situations where the categories cannot be considered in isolation, and yet, are not similar enough to be merged together. This generalizes the existing uncertainty measure, in the sense that when the knowledge regarding the relation between various conditions is completely absent, it is identical to Shannon's Entropy.

Two applications of the proposed measure, namely categorical clustering and measuring diversity, are highlighted. These are areas where Shannon's Entropy has been widely used, and our experimental results demonstrate how powerful a tool sim-adjusted entropy can be in the hands of a domain expert. Employing sim-adjusted entropy as the objective function to be minimized for categorical clustering, one may guide the clustering algorithm towards grouping points with similar features together. Measuring user diversity by using the proposed measure instead of Shannon's entropy, one tends to identify situations where more users are from dissimilar categories as more diverse.

The proposed measure is introduced, along with some motivational examples, in Section 2. Section 3 deals with applications of sim-adjusted entropy, experiments on which are described in Section 4. A brief discussion on further extensions of this work appears in Section 5.

2. REDUCING UNCERTAINTY BY KNOWING THE SIMILARITY STRUCTURE

Before we propose a generalization of the classical entropy measure $H(p_1, p_2, \ldots, p_k) = -\sum_{i=1}^{k} p_i \log p_i$, we provide some motivational examples to demonstrate what the generalization tries to achieve. The following are various cases where just considering the probability distribution does not suffice to quantify the uncertainty involved.

2.1 Motivation

- Incorporating domain knowledge: The function H, which is symmetric in its arguments, does not depend on the underlying x_i's. So, when the x_i's are known to have some relation amongst themselves, how can one modify the definition of entropy to make use of this relation?

CIKM'11, October 24–28, 2011, Glasgow, Scotland, UK.

The definition of variance, for example, makes use of both the x_i values, as well as, the corresponding p_i's. In [3], diversity is computed based on variance for numeric attributes, and based on entropy for categorical (or nominal) attributes. Is there a way to utilize additional information about the x_i's while computing entropy?

- Continuity: Let $k = 3$, so X assumes the values x_1, x_2, and x_3, with probabilities p_1, p_2, and p_3, respectively. The uncertainty associated with X is $H(p_1, p_2, p_3)$. Now, if it becomes known that x_2 and x_3 are identical (or indistinguishable from each other), X would assume just two values x_1 and x_2 with probabilities p_1 and $p_2 + p_3$, respectively. Consequently, the uncertainty of X reduces to $H(p_1, p_2+p_3)$. To give a numeric example, if $p_i = \frac{1}{3}, i = 1, 2, 3$, then the knowledge that x_2 and x_3 are identical reduces the uncertainty of X from $\log 3$ to $\log 3 - \frac{2}{3}\log 2$. What is to be done when x_2 and x_3 are not entirely identical but are not entirely dissimilar either?
- Ordinal values: When measurements are made on the ordinal scale, neighboring values are more similar to each other than distant ones. For example, in the case of Likert Scale [7] "strongly agree" is more similar to "agree" than to "disagree".

2.2 Proposed uncertainty measure

We now put forward a measure that generalizes Shannon's entropy [5] by incorporating the notion that information gained through x_i is reflected on x_j proportional to the similarity between them. Let $A = ((a_{ij}))_{1 \le i,j \le k}$ be a similarity matrix, possibly based on a similarity function [8], with $a_{ij} = 1$ signifying that x_i and x_j may be considered identical. We observe that

$$G(p_1, p_2, \ldots, p_k; A) = -\sum_{i=1}^{k} p_i \log\left(\sum_{j=1}^{k} a_{ij} p_j\right). \quad (1)$$

is one generalization of $H(\underset{\sim}{p})$ that satisfies the continuity criterion, and propose $-\log\left(\sum_{j=1}^{k} a_{ij} p_j\right)$ as the unit of information given the similarity matrix A. In other words, this is the amount of information gained by knowing that X has taken the value x_i, which indicates that not only did we get to know completely about x_i, but also partially about other values, too. G is the expectation of this unit of information. We shall refer to $G(p_1, p_2, \ldots, p_k; A)$ by $G(\underset{\sim}{p}; A)$, G_A or just G, whenever clear from the context.

3. APPLICATIONS

The proposed measure G being a generalization of entropy, may replace it in situations where additional information is available about the categories. In particular, sim-adjusted entropy may be used as a measure of diversity. Two diversity-related applications, namely, categorical clustering and measuring user diversity, are presented here.

3.1 Clustering Categorical Data

Categorical (or nominal) data clustering needs special treatment as distances between points are not always computable. There have been many attempts at clustering categorical data [4], and a common approach is to assume that all the features are equally important and that there is no similarity between the features. That way, one just needs to pay attention to only the feature counts of individual points, as well as, the clusters, for obtaining a criterion for determining a good clustering. Entropy of the feature proportions in each cluster is a commonly used criterion to segregate the points based on the feature counts [2, 6].

In practice, however, some categorical attributes and their values may be similar to one another. Existing methods deal with this by explicitly merging these features. However, merging features introduces other problems that need special attention. First, one needs to perform some thresholding in order to decide which features are similar enough to deserve being treated as identical, and this now requires additionally addressing the problem of how these thresholds are to be chosen. Also, one may encounter the chaining effect, whereby even if merging the feature pair $(1, 3)$ does not make sense, it might happen because the pairs $(1, 2)$ and $(2, 3)$ are merged together.

Replacing entropy by sim-adjusted entropy seems quite natural in this situation as one does not need to create entirely dissimilar features artificially. The features, and their counts, remain unchanged (i.e., without thresholding) while the similarity information is incorporated into the clustering criterion directly. This allows one to guide the clustering algorithm in a *systematic* manner towards including similar features in the same cluster.

As in [6], the clustering is performed by minimizing the total system sim-adjusted entropy using a Markov Chain Monte Carlo approach – iteratively picking a point at random from one cluster and moving it to a randomly picked cluster if it reduces the system entropy. We improvise on this by moving all identical points at the same time, thereby reaching the global optimum in fewer iterations.

3.2 Measuring Audience/User Diversity

Audience or user diversity is an important metric for measuring the health of an online network (e.g., Yahoo!) and various properties under it (e.g., Yahoo! Finance, Yahoo! Sports, etc.), and it may be measured along various user dimensions, such as demographics (age, gender, geo, *etc.*), behavior (page views and clicks on various properties, *etc.*), and the monetary value of a user to the network. Observing a lack of diversity may prompt actions of two kinds from property owners: (a) tune content towards catering to the dominant category, and (b) devise strategies for attracting the user groups currently in a minority.

Traditionally, Shannon entropy was used to measure how varied the audience is, but it is not always adequate. For example, when measuring diversity by the age of users, whether the audience is equally split between teenagers and middle-aged users, or equally split between teenagers and baby boomers, the diversity value is computed as the same. Intuitively, however, the second case appears to be more diverse. The following is a real-life example of this situation.

Suppose, diversity is computed based on the distribution across three age categories, namely, 0–29, 30–44, and 45+, denoted by A_1, A_2, and A_3, respectively. The proportions of users of Property A are 35%, 31%, and 34%, respectively, whereas, the corresponding numbers for Property B[1] are

[1]Properties A and B are real websites, and are being referred to in an anonymized manner only due to Yahoo!'s corporate policies regarding revealing demographic information

30%, 35%, and 35%. It may be noted that the proportions for B are nearly a permuted version of those for A, and so, diversity as computed by Shannon's entropy is about the same for both properties. This diversity measure does not consider the meaning of the classes, however, and would come up with the same value, say, even if the third category is for a different age group. We argue that, given that the classes are age groups, and since users with similar age are expected to behave similarly, the diversity is higher for A where more mass is in the disparate categories (young and old) than for B. Similar arguments hold along other dimensions, as it would be very difficult to have unrelated categories purely by design. This provides the motivation for incorporating additional information into the diversity computation.

Sim-adjusted entropy, which discounts the diversity value if the user base is split among similar categories rather than dissimilar categories, may be used instead to measure diversity. In [3], entropy was used for categorical variables while variance was preferred for numeric attributes. Sim-adjusted entropy is suited for nominal variables with an associated similarity structure. Of course, some effort is required for obtaining the similarity values themselves, but this is a tradeoff that a property owner would need to make in order to be able to measure diversity more accurately and avoid reaching wrong conclusions about the health of the property. After all, the perceived similarity between various age groups might vary from one property to another. Similar arguments apply to other dimensions (e.g., geo location).

4. EXPERIMENTAL RESULTS

Experimental results are now presented to demonstrate the utility of sim-adjusted entropy. Each application listed earlier is dealt with in a separate subsection.

4.1 Categorical Clustering

We now provide details on the application of sim-adjusted entropy on clustering categorical data, and demonstrate the efficacy of our approach in enhancing the semantic richness of the clusters obtained. We experiment with datasets from Yahoo! Answers to illustrate the application of sim-adjusted entropy for clustering. Another experiment on the Plants database yielded similar results, but is not included here for want of space.

First, we consider a snapshot of users' activities from Yahoo! Answers that range from May 2006 to Aug 2009. We chose four factoid categories, namely, 1) Maintenance and Repairs, 2) Motorcycles, 3) Cameras, 4) Cam-corders, as these had high quality answers compared to high activity categories like Dating or Polls & Surveys. Note that categories 1 and 2 are similar and so are 3 and 4. We selected the resolved questions from these categories, where the best answers were chosen by the asker. We preferred not to consider the best answers that were chosen by community votes as these could be from spammers. Each of the best answers was rated by the asker from 1 to 5. Aggregated data per answerer had $4(categories) \times 5(ratings) = 20$ features, and a total of 306354 answers from 93984 answerers.

Next, we describe an experiment that leverages domain expertise using similarity among the features to enhance the cluster diversity.

We tested the robustness of our approach on the Maintenance category from Yahoo! Answers [1], which had 151849 answers with 4938, 4612, 22288, 43836, and 76175 answers of ratings 1 to 5, respectively from 48272 users. We computed the proportional reduction in system entropy $(S_0 - S)/S_0$ (where S_0 is the initial system entropy without any clustering) with varied number of clusters for different similarity matrices. The matrices, symmetric and with all the diagonal entries equal to 1, were input in sparse matrix format (off-diagonal entries not mentioned are 0) are as follows:

A: a_{12}=0.2; a_{23}=0.1; a_{45}=0.3;
B: b_{12}=0.5; b_{23}=0.5; b_{45}=0.5;
C: c_{12}=0.9; c_{23}=0.6; c_{45}=0.9;
D: d_{12}=1.0; d_{23}=0.5; d_{45}=1.0;

The reduction in entropy increased with both the number of clusters and the similarity values.

While clustering of Yahoo! Answers dataset without considering any side information does lead to category specific users in each cluster, the authority of the users is not captured in the clusters. This is mainly due to all the ratings being treated as independent and unrelated. For example, consider two users from the category Cameras, with one having ratings ranging between 3 and 5, while the other's range from 1 to 3. The clustering process with unrelated ratings may put these two users in the same cluster, hence diluting the authority levels. However if we treat ratings 3, 4, and 5 as being similar to one another but not to 1 or 2, the authoritative users in each category may be discovered separately. By imposing similarity on categories along with ratings, we can bias or guide the clustering to get authoritative set of users in similar categories.

In this experiment, we use the notion of Sim-adjusted entropy to group together equally authoritative users of similar categories. We assigned a similarity of 0.5 to ratings in Cameras and Cam-Corders, and a similarity of 0.6 to those in Motorcycles and Maintenance. Within each category, we assigned similarity values of 0.9, 0.6, and 0.9 to the rating pairs (1,2), (2,3), and (4,5), respectively. The number of clusters was fixed at 8, accounting for high and low expertise in each of the four categories. With no similarity, the clustering procedure was able to find clusters of users in the *individual* categories. This may be seen in Fig. 1 where we plot the overall fraction of the features (in bubble size) for each of the clusters obtained. It may be noted that, clusters 3, 4 and 8 had users who answered in Cameras, Cam-Corders and Maintenance category, respectively. Users in Motorcycles category were clustered into high and low ratings in clusters 7 and 5, respectively. On the other hand, using *sim-adjusted entropy*, users are naturally clustered in *related* categories. In Fig. 1, clusters 3 and 4 had users with low quality answers (ratings of 1,2,3) across similar categories. Users from Cam-corders category are divided based on high (cluster 5) and low (cluster 4) quality ratings, as opposed to all of them being grouped together in the no similarity case. Similar observations may be made for other clusters/categories as well.

4.2 Audience Diversity

This section presents results that demonstrate the utility of the proposed diversity measure. As in Section 3.2, the age groups A_1, A_2, and A_3 are as defined as 0–29, 30–44, and 45+, respectively. Age distributions over these age groups were obtained from an internal reporting system at Yahoo! for the top 200 Yahoo! properties, both in terms of unique

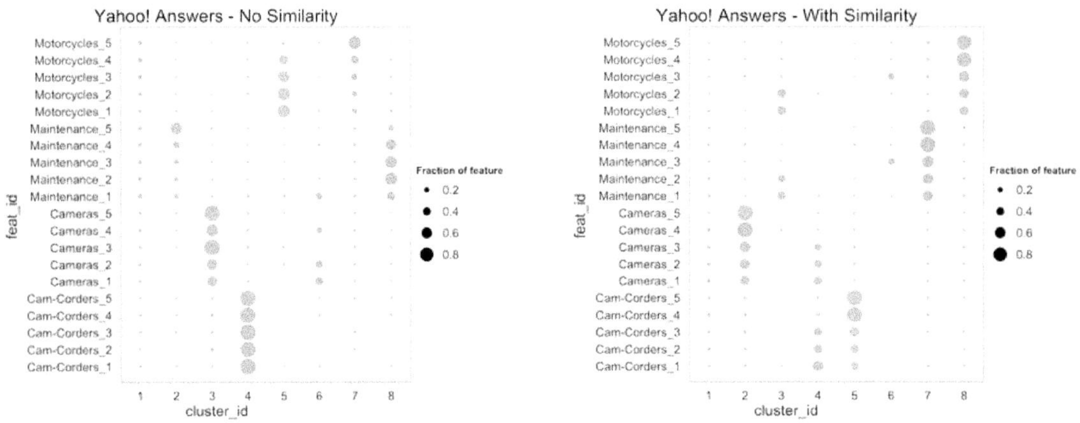

Figure 1: Cluster results for Yahoo! answers data, with overall fraction of features in each cluster

Table 1: Examples of age distributions for properties where H and $G_{0.5}$ differ vastly

Property	Metric	Distrib.	H	$G_{0.5}$
Property C	UUs	21:55:24	1.002	0.454
Property D	UUs	54:28:18	1.002	0.542
Property E	PVs	32:44:24	1.068	0.527
Property F	PVs	44:24:32	1.068	0.630
Property G	PVs	52:41:7	0.900	0.406
Property H	PVs	71:19:10	0.783	0.410

users and page views. For the sake of simplicity, we assume in this set of experiments that (a) $Sim(A_1, A_3) = 0$, and (b) $Sim(A_1, A_2) = Sim(A_2, A_3) = a$. In this assumption, the value of a signifies how much similarity exists between users of similar age. The diversity measure shall be denoted G_a (with $G_0 \equiv H$). For want of space, we only present experiments where $a = 0.5$.

Kendall's τ between H and $G_{0.5}$ is 0.78, that is, the two measures do not agree about 22% of the time on which property has more age diversity. Some examples are also provided in Table 1[2] to depict how $G_{0.5}$ better matches our intuition about diversity than G_0. One may note that $G_{0.5}$ shows a 19% change between Property C and Property D although they have the same entropy. This is a result of the latter having 72% of the mass in the extremes as opposed to just 45% for the former. Similar is the case for Properties E and F. In contrast, while entropy changes significantly due to the change in distributions of Properties G and H, $G_{0.5}$ does not change much because the distributional changes are mostly restricted between similar age groups.

5. CONCLUSIONS AND DISCUSSION

A novel measure based on the premise that additional information about the relationship between various categories helps reduce uncertainty has been proposed in this work. A simple generalization of the entropy measure, called similarity adjusted entropy, has been put forward, and its basic characteristics have been studied. Two applications, namely, categorical data clustering and user diversity measurement, were described in detail. Experimental results convincingly demonstrate the utility of the proposed approach.

One may observe that, throughout this article, the focus was always on how to incorporate a given similarity structure into the definition of entropy, rather than determining the similarity itself. So, this approach provides a simple alternative for measuring diversity to someone already armed with additional information over what is used by the classical Shannon's entropy. Another point to be noted is that the proposed measure is just one of several possible generalizations of entropy of the desired form.

In future, once the proposed measure is established as a measure of diversity, we would like to present it as a measure of information. That would give rise to notions of sim-adjusted information gain and maximum sim-adjusted entropy, and may have other machine learning applications like classification, decision trees, *etc.*

[2]names of the properties anonymized as mentioned in Section 3.2

6. REFERENCES

[1] L. A. Adamic, J. Zhang, E. Bakshy, and M. S. Ackerman. Knowledge sharing and Yahoo Answers: everyone knows something. In *WWW'08*, pages 665–674, New York, NY, USA, 2008.

[2] D. Barbara, J. Couto, and Y. Li. COOLCAT: an entropy-based algorithm for categorical clustering. In *CIKM'02*, pages 582–589, 2002.

[3] M. A. Bedau, M. Zwick, and A. Baham. Variance and uncertainty measures of population diversity dynamics. *Advances in System Science and Applications Special Issue I*, pages 7–12, 1995.

[4] P. Berkhin. Survey of clustering data mining techniques. Technical report, 2002.

[5] T. M. Cover and J. A. Thomas. *Elements of Information Theory*. Wiley & Sons, 1991.

[6] T. Li, S. Ma, and M. Ogihara. Entropy-based criterion in categorical clustering. In *ICML'04*, pages 68–75, 2004.

[7] R. Likert. A technique for the measurement of attitudes. *Archives of Psychology*, 140:1–55, 1932.

[8] S. Santini and R. Jain. Similarity measures. *IEEE Trans. PAMI*, 21(9):871–883, September 1999.

Mining Query Structure from Click Data: A Case Study of Product Queries

Julia Kiseleva*
Saint-Petersburg State University
Russia, Saint-Petersburg
julianakiseleva@gmail.com

Eugene Agichtein
Emory University
Atlanta, Georgia 30322, USA
eugene@mathcs.emory.edu

Daniel Billsus
Shopping.com
Brisbane, CA 94005
dbillsus@shopping.com

ABSTRACT

Much of the information on the Web is inherently structured, product pages of large online shopping sites such as Amazon.com being a typical example. Yet, unstructured keyword queries are still the most common way to search for such structured information, which can introduce ambiguity and noise into the search results. This problem can be resolved by *query segmentation*, that is, transformation of unstructured keyword queries into *structured* queries. The resulting queries can be used to search product databases more accurately, and to improve result presentation and query suggestion. The main contribution of our work is a novel approach to query segmentation based on weakly supervised machine learning, trained on the existing structured data (e.g., product tables) and the associated query and click logs. Extensive experiments over a large query and click log from a leading shopping engine demonstrate that our approach significantly outperforms previously reported methods.

Categories and Subject Descriptors

H.3.3 [**Information Search and Retrieval**]: Information Storage and Retrieval – *Search Process*

General Terms

Performance, Design, Experimentation.

Keywords

Query segmentation, attribute extraction, product search.

1. INTRODUCTION

A large fraction of the available data on the Web originally exists in structured databases, such as product catalogs. In contrast, unstructured keyword queries represent the most common way to search for information. Clearly, using unstructured queries to retrieve structured data represents a mismatch of retrieval paradigms, which is the central problem we are addressing in this paper. In short, the goal of our work is to use unsupervised machine learning techniques to automatically learn to transform unstructured into structured queries.

*Work done while visiting Emory University and Shopping.com

CIKM'11, October 24–28, 2011, Glasgow, Scotland, UK.

The tension between structured and unstructured modes of representing and accessing information on the Web has sparked a lot of attention leading to many recent contributions in the area of information extraction. In particular, unsupervised techniques for fact extraction are an emerging field of critical importance. Shopping sites and specialized crawlers (e.g. those powering comparison shopping sites) are often able to obtain information directly from the original product databases, and store product characteristics in a structured form. Similarly, the users searching these shopping sites (e.g., Shopping.com or Amazon.com) often have a particular product and characteristics in mind. Hence, understanding the implied query structure could help better map the (implicitly structured) query submitted by a user to the appropriate products stored in the (explicitly structured) database. In turn, this would improve the quality of the result ranking, query suggestion, and potentially results presentation.

This paper focuses on the problem of detecting and labeling structured attribute values in keyword search queries to enable structured querying of product databases. For example, a keyword query *'dell inspiron 15 2gb'* could be converted to a structured form, such as *{'dell'*:BRAND, *'inspiron'*:FAMILY LINE, *'15'*: DISPLAY SIZE, *'2gb'*: INSTALLED MEMORY*}*. This structured query would more likely retrieve relevant results against a structured product database, compared to resorting to a keyword-based search only.

To accomplish this segmentation we follow the machine learning-based approach to information extraction and text segmentation. This approach is attractive since it allows the system to be retrained as the underlying data changes. This requires obtaining a high-quality training set (TS) used for tuning the extraction system. The classical approach of manually labeling thousands or perhaps millions of queries is not feasible and to some degree futile because the labels can become obsolete as the queries and the product database contents change. Instead, we propose to *generate* this training set *automatically* and *robustly*, using only user clicks and the existing structured product databases to guide the training process.

That is, our idea, similar to [1], is to use the *clicks on product records* as indicators of a connection between the unstructured query text and the structured product description, and use this connection to construct labels for the query terms. However, unlike in the previous work we recognize that clicks are *noisy* (often users click on results by accident) and *sparse* (many *tail* records in the database are *never* clicked). Thus, the main contribution of this paper is development of a *novel*, *robust* and *effective* method of an unsupervised machine learning technique to train the query segmentation system. Our method requires no manual labeling for building a training set, which can be time consuming for a large number of domains. At the same time our method is able to capture *approximate* matches between query terms and target attribute values, thus increasing the *coverage* of the TS. Finally, our approach allows for elegantly trading off between different performance characteristics through controlling the parameters of the automatic labeling process.

2. RELATED WORK

Many semi-supervised or unsupervised methods for sequence labeling have been proposed. A few dealt with search query segmentation (e.g., [1]). Several semi-supervised approaches to text segmentation, particularly to methods based on conditional random fields (CRFs) and Hidden Markov Models (HMMs) have been proposed. One common approach makes a typical assumption that in addition to a small amount of labeled data there is a large amount of unlabeled data. In this setting it is natural to apply self-training which combines a multi view and semi-supervised learning in different ways. It trains a model using the labeled data, and afterwards iteratively uses high-confidence predictions with the unlabeled data to expand the training set.

Previous work has shown that the results were improved by adding a dictionary as a feature for HMM. A similar approach to CRF was presented and shown successful for text segmentation (e.g., in reference [5]). This semi-supervised learning method aims to maximize the conditional log-likelihood of labeled data while minimizing the conditional entropy of the model predictions on unlabeled data. Previous approaches to context-aware sequential labeling have used Conditional Random Field (CRF) models [4] that allow modeling dependencies between states (e.g. attributes) and observations (e.g. tokens in a query). Moreover, previous works demonstrated that user product search queries do display statistically significant patterns that can help sequential labeling.

Unfortunately, CRFs and other supervised models require significant amounts of human annotated data for the training to achieve production-level accuracy. This process can be expensive and not scalable, especially for a general-domain setting where training a system for thousands of product/attribute domain categories is simply not feasible. Additionally, there is a fairly large amount of work on using additional resources for semi- or unsupervised information extraction in general. Click data together with databases was used in [1] for a semi-supervised CRF-based model. In our work we also use click data to decrease ambiguity. It was shown in [7] that clicked pages are important for uncovering the query intent. The unsupervised machine learning method for query segmentation was presented in reference [2]. The authors use *click data* and *product database* to reduce term ambiguity in segmentation process. This paper builds on that work and extends it significantly by improving the training set generation process and the training methodology, resulting in substantial accuracy improvements.

3. QUERY SEGMENTATION APPROACH

We now present our novel weakly supervised machine learning method for query segmentation problem, which is composed of two novel components: *automatic query labeling algorithm (AQLA), synthetic queries generation algorithm (SQGA)* which are used for *training* the *segmentation system (TSS).*

AQLA: the goal of this component is to map unstructured query terms to product names and attributes based on the click data. The click data comes from users interacting naturally with a product search engine. The searchers run queries (e.g. '*sony vaio*', '*dell inspiron 4gb*', etc.) against a product search engine and click on product listings from the search results. Each click event is recorded to the *clicks logs* in the form of a *(query, product name)* tuple. The products are stored in a database where each product consists of its name, textual description, and structured attribute values. The *AQLA* uses *clicks logs* and *product database* as an input sources to derive a set of structured queries. The algorithm assigns a target attribute to each term in the query with a confidence estimation in range [0,1] corresponding to the certainty that a query term in fact corresponds to that attribute value. The method will mark the word using a specific label *'Unknown'* if it cannot detect any suitable target attributes for this term. This process follows the method previously described in reference [2] but the is enhanced by post-processing techniques to reduce the *sparsity* in the resulting training set, as described next.

SQGA: the goal of this component is to substantially enhance the training set size and comprehensiveness by automatically generating a *synthetic* set of queries to be used for training the attribute extractors.

First, SQGA computes the observed distribution of transition probabilities between attributes; the transition probability distribution is represented by a transition matrix (P), where:

$$P(i,j) = Pr(attribute_{n+1=j} \mid attribute_{n=i}) \quad (1)$$

The distribution is calculated based on the automatic labeled query set which is derived by AQLA. The clicked products have the following form: *Clicked products = {product name, set of attributes description}*. For example, the product ***'sony vaio 1.33ghz 2gb 260gb 8in'*** has the following set of attribute*:*

{(attr: ***brand****, attr_name:* ***sony****), (attr:* ***family line****, attr_name:* ***vaio****), (attr:* ***processor speed****, attr_name:* ***1.33 ghz****), (attr:* ***installed memory****, attr_name:* ***2 gb****)}* (2).

Using the observed distribution of attribute value sequences in real queries, SQGA takes clicked products and generates a larger set of *synthetic queries* (SQ) using an attributes description and the distribution of transition probability to generate queries similar to real ones, but including queries for all products in the database, including the tail ones. To deal with rare terms, SQGA uses simple additive smoothing.

Training the Segmentation System: The CRF model (using the Mallet implementation) is used for the actual segmentation of new queries. The key idea is to use for training the system the union of automatically labeled queries (from AQLA) and the synthetically generated queries (from SQGA). Otherwise, the CRF training proceeds in the standard fashion.

4. SYSTEM IMPLEMENTATION

Detecting Target Attributes: The common challenge of the large database data is a duplicate detection [6]. Our problem is somewhat different: there are many nearly-duplicate attributes (e.g. *'release-year'* and *'release date'*). We propose to detect such attribute duplicates by comparing the attribute values, using a bag-of-words representation we call an *'attribute document'*:

$$attribute\_document = \{a_j\}_{j=1}^{m}, \text{ where}$$

$$a_j = \{(t_1, freq(t_1)), (t_2, freq(t_2)), ..., (t_n, freq(t_n))\} \quad (3).$$

The *'attribute document'* is represented by a set of words that appear as attribute values. For example, a *'brand_document'* contains all observed terms from all textual description of the attribute *'brand'* and their frequencies, which are derived across all clicked products, e.g. *brand_document = ('dell':14, 'lenovo':9, 'asus':7)*.

Attribute duplicate detection measures closeness between each pair of attributes by calculating a cosine similarity value between their dictionaries. Therefore, each term in the attribute document is weighted using a *tf*idf* metric, where *tf* is the count of times the term appeared inside the given attribute value, and *idf* is the inverse of the count of different *attributes* where the term appeared. A threshold for the cosine similarity value was used to decide whether two attributes are duplicates. The threshold was optimized empirically and set to 0.7 for all subsequent experiments.

This process of duplicates detection reduced the number of *target attributes* from **65** to **41**. Thus, it significantly reduced the target attribute space, increasing accuracy of segmentation without degrading the user experience.

Automatic Query Labeling: The AQLA uses the following input sources:

1. **User clicks logs** consist of click events e.g. *(*QUERY = *dell inspiron 14 black,* CLICKED PRODUCT NAME = dell inspiron i1464-4382obk 1464 **14**-inch laptop obsidian black*)*, *(*QUERY = *sony vaio,* CLICKED PRODUCT NAME = sony vaio 1.33ghz 2gb 260gb 8i).
2. **Product database** contains the names and attribute values of the products, with some values containing text.
3. **Brand dictionary (BD)** contains all brand names, brand synonyms and brand abbreviations and is built manually. E.g. *'hp'* is an abbreviation for the brand *'Hewlett Packard'*, *'mac'* is synonym for *'mackintosh'*, etc.

AQLA examines every click event (*query, product name)* and quantifies the matching degree between each query term and a product attribute descriptions using a cosine similarity. *Tf*idf*-measure is used for weighting terms, but we used a modified conception of a *'document'*. Our schema of the *'document'* is presented as in formula (3). Every query term is referred to a particular attribute in the final labeled query set. The derived pair is characterized by the weight (cosine similarity) in range [0, 1]. AQLA assigns a *zero* weight to a query term which is labeled as '*unknown*'. Thereafter we notice that the matched data is very sparse, meaning that a large number of queries contains terms which are defined as '*unknown*'. This phenomenon happens because some product attribute descriptions do not contain a particular term. The described phenomenon significantly decreases the quality of derived labeled queries. Therefore we introduce a novel method to avoid such situations. This method constructs a dictionary for each attribute which includes terms and posterior probabilities. Posterior probabilities *(post_pr)* of belonging to a particular attribute dictionary are calculated for each query term during the automatic query labeling process. Then a dictionary of posterior probabilities for each attribute is derived in the following form: $\{attribute_j \rightarrow \{(term_i, post\_pr_i)\}_{i=1}^{n}\}_{j=1}^{m}$ (4).

This dictionary is used for an *updating algorithm* (UA) which cleans up automatically labeled queries. Note that the value of posterior probability of belonging to a particular attribute is assigned as an updated attribute weight for the term.

The *SQ* are needed to extend a training TS for CRFs model. The distribution from formula (1) is supplemented with two special symbols: *$begin* and *$end* which are the beginning and the end of the query respectively. The *SQGA* uses this distribution and textual descriptions of attributes to simulate the process of how a human being generates the product search query, generating a large synthetic training set SQ. Each *(term, attribute)* pair has a weight which equals a *post_pr* from formula (4). We consider this metric as a similarity value between term and attribute.

CRF Model for Segmentation System: The training set for CRF learning is a union of automatically labeled queries and SQ. The system trains the CRFs model to segment the queries into attribute-value pairs. The set of target attributes was extended to label a sequence of terms like '*Hewlett Packard*' which are both '*brand*' more precisely. We use the common approach of information extraction which introduces two types of attribute names: with suffixes '*_BEGIN*' and '*_CONTINUE*'. Specifically, the CRF model is trained separately for each product sub-category because every product in our TS is already pre-classified into a distinct sub-category.

Segmentation features: We introduce two types of features for the process of training the CRFs model: *general features* and *dictionary features.* **General Features** include*:*

- *Boolean features* that represent a presence or an absence of: *terms* and *ngram (unigram+bigram)* ;
- *Regular expressions* (*regexp*) *features* that match different types of the term such as numbers, words and mixed terms. Let us show an example of mixed terms: 4gb, 320gb and sd850 all match the regular expression: '[a-z]+[0-9]+' or '[0-9]+[a-z]+' (in the pattern matching language):
  - ✦ if the system detects that the term is a *number*, it adds a feature which shows a range of this number.
  - ✦ if the term is defined as a *mixed term* the system splits it up into the *number* and the *word*. Then the system defines a range of the derived *digit* and constructs new feature. The derived word is a separate feature.
- *Context information of the term* that shows the preceding and the subsequent terms.

Dictionary features:

- *Brand feature* that shows if a particular term is a brand or not The system uses a brand catalog from the database for implementation of this.
- *Dictionary for the attribute names.* The system creates a dictionary for every attribute name where all terms are associated with a set of attributes and every term is associated with a posterior probability of belonging to a particular attribute. The system can detect an attribute for an incoming term using this dictionary.

5. EXPERIMENTAL SETUP

There is no generally accepted benchmark to evaluate product query segmentation. In the section of related work we mentioned several evaluated results of the query segmentation system which were introduced by other authors. There is no generally accepted benchmark to evaluate product queries segmentation and we cannot make a straightforward comparison of our results with previously reported semi-supervised approach [1] as we have no access to the datasets used in reference [1]. Therefore we provide evaluation experiments using a strong baseline, based on [1], and our own 'ground truth' datasets, described below.

Data Description: The data for the experiments is a union of query and click logs to the Shopping.com site which were collected from following months: September 2009, December 2009, March 2010. The total number of queries is *29,257*. These include clicks on products from *computers* categories which combine five sub-categories: *Laptops*, *Software*, *Hard Drives*, *Printers*, and *Laptop Accessories*.

Ground Truth: We select 450 unique queries from our search query log described above to construct 'ground truth'. We impose the constraints that queries in 'gold standard' should have length more than one word but less than six.

The human 'ground truth' judgments were obtained by using the Amazon Mechanical Turk workers, in batches of 50 queries per assignment, resulting in 450 queries labeled overall. Up to 10 workers per batch were assigned. We developed a detailed guide for MT users which contains an explanation with examples of how labeling should be performed. Ten (distinct) queries from pre-evaluated dataset were injected into each batch, in order to provide a calibration baseline to discard poor-quality work. As a result, the work of the annotators with ratings that correlated less than 65% on the pre-evaluated subset of the batch, or those that failed the rule was discarded (approximately 30% of the submitted ratings were discarded through this procedure). Hence the ground truth includes evaluation results from reliable users we can assert that we use a high quality 'ground truth' for our evaluation.

Training Set Construction: The final training set is a combination of real queries, automatically labeled using AQLA, and the SQ set. The set of automatically labeled queries was evaluated using the constructed 'ground truth'. We empirically measure precision, recall and f1-measure for distinct cosine similarity values. The f1-measure obtains a maximum value where the similarity between term and attribute equals to **0.3**. Therefore we suggest the following constraints to create the final TS: (1) each term in the derived query should be defined by target attributes with weight over **0.3**, (2) the derived query could contain terms which are defined as *'unknown'*, but at least two terms must have target attribute. Table 1 presents derived metrics for the enhanced AQ-LA which uses the additional data sources UA (Section 3) and BD (Section 3). The relative improvements are shown in the brackets. All derived metrics are reported across all sub-categories. Precision increases due to introducing UA and BD. Recall increases due to the using of UA.

Table 1. Relative improvements of AQLA on the automated query labeling task (Category : Computers).

Method	*Precision (%)*	*Recall (%)*	*F1 (%)*
Baseline	78	47	57
AQLA	**86 (+10.3)**	**63 (+34)**	**72 (+26.3)**

6. EXPEREMENTAL RESULTS AND DISSCUSSION

Query Segmentation Evaluation: The developed query segmentation system derives results with a computed confidence level (marginal probability) *(CL)* in range [0, 1]. Our hypothesis is that it shows *'assurance'* for a particular prediction and could be used as a filter. The baseline algorithm for segmentation process builds a dictionary of the terms form database for every attribute and calculates posterior probability for each term in this dictionary. It assigns to every given term an attribute with the highest posterior probability. The different TSs were used to teach CRFs model: **(1) TS1** is a subset of set of automatically labeled queries which does not contain the queries with terms defined as *'unknown'* and **(2) TS2** is a combination of labeled queries which contain *'unknown'* and SQ. The evaluation was performed across all five sub-categories and the results are presented in Table 2. The f1-meassure is maximized at CL value equals to **0.3.** The derived evaluation result proves that the adding of SQ into TS significantly increases the quality of the segmentation system. The obtained segmentation result looks better compared to our baseline. The described new feature set improves overall result of prediction by **5-6%** relative to the method of training CRF over the TS1.

Table 2. Relative improvements on the query segmentation task (Category : Computers).

Method	*Precision (%)*	*Recall (%)*	*F1 (%)*
Baseline	70	51	59
TS1+CRF	65 (-7)	36 (-29)	47 (-20)
TS2+CRF	**75 (+7.1)**	**53 (+4)**	**62 (+5)**

The presented unsupervised machine learning approach outperforms the previous state of the art baseline, based on reference [1]. Our experiments have shown that the segmentation method obtains precision of 75%, which is higher than both our baseline and the reported result of 72% reported in reference [1] for the comparable *'computer'* category.

7. CONCLUSIONS AND FUTURE WORK

We proposed a novel unsupervised machine learning approach to structure search queries with product intent. Our approach is scalable, in that it relies primarily on query and click logs and does not require human-annotated training data. Specifically, we introduced two innovations: first, a new method, AQLA, for automated and robust training dataset construction that uses a product database and click events, and SQGA, which uses the observed data distribution to generate synthetic comprehensive training data for rare items that may not have appeared in the query logs in the past. Second, we proposed a new method for generating a feature set for training a query segmentation model. Possible future directions include making the system even more general to allow applications of our method to other vertical domains without additional tuning.

8. REFERENCES

[1] Li X., Wang Y.-Y. and Acero A. A Extracting structured information from user queries with semi-supervised Conditional Random Fields. In *SIGIR* (2009). Pages 672-579.

[2] Kiseleva J., Agichtein E., Guo Q., Billsus D., Chai W. Unsupervised Query Segmentation Using Click Data: Preliminary Results. In *WWW* (2010). Pages 1131-1132.

[3] Amini M.-R., Goutte C., Usunier N. Combining coregularization and consensus-based self-training for multilingual text categorization. In *SIGIR* (2010). Pages 475-482.

[4] Bradley J. K., Guestrin C. Learning Tree Conditional Random Fields. In *ICML* (2010).Pages 127-134.

[5] Mann G., McCallum A. Efficient Computation of Entropy Gradient for Semi-Supervised Conditional Random Fields. In *HLT/NAACL* (2007). Pages 109-112.

[6] Mikhail Bilenko and Raymond J. Mooney. Adaptive Duplicate Detection Using Learnable String Similarity Measures. In *KDD* (2003). Pages 39-48.

[7] Li X., Wang Y.-Y. and Acero A. Learning query intent from regularized click graph. In SIGIR (2008). Pages 339-346

Towards Expert Finding by Leveraging Relevant Categories in Authority Ranking

Hengshu Zhu[1,2] Huanhuan Cao[2] Hui Xiong[3] Enhong Chen[1] Jilei Tian[2]
[1]University of Science and Technology of China [2]Nokia Research Center [3]Rutgers University
[1]{zhs, cheneh}@ustc.edu.cn [2]{happia.cao, jilei.tian}@nokia.com [3]hxiong@rutgers.edu

ABSTRACT

How to improve authority ranking is a crucial research problem for expert finding. In this paper, we propose a novel framework for expert finding based on the authority information in the target category as well as the relevant categories. First, we develop a scalable method for measuring the relevancy between categories through topic models. Then, we provide a link analysis approach for ranking user authority by considering the information in both the target category and the relevant categories. Finally, the extensive experiments on two large-scale real-world Q&A data sets clearly show that the proposed method outperforms the baseline methods with a significant margin.

Categories and Subject Descriptors

H.3.3 [**Information Search and Retrieval**]: Search process; H.3.5 [**Online information services**]: Web-based services

General Terms

Algorithms, Experimentation

Keywords

Authority Ranking, Expert Finding, Category Relevancy, Topic Models

1. INTRODUCTION

A critical challenge in knowledge sharing social networks, such as online forums and Question Answering (Q&A) communities is how to find experts, i.e., a group of authoritative users with special skills or knowledge for a specific category. Indeed, the problem of expert finding has attracted a lot of attention in the literature and a central issue of expert finding is how to perform effective authority ranking.

However, when performing authority ranking for expert finding, most of the state-of-the-art works only take the information in the target category into consideration. Indeed, every target category usually has some very relevant categories. The information in these relevant categories might be exploitable for improving the performance of authority ranking for the target category.

To this end, we propose to exploit the information in both target and relevant categories for improving the performance of authority ranking. The first task along this line is to measure category relevancies. In this paper, we propose to exploit topic models for representing categories as topic distributions and then measure the relevancies between categories by normalized Kullback Leibler (KL) divergence. In addition, we develop a link analysis approach, which is based on the Topical Random Surfer model [4], to collectively exploit the information in both target and relevant categories for authority ranking. Finally, we perform extensive experiments on two large-scale real-world data sets collected from two major commercial Q&A web sites. The results demonstrate the efficiency and effectiveness of the proposed approach.

CIKM'11, October 24–28, 2011, Glasgow, Scotland, UK.

2. PROBLEM STATEMENT

In this paper we propose a new framework for expert finding, namely, category relevancy based authority ranking. To be specific, here we first introduce the traditional authority ranking problem, and then formally define the problem of category relevancy based authority ranking.

Traditional Authority Ranking: Given a category set $C = \{c_1, c_2, ..., c_n\}$ and a user set $U = \{u_1, u_2, ..., u_m\}$, the category link graph G_c ($c \in C$) for a given knowledge sharing social network S is denoted as $G_c = (V_c, E_c, W_c)$, where

- $V_c = \{u_i\}$ is a set of user nodes, where each user in V_c made or replied the posts which are labeled with category c in S.
- $E_c = \{e_{ij}\}$ is a set of directed edges, where e_{ij} indicates that user u_j replied the posts which are labeled with category c and made by user u_i in S.
- $W_c = \{w_{ij}^c\}$ is a set of weights for the edges in E_c, where w_{ij}^c indicates the frequency that user u_j replied the posts which are labeled with category c and made by user u_i in S.

Given a knowledge sharing social network S, the task of the traditional authority ranking for category c is to find top K authoritative users from G_c. In this way, only the information in target categories are taken into account. In contrast, we introduce a new approach for authority ranking by exploiting the information in both target and relevant categories. Next, we first present some notations as follows.

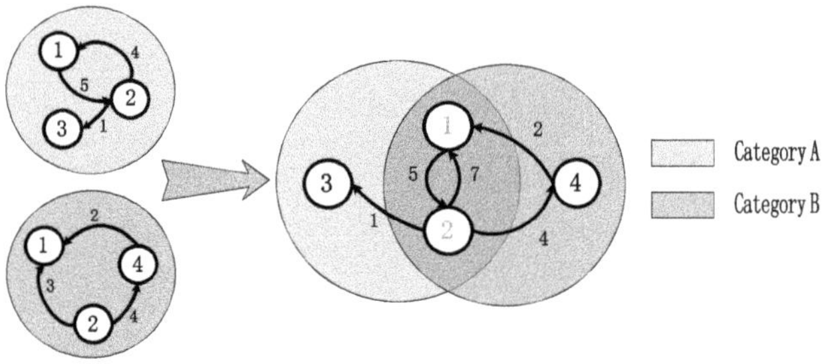

Figure 1: An example of extended category link graph in a Q&A community. A node denotes a user, and an edge from user u_i to user u_j denotes that u_j has answered a question posted by u_i.

DEFINITION 1. (EXTENDED CATEGORY SET, EXTENDED CATEGORY LINK GRAPH). *An* ***extended category set*** $\Upsilon_c = \{c\} \cup R_c$, *where* R_c *denotes the set of relevant categories of category* c.

An ***extended category link graph*** $G_{\Upsilon_c} = (V_{\Upsilon_c}, E_{\Upsilon_c}, W_{\Upsilon_c})$ *is the extension of the category link graph* G_c, *where* $V_{\Upsilon_c} = \bigcup_{c' \in \Upsilon_c} V_{c'}$, $E_{\Upsilon_c} = \bigcup_{c' \in \Upsilon_c} E_{c'}$, *and* $W_{\Upsilon_c} = \{w_{ij} | w_{ij} = \sum_{c' \in \Upsilon_c} w_{ij}^{c'}\}$ *is the corresponding weight set.*

Figure 1 illustrates an example of extended category link graph in a Q&A community. With above notions, the problem of category relevancy based authority ranking is formally defined as follows.

DEFINITION 2. (CATEGORY RELEVANCY BASED AUTHORITY RANKING). *Given a category c, the task of* ***category relevancy based authority ranking*** *is to build the extended category link graph* G_{Υ_c} *and then find top* K *authoritative users for category* c *in* G_{Υ_c}.

Therefore, the problem of category relevancy based authority ranking can be divided into two sub-problems as follows. The first problem is how to find the relevant category set R_c to extend the original category link graph G_c. The second problem is how to rank user authority for category c in the extended category link graph G_{Υ_c}. In the following sections, we present the technical details of our solutions for the two sub-problems, respectively.

3. INFERRING CATEGORY RELEVANCY THROUGH TOPIC MODELS

In this paper, we propose to leverage topic models for inferring category relevancies. The basic assumption is that two categories are relevant because their probabilities of belonging to the same latent topic are similar. For example, the categories "Singing", "Pop Music" and "Instruments" are related because they all belong to the latent topic *Music*.

3.1 Inferring Latent Topics by LDA

Topic models assume that there are several latent topics for a corpus D and a document d in D can be represented as a bag of words $\{w_{d,i}\}$ which are generated by these latent topics. We first define a *user interactive log* consists of a set of category labels where the user made or replied the posts with these category labels and the corresponding frequencies. Then intuitively, if we take category labels as words, take user interactive logs as documents we can directly take advantage of topic models for inferring latent topics of categories. Then we can represent each category c as a conditional probabilistic distribution $P(z|c)$ which denotes the probability of category c being labeled with topic z.

Among several existing topic models, we use the Latent Dirichlet Allocation model (LDA) [2] in our approach. According to LDA, a user interactive log L_i is generated as follows. Firstly, a prior topic distribution θ_i is generated from a prior Dirichlet distribution α. Secondly, a prior category distribution ϕ_i is generated from a prior Dirichlet distribution β. Therefore, for the j-th category c_j in L_i, the model generates a topic $z_{i,j}$ from θ_i and then generates c_j from ϕ_i.

The main requirement for our approach is to estimate the probability $P(z_i|c)$, which cannot be obtained directly from LDA. However, according to the Bayes formula we can calculate $P(z_i|c)$ by $P(z_i|c) = \frac{P(c|z_i)P(z_i)}{\sum_i P(c,z_i)}$, where $P(c|z_i)$ and $P(z_i)$ can be obtained from LDA. In this paper, we use Gibbs sampling method to estimate $P(c|z_i)$ and $P(z_i)$. After several rounds of Gibbs sampling, we can get the estimated value $\widetilde{P}(c|z_i)$ by $\widetilde{P}(c|z_i) = \frac{n_i^{c} + \beta}{n_i^{\cdot} + |C|\beta}$, where $n_i^{(c)}$ indicates the frequency that category c has been assigned to topic z_i, $n_i^{(\cdot)}$ indicates the frequency that any category is assigned to topic z_i, and $|C|$ indicates the total number of unique categories. Similarly, the estimated value $\widetilde{P}(z_i)$ can be calculated by $\widetilde{P}(z_i) = \frac{n_i^{\cdot}}{\sum_i n_i^{\cdot}}$

LDA model needs a predefined parameter Z to indicate the number of latent topics. How to select an appropriate Z for LDA is an open question. In terms of guaranteeing the performance of expert finding, in this paper we utilize the method proposed by Bao et al [1] to estimate Z.

3.2 Building Category Relevancy Matrix

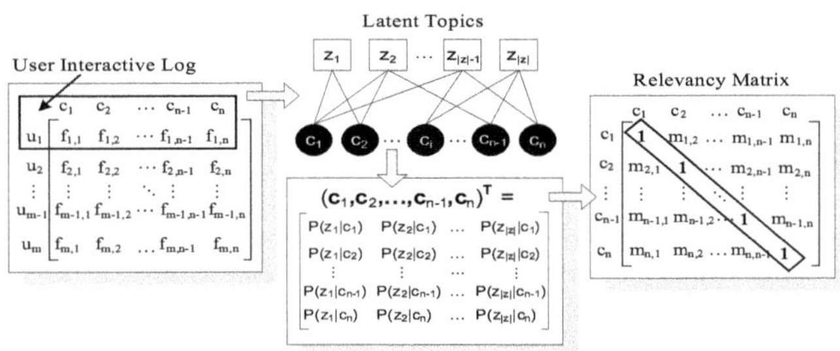

Figure 2: Category relevancy matrix generation.

By utilizing LDA, each category c can be represented as a Z-dimension vector of topic distribution $P(z|c)$. Thus, the task of estimating category relevancy is converted to calculate the distance between vectors. In this paper, we propose to use normalized Kullback Leibler (KL) divergence, which is an asymmetric measure, for measuring category relevancies. The KL-divergence from category c_i to category c_j is computed by $KL(c_i||c_j) = \sum_z P(z|c_i) log \frac{P(z|c_i)}{P(z|c_j)}$.

Then we calculate the relevancy between categories c_i and c_j by $Rel(c_i||c_j) = 1 - \frac{KL(c_i||c_j)}{Max(KL(c_j))}$, where $Max(KL(c_j))$ denotes the maximum KL-divergence from other categories to category c_j. The bigger $Rel(c_i||c_j) \in [0,1]$, the more relevant c_i is for c_j.

After calculating the relevancies between each pair of categories, we can obtain the category relevancy matrix $M_C = \{m_{ij} = Rel(c_i||c_j)\}$, where $i, j \in [1, n]$. Figure 2 illustrates an example of generating the category relevancy matrix.

From M_C, we can easily find the relevant categories for a given category through a predefined relevancy threshold τ. In Section 6, we analyze the robustness of expert finding when given varying parameters τ and Z.

4. AUTHORITY RANKING THROUGH LINK ANALYSIS

By finding relevant categories from the category relevancy matrix, we can build the extended category link graph for a target category. Compared with a normal category link graph, in an extended category link graph the authority propagation in the target category between two users may be impacted by their different original expertise in the target category before authority propagation. To this end, we extend the Topical Random Surfer (TRS) model [4] to rank user authority in extended category link graphs for considering their different original expertise in the target category.

The TRS model is originally proposed for web page ranking. Its basic idea is similar to the "random surfer" process described in PageRank model and the special property is that the "random surfer" is sensitive to different topics of web pages. Specifically, in the TRS model, there are two possible ways to move to another web page v' for a web surfer who is browsing a web page v for the interesting topic z. The first is with probability $(1-d)$ to follow a outgoing link on the current page v (e.g., clicking a hyper-link). Another is with probability d the surfer will jump to a random page from the entire web W (e.g., directly typing an url in the address field). Moreover, for each new page v', the surfer will browse it either because of the same interesting topic z with probability $\psi_{v,z}$ or any other interesting topic z' with probability $(1-\psi_{v,z})$. Therefore, there are total three reasons for the web surfer to browse a new web page v', namely, 1) following a link for the same interesting topic z, 2) following a link for any other interesting topic ($z' \neq z$) and 3) jumping to another page for any interesting topic z'. To facilitate expression, TRS model names these three reasons as "F_S", "F_J" and "J_J", respectively.

To utilize TRS model for our authority ranking problem, we take the extended category link graph G_{Υ_c} as a web page link graph G, let each $u \in G_{\Upsilon_c}$ correspond to a web page v and let the original expertise of each user in different categories (without considering the authority propagation) correspond to different topics of a web page. Moreover, in our problem "F_S", "F_J" and "J_J" denote 1) following a link to select the next user as the authoritative user for the same category c, 2) following a link to select the next user as the authoritative user for any other interesting category c' ($c' \neq c$), and 3) randomly select a user as the authoritative user for any category c', respectively. Therefore, we have the following equations according to the TRS model.

$$\begin{cases} P(F_S|u,c) = (1-d)\psi_{u,c} \\ P(F_J|u,c) = (1-d)(1-\psi_{u,c}) \\ P(J_J|u,c) = d \\ P(u',c'|u,c',F_S) = D(u,u') \\ P(u',c'|u,c,F_J) = D(u,u')\psi_{u,c'} \\ P(u',c'|u,c,J_J) = \dfrac{1}{|V_{\Upsilon_c}|}\psi_{u',c'} \end{cases}, \quad (1)$$

where $P(*|u,c)$ denotes the conditional probability of next choice of the surfer denoted as $*$ given that the surfer has selected u as the authoritative user for category c, $P(u',c'|u,c,*)$ denotes the conditional probability of selecting u' as the authoritative user for category c given that the surfer selected u as the authoritative user for category c previously and then selected the choice $*$, $D(u,u') = \frac{w_{u,u'}}{\sum_{u^*:u \to u^*} w_{u,u^*}}$ and $\psi_{u,c} = P(c|u) = P(z|u)P(c|z)$ can be directly estimated by the LDA model trained in the stage of calculating category relevancies.

According to above equations, we can calculate the joint probability $P(u',c')$ which denotes the probability that the surfer is selecting user u' as an authoritative user for category c' by

$$\begin{aligned} P(u',c') =& f(F_S, F_J, J_J) \\ =& \sum_{u:u \to u'} D(u,u')P(u,c')(1-d)\psi_{u,c'} + \\ & \sum_{u:u \to u'} \sum_{c} D(u,u')\psi_{u,c'}(1-d)(1-\psi_{u,c})P(u,c) + \\ & \sum_{u \neq c'} \sum_{c} \frac{d}{|V_{\Upsilon_c}|}\psi_{u',c'}P(u,c). \end{aligned}$$

Therefore, we can iteratively calculate $P(u,c)$ for each user u for the target category c. In the first round of propagation, we let $P(u',c') = \frac{1}{|V_{\Upsilon_c}| \times |C|}$. Then the result will converge after several rounds of propagation. Therefore, we can rank all users' authority in G_{Υ_c} for category c by $P(u,c)$.

5. EXPERIMENTAL RESULTS

In this section, we demonstrate the experimental results of 1) the performance comparison between our **C**ategory **R**elevancy based **A**uthority **R**anking (CRAR) approach and baselines, 2) robustness analysis of parameter setting.

Data Sets. The data sets used in the experiments are collected from two major commercial Q&A web sites. The first one is a public data set collected from Yahoo! Answers (`http://answers.yahoo.com`) by Liu et al. [3]. There are 100 categories, 216,563 questions, and more than 1.9 million answers posted by 171,266 users in this data set. Another data set was collected from a major Chinese Q&A service web site named Tianya Wenda (`htpp://wenda.tianya.cn`). This data set contains 595 categories, more than 1.3 million questions, and 5.5 million answers posted by 274,896 users. In both data sets, all questions are resolved questions which contain a best answer voted by the question author. Moreover, each data set contains a predefined two-level category taxonomy. To avoid category overlap, we only use the leaf categories in the taxonomy in the experiments. In total, there are 94 leaf categories in the Yahoo! Answers data set and 595 leaf categories in the Tianya wenda data set.

Benchmark Methods. To evaluate the performance of the CRAR, we chose three baseline methods as follows. *Degree* is a simple statistical measure which ranks user authority in the order of the in-degrees of the according user node in the category link graph. *HITS* is an iterative approach which assigns two scores for each node in the category link graph, namely, hub score and authority score. *ExpertiseRank* [5] is extended from PageRank. *TRSO* stands for TRS for original category link graph. It is an topical link analysis approach by leveraging TRS model in the original category link graphs but not the extended category link graphs.

Evaluation Metrics. To evaluate the performance for

expert finding, we used three widely-used metrics as follows. *Average Precision@K* (Avg. P@K) denotes the average ratio of real experts in top K identified authoritative users for each category. In the experiments, K is 10. *Mean Reciprocal Rank* (MRR) is the multiplicative inverse of the rank of the first mined authoritative user in each category. *Mean Average Precision* (MAP) is the mean of the average precision scores for each category.

Since both data sets have no principle benchmark for who are real authoritative users for a given category, we manually inspect the expert finding results. To be specific, firstly we carry out each measuring approach to find top K users as expert candidates for all target categories. Then, for each mined expert candidate u for category c, we ask three human evaluators to check whether u is a real expert for the category c by comprehensively considering the interactive history of u including the number of posted answers, the number of best answers, the voting from another users for the posted answers. Each identified authoritative user is voted by three evaluators with label **Yes** (the user is a real expert) or **No** (the user is not a real expert). It is worth noting that when the evaluators count the answers of a user for category c, they are asked to manually check each answer in the history of the user whether it is relevant to category c other than only consider the answers with the category c.

Table 1: The performance of expert finding.

Yahoo! Answers			
	Avg. P@10	MRR	MAP
Degree	0.434	0.853	0.642
HITS	0.547	0.885	0.699
ExpertiseRank	0.558	0.915	0.732
TRSO	0.569	0.917	0.753
CRAR	**0.619**	**0.953**	**0.808**
Tianya Wenda			
	Avg. P@10	MRR	MAP
Degree	0.523	0.883	0.687
HITS	0.586	0.916	0.724
ExpertiseRank	0.606	0.935	0.756
TRSO	0.625	0.942	0.771
CRAR	**0.669**	**0.973**	**0.828**

Overall Results of Expert Finding. According to the method introduced in [1], the numbers of topics Z are set to be 30 for the Yahoo! Answers data set and 100 for the Tianya Wenda data set. The two parameters α and β were empirically set to be $50/Z$ and 0.2. We randomly select 100 categories in Tianya Wenda to test the overall performance of our approach and other baselines for expert finding. For the Yahoo! Answers data set, we evaluate the performance for all categories. In addition, *as PageRank usually does, d is set as 0.15 here* [4]. Table 1 shows the average experimental results for all test categories with respect to different metrics. From this table we can see that our approach consistently outperforms other baselines with respect to varying metrics on both data sets. Moreover, we also observe that the topical analysis in original category link graphs can only slightly improve the performance of expert finding than ExpertiseRank. It is because that the number of relevant users to the target category are limited in the original category link graphs, thus the topical related information from other users cannot be fully taken advantage of.

Robustness Analysis. The CRAR approach needs two parameters, namely, the latent topic number Z and the extension rate τ of categories. Figure 3 (a) and (b) show the Avg. P@10 of CRAR with varying topic numbers and extension rates for each data set, respectively. From these figures we can see that the setting of Z in this paper estimated by perplexity is reasonable. Moreover, we also can find that the performance of CRAR for expert finding is stable for extension rates with the large topic numbers. However, if a small topic number is used, the extension rate can dramatically impact the performance of CRAR. The phenomenon is reasonable because large topic numbers will cause stricter relevancy metrics while small topic numbers will make the relevancy metric weak. Then, a number of the irrelevant categories will be involved as noise information and will dramatically impact the performance of expert finding. In another case, if the relevancy metric which are strict enough the benefit from other relevant categories is very limited and the performance of CRAR is similar as the TRSO.

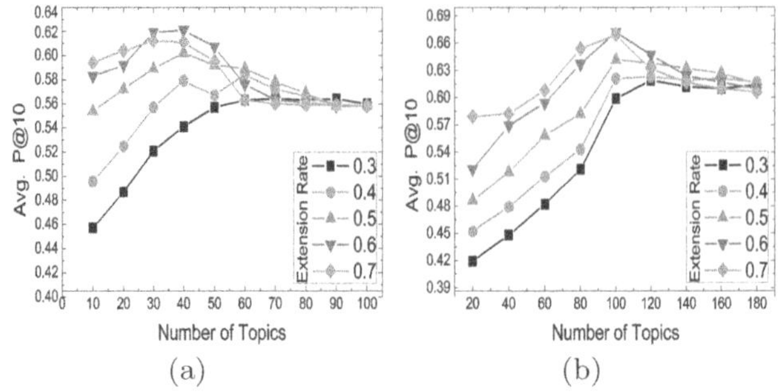

Figure 3: The Avg. P@10 of expert finding versus varying numbers of topics and extension rates in (a) Yahoo! Answers, (b) Tianya Wenda.

6. CONCLUDING REMARKS

In this paper, we investigated how to exploit the information in both target and relevant categories for enhancing authority ranking in expert finding. Specifically, we first provided a method for measuring category relevance by utilizing topic models and KL-divergence. Then, a multiple-category-based link analysis approach was extended from the TRS model for ranking user authority in extended category link graphs. Finally, we performed extensive experiments on two large-scale real-world Q&A data sets and results clearly show that our CRAR approach can significantly improve the performance of authority ranking for expert finding.

Acknowledgement. This work is supported by grants from Natural Science Foundation of China (No. 61073110), Key Program of National Natural Science Foundation of China (No. 60933013), National Major Special Science & Technology Projects (No. 2011ZX04016-071), Research Fund for the Doctoral Program of Higher Education of China (No. 20093402110017) and Nokia.

7. REFERENCES

[1] T. Bao, H. Cao, E. Chen, J. Tian, and H. Xiong. An unsupervised approach to modeling personalized contexts of mobile users. In *ICDM'10*.

[2] D. M. Blei, A. Y. Ng, and M. I. Jordan. Lantent dirichlet allocation. In *Journal of Machine Learning Research*.

[3] Y. Liu, J. Bian, and E. Agichtein. Predicting information seeker satisfaction in community question answering. In *SIGIR'08*.

[4] L. Nie, B. D. Davison, and X. Qi. Topical link analysis for web search. In *In SIGIR'06*.

[5] J. Zhang, M. S. Ackerman, and L. Adamic. Expertise networks in online communities: structure and algorithms. In *WWW'07*.

Joint Inference for Cross-document Information Extraction

Qi Li, Sam Anzaroot, Wen-Pin Lin, Xiang Li, Heng Ji
Computer Science Department, Queens College and Graduate Center
City University of New York
New York City, NY, USA
{liqiearth, samanzaroot, danniellin, jackieiuu729, hengjicuny}@gmail.com

ABSTRACT

Previous information extraction (IE) systems are typically organized as a pipeline architecture of separated stages which make independent local decisions. When the data grows beyond some certain size, the extracted facts become inter-dependent and thus we can take advantage of information redundancy to conduct reasoning across documents and improve the performance of IE. We describe a joint inference approach based on information network structure to conduct cross-fact reasoning with an integer linear programming framework. Without using any additional labeled data this new method obtained 13.7%-24.4% user browsing cost reduction over a state-of-the-art IE system which extracts various types of facts independently.

Categories and Subject Descriptors

I.2.7 [**Natural Language Processing**]: Text analysis; H.3.4 [**Systems and Software**]: Information networks, Question-answering (fact retrieval) systems

General Terms

Algorithms

Keywords

Information extraction, global reasoning, Integer Linear Programming

1. INTRODUCTION

One of the initial goals for Information Extraction (IE) was to create a knowledge base from the entire input corpus, such as a profile or a series of activities about any entity, and allow further logical reasoning on the knowledge base. Unfortunately the knowledge base constructed from a typical IE pipeline often contains lots of erroneous and conflicting facts. Interestingly, when the data grows beyond some certain size, the extracted facts become inter-dependent and thus we can take advantage of information redundancy to conduct reasoning across documents and improve the performance of IE. Some recent work conducted inference to achieve extraction consistency across documents [4], entities [3], relations [11, 6] and events [7].

In this paper we propose to apply the new structure called "Information Networks" to conduct more complete and robust inference. An Information Network (InfoNet) is a heterogeneous network that includes a set of "information graphs" $G = G_i(V_i, E_i)$, where V_i is the collection of entity nodes, and E_i is the collection of edges linking one entity to the other, labeled by relation or event attributes, such as "Member_of" and "Family". This structured networked representation characterizes a dense graph of relations/events among all entities provides a strong graph theoretical framework to enable effective inference and propagation. From the InfoNet point of view, it's clear that most previous inference work addressed partial structures, such as the inferences between repeated nodes/links [4], a pair of nodes [3], or a pair of links [7]. The goal of this paper is to develop a uniformed global inference framework across all of the nodes and links in the entire InfoNet.

When a user distills knowledge from the IE output, coherent facts are preferred because they include fewer conceptual gaps and thus require fewer inferences and less prior knowledge to understand [9]. Based on this intuition, we propose the following hypothesis: if an extracted fact is more consistent with other facts to tell a *coherent* story, it's more likely to be correct. For example, Figure 1 depicts a partial InfoNet connecting inter-dependent relations. The solid lines present correct relations, while dash lines indicate incorrect relations. From this figure, we can observe that contradictions may happen due to the relational dependencies, for instance, *George W. Bush* is detected as the member of both *Republican Party* and *Hamas*, while these two organizations are located in different countries (*United States of America* vs. *Hamas*). Based on one possible global constraint that an organization and its members are unlikely to locate in different countries, we can determine that *George W. Bush* is unlikely to be a member of *Hamas*.

We propose a joint inference method based on cross-fact constraints in InfoNets to approach this goal. We gather together IE results from a large collection of documents, and then impose constraints in an integer linear programming framework to reach global optimization. The inference knowledge includes constraints among all kinds of IE stages. To demonstrate the power and generality of this approach, we evaluate it for two distinct relation types: membership and family relations. The effectiveness of this framework is demonstrated by substantially improving the performance of both relation types.

2. RELATED WORK

Some recent IE research has raised much interest in global inference [8, 4, 1, 2, 12, 7, 10, 3] based on integer linear programming,

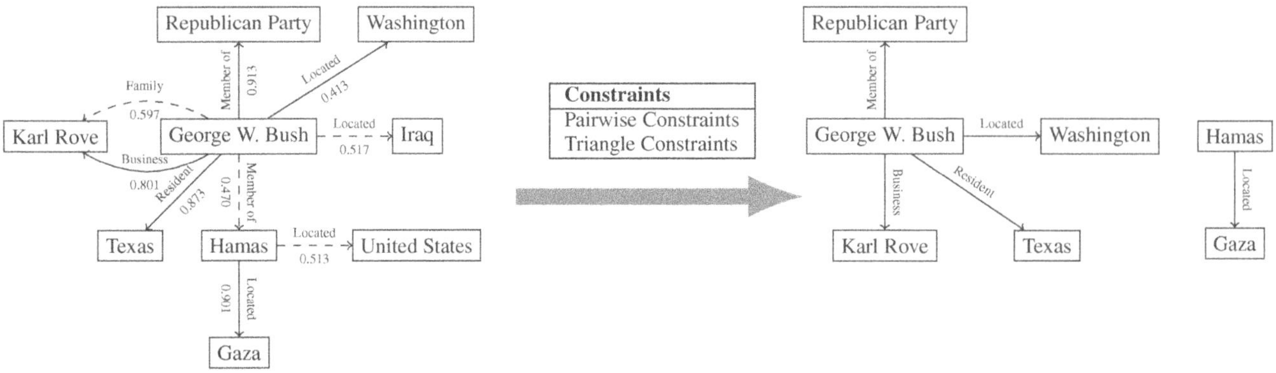

Figure 1: Inference on a partial graph connecting inter-dependent relations

heuristic rules or Markov Logic. In this paper, we extend the idea of global inference to the cross-document paradigm for enhancing IE performance. We also leverage relational constraints among all kinds of facts on diverse levels through a new information network representation. In addition, we have generalized the constraints to various categories, so that in the future one only needs to materialize these categories to new types of facts.

3. TASK AND BASELINE SYSTEM

We define a new cross-document IE task on top of the terminologies specified in the NIST ACE program. ACE defined 7 types of entities (persons, geo-political entities, locations, organizations, facilities, vehicles and weapons), 18 types of relations (e.g., "a town some 50 miles south of Salzburg" indicates a "Located" relation.); and 33 distinct types of relatively dynamic events (e.g., "Barry Diller on Wednesday quit as chief of Vivendi Universal Entertainment." indicates a "Personnel-start" event). We extend the ACE terminology from single document to cross-document setting as follows: Given a collection of source documents, our cross-document IE system should produce a networked knowledge base including unique (i.e. redundancy must be removed) facts.

We apply a state-of-the-art English ACE single-document IE system [4] as our baseline to extract facts from individual documents. This IE system includes Hidden Markov Model based name tagging, and Maximum Entropy based nominal mention tagging, entity coreference resolution, time expression extraction and normalization, relation extraction and event extraction , incorporating diverse lexical, syntactic, semantic and ontological knowledge. Finally a cross-document entity linking component based on graph clustering is applied to aggregate facts from different documents. Each component produces reliable confidence values.

4. GLOBAL INFERENCE

In this section, we will discuss the dependency and constraints of the IE outputs in detail, then present a novel cross-document global reasoning approach to enhance IE performance, based on Integer Linear Programming.

4.1 Dependency Constraints

We explore typical constraints to be defined across various types of facts. Usually there are heterogeneous relations and events existing among entities, as well as complex interaction patterns. We summarize the constraints on a more abstract level so that one can design domain-specific constraints with the map. Let L_i denote a unique relation or event linking two entities A and B. In this paper we consider pairwise and triangle dependency relations among various types of entities and link types, as depicted in Figure 2.

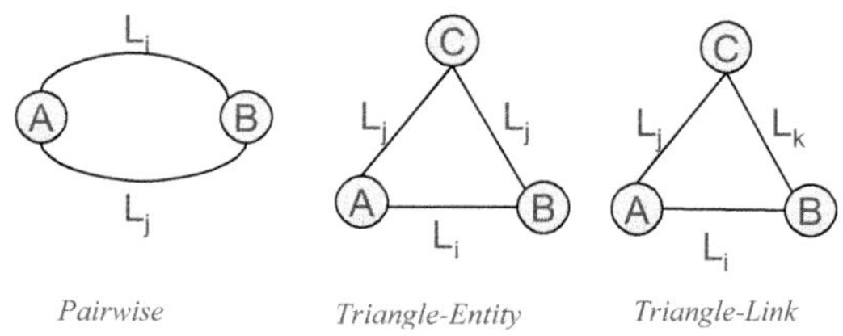

Figure 2: Dependency Constraints among Entities, Relations and Events

We compute pointwise mutual information (PMI) to automatically estimate the pairwise dependency between any two types of links from ACE2005 training data:

$$PMI(L_i, L_j) = log\frac{p(L_i, L_j)}{p(L_i)p(L_j)} \quad (1)$$

where $p(L_i)$ and $p(L_j)$ are the frequency of L_i and L_j respectively, and $p(L_i, L_j)$ is the co-occurence frequency of $L_i(A, B)$ and $L_j(A, B)$, for any two entities A and B.

Similarly, we apply a multivariate generalization form of PMI [13], total correlation, to the triangle dependency:

$$PMI(L_i, L_j, L_k) = log\frac{p(L_i, L_j, L_k)}{p(L_i)p(L_j)p(L_k)} \quad (2)$$

for any two entities A and B or three entities A, B and C as shown in Figure 2.

If the PMI value is lower than a certain threshold (in our experiment we used -2.0 for pairwise and -3.0 for triangle), the links are considered as incompatible and used as a constraint for global inference.

In total we learned 34 pairwise constraints and 16 triangle constraints. Some constraint examples are listed in Table 1. For example, *Ariel Sharon* and *Mahmoud Abbas* are frequently involved in Contact.Meet events, so they are unlikely to be members of the same organization according to the pairwise constraint. If *Osama bin Laden* and *George W. Bush* are involved in a Conflict event with high confidence, then they are unlikely to be the members of the same organization according to the triangle-entity constraint. If *Washington* and *Iraq* are involved in a *Transport* event, then any member of *Washington* is unlikely to be located in *Iraq* according to the triangle-link constraint.

Pairwise	L_i	L_j	
	Person A founded Organization B	Organization B hired Person A	
	Person A has a Business relation with Person B	Person A has a Person-Social relation (e.g. family) with Person B	
Triangle-Entity	L_i	L_j	
	Organization A is involved in a Justice/Conflict/Transaction event with Organization B	Person C is affiliated with/member of both Organization A and Organization B	
Triangle-Link	L_i	L_j	L_k
	Entity A is involved in a Transport event originated from Location B	Person C is affiliated with/member of Entity A	Person C is located in Location B

Table 1: Examples for Incompatible Constraints

4.2 Integer Linear Programming

Motivated by the intuition that facts are often dependent on each other, we consider the global inference as an optimization problem of all local predication confidence values, using the constraints automatically learned from the above PMI method as hard rules. These hard rules or constraints are designed to guarantee that the facts extracted from different documents are consistent with each other, hence weak predications which violate constraints can be filtered out.

First of all, we shall introduce the objective of our optimization problem. Assume we have a set of local outputs, $\mathcal{R} = \{r_i\}$, of inter-dependent relations and events, each output r_i is associated with a number of entities $r_{i,j}$ with local confidence values $p_{i,j}$, where $p_{i,j} \in (0, 1]$.

From cross-document point of view, a reliable output should have high local confidence value as well as high global frequency. A correct fact may appear rarely within a single document but often appears frequently across documents. In contrast, an invalid fact often has low-frequency, simply because some entities accidentally co-occur in mis-leading contexts. We incorporate this hypothesis into a Integer Linear Programming framework by solving the following optimization problem:

$$
\begin{aligned}
& max \sum_{i=0}^{N} (x_i \cdot \sum_{j=0}^{M} p_{i,j}^{\theta}) \\
& \text{subject to :} \\
& x_i \in \{0, 1\} \quad \forall x_i \\
& \forall x_a \text{ and } x_b \text{ violate a pairwise constraint :} \\
& \qquad x_a + x_b \leq 1 \\
& \forall x_a, x_b, x_c \text{ violate a triangle constraint :} \\
& \qquad x_a + x_b + x_c \leq 2
\end{aligned} \tag{3}
$$

Where x_i is a binary value: 1 indicates r_i is selected in the final output and 0 indicates r_i is removed. θ determines to which extent we penalize low confidence values. If θ equals 0 then any confidence value should be considered equally as 1, since $p^0 = 1$ by definition. As θ grows, it gives more penalty to lower confidence values; a special case is θ equals 1, where p^{θ} equals p itself.

5. EXPERIMENTS

In this section we present the results of applying this joint inference method to improve cross-document information extraction.

5.1 Data and Scoring Metric

We use the data set from the DARPA GALE distillation task, which contains 381,588 newswire documents, for our experiment. The baseline IE system extracted 18,386 person entities, 21,621 geo-political entities and 18,792 organization entities. Without loss of generality, we ask human annotators to evaluate the quality of all of the 1128 *Family* relations and 2854 *Member_of* relations (including ORG-Aff.Employment, ORG-Aff.Membership defined in ACE).

It's important to measure how well a system performs at extracting facts across documents accurately. However, it's time-consuming to manually extract all possible facts from a large collection of documents, and thus it's difficult to measure recall. To solve this problem, we apply the Browsing Cost metric defined in [5] to evaluate cross-document IE performance:

Browsing Cost (i) = the number of incorrect or redundant facts that a user must examine before finding *i* correct facts.

In our experiment, we consider a fact as a link $L^i(A, B)$, which is judged as correct if and only if both A and B have correct boundaries and entity types and L^i has correct relation or event type.

5.2 Overall Performance

Figure 3 and 4 demonstrate the browsing costs. Compared to the baseline, on average our approach resulted in a 13.7% user browsing effort reduction for *Family* relations and a 24.4% user browsing effort reduction for *Member_of* relations.

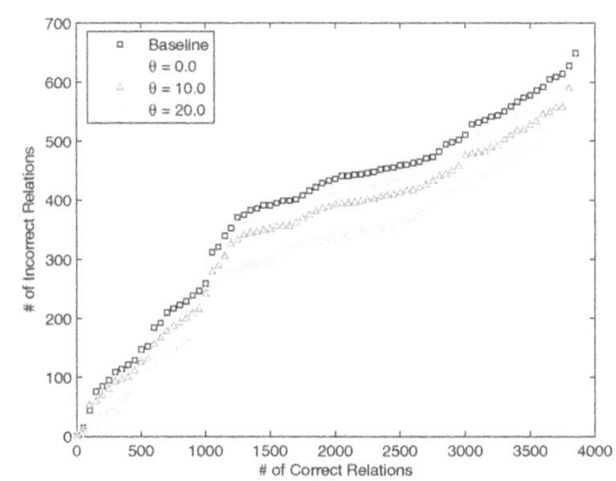

Figure 3: Browsing cost comparison of *Member_of* relation.

5.3 Discussion

Figure 5 depicts the correctness of the removal operations (i.e. the number of unique facts are removed corectly/incorrectly) for *Family* relation, varying the parameter θ of the objective function. Although our method mistakenly removed a few correct facts, it successfully removed many more incorrect instances using any parameter. For example, it removed the *Family* relation between "*Jack Straw*" and "*Tony Blair*" because they were involved in the *Business* relation ("*Jack Straw*" was in "*Tony Blair*"'s Cabinet). It occasion-

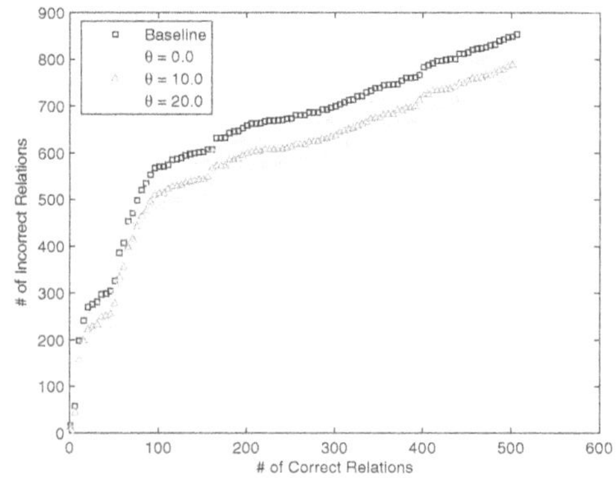

Figure 4: Browsing cost comparison of *Family* relation.

ally removed a few correct relations involving two person entities with multiple types of relations. For example, "*Mohammed Bakir Al-hakim*" and "*Abdul Aziz Al-hakim*" are family members as well as colleagues in the Iraqi government. Clearly overall the rewards of using joint inference significantly outweigh the risks.

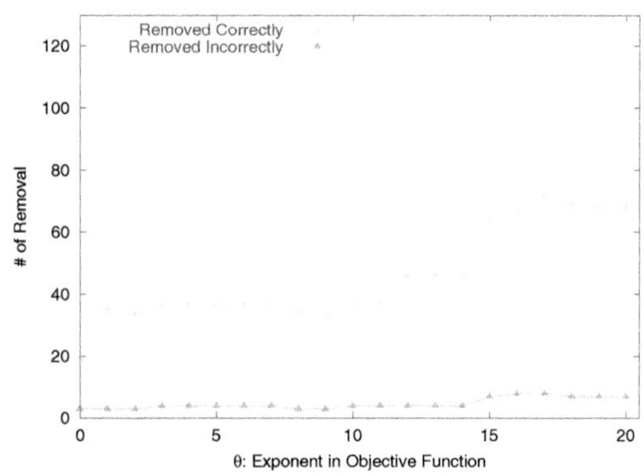

Figure 5: Removal curve of *Family* relation w.r.t parameter θ.

In order to evaluate the impact of each constraint, we also conducted experiments using each constraint independently in the ILP model with $\theta = 20$ for *Family* relation. The results are presented in Table 2.

Constraint type	# removed correctly	# removed incorrectly
Pairwise	52	7
Triangle	64	5

Table 2: Impact of different types of constraints on *Family* relation.

6. CONCLUSION AND FUTURE WORK

Most previous IE research considered various types of relations and events independent of each other, and focused on individual predictions using local information. As a result, it's inevitable that contradictory facts can be extracted and the incorrect ones must then be removed in an effective way. We incorporated the interdependencies among various types of facts as latent constraints in an information network based inference framework using integer linear programming. Such joint inference analysis allowed us to incorporate information from a much wider context, going across documents and fact types, and utilize deeper semantic inferences to significantly enhance the extraction performance. In the future we are interested in applying statistical relational learning algorithms to capture more implicit constraints and soft inference rules. Finally in this paper we assumed that the constraints are relatively static, however, some facts may change over time (e.g. a person's employment or residence relation). Therefore we are also interested in extending our joint inference framework to capture temporal constraints.

7. ACKNOWLEDGMENTS

This work was supported in part by the U.S. Army Research Laboratory under Cooperative Agreement No. W911NF-09-2-0053 (NS-CTA), the U.S. NSF CAREER Award under Grant IIS-0953149 and PSC-CUNY Research Program. The views and conclusions contained in this document are those of the authors and should not be interpreted as representing the official policies, either expressed or implied, of the U.S. Government. The U.S. Government is authorized to reproduce and distribute reprints for Government purposes notwithstanding any copyright notation here on.

8. REFERENCES

[1] N. Chambers and D. Jurafsky. Jointly combining implicit constraints improves temporal ordering. In *EMNLP*, pages 698–706, 2008.

[2] P. Gupta and H. Ji. Predicting unknown time arguments based on cross-event propagation. In *Proc. ACL-IJCNLP2009*, 2009.

[3] Y. Hong, J. Zhang, B. Ma, J. Yao, G. Zhou, and Q. Zhu. Using cross-entity inference to improve event extraction. In *Proc. ACL2011*, 2011.

[4] H. Ji and R. Grishman. Refining event extraction through cross-document inference. In *Proc. ACL*, 2008.

[5] H. Ji, R. Grishman, Z. Chen, and P. Gupta. Cross-document event extraction, ranking and tracking. In *Proc. RANLP*, 2009.

[6] H. Ji, D. Westbrook, and R. Grishman. Using semantic relations to refine coreference decisions. In *Proc. HLT/EMNLP2005*, 2005.

[7] S. Liao and R. Grishman. Using document level cross-event inference to improve event extraction. In *Proc. ACL2010*, 2010.

[8] A. Mccallum. Information extraction, data mining and joint inference. In *Proc. KDD2006*, 2006.

[9] D. S. McNamara. Reading both high-coherence and low-coherence texts: Effects of text sequence and prior knowledge. In *Canadian Journal of Experimental Psychology*, 2001.

[10] H. Poon and L. Vanderwende. Joint inference for knowledge extraction from biomedical literature. In *HLT-NAACL*, pages 813–821, 2010.

[11] D. Roth and W. tau Yih. A linear programming formulation for global inference in natural language tasks. In *Proc. CoNLL*, pages 1–8, 2004.

[12] M. Tatu and M. Srikanth. Experiments with reasoning for temporal relations between events. In *Proc. COLING2008*, 2008.

[13] Van de Cruys Tim. Two Multivariate Generalizations of Pointwise Mutual Information. In *Proc. ACL2011*, 2011.

Building a Generic Debugger for Information Extraction Pipelines

Anish Das Sarma
Yahoo, CA, USA
anish.dassarma@gmail.com

Alpa Jain
Yahoo, CA, USA
alpa@yahoo-inc.com

Philip Bohannon
Yahoo, CA, USA
plb@yahoo-inc.com

ABSTRACT

Complex information extraction (IE) pipelines are becoming an integral component of most text processing frameworks. We introduce a first system to help IE users analyze extraction pipeline semantics and operator transformations interactively while debugging. This allows the effort to be proportional to the need, and to focus on the portions of the pipeline under the greatest suspicion. We present a generic debugger for running post-execution analysis of any IE pipeline consisting of arbitrary types of operators. For this, we propose an effective provenance model for IE pipelines which captures a variety of operator types, ranging from those for which full to no specifications are available. We have evaluated our proposed algorithms and provenance model on large-scale real-world extraction pipelines.

Categories and Subject Descriptors: H.4.0 Information Systems Applications: General

General Terms: Algorithms

Keywords: Information extraction, provenance

1. INTRODUCTION

Information extraction (IE) systems identify structured information and, not surprisingly, IE systems are becoming a critical first-class operator in a large number of text-processing frameworks. As a concrete example, search engines are moving beyond a "keyword in, document out" paradigm to providing structured information relevant to users' queries (e.g., providing contact information for businesses when user queries involve business names). For this, search engines typically rely on having available large repositories of structured information generated from web pages or query logs using IE systems. With the increasing complexity of IE pipelines, a critical exercise for IE developers and even users is to *debug*, i.e., perform a thorough post-mortem analysis of the output generated by running an entire or partial extraction pipeline. Despite the popularity of IE pipelines, very little attention has been given to building effective ways to trace the control or data flow through an extraction pipeline.

Prior work [14] recognizes the need for interactive debuggers and proposes methods that use complete knowledge of how each operator functions. However, prior information regarding the specifications of the operators may not be available (e.g., off-the-shelf black-box operators). In the absence of full function specifications of an operator, the only (straightforward) approach to debugging is exploring all data in the pipeline. However, such an approach is clearly infeasible due to the sheer volume of data. For instance, debugging a simple pipeline involving 10 operators with 10,000 input records per operator would require 100K records to be manually examined; typical data sizes are even larger.

This paper presents PROBER (for Provenance-Based Debugger), the first generic framework for debugging information extraction pipelines composed of arbitrary ("black-box") operators. A critical task towards building debuggers is that of tracing and linking output records from each operator and understanding their transformations across different operators in the pipeline. To trace the lineage of any arbitrary record in the output, we propose a novel provenance model for IE pipelines. With debugging in mind, our provenance model tries to minimize the amount of user effort necessary in resolving the fate of the records in the output. For example, provenance for (incorrect) output records *only* refer to input tuples that impacted this output record.

2. PROBLEM FORMULATION

While IE pipelines may vary in their implementation logic [1, 11, 12, 13] several underlying common components can be abstracted from the implementation details. We characterize information extraction pipelines for the task of performing post-mortem analysis.

DEFINITION 2.1. **[Record]** *A* record r *is a basic unit of data (e.g., a tuple), consisting of a globally unique identifier* $I(r)$*, and value* $V(r)$*. We use* R *to denote the set of all records.* □

DEFINITION 2.2. **[Operator]** *An* operator *is defined by a function* $O : (I_1, I_2, \cdots, I_N) \rightarrow R$*, where each* $I_i \subseteq R$ *is a set of records. In practice, the function* O *may be unknown to us.* □

Intuitively, an operator takes as input an N-tuple of sets of records and outputs one set of records. Specifications on how an operator generates an output record may be available in

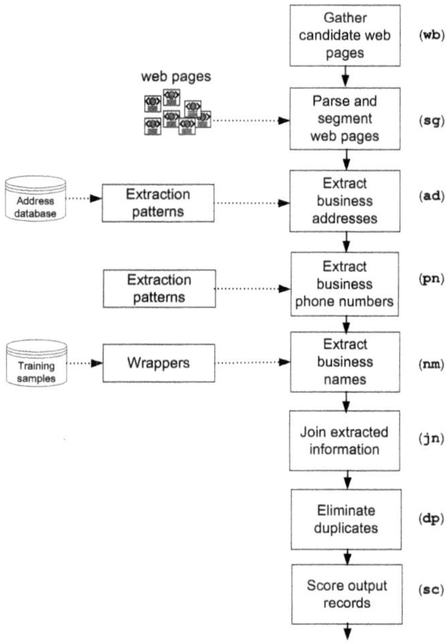

Figure 1: Example of an IE pipeline to generate business names and their contact information.

varying forms. Specifically, we consider the following four scenarios involving operator specifications.

An operator is said to be a *black-box* if we have no information about it. In this case, naturally, the only way to gain information about a black-box operator is by executing it on input sets of records. In contrast, we have *exact* information about an operator O if we know precisely *which* input records contributed to each output record, *and how*. We have *Input-Output (IO) specifications* when for each output record, we know which input records were used to construct it, however exactly how a record is generated is unknown to us. Finally, we may have *integrity constraints*, e.g., key-foreign key relationships, satisfied by the input and output records. For instance, an operator may support a 'debug' mode where each output record is assigned an id associated with the input records that generated it. Effectively, using key-foreign keys we have the same information as that in IO specifications, but this information is (indirectly) available using dependencies on the values of *fields* in input and output records.

Next, we define various (standard) properties of an operator, that help design specialized algorithms for building provenance and debugging effectively. As we will see later, these properties may be learned by sampling or the operator specifications (when available) described above.

DEFINITION 2.3. **[Properties]**

- `monotonic`: *Operator* O *is* `monotonic` *iff* $\forall I_1, I_2 \subset R : (I_1 \subseteq I_2) \Rightarrow (O(I_1) \subseteq O(I_2))$.
- `one-to-one`: *Operator* O *is* `one-to-one` *iff: (a)* $\forall I \subset R : O(I) = \bigcup_{r \in I} O(\{r\})$; *(b)* $\forall r \in R$: $|O(\{r\})| \leq 1$.
- `one-to-many`: *Operator* O *is* `one-to-many` *iff* $\forall I \subset R : O(I) = \bigcup_{r \in I} O(\{r\})$.
- `many-to-one`: *Operator* O *is* `many-to-one` *iff* $\forall I \subset R$, $\exists$ *a partition* $P_I = \{I_1, \ldots, I_n\}$ *of* I[1] *such that: (a)* $O(I) = \bigcup_{i=1}^{n} O(I_i)$; *and (b)* $\forall i : |O(I_i)| \leq 1$.

□

[1](a) $I = \bigcup_{i=1}^{n} I_i$ (b) $\forall i \neq j : (I_i \cap I_j) = \emptyset$.

DEFINITION 2.4. **[Extraction Pipeline]** *An extraction pipeline* P *is defined by a DAG* $G(V, E)$ *consisting of a set* V *of nodes and a set* E *of edges where each node* $v \in V$ *corresponds to an operator* O *in the pipeline. An edge* $a \rightarrow b$ *between nodes* a *and* b *indicates that the output from the operator represented by* a *is input to operator represented by* b. *We have a single special node* $s \in V$ *with no incoming edges representing the operator that takes input to the pipeline, and one special node* $t \in V$ *with no outgoing edges representing the operator that outputs the final set of records.* □

3. MOTIVATING EXAMPLE

Figure 1 shows a real-world extraction pipeline, `Business`, for building a large collection of businesses by extracting records of the form $\langle n, a, p \rangle$, where business n is located at address a with contact number p. The first step is to build a set of web pages likely to contain information regarding businesses which is done using a variety of document retrieval strategies. Specifically, we issue manually generated domain-dependent queries (e.g., "Toyota car dealership locations") as well as use form filling methods where entries such as model, make, and zipcode may be filled in order to fetch a list of car dealerships. This operator, denoted by `wb` is an example of a black-box operator with arbitrary properties.

Given a collection of web pages, operator `sg` parses the html page and identifies appropriate segments of text in this page, where ideally, each segment contains a complete target record (see Figure 2 for a real-world example). These segments are then processed by operators, `ad` and `pn`, which respectively identify an occurrence of an address and a phone number. The annotation from one operator is used by the subsequent operator to identify regions of text that should not be processed. `ad` and `pn` are implemented using hand-crafted patterns based on a dictionary of address formats. The `nm` operator on the other hand needs to identify names of business which may be arbitrary strings and for this, we follow a wrapper-induction approach. In particular, using some training examples we learn a wrapper rule to identify candidate business names; these rules are based on the document structure of the html content. Of course, several other implementations for each of these operators are possible and the implementation details are orthogonal to our discussion since our goal is to build debuggers for pipelines with black-box operators where no implementation information may be available. The `jn` operator joins outupt from `ad`, `pn`, and `nm` to build candidate output records which are, in turn, processed by `dp` to eliminate duplicates. The final operator, assignes a confidence score `sc` to each output record.

We note that all our implementations of the above operators are monotonic. (Obviously, there may be non-monotonic implementations in other pipelines, but we primarily consider monotonic operators in this paper.) Although monotonic, the operators from the pipeline span a variety of properties, e.g., segmentation is a `one-to-many` operation, and by design one address is extracted from each segment, so address extraction is `one-to-one`, while deduplication is `many-to-one`. Candidate webpage generation and wrapper training, on the other hand are arbitrary, i.e. "`many-to-many`".

Given unexpected output records, an IE developer may want to answer some natural questions about the output [14]. (Figure 2 shows an example where `sg` generates an incorrect segment that leads to missing one address and

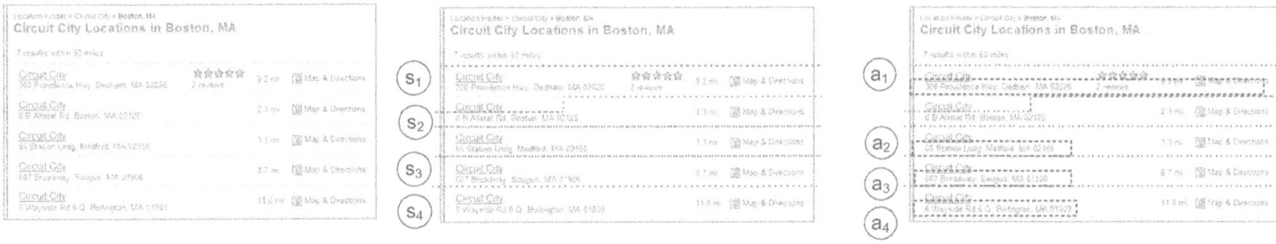

Input web page | Segments identified on the page | Addresses identified on the page

Figure 2: Sample input output for three steps, namely, sg, ad, and pn, in our extraction pipeline.

extracting one incorrect address.) Specifically, a developer may be interested in tracing all or part of the input records that contributed to a particular output record. For instance, given an incorrectly extracted record, we would like to know only the relevant subset of webpages and training data that impacted it, i.e., the *minimal* amount of input data necessary to identify the error. Motivated by the above observations, we focus on the following problem in the PROBER system.

PROBLEM 3.1. *Given a pipeline P, input I, and partial information about operators in P, we would like to (1) build* provenance *for the set of (intermediate and final) records in the pipeline; (2) expose provenance to developers through a query language and guide them in debugging the pipeline.*

4. PROVENANCE FOR IE PIPELINES

The notion of provenance is relatively well-understood for traditional relational databases (refer [6, 16]). A commonly advocated model [2] is to use a boolean-formula provenance, e.g., $S_1 \wedge (S_2 \vee \neg S_3)$. For the purpose of debugging extraction pipelines, such provenance models are not appropriate for two main reasons. First, unlike relational queries where the exact specifications of each operator are known, we may have black-box operators in our extraction pipeline. Second, for debugging, ideally we would like to limit the number of records (and simplify their interdependencies typically represented as boolean formulas for relational operators) a human has to assess in order to understand the issue at hand. With these in mind, we define a provenance model based on *minimal subsets* of operator inputs that capture necessary information (Section 4.1) and extend this basic model to operators where multiple minimal subsets may exist (Section 4.2) .

4.1 MISet: Basic Unit of Provenance

To define the provenance of an IE pipeline P, we begin by defining the provenance for each operator in P; we omit details on how to construct the provenance for each operator in P due to space constraints. We confine ourselves to extraction pipelines consisting of only monotonic operators (see Definition 2.3), which are a common case in practice (as in our motivating example from Section 2). We define the provenance of a monotonic extraction operator O based on the provenance for each output record $r \in R$ for O as in the definition below:

Ideally, we would like the provenance of r to represent precisely the set of records that contributed to r, however, as we will see, in practice it may not be possible to always determine the precise set of contributing records (e.g., in the absence of exact information about O), and even if possible it may be computationally intractable. For our goal of building a debugger, we observe that one of the main operations we expect users to perform is look at an (erroneous) output record r, and explore its provenance to determine the cause of this error. Therefore, a suitable provenance model is one that enables users to examine the fewest records required to decide the fate of an output record r. Formally, we define a basic unit of provenance, called MISet as follows:

DEFINITION 4.1. **[MISet]** *Given an operator O, its input I and output R, we say that $I_s \subseteq I$ is a* Minimal Subset *(MISet) of $r \in R$ if and only if: (1) $r \in O(I_s)$; and (2) $\forall I' \subset I_s : r \notin O(I')$. We use $M_{all}(O, I, r \in R)$ to denote the set of all MISets of O for input I and output record $r \in R$.* □

Intuitively, an MISet gives the fewest input records required for a particular output record r to be present. Therefore, an MISet provides users with one possible reason for the occurrence of r. This, in turn, reduces the burden of manual annotation on the users; in the absence of MISets, a user may have to explore the entire input to understand what caused an error in the output. The notion of MISets primarily focuses on debugging the *presence* of records in the output.

We note that the notion of MISets has been proposed in the past [4] in the context of relational operations (called *minimal witnesses*). In practice, we may have more than one MISet possible for an output record as shown by the following example. Therefore, in the context of debugging extraction operators, we study the handling of non-uniqueness of MISets, and propose provenance definitions and construction algorithms based on combinations of MISets to facilitate debugging.

In practice, we may have more than one MISet possible for an output record as shown by the following example.

EXAMPLE 4.1. *Consider a (simple) record validation operator (e.g.,* sc *in Figure 1) that computes the "support" of each record and outputs only records with sufficient support. Suppose* sc *outputs a record r if there are atleast 50 input records supporting it. Given an input of 100 records that could support r, the MISet for r is* any *subset of the input records of exactly 50 records.* □

When multiple MISets are available, several ways of building provenance are possible, each differing in the extent to which they impact information and execution speed.

4.2 Handling Multiple MISets

Several formalisms for provenance model are possible when multiple MISets are available. We rigorously examine compositions of MISets, while capturing the spectrum of complete (and potentially intractable) provenance, to more tractable (but approximate) provenance.

Consider an operator O which consumes input I and generates output R; for a record $r \in R$, we denote the provenance of r as $P(O, I, r)$. We use subscripts P_* to capture various types of provenance and when clear from the context, we simply use $P_*(r)$ to denote $P_*(O, I, r)$.

All- and Any-provenance: Ideally for any output record, we would like to provide all possible information using MISets, i.e., capture all possible "causes" of an output record.

DEFINITION 4.2. **[All-provenance]** *Given an operator O, input I, output R, and $r \in R$, we define* all-provenance *as $P_{all}(r) = M_{all}(O, I, r \in R)$.* □

In many cases P_{all} may be intractable to compute or store, and we may need to resort to "approximations" of it, presented shortly. Alternatively, we may want to find any one (or k) MISets.

DEFINITION 4.3. **[Any-provenance]** *Given integer $k > 0$, operator O, input I, output R, and $r \in R$, we define* any-provenance *as any $P_{any}(r) \subseteq P_{all}(r)$ of size* $\min(k, |P_{all}(r)|)$. □

Impact-provenance: Given restricted amount of editorial resources, we may want to explore the most *impactful*, i.e., top-l input records sorted by their impact instead of any-k MISets. Our next definition of provenance ranks tuples based on their expected impact on the output record, measured by the number of MISets in which a tuple is present.

DEFINITION 4.4. **[Impact-provenance]** *Given an operator O, input I, output R, and $r \in R$, we define* impact-provenance *as* $P_{imp}(r) = \{(i, c_i) | \exists M \in P_{all}, i \in M, c_i = \sum_{M \in P_{all}, i \in M} 1\}$. □

Union- and Intersection-provenance: Our next goal is to summarize P_{all} using two approximations: (1) We obtain an "upper bound" provenance that captures the set of all inputs *possible* for r, instead of exact combinations of inputs. Therefore, we define the union-provenance of r to be the union of all its MISets. (2) We obtain a "lower bound" provenance that captures the set of all possible inputs *necessary* for r; we define the intersection-provenance of r to be the common input records among all MISets.

DEFINITION 4.5. **[Union-Provenance]** *Given an operator O, input I, output R, and $r \in R$, we define* union-provenance *as* $P_{uni}(o) = \bigcup_{I_s \in M_{all}(O,I,r \in R)} I_s$. □

DEFINITION 4.6. **[Intersection-Provenance]** *Given an operator O, input I, output R, and $r \in R$, we define* intersection-provenance *as* $P_{int}(o) = \bigcap_{I_s \in M_{all}(O,I,r \in R)} I_s$. □

It can be seen easily that for operators with unique MISets, P_{uni} and P_{int} coincide.

5. RELATED WORK

Recent work [7, 8, 9, 10, 15] has looked at providing *exploration* phases to determine if a text database is appropriate for an IE task, but little or no insight is provided into why unexpected results are produced, and how to debug them. There is a large body of work on provenance for relational data (refer [6, 16]), and more recently [3] on understanding provenance information, which not address the problem of building provenance for black-box operators to facilitate IE debugging with minimal editorial effort, the primary goal of our work. Our recent work [14] considered debugging for iterative IE, and [5] looked at provenance for *non-answers* in results of extracted data. However, these papers assumed complete knowledge of each operator in some form. Also, in [14], we considered a specific type of extraction, namely iterative information extraction and studied how a simple 'provenance structure' helped debugging. In this paper, we provide a system for constructing provenance for *ad-hoc debugging tasks* for *any* extraction pipeline with black-box operators.

6. REFERENCES

[1] E. Agichtein and L. Gravano. Snowball: Extracting relations from large plain-text collections. In *DL*, 2000.

[2] O. Benjelloun, A. Das Sarma, A. Halevy, and J. Widom. ULDBs: Databases with uncertainty and lineage. In *VLDB*, 2006.

[3] A. Chapman and H. V. Jagadish. Understanding provenance black boxes. *Distributed and Parallel Databases*, 27(2), Apr. 2010.

[4] J. Cheney, L. Chiticariu, and W.-C. Tan. Provenance in databases: Why, how, and where. *Foundations and Trends in databases*, 1, 2009.

[5] J. Huang, T. Chen, A. Doan, and J. F. Naughton. On the provenance of non-answers to queries over extracted data. *PVLDB*, 1(1), 2008.

[6] R. Ikeda and J. Widom. Data lineage: A survey. Technical report, Stanford University, 2009.

[7] A. Jain, A. Doan, and L. Gravano. Optimizing SQL queries over text databases. In *ICDE*, 2008.

[8] A. Jain and P. G. Ipeirotis. A quality-aware optimizer for information extraction. *ACM Transactions on Database Systems*, 2009.

[9] A. Jain, P. G. Ipeirotis, A. Doan, and L. Gravano. Join optimization of information extraction output: Quality matters! Technical Report CeDER-08-04, New York University, 2008.

[10] A. Jain and D. Srivastava. Exploring a few good tuples from text databases. In *ICDE*, 2009.

[11] G. Kasneci, S. Elbassuoni, and G. Weikum. Ming: mining informative entity relationship subgraphs. In *CIKM*, 2009.

[12] M. Paşca, D. Lin, J. Bigham, A. Lifchits, and A. Jain. Organizing and searching the world wide web of facts - step one: The one-million fact extraction challenge. In *Proceedings of AAAI-06*, 2006.

[13] P. Pantel and M. Pennacchiotti. Espresso: leveraging generic patterns for automatically harvesting semantic relations. In *Proc. of ACL*, 2006.

[14] A. D. Sarma, A. Jain, and D. Srivastava. I4E: Interactive investigation of iterative information extraction. In *SIGMOD*, 2010.

[15] W. Shen, A. Doan, J. Naughton, and R. Ramakrishnan. Towards best-effort information extraction. In *SIGMOD*, 2008.

[16] W.-C. Tan. Provenance in Databases: Past, Current, and Future. *IEEE Data Engineering Bulletin*, 2008.

Fast Supervised Feature Extraction by Term Discrimination Information Pooling

Amara Tariq
Dept. of Computer Science
LUMS School of Science and Engineering
Lahore, Pakistan
09060012@lums.edu.pk

Asim Karim
Dept. of Computer Science
LUMS School of Science and Engineering
Lahore, Pakistan
akarim@lums.edu.pk

ABSTRACT

Dimensionality reduction (DR) through feature extraction (FE) is desirable for efficient and effective processing of text documents. Many of the techniques for text FE produce features that are not readily interpretable and require super-linear computation time. In this paper, we present a fast supervised DR/FE technique, named FEDIP, that is motivated by the notion of relatedness of terms to topics or contexts. This relatedness is quantified by using the discrimination information provided by a term for a topic in a labeled document collection. Features are constructed by pooling the discrimination information of highly related terms for each topic. FEDIP's time complexity is linear in the size of the vocabulary and document collection. FEDIP is evaluated for document classification with SVM and naive Bayes classifiers on six text data sets. The results show that FEDIP produces low-dimension feature spaces that yield higher classification accuracy when compared with LDA and LSI. FEDIP is also found to be significantly faster than the other techniques on our evaluation data sets.

Categories and Subject Descriptors

I.7.m [**Document and Text Processing**]: Miscellaneous; H.2.8 [**Database Management**]: Database Applications—*Data Mining*

General Terms

Algorithms, Theory

1. INTRODUCTION

Dimensionality reduction (DR) via feature extraction (FE) is an important step in many textual information retrieval and text mining applications. It often produces more efficient and effective solutions, and in certain applications, can ensure the practical feasibility of a solution because of its efficiency. A popular text mining application is that of document classification where labeled documents are used to learn a classifier for labeling new documents. Feature extraction for document classification can yield classifiers that are more robust to noise and shifts in distributions. Another popular application is document understanding and visualization. A fast FE technique can enable interactive visualizations of documents and their features.

In this paper, we propose a fast and effective supervised feature extraction technique for textual information. Our technique, named FEDIP, is motivated by the notion of relatedness of terms to topics or contexts in which they occur. This notion of relatedness has been shown to play a significant role in human comprehension of text [3, 5]. For instance, humans can easily associate terms with a particular topic after reading a few documents discussing that topic. We use discriminative term weights, computed via the relative risk of a term in a topic-labeled document collection, to quantify the relatedness of terms to topics. Features are constructed by pooling the discrimination information of highly related terms for each topic. We evaluate FEDIP for document classification, comparing it with Latent Semantic Indexing (LSI) [2] and Linear discriminant Analysis (LDA) [8] on six data sets. The results show that FEDIP produces low-dimension feature spaces in which document classification is more accurate and efficient. FEDIP represents a new semantically motivated term pooling approach for text FE that supports efficiency and effectiveness in text mining.

The remainder of this paper is organized as follows. In Section 2, we outline the motivation for our feature extraction technique. Section 3 presents our fast supervised technique for feature extraction. We discuss the experimental evaluation of our technique in Section 4. Finally, we present our concluding remarks in Section 5.

2. MOTIVATION: EXPLOITING THE RELATEDNESS OF TERMS TO TOPICS

Typically in text mining and information retrieval, the notion of relatedness refers to the semantic relatedness between pairs of terms (e.g. words). Accordingly, two terms are said to be related when they are linked by semantic relationships. Usually these are the so-called classical lexical relationships like synonymy, antonymy, and hypernymy. Numerous semantic relatedness measures of this type have been proposed and evaluated in the literature. However, these measures have been developed for and are used primarily for natural language processing tasks like word sense disambiguation [6, 7].

On the other hand, the notion of relatedness of terms to contexts or topics is less known. Nonetheless, this notion of relatedness is more powerful for some applications where contexts are pre-defined or known. Furthermore, this notion of relatedness has been linked to humans' comprehension of text by association of terms with their contexts. In a study by [5], it has been argued that readers develop non-classical relationships between terms by grouping terms associated to common contexts. These groups of terms may then serve as units of understanding of the respective contexts [3].

These observations indicate that groups of terms that are related to a particular context convey meaning about that context or topic. Thus, if we can find such groups of terms then we can pool their information content to construct features. These features will better capture the meaning of the text and aid in document understanding and document classification. Our FE technique, FEDIP, uses term discrimination information as a measure of its relatedness to a context in a labeled document collection, and constructs features by pooling the discrimination information of terms related to each context.

3. FEDIP – OUR FEATURE EXTRACTION TECHNIQUE

We describe the key steps of our feature extraction technique, FEDIP (Feature Extraction by [Term] Discrimination Information Pooling), in the following subsections. Here, we define the problem setting and notations.

Let $\mathcal{D} = \{d_1, d_2, d_3, \ldots, d_N\}$ be the set of documents and $\mathcal{V} = \{t_1, t_2, t_3, \ldots, t_M\}$ be the vocabulary of terms in these documents. The context or topic of a document d is identified by the context label $cont(d) \in \{c_1, c_2, c_3, \ldots, c_K\}$, where K is the total number of topics in $\mathcal{D}$ (usually $K \ll N$). The weight of term t_j in document d_i is identified by $x_{ij} = tw(t_j, d_i)$, which is always greater than or equal to zero. In practice, this term weight can be a 0/1 value (e.g. term occurrence), an integer value (e.g. term count), or a positive real number (e.g. term frequency inverse document frequency or TFIDF).

Given the above setting, a document d_i is represented by the vector $\mathbf{x}_i = \langle x_{i1}, x_{i2}, \ldots, x_{iM}\rangle$ in the input space $\mathcal{X} \subset \Re^M$. After dimensionality reduction, document d_i is represented by the vector $\mathbf{y}_i = \langle y_{i1}, y_{i2}, \ldots, y_{iR}\rangle$ in the feature space $\mathcal{Y} \subset \Re^R$. For our technique, the dimension R can range from K, the number of context labels, to M, the number of dimensions in the input space (i.e. $K \leq R \leq M$).

3.1 Discriminative Term Weights

Measures of discrimination information can be used to quantify the discriminative power provided by a term for a given context over all other contexts. They can also be viewed as the strength of the evidence or opinion that a term provides for a given context. Measures of discrimination and association have been studied for different purposes in the literature including feature selection, association rule mining, and text classification. The idea of discriminative term weights is introduced in [4] for quantifying the discrimination information provided by terms for classification purposes. Three measures (Kullbach-Leibler divergence, relative risk, and log relative risk) are evaluated and it is reported that the relative risk of a term provides robust classification performance.

In this work, we use the relative risk of a term to quantify its discrimination information for a given context over the others. Accordingly, the discriminative term weight of term t_j for context c_k is defined as

$$dtw(t_j, c_k) = \frac{p(t_j|c_k)}{p(t_j|\bar{c}_k)} \quad (1)$$

where $p(t_j|c_k)$ denotes the probability of term t_j in documents belonging to context c_k and $\bar{c}_k$ refers to documents in all contexts but c_k. If $dtw(t_j, c_k) > 1$ then term t_j provides positive discrimination information for context c_k, with larger values signifying higher discriminative power.

The probabilities in Equation 1 are computed from the set of labeled document $\mathcal{D}$ via maximum likelihood estimation (MLE). We evaluate two document models in this work: (a) documents' terms follow a Multinomial distribution and (b) each term follows a Bernoulli distribution.

Once the discriminative term weights are estimated, we can identify all the terms that provide significant positive discrimination information for a given context. Specifically, the set of terms $\mathcal{V}_k$ providing significant positive discrimination information for context c_k is defined as

$$\mathcal{V}_k = \{t_j \| dtw(t_j, c_k) > T \ \forall j\} \quad (2)$$

where $T \geq 1$ is a term selection parameter controlling the exclusion of insignificant terms. It is important to note that, in general, $\mathcal{V}_k \cap \mathcal{V}_l \neq \emptyset$ for all k and l. Also, depending on the value of T, $\cup_k \mathcal{V}_k \neq \mathcal{V}$ as some terms may not provide significant discrimination information for any context.

3.2 Relatedness of Terms to Contexts

Cai and van Rijsbergen [1] define the relatedness of a term to a context/topic as the product of a weight of the term in the context and a discrimination information measure of the term for the context. Following their framework, we define the relatedness of term t_j to context c_k as follows:

$$rel(t_j, c_k) = p(t_j|c_k) \times dtw(t_j, c_k) \quad (3)$$

Thus, the weight of a term in the context c_k is taken to be the probability of the term in documents belonging to context label c_k. Intuitively, a term is more related to a context if its discriminative term weight is larger and if it occurs frequently in documents belonging to the context.

This choice of the weight of a term in a context leads to the interpretation that the relatedness of a term to a context (Equation 3) is the term's contribution towards the expected discrimination information provided by all significant terms for that context. The expected discrimination information provided by all terms $t \in \mathcal{V}_k$ for context c_k over the other contexts can be written as

$$E_k = \sum_{t_j \in \mathcal{V}_k} p(t_j|c_k) \times dtw(t_j, c_k) = \sum_{t_j \in \mathcal{V}_k} rel(t_j, c_k). \quad (4)$$

In words, E_k is the expectation of the discrimination information for context c_k based on terms in the labeled document collection. And, the relatedness of a term to this context represents its contribution to the expected value E_k; the stronger the relatedness, the larger the contribution to E_k.

3.3 Feature Construction

In the previous subsections, we have defined the relatedness of a term to a context (Equation 3) and identified all terms that are related to a given context (Equation 2). Given this setup, we can construct features by pooling the discrimination information provided by terms in $\mathcal{V}_k$ ($k = 1, K$). Consider a document d_i represented in the input space by the vector $\mathbf{x}_i$. The representation of this document in the feature space $\mathbf{y}_i$ is defined as follows:

$$y_{ik} = \frac{\sum_{t_j \in \mathcal{V}_k} tw(t_j, d_i) \times dtw(t_j, c_k)}{\sum_{t_j \in \mathcal{V}_k} tw(t_j, d_i)} \quad k = 1, K \qquad (5)$$

This expression will create $R = K$ features, where K is the total number of contexts in the document collection. Each feature represents the linear opinion pool or ensemble average of the discrimination information provided by terms in the document. If a term does not occur in a document, then the discrimination information or opinion of that term is not included. The larger the value of y_{ik} the greater is the chance that document d_i belongs to context c_k. The extension for $R > K$ features is omitted from this shortened paper.

3.4 Algorithm and its Computational Complexity

Algorithm 1 FEDIP

1: **Input:** $\{d_i\}_{i=1}^N$ (documents), $\mathcal{V} = \{t_j\}_{j=1}^M$ (term vocabulary), $cont(d_i)\forall i$ (contexts of documents), K (no. of contexts), $tw(t_j, d_i)\forall j, i$ (document-term weights), $R = K$ (no. of features)
2: **Output:** $\{\mathbf{y}_i\}_{i=1}^N$ (feature vectors of length R)
3:
4: **for** $k = 1 \to K$ **do**
5:   **for** $j = 1 \to M$ **do**
6:     $dtw(t_j, c_k) \leftarrow$ discriminative term weight of term t_j for context c_k (Eq. 1)
7:   **end for**
8:   $\mathcal{V}_k \leftarrow$ significant terms for context c_k (Eq. 2)
9: **end for**
10:
11: **for** $i = 1 \to N$ **do**
12:   **for** $r = 1 \to R$ **do**
13:     $y_{ir} \leftarrow$ linear opinion pool of terms in $\mathcal{V}_r$ (Eq. 5)
14:   **end for**
15: **end for**

The steps in FEDIP are given in Algorithm 1. There are two main processing blocks in FEDIP. The first code block (lines 4– 9) finds the discriminative term weights and constructs the term pool for each context. The estimation of the discriminative term weight (line 6) for a given term and context requires one pass over the set of labeled documents. Hence, the time complexity of this block of processing is $O(KMN)$.

The second block of processing (lines 11 – 15) computes the desired features by outputting a feature value for each context. The time complexity of this processing is $O(RMN)$. The overall worst-time complexity of FEDIP is $O(KMN) + O(RMN)$. This expression shows that FEDIP's time complexity depends linearly upon the data parameters N and M, and since $K = R$ is usually much smaller than both M and N, FEDIP is computationally very efficient in practice.

4. EMPIRICAL EVALUATION

We evaluate FEDIP for document classification using six text data sets. Its performance is compared with Latent Semantic Indexing (LSI) and Linear Discriminant Analysis (LDA) under Support Vector Machine (SVM) and Naive Bayes (NB) classifiers. Our experiments are conducted in the MATLAB environment (LSI, NB). For SVM we use the LIBSVM[1] implementation, and for LDA we use the LDA/QR[2] implementation [8]. In all our experiments, the term selection parameter T is set equal to one.

Table 1: Key characteristics of the evaluation data sets

Name	Docs (N)	Terms (M)	Contexts (K)
MReview	2000	31296	2
Hitech	2301	13170	6
TR31	927	10128	7
TR41	878	7454	10
RE0	1504	2886	13
WAP	1560	8460	20

The names and key characteristics of the selected data sets are given in Table 1. The first data set is taken from a Cornell University page[3], while the remaining five data sets are available from Karypis Lab at University of Minnesota[4]. Brief descriptions of these data sets can be found on the respective Web sites.

FEDIP preserves the topic or context information in the reduced feature space. This characteristic is highly desirable for visualization of document collections and document classification. We illustrate this in Figure 1. In this figure, the left plot shows the Movie Review data set in the 2-dimensional feature space produced by FEDIP, while the right plot shows the same for LSI. The separation of documents belonging to the two contexts is evident in the feature space produced by FEDIP. Furthermore, the feature values produced by FEDIP are readily interpretable as relevance of documents to the respective contexts. In general, the scatter plots of documents in the 2-dimensional feature space produced by FEDIP have documents belonging to one context spread along one axis and documents belonging to the other context spread along the other axis with some overlap along the diagonal. This representation suggests that a linear discriminant passing through the origin can produce accurate classification.

Table 2 gives the classification performance (average percent accuracy and standard deviation obtained from five random train/test runs in which the size of the test set is 33% of the total data size) of SVM and NB classifiers in the feature space. The number of features is equal to the number of contexts ($R = K$) of the data sets, except for LDA/QR, for which $R = K - 1$. FEDIP-a is the variant based on the Multinomial model and FEDIP-b is the variant based on the Bernoulli model.

The following observations and interpretations can be made from these results. (1) FEDIP's feature spaces yield higher classification accuracy for the majority of the data sets. FEDIP's performance is much better for data sets with fewer contexts when compared to LDA/QR. (2) The performance gap between FEDIP and LDA/QR decreases as the number

[1]http://www.csie.ntu.edu.tw/ cjlin/libsvm/
[2]http://sites.google.com/site/mydemossite/
[3]http://www.cs.cornell.edu/people/pabo/movie-review-data/
[4]http://glaros.dtc.umn.edu/gkhome/cluto/cluto/download

Table 2: Classification performance of different feature extraction techniques when paired with SVM and NB classifiers

Data	NB Classifier				SVM Classifier			
	FEDIP-a	FEDIP-b	LSI	LDA/QR	FEDIP-a	FEDIP-b	LSI	LDA/QR
MReview	79.19 ± 0.63	$\mathbf{82.16 \pm 0.73}$	56.01 ± 3.76	65.98 ± 3.61	78.92 ± 0.67	81.89 ± 0.92	48.59 ± 0.57	66.13 ± 4.21
Hitech	70.3 ± 1.21	67.81 ± 0.66	53.91 ± 1.82	68.36 ± 0.95	$\mathbf{71.58 \pm 1.19}$	67.66 ± 0.92	31.37 ± 0.78	69.93 ± 1.32
TR31	95.5 ± 0.85	96.89 ± 0.995	77.09 ± 1.15	71.59 ± 6.5	97.73 ± 0.46	$\mathbf{98.38 \pm 0.46}$	55.02 ± 2.48	91.34 ± 2.39
TR41	93.33 ± 0.71	93.26 ± 1.10	84.12 ± 2.01	82.27 ± 1.91	95.26 ± 0.77	$\mathbf{95.81 \pm 0.96}$	44.19 ± 3.63	94.02 ± 1.33
RE0	78.84 ± 2.00	76.92 ± 2.30	60.88 ± 2.23	73.49 ± 2.50	$\mathbf{85.15 \pm 1.49}$	81.16 ± 1.75	42.28 ± 0.91	81.92 ± 2.02
WAP	73.95 ± 1.57	77.46 ± 1.98	67.94 ± 1.98	75.92 ± 1.30	78.65 ± 1.61	78.57 ± 0.89	29.59 ± 0.91	$\mathbf{81.5 \pm 1.24}$

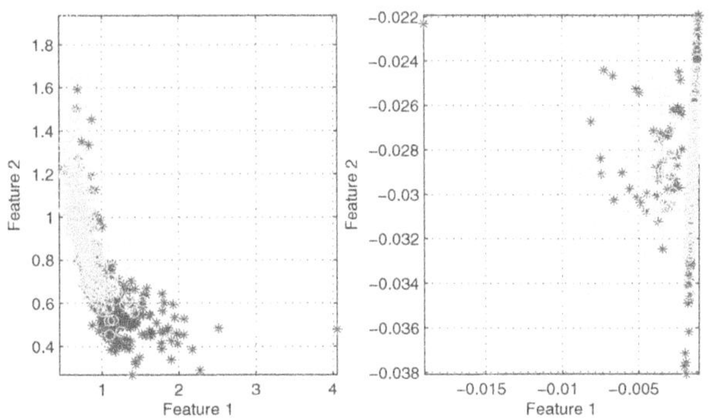

Figure 1: Scatter plot of Movie Review data set in 2-D feature space. Left plot is for FEDIP and right plot is for LSI. The two categories are identified by different color markers.

of contexts increases. (3) LSI's feature spaces produce poor classification accuracy, especially when paired with SVM. Since LSI is unsupervised, it is not able to preserve the category separation in the low-dimension feature space. Moreover, linear SVM, which is discriminative in nature, does poorly when compared to NB, which is generative in nature, in LSI feature spaces. (4) FEDIP-a and FEDIP-b can produce slightly different classification accuracies, and no clear winner is observable from our evaluation.

We now compare the computation times required by FEDIP, LSI, and LDA/QR on our evaluation data sets. Instead of providing absolute run-time values, which depend heavily upon the computing environment, we provide the relative run-times on our computing setup. We observed the run-times for all data sets and found that LDA/QR is at least 4 times slower than FEDIP and LSI is at least 15 times slower than FEDIP. Even though LDA/QR has a theoretical worst-case time complexity identical to that of FEDIP [8], in practice we found it to be significantly slower than FEDIP.

5. CONCLUDING REMARKS

Motivated by the notion of relatedness of terms to topics or contexts, we develop and evaluate a supervised feature extraction technique for text, named FEDIP, based on discriminative term weighting and term pooling. FEDIP produces features that are readily interpretable as the strength of the discrimination information provided by the term pool for a given context. The computational complexity of FEDIP is linear in M (number of terms) and N (number of documents). These characteristics of FEDIP are evaluated on six text data sets and its performance compared with LSI and LDA/QR using naive Bayes and SVM text classification. FEDIP outperforms LSI and LDA/QR especially when the dimensions have been reduced significantly.

This work demonstrates that term pooling is a practically effective technique for text dimensionality reduction. It also highlights the use of relatedness of terms to contexts. There is much potential for future research in this direction. Specifically, it is worth investigating the use of knowledge-based measures of relatedness (in addition to the corpus-based measure used in this work) for term pooling. We also feel that term selection, via the term selection parameter T, can improve the quality of the feature spaces produced by FEDIP.

6. REFERENCES

[1] D. Cai and C. J. van Rijsbergen. Learning semantic relatedness from term discrimination information. *Expert Systems with Applications*, 36:1860–1875, 2009.

[2] S. C. Deerwester, S. T. Dumais, T. K. Landauer, G. W. Furnas, and R. A. Harshman. Indexing by Latent Semantic Analysis. *Journal of the American Society of Information Science*, 41(6):391–407, 1990.

[3] M. A. K. Haliday and R. Hassan. *Cohesion in English*. Longman, London, UK, 1976.

[4] K. Junejo and A. Karim. A robust discriminative term weighting based linear discriminant method for text classification. In *Proceedings of Eighth IEEE International Conference on Data Mining (ICDM '08)*, pages 323 –332, 2008.

[5] J. Morris and G. Hirst. Non-classical lexical semantic relations. In *Proceedings of the HLT-NAACL Workshop on Computational Lexical Semantics*, CLS '04, pages 46–51. Association for Computational Linguistics, 2004.

[6] P. Resnik. Using information content to evaluate semantic similarity. In *Joint Conference on Artificial Intelligence*, pages 448–453, Montreal, Canada, August 1995.

[7] G. Tsatsaronis, I. Varlamis, and M. Vazirgiannis. Text relatedness based on a word thesaurus. *Journal of Artificial Intelligence Research*, 37:1–39, 2010.

[8] J. Ye and Q. Li. A two-stage linear discriminant analysis via QR-decomposition. *IEEE Transactions on Pattern Analysis and Machine Intelligence*, 27:929–941, 2005.

Constructing Efficient Information Extraction Pipelines

Henning Wachsmuth
Universität Paderborn, s-lab
Paderborn, Germany
hwachsmuth@s-lab.upb.de

Benno Stein
Bauhaus-Universität Weimar
Weimar, Germany
benno.stein@uni-weimar.de

Gregor Engels
Universität Paderborn, s-lab
Paderborn, Germany
engels@upb.de

ABSTRACT

Information Extraction (IE) pipelines analyze text through several stages. The pipeline's algorithms determine both its effectiveness and its run-time efficiency. In real-world tasks, however, IE pipelines often fail acceptable run-times because they analyze too much task-irrelevant text. This raises two interesting questions: 1) How much "efficiency potential" depends on the scheduling of a pipeline's algorithms? 2) Is it possible to devise a reliable method to construct efficient IE pipelines? Both questions are addressed in this paper. In particular, we show how to optimize the run-time efficiency of IE pipelines under a given set of algorithms. We evaluate pipelines for three algorithm sets on an industrially relevant task: the extraction of market forecasts from news articles. Using a system-independent measure, we demonstrate that efficiency gains of up to one order of magnitude are possible without compromising a pipeline's original effectiveness.

Categories and Subject Descriptors: I.2.7 [AI]: Natural Language Processing—*Text analysis* H.3.4 [Information Storage and Retrieval]: Systems and Software—*Performance evaluation (efficiency and effectiveness)*
General Terms: Algorithms, Performance
Keywords: information extraction, run-time efficiency

1. INTRODUCTION

Information Extraction (IE) will improve today's possibilities of knowledge and information acquisition. Yet, the number of industrial applications is still limited. Typical IE tasks require several analysis stages ranging from preprocessing over the extraction of entities, attributes, relations, and events to reference resolution and normalization. "Conventional" pipelines for these tasks execute all analyses on the whole input and tend to run into efficiency problems, i.e., they fail to meet some required response time. We use the term *efficiency* here only to address such run-time concerns. Accordingly, we use *effectiveness* to describe the quality of an algorithm, such as its accuracy. Existing approaches to increase efficiency focus on faster algorithms for single analyses within a pipeline. However, more effective algorithm sets normally lead to a decrease in efficiency as illustrated in Figure 1a. In contrast, we aim to increase efficiency without

CIKM'11, October 24–28, 2011, Glasgow, Scotland, UK.

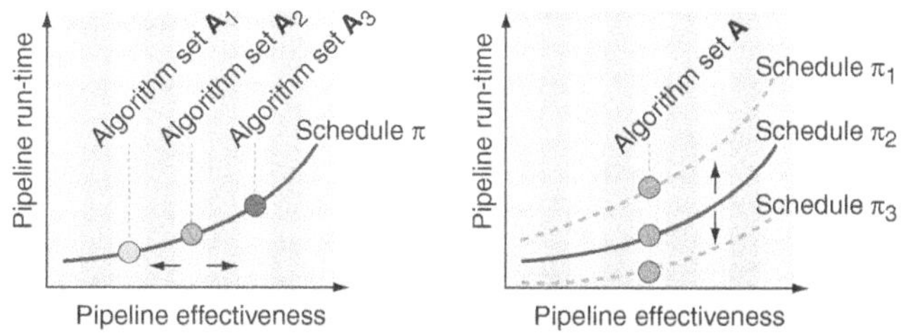

Figure 1: (a) Typical growth curve of the run-time of an IE pipeline; more effective sets of algorithms improve the pipeline's effectiveness but entail higher run-time. (b) A smart scheduling of a pipeline's algorithms can improve its efficiency without impairing its effectiveness.

losing effectiveness by optimizing the pipeline itself: instead of changing the pipeline's algorithms we introduce filtering stages and rearrange the pipeline's schedule (Figure 1b).

Within an IE task, different analyses $\mathcal{A}_1, ..., \mathcal{A}_k$ take place, e.g. tokenization or person entity recognition, whereas each analysis $\mathcal{A}_i$ can be operationalized by alternative IE algorithms. We call an ordered subset $\pi = (\mathcal{A}_1, ..., \mathcal{A}_k)$ of analyses an *analysis schedule* and denote the employed set of algorithms as $\mathbf{A}$. The tuple $\Pi = \langle \mathbf{A}, \pi \rangle$ constitutes an *Information Extraction pipeline.* Each algorithm $A \in \mathbf{A}$ needs information of certain input types in order to work properly, and A provides information of certain output types. Consequently, only a subset of the $k!$ possible analysis schedules fulfill the input constraints for all algorithms in $\mathbf{A}$. While some algorithms will fail completely if their requirements are not met, others may degrade significantly in their effectiveness. We hence consider only pipelines whose schedules comply with all input constraints imposed by the employed algorithms. We call such pipelines *admissible.* If admissibility is maintained, the exchange of a pipeline's schedule does not impair the pipeline's effectiveness.

Contributions In this paper, we present a generic method to construct efficient IE pipelines based on four paradigms: 1) a *maximum decomposition* of the given IE task into single analyses, 2) *early filtering* of relevant information, 3) *lazy evaluation* of the applied algorithms, and 4) an *optimized scheduling* of the resulting filtering stages. We have evaluated our method on a subtask of the market forecast extraction task [13]. To make the efficiency of pipelines comparable beyond system bounds, we use a new measure of efficiency that relies on an internal comparison of the algorithms in a pipeline. The results indicate that our method can speed up conventional IE pipelines up to an order of magnitude, while maintaining effectiveness.

Related Work The limited industrial usage of IE has recently been discussed in [14]. The authors identify the lack of reusability as one major problem and introduce a component-based IE approach. We also exploit a decomposition into components, but we address another major problem of IE: efficiency. Run-time efficiency has always been a main aspect of algorithm research, but we observe that most rewarded research in IE and in Natural Language Processing (NLP) focuses on effectiveness as do the leading evaluation tracks, namely, MUC, ACE, and the CoNLL Shared Task. While effectiveness is the key to making information processable, we argue that the success of IE systems in the wild is decided by their response times.

Efficiency is by far not an unknown topic in IE and NLP. For instance, greedy decoding has been shown to be competitive with exact inference in entity recognition [10] and machine translation [7]. Other research uses hashing or heuristic search for feature extraction [6] and parsing [4, 8], while Petrov [9] studies efficiency under an iterative refinement of the complexity of NLP models. Like in these examples most research concentrates on *single analyses*. In contrast, we aim to develop efficient *analysis pipelines*. Pipelines that operate on large sources first need to efficiently filter candidate texts, which has been done with fast text categorization [12] or querying techniques trained on text with the relations of interest [1]. The KnowItNow system builds specialized index structures to speed up the IE process [5], and a schedule designed with efficiency in mind is given in [2]. In both cases, the authors focus on retrieval aspects. Instead, we investigate the core IE algorithms for text analysis.

2. PIPELINE OPTIMIZATION

For the purpose of this paper, we first introduce two definitions in order to quantify the efficiency of IE algorithms and pipelines. On this basis, we then present the essential steps to optimize the efficiency of IE pipelines.

Definition 1. Let A be an IE algorithm and D a text collection with n sentences. If A needs time $T_D(A)$ to process all sentences of D on a system Σ, then the *average sentence response time* of A on Σ is $t(A) = T_D(A)/n$.

Definition 1 can be adopted to $t(\Pi)$ for an IE pipeline Π. However, response times are not meaningful by themselves: usually, run-time complexities are defined in a relative manner, by measuring the run-time in unit cost steps that are accepted over system bounds, programming environments, and the like. In this regard we employ $t(A_0)$ of a tokenization algorithm A_0 on the given system Σ as unit cost step. Thereby, we normalize $t(A)$ with respect to IE tasks and cancel out many system-specific side effects.

Definition 2. Let τ be an IE task, Π a pipeline to tackle τ, $\mathcal{E}$ the effectiveness of Π on τ, and A_0 a tokenization algorithm. Then, the *averaged efficiency of* Π *to tackle* τ *at effectiveness* $\mathcal{E}$ is $\mathcal{F}@\mathcal{E} = t(\Pi)/t(A_0)$.

$\mathcal{F}@\mathcal{E}$ allows to estimate $t(\Pi)$ system-independently. In general, $t(\Pi)$ follows from the response times of the algorithms and the number of processed sentences. While $t(A)$ is inherent to an algorithm A, the number of processed sentences depends on a pipeline's schedule. To construct a preferably efficient pipeline, we now introduce four paradigms that yield a tailored scheduling of its algorithms, and that can be seen as operational steps of a method.

Paradigm 1: Maximum Decomposition The deeper a task τ is decomposed into single analyses, the better a pipeline for τ can be optimized. Some analyses have a predefined order, though. Also, some algorithms may be bundled in off-the-shelf tools, which can only be used in a black-box manner. In preprocessing, decomposition means to separate the analyses for sentence splitting, tokenization, the decoding of sequence information (e.g. part-of-speech-tagging), and the creation of syntactic tree structures (e.g. dependency parsing). Similarly, decomposing the recognition of different entity, attribute, and relation types supports optimization. Some of these are *required*, whereas others are *optional*. Finally, IE pipelines extract information on specific events, which relate to *statements* in the text, i.e., text windows of $w > 0$ sentences. Such a statement is only relevant if it comprises an anchor for an event of interest.

Paradigm 2: Early Filtering It is reasonable to focus only on information that probably satisfies a given information need. Thus, filters are inserted after each core IE analyses. In particular, statements without instances of a required entity, attribute, or relation type are discarded as well as statements that are classified not to refer to an event of interest. Also, statements are only kept if the required entities and attributes can be normalized. We call the combination of preprocessing, IE analysis, and filter a *filtering stage*. While filtering can drastically reduce the amount of data to be processed, we thereby miss statements where entities and attributes are spread across the text. This tradeoff can be influenced by adjusting the statement size w.

Paradigm 3: Lazy Evaluation Based on the filtering stages, a simple but effective paradigm can be applied: each analysis is delayed until its results is needed, and it is executed only on possibly relevant text windows. Of course, no analysis is performed more than once. The rationale is that, the more filtering takes place before the execution of an algorithm A, the less data A will process.

Paradigm 4: Optimized Scheduling Finally, the filtering stages are arranged in the most efficient way. Assume that we have implementations of two stages F_1 and F_2 with $t(F_1)$ and $t(F_2)$. If F_1 is applied to n sentences, it filters a number $m(F_1)$ of the n sentences on average, while F_2 filters $m(F_2)$ sentences. In order to minimize the response time of both stages in sequence, F_1 is then applied before F_2 iff

$$t(F_1) + m(F_1)/n \cdot t(F_2) < t(F_2) + m(F_2)/n \cdot t(F_1). \quad (1)$$

While the *filter ratios*, such as $m(F_1)/n$, can be estimated based on a training set, they may change after each applied filter. For simplicity, we approximate the optimized schedule in Section 3 by only pairwise computing the most efficient schedule of two filters using their initial filter ratios.

3. EVALUATION

The Task We evaluated the following subtask τ of the market forecast extraction task [13]: *Extract all related time and money entities that refer to a revenue forecast.* An example for such a relation is: "In 2009, market analysts expected touch screen revenues to reach $[\$9B]_{\text{money}}$ $[\text{by } 2015]_{\text{time}}$." While τ is quite new and non-standard, the implications of the evaluation can be transferred to other tasks as well.

The Data We used the *Revenue Corpus* introduced in [13] and processed its training set to develop and train algorithms, to measure their response times, and to estimate

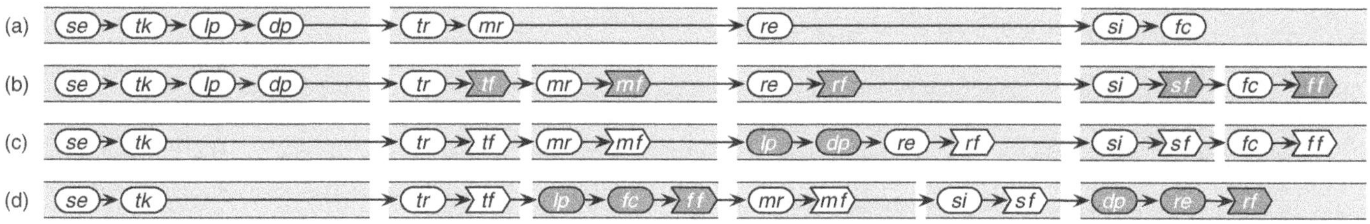

Figure 2: Construction of an optimized schedule following the four paradigms: (a) Maximum decomposition. (b) Early filtering. (c) Lazy evaluation. (d) Optimized scheduling (here, according to algorithm set $\mathbf{A}_2$).

the initial filter ratios of the filtering stages.[1] On the test set, we evaluated the efficiency and the effectiveness of all constructed pipelines. In this set, all 347 of the 6,038 sentences, in which both a time and a money entity relate to revenue, are manually annotated as statements on revenue, among them 104 forecasts. Hence, we set the statement size w (cf. Section 2) of all evaluated algorithms to 1.

Analyses and Algorithms Following paradigm 1, we decomposed τ into the following nine analyses (cf. Figure 2a):

- *se* Split the input text into sentences.
- *tk* Tokenize the sentences.
- *lp* Lemmatize the tokens and tag their part-of-speech.
- *dp* Parse dependencies of the tokens in the sentences.
- *tr* Recognize all time entities in the sentences.
- *mr* Recognize all money entities in the sentences.
- *re* Extract relations between time and money entities.
- *si* Identify statements on revenue.
- *fc* Classify whether a sentence is a forecast or not.

As we only needed lemmas and tags together, we did not decompose *lp*. Table 1 lists the algorithms that we evaluated for the nine analyses. We used the *TreeTagger*[2] [11] and the *mate-tools*[3] [3, 4] for lemmatization, tagging, and parsing. Where no reference is given, we measured effectiveness on the test set. Since we had more than one algorithm for *lp*, *dp*, *re*, and *si*, we investigated three algorithm sets:

$$\mathbf{A}_1 = \{\mathrm{se}_1, \mathrm{tk}_1, \mathbf{lp_1}, -\;\;, \mathrm{tr}_1, \mathrm{mr}_1, \mathbf{re_1}, \mathbf{si_1}, \mathrm{fc}_1\}$$
$$\mathbf{A}_2 = \{\mathrm{se}_1, \mathrm{tk}_1, \mathbf{lp_1}, \mathbf{dp_1}, \mathrm{tr}_1, \mathrm{mr}_1, \mathbf{re_2}, \mathbf{si_2}, \mathrm{fc}_1\}$$
$$\mathbf{A}_3 = \{\mathrm{se}_1, \mathrm{tk}_1, \mathbf{lp_2}, \mathbf{dp_2}, \mathrm{tr}_1, \mathrm{mr}_1, \mathbf{re_2}, \mathbf{si_2}, \mathrm{fc}_1\}$$

Differences are marked in bold. Because of a very simple relation extractor, $\mathbf{A}_1$ needs no dependency parsing at all.

Filtering Stages For paradigm 2, we inserted a filter after each IE analysis (cf. Figure 2b). The results of *dp* are used for *re*, whereas *dp* itself requires lemmas and tags from *lp* as input. So, for lazy evaluation, we delayed *lp* and *dp* to execute them right before *re* (cf. Figure 2c).

Schedules and Pipelines The last step is to derive an optimized schedule, which we sketch for $\mathbf{A}_2$. As follows from the dependencies in Table 1 the filtering stages $F_t = (tr, tf)$ and $F_m = (mr, mf)$ have to precede $F_r = (lp, dp, re, rf)$ and $F_s = (si, sf)$ for admissibility, and F_t also has to precede $F_f = (fc, ff)$. We pairwise computed the most efficient schedule of two stages using inequation 1. As a result, we moved F_f before F_r and inserted *lp* before *fc*. Also, we postponed F_r after F_s as illustrated in Figure 2d. Altogether, we finished with the optimized schedule π_2^* for $\mathbf{A}_2$:

[1]Revenue Corpus, http://infexba.upb.de
[2]TreeTagger, http://code.google.com/p/tt4j
[3]mate-tools, http://code.google.com/p/mate-tools

Table 1: The evaluated algorithms A for analysis $\mathcal{A}$, the analyses each A depends on, its average sentence response time $t(A)$ in milliseconds, and its effectiveness $\mathcal{E}(A)$ if applied in isolation (accuracy Acc, labeled attachment score LAS, precision P, recall R).

$\mathcal{A}$	A	approach	depends on	$t(A)$	$\mathcal{E}(A)$
se:	se_1	rule-based	–	0.46	Acc 0.95
tk:	tk_1	rule-based	*se*	0.60	Acc 0.98
lp:	lp_1	*TreeTagger*	*se, tk*	0.34	Acc 0.97 [11]
	lp_2	*mate-tools*	*se, tk*	21.87	Acc 0.98 [3]
dp:	dp_1	*mate-tools*	*se, tk, lp*	54.61	LAS 0.87 [4]
	dp_2	*mate-tools*	*se, tk, lp*	166.14	LAS 0.88 [4]
tr:	tr_1	regex	*se, tk*	0.37	P 0.91, R 0.97
mr:	mr_1	regex	*se, tk*	0.70	P 0.99, R 0.95
re:	re_1	rule-based	*se, tk, tr, mr*	0.02	P 0.69, R 0.88
	re_2	SVM	*se, tk, lp, dp, tr, mr*	1.39	P 0.75, R 0.88
si:	si_1	lexicon	*se, tk*	0.02	P 0.86, R 0.93
	si_2	SVM	*se, tk, tr, mr*	1.43	P 0.87, R 0.93
fc:	fc_1	SVM	*se, tk, lp, tr*	0.27	Acc 0.93

Table 2: Precision (P), recall (R), and F_1-score (F_1) of all admissible pipelines $\Pi_{i,j} = \langle \mathbf{A}_i, \pi_j \rangle$.

π	P	R	F_1	P	R	F_1	P	R	F_1
	algorithm set $\mathbf{A}_1$			*algorithm set* $\mathbf{A}_2$			*algorithm set* $\mathbf{A}_3$		
π_a	0.65	0.56	0.60	0.72	0.58	0.65	0.75	0.61	0.67
π_b	0.65	0.56	0.60	0.72	0.58	0.65	0.75	0.61	0.67
π_c	0.65	0.56	0.60	0.72	0.58	0.65	0.75	0.61	0.67
π_1^*	0.65	0.56	0.60	–	–	–	–	–	–
π_2^*	0.65	0.56	0.60	0.71	0.58	0.64	0.75	0.61	0.67
π_3^*	0.65	0.56	0.60	0.71	0.58	0.64	0.75	0.61	0.67

$$\pi_2^* = (se, tk, tr, tf, lp, fc, ff, mr, mf, si, sf, dp, re, rf)$$

For $\mathbf{A}_1$ and $\mathbf{A}_3$, we accordingly obtained π_1^* and π_3^*:

$$\pi_1^* = (se, tk, si, sf, tr, tf, mr, mf, lp, fc, ff, re, rf)$$
$$\pi_3^* = (se, tk, tr, tf, mr, mf, si, sf, lp, fc, ff, dp, re, rf)$$

As baselines, we used all pipelines with one of the schedules π_a, π_b, and π_c from Figure 2a–c. In fact, π_c resembles the schedule from [2]. Except for π_1^*, we implemented a pipeline $\Pi_{i,j}$ in Java for each $\mathbf{A}_i$ and π_j. π_1^* applies *si* before *tr* and *mr*. Thus, a pipeline with π_1^* is only admissible for $\mathbf{A}_1$, which contains si_1 for *si*. We ran all pipelines five times on the test set using a *2 GHz Intel Core 2 Duo MacBook* with *4 GB RAM* and averaged over the response times.

Effectiveness Results The effectiveness of each pipeline is given in Table 2. Precision and recall increase from $\mathbf{A}_1$ to $\mathbf{A}_3$ significantly. Only in case of $\mathbf{A}_2$, the optimization impaired the effectiveness: the F_1-scores of both $\Pi_{2,2} = \langle \mathbf{A}_2, \pi_2^* \rangle$ and $\Pi_{2,3} = \langle \mathbf{A}_2, \pi_3^* \rangle$ are one point lower than for the baselines. However, this is noise from the TreeTagger, which operates

Table 3: The average sentence response time $t(\Pi_{i,j})$ with standard deviation $\sigma_{i,j}$ of each admissible pipeline $\Pi_{i,j} = \langle \mathbf{A}_i, \pi_j \rangle$ measured in milliseconds.

π_j	$t(\Pi_{1,j})$	$\sigma_{1,j}$	$t(\Pi_{2,j})$	$\sigma_{2,j}$	$t(\Pi_{3,j})$	$\sigma_{3,j}$
	algorithm set $\mathbf{A}_1$		*algorithm set* $\mathbf{A}_2$		*algorithm set* $\mathbf{A}_3$	
π_a	3.23	0.07	51.05	0.40	168.40	0.57
π_b	2.86	0.09	49.66	0.28	167.85	0.70
π_c	2.54	0.08	15.54	0.23	45.16	0.53
π_1^*	**2.44**	0.03	–	–	–	–
π_2^*	2.47	0.15	**4.77**	0.06	16.25	0.15
π_3^*	2.62	0.05	4.95	0.09	**10.19**	0.05

on token-level. For such algorithms, filtering may influence the feature values of tokens near sentence boundaries.

Efficiency Results Table 3 lists $t(\Pi_{i,j})$ of each $\Pi_{i,j}$. For $\mathbf{A}_1$, our method led to a decrease from 3.23 ms to 2.44 ms. This improvement seems small, but note that se_1 and tk_1 already need over 1 ms (cf. Table 1). In case of $\mathbf{A}_2$, the response time was reduced to less than 1/10 of $t(\Pi_{2,a})$ and to less than 1/3 of $t(\Pi_{2,c})$. For $\mathbf{A}_3$, the pipeline $\Pi_{3,3}$ with $t(\Pi_{3,3}) = 10.19$ ms is over 4 times as fast as the most efficient baseline $\Pi_{3,c}$. Moreover, $\Pi_{3,3}$ clearly outperforms $\Pi_{3,2}$. This offers evidence for the benefit of paradigm 4, while especially the scheduling of $\mathbf{A}_1$ profits most from paradigm 1 and 2. Accordingly, looking at the standard deviations, we see that π_b is significantly faster than π_a only for $\mathbf{A}_1$.

Efficiency at Effectiveness Using the F_1-score as effectiveness $\mathcal{E}$, we plotted $\mathcal{F}@\mathcal{E}$ for the three algorithm sets and the six schedules in Figure 3. The interpolated curves of the schedules have the shape introduced in Section 1, and we observe only a moderate slope for the optimized schedules. Also, $\mathcal{F}@\mathcal{E}$ cancelled out effects of high memory load from applying complex algorithms, such as dp_2, to many sentences. For instance, this yielded $\mathcal{F}(\Pi_{3,a})/\mathcal{F}(\Pi_{3,3}) = 15.1$ as opposed to $t(\Pi_{3,a})/t(\Pi_{3,3}) = 16.5$.

Discussion The three algorithm sets mainly differ in the uniformity of the algorithms' response times (cf. Table 1), which gives rise to the potential of lazy evaluation and optimized scheduling. In general, the room for improvement depends on the density and distribution of task-relevant information in input texts. The more dense relevant information occurs, the less improvement through filtering can be expected, and, the more spread event-related information is across the text, the larger the statement size w must be in order to achieve high recall. Still, our method is generic in that it allows to integrate arbitrary text analysis algorithms and in that it can, in principle, be applied to any IE task.

4. CONCLUSION

Existing approaches to run-time efficiency in IE mostly rely on the development of fast *algorithms*. In contrast, we presented a method to increase the efficiency of IE *pipelines*. Using a system-independent measure, we showed for a complex IE task and three algorithm sets that a pipeline can be significantly sped up without impairing its effectiveness. The improvement is especially high if the response times of the employed algorithms differ largely. Also, the impact depends on the density and the distribution of task-relevant information. These observations—along with the four optimization paradigms of our method—are a step towards a theory of efficiency in IE, which we plan to extend and underpin within forthcoming research.

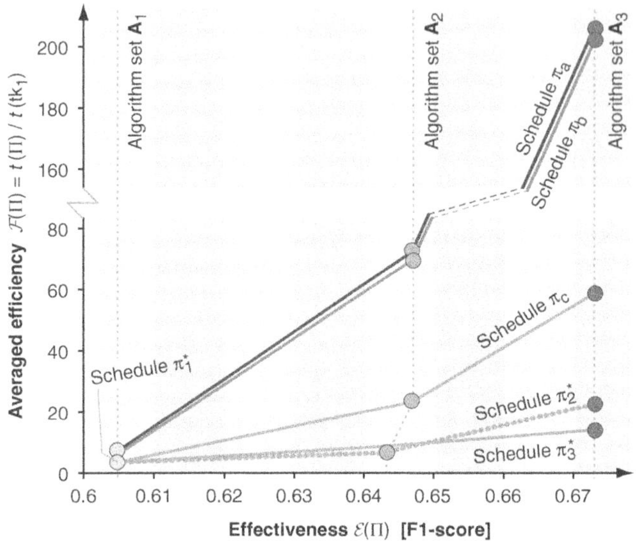

Figure 3: Averaged efficiency at effectiveness $\mathcal{F}@\mathcal{E}$ of all admissible pipelines $\Pi_{i,j} = \langle \mathbf{A}_i, \pi_j \rangle$ at the three effectiveness levels represented by $\mathbf{A}_1$, $\mathbf{A}_2$, and $\mathbf{A}_3$.

5. REFERENCES

[1] E. Agichtein and L. Gravano. Querying Text Databases for Efficient Information Extraction. In *ICDE*, pp. 113–124, 2003.

[2] E. Agichtein. Scaling Information Extraction to Large Document Collections. *Bulletin of IEEE-CS Technical Committee on Data Engineering*, 28:3–10, 2005.

[3] A. Björkelund, B. Bohnet, L. Hafdell, and P. Nugues. A High-Performance Syntactic and Semantic Dependency Parser. In *COLING: Demonstrations*, pp. 33–36, 2010.

[4] B. Bohnet. Very High Accuracy and Fast Dependency Parsing is not a Contradiction. In *COLING*, pp. 89–97, 2010.

[5] M.J. Cafarella, D. Downey, S. Soderland, and O. Etzioni. KnowItNow: Fast, Scalable Information Extraction from the Web. In *HLT and EMNLP*, pp. 563–570, 2005.

[6] G. Forman and E. Kirshenbaum. Extremely Fast Text Feature Extraction for Classification and Indexing. In *CIKM*, pp. 1221–1230, 2008.

[7] U. Germann, M. Jahr, K. Knight, D. Marcu, and Y. Yamada. Fast Decoding and Optimal Decoding for Machine Translation. In *ACL*, pp. 228-235, 2001.

[8] A. Pauls and D. Klein. k-best A* Parsing. In *ACL and IJCNLP*, pp. 958–966, 2009.

[9] S. Petrov. *Coarse-to-Fine Natural Language Processing.* PhD Thesis, University of California at Berkeley, 2009.

[10] L. Ratinov and D. Roth. Design Challenges and Misconceptions in Named Entity Recognition. In *CoNLL*, pp. 147–155, 2009.

[11] H. Schmid. 1995. Improvements in Part-of-Speech Tagging with an Application to German. In *ACL SIGDAT-Workshop*, pp. 47–50.

[12] B. Stein, S. Meyer zu Eissen, G. Gräfe, and F. Wissbrock. Automating Market Forecast Summarization from Internet Data. In *WWW/Internet*, pp. 395–402, 2005.

[13] H. Wachsmuth, P. Prettenhofer, and B. Stein. Efficient Statement Identification for Automatic Market Forecasting. In *COLING*, pp. 1128–1136, 2010.

[14] D.C. Wimalasuriya and D. Dou. Components for Information Extraction: Ontology-Based Information Extractors and Generic Platform. In *CIKM*, pp. 9–18, 2010.

CoRankBayes: Bayesian Learning to Rank under the Co-training Framework and Its Application in Keyphrase Extraction

Chen Wang
wangche386@gmail.com

Sujian Li
lisujian@pku.edu.cn

Key Laboratory of Computational Linguistics, Peking University
Ministry of Education, 100871, Beijing, China

ABSTRACT

Recently, learning to rank algorithms have become a popular and effective tool for ordering objects (e.g. terms) according to their degrees of importance. The contribution of this paper is that we propose a simple and fast learning to rank model RankBayes and embed it in the co-training framework. The detailed proof is given that Naïve Bayes algorithm can be used to implement a learning to rank model. To solve the problem of two-model inconsistency, an ingenious approach is put forward to rank all the phrases by making use of the labeled results of two RankBayes models. Experimental results show that the proposed approach is promising in solving ranking problems.

Categories and Subject Descriptors

H.3 [**Information storage and retrieval**]: Content Analysis and Indexing

General Terms

Algorithms, Experimentation

Keywords

Learning to rank, Naïve Bayes, Co-training framework, Keyphrase extraction

1. INTRODUCTION

Ranking, which is to order objects according to their degrees of importance, is a key problem to many applications, such as information retrieval, document summarization, collaborative filtering and so on. Recently the learning to rank methods are widely used for ranking tasks [1]. The commonly used approaches are pairwise, which model all the object pairs with a binary classification problem and establish the relative importance relations between two objects [2]. To get a better performance, however, pairwise learning to rank approaches still need a larger corpus of training data. Joachims collected the training data automatically by analyzing the click-through logs and used them to train a pairwise learning to rank method – Ranking SVM in search engine [4]. For the keyphrase extraction task, it is difficult to get a complete ranking of all phrases as training corpus, though a few documents labeled with keyphrases can be collected. To apply the learning to ranking strategy, we can collect all the <keyphrase, non-keyphrase> pairs as training data and it is obvious each keyphrase has higher relative importance than non-keyphrases. Jiang also verifies that the learning to rank method is more appropriate for keyphrase extraction than the conventional classification methods [3].

CIKM'11, October 24-28, 2011, Glasgow, Scotland, UK.

To make full use of the training data and further enhance the learning to rank model, the introduction of co-training framework [1] where two base rankers learn each other, is a better option. In this paper, we propose to apply the co-training idea on two learning to rankers for the keyphrase extraction task. However, the co-training learning to rank framework should consider two problems: co-training speed and two-model inconsistency.

It is known that the co-training process needs a number of iterations to reach the convergence. Most learning to rank models like RankSVM and RankNet, which respectively use SVM and Artificial Neutral Network, cost a great deal of time in each iteration. To speed up the co-training process, we put forward a simple learning to rank model - RankBayes, which adopts Naive Bayes to rank the relative importance of any two objects. Herbrich mentioned that the traditional Bayesian approaches may not be fit for a learning to rank model, because the properties of transitivity and asymmetry may be violated due to the problem of stochastic transitivity [2]. However, for our specific keyphrase extraction task, we can give a detailed proof that the Naïve Bayes algorithm can be used to implement a learning to rank model, meaning that it will not yield inconsistent relative importance relations. Next, we propose the CoRankBayes model, which embeds two RankBayes models under the co-training framework.

Two RankBayes models may produce inconsistency among the relative importance relations. For example, for two objects a and b, we use the symbol $\succ$ to denote the relative importance relation, and the two models may respectively generate $a \succ b$, and $b \succ a$ which are inconsistent to rank these two objects. In this paper, we propose an efficient approach, which can tackle the inconsistent relative importance relations and make use of the labeled results calculated by the two RankBayes models to rank all the objects.

2. RELATED WORK

For the keyphrase extraction task, point-wise ranking has been the research focus. Turney implemented a system called GenEx and adopted the genetic algorithm to rank the importance of each phrase based on frequency and position features [6]. Witten implemented another system named KEA with the Bayesian approach [7]. Due to the difficulty of obtaining training corpus, pairwise learning to rank methods have recently attracted the researchers' attention. Jiang brought the Ranking SVM algorithm to the keyphrase extraction task and achieved satisfying results [3].

Ranking SVM was first used in the field of information retrieval, which demonstrates that the learning to rank strategy can well model the ranking orders and optimize the retrieval quality [2, 4].

Also in the field of information retrieval, Tan further proposed to use the ranking SVM models in the co-training framework (RSCF) [5], which however does not involve much the problems of time efficiency and two-model inconsistency. To improve the co-training efficiency, Zhao proposed the feature fusion and sample selection strategies in the co-training Rank SVM framework [8]. In this paper, we will first introduce the co-training learning to rank framework into the keyphrase extraction task. With the research focus on the co-training speed and two-model inconsistency, we propose the CoRankBayes model.

3. CORANKBAYES

In this section, we introduce the general architecture of CoRankBayes as illustrated in Figure 1. The basic idea of CoRankBayes does not make much difference to a standard co-training algorithm, where two models learn from each other by making use of both unlabeled data and labeled data. Next, we will address the consistency of RankBayes, the selection of the most confident labeled pairs to update L_1 and L_2 during the co-training process, and the rank-ordering approach using two sets of relative importance relations.

Algorithm 1: CoRankBayes

Input: A set of labeled pairs L, A set of unlabeled pairs U (including unlabeled training data and test data)

Output: absolute importance ordering list

$L_1 = L_2 = L$; $U_1 = U_2 = U$;

Loop for K iterations

1. Train RankBayes model Φ_1 from L_1, RankBayes model Φ_2 from L_2
2. Allow Φ_1 to label the unlabeled pairs in U_1, Φ_2 to label the unlabeled pairs in U_2
3. Add Φ_1's N most confidently labeled pairs to update L_2 consistently and remove the pairs from U_1
4. Add Φ_2's N most confidently labeled pairs to update L_1 consistently and remove the pairs from U_2

Loop end

5. Allow Φ_1 to label all the pairs in U_1, and add them to L_2; Allow Φ_2 to label all the pairs in U_2, and add them to L_1
6. Order the ranks for all the phrase according to L_1 and L_2

Figure 1. CoRankBayes Algorithm

3.1 RankBayes

We choose the Naïve Bayes algorithm in the pairwise learning to rank model due to its pretty good performance and fast training speed. What we need do is to prove it won't lead to ranking inconsistency. We define the phrase set as ($X = \{\overrightarrow{x_1}, \overrightarrow{x_2}, \dots, \overrightarrow{x_n}\}$) where $\overrightarrow{x_i}$ is a D-dimension feature vector for phrase x_i, if we suppose there are D features such as position, term frequency and so on. The vector difference $\overrightarrow{x_{i,j}} = \overrightarrow{x_i} - \overrightarrow{x_j}$ is usually used as the input of a binary classification function to determine the relative importance of two phrases x_i and x_j. To conform to the Naïve Bayes algorithm, through discretizing each dimension of the vector difference, we construct a set of new binary features F. For example, the maximum and minimum values of term frequency are 50 and 0 respectively, the frequency difference is thereby ranged from -50 to 50, and a binary feature can be designed as fd_10 , whose value is 1 if the term frequency difference equals to 10, 0 otherwise. Next, for the n phrases in X, we construct a set $X^* = \{\overrightarrow{x_{1,2}}, \dots, \overrightarrow{x_{1,n}}, \overrightarrow{x_{2,3}}, \dots, \overrightarrow{x_{n-1,n}}\}$ which comprises of $m = \frac{n(n-1)}{2}$ pairs of comparable phrases and $\overrightarrow{x_{i,j}}$ is a $|F|$-dimension binary feature vector. Then we construct the classification function $\Phi: X^* \rightarrow \{-1, 1\}$, where 1 means that phrase x_i has higher relative importance than x_j ($x_i \succ x_j$) denote the relative importance relation) while -1 means the opposite ($x_j \succ x_i$). Next we need to prove that the $\succ$ relation determined by the Naïve Bayes classification function is partial ordering. With the Naive Bayes algorithm, we get:

$$P(c|\overrightarrow{x_{i,j}}) \propto P(c) \prod_{x_{i,j}^{(f)}=1, 1 \le f \le |F|} P\left(x_{i,j}^{(f)} = 1|c\right) \quad (1)$$

where c means the class being 1, $x_{i,j}^{(f)} = 1$ represents one discretized feature of $\overrightarrow{x_{i,j}}$ with feature value as 1, and $|F|$ denotes the number of all binary features. We obtain for the log odd-ratio:

$$log \frac{P(c|\overrightarrow{x_{i,j}})}{P(\bar{c}|\overrightarrow{x_{i,j}})} = log \frac{P(c)}{P(\bar{c})} + \sum_{x_{i,j}^{(f)}=1, 1 \le f \le |F|} log \frac{P\left(x_{i,j}^{(f)}=1|c\right)}{P\left(x_{i,j}^{(f)}=1|\bar{c}\right)} \quad (2)$$

where $\bar{c}$ means not being classified to class c. It follows that class c is chosen if the log value is greater than 0, otherwise $\bar{c}$. According to the log equation, we can get a separating hyperplane:

$$\overrightarrow{W}^T \overrightarrow{x_{i,j}} = b$$

(3)

where $\overrightarrow{W}$ weights all the features with

$$W_{x_{i,j}^{(f)}} = log \frac{P\left(x_{i,j}^{(f)}=1|c\right)}{P\left(x_{i,j}^{(f)}=1|\bar{c}\right)}.$$

Since the phrase pairs are selected randomly, the probability of classifying to c or $\bar{c}$ is equal, and then the hyper-plane is further written as:

$$\overrightarrow{W}^T \overrightarrow{x_{i,j}} = 0 \quad (4)$$

Equation (4) shows that the Naïve Bayes classifier is linear for a pairwise learning to rank task. And we prove that the $\succ$ relation satisfies the properties of asymmetry and transitivity respectively as follows:

$$\overrightarrow{X_a} \succ \overrightarrow{X_b},\ \overrightarrow{X_a} \ne \overrightarrow{X_b} \Rightarrow \overrightarrow{W}^T(\overrightarrow{X_a} - \overrightarrow{X_b}) > 0 \Rightarrow \overrightarrow{W}^T(\overrightarrow{X_b} - \overrightarrow{X_a}) \ngtr 0 \Rightarrow \overrightarrow{X_b} \nsucc \overrightarrow{X_a}$$

$$\overrightarrow{X_a} \succ \overrightarrow{X_b},\ \overrightarrow{X_b} \succ \overrightarrow{X_c} \Rightarrow \overrightarrow{W}^T(\overrightarrow{X_a} - \overrightarrow{X_b}) > 0,\ \overrightarrow{W}^T(\overrightarrow{X_b} - \overrightarrow{X_c}) > 0$$

$$\Rightarrow \overrightarrow{W}^T(\overrightarrow{X_a} - \overrightarrow{X_c}) > 0 \Rightarrow \overrightarrow{X_a} \succ \overrightarrow{X_c}$$

#

That is to say, the $\succ$ relation is quasi-linear, which can sort all the objects naturally and consistently.

3.2 Co-training of Two RankBayes Models

During the co-training process, two RankBayes models update their training set L_1 and L_2 iteratively by adding some phrase pairs with relative importance relation labeled by the other RankBayes model, as illustrated in Step 3 and Step 4 of Figure 1. With L_1 and L_2 updated, two RankBayes models Φ_2 and Φ_1 are respectively tuned. First of all, we should select those most confidently labeled phrase pairs for refining the RankBayes models. As in Equation (2), during the kth iteration, Φ_1 labels the phrase pair $\overrightarrow{x_{i,j}^{(1)}}$ with:

$$S^{(1)}\left(\overrightarrow{x_{i,j}^{(1)}}\right) = log\frac{P\left(c|\overrightarrow{x_{i,j}^{(1)}}\right)}{P\left(\bar{c}|\overrightarrow{x_{i,j}^{(1)}}\right)} \quad (5)$$

and Φ_2 labels $\overrightarrow{x_{i,j}^{(2)}}$ with:

$$S^{(2)}\left(\overrightarrow{x_{i,j}^{(2)}}\right) = log\frac{P\left(c|\overrightarrow{x_{i,j}^{(2)}}\right)}{P\left(\bar{c}|\overrightarrow{x_{i,j}^{(2)}}\right)} \quad (6)$$

where $\overrightarrow{x_{i,j}^{(1)}}$ and $\overrightarrow{x_{i,j}^{(2)}}$ mean the feature vector represented respectively by the two RankBayes models. We call $S^{(1)}\left(\overrightarrow{x_{i,j}^{(1)}}\right)$ and $S^{(2)}\left(\overrightarrow{x_{i,j}^{(2)}}\right)$ as the confidence scores, whose sign (positive or negative) denotes one relative importance relation, and absolute value denotes the confidence degree of labeling the relation. Thus, we list the phrase pairs in decreasing order by the absolute values of the confidence scores, and select the top N phrase pairs for updating L_1 or L_2.

With training data updated, the two models changed iteration by iteration. Thus, even for one model, we cannot assure that the labeled results from different iterations are consistent. Then, in the updating process, L_1 and L_2 must be guaranteed their consistency as the training data of the next iteration. Since the updating of L_1 and L_2 are the same, we take L_2 as example. With the assumption that the phrase pairs entering into L_2 in earlier rounds are more confidently labeled than those in later rounds, we will not select those phrase pairs when they are not consistent with those pairs already in L_2. In our detailed implementation, we check each relative importance pair $x_i \succ x_j$ produced by Φ_1 using the recursive algorithm in Figure 2.

Algorithm 2: CheckInconsistency ($x_i \succ x_j$, L_2)

A set of labeled pairs in L_2, a phrase pair with the relative importance relation $x_i \succ x_j$. Return *True*, if inconsistency exists; *False*, otherwise.

If $x_i \prec x_j \in L_2$ return *True*
Loop for all phrase x_t in $\{ x_t \mid x_t \succ x_i \in L_2 \}$
  If CheckInconsistency($x_t \succ x_j$, L_2) = *True*
    return *True*
Loop end
Loop for all phrase x_t in $\{ x_t \mid x_j \succ x_t \in L_2 \}$
  If CheckInconsistency($x_i \succ x_t$, L_2) = True
    return *True*
Loop end
return *False*

Figure 2. Check Inconsistency Algorithm

3.3 Rank-Ordering Approach

After the co-training process, the performance of the two RankBayes models reaches their stable states, and both L_1 and L_2 include the phrase pairs most confidently labeled by Φ_2 and Φ_1. As not all the unlabeled pairs enter into L_2 and L_1, we use Φ_1 and Φ_2 to respectively label the phrase pairs left in U_1 and U_2, and add the labeled results to L_2 and L_1, just as Step 5 describes in Figure 1. Now, we know L_1 and L_2 respectively include $m = \frac{n(n-1)}{2}$ phrase pairs with confidence scores, which may have much inconsistency for the final ranking of all the phrases. Here we propose a simple and efficient approach to ignore the inconsistency and rank the n phrases. First, in L_1 and L_2 we respectively regularize the confidence scores by dividing the maximum absolute value of the confidence scores. It follows that the regularized values range from -1 to 1. Take any phrase pair < x_i, x_j > for example, its regularized confidence scores in L_1 and L_2 are named as $S_r^{(1)}(i,j)$ and $S_r^{(2)}(i,j)$ respectively. If these two values have the same sign: positive means that both the two models agree $x_i \succ x_j$ and negative means $x_j \succ x_i$, we will choose the one with the larger absolute value as the confidence score. If these two values have different signs meaning the two models disagree with each other, we reduce the confidence score by directly averaging these two values. Finally, we compute a new confidence score $S_r(i,j)$ for each pair <x_i , x_j>.

According to the final confidence scores, we calculate an importance score for each phrase. For a phrase pair <x_i, x_j> with $S_r(i,j)$, we think that $S_r(i,j)$ contributes to the importance scores of both x_i and x_j. Then the importance score of x_i is summed by adding $S_r(i,j)$ and the importance score of x_j is simultaneously subtracted from $S_r(i,j)$. In the same way, all the phrase pairs are traversed and each phrase gets its importance score, according to which all phrases are ranked and those higher ranked phrases are selected as keyphrases.

4. EXPERIMENTS

We use two datasets to evaluate our approach: Dataset 1 contains 244 scientific articles from Task 5 (named: Automatic keyphrase extraction from scientific articles) of SemEval-2[1], where 8 to 37 keyphrases are given as the standard answer for each document and the average number of the keyphrases is 15.1 per document; Dataset 2 is composed of 90 pieces of news, which we collect from well-known English media and manually label 1 to 8 keyphrases in each news document with the average number 4.6 keyphrases per document. To represent phrases, a set of commonly used features are designed as illustrated in Table 1. And we use Weka[2] to discretize the continuous features for getting binary features used in CoRankBayes.

Table 1. Feature Design

Feature	Description
TF	Term Frequency
IDF	Inverse document frequency
TF×IDF	Product of TF and IDF
ISF	Inverse sentence frequency
IfCap	If a candidate is capitalized
SentPos	Position of a candidate in the sentence
DocPos	Position of a candidate in the document
IfTitle	If the title contains the candidate

The micro-averaged Precision, Recall, F-measure metrics are adopted for evaluation. According to SemEval-2, we respectively evaluate the top 5(@5), top 10 (@10), top 15 (@10) candidates in the ranking list.

4.1 Experiments on Dataset 1

For scientific articles, it is often difficult to recognize the terminology so that we use the Stanford Parser[3] to parse the noun

[1] http://semeval2.fbk.eu/semeval2.php?location=tasks

[2] http://www.cs.waikato.ac.nz/ml/weka/

[3] http://nlp.stanford.edu/software/lex-parser.shtml

phrases (tagged as NN, NNS, NNP and NNPS[4]) for ranking. All the scientific articles are divided into: 144 articles as training data and 100 articles as test data. From the training data, we obtain 202,344 <keyphrase non-keyphrase> pairs as the initial labeling data for CoRankBayes. In each iteration, the number (N) of phrase pairs selected for updating L_1 and L_2 cannot be too large or too small and is assigned an experience value 100. We try to keep the independence of two RankBayes models, and choose 4 features (TF, IDF, TF × IDF, IfCap) for Φ_1 and 3 features (SentPos, DocPos, IfTitle) for Φ_2. For comparison, a RankBayes model and a linear Ranking SVM model are implemented to extract keyphrases using all the 7 features, and the two baselines (using Naïve Bayes and Maximum Entropy approaches respectively) provided by SemEval-2 are also given. In total, 1,830,371 phrase pairs need to be labeled where only 202,344 pairs have been labeled for all the models. Table 2 compares their training time[5], test time and F@15. We can see that the performance of RankBayes is similar to that of RankSVM since they both in nature adopt a linear classification strategy in the pairwise learning to rank models. And CoRankBayes reaches a satisfying performance with a tolerable speed after it further improves the RankBayes under the co-training framework.

Table 2. Performance Comparison on Dataset 1

	Train Time(s)	Test Time(s)	F@15
CoRankBayes	0	957	21.04%
RankBayes	53	348	19.96%
RankSVM	3,434	8,581	19.89%
Baseline1	-	-	14.70%
Baseline2	-	-	14.70%

To observe the co-training process, we control the iteration times K. Figure 3 displays the F@5, F@10, F@15 performance of the CoRankBayes model with K increasing. We can see that each RankBayes model improves itself by learning each other, and the combination approach furthermore promotes the performance.

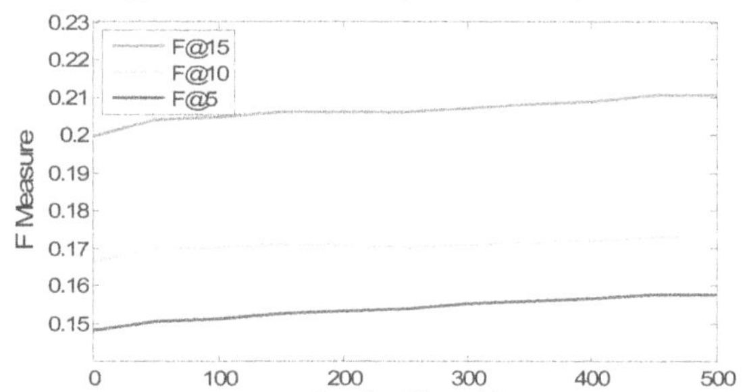

Figure 3. Performance with K Increasing

4.2 Experiments on Dataset 2

For news documents, the phrases are identified with the help of a dictionary which collects all the Wikipedia terms. The word sequences that occur in the dictionary are identified as phrases and a finite-state automaton is used to accomplish this task to avoid the imprecision of preprocessing by POS tagging or chunking. We choose 3 features (IDF, TF × IDF, ISF) for Φ_1 and 3 features (IfCap, DocPos, IfTitle) for Φ_2. 30 documents serve as training data, with 28,744 <keyphrase, non-keyphrase> pairs as the initial labeled data of CoRankBayes. Since the average of keyphrase number is no more than 5, we only evaluate the top 5 candidates. Table 3 compares CoRankBayes with other approaches, which shows RankBayes also has a similar performance with RankSVM and CoRankBayes can be easily transferred to other corpus, with a comparable performance.

Table 3. Performance Comparison on Dataset 2

	P@5	R@5	F@5
CoRankBayes	30.67%	33.45%	32.00%
RankBayes	29.67%	32.36%	30.96%
RankSVM	29.00%	31.63%	30.26%

5. CONCLUSIONS

In this paper, we propose the CoRankBayes model: a feasible co-training framework which combines two Naïve Bayes based learning to rank models. We prove that the Naïve Bayes algorithm can be used to implement a learning to rank model with a fast speed. To solve the two-model inconsistency, an ingenious approach is proposed to rank all the phrases by using the labeling confidence of two RankBayes models. Experimental results also show CoRankBayes is promising in solving ranking problems.

6. ACKNOWLEDGEMENTS

This research was supported in part by the National Science Foundation of China grants (No: 60875042 and 90920011), National Social Science Foundation grant (No: 10CYY023).

7. REFERENCE

[1] Blum, A. and Mitchell, T.. 1998. *Combining Labeled and Unlabeled Data with Co-Training.* In Proceedings of the eleventh annual conference on Computational learning theory, NY, USA.

[2] Herbrich, R., Graepel, T., and Obermayer, K.. 2000. *Large Margin Rank Boundaries for Ordinal Regression.* Advances in Large Margin Classifiers, 115–332.

[3] Jiang, X., Hu, Y., and Li, H. 2009. A Ranking Approach to Keyphrase Extraction. In proceedings of SIGIR 2009.

[4] Joachims, T. 2002. *Optimizing search engines using clickthrough data.* In Proceedings of the eighth ACM SIGKDD international conference on Knowledge discovery and data mining, NY, USA.

[5] Tan, Q., Chai, X., Ng, W. and Lee, D.L. 2004. *Applying Co-training to Clickthrough Data for Search Engine Adaptation.* In Lecture Notes in Computer Science, Volume 2973/2004, 519-532.

[6] Turney, P.D. 1999. *Learning to Extract Keyphrases from Text.* Technical Report ERB-1057, National Research Council, Institute for Information Technology.

[7] Witten, I.H., Paynter, G.W., Frank, E., Gutwin, C., and Nevill-Manning, C.G. 1999. *Kea: Practical Automatic Keyphrase Extraction.* In Proceedings of the 4th ACM Conference on Digital Libraries.

[8] Zhao, C., Yan, J. and Liu, N. 2008. *Improve Web Search Ranking by Co-Ranking SVM.* In proceedings of Fourth International Conference on Natural Computation.

---

[4] http://www.comp.leeds.ac.uk/amalgam/tagsets/upenn.html

[5] Hardware: Inter ® Core™ i5-540M Processor, 4GB RAM

Discovering Trending Phrases on Information Streams

Krishna Y. Kamath
Texas A&M University
College Station, TX 77843
kykamath@cs.tamu.edu

James Caverlee
Texas A&M University
College Station, TX 77843
caverlee@cse.tamued.u

ABSTRACT

We study the problem of efficient discovery of trending phrases from high-volume text streams – be they sequences of Twitter messages, email messages, news articles, or other time-stamped text documents. Most exisiting approaches return top-k trending phrases. But, this approach neither guarantees that the top-k phrases returned are all trending, nor that all trending phrases are returned. In addition, the value of k is difficult to set and is indifferent to stream dynamics. Hence, we propose an approach that identifies all the trending phrases in a stream and is flexible to the changing stream properties.

Categories and Subject Descriptors: H.3.4 [**Information Storage and Retrieval**]: Systems and Software—*Current awareness systems*

General Terms: Algorithms, Experimentation

Keywords: trending phrases, social media, real-time web

1. INTRODUCTION

High-volume text information streams have grown at an astonishing rate in the past several years. As one example, Twitter has rapidly grown from handling 5,000 tweets per day in 2007 to 50 million tweets per day in 2010 to 140 million per tweets per day in 2011. Making sense of these high-volume text streams offers rich opportunities and there is a growing body of research aimed at mining these streams, e.g., [3, 7, 8, 9]. In this paper, we explore the possibility of extracting trending phrases from these streams for understanding the relationship among phrases, topics, and keywords as they rapidly evolve over time.

2. RELATED WORK

The database community has long studied stream operations, like finding aggregates on time-ordered data streams, say for performing counts, calculating averages, and so forth about stream objects. The *trending phrase discovery* approach at the core of the method described in this paper is similar to the frequent items (FI) finding problem. In the FI problem, a data structure maintains the score of objects seen on the stream, with which the top-k items may be determined. Cormode and Hadjieleftheriou in [3] give details of several algorithms that have been proposed for the FI problem. Based on [3], the solutions to the FI problem can be split into counter-based algorithms [9, 7, 8], quantile algorithms [5, 10] and sketches [2]. Several approaches have been proposed to deal with a variant of the FI problem that decays items over time using a sliding window [4, 1, 6]. We will describe later in the paper how FI problem is different from the problem we are dealing with.

CIKM'11, October 24–28, 2011, Glasgow, Scotland, UK.

3. TRENDING PHRASES DISCOVERY

In this section, we first describe some concepts and then formally define the trending phrases discovery problem. We then propose our solution to this problem using trend threshold parameters.

DEFINITION 3.1. ***(Information Stream)*** *An information stream $D = \{(d_1, t_1), (d_2, t_1), (d_3, t_2) \ldots\}$ is an ordered set of document tuples. The stream D is of infinite size and is ordered in a non-decreasing fashion by time-stamp values of the documents. Note that, there might be multiple documents in the stream that share the same time-stamp.*

Examples of streams that satisfy this property are high volume sequence of Twitter messages, email messages, news articles, or other time-stamped text documents. Our ultimate goal is to map from a stream to a time-sensitive concept hierarchy reflecting the relationship among concepts for a particular degree of temporal granularity (e.g., by minute, hour, or day):

DEFINITION 3.2. ***(Candidate Phrase)*** *Consider a document $d \in D$, where $|d|$ equal to the number of terms in the document. Let P_k be a set of phrases of length k. Then, d can be represented using the set of phrases $P = P_1 \cup P_2 \cup \cdots \cup P_{|d|}$. Such a phrase $p \in P$ is called a candidate phrase and the set of all the candidate phrases, observed in the information stream up until time t, is denoted C_t.*

For example, the document "Packers win Superbowl" can be represented by P = {"packers", "win", "superbowl", "packers win", "win superbowl", "packers win superbowl"}. The phrases "superbowl", "packers win", etc are examples of candidate phrases and $P \subseteq C$. A single candidate phrase p may appear multiple times in the stream. Each such instance of the phrase p_i is called a *candidate phrase instance*. For example, consider the document tuples ("Packers win", t_1) and ("Champions packers ", t_2). In this case, the candidate phrase "packers" has two instances each with time-stamp t_1 and t_2 respectively. Similarly, "win" and "champions" have single instances.

PROBLEM 1. ***(Trending Phrases Discovery Problem)*** *Given an infinite information stream D and the set of candidate phrases C_t observed in D, the trending phrases discovery problem is to identify the subset of phrases $\Gamma_t \subseteq C_t$ that are trending at time t.*

One straightforward solution approach is to map this problem to the frequent items finding (FI) problem, where the item score decay with time, and select top-k items as trending phrases. But this approach neither guarantees that the top-k phrases returned are all trending, nor that all trending phrases are returned. In addition, the value of k is difficult to set and is indifferent to stream dynamics. Hence, we propose an approach that identifies all the trending phrases in a stream and is flexible to the changing stream properties.

3.1 Our Solution

The approach we take to identify trending phrases is to associate with each candidate phrase p a score at a particular time $S(p,t)$ and to keep only phrases with a score greater than some threshold, where the threshold may vary in time (as the stream becomes more or less bursty, or as more phrases become "activated"). The challenge is to compute this score efficiently (ideally O(1) time).

Formally, every candidate phrase instance p_i is associated with a score, that decreases as the phrase ages, and a time-stamp t_i of the document in which the instance was observed. The score $S(p_i,t)$ for p_i at time t is given by:

$$S(p_i,t) = \lambda_c^{t-t_i} \qquad (1)$$

where $\lambda_c \in (0,1)$ is a constant know as the *phrase score decay rate*. In a stream we can observe several instances of a candidate phrase p. Let $E(p,t)$ be the set of all the instances of p that have been observed until time t. Then, the *candidate phrase score* at t, $S(p,t)$ is defined as the sum of all the candidate phrase instances of P.

$$S(p,t) = \sum_{p_i \in E(p,t)} S(p_i,t) = \sum_{p_i \in E(p,t)} \lambda_c^{t-t_i}$$

Unfortunately, this definition of $S(p,t)$ requires all of the previous observed instances $E(p,t)$ for p and its calculation takes $O(|E(p,t)|)$ time, which is inefficient for high-volume text information streams with a large number of candidate phrases. However, we can prove a proposition that will help us calculate this score efficiently in O(1) time and does not have the requirement of storing $E(p,t)$. The proof of the proposition is dropped because of space constraints.

PROPOSITION 3.1. *Given a candidate phrase p with score $S(p,t_l)$ at time t_l, if a phrase instance p_i for p is observed at time t_n, where $t_n > t_l$ then the new score for p at t_n, $S(p,t_n)$ is given as:*

$$S(p,t_n) = \lambda_c^{t_n-t_l} S(p,t_l) + 1$$

Given the scores for all candidate phrases, we can easily determine if a candidate phrase p is a trending phrase if its score is greater than a *trending threshold* θ_{tt}, which yields the set of all trending phrases Γ_t:

$$\Gamma_t = \{p \mid S(p,t) \geq \theta_{tt} \forall p \in C_t\} \qquad (2)$$

Note that the value of θ_{tt} is dependent on the number of candidate phrases in C_t and so can vary with the temporal changes in the information stream.

For example, Figure 1(a) shows the scores for two candidate phrases "super bowl" and "Grammys" over time. To keep the example simple we assume that the phrase rate in the information stream does not change and hence the value of θ_{tt} is unchanged. So, using (2) we have, Γ_{t_1} = {"super bowl"}, Γ_{t_2} = {"super bowl", "Grammys"} and Γ_{t_3} = {"Grammys'}.

Pruning Candidate Phrases: In real-world applications, the number of candidate phrases C_t can become very large, meaning that finding Γ using (2) will become expensive. Hence, we can further prune the set of candidate phrases using a *pruning threshold* θ_{pt} , where $C'_t \subseteq C_t$. Like the trending threshold, the pruning threshold is also dependent on C_t. Using the candidate phrase score, the two thresholds – θ_{tt} and θ_{pt} – divide the candidate phrases C_t into 3 disjoint sets: (i) trending; (ii) transitional; and (iii) non-trending. An example of this is shown in Figure 1(a). Though the candidate phrases to prune are in the non-trending set, not all the phrases in this set can be pruned since the candidate phrases that are in the non-trending set can either be trending up or trending down. Figure 1(a) shows both the cases for the phrase "Super bowl".

The phrases to be pruned are the ones that are trending down, but we cannot determine the direction of the trend just based on the candidate phrase score. Hence, we adopt a heuristic to prune the candidate phrases. For a candidate phrase $p \in C_t$ that is in the non-trending set we use the last time a phrase instance of p was observed, t_p to decide if it should be pruned. To determine C'_t, we propose two approaches that use t_p: (i) a deterministic approach; and (ii) a randomized approach. Both approaches also use a parameter *maximum phrase inactivity time* T_{pi}.

Using the deterministic approach C' is defined as follows:

$$C'_t = \{p \mid S(p,t) \leq \theta_{pt} \ and \ (t - t_p) \geq T_{pi} \ \forall p \in C_t\} \qquad (3)$$

The randomized approach uses a function $R(p,t)$ $\forall p \in C_t$ defined as:

$$R(p,t) = \begin{cases} 0 & \text{if } t - t_p < T_{pi} \\ 1 & \text{if } t - t_p \geq 2T_{pi} \\ coinFlip(\frac{t-t_p}{2T_{pi}}) & \text{Otherwise} \end{cases}$$

where, $coinFlip : [0,1] \rightarrow \{0,1\}$, is a function where the probability of 1 increases as input is closer to 1. Now, C'_t is defined as follows:

$$C'_t = \{p \mid S(p,t) \leq \theta_{pt} \ and \ R(p,t) = 1 \ \forall p \in C_t\} \qquad (4)$$

3.2 Trend Threshold Parameters

In the previous section we showed how we can efficiently identify trending phrases given some stream-dependent threshold parameters θ_{tt} and θ_{pt}. But how are these parameters determined in the first place? A poor selection can impact the quality and efficiency of concept extraction. A high value

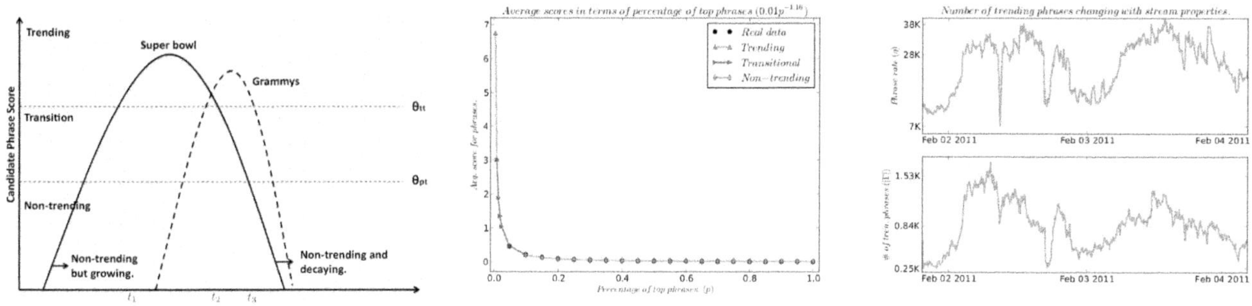

(a) Examples for trending phrases discovery problem.

(b) Phrase scores distribution

(c) Tren. phrases changing with stream

Figure 1

of θ_{tt} may result in false negatives (i.e., incorrectly excluding from concept hierarchy generation a legitimately important concept), while a low value for θ_{tt} may result in false positives (i.e., incorrectly including non-trending phrase concepts). Similarly, a low value of θ_{pt} can result in a large set of candidate phrases C_t making the determination of Γ expensive, while a large value of θ_{pt} results in removal of phrases that could trend in the future, thereby reducing the quality of the results.

Hence, it is important that these trend threshold parameters by determined carefully. Concretely, we first state a lemma that gives us the upper bound on the sum of scores for all the candidate phrase instances that have been observed on the information stream. We will state a theorem, which can be proved using the lemma, that guides the determination of thresholds. The proof of the lemma and theorem are dropped because of space constraints.

LEMMA 3.1. *Given an information stream D with a phrase rate of η and the set of all candidate phrase instances P_t that have been observed on D during time intervals $0, 1, ...t$, we have:*

$$\sum_{p_i \in P_t} S(p_i, t) \leq \frac{\eta}{1-\lambda_c} \quad \text{and} \quad \lim_{t \to \infty} \sum_{p_i \in P_t} S(p_i, t) = \frac{\eta}{1-\lambda_c}$$

THEOREM 3.1. *Given an information stream D at a phrase rate η and the set of candidate phrases C_t at time t, the trending threshold θ_{tt} and the pruning threshold θ_{pt} are given as:*

$$\theta_{tt} = \frac{\eta S_t}{|C_t|(1-\lambda_c)} \quad \text{and} \quad \theta_{pt} = \frac{\eta S_p}{|C_t|(1-\lambda_c)}$$

where, $S_t > 1$ and $S_p < S_t$ are stream specific constants.

To summarize, this section has shown how we can efficiently identify the significant base conceptual units (phrases) from an information stream. The two critical trend threshold parameters guiding this identification can be calculated with little overhead and can be tailored for stream and application-specific properties.

4. EXPERIMENTS

In this experiments section, our goal is to see if we can discover trending phrases over a real high-volume text information stream. We want to see if we can estimate the stream parameters required to do such discovery and analyze the properties of the trending phrases discovered.

We begin by examining the algorithm presented in Section 3 to extract trending phrases. Recall that the algorithm requires threshold parameters θ_{tt} and θ_{pt} to determine which phrases to extract, and that these parameters are dependent on stream-specific constants S_t and S_p, respectively. We use a sample of 3.4 million Twitter messages collected from the Twitter Streaming API, resulting in 640 messages per minute.

Phrase Score Distribution: First, we analyze the distribution of phrase scores in a sample from the trending topic stream, updating the phrase scores using equation Proposition 3.1. How are these scores distributed? Our goal is to identify a reasonable expected split for trending, transitional, and non-trending phrases (Recall Figure 1(a)).

We set the phrase score decay rate $\lambda_c = 0.80$ and process the stream for 2.5 hours (150 minutes), noting down the phrase scores in C_t every 5 minutes. We then take these 30 sets of phrase scores and sort all of them to calculate the average phrase scores at different levels of top phrases as shown in Figure 1(b). Based on this figure we see that the scores follow a skewed distribution, with most phrases having very low scores (and hence, being of less importance at a particular time in the stream). Based on this score distribution, we fix the following split: (i) Trending (green): top-0.5% phrases (ii) Transitional (blue): middle 0.5 – 10% phrases (iii) Non-trending (red): bottom 90%.[1]

Parameter Estimation: With these splits in mind, we next estimate the stream-specific constants S_t and S_p which guide the threshold parameters θ_{tt} and θ_{pt} for trending phrase discovery as the stream rate (and burstiness) changes over time. To estimate the value of S_t we process the messages from the trending topic stream, and for every 5 minutes interval, we calculate the percentage of phrases above θ_{tt}, calculated using Theorem 3.1. We calculate θ_{tt} for different values of S_t. The values for η and C_t are obtained from the stream, and we set the phrase score decay rate $\lambda_c = 0.80$. The variation of percentage of trending phrases above θ_{tt} with S_t is shown in Figure 2(a). Using this curve we get S_t as a function of the percentage of trending phrases p.

$$S_t = \left(\frac{10.71}{p}\right)^{\frac{1}{2.61}}$$

[1] Note that the choice of split is application-dependent. For clarity of presentation in the rest of the paper we select these guideposts for trending phrase discovery.

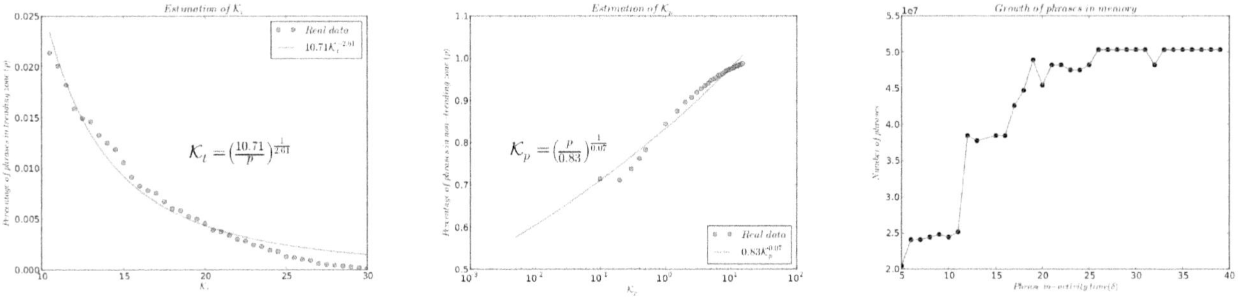

(a) Estimation of S_t (b) Estimation of S_p (c) Estimation of T_{pi}

Figure 2: Parameter estimation.

Hence, if our goal is to consider the top-0.5% of phrases as trending phrases, then for $p = 0.005$ we have the stream-specific constant $S_t = 18.96$.

Similar to S_t, to can calculate S_p over the stream by calculating θ_{pt} for different values of S_p (according to Theorem 3.1). At every 5 minutes interval, we calculate the percentage of phrases that are below θ_{pt}. The variation of percentage of top phrases below θ_{pt} with S_p is shown in Figure 2(b). Using this curve we get S_p as a function of percentage of trending phrases p.

$$S_p = \left(\frac{p}{0.83}\right)^{\frac{1}{0.07}}$$

Hence, for a choice of 90% phrases as non-trending, we have for $p = 0.9$ a score of $S_p = 3.02$.

The values we determined for S_t and S_p are interesting because, using the definitions for threshold parameters θ_{tt} and θ_{pt}, defined in Theorem 3.1, we realize that phrases that have a score more than 19 times the average score are trending while phrases that have score lesser than 3 times the average score can be pruned.

Finally, recall that the set of candidate phrases C_t can be pruned occasionally to remove inactive phrases. The last parameter to be estimated is the maximum phrase inactivity time T_{pi} which guides this pruning. If T_{pi} is low, then the phrases are not allowed to trend, while if it is very high C_t could become too large. Hence, we show in Figure 2(c) the variation of the size of C_t with increasing T_{pi}. We see that the choice of T_{pi} results in a quasi-stepwise change in C_t, and so for this case a choice of $T_{pi} = 7$ minutes would result in a smaller C_t with confidence that the choice is fairly stable.

Stream Properties Vs Trending Phrases: To verify the robustness of our approach to changing stream properties, we observe the number of trending phrases identified by our approach as the input stream changes. This comparison is shown in Figure 1(c). The top plot in the figure shows variation of phrase rate in the input stream for 2 days. We observe that the number of trending phrases identified for concept hierarchy detection (shown in the bottom plot of the figure) correlates with top plot, since the trending threshold θ_{tt} is defined as a function of the phrase rate η.

Sample Trending Phrases: A sample of trending phrases discovered during the first week of Feb, 2011 is shown in Table 1.

Day	Trends
2011-02-01	fernando torres, jan25, human rights
2011-02-02	mubarak, tcyasi, news
2011-02-03	cairo, news, square
2011-02-04	imgood, search google, super bowl
2011-02-05	search google, cowboys, bielsa
2011-02-06	church lady, femme fatale, jon jones
2011-02-06	sb45, chelsea liverpool, lil wayne
2011-02-07	christina aguilera, tomlin, darth vader

Table 1: Sample trend for first week of Feb, 2011

5. CONCLUSION

We have studied the problem of efficient discovery of trending phrases from high volume text information streams. We have seen how the proposed method can efficiently identify significant phrases from high-volume information streams. For our future work we are interested in developing applications that use the solution proposed in this paper to discover trending phrases. In this table, we observe various events of the week like Middle East revolution, Super Bowl, transfer of Fernando Torres to Chelsea from Liverpool, etc.

6. REFERENCES

[1] A. Arasu. Approximate counts and quantiles over sliding windows. In *In PODS*, pages 286–296, 2004.

[2] M. Charikar, K. Chen, and M. Farach-Colton. Finding frequent items in data streams. In *Proceedings of International Colloquium on Automata, Languages and Programming*, ICALP '02. Springer-Verlag, 2002.

[3] G. Cormode and M. Hadjieleftheriou. Methods for finding frequent items in data streams. *The VLDB Journal*, 19:3–20, February 2010.

[4] M. Datar, A. Gionis, P. Indyk, and R. Motwani. Maintaining stream statistics over sliding windows (extended abstract), 2002.

[5] M. Greenwald and S. Khanna. Space-efficient online computation of quantile summaries. In *In SIGMOD*, pages 58–66, 2001.

[6] L. K. Lee and H. F. Ting. A simpler and more efficient deterministic scheme for finding frequent items over sliding windows. PODS '06, pages 290–297, 2006.

[7] G. S. Manku and R. Motwani. Approximate frequency counts over data streams, 2002.

[8] A. Metwally, D. Agrawal, and A. E. Abbadi. Efficient computation of frequent and top-k elements in data streams. In *IN ICDT*, pages 398–412, 2005.

[9] J. Misra and D. Gries. Finding repeated elements. Technical report, Ithaca, NY, USA, 1982.

[10] N. Shrivastava, C. Buragohain, D. Agrawal, and S. Suri. Medians and beyond: New aggregation techniques for sensor networks. pages 239–249. ACM Press, 2004.

Review Recommendation: Personalized Prediction of the Quality of Online Reviews

Samaneh Moghaddam
School of Computing Science
Simon Fraser University
Burnaby, BC, Canada
sam39@cs.sfu.ca

Mohsen Jamali
School of Computing Science
Simon Fraser University
Burnaby, BC, Canada
sja25@cs.sfu.ca

Martin Ester
School of Computing Science
Simon Fraser University
Burnaby, BC, Canada
ester@cs.sfu.ca

ABSTRACT

The problem of identifying high quality and helpful reviews automatically has attracted many attention recently. Current methods assume that the helpfulness of a review is independent from the readers of that review. However, we argue that the quality of a review may not be the same for different users. In this paper, we employ latent factor models to address this problem. We evaluate the proposed models using a real life database from Epinions.com. The experiments demonstrate that the latent factor models outperform the state-of-the-art approaches and confirms that the helpfulness of a review is indeed not the same for all users.

Categories and Subject Descriptors

H.2.8.d [**Information Technology and System**]: Database Application—*Data Miming*; G.3 [**Mathematics of Computing**]: Probability and Statistics—*Statistical Computing, Multivariate Statistics*

General Terms

Algorithms, Design, Experimentation

Keywords

Personalized Review Quality Prediction, Review Recommendation, Matrix Factorization, Tensor Factorization

1. INTRODUCTION

Other people's opinions have always played an important role in decision-making process. As online commerce activity continues to grow, the role of online reviews is expected to become increasingly important [7, 8]. However, due to the fact that most online reviews are written by non-professional authors, they tend to be of very different quality. The growing importance of online reviews in the purchasing decision making process of users has also led to the creation of an ever growing number of spam reviews, which try to mislead online users. Given the huge number of online reviews available and their greatly varying quality, it becomes more and more difficult to find high-quality, helpful reviews.

Most previous works [3, 4, 11] attempt to predict the quality of reviews by extracting textual features (e.g. total number of tokens, ratio of nouns, adjectives, etc.) and learning a function of these features for predicting review quality. There are also some recent works [5, 10] utilizing social features (e.g. number of past reviews by reviewer, PageRank of the reviewer, etc.) in addition to the textual features to assess the quality of reviews.

To the best of our knowledge, all of the existing methods assume that the helpfulness of a review is the same for all users and determine the quality of a review in general (i.e. in a user unspecific way). However, this assumption may not be true in all cases. We argue that the quality of the same review may not be the same for different users. For example, a professional and an amateur photographer may rate the helpfulness of a review very differently because of their different evaluation criteria. We believe differences in the users' criteria may result in different evaluations of a review.

In this paper, we introduce the new problem of personalized review quality prediction for recommendation of helpful reviews. To address this problem, we employ two latent factor models based on the assumption that the observed review ratings depend on latent features of the reviews, reviewers, raters, and products. We first present a model based on probabilistic Matrix Factorization (MF) (Section 2.1). The underlying assumption of this model is that both reviews and raters (review readers) can be modeled by a set of latent features. The MF model personalizes review quality prediction by decomposing the $rater \times review$ matrix and learning latent factors for each rater and each review. We also employ the concept of Tensor Factorization (TF) (Section 2.2). The TF based model assumes that the latent feature vector of each review is generated in a probabilistic way by aggregating the latent feature vector of its reviewer and the latent feature vector of the corresponding product (since each review is written by a reviewer about a product). That is, the $rater \times review$ two-dimensional matrix is converted into a three-dimensional tensor $rater \times reviewer \times product$.

We empirically verify that the TF model improves MF, which does not take into account the product and reviewer factors. In addition, our experiments demonstrate that latent factor models outperform the state-of-the-art non-personalized approaches using textual and social features. Thus,

CIKM'11, October 24–28, 2011, Glasgow, Scotland, UK.

our experiments confirm that the helpfulness of a review is indeed not the same for all users, and there are some latent factors that affect a user's evaluation of review quality.

2. PROBABILISTIC FACTOR MODELS

In this section, we present two factor models for estimating review quality: A probabilistic matrix factorization (MF) model, and a tensor factorization (TF) model. Note that, while MF and TF have already been used in the literature for item recommendation [1, 2], these methods have not yet been explored for review recommendation.

In the following models, p, v, u, and r denote the latent variables for product, reviewer, rater, and review, respectively.

2.1 Matrix Factorization Model

In this section we employ MF to factorize the *rater* $\times$ *review* matrix for predicting review quality. The underlying assumption of this model is that both raters and reviews can be modeled by a set of latent features, which together determine the rating of a review in a probabilistic way.

Suppose we have a set of N_u raters and a set of N_r reviews. The quality ratings expressed by raters on reviews are given in a matrix $q = [q_{ij}]_{N_u \times N_r}$. In this matrix q_{ij} represents the quality rating of rater u_i for review r_j. q_{ij} can be any real number, but often ratings are integers in the range $[1, 5]$. In this paper, without loss of generality, we map the ratings to the interval $[0, 1]$ by normalizing the ratings. Let $u \in \mathbb{R}^{K \times N_u}$ and $r \in \mathbb{R}^{K \times N_r}$ be latent rater and review feature matrices, with column vector u_i representing K-dimensional rater-specific latent feature vectors of rater u_i and column vector r_j representing K-dimensional review-specific latent feature vectors of review r_j. The goal of MF is to learn these latent variables and exploit them for recommendation. The conditional probability of the observed ratings in our MF model is defined as:

$$P(q|u, r, \sigma_q^2) = \prod_i^{N_u} \prod_j^{N_r} [\mathcal{N}(q_{ij}|g(u_i^T r_j), \sigma_q^2)]^{I_{ij}^q} \quad (1)$$

where $\mathcal{N}(x|\mu, \sigma^2)$ is the probability density function of the Gaussian distribution with mean μ and variance σ^2, and I_{ij}^q is the indicator function that is equal to 1 if rater u_i rates review r_j (q_{ij} is observed) and equal to 0 otherwise. The function $g(x)$ is the logistic function $g(x) = 1/(1+exp(-x))$, which bounds the range of $u_i^T r_j$ within $[0, 1]$. We also place a zero-mean spherical Gaussian prior on rater and review feature vectors:

$$P(u|\sigma_u^2) = \prod_i^{N_u} \mathcal{N}(u_i|0, \sigma_u^2 \mathbf{I}) \quad (2)$$

$$P(r|\sigma_r^2) = \prod_j^{N_r} \mathcal{N}(r_j|0, \sigma_r^2 \mathbf{I}) \quad (3)$$

Through a Bayesian inference, the log of the posterior distribution over rater and review features can be obtained as follows:

$$\begin{aligned} \ln P(u, r|q, \sigma_q^2, \sigma_u^2, \sigma_r^2) = \\ -\frac{1}{2\sigma_q^2} \sum_i^{N_u} \sum_j^{N_r} I_{ij}^q (q_{ij} - g(u_i^T r_j))^2 - \frac{1}{2\sigma_u^2} \sum_i^{N_u} u_i^T u_i \\ -\frac{1}{2\sigma_r^2} \sum_j^{N_r} r_j^T r_j - \frac{1}{2} (\sum_i^{N_u} \sum_j^{N_r} I_{ij}^q) \ln \sigma_q^2 \\ -\frac{1}{2}(N_u \times K) \ln \sigma_u^2 - \frac{1}{2}(N_r \times K) \ln \sigma_r^2 + C \quad (4) \end{aligned}$$

where C is a constant that does not depend on the parameters. Maximizing the log-posterior over latent rater and review variables with hyper-parameters kept fixed is equivalent to minimizing the following sum-of-squared-errors loss function with regularization terms:

$$\begin{aligned} E_{MF} = \frac{1}{2} \sum_i^{N_u} \sum_j^{N_r} I_{ij}^q (q_{ij} - g(u_i^T r_j))^2 \\ + \frac{\lambda_u}{2} \sum_i^{N_u} \|u_i\|_{Fro}^2 + \frac{\lambda_r}{2} \sum_j^{N_r} \|r_j\|_{Fro}^2 \quad (5) \end{aligned}$$

where $\lambda_u = \sigma_q^2/\sigma_u^2$, $\lambda_r = \sigma_q^2/\sigma_r^2$ and $\|.\|_{Fro}^2$ denotes the Frobenius norm. A local minimum of this objective function can be found by performing stochastic gradient descent.

2.2 Tensor Factorization Model

In this section, we employ TF to personalize review quality prediction. The underlying assumption of our model is that since each review is written by a reviewer about a product, the latent feature vector of a review can be generated in a probabilistic way by aggregating the latent feature vector of its reviewer and the latent feature vector of the corresponding product. That is, the *rater* $\times$ *review* two-dimensional matrix used as input in MF is converted into three-dimensional tensor *rater* $\times$ *reviewer* $\times$ *product*. Note that, in contrast to most of the TF-based recommendation system approaches which add a third dimension to the traditional user-item matrix, we propose to replace the *review* dimension in MF with *reviewer* $\times$ *product* in TF.

Suppose we have a set of N_u raters, a set of N_v reviewers, and a set of N_p products. The quality ratings expressed by raters on reviews written by reviewers about different products are given in a three-dimensional tensor $q = [q_{ijk}]_{N_u \times N_v \times N_p}$. In this tensor q_{ijk} represents the quality rating of rater u_i for the review written by reviewer v_j about product p_k. The three-dimensional tensor is factorized into three matrices and one central tensor. Let $u \in \mathbb{R}^{K \times N_u}$, $v \in \mathbb{R}^{K \times N_v}$, and $p \in \mathbb{R}^{K \times N_p}$ be latent rater, reviewer, and product feature matrices, with column vector u_i representing K-dimensional rater-specific latent feature vector of rater u_i, column vector v_j representing K-dimensional reviewer-specific latent feature vector of reviewer v_j, and column vector p_k representing K-dimensional product-specific latent feature vector of product p_k. Let also $s \in \mathbb{R}^{K \times K \times K}$ be the central tensor where K is the dimension of the model latent factors. The goal of tensor factorization is to learn these latent variables and exploit them for rating prediction. Given the feature matrices and the central tensor, the prediction can be made as follows:

$$h_{ijk} = \sum_{x=1}^{K}\sum_{y=1}^{K}\sum_{z=1}^{K} s_{xyz} u_{ix} v_{jy} p_{kz} \quad (6)$$

where h_{ijk} is the predicted value for q_{ijk}. To simplify Equation 6, we use the tensor-matrix product operator $\times_a$ to multiply a matrix on dimension a with a tensor [2], e.g. $t = s \times_u u_i$ is a $K \times K$ matrix where $t_{yz} = \sum_{x=1}^{K} s_{xyz} u_{ix}$. So, the prediction is made by multiplying the three feature matrices and the central tensor:

$$h_{ijk} = s \times_u u_i \times_v v_j \times_p p_k \quad (7)$$

Similar to MF, we minimize the sum-of-squared-errors between the observed rating q_{ijk} and the predicted rating $g(h_{ijk})$ [2]. We also add regularization terms to avoid overfitting. So, the objective function for the minimization problem is as follows:

$$\begin{aligned} E_{TF} = \frac{1}{2}\sum_{i}^{N_u}\sum_{j}^{N_v}\sum_{k}^{N_p} I_{ijk}^{q}(q_{ijk} - g(h_{ijk}))^2 \\ + \frac{\lambda_u}{2}\sum_{i}^{N_u}\|u_i\|_{Fro}^2 + \frac{\lambda_v}{2}\sum_{j}^{N_v}\|v_j\|_{Fro}^2 \\ + \frac{\lambda_p}{2}\sum_{k}^{N_p}\|p_k\|_{Fro}^2 + \frac{\lambda_s}{2}\sum_{ijk}\|s_{ijk}\|_{Fro}^2 \end{aligned} \quad (8)$$

where I_{ijk}^{q} is the indicator function that is equal to 1 if q_{ijk} is observed (i.e. rater u_i rates the review written by reviewer v_j about product p_k) and equal to 0 otherwise. The function $g(x)$ is the logistic function defined in Section 2.1 which bound the range of h_{ijk} within $[0, 1]$. Again, to minimize the objective function, we perform stochastic gradient descent.

3. EXPERIMENTAL EVALUATION

In this section, we describe the real-life dataset we used for our experiments and present the results of our experimental evaluation and comparison with state-of-the-art methods.

3.1 Dataset

To evaluate the proposed models, we performed experiments on a dataset from the popular reviewing website Epinions.com. Epinions.com is a consumers opinion website where users can write reviews about products (such as digital cameras, laptops, books, movies, software, etc.) and assign them numeric ratings in the range from 1 to 5. It also allows users to express their feedback about the helpfulness of a review using numeric quality ratings. We used the version of the Epinions' dataset[1] published by the authors of [6]. This dataset was given directly by Epinions staff to the authors and, different from other publicly available Epinions datasets, contains ratings of reviews assigned by different users. This dataset does not have the text of the reviews, but it provides the review identifiers. We enhanced this dataset by downloading the review text from the Epinions website (using the available identifiers). This dataset is very large and covers a very wide range of more than 200,000 products from different categories which can be considered as a collection of several review datasets.

[1] http://www.trustlet.org/wiki/Extended_Epinions_dataset

Table 1: Statistics of the dataset

#Reviews	1,560,144
#Products	200,953
#Reviewers	326,983
#Raters	120,492
#Rated Reviews	755,760
#Ratings	13,668,320

Table 1 presents some statistics of our Epinions dataset. We can see that about 50% of the reviews have been rated by at least one rater. It is also shown that on average each rated review has been rated by 18 different raters which indicates the richness of this dataset.

3.2 Experimental Setup

As pointed out already, all of the current works have formulated the problem of determining review quality as a classification or regression problem using a set of observed features, i.e. textual and/or social features. Classification-based approaches mainly employ SVM for classifying reviews [10, 4]. Our proposed models, on the other hand, predict real-value ratings which cannot be compared with the classification results. For a fair comparison, we use the regression version of SVM, Support Vector Regression (SVR), which is also used in some regression-based approaches [3, 11]. Since other regression-based approaches mainly apply Linear Regression (LR) [5, 11] to predict the quality rating of reviews, we use LR as another comparison partner.

Each of the current works has defined a set of features to predict the quality of reviews. Most of them only use textual features [3, 4, 11] , while some of them combined both textual and social features [5, 10, 9]. Our proposed models do not use observed features, however our comparison partners need them to be learned. We use textual and social features defined in the most recent work [5] to implement our comparison partners. Textual features include total number of tokens and sentences, ratio of positive and negative sentiment words, ratio of verbs, adverbs, etc. Social features include number of past reviews by the reviewer, in-degree and out-degree of the reviewer, PageRank score of the reviewer, etc. For the sake of clarity, we list all comparison partners as follows:

LR-Text Features: Linear Regression on textual features.

LR-Social Features: Linear Regression on social features.

LR-All Features: Linear Regression on textual and social features.

SVR-Text Features: Support Vector Regression on textual features.

SVR-Social Features: Support Vector Regression on social features.

SVR-All Features: Support Vector Regression on textual and social features.

Matrix Factorization: Matrix factorization model described in Section 2.1.

Tensor Factorization: Tensor Factorization model described in Section 2.2.

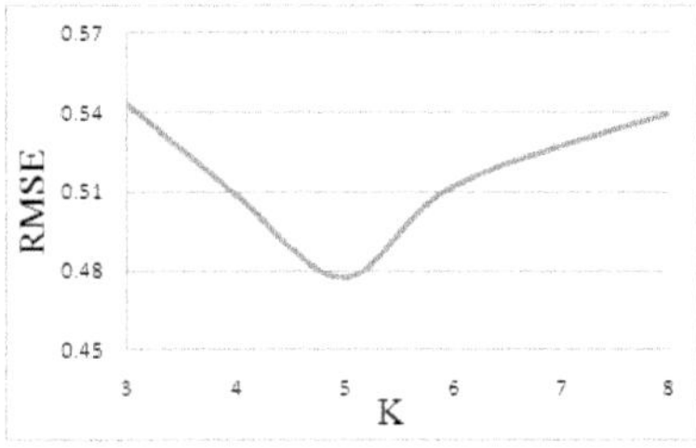

(a) RMSE of MF

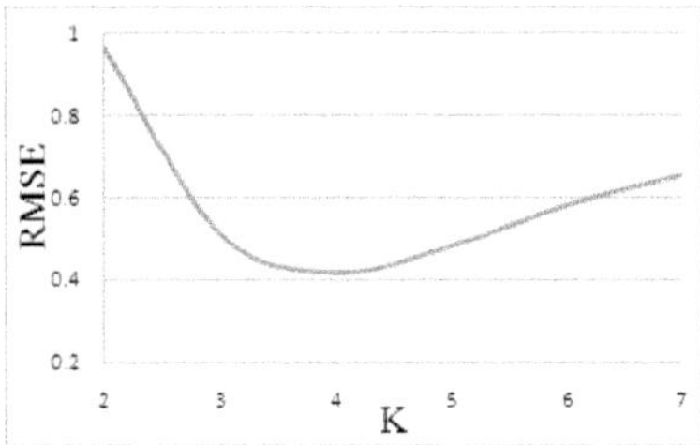

(b) RMSE of TF

Figure 1: Sensitivity analysis for RMSE of MF and TF models for different values of K

In our proposed models, the dimension of the latent factors, K, need to be specified as input. We perform sensitivity analysis to find the optimum value for K. Figure 1 shows the RMSE of MF and TF models for different values of K. MF performs best at $K = 5$ and TF reaches its minimum RMSE at $K = 4$. It should be noted that in our experiments we set all regularization parameters (λ's) to 0.1.

3.3 Experimental Results

In this section, we report the results of our experimental evaluation for the comparison partners listed in Section 3.2. For evaluation, we performed 10-fold cross validation on the Epinions dataset. In each fold we used 90% of the data as the training set and the remaining 10% as the test set. The evaluation metric is Root Mean Squared Error (RMSE), the standard metric for evaluation of recommender systems, which is defined as:

$$RMSE = \sqrt{\frac{\sum_{D_{test}}(q-h)^2}{|D_{test}|}} \quad (9)$$

where q is the actual quality rating of a review for a specific user in the test set, h is the predicted value for q, and $|D_{test}|$ is the number of ratings in the test set.

Analyzing the RMSE results (Table 2) confirms the finding from the literature [5] that using the combination of textual and social features can improve the accuracy of prediction over the text-only and social-only methods. The MF model, which is learned based on rater and review latent factors, outperforms all of the existing non-personalized methods, showing the superior ability of latent factor models in personalized review quality prediction. As expected, the TF model outperforms the MF model, since TF decomposes the review latent factor into reviewer and product latent factors, providing a richer model of the effects underlying the observed data.

Table 2: RMSE of the proposed models and comparison partners

Method	RMSE
LR-Text Features	0.6339
LR-Social Features	0.5331
LR-All Features	0.5230
SVR-Text Features	0.5665
SVR-Social Features	0.5176
SVR-All Features	0.5018
Matrix Factorization	0.4774
Tensor Factorization	0.4164

4. CONCLUSION

In this paper, we introduce the problem of personalized review quality prediction. To address this problem, we have employed two probabilistic factorization models, MF and TF. Experiments on a real-life dataset from Epinions.com demonstrate that the latent factor models outperform state-of-the-art comparison partners using observed features (LR and SVR). We also observed that TF performs better than MF by replacing the review latent factor with the reviewer and product latent factors. Finally, our experiments confirm that the helpfulness of a review is indeed not the same for all users and personalized predictions are more accurate.

5. REFERENCES

[1] M. Jamali and M. Ester. A matrix factorization technique with trust propagation for recommendation in social networks. In *ACM RecSys '10.*

[2] A. Karatzoglou, X. Amatriain, L. Baltrunas, and N. Oliver. Multiverse recommendation: n-dimensional tensor factorization for context-aware collaborative filtering. In *ACM RecSys '10.*

[3] S.-M. Kim, P. Pantel, T. Chklovski, and M. Pennacchiotti. Automatically assessing review helpfulness. In *EMNLP '06.*

[4] J. Liu, Y. Cao, C.-Y. Lin, Y. Huang, and M. Zhou. Low-quality product review detection in opinion summarization. In *EMNLP-CoNLL'07.*

[5] Y. Lu, P. Tsaparas, A. Ntoulas, and L. Polanyi. Exploiting social context for review quality prediction. In *WWW'10.*

[6] P. Massa and P. Avesani. Controversial users demand local trust metrics: an experimental study on epinions.com community. In *Proceedings of the 20th national conference on Artificial intelligence*, 2005.

[7] S. Moghaddam and M. Ester. Ilda: Interdependent lda model for learning latent aspects and their ratings from online product reviews. In *SIGIR '11.*

[8] S. Moghaddam and M. Ester. Opinion digger: An unsupervised opinion miner from unstructured product reviews. In *CIKM '10.*

[9] M. P. O'Mahony and B. Smyth. Learning to recommend helpful hotel reviews. In *ACM RecSys '09.*

[10] Y.-D. Tseng and C. C. Chen. Using an information quality framework to evaluate the quality of product reviews. In *AIRS '09.*

[11] Z. Zhang and B. Varadarajan. Utility scoring of product reviews. In *CIKM'6.*

Improving K-Nearest Neighbors Algorithms: Practical Application of Dataset Analysis

Fidel Cacheda, Victor Carneiro, Diego Fernández, Vreixo Formoso
University of A Coruña
Campus de Elviña s/n
15071 A Coruña SPAIN
{fidel, viccar, diego.fernandez, vformoso}@udc.es

ABSTRACT

In the last years, recommender systems have achieved a great popularity. Many different techniques have been developed and applied to this field. However, in many cases the algorithms do not obtain the expected results. In particular, when the applied model does not fit the real data the results are especially bad. This happens because many times models are directly applied to a domain without a previous analysis of the data. In this work we study the most popular datasets in the movie recommendation domain, in order to understand how the users behave in this particular context. We have found some remarkable facts that question the utility of the similarity measures traditionally used in k-Nearest Neighbors (kNN) algorithms. These findings can be useful in order to develop new algorithms. In particular, we modify traditional kNN algorithms by introducing a new similarity measure specially suited for sparse contexts, where users have rated very few items. Our experiments show slight improvements in prediction accuracy, which proves the importance of a thorough dataset analysis as a previous step to any algorithm development.

Categories and Subject Descriptors

H.3.3 [**Information Search and Retrieval**]: Information filtering

General Terms

Algorithms, Experimentation, Theory

Keywords

Collaborative Filtering, Dataset analysis, Nearest Neighbors

1. INTRODUCTION

Collaborative Filtering is one of the most popular recommendation techniques. It is based on the opinions of users, usually expressed with numerical ratings. The idea is that, given a user, the opinions of other users with similar tastes are valuable to predict which items the former user would like. The ratings or opinions are stored in a table known as the rating matrix. Collaborative Filtering algorithms process the information in that matrix in order to extract information about user tastes, thus offering personalized recommendations.

In the literature we can find many examples of this kind of algorithms. Although many of them obtain very good results, a lot of algorithms are developed based on ideas or models applied in other domains, without paying attention to the actual data. Many times, it is just the evaluation of the results what lets developers know whether the algorithm fits the data. In that case, problems with the methodology of evaluation or the metrics can lead to wrong conclusions.

To the best of our knowledge, very few works actually develop an algorithm based on a previous analysis of the data. In most of papers, authors analyze the data just for providing a context of the domain. Some particular cases have shown the utility of dataset analysis. For example, in some contexts ratings are not available and must be inferred from the behavior of the users [3]. Moreover, recent works have described the evolution of the ratings, users and items over time [5].

This paper is organized as follows. First, we study the most popular datasets in the movie recommendation domain. We analyze several of the design weakness of traditional user-based algorithms, and we try to figure out, based on the information that is available in those datasets, how to overcome these limitations. Our study is presented in Section 2. With the conclusions obtained from this study, in Section 3 we propose several enhancements to traditional kNN algorithms. In Section 4, we evaluate our approach. In Section 5 we discuss the importance of doing a dataset analysis previously to any algorithm design, and we introduce several future improvements.

2. ANALYZING MOVIE RECOMMENDER DATASETS

We have analyzed two of the most popular datasets in the movie recommendation domain: Netflix and Movielens 10M.

2.1 Limitations of traditional similarity measures

An important step in kNN algorithms is to find the neighborhood, that is, the set of users most similar to the active user. A similarity measure such as Pearson correlation is used to compute the degree of similarity between each pair

CIKM'11, October 24–28, 2011, Glasgow, Scotland, UK.

of users. Theoretically, most similar users are the best predictor for the user rating. However, several authors [4, 1] have empirically demonstrated that using few and highly correlated neighbors actually worsens the algorithm accuracy. Indeed, we think that in the movie recommendation domain such strong correlations do not appear frequently. That is because user tastes are generally different: the fact that two users like the same movies does not imply they will agree on all movies.

To study this fact, we have analyzed around 25,000 user-user relationships randomly chosen from the Movielens 10M dataset. In Figure 1, we plot the histogram for Pearson correlation. It can be seen that most users present a very low correlation, around 0.0. That is expected and proves that most users have different tastes so they are not correlated at all. Many users also present a strong correlation (around −1.0 and 1.0), which might seem surprising and apparently contradicts the previous statement claiming that strong correlations do not exist in movie domains. However, strong correlation is only achieved between users who have rated very few items in common. In this case, of course, the computed similarity does not really reflect the actual user similarity.

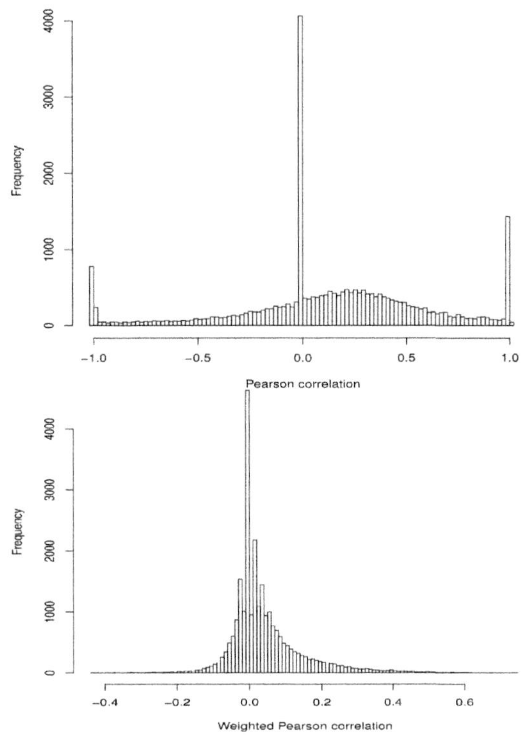

Figure 1: Histograms for Pearson and weighted Pearson correlations

To avoid this problem, some authors have proposed to weight the correlation according to the number of items it is based on. A well-known approach is the weighted Pearson correlation. This technique mitigates the discussed problem, by removing those incorrect high correlations. However, the actual effect is that highly correlated users disappear, as can be seen in Figure 1. So, the actual problem is not fixed at all[1].

[1]Item correlations have the same problem

There exist two possible explanations for this problem. First, the lack of information. Given that rating matrix is too sparse, it might be happening that correlated users are not found just because they have rated very few items in common. In fact, in the vast majority of user-user pairs both users only have between and 0 and 10% of items in common. Second, the differences among users. Two users with different tastes would probably watch (and thus rate) different movies. Moreover, for many pairs of users that have rated quite a big number of items in common, the percentage of items both have rated is still small.

Thus, the study of the data seems to confirm that traditional correlation-based similarity measures are not always the best alternative. These observations lead us to think that approaches that are less strict relating users may obtain better accuracy.

2.2 About the (lack of) importance of the popular items

As some authors have shown [2], most ratings in commercial datasets are condensed in a small number of popular items. In particular, on both Movielens 10M and Netflix datasets, more than 20% of ratings belong to just 1% of items. Usually, it is worthless to recommend such popular items, as probably the user already knows about them. That observation is not taken into account when dealing with the annotation in context task, because it is still needed to predict a rating for those movies if the user request it.

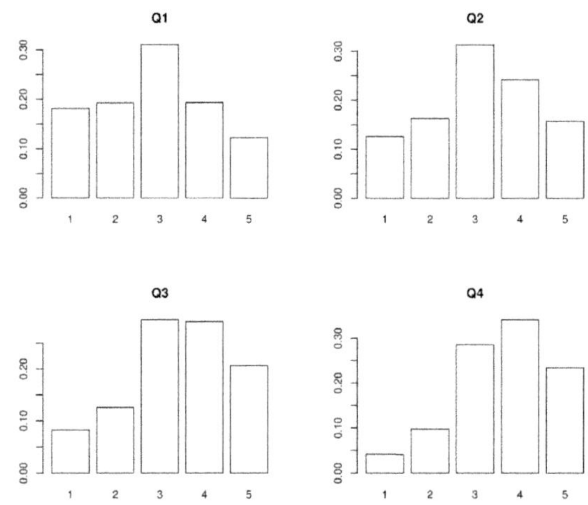

Figure 2: Rating distribution for each number of ratings quartile, on Netflix dataset. Q1 are the items with less ratings, while Q4 are the most popular items.

However, those popular items may not be so useful to compute the similarity between users. It seems logical to think that not all items give the same information about user similarity. For example, a coincidence in a very popular movie is less important than a coincidence in an old and hard to find movie. The reason is that popular movies are usually considered good by most users, which is logical since a bad movie hardly becomes popular. So, many users will agree in the movie rating, but that does not mean the users are really similar. That can be seen if we analyze the rating distribution for both popular and non popular items. In Figure 2 we have plotted the rating distribution on Netflix dataset (it is similar on Movielens 10M), classified according to the number of users that have rated the item. In particular, we have used the quartiles of the number of ratings. It can be seen that items in the fourth quartile (Q4), that are the most popular items, have received mostly good ratings. On the other hand, items in the first quartile (Q1) have received many bad ratings too. That is, most users tend to agree on their opinion about popular items, but they show many different opinions about less popular items. So, a coincidence in a popular item does not really mean that two users are in fact similar, while a coincidence in a rare, non popular item may. That should be taken into account by similarity measures. However, to the best of our knowledge no study has been carried out about the utility of such popular items to compute similarity between users.

3. IMPROVING KNN ALGORITHMS

From the dataset analysis presented in the previous section, we propose a new similarity measure for dealing with the limitations of the traditional similarity measures. This new measure is based on two criteria: the items in common and the coincidences in the ratings.

Traditional measures are very strict and try to compute the similarity using the actual numerical value of ratings. When handling users that have rated few items, the available data is too sparse, and, therefore, using numerical ratings in these conditions is not suitable, because there are not enough items in common. Instead, we propose to take into account only the items rated in common by each pair of users, as showed in Equation 1. With traditional correlation-based measures, it is probable that two users that share few ratings are given a high similarity. However, the coincidences in the ratings could be just by chance (they might not be really similar users). By taking into account the number of items rated in common, our measure avoids this problem.

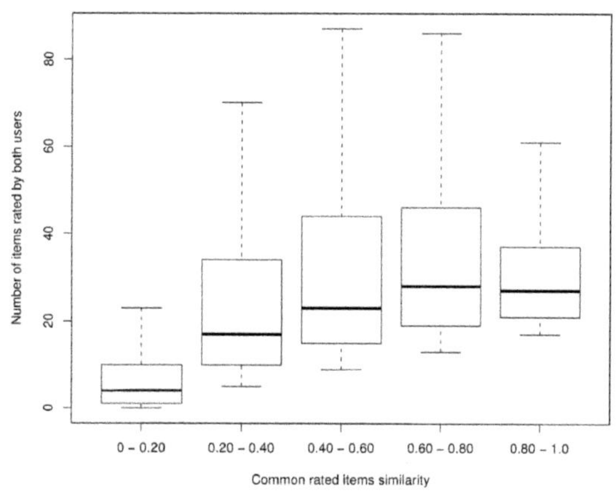

Figure 3: Number of items rated by both users, by common rated items similarity.

In fact, as observed in Figure 3, with this measure high similarity is achieved not only with users who have rated few items in common, but also with many users who have rated quite a few items in common. This is an important difference with respect to Pearson correlation, and one of the main advantages of this measure.

As the number of ratings in common increases, it is possible to begin to use more complex techniques in addition to this measure, in order to extract as much information as possible. In particular, if the number of coincidences in the ratings between users is high, it is probably because they actually are similar users. Therefore, the more the number of items in common between two users, the more useful the coincidences in the ratings. So, we propose an alternative similarity measure that takes into account this fact, according to the Equation 2. However, not all coincidences are equally significant. In order to measure the similarity between two ratings, it is worth weighting it by the importance of the item. Inverse user frequency (iuf) represents this importance and it is defined in Equation 3. We have also analyzed two simple alternatives for the similarity between ratings ($s_{ratings}$). In the first one, called *distance-based measure*, we just calculate the difference between two ratings weighted by the range of R (Equation 4). In the second alternative, called *level-based measure*, two ratings are considered similar if they belong to the same group, as defined in Equation 5[2].

$$s_{common}(a,u) = \frac{|I_a \cap I_u|}{|I_a|} \tag{1}$$

$$s_{coinc}(a,u) = \frac{\sum_{i \in I_a \cap I_u} s_{ratings}(v_{ai}, v_{ui}) * iuf(i)}{\sum_{i \in I_a \cap I_u} iuf(i)} \tag{2}$$

$$iuf(i) = log\frac{|U|}{|U_i|} \tag{3}$$

$$s_{ratings}(v_1, v_2) = 1 - \frac{|v_1 - v_2|}{r_{max} - r_{min}} \tag{4}$$

$$s_{ratings}(v_1, v_2) = \begin{cases} 1 & v_1 < \theta \wedge v_2 < \theta \\ 1 & v_1 \geq \theta \wedge v_2 \geq \theta \\ 0 & otherwise \end{cases} \tag{5}$$

We thus propose a similarity measure (defined in Equation 6) that combines the items rated in common with the actual coincidence in ratings. This way, we tackle the mentioned limitations of the traditional measures.

$$s(a,u) = \beta * s_{common}(a,u) + (1-\beta) * s_{coinc}(a,u) \tag{6}$$

4. EXPERIMENTS

We have performed our experiments using Movielens 10M dataset, that was previously analyzed in Section 2. We have divided the dataset into a training subset and an evaluation subset, and we have evaluated the annotation in context task using kNN algorithms to predict the selected ratings.

4.1 The influence of the parameters

First of all, we have studied the influence of the β parameter. As seen in Figure 4, with a small percentage of ratings as training subset, best results are achieved with β set to a high value. The reason is that, when the information is extremely sparse, there is no point in having a complex similarity measure, because it has no information to work with. In those cases, information is often misunderstood,

[2]We have used a threshold $\theta = 4$.

leading to bad results, so it is worth using a simpler measure. In particular, results show that our choice, based on the items rated instead of the actual rating value, is a good alternative. On the other hand, with higher density, the best results are achieved with low β values, which proves that in that case the more complex measures outperform the simple alternative based on the number of common rated items.

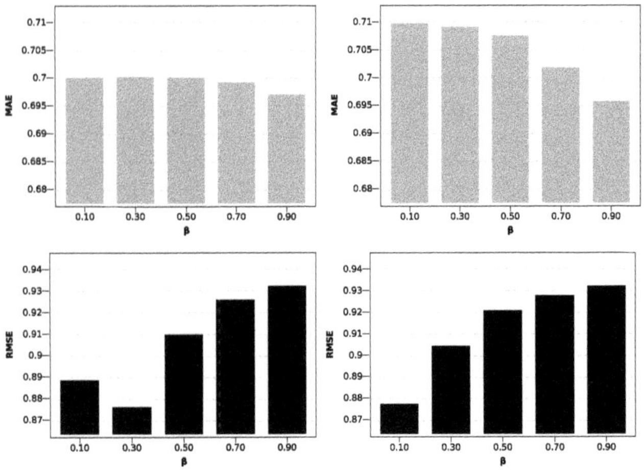

Figure 4: MAE and RMSE for different β values with 10% and 90% of the ratings as training subset, respectively. On the left the level-based similarity and on the right the distance-based similarity.

Regarding the influence of the N parameter[3], that controls the number of neighbors, the results are compatible with those presented by traditional user-based approaches. That is, the results worsen notably when N is set to a low value.

Finally, the results show that the overall impact of the iuf factor is almost imperceptible.

4.2 Comparison with correlation-based measures

We have compared our results with those obtained with two traditional correlation-based techniques: Pearson correlation and cosine vector similarity.

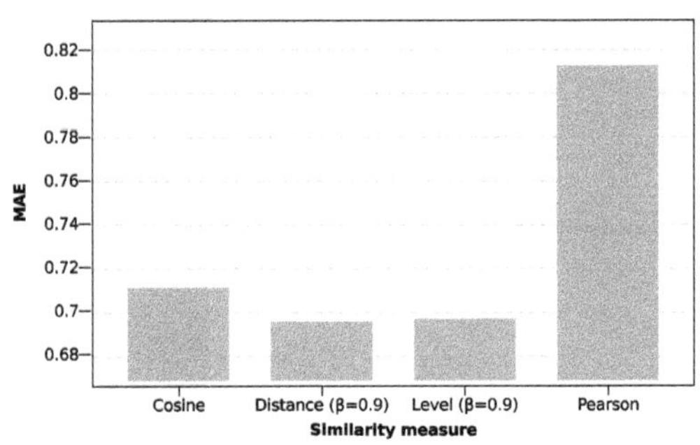

Figure 5: Comparison of different similarity measures, with 10% of the ratings as training set.

As shown in Figure 5, when the available information is scarce, our simple approach outperforms traditional measures. Note that distance-based and level-based variants obtain pretty similar results, as expected, because only 10% of the final similarity value depends on them. On the other hand, with 90% of the ratings as training set, cosine vector similarity obtains slightly better results.

The results obtained were expected and confirm what we have said previously. Traditional measures are too strict, and when the available information is scarce, that leads to wrong results. However, they also show that distance-based and level-based measures do not improve traditional measures. So, a better approach could be to combine our simple measure based on the number of items rated in common with a traditional, more complex, approach.

[3] N has been set to 50

5. CONCLUSIONS AND FUTURE WORK

In this paper we have shown how a design methodology that includes a previous analysis of the domain data can be helpful to develop Collaborative Filtering algorithms. We have confirmed that many of the problems presented in traditional user-based algorithms can be explained by means of a study of the data. We have also proposed several improvements to those algorithms.

It has been shown how dataset analysis is specially useful to understand user behavior in a particular domain. That information can be used for improving the algorithm design and avoid common pitfalls introduced because of a misunderstanding of data peculiarities in a particular domain.

We plan to combine traditional similarity measures with our measure based on the number of items rated in common. We will also focus on a new similarity measure based on a dynamic β parameter according to the conclusions obtained in this work. That is, using a different β for each user depending on the number of items he has rated.

Moreover, the conclusions obtained from our dataset analysis can be used to develop new models that could fit the data better than existing approaches.

6. ACKNOWLEDGMENTS

This research was supported by the Ministry of Education and Science of Spain and FEDER funds of the European Union (Project TIN2009-14203).

7. REFERENCES

[1] F. Cacheda, V. Carneiro, D. Fernández, and V. Formoso. Comparison of collaborative filtering algorithms: Limitations of current techniques and proposals for scalable, high-performance recommender systems. *ACM Trans. Web*, 5:2:1–2:33, February 2011.

[2] P. Cremonesi, Y. Koren, and R. Turrin. Performance of recommender algorithms on top-n recommendation tasks. In *RecSys '10: Proceedings of the fourth ACM conference on Recommender systems*, pages 39–46, New York, NY, USA, 2010. ACM.

[3] M. Hahsler. Developing and testing top-n recommendation algorithms for 0-1 data using recommenderlab, 2010.

[4] J. Herlocker, J. A. Konstan, and J. Riedl. An empirical analysis of design choices in neighborhood-based collaborative filtering algorithms. *Inf. Retr.*, 5(4):287–310, 2002.

[5] Y. Koren. Collaborative filtering with temporal dynamics. *Commun. ACM*, 53:89–97, April 2010.

Structured Collaborative Filtering

Alejandro Bellogín
Universidad Autónoma de Madrid
Madrid, 28049 Spain
alejandro.bellogin@uam.es

Jun Wang
University College London
Malet Place, London WC1E 6BT, UK
j.wang@cs.ucl.ac.uk

Pablo Castells
Universidad Autónoma de Madrid
Madrid, 28049 Spain
pablo.castells@uam.es

ABSTRACT

In a general collaborative filtering (CF) setting, a user profile contains a set of previously rated items and is used to represent the user's interest. Unfortunately, most CF approaches ignore the underlying structure of user profiles. In this paper, we argue that a certain class of interest is best represented jointly by several items, drawing an analogy to "phrases" in text retrieval, which are not equivalent to the separate meaning of their words. At an alternative stance, we also consider the situation where, analogously to word synonyms, two items might be substitutable when representing a class of interest. We propose an approach integrating these two notions as opposing poles on a continuum spectrum. Upon this, we model the underlying structure in user profiles, drawing an analogy with text retrieval. The approach gives rise to a novel structured Vector Space Model for CF. We show that item-based CF approaches are a special case of the proposed method.

Categories and Subject Descriptors

H.3.3 [**Information Search and Retrieval**]: Information filtering

General Terms

Algorithm, Performance, Experimentation

Keywords

Recommender systems, Collaborative filtering, synonymy

1. INTRODUCTION

Most Collaborative Filtering (CF) algorithms disregard the fact that the rating data shows some structure. For example, in an item-based approach, the candidate item's preference is commonly predicted by independently evaluating its similarity to each individual items in the profiles and then averaging them together to obtain the final score. However, the items in the system may have explicit relations among them, such as sharing the director (for movies), or belonging to the same genre (movies, music, books). Dealing properly with this structure is a challenge for the community. Most of the works assume some kind of clustering is performed on the users or the items, and then, predictions are performed using only these subsets of the collection [4, 1]. Obviously, this would increase the sparsity of the system, which turns out to be a serious problem for real-world systems. On the other hand, some works propose to use clustering for avoiding the sparsity, although it is not clear how the structure is kept in this situation [8].

Recently, different papers have explicitly linked CF algorithms with Information Retrieval (IR) techniques, and apply them successfully for recommendation. In [7], the authors find an analogy between implicit CF and IR, applying the Probability Ranking Principle from IR to CF. More recently, [2] proposes a framework in which any IR scoring function could be used with CF rating data. In [3], the authors reformulate the recommendation problem and use algorithms from IR, namely a model based on Discrete Fourier Transform and the Vector Space Model (VSM).

In the proposed approach, we adapt, upon the already found analogies between IR and CF, the extended Boolean retrieval model presented in [6]. In that work, the authors introduce a generic model in which intermediate systems between Boolean and VSM models appears naturally. In particular, they acknowledge that the query structure should be altered in order to distinguish between compulsory terms (phrases) and alternative words (synonynms), whereas the Boolean strategy requires a very strict interpretation of such structure, the VSM model completely loses this distinction and the terms are considered independent of each other.

The proposed approach defines a method for providing structure to user profiles in CF. The extended model is applied to two particular tasks: a) *user profile expansion*, which consists of propagating user ratings to other similar (or synonym) items; and b) user profile decomposition into area-specific subprofiles, as an enhanced structure enabling recommendation performance improvements. We report empirical results confirming that structured user profiles in CF outperform the standard item-based approach, which is a particular case of our model with plain profiles and no synonymy expansion.

2. STRUCTURED FILTERING MODEL

The main idea of this work is inspired by the Salton's classic paper [6]. The novelty here lies in the use of the analogy between IR and CF proposed in [2] to address the structure problem in CF. In the next subsections, we propose how structure could be added to CF, by adapting the methods proposed in [2] so that more advanced models such as [6] could be used.

2.1 A Vector-Space Representation

As already proposed in [2], we can obtain a new insight into the current CF approaches by reformulating them using a Vector Space Model [5]. Formally, a user profile can be

CIKM'11, October 24–28, 2011, Glasgow, Scotland, UK.

Table 1: "AND" and "OR" representations of a user interest

(a) using Boolean retrieval.

	Query items		user interest representation	
	a	b	a OR b	a AND b
item 1	1	1	1	1
item 2	1	0	1	0
item 3	0	1	1	0
item 4	0	0	0	0

(b) using extended Boolean retrieval ($p = 2$).

	Query items		user interest representation	
	a	b	a OR b	a AND b
item 1	1	1	1	1
item 2	1	0	$1/\sqrt{2}$	$1 - 1/\sqrt{2}$
item 3	0	1	$1/\sqrt{2}$	$1 - 1/\sqrt{2}$
item 4	0	0	0	0

regarded as a query. Each of the rated items in the profile is considered as a query term. Therefore, we could use a vector to represent a user profile as follows:

$$\mathbf{Q}^u = (i_1, r^u_{i_1}; \ldots; i_k, r^u_{i_k}; \ldots; i_n, r^u_{i_n}) \quad (1)$$

where $\mathbf{Q}^u$ denotes a user profile u. $r^u_{i_k}$ represents the rating of item k by this user, where $k \in \{1, n\}$. It is equal to 0 when item k is not rated by u. In practice, the ratings are normalized with respect to the users' mean or items' mean.

By contrast, the item representation is different to the text retrieval. In CF, we do not have a common feature space. Thus, we should project each item into the same feature space as queries by using its similar items. That is

$$\mathbf{I}^j = (i_1, s^j_{i_1}; \ldots; i_k, s^j_{i_k}; \ldots; i_n, s^j_{i_n}) \quad (2)$$

where s_{i_k} is the similarity between the candidate item j and item k, using, for instance, the Pearson's similarity.

Given the vector representations of Eq. (1) and Eq. (2), a query-item similarity value may be obtained by comparing the corresponding vectors, using for example the conventional vector product:

$$\text{Sim}(u, i) = \text{Sim}(\mathbf{Q}^u, \mathbf{I}^j) = \sum_{k=1}^{n} s^j_{i_k} \cdot r^u_{i_k} \quad (3)$$

The system could provide a ranked recommendation output in decreasing order of the computed similarities between $\mathbf{Q}^u$ and $\mathbf{I}^j$. In practice, it is also needed to predict the user's rating of an unspecified item. The similarity score should be normalized to produce a rating in the proper range:

$$\hat{r}^u_j = \frac{\sum_{k=1}^{n} s^j_{i_k} \cdot r^u_{i_k}}{\sum_k s^j_{i_k}} = \sum_{k=1}^{n} \bar{s}^j_{i_k} \cdot r^u_{i_k} \quad (4)$$

where $\bar{s}^j_{i_k} = \frac{s^j_{i_k}}{\sum_k s^j_{i_k}}$. It can be easily seen that Eq. (4) is indeed an item-based CF approach, but rather in a vector space formulation.

2.2 An Extended Vector-Space Representation

As we discussed previously, the user profile represented by independently rated items is problematic. We shall illustrate it by considering the following Boolean retrieval example. Suppose we have a class of user interest, and it is represented jointly by two items a and b. In a Boolean retrieval model, we would use an "AND" rule, meaning that a candidate item should be similar to both of them. By contrast, if a class of user interest is represented by either of two items, an "OR" rule may be applied. Table 1(a) illustrates the results from the Boolean Retrieval model for the four different types of items. Note that for simplicity, the binary similarity is assumed.

From the table, we can see that the Boolean retrieval is too rigid in terms of producing the ranking score, either too loose or tight. And in practice, the interest representation is between "AND" and "OR". An extension of the Boolean model was given in [6]. The idea was to apply a more discriminative ranking formula by calculating the distance towards the most desired point in the vector space. Let us define how we represent the query and documents in the extended model by using a regular expression, where n is the number of terms in the collection:

$$\mathbf{Q} := \begin{matrix}\text{and}\\ \text{or}\end{matrix} (p_1) \left[\begin{matrix}\text{and}\\ \text{or}\end{matrix} (p_2)[Q]^+, cw \right]$$

$$\mathbf{Q} := (\text{qw}_1, \ldots, \text{qw}_n)$$

$$\mathbf{D}^i := (\text{dw}_{i,1}, \ldots, \text{dw}_{i,n})$$

In this definition, a clause query is a combination of simple queries (as in VSM, where qw_i is the weight given for that query to the term t_i) by means of connectives and clause weights (cw). Besides, each connective has an associated p-value, in this case, we denote p_2 as the inner value and p_1 as the outer one. Documents are simply represented as in the standard VSM, where $\text{dw}(i, j)$ is the weight between document D_i and term t_j. Using this notation, the similarity between a query and a document can be computed recursively until a simple query is found, by using cw to weight the importance of the similarity between the subqueries and the document (more details in [6]). Depending on the connective, similarity between a document and a simple query is calculated as follows:

$$sim(\mathbf{Q}_{or(p)}, \mathbf{D}^i) = \left[\frac{(\text{qw}_1\, \text{dw}_{i,1})^p + \ldots + (\text{qw}_n\, \text{dw}_{i,n})^p}{(\text{qw}_1)^p + \ldots + (\text{qw}_n)^p}\right]^{1/p}$$

$$sim(\mathbf{Q}_{and(p)}, \mathbf{D}^i) = 1 - \left[\frac{(\text{qw}_1(1-\text{dw}_{i,1}))^p + \ldots + (\text{qw}_n(1-\text{dw}_{i,n}))^p}{(\text{qw}_1)^p + \ldots + (\text{qw}_n)^p}\right]^{1/p}$$

where $p \in [1, +\infty)$ is the corresponding connective p-value. Note that when $p = 1$ we have $sim(\mathbf{Q}_{or}, \mathbf{D}_i) = sim(\mathbf{Q}_{and}, \mathbf{D}_i)$.

In this way, depending on the value of p we can generalize different retrieval systems. For instance, when $p = \infty$ (assuming binary weights) a standard Boolean scoring is performed, for $p = 1$ a VSM is obtained, and the rest of the values produce intermediate extended retrieval models.

Furthermore, as stated in [6], each p-value has a *semantic* interpretation in IR, depending on the connectives used. With $p = \infty$ and the "AND" connective, then a strict **phrase** has to be matched, i.e., the document is not retrievable unless all phrase components are present. If, on the other hand, the connective is an "OR", then a strict **thesaurus** feature is used, i.e., all the connected terms are substitutable for one another. When the p-value is lower, these constraints are less strict, in the sense that, for the "AND" connective, the presence of every term is worth more than the presence of only some of them, but they are not compulsory; similarly, for the "OR" connective, the presence of several terms from a given class is more important than the presence of only one term. Finally, when $p = 1$ both connectives are equivalent and the distinction between phrase and thesaurus disappears, thus only the presence or absence of the terms is considered, i.e., the terms are independent of each other.

2.3 Modelling Structured User Profiles

We have seen in the previous section that documents need no further modification. Thus, in the context of CF, this means that only the user profile (query) has to be expressed as a set of clause queries by using different connectives, and the items (documents) may be represented as in Section 2.1. Since the equivalence presented in that section corresponds with a VSM in IR, the representation of the constituent elements in the extended model is simply as follows, where n now is the number of items in the system:

$$\mathbf{Q}^u = \text{and}(1)\,[\text{and}(1)((i_1, r^u_{i_1}), \ldots, (i_n, r^u_{i_n}), 1)] \quad (5)$$

$$\mathbf{I}^j = \left(s^j_{i_1}, \ldots, s^j_{i_n}\right)$$

In this situation, the query is defined as an "AND" rule with $p = 1$. As we have already noted, for this value of p, the similarity formula of an "AND" rule is equivalent to that of an "OR" rule, so we can define the queries with or(1) instead of and(1). Besides, we have to note that Eq. (4) is not completely equivalent with the formulation presented herein, since standard item-based CF normalizes with respect to the similarity values, which are encoded in the document vector, while in IR the model is normalized using the query weights. Both representations, nonetheless, could be equivalent with a slight modification of the extended model.

2.4 Exploiting Structured Profiles

Once an extended user profile representation is available for recommendation by adapting the extended retrieval model, we envision two main applications. First, performing expansions over the user profiles, in a similar way as IR researchers include synonyms and related words when expanding queries. Second, providing structure to the profiles based on implicit similarities found between the items in the system. In the following, we explain how these two applications may be performed in CF.

2.4.1 *Profile expansion*

In any recommendation system, there are some items which tend to occur very frequently together, such as movie series (e.g., Lord of the Ring, Star Wars, or Star Trek), or movies by some particular director. These movies could be considered close *synonyms*, in the sense that people tend to like them all or none of them. If this assumption holds, once one item belonging to a particular group is rated in a profile, the rating could be propagated to the rest of synonyms in the system, by using an "OR". In this way, the rating sparsity would be reduced, since each user would contain in her profile additional items, implicitly derived through the synonym relation.

A very important parameter in this setting would be the expansion size, that is, how many synonyms are incorporated into the user profile. As a first attempt, we can expand all the user profiles in the same way. However, as in query expansion, it seems clear that some users could benefit more from the expansion than others. Query performance techniques, which have been frequently applied to query expansion, can be very useful in order to determine the strength of the expansion on a per-user basis. Another important parameter is the p-value, which, for instance, could be set based on the co-occurrence strength between each pair of items, or any function which manipulates those co-occurrences, such as normalization by the average, minimum, or maximum value.

2.4.2 *Inferring profile structure*

It often makes sense to find subprofiles within user profiles. This is a very recurrent idea in recommender systems, with different motivations, such as when two users A and B have very similar movie tastes, but very different in music. Their music dissimilarity should not obscure their movie similarity, so that A and B can get area-specific recommendations from each other based on their area-specific common tastes. Preference clusters can be created automatically and used in many ways (see [4, 8] among others).

In this view, user profile vectors could be decomposed into a soft "OR" of cohesive subprofiles or *phrases* (music tastes, movie tastes, sports, etc.), where subprofiles are also soft "OR"s of item ratings, and the outer "OR" should have a higher p than the inner "OR". Different options arise when defining this structure with respect to how the clusters are defined and how to set the inner and outer p values.

Clusters within a user profile can be created using predefined clusters over the item space, and these clusters can be found using classic clustering algorithms (such as K-means) or any other alternative strategy. Pearson correlation can be used as distance between items, and external features such as genre or actor information apart from ratings may be taken as input data.

Inner p-values can be set in many different ways: they can be fixed or depend on the average (or minimum, maximum) similarity in the cluster or its centroid, using an additional step function discretizing those values, in such a way that the higher the cohesion in the cluster, the higher the inner p-value. The outer p-value can have a fixed, low value since we want to retrieve documents matching any of the subprofiles, however if we want to boost those documents matching more than one subprofile, a higher p-value should be used instead. Actually, the outer "OR" rule may be replaced by an "AND" rule in order to check if documents matching every subprofile are more likely to be relevant to the user or not.

3. EXPERIMENTS

The experiments have been carried out using the publicly available dataset called *Movielens 100K*[1]. This dataset contains 943 users, 1682 items and 100000 ratings. We performed a 5-fold cross validation using the splits contained in the public package, these splits retain the 80% of the data for training, and the rest for testing.

The evaluation was performed as explained in [2], that is, for each user, a ranking is generated by predicting a score for every item in the test set. We then measure the performance of this ranking, using the *trec_eval* program.

Now, we present the results obtained in the two tasks where the extended retrieval model has been applied: expanding the user profiles and inferring profile structure.

3.1 User profile expansion

In this experiment, we analyze the recommendation performance variations that result from introducing different amounts of profile expansion, compared to a plain item-based recommender baseline without expansion ($S = 0$). Besides, as noted in Section 2.4.1, we consider the expanded items as synonyms, and thus, we include an infinity inner p-value, in order to have the standard Boolean behaviour for the "OR" connective. As shown in Table 2(a), we may observe a significant improvement when user profiles are expanded with similar items, and the more synonyms are used in the expansion, the better the performance. It is worth noting that changing the order of the connectives (bottom row) leads to poor results, showing that profiles built this way make little sense.

The baseline in the table is the method presented in Section 2.1, which corresponds to the standard item-based CF approach. We can see that properly using the extended model leads to outperforming the baseline formulation. In contrast with [2], we have not yet experimented with different normalization techniques, in order to keep the extended model as close to the original as possible. The results suggest, nonetheless, that a combination of both methods might result in higher, more significant performance improvements, since they may be used complementarily: while our method expands the profiles, the method described in [2] explores different techniques inspired by IR scoring functions.

[1]Available at http://www.grouplens.org/node/73

Table 2: Results. Outer and inner connectives in the user profile representation are presented in this order.

(a) Performance values for the profile expansion experiment. S is the expansion size.

Method	P@1	P@3	P@5	P@10	NDCG@3	NDCG@5	NDCG@50	MRR
Baseline	0.002	0.004	0.005	0.007	0.002	0.003	0.009	0.027
$S = 1$, and(1), or(∞)	0.129	0.121	0.120	0.114	0.099	0.099	0.126	0.243
$S = 2$, and(1), or(∞)	0.149	0.138	0.130	0.119	0.113	0.110	0.128	0.260
$S = 5$, and(1), or(∞)	0.190	0.166	0.155	0.141	0.140	0.134	0.146	0.304
$S = 10$, and(1), or(∞)	0.197	0.171	0.161	0.147	0.146	0.140	0.151	0.313
$S = 5$, or(∞), and(1)	0.004	0.005	0.005	0.005	0.002	0.003	0.010	0.028

(b) Performance values for the dynamic user profile expansion.

Method	P@1	P@3	P@5	P@10	NDCG@3	NDCG@5	NDCG@50	MRR
Threshold found by median	0.183	0.167	0.157	0.145	0.137	0.132	0.158	0.302
Threshold found by average	0.186	0.165	0.158	0.146	0.137	0.133	0.157	0.303

(c) Performance values for structured profiles.

Method	P@1	P@3	P@5	P@10	NDCG@3	NDCG@5	NDCG@50	MRR
Baseline	0.002	0.004	0.005	0.007	0.002	0.003	0.009	0.027
K-means genre or(1), or(2)	0.013	0.016	0.017	0.018	0.010	0.011	0.032	0.061
K-means genre or(2), or(2)	0.005	0.006	0.006	0.006	0.003	0.004	0.011	0.030
K-means sim or(1), or(2)	0.008	0.011	0.014	0.016	0.007	0.009	0.023	0.047
K-means sim or(2), or(2)	0.006	0.006	0.006	0.008	0.004	0.004	0.012	0.031

In Table 2(b), we present further experiments with a dynamic profile expansion strategy. In this experiment, the parameter S is not fixed for all the users in the system, but depends on each user's characteristics. In particular, and as a first attempt, we assume that the size of the user profile might be an indicator of the demand for more or less items in the expanded model —in the same way as the query length may be used in IR for deciding whether or not to expand the query. In this context, we only expand those users which are below some threshold. In the table, we show the results when the threshold is the average or the median of the number of ratings in the system. These two methods obtain very similar results, and compared with the previous methods, they outperform static expansion when the cutoff value is high, e.g., P@10 and NDCG@50.

3.2 Inferring user profile structure

In order to compare whether structured profiles improve the performance, we compare against the baseline method presented in Section 2.1, which simply uses plain profiles (no structure). Furthermore, to provide structure to the item profiles, two clustering algorithms were used: K-means and X-means (as implemented by Weka library[2]). These algorithms have been trained on different data related with items, more specifically, on genre information and similarity values among items. Different values for the number of clusters with K-means were tried, and an optimal $K = 50$ was found and used in our experiments.

Table 2(c) shows the results of this experiment. We have tried a uniform p for all the subprofiles, which corresponds to the clusters found by the clustering algorithm. In the future, a different p depending on the intracluster similarity might be considered. Results with the X-means algorithm are not reported here because it always performed worse than K-means. As we can see in this table, structured profiles obtain better performance than plain profiles. Besides, we have found no significant differences when changing the inner p-value, since or(2) and or(5) gave the same result. Furthermore, clustering genre information about items provides better results than clusters generated using similarity between items. This may be due to the relatively higher amount of noise when using item similarity, in comparison to explicit external information such as item genres.

[2]Available at http://www.cs.waikato.ac.nz/~ml/weka/

4. CONCLUSION AND FUTURE WORK

We have presented a method for incorporating structure into the user profiles of CF algorithms. Upon the work described in [2], we apply an extended retrieval model which allows for incorporating such structure. We report two applications for this approach: user profile expansion and inference of profile structure. Empirical results show that our methods introduce significant performance improvements over an item-based CF baseline, which can be simply represented in our framework as a method where the items are considered independent from each other. Therefore, taking into account the structure of the user profiles seems to lead to better performing CF algorithms, while it opens up new possibilities and applications.

As future work, we plan to investigate a formal way for calculating automatically the p-values, instead of the fixed values used so far. This would provide insights about the real meaning in CF of the IR concepts of synonymy and phrase. More generally, the proposed model may provide a flexible ground for the exploration of further potential applications.

5. ACKNOWLEDGMENTS

This work was supported by the Spanish Ministry of Science and Innovation (TIN2008-06566-C04-02), University Autónoma de Madrid and the Community of Madrid (CCG10--UAM/TIC-5877).

6. REFERENCES

[1] L. Baltrunas and F. Ricci. Context-based splitting of item ratings in collaborative filtering. In *RecSys*, pages 245–248. ACM, 2009.

[2] A. Bellogín, J. Wang, and P. Castells. Text retrieval methods for item ranking in collaborative filtering. In *ECIR*, pages 301–306. Springer, 2011.

[3] A. Costa and F. Roda. Recommender systems by means of information retrieval. In *WIMS*, pages 57:1–57:5. ACM, 2011.

[4] M. O'Connor and J. Herlocker. Clustering items for collaborative filtering. In *ACM SIGIR Workshop on Recommender Systems*, 1999.

[5] G. Salton and C. Buckley. Term weighting approaches in automatic text retrieval. Technical report, 1987.

[6] G. Salton, E. A. Fox, and H. Wu. Extended boolean information retrieval. *Commun. ACM*, 26(11):1022–1036, 1983.

[7] J. Wang, S. Robertson, A. de Vries, and M. Reinders. Probabilistic relevance ranking for collaborative filtering. *Information Retrieval*, 11(6):477–497, 2008.

[8] G. R. Xue, C. Lin, Q. Yang, W. Xi, H. J. Zeng, Y. Yu, and Z. Chen. Scalable collaborative filtering using cluster-based smoothing. In *SIGIR*, pages 114–121. ACM, 2005.

User Oriented Tweet Ranking: A Filtering Approach to Microblogs

Ibrahim Uysal
uysal@cs.umass.edu

W. Bruce Croft
croft@cs.umass.edu

Center for Intelligent Information Retrieval
Department of Computer Science
University of Massachusetts, Amherst, MA

ABSTRACT

The increasing volume of streaming data on microblogs has re-introduced the necessity of effective filtering mechanisms for such media. Microblog users are overwhelmed with mostly uninteresting pieces of text in order to access information of value. In this paper, we propose a personalized tweet ranking method, leveraging the use of retweet behavior, to bring more important tweets forward. In addition, we also investigate how to determine the audience of tweets more effectively, by ranking the users based on their likelihood of retweeting the tweets. Finally, conducting a pilot user study, we analyze how retweet likelihood correlates with the interestingness of the tweets.

Categories and Subject Descriptors

H.2.8 [**Database Management**]: Data Mining; J.4 [**Computer Applications**]: Social and Behavioral Sciences

General Terms

Algorithms, Experimentation, Human Factors

Keywords

Twitter, Retweet behavior, Filtering

1. INTRODUCTION

Although microblogs serve as a useful medium for various activities, the excessive number of posts users receive reduces their utility. In order to find interesting tweets, for example, users must scan potentially hundreds of less relevant posts every day from the people they subscribe to. This situation shows the potential value of an effective filtering system for microblogs.

Information filtering requires some criteria as the basis for the filtering process. In the case of Twitter, one of the potential criteria is whether a tweet is being disseminated by the users who read it. The practice of propagating a tweet from another user is called *retweeting*. Since the practice of retweeting includes reading the tweet, deciding that it is worthwhile to share, and then acting on it; we can use retweet (RT) behavior as an explicit signal that the user considers the tweet to contain useful or interesting information.

In this paper, we approach the problem of reducing information overload in Twitter from two directions. First, we train a model using a coordinate ascent algorithm to rank the incoming tweets based on the likelihood that the user will RT them. Secondly, for a given tweet, we rank the users who receive that tweet, so that the user who is more likely to RT the given tweet will appear at the top of the ranking. Finally, we analyze how the tweet ranking approach based on RT likelihood correlates with the actual user preference by conducting a pilot user study.

2. RELATED WORK

One way to address the problem of improving the attractiveness of incoming tweets is choosing which user to follow in a more selective manner. The idea is that if a user receives the tweets of the right users, then she is less likely to get lost among uninteresting tweets. A few papers propose effective user recommendation approaches to overcome this issue. Hannon et al. utilize content and collaborative based approaches to evaluate a range of different user profiling and recommendation strategies [4]. In another paper, Golder et al. investigate a number of user similarity measures to be used in contact recommendation in Twitter [3]. Discovering both global and topic-sensitive influential users is also studied [12, 13].

A number of papers have studied how to classify tweets to improve information filtering. Sriram et al. trained a Naive-Bayes classifier to determine which predefined class a tweet falls into [10]. In their paper, they used categories such as news, events, opinions, deals, and private messages. Classifying the tweets solely on their news-relatedness was studied in [2, 9]. All these classifications are generic, not user oriented.

In order to shed light on what sort of information people propagate on Twitter, several studies investigated the RT behavior of the users. Boyd et al. focused on the qualitative aspect of the RT behavior and gave answers to the questions like "Why people retweet?" and "What people retweet?" [1]. Having a similar motivation to this paper, Suh et al. analyzed 9 features to see how they correlate with the retweetability of a tweet [11]. Their hypothesis is that recommen-

CIKM'11, October 24–28, 2011, Glasgow, Scotland, UK.

dation and personalization could help to optimize the information diffusion, and help the users to catch interesting tweets. Apart from the global statistical analysis of these features, they did not build a personalized user model using the RT prediction.

To the best of our knowledge, there are four papers extending the analysis to building a retweet prediction model. Yang et al. used 22 features for observation, then built an RT prediction model using a factor graph model [14]. In another study, Zaman et al. used a probabilistic collaborative filtering model, called Matchbox, to make RT predictions [15]. Hong et al. used 5 features to train a logistic regression model and achieved a performance with relatively low recall score: 0.44 [5]. Lastly, Petrovic et al. introduced a few more features such as novelty of a tweet and the number of times the author is listed, to train a model using a passive aggressive algorithm [6]. All these papers approach the RT prediction problem from a global perspective, answering the question of "Whether a given tweet will be retweeted by anyone or not?". Thus, they fail to capture which tweets are more retweetable from a user-centric perspective. In this paper, we build a model which is adaptable for individual users.

Finally, Ramage et al. investigated which topics users are interested in using a Labeled-LDA approach, to classify the tweets based on whether each one is worth to be read or not [8]. They also addressed the user recommendation task, however, what they do is basically deciding whether a user is in the followee list of a given user or not.

3. PROPOSED METHODS

The goal of ranking the Twitter feed of individual users is to display incoming tweets in a descending order based on their likelihood of being retweeted by the specific user. An effective ranking will help the user to find potentially more interesting tweets. Compared to a filtering approach where the incoming information either passes or fails the filter, the ranking method is more conservative in that all the relevant information is presented to the user in a more organized way.

Another approach for reducing the information overload is presenting the posted tweets to the potential audiences more selectively. Twitter already addresses this issue by hiding personal conversations from other users' timelines. However, this is just a small step towards filtering out uninteresting tweets. Our approach for this problem is to rank the potential audience (users) of a tweet based on their likelihood of retweeting that tweet.

In the next two subsections, we explain our approach and experiments in detail.

3.1 Ranking Incoming Tweets

As a preliminary experiment, we trained a decision tree based classifier (J48), using the WEKA[1] toolkit, to see how accurately we can classify the tweets as retweetable or not for a specific user. To train the classifier, we used four groups of features explained below. Then, with the same set of features, we took a learning to rank approach using the Coordinate Ascent (CA) algorithm. The experimental setup and the results are explained below as well. In all our experiments, we used 5-fold cross-validation to split the training and test sets.

3.1.1 Features

Author-based: These are basically the features that appear on or can be inferred through the user profile: Is the author locally elite (i.e. the # of followers she has is in the range of (10K - 50K)), is she globally elite (i.e. she has more than 50K followers), followers count, friends count, age (i.e. # of days since the creation of her account), statuses count, favourites count, her tweet rate (i.e. avg. tweet count per week), # of times she is listed, is she a verified user, does she have a description, does she have a url, is her language English.

Author-related features mainly give clues about the authority of the author and how active user she is.

Tweet-based: These are the syntactic features of the tweet: Does it contain hashtags (#xyz), urls (http://xyz..), mentions (@user), question mark (?), exclamation mark (!), quotation mark ("), first person pronoun (I), same character consecutively three times (e.g. cooool), emoticons (e.g. :P), is the tweet retweeted by anyone, is the tweet an RT itself, the length of the tweet, and the tf-idf score of the tweet.

Some of these features give implications about how well-written the tweet is, the category, the audience, and the popularity of the tweet.

Content-based: Content based features are the ones related to the information contained by the tweet. These are the novelty of the tweet (i.e. minimum cosine distance to the other tweets that appear on the user's timeline in the last week), the unexpectedness of the tweet from the author (i.e. minimum cosine distance to the other tweets of the author), and the Query Likelihood (QL) [7] score of the author based on the Language Model (LM) of her tweets.

User-based: These features are related to the user whose Twitter feed is being ranked. From the user's point of view, the features are as follows: Is the author my friend (i.e. is she also following me), is the author my conversation friend (i.e. did we mention each other before), did I RT her before, did I list her, did I use the hashtag in the tweet (if any), did I use the url domain in the tweet (if any), is the tweet mentioning me, did I mention the any of the users mentioned in the tweet (if any).

The first four features show how closely the author and the user is interacting with each other. The remaining ones indicate how the tweet is related to the user and her interests.

3.1.2 Experimental Setup

Dataset: We used the Twitter REST API[2] to crawl information about the users and their tweets. To train the classifier, we need both positive and negative examples. The positive examples in our case are obvious: the user retweeting a given tweet. However, the negative examples are a little bit problematic since we do not know whether the user did not retweet a given tweet on purpose or she did not even see that tweet. In order to make sure that the latter is not the case, we randomly chose seed users who are considered as "ordinary". We assumed that if a user has (10-1,000) friends/followers, tweets (1-200) times a week, and has tweeted more than 10 times so far, then she is considered to be an ordinary user. Most active Twitter users fall into this category. These users are periodically logging into

[1]http://www.cs.waikato.ac.nz/ml/weka/

[2]http://apiwiki.twitter.com/w/page/22554679/Twitter-API-Documentation

Table 1: Classification results for predicting retweetability of the tweets. The metrics are based on the positive instances.

Features	Precision	Recall	F-Measure
All	0.771	0.683	0.724
Tweet-based	0.771	0.369	0.499
Author-based	0.636	0.201	0.305
User-based	0.728	0.191	0.302
Content-based	0.690	0.019	0.037

Table 2: Tweet ranking results based on the retweetability.

Features	NDCG@1	NDCG@5	NDCG@10
All	0.814	0.834	0.809
Tweet-based	0.797	0.722	0.718
User-based	0.306	0.381	0.392
Content-based	0.376	0.326	0.339
Author-based	0.239	0.263	0.277
Random_baseline	0.095	0.099	0.111

Twitter (i.e. tweeting 1-200 times a week), therefore, they are less likely to skip the tweets appearing on their timelines. Yet, we cannot guarantee that they read all their tweets.

We crawled 242 ordinary seed users, all their followees and tweets. Then, for each seed user, we randomly selected 100 tweets that would appear on her Twitter feed. All together, we had 24,200 tweets, 2,547 of which were retweeted by the seed users. For each of the 24,200 tweets, we extracted the features using information from the author of the tweet, the tweet itself, and the user who is receiving that tweet. We followed the "RT @username" convention on deciding whether a tweet is RT or not. Twitter's "retweet" button also adheres to this convention implicitly.

Results: The classification results using each group of features are shown in Table 1. *Precision* and *recall* metrics are used in the evaluation. The metrics are evaluated based on the positive instances. Since the RT ratio is almost 0.1 in our corpus, building an effective classifier on the positive instances is quite challenging. Nevertheless, the results obtained are reasonable.

Among the feature groups, the tweet-based ones have better performance. Since the tweet-based features are quite common in other microblogging services, this is a useful result. On the other hand, none of the feature groups gives satisfactory results alone.

We also applied the "leave-one-out" technique to see which features are more useful. From the tweet-based features, the presence of a URL, whether the tweet is retweeted, and the tf-idf score of the tweet were the most effective features. In addition, the "is she my conversation friend?" and "Did I use that URL domain" features from the user-based category are also useful features.

In the main part of the experiments, we ranked the incoming tweets for the 242 users to optimize the retweetability probability of the top ranked tweets. The results are shown in Table 2. For this part of the experiments, we used the *NDCG@k* metric. The relevance score for a tweet is 1 if the user retweets it later, 0 otherwise. Along with the results using each set of features, we also listed the performance of a random baseline, which is quite similar to how Twitter would rank the tweets. Again, tweet-based features outperform other groups of features. Using all the features, it is possible to achieve very effective ranking of the tweets for retweetability. In other words, the Coordinate Ascent algorithm can learn how to rank the tweets to place the the ones that will be retweeted on the top.

Table 3: Classification results for predicting whether a user will retweet a given tweet.

Features	Precision	Recall	F-Measure
All	0.965	0.668	0.789
User-based	0.976	0.629	0.765
Author-based	0.679	0.095	0.166
Content-based	0.0	0.0	0.0

3.2 Ranking Targeted Users

Similar to the previous section, we attempted to answer the following two questions: "Can we classify the users based on whether they retweeted a given tweet?" and "Can we rank the users to potentially identify which users should receive a tweet?". Again, we used the same classifier and learning to rank algorithm with a slightly different set of features. 5-fold cross-validation is also applied to split the dataset.

3.2.1 Features

Author-based: From the author's point of view, the features are as follows: Is the user my friend (i.e. am I also following her), is the user my conversation friend, did I RT her before, did she RT me before, did she use the hashtags in the tweet (if any), am I mentioning her in the tweet.

Content-based: Novelty of the tweet (i.e. minimum cosine distance of this tweet to the user's previous tweets) and the QL score of the user based on the LM of her tweets, where the tweet is the query.

User-based: We used the same set of author-based features with the tweet ranking task, which are applied to the users, not to the author of the given tweet.

We did not consider the tweet-based features here because our main focus is ranking the users and tweet-related features would be the same for all the users seeing this tweet.

3.2.2 Experimental Setup

Dataset: In this part of the experiments, we randomly selected 665 tweets which were retweeted at least by one user. For each tweet, we crawled all the users who follow the author of the tweet. The total number of users were 53,136. Due to the problem we stated about the negative instances of retweeting, we eliminated non-ordinary users from this pool. In addition to the described ordinary user criteria, we also enforced these users to tweet at least 10 times a week, to make sure that they are more likely to read all their incoming tweets. Finally we had 20,397 followers for the 655 tweets.

Results: Table 3 lists the classification results, where the the task was to decide whether a user will retweet a given tweet or not. This problem is more challenging than the previous classification task, because out of 20,397 people, just 780 retweeted something. In other words, the average number of RTs for the selected 665 tweets is 1.17. Even so, our classifier managed to achieve a relatively high F-measure. User-based features dominated other features, but still benefited from them in the overall model. The content-

Table 4: User ranking results based on the retweet likelihood.

Features	Best@1	Best@5	Best@10	RR@10
All	0.602	0.756	0.828	0.684
User-based	0.602	0.657	0.736	0.637
Author-based	0.528	0.675	0.782	0.592
Content-based	0.362	0.676	0.795	0.508

based features had unacceptably poor performance on the positive instances. Our feature analysis through "leave-one-out" technique revealed that the best feature was the tweet-rate of the users. From the author-based features, "did she use the hashtags in the tweet (if any)" and "am I mentioning her in the tweet" also proved to be effective.

Considering that approximately one follower retweets each tweet, instead of *NDCG@k*, we used *Best@k* and *Reciprocal Rank* metrics for evaluating how effectively we can rank the users. The results are demonstrated in Table 4. We can infer that, for instance, 75% of the times, the user who will RT the given tweet will appear on the top 5 rankings (e.g. Best@5: 0.756). It is also shown that the retweeter appears either on the top, or the 2nd position in the list on average (e.g. RR@10: 0.684). Although the feature groups do not have significant variances in performance, it is notable that the content-based features do work here even when used alone.

4. PILOT USER STUDY

In order to understand whether RT prediction can be an indicator of the interestingness of the tweets, we conducted a pilot user study on 10 volunteers. In the study, the participants rated a total of 700 tweets that they see on their Twitter feed, based on the following rating scheme:

2: I'm glad seeing this tweet.

1: I don't mind seeing this tweet. I may enjoy reading it if I have time.

0: I prefer not to see this tweet at all. It's a waste of my time.

The average rating was 0.95.

We then applied the tweet ranking model described in Section 3.1 to the tweets presented to the participants. As shown in Table 5, when the tweets are ranked temporally (as Twitter does), the NDCG values are lower than our method of ranking the tweets. The size of the pilot study is too small to make sound conclusions. Nevertheless, ranking the incoming tweets based on their likelihood of being retweeted by a specific user yields promising results in this user study, which supports our motivation.

5. CONCLUSIONS

In this paper, we proposed two methods for tackling the information overload problem in microblogs. Using four groups of features, we trained a Coordinate Ascent learning to rank algorithm to rank the incoming tweets to help the users interact with the tweets they are more likely to retweet. Additionally, we ranked users given a tweet, so that the users who are more likely to retweet have higher ranks. While our first approach effectively ranks the tweets, the second approach can help to decide the priority of a tweet for a specific user at an earlier stage. Finally, conducting a pilot user study, we observed that the tweets users want to read correlates with the ones they are likely to retweet.

Table 5: Performance of the RT likelihood based tweet ranking on interestingness.

Features	NDCG@1	NDCG@5	NDCG@10
Our model	0.4	0.543	0.541
Twitter	0.45	0.449	0.444

6. ACKNOWLEDGMENTS

This work was supported in part by the Center for Intelligent Information Retrieval. Any opinions, findings and conclusions or recommendations expressed in this material are those of the authors and do not necessarily reflect those of the sponsor.

7. REFERENCES

[1] D. Boyd, S. Golder, and G. Lotan. Tweet, tweet, retweet: Conversational aspects of retweeting on twitter. In *HICSS*, 2010.

[2] C. Castillo, M. Mendoza, and B. Poblete. Information credibility on twitter. In *WWW*, 2011.

[3] S. A. Golder, A. Marwick, and S. Yardi. A structural approach to contact recommendations in online social networks. In *Workshop on Search in Social Media at ACM SIGIR*, 2009.

[4] J. Hannon, M. Bennett, and B. Smyth. Recommending twitter users to follow using content and collaborative filtering approaches. In *RecSys*, 2010.

[5] L. Hong, O. Dan, and B. D. Davison. Predicting popular messages in twitter. In *WWW*, 2011.

[6] S. Petrovic, M. Osborne, and V. Lavrenko. Rt to win! predicting message propagation in twitter. In *ICWSM*, 2011.

[7] J. M. Ponte and W. B. Croft. A language modeling approach to information retrieval. In *SIGIR*, 1998.

[8] D. Ramage, S. T. Dumais, and D. J. Liebling. Characterizing microblogs with topic models. In *ICWSM*, 2010.

[9] J. Sankaranarayanan, H. Samet, B. E. Teitler, M. D. Lieberman, and J. Sperling. Twitterstand: news in tweets. In *GIS*, 2009.

[10] B. Sriram, D. Fuhry, E. Demir, H. Ferhatosmanoglu, and M. Demirbas. Short text classification in twitter to improve information filtering. In *SIGIR*, 2010.

[11] B. Suh, L. Hong, P. Pirolli, and E. H. Chi. Want to be retweeted? large scale analytics on factors impacting retweet in twitter network. In *SOCIALCOM*, 2010.

[12] J. Weng, E.-P. Lim, J. Jiang, and Q. He. Twitterrank: finding topic-sensitive influential twitterers. In *WSDM*, 2010.

[13] Y. Yamaguchi, T. Takahashi, T. Amagasa, and H. Kitagawa. Turank: Twitter user ranking based on user-tweet graph analysis. In *WISE*. 2010.

[14] Z. Yang, J. Guo, K. Cai, J. Tang, J. Li, L. Zhang, and Z. Su. Understanding retweeting behaviors in social networks. In *CIKM*, 2010.

[15] T. R. Zaman, R. Herbrich, J. Van Gael, and D. Stern. Predicting information spreading in twitter. In *Workshop on Computational Social Science and the Wisdom of Crowds at NIPS*, 2010.

A Semi-Supervised Hybrid System to Enhance the Recommendation of Channels in Terms of Campaign ROI

Julie Séguéla
Cedric-CNAM & Multiposting.fr
292, rue Saint-Martin
75141, Paris, France
jseguela@multiposting.fr

Gilbert Saporta
Cedric-CNAM
292, rue Saint-Martin
75141, Paris, France
gilbert.saporta@cnam.fr

ABSTRACT

In domains such as Marketing, Advertising or even Human Resources (sourcing), decision-makers have to choose the most suitable channels according to their objectives when starting a campaign. In this paper, three recommender systems providing channel ("user") ranking for a given campaign ("item") are introduced. This work refers exclusively to the new item problem, which is still a challenging topic in the literature. The first two systems are standard content-based recommendation approaches, with different rating estimation techniques (model-based vs heuristic-based). To overcome the lacks of previous approaches, we introduce a new hybrid system using a supervised similarity based on PLS components. Algorithms are compared in a case study: purpose is to predict the ranking of job boards (job search web sites) in terms of ROI (return on investment) per job posting. In this application, the semi-supervised hybrid system outperforms standard approaches.

Categories and Subject Descriptors

H.3.1 [**Content Analysis and Indexing**]: Indexing methods; I.2.6 [**Learning**]: Knowledge acquisition

General Terms

Algorithms, Experimentation

Keywords

Recommender systems, feature extraction, PLS, channels

1. INTRODUCTION

With the expansion of internet to advertise, the number of potential channels (and targets) is exponentially growing. Today, a great challenge common to several research domains is the development of intelligent tools to support (or to replace) users in their choices. In this context, we are introducing algorithms which aim at providing a ranking of channels according to the expected ROI, in order to help decision-makers to identify the best channels. To do that, we resort to an innovative application of recommender system, in which items are assumed to be campaigns, users are assumed to be channels, and ratings are assumed to be observed returns of campaigns on channels. The type of recommender studied is very specific: since each campaign is different, we don't have any explicit preference on items of interest. Consequently, traditional collaborative methods are excluded: we have to face to item cold-start problem, which is still a challenging topic in the literature. In order to simplify and to compare the effectiveness of algorithms on high dimensional data, items are only described by textual data. Background is presented in Section 2. Algorithms and performance indicators are described in Section 3. Section 4 is dedicated to a case study: identify the most effective sourcing channels to support recruiters in their choice.

CIKM'11, October 24–28, 2011, Glasgow, Scotland, UK.

2. BACKGROUND

2.1 Feature extraction

As previously mentioned, campaigns are characterized by a text. To extract a set of features from the text we will use several common techniques in Information Retrieval and compare them. First, we use the well-known Vector Space Model in order to obtain a vector of term frequencies for each campaign. To improve text representation we will use TF-IDF weighting, which decreases weights of keywords appearing in many documents and not useful to distinguish a relevant document from an irrelevant one. After weighting, documents will be indexed by Latent Semantic Analysis, a dimensionality reduction technique through a singular value decomposition of term-document matrices [4].

2.2 Recommender systems

Recommender systems are usually classified into three main categories: content-based recommendations, collaborative recommendations, and hybrid approaches [1]. The first approach proposed is a content-based algorithm which recommendation technique is based on a model (PLS regression, see 2.3). The second approach uses a heuristic-based recommendation technique (computing of a feature-based similarity measure) in a content-based approach. In addition to these two basic approaches, we introduce a hybrid recommender (output produced by a content-based model is used as an input in a collaborative approach) based on a heuristic technique to estimate ratings. Hybridization strategy used is the same as in [5] or [2], also called "collaboration through content".

2.3 PLS Regression

Partial Least Squares Regression (PLS-R), introduced by [9], is a technique that generalizes and combines features from principal component analysis and multiple regression. This method is used when the number of predictors is large, and also large compared to the number of observations. The higher the number of predictors is, the higher the risk of important correlations between variables is. In case of high correlations between predictors, standard regression methods fail in estimating coefficients. As an alternative, PLS-R provides robust components (linear combinations of predictors), independent and highly correlated with the dependent variable. In this work, we have to cope with a large number of predictors (number of features extracted from campaign descriptions) and high correlations, so PLS-R seems to be a very suitable technique.

3. RECOMMENDATION APPROACHES

3.1 Extraction of PLS components

One part of PLS-R algorithm consists in computing non-correlated components, highly correlated with the dependent variable. The computing of components is based on NIPALS algorithm, first introduced by [8] for principal component analysis. Considering $(x_1, ..., x_p)$ a set of features, potentially highly correlated, and a dependent variable r, the first component is: $t_1 = w_{11}x_1 + \cdots + w_{1p}x_p$, where $w_{1j} = \frac{cov(x_j, r)}{\sqrt{\sum_{j=1}^{p} cov^2(x_j, r)}}$. Residual r_1 is obtained by regressing r on t_1. The second component t_2 is a linear combination of x_{1j}, residuals coming from the regressions of x_j on t_1: $t_2 = w_{21}x_{11} + \cdots + w_{2p}x_{1p}$, where $w_{2j} = \frac{cov(x_{1j}, r_1)}{\sqrt{\sum_{j=1}^{p} cov^2(x_{1j}, r_1)}}$. The regression of r on t_1 and t_2 gives the residual r_2. This iterative process continues until reaching H components, where H is determined by cross validation [3].

3.2 Recommender algorithms

Let $r_{u,i}$ and $p_{u,i}$ be respectively actual and predicted rating of user u for item i.

3.2.1 *Model-based recommender: PLS-R*

The first approach is content-based, and ratings are estimated by a PLS regression model learned on each user. After computing of PLS components (see 3.1), a linear regression is applied: $r = c_1t_1 + \cdots + c_Ht_H + r_{H+1}$, where c_h are the regression coefficients. PLS components and predictions $p_{u,i}$ are computed by *10-fold* cross-validation.

3.2.2 *Heuristic feature-based recommender*

The second approach is also content-based but ratings are predicted by an heuristic technique. The similarity of the new item with respect to all past items is computed. It is a feature-based similarity since no rating is known for this new item. This approach assumes that similar items regarding to their features should have a similar rating for a given user. Four similarity measures between items i_1 and i_2 are tested. Since we are working on textual data, cosine similarity measure will be used. As a particular case, we will test constant similarity measure. The following similarity functions are based on Euclidean distance: d_{i_1,i_2}(the lower the Euclidean distance, the greater the similarity). We use the same method as [6] for generating a third similarity measure: $sim(i_1, i_2) = \max_{i_k \in K}(d_{i_1,i_k}) - d_{i_1,i_2}$, where K is the set of $|K|$ nearest neighbors of i_1 according to d_{i_1,i_2}. Finally, the fourth similarity function is inverse proportional to Euclidean distance: $sim(i_1, i_2) = 1/d_{i_1,i_2}$.

Ratings are then estimated thanks to an aggregating function [1], computed on item neighborhood. Expected rating of user u for item i_1 is given by:

$$p_{u,i_1} = \frac{\sum_{i_{k'} \in K} sim(i_1, i_{k'}) \times r_{u,i_{k'}}}{\sum_{i_{k'} \in K} sim(i_1, i_{k'})} \quad (1)$$

where K is the set of $|K|$ nearest neighbors of i_1 with respect to the correspondent similarity measure. For constant similarity, which means computing average rating on i_1 neighborhood, nearest neighbors are determined by Euclidean distance.

3.2.3 *Semi-supervised hybrid recommender*

While recommender introduced in Section 3.2.2 is based on a "naive" similarity, this approach is based on a supervised similarity measure which allows to identify nearest neighbors with respect to relevant features. Instead of computing Euclidean distance on item features, it is computed on PLS components which are extracted so as to explain as much as possible actual ratings. Similarity measures are computed as defined in Section 3.2.2. Cosine similarity is not used because in practice, the number of components kept is very low (1 to 12). Similarities are then taken as inputs in a collaborative approach by respecting (1) formula.

These three approaches will be respectively named $S1$, $S2$, and $S3$ in the rest of the paper. The third algorithm is built so as to overcome weaknesses of the first two approaches. PLS-R implies a linear constraint between components and the dependent variable, whereas other approaches are non-linear. In addition, the risk of overfitting is high (because of the high number of input variables) while it is low or absent in other approaches. We appreciate the ability of $S1$ and $S3$ to provide interpretation tools of variable impact (at the PLS modeling step), absent in $S2$.

3.3 System evaluation

Recommender systems are systematically compared with the performance of the "average" recommender (AR). The latter provides channel recommendations based on their average rating (computed on all past campaigns) and does not take campaign features into account.

3.3.1 *Mean Absolute Error*

Mean Absolute Error (MAE) or Root Mean Squared Error (RMSE) are commonly used to assess the capability of a system to provide good rating estimations. In our context, users have big differences in the number of rated items. This can bias our estimator because of the high variability between average ratings of users. Consequently, the mean of users MAE is used to compare system performances on the prediction task: $\overline{MAE} = \frac{1}{|U|} \sum_{u \in U} \frac{\sum_{i \in D_u} |p_{u,i} - r_{u,i}|}{|D_u|}$, where U is the set of users and D_u the set of items previously rated by user u.

3.3.2 *Ranking error and return loss*

Although providing an accurate prediction is important, professionals want to choose channels with the best ROI under their budget constraint. The estimated return on investment of campaign i on channel u is: $ROI_{u,i} = \frac{p_{u,i}}{c_u}$, given that the cost of a channel c_u is independent from the campaign. Since the cost is fixed for a given channel, ROI is deducted in an obvious way from the estimated return $p_{u,i}$. In order to simplify and without loss of generality towards performance evaluation, we consider a fixed cost c for all channels. Consequently, classifying estimated returns in decreasing order is sufficient to give us the ranking of channels. In order to assess system performances on a domain-driven way, we are interested in return loss generated by an error in channel ranking. In this case study, we focus on the first rank channel because it is by definition that with the most important return. Two measures of performance are considered: the ability of system to find the first rank channel, and the reduction of return loss when using an alternative recommender S instead of using average recommender AR. Let a be the number of campaigns for which first rank channel is correctly identified, and $a+b$ the number of campaigns, the first evaluation measure for recommender S is: $Precision_S = \frac{a}{a+b}$. Let r_{R1} be the return associated with actual first rank channel and $r_{P1,S}$ the return associated with first rank channel predicted by system S. Per se, $r_{R1} \geq r_{P1,S}$, equality being true when the first channel is correctly predicted. The second indicator is defined by: $Loss\ reduction_S = \frac{\sum(r_{R1}-r_{P1,AR})-\sum(r_{R1}-r_{P1,S})}{\sum(r_{R1}-r_{P1,AR})}$.

4. EXPERIMENTS: JOB BOARD RECOMMENDATION FOR JOB POSTINGS

The increasing number of online job boards has made crucial the introduction of decision-making tools adapted to recruiter needs. On a job board, a job posting ROI can be measured by the number of applications received per currency unit spent (or symmetrically the cost per application received). We consider that each job board has the same cost and focus on the number of applications received on channels. The purpose of application is to provide a tool which automatically recommends the best job board with respect to the expected return. To our knowledge, this kind of data has never been studied in the recommender system literature. Data are provided by *Multiposting.fr*, an online job posting distributor, and concern generalist and specialized job boards.

4.1 Dataset description

This kind of dataset is quite unusual in recommender system literature: only few users (31 job boards), very small dataset (about 30 500 ratings), and high rating variability inside and between users. Return on a job board is not limited contrary to usual recommenders where ratings take values between 0 and 5, which explains that our collaborative recommendation approaches are item-based. The number of items is reasonable with about 7 730 jobs posted on 4 different job boards in average. We are studying job boards with 100 postings and more.

4.2 Feature extraction

The first step is the preprocessing of job offer texts to obtain "bag-of-words" representation: lemmatization and tagging, filtering according to grammatical category, filtering words occurring in less than five postings. Before preprocessing, a posting is in average 165 tokens long, and the total size of vocabulary is about 20 000 distinct words. After preprocessing, a posting is in average 92 tokens long, and the vocabulary size is reduced to 5 000 distinct words. During experiments, several text representation techniques are tested: term frequency (TF), TF-IDF weighting, LSI (with TF-IDF weighting). Since $S2$ is a non supervised system, the number of dimensions kept with LSI can impact the recommender performance: experiments lead us to keep 50 dimensions (highest *loss reduction*).

Table 1: PLS-R (S1) results

Feature representation	$\overline{MAE}$	Precision (%)	Loss reduction (%)
AR	10.18	62.8	.
TF	7.80	63.3	27.7
TF-IDF	7.64	62.7	23.3
LSI	7.98	61.8	27.8

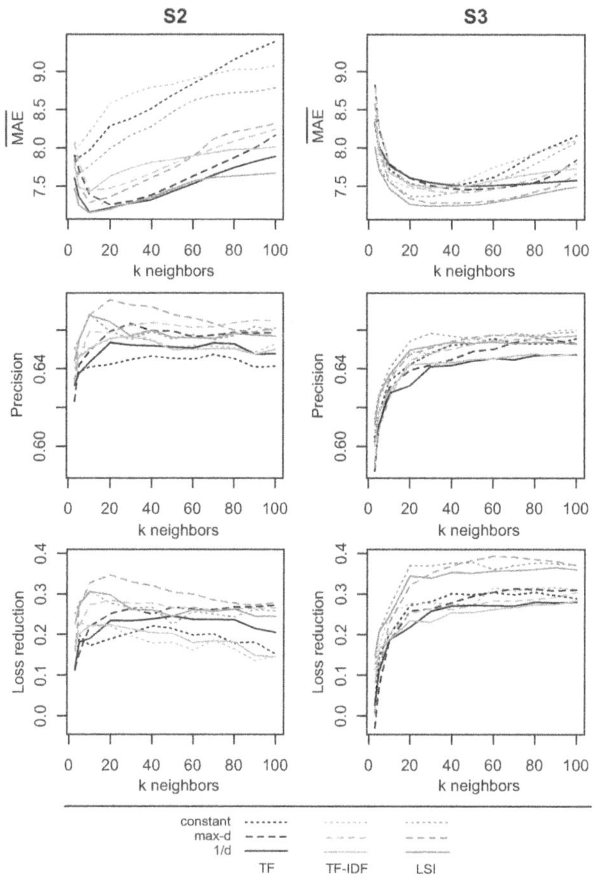

Figure 1: S2 and S3 performance according to feature representation method and similarity measure.

4.3 Results

Loss reduction will be used to identify the best recommenders while other indicators, $\overline{MAE}$ and *Precision*, have an illustrative purpose. Table 1 shows $S1$ results according to model input data, and average recommender (AR) results. $S1$ globally outperforms average recommender and differences associated with different feature representation techniques are very slight. Results of experiments for $S2$ and $S3$ systems are presented in Figure 1. Results obtained

Table 2: **Best recommender for each approach**

Approach	$\overline{MAE}$	Precision (%)	Loss reduction (%)
AR	10.18	62.8	.
S1	7.98	61.8	27.8
S2($k = 20$)	7.36	**67.6**	34.6
S3($k = 60$)	**7.31**	65.7	**39.2**

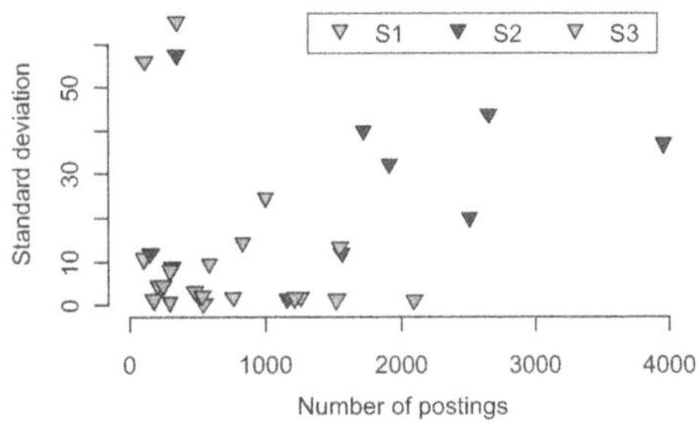

Figure 2: The best system for each job board according to the number of postings and return variability.

with cosine similarity are not represented because they are very close to those obtained with average on neighborhood (constant similarity). Whatever the similarity measure, for both $S2$ and $S3$ approaches, LSI representation allows to obtain the best performance indicators (except for $\overline{MAE}$ in $S2$ approach where TF representation performs equally). Assuming that LSI provides the most relevant features to explain the job board return, we now focus on loss reduction criterion and comment the impact of similarity measure. While $max - d$ is better than other similarities in approach $S2$, the three measures are fairly equivalent in approach $S3$. The highest loss reduction is reached with $max - d$ similarity in both approaches, so we choose it for a general comparison of recommender performances (Table 2). The three approaches outperform average recommender. $S2$ allows to reach a higher loss reduction than $S1$, but $S3$ is the best recommender with regard to this performance indicator.

In the non supervised approach ($S2$), the optimal number of neighbors is very low: 20 or less. Especially with constant similarity (average prediction), $\overline{MAE}$ increases drastically with the number of neighbors. That measure gives too much importance to distant neighbors (contrary to $1/d$ weighting). In the semi-supervised approach ($S3$), indicators are more stable from 20 to 100 neighbors. PLS components operate as an information smoothing method.

4.4 Discussion

In Figure 2, each point represents a job board and color designates the winner recommender (that which has provided the lowest MAE on the channel). $S1$ is the best recommender on only 2 job boards, $S2$ on 10 job boards and $S3$ is winning on 19 job boards. While $S3$ seems to be efficient on job boards with few postings, on the contrary, $S2$ seems to perform better on job boards with a high number of postings (the highest the number of postings, the highest the probability to find a very similar offer on the job board). Since we have kept a selection of features (and not all features) as input in PLS modeling, some information has been lost in the process. But when job boards have few postings, generalization power of PLS provides better results.

5. CONCLUSION AND FUTURE WORK

We have introduced a hybrid recommender suitable in the cold-start case. This system outperforms content-based (model-based and heuristic-based) approaches, by combining the understanding of campaign features impact on channel ROI and the usage of collaborative knowledge. The evaluation of system performances on the basis of channel returns ensures relevant results in practice for similar applications.

Campaigns are described by texts but we could add other information to the vector of descriptors. In this latter case, $S3$ would be a suitable recommendation approach (fitting of predictor weights according to their power of explanation) contrary to $S2$. Weights of variables could be even more controlled with techniques such as multiblock PLS [7]. In the future, we will test other similarity functions (e.g. gaussian) under a nonparametric theoretical framework.

6. ACKNOWLEDGMENTS

We would like to thank Stéphane Le Viet and Gautier Machelon (*Multiposting.fr* company) for supporting this work. We also thank Guillaume Bandet (*Multiposting.fr* company) for his many helpful comments on this paper.

7. REFERENCES

[1] G. Adomavicius and A. Tuzhilin. Toward the next generation of recommender systems: A survey of the state-of-the-art and possible extensions. *IEEE Transactions on Knowledge and Data Engineering*, 17(6):734–749, 2005.

[2] M. Balabanovic. An adaptive web page recommendation service. In *Agents 97: Proceedings of the 1st International Conference on Autonomous Agents*, pages 378–385, 1997.

[3] A. Höskuldsson. PLS regression methods. *Journal of Chemometrics*, 2:211–228, 1988.

[4] D. I. Martin and M. W. Berry. Mathematical foundations behind latent semantic analysis. In T. K. Landauer, D. S. McNamara, S. Dennis, and W. Kintsch editors, *Handbook of Latent Semantic Analysis*, pages 35–55. Lawrence Erlbaum Associates, 2007.

[5] M. J. Pazzani. A framework for collaborative, content-based and demographic filtering. *Artificial Intelligence Review*, 13(5/6):393–408, 1999.

[6] U. Shardanand. *Social Information Filtering for Music Recommendation.* MIT EECS M. Eng. thesis, 1994.

[7] L. E. Wangen and B. R. Kowalski. A multiblock partial least squares algorithm for investigating complex chemical systems. *Journal of Chemometrics*, 3(1):3–20, 1989.

[8] H. Wold. Estimation of principal components and related models by iterative least squares. In P. R. Krishnaiaah editor, *Multivariate Analysis*, pages 391–420. New York: Academic Press, 1966.

[9] S. Wold, H. Martens, and H. Wold. The multivariate calibration problem in chemistry solved by the pls method. In *Proceedings of the Conference on Matrix Pencils*, pages 286–293, 1983.

YANA: An Efficient Privacy-Preserving Recommender System for Online Social Communities

Dongsheng Li[†], Qin Lv[§], Li Shang[‡], Ning Gu[†]

†School of Computer Science
Fudan University
Shanghai 200433 P.R.China
dongshengli@fudan.edu.cn
ninggu@fudan.edu.cn

§CS Department
University of Colorado at Boulder
Boulder, CO 80309 USA
qin.lv@colorado.edu

‡ECEE Department
University of Colorado at Boulder
Boulder, CO 80309 USA
li.shang@colorado.edu

ABSTRACT

Many recommender systems use collaborative filtering, a method that makes recommendations based on what are liked by other users with similar interests. Serious privacy issues may arise in this process, especially for online social communities, as sensitive personal information (e.g., content interests) may be collected and disclosed to other parties. In this paper, we propose *YANA* (short for "you are not alone"), a group-based content recommender system for online social communities, which protects users' interest privacy via interest-based groups and pseudo users. We have developed a prototype system on desktop and mobile devices, and evaluated it using real-world data. The results demonstrate that YANA can effectively protect users' privacy, while achieving high recommendation quality and energy efficiency.

Categories and Subject Descriptors

H.3.3 [**Information Search and Retrieval**]: Information filtering; K.4.1 [**Public Policy Issues**]: Privacy

General Terms

Algorithms, Experimentation

Keywords

Collaborative filtering, Privacy, Efficiency

1. INTRODUCTION

Many recommender systems [3, 2, 6]) adopt *collaborative filtering* (CF), a popular recommendation method that has high accuracy, low overhead, and is generally applicable to various domains. In CF-based systems, the server collects user information and predicts a user's interest on an item based on the decisions (or ratings) of other similar users. In this process, users' personal interests are exposed to the recommender server, which raises several privacy concerns.

Recent research efforts towards privacy-preserving collaborative filtering (PPCF) have generated solutions in two main categories. One is based on secure multi-party computation (SMPC) [5, 9], and the other is based on randomization [4, 10]. SMPC-based methods require a large amount of computation and communication in order for users to jointly compute a value (e.g., overall rating for an item) without disclosing their individual values. This is inefficient for online social communities, where the number of users and items can be millions or even billions. What is more, many users tend to access online social communities via their smartphones or tablet PCs, which have limited computation capability and battery capacity. The efficiency of PPCF is thus critical. Randomization-based methods trade accuracy for privacy, which means users will receive lower-quality recommendation in order to protect their privacy.

In this paper, we propose *YANA* (short for "you are not alone"), a privacy-preserving content recommender system for online social communities. YANA can protect user privacy, while at the same achieving high recommendation quality and energy efficiency. YANA is group based – it automatically organizes users into groups with diverse interests such that each user's private interests can be hidden among a set of users. A number of pseudo users are created for each group, each representing a unique interest and the union of them covers all interests of the group. The pseudo users communicate with the recommender server on behalf of the real users. The real users can then obtain personalized recommendations based on the server's recommendations to the pseudo users, without exposing their private data to the server. To the best of our knowledge, this is the first work that targets efficient privacy-preserving collaborative filtering for recommender systems in online social communities.

2. SYSTEM OVERVIEW

Targeting the large-scale users and items in online social communities, YANA is designed to be highly efficient and scalable. As illustrated in Figure 1, YANA consists of three key components:

- **User groups**. YANA automatically organizes users into groups with diverse content interests, and individual users' content interests are hidden and aggregated within each group. Thus, user privacy is protected from the server. Inside each user group, users collaborate via privacy-preserving mechanisms, including efficient secure multi-party computation (SMPC), to protect user privacy from being inferred by other members in the group.

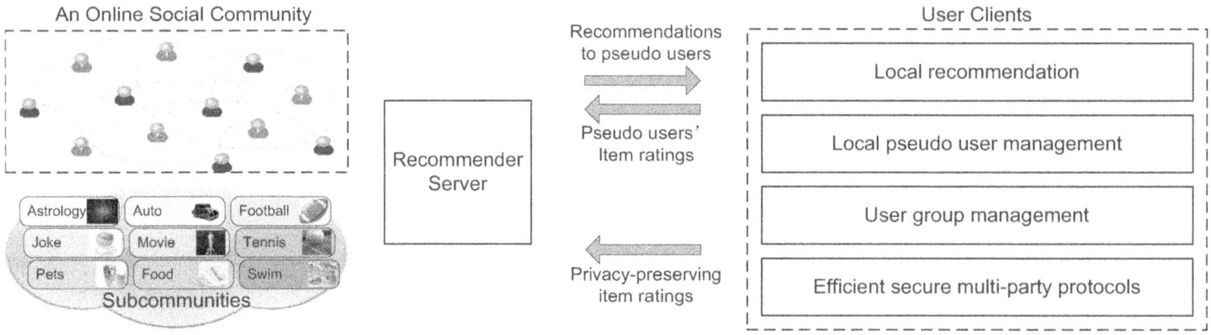

Figure 1: YANA: Group-based privacy-preserving recommendation for online social communities.

- **Pseudo users**. To obtain recommendations, the users in a group maintain a set of local pseudo users, each of which represents a unique interest liked by at least one group member. The pseudo users together cover all interests of the group members. The server makes recommendations to the pseudo users based on their interests, and the real users can re-calculate their personalized recommendations based on their own interests distribution and the server's recommendations to the pseudo users.
- **Recommendation algorithm**. To make recommendations, the server first needs to collect users' item ratings. We achieve this through efficient secure multi-party computation inside each group, and the aggregated decisions of each group are sent to the server via pseudo users. The server then runs the proposed collaborative filtering algorithm to make recommendations to the pseudo users. These recommendations to pseudo users are used by the real users to calculate their own personalized recommendations.

3. USER GROUPING

3.1 User Group Definition

We leverage *user groups* to hide individual users' content interests among a set of users with diverse interests, such that no one can associate any specific interest with a particular user. A user group is defined as following:

DEFINITION 1 (USER GROUP). *A user group g is a 4-tuple: $\{\mathcal{U}_g, \mathcal{WU}_g, \mathcal{S}_g, \mathcal{P}_g\}$, in which $\mathcal{U}_g$ is a set of users who have joined g and collaborate together to hide the privacy of each other, $\mathcal{WU}_g$ is a set of users who want to join the group (i.e., on the waiting list of g), $\mathcal{S}_g$ is the set of interests that users in $\mathcal{U}_g$ have, and $\mathcal{P}_g$ is a set of pseudo users who communicate with the server on behalf of the real users.*

3.2 User Group Construction

Given the user group definition above, we propose a method to automatically organize users into groups with diverse interests in a distributed and privacy-preserving way. The basic process of user group construction works as follows: 1) some random users are chosen to host groups; 2) other users choose the groups that are hosted/joined by their friends; 3) users in groups check if their privacy requirements (e.g., the number of users and the number of interests inside a group) are satisfied via distributed privacy-preserving computation.

Condition checking in Step 3) can be reduced to computing the sum of n real values privately held by n parties. To achieve secure n-party computation, we adopt an efficient secure multi-party summation protocol **SecureSum** [8]. The basic idea is as follows: 1) users randomly divide their local value into r parts with the property that the sum of the r parts equals their local value; 2) users randomly send/receive parts to/from other random users (i.e., random shuffling of the split parts); 3) after some rounds, each user sums its local parts and sends the sum to a host; 4) the host sums all values and returns the final result to all users.

4. PSEUDO USER MANAGEMENT

After user grouping, pseudo users are generated to protect user privacy and provide recommendations to real users. Real users interact with servers through the pseudo users, and all the information sent to the server by the pseudo users are the aggregated results of a group of users, so that the server cannot identify the information of individual real users. Each pseudo user acts as a "delegate" for a particular interest, and the recommendations to the pseudo user can be utilized by real users who have that interest.

Local pseudo users are formed based on the interests of the users inside each group. Let $\mathcal{S}_g$ be the set of interests for a given group g. Then the group members will construct $|\mathcal{P}_g| = |\mathcal{S}_g|$ pseudo users. For each pseudo user p with interest s_p, the items that p likes is the union of the items liked by users in the group who have interest s_p. One issue in maintaining local pseudo users is to update the interest profiles of the pseudo users as new items are generated in online social communities. This step is important, as we rely on the pseudo users' item decisions (or ratings) to make recommendations to pseudo users (with similar interest) in other user groups. Given a new item x, whether x is liked by pseudo user p depends on the number of real users who share interest with p and like x:

$$w_{x,p} = \sum_{u \in \mathcal{U}_g \text{ and } p \in \mathcal{P}_g} w_{x,u} * \lambda(u, s_p) \qquad (1)$$

where $w_{x,u} = 1$ if u has read x, and 0 otherwise. s_p is the interest of pseudo user p, and $\lambda(u, s_p) = |X_{s_p} \cap X_u|/|X_u|$ (where X_u is the set of items that u is interested in). Equation 1 can be computed securely by the **SecureSum** protocol among a group of users. Item x is then assigned to the pseudo user with the highest non-zero $w_{x,p}$ value.

5. PRIVACY-PRESERVING CONTENT RECOMMENDATION

After the generation of local pseudo users, the server can collect the interest profiles of local pseudo users of all groups. The server can then make recommendations to the pseudo users based on the item ratings of other pseudo users. However, the use of pseudo users and user groups, while protecting user interest privacy, introduces new challenges to the recommendation process:

- **Group ratings of new items.** Given a group g with K users. Each pseudo user represents a specific content interests, and some real users may have shared interests. How to measure the importance of an item within a group g is challenging. To determine the rating of an item inside a group, we need to consider two factors: 1) how the users in the group like it, and 2) the importance (or "expertise") of the users in the group for that kind of items. The first factor can be measured by $w_{x,p}$ in Equation 1, as higher value indicates that the item is more popular in the group. The second factor can be measured similarly as follows. Since the pseudo user p represents a specific interest s_p, the importance of user u with regard to s_p can be measured by the fraction of items liked by u that belong to s_p. Moreover, the weight of the users who do not like s_p will be 0, which means that the "non-experts" will not influence the rating of an item. Thus, the rating of item x by the users in group g can be computed as follows:

$$v_{x,g} = \sum_{u \in \mathcal{U}_g} \lambda(u, s_{\tilde{p}}) \tag{2}$$

where $\tilde{p} = \arg\max_{p \in \mathcal{P}_g} \{w_{x,p}\}$. The user who maintains pseudo user $\tilde{p}$ will send the pair $(w_{x,\tilde{p}}, v_{x,g})$ to the server.

- **Server-side recommendation.** The server cannot get a standard user-item matrix, which is required in the standard collaborative filtering algorithm. Thus, another challenge is how to adapt the standard collaborative filtering algorithm to work in the new form of data. The server generates the rating of item x for pseudo user q as follows:

$$\gamma(x, p) = \frac{\sum_{p' \in P} w_{x,p'} \times sim(p, p')}{\sum_{p' \in P} v_{x,g_{p'}} \times sim(p, p')} \tag{3}$$

where P is the set of all pseudo users, $g_{p'}$ is the group that pseudo user p' belongs to, $sim(p, p')$ is the Jaccard Similarity between pseudo user p and p'. $w_{x,p'}$ and $v_{x,g_{p'}}$ are obtained from the pseudo user p'. After the calculation of $\gamma(x, p)$, the server will recommend highly-rated items to pseudo user p.

- **Client-side recommendation.** In our system, the server makes recommendations only to the pseudo users, each of which stands for a unique interest. But the real users may have diverse interests. How to generate personalized recommendations for each real user based on the recommendations for the pseudo users is another challenge. As an item may have different ratings for different pseudo users, and real users also have different levels of interests for different pseudo users. We combine the ratings as follows:

$$\hat{\gamma}(x, u) = \sum_{p \in \mathcal{P}_g} \lambda(u, s_p) \times \gamma(x, p) \tag{4}$$

where $\mathcal{P}_g$ is the set of pseudo users in u's group, and s_p is the interest of pseudo user p.

6. EXPERIMENTAL RESULTS

We have developed a prototype system of YANA and conducted detailed evaluation using *Fudan* BBS [1], a popular online social community with mobile client support. YANA emphasizes high-quality, high-efficiency, and privacy-preserving content recommendation. We compare YANA with two state-of-the-art CF solutions. One is a privacy-preserving SVD-based collaborative filtering framework proposed by Canny [5]. The other is a probabilistic latent semantic indexing (PLSI) based collaborative filtering algorithm proposed by Hofmann [7], and later adopted by Google News [6].

6.1 Experimental Setup

YANA is implemented both on desktop and mobile devices using Java. The mobile client is implemented on HTC Magic smartphones. The HTC Magic runs Android 2.1 operating system with 528 MHz CPU and 288 MB Ram. It supports Wi-Fi of IEEE 802.11 b/g. And the battery capacity is 1340 mAh. The energy consumption of YANA is measured by monitoring the run-time battery capacity of the mobile phone. The recommendation server is also developed using Java on workstation, which collects pseudo users' information, clusters items, and computes item recommendations for the pseudo users.

YANA is tested with *Fudan* BBS, a popular online social forum among Chinese universities. It has over 60,000 users and supports various content-related user interactions, including posting, reading, and replying to articles and multimedia content. Everyday, there are approximately 20,000 new posts, and over 180,000 reads. *Fudan* BBS has over 100 subcommunities, and our experiments are conducted on 10 of the most popular subcommunities. We have collected data over three consecutive weeks, and divided the data into training set (Weeks 1 and 2) and testing set (Week 3). The training set is used to construct user groups and pseudo user profiles, and the testing set is used to evaluate the quality and efficiency of recommendations.

6.2 Recommendation Quality

Figure 2 shows the recommendation quality of YANA compared with the SVD and PLSI algorithms [1]. Please note that, higher precision at the same recall indicates better recommendation quality. As we can see, YANA outperforms PLSI in all the 10 subcommunities (by 23.2% on average), and outperforms SVD in 8 of the 10 subcommunities (by 16.3% on average), and achieves comparable quality in the other 2 subcommunities. The improvement is achieved through the accurate interest grouping and the novel interest based recommendation, which can accurately identify user interests, reduce false negative user decisions, and improve the overall recommendation quality of less popular items.

6.3 Recommendation Efficiency

To evaluate recommendation efficiency, we compare YANA with SVD, both of which are privacy-preserving collaborative filtering algorithms. The computation and communication complexities of SVD are both $O(k'm \log n)$ per user, where k' is the decomposition factor of SVD, m is the number of items, and n is the number of users. In contrast, the computation and communication complexities of YANA are both $O(km)$ per user. Since k' and k have similar order and n is usually big for online social communities, YANA can be much more efficient than SVD in terms of computation and communication complexities.

Latency. Figure 3 shows the overall latency of recommending each item to a user. We only consider the overall client-side latency as it would be the bottleneck of the whole system. Please note that, for the SVD solution, we cannot

[1]The number of users per group K is set to 10 in these experiments. We have also tested with different K values (from 10 to 50) and the quality results are similar.

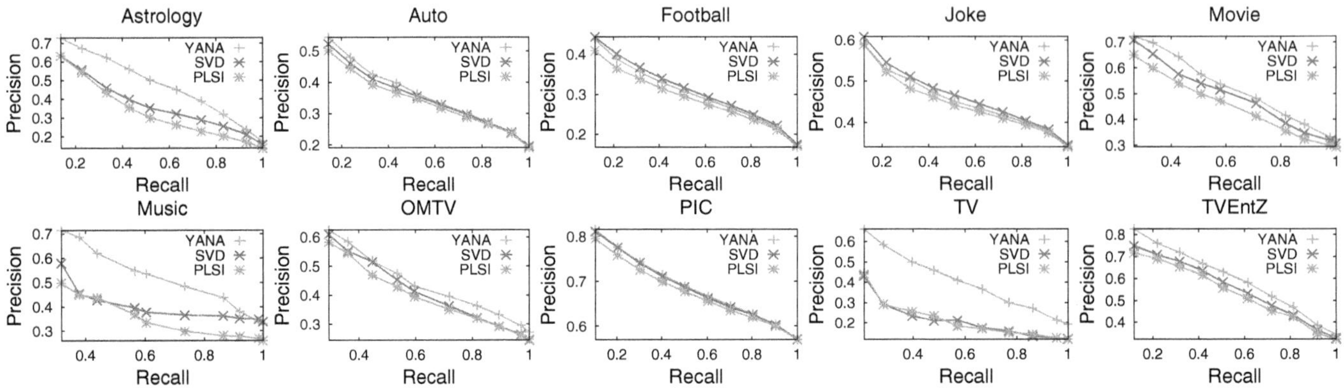

Figure 2: Recommendation quality comparison of YANA, SVD and PLSI in ten subcommunities.

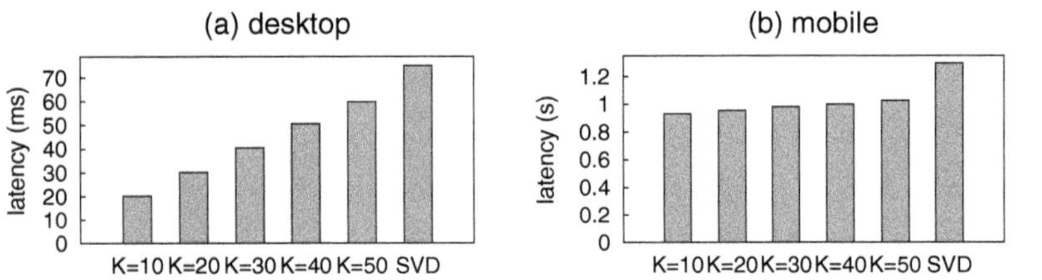

Figure 3: Comparison of recommendation latency (per user and per item) between YANA (with different group size K) and SVD.

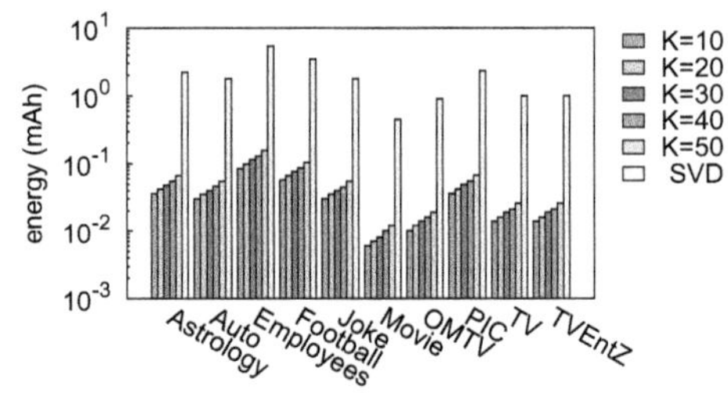

Figure 4: Daily energy consumption comparison of YANA and SVD.

measure its communication latency, as it requires a large-scale ($O(k'm \log n)$) peer-to-peer communication. Thus, we only measure the computation latency of the clients of SVD. Still, we can see that YANA outperforms SVD both on desktop and mobile devices in all the cases by at least 30%. The latency of YANA on desktop is between 20 and 60 milliseconds, which is fairly efficient. The latency on mobile devices is around 1 second, which is also reasonable and practical for users of mobile devices.

Energy Efficiency. Figure 4 shows the daily energy consumption of YANA mobile clients in the ten subcommunities, as compared with SVD. The daily energy consumption of YANA ranges from less than $0.01mAh$ to $0.16mAh$, which is really small compared with the total capacity of the battery ($1340mAh$). In contrast, the energy consumption of SVD ranges from about $0.6mAh$ to $5.36mAh$, which is over 30 times higher than that of YANA. The high energy consumption of SVD is due to its encryption and decryption operations in the singular value decomposition process, which is both time consuming and energy expensive.

7. CONCLUSION

In this work, we propose YANA, a group-based privacy-preserving content recommender system for online social communities. YANA automatically organizes users into groups with diverse content interests, which help protect individual users' private interests from the server. Inside the groups, efficient secure multi-party computation protocols are adopted to ensure privacy among group members. Pseudo users are created within each group to communicate with the server on behalf of real users, and the recommendations they receive from the server can be re-calculated locally to provide customized recommendation for individual real users. We have developed a prototype system and evaluated it using real-world traces of an online social community. The experimental results demonstrate that YANA can protect user interest privacy, achieve better recommendation quality, and is much more efficient compared against state-of-the-art collaborative filtering solutions.

Acknowledgment

This work was supported in part by the National Natural Science Foundation of China under Grant No. 60736020 and No. 60803118, the Shanghai Leading Academic Discipline Project under Grant No. B114, and the National Science Foundation of USA under Grant No. CNS–0910995.

8. REFERENCES

[1] Fudan BBS. `http://bbs.fudan.edu.cn`.
[2] NetFlix. `http://www.netflix.com/`.
[3] G. Adomavicius and A. Tuzhilin. Toward the next generation of recommender systems: A survey of the state-of-the-art and possible extensions. *IEEE Trans. on Knowl. and Data Eng.*, 17(6):734–749, 2005.
[4] S. Berkovsky, Y. Eytani, T. Kuflik, and F. Ricci. Enhancing privacy and preserving accuracy of a distributed collaborative filtering. In *RecSys '07*, pages 9–16, 2007.
[5] J. Canny. Collaborative filtering with privacy. In *S&P '02*, pages 45–57, 2002.
[6] A. S. Das, M. Datar, A. Garg, and S. Rajaram. Google news personalization: scalable online collaborative filtering. In *WWW '07*, pages 271–280, 2007.
[7] T. Hofmann. Latent semantic models for collaborative filtering. *ACM Trans. on Info. Sys.*, 22(1):89–115, 2004.
[8] D. Li, Q. Lv, H. Xia, L. Shang, T. Lu, and N. Gu. Pistis: A privacy-preserving content recommender system for online social communities. In *WI '11*, 2011.
[9] H. Polat and W. Du. Privacy-preserving top-n recommendation on horizontally partitioned data. In *WI '05*, pages 725–731. IEEE Computer Society, 2005.
[10] S. Zhang, J. Ford, and F. Makedon. A privacy-preserving collaborative filtering scheme with two-way communication. In *EC '06*, pages 316–323, 2006.

More Influence Means Less Work: Fast Latent Dirichlet Allocation by Influence Scheduling

Mirwaes Wahabzada, Kristian Kersting, Anja Pilz, Christian Bauckhage
Fraunhofer IAIS, Sankt Augustin, Germany
{firstname.lastname}@iais.fraunhofer.de

ABSTRACT

There have recently been considerable advances in fast inference for (online) latent Dirichlet allocation (LDA). While it is widely recognized that the scheduling of documents in stochastic optimization and in turn in LDA may have significant consequences, this issue remains largely unexplored. Instead, practitioners schedule documents essentially uniformly at random, due perhaps to ease of implementation, and to the lack of clear guidelines on scheduling the documents. In this work, we address this issue and propose to schedule documents for an update that exert a disproportionately large influence on the topics of the corpus before less influential ones. More precisely, we justify to sample documents randomly biased towards those ones with higher norms to form mini-batches. On several real-world datasets, including 3M articles from Wikipedia and 8M from PubMed, we demonstrate that the resulting influence scheduled LDA can handily analyze massive document collections and find topic models as good or better than those found with online LDA, often at a fraction of time.

Categories and Subject Descriptors

H.3.3 [**Information Storage and Retrieval**]: Information Search and Retrieval; I.2.7 [**Artificial Intelligence**]: Natural Language Processing

General Terms

Algorithms

Keywords

Latent Dirichlet Allocation, Stochastic Gradient

1. INTRODUCTION

LDA has recently become popular due to its effectiveness at extracting low-dimensional representations from sparse high-dimensional data, with numerous applications in areas such as text analysis and computer vision [1]. Unfortunately, fitting a LDA topic model given a set of training documents requires approximate inference techniques that are computationally expensive. This makes it challenging to apply LDA to large-scale document collections that nowadays become increasingly common.

A promising approach to scaling LDA to large datasets are online variants, see e.g. [5] and references in there, that incrementally build topic models when a new document (or a set of documents) appears. Specifically, Hoffman *et al.* [5] presented an online variational Bayes (VB) algorithm for LDA based on online stochastic optimization with a natural gradient step that can easily analyze massive document collections. Here, we explore another avenue opened up by online LDA (oLDA) algorithms, namely, to view LDA as a search process and to ask the question whether we can improve it by scheduling documents respectively mini-batches for processing. Somewhat surprisingly, there has been virtually no attempt to study the question of determining a good order for documents to be processed. While it is widely recognized that the scheduling of documents in stochastic optimization of LDA topic models may have significant consequences, this issue remains largely unexplored. Instead, practitioners schedule documents essentially uniformly at random, due perhaps to ease of implementation, and to the lack of clear guidelines on scheduling the documents. In this work, we address the question of how to schedule documents and show that convergence can be reached faster.

2. ONLINE LDA

LDA is a Bayesian probabilistic model of collections of text documents [1]. It assumes a fixed number of K underlying topics in a document collection. Topics are assumed to be drawn from a Dirichlet distribution, $\beta_k \sim Dir(\eta)$, which is a convenient conjugate to the multinomial distribution of words appearing in documents. According to LDA, documents are generated by first drawing topic proportions according to $\theta_d \sim Dir(\alpha)$, where α is the parameter of the Dirichlet prior on the per-document topic distributions. Then for each word i a topic is chosen according to $z_{di} \sim Mult(\theta_d)$ and the observed word w_{di} is drawn from the selected topic, $w_{di} \sim Mult(\beta_{z_{di}})$.

In this paper, we focus on variational Bayesian (VB) inference. Here, the true posterior is approximated using a simpler, fully factorized distribution q. Following [1, 5], we choose $q(z, \theta, \beta)$ of the form $q(z_{di} = k) = \phi_{dw_{di}k}$, $q(\theta_d) = Dir(\theta_d, \gamma_d)$, and $q(\beta_k) = Dir(\beta_k, \lambda_k)$. The variational parameters ϕ, γ, and λ are optimized to maximize the Evidence

CIKM'11, October 24–28, 2011, Glasgow, Scotland, UK.

Lower BOund (ELBO) $\log p(w \mid \alpha, \eta) \geq \mathcal{L}(w, \phi, \gamma, \lambda) \triangleq \mathbb{E}_q[\log p(w, z, \theta, \beta \mid \alpha, \eta)] - \mathbb{E}_q[\log q(z, \theta, \beta)]$, which is equivalent to minimizing the Kullback - Leibler divergence between $q(z, \theta, \beta)$ and the true posterior $p(z, \theta, \beta \mid w, \alpha, \eta)$.

Based on VB, Hoffman *et al.* [5] have introduced an online variant that we here present for the batch case running over mini-batches (chunks of multiple observations). That is, we assume that the corpus of documents has been sorted according to some schedule, i.e. permutation π and chunked into l mini-batches $B_1, B_2, \ldots, B_l$ of size S. That is, the ELBO $\mathcal{L}$ is set to maximize $\mathcal{L}(w, \phi, \gamma, \lambda) \triangleq \sum_{B_i} \sum_{d \in B_i} \ell(n_d, \phi_d(n_d, \lambda), \gamma_d(n_d, \lambda), \lambda)$, where n_d is the word count vector and $\ell(n_d, \phi_d(n_d, \lambda), \gamma_d(n_d, \lambda), \lambda)$ denotes the contribution of document d to the ELBO. As Hoffman *et al.* [5] have shown this mini-batch VB-LDA corresponds to a stochastic natural gradient algorithm on the variational objective $\mathcal{L}$. Using mini-batches reduces the noise in the stochastic gradient estimation as we consider multiple observations per update: $\tilde{\lambda}_{kw} = \eta + D/S \sum_{s \in B_i} n_{sw} \phi_{skw}$ where n_{sw} is the s-th document in the i-th mini-batch and D denote the number of documents.

3. INFLUENCE SCHEDULED (O)LDA

It is known that LDA and its precursor probabilistic latent semantic analysis (pLSA) are closely related. In particular, one can show that pLSA is tantamount to LDA with a uniform prior [4]. Moreover, it is well known that pLSA is deeply connected to instances of the problem of non-negative matrix factorization [2]. Putting both results together, there is a relation between LDA and certain settings of low-rank matrix factorization. Thus, it is natural to ask: "*Can we improve LDA by adapting techniques developed for matrix factorization?*" Here, we show that this is actually the case. Specifically, we utilize randomized matrix factorization approaches, see e.g. [3, 6]. That is, we approximate a given matrix A by S rescaled rows/columns sampled from A. To do so, we compute an "importance score" for each row, and sample rows using that score as an importance sampling probability distribution.

A common score is $p(i) = \sum_j n_{ij}^2 / \sum_{i,j} n_{ij}^2$, and the rescaling factor is $1/\sqrt{p(i) \cdot S}$. This importance score depends on the whole corpus and intuitively captures the "influence" of a given document on the LDA topic model. By preferentially choosing documents that exert a disproportionately large influence on the topic model, we expect to capture the important part of a given corpus at hand.

Our key idea now is to apply the importance sampling procedure to LDA. However, whereas the randomized matrix factorization approaches sample a subset of documents with replacement, we want to keep all documents exactly once. Consequently, we schedule documents by sampling all documents with replacement biased towards those ones with higher norms. In other words, the documents with higher entry values will have higher chance to be processed earlier.

We compute a schedule, i.e., a permutation π of the document collection $\{d_1, d_2, \ldots, d_n\}$ by sweeping through the list of documents in order of increasing indices until all documents have been selected. To decide whether the current document d_i should be placed at position $\pi(idx)$ of the schedule π, we draw a random number in $[0, 1]$ and check whether it is larger than the influence score $p(i)$ of d_i. If that is not the case, we place d_i at position $\pi(idx)$ of the schedule π. Alternatively, we just sort the documents according to their norm, from large to small documents. Setting π to a random permutation would recover oLDA.

Putting everything together results in *influenced* scheduled LDA (isLDA): Compute $p(i)$, rescale and shuffle the documents according to π, and build mini-batches as described earlier — and then run online variational Bayes inference using these mini-batches. Because we only change the schedule in which documents are considered, we do not change the expected number of times a document is seen. In turn, the analysis of [5] carries over to isLDA: isLDA converges to a stationary point of the objective $\mathcal{L}(w, \phi, \gamma, \lambda)$.

As we will show now, influence scheduling can be seen as a stochastic search problem [7]. More formally, assume that we have a distribution $p(\mathbf{z}|\theta)$ over search directions, i.e., gradients parameterized by θ. In each iteration, we generate m samples of search directions $\mathbf{z}_1, \ldots, \mathbf{z}_m$ and use some fitness function to evaluate them — such as the contribution ℓ of document d to the ELBO — to evaluate and in turn to adjust the parameters θ of the search distribution.

Let $J(\theta)$ be the expected fitness under search distribution $p(\mathbf{z}|\theta)$, namely $J(\theta) = \int f(\mathbf{z}) p(\mathbf{z}|\theta) d\mathbf{z}$. We now want to adjust θ such that the expected fitness $J(\theta + \delta\theta)$ is increased. The most straightforward way to do this is to set $\delta\theta = \nabla_\theta J(\theta) = \int p(\mathbf{z}|\theta) \cdot (f(\mathbf{z}) \nabla_\theta \ln p(\mathbf{z}|\theta) d\mathbf{z})$. Using Monte Carlo, we can approximate the last term as $\nabla_{\theta}{}^{s} J(\theta) = (1/m) \sum_{i=1}^{m} f(\mathbf{z}_i) \nabla_\theta \ln p(\mathbf{z}_i|\theta)$. Apriori, i.e., when have not seen any document, it is natural to assume the fitness $f(\mathbf{z}_i)$ is identical for all search directions, for the ease of simplification say $f(\mathbf{z}_i) = 1$ for $i = 1, \ldots, m$. The last equation simplifies to $\nabla_{\theta}{}^{s} J(\theta) = (1/m) \sum_{i=1}^{m} \nabla_\theta \ln p(\mathbf{z}_i|\theta)$. So, what is $\nabla_\theta \ln p(\mathbf{z}_i|\theta)$? With a rough approximation, one can assume all the search directions are independent and identically distributed. The central limit theorem then gives $\mathbf{z} \sim \mathcal{N}(\mathbf{x}, (C/m))$ where $\mathbf{x}$ represents the mean and C is the covariance matrix of the search directions. Again, if we have not seen any document it is sensible to assume $\tilde{C}$ is the identity matrix. Now, it is easy to show that $\nabla_{\mathbf{x}} \ln p(\mathbf{z}|\theta) = C^{-1}(\mathbf{z} - \mathbf{x}) = \mathbf{z} - \mathbf{x}$.

What do we gain by this? It allows us to see isLDA as an offline, greedy search learning approach and in turn that it has close links to well-known active learning approaches. Specifically, we have a set of i.i.d. documents simultaneously available. Then, isLDA queries documents so as to attempt to improve the ELBO as much as possible without computing the ELBO. Actually, isLDA takes a myopic approach that greedily chooses the next query based on this criterion. To see this, assume that the expected variational parameters are uniform for documents not seen, i.e., $\phi_{dwk} = K^{-1}$. Now, the expected influence of an unseen document d to $\tilde{\lambda}$ is $\xi_d = \sum_k \sum_w n_{dw} \phi_{dwk} = \sum_k \sum_w n_{dw} K^{-1} = \sum_w n_{dw}$, i.e. the number of words in the document. This tells us that the document with the largest norm will have the greatest expected impact on the search distribution. The sampling implements a simple exploration and exploitation strategy. Because the norm of a document is not changing, we can stick to the corresponding schedule after having seen each document once and continue running batch LDA following the computed schedule. This essentially proves:

THEOREM 3.1. *isLDA is a myopic stochastic search policy assuming all documents are i.i.d. and uncorrelated.*

Moreover, we can generalise isLDA to the online case. Intu-

Algorithm 1 Influence Scheduled Online LDA (isoLDA)

Define $\rho_t \triangleq (\tau_0 + t)^{-\kappa}$ with $\kappa \in (0.5, 1]$
Initialize $\boldsymbol{\lambda}$ randomly and set $t = 0$
repeat
  Randomly select a batch B of documents
  Compute a schedule π for B
  Sort the documents in B according to schedule π
  Build mini-batches $B_1, B_2, \ldots, B_l$ according to π
  for each batch B_i in turn **do**
    for each document s in B_i **do**
      Initialize $\gamma_{sk} = 1$. */*The const. is arbitrary*/*
      repeat
        Set $\phi_{swk} \propto \exp\{\mathbb{E}_q[\log\theta_{sk}] + \mathbb{E}_q[\log\beta_{kw}]\}$
        Set $\gamma_{sk} = \alpha + \sum_w \phi_{swk} n_{sw}$
      until $\frac{1}{K}\sum_k |\text{change in } \gamma_{sk}| < 0.00001$
    Compute $\tilde{\lambda}_{kw} = \eta + \frac{D}{S}\sum_{s \in B_i} n_{sw}\phi_{swk}$
    Set $\boldsymbol{\lambda} = (1-\rho_t)\boldsymbol{\lambda} + \rho_t\tilde{\boldsymbol{\lambda}}$
    Increment $t = t + 1$
until converged

itively, we draw a batch of documents at random, apply one iteration of isLDA on this batch, and iterate. That is, we draw again randomly a batch, apply one iteration of isLDA, and so on. This *influence scheduled oLDA* (isoLDA) is summarized in Alg. 1.

The benefits of isoLDA are manifold. In contrast to isLDA, it does not require a full pass through the entire corpus in order to schedule documents for an update. Instead, it realizes a dynamic scheduling by scheduling each random batch again and again. In turn, it can be quite fast and flexible when applying to massive datasets. Finally, it has a constant memory consumption and naturally applies to growing datasets. In a nutshell, it combines the benefits of isLDA and oLDA: faster convergence and better quality. And, since we sample batches uniformly at random, the analysis of [5] again carries over:

THEOREM 3.2. *isoLDA converges to a stationary point of the objective $\mathcal{L}(w, \phi, \gamma, \lambda)$.*

4. EXPERIMENTAL EVALUATION

Our intention here is to investigate the following questions: **Q1** Can isLDA be faster than batch LDA and oLDA on small and medium scale datasets? **Q2** If so, does isLDA find solutions that are as good as the ones of batch LDA and oLDA for small and medium scale datasets? **Q3** Does isLDA scale also well to large datasets? **Q4** If not, does isoLDA scale better than isLDA and oLDA?

To this aim, we implemented batch LDA and all isLDA variants in Python based on Hoffman *et al.*'s [5] Python code[1] for oLDA and evaluated their performances on several datasets. Specifically, we considered the following datasets where **D** denotes the number of documents, **W** the number of unique words, and **N** the total number of words.

The **WebKB**[2] dataset consists of webpages of various universities with four different categories (student, course, faculty, project) with **D** = 3,869 and **N** = 217,671. We chose a vocabulary of **W** =3,000 unique words consisting of the terms with the highest TFIDF. Finally, we also used the 20-newsgroups[3] dataset (**20N**) with **D** = 18,576, **N** =1,847,456, and **W** = 10,000. From all corpora, we removed documents with less than six words. For the scaling experiment (**Q3**,

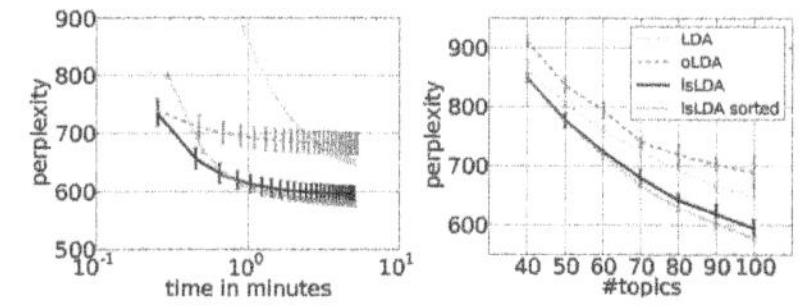

K	is-o	iss-o	is-iss
40	↓	↑ •	↓ •
50	↓ •	↓	↓
60	↑ •	↑	↑
70	↓	↑ •	↓ •
80	↑	↑ •	↓ •
90	↑	↑ •	↓
100	↑	↑	↑

(a) **WebKB**: Time - #Topics - Classification

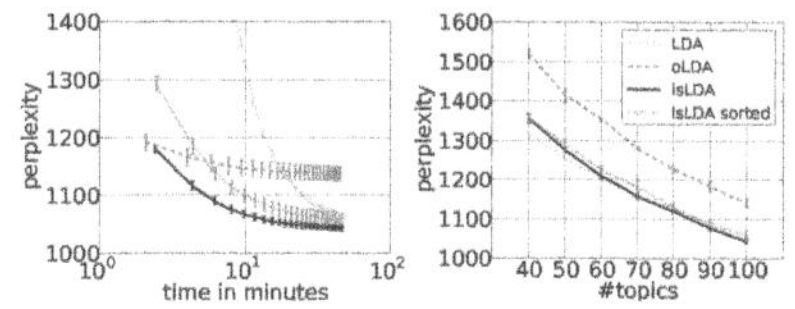

K	is-o	iss-o	is-iss
40	↑ •	↑ •	↓ •
50	↑ •	↑ •	↓ •
60	↑ •	↑ •	↓ •
70	↑ •	↑ •	↓
80	↑ •	↑ •	↑ •
90	↑ •	↑ •	↓ •
100	↑ •	↑ •	↓

(b) **20N**: Time - #Topics - Classification

Figure 1: (Left and middle col.) Perplexity vs. CPU time (sec.; $K = 100$; in log scale) resp. the number of topics. (Right col.) Influence scheduling yields competitive classification performance. Here, is = isLDA, iss = isLDA (sorted), and o = oLDA. A ↑ (↓) denotes that the first (second) algorithm achieved a higher mean. A • denotes significant differences (paired t-test, $p = 0.05$). (Best viewed in color)

Q4), we crawled our own **Wiki**pedia (english) corpus of **D** = 3,295,656 documents with **N** ≈ 294,000,000 and a fixed vocabulary of **W** =7,686 words. We preprocessed the crawled Wikipedia articles as done in [5], using the provided positive-list vocabulary to remove terms not appearing in our articles. Additionally we used PubMed (**PM**) abstracts from the UCI repository with **D** = 8,200,000 documents with **N** ≈ 737,000,000 and a vocabulary of **W** =141,043 words. And finally, to compare the influence of different parameter settings, we use the NY Times (**NYT**) news articles from UCI with **D** = 300,000 documents with **N** ≈ 100,000,000 and a vocabulary of **W** = 102,660 words. For both (after stoppword removal), the vocabulary was reduced by keeping just words which appeared more than ten times, and additionally for **NYT** we excluded all multi token phrases.

For **WebKB** and **20N**, we held out 500 randomly selected documents for evaluation purposes; 1000 documents for the **Wiki**, **PM** and **NYT** datasets. On the test sets, we computed perplexity (the lower, the better) to measure the model's ability to generalise to unseen data [1]. Additionally, we evaluated all approaches in a classification setting for **WebKB** and **20N**. Specifically, we used the 7 first-level classes for **20N** and all classes for **WebKB**. Then, we used a multi-class linear support vector machine[4] to predict the class labels merely using the topic distributions of the documents as estimated by the learned LDA models. We report on the average accuracy achieved in a 5-fold cross-validation.

For all experiments, we set κ close to 0.5 as suggested in [5] and $\tau_0 = 4$ for the small and medium corpora (determined by cross-validation on the training set of **20N** but used for all experiments). To set the mini-batch size for isLDA on the small datasets we used the following heuristic: $S = \frac{\mathbf{D}\cdot\|D\|_2}{\sum_i \|d_i\|_2}$, where $\|d_i\|_2$ resp. $\|D\|_2$ denotes the Frobenius norm of document i resp. the whole corpus. Intuitively, it measures how many documents are required to capture

[1] http://www.cs.princeton.edu/~mdhoffma

[2] http://web.ist.utl.pt/~acardoso/datasets/

[3] http://www.kyb.tuebingen.mpg.de/bs/people/pgehler/rap/

[4] We used PyML http://pyml.sourceforge.net/ with the default parameter settings.

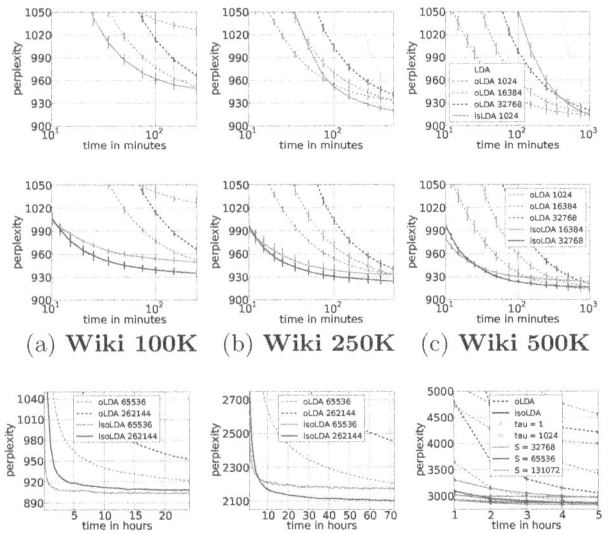

(a) **Wiki 100K** (b) **Wiki 250K** (c) **Wiki 500K**

(d) **Wiki** (e) **PM** (f) **NYT**

Figure 2: Perplexity vs. CPU time on Wiki subsets (min.; $K = 100$; upper two rows) resp. for (d) Wiki and (e) PM (h.; $K = 100$). (f) isoLDA is more stable for different parameter settings than oLDA: Perplexity on NYT after 5 hours. The numbers behind (is)(o)LDA indicate the batch sizes used. (Best viewed in color)

the important part of a corpus. We always stopped when each document was seen 25 times. We used fixed symmetric hyperparameters $\alpha = 0.01$ and $\eta = 0.01$.

Q1, Q2: Small and Medium Corpora The perplexity results are summarized in Fig. 1. As one can see, isLDA approaches find solutions in the range of the batch algorithm's solution with much less computation. For small corpora, the higher bias of isLDA (sorted) results in significantly better performance compared to isLDA and oLDA. With increasing sizes of the corpora, however, isLDA catches up. Taking all experiments together, either influence scheduling outperforms oLDA on all document selections. We note, however, that batch LDA's perplexity can drop below the ones of the mini-batch approaches. The accuracies of the classification experiments as summarized in Fig. 1 clearly show that influence scheduling yield competitive predictive accuracies. In 8 cases, isLDA produced significantly higher classification accuracies than oLDA. Only in one case oLDA produced a significantly higher classification accuracy.

Q3, Q4: Scaling Experiments The results so far suggest that isLDA finds solutions in the range of (o)LDA but much faster. To investigate this further for large datasets, we ran experiments on several subsets of the Wikipedia corpus ranging from 100K to 500K documents using the optimal parameters as determined by Hoffman *et al.* [5]. For isoLDA, we used a mini-batch size of 1024. The results are summarized in Fig. 2. As one can see, isLDA does not scale well. It actually slows down for larger document collections. In contrast, isoLDA scales well. To further investigate if isoLDA scales better than oLDA we conducted experiments on two massive datasets with approx. 3.3M (**Wiki**) respectively 8.2M (**PM**) documents. Here, we used $|B|/64$ to set the mini-batch size for isoLDA given that oLDA used a batch size $|B|$. For **Wiki** we set $\tau_0 = 1$ based on the proposed settings in [5] for large batch sizes. For **PM** we set $\tau_0 = 1024$ to account for its large vocabulary size. We considered large batch sizes of $|B| = 65536$ and $|B| = 262144$ as we can expect to find models of higher quality for them. The results are summarized in Fig. 2. On **Wiki**, isoLDA converged after about only 4 hours to a model with a lower perplexity than the model oLDA found after 24 hours. On **PM**, this difference in performances is even more pronounced. Moreover, the learning curves are much more stable compared to oLDA. That isoLDA is more stable w.r.t. to different parameter settings is also confirmed by our final experiment on the **NYT** corpus. Fig. 2 shows learning curves for several different parameter settings. Clearly, the variance is much lower for isoLDA than for oLDA.

Putting all experimental results together, we can clearly answer questions **Q1**, **Q2** and **Q4** affirmatively.

Conclusion

Triggered by the recent success stories of oLDA approach for the problem of inferring topics in growing document collections, we revisited batch LDA. We turned batch LDA into a quasi-online LDA approach that forms mini-batches of highly influential documents first and processes them before less influential ones, called isLDA. Then, we turned isLDA into a novel, easy-to-implement oLDA approach, called isoLDA, that scales well to massive and growing datasets by applying influence scheduling to randomly formed batches. Based on the results of the present paper, [8] have recently developed the first active LDA.

Acknowledgements: MW and KK were supported by the Fraunhofer ATTRACT fellowship STREAM. AP was funded by the German Federal Ministry of Economy and Technology (BMWi) under the THESEUS project.

References

[1] D.M. Blei, A. Ng, and M. Jordan. Latent dirichlet allocation. *JMLR*, 3:993–1022, 2003.

[2] C. Ding, T. Li, and W. Peng. NMF and PLSI: Equivalence and a Hybrid Algorithm. In *Proc. SIGIR*, 2006.

[3] A. Frieze, R. Kannan, and S. Vempala. Fast monte-carlo algorithms for finding low-rank approximations. *Journal of the ACM*, 51(6):1025–1041, 2004.

[4] M. Girolami and A. Kaban. On an Equivalence between PLSI and LDA. In *Proc. SIGIR*, 2003.

[5] M. Hoffman, D.M. Blei, and F. Bach. Online learning for latent dirichlet allocation. In *Proc. NIPS*, 2010.

[6] M.W. Mahoney and P. Drineas. Cur matrix decompositions for improved data analysis. *Proceedings of the National Academy of Sciences of the United States of America (PNAS)*, 106(3):697–703, 2009.

[7] Y. Sun, D. Wierstra, T. Schaul, and J. Schmidhuber. Stochastic search using the natural gradient. In *Proceedings of ICML*, page 146, 2009.

[8] M. Wahabzada and K. Kersting. Larger residuals, less work: Active document scheduling for latent dirichlet allocation. In *Proceedings of ECML PKDD*, 2011.

Utility-Driven Anonymization in Data Publishing*

Mingqiang Xue⋆ Panagiotis Karras◇ Chedy Raïssi§ Hung Keng Pung⋆
⋆National University of Singapore ◇Rutgers University §INRIA, Nancy Grand-Est

ABSTRACT

Privacy-preserving data publication has been studied intensely in the past years. To date, all existing approaches transform data values by random perturbation or generalization. In this paper, we introduce a radically different data anonymization methodology. Our proposal aims to maintain a certain amount of *patterns*, defined in terms of a set of properties of interest that hold for the original data. Such properties are represented as linear relationships among data points. We present an algorithm that generates a set of anonymized data that strictly preserves these properties, thus maintaining specified *patterns* in the data. Extensive experiments with real and synthetic data show that our algorithm is efficient, and produces anonymized data that affords high utility in several data analysis tasks while safeguarding privacy.

Categories and Subject Descriptors

H.2.7 [**Database Management**]: Database Administration—*Security, integrity, and protection*; H.2.8 [**Database Management**]: Database Applications—*Data Mining*; K.4.1 [**Computers and Society**]: Public Policy Issues—*Privacy*

General Terms

Algorithms, Security, Experimentation

1. INTRODUCTION

Organizations often possess data that need to be made public for the common good. Yet such data may contain sensitive personal information. Several methodologies for data anonymization have been proposed, with the aim of protecting the privacy of persons involved while maintaining as much of the utility of the published data as possible. Existing approaches for data anonymization transform the data by either *generalizing* or *perturbing* data values. Generalization-based approaches [10, 9, 2] group records into *equivalence classes* (ECs), and render the records within the same EC indistinguishable by *generalizing* their values on some pre-selected quasi-identifying attributes (QIs) to the same range(s).

*Work supported by Singapore's MOE AcRF grant T1 251RES0807.

CIKM'11, October 24–28, 2011, Glasgow, Scotland, UK.

id	*age*	*weight*	*disease*	
1	42	66	Gastritis	●
2	40	76	Diabetes	○
3	49	73	Pneumonia	⊕
4	54	68	Gastritis	●
5	55	53	Pneumonia	⊕
6	60	66	Alzheimer	⊗

Table 1: Sample medical micro-data

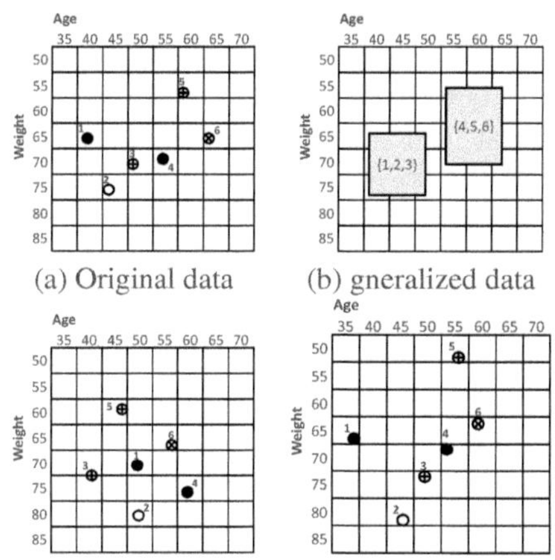

(a) Original data (b) gneralized data

(c) Perturbed data (d) Our approach

Figure 1: Comparison of anonymization paradigms

Table 1 shows a sample of medical microdata records. *Age* and *Weight* are *quasi-identifying attributes* [12]; knowledge of those attributes' values allows an adversary to re-identify the person involved. *Disease* is a *sensitive attribute*; it contains information that entails a privacy risk for the persons concerned. Figure 1(a) visualizes these microdata in the two-dimensional space formed by the two quasi-identifiers [5], *Age*×*Weight*. An *anonymization* of these data by the generalization-based k-anonymity model with $k = 3$ could form two ECs out of them, one containing records $\{1, 2, 3\}$ and one out of $\{4, 5, 6\}$. Figure 1(b) presents these two ECs as rectangular regions in the two-dimensional QI-space. All records within the same generalized region become indistinguishable as far as their QIs are concerned. Following the paradigm of random perturbation [1], an attribute value is modified by adding to the original value a random variable uniformly or normally distributed in a predefined interval $[-\alpha, +\alpha]$. This perturbation effectively contains an adversary's capacity to re-identify the record of a specific person. In the running example, Figure 1(c) presents an example of how the published data may look after random perturbation.

A careful examination of Figures 1(b) and (c) reveals that, though the anonymized data obtained from generalization and perturbation achieves privacy objectives, important topological relationships between the data points are lost. In generalization, topological information is completely obscured within the generalized regions; in perturbation, topological information is destroyed due to blind modification. However, topological information is essential in data mining tasks such as ranking, clustering or skyline queries. Hence, the data obtained from generalization or perturbation is not suitable for these tasks. Popular generalization-based approaches [12, 10, 8, 9, 2] and random perturbation-based approaches [1, 4, 11, 3, 14, 6] all inherit such shortcomings.

In this paper, we propose a novel data anonymization paradigm that addresses the above drawbacks. Given a microdata table $\mathcal{T}$, we define a process that specifies certain *properties of interest* (PoIs) among the QI attributes of $\mathcal{T}$. The set of PoIs describes the data characteristics that the anonymization should maintain. Each PoI is expressed as a linear relationship between a subset of QI attribute values. We develop a scheme to obtain an anonymized table $\mathcal{T}^A$ that satisfies all defined PoIs. $\mathcal{T}^A$ is nearly randomly and uniformly sampled the space for all possible data that satisfy the PoIs, so as to afford privacy for the original data. With our approach, we get a result as in Figure1(d) for the sample medical data. Notably, the data pattern in (d) preserves the original pattern in (a) much more faithfully than that in (b) and (c). Still, the data values in (d) are modified in a way that preserves privacy, and they do not appear exactly the same as the original data.

2. NOTATIONS AND DEFINITIONS

Let $\mathcal{T}$ be a table with n data records and m QI attributes. Entry $t_{i,j}$ refers to the data value in the ith row and j^{th} column in $\mathcal{T}$. We first focus on describing the scheme for anonymzing 1D data, and later generalize it to work for a table with multiple QIs. Let $D = \{d_1, \ldots, d_n\}$ be a particular 1D data vector (i.e., a QI column of $\mathcal{T}$) that is subject to anonymization and $X = \{x_1, \ldots, x_n\}$ be the corresponding set of variables that express the anonymized form of D. Then we define a *property of interest* as follows.

DEFINITION 1. *A property of interest (PoI) on data vector D is a linear relationship of the form $\sum_i^{d_i \in D} c_i d_i \leq \lambda$ among values in D, where c_i is the coefficient of d_i and $\lambda \in \mathbb{R}^+$ is a user-defined constant.*

Our scheme operates in two phases, the *properties extraction phase* and the *value substitution phase*, to find a set of new data $D^A = \{d_1^A, \ldots, d_n^A\}$ for the variables in X that satisfy $\mathcal{Q}$.

3. PROPERTIES EXTRACTION PHASE

Our overall proposal does not constraint the types of linear relationships that may be defined as PoIs. It is up to the data vendor and legitimate data recipients to decide what form of PoIs are important. However, in order to make our proposal concrete and illustrate the *properties extraction phase*, we introduce a particular type of PoIs that we use in the rest of this paper, *locality*.

DEFINITION 2 (LOCALITY). *The* locality *of data values d_i and d_k with respect to data value d_j, denoted as $loc_{d_j}(d_i, d_k)$ is a linear relationship of the form $|d_i - d_j| \odot |d_j - d_k|$, where $\odot \in \{\geq, \leq\}$ makes the relationship true.*

Locality captures relative distance information of two data values with respect to a third data value. The distance between d_i and d_j is denoted as $d_{i,j}$. Without loss of generality, we assume that $d_i < d_k$. A locality property is most informative when d_j lies between d_i and d_k, i.e. $d_i \leq d_j \leq d_k$. Otherwise, it suffices to know whether $d_j < d_i$ or $d_j > d_k$ to deduce the property that holds, independently of the value of d_j.

3.1 Extraction of Localities

Without loss of generality, we assume that D is sorted in non-decreasing order. At first glance, each combination of i, j and k can form a *locality*; thus, the total number of *locality* properties is $\binom{n}{3}$. A naive *locality* extraction algorithm would have to enumerate all possible combinations of i, j, k in $O(n^3)$. Still, some of the *localities* generated by such a process would be *redundant*. For example, from $d_{1,3} \leq d_{3,4}$ we can infer $d_{1,3} \leq d_{3,5}$. We utilize the following two rules for pruning redundant localities:

- *Rule 1:* If $d_i < d_k$ and $d_{i,j} \leq d_{j,k}$, then $d_{i,j} \leq d_{j,k'}$, $\forall k' > k$ and $d_{i',j} \leq d_{j,k}, \forall i' \in [i, k]$.
- *Rule 2:* If $d_i < d_k$ and $d_{i,j} \geq d_{j,k}$, then $d_{i,j} \geq d_{j,k'}$, $\forall k' \in [i, k]$ and $d_{i',j} \geq d_{j,k}, \forall i' < i$.

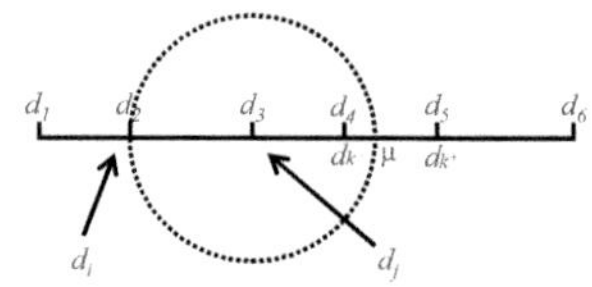

Figure 2: Illustration of locality extraction

Based on the two pruning rules, we propose an algorithm that generates a complete set of *localities*, $\mathcal{P}_{locs}$, whose size is $O(n^2)$. We use the following simple example to illustrate the rationale behind the algorithm. Figure 2 shows a set of data values $D = \{d_1, \ldots, d_6\}$ from which localities are to be extracted. Suppose we wish to retrieve localities for $i=2$ and $j=3$. A naive approach would try all possible values of $k > j$ (i.e., $k = 4, 5$ or 6) to determine $loc_{d_3}(d_2, d_4)$, $loc_{d_3}(d_2, d_5)$ and $loc_{d_3}(d_2, d_6)$, respectively. However, we can avoid this enumeration thanks to a simple geometrical observation: A circle centered at d_j with radius $d_j - d_i$, intersecting the D axis at breakpoint μ, implies that for all k values such that $d_k \leq \mu$, it is $d_j - d_i \geq d_k - d_j$. Similarly, for all k values such that $d_k \geq \mu$, $d_j - d_i \leq d_k - d_j$. Let d_{k^-} be the largest value in D less than μ and d_{k^+} be the smallest value in D that is greater than μ. In our example, d_{k^-} is d_4 and d_{k^+} is d_5 (Figure 2). It then suffices to derive the localities $d_j - d_i \geq d_{k^-} - d_j$ and $d_j - d_i \leq d_{k^+} - d_j$, instead of generating one for each possible k. Algorithm 1 shows a pseudocode for our *locality* extraction algorithm. Arguably, a small subset of *localities* $\mathcal{P} \subset \mathcal{P}_{locs}$ can provide a balance between utility and privacy, where $\mathcal{P}$ can be creating by sampling from $\mathcal{P}_{loc}$, or via other selection algorithms.

Algorithm 1: Locality Extraction Algorithm

```
Data: Original data D
Result: a set of localities P_locs
μ, k⁻, k⁺ ← 0;
for j ← 2 to n do
    for i ← 1 to j − 1 do
        μ ← 2d_j − d_i;
        if μ ≤ d_n then
            j* ← min{ℓ | d_ℓ ≥ μ};
            k⁻ ← j* − 1;
            k⁺ ← j*;
            P_locs.add({i, j, k⁻, ≥});
            P_locs.add({i, j, k⁺, ≤});
        else
            P_locs.add({i, j, n, ≥});
return P_locs;
```

4. VALUE SUBSTITUTION PHASE

In this section, we tackle the second step of our anonymization scheme, i.e., the value substitution phase. The problem we face is to find a set of values for the variables in X so that all the constraints in $\mathcal{Q}$ are satisfied. In addition, we also aim to find a solution in which the *correlation* between the anonymized and the original data is weak. The value substitution algorithm should ideally give a solution *randomly* and *uniformly* sampled from the solution space.

To achieve our goal, we propose a *Random Walk* algorithm. In this algorithm, D and X are viewed as vectors in a n-dimensional space $\mathbb{R}^n$, i.e. $D = (d_1\ d_2\ \ldots\ d_n)^T$ and $X = (x_1\ x_2\ \ldots\ x_n)^T$. In addition, we introduce a set of constraints $\mathcal{H}$ that defines the domain values of the attributes: $\mathcal{H} : \gamma_{min} \leq X^T \leq \gamma_{max}$. For instance, we can use $\mathcal{H}$ to ensure *Age* values are bounded between 1 and 120. Trivially, the set of all constraints on X, $\tilde{\mathcal{Q}} = \mathcal{Q} \cup \mathcal{H}$, defines a bounded polyhedron $\mathcal{S}$ in $\mathbb{R}^n$. Any point in $\mathcal{S}$ is a feasible assignment to X that satisfies the constraints $\tilde{\mathcal{Q}}$. Thus, our problem is to randomly select a point in $\mathcal{S}$. Our algorithm exploits the fact that D is an already known solution in $\mathcal{S}$; it initiates a random walk from D and arrives at another internal point within $\mathcal{S}$. We ensure that the random walk always stays within the bounds of $\mathcal{S}$; thus, the arrival point corresponds to an acceptable value assignment to all the variables in X. To minimize the correlation of the destination point to the original data D, the *Random Walk* algorithm operates in an iterative manner. As the number of iterations increases, the probability distribution of the location of the final destination tends to be uniform [13].

We now elaborate on the details of the random walk within $\mathcal{S}$. Each random walk iteration is characterized by two parameters: its direction, ΔX, and the length of walk in the direction, θ. In the following we describe the derivation of ΔX and θ:

- *Walking direction* ΔX. Let $\Delta X = (\Delta x_1\ \Delta x_2 \ldots\ \Delta x_n)$. First, n numbers are randomly chosen from a normal distribution to form a directional vector. Then, the directional vector is normalized to a unit vector and returned.
- *Walking length* θ. The walking length is bounded by a maximum value l in direction ΔX, beyond which the walk leads to a point outside the solution space. The actual walking length θ is then randomly and uniformly chosen from $[0, l]$.

In the following, we derive the maximum walking length l.

4.1 Maximum Walking Length

To calculate l, we convert the linear inequalities in $\mathcal{Q}$ to a set of linear equalities by adding a non-negative slack variable v_i to the left-hand side of each inequality:

$$\textstyle\sum_j^{1\leq j\leq n} c_{i,j} \cdot x_j + v_i = \lambda_i, \text{ where } v_i \geq 0 \qquad (1)$$

Let V be the set of all slack variables, i.e. $V = \{v_1, \ldots, v_{|\mathcal{Q}|}\}$. (X, V) represents the vector for all variables in the system.

Similar to the walking direction ΔX for the variables in X, we can also introduce a direction vector $\Delta V = (\Delta v_1\ \ \ldots\ \Delta v_{|\mathcal{Q}|})$ for the slack variables V. ΔV. Then $(\Delta X, \Delta V)$ is the direction vector in a particular random walk. In the following, we try to express each Δv_i in terms of ΔX. As the destination of the random walk is within $\mathcal{S}$, the following equation holds after the walk:

$$\textstyle\sum_j^{1\leq j\leq n} c_{i,j}(x_j + \theta \cdot \Delta x_j) + (v_i + \theta \cdot \Delta v_i) = \lambda_i \qquad (2)$$

From Equations 1 and 2, we derive:

$$\textstyle\sum_j^{1\leq j\leq n} c_{i,j} \Delta x_j + \Delta v_i = 0 \qquad (3)$$

The above equality can be rewritten to express Δv_i as:

$$\Delta v_i = -\textstyle\sum_j^{1\leq j\leq n} c_{i,j} \Delta x_j \qquad (4)$$

Since $V^T \geq 0$ is always required and the values in X should always be in their predefined ranges, the following system of inequalities is formed:

$$\begin{cases} V + \theta \cdot \Delta V \geq 0 \\ \gamma_1 \leq X + \theta \cdot \Delta X \leq \gamma_1 \end{cases} \qquad (5)$$

Let $[\theta_{min}, \theta_{max}]$ be the interval that defines the feasible range of θ in the above system; then $l = \max\{0, \theta_{max}\}$.

4.2 Table Anonymization

The anonymization scheme we have developed applies to 1D data vectors. To anonymize a table, we anonymize each QI attribute column independently. Moreover, instead of treating a single column as a single 1D data set, we partition it to segments, and treat each segment independently. We emphasize that this approach does not contribute to the anonymization itself; it is only a mechanism to assist in defining PoIs and processing the data efficiently.

5. EXPERIMENTAL EVALUATION

We now conduct experiments of our anonymization scheme, using both real and synthetic data. Our first data set is a sample of the IPUMS USA census data[1] for the year 2008. It consists of 75K data records; we extract *Age*, *Birth place*, and *Occupation* as QIs. Our second data set is a synthetic one created by the randdataset tool[2]. We create a table with 3 columns and 10K rows, where the columns are independently selected from [0, 1], treated as normalized values of the same four attributes as in the IPUMS data. To compare with ℓ-diversification schemes, we employ the Adult dataset[3]; we extract its first 30K tuples, and treat attributes *Age*, *Final weight* and *Education years* as QIs, and *Occupation* as the $\mathcal{SA}$. All algorithms were developed in Java, and experiments ran on a 3GHz CPU, 2GB RAM machine running Windows XP.

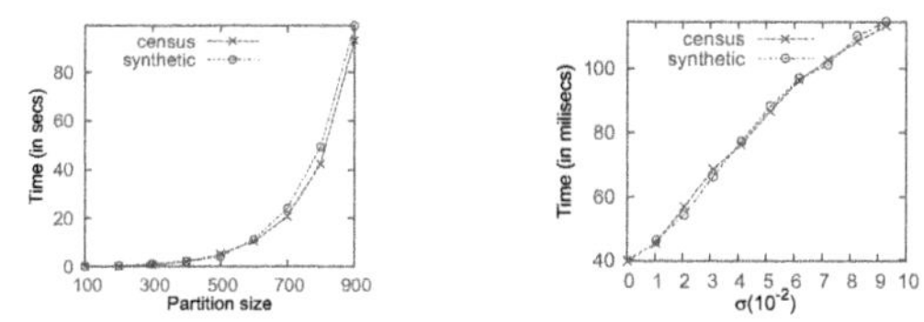

(a) Properties extraction time (b) Value substitution time

Figure 3: Algorithm runtime

5.1 Running Time

We start by measuring the runtime of our algorithm. We increase the partition size from 100 to 900, and measure the average time for extracting all the localities for a partition with Algorithm 1. Figure 3(a) plots our results for both the census and synthetic data. As expected, time grows quadratically in partition size. Still, locality extraction runs in reasonable time even for large partition sizes.

In our next experiment, we fix the partition size to be 100; we run property extraction and randomly sample a number out of the set of all *localities* produced in a partition. We denote the percentage of sampled PoIs as σ. Then, we run our value substitution algorithm with the chosen set of localities as constraints, taking 4000 random-walk iterations. Figure 3(b) shows our results. The runtime grows linearly in the number of PoIs, as our analysis in Section 4 predicts.

5.2 Clustering Quality

In this experiment, we evaluate our method by conducting a popular data mining operation, k-means clustering, over the anonymized data set. We produce anonymized forms $\mathcal{T}^A$ of the same original data table $\mathcal{T}$ using our approach, and a random perturbation-based scheme [1], ensuring that both of them effect the same amount

[1] http://usa.ipums.org/usa/

[2] http://pgfoundry.org/projects/randdataset

[3] http://archive.ics.uci.edu/ml/datasets/Adult

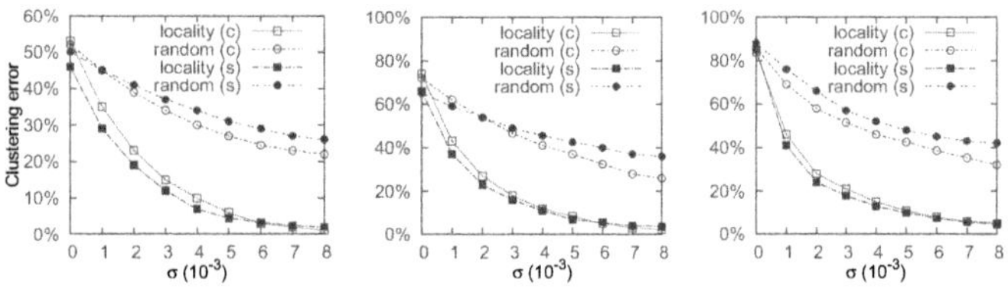

(a) 2-clustering (b) 4-clustering (c) 6-clustering

Figure 4: Data quality for clustering

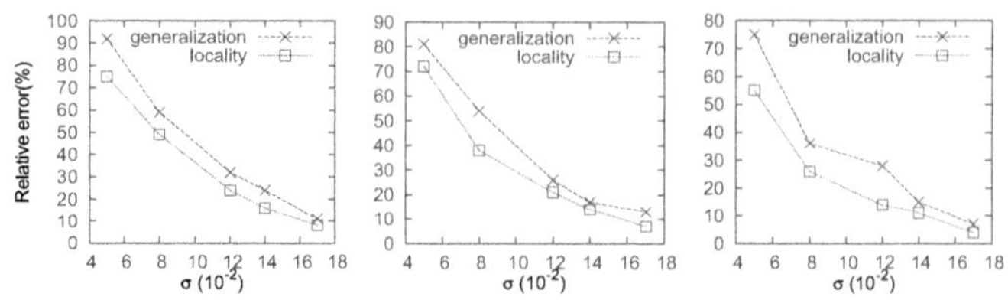

(a) Query 1 (b) Query 2 (c) Query 3

Figure 5: Answering aggregate queries

of *distortion* on the data. The distortion is assessed as follows:

$$Dst(\mathcal{T},\mathcal{T}^A)=\frac{\sum_{i=1}^{n}\sum_{j=1}^{m}\left|\frac{t_{i,j}-t_{i,j}^A}{t_{i,j}}\right|}{m\cdot n} \quad (6)$$

This metric measures the average relative error in each entry of the anonymized data with respect to the original data. We first set the size of randomly sampled PoIs σ for our scheme and measure the distortion Dst it incurs; then, we tune the perturbation interval in [1] so that it effects the same (or less) distortion Dst', allowing for a small divergence ϵ. Both compared schemes maintain exact data values, hence their results are amenable to clustering. As grounds of assessment we use the following clustering error metric:

$$CE(\mathcal{T},\mathcal{T}^A)=\frac{1}{2n}\sum_{i=1}^{k}|C_i(\mathcal{T})\cup C_i(\mathcal{T}^A)|-|C_i(\mathcal{T})\cap C_i(\mathcal{T}^A)|$$

where $C_i(\mathcal{T})$ and $C_i(\mathcal{T}^A)$ are the sets of data records in the ith cluster based on the original data $\mathcal{T}$ and the anonymized data $\mathcal{T}^A$, respectively. The clustering error measures the percentage of data records that fail to be grouped in the correct cluster. We measure this error as a function of the size of sampled PoIs σ for our scheme, on which the amount of effected distortion for both methods depends. The partition size is 100, and the random walk makes 4000 iterations. The results are shown in Figure 4, for 3 different k values in k-means clustering, for both the census (c) and synthetic (s) data. Our scheme consistently outperforms the one based on random perturbation.

5.3 Answering Aggregate Queries

Next, we study the suitability of using the anonymized data generated with our approach for answering aggregate queries using the Adult dataset. We compare the results derived with our scheme against the generalization-based Mondrian algorithm for ℓ-diversity [7]. We design three types of aggregate queries:

- *Query 1:* SELECT AVG(*Age*) FROM $\mathcal{T}$ WHERE *Fw* $> \tau_{fw}$ AND *Edu* $> \tau_{edu}$ AND (*Occ* = o_1 OR ... OR *Occ* = o_b)
- *Query 2:* SELECT AVG(*Fw*) FROM $\mathcal{T}$ WHERE *Age* $> \tau_{age}$ AND *Edu* $> \tau_{edu}$ AND (*Occ* = o_1 OR ... OR *Occ* = o_b)
- *Query 3:* SELECT AVG(*Edu*) FROM $\mathcal{T}$ WHERE *Age* $> \tau_{age}$ AND *Fw* $> \tau_{fw}$ AND (*Occ* = o_1 OR ... OR *Occ* = o_b)

For each query, the parameters τ_{age}, τ_{fw} and τ_{edu} take the values that are randomly chosen from their attribute domains. The set $\{o_1,\ldots,o_b\}$ is a random subset of all possible occupation values of random size $b\in[1,14]$. Each query asks for the average value of one QI attribute based on predicates on other attributes.

We first anonymize the Adult dataset using generalization with $\ell=4,6,8,10$ and 12. We measure the relative errors obtained with generalization with respect to the *distortion* (Equation 6). To measure the distortion of generalized data, we select the mean value of each attribute within the EC as its representative value. Hence, for each version of anonymized dataset $\mathcal{T}^\ell$ under a particular value of ℓ, we can compute a distortion value Dst_ℓ. Then, for each Dst_ℓ value, we tune the amount of PoIs σ used in our approach, until we arrive at an anonymized data set having the same or just a bit more distortion than Dst_ℓ. The partition size is 20, and the number of random walking iterations is $40,000$. Next, we create 2,000 instances for each of the three queries, execute them over these data, and average the accuracy results for each query type. When estimating the answers to range predicates with ℓ-diversified data, we assume that QI values are uniformly distributed within their ECs, and calculate the estimates accordingly. The accuracy of a query answer is assessed by the relative error $\frac{|\phi-\phi^A|}{\phi}$, where ϕ (ϕ_A) is the answer based on the original (anonymized) data.

Our results are shown in Figure 5. Remarkably, for all three queries, the results with our scheme are more accurate than those by ℓ-diversification, even though both incur the same distortion. This result shows that our method preserves more utility than Mondrian.

6. CONCLUSION

This paper has proposed a simple, yet effective, methodology for data anonymization, which allows a data owner to publish *exact*, instead of generalized, values, yet also preserves patterns among the data. Our scheme extracts a set of properties of interest as linear inequalities, which the anonymized data, generated by a random walk process, preserve. As opposed to traditional *privacy-driven* approaches, our approach is *utility-driven*. Our experiments verify that data anonymized by our approach allows for better or similar performance in data analysis tasks compared to data undergoing the same distortion under other anonymization methods.

7. REFERENCES

[1] R. Agrawal and R. Srikant. Privacy-preserving data mining. *SIGMOD Rec.*, 29(2):439–450, 2000.

[2] J. Cao, P. Karras, P. Kalnis, and K.-L. Tan. SABRE: a Sensitive Attribute Bucketization and REdistribution framework for t-closeness. *The VLDB Journal*, 20(1):59–81, 2011.

[3] K. Chen, G. Sun, and L. Liu. Towards attack-resilient geometric data perturbation. In *SDM*, 2007.

[4] A. V. Evfimievski, J. Gehrke, and R. Srikant. Limiting privacy breaches in privacy preserving data mining. In *PODS*, 2003.

[5] G. Ghinita, P. Karras, P. Kalnis, and N. Mamoulis. A framework for efficient data anonymization under privacy and accuracy constraints. *ACM TODS*, 34(2):1–47, 2009.

[6] M. Hay, V. Rastogi, G. Miklau, and D. Suciu. Boosting the accuracy of differentially private histograms through consistency. *PVLDB*, 3(1), 2010.

[7] K. LeFevre, D. J. DeWitt, and R. Ramakrishnan. Mondrian multidimensional k-anonymity. In *ICDE*, 2006.

[8] N. Li, T. Li, and S. Venkatasubramanian. t-closeness: Privacy beyond k-anonymity and ℓ-diversity. In *ICDE*, 2007.

[9] N. Li, T. Li, and S. Venkatasubramanian. Closeness: A new privacy measure for data publishing. *IEEE TKDE*, 22(7):943–956, 2010.

[10] A. Machanavajjhala, J. Gehrke, D. Kifer, and M. Venkitasubramaniam. ℓ-diversity: Privacy beyond k-anonymity. In *ICDE*, 2006.

[11] S. Mukherjee, Z. Chen, and A. Gangopadhyay. A privacy-preserving technique for euclidean distance-based mining algorithms using fourier-related transforms. *The VLDB Journal*, 15(4):293–315, 2006.

[12] P. Samarati. Protecting respondents' identities in microdata release. *IEEE TKDE*, 13(6):1010–1027, 2001.

[13] R. L. Smith. Efficient monte carlo procedures for generating points uniformly distributed over bounded regions. *Operations Research*, 32(6):1296–1308, 1984.

[14] Y. Tao, X. Xiao, J. Li, and D. Zhang. On anti-corruption privacy preserving publication. In *ICDE*, pages 725–734, 2008.

Privacy Preserving Feature Selection for Distributed Data Using Virtual Dimension

Madhushri Banerjee
Georgia Gwinnett College
Lawrenceville, GA, USA
mbanerje@usg.ggc.edu

Sumit Chakravarty
Stinger & Ghaffarian Technologies Inc.
Greenbelt, MD, USA
schakravarty@sgt-inc.com

ABSTRACT

Data Mining often suffers from the curse of dimensionality. Huge numbers of dimensions or attributes in the data pose serious problems to the data mining tasks. Traditionally data dimensionality reduction techniques like Principal Component Analysis have been used to address this problem. However, the need might be to remain in the original attribute space and identify the key predictive attributes instead of moving to a transformed space. As a result feature subset selection has become an important area of research over the last few years.

With the advent of network technologies data is sometimes distributed in multiple locations and often with multiple parties. The biggest concern while sharing data is data privacy. Here, in this paper a secure distributed protocol is proposed that will allow feature selection for multiple parties without revealing their own data. The proposed distributed feature selection method has evolved from a method called virtual dimension reduction used in the field of hyperspectral image processing for selection of subset of hyperspectral bands for further analysis. The experimental results with real life datasets presented in this paper will demonstrate the effectiveness of the proposed method.

General Terms

Algorithms

Categories and Subject Descriptors

H.2.8 [**Database Applications**]: Data Mining;
C.2.4 [**Distributed Systems**]: Distributed applications, Distributed databases

Keywords

Privacy preserving distributed data mining, feature selection,virtual dimensionality reduction

1. INTRODUCTION

The curse of dimensionality is referred to the scenario where huge amount of attributes present in the dataset makes statistical analysis of the data extremely difficult. Various dimensionality reduction techniques are used to address this problem like Principal Component Analysis, Singular Value Decomposition etc. These methods have been widely used in privacy preserving data mining because they provide data transformation as well as the orthogonality of the resultant data eliminates the risk of correlation attack. However, there might be a need to retain the original attribute space. In this case feature selection is done using some systematic approach to retain only the attributes that will lead to accurate statistical analysis and all other attributes are eliminated. The most appropriate feature subset selection method would be to try all combinations of the attributes by construction of the powersets of the attributes and then select the subset that is most effective. But, this method of exhaustive search is impractical with high dimensionality, e.g., in case of n attributes the number of combination would be 2^n.

In this paper we will use a feature subset selection method called virtual dimensionality reduction [1] which is used in hyperspectral image processing to select hyperspectral bands that are relevant for further analysis and eliminates all other redundant bands. The details of this method are presented later in this paper in section 2. Here, we use this method in a privacy preserving distributed data setting.

The greatest concern while sharing data is privacy. The privacy and security risks associated with data mining often thwarts the utility of data mining. Data can be distributed either horizontally or vertically. When the data is horizontally partitioned each party involved in data sharing has information about all the attributes but for different sets of objects whereas when the data is vertically partitioned each party has partial information about all the objects. An example of horizontal partitioning can be where more than one banks have data from their corresponding sources about fraud detection and will benefit from collaborative analysis but is unwilling or not allowed to reveal their business data. The data at different banks have the same attributes but contain different records. An example of vertical partitioning can be where a hospital and the environmental department wish to collaborate in order to analyze outbreak of certain diseases in certain areas without actually revealing their data. Here, both data sets are about the same locations or areas, but have different attributes.

There exists a rich body of work in privacy preserving distributed data mining based on Secure Multi-Party Computation techniques. Surveys can be found in [7]. The secure distributed protocols are often derived from various cryptographic techniques [6,10]. The privacy preserving distributed data mining techniques develop algorithms that will work in a distributed scenario and will not reveal critical information of the parties involved. There has been extensive research in classification, clustering etc. for a privacy preserving distributed data setting [5,8,9]. However to the best of our knowledge not many research in this area handle feature selection. In this paper we address this shortcoming by proposing an algorithm for feature selection that deals with both horizontally and vertically partitioned data. As the method is unsupervised, it can be used as a preprocessing step for any data mining task that will follow. The proposed algorithm explores a very different approach for feature subset selection called virtual dimensionality reduction. Extensive experiments have been conducted to validate the effectiveness of the proposed algorithm.

The rest of the paper is organized as follows. Section 2 presents the virtual dimensionality reduction technique. Section 3 provides details about our methodology. Section 4 presents the extensive experimental results. Section 5 concludes the paper.

2. VIRTUAL DIMENSIONALITY REDUCTION

This section presents the virtual dimensionality reduction method briefly. Harsanyi,Farrand and Chang in recent past developed an eigen thresholding method referred to as Harsanyi-Farrand-Chang(HFC) to determine the number of spectral endmembers of a hyperspectral data. The concept of this method is based on the Neyman Pearson detection theory and can be briefly described as follows.

Since the data dimensionality is equal to the total number of its eigenvalues, each eigenvalue specifies a data dimension with a certain level of significance provided by that particular attribute in terms of energy or variance. If there is no effective value contained in an attribute, its corresponding correlation-eigenvalue and covariance-eigenvalue should reflect only noise energy, in which case, both correlation-eigenvalue and covariance-eigenvalue must be equal. This fact allows to formulate the difference between the correlation-eigenvalue and the covariance-eigenvalue as a binary composite hypothesis testing problem where the null hypothesis represents the case of the zero difference while the alternative hypothesis being the case that the difference is greater than zero. When the Neyman-Pearson test is applied to each pair of a correlation-eigenvalue and its corresponding covariance-eigenvalue, the number of times the test fails indicates how many significant attributes are present in the data. The cardinality of this reduced set of attributes is termed as the virtual dimension of the data.

HFC method, which is conceptually described above can be mathematically represented as follows. Let $\lambda_1^c \geq \lambda_2^c \geq \lambda_3^c \ldots \lambda_L^c$ and $\lambda_1^v \geq \lambda_2^v \geq \lambda_3^v \ldots \lambda_L^v$ be two sets of eigenvalues generated by $CORR_{L\times L}$ and $COV_{L\times L}$, called correlation eigenvalues and covariance eigenvalues respectively. Assume that the significant attributes have positive energies and noise variance in attribute l is given by σ_l^2.

$$\lambda_l^c - \lambda_l^v > 0 \; for \; l=1,2........ VD \quad (1)$$

and

$$\lambda_l^c - \lambda_l^v = 0 \; for \; l=VD+1,VD+2,........ L \quad (2)$$

where $\lambda_l^c = \lambda_l^v + \sigma_l^2$ for $l = 1, 2 \ldots VD$ and $\lambda_l^c = \lambda_l^v = \sigma_l^2$ for $l = VD+1, VD+2 \ldots L$

In order to determine significant dimensionality, [3] formulated the problem outlined by equations 3 and 4 as a binary hypothesis problem as follows.

$$H_0 : z_l = \lambda_l^c - \lambda_l^v = 0 \quad (3)$$

$$H_1 : z_l = \lambda_l^c - \lambda_l^v > 0 \quad (4)$$

for $l = 1, 2 \ldots L$ and where H_0 is the null hypothesis and the alternative hypothesis is H_1.

3. OUR APPROACH

Algorithm 1 Algorithm: Virtual Dimensionality Reduction

Input: Dataset D, threshold δ
Output: Retained attributes A

```
Compute the covariance of D; cov = covariance(D)
Compute the correlation of D; cor = correlation(D)
Compute the eigen values of covariance matrix; eigcov = eigen(cov)
Compute the eigen values of correlation matrix; eigcor = eigen(cor)
A={}
for each attribute i do
   if eigcor(i) − eigcov(i) > δ then
      Retain i; A = A ∪ i
   else
      Discard i
   end if
end for
return A
```

The generic algorithm of the feature selection method using virtual dimensionality reduction [1] is presented in algorithm 1. Algorithm 1 basically computes the covariance matrix and correlation matrix of the datasets followed by the eigen value decomposition of both the covariance and the correlation matrices. Then the eigen values of the covariance and the correlation matrices are compared with a predetermined threshold δ for each attribute to identify the significance of that attribute. The threshold is basically used to regulate the number of attributes filtered. From algorithm 1 it is apparent that if we can compute the following statistics from the data for horizontal as well as vertical partitioning in a secure way we can compute both covariance and correlation of the whole dataset. Then the eigen value decomposition can be done locally by each party which will reduce the communication cost drastically. However, the parties will have to agree on a threshold value δ beforehand to compute the filtering locally. More details on the algorithm for horizontal and vertical partitioning is presented below.The statistics that needs to be computed are as follows:

- Number of data elements in the distributed data $N(D)$.
- For each attribute j, sum of corresponding values in j, $FS_j(D)$; this is the first order sum.
- For each attribute j, the standard deviation of the corresponding values in j, $\sigma(j)$.
- For each pair of attributes i and j, sum of the product of corresponding attribute values; denoted by $SS_{ij}(D)$; this is the second order sum.

The covariance between attributes i and j is:

$$COV(i,j) = SS_{ij}(D)/N(D) - FS_i(D) \cdot FS_j(D)/N(D)^2 \quad (5)$$

The correlation between attributes i and j is:

$$CORR(i,j) = COV(i,j)/(\sigma(i) \cdot \sigma(j)) \quad (6)$$

Horizontally Partitioned Data: The algorithm for horizontal partitioning is presented in algorithm 2. In case of horizontal partitioning computing these statistics is relatively simple as each party p can compute the share of their local data $N^p(D)$, $FS^p(D)$ and $SS^p(D)$ and then engage in a secure sum protocol to compute the global statistics for all parties involved. The next step is to compute the standard deviation of each attribute. Once $N(D)$ and $FS(D)$ are known to each party, mean of each attribute j, $\mu_j(D)$ can be computed locally. Each party p then computes their local share of the standard deviation $\sigma^p(D)$ and then engages in a secure sum protocol to compute the global standard deviation $\sigma(D)$.

Algorithm 2 Algorithm: Secure Feature Selection for Horizontally Partitioned Data

---

Input: Dataset D (n rows and m columns) distributed as $D_1, D_2....D_p$ in p participating parties; predetermined threshold δ

1: Each party p computes local share $N^p(D)$ and then all parties engage in secure sum protocol to compute $N(D)$
2: Each party p computes local share ${FS_j}^p(D)$ where $1 \leq j \leq m$ and then all parties engage in secure sum protocol to compute $FS_j(D)$
3: Each party locally computes the mean of each attribute j, $\mu_j(D) = FS_j(D)/N(D)$
4: Each party computes local share of standard deviation $\sigma_j(D)$ for each attribute j by computing $\sigma_j(D)^p = \sum(D_j^p - \mu_j(D))^2$ then all parties engage in secure sum protocol to compute $\sigma_j(D)$
5: Each party p computes local share ${SS_{ij}}^p(D)$ where $1 \leq i \leq m$, $1 \leq j \leq m$ and $i \neq j$ and then engage in secure sum protocol to compute $SS_{ij}(D)$
6: Each party then locally computes $cov(D)$, $corr(D)$, $eigcov = eigen(cov(D))$ and $eigcor = eigen(cor(D))$ and performs feature selection following steps 5 to 13 of algorithm 1

Vertically Partitioned Data: In case of vertical partitioning the number of data elements in the whole dataset $N(D)$ is known to each party and $FS_j(D)$ and $sigma_j(D)$ for each attribute j where $1 \leq j \leq m$ and m is the number of attributes in the dataset can be computed locally. The computation of the second order sum $SS_{ij}(D)$ for each pair of attributes i, j, is relatively complex as attributes are distributed among p parties. If attribute i and j belong to the same party $SS_{ij}(D)$ can be computed locally. However, if i and j belong to two different parties p and t, then p and t will have to engage in a secure dot product protocol [5] in order to compute the second order sum for attribute pair i, j. The algorithm for secure feature selection for vertical data partitioning is presented in algorithm 3.

Security Analysis for Horizontal and Vertical Partitioning: We follow the semi-honest adversarial model as presented in [7]. Therefore, our main concern is to restrict the amount of information revealed in the intermediate steps. We also assume that individual data is sensitive but global statistics is not. We also follow the 'composition theorem' as mentioned in [7] which states that if each sub protocol is secure, the entire protocol is secure.

Algorithm 3 Algorithm: Secure Feature Selection for Vertically Partitioned Data

---

Input: Dataset D (n rows and m columns) distributed as $D_1, D_2....D_p$ in p participating parties, predetermined threshold δ

1: $N(D)$ is known to each party
2: $FS_j(D)$ where $1 \leq j \leq m$ can be computed locally by each party.
3: Each party locally computes the standard deviation for each attribute j, $\sigma_j(D)$
4: **for** each attribute pair i, j where $1 \leq j \leq m$, $1 \leq j \leq m$ and $i \neq j$ **do**
5:   **if** i and j belong to same party p **then**
6:     Party p computes the second order sum $SS_{ij}(D)$ locally
7:   **else**
8:     i and j belong to party p and party t respectively and party p and party t engage is secure dot product protocol [5] to compute $SS_{ij}(D)$
9:   **end if**
10: **end for**
11: All parties share their part of the statistics with all other parties and each party locally computes $cov(D)$, $corr(D)$, $eigcov = eigen(cov(D))$ and $eigcor = eigen(cor(D))$ and performs feature selection following steps 5 to 13 of algorithm 1

In case of horizontally partitioned data Step 1, 2, 3 and 5 in algorithm 2 uses secure sum protocol to compute the required statistics. Since, secure sum protocol is secure all these steps are secure. For vertically partitioned data in the algorithm 3 the only step where data is being shared by multiple parties is step 8. Secure dot product protocol [5] is used to compute step 8 and since this is proved to be secure, step 8 can be considered secure. In step 11 all the parties share their part of the statistics with all other parties but since the only information shared is the statistics the individual data elements are not divulged. If the parties are unwilling they can use more stringent cryptographic techniques for this part with increased communication cost.

Communication Cost Analysis for Horizontal and Vertical Partitioning: Let n be the number of records, m be the number of attributes and p be the number of parties. The only secure protocol used in case of horizontal partitioning is secure sum protocol. Each party is computing a vector of it's local share for m attributes and using secure sum protocol to compute the global statistics. Therefore, the communication cost for horizontal partitioning is in the order of $O(mp)$. Whereas, the only secure protocol used in case of vertical partitioning is secure dot product protocol. If a pair of attribute i, j is located in two different parties, the parties engage in secure dot product protocol to compute the global second order sum for attribute i and j. Therefore, the communication cost for vertical partitioning is in the order of $O(m^2np)$.

4. EXPERIMENTS

This section presents experimental evaluation of the proposed method. The experiments were conducted on a machine with Pentium Dual Core, 2.0 GHz CPU, 3.0 GB of RAM, and running Windows Vista. All algorithms were implemented using Matlab 7.0.

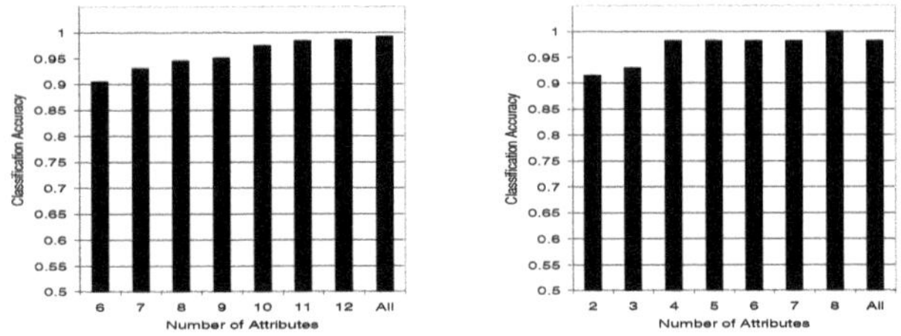

(a) Pendigits (b) Breast Cancer

Figure 1: Classification Accuracy for Pendigits and Breast Cancer after Feature Selection

Datasets: The experiments were run over four real life datasets. Three of the datasets are from UCI Machine learning Repository namely Pendigits, Breast Cancer Wisconsin and Ionosphere [2]. A real life dataset for Agriculture data [4] has been used as well. The Agriculture dataset is a time series data consisting of annual yield of grain on Broadbalk field at Rothamsted from 1852 to 1925 for 34 neighboring plots.

Metrics: We measure the quality of mining. We ran the linear regression in WEKA 3.6 with 10 fold cross validation for Agriculture data after feature subset selection (where we tried to predict the yield of grain for the year of 1925 based on the previous years) and reported the correlation coefficient. For Pendigits, Breast Cancer and Ionosphere we randomly selected 10% of the data as test data and ran K-nearest neighbor classification in MATLAB after applying feature selection method.

Results: We implemented algorithm 1 and tested with the above mentioned four datasets. The threshold δ is varied between 0 to 1 to gradually increase the number of selected attributes, with zero selecting no attributes and 1 selecting all attributes. The results are presented in figure 1 for Pendigits and Breast Cancer datasets and figure 2 for Ionosphere and Agriculture datasets. The number of attributes is presented in the X-axis while the mining quality is presented in the Y-axis.

As apparent from the figures for all the datasets mining accuracy comparable with mining on the original data can be achieved for much lower number of attributes. The reason for Pendigits requiring more number of attributes can be since the number of class labels in Pensigits is 10. The results are pretty convincing for Breast Cancer and Ionosphere, each requiring approximately 10% of their actual number of attributes. Also, for Breast Cancer dataset the mining accuracy after feature selection improves when the number of attributes is equal to 8. The result is probably most satisfactory for the time series data of Agriculture where we are trying to predict the production of grain for the 74th year from the previous 73 consecutive years using linear regression. The figures for Breast Cancer and Agriculture datasets also show that the mining accuracy is often decreasing with increasing the number of selected features which can be explained as including of not so significant attributes can often decrease the mining accuracy. Therefore, the threshold δ can be used to find the ideal number of selected attributes.

5. CONCLUSION

In this paper we have proposed a distributed privacy preserving method to perform feature subset selection that handles both horizontal as well as vertical data partitioning.

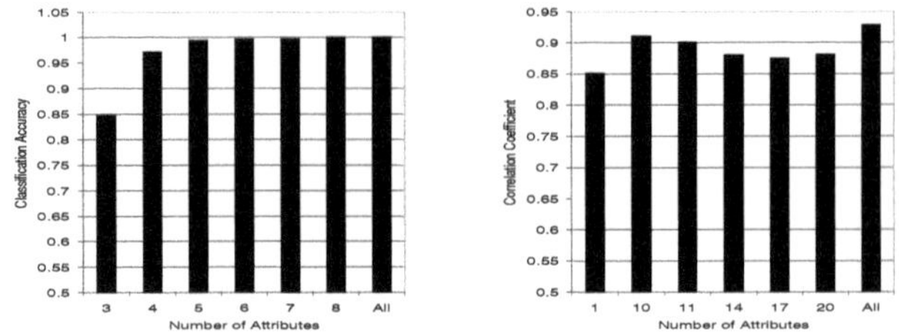

(a) Ionosphere (b) Agriculture

Figure 2: Classification Accuracy for Ionosphere and Agriculture Data after Feature Selection

Our research is inspired from a method that is used for band selection in hyperspectral image processing. The experimental results prove the efficiency of this method for real life datasets including time series data. Therefore, our contributions can be summarized as exploring a new technique for feature selection and applying this feature selection technique in a privacy preserving distributed data setting.

As the future direction of this research we would like to try more real life datasets, specifically more time series datasets. We would also like to explore various noise whitening methods as a preprocessing step to the feature selection method to see if the feature subset selection method can be improved.

6. REFERENCES

[1] C. I. Chang, Hyperspectral Imaging: Techniques for Spectral Detection and Classification, Springer, 2003. URL `http://books.google.com/books?id=JhBbXwFaA6sC`

[2] A. Frank, A. Asuncion, UCI machine learning repository (2010). URL `http://archive.ics.uci.edu/ml`

[3] J. Harsanyi, W. Farrand, C.-I. Chang, Detection of subpixel spectral signatures in hyperspectral image sequences, in: Annual Meeting, American Society of Photogrammetry and Remote Sensing, 1994.

[4] R. Hyndman, Time series data library (Accessed on May 2011). URL `http://robjhyndman.com/TSDL`

[5] G. Jagannathan, R. N. Wright, Privacy-preserving distributed k-means clustering over arbitrarily paritioned data, in: SIGKDD'05, Chicago, IL, 2005.

[6] Y. Lindell, B. Pinkas, Privacy preserving data mining, Advances in Cryptology (CRYPTO'00), Lecture Notes in Computer Science 180 (2000) 36–53.

[7] J. Vaidya, C. Clifton, M. Zhu, Privacy Preserving Data Mining, Springer-Verlag, 2005.

[8] J. Vaidya, M. Kantarcioglu, C. Clifton, Privacy-preserving naïve bayes classification, The VLDB Journal 17 (4) (2008) 879–898.

[9] J. S. Vaidya, C. Clifton, Privacy preserving association rule mining in vertically partitioned data, in: 8th ACM SIGKDD, Edmonton, Canada, July 2002.

[10] A. C. Yao, How to generate and exchange secrets, in: 27th IEEE Symposium on Foundations of Computer Science, 1986.

Switch Detector: An Activity Spotting System for Desktop

Hamid Turab Mirza, Ling Chen, Gencai Chen, Ibrar Hussain, Xufeng He
College of Computer Science, Zhejiang University, Hangzhou, 310027, P.R. China.
{hamid306, lingchen, chengc, ibrar, hxf0704}@zju.edu.cn

ABSTRACT
An average white-collar worker deals with enormous amount of digital information on daily basis. Recently, there has been a growing interest to support their work. However, in order to be really supportive there is a need to know the current activity of the user at all times. In this paper we present a new technique that takes advantage of temporal aspects of user activity behavior to infer when it is most likely that an activity switch is occurring. We then describe "Activity Switch Detector" an interactive switch notification system embodying these ideas, and an extensive user study by ten participants to test the validity of the approach and present its results.

Categories and Subject Descriptors
H.1.2 [**User/Machine Systems**]: Human factors; H.5.2 [**Information Interfaces and Presentation**]: User Interfaces—Graphical user interfaces

General Terms
Algorithms, Experimentation, Human Factors.

Keywords
Activity switching, modeling and prediction of user behavior, user interaction.

1. INTRODUCTION
In today's world, knowledge work plays an ever more important role in organizations of all sorts. An average white-collar worker deals with enormous amount of digital information on daily basis. Previously efforts have been made to support their work by employing different indexing and search tools that make information more accessible. However, recently it has been realized that to be really supportive all these systems have to take user's context into account. Awareness of the user's current context, i.e., the 'activity' that a user resides in, allows various ways of support, like for example activity management and recovery, ranked search results, providing workflow guidance and suggesting experts.

In this work, our goal is to automatically identify and distinguish users' activities from their everyday desktop interactions. The work is primarily based on the assumption that; user activities can be characterized by actions that are executed with in a close temporal proximity to each other. Following are the definitions of the terms used in this paper:

Action (Ac): An action is an interaction that a user performs with desktop every day. Each action is a couple $Ac = Ac\ (a\ ,\ t)$, where a corresponds to a desktop event, such as opening a file, bringing a focus to an application window, clicking a hyperlink, sending an e-mail; associated with a time stamp t.

Interaction History (H): Let an individual's desktop interaction history H be represented as a sequence of actions he/she has performed with corresponding transition time Δt_i ($1 \leq i \leq n$) and is defined as $H = \{Ac_1, Ac_2, Ac_3, \ldots, Ac_n\}$, where $\Delta t_i = t_i - t_{i-1}$ is the time interval between two actions.

Activity (At): In an interaction history H, Activity At is characterized by a set of consecutive actions Ac that have been performed by a user in a close temporal proximity, and is defined as $At = \{Ac_1, Ac_2, \ldots, Ac_m\}$ where $m \leq n$.

2. RELATED WORK
Recently, systems such as TaskTracer [1] and SWISH [2] have used sophisticated methods to automatically identify current activities and adapt to user behavior. TaskTracer uses machine learning to detect undeclared activity switches and predict the correct activity switches. SWISH system recognizes users' activities by analyzing the windows switching history and tf-idf extracted terms from windows titles. However, these works have not utilized the time distances between users' actions and have used predefined time windows of fixed lengths. Whereas we believe that duration information is crucial in identifying the activity switches.

Our work is closely related to [3] that draw on the frequency of user interaction with desktop windows to infer the occurrence of activity switch. However for detecting the switch they have used a simple heuristic of using the moving average between the last k user interactions. Moreover, again they have enforced a fixed five minutes interval before notifying the user that an activity switch might have occurred. In our work, we have studied average time distance between actions on a daily and weekly basis. Moreover, application specific focus time behavior is also analyzed and incorporated into a real time activity switch detection system.

3. SYSTEM DESIGN
The framework of switch detector consists of three steps. First we log system wide user desktop interactions. Next; filtered user actions are fed to the time-based switch detection algorithm. In the last step the detected activity switches are presented to the user through a real time user interface for analysis and evaluation purposes. Below we discuss each step in detail.

3.1 Interaction Logging
While designing the logging mechanism, we had three considerations in mind: First, *How to gather user interaction data in a most unobtrusive way?* For this, we opted for an implicit feedback approach for recording the user actions. An adaptation of a logging utility developed by [4] is used to automatically log user actions without interrupting their workflow and no explicit input is required at any stage.

CIKM'11, October 24–28, 2011, Glasgow, Scotland, UK.

Second, *What data should be collected for best possible user activity analysis?* Keeping in view the diversity of knowledge work environment, an attempt has been made to acquire cross application data from file system, web browsers, office tools and instant messengers (see Figure 1).

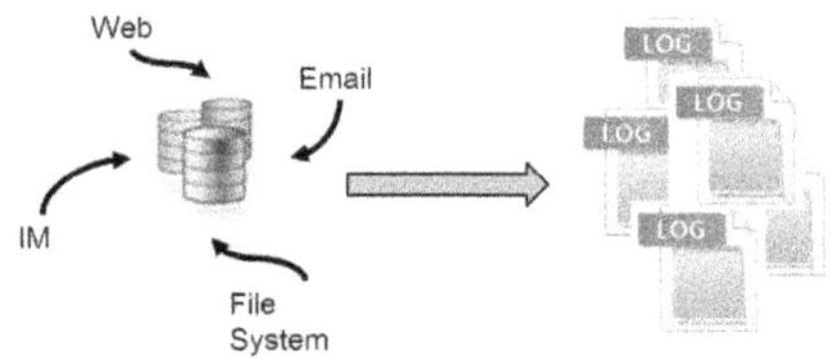

Figure 1. Logging cross application data

Third, *How to preserve user's privacy while logging interaction data?* Since the logged data is very personal and represents user's interaction history in detail, therefore it also raises many privacy concerns. An effort has been made to alleviate those concerns by keeping the log files at the user specified location on his/her computer and it is up to them to release the data to anyone in any form. Moreover the log is kept in a simple human readable plain text file format, so that the user can easily edit or delete any private entries from it.

3.2 Detection Algorithm

Our system begins by filtering the user activity log, any actions that are not explicitly performed by the user e.g. system calls and repeated consecutive actions with any single resource are filtered out. The timestamps are then used to calculate average time distance between user actions for last one week.

Word-09:12 Notepad-09:14 Word-09:17 Excel-09:20

2 minutes 3 minutes

Figure 2. Calculating application specific focus time

The system also calculates the application specific focus time averages for the same period of time; e.g. Figure 2 illustrates a scenario where we calculate the focus time of the actions that were performed using MS Word.

Algorithm Detect_Switch (*log, week_avg, app_avg*)

```
1:  Current_Activity = Ø
2:  last action Ac
3:  add Ac to Current_Activity
4:  for each action Ai in log
5:    current action Ac = Ai
6:    if app_avg is not null
7:         Td = app_avg
8:    else
9:         Td = week_avg
10:   end if
11:   if interval (Ac, Ai) < Td
12:     add Ac to Current_Activity
13:   else
14:     add Ac to New_Activity
15:     Current_Activity is null
16:     Ac = Ai
17:     add Ac to Current_Activity
18:   end if
19: end for
```

Figure 3. Switch detection algorithm

The algorithm in Figure 3 takes as input the filtered interaction log '*log*', average time distance between last one week's actions '*week_avg'* and application specific average focus time for different applications '*app_avg*'. In case the focus time of the currently used application type is not known then weekly average time distance is used (lines 6 to 10). Any two consecutive actions whose time distance is less than computed average time distance 'T*d*' are grouped together in one activity (lines 11 and 12). On the other hand, whenever two actions have a time distance more than the threshold a new activity is created (lines 14 to 17).

3.3 User Interface

The purpose of the interface is to evaluate the accuracy of different activity switch detection methods. The system as illustrated in Figure 4, presents the real time user activities at the bottom of the screen (just above the Windows OS task bar) and notifies the identified activity switches to the user. The user can simply respond by clicking once on the separator bar to reject the detected switch (bar turns red) or clicking again to revert back to accept (bar turns green). The system registers and remembers the user's decision.

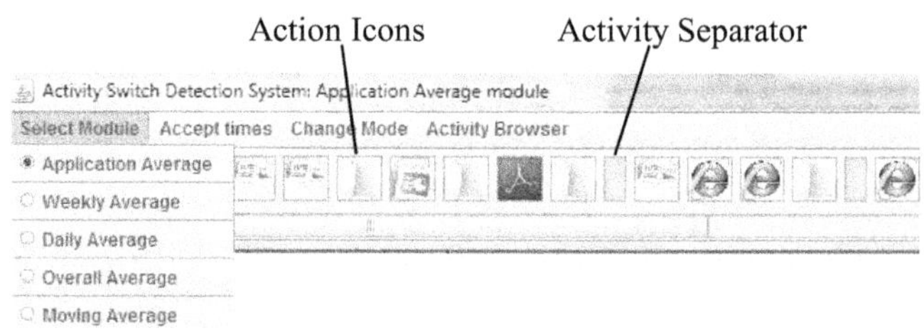

a) Switch identified and activity separated by green bar

b) User views the activity details and rejects the identified switch

Figure 4. Interaction between Switch Detector and the user

Also user can scroll through the activities before making a decision. One can either hover the mouse over a single action to view its information or double click the activity separator (green or red bar) to view the details of whole activity (see Figure 4b). Activity start/end times and all the actions of the activity are displayed. Moreover, to help the user better analyze the activities we allocate each activity to a category by using some static rules e.g. resources accessed with MS Word and Notepad are allocated to editing category. Also activity keywords are extracted from its action titles by using keyphrase extraction algorithm (Kea) [5].

We also implemented a more interactive user interface with a sliding activity separator; through which user can correct the detected activity switch by sliding it between different actions. Figure 5 illustrates a scenario where the user felt that identified activity switch is not precise and corrects it by sliding the separator bar between a MS Word and MS PowerPoint resource. All changes are reflected in background files and remembered by the currently implemented system. However, if the user feels that automatically detected switch is correct then no action is required.

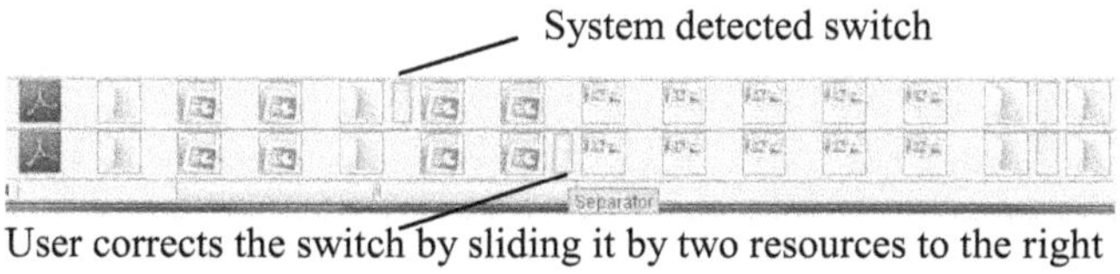

Figure 5. User providing feedback by correcting the switch

Since by correcting the switch user is providing us with ground truth, therefore system can learn from this rich contextual information. Though in our current implementation we have not used any learners for switch prediction, however we have identified and recorded the following activity specific features [6] that might indicate that activity switch is occurring: (a) Window captions and associated application types of resources accessed in an activity, to see if user follows a certain pattern for carrying out activities. (b) No of resources closed in the last s seconds, if a user is closing windows it is likely to be an end of activity. (c) No of actively accessed resources in the last *s* seconds, if the user is actively accessing open resources it is unlikely to be an activity switch. (d) Time duration of an activity and no of actions performed in that time span. (e) Time distance between the last and first action of any two consecutive activities.

4. EXPERIMENTAL EVALUATION

The goal of the experiments was to study the temporal aspects of participant's desktop interaction behavior. Specifically, for the purpose of activity switch detection, we studied the suitability of using the daily and weekly average time distances between the users' actions. Also we analyzed the significance of using average focus time of specific application types for deciding when the switch is probably occurring.

4.1 Data Collection

We collected desktop activity data from ten participants; the participants consisted of Masters and PhD students in a computer science laboratory. Data was collected for an average of 55 active working days per participant, the days when the user performed some desktop actions with the activity logger running in the background. A total of 5,19,449 actions were recorded. Table 1 illustrates the fields of the activity log.

Table 1. Fields of the user interaction log

Name of Field	Example Values
Operation Type	Created; Activated; Destroyed
Timestamp	2011-05-25T19:53:09+08
Window Handle	A058A; 401F8
Application Name	AcroRd32.exe, iexplore.exe
Window Caption	Switch PaperV1.3–MS Word; My Documents
File Path	URL=http://www.google.com

4.2 Time Distance between Actions

A simple comparison (see Table 2) among the daily and weekly average time distance between actions of different participants shows that for each participant there is a significant amount of deviation between his/her daily behavior. However in comparison, week wise result exhibits a much more consistent behavior with negligible deviation for most of the participants. Also, Figure 6 shows a clear pattern in activity behavior of three different users over a period of ten weeks. These results justify our choice of using the last week's average time distance to determine the current activity switches.

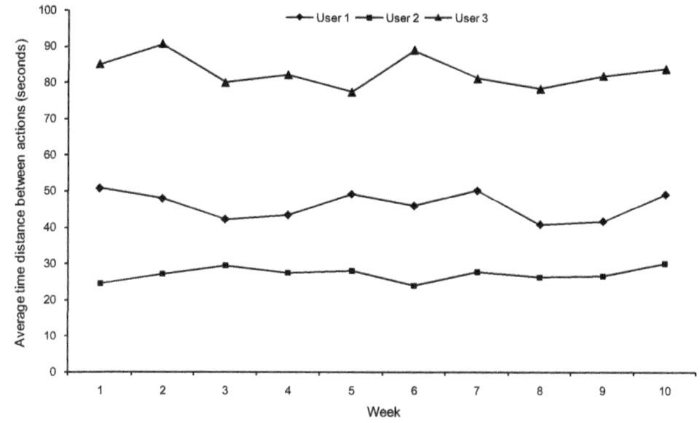

Figure 6. Week wise average time distance between actions

4.3 Focus Time of Applications

We also analyzed the temporal aspects of application specific usage behavior of individual users e.g. typically how much more time (focus time) user spends on editing tools than web browsers? The results in Table 3 depict that there is a significant variation in time spent by different participants on different applications. For instance, on average Participant 3 when using the editing tools e.g. MS Word spends 57% more time (i.e. focus time for that application) than when using the web browsers. On the other hand, on average Participant 4 spends 61% more time on web browsing than editing.

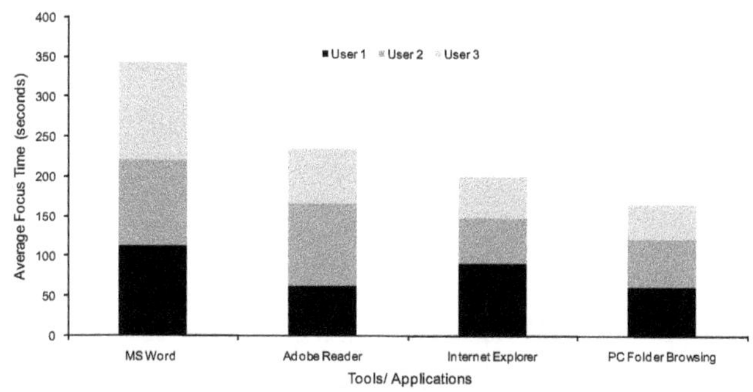

Figure 7. Application specific average focus time

Figure 7 shows average focus times of different applications for three participants. Overall, it can be observed that MS Word i.e. editing tools stay in focus for longer time spans than other categories and there are more chances that users when working with editing tools will stay focused for longer time span before switching the activity. This observation motivated us to use application specific behavior knowledge for deciding an activity switch, however in case of a new application type where prior user interaction experience is not available then we opt for week wise average time distance.

4.4 Study Design and Findings

We evaluated the switch detection system by deploying it with five users from the original pool of ten participants. All participants were proficient in computer use, two of them were using Windows 7 and other three were using Windows Vista as

Table 2. Day and Week wise Average Time Distance between User Actions

Participant ID		1	2	3	4	5	6	7	8	9	10
Daily Behavior	Average	46.48	43.01	59.33	26.87	55.73	64.73	66.75	57.71	48.66	24.61
	Std. Dev	11.43	15.98	10.31	4.86	15.09	31.39	35.51	17.43	12.54	7.65
Weekly Behavior	Average	45.86	45.00	63.12	26.15	54.88	72.12	82.17	59.12	47.3	21.65
	Std. Dev	4.7	6.26	5.84	2.37	9.04	18.6	21.63	8.07	5.99	3.58

Table 3. Average Focus Times for different Applications/ Tools

Participant ID		1	2	3	4	5	6	7	8	9	10
Editing Tools e.g. MS Word	Average	112.75	108.91	121.41	55.99	116.65	68.16	76.29	141.74	84.20	55.75
	Std. Dev	32.01	29.53	34.13	10.08	31.21	16.63	14.25	36.51	23.94	12.73
Document Readers e.g. Adobe Reader	Average	63.39	102.53	69.68	77.17	76.49	86.71	42.53	78.52	75.16	74.80
	Std. Dev	15.31	25.83	11.25	18.81	21.97	19.83	7.11	17.86	15.49	16.11
Web Browser e.g. Internet Explorer	Average	90.73	56.94	51.89	146.55	95.03	55.99	107.57	124.55	100.73	46.48
	Std. Dev	24.10	12.61	10.17	41.81	24.05	12.84	26.75	33.32	23.21	13.77
PC Folder Browsing	Average	60.90	60.44	43.94	49.87	43.25	57.57	32.57	65.85	44.98	32.85
	Std. Dev	16.22	18.28	12.10	11.67	9.94	15.37	8.58	18.12	10.60	6.67

their main operating system. Each participant interacted with the interface for two hours and during this time they were not manually shadowed and were encouraged to carry out their normal work activity.

By the end of the study, for all the users our proposed method detected 92 switches with 54 (58.69%) being accepted. Whereas the moving average method [3] detected 165 switches with 73 (44.24%) being accepted and the commonly used 5 minutes fix time window method detected 126 switches with only 43 (34.12%) being accepted.

Table 4. Comparison of Switch Detection methods

Participant ID		1	2	3	4	5	Accuracy
Proposed Method	Accept	8	10	11	17	8	58.69%
	Reject	13	6	7	9	3	
Moving Average Method [3]	Accept	16	16	13	19	9	44.24%
	Reject	18	25	24	12	13	
5 Minutes Fix Time Window	Accept	7	9	11	10	6	34.12%
	Reject	19	15	14	15	20	

Table 4 shows the individual results for five participants. It can be seen that acceptance rate varies among different users with Participant 1 accepting only 38% of the switches across all methods whereas Participant 4 accepted 56% switches. This observed variation can be explained by the differences in work patterns. However, despite of the variation in the accuracy, this study has demonstrated the feasibility of using temporal aspects of user interaction behavior for detecting activity switches.

5. CONCLUSIONS

This paper introduced a new technique that takes the advantage of temporal aspects of user activity behavior to infer when it is most likely that an activity switch is occurring. Implementation of the "Activity Switch Detector" an interactive switch notification system allowed us to present the notifications in an effective way. Our findings show that temporal aspects of user activity, specifically the application specific behavior is very effective in identifying the user activity switches. Additionally, the computational cost of calculating simple averages is much lower than traditional machine learning based techniques.

6. ACKNOWLEDGMENTS

This research was funded by the Natural Science Foundation of China (No. 60703040), the Zhejiang Provincial Natural Science Foundation of China (No. Y107178), Science and Technology Department of Zhejiang Province (No.2007C13019), and the Ministry of Industry and Information Technology of China (No.2010ZX01042-002-003-001).

7. REFERENCES

[1] J. Shen, L. Li, and T. G. Dietterich. Real-time detection of task switches of desktop users. In *Proceedings of International Joint Conference on Artificial Intelligence*, pages 2868-2873, 2007.

[2] N. Oliver, G. Smith, C. Thakkar, and A. C. Surendran. SWISH: semantic analysis of window titles and switching history. In *Proceedings of the 11th international conference on Intelligent User Interfaces*, pages 194-201, 2006.

[3] R. Nair, S. Voida, and E. Mynatt. Frequency-based detection of task switches. In *Proceedings of the 19th British HCI Group Annual Conference*, pages 94-99, 2005.

[4] S. Chernov, G. Demartini, E. Herder, M. Kopycki, and W. Nejdl. Evaluating personal information management using an activity logs enriched desktop dataset. In *Proceedings of the 3rd Workshop on Personal Information Management,* 2008.

[5] I. H. Witten, P. Gordon, F. Eibe, G. Carl, and G. C. Nevill-Manning. KEA: Practical automatic keyphrase extraction. In *Proceedings of the 4th ACM International Conference on Digital Libraries*, pages 254–255, 1999.

[6] J. Shen , J. Irvine , X. Bao , M. Goodman , S. Kolibaba , A. Tran , F. Carl , B. Kirschner , S. Stumpf , and T. G. Dietterich. Detecting and correcting user activity switches: algorithms and interfaces, In *Proceedings of the 13th international conference on Intelligent User Interfaces*, pages 117-126, 2009.

LSH Based Outlier Detection and Its Application in Distributed Setting

Madhuchand Rushi Pillutla, Nisarg Raval, Piyush Bansal,
Kannan Srinathan and C. V. Jawahar
International Institute of Information Technology Hyderabad, India
{rushi.pillutla, nisarg.raval, piyush_bansal}@research.iiit.ac.in
{srinathan, jawahar}@iiit.ac.in

ABSTRACT

In this paper, we give an approximate algorithm for distance based outlier detection using Locality Sensitive Hashing (LSH) technique. We propose an algorithm for the centralized case wherein the entire dataset is locally available for processing. However, in case of very large datasets collected from various input sources, often the data is distributed across the network. Accordingly, we show that our algorithm can be effectively extended to a constant round protocol with low communication costs, in a distributed setting with horizontal partitioning.

Categories and Subject Descriptors

H.2.8 [**Database Management**]: Database Applications

General Terms

Algorithms, Performance

1. INTRODUCTION

Our outlier detection scheme is based on the definition introduced by Knorr *et al.* [2], which says that an object o is an outlier if a very large fraction p_t of the total objects in the dataset D lie outside the radius d_t from o. In our approach, we use the converse of this idea and say an object to be a non-outlier if it has enough neighbors within the radius d_t. This way, all those non-outliers in the data which have many near neighbors can be identified easily, without calculating the distances to every other object in the dataset. Moreover, in our approach whenever we identify a non-outlier we will be able to say most of its neighbors as non-outliers without even considering those objects separately. Thus, we obtain a very efficient pruning technique where, most of the non-outliers in the dataset can be easily pruned and a very small percent of the objects in the dataset need to be processed after pruning. In order to efficiently find the near neighbors in a large dimensional data, we use the Locality Sensitive Hashing(LSH) scheme. The idea of Locality Sensitive Hashing was first introduced in [1]. The basic concept of LSH is to hash all the objects such that similar objects are hashed to the same bin with high probability. Mathematically, this idea is formalized as follows [1]:

Definition 1. A family $H = h : S \rightarrow U$ is called (r_1, r_2, p_1, p_2) - sensitive if for any two objects p, q in S:

$$if\ d(p,q) \leq r_1 : Pr[h(p) = h(q)] \geq p_1 \quad (1)$$

$$if\ d(p,q) \geq r_2 : Pr[h(p) = h(q)] \leq p_2 \quad (2)$$

where $d(p,q)$ is the distance between objects p and q. For the hashing scheme to be locality sensitive, two conditions to be satisfied are $r_2 > r_1$ and $p_2 < p_1$. In order to amplify the gap between the probabilities p_1 and p_2, standard practice is to concatenate several hash functions to obtain a function family $G = \{g : S \rightarrow U^k\}$ such that $g(p) = (h_1(p), h_2(p), ..., h_k(p))$; where k is the width of each hash function and $h_i \in H$. For a hash function family G, the probabilities in Equation 1 and 2 are modified as:

$$if\ d(p,q) \leq r_1 : Pr[g(p) = g(q)] \geq p_1^k \quad (3)$$

$$if\ d(p,q) \geq r_2 : Pr[g(p) = g(q)] \leq p_2^k \quad (4)$$

During LSH, each object $o \in D$ is stored in the bins $g_j(o)$ for $j = 1, 2...L$; where each g is drawn independently and uniformly at random from G i.e., each object is hashed using L hash functions drawn from G and stored in the corresponding bins. Recently Wang *et al.* [4] proposed an outlier detection method using LSH, but unlike our approach their scheme uses the definition of an outlier given by [3].

2. ALGORITHMS

In this section we describe our algorithms for both centralized as well as distributed scheme in detail.

2.1 Centralized Setting

The algorithm for outlier detection in the centralized setting takes as input the dataset D, distance threshold d_t, point threshold p_t and outputs the outlier set M. The algorithm for centralized setting is executed in three phases.

In the First phase, initially the parameters $R = r_1 = d_t/(1+\epsilon)$ and $p'_t = (1-p_t) \times |D|$ are computed. Here $\epsilon > 0$ is an approximation factor. The LSH scheme is applied on the dataset with the parameter R, the output of which is an $L \times H$ array of bins with each bin containing the set of objects hashed to that bin. In the Second phase *ApproximateOD*

*This work was partly supported by Naval Research Board, India.

CIKM'11, October 24–28, 2011, Glasgow, Scotland, UK.

Algorithm 1 CentralizedOD

Input: Dataset D, Distance Threshold d_t, Point Threshold p_t, Threshold ϵ
Output: Outliers M

$p'_t = (1 - p_t) \times |D|$
$R = r_1 = d_t/(1 + \epsilon)$
$T_{L \times H} = LSH(D, R)$
Compute b_t // using Equation 5
$M' = ApproximateOD(D, T_{L \times H}, p'_t, b_t)$
$M = BrutForceOD(D, M', d_t, p_t)$

Algorithm 2 ApproximateOD

Input: Dataset D, Hash Table $T_{L \times H}$, Point Threshold p'_t, Bin Threshold b_t,
Output: Outliers M'

$M' = \{\}$
$\forall o \in D$, $flag[o] = 0$ // mark all objects as outliers
for each object o in D **do**
  if $flag[o] = 0$ **then**
    $l_o = \{g_i(o) | i = 1 \text{ to } L\}$
    $S' = FindNeighbors(D, T_{L \times H}, o, l_o, b_t)$
    if $|S'| > p'_t$ **then**
      $\forall o' \in S'$, $flag[o'] = 1$ // mark objects in S' as non-outliers
    else
      $M' = M' \cup \{o\}$ // add current object into set of probable outliers M'
    end if
  end if
end for

(Algorithm 2), using the LSH binning structure, most of the non-outliers in the dataset are pruned. We consider an object o and find all L bins to which it is hashed by LSH. We then construct the set S of all the objects stored in those L bins (without removing duplicates). The objects in this set are the probable neighbors of o. More precisely, from Equation 4, we know that each object in S is within the distance $r_2 = (1 + \epsilon) \times r_1 = d_t$ from o, with a probability at least $(1 - p_2^k)$. To boost this probability, we consider only those objects which are repeated at least $b_t (b_t \leq L)$ times in the L bins and store only those objects in a new set S'. In other words, we are reducing the error probability

Algorithm 3 FindNeighbors

Input: Dataset D, Hash Table $T_{L \times H}$, object o, hash labels l_o, Bin Threshold b_t
Output: Set S' of objects satisfying Bin Threshold criteria

$S = S' = \{\}$
for $i = 1$ to $|l_o|$ **do**
  $S = S \| T[i, l_o[i]]$
end for
$\forall o' \in D$, $count[o'] = 0$
for each object $o' \neq o$ in S **do**
  $count[o'] = count[o'] + 1$
  if $count[o'] \geq b_t$ **then**
    $S' = S' \cup \{o'\}$
  end if
end for

of considering an actual non-neighbor as a neighbor of the object o. Here, b_t is a *bin threshold* which can be computed based on the desired false negative probability as explained latter in this section.

If the cardinality of S', returned by the *FindNeighbors* (Algorithm 3) protocol is greater than the modified point threshold $p'_t = (1 - p_t) \times |D|$, with a very high probability o cannot be an outlier since it has sufficient neighbors within distance d_t. Moreover, this holds true for all the objects in S' i.e., every object other than o also has more than p'_t neighbors with in the distance d_t, so it can not be an outlier (with a very high probability). Hence, all the objects in S' are marked as non outliers. If, on the other hand the cardinality of S' is less than or equal to the point threshold p'_t, we consider the object o as a probable outlier. This procedure is repeated till all the objects are either marked as non-outliers or probable outliers. We denote the number of objects for which the *FindNeighbors* protocol is queried as N_q and in the Section 3, we show that this value is very less (less than 1%) compared to the total dataset size. The resulting set of probable outliers M' can have a few false positives and negligible amount of false negatives. In the final phase *BruteForceOD* (Algorithm 4), the false positives are removed and the final set of approximate outliers M is returned.

The overall computational complexity of Algorithm 1 is $O(ndL)$; where $n = |D|$, d is the dimensionality of the dataset and $L = n^{1/(1+\epsilon)}$.

Algorithm 4 BruteForceOD

Input: Dataset D, Probable Outliers M', Distance Threshold d_t, Point Threshold p_t
Output: Outliers M

$M = \{\}$
for each object o' in M' **do**
  $count = 0$
  for each object o in D **do**
    if $Dist(o', o) > d_t$ **then**
      $count = count + 1$
    end if
  end for
  if $count \geq p_t$ **then**
    $M = M \cup \{o'\}$
  end if
end for

False Positives and False Negatives: In the context of outlier detection, a false positive (fp) is to label a non-outlier as an outlier and false negative (fn) is to label an outlier to be a non-outlier. In this section we give a bound on the probabilities of both based on the value of the bin threshold parameter b_t. Consider a LSH scheme where each object is hashed using L hash functions each of width k. The probability of two objects at a distance greater than $r_2 = r_1 \times (1 + \epsilon) = d_t$, to be hashed to the same bin is at most p_2^k. Consider the worst case scenario where an actual outlier has exactly p'_t neighbors. Hence, counting one non-neighbor as a neighbor will lead to a false negative. In our scheme, for a non-neighbor to be counted as a neighbor of an object o, it should hash to the same bin as o for at least b_t times out of L times. The probability that this happens for exactly b_t times out of L is given by the binomial probability:

$$Pr'[fn] \leq \binom{L}{b_t} P_2^{kb_t} (1 - P_2^{kb_t})^{L - b_t}$$

Hence, probability for a false negative is upper bounded by:

$$Pr[fn] < (L - b_t) \times \binom{L}{b_t} P_2^{kb_t}(1 - P_2^{kb_t})^{L-b_t} \tag{5}$$

Similarly, the probability that two objects within a distance R being hashed to two different bins is at most $(1-p_1^k)$. The probability that this will happen at least $(L - b_t)$ times out of L times is given as:

$$Pr[fp] < b_t \times \binom{L}{L - b_t}(1 - p_1^{k(L-b_t)})p_1^{kb_t} \tag{6}$$

This gives an upper bound for the probability of a false positive.

Bin Threshold: As seen from the Equations 5 and 6, both the false negative and false positive probabilities depend on the bin threshold. Increasing the bin threshold has an effect of decreasing the false negatives at the cost of an increase in the false positives and vise versa. An optimal value for b_t would be one which would remove the false negatives at the cost of introducing minimal false positives. In our scheme, the user has the flexibility to fix b_t, based on the false negative probability desired, using Equations 5.

2.2 Distributed Setting

We consider the horizontal distribution where each player has a subset of the total number of objects. The distributed algorithm is given in two player setting, which can be easily extended to a p player setting. Consider two players denoted by P^A and P^B with local datasets D^A and D^B respectively.

Algorithm 5 DistributedOD

Input: Player P^A with Dataset D^A, Player P^B with Dataset D^B, Distance Threshold d_t, Point Threshold p_t, Threshold ϵ

Output: Player P^A Outliers M^A

At P^A :
P^A sends $|D^A|$ to P^B
At P^B :
$n = |D^A| + |D^B|$
P^B sends n to P^A
At P^A :
$p'_t = (1 - p_t) \times n$
$R = d_t/(1 + \epsilon)$
$T^A_{L\times H} = LSH(D^A, R)$
compute b_t
$M'^A = ApproximateOD(D^A, T^A_{L\times H}, p'_t, b_t)$
$M''^A = GlobalApproxOD(M'^A)$
$M^A = GloabalOD(M''^A)$

We present the algorithm such that one player, say P^A will be able to compute its subset of the global outliers at the end of the algorithm. Similarly the algorithm can be used to enable P^B to compute its subset of the global outliers by simply interchanging the roles of P^A and P^B in the algorithm. Before giving a detailed description of the algorithm, we give the following definitions.

Definition 2. local outlier: Given a distance threshold d_t and a point threshold p_t, an object o with player P^i is a local outlier if the number of objects in the local dataset D^i lying at a distance greater than d_t is at least a fraction p_t of the total dataset D.

Definition 3. global outlier: Given a distance threshold d_t and a point threshold p_t, an object o in a dataset D is a global outlier if at least fraction p_t of the objects in D lie at a distance greater than d_t from o.

Algorithm 6 GlobalApproxOD

Input: Players P^A and P^B, Player P^A Dataset D^A, Player P^B Dataset D^B, Point Threshold p'_t, Bin Threshold b_t, Player P^A Hash Table $T^A_{L\times H}$, Player P^B Hash Table $T^B_{L\times H}$, Player P^A Local Approximate Outliers M'^A

Output: Player P^A Global Approximate Outliers M''^A

At P^A :
for each object o in M'^A **do**
  $l^A_o = \{g_i(o)|i = 1 \text{ to } L\}$
end for
send l^A to P^B
At P^B :
$\forall l \in l^A$, $c^B[l] = 0$
for each label l in l^A **do**
  $S' = FindNeighbors(D^B, T^B_{L\times H}, null, l, b_t)$
  $c^B[l] = |S'|$
end for
send c^B to P^A
At P^A :
$M''^A = \{\}$
for each object o' in M'^A **do**
  $l_o = \{g_i(o)|i = 1 \text{ to } L\}$
  $S' = FindNeighbors(D^A, T^A_{L\times H}, o', l_o, b_t)$
  $count = |S'| + c^B[o]$
  if $count \leq p'_t$ **then**
    $M''^A = M''^A \cup \{o'\}$
  end if
end for

In the first phase, player P^A sends the size of his dataset to P^B and gets the size of the entire dataset (i.e. $|D^A|+|D^B|$). Player P^A locally computes its local probable outliers M'^A by running the centralized algorithm on its dataset D^A. In the second phase, for each object o in the set M'^A, P^A forms the set l^A_o which is the set of L labels of the bins to which o is hashed to (these labels are stored while performing LSH). P^A sends the set l^A to P^B. Player P^B considers each element l in l^A and runs the *FindNeighbors* algorithm on its local dataset. P^B then counts the cardinality of the sets returned by *FindNeighbors* and sends the set of counts to P^A. Player P^A considers each object o in M'^A and runs the *FindNeighbors* algorithm to obtain its count of the number of objects repeating more than b_t times (this step is actually redundant if P^A stores this count in first phase). P^A then computes the sum of this count and the corresponding count in c^B, and if this sum is less than or equal to point threshold P'_t, P^A stores o in the set M''^A of global probable outliers.

The set M''^A contains some false positives which can be removed in third phase with another round of communication as follows: P^A sends the set M''^A to P^B. Player P^B considers each object o in M''^A and computes the distance to each object in its dataset D^B and counts the number of objects which lie at distance greater than the distance threshold d_t from o. P^B sends all the counts back to P^A. P^A then considers each object o in M''^A and computes the distance to each object in its dataset D^A and counts the number of objects lying at distance greater than d_t. P^A

then computes the sum of this count and the corresponding count received from P^B and if this count is greater than or equal to fraction p_t of n, marks the object o as an outlier.

The computational complexity of player P^A is $O(n^A dL)$. The overall communication complexity of player P^A would be $O(m'^A L + m''^A d)$, where $m'^A = |M'^A|$ and $m''^A = |M''^A|$.

Algorithm 7 GlobalOD

Input: Players P^A and P^B, Player P^A Dataset D^A, Player P^B Dataset D^B, Distance Threshold d_t, Point Threshold p_t, Player P^A Global Approximate Outliers M''^A
Output: Player P^A Global Outliers M^A

send M''^A to P^B
At P^B :
$\forall o'' \in M''^A$, $c^B[o''] = 0$
for each object o'' in M''^A **do**
  for each object o in D^B **do**
    if $Dist(o'', o) > d_t$ **then**
      $c^B[o''] = c^B[o''] + 1$
    end if
  end for
end for
send c^B to P^A
At P^A :
for each object o'' in M''^A **do**
  $count = 0$
  for each object o in D^A **do**
    if $Dist(o'', o) > d_t$ **then**
      $count = count + 1$
    end if
  end for
  $count = count + c^B[o'']$
  if $count \geq p_t$ **then**
    $M^A = M^A \cup \{o''\}$
  end if
end for

3. EXPERIMENTS

All experiments are performed on Intel(R) Core $i7$ CPU $3.33GHz$ machine, using various datasets[1] listed in Table 1.

Centralized: Table 1 outline the performance of proposed *CentralizedOD* algorithm. First 3 columns lists the various datasets with respective number of objects and dimensions. The execution time (in seconds) averaged over multiple runs of our algorithm in centralized setting is tabulated in column 4. We computed the optimal bin threshold b_t (listed in column 5) as described in Section 2 for mentioned datasets and ran our algorithm using the same bin threshold. By setting bin threshold to the optimal value, we achieved very low false positive rate as shown in the column 6. The final phase of removing false positives can be avoided if this false positive rate is acceptable. Even if the false positives needs to be removed, the low false positive rate ensures that the brute force needs to process only few objects. The false negative rate is not mentioned in the table as it is 0 in case of optimal Bin Threshold. In other words, we achieved 100% detection rate on optimal bin threshold.

For each dataset considered, we computed the percentage of objects for which the *FindNeighbors* protocol is invoked.

[1]All datasets are taken from UCI Machine Learning Repository. http://archive.ics.uci.edu/ml

Table 1: Performance of CentralizedOD

Dataset	Objects	Dim	Time	b_t	FP
Letter	20000	16	7.53	2	0.12
Corel	68040	32	32.27	20	0.09
MiniBooNE	130064	50	29.86	4	0.01
Server	494021	5	41.93	22	0.02
YearPrediction	515345	90	193.11	4	0.03

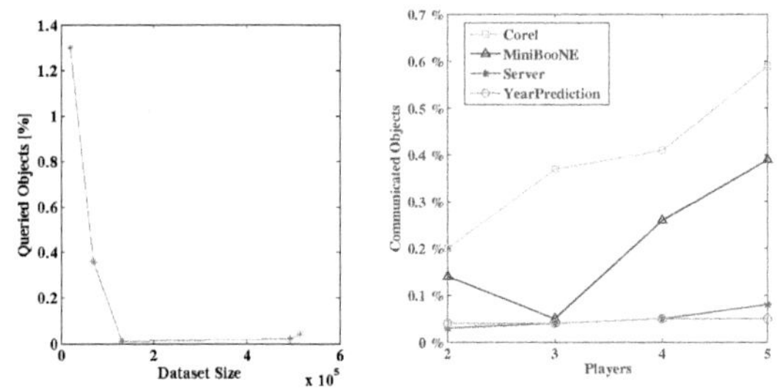

(a) (b)

Figure 1: (a) Queried Objects N_q (b) Communication Cost in Horizontal Distribution

The results are shown in Figure 1(a). For small datasets the percentage of queried objects is close to 1%, but as the dataset gets larger this value keeps decreasing rapidly which is evident from the figure.

Distributed: For the distributed case, we have uniformly distributed all the objects in a dataset among the players. For all datasets, the union of the outliers found at each player is equivalent to the set of outliers returned by the centralized algorithm run on the same dataset. This shows that functionality is preserved in the distributed setting also. We have repeated the experiment by varying the number of players from 1 to 5 and studied the effect on the communication cost. The results are given in Figure 1(b). It can be seen that the percentage of the communicated objects is indeed very less.

4. CONCLUSIONS

In this paper, we have proposed an approximate algorithm for distance based outlier detection. Our approach uses the Locality sensitive hashing (LSH) to achieve an efficient pruning technique. Further, we have extended our scheme to horizontally distributed setting and proved it to be highly efficient in terms of the communication cost.

5. REFERENCES

[1] P. Indyk and R. Motwani. Approximate nearest neighbors: towards removing the curse of dimensionality. In *STOC*, pages 604–613, 1998.

[2] E. M. Knorr and R. T. Ng. Algorithms for mining distance-based outliers in large datasets. In *VLDB*, pages 392–403, 1998.

[3] S. Ramaswamy, R. Rastogi, and K. Shim. Efficient algorithms for mining outliers from large data sets. *SIGMOD Rec.*, 29:427–438, 2000.

[4] Y. Wang, S. Parthasarathy, and S. Tatikonda. Locality sensitive outlier detection: A ranking driven approach. In *Proc. ICDE 2011*, 2011.

Authormagic – An Approach to Author Disambiguation in Large-Scale Digital Libraries

Henning Weiler*
University
Erlangen-Nuremberg and
CERN
henning.weiler@cern.ch

Klaus Meyer-Wegener
University
Erlangen-Nuremberg
kmw@cs.fau.de

Salvatore Mele
CERN
salvatore.mele@cern.ch

ABSTRACT

A collaboration of leading research centers in the field of High Energy Physics (HEP) has built INSPIRE, a novel information infrastructure, which comprises the entire corpus of about one million documents produced within the discipline, including a rich set of metadata, citation information and half a million full-text documents, and offers a unique opportunity for author disambiguation strategies. The presented approach features extended metadata comparison metrics and a three-step unsupervised graph clustering technique. The algorithm aided in identifying 200'000 individuals from 6'500'000 author signatures. Preliminary tests based on knowledge of external experts and a pilot of a crowd-sourcing system show a success rate of more than 96% within the selected test cases. The obtained author clusters serve as a recommendation for INSPIRE users to further clean the publication list in a crowd-sourced approach.

Categories and Subject Descriptors

H.3.3 [**Information Search and Retrieval**]: Clustering; I.2.6 [**Learning**]: Knowledge acquisition

General Terms

Algorithms, Human Factors

Keywords

Author disambiguation, entity resolution, digital libraries, knowledge management

1. INTRODUCTION

For decades, knowledge about the attribution of scholarly artifacts to individuals, in the frequent cases of name ambiguity, has been with the authors' peers or knowledgeable experts in libraries and has since been a known and systematic problem for repositories of all kinds and sizes. The digitization of scholarly communication, public interest in science, the international expansion of the scientific community and other factors constitute to a substantial growth of the information environment in both quantity and complexity. In turn, these advances make unambiguous attribution of scholarly artifacts an even harder task, while making it all the more valuable for the discovery and retrieval of information in the environment of scholarly communication and the increased market for evaluation of scientific productivity.

A collaboration of leading research centers in the field of High-Energy Physics (HEP) has developed INSPIRE[1], a complete digital library of all HEP publications. INSPIRE follows in the steps of the HEP tradition of community-based scientific information infrastructures [8] and offers unique opportunities for author disambiguation. The data set comprises the entire corpus of documents produced within the discipline including a comprehensive citation database.

Data quality is becoming ever more important and automated systems aid human experts in increasing the overall quality of metadata in digital libraries. Novel and dynamic approaches to identify metadata similarities are required to make better decisions in the attribution of scholarly artifacts. Author disambiguation is a long-standing challenge with various approaches in different disciplines [5, 6, 7, 9, 10, 11]. The algorithm described in this document has been designed and implemented to identify which individual researcher wrote which particular documents when, where, with whom and about what. The algorithm determines metadata similarities of an author's name, affiliation, coauthors and citations between all author signatures (author names along with describing metadata on documents). Unsupervised clustering of this related-authors-graph results in potential author clusters.

The final clustering result is used as a recommendation in a crowd-sourcing approach to author disambiguation, which empowers users of INSPIRE to participate in the task of keeping publication and citation lists as up-to-date as possible. Precise knowledge of authorship yields the design of unexampled services in information discovery and knowledge extraction (e.g. extended author-based analyses of citation or co-authorship graphs). It also enables meaningful author-centric scientometric information and removes uncertainties from attempts to use bibliographic and citation data to evaluate scientific quality of an individual.

*Supported by the Wolfgang-Gentner-Programme of the *Bundesministerium für Bildung und Forschung (BMBF)*

[1]http://inspirehep.net

2. RELATED WORK

Recent years have shown advances in automated and collaborative approaches to author disambiguation. Some solutions involve manual assignments of author data by librarians and collaborative approaches, e.g. "ACM Author Pages"[2], "The Names Project"[3] or, as one of the most promising collaborative approaches involving research institutes, universities and publishers alike, ORCID[4].

Name ambiguity is a special instance of *identity uncertainty* and several approaches aim for an automated solution to the challenge [11]. Computer-aided approaches employ unsupervised clustering strategies [3, 9, 10] and supervised techniques [4, 7] or a hybrid of those [6].

Supervised strategies to author disambiguation require training data to allow for a compilation of the set of documents an author produced [4, 11] or to predict the authorship of a document [7]. Training sets are tedious to maintain and mostly do not cover all the cases needed to perform author disambiguation [3].

Different similarity measures have been proposed in various author clustering scenarios to compare metadata of documents [3, 10, 11, 9]. The selection of metadata similarity measures is mostly limited to the comparison of either name strings, coauthors or citations mentioned on a document, while disregarding the usefulness of combining various pieces of information.

The ideas closest to this work are probably [10, 3] due to their approach to solve name ambiguity though graph manipulations. The presented approach is different in such that the graph clustering strategy uses another approach and that the overall comparison strategy is focused on a broader selection of metadata.

3. AUTHORMAGIC ALGORITHM

As a preparation, potentially ambiguous name data is unified for better comparability. This is accomplished by splitting each name in several parts: *last name(s)*, *initial(s)* and *first name(s)*. The identification of the last name in a name string is a challenge in itself [2]. The following rules are applied to identify the last name in a name string: *1)* The last name is the first part of a comma-separation or *2)* the last name is spelled in all caps or *3)* if no other rule applies, the last substring of a name string is used to denote the last name.

In a *first* step, *author signatures* are partitioned into groups of similar last names to reduce the total number of comparisons. A regular expression aids in finding commonly misspelled names as well as compound names with different compound characters, e.g. *t'hooft* vs. *thooft* vs. *'t Hooft* or *Ruiz-Perez* vs. *Ruiz Perez.*

The *second* step comprises of pair-wise comparisons of all author signatures within a last name group. These comparisons allow the identification of *potential authors* through transitive graph clustering as explained in section 3.1.

The *third* and last step performs comparisons of individual author signatures that have not been connected in step 2, with the aggregated information of a potential author entity as explained in section 3.2.

[2]http://plone.acm.org/membership/author_pages
[3]http://names.mimas.ac.uk
[4]http://orcid.org

Algorithm 1 Authormagic algorithm pseudo code

```
Ensure: All names are unified. {cf. section 3}
  for all lastnames from the dataset as lname do
    AS ← find all author signatures with lname
    M ← sparse matrix of size |AS| × |AS|
    for all AS as a do
      for all AS as b do
        M[a,b] ← compare(a, b)
      end for
    end for
    PA ← cluster AS in M {cf. section 3.1}
    AS_n ← find all AS not connected to any PA
    for all AS_n as n do
      compare n to each PA
      connect n to most compatible PA {cf. section 3.2}
    end for
  end for
```

3.1 Identify Potential Authors

To identify a potential author PA, it is necessary to compute the similarity between all author signatures AS within their respective last name groups. Similarity metrics are applied on the following metadata attached to each AS: common co-authors, affiliations, names, publication dates and keywords. It is also assessed if two AS appear on one document, which yields absolute inequality. These metrics are then combined to a total result $p_{pair}(AS_1, AS_2)$ following formula 1. n_p is the count of metrics of total inequality f^p, while n_s is the count of metrics f^s with the metrics' respective weight w_i. n^+ describes the number of metrics that resulted in a probability > 0 (This is done to address possible metadata deficiencies). All weights of the similarity functions have been determined by librarians according to the importance of each function in the manual disambiguation process.

$$\frac{\left(\sum_{i=1}^{n_s} w_i f_i^s(AS_1, AS_2)\right) \times \left(\prod_{i=1}^{n_p} w_i f_i^p(AS_1, AS_2)\right)}{max(n^+, 1)} \quad (1)$$

The pair-wise comparisons will form a fully-connected graph between all ASs. The edges describe the similarity between the two ASs. with the compatibility between each node as a weighted edge. To identify a PA, the transitive sub-tree around each node is formed. A minimum similarity $> .78$ is required to be part of the transitive sub-tree. The threshold has been chosen to be a constant slightly above the average distance of all author signatures from a hand-labeled test set to ensure a high cluster quality.

3.2 Attach Unclustered Author Signatures

Upon completion of the previous step (cf. section 3.1), single AS nodes may remain, which are then compared with all the PAs.

An average of the similarity values of the single node AS and all ASs in a PA cluster is computed first using the cached results of the pair-wise comparisons. The second computation compares the metadata information of the AS to the aggregated metadata information of all AS nodes within the PA cluster. Metrics for aggregated information include comparisons of frequent co-authors and most frequent citations of all AS in a PA.

Formula 2 describes the computation. λ will set the en-

AS	0	1	2	3	4	5	6	7
0	1							
1	0.82	1						
2	0.5	0.69	1					
3	0.14	0.29	0.83	1				
4	0.14	0.61	0.18	0.55	1			
5	0.34	0.56	0.44	0.66	0.56	1		
6	0.43	0.86	0.77	0.2	0.61	0.49	1	
7	0.85	0.48	0.17	0.61	0.42	0.26	0.33	1

Figure 1: A clustered graph in matrix representation. The dark and light gray parts form the two transitive clusters $\{0, 1, 6, 7\}$ and $\{2, 3, 5\}$, while node 4 is not connected to a cluster. The thresholds $d = 0.8$ and $\varphi = 0.5$ were used for this simplified example.

tire equation to zero if absolute inequalities are detected in the pair-wise comparisons. n_a indicates the total number of metrics for aggregated information computations f_i^a along with the respective weights w_i and n^+, the count of metric results that returned a similarity of > 0. Formula 2 results in p_c in the range $[0..1]$.

A second threshold, $\varphi = 0.59$ is introduced to regulate the connection of any AS to a PA cluster. φ has been chosen slightly beneath the result of a comparison that only features the name comparison without support from other metrics to prevent under-clustering of initial-only names. A connection happens iff $p_c \geq \varphi$ and only when all comparisons of all single nodes with all PAs have finished. Nodes that fit either multiple or none of the clusters are left disconnected to form their own PA.

Figure 1 shows a clustering based on simplified thresholds. Author signatures $\{0, 1, 6, 7\}$ and $\{2, 3, 5\}$ are clustered together in the described two steps. Node $\{4\}$ remains disconnected and will form a potential author by itself.

$$\lambda \times \frac{1}{2} \times \left(\frac{\sum \forall_r AS_{PA} : p_{pair}(AS, r)}{|AS_{PA}|} + \frac{\sum_{i=1}^{n_a} w_i f_i^a(AS, PA)}{max(n^+, 1)} \right) \quad (2)$$

4. RESULTS AND EVALUATION

This section presents results that were obtained from using the algorithm on a real-world set of scientific documents in HEP. The accuracy of the algorithm and the impact of additional metrics on the computation shall be shown on the example of a hand-labeled subset.

4.1 Data Collection

The total data set comprises of 6'380'821 author signatures on 892'318 documents with a total of 407'626 different name strings. Each author signature holds information about an author's name, affiliation, co-authors, outgoing citations, the date of publication and the ID of the document the author is listed on.

A subset of these documents has been hand-labeled by librarians of the INSPIRE collaboration. This subset of 15'744 documents will be referred to as *control set* $\mathcal{C}$. It holds hand-checked data of 127 distinct authors with 611 name variations across 103 last names with 24 authors sharing a last name.

Table 1 shows the selected test groups alongside their

Table 1: Overview of control set $\mathcal{C}$

Name group	#papers	#authors
Dvali, G	171	3
Ellis, J	892	3
Fabian, A	549	3
Thomas, A	629	3
Williams, A	259	3

number of hand-tagged documents and the number of known authors in the control set $\mathcal{C}$. **NOTE** that the number of authors only represents the hand-labeled authors to perform the evaluation on; each name group includes far more than three authors to be disambiguated by the algorithm to form the reseult set $\mathcal{R}$.

4.2 Evaluation Metrics

F1–Precision/Recall

The *F1* metric featuring precision and recall measures is used for the cluster evaluation. Due to the nature of the algorithm in using aggregated information of clusters, it is not feasible to use a strictly pair-wise F1 measure. To counteract this limitation, the cluster with the highest number of true positives is chosen as a reference for the computation of precision and recall as it is defined in [1]. The F1 measure is calculated for each cluster in $\mathcal{R}$ in accordance to $\mathcal{C}$ using the formula $F = 2 \cdot \frac{\text{precision} \cdot \text{recall}}{\text{precision} + \text{recall}}$

C-Measure

An experimental cluster evaluation method is proposed as an external criteria for the evaluation of cluster quality. The proposed *C-Measure* is a contextualized metric for the area of document attribution tasks, where the result set might be split in distributed clusters.

Let each AS on each paper be identified by a unique integer number n; each AS can thus be represented by it's own unique string pn. If the set of all available signatures in $\mathcal{R}$ is called $\mathcal{S}$: $\mathcal{S} = \{"pn" \mid \exists \text{ signature } n\}$ the definition of the control set $\mathcal{C}$ follows straightforward as a set of sets, each containing elements from $\mathcal{S}$; each labeled as "C_x" with $x \in (a|b|...|z)[a, b - z]^*$. Formally, $\mathcal{C} = \{\mathcal{K} \text{ as } C_k \mid \mathcal{K} \subseteq \mathcal{S}\}$ with $C_x \bigcap C_z = \emptyset$ for each $x \neq z$. In a similar way, the results set $\mathcal{R}$ can be defined as $R = \{\mathcal{K} \text{ as } R_k \mid \mathcal{K} \subseteq S\}$. Empty intersections between all the subsets can be requested but is not a strict requirement.

The idea is to define the correctness of a clustering $\mathcal{R}$ with respect to a control set $\mathcal{C}$ in terms of average distance between the two. The total distance is computed averaging the distances between each set C_k and all the respective sets R_k, for it may happen that elements of C_k are spread among more than one set in $\mathcal{R}$.

Summarizing: for each C_k find all R_s in such that $C_k \cap R_s \neq \emptyset$; for each R_s compute a distance $E(C_k, R_s)$ and average in $E(C_k)$, which will then be used to compute the average total distance.

The average error is defined as: $\bar{E}_C = \sum_{C_k \in \mathcal{C}} E(C_k)/|\mathcal{C}|$ in which $E(C_k)$ is defined as the average error for that cluster. In particular: $E(C_k) = \sum_{R_s \in \mathcal{K}_{C_k}} (E(C_k, R_s)/|\mathcal{K}_{C_k}|)$ where $\mathcal{K}_{C_k}$ is the set of overlapping clusters. Formally defined: $\mathcal{K}_{C_k} = \{R_s \mid R_s \cap C_k \neq \emptyset\}$

The distance metric $E(C_k, R_s)$ is defined as the euclidean distance between two vectors. For each couple (C_k, R_s), from $A_{ks} = C_k \cup R_s$ a n-dimensional space $\mathcal{P}^n$ with $n = |A_{ks}|$ is defined, thus each element of A_{ks} may be located on a different dimension of $\mathcal{P}^n$. It is now possible to define the vectors $v, w \in \mathcal{P}^n$ such that $v_i = 1$ iff $i \in C_k$ and $w_i = 1$ iff $i \in R_s$, for $i \in A_{ks}$. The distance $E(C_k, R_s)$ is then simply defined as the standard euclidean distance: $E(C_k, R_s) = \|v - w\|_2$

4.3 Results

To measure the impact of the comparison methods that compare single author signatures with the aggregated information in a potential author cluster, the results are divided into two scenarios; executions of the algorithm *with* and *without* the additional metrics. The evaluation metrics described in section 4.2 are used to measure the respective accuracy of each run. The algorithm has been executed 10 times with a randomly shuffled processing queue for each scenario to determine a bias towards the order of computation. The results of all runs were invariant.

Table 2 shows the results of the test runs. With $Q = 1 - \bar{E}_C$, it can be defined that $F^\dagger$ and $Q^\dagger$ denote the results from runs without the metrics for aggregated information. $F^\ddagger$ and $Q^\ddagger$ denote the runs that did use the metrics for aggregated information. The results obtained from the cluster quality measures F and Q in table 2 show a slight increase in clustering accuracy while employing the additional metrics and suggest further exploration in the direction of mining aggregated information for the purpose of author disambiguation. Preliminary results from a pilot project, further described in section 5, indicate that more than 96% of all documents the users claimed ownership of were recommended correctly.

Table 2: Cluster quality results

Ambiguous Group	$F^\dagger$	$Q^\dagger$	$F^\ddagger$	$Q^\ddagger$
Dvali, G	0.931	0.852	0.995	0.895
Ellis, J	0.897	0.818	0.962	0.855
Fabian, A	0.881	0.801	0.922	0.829
Thomas, A	0.784	0.722	0.851	0.791
Williams, A	0.904	0.831	0.926	0.815

5. CONCLUSIONS AND OUTLOOK

Since each information system, digital library or digital repository features a different set of complex requirements, curation strategies and data quality management ideas, there is no universal response to the challenge of name ambiguity. The increasing amount of metadata about digital objects offers new possibilities in disambiguation strategies.

The 200'000 author clusters, obtained from the corpus of documents in HEP using the discussed approach, are currently used to pre-populate author profiles within INSPIRE. The user and owner of the profile is then presented with a set of tools to actively participate in the author data curation process by claiming or repealing authorship of a given document. Actions that users have taken in attributing documents to themselves or other researchers will have an effect on the algorithm: The information about authorship attribution supplied by the user feeds back into the algorithm and serves as an unquestionable reference point for future author disambiguation tasks making it a deterministic, yet evolutionary approach in the long-term. This data also allows for more comprehensive evaluations of the matching accuracy of the Authormagic algorithm to further tweak the metrics towards an improved matching quality.

Although a purely algorithmic approach to solve uncertainties in authorship attribution may never reach 100% accuracy, it is a great step towards a high-quality data set that enables novel user- and author-centric services. With a little help of the users to clean the last nuggets of precious information, extended scientometric and meaningful bibliometric evaluations in scholarly communication will emerge.

6. REFERENCES

[1] R. Baeza-Yates and B. Ribeiro-Neto. *Modern Information Retrieval.* Addison Wesley, 1999.

[2] W. Cohen, P. Ravikumar, and S. Fienberg. A comparison of string distance metrics for name-matching tasks. In *Proceedings of the IJCAI-2003 Workshop on Information Integration on the Web (IIWeb-03)*, pages 73–78. Citeseer, 2003.

[3] R. G. Cota, A. A. Ferreira, C. Nascimento, M. A. Gonçalves, and A. H. F. Laender. An Unsupervised Heuristic-Based Hierarchical Method for Name Disambiguation in Bibliographic Citations. *Journal of the American Society for Information Science*, 61(May):1853–1870, 2010.

[4] A. Culotta, P. Kanani, R. Hall, M. Wick, and A. Mccallum. Author Disambiguation using Error-driven Machine Learning with a Ranking Loss Function. In *Sixth International Workshop on Information Integration on the Web (IIWeb- 07)*, 2007.

[5] A. Dai and A. Storkey. Author disambiguation: a nonparametric topic and co-authorship model. *NIPS Workshop on Applications for Topic Models Text and Beyond*, pages 1–4, 2009.

[6] A. A. Ferreira, A. Veloso, M. A. Gonçalves, and A. H. Laender. *Effective self-training author name disambiguation in scholarly digital libraries.* ACM Press, New York, New York, USA, June 2010.

[7] H. Han, L. Giles, H. Zha, C. Li, and K. Tsioutsiouliklis. *Two supervised learning approaches for name disambiguation in author citations.* JCDL '04. ACM Press, New York, New York, USA, 2004.

[8] R.-D. Heuer, A. Holtkamp, and S. Mele. Innovation in scholarly communication: Vision and projects from High-Energy Physics. *Information Services and Use*, 28(2):83–96, Apr. 2008.

[9] I. Kang, S. Na, S. Lee, H. Jung, P. Kim, W. Sung, and J. Lee. On co-authorship for author disambiguation. *Information Processing & Management*, 45(1):84–97, Jan. 2009.

[10] B.-W. On, E. Elmacioglu, D. Lee, J. Kang, and J. Pei. *An effective approach to entity resolution problem using quasi-clique and its application to digital libraries.* ACM Press, New York, New York, USA, June 2006.

[11] V. Torvik and N. Smalheiser. Author name disambiguation in MEDLINE. *ACM Transactions on Knowledge*, 3(3):1–29, 2009.

DIGRank: Using Global Degree to Facilitate Ranking in an Incomplete Graph

Xiang Niu
State Key Lab of Software Development Environment
Beihang University
nx.niuxiang@gmail.com

Lusong Li
State Key Lab of Software Development Environment
Beihang University
lilusong@gmail.com

Ke Xu
State Key Lab of Software Development Environment
Beihang University
kexu@nlsde.buaa.edu.cn

ABSTRACT

PageRank has been broadly applied to get credible rank sequences of nodes in many networks such as the web, citation networks, or online social networks. However, in the real world, it is usually hard to ascertain a complete structure of a network, particularly a large-scale one. Some researchers have begun to explore how to get a relatively accurate rank more efficiently. They have proposed some local approximation methods, which are especially designed for quickly estimating the *PageRank* value of a new node, after it is just added to the network. Yet, these local approximation methods rely on the *link server* too much, and it is difficult to use them to estimate rank sequences of nodes in a group. So we propose a new method called *DIGRank*, which uses global Degree to facilitate Ranking in an Incomplete Graph and which takes into account the frequent need for applications to rank users in a community, retrieve pages in a particular area, or mine nodes in a fractional or limited network. Based on experiments in *small-world* and *scale-free* networks generated by models, the *DIGRank* method performs better than other local estimation methods on ranking nodes in a given subgraph. In the models, it tends to perform best in graphs that have low average shortest path length, high average degree, or weak community structure. Besides, compared with an local *PageRank* and an advanced local approximation method, it significantly reduces the computational cost and error rate.

Categories and Subject Descriptors

D.3.3 [**Information Search and Retrieval**]: Retrieval models; Information filtering

General Terms

Algorithm, Experimentation

Keywords

PageRank, Small-world, Scale-free, Online Social Network

1. INTRODUCTION

Recently, *PageRank* [1] has been widely used in ranking retrieval results on the web, such as finding the top influential papers in citation networks or valuable users in online social networks (OSNs). Although, in theory, *PageRank* is an excellent method to accomplish those jobs, in practice, there are some limitations. For instance, the webs and OSNs are continually expanding, it is not possible to know a network's complete structure at any one time. Search engines must crawl through pages and update methods repeatedly to prevent rank values of nodes from being outdated. However, repeatedly updating the value of all the nodes in the network is too costly. Besides, in many cases, it is sufficient to just quickly ascertain a new node's approximate value. So a more efficient method is needed to estimate rank values.

To avoid performing a large-scale computation on the entire graph, Chen *et al.* proposed an *influence method* [2]. This method focused on estimating the *PageRank* score of a particular webpage using only a small subgraph of the entire web. Then, Bar-Yossef *et al.* further investigated and gave a more advanced method by pruning [3]. These local *PageRank* methods can quickly and accurately estimate the global *PageRank* value of a target node by crawling its adjacent nodes, and do so with a relatively moderate convergence rate. Yet, they are not suitable for some other applications. First, they strongly rely on the accessibility to the adjacent nodes through a *link server*, and would become infeasible if the server is blocked. Second, they do not emphasize the accuracy of rank sequences among nodes, which is important in many applications. Third, it takes a long time to accomplish this type of ranking because there are a lot of high in-degree nodes that have to be crawled repeatedly.

Other researchers hope to estimate global rank values of nodes by their global in-degrees, which have been proven to have a high correlation to global *PageRank* when using a *mean field approach* [4]. But Fortunato *et al.* [4] found that nodes with the same global degree may still differ in their ranking. Meanwhile, other researchers estimate the value of nodes only by computing *PageRank* of the local incomplete network (PR*). But this method also produces skewed rankings because the local network doesn't take into account the link structure of the network as a whole. Therefore, it is insufficient to use only a subgraph's global degree or incomplete structure to make an estimation.

Motivated by the above investigations and analyses, we propose a new method called *DIGRank*, which exploits both global degree and incomplete structural information. Doing so avoids the aforementioned structural shortcomings and,

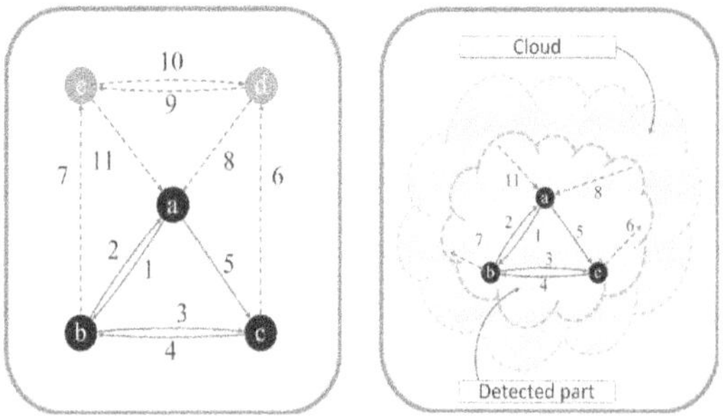

(a) complete graph (b) cloud graph

Figure 1: A sample of node structure graphic. (a) is a complete graph, while (b) is a cloud graph.

thus, is a more reliable method. To test the adaptability of *DIGRank*, we analyze its performance characteristics using different parameters based on several topological models, such as *WS* and *BA*. The results show our new method is suitable for *scale-free* [5] and *small-world* [6] graphs, both of which are present in most real world networks.

Compared with Bar-Yossef *et al.*'s Local *PageRank* Approximation *LPRA*, our method has several advantages. First, it relies on only the structure of a given local graph and global degrees of local nodes, instead of running endless crawling through the *link server*. Second, compared with *LPRA*, our method reduces the computational cost by 50% and the error rate by 56% in a data set on which *LPRA* performs well.

2. ALGORITHM

As mentioned above, it is necessary to find a method to rank nodes in an incomplete graph when the complete graph is hard to obtain. Figure 1(a) shows an example of a complete graph. Including all nodes and links. The complete graph consists of a detected part and an undetected part. The incomplete graph (only the detected part) contains nodes a, b and c. The links are shown as solid lines.

To rank nodes in the incomplete graph, people usually use a simple local *PageRank* method. But, because the structure of the complete and incomplete graphs differ, their final rankings will also differ.

In order to improve the consistency of such rankings, we are proposing a method called *DIGRank* which is used in a *cloud graph* as shown in Figure 1(b). In the *cloud graph*, we see the undetected part as a *Cloud*, and assume every undetected link end connects to the *Cloud*. Thus, there may be more than one link between the Cloud and a node. For example, both 8 and 11 are links from the *Cloud* to the node a. To decrease the redundancy of links, we replace multi-links as 8 and 11 by one weighted link (the weight of this weighted link equals to the number of multi-links from the *Cloud* to the node a) . Fortunately, the number of links between the *Cloud* and each node equals the degree of the node in the incomplete graph minus the complete graph. Thus, we only need to know in-degrees of all nodes in the incomplete graph LI and the complete graph GI, and out-degrees of those in the incomplete graph LO and the complete graph GO, to count the weight of each link. Supposing that there are n nodes in an incomplete graph, based on the basic *PageRank* algorithm, we initiate the rank value of each detected node as $1/N$ (N is the number of nodes in the complete graph) and that of the *Cloud* as the subtraction of n/N, the value of all detected nodes, from 1. Then we transform the incomplete graph into a weighted *cloud graph*, and compute the rank value of each detected node iteratively as Algorithm 1 shows.

Table 1: Ranking methods

	a	b	c	d	e	Rank
PR	0.2392	0.2126	0.1924	0.1852	0.1708	a>b>c
PR*	0.2380	0.4287	0.3333	-	-	b>c>a
DR	0.2942	0.2470	0.2236	0.2352		a>b>c

Algorithm 1: Ranking nodes by adding a *Cloud*

```
input  : E, weighed edges of the Cloud Graph
output: R, a list of rank scores {r_1, ..., r_n} of nodes
for i ∈ [1, n] do
    r_i = 1/N;
    if GI_i > LI_i then
        E(0, i) = GI_i − LI_i; /*edge from 0 to i, 0
        represent the cloud*/
    if GO_i > LO_i then
        E(i, 0) = GO_i − LO_i; /*edge from i to 0*/
r_0 = 1 − n/N;
R = WeightedRank(E, R);
delete r_0 from R;
sort R by rank score;
return R;
function WeightedRank(E, R)
R* = R, R = {0, ..., 0};
while |R* − R| > ε, ε → 0 do
    R = R*, R* = {0, ..., 0};
    for every E(i, j) in E do
        r*_j = r*_j + r_i * (E(i, j)/GO_i); /* distribute
        score from r_i to r*_j */
return R;
```

In Table 1, we rank nodes of Figure 1 by *PageRank* (*PR*) in a complete graph, by simple local *PageRank* (*PR**) in an incomplete graph, and by *DIGRank* (*DR*) in a *Cloud Graph*. We can see that *PR**'s ranking sequence is different with *PR*, while *DR*'s ranking sequence is the same as *PR*.

3. SIMULATED GRAPH ANALYSIS

Because most real networks contain *small-world* and *scale-free* characteristics, we generate two groups of such simulated graphs and conduct measurements to test *DIGRank*'s performance.

3.1 Measurement

In the evaluation, we use *unsortedness ratio* U to measure correspondence between estimated sequences in a subgraph and real sequences by *PageRank* in the complete graph.

$$U = \frac{\sum_{i=1}^{n} \sum_{j=2, i<j}^{n} P_{ij}}{n * (n-1)/2} \tag{1}$$

Boolean variable P_{ij} means coherence between two pair sequences. If matched, P_{ij} is 0; otherwise, P_{ij} is 1. U measures the *unsortedness ratio*, $U \in [0, 1]$. $U = 0$ means the two sequences are identical, $U = 1$ means one is in

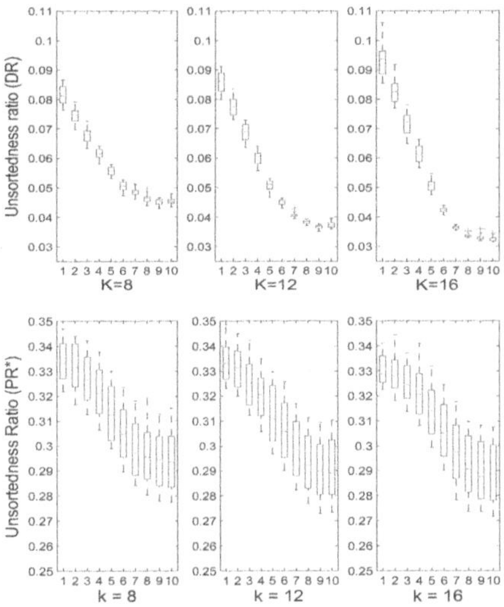

Figure 2: Small-world Graphs

reverse order of the other. For instance, in Table 1, the sequences $\langle b, a\rangle$, $\langle c, a\rangle$ of PR^* are different with that $\langle a, b\rangle$, $\langle a, c\rangle$ of PR, which means $P_{ab} = 1$, $P_{ac} \doteq 1$, $P_{bc} = 0$ and $U_{PR*} = (1 + 1 + 0)/(3 * (3 - 1)/2) = 2/3$.

3.2 Small-world Graph

We generate 250 WS graphs with different parameters, k (average degree), p (random reconnection coefficient), N (number of nodes). Then we extract 200 subgraphs by BFS from each WS graph: 50 in which the nodes amount to 5% of the whole WS graph, 50 at 10%, 50 at 15%, and 50 at 20%. The total number of subgraphs analyzed is 50,000. We apply local estimating methods to these data, compute *unsortedness ratio* of all subgraphs, and get the average value of every 50 subgraphs with the same r of each WS graph. In Figure 2, each box contains 5 ($N = 2000, 4000, 6000, 8000, 10000$)*4 ($r = 5\%, 10\%, 15\%, 20\%$) *unsortedness ratio* values. We find that the gaps among these values in each box are small, which means the graph scale N and extracting ratio r have little impact on the accuracy of *DR*.

The horizontal axis x represents different values of $p = 0.1, 0.2, ..., 1$ ($x = 1$ means $p = 0.1$) in Figure 2. We find that *unsortedness ratio* decreases as p increases, which means the lower average shortest path length [1] the graph has, the better accuracy the *DIGRank* has. We also find that, when k increases, the range of accuracy variation becomes larger.

Using these generated WS graphs, we test how the community structure of a graph affects DIGRank's accuracy. Module degree Q [7] is a value to indicate the tendency of a graph to be divided into different communities. A graph that is easily divided is said to have high modularity. Figure 3 shows that *unsortedness ratio* increases as Q increases, which means the algorithm would have a better performance if the community characteristic of a graph is not notable.

3.3 Scale-free Graph

We also generate a group of BA graphs with different parameters, m (number of nodes to be linked by each added node), N (number of nodes in the final graph). Then we extract 200 subgraphs by BFS at a different ratio r. Similar to WS graphs, the accuracy of *DIGRank* is relative to average degree of a graph rather than the graph scale N and extracting ratio r. Specially, in Figure 4, the accuracy of *DIGRank* behaves a power-law relationship with average degree. Thus, with the increase of average degree of the network, *DIGRank* would perform even better.

[1]In WS model, average shortest path length and cluster coefficient has positive correlation with p

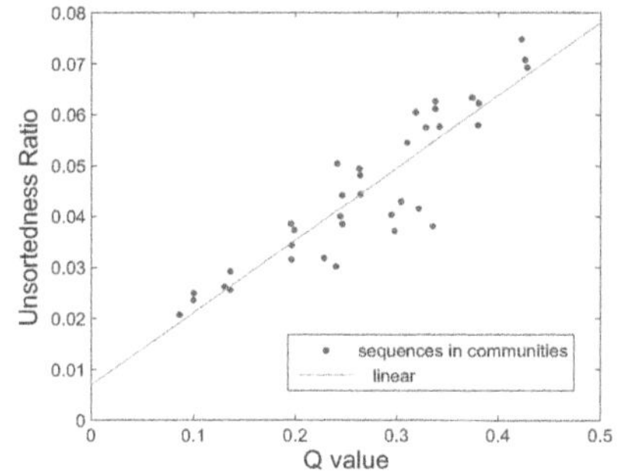

Figure 3: Relationship between U and Community Structure

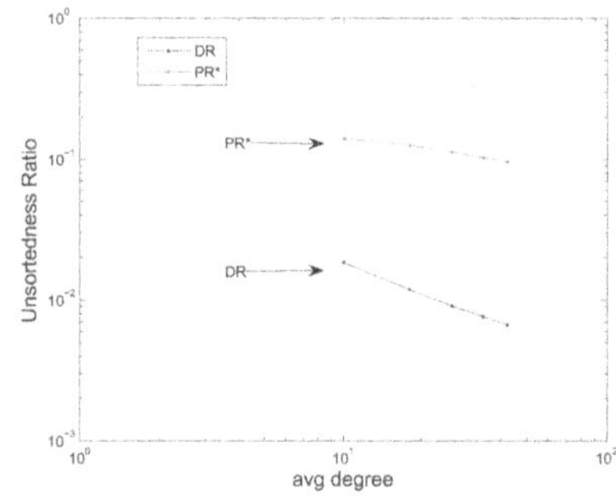

Figure 4: Scale-free Characteristic

In this section, we find some characteristics of our method. First, its performance is independent with the graph scale and extracting rate at some extent. Second, with increase of random reconnection coefficient and average degree, the error rate decreases. Moreover, compared with PR^*, our method reduces the error rate by more than 70% in both *small-world* and *scale-free* graphs. Thus, we assume that *DIGRank* would be suitable for many real networks which contain *small-world* and *scale-free* characteristics.

4. COMPARISON IN REAL NETWORK

4.1 Other Advanced Methods

Beyond the simple local *PageRank*, Chen *et al.* proposed an *influence method*; later on, Bar-Yossef *et al.* further researched on it and gave a more advanced method Local *PageRank* Approximation *LPRA*. This advanced method crawls all adjacent nodes of a target node layer by layer, and computes the influences of them on the target node. It has been used for quickly estimating global rank value of a target node. Yet, it still has some disadvantages.

First, *LPRA* strongly relies on the accessibility to the adjacent nodes of a target one through a *link server*. If not all the adjacent nodes are accessible to the crawler, accuracy

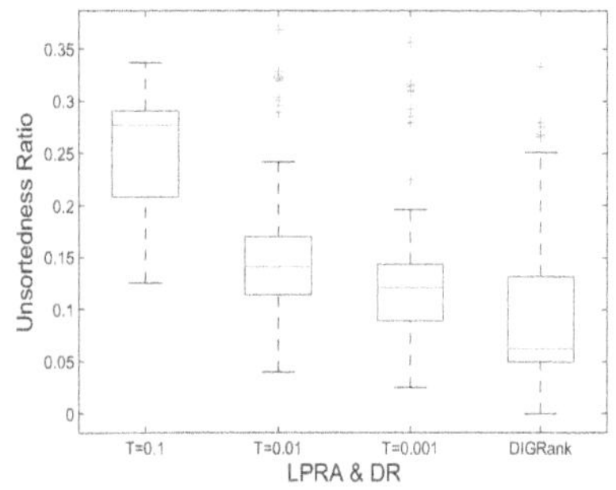

Figure 5: Accuracy comparison.

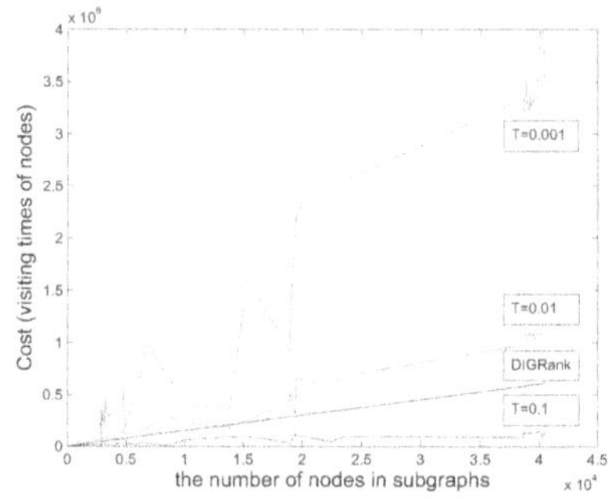

Figure 6: Computational cost comparison.

will decrease. Second, they do not put an emphasis on the accuracy of sequences of nodes, which is important in many applications. Third, the cost of *LPRA* is still not low when dealing with local graphs.

4.2 Dataset

We compare our method *DR* with *LPRA* based on a 280,000 page crawl of the `www.stanford.edu` domain performed in 2002 by the `WebBase project`[2]. The data is considered suitable to test the *LPRA* and even able to represent large connected components of the web graph to some extent.

We randomly extract 100 subgraphs by *BFS* with size smaller than 20% of the whole graph. In each subgraph, we run the *DR* and *LPRA* with different threshold [3] value T range from 0.001 to 0.1.

4.3 Comparison

Figure 5 shows *unsortedness ratio* comparison of the two methods in all subgraphs. $T = 0.1$ means using *LPRA* with threshold 0.1 to compute each subgraph. We see that with the decrease of T, the decrease of the error rate becomes slower. Yet, even when we choose a much lower threshold $T = 0.001$, the error rate of *LPRA* is still much higher than that of *DR*. We see that the median of the error rate of *DR* is reduced by 49% compared with $T = 0.001$, 56% compared with $T = 0.01$ and 78% compared with $T = 0.1$.

Figure 6 shows the comparison of computational cost for methods in all subgraphs whose numbers of nodes range from 100 to 45000. Computational cost is the sum number of times all the nodes are visited after a method completes all of its scans. *LPRA* prunes away and ignores some nodes after several scans, saving time and resources, but its computational cost is still high because many influential nodes are visited dozens or hundreds of times. To compute the cost of *DR*, we multiply 15 scans [4] by the number of nodes in the subgraph because in each iterative process, all these nodes are visited. In Figure 6, the cost of *DR* is a bit higher than that of *LPRA* with $T = 0.1$, but much lower than that of *LPRA* with $T = 0.01$ and $T = 0.001$. In addition, as T decreases, the cost increases rapidly. For example, the cost of $T = 0.001$ is much higher than that of other thresholds.

In this section, we find that $T = 0.01$ is an acceptable tradeoff for LPRA which is similar to Chen *et al.*'s result [5]. Compared with LPRA($T = 0.01$), our approach reduces the cost by 50%, and error rate by 56%.

5. CONCLUSIONS

In this paper, we propose a new algorithm called *DIGRank*, which is specially designed for ranking the nodes in local graphs. Compared with the simple local PageRank, our method is very suitable for *small-world* and *scale-free* graphs which contain similar characteristics with many real networks. Compared with the advanced local *PageRank* approximation method, *DIGRank* significantly reduces the computational cost and error rate.

6. ACKNOWLEDGMENTS

The research was supported by the fund of the State Key Laboratory of Software Development Environment (SKLSDE-2011ZX-02).

7. REFERENCES

[1] Lawrence Page, Sergey Brin, Rajeev Motwani, and Terry Winograd. The pagerank citation ranking: Bringing order to the web. Technical report, Stanford InfoLab, November 1999.

[2] Yen-Yu Chen, Qingqing Gan, and Torsten Suel. Local methods for estimating pagerank values. In *Proceedings of the thirteenth ACM international conference on Information and knowledge management*, CIKM '04, pages 381–389, New York, NY, USA, 2004. ACM.

[3] Ziv Bar-Yossef and Li-Tal Mashiach. Local approximation of pagerank and reverse pagerank. In *Proceeding of the 17th ACM conference on Information and knowledge management*, CIKM '08, pages 279–288, New York, NY, USA, 2008. ACM.

[4] Santo Fortunato, Marián Boguñá, Alessandro Flammini, and Filippo Menczer. How to make the top ten: Approximating pagerank from in-degree. *CoRR*, abs/cs/0511016, 2005. informal publication.

[5] A. L. Barabasi and R. Albert. Emergence of scaling in random networks. *Science*, 286:509–512, 1999.

[6] D. J. Watts and S. H. Strogatz. Collective dynamics of "small-world" networks. *Nature*, 393:440–442, 1998.

[7] M. E. J. Newman and M. Girvan. Finding and evaluating community structure in networks. *Physical Review E*, 69(2):026113, February 2004. PT: J; PN: Part 2; PG: 15.

[2] vlado.fmf.uni-lj.si/pub/networks/data/mix/mixed.htm.

[3] Bar-Yossef *et al.*'s local *PageRank* approximation used a pruning method to cut low influence nodes whose influences are below threshold value T. With decrease of the threshold, the error rate decreases while the cost increases. Chen *et al.*'s *influence method* also focused on the tradeoff between the error rate and the cost.

[4] In most graphs, *PageRank* is convergent after 10 to 20 iterations.

[5] Chen *et al.*'s simple *influence method* showed when the threshold below a certain value such as 0.005, the average error will decrease much slower than before and will keep stable after *T=0.001*.

On Selection of Objective Functions in Multi-Objective Community Detection

Chuan Shi
Beijing University of Posts and Telecommunications
Beijing China 100876
shichuan@bupt.edu.cn

Philip S. Yu
University of Illinois at Chicago
IL USA 60607-7053
psyu@uic.edu

Yanan Cai
Beijing University of Posts and Telecommunications
Beijing China 100876
diandacainan@gmail.com

Zhenyu Yan
Fair Isaac Corporation(FICO)
CA USA 94903
yan_zhen_yu@hotmail.com

Bin Wu
Beijing University of Posts and Telecommunications
Beijing China 100876
wubin@bupt.edu.cn

ABSTRACT

There is a surge of community detection of complex networks in recent years. Different from conventional single-objective community detection, this paper formulates community detection as a multi-objective optimization problem and proposes a general algorithm NSGA-Net based on evolutionary multi-objective optimization. Interested in the effect of optimization objectives on the performance of the multi-objective community detection, we further study the correlations (i.e., positively correlated, independent, or negatively correlated) of 11 objective functions that have been used or can potentially be used for community detection. Our experiments show that NSGA-Net optimizing over a pair of negatively correlated objectives usually performs better than the single-objective algorithm optimizing over either of the original objectives, and even better than other well-established community detection approaches.

Categories and Subject Descriptors

H.2.8 [**Database Management**]: Database Applications-Data Mining

General Terms

Algorithm

Keywords

Complex network, community detection, multi-objective optimization, evolutionary algorithm

1. INTRODUCTION

Recently a large amount of research has been devoted to the task of defining and identifying communities in social and information networks. Loosely speaking, communities are groups of nodes that are densely interconnected but only sparely connected with the rest of the network [3]. To extract such groups of nodes, one typically chooses an objective function that captures the intuition of a community as a group of nodes with better internal connectivity than external connectivity. As a consequence, the community detection problem (Ω, O) can be formally defined as a Single-objective Optimization Problem (SOP): determine the partition C^* for which

$$O(C^*) = \min_{C\in\Omega} O(C) \tag{1}$$

where Ω is the set of feasible partitions, C is a community structure of a given network G and $O : \Omega \rightarrow R$ is an objective function. Without loss of generality, we assume O is to be minimized. Most conventional community detection algorithms are based on the SOP. Different algorithms vary in the objective function O and optimization techniques.

These single-objective community detection algorithms have been widely applied to both artificial and real problems. However, they also face some fundamental difficulties. These single-objective algorithms attempt to optimize just one objective function and this confines the solution to a particular community structure property. Moreover, these algorithms may fail when the optimized objectives are inappropriate. In addition, one single fixed community partition returned by the single-objective algorithms may not be suitable for the networks with multiple potential structures (e.g., hierarchical and overlapping structures).

It might be more natural and reasonable to consider the community structure from different angles (i.e. multiple optimized objectives) at the same time. That is, in the multi-objective community detection problem $(\Omega, O_1, O_2, \cdots, O_t)$, we aim to discover the community structure C^* for which

$$O(C^*) = \min_{C\in\Omega}(O_1(C), O_2(C), \cdots, O_t(C)) \tag{2}$$

where t is the number of objectives and O_i represents the i-th objective. With the introduction of multi-objective, there is usually no single best solution for this optimization task, but instead, the notion of Pareto optimality should be embraced. For two partitions $C_1, C_2 \in \Omega$, the partition C_1 is said to dominate the partition C_2 (denoted as $C_1 \preceq C_2$) if and only if

$$\begin{aligned} &\forall i \in \{1, \cdots, t\}\ O_i(C_1) \leq O_i(C_2) \\ &\wedge \exists i \in \{1, \cdots, t\}\ O_i(C_1) < O_i(C_2) \end{aligned} \tag{3}$$

A partition $C \in \Omega$ is said to be Pareto optimal if and only if there is no other partition dominating C. The set of all Pareto optimal partitions is the Pareto optimal set and the corresponding set in the objective space is called the non-dominated set, or Pareto front.

Compared to single-objective approaches, the multi-objective community detection has many advantages. (1) The optimal solutions of the single-objective community detection problems defined by $(\Omega, O_1), \cdots, (\Omega, O_t)$ are always comprised by the Pareto optimal set of the multi-objective problem defined by $(\Omega, O_1, \cdots, O_t)$. (2) The multiple objectives can measure characteristics of community structure from different angles, and thus it helps to avoid the risk that one single objective may only be suitable to a certain kind of networks. (3) The multi-objective community detection usually returns a set of community partitions according to the multiple optimized objectives. These community partitions reveal community structure from different angles, which help to discover complex and comprehensive community structures.

In order to effectively solve the Multi-objective Optimization Problem (MOP), we propose a general solution, NSGA-Net, which simultaneously optimizes multiple objective functions with an evolutionary algorithm. As a general multi-objective community detection solution, NSGA-Net can optimize over any multiple objective functions. For this new community detection paradigm, one important issue is that what type of objective functions should be optimized to improve the accuracy of community partition. To solve this issue, we first study correlation relations among 11 popular objective functions and divide the relations between any two objective functions into three categories: positively correlated, independent, and negatively correlated. Then we compare NSGA-Net optimizing over six pairs of objective functions from these three types of correlations (two pairs for each type) to a SOP based approach optimizing over the original single objective. Experiments demonstrate that NSGA-Net only with negatively correlated objectives usually leads to a better performance than that can be achieved by any of the original objectives. We also show that with a pair of negatively correlated objectives, the NSGA-Net performs better than most conventional community detection algorithms.

2. NSGA-NET

In order to effectively solve the multi-objective community detection problem, we propose the NSGA-Net solution based on Evolutionary Algorithm (EA). EA has been proven to be an effective method for MOP. Evolutionary Multi-objective Optimization (EMO) has become one of the main research fields in the EA community, which has also been applied in data mining [11]. Conventional EMO algorithms are designed for numerical optimization problems. When we solve a real problem with EMO, many components of EA need to be redesigned.

Multi-objective optimization mechanism. In this paper, we select NSGA-II [2] as the multi-objective optimization mechanism in NSGA-Net. Four parameters govern the run of NSGA-Net: the population size $popSize$, the running generation gen, the ratio of crossover $croRat$ and the ratio of mutation $mutRat$.

Genetic representation. We apply the *locus-based adjacency* [4] to represent a partition. In this graph-based representation, each genotype g consists of n genes $g_1, g_2, \cdots, g_n$ and each g_i can take one of the adjacent nodes of node i. Thus, a value of j assigned to the i-th gene, is then interpreted as a link between node i and j. In the resulting solution, they will be in the same community. The decoding of this representation requires the identification of all connected components. All nodes belong to the same connected component are then assigned to one community.

Genetic operation and initialization. The uniform two-point crossover is employed. In the mutation operation, NSGA-Net randomly selects some genes and assigns them with other randomly selected adjacent nodes. In the initialization process, we randomly generate some individuals. For each individual, each gene g_i randomly takes one of the adjacent nodes of node i.

Model selection. NSGA-Net returns a set of solutions, which provides Decision Makers (DMers) with more choices. Sometimes DMers may desire that the set of candidate solutions could be narrowed down to those of most interest. In this paper, we therefore propose the novel *Max-Min Distance* model section method to select one single recommendation solution from the Pareto front. Inspired by Gap statistic [4], the *Max-Min Distance* method selects the solution model that mostly deviates from the null models generated by NSGA-Net by running on random networks with the same distribution. Concretely, NSGA-Net firstly runs on the real network and randomly generated networks with the same scale. Thus the optimal solution set on the real network (called $CandSet$) and the corresponding random network (called $RandSet$) can be obtained, respectively. For each solution in $CandSet$, we calculate the minimum-distance with solutions in $RandSet$, and then we select the solution in $CandSet$ with the maximum minimum-distance as the recommendation solution. Here, Euclidean distance is employed. Intuitively, the recommendation solution is the most different one from the solutions in $RandSet$.

Objective function. Still NSGA-Net has an important component unsolved: objective functions. As a general multi-objective community detection solution, NSGA-Net can apply any multiple objective functions. With NSGA-Net, we will examine the general performance of the multi-objective community detection. Furthermore, we explore what type of objectives is suitable for the multi-objective paradigm.

3. PERFORMANCES OF MULTI-OBJECTIVE COMMUNITY DETECTION

3.1 Objective Functions

Many objective functions have been proposed to capture the intuition of communities. We summarize 11 objective functions that are already widely used in community detection literatures or can be potentially used for community detection.

- **Conductance** (Q_1) measures the fraction of total edge volume that points outside the cluster [6].
- **Expansion** (Q_2) measures the number of edges per node that point outside the cluster [6].

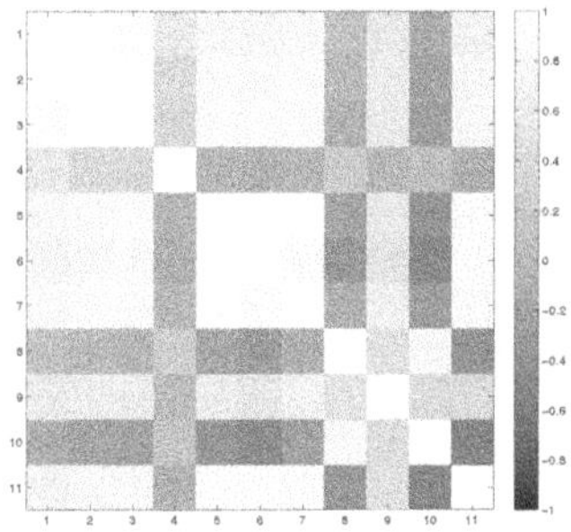

Figure 1: Pearson correlative coefficients of the 11 objectives. 1-11 represent the objective functions $O_1 - O_{11}$, respectively.

- **Cut Ratio** (Q_3) is the fraction of all possible edges leaving the cluster [6].
- **Normalized Cut** (Q_4) is the normalized fraction of edges leaving the cluster [6].
- **Maximum-ODF(Out Degree Fraction)** ((Q_5)) is the maximum fraction of edges of a node pointing outside the cluster [6].
- **Average-ODF** (Q_6) is the average fraction nodes' edges pointing outside the cluster [6].
- **Flake-ODF** (Q_7) is the fraction of nodes in S that have fewer edges pointing inside than to the outside of the cluster [6].
- **Q** (Q_8) measures the number of within-community edges, relative to a null model of a random graph with the same degree distribution [8].
- **Description Length** (Q_9) is the number of edges between the community i and j. The objective regards the community as a optimal compression of network's topology [7].
- **Community Score** (Q_{10}) measures the density of a sub-matrices based on volume and row/column means [9].
- **Internal Density** (Q_{11}) is the internal edge density of the cluster [6].

We roughly classify the objective functions into three categories. The first category contains the first four objectives from graph theory community, which are called the cut-based objectives. The three objectives ended with "ODF" are called the degree-based objectives. Finally, the remaining objectives are classified into one category. These objective functions come from different research fields, such as graph theory and physics. All these objectives attempt to capture a group of nodes with better internal connectivity than external connectivity, and thus they all can be potentially used in community detection.

3.2 Objective Correlations

We can observe that the definitions of some objectives are similar, such as the cut-based objectives. Namely, these objectives are correlated. Here we apply the Pearson correlation coefficients to describe their relations. Because it is difficult to analyze their correlations from the definitions directly, we perform experiments to estimate the Pearson correlation coefficients. The experiments are done with the following steps. (1) For a given network, we generate a set of random partitions. (2) For each partition, we calculate the values of the different objective functions. Thus each objective function has a vector of random samples. (3) We estimate the Pearson correlation coefficients among these objective vectors. (4) In order to reduce the estimation variance, we repeat step 1 to 3 many times and get the average values.

The results are illustrated in Figure 1. We can observe that the cut-based objectives are highly correlated (especially $O_1 - O_3$). It is the same case for the degree-based objectives. In addition, we notice that *InternalDensity* is negatively correlated with Q and *CommunityScore*. The relations of these objectives can be roughly classified into three categories in terms of their correlation coefficients: positively correlated (e.g., $\{O_1, O_2, O_3, O_4\}$, $\{O_5, O_6, O_7\}$, $\{O_8, O_9, O_{10}\}$), independent (e.g., $\{O_1, O_8\}$, $\{O_1, O_{10}\}$, $\{O_4, O_9\}$), and negatively correlated (e.g., $\{O_8, O_{11}\}$, $\{O_{10}, O_{11}\}$).

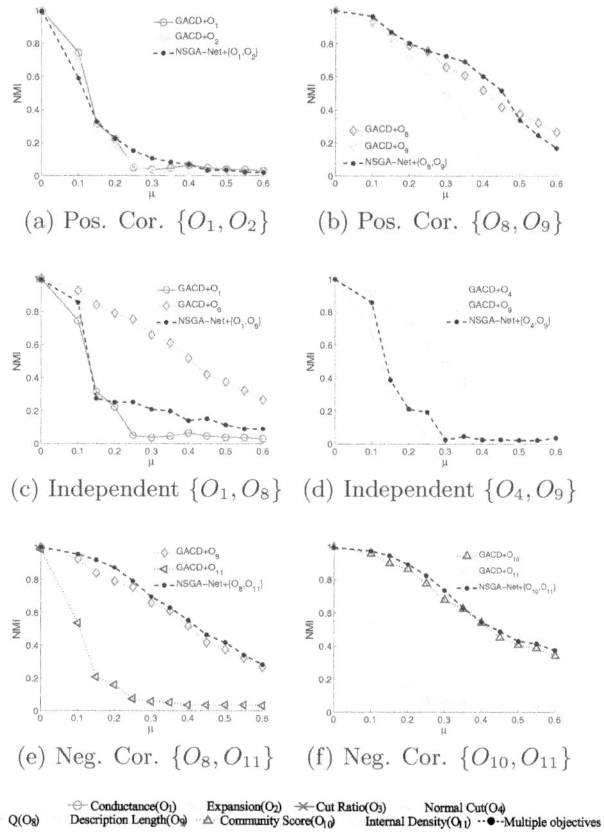

(a) Pos. Cor. $\{O_1, O_2\}$ (b) Pos. Cor. $\{O_8, O_9\}$ (c) Independent $\{O_1, O_8\}$ (d) Independent $\{O_4, O_9\}$ (e) Neg. Cor. $\{O_8, O_{11}\}$ (f) Neg. Cor. $\{O_{10}, O_{11}\}$

Figure 2: The NMI comparison of NSGA-Net optimizing over three types of objective functions (i.e., positively correlated, independent, negatively correlated) and GACD optimizing over original single objectives on artificial networks. The larger the NMI, the better the performance.

3.3 Performance Effect of Objective Selection

In this section, we will test the performances of the multi-objective community detection method (i.e., NSGA-Net) and find what kind of objectives are suitable for the method. Here we only consider two objectives, rather than more objectives, in order to focus on the effectiveness of the multi-objective method and reduce the complexity. From each of the three categories of objective correlations, we select two pairs as the optimized objectives in NSGA-Net. Particularly, for the positively correlated objectives we choose $\{O_1, O_2\}$, $\{O_8, O_9\}$; the independent objectives, $\{O_1, O_8\}$, $\{O_4, O_9\}$; and the negatively correlated objectives, $\{O_8, O_{11}\}$, $\{O_{10}, O_{11}\}$. For the SOP: $\min_{C \in \Omega} O(C)$, we choose GACD [12] as the single-objective community detection optimizer. NSGA-Net is equipped with the same parameters with GACD for a fair comparison. That is, $popSize = gen = 200$; $croRat = 0.6$; and $mutRat = 0.4$.

We use a popular artificial network with a known commu-

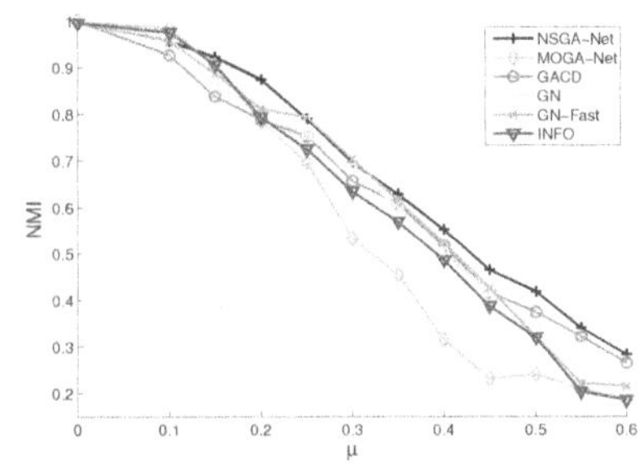

Figure 3: The comparison of NSGA-Net with a pair of negatively correlated objectives (i.e., O_8 and O_{11}) with other popular algorithms on artificial networks.

nity structure [5], which has the heterogeneity in the distributions of node degrees and community sizes. Same in ref. [5], each node in the benchmark graphs share a fraction $1-\mu$ of its links with the other nodes of its community and a fraction μ with the other nodes of the network. As μ increases, it becomes harder and harder to identify the community structure. To compare the built-in modular structure with the one delivered by different objectives, we adopt the Normalized Mutual Information (NMI), a measure of similarity of partitions borrowed from information theory [5].

We first run NSGA-Net on the artificial networks. The comparison results of NSGA-Net optimizing over six pairs of objectives and GACD optimizing over original single objectives are shown in Figure 2. When the optimized objectives are positively correlated or independent, NSGA-Net's performances have no obvious differences from the performances of the optimization on each single objective with GACD. Most results of NSGA-Net are between those of the single objectives. However, it is obvious that NSGA-Net with a pair of negatively correlated objectives has better performance than the optimization on the original single objective, since their NMI are larger than those of the single objective in most conditions.

3.4 Comparison with Other Algorithms

We further validate the performance of NSGA-Net through comparing it with representative community detection algorithms. NSGA-Net is equipped with a pair of negatively correlated objectives O_8 and O_{11}. Other five algorithms are included in the experiments. It includes the betweenness-based heuristic algorithm [8] (named GN) and its improved version [1] (named GN Fast). The EA-based optimization algorithm [12] (named GACD) optimizes the O_8. The information-theoretic framework based algorithm (named INFO) [7] optimizes the O_9. Another multi-objective method MOGA-Net [10] is also included. In order to obtain one single recommendation solution, MOGA-Net also employs the *Max-Min distance* model selection method. NSGA-Net and MOGA-Net are set as the same parameters with GACD. The benchmark is the same artificial networks as before.

The experimental results are shown in Figure 3. In most conditions, NSGA-Net obviously performs better than other five algorithms including not only the single-objective algorithms but also the multi-objective method, MOGA-Net. An important difference between NSGA-Net and MOGA-Net lies in the objective functions. We think the absence of the sufficient negative correlation between objectives in MOGA-Net causes its bad performances.

4. CONCLUSION

In this paper, we study the multi-objective community detection problem and propose a novel solution NSGA-Net. Aiming to exploit the universal validity of the multi-objective solution for community detection and its requisition on objective functions, we first analyze the intrinsic correlations among 11 objectives. Then we compare the performances of NSGA-Net optimizing over different types of objectives to those of a single-objective based approach optimizing over the original single objective. The experiments show that NSGA-Net only with a pair of negatively correlated objectives remarkably improve the performance.

5. ACKNOWLEDGMENTS

It is supported by the National Natural Science Foundation of China (No. 60905025, 61074128, 61035003) and the 863 Program of China No.2009AA04Z136.

6. REFERENCES

[1] A. Clauset, M. E. J. Newman, and C. Moore. Finding community structure in very large networks. *Physical Review E*, 70(06611), 2004.

[2] K. Deb, A. Pratab, S. Agarwal, and T. MeyArivan. A fast and elitist multiobjective genetic algorithm: Nsga-ii. *IEEE Transaction on Evolutionary Computation*, 6(2):182–197, 2002.

[3] M. Girvanl and M. E. J. Newman. Community structure in social and biological networks. *Proceedings of the National Academy of Sciences*, 99(12):7821–7826, 2002.

[4] J. Handle and J. Knowles. An evolutionary approach to multiobjective clustering. *Transaction on Evolutionary Computation*, 11(1):56–76, 2007.

[5] A. Lancichinetti, S. Fortunato, and F. Radicchi. Benchmark graphs for testing community detection algorithms. *Physical Review E*, 78(046110), 2008.

[6] J. Leskovec, K. J. Lang, and M. W. Mahoney. Empirical comparison of algorithms for network community detection. In *WWW2010*, pages 631–640, 2010.

[7] R. Martin and T. B. Carl. An information-theoretic framework for resolving community structure in complex networks. *Proceedings of the National Academy of Sciences*, 104(18):7327–7331, 2007.

[8] M. E. J. Newman and M. Girvan. Finding and evaluating community structure in networks. *Physics Review E*, 69(026113), 2004.

[9] C. Pizzuti. Ga-net: a genetic algorithm for community detection in social networks. In *PPSN2008*, pages 1081–1090, 2008.

[10] C. Pizzuti. A multi-objective genetic algorithm for community detection in networks. In *ICTAI09*, pages 379–386, 2009.

[11] C. Shi, X. Kong, P. S. Yu, and B. Wang. Multi-label ensemble learning. In *ECML/PKDD 2011*, 2011.

[12] C. Shi, Z. Y. Yan, Y. Wang, Y. N. Cai, and B. Wu. A genetic algorithm for detecting communities in large-scale complex networks. *Advance in Complex System*, 13(1):3–17, 2010.

Suggesting Ghost Edges for a Smaller World

Manos Papagelis
University of Toronto
papaggel@cs.toronto.edu

Francesco Bonchi
Yahoo! Research
bonchi@yahoo-inc.com

Aristides Gionis
Yahoo! Research
gionis@yahoo-inc.com

ABSTRACT

Small changes in the network topology can have dramatic effects on its capacity to disseminate information. In this paper, we consider the problem of adding a small number of *ghost edges* in the network in order to minimize the average shortest-path distance between nodes, towards a smaller-world network. We formalize the problem of suggesting ghost edges and we propose a novel method for quickly evaluating the importance of ghost edges in sparse graphs. Through experiments on real and synthetic data sets, we demonstrate that our approach performs very well, for a varying range of conditions, and it outperforms sensible baselines.

Categories and Subject Descriptors [H.3.4]: Systems and Software - *Information networks*
General Terms Algorithms, Peformance, Human Factors
Keywords Graph Augmentation, Social Networks, Small World

1. INTRODUCTION

The way that information disseminates in a social network depends, to a great extent, on its topology. As a matter of fact, small changes in the network topology can have dramatic effects on how efficiently information spreads among individuals. In this paper, we consider the problem of adding a small number of *ghost edges*, i.e., edges between existing nodes in the graph that could exist but have not yet been realized, with the objective of improving the network efficiency of information propagation. While having plenty of choices for measuring the network efficiency, we focus on a structural feature, namely the *average all-pairs shortest path distance* $\bar{L}(G)$. Minimizing $\bar{L}(G)$ gives smaller-world networks [4], in which information can travel from one node to another by traversing a smaller number of intermediate edges, and distinguishes an easily negotiable network from one which is inefficient, with a network with shorter $\bar{L}(G)$ being more desirable. Now, let $G(V, E)$ be a connected undirected graph and assume that we are allowed to augment G with a small number of edges. Note that, adding edges in a network results in altering some of the shortest paths for some pairs of nodes in the graph. It is worth noting that while adding long-haul edges may bring a large gain in terms of connectivity for some node pairs (the new shortest path connecting them will be much shorter), long-haul edges are likely to affect the shortest path of only a few pairs. On the other hand, suggesting short-haul, intra-community edges is likely to affect the shortest path length of many node pairs, but the gain in connectivity for each of them might be limited (the new shortest path connecting them will not be much shorter). Therefore in trying to suggest edges to be added to G we are facing an interesting trade-off. We are now in position to formally define the problem of interest in this paper:

CIKM'11, October 24–28, 2011, Glasgow, Scotland, UK.

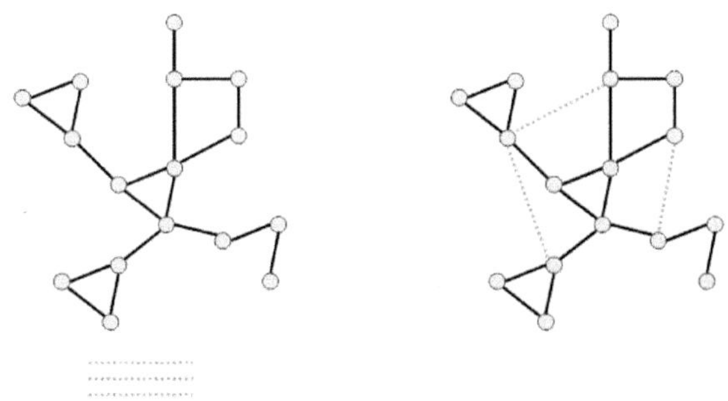

(a) $G = (V, E)$, $|R| = k$ (b) $G_{aug} = (V, E \cup R)$

Figure 1: The problem: (a) the input consists of G and an integer k, (b) the augmented graph G_{aug} is a possible output. The goal is to find the set of ghost edges R that minimizes $\bar{L}(G_{aug})$.

PROBLEM 1. *Let $G(V, E)$ be a connected, undirected graph, and let $\bar{L}(G)$ be the average all-pairs shortest path length in G. Let $R \subseteq V \times V \setminus E$ where $|R| \leq k$ be a set of candidate ghost edges for augmentation. If $G_{aug} = (V, E \cup R)$ is the augmented graph of G, then the objective is, given G and an integer k, to determine the subset of edges R that minimizes $\bar{L}(G_{aug})$.*

This is a challenging problem, as traditional graph augmentation problems, where we ask to find a minimum-cost set of edges to add to a graph to satisfy a specified property, such as biconnectivity, have been shown to be NP-complete [2, 7]. In the case that the problem is considered with a hard limit on the number of edges to be added, such as in [1, 5], authors observe a relation between the single-source version of the problem, where we want to minimize the largest distance from a given source vertex, and the well-known k-median problem. In [1], the focus is on minimizing the diameter of the network, while in [5] the suggested edges are all incident to a single node. The problem draws connections, as well, to the *link revival* problem [6]. Our methods can be adopted in a variety of strategies for speeding up communication or increasing the reliability of a network, and as such, can form the core component of many interesting applications. To name a few, they can be used in algorithms that suggest friends in a social network with the global objective of bringing anyone closer enabling efficient information dissemination or in algorithms that suggest new edges in a network with the global objective of destroying its clustering structure.

2. ALGORITHMS

In this section, we describe algorithms that solve the problem of interest; they take as input a graph G and a constant k and return a set R of the top-k ghost edges for augmentation. Central to the algorithms is the concept of the utility of an edge. Let U_{xy} represent a measure of the utility of adding an edge $(x, y) \in C = V \times V \setminus E$ in G. The measure of the utility U_{xy} represents the gain in decreasing the average shortest path length of the network. To evaluate U_{xy}, we need to recompute the shortest paths between all pairs of vertices $s, t \in V$. This is because a previously shortest path connecting s, t may now need to include the newly added edge (x, y). Let $\ell(x, y)$ and $\ell'(x, y)$ represent the length of the shortest path between x and y in G and G_{aug} respectively. It is easy to see that addition of an edge (x, y) will always decrease the average shortest path length of the network. We can compute the utility U_{xy} of adding an edge (x, y) by summing up the differences in the shortest path length of any pair $s, t \in V$ in G and G_{aug} respectively:

$$U_{xy} = \sum_{(s,t) \in V \times V \setminus E} (\ell(s,t) - \ell'(s,t))$$

2.1 Greedy Algorithm

We first describe a general greedy algorithm where all possible candidate ghost edges are considered and an edge is selected in each iteration that lowers the average shortest path length of the graph as much as possible (locally optimal choice). The algorithm operates in k rounds. In each round i, the algorithm determines the edge with the highest utility and adds it to the set of the top-k edges to be suggested for augmentation. Equivalently, this means that the edge selected in round i is the one that minimizes the average shortest path length in this round and for this graph. To find this edge, the algorithm iterates over all candidate ghost edges $e \in C$ and estimates the associated utility U_e by adding the edge to the graph and recomputing the new average shortest path length in the augmented graph. Computation of the utility of each candidate ghost edge takes $O(n^3)$ time (equivalent to running the Floyd-Warshall algorithm one time), there are $|C| = n(n-1)/2$ candidate ghost edges to be considered in each round i, i.e., $O(n^2)$, and there are k rounds, thus the Greedy algorithm takes $O(kn^2n^3)$ or $O(kn^5)$ time to complete. However, it is possible to omit k if instead of computing the best ghost edge, one at a time, we use the already computed edge utilities from the first iteration and determine the best k ghost edges all at once (batch processing). While this variant is expected to be faster, it will affect the quality of edges suggested, as inclusion of a candidate ghost edge may lower the utility of a subsequent ghost edge.

2.2 Heuristic Method

It's easy to see, that in the general case the addition of an edge (x, y) to G, alters the shortest path lengths for many pairs of vertices (s, t) with $s \in V$ and $t \in V$. However, a large number of the shortest paths are not affected by the addition. Let us now make a simplifying assumption that if $p_{st} =< x_1, x_2, ..., x_n >$ is the shortest path between s and t in G then both x and y belong in p_{st} (i.e., they are nodes in the existing shortest path between s and t) (see Figure 2). The premise of our assumption is that at least as good candidate ghost edges can still be found despite the fact that we constrain the set of (s, t) pairs that depend on edge (x, y) to be pairs that their existing (s, t)-shortest path in G passes through both nodes x and y. Let this smaller set of (s, t) pairs that depend on a candidate edge (x, y) be $D(x, y)$. It's easy to see that this assumption does not always hold (see Figure 2), however, this assumption

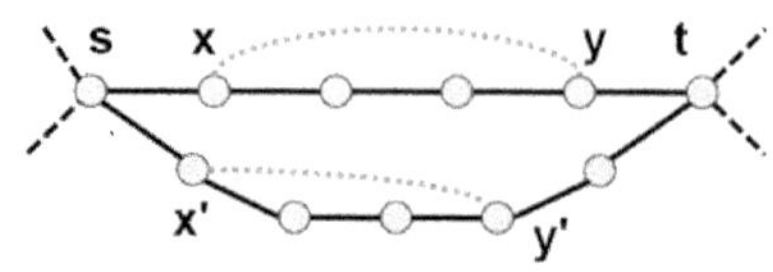

Figure 2: The (s, t) pair would benefit from both the ghost edge (x, y) and (x', y'). But due to our simplifying assumption (s, t) belongs to $D(x, y)$ and not to $D(x', y')$.

is unlikely to harm the final solution set. This is especially true in the case of sparse graphs where the shortest paths between any two nodes are more prominent. We show in the experimental evaluation that our algorithm performs very well in practice. This assumption suggests large savings in the computation of the utility U_{xy}, since now we need to only sum up the differences in the shortest path length of a much smaller set of pairs $(s, t) \in D(x, y)$, as follows:

$$\begin{aligned} U_{xy} &= \sum_{(s,t) \in D(x,y)} (\ell(s,t) - \ell'(s,t)) \\ &= \sum_{(s,t) \in D(x,y)} ((\ell(s,x) + \ell(x,y) + \ell(y,t)) \\ &\qquad - (\ell(s,x) + \ell'(x,y) + \ell(y,t))) \\ &= \sum_{(s,t) \in D(x,y)} (\ell(x,y) - \ell'(x,y)) \\ &= \sum_{(s,t) \in D(x,y)} (\ell(x,y) - 1) \end{aligned}$$

Note that the utility U_{xy} eventually depends on two factors: (a) the size of the set $D(x, y)$ (i.e., the number of (s, t) shortest paths affected by (x, y) in G_{aug}), and (b) the length $\ell(x, y)$ in G (i.e., the shortest path length of x, y in G).

We are now in position to describe our heuristic algorithm (see Algorithm 1) that can speed up the process of finding a good enough solution to the problem by incrementally computing the utility U_{xy} of each candidate edge. The algorithm first uses a modification of the classic Johnson's Algorithm that does not only provide the lengths of the paths between all pairs of vertices, but also reconstructs the actual path between any two endpoint vertices. The algorithm works in $O(n^3)$ time and stores all (s, t) paths of G in P. For each path $p \in P$ the algorithm uses a δ-size window to determine the x and y endpoints of a candidate edge (x, y) and incrementally updates its utility U_{xy}. Each time a ghost edge (x, y) is encountered in a path p an increment equal to $(\delta - 1)$ is contributed to its total utility. Note that δ is a variable that defines the size of the current δ-size window, and that for each path $p \in P$ takes values that range from $\delta = 2$ (i.e., consider ghost edges between not adjacent nodes in G) to $\delta = l$, where l is the length of the current path p. It's easy to see that the maximum δ to be considered in the whole process will be equal to the *diameter* d of G, which is defined as the longest shortest path between any two nodes in G, so the range of values of δ is $2 \leq \delta \leq d$. In the end of the procedure, for each candidate ghost edge (x, y) considered, the algorithm has associated a utility value U_{xy}. Finally, the algorithm determines the top-k candidate edges by sorting the edges on their U_{xy} value and returning the first k.

Algorithm 1 takes $O(n^3) + O(n^2\bar{L}(G)\bar{L}(G))$ or just $O(n^3)$) time to complete. First, it requires $O(n^3)$ time to find all paths in G (equivalent to running the Floyd-Warshall algorithm one time). Then for each path (i.e., $O(n^2)$) needs to vary the δ-size of the window (i.e, $O(\bar{L}(G))$) and slide the window over the path p (i.e., $O(\bar{L}(G))$).

Algorithm 1 Heuristic (G, k)

1: **procedure** HEURISTIC(G, k)
2: G: Social Graph $G(V, E)$
3: C: The set of candidate edges for addition
4: $TopK \leftarrow \emptyset$
5: $C \leftarrow \emptyset$
6: $P = getAllPairsShortestPaths(G)$
7: **for all** $p \in P$ **do**
8: $l = length(p)$
9: /* Variable size of window */
10: **for** $\delta = 2$ to l **do**
11: /* Slide a δ-size window over nodes of p */
12: **for** $i = 0$ to $l - \delta$ **do**
13: $x = p[i]$
14: $y = p[i + \delta]$
15: **if** $(x, y) \notin C$ **then**
16: $U_{xy} = (\delta - 1)$
17: add $< (x, y), U_{xy} >$ in C
18: **else**
19: update $< (x, y), U_{xy} + (\delta - 1) >$ in C
20: Sort C on the U_{xy} value *descending*
21: return $Top - k$ in C

2.3 Heuristic Sampling-based Method

Our *Heuristic* algorithm is much faster than the *Greedy* algorithm, but it's still impractical for very large graphs as it requires that all-pairs shortest paths can be efficiently computed ($O(n^3)$). In this section we describe a sampling-based variant of our heuristic, based on the assumption that even a limited number of shortest paths could provide a good approximation of the utility of each edge U_{xy}. Our sampling method works as follows: we first uniformly sample Q sources $Q = \{q_1, ..., q_q\}$; then, starting from a source q_i, $i = 1, ..., q$, we execute the Dijkstra algorithm and compute the single source shortest path tree from all q_i to all nodes x in the graph. Ideally, we would like to sample uniformly at random a few shortest paths from the set of all available ones. However, the way we perform the sampling is likely to introduce bias, as some paths are more likely to exist in the shortest path trees of sampled sources [3]. But, in our setting, we are only interested in suggesting a few ghost edges with very high utility, and these edges are expected to be part of many shortest paths, so it's expected that they will be sufficiently represented in the sampled paths. We experimentally assessed the effect of this bias and found it to be minor. Once we have obtained a set of shortest paths using our sampling method, we feed the Algorithm 1 (line 6). The rest of the algorithm remains the same. The point is that the above computation is relatively efficient, since instead of computing all-pairs shortest paths, computes q times the single-source shortest-path Dijkstra. So the overall running time is $O(q(m + nlogn))$.

3. EXPERIMENTAL EVALUATION

For the needs of our experimental evaluation we consider both real (*karate*, *dolphins*, *football*, *netscience*, *yeast*) and synthetic (*ba-s*, *ba-m*, *ba-l*) *network topologies* that represent connected, undirected, unweighted graphs (Table 1). We assess the performance of the various methods according to *accuracy* (how well a method suggests a set of k ghost edges) and *efficiency* (how fast a method suggests a set of k ghost edges) measures. To assess the accuracy we define a *gain* metric, which expresses the percentage change of $\bar{L}(G)$ before and after augmention. To assess the efficiency we measure the execution time, in *milliseconds*. Given G and k, we assess the performance of the following methods:

Table 1: Networks

Name	Nodes	Edges	Ghost Edges	Density	L(G)
karate	34	78	483	0.139	2.408
dolphins	62	159	1732	0.084	3.357
football	115	616	5939	0.093	2.508
netscience	379	914	70717	0.012	6.042
yeast	2224	7049	2464927	0.003	4.376
ba-s	50	49	1176	0.040	4.640
ba-m	500	499	124251	0.004	7.398
ba-l	1000	999	498501	0.002	8.132

Greedy-S: This is the greedy method described in paragraph 2.1.
Greedy-B: This is the *batch variant* of the *Greedy-S* method.
Heuristic: This is our heuristic method described in Algorithm 1.
Random: This is a baseline method that randomly selects k ghost edges to add in G.
Rand Star: This is a more sensible baseline method that selects k ghost edges to add in G that resemble the topology of a star. The intuition behind this method is that stars are network topologies with very small average shortest path distance [5].

We evaluate the accuracy and efficiency of our heuristic method against the greedy methods, for a varying range of network topologies and number of ghost edges k to be added. More specifically, we experiment with *karate*, *dolphins*, *football* and *ba-s* and we want to suggest 1, 5, 10 and 20 ghost edges. We had to limit our experiments on very small networks; this is because *Greedy-S* is extremely slow as we discuss below.

Accuracy: Figure 3 presents the accuracy results for the various networks. In all instances, *Greedy-S* performs better than any other method; this is because it evaluates any of the k ghost edges one at a time. Even if this method is still suboptimal, it ensures that at each iteration the correct utility for each of the subsequent ghost edges is computed, taking into consideration the previously suggested edges. As such, it avoids suggesting ghost edges that are gainful for overlapping sets of st-shortest paths. On the other hand, *Random* performs poorly in all instances, as expected, and forms a baseline for the performance of the other methods. The accuracy performance of the rest three methods, *Greedy-B*, *Heuristic*, *Rand Star* is comparable. They all perform worse than *Greedy-S*, and outperform *Random*. However, from the three, *Rand Star*, is inconsistent, as its performance largely depends on the random process with which the center node and its incident edges are selected. Overall, in terms of accuracy, the performance of *Heuristic* is always comparable and even better than that of the *Greedy-B* method. On another point it is important to note that the difference between the performance of *Greedy-S* and the other methods is becoming more evident as the number of ghost edges to be added, k, is increasing. This is to be expected; as all the other methods suggest edges on a batch way, the larger the number of suggested edges is, the larger the likelihood that these edges share overlapping st-shortest paths will be, rendering the overall gain to be smaller.

Efficiency: Table 2 presents the efficiency results for the various networks. Note that, for all methods other than the *Greedy-S* it's enough to report only one value for each network, since these methods will evaluate the utility of all edges only once. On the other hand, for the case of *Greedy-S* we report values for all different instantiations of k (i.e., *Greedy-S-1*, *Greedy-S-5*, *Greedy-S-10*, *Greedy-S-20*). It becomes obvious from Table 2 that *Greedy-S* is very inefficient, as it suggests one edge at a time, and in fact, it is (almost) k times slower than *Greedy-B*. More importantly, our method, *Heuristic*, runs multitude times faster than *Greedy-B*. The gain in effi-

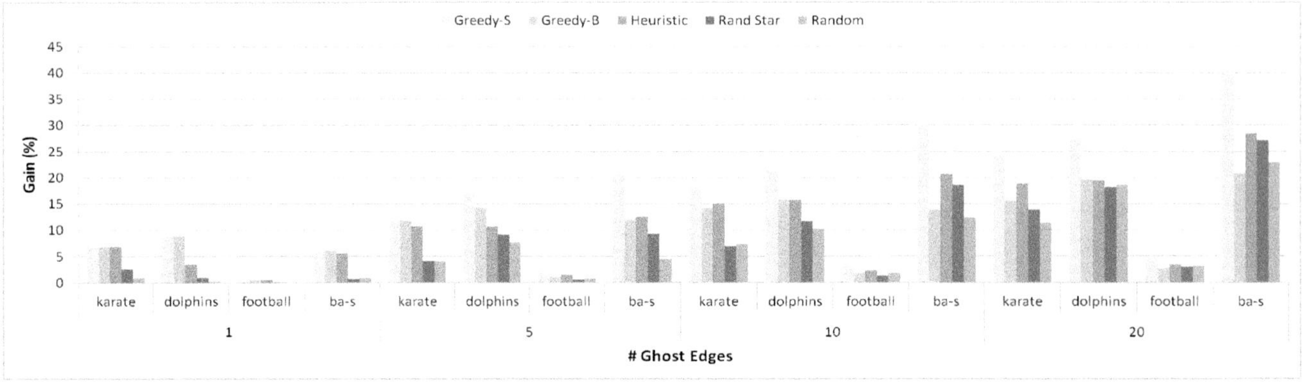

Figure 3: Heuristic Performance: Accuracy

Table 2: Heuristic Performance: Efficiency

Method	karate	dolphins	football	ba-s
Greedy-S-1	3288	39931	809550	12745
Greedy-S-5	16412	205175	4046788	62284
Greedy-S-10	32372	403252	8094511	127333
Greedy-S-20	65359	816703	16191000	257063
Greedy-B	3891	55203	956579	13188
Heuristic	**47**	**110**	**375**	**32**
Random	2	2	2	2
Rand Star	2	2	2	2

Table 3: Efficiency of Heuristic in Figure 5 (msec)

dolphins	netscience	yeast	ba-s	ba-m	ba-l
63	3156	133078	31	4828	25078

ciency is due to the fact that, while *Greedy-B* will need to compute the utility of all possible ghost edges, *Heuristic* will constrain the search space and look for ghost edges that connect nodes of already existing shortest paths. As such, our method suggests huge savings in the computation of the importance of ghost edges.

Heuristic Sampling-based (HSB) Performance: We have demonstrated that *Heuristic* is much faster than *Greedy-S* and *Greedy-B*, while maintaining high levels of accuracy. Now, we assess the performance of the sampling based variant of our heuristic *HSB* against the *Heuristic* method that serves as the ground truth and the *Random* method that serves as the baseline for our sampling based method. We experiment in real and synthetic networks of varying size and for varying number of ghost edges to be added, as well as, varying sample size. In particular, for each network, we experiment with sample sizes of 10%, 20% and 30% of the total nodes in network that define the methods *HSB (10%)*, *HSB (20%)* and *HSB (30%)* respectively. Figure 4 presents the accurracy results for the various instances of real and synthetic networks when adding 5% of the total number of ghost edges. In all cases, *HSB* has a better accuracy than *Random* and it's accuracy is slightly lower than the accuracy of *Heuristic*. Moreover, the accuracy of HSB increases with the sample size; this behavior is expected, as more shortest paths are evaluated in larger samples. Figure 5 presents the efficiency results for the various methods in varying networks. Note that for demonstration issues, we report on the relative time, where the execution time of the *Heuristic* represents the time of the slower method. We also report the actual execution times of *Heuristic* in Table 3 to complement Figure 5. For example, while the *Heuristic* method requires almost 25sec for suggesting ghost edges in the *ba-l* network, *HSB-10* requires less than 5sec (i.e., less than 20% relative time). Overall, *HSB* can be used to boost the performance of *Heuristic*, without duly affecting its accuracy, and as such, it's the method we propose to use for suggesting edges in larger networks.

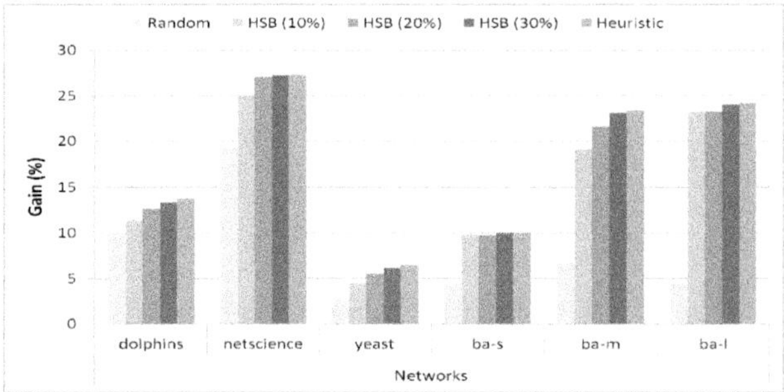

Figure 4: HSB Performance: Accuracy

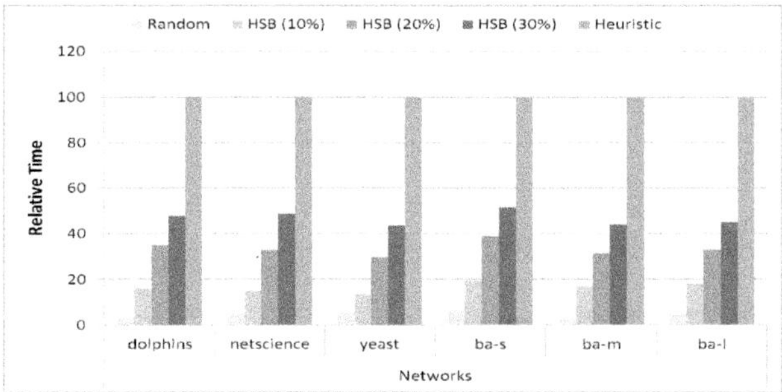

Figure 5: HSB Performance: Efficiency

4. REFERENCES

[1] E. D. Demaine and M. Zadimoghaddam. Minimizing the diameter of a network using shortcut edges. In *SWAT*, 2010.

[2] K. P. Eswaran and R. E. Tarjan. Augmentation problems. *SIAM J. Comput.*, 5(4), 1976.

[3] S. Kandula and R. Mahajan. Sampling biases in network path measurements and what to do about it. In *IMC*, 2009.

[4] J. Kleinberg. The small-world phenomenon: an algorithm perspective. In *STOC*, 2000.

[5] A. Meyerson and B. Tagiku. Minimizing average shortest path distances via shortcut edge addition. In *APPROX-RANDOM*, 2009.

[6] Y. Tian, Q. He, Q. Zhao, X. Liu, and W.-c. Lee. Boosting social network connectivity with link revival. In *CIKM*, 2010.

[7] T. Watanabe and A. Nakamura. Edge-connectivity augmentation problems. *J. Comput. Syst. Sci.*, 35, 1987.

Examining the "Leftness" Property of Wikipedia Categories

Karl Gyllstrom
karl.gyllstrom@cs.kuleuven.be

Marie-Francine Moens
sien.moens@cs.kuleuven.be

Department of Computer Science
Katholieke Universiteit Leuven
Leuven, Belgium

ABSTRACT

Wikipedia's rich category structure has helped make it one of the largest semantic taxonomies in existence, a property that has been central to much recent research. However, Wikipedia's category representation is simplistic: an article contains a single list of categories, with no data about their relative importance. We investigate the ordering of category lists to determine how a category's position in the list correlates with its relevance to the article and overall significance. We identify a number of interesting connections between a category's position and its persistence within the article, age, popularity, size, and descriptiveness.

Categories and Subject Descriptors

H.4.0 [**Information Systems Applications**]: General

General Terms

Experimentation, Measurement

1 Introduction

A typical Wikipedia article contains a list of categories (e.g., "21st century actors"), which serve to place the article within the semantic, conceptual structure of Wikipedia. Categories, in turn, are implemented as special Wikipedia pages, which list all of the pages for which the category label is assigned. There is a many-to-many relationship between articles and categories, and they are intended as a way for users to navigate among articles (e.g., by selecting a category through which to find related articles). As with normal Wikipedia content, categories are added or removed to a page by edits from the community of Wikipedia authors (i.e., the general public). Hence, they reflect a form of editorial consensus; an aggregate human view of how an article fits within the conceptual space.

In this work, we examine the role played by the order of an article's category list. As stated by Wikipedia's editing guidelines:

> *The order in which categories are placed on an article is not governed by any single rule [...] Normally the most essential, significant categories appear first.* [2]

We investigate the reliability of this guideline. In particular, we consider how a category's *leftness*, or how early it appears in an article's category list (i.e., earlier/lower list position), correlates with various attributes connected to its importance to an article and overall significance.

This work contributes an analysis of Wikipedia categories which may help guide other work that makes use of categories. The use of Wikipedia in research is widespread; in particular, categories have been central to a number of works (e.g, [3–6]). For example, Koolen and Kamps use categories to measure the semantic relationship among articles, but consider all categories equally [4]. Ponzetto and Strube derive a linguistic taxonomy using the Wikipedia category structure, also treating categories equally [5]. Our work suggests that categories are not equal and, in particular, the leftmost categories should be given significant priority. To our knowledge, no such examination yet exists.

2 Leftness examined

We used a collection of Wikipedia articles, selected as the 3000 most frequently viewed articles during an hour of August 25th, 2010, which we refer to as *Wikitop*, downloaded from a public Wikipedia page access repository [1]. For each article, we examined its entire edit history, recording when the category list was changed, and how it was changed.

2.1 Category modifications

Category changes are infrequent. Across 347,438 article modifications, only 24,398 (6.6%) included changes to the category list itself. The occurrences of different types of changes are depicted in Table 1. We observe that insertions to and deletions from the category lists dominate the number of operations. Reordering, in which at least one category changes position in the list, is relatively infrequent. Pure reorders, where the only change is a reorder (i.e., no coinciding a insertions or deletions) are even less common. Category positions appear to be relatively stable once established.

2.2 Duration and age

In this section we investigate two temporal properties of position: (1) the duration over which a category is present in

Type	#	Portion
Insert	11637	0.477
Delete	11264	0.462
Insert+Delete	941	0.039
Duplicate inserted/deleted	422	0.017
Reorder	436	0.018
Pure reorder	134	0.005

Table 1: Operations. As some operations can coincide with others, the portion sum is > 1.

an article, and (2) the age of the category (as defined by time since the category was created). Conceptually, the longer a category exists within an article, the more scrutiny it persists, and the older a category article, the more established it is within Wikipedia's category structure.

For each article in *Wikitop*, we examined its current list of categories (i.e., the list appearing in the most recent version), and measured the duration over which each category in this list was present in the article. For each category position from 0-14 (with 0 being leftmost), we recorded the mean duration for categories at that position across all articles in *Wikitop*, depicted in Figure 1[1]. In other words, the value at position 0 reflects the mean duration of categories appearing at position 0 across all articles in *Wikitop*. A category at position 0 appears, on average, within its article for about 73% of the article's lifetime. As position increases, we observe a large decline in the duration for which categories at that position are present in the article. Figure 2 depicts the mean age of categories over position. As in Figure 1 we see a decline as position increases. This indicates that older and more persistent categories are placed in lower positions.

2.3 Popularity and Size

We report the connection between position and category popularity and size. Popularity is defined by number of times web surfers accessed the category article directly (e.g., `http://en.wikipedia.org/wiki/Category:1975_births`) over a given time period[2]. The size of a category is defined by the number of articles it contains.

Figure 3 depicts the popularity of articles across position. We observe an overall general though variable decline of popularity with position[3].

Figure 4 depicts the mean size of categories across position. We observe a sharp decline among the first few positions. This could indicate that categories placed in leftmost positions are more applicable overall (as they have more articles) or are generally more favored by Wikipedia authors.

2.4 Descriptiveness

In this section we examine the relationship between position and category descriptiveness, which indicates how well a category describes a particular article. We examine this property in three ways.

[1]Around 85% of articles have 15 or fewer categories, so we chose this as the number of category positions to consider.

[2]We aggregated access data from the repository, obtained from three one hour periods [1].

[3]In Figure 3 and Figure 4, we omit data pertaining to the *Living people* category, an exceptionally large outlier.

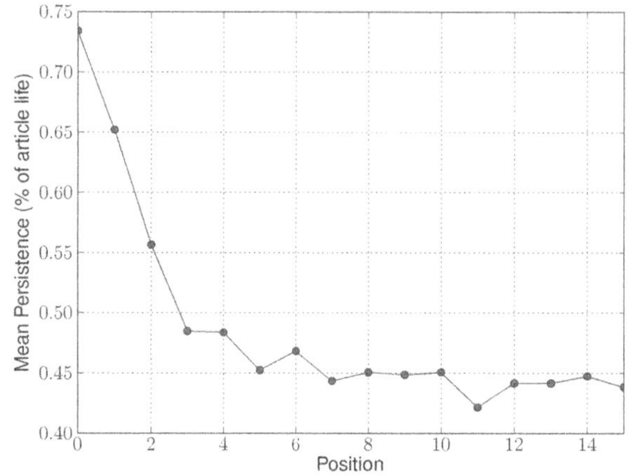

Figure 1: Duration existing in article at position.

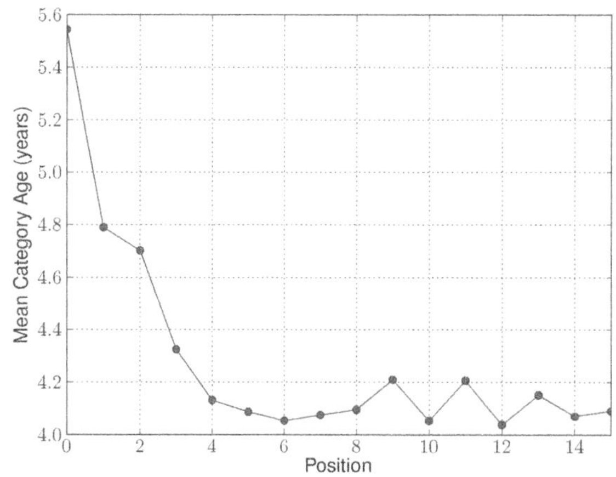

Figure 2: Category age across position.

2.4.1 *Mean category count*

First, we consider the mean number of categories per article within a category. For example, articles within the category *Zoos* have a mean of 3.72 categories per article. Our hypothesis is that this reflects the exclusivity of a category: when its articles have few other suitable categories, it is likely the category itself is a better descriptor of the article. For each article in *Wikitop*, we compute the *mean category count* (MCC) for each category by calculating the mean number of categories per article within the category. Note that the number of articles considered in this calculation (1,002,937) is much higher than the number of articles in *Wikitop*. We then aggregate MCC scores by position number. Figure 5 depicts MCC across position; we observe that as categories appear at higher positions, they are more likely to contain pages with higher number of categories, indicating that they become less effective descriptors.

2.4.2 *Mean position*

Next, we assign a positional score to categories, defined as the mean position of the category within articles in which it appears. Assuming a connection between position and

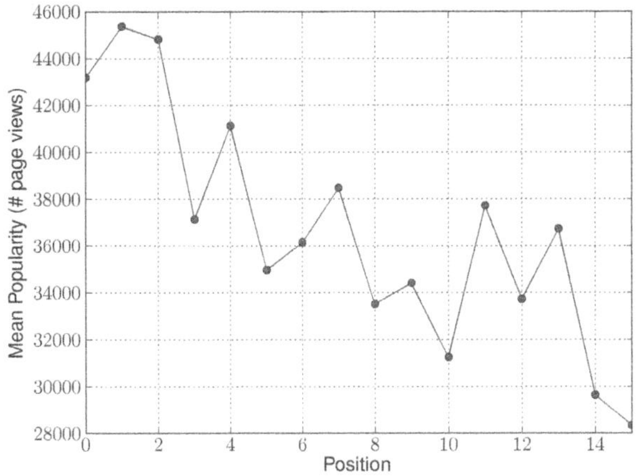

Figure 3: Category popularity across position.

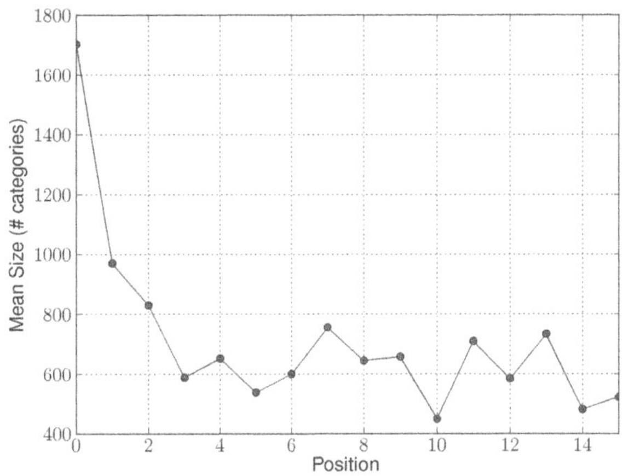

Figure 4: Category size across position.

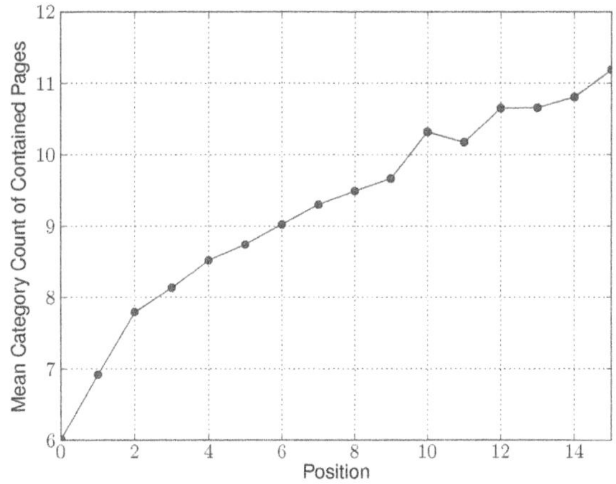

Figure 5: Mean category count across position.

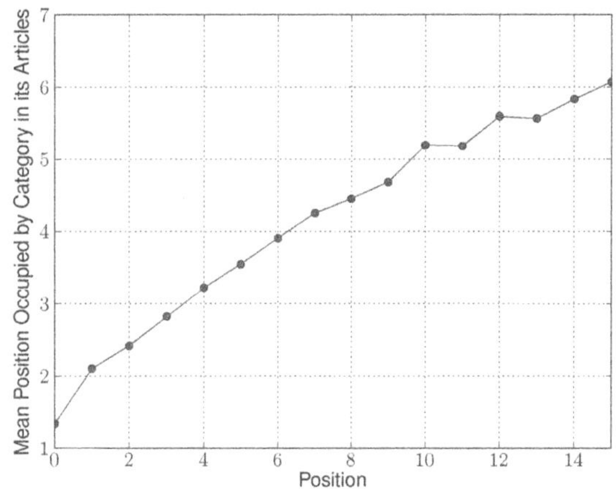

Figure 6: Mean position of category articles across position.

category importance, a category with a lower mean position across all of its articles is likely to be more significant overall. Figure 6 depicts the mean leftness of categories across position, revealing that the mean leftness of a category increases with position. In other words, categories that tend to appear at a higher position in *Wikitop* also tend to appear in higher positions in all of the articles they contain, indicating that they are generally subordinate categories.

2.4.3 *Similarity*

The next score we consider is categorical similarity. We consider a category to be a more specific descriptor if the articles with which it is associated tend to be more similar to each other. We measure this via the mean similarity of a category's articles among each other, with similarity calculated by the Jaccard coefficient:

$$similarity(P_1, P_2) = \frac{|Categories_{P_1} \cap Categories_{P_2}|}{|Categories_{P_1} \cup Categories_{P_2}|}$$

In other words, it is the proportion of category overlap among categories in a pair. For each category, we calculated the mean similarity score among each pair of articles within it, capping at 200 articles where necessary to ease computation.

Figure 7 depicts the relationship of position and categorical similarity. As position increases, the similarity among articles decreases, indicating that it is less coherent as a descriptor. One challenge to this interpretation is that the overall number of common categories remains stable across position, but as MCC increases with position, the similarity score necessarily declines. We believe that this still reflects an overall decline in similarity, as each category should be considered less individually descriptive, therefore fewer categories in common relative to total categories still achieves a reasonable approximation of overall similarity.

2.5 Parent categories

A category may have parent categories, which represent its generalizations. For example, the category *1975_births* has *1970s_births* as one of its parent categories. Figure 8 depicts the mean number of parent categories across position. We observe the 0th position containing a much higher number of parent categories, with a slight, general increase in parent category count across position. Figure 9 depicts the mean

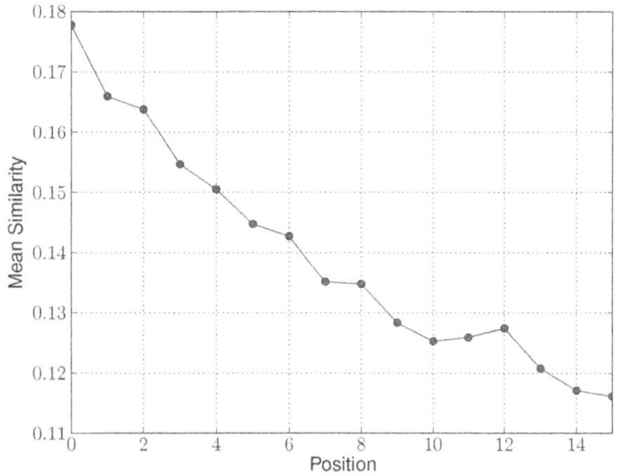

Figure 7: Mean similarity across position.

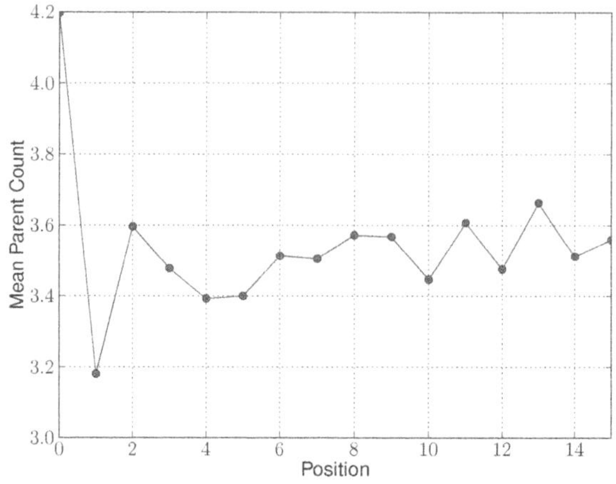

Figure 8: Mean number of parent categories across position.

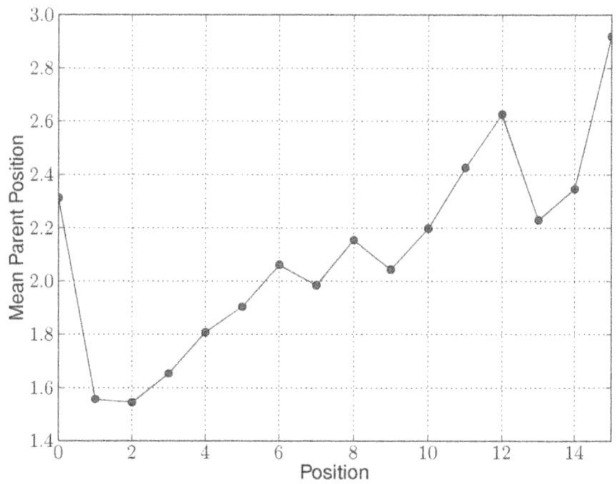

Figure 9: Mean parent position in its pages (see Figure 6).

position of a category's parents within the articles they contain. This echoes the trend in Figure 6, indicating parent categories can also be distinguished by relative importance. We are uncertain about the implications of Figure 8; our intuition is that categories with many parent categories are likely to be more specific while also less independently useful. Nonetheless, the exceptional value for the 0th position in both cases should be noted.

3 Concluding remarks

This work represents a preliminary analysis of some Wikipedia category attributes, specifically with respect to their position in category lists. We identified a number of connections to position; at lower positions, categories tend to be (1) those which persisted for longer durations in the article, (2) older, (3) more popular, and (4) larger. Our analysis of descriptiveness also indicates that categories at lower positions (5) contain articles with fewer categories, hence their categories are more exclusive; (6) generally appear at lower positions across all the articles they contain; and (7) contain articles that are more similar to each other in terms of category overlap. With respect to (1), (2), (4), and (5), the drop off after position 0 is dramatic, indicating that there is increased importance on the first few listed categories, especially at the leftmost position. Though our work is at an early stage, we believe these results provide support that Wikipedia's guidelines are generally followed, and we advocate the emphasis of leftmost categories among researchers who make use of Wikipedia categories.

We plan to continue this work. First, we intend to execute a user evaluation in which category quality – especially with respect to article assignments – is assessed by human raters. Next, we seek to continue the analysis on (1) less popular and (2) lower quality articles (as indicated by improvement flags placed by editors) to find if the observations hold. Finally, we desire to apply our discoveries in a set of ranking functions, which can help determine the best category for an article based on a preference metric, such as quality, comprehensiveness, exclusivity, or descriptiveness.

References

[1] Wikipedia traffic. `http://dammit.lt/wikistats/`.

[2] Wikipedia:Categorization. `http://en.wikipedia.org/wiki/Wikipedia:Categorization`.

[3] S. Auer, C. Bizer, G. Kobilarov, J. Lehmann, R. Cyganiak, and Z. Ives. DBpedia: A nucleus for a web of open data. In *ISWC*, pages 722–735. Springer, 2007.

[4] M. Koolen and J. Kamps. Are semantically related links more effective for retrieval? In *ECIR*, pages 92–103. Springer, 2011.

[5] S. P. Ponzetto and M. Strube. Deriving a large-scale taxonomy from Wikipedia. In *AAAI*, pages 1440–1445, 2007.

[6] F. M. Suchanek, G. Kasneci, and G. Weikum. Yago: a core of semantic knowledge. WWW '07, pages 697–706, New York, NY, USA, 2007. ACM.

Detection of Text Quality Flaws as a One-class Classification Problem

Maik Anderka Benno Stein Nedim Lipka

Bauhaus-Universität Weimar
99421 Weimar, Germany
<first name>.<last name>@uni-weimar.de

ABSTRACT

For Web applications that are based on user generated content the detection of text quality flaws is a key concern. Our research contributes to *automatic quality flaw detection*. In particular, we propose to cast the detection of text quality flaws as a one-class classification problem: we are given only positive examples (= texts containing a particular quality flaw) and decide whether or not an unseen text suffers from this flaw. We argue that common binary or multiclass classification approaches are ineffective in here, and we underpin our approach by a real-world application: we employ a dedicated one-class learning approach to determine whether a given Wikipedia article suffers from certain quality flaws. Since in the Wikipedia setting the acquisition of sensible test data is quite intricate, we analyze the effects of a biased sample selection. In addition, we illustrate the classifier effectiveness as a function of the flaw distribution in order to cope with the unknown (real-world) flaw-specific class imbalances. Altogether, provided test data with little noise, four from ten important quality flaws in Wikipedia can be detected with a precision close to 1.

Categories and Subject Descriptors: H.3.3 [Information Storage and Retrieval]: Information Search and Retrieval; H.5.3 [Information Interfaces and Presentation]: Group and Organization Interfaces— *Evaluation/methodology*

General Terms: Measurement, Algorithms, Experimentation

1. INTRODUCTION

The machine-based assessment of text quality is becoming a topic of enormous interest. This fact is rooted, among others, in the increasing popularity of user generated Web content [3] and the (unavoidable) divergence of the delivered content's quality. Most of the relevant literature on automatic text quality assessment deals with the classification of texts in predefined abstract quality schemes, see for instance [2, 6, 11]. Only a few approaches focus on quality flaw *detection* and try to give precise indications in which respects a text needs improvement [1, 7]. A general finding of our literature review (from which we can show only a tiny excerpt here) is the fact that the detection of text quality flaws in general has not yet been operationalized.

CIKM'11, October 24–28, 2011, Glasgow, Scotland, UK.

The paper in hand focuses on detection issues, whereas our contributions are as follows: Firstly, in the remainder of this section, we argue that the detection of text quality flaws is essentially a one-class classification problem and give a respective problem definition. Secondly, we employ a one-class machine learning approach to detect quality flaws in Wikipedia articles (Section 2). Thirdly, we perform comprehensive analyses to assess the effectiveness of our approach (Section 3).

Problem Definition Let D be a set of text documents and let F be a set of text quality flaws. A document $d \in D$ can contain up to $|F|$ flaws, where, without loss of generality, the flaws in F are considered as being uncorrelated. A classifier c hence has to solve the following multi-labeling problem:[1]

$$c : \mathbf{D} \rightarrow 2^F,$$

where 2^F denotes the power set of F. A document d is represented by a feature vector $\mathbf{d}$, called document model, where $\mathbf{D}$ denotes the set of document models for D.

Basically, there are two strategies to tackle multi-labeling problems: (1) by multiclass classification, where a single classifier is learned on the power set of all classes, and (2) by multiple binary classification, where a specific classifier $c_i : \mathbf{D} \rightarrow \{1, 0\}$ is learned for each class $f_i \in F$. Since the high number of classes under a multiclass classification strategy entails a very large number of training examples, the second strategy is favorable.

In most classification problems training data is available for all classes that can occur at prediction time, and hence it is appropriate to train a classifier c_i with (positive) examples of the target class f_i and (negative) examples from the classes $F \setminus f_i$. However, in the case of detecting text quality flaws an unseen document can either belong to the target class f_i or to some unknown class that was not available during training. I.e., the standard discrimination-based classification approaches (binary or multiclass) are not applicable to learn a class-separating decision boundary: given a flaw f_i, its target class is formed by those documents that contain (among others) flaw f_i—but it is impossible to model the "co-class" with documents *not* containing f_i. Even if many counterexamples were available, they could not be exploited to properly characterize the universe of possible counterexamples. As a consequence, we model the classification $c_i(\mathbf{d})$ of an document $d \in D$ with respect to a text quality flaw f_i as the following one-class classification problem: Decide whether or not d contains f_i, whereas a sample of documents containing f_i is given.

The following example may serve as an additional illustration: Wikipedia articles should be written in a formal tone[2], and hence

[1] Possibly existing correlations among the flaws in F will not affect the nature of the multi-labeling problem.

[2] http://en.wikipedia.org/wiki/Wikipedia:Tone#Tone

"inappropriate tone" is a text quality flaw in this particular context. An even large sample of articles that suffer from this flaw can be compiled without problems (consider articles containing slang, jargon, etc.). However, it is impossible to compile a representative sample of articles that are written in a formal tone. Though there definitely exist outstanding articles written in a formal tone, they cannot be considered as a representative sample.

For an in-depth discussion of one-class classification and a survey of respective methodologies see [14, 9]. Typical one-class problems in the information retrieval domain include typist recognition [8], authorship verification [10], plagiarism analysis [12], and anomaly detection [5].

2. QUALITY FLAWS IN WIKIPEDIA

In previous research we analyzed cleanup template messages in the English Wikipedia and compiled a set of quality flaws of Wikipedia articles that have been tagged by the community [1]. This analysis is restricted to a specific subset of cleanup template messages. By applying the same approach without these restrictions to a more recent Wikipedia snapshot from January 2011 we extracted 388 quality flaws, which form the set F; the 3 557 468 articles of the snapshot form the set D. We distinguish different subsets of D, see Figure 1: The set D^- comprises 979 299 articles that have been tagged with at least one of the flaws from F, which corresponds to 27.5% of D. Notice that we have no knowledge about the articles in $D \setminus D_i^-$; these articles either do not contain the flaw f_i or have not yet been evaluated with respect to f_i.[3]

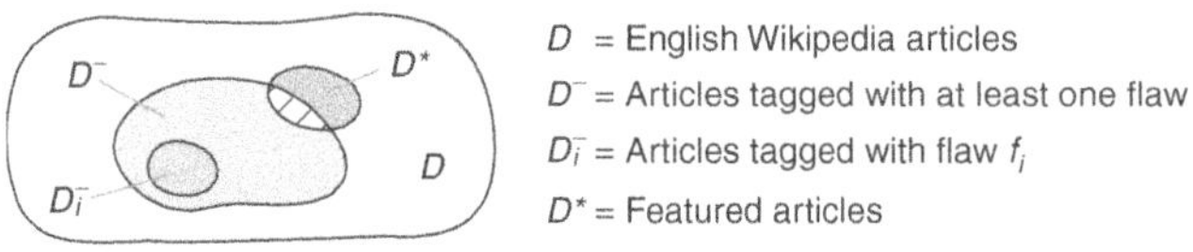

Figure 1: The sets of Wikipedia articles which we distinguish in this paper. Without loss of generality we assume in our experiments that the hashed area $D^- \cap D^*$ is empty, i.e., featured articles are flawless.

We make two assumptions in order to estimate the actual frequency of a flaw f_i: (1) each article in D^- is tagged completely, i.e. with all flaws that it contains (Closed World Assumption), and (2) the distribution of f_i in D^- is identical to the distribution of f_i in D. Based on these assumptions we estimate the actual frequency of a flaw f_i by the ratio of articles in D_i^- and articles in D^-.

We model the quality flaws of an article $d \in D$ by a feature vector $\mathbf{d}$, where each dimension in $\mathbf{d}$ quantifies a quality-specific characteristics of d. Our document model employs state-of-the-art features that have been proposed in the relevant literature [6, 11, 13] as well as new quality flaw predictors that quantify the usage of in-links, templates, lists, and special words, among others.

We employ a one-class classification approach as proposed by [8], which combines density estimation with class probability estimation. The idea is to use a reference distribution to model the probability $P(\mathbf{d} \mid f_i')$ of an artificial class f_i', and to generate (artificial) data governed by the distribution characteristic of f_i'. For a flaw f_i let $P(f_i)$ and $P(f_i \mid \mathbf{d})$ be the a-priori probability and the class probability function respectively. According to Bayes' theorem the class-conditional probability for f_i is given as follows:

$$P(\mathbf{d} \mid f_i) = \frac{(1 - P(f_i)) \cdot P(f_i \mid \mathbf{d})}{P(f_i) \cdot (1 - P(f_i \mid \mathbf{d}))} \cdot P(\mathbf{d} \mid f_i')$$

$P(f_i \mid \mathbf{d})$ is estimated by a class probability estimator (a classifier whose output is interpreted as probability). Since we are in a one-class situation we have to rely on the face value of $P(\mathbf{d} \mid f_i)$; more specifically, $P(\mathbf{d} \mid f_i)$ cannot be used to determine a maximum a-posterior (MAP) hypothesis among the $f_i \in F$. As a consequence, given $P(\mathbf{d} \mid f_i) < \tau$ with $\tau = 0.5$, the hypothesis that d suffers from f_i could be rejected. However, because of the approximative nature of $P(f_i \mid \mathbf{d})$ and $P(f_i)$ the estimation for $P(\mathbf{d} \mid f_i)$ is not a true probability, and the threshold τ has to be chosen empirically. In practice, the threshold τ is derived from a user-defined target rejection rate, trr, which is the rejection rate of the target class training data.

[3] A special case is the set D^*, which will be discussed later on.

3. ANALYSIS

We report on experiments to assess the effectiveness of our classification approach in detecting ten of the most frequent quality flaws of Wikipedia articles. The evaluation treats the following issues:

1. Since a bias may not be ruled out when collecting outlier examples for a classifier's test set, we investigate the consequences of the two extreme (overly optimistic, overly pessimistic) settings (Section 3.1).
2. Since users (Wikipedia editors) have different expectations regarding the classification effectiveness given different flaws, we analyze the optimal operating point for each flaw-specific classifier within the controlled setting of a balanced class distribution (Section 3.2).
3. Since the true flaw-specific class imbalances in Wikipedia can only be hypothesized, we illustrate the effectiveness of the classifiers in different settings, this way enabling users (Wikipedia editors) to assume an optimistic or a pessimistic position (Section 3.3).

3.1 Outlier Selection

Recall that no articles are available that have been tagged to *not* contain a quality flaw $f_i \in F$. Thus a classifier c_i can be evaluated only with respect to its recall, whereas a recall of 1 can be achieved easily by classifying all examples into the target class of f_i. In order to evaluate c_i with respect to its precision one needs a representative sample of examples from outside the target class, so-called outliers. As motivated above, in a one-class situation it is not possible to compile a representative sample, and one way out of the dilemma is the generation of uniformly distributed outlier examples [14]. Here, we pursue two strategies to derive examples from outside the target class, which result in the following settings:

1. *Optimistic Setting.* Use of featured articles as outliers. This approach is based on the hypothesis that featured articles do not contain a quality flaw at all, see Figure 1.[4] Under this setting one introduces some bias since featured articles cannot be considered as a representative sample of Wikipedia articles.
2. *Pessimistic Setting.* Use of a random sample from $D \setminus D_i^-$ as outliers for each f_i. This approach may introduce considerable noise since the set $D \setminus D_i^-$ is expected to contain untagged articles that suffer from f_i.

The above settings address two extremes: classification under laboratory conditions (overly optimistic) versus classification in the wild (overly pessimistic). The experiment design is owing to the

[4] The hypothesis may hold in many cases but not always: the snapshot comprises 13 featured articles that have been tagged with some flaw. We discarded these articles in our experiments.

facts that "no-flaw features" cannot be stated and that the number of false positives as well as the number of false negatives in the set D^- of tagged articles are unknown.

3.2 Effectiveness of Flaw Detection

We use the English Wikipedia snapshot from January 15, 2011.[5] The articles' plain texts and wikitexts are extracted in a preprocessing step by processing the "pages-articles" XML dump on an Apache Hadoop cluster using Google's MapReduce. Furthermore, a local copy of the Wikipedia database is established by importing the database dumps into a MySQL database. The plain texts, the wikitexts, and the local Wikipedia database form the basis to compute the features of our document model.

Experiment Design The evaluation is performed for the set $F' \subset F$ of the ten most frequent quality flaws that show the following three properties: they describe a single and specific quality aspect, they refer to an article as a whole, and they are not restricted to a particular domain, language, or user group (see Table 1). About 70% of the articles in D^- suffer from these flaws. In the optimistic setting 1 000 outliers are randomly selected from the 3 128 featured articles in the snapshot. In the pessimistic setting 1 000 outliers are randomly selected for each flaw $f_i \in F'$ from $D \setminus D_i^-$. We evaluate our approach under both settings by applying the following procedure: For each flaw $f_i \in F'$ the one-class classifier c_i is evaluated with 1 000 articles which are randomly sampled from D_i^- and the respective 1 000 outliers, applying tenfold cross-validation. Within each run the classifier is trained with 900 articles from D_i^-, whereas testing is performed with the remaining 100 articles from D_i^- plus 100 outliers. Note that c_i is trained exclusively with the examples of the respective target class, i.e., the articles in D_i^-: The training of c_i is neither affected by the class distribution nor by the outlier selection strategy that is used in the respective setting.

The one-class classifier is built as follows: a class with artificial examples is generated, whereas the feature values obey a Gaussian distribution with $\mu = 0$ and $\sigma^2 = 1$. The Gaussian distribution is employed in favor of a more complex reference distribution to underline the robustness of the approach. The proportion of the generated data is 0.5 compared to the target class. As class probability estimators we apply bagged random forest classifiers with 1 000 decision trees and ten bagging iterations. A random forest is a collection of decision trees that differ with respect to their features, and a voting over all trees is run in order to obtain a classification decision (for further details see [4]).

Operating Point Analysis For the major part of the relevant use cases precision is the determining measure of effectiveness; consider for instance a bot that autonomously tags flawed articles. The precision of the one-class classifier is controlled by the hyperparameter target rejection rate. We empirically determine the optimal operating point for each of the ten flaws under both the optimistic and the pessimistic setting. Here, the optimal operating point corresponds to the target rejection rate of the maximum precision classifier. Figure 2 illustrates the operating point analyses exemplary for the flaw *Unreferenced*: with increasing target rejection rate the recall value drops while the precision values increase. Observe that the recall is the same in both settings, since it solely depends on the target class training data. For the flaw *Unreferenced* the optimal operating points under the optimistic and the pessimistic setting are at a target rejection rate of 0.1 and 0.35 respectively (with precision values of 0.99 and 0.63).

The precision of a one-class classifier cannot be adjusted arbitrarily since the target rejection rate controls only the probability

[5]Wikimedia downloads: http://download.wikimedia.org/enwiki.

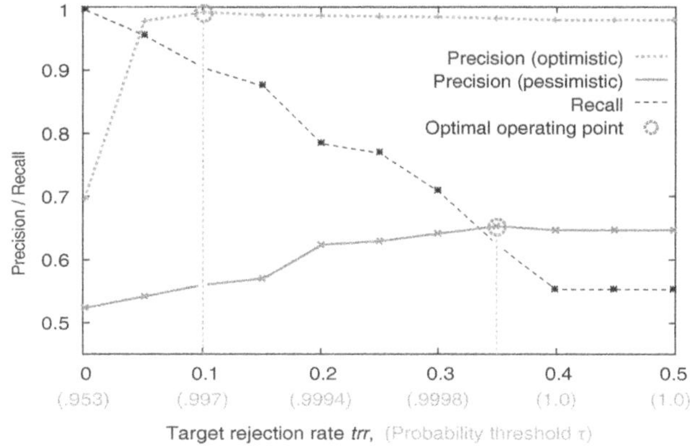

Figure 2: Precision and recall over target rejection rate for the flaw *Unreferenced*. The figure illustrates the difference in terms of precision under the optimistic setting, using featured articles as outliers, and the pessimistic setting, using random articles as outliers. The recall is the same under both settings. The optimal operating points correspond to the target rejection rates that maximizes classifier precision.

threshold τ for the classification decision. For instance, a target rejection rate of 0.1 means that a τ is chosen such that 10% of the target class training data will be rejected, which results in a classifier that performs with an almost stable recall of 0.9. Increasing the target rejection rate entails an increase of τ. However, if τ achieves its maximum no further examples can be rejected, and hence both the precision and the recall remain constant beyond a certain target rejection rate (which is 0.4 for the flaw *Unreferenced*, see Figure 2).

Results and Discussion Table 1 shows the performance values for the ten quality flaws. The values correspond to the performances at their optimal operating points; the performance is quantified as precision (*prec*) and recall (*rec*). We also report the area under ROC curves (AUC), which is important to assess the tradeoff between specificity and sensitivity of a classifier: an AUC value of 0.5 means that all specificity-sensitivity-combinations are equivalent, which in turn means that the classifier is random guessing.

Under the optimistic setting four flaws can be detected with a nearly perfect precision. For the flaw *Notability* even the achieved recall value is very high, which means that this flaw can be detected exceptionally well. As expected, the effectiveness of the one-class classifiers deteriorates under the pessimistic setting. However, the classifiers still achieve reasonable precision values, and even in the noisy test set the flaw *Orphan* can be detected with a good precision. Notice, however, that the expected performance in the wild lies in between the two extremes. For some flaws the effectiveness of the one-class classifiers is pretty low under both settings, including *Original research*. We explain this behavior as follows: (1) Either the document model is inadequate to capture certain flaw characteristics, or (2) the hypothesis class of the one-class classification approach is too simple to capture the flaw distributions.

3.3 Flaw-specific Class Imbalances

The performance values in Table 1 presume a balanced class distribution, i.e., the one-class classifiers are evaluated with the same number of flawed articles and outliers. The real distribution of flaws in Wikipedia is unknown (cf. Section 2), and we hence report precision values as a function of the class imbalance. Given the recall and the false positive rate (*fpr*) of a classifier for the balanced setting, its precision for a class size ratio of 1:n (flawed articles : flawless articles) computes as follows:

$$prec = \frac{rec}{rec + n \cdot fpr}$$

Table 1: **Individual performance for each of ten quality flaws at the optimal operating point, using featured articles as outliers (optimistic setting) and using random articles as outliers (pessimistic setting). The class distribution is balanced under both settings. The flaw ratio 1:n (flawed articles : flawless articles) corresponds to the estimated actual frequency of a flaw.**

Flaw name	Flaw ratio	Optimistic setting			Pessimistic setting		
		prec	*rec*	AUC	*prec*	*rec*	AUC
f_1 Unreferenced	1:3	0.99	0.90	0.95	0.63	0.63	0.63
f_2 Orphan	1:5	1.00	0.90	0.95	0.72	0.59	0.68
f_3 Refimprove	1:10	0.83	0.87	0.85	0.57	0.56	0.57
f_4 Empty section	1:21	0.90	0.70	0.82	0.74	0.70	0.72
f_5 Notability	1:26	0.99	0.96	0.98	0.66	0.61	0.65
f_6 No footnotes	1:36	0.82	0.87	0.84	0.59	0.59	0.58
f_7 Primary sources	1:44	0.94	0.90	0.92	0.61	0.59	0.61
f_8 Wikify	1:68	0.96	0.87	0.92	0.64	0.58	0.63
f_9 Advert	1:136	0.86	0.91	0.88	0.65	0.58	0.63
f_{10} Original research	1:147	0.76	0.64	0.71	0.56	0.80	0.59

The false positive rate is the ratio between the detected negative examples and all negative examples, and hence it is independent from the class size ratio; the same argument applies to the recall. Figure 3 shows the precision values as a function of the flaw distribution under the optimistic setting.

Observe that the expected precision values for the flaws *Unreferenced*, *Orphan*, and *Notability* are still high. The flaw ratio of the flaw *Unreferenced* is 1:3, and thus the expected precision is close to that of the 1:1 ratio. The flaw *Orphan* can be detected with a precision of 1, i.e., the false positive rate is 0, and hence the detection performance is independent of the class imbalance. Although the flaw ratio of the flaw *Notability* is 1:26, the expected precision is still about 0.9, which shows that the respective one-class classifier captures the characteristics of the flaw exceptionally well. The expected precision values for those flaws with a flaw ratio 1:n where $n > 40$ are lower than 0.2. Aside from conceptual weaknesses regarding the employed document model, the weak performance indicates also that the training set of the respective one-class classifiers might be too small.

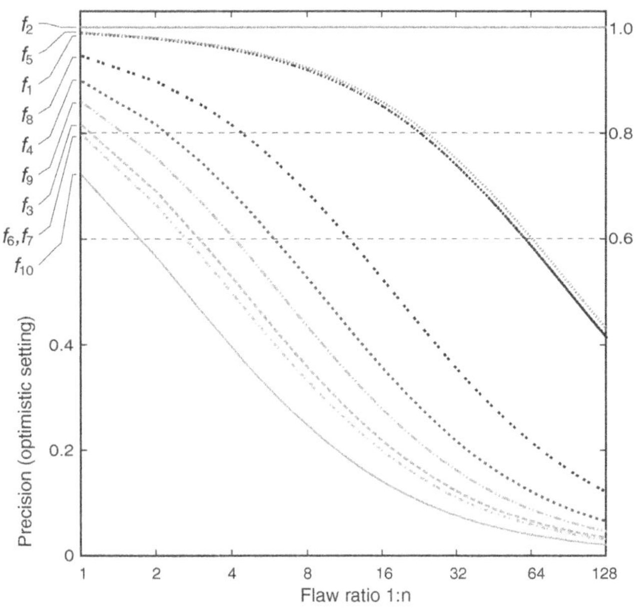

Figure 3: Precision in the optimistic setting over flaw ratio for ten quality flaws: 1:n $\sim$ with flaw : without flaw, with n $\in [1; 128]$. The figure puts the classification performances reported in Table 1 into perspective, since it considers imbalances in the test sets that might occur in the wild.

4. CONCLUSIONS AND OUTLOOK

We treat the detection of text quality flaws as a process where for each known flaw an expert is asked whether or not a given document suffers from it; the experts in turn are operationalized by one-class classifiers. This approach is applied to detect text quality flaws in the English Wikipedia. Our evaluation is based on a corpus comprising 10 000 human-labeled Wikipedia articles. We report on precision values close to 1 for four out of ten important quality flaws—presuming an optimistic test set with little noise and a balanced flaw distribution. Even for a class size ratio of 1:16 three flaws can still be detected with a precision of about 0.9.

We are convinced that the presented or similar approaches will help to simplify Wikipedia's quality assurance process by spotting weaknesses within articles. Our current research on quality flaw detection in Wikipedia targets the investigation of tailored one-class classifiers for each flaw, as well as the development of flaw-specific document models that combine expert rules, multi-level filtering, and feature selection.

5. REFERENCES

[1] M. Anderka, B. Stein, and N. Lipka. Towards automatic quality assurance in Wikipedia. In *Proceedings of WWW'11*, pages 5–6, 2011. ACM.

[2] E. Agichtein, C. Castillo, D. Donato, A. Gionis, and G. Mishne. Finding high-quality content in social media. In *Proceedings of WSDM'08*, pages 183–194, 2008. ACM.

[3] R. Baeza-Yates. User generated content: how good is it? In *Proceedings of WICOW'09*, pages 1–2, 2009. ACM.

[4] L. Breiman. Random forests. *Machine Learning*, 45(1):5–32, 2001.

[5] V. Chandola, A. Banerjee, and V. Kumar. Anomaly detection: a survey. *ACM Computing Surveys*, 41(3):15:1–15:58, 2009.

[6] D. Dalip, M. Gonçalves, M. Cristo, and P. Calado. Automatic quality assessment of content created collaboratively by Web communities: a case study of Wikipedia. In *Proceedings of JCDL'09*, pages 295–304, 2009. ACM.

[7] L. Gaio, M. den Besten, A. Rossi, and J. Dalle. Wikibugs: using template messages in open content collections. In *Proceedings of WikiSym'09*, pages 1–7, 2009. ACM.

[8] K. Hempstalk, E. Frank, and I. Witten. One-class classification by combining density and class probability estimation. In *Proceedings of ECML/PKDD'08*, pages 505–519, 2008. Springer.

[9] V. Hodge and J. Austin. A survey of outlier detection methodologies. *Artificial Intelligence Review*, 22(2):85–126, 2004.

[10] M. Koppel and J. Schler. Authorship verification as a one-class classification problem. In *Proceedings of ICML'04*, pages 1–7, 2004. ACM.

[11] N. Lipka and B. Stein. Identifying featured articles in Wikipedia: writing style matters. In *Proceedings of WWW'10*, pages 1147–1148, 2010. ACM.

[12] B. Stein, N. Lipka, and P. Prettenhofer. Intrinsic plagiarism analysis. *Language Resources and Evaluation*, 45(1):63–82, 2011. Springer.

[13] B. Stvilia, M. Twidale, L. Smith, and L. Gasser. Assessing information quality of a community-based encyclopedia. In *Proceedings of ICIQ'05*, pages 442–454, 2005. MIT

[14] D. Tax. *One-Class Classification*. PhD thesis, Delft University of Technology, 2001.

Two Birds with One Stone: Learning Semantic Models for Text Categorization and Word Sense Disambiguation

Roberto Navigli, Stefano Faralli
Dipartimento di Informatica
Sapienza Università di Roma
Roma, Italy
{navigli,faralli}@di.uniroma1.it

Aitor Soroa, Oier de Lacalle, Eneko Agirre
IXA NLP Group
University of the Basque Country
Donostia, Spain
{a.soroa,oier.lopezdelacalle,e.agirre}@ehu.es

ABSTRACT

In this paper we present a novel approach to learning semantic models for multiple domains, which we use to categorize Wikipedia pages and to perform domain Word Sense Disambiguation (WSD). In order to learn a semantic model for each domain we first extract relevant terms from the texts in the domain and then use these terms to initialize a random walk over the WordNet graph. Given an input text, we check the semantic models, choose the appropriate domain for that text and use the best-matching model to perform WSD. Our results show considerable improvements on text categorization and domain WSD tasks.

Categories and Subject Descriptors

I.2.7 [**Natural Language Processing**]: Text analysis

General Terms

Algorithms

Keywords

Word Sense Disambiguation, Text Classification

1. INTRODUCTION

In everyday life the use of natural language is often confined to specific fields of knowledge. Examples include newspaper sections (crime, sports, finance, etc.), blogs and Web sites on specific topics, business documents, etc. Performing a semantic analysis of domain text is thus a crucial Natural Language Processing (NLP) task that can boost applications such as Question Answering, Information Retrieval and Information Extraction.

The first step in determining the content of an input text is to assign it a domain or topic label, a task referred to as Text Classification (TC). Text classification is a widely studied topic in machine learning and NLP, and has attracted the use of a wide range of machine learning algorithms and text processing approaches. More recently the use of encyclopedic knowledge resources such as Wikipedia for classification purposes has received considerable attention in the scientific community. In fact, Wikipedia contains a vast amount of information covering virtually all domains of knowledge. Wikipedia has been used to enrich shallow text representations with concepts in order to improve supervised text classification [16] and concept-based kernels have been developed to perform semantically-informed supervised text categorization [15].

In the last few years attention has also been paid to the semantic analysis of domain texts at the lexical level, a task called Domain Word Sense Disambiguation (WSD). The automated association of meanings with words occurring in a domain context can benefit from domain cues such as topic words. Current approaches either exploit supervised techniques [2] or are based on unsupervised models of domains [5] and word sense dominance [10, 9]. However, the former rely on sense-annotated corpora for many domains, whereas the latter do not achieve high performance (unless a very large knowledge resource is available [12]). Although intermediate solutions have recently been proposed [7], sense-tagged data are still needed for accurate domain WSD.

In this paper we present a novel approach to the semantic analysis of domain texts. For each domain of interest we automatically learn a so-called semantic model vector for that domain. To this end we extract relevant terms from selected texts in the domain, determine their meaning and then use this information to initialize a random walk over the WordNet [3] graph. This yields a semantic model for each domain, represented as a vector of probabilities over WordNet nodes. Given an input text we identify the best-matching model, i.e., domain, for that text. As a result, the corresponding semantic model is used to disambiguate the words in the text, assigning the senses that are best fit to the context of occurrence **and** the domain of the text. The strength of our work lies in the use of the same semantic model to perform two different tasks, namely Text Classification and Word Sense Disambiguation. In fact, our experiments show that our approach achieves high performance in both tasks.

2. SEMANTIC MODEL VECTORS

We first learn a semantic representation for each domain in the form of Semantic Model Vectors. To this end we perform the following steps:

1. Analyse the training documents in each domain and produce for each **a weighted list of terms**, where the weight is higher for those terms which are most important in that domain.
2. Use these lists of terms to obtain **a weighted list of synsets for each domain**, where the weight is higher for those synsets which are most important in that domain.
3. For each domain perform a random walk over the WordNet graph, thus spreading domain information across the graph. We use **Personalized PageRank** [1] for the random walk and the above weighted synset list for initialization.
4. Reweight synsets according to their prominence **across domains**, demoting synsets with similar prominence in all domains, and promoting synsets which are only prominent in few domains.

CIKM'11, October 24–28, 2011, Glasgow, Scotland, UK.

5. We thus obtain a semantic model for each domain in the form of a weighted list of synsets, which we call the **Semantic Model Vector** (SMV) for that domain.

2.1 Weighting domain terms

Given a domain d, we first extract candidate domain terms from the training document collection for that domain, and weight them according to TFIDF:

$$\text{TFIDF}_d(t) = \text{TF}_d(t) \cdot log_2 \frac{N_d}{n_{d,t}} \tag{1}$$

where $\text{TF}_d(t)$ is the frequency of term t in the document collection for domain d, N_d is the number of documents in the domain collection, and $n_{d,t}$ is the number of domain documents in which t occurs.

2.2 Weighting domain synsets

Given the weighted list of domain terms, we produce a weighted list of synsets in two different ways.

The **uniform** method is to distribute the TFIDF weight of each word across all synsets that are denoted by the word (i.e., all its senses) uniformly. Let s be a synset, $Synonyms(s)$ the set of words (i.e., synonyms) in the synset s, $\text{TFIDF}_d(w)$ the TFIDF value of a word w in domain d and $Synsets(w)$ the set of synsets (i.e., senses) for the word w. Then, the uniform method assigns the following score to synset s:

$$UniformScore_d(s) = \sum_{w \in Synonyms(s)} \frac{\text{TFIDF}_d(w)}{|Synsets(w)|}. \tag{2}$$

We also tried a more sophisticated method based on **related words**. In this method we use the information about related words to compute the synset relevance to the domain. We first define a set of related words for each synset s as follows:

$$RW_d(s) = \bigcup_{s' \in R(s)} Synonyms(s') \cup GlossWords(s') \tag{3}$$

where $R(s)$ is the set of WordNet synsets directly related to s by any lexical or semantic relation, also including s itself, and $Synonyms(s)$ and $GlossWords(s)$ are the set of content words which denote s and appear in the gloss of s, respectively. Then, we define a score for synset s given by the normalized sum of the domain TFIDF values of the words in the set of related words of s:

$$RelWordsScore_d(s) = \frac{\sum_{w \in RW_d(s)} \text{TFIDF}_d(w)}{|RW_d(s)|} \tag{4}$$

Finally, we normalize the domain scores to range between zero and one, and produce a weighted list of synsets for each domain d.

2.3 Applying Personalized PageRank

Given the graph-based representation of WordNet, we apply Personalized PageRank to each domain, obtaining a probability distribution over WordNet synsets for each domain d, the Semantic Model Vector SMV_d. For initializing the random walk we set the so-called reset distribution, which defines which synsets are most relevant for the domain of interest (cf. [1] for further details on Personalized PageRank). We tried two different reset distributions: the weighted list of synsets for each domain, as produced by the **uniform** and the **related words** method in Section 2.2.

2.4 Cross-domain reweighting (CDR)

In the previous step we obtained an SMV for each domain. Ideally, domain-specific synsets will rank high in the corresponding domain SMV, and low in the others.

However, some synsets are very central in the WordNet graph (i.e., they are linked to synsets which also have a high number of relations) and receive high scores on most domains. Examples include synsets such as individual_n^1 or britain_n^1. Thus, we decided to reweight the SMVs obtained in the previous step, trying to promote domain specific synsets and demote general-purpose synsets (i.e., those concepts with similar scores in all domains).

Let SMV_d be the SMV vector for domain $d \in$ Domains, so that $\text{SMV}_d(s)$ is the score of synset s in the domain d. We calculate the entropy for s using the formula:

$$\text{ent}(s) = - \sum_{d \in \text{Domains}} \text{SMV}_d(s) \cdot \log(\text{SMV}_d(s)) \tag{5}$$

Senses with high scores in some domains but low scores in other domains will receive a low entropy. In contrast, senses with high (or low) values on all domains will receive high entropy.

After calculating the entropy, we obtain new SMV'_d vectors by dividing each synset score by the synset's entropy:

$$\text{SMV}'_d(s) = \text{SMV}_d(s) \cdot \frac{1}{\text{ent}(s)}. \tag{6}$$

2.5 Text Classification

Given a test document and the SMVs for each domain (either SMV_d or SMV'_d, see Sections 2.3 and 2.4), we combine the information coming from the TFIDF from each domain (cf. Section 2.1) and the SMVs. Given the fact that the synsets with lowest weights might confuse the classification algorithm, we decided to keep the synsets with words having high TFIDF, and assign a zero weight to the rest. For a domain d, we first select the set top_K of K top-ranking words according to their TFIDF_d values. We then keep the synsets in each SMV_d that contain at least one word in top_K, zeroing the rest and normalizing, yielding a new vector SMV_d^K. This vector is very close to SMV_d, but synsets with low TFIDF words are assigned a zero weight. Finally we select the best domain d_{BEST} for document doc as follows:

$$d_{\text{BEST}} = \underset{d \in Domains}{\text{argmax}} \sum_{w \in doc} \max_{s \in Synsets(w)} \text{SMV}_d^K(s) \tag{7}$$

where $Synsets(w)$ returns the synsets denoted by w.

2.6 Domain Word Sense Disambiguation

In order to perform Word Sense Disambiguation of the words in a test document, we first classify the document as described above. For each content word to be disambiguated in the document we then combine the information in the chosen SMV and the context(s) of the target word. We thus create a large context by joining all the sentences where the word occurs in the document, set the reset distribution with the content words in the context, and run Personalized PageRank, yielding a Personalized Pagerank vector for the word (PPV_w).

We then select the best sense of the word as follows:

$$sense_{\text{BEST}}(w) = \underset{s \in Synsets(w)}{\text{argmax}} \text{SMV}_d(s) \cdot \text{PPV}_w(s) \tag{8}$$

where w is the word to be disambiguated, $Synsets(w)$ are the synsets of word w, d is the chosen domain, SMV_d is the SMV of domain d and PPV_w is the PPV of the word's context.

3. EXPERIMENTAL SETUP AND RESULTS

We first describe our general experimental setup, which we used to perform experiments on text classification (Section 3.3) and WSD (Section 3.4).

3.1 Target Domains and Training Set

We first chose the set of target domains. We selected the 29 domain labels used in featured Wikipedia articles – a list of the best articles in Wikipedia, as determined collectively by its editors.[1] The domain labels cover a wide variety of topics, including business, arts, computing, sport, etc.

For each domain, we randomly picked up 30 featured articles, thus totalizing $30 \cdot 29 = 870$ articles. Each article in the dataset has a single correct domain label. Note that we use Wikipedia only to define the training and test dataset (i.e., a fixed set of domains and the corresponding articles), but that our semantic model is solely based on WordNet.

3.2 Semantic Model Construction

To build our semantic models we extracted the terms from the training set and calculated their TFIDF scores for each domain. For each domain d, we then used the TFIDF domain scores to weight synsets and built the SMV_d and the corresponding model with cross-domain reweighting.

3.3 Text Classification

3.3.1 Test set

To perform text classification, we prepared a dataset of 290 Wikipedia articles (10 for each of the 29 domains defined for the training set, cf. Section 3.1) that were collaboratively classified as "good articles"[2], i.e., of good quality but that are not yet, or are unlikely to reach, featured article quality. Similarly to the training set, the test set is single-labeled.

3.3.2 Systems

We experimented with four variants of our SMVs, each obtained by selecting a specific combination of the **reset distribution** (either the **Uniform** or the **Related Words** strategy) and **cross-domain reweighting (CDR)** (entropy-based reweighting either enabled or disabled).

3.3.3 Parameters

Our approach has only one parameter, that is, the K constant used for selecting the top domain terms in each SMV_d for text classification. In order to choose the best value of K, we created a tuning dataset by randomly sampling a set of 58 "good" Wikipedia articles (2 articles per domain), with no overlap with our training and test sets. We then ran our classification algorithm on this tuning set and found the optimal values for each variant of our method (1250 and 750 respectively for Uniform SMVs with and without cross-domain reweighting; similarly, 400 and 1350, respectively, for RelWords SMVs).

3.3.4 Baselines and skyline

As a first baseline we calculated the **random baseline**, which selects a random domain label. We also constructed a baseline TFIDF-based classification system. Given the test document, we select the domain that maximizes the sum of the TFIDF scores for the terms in the document:

$$d_{\text{BEST}} = \operatorname*{argmax}_{d \in Domains} \sum_{w \in doc} \mathrm{TFIDF}_d(w). \quad (9)$$

In order to give a reference for the results of a state-of-the-art machine learning technique, we chose Support Vector Machines (SVM) [6] as the skyline. Given that we are working on many domains, we adopt the *one versus all* paradigm.

We used a linear kernel, whose C parameter was set to 0.5, after using the tuning dataset for optimization (cf. Section 3.3.3). The features were composed of word stems and their normalized TFIDF weights, following the widely used bag-of-words approach.

3.3.5 Results

In Table 1 we report the results of our systems in the classification task. We show recall@k, i.e., the ratio of examples where the correct answer is found among the system's top k domain labels ($k = 1, 2, 3$). The main evaluation measure is recall@1, which is equivalent to recall, precision, F1 and Break-Even Point (BEP) in this dataset.

Table 1: Classification results on Wikipedia (†: signif. diff. from RelWords SMV+CDR, $p < 0.001$).

System	Recall@k		
	k=1	k=2	k=3
Uniform SMV	58.0†	72.9	79.9
Uniform SMV + CDR	64.6†	76.3	80.5
RelWords SMV	64.2†	75.7	81.9
RelWords SMV + CDR	**67.0**	**76.7**	**83.7**
Random baseline	3.5†	-	-
TFIDF baseline	60.4†	71.9	79.5
SVM skyline	68.2†	76.8	81.7

Three of our best SMV variants surpass the TFIDF baseline by several points for all three values of k, showing that our classification performance is generally good. The results show that CDR is beneficial in all cases.

We observe that a 67% recall@1 obtained with our RelWords+CDR SMV on this dataset is a significant result, considering that we have 29 classes with identical prior probabilities (the performance of the random baseline is extremely low, a mere 3.5%).

3.3.6 Analysis

Note that our method is basically the TFIDF baseline with WordNet information added on top of it. The improvement of our systems over the TFIDF baseline could be caused by the use of cutoffs alone (cf. Section 3.3.3). We thus compared our systems against a TFIDF baseline with cutoff on the top-ranking K words (the best value for K was selected on the tuning dataset). The result for this TFIDF top K baseline is 61.1 recall@1, only one point above the unthresholded baseline, showing that semantic information from WordNet can improve results beyond the keyword level.

In a related experiment, we used the result of the "weighting domain synsets" step (cf. Section 2.2) directly. This would shed some light on the usefulness of the Personalized PageRank step when constructing the SMVs. The synset weights provided by the related words approach, when used by our TC algorithm without CDR, yields a recall@1 of 60.8 when used directly, well below the 64.2 attained by our SMV with no CDR ("RelWords SMV" row in Table 1). The only difference between the two runs is the use of PPR, beneficial when building SMVs. We attribute such positive difference to the semantic spreading effect of PPR.

3.4 Word Sense Disambiguation

3.4.1 Test set

For our domain WSD experiment we used the gold standard dataset released by Koeling *et al.* [8]. This dataset comprises examples of 41 words retrieved from the Sports and Finance sections of the Reuters corpus, and also from the balanced British National Corpus (BNC). The selected words are quite polysemous and thus difficult to disambiguate, with an average polysemy of 6.7 senses, ranging from 2 to 13 senses. We created a pseudo-document for each word containing all its contexts, classified this pseudo-document into one of the domains, and proceeded as in Section 2.6.

3.4.2 Baselines and skyline

As baselines we adopted two well-known strategies, i.e., the **random baseline** – which selects a random sense for each word item to disambiguate, and the **SemCor Most Frequent Sense (MFS) baseline** – based on sense occurrence counts within the largest sense-tagged corpus. As a skyline we applied the **test MFS**, i.e., we assigned to each

[1] http://en.wikipedia.org/wiki/Wikipedia:Featured_articles

[2] http://en.wikipedia.org/wiki/Wikipedia:Good_articles

Table 2: **WSD results on Finance and Sports (†: signif. diff. from RelWords SMV + CDR, $p < 0.001$).**

System	Sports	Finance
Uniform SMV	29.4†	51.2†
Uniform SMV + CDR	41.5†	54.2†
RelWords SMV	27.7†	52.6†
RelWords SMV + CDR	**52.7**	**58.2**
UKB	40.3†	49.9†
Random baseline	19.2†	19.5†
SemCor MFS	19.6†	37.1†
Test MFS skyline	77.8†	82.3†

word its most frequent sense as taken from the test set. This skyline is hard to beat, even for supervised systems [8].

3.4.3 *Systems*

We experimented our **Uniform** and **RelWords SMV** methods with and without cross-domain reweighting (CDR). Note that no additional parameter tuning is needed for WSD. We compared our systems with **UKB** [1], a state-of-the-art WSD system based on Personalized PageRank.

3.4.4 *Results*

We calculated recall on the two domain test sets (see Table 2). Our RelWords SMV + CDR outperforms all baselines and the UKB method by 12 points on Sports and 8 points on Finance (relative improvement of 31.5% and 16.6% respectively), and achieves state-of-the-art performance.

We remark that the same configuration, i.e., RelWords SMV + CDR, attains the best performance in both categorization and WSD tasks, which provides an added value to our system. Interestingly, Uniform SMV + CDR also outperforms UKB – by a small margin on Sports and many points on Finance – but other variants obtain lower performance.

4. RELATED WORK

Text Classification. The state of the art in text classification uses word-based features and sophisticated machine learning algorithms such as Support Vector Machines or logistic regression among others. Much work tries to improve TC by enriching the documents with semantic information, e.g., with limited information from WordNet [14]. In contrast, our approach uses the rich structure of WordNet, and yields improvement over the text-only baseline using just the semantic model.

Subsequent work focused on Wikipedia [4, 16], which has been used to augment the text representation with semantic features with a larger coverage of named entities. In contrast to the above approaches, in which Machine Learning is combined with bags of words, we show that a semantics-only representation improves over a bag-of-words representation.

Domain Word Sense Disambiguation. Domain WSD is often performed in a type-based fashion, i.e., by assigning a single sense per word. Distributionally similar neighbors in raw text can be used as cues to determine the predominant sense of a target word using a semantic similarity measure [8, 9]. Other distributional methods use word-category matrices and synonym occurrence counts (see [11] for a survey).

Knowledge-based approaches – which exploit the semantic structure of resources such as WordNet – take the middle ground between domain-driven [13] and supervised methods [7], and have been shown to perform equally well on domain texts [1, 12]. In this paper we go one step further: we propose an approach with little human intervention which first classifies a word context and then uses the selected SMV for WSD. In contrast to state-of-the-art WSD [12], we do not use the MFS as a backoff strategy, thanks to our effective combination of the classification and disambiguation steps.

5. CONCLUSIONS

In this paper we presented a unified approach for categorizing Wikipedia pages and performing Domain Word Sense Disambiguation. Key to our approach is the automatic acquisition of semantic models for multiple domains which we then use to perform semantic analysis of input texts.

The crucial fact that we provide a unified approach with remarkably good results in **both tasks** opens an exciting direction of research, thus enabling deeper understanding and hopefully boosting performance on applications such as Question Answering and Information Retrieval.

Acknowledgments

The first author gratefully acknowledges the support of the ERC Starting Grant MultiJEDI No. 259234.

6. REFERENCES

[1] E. Agirre, O. L. de Lacalle, and A. Soroa. Knowledge-based WSD on specific domains: performing better than generic supervised WSD. In *Proc. of IJCAI 2009*, pages 1501–1506, Pasadena, California, USA, 2009.

[2] E. Agirre and O. Lopez de Lacalle. Supervised domain adaption for WSD. In *Proc. of EACL 2009*, pages 42–50, Athens, Greece, 2009.

[3] C. Fellbaum, editor. *WordNet: An Electronic Database*. MIT Press, Cambridge, MA, 1998.

[4] E. Gabrilovich and S. Markovitch. Wikipedia-based semantic interpretation for natural language processing. *Journal of Artificial Intelligence Research*, 34:443–498, March 2009.

[5] A. Gliozzo, C. Strapparava, and I. Dagan. Unsupervised and supervised exploitation of semantic domains in lexical disambiguation. *Computer Speech and Language*, 18(3):275–299, 2004.

[6] T. Joachims. *Learning to Classify Text Using Support Vector Machines – Methods, Theory, and Algorithms.* Kluwer/Springer, 2002.

[7] M. Khapra, A. Kulkarni, S. Sohoney, and P. Bhattacharyya. All words domain adapted WSD: Finding a middle ground between supervision and unsupervision. In *Proc. of ACL 2010*, pages 1532–1541, Uppsala, Sweden, July 2010.

[8] R. Koeling, D. McCarthy, and J. Carroll. Domain-specific sense distributions and predominant sense acquisition. In *Proc. of HLT-EMNLP 2005*, pages 419–426, Vancouver, Canada, 2005.

[9] D. McCarthy, R. Koeling, J. Weeds, and J. Carroll. Unsupervised acquisition of predominant word senses. *Computational Linguistics*, 33(4):553–590, 2007.

[10] S. Mohammad and G. Hirst. Determining word sense dominance using a thesaurus. In *Proc. of EACL 2006*, pages 121–128, Trento, Italy, 2006.

[11] R. Navigli. Word Sense Disambiguation: A survey. *ACM Computing Surveys*, 41(2):1–69, 2009.

[12] S. P. Ponzetto and R. Navigli. Knowledge-rich Word Sense Disambiguation rivaling supervised system. In *Proc. of ACL 2010*, pages 1522–1531, Sweden, 2010.

[13] C. Strapparava, A. Gliozzo, and C. Giuliano. Pattern abstraction and term similarity for word sense disambiguation: Irst at senseval-3. In *Proc. of Senseval-3*, pages 229–234, Barcelona, Spain, 2004.

[14] L. Ureña-López, M. de Buenaga Rodríguez, and J. Gómez. Integrating linguistic resources in TC through WSD. *Computers and the Humanities*, 35(2):215–230, 2001.

[15] P. Wang and C. Domeniconi. Building semantic kernels for text classification using wikipedia. In *Proc. of KDD 2008*, pages 713–721, Nevada, 2008.

[16] P. Wang, J. Hu, H.-J. Zeng, and Z. Chen. Using wikipedia knowledge to improve text classification. *Knowledge Information Systems*, 19(3):265–281, 2009.

More or Better: On Trade-offs in Compacting Textual Problem Solution Repositories

Deepak P
IBM Research - India,
Bangalore, INDIA
deepak.s.p@in.ibm.com

Sutanu Chakraborti
IIT Madras, Chennai, INDIA
sutanuc@iitm.ac.in

Deepak Khemani
IIT Mandi, Himachal Pradesh,
INDIA
khemani@iitm.ac.in

ABSTRACT

In this paper, we look into the problem of filtering problem solution repositories (from sources such as community-driven question answering systems) to render them more suitable for usage in knowledge reuse systems. We explore harnessing the fuzzy nature of usability of a solution to a problem, for such compaction. Fuzzy usabilities lead to several challenges; notably, the trade-off between choosing *generic* or *better* solutions. We develop an approach that can heed to a user specification of the trade-off between these criteria and introduce several quality measures based on fuzzy usability estimates to ascertain the quality of a problem-solution repository for usage in a Case Based Reasoning system. We establish, through a detailed empirical analysis, that our approach outperforms state-of-the-art approaches on virtually all quality measures.

Categories and Subject Descriptors: H.3 [Information Systems]: Information Storage and Retrieval – *Content Analysis and Indexing, Information Search and Retrieval*

General Terms: Algorithms

Keywords: Compaction, QA, Case-based Reasoning

1. INTRODUCTION

Internet based knowledge markets[1] have been increasingly gaining popularity in recent years. Of these, community driven QA (CQA) sites are considered a valuable source of *opinions*, *facts* and *experiences*[2], whereas Wikipedia-like sources are mostly for *facts*. Here, we focus on approaches for pre-processing problem-solution datasets to filter out knowledge based on the *quality* and *genericity* criteria that we will outline. Research on the *utility problem* in CBR systems [1] suggests that such compaction is necessary for building efficient Case-Based Reasoning (CBR) systems. Data from CQA websites contain multiple solutions to each problem, with each solution tagged with the number of votes it has acquired through user voting.

[1] http://en.wikipedia.org/wiki/Knowledge_market

[2] http://answers.yahoo.com/info/product_tour

CIKM'11, October 24–28, 2011, Glasgow, Scotland, UK.

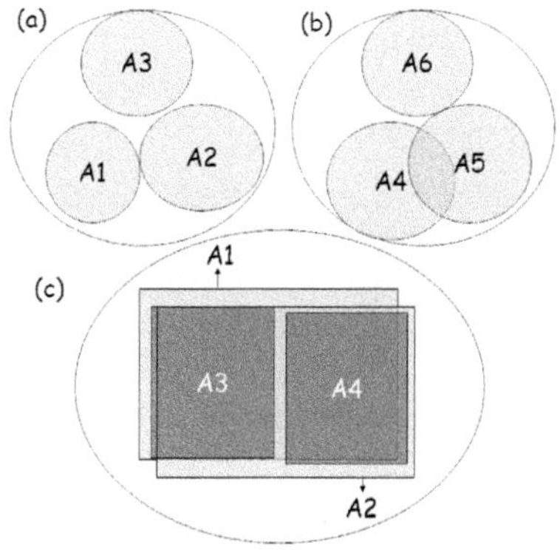

Figure 1: Example

We motivate the problem using a series of examples. The outer black boundary in Figure 1(a) is meant to represent a space of problems. A1, A2 and A3 represent solutions; corresponding ovals represent the subset of problems (called the *coverage space*) that they can *solve*. Assuming all solutions are of indistinguishable quality, consider the problem of choosing two solutions from among them. One woul intuitively want to choose A2 and A3 since they have the largest coverages. The same approach, applied to Figure 1(b) would choose A4 and A5. However, the large overlap between the coverage spaces of A4 and A5 does not augur well with our rather intuitive intent of preserving solutions that together solve as many problems as possible; one may want to choose $A4$ and $A6$ hence. A greedy incremental heuristic [2] starts from an empty set of solutions, and keeps adding solutions that are useful for the maximum number of problems outside the set of problems already covered by the solutions selected so far. Similar effects could also be achieved by weighing problems in the intersection of A4 and A5 half as much as those which are in the coverage area of only one solution [3].

Unlike Figure 1(a&b), *usabilities* of solutions to problems are often fuzzy. Consider an example in Figure 1(c); the degree of darkness of the coverage area is directly related to the usability of the solution to that problem subset. Let the coverage areas of A1 and A2 be roughly the same ($\approx$60% of the problem space) and their darkness representing *medium* usability; on the other hand, A3 and A4 cover two disjoint 30% regions with *high* usability. Consider choosing one solution from among $\{A1, A2, A3, A4\}$. We could choose one from either of $\{A1, A2\}$ or $\{A3, A4\}$; the former leads to preserving a *medium* usability solution for 60% of the problems, and the latter preserves a *high* usability solution for half as many.

This trade-off is tricky, and depends on the intelligence in the downstream *adaptation* engine (that adapts the retrieved solution to help solve the user posed problem), user preferences etc.

Now, consider choosing two solutions from $\{A1, A2, A3, A4\}$; each combination of two solutions leads to a coverage of 60% of the problem space. One option is to choose A1 and A2 that leads to retaining *two medium usability solutions* for each problem in that 60% space; at the other extreme is choosing A3 and A4 that retains *one high usability solution* for each problem in the same space. The choice between these is dependent on various factors. Real scenarios are often more complex than that in Figure 1(c); a solution that is of medium usability for a part of the problem space may be of high usability to other problems. Thus, coverage areas for solutions are often composed of various shades. This trade-off between solution *usability* and solution *abundance* is at the core of the problem addressed in this paper.

2. PROBLEM SETTING

Problem-Solution pairs are often referred to as *cases* in CBR literature; case bases are collections of cases. Consider a case base $\mathcal{D}$ that contains objects of the form $d_i = \{p_i, s_i\}$. Each object d_i is composed of a problem p_i and a set of solutions s_i (we model s_i as a set since multiple solutions to a problem is typical of CQA systems). We would like to condense $\mathcal{D}$ to a form $\mathcal{D}'$ whose objects are of the form $d'_i = \{p_i, s'_i\}$ where $\forall i, s'_i \subseteq s_i$. *Informally, we would like to remove some solutions from the solution set of each object in $\mathcal{D}$ based on a user-specified preference of the quality-abundance trade-off.* Our compaction process decides on which solutions are to be removed from $\mathcal{D}$ based on a user-specified trade-off between *usability* and *abundance* of solutions; we allow the user to specify this using a parameter γ, a high value for γ indicating that the usage of the compacted dataset $\mathcal{D}'$ would be in scenarios where the user is interested in getting *more* solutions (even at the expense of some reduction in usability) to newly posed problems and vice versa.

$p(\alpha)$ denotes the problem associated with a particular solution, α. In heeding to the user specified trade-off, we would make use of usability estimates for solutions to specific problems. The usability of a solution α to a problem p_j is denoted by $u(\alpha, p_j)$. Usability of a solution to its own problem (i.e., values for $u(\alpha, p(\alpha))$) is often readily available from user voting systems such as those in *Yahoo! Answers*; more votes correspond to more usability. We will elaborate on our notion of usability and how we estimate it in the absence of voting data, in Section 4.

We do not remove any problems from $\mathcal{D}$ since retrieving similar problems to a new problem is a text retrieval problem and state of the art techniques for text retrieval easily scale to terabytes[3]; the utility problem is more manifested in downstream processes that are handled by the CBR system core, making the compactness of the solution set an important priority.

3. RELATED WORK

The *utility problem* in case-based reasoning systems [1] suggests that the efficiency of a case based reasoning system often degrades when the size of the case-base increases. In response, case-base compaction techniques have been developed considering aspects such as *classification accuracy* [4, 5], coverage and reachability [6], retrieval models [7] and competence retention [8]. In this paper, we focus on certain trade-offs in case base compaction that stem from the nature of fuzzy usability of solutions. Fuzzy usability scores are not unique to unstructured problem-solution pairs; even in structured cases, assessments of whether a plan would work for a travel request may be subjective, leading to fuzzy usability assessments. *To the best of our knowledge, case base compaction with fuzzy usability scores is being considered for the first time.* We will elaborate on the notion of usability in Section 4.

[3]http://www-nlpir.nist.gov/projects/terabyte/

4. NOTION OF USABILITY

Usability of a solution for a problem quantifies the ease of adapting the solution for solving the problem. The CBR system relies on the assumption that similar problems have similar solutions. Thus, given a new problem, a CBR system retrieves solutions of similar problems since they are *deemed to be usable*. However, it could so happen that such solutions are not so usable; thus, the real usability of the solution is determined based on voting systems where users vote whether the deemed to be usable solutions presented to them are really usable or not. Thus, this actual usability, a supervised concept (derived from user feedback), is distinct from deemed usability, an unsupervised measure.

CQA systems often have voting scores for problem-solution pairs where the solution was proposed for the problem; we use these as a proxy for the usability. We have to fall back to using statistical measures to estimate the usability of an solution α to a different problem p_j (i.e., $p_j \neq p(\alpha)$). We compute the usability of the solution $\alpha \in s_i$, to the problem p_j (whose true solutions are available as s_j) as:

$$u(\alpha, p_j) = max\{s(\beta) * sim(\alpha, \beta) | \beta \in s_j\} \quad (1)$$

where $sim(.,.)$ is a text similarity function such as cosine[4]. We use $s(\beta)$ as a shorthand for $u(\beta, p(\beta))$ and will follow the convention of using $s(.)$ when the usability is estimated from user feedback such as votes and $u(.,.)$ when the usability is estimated using statistical measures as above. The above formulation is based on the intuition that α is more usable for p_j if it is *highly* similar to *highly* usable solutions associated with p_j.

Usage of a CBR system starts with receiving a user-posed problem and invoking a retrieval engine to retrieve the top-k similar problems. Thus, the usabilities of solutions associated with problems that are not retrieved need to be squished to zero. Thus, our refined formulation (that also uses a threshold, β, that we set to 1.0) stands as:

$$u(\alpha, p_j) = \begin{cases} u(\alpha, p_j), & \text{if } p(\alpha) \in top\text{-}k(p_j) \wedge \\ & u(\alpha, p_j) \geq \beta \\ 0, & \text{otherwise} \end{cases}$$

We use $u(.,.)$ to denote this refined notion hereafter.

5. THE TRADE-OFF PARAMETER

As outlined in Section 2, we would like to design a compaction technique that can make use of a user parameter specifying the trade-off between *solution usability* and *solution abundance*. At one extreme, the users of the target CBR system are only interested in getting the *maximally usable solution* to their queries; at the other, they are interested in getting *as many usable solutions as possible*. Instead of modeling it as an awkward parameter ranging from 0 to 1 (the ends for each extreme), we model the trade-off parameter as the *tipping point*, the number of solutions upto which a user may consider abundance useful. For example, a user may suggest that she may be interested in looking at *upto* 3 different

[4]http://en.wikipedia.org/wiki/Cosine_similarity

solutions, beyond which she attaches no value for abundance; the compaction engine could then focus on enough abundance that ensures close to 3 solutions for problems from the problem space, beyond which it could optimize usability. When the parameter is set to 4, the end-user could then expect to receive more number of solutions (closer to 4); however, the trade-off forces it to deliver solutions of lesser usability than the former case with 3.

6. EVALUATION MEASURES

We now lay down evaluation criteria to measure the goodness of compaction. These are run-time characteristics, that would be measured for problems from the test set posed to a CBR system built on the compacted dataset. The evaluation is done on a test dataset of cases for which true solutions are known; more specifically, the criteria that we describe here all make use of usability scores that are estimated using the true solutions of the test problem (these true solutions come with user feedback data such as # votes). Consider a set of test problems, $\mathcal{T} = \{t_1, t_2, \ldots, t_k\}$. Let the set of solutions returned by the CBR system for a test problem t_i be denoted by $R(t_i)$. We evaluate the various compaction techniques on how they perform on these measures, based on the average of these measures across problems in $\mathcal{T}$.

Usability of the Maximally Usable Solution*(max):*
$max(t_i, R(t_i)) = max\{u(\alpha, t_i) | \alpha \in R(t_i) \wedge u(\alpha, t_i) \geq \beta\}$
where $u(.,.)$ is estimated as shown in Section 4.

Number of Usable Solutions Presented*(#ans):*
$\#ans(t_i, R(t_i)) = |\{\alpha | \alpha \in R(t_i) \wedge u(\alpha_{ij}, t_i) \geq \beta\}|$

Total Usability of Solutions*(tot):*
$tot(t_i, R(t_i)) = \sum_{\alpha \in R(t_i)\ where\ u(\alpha, t_i) \geq \beta} u(\alpha, t_i)$

Coverage*(cov):* This measures the number of solutions that pass the usability threshold (which we set to 1.0, the quantity equivalent to one user vote)
$cov(\mathcal{T}) = \frac{|\{t_i | \#ans(t_i, \{\alpha_{i1}, \ldots, \alpha_{il_i}\}) \geq 1\}|}{|\mathcal{T}|} * 100$
cov precisely denotes the notion of *competence* of case bases [7]; this is mostly the only metric used in evaluating case base compaction techniques in lietarature.

Diversity*(div):* This measures the diversity of the solution set; diverse result sets may be intuitively preferred.
$div(t_i, R(t_i)) = \frac{\sum_{\alpha_x \in R(t_i), \alpha_y \in R(t_i), x \neq y} (1 - sim(\alpha_x, \alpha_y))}{|R(t_i)|}$

7. OUR APPROACH

Our approach is a simple greedy decremental approach that removes solutions one-by-one, each iteration removing the solution that minimally affects a specified objective function.

Consider an intermediate dataset $\mathcal{D}^\circ$ ($\mathcal{D}^\circ$ is to be understood as $\mathcal{D}$ after removal of some solutions) and the input compaction parameter γ. Since the specification of the compaction parameter suggests that the user is interested only in the top-γ solutions for a problem, our objective function will also concern with only the top-γ solutions. Consider a case d_i° (used to denote the case corresponding to d_i in $\mathcal{D}$) from $\mathcal{D}^\circ$ whose problem p_i is posed to a CBR system built on $\mathcal{D}^\circ - \{d_i^\circ\}$. Our objective function for this specific p_i is defined as the following:

$$\mathcal{O}(\mathcal{D}^\circ, p_i) = max(p_i, R'(p_i)) + tot(p_i, R'(p_i))$$

where $R'(p_i)$ denotes the top-γ solutions to p_i when posed on a CBR system that works on the dataset $\mathcal{D}^\circ - \{d_i^\circ\}$. We use the original solution set s_i (from $\mathcal{D}$, Ref. Section 2) to estimate the $u(.,.)$ for usage in computation of $max(.,.)$, $tot(.,.)$ and $R'(.)$. The design of $\mathcal{O}(\mathcal{D}^\circ, p_i)$ counts the usability of the maximally usable solution twice, once in the first term and once in the second term; the other solutions are only counted once (in the second term, as part of the $tot(.,.)$). For very high γ, the overall sum is contributed to, by mostly the second term since $|R'(.)|$ increases with γ leading to a corresponding increase in $tot(., R'(.))$. This property reduces the relative contribution by the maximally usable solution for high γ. The overall measure of fit for $\mathcal{D}^\circ$ is then defined as:

$$\mathcal{O}(\mathcal{D}^\circ) = \sum_{p \in \{p_i | d_i^\circ \in \mathcal{D}^\circ\}} \mathcal{O}(\mathcal{D}^\circ, p)$$

Let κ be the number of solutions desired in the compacted dataset $\mathcal{D}'$; the greedy decremental algorithm is given in Algorithm 1.

Alg. 1 ***Greedy Decremental Optimization***

Input. $\mathcal{D}, \kappa, \gamma$
Output. $\mathcal{D}'$

1. $\mathcal{D}^\circ = \mathcal{D}$
2. while $\mathcal{D}^\circ$ has more than κ solutions
3. $\quad a = \underset{\alpha \in Solutions(\mathcal{D}^\circ)}{\text{argmin}} \; (\mathcal{O}(\mathcal{D}^\circ) - \mathcal{O}(\mathcal{D}^\circ \backslash \alpha))$
4. $\quad$ remove a from among the solutions in $\mathcal{D}^\circ$
5. return $\mathcal{D}^\circ$ as $\mathcal{D}'$

Although the objective function only includes $max(.,.)$ and $tot(.,.)$, Algorithm 1 indirectly optimizes on coverage. This is because the removal of the only usable solution to a problem (i.e., the operation that would reduce coverage) would affect the objective function through both the $max(.,.)$ and $tot(.,.)$ (whereas most other operations only affect $tot(.,.)$) and hence is less preferred by design. This is so since the only solution is also the maximally usable solution. The objective function and the algorithm are not designed to optimize for $div(.,.)$; however, we will see that the resultant dataset $\mathcal{D}'$ fares well on the diversity of solutions too.

7.1 Baselines

Making use of fuzzy solution usabilities in case base compaction is a new problem, and has not been addressed in literature. *Thus, we can only compare our techniques with those that work with crisp usabilities by quantizing the fuzzy usability with a threshold.* We use the incremental approach from [9] (ADD) and the decremental approach from [6] (DEL) as baseline techniques to compare our technique to. We incorporate the γ parameter in these approaches by assigning the utility of adding (or penalty of removing) a solution which is usable for a problem that has fewer than γ solutions to 0.5. The raw version of these approaches are equivalent to assigning utility of 0.0 to any solution beyond the first.

8. EXPERIMENTAL EVALUATION

8.1 Datasets

We use three datasets; (1) MSR QA Dataset[5] (*encarta*), (2) Yahoo! Answers Data from the *Lincoln cars* category (*lincoln*) and (3) Yahoo! Answers Data from the *Delhi and NCR* category (*delhi*). Each of these have thousands of problems and multiple solutions

[5] http://research.microsoft.com/en-us/downloads/88c0021c-328a-4148-a158-a42d7331c6cf/default.aspx

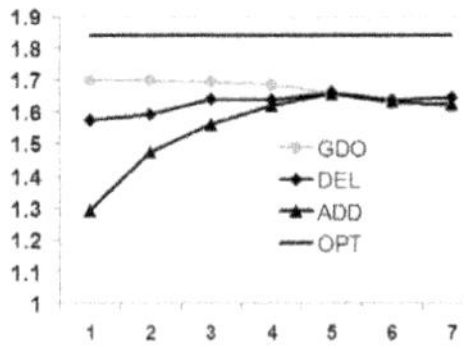

Figure 2: *max* **vs.** γ

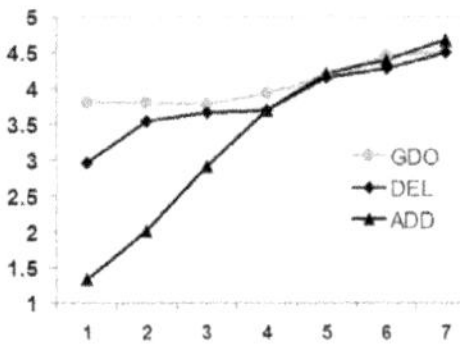

Figure 3: *#ans* **vs.** γ

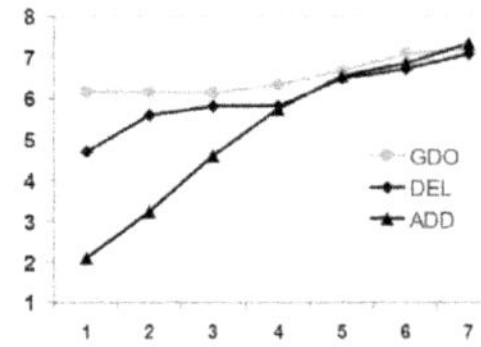

Figure 4: *tot* **vs.** γ

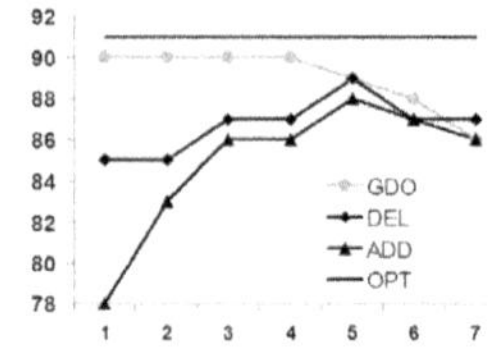

Figure 5: *cov* **vs.** γ

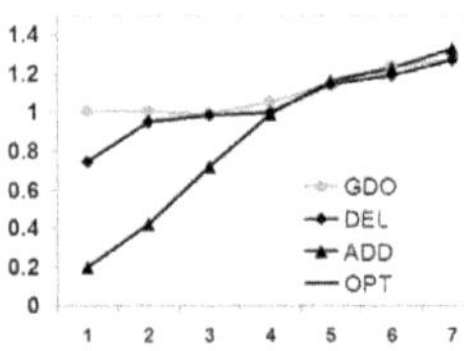

Figure 6: *div* **vs.** γ

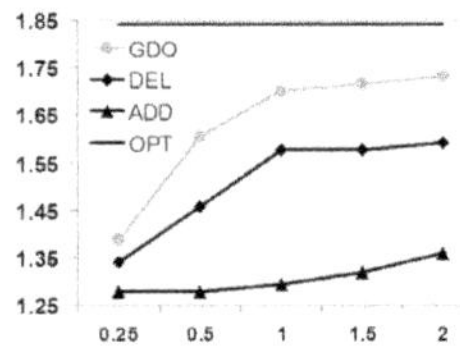

Figure 7: *max* **vs. fraction (encarta) (**γ**=1)**

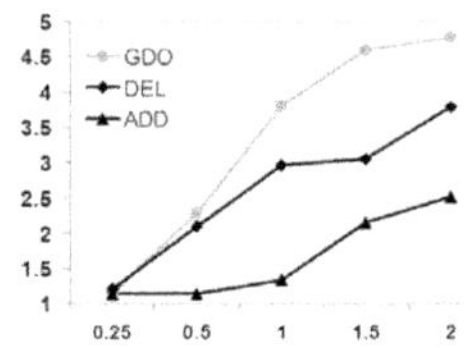

Figure 8: *#ans* **vs. fraction (encarta) (**γ**=1)**

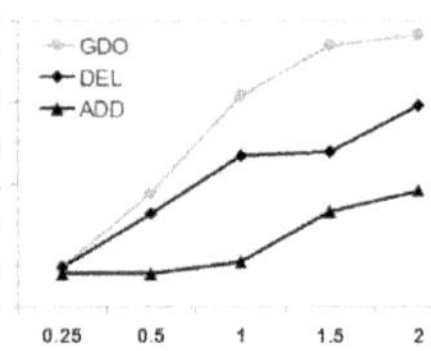

Figure 9: *tot* **vs. fraction (encarta) (**γ**=1)**

per problem. We randomly chose 100 problems for each to use as the test set, and report the performance on the evaluation measures averaged over the test problems. We present charts only on the *encarta* dataset since the trends were mostly similar across datasets.

8.2 Performance with Varying γ

Firstly, we analyze the performance of the various techniques with varying γ. *We set the number of solutions to be preserved to be equal to the number of problems in $\mathcal{D}$ ensuring one solution per problem in $\mathcal{D}'$, on an average.* We expect that the performance on the *max* measure would deteriorate with increasing γ, since *more* and *better* are often contradictary goals. We plot the performance of the various techniques on the *encarta* dataset in Figures 2,3,4,5 and 6 (γ is plotted on the X-Axis). The OPT line (wherever it is visible on the scale) shows the value of the appropriate metric when no compaction has been performed on the dataset; this signifies the upper bound. From the charts, it is easy to see that GDO is seen to outperform the other techniques on each and every measure for small values of γ, while the difference between the various techniques starts to fade away at high values of γ. The GDO technique remained the absolute best on each of the settings on the other datasets; the quantum of improvements is summarized in Table 1. It is interesting to note that heeding to the usability while compaction also automatically optimizes better on the $\#ans$ and div measure as compared to DEL and ADD that seek to optimize only $\#ans$ (since they do not use the fuzzy usability scores). This underlines the importance of heeding to fuzzy usabilities since it leads to more and diverse result sets across problems.

8.3 Performance with Varying Compactions

We now analyze the performance of the compaction techniques with varying ratios of $\frac{\#solutions}{\#problems}$ in the compacted dataset, $\mathcal{D}'$. We run two sets of experiments, one on a dataset compacted with γ=1 and the other with γ=3. The charts for the *encarta* dataset with γ=1 are plotted against the ratio of solutions to problems (in $\mathcal{D}'$) in Figures 7,8,9, 10 and 11 (ratio is plotted in the X-axis). The difference in effectiveness between the techniques manifest more as more solutions can be chosen for retention. GDO still outperforms the other techniques in each and every measure of interest.

9. CONCLUSIONS AND FUTURE WORK

In this paper, we considered the novel problem of harnessing fuzziness in the usability of solutions to problems in compacting problem solution repositories. We outline various evaluation measures, and show that the technique we propose outperforms the state of the art techniques in each of them. This underlines the importance of heeding to any available fuzzy usability scores, while performing compaction of problem solution repositories.

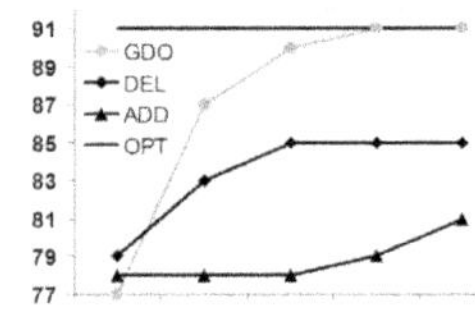

Figure 10: *cov* **vs. fraction (encarta) (**γ**=1)**

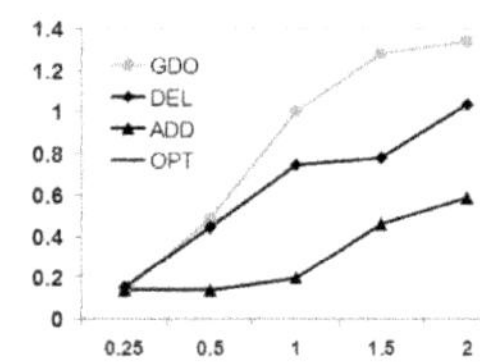

Figure 11: *div* **vs. fraction (encarta) (**γ**=1)**

Dataset	max	#ans	tot	cov	div
encarta	9%	30%	30%	6%	34%
lincoln	3%	15%	17%	1%	28%
delhi	2%	8%	7%	3%	14%

Table 1: γ**=1 (%age GDO is better than** 2nd **best)**

10. REFERENCES

[1] Smyth, B., Cunningham, P.: The utility problem analysed: A case-based reasoning perspective. In: EWCBR. (1996)

[2] Yang, Q., Zhu, J.: A case-addition policy for case-base maintenance. Computational Intelligence **17** (2001) 250–262

[3] Smyth, B., McKenna, E.: Building compact competent case-bases. In: In Proceedings of the Third International Conference on Case-Based Reasoning, Springer (1999) 329–342

[4] Kibler, D., Aha, D.W.: Learning representative exemplars of concepts: an initial case study. In: International Workshop on Machine Learning. (1987)

[5] Aha, D.W., Kibler, D.: Instance-based learning algorithms. In: Machine Learning. (1991) 37–66

[6] Smyth, B., Keane, M.T.: Remembering to forget: A competence-preserving case deletion policy for case-based reasoning systems. In: IJCAI. (1995)

[7] Smyth, B., McKenna, E.: Modelling the competence of case-bases. In: Advances in Case-Based Reasoning:Proceedings of the Fourth European Workshop on Case-Based Reasoning, Springer-Verlag (1998) 208–220

[8] Pan, R., Yang, Q., Pan, S.J.: Mining competent case bases for case-based reasoning. Artif. Intell. **171** (2007) 1039–1068

[9] Zhu, J., Yang, Q.: Remembering to add: competence-preserving case-addition policies for case-base maintenance. In: IJCAI. (1999)

Mining Frequent Patterns Across Multiple Data Streams

Jing Guo[⋆,†], Peng Zhang[⋆], Jianlong Tan[⋆], Li Guo[⋆]

[⋆] Institute of Computing Technology, Chinese Academy of Sciences, Beijing, 100190, China
[†] Beijing University of Posts and Telecommunications, Beijing, 100876, China
guojing@software.ict.ac.cn, {zhangpeng, tjl, guoli}@ict.ac.cn,

ABSTRACT

Mining frequent patterns from data streams has drawn increasing attention in recent years. However, previous mining algorithms were all focused on a single data stream. In many emerging applications, it is of critical importance to combine multiple data streams for analysis. For example, in real-time news topic analysis, it is necessary to combine multiple news report streams from different media sources to discover *collaborative frequent patterns* which are reported frequently in all media, and *comparative frequent patterns* which are reported more frequently in a media than others. To address this problem, we propose a novel frequent pattern mining algorithm *Hybrid-Streaming*, H-Stream for short. H-Stream builds a new Hybrid-Frequent tree to maintain historical frequent and potential frequent itemsets from all data streams, and incrementally updates these itemsets for efficient collaborative and comparative pattern mining. Theoretical and empirical studies demonstrate the utility of the proposed method.

Categories and Subject Descriptors

H.2.8 [**Database Management**]: Database Applications—*Data Mining*

General Terms

Algorithm

Keywords

Multiple data streams, Data stream mining, Frequent pattern mining

1. INTRODUCTION

Data stream mining has drawn increasing attention in recent years [1, 2, 3, 4, 5]. Mining frequent patterns from data streams represents one of the most important directions in data stream mining community [1]. Due to the rapid growth of data volumes, frequent pattern mining on data streams needs to mine from large volumes of continuous stream data in limited memory. To this end, many data stream frequent pattern mining algorithms have been proposed recently, such as the FP-Stream algorithm [1], Lossy Counting algorithm [2], Count Sketch algorithm [3], to name a few. Although these algorithms have demonstrated their effectiveness, a limitation is that they were all designed for mining a single data stream. In many emerging applications, stream data are often generated and collected from multiple sources, and it is necessary to combine multiple data streams for mining.

CIKM'11, October 24–28, 2011, Glasgow, Scotland, UK.

EXAMPLE 1. *Let us take a real-time news topic analysis system for example. The system collects news report streams from three public social media: BBC, New York Times, and The Globe And Mail. The essential goal of the system is to analyze some interesting and insightful patterns. Specifically, the following four tasks need to be addressed:*

(1) Which topics were reported frequently by all the three media in the last 12 hours?

(2) Which topics were reported frequently by The Globe And Mail, while infrequently by BBC and New York Times in the last 12 hours?

(3) Which topics were not only reported frequently by The Globe And Mail in the last 12 hours, but were also reported frequently by BBC and New York Times in the last 24 hours?

(4) Which topics were reported frequently by all the three media, while more frequently by BBC in the last 12 hours?

Tasks (1) and (3) are defined as mining collaborative frequent patterns, *as they aim to find the common frequent patterns across multiple data streams. Tasks (2) and (4) are defined as mining* comparative frequent patterns, *as they aim to find contradicting frequent patterns across multiple data streams.*

In order to solve these tasks, it is necessary to combine multiple data streams for analysis. Combining multiple data streams for mining has been studied previously. For example, clustering multiple streams [6], classifying multiple data streams [7], analyzing correlations among multiple streams [8], and privacy preserving mining across multiple data streams [9]. However, none of them considers the problem of mining collaborative and comparative frequent patterns across multiple data streams. On the other hand, although some previous work [10] considered mining frequent patterns across multiple databases, the method cannot be directly used in data streams.

In order to discover frequent patterns across multiple data streams, an intuitive method is to maintain and update the frequencies of all historical stream data into a summary structure, based on which all the collaborative and comparative patterns can be retrieved accordingly. However, with this method, the following concerns need to be addressed:

(1) How to efficiently maintain historical frequent itemsets from all data streams? A simple solution is to extend the single data

stream frequent mining structure (e.g., FP-Stream structure [1]) to multiple data streams. In other words, each data stream can be maintained in an independent FP-Stream structure, and the results from each FP-Stream can be combined for mining. Although this method is very easy to implement, a limitation is that its memory cost increases linearly with the number of streams. For example, in order to mine from one hundred data streams, we have to build one hundred FP-Stream structures. This is unaffordable for many applications. A better alternative method is to construct a single global data structure to make full use of shared itemsets across all the data streams.

(2) How to update historical frequent itemsets? In data streams, an infrequent itemset has the potential to grow into a frequent itemset. Thus, we cannot delete an infrequent itemset at each given time point. On the other hand, due to the huge number of infrequent itemsets in data streams, it is impractical to maintain them all in memory during mining. Thus, it is necessary to find a compromise solution between accuracy and memory cost.

(3) Based on the historical itemsets, how to design an effective method to discover collaborative and comparative patterns across all streams. The algorithm should be able to discover these complex patterns not only from the same time interval, but also from different time intervals.

In summary, in order to discover collaborative and comparative frequent patterns across multiple data streams, the following concerns need to be addressed:

- How to design an efficient data structure to maintain historical frequent itemsets from all streams?
- How to design an approximate updating algorithm to efficiently update the frequent itemsets from all streams?
- How to retrieve collaborative and comparative frequent patterns from the designed data structure?

To address these challenges, an novel *Hybrid-Streaming* algorithm (H-Stream for short) is proposed to discover collaborative and comparative frequent patterns across multiple data streams. H-Stream first employs a new *Hybrid-Frequent Tree* (H-tree for short) to maintain historical frequent and potential frequent itemsets for all streams, and then it incrementally updates these itemsets under the Chernoff bound. Based on the maintained itemsets in H-tree, the collaborative and comparative patterns can be efficiently retrieved by traversing the tree. Theoretical and empirical studies demonstrate the utility of the proposed method.

The rest of this paper is organized as follows. Section 2 introduces the H-Stream algorithm and analyzes its performance. Section 3 reports experimental results and comparisons. We conclude the paper in Section 4.

2. THE H-STREAM ALGORITHM

In this section, we first introduce the H-tree structure in Section 2.1, based on which we design the H-Stream algorithm in Section 2.2. We analyze the performance of the algorithm in Section 2.3.

2.1 The H-tree structure

Structurally, H-tree consists of three components:

(1) A *Tree* (T) that maintains frequent and potential frequent itemsets discovered from all streams. Itemsets in data streams are categorized into three types: *frequent itemset* whose current support is larger than δ, where δ is the min-support; *infrequent itemset* whose current support is lower than $(\delta - \epsilon)$, where ϵ is the error

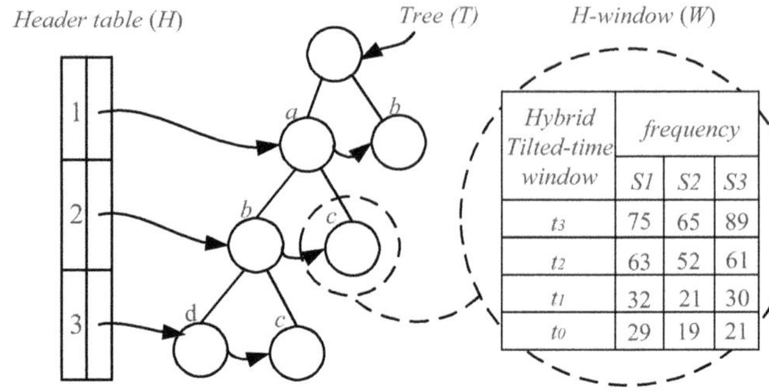

Figure 1: An illustration of the H-tree structure.

bound; and *potential frequent itemset* whose current support lies between parameters δ and (δ-ϵ). We will discuss this parameter later in Section 2.3.

Ideally, all these three types of itemsets can be maintained for accurate mining. But due to the limited memory, only the frequent and potential frequent itemsets will be maintained in the tree.

(2) A *Hybrid-window* (W) that records the frequencies of the maintained itemsets in each time interval. Moreover, to further reduce the memory cost of H-tree, a logarithmic tilted window [1] can be used here.

(3) A *Headertable* (H) that consists of an array of pointers that point to the itemsets in distinct level of tree. By using table H, the frequent and potential frequent itemsets can be efficiently retrieved from tree T. This will reduce the overall update time of H-tree.

Compared to maintain each data stream independently, H-Tree can achieve a more compacted memory cost by making full use of the overlapping structures among all maintained itemsets.

2.2 Algorithm Description

Algorithm 1 shows the whole procedure of the H-Stream algorithm. Obviously, H-Stream mainly consists of three steps. In the first step, it builds an H-tree structure to maintain the frequent and potential frequent itemsets from all streams. Note that the numbers of these itemsets are controlled by parameters δ and ϵ. In the second step, H-Stream continuously updates H-tree by inserting new emerging frequent and potential frequent itemsets, meanwhile deleting itemsets that have become infrequent. In the last step, H-Stream traverses the tree to retrieve collaborative and comparative frequent patterns.

There are five inputs of Algorithm 1. Parameter δ controls the number of frequent itemsets. The lower value of δ, the more frequent itemsets we can obtained. Parameter ϵ controls the tree prune rate. The lower value of ϵ, the more infrequent itemsets will be deleted. Besides, we assume the m data streams S are processed batch-by-batch, and data from the jth stream $(1 \leq j \leq m)$ during time interval t_i $(i \geq 1)$ is denoted by B^i_j. The collaborative parameter set α and the comparative parameter set β vary case by case. They can be manually set by end users.

In the first step of Algorithm 1, H-Stream uses the first batch data B^1_j $(1 \leq j \leq m)$ to construct an H-tree. This can be further split into two sub-steps: (1) Discover frequent and potential frequent itemsets from B^1_j. Specifically, frequent itemsets U (i.e., $sup(U) \geq \delta$), and potential frequent itemsets V (i.e.,$sup(V) \geq \delta - \epsilon$) will be extracted from all B^1_j $(1 \leq j \leq m)$ using FP-growth algorithm [11]; (2) Initialize the three components of H-tree. Assume all items distribute uniformly in the streams, and all the distinct items in the first batch can be observed. We calculate the average frequencies for all the distinct items to get an item list in descending order. To

Algorithm 1: The H-Stream Algorithm

Input : (1) min-support δ ,
(2) error-rate ϵ,
(3) m data streams $\mathcal{S}$,
(4) collaborative parameter set α,
(5) comparative parameter set β

Output: the collaborative and comparative patterns Θ

// step 1. construct H-tree
$U, V \longleftarrow \Phi$;
$i \longleftarrow 1$;
for j=*1 to m* **do**
    $U \longleftarrow U \bigcup Fp\text{-}growth(B^i_j, \delta)$;
    $V \longleftarrow V \bigcup Fp\text{-}growth(B^i_j, \delta, \epsilon)$;
$Tree \longleftarrow Initialize\_H\_Tree(U, V)$;

// step 2. update H-tree
while $\mathcal{S} \neq \Phi$ **do**
    $X \longleftarrow \Phi$;
    $i \longleftarrow i + 1$;
    $C^i_1, ..., C^i_m \longleftarrow Preprocess(B^i_1, ..., B^i_m, Tree, \delta, \epsilon)$;
    for j=*1 to m* **do**
        $X \longleftarrow X \bigcup Fp\text{-}growth(C^i_j)$;
    $Tree \longleftarrow Insert\_H\_Tree(X)$;
    $Tree \longleftarrow Prune\_H\_Tree(Tree, \delta, \epsilon)$;

// step 3. mining across multiple streams
$\Theta \longleftarrow Collabrative\_Mining(\alpha)$;
$\Theta \longleftarrow \Theta \bigcup Comparative\_Mining(Tree, \beta)$;
Output Θ

initialize the H-tree, we insert all elements $e \in \{U \bigcup V\}$ into the tree T with it's frequencies of all streams into the window W, the items in e are sorted by the item list. By doing so, we can obtain an H-tree with minimal size [1]. Besides, we add a pointer in the Headertable H pointing to the element e in the tree.

In the second step, H-Stream updates H-Tree based on new stream data. This can be categorized into four sub-steps: (1) Preprocess new stream data. For any item infrequent in all streams, if it is either not in the tree structure, it will be removed in the preprocessing stage; (2) Discover itemsets X. For each preprocessed stream, discover itemsets X from it without any prune. (3) Insert itemsets X. For each itemset e, if e has already been maintained in the tree, we update its corresponding value in H-Window. Otherwise, if itemset $e \in U \bigcup V$, we insert it into H-tree by updating all the three components of H-tree. Besides, for each itemset in H-tree, if it is not updated in the current time interval, we set its corresponding frequency to 0 in H-window. (4) Delete infrequent itemsets from H-tree. Call a *tail prune* function to tailor the H-window. A tail prune function will delete all the infrequent itemsets from H-window in a bottom-up manner.

In the last step, collaborative and comparative patterns can be retrieved by traversing H-tree. Given a query as in Example 1, H-Stream traverses H-Tree using a depth-first search until all the collaborative and comparative patterns are retrieved. Due to the limit of space, we omit the details here.

2.3 H-Stream Performance Analysis

We study H-Stream's performance from both accuracy loss and memory cost pointviews. As we discussed above, H-Stream uses parameters (δ-ϵ) to prune H-tree. Thus, we analyze H-Stream's performance under this prune method.

We use the *Chernoff bound* to analyze H-Stream's accuracy loss. Formally, each transaction in data streams can be considered as an observation. Suppose x is the expected support of an itemset X, $\overline{x}$ is the observed support of X from n transactions, and ϵ is the error bound that denotes the degree of $\overline{x}$ deviating from x. According to the Chernoff bound, we have the following Eq. (1),

$$pr\{|\overline{x} - x| \leq \epsilon\} \geq 1 - 2e^{\frac{-n\epsilon^2}{2x}}. \qquad (1)$$

Replace the right side of Eq. (1) with probability p, and let x equal to the min-support δ, we have Eq. (2) as follow,

$$\epsilon = \sqrt{\frac{2\delta \ln(2/(1-p))}{n}}. \qquad (2)$$

Since the transactions number per batch in each stream may be different, it is difficult to get the optimal ϵ for all streams. An alternative method is to set a global satisfactory solution for ϵ using the above Chernoff bound as in Eq. (3),

$$\epsilon = \sqrt{\frac{2\delta \ln(2/(1-p))}{min(||B_j||)}}. \qquad (3)$$

where $||B_j||$ denotes transactions number per batch in each stream. From Eq. (3), we can come to the conclusion that all frequent itemsets will be output with the accuracy loss of $(1 - p)$ at worst.

We use the *downward closure property* of the frequent itemsets to analyze H-Stream's memory cost. Suppose streams are composed of L items, and the average length of transactions is $\overline{S}$. Then we have Theorem 1. Due to the limit of space, we omit the proof.

THEOREM 1. *The upper boundary of the number of tree nodes in H-Tree is* $(2^{\lfloor \frac{1}{\delta - \epsilon} \rfloor \times \overline{S}} - 1) \times m$.

For example, let $\delta = 0.2$, $\epsilon \approx 0$, $L = 1000$, $m = 5$, $\overline{S} = 3$, the H-tree will maintain no more than $2^{15} \times 5$ nodes. This is much more efficient than the exact algorithm [1] that need to maintain a total number of $2^{1000} - 1$ nodes at most. So we can conclude that H-Stream scales well to multiple data streams.

3. EXPERIMENTS

News Report Streams were collected from three public social media: BBC, The Globe And Mail, and New York Times from July 22 to July 29, 2011. The news titles span over politics, technology, entertainment, and sports. In our experiments, a news title is taken as a transaction.

Table 1: Parameters used in the IBM data generator.

Parameter	S_1	S_2	S_3	S_4	S_5	S_6	S_7
tlen	3	3	3	3	3	3	3
nitems	7	7	8	8	6	6	7
npats	20	22	25	23	25	24	21

The IBM Quest Market-Basket Synthetic Data Streams were generated by IBM Quest Market-Basket Synthetic Data Generator [12]. The parameters of the data generator are listed in Table 1. We generated seven data streams, each having a batch size of 10,000 transactions.

[1]The exact algorithm maintains all the transactions in data streams for mining, which is supposed to be the best algorithm in term of mining accuracy.

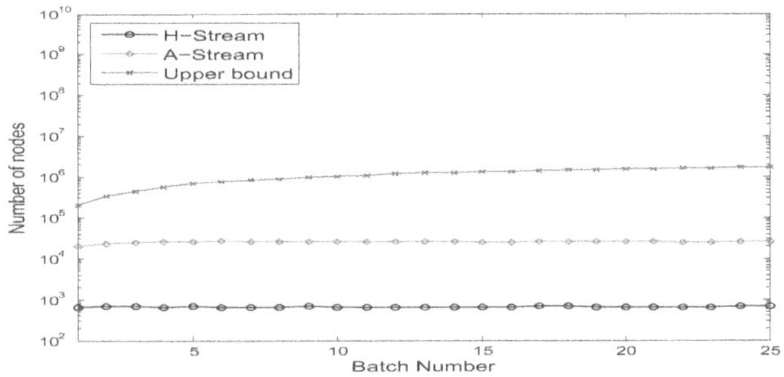

Figure 2: Parameter study on ϵ.

Benchmark Method We compare H-Stream with another Approximation Stream mining algorithm, A-Stream for short. A-Stream is a variation of H-Stream. Different from H-Stream that uses both ϵ and δ to prune H-tree, A-Stream uses only ϵ for pruning. In so doing, A-Stream can maintain more potential frequent itemsets.

Parameter Study on ϵ The error rate ϵ is an important parameter for pruning H-tree. The comparison results are shown in Table 2 and Fig. 2. From Table 2, we can observe that H-Stream and A-Stream perform almost equally well. From Fig. 2, we can observe that H-Stream maintains much fewer nodes than A-Stream. This also validates our claim in Theorem 1.

Table 2: Comparisons w.r.t. different ϵ values.

parameter	Stream	A-Stream		H-Stream	
	$s_1 - s_3$	Precision	Recall	Precision	Recall
$\epsilon = 0.0005$	s_1	0.912621	1	1	0.978723
	s_2	0.868000	1	1	1.000000
	s_3	1.000000	1	1	1.000000
$\epsilon = 0.001$	s_1	0.844311	1	1	1.000000
	s_2	0.733108	1	1	1.000000
	s_3	1.000000	1	1	1.000000
$\epsilon = 0.0015$	s_1	0.798867	1	1	1.000000
	s_2	0.638235	1	1	1.000000
	s_3	1.000000	1	1	1.000000

Parameter Study on m From Table 3, we can observe that H-Stream outperforms A-Stream in terms of Precision rate, and performs almost as well as A-Stream in terms of Recall rate.

Table 3: Comparisons w.r.t. different m values

parameter	Stream	A-Stream		H-Stream	
	$s_1 - s_7$	Precision	Recall	Precision	Recall
$m = 7$	s_1	0.912621	1	1	0.978723
	s_2	0.868000	1	1	1.000000
	s_3	1.000000	1	1	1.000000
	s_4	0.996296	1	1	1.000000
	s_5	1.000000	1	1	1.000000
	s_6	0.992620	1	1	1.000000
	s_7	0.902953	1	1	1.000000

Mining results from the real world news report streams Stream news received in one day will be taken as a batch. A keyword will be taken as a frequent item if it is reported no less than three times a day. Due to space limitation, we only summarize four interesting patterns as follows.

(1) The keyword *Norway* was reported frequently by all the three media from July 26 to July 27, 2011 (*collaborative frequent pattern*).

(2) The keyword *Olympic* was reported frequently by BBC, while infrequently by New York Times and The Globe And Mail from July 25 to July 29, 2011 (*comparative frequent pattern*).

(3) The keyword *China* was not only reported frequently by New York Times and BBC from July 26 to July 27, 2011, but was also reported frequently by The Globe And Mail from July 22 to July 25, 2011 (*collaborative frequent pattern*).

(4) The keyword *debt* was reported frequently by all the three media, while more frequently by New York Times from July 22 to July 29, 2011 (*comparative frequent pattern*).

4. CONCLUSIONS

In this paper, we study a novel problem of mining collaborative and comparative frequent patterns across multiple data streams. To achieve this goal, we propose a new frequent pattern mining algorithm called H-Stream. H-Stream uses a new H-tree to maintain historical frequent and potential frequent itemsets, and incrementally updates these itemsets for efficient collaborative and comparative mining. Theoretical and empirical studies have demonstrated the utility of the proposed method.

5. ACKNOWLEDGMENTS

This research was supported by the National Science Foundation of China (NSFC) under Grant No. 61003167, Basic Research Program of China (973 Program) under Grant No. 2007CB311100.

6. REFERENCES

[1] C. Giannella, J. Han, J. Pei, X. Yan, and P. S. Yu. *Mining Frequent Patterns in Data Streams at Multiple Time Granularities*. AAAI/MIT, 2003.

[2] G. Manku and R. Motwani. Approximate frequency counts over data streams. In *Proc. of VLDB 2002*.

[3] M. Charikar, K. Chen, and M. Colton. Finding frequent items in data streams. *Theoretical Computer Science*, 312, 2004.

[4] P. Zhang, J. Li, P. Wang, B. Gao, X. Zhu, and L. Guo. Enabling fast prediction for ensemble models on data streams. In *Proc. of KDD 2011*.

[5] P. Zhang, X.Zhu, Y. Shi, L.Guo, and X. Wu. Robust ensemble learning for mining noisy data streams. *Decision Support Systems*, 50(2):469–479, 2011.

[6] M. Yeh and et al. Clustering over multiple evolving streams by events and correlations. *IEEE TKDE*, 19, 2007.

[7] P. Zhang, X. Zhu, J. Tan, and L. Guo. Skif: A data imputation framework for concetp drifting data streams. In *Proc. of CIKM 2010*.

[8] V. Hristidis and et al. Information discovery across multiple streams. *Information Sciences*, 179(19):3268–3285, 2009.

[9] Y. Xu, K. Wang, A. Fu, R. She, and J. Pei. *Privacy-Preserving Data Mining, Models and Algorithms*. Springer, 2008.

[10] X. Zhu and X. Wu. Discovering relational patterns across multiple databases. In *Proc. of ICDE 2007*.

[11] J. Han, J.Pei, and Y. Yin. Mining frequent patterns without candidate generation. In *Proc. of SIGMOD 2000*.

[12] http://www.cs.indiana.edu/ cgiannel/assoc_gen.html.

SILA: a Spatial Instance Learning Approach for Deep Web Pages

Ermelinda Oro
Institute of High Performance Computing and Networking
of the Italian National Research Council
Via. P. Bucci, 41/C, University of Calabria
87036, Rende (CS), Italy
oro@icar.cnr.it

Massimo Ruffolo
Institute of High Performance Computing and Networking
of the Italian National Research Council
Via. P. Bucci, 41/C, University of Calabria
87036, Rende (CS), Italy
ruffolo@icar.cnr.it

ABSTRACT

Deep Web pages convey very relevant information for different application domains like e-government, e-commerce, social networking. For this reason there is a constant high interest in efficiently, effectively and automatically extracting data from Deep Web data sources. In this paper we present SILA, a novel Spatial Instance Learning Approach, that allows for extracting data records from Deep Web pages by exploiting both the spatial arrangement and the presentation features of data items/fields produced by layout engines of Web browsers in visualizing Deep Web pages on the screen. SILA is independent from the internal HTML encodings of Web pages, and allows for recognizing data records in pages having multiple data regions in which data items are arranged by many different presentation layouts. Experimental results show that SILA has very high precision and recall and that it works much better than MDR and ViNTs approaches.

Categories and Subject Descriptors

[**Knowledge Management (KM)**]

General Terms

Algorithms, Experimentation

Keywords

Web Information Extraction, Deep Web, Instance Learning, Web Wrapping

1. INTRODUCTION

The Deep Web is the part of the Internet that is not accessible by conventional search engines. Deep Web pages are dynamically generated from databases in response to queries submitted via search forms filled in by keywords. The Deep Web continue to grow as organizations and companies, operating in fields like e-government, e-commerce and social networking, make available their large amounts of data by providing Web-access facilities to their databases. Consequently, there is a constant high interest in efficiently extracting data from Deep Web data sources.

A large body of work on approaches for extracting data from Deep Web sources is already available in literature. Already existing approaches can be classified, for the scopes of this paper, in two main groups: (i) approaches that mainly use the internal representation of Deep Web pages [1, 5, 6], and (ii) approaches that exploit the visual appearance of Deep Web pages [2, 7]. Approaches in both groups are still limited in many aspects. Methods based on the internal structure of Deep Web pages suffer of the complexity of today Web pages encodings. In fact, they need to be updated for facing the adoption of new standards and tags. In particular, the growing adoption of scripts and CSS style sheets, for presenting data to human users, makes Web pages more complex than ever. Even if the layout of information on Web pages provides visual cues that help human readers to make sense of Web pages contents, current approaches that exploit the visual appearance of Web pages adopt page segmentation algorithms and heuristics that require specific and, sometime, complex tunings.

In this paper we present a novel spatial instance learning approach for Deep Web pages that exploits both the spatial arrangement and the presentation features of data records and data items/fields produced by layout engines of Web browsers. Main contributions are: (i) The definition of a novel spatial data model for Web pages named PDOM, i.e. Positional Document Object Model. (ii) A novel visual similarity measure that computes similarity between sets of PDOM nodes by exploiting their spatial and presentation features. (iii) The definition of an efficient and effective instance learning algorithm, based on a hierarchical clustering technique and heuristic aggregation methods, that allows for recognizing data records and data items in Deep Web pages independently from their visual arrangement.

The SILA algorithm has been tested on a dataset of 210 Deep Web pages randomly selected from most known Deep Web sites. Experimental results have shown the effectiveness of SILA. In particular, carried out experiments have shown that SILA: (i) allows for recognizing data records and items having any spatial arrangement and spread on multiple (data) regions of a single page. (ii) has very high precision and recall and works much better than already existing and well known MDR [1], and ViNTs [7] approaches.

CIKM '11, October 24-28, 2011, Glasgow, Scotland, UK.

2. A SPATIAL DATA MODEL FOR WEB PAGES

In this section we firstly introduce the notion of *Positional Document Object Model* (PDOM) of Web pages. Then we describe how PDOMs are created by considering both the traditional DOM representation and the spatial arrangement of Web pages obtained from layout engines of Web browsers.

A Web page can be seen as a 2-dimensional Cartesian plane on which are placed 2-dimensional objects (e.g. data records and items) surrounded by *Minimum Bounding Rectangles* (MBRs), as shown in Figure 1. In spatial reasoning [3], MBRs are the most common approximations of 2-dimensional objects because they need only two points for their representation in the Cartesian space. The concept of MBR is defined as follows.

Definition 1. Minimum Bounding Rectangle. Let o be a 2-dimensional object, the *minimum bounding rectangle* (MBR) of o is the minimum rectangle r that surrounds o and has sides parallel to the axes (x and y) of the Cartesian plane. We call r_x and r_y the segments that are obtained as the projection of r on the x-axis and the y-axis respectively. Then, each side of the rectangle is represented by the segments (r_x^-, r_x^+) and (r_y^-, r_y^+), where r_x^- (resp. r_y^-) denote the *infimum* on the x-axis (y-axis) and r_x^+ (resp. r_y^+) denote the *supremum* on the x-axis (y-axis) of the segments r_x and

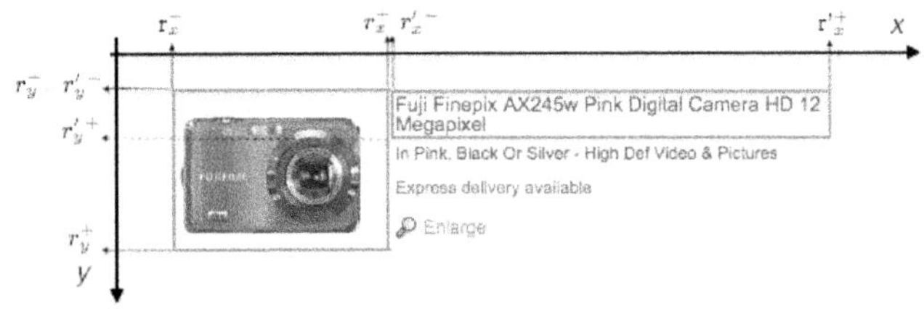

Figure 1: MBRs of DOM nodes

Considering MBRs, directional and containment relations among 2-dimensional objects can be simply modeled. For representing directional relations we adopt the *Rectangular Cardinal Relation* (RCR) spatial reasoning model [3].

We define the *Positional Data Object Model* (PDOM) of Web pages which the proposed spatial instance learning approach is based on. A PDOM is a tree structure where: (i) the parent-child relation represents spatial containment between nodes (PNodes) and (ii) each PNode, named *positional node* (PNode), represents one or more DOM nodes laid out on the screen by the layout engine of a Web browser. PNodes are equipped by both spatial (i.e. the position in which DOM nodes are visualized on the screen by the layout engine of a Web browser) and presentation features (i.e. font color, font or image size, font style, background color, borders, etc.). In order to explain why we adopt a spatial representation of Deep Web pages we point out that Web designers frequently use very involved and undergoing HTML structures for obtaining visual appearance of data records in Deep Web pages that make sense for human readers, as already discussed in [4]. Such structures pose many problems to already existing instance learning and wrapper induction techniques. At the contrary, the PDOM, allows for representing Web pages in a quite simple way. So, pages that show the same visual pattern to human readers, may have very different internal HTML encodings, as shown in Figure 2a-b. By the PDOM representation such pages can be made more easy to process for instance learning and wrapper induction approaches. Furthermore, frequently it is possible to obtain the same PDOM represetation for different pages as shown in Figure 2c-d.

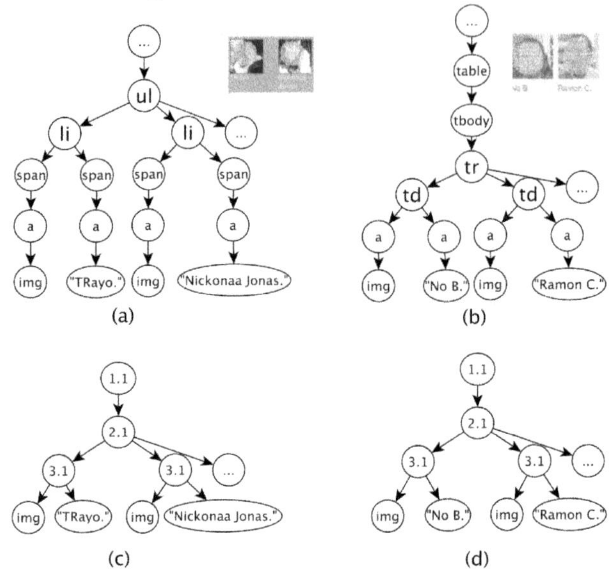

Figure 2: DOMs fragments of Web pages representing friend lists in social networks: (a) Care2.com, and (b) Bebo.com. PDOMs - (c) and (d) - representing the visual arrangement for page fragments in (a) and (b) respectively.

It is worthwhile noting that in Deep Web pages data records are usually arranged either as lists or matrices where data items can be indifferently organized in vertical or horizontal way as depicted in Figure 2.

A human-oriented visual pattern for data records can be obtained from very different HTML encodings. The PDOM has the property to generalize different possible HTML encodings by combinations of only four different structural patterns that we call: *standard*, *flat*, *nested*, and *non-contiguous*. In the *standard* PDOM record pattern, each data record is represented by a single PNode which subtree constitute all data items of the data record as depicted in Figure 4a. In the *nested* PDOM record pattern, groups of data records have a common parent PNode, as sketched in Figure 4b. In the *flat* PDOM record pattern, data items of data records of a data region have the same parent PNode, as shown in Figure 4c. Finally, in the *non-contiguous* PDOM record pattern, groups of data items of different data records can have different parents as shown in Figure 4d.

PNodes and the PDOM are formally defined as follows.

Definition 2. PNode. A PNode is a 3-tuple of the form:

$$PNode = \langle value, mbr, Style \rangle$$

where:

- *value* is the value of the PNode. The value is either a string or an url of an image.
- $mbr = \langle (r_x^-, r_y^-), (r_x^+, r_y^+) \rangle$ is the MBR (as defined in Definition 1) of the PNode. The MBR define the absolute position of the PNode on the screen.
- *Style* is the set of presentation features of the PNode.

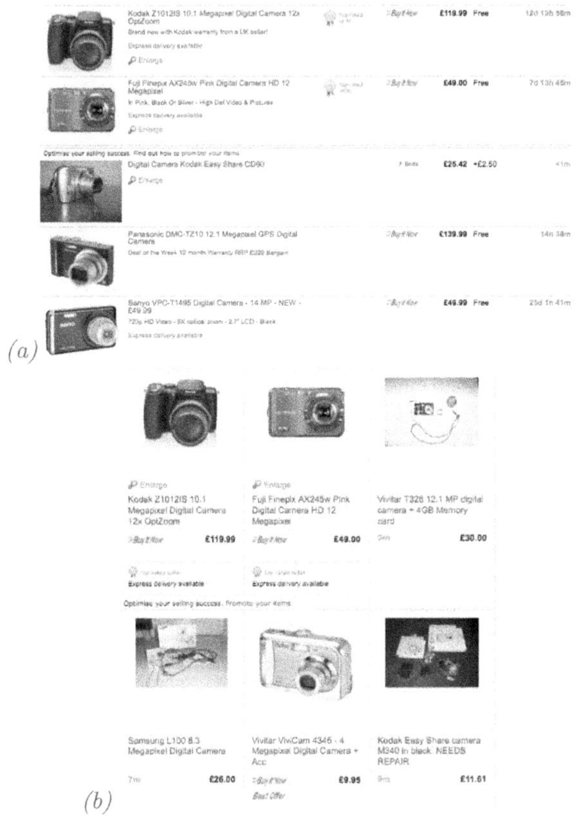

Figure 3: Examples of visual arrangements of data records in deep web pages: (a) list arrangement and (b) matrix arrangement

Definition 3. PDOM. A PDOM is a 3-tuple of the following form:

$$PDOM = \langle V, root, C \rangle$$

where:

- V is a set of PNodes (as defined in Definition 2).
- *root* is an unary relation, which contains the root PNode of the tree.
- $C \subseteq V \times V$ is the set of *containment relations* between PNodes. Let u and w be two PNodes in V, and $c \in C$ a containment relation, $u\ c\ w$ holds iff $mbr(u)$ contains $mbr(w)$ and there is not a third node v such that $mbr(u)$ contains $mbr(v)$ and $mbr(v)$ contains $mbr(w)$.

For computing the PDOM, the SILA system embeds the Mozilla browser by exploiting the Mozilla XULRunner[1] application framework that allows for implementing the function *mbr* (see Definition 1).

In the DOM there are chains of nodes that are rendered in the same MBR. For this reason, a PNode p can represents more DOM nodes. Let D be a DOM, a PDOM P is built on the base of the containment relations among the MBRs of nodes in D, starting from the root node of D. More in detail, for each pair of nodes u and v in D, we have:

[1]https://developer.mozilla.org/en/XULRunner_1.9.2_Release_Notes

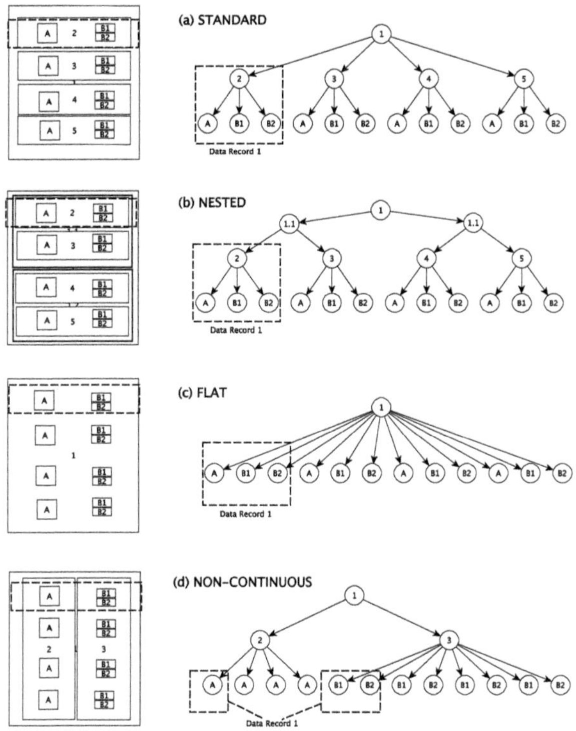

Figure 4: Structural PDOM patterns that represent the same visual arrangement of data records.

- iff $mbr(u) = mbr(v)$, then u and v are represented by the same PNode p.
- iff $mbr(u)$ *contains* $mbr(v)$, then u corresponds to a PNode p_1 and v correspond to a PNode p_2 and $mbr(p_1)$ *contains* $mbr(p_2)$.
- iff $mbr(v)$ *contains* $mbr(u)$, then v corresponds to a PNode p_1 and u correspond to a PNode p_2 and $mbr(p_1)$ *contains* $mbr(p_2)$.
- else, there exists two PNodes p_1 and p_2 such that $mbr(p_1)$ do not intersect $mbr(p_2)$.

3. VISUAL SIMILARITY

In this section we present a novel visual similarity measure that is one of the pillars which the instance learning approach proposed in this paper is based on. The main ideas which the visual similarity measure if founded on are: (i) a data record can be seen as a set of visually similar PNodes; (ii) two set of PNodes are visually similar if they contain nodes which leafs are spatially arranged in similar way on the rendered Web page and that have similar presentation features. Spatial arrangement of PNodes are computed by using the Rectangular Cardinal Relation model (RCR) [3] widely adopted in spatial reasoning. Roughly speaking, given a set of PNodes, the spatial context represents, for each pair of PNodes in the set, reciprocal RCRs. The spatial context of a set of PNodes is computed by means the function $Context : 2^V \rightarrow 2^{V \times V \times RCR \times RCR}$, that for each pair of PNodes in the input set of PNodes compare coordinates and computes direct and inverse RCR relations.

4. THE SILA ALGORITHM

In this section we present the spatial instance learning algorithm that extracts data records and items from Deep Web pages by exploiting visual patterns created by Web designers in order to help human readers in making sense of Deep Web pages contents. The Algorithm 1 takes as input a PDOM and returns a set of data records instances with aligned data items.

Algorithm 1. InstanceLearner
Input: A PDOM P;
Output: A set I of data records instances with aligned data items.
1.1: $Rs :=$ `findDataRegions`(P, λ);
1.2: $R :=$ `maxRegion`(Rs, μ);
1.3: $Rs' :=$ `similarRegions`$(R, (Rs - R))$;
1.4: **for all** $(R \in Rs')$ **do** $rs := rs \cup R.records$;
1.5: $I :=$ `getDataItems`(rs);
1.6: **return** I;

Algorithm 1 consists of the two steps described below:

1. *Data region and data record identification.* In this step (instructions 1.1-1.3), the PDOM of a Deep Web page is taken as input and a set of data regions, which are portions of Deep Web pages containing similar data records, are returned. The procedure **`findDataRegions`** collects PNodes that represent data regions by performing a depth-first search in the PDOM in input. The procedure **`maxRegion`** takes as input found data regions and a threshold μ, that represents the minimum number of records admitted for a data region, and chooses the region R that has the greatest area. Such a choice is due to the fact that in Deep Web pages the size of the most important data region is larger than the size of the areas of other possible data regions. Since, smaller data regions can contain the same type of records that are in the main region, the method **`similarRegions`** founds smaller regions similar to R. This way the instance learning algorithm allows for finding data records spread in multiple regions and discards only not relevant information.

2. *Data records and data item extraction.* In this step (instructions 1.4-1.6), the algorithm constructs final data records in which data items of the same semantics are aligned by means of the procedure **`getDataItems`**.

5. EXPERIMENTS AND DISCUSSION

The instance learning approach presented in the paper has been experimentally evaluated on a dataset of 210 Deep Web Pages randomly selected from most known Deep Web Sites[2]. Table 5 shows results obtained by applying the SILA algorithm, and compares such results with those obtained on the same dataset by applying MDR [1] and ViNTs [7] approaches. It is noteworthy that versions of MDR and ViNTS available on the Web allow for performing only data record extraction. Precision and Recall of SILA, in extracting data records, have been 99,79%, and 98,19% respectively. Whereas, MBR has Precision 25,61%, and Recall 46,75%, and ViNTs has Precision 53,57%, and Recall 50,47%. Precision and Recall of SILA, in extracting data items, have been 95,68%, and 99,40% respectively. Whereas MDR and ViNTs are unable to extract data items.

Sites	Data Records Extraction						Data Items Extraction	
	SILA		MDR		VINTS		SILA	
	P	R	P	R	P	R	P	R
Average	99,79	98,19	25,61	46,75	53,57	50,47	95,68	99,40

Table 1: Precision and Recall Scores for 210 pages from 70 Deep Web sites

6. CONCLUSIONS AND FUTURE WORK

In this paper has been presented SILA a novel spatial instance learning approach for Deep Web pages. SILA is based on: (i) the novel Positional Document Object Model (PDOM) that represents both spatial and presentation features of data records and data items/fields produced by layout engines of Web browser in rendering Deep Web pages; (ii) the novel visual similarity measure that computes similarity between sets of PDOM nodes by exploiting their spatial and presentation features. Such a measure considers two set of PDOM nodes similar if leaf nodes they contain have a similar spatial arrangement and similar presentation features on the Deep Web page. This visual similarity measure exploits the rectangular cardinal relation model [3] widely adopted in spatial reasoning. So at the best of our knowledge this is the first paper in which models and results coming from the spatial reasoning fields have been applied to automatic instance learning on the Web and Web information extraction. Experiments carried out on 210 Deep Web pages randomly selected from well known Deep Web sites, show very high precision and recall.

7. REFERENCES

[1] B. Liu, R. Grossman, and Y. Zhai. Mining data records in web pages. In *KDD '03: Proceedings of the ninth ACM SIGKDD international conference on Knowledge discovery and data mining*, pages 601–606, New York, NY, USA, 2003. ACM.

[2] W. Liu, X. Meng, and W. Meng. Vide: A vision-based approach for deep web data extraction. *IEEE Trans. on Knowl. and Data Eng.*, 22(3):447–460, 2010.

[3] I. Navarrete and G. Sciavicco. Spatial reasoning with rectangular cardinal direction relations. In *ECAI*, pages 1–9, 2006.

[4] E. Oro, M. Ruffolo, and S. Staab. Sxpath - extending xpath towards spatial querying on web documents. *PVLDB*, 4(2):129–140, 2010.

[5] N. K. Papadakis, D. Skoutas, K. Raftopoulos, and T. A. Varvarigou. Stavies: A system for information extraction from unknown web data sources through automatic web wrapper generation using clustering techniques. *TKDE*, 17(12):1638–1652, 2005.

[6] Y. Zhai and B. Liu. Structured data extraction from the web based on partial tree alignment. *TKDE*, 18(12):1614–1628, 2006.

[7] H. Zhao, W. Meng, Z. Wu, V. Raghavan, and C. Yu. Fully automatic wrapper generation for search engines. In *Proceedings of the 14th international conference on World Wide Web*, WWW '05, pages 66–75, New York, NY, USA, 2005. ACM.

[2]The adopted dataset, and a more complete version of experimental results, are available at www.icar.cnr.it/ruffolo/SILA/dataset

A Geographic Study of Tie Strength in Social Media

Jeffrey McGee, James Caverlee, Zhiyuan Cheng
Department of Computer Science and Engineering
Texas A&M University
College Station, TX, USA
jeffamcgee@tamu.edu, caverlee@cse.tamu.edu, zcheng@cse.tamu.edu

ABSTRACT

In this paper, we investigate the interplay of distance and tie strength through an examination of 20 million geo-encoded tweets collected from Twitter and 6 million user profiles. Concretely, we investigate the relationship between the strength of the tie between a pair of users, and the distance between the pair. We identify several factors – including following, mentioning, and actively engaging in conversations with another user – that can strongly reveal the distance between a pair of users. We find a bimodal distribution in Twitter, with one peak around 10 miles from people who live nearby, and another peak around 2500 miles, further validating Twitter's use as both a social network (with geographically nearby friends) and as a news distribution network (with very distant relationships).

Categories and Subject Descriptors: H.2.8 [**Database Management**]: Database Applications—*Data Mining*; J.4 [**Computer Applications**]: Social and Behavioral Sciences—*Sociology*;

General Terms: Measurement, Experimentation

Keywords: location prediction, spatial data mining, Twitter

1. INTRODUCTION

Online social networks are increasingly getting "geographical." Millions of online social network users are voluntarily sharing their location through location sharing services like Foursquare, short text status updates through real-time microblogs, and photos in online image hosts. This location information is increasingly being incorporated in social media for providing localized content, location-aware recommendations, and other geo-spatial enabled services. The access to the trails and connections among millions of social media users provides an unprecedented opportunity to study the relationship between the geographical properties of social media users and the social relations connecting them.

CIKM'11, October 24–28, 2011, Glasgow, Scotland, UK.

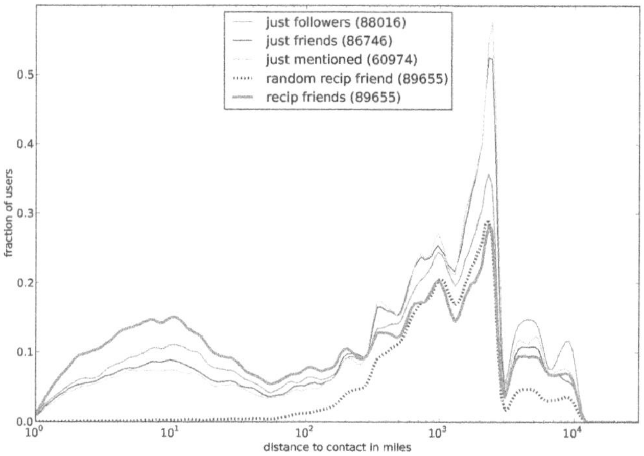

Figure 1: Smoothed histogram of distance to users for different types of relationships. The dotted black line was created by calculating the distance between random, unrelated users.

The study of geographical properties of online social media users has drawn intensive attention in recent years. Characterizing network properties in relation to local geography has been studied in [7]. Lindqvist [5] analyzed how and why people use location sharing services, and discussed the privacy issues related to location sharing services. Scellato et al. [6] used data from three location based social networks to investigate the relationship between distance and location, and they show that connections are not purely caused by geographical or social factors. Instead, the show that it is a mix of the two. We know of two previous systems that attempted to estimate the location of users on social networking sites: [1] and [2].

In this paper, we extend these works by investigating the interplay of distance and tie strength through a fine-grained examination of 20 million geo-encoded tweets and 6 million user profiles collected from Twitter. Concretely, we investigate the relationship between the strength of the tie between a pair of users and the distance between the pair. We identify several factors – including following, mentioning, and actively engaging in conversations with another user – that can strongly reveal the distance between a pair of users.

We find a bimodal distribution in the distance between Twitter users, with one peak around 10 miles from people who live nearby, and another peak around 2500 miles, further validating Twitter's use as both a social network (with geographically nearby friends) and as a news distribution network (with very distant relationships). Figure 1 gives a preview of this bimodal distribution for four basic types of relationships. The red curve represents a strong, reciprocal friendship whereas the cyan line represents a relatively weak relationship. The red curve has more users at a distance of ten miles than the cyan line, indicating that reciprocal friendships are more likely to be local.

2. DATA COLLECTION

To investigate how social relation and geographical distance between the relations correlate, we sample a dataset from Twitter. We first define a few terms to simplify the process of explaining how the data was collected. **Contacts** are defined to be the set of a user's friends, followers, and people who a user mentioned in her tweets (i.e., people the user speaks to). Twitter does not provide a mechanism to determine who mentioned a given user. Thus, only one-directional conversation is considered.

Any given contact can be categorized into precisely one of these four disjoint sets:

reciprocal friend The geo-located user follows this user and is followed back.

just friend The geo-located user follows this user and is not followed back.

just follower The geo-located user is followed by this user, but does not follow them.

just mentioned The users do not follow each other, but the geo-located user mentioned the name of the other user in a tweet.

We built a crawler to find these contacts for users who used Twitter's Location Feature to disclose their location.[1] The crawler sampled 19,877,804 geo-coded tweets by monitoring Twitter's public Streaming API between April 7 until April 16, 2011. In the dataset, users are filtered who have strict privacy settings, have neither friends nor followers, or posted fewer than two tweets in the sampled dataset. For each user in the geo-coded tweets, we use the median latitude and median longitude of locations of the user's tweets as an approximation of her home location. Some Twitter accounts, such as accounts that posted jobs, would move around faster than a human could possibly move. To account for this, the crawler calculated the distance between each tweet and the user's home location. The crawler ignored users if the median distance from their tweets to their home location was greater than 50 miles.

Users are considered to be in the US based on a simple bounding box, yielding 104,214 geo-located users. For all of the geo-located users with a home location in the US, the crawler used Twitter's API to download the users' friends, followers, and 100 most recent tweets. The crawler also downloaded the profiles for up to 2000 friends, followers, and people they mention in their tweets. If they had over 2000, it chose a random sample of 2000 profiles that included at least 25 of each of the four categories listed below. From the profiles, the crawler kept the users with a decodable location field and threw away the rest. From what was left,

[1]The crawler and scripts used for the investigation are available online: `https://github.com/jeffamcgee/friendloc`

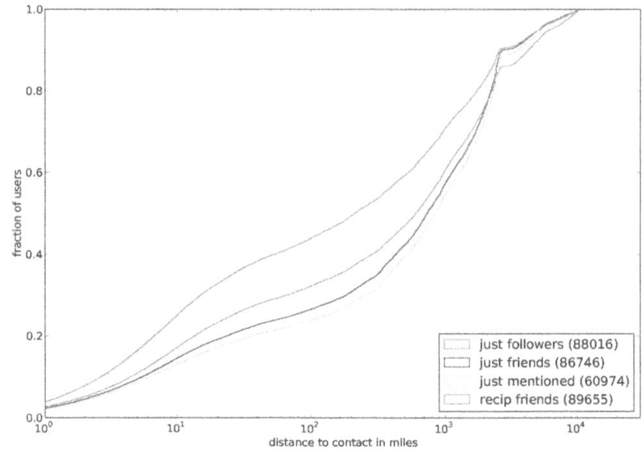

Figure 2: CDF of distance from geo-located users to users they have some contact with. The curves in this figure are the integrals of the curve in Figure 1.

the crawler randomly picked one Friend, one Follower, one Just Mentioned, and up to seven reciprocal friends. For each of these contacts, the crawler stored their friends, followers, and 100 most recent tweets.

We additionally geocoded each user's location field through a combination of extracting latitude/longitude coordinates via regular expression and by using Gisgraphy, which does full-text search on the GeoNames database using Lucene.

3. INVESTIGATION

In this section, we investigate how various types of contacts correlate with proximity. All of the analysis in this section was done on the contacts of 104,214 users with a home location inside the US bounding box.

3.1 What type of contact is closest?

Figure 2 shows the cumulative distribution function(CDF) of the distance between a geo-located user and several types of contacts. Distance is plotted on a logarithmic scale to show both local and global effects.

In general, reciprocal friends are the closest, followed by followers, friends, and finally users who are just mentioned. 34% of reciprocal friends live within 25 miles while only 18% of users who are just mentioned live within that radius. While it may seem that since being followed by someone and following someone should be identical, they are not. Celebrity and news accounts on Twitter often have large numbers of followers, but they normally do not follow a large number of users. Since the geo-located user was selected randomly, they are usually an average user and not a celebrity. If they follow someone, it might be a celebrity; however, if someone follows them, it is probably someone who knows them.

There is a strange corner in the top right corner of all the graphs at approximately 2500-2750 miles. This is caused by the large population living on the coast, and the minuscule number of people posting tweets from the Atlantic and Pacific oceans.

3.2 What is the distribution of contacts?

To understand the distribution of contacts, we created a

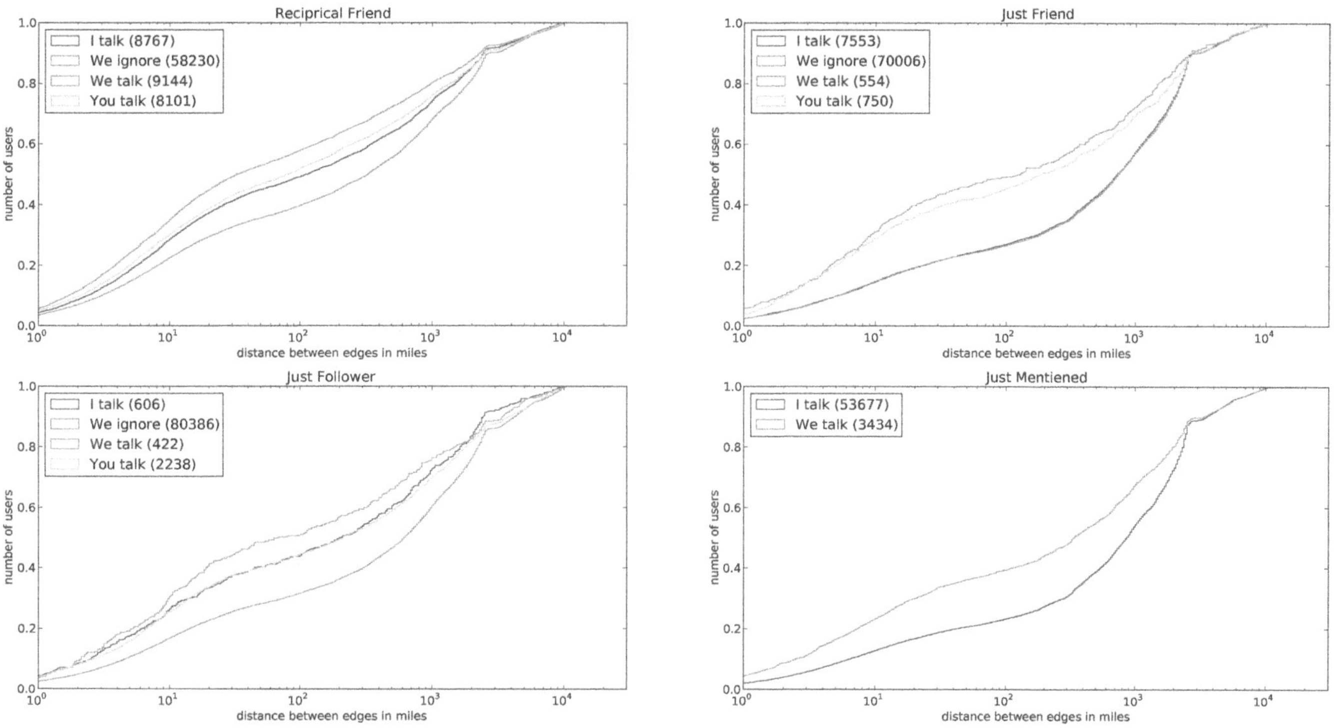

Figure 3: CDF of the distance between a geo-located user and various types of contacts piloted on a logarithmic scale. In these graphs, "I" refers to the geo-located user. "You" refers to their contact.

smoothed histogram. First, the distances between contacts are sorted into 200 logarithmically scaled bins (40 bins for each power of 10). Next, the curve is smoothed by convoluting it with a seven element triangular window. Figure 1 (on page 1) shows the result of plotting the smoothed histogram. All four types of contacts follow roughly the same bimodal distribution: one peak around 10 miles from people who live nearby, and another peak around 2500 miles, which is approximately the distance from coast to coast.

The geo-located users and their reciprocal friends were shuffled so that they would be paired with someone who was probably not their friend and then calculated the distance between the pair. The dotted black line shows the results of this procedure. For distances greater than around five hundred miles, the red line and the black line have roughly the same shape, which suggests that people when people are far away, their physical location no longer matters. The random line also has a similar shape to the other curves for distances greater than 100 miles.

One reasonable explanation for this is that Twitter is not just a social network; it is also a news distribution network (echoing the findings in [4]). This bimodal distribution suggests that users have two types of contacts: people who they met in real life, and people who they met online or know about via mainstream media. The former group is useful for predicting location and the latter group is not.

3.3 Are users closer to people they communicate with?

Figure 3 shows the relationship between various types of communication patterns between the geo-located users and their contacts. Each of the four graphs visualize the same number of edges on the social graph with the exception of the Just Mentioned graph. Approximately one-third of our geo-located users never mentioned someone who was not a friend or a follower, so the sample size is smaller.

In almost every case, increased communication increases the probability that two users live near each other. There is one exception: when an average user mentions someone they follow who does not follow them back, it has no effect. In other words, if a random user mentions a celebrity who does not bother to reply, they probably do not live in the same area. This can be seen by the blue and green lines that are right on top of each other in the Just Friend graph. On the other hand, in the rare event that someone who is just a friend replies to their follower, then the probability that they live near each other is much higher.

The weakest type of contact is for users who were just mentioned, but never replied to, but if the person is mentioned, then 31% of users with no friend/follow relationship who have a conversation live within 25 miles. This is approximately equal to the 31% of reciprocal friends who ignore each other and live within 25 miles. Unsurprisingly, the strongest type of connection is reciprocal friends who communicate.

3.4 Are users closer to private accounts?

Like many social networks, Twitter allows users to mark their account as protected. The specifics differ from network to network, but in Twitter's case a user has to be approved to follow a protected user. There are demographic differences between public and protected accounts. For example, Gilbert [3] demonstrates that rural users are more likely to make their accounts private than public accounts. In the case of protected accounts on Twitter, basic information

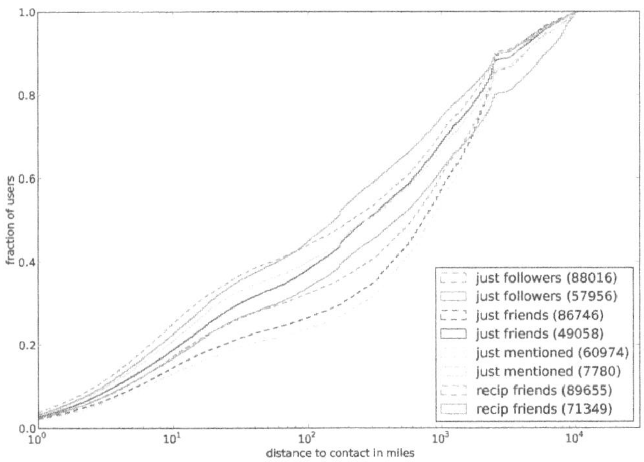

Figure 4: Solid lines represent protected accounts, and dashed lines represent public accounts. If a user follows a protected account, they tend to be closer.

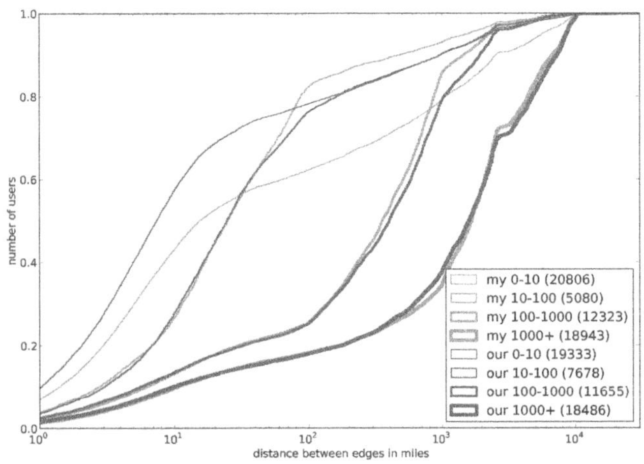

Figure 5: Comparison between distance to a mutual friend, labeled "our", and someone who is not a mutual friend, labeled "my".

about their profile such as their location and the number of friends and followers is public, but their friends list, followers list, and the text of their tweets is private, and not available for analysis.

Figure 4 shows the effect of protected accounts on proximity. The most dramatic difference between private and public occurs if a user follows a protected account. Since users generally only allow people they know to follow a protected account, this brings the users almost as close together as if they were reciprocal friends. On the other hand, if a protected account follows the geo-located user, this is almost insignificant.

3.5 If two of your friends live near each other, does that increase the chance that they live near you?

In this section, we turn our attention to triangles of users. Finding useful relationships between the edges of a social triangle is tricky because the three distances depend on each other. Unfortunately, it is fairly simple to show using the triangle inequality that if two users are 1000 miles apart, then the third member of the triangle has to be at least 500 miles from one of the other two. Since this isn't a useful result, we designed a more complex experiment to analyze the relationship between the sides of the triangle. A script searched for a specific pattern in the social network of the reciprocal friends. It needed four users who fit the following criteria: (i) "me" is the geo-located user; (ii) "you" is reciprocal friends with "me"; (iii) "my" has no relationship with "you" and is reciprocal friends with "me"; and (iv) "our" is reciprocal friends with both "me" and "you". It found this pattern in 57152 of the users in the training set. If a user had multiple instances of this pattern, it picked one of them randomly so that particular users would not bias the results.

Figure 5 shows a comparison between the "my" users and the "our" users. For each of the "my" users and the "our" users, we put them into one of four logarithmically scaled bins based on their distance from the "you" user. Then we plot the CDF for the distance to "me" for each user in the set. This allows us to investigate the effect of mutual friendship on distance. We report one very simple result: if two of your friends are close (within 10 miles), then whether they know each other or not is strongly affects how close you are to them. If they are farther apart, it doesn't matter.

4. CONCLUSIONS AND FUTURE WORK

We demonstrated that some types of relationships tend to be closer than others, identified some features of relationships that are correlated with physical proximity, and investigated how social triangles relate to physical location. Our analysis showed that people who have stronger ties such as reciprocal friendship and reciprocal communication are more likely to live near each other than people who have weak ties.

We are currently working on using the results of this paper to build a system for location prediction. We may be able to combine the results of tie strength with other factors such as the words users choose to use as described by Cheng [2].

5. REFERENCES

[1] L. Backstrom, E. Sun, and C. Marlow. Find me if you can: improving geographical prediction with social and spatial proximity. In *WWW 2010*.

[2] Z. Cheng, J. Caverlee, and K. Lee. You are where you tweet: a content-based approach to geo-locating twitter users. In *CIKM 2010*.

[3] E. Gilbert, K. Karahalios, and C. Sandvig. The network in the garden: an empirical analysis of social media in rural life. In *SIGCHI 2008*.

[4] H. Kwak, C. Lee, H. Park, and S. Moon. What is twitter, a social network or a news media? In *WWW 2008*.

[5] J. Lindqvist, J. Cranshaw, J. Wiese, J. Hong, and J. Zimmerman. I'm the mayor of my house: Examining why people use foursquare-a social-driven location sharing application. SIGCHI, 2011.

[6] S. Scellato, A. Noulas, R. Lambiotte, and C. Mascolo. Socio-spatial properties of online location-based social networks. In *ICWSM 2011*.

[7] S. Yardi and D. Boyd. Tweeting from the town square: Measuring geographic local networks. In *ICWSM 2010*.

Named Entity Recognition using a Modified Pegasos Algorithm

Changki Lee
ETRI
138 Gajeongno, Yuseonggu, Daejeon
305-700, Korea
+82-42-860-6879
leeck@etri.re.kr

Pum-Mo Ryu
ETRI
138 Gajeongno, Yuseonggu, Daejeon
305-700, Korea
+82-42-860-5327
pmryu@etri.re.kr

HyunKi Kim
ETRI
138 Gajeongno, Yuseonggu, Daejeon
305-700, Korea
+82-42-860-5965
hkk@etri.re.kr

ABSTRACT

In this paper, we describe a named entity recognition using a modified Pegasos algorithm for structural SVMs. We show the modified Pegasos algorithm significantly outperformed CRFs and the training time for the modified Pegasos algorithm is reduced 17~26 times compared to CRFs.

Categories and Subject Descriptors

I.2.7 [**Natural Language Processing**]: Text analysis.

General Terms

Algorithms, Experimentation, Languages.

Keywords

Modified Pegasos algorithm, named entity recognition.

1. INTRODUCTION

The named entity recognition (NER) task is one of the most important subtasks in natural language processing (NLP) and information extraction (IE). It is defined as the identification and classification of named entities in natural language text. While early studies were mostly based on handcrafted rules, most recent ones use supervised machine learning as a way to automatically induce rule-based systems or sequence labeling algorithms starting from a collection of training examples. Supervised machine learning techniques include Hidden Markov Models [1], Maximum Entropy Models [2], Support Vector Machines (SVM) [3], and Conditional Random Fields (CRF) [4].

In this paper, we present a NER using a modified Pegasos algorithm for structural SVMs. First, we describe structural SVMs [5][6][7] for NER. Then we extend the Pegasos algorithm originally designed to fit binary classification SVMs [8] to structural SVMs.

2. NAMED ENTITY RECOGNITION

2.1 Structural SVMs for NER

Structural SVMs are proposed for structured prediction problem by Tsochantaridis et al. [5]. Joachims et al. proposed 1-slack formulation to structural SVM [6]. It is based on an alternative formulation of the SVM optimization problem that exhibit a different form of sparsity compared to the conventional formulation. The 1-slack algorithm is substantially faster than existing methods like SMO and SVM-light.

Let $\mathbf{x} = \langle x_1, x_2, \ldots x_T \rangle$ be a sequence of words of sentences in a document. Let $\mathbf{y} = \langle y_1, y_2, \ldots y_T \rangle$ be some sequences of labels, each of which is associated with a named entity class and a boundary tag (i.e. B-Per, I-Per, B-Loc, I-Loc, B-Org, I-Org, O). Here is an example:

x:	U.N.	official	Ekeus	heads	for	Baghdad	.
y:	B-Org	O	B-Per	O	O	B-Loc	O

We used the margin rescaling formula of 1-slack structural SVMs for named entity recognition as follows:

$$\min_{w,\xi} \frac{1}{2}\|\mathbf{w}\|^2 + C\xi \text{ , } s.t. \text{ } \xi \geq 0 \quad (1)$$
$$\forall(\hat{\mathbf{y}}_1,\ldots,\hat{\mathbf{y}}_n) \in Y^n : \frac{1}{n}\mathbf{w}^T \sum_{i=1}^{n} \delta\Psi_i(\mathbf{x}_i, \hat{\mathbf{y}}_i) \geq \frac{1}{n}\sum_{i=1}^{n} L(\mathbf{y}_i, \hat{\mathbf{y}}_i) - \xi.$$

where C is a regularization parameter, $(\mathbf{x}_i,\mathbf{y}_i)$ is a training example, $\delta\Psi_i(\mathbf{x}_i,\mathbf{y}) = \Psi(\mathbf{x}_i,\mathbf{y}_i)-\Psi(\mathbf{x}_i,\mathbf{y})$, $\Psi(\mathbf{x},\mathbf{y})$ is a feature vector function, and $L(\mathbf{y}_i,\mathbf{y})$ is a Hamming loss function that counts the number of mislabelings for output $\mathbf{y}$ relative to the correct output, $\mathbf{y}_i$. Unlike regular SVMs, structural SVMs can predict complex $\mathbf{y}$ outputs such as trees, sequences, or sets.

Algorithm 1. 1-Slack Cutting Plane Algorithm

1: Input: $(\mathbf{x}_1,\mathbf{y}_1), \ldots, (\mathbf{x}_n,\mathbf{y}_n), C, e$
2: $S \leftarrow \emptyset$
3: **repeat**
4: $(\mathbf{w}, \xi) \leftarrow \arg\min_{\mathbf{w},\xi>0} \frac{1}{2}\|\mathbf{w}\|^2 + C\xi$
   $s.t. \forall(\hat{\mathbf{y}}_1,\cdots,\hat{\mathbf{y}}_n) \in S:$
   $\frac{1}{n}\mathbf{w}^T \sum_{i=1}^{n} \delta\Psi_i(\mathbf{x}_i,\hat{\mathbf{y}}_i) \geq \frac{1}{n}\sum_{i=1}^{n} L(\mathbf{y}_i,\hat{\mathbf{y}}_i) - \xi$
5: **for** i=1,...,n **do**
6: $\hat{\mathbf{y}}_i \leftarrow \arg\max_{\mathbf{y}\in Y}\{L(\mathbf{y}_i,\mathbf{y}) + \mathbf{w}^T\Psi(\mathbf{x}_i,\mathbf{y})\}$
7: **end for**
8: $S \leftarrow S \cup \{(\hat{\mathbf{y}}_1,\cdots,\hat{\mathbf{y}}_n)\}$
9: **until** $\frac{1}{n}\sum_{i=1}^{n} L(\mathbf{y}_i,\hat{\mathbf{y}}_i) - \frac{1}{n}\mathbf{w}^T\sum_{i=1}^{n}\delta\Psi_i(\mathbf{x}_i,\hat{\mathbf{y}}_i) \leq \xi + e$
10: return $(\mathbf{w}, \xi)$

To find this solution, Joachims et al. proposed 1-slack cutting plane algorithms [6]. The pseudo code of the algorithm is given in algorithm 1.

2.2 Modified Pegasos algorithm for structural SVMs

The Pegasos algorithm is a stochastic gradient decent (SGD) method that is originally designed to fit binary classification SVMs [8]. SGD methods use approximate gradients estimated from subsets of the training data and update the weights of the features in an online fashion. For large-scale problems, SGD methods are claimed to be sufficiently precise while delivering the best performance vs. training time trade-off [9]. Among SGD methods, the Pegasos algorithm has shown a promising performance for binary classification SVMs. The Pegasos algorithm shares the simplicity and speed of online learning algorithms but is guaranteed to converge to an actual binary SVM solution. The Pegasos algorithm minimizes the following objective function for binary classification SVMs.

$$f(\mathbf{w}; A_t) = \frac{\lambda}{2}\|\mathbf{w}\|^2 + \frac{1}{k}\sum_{(\mathbf{x}_i, y_i)\in A_t} l(\mathbf{w}; (\mathbf{x}_i, y_i)) \tag{2}$$

where $l(\mathbf{w}; (\mathbf{x}_i, y_i)) = \max\{0, 1 - y_i \mathbf{w}^T \mathbf{x}_i\}$ and $y_i = \pm 1$.

Parameter k is the number of examples used for calculating the subgradients, and A_t is the subset of training set $S=\{(\mathbf{x}_i,y_i): i=1,2,\ldots,m\}$ ($|A_t| = k$). The subgradient of $f(\mathbf{w}; A_t)$ is

$$\nabla f(\mathbf{w}; A_t) = \lambda \mathbf{w} - \frac{1}{|A_t|}\sum_{(\mathbf{x}_i, y_i)\in A_t} y_i \mathbf{x}_i. \tag{3}$$

The Pegasos consists of two major steps in updating $\mathbf{w}_t$: 1) substeepest gradient update $\mathbf{w}_{t+1/2}$ and 2) projection step. Specifically, in each iteration, the Pegasos looks for a steepest gradient search direction given A_t and projects the updated $\mathbf{w}_{t+1/2}$ onto the set $\{\mathbf{w}:\|\mathbf{w}\| \leq 1/\mathrm{sqrt}(\lambda)\}$.

We extend the Pegasos algorithm for structural SVMs. We replace the objective of Pegasos with an approximate objective function of structural SVMs by setting $\lambda=1/C$ (C is a regularization parameter):

$$f(\mathbf{w}; A_t) = \frac{\lambda}{2}\mathbf{w}^T\mathbf{w} + \frac{1}{k}\sum_{(\mathbf{x}_i, \mathbf{y}_i)\in A_t} l(\mathbf{w}; (\mathbf{x}_i, \mathbf{y}_i)) \tag{4}$$

where $l(\mathbf{w}; (\mathbf{x}_i, \mathbf{y}_i)) = \max_{\mathbf{y}}\{L(\mathbf{y}_i, \mathbf{y}) - \mathbf{w}^T \delta\Psi_i(\mathbf{x}_i, \mathbf{y})\}$

$\delta\Psi_i(\mathbf{x}_i,\mathbf{y}) = \Psi(\mathbf{x}_i,\mathbf{y}_i)-\Psi(\mathbf{x}_i,\mathbf{y})$, $\Psi(\mathbf{x},\mathbf{y})$ is a feature vector function and $L(\mathbf{y}_i,\mathbf{y})$ is a Hamming loss function that counts the number of mislabelings for output $\mathbf{y}$ relative to the correct output, $\mathbf{y}_i$. The subgradient of $f(\mathbf{w}; A_t)$ is

$$\nabla f(\mathbf{w}; A_t) = \lambda \mathbf{w} - \frac{1}{|A_t|}\sum_{(\mathbf{x}_i, \mathbf{y}_i)\in A_t} \delta\Psi_i(\mathbf{x}_i, \hat{\mathbf{y}}_i) \tag{5}$$

where $\hat{\mathbf{y}}_i = \arg\max_{\mathbf{y}}\{L(\mathbf{y}_i, \mathbf{y}) - \mathbf{w}^T \delta\Psi_i(\mathbf{x}_i, \mathbf{y})\}$

If we choose $A_t=S$ (i.e. $k=m$) on each round t, then we obtain the subgradient projection method. For the case of $k=1$, we obtain a variant of the stochastic gradient method.

A pseudocode of the modified Pegasos for structural SVMs (Pegasos-struct) is depicted in algorithm 2. The algorithm receives as input two parameters: T, the number of iterations to perform; and k, the number of examples to use for calculating the subgradients. Initially, we set $\mathbf{w}_1$ to any vector whose norm is at most $1/\mathrm{sqrt}(\lambda)$. On iteration t, the algorithm first chooses set A_t of size k in S (line 4), finds the "most violated" sequence of labels $\hat{\mathbf{y}}_i$ for $(\mathbf{x}_i,\mathbf{y}_i)$ in A_t (line 5), sets the learning rate (line 6), calculates $\mathbf{w}_{t+1/2}$ (line 7), and sets $\mathbf{w}_{t+1}$ to be the projection of $\mathbf{w}_{t+1/2}$ onto the set $\{\mathbf{w}:\|\mathbf{w}\| \leq 1/\mathrm{sqrt}(\lambda)\}$ (line 8). In line 5, $\hat{\mathbf{y}}_i$ can be found using the same inference algorithms (i.e. Viterbi algorithm) as $\mathbf{y}^* = \arg\max_{\mathbf{y}} \mathbf{w}^T\Psi(\mathbf{x}_i, \mathbf{y})$ because $L(\mathbf{y}_i,\mathbf{y})$ decomposes over variable subsets no larger than the subsets in the decomposition of $\Psi(\mathbf{x}_i,\mathbf{y})$. We adapted the Viterbi algorithm to solve the *argmax* in line 5.

Algorithm 2. A modified Pegasos algorithm for structural SVMs (Pegasos-struct).

```
1: Input: S, λ, T, k
2: Initialize: Choose w_1 s.t. ||w_1|| ≤ 1/√λ
3: For t = 1,2,…,T
4:   Choose A_t ⊆ S, where |A_t| = k
5:   ∀(x_i, y_i) ∈ A_t : ŷ_i = arg max_y {L(y_i, y) + w^T Ψ(x_i, y)}
6:   η_t = 1/λt
7:   w_{t+1/2} = (1 − η_t λ) w_t + (η_t / k) Σ_{(x_i, y_i)∈A_t} δΨ_i(x_i, ŷ_i)
8:   w_{t+1} = min{1, (1/√λ) / ||w_{t+1/2}||} w_{t+1/2}
9: Output: w_{T+1}
```

3. EXPERIMENTS

We used a Korean named entity data set that were annotated into 15 NE categories: *person*, *location*, *organization*, *artifacts*, *study fields*, *theory*, *civilization*, *date*, *time*, *quantity*, *event*, *animal*, *plant*, *material*, and *term*. We used two domains: a TV domain (TV scripts) and a food domain (food and restaurant articles). In the TV domain, we used 2,900 documents as a training set and 100 documents as a test set, respectively. In the food domain, we used 1,500 documents as a training set and 50 documents as a test set, respectively. Table 1 summarizes the characteristics of the data sets.

Table 1. Data set used in the NER experiments

Data set	Training data (#sent.)	Test data (#sent.)	#class	#feature
TV domain	105,265	3,719	31	281,696
Food domain	27,628	3,719	31	136,281

Because of the lack of capitalization in Korean orthography to mark a named entity, we could not use capitalization features. We use the following features for Korean NER:

- Word feature: orthographical features for words at position {-2,-1,0,1,2}.
- Suffix feature: suffixes of length 1~3 for words at position {-2,-1,0,1,2}.

- Part-of-speech (POS) tag feature: POS tag for words at position {-2,-1,0,1,2}.
- List lookup feature: list of entities and list of entity cues.
- Character level regular expression feature: such as [A-Z]*, [0-9]*, [0-9][0-9], [0-9][0-9][0-9][0-9], [A-Za-z0-9]*, …

We used 1-slack structural SVMs using a modified FSMO [10][11][12]. We implemented Pegasos-struct algorithm in C++. For all experiments, a linear kernel was used. Regularization constant C from {10, 100, 1000, 10000, 100000} was chosen based on optimization of the test set for all experiments. For a precise stopping condition, we set $e = 0.1$. In Pegasos-struct algorithm, we use $k = 100$ and $\lambda = 1/C$. For comparison, we also implemented the CRFs using L-BFGS algorithm. Gaussian prior for CRFs from {0.01, 0.1, 1, 10, 100} was chosen based on optimization of the test set for all experiments. We performed 500 iterations for training. All experiments were conducted on an Intel Core i7 CPU PC with 3.33 GHz and 12 GB of RAM.

Table 2. Performance of NER on TV domain

Method	Training Time (second)	Accuracy	F1
CRFs (baseline)	16,738	96.78	84.99
1-slack S-SVMs	11,239	96.92	85.14
Pegasos-struct	**649**	**96.94**	**85.43**

Table 2 shows the performance of NER on TV domain. We obtained the performance, 84.99% F1, 85.14% F1, and 84.3% F1 using CRFs, 1-slack structural SVMs, and Pegasos-struct respectively. We found 1-slack structural SVMs and Pegasos-struct significantly outperforms CRFs. The improvement of 1-slack structural SVMs over CRFs is highly significant with a significance level less than 0.01 using a paired t-test[1] (the two-tailed p-value is 0.0037). Pegasos-struct's improvement over CRFs is also highly significant with a significance level less than 0.01 using a paired t-test (the two-tailed p-value is 0.0018). However, the difference of Pegasos-struct and 1-slack structural SVMs is not significant (the two-tailed p-value is 0.69). Moreover, the training time for Pegasos-struct is reduced 26 times and 17 times compared to CRFs and 1-slack structural SVMs, respectively.

Table 3 shows the performance of NER on food domain. The improvement of Pegasos-struct over CRFs is highly significant with a significance level less than 0.05 using a paired t-test (the two-tailed p-values are 0.038). However, the improvement of 1-slack structural SVMs over CRFs is not significant with a significance level less than 0.05 (the two-tailed p-values are 0.102 respectively). The difference of Pegasos-struct and 1-slack structural SVMs is not significant (the two-tailed p-value is 0.38). The training time for Pegasos-struct is reduced 17 times and 3 times compared to CRFs and 1-slack structural SVMs, respectively.

[1] We used a paired t-test on labeling disagreements. We compared the correctness of the labeling decisions of two methods. The null hypothesis is that the disagreements (correct vs. incorrect) are due to chance.

Table 3. Performance of NER on Food domain

Method	Training Time (second)	Accuracy	F1
CRFs (baseline)	4007	96.83	88.54
1-slack S-SVMs	718	97.05	89.18
Pegasos-struct	**239**	**97.12**	**89.46**

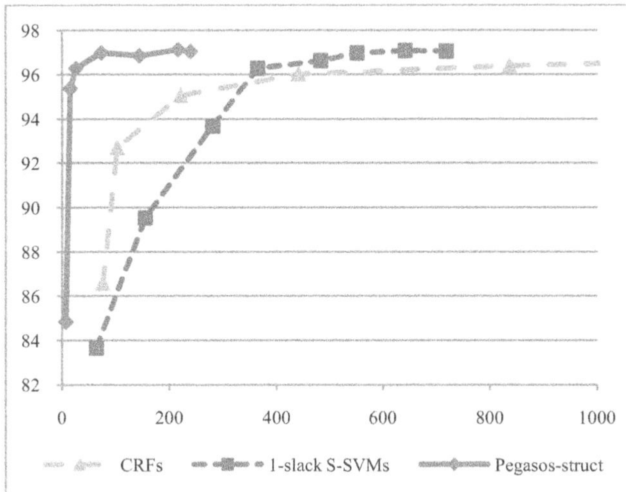

Figure 1. Accuracies of CRFs, 1-slack S-SVMs, and Pegasos-struct vs. training time (second) on Food domain.

Figure 1 compares the performances and training time of Pegasos-struct, 1-slack S-SVMs, and CRFs on the food domain. The Pegasos-struct and 1-slack S-SVMs have similar performance, but the Pegasos-struct is much faster than the 1-slack S-SVM and CRFs. We think that this is because the Pegasos-struct shares the speed of online learning algorithms but is guaranteed to converge to the actual structural SVM solution.

From our observations, we can conclude that Pegasos-struct and 1-slack structural SVMs significantly outperformed CRFs and the difference of Pegasos-struct and structural SVMs is not statistically significant. Moreover, the training time for the modified Pegasos algorithm is reduced 17~26 times and 3~17 times compared to CRFs and 1-slack structural SVMs, respectively.

4. CONCLUSION

In this paper, we described a named entity recognition using a modified Pegasos algorithm for structural SVMs. We showed that the modified Pegasos algorithm for structural SVMs significantly outperforms CRFs and the difference of the modified Pegasos algorithm and structural SVMs is not statistically significant. Moreover, the training time for the modified Pegasos algorithm is reduced 17~26 times compared to CRFs.

5. REFERENCES

[1] Daniel M. Bikel, Scott Miller, Richard Schwartz and Ralph Weischedel. 1997. Nymble: a High-Performance Learning Name-finder. In Proc. Conference on Applied Natural Language Processing, pp.194-201.

[2] Andrew Borthwick, John Sterling, Eugene Agichtein and Ralph Grishman. 1998. NYU: Description of the MENE Named Entity System as used in MUC-7. In Proc. Seventh Message Understanding Conference.

[3] Masayuki Asahara and Yuji Matsumoto. 2003. Japanese Named Entity Extraction with Redundant Morphological Analysis. In Proc. Human Language Technology conference, pp.8-15.

[4] Andrew McCallum and Wei Li. 2003. Early Results for Named Entity Recognition with Conditional Random Fields, Features Induction and Web-Enhanced Lexicons. In Proc. Conference on Computational Natural Language Learning, pp.188-191.

[5] Ioannis Tsochantaridis, Thomas Hofmann, Thorsten Joachims and Yasemin Altun. 2004. Support Vector Machine Learning for Interdependent and Structured Output Spaces. In Proc. International Conference on Machine Learning.

[6] Thorsten Joachims, Thomas Finley and Chun-Nam John Yu. 2009. Cutting-Plane Training of Structural SVMs. Machine Learning, vol. 77, no. 1., pp.27-59.

[7] Changki Lee and Myung-Gil Jang. 2009. Fast Training of Structured SVM Using Fixed-Threshold Sequential Minimal Optimization. ETRI Journal, vol. 31, no. 2, pp.121-128.

[8] Shai Shalev-Shwartz, Yoram Singer and Nathan Srebro. 2007. Pegasos: Primal Estimated sub-GrAdient SOlver for SVM. In Proc. International Conference on Machine Learning, pp.807-814.

[9] Leon Bottou and Olivier Bousquet. 2008. The Tradeoffs of Large Scale learning. In Proc. Advances in Neural Information Processing Systems.

[10] Changki Lee and Myung-Gil Jang. 2010. A Modified Fixed-Threshold SMO for 1-Slack Structural SVMs. ETRI Journal, vol. 32, no. 1, pp.120-128.

[11] Changki Lee, Soojong Lim and Myung-Gil Jang. 2010. Large-Margin Training of Dependency Parsers Using Pegasos Algorithm. ETRI Journal, vol. 32, no. 3, pp.486-489.

[12] Changki Lee and Myung-Gil Jang. 2011. A Prior Model of Structural SVMs for Domain Adaptation. ETRI Journal, (in press).

WikiLabel: An Encyclopedic Approach to Labeling Documents en masse

Tadashi Nomoto
National Institute of Japanese Literature
10-3 Midori Tachikawa
Tokyo 190-0014 Japan
nomoto@acm.org

ABSTRACT

This paper presents a particular approach to collective labeling of multiple documents, which works by associating the documents with Wikipedia pages and labeling them with headings the pages carry. The approach has an obvious advantage over past approaches in that it is able to produce fluent labels, as they are hand-written by human editors. We carried out some experiments on the TDT5 dataset, which found that the approach works rather robustly for an arbitrary set of documents in the news domain. Comparisons were made with some baselines, including the state of the art, with results strongly in favor of our approach.

Categories and Subject Descriptors: H.3 [**Information Storage and Retrieval**]: Information Search and Retrieval // **General Terms**: Algorithms // **Keywords**:TDT-5, Cluster Labeling, Topic Detection

1. INTRODUCTION

One curious aspect of the TDT (Topic Detection and Tracking) program organized by NIST [1], which ran from late 1990s to early 2000s is that it had completely shied away from addressing how to *name* topics or how one would give a verbal expression to what the topic is given a set of related stories, though its name suggests otherwise. One would suspect that the irregularity may have risen from the general difficulty at the time of labeling a set of documents in any systematic way. However, as pointed out in the past literature [6, 7, 2], in order for humans to make sense of document clusters, which usually amount to no more than a bag of words, it is critically important to label clusters with linguistically coherent expressions that would give a general idea of what the content is about.

Take for instance, two cluster labels A and B.

A	euro, debt, moody, greece, rating, european, bailout
B	European sovereign debt crisis

While it would be some challenge to make sense of A unless you are familiar with the European financial situation, B is more straightforward, quite sensible even if you are not a financial expert. The goal of the paper is to develop a systematic way of creating a readable label such as B, for a document cluster, through the use of Wikipedia. In contrast to the prior work [6, 2], which focus on constructing labels from textual resources in documents, we seek to create labels not by manipulating documents in question, but by deconstructing the Wikipedia into a collection of highly focused mini pages, and reusing their headings. Our work closely parallels yet differs from Syed et al. [7] in that we pursue an aggressive re-organization of Wikipedia pages to leverage concept generation.

Typically, a Wikipedia page (or Wiki page, hereafter) is organized into a hierarchical structure, with headings for sections, subsections, sub-subsections, and even smaller sections. Our idea is to break apart or 'deconstruct' the page along the hierarchical structure to create smaller segments focused on particular aspects of the concept that the page represents, and label a cluster of documents by retrieving a segment from the deconstructed Wiki that best matches the cluster and assigning it to a heading that the segment carries.

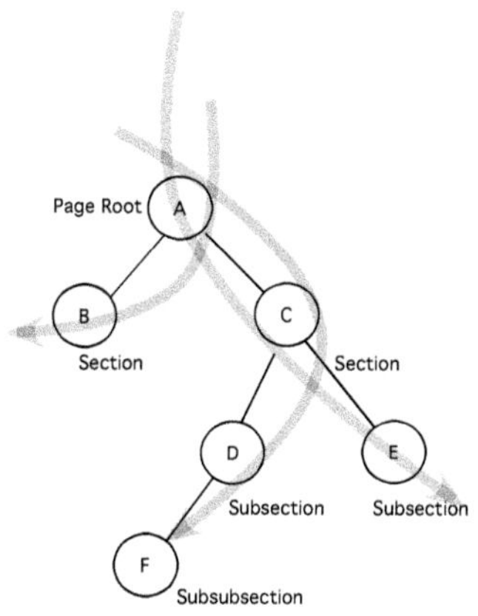

Figure 1: Deconstructing the Wiki page

2. DECONSTRUCTING WIKIPEDIA

Figure 1 gives a graphic view of how we deconstruct a Wiki page. Given a Wiki page consisting of one main section (A), followed by two sections (B, C), with C dominating two subsections (D, E) and D containing one subsubsection (F), we tear apart the page along the path from the page root to a terminated or non-terminated sectional node,[1] which leads to the creation of the following subpages, among others.

[1]A section node here is thought of as an XML node spanning a given region of text. A terminated (or non-terminated) node refers to one that does not contain any further sectional parts (or one that contains one or more subordinate sections).

CIKM'11, October 24–28, 2011, Glasgow, Scotland, UK.

$$p_1 = \langle \text{A} \rangle$$
$$p_2 = \langle \text{A B} \rangle$$
$$p_3 = \langle \text{A C} \rangle$$

p_1 denotes a subpage consisting of paragraphs appearing in the main section, i.e., a part that appears immediately after the main title. p_2 denotes a subpage consisting of the main section and a part of the page that immediately follows the section heading of B, i.e., a text fragment directly dominated by B. And similarly for $p_4 = \langle \text{A C D} \rangle$, $p_5 = \langle \text{A C E} \rangle$ and $p_6 = \langle \text{A C D F} \rangle$.

More precisely, we define the content $\mathcal{D}$ of a subpage p_i as combined contents of sectional nodes found on its corresponding path $\langle p_i \rangle$,

$$\mathcal{D}(p_1) = \mathcal{C}^+(A)$$
$$\mathcal{D}(p_2) = concat(Text(A), \mathcal{C}^+(B))$$
$$\mathcal{D}(p_3) = concat(Text(A), \mathcal{C}^+(C))$$

and its title $\mathcal{T}$ as combined titles associated with sectional nodes on $\langle p_i \rangle$

$$\mathcal{T}(p_1) = H(A)$$
$$\mathcal{T}(p_2) = concat(H(A), H(B))$$
$$\mathcal{T}(p_3) = concat(H(A), H(C))$$

where we set

$$concat(s_1, \ldots, s_n) = s_1 \ldots s_n,$$

and

$$\mathcal{C}^+(n) = \bigcup_{i \in D(n)} \{\mathcal{C}^+(i), Text(n)\},$$

where $D(n)$ denotes child nodes immediately dominated by n, and $Text(n)$ a span of text that immediately follows n's section heading. $H(x)$ indicates a title (heading) associated with a section node x. The deconstruction of a Wiki page in Figure 1 gives rise to mini Wiki pages, each corresponding to one of the paths $p_1, \ldots, p_6$, and each consisting of two elements $\mathcal{T}(p_i)$ and $\mathcal{D}(p_i)$. For the current work, we assume a section node to be that marked by the equal signs, namely, tags that mark section headings in Wikipedia.[2] In what follows, we refer to a deconstructed version of Wikipedia as a 'DeWiki.'

Obviously, there are as many DeWikis as there are ways to deconstruct Wikipedia: one may create a DeWiki solely made up of sectional nodes one edge away from the root, or one that includes nodes at the full depth. Wikipedia itself is considered a DeWiki which happens to keep the original structure intact (call it the first-order DeWiki). A DeWiki is said to be of second order if it consists of pages made up of the root and its immediate child nodes. We say that a DeWiki is of infinite order if its pages involve the deconstruction to the fullest extent, where each page has its paths expanded to the fullest. We stipulate that the n-th order DeWiki include pages whose path terminates earlier than n, in addition to those of the n-th order. Suppose we have a Wikipedia consisting of a single page shown in Figure 1. Then $\mathcal{W}^1 = \{p_1\}$, $\mathcal{W}^2 = \{p_2, p_3\}$, $\mathcal{W}^3 = \{p_2, p_4, p_5\}$, $\mathcal{W}^\infty = \{p_2, p_5, p_6\}$, where $\mathcal{W}^n$ denotes the n-th order DeWiki.

Given a set of documents, we are interested in generating their collective label through the deconstruction of Wikipedia. The label generation happens in three steps: (1) select terms representative of a group of documents; and (2) query the DeWiki using the terms; and (3) take titles of pages the DeWiki considers best matches for the query as a label for the document cluster. The advantage of using the DeWiki to generate labels lies in its strong ability to generate fluent and readable labels, though not much of a surprise, given that they are hand-created by human editors. However it is not immediately clear how robust it is against an arbitrary set of documents. We turn to this question in the experiment section.

[2]http://en.wikipedia.org/wiki/Wikipedia:Manual_of_Style

Table 1: TDT-5 Topic Profile

TOPIC ID:	55016
TITLE:	Gay Bishop
WHO:	Jeffrey John
WHAT:	Jeffrey John is appointed as Bishop of Reading, England
WHEN:	05/20/2003
WHERE:	Reading, England
TERMINOLOGY:	Reverend Canon Jeffrey Philip Hywel John Archbishop of Canterbury Rowan Williams

Table 2: Answer keys for link detection in lnk_SR= nwt_TE= mul,eng.key

Language	# topics	# on-topic docs	
English	100	4,501	
	# on-topic docs		
Language	min	max	avg
English	3	244	45.01

Assuming that θ represents a vector space model for a document cluster D, we define l^*_θ, a likely label for D, as follows.

$$l^*_\theta = \underset{l:p[l] \in \mathcal{W}^M}{\arg\max}\ Score(p[l], \theta|_N), \tag{1}$$

where

$$Score(p[l], \theta|_N) = \lambda \mathsf{COS}(p[l], \theta|_N) + (1-\lambda)\mathsf{OVL}(l, \theta|_N). \tag{2}$$

$\mathcal{W}^M$ represents the m-th order DeWiki, $\theta|_N$ a vector space model restricted to top N terms; $p[l]$ stands for a Wiki page with a title l such that $\mathcal{T}(p) = l$. $\mathsf{COS}(\mathbf{r},\ )$ indicates a cosine similarity between $\mathbf{r}$ and , while $\mathsf{OVL}(l,\ )$ represents a measure for the lexical overlap between l and . More specifically, we set

$$\mathsf{COS}(\mathbf{r},\ ) = \frac{\langle \mathbf{r},\ \rangle}{\sqrt{\langle \mathbf{r}, \mathbf{r} \rangle}\sqrt{\langle\ ,\ \rangle}}, \tag{3}$$

and

$$\mathsf{OVL}(l,\ ) = \frac{\sum_{i \in \mathcal{U}(l)} \sum_{j \in \mathbf{v}} w_j \cdot \delta(i,j)}{\sum_{j \in \mathbf{v}} w_j}. \tag{4}$$

$\mathcal{U}(l)$ indicates a set of unique tokens that appear in the string l, δ represents Kronecker's delta function, and w_j denotes a weight associated with the term j. We set λ to 0.5 unless otherwise stated. The model in Eqn. 1 takes a most likely label for a cluster D to be one whose page ranks highest among those found in the m-th order DeWiki, by the measure that $Score$ defines. $Score$ is akin to what [2] proposes, but unlike [2], it is designed to favor Wiki pages that closely match θ, as a measure against the semantic drift.

3. EXPERIMENT SETUP

We conducted evaluation using the TDT-5 corpus, which contains some 400,000 news stories, collected from Chinese, Arabic, English news sources including Agence France Presse (AFP), An-Nahar, Xinhua, CNN, the New York Times, from April to September 2003 [4]. TDT-5 comes with human judgments on relevance of news stories to a pre-defined set of 250 topics: TDT defines a topic as an event or an activity occurring at a specific point in time and space; Table 1 shows part of what is called a 'topic profile,' an event description intended to help the annotator decide whether a story fits a given topic [4].

Our experiment made use of a particular answer key set called "lnk_SR =nwt_TE=mul, eng .key," provided as part of TDT-5. The set consists of gold standard 'links,' each of which consists of a pair of story identifiers and a decision made by humans on whether they are related to a particular topic. Although the file contains links within and across several different languages, we decided to restrict ourselves to English links, i.e., links involving only English stories, since we were interested in using the English Wikipedia as part of WikiLabel (which denotes our approach). We created document clusters out of TDT-supplied links by grouping documents by their associated topics, and discarded documents not linked to any topic. This had left us with 4,501 documents, which together comprised 100 topic clusters. The clusters varied in length from 3 to 244 documents, containing 45.01 documents on average (Table 2). Following a labeling practice common in journalism,[3] we take a label for a news event to be a name of person, entity or incident closely associated with, or evocative of the event in question, in particular those that appear in title, who, what, and terminology sections of the TDT topic profile. Thus possible labels for the topic 55016 in Table 1 would include *'Gay ishop,'* *'Jeffrey John,'* *'Jeffrey John is appointed as ishop of Reading, England,'* *'Reverend Cannon Jeffrey Phillip Hywel John,'* and *'Archbishop of Canterbury Rowan Williams, '* and not '05/20/2003' or 'Reading, England,' as a date or a place name rarely becomes associated with a news event, except perhaps for '9/11.' In what follows, we call topic labels found in the TDT topic profiles 'TTLs.'

In order to put things into a perspective, we make empirical comparisons to some of the approaches either proposed or used as a baseline in the prior literature. In particular, we will look at TFIDF, T-score [2, 6] and an approach based on Kullback-Leibler (KL) divergence [6]. TFIDF represents an approach which consists of choosing k terms with highest scores in TFIDF from a cluster and presenting them in the order of their scores as a possible label for the cluster. On the other hand, T-score works by ranking bigrams found in a cluster, based on t-statistic and choosing as potential labels, bigrams whose internal words are found to be closely associated [3]. Mei et al. [6] took a step further when they introduced the KL divergence into the picture, providing the way to exploit the distributional similarity between a label and a cluster in cluster labeling. After some tinkering with their model, they arrived at the following formula (which we simplified for the sake of readability).

$$Score(l, \theta_i) = \lambda E_{\theta_i}[\mathsf{PMI}(w, l)] - \gamma \sum_{j \in S/i} E_{\theta_j}[\mathsf{PMI}(w, l)] \quad (5)$$

θ_i represents a multinomial topic model, i.e., a probability distribution of words in a cluster, l denotes a bigram label. PMI represents a pointwise mutual information. w stands for a word in a cluster. E_{θ_j} represents an expectation under θ_j. λ and γ are mixing parameters. S denotes a a set of clusters and S/i an S with a cluster i removed. In words, what the formula says is that a most likely label for a cluster θ_i is one that has a strong tie with θ_i in terms of PMI, and least tie with the rest of the clusters in S. The experiments below will look at how WikiLabel compares against the three baselines, TFIDF, T-score and the KL divergence on TDT-5.

[3]In its weekly report of trends in news coverage, PEJ (PEW Center for Excellence in Journalism) refers to stories covering events related to the Gulf oil disaster in 2010, collectively as 'BP oil spill,' or 'Oil spill,' those on the leak of classified war reports as 'WikiLeaks,' and those on incidents involving Sarah Palin simply as 'Sarah Palin' (http://www.journalism.org).

Table 3: DeWikis

SOURCE: English Wikipedia dump version 0406/2011	
ORDER	NUMBER OF PAGES
$\mathcal{W}^1$	3,914,761
$\mathcal{W}^2$	5,674,922
$\mathcal{W}^\infty$	7,583,458

Table 4 : Long vs. short labels

MAJOR	MINOR
Channel Islands	· History · 20th Century · World War II

Table 5: Performance with $\mathcal{W}^1$

k	TFIDF	WikiLabel	T-score	Mei et al. (2007)
1	0.1240	**0.3103**	0.1485	0.0761
3	0.1858	**0.4456**	0.2155	0.1063
5	0.1999	**0.4860**	0.2320	0.1153

Table 6: Short-label results with $\mathcal{W}^2$

k	TFIDF	WikiLabel	T-score	Mei et al. (2007)
1	0.1520	**0.3757**	0.1683	0.0971
3	0.1756	**0.4515**	0.2084	0.1119
5	0.1879	**0.4789**	0.2212	0.1194

Table 7: Short-label results with $\mathcal{W}^\infty$

k	TFIDF	WikiLabel	T-score	Mei et al. (2007)
1	0.1474	**0.3325**	0.1694	0.0907
3	0.1691	**0.4148**	0.2037	0.1074
5	0.1846	**0.4501**	0.2195	0.1188

Table 8: Long-label results with $\mathcal{W}^2$

k	TFIDF	WikiLabel	T-score	Mei et al. (2007)
1	0.1035	**0.2041**	0.1569	0.0704
3	0.1290	**0.2620**	0.2098	0.1012
5	0.1411	**0.2720**	0.2163	0.1089

Table 9: Long-label results with $\mathcal{W}^\infty$

k	TFIDF	WikiLabel	T-score	Mei et al. (2007)
1	0.0817	0.1409	**0.1470**	0.0572
3	0.1026	**0.1821**	0.1706	0.0843
5	0.1186	**0.2026**	0.1930	0.0969

4. RESULTS

Tables 5 through 9 show main results. Numbers given in each table represent ROUGE [5], a metric widely used in the IR and Natural Language Processing communities to measure the quality of a machine generated summary. In this study, we made use of a particular version of ROUGE called ROUGE-W, which estimates the degree of similarity between a pair of strings in terms of the normalized length of a longest subsequence that the two strings have in common. The value of ROUGE-W ranges from 0 (zero match) to 1 (perfect match). For each topic profile, we compute the string similarity $\mathcal{R}$ between labels ($\mathcal{C}$) generated by a model in Eqn. 1 and TTLs ($\mathcal{L}$) associated with that profile.[4] $\mathcal{R}$ seeks the best match between a candidate label and a TTL, and takes its ROUGE as an indicator of a model's performance.[5] Figures we report in

[4]We define $\mathcal{R}$ as $\mathcal{R}(\mathcal{C}|_k, \mathcal{L}) = \max_{i \in \mathcal{C}|_k} \mathsf{ROUGE}(i, \mathcal{L})$, where $\mathcal{C}|_k$ denotes top k candidate labels generated by Eqn. 1. Moreover, we let $\mathsf{ROUGE}(i, \mathcal{L}) = \max_{j \in \mathcal{L}} \mathsf{ROUGE\text{-}W}(i, j)$.

[5]Note that $\mathcal{R}$ gives a score based on the one-on-one similarity between a label and a TTL that best matches that label. This is because in contrast to text summarization where we need to recover as much of content in the original summary as possible, we do not need all the TTLs to make a sensible label for a cluster: we chose to limit ourselves to one TTL here.

Tables 5 through 9 represent $\mathcal{R}$ scores averaged over 100 topics. Table 3 gives some details on how large DeWikis we used were. The infinite order DeWiki has grown about twice as large as the first order DeWiki. As a seed Wikipedia, we made use of an English Wikipedia dump created on 04/06, 2011.

Table 5 shows performance of WikiLabel, run with the first-order DeWiki, along with the baselines. Note that labels generated by the baselines are made as long or as short as those generated by WikiLabel, which may vary in length. The results clearly indicate that WikiLabel is by far the most successful among the competing models. Table 6 shows short label performance with WikiLabel running with the second order DeWiki. 'Short label' means that WikiLabel outputs labels composed entirely of a main page heading. Shown in Table 4 are some headings from a Wiki page on Channel Islands. The main heading is 'Channel Islands,' followed by some minor headings. We refer to a full-length title (which includes all the relevant minor headings) as a long label. Of particular note in Table 6 is that WikiLabel produces a ROUGE score of 0.3757 at $k = 1$ for $\mathcal{W}^2$, which is much higher than the corresponding score in $\mathcal{W}^1$ (i.e., seed Wiki) of 0.3103, demonstrating the effectiveness of deconstruction. As we go further with the deconstruction, however, we gradually lose the lead over WikiLabel with $\mathcal{W}^1$, though we sustain the edge over $\mathcal{W}^1$ at $k = 1$ with $\mathcal{W}^\infty$. We find that the use of a long label, which retains all headings in a Wiki page, results in performance far worse than short labels. This may be an indication that minor headings, being made up of attributional expressions such as 'history,' 'geography,' are rarely of use in predicting TTLs.

5. DETECTING MEDIA EVENTS

In order to see how well WikiLabel works for live data, we conducted a run of 'more informal' experiments where we applied WikiLabel to 5,759 news stories collected mostly from online media outlets in the US, during July 26 - August 1, 2010. The sources included the New York Times, Yahoo! News, CNN, MSNBC, Fox, Washington Post, ABC, BBC, and Reuters. We randomly created 1,000 clusters, using Apache Mahout/Kmeans.[6] For each of the clusters we created, we ran WikiLabel, harnessed with the second order DeWiki ($\mathcal{W}^2$), and assigned it to a top scoring short label WikiLabel generated for the cluster (i.e., $\mathcal{C}|_1$).

For the validity of labels assigned to clusters, we tuned to PEJ, a non-profit media watchdog based in the US, which manually creates on a weekly basis, a quantitative measure of how much the US media covered on particular news topics, known as News Coverage Index (NCI).[7] We examined how closely labels generated by WikiLabel correspond to news topics NCI identified.

The top panel in Figure 2 shows some of the labels assigned by WikiLabel, ordered in accordance to the size of the associated cluster. The y-axis represents the number of stories that fell under a given label. The bottom panel indicates the NCI for July 26 - August 1, 2010.[8] The y-axis represents the proportion of media coverage on a given topic. In its analysis of NCI for the week, PEJ explains that topic 'WikiLeaks' is meant to represent coverage related to the leak of massive US war reports in Afghanistan, while 'Immigration' is about the debate on a new immigration law in the US, aka Arizona SB 1070. The third leading topic, 'Oil spill' refers to the media coverage on the oil spill caused by an accident at BP's Deepwater Horizon oil rig in the Gulf of Mexico. Tony Hayward was a president of BP at the time. As it turns out, some of the major topics detected by WikiLabels such as *'Afghan War documents leak,' '(Timeline of the) Deepwater Horizon oil spill,' 'Illegal immigration to the United States,' 'Arizona S 1070,'* are fairly close to those found by PEJ, which could be considered an important, though informal, vindication of the former.

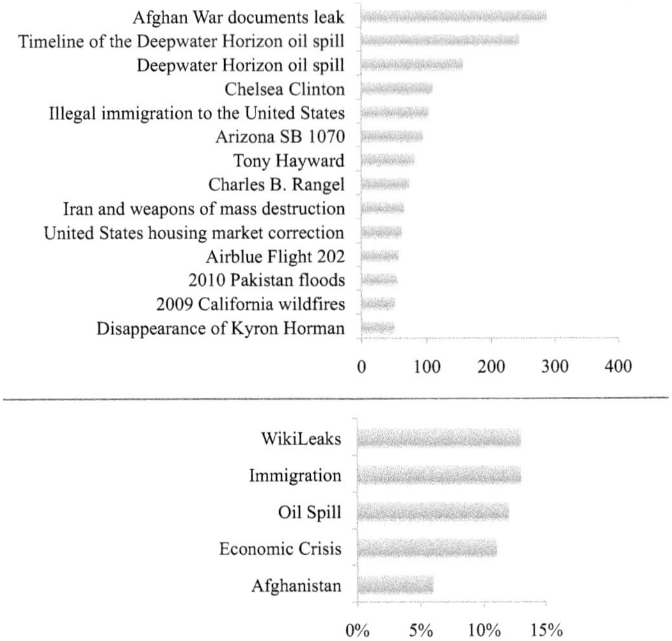

Figure 2: WikiLabel ($\mathcal{W}^2$) vs. PEJ's NCI

6. CONCLUSIONS

This paper has presented a novel approach to collectively labeling a cluster of documents, which essentially views cluster labeling as search over the deconstructed Wikipedia for a page that fits terms representative of the cluster. The approach is a departure from the past work, in that it seeks to create labels not by manipulating documents in question, as most prior work did, but by manipulating the Wikipedia, in particular transforming it into a collection of highly focused mini pages. The experiments with TDT-5 found the significant lead of the present approach over the baselines. Also preliminary experiments with the real world data seem to indicate that our approach is generally on a par with manual labeling.

7. REFERENCES

[1] J. Allen, editor. *Topic Detection and Tracking Event-based Information Organization.* Springer, 2002.

[2] D. Carmel, H. Roitman, and N. Zwerding. Enhancing cluster labeling using wikipedia. In *Proc. of SIGIR'09*, 2009.

[3] K. Church, W. Gale, P. Hanks, and D. Hindle. Using statistics in lexical analysis. In U. Zernik, editor, *exical Acquisition Exploiting On- ine Resources to uild a exicon.* 1991.

[4] M. Glenn, S. Strassel, J. Kong, and K. Maeda. TDT5 Topics and Annotations, 2006. Linguistic Data Consortium.

[5] C.-Y. Lin. Rouge: a package for automatic evaluation of summaries. In *Proc. of WAS 2004*, 2004.

[6] Q. Mei, X. Shen, and C. Zhai. Automatic labeling of multinomial topic models. In *Proc. of KDD'07*, 2007.

[7] Z. S. Syed, T. Finin, and A. Joshi. Wikipedia as an ontology for describing documents. In *Proc. of the Second Conference on Weblogs and Social Media*, 2008.

[6]http://www.mahout.apache.org

[7]http://www.journalism.org/about_news_index/methodology

[8]PEJ does not provide NCIs for topics that rank below top 5.

Towards Noise-Resilient Document Modeling

Tao Yang
The Pennsylvania State University
University Park, PA 16802, USA
tyang@ist.psu.edu

Dongwon Lee*
The Pennsylvania State University
University Park, PA 16802, USA
dongwon@psu.edu

ABSTRACT

We introduce a generative probabilistic document model based on latent Dirichlet allocation (LDA), to deal with textual errors in the document collection. Our model is inspired by the fact that most large-scale text data are machine-generated and thus inevitably contain many types of noise. The new model, termed as TE-LDA, is developed from the traditional LDA by adding a switch variable into the term generation process in order to tackle the issue of noisy text data. Through extensive experiments, the efficacy of our proposed model is validated using both real and synthetic data sets.

Categories and Subject Descriptors

H.1.0 [**Information Systems**]: Models and Principles

General Terms

Algorithms, Theory

Keywords

Topic Models, Textual Errors

1. INTRODUCTION

Probabilistic topic models are stochastic models for text documents, which explicitly model topics in the document corpus. As generative models, they describe a procedure for generating documents using a series of probabilistic steps. Since it was introduced in 2003 [1], the latent Dirichlet allocation (LDA) model has quickly become a powerful tool for statistical analysis of text documents. LDA assumes that text documents are mixtures of hidden topics and applies Dirichlet prior distribution over the latent topic distribution of a document having multiple topics. Also, it assumes that topics are probability distribution of words and words are sampled independently from a mixture of multinomials. Therefore, LDA is a widely used Bayesian topic model which can model the semantic relations between topics and words for document corpora.

(a) typewritten text

OCR A: RAILWAY mmmSBZ
OCR B: RAILWAY ANSP
OCR C: RAILWAI TRANSPORT

(b) OCR output

Figure 1: Three examples of erroneous OCR output of a poor quality typewritten text (taken from [2]). Erroneous outputs are underlined.

LDA requires accurate counts of the occurrences of words in order to estimate the parameters of the model, Therefore, it assumes that the entire document corpus is clean in order to ensure correct calculation of frequencies of words. However, as text data become available in massive quantities, textual errors are appearing inevitable in large-scale document corpora. These textual errors include typos, spelling errors, transcription errors caused by text or speech recognition tools, digitization errors of Google Books and Internet Archives, etc. For example, Walker et al. [2] point out that although researchers are having increasing levels of success in digitizing hand-written manuscripts, error rates remain significantly high. Figure 1 shows an example of typewritten documents and output by three Optical Character Recognition (OCR) engines. Even on clean data, LDA will often do poorly if the very simple feature selection steps of removing stop-words is not performed first. It is shown that the performance in terms of accuracy declines significantly as word error rates increase [2], which highlights the importance of taking into account the noisy data issue in document modeling.

Motivated by the above observations, in this paper, we introduce our new model to tackle the issue of noisy data. In particular, we propose a new LDA model termed as TE-LDA to take into account textual errors in the document generation process. We compare the performance of our new model against the traditional LDA model and report promising results of our proposal in terms of perplexity. Through extensive experiments, the efficacy of our proposed models is validated using both real and synthetic data sets.

*Partially supported by NSF DUE-0817376 and DUE-0937891 awards.

CIKM'11, October 24–28, 2011, Glasgow, Scotland, UK.

2. RELATED WORK

Probabilistic document modeling has recently received tremendous attention in the data mining community. A series of probabilistic models including the Naive Bayesian model and the Probabilistic Latent Semantic Indexing (PLSI) model have been introduced to simulate the document generation process. The LDA model has become most popular in the data mining and information retrieval community due to its solid theoretical statistical foundation and promising performance. A wide variety of extensions of LDA model have been proposed for different modeling purposes in different contexts. For example, the correlated LDA model learns topics simultaneously from images and caption words [3].

However, topic modeling techniques require clean document corpus. This is to prevent the model from confusing patterns which emerge in the noisy data. Recent work by Walker [2] is the first comprehensive study of document clustering and LDA on synthetic and real-word Optical Character Recognition data. The character-level textual errors introduced by OCR engines serve as baseline document corpora to understand the accuracy of document modeling in erroneous environment. The study shows that the performance of topic modeling algorithms degrades significantly as word error rates increase.

3. LDA MODEL

In this section, we give a brief overview of the LDA model. Blei et al. [1] introduced it as a semantically consistent topic model, which attracted a considerable interest from both the statistical machine learning and natural language processing communities. LDA models documents by assuming that a document is composed by a mixture of hidden topics and that each topic is characterized by a probability distribution over words. The model is shown as a graphical model in Figure 2(a). The notation is shown in Table 1. θ_d denotes a T-dimensional probability vector and represents the topic distribution of document d. ϕ_t denotes a W-dimensional probability vector where $\phi_{t,w}$ specifies the probability of generating word w given topic t. $Multi(.)$ denotes multinomial distribution. $Dir(.)$ denotes Dirichlet distribution. α is a T-dimensional parameter vector of the Dirichlet distribution over θ_d, and β is a W-dimensional parameter vector of the Dirichlet distribtion over ϕ_t. The process of generating documents is shown in Algorithm 1.

Algorithm 1: LDA Model.

1. For each of the T topics t, sample a multinomial distribution ϕ_t from a Dirichlet distribution with prior β;
2. For each of the D documents d, sample a multinomial distribution θ_d from a Dirichlet distribution with prior α;
3. For each word $w_{d,i}$ in document d, sample a topic $z_{d,i}$ from the multinomial distribution θ_d;
4. Sample word $w_{d,i}$ from the multinomial distribution $\phi_{z_{d,i}}$.

4. PROPOSED MODEL

To overcome the constraints of the above traditional LDA topic model, in this section, we propose a new LDA model

Table 1: Notations

Symbol	Description
D	total number of documents
W	total number of word tokens
T	total number of topics
N_d	the number of words in document d
$w_{d,i}$	ith word in document d
$z_{d,i}$	latent topic at ith word in document d
$\theta_{d,i}$	probability of topic i in document d
$\phi_{t,w}$	probability of word w in topic t

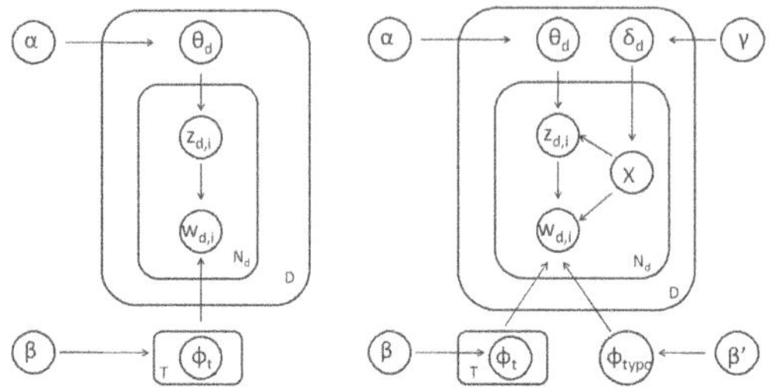

(a) LDA Model. (b) TE-LDA Model.

Figure 2: Comparison between our model vs. LDA model.

termed as TE-LDA (LDA with **T**extual **E**rrors) to take into account noisy data in the document generation process. In this model, we distinguish the words in the documents and separate them as tokens and typos. Given a document, each word has a probability to be an error and we want to capture this probability structure in the term generation process. In order to reflect the nature of textual errors in the generative model, we adopt a switch variable to control the influence of errors on the term generation. The proposed model is illustrated in Figure 2(b). N_d is the total number of words in document d (with $N_d = N_{term} + N_{typo}$, the sum of all the true terms and typos). α, β and β' are Dirichlet priors, θ_d is the topic-document distribution, ϕ_t is the term-topic distribution. ϕ_{typo} is the term distribution specifically for typos. We include an additional binomial distribution δ with a Beta prior of γ which controls the fraction of errors.

For each word w in a document d, a topic z is sampled first and then the word w is drawn conditional on the topic. The document d is generated by repeating the process N_d times. To decide if each word is an error or not, a switch variable X is introduced. The value of X (which is 0 or 1) is sampled based on a binomial distribution δ with a Beta prior of γ. When the sampled value of X equals 1, the word w is drawn from the topic z_t which is sampled from the topics learned from the words in document d. When the value of X equals 0, the word w is drawn directly from the term distribution for errors. Overall, the generation process for TE-LDA can be described in Algorithm 2. We omit the derivation of parameter estimation due to space limit.

5. EXPERIMENTAL VALIDATION

We trained our new model as well as the traditional LDA model on both synthetic and real text corpora to compare the generalization performance. Each model was trained on 90% of the documents in each data set and the trained model was used to calculate the estimates of the marginal log-likelihood of the remaining 10% of documents.

Algorithm 2: TE-LDA Model.

For each of the D documents d , sample $\theta_d \sim$ Dir(α)and $\delta_d \sim$ Beta(γ);
For each of the T topics t, sample $\phi_t \sim$ Dir(β);
Sample $\phi_{typo} \sim$ Dir(β');
foreach N_d *words* $w_{d,i}$ *in document* d **do**
    Sample a flag $X \sim$ Binomial(δ_d);
    if $X = 1$ **then**
        Sample a topic $z_{d,i} \sim$ Multi(θ_d);
        Sample a word $w_{d,i} \sim$ Multi($\phi_{z_{d,i}}$);
    endif
    if $X = 0$ **then**
        Sample a word $w_{d,i} \sim$ Multi(ϕ_{typo});
    endif
endfch

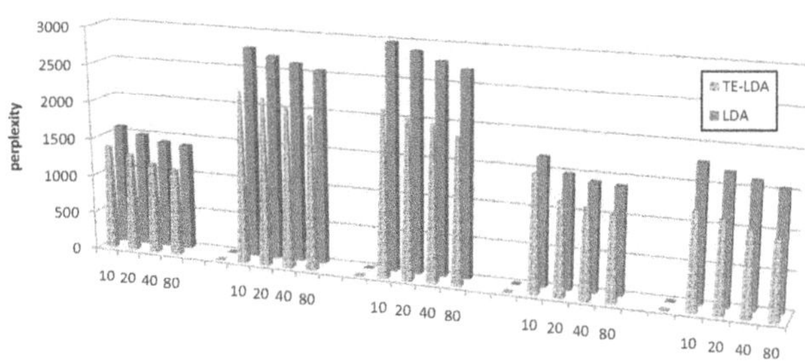

Figure 3: Perplexity of different models in `Unlv` data set. From left to right, the subsets are `Business`, `Magazine`, `Legal`, `Newspaper`, `Magazine2`.

5.1 Data Sets

In our experiment, we used three benchmark data sets `TREC AP`, `NIPS`, and `Reuters-21578` in the document modeling literature. The TREC Associate Press (AP) data set[1] contains 16333 newswire articles with 23075 unique terms. The `NIPS` data set[2] consists of the full text of the 13 years of proceedings from 1988 to 2000 Neural Information Processing Systems (NIPS) Conferences. The data set contains 1740 research papers with 13649 unique terms. The `Reuters-21578` data set[3] consists of newswire articles classified by topic and ordered by their date of issue. The data set contains of 12902 documents and 12112 unique terms. For all the above data sets, we synthetically generated noisy text data to simulate different levels of Word Error Rates (WER). We also conducted experiments on one real OCR data set `Unlv`[4] with five subsets, namely `Business`, `Magazine`, `Legal`, `Newspaper`, `Magazine2`. The average document WER generated by the OCR engine is around 30%.

5.2 Evaluation Metrics

We calculated the *perplexity* of a held-out test set to evaluate the models. A lower perplexity score corresponds to better generalization performance of the document model. Formally, for a test data of D_{test} documents the perplexity score is calculated as follows [1]. Note that the probability $p(w_d|z_k)$ is learned from the training process and $p_{test}(z_k|d)$ is estimated on the test data based on the parameters ϕ, θ and δ learned from training data.

$$perplexity(D_{test}) = \exp\{\frac{-\sum_{d=1}^{D_{test}} \log p(\mathbf{w}_d)}{\sum_{d=1}^{D_{test}} N_d}\} \quad (1)$$

$$p(\mathbf{w}_d) = \sum_{k=1}^{K} p(w_d|z_k) p_{test}(z_k|d) \quad (2)$$

5.3 Experimental Results

We first compare the performance of our proposed model with the baseline LDA model on the real OCR dataset. Figure 3 show the perplexity of TE-LDA as a function of the number of hidden topics in the five subsets of `Unlv` corpus. At different levels of WER for each subset, our TE-LDA model consistently outperforms the traditional LDA model.

We then systematically compare the performance of our model with LDA on the synthetically generated noisy corpora. In this experiment, we simulate different levels of word error rates (WER= 0.01, 0.05, 0.1). Figures 4(a)-(c) show the perplexity of TE-LDA model as a function of the number of hidden topics in the document corpus on `AP` data set. As we can see from Figures 4(a)-(c), at different levels of WER, our TE-LDA model consistently outperforms the traditional LDA model. Furthermore, as WER increases, the margin of improvement increases. This is due to explicit modeling of textual errors during the generation of terms in the document modeling process. In Figures 4(d)-(f), we fix the number of topics T and demonstrate how the different models perform as the word error rates increase. An interesting finding here is that the perplexity of LDA increases as the word error rates increase while the perplexity of TE-LDA models decreases as the word error rates increase. This is because LDA does not consider the textual errors in the term generation where the accuracy of calculation of word frequencies is affected significantly in the noisy text environment. In summary, our TE-LDA outperforms LDA and the margin of improvement increases as the word error rates increase. Figures 4(g)-(l) and Figures 4(m)-(r) show similar patterns on `NIPS` data set and `Reuters` data set respectively.

6. CONCLUSION AND FUTURE WORK

In this paper, we extend the traditional LDA model to account for noisy text data in latent document modeling. Our TE-LDA adopts a switching mechanism to explicitly determine whether the word is generated from the topic-document distribution through the general topic generation route or from a special word distribution through the typo processing route. We show that our proposed model achieves better generalization performance than the LDA model.

7. REFERENCES

[1] D. M.Blei et al., *Latent Dirichlet Allocation*, In Journal of Machine Learning Research, 2003.

[2] D. D.Walker et al., *Evaluating Models of Latent Document Semantics in the Presence of OCR Errors*, In EMNLP, 2010.

[3] X. Chen et al., *Probabilistic Models for Topic Learning from Images and Captions in Online Biomedical Literatures*, In CIKM, 2009.

[1] http://www.daviddlewis.com/resources/testcollections/trecap/
[2] http://www.cs.nyu.edu/ roweis/data.html
[3] http://kdd.ics.uci.edu/databases/reuters21578/reuters21578.html
[4] http://code.google.com/p/isri-ocr-evaluation-tools/updates/list

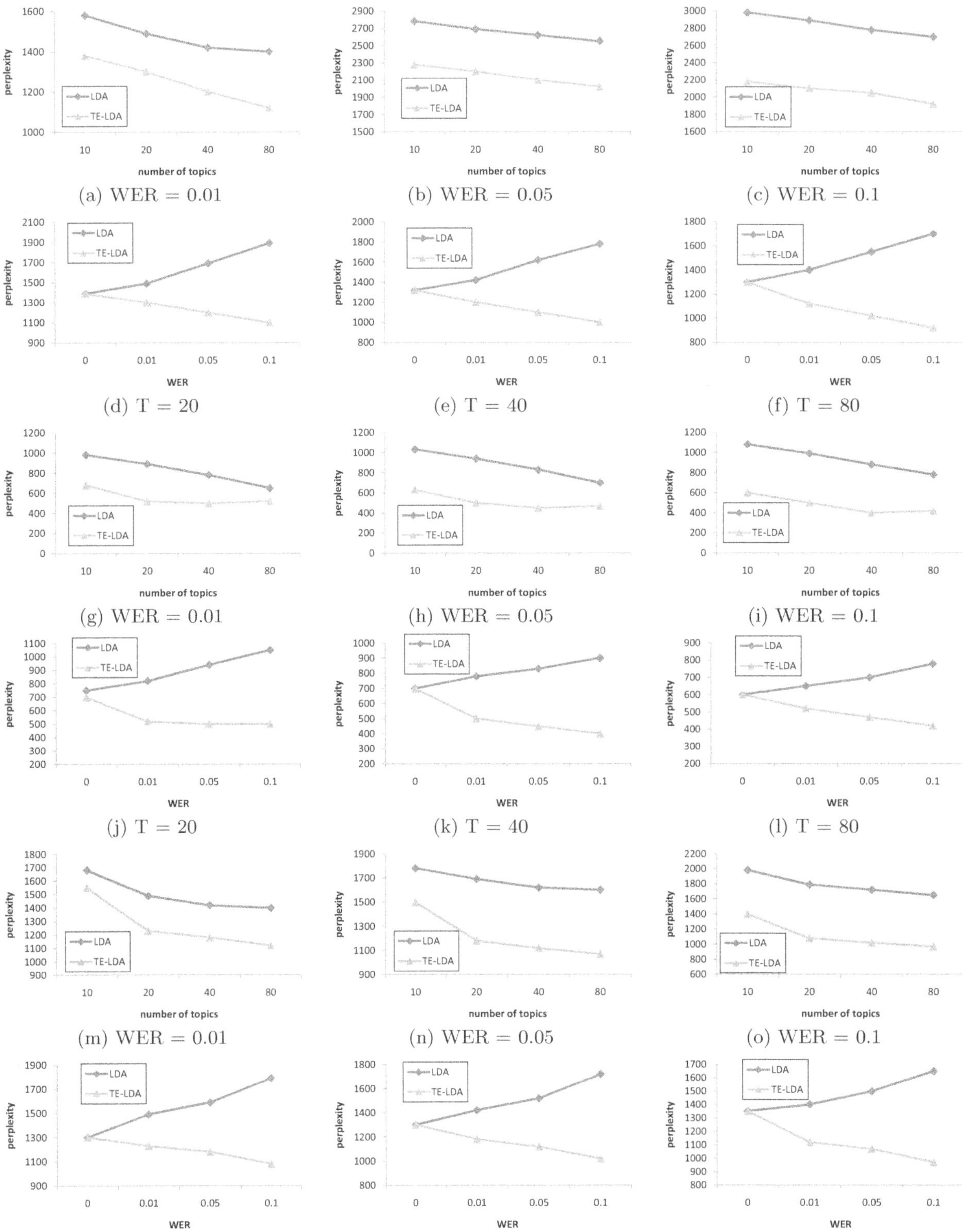

(a) WER = 0.01 (b) WER = 0.05 (c) WER = 0.1

(d) T = 20 (e) T = 40 (f) T = 80

(g) WER = 0.01 (h) WER = 0.05 (i) WER = 0.1

(j) T = 20 (k) T = 40 (l) T = 80

(m) WER = 0.01 (n) WER = 0.05 (o) WER = 0.1

(p) T = 20 (q) T = 40 (r) T = 80

Figure 4: (a)-(c),(g)-(i) and (m)-(o): Perplexity of different models as a function of the number of topics in `TREC AP`, `NIPS` and `Reuters` data sets respectively. (d)-(f), (j)-(l) and (p)-(r): Perplexity of different models as a function of WER in `TREC AP`, `NIPS` and `Reuters` data sets respectively.

Probabilistic Model for Discovering Topic based Communities in Social Networks

Mrinmaya Sachan Danish Contractor Tanveer A. Faruquie L. V. Subramaniam
IBM Research India
New Delhi, India
{mrsachan,dcontrac,ftanveer,lvsubram}@in.ibm.com

ABSTRACT

Social graphs have received renewed interest as a research topic with the advent of social networking websites. These online networks provide a rich source of data to study user relationships and interaction patterns on a large scale. In this paper, we propose a generative Bayesian model for extracting latent communities from a social graph. We assume that community memberships depend on topics of interest between users and the link relationships between them in the social graph topology. In addition, we make use of the nature of interaction to gauge user interests. Our model allows communities to be related to multiple topics and each user in the graph can be a member of multiple communities. This gives an insight into user interests and topical distribution in communities. We show the effectiveness of our model using a real world data set and also compare our model with existing community discovery methods.

Categories and Subject Descriptors

H.2.8 [**Information Systems**]: Database ApplicationsData mining; G.3 [**Probability and Statistics**]: Probabilistic algorithms

General Terms

Algorithms

Keywords

Community Detection, Social Networks, Probabilistic methods

1. INTRODUCTION

With the rise of online social networking websites, Social Network Analysis has gained renewed interest. A Social Network is a graph that develops with interaction between users who may be friends, acquaintances, colleagues, etc. in the real world and/or those who share similar interests, likes or dislikes.

CIKM'11, October 24–28, 2011, Glasgow, Scotland, UK.

These online social graphs provide a rich source of data for studying community and user relationships. A network feature that has been emphasized in recent works is community structure i.e. the gathering of vertices into groups such that there is higher relatedness among vertices within a group. The discovery of communities in a social graph consisting of "similar" users is an important problem and finds applications in many areas as diverse as sociology, biology and computer science where systems are often represented as graphs.

In this paper, we propose a generative Bayesian model for extracting latent communities from a social graph. It assumes that community memberships are dependent on the topics of interest amongst users and their link relationships in the social graph. Users can belong to multiple communities and a community can be related to multiple topics. Further, a user may be interested in multiple topics based on his interest. This is useful in modelling user interests or roles they play in the network.

Finally, we observe that the "type" of interactions between users can be used to emphasize their interest in topics, and thus community membership. For example, two users engaging in conversations related to politics (posting "replies" to each other) would be more likely to be members of a community on politics than someone who has occasionally "broadcasted" posts on politics (for example, during the elections in a country). Hence, we also model communication types. To the best of our knowledge we are the first to use all the three q: topics, social graph topology and nature of user interactions in the discovery of latent communities from a social graph.

The paper is structured as follows: In Section 2, we review some prior work on latent community discovery. In section 3, we describe the TURCM model and present Gibbs sampling equations to infer its parameters. In section 4, we give experiments to validate the model. Section 5 concludes.

2. PRIOR WORK

Traditionally, community detection has dealt with a hard-partitioning of nodes in the graph and do not allow nodes (users) to have membership in multiple communities. Also, they do not account for inter-user interactions outside the graph link. Recently, with the popularity of LDA, there has been significant interest in Bayesian probabilistic models for community discovery like Simple Social Network LDA (SSN-LDA) [8], Generic Weighted network LDA (GWN-LDA) [7], Hybrid Community Discovery Framework (HCDF) [2] and Hierarchical Social Network-Pachinko Allocation Model (HSN-

PAM) [6]. Although they allow for mixed community memberships, they too rely primarily on the link structure in a social graph to learn communities.

Some community discovery methods have tried to utilize the semantic content of social graphs. In [9] the authors propose the CUT (Community-User-Topic) model which uses the semantic content to discover communities in an email social graph. Communities are modelled as random mixtures over users who are in turn modelled by their interests (represented by the *topical* distribution concerning them). The model, however, does not utilize the link information in a graph while discovering communities. While models like CUT are suitable when community members communicate actively with each other, models like SSN-LDA assume that users that are inter-connected share similar interests. However, this is not always true in real world scenarios. For example, in social networks there are many users who are members of communities but do not actively contribute in them. Thus, both the graph structure and the interactions between users should be used to model the formation of communities.

Recently, researchers have started looking for one integrated probabilistic model that combines both content and link information available in social networks. The Community-Author-Recipient-Topic (CART) model [5], was one of the first attempts to combine previous link based community discovery methods with content based community discovery. Though, both the CART model and our models use topics and social graph topology to model communities, the generative process in both is significantly different. While our models assume that communities are generated based on users, recipients, topics and links connecting them, the CART model generates authors(users) and recipients of a post from latent communities.

Since CART, there have been few more attempts to combine content and link to obtain community structures more effectively ([4] [1]). These models assume links as binary. Whereas, our model utilizes the nature of interactions between users while modelling communities. This is synonymous to using weights in a graph for community discovery.

3. COMMUNITY DISCOVERY MODELS

Notation: Let $\mathbf{U}$ be the set of users in the social network under consideration. Let $\mathbf{R_i}$ be the set of neighbors (recipients) of user (sender) $u_i \in \mathbf{U}$. For a given user (sender) $u_i \in \mathbf{U}$ and its neighbor (recipient) $u_j \in \mathbf{R_i}$, let $\mathbf{P_{ij}}$ be the set of posts (messages) sent by u_i to u_j. Overall, let $\mathbf{P_i} = \bigcup_{u_j \in \mathbf{R_i}} \mathbf{P_{ij}}$ be the set of posts (messages) sent by user(sender) u_i. Let N_p be the number of words in a given post p, $p \in \{ \bigcup_{u_i \in \mathbf{U}} \mathbf{P_i}\}$. Also let the cardinality of all these sets (in boldface) be represented by their corresponding capitalized symbols. The sender u_i, recipient u_j, the set of words $\mathbf{W_p}$ for each post p and the type of posts X_p are observable variables, while the communities, c, and topics, z, are considered as latent variables.

3.1 Topic User Recipient Community Model

In this section we describe our generative model : Topic User Recipient Community Model (TURCM) for latent community discovery in such networks. TURCM tries to discover communities by integrating the content being discussed by users in the form of latent topics and the type of posts generated by them. User interests are modelled via topics of mutual interest to both the sender as well as the recipient. We use a mixture of unigrams approach in our work, essentially assuming that the entire post is on one topic. As we shall see later, this is a reasonable assumption and allows our model to scale much better. Consequently, we experienced a significant decrease in training time over CUT and CART. Scalability is a major issue in the application of such probabilistic approaches in Social Network Analysis.

We also use the "type" of communication to improve community discovery. The idea being that two users who share a series of posts (messages) with each other, are likely to be communicating on certain common topics, indicating similar interests and therefore, can be members of the same community. The type of communication indicates the strength of association between two users and their interest in a topic. The type of interaction varies from one social graph to another. User uploads/downloads, comments, wall posts, shared photographs, tags, etc. can be considered as interactions in social networks. For example, in the traditional model of email, an initiated email, a reply, or a forwarded email could be types. We can also include email list subscriptions, bulk-emails, etc. also into types if we have the required information.

Motivated by SSN-LDA [8], we represent every user as a combination of his interaction space. Each user (u_i) is characterized by a social interaction profile representing all its P_i interactions (post types): $SIP(u_i) = \{X_1 \ldots X_{P_i}\}$. The social interaction profile of users is represented as random mixtures over latent community variables. Each community is in turn defined as a distribution over the interaction space. This idea is analogous to LDA, where the social interaction profile is a document, interactions are words in that document and communities are latent topics.

The number of topics Z, and the number of communities C, to be discovered are specified apriori as model parameters. Let the size of the vocabulary from which the communications between users are composed be V. The number of different type of communications is K. Let $Dir_X(\alpha)$ denote a X-dimensional symmetric Dirichlet with scalar parameter α and $Mult(.)$ denote the discrete multinomial distribution.

1. For each of the topics, $1 \leq z \leq Z$, sample a V dimensional multinomial, $\vec{\lambda}_z \sim Dir_V(\delta)$.
2. For each of the communities, $1 \leq c \leq C$ sample a K dimensional social interaction mixture $\vec{\phi}_c \sim Dir_K(\beta)$.
3. For the ith user u_i, $1 \leq u_i \leq U$:
   (a) For each neighbor/recipient $1 \leq u_j \leq N_i$:
      i. Sample a Z dimensional vector of topic proportions, $\vec{\eta}_{u_i,u_j} \sim Dir_Z(\nu)$. This represents that the post is of a mutual interest to the sender and the recipient.
      ii. For each topic $z \in Z$, sample a C dimensional multinomial, $\vec{\theta}_{u_i,u_j,z} \sim Dir_C(\alpha)$, representing the community proportions for that topic and the sender-recipient pair.
      iii. For each post p ($1 \leq p \leq P_{ij}$) sent by u_i to u_j, having N_p words:
         A. Choose a topic assignment $z_p \sim Mult(\vec{\eta}_{u_i,u_j})$ $z_p \in [1 : Z]$ for the post.

B. Choose a community assignment: $c_p \sim Mult(\vec{\theta}_{u_i,u_j,z_p})$ $c_p \in [1:C]$.

C. Choose a social interaction type $X_p \sim Mult(\vec{\phi}_{c_p})$, $X_p \in [1:K]$ for the post.

D. For every slot j, $1 \leq j \leq N_p$ in p, choose a word $w_j \sim Mult(\lambda_{z_p})$.

Let $\mathbf{W}$ be the set of observable words in the corpus, $\mathbf{X}$ be the set of interaction types observed on the social graph among the $\mathbf{U}$ set of users (senders) and $\mathbf{R}$ recipients. Let $\mathbf{Z}$ and $\mathbf{C}$ be the latent topic and community assignments for every post. The generative process for the model is given below. The joint likelihood of users, recipients, posts, interaction types, topic and community assignments given by the TURCM model is

$$L = P(\mathbf{W}, \mathbf{X}, \mathbf{U}, \mathbf{R}, \mathbf{Z}, \mathbf{C}, \theta, \phi, \eta, \lambda | \alpha, \beta, \nu, \delta)$$

This can be factorized into:

$$\begin{aligned} L = \quad & P(\mathbf{W}|\mathbf{Z};\lambda)P(\mathbf{X}|\mathbf{C};\phi)P(\mathbf{Z}|\mathbf{U},\mathbf{R};\eta) \\ & P(\mathbf{C}|\mathbf{Z},\mathbf{U},\mathbf{R};\theta)P(\theta|\alpha)P(\phi|\beta)P(\eta|\nu)P(\lambda|\delta) \end{aligned}$$

Next, we give a Gibbs Sampling based approach to infer TURCM's parameters. We represent $\bar{\mathbf{W}}_\mathbf{p}$ as the set of words in a given post p, N_p as the number of words in the post and N_w^p as the number of times a given word w occurs in p. Let $\mathbf{C}_{-\mathbf{p}}, \mathbf{X}_{-\mathbf{p}}, \mathbf{Z}_{-\mathbf{p}}$ and $\bar{\mathbf{W}}_{-\mathbf{p}}$ represent the community, post type, topic assignments and the set of words except post p. The Gibbs update equations are:

$$P(c_p = c|\mathbf{C}_{-\mathbf{p}}, \mathbf{Z}, \mathbf{U}, \mathbf{R}) = \frac{n_{c(urz)}^{-p} + \alpha}{\sum_{c'} n_{c'(urz)}^{-p} + C\alpha}$$

$$P(x_p = x|\mathbf{X}_{-\mathbf{p}}, \mathbf{C}) = \frac{n_{xc}^{-p} + \beta}{\sum_{x'} n_{x'c}^{-p} + X\beta}$$

$$P(z_p = z|\mathbf{Z}_{-\mathbf{p}}, \mathbf{U}, \mathbf{R}) = \frac{n_{z(ur)}^{-p} + \nu}{\sum_{z'} n_{z'(ur)}^{-p} + Z\nu}$$

$$P(\bar{\mathbf{W}}_\mathbf{p} = \bar{\mathbf{w}}|\bar{\mathbf{W}}_{-\mathbf{p}}, \mathbf{Z}) = \frac{\prod_{w \in \bar{\mathbf{W}}_\mathbf{p}} \prod_{i=0}^{N_w^p} (n_{wz}^{-p} + i + \delta)}{\prod_{i=0}^{N_p - 1} (\sum_{w'} (n_{w'z}^{-p} + i + V\delta))}$$

where $n_{a(b_1 \ldots b_v)}^{-p}$ represents the number of times a,$(1 \leq a \leq A)$ is generated from the combination of variables $b_1 \ldots b_v$ in the model, $(1 \leq b_i \leq B_i$, $1 \leq i \leq v)$ excluding post p.

The topics $P(w|z)$, community memberships $P(u|c)$ and topic proportions for a community $P(z|c)$ are estimated using a Maximum Likelihood estimate. The $P(u|c)$ computation gives us the community as a distribution over users while $P(z|c)$ gives us the topical interest in a community.

4. EXPERIMENTS

In this section, we evaluate the TURCM model on the ENRON email corpus and compare it with CUT and CART models. For all our simulations, we set the number of communities C at 10 and topics Z at 20. These choices are later proved to be close to the optimal in Sections 4.1 and 4.2. We ran 1000 iterations in the burn-in period and took 250 samples (every fourth sample) in the next 1000 iterations. In Table 1, we list a few topics $(\vec{\lambda}_z)$ discovered by TURCM. We give top 5 words to visualize each topic. Here "calpx" is the California Power Corporation, "transco" is a gas transportation company and "nymex" is the New York Mercantile Exchange. We see that TURCM is able to discover meaningful topics, thus validating the assumption that each post is often associated with a single topic.

California Power	Gas Transportation	Trading	Deals
power	gas	price	meeting
transmission	energy	market	contract
energy	enron	dollar	report
calpx	transco	nymex	enron
california	chris	trade	deal

Table 1: Topics extracted from Enron

Number of Communities	6	8	10	12	14
TURCM	0.198	0.271	0.339	0.331	0.283
CART	0.152	0.249	0.302	0.294	0.255
CUT	0.133	0.231	0.266	0.278	0.227

Table 2: Fuzzy modularity on the Enron dataset

4.1 Community Analysis

Next, we evaluate the quality of communities discovered by the TUCM and TURCM models against the communities discovered by the CUT and the CART models.

Newman proposed modularity, a measure of goodness for community structure. Unlike most other works, it assumes that a good division of the network is not merely one in which the number of edges running between groups is small. Rather, it is one in which the number of edges between groups is smaller than expected. Since the output of all these probabilistic models(TURCM, CART and CUT) is a fuzzy community structure, in which each node has a certain probability of belonging to a certain community; we use a fuzzy version of modularity proposed in [3]. Table 2 compares the fuzzy modularity of the TURCM model with its peers(CUT and CART). The high modularity values support our assumption that people who share common interests and are inter-connected with each other in the social graph often form communities. Modularity is important as one is always interested in strong-knit communities where people know each other as well as share common interests for reasons such as networking and task assignment. Methods that form communities purely on interest can end up with disparate people (who dont know each other and are disconnected in the graph) in one community. This is shown by much weaker numbers for the CUT model. The number of topics was set to 20 for these experiments.

4.2 Perplexity Analysis

Next, we explore the perplexity of our model. We choose two previous probabilistic models for community discovery (CUT and CART) and compare our models with them in terms of perplexity. Figure 1 gives perplexity comparison establishing a significant improvements by the TURCM model.

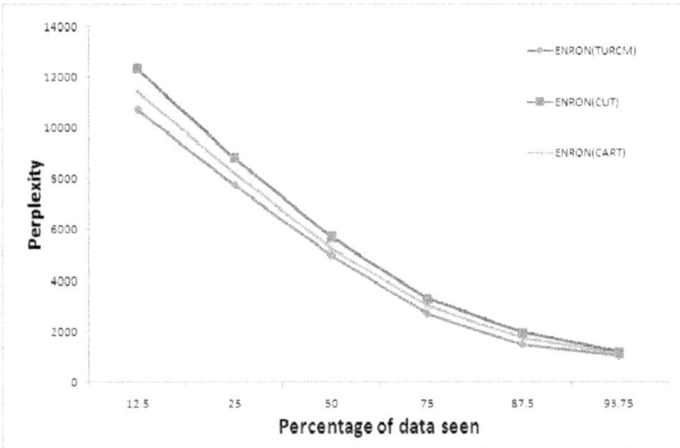

Figure 1: Perplexity comparison on the ENRON dataset

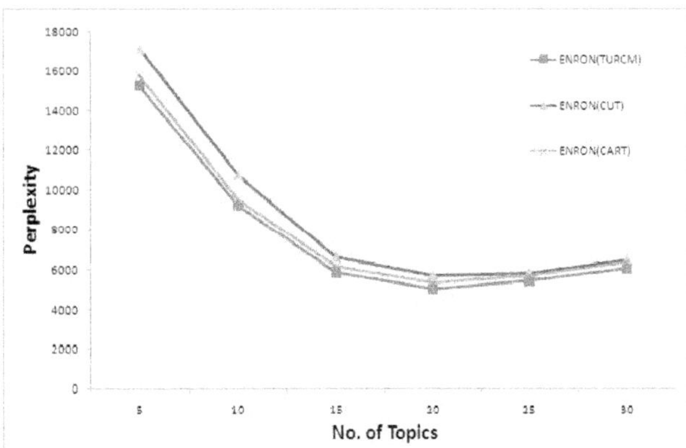

Figure 2: Perplexity on the Enron dataset against the number of topics

This is because the TURCM model generates topic based communities and accounts for link types which are important descriptors of the strength of relationship between users. The results also confirm to our intuition that the post topics should model the joint interest of the sender and the recipient. For these reasons, CUT doesn't perform well.

Finally, in order to comment on the model parameters (number of topics and communities), we analyze how model perplexities behave as the model parameters are changed. Figure 2 plots the perplexities against the number of topics. The number of communities was set to 10 for this experiment. It can be roughly concluded that the peplexities attain their minimum at around 20-25 topics. Figure 3 plots the perplexities against the number of communities. The number of topics was set to 10 for this experiment. Again, it can be roughly concluded that the perplexities attain their minimum at around 10 communities. Similar insights could be obtained about the number of communities from Table 2 where the fuzzy modularities optimize around 10 communities for both datasets. This analysis not only helps us in concluding that our model outperforms the two baselines (CUT and CART) independent of the model parameters (number of topics and number of communities) but also get an estimate on optimal model parameter settings.

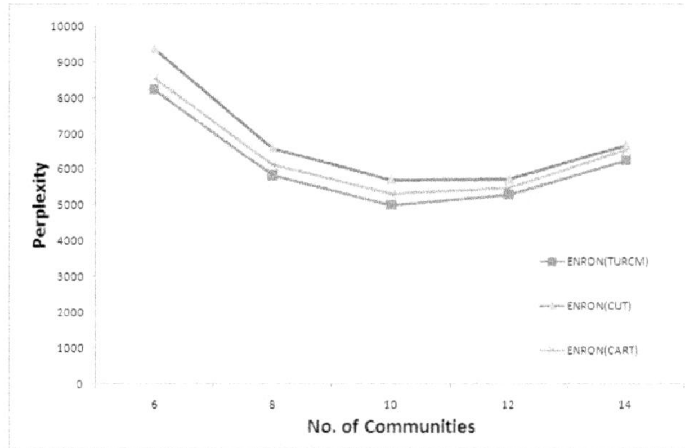

Figure 3: Perplexity on the Enron dataset against the number of communities

5. CONCLUSION

We posited that communities are formed by users who communicate on topics of mutual interest, are connected to each other in the social graph and share frequent communication of certain types. Then, we argued that interaction types are important indicators of the strength of association between users and proposed a probabilistic scheme that incorporates all these three features to discover communities more effectively. Finally, we showed superior community discovery results over our closest peers.

6. REFERENCES

[1] J. Chang and D. Blei. Relational topic models for document networks. In *AIStats*, 2009.

[2] K. Henderson, T. Eliassi-Rad, S. Papadimitriou, and C. Faloutsos. Hcdf: A hybrid community discovery framework. In *SDM 10*, 2010.

[3] J. Liu. Fuzzy modularity and fuzzy community structure in networks. *The European Physical Journal B - Condensed Matter and Complex Systems*, 77:547–557, 2010. 10.1140/epjb/e2010-00290-3.

[4] Y. Liu, A. Niculescu-Mizil, and W. Gryc. Topic-link lda: joint models of topic and author community. In *Proceedings of the 26th Annual International Conference on Machine Learning*, ICML '09, pages 665–672, New York, NY, USA, 2009. ACM.

[5] N. Pathak, C. DeLong, A. Banerjee, and K. Erickson. Social topics models for community extraction. In *Proceedings of the 2nd SNA-KDD Workshop*, 2008.

[6] H. Zhang. Hsn-pam: Finding hierarchical probabilistic groups from large-scale networks, 2010.

[7] H. Zhang, C. L. Giles, H. C. Foley, and J. Yen. Probabilistic community discovery using hierarchical latent gaussian mixture model. In *Proceedings of the Conference on Artificial intelligence*, 2007.

[8] H. Zhang, B. Qiu, C. L. Giles, H. C. Foley, and J. Yen. An lda-based community structure discovery approach for large-scale social networks. In *In IEEE Conference on Intelligence and Security Informatics*, pages 200–207, 2007.

[9] D. Zhou, E. Manavoglu, J. Li, C. L. Giles, and H. Zha. Probabilistic models for discovering e-communities. In *Proceedings of the International Conference on World Wide Web*, 2006.

Scalable Entity Matching Computation with Materialization

Sanghoon Lee, Jongwuk Lee, Seung-won Hwang
Department of Computer Science and Engineering
Pohang University of Science and Technology (POSTECH)
Pohang 790-784, Republic of Korea
{sanghoon, julee, swhwang}@postech.edu

ABSTRACT

Entity matching (EM) is the task of identifying records that refer to the same real-world entity from different data sources. While EM is widely used in data integration and data cleaning applications, the naive method for EM incurs quadratic cost with respect to the size of the datasets. To address this problem, this paper proposes a scalable EM algorithm that employs a pre-materialized structure. Specifically, once the structure is built, our proposed algorithm can identify the EM results with sub-linear cost. In addition, as the rules evolve, our algorithm can efficiently adapt to new rules by selectively accessing records using the materialized structure. Our evaluation results show that our proposed EM algorithm is significantly faster than the state-of-the-art method for extensive real-life datasets.

Categories and Subject Descriptors

H.2.m [**Database Management**]: Miscellaneous.data cleaning; H.2.8 [**Database Management**]: Database Applications.data mining

General Terms

Algorithms, experimentation, performance

Keywords

Entity matching, resolution, materialization, rule evolution

1. INTRODUCTION

Entity matching (EM) is the process of identifying records that come from different data sources but represent the same real-world entity. EM is also known as entity resolution [1], reference reconciliation [3], record linkage [5], or object identification [10]. EM is widely used in various real-world applications such as data integration and data cleaning: (1) When entities are stored in a distributed manner across heterogeneous databases, we need to maintain those databases for data integration. (2) When many records in a single database may indicate the same entity, we need to eliminate redundant records for data consistency.

CIKM'11, October 24–28, 2011, Glasgow, Scotland, UK.

1.1 Basic Model of EM

We first introduce basic notations to define the EM problem. We assume two finite sets $\mathcal{P}$ and $\mathcal{Q}$ of records from different sources, *i.e.*, $\mathcal{P} = \{p_1, \ldots, p_m\}$ and $\mathcal{Q} = \{q_1, \ldots, q_n\}$, as input. Each record has a finite set of fields (or attributes) with various data types such as numbers and strings. For simplicity, we assume that $\mathcal{P}$ and $\mathcal{Q}$ have compatible schemas: the records from $\mathcal{P}$ and $\mathcal{Q}$ have corresponding values for some fields.

We then formalize a *match function* (or a *matcher*) to compare records in a pair-wise manner. Specifically, we follow a *join model* over $\mathcal{P} \times \mathcal{Q}$. A join operation takes two sets $\mathcal{P}$ and $\mathcal{Q}$ as input, and returns a set of record pairs $(p, q) \in \mathcal{P} \times \mathcal{Q}$, referring to the same real-world entity, along with a match function $\mathcal{M}$. The match function can thus be represented by a Boolean condition for the same fields of $\mathcal{P}$ and $\mathcal{Q}$ if $\mathcal{M}(p, q)$ is true, p and q indicate the same entity; otherwise, they are different. Without loss of generality, we define the match function $\mathcal{M}$ as:

$$\mathcal{M}(p,q) \leftarrow \begin{cases} 1, & \text{if } \mathcal{F}(p,q) \leq \delta, \\ 0, & \text{otherwise,} \end{cases}$$

where $\mathcal{F}(p, q)$ is a user-specific function calculating the similarity between records and δ is a threshold parameter.

Considering the match function $\mathcal{M}$ as a *user-specific rule*, we can define the *rule-based EM problem* [1, 7, 9, 11].

Definition 1 (Entity matching) Given two sets $\mathcal{P}$ and $\mathcal{Q}$ of records and a match function $\mathcal{M}$, *entity matching* is to identify a set $\mathcal{S}$ of record pairs $(p, q) \in \mathcal{P} \times \mathcal{Q}$ such that $\mathcal{S} = \{(p,q) | p \in \mathcal{P}, q \in \mathcal{Q}, \mathcal{M}(p,q) = 1\}$.

To support a sophisticated matching rule $\mathcal{M}$ we exploit $\mathcal{F}$ by using an *aggregate function* combining multiple fields, as commonly adopted in the EM literature [7]. For simplicity, we assume that $\mathcal{F}$ is *monotone* [4].

$$\mathcal{F}(p,q) = \sum_{f \in \Omega} w_f \times f(p,q),$$

where Ω is a space of all possible similarity functions, and $f(p, q)$ is the similarity function between p and q. Also, w_f is a weight vector reflecting the importance of function $f(p, q)$.

For example, we describe the toy datasets related to restaurants (Table 1). For the first three fields *name*, *address* and *type*, we can exploit well-known string similarity functions such as *Levenshtein* distance and *Jaro-Winkler* distance. For the fourth field, *coordinate*, we can make use of numeric similarity functions such as *Manhattan* distance and *Euclidean* distance.

Table 1: Toy datasets from Fodor's and Zagat's restaurant resources

id	*name*	*address*	*type*	*coordinate*
p_1	Fringale	570 4th St. San Francisco	French	[37.778483, -122.396783]
p_2	Philippe's The Original	1001 N. Alameda St. Los Angeles	American	[34.059619, -118.237073]
p_3	Ocean Avenue	1401 Ocean Ave. Santa Monica	American	[34.014045, -118.497473]

(a) Dataset $\mathcal{P}$ from Fodor's restaurant resource

id	*name*	*address*	*type*	*coordinate*
q_1	Ocean Park Cafe	3117 Ocean Park Blvd. Santa Monica	American	[34.021079, -118.452519]
q_2	Fringale	570 Fourth St. San Francisco	French Bistro	[37.778559, -122.39718]
q_3	Philippe The Original	1001 N. Alameda St. Chinatown	Cafeteria	[34.059673, -118.23702]

(b) Dataset $\mathcal{Q}$ from Zagat's restaurant dataset resource

1.2 Challenges of EM

Once the match function $\mathcal{M}$ is determined, we identify a pair of records that refer to the same entity over $\mathcal{P} \times \mathcal{Q}$. The brute-force approach for EM first enumerates all possible record pairs $(p, q) \in \mathcal{P} \times \mathcal{Q}$, and then checks whether p and q match: if $\mathcal{M}(p, q)$ is true, (p, q) is inserted into an EM result set; otherwise, (p, q) is skipped.

We describe how this naive method works using toy datasets. We generate nine possible record pairs over $\mathcal{P} \times \mathcal{Q}$ (Table 2). Suppose that similarity functions f_{name} and f_{type} are defined as *Levenshtein* distance, f_{addr} is defined as *Jaro-Winkler* distance, and f_{coord} is defined as *Manhattan* distance. On the basis of some background knowledge, we set the weight vector w used in $\mathcal{F}$ as $\langle 0.1, 5, 0.02, 0.1 \rangle$ and the threshold δ as 1. The aggregate function values for each pair are given in the last column in Table 2. Finally, we can identify the EM result as $\{(p_1, q_2), (p_2, q_3)\}$, *i.e.*, "Fringale" and "Philippe The Original" and are correctly resolved.

Table 2: All possible record pairs and their aggregated scores with weight vector $\langle 0.1, 5, 0.02, 0.1 \rangle$

record pair	*distance score*				*aggregated score*
	f_{name}	f_{addr}	f_{type}	f_{coord}	
(p_1, q_1)	12	0.431	6	7.702	4.244
(p_1, q_2)	0	0.091	7	0.000	0.594
(p_1, q_3)	18	0.414	8	7.879	4.819
(p_2, q_1)	20	0.449	0	0.254	4.272
(p_2, q_2)	20	0.462	11	7.879	5.317
(p_2, q_3)	2	0.115	7	0.306	0.948
(p_3, q_1)	8	0.250	0	0.052	2.054
(p_3, q_2)	10	0.421	11	7.664	4.090
(p_3, q_3)	18	0.295	7	0.306	3.444

To provide exact EM results, it is critical to determine meaningful similarity functions $f \in \Omega$ and tune the user-specific parameters w and δ. To address these needs, rules can continuously evolve either by adding/removing functions from Ω or adjusting w and δ. Efficient support for evolving rules has also been emphasized by Whang and Garcia-Molina [11]. However, their proposed solution makes restrictive assumptions, *e.g.*, rule monotonicity, and suffers in performance when rules evolve significantly. Even when their assumptions hold (as we empirically study later), our proposed algorithm significantly outperforms the other solution, which still incurs a prohibitive cost for intermediate EM results.

1.3 Our Contributions

We propose a scalable EM algorithm using a materialization structure. Specifically, we observe that the process of finding EM results satisfying a threshold condition is similar to that of *top-k queries* [2, 4, 6], which identify the best k records with the highest scores. We thus adopt the *materialized lists* used for top-k processing without accessing all records. The materialized lists for EM store the similarity values of all record pairs for single-field functions as a basic access unit for EM. By accessing records in materialization lists at a time, we can identify a final EM result with sub-linear cost. Furthermore, we can interactively evolve various rules and efficiently obtain EM results with high accuracy.

2. ALGORITHM

This section proposes a scalable EM algorithm that identifies EM results using a pre-materialized structure. Towards this goal, we first introduce a *threshold algorithm* (*TA*) [4] that identifies the top-k results by performing a fuzzy join with sub-linear cost. With similar intuition, we then adopt the materialization used in TA-family algorithms, and develop an EM algorithm that efficiently evolves for new rules.

2.1 Threshold Algorithm (TA)

We first provide the overview of top-k query computation. A top-k query aims to identify the best k records with respect to a user-specific *scoring function* $\mathcal{F}$. Suppose that the function $\mathcal{F}$ is represented by a linear combination of d attributes, *i.e.*, $\mathcal{F}(f_1(A_1), \ldots, f_d(A_d))$, where $f_i(A_i)$ is the scoring function of attribute A_i. The naive approach to finding the top-k results requires to access all records in the worst case.

To address this problem, TA exploits a pre-computed data structure. Specifically, they first maintain d sorted lists in increasing order of $f_i(A_i)$, where smaller scores are better. On these sorted lists, they then access records by performing *sorted access* or *random access* until the top-k records with the highest scores are identified.

TA keeps the current top-k records found thus far while accessing the sorted lists. When the aggregated score of the kth ranked record is larger than the aggregated score of the last seen attribute values in the sorted lists, TA stops attempting to access further records and returns the current top-k records as an answer. Because this early-termination condition avoids searching the whole dataset, it is enough to consider few records distributed at the heads of sorted lists.

This key idea of TA can be applied to the EM problem in the sense that both problems only deal with some of the records satisfying a threshold condition. Therefore, we can get the EM results quickly by probing a small number of record pairs.

2.2 Threshold-Based EM Algorithm

We first devise a materialization structure inspired by TA. Before starting an EM algorithm, we construct lists for each similarity function $f_i(p, q)$. These lists are sorted in increasing order of function values, *i.e.*, the most similar record pairs are accessed first. We call them *materialized lists*, denoted as M_i for $f_i(p, q)$.

Algorithm 1 $TEM(\mathcal{M}, w, \delta, \mathcal{H})$

Input: set of materialized lists $\mathcal{M} = \langle M_1, \ldots, M_d \rangle$, weight vector $w = \langle w_1, \ldots, w_d \rangle$, threshold δ and EM history $\mathcal{H}$
Output: set of record pairs representing the same entity, $\mathcal{S}$

1: $\langle t_1, \ldots, t_d \rangle \leftarrow 0$ // *a threshold vector for seen records*
2: $\mathcal{S} \leftarrow \{\}$
3: **if** $\mathcal{H}.w \prec w$ **then**
4: $\quad \mathcal{S} \leftarrow \mathcal{H}.\mathcal{S}$ // *start from the result of history*
5: $\quad$**for** $\forall M_i \in \mathcal{M}$ **do**
6: $\quad\quad M_i$.access-point $\leftarrow \mathcal{H}.M_i$.access-point
7: $\quad$**end for**
8: **end if**
9: **while** $\sum_{i=1}^{d} w_i \cdot t_i \leq \delta$ **do**
10: $\quad$**for** $\forall M_i \in \mathcal{M}$ **do**
11: $\quad\quad \langle (p,q), r_i \rangle \leftarrow$ sorted-access(M_i) // *get record pair with the next largest similarity for f_i, and its score*
12: $\quad\quad t_i \leftarrow r_i$
13: $\quad\quad$**for** $\forall M_j \in \mathcal{M}, j \neq i$ **do**
14: $\quad\quad\quad r_j \leftarrow$ random-access$(M_j, (p,q))$ // *get similarity score of (p,q) for f_j*
15: $\quad\quad$**end for**
16: $\quad\quad$**if** $\sum_{i=1}^{d} w_i \cdot r_i \leq \delta$ **then**
17: $\quad\quad\quad \mathcal{S} \leftarrow \mathcal{S} \cup (p,q)$ // *(p,q) is a matched record pair*
18: $\quad\quad$**end if**
19: $\quad$**end for**
20: **end while**
21: **return** $\mathcal{S}$

For example, we describe the materialized lists using the toy datasets in Table 2. For ease of representation, suppose that three similarity functions on the fields of *name*, *address*, and *coordinate* are used for EM. We calculate all possible pair-wise similarities and sort them (Table 3).

Table 3: Materialized lists built from 3 similarity function values of pair-wise records in Table 2

M_{name}		M_{addr}		M_{coord}	
pair	f_{name}	*pair*	f_{addr}	*pair*	f_{coord}
(p_1,q_2)	0	(p_1,q_2)	0.091	(p_1,q_2)	0.000
(p_2,q_3)	2	(p_2,q_3)	0.115	(p_3,q_1)	0.052
(p_3,q_1)	8	(p_3,q_1)	0.250	(p_2,q_1)	0.254
(p_3,q_2)	10	(p_3,q_3)	0.295	(p_2,q_3)	0.306
(p_1,q_1)	12	(p_1,q_3)	0.414	(p_3,q_3)	0.306
(p_1,q_3)	18	(p_3,q_2)	0.421	(p_3,q_2)	7.664
(p_3,q_3)	18	(p_1,q_1)	0.431	(p_1,q_1)	7.702
(p_2,q_1)	20	(p_2,q_1)	0.449	(p_1,q_3)	7.879
(p_2,q_2)	20	(p_2,q_2)	0.462	(p_2,q_2)	7.879

We then develop a *threshold-based EM algorithm* (*TEM*) using the materialized lists. In a method similar to TA, we use two access modes: sorted access and random access. Algorithm 1 describes the pseudo code of *TEM*. Let d denote the number of fields used in EM. Specifically, the overall procedure of *TEM* is as follows:

1. We do sorted access on each materialized list. If a new record pair (p,q) appears in M_i, we do random access on the other materialized lists to identify unseen similarity scores. Then, we compute the overall similarity function score $\mathcal{F}(p,q)$ and check whether $\mathcal{F}(p,q)$ is less than or equal to δ. If p and q are matched, we can insert (p,q) into an EM result set.
2. For each list M_i, let t_i be the last similarity score seen by sorted access. We compute a threshold $\sum_{i=1}^{d} w_i \cdot t_i$ such that $t = \langle t_1, \ldots, t_d \rangle$. If $\sum_{i=1}^{d} w_i \cdot t_i$ is smaller than δ, return to step 1.
3. Return all matched record pairs as EM results.

In addition to the above basic procedure, we can also exploit the EM history $\mathcal{H}$ and evolve from an old rule. If a weight vector of $\mathcal{H}$ is dominated by w (line 3), the result in the history will also be a part of the result for w. Therefore, we reuse results for the old rule (line 4) and save access costs by restarting from the last access points of $\mathcal{H}$ (lines 5–7).

We prove the correctness of *TEM* as follows.

THEOREM 1 (CORRECTNESS OF *TEM*) Given a match function $\mathcal{M}$, *TEM* correctly returns all record pairs such that $\mathcal{M}(p,q) = 1$.

PROOF. Suppose there is a matched record pair (p', q'), but *TEM* does not return it as an answer. That is, (p', q') is not applied to a match function, since it is not visible by sorted access on the materialized lists. This means that any similarity function value of (p', q') is not smaller than the corresponding value of the last seen similarity score t_i. By the definitions of the aggregate and match functions, $\mathcal{F}(p', q') \geq \sum_{i=1}^{d} w_i \cdot t_i > \delta$. This contradicts the supposition that (p', q') is a matched record pair. Therefore, there does not exist a false negative such as (p', q'), and *TEM* correctly returns all matched record pairs. $\square$

We explain *TEM* using materialized lists (Table 3). Suppose an aggregation function $\mathcal{F}$ consists of $w = \langle 0.1, 5, 0.1 \rangle$, and δ is 1. The threshold vector t is initially a zero vector. Then, we access the materialized lists from M_{name} to M_{coord}. The first sorted access steps for the three materialized lists retrieve (p_1, q_2), whose aggregate score $\mathcal{F}$ is smaller than the threshold $\delta = 1$, and we insert (p_1, q_2) into an EM result set. Then t is updated to $\langle 0, 0.091, 0 \rangle$. The second sorted access and random access steps calculate $\mathcal{F}(p_2, q_3)$ and $\mathcal{F}(p_3, q_1)$. The (p_2, q_3) pair is matched and inserted into the result set. Now, t is updated to $\langle 2, 0.11, 0.052 \rangle$ and $\mathcal{F}(t) < \delta$, so we continue. The third access steps get (p_3, q_1) and (p_2, q_1). The pair (p_3, q_1) is was already addressed at the second step, and $\mathcal{F}(p_2, q_1) > \delta$; thus, we dismiss them. At this moment, t is $\langle 8, 0.250, 0.254 \rangle$ and $\mathcal{F}(t) = 2.075 > \delta$. Finally, we stop accessing the materialized lists and return the result set $\{(p_1, q_2), (p_2, q_3)\}$.

3. EVALUATION

This section shows experimental results for our proposed EM algorithm using extensive real-life datasets. Specifically, we exploited four datasets used in existing EM experimental study [8] (Table 4). Two dataset pairs, Abt-Buy and Amazon-GoogleProducts are used in e-commerce applications, where they consist of four fields, *product name*, *description*, *manufacturer*, and *price*. The other pairs DBLP-ACM and DBLP-Scholar are used in the bibliographic domain, where they consist of four fields, *title*, *authors*, *venue*, and *year*. For simplicity, we used *Levenshtein* distance as the similarity function for each field. (By carefully designing similarity functions, we can further improve the accuracy of EM results.)

Our experiments were conducted using a 64-bit Linux server with an Intel Core i7 Processor (2.8 GHz) and 24 GB of RAM. All the algorithms were implemented in Java.

Figure 1 depicts the execution time for two EM tasks. Note that these figures have a log-scaled y-axis. When constructing the initial EM task (Figure 1a), the *TEM* execution time is the sum of those for both building materialization lists and computing EM results. Nevertheless, our

Table 4: Four real-life datasets used in evaluation of *TEM*

real-life dataset pairs	*dataset size*		*search space*	*perfect*
	$\|\mathcal{P}\|$	$\|\mathcal{Q}\|$	$\|\mathcal{P} \times \mathcal{Q}\|$	*mapping size*
$\mathcal{D}_1$ (Abt-Buy)	1,081	1,092	1,180,452	1,097
$\mathcal{D}_2$ (Amazon-GoogleProducts)	1,363	3,226	4,397,038	1,300
$\mathcal{D}_3$ (DBLP-ACM)	2,616	2,294	6,001,104	2,224
$\mathcal{D}_4$ (DBLP-Scholar)	2,616	64,263	168,112,008	5,347

algorithm is two to seven times faster than the state-of-the-art EM algorithm *R-Swoosh* [1]. Although *R-Swoosh* focuses on reducing the search space for all possible pairs without additional indices, as a hierarchical tree structure it inherently requires a large number of comparisons to obtain intermediate EM results. These comparisons can deteriorate the overall performance. In contrast, after building sorted lists, our algorithm selectively accesses records to minimize unnecessary computation.

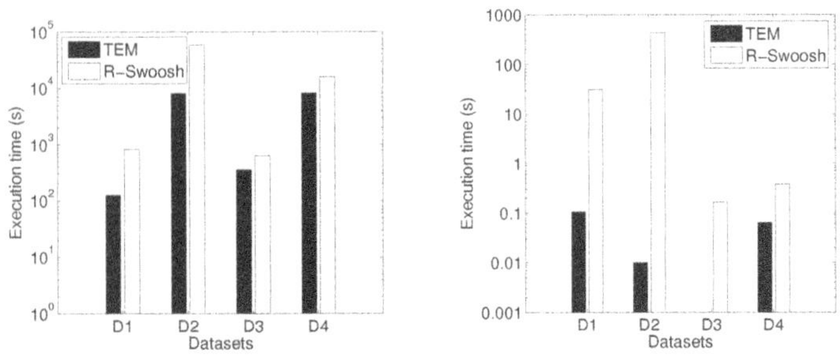

(a) Initial EM task (b) Evolving EM task

Figure 1: Execution times to perform an EM task from scratch[1] and to evolve for a new rule[2]

We also report on the execution time for evolving rules after the materialized lists are built up. We compared our algorithm with the rule evolution algorithm HC_{DS} [11] based on *R-Swoosh*. We generated evolving rules satisfying some constraints, *i.e.*, *rule monotonicity* and *rule-context free*, mentioned the previous study [11]. Note that these rule generation constraints are unfavorable for our work, which does not have these restrictions. In addition, the *TEM* used in this experiment does not exploit the history. However, for all datasets, our algorithm is up to two orders of magnitude faster than the existing algorithm. This implies that our algorithm selectively accesses small portions of the materialization lists over an extensive set of rules.

Table 5: Ratio of sorted accesses in materialized lists

datasets	*#record pairs (a)*	*#access pairs (b)*	*access ratio (b/a)*
$\mathcal{D}_1$	1,180,452	1,995	0.0017
$\mathcal{D}_2$	4,397,038	22,079	0.0050
$\mathcal{D}_3$	6,001,104	3,540	0.0006
$\mathcal{D}_4$	168,112,008	11,655	0.0001

Specifically, Table 5 reports on the ratio of accessed tuples in the materialized lists. This ratio determines the execution time to resolve entities for our proposed method. Empirically, sorted access of less than 0.5% of the materialized lists is sufficient to obtain EM results.

[1] Weight vectors for $\mathcal{D}_1, \mathcal{D}_2, \mathcal{D}_3$, and $\mathcal{D}_4$ are ⟨1.87, 0.06, 0.04⟩, ⟨1.10, 0.32, 0.17, 0.18⟩, ⟨1.34, 0.61, 0.32, 2.06⟩, and ⟨1.55, 0.94, 0.14, 0.08⟩, respectively.

[2] Weight vectors for $\mathcal{D}_1, \mathcal{D}_2, \mathcal{D}_3$, and $\mathcal{D}_4$ are ⟨1.98, 0.07, 0.04⟩, ⟨1.16, 0.34, 0.18, 0.19⟩, ⟨1.41, 0.64, 0.34, 2.17⟩, and ⟨1.63, 0.99, 0.15, 0.08⟩, respectively. This is the best rule among rules with <5% weight difference. Although our work is not constrained by this condition, we add it to accommodate *R-Swoosh* building on this constraint.

Finally, we report on the accuracy of our algorithm using F_1 *score* (Table 6). We evolved rules by changing a weight vector w in a simple hill-climbing manner, where the functions and threshold δ are fixed. In clear contrast to previous methods, our algorithm achieved comparable accuracy from $\mathcal{D}_3$ and $\mathcal{D}_4$ in the benchmark set in addition to adapting to rule changes efficiently. These algorithms require complete re-training to try out new matching techniques, which can also be repeated until convergence.

Table 6: Accuracy comparisons (F_1 *score*) for ours and ML-based EM algorithms

datasets	*TEM*	*PPJoin+*	*FEBRL*	*MARLIN*
$\mathcal{D}_3$	0.965	0.919	0.976	0.974
$\mathcal{D}_4$	0.854	0.778	0.876	0.894

4. CONCLUSION

This paper has addressed the scalability of EM. Towards this goal, we exploited a materialization structure inspired by top-k query processing. Using the materialization, we developed a scalable EM algorithm for evolving rules. Our evaluation demonstrated that our proposed algorithm is two to seven times faster than existing ER algorithms. In addition, when rules are evolved, our algorithm is two orders of magnitude faster than existing algorithms.

Acknowledgement

This work was supported by Microsoft Research Asia and the Ministry of Knowledge Economy (MKE), Korea under Information Technology Research Center (ITRC) support program supervised by the National IT Industry Promotion Agency (NIPA-2011-C1090-1131-0009).

5. REFERENCES

[1] O. Benjelloun, H. Garcia-Molina, D. Menestrina, Q. Su, S. E. Whang, and J. Widom. Swoosh: a generic approach to entity resolution. *VLDB Journal*, 18:255–276, 2009.

[2] K. C. Chang and S. Hwang. Minimal probing: supporting expensive predicates for top-k queries. In *SIGMOD*, pages 346–357, 2002.

[3] X. Dong, A. Halevy, and J. Madhavan. Reference reconciliation in complex information spaces. In *SIGMOD*, pages 85–96, 2005.

[4] R. Fagin, A. Lotem, and M. Naor. Optimal aggregation algorithms for middleware. In *PODS*, pages 102–113, 2001.

[5] I. P. Fellegi and A. B. Sunter. A theory for record linkage. *Journal of the American Statistical Association*, 64(328):1183–1210, 1969.

[6] S. Hwang and K. C. Chang. Optimizing top-k queries for middleware access: A unified cost-based approach. *ACM Trans. Database Syst.*, 32(1), 2007.

[7] H. Köpcke and E. Rahm. Frameworks for entity matching: A comparison. *Data Knowl. Eng.*, 69(2):197–210, 2010.

[8] H. Köpcke, A. Thor, and E. Rahm. Evaluation of entity resolution approaches on real-world match problems. *PVLDB*, 3(1):484–493, 2010.

[9] D. Menestrina, S. E. Whang, and H. Garcia-Molina. Evaluating entity resolution results. *PVLDB*, 3:208–219, 2010.

[10] S. Tejada, C. A. Knoblock, and S. Minton. Learning object identification rules for information integration. *Inform. Syst.*, 26:607–633, 2001.

[11] S. E. Whang and H. Garcia-Molina. Entity resolution with evolving rules. *PVLDB*, 3:1326–1337, 2010.

Predicting the Optimal Ad-hoc Index for Reachability Queries on Graph Databases

Jintian Deng, Fei Liu, Yun Peng, Byron Choi, and Jianliang Xu
Department of Computer Science, Hong Kong Baptist University
Hong Kong, China
{jtdeng, d8050813, ypeng, bchoi, xujl}@comp.hkbu.edu.hk

ABSTRACT

Due to the recent advances in graph databases, a large number of ad-hoc indexes for a fundamental query, namely, reachability query, have been proposed. The structures and performances of these indexes on different graphs have known to be very different. Worst still, deriving an accurate cost model for selecting the optimal index of a graph database has been a daunting task. In this paper, we propose a hierarchical prediction framework, based on neural networks and a set of graph features and a knowledge base on past predictions, to select the optimal index for a graph database. For ease of presentation, we discuss our framework with three structurally distinguishable indexes. Our preliminary experiments show that our framework is 90% accurate on thousands of synthetic graphs.

Categories and Subject Descriptors: H.2.4 [Systems]: Query processing

General Terms: Experimentation, Performance

Keywords: Graph indexing, Neural networks, Reachability queries

1. INTRODUCTION

Recent applications on graph data, for example, social networks, Web ontology, the Semantic Web and XML, have sparked a renewed interest on graph-structured databases. For example, there has been work on XML repositories [6], biological databases [5], ontology data on the Web [8], graph networks [2] and classical graph databases with recursive query language support.

A fundamental query on graphs is reachability queries. Specifically, given two nodes u and v of a graph, the query returns true if and only if v is reachable from u. For all the reasons that reachability queries are important in classical graph databases, there has been a large body of work on its recent applications. For instance, the descendant axis ("//") in XPath, a query language for XML, can be considered as a special application of reachability queries. The descendant axis in XPath can be readily implemented by extending the reachability query to support sets of nodes, e.g., [7]. In addition, reachability queries have also been one of the components in querying the Semantic Web [9]: Information on resources on Semantic Web can be naturally represented as a graph with Resource Description Framework (RDF) [10]. Query languages for the Semantic Web, e.g., SPARQL (a W3C recommendation), involve subgraph matching, where reachability queries are intrinsically a part of the matching.

A wide range of indexes has been proposed for optimizing the performance of reachability queries, which includes interval labeling [1], 2-hop labeling [4] and prime labeling [7, 11], among others. These indexes are often very different in structure and often appear to be fairly ad-hoc. In addition, the asymptotic analysis of the indexes might tell little about the actual performance. For example, the interval labeling's query time is $O(n)$ and index size is $O(n^2)$; and 2-hop labeling's query time is $O(\sqrt{m})$ with index size $O(n\sqrt{m})$, where n and m are nodes number and edges number in graphs, respectively. Worst still, since the structure of these indexes/labels are fairly different, deriving an accurate cost model for the relative performances of the indexes has been a daunting task. A concrete example from our preliminary experiments is that given 100 random reachability queries, 2-hop labeling can be 2 times slower than interval labeling in one data graph but 1.74 times faster in another. As more ad-hoc indexes are proposed, the selection of the optimal index can be expected increasingly challenging. Therefore, what is desirable is *an accurate and practical method to determine the optimal index for a given graph database.*

In this paper, we leverage machine learning technology to solve an important problem in databases. Specifically, we leverage artificial neuron networks (a.k.a neural networks) to predict the optimal labeling based on some graph features, where the networks are trained *offline* and the features are presented in the original proposals of the indexes used. A unique challenge of our prediction problem is that our framework may adapt to predict new graphs, whose features may not be encountered before. Instead of using online neural networks as a black box, we propose a hierarchical framework with a knowledge base of past predictions, which gives more flexibility and extensibility in adapting to recent predictions.

In all, the contributions of the paper are summarized as follows. (i) We propose a framework for predicting the optimal index for reachability queries of a given graph database on-the-fly; and (ii) We conduct an experimental comparison of performance among three structurally-distinguishable indexes under different circumstances.

CIKM'11, October 24–28, 2011, Glasgow, Scotland, UK.

2. BACKGROUND ON AD-HOC INDEXES

A large number of indexes has been proposed recently to support reachability queries on trees or arbitrary graphs. (Since indexes often associate labels with nodes, we may use the term *indexes* and *labels* interchangeably.) Here, we review three selected indexes for two major reasons. Firstly, the indexes are clearly structurally distinguishable, which show the difficulties in deriving an accurate formula to dictate their relative performances. Secondly, the implementation of the indexes are available for our experiments.

(1) Interval labeling has been widely used for trees possibly because of its query efficiency and ease for implementation. The construction involves a traversal on an input tree and labels each node with an interval (i, j), where i is the node's preorder number and j is its postorder number. Node w is reachable from node v, iff v's interval contains w's interval. [1] proposes to extend this labeling to support reachability queries on DAGs. In particular, each node may be associated with multiple intervals, as there may be multiple paths between any two nodes. However, determining reachability query could then be potentially time-consuming.

(2) 2-hop labeling [4] is a popular index to test reachability on arbitrary graphs. 2-hop labeling associates each node v with two labels $L_{in}(v)$ and $L_{out}(v)$, where $L_{in}(v)$ contains *some* nodes that can reach v and similarly, $L_{out}(v)$ consists of some nodes that v can reach. Node v can reach node w, iff $L_{out}(v) \cap L_{in}(w) \neq \emptyset$. Determining the 2-hop labeling with the minimum size is NP-hard, and its approximate construction is often computation intensive as well. However, its desirable index size still makes it a reasonable choice for large (cyclic) graphs applications.

(3) Prime number labeling (or simply prime labeling) [11] uses prime numbers to encode reachability information of trees. A subsequent work [7] extends this work to support reachability test on arbitrary graphs. Prime labeling associates each node with a product of prime numbers and node w is reachable from node v, iff v's label is divisible by w's label. In comparison to 2-hop labeling, prime labeling of graphs could be efficiently constructed. However, for graphs with large depth, prime labeling may results in large product, which leads to large labeling size.

3. DEFINITIONS AND PRELIMINARIES

We begin with the definitions and notations used in this paper.

Data Model and Queries. In this paper, we study directed rooted data graphs, or simply *graphs* in the subsequent discussions. A graph can be defined as $G = (V, E, r, \Sigma, \lambda)$, where V is a set of nodes and $E : V \times V$ is a set of edges, $r \in V$ is a root node, Σ is a set of tags and $\lambda : V \rightarrow \Sigma$ is a function that returns the tag of a node. For simplicity, we may denote a graph as (V, E) when others are irrelevant. Also, we may use *query* to refer to reachability query as it is often clear from the context. In this paper, we often use the *expected query time (EQT)* of a particular labeling (defined below) to refer to query performance.

Definition 3.1: Given a graph G and its label L_G, the *expected query time (EQT)* of L_G is the average time of all possible reachability queries on G. □

Next, we are ready to present the problem studied in this paper.

Problem statement. *Given a graph and a set of labeling techniques, we want to predict the labeling technique for the graph that results in the smallest EQT.*

Artificial Neuron Network. This paper adopts Artificial Neuron Network (ANN), or simply neural network, to predict an optimal index. The ANN takes feature vectors of user-interested objects as input and produces predictions, for example, class labels of objects, as output. The task of ANN learning is to find a satisfactory assignment of its weighted variables, based on training samples, such that prediction error is minimized. The objects of our interest is graph databases and the prediction is labeling types.

Features of Graphs. The structure of a graph database is represented by a set of features for training an ANN. There have been admittedly many possible features which cannot be included in this paper. We however study the performance analysis (both asymptotical and experimental) of the index proposals to summarize a number of features, which have been considered relevant by the inventors of the indexes. Specifically, the features of graph $G = (V, E)$ are the following: (i) the number of nodes, $|V|$; (ii) the number of edges, $|E|$; (iii) the number of strongly connected components (`SCCs`) ; (iv) the acyclicity: if a graph contains at least one cycle, we say the acyclicity of the graph is false; it is true, otherwise; (v) the average fan-out of nodes: the fan-out of a node is the number of outgoing edges; (vi) the depth: the depth of a graph is defined to be of the "deepest" spanning tree of the graph (vii) the non-tree density: $(|E| - |V| - 1)/|E|$ (viii) the graph density: $|E|/|V|^2$ (ix) the cut nodes density: the number of cut nodes divided by the number of nodes; and (x) the "cycle-edge" density: the number of edges that are on at least one cycle over the number of edges.

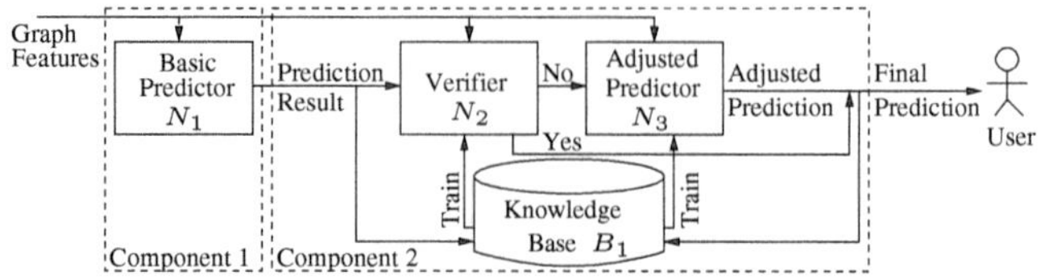

Figure 1: Overview of the basic prediction model

4. BASIC PREDICTION MODEL

In this section, we present the details of the basic prediction model. In a nutshell, the model has two components. The first component contains a single neural network namely the basic predictor, denoted as N_1, and the second component consists of a knowledge base, denoted as B, and two neural networks, namely the verifier and the adjusted predictor, denoted as N_2 and N_3, respectively. We illustrate the overall framework with Fig. 1.

The first component takes the features of a graph G as input and produces a prediction for the optimal index on G as output. This prediction may be accepted as the final prediction. However, when the graphs for prediction have not been encountered in training, the first component alone may no longer be accurate. To address these, we introduce the second component to assess the prediction and if necessary, to adjust the prediction based on previous predictions. In the following, we discuss the details of these two components.

4.1 The Basic Predictor

The basic predictor is a single neural network N_1. Its input layer has ten neurons, each of which represents a graph feature. The hidden layer has m neurons, where m is a tunable parameter to balance prediction accuracy and computational cost. The output layer has a neuron for each labeling to determine the confidence of being selected as output. We may simply take the labeling with the highest confidence as the optimal index prediction. In this paper, we used three labelings for illustration and therefore the output layer consists of three neurons.

4.2 The Verifier and the Adjusted Predictor

The second component performs two tasks. The first task is to verify the correctness of the prediction of N_1. The other task is to adjust the prediction, if the prediction of N_1 cannot pass the assessment. Fig. 1 shows that this component comprises two neural networks N_2 and N_3 and a knowledge base B_1. The verifier N_2 takes the prediction of N_1 combining with graph features as input and predicts whether N_1's prediction is correct or not. If it is correct, N_1's prediction is final. Otherwise, N_2 passes graph features to N_3 for an adjusted prediction.

To construct the second component, we maintain the knowledge base B_1 to record the correctness of previous predictions. The

Table 1: **Possible predictions of the basic prediction model**

N_1	N_2	N_3	N_1	N_2	N_3
0	0	0	0	1	1
0	0	1	1	0	1
0	1	0	1	1	0
1	0	0	1	1	1
correct final result			erroneous final result		

correctness of previous predictions can be either directly provided by users or verified by experiments offline. Subsequently, N_2 is trained with the knowledge base and N_3 is trained with the cases where N_2 declared N_1 incorrect. The accuracy of N_1 may drop when the graph features in the input graph have not been encountered before, which are required to identify by N_2. We remark that the prediction of the verifier N_2 is much simpler than that of N_1, which only involves a binary output. In addition, N_3 is specially trained to adjust incorrect predictions.

Error Analysis. Next, we analyze the expected prediction error of the basic prediction model and compare it with that of a naive method. We first define some notations for the analysis. Abusing the notations slightly, we use N_1, N_2 and N_3 to denote the correctness of the prediction of the neural networks N_1, N_2 and N_3, respectively. We use the value 0, e.g., $N_i = 0$, to denote a correct prediction of N_i, where $i \in \{1,2,3\}$. Similarly, an incorrect prediction of N_i is denoted as $N_i = 1$. Since we have three neural networks in the basic prediction model, we have eight cases, listed in Tab. 1. In Tab. 1, the four cases of the LHS (respectively, the RHS) shows that the final prediction of the model is correct (respectively, incorrect). For instance, in the case where $N_1 = 1$, $N_2 = 0$, $N_3 = 0$, N_1 predicts incorrectly, N_2 detects the incorrect prediction and N_3 determines the correct prediction to users.

Proposition 4.1: *Suppose* $P(N_i = 0) > k$, $1 \geq k > 0.5$, $i = \{1, 2, 3\}$, *the basic prediction model outperforms a naive method (i.e., a single neural network) and the performance improvement increases with the growth of k.* □

PROOF. Let P_1 denote the error probability of the naive method and P_2 that of the basic append model. P_1 and P_2 are as follows:

$$P_1 = P(N_1 = 1)$$

$$\begin{aligned} P_2 = &(P(N_1 = 0) \times P(N_2 = 1) \times P(N_3 = 1)) \\ &+ (P(N_1 = 1) \times P(N_2 = 0) \times P(N_3 = 1)) \\ &+ (P(N_1 = 1) \times P(N_2 = 1) \times P(N_3 = 0)) \\ &+ (P(N_1 = 1) \times P(N_2 = 1) \times P(N_3 = 1)). \end{aligned}$$

It follows that

$$\begin{aligned} P_1 - P_2 = &P(N_1 = 1)P(N_2 = 0)P(N_3 = 0) \\ &- P(N_1 = 0)P(N_2 = 1)P(N_3 = 1). \end{aligned} \tag{1}$$

For simplicity, let x, y, z denote $P(N_1 = 0)$, $P(N_2 = 0)$, and $P(N_3 = 0)$, respectively. (1) is rewritten as

$$P_1 - P_2 = (1 - x)yz - x(1 - y)(1 - z) \tag{2}$$

Let the LHS of (2) be 0. We obtain a surface in the 3-d space:

$$z = \frac{x(1-y)}{(1-x)y + x(1-y)} \tag{3}$$

$$P_1 - P_2 > 0 \Leftrightarrow z > \frac{x(1-y)}{(1-x)y + x(1-y)} \tag{4}$$

Since $P(N_i = 0) \in (0, 1)$, i={1,2,3}, it is evident that the probability of $P_1 > P_2$ is the volume *above the surface* of the cube:

$$P(P_1 - P_2 > 0) = \int_0^1 \int_0^1 \frac{x(1-y)}{(1-x)y + x(1-y)} dxdy \tag{5}$$

Since $x, y > k, k \in (0.5, 1)$ by assumption, the space volume above the surface in the cuboid $x, y \in (k, 1), z \in (0, 1)$ is

$$\int_k^1 \int_k^1 \frac{x(1-y)}{(1-x)y + x(1-y)} dxdy$$

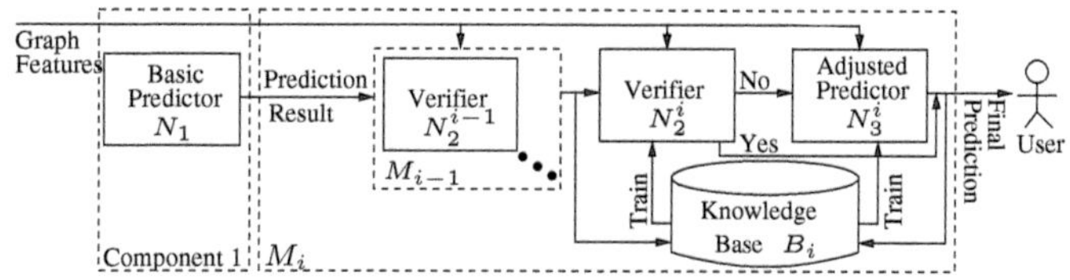

Figure 2: Overview of the hierarchical prediction model

and the cuboid's volume is $(1 - k)^2$. Therefore, the probability of $P_1 > P_2$ is

$$P(P_1 - P_2 > 0) = \frac{\int_k^1 \int_k^1 \frac{x(1-y)}{(1-x)y+x(1-y)} dxdy}{(1-k)^2} \tag{6}$$

And if we restrict $z > k$, it follows

$$P(P_1 - P_2 > 0) = \frac{\int_{\frac{k^2}{2k^2-2k+1}}^1 \int_k^{\frac{(1-k)x}{k-(2k-1)x}} \frac{x(1-y)}{(1-x)y+x(1-y)} dxdy}{(1-k)^3} \tag{7}$$

To simplify calculation, we rewrite the surface (3) as

$$x = \frac{yz}{(1-y)(1-z) + yz} \tag{8}$$

and alter integration variables from x, y to y, z. (7) becomes

$$P(P_1 - P_2 > 0) = \frac{\int_k^1 \int_k^1 \frac{yz}{(1-y)(1-z)+yz} dydz - k(1-k)^2}{(1-k)^3} \tag{9}$$

Since the differential of Formula (9) with respect to k is positive when $k > 0.5$, $P(P_1 - P_2 > 0)$ increases as k increases. □

5. HIERARCHICAL PREDICTION MODEL

In the context of graph databases, it is often unrealistic to assume the training data graphs are always representative enough. That is, one may need to determine the optimal index for data graphs that have not been encountered in training. Such new graphs often notably reduce the accuracy of any prediction model. In this section, we generalize the basic prediction model in order to further enhance the prediction accuracy.

In a nutshell, we organize the second component of the basic prediction model in a hierarchy. An overview of the hierarchical model is illustrated in Fig. 2. Specifically, the verifier at level i (denoted as N_2^i) is connected from the hierarchical prediction model at level $i - 1$ (i.e., M_{i-1}) and M_0 is simply the second component of the basic prediction model. Such an organization of neural networks allows the prediction of the model at the lower level to be adjusted by that at the upper level.

More specifically, M_i is composed of three elements: (i) two neural networks N_2^i and N_3^i, (ii) the prediction model at the lower level M_{i-1} and (iii) a knowledge base B_i to record the prediction correctness of M_{i-1}. Similar to the basic model, N_2^i takes M_{i-1}'s prediction as input and assesses its prediction. If the assessment passes, M_{i-1}'s prediction is delivered to the user. Otherwise, the prediction together with graph features are delivered to N_3^i for further adjustment. The adjusted prediction is delivered to the user.

We remark that our approach has a flexibility on the levels of the hierarchy needed for prediction and the refresh frequency of verifiers and adjusted predictors. In comparison, adopting an online neural network (as a black box) does not give us such a flexibility.

Error Analysis. Similar to the analysis on the basic model, we analyze the accuracy of the hierarchical model below.

Proposition 5.1: *Suppose the neural networks' accuracies are larger than k, where* $0.5 < k \leq 1$, *prediction accuracy increases with the hierarchy level i.* □

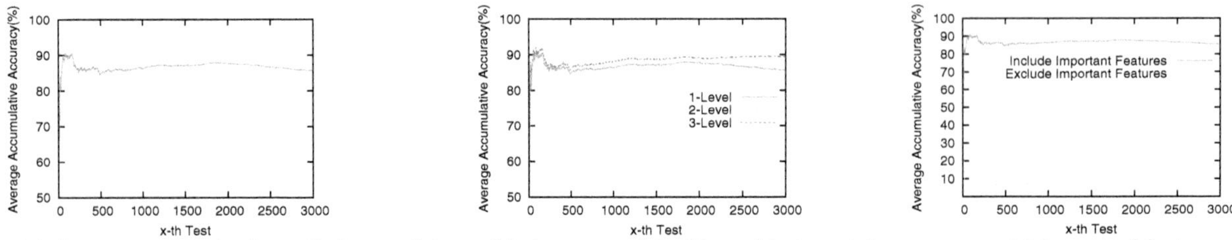

(a) Accuracy of the basic prediction model (b) Accuracy of the hierarchical model (c) Impact of features

Figure 3: Prediction accurarcies

PROOF. To prove the proposition, we need to argue M_i outperforms M_{i-1}, for any $i \geq 1$. Similar to the proof of Proposition 1, we calculate the error probabilities of model with M_{i-1} and M_i, respectively, as

$$P_1 = P(M_{i-1} = 1)$$

and

$$\begin{aligned} P_2 = & P(N_1 = 0)P(N_2^i = 1)\big(P(N_3^i = 1) + P(N_3^i = 0)\big)P(M_{i-1} = 1) \\ & + P(N_1 = 1)P(N_2^i = 1)\big(P(N_3^i = 1) + P(N_3^i = 0)\big) \\ & + P(N_1 = 1)P(N_2^i = 0)\big(P(N_3^i = 1) + P(N_3^i = 0)\big)P(M_{i-1} = 1), \end{aligned}$$

where $M_i = 1$ means "M_i produces erroneous result". It follows that

$$\begin{aligned} P_1 - P_2 = & P(N_1 = 0)P(N_2^i = 0)P(M_{i-1} = 1) \\ & + P(N_1 = 1)P(N_2^i = 1)P(M_{i-1} = 0). \end{aligned}$$

It is of the same form of Equation (1). Hence, we can readily draw the conclusion that $P(P_1 - P_2 > 0)$ is larger than 0.5 and increases monotonously with the increase of the accuracy lower bound of N_1, N_2^i, N_3^i and M_{i-1}. □

6. EXPERIMENT EVALUATION

This section presents a preliminary experiment that verifies the effectiveness of our proposed method.

Hardware and software. We ran our experiments on a machine with a Core2 Quad 2.33GHz CPU and 4GB RAM running Windows Vista. We used the interval labeling implementation from Zhu *et al* [12] written in C, prime labeling implementation from Peng *et al* [7] written in Java and the 2-hop labeling implementation from Bramandia *et al* [3] written in C++. We used JDK 1.6 and Microsoft Visual Studio 2008 as the running environment.

Datasets and query workload. We used the synthetic graph generator from Zhu *et al* [12]. We generated 8000 graphs with vertices and fanouts ranging from 1000 to 5000 and from 5 to 20, respectively. We divided the graphs randomly into two sets: (i) 5000 for training and (ii) 3000 for testing. For each graph, we estimated the **EQT** of each indexing technique by measuring the runtime of 100 random reachability queries. We then used the graph features together with the **EQT** of each index to train the basic prediction model. The correctness of the prediction is compared with the real optimal one. The prediction times were negligible (less than 20 milliseconds) and therefore omitted here.

Performance results. We first tested the accuracy of the basic predictor. The accuracy is given in terms of of the average accuracy among the testing graphs so far. We refer the accuracy as the *average accumulative accuracy*. The result is shown in Fig. 3(a). The figure shows that the average accumulative accuracy of the basic prediction model is often higher than 85% for the testing graphs.

Next, we conducted an experiment on the hierarchy prediction model. We trained and tested the accuracies of 1-level, 2-level and 3-level models. The results are shown in Fig. 3(b). The performances of 2-level and 3-level are 5% more accurate than that of the basic predictor. However, in our particular experiment settings, the improvement of introducing the third level was not significant, as we only tested the hierarchical framework with 3000 graphs. The graphs for training the third level (the knowledge base B_3) and testing the adjusted predictor at the third level are relatively small.

Finally, to illustrate that there are in fact some important features for our index selection problem, we trained the ANN by using classical feature selection algorithm. In particular, we trained our model with the important features, which are $|E|$, $|V|$, the graph density, and the average fanout. The accuracy of the model is reported in Fig. 3(c). It shows that the accuracy is still high when compared to Fig. 3(a) and Fig. 3(c) shows that the model trained without these five features are clearly inaccurate.

7. FUTURE WORK

In this paper, we propose a hierarchical model to predict the optimal index for reachability queries of a graph database and evaluate it with our preliminary experiments. As for future work, we are extending the experiments and analysis on more features, graphs and queries. We are studying how this model is extended to the indexes of other query formalisms, e.g., subgraph isomorphism.

Acknowledgement. This work is partly supported by FRG2/08-09/091 and FRG2/09-10/054. We are thankful to the members of the Database Group of Hong Kong Baptist University for helpful discussions. We are grateful to Rui Shi for her initial implementations.

8. REFERENCES

[1] R. Agrawal, A. Borgida, and H. V. Jagadish. Efficient management of transitive relationships in large data and knowledge bases. In *SIGMOD*, pages 253–262, 1989.

[2] V. Batagelj and A. Mrvar. Pajek datasets. *http://vlado.fmf.uni-lj.si/pub/networks/data/*, 2006.

[3] R. Bramandia, B. Choi, and W. K. Ng. Incremental maintenance of 2-hop labeling of large graphs. *IEEE Trans. Knowl. Data Eng.*, 22(5):682–698, 2010.

[4] E. Cohen, E. Halperin, H. Kaplan, and U. Zwick. Reachability and distance queries via 2-hop labels. In *SODA*, pages 937–946, 2002.

[5] I. Keseler, J. C. Vides, S. G. Castro, J. Ingraham, S. Paley, I. Paulsen, M. Peralta-Gil, and P. Karp. Ecocyc: a comprehensive database resource for escherichia coli. *Nucleic Acids Research*, vol. 33:pp. D334–D337, 2005.

[6] G. Miklau. UW XML repository. *http://www.cs.washington.edu/research/xmldatasets/*, 2009.

[7] Y. Peng, B. Choi, and J. Xu. Selectivity estimation of twig queries on cyclic graphs. In *ICDE*, 2011.

[8] QuickGo: GO Browser. Web interface. *European Bioinformatics Inst, http://www.ebi.ac.uk/ego/*, 2009.

[9] W3C. Semantic web activity. *http://www.w3.org/2001/sw/*, 2007.

[10] W3C. Resource description framework (RDF). *W3C, http://www.w3.org/RDF*, 2009.

[11] X. Wu, M. L. Lee, and W. Hsu. A prime number labeling scheme for dynamic ordered xml trees. In *ICDE*, pages 66–, 2004.

[12] L. Zhu, B. Choi, B. He, J. Yu, and W. Ng. A Uniform Framework for Ad-Hoc Indexes to Answer Reachability Queries on Large Graphs. In *DASFAA*, pages 138–152, 2009.

Collection-Based Compression using Discovered Long Matching Strings

Andrew Peel[1,2] a.peel@student.unimelb.edu.au
Anthony Wirth[1] awirth@unimelb.edu.au
Justin Zobel[1,2] jzobel@unimelb.edu.au

[1] Dept. Computer Science & Software Engineering, The University of Melbourne, Australia
[2] National ICT Australia (NICTA), Victoria Research Laboratory, The University of Melbourne, Australia

ABSTRACT

Many collections of data contain items that are inherently similar. For example, archives contain files with incremental changes between releases. Long-range inter-file similarities are not exploited by standard approaches to compression. We investigate compression using similarity from all parts of a collection, *collection-based compression* (CBC). Input files are delta-encoded by reference to long string matches in a source collection. The expected space requirement of our encoding algorithm is sublinear with the collection size, and the compression time complexity is linear with the input file size. We show that our scheme achieves better compression for large input files than existing differential compression systems, and scales better. Also, we achieve significant compression improvement compared to compressing each file individually using standard utilities: our scheme achieves several times the compression of `gzip` or `7-zip`. The overall result is a dramatic improvement on compression available with existing approaches.

Categories and Subject Descriptors

E.4 [**Coding and Information Theory**]: Data Compaction and Compression

General Terms

Algorithms, Experimentation, Performance

Keywords

Compression, data representation, repository storage

1. INTRODUCTION

Many data collections contain vast quantities of repeated material. Examples include version repositories for software, web site archives, and collections of genomes. It is attractive to compress large collections to reduce the cost of storage and synchronisation, but most compression methods require a representation of the data in memory.

In this paper we explore ways of using an entire collection as a reference against which new material can be compressed. We describe this as *collection-based compression* (CBC), an approach that generalises previous methods based on coding similarities with a previous file or small set of files. A successful CBC system: (1) has the ability to compress a *query* string or file using information from every location in the collection; (2) has running time growing in proportion to the size of the file being compressed; and (3) operates within fixed or limited memory.

We present `cobald`, a simple, but effective, CBC scheme using two stages. The first stage uses hash-based string search to find long matching substrings in the collection, and produces a *delta encoding* of the query file in which the string matches are replaced with references to the collection, thus taking advantage of long-range similarities. In the second stage, the delta encoding is compressed using a standard compression tool, thus taking advantage of local similarities. Our scheme differs from previous approaches in two key aspects. It uses a permanent index, consisting of hashes of large substrings, to support the search during delta encoding; and it employs a novel encoding algorithm.

A benefit of our approach is that encoding a new file does not require large parts of the collection to be re-read. Overall compression time is comparable to that with a standard compressor alone, and often is faster. Our experiments demonstrate that our approach achieves a several-fold compression improvement compared to standard tools.

2. BACKGROUND

Differential encoding, also known as delta encoding, is the process of encoding one string or file in terms of another. The resulting delta represents a sequence of instructions to reconstruct, or *decode*, a query string from a reference string. (In some literature, the query string is referred to as the 'version' or 'target', and the delta as a 'patch'.)

Existing LZ compression utilities build a dictionary of the strings contained in a sliding window from the input file. `Gzip` uses a 32 kB window, whereas `7-zip` achieves better compression using a window up to 4 GB in size. Techniques for exploiting similarity in the data beyond the compression window typically employ hash-based string search, such as the Karp-Rabin string search algorithm [5]. The strings of length n, or *n-grams*, in the reference and query strings are hashed, then matching strings are located by finding matching hashes. However, as string matches shorter than n will not be found, the delta is no longer optimal. We refer to this string search method as *n-gram search*.

The **rzip** program [8] performed a long-range search over a 900 MB window for duplicate 32-byte blocks, which were hashed using **rsync**. The resulting delta was compressed using **bzip2**. Bentley and McIllroy [3] reduced the space requirement of hash-based search by inserting every k^{th} n-gram hash of the reference string into the hash table, and discarding the rest; a technique we refer to as a *sampled hash index*. The search algorithm using a sampled hash index is more complicated. Each n-gram of the query string was hashed and queried in the hash table to identify potential matches in the reference string. A matching n-gram found in the index is likely to occur partway through a longer matching string, so the matching n-gram is then *extended* backwards and forwards using a symbol-by-symbol comparison of the strings to find the complete matching substring. Their delta was then compressed using **gzip**.

While these approaches compress a single file, utilising matching data from another file may be achieved using differential encoding. **Vdelta** [4] processes a concatenation of the reference string followed by the query string, constructing an index of n-gram hashes in a single pass. By applying compression techniques such as efficient coding of the instructions in the delta, Hunt et al. [4] developed the concept of *differential compression*. This has been incorporated into the VCDIFF format (RFC3284) [6] for differentially compressed data. **Vdelta** is not suitable for CBC without modification as each consecutive unmatched n-gram is indexed, which requires more space than the unmatched input symbols themselves. The **xdelta** program [7] constructs a delta using constant memory. As the n-gram hashes are indexed, a new hash replaces a duplicate hash in the hash table. The compression performance may be expected to degrade for larger inputs as a larger proportion of n-grams will have been deleted from the index.

Delta compression techniques have been applied to file system backup and archiving file system snapshots. The '1.5-pass' algorithm of Ajtai et al. [2] also uses hash-based search in constant memory by only indexing a single n-gram reference for each hash. The **hsadelta** [1] algorithm achieves constant space using a different approach. It uses a sampled hash index in which every n^{th} n-gram is indexed, and varies n with the input size so that the number of index entries is constant. Consequently, we expect gradually worse compression with increasing collection size. However, **hsadelta** includes features that are likely to be useful for CBC. It uses hash sampling with a fixed sampling period in order to reduce the index size to a fraction of the input. The problem of false negative index queries is addressed by including several data structures intended to quickly answer most queries for hashes which are not in the index. Another feature is that it uses a larger hash space of $2^{64} - 1$ to obtain a very small probability of hash collisions. This index is sparsely populated even for multi-terabyte collections, so a tree structure is used for the index, rather than a hash array. As **hsadelta** records duplicate hashes, it is able to locate all instances of a repeated string. It searches for the longest of these string matches by finding sequential references in the hash table.

An alternative approach to CBC is to encode the query file as a delta with respect to a small selection of reference files which are most similar to the query file. The principal challenge of this approach is to find methods to identify the files in a collection which are most similar to the new query file. We do not pursue this approach as we expect similarity to be dispersed over multiple fragments of collection files.

3. DESCRIPTION OF OUR SCHEME

Cobald compresses using a two-stage pipeline with an encode operation followed by a compress operation. In the *encode operation* the query string is differentially encoded in terms of the files already in the collection. An index of n-gram hashes is constructed and then used to locate strings in the collection matching substrings of the query string. The constructed index is a subset of the *hash list file* which is maintained on external storage. The encode operation also reads data from the collection when checking for hash collisions and extending string matches. The output of the encode operation is a delta file which is input to both the compress and insert operations. In the *insert operation*, an encoded delta file is indexed by appending its n-gram hashes to the hash list file. In the *compress operation* a standard compression utility (we present results using **gzip** and **7-zip**) is applied to the delta file to produce the final compressed version of the query string.

In order to search a reference collection, **cobald**'s encode operation uses several of the previously-described modifications of the hash-based n-gram search algorithm. Similarly to **hsadelta** and the system of Bentley and McIllroy [3], **cobald** uses a sampled hash index, sampling every n^{th} n-gram. Like **vdelta** and **xdelta**, in **cobald** we select the first match found, rather than searching for the longest match. By discarding references to duplicate n-grams from the index, the space complexity of **cobald** is proportional to the unmatched data in the collection files and the query string.

The following scenario illustrates the system operation. A *collection* consisting of several *data sets*, each containing multiple files, is to be compressed. Initially, the hash list file is empty. The first file is encoded, perhaps identifying some duplicate substrings within itself and achieves a modest reduction in size. The encoded file is then inserted into the index; a sample (every n^{th}) of its string hashes is appended to the hash list file. A second file is then encoded, replacing strings matched to duplicates found in the first file, or earlier in itself. The encoded second file is then inserted. This process continues for subsequent files: each file is able to refer to previous occurrences of duplicate strings, either in a previously-inserted file, or in itself. Once an input file has been encoded and inserted, it is compressed using **gzip** or another compression utility.

In order to retrieve a compressed file from the collection, it is decompressed and decoded, which requires retrieving its references to other encoded files in the collection. These referenced files must also be decompressed, but they do not need to be decoded as the delta references are to matching strings in other delta files.

The scenario highlights several desirable aspects of the compression system. First, the entire collection does not need to be read when encoding or inserting a new file. Second, a file may be decoded without needing to decode other files in the collection (although they will need to be decompressed), and consequently decoding may be expected to be fast. Third, as the encoded file is subsequently compressed using a standard compression tool, the first stage can use an inefficient coding method for the match references in the encoded file.

Table 1: Comparison of compression achieved by `cobald`, `hsadelta`, `xdelta` and `open-vcdiff`. For each trial, the top number is the size of the compressed delta file in megabytes, and the bottom number is the compressed delta file size as a percentage of the query file size. The last trial has some entries as 'n/a' as these systems where unable to compress the 6 GB file.

query file *reference file*	*Size* *(MB)*		`cobald` $n = 256$	`cobald` $n = 1024$	`hsadelta`	`xdelta`	`vcdiff`
Drosophila-r56.stripped.tar	1,200	MB	18.3	41.9	78.8	18.9	**10.2**
w.r.t. Drosophila-r55.stripped.tar	1,140	%	1.53	3.50	6.58	1.58	**0.85**
ABCwebCrawl.table1.week2	1,910	MB	**5.81**	7.58	7.54	18.1	9.28
w.r.t. ABCwebCrawl.table1.week1	1,910	%	**0.30**	0.40	0.40	0.95	0.49
ABCwebCrawl.week2.tar	6,470	MB	**14.7**	23.9	n/a	n/a	n/a
w.r.t. ABCwebCrawl.week1.tar	6,540	%	**0.23**	0.37			

The delta file begins with an array of the names of all collection files referred to by the COPY commands in the delta. The delta commands follow as a sequence of blocks. A *COPY block* describes a COPY command to locate the matching string in a collection file and consists of a triple ⟨*file id, length, offset*⟩ where *file id* is the index of the file name array in the header, *length* is the number of bytes of the matching string and *offset* is the position in the file of the first byte. An *ADD block* describes an ADD command and contains a variable-length string of verbatim data to be inserted into the decoded string.

The hash list file contains triples ⟨*hash, match set, offset*⟩ for every k^{th} n-gram in each file in the collection, which are appended as the file is inserted. To ensure complete coverage of the data, we set $k = n$. The hashes are calculated over substrings of fixed length n, using the Karp-Rabin rolling hash function [5] with the maximum hash being a large prime less than 2^{28}. During insertion, hash matches are resolved by comparing the new n-gram with n-grams in the collection files. Matching n-grams are assigned the same *match set* identifier, and a match set defines a set of references to identical n-grams in the collection files. In many cases, several match sets are associated with a single hash value, a consequence of hash collisions. *Offset* is the position in the collection file of the first byte of the n-gram. This process is modified slightly for the special case of inserting a delta file; to avoid attempting to match a string containing a COPY block, only the hashes from ADD blocks are appended to the hash list file, and the count for the kth n-gram is restarted at the beginning of each block.

Index construction. Before searching the collection, the encode operation constructs an index in memory from the hash list file. We use a separately-chained hash table. The first occurrence of each match set in the hash list file is inserted into the hash table, and subsequent matching n-grams, which have the same match set identifier, are discarded. This has the effect of preferring the oldest occurrences of a duplicate n-gram as file indexes are appended to the hash list file in chronological order.

Encoding algorithm. When a hash match is found, the n-gram references in the index are retrieved from the collection files and compared to the n-gram in the query string. A successful match is extended forwards and backwards to find the complete matching substring. This match reference is then appended to a *match list*, and the search resumes from the end of the match in the query string. Once the search of the query string is complete, the match list is traversed to remove overlapping references, which occur when a reference has been extended backwards to overlap previous references. Then the delta is created by writing the references from the match list as COPY blocks and inserting ADD blocks in the gaps between matches.

4. TEST DATA

Results are presented using two data collections: *web snap-shots* and *genome*. Each *collection* contains several *data sets*, each containing multiple files. The data sets in each collection were created sequentially as a revision of the previous data set. Therefore a substantial proportion of the data will be unchanged between data sets, as might be expected from a sequence of archival snap-shots.

The *web snap-shots* collection is eight web crawls of a media web site (`abc.net.au`) taken one week apart over a two-month period. It contains only the (untruncated) html files; media files such as images have been discarded. It consists of 8 data sets, ranging from 6,450 to 7,850 MB in size, with a total size of 55,714 MB.

The *genome* data collection comprises releases 36 to 56 of the *Drosophila melanogaster* genome from the Ensembl project (`ftp.ensembl.org`). It consists of 21 data sets, ranging from 1,100 to 1,400 MB in size, with a total size of 26,141 MB. The data consists of nucleotide sequences with annotations describing aspects such as protein and RNA expression. Each release is an update of the data from the previous release, incorporating new results from the genomic research community.

5. RESULTS

We compared `cobald` to other delta-encoders by encoding and compressing a query file with respect to a collection containing a single reference file. In trials conducted using smaller files ($<$ 1 GB) (results not shown), `hsadelta` and `vcdiff` (an open source implementation of `vdelta`) achieved the best compression. The files compressed using `cobald` ($n = 256$) were approximately 15% larger, and using `cobald` ($n = 1024$) and `xdelta` were approximately 30 to 60% larger than the compression achieved by `hsadelta` and `vcdiff`.

For larger files, we found that `cobald` achieves comparable, and often better, compression than the other tools. Some compression results for larger files are presented in Table 1. This compression improvement with input size is

Table 2: **Total compressed collection file size in megabytes, including the hash list file size and compressed collection file sizes, using gzip and 7-zip for the second compression stage in cobald with $n = 1024$. The unencoded rows show the compression by gzip and 7-zip without prior encoding by cobald.**

Collection	*uncompressed*	gzip	7-zip
Web snap-shots			
unencoded	55,714	6,564	2,618
cobald	5,902	1,067	701
Genome			
unencoded	26,100	7,060	5,680
cobald	1,710	408	321

expected as the other tools contain limits on their index sizes as described in Section 2.

To evaluate cobald for CBC, we compressed the data collections and used gzip and 7-zip for the second compression stage. The results presented were obtained using $n = 1024$. While a smaller value for n will yield better compression, a larger index file is required; as n decreases the additional index storage exceeds the marginal improvement in compression. We found that $n = 1024$ required the least external storage (the total sizes of the compressed collection files and the index file). The compression results using other values for n will be presented in a full version of this article.

Table 2 shows the total file space used for the compressed web snap-shots and genome collections. We see that our scheme is of considerable benefit. For example, combining cobald with 7-zip reduces the total size of the web snapshots collection to less than 30% of the archive made when 7-zip is used alone. Compression of the genome collection was more than 15 times that achieved by 7-zip alone.

Compression of individual data sets in the *genome* collection is shown in Figure 1. We observe that, after the first data set has been inserted into the index, the compression of subsequent data sets is in the range of 0.5% to 2%. Looking at individual data sets, the compression is not uniform. For releases 49 and 56, for instance, the compressed file sizes are significantly larger, most likely because of major updates to the database. Even then, our encoding scheme achieves a gain close to a factor of ten.

6. CONCLUSIONS

Our scheme, cobald, is a practical approach to collection-based compression. It compresses the large collections we have tested six to ten times more than is achieved by compressing the collection files individually. Additional files may readily be added to the collection and files are decompressed faster than with 7-zip. Recalling the desirable properties of a CBC system described in Section 1, our scheme avoids the need to read the entire collection when encoding a new file by maintaining the hash list file and constructing an index. Cobald achieves similar compression to mature delta encoding systems, and demonstrates some advantage with larger input files.

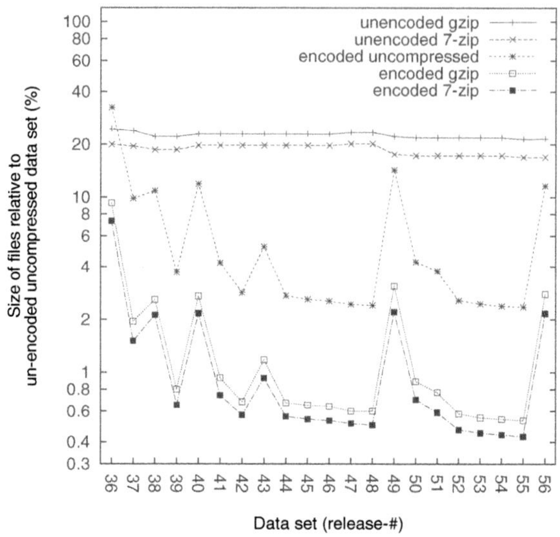

Figure 1: Compressed sizes of each data set in the genome collection using cobald with $n = 1024$.

Acknowledgements

We thank Halil Ali for providing the *web snap-shots* data collection, and Kerri Morgan for her thorough feedback on the paper. We also thank Shir Peled and Kevin Fray.

NICTA is funded by the Australian Government as represented by the Department of Broadband, Communications and the Digital Economy and the Australian Research Council through the ICT Centre of Excellence program.

7. REFERENCES

[1] R. C. Agarwal, K. Gupta, S. Jain, and S. Amalapurapu. An approximation to the greedy algorithm for differential compression. *IBM Journal of Research and Development*, pages 149–166, Jan. 2006.

[2] M. Ajtai, R. Burns, R. Fagin, D. D. E. Long, and L. Stockmeyer. Compactly encoding unstructured inputs with differential compression. *Journal of the ACM*, 49(3):318–367, May 2002.

[3] J. Bentley and D. McIlroy. Data compression with long repeated strings. *Information Sciences*, 135(1-2):1–11, 2001.

[4] J. J. Hunt, K.-P. Vo, and W. F. Tichy. Delta algorithms: an empirical analysis. *ACM Trans. Software Engineering Methodology*, 7(2):192–214, 1998.

[5] R. M. Karp and M. O. Rabin. Efficient randomized pattern-matching algorithms. *IBM Journal of Research and Development*, 31(2):249–260, 1987.

[6] D. G. Korn and K.-P. Vo. Engineering a differencing and compression data format. In *Proc. USENIX Annual Technical Conference*, 2002.

[7] J. P. MacDonald. File system support for delta compression. Master's thesis, University of California at Berkeley, Dept. Electrical Engineering and Computer Sciences, Berkeley, CA, USA, 2000.

[8] A. Tridgell. *Efficient Algorithms for Sorting and Synchronization*. PhD thesis, Australian National University, Canberra, Australia, 1999.

A Robust Index for Regular Expression Queries

Dominic Tsang
University of Sydney
City Road
Sydney, Australia
dtsa3820@uni.sydney.edu.au

Sanjay Chawla
University of Sydney
City Road
Sydney, Australia
sanjay.chawla@uni.sydney.edu.au

ABSTRACT

The `like` regular expression predicate has been part of the SQL standard since at least 1989. However, despite its popularity and wide usage, database vendors provide only limited indexing support for regular expression queries which almost always require a full table scan.

In this paper we propose a rigorous and robust approach for providing indexing support for regular expression queries. Our approach consists of formulating the indexing problem as a combinatorial optimization problem. We begin with a database, abstracted as a collection of strings. From this data set we generate a query workload. The input to the optimization problem is the database and the workload. The output is a set of multigrams (substrings) which can be used as keys to records which satisfy the query workload. The multigrams can then be integrated with the data structure (like B+ trees) to provide indexing support for the queries. We provide a deterministic and a randomized approximation algorithm (with provable guarantees) to solve the optimization problem. Extensive experiments on synthetic data sets demonstrate that our approach is accurate and efficient.

We also present a case study on PROSITE patterns - which are complex regular expression signatures for classes of proteins. Again, we are able to demonstrate the utility of our indexing approach in terms of accuracy and efficiency. Thus, perhaps for the first time, there is a robust and practical indexing mechanism for an important class of database queries.

Categories and Subject Descriptors

H.2.4 [**Database Management**]: Query processing; D.2.10 [**Software**]: Methodologies

General Terms

Design, Performance

CIKM'11, October 24–28, 2011, Glasgow, Scotland, UK.

1. INTRODUCTION

Consider a simple database query:

```
SELECT doc.id FROM doc where doc.text LIKE '%har%'
```

Current database systems have to carry out a full table scan to answer the above query. For large databases (like collections of documents) this can be extremely time consuming rendering the use of regular expression queries almost infeasible.

In the above query, the query poser may be searching for documents which contain the text **share** or **shard** or something else. To speed up query processing, the database designer could potentially create an index where the keys are multigrams (substrings) which point to all records that contain that multigram themselves (the **posting list** of the multigram). In this instance, there are several choices that could be made. For example, the index algorithm may decide to select the multigram **har** or **ha** or **ar** or nothing at all.

To process the query, the query engine will determine if there is any of the text fragments in the regular expression query belong to the key set of the index. If so, then the index will be scanned to retrieve the posting list for that multigram. The query engine then will apply the regular expression template on each record of the posting list and select those that are matched. The query processing framework is shown in Figure 1.

The key challenge is in deciding what to index. For example, the advantage of indexing **har** over **ha** is efficiency: the database records which contain the text **har** is a subset of those which contain **ha** resulting in lower IO cost for queries which contain **har**. The disadvantage is that fewer queries are likely to use this key compared to **ha**. Thus the index designer has to (i) control the size of the index by bounding the maximum number of multigrams that can be indexed, (ii) balance the trade-off between the likelihood of a multigram being used by a query and the size of its posting list.

The paper makes four significant contributions. (1) We present a novel integer program algorithm to select the multigrams to index. (2) Using the above algorithm, we have implemented a fully functional regular expression query framework on top of a commercial database. (3) We have carried out extensive experiments to test for the accuracy, efficiency and robustness. (4) We present a novel case study using protein data where regular expression patterns are used routinely to classify families of proteins.

The rest of the paper is organized as follows. In Section 2

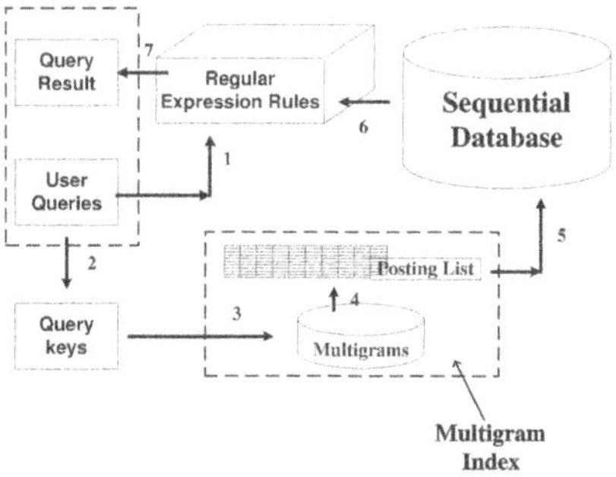

Figure 1: A generic indexed query framework consists of 7 steps. Whereas, if no indexes are employed, steps 2 to 5 will be skipped

we report on related work. Section 3 formalizes the index selection problem. Section 4 presents the Linear Programming Multigram Selection (LPMS) algorithm and the related theory. In Section 5 we present our experiments and case study. We conclude in Section 6 with a summary and directions for future research.

2. RELATED WORK

Traditionally a regular expression query is processed by constructing a non-deterministic finite automata (NFA) which recognizes the language defined by the regular expression pattern [3]. The entire database needs to be processed.

More recently, a relatively different research strand has been developed to support regular expression querying. The initial work in this area was carried out by Cho and Rajgopalan - the authors who denote their index as FREE multigram[2].

The objective of the Free model is to select the **minimal useful** multigram set. A multigrams is considered **useful** as long as the number of data records containing the multigrams that are smaller than a threshold (namely selectivity or support). The FREE algorithm is designed so that the set of useful multigrams selected are **prefix-free**.

The key insight of the **FREE prefix-free** algorithm is that *the size multigram index is always bounded above by the database size*. This is an important property that all regular expression indexes should enforce. Since FREE selects low support multigrams, queries which use FREE always take less time than queries which employ a full table scan. However the disadvantage of FREE is that it does not take any query workload into account and thus many queries are unlikely to utilize the index.

To overcome the weakness of **FREE**, Hore et. al. in [4] proposed a multigram selection algorithm called **BEST** which takes both the database and query workload into consideration. In the BEST algorithm, each multigram is associated with a cost factor c (equivalent to the support) and at the same time associated with the query set by a benefit factor, b. The main advantage of **BEST** is select multigrams which increase the cost factor and also the benefit factor at the same time. However, a major weakness of the BEST algorithm is that it neither scales to large datasets nor large query workloads because it uses a cartesian product of query workload and database as the search space.

Our approach is inspired by both **FREE** and **BEST**. Like the **BEST** algorithm we take both the database and query workload into consideration but unlike **BEST** we generate a representative workload from the database. The advantage of having both a database and workload is that we can formalize the problem in a *combinatorial optimization framework*. We also formalize the problem in a way which ensures that the set of multigrams selected are prefix-free. Thus we are able to bound the size of the index and guarantee that the running time of a query using the index will be less than the full database scan.

3. PROBLEM DEFINITION

In this section we will use the integer programming framework to formalize the index selection problem. To recall we are given a database, abstracted as a collection of strings, and a set of regular expression queries Q. Our objective is to select a set of multigrams which will be used as keys of an index for efficiently answering the queries Q.

The index will be used to retrieve a set of candidate records from the database which may satisfy the query. After the candidate records are selected, the actual regular expression matching is done in memory to select the exact set of records which satisfy the query.

For the purpose of indexing we will treat each query q as a set of multigrams M_q. Let $\bar{M}_q$ be the set M_q and all the substrings of length at least one which appear within each multigram in M_q.

Let $G = \bigcup_{q \in Q} \bar{M}_q$ be the universe of candidate multigrams. It is from G that we will select a subset G_I which will form the index. For example, suppose the set Q consists of a single query $q = (ex).\{1,3\}(ess)$. Then $M_q = \{ex, ess\}$ and $\bar{M}_q = \{ex, es, ss, ess\}$.

To formalize the index selection problem as an integer program (IP) we need to define (i) integer variables (x), (ii) the constraints (A, b) and (iii) the objective function (c) and set up the problem as follows:

$$\begin{array}{ll} \text{minimize} & \sum_{g \in G} c_g x_g \\ \text{subject to} & Ax \geq b \quad , x \in \{0,1\} \end{array} \tag{1}$$

For each multigram g in G we associate an integer binary variable $x_g \in \{0,1\}$. The variable x_g will be set to one if the multigram g is selected to be part of the index. To formalize the constraints we will construct a $|Q| \times |G|$ matrix A such that

$$A_{i,j} = \left\{ \begin{array}{ll} s(g_j) & \text{if } g_j \in \bar{M}_{q_i}; \\ 0 & \text{otherwise.} \end{array} \right\} \tag{2}$$

Here $s(g)$ is the *support* or the number of rows in the database in which the multigram g appears at least once. It is through the definition of A that the integer program captures the characteristics of the underlying database. We also need to define the $|Q|$ dimensional vector b which defines the right hand side of the system $Ax \geq b$. Here we define

$$b_i = \min_{g \in \bar{M}_{q_i}} s(g) \ \ \forall i \tag{3}$$

The definition of b_i can be interpreted as follows. Each row of A represents a query. The row constraint captures the smallest number of database records that must be returned if the query will use the index. This is captured with multigram g with the smallest support contained in the *expanded* query $\bar{M}_q$.

Table 1: Road map of the four experiments and one case study performed to evaluate the LPMS multigram index. The details are reported in [6]

	Objective and Description	Data Set Description	Results
1	Compare: Accuracy and Performance of LPMS-R, LPMS-D, RDB and FREE[2]	Synthetic data sets with varying support distribution of multigrams	The recall of LPMS-D and LPMS-R are close to 1 with LPMS-D > LPMS-R >> FREE. While the precision of FREE > LPMS-R > LPMS-D.
2	Evaluate: Scalability of LPMS-R and LPMS-D	Synthetic data sets with varying data and query workload size	The overall build time of both LPMS-R and LPMS-D scales linearly with the database size and super-linearly with the query workload size.
3	Evaluate: Quality of LPMS-R relaxation vis-a-vis optimal Integer Program (IPMS) and BEST[4]	Same as Experiment 2	The optimal posting list size of LPMS-R and BEST are 26 and 94 times of IMPS respectively.
4	Evaluate: Robustness of index as query workload change	Synthetic data sets with varying alphabet size	The recall of LPMS-D and LPMS-R are both high against all query perturbations.
5	Case Study: Prosite protein patterns using LPMS-D	Protein database[1] and Prosite pattern query[5]	Figure 2

We now define the objective function which is typically of the form : $\sum_{g \in G} c_g x_g$.

The objective should capture the trade-off between the coverage of a multigram and it is support in a database. By coverage we mean that one multigram can be used by several queries. On the other hand if the support of this multigram is high (relative to the size of the database) then the index is not necessarily useful as a full table scan may only be slightly less efficient.

Since we want to cast the IP as a minimization problem we want to select multigrams which have low support and at the same time we want the selected multigram to be used by as many queries as possible. Thus we define

$$c_g = \frac{s(g)}{|g| \sum_{q \in Q} \imath(g \in \bar{M}_q)} \quad (4)$$

where $\imath(g \in \bar{M}_q)$ is an indicator function. Thus the numerator of c_g is the support of the multigram g and we want multigrams with small support (making the index more efficient) and at the same time we want to select multigrams with high coverage so fewer multigrams need to selected to form the index.

THEOREM 1. *The solution vector x returned by the integer program represents a set of multigrams which form a prefix-free set. We presented the proof in [6] for interested readers.*

The importance of having a prefix-free index set has been noted (and proved) before by Cho and Rajgoplan [2]. Essentially the **prefix-freeness** guarantees that the size of the index is bounded by the size of the database. More formally (and in our notation):

THEOREM 2. *If x is the vector returned by the integer program and $|R|$ is the size of the underlying database then*

$$\sum_{\{g: x_g = 1\}} s(g) \leq |R|$$

The importance of Theorem 1 and 2 cannot be underestimated. For the first time we have a principled way of selecting a set of multigrams to index. The definition of the problem gives us **prefix-freeness**. As a result the constraint on the size of the index is now *endogenous* to the problem as opposed to providing an exogenous (budget) constraint as in the BEST method [4].

4. THE LP RELAXATION

In the previous section we have presented a model for the multigram selection problem based on integer programming. We proved that the the resulting multigrams form a prefix-free set.

However theoretically the general integer program problem is NP-Hard and even in practice algorithms for IP programs require exponential time for most instances. This is because unlike linear programming problems where convexity of the problem can be exploited (local optima are global optima), for integer programming the full lattice of feasible points has to be explored.

A common approach to get around the complexity of integer programs is to relax them to linear programs which can then be solved efficiently (in polynomial time). The solution of the linear program provides a natural lower bound (for minimization problems) for the integer program. There are two approaches for carrying out the conversion. The first approach is to select a deterministic threshold and use that to round the solutions. The second approach is to interpret the solution vector (typically between 0 and 1) as probabilities and carry out a randomized rounding.

THEOREM 3. *Let $s_{\max}$ and $s_{\min}$ be the multigram in G with the largest and smallest non-zero support respectively. Furthermore let $m^* = \max_{q \in Q} |\bar{M}_q|$. If x_l is the solution of the relaxed linear program and we convert it to an integer solution by rounding up all elements in x_l which are greater than $\frac{s_{\min}}{s_{\max} m^*}$ then the rounded solution is a feasible solution of the integer program and achieves a constant approximation to the original integer program. We presented the proof in [6] for interested readers.*

The above theorem simplify states that $x_l^D = 1$ if $x_l > s_{\max} m^* \frac{s_{\min}}{s_{\max} m^*}$. Otherwise, $x_l^D = 1$. This will be used as a basis for designing a deterministic rounding algorithm LPMS-D.

While LP relaxation and rounding mechanism allows us to overcome the exponential runtime complexity of integer programs, it does not guarantee that the resulting multigram set is a prefix-free. The resulting size of the index may not be bounded by the database size. In order to overcome this shortcoming, we enforce the prefix-free constraint by proposing an iterative algorithm- LPMS.

Algorithm 1 outlines the LPMS multigram prefix-free selection process. Firstly, the expandSet starts with an element ".". Secondly, each element in it is expanded by ap-

ALGORITHM 1: LPMS multigram selection algorithm

Input: string database (R), query set (Q), alphabet set (Σ)
Output: Multigram index (G)
expandSet = {.};
repeat
  For each multigram in the expandSet, append a member in Σ and save to the childrenSet;
  Remove all multigram g $\in$ childrenSet if g $\notin \bar{M}_{k,q}$ $\forall$ k;
  Populate matrix A, b, c of the LP model using formulae (2), (3) and (4) respectively;
  Apply LPMS-D or LPMS-R to find the vector x;
  Move all multigrams whose associated value in the vector x = 1 to G;
  Those multigrams remaining will become the expandSet;
until *(expandSet = {})*;

pending one element from the alphabet set, Σ, which will form the childrenSet. Thirdly, all query keys contained in the query set, Q, are consolidated to generate the $\bar{M}_{k,q}$ set. Fourthly, any multigrams in the childrenSet that are not present in the $\bar{M}_{k,q}$ set will be removed. Fifthly, the refined childrenSet and set Q will be applied to the LP solver to produce the linear programming solution, x. Finally, x is relaxed by applying either LPMS-D or LPMS-R. Those multigrams with its associated x value equals to "1" will be selected as the multigram and save in set G. All unselected multigrams will then replace the current expandSet. The process will be repeated continuously until all the multigrams are being selected.

For the rest of the paper, the solution of multigram selection problem obtained using the integer program will be referred as IPMS (Integer Program Multigram Selection). Similarly those obtained from deterministic and randomized rounding of the linear program will form the basis of the LPMS-D and LPMS-R algorithms respectively.

5. EXPERIMENTS AND CASE STUDY

We have carried out four extensive experiments and one case study to evaluate the LPMS multigram. The experiment road map is shown in Table 1. For each of the four experiments we generate a different synthetic data set to vary conditions appropriate for that particular experiment. The details of the experiments are reported in [6].

The result in experiment 1, 3 and 4 showed that the recall and precision of LPMS multigram is consistently high. This allows us to conclude that LPMS multigram is highly accurate, efficient and robust. In experiment 2, the result showed that the LPMS build time scales nearly linearly with both database size and query workload size thus making LPMS feasible and practical.

The case study is to apply the LPMS multigram on a real data and contemporary application. Figure 2 shows the data flow of the LPMS-D multigram index Prosite-Protein application. The test data is protein sequences which are downloaded from the PFAM-A protein database [1]. Each sequence is composed of 20 distinct amino acids (alphabet) with length ranging from 4 to 2750. The query workload is the Prosite signatures [5]. Each Prosite signature defining a protein class represents a classic regular expression.

One hundred Prosite queries were tested with 100k protein sequences with and without the LPMS-D index. The recall of this test was equal to 1, which demonstrates that the LPMS-D index is 100% accurate.

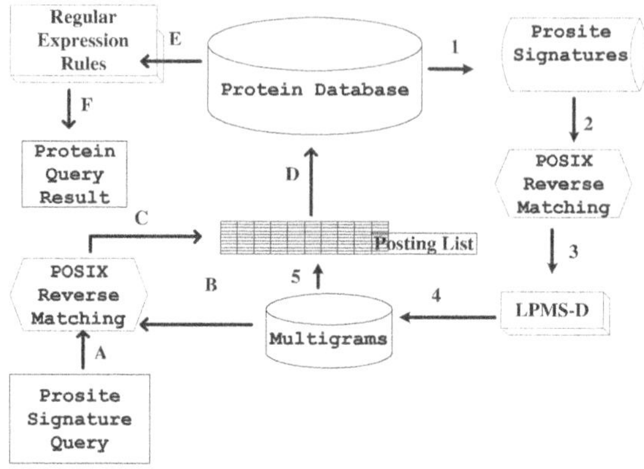

Figure 2: Case study: In the Full POSIX Prosite-Protein application, Step 1 to 5 and step A to E represents the LPMS-D Multigram index construction and query process respectively.

6. SUMMARY AND CONCLUSION

While modern database management systems support forms of regular expression querying, they do not provide any indexing support for such queries. Thus, a regular expression query requires a full database scan to find the matching records. This is a severe limitation as the database size will continue to increase and applications for such queries (e.g., bioinformatics) proliferate.

In this paper, we have proposed a robust, scalable and efficient approach to design an index for such queries. The heart of our approach is to model the multigram selection problem as an integer program (IP) and show that the approximate solutions of the IP have many of the properties we desire: accuracy robustness and efficiency. Extensive set of experiments on both synthetic and real datasets demonstrate our claimed contributions.

For future work we will replace the current linear programming solver by using a primal-dual approach which will make the approach handle very large query workloads. Furthermore we will test our approach in other application domains including intrusion detection systems.

7. REFERENCES

[1] Pfam-a database. `http://pfam.sanger.ac.uk`, 2008(accessed 2011).

[2] J. Cho and S. Rajagopalan. A fast regular expression indexing engine. *Proceedings 18th International Conference on Data Engineering*, 2002.

[3] J. E. Hopcroft, R. Motwani, and J. D. Ullman. *Introduction to Automata Theory, Language, and Computation*. Addison-Wesley, 2001.

[4] B. Hore, H. Hacigumus, and B. Lyer. Indexing text data under space constraints. *CIKM 04 November 8-13, Washington, DC, USA*, 2004.

[5] C. J. A. Sigrist, L. Cerutti, N. Hulo, A. Gattiker, and L. Falquet. Prosite: A documented database using patterns and profiles as motif descriptors. *Henry Stewart Publications*, 3:265–274, September 2002.

[6] D. Tsang and S. Chawla. An index for regular expression querying: Design and implementation. http://arxiv.org/abs/1108.1228.

Integrating and Querying Web Databases and Documents

Carlos Garcia-Alvarado
University of Houston
Houston, TX 77204, USA

Carlos Ordonez
University of Houston
Houston, TX 77204, USA

ABSTRACT

There exist many interrelated information sources on the Internet that can be categorized into structured (database) and semistructured (documents). A key challenge is to integrate, query and analyze such heterogeneous collections of information. In this paper, we defend the idea of building web metadata repositories using relational databases as the main source and central data management technology of structured data, enriched by the semistructured data surrounding it. Our proposal rests on the assumption that heterogeneous relational databases can be integrated (i.e. entity resolution is assumed to work well) and thus can serve as references for external data. That is, we tackle the problem of integrating information in the deep web, departing from databases. We discuss a prototype system that can integrate and query metadata and related documents, based on relational database technology. Metadata includes database ER model elements like database name, table, and column (entity, attribute). Web document data include files, documents and web pages. Links between metadata and external documents are built with SQL queries. Once databases and documents are linked, they are managed and queried with SQL. We discuss an interesting scientific application of our solution with a water pollution database.

Categories and Subject Descriptors

H.3.3 [**Information Systems**]: Information Storage and Retrieval—*Information Search and Retrieval*

General Terms

Algorithms, Experimentation

Keywords

Database, Documents, Integration

CIKM'11, October 24–28, 2011, Glasgow, Scotland, UK.

1. INTRODUCTION

Information retrieval (IR) and databases (DB) are two different major technologies for managing and searching for information that are slowly approaching each other. As stated in [3], almost any application that manages information requires the joint capabilities of IR and database systems to provide the users with a complete application [9]. The defining feature of a database is structure, and such structure has meaning (i.e. semantics), typically captured in an ER model. In contrast, in IR systems, there is some structure, but extracting the semantic information from the semistructured is a difficult task. Semistructured data sources (i.e. documents, web pages, files) are valuable for describing and enriching structured data. Managing and querying semistructured data sources is more challenging than self-described structured data (i.e. tables in a DBMS). Therefore, linking IR and DBMS is even more challenging.

We defend the idea of using a relational database as a central repository to store metadata and to integrate both technologies. The main advantage is that the integration can be done efficiently inside the DBMS by using SQL and extensibility features. The resulting repository can then be managed efficiently inside the DBMS due to the fact that the links can be represented in a relational form. With such motivation in mind, we built a novel hybrid DB-IR model integrating two previous separate approaches [8, 4]. Our new system finds and explores links between databases and documents, and then ranks them in a search engine fashion with a DBMS with primitive IR capabilities. Our system incorporates new optimizations, including efficient and approximate matching, link ranking and adapting the Rank-Join approach for top-k querying [6]. Our system enables discovering unknown links that go beyond simple keyword matching. Our goal is to find a core set of links between database metadata, database content, and documents, which can be efficiently managed and queried in a DBMS, instead of searching the document collection while lacking information links to the database. In addition, it is possible to extract information that it is not possible to find if both sources are queried independently.

We tested our application with a scientific database containing water pollution data and a collection of documents from the Texas Commission on Environmental Quality. The user can get insightful answers to non-trivial questions such as, "Which database tables are highly related to arsenic measurement?", "Which information in the database is related to a specific section of a document?" or "Which researchers query a particular table?"

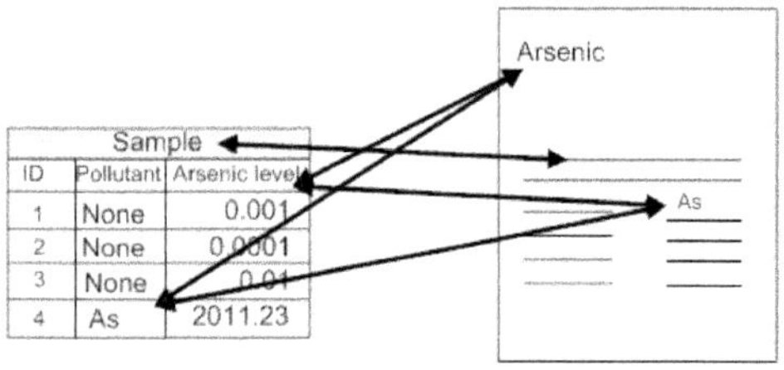

Figure 1: Links between database and documents.

2. LINKING AND QUERYING WEB DATABASES AND DOCUMENTS

Our approach can be divided into building the metadata repository (finding links), and ranking and querying this repository with relational queries.

2.1 Finding Links

Structured metadata is represented by table and column names. Database records (or rows) represent the basic atoms of information content, following a fixed table schema. Semistructured data are given by all the words contained in any external document, outside of the database. All documents are considered to have some structure that helps focus on a set of keywords in a particular portion of the document. This is particularly evident in web pages due to the fact that titles and paragraphs are specified by HTML tags. Additionally, documents' metadata, such as author, filename and title, can be extracted to establish additional links with this information. All of this information is then stored in the database and ranked based on discovered links from the matching process with a classical IR model. In summary, metadata and content from structured data and semistructured data are matched. Notice that assuming a perfect match scenario is unrealistic. As such, we decided to look for approximate matches. Three complementary types of links are generated: high, specific, and content-level links. These links differ in the level at which they match information metadata and data elements (see Figure 1). High level metadata links are based on describing a link between a table and a document. These links are found by finding matches between annotations describing the tables, as well as tablenames and information surrounding a document, such as filename, author, or even a description name, if available. Specific links relate sections or subsections in the document and columns in a table schema. Examples of these types of links are the keywords inside the header, <h2></h2> tags in HTML, and the column names. Finally, content links represent the most complex type of atomic granularity; they are the result of matching the content of structured data records and document keywords (e.g. keywords inside the <p></p> tags).

In more detail, this matching is performed by exploiting a set of known concepts given by the user (e.g. arsenic, water pollution) and synonyms (e.g. {arsenic, AS},{pollutant, contaminant}), and then applying an efficient keyword matching algorithm in order to generate these links between parts of the database and certain parts of a document. As stated previously, we focus on approximate matching (e.g. keywords that match at least 90% of the given keyword) using the Approximate Boyer-Moore algorithm in order to obtain similar keywords (e.g. pollutant and pollutants). The main advantage of finding such links is that it is possible to explore integrated information at different granularity levels within a database, following the information on web documents, using high level links. Also notice that the generation of these links (or source integration) can be performed on a particular granularity. High level metadata links are generated much faster than specific links and in a similar fashion. Specific links are obtained much faster than content links. Also notice that the resulting number of links grows as we drill down into the integration of both sources.

L		E	
kid	k	kid	Database Location
1	sample	1	$\{T = sample\}$
2	arsenic	2	$\{T = arsenic\}$
. . .		2	$\{T = sample, c = pollutant, PK = 4\}$
5	pollutant	5	$\{T = sample, c = pollutant\}$
6	arsenic level	6	$\{T = sample, c = arsenic\ level\}$
. . .		. . .	

Table 1: Example of E and L.

When desired, the user can explore in more detail all documents related to a particular matched table or drill down into such a table. Thus, the user can query and explore both documents and the databases that relate to them.

loc. in db	keyword in db.	concept	doc.	keyword in doc.	loc. in doc.
High level					
db1:arsenic	arsenic	arsenic	1	arsenic	filename
db1:As	As	arsenic	3	As	metadata
Specific level					
db1:chemical	arsenic	arsenic	1	arsenic	title
db1:chemical	arsenic	arsenic	3	As	paragraph
Content level					
db1:sample: record1	As	arsenic	1	arsenic	title
db1:sample: record1	As	arsenic	3	As	paragraph

Table 2: Examples of high level, specific level, and content level links.

The main algorithms for performing such an exploration are detailed in [5], in which the main idea is to keep a list with all the unique keywords to integrate in both sources (given as a set of valid concepts and synonyms). These concepts are then matched to elements in the database (storing their location) and then performing a similar search within the corpus. An important characteristic is that when a keyword is not found in either the database or the corpus, this concept is dropped from the search list to avoid looking into the rest of the sources. Upon completion of this process, the set of approximate matches of both sources is matched to obtain the links. In order to avoid repeating computations, it is preferable to search for all the links (high level, specific links or content links) at the same computation.

2.2 Processing with Relational Queries

The basic IR system in SQL is introduced in [4]. The application was developed using SQL statements and in-DBMS extensibility mechanisms, such as User-Defined Functions (UDFs) for stemming, SQL statements for cleaning, storing and obtaining the links, and UDFs for parsing and ranking [4]. Notice that unlike [4], our ranking is focused on the newly discovered links and not on keywords. Therefore, links are weighted considering whether they match metadata or actual data content, as well as how close they match it (due to the approximate matching result). If links connect metadata elements, then the links can be weighted computing a measure summarizing actual content (similar to applying the Vector Space Model). If links are connecting content, then they are weighted based on the number of links associated with a particular concept (using a summarization). For example, if a link matches a document and a table, these two elements are composed of a set of keywords that can be used to compute a cosine similarity. On the other hand, when links are connecting a record in the database (in the content level) and a keyword in a document, they will have to be ranked based on the number of links associated with that particular record. Once an appropriate ranking function has been defined, the retrieval of top-k links can be done efficiently (e.g. using the Rank-Join algorithm).

Links between the database and documents are built as follows: an input table with basic keywords (representing concepts), is given to perform matching. An auxiliary table is used to represent concept synonyms. These keywords are then matched between every element in the database and then for every keyword in the corpus. This matching is performed using user-defined functions in order to keep in-main memory all the data structures used to obtain the edit distance for every concept and every given string coming from the database or a document in the corpus. This matching step is the bottleneck of the link matching. However, to ease the processing, we perform the matching in batches. In other words, a set of elements in the DBMS or documents is scanned simultaneously to avoid I/Os. The size of the batches, as well as a valid approximate match, are parameters that need to be tuned by the user. A sample list of the concepts L and the elements found in the database E are presented in Table 1. Summary tables are created to avoid repeated searches on a particular data source and they include the location of the concept in the database and in the corpus. By using these summary tables, it is possible to build metadata and content links by performing a join on the matching keywords. The join on the matching keyword is performed by using a hash join on the concept id that was assigned during the matching phase. The resulting hash join is quite efficient due to the keyword indexes.

Notice that the type of link is based on the location of the elements in the database and the keywords in the corpus. By joining these two summary tables containing the concept match and the location of the match between the two sources, we can find that there are indeed two metadata links pointing to a table name and a column name. Also, during this phase, the concepts that do not have a corresponding link between the database and the documents must be removed from the list. Additionally, the number of links associated with particular concept must be computed (used to rank content links). A final step for link creation is assigning a weight to every content keyword that can be associated with a corresponding match in the corpus. By doing so, it is feasible to rank all metadata links.

Exploring (ad-hoc querying) links is less computationally expensive due to the links that have already been found, and thus work on materialized views. The querying is performed on these smaller indexed tables by using selection predicates p to find matching keywords given in a query, and the ranking is obtained by computing the corresponding weights for every concept (see Figure 2). Notice that p is a subquery that selects the keywords from the list L that approximately match a given concept. We should point out that ranking can be performed with any information retrieval ranking method. Due to their solid theoretical foundation, we used the vector space model and the Rank-Join algorithm for returning the top-k concepts. The Rank-Join algorithm was pipelined as an operation using a user-defined function and managed as an approximation for efficiency purposes.

```
SELECT P.kid, R.i, E.level, P.d
FROM
   L_predicate P
   INNER JOIN database_keyword E
     ON  (P.kid = E.kid)
   INNER JOIN document_keyword R
     ON  (R.kid = E.kid)
ORDER BY  E.level, R.i, P.d DESC
```

Figure 2: Querying the link repository.

3. APPLICATION ON SCIENTIFIC DATA

Our system is a Web DBMS Client Application with a client-server architecture. The processing works entirely inside the DBMS exploiting efficient SQL queries. These SQL queries are also enhanced by efficient extensibility features for complex processing (e.g. matching or parsing). Therefore, the front-end is a thin layer of SQL generation, which connects to the DBMS via ODBC and displays the final results. The front-end was developed with ASP .NET. The user interface allows searching documents utilizing the links involving Users, Tables, Documents, Columns and Fields, as well as the document abstracts. The output shows the results that are part of the database schema (e.g. columns), the results that are part of the semistructured world (e.g. authors) and the SQL associated to obtain those results. The front-end also allows the user to define the settings of the application, such as the document loading options, on-demand links search, and the top-k implementation (exact built-in top-k or UDF Rank-Join).

We are currently using our system on a scientific database containing water pollution data from wells in Texas (TWWD). The goal is to determine if water is polluted by humans or if it is naturally polluted. This database consists of 32 tables with up to 214 columns, where each table has an average size of 111,488 rows. Tables contain measurement information regarding chemicals found in water samples, such as concentration and units of measurement, as well as the geographical location of the well and associated descriptions and measurements of the results of several water samples. Due to the complexity of establishing semantics of numeric data, we are currently ignoring numbers during the linking process, but that is an area for future research. Associated with this database, we analyzed a pre-processed (stop words removed, stemmed) collection of documents describing scientific findings regarding the causes for water pollution.

In these two data sources, we applied two phases: (1) finding links and (2) navigating interrelated documents. Phase 1 is the most difficult and time consuming, especially while factoring in semantics. Phase 2 includes top-k selection, exploration of the links, and monitoring performance. An example of discovered links associated with the concept "arsenic" is shown in Table 2. In addition, in Table 3 we also show the resulting links found using the query presented in Figure 2. Our system allows more complex queries by weighting using the content of the metadata or faster alternatives such as the Rank-Join.

kid	i	f	δ	Database Location
2	1	1	0	$\{T = arsenic\}$
2	2	1	0	$\{T = arsenic, c = pollutant, PK = 4\}$

Table 3: Ranking Links (query = "arsenic").

4. RELATED WORK

Heterogeneous source integration has been approached in similar research. EROCS is one of the few attempts at obtaining a linkage between structured and unstructured data [2]. EROCS focuses on linking transactions and then performing data mining operations over the newly discovered links. The linkage is performed using templates for identifying entities. However, unlike our approach, EROCS does not extend the DBMS functionalities using user-defined functions, nor does it deal with approximate matching. In [10, 7] the authors have a similar objective of linking structured and unstructured sources. This is probably the closest work to our research. However, in their approach, the DBMS is analyzed as a graph and then clustered. The final result is a traditional rank on top of the nodes of a graph. Similar to EROCS, their system does not take advantage of the extensibility features of the DBMS and avoids approximate matching. In addition, the ranking is performed on the extracted concepts and the weights are not assigned based on the frequency of appearance or location of these concepts.

Finally, in [8, 6], the authors suggest a method of relating schema-keywords with keywords in the documents, and generating macro and micro relationships. The matching between both sources is done using an Object Data Model, as presented in [1], and the unstructured sources were managed using XML. We integrated the schema matching and keyword search ideas to present a more complete solution on the existing types of links between elements and documents and present a novel idea on how to rank documents given these relationships within the DBMS. In addition, we do not require a given Object Data Model for discovering these links between the structured and unstructured sources, and our linkage is performed only with concept and synonym lists. Finally, this paper extends the ideas presented in [5] by limiting the high level links to relate only metadata, the specific links to relate certain sections of the keywords in the documents, and provides a ranking based on the content of the high or specific links. The objective of these modifications was to obtain efficient metadata linkage and allow a drill down exploration through more granular links.

5. CONCLUSIONS

In this paper, we presented a process for discovering "links" between the elements of a central database and a collection of documents. To the best of our knowledge, this research is one of the few efforts to obtain, manage, and rank links between these sources. The links are defined in different levels of granularity based on the elements they link. High links relate a document and a table, and specific links relate a column of a table and a section or subsection of a document. The content links match the actual rows of the database to specific keywords within the content of the semistructured source. In addition, an algorithm for discovering such relations was presented. We proposed an approximate search which provides a fair policy for obtaining matching concepts. We also found that that the bottleneck of the algorithm is in searching for the elements in the database when a set of keywords is given. In addition, the search of approximate keywords appears to be a target for future optimizations. The algorithms perform efficiently because the search is performed in small and indexed data structures containing the set of valid relationships and summarized tables. We also propose a data layout, indexing and querying strategies that optimized retrieval times.

Future work in this area includes thorough experiments for verifying the reliability of the extracted links. In addition to some comparisons with similar integration approaches and exploring a parallel implementation of the proposed algorithms, which can speed up the execution of both tasks (preprocessing and retrieval). The optimization for approximate string matching with multiple keywords appears as an interesting area of research. Finally, the combination of more complex weighting techniques of the elements in the database, as well as formalizing the complexity and computability of finding links, remain as open problems for future research.

Acknowledgments

This work was supported by NSF grants CCF 0937562 and IIS 0914861.

6. REFERENCES

[1] S. Bergamaschi, S. Castano, and M. Vincini. Semantic integration of semistructured and structured data sources. *ACM Sigmod Record*, 28(1):54–59, 1999.

[2] M. Bhide, V. Chakravarthy, A. Gupta, H. Gupta, M. Mohania, K. Puniyani, P. Roy, S. Roy, and V. Sengar. Enhanced Business Intelligence using EROCS. In *Proc. of ICDE*, pages 1616–1619. IEEE Computer Society Washington, DC, USA, 2008.

[3] S. Chaudhuri, R. Ramakrishnan, and G. Weikum. Integrating DB and IR technologies: What is the sound of one hand clapping. In *Proc. of CIDR*, 2005.

[4] C. Garcia-Alvarado and C. Ordonez. Information retrieval from digital libraries in SQL. In *WIDM 2008*. ACM New York, NY, USA, 2008.

[5] C. Garcia-Alvarado and C. Ordonez. Keyword Search Across Databases and Documents. In *Proc. ACM SIGMOD Workshop on Keyword Search on Structured Data (KEYS)*, 2010.

[6] C. Garcia-Alvarado, C. Ordonez, and Z. Chen. DBDOC: Querying and Browsing Databases and Interrelated Documents. In *Proc. ACM SIGMOD Workshop on Keyword Search on Structured Data (KEYS)*, 2009.

[7] G. Li, B.C. Ooi, J. Feng, J. Wang, and L. Zhou. EASE: an effective 3-in-1 keyword search method for unstructured, semi-structured and structured data. In *Proc. of ACM SIGMOD*, pages 903–914. ACM, 2008.

[8] C. Ordonez, Z. Chen, and J. García-García. Metadata management for federated databases. In *ACM CIMS Workshop*, pages 31–38, 2007.

[9] L. Qin, J.X. Yu, and L. Chang. Keyword search in databases: the power of RDBMS. In *Proc. of SIGMOD*, pages 681–694, 2009.

[10] Q.H. Vu, B.C. Ooi, D. Papadias, and A.K.H. Tung. A graph method for keyword-based selection of the top-K databases. In *SIGMOD*, pages 915–926. ACM, 2008.

Processing the Signature Quadratic Form Distance on Many-Core GPU Architectures

Martin Kruliš ○ Jakub Lokoč ○ Christian Beecks • Tomáš Skopal ○ Thomas Seidl •
○SIRET Research Group, Faculty of Mathematics and Physics, Charles University in Prague, Czech Republic
○{krulis,lokoc,skopal}@ksi.mff.cuni.cz
•Data Management and Data Exploration Group, RWTH Aachen University, Germany
•{beecks,seidl}@cs.rwth-aachen.de

ABSTRACT

The Signature Quadratic Form Distance on feature signatures represents a flexible distance-based similarity model for effective content-based multimedia retrieval. Although metric indexing approaches are able to speed up query processing by two orders of magnitude, their applicability to large-scale multimedia databases containing billions of images is still a challenging issue. In this paper, we propose the utilization of GPUs for efficient query processing with the Signature Quadratic Form Distance. We show how to process multiple distance computations in parallel and demonstrate efficient query processing by comparing many-core GPU with multi-core CPU implementations.

Categories and Subject Descriptors

H.3.1 [**Content Analysis and Indexing**]: Indexing Methods; C.1.4 [**Processor Architectures**]: Parallel Architectures

General Terms

Performance, Design, Algorithm

Keywords

GPU, many-core, quadratic form distance, similarity search

1. INTRODUCTION

Multimedia retrieval systems frequently store billions of images and provide users with different ways of searching and browsing (e.g., catalog-based or keyword-based search). However, effective yet efficient techniques for content-based similarity search are still a big issue. To this end, multimedia retrieval systems are designed based on advanced similarity models consisting of image representations and similarity/distance measures. A flexible way to represent the content of an image is by means of *feature signatures* [7].

CIKM'11, October 24–28, 2011, Glasgow, Scotland, UK.

In general, a feature signature of an image is a set consisting of multiple local image features, where the length of a feature signature is not fixed (to distinguish more or less complex images). However, the comparison of feature signatures requires more sophisticated and computationally expensive adaptive distance measures [2], such as the Earth Mover's Distance (EMD) [7] or the Signature Quadratic Form Distance (SQFD) [3]. In this paper, we focus on the latter, as the SQFD shows high retrieval quality and lower time complexity compared to the EMD ($O(n^2)$ vs. $O(n^4)$).

In order to reduce the computational effort, *metric indexing* [8] approaches have been applied to the SQFD. It has been shown, that pivot tables [1] and ptolemaic indexing [5] reach a speed-up of over two orders of magnitude with respect to the sequential scan. Nevertheless, by using metric indexing approaches, this speed-up is generally limited due to the intrinsic dimensionality [8]. Thus, in order to use the SQFD for large-scale image retrieval, we propose to parallelize the SQFD query processing.

In this paper, we consider many-core GPU devices for parallel SQFD query processing. While parallel multi-core CPU processing is straightforward and supported by many development tools, designing efficient algorithms for GPUs is a challenging task for content-based retrieval purposes. Although GPUs generally contain more cores than CPUs, they suffer from slow data transfer rates and code execution restrictions. We discuss GPU processing limitations and introduce a new schema for efficient SQFD query processing utilizing the combination of metric indexing approaches and the computational power of GPUs.

The paper is organized as follows. Section 2 describes the SQFD. Section 3 discusses the most important aspects of GPU architectures, while Section 4 describes our SQFD implementation for GPUs. Section 5 presents the experimental results, and Section 6 concludes this paper.

2. SIGNATURE QUADRATIC FORM DIST.

The Signature Quadratic Form Distance (SQFD) [3] is an adaptive distance-based similarity measure for feature signatures. It is defined as follows.

DEFINITION 1 (SQFD). *Given two feature signatures $S^q = \{\langle r_i^q, w_i^q \rangle\}_{i=1}^n$ and $S^o = \{\langle r_i^o, w_i^o \rangle\}_{i=1}^m$ and a similarity function $f_s : \mathbb{F} \times \mathbb{F} \to \mathbb{R}$ over a feature space $\mathbb{F}$, the signature quadratic form distance SQFD_{f_s} between S^q and S^o is defined as:*

$$\mathrm{SQFD}_{f_s}(S^q, S^o) = \sqrt{(w_q \mid -w_o) \cdot A_{f_s} \cdot (w_q \mid -w_o)^T},$$

where $A_{f_s} \in \mathbb{R}^{(n+m)\times(n+m)}$ is the similarity matrix arising from applying the similarity function f_s to the corresponding feature representatives, i.e., $a_{ij} = f_s(r_i, r_j)$. Furthermore, $w_q = (w_1^q, \ldots, w_n^q)$ and $w_o = (w_1^o, \ldots, w_m^o)$ form weight vectors, and $(w_q \mid -w_o) = (w_1^q, \ldots, w_n^q, -w_1^o, \ldots, -w_m^o)$ denotes the concatenation of weights w_q and $-w_o$.

The similarity function f_s is used to determine similarity values between all pairs of representatives from the feature signatures. In our implementation we use the similarity function $f_s(r_i, r_j) = e^{-\alpha L_2(r_i, r_j)^2}$, where α is a constant for controlling the precision-indexability tradeoff, as investigated in our previous works [1, 5], and L_2 denotes the Euclidean distance.

3. GPU FUNDAMENTALS

In general, GPU architectures [6] differ from CPU architectures in multiple ways. In the remainder of this section, we describe two major differences, the *thread execution* and *memory organization*, which have direct impact on the design of our SQFD implementation.

3.1 Thread Execution

The first difference is the specific program execution. Portions of code, which are executed on the GPU, are called *kernels*. A kernel is a function that is invoked multiple times simultaneously, so that all spawned threads execute the same code. Each spawned thread gets the same set of calling arguments and a unique identifier, which is used to select proper parts of the parallel work.

The thread managing and context switching capabilities of the GPU are very advanced. Thus, it is usually better to create a multitude of threads, even if they execute only a few instructions each, in order to optimize the load balancing. In addition, fast context switching capabilities of the GPU are used to hide latency of global memory transactions.

Threads are aggregated into small bundles called groups. A group usually contains tens to hundreds of threads which execute the kernel in SIMT[1] or virtual SIMT fashion. Every thread executes the same instruction, but it has its own set of registers, thus working on different portions of the data. The SIMT execution suffers from branching problems when different threads in the group choose different branches, for instance when executing 'if' statements. To execute conditional code properly, all branches must be executed by all threads and each thread masks instruction execution according to local result of the condition. On the other hand, the SIMT approach eases synchronization within the group and allows threads to communicate and collaborate through shared local memory.

3.2 Memory Organization

The second difference is the memory organization, which is divided into the following memory address spaces:

- host memory,
- global memory,
- local memory,
- and private memory.

In fact, the *host memory* is the operational memory of the computer. It is directly accessible by the CPU, but it cannot be accessed by any peripheral device such as the GPU. Input data needs to be transferred from the host memory to the graphic device memory (global memory), and the results need to be transferred back when the kernel execution finishes. This transfer uses the PCI-Express bus, which is rather slow in comparison with the internal memory bus.

The *global memory* is directly accessible from GPU cores. Input data and computed results of a kernel are stored here. The global memory bus shows both high latency and high bandwidth. In order to access the global memory optimally, threads in one group are encouraged to use *coalesced loads*. A coalesced load is performed when all threads of a group load or store a contiguous memory area, so that each thread transfers a single 4-byte word of this block.

The *local memory* is shared among threads within one group. It is very small (tens of kB) but almost as fast as GPU registers. The local memory can play role of program-managed cache for global memory, or the threads may share intermediate results in here while they cooperate on a task.

Finally, the *private memory* exclusively belongs to a single thread and corresponds to the GPU core registers. Private memory size is very limited (tens to hundreds of words), therefore it is suitable just for a few local variables.

4. QUERYING BY SQFD ON A GPU

In our approach, we consider both the parallel execution of multiple SQFD computations during the query evaluation as well as the parallel computation of a single SQFD between two feature signatures.

4.1 Multiple SQFD Computations

Since the SQFD is computed between the query signature and each database signature, it would be ineffective to execute each computation separately on the GPU due to the latencies caused by data transfer and kernel executions. Therefore, we perform a block-wise computation of multiple SQFDs in parallel. Each block contains $N + 1$ feature signatures. The first feature signature is the query signature and remaining N feature signatures are database signatures, thus each block yields a vector of N distances as a result. The choice of N is essential for good performance. In general, a large number of N performs better. However, at least two blocks of feature signatures must fit each GPU device in order to process the first block and transfer the data of the other one.

Each SQFD is computed by a group of 256 threads, thus $256 \times N$ threads are spawned for one block. The constant 256 was selected based on current hardware capabilities. We have assigned one thread group to compute a single SQFD in a block, because these threads benefit from shared local memory, as the group does cache the input data from global memory and keeps intermediate results. Using multiple groups to compute one SQFD would be problematic as the groups do not have any effective means of communication. The opposite approach (using one group to compute multiple SQFDs) is feasible. However, the parallelism would not be exploited any further and many technical complications would arise due to the limited size of local memory.

4.2 Computing The Distance in Parallel

The SQFD between two feature signatures has been defined in Definition 1. For the sake of parallelism, we compute the items of the similarity matrix A_{f_s}, and multiply them directly with the corresponding weights of $(w_q \mid -w_o)$. Fi-

[1]Single Instruction Multiple Threads

nally, we compute a sum of every item in the matrix and we find its square root. Our algorithm has the following phases:

1. Load feature signatures into local memory
2. Compute the similarity matrix A_{f_s} and multiply its entries by corresponding entries in the weight vectors
3. Sum up items in the matrix and yield the square root

Data are loaded into local memory, since they are required multiple times and it would be ineffective to load them from global memory each time. Furthermore, the loading is more efficient when all threads cooperate in coalesced loads.

The similarity matrix has $(m+n) \times (m+n)$ entries, where m and n are the numbers of feature representatives in S^q and S^o, respectively. Since $m + n$ is usually smaller than 256 and varies for each feature signature, we use an irregular mapping of similarity matrix items to threads.

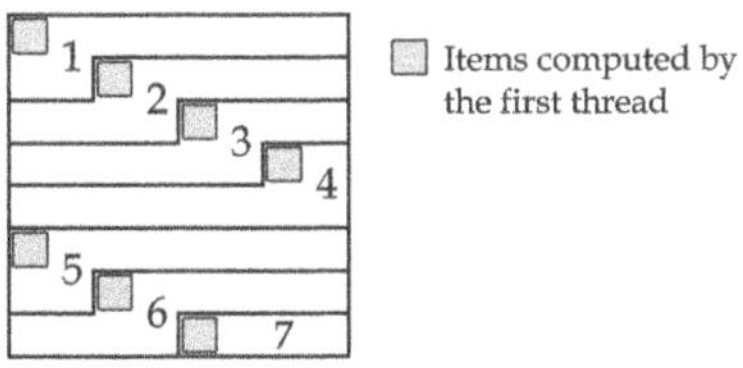

Figure 1: Matrix work decomposition

Figure 1 depicts the mapping scheme, where each area represents items being computed simultaneously. The numbers indicate in which step the items will be processed. In the last step, the remaining part of the similarity matrix may be smaller than total number of threads. In such case, some threads will remain idle in this step.

The entire similarity matrix is not stored in memory since only a sum of its items is required. When a thread computes a new item in the similarity matrix, its value is added to a partial sum and the item itself is discarded. Even though this method requires significantly less memory, it creates a synchronization problem as multiple items are computed and added to the partial sum concurrently. To avoid explicit synchronization, every thread is provided with its own instance of partial sum.

When the second phase terminates, the total sum of the partial sums of each thread is computed. This total sum is only computed by the first thread, which is also responsible for finding the square root and for writing the computed distance into the global memory. The total sum can also be computed cooperatively by all threads in logarithmic time; however, such improvement has no measurable impact on the performance as the time required by the second phase dominates significantly over the time required by the final summation.

4.3 Integration to Query Evaluation System

We have described how to compute distances between a query signature and a block of database signatures on the GPU. How to integrate this functionality into a system that computes range and kNN queries is explained in the remainder of this section.

The rest of the query processor treats our SQFD implementation as an asynchronous operation that does not block the CPU when started, and the system can wait for its termination. The system may start as many operations as required, and the operations are queued and distributed over available GPU devices equally. The architecture is flexible, thus it can be easily used with any type of distance-based index.

4.3.1 Range Query

The sequential range query algorithm is easy to implement. The database is divided into blocks of appropriate size[2] and all blocks are enqueued for GPU processing. The system waits for all SQFD computations to complete, and the computed distances are filtered on the CPU to exclude objects outside of the query range from the result.

This method can be improved easily with pivot table indexing (either metric or ptolemaic variant). First, distances from the query to all pivot objects are computed on the GPU. Afterwards, the CPU prefilters database objects using the pivot table. The objects which are not excluded in the prefiltering step are formed into blocks. A block is passed to the GPU as soon as it has a sufficient number of objects (we use 8,000, observed empirically as optimal).

4.3.2 kNN Query

The kNN query evaluation is slightly more complicated. When no indexing is used, it works very much like sequential range query. When the pivot table indexing is employed, some additional modifications are required. The problem is that the kNN query has no fixed query range for the pivot table prefiltering, as this range is dynamically refined during the kNN query processing using heuristics.

In order to adapt to the heuristics, we have limited the block size to a value of 64. Also, there are at most $2g$ blocks pending where g is the number of GPU devices available. These constants have been chosen empirically[3]. When the limit of pending blocks is reached, the system waits for the first enqueued block to finish, its results are taken, and the query range is refined. This way a pipeline effect is achieved, so that the CPU prefilters the database objects and refines the kNN set while the GPU computes the SQFD.

5. EXPERIMENTS

We conduct GPU and CPU tests with up to 12 cores on a desktop PC based on six-core Intel Core i7 870 CPU with hyper-threading clocked at 2.93 GHz. The machine was equipped with 16 GB of RAM and two NVIDIA GTX 580 GPU cards with 512 CUDA cores and 1.5 GB of RAM each. More extensive multi-core CPU tests for 48 cores were executed on a Dell M910 server with four six-core Intel Xeon E7540 processors with hyper-threading (i.e., 48 logical cores) clocked at 2.0 GHz. The server was equipped with 128 GB of RAM organized as 4-node NUMA. A RedHat Enterprise Linux 6 was used as operating system on both machines.

Our approach was tested on the ALOI database [4] which consists of 72,000 images. Although the selected database was not very large, its size was sufficient to demonstrate the speed-up of our method. To perform test using Pivot tables, we have randomly selected 32 pivots from the database. The queries were selected as 100 random objects from the database (and excluded from indexing). All tests were performed for $\alpha \in \{3, 0.2, 0.01\}$, where $\alpha = 3$ exhibits the best

[2]We use as large blocks as possible that fit the GPU memory.

[3]Actually, these constants are suitable only for $\alpha = 0.2$ and $\alpha = 0.01$. The value $\alpha = 3$ requires the largest possible blocks since it does not benefit much from indexing.

precision, $\alpha = 0.01$ offers the best indexability, and $\alpha = 0.2$ is the best compromise between precision and indexability.

5.1 Simple Sequential Scan

The first test demonstrates the behavior of the sequential scan, i.e. either range or kNN query, without pivot table indexing. The measured values represent real times required for computing a vector of distances between the query object and all database objects. Each test was performed for 32 randomly chosen objects and the presented values are arithmetic averages of the measured times. Each test is denoted as follows. The n CPU stands for SQFD running on n processor cores and m GPU means that the test was using m GPU devices (512 cores each). The data type in brackets indicates the floating point precision used for intermediate results.

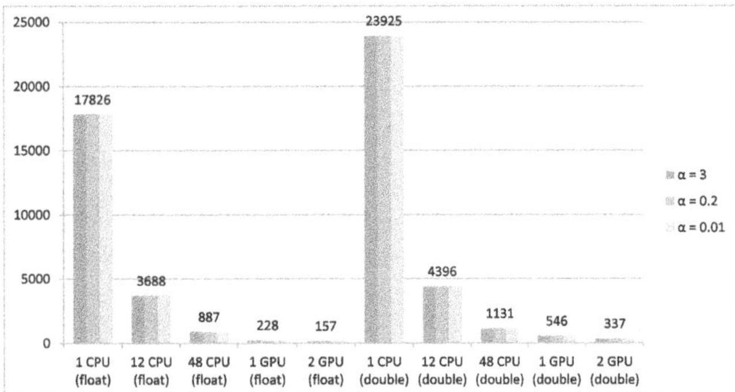

Figure 2: Times[ms] of sequential scan

Figure 2 clearly indicates that the GPU approach is faster by two orders of magnitude than sequential version of the algorithm running on CPU. Furthermore, the GPU is significantly faster (5.6× in float and 3.4× in double) than 4-CPU NUMA server with 48 logical cores (which is financially an order of magnitude more expensive than a desktop PC with GPU cards). We have also observed that different values of α have no effect on the evaluation speed.

5.2 SQFD with Ptolemaic Indexing

In the second experiment, we have tested the GPU acceleration for kNN queries, where objects are prefiltered using Ptolemaic indexing on CPU [5]. The results are denoted as in the previous test, except for only float precision was used for intermediate results.

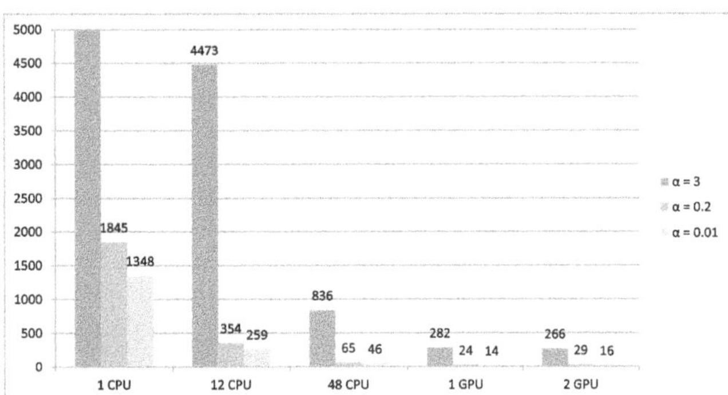

Figure 3: Times[ms] of 10NN with ptolemaic index

Figure 3 verifies that 10NN queries with indexing can be accelerated by computing SQFD on GPU, although the speed-up is slightly less significant than in the previous test. The average speed-up of a GPU w.r.t. 48 CPU cores (2.98×) proves that GPU can accelerate also indexing methods significantly. Despite our efforts, the 2-GPU version was slower than one-GPU for $\alpha \in \{0.2, 0.01\}$. We belive that this was the result of fragile balance between CPU and GPU workload at the moment the CPU prefilters the database objects. We are planning to study this phenomenon further and improve our method by moving the index prefiltering to GPU as well.

6. CONCLUSIONS

In this paper, we have shown how to exploit the computational power of GPUs for an efficient similarity query processing for multimedia retrieval models utilizing the Signature Quadratic Form Distance. We have experimentally proved that the speedup is considerable even in comparison with expensive NUMA server.

In the future, we plan to employ GPUs in other operations (such as index filtering) and to create a sophisticated large-scale multimedia retrieval system utilizing SQFD on feature signatures as similarity model.

7. ACKNOWLEDGMENTS

This research has been supported by Czech Science Foundation (GAČR) projects 201/09/0683 and 202/11/0968, by the grant agency of Charles University (GAUK) project no. 277911, and by the Deutsche Forschungsgemeinschaft within the Collaborative Research Center SFB 686.

8. REFERENCES

[1] C. Beecks, J. Lokoč, T. Seidl, and T. Skopal. Indexing the signature quadratic form distance for efficient content-based multimedia retrieval. In *Proc. ACM Int. Conf. on Multimedia Retrieval*, pages 24:1–24:8, 2011.

[2] C. Beecks, M. S. Uysal, and T. Seidl. A comparative study of similarity measures for content-based multimedia retrieval. In *Proc. IEEE ICME*, pages 1552–1557, 2010.

[3] C. Beecks, M. S. Uysal, and T. Seidl. Signature quadratic form distance. In *Proc. ACM CIVR*, pages 438–445, 2010.

[4] J.-M. Geusebroek, G. J. Burghouts, and A. W. M. Smeulders. The Amsterdam Library of Object Images. *IJCV*, 61(1):103–112, 2005.

[5] J. Lokoč, M. Hetland, T. Skopal, and C. Beecks. Ptolemaic indexing of the signature quadratic form distance. In *Proceedings of the Fourth International Conference on SImilarity Search and APplications*, pages 9–16. ACM, 2011.

[6] NVIDIA. Fermi GPU Architecture. http://www.nvidia.com/object/fermi_architecture.html.

[7] Y. Rubner, C. Tomasi, and L. J. Guibas. The Earth Mover's Distance as a Metric for Image Retrieval. *IJCV*, 40(2):99–121, 2000.

[8] P. Zezula, G. Amato, V. Dohnal, and M. Batko. *Similarity Search: The Metric Space Approach (Advances in Database Systems)*. Springer-Verlag New York, Inc., Secaucus, NJ, USA, 2005.

Top-k Most Influential Location Selection

Jin Huang
South China Univ. of Tech.
Guangzhou, China
jin.h@iojin.com

Zeyi Wen
University of Melbourne
Melbourne, Australia
wenzeyi@gmail.com

Jianzhong Qi
University of Melbourne
Melbourne, Australia
jiqi@csse.unimelb.edu.au

Rui Zhang
University of Melbourne
Melbourne, Australia
rui@csse.unimelb.edu.au

Jian Chen
South China Univ. of Tech.
Guangzhou, China
ellachen@scut.edu.cn

Zhen He
La Trobe University
Bundoora, Australia
z.he@latrobe.edu.au

ABSTRACT

We propose and study a new type of facility location selection query, the *top-k most influential location selection query*. Given a set M of customers and a set F of existing facilities, this query finds k locations from a set C of candidate locations with the largest influence values, where the influence of a candidate location c ($c \in C$) is defined as the number of customers in M who are the reverse nearest neighbors of c. We first present a naive algorithm to process the query. However, the algorithm is computationally expensive and not scalable to large datasets. This motivates us to explore more efficient solutions. We propose two branch and bound algorithms, the *Estimation Expanding Pruning (EEP)* algorithm and the *Bounding Influence Pruning (BIP)* algorithm. These algorithms exploit various geometric properties to prune the search space, and thus achieve much better performance than that of the naive algorithm. Specifically, the EEP algorithm estimates the distances to the nearest existing facilities for the customers and the numbers of influenced customers for the candidate locations, and then gradually refines the estimation until the answer set is found, during which distance metric based pruning techniques are used to improve the refinement efficiency. BIP only estimates the numbers of influenced customers for the candidate locations. But it uses the existing facilities to limit the space for searching the influenced customers and achieve a better estimation, which results in an even more efficient algorithm. Extensive experiments conducted on both real and synthetic datasets validate the efficiency of the algorithms.

Categories and Subject Descriptors

H.2.8 [**Database Management**]: Database Applications—*Spatial databases and GIS*

General Terms

Algorithms, Performance, Theory

Keywords

Location Selection, Top-k Query, Reverse Nearest Neighbors

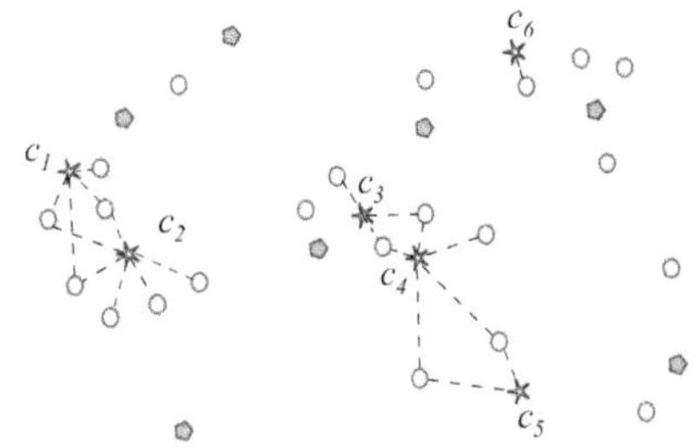

Figure 1: The top-k most influential location selection problem

1 Introduction

A common problem many businesses and organizations share is finding a suitable place for the establishment of a new facility. For example, McDonald's may want to add a new restaurant to compete with other restaurants; a wireless service provider may want to add a hotspot to a densely populated area to improve the quality of service. In most cases, there is a set of candidate locations to select from (e.g., real estate agents have databases of places for lease or sale). Then, an important business decision (for McDonald's or a wireless service provider) is to select a location that attracts as many customers as possible. Sometimes, one may want to first have a number (k) of such locations and then make decisions with further considerations. In this paper, we investigate this problem of finding the top-k candidate locations that attract the largest numbers of customers, where k is a user input parameter. These k candidate locations can then be fed to further decision making procedures for selecting an overall best location for the new facility. Here, we assume a customer is attracted by her nearest facility and the business has the knowledge of customer distribution from surveys or past sales records.

In urban development simulation, very often urban planners need to simulate the above facility location selection procedure, so that the influence of establishing a new public facility or business center on the residents can be observed. Figure. 1 gives an example, where circles, pentagons and stars denote customers, existing facilities and candidate locations (labeled as $c_1, ..., c_6$), respectively. First, for every candidate location c_i, we compute the number of customers c_i can attract. For example, if a new facility is established at c_1, then it will attract 4 customers. Similarly, we can compute the numbers for c_2, c_3, c_4, c_5 and c_6, which are 6, 3, 5, 2 and 1, respectively. Suppose now we want to have the top-3 candidate locations that attract the largest numbers of customers, i.e., $k = 3$. Then, c_2, c_4 and c_1 are returned as the answer set.

The above location selection problem aims at maximizing the "influence" of the candidate locations, where the influence of a candidate location c denotes the number of customers whose respective nearest facility will be c if a new facility is established at c. This problem is frequently raised in applications like urban development simulation. Thus, we formulate it as the top-k most influential location selection query. We propose algorithms to process this query efficiently and make the following contributions.

- We formulate the top-k most influential location selection query.
- We analyze the properties of the query and propose pruning techniques to reduce the search space for processing the query.
- Based on the proposed pruning techniques, we propose two algorithms, namely, the Estimation Expanding Pruning algorithm (EEP) and the Bounding Influence Pruning (BIP) algorithm, to efficiently process the query.
- We perform an extensive experimental study. The results confirm the effectiveness of the proposed pruning techniques and the efficiency of the proposed algorithms.

The rest of the paper is organized as follows. § 2 reviews previous studies on related topics. § 3 defines the problem and presents the naive algorithm. § 4 and 5 describe our EEP algorithm and BIP algorithm, respectively. § 6 presents the experimental results and § 7 concludes the paper.

2 Related Work

The studied problem is based on the concept of *reverse nearest neighbor (RNN)* query [10], which finds for a query object o a set of objects, who perceive o as their nearest neighbors. Since it was proposed, various techniques [14, 16, 1] have been proposed to process this type of query and its variants under different settings. For example, a most relevant RNN variant, the *reverse k nearest neighbor (RkNN)* query, extends the answer set to include objects who perceive the query object as among their k nearest neighbors. Wu et al. [16] study the RkNN query on continuously moving objects, which correlates two sets of moving objects according to their closeness. The continuous join query on moving objects [18] also correlates multiple sets, but it focuses on intersection of objects with a time constraining technique rather than closeness. While these studies work well for processing a single R(k)NN query, they are not designed to compute R(k)NNs for large amount of objects at the same time, which is one of the key difficulties in our study.

Regarding to facility location problems, the most relevant study [8] ranks the candidate locations according to their influence values. However, the proposed solution cannot find the top-k locations and then early terminates the algorithm. Therefore, it does not solve our problem, while our proposed algorithms can be used to rank the locations by setting k to the number of candidate locations. Other studies on facility location problems have quite different problem settings. Cabello et al. [2] propose a facility location problem based on the MAXCOV optimization criterion, which is to find regions in the data space to maximize the numbers of RNNs for the points in these regions. The study gives a theoretical analysis, but no efficient algorithm is presented. Chen et al. [4] study this problem further and propose an efficient solution for finding the nearest facilities. Xia et al. [17] propose the top-t most influential sites problem, which finds the top-t most influential existing sites within a given region Q. Unlike our study, they do not consider any candidate locations. Du et al. [5] propose to find a point from a continuous candidate region that can maximize the influence value. They use L_1 as the distance metric and have a strong assumption that all the roads are either horizontal or vertical. We consider L_2 distance, which is a more general problem setting. More importantly, *we consider a candidate location set instead of a candidate region. This is a more practical problem setting because in many real applications, we can only choose from some candidate locations (e.g. a McDonald's restaurant can only be opened at a place for lease or sale rather than anywhere in a region).* Cheema et al. [3] propose to find an influence zone for a query location c, where customers inside this zone form exactly the RkNN query result of c. They compute *Voronoi cells* on the fly for the query location to obtain its RkNNs. Similarly, Wong et al. [15] propose to find the optimal region in which all query objects are of the maximum influence. Compared with this problem, our problem focuses on the numbers of RNNs of the candidate locations instead of specific locations of the RNNs. These problems use different settings from ours. Therefore, their solutions do not apply.

3 Preliminaries

3.1 Problem Definition

We assume three object sets, namely, a set of customers M, a set of existing facilities F and a set of candidate locations C. All the data objects (customers, existing facilities or candidate locations) are represented by points in an Euclidean space. We may refer to a data object as a data point or simply as a point. The distance between two points p_1 and p_2 is denoted as $d(p_1, p_2)$.

Given a customer $m \in M$, we denote her nearest existing facility as $nf(m)$, and call the distance between m and $nf(m)$, $d(m, nf(m))$, the *nearest facility distance (NFD)* of m. We say that customer m is attracted by a candidate location $c \in C$ if the distance between m and c is less than the nearest facility distance of m, i.e., $d(m, c) < d(m, nf(m))$. In this case, if we add a facility at c, it will become the new nearest facility of m.

A candidate location $c \in C$ may attract multiple customers. The number of these attracted customers defines the *influence* of c, $inf(c)$. Formally, $inf(c) = |\{m \in M | d(m, c) < d(m, nf(m))\}|$.

The top-k most influential location selection query is to find k candidate locations that attract the largest numbers of customers.

DEFINITION 1. *Top-k Most Influential Location Selection (TILS) Query: Given a constant k, a set of points M as customers, a set of points F as existing facilities and a set of points C as candidate locations, the top-k most influential location selection query finds a set $C' \subset C$ with k points, so that $\forall c_i \in C', c_j \in C \setminus C'$: $inf(c_i) \geq inf(c_j)$.*

We call the subset C' the *top-k most influential location set* and denote it as TOPINF(K,M,F,C)[1]. Next, we present a naive algorithm to find this subset.

3.2 A Naive Algorithm

A *naive algorithm (NA)* to process the TILS query is to first compute the nearest facility distance for every $m \in M$, which is done by scanning F to find m's nearest existing facility. Then, for every candidate location $c \in C$, we scan the customer set M. If the distance between c and a customer m, $d(c, m)$, is less than the nearest facility distance of m, i.e., c attracts m, then we increment the influence value of c. After we have scanned every pair of c and m, we obtain the influence value for every c. We then sort the candidate locations according to their influence values, and output the first k candidate locations in the sorted result as the query answer set.

The NA algorithm is inefficient in that it has to scan every pair of customer and existing facility to find customers' nearest existing facilities, and every pair of candidate location and customer to compute candidate locations' influence values. This motivate us

[1] Note that there may be ties in the influence values. To simplify our discussion, we always return the first k candidate locations found that have the largest influence values.

to explore effective pruning techniques to reduce the search space. We assume that the datasets are maintained in spatial indexes [2] and propose two algorithms utilizing different geometric properties to achieve effective pruning. In what follows, we present the overall ideas of these two algorithms. Technical details are omitted due to space limit and they are given in a technical report [9].

4 Estimation Expanding Pruning

In this section, we propose an algorithm that estimates the distances to the nearest existing facilities for the customers and the numbers of influenced customers for the candidate locations, and gradually refines these estimations to obtain k candidate locations with the largest influence values. We use two R-trees and an R-tree variant to index the three datasets. The **estimations** and the refinement are performed during a traversal on the trees (**expanding** tree nodes), where the *importance* value is introduced to help achieve a best first tree traversal while branch and bound techniques are introduced to **prune** the search space. We call this algorithm the *Estimation Expanding Pruning (EEP)* algorithm.

EEP indexes the set of existing facilities F and the set of candidate locations C with two R-trees tr_F and tr_C, respectively. It indexes the set of customers M with an R-tree variant called the *aggregate R-tree (aR-tree)* [11] tr_M, where a tree node stores the number of data objects that are enclosed by its MBR in addition to what is stored in a regular R-tree node. These three trees are traversed simultaneously. The traversal is managed using three auxiliary lists L_M, L_F and L_C, which store objects (either nodes or data objects) from tr_M, tr_F and tr_C, respectively. For an object O in an auxiliary list, we define its *importance* value with its estimated distance to its nearest existing facility (if O is an object in the customer tree tr_M) or estimated number of influenced customers (if O is an object in the existing facility tree tr_F or the candidate location tree tr_C). We use the importance value to determine which objects should be accessed first, and which objects should be pruned. Every object in these lists stores some *influence relation information* that indicates its position relation with the objects in other lists and will be used for importance value computation. Initially, each of these three lists contains only the root node of the corresponding tree. Then, these three lists are accessed repeatedly in the order of L_M, L_F and L_C.

Every time a list L is accessed, EEP computes the importance value $imp(O)$ for every object O contained in L. The object in L with the largest importance value is accessed first. If the accessed object O is a node, the following 5 steps are performed: (i) O's child objects (either nodes or data objects) use O's influence relation information to compute their own influence relation information according to their positions; (ii) EEP prunes a child object O' of O if the influence relation information of O' indicates that the data objects enclosed in O' will not influence or be influenced by the data objects enclosed in the objects of other lists; (iii) if O is a node in tr_C, we compute an influence value upper bound for each of its child objects O', denoted by $maxinf(O')$, which is an upper bound of the influence value for all the candidate locations enclosed by O'. We prune O' if $maxinf(O') < inf_{pr}$, where inf_{pr} is an influence threshold value used for pruning objects in tr_C from further consideration. (iv) the unpruned child objects are used to update the influence relation information of the objects in other lists and further prune some of the objects. (v) EEP removes O and inserts the unpruned child objects of O into L. If the accessed object O is a candidate location $c \in C$, EEP computes the maximum and minimum possible influence values for c, denoted by $maxinf(c)$ and $mininf(c)$, and compare $mininf(c)$ with the largest $maxinf$ value, inf_{mx}, for all the objects in L_C. If $mininf(c) \geq inf_{mx}$, then c is put in the query answer set TOPINF(K,M,F,C) and the pruning influence value inf_{pr} is updated to $mininf(c)$. If O is an existing facility or a customer, there is no computation required for processing O. However, we cannot simply remove O because there are objects in other lists that are related to O. Therefore, EEP skips it and continues to access objects in other lists. The algorithm terminates when TOPINF(K,M,F,C) is filled with k candidate locations and no other candidate location can have larger influence values than those obtained so far.

[2]We assume the R-tree [6] (or its variant), although our algorithms apply to any hierarchical index.

5 Bounding Influence Pruning

This section proposes a second strategy to estimate and refine the influence values for candidate locations. This strategy employs the concept of *influencing region*, which is a region computed from the existing facilities near a candidate location c to enclose all the customers who are influenced by c. The number of customers in this region forms an upper bound for c's influence value. By gradually refining the influencing region (**pruning** customers), we reduce c's **influence** value upper **bound** until we get c's exact influence value.

We present a branch and bound algorithm called the *Bounding Influence Pruning (BIP)* algorithm that utilizes the above strategy to process the TILS query. Like the EEP algorithm, the BIP algorithm also indexes the set of candidate locations C and the set of existing facilities F with two R-trees tr_C and tr_F. It indexes the set of customers M with an aR-tree tr_M. BIP also takes a best first approach. The algorithm uses a priority queue Q_C to perform a best first traversal on tr_C, where each queue element is a node N_C from tr_C, associated with a set of *relevant F nodes* $N_C.R_F$ from tr_F for influencing region computation, a set of relevant M nodes $N_C.R_M$ from tr_M for influence value estimation, and an estimated upper bound for the influence values of the candidate locations enclosed by the MBR of N_C as N_C's priority. To simplify the discussion, we call this upper bound the influence value upper bound of N_C. Initially, Q_C only contains the root node of tr_C, denoted as $root_C$, with $root_C.R_F = \{root_F\}$ and $root_C.R_M = \{root_M\}$, where $root_F$ and $root_M$ denote the root nodes of tr_F and tr_M.

Every time Q_C is accessed, the first node N_C in Q_C is popped out. If N_C is a non-leaf node, the algorithm (i) retrieves N_C's child nodes, (ii) constructs their own sets of relevant nodes according to $N_C.R_F$ and $N_C.R_M$, (iii) computes their influencing regions and influence value upper bounds, (iv) removes a child node if its influence value upper bound is less than the smallest influence value of the candidate locations in TOPINF(K,M,F,C), inf_{pr}, and (v) pushes the unpruned child nodes into Q_C. If N_C is a leaf node, the algorithm (i) retrieves the candidate locations indexed in N_C, (ii) computes their own influencing regions and exact influence values using $N_C.R_F$ and $N_C.R_M$, (iii) inserts a candidate location into TOPINF(K,M,F,C) if its influence value is larger than inf_{pr}, and (v) updates inf_{pr}. The algorithm stops when $Q_C = \emptyset$.

6 Performance Study

6.1 Experimental Settings

All experiments were conducted on a PC with a 2GHz CPU and 2GB RAM. R-trees and aR-trees are used to index the datasets. With practical cardinalities of the three datasets, the total data size is less than 100MB. Given the current computer memory size, it is reasonable to assume that all the datasets reside in the memory and our performance measurement focuses on the total response time. We also measure the number of distance metric computations of the algorithms, which is a good indicator of their pruning power.

We conduct experiments on both synthetic and real datasets. Syn-

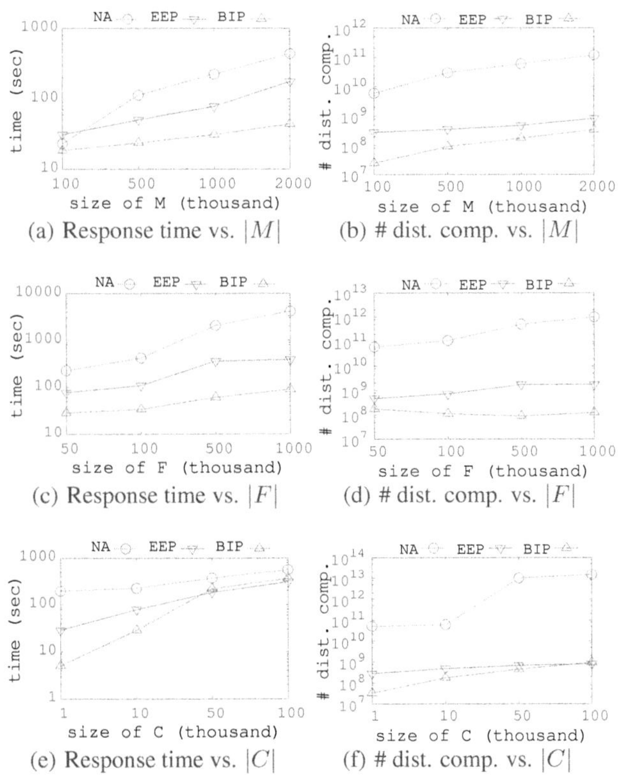

Figure 2: Effect of dataset cardinality on the total response time

thetic datasets are generated in a space domain of 1000×1000. The dataset cardinalities range from 1,000 to 2,000,000. To simulate real-life scenarios, where residents and facilities' distributions are skewed while candidate locations' distribution is relatively uniform, we generate M and F with Zipfian distribution with $\alpha = 1.2$, and C with uniform distribution. To verify the effect of the value of k, we use values ranging from 10 to 5,000. As previous studies [13, 7, 19] on main memory databases show, the tree node size of main memory index has a significant impact on the index performance. Therefore, we vary the node size ranging from 1K to 4K to study the effect of node size. By default, we use $k = 10$ and 2K as the tree node size. The real dataset we use is the North East dataset [12]. which contains 123,593 postal addresses representing three metropolitan areas of the USA. We uniformly sample from this dataset to generate M, F and C, with dataset cardinalities ranging from 500 to 100,000.

6.2 Effect of Dataset Cardinality

Figure 2 shows the results of the experiments varying the dataset cardinalities on the synthetic datasets. When varying the cardinality of one dataset, we set the cardinalities of the other two datasets to their default values. The default values used are $|M|$ = 1M, $|F|$=50K and $|C|$ = 10K.

From the figure, we can see that both the EEP and BIP algorithms consistently outperform the NA algorithm in terms of the total response time and the number of distance metric computations. This is because of the pruning techniques used by EEP and BIP to reduce the search space. We can also make other observations as follows. (i) With the increase in the customer set cardinality, EEP and BIP keep relatively stable performance, while NA's performance deteriorates drastically (please note the logarithmic scale in the figures). The reason is that NA sequentially scans all the datasets, and the dataset cardinality directly affect the number of distance computations. In contrast, EEP and BIP use pruning techniques to keep relatively small search spaces and thus achieve much better performance. (ii) With the increase in the number of existing facilities, the number of distance metric computations of BIP becomes smaller. This is because BIP uses the set of F to prune some of the nodes in tr_F as well as tr_M. More existing facilities means larger search space can be pruned and BIP achieves better performance.

We have also performed similar experiments on real datasets, experiments on the effect of tree node size, and experiments on the effect of the value of k. The comparative performance of the different methods are very similar to the above experiments. We omit presenting the results due to space limit.

7 Conclusions

We formulated the top-k most influential location selection query and conducted a comprehensive study on processing this query. We first analyzed the basic properties of this query type and proposed a naive algorithm (NA) to process the query. However, the NA algorithm is inefficient due to repeated scanning on datasets. Motivated by this, we explored geometric properties of spatial data objects, and proposed techniques to prune the search space. This resulted in two algorithms, the EEP algorithm and the BIP algorithm. Experimental results show that the proposed pruning techniques are effective and the proposed algorithms outperform the naive algorithm significantly. In most cases, BIP performs better than EEP.

8 Acknowledgments

We thank Google for funding a travel award that enabled Jianzhong Qi to attend the conference. This work is supported by the Australian Research Council's Discovery funding scheme (project number DP0880250). Zeyi Wen is supported by the Commonwealth Scientific and Industrial Research Organization (CSIRO).

9 References

[1] E. Achtert, H.-P. Kriegel, P. Kröger, M. Renz, and A. Züfle. Reverse k-nearest neighbor search in dynamic and general metric databases. In *EDBT*, 2009.

[2] S. Cabello, J. M. D, S. Langerman, and C. Seara. Reverse Facility Location Problems. In *CCCG*, 2006.

[3] M. A. Cheema, X. Lin, W. Zhang, and Y. Zhang. Influence Zone : Efficiently Processing Reverse k Nearest Neighbors Queries. In *ICDE*, 2011.

[4] Y. Chen and J. M. Patel. Efficient Evaluation of All-Nearest-Neighbor Queries. In *ICDE*, 2007.

[5] Y. Du, D. Zhang, and T. Xia. The Optimal-Location Query. *Advances in Spatial and Temporal Databases*, 3633:163–180, 2005.

[6] A. Guttman. R-Trees: A Dynamic Index Structure for Spatial Searching. In *SIGMOD*, 1984.

[7] R. A. Hankins and J. M. Patel. Effect of node size on the performance of cache-conscious b+-trees. In *SIGMETRICS*, 2003.

[8] J. Huang, Z. Wen, M. Pathan, K. Taylor, and R. Zhang. Ranking Locations for Facility Selection based on Potential Influences. In *the 37th Annual Conference of the IEEE Industrial Electronics Society*, 2011.

[9] J. Huang, Z. Wen, J. Qi, R. Zhang, J. Chen, and Z. He. Top-k most influential location selection. *http://ww2.cs.mu.oz.au/~zeyiw/TR_TkMIL.pdf.*

[10] F. Korn and S. Muthukrishnan. Influence Sets Based on Reverse Nearest Neighbor Queries. *ACM SIGMOD Record*, 29(2):201–212, June 2000.

[11] D. Papadias, P. Kalnis, J. Zhang, and Y. Tao. Efficient OLAP Operations in Spatial Data Warehouses. *Advances in Spatial and Temporal Databases*, 2121:443–459, 2001.

[12] R.-T. Portal. http://www.rtreeportal.org/.

[13] J. Rao and K. A. Ross. Cache conscious indexing for decision-support in main memory. In *VLDB*, 1999.

[14] I. Stanoi, M. Riedewald, D. Agrawal, and A. E. Abbadi. Discovery of Influence Sets in Frequently Updated Database. In *VLDB*, 2001.

[15] R. C.-w. Wong, M. T. Ozsu, P. S. Yu, A. W.-c. Fu, and L. Liu. Efficient Method for Maximizing Bichromatic Reverse Nearest Neighbor. In *VLDB*, 2009.

[16] W. Wu, F. Yang, C. Y. Chan, and K.-L. Tan. Continuous Reverse k-Nearest-Neighbor Monitoring. In *Proc. of MDM*. Ieee, Apr. 2008.

[17] T. Xia, D. Zhang, E. Kanoulas, and Y. Du. On Computing Top-t Most Influential Spatial Sites. In *VLDB*, 2005.

[18] R. Zhang, D. Lin, K. Ramamohanarao, and E. Bertino. Continuous Intersection Joins Over Moving Objects. In *ICDE*, 2008.

[19] R. Zhang and M. Stradling. The hv-tree: a memory hierarchy aware version index. *Proc. VLDB Endow.*, 3:397–408, September 2010.

Defining Isochrones in Multimodal Spatial Networks *

Johann Gamper[1] Michael Böhlen[2] Willi Cometti[1] Markus Innerebner[1]
[1] Free University of Bolzano-Bozen [2] University of Zurich
{gamper,cometti,innerebner}@inf.unibz.it boehlen@ifi.uzh.ch

ABSTRACT

An isochrone in a spatial network is the minimal, possibly disconnected subgraph that covers all locations from where a query point is reachable within a given time span and by a given arrival time. In this paper we formally define isochrones for multimodal spatial networks with different transportation modes that can be discrete or continuous in, respectively, space and time. For the computation of isochrones we propose the multimodal incremental network expansion (MINE) algorithm, which is independent of the actual network size and depends only on the size of the isochrone. An empirical study using real-world data confirms the analytical results.

Categories and Subject Descriptors

H.2 [**Database Management**]: Database Applications—*Spatial Databases and GIS*

General Terms

Algorithms

1. INTRODUCTION

Reachability analyses are important in many applications of spatial network databases. For example, in urban planning it is important to assess how well a city is covered by various public services such as hospitals or schools. An effective way to do so is to compute isochrones. An *isochrone* is the minimal, possibly disconnected subgraph that covers all locations from where a query point, q, is reachable within a given time span. When schedule-based networks, such as the public transport system, or time-dependent edge costs are considered, isochrones depend additionally on the arrival time at q. Isochrones can also be used as a primitive to efficiently answer other spatial network queries, such as range queries, by retrieving all objects within the isochrone without the need to compute the distance to the individual objects. For instance, by joining an isochrone with an inhabitants database, the citizens living in the area of the isochrone or the (number of) kids who can reach a school in 10 minutes can be determined.

*This work is partially funded by the Municipality of Bolzano.

Figure 1 shows the 10 min isochrone at 10:00 am for a query point (*) in Bolzano-Bozen. The isochrone consists of the bold street segments that cover all points from where the query point is reachable in less than 10 minutes, starting at 09:50 am or later and arriving at 10:00 am or before. A large area around the query point is within 10 minutes walking distance. Smaller areas are around bus stops, from where the query point can be reached by first walking to the bus stop and then taking the bus towards the query point. The box in the lower right corner shows the number of inhabitants in the isochrone area.

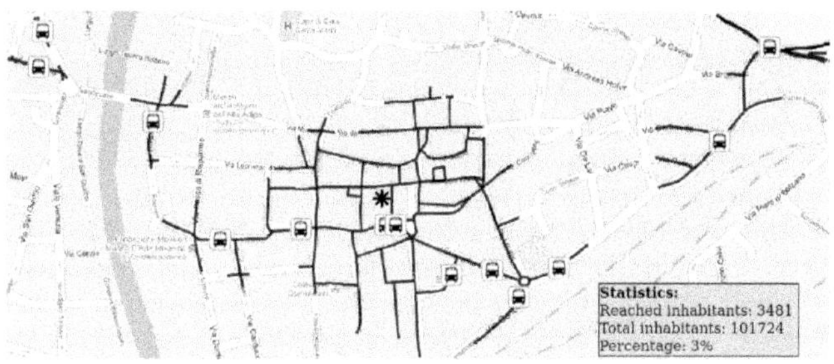

Figure 1: Screenshot of an Isochrone.

Spatial networks can be classified as *continuous* or *discrete* along, respectively, the space and the time dimension. Continuous space means that all points on an edge are accessible, whereas in a discrete space network only the vertices can be accessed. Continuous time networks can be traversed at any point in time, discrete time networks follow an associated schedule. For instance, the pedestrian network is continuous in time and space, whereas public transport systems are discrete in both dimensions.

Most of the past research work in spatial network databases is on shortest path (SP), nearest neighbor (NN), and range queries, predominantly in continuous road networks, e.g., [5, 6, 9, 12, 14]. Dijkstra's [6] incremental network expansion algorithm is the most basic solution to the SP problem and influenced much of the later works. The A^* algorithm [9] uses a lower bound estimate of the SP to get a more directed search with less vertex expansions. Papadias et al. [14] present two disk-based frameworks for different network queries: Incremental Euclidean Restriction (IER) repeatedly uses the Euclidean distance to reduce the number of objects for which the network distance is computed; Incremental Network Expansion (INE) is an adaptation of Dijkstra's SP algorithm. Deng et al. [5] improve over Papadias et al. [14] by exploiting the incremental nature of the lower bound to limit the number of distance calculations to only vertices in the final result set. Almeida and Güting [4] present an index structure and an algorithm for kNN queries to allow a one-by-one retrieval of objects. Other approaches take advantage of partitioning a network and pre-computing all or some of the SPs to save computation cost at query time. Examples are Voronoi regions [13], shortest path quadtrees [16], precomputed NN lists [3], and hierarchically organized subgraphs [1, 11]. For traffic networks that are too large for exact solutions in reasonable time, efficient approximation techniques have been proposed, most prominently based on the landmark embedding technique and sketch-based frameworks, e.g., [8, 15]. While most of the works assume a fixed cost value associated with each edge, only a few models support time-varying edge costs [7, 12]. There is far less work on schedule-based transportation networks and networks that support different transportation modalities [10].

In this paper we formally define isochrones for multimodal spatial networks that support different classes of transport modes, namely continuous and discrete in space and/or time, respectively, and we provide a disk-based evaluation algorithm. Isochrones constitute a new query type in spatial network databases. An isochrone query returns the possibly disconnected minimal subgraph that covers all space points in the network from where q is reachable within a given time span d_{max} and by a given arrival time t (i.e., space points with a time-dependent SP to q that is smaller than d_{max}). Isochrones are closest to range queries which return all *objects* that are within a given distance, whereas isochrone queries return all *space points* within a given distance. Indeed, by joining an isochrone with a relation of objects, range queries can be answered without the need to compute the distance to the individual objects. At the algorithmic level, the major difference to range queries (and other network queries) is that most optimization techniques are not effective for isochrones. For instance, search space pruning is not applicable since all edges that are (partially) reachable need to be explored. In contrast, in Papadias et al. [14] the search is driven by candidate objects that are computed using the Euclidean distance. Early termination of the search is possible if all candidates are explored, and a more directed search for the computation of the network distance to the candidate objects can be applied.

Isochrones have been introduced informally by Bauer et al. [2] together with a main memory evaluation algorithm that suffers from a high initial loading cost and is limited by the available memory since the entire network is loaded. In this paper we provide a precise formalization of isochrones in multimodal networks, and give a disk-based, multimodal incremental network expansion (MINE) algorithm that leverages Dijkstra's SP algorithm to the computation of isochrones and overcomes the major limitations of the main memory algorithm. Since only network portions are loaded that eventually will be part of the result, MINE's runtime and space complexity is independent of the actual network size and depends only on the size of the isochrone, i.e., $\mathcal{O}(|V^{iso}|)$, where $|V^{iso}|$ is the number of vertices in the isochrone.

The technical contributions can be summarized as follows:

- We formally define isochrones for multimodal spatial networks that can be discrete or continuous in, respectively, time and space. An isochrone is a new query type and can be used as a primitive operation for other spatial network queries.
- We propose a disk-based multimodal network expansion algorithm, termed MINE, that is independent of the network size and depends only on the isochrone size.
- We report the results of an empirical evaluation on real-world data that confirm the analytical results.

The rest of the paper is organized as follows. In Section 2 we formally define isochrones for multimodal networks. Section 3 presents the MINE algorithm. Section 4 reports experimental results. Section 5 concludes the paper and points to future work.

2. ISOCHRONES IN MULTIMODAL SPATIAL NETWORKS

In this section we provide a formal definition of isochrones in multimodal spatial networks that support different transport modes.

Definition 1. (*Multimodal Network*) A *multimodal network* is a seven-tuple $\mathsf{N} = (G, R, S, \rho, \mu, \lambda, \tau)$. $G = (V, E)$ is a directed multigraph with a set V of vertices and a multiset E of ordered pairs of vertices, termed edges. R is a set of transport systems. $S = (R, TID, W, \sigma_a, \sigma_d)$ is a schedule, where TID is a set of trip identifiers, $W \subseteq V$, and $\sigma_a : R \times TID \times W \mapsto \mathbb{T}$ and $\sigma_d : R \times TID \times W \mapsto \mathbb{T}$ determine arrival and departure time, respectively ($\mathbb{T}$ is the time domain). Function $\mu : R \mapsto \{'csct', 'csdt', 'dsct', 'dsdt'\}$ assigns to each transport system a transport mode, and the functions $\rho : E \mapsto R$, $\lambda : E \mapsto \mathbb{R}^+$, and $\tau : E \times \mathbb{T} \mapsto \mathbb{R}^+$ assign to each edge transport system, length, and transfer time, respectively.

A multimodal network allows to represent several transport systems, R, with different modalities in a single network: continuous space and time mode, $\mu(.) =$ '*csct*', e.g., pedestrian network; discrete space and time mode, $\mu(.) =$ '*dsdt*', e.g., the public transport system such as trains and buses; discrete space continuous time mode, $\mu(.) =$ '*dsct*', e.g., moving walkways or stairs; continuous space discrete time mode, $\mu(.) =$ '*csdt*', e.g., regions or streets that can be passed by pedestrians or cars only in specific time slots. Vertices represent crossroads of the street network and/or stops of the public transport system. Edges represent street segments, transport routes, moving walkways, etc. The schedule stores for each discrete time ('*dsdt*', '*csdt*') transport system in R the arrival and departure time at the stop nodes for the individual trips. For an edge $e = (u, v)$, function $\tau(e, t)$ computes the time-dependent transfer time that is required to traverse e, when starting at u as late as possible yet arriving at v no later than time t. For discrete time edges, the transfer time is the difference between t and the latest possible departure time at u according to the given schedule in order to reach v before or at time t. This includes a waiting time should the arrival at v be before t. For continuous time edges, the transfer time is modeled as a time-dependent function that allows to consider, e.g., different traffic conditions during rush hours.

Figure 2 shows a multimodal network with two transport systems, $R = \{'P', 'B'\}$, representing the pedestrian network with mode $\mu('P') =$ '*csct*' and bus line B with mode $\mu('B') =$ '*dsdt*', respectively. Solid lines are street segments of the pedestrian network, e.g., edge $e = (v_1, v_2)$ with $\rho(e) =$ 'P'. An undirected edge is a shorthand for a pair of directed edges in opposite directions. Pedestrian edges are annotated with the edge length, which is the same in both directions, e.g., $\lambda((v_1, v_2)) = \lambda((v_2, v_1)) = 300$. For simplicity, we assume a constant walking speed of 2 m/s, yielding a fixed transfer time, $\tau(e, t) = \frac{\lambda(e)}{2\,\mathrm{m/s}}$. Dashed lines represent bus line B. An excerpt of the schedule is shown in Fig. 2(b), e.g., $TID = \{1, 2, \dots\}$, $\sigma_a('B', 1, v_6) = \sigma_d('B', 1, v_6) =$ 05:33:00. The transfer time of a bus edge $e = (u, v)$ is computed as $\tau(e, t) = t - t'$, where $t' = \max\{\sigma_d('B', tid, u) \mid \sigma_a('B', tid, v) \leq t\}$ is the latest departure time at u.

A *location* in a multimodal network N is any point on an edge $e = (u, v) \in E$ that is accessible. We represent it as $l = (e, o)$, where $0 \leq o \leq \lambda(e)$ is an offset that determines the relative position of l from u on edge e. A location represents vertex u if $o = 0$ and vertex v if $o = \lambda(e)$; any other offset refers to an intermediate point on edge e. In continuous space networks all points on the edges are accessible. Since a pedestrian segment is modeled as a pair of directed edges in opposite direction, any

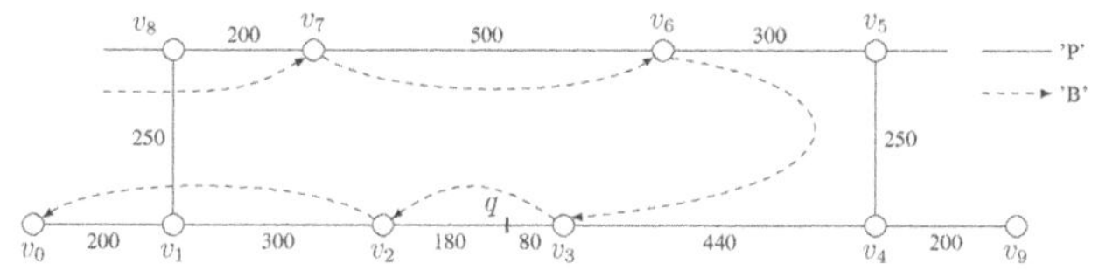

(a) Network

R	TID	Stop	Arrival	Departure
B	1	v_7	05:31:30	05:32:00
B	1	v_6	05:33:00	05:33:00
	⋮	⋮	⋮	⋮
B	2	v_7	06:01:30	06:02:00
B	2	v_6	06:03:00	06:03:00
B	2	v_3	06:05:00	06:05:30

(b) Schedule

Figure 2: Multimodal Network.

point on it can be represented by two locations, $((u, v), o)$ and $((v, u), \lambda((u, v)) - o)$, respectively. For instance, in Fig. 2 the location of q is $l_q = ((v_2, v_3), 180) = ((v_3, v_2), 80)$. In discrete space networks only vertices are accessible, thus $o \in \{0, \lambda(e)\}$ and locations coincide with vertices.

An *edge segment*, (e, o_1, o_2), with $0 \leq o_1 \leq o_2 \leq \lambda(e)$ represents the contiguous set of space points between the two locations (e, o_1) and (e, o_2) on edge e. We generalize the length function for edge segments to $\lambda((e, o_1, o_2)) = o_2 - o_1$.

Definition 2. (*Path, Path Cost*) A *path* from a source location $l_s = ((v_1, v_2), o_s)$ to a destination location $l_d = ((v_k, v_{k+1}), o_d)$ is defined as a sequence of connected edges and edge segments, $p(l_s, l_d) = \langle x_1, \ldots, x_k \rangle$, where $x_1 = ((v_1, v_2), o_s, \lambda((v_1, v_2)))$, $x_i = (v_i, v_{i+1})$ for $1 < i < k$, and $x_k = ((v_k, v_{k+1}), 0, o_d))$. With arrival time t at l_d, the *path cost* is

$$\gamma(\langle x_1, \ldots, x_k \rangle, t) = \begin{cases} \tau(x_k, t) & k=1, \\ \gamma(\langle x_k \rangle, t) + \\ \gamma(\langle x_1, \ldots, x_{k-1} \rangle, t - \gamma(\langle x_k \rangle, t) & k>1. \end{cases}$$

The first and the last element in a path can be edge segments, whereas all other elements are entire edges. Since isochrones depend on the arrival time at the query point, we define the path cost recursively as the cost of traversing the last edge (segment), x_k, considering the arrival time t at the destination l_d, plus the cost of traversing $\langle x_1, \ldots, x_{k-1} \rangle$, where the arrival time at v_k (the target vertex of edge x_{k-1}) is determined as t minus the cost of traversing x_k. The cost of traversing a single edge is the transfer time τ. Edges along a path may belong to different transport systems, which enables the changing of transport system along a path.

In Fig. 2, a path from v_7 to q is to take bus B from v_7 to v_3 and then walk to q, i.e., $p(v_7, l_q) = \langle x_1, x_2, x_3 \rangle$, where $x_1 = (v_7, v_6)$ and $x_2 = (v_6, v_3)$ are complete edges and $x_3 = ((v_3, v_2), 0, 80)$ is an edge segment. With arrival time $t = $ 06:06:00, the path cost is $\gamma(p(v_7, l_q), t) = (06{:}03{:}00 - 06{:}02{:}00) + (06{:}05{:}20 - 06{:}03{:}00) + 80/2 = 240\,\mathrm{s}$. To reach q at 06:06:00, the bus must arrive at v_3 no later than 06:05:20. Since the latest bus that matches this constraint arrives at 06:05:00, we have a waiting time of 20 s at v_3.

The *network distance*, $d(l_s, l_d, t)$, from a source location l_s to a destination location l_d with arrival time t at l_d is defined as the minimum cost of any path from l_s to l_d with arrival time t at l_d if such a path exists, and ∞ otherwise.

We proceed with the definition of an isochrone as the minimal subgraph of a multimodal spatial network that covers all locations from where a query point q is reachable under the given time constraints.

Definition 3. (*Isochrone*) Let $\mathsf{N} = (G, R, S, \mu, \rho, \lambda, \tau)$ with $G = (V, E)$ be a multimodal network, q be the query point with arrival time t, and $d_{max} > 0$ be the time span. An *isochrone*, $N^{iso} = (V^{iso}, E^{iso})$, is defined as the minimal and possibly disconnected subgraph of G that satisfies the following conditions:

- $V^{iso} \subseteq V$,
- $\forall l (l = (e, o) \wedge e \in E \wedge d(l, q, t) \leq d_{max}$
  $\Leftrightarrow \exists x \in E^{iso} (x = (e, o_1, o_2) \wedge o_1 \leq o \leq o_2))$.

The first condition requires the vertices of the isochrone to be a subset of the vertices of the multimodal network. The second condition constrains an isochrone to cover exactly those locations l that have a network distance $d(l, q, t)$ to q that is smaller or equal than d_{max}, taking into consideration the arrival time t. Notice the use of edge segments in E^{iso} to represent edges that are only partially reachable. Whenever an edge e is entirely covered by an isochrone, we use e instead of $(e, 0, \lambda(e))$.

In Fig. 3, the subgraph in bold represents the isochrone for $d_{max} = 5$ min and $t = $ 06:06:00. The numbers in parentheses are the network distance to q. Edges close to q are entirely reachable, whereas edges on the isochrone border are only partially reachable. For instance, (v_0, v_1) is only reachable from offset 80 to v_1. Bus edges are not included in the isochrone since intermediate points on bus edges are not accessible. Formally, the isochrone in Fig. 3 is represented as $N^{iso} = (V^{iso}, E^{iso})$ with $V^{iso} = \{v_0, \ldots, v_9\}$ and $E^{iso} = \{((v_0, v_1), 80, 200), ((v_8, v_1), 150, 250), (v_1, v_2), (v_2, v_1), (v_2, v_3), (v_3, v_2), (v_3, v_4), (v_4, v_3), ((v_5, v_4), 170, 250), ((v_9, v_4), 120, 200), ((v_5, v_6), 60, 300), ((v_7, v_6), 260, 500), ((v_6, v_7), 380, 500), ((v_8, v_7), 80, 200)\}$.

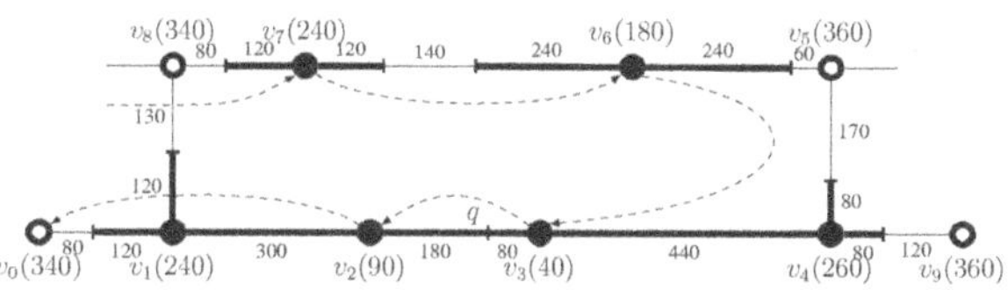

Figure 3: Isochrone in Multimodal Network.

3. MINE ALGORITHM

Algorithm 1 shows the incremental network expansion algorithm (MINE) for computing isochrones in multimodal networks. It maintains two sets of vertices: closed vertices (C) that have already been expanded and open vertices (O) that have been encountered but are not yet expanded. For each vertex $v \in O \cup C$, we maintain the distance $d(v, q, t)$ to q. C is initialized to the empty set. O is initialized to q with $d(q, q, t) = 0$ (without loss of generality we assume that q coincides with a vertex). O is maintained as a priority queue. During the expansion phase, vertex v with the smallest network distance is dequed from O and added to C. All incoming edges, $e = (u, v)$, are retrieved from the database and considered in turn. If vertex u is visited for the first time, it is added to O with a distance of ∞. The distance of u when traversing e is incrementally updated. If e is a continuous space edge, the reachable part of e is added to the result. Discrete space edges produce no direct output, since they have no accessible locations except the end vertices that are added when the incoming continuous space edges are processed. The algorithm terminates when O is empty or the network distance of the closest vertex in O exceeds d_{max}.

Algorithm 1: MINE($\mathsf{N}, q, t, d_{max}$)

input : network N, query point q, arrival time t, time span d_{max}
output: Isochrone N^{iso}

$C \leftarrow \emptyset$; $O \leftarrow \{(q, 0)\}$;
while $O \neq \emptyset$ *and first element has distance* $\leq d_{max}$ **do**
  $(v, d_v) \leftarrow$ first element from O;
  $O \leftarrow O \setminus \{v\}$; $C \leftarrow C \cup \{v\}$;
  foreach $e = (u, v) \in E$ **do**
    if $u \notin O \cup C$ **then** $O \leftarrow O \cup \{(u, \infty)\}$;
    $d'_u \leftarrow \tau(e, t - d_v) + d_v$;
    $d_u \leftarrow \min(d_u, d'_u)$;
    if $\mu(\rho(e)) \in \{$'csct', 'csdt'$\}$ **then**
      if $d'_u \leq d_{max}$ **then** Output $(e, 0, \lambda(e))$;
      else Output $(e, o, \lambda(e))$, where $d((e, o), q, t) = d_{max}$;

return;

4. EMPIRICAL EVALUATION

We compare MINE with Dijkstra's algorithm [6], which initially loads the entire network in memory, and Incremental Euclidean restriction (IER) [14], which instead of loading the entire network uses the Euclidean lower bound property to incrementally load smaller network chunks. The networks together with the schedules are stored in an Oracle Spatial 11g Enterprise database. All experiments run in a virtual machine on a dual processor Intel Xeon 2.67 GHz with 3 GB RAM. We test two real-world street and public transport networks: San Francisco/SF ($|V| = 33$ K, $|E| = 96$ K) and Bozen-Bolzano/BZ ($|V| = 3$ K, $|E| = 8$ K).

Figures 4(a)–4(b) analyze the memory requirements. As expected, MINE's memory consumption is independent of the network size and depends only on the isochrone size. It grows quadratically in d_{max} until the isochrone approaches the network border, where the growing slows down. The memory of Dijkstra is equal to the size of the entire network. IER is in between since many vertices are loaded that eventually will not be part of the isochrone.

Figures 4(c)–4(d) show the results of the runtime analysis for a central query point with arrival time 9:50 am on a weekday. For small values of d_{max} and small isochrones, Dijkstra has the worst performance due to the initial loading of the entire network. For large d_{max}, Dijkstra (though limited by the available memory) is more efficient since the initial loading of the network using a full table scan is faster than the incremental loading in MINE and IER. IER performs worse than MINE due to multiple loadings of edges.

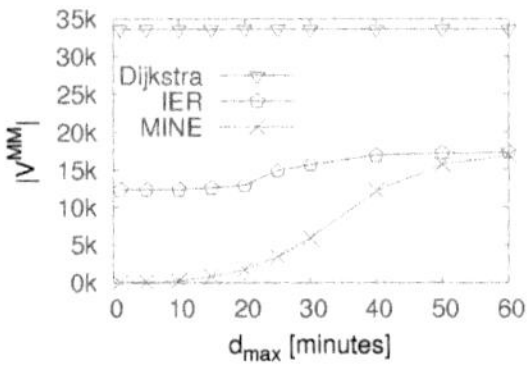

(a) Memory SF

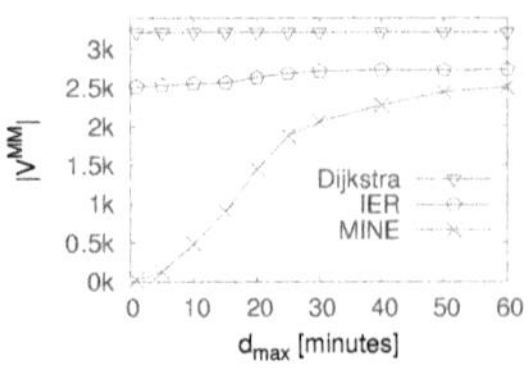

(b) Memory BZ

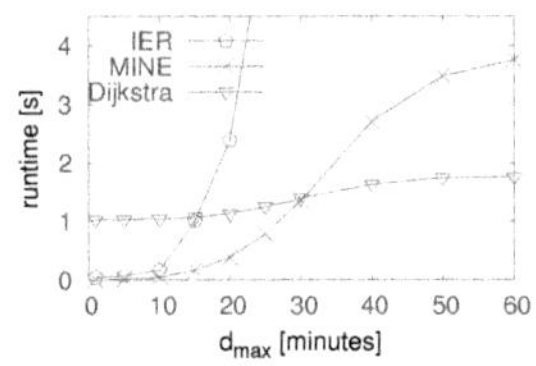

(c) Runtime SF

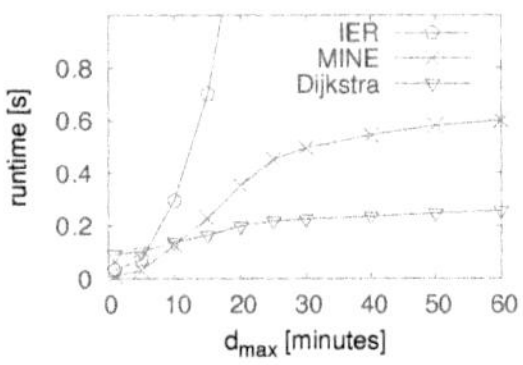

(d) Runtime BZ

Figure 4: Memory Requirements and Runtime.

5. CONCLUSION AND FUTURE WORK

In this paper we formally defined isochrones for multimodal spatial networks that can be discrete or continuous in, respectively, space and time. We proposed the MINE algorithm to compute isochrones, which is independent of the network size and depends only on the isochrone size. An empirical study confirmed the analytical results.

Future work includes the study of various optimization techniques in MINE as well as approximation algorithms. We will also study the use of isochrones in new application scenarios.

6. REFERENCES

[1] V. Balasubramanian, D. V. Kalashnikov, S. Mehrotra, and N. Venkatasubramanian. Efficient and scalable multi-geography route planning. In *EDBT*, 2010.

[2] V. Bauer, J. Gamper, R. Loperfido, S. Profanter, S. Putzer, and I. Timko. Computing isochrones in multi-modal, schedule-based transport networks. In *ACMGIS*, 2008.

[3] H.-J. Cho and C.-W. Chung. An efficient and scalable approach to CNN queries in a road network. In *VLDB*, 2005.

[4] V. T. de Almeida and R. H. Güting. Using Dijkstra's algorithm to incrementally find the k-nearest neighbors in spatial network databases. In *SAC*, pages 58–62, 2006.

[5] K. Deng, X. Zhou, H. T. Shen, S. W. Sadiq, and X. Li. Instance optimal query processing in spatial networks. *VLDB J.*, 18(3):675–693, 2009.

[6] E. W. Dijkstra. A note on two problems in connexion with graphs. *Numerische Mathematik*, 1(1):269–271, 1959.

[7] B. Ding, J. X. Yu, and L. Qin. Finding time-dependent shortest paths over large graphs. In *EDBT*, 2008.

[8] A. Gubichev, S. Bedathur, S. Seufert, and G. Weikum. Fast and accurate estimation of shortest paths in large graphs. In *CIKM*, pages 499–508, New York, NY, USA, 2010. ACM.

[9] P. Hart, N. Nilsson, and B. Raphael. A formal basis for the heuristic determination of minimum cost paths. *IEEE Transations on Systems Science and Cybernetics*, 4(2):100–107, 1968.

[10] R. Huang. A schedule-based pathfinding algorithm for transit networks using pattern first search. *GeoInformatica*, 11(2):269–285, 2007.

[11] N. Jing, Y.-W. Huang, and E. A. Rundensteiner. Hierarchical encoded path views for path query processing: An optimal model and its performance evaluation. *IEEE Trans. Knowl. Data Eng.*, 10(3):409–432, 1998.

[12] E. Kanoulas, Y. Du, T. Xia, and D. Zhang. Finding fastest paths on a road network with speed patterns. In *ICDE*, 2006.

[13] M. R. Kolahdouzan and C. Shahabi. Voronoi-based k nearest neighbor search for spatial network databases. In *VLDB*, pages 840–851, 2004.

[14] D. Papadias, J. Zhang, N. Mamoulis, and Y. Tao. Query processing in spatial network databases. In *VLDB*, 2003.

[15] M. Potamias, F. Bonchi, C. Castillo, and A. Gionis. Fast shortest path distance estimation in large networks. In *CIKM*, pages 867–876, 2009.

[16] H. Samet, J. Sankaranarayanan, and H. Alborzi. Scalable network distance browsing in spatial databases. In *SIGMOD Conference*, pages 43–54, 2008.

On the Elasticity of NoSQL Databases over Cloud Management Platforms

Ioannis Konstantinou, Evangelos Angelou, Christina Boumpouka,
Dimitrios Tsoumakos, Nectarios Koziris
Computing Systems Laboratory, School of Electrical and Computer Engineering
National Technical University of Athens, Greece
{ikons, eangelou, christina, dtsouma, nkoziris}@cslab.ece.ntua.gr

ABSTRACT

NoSQL databases focus on analytical processing of large scale datasets, offering increased scalability over commodity hardware. One of their strongest features is elasticity, which allows for fairly portioned premiums and high-quality performance and directly applies to the philosophy of a cloud-based platform. Yet, the process of adaptive expansion and contraction of resources usually involves a lot of manual effort during cluster configuration. To date, there exists no comparative study to quantify this cost and measure the efficacy of NoSQL engines that offer this feature over a cloud provider. In this work, we present a cloud-enabled framework for adaptive monitoring of NoSQL systems. We perform a study of the elasticity feature on some of the most popular NoSQL databases over an open-source cloud platform. Based on these measurements, we finally present a prototype implementation of a decision making system that enables automatic elastic operations of *any* NoSQL engine based on administrator or application-specified constraints.

Categories and Subject Descriptors

H.3.4 [**Systems and Software**]: Distributed Systems

General Terms

Design, Performance

Keywords

Cloud Computing, NoSQL, HBase, Cassandra, Riak.

1. INTRODUCTION

Computational and storage requirements of applications such as business intelligence and social networking over peta-byte datasets have pushed sql-like centralized databases to their limits [8]. This led to the development of horizontally scalable, distributed non-relational data stores, called No-SQL databases, such as Google's Bigtable [9] and its open-source implementation HBase [5] and Facebook's Cassandra [12]. NoSQL systems exhibit the ability to store and index arbitrarily big data sets while enabling a large amount of concurrent user requests. They are perfect candidates for IaaS clouds such as Amazon's EC2 [1] or its open-source alternative, OpenStack [6]: NoSQL admins can utilize the cloud API to throttle the number of acquired resources (i.e., number of virtual machines – VMs and storage space) according to application needs.

This is highly-compatible with NoSQL stores that offer *elasticity* and *sharding*. The former refers to the ability to expand or contract resources in order to meet the exact demand. The latter refers to the horizontal partitioning over a shared-nothing architecture. It is obvious that these two properties (henceforth referred to as *elasticity*) are intertwined: as computing resources grow and shrink, data partitioning must be done in such a way that no loss occurs and the right amount of replication is conserved.

Many NoSQL systems (e.g., [5, 12, 7]) claim to offer adaptive elasticity according to the number of participant commodity nodes. Nevertheless, the "throttling" is usually performed manually, making availability problems due to unanticipated high loads not infrequent (e.g., the recent Foursquare outage [3]). Adaptive frameworks are offered by major cloud vendors as a service: Amazon's SimpleDB [2] and Google's AppEngine [4] are proprietary systems offering (virtually) unlimited processing power and storage. However, these services run on dedicated servers, their architecture is not publicly documented, their cost is prohibitive and their performance is questionable [11].

Recent works [11, 10] have dealt with the performance of various analytics platforms, without dealing with elasticity in virtualized cloud resources. The studies presented in [13, 15] deal with this feature but do not address NoSQL databases. Thus, although both NoSQL and cloud infrastructures are inherently elastic, there exists no actual study to report how effective this is in practice. To the best of our knowledge, there also exists no actual system that combines these two technologies to offer automated NoSQL cluster resize according to dynamic workload changes.

Having reviewed the most popular NoSQL solutions and the OpenStack IaaS [6], our contributions are the following: We provide a generic control module that monitors No-SQL clusters, We identify how each metric of interest (CPU, RAM, etc) varies under various workload types and rates. We document the costs and gains after a cluster resize. We register the performance gains when increasing the cluster size in varying workloads. We demonstrate the applicability of our framework by presenting a prototype implementation that allows for adaptive and automatic cluster resize. To show our framework's modularity, we incorporate three popular NoSQL implementations, HBase [5], Cassandra [12]

CIKM'11, October 24–28, 2011, Glasgow, Scotland, UK.

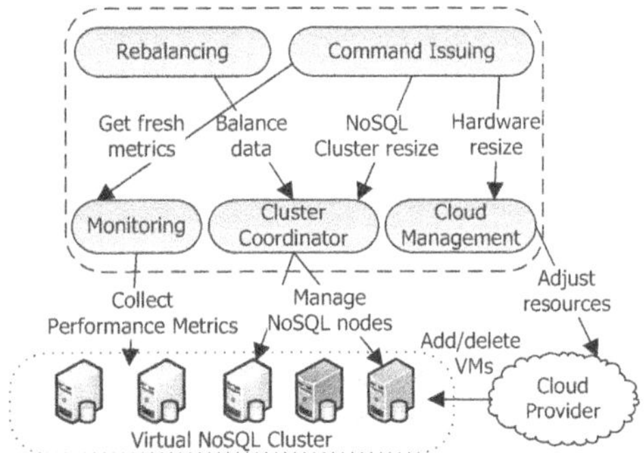

Figure 1: Architecture of our Cloud-based NoSQL elasticity-testing framework.

and Riak [7] that support elasticity and we utilize YCSB [10], Yahoo's open-source client. Our findings are presented more thoroughly in the following technical report[1].

2. ARCHITECTURE

Our elasticity-testing framework, an open-source project[2] with over 2K lines of Python code, features an architecture that is illustrated in Figure 1. The *Command Issuing* module is used to initiate a cluster resize operation. It interacts with the *Cloud Management* module that contacts the cloud vendor to adjust the cluster's physical resources by releasing or acquiring more virtual machines. The *Rebalancing* module makes sure that newly arrived nodes join the cluster contributing an equal share of the work. The *Cluster Coordinator* module executes higher level add, remove and rebalance commands according to the particular NoSQL system used. Finally, the *Monitoring* module maintains up-to-date performance metrics that collects from the cluster nodes. Below we describe the modules in detail:

Command Issuing Module: This is the 'coordinator' module. In the current implementation phase, this module requests addition or removal of a number of VMs using the Cloud Management and Cluster Coordinator modules.

Monitoring Module: Our system receives data from Ganglia [14], a scalable distributed system monitoring tool that allows the user to remotely collect live or historical statistics (such as CPU load averages, network, memory or disk space utilization) through its XML API and present them through its web front-end via real-time dynamic web pages. Apart from general operating-system statistics, Ganglia may also gather NoSQL performance metrics such as the current number of open client threads, number of served operations per second, etc.

Rebalancing Module: The rebalancing module is activated after a newly arrived virtual machine from the cloud vendor has successfully started (i.e., has booted and received a valid IP). When this happens, the module executes a "global rebalance" operation, in which client requests are spread equally among the cluster nodes according to the specific NoSQL implementation and semantics.

Cloud management: Our system interacts with the cloud vendor using euca-tools, an Amazon EC2 compliant REST-based client library. The command issuing module interacts with this module when it commands for a resize in the physical cluster resources, i.e., the number of running VMs. The use of euca-tools guarantees that our system can be deployed in Amazon's EC2 or in any EC2-compliant IaaS cloud. We have created an Amazon Machine Image (AMI) that contains pre-installed versions of the supported NoSQL systems along with the Ganglia monitoring tool.

Cluster coordinator: The coordination of the remote VMs is done with the remote execution of shell scripts and the injection of on-the-fly created NoSQL specific configuration files to each VM. A higher level "start cluster", "add NoSQL node" and "remove NoSQL node" command is translated in a workflow of the aforementioned primitives. Our framework implementation makes sure that each step has succeeded before moving to the next one.

For instance, the Command Issuing module requests an "add virtual machine" command using the euca-tools API and waits until it is started and has been assigned with an IP. After this, the Cluster Coordinator creates the appropriate configuration scripts on-the-fly, transfers them to the new VM, and remotely starts the NoSQL service along with the Ganglia tool. The Rebalancer module inserts the node to the cluster and rebalances client requests among the server nodes. Our framework currently incorporates HBase, Cassandra and Riak. Yet, the system is extensible enough to include more engines that support elastic operations by implementing the system's abstract primitives in the Cluster Coordinator module and by including the system's binaries to the existing AMI virtual machine image. The precooked AMI is available for download from the project's web site.

3. EXPERIMENTAL RESULTS

Our experimental setup consists of an OpenStack private cluster of 16 worker nodes and a single cluster controller. We were allocated enough resources for a cluster of 20 client VMs (load generators) and 28 server VMs (each with 4 vCPUs and 8GB RAM). First, we identify the affected performance metrics under heavy load, second, we measure the performance gain/loss after cluster resize for various workloads and resize choices and finally we present a prototype, fully automated system setup where resources are adaptively resized according to user-defined policies.

Clients and workloads used: We utilize fixed HBase (v. 0.20.6) Cassandra (v. 0.7.0 beta) and Riak (v. 0.14.0) initial 8 node clusters with default configurations which are loaded with 20M 1KB objects (i.e., 20GB of plain raw data) by utilizing the YCSB [10] load function. We use 4 workloads (namely UNIFORM_READ, ZIPFIAN_READ, UNIFORM_UPDATE and UNIFORM_RMW) with fixed query arrival rates λ in order to better understand the behaviour of the databases for different types of load. These correspond to uniform and zipfian random reads, and uniform random updates and read-modify-writes respectively.

For the 8-node clusters, we first identified the maximum sustained query throughput in a simple UNIFORM_READ workload. The HBase, Cassandra and Riak clusters achieved a maximum throughput of 80, 13 and 10 Kreqs/sec for a λ of 80, 20 and 10 Kreqs/sec respectively. Cluster CPU usage increased as throughput increased, reaching a 50% and 75% usage in their maximum throughput. For higher λ rates (up to 280 Kreqs/sec) query throughput remained the same while query latencies increased linearly for HBase and Cassandra, with HBase being constantly faster than Cassandra. Riak servers became unresponsive above 10 Kreqs/sec, therefore we did not include Riak in the following experiments. For the zipfian read and uniform update workloads, with a λ of 180 Kreqs/sec, Cassandra had an average CPU usage of 68% and 55% respectively, whereas HBase had 55%

[1] http://www.cslab.ntua.gr/~ikons/elastic_nosql.pdf
[2] http://tiramola.googlecode.com

Table 1: Data rebalancing effect for a 8+8 resize

Metric \ Cluster	HBase		Cassandra		Riak
	Reb	No	Reb	No	Reb
Completion time (min)	98	5	665	5	150
Data moved (GB)	22.5	-	87.7	-	44.8
Througput (Kreqs/s)	154.5	129.6	18.3	14.9	18
Avg. Latency (s)	0.7	1.1	7.1	9.3	0.2

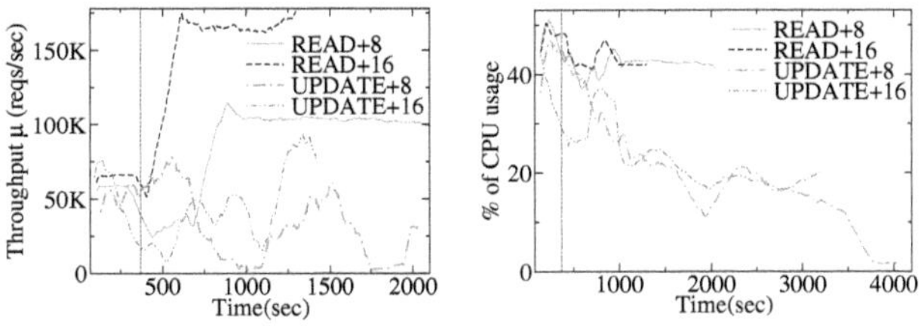

Figure 2: Query throughput and CPU usage for an HBase cluster of 8 nodes after adding 8 and 16 more nodes for the UNIFORM_READ and UNIFORM_UPDATE workload with $\lambda = 180$ Kreqs/sec

and 45%. Average query throughput was 77 and 8 Kreqs/sec respectively for the zipfian read, whereas for the update it was 30 and 12 Kreqs/sec.

Cluster resize performance measurements: Our first concern on the costs and gains of a resize operation relates to the rebalancing of the database data. Since data rebalancing is by itself a resource intensive procedure, we only perform node additions and data migration in an idle cluster for this case. This scenario is valid, since data rebalancing is usually scheduled for off-peak time periods. Nevertheless, in our experiments conducted with extra client workload during data rebalance, all systems exhibited erratic behaviour. In Table 1 we present our results. We have started an 8-node cluster in each case and added 20M tuples. We then expanded each cluster by adding 8 more nodes and applied a UNIFORM_READ workload with a $\lambda = 180$ Kreqs/sec ("No" column for every database - for Riak that rebalances data automatically as soon as a new node joins the ring, this is not applicable). After this, we manually rebalanced data in HBase and Cassandra. When data rebalancing finishes, we applied the same workload $\lambda = 180$ Kreqs/s for HBase, Cassandra and 18 Kreqs/s for Riak (Riak could not operate with a higher workload). The results for this setup are presented in the "Reb" column.

The data rebalancing costs far outweigh its benefits for the cases of HBase and Cassandra. For HBase a net gain of about 20% in throughput was achieved compared to a non-rebalanced 16 node cluster, which could be easily offset by adding two extra nodes without using data rebalancing. The results were better for Cassandra with a net gain of 22% for the average throughput. In terms of latency, similar performance benefits were achieved (33% and 23% for HBase and Cassandra respectively). The data moved during data rebalancing for HBase is 25% of the entire dataset. In Cassandra's case the whole dataset was moved. HDFS's centralized balancer is more advanced than Cassandra's decentralized balancer. Riak rebalancing is also a costly operation (43% of the dataset was transferred). Given the large time costs for data rebalancing operations (93, 660 and 150 minutes in HBase, Cassandra and Riak respectively), and the fact that simple caching can do the work (see the following analysis) we conclude that gains do not outweigh costs.

We continue our evaluation with node additions in an initial 8-node cluster without data rebalancing for HBase and Cassandra. We utilize a high load of $\lambda = 180$ Kreqs/sec for two workload types: UNIFORM_READ and UNIFORM_UPDATE (referred to as READ and UPDATE henceforth). For each workload and database combination we perform an addition of 8 and 16 nodes. The cluster resize occurs at about $t = 370$ sec.

Figure 2 shows the HBase results. Legends refer to the workload type along with the resizing action (e.g., READ+8 represents a read workload with an 8-node resize). Regarding mean query latency (graph omitted due to lack of space), adding nodes during READ loads has a transient negative effect, attributed to the HMaster table region reassignment. Clients cache region locations which however change during cluster resizing. As a result, latency increases due to client cache misses. In the updates we notice an oscillation due to the compaction and caching mechanisms of HBase. Incoming data is cached in memory (i.e., low latency) but when the memory is full and a I/O flush occurs with a compaction, the latency is increased. Throughput μ increases in read workloads: adding 16 nodes results in about 170 Kreqs/sec in the steady state and 100 Kreqs/sec for the READ+8 case (compared to about 55K before additions). More servers are able to simultaneously handle more requests that results in a higher throughput (roughly doubling and tripling it respectively). Although items are not actually transferred, this speed is due to the caching effect of the RegionServers. Regarding updates, since they are I/O-bound operations, μ is not significantly altered.

The final graph reports the aggregate cluster CPU usage. In the read workloads we notice that the initial load of around 55% is reduced to around 42% in both cases since new nodes immediately start handling incoming queries. The addition of 16 against 8 nodes does not result in a further decrease in the average CPU, as the load is still large enough for all servers to contribute. The extra 8 nodes make a difference in terms of throughput, as shown in the second graph. In the update workloads, we notice that in both experiments the initial CPU load continues to drop until run completion since servers freeze incoming requests until the updated regions are flushed to the file system.

In Figure 3 we present the Cassandra results. The first graph presents query latency. In both READ cases, we notice that the latency drops from 22 secs to 10 secs and 8 secs respectively. New servers are assigned half of the data partitions of existing servers, they cache portions of their data and answer queries on their behalf. The larger the resize, the bigger the decrease in latency. The same hold for the update workloads. We notice here that writes are faster than reads, due to the weak consistency model followed by Cassandra. Query throughput μ shows a similar linear trend in reads and updates. Extra servers immediately join the p2p ring and take portions of the applied workload. Finally, in the third graph of Figure 3 we present the CPU usage. In the read case adding 8 nodes decreases CPU usage to around 60%, whereas adding 16 servers decreases CPU load to around 50%. The same trend holds for the updates.

Both NoSQL systems take advantage of extra nodes: HBase exhibits very fast concurrent reads compared to Cassandra. On the other hand, Cassandra is more efficient with object updates because of the weak consistency model. Finally, we notice that Cassandra does not exhibit a negative transient effect when new nodes enter the ring. Its decentral-

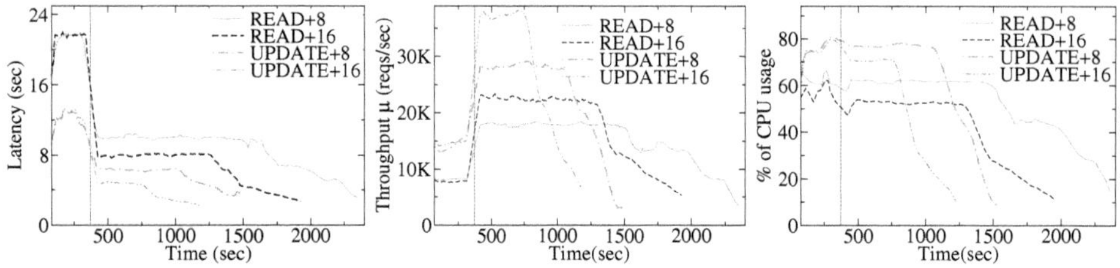

Figure 3: Query latency, query throughput and CPU usage per time for a Cassandra cluster of 8 nodes after adding 8 and 16 more nodes for the UNIFORM_READ and UNIFORM_UPDATE workload with a query rate of $\lambda = 180$ Kreqs/sec

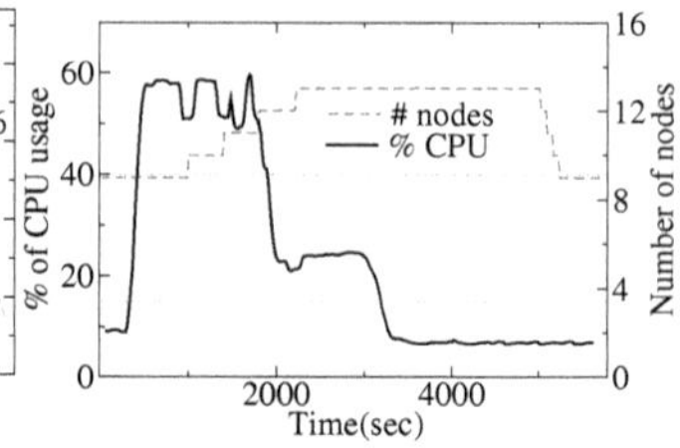

Figure 4: CPU usage for an HBase cluster of 8 nodes under dynamic load changes.

ized nature allows for a transparent cluster resize, whereas in HBase the HMaster coordinates the whole procedure.

Elasticity-provisioning prototype: We now present some initial results achieved using our framework to deploy a fully automatic cluster resize system. We utilize a long running read-heavy load, for a total load of 9 Kreqs/sec on an 8-node HBase cluster. After 7 min, an additional high load of 180 Kreqs/sec is created for a short period of time. Utilizing the experience from our previous experiments, we trigger node additions when CPU usage is over 40%, for *any* one server on the cluster and we remove nodes when the CPU usage is 15% or lower for *all* nodes in the cluster. To avoid oscillations, we utilize a 5 minute running average of the load. In Figure 4 we show our results. The low initial load stresses the servers enough to avoid a node removal but not enough for a node addition. When load increases, CPU increases dramatically and 10 minutes are needed for the new node to be fully operational and monitored. The high load requests complete before the addition of the fourth extra node. At this point the total load decreases significantly, but not substantially for a new node addition. The system continues its normal operation, since the medium load is just enough to prevent node removal. Once the load drops under the lower threshold, node removal proceeds. Node removal is much faster than node addition, thus the system returns to its original size in about 5 minutes. CPU usage does not drop during single node addition, as there are not enough nodes added to accommodate the high load.

4. DISCUSSION AND CONCLUSIONS

In the following section, we argue on the design choices, we offer recommendations based on our experience in setting up this system and we conclude our work.

Concerning monitoring, the selected metrics are important: We showed that we can accurately distinguish the system's critical state using passive, general purpose metrics. Finally, Ganglia's rich set of available metrics and ease of use enable the automatic decision making module to take accurate and prompt decisions.

Regarding region rebalancing, in HBase it is performed automatically when new nodes are added or removed from the cluster. HBase is extremely elastic, as all new nodes can quickly assume load, increasing the cluster's performance in very short time, as reported. Conversely, Cassandra does not split data into regions of equal size. It reassigns regions on a per node basis, i.e., region rebalancing is performed in node pairs between newly arrived and previously existing ones by splitting the key-space in half. Riak divides data space into partitions and as new nodes are added, they claim an equal slice of partitions. However, the fact that the cluster turns unresponsive for a throughput higher than what its nodes can handle, prevents us from examining its elasticity under high load. Concerning data rebalancing, it should only be performed when the system administrator can accurately predict a constant load for a large amount of time, that is in the order of days. In this case, even if the performance is affected for a while, the overall gain justifies this transient rebalancing cost. On the contrary, variable and unpredictable short-term load does not justify such an expensive of operation, and should be avoided.

In this work we quantified and analyzed the costs and gains of various NoSQL cluster resize operations, utilizing three popular NoSQL implementations. HBase is the fastest and scales with node additions (only for reads though); Cassandra performs fast writes and scales also, without any transitional phase during node additions; Riak was unresponsive in high request rates, could scale only at lower rates but rebalances automatically; all three achieve small gains from a data rebalance, provided they are under minimal load. Based on our findings, we offered a prototype implementation of our automatic cluster resize module, that matches the number of provisioned resources against the total demand and the application expert's rules of required operation. Our open-source implementation can provide a good basis on which numerous applications can test their adaptivity at very-high scale.

5. REFERENCES

[1] Amazon EC2. http://aws.amazon.com/ec2/.

[2] Amazon SimpleDB. http://aws.amazon.com/simpledb/.

[3] Foursquare Outage Post Mortem. http://bit.ly/gjA2IK.

[4] Google AppEngine. code.google.com/appengine.

[5] HBase Homepage. http://hbase.apache.org.

[6] OpenStack. http://openstack.org.

[7] Riak Homepage. http://wiki.basho.com/.

[8] D. J. Abadi. Data Management in the Cloud: Limitations and Opportunities. *IEEE Data Eng. Bull*, 32(1):3–12, 2009.

[9] F. Chang et al. Bigtable: A Distributed Storage System for Structured Data. In *OSDI*, 2006.

[10] B. F. Cooper et al. Benchmarking Cloud Serving Systems with YCSB. In *ACM SOCC*, 2010.

[11] D. Kossmann et al. An Evaluation of Alternative Architectures for Transaction Processing in the Cloud. In *SIGMOD*, 2010.

[12] A. Lakshman and P. Malik. Cassandra: A Decentralized Structured Storage System. *SIGOPS*, 2010.

[13] P. Marshall, K. Keahey, and T. Freeman. Elastic Site: Using Clouds to Elastically Extend Site Resources. In *CCGRID*, 2010.

[14] M. L. Massie, B. N. Chun, and D. E. Culler. The Ganglia Distributed Monitoring System: Design, Implementation, and Experience. *Parallel Computing*, 30(7):817–840, 2004.

[15] P. Xiong et al. Intelligent Management of Virtualized Resources for Database Systems in Cloud Environment. In *ICDE*, 2011.

Continuous Data Stream Query in the Cloud

Jun Li[†,‡], Peng Zhang[†], Jianlong Tan[†], Ping Liu[†], Li Guo[†]

[†] Institute of Computing Technology, Chinese Academy of Sciences, Beijing, 100190, China
[‡] Department of Computer Science, Beijing University of Posts and Telecommunications, Beijing,100876, China
lijun@software.ict.ac.cn, {zhangpeng, tjl, liuping, guoli}@ict.ac.cn

ABSTRACT

Cloud computing represents one of the most important research directions for modern computing systems. Existing research efforts on Cloud computing were all focused on designing advanced storage and query techniques for *static data*. None of them consider the problem that data in a Cloud may appear as continuous and rapid *data streams*. To address this problem, in this paper we propose a new *LCN-Index* framework to handle continuous data stream queries in the Cloud. LCN-Index uses the *Map-Reduce* computing paradigm to process all the queries. In the Mapping stage, it divides all the queries into a batch of predicate sets which are then deployed onto mapping nodes using *interval predicate index*. In the reducing stage, it merges results from the mapping nodes using *multi-attribute hash index*. In so doing, a data stream can be efficiently evaluated by traversing through the LCN-Index framework. Experiments demonstrate the utility of the proposed method.

Categories and Subject Descriptors

H.2 [**Information Systems**]: DATABASE MANAGEMENT; H.2.4 [**Systems**]: Query Processing

General Terms

Algorithms, Design

Keywords

Cloud, Data Stream, Index

1. INTRODUCTION

Cloud service has drawn increasing attention in recent years. A wide spectrum of commercial applications, such as Google Docs, Amazon WebStore and Facebook, are using Cloud as their fundamental solution for the unprecedented amount of data problem [5, 6, 9, 10, 1].

Although the successes of Cloud systems, existing research efforts were merely focused on *static data* queries in the Cloud. For many emerging applications where data appear as continuous *data streams*, it is urgent to design stream-based query techniques for the Cloud systems.

CIKM'11, October 24–28, 2011, Glasgow, Scotland, UK.

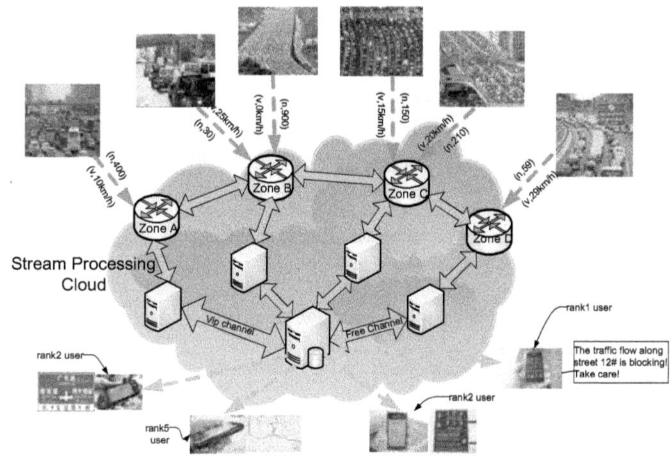

Figure 1: An illustration of the online traffic management system used in Example 1.

EXAMPLE 1. *Let us consider an online traffic management system as shown in Fig. 1. The essential goal of the system is to provide real-time traffic information for all connected users. In this system, on one hand, real-time traffic conditions are monitored by on-street cameras and uploaded to servers deployed in the Cloud; on the other hand, users can submit queries to the system, and get continuous real-time traffic information from the system. Note that different users have different levels of services. A VIP user can get much richer information in a more friendly way than a free user, even if they both submit the same query. For example, the system will return a VIP user a virtual electronic map with some recommendations. In contrast, a free user can only get a textual description.*

Obviously, the above example represents a new class of *data stream* applications in the Cloud. Compared to traditional data stream query and distributed stream query, data stream query in the Cloud faces the following new challenges:

- Large and complex queries. Traditional data stream processing methods [8, 2, 3, 4] usually make an assumption that the number of queries is not very large (e.g., no more than 2,000). Besides, each query has a very low dimensionality. In the Cloud, however, the number of queries will be very large, and each query often has a very high dimensionality.

For instance, in Example 1, there are probably more than 1 million users accessing the system simultaneously, each user submitting a very complex query.

- Dynamic changing queries. The number of queries usually changes over time in the Cloud, demanding elastic computing techniques. Existing distributed stream processing methods [8, 2, 3, 4] usually predefine the number of computing nodes, which are inapplicable.

- Real time response. It is a must to design efficient algorithms that can make timely responses, especially when the queries are very complex, e.g., having a very high dimensionality.

In light of the above challenges, in this paper we design a new LCN-Index framework for the stream queries in the Cloud. LCN-Index is on the basis of the Map-Reduce computing paradigm. In the Map stage, it decomposes all the queries into a batch of predicate sets which are then deployed onto mapping nodes using the interval predicate index. In the Reduce stage, it merges the intermediate results from all the mapping nodes using multi-attribute hash index. In addition, the LCN-Index can dynamically add (or delete) computing nodes during processing. In so doing, data streams can be efficiently evaluated under the LCN-Index framework. Experiments demonstrate the utility of the proposed method.

The main contributions of the study are threefold:

1. We address a new problem of continuous data stream query in the Cloud.

2. We propose a new scalable index framework, LCN-Index, to efficiently evaluate a large number of continuous queries in the Cloud. By using the Map-Reduce computing paradigm, LCN-Index is able to evaluate data streams efficiently.

3. We conduct empirical studies to demonstrate the utility of the proposed LCN-Index framework.

The rest of the paper is organized as follows. Section 2 introduces the LCN-Index framework. Section 3 studies the performance of LCN-Index. Section 4 conducts experiments and comparisons. We conclude the paper in Section 5.

2. THE LCN-INDEX FRAMEWORK

Consider n continuous queries $Q = \{Q_1, Q_2, \cdots, Q_n\}$ registered on a data stream $S = \{T_1, \cdots, T_k, \cdots\}$. Assume each stream tuple T_i has d dimensions $\{r^1, r^2, \cdots, r^d\}$, where each $r^j \in [l_j, u_j]$, and l_j and u_j are the lower and upper boundaries. Besides, assume each query Q_i $(1 \le i \le n)$ spans over all the d dimensions, i.e., $Q_i = \{q_i^1, q_i^2, \cdots, q_i^d\}$, where each q_i^j $(1 \le j \le r)$ is an interval query on the jth attribute, e.g., to evaluate if $q_i^j \in [x, y]$, where x and y are given boundaries. The ultimate goal is to efficiently evaluate all the n queries with respect to each stream tuple $T_k \in S$.

To achieve the above goal, we propose a new data stream query system in the Cloud as shown in Fig.2. The system consists of two components: an off-line index construction part, and an on-line stream processing part. In the off-line part, the n continuous queries are decomposed into predicate sets that are then indexed on both Mapper (using predicate index) and Reducer (using multi-attribute hash index). In the on-line part, to evaluate all the queries with respect to each stream tuple, LCN-Index first retrieves from the mapping nodes all the matched predicates, which are then merged together on the Reducer using multi-attribute hash index.

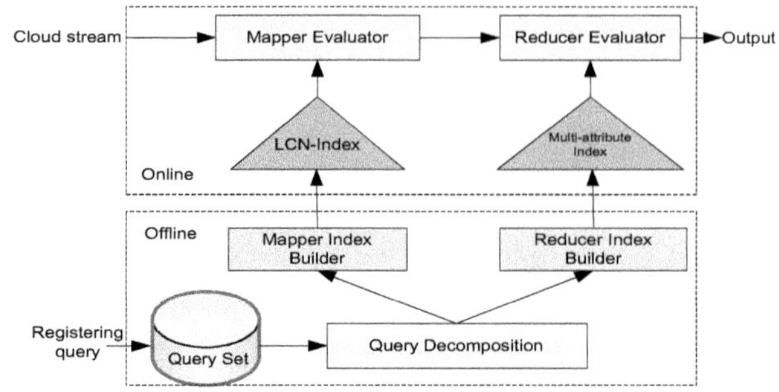

Figure 2: An illustration of the data stream query system in the Cloud.

The whole procedure of the LCN-Index framework is shown in Algorithm 1. The key step of the algorithm is to index the interval predicates that are deployed on the mapping nodes. An intuitive method is to compare each attribute value with the boundaries of all the predicates, which needs $O(log(n))$ time, where n is the number of predicates. Obviously, this is time-consuming when the query number is very large. Thus, we use a new *indirect indexing* approach instead. This method is based on the *Standard Interval Unit*(SIU for short) [1]. First of all, a set of SIU is predefined and labeled, and then each predicate is split into a couple of SIUs. Each predicate will be assigned a unique ID, named *PredId*, which are then inserted into the *Id Listes* associated with the decomposed SIUs. Given an attribute value X, the search procedure can be executed indirectly by using the SIUs. *In so doing, the search time will be independent of the number of predicates, and it is unnecessary to compare each attribute value of* X *with all the predicates' boundaries.*

Algorithm 1 The workflow of the LCN-Index Framework

```
Require: Query set Q, Data stream S
  //off-line index construction
  Partition Q into a batch of predicate sets P.
  Build interval index and multi-attribute hash index based on P.
  Deploy the indexes on both Mapper and Reducer.
  //on-line stream processing
  for each incoming tuple T_i ∈ S do
    if T_i ≠ Φ then
      Search the interval index on Mapper.
      Merge the results from Mapper on Reducer.
      Output satisfied queries in Q.
    end if
  end for
```

Now we explain how to partition each attribute of a query Q into a predicate set for efficient search. For each attribute r^j $(1 \le j \le d)$ in a query, we partition r^j into r/L segments, where L is a predefined length. Thus, each segment can be denoted as s_i,where $i = \{0, 1, \cdots, \frac{(u_j - l_j)}{(L-1)}\}$. In so doing, for each segment, we can define a $(2L - 1)$ Standard Interval Unit(SIU) as follows:

(1) Use only one SIU with length L to describe the entire segment;
(2) Partition the segment into two SIUs, each having length $L/2$;
(3) Build four SIUs, each having a length of $L/4$;
(4) Each SIU have the shortest length of 1.

Fig. 3 gives an illustration of the local ID labeling on each interval predicate. The unit-length is set to $L = 2^k$. The interval is divided into unit-length segments. In each segment, $2^k - 1$ SIUs are

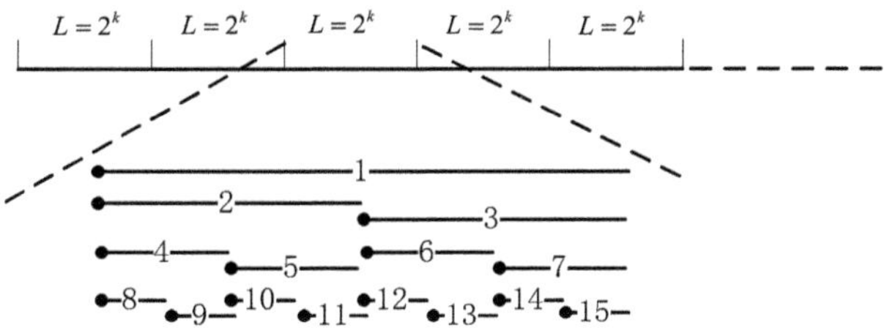

Figure 3: An illustration of the labeling on a predicate interval.

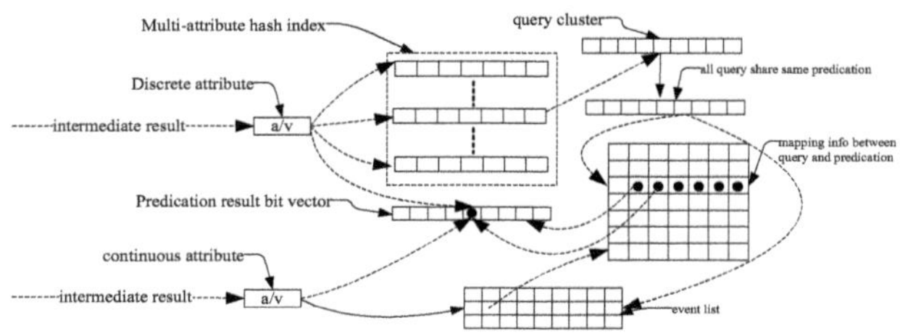

Figure 4: The merging procedure in the Reducer.

built for indexing. The local IDs of all these SIUs range from 1 to $(2^{k+1}-1)$.

On the other hand, the **Reducer** merges all intermediate search results from Mappers. The merging algorithm uses the multi-attribute hash index. For each incoming stream tuple, the multi-attribute index can help find all the satisfied queries efficiently and accurately. In this index structure, the *equality predicates* are used as trigger predicates. A trigger predicate p is associated with a list of query clusters. When an equality predicate is triggered, all the queries associated with the trigger predicates will be examined. In addition, a bit vector is used to record results of all predicates. The query clusters examine all satisfied queries sharing the same predicates. In so doing, for each incoming intermediate search result from Mapper, its attribute ID will be examined in the multi-attribute index. If all the predicates of a query are estimated TRUE, this query will be taken as matched with respect to the current stream tuple.

Fig.4 describes a query cluster for queries sharing the same equality predicate p. A query cluster is a vector of query structures. It consists of a collection of all predicate results and a bit vector which denotes the identifier of the query. An Entry $[i, j]$ of a query cluster contains a bit vector that refers to the ith predicate of the jth attribute in the query cluster. If all the bit vector entries are estimated TRUE, the jth attribute in query cluster will be taken as TRUE.

3. PERFORMANCE ANALYSIS

In this section, we analyze time and memory costs for evaluating each stream tuple. When a tuple arrives, it needs to go through the whole LCN-Index framework to answer all registered queries. Since the merging operation dominates the query time, we mainly discuss the time cost from this step.

Formally, consider a query set Q, a query cluster C generated from Q, and a multi-attribute hashing function H. The cost of merging a stream event with respect to all queries in Q needs the following three steps:

(1) retrieving relevant multi-attribute index results for the incoming stream tuple.
(2) hashing each indexes using H.
(3) examining all mapping functions between the triggering predicates and queries.

To sum up, the processing time can be described in Eq. (1):

$$sum = idx\_scanning(H) + \sum_{h\in H} hashing(h) + \sum_{p\in TP(C)} v(p) * scanning(p, Q) \quad (1)$$

where $idx\_scanning(H)$ is the cost from scanning the multi-attribute indexes, $hashing(h)$ is the cost from executing a hashing function $h \in H$, and $sccanning(p, Q)$ is the cost from trigger predicates p.

In order to solve Eq. (1), without loss of generality, we make the following three assumptions.

(1) retrieving the relevant indexes needs a linear time with respect to the number of *Hashing Combination.*
(2) the hashing function takes linear time with respect to the size of the *Hashing Combination.*
(3) examining a set of queries has a linear time complexity with respect to the number of queries.

Under these assumptions, Eq. (1) can be converted to Eq.(2),

$$sum = |H| * C_{idx} + \sum_{h\in H} \lambda(h) * (C_h + \mu * A(h)) + \sum_{p\in TP(C)} v(p) * \lambda_p * \kappa_p * n \quad (2)$$

where C_{idx} is the average size of each multi-attribute index, $A(h)$ represents the size of the schema of h. λ_p represents the popularity of the trigger predicate p, κ_p is the width of trigger predicate p, and n is the scale size of the query set Q.

The memory cost of the merging algorithm on query set Q mainly comes from the following two parts:

(1) the cost from buffering the hashing indexes.
(2) the cost from storing the mapping functions between predicates and queries.

To sum up, the memory cost can be described in Eq.(3) as follow,

$$sum = \sum_{h\in H} M_{init}(h) + \sum_{p\in TP(H)} M_{insert}(p) + \sum_{p\in TP(H)} M_{mapping}(Q) \quad (3)$$

where M_{init} is the initial memory to create an empty multi-attribute index, M_{insert} is the space for maintaining all entries of the trigger predicates, and $M_{mapping}$ denotes the memory cost from storing the mapping information between trigger predicates and queries set Q.

4. EXPERIMENTS

Our testing infrastructure consists of 16 Redhat server 5.2 systems. Each machine has a 3.00GHz Inter Core2 CPU and 4G memory. The last system is used as the master.

Benchmark data Three real world data sets are used. Table 1 lists the real world data sets. All these data sets were crawled from Internet. Due to space limitation, we omit the detailed introduction here. All queries are generated using *Zipf* distribution, under which the popularity of a predicate is inversely proportional to its rank.

Table 1: Real world data streams

Name	Continuous	Queries	Discrete
stock data analysis	400	10,000,000	200
spam detection	800	10,000,000	210
malicious url detection	1200	10,000,000	320

Benchmark methods & Measures A distributed multi-dimension index, which is similar to R-Tree [7, 11, 12], denoted by *Dis-*

tributeRTree, is used as the benchmark method. Each query is taken as a multi-dimensional matrix and inserted into the tree.

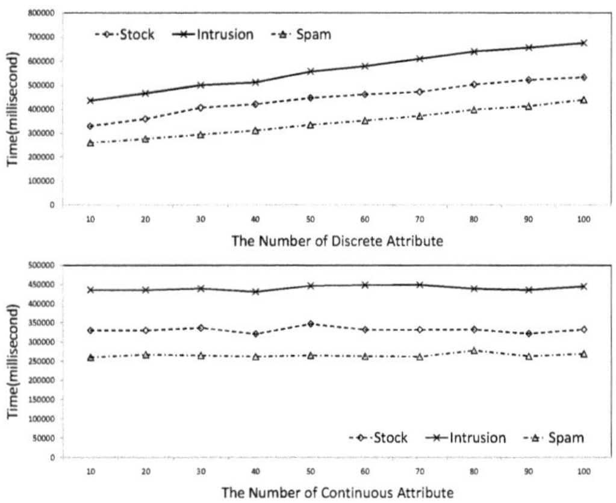

Figure 5: Comparisons under different attribute numbers.

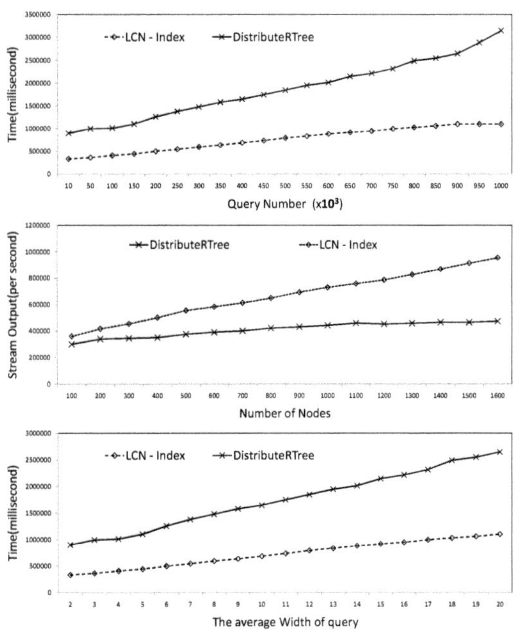

Figure 6: Comparisons with respect to different (a)query number, (b) Cloud size, and (c) query width.

Experimental results In our experiments, the default node number is 100. The number of queries is set to 10 million.

Query number Fig.6 (a) shows comparisons with respect to different query numbers. Obviously, our LCN-Index always performs better than the DistributeRTree. In LCN-Index, each stream tuple will be processed on multiple mapping nodes in a parallel way. However, in the DistributeRTree, the parallel search is inapplicable, because the query is represented by a matrix and has been randomly distributed in the Cloud.

Node number From Fig.6 (b), we can observe that when the number of computing node increases, LCN-Index outperforms DistributeRTree. For example,in the stock data stream, when the computing node n equals to 1000, DistributeRTree outputs 379,166 tuples, whereas the LCN-Index emits as much as 772,937 tuples.

Attribute numbers Fig.5 shows the comparisons with respect to different attribute numbers. We can observe that the cost of the LCN-Index framework decrease with respect to the discrete attribute number. This is because LCN-Index can be estimated in a parallel way, and is impervious to the number of continuous attributes.

Query width The comparison results are listed in Fig.6 (c). From the results, we can come to several important conclusions: (1) LCN-Index can significantly reduce the query costs in terms of both time and memory. (2) when increasing w, the cost of DistributeRTree increases faster than that of LCN-Index.

5. CONCLUSIONS

Cloud data stream query is a challenging problem. In this paper we propose a new LCN-Index framework to support a huge number of complex stream queries in the Cloud. LCN-Index uses the *Map-Reduce* computing paradigm to organize all the queries. In so doing, a data stream can be efficiently evaluated by traversing through the LCN-Index framework. Experiments on real world data streams demonstrate that our approach is efficient, elastic, and scalable.

6. ACKNOWLEDGMENTS

This research was supported by the National Science Foundation of China (NSFC) under Grant No. 61003167, Basic Research Program of China (973 Program) under Grant No. 2007CB311100.

7. REFERENCES

[1] D. J. A. A. R. A. Abouzeid, K. Bajda-Pawlikowski and A. Silberschatz. Hadoopdb: An architectural hybrid of mapreduce and dbms technologies for analytical workloads. *Proc. of VLDB 2009*.

[2] R. Avnur and J. Hellerstein. Eddies: Continuously adaptive query processing. *Proc. of SIGMOD 2000*.

[3] S. Babu and J. Widom. Streamon: An adaptive engine for stream query processing. *Proc. of SIGMOD 2004*.

[4] J. W. Chris Olston, Jing Jiang. Adaptive filters for continuous queries over distributed data streams. *Proc. of SIGMOD 2003*.

[5] J. W. et al. Indexing multi-dimensional data in a cloud system. *Proc. of SIGMOD 2010*.

[6] S. W. et al. Efficient b-tree based indexing for cloud data processing. *Proc. of VLDB 2010*.

[7] A. Guttman. R-trees: A dynamic index structure for spatial searching. *Proc. of SIGMOD 1984*.

[8] F. Y. J.Chen, D. J.DeWitt. Niagracq : A scalable continuous query system for internet databases. *Proc. of SIGMOD 2000*.

[9] J.Dean and S.Ghemawat. Mapreduce: Simplified data processing on large clusters. *Proc. of OSDI 2004*.

[10] P.-A. L. B. R. D. S. S. W. R. Chaiken, B. Jenkins and J. Zhou. Scope: easy and efficient parallel processing of massive data sets. *Proc. of VLDB 2008*.

[11] P. Zhang, J. Li, P. Wang, B. Gao, X. Zhu, and L. Guo. Enabling fast prediction for ensemble models on data streams. In *Proc. of KDD 2011*.

[12] P. Zhang, X.Zhu, Y. Shi, L.Guo, and X. Wu. Robust ensemble learning for mining noisy data streams. *Decision Support Systems*, 50(2):469–479, 2011.

A Cluster based Mobile Peer to Peer Architecture in Wireless Ad Hoc Networks

He Li
Chungbuk National University
Cheongju, Korea
lihelol@gmail.com

KyoungSoo Bok
Chungbuk National University
Cheongju, Korea
ksbok@chungbuk.ac.kr

JaeSoo Yoo*
Chungbuk National University
Cheongju, Korea
yjs@chungbuk.ac.kr

ABSTRACT
With the rapid development of wireless communication technologies and mobile devices, the mobile peer to peer (MP2P) network has been emerged. Since the existing MP2P architectures have high management cost, in this paper, we propose a hierarchical MP2P architecture using clustering mobile peers. The proposed method clusters the mobile peers by considering three aspects like the maximum connection time, the minimum hop count and the number of the connected peers. The connection times between the connected peers can be determined by the location, velocity vector and communication range of the mobile peers. Since the maximum connection time of the connected peers are considered, the network topology is relatively stable. Therefore, the management cost of the network is decreased and the success rate of contents search is increased. Experiments have shown that our proposed method outperforms the existing schemes.

Categories and Subject Descriptors
C.2.1 [**Network Architecture and Design**]: Distributed networks

General Terms
Algorithms, Performance.

Keywords
Mobile P2P, Ad-hoc network, Hierarchical architecture, Clustering.

1. INTRODUCTION
Recently, the MP2P over ad-hoc networks have received much attraction since the contents sharing among PDA, smart phone and pocket PC have emerged over ad hoc networks[1-4]. In such networks, the contents search is based on multi-hop wireless communication via IEEE 802.11, Bluetooth, UWB among mobile peers. Since the mobile peers can frequently change their physical locations and establish connections with other neighbor peers, the maintenance of the network topology and searches through these networks have high expensive overheads and low success rate.

A typical mobile P2P technique based on two mobile routing protocols DSR [5] and AODV [6] is called the optimized routing independent overlay network (ORION) [1]. Since it needs to broadcast a query in the whole network for searching contents, this method is not competent for large networks. To efficiently search contents in large networks, the distributed hash table (DHT) based mobile P2P methods were proposed such as M-Chord [7], M-Can [8] and Virtual Ring Routing [9]. In DHT based methods, content is associated with a unique key by hashing, and each peer is responsible for storing certain ranges of keys. Such methods can significantly decrease the search costs in a large network. However, due to the characteristics of mobile environment, the maintenance of the overlay network is high expensive.

Recently, some hierarchical methods were proposed to reduce the management cost of mobile peers in dynamic network environments. These methods classify the peers into super peer and sub peer. Each super peer maintains the contents and routing of its sub peers. Therefore, the content search is only traversed through super peers. In [10], D. T. Ahmed, et al. proposed a multi-level hashing for peer to peer system in wireless ad hoc environment. However, this method did not consider the movement of the peers at the first level. In general environment, all of the peers are mobile peers. The super peer based method [11] and group P2P [12] are proposed in the completely mobile environment. But the connections between each connected peers will break and establish frequently, which results in high update overhead. Especially, when the mobile peers have high speed or different direction the update overhead is horrendous.

In this paper, we propose a hierarchical MP2P architecture that clusters the mobile peers according to the network connectivity and the mobility of peers. The proposed scheme organizes MP2P network based on three criteria, the maximum connection time of connected peers, the hop count with super peer, and the number of connected peers of the super peer. A new join peer selects the super peer which can connect for a longer time to register. The connection time between each connected peers can be determined by the location, velocity vector and communication range of each peer. Therefore, in this network, the frequent update overheads are avoided and the success rate of content search is promoted.

The remainder of the paper is organized as follows. Section 2 introduces the related works. Section 3 presents the details of the proposed method. Section 4 contains experimental evaluation that demonstrates the superiority of our proposed method. Finally, Section 5 concludes this paper.

2. RELATED WORK
There has been a large amount of work on the MP2P network. The existing MP2P systems can be classified into two main types: the structured systems and unstructured systems.

In structured MP2P systems, in order to form an overlay network, the participating peers are organized into a specified structure (e.g.

*: corresponding author

CIKM'11, October 24–28, 2011, Glasgow, Scotland, UK.

the virtual ring or tree). For these systems, the distributed hash table (DHT) is the most effective method. The content is associated with a unique key by a specified hashing function, and each peer is responsible for storing certain range of keys. Each participating peer stores a content item with a hash value that is close to its key range. The content search request is forwarded to the intermediated peers whose hash value is close. M-Chord [7], M-Can [8] and Virtual Ring Routing [9] are typical DHT based methods. Such methods can efficiently decrease search cost in a large network. However, the maintenance of the overlay network over mobile environments is high expensive.

The unstructured MP2P systems need not to maintain the overlay network, but they have no knowledge of the location of the contents. There are some wireless routing protocols that can be used for unstructured MP2P systems, such as DSR [5] and AODV [6]. The optimized routing independent overlay network (ORION) [1] is a typical MP2P technique based on these protocols. Each peer has the information of its neighbor peers, and the search message is flooded in the system until the required content is found or the specified maximum hop count is reached. If the network is large, a great number of bandwidth is needed. In [10], D. T. Ahmed, et al proposes a multi-level hashing for peer to peer system in wireless ad hoc environments. It considers that the participating peers either as mobile peers or stationary peers. The stationary peer represents a home region of the entire regions and provides useful information to its local mobile peers. However, in this paper we assume that all of the participated peers are mobile peers.

To reduce the maintenance cost and the requirement of bandwidth, some hierarchical methods have been proposed, such as super peer based method [11] and group P2P [12]. In this network, the peers are classified into super peers and sub peers. Each super peer maintains the information of its sub peers and the contents search is only traversed through super peers. However, both super peer based method [11] and group P2P [12] have a high update overhead to maintain the network. This is because the connections between each paired peers can be broken and must be reestablished frequently when the mobile peers have high-speed or opposite direction. Therefore, in this paper, we propose a maximum connection time based MP2P network.

3. THE PROPOSED MP2P ARCHITECTURE

3.1 Overview

In this section, we present an overview of our proposed MP2P architecture. The proposed architecture is composed of peers through multiple hops. The mobile peers in this network are divided into normal peers and super peers. We divide these mobile peers into clusters according to the following three criteria:

- The maximum connection time with the super peer
- The maximum hop count with the super peer
- The total number of the connected peers of each super peer is limited within a predefined threshold value

Since establishing and disconnecting connections of the mobile peers is a significant reason that causes the update overhead of the network, we construct the MP2P network by considering the maximum connection time between the normal peers and its super peers. The mobile peers with similar velocity vector and near physical location are put into the same cluster. By doing this, the frequency of disconnecting and re-establishing connections can be reduced. The hop count between normal peer and its super peer significantly impacts the efficiency of contents search and the cost of the network management. Therefore, when the maximum connection time is similar, the minimum hop count between normal peer and its super peer is selected. In order to balance the load of super peers, the total number of the connected peers of each super peer is limited within a predefined threshold value.

The super peer communicates with the other super peers via the connected boundary peers. The normal peer communicates with its super peer via intermediated peers. Without loss of generality, we assume that the capability of the super peer is the same as the normal peer and each normal peer can become a super peer.

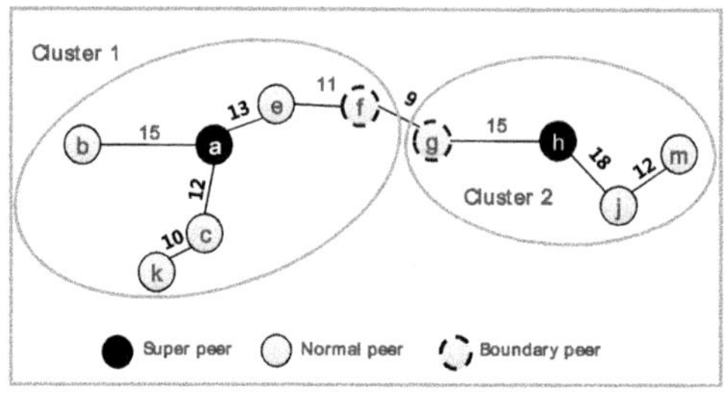

Figure 1. The proposed MP2P architecture.

In this network, each peer has its own information <*Pid*, *Cid*, *Ptype*, *Connectivity*, (x,y), (v_x,v_y)>, where *Pid* is the peer id, *Cid* denotes the cluster id it belongs to, *Ptype* is used to distinguish whether the peer is a normal peer, super peer or boundary peer, *Connectivity* is the number of connected peers, and (x,y) and (v_x,v_y) denotes the location and velocity vector of the peer. The velocity and direction of each peer is represented by velocity vector. The normal peers contain the contents and routing information of its neighbor peers and super peers. The super peers have all of the routing and contents information of the connected normal peers. Figure. 1 shows the proposed MP2P architecture, where the values between the connected peers represent the connection times. The connection time of two peers can be obtained by solving the equations (1), (2), and (3) detailed in 3.2.

3.2 The Join of a Peer

Now we describe how a new peer joins a cluster in the MP2P network. At first, a new coming peer broadcasts a hello message to find an entry peer to join a cluster. If there is no response, the new peer becomes a super peer and a new cluster is created. Otherwise, the new peer uses the response peer as an entry peer to join its cluster. However, if the new peer receives the multiple responses from different clusters, it selects the optimal one to join. In order to make the network relatively stable, the super peer which has a maximum connection time is selected. Since a normal peer communicates with its super peer via multiple hops, the hop count will directly affect the efficiency. Then, the maximum hop count of a normal peer with its super peer is limited within a predefined threshold range value. To balance the load of each super peer, the reasonable number of connected peers of each super peer is considerable. And then, the new peer becomes a boundary peer. The other peers use the same method to participate in a cluster. The connection time of paired peers can be computed according to their velocity and location information. For example, at time t, there are a mobile peer p at position (x,y) with velocity vector (v_x,v_y) and another mobile peer q at position (x',y') moving with $(v_{x'},v_{y'})$. $pos_{t_i}(p_x)$ denotes the x coordinate position of peer p at time t_i, and the communication radius is r. The communication time t can be obtained by solving the below equations (1), (2), and (3).

$$\mathrm{pos}_{t_i}(\mathrm{p_x}) = x + v_x(t_i - t);\ \mathrm{pos}_{t_i}(\mathrm{q_x}) = x' + v_{x'}(t_i - t)\ (1)$$

$$\mathrm{pos}_{t_i}(\mathrm{p_y}) = y + v_y(t_i - t);\ \mathrm{pos}_{t_i}(\mathrm{q_y}) = y' + v_{y'}(t_i - t)\ (2)$$

$$dist_{t_i}(p,q) = \sqrt{(\mathrm{pos}_{t_i}(\mathrm{p_x}) - \mathrm{pos}_{t_i}(\mathrm{q_x}))^2 + (\mathrm{pos}_{t_i}(\mathrm{p_y}) - \mathrm{pos}_{t_i}(\mathrm{q_y}))^2} \le r \quad (3)$$

A simple example of a new peer join is illustrated in Figure 2. The connection times between each paired peers are computed respectively. The connection time (CT) between *e* and *a* is 13, *f* and *e* is 10, and *g* and *h* is 15. When a new peer *n* arrives, its connection time with peer *f* is 15 and peer *g* is 10, therefore, both the connection times of the new peer *n* with super peer *a* and *h* is 10. Since the hop count to *a* is 3 and *h* is 2, the new peer *n* selects *cluster 2* to join.

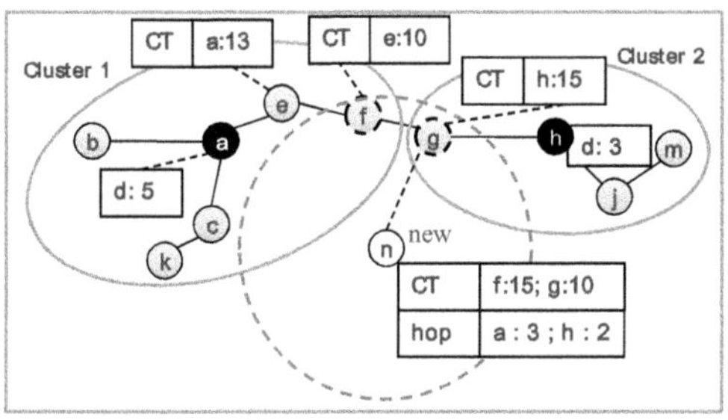

Figure 2. An example of peer join.

3.3 The Leave of a Peer

Due to battery or other reasons, peers may leave the network. There are two kinds of cases to be considered, the leaving peer sending a leaving message to its connected peers before leave or without sending a leave message before leave. For the first case, if the leaving peer is a normal peer and do not affect the routing of the other peers, it only send a leaving message to its connected peers and super peer to update their routing and contents tables. However, if the leaving peer is a super peer or an intermediate peer, the remaining peers connected with it need to be re-organized. The remaining peers who receive the leaving message broadcast each other to select the other clusters to join. If not exist the appropriate cluster to join, the new super peer is elected. The peer with a higher expectation value is selected as the new super peer. The expectation value *e* takes the connection time (*CT*), the hop count (*H*) and the degree (*D*) into account, where the maximum maintenance time, minimum hop count, and maximum degree is preferable. The expectation value can be obtained by solving the equations (4).

$$f(i) = w_0 \frac{\min_{0<m\le D} CT_{im}}{\max_{0<m\le D} CT_{im}} + w_1 \frac{\min_{0<n\le D} H_{in}}{\max_{0<m\le D} H_{im}} + w_2 \frac{D_i}{\max_{0<m\le D} D_{im}} \quad (4)$$

Let $f(i)$ denote the expectation value of peer *i*; *w* is the weight factor that adjusts the priority, $w \in [0, 1]$ and $w_0 + w_1 + w_2 \le 1$. A large value w_0 gives more weight to the peer's connection time than its hop count and degree, where w_1 and w_2 are as same as w_0. The $\max_{0<m\le D} CT_{im}$, $\max_{0<m\le D} H_{im}$ and $\max_{0<m\le D} D_{im}$ is the maximum maintenance time, maximum hop count and maximum degree of peer *i* and its neighbor peers.

For the second case, in order to prevent the leave of the peers without sending leaving message, the peers send confirming messages periodically to detect the status of their connected peers. When the peer finds the disconnection with its super peer or connected peers, it broadcasts to find a new super peer to join or become a new super peer. The processing is similar to the join of the peer.

4. EXPERIMENTAL EVALUATION

In this section, we compare the proposed scheme with group P2P [12] in terms of the update overhead and the success rate of search. The results of super peer based method [11] are omitted as it is similar to [12]. All of the experiments were coded in Java. The mobile objects are generated by the network-based generator [13] and the arrival and departure occurs randomly. The contents are randomly assigned with each participated peers. Table 1 summarizes the parameters for this performance evaluation.

Table 1. The values of parameters

Parameter	Values
Deployment area	$100*100m^2$ / $500*500m^2$
Simulation time	400s
Maximum speed of peers	(0~5)m/s
The total number of peers	500
Communication range	30m

The update overhead is measured as how many times the network topologies update during the period of simulation time. The high update frequency of the network topology will cause high bandwidth and battery cost. The search success rate is measured as the ratio of the search success times and the total search times. The search success means that a peer can connect to the peer that has the searched contents. In the first experiment, we evaluate the update overhead and success rate according to the variation of communication range. The development area is set to $100*100m^2$, and the maximum speed of each peer is 3m/s. Figure 3 shows that the update overhead and success rate increase with the increase of communication range. This is because when the communication range increases the mobile peers can communicate with more peers. But when the communication range reaches to 30m, the success rate is almost saturated.

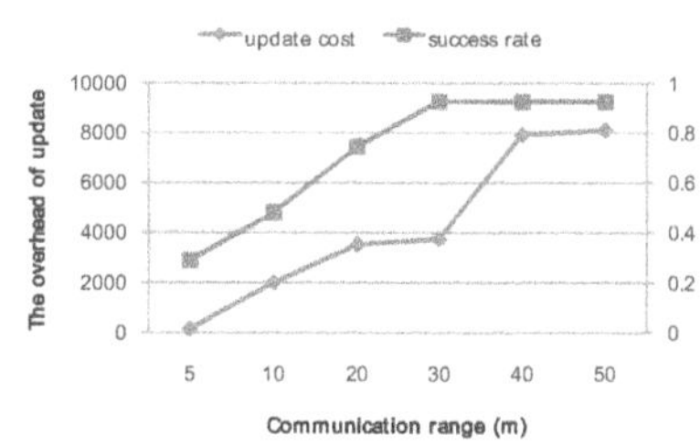

Figure 3. The effect of communication range.

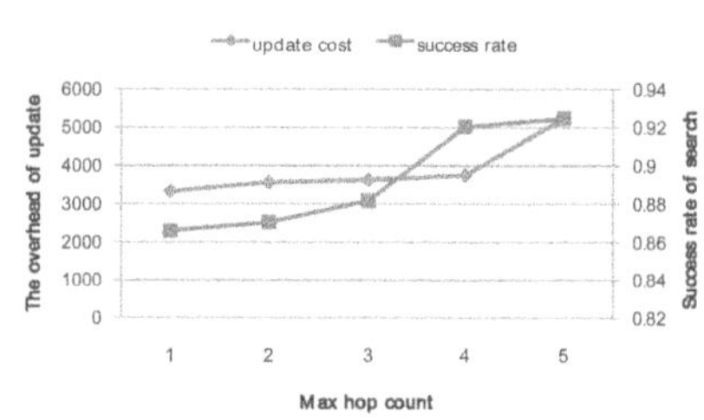

Figure 4. The effect of maximum hop count.

In the second experiment, we compare the effect of the hop count. The development area is set to $100*100m^2$, the maximum speed of each peer is 3m/s and the communication range is 30m. As shown in Figure 4, with the increase of the hop count, the update overhead and content search rate increase. This is because the connected peers of a super peer will increase which increase the amount of contents in a cluster but decrease the connection time of the network. We obtain the balance value at the hop count 3.

Figure 5 compare the group P2P and the proposed method according to the max speed of the mobile peers. The results show that the group P2P is not suitable for high-speed movement of the mobile peers. The experiments are performed in the area of 500x500m^2. From the results we can see that the update cost increases fast with the increase of the max speed of the mobile peers. This is because the faster the movement of the mobile peers, the higher the frequency of the network re-organizing. The group P2P uses RSSI to form the network which may interrupt soon by the high-speed or the opposite direction of the mobile peers. Since the proposed method adopts the maximum connection time to form the network, the performance of update overhead is better than the group P2P.

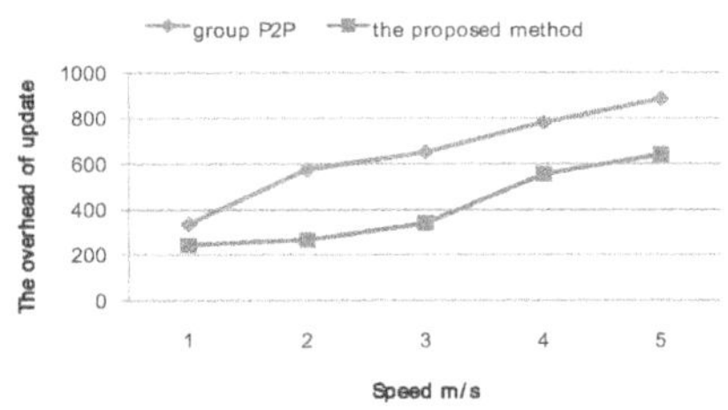

Figure 5. The maximum speed of mobile peers.

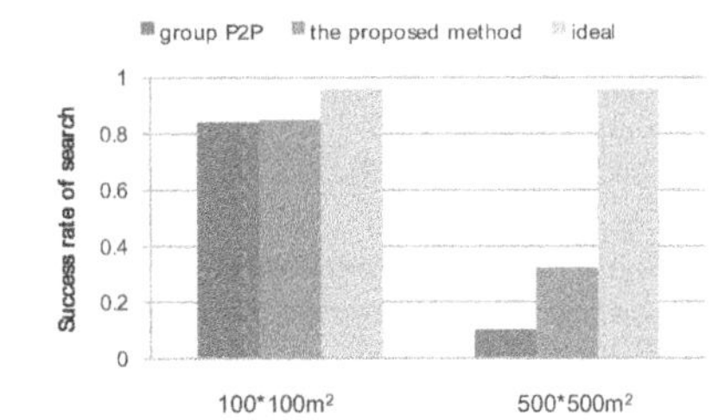

Figure 6. The success rates according to different areas.

The success rates of content search in different areas are shown in Figure 6. In this experiment, the speed of mobile peers is set to 3m/s and the 10000 queries are issued from the participant mobile peers randomly. The experiment is executed in 100*100m^2 and 500*500m^2. From the results, we can see that the search success rate of our proposed method is similar to group P2P in 100*100m^2. However, our proposed method is 3 times higher than the group P2P in 500*500m^2. This is because, in a wider area, the stable connection can improve the success rate of search. The ideal method that uses a central server is efficient but is not suitable for a large network.

5. CONCLUSIONS

In this paper, we proposed a cluster based MP2P architecture over mobile networks. The proposed method utilizes the location and velocity vector of each mobile peer to determine the maximum connection time. The network is constructed based on the proposed three criteria. Since the network is relatively stable, the update overhead is reduced and the success rate of content search is increased. The experimental results have shown that the proposed method is more efficient than the existing methods.

6. ACKNOWLEDGMENTS

This work was supported by the Ministry of Education, Science and Technology Grant funded by the Korea Government (The Regional Research Universities Program/Chungbuk BIT Research-Oriented University Consortium) and the Basic Science Research Program through the National Research Foundation of Korea(NRF) grant funded by the Korea government(MEST)(No. 2009-0080279).

7. REFERENCES

[1] Klemm, A. Lindemann, C. and WaldhorstK, O. P. 2003. A Special-Purpose Peer-to-Peer File Sharing System for Mobile Ad Hoc Networks, In *Proceedings of the VTC*, 2758-2763.

[2] Wu, H. Cheng, C. and Zhong, Z. 2010. A RESOURCE DISCOVERY STRATEGY FOR MOBILE. PEER-TO-PEER NETWORKS, In *Proceedings of the WINSYS*, 1-5.

[3] Li, B. Wang, K. and Hsieh, Y. 2010. A Hierarchical Social Network-based P2P SIP System for Mobile Environments, In *Proceedings of the 21st IEEE Int'l Conf on Personal Indoor and Mobile Radio Communications*, 2581-2585.

[4] Dutta, N. 2010. A Peer to Peer based Information Sharing Scheme in Vehicular Ad Hoc Networks. In *Proceedings of the MDM*, 309-310.

[5] Johnson, D. Maltz, D. and Broch, J. 2001. DSR: The Dynamic Source Routing Protocol for Multi-Hop Wireless Ad Hoc Networks. Addison-Wesley, 139-172.

[6] Perkins, C. and Royer, E. 1999. Ad-hoc On-Demand Distance Vector Routing. In *Proceedings of the second IEEE workshop on Mobile Computing Systems and applications*, 90-100.

[7] Lin, M. Chen, E. Sheu, P. C. 2006. M-Chord: A Chord-based Novel Mobile Peer to Peer File Sharing Protocol. In *Proceedings of the APWEB 2006*, 806-811.

[8] Peng, G. Li, S. Jim, H. Ma, T. 2004. M-CAN: a Lookup Protocol for Mobile Peer-to-Peer Environment. In *Proceedings of the ISPAN*.

[9] Caesar, M. Castro,M. Nightingale,E. B. O'Shea, G. and Rowstron, A. 2006. Virtual Ring Routing: Network Routing Inspired by DHTs. In *Proceedings of the SIGCOMM 06*.

[10] Ahmed, D. T. and Shirmohammadi, S. 2007. Multi-level Hashing for Peer to Peer System in Wireless Ad Hoc Environment. In *Proceedings of the PERCOMW*, 126-131.

[11] Han, S. Lee, J. Song, W. and Yang, B. 2008. Mobile Peer-to-Peer systems using Super Peers for Mobile Environments. In *Proceedings of the ICOIN*, 1-4.

[12] Haw, R. Hong, C. and Kim, D. 2009. Group P2P Network organization in mobile Ad-Hoc Network. In *Proceedings of the APNOMS*, 477-480.

[13] Thomas B. 2002. A Framework for Generating Network-Based Moving Objects. *GeoInformatica*, 6, 2, 153-180.

Block-based Load Balancing for Entity Resolution with MapReduce

Lars Kolb, Andreas Thor, Erhard Rahm
Database Group
University of Leipzig, Germany
{kolb,thor,rahm}@informatik.uni-leipzig.de

ABSTRACT

The effectiveness and scalability of MapReduce-based implementations of complex data-intensive tasks depend on an even redistribution of data between map and reduce tasks. In the presence of skewed data, sophisticated redistribution approaches thus become necessary to achieve load balancing among all reduce tasks to be executed in parallel. For the complex problem of entity resolution with blocking, we propose BlockSplit, a load balancing approach that supports blocking techniques to reduce the search space of entity resolution. The evaluation on a real cloud infrastructure shows the value and effectiveness of the proposed approach.

Categories and Subject Descriptors

H.2.4 [**Systems**]: Distributed Databases; H.3.4 [**Systems and Software**]: Distributed Systems

General Terms

Algorithms, Performance

Keywords

MapReduce, Entity Resolution, Load Balancing, Data Skew

1. INTRODUCTION

Cloud computing has become a popular paradigm for efficiently processing computational- and data-intensive tasks. Such tasks can be executed on demand on powerful distributed hardware and service infrastructures. The MapReduce (MR) model [2] supports the transparent parallel execution of complex tasks on cloud infrastructures. However, the (cost-) effectiveness and scalability of MR programs depend on effective load balancing approaches to evenly utilize available nodes. This is particularly challenging for data-intensive tasks where skewed data redistribution may cause node-specific bottlenecks and load imbalances.

We propose and evaluate an effective load balancing approach to data skew handling for MR-based entity resolution (ER). Note that MR's inherent vulnerability to load imbalances due to data skew is relevant for all kind of pairwise similarity computation, e.g., document similarity computation [4] and set-similarity joins [9]. Such applications can therefore also benefit from our load balancing approach though we study MR-based load balancing in the context of ER only. ER is the task of identifying entities referring to the same real-world object [7]. It is a pervasive problem and of critical importance for data quality and data integration, e.g., to match product offers for price comparison portals. ER techniques usually compare pairs of entities by evaluating multiple similarity measures. Naïve approaches examine the Cartesian product of n input entities. However, the resulting complexity of $O(n^2)$ is inefficient for large datasets. The common approach to improve efficiency is to adopt so-called blocking techniques [1]. They utilize a blocking key based on the values of one or several entity attributes to partition the input data into multiple partitions (blocks) and restrict the subsequent matching to entities of the same block. For example, it is sufficient to compare entities of the same manufacturer when matching product offers.

Even with blocking, ER remains a costly process that can take up to days for large datasets [8]. The MR model is well suited to execute blocking-based ER in parallel. Several map tasks can read the input entities in parallel and redistribute them among several reduce tasks based on the blocking key. This guarantees that all entities of the same block are assigned to the same reduce task so that different blocks can be matched in parallel by multiple reduce tasks. However, such a basic MR implementation is susceptible to severe load imbalances due to skewed block sizes since the match work of an entire block is assigned to a single reduce task. As a consequence, large blocks prevent the utilization of more than a few nodes. The absence of skew handling mechanisms can therefore tremendously deteriorate runtime efficiency and scalability of MR programs. Furthermore, idle nodes may produce unnecessary costs because public cloud infrastructures usually charge per utilized machine hours.

We therefore propose BlockSplit, a general load balancing approach that addresses the mentioned skew problems. It takes the size of blocks into account and assigns entire blocks to reduce tasks if this does not violate load balancing constraints. Larger blocks are split into smaller chunks based on the input partitions to enable their parallel matching within multiple reduce tasks. The evaluation uses real-world data and demonstrates the importance of skew handling for MR-based ER and the efficiency of BlockSplit.

CIKM'11, October 24–28, 2011, Glasgow, Scotland, UK.

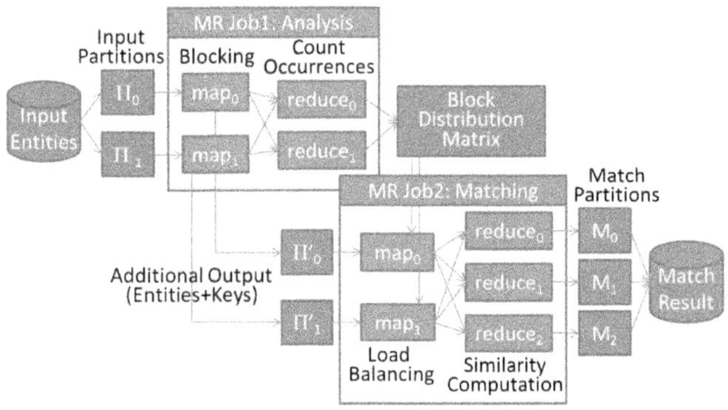

Figure 1: Schematic overview of the MR-based matching process with load balancing.

2. MAPREDUCE AND ENTITY RESOLUTION

MapReduce (MR) is a programming model designed for parallel data-intensive computing in cluster environments with up to thousands of nodes [2]. A computation is expressed with two user defined functions, map and reduce, that are executed in parallel on disjoint partitions of the input data. The map function transforms input entities to key-value pairs whereas reduce is called for each key that occurs as map output. Within the reduce function, one can access the list of all corresponding values. A MR cluster consists of a set of nodes that run a fixed number of map and reduce processes. For each MR job execution, the number of map tasks (m) and reduce tasks (r) is specified. Each process can execute only one task at a time. After a task has finished, another task is automatically assigned to the released process using a framework-specific scheduling mechanism.

Besides map and reduce, a MR dataflow relies on three further functions. First, the function part partitions the map output and thereby distributes it to the available reduce tasks. All keys are sorted with the help of a comparison function comp. Finally, each reduce task employs a grouping function group to determine the data chunks for each reduce function call. Each of these functions operates only on (parts of) the key of key-value pairs and does not take the values into account. The use of extended (composite) keys and an appropriate choice of part, comp, and group supports sophisticated partitioning and grouping behavior and will be utilized in our load balancing approach.

As discussed in the introduction, parallel ER using blocking can be easily implemented with MR. The map function can be used to determine for every input entity its blocking key and to output a key-value pair (blocking_key, entity). The default hash partitioning strategy would use the blocking key to distribute key-value pairs among reduce tasks so that all entities sharing the same blocking key are assigned to the same reduce task. Finally, the reduce function is called for each block and computes the matching entity pairs within its block. We call this straightforward approach Basic. However, the Basic strategy is vulnerable to data skew due to blocks of varying size. Therefore, the execution time may be dominated by a single or a few reduce tasks.

3. BLOCK-BASED LOAD BALANCING

We describe our load balancing approach BlockSplit for

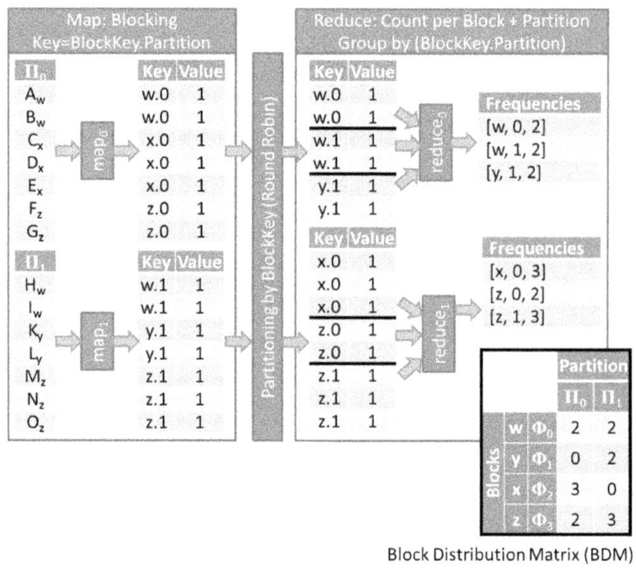

Figure 2: Example dataflow for computation of the block distribution matrix (MR Job1 of Figure 1).

ER for one data source R. The input is a set of entities and the output are the entity pairs that are considered to be the same. We perform ER processing within two MR jobs as illustrated in Figure 1. Both jobs are based on the same number of map tasks and the same partitioning of the input data. The first job calculates a so-called block distribution matrix (BDM) that specifies the number of entities per block separated by input partitions. The matrix is used by the map phase of the second MR job to tailor entity redistribution for parallel matching of blocks of different size.

BlockSplit generates one or several so-called match tasks per block and distributes match tasks among reduce tasks. Furthermore, it uses the following two ideas:

- Small blocks are processed within a single match task similar to Basic. Large blocks are split according to the m input partitions into m sub-blocks. All entities within the same sub-block are compared with each other. Furthermore, pairs of sub-blocks are processed to evaluate their Cartesian product. This ensures that all comparisons of the original block will be computed.
- BlockSplit determines the number of comparisons per match task and assigns match tasks in descending size among reduce tasks. This implements a greedy load balancing heuristic ensuring that the largest match tasks are processed first and makes it unlikely that two large match tasks are processed by the same reduce task.

In the following, we describe the computation of the BDM and our BlockSplit strategy. Further information including pseudo-code can be found in [5].

3.1 Block Distribution Matrix

The block distribution matrix (BDM) is a $b \times m$ matrix that specifies the number of entities of b blocks across m input partitions. The BDM computation using MR is straightforward as illustrated by Figure 2 for an example dataset. The 14 entities (A-O) are divided into two input partitions Π_0 and Π_1 and each entity has a blocking key (w-z) that is denoted as index. For example, the map output key of

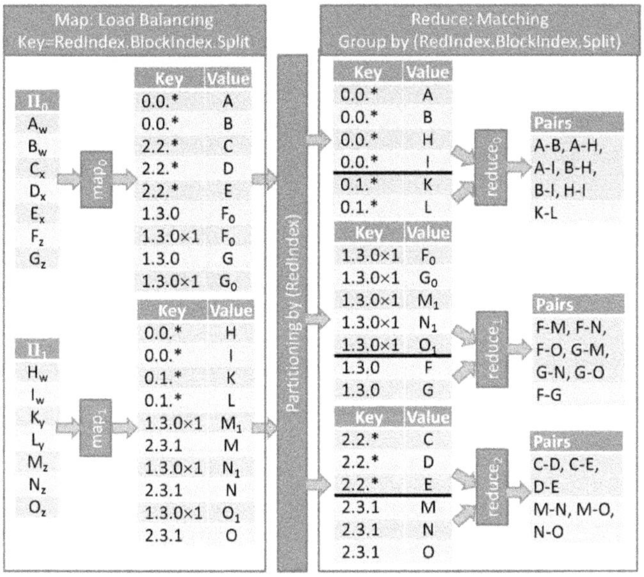

Figure 3: Example dataflow for the load balancing strategy BlockSplit (MR Job2 of Figure 1).

M is $z.1$ because M's blocking key equals z and M appears in the second partition (partition index=1). This key is assigned to the last reduce task that outputs $[z, 1, 3]$ because there are 3 entities in the second partition for blocking key z. The combined reduce outputs correspond to the BDM. To assign block keys to rows of the BDM, we use the order of the blocks from the reduce output, i.e., we assign the first block (key w) to block index position 0, etc.

The block sizes in the example vary between 2 and 5 entities. The match work to compare all entities per block with each other thus ranges from 1 to 10 comparisons; the largest block with key z entails 50% (10 of 20) of all comparisons although it contains only 35% (5 out 14) of all entities.

As illustrated in Figure 1, map produces an additional output Π'_i per input partition that contains the original entities annotated with their blocking keys. This output is not shown in Figure 2 to save space but used as input in the second MR job (see Figure 3).

3.2 BlockSplit

The realization of BlockSplit makes use of the BDM as well as of composite map output keys. Map generates a carefully constructed composite key that (together with associated partition and group functions) allows a balanced load distribution. The composite key thereby combines information about the target reduce task(s), the block of the entity, and the entity itself. The map function may generate multiple keys per entity if this entity is supposed to be processed by multiple reduce tasks. The reduce phase performs the actual ER and computes match similarities between entities of the same block. Since the reduce phase consumes the vast majority of the overall runtime (~95% in our experiments), our load balancing strategy solely focusses on data redistribution for reduce tasks. Other MR-specific performance factors as data locality are therefore not considered.

Map outputs key-value pairs with key=(reduce_index $\odot$ block_index $\odot$ split) and value=(entity). The reduce task index has a value between 0 and $r-1$ and is used by part to realize the desired assignment to reduce tasks. Grouping is done on the entire key and – since the block index is part of the key – ensures that each reduce function only receives entities of the same block. The split value indicates what match task has to be performed by the reduce function, i.e., whether a complete block or sub-blocks need to be processed.

During the initialization, each of the m map tasks reads the BDM and computes the number of comparison per block and the total number of comparisons P over all b blocks Φ_k: $P = \frac{1}{2} \cdot \Sigma_{k=0}^{b-1} |\Phi_k| \cdot (|\Phi_k| - 1)$. For each block Φ_k, it also checks if the number of comparisons is above the average reduce task workload, i.e., if

$$\frac{1}{2} \cdot |\Phi_k| \cdot (|\Phi_k| - 1) > P/r.$$

If the block Φ_k is *not* above the average workload it can be processed within a single match task (denoted as $k.*$ in the block_index and split components of the map output key). Otherwise, it is split into m sub-blocks based on the m input partitions leading to the following $\frac{1}{2} \cdot m \cdot (m-1) + m$ match tasks:

- m match tasks, denoted with key components $k.i$, for the individual processing of the ith sub-block for $i \in [0, m-1]$
- $\frac{1}{2} \cdot m \cdot (m-1)$ match tasks, denoted with key components $k.i{\times}j$ with $i, j \in [0, m-1]$ and $i < j$, for the computation of the Cartesian product of sub-blocks i and j

Note that the BDM holds the number of entities per (block, partition) pair and map can therefore determine which input partitions contain *no* entities of Φ_k, resulting in less match tasks. However, in favor of readability we assume that all m input partitions contain at least one entity. To determine the reduce task for each match task, all match tasks are first sorted in descending order of their number of comparisons. Match tasks are then assigned to reduce tasks in this order so that the current match task is assigned to the reduce task with the lowest number of already assigned pairs. In the following, we denote the reduce task index for match task $k.x$ with $R(k.x)$.

After the described initialization phase, the map function is called for each input entity. If the entity belongs to a block Φ_k that has *not* to be split, map outputs one key-value pair with composite key=$R(k.*).k.*$. Otherwise, map outputs m key-value pairs for the entity. The key $R(k.i).k.i$ represents the individual sub-block i of block Φ_k and the remaining $m-1$ keys $R(k.i).k.i \times j$ (for $j \in [0, m-1]$ and $j \neq i$) represent all combinations with the other $m-1$ sub-blocks. This indicates that entities of split blocks are replicated m times to support load balancing. The map function emits the entity as value of the key-value pair; for split blocks we annotate entities with the partition index for use in the reduce phase.

In our running example, only block Φ_3 (blocking key z) is subject to splitting into m=2 sub-blocks. The BDM (see Figure 2) indicates for block Φ_3 that Π_0 and Π_1 contain two and three entities, respectively. The resulting sub-blocks $\Phi_{3.0}$ and $\Phi_{3.1}$ lead to the three match tasks *3.0*, *3.0×1*, and *3.1* that account for 1, 6, and 3 comparisons, respectively. The resulting ordering of match tasks by size (*0.**, *3.0×1*, *2.**, *3.1*, *1.**, and *3.0*) leads for three reduce tasks to the distribution shown in Figure 3. The replication of the five entities for the split block leads to 19 key-value pairs for the 14 input entities. Each reduce task has to process between six and seven comparisons indicating a good load balancing for the example.

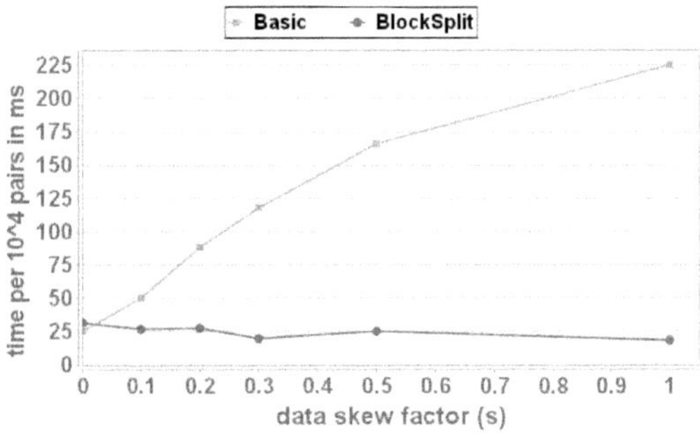

Figure 4: Execution times for different data skews using 114,000 entities.

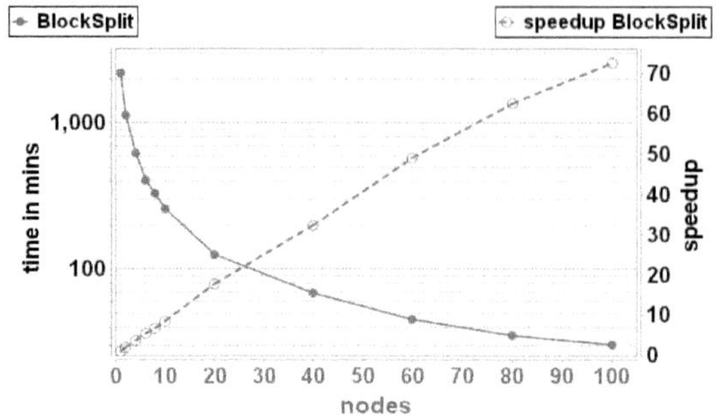

Figure 5: Execution times and speedup of the BlockSplit strategy.

4. EVALUATION

In the following we evaluate our BlockSplit strategy regarding the degree of data skew and the number of available nodes (n). We ran our experiments with real-world datasets on the Amazon EC2 cloud infrastructure using Hadoop.

We first evaluate the robustness of our load balancing strategies against data skew for a dataset containing about 114,000 product descriptions. To this end, we control the degree of data skew by generating block distributions that follow an exponential distribution. Given a fixed number of blocks b=100, the number of entities in the kth block is proportional to $e^{-s \cdot k}$. The skew factor $s \geq 0$ thereby describes the degree of data skew. Note that the data skew, i.e., the distribution of entities over all blocks, determines the overall number of entity pairs. We are therefore interested in the average execution time *per entity pair* when comparing load balancing strategies for different data skews.

Figure 4 shows the average execution time per 10^4 pairs for different data skews (n=10, m=20, r=100). The Basic strategy explained in Section 2 is not robust against data skew because a higher data skew increases the number of pairs of the largest block. For example, for s=1 Basic needs 225ms per 10^4 comparisons which is more than 12 times slower than BlockSplit. However, the Basic strategy is slightly faster for a uniform block distribution (s=0) because it does not suffer from the additional BDM computation and load balancing overhead. The BDM influence becomes insignificant for higher data skews because the data skew does not affect the time for BDM computation but the number of pairs. This is why the execution time per pair is reduced for increasing s. In general, BlockSplit is stable across all data skews.

To analyze the scalability of BlockSplit, we use a larger dataset of approx. 1.4 million publication records. The blocking is formed by the first three letters of the publication title. We vary the number of nodes from 1 up to 100. For n nodes, the number of map tasks is set to $m = 2 \cdot n$ and the number of reduce tasks is set to $r = 10 \cdot n$, i.e., adding new nodes leads to additional map and reduce tasks.

The resulting execution times and speedup values are shown in Figure 5. In contrast to Basic, BlockSplit shows its ability to evenly distribute the workload across available nodes. It scales almost linearly up to 40 nodes. For larger n the speedup increase slightly alleviates due to the decreasing workload (number of entity comparisons) per reduce task. At the same time, the relative fraction of the MR overhead for task initialization and task shutdown is increasing.

5. RELATED WORK

Load balancing and skew handling are well-known data management problems and MR has been criticized for having overlooked the skew issue [3]. MR's inherent vulnerability to data skew is relevant for all kind of pairwise similarity computation, e.g., pairwise document similarity [4] or set-similarity joins [9]. MR has already been employed for ER (e.g., [10]) but we are only aware of one load balancing mechanism. [6] studies load balancing for Sorted Neighborhood that is by design less vulnerable to skewed data.

6. SUMMARY AND OUTLOOK

We proposed a load balancing approach, BlockSplit, for parallelizing blocking-based entity resolution using the widely available MapReduce framework. The approach is capable to deal with skewed blocking key distributions and effectively distributes the workload among all reduce tasks by splitting large blocks. Our evaluation in a real cloud environment demonstrated that it is robust against data skew and scales with the number of available nodes.

In future work we will extend our approach to multi-pass blocking that assigns multiple blocks per entity. We will further investigate how our load balancing approach can be adapted for MapReduce-based implementations of other data-intensive tasks, such as join processing or data mining.

7. REFERENCES

[1] R. Baxter, P. Christen, and T. Churches. A comparison of fast blocking methods for record linkage. In *Workshop Data Cleaning, Record Linkage, and Object Consolidation*, 2003.

[2] J. Dean and S. Ghemawat. MapReduce: Simplified Data Processing on Large Clusters. In *OSDI*, 2004.

[3] D. J. DeWitt and M. Stonebraker. MapReduce: A major step backwards, 2008.

[4] T. Elsayed, J. Lin, and D. W. Oard. Pairwise Document Similarity in Large Collections with MapReduce. In *ACL*, 2008.

[5] L. Kolb, A. Thor, and E. Rahm. Load Balancing for MapReduce-based Entity Resolution. *ArXiv*, 2011.

[6] L. Kolb, A. Thor, and E. Rahm. Multi-pass Sorted Neighborhood Blocking with MapReduce. *CSRD*, 2011.

[7] H. Köpcke and E. Rahm. Frameworks for entity matching: A comparison. *Data Knowl. Eng.*, 69(2), 2010.

[8] H. Köpcke, A. Thor, and E. Rahm. Evaluation of entity resolution approaches on real-world match problems. *PVLDB*, 3(1), 2010.

[9] R. Vernica, M. J. Carey, and C. Li. Efficient parallel set-similarity joins using MapReduce. In *SIGMOD*, 2010.

[10] C. Wang et al. MapDupReducer: Detecting near duplicates over massive datasets. In *SIGMOD*, 2010.

PCMLogging: Reducing Transaction Logging Overhead with PCM

Shen Gao Jianliang Xu
Hong Kong Baptist University
{sgao, xujl}@comp.hkbu.edu.hk

Bingsheng He
Nanyang Technological University
bshe@ntu.edu.sg

Byron Choi Haibo Hu
Hong Kong Baptist University
{haibo, bchoi}@comp.hkbu.edu.hk

ABSTRACT

Phase Changing Memory (PCM), as one of the most promising next-generation memory technologies, offers various attractive properties such as non-volatility, bit-alterability, and low idle energy consumption. In this paper, we present PCMLogging, a novel logging scheme that exploits PCM devices for both data buffering and transaction logging in disk-based databases. Different from the traditional approach where buffered updates and transaction logs are completely separated, they are integrated in the new logging scheme. Our preliminary experiments show an up to 40% improvement of PCMLogging in disk I/O performance in comparison with a basic buffering and logging scheme.

Categories and Subject Descriptors

H.2.4 [Database Management]: Transaction Processing

General Terms

Algorithm, Performance

Keywords

Transaction Management, Logging, Database Recovery, PCM

1. INTRODUCTION

Over decades, non-volatile random access memory (NVRAM) has been actively investigated as the next-generation memory technology. The goal of the NVRAM technology is to take the best of the hard disk and DRAM: with non-volatility like the hard disk and with read/write speeds like DRAM. Recently, PCM has been considered one of the most promising NVRAM technologies. PCM is not only a persistent fast random-access memory but also has a higher density than the floating-gate based memory. Manufacturers have already started the mass production of PCM at a reasonable price. For example, Numonyx (later acquired by Micron) and Samsung released their first PCM products in 2010 [4, 5]. It has been envisioned that PCM will be integrated into the memory/storage hierarchy in the near future [2]. An important question brought by a recent research on using PCM in databases [1] is "how should database systems be modified to best take advantage of this emerging trend towards PCM?" In this paper, we study how PCM can be leveraged to improve the transaction processing performance in disk-backed relational databases.

Compared with DRAM and recently popular flash memory, PCM offers various attractive hardware features to database transaction processing. Compared with DRAM, PCM has the advantage of persistence with a comparable read speed. Compared with flash memory, PCM has over two orders of magnitude faster read/write speeds. Unlike flash memory with an erase-before-write constraint, PCM is bit-alterable without a separate erase step [5]. These unique hardware features of PCM motivate us to revisit and improve the core components in transaction processing.

Previous work [3] has demonstrated that logging is a critical component for transaction processing in disk-based databases. Therefore, we consider leveraging PCM to reduce the transaction logging overhead. In general, PCM can be used for both data buffering and transaction logging. Owing to its fast data access performance, dirty pages evicted from main memory can be buffered in PCM to minimize disk I/Os. Meanwhile, the non-volatile nature of PCM makes it an ideal place for archiving transaction log records. Hence, a simple design is to divide the PCM into a buffer pool and a log pool. However, this simple scheme has several drawbacks. First, buffering a full page in PCM may not be very cost-efficient since most updates in OLTP workload are small writes. Second, a transaction update kept in the log might also be buffered in a dirty page, which leads to data redundancy. Third, the space management of the PCM becomes a challenge as it is shared by the buffer pool and the log pool.

To address the drawbacks of the basic scheme, we propose a new logging scheme called PCMLogging. In this scheme, we eliminate the explicit logs, such as REDO and UNDO logs, by integrating implicit logs into buffered updates to ensure durability and atomicity of database transaction processing. Meanwhile, this makes checkpoint unnecessary and enables a simple and cheap recovery algorithm. We also develop a trace-driven simulator to study the performance of PCMLogging. The evaluation results based on a TPC-C benchmark trace show that, compared to the basic scheme mentioned above, PCMLogging saves up to 40% I/Os to the external disk and 97% write traffic to the PCM device.

The rest of this paper proceeds as follows. In Section 2, we give some background of PCM and review the related work. Section 3 presents the PCMLogging scheme. In Section 4, we report our performance evaluation results. Finally, Section 5 concludes the paper and points out some future directions.

2. BACKGROUND AND RELATED WORK

PCM is based on a new storage material called *chalocogenide glass*, which retains information by a large resistance contrast between two states, namely *amorphous* and *crystalline*. To switch between these two states, different kinds of electronic currents are applied on chalocogenide glass. To crystallize the phase change material, a *set* current pulse is applied to heat chalocogenide glass for a sufficiently long time. On the other hand, a *reset* current is a sudden pulse which melts chalocogenide glass to largely increase its resistance. Sensing the resistance and retrieving the information requires only a very low current.

Table 1 summarizes the hardware performance of several current storage technologies including DRAM, NAND flash, PCM, and hard disk [1]. Besides non-volatility and higher density, PCM has the following hardware features [1, 2, 5]:

CIKM'11, October 24–28, 2011, Glasgow, Scotland, UK.

Parameter	DRAM	NAND Flash	Hard Disk	PCM
Density	1X	4X	N/A	2-4X
Read latency (granularity)	20-50ns (64B)	~25μs (4KB)	~5ms (512B)	~50ns (64B)
Write latency (granularity)	20-50ns (64B)	~500μs (4KB)	~5ms (512B)	~1μs (64B)
Endurance	N/A	10^4~10^5	∞	10^6~10^8

Table 1: Comparison of Storage Technologies [1]

- *Finer-grained access granularity.* PCM has an access granularity as small as DRAM. Compared to other non-volatile memory technologies such as flash, it breaks the constraints of erase-before-write and page-based access. It is byte-addressable (or word-addressable) and bit-alterable. This feature enables PCM to support small in-place updates.
- *Asymmetric read/write latency.* The write speed of PCM is about 20 times slower than the read speed.
- *Endurance limitation.* Similar to flash memory, PCM endures a limit number of writes, on the scale of 10^6 to 10^8 writes on each unit.

Recently, system researchers have started revisiting system design and optimizations with PCM. Fig. 1 shows two representative architectures of using PCM in the memory hierarchy [2]: a) PCM as an auxiliary memory attached to the main memory; b) PCM as the whole main memory. Based on the storage properties of PCM, the former method using PCM as an auxiliary memory might be more practical. The first reason is that PCM has endurance limitation, and its write latency is still much higher than DRAM. Secondly, the capacity of PCM is still small in the coming few years, compared with DRAM. In this study, we mainly consider the memory architecture of using PCM as an auxiliary memory.

There has been research on how to take advantages of non-volatile memory for improving database performance. Early work focused on the use of non-volatile memory as an extension of the storage hierarchy [6]. As the technology matures, in 2011, Chen *et al.* [1] presented a pioneer study on how database algorithms should be adapted to PCM technology. They improved two fundamental database algorithms, *i.e.*, B+-tree and hash join, by reducing their write operations to PCM. In contrast, in this study we focus on how PCM can be used to improve transaction processing performance in disk-based databases.

3. PCMLOGGING

We consider the memory architecture as shown in Fig. 1(a). Without modifying the buffer manager of the main memory (DRAM), we develop a new scheme, called PCMLogging, where the buffered updates and transaction logs are combined.

3.1 Overview

The basic idea of PCMLogging is to integrate the transaction logs into buffered updates, by exploiting the persistency feature of PCM storage. For ease of exposition, we assume that the PCM buffering granularity is a page in this section. We also assume that the concurrency control is on a page level. That is, a page is updated by at most one transaction at one time. To further improve the transaction processing performance, we extend the design to tuple-based buffering and tuple-level concurrency control in Section 3.3.

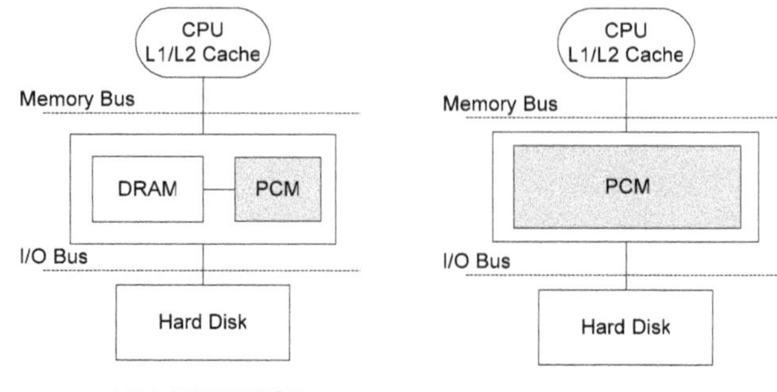

Fig. 1: Memory Architecture Alternatives

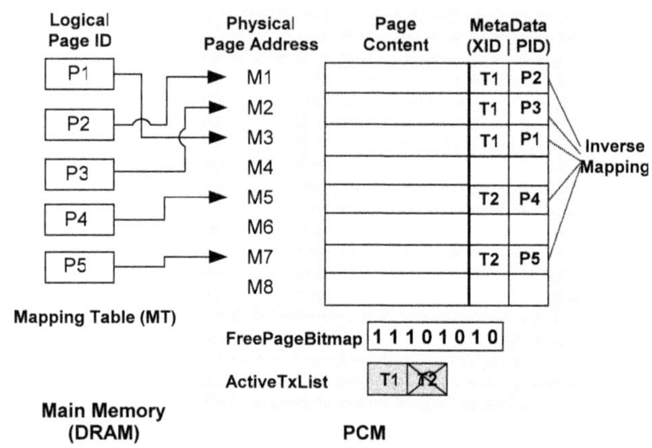

Fig. 2: Page Format and Mapping Table

To support buffering in PCM, we maintain a *Mapping Table* in the main memory to map logical page IDs to physical PCM addresses, as well as *Inverse Mapping* and *FreePageBitmap* in the PCM (see Fig. 2). Inverse Mapping is used to construct the Mapping Table at the boot time and FreePageBitmap is used to keep track of the free page slots. Note that in PCMLogging, only dirty pages evicted from the main memory are buffered in order to minimize the disk write I/Os.

An overview of the PCMLogging scheme is as follows. To achieve atomicity and durability of transactions, an *ActiveTxList* is maintained in PCM to record the in-progress transactions that have dirty pages buffered in the PCM; each buffered page records the XID of the last transaction that caused the page to be dirty. To guarantee atomicity, before the first dirty page of a transaction is written to the PCM, its corresponding XID should be recorded in the ActiveTxList. The XID is not removed until the transaction is requested to commit and all its dirty pages have been flushed to the PCM. Thus, during recovery, if the XID of a transaction is found in the ActiveTxList, it implies that the transaction is not committed before the crash; otherwise, the transaction is committed. Consequently, each PCM page can be recovered according to the status of the corresponding transaction. For example, if the PCM appears as shown in the right part of Fig. 2, during recovery, we can infer that *T1* is not yet committed while *T2* is committed. Thus, the pages stored in *M1~M3* would be discarded while the pages stored in *M5* and *M7* would be retained. Accordingly, the FreePageBitmap should be updated to "00001010". We note that, to avoid the hot-spot on the PCM, dynamic space allocation and wear-leveling techniques can be adopted to evenly distribute writes across the PCM space, which is, however, an orthogonal issue to our PCMLogging scheme.

As can be seen, PCMLogging totally eliminates the explicit transaction logs by integrating them into the dirty pages buffered in the PCM. This integrated design has several advantages. First, the data redundancy between buffered updates and transaction logs is minimized. Second, it avoids the challenging space management issue, which is a must if they are separated. Third, checkpoint becomes unnecessary since we do not maintain explicit logs. In addition, the recovery process becomes extremely simple and efficient. In the following, we detail the PCMLogging operations such as flushing, commit, abort, and recovery.

3.2 PCMLogging Operations

In PCMLogging, durability is achieved by forcing the corresponding dirty pages to the PCM when a transaction is requested to commit. Meanwhile, a *steal* buffer policy of the main memory allows a dirty page to be flushed to the PCM before the transaction commits. To ensure atomicity, undo operations will be needed if the transaction is finally aborted. To efficiently support such undo operations, we maintain two additional data structures in the main memory:

- *Transaction Table (TT).* This table records all in-progress transactions. For each in-progress transaction, it keeps track of all its dirty pages stored in the main memory and PCM. The purpose is to quickly identify the relevant pages when the transaction is committed or aborted.
- *Dirty Page Table (DPT).* This table keeps track of the previous version for each PCM page "overwritten" by an in-progress transaction. This is necessary for restoring the original page content in the event of a rollback. A dirty page entry will be removed from the table once the in-progress transaction is committed or aborted.

Flushing Dirty Pages to PCM. When the main memory becomes full or a transaction is committed, some dirty pages may need to be flushed to the PCM. We first check the ActiveTxList in the PCM. For each dirty page, if the corresponding XID is not yet in the ActiveTxList, we add it to the list before flushing. In case a page *P* already exists in the PCM, we do not overwrite it in place. In order to support undo, instead, we create an out-of-place copy *M'* with the current timestamp. Then, *M'* is added to the Dirty Page Table and *P* is mapped to *M'* in the Mapping Table. Finally, the Transaction Table is updated.

Commit. Upon receiving a commit request, we first force all its dirty pages that are still buffered in the main memory to the PCM, by checking the Transaction Table. After that, we remove the XID from the ActiveTxList and indicate the transaction is committed. Next, if any of its pages is contained in the Dirty Page Table, the previous version is discarded. Finally, we clear the relevant entries in the Transaction Table and Dirty Page Table.

Abort. When a transaction is aborted, all its dirty pages are discarded, by checking the Transaction Table. If any of its pages is contained in the Dirty Page Table, the previous version should be restored. Finally, we clear the XID in the ActiveTxList and the relevant entries in the Transaction Table and Dirty Page Table.

An Example: *Consider the example shown in Fig. 2, where T1 is in progress and T2 is committed. Suppose now a new transaction T3 updates the page P5. Before this dirty page is flushed, T3 points to the page P5 kept in the main memory (see Fig. 3(a)). When it is flushed to the PCM slot M8, T3 is added to the ActiveTxList in PCM (see Fig. 3(b)). After that, P5 is mapped to M8, T3 points to M8, and the previous version M7 is kept in the Dirty Page Table. Finally, if T3 is requested to commit, it is removed from the ActiveTxList; the previous version is discarded (the corresponding bit becomes 0 in the FreePageBitmap); and the relevant entries are removed from the Transaction Table and Dirty Page Table (see Fig. 3(c)). Otherwise, if T3 is finally aborted, the current version is discarded (the corresponding bit becomes 0 in the FreePageBitmap) and the previous version is restored in the Mapping Table; and the relevant entries are also removed from the ActiveTxList, Transaction Table, and Dirty Page Table (see Fig. 3(d)).*

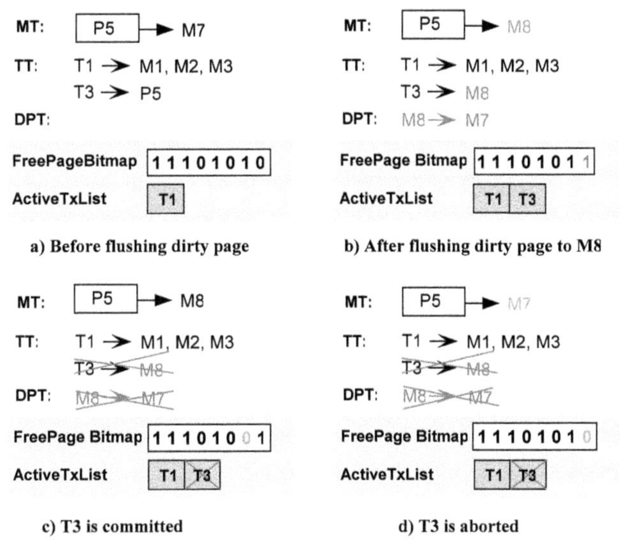

Fig. 3: An Example of PCMLogging

Recovery. A recovery process is invoked when the system restarts after a failure. It identifies the last committed version for each PCM page and constructs the Mapping Table. To do so, the recovery reads all valid pages based on the FreePageBitmap and the XIDs of the in-progress transactions from the ActiveTxList. We then simply discard the pages that belong to the in-progress transactions. Note that this process does not involve any disk I/Os.

Replacement in PCM. When the PCM is full (or the disk system is idle), we will select some committed pages and write them back to the external disk. Thus, some replacement policy (*e.g.*, LRU) can be used to select the victims.

3.3 Tuple-based Buffering

Recall that PCM supports byte-addressability and bit-alterability. Thus, in response to small writes in OLTP workload and tuple-based concurrency control, we propose to buffer dirty tuples, instead of dirty pages, in the PCM. The proposed PCMLogging scheme can be easily extended to tuple-based buffering. It works similarly except the following modifications: 1) In the PCM, the buffer slots should now be managed in the unit of tuples, rather than pages. To manage the free space, if the tuples are of variable size, a bitmap does not work; instead we may employ a slotted directory. 2) In the Mapping Table, we still keep track of dirty pages, but maintain the mappings for the buffered tuples in each dirty page. 3) If a read/write request is on a tuple granularity, the tuple can be accessed from the PCM directly, if available. Otherwise, we have to load the corresponding page from the external disk and merge it with the latest contents of the buffered tuples in the page. Note that loading page contents from the external disk and the PCM is a parallel process and the access latency of the PCM is negligible. 4) When a committed tuple is moved from the PCM to the external disk, we have to first load the corresponding page from the external disk, and then merge it with the tuple before writing back.

4. PERFORMANCE EVALUATION

In this section, we report the preliminary results we obtained via simulation experiments. We have developed a trace-driven simulator based on DiskSim (http://www.pdl.cmu.edu/DiskSim/). We implemented a transaction processing model and a PCM model on top of a simulated disk. In the transaction processing model, we employ the strict two-phase locking protocol for concurrency control at a tuple level. Deadlocks are detected and resolved whenever a transaction is blocked. If a deadlock is discovered, the youngest transaction in the deadlock is restarted after a random backoff time. In the PCM model, the current implementation assumed only one memory chip [5]. The data access granularity in the PCM was fixed at 64B. We set its write latency at 1μs, and its read latency the same as that of DRAM access (*i.e.*, 50 ns).

The database trace on disk I/O accesses was obtained by running PostgreSQL 8.4 with the TPC-C benchmark for four hours. We set the client number at 50 and the number of data warehouses at 20. As the database size is 2.4GB, we fixed the size of DRAM main memory at 64MB (*i.e.*, ~2.6% of the database size). For simplicity, we assumed that each tuple has a size of 128B. We conducted our simulation study on a desktop computer running Windows XP SP2 with an Intel Quad 2.4GHz CPU. For a fair comparison, the results were collected after a fixed warmup period (*i.e.*, after the PCM becomes full under all schemes).

Fig. 4 shows the disk I/O performance when we vary the PCM size from 8MB to 64MB. We compare the PCMLogging scheme with tuple-based buffering (denoted as *PCMLogging*) to the basic scheme (denoted as *PCMBasic*) presented in the Introduction. For PCMBasic, to minimize the disk I/Os, checkpoint is triggered whenever the log pool becomes full; under each PCM size setting, we tried different space partitions between the buffer pool and the log pool and plotted the result with the best partition. As a reference, we also include a scheme without PCM support (denoted as *NoPCM*).

As shown in Fig. 4(a), both PCMBasic and PCMLogging achieve a better I/O performance than the NoPCM scheme, as expected. PCMLogging greatly improves the performance when the PCM size is larger than 16MB. At a PCM size of 64MB, it outperforms PCMBasic by 40%. However, PCMLogging is slightly worse than PCMBasic at a PCM size of 8MB. To explain this, we plot the I/O breakdown and PCM miss rate in Figs. 4(b) and 5(a), respectively. We can observe that when the PCM size is 8MB, the miss rate is high and hence not many read and write requests can be served by the buffered copies. Thus, the read I/Os are not much reduced, as compared with the NoPCM scheme (see Fig. 4(b)). On the other hand, due to a small size, PCM replacement happens frequently. Recall that PCMLogging incurs an extra read I/O (counted in write in Fig. 4(b)) when writing buffered tuples to the disk during PCM replacement. This makes its write performance even worse than NoPCM, thereby incurring a worse overall performance. When the PCM size increases, the miss rate is significantly reduced, especially for PCMLogging. For example, at 64MB, PCMLogging reduces the miss rate to 63% (vs. 81% for PCMBasic), as shown in Fig. 5(a). Moreover, PCMLogging has a larger buffering capacity with a tuple-based buffering granularity. As a result, PCMLogging gets much fewer disk I/Os for both reads and writes, as shown in Fig. 4(b).

Next, we investigate the write traffic to the PCM, which may affect its lifetime. As shown in Fig. 5(b), the write traffic of PCMLogging is greatly reduced; it is only 2.7% of PCMBasic on average.

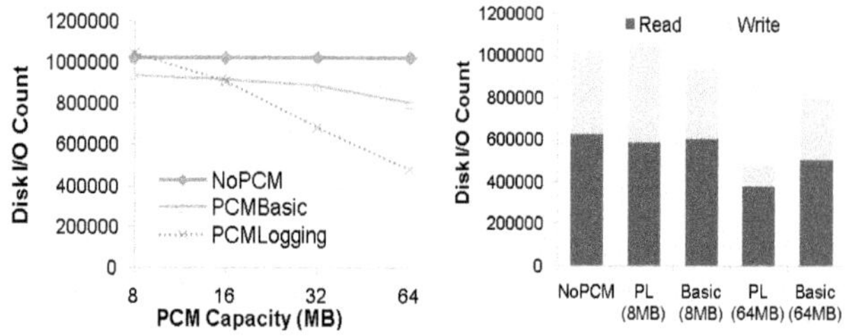

(a) Disk I/O Count (b) I/O Breakdown

Fig. 4: Disk I/O Performance (PL=PCMLogging)

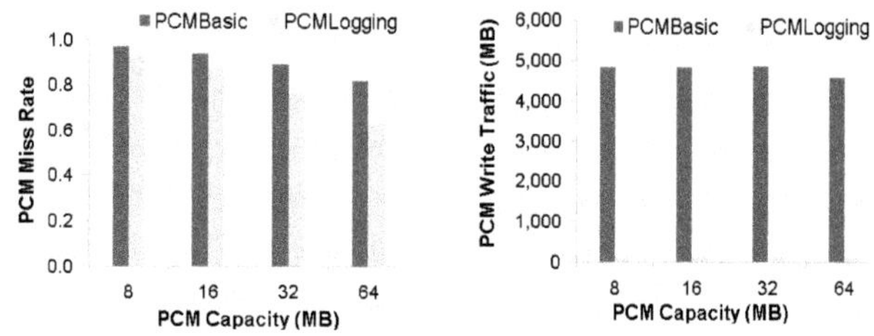

(a) Write Hit Rate on PCM (b) Write Trafic on PCM

Fig. 5: PCM Write Traffic

This is mainly because that the updates in OLTP workloads are mostly small writes, buffering only the dirty tuples in PCMLogging can avoid writing the clean part of a page. This result indicates that the lifetime of PCM can be significantly improved by PCMLogging.

5. CONCLUSIONS AND FUTURE WORK

In this paper, we have presented a study on leveraging PCM to support efficient transaction processing. We have developed a new PCMLogging scheme that combines the buffered updates and log records, by taking advantage of the PCM hardware features. The preliminary results have been encouraging. It is shown that PCMLogging saves up to 40% disk I/Os and 97% PCM write traffic in comparison with the basic buffering and logging scheme.

This paper represents an initial step of our work towards improving database transaction performance with PCM. For future work, we will enhance the simulation experiments. We also plan to further improve our work in a number of directions, such as advanced PCM replacement policies, fine-grained tuple-based mapping, wear-leveling techniques, multi-version concurrency control, and integration with flash-memory technology.

Acknowledgement. This work is partially supported by GRF Grants HKBU210808 and HKBU211510.

6. REFERENCES

[1] S. Chen, P. Gibbons, and S. Nath. Rethinking database algorithms for phase change memory. In CIDR, 2011.

[2] J. Condit, E. B. Nightingale, C. Frost, E. Ipek, B. C. Lee, D. Burger, and D. Coetzee. Better I/O through byte-addressable, persistent memory. In SOSP, 2009.

[3] R. Johnson, I. Pandis, R. Stoica, M. Athanassoulis, and A. Ailamaki. Aether: A scalable approach to logging. VLDB, 2010.

[4] Samsung Press Release. Samsung ships industry's first multi-chip package with a PRAM chip for handsets, April 2010.

[5] Micron 128Mb P8P Parallel PCM Data Sheet, March 2011.

[6] E. Rahm. Performance evaluation of extended storage architectures for transaction processing. In SIGMOD, 1992.

A Continuous Query Evaluation Scheme for a Detection-Only Query over Data Streams

Hong Kyu Park
Department of Computer Science, Yonsei University
134 Shinchon-dong Seodaemun-gu
Seoul, 120-749, Korea
+82-2-2123-2716
gladiator11@database.yonsei.ac.kr

Won Suk Lee
Department of Computer Science, Yonsei University
134 Shinchon-dong Seodaemun-gu
Seoul, 120-749, Korea
+82-2-2123-2716
leewo@database.yonsei.ac.kr

ABSTRACT
In a data stream environment, a multi-way join continuous query is employed to monitor a considerable number of source data streams from various remote sites in real-time. One key role of a continuous query is detecting only the invocation of a particular event corresponding to the specifications of the query. The evaluation of such a *detection-only query* does not require to produce either an intermediate tuple or a final result tuple, which not only shortens the processing time of a query but also reduces the usage of memory space. However, there has been no special effort to deal with a query of this type. This paper proposes a new evaluation framework which efficiently processes a multi-way detection-only query without generating any intermediate result tuple explicitly.

Categories and Subject Descriptors
H.2.4. [**DATABASE MANAGEMENT**]: Systems – *Query processing*

General Terms
Algorithms, Management, Experimentation

Keywords
Data stream, Continuous query, multi-way join processing, Detection-only query

1. INTRODUCTION
Many recent researches for emerging applications such as web click monitoring, sensor data processing and network traffic analysis often need to deal with a data stream which is a massive unbounded sequence of data elements continuously generated at a rapid rate. In these applications, a continuous query represents a specific event and it is generally used to monitor the ongoing change of recent information over infinite data streams. A multi-way join query is employed to monitor a considerable number of source data streams from various remote sites in real-time. Most previous researches [1,2,3,4,5,7,9] focus on devising an efficient multi-way join processing mechanism because a join operator is a blocking operator and it is more expensive than a unary operator like a selection or projection operator. Basically, they use a tree-structured execution plan employed in a conventional database management system. Since the selectivity of a join operation over infinite data streams is mostly unpredictable, they required to employ an adaptive query re-optimization scheme to reorder the evaluation order of the join operations in a query dynamically [6,7,8]. This causes a serious run-time burden because finding the optimal execution plan of a query is NP-complete [6].

A continuous query can be classified into two different types according to its intended usage. One is a *general-purpose continuous query* which produces its results as an output data stream. The result tuples of this type are required explicitly to perform a subsequent task. The other is a *detection-only continuous query* which only monitors the invocation of a particular event corresponding to the specifications of the query. For a query of the second type, neither an intermediate tuple nor a final result tuple needs to be produced, which not only shortens the processing time of a query but also reduces the required usage of memory space. However, there has been no special effort to deal with this type of a query.

This paper proposes a new query evaluation scheme for a detection-only continuous query. In order to present its basic ideas, this paper focuses on how a multi-way path join query is evaluated without generating any intermediate result tuple explicitly as well as reoptimizing its execution plan. First, a matrix-based synopsis is constructed for each source stream of an n-way path join query in which at least one and at most two join predicates are specified on every source stream. Depending on the number of join attributes specified in a source stream, either one or two dimensional matrix-based synopsis is constructed. In addition, a hash function is defined for each join attribute domain. The number of entries in a synopsis is determined in compile time by the number of buckets in the hash function(s) of the join attribute(s) in its corresponding source stream. Every incoming tuple of a source stream is hashed into an entry of its corresponding matrix-based synopsis with respect to its join attribute value(s). Each entry of a matrix-based synopsis for a source stream keeps track of the number of tuples whose join attribute values are currently hashed into the entry.

The proposed scheme employs a *query equation,* a sequence of multiplication operations on matrix-based synopses constructed for the source streams of a query. Based on the order of a query equation, a chunk of newly incoming tuples of each source stream are batch-processed together against those tuples in the windows of the other source streams. For a new batch of each stream, the final result of the equation contains the maximum possible number of the final results for the batch. Therefore, the proposed scheme makes it possible to efficiently detect the invocation of the event that satisfies the specifications of a detection-only query. In addition, the proposed scheme eliminates the need of run-time query re-optimization. This is because the optimal order of matrix multiplication operations in a query equation is determined in compile time. Therefore, a considerable amount of run-time overhead can be avoided. However, the result of a query equation may contain some false positive errors. To guarantee the accuracy of a detection-only query, the accurate final result tuples of the query can be explicitly generated when the result of the proposed scheme fails to satisfy a required accuracy level.

2. Basic Constructs

2.1 Matrix-based synopses

Given an n-way path join query with n source streams $\{S_1, S_2, ..., S_n\}$, a $1 \times m$ matrix-based synopsis M_i is constructed for a source stream S_i which only has a single join attribute A. In order to assign a tuple of the source stream S_i to an entry of the synopsis M_i, a hash function $h(k)$ with m buckets is employed for the attribute A. In other words, a tuple x of S_i is assigned to the $h(x.A)^{th}$ entry of M_i, i.e. $M_i[h(x.A)]$ where $x.A$ denotes the value of the attribute A in x. Likewise, for a source stream S_j with two join attributes 'A_1' and 'A_2', an $m_1 \times m_2$ matrix-based synopsis M_j is constructed. In order to assign a tuple of the source stream S_j to an entry of its synopsis, two distinct hash functions $h_1(k)$ and $h_2(k)$ with m_1 and m_2 buckets are employed for the join attributes A_1 and A_2 respectively. A tuple y of S_j is assigned to the entry $M_j[h_1(y.A_1), h_2(y.A_2)]$ where the attribute A_1 is called as a row attribute of the synopsis while A_2 is called as a column attribute. When two or more attributes of a source stream are used to express a join predicate, a multiple-key hashing function is employed.

Given a hash function h for a join predicate $R.a=S.b$ on two streams R and S, a tuple x of R and a tuple y of S are *buddy tuples* if the hash values of the two tuples x and y are the same, i.e. $h(R.a)=h(S.b)$. Apparently, a pair of two buddy tuples does not always satisfy the join predicate since two or more distinct attribute values can have the same hash value. However in order to satisfy the join predicate, a pair of two tuples should be buddy tuples. Therefore, a concatenated tuple of successive buddy tuples for a path join query can be a candidate for a final result tuple of the query. Such a tuple is called as a *connecting sequence* formally defined in Definition 1.

Definition 1. Connecting sequences

Given a sequence of source streams $<S_1,S_2,...,S_n>$ for an n-way path join query Q whose (n-1) join predicates are $S_1.a_1= S_2.a_1$, $S_2.a_2= S_3.a_2$ ... and $S_{n-1}.a_{n-1}= S_n.a_{n-1}$, a *k-partial connecting sequence* is a list of k source tuples $cs=<c_1,c_2,...c_k>$ each of which is a tuple of a source stream up to the kth stream ($k \le n$). Every tuple in cs is a buddy tuple to adjacent tuple(s). An n-partial connecting sequence is called as a *complete connecting sequence.* □

For example, consider a four-way path join query Q whose predicates are *Stdt.name=Sbj.name, Sbj.sid=Dept.sid and Dept.dept=Prof.dept* over source streams Student *Stdt*, Subject *Sbj*, Department *Dept* and Professor *Prof.* Suppose that the domains of the join attributes *sname, sid* and *dname* are {*Adam, Bill, Sera, John*}, {*C01, C02,...C06*} and {*Math, EE, CS*} respectively. Let the number of buckets for the hash functions of the domains of these attributes be 4, 2 and 3 respectively. Let the current windows of the source streams are shown in Figure 2-(a) where r_i, s_i, t_i and u_i ($1 \le i \le 4$) denote the pointers to the tuples in the window of the source streams. The window synopsis W of a source stream is a matrix-based synopsis for those tuples that are currently in the window of the stream. For the source streams *Stdt, Sbj, Dept* and *Prof*, 1×4, 4×2, 2×3 and 1×3 window synopses are constructed as shown in Figure 2-(c) when the three hash functions of the attribute domains are illustrated in Figure 2-(b).

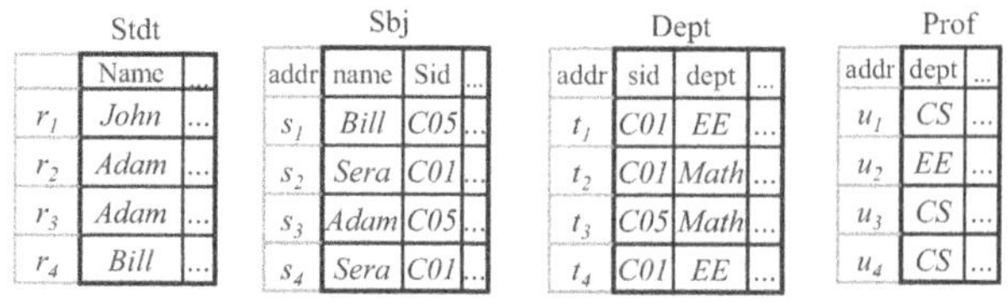

(a) The current windows of source data streams

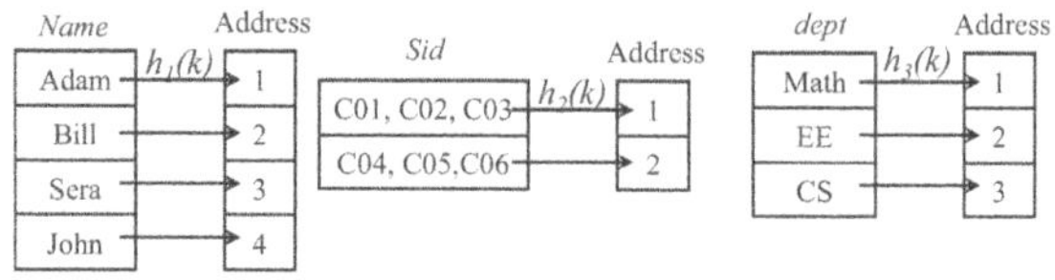

(b) Hash mapping

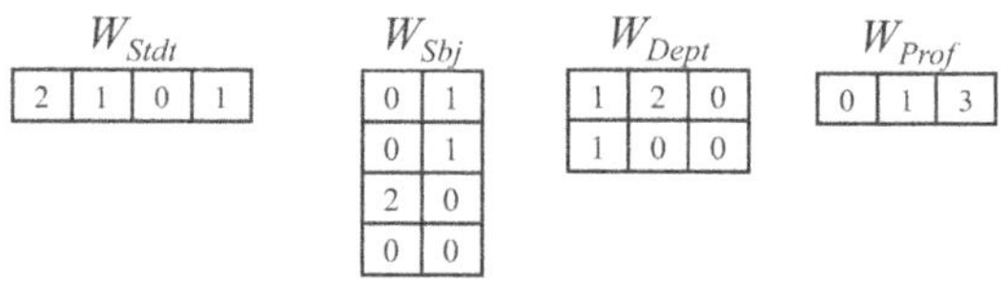

(c) Window synopses

Figure 1. An example of window synopses

2.2 Query equations

The proposed scheme employs two different types of a multiplication operation, *matrix multiplication* (×) and *element-wise array multiplication* (⊗) as follows:

1) Matrix multiplication '×':

Given a $1 \times m_1$ vector synopsis X and an $m_1 \times m_2$ matrix synopsis Y, a $1 \times m_2$ result vector Z is produced by a matrix multiplication $Z = X \times Y$ as follows:

$$Z[j] = \sum_{i=1}^{i=m_1} X[i] \times Y[i,j] \ , \ 1 \le j \le m_2$$

2) Element-wise array multiplication ⊗:

Given two $1 \times m$ vector synopses X and Y, a $1 \times m$ result vector Z is produced by an element-wise array multiplication $Z = X \otimes Y$ as follows:

$$Z[i] = X[i] \times Y[i], \ 1 \le i \le m$$

To estimate the total number of the final result tuples of a query, a *query equation* defined in Definition 2 is formulated.

Definition 2. Query equation

Given an n-way path join query Q whose (n-1) join predicates are $S_1.a_1= S_2.a_1$, $S_2.a_2= S_3.a_2$ ... and $S_{n-1}.a_{n-1}= S_n.a_{n-1}$, its query equation $E(Q)$ is a sequence of multiplication operations (*) on all the window synopses of the query Q by the same order as in the join path of the query as follows:

$$E(Q) = W_1 * W_2 * ... * W_n^T$$ □

The kth multiplication operation (*) in $E(Q)$ becomes an element-wise array multiplication operation (⊗) if W_{k+1} is a $1 \times m$ vector synopsis. Otherwise, it becomes a matrix multiplication operation (×).

3. Query Evaluation

A sliding-window join operation [2] is a typical way of evaluating a join operation over infinite data streams. It is composed of three tasks: *inserting*, *probing* and *invalidating*. In the proposed scheme, a number of consecutive tuples of a source stream form a batch which is a unit of a task. The minimum size of a batch is a single tuple but the size of a batch can be adjusted depending on the current workload. The information about the newly incoming tuples of the new batch of each source stream is maintained separately. For this purpose, an additional matrix-based synopsis for the batch, namely *batch synopsis* (B) is constructed for each source stream. Given an n-way join query Q, to evaluate its query equation $E(Q)$ for the new batch ΔS_i of a source stream $S_i(1 \le i \le n)$, the window synopsis W_i of the stream S_i is replaced by its batch synopsis B_i. This modified query equation is called as a *batched query equation* $E(Q|\Delta S_i)$. The multiplication operations up to the kth synopsis of $E(Q|\Delta S_i)$ result in a partial result vector V_k. Each entry of V_k maintains the number of k-partial connecting sequences hashed into the entry. As a result, the last result vector V_n maintains the total number of complete connecting sequences for the current batch of the query. Therefore, it indicates the maximum possible number of final result tuples.

For a new batch ΔS_i, the following three tasks are performed in sequence for the evaluation of a batched query equation $E(Q|\Delta S_i)$. (1) (*Inserting*) Reset all the entries of B_i. Hash the tuples of the new batch ΔS_i one by one and increment the hashed entries of B_i and W_i respectively. Insert the tuples of ΔS_i into the window of the source stream S_i; (2) (*Matrix multiplying*) Evaluate the batched query, (3) (*Invalidating*) Hash the out-of-window tuples in the window of the source stream S_i one by one and decrement the hashed entry of W_i. Finally, delete the out-of-window tuples.

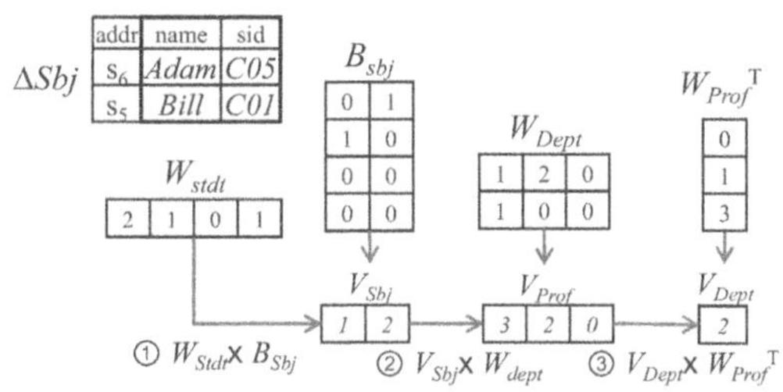

Figure 2. Evaluation of a query equation

```
Input : a batched query equation E(Q|ΔSx) = K1*K2,...,*Km^T
Output : result vectors Vm
Algorithm StaMe
V1 = K1
for i=1 to m-1 do
  If Ki+1 is an 1×n row vector then
    Vi+1 = element-wise-multiplication(Vi, Ki+1);
  Else
    Vi+1 = matrix-multiplication(Vi, Ki+1);
  End if
End for
Return V
```

Figure 3. Pseudo code of the proposed scheme

For example, when a new batch Δsbj in Figure 2 is processed, the batched query equation $E(Q|\Delta sbj) = W_{Stdt} \times B_{Sbj} \times W_{Dept} \times W_{Prof}$ of the query Q is processed as shown in Figure 2. The first matrix multiplication $W_{Stdt} \times B_{Sbj}$ generates a result vector $V_{Sbj}=[1,2]$. This result vector indicates there are 3 partial connecting sequences up to the stream *sbj*. The subsequent matrix multiplication $V_{Sbj} \times W_{Dept}$ produces $V_{Dept}=[3, 2, 0]$. Finally, $V_{Dept} \times W_{Prof}^{T}$ produces $V_{Prof} = [2]$ which indicates there are 2 final connecting sequences. In Figure 3, the precise steps of the proposed scheme are presented.

When the final result vector obtained by the batched query equation $E(Q|\Delta S_x)$ of a query is zero, the query is not satisfied by the new batch ΔS_x. On the other hand, even though the final result vector is non-zero, it cannot guarantee that the query is really satisfied for ΔS_x because the result of the query equation may contain some false positive errors. There are two different causes for the false positive errors. The first one is due to the collisions of a hash function. To measure the effects of this type, the packing density ρ of a window or batch synopsis K is defined as follows:

$$\rho(K) = |K| \big/ v_K$$

where $|K|$ denotes the number of tuples hashed into K and v_K denotes the number of entries in K. As in a hash index, the packing density of a window or batch synopsis influences on the error rate of this type. Therefore, given *a predefined threshold* ε, in order to guarantee the accuracy of the proposed scheme for a detection-only query, the accurate final result tuples of the query should be explicitly generated as in a general-purpose continuous query if the average packing density of the synopses of a batched query equation becomes higher than ε.

The other type of an error is due to batch processing. Since a batch is a unit of invalidating, the window of a source stream may include some out-of-window tuples. These tuples are not deleted because the oldest batch for invalidating has not been fully populated yet. Consequently, the entries of a window synopsis may contain some false positive counts. There is a trade-off between the error rate of this type and the processing time of the proposed scheme, i.e. as the size of a batch gets larger, the error rate is increased while the processing time is shortened.

If a query is not a path join query, it can be divided into a number of sub-queries each of which is a path join query. For each sub-query, its sub-query equation is constructed and every sub-query equation is evaluated individually as described above. Among the final result vectors of these sub-query equations, if at least one result vector is zero, the original query is not satisfied.

4. Performance Evaluation

To illustrate the characteristics of the proposed scheme, the performance of an n-way path join detection-only query is experimented on two synthetic datasets and one real data set [10] obtained by EPFL's SensorScope team. In the synthetic datasets, every data stream has three integer attributes whose values are uniformly distributed in a range $[1,...D_{max}]$ where D_{max} is a join attribute domain. In the experiments, a matrix-based synopsis is additionally implemented by a *bitmap*. A $1 \times m$ synopsis is implemented by a bit vector of m bits. Likewise, an $m \times n$ synopsis is implemented by n bit vectors of m bits. The ith bit of the jth bit vector indicates whether there exists at least one tuple assigned to the $(i,j)^{th}$ entry of the synopsis. This is because there is no need to maintain the actual number of tuples for each entry of a matrix-based synopsis. Only a flag bit is enough for each entry to indicate whether the entry has at least one connecting tuple for the current batch or not. The implementation can significantly speed up the evaluation of a batched query equation because a bitwise *AND* operation is much faster than a matrix multiplication operation. All the algorithms are implemented in C and all the experiments are executed on a Pentium 4 CPU 2.66GHz system with 4GB RAM. The system runs Linux with a 2.6 kernel and gcc 3.3.2.

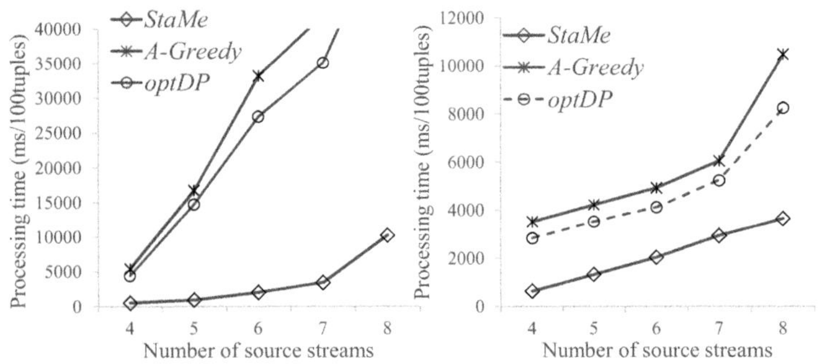

(a) $D_{max} = 200$ (b) $D_{max} = 1000$

Figure 4. Effects of the number of source streams on a synthetic data set

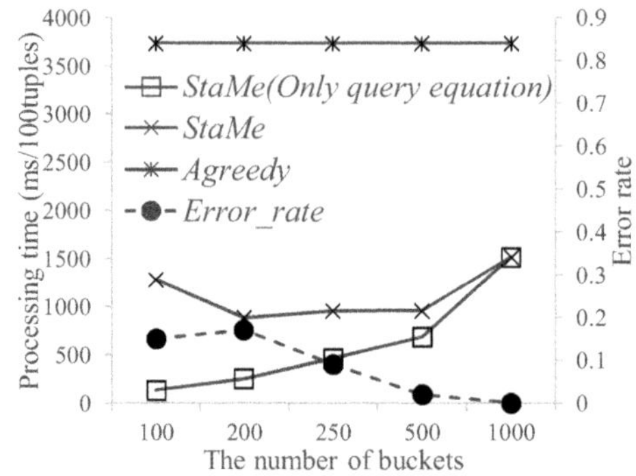

Figure 6. Effects of the number of buckets (D_{max}=1000)

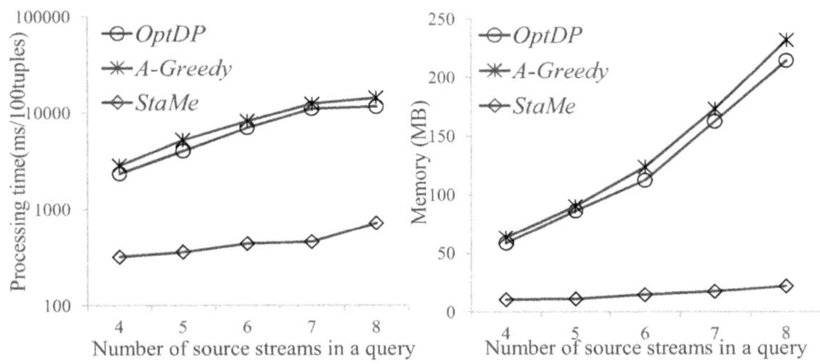

(a) Processing time (b) Memory usage

Figure 5. Effects of the number of source streams on a real data set

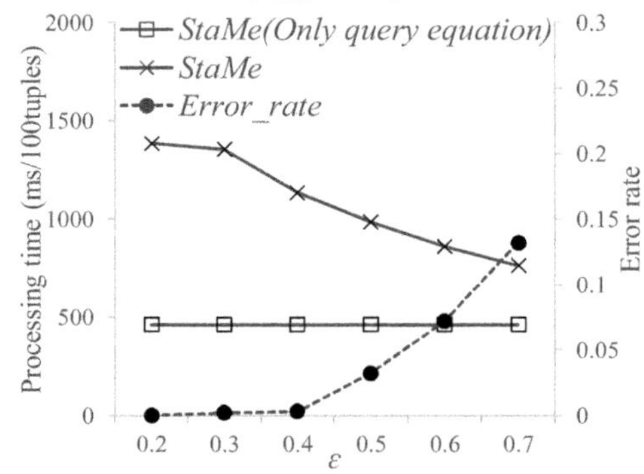

Figure 7. Effects of a packing density threshold (D_{max} = 1000, m = 250)

Figure 4 and Figure 5 illustrate the effects of the number of source streams on synthetic data sets and a real data set respectively. As the number of source streams per query is increased, the proposed scheme *StaMe* performs better than two other algorithms *A-Greedy* [7] and *optDP* [*8*] do in terms of both processing time and memory usage. This is because it only evaluates a query equation without generating any result tuple explicitly.

As mentioned in Section 3, the *StaMe* scheme should generate its result tuples explicitly when its accuracy is not guaranteed. Figure 6 illustrates the overall processing time of the proposed scheme when $\varepsilon = 0.6$ and $D_{max} = 1000$. In this experiment, the input rate of each source stream is varied from 1 to 30 tuples/sec. As the number of buckets for a join attribute domain is increased, the packing density of a join attribute synopsis is decreased, so that the error rate is decreased. However, the processing time of the proposed scheme is increased. Since *A-Greedy* is irrelevant to this factor, its performance remains the same. Figure 7 illustrates the effects of a packing density threshold ε. The error rate of the proposed scheme is increased as this threshold gets larger. This is because generating query result tuples explicitly is less frequently invoked.

5. Conclusion

This paper proposes a new framework for the evaluation of a detection-only query. Based on a query equation of matrix-based synopses, the proposed scheme can avoid generating query result tuples explicitly as well as re-optimizing the execution plan of a query dynamically. Therefore, it can reduce the run-time overhead of continuous query evaluation greatly.

Acknowledgements

"This work was supported by core research program (No. 2011-0016648) and NRL Program (No.2010-0008007) of the Korea Science and Engineering Foundation(KOSEF) grant funded by the Korea government(MEST)."

6. REFERENCES

[1] Y. Yang, D. Papadias "Just-In_Time Processing of Continuous Queries", In ICDE, 2008.

[2] J. Kang, J. F. Naughton, and S. Viglas, "Evaluating window joins over unbounded streams", In ICDE, 2003.

[3] S.Madden, J.M.Hellerstein and et al, "Continuously adaptive continuous queries over streams", In SIGMOD, 2002.

[4] The STREAM groups, "STREAM: The Stanford Stream Data Manager", IEEE Data Engineering Bulletin, 2003.

[5] D.J.Abadi and et al. "Aurora: A New Model and Architecture for Data Stream Management" VLDB Journal, 2003.

[6] H.K.Park, W.S.Lee, Adaptive Continuous Query Re-optimization over Data Streams, IEICE Transactions on Information and Systems E92.D(7), 1421-1428, 2009

[7] S. Babu, R. Motwani, K. Munagala, Adaptive Ordering of Pipelined Stream Filters, ACM, SIGMOD, June 2004.

[8] J. Gomes, H. Choi, Adaptive optimization of join trees for multi-join queries over sensor streams, Information Fusion, Vol. 9. Issue 3. Pp.412-424, 2008.

[9] M.Stern, K.Bohm, E.Buchmann, "Processing Continuous Join Queries in Sensor Networks: a Filtering Approach", In *SIGMOD*, pp.267-278, 2010.

[10] G. Baraenetxea, F. Ingelrest, and et al, Sensorscope: Out-of-the-box environmental monitoring, In IPSN, 2008.

Subject-oriented Top-k Hot Region Queries in Spatial Dataset

Junling Liu
Northeastern University
Shenyang Jianzhu University
Shenyang, China
liujl@sjzu.edu.cn

Ge Yu
Northeastern University
Shenyang, China
yuge@mail.neu.edu.cn

Huanliang Sun
Shenyang Jianzhu University
Shenyang, China
sunhl@sjzu.edu.cn

ABSTRACT

This paper proposes and solves a novel type of spatial queries named *Subject-oriented Top-k hot Region* (STR) queries. Given a subject S defined by a feature set R and features importance denoted by weights, an STR query retrieves k non-overlapping regions that have the highest scores computed by the number of feature objects and their weights. As an example, the culture subject is defined by exhibition halls, libraries and museums. On the subject, an STR query finds cultural centers intensively distributed feature objects. In this paper, we propose two efficient algorithms, single-partition (SP) algorithm and dual-partition (DP) algorithm, to process STR queries. Extensive experiments evaluate the proposed solutions under a wide range of parameter settings.

Categories and Subject Descriptors

H.2.8 [**DATABASE MANAGEMENT**]: Database applications—*Spatial databases and GIS*

General Terms

Algorithms, Performance

Keywords

hot region, top-k, spatial query

1. INTRODUCTION

Spatial query processing has widely been applied to Geographic Information System(GIS), location-based services, the facility location, etc. Typical spatial queries involve: (1) fundamental queries including the spatial point queries, spatial join, range queries etc. [4]; (2) some complex queries such as nearest neighbor and reverse nearest neighbor queries [8]; (3) advanced queries based on spatial attributes, including site rankings and density queries used to locate facilities, spatial decision support applications [3, 9, 11].

In this paper, we study a new type of spatial queries, named *Subject-oriented Top-k hot Region* (STR) queries defined by definition 1. A query region is a square with $l_q \times l_q$ and the length l_q of a square can be a user-specified parameter. We assume $l_q \geq l$, where l is the line length of grid cells.

Definition 1. (**Top-k Hot Region Query**): Given a query region q, subject S. Top-k hot region query retrieves k non-overlapping regions that have the highest subject region scores computed by the number of feature objects and their weights.

Consider an example, we hope to find some cultural centers in a city. Domain experts have provided us the knowledge for defining a culture center. The knowledge describes what spatial objects are considered as features of a cultural center and their importance evaluation contributing to the culture center. Assuming features on this subject include exhibition halls, libraries and museums, and their weights are 0.5, 0.3 and 0.2 represented by different symbols as shown in figure 1. For a square region r, we compute the score according to the numbers of feature objects and their weights. Figure 1 indicates top-3 hot regions are A, B and C with highest scores 1.4, 1.3 and 1.0 respectively. an STR query retrieves k non-overlapping regions with the highest scores at an arbitrary location.

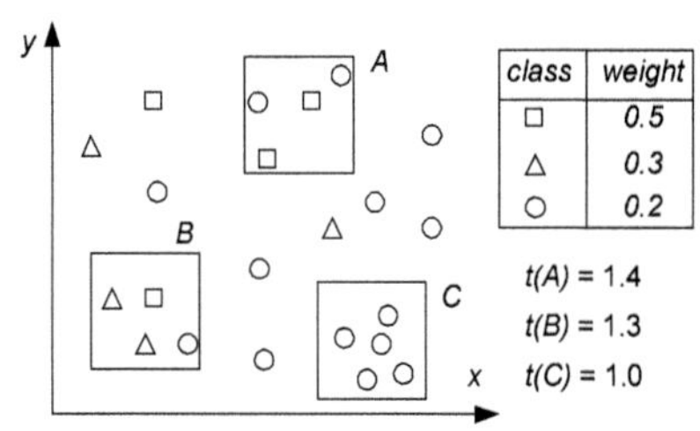

Figure 1: An example of STR query

A typical application of STR query is to evaluate the development of regions on any subject. Also, it can help us to locate services and facilities considering multiple features. STR queries are important in geographic information systems, location-based services, and spatial decision support systems.

Despite the usefulness of STR query, to our knowledge, it has not been studied in the past. The challenge of the problem is to rank regions at any location by multiple feature datasets. The intuitive way is to move a square-shaped window in the space, and to accumulate the scores of all locations by feature objects falling in this window. If there are N feature objects in the space, the basic way will examine N^2 locations, which will spend excessive I/O and CPU cost. As discussed in related work, existing methods can not be applied to solve the problem directly.

As a ranking problem, a progressive processing is an efficient strategy, which first initializes k candidates, updates candidates and prunes the searching regions gradually. The processing efficiency is dominated by two factors including the quality of k candidates and the size of the searching region. Therefore, the targets of this paper are to get k candidates with as high scores as possible and to reduce the searching region.

We propose two efficient algorithms, single-partition (SP) algorithm and dual-partition (DP) algorithm, to process STR queries. Based on a single partitioning, the paper introduces a filtering-refinement algorithm. The algorithm sorts extensive regions by their scores. To get high ρ_k, SP algorithm first visits regions with high scores, which improves the processing efficiency. Furthermore, we explore an optimized algorithm (DP) based on the dual-partition to the space. DP algorithm executes a fine partition on candidate regions intensively distributed feature objects, and shrink candidate regions further by cutting borders not containing results. DP algorithm improves by reducing the searching region and providing a tight pruning bound.

The paper also reports on extensive experimental studies of the proposed algorithms. The results denote that DP algorithm offers an improvement of a factor of in terms of I/O, compared with SP algorithm.

2. RELATED WORK

The object ranking is a popular retrieval task in various applications. [9] processes the problem of ranking top-k sites (service facilities, e.g., supermarkets) based on their influence on feature points(served objects, e.g., residential buildings). The influence of a site p is defined by the sum of weights of feature points considering p as their nearest site. The optimal location queries in [3] retrieves the optimal location in a space based on an objective function. Top-k spatial preference query is a kind of site ranking queries [10].Site ranking queries evaluate the quality of a single point location, not a region, according to surrounding feature objects. However, STR queries evaluate a region by sweeping a square window in the space.

Density queries [7] find regions with a high concentration of objects. The density query is used for monitoring moving objects and identifying regions with traffic jams. STR query is a ranking problem, however, density queries find regions whose density are not lower than a threshold.

Clustering algorithms [1] group objects into clusters by some criteria. Clustering does not focus on the ranking of groups and clusters have non-fixed size and shape. However, STR queries rank regions with a fixed size and shape. As the extension of clustering problems, hot spots detection finds point-event patterns [2]. In hot spots detection, the event frequency or attribute values, e.g., temperature or pressure can be evaluated for clustering hot spots. However, hot region queries evaluate a region by feature object numbers and their weights defined by a subject.

3. ALGORITHMS

We use the grid index to keep the statistics information of feature objects. The information can provide the pruning mechanism. Given a query region q, we can define an extensive region C on the grid index that contains q. If the score of an extensive region C is less than the score ρ_k of $k-th$ current candidate, then C can not generate any result.

The whole space is divided into non-overlapping cells. Cell $c_{i,j}$ denotes the cell on the i row and j column position. For each cell c, we only maintain numbers of feature objects falling in c, denoted by $(n_1,n_2,...,n_m)$. The score of a cell on a subject can be computed by object numbers and weights of related features. We can construct bounds by these scores to prune regions that can not generate results. Each feature dataset is indexed by a single R-tree.

For one cell $c_{i,j}$, we define an extensive region $C_{i,j}$ as definition 2. Extensive region $C_{i,j}$ of cell $c_{i,j}$ is the union of cells that contains cell $c_{i,j}$. $C_{i,j}$ is obtained by extending the breadth of one cell on both width and length, whose size is $(l_q + l) \times (l_q + l)$.

Definition 2. **(Extensive Region)**: The extensive region $C_{i,j}$ of cell $c_{i,j}$ corresponding to q is the union of cells $c_{u,v}$ for which $i \le u \le (i + l_q/l)$ and $j \le v \le (j + l_q/l)$.

Here, we introduce a sweep procedure named as Sweep(C,q,ρ_k), which returns a region r with the highest score ρ_r in C, and ρ_r is larger than ρ_k. If a candidate can not be found in C, a null region is returned. This is a fundamental process for any algorithm proposed later. The algorithm first sorts objects by coordinate x. Then, we move query window from left to right and from bottom to top. At any location, when an object passes the sweep lines (the left and bottom lines of a query window), we count the number of objects and their types, and compute the score. If the score ρ_q is larger than the current maximal score ρ_{max}, then q is assigned to r. After sweeping all location, the algorithm returns r.

3.1 Single-Partition Algorithm (SP)

We will propose a filtering-refinement algorithm by using a single granularity grid. The filtering phase finds top-k candidates in extensive regions. The output of this phase is a list of grid cells of the same sizes as the query region size. The refinement phase find top-k results.

The algorithm examines every extensive region of cells in the order from left to right and from bottom to top to find top-k non-overlapping regions as candidates. For each extensive region C of cell c, the algorithm computes the score ρ_C of C. If ρ_C is larger than ρ_k, it is possible to get a candidate in C. Then, SP executes a sweep procedure to find a region r with the highest score in C. If the score of r is larger than the $k-th$ candidate and does not overlap with candidates, the algorithm inserts r into result list L_c and delete the $k-th$ candidate. If r overlaps with r_i and ρ_r is larger than ρ_i, then update r_i with r. Otherwise, r is discarded.

At the refinement phase, the algorithm finds the results according to the candidates generated at the filtering stage. As discussed above, to output one region in an extensive region will generate overlapping results. In order to find non-overlapping results, we need search a global highest score region k times. After finding a result, the algorithm removes the region of the result, and searches the remaining space to find the next result.

3.2 Dual-Partiton algorithm(DP)

In this section, we will introduce a method, Dual-Partiton algorithm(DP), to improve the processing of STR queries. Algorithm 1 illustrates the details of DP. First, DP sorts 4-cell extensive regions by score descending, and then groups extensive regions with high scores into clusters. For each cluster, the algorithm iteratively calls function $SweepCluster$. After obtaining k candidates and ρ_k, we perform the second clustering, and calls function $SweepCluster$ for searching the other regions.

Before each stage, DP groups connected extensive regions into clusters, and searches in each cluster. DP executes the clustering procedure twice. The first clustering forms some groups that can generate k candidates. When the area of MBRs is larger than k times of the query region, this clustering ends. Next, in these clusters, we finds k candidates. Then, we cluster the other extensive regions whose scores are larger than ρ_k.

Algorithm 1: Dual-partition Algorithm(DP)

input : query region q, grid index, feature objects.
output: k results

sorting 4-cell extensive regions by score descending L_C ;
initial clustering for k candiates;
for *each cluster* G **do**
  invoke SweepCluster(G,q,ρ_k);
clustering extensive regions whose scores are larger than ρ_k;
for *each cluster* G **do**
  invoke SweepCluster(G,q,ρ_k);

Similar to density-based clustering method [6], an extensive region cluster combines all connected extensive regions whose scores exceed a threshold ρ. An extensive region cluster G is represented by the minimum bounding rectangle of all extensive regions in G.

Figure 2 shows 3 clusters G_1, G_2 and G_3 are created, where G_1 is a single 4-cell extensive region, G_2 is formed from 4 extensive regions $C_{1,0}$, $C_{0,1}$, $C_{3,1}$ and $C_{2,2}$, etc. A cluster is denoted by a rectangle boundary similar to MBR in R-tree. In G_1 and G_2, one non-overlapping at most candidate can be output respectively, and G_3 can generate 4 candidate at most. Therefore, in this example, three clusters can create 6 candidates.

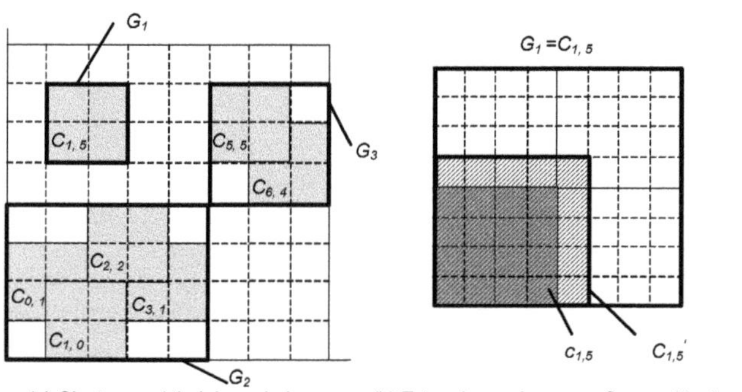

(a) Clusters and their boundaries (b) Extensive regions on a fine partitioning

Figure 2: Clustering and a fine partition

For each cluster G, we partition its MBR by a fine granularity. For instance, a cell is divided into 4×4 cells, cluster G_1 in figure 2(a) is partitioned further into 16×16 cells as shown in figure 2(b). Based on fine partitioning, we can define smaller extensive regions than 4-cell regions. Figure 2(b) shows a new extensive region $C'_{1,5}$ corresponding to cell $c_{1,5}$. In this example, a sweeping region $C'_{1,5}$ with $25/16$ times of the query window is far smaller than $C_{1,5}$ that 4 times of the query window in algorithm 2. Although the method needs to process small extensive regions due to finer partitioning, it also benefits a lots from dealing less objects in small extensive regions.

Algorithm 2 processes a cluster G, and outputs all results in G. First, a shrink procedure is called described in algorithm 3, which gets a small cluster G'. The algorithm sweeps G', if finding a region r, then updates the candidate list L_c and ρ_k by r. A cluster may generate more than one result. After one result is output, $SweepCluster$ processes other regions larger than the query window described in algorithm 2.

Algorithm 3 introduces a shrink function, which is called in algorithm 2. An input cluster G is reduced to a small one G' by cutting boundary region not containing results from four directions. A border b with width of one fine cell can be cut when scores of all extensive regions containing the border cells are less than ρ_k.

Algorithm 2: SweepCluster(G,q,ρ_k)

input : cluster G, q, ρ_k.
output: k non-overlap candidates L_c

G'=Shrink(G,q,ρ_k);
$r \leftarrow$Sweep(G',q,ρ_k);
if $\rho_r > \rho_k$ **then**
  update L_c by r;
  update ρ_k by ρ_r;
  divide G into subclusters;
  for *each subcluster* G_s *larger than* q **do**
    SweepCluster(G_s,q,ρ_k);

Algorithm 3: Shrink(G,q,ρ_k)

input : cluster G, q, ρ_k.
output: a shrinked cluster G

partition G by a fine granularity l_f;
$\rho_{max} \leftarrow \rho_k$;
find C_{max} with the highest score;
$r \leftarrow$Sweep(C_{max},q,ρ_k);
if $\rho_r > \rho_k$ **then**
  $\rho_k \leftarrow \rho_r$;
for *each border b of G from four directions* **do**
  if *scores of all small extensive regions containing cells on b is less than* ρ_k **then**
    $G \leftarrow G$-b;
return G;

Compare with SP algorithm, DP algorithm can obtain the pruning threshold ρ_k and provides tighter pruning bounds. First, DP visits clusters grouped by extensive regions with high scores so that ρ_k can be obtained quickly. Then, large ρ_k benefits the pruning processing. On the other hand, sweeping small extensive regions decreases I/O cost, and provides tighter pruning bounds. In SP algorithm, the pruning condition is the score of a 4-cell extensive region is larger than ρ_k. However, in DP algorithm, the finer partitions provide the tighter bounds. When a cell is divided into 16 parts, the pruning condition is to compare the score in a region of 25/16 times of one cell with ρ_k. If dividing a cell into 16 parts, 81/64 times of one cell, far less than 4 times, is considered.

4. PERFORMANCE EVALUATION

We will evaluate the efficiency and effectiveness of the proposed algorithms, including:SP and DP for top-k hot region queries. All algorithms were implemented in C++, and the experiments were conducted on a Intel(R) Core(TM)2 Duo CPU P8700 2.53 Ghz PC with 3.0GB memory, Window XP Pro. We first describe the experimental settings, and then, introduce the experimental results and findings.

4.1 Experimental settings

We have used both real and synthetic datasets in the experiments and normalize the coordinates of each dimension to $[0, 1]$. The dataset is POI data of California [5], which includes 64 features and 64000 objects expressed by longitude and latitude. We choose some features including school, church, park, building and hospital.

Table 1: Parameter Settings

Parameter	Settings	Default
k	1,5,10,15,20	5
query region size l_q	0.01	0.01
grid size l	0.01	0.01
fine grid size l_f	0.01/8	0.01/8
feature number m	1,2,3,4,5	3
R-tree page size	4k	4k
R-tree buffer number	50	50

We investigate the performance of our proposed algorithms under various settings parameters. The I/O cost and the query cost(CPU) are employed as the major performance metrics. We measure the I/O cost by the number of accessed nodes(containing intermediate nodes and leaf nodes) and the CPU cost by the average response time of an STR query. The parameters used are listed in table 1. In order to evaluate the impact of each parameter, we vary one parameter and fix the others at their default values in each experiment.

Each feature dataset is indexed by R*-tree with 4k page size. The grid index is kept in memory, in which summarized information is stored. When executing a sweeping processing, the algorithm visits objects indexed on R*-tree.

4.2 Performance Study

In order to testify the effectiveness of the algorithms, we list the result of an STR query, where k is 5, $l_q = 0.01$, three features (school, church and park) are included. On POI data of California, we also study the impact of the number of features m and the number of results k by fixing query region size l_q on the efficiency of the algorithm. We vary m between 2 and 5 corresponding to 4 subjects.

Figure 3(a),(b) compare the cost of the algorithms by varying the number of features m. The costs for two methods increases with m, because more feature objects are involved for computing the scores. On I/O cost, DP slightly outperforms SP, because SP need to search a larger area shown in figure 3(a). Figure 3 (b) shows DP spends less CPU time than SP when m increases, because SP induces more computations.

Figure 3(c),(d) compares the performance of SP and DP versus the number of results k. Similar to the experimental results on the single dataset, with the increase of k, the more candidates are kept, which enlarges the searching space of algorithms. So two algorithms spend more I/O and CPU cost when k increases. However, DP is better than SP.

5. CONCLUSIONS

We introduced and solved a new form spatial queries named top-k hot region(STR) queries, which can be applied to regional evaluation and subject findings based on feature objects in spatial datasets. Our contribution is to solve the problem of ranking regions at any location by multiple feature datasets. We proposed an algorithm SP based on a single partition on the space that prunes the regions not containing results by 4-cell extensive regions. An improved algorithm SP was proposed to reduce searching regions further by a fine partition on regions concentrated lots of feature objects. Our experimental results showed that DP outperforms SP since DP applies a dual-partition to shrink searching regions.

6. ACKNOWLEDGMENTS

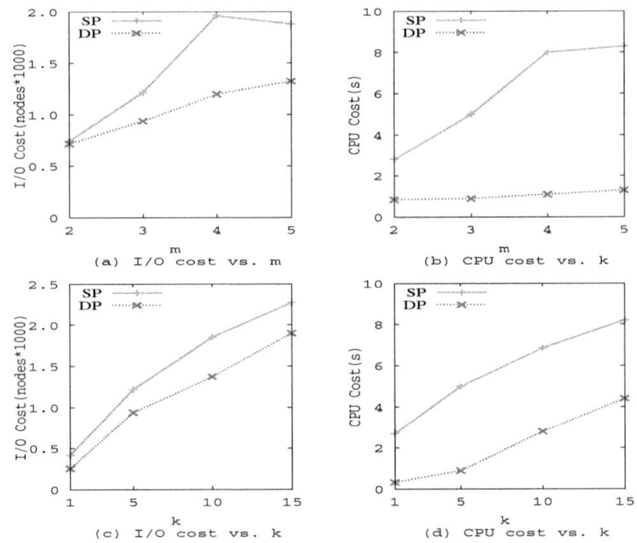

Figure 3: Effects of m and k on POI data

The authors would like to thank all the anonymous reviewers for their helpful comments. The work reported is partially supported by the National Natural Science Foundation of China (61033007, 61070024), the Fundamental Research Funds for the Central Universities(N090104001) and National Key Technology R&D Program of China(2008BAJ08B08).

7. REFERENCES

[1] J. D., E. C.F., and C. C. On supervised density estimation techniques and their application to clustering. In *Proc. of the 15th Annual ACM International Symposiumon Advances in Geographic Information Systems*, 2007.

[2] W. Ding, T. F.Stepinski, R. Parmar, D. Jiang, and C. F. Eick. Discovery of feature-based hot spots using supervised clustering. *Computers and Geosciences*, 35(7), 2009.

[3] Y. Gao, B. Zheng, G. Chen, and Q. Li. Optimal-location-selection query processing in spatial databases. *IEEE Trans. Knowledge and Data Engineering (TKDE)*, 21(8):1162–1177, 2009.

[4] G. R. Hjaltason and H. Samet. Distance browsing in spatial databases. *ACM Trans. Database Systems (TODS)*, 24(2):265–318, 1999.

[5] F. Li, D. Cheng, M. Hadjieleftheriou, G. Kollios, and S.-H. Teng. On trip planning queries in spatial databases. In *Proc. of SSTD*, pages 273–290, 2005.

[6] J. S. X. X. M. Ester, H. P. Kriegel. A density-based algorithm for discovering clusters in large spatial databases. In *Proc. of KDD*, pages 226–231, 1996.

[7] J. Ni and C. Ravishankar. Pointwise-dense region queries in spatio-temporal databases. In *Proc. of ICDE*, 2007.

[8] W.Wu, F.Yang, C.Y.Chan, and K.L.Tan. Finch: Evaluating reverse k-nearest-neighbor queries on location data. In *Proc. of VLDB*, 2008.

[9] T. Xia, D. Zhang, E. Kanoulas, and Y. Du. On computing top-t most influential spatial sites. In *Proc. of VLDB*, 2005.

[10] M. L. Yiu, X. Dai, N. Mamoulis, and M. Vaitis. Top-k spatial preference queries. In *Proc. of ICDE*, 2007.

[11] D. Zhang, Y. Du, and L. Hu. On monitoring the top-k unsafe places. In *Proc. of ICDE*, 2008.

k-Nearest Neighbor Query Processing Method Based on Distance Relation Pattern

Yonghun Park
Dept. of Information and Communication Engineering
Chungbuk National University, Cheongju, Korea
yhpark1119@chungbuk.ac.kr

Dongmin Seo
Dept. of Information Technology Research
Korea Institute of Science and Technology Information
Daejeon, Korea
dmseo@kisti.re.kr

Kyoungsoo Bok
Dept. of Information and Communication Engineering
Chungbuk National University, Cheongju, Korea
ksbok@chungbuk.ac.kr

Jaesoo Yoo*
Dept. of Information and Communication Engineering
Chungbuk National University, Cheongju, Korea
yjs@chungbuk.ac.kr

ABSTRACT

The k-nearest neighbor (*k*-NN) query is one of the most important query types for location based services (LBS). Various methods have been proposed to efficiently process the *k*-NN query. However, most of the existing methods suffer from high computation time and larger memory requirement because they unnecessarily access cells to find the nearest cells on a grid index. In this paper, we propose a new efficient method, called Pattern Based *k*-NN (PB-*k*NN) to process the *k*-NN query. The proposed method uses the patterns of the distance relationships among the cells in a grid index. The basic idea is to normalize the distance relationships as certain patterns. Using this approach, PB-*k*NN significantly improves the overall performance of the query processing. It is shown through various experiments that our proposed method outperforms the existing methods in terms of query processing time and storage overhead.

Categories and Subject Descriptors

H.2.4[Systems]: Query processing

General Terms

Algorithms, Performance

Keywords

Location based services, *k*-Nearest Neighbor queries, query processing methods

1. INTRODUCTION

The Location Based Service (LBS) provides users or other objects with their position related information. Accordingly, the LBS can be applied to various value-added services such as taxi, delivery, and rental services that require the tracking and monitoring of objects. Recently, due to the wide use and development of mobile devices and positioning technologies, the interests in LBS and related technologies from many researchers in different fields have been greatly increased.

In this paper, we propose a new main memory based *k*-NN query processing method. A *k*-NN query can be applied to many LBS applications. For example, when a customer calls a taxi company to take a taxi, the company can find the nearest taxi to the customer and direct it to her or him.

Many different query processing approaches have been proposed. YPK-CNN [1] processes a *k*-NN query in a grid index structure. To get the result of a *k*-NN query, it searches cells overlapped with a certain rectangle while extending the size of its all sides such as top, down, right, and left until the initial *k*-NN is found. CPM [2][3] was proposed to solve the problems of YPK-CNN by applying the best-first search approach to a grid index structure. This method guarantees to visit the nearest cells in the order of the distance between the query point and the cells. To reduce the cost to manage the heap, it inserts the virtually grouped cells around the cell containing the query point. The groups are treated as the internal nodes of a tree index structure. CircularTrip [4] was proposed to resolve the problems of CPM by improving the query performance and by saving the memory resource. CircularTrip also uses a range query processing approach. However, CircularTrip uses circles to find nearest cells while YPK-CNN uses rectangles. In addition, CircularTrip uses a heap structure with the cells overlapped with the circle range to sort the cells in the distance order. Therefore, the method does not search all cells in the heap.

We propose a new Pattern Based *k*-NN (PB-*k*NN) query processing method that overcomes the problems of the existing methods. The proposed method utilizes the Distance Relation Patterns (DRP) for processing a *k*-NN query efficiently. DRP is a set of relative coordinates sorted by the distance between a point in a cell and a point in another cell in ascending order so that the pre-sorted cell lists to be visited can be used in processing a *k*-NN query. In addition, we propose a query index structure using the DRP to reduce the computation cost needed to find the nearest cells in the distance order. In order to show the superiority of the proposed method, we conduct the performance evaluation of PB-*k*NN, CPM and CircularTrip.

The rest of this paper is organized as follows. Section 2 proposes DRP and the new query processing method using DRP. The results of performance evaluation are shown in Section 3. Finally, Section 4 concludes the paper.

* : corresponding author

2. THE PROPOSED *k*-NN QUERY PROCESSING METHOD

The key idea of the proposed method is to make it possible to efficiently visit the nearest cells in sequence using the DRP in the grid structures. By using the pre-sorted cell lists to be visited instead of heap, the proposed method requires much less storage and computation to find the nearest cells than CPM and CircularTrip. Table 1 represents the notations used in this paper.

Table 1. Notations

Notations	Descriptions
PC(p)	The coordinates of point *p* in a cell
CP(r)	The center point of rectangle *r*
ACL(p)	The absolute coordinates list of cells in the order of the closeness from point *p*.
RCL(p)	The relative coordinates list of cells in the order of the closeness from point *p*.
MINDIST()	The minimum distance between two points or a point and a cell
MAXDIST()	The maximum distance between two points or a point and a cell

2.1 Distance Relation Pattern (*DRP*)

DRP is the list of the relative coordinates of cells in the distance order from a certain point in a cell to another point in other cells. We formally define DRP as follows.

Property 1: Given two points p_n and pm in different cells in a grid space, if $PC(p_n) = PC(p_m)$, then $ACL(p_n) \neq ACL(p_m)$ but $RCL(p_n) = RCL(p_m)$.

The property indicates that if arbitrary two points in different cells have the same positions in their cells, their distance relations with other relative cells are the same. Figure 2 shows an example of property 1. Figure 2(a) shows two point p_1, and p_2 that are in different cells but have the same positions in their cells. Figure 2(b) represents the Absolute Coordinate List (ACL) and Relative Coordinate List (*RCL*) of p_1 and p_2, respectively. As shown in Figure 2, $ACL(p_1)$ and $ACL(p_2)$ are not the same but $RCL(p_1)$ and $RCL(p_2)$ are the same.

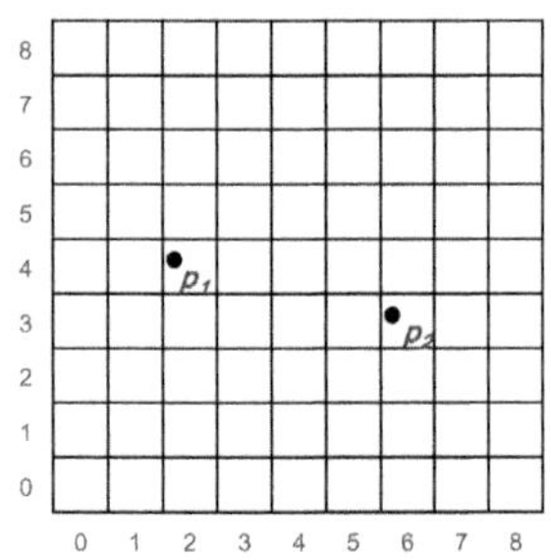

(a) Two points in the index space

Closest Cell list of p_1

$ACL(p_1)$	$RCL(p_1)$
C(2,4)	(0,0)
C(1,4)	(-1,0)
C(2,5)	(0,+1)
C(1,5)	(-1,+1)
C(2,3)	(0,-1)
...	...

Closest Cell list of p_2

$ACL(p_2)$	$RCL(p_2)$
C(6,3)	(0,0)
C(5,3)	(-1,0)
C(6,4)	(0,+1)
C(5,4)	(-1,+1)
C(6,2)	(0,-1)
...	...

(b) *ACL* and *RCL* of p_1 and p_2

Figure 2. Difference between *ACL* and *RCL*

Therefore, all the points with the same coordinates in different cells have the same *RCL* but have the different *ACL*. Using the characteristics, if *RCLs* for all the points in a cell are pre-computed and maintained, it is quite easy to identify the nearest cells sequentially from any points in the grid. But it is infeasible to maintain all *RCLs* because the number of points in a cell is infinite. Therefore, we select only a few points that can be the representatives of the cell space and maintain only a set of *RCLs* for the points.

Here *RCL* is defined as Distance Relation Pattern (*DRP*). We predefine the number of *DRPs* and denote it by N_{drp}. We divide a cell into N_{drp} sub-cells virtually and call the sub-cell *VDC* (Virtually Divided Cell). *DRP* is created only for the center point of each *VDC*. Therefore, the accuracy and storage cost of *DRP* depend on N_{drp}.

2.2 *k*-Nearest Neighbor Query Processing

We propose a *k*-NN query processing method using DRP in this paper. The form of a *k*-NN query is <*qid, query_point, k*>, where *qid* denotes the identifier of the query, *query_point* is its coordinates, and *k* is the number of nearest neighbors. The proposed method also uses additional data structures such as *drp*, *k-dist* and *result_set*, where *drp* is one of DRPs chosen by the *VDC*, *k-dist* is the distance between *query_point* and the kth nearest neighbor, and *result_set* is the set of objects in the *k-dist* from *query_point*. Query processing consists of the following three steps.

Step 1. Creation of *DRPs*

We create a set of *DRPs* according to the predefined N_{drp}. Once the *DRP* is created, it is used permanently because the shape of a grid is never modified.

Step 2. Assignment of a *DRP*

We assign a *drp*, one of the *DRPs* created in Step 1, to the query when the query is requseted. The *drp* is chosen by the *VDC*.

Step 3. Query processing using the *DRP*

Third, the *k*-NN query is processed by using the *drp* assigned in Step 2. Following the relative coordinates in the *drp*, the cells around the *query_point* are visited sequentially until *k*-nearest objects are found.

Figure 4 shows how to process a *k*-NN query using *DRP*. As shown in Figure 4(a), the cells around the *query_point* of a query *q* are visited sequentially based on the assigned *drp* until *k* objects are found. Then, we compute the *k-dist* of *q* and compare the *k-dist* with the distance between the last visited cell and the *query_point*. If the *k-dist* is larger than the distance, the method finds additional cells continuously until the cell whose distance from the *query_point* is less than the *k-dist* is found in the *drp* to guarantee the correct result. This process is shown in Figure 4(b).

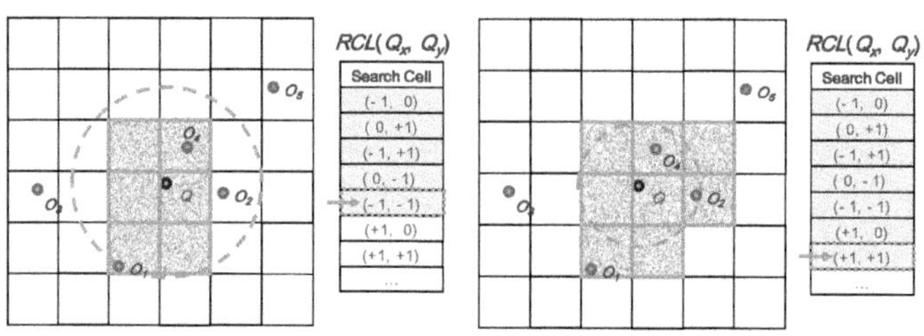

(a) finding 3 objects using *DRP* (b) additional search to guarantee the result

Figure 4. Processing 3-NN queries using *DRP*

The query processing using *DRP* incurs the incorrect distance because of the difference between the *query_point* and the reference point of *DRPs*. We denote the difference by *error_dist*.

To correct the *error_dist*, we use *search_dist*. Equation 1 represents the *search_dist*, where $EQ(q)$ denote the error_dist of a query q. Given a query q, Figure 5 shows the difference between the maximum error distance E and the *error_dist* of q denoted by $EQ(q)$. The *error_dist* is described in Section 2.3 in detail.

$$search\_dist(q) = q.k - dist + EQ(q) \quad (1)$$

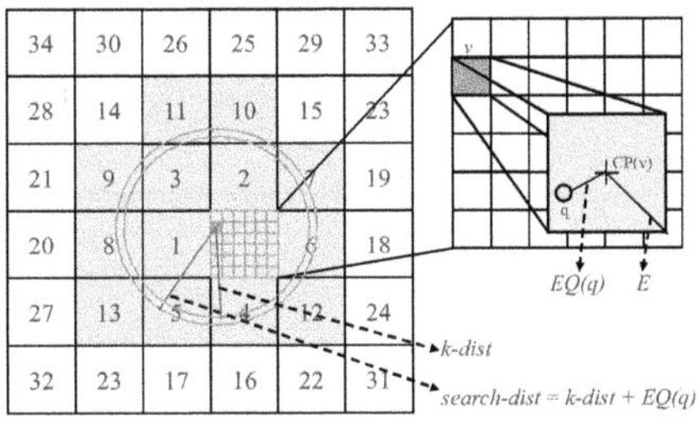

Figure 5. Searching area considering *search-dist*

Figure 6 shows the algorithm to process a *k*-NN query. Once *k*-NN query *q* is requested, we assign a DRP *drp* as specified in line 01 of the algorithm and find the cell C_q which contains the *query_point* (Line 02). Then, the cells are visited sequentially following the *drp* until *k* objects are found. The *k* objects are inserted into *result_set* (Line 05~07). After finding *k* objects, we calculate and update *k-dist* (Line 08). Next, to guarantee that *k* objects are the *k*-NN, the cell search is continued while the condition '$MINDIST(q, drp[q.p_{clr}]) < search\_dist(q)$' is satisfied (Line 09). While visiting the additional cells, *result_set* and *k-dist* are updated whenever the objects that are closer to *q* than *k-dist* are found (Line 14~18).

```
k-NN_Query Processing(q)
// Input = query q
// Output = query result
01 drp = DRP(q)
02 C_q = a cell which contains q.query_point
03 While (k > |q.result_set|)
     // AC makes the coordinates of the cell with the coordinates of drp
04   Ccur = AC(C_q, drp[q.p_drp])
     // OL(c) is the objects list in a cell c
05   For each object o ∈ OL(C_cur)
06     Insert o into q.result_set
07   q.p_drp++
08 Update q.k-dist
09 While (MINDIST(q, drp[q.p_drp]) < search_dist(q))
10   If (q.k-dist < MINDIST(q, C_cur))
11     q.p_drp++
12     continue
13   Ccur = AC(C_q, drp[q.p_drp])
14   For each o, ∀ o ∈ OL(C_cur)
15     If (q.k-dist > MINDIST(o, q))
16       Remove o^k-th from q.result_set
17       Insert o into q.result_set
18       Update q.k-dist
19   q.p_drp++
20 Return q.result_set
```

Figure 6. *k*-NN query processing algorithm

2.3 Error Distance of *DRP*

DRP has little error distance because of the difference between the reference point of the *DRP* and the other points in the same *VDC*. We propose and use *error_dist* to correct the result. Given query *q*, we define the *error_dist* of *q* as Equation 3, where P_{query} is the query point of *q* and P_{ref} is the reference point of the *DRP* of *q*.

$$error\_dist = MINDIST(P_{ref}, P_{query}) \quad (2)$$

The *error_dist* is computed by the triangle-determining conditions. More specifically, given arbitrary three points p_1, p_2, and p_3 on a two dimensional plane, $MINDIST(p_1, p_3) \le MINDIST(p_1, p_2) + MINDIST(p_2, p_3)$ is guaranteed by triangle-determining conditions. To apply the conditions to the relation between points and rectangles, given two points p_1 and p_2 in the same cell and a certain rectangle *b* out of the cell, $MINDIST(p1, b) \le MINDIST(p_1, p_2) + MINDIST(p_2, b)$ is also guaranteed. Therefore, given query *q* and cell *c* that does not include *q.query_point*, and P_{ref} that denotes the reference point of the *DRP* of *q*, the condition $MINDIST(q.query\_point, c) \le MINDIST(q.query\_point, P_{ref}) + MINDIST(c, P_{ref})$ is guaranteed. So that, after visiting all cells on the DRP of q until a cell which is farther than the sum of *k-dist* and *error_dist* is found, there are no cells closer than *q.k-dist* to *q.query_point*. If a side length of a cell is denoted by α, the *error_dist* of a query q and the maximum error distance *E* of the *DRP* when N_{drp} is 4 are shown in Figure 7.

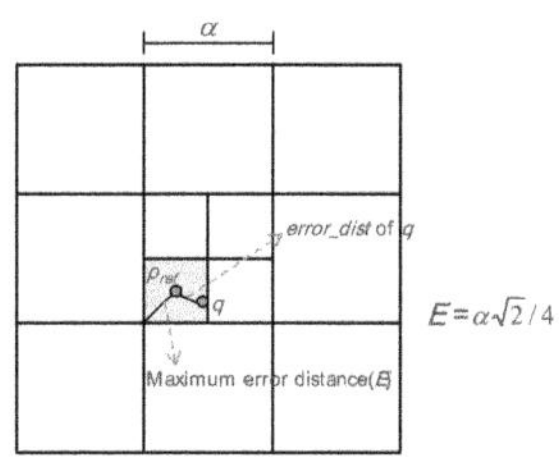

Figure 7. Error distance of *DRP* when N_{drp} is 4

3. PERFORMANCE EVALUATION

In this section, we conducted the performance evaluation to show the characteristics of the *DRP* based *k*-NN query processing method in various environments. For all simulations, we use IBM xSeries 336, 3.2GHz CPU with 2Gbyte memory. The proposed method is denoted by PB-*k*NN.

We measured the effects of storage cost and computation cost according to N_{drp}. Figure 8 shows the relation between the costs and N_{drp}. If N_{drp} is increased, the storage cost is increased. However, a *VDC* becomes smaller and the possible error distance also becomes shorter. It leads to decrease the computation cost since the number of cells to be visited additionally is decreased. The query processing time is very slightly changed since N_{drp} is 4, and the storage cost is increased continuously as N_{drp} is increased. As a result, we decide the default value of N_{drp} as 4.

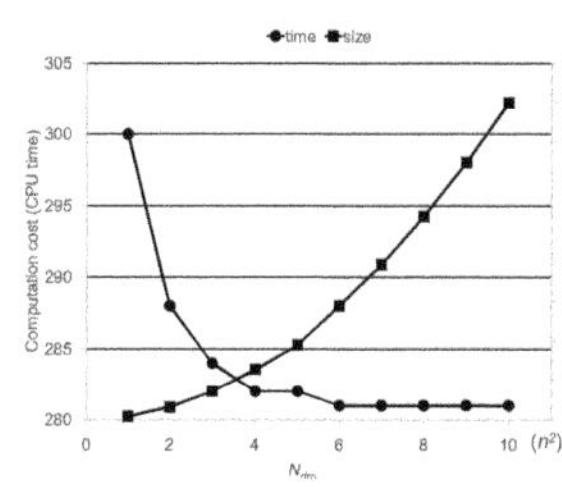

Figure 8. Storage cost and computation cost according to N_{drp} and grid resolution

To decide the appropriate grid resolution, we measure the effects of storage and computation costs according to the grid resolution. Figure 9(a) shows the effects of computation costs according to the grid resolution. As a result, we can see that PB-*k*NN is faster than CPM and CircularTrip regardless of the resolution. If the resolution is too low or high, CPM and CircularTrip become slow because the number of the visited cells to process a query and the number of the objects in a cell are increased. PB-*k*NN is less affected by the resolution of the grid than CPM and CircularTrip. In the experiments, since the most appropriate resolution is 256 x 256 for the environments, we chose the resolution 256x256 as the default resolution of the grid. Figure 9(b) shows the effect of the storage cost required to process queries according to the grid resolution. *BASE* denotes the storage cost without the storage of the query table and *DRPs*. In other words, *BASE* includes only the storage costs for grid and the object table. The data structure of the query table depends on the query processing methods. The query table of CPM keeps the priority queue to find the nearest cells sequentially and the visit list to be used when a query are reevaluated. CircularTrip is the same as CPM except that the query table of CircularTrip does not include the visit list and priority queue. PB-*k*NN uses *DRP* instead of the visit lists and priority queues. However, the storage cost for *DRP* is unlikely to affect the total storage cost because all queries share *DRP*. The storage costs of CPM increase significantly when the grid resolution becomes high since the number of the visited cells is increased and the visited cells are maintained in main memory during the query processing. In the environments, it is shown that PB-*k*NN requires less storage and higher scalability than CircularTrip and CPM.

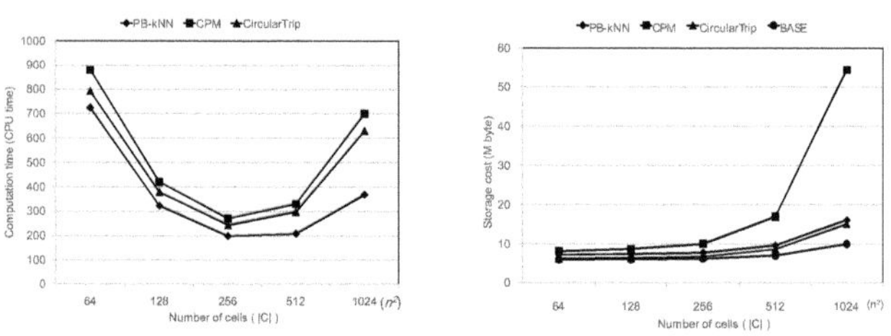

(a) Computation cost (b) Storage cost

Figure 9. Computation and storage cost according to the grid resolution

Figure 10(a) shows the effect of the computation cost according to the number of objects. If the density of objects rises, the computation cost to find the nearest cells decreases because the number of visited cells is increased. This phenomenon occurs in all methods. The computation cost of CPM decreases approximately from 2700 to 270 and the computation cost of CircularTrip decreases approximately from 2400 to 270 while the computation cost of PB-*k*NN decreases approximately from 500 to 200. The query processing time of PB-*k*NN is at least 1.3 and 5 or more times faster than those of CPM and CircularTrip. As a result, it is shown that PB-*k*NN is faster than CPM in all situations regardless of the density of the objects. Figure 10(b) shows the effect of computation cost according to the number of NNs(*k*). We measure the CPU times of the query processing methods when the value *k* changes from 1 to 256. As *k* increases, the query processing times of CPM, CircularTrip, and PB-*k*NN increase as well. However, the increase rates of the query processing time in CPM and CircularTrip are changed more sharply than that in PB-*k*NN. When the value of *k* is 256, PB-*k*NN is about 4 times faster than CPM and CircularTrip. It is expected in the evaluation that the more *k* increases, the more the difference between the computation costs of PB-*k*NN and the existing methods increases.

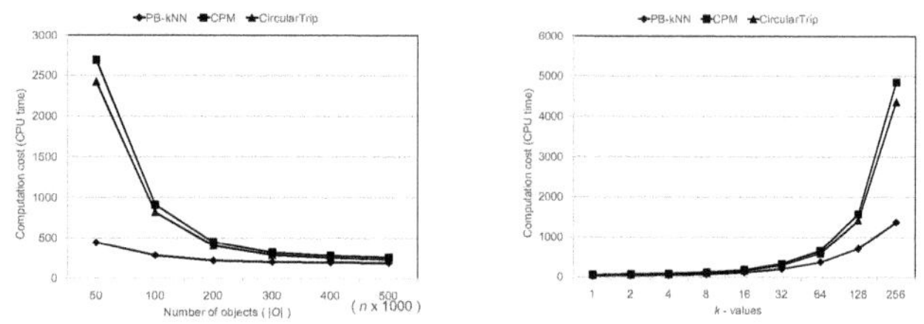

(a) According to the number of objects (b) According to the Number of NNs(k)

Figure 10. Computation cost according to the number of objects and NNs(*k*)

4. CONCLUSTIONS

We have proposed a new method called PB-*k*NN to efficiently process the *k*-NN queries in grid environments utilizing *DRP*, that is, a set of relative coordinates sorted by the distance between certain points in a cell and other cells. Based on our various experiments, the proposed method, PB-*k*NN outperforms the existing methods CPM and CircularTrip. In the future, we will study on other query processing algorithms such as reverse NNs using *DRP*

5. ACKNOWLEDGMENTS

This work was supported by the Ministry of Education, Science and Technology Grant funded by the Korea Government (The Regional Research Universities Program/Chungbuk BIT Research-Oriented University Consortium) and Basic Science Research Program through the National Research Foundation of Korea (NRF) grant funded by the Korea government (MEST)(No. 2009-0080279).

6. REFERENCES

[1] X. Yu, K. Pu, and N. Koudas, Monitoring k-nearest Neighbor Queries over Moving Objects, In Proc. Intl. Conf. Data Engineering, pp.631-642, 2005.

[2] K. Mouratidis, M. Hadjieleftheriou, and D. Papadias, Conceptual Partitioning: An Efficient Method for Continuous Nearest Neighbor Monitoring, In Proc. ACM Conf. Management of Data, pp. 634-645, 2005.

[3] K. Mouratidis and D. Papadias, Continuous Nearest Neighbor Queries over Sliding Windows, IEEE Transactions on Knowledge and data Engineering (TKDE), 19(6), pp.789-803, 2007.

[4] M. A. Cheema, Y. Yuan, and X. Lin, CircularTrip: An Effective Algorithm for Continuous kNN Queries, In Proc, Intl. Conf. Database systems for Advanced Applications (DASFAA), 2007.

Efficient Query Rewrite for Structured Web Queries

Sreenivas Gollapudi Samuel Ieong Alexandros Ntoulas Stelios Paparizos
Microsoft Research, Silicon Valley
{sreenig, saieong, antoulas, steliosp}@microsoft.com

ABSTRACT

Web search engines incorporate results from structured data sources to answer semantically rich user queries, i.e. '`Samsung 50 inch led tv`' can be answered from a table of television data. However, users are not domain experts and quite often enter values that do not match precisely the underlying data, so a literal execution will return zero results. A search engine would prefer to return at least a minimum number of results as close to the original query as possible while providing a time-bound execution guarantee. In this paper, we formalize these requirements, show the problem is NP-Hard and present approximation algorithms that produce rewrites that work in practice. We empirically validate our algorithms on large-scale data from a major search engine.

Categories and Subject Descriptors: H.3.3 [Information Search and Retrieval]: Information Search and Retrieval—Retrieval model

General Terms: Algorithms, Experimentation

1. INTRODUCTION

Web users commonly look for results beyond the traditional web pages and often their need is covered via the use of semantic information that comes from (semi-)structured data sources. For example, consider queries such as electronic goods (e.g. '`50 inch samsung led tv`'), fashion (e.g. '`$1600 prada handbags`'), or movie-showtimes listings (e.g. '`avatar showtimes near san francisco`').

A major challenge in using structured data to answer keyword queries is that users often lack domain expertise and may pose queries that lead to very few or no results. For example, consider the query '`50 inch samsung led tv`'. There exists work in the literature [9] that can correctly classify and semantically interpret the query to attribute-value pairs that correspond to underlying structured attributes. So the query can be thought as (`50 inch` ⇒ `display size`, `Samsung` ⇒ `Brand`, `led tv` ⇒ `display type`). However, if the query is directly evaluated as specified, there will be no results that can satisfy the interpretation as Samsung does not make 50-inch LED TVs. On the other hand, Samsung makes *46-inch* and *55-inch LED* TVs and 50-inch *PLASMA* TVs. Arguably, the users would prefer to see such results that are close to their original query instead of looking at an empty page with no results because they did not know the appropriate precise values when typing the query.

We are interested in rewriting the queries through semantic term expansion. For example, the above query may be rewritten as '`(46 to 55 inch) (samsung or sony) (led or plasma) tv`'. The quality of the rewrites depends on two factors. First, the rewritten query should preserve the meaning of the original query as closely as possible. We measure the fidelity of the rewrite by computing how far away the set of results retrieved are to the original query, as estimated by user preferences learned through click logs. Second, the rewritten query should ensure there are sufficiently many results returned to the user. We measure the coverage of the rewrite by counting how many times when a certain number of results is requested, the expectation is met.

If efficiency had not been an issue, a candidate solution would have been to expand the terms a little at a time, issue the rewritten query to the index, and repeat as necessary until the minimum number of results requested is retrieved. This solution would not be applicable to web search, however, as users expect results to be returned in half a second or less, thus placing a strict performance requirement on the query rewriting component. Hence, many search engines place a restriction on the number of re-written queries that can be issued to the index as part of the original query execution. To ensure this requirement is met, we require that the techniques may only use precomputed statistics of the index but may not access the index at run time more than once to execute the final query. Similarly, we also require that the techniques can take an input parameter that limits the number of alternative rewrites they can examine.

In this paper, we formulate the above problem as time-bound query rewriting for structured web queries. As part of our contributions we formally describe an optimization framework that takes as input a candidate query q, a desired number of results k, and a parameter T that governs how many rewrites can be considered, and produces a rewritten query that aims to retrieve at least k results as close to the original query as possible. We show that finding the optimal solution to this problem is NP-Hard and introduce a greedy and a dynamic programming solution that rewrite the query in a principled and controlled fashion. We evaluate the proposed solution using real queries from a commercial search engine's shopping vertical against a prototype commerce search engine.

CIKM'11, October 24–28, 2011, Glasgow, Scotland, UK.

2. RELATED WORK

Structured data is abundant on the web, and there have been studies on how to retrieve them in a manner suitable to web search [3, 4]. Fontoura *et al.* proposed a method to relax text queries using taxonomies [5]. Finally, given a query and a distance function, one can think of the problem we are trying to solve as a nearest neighbor problem. Nearest neighbor problems have been studied in the past, for example [8]. Similar to the k-nearest neighbors, but from a join relaxation problem in databases is the work described in [6]. We find such work very valuable in relaxing the user query and finding good quality results within a reasonable distance around what was specified in the query. However, it is not clear how these techniques will perform under strict time constraints like ours.

3. PROBLEM FORMULATION

We first describe a model of structured web queries, and assumptions on how they are parsed, and how items are evaluated with respect to the parsed queries. We then formally define the problem of time bound query rewrites.

3.1 Model

Given a keyword web query, we assume the existence of a semantic parser that identifies the attributes requested in the query and extracts their associated desired values, based on past work such as [9]. For example, the query '`50 inch samsung led tv`' is parsed as a *structured query* {*table:TV, brand:Samsung, type:LED, diagonal:50*}. Denote a generic parsed query by its attribute-value pairs, $q = \{a_1 : v_1, a_2 : v_2, \ldots, a_m : v_m\}$. Denote the value of attribute a_i in query q by q_{a_i}. For our example query, q_{brand} = Samsung. Consistent with the interpretation of web queries as conjunctions of keywords, we interpret the structured query under the AND-semantics as well.

Let P be a database of items, from which we retrieve results to serve the query. For each item $p \in P$, we represent it as a set of attribute-value pairs $\{a_1 : w_1, a_2 : w_2, \ldots, a_n : w_n\}$, and the value of attribute a_i by p_{a_i}. We assume that the semantic parser will only identify attributes for which we have data, hence the query specifies the values of a subset of these n attributes. Henceforth, given a query, we only focus on the m attributes mentioned.

As discussed in the Introduction, users may lack domain expertise and may be unfamiliar with the attribute specification of the underlying structured data. As a result, they may issue queries for which there exists no match in the database. Nonetheless, it is desirable that a search engine should return results that are close to the query. Our objective is to develop a formal framework that allows one to investigate how best to rewrite the user query in order to retrieve good results for the user efficiently.

To make the discussion formal, denote the domain of attribute a_i by A_i. Let the function $d_i : A_i \times A_i \to [0, 1]$, $d_i(v, w)$ measures the distance of attribute value w from attribute value v. When $d_i(v, w)$ is small, it means that attribute value w is similar to attribute value v. We note that our solution does not depend on assumptions such as symmetry or triangle-inequality about the distance function.

An aggregate distance function $ad : P \times Q \to \mathbb{R}$, $ad(p, q)$ measures how well item p matches query q. When $ad(p, q)$ is small, it means item p matches the query q well. We assume that the function depends only on the attribute values of the item and the query. We next define a basic yet fundamental property of aggregate distance functions that we assume throughout the paper.

DEFINITION 1 (MONOTONICITY). *An aggregate distance function, $ad(\cdot)$, is* monotonic *if for any query $q = \{a_1 : v_1, a_2 : v_2, \ldots, a_m : v_m\}$, any two items p^1 and p^2, if*

$$\forall 1 \leq i \leq m, \qquad d_i(v_i, p^1_{a_i}) \geq d_i(v_i, p^2_{a_i}) \ ,$$

then $ad(p^1, q) \geq ad(p^2, q)$.

Monotonicity ensures that an item closer to the query in each of the attributes will also be closer to the query in aggregate distance. This is a natural property that should be satisfied when the attribute distances determine how well an item matches a query.

3.2 Query Rewrite Formulation

Given a query q, our ultimate goal is to find the top-k items that match the query within a fixed time window. In order to find the top-k items, we must first be able to select at least k items from the database. This may not be possible when there are less than k items that match all the desired attribute values. The focus of our work is on how to rewrite the query in a principled way so as to ensure sufficiently many items are returned, keeping fidelity to the original query, while respecting the time constraints imposed on the individual components of a search engine.

For a given attribute-value pair $a_i : v$ and value $\delta \in [0, 1]$, let $B_i(v, \delta)$ be the set of attribute values that is δ-close to v, i.e.,

$$B_i(v, \delta) = \{w \in A_i | d_i(v, w) \leq \delta\} \ . \qquad (1)$$

In other words, $B_i(v, 0)$ are the set of attribute values that are equivalent to v, whereas $B_i(v, 1)$ are the set of all attribute values.

Denote a *relaxed query* q by $\{a_1 : v_1 \pm \delta_1, a_2 : v_2 \pm \delta_2, \ldots, a_m : v_m \pm \delta_m\}$. An item p matches q if and only if

$$\forall 1 \leq i \leq m, \qquad p_{a_i} \in B_i(v_i, \delta_i) \ .$$

The goal of the rewriting structured web query is to take an input query and find a relaxed query that will result in at least k matches in the database. If time had not been an issue, a simple solution would be to iteratively make small relaxation to the query, issue it to the database to find out the number of matches, and repeat until we have found k results. However, due to the performance requirement imposed by web search, this approach is infeasible as database access is costly. Indeed, an algorithm may only be able to carry out a few computations within the time envelope.

To capture these limitations, we propose to bound the time of any solution by the *number of different relaxed queries* it considers, and include this as an explicit parameter to the problem specification. To ensure that this meaningfully reflects the performance requirement and is helpful in differentiating among solutions, we require that the amount of time it takes to evaluate each relaxed query to be constant. Note that different forms of evaluating the relaxation will lead to different classes of problems.

In this paper, we focus on evaluating the relaxed query using database histograms. Histograms are one of the most common and important statistics of an attribute used in databases. We now describe how they can be used to estimate the number of potential matches to a query without direct database access.

Formally, let the histogram of attribute a_i be h_i, and that for a set of attribute values $V \subseteq A_i$, $h_i(V)$ returns the number of items that have the corresponding attribute value.

Assuming the attributes in the query are independent, one can estimate the number of matches to a relaxed query as follows. For a query $q = \{a_1 : v_1 \pm \delta_1, a_2 : v_2 \pm \delta_2, \ldots, a_m : v_m \pm \delta_m\}$, the estimated number of matches equals

$$\textsc{Est}(q) = |P| \prod_{i=1}^{m} \frac{h_i(B_i(v_i, \delta_i))}{|P|} . \quad (2)$$

When attributes are dependent, the estimate could be misleading. Functional dependencies may help to improve the estimate. A discussion of how they can help with estimation is beyond the scope of this paper.

Using histograms, we define our time-bound query rewrite problem using histogram statistics as follows.

DEFINITION 2 (QUERY-REWRITE-HISTOGRAMS). *Given*
(1) A query $q = \{a_1 : v_1, a_2 : v_2, \ldots, a_m : v_m\}$;
(2) Database size $|D|$;
(3) Histograms h_i *for each attribute* a_i;
(4) The minimum number of items to return, k;
(5) The maximum number of relaxed queries considered, T.
Find a relaxed query $q' = \{a_1 : v_1 \pm \delta_1, a_2 : v_2 \pm \delta_2, \ldots, a_m : v_m \pm \delta_m\}$ *with at most* T *relaxed queries considered, such that* $\textsc{Est}(q')$ *is at least* k, *and that the total amount of relaxation,* $tr(q') = \sum_{i=1}^{m} \delta_i$, *is minimized.*

Note that ideally we would like to minimize the maximum aggregate distances of the set of selected items to a query. Unfortunately, the maximum aggregate distance cannot be estimated using histograms alone. Therefore, we instead focus on bounding the aggregate distance by controlling the total amount of relaxation as defined above.

We end by noting that the problem of QUERY-REWRITE-HISTOGRAMS is closely related to knapsack problems, and is hard to solve optimally.

THEOREM 1. QUERY-REWRITE-HISTOGRAMS *is NP-hard, even when there is no limit on the number of relaxations.*

4. ALGORITHMS FOR QUERY REWRITES

We present two algorithms for QUERY-REWRITE-HISTOGRAMS and discuss their trade-offs.

Greedy-Rewrite. A general template for solving QUERY-REWRITE-HISTOGRAMS is to (1) select an attribute based on some criteria, (2) relax it by a small amount ϵ to get relaxed query q, (3) compute the estimate $\textsc{Est}(q)$, and (4) repeat as long as $\textsc{Est}(q) < k$. Different selection criteria give rise to different heuristics.

In GREEDY-REWRITE, we select an attribute to relax based on how constraining the attribute is. Formally, for a relaxed query $q = \{a_1 : v_1 \pm \delta_1, a_2 : v_2 \pm \delta_2, \ldots, a_m : v_m \pm \delta_m\}$, we pick the most constraining attribute, a_i where

$$h_i(B_i(v_i, \delta_i))$$

is the smallest to relax.

If at the end of having evaluated T relaxed queries and none is found to have an estimated number of matches of at least k, the last relaxed query (i.e., the one with the largest amount of relaxation) is returned.

DP-Rewrite. Drawing on ideas similar to the dynamic program for knapsack-style problems, we also consider a dynamic programming heuristic DP-REWRITE. For a query $q = \{a_1 : v_1, a_2 : v_2, \ldots, a_m : v_m\}$, let

$F(j, d)$ = Maximum fraction of products satisfying the relaxed query on attributes $a_1, \ldots, a_j$ with total relaxation $\sum_{i=1}^{j} \delta_i \le d$.

Let ϵ be a parameter to the heuristic that determines the step size, i.e., by what increment we increase the relaxation of an attribute. For each cell in $F(\cdot, \cdot)$, we need to consider one new relaxation. Therefore, for a given maximum number of relaxations T, we can consider only $\rho = \lfloor \frac{T}{m} \rfloor$ different values for each attribute. Hence, we compute $F(j, d)$ using dynamic programming as described in Algorithm 1.

Algorithm 1 Dynamic program for Query Rewrite Using Histograms, with step size ϵ and $\rho = \lfloor \frac{T}{m} \rfloor$.

for $d \leftarrow 0, \epsilon, 2\epsilon, \ldots, \min(\rho\epsilon, 1)$ **do**
  $F(1, d) \leftarrow \frac{h_1(B_1(v_1, d))}{|P|}$
end for
for $j \leftarrow 2$ to m **do**
  for $d \leftarrow 0, \epsilon, 2\epsilon, \ldots, \min(\rho\epsilon, j)$ **do**
    $F(j, d) \leftarrow \max_{d'=0,\epsilon,\ldots,\min(d,1)} \left(\frac{h_j(B_j(v_j, d'))}{|P|} F(j-1, d-d') \right)$
  end for
end for

The optimal solution is given by $\min_{d'} F(m, d')$ for which the value is at least $\frac{k}{|D|}$. The amount of relaxation for each attribute can be kept track of by an auxiliary table.

Similar to GREEDY-REWRITE, if no relaxed query with an estimated number of matches of at least k is found at the end of having evaluated T relaxed queries, the relaxed query with the largest amount of relaxation is returned.

Trade-off Between the Algorithms. There is a trade-off between the algorithms. On the one hand, for any fixed ϵ, if the number of relaxed queries allowed is large, DP-REWRITE is guaranteed to find a relaxed query q with $tr(q)$ no larger than the one found by GREEDY-REWRITE. However, when the number of relaxed queries allowed is small, DP-REWRITE will only be able to investigate solutions of small total amount of relaxation, and may fail to find a solution when GREEDY-REWRITE may succeed.

5. EXPERIMENTAL EVALUATION

In this section, we study the behavior and performance of our algorithms on effectively rewriting real user queries.

5.1 Experimental Setup

For our experimental evaluation we built a prototype search engine and we populated it with real data from the shopping vertical of a commercial search engine. To this end, we downloaded the detailed descriptions for about 5 million products related to 73 categories about electronics (such as Televisions, Equalizers, GPS Receivers, etc.) from [2]. Each product was retrieved in structured form, with its attribute and values clearly specified (e.g. [1]). We indexed the product details and computed the histograms for their attributes.

We randomly sampled $1K$ commerce queries from the logs of a commercial search engine and selected the 343 queries that returned too few results as our test set.

For our performance metric we used the average distance of all items within our result set (MEAN-DIST). The distance is computed as the average of pair-wise attribute distances between a given product and the query. The distances

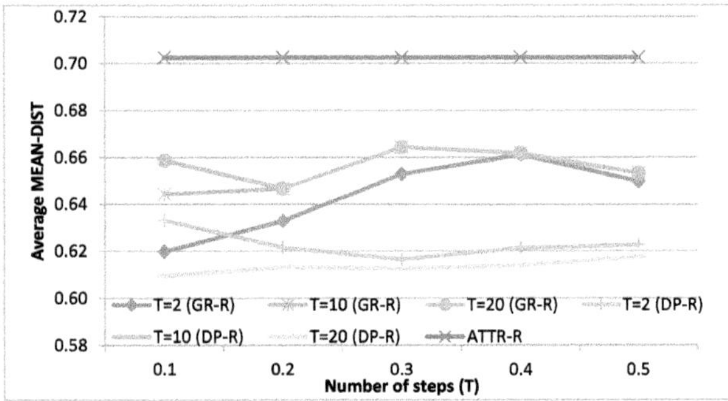

Figure 1: Effect of step size ϵ on avg Mean-Dist

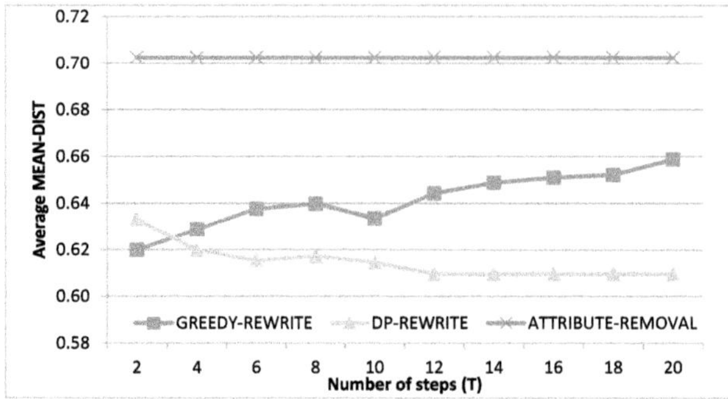

Figure 2: Change in avg Mean-Dist with time steps

between attribute values are estimated from search logs using the technique described in [7]. In general, the lower the MEAN-DIST the better the performance of an algorithm. Finally, we set the number of returned results to 10.

As a baseline, we implemented an approach similar to that of `amazon.com`, named ATTRIBUTE-REMOVAL. This approach rewrites a query that returns few results by directly dropping keywords. In our case, we implemented a version that removes attributes from the structured interpretation of the query. More specifically, we select the attrbute which is the most constraining to be dropped from the query.

5.2 Results

We start our experimental evaluation by studying the effect of the step size ϵ in the performance of our query rewrite algorithms. Both GREEDY-REWRITE and DP-REWRITE use a parameter ϵ that determines the amount of relaxation of an attribute at a step of the algorithm. To study this effect in more detail, we evaluate our algorithms over our data and we plot the graphs shown in Figure 1. The results for ATTRIBUTE-REMOVAL are not affected by the step size ϵ or the number of steps T. We evaluated our algorithms for increasing amounts of rewrites with a maximum of 20. Our goal was to ensure that they would consider rewrites that would return at least 10 results. Overall, for GREEDY-REWRITE, we observe that an increasing step size leads to lower performance for all number of steps allowed.

For DP-REWRITE however, we observe two different trends. First, for small number of steps, DP-REWRITE faces a trade-off in choosing the step size. When the step size is small, DP-REWRITE fails to find rewrites that retrieve at least 10 results. However, when it is larger, DP-REWRITE finds rewrites that obtain at least 10 results, but with large total amount of relaxation across all attributes. Hence, we observe a U-shaped curve for smaller number of steps. When the number of steps is larger, the performance of DP-REWRITE is closer to monotonically increasing with the step size, as relaxations of at least 10 results are found for any step size, and hence smaller step sizes lead to better performance.

We now turn to study the performance of our algorithms in terms of the number of steps that they are allowed. To this end, we fixed the step size to 0.1 and examined the performance for increasing step values. We show the results in Figure 2. Our first observation is that both GREEDY-REWRITE and DP-REWRITE perform substantially better than ATTRIBUTE-REMOVAL. The second observation is that more steps do not necessarily translate to better performance. GREEDY-REWRITE performs worse as the number of steps increases. This is an artifact of the understimation of the number of results during the relaxation. In this case, GREEDY-REWRITE will continue to relax beyond the point necessary, leading to a set of results with higher MEAN-DIST, even though a run with smaller number of steps would terminate with a relaxed query leading to lower MEAN-DIST. Indeed, the performance of GREEDY-REWRITE deteriorates after 10 steps since the additional relaxation of the attributes only adds more unrelated results to the final set.

In contrast, for DP-REWRITE, increasing the number of steps leads to steady improvements in MEAN-DIST. While in principle DP-REWRITE may be affected by the aforementioned problem for GREEDY-REWRITE due to underestimation, it is less affected by poor estimation compared to GREEDY-REWRITE because it explores the space of relaxed queries more broadly. Nonetheless, after about 12 steps, the quality of results does not gain any further improvement improve since the algorithm seems to identify the same relaxed query regardless of the number of steps.

6. CONCLUSION

In this paper we propose a query-rewrite framework for answering structured web queries when users pose queries that would have led to very few results. Our framework takes into account the stringent time requirement of answering web queries, and balances it with the need of retrieving results close to the user queries. We describe two approaches to solving this problem, and show experimentally that both solutions produce meaningful results given our constraints.

7. REFERENCES

[1] Msn shopping xml api: Specs. `http://shopping.msn.com/xml/v1/getspecs.aspx?itemid=1202956773`.

[2] Msn shopping xml api: Televisions. `http://shopping.msn.com/xml/v1/getresults.aspx?bcatid=4724`.

[3] M. Bergman. The deep web: Surfacing hidden value. *Journal of Electronic Publishing*, 7(1), 2001.

[4] M. J. Cafarella, A. Y. Halevy, D. Z. Wang, E. W. 0002, and Y. Zhang. Webtables: exploring the power of tables on the web. *PVLDB*, 1(1):538–549, 2008.

[5] M. Fontoura, V. Josifovski, R. Kumar, C. Olston, A. Tomkins, and S. Vassilvitskii. Relaxation in text search using taxonomies. *PVLDB*, 1(1):672–683, 2008.

[6] N. Koudas, C. Li, A. K. H. Tung, and R. Vernica. Relaxing join and selection queries. In *VLDB*, 2006.

[7] D. Panigrahi and S. Gollapudi. Result enrichment in commerce search using browse trails. In *WSDM*, 2011.

[8] N. Roussopoulos, S. Kelley, and F. Vincent. Nearest neighbor queries. In *Proc. SIGMOD Conf.*, June 1995.

[9] N. Sarkas, S. Paparizos, and P. Tsaparas. Structured annotations of web queries. In *SIGMOD Conf.*, 2010.

Rule-based Construction of Matching Processes

Eric Peukert
SAP Research Center Dresden
01187 Dresden, Germany
eric.peukert@sap.com

Julian Eberius
Dresden University of Technology
Dresden, Germany
julian.eberius@tu-dresden.de

Erhard Rahm
University of Leipzig
Leipzig, Germany
rahm@informatik.unileipzig.de

ABSTRACT
Semi-automatic schema matching systems have been developed to compute mapping suggestions that can be corrected by a user. However, constructing and tuning match strategies still requires a high manual effort. We therefore propose a self-configuring schema matching system that is able to automatically adapt to the given mapping problem at hand. Our approach is based on analyzing the input schemas as well as intermediate match results. A variety of matching rules use the analysis results to automatically construct and adapt an underlying matching process for a given match task. The evaluation shows that our system is able to robustly return good quality mappings across different mapping problems and domains.

Categories and Subject Descriptors
D.2.12 [**Interoperability**]: Data mapping

General Terms
Algorithms

Keywords
Matching system, rewrite rules, features, matching process

1. INTRODUCTION
Finding mappings between complex metadata structures is a critical task in a number of domains such as data integration, ontology alignment or model transformation. A multitude of schema matching systems and matching algorithms were proposed (see [1] for an overview) to speed up that process. Except for some domain-specific matchers, the algorithms used in the different systems are often similar, e.g. they consider the linguistic and structural similarity of schema elements or the similarity of instance data. Many systems are constructed for a single schema type or domain and may even be tuned for specific benchmarks such as the OAEI Benchmark [5]. Moreover, schema matching publications typically report the maximally achieved quality of automatically computed mapping suggestions using some specially tuned parameter configuration. This construction and tuning is a complex, manual and time-consuming task that often requires substantial matching experience and expert knowledge as well as given perfect mappings.

However, such an approach cannot be adopted for applying a schema matching system in practice onto fully unknown matching problems. Additionally, given default configurations may not be robust enough to cope with largely differing matching problems of diverse domains. Hence, there is a need for adaptive and robust matching systems that return good mappings across different matching problems without manual tuning.

There have already been some attempts to make parts of a matching system more adaptive and self-tuning [9][13][10]. However, these adaptations are typically fixed in the code or seem tailored to specific tasks. Other approaches like eTuner [14] perform tuning based on a synthetically constructed gold standard. However, this approach seems not applicable in practice since a synthetic gold standard could differ a lot from the given mapping problem. Learning techniques like YAM [3] or [7] were also proposed, but in practice, gold mappings for learning are not available. The concept of meta-level learning already aims at adaptive matching processes based on schema features [4]. However they still rely on learning from existing mappings.

We aim at a comprehensive approach for a fully self-configuring schema matching system that can automatically construct and adapt a matching process for a given mapping problem. To this end, we make the following contributions:

- We introduce so-called *features* that are computed from the input schemas as well as from intermediate mapping results.
- Based on the features, we introduce the concept of *matching rules* that represent expert knowledge on how to define or adapt a schema matching process.
- We propose an adaptive matching approach that integrates features and matching rules. A matching process is iteratively extended, rewritten and executed.
- We evaluate our approach on different match problems and show its robustness.

2. PRELIMINARIES
We first provide some preliminaries on the assumed model of schemas and schema matching.

A **schema** consists of a number of schema elements. Each element carries a name, a data type, and optionally a description (called annotation) as well as instances. The kind of schema is not restricted and can refer to any metadata structure such as XML schema trees, ontologies, database schemas or meta-models. The goal of a schema matching system is to compute a mapping suggestion between a source schema S and a target schema T. For computing the mapping, most matching systems use several matchers as well as other operators for aggregation and selection.

The **matcher** operator computes a similarity value for each pair of schema elements from the source schema S and the target schema T and constructs a **similarity matrix** as output. An entry in the similarity matrix is a value between 0 and 1 representing the similarity between two elements with 0 representing low and 1 representing high similarity. An **aggregation** operator is used to combine multiple similarity matrices computed by different

CIKM'11, October 24–28, 2011, Glasgow, Scotland, UK.

matchers to a single aggregated similarity matrix. Finally, a **selection** operator extracts the most probable element pairs from a similarity matrix and sets all other values to zero (see [15] for an overview to selection strategies). From the finally selected matrix a **mapping** between a source schema S and a target schema T can be constructed. A mapping consists of a set of correspondences (s, t, sim) referring to a source- and a target element as well as a similarity value.

Matching systems not only differ in the implementation of these basic operators but also by the order in which these operators can be executed. In this paper we adopt the notion of matching processes similar to eTuner [14]. A **matching process** (or matching strategy) is represented by a directed acyclic graph describing the execution order of operators such as match, aggregation or selection. It contains all steps necessary to come from two input schemas to a final mapping. Operators in the graph have one or more similarity matrices as input and return a similarity matrix as output. The topology of a matching process can be very different. Simple topologies that are commonly used are parallel, sequential and iterative execution of matchers. These basic topologies may also be combined in more sophisticated match strategies.

In general, tuning a matching system involves defining the underlying matching process structure, selecting the appropriate operators and parameterizing individual operators. Our system should be able to automatically choose promising matchers, aggregation and selection operations and their parameters. Also the structure of a matching process should be automatically adaptable.

3. ADAPTIVE MATCHING SYSTEM

We took inspiration from how a matching expert would interactively develop and execute a matching process. She analyzes the source and target schema, selects appropriate matchers and constructs an initial matching process. The process is executed and the result is inspected. Depending on that result, certain parts or parameters of the matching process can be changed and extended manually.

Our approach performs similarly but in an automatic way. In order to automate the analysis step, we rely on so-called features. These are computed from the input schemas but also from intermediate mapping results. Features try to give some indication about schema properties or the quality of a mapping. Computed features are used by so-called *matching rules* representing expert knowledge about a relation between features and operators or process patterns. Finally, an adaptive process execution system (see Figure 1) selects and applies rules and incrementally executes the constructed process. Our adaptive matching system gets two schemas as input and returns a mapping as output. Ideally, no further parameterization input should be needed when running the system. All necessary parameters should be defined automatically.

The system consists of a registry that contains a number of so called feature analyzers, matching rules as well as an operator library that contains all necessary operators in particular the matchers, aggregation or selection operators. The core component of the system is the adaptive process construction that implements a staged rule application approach that we describe below. In a preprocessing step all schema features of the input schemas are computed. The adaptive process construction starts with an empty process and applies rewrite rules to add or change operators. After every change of the process the matching process execution is called to execute the new operators. This creates new intermediate similarity matrices that can be analyzed by matrix feature analyzers.

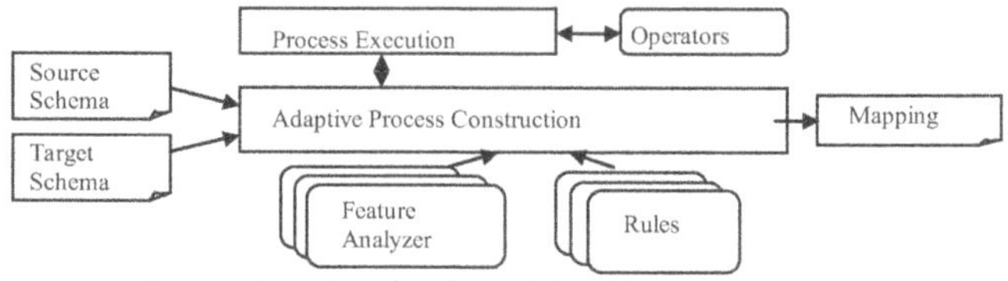

Figure 1: Adaptive Matching System

In the following, each of the components is described (Please see extended version for more details[1]).

3.1 Features

In general a **feature** takes one or several schemas or similarity matrices as input and computes a value between 0 and 1 as output. We distinguish between schema features, and matrix features. The notion of matrix features is newly introduced by this paper.

Schema features try to describe properties of schemas that can be computed in a preprocessing step before actually executing a matching process. In simple cases they reflect the schema size or the relative frequency of schema element properties such as the availability of element descriptions or data type information. More complex features rely on value distributions of schema elements or structural properties. For instance, the average length of paths in a schema tree gives some indication of whether to use a path matcher evaluating the name similarity of elements and their predecessors. Some schema features evaluate the degree of similarity between both input schemas. For example the structural and linguistic schema similarity can be used to decide about the appropriateness of applying a structure-based or name-based matcher [9].

We additionally analyze intermediate similarity matrices after executing operators of the matching process to derive **matrix features**. They are used to evaluate the quality or similarity value distributions of similarity matrices. For instance a so-called Noise feature computes the number of low valued entries in a similarity matrix in relation to the top-1 values in each row and column. The resulting feature can be used to evaluate the quality of a matrix and thus the operator that has generated it. Some matrix features take more than two matrices as input to describe the degree of commonalities and differences between them. For instance a feature could measure the overlap of top-1 values of different similarity matrices. If the overlap is higher, more confidence could be put in the different matrices.

3.2 Matching Rules

We use schema and matrix features within so-called matching rules. A matching rule captures a design decision a matching process expert would take, e.g. to select and add matchers..

A **matching rule** consists of the following parts:

- A **pattern** that describes a part of a process graph where the rule can be applied to. The pattern can be empty, in particular within rules that start the process construction.

[1] http://arxiv.org/abs/1108.1925

- An **action** that applies a defined change to instances of the found process pattern, e.g. additions and changes of operators.
- A **relevance** function that computes the relevance of the respective rule for the current matching process and match task. It is based on computed schema and matrix features on the input schemas and already computed similarity matrices and computes a relevance value between 0 and 1. The relevance is used to decide whether a rule is executed.
- An optional **check** function that is used after a rule was applied to a process. It rates the quality of the changes that were introduced by the action. It also relies on matrix features to compute a value between 0 and 1.

We identified different types of matching rules that are starting-, aggregation-, rewrite-, refine and selection rules. **Starting rules** can be applied to an empty process when no intermediate matrix was computed yet. Each application of a starting rule creates so called dangling nodes that are possible end-points of the process and do not have following nodes. **Aggregation rules** add aggregation operators to a process and combine a number of dangling operators from a matching process. **Rewrite rules** change the structure of a given process without changing the input and dangling output nodes. For instance the order of operators could be changed or additional operations can be added in between others. Selection Rules are used to add a selection operator to the last dangling node of the current matching process.

3.3 Adaptive process construction

The different kinds of rules are applied in a certain order to control the degree of process adaptations. Different rule classes depend on each other since some rules add operators and others combine the output of several operators as done by the aggregation rule. In order to restrict complexity we perform the application of rules only within a fixed number of stages as shown in the left part of Figure 2. This reduces the structural diversity an adaptively created process can have but simplifies the rule selection process significantly. If all rules would be able to compete in all stages of the process side-effects of rule application could not be controlled and termination could not be ensured.

The process starts with importing the input schema and analyzing them to compute the schema features. An empty matching process is created. In the next stage starting rules can be selected and applied. Starting rules mostly add element-based matchers. However, also more complex starting rules can be defined that already construct an advanced matching process structure, e.g. to enforce the sequential execution of several matchers. In the next stage the dangling nodes from applying the starting rules need to be combined and the result matrices are aggregated. After the aggregation, rewrite rules can be applied. If no relevant rewrite rules can be found, a selection rule is applied. Based on the selection result the process can be finished or refine rules can be applied iteratively.

Within each stage of the process a predefined rule selection process is started (see right state chart from Figure 2). The selection process begins with filtering all rules that can be executed within the current stage. This set of rules is only created once within a stage. If the remaining set of rules is empty the stage can be finished directly. If there are rules left to be applied, their relevance is computed for each rule using the rules relevance functions. The most relevant rule is selected and applied.

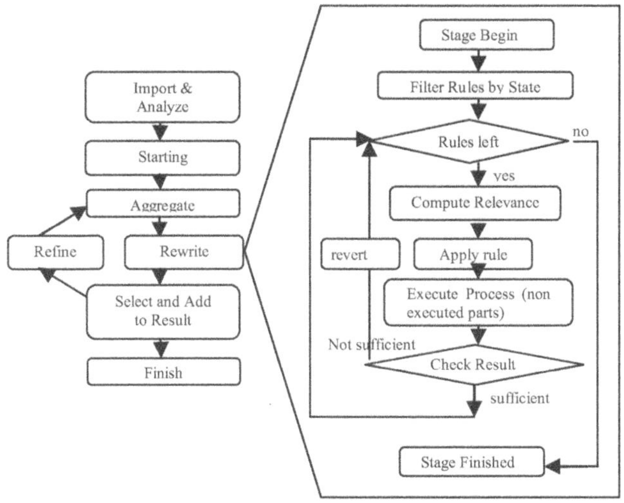

Figure 2: Stages and rule selection

Applying a rule implies changes to the current matching process. After that the current process is executed. However no operator is executed twice and only new or changed parts are executed. The matrix result of executing the most recently applied rule is evaluated using the rules check function. It often happens that rules are rated as relevant due to the existence of certain attributes in the source and target schema. However, after executing the matchers that were added by the rule the matrix result quality is sometimes very low, indicating that the most recent rule should be ignored. For that purpose the most recent rule effect is reverted. After executing a rule it is removed from the remaining list of rules. Again the most relevant rule is selected and the process runs on until the rule set is empty.

3.4 Example

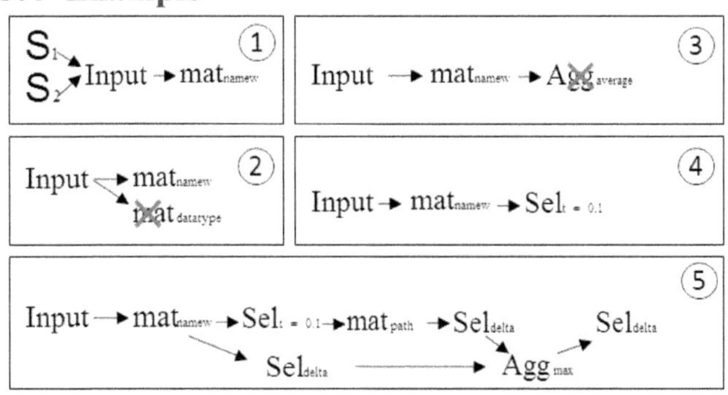

Figure 3: Example adaptive construction

For illustration we explain the adaptive process construction for matching two anatomy taxonomies that are also used in our evaluation. In Figure 4 different states of the adaptive construction are visualized. Our system starts with constructing a new process with an input node that imports the source and target schemas and computes the schema features. In (1) a starting rule is applied that measures the number of repeating tokens in element names and selects a name matcher with term weighting. In (2) a rule adds the datatype matcher and executes it. However it is then removed due to a low quality detected by the check function. After all relevant starting rules are executed, an aggregation rule is executed (3) that combines multiple dangling nodes (these are operators that need to be consumed by other operators to complete the matching process). In the example, only one dangling node exists so that the

Aggregation operator can be removed. In (4) a rewrite rule has been found relevant and applied; it adds a selection operator after the matcher operator. In (5) a refine rule that adds a path matcher after the dangling selection to refine the intermediate match result. Finally an aggregate/selection rule is applied that combines the results of both matchers.

4. EVALUATION

In the evaluation we want to investigate the effectiveness and robustness of our approach. For that reason we compare our adaptive schema matching system to currently known alternative approaches for diverse problems. We currently have implemented 20 feature analyzers and 18 rules. For details, please refer to the extended version of the paper.

We consider a wide range of schema mapping problems from different domains. To be comparable to existing work we include the OAEI-Benchmark and Anatomy as well as the ModelCVS Benchmark [6] in our evaluation. The Purchase Order dataset and mappings were already used in the early evaluations from COMA [2] and they are publicly available. We also use them for computing a default configuration to compare against.

We precomputed a best configuration for the Purchase Order dataset similar to the way the default strategy proposed in [2] was computed. We call this computed strategy our DEFAULT configuration. It consists of the matchers WeightedName, Path, Children, Leaf, Sibling and Datatype. The best selection strategy found was parameterized with delta=0.021 and a threshold=0.5 (see [2] for details on selection strategies).

Secondly we implemented the Meta-level learning proposed in [4]. This approach is a valid comparison since it includes schema features in a learning process of a decision tree to increase adaptivity. The learning also takes the Purchase Order dataset as gold mappings. We include all schema features in the learning process. The learning was implemented using the weka[2] library. The computed decision trees are then translated into matching processes without loss of information. In order to reduce possible overfitting we restricted the size of the decision tree. We then executed the default configuration, the decision tree and our new adaptive matching system with all provided mapping problems.

4.1 Results

The results of our evaluations are summarized in Figure 4.

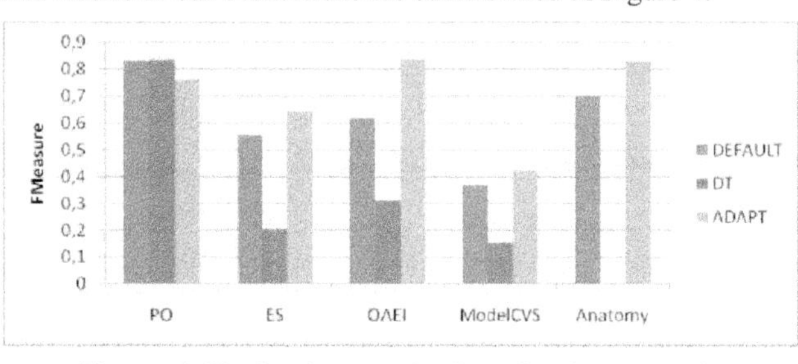

Figure 4: Evaluation results for adaptive execution

For each dataset we compared the average achieved F-Measure of the individual approaches DEFAULT, DT and ADAPT. Our adaptive approach (ADAPT) returned good results across all different test cases and thus proved its viability. For the Purchase Order data set ADAPT is only closely behind the DEFAULT configuration and the computed decision tree (DT). The slightly better outcome for DEFAULT is not surprising since DEFAULT was tuned on this data set by testing all possible parameter configurations. DT had problems to learn a good process since the diversity of matches is too big to derive a representative rule in a decision tree. We also experienced strong overfitting which was already experienced by the authors of [4].

5. CONCLUSIONS

We proposed a new self-configuring and adaptive schema matching system. It uses a series of schema and matrix features and different matching rules to automatically construct and adapt matching processes. Our evaluations show that the approach is able to return good results for diverse match problems and that it can compete with manually tuned approaches.The proposed approach is in its initial version and we plan further improvements, e.g. to support more complex adaptations.

6. REFERENCES

[1] Rahm, E. and Bernstein, P. A. 2001. A survey of approaches to automatic schema matching. The VLDB Journal 10.

[2] Do , H. H. and Rahm, E. 2002. COMA - A System for Flexible Combination of Matching Approaches. VLDB Proc.

[3] Duchateau, F., et. al. 2009. YAM: a schema matcher factory, CIKM.

[4] Eckert, K., Meilicke C., Stuckenschmidt, H. 2009. Improving ontology matching using meta-level learning. In ESWC 2009.

[5] Euzenat, J., et. al. 2010. Results of the Ontology Alignment Evaluation Initiative 2010. Workshop on Ontology Matching.

[6] Falleri, J.-R., et. al. 2008. Metamodel matching for automatic model transformation generation. MoDELS '08

[7] Gal, A., and Sagi, T., 2010, Tuning the Ensemble Selection Process of Schema Matchers, Information Systems 35

[8] Gusfield, D., Irving, R. W. 1989. The stable marriage problem: structure and algorithms. MIT Press.

[9] Hu, W. and Qu, Y. 2008. Falcon-AO: A practical ontology matching system. Web Semant., 6(3).

[10] Li, J. et al. 2009. RiMOM: A Dynamic Multistrategy Ontology Alignment Framework. IEEE Transactions on Knowledge and Data Engineering, 21(8).

[11] Meilicke, C., Stuckenschmidt, H. 2007. Analyzing Mapping Extraction Approaches. ISWC - Workshop on Ontology Matching.

[12] Noy, N. F. and Musen, M. A. 2003. The PROMPT Suite:Interactive Tools for Ontology Merging and Mapping. Int. J. Hum.-Comput. Stud.

[13] Pirrò, G.,Talia, D., 2010: UFOme: An ontology mapping system with strategy prediction capabilities. Data Knowl. Eng. 69(5)

[14] Y. Lee et. al. 2007. eTuner: tuning schema matching software using synthetic scenarios. The VLDB Journal, 16(1).

---

[2] http://www.cs.waikato.ac.nz/~ml/weka/index.html

A Taxonomy of Local Search: Semi-Supervised Query Classification Driven by Information Needs

Jiang Bian
Yahoo! Labs
Sunnyvale, CA 94089
jbian@yahoo-inc.com

Yi Chang
Yahoo! Labs
Sunnyvale, CA 94089
yichang@yahoo-inc.com

ABSTRACT

Local search service (e.g. Yelp, Yahoo! Local) has emerged as a popular and effective paradigm for a wide range of information needs for local businesses; it now provides a viable and even more effective alternative to general purpose web search for queries on local businesses. However, due to the diversity of information needs behind local search, it is necessary to use different information retrieval strategies for different query types in local search. In this paper, we explore a taxonomy of local search driven by users' information needs, which categorizes local search queries into three types: *business category*, *chain business*, and *non-chain business*. To decide which search strategy to use for each category in this taxonomy without placing the burden on the web users, it is indispensable to build an automatic local query classifier. However, since local search queries yield few online features and it is expensive to obtain editorial labels, it is insufficient to use only a supervised learning approach. In this paper, we address these problems by developing a semi-supervised approach for mining information needs from a vast amount of unlabeled data from local query logs to boost local query classification. Results of a large scale evaluation over queries from a commercial local search site illustrate that the proposed semi-supervised method allow us to accurately classify a substantially larger proportion of local queries than the supervised learning approach.

Categories and Subject Descriptors

H.3.3 [**Information Systems**]: Information Search and Retrieval

General Terms

Algorithms, Experimentation, Measurements

Keywords

Local query taxonomy, Local search, Semi-supervised learning

1. INTRODUCTION

Local search site is a viable method for seeking information about geographically constrained local businesses, products, and services online. Beyond general purpose web search engines, local search sites, such as Yelp [1] and Yahoo! Local [2], provides a more effective alternative for web users' queries on local businesses. As general purpose web search is driven by users' information needs [4, 8], the central tenet of local search is that web users are driven by *location-targeted* information needs. However, those information needs behind local search queries are usually diverse. For example, some local search queries, such as '*walmart*' and '*cheesecake factory*', intend to retrieve the information of the certain business near the user-specified geographical location, while other local search queries, such as '*Italian restaurant*' and '*gas stations*', infer users' intents to find businesses of the certain category near the user-specified location. Note that, in local search sites, usually the location information is specified by users as one of search settings and not included in the query.

Due to the diversity of information needs behind local search queries, it is inadequate to use a single information retrieval approach to serve all local search queries. For example, to retrieve relevant results for the query '*walmart*', the feature of textual matching between the query and the name of the business might be more essential than others; while, for the query '*Italian restaurant*', the search strategy might count more on the correlation between the query and the topical taxonomy of the business. Therefore, in order to better serve local search, it is necessary to employ different strategies to deal with the various information needs of web users. And, the indispensable prerequisite is to introduce a taxonomy for local search which can categorize local search queries according to diverse information needs.

In this paper, we propose and deeply analyze a taxonomy of local search, which classifies local queries into hierarchical categories according to the hierarchical information needs:

- Business category query
- Business name query
  - Chain business query
  - Non-chain business query

where a business category query, such as '*Italian restaurant*', represents the user's intent to find business of a certain category; a business name query represents the user's intent to retrieve a specific business, which is further categorized into chain business query (e.g. '*walmart*') v.s. non-chain business query (e.g. '*uc berkeley*').

Better understanding of the information needs of queries in terms of the proposed taxonomy can significantly benefit local search, since correct query categorization results in higher relevance with reduced computation for local search service via selecting different search strategies for different query categories. With the goal of automatically and precisely classifying the local search query stream, using solely supervised learning techniques is too limited to be of much practical use since local search queries yield very few online features and it is too expensive to obtain enough editorial la-

CIKM'11, October 24–28, 2011, Glasgow, Scotland, UK.

[1] http://yelp.com
[2] http://local.yahoo.com

bels to train an accurate classifier. In this paper, to address these problems, we develop a semi-supervised approach, which mines large scale local search engine query logs as the source of unlabeled data to aid in automatic classification. In particular, based on analysis over search logs using a small set of labeled queries, we propose a click-based as well as a location-based label propagation method to automatically generate query category labels for unlabeled queries from search logs. Results of a large scale evaluation demonstrate that our semi-supervised method can substantially boost the accuracy of local query classification over the supervised learning approach. Moreover, our method is quite efficient since it only requires very little labeling effort and uses very cheap word unigram features. The specific contributions of this paper include: (1) A general taxonomy for local search driven by local information needs (Section 2). (2) Deep-dive analysis on local search logs. (3) A click-based and a location-based label propagation technique for semi-supervised query classification (Section 3).

2. A TAXONOMY OF LOCAL SEARCH

The information needs behind local search queries are quite different in nature from most of those in general purpose web search, since users of local search sites target finding geographically constrained local businesses rather than traditional web-pages. After observing large scale local search query logs from a commercial local search site, we generalize local search queries into a hierarchical taxonomy according to users' intents:

- **Business category queries:** The purpose of such queries is to search for local businesses of a certain category that the user has in mind. The user will select the specific business after comparing the retrieved ones of the same category. Some examples are '*Italian restaurant*', '*gas station*', '*car dealer*', etc.
- **Business name queries:** The purpose of such queries is to reach the specific business that the user intends to find around a geographically constrained location. According to the scale of such specific business, these queries can be further classified into two sub-categories:
  - **Chain business queries:** The specific business that user intend to reach is of large scale and has many chain stores, such as '*walmart*', '*cheesecake factory*', '*citi*', etc.
  - **Non-chain business queries:** The specific business that user intend to reach is not a chain, such as '*mass general hospital*', '*stanford university*', '*san bruno library*', etc.

3. SEMI-SUPERVISED CLASSIFICATION

Automatic accurate local query classification can benefit local search since it allows us to employ various search strategies to serve different types of information needs. Supervised learning methods [6, 8, 5, 1] have demonstrated their success in building accurate query classifier, however, they usually require high quality features and much human labeling effort, both of which are expensive to obtain. To address these problems, some of previous studies [3, 2] have investigated mining the vast amount of unlabeled data in web query logs to improve automatic web query classification. In this section, we will first conduct a deep analysis on the local search query logs and then develop automatic classifiers by leveraging click and location related information mined from local search logs. It is naturally a semi-supervised learning approach based on label propagation. And, the proposed method can use only cheap features, such as unigram word features, during learning.

3.1 Analysis on Local Search Logs

Local search query logs record the activities of users and reflect the users' actual information needs when conducting local search. They generally have the following information: text queries that users submitted, the URLs displayed to users after they submit the queries, the activities (click or not) of users on URLs, the timestamp of users' activities, and especially the locations that users search for the businesses nearby. Local search logs are separated by sessions, each of which represent one user's single search activity and thus includes one query, one location and all the URLs displayed to the user. Note that the location information can be identified either explicitly by users or implicitly by IP address. The schema and examples of local search logs is shown in Figure 1.

Session	Query	Location	URL	Activity	Time
S_1	Q_1	L_1	D_1^1	view/click	xxxx
S_1	Q_1	L_1	D_2^1	view/click	xxxx
...	...	...	...	...	...
S_2	Q_2	L_2	D_1^2	view/click	xxxx
...	...	...	...	...	...

Figure 1: The schema and example entries of local search logs

Our idea of using local search logs to improve local query classification is to treat these logs as past history of users' information needs, extract more critical information from these logs for better describing diverse information needs, and leverage such a critical information to propagate existing query taxonomy labels to larger set of unlabeled local queries.

In particular, to classify between business category and business name queries, we consider the click information critical: the number of clicks per search session of business name queries is much more likely to be smaller than that of business category queries, because each business name query is intended to reach one specific business that the user has in mind, but users with business category queries tend to compare (click) several search results before selecting her/his favorite business. Moreover, to distinguish between chain and non-chain business queries, the diversity of users' locations becomes vital: chain business queries are submitted by users from more locations since chain businesses have larger geographic scale, but non-chain ones are likely to be bound to fewer locations.

To examine these two intuitions, we analyze a large amount of local search logs from a commercial local search site. In particular, we collect all the search logs from Jan, 2010 to Nov, 2010. Then, we randomly sampled 5074 local queries which occur frequently in the logs and asked human experts to give the editorial taxonomy labels for all the 5074 queries. As a result, there are 1874 queries labeled as business category, 1998 labeled as chain business, and 1202 labeled as non-chain business. Then, we compute the average numbers of clicks per session for all three query categories using different timespans, as shown in Table 1. From the table, we can see that the average clicks per session of business category queries is explicitly larger than that of business name queries, while chain business and non-chain business queries have very close average clicks per session, and that each query category yields very small variance. All these observations indicate that average clicks per session can be used as an effective signal to distinguish between business category queries and business name ones.

Table 1: Average clicks per session for all query categories

Timespan	Category	Aver clicks/session (variance)
1 month (Nov, 2010)	Business category	1.484 (0.554)
	Chain business	1.098 (0.0090)
	Non-chain business	1.105 (0.027)
3 month (Sep-Nov, 2010)	Business category	1.481 (0.581)
	Chain business	1.101 (0.0088)
	Non-chain business	1.103 (0.030)
12 month (Jan-Nov, 2010)	Business category	1.482 (0.574)
	Chain business	1.099 (0.0087)
	Non-chain business	1.102 (0.026)

Additionally, we count the average number of different locations where one query occurs per month for all business name queries, as shown in Table 2. In our work, we use each distinct city to denote one specific location. The table shows that chain and non-chain business queries have very distinct average numbers of locations per month. Although their respective variances are relatively large,

Table 2: **Average number of different locations per month for all query categories**

Category	Aver num of locations per month (variance)
Chain business	248.16 (2.88×10^3)
Non-chain business	65.36 (4.65×10^2)

we will illustrate in our experiments that this location-based information can be still used as a vital signal to distinguish between chain and non-chain business queries.

In the following, we will introduce how to take advantage of click-based signals to propagate labels of business category and business name to unlabeled queries from search logs, as well as how to leverage location-based signals to automatically assign labels of chain and non-chain business to queries from search logs.

3.2 Click-based Label Propagation

As Table 1 shows, business category queries tend to attract more clicks per session than business name queries; we propose a **click-based label propagation** method to automatically assign labels of business category or business name to unlabeled queries from search logs. In particular,

> *Queries whose average number of result clicks per session is more than a threshold will be labeled as business category; otherwise, they will be labeled as business name.*

The threshold can be decided based on analyzing those queries labeled by human judgments. Specifically, we use this click-based label propagation to automatically generate new class labels for those human labeled queries. We use human labels as truth and select the threshold which can optimize the recall of both query categories based on the new generated labels.

In our experiments, we evaluate the recall of two query categories on those 5074 queries when using the click-based label propagation with different thresholds. The results are shown in Table 3, where the average clicks per session is computed based on three months (Sep-Nov,2010) of local search logs. From the table, we

Table 3: Recall of two query categories (CAT: business category, BIZ: business name) when using the click-based label propagation method with different threshold values.

Threshold	1.1	1.15	**1.2**	1.25	1.3	1.4
CAT recall	0.959	0.929	0.905	0.849	0.797	0.636
BIZ recall	0.646	0.840	0.916	0.956	0.969	0.980
Weighted recall	0.802	0.884	**0.911**	0.902	0.883	0.808

can find that the clicked-based label propagation method can reach nearly optimal performance when we set the threshold as 1.2. We will use this threshold in the following experiments. Note that, with finer selection, we may find more precise thresholds than 1.2, but the following evaluations show that we can achieve good enough accuracy using 1.2 as the threshold.

3.3 Location-based Label Propagation

As shown in Table 2, chain business queries tend to occur at different locations compared to non-chain business queries, thus, we propose a **location-based label propagation** method to automatically assign labels of chain or non-chain business to unlabeled queries from search logs. In particular,

> *Queries which on average occur at more than a certain number (threshold) of locations will be labeled as chain business; otherwise, they will be labeled as non-chain business.*

Similar to Section 3.2, this threshold can be decided by analyzing our set of 5074 human labeled queries. Specifically, we apply this location-based label propagation to generate new class labels for those human labeled queries, and we use human labels as truth and select the threshold which can optimize the recall of both query categories based on new generated labels.

Algorithm 1 Semi-Supervised Local Query Classification

Inputs: Q_E: queries with existing editorial judgments
Q_L: more queries from search logs without editorial judgments
L: a large scale local search log

Outputs: M_{lev_1}: the classifier at 1st level to classify between business category and business name queries.
M_{lev_2}: the classifier at 2nd level to classify between chain and non-chain business queries.

Algorithms:

Step1: Decide the thresholds of click-based and location-based label propagation by using the labeled queries Q_E and search log Q_L.

Step2: Assign the label *business category* or *business name* to each query in Q_L based on click-based label propagation method.

Step3: Train M_{lev_1} based on human labeled Q_E and automatically labeled Q_L.

Step4: For those queries labeled as *business name* in *Step 2*, assign the label *chain* or *non-chain* based on location-based label propagation method.

Step5: Train M_{lev_2} based on human labeled Q_E and automatically labeled Q_L.

We evaluate the recall of two query categories when using the location-based label propagation with different thresholds to generate new labels. As shown in Table 4, the location-based label

Table 4: Recalls of two query categories (BIZ-CH: chain business, BIZ-NC: non-chain business) when using the location-based label propagation with different threshold values.

Threshold	27	28	**29**	30	31	32
BIZ-CH recall	0.720	0.712	0.703	0.694	0.688	0.681
BIZ-NC recall	0.691	0.702	0.718	0.723	0.729	0.734
Weighted recall	0.706	0.707	**0.711**	0.709	0.709	0.708

propagation method can reach nearly optimal performance when setting the threshold to 29. We will use this threshold value in the following evaluations. Also note that we may find more precise thresholds via finer selection, but the following evaluations show that we can achieve good enough accuracy using this threshold.

3.4 Semi-Supervised Classification

Using the above two label propagation methods, we can collect large amounts of automatically labeled local search queries for training more reliable classifiers to categorize queries into the taxonomy introduced in Section 2. In particular, we develop a hierarchical classification system which consists of two classifiers: the first one takes charge of classifying queries between business category and business name, while the second one is used for classification between chain and non-chain business if the result of first classifier is business name. Both of these two classifiers follow the standard classification framework: we derive only cheap unigram word features to represent each query; the label of each query is assigned either by existing human judgments or by automatic label propagation methods. The whole semi-supervised classification framework is generalized in Algorithm 1. For learning method, we will explore three families: SVM, Naive Bayes, and Decision Trees, all using implementations from the Weka [7] framework.

4. EXPERIMENTS

4.1 Datasets

All the queries in our datasets are collected from a commercial local search site. We first sample 5074 queries and ask human experts to give the editorial class labels. Then, to enrich the training data, we collect all local queries in three months (Sep-Nov, 2010), about 405K queries in total, on which we apply our proposed label propagation methods with the thresholds decided by analyzing those 5074 labeled queries in search logs. About 37% of

Table 5: **Accuracy of the 1st level semi-supervised classifier (implemented by Naive Bayes(NB), SVM, and Decision Trees(DT)), compared with supervised method trained with small training set.**

Classifier	Business category			Business name		
	Precision	Recall	F1	Precision	Recall	F1
Baseline	0.667	0.583	0.622	0.773	0.830	0.800
NB	0.969	0.825	0.891	0.786	0.992	0.877
SVM	0.949	0.940	0.945	0.984	0.986	**0.985**
DT	0.936	0.958	**0.947**	0.988	0.943	0.972

Table 6: **Accuracy of the 2nd level semi-supervised classifier (implemented by Naive Bayes(NB), SVM, and Decision Trees(DT)), compared with supervised method trained with small training set.**

Classifier	Chain business			Non-chain business		
	Precision	Recall	F1	Precision	Recall	F1
Baseline	0.702	0.518	0.596	0.636	0.744	0.686
NB	0.923	0.836	0.877	0.802	0.942	0.866
SVM	0.974	0.909	0.941	0.889	0.968	**0.927**
DT	0.969	0.917	**0.942**	0.882	0.958	0.918

those queries are automatically labeled as *business category*, about 40% as *chain business*, and 23% as *non-chain business*. All the log queries and 5074 human-labeled ones are used as the training set in the experiments. We additionally sample another 3023 local search queries and ask human experts to assign editorial class labels, which are used as the testing set in the evaluations. In total, this testing set contains 508 *business category* queries, 1448 *chain business*, and 1027 *non-chain business* queries.

4.2 Evaluation Metrics

Since our local search query classification system consists of two level classifiers, we can evaluate the performance of each classifier separately. We use standard evaluation metrics in classification, *Precision* and *Recall*. *Precision* of one query class is the ratio of the number of queries correctly assigned to this class divided by the total number of queries assigned to this class. *Recall* of one class is the ratio of the number of queries correctly assigned to this class as compared with the total number of queries truly in this class. We also compute the *F-measure*, which combines two metrics into a single number, the geometric mean of precision and recall, computed as $\frac{2\times\text{precision}\times\text{recall}}{\text{precision}+\text{recall}}$.

4.3 Classification Results and Analysis

In our experiments, we train the two-level classifiers. For the first one, we use 5074 human-labeled queries with 405K automatically labeled queries from three month of search logs as our training set and use another 3023 human-labeled queries as our testing set; for the second classifier, we use all business name queries from those 5074 queries with all logs queries that are automatically labeled as business name as our training set and use all business name queries from 3023 human-labeled queries for testing.

Table 5 reports the accuracy of our semi-supervised first level classifier with different implementations of classification algorithms (Naive Bayes, SVM, and Decision Trees), compared with the supervised baseline which utilizes only 5074 human-labeled queries for training and 3023 queries for testing. The supervised baseline is implemented with Decision Trees which performs best among three algorithms. From the table, we can find that semi-supervised methods can achieve much better accuracy than the supervised baseline, which indicates the effectiveness of our click-based label propagation method for classifying between business category and business name queries. We can also observe that semi-supervised methods implemented by SVM and Decision Trees can result in similar performance. We will use SVM in further analysis since it costs less time for training than Decision Trees.

Table 6 demonstrates the accuracy of our second level classifier with different implementations of classification algorithms, compared with the supervised baseline implemented with Decision Trees. From the table, we can find that the semi-supervised methods can achieve much better performance than the supervised baseline, indicating the effectiveness of our location-based label propagation method for classifying between chain and non-chain business queries. Similarly, since SVM reaches similar accuracy compared to Decision Trees but costs much less time, we use SVM in further analysis.

In our semi-supervised learning methods, the threshold of average number of clicks per session for click-based label propagation and that of average number of unique locations associated for location-based label propagation are essential for the classification accuracy. To examine whether optimizing the thresholds, which are decided based on analyzing the corresponding characteristics of relatively small set of human-labeled queries in the search logs, can result in better performance, we compare the classification accuracy against varying thresholds during label propagation. Figure 2 demonstrates the classification accuracy in terms of F-

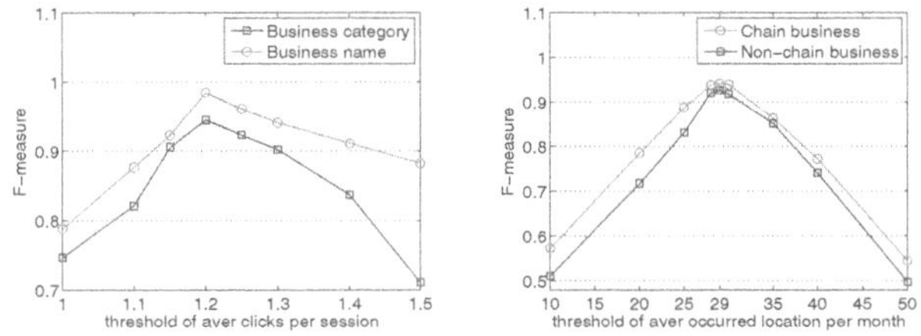

(a) Varying threshold of average clicks per session

(b) Varying threshold of average occurred locations per month

Figure 2: Classifiers' accuracy in terms of F-measure against varying values of two thresholds

measure when we use different values for the two thresholds for label propagation during training, respectively. From these figures, we can find that if we select the values of these two thresholds (i.e. 1.2 for first-level classifier and 29 for second-level classifier) based on analyzing the corresponding characteristics of human labeled queries in search logs, respectively, we can reach the better accuracy of both two classifiers than using different threshold values.

5. CONCLUSION

In this paper we presented, to our knowledge, the first attempt to define a taxonomy of local search driven by users' diverse information needs. To automatically decide the classes of information need for local search queries, we propose a semi-supervised approach for mining the large amount of local search logs to boost local query classification. Our evaluations using queries from a commercial local search site demonstrate that our proposed methods can substantially outperform the state-of-the-art supervised learning methods. In the future, we will study quantitatively on how such local search taxonomy and corresponding accurate classification can benefit the relevance of local search.

6. REFERENCES

[1] S. Beitzel, E. Jensen, A. Chowdhury, D. Grossman, and O. Frieder. Hourly analysis of a very large topically categorized web query log. In *Proc. of SIGIR*, 2004.

[2] S. Beitzel, E. Jensen, D. Lewis, A. Chowdhury, A. Kolcz, O. Frieder, and D. Grossman. Automatic web query classification using labeled and unlabeled training data. In *Proc. of ICDM*, 2005.

[3] S. Beitzel and D. Lewis. Improving automatic query classification via semi-supervised learning. In *Proc. of ICDM*, 2005.

[4] A. Broder. A taxonomy of web search. In *SIGIR Forum*, 2002.

[5] A. Broder, M. Fontoura, E. Gabrilovich, A. Joshi, V. Josifovski, and T. Zhang. Robust classification of rare queries using web knowledge. In *Proc. of SIGIR*, 2007.

[6] L. Gravano, V. Hatzivassiloglou, and R. Lichtenstein. Categorizing web queries according to geographical locality. In *Proc. of CIKM*, 2003.

[7] M. Hall, E. Frank, G. Holmes, B. Pfahringer, P. Reutemann, and I. H. Witten. The weka data mining software: An update. In *SIGKDD Explorations*, 2009.

[8] I. Kang and G. Kim. Query type classification for web document retrieval. In *Proc. of SIGIR*, 2003.

ONTOCUBE: Efficient Ontology Extraction using OLAP Cubes

Carlos Garcia-Alvarado
University of Houston
Dept. of Computer Science
Houston, TX 77204, USA

Zhibo Chen
University of Houston
Dept. of Computer Science
Houston, TX 77204, USA

Carlos Ordonez
University of Houston
Dept. of Computer Science
Houston, TX 77204, USA

ABSTRACT

Ontologies are knowledge conceptualizations of a particular domain and are commonly represented with hierarchies. While final ontologies appear deceivingly simple on paper, building ontologies represents a time-consuming task that is normally performed by natural language processing techniques or schema matching. On the other hand, OLAP cubes are most commonly used during decision-making processes via the analysis of data summarizations. In this paper, we present a novel approach based on using OLAP cubes for ontology extraction. The resulting ontology is obtained through an analytical process of the summarized frequencies of keywords within a corpus. The solution was implemented within a relational database system (DBMS). In our experiments, we show how all the proposed discrimination measures (frequency, correlation, lift) affect the resulting classes. We also show a sample ontology result and the accuracy of finding true classes. Finally, we show the performance breakdown of our algorithm.

Categories and Subject Descriptors

H.2.8 [**Database Management**]: Database applications—*Data mining*

General Terms

Algorithms, Experimentation

Keywords

OLAP, Ontologies, DBMS

1. INTRODUCTION

Ontologies model a view of a continuously evolving world. However, this formal specification of a shared conceptualization, made into a machine readable format, is dependent on a specific context and point of view [1]. Due to this specialization, it is required that multiple ontologies be created for every world's view, giving as a result a huge task that normally undergoes human supervision, creating a knowledge acquisition bottleneck. In this paper, we focus on the problem of extracting the main concepts of a set of documents stored in a DBMS and then using them to build an ontology. The problem of extracting concepts is not trivial and has been tackled through natural language processing, clustering, singular value decomposition (SVD), and statistics, among many other proposed solutions [1]. The main problem with these approaches is that they are time-consuming or require previous knowledge to be provided. Moreover, it has been shown that these proposals are not the ultimate answer for ontology extraction.

Online Analytical Processing (OLAP) can be used to efficiently obtain these frequency summarizations' and keywords' correlation in order to extract and organize the most representative concepts in a corpus. The main characteristic of this approach is that the ontology can be built without the need of a given pattern or a set of rules in an automated form. However, OLAP has never been exploited to build ontologies. The ontology construction process can be summarized as the extraction of concepts (classes) and the relations between them based on an analysis of the keywords of a corpus. The documents within the corpus are initially preprocessed, transformed and analyzed, and finally organized to build an ontology. The result of the analysis phase is a set of concepts built from a group of keywords. The analysis phase determines the concepts and properties that characterize each concept. In a similar manner, basic relations, such as "has a" or "is a" can be inferred with the analysis of the preprocessed data set. The final phase builds the ontology by organizing the extracted relations and classes. In this research, we present how all these steps can be included within the OLAP process in order to generate efficiently, in an automated fashion, an ontology from a given set of documents stored in a DBMS. This paper is organized as follows: Section 2 presents the notation of the main concepts of ontologies and OLAP. Section 3 shows our OLAP process for building ontologies. In Section 4, the quality and performance results are presented. Similar works are discussed in Section 5. Finally, in Section 6, we make our final remarks.

2. PRELIMINARIES

Let us focus on defining the notation that will be used throughout this paper. Let C be a collection, or corpus, of n documents $\{d_1, d_2, \ldots, d_n\}$, where each document d_i is composed of a set of keywords t_{ij}. In addition, let x_i be a frequency vector of all the different keywords in C for each

CIKM'11, October 24–28, 2011, Glasgow, Scotland, UK.

document d_i. We assume that C is stored in a vertical list format. This list is stored in a vtf table that contains the document id, keyword, and position in the ith document. A summarization table tf is computed from vtf as a table with the document id i, the keyword t, and the term frequency f stored. The backbone data structure for OLAP data cubes is the dimensional lattice, which has a size of $2^{\hat{t}-1}$, where $\hat{t}$ is the number of selected keywords. One level (or depth in the lattice) of the cube is denoted by $\binom{|\hat{t}|}{level}$, s.t. $level \leq |\hat{t}|$.

2.1 Ontologies

Regardless of the ontology language, all these knowledge representations rely on the specification of the main concepts in the given context. Every concept is defined as a class with a set of properties and interactions between the classes, subclasses, and their properties. A class (e.g. owl:Class) is a classification of individuals (instances) that share common characteristics. This class classification is obtained through a taxonomy (hierarchy). In the case of individuals, the relationship between them is given by the specification of properties, which can be represented by an object (e.g. owl:ObjectProperty) and by a datatype (e.g. owl:DatatypeProperty). In this work, we do not focus on the language, but on the extraction of classes and relations.

2.2 OLAP Cubes

While normal applications of OLAP include business reports and financial analysis [2], we believe that the OLAP dimensional lattice can be used to efficiently obtain classes and their relations. In this case, the data is represented by the collection of keywords and documents while the level of aggregation allows us to obtain various combinations of these keywords to generate concepts.

While traditional OLAP accepts inputs that are horizontal, in our system, vtf has a vertical format, with each row containing a single keyword. This presents a challenge to aggregations because we are unable to use the normal techniques, such as slicing, with the vertical format. Despite this, we are only analyzing a small subset (the most frequent keywords), $\hat{t}$, of all keywords in the collection.

We developed an algorithm that can obtain the necessary aggregations and perform the required auxiliary computations with the associated keyword frequency (correlations and lift) directly from the vertical format. In this case, a data cube is computed from the list of keywords in order to form sets of words. OLAP is the perfect tool because it is able to use data cubes that allow for quick access.

2.3 Correlation

We also utilize correlation, which will represent how related the frequency of a keyword is with another in terms of the whole collection. In addition to the previous definitions, let L be an additional set containing the total sum of all the different terms in the collection ($L = \sum_{i=1}^{n} x_i$). Moreover, let Q be a lower triangular matrix containing the squared measures between the terms $Q = \sum_{i=1}^{n} x_i x_i^T$ (see [7]). In the last step, the correlation of a pair of keywords a and b is obtained by computing equation $\rho_{ab} = \frac{nQ_{ab} - L_a L_b}{\sqrt{nQ_{aa} - L_a^2}\sqrt{nQ_{bb} - L_b^2}}$. An additional measure to evaluate a pair of keywords is obtained through lift, λ. λ represents how often these two keywords appear in the collection. This value is computed as $\lambda = \frac{n_{a,b}}{Max(n_a, n_b)}$, where n_a and n_b are the number of documents containing keywords a and b, respectively.

```
Input: level , t̂
Set of Classes S
Init List_tf
foreach<i,t̂,p> r in vtf sorted by i
    if i changed
        C ← GetNextCombo(List_tf, level)
        DoWhile (C!=null)
            S_C.freq++
            S_C.pos+=r.p
            C ← GetNextCombo(List_tf, level)
        endwhile
    else
        List_tf ← {r.t, r.p}
    endif
endforeach
return S
```

Figure 1: Ontocube.

3. ONTOCUBE

In this section, we detail the ontology extraction process and every optimization performed to obtain classes and build the ontology.

3.1 Concept extraction

A one-time preprocessing step is required for setting the environment for obtaining the frequency of the keywords. The data set was preprocessed by removing the stopwords and assigning a position for every keyword in every document. Our proposed process for extracting concepts is the result of analyzing the most frequent keywords and generating combinations with these keywords. The frequencies of these combinations are also computed, as well as the correlation and lift of these pairs of keywords. The classes are obtained from the combinations by answering these questions: (1) Do the keywords appear in the same documents frequently? (2) Are the set of keywords close to each other? (3) How often do they appear together within the corpus? (4) How often is one keyword found in a document but not the other? The first question addresses the problem of finding keywords that appear in the same documents. In addition to this, we are required to know if they appear in the same proportion within the collection. As such, the correlation of each combination is computed. In the second question, we are interested in finding how close the keywords appear to each other. This distance between keywords is obtained as the difference between the positions of the keywords. The last two questions try to identify those sets of keywords that commonly appear together throughout the collection, or those that do not. The rationale behind this is that the core concepts appear consistently together throughout the collection. On the other hand, there are concepts that may appear strong when present together, but are often found in separate areas. Both of these questions can be answered by observing the lift of the concept.

Efficient summarization is performed in one-pass by creating the keyword combinations "on-the-fly" during the OLAP cube aggregation. The final result for this step is a set of classes from which the ontology will be extracted. The algorithm for obtaining such classes is as follows: (1) obtain all available classes by pairing all keywords within each document, (2) for each class, determine the frequency of occurrence and average position gap within the corpus, (3) filter out all classes whose keywords have a position gap greater than a user-defined threshold, $pDiff$, and (4) filter out all classes whose frequency, correlation, or lift does not meet user-defined thresholds.

The pseudocode for the first two steps is shown in Figure 1. The remaining two steps can be accomplished by traversing S and removing those classes that do not meet the user-defined thresholds. We are only interested in the classes formed by keywords within a specific document. As a result, we found it is easiest to first gather all the keywords within a document into $List_{vtf}$ before processing them once the document id, i, changed. Notice that this algorithm would not generate the combinations of keywords that are not present in the data set.

We adapted an efficient one-pass method to compute the correlation values of unique terms in the collection similar to the one presented in [2, 6]. The correlation and lift values are computed with the resulting aggregations from the summarization step. As a result, the vtf table is not scanned again to compute both values. Instead, we only used a summarization table. The lift values for each set of terms are computed from a separate aggregation step where we stored the number of documents that each term appears in.

3.2 Ontology building

The ontology is built from the pool of classes generated from the previous step. We then proceed to build links between the individual classes. Initially, we pair each class with all other classes within the pool. Let each set of two classes be a relationship. For each of these relationships, we extracted the correlation and lift of each set of two keywords. For example, suppose we have the relationship $\{A, B\}, \{C, D\}$. We would need to obtain the correlation and lift for the following set of keywords: (A,C), (A,D), (B,C), (B,D). These values would allow us to observe how closely related these two classes are to one another. A high correlation and a high lift from any one of these four subsets would confirm that this is a valid relationship. Otherwise, if these four subsets do not show a high connection, we would discard this relationship.

Upon completion of this process, we have a set of valid relationships, each formed from two classes. The final step is identification of relations of the form "has a", which define a hierarchy. In other words, we are only concerned with parent-child relationships to build a vertical ontology. The parent is determined with a heuristic based on the frequency of appearance of these classes. We considered a class (A) to be the parent of another class (B) in a relationship if the following criteria is satisfied: (1) Number of documents containing A - Number of documents containing B $<$ 10% of total documents, (2) Number of classes containing keywords in class A $>$ Number of classes containing keywords in class B. If class A passes both criteria, then we consider it to be a parent of class B.

4. EXPERIMENTS

Our experiments were run on an Intel Xeon E3110 server at 3.00 GHz with a 750 GB in hard drive and 4 GB of RAM. The server was running an instance of SQL SERVER 2005. The OLAP algorithm was implemented entirely with SQL. We tested our approach with a real data set comprised of a corpus of sports articles centered around the Boston Celtics basketball team. There are a total of 50 documents based on game recaps with a total of nearly 15K individual terms.

Table 1: Num. of Classes varying corr, lift, and freq.

$Corr$	$Freq$	$Lift$	$No.\ t$	$Corr$	$Freq$	$Lift$	$No.\ t$
0.6	10	0.0	3765	0.8	10	0.0	2383
0.6	10	0.5	146	0.8	10	0.5	48
0.6	20	0.0	1122	0.8	20	0.0	529
0.6	20	0.5	83	0.8	20	0.5	22
0.6	40	0.0	229	0.8	40	0.0	91
0.6	40	0.5	42	0.8	40	0.5	5

Table 2: Sample Ontology Result.

Parent	Child	Parent	Child
Boston Celtics	Rajon Rondo	Box Score	Ray Allen
Boston Celtics	Ray Allen	Box Score	Kevin Garnett
Boston Celtics	Doc Rivers	Key Moment	Ray Allen
Boston Celtics	Kevin Garnett	Key Moment	Rajon Rondo
Box Score	Rajon Rondo	Key Score	Kevin Garnett

4.1 Summarization

Table 1 displays the total number of classes that are found when the shown thresholds are applied. These are the classes that form the pool from which the ontologies are later extracted. It is important to note that the total number of possible classes is 786382. Thus, even with minimal thresholds, we are still able to filter more than 99% of the possible classes. We can also observe that most influential threshold on the number of classes is lift. An important property that we observed during the experiments is that the larger the collection of documents, the fewer the number of incorrect classes we obtain. The rationale behind this is that true concepts tend to be more consistent throughout the collection.

4.2 Ontologies

The next step is to extract meaningful ontologies from this set of classes. Table 2 shows several examples of meaningful ontologies that were extracted. We were able to extract several key players from the Celtics team and also apply the correct parent-child relationship. Rondo, Allen, and Garnett are all players, while Rivers is the coach of the Celtics. The link of Box Score to the actual players makes perfect sense, since each player would have their own set of scores. The last three relationships are the most interesting because they provide us with descriptive terms. From them, we can surmise that the writers of these documents consider both Allen and Rondo to be vital in Key Moments while Garnett is a Key Scorer. We conducted additional verification on these discoveries and found them to be true.

It is also important to look at how many erroneous links are formed. To showcase this, we studied the accuracy of our resulting ontologies. In this case, accuracy represents whether a certain link makes sense or not. For example, Boston Celtics $\rightarrow$ Rajon Rondo is correct because Rondo is a player on the Celtics. Had the relationship been reversed, then this would be considered incorrect. The final tally of the accuracy is shown in Table 3. We can see that parents that are players consistently had lower accuracies than parents that represented items or stats. This can be explained by the fact that the documents we obtained were all game recap articles. As such, those articles contain a wide variety of players and teams, but are quite consistent in reporting the scores and stats of each game. The classes Key Box and Key Line obtained 0% accuracy because these classes themselves do not represent viable sets. We believe that with a larger and more varied pool of documents, the accuracies would improve.

Table 3: Accuracy of Results

Parent	No. Ch.	Acc. (%)	Parent	No. Ch.	Acc. (%)
Boston Celtics	19	89	Key Moment	11	91
Box Line	11	82	Key Score	12	83
Box Score	12	75	Paul Pierce	6	50
Doc Rivers	3	0	Points Rebounds	9	88
Game Celtics	17	100	Rajon Rondo	6	50
Glen Davis	1	100	Ray Allen	4	50
Kevin Garnett	3	33	Score Line	12	83
Key Box	11	0	Score Points	7	43
Key Line	11	0			
Overall	155	67			

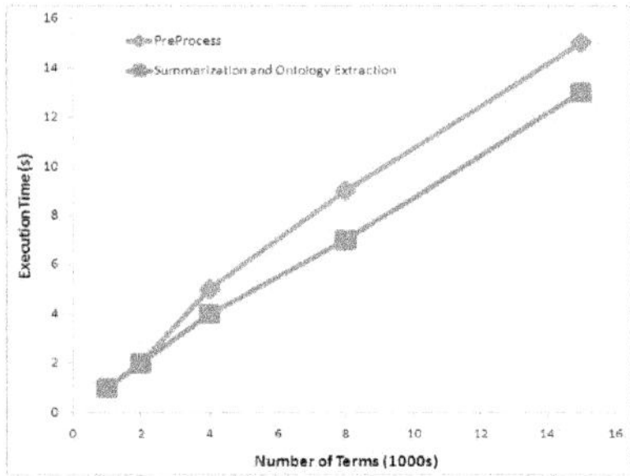

Figure 2: Ontology generation varying no. of terms.

4.3 Performance

Performance is a key factor in determining the usefulness of an algorithm. Thus, we provide two performance indicators. First, in Table 2, we show the general trend for both the preprocessing steps and the summarization/ontology extraction steps as we vary the number of initial terms. We can observe that the trend is linear with respect to the number of terms. This is to be expected since we are mostly using self-joins and table scans, so the number of terms should not exponentially affect the execution time.

We show a breakdown of the times for executing our algorithm with an initial term size of 15K in Table 4. We can see that the most heavily-weighted steps are the preprocessing step and the validating pairs step. We expected these two steps to be the most costly because of the self-join that is present in both steps. The preprocessing step includes the NLQ calculation for pairs of terms while the other step involves the actual pairing of the terms to produce the classes.

5. RELATED WORK

The need to automate the time-consuming generation of ontologies has led to multiple solutions that rely on previous knowledge or time-consuming tasks. OntoLT [1] is a plug-in for the Protégé ontology tool. It allows the user to define a set of rules for extracting an ontology from annotated text collections. Data mining approaches, such as [3], propose using a C4.5 decision tree to extract the main concepts. The non-leaf nodes are classes and the leaf nodes are individuals. In contrast to our approach, we perform this class extraction in one pass through the data. Ontobuilder is a ontology extractor based on a schema matching approach [5]. The ontology extractor is based on heuristic methods. Doddle-OWL [4] reuses given knowledge to extracts classes and relations (mostly WordNet). Then it relies on a refinement (feedback) to build a final ontology.

In [6], we realized that our query recommendation algorithm could also discover the main ontology concepts behind a particular topic. Our main contribution is that we are able to obtain classes and relations based only on efficient computations of several discrimination values (correlation and lift.) Unlike the proposed solutions, we require minimal human intervention and only a few parameters to be tuned.

Table 4: Breakdown of computation time (in secs).

Step	*Time*	*Percentage*
PreProcessing	11.0	40
Corr and Lift	2.3	8
Pairing Terms	11.9	44
Ontology	2.3	8

6. CONCLUSIONS

We presented an algorithm for ontology extraction with OLAP cubes. The core of the proposal is the obtaining of an efficient keyword frequency summarization with a one-pass algorithm for computing the correlation and lift from pairs of keywords from a corpus. Once this analysis has been performed, a set of heuristics are used to create a hierarchy and find the relation between the classes. Our experiments show that our candidate classes are pruned early with minimal thresholds for lift and correlation to obtain meaningful classes. We observed that most influential threshold on the number of classes is lift, with frequency and correlation having similar selectivity effects. We also found that the most of the classes are quite relevant, and the overall hierarchy accuracy had an overall performance of 67% with a few misclassified concepts decreasing the overall average. However, for most of the concepts, the hierarchy achieved outstanding results of 75% or higher. The algorithm also showed linear scalability with term pairing and preprocessing as the most costly steps, respectively. Future research includes hybrid approaches (NLP, ML, OLAP), trying other heuristics, and finding other types of relationships between classes.

Acknowledgments

This work was supported by NSF grants CCF 0937562 and IIS 0914861.

7. REFERENCES

[1] P. Buitelaar, D. Olejnik, and M. Sintek. OntoLT: A protégé plug-in for ontology extraction from text. In *Proc. of ISWC*, 2003.

[2] Z. Chen and C. Ordonez. Efficient OLAP with UDFs. In *Proc. ACM DOLAP Workshop*, pages 41–48, 2008.

[3] A. Elsayed, S. El-Beltagy, M. Rafea, and O. Hegazy. Applying Data Mining for Ontology Building. In *Proc. of ISSR*, 2007.

[4] N. Fukuta, T. Yamaguchi, T. Morita, and N. Izumi. DODDLE-OWL: Interactive Domain Ontology Development with Open Source Software in Java. *IEICE TOIS*, 91(4):945–958, 2008.

[5] A. Gal, G. Modica, and H. Jamil. Ontobuilder: Fully automatic extraction and consolidation of ontologies from web sources. In *Proc. of ICDE*, page 853, 2004.

[6] C. Garcia-Alvarado, Z. Chen, and C. Ordonez. OLAP-based query recommendation. In *Proc. of ACM CIKM*, pages 1353–1356, 2010.

[7] C. Ordonez. Statistical Model Computation with UDFs. *IEEE TKDE*, 2010.

An Algorithm for Axiom Pinpointing in EL$^+$ and its Incremental Variant

Xiaojun Cheng, Guilin Qi
School of Computer Science and Engineering
Southeast University,Nanjing, China

ABSTRACT

Axiom pinpointing plays an important role in the development and maintenance of ontologies. It helps the user to comprehend an unwanted entailment of an ontology by presenting all minimal subsets of the ontology which are responsible for the entailment (called MinAs). In this paper, we consider the problem of axiom pinpointing in description logic EL^+, which underpins OWL 2 EL, a profile of the latest version of Web Ontology Language (OWL). We propose a novel method to compute all MinAs that utilizes the hierarchy information obtained from the classification of an EL$^+$ ontology. The advantage of our method over an existing *labeled classification* based method is that we do not attach labels to entailed subsumptions, which can be memory exhaustion for large scale ontologies. We further consider axiom pinpointing in EL$^+$ when ontologies change. An incremental algorithm is given to compute all MinAs by reusing MinAs previously computed.

Categories and Subject Descriptors

F.3.m [**Theory of Computation**]: Logic and Meanings of Program

General Terms

Algorithms, Management, Theory

Keywords

Ontologies, Description Logics, Axiom pinpointing

1. INTRODUCTION

Ontologies play a key role in many domain, such as biomedicine, petroleum, healthcare, and Semantic Web. However, the development and maintenance of an ontology are complex and error-prone. Some unwanted entailments may be inferred from an ontology containing errors. When an unwanted entailment is inferred, it is important to provide with the user some explanation services to understand this entailment. In the last few years, there is an increasing interest in axiom pinpointing in description logics (DL for short), which underpin web ontology language OWL. Given an unwanted entailment of an ontology, axiom pinpointing computes all minimal subsets of the ontology that have the entailment (called MinAs) which can be used to explain the entailment. It is also called finding justifications in some works (i.e., [5])

Existing methods for axiom pinpointing can be roughly classified into two categories: glass-box methods and black-box methods. Glass-box methods are based on the reasoning algorithm of a DL. The advantage of a glass-box method is that it can find all MinAs of an entailment by a single run of a modified reasoner. Most of the glass-box algorithms are obtained as extension of tableau-based algorithms for checking satisfiability of a DL-based ontology [7, 6]. It has been pointed out in [5] that one problem for the tableau-based algorithms is that some important blocking techniques cannot be used. In contrast, black-box methods treat a DL reasoner as a "black-box" or an "oracle" and uses it to check satisfiability of an ontology [6, 4, 5]. These methods are reasoner-independent, in the sense that the DL reasoner is solely used as an oracle to determine concept satisfiability with respect to an ontology. The disadvantage of this approach is that it needs to call the reasoner an exponential number of times in the worst case, thus cannot handle large ontologies.

In recent years, EL^+, as a lightweight DL, has gained widespread concerns due to several reasons. First, many important medical ontologies can be formalized in EL^+, such as SNOMED CT and Galen. Second, the reasoning in EL^+ and some of its extensions is tractable when dealing with terminologies. Third, EL^+ provides a logical underpinning of OWL 2 EL, which is an important profile of latest version of OWL, called OWL 2. As some works (i.e., [3]) suggest, unwanted entailments can occur in EL^+ ontologies, such as SNOMED CT. For example, by classifying SNOMED CT, one can get the unintended subsumption relationship between "amputation of finger" and "amputation of upper limb". Several methods have been developed to find all MinAs of an entailment in EL^+, including black-box methods [3, 8] and a glass-box method [2, 8]. The glass-box method is based on the well-known polynomial time *subsumption algorithm* given in [1] by attaching a label to each axiom in the original ontology and propagated it to inferred axioms through completion rules. As was shown in [2, 8],

CIKM'11, October 24–28, 2011, Glasgow, Scotland, UK.

this method is not efficient as too much space is needed to store labels.

In this paper, we propose a novel method to compute all MinAs that utilizes the hierarchy information obtained from the classification of an EL^+ ontology without attaching labels to entailed subsumptions. We further consider axiom pinpointing in EL^+ when ontologies change. An incremental algorithm is given to compute all MinAs by reusing MinAs previously computed.

2. PRELIMINARY

In this section, we introduce some basic notions in EL^+ and the notion of an MinA.

DEFINITION 1. *[1] **(Syntax and Semantics of EL^+)** Let CN_O and RN_O be two disjoint sets of concept and role names, respectively. Then, we can define* concept descriptions *or* concepts *inductively by using the four constructors shown in the left upper part of Table 1. The definition of general concept inclusions or axioms in EL^+ is shown in the left lower part of Table 1.*

An interpretation $\mathbf{I} = (\triangle^{\mathbf{I}}, \cdot^{\mathbf{I}})$ consists of $\triangle^{\mathbf{I}}$ and $\cdot^{\mathbf{I}}$, where $\triangle^{\mathbf{I}}$ is the domain of $\mathbf{I}$ which is a non-empty set, and $\cdot^{\mathbf{I}}$ is a function mapping each concept name A (resp. role name r) to a subset $A^{\mathbf{I}}$ (resp. a subset $r^{\mathbf{I}}$) of $\triangle^{\mathbf{I}}$ (resp. $\triangle^{\mathbf{I}} \times \triangle^{\mathbf{I}}$). The interpretation function can be extended to arbitrary concept and role descriptions as shown in right part of Table 1.

Table 1: syntax and semantics of EL^+

Name	Syntax	Semantics
top concept	$\top$	$\triangle^I$
bottom concept	$\bot$	$\emptyset$
conjunction	$C \sqcap D$	$C^I \sqcap D^I$
existential restriction	$\exists r.C$	$\{x \in \triangle^I \mid \exists y \in \triangle^I : (x,y) \in r^I \wedge r \in C^I\}$
general concept inclusion	$C \sqsubseteq D$	$C^I \subseteq D^I$
role inclusion	$r_1 \circ ... \circ r_k \sqsubseteq r$	$r_1^I \circ ... \circ r_k^I \subseteq r^I$
transitivity	$transitive(r)$	$\forall d,e,f \in \triangle^I : (d,e),(e,f) \in r^I \longrightarrow (d,f) \in r^I$
reflexivity	$reflexivity(r)$	$\forall d \in \triangle^I : (d,d) \in r^I$
range restriction	$range(r) \sqsubseteq C$	$\{e \in \triangle^I \mid \exists d : (d,e) \in r^I\} \subseteq C^I$
domain restriction	$domain(r) \sqsubseteq C$	$\{d \in \triangle^I \mid \exists e : (d,e) \in r^I\} \subseteq C^I$
role hierarchy	$r \sqsubseteq s$	$r^I \subseteq s^I$

Given an EL^+ ontology, the subsumption algorithm given in [1] first normalizes the ontology as follows by applying some normalization rules:

- all concept inclusions are in one of the following forms: $A_1 \sqcap A_2 \sqcap ... \sqcap A_n \sqsubseteq B$, $A \sqsubseteq \exists r.B$, $\exists r.A \sqsubseteq B$
- role inclusions are in one of the following forms: $r \sqsubseteq s$, $r \circ s \sqsubseteq t$

Then, we classify the normalized ontology by using the completion rules given as follows [1].

CR1 if $A_1, ..., A_n \in S(X)$, $A_1 \sqcap A_2 \sqcap ... \sqcap A_n \sqsubseteq B \in O$ and $B \notin S(X)$ then $S(X) := S(X) \cup B$

CR2 if $A \in S(X)$, $A \sqsubseteq \exists r.B \in O$ and $(X,B) \notin R(r)$ then $R(r) := R(r) \cup (X,B)$

CR3 if $(X,Y) \in R(r)$, $A \in S(Y)$, $\exists r.A \sqsubseteq B \in O$ and $B \notin S(X)$ then $S(X) := S(X) \cup B$

CR4 if $(X,Y) \in R(r)$, $\bot \in S(Y)$ and $\bot \notin S(X)$ then $S(X) := S(X) \cup \bot$

CR5 if $(X,Y) \in R(r)$, $r \sqsubseteq s \in O$ and $(X,Y) \notin R(s)$ then $R(s) := R(s) \cup (X,Y)$

CR6 if $(X,Y) \in R(r)$,$(Y,Z) \in R(s)$, $r \circ s \sqsubseteq t \in O$ and $(X,Z) \notin R(t)$ then $R(t) := R(t) \cup (X,Y)$

DEFINITION 2. ***(MinA)** Let O be an EL^+ ontology, and σ a logical entailment of O, i.e., $O \models \sigma$. Then, a subset $S \subseteq O$ is a minimal axiom set (MinA) for σ w.r.t. O, if, and only if $S \models \sigma$, and for every $S' \subset S$, $S' \not\models \sigma$.*

3. AN ALGORITHM FOR AXIOM PINPOINTING IN EL^+

It is easy to see that an axiom of the form $C \sqsubseteq D$ is added to the classification of an EL^+ ontology only by applying completion rule CR1, CR3 or CR4, and an axiom of the form $C \sqsubseteq \exists r.D$ is added to the classification of an EL^+ ontology only by applying rule CR2, CR5 or CR6. We use $C \sqsubseteq_O D$ to denote $O \models C \sqsubseteq D$. Then, we have the following observation.

- Suppose $C \sqsubseteq_O D$ is obtained by applying rule CR1, CR3 or CR4, at least one of the following two conditions is satisfied:

  (1.1) there exists an axiom $A_1 \sqcap A_2 \sqcap ... \sqcap A_n \sqsubseteq D \in O$ such that $C \sqsubseteq_O A_1$,...,$C \sqsubseteq_O A_n$

  (1.2) there exists an axiom $\exists r.A \sqsubseteq D \in O$ such that $C \sqsubseteq_O \exists r.A$

- Suppose $C \sqsubseteq_O \exists r.D$ is obtained by applying rule CR2,CR5 or CR6, at least one of the following three conditions is satisfied:

  (2.1) there exists an axiom $Y \sqsubseteq_O D$ such that $C \sqsubseteq_O \exists r.Y$ or there exists an axiom $C \sqsubseteq_O Y$ such that $Y \sqsubseteq_O \exists r.D$

  (2.2) there exists an axiom $s \sqsubseteq r \in O$ such that $Y \sqsubseteq_O \exists s.D$

  (2.3) there exists an axiom $s \circ t \sqsubseteq r \in O$ and an concept name Y such that $C \sqsubseteq_O \exists s.Y$, $Y \sqsubseteq_O \exists t.D$

Based on the above observation, we present a pinpointing algorithm (see Algorithm 1) for EL^+. We assume that ontology O has been classified by using the classification algorithm given in [8], so we can obtain the hierarchy information $\mathcal{C}_O$, $\mathcal{C}_O = \bigcup_{A \in CN_O} (S_O^+(A) \cup S_O^-(A)) \cup \bigcup_{r \in RN_O} R_O(r)$.

$$S_O^+(A) = \{\ C \in CN_O \mid A \sqsubseteq_O C\ \}$$

$$S_O^-(A) = \{\ C \in CN_O \mid C \sqsubseteq_O A\ \}$$

$$R_O(r) = \{(C,D) \mid C \sqsubseteq_O \exists r.D, C, D \in CN_O, r \in RN_O\}$$

Then, we define an operator $\otimes$. Suppose S_i, T_j are sets of axioms ($1 \le i \le m, 1 \le j \le n$), $S = \{S_1, S_2, ..., S_m\}$ and $T = \{T_1, T_2, ..., T_n\}$ we have

$$S \otimes T \equiv \{ \; S_1 \cup T_1, S_2 \cup T_1, ..., S_m \cup T_1, \; S_1 \cup T_2, S_2 \cup T_2, ..., S_m \cup T_2, \; ..., \; S_1 \cup T_n, S_2 \cup T_n, ..., S_m \cup T_n \; \}$$

The input of our algorithm consists of an ontology O, its entailment $C \sqsubseteq D$ and the hierarchy information $\mathcal{C}_O$. The first and second **for**-loops of the procedure **MinAs** correspond to (1.1). The third **for**-loop corresponds to (1.2). The procedure **MinAsEdge** is called by **MinAs** to compute all MinAs for the subsumption of the form $C \sqsubseteq \exists r.D$. The first and second **for**-loops of the procedure **MinAsEdge** correspond to (2.1). The third and fourth **for**-loops correspond to (2.2) and (2.3) respectively.

The correctness of our algorithm is clear based on our previous observation. Formally, we have:

THEOREM 1. *Given an ontology O and the hierarchy information $\mathcal{C}_O$, suppose $C \sqsubseteq D$ is its entailment and , Algorithm 1 returns all the MinAs of $C \sqsubseteq D$.*

We also consider an optimization in Algorithm 1. In our algorithm, if all MinAs for a concept subsumption are returned, we label the state of this concept as "computed". When the procedures **MinAs** and **MinAsEdge** are called iteratively, we do not compute the MinAs of a subsumption repeatedly but return the computed all MinAs directly when a subsumption is labelled as "computed".

EXAMPLE 1. *Let O be an EL^+ ontology consisting of the following axioms:*

$\alpha_1 : A \sqsubseteq P_1$ $\quad \alpha_2 : A \sqsubseteq \exists r.P_2$ $\quad \alpha_3 : r \sqsubseteq s$
$\alpha_4 : P_2 \sqsubseteq P_1$ $\quad \alpha_5 : \exists s.P_1 \sqsubseteq P_3$ $\quad \alpha_6 : P_1 \sqsubseteq B$
$\alpha_7 : P_3 \sqsubseteq B$ $\quad \alpha_8 : \exists r.P_4 \sqsubseteq B$

After classifying O we get the following hierarchy information:

$S^+_O(A) = \{P_1, P_3, B\}$ $\quad S^+_O(P_1) = \{B\}$
$S^+_O(P_2) = \{P_1, B\}$ $\quad S^+_O(P_3) = \{B\}$
$S^-_O(P_1) = \{A, P_2\}$ $\quad S^-_O(P_3) = \{A\}$
$S^-_O(B) = \{A, P_1, P_2, P_3\}$
$R_O(r) = \{(A, P_2), (A, P_1)\}$ $\quad R_O(s) = \{(A, P_2), (A, P_1)\}$

It is clear that $A \sqsubseteq B$ is inferred from O. We use Algorithm 1 to compute all MinAs of $A \sqsubseteq B$:

- *since $S^+_O(A) \cap S^-_O(B) = \{P_1, P_3\}$, we have:*
  $J_1 = MinAs(A \sqsubseteq P_1, O, \mathcal{C}_O) \otimes MinAs(P_1 \sqsubseteq B, O, \mathcal{C}_O)$
  $J_2 = MinAs(A \sqsubseteq P_3, O, \mathcal{C}_O) \otimes MinAs(P_3 \sqsubseteq B, O, \mathcal{C}_O)$
  $MinAs(A \sqsubseteq B, O, \mathcal{C}_O) = J_1 \cup J_2$, *and it is clear that*
  $MinAs(A \sqsubseteq P_1, O, \mathcal{C}_O) = \{\{\alpha_1\}\}$ *and*
  $MinAs(P_1 \sqsubseteq B, O, \mathcal{C}_O) = \{\{\alpha_6\}\}$, *so we have*
  $J_1 = \{\{\alpha_1, \alpha_6\}\}$.
- *since $\alpha_5 : \exists s.P_1 \sqsubseteq P_3 \in O$ and $(A, P_1) \in R_O(s)$, we have*
  $MinAs(A \sqsubseteq P_3, O, \mathcal{C}_O) =$
  $MinAsEdge(A, s, P_1, O, \mathcal{C}_O) \otimes \{\{\alpha_5\}\}$
- *since $P_2 \in S^-_O(P_1)$ and $(A, P_2) \in R_O(s)$, we have*
  $MinAsEdge(A, s, P_1, O, \mathcal{C}_O) =$
  $MinAsEdge(A, s, P_2, O, \mathcal{C}_O) \otimes MinAs(P_2 \sqsubseteq P_1, O, \mathcal{C}_O)$
- *since $\alpha_3 : r \sqsubseteq s \in O$ and $(A, P_2) \in R_O(r)$, we have*
  $MinAsEdge(A, s, P_2, O, \mathcal{C}_O) =$
  $MinAs(A, r, P_2, O, \mathcal{C}_O) \otimes \{\{\alpha_3\}\}$

then it is clear that
$MinAsEdge(A, r, P_2, O, \mathcal{C}_O) = \{\{\alpha_2\}\}$, *so*
$MinAsEdge(A, s, P_2, O, \mathcal{C}_O) = \{\{\alpha_2, \alpha_3\}\}$, *and since*
$MinAs(P_2 \sqsubseteq P_1, O, \mathcal{C}_O) = \{\{\alpha_4\}\}$, *we have*
$MinAsEdge(A, s, P_1, O, \mathcal{C}_O) = \{\{\alpha_2, \alpha_3, \alpha_4\}\}$,
$MinAs(A \sqsubseteq P_3, O, \mathcal{C}_O) = \{\{\alpha_2, \alpha_3, \alpha_4, \alpha_5\}\}$,
$MinAs(P_3 \sqsubseteq B, O, \mathcal{C}_O) = \{\{\alpha_7\}\}$, *so*
$J_2 = \{\{\alpha_2, \alpha_3, \alpha_4, \alpha_5, \alpha_7\}\}$
$J = J_1 \cup J_2 = \{\{\alpha_1, \alpha_6\}, \{\alpha_2, \alpha_3, \alpha_4, \alpha_5, \alpha_7\}\}$

Algorithm 1 Computing All the MinAs

procedure MinAs($C \sqsubseteq D$, O, $\mathcal{C}_O$)
Input:
O: an ontology
$C \sqsubseteq D$: a subsumption
$\mathcal{C}_O$: the hierarchy information for O
Output:
J: the set of all the MinAs for $C \sqsubseteq D \in O$
J:=$\{\emptyset\}$
if $C \sqsubseteq D \in O$ **then**
  J:=$\{\{C \sqsubseteq D\}\}$
end if
for every concept name $A \in (S^+_O(C) \cap S^-_O(D))$ **do**
  J:=$J \cup$ (MinAs($C \sqsubseteq A$, O, $\mathcal{C}_O$)$\otimes$MinAs($A \sqsubseteq D$, O, $\mathcal{C}_O$)) //**(1.1)**
end for
for every axiom $\alpha \in O$ in the form of $A_1 \sqcap A_2 \sqcap ... \sqcap A_n \sqsubseteq D$, $n \ge 2$ **do**
  if $A_1 \in S^+_O(C)$, $A_2 \in S^+_O(C)$, ..., $A_n \in S^+_O(C)$ **then**
    J_1:=MinAs($C \sqsubseteq A_1$, O, $\mathcal{C}_O$) //**(1.1)**
    ...
    J_n:=MinAs($C \sqsubseteq A_n$, O, $\mathcal{C}_O$)
    J:=$J \cup (J_1 \otimes J_2 \otimes ... \otimes J_n \otimes \{\{\alpha\}\})$
  end if
end for
for every axiom $\beta \in O$ in the form of $\exists r.A \sqsubseteq D$ **do**
  if $(C, A) \in R_O(r)$ **then**
    J':=MinAsEdge(C, r, A, O, $\mathcal{C}_O$) //**(1.2)**
    J:=$J \cup (J' \otimes \{\{\beta\}\})$
  end if
end for
return J

Procedure MinAsEdge(C, r, A, O, $\mathcal{C}_O$) //$C \sqsubseteq \exists r.A$
J:=$\{\emptyset\}$
if $(C, A) \in R_O(r)$ **then**
  J:=$\{\{C \sqsubseteq \exists r.A\}\}$
end if
for every concept name $B \in S^-_O(A)$) **do**
  if $(C, B) \in R_O(r)$ **then**
    J:=$J \cup$(MinAsEdge(C, r, B, O, $\mathcal{C}_O$) $\otimes$ MinAs($B \sqsubseteq A$, O, $\mathcal{C}_O$)) //**(2.1)**
  end if
end for
for every concept name $B \in S^+_O(C)$) **do**
  if $(B, A) \in R_O(r)$ **then**
    J:=$J \cup$(MinAsEdge(B, r, A, O, $\mathcal{C}_O$) $\otimes$ MinAs($C \sqsubseteq B$, O, $\mathcal{C}_O$)) //**(2.1)**
  end if
end for
for every axiom $\alpha \in O$ in the form of $s \sqsubseteq r$ **do**
  if $(C, A) \in R_O(s)$ **then**
    J':=MinAsEdge(C, s, A, O, $\mathcal{C}_O$)$\otimes\{\{\alpha\}\}$
    J:=$J \cup J'$ //**(2.2)**
  end if
end for
for every axiom $\beta \in O$ in the form of $s \circ t \sqsubseteq r$ **do**
  for every concept name $Y \in O$ such that $Y \sqsubseteq \exists t.A$ **do**
    if $C \sqsubseteq \exists s.Y$ **then**
      J_1:=MinAsEdge(C, s, Y, O, $\mathcal{C}_O$) //**(2.3)**
      J_2:=MinAsEdge(Y, t, A, O, $\mathcal{C}_O$)
      J:=$J \cup \{J_1 \otimes J_2 \otimes \{\{\beta\}\}\}$
    end if
  end for
end for
return J

4. AN INCREMENTAL PINPOINTING ALGORITHM

Ontologies are typically not static entities, but they evolve over time and need to be modified. Changes to an ontology may be caused, e.g., by modifications in the application domain, the reorganization of existing information, or the incorporation of additional knowledge according to changes in the users' needs. Errors can naturally occur when ontologies evolve. Axiom pinpointing during ontology evolution raises some new challenges. Instead of computing all MinAs of an entailment from scratch, it is highly desirable to reuse computed MinAs of the entailment if available. That is, we want to incrementally compute all MinAs when ontologies change. In this section, we propose an incremental pinpointing algorithm which is based on our proposed pinpointing algorithm (see Algorithm 2).

Algorithm 2 Incremental Finding All the MinAs

procedure inc_MinAs($C \sqsubseteq D$, O, $\triangle O^+$, $\triangle O^-$)
Input:
O: an ontology
$\triangle O^+$: added axioms
$\triangle O^-$: removed axioms
Output:
J: the set of all the MinAs for $C \sqsubseteq D \in (O \cup \triangle O^+ - \triangle O^-)$
1: *inc_classify*(O, $\triangle^+ O$)
2: J = MinAs($C \sqsubseteq D$, $O \cup \triangle O^+$, $\mathcal{C}_{O \cup \triangle O^+}$)
3: **for** every set $S \in J$ **do**
4: **if** exist axiom $\gamma \in \triangle O^-$ and $\gamma \in S$ **then**
5: $J = J - \{S\}$
6: **end if**
7: **end for**
8: return J

We first consider the case when new axioms are added to an ontology. We slightly modify the duo-ontology classification algorithm in [8] to incrementally classify the new ontology (see function *inc_classify* in Algorithm 2). That is, for every axiom which can be inferred by the original ontology O, if it is inferred again during the process of incremental classification (i.e., it is inferred by new added axioms and some axioms in the original ontology), and all its MinAs have been calculated, we label it as "non-computed". Then we call MinAs($C \sqsubseteq D$, $O \cup \triangle O^+$, $\mathcal{C}_{O \cup \triangle O^+}$) (line 2), which will reuse previously computed MinAs and continue to compute new MinAs. Otherwise, if $C \sqsubseteq D$ cannot be inferred again during the process of incremental classification, the label of its MinAs set is still "computed". In this case, we can just return the computed MinAs for $C \sqsubseteq D$ directly.

When deleting axioms, we simply delete those MinAs which contain one or more deleted axiom(s) (lines 3-7).

EXAMPLE 2. *(Example 1 continues) We add a new axiom* α_9*:* $A \sqsubseteq \exists r.P_4$ *and delete the axiom* α_3*:* $r \sqsubseteq s$*. By applying the incremental classification algorithm, axiom* $A \sqsubseteq B$ *will be inferred again by* α_8 *and* α_9*, according to Example 1, MinAs(*$A \sqsubseteq B$*,* O*,* $\mathcal{C}_O$*) is labelled as "computed", so we label it as "un-computed". Then we use Algorithm 1 to compute new MinAs for* $A \sqsubseteq B$*:*

Since $S^+_{O \cup \triangle O^+}(A) \cap S^-_{O \cup \triangle O^+}(B) = \{P_1, P_3\}$*, we have* J_1 *= MinAs(*$A \sqsubseteq P_1$*,* $O \cup \triangle O^+$*,* $\mathcal{C}_{O \cup \triangle O^+}$*)*$\otimes$ *MinAs(*$P_1 \sqsubseteq B$*,* $O \cup \triangle O^+$*,* $\mathcal{C}_{O \cup \triangle O^+}$*), and* J_2 *= MinAs(*$A \sqsubseteq P_3$*,* $O \cup \triangle O^+$*,* $\mathcal{C}_{O \cup \triangle O^+}$*)*$\otimes$ *MinAs(*$P_3 \sqsubseteq B$*,* $O \cup \triangle O^+$*,* $\mathcal{C}_{O \cup \triangle O^+}$*). It is clear*

MinAs($A \sqsubseteq P_1$*,* $O \cup \triangle O^+$*,* $\mathcal{C}_{O \cup \triangle O^+}$*)* $= \{\{\alpha_1\}\}$*, and*

MinAs($P_1 \sqsubseteq B$*,* $O \cup \triangle O^+$*,* $\mathcal{C}_{O \cup \triangle O^+}$*)* $= \{\{\alpha_6\}\}$*.*

So $J_1 = \{\{\alpha_1, \alpha_6\}\}$*. We also have*

MinAs($A \sqsubseteq P_3$*,* $O \cup \triangle O^+$*,* $\mathcal{C}_{O \cup \triangle O^+}$*)* $= \{\{\alpha_2, \alpha_3, \alpha_4, \alpha_5\}\}$*, and*

MinAs($P_3 \sqsubseteq B$*,* $O \cup \triangle O^+$*,* $\mathcal{C}_{O \cup \triangle O^+}$*)* $= \{\{\alpha_7\}\}$*.*

So $J_2 = \{\{\alpha_2, \alpha_3, \alpha_4, \alpha_5, \alpha_7\}\}$*. Since* $\alpha_8 : \exists r.P_4 \sqsubseteq B \in O$ *and* $(A, P_4) \in R_O(r)$*, we have* J_3 *= MinAsEdge(*A*,* r*,* P_4*,* $O \cup \triangle O^+$*,* $\mathcal{C}_{O \cup \triangle O^+}$*)*$\otimes \{\{\alpha_8\}\}$*. It is clear*

MinAsEdge(A*,* r*,* P_4*,* $O \cup \triangle O^+$*,* $\mathcal{C}_{O \cup \triangle O^+}$*)* $= \{\{\alpha_9\}\}$*.*

So $J_3 = \{\{\alpha_8, \alpha_9\}\}$*. Therefore,* $J = \{\{\alpha_1, \alpha_6\}, \{\alpha_2, \alpha_3, \alpha_4, \alpha_5, \alpha_7\}, \{\alpha_8, \alpha_9\}\}$*. Finally, after deleting axiom* α_3 $r \sqsubseteq s$*, we have* $J = \{\{\alpha_1, \alpha_6\}, \{\alpha_8, \alpha_9\}\}$*.*

5. CONCLUSION

In this paper, we proposed a novel method for axioms pinpointing in EL^+ by using the hierarchy information obtained during classification of an ontology. We also proposed an optimization technique to avoid repeated computation of MinAs in our algorithm. We then considered axiom pinpointing when ontologies evolve. Based on our pinpointing algorithm and the incremental classification algorithm given in [8], we presented an incremental pinpointing algorithm to reuse computed MinAs of an entailment.

6. ACKNOWLEDGEMENT

This work is supported by NSFC (61003157), Jiangsu Science Foundation (BK2010412), and the Key Laboratory of Computer Network and Information Integration (Southeast University).

7. REFERENCES

[1] F. Baader, S. Brandt, and C. Lutz. Pushing the el envelope. In *Proc. of IJCAI'05*, pages 364–369, 2005.

[2] F. Baader, R. Peñaloza, and B. Suntisrivaraporn. Pinpointing in the description logic EL$^+$. In *Proc. of KI'07*, pages 52–67, 2007.

[3] F. Baader and B. Suntisrivaraporn. Debugging SNOMED CT using axiom pinpointing in the description logic EL$^+$. In *Proc. of KR-MED'08*, 2008.

[4] G. Friedrich and K. M. Shchekotykhin. A general diagnosis method for ontologies. In *Proc. of 4th International Conference on Semantic Web*, pages 232–246, 2005.

[5] A. Kalyanpur, B. Parsia, M. Horridge, and E. Sirin. Finding all justifications of OWL DL entailments. In *Proc. of ISWC/ASWC'07*, pages 267–280, 2007.

[6] A. Kalyanpur, B. Parsia, E. Sirin, and J. Hendler. Debugging unsatisfiable classes in OWL ontologies. *Journal of Web Semantics*, 3(4):268–293, 2005.

[7] S. Schlobach and R. Cornet. Non-standard reasoning services for the debugging of description logic terminologies. In *Proc. of IJCAI'03*, pages 355–362. 2003.

[8] B. Suntisrivaraporn. *Polynomial-Time Reasoning Support for Design and Maintenance of Large-Scale Biomedical Ontologies*. PhD thesis, Technical University of Dresden, 2009.

Folksonomy-Based Term Extraction for Word Cloud Generation

David Carmel, Erel Uziel, Ido Guy, Yosi Mass, Haggai Roitman
IBM Research, Haifa lab
Haifa, 31905, Israel
{carmel,erelu,ido,yosimass,haggai}@il.ibm.com

ABSTRACT

In this work we study the task of term extraction for word cloud generation. We present a folksonomy-based term extraction method, called *tag-boost*, which boosts terms that are frequently used by the public to tag content. Our experiments with tag-boost-based term extraction over different domains demonstrate tremendous improvement in word cloud quality, as reflected by the agreement between extracted terms and manually assigned tags of the testing items. Additionally, we show that tag-boost can be effectively applied even in non-tagged domains, by using an external rich folksonomy borrowed from a well-tagged domain.

Categories and Subject Descriptors: H.3.3 [Information storage and retrieval]: Information search and retrieval

General Terms: Algorithms, Experimentation

Keywords: Word-cloud generation, Term extraction, Tag-boost

1. INTRODUCTION

The emergence of social media applications in recent years has encouraged people to be actively involved in content creation and classification. Collaborative bookmarking systems such as Delicious (*delicious.com*) and Dogear for the enterprise [12], as well as many other content sharing sites, encourage users to tag available content for their own use, as well as for the public.

Tags annotated by users form a taxonomy of the tagged items, commonly referred to as a *folksonomy*. The value of a folksonomy is derived from the unique vocabulary and explicit meanings added by the people who tag the items. Folksonomies have been found to be extremely useful for many information retrieval (IR) applications, including tag cloud representation of social media items, query refinement, and search and browse enhancement [6, 4].

A word cloud is a visual depiction, typically used to provide a visual summary or a semantic view of an item or a cluster of items that have something in common (e.g., the search results for a specific query). Clouds are usually generated using the tags assigned to an item (referred to as *tag clouds*), or important terms extracted from the item's description (referred to as *word clouds*). Clearly, meaningful, high-quality tag clouds can be generated in well-tagged domains where the resources are widely tagged. An item can be successfully represented by a tag cloud that is based on its own tags, or on tags associated with similar items. However, when manual (user-provided) tags are not available, feature selection techniques can be used to extract meaningful terms from the item's content or from other textual resources that are related to the item, such as anchor text or the item's metadata [5]. These extracted terms can be used to create a word cloud [10, 9]. Word clouds, however, are usually inferior to tag clouds, since significant terms, from a statistical perspective, do not necessarily serve as good labels for the content from which they were extracted [3]. Recently, word clouds have been popularized by leading social media sites such as *Twitter* and *Facebook*, as an alternative to tag clouds due to the sparseness of manual tags in these domains.

CIKM'11, October 24–28, 2011, Glasgow, Scotland, UK.

2. WORD CLOUD GENERATION

In this section, we describe the technique we used for word cloud generation, based on a tag-cloud generation technique originally described by Amitay et al. [1]. This method proved to perform properly when applied on manual tags of well-tagged items and therefore provides a basis for our work.

Most cloud generation techniques that are based on existing manual tags, rank the tags associated with the items in order to create a cloud from the top-ranked tags. In many cases, tags are ranked according to the number of times they were used to tag an item. Let e be an item tagged by k manual tags, $(t_1, \ldots, t_k)$, then a tag cloud (a ranked list of representative tags) can be generated by ranking the tags according to the tag score, $s(t,e) = tf(t,e) \cdot ief(t)$, where $tf(t,e) = \log(freq(t,e) + 1)$ is proportional to $freq(t,e)$, the number of times e was tagged by t; $ief(t) = \log \frac{N}{N_t}$ is the *inverse entity frequency* of the tag t, where N is the total number of items, and N_t is the number of items tagged by t. Such a weighting scheme is analogous to the popular vector-space *tf-idf* weighing approach. Thus, a highly used tag (high tf), which is assigned to only a few items in the collection (high ief), is ranked higher in the cloud.

A cloud for a cluster of tagged items is generated by ranking the tags assigned to all items in the cluster. Let $S = \{e_1 \ldots, e_n\}$ be a list of tagged items, ranked according to an arbitrary score function, *Score*(e). Each item e_i is associated with a list of tags $(t^i_1, \ldots, t^i_{k_i})$, $k_i \geq 0$ (for a non-tagged item e_j, $k_j = 0$). The aggregated score of a tag, with respect to S, is determined as follows:

$$s(t, S) = \sum_{e \in S} Score(e) \cdot s(t, e). \quad (1)$$

Thus, tags that are frequently assigned to many highly scored items are ranked higher in the tag-cloud.

The same formula can be used for word cloud generation. Given a set of items, each associated with a set of extracted terms, then a word cloud can be generated using Equation 1, where the term score per item, $s(t, e)$, is determined by the the term extraction method.

Term extraction

Term extraction is strongly related to feature selection, which is the process of selecting a set of terms for text representation. We experimented with four fundamental extraction techniques [11]: 1) *tf-idf*, which selects terms from the item textual description with maximum *tf-idf* weights; 2) *Mutual Information* (MI), which measures how much information the presence/absence of a term contributes to the item description; 3) χ^2, which measures the statistical independence of the occurrence of the term in the item description and its occurrence in the collection; and 4) *Kullback-Leibler divergence* (KL), which looks for a set of terms that maximize the KL divergence between the language model of the item's content and the language model of the entire collection [2].

We can also consider more sophisticated combination policies between tags and terms, like measuring the mutual relationships between them [14]. However, existing methods assume the existence of sufficient associated tags. Advanced integration approaches of terms and tags in sparsely-tagged domains have not yet been studied, to the best of our knowledge, and we suggest this as a direction for future work.

Tag-boost enhancement

Internal extracted terms are very useful for IR applications such as text clustering and categorization [11]. However, in general, extracted terms are not always optimal for tagging. Carmel et al. [3] showed that in many cases, even when manually associated tags appear in the text, pure statistical methods have difficulty in identifying them as good descriptors. An important term, as determined by common statistical criteria, is not always considered a good label by humans. Therefore, our main hypothesis is that terms considered as good labels by humans have specific characteristics that are not always exposed by standard statistical extraction approaches. We attempt to measure the likelihood of a term being considered by humans as a good tag.

Let C be a collection of items, and let w be a term. Let $C_w \subseteq C$, and $T_w \subseteq C$ be the set of items containing w, and the set of items tagged by w, respectively. We mark $w \in e$, if term w appears in e's description. We mark $tag(w, e)$, when w is used to tag e. We mark $tag(w)$ if w is used to tag any item in C.

The probability of term w to tag an item e when appearing in its description can be approximated by *maximum likelihood estimation* (MLE): $Pr_C(tag(w, e)|w \in e) \stackrel{def}{=} \frac{|C_w \cap T_w|}{|C_w|}$. $Pr_C(tag(w, e)|w \in e)$ estimates the probability that a term w found in the item's description will also be used to tag that item. Thus, terms with high values should be biased for word cloud generation.

The second measure we apply approximates the global likelihood of a term to be used as a tag. Our approximation is based on the assumption that a term w, used to tag many items in the collection, is more likely to be used as a tag for **any** item in the collection, compared to terms which are rarely used as tags: $Pr_C(tag(w)) \stackrel{def}{=} \frac{|T_w|}{|C|}$.

When estimating probabilities based on a limited amount of data, smoothing is a fundamental approach to adjust the maximum likelihood estimator and thereby correct the inaccuracy due to data sparseness [13]. For example, a term that has never been used to tag the items to which it belongs ($Pr_C(tag(w, e)|w \in e) = 0$), should still be considered a good candidate for tagging when it is frequently used to tag other items in the collection (with high $Pr_C(tag(w))$). Therefore, the tag-boost probability we apply is based on the *Jelinek-Mercer* smoothing of the two estimators:

$$Pr_C^{smooth}(tag(w, e)|w \in e) \stackrel{def}{=} \quad (2)$$
$$\lambda \cdot Pr_C(tag(w, e)|w \in e) \quad + \quad (1 - \lambda) \cdot Pr_C(tag(w)).$$

The smoothing coefficient λ, can be optimally tuned for each individual collection. In our experiments, described in Section 3, we set λ to 0.9 as it seems to perform well for all collections with which we experimented.

Finally, we boosted each term extracted from the item's description, by any statistical term extraction technique, by multiplying its (statistical) weight by the estimated tag-boost probability. We then selected terms with the maximum boosted score for word cloud representation:

$$s_{boost}(w, e) = s(w, e) \cdot Pr_C^{smooth}(tag(w, e)|w \in e). \quad (3)$$

We also note that both estimators of the term-tagging characteristics can be inferred from any collection of tagged items. Thus, as we will show, it is possible to estimate those probabilities from an external well-tagged collection, to boost terms in a sparsely-tagged collection that suffers from insufficient statistics.

3. EVALUATION

The main assumption behind our evaluation approach is that manual tags assigned to an item are good labels for summarizing its main characteristics. Therefore, given a testing item associated with good manual tags, the quality of a word cloud generated for that item can be estimated by measuring the number of manual tags retrieved, as well as their relative position in the ranked list of extracted terms. The average precision (AP) measure estimates the quality of a ranked list of terms by measuring the number and rank of the manual tags in the list. MAP, the mean AP over a set of testing items, is the main evaluation measure we used for this work. We also used P@10, the relative frequency of manual tags in the top ten retrieved terms, as a complementary measurement.

Data. We experimented with term extraction methods over four social media datasets, described in Table 1.

Delicious is a dataset made up of 144.5K unique web pages, all of them with their corresponding social tags retrieved from *Delicious* during June 2008[1]. This is a well-tagged dataset with 1.85M tags (67K unique tags). All documents (web-pages) are assigned at least one tag.

[1]http://nlp.uned.es/social-tagging/delicioust140/

	#items	#unique tags	avg. tags/item	median tags/item
Delicious	144.5K	67K	12.8	11
CiteULike	235K	54K	3.5	3
Dogear	198K	47K	3.8	2
BlogCentral	119K	24K	2.9	2

Table 1: Social media datasets

Collection	Term Ext. Method	MAP	
		no-boost	tag-boost
Delicious	*tf-idf*	0.16	0.25 (+56%)
	χ^2	0.11	**0.27** (+145%)
	MI	0.16	0.26 (+62%)
	KL	0.16	0.25 (+56%)
CiteULike	*tf-idf*	0.17	0.21 (+24%)
	χ^2	0.14	**0.24** (+71%)
	MI	0.17	0.23 (+35%)
	KL	0.17	0.23 (+35%)
Dogear	*tf-idf*	0.19	0.21 (+11%)
	χ^2	0.16	**0.25** (+56%)
	MI	0.19	0.23 (+21%)
	KL	0.19	0.22 (+16%)
BlogCentral	*tf-idf*	0.15	0.26 (+73%)
	χ^2	0.14	**0.27** (+93%)
	MI	0.18	0.27 (+50%)
	KL	0.18	0.26 (+44%)

Table 2: Word cloud quality of several term extraction methods, with and without tag-boost

CiteULike is an online bookmarking service that allows users to bookmark academic articles. For our experiments, we used a random sample of 235K documents, with a total of 209K tags (54K unique tags).

Dogear is an enterprise social bookmarking system [12], popularly used by thousands of employees, to organize their bookmarks of both intranet and Internet documents. The *Dogear* dataset contains 198K web pages, bookmarked with a total of 743K tags (47K unique tags).

BlogCentral is an enterprise blog service allowing employees to publish personal blogs within the intranet and to comment on other people blogs [7]. The dataset contains 119K blog posts, tagged with a total of 350K tags (24K unique tags).

Word cloud generation for a single item. In our first experiment, we evaluated several term extraction methods for a single item, with and without tag-boost over the four domains. For each domain, we randomly selected 1000 items, each assigned with at least 5 unique tags for testing. For each item, we generated a word cloud by extracting the most important terms from the item's content. We measured its quality according to the manual tags of that item. The (statistical) term extraction methods select the most informative terms from the item's content; we then boosted each term by the tag-boost probability, according to Equation 3. Table 2 represents the MAP achieved by the different term extraction methods over the four domains.

The results reveal no significant difference in performance among the different statistical methods, in terms of the agreement between the generated word cloud and the manual tags assigned to an item, as measured by MAP. However, tag-boost improved that agreement significantly for all methods, particularly for *Delicious* (80% on average for MAP). The improvement was less impressive for the other domains but still significant (65% for *BlogCentral*, 23% for *Dogear* and 41% for *CiteULike*). In all domains, the improvement achieved by tag-boost was statistically significant (paired t-test $p < 0.001$). Interestingly, χ^2, which is the inferior method over all collections, outperformed all other methods (albeit insignificantly) when combined with tag-boost.

Since no significant difference in performance was measured among the term extraction methods, we focused the following experiments on the KL extraction method as a representative for statistical term extraction.

Word cloud generation for a cluster of items. Clouds are usually created for a set of items, rather than for an individual item, due to the sparseness of manual tags per item, even in well-tagged domains. We now describe two experiments that evaluate term extraction methods for word cloud generation for a cluster of items.

In the first experiment, we measured the quality of a word cloud created for the result list of a query. For each domain, we ran 100 text queries, randomly selected from a query log, and created two clouds for the top-10 results per query. We created the manual tag-cloud from the tags of retrieved items according to Equation 1. We then created the term-based word cloud by the same formula, using the 30 terms per item extracted from its content. We used the top 10 tags of the manual tag cloud to measure the precision of the word cloud. Table 3 shows the quality of the word cloud, while using KL and tag-boost-based KL (KL+TB) for term extraction, over the four domains. Tag-boost significantly improved the word cloud quality (by more than 200% on *Delicious*!), to better agree with manual based tag clouds.

Collection	Term Extr. method	MAP	P@10
Delicious	KL	0.14	0.41
	KL+TB	0.44 (+214%)	0.87 (+112%)
CiteULike	KL	0.13	0.40
	KL+TB	0.29 (+123%)	0.69 (+73%)
Dogear	KL	0.13	0.43
	KL+TB	0.23 (+77%)	0.60 (+40%)
BlogCentral	KL	0.15	0.42
	KL+TB	0.27 (+80%)	0.56 (+33%)

Table 3: Quality of word clouds generated for result lists of queries

In the second experiment we measured the quality of a word cloud generated for a cluster of items tagged by a person. The word cloud's quality was measured using the person's in-tags (terms used to tag that user by others). This evaluation is highly reliable since a person's in-tags, provided by other users, represent well the person's topics of interest, while they are also independent of the tagged items. Therefore, the higher the agreement of the word cloud generated for the person's items with her in-tags, the higher its quality.

We selected 1000 people for testing in the *Dogear* and the *BlogCentral* domains, each associated with at least 5 in-tags[2]. Table 4 shows the quality of the different term extraction methods used for word cloud generation. The last row shows the quality of the manual-based tag cloud

[2]We could not run this experiment on *Delicious* and *CiteULike* since we do not have the in-tags for users in these domains.

of those items, which is given for reference. While the KL-based extraction method fails to agree with the users' in-tags, using tag-boost improves the quality by more than 100% on *Dogear*, and by 60% on *BlogCentral*, performing almost as well as manual tags.

Collection	Term Extr. method	MAP	P@10
Dogear	KL	0.06	0.12
	KL+TB	0.12 (+100%)	0.23 (+92%)
	Manual Tags	0.15	0.30
BlogCentral	KL	0.15	0.30
	KL+TB	0.24 (+60%)	0.46 (+20%)
	Manual Tags	0.25	0.50

Table 4: Quality of word clouds generated for clusters of items, all tagged by the same person

Using an external folksonomy for tag-boosting. In the final experiment, we examined whether an external folksonomy can be used for word cloud generation. The data we used was taken from *Twitter*. Users can tag their tweets by *hashtags*; however, less than 30% of the tweets are tagged, and many of the hashtags are used for marking a thread of discussion rather than for labeling [8]. Consequently, manual tags in *Twitter* are useless for cloud generation. Moreover, its poor folksonomy cannot even be used for tag-boosting. Therefore, *Twitter* is an excellent example for a sparsely-tagged domain.

We used the *Twitter* domain to examine whether an external folksonomy can be effectively used to replace the useless folksonomy for tag-boosting. Existing hashtags were treated as regular terms while the *Delicious* and *CiteULike* folksonomies were used for tag-boosting. In order to evaluate the word cloud quality in this case, we manually tagged a random sample of 1000 tweets, extracted from a collection of 100K tweets that we collected during one week in November 2010. Tweets were tagged according to their content, while considering their hashtags and urls (when they existed). The average number of manual tags per tweet was 2.5 and about 20% of the tweets were not tagged due to difficulties in understanding their underlying topics.

The word-cloud quality was measured in two cases. First, we extracted 5 terms from each tweet's content, using KL with and without tag-boost, and measured the agreement between them with the tweet's manual tags. Second, we ran 100 randomly selected queries and measured the quality of the word cloud generated for the top-10 results for each query, based on these extracted terms. Table 5 shows the effectiveness of tag-boost for the *Twitter* domain, first using the *Delicious* folksonomy, and then using the *CiteULike* folksonomy. In both cases, tag-boost significantly improved the quality of extracted terms, using the two folksonomies, despite the fact that both folkosonomies were borrowed from different domains. The *Delicious* folksonomy was superior to the *CiteULike* folksonomy for tag-boosting, since it is more general and presumably better fits the *Twitter* domain.

	Term Extr. Method	MAP	P@5
Single items	KL	0.39	0.26
	KL+TB(Del.)	0.54(+38%)	0.44(+69%)
	KL+TB(CUL)	0.47(+21%)	0.36(+38%)
Cluster items	KL	0.11	0.36
	KL+TB(Del.)	0.27(+145%)	0.62(+72%)
	KL+TB(CUL)	0.21(+91%)	0.58(+61%)

Table 5: Quality of the word clouds generated for *Twitter* items, using the *Delicious* (Del.) and the *CiteULike* (CUL) folksonomies for tag-boosting

4. SUMMARY

In this work we studied the task of term extraction for word cloud generation in sparsely-tagged domains, in which manual tags are scarce. We presented the tag-boost enhancement approach for term-extraction methods, which boosts terms that are frequently used by the public to tag content. Our experiments with tag-boost enhancement, over several enterprise and non-enterprise domains, demonstrated a tremendous improvement in word cloud quality, as reflected by the agreement between the generated word clouds and the corresponding manual tags of the testing items. Moreover, we showed that tag-boost can even be applied in non-tagged domains, by using an external folksonomy borrowed from a well-tagged domain.

For future work we intend to investigate the contribution of tag-boost-based term extraction for other applications. We also intend to explore mutual relations between tags and terms in sparsely-tagged domains, in which manual tags (if they exist) and internal terms can be mixed to provide a better cloud representation.

5. REFERENCES

[1] E. Amitay, D. Carmel, N. Har'El, S. Ofek-Koifman, A. Soffer, S. Yogev, and N. Golbandi. Social search and discovery using a unified approach. In *Proceedings of HyperText*, pages 199–208, 2009.

[2] A. Berger and J. Lafferty. Information retrieval as statistical translation. In *Proceedings of SIGIR*, pages 222–229, 1999.

[3] D. Carmel, H. Roitman, and N. Zwerdling. Enhancing cluster labeling using wikipedia. In *Proceedings of SIGIR*, pages 139–146, 2009.

[4] P. Heymann, G. Koutrika, and H. Garcia-Molina. Can social bookmarking improve web search? In *Proceedings of WSDM*, pages 195–206, 2008.

[5] P. Heymann, D. Ramage, and H. Garcia-Molina. Social tag prediction. In *Proceedings of SIGIR*, pages 531–538, 2008.

[6] A. Hotho, R. Jäschke, C. Schmitz, and G. Stumme. Information retrieval in folksonomies: Search and ranking. In *The Semantic Web: Research and Applications, ESWC 2006*, pages 411–426, 2006.

[7] J. Huh, L. Jones, T. Erickson, W. A. Kellogg, R. K. E. Bellamy, and J. C. Thomas. Blogcentral: the role of internal blogs at work. In *Proceedings of CHI*, pages 2447–2452, 2007.

[8] H. Kwak, C. Lee, H. Park, and S. Moon. What is twitter, a social network or a news media? In *Proceedings of WWW*, WWW '10, pages 591–600, 2010.

[9] Y. Liu, M. Liu, X. Chen, L. Xiang, and Q. Yang. Automatic tag recommendation for weblogs. In *Proceedings of ITCS*, pages 546–549, 2009.

[10] Y.-T. Lu, S.-I. Yu, T.-C. Chang, and J. Y.-j. Hsu. A content-based method to enhance tag recommendation. In *Proceedings of IJCAI*, pages 2064–2069, 2009.

[11] C. D. Manning, P. Raghavan, and H. Schutze. *Introduction to Information Retrieval.* 2008.

[12] D. R. Millen, J. Feinberg, and B. Kerr. Dogear: Social bookmarking in the enterprise. In *Proceedings of CHI*, pages 111–120, 2006.

[13] C. Zhai and J. Lafferty. A study of smoothing methods for language models applied to ad hoc information retrieval. In *Proceedings of SIGIR*, pages 334–342, 2001.

[14] X. Zhang, L. Yang, X. Wu, H. Guo, Z. Guo, S. Bao, Y. Yu, and Z. Su. sdoc: exploring social wisdom for document enhancement in web mining. In *Proceedings of CIKM*, pages 395–404, 2009.

Efficient Association Discovery with Keyword-based Constraints on Large Graph Data

Mo Zhou
Indiana University, USA
mozhou@cs.indiana.edu

Yifan Pan
Indiana University, USA
panyif@cs.indiana.edu

Yuqing Wu
Indiana University, USA
yuqwu@cs.indiana.edu

ABSTRACT

In many domains, such as social networks and chem-informatics, data can be represented naturally in graph model, with nodes being data entries and edges the relationships between them. We study the application requirements in these domains and find that discovering *Constrained Acyclic Paths* (CAP) is highly in demand. In this paper, we define the CAP search problem and introduce a set of quantitative metrics for describing keyword-based constraints. We propose a series of algorithms to efficiently evaluate CAP queries on large-scale graph data. Extensive experiments illustrate that our algorithms are both efficient and scalable.

Categories and Subject Descriptors

H.3.3 [**Information Systems**]: Information Storage and Retrieval—*Information Search and Retrieval (Search process)*

General Terms

Algorithms

Keywords

Keyword-based Association Discovery, Search Algorithm, Coverage, Relevance

1. INTRODUCTION

RDF (Resource Description Framework) [13] is a W3C recommended language for describing linked data of the Semantic Web in the form of triples. RDF data can be represented by node and edge labeled graphs. The simplicity and flexibility of the graph-based data representation model facilitate the wide adoption of Semantic Web technologies in domains such as social network and cheminformatics. Applications in these domains pose challenges and opportunities for managing and searching data on the Semantic Web, as witnessed by new technologies proposed in semantic association discovery [4] and keyword search [11, 15].

The semantic association discovery problem aims to answer questions such as "what are possible relationships between X and Y" and the results are usually paths connecting the two nodes corresponding to the two entities in the graph [4]. The keyword search problem aims to answer questions such as "how do the data entities that match keywords X, Y and Z relate to each other" and the results are usually trees/sub-graphs with the labels of their nodes and edges covering all of the keywords [8, 11, 15].

Discovering acyclic paths between data entities under constraints, such as appearance of nodes, edges and patterns, and the length of paths, is at the core of many applications, such as drug discovery [7, 14] in cheminformatics and research/social networks [18]. How to express such search queries precisely and how to answer such search queries efficiently are critical problems, but are yet fully studied in the literature.

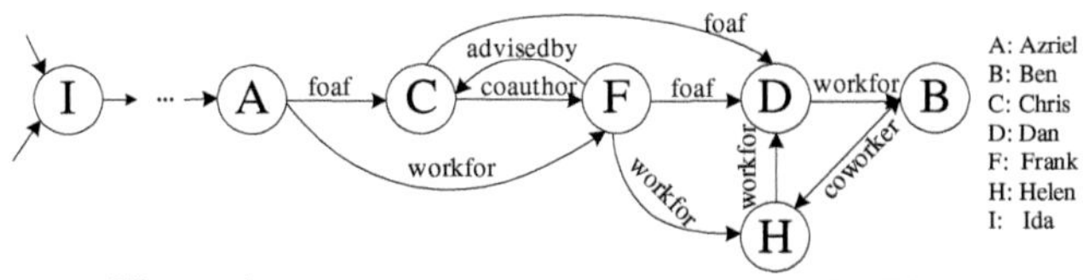

Figure 1: Graph Representation of a Sample RDF Data

EXAMPLE 1. *Figure 1 shows the graph representation of a sample RDF data representing the relationships among people in the social networks. Let's consider the following search requests:*
case1. *Find how* Azriel *connects to* Ben *through* Chris *or* Dan*;*
case2. *Find how* Azriel *connects to* Ben *through at least two people from* Chris, Dan *and* Ida *within four steps.*
case3. *Find* Azriel*'s close (within 4 steps) professional connections (e.g. relationships such as* workfor, coworker, coauthor*) to* Ben*;*
case4. *Find* Azriel*'s close semi-professional connections to* Ben *(i.e. half of the relationships in any tie should be professional);*

Query languages, such as SPARQL [16], have been proposed to query data on the Semantic Web. Later, the notions of semantic association [4], label-constraint reachability [17], and semantic keyword search [11, 15] were proposed. Extending SPARQL with regular expressions [3] enhances it with the capability to express complex patterns satisfying strictly defined constraints, e.g. cases 1 & 3. However, search requests as those in cases 2 & 4 cannot be expressed by any existing language or language extension.

Significant amount of research has been done in RDF data storage, indexing and query evaluation for answering SPARQL queries efficiently [2, 10]; however, the focus was on accelerating graph pattern matching, rather than finding arbitrary paths between data entries. Many graph searching algorithms were proposed for answering keyword searches in graph data [11, 15]; but they are searching for trees whose node/edge labels cover all keywords and cannot be applied to answering CAP queries efficiently. Traversal-based approaches such as DFS, BFS, and bidirectional search [12] were proposed for finding paths satisfying given regular expressions between two end nodes [3]. These algorithms, trailed by a filtering process, can be used to answer CAP queries in Exp. 1, but inefficiently, due to their poor scalability with respect to the size and complexity of the graph data.

CIKM'11, October 24–28, 2011, Glasgow, Scotland, UK.

We study and tackle the problem of precisely specifying and efficiently answering CAP queries. Particularly,

• we introduce the notions of *coverage* and *relevance* for precisely describing the correlation between a resultant path and a keyword set in a CAP query (Sec. 2);

• we propose a set of efficient CAP query answering algorithms, including a family of DFS-based algorithms, which takes advantage of the keyword-based constraints to eliminate unpromising search branches (Sec. 3.1), and a novel *Search-and-Join* algorithm in which a CAP search is broken into a sequence of mini-searches and their results are *joined* to answer the CAP query and its efficiency is guaranteed by carefully designing bookkeeping and pruning (Sec. 3.2);

• we conduct extensive empirical study to understand the strengths and limits of our algorithms (Sec. 4); and

• we explore the application of CAP search queries, in stand-alone domain-specific applications, and in a new SPARQL extension, cSPARQL (Sec. 5).

2. CONSTRAINED ACYCLIC PATH DISCOVERY PROBLEM

In this section, we formally define the *Constrained Acyclic Path Discovery* problem whose applications have been illustrated in Sec. 1.

2.1 Preliminary

Let $\mathcal{L}$ be an infinite set of literals and $\mathcal{U}$ be an infinite set of URIs disjoint with $\mathcal{L}$. We represent RDF data as a node and edge labeled directed graph $G = (V, E, \lambda)$ where V is a set of nodes, $E \subset V \times V$ is a set of edges, and λ is a labeling function that maps items in $V \cup E$ into a finite set of labels and literals.

We represent a path between two nodes of graph G as a sequence of interleaving nodes and edges. Frequently, we are interested in partial paths, which we call *fragments*. In particular, we are interested in two types of fragments: e-fragment (denoted f_e) which starts and ends with an edge, and en-fragment (denoted f_{en}) which starts with an edge and ends with a node.

Given source and destination nodes, $n_s, n_d \in V$ of G, in search queries looking for paths from n_s to n_d, frequently only acyclic paths are of interest to users. In the rest of the paper, we will focus only on acyclic paths, and as the two end nodes are known, we focus on the e-fragments and use $\mathcal{F}_e(n_s, n_d)$ to represent all acyclic e-fragments from n_s to n_d in G.

To facilitate the discussion of constraints on paths, we use $nodes(f)$ ($edges(f)$) to represent the set of nodes (edges) in fragment f, and $|f|$ the length of f, defined as $|edges(f)|$. We overload the mapping function λ to map a set of nodes (edges) to their corresponding labels.

2.2 Set-based Constraints

As shown in Exp. 1, when users search for paths between a pair of nodes, it is frequently the case that the constraints are expressed in the form of a *keyword set* (denoted $\mathcal{S}$), where a keyword is a label in $\mathcal{U}$. Keyword-based constraints as discussed in [5, 17] are quite limited in terms of what can be in the keyword set and how the results are regulated by it. We generalize the keyword set to include keywords that can be mapped to labels of both nodes and edges and extend how the results are confined by the keyword set.

Definition 1. Given a finite keyword set $\mathcal{S} \subseteq \mathcal{U}$ and an e-fragment $f_e \in \mathcal{F}_e(n_s, n_d)$,

1. if $\mathcal{S} \subseteq (\lambda(nodes(f_e)) \cup \lambda(edges(f_e)))$, we say f_e satisfies *presence constraint* w.r.t. $\mathcal{S}$;
2. if $\mathcal{S} \supseteq (\lambda(nodes(f_e)) \cup \lambda(edges(f_e)))$, we say f_e satisfies *context constraint* w.r.t. $\mathcal{S}$;
3. if $\mathcal{S} \cap (\lambda(nodes(f_e)) \cup \lambda(edges(f_e))) \neq \emptyset$, we say f_e satisfies *intersection constraint* w.r.t. $\mathcal{S}$.

Using this definition, we can express the search request in Exp. 1 case1 as "find e-fragments from *Azriel* to *Ben* that satisfy the *intersection constraint* w.r.t. keyword set $\{Chris, Dan\}$".

2.3 Quantitative Metrics

Among a possible large number of resultant e-fragments of a search request, shorter ones tend to express stronger and more meaningful relationship between the two end nodes than the longer ones do [4, 11]. The *length constraint* which restricts the length of the resultant e-fragments has been studied in [3, 5], and can be used to express the search request in Exp. 1 case 2 & 3. However cases 2 & 4 require a more subtle description of the relationship between an e-fragment and a keyword set than the *all-or-nothing* set-based constraints described in Def. 1. For this purpose, we introduce quantitative metrics *coverage* and *relevance*.

Intuitively, *coverage* describes the fraction of the keyword set that appears in the label set of an e-fragment, while *relevance* describes the fraction of the labels of an e-fragment that are in the keyword set. In an RDF graph, each node has its unique label, while more than one edge may have the same label. Therefore, we refine *coverage* and *relevance* further into *node-coverage* and *node-relevance* for keyword sets to be applied only on nodes, *edge-coverage* and *edge-relevance* for edges, and use *coverage* and *relevance* for the constraints in which keywords can be mapped to both nodes and edges.

Definition 2. Given a graph G, two nodes $n_s, n_d \in V$ and a finite keyword set $\mathcal{S} \subseteq \mathcal{U}$, for an e-fragment $f_e \in \mathcal{F}_e(n_s, n_d)$,

$$Coverage(f_e, \mathcal{S}) = \frac{|\mathcal{S} \cap (\lambda(nodes(f_e)) \cup \lambda(edges(f_e)))|}{|\mathcal{S}|} \quad (1)$$

$$Relevance(f_e, \mathcal{S}) = \frac{|\mathcal{S} \cap \lambda(nodes(f_e))| + \Sigma_{l \in \mathcal{S}} cntE(l, f_e)}{|nodes(f_e)| + |edges(f_e)|} \quad (2)$$

$cntE(l, f_e)$ is the total number of edges in f_e with label l.

The coverage and relevance for only nodes or edges can be easily inferred.

Now, taking advantage of the quantitative metrices defined above, we are able to express all constrains in Exp. 1. For example, case 4: $\{f_e \mid f_e \in \mathcal{F}_e(\text{Azriel, Ben}) \wedge EdgeRelevance(f_e, \{\text{workfor, coworker,coauthor}\}) \geq 0.5\}$.

All the constraints we defined in Def. 1 can be expressed using the quantitative metrics defined in Def. 2.

$$Presence(f_e, \mathcal{S}) \iff Coverage(f_e, \mathcal{S}) == 1 \quad (3)$$
$$Context(f_e, \mathcal{S}) \iff Relevance(f_e, \mathcal{S}) == 1 \quad (4)$$
$$Intersection(f_e, \mathcal{S}) \iff Relevance(f_e, \mathcal{S}) > 0 \quad (5)$$

Similarly, we can define the node/edge version of these functions.

2.4 Problem Definition

We define the Constrained Acyclic Path (CAP) search query:

> *A CAP search query $CAP(n_s, n_d, \tau)$ on an RDF graph G involves two end nodes $n_s, n_d \in V$, and constraint τ expressed using zero to many quantitative metrics functions that involve zero or many keyword sets, and returns the e-fragment(s) from n_s to n_d that satisfy τ.*

In this paper, we tackle the problem of efficiently evaluating CAP searches, and discuss the applications of CAP searches.

3. CAP DISCOVERY

We will first focus on the evaluation of a critical subset of CAP queries, *core CAP* queries, in which τ contains conjunctive predicates featuring only one keyword set. We use $\mathcal{S}$ to represent the single keyword set in τ, and use τ_l, τ_c, τ_r, τ_{nc}, τ_{ec}, τ_{nr} and τ_{er}

to represent the length, coverage, relevance, node/edge coverage, node/edge relevance constraints respectively, each of which is defined as an interval, for example, $\tau_l = [\tau_{l_{min}}, \tau_{l_{max}}]$.

Certainly one solution, which we call *Search-and-Filter approach* (S&F), is to first find all acyclic e-fragments in $\mathcal{F}_e(n_s, n_d)$, then eliminate those not satisfying τ. However this approach is not practically efficient because generating $\mathcal{F}_e(n_s, n_d)$ is very time and space consuming and the search cost is mostly wasted since the CAP query results are usually a very small subset of $CAP(n_s, n_d, \emptyset)$.

3.1 Constrained DFS Algorithm

Depth First Search (DFS) is a commonly adopted approach for generating paths between two nodes. In DFS, to generate an e-fragment, en-fragments are generated one step at a time. To minimize the DFS search space in answering core CAP query, we want to stop the expansion of an intermediate result f_{en} if we are certain that the expansion will not lead to any final results. The basic idea is to calculate projected value ranges of the quantitative metrics' values by considering the best and worst cases of $f_e \in \mathcal{F}_e(n_s, n_d)$ which has f_{en} as prefix. If the projected value ranges of the quantitative metrics do not overlap with those in τ, we can safely stop the expansion of f_{en}.

LEMMA 1. *Given an en-fragment f_{en} generated in the DFS of $CAP(n_s, n_d, \emptyset)$ and a keyword set $\mathcal{S}$, for any e-fragment $f_e \in \mathcal{F}_e(n_s, n_d)$ having f_{en} as prefix,*

$$\frac{|\mathcal{S} \cap (\lambda(nodes(f_{en}))|}{|\mathcal{S}|} \le NodeCoverage(f_e) \le \begin{cases} \frac{|\mathcal{S}\cap(\lambda(nodes(f_{en}))|+|f_e|-|f_{en}|-1}{|\mathcal{S}|} & * \\ 1 & Otherwise \end{cases} \quad (1)$$

$$\frac{|\mathcal{S} \cap (\lambda(nodes(f_{en}))|}{|f_e|-1} \le NodeRelevance(f_e) \le \begin{cases} \frac{|\mathcal{S}\cap(\lambda(nodes(f_{en}))|+|f_e|-|f_{en}|-1}{|f_e|-1} & * \\ \frac{|\mathcal{S}|}{|f_e|-1} & Otherwise \end{cases} \quad (2)$$

$$* \quad |f_e| \le |\mathcal{S}| + (|f_{en}| - |\mathcal{S} \cap (\lambda(nodes(f_{en}))|) + 1$$

We then propose two DFS-based algorithms: constraintDFS (cDFS) and enhanced-cDFS (ecDFS).

constraintDFS (cDFS) is based on the non-recursive DFS. In cDFS, we start a DFS from the source node n_s. At each step of the DFS process, we (1) identify a resultant e-fragment when the destination node n_d is reached; (2) detect loops in a fragment generated and eliminate the fragment in question; and (3) calculate projected value ranges of the quantitative metrics by applying the formulae of Lemma 1 and eliminate a fragment if its projected value ranges do not overlap with those specified in τ.

Enhanced-cDFS (ecDFS) overcomes the extra overhead brought by the cDFS algorithm, in which the projected value ranges of the quantitative metrics are computed and compared with τ for every en-fragment generated. In ecDFS, at the time when the project value ranges are estimated for an en-fragment, we also estimate, under the worst-case scenario, for how many more steps the generated en-fragments can remain promising. This allows us to skip the calculation and comparison for the en-fragments generated in these search steps, hence further improve the performance.

3.2 Localized Search and Join

Targeting an important class of CAP queries, in which the keyword-based constraints are specified on nodes, we propose the *Search&Join* (S&J) algorithm. It leverages the local information around the nodes containing the keywords to calculate more accurate projected value ranges, and thus conducts more efficient pruning.

We first introduce a few notions that are critical for this algorithm. We use $\mathcal{S}_k$ to denote a set of nodes containing keywords in $\mathcal{S}$. We define *query nodes* as $\mathcal{S}_k \cup \{n_s, n_d\}$. A *query node sequence* (QNS) is a sequence of query nodes which always starts with n_s, ends with n_d, and consists of a subset of $\mathcal{S}_k$. We are interested in a special type of e-fragment, *exclusive* e-fragment (xe-fragments), which links two query nodes but does not go through any query node. The *constrained sequence join* operation takes as input τ from a CAP query, a set of QNSs based on the keywords in τ, and sets of exclusive e-fragments between every pairs of query nodes, and computes the e-fragments that satisfy the CAP query by concatenating the xe-fragments with the guidance from the QNSs and validating the constraints τ.

The *Search & Join* (S&J) algorithm has two phases: the *search* phase takes as input the data graph G and the query $CAP(n_s, n_d, \tau)$, computes the QNSs, and issues mini-searches on pairs of query nodes to find the set of xe-fragments for each pair of query nodes; the *join* phase then produces the query results by conducting constrained sequence join on the QNSs and xe-fragment sets generated in the *search* phase.

Clearly, not all QNSs lead to valid e-fragments that satisfy τ. In addition, given a QNS qns that yields non-empty results, not all the xe-fragments between all pairs of adjacent query nodes in qns contribute to the final results. Following the "selection-push-down" scheme widely used in database system design, it is critical to minimize the cardinality of the participants of constrained sequence join. We accomplish so by
(1) identify and eliminate invalid QNSs, e.g. QNSs whose constrained sequence join result is empty; and
(2) for each QNS that may generate non-empty constrained sequence join results, identify and eliminate the xe-fragments that have no chance contributing to the results.

Given a QNS qns, qns is guaranteed to be invalid if there is no xe-fragment between a pair of adjacent nodes in qns, or the sum of the minimum lengths of the xe-fragments of adjacent node pairs in qns exceeds $\tau_{l_{max}}$, or the combined projected value ranges of the node coverage or relevance are guaranteed to fall outside of the ranges specified in τ. When a QNS is deemed invalid, it can be pruned immediately.

Beside generating minimal QNSs and xe-fragment sets, we also aim at exploiting minimum number of data nodes/edges in the search phrase in order to limit the search space, hence improving the performance. We accomplish this by carefully design the search steps and bookkeeping mechanism:
(1) For all node pairs that share the same starting node, one single BFS search is issued for generating the xe-fragments for all these node pairs.
(2) After each BFS expansion, the QNSs are evaluated to have the invalid ones pruned, and the newly generated intermediate e-fragments are leveraged to tighten constraints for all mini-searches.
(3) Each time, one BFS is picked to expand its intermediate e-fragments. The criteria is that we always pick the BFS search such that the expansion has the potential to prune the maximum number of invalid QNSs and restricts the search ranges of the BFSs of itself and other query nodes most sharply.

4. EXPERIMENTAL EVALUATION

We conducted extensive experiments to study the performance of our algorithms, constraintDFS (*cDFS*), enhanced-constraintDFS (*ecDFS*), and Search-and-Join(*S&J*), as well as existing Search-and-Filter algorithms based on Depth First Search (*S&F-DFS*) and Bi-directional Search (*S&F-BIS* [12]). The experiments were carried out on a desktop PC running Red Hat 4.1.2 with dual Intel(R) Core(TM)2 2.40GHz CPU and 4GB memory.

Our experiments were conducted on two RDF datasets: *DBpedia* (1504K nodes, 5.4M edges) [1] and *Chem2Bio2RDF* (139K nodes, 1.8M edges) [7]; both have been widely used in the literature. We tested the algorithms on many randomly generated CAP queries, varying source and destination nodes, keyword sets and constraints. Same trends were observed. Due to space limitation, we will report our experimental results only on the Chem2Bio2RDF dataset, as the paths in this dataset are much longer, putting significantly more stress on our algorithms and highlighting the impact of various parameters to the algorithms, and with only queries in which the parameters on node coverage and node relevance vary. Please note that queries in each category shares the same $\tau_{l_{max}}$ and S:

We compared the hot run of the algorithms and measured the elapsed time in *ns*. Please note that as our algorithms improve the performance over the S&F algorithms by several orders of magnitude, to better illustrate the difference, we plot the results in logarithmic scale.

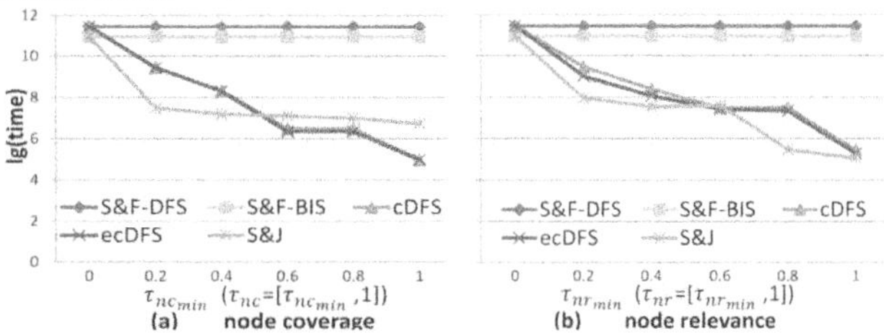

Figure 2: Performance Comparison: Varying τ_{nc} and τ_{nr}

As shown in Fig. 2(a) and 2(b), keyword-based constraints have no impact to the S&F algorithms. Our algorithms, which take advantage of such constraints, significantly outperform them, especially when the constraint is strict, e.g. $\tau_{nc_{min}}$ (or $\tau_{nr_{min}}$) is close to 1, as more intermediate results are pruned. Even when the constraint is loose, the performance of the S&J algorithm is significantly better than others, as it has much smaller search scope, thanks to the local information it takes into account. It is also worth pointing out that our DFS-based algorithms and S&J algorithm react differently when $\tau_{nc_{min}}$ changes: when the node constraint becomes tighter, e.g. closer to 1, cDFS and ecDFS are very efficient, due to their strong pruning power and small overhead; but when the constraint is relatively relaxed, e.g. < 0.5, the S&J algorithm is able to take advantage of local information around the query nodes to limit the search space and thus is much more efficient (by two orders of magnitude) than cDFS and ecDFS.

5. APPLICATIONS

CAP search can be used as a stand-alone search tool in domain-specific applications, such as drug discovery, as well as integrated into a high level query language to enhance its expressiveness.

In cheminformatics, a drug could affect a disease by affecting proteins and genes in a treatment process. By examining the paths from a drug to a disease, domain experts can assess the effectiveness of the drug before conducting chemical experiments [7]. Existing path discovery tools on Chem2Bio2RDF [7] can only find all paths between drug and disease, leaving the domain experts doing the filtering manually or relying on other tools to do so, rendering them impractical in dealing with the large data set and the subtle constraints demanded by the domain experts. Based on the research presented in this paper, we developed a tool that features CAP search queries [20], which enables the domain experts to compose CAP search queries, execute it, get results instantly, and adjust the constraints to alter the results as the research leads them.

If a drug is considered to be effective in treating certain disease, its side-effect should also be considered [14]. As such data entries do not appear directly on the paths between drug and disease, more complex pattern matching is required in addition to path finding to integrate constraints about side-effects into the CAP search queries for drug discovery. We propose cSPARQL to integrate the CAP search into the structured search of SPARQL [16] by introducing (1) *path variables* for expressing arbitrary e-fragments in a graph pattern; and (2) a set of quantitative metrics functions as defined in Sec. 2 for specifying the length and keyword-based constraints. More details about cSPARQL can be found in [19].

6. SUMMARY AND FUTURE WORK

In this paper we identify the problem of discovering acyclic paths between two given nodes in a directed graph under keyword-based constraints (CAP). We introduce the notions of coverage and relevance for specifying subtle relationship between paths and the keyword set. We propose algorithms, including cDFS, ecDFS and S&J, to efficiently evaluate CAP queries. Our empirical evaluation proved that our algorithms outperform existing Search-and-Filter algorithms using both DFS and bidirectional search and improve the performance by several orders of magnitude. We further discuss the applications of CAP queries and propose cSPARQL, an extension of SPARQL, to integrate CAP queries and the structured search on graph data.

7. REFERENCES

[1] http://wiki.dbpedia.org

[2] D. Abadi, *et al.* SW-Store: a Vertically Partitioned DBMS for Semantic Web Data Management. In *VLDBj*, 2009.

[3] F. Alkhateeb, *et al.* Constrained Regular Expressions in SPARQL. In *SWWS*, 2008.

[4] K. Anyanwu, *et al.* ρ-Queries: Enabling Querying for Semantic Associations on the Semantic Web. In *WWW*, 2003.

[5] K. Anyanwu, *et al.* SPARQ2L: Towards Support for Subgraph Extraction Queries in RDF Databases. In *WWW*, 2007.

[6] K. Anyanwu, *et al.* Structure Discovery Queries in Disk-Based Semantic Web Databases. In *DOI*, 2008.

[7] C. Bin, *et al.* Chem2Bio2RDF: a Semantic Framework for Linking and Data Mining Chemogenomic and Systems Chemical Biology Data. In *BMC Bioinformatics*, 2010.

[8] G. Bhalotia, *et al.* Keyword Searching and Browsing in Databases using BANKS. In *ICDE*, 2002.

[9] B. Dalvi, *et al.* Keyword Search on External Memory Data Graphs. In *VLDB Endowment*, 2008.

[10] G. Fletcher, *et al.* Scalable Indexing of RDF Graphs for Efficient Join Processing. In *CIKM*, 2009.

[11] H. He, *et al.* BLINKS: Ranked Keyword Searches on Graphs. In *SIGMOD*, 2007.

[12] V. Kacholia, *et al.* Bidirectional Expansion For Keyword Search on Graph Databases. In *VLDB*, 2005.

[13] K. Kochut, *et al.* SPARQLeR: Extended SPARQL for Semantic Association Discovery. In *ESWC*, 2007.

[14] S. Lee, *et al.* Building the Process-drug-side Effect Network to Discover the Relationship Between Biological Processes and Side Effects. In *BMC Bioinformatics*, 2011.

[15] G. Li, *et al.* EASE: An Effective 3-in-1 Keyword Search Method for Unstructured, Semi-structured and Structured Data. In *SIGMOD*, 2008.

[16] E. Prud'hommeaux, *et al.* SPARQL Query Language for RDF. In *W3C Recommendation*, 2008.

[17] J. Ruoming, *et al.* Computing Label Constraint Reachability in Graph Databases. In *SIGMOD*, 2010.

[18] L. Zhang, *et al.* An Enhanced Model for Searching in Semantic Portals. In *WWW*, 2005.

[19] M. Zhou, *et al.* Efficient Association Discovery with Keyword-based Constraints on Large Graph Data. *Tech. Report, IUB*, 2011.

[20] M. Zhou, *et al.* Conkar: Constraint Keyword-based Association Discovery. *CIKM Demo*, 2011.

AWETO: Efficient Incremental Update and Querying in RDF Storage System

Xu Pu
Department of Computer Science and Technology, Tsinghua University
bertpu@gmail.com

Jianyong Wang
Department of Computer Science and Technology, Tsinghua University
jianyong@tsinghua.edu.cn

Ping Luo
HP Labs China
ping.luo@hp.com

Min Wang
HP Labs China
min.wang6@hp.com

ABSTRACT

With the fast growth of the knowledge bases built over the Internet, storing and querying millions or billions of RDF triples in a knowledge base have attracted increasing research interests. Although the latest RDF storage systems achieve good querying performance, few of them pay much attention to the characteristic of dynamic growth of the knowledge base. In this paper, to consider the efficiency of both querying and incremental update in RDF data, we propose a hAsh-based tWo-tiEr rdf sTOrage system (abbr. to AWETO) with new index architecture and query execution engine. The performance of our system is systematically measured over two large-scale datesets. Compared with the other three state-of-the-art RDF storage systems, our system achieves the best incremental update efficiency, meanwhile, the query efficiency is competitive.

Categories and Subject Descriptors

H.2.2 [**Database Management**]: Physical Design—*Access methods*; H.2.4 [**Database Management**]: Systems—*Query processing*; H.3.1 [**Information Storage and Retrieval**]: Content Analysis and Indexing—*Indexing methods*

General Terms

Algorithms, Design, Performance

Keywords

AWETO, RDF, Index, Incremental Update, Query

1. INTRODUCTION

The RDF (Resource Description Framework) [5] data model, recommended by W3C, is widely adopted to represent the relationships in a knowledge base. With the much efforts in extracting relationships over the Internet in recent years, storing and querying these relationships, represented by the RDF triples, have attracted increasing research interests. Current research on large-scale RDF storage system mainly focuses on query efficiency of the system but considers little on incremental update, which is essentially required by the increasing size of knowledge bases. Therefore, considering the dynamic nature of the built knowledge base, a well-designed RDF storage system is extremely needed for fast incremental update and querying of RDF triples. In this paper, we propose a new RDF storage system AWETO (abbr. for a hAsh-based tWo-tiEr rdf sTOrage system) with new index architecture and query execution engine which considers the efficiency of both querying and incremental update. In AWETO, a hash-based string-ID mapping strategy is firstly developed which maps the string representation of triples to their ID representation in a hash manner. Secondly, instead of creating big clustered B+ tree indices for all triples, we group the triples according to different atoms and different roles (subject, predicate or object) of atoms to create a two-tier index. The above two designs of the index architecture benefits the incremental update procedure, in the meantime the query performance is also competitive. Due to our new index architecture, new query execution engine is developed for fast access of the index. Note that incremental update only refers to incremental bulk load of the RDF triples in this paper, and other update operations such as triple deletion are for future work.

2. STRING-ID MAPPING APPROACH

Before the creation of the ID-based triple index, we convert the triples to their ID representation. Most of the RDF storage systems do the transformation because it decreases the index size and improves query efficiency.

Typically, while performing incremental update, the RDF storage system will look up each string in the input data to generate ID-based triples. This approach will cause vast disk look up because each string in the input data file need to be looked up in the in-disk string-ID mapping table, which causes performance degradation. We adopt a hash-based approach in our system, however it is different from those in previous work. We use an in-disk ID-to-string mapping table and an in-memory *conflict map* rather than only the in-disk string-ID mapping table to efficiently resolve the string-ID mapping. With the in-memory *conflict map*, our approach can efficiently resolve the string-ID mapping in a fast and bulk manner, which cannot be accomplished in previous work.

During initial bulk load, we generate a temp file which contains all different strings with their IDs and the file is sorted by IDs. The IDs in the file are generated by the hash lookup algorithm [1]. Then, for each (*id, string*) pair in the temp file, we determine whether *id* equals to the ID in the previous pair in the file. If it does not, we add the pair into an in-disk ID-to-string mapping table (denoted as $itsTable$). Otherwise, we know that the *id* has already been assigned to another string. On this occasion, we use a *conflict map* (denoted as $conflictMap$) to record all such strings, which is called *conflict string*. Another ID $newID$ is assigned and the ($newID$, *string*) pair is added both to the $itsTable$ and $conflictMap$.

When an ID-to-string look up is needed, we use $itsTable$ to look up strings. In our current implementation, we adopt the Tokyo Cabinet [4] B+ tree as the ID-to-string mapping table. To improve the performance of $itsTable$, a *Bloom filter* [9] is added above $itsTable$. For *conflict map*, the number of *conflict strings* is small when a good hash function, is adopted even for large RDF data, thus, the *conflict map* can be located in memory for fast access.

For the sequential string-ID mapping approach, a string-to-ID mapping table must exist in disk to get the ID of a specific string. However, in our approach, the in-disk string-to-ID mapping is not essential which saves a lot of disk space. When we need to convert a string s into its ID representation, we first look up s in $conflictMap$. If $conflictMap$ contains s, we naturally get the ID, otherwise, $h(s)$ is computed. If we are sure that s exists in the string-ID mapping, $h(s)$ is naturally the ID representation for s. It can be used for generating ID-based triples after the string-ID mapping. If we are not sure the existence of s, $h(s)$ is looked up in $itsTable$. If we get exactly the string s by the look up, we can conclude that $h(s)$ is the ID representation of s, otherwise, we know that s does not exist in the string-ID mapping.

Differently from initial bulk load, during incremental update, the *conflict strings* cannot be retrieved by the temp file mentioned above because there have already existed many strings in the string-ID mapping. In this case, we generate a temp file which only contains all different strings of the new triples to be inserted, sorted by $h(s)$. Then, for each string s in the temp file, we look up if s is contained by string-ID mapping. If it is, nothing will be done, otherwise, we need to check if s is a new *conflict string*. If it is, we assign a new unused ID $newID$ for it and add $(newID, s)$ into both $itsTable$ and $conflictMap$, otherwise, $(h(s), s)$ is added into $itsTable$.

Compared with the traditional ID assignment approaches, which looks up each string in the new triples in string-ID mapping, we propose a two-step string-ID mapping approach. The first step resolves all the strings to their ID representation which is depicted above; the second step performs a sequential scan of the input data and generates ID-based triples. Our approach achieves high efficiency for the following two reasons. Firstly, in the first step, the number of different strings is much smaller than that of all the strings in the source file, less I/O operation is required to look up the strings. Bloom filter is adopted which also decreases the number of I/O operations. Secondly, in the second step, all the strings in the new triples have been already resolved and added to our string-ID mapping. On this occasion, each string is looked up extremely fast because no I/O operation for looking up string-ID mapping is needed. We only need to perform look ups in the in-memory *conflict map* and calculate the hash values of the strings.

3. TRIPLE INDEX

Traditionally, several big clustered B+ trees are used to store different orders of the ID-based triples. During the incremental update procedure, large number of triples with their ID form will be inserted into the B+ trees which causes heavy maintenance burden. If the number of insertions could be decreased, it could improve the performance of incremental update. Based on this consideration, differently from previous work, we adopt a new two-tier index architecture. The upper tier is called *atom position index* (*AP index*) which is actually a small B+ tree index, and the lower tier is called *binary tuple index* (*BT index*) which adopts our own index strategy that can be efficiently maintained.

Our triple index consists of four different index orders: S-PO, P-SO, P-OS, and O-PS. The basic idea is to separate a triple into a single atom and a two-atom tuple, which is called *binary tuple*. The separated atom is stored in *AP index* with some information related to it. All the *binary tuples* associated with each separated atom are sorted and stored in *BT index*.

The *AP index* is a key-value store in disk which is implemented by B+ tree. For each atom that appears in each role of a triple, we add a data item into *AP index*. The key is a 9-byte (*flag, atom*) pair (*FA pair*). The first byte is a flag byte, which indicates not only the role of the atom, but also the order of the associated *binary tuples* in *BT index*. The following 8 bytes after the flag byte contain the ID representation of the atom. The value associated with the key contains all the (*position, length*) pairs which indicate where the *binary tuples* associated with the *FA pair* are stored in *BT index*.

The *BT index* is a file located in disk. We divide the disk space into *blocks*, which is the basic unit for allocating disk space in *BT index*. The length of a *block* should be small, especially for the orders of S-PO and O-PS, because *binary tuples* associated with different *FA pairs* use different *blocks*, if *block* size is big, too much *internal fragmentation* will be made. Note that, due to the small size of *block*, it is only used for allocating disk space, not used for reading and writing data in disk.

Although *blocks* may be incontinuous in disk, for each *FA pair*, the *blocks* associated with it can be seen as *logically continuous*. We group each n *logically continuous blocks* into a *segment*, where n is called *segment size*. To support fast query execution, for each *FA pair*, except storing (*position, length*) pair, we also store the range information of the *binary tuples* for each *segment* in the value field of the *FA pair*, which is used by our query execution engine. *Segment* is treated as the basic unit of operating on the indexed data in *BT index*, including data compression/decompression, atom filtering (discussed in Section 4) and U-SIP [13] pruning.

Compression is needed for both the *AP index* and *BT index*. For *AP index*, we adopt the famous *variable-byte coding* [17] for the value field of *AP index*. For *BT index*, instead of storing the original *binary tuples*, we adopt our own compression scheme which is similar to [12]. We omit the details for space limitation.

When performing incremental update, we sort the new ID-based RDF triples into four different orders, i.e., SPO, PSO, POS and OPS to get the *FA pairs* and sorted *binary tuples* associated with them. For each of the *FA pairs* and the associated *binary tuples* bt_{new}, we get the *binary tuples* bt_{old} which have the same role and atom with bt_{new} in triple index. Then we perform a merge union operation to merge the bt_{old} and bt_{new}. After that, we write the merged data into disk using the space that has already been allocated to bt_{old}. If the space is not sufficient, new space will be allocated. If the old *AP index* does not contain the new *FA pair*, we directly allocate new space and write bt_{new} into disk. Finally, we update the value field of *AP index*.

4. QUERY EXECUTION

Our query execution engine executes queries in a pipelining way; query is executed by an *operator tree*. Each operator gets part of data from its children and achieves its own logic. Due to our new index architecture, the *index scan operator* is different from that in previous work. In our system, the *index scan operator* reads and decompresses data from disk by *segment*. We take the S-PO order for example. There are four kinds of *simple access patterns* (SAPs) related to S-PO order: $(s, ?p, ?o)$, $(s, p, ?o)$, (s, p, o), and $(?s, ?p, ?o)$.

For SAPs like $(s, ?p, ?o)$, we firstly look up the *AP index* using atom s, then according to the positions and lengths information got from *AP index*, the bindings for $?p$ and $?o$ can be naturally retrieved. For $(s, p, ?o)$ and (s, p, o), we also firstly look up *AP index* using s. However, among all the bindings of $(s, ?p, ?o)$, we must get the bindings that satisfy $?p = p$ for $(s, p, ?o)$ or $?p = p, ?o = o$ for (s, p, o). Here, we adopt an efficient *atom filter* to accomplish this task. It first filters in the *segment* level and skips useless *segments* according to the range information before reading the *segments*, then only the data in the first and last read *segments* need to be filtered after the skips. At last, for the special case $(?s, ?p, ?o)$, we perform a full scan on the *AP index* to get all the bindings of $?s$. Then for each binding of $?s$, the operation is the same as $(s, ?p, ?o)$.

5. EXPERIMENTAL EVALUATION

In order to evaluate the performance of our system, we compared both the query runtime and incremental update efficiency to other systems. All the experiments were done on an IBM System x3650 server (eight 1.66GHz CPU cores, 20GB memory) with 64-bit Linux. Two datasets are used, YAGO2 [6] (the core version) and LUBM [11]. YAGO2 contains 15,820,985 different strings and 32,393,226 different triples. For LUBM, we generated a dataset which consists of 500 universities by the UBA 1.7 data generator with *index* = 0 and *seed* = 0. The dataset contains totally 16,439,335 different strings and 66,751,196 different triples. Because LUBM is a synthetic dataset, the triple order in it has fixed and regular pattern. Thus, we disorganized the triple order in the dataset to make it more natural. In all the tests, the *block* size is set to 32 bytes. *Segment size* is set to 32 for YAGO2 and 512 for LUBM.

The RDF-3X system introduced in [12, 13, 14, 15] is the primary competitor of our system because it has achieved

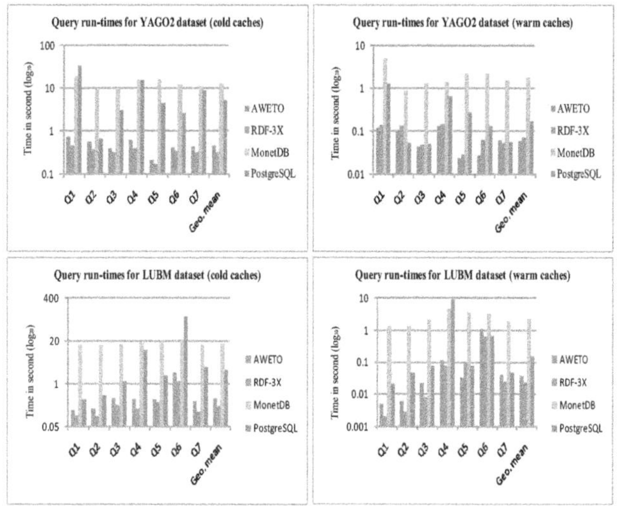

Figure 1: Query run-times evaluation

the best performance among all the current RDF storage systems. The second baseline system is column-store-based vertical partitioning approach introduced in [8, 7], which has gained the best performance among all other approaches based on DBMS. Differently from vertical partitioning approach, we used MonetDB [2] instead of C-Store [16] as the underlying column store suggested by the authors of C-Store. The third baseline is the PostgreSQL [3] database system acting as *triple store*. The indices were built with the orders SPO, PSO and POS which belong to the Sesame-style storage system [10].

The query evaluation for YAGO2 and LUBM are shown in Figure 1. For YAGO2, RDF-3X storage system achieves the best performance in cold caches and our system performs the best in warm caches. In cold caches, RDF-3X outperforms our system by an average factor of about 1.4, while in warm caches, our system performs better than RDF-3X by an average factor of about 1.2. The main reason for the slowness of our system in cold caches is that our system takes both querying and incremental update into consideration. The big ID range of hash-based string-ID mapping influences the compression efficiency of *binary tuples*, thus slows down the I/O read time. Our system performing well in warm caches benefits from our well-designed query execution engine. For MonetDB and PostgreSQL, our system achieves much higher efficiency than the two systems. Our system outperforms PostgreSQL by an average factor of 11.8, sometimes by more than 47.1 in cold caches and an average factor of 2.9, sometimes by more than 12.2 in warm caches. Differently from performance reported in [8], MonetDB performs the worst because we have included the time for converting the string representation of atoms in the SPARQL query into their ID representation. MonetDB consumes much of the time for this conversion which has dominated the query time.

LUBM has similar result. RDF-3X storage system achieves the best performance and our system is the runner-up. RDF-3X outperforms our system by an average factor of about 1.7 in cold caches and about 1.5 in warm caches. For Post-

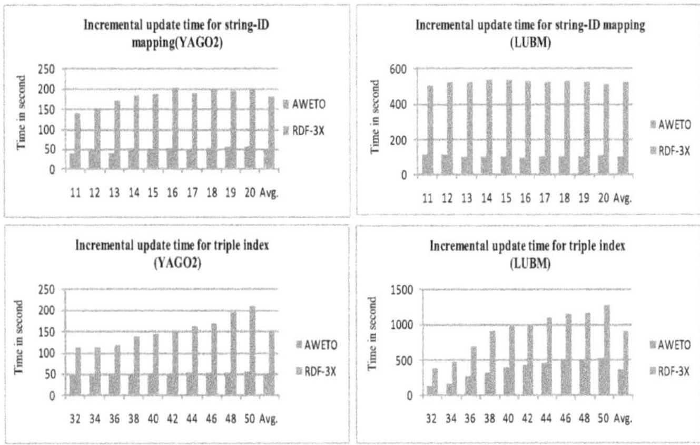

Figure 2: Incremental update evaluation

greSQL, our system outperforms PostgreSQL by an average factor of 7.7, sometimes by more than 49 in cold caches and an average factor of 4, sometimes by more than 78 in warm caches. For MonetDB, string-to-ID mapping also dominates the whole query time.

To evaluate incremental update efficiency, for all the systems, we take the N3 file as input. Our system has full ability to accomplish incremental update. For RDF-3X system, although the authors have implemented incremental update in their system, it cannot work well according to our experiment. Furthermore, our system and RDF-3X uses different programming language and B+ tree implementation. To make a fair comparison, we implemented the basic idea of incremental update procedure of RDF-3X in Java and used Tokyo Cabinet which is the same as AWETO and tried our best to make the code the most efficient. We reduced the number of triple indices in RDF-3X from fifteen to four, which makes RDF-3X have the same number of indices with our system. For MonetDB and PostgreSQL, we found the incremental update operation is much slower than that of our system and RDF-3X, thus we only report the incremental update performance of our system and RDF-3X.

We assume the following scenario of incremental update. For YAGO2 dataset, the initial size of the knowledge base is set to 10 million triples. We repeat 10 batches of incremental update, 1 million triples in each batch. For LUBM we set the initial size to 30 million triples and repeat 10 batches of incremental update, 2 million triples per batch.

The experimental results of string-ID mapping strategy and triple index for our system and RDF-3X are shown in Figure 2. The X-axis indicates the number of triples (in million) in the knowledge base after the incremental update. For both the string-ID mapping and triple index, our system achieves the best incremental update efficiency and outperforms RDF-3X a lot with both of the two datasets. For string-ID mapping, our system outperforms RDF-3X by an average factor of 3.638/4.962 by adopting our hash-based String-ID mapping approach using YAGO2/LUBM dataset. Also, our system outperforms RDF-3X by a factor of 2.964/2.453 by adopting our triple index using YAGO2/LUBM. Therefore, both our hash-based String-ID mapping approach and the triple index are optimized for incremental update and more time-efficient compared with previous work.

6. CONCLUSION

In this paper, we propose a new RDF storage system AWETO which considers both the performance of querying and incremental update. For string-ID mapping, we adopt a hash-based approach with in-memory *conflict map* which achieves high performance in incremental update. For triple index, a new two-tier index approach is proposed which optimizes the incremental update efficiency. For query execution, our highly-efficient operators achieve high efficiency while performing queries. Experimental results show that our system is competitive in querying and outperforms all other three state-of-the-art storage systems when performing incremental update.

7. ACKNOWLEDGMENT

This work was supported in part by the National Basic Research Program of China (973 Program) under Grant No. 2011CB302206, National Natural Science Foundation of China under grant No. 60833003 and 60873171, an HP Labs Innovation Research Program award, and the Program for New Century Excellent Talents in University under Grant No. NCET-07-0491, State Education Ministry of China.

8. REFERENCES

[1] A hash function for hash table lookup. http://burtleburtle.net/bob/hash/doobs.html.
[2] MonetDB. http://monetdb.cwi.nl.
[3] PostgreSQL: the world's most advanced open source database. http://www.postgresql.org.
[4] Tokyo cabinet: a modern implementation of DBM. http://fallabs.com/tokyocabinet.
[5] W3C: Resource description framework(RDF). http://www.w3.org/RDF.
[6] YAGO2. http://www.mpi-inf.mpg.de/yago-naga/yago.
[7] D. J. Abadi, A. Marcus, S. Madden, and K. Hollenbach. Sw-store: a vertically partitioned dbms for semantic web data management. *VLDB J.*, 18(2):385–406, 2009.
[8] D. J. Abadi, A. Marcus, S. Madden, and K. J. Hollenbach. Scalable semantic web data management using vertical partitioning. In *VLDB*, pages 411–422, 2007.
[9] B. H. Bloom. Space/time trade-offs in hash coding with allowable errors. *Commun. ACM*, 13(7):422–426, 1970.
[10] J. Broekstra, A. Kampman, and F. van Harmelen. Sesame: An architecture for storing and querying rdf data and schema information. In *Spinning the Semantic Web*, pages 197–222, 2003.
[11] Y. Guo, Z. Pan, and J. Heflin. Lubm: A benchmark for owl knowledge base systems. *J. Web Sem.*, 3(2-3):158–182, 2005.
[12] T. Neumann and G. Weikum. Rdf-3x: a risc-style engine for rdf. *PVLDB*, 1(1):647–659, 2008.
[13] T. Neumann and G. Weikum. Scalable join processing on very large rdf graphs. In *SIGMOD Conference*, pages 627–640, 2009.
[14] T. Neumann and G. Weikum. The rdf-3x engine for scalable management of rdf data. *VLDB J.*, 19(1):91–113, 2010.
[15] T. Neumann and G. Weikum. x-rdf-3x: Fast querying, high update rates, and consistency for rdf databases. *PVLDB*, 3(1):256–263, 2010.
[16] M. Stonebraker, D. J. Abadi, A. Batkin, X. Chen, M. Cherniack, M. Ferreira, E. Lau, A. Lin, S. Madden, E. J. O'Neil, P. E. O'Neil, A. Rasin, N. Tran, and S. B. Zdonik. C-store: A column-oriented dbms. In *VLDB*, pages 553–564, 2005.
[17] H. E. Williams and J. Zobel. Compressing integers for fast file access. *Comput. J.*, 42(3):193–201, 1999.

Insert-friendly XML Containment Labeling Scheme

Canwei Zhuang
Department of Computer Science
Xiamen University
Xiamen 361005, China
cwzhuang0229@163.com

Ziyu Lin[+]
Department of Computer Science
Xiamen University
Xiamen 361005, China
ziyulin@xmu.edu.cn

Shaorong Feng
Department of Computer Science
Xiamen University
Xiamen 361005, China
shaorong@xmu.edu.cn

ABSTRACT
The labeling scheme is designed to label the XML nodes so that both ordered and un-ordered queries can be processed without accessing the original XML file. When XML data become dynamic, it is important to design a labeling scheme that can facilitate updates and support query processing efficiently. In this paper, we propose a novel containment labeling scheme called DXCL (Dynamic XML Containment Labeling) to effectively process updating in dynamic XML data. Compared with the existing dynamic labeling schemes, a distinguishing feature of DXCL is that DXCL is compact and efficient regardless of whether the documents are updated or not. DXCL uses fixed length integer numbers to label initial XML documents and hence yields compact label size and high query performance. When updates take place, DXCL also has high performance on both label updates and query processing especially in the case of skewed insertions. Experimental results conform the benefits of our approach over the previous dynamic schemes.

Categories and Subject Descriptors
H.2.4 [**Database Management**]: Systems – Query processing

General Terms
Algorithms, Performance.

Keywords
Dynamic XML Data, Containment Labeling scheme, Update.

1. INTRODUCTION
XML becomes an important standard for data representation and exchange on the web and elsewhere. Labeling schemes have been wildly adopted to process query over XML data which conform to an ordered tree-structured data model. Labeling schemes facilitate XML query processing by assigning a unique label to each node in the XML tree. In such a way, the structural relationships of the nodes such as ancestor/descendant, parent/child can be efficiently established.

Containment labeling scheme [1] is popular in many XML database management systems. It provides several advantages over prefix labeling scheme [2]. The label size of containment scheme is not affected by the structure of the XML documents; whereas the sizes of prefix labels increase linearly with the depths of XML document, which makes prefix labeling scheme performs poorly if XML documents are deep and complex. In addition, when querying XML data, the prefix based scheme needs a prefix comparison for the determination of the structural relationships, which spends more time than ordering operations.

While containment labeling scheme works well for static XML documents, an insertion of a node incurs re-labeling of large amounts of nodes, which is costly and becomes a bottleneck. The existing approach to design dynamic containment labeling scheme is based on the notion of encoding, which includes CDBS [3] and QED [4]. The encoding approaches transform the original containment labels to some dynamic formats which can avoid re-labeling when updates take places. However, the encoding schemes are no entirely satisfactory. Firstly, transforming labels into dynamic formats incurs extra labeling cost and larger label size. In addition, since encoding approaches generate the codes not sequentially, they all require creating encoding table with size O(N) for labeling N nodes. It may fail to process large-scale XML documents when limited memory is available.

The dynamic labeling schemes and traditional static labeling scheme both have advantages and disadvantages: the dynamic labeling schemes are preferred for XML documents that are frequently updated, in which case the performances of static labeling schemes degrade significantly as large amounts of nodes need relabeling; in contrast, when the XML documents are not or rarely updated, the static documents are more efficiently supported by the static labeling schemes as applying dynamic schemes to documents would result in extra encoding cost and querying inefficiency. For getting better performance, we should choose between the static schemes and the dynamic schemes to label the XML document in accordance with its updating frequency. In practice, however, the line between static and dynamic XML documents is often blurred since the updating frequency of a document varies according to time. Hence making a choice between the static schemes and the dynamic schemes is not an easy thing and in many cases it may turn out to be contrary to one's expectations. It is of great interest to design a labeling scheme tailored for both static and dynamic XML documents.

In this paper, we propose a novel dynamic containment labeling scheme called DXCL which doesn't need transform the original labels to dynamic format but can effectively process updating in dynamic XML data. DXCL labels initial XML document based on integer numbers which are stored with fixed bits, and therefore yields cheap label costs as well as compact label size and high query performance. Moreover, when XML becomes dynamic, DXCL completely avoids relabeling and its label quality is resilient to skewed insertions.

2. RELATED WORK
Due to space constraint, we only focus on XML labeling and encoding techniques related to containment labeling scheme.

[+]Corresponding author.

CIKM'11, October 24–28, 2011, Glasgow, Scotland, UK.

Containment Labeling Scheme In containment labeling scheme [1], every node is assigned three values: *start*, *end* and *level*, where *start* and *end* denote an interval and *level* refers to the level in the XML document tree. For any two nodes *u* and *v*, *u* is an ancestor of *v iff* the interval of *v* is contained in the interval of *u*. Additionally, with using the *level* of a node, the parent-child relationship can be determined efficiently. Document order can also be deduced well by the comparison of *start* values. However, containment labeling scheme can not support updates efficiently. An insertion of a node incurs relabeling of all its ancestor nodes and all the nodes after this node in document order.

Encoding Schemes are proposed to avoid the re-labeling when XML updating. By applying an encoding scheme to containment labeling scheme, the original labels are transformed to some dynamic codes which can efficiently process updates. QED[4] encoding scheme transforms labels to QED codes. Given three integer numbers 1,2, 3 where each number is stored with 2 bit, i.e. 01, 10 and 11, a QED code is a sequence of these numbers which ends with 2 or 3. QED codes are compared based on lexicographical order and robust enough to allow insertions without re-labeling. For example, "22" can be inserted between "2" and "3" whereas "212" can be inserted between "2" and "22". In additional, QED completely avoids the overflow problem as the number 0 does not appear in QED code itself and can be served as the separator of the different codes. However, the sizes of QED codes increase fast for skewed insertions. For example, suppose there are many codes that are required to be inserted one by one before a QED code "332", then each insertion requires that two more bits should be added for the new inserted code, i.e., the new codes will be "3312", "33112", "33112" etc. The fast increase of code lengths make QED perform poorly. The other encoding scheme CDBS [3] is similar to QED except that its encoding unit is binary bit. Compared with QED, CDBS is compact and its labeling cost is small, but CDBS cannot completely solve the re-labeling problem in frequent updates due to its overflow problem.

P-Containment In [3], a variant of the containment labeling scheme called P-Containment is proposed. Rather than storing the *level* information, P-Containment scheme stores the *start* value of the parent of the node. With the parent information, the parent-child relationship can be determined faster and the sibling relationship can be determined much faster. Furthermore, when dynamic encoding schemes are applied, P-Containment can efficiently process the internal node insertions. Prefix labeling schemes, however, cannot intrinsically avoid re-labeling when an insertion takes place between child and parent nodes.

3. DXCL

Our labeling scheme DXCL is based on P-Containment (see Sec.2), and solves the update sensitive problem.

3.1 DXCL code

We first introduce some correlative conceptions on DXCL code.

Definition 1 (Quaternary String, QS) *Given a set of integer numbers $A=\{1,2,3\}$ where each number is stored with 2 bit, i.e. "01", "10" and "11". A quaternary string is $(q_1q_2...q_t)$, where t is the code size; $q_t \in \{2, 3\}$ and $q_i \in A$, $1 \leq i \leq t-1$.*

Definition 2 (DXCL Code, DC) *DXCL Code is a integer number N concatenating a quaternary string, i.e. $DC=N \oplus QS=(N.q_1q_2...q_t)$, where N is store with fixed bits and $t \geq 0$.*

Note that: (1).When t=0, the DXCL code is just a integer number and therefore we can apply the integer number to label initial XML document;(2).The delimiter "." in a DXCL code $(N.q_1q_2...q_t)$ is not needed to be stored since the integer number N is of fixed length; (3). The same as that of QED [4], number 0 (stored with 2 bits, i.e. "00") does not appear in the quaternary string field because it servers as the separator to identify the different DXCL codes. In such a way, DXCL could never encounter the overflow problem.

Example 1 DXCL uses the number 0 (2 bits) to separate different codes. For example, "9.2209.230" will be separated to "9.22" and "9.23". Importantly, it avoids the overflow problem in this way.

DXCL codes are compared by lexicographical order.

Definition 3 (Lexicographical order $\prec$) *Given two DXCL codes S_L:$M.p_1p_2...p_s$, and S_R:$N.q_1q_2...q_t$, $S_L \prec S_R$ if and only if one of the following three conditions holds:*
C1. $M<N$;
C2. $M=N$, $s<t$ and $p_1=q_1$, $p_2=q_2$, ..., $p_s=q_s$;
C3. $M=N$ and $\exists\, k \leq min(s, t)$, such that $p_1=q_1$; $p_2=q_2$; ...; $p_{k-1}=q_{k-1}$ and $p_k<q_k$.

Example 2 We have "9" $\prec$ "10" based on condition *C1*. "9" $\prec$ "9.2" since "9" is a prefix of "9.2", which satisfies *C2*. Based on *C3*, "9.233" $\prec$ "9.3" because the comparison is from left to right.

3.2 Initial labeling

DXCL labels the initial XML tree based on integer numbers which are stored with fixed bits. Suppose the total number of the nodes in an XML tree is *K*. Since we should assign *start* and *end* values to total *K* nodes, we need to generate *2K* consecutive integer numbers, and the size to store each integer is $\log_2 2K$ bits. Fig.1 shows an example of an XML tree labeled by DXCL. Note that each integer in Fig.1 is stored with 4 bits.

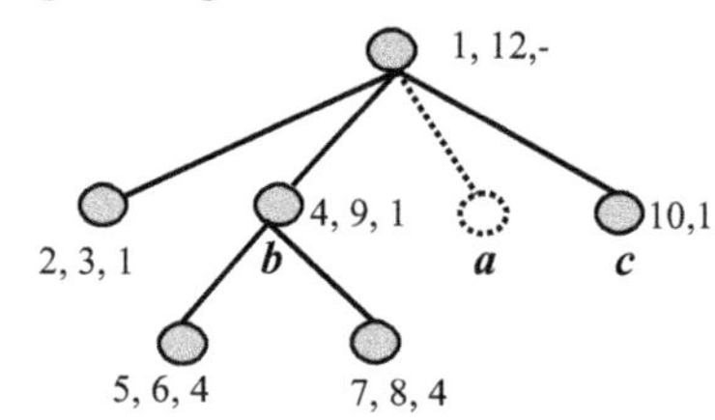

Fig. 1 DXCL scheme ("*a*" is an inserted node)

3.3 Updates processing

We start by introducing two primitive functions to determine a new quaternary string that precedes or follows a given quaternary string *S* in lexicographical order. Suppose a sequence *SEQ* containing all the quaternary strings with size equal to that of *S* is arranged in increasing lexicographical order. We define ***BEF(S)*** to get the string before *S* and ***AFT(S)*** to get the string after *S* in this sequence. Specially, when *S* is the first string in *SEQ*, i.e. $S=1^{size(S)-1} \oplus 2$ (we use "i^k" to represent the *k* "*i*"s in this paper), we define $BEF(S)= 1^{size(S)} \oplus 3^{size(S)}$; when *S* is the last string in *SEQ*, i.e. $S=3^{size(S)}$, we define $AFT(S)= 3^{size(S)} \oplus 1^{size(S)-1} \oplus 2$.

Example 3 Let 23 be a quaternary string, then *SEQ* is 12, 13, 22, 23, 32,33. Based on our definition, we have *AFT*(23)=32 and *BEF* (23)=22. Likewise, *AFT*(12)=13, *AFT*(13)=22,...; and *BEF*(33)= 32, *BEF*(32)=23,....Specially, *AFT*(33)=3312 and *BEF* (12)=1133.

It is verifiable that $BEF(S) \prec S \prec AFT(S)$ lexicographically. The implements of *AFT* and *BFE* are shown in Algorithm 1 and Algorithm 2.

Algorithm 1 ***AFT*(S)**

if S= "$3^{size(S)}$" **then return** $3^{size(S)} \oplus 1^{size(S)-1} \oplus 2$;
else if the last symbol of S is "2"
  then return S with the last symbol changed to "3";
else if the last symbol of S is "3"
  denote the position of the lastly encountered "1" or "2" in S as p
  if $substring(S, p, p)$= "1"
    then return $substring(S, 1, p\text{-}1) \oplus 2 \oplus 1^{size(S)\text{-}p\text{-}1} \oplus$ "2";
  else // the case $substring(S, p, p)$= "2"
    return $substring(S, 1, p\text{-}1) \oplus 3 \oplus 1^{size(S)\text{-}p\text{-}1} \oplus$ "2";

Algorithm 2 ***BEF*(S)**

if S= "$1^{size(S)\text{-}1}$" $\oplus$ "2" **then return** $1^{size(S)} \oplus 3^{size(S)}$;
else if the last symbol of S is "3"
  then return S with the last symbol changed to "2"
else if the last symbol of S is "2"
  $S_T \leftarrow substring(S, 1, size(S)\text{-}1)$;
  denote the position of the lastly encountered "2" or "3" in S_T as p
  if substring(S, p, p)= "2"
    then return $substring(S, 1, p\text{-}1) \oplus 1 \oplus 3^{size(S)\text{-}p}$
  else // the case $substring(S, p, p)$= "3"
    return $substring(S, 1, p\text{-}1) \oplus 2 \oplus 3^{size(S)\text{-}p}$

We then propose the algorithm that can always insert a DXCL code between two ordered DXCL codes, which guarantees that we can update the XML document without re-labeling.

Algorithm 3 ***GetInsertedCode*(S_L, S_R)**

Input: DXCL codes S_L and S_R
Output: DXCL code S_M, such that $S_L \prec S_M \prec S_R$
1 **if** $size(S_L) = size(S_R)$ **then** $S_M \leftarrow S_L \oplus$ "2"
2 **else if** $size(S_L) < size(S_R)$ **then**
3   $S_T \leftarrow substring(S_R, size(S_L)+1, size(S_R))$
4   $S_M \leftarrow S_L \oplus BEF(S_T)$
5 **else** $S_T \leftarrow substring(S_L, size(S_R)+1, size(S_L))$
6   $S_M \leftarrow substring(S_L, 1, size(S_R)) \oplus AFT(S_T)$
    //we define $substring(S, 1, 0)=NIL$
7 **end**
8 **return** S_M

Theorem 1 *Given any two DXCL codes S_L and S_R which satisfies $S_L \prec S_R$, we can always find a new DXCL code S_M based on Algorithm 3 such that $S_L \prec S_M \prec S_R$ lexicographically.*

Proof If $size(S_L) = size(S_R)$, then S_M=$S_L \oplus$"2" and $S_L \prec S_M \prec S_R$; If $size(S_L)<size(S_R)$, then $S_L \prec =substring(S_R, 1, size(S_L))$ as $S_L \prec S_R$. Moreover, let S_T=$substring(S_R, size(S_L)+1, size(S_R))$, then S_T is a quaternary string and we can get $BEF(S_T)$ which is smaller than S_T lexicographically. Thus $S_L \prec S_L \oplus BEF(S_T) \prec S_L \oplus S_T \prec =substring(S_R, 1, size(S_L)) \oplus S_T = S_R$. Let S_M=$S_L \oplus BEF(S_T)$, then $S_L \prec S_M \prec S_R$; If $size(S_L)>size(S_R)$, then $substring(S_L, 1, size(S_R)) \prec S_R$ as $S_L \prec S_R$; In additional, let S_T=$substring(S_L, size(S_R)+1, size(S_L))$, then S_T is a quaternary string and we can get $AFT(S_T)$ which is larger than S_T lexicographically. Thus S_L = $substring(S_L, 1, size(S_R)) \oplus S_T \prec substring(S_L, 1, size(S_R)) \oplus AFT(S_T) \prec S_R \oplus AFT(S_T) \prec S_R$. Let S_M= $substring(S_L, 1, size(S_R)) \oplus AFT(S_T)$, then $S_L \prec S_M \prec S_R$. □

Example 4 To insert a code between "9" and "10", since they are of same size, we concatenate one more "2" after "9" to get the inserted code, which is "9.2". To insert a code between "9" and "9.2", since the size of "9" is smaller than that of "9.2", we get S_T = "2" (see line 3 in Algorithm 3) and then concatenate $BEF(S_T)$ = "12" after "9" to get the inserted code, which is "9.12". Similarly, we can get the inserted code "9.3" between "9.2" and "10".

The same as that of QED [4], we require the last symbol of the quaternary string field in a DXCL code to be "2" or "3". We use an example to show the reason.

Example 5 Suppose there are two codes "9.1" and "9.11". We have "9.1" $\prec$ "9.11", but we can not insert anther code S_M such that "9.1" $\prec S_M \prec$ "9.11". Hence we require the quaternary string field in a DXCL code to be ended with "2" or "3".

Based on Algorithm 3 and Theorem 1, DXCL can process XML updating without re-labeling the existing labels.

Example 6 To insert a node "*a*" in Fig. 1, we should insert 2 DXCL codes between the *end* of node *b* "9" and the *start* of the node *c* "10". If we use the original containment scheme, we can not insert a code between "9" and "10" and we must re-label the existing nodes. Based on our *GetInsertedCode* algorithm, we insert a code "9.2" between "9" and "10", and then the *start* value of the inserted node "*a*" is "9.2". The *end* value of node "*a*" is an insertion between the code "9.2" and "10", which is"9.3". We don't need to re-label any node but can keep the labeling scheme working correctly. It is similar for the insertions in other positions.

DXCL has high resilience to skewed insertions. We use an example to analyze the DXCL label size after skewed insertions.

Example 7 Suppose there are 2000 nodes which are required to be inserted repeatedly before the node "*c*" in Fig.1. Then we should generate 4000 DXCL codes one by one between "9" and "10". Based on our algorithm, the first 2 codes are "9.2" and"9.3", which can be stored with 8 bits(equal to $4+2 \times 1+2$, where the last 2 is the size of the separator 0);Likewise, the following 2 codes are "9.32" and "9.33" stored with size 10; 6 codes "9.3312", "9.3313", "9.3322", "9.3323", "9.3332" and "9.3333" are stored with size 14; 54 codes "9.33331112",..., "9.33333333" are stored with size 22; and all the rest codes are stored with size 38. It can be seen that the label size of DXCL is little affected by ordered insertion sequence. In contrast, the sizes of CDBS and QED codes increase at 1 or 2 bits per insertion.

[5] has proved that the label size of any deterministic labeling scheme which does not re-label nodes must increases linearly in the worst case. DXCL cannot escape from this claim also. DXCL needs to assign labels of size $O(n)$ when n nodes are inserted between two consecutive nodes *left* and *right* as follows: the first node M is inserted between *left* and *right*; then the second node is inserted between *left* and M; the insertion of the ith node($3 \le i \le n$) takes place between the $(i\text{-}2)^{th}$ inserted node and the $(i\text{-}1)^{th}$ inserted node. Clearly, this is normally extremely rare in practice.

4. EXPERIMENT AND RESULTS

We evaluate DXCL against CDBS and QED using P-Containment labels. We don't compare DXCL against Ordpaths(see SIGMOD 2004) and DDE(see SIGMOD 2009) as they are prefix-based schemes. Table 1 shows the test datasets.

Table 1. Test datasets

Dataset	Doc.	No. of nodes	Max/average depth
D1	Hamlet	6,636	6/4.79
D2	Allshakes	179,690	7/5.58
D3	Nasa	476,646	8/3.16
D4	Lineitem	1,022,976	3/2.94
D5	Treebank	2,437,666	36/7.87

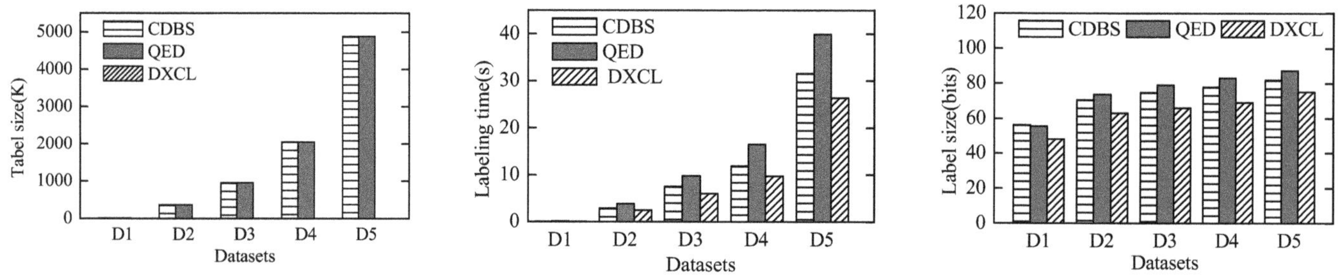

(a) Memory usage (b) Labeling time (c) Label size

Fig. 2 Performance study on initial labeling

4.1 Initial Labeling

We test the performances of different schemes labeling on D1-D5.

Memory Usage We compare the memory usage dominated by the size of the encoding table and show the result in Fig.2 (a). We observe clear difference of memory usages between difference schemes. This result conforms to our previous discussions that DXCL need no encoding table whereas both CDBS and QED need a tables of size $O(N)$ where N is the nodes number. DXCL can process large XML documents with limited memory available.

Labeling Time Fig.2 (b) shows the different initial labeling time of different containment schemes. DXCL spends smallest time since it doesn't need to transform labels into dynamic formats as those of CDBS and QED. Additionally, QED needs longest encoding time since QED encodes longer strings and has time-consuming division operation by "3".

Label Sizes As is shown in Fig.2(c), QED has largest average label size as QED is stored with quaternary string and "0" cannot appear in the QED code itself, which is a waste. Compared with CDBS codes which are stored with variable length, DXCL is more compact.

4.2 Frequent Updates

We discuss the performances of two kinds of frequent updates.

Uniform Insertions We test the cases that 2^n-1(n=1, 2,…,20) nodes are uniformly inserted between two consecutive nodes *left* and *right* where the *end* value of the node *left* and the *start* value of the node *right* both are *NIL*. The 2^n-1 nodes are inserted by n times. At the first time, one node M is inserted between *left* and *right*. At the second time, another 2 new nodes are inserted between every two consecutive nodes which lie between *left* and *right*, i.e., one is inserted between *left* and M and the other between M and *right*. At the kth time (k=1, 2,…, n), 2^k new nodes are inserted similarly. We study the average label size of new inserted nodes after uniform insertions. As is shown in Fig.3 (a), the label size of DXCL shows a little overhead compared with that of QED. However, the difference is negligible. Both DXCL and QED assign labels to updated nodes using quaternary strings and thus their label sizes are approximately the same. Though the label size of CDBS is smallest, it cannot avoid re-labeling in XML frequent updates.

Skewed Insertions are common in practice. CDBS easily encounter overflow problem in the case of skewed insertions as it uses fixed bits to represent its size. Therefore we just compare our DXCL against QED. We test the case that n nodes are inserted one by one before a particular node of which the *start* value is *NIL*. Fig.3 (b) shows the different label sizes after skewed insertions. The size of DXCL labels only increases slightly whereas the size of QED labels has showed a much higher increase. This result illustrates the significant advantage of DXCL.

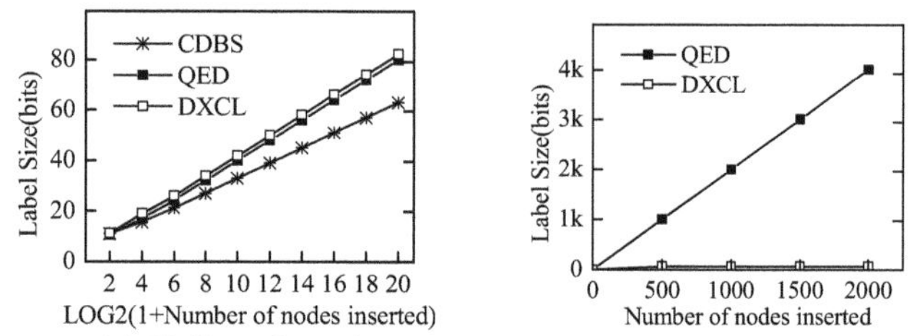

(a) Uniform insertions (b) Skewed insertions

Fig. 3 Performance study on frequent updates

4.3 Query Performances

Since all the three schemes compare labels based on lexicographical order, the label size is the primary factor in determining the query performances. We ignore the diagrams of the comparison of query performances here as they show the similar trends to that of Fig.2(c), Fig.3 (a) and Fig.3 (b). DXCL has high performance on query processing especially in the case of skewed insertions.

5. CONCLUSION

In this paper, we have presented a novel containment labeling scheme DXCL which not only completely avoids re-labeling when updating, but also has compact size and high query performance. DXCL has controllable size for skewed insertions in which case the existing labeling schemes perform poorly. Experimental results have demonstrated the benefits of our proposed labeling scheme compared to previous approaches.

6. ACKOWLEDGEMENT

This research was supported by the Fundamental Research Funds for the Central Universities under Grant No. 2011121049.

REFERENCES

[1] C. Zhang, J. F. Naughton, D. J. DeWitt, Q. Luo, and G. M. Lohman. On supporting containment queries in relational database management systems. In SIGMOD, 2001.

[2] I. Tatarinov, S. Viglas, K. S. Beyer, J. Shanmugasundaram, E. J. Shekita, and C. Zhang. Storing and querying ordered XML using a relational database system. In SIGMOD, 2002.

[3] C. Li, T. W. Ling, and M. Hu. Efficient updates in dynamic XML data: from binary string to quaternary string. VLDB J, 2008.

[4] C. Li and T. W. Ling. QED: a novel quaternary encoding to completely avoid relabeling in XML updates. In CIKM,2005.

[5] E. Cohen, H. Kaplan, and T. Milo. Labeling Dynamic XML Trees. In PODS, 2002.

A Pretopological Framework for the Automatic Construction of Lexical-Semantic Structures from Texts

Guillaume Cleuziou
LIFO - Université d'Orléans
Orléans, France
guillaume.cleuziou@univ-orleans.fr

Davide Buscaldi
LIFO - Université d'Orléans
Orléans, France
davide.buscaldi@univ-orleans.fr

Vincent Levorato
LIFO - Université d'Orélans
Orléans, France
vincent.levorato@univ-orleans.fr

Gaël Dias
HULTIG - Universidade da Beira Interior
DLU - Université de Caen Basse-Normandie
ddg@hultig.di.ubi.pt

ABSTRACT

In this paper, we present a new approach for the automatic generation of lexical-semantic structures from texts. In particular, we propose a pretopological framework to formalize and combine various hypotheses on textual data in order to automatically derive a structure similar to common lexical-semantic knowledge bases such as WordNet. In addition, we define a new metric to intrinsically evaluate structures.

Categories and Subject Descriptors: I.2.4 [**Artificial Intelligence**]: Knowledge Representation Formalisms and Methods; I.2.7 [**Artificial Intelligence**]: Natural Language Processing

General Terms: Algorithms, Experimentation

Keywords: Lexical-Semantic Structures; Pretopology; Evaluation

1. INTRODUCTION

Coding the semantic relationships between concepts of discourse into a lexical-semantic structure may enrich the reasoning capabilities of Information Retrieval and Natural Language Processing applications. However, their development is largely limited by the efforts required for their construction. To reduce the amount of work needed, many research have appeared in recent years to learn such structures from texts, fostering new surveys in the field [1, 5]. Learning lexical-semantic resources from texts instead of manually creating them has undeniable advantages. First, creating resources from texts within a domain may fit the semantic component neatly and directly, which will never be possible with general-purpose resources. Second, the cost per entry is greatly reduced, giving rise to much larger resources than an advocate of a manual approach could ever afford.

Different learning methods have been proposed to automatically build lexical-semantic structures. They can be grouped into three main classes: the similarity-based methods [12, 3], the set-theoretical approaches [9, 4] and the associative frameworks [13, 7]. In this paper, we aim at learning terminological ontologies following the associative framework but **relieving the frequency problem** evidenced in [13, 7]. For that purpose, we propose to analyze the topology of the graph structure between terms induced by associative measures. Within this context, we propose an **unsupervised methodology** based on Pretopology, which automatically learns lexical-semantic structures. Thus, from a given set of terms from potentially different domains and any domain corpus, we assess the asymmetric proximity between terms using asymmetric similarity measures. From the resulting proximity matrix, we present a Pretopological framework to obtain a non-triangular directed acyclic graph corresponding to the semantic structure of the domains.

The evaluation of learned structures is a rather complicated task. Indeed, [14] claims that there are several possibilities of conceptualizations for one domain that might differ in their usefulness for different groups of people, but not in their soundness and justification. In this paper, we propose an exhaustive intrinsic evaluation of the learned lexical-semantic structures by comparing them to the state-of-the-art approach [13]. For that purpose, we take as baseline the work done by [11] and propose an alternative solution to overcome some evidenced drawbacks as well as we present an original methodology for a "fair" comparison.

2. PRETOPOLOGICAL FRAMEWORK

The links between elements of a population can be modeled in several ways, e.g. Topology. However, topological axioms and properties are too restrictive to model a space in concrete terms. Instead, Pretopology models proximity in a more general way. So, we propose to use this theoretical framework to model a "lexical space" with pretopological relations and derive a structure with propagation strategies.

CIKM'11, October 24–28, 2011, Glasgow, Scotland, UK.

2.1 Notions of Pretopology

We can define a pretopological space by a family of neighborhoods. Let (E, a) be a pretopological space [2] where $a(.)$ is a pseudo-closure function and E a non-empty set. A neighborhood $N(x)$ of $x \in E$ is a subset of E containing x and a family of neighborhoods $\mathcal{N}(x)$ for x can be defined by the union of neighborhoods as $\mathcal{N}(x) = \{N \subseteq E | x \in N\}$. We then construct the pseudo-closure function based on the family of neighborhoods as $\forall A \in \mathcal{P}(E), a(A) = \{x \in E | \forall N \in \mathcal{N}(x), N \cap A \neq \emptyset\}$. Within our context, a pretopological space is defined by a vocabulary E (set of terms) and a pseudo-closure operator $a(.)$ supposed to model the propagation of semantic dependencies over term sets. The way to define the family of neighborhoods is crucial for the modeling. For example, the approach proposed by [13] can be instantiated in our pretopological framework by considering a family composed of two neighborhoods $\mathcal{N}_{OHC}(x) = \{N_O(x), N_{HC}(x)\}$ matching the two properties (high confidence and order respectively) used in the subsumption definition of [13] i.e. $N_{HC}(x) = \{y \in E | P(y|x) > t\}$ and $N_O(x) = \{y \in E | P(y|x) \geq P(x|y)\}$.

As the pseudo-closure function is not idempotent, its successive applications lead to the achievement of closed subsets. These closed subsets represent interdependent subsets related to the pseudo-closure function. As a consequence, a structure is induced by the elementary closed subsets and maximal closed subsets can be seen as the less homogeneous groups of E. The nature of these particular subsets is interesting in terms of space analysis, as we can consider an inclusion relation between them, leading to a structural analysis algorithm. Such a structure can be obtained with the pretopological algorithm proposed by [10]. In particular, we proposed a top-down version of this algorithm in [6]. So, when using $\mathcal{N}_{OHC}$, the algorithm provides a non-triangular directed acyclic graph that is exactly the final structure obtained by [13]. In the next section, we take advantage of this general framework to propose new neighborhoods relevant for lexical space modeling.

2.2 Lexical Space Modeling

Various pretopological neighborhoods may exist to model the proximity relations between elements in the vocabulary.

2.2.1 *K-Nearest Neighbors*

A k-Nearest Neighbors pretopological space (k-NN) consists in defining the neighborhood of an element x by the subset composed of the k elements having the highest proximity with x. For the lexical application, we choose as neighborhood for a term x, the terms y with the highest confidences using $P(y|x)$. As such, we define the following family of neighborhoods: $\mathcal{N}_{kNN}(x) = \{N_{kNN}(x), N_O(x)\}$ where $N_{kNN}(x) = \{y \in E | y \in kNN_E(x)\}$. The family $\mathcal{N}_{kNN}$ leads to a pseudo-closure operator $a(.)$ such that $a(x)$ is the set $\{x\}$ extended by its more general terms (N_O), which have x among its k best direct predecessors (N_{kNN}).

2.2.2 *Directed Relative Neighborhood (DRN)*

The second modeling is based on a statistical property observed on lexical structures. Given a benchmark structure $\mathcal{S}_r$ as reference and a corpus on the domain of $\mathcal{S}_r$, we performed an analysis on the distribution of the confidence values along the paths from a root to a leaf on the reference. Several intuitive hypotheses have been tested and one of them appeared to be statistically relevant. Let $x_1, x_2, \ldots, x_n$ be a path in the reference structure such that x_i subsumes x_{i+1}. We observed that a term x_i in the path has a higher minimal confidence with its predecessors than its successors have with their own predecessors. This statement can be formalized by the following property: $\forall i,\ min\{P(x_j|x_i)\}_{j=1}^{i-1} \geq min\{P(x_j|x_{i+1})\}_{j=1}^{i}$. By applying this property locally on a triplet (w, x, y), y is a neighbor of x if and only if any w satisfies the property to be a successor of x in the path (x, y) i.e. $N_{DRN}(x) = \{y \in E | \forall w \in E,\ P(y|x) \geq min\{P(x|w), P(y|w)\}\}$. As a consequence, a new family of neighborhoods is proposed $\mathcal{N}_{DRN}(x) = \{N_{DRN}(x), N_O(x)\}$. In particular, the pseudo-closure operator derived from $\mathcal{N}_{DRN}$ extends a term singleton $\{x\}$ with its more general terms (N_O) satisfying the extended ultrametric property (N_{DRN}). The interesting property of $\mathcal{N}_{DRN}$ is that it is free of parameter. However, it leads on practice to over-sized neighborhoods. A way to adjust the neighborhoods consists in introducing the high confidence parameter such that $\mathcal{N}_{HC\_DRN}(x) = \{N_{DRN}(x), N_O(x), N_{HC}(x)\}$. Another solution that avoids the threshold problem is presented in the next section.

2.2.3 *K-Nearest DRN*

As mentioned above, the *Directed Relative Neighborhood* produces over-sized neighborhoods. However, it could be used as a relevant "filter" and force other neighborhood functions to select elements satisfying a property observed on expected structures. In that sense, we define a new neighborhood that combines on the one hand the structural benefits and the simplicity of the parametrization of the kNN approach and on the other hand the statistical property of the DRN topology such that $N_{kN\_DRN}(x) = \{y \in E | y \in kNN_{N_{DRN}(x)}(x)\}$. Finally, the new family of neighborhoods is given by $\mathcal{N}_{kN\_DRN}(x) = \{N_{kN\_DRN}(x), N_O(x)\}$.

3. INTRINSIC EVALUATION

Two benchmarks have been used as references to tackle two different semantic relationships: synonymy and meronymy. First, we used the UMLS[1] from which four distinct sub-domains have been selected (cardiovascular (CS), digestive (DS), respiratory (RS) and nervous (NS)). In particular, each sub-domain is represented by its own lexical structure present in the meta-thesaurus using the hypernym/hyponym relation. The second reference ontology was obtained from WordNet by considering all geographical places deriving from the concept "United States of America" by means of the meronymy relation. We call it GEO-WordNet. For each reference, we retrieved the proximities between terms from two different corpora. For the UMLS, we used (1) PubMed[2] and (2) BioMed[3]. For the GEO-WordNet, we exploited the Glasgow Herald (GH95) and Los Angeles Times (LAT94) both used in the GeoCLEF evaluation campaigns[4], where toponyms have been identified with the Stanford Named Entity Recognition (NER) [8] and disambiguated using a conceptual-density based method.

[11] proposed a way to compare ontologies at the structural level (the J_1 measure). Given a set of terms E and two

[1]http://www.nlm.nih.gov/research/umls/
[2]http://www.ncbi.nih.gov/pubmed/
[3]http://www.biomedcentral.com/
[4]http://ir.shef.ac.uk/geoclef

ontologies $\mathcal{O}_1$ and $\mathcal{O}_2$ structuring E, the general principle is to compare for each entry $x \in E$ the matching between the super/subconcepts of x in $\mathcal{O}_1$ and the super/subconcepts of x in $\mathcal{O}_2$. This evaluation approach is also suitable in our context by quantifying the matching between the predecessors $Preds_{\mathcal{S}}(x)$ and successors $Succs_{\mathcal{S}}(x)$ of a term x in the two lexical structures $\mathcal{S}_1$, $\mathcal{S}_2$. However, the main drawback of J_1 is its insensitivity to the direction of the relations into the structures. Such, two structures with full inversion would have a perfect matching according. To avoid the inversion problem, we propose to consider separately predecessors and successors in the matching evaluation. A new J_2 matching index is proposed as the (geometric) mean of two Jaccard indices for which a perfect matching of 1 implies strictly identical structures as shown in Equation 1.

$$J_2(\mathcal{S}_1, \mathcal{S}_2) = \frac{1}{|X|} \sum_{x \in E} \left(\frac{|Preds_{\mathcal{S}_1}(x) \cap Preds_{\mathcal{S}_2}(x)|}{|Preds_{\mathcal{S}_1}(x) \cup Preds_{\mathcal{S}_2}(x)|} \right)^{1/2} \cdot \left(\frac{|Succs_{\mathcal{S}_1}(x) \cap Succs_{\mathcal{S}_2}(x)|}{|Succs_{\mathcal{S}_1}(x) \cup Succs_{\mathcal{S}_2}(x)|} \right)^{1/2} \quad (1)$$

In order to evaluate the acquired structure with the intrinsic J_2 measures, we need to fix the parameter k or the threshold t depending on the pretopological space used. In our experiments, we noticed two generic phenomena: (1) the best structures are obtained with small-sized neighborhood and (2) the size of the neighborhoods must be comparable to be fair in the comparison of the different pretopological spaces. The first observation corroborates the intent of [13] to filter only very high confidence values by means of a strong threshold (e.g. $t = 0.8$). This is illustrated by Figure 1 that reports the J_2 scores obtained by the $\mathcal{N}_{OHC}$ pretopological space when the number of confidence values retained grows (i.e. threshold t decreases). Furthermore, such a threshold cannot be universal and must be adjusted for each corpus. For example, the proportion of confidence values greater than 0.8 is about 1% for the CS sub-domain of the UMLS on the BioMed corpus, but only 0.07% for the GEO-WordNet observed on the LAT94 corpus.

Based on these findings, we chose two heuristics for the parametrization of the pretopological spaces. Let n be the size of the vocabulary E to structure, the threshold t is adjusted in such a way that only n (first heuristic) and $2n$ (second heuristic) confidence values exceed t. The two heuristics are used for high confidence-based pretopological spaces (i.e. $\mathcal{N}_{OHC}$ and $\mathcal{N}_{HC\_DRN}$). For the nearest neighbors-like spaces (i.e. $\mathcal{N}_{kNN}$ and $\mathcal{N}_{kN\_DRN}$) neighbors with comparable sizes are obtained with parameters $k = 1$ and $k = 2$ respectively. Table 1 reports the structural evaluation of each acquired structure compared to the corresponding reference.

Important variations on the J_2 index are observed depending of the benchmark and the corpus. Very poor matching are obtained for example on the RS with PubMed where the scores are sometimes lower than 0.10 and strong promising matching are obtained for example on the NS sub-domain and the Geographical domain where the scores are closed or higher than 0.40. Such variations can be explained by the nature of the reference used and especially the kind of semantic relations into consideration. Some of the domains are structured based exclusively on the *Part-of* relation (e.g. Geo-WordNet) or the *Is-a* relation (e.g. NS sub-domain), while other references mix up both types of relations such as the CS sub-domain (and the global UMLS reference by extension). It seems to be incontestable that such an heterogeneity in the semantic structuring of the vocabulary is a problem that current approaches do not transcend.

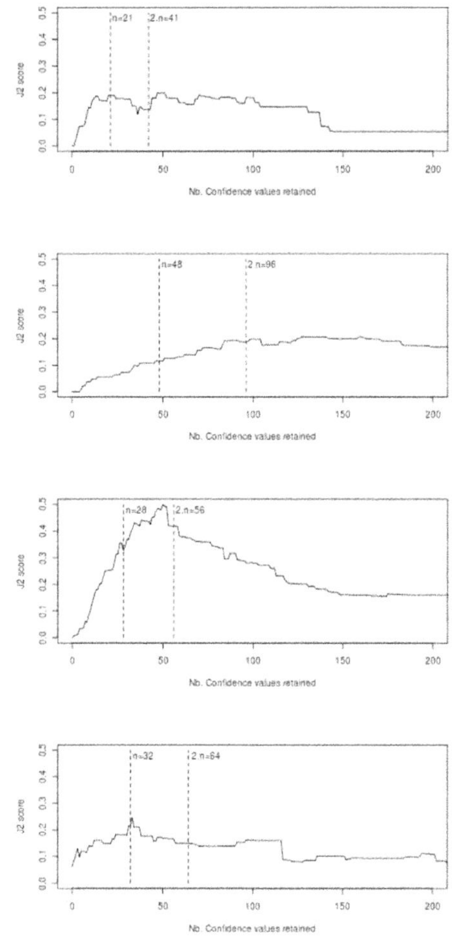

Figure 1: J_2 scores with the baseline approach of [13] on the BioMed corpus: CS, DS, NS and RS sub-domains in the top-down order.

The corpus used and the way to exploit the text collection also have a significant impact on the quality of the retrieved statistics and then on the acquired lexical structure. Indeed, the matching scores are lower overall when using the PubMed corpus compared to BioMed. It is mainly due to the fact that only abstracts of the scientific papers have been used for the statistics computation with PubMed whereas full text retrieval has been performed on BioMed, thus providing more confidence in the extracted statistics.

Table 1 also reports the comparison between the structures obtained from different pretopological spaces. Bold values in the table distinguish the modeling that leads to the best matching for a benchmark and a corpus. It is interesting to observe that even if the ultrametric topological space ($\mathcal{N}_{HC\_DRN}$) never leads to the best matching, the filter performed by this space is profitable to the nearest neighbors-like space since the $\mathcal{N}_{kN\_DRN}$ modeling obtains best results on four experiments. As a summary one can notice that the new proposed $\mathcal{N}_{kN\_DRN}$ modeling outperforms the baseline proposed by [13] in two thirds of the experimented contexts

Corpora	Domain	n	$\mathcal{N}_{OHC}$		$\mathcal{N}_{kNN}$		$\mathcal{N}_{HC\_DRN}$		$\mathcal{N}_{kN\_DRN}$	
			n	$2n$	k=1	k=2	n	$2n$	k=1	k=2
BioMed	Cardiovascular system	21	0.191	0.138	0.189	**0.304**	0.192	0.133	0.144	0.136
	Digestive system	48	0.116	**0.187**	0.104	0.137	0.116	0.175	0.110	0.116
	Nervous system	28	0.328	0.419	**0.428**	0.382	0.344	0.392	**0.428**	0.414
	Respiratory system	32	0.215	0.149	0.188	0.240	0.220	0.138	0.154	**0.251**
	UMLS (4 sub-domains)	128	0.172	**0.218**	0.151	0.162	0.184	0.213	0.180	0.173
PubMed	Cardiovascular system	21	0.100	**0.173**	0.133	0.147	0.097	0.162	0.133	0.166
	Digestive system	48	0.130	0.107	0.123	0.111	0.117	0.138	**0.243**	0.188
	Nervous system	28	0.196	0.258	**0.440**	0.401	0.208	0.257	0.429	0.381
	Respiratory system	32	0.095	0.119	**0.143**	0.139	0.092	0.127	0.131	0.101
	UMLS (4 sub-domains)	128	0.102	0.132	0.165	0.142	0.096	0.145	0.169	**0.171**
LAT94	GEO-WordNet (USA)	150	0.207	0.312	**0.392**	0.332	0.183	0.276	0.386	0.347
GH95		131	0.305	0.372	**0.399**	0.382	0.289	0.312	0.391	0.382

Table 1: Structural matching of each acquired structure with its reference using the J_2 index.

and sometimes with strong improvements as for example on the geographical benchmark with a score increased by 87% at the very most.

4. CONCLUSIONS

In this paper, we presented a new framework to automatically build terminological ontologies based on the formalism of Pretopology. In particular, Pretopology proposes a well-founded mathematical framework to model the degree of generality/specificity as well as the semantic closeness between terms based on an asymmetric proximity measure. Unlike similarity-based and set-theoretic approaches, we deal with asymmetry in NLP based on the associative framework, which allows domain and language independency and opens new research directions. In particular and compared to the work of [13], we proposed to focus on the topology of the structure obtained from the proximity measure thus avoiding isolated terms and simplifying the parametrization. We also proposed an exhaustive intrinsic evaluation of the learned lexical-semantic structures based on a new metric called the J_2 index, which proposes a solution to the ontology inversion problem untreated by [11]. We validated our model based on two benchmarks: the UMLS referential medical ontology over the PubMed and BioMed corpora, and the GEO-WordNet referential over two news stories collections. We compared it to the best-so-far state-of-the-art methodology proposed by [13]. The results showed that the pretopological structuralist formalism outperforms the methodology of [13] in the majority of the cases.

5. REFERENCES

[1] C. Biemann. Ontology learning from text – a survey of methods. *LDV-Forum*, 20(2):75–93, 2005.

[2] M. Brissaud. Les espaces prétopologiques. *Compte-rendu de l'Académie des Sciences*, 280(A), 1975.

[3] P. Cimiano, A. Hotho, and S. Staab. Comparing conceptual, partitional and agglomerative clustering for learning taxonomies from text. In *Proceedings of the European Conference on Artificial Intelligence (ECAI 2004)*, pages 435–439, 2004.

[4] P. Cimiano, A. Hotho, and S. Staab. Learning concept hierarchies from text corpora using formal concept anaylsis. *Journal of Artificial Intelligence Research*, 24:305–339, 2005.

[5] P. Cimiano, A. Mädche, S. Staab, and J. Völker. Ontology learning. In *Handbook of Ontologies*, pages 245–267. Springer Verlag, 2009.

[6] G. Cleuziou, G. Dias, and V. Levorato. Acquisition de structures lexico-sémantiques à partir de textes : un nouveau cadre de travail fondé sur une structuration prétopologique. In *Proceedings of the 11ème Conférence Internationale Francophone sur l'Extraction et la Gestion des Connaissances*, 2011.

[7] G. Dias, R. Mukelov, and G. Cleuziou. Unsupervised graph-based discovery of general-specific noun relationships from web corpora frequency counts. In *Proceedings of the 12th International Conference on Natural Language Learning (CoNLL 2008)*, 2008.

[8] J. Finkel, T. Grenager, and C. Manning. Incorporating non-local information into information extraction systems by gibbs sampling. In *Proceedings of the 43rd Annual Meeting of the Association for Computational Linguistics on Computational Linguistics (ACL 2005)*, pages 363–370, 2005.

[9] B. Ganter and R. Wille. *Formal Concept Analysis: Mathematical Foundations.* 1998.

[10] C. Largeron and S. Bonnevay. A pretopological approach for structural analysis. *Information Sciences*, 144:169–185, 2002.

[11] A. Maedche and S. Staab. Measuring similarity between ontologies. In *Proceedings of the 13th International Conference on Knowledge Engineering and Knowledge Management. Ontologies and the Semantic Web (EKAW 2002)*, pages 251–263, 2002.

[12] G. Paaß, J. Kindermann, and E. Leopold. Learning prototype ontologies by hierachical latent semantic analysis. In *Proceedings of the 15th Joint Conference European Conference on Machine Learning and Principles and Practice of Knowledge Discovery in Databases (ECML/PKDD 2004)*, 2004.

[13] M. Sanderson and D. Lawrie. Building, testing, and applying concept hierarchies. In W. B. Croft, editor, *Advances in Information Retrieval*, pages 235–266. Kluwer Academic Publishers, 2000.

[14] B. Smith. Ontology. In *The Blackwell Guide to Philosophy of Computing and Information*, pages 155–166. Malden: Blackwell, 2004.

Leveraging Web 2.0 Data for Scalable Semi-supervised Learning of Domain-specific Sentiment Lexicons

Raymond Y.K. Lau and C. L. Lai
Department of Information Systems
City University of Hong Kong
Tat Chee Avenue, Kowloon, Hong Kong SAR
(raylau,chunlai)@cityu.edu.hk

Peter D. Bruza
Faculty of Science and Technology
Queensland University of Technology
Brisbane QLD 4001, Australia
p.bruza@qut.edu.au

K.F. Wong
Department of Systems Eng. & Eng. Mgt.
Chinese University of Hong Kong
Shatin, Hong Kong SAR
kfwong@se.cuhk.edu.hk

ABSTRACT

Since manually constructing domain-specific sentiment lexicons is extremely time consuming and it may not even be feasible for domains where linguistic expertise is not available, research on automatic construction of domain-specific sentiment lexicons has become a hot topic in recent years. The main contribution of this paper is the illustration of a novel semi-supervised learning method which exploits both term-to-term and document-to-term relations hidden in a corpus for the construction of domain-specific sentiment lexicons. More specifically, the proposed two-pass pseudo labeling method combines shallow linguistic parsing and corpus-base statistical learning to make domain-specific sentiment extraction scalable with respect to the sheer volume of opinionated documents archived on the Internet these days. Our experiments show that the proposed method can generate high quality domain-specific sentiment lexicons according to users' evaluation.

Categories and Subject Descriptors

I.2.6 [**Artificial Intelligence**]: Learning; I.2.7 [**Artificial Intelligence**]: Natural Language Processing
; H.3.3 [**Information Search and Retrieval**]: Text Mining

General Terms

Algorithms, Performance, Experimentation

Keywords

Sentiment Lexicon, Sentiment Analysis, Text Mining, Statistical Learning

1. INTRODUCTION

Sentiment analysis or opinion mining is a hot research topic given the sheer volume of user-contributed opinionated documents in the era of Web 2.0 [14, 17, 20, 21]. Utilizing sentiment lexicons, also called polarity lexicons or opinion lexicons, to identify the sentiments embedded in opinionated documents and predicting the polarities (i.e., orientations) of these sentiments has been a widely used approach [3, 4, 19]. Nevertheless, manually constructing sentiment lexicons for various domains is extremely labor intensive. More recently, researchers have examined various methods such as linguistic-based methods [7, 16], lexical graph-based propagation methods [18], and corpus-based statistical learning methods [1, 5] to automatically construct sentiment lexicons. Nevertheless, solely based on linguistic rules to identify sentiments and predict their polarities may lead to the low recall problem, i.e., many sentiment words may be missed out due to the extreme flexibility of language usages for most natural languages. On the other hand, supervised machine learning methods suffer from the problem of low autonomy (e.g., large human effort is often involved in labeling training examples) [14, 21]. Semi-supervised sentiment lexicon construction methods seem promising since they strives for optimizing two probably contradictory requirements, that is, high recall and high learning autonomy.

2. SEMI-SUPERVISED LEARNING FOR SENTIMENT LEXICON BUILDING

The main intuition behind the proposed computational method for domain-specific sentiment lexicon learning is depicted in Figure 1. The observable layer represent the reality (e.g., labeled or unlabeled opinionated documents and the terms contained within them) that the proposed computational method can inspect to extract the domain-specific sentiments which are captured by the hidden layer. Figure 1 also highlights the "distributional characteristic" of sentiments in positively and negatively opinionated documents, respectively. Basically, a positively opinionated document tends to contain more positive sentiments than negative sentiments; this is also the reason why the document is regarded as positive in the first place. The same concept is applied to negatively opinionated documents. When a sheer volume of opinionated documents is readily available (the reality in the era of Web 2.0), an effective lexicon learning mechanism can exploit the distributional characteristics of a term in positively and negatively opinionated documents (the observable layer) to estimate the probability of the term having a specific polarity (the hidden layer).

Moreover, term relationships exist among sentiments since they may be semantically related (e.g., "love" and "like"). However, these relationships may be hidden in a corpus. An effective lexicon learning mechanism should also explore term relationships to discover new sentiments based on the known seeding sentiments. In addition, Figure 1 pinpoints the domain-specific nature of sentiments. A sentiment deemed negative in one domain (e.g., "small" hotel room) may well be regarded as positive in another domain (e.g., "small" physical size of a netbook). It is true that not all opinionated documents are labeled (e.g., financial news). The proposed sentiment lexicon construction method can exploit the hidden term relationships between seeding sentiments and candidate sentiments of a corpus to discover the initial domain-specific sentiments. These sentiments can then be use to tentatively label (i.e., pseudo labeling) opinionated documents in order to extract more domain-specific sentiments.

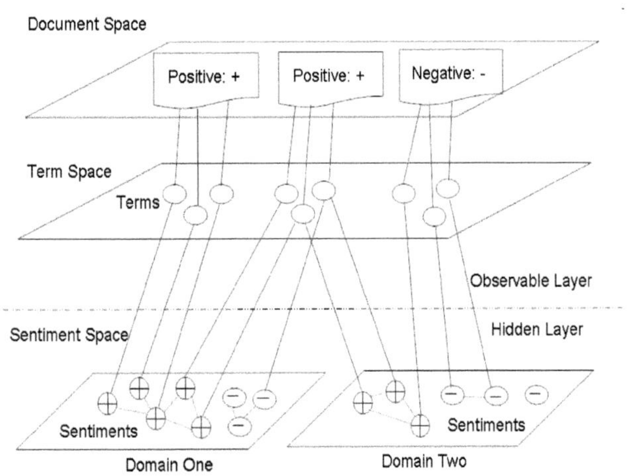

Figure 1: The Intuition of the Pseudo Labeling Method

The proposed semi-supervised computational method for two-pass domain-specific sentiment lexicon construction can be summarized with the following steps:

1. Extract domain-independent sentiments based on existing linguistic resources such as OpinionFinder [19];
2. Apply the principle of "context coherence" to extract initial domain-specific sentiments from a corpus;
3. Apply the proposed SMI measure to identify statistically associated terms with the initial domain-specific sentiments and the domain-independent sentiments;
4. Pseudo label the opinionated documents of a corpus;
5. Apply the proposed statistical learning method SE to extract more domain-specific sentiments;

One can use the manual labels such as "strong subjective" in OpinionFinder [19] or a high sentiment score in SentiWordNet [4] to extract the domain-independent sentiments. To promote language independency of the proposed method, we do not rely on fragile language specific rules nor sentence dependency parsing method to extract domain-specific sentiments; instead only the general principle of "contextual coherence" is applied. In particular, we assume that sentiments appearing within the same sentence should have the same polarity unless contrary indicators such as "not", "no", "but", "except", etc. appear around the candidate sentiment. Both the domain-independent sentiments extracted from a generic sentiment lexicon and the contextually inferred domain-specific sentiments from a specific review corpus are used to construct an initial domain-specific sentiment lexicon. PMI has been applied to extract sentiments statistically correlated with the seeding sentiments from a Web corpus [20]. To extract candidate sentiments statistically associated with the sentiments captured in the initial domain-specific sentiment lexicon, we extend the PMI measure to develop the sentiment mutual information estimator (SMI). The extended PMI measure has been successfully applied to concept extraction in ontology discovery [12, 9].

Through contextual inference and statistical inference, initial domain-specific sentiments are discovered. These initial domain-specific sentiments and the domain-independent sentiments extract from a generic sentiment lexicon are applied to assign pseudo polarity labels to opinionated documents of a corpus (e.g., online financial reviews). In the field of information retrieval (IR), the distributional characteristic of terms in relevant and non-relevant documents have been explored to induce an information seeker's real interests [8, 10, 11]. The basic assumption is that terms occur more often in the set of relevant documents are likely representing the information seeker's need. Accordingly, the measure of Keyword Classifier (KC) has been developed to extract positive, negative, and neutral terms representing the information seeker's positive, negative, or neutral information needs [8]. The KC measure has been successfully applied to induced the beliefs for adaptive information filtering later on [10, 11]. For our research, we adapt the KC measure to develop a statistical learning mechanism called sentiment extractor (SE). The formulations of our SE method are shown as follows:

$$\begin{aligned} SE(t) = \; & [\frac{df(t)}{\varpi_{pos}} \times \Pr(pos|t) \times \log_2 \frac{\Pr(pos|t)}{\Pr(pos)}] - \\ & [\frac{df(t)}{\varpi_{neg}} \times \Pr(neg|t) \times \log_2 \frac{\Pr(neg|t)}{\Pr(neg)}] \end{aligned} \quad (1)$$

$$polarity(t) = \begin{cases} \frac{1}{1+e^{-|SE(t)|}} & \text{if } SE(t) > \phi \\ -\left(\frac{1}{1+e^{-|SE(t)|}}\right) & \text{if } SE(t) < -\phi \\ 0 & \text{otherwise} \end{cases} \quad (2)$$

where $SE(t)$ indicates how likely the term t is a sentiment; the higher the sentiment estimation score, the more likely the term is a sentiment. The term t carries a specific POS such as Adjective; this is one of the ways to prune noisy sentiments. The parameters $\varpi_{pos} = \pi_{pos} \times |D|$ and $\varpi_{neg} = \pi_{neg} \times |D|$ control the learning rates for positive and negative sentiments, respectively. The set $D = D^+ \cup D^-$ represents the corpus of opinionated documents, whereas D^+ (D^-) is the set of positively (negatively) rated documents; the document label can be generated though pseudo labeling or directly retrieved from Web 2.0 sites. The term $Pr(Pos|t) = \frac{df(D_t^+)}{df(t)}$ is the estimated conditional probability that a document is rated positive given that it contains a candidate sentiment term t. It is expressed as the fraction of the number of positive documents (i.e., document frequency df) which contain the term t (i.e., $df(D_t^+)$) over the total number of documents which contain t (i.e., $df(t)$). Similarly, $Pr(Neg|t) = \frac{df(D_t^-)}{df(t)}$ is the estimated conditional probability that a document is rated negative when it contains the term t. In addition, $Pr(Pos) = \frac{|D^+|}{|D^+|+|D^-|}$ is the estimated priori probability that a document is positive, whereas $Pr(Neg) = \frac{|D^-|}{|D^+|+|D^-|}$ is the estimated priori probability that a document is negative in the collection.

Basically, Eq. 2 is applied to prune noisy sentiments. In particular, only the candidate terms with the $|SE(t)|$ score greater than a threshold ϕ will be identified as positive or negative sentiments. The parameters π_{pos}, π_{pos}, and ϕ are empirically established based on the training corpus of a specific domain. For the experiments reported in this paper, we adopted the following values: $\pi_{pos} = 0.02\%$, $\pi_{pos} = 0.01\%$, and $\phi = 0.05$. The computational complexity of the proposed Pseudo Labeling method can be characterized by $O(L_s L_d |D|)$, where L_s is the number of seeding sentiments, and L_d is the average document length of a corpus; $|D|$ is the size of the corpus. It has a linear time complexity with respect to the size of the input document collection and the number of seeding sentiments. To predict the polarity of an unseen opinionated document (e.g., an online financial news), the automatically constructed domain-specific sentiment lexicon is referred to. We apply the unigram language model originally developed in the field of IR to develop a probabilistic measure to estimate the strength of polarity of an opinionated document [15].

3. SYSTEM EVALUATION

Similar to previous studies [2, 16], we retrieved real-world opinionated documents from the Web to build our evaluation data set. More specifically, we downloaded online reviews from amazon.com, tripadvisor.com, mldb.com, and resuters.com using the provided APIs (e.g., amazon.com and tripadvisor.com) or invoking our crawler programs (e.g., for mldb.com and reuters.com). A total of 993,324 positive reviews and 358,144 negative reviews were used in our experiment. For amazon.com and tripadvisor.com, the reviews with user rating 4 and 5 were treated as positive documents, and the reviews with user rating 1 were taken as negative documents. The products reviews of books, automotive gears, computers (PC hardware), digital cameras, music, and health care products extracted from amazon.com represent six different application domains. For movie reviews extracted from mldb.com, a review with user ratings 8 to 10 was considered positive, and a review with user ratings 1 to 3 was considered negative. Nevertheless, user-contributed label was not available for the financial news retrieved from reuters.com.

We examined the intrinsic quality of the domain-specific lexicons generated by the proposed system. More specifically, we applied the P@100 (precision at 100 documents) measure to evaluate the quality of the domain-specific sentiments generated by the system when compared to the ground truths provided by three human annotators. A similar approach was adopted to evaluate a topic-specific sentiment lexicon construction method before [6]; a performance measure similar to P@10 (precision at 10 documents) adopted in the TREC Blog Track [13] was applied to our experiment. 513 positive and 527 negative seeding sentiments were manually extracted from OpinionFinder [19] by three human annotators. These sentiments were considered generic and applicable to different domains. The same annotators also assessed the quality of the sentiment lexicons generated by the proposed method. Each human annotator examined the positive and the negative lists of sentiments generated by the proposed Pseudo Labeling (PL) method individually. If there was a disagreement about the polarity of a system generated sentiment, the third annotator's judgment would be used to determine the final ground truth. The inter-rater agreement of these annotators was $\kappa = 0.81$ according to Cohen's Kappa statistic. The high inter-rater agreement of our annotators shows that their judgment is reliable, and our κ value is close to that obtained in a previous study [7].

Table 1: The Intrinsic Evaluation of Sentiment Lexicons

Application Domain	P@100 PL	P@100 UL	Lexicon Size	P@100 Diff.
Automotive	0.830	0.840	4,165	−1.2%
Book	0.825	0.845	4,687	−2.4%
Camera	0.825	0.825	3,712	0.0%
Computer	0.840	0.845	4,789	−0.6%
Health Care	0.815	0.830	4,019	−1.8%
Music	0.855	0.860	4,228	−0.6%
Movie	0.800	0.820	3,481	−2.5%
Hotel	0.825	0.840	3,804	−1.8%
Finance	0.835	-	4,514	-
Average	0.828	0.838	4,155	−1.4%

The results of the intrinsic assessment of the domain-specific lexicons generated by the PL system are listed in Table 1. The figures represent the average precision for the system generated positive and negative sentiments. The results achieved by using user labeled (UL) opinionated documents for domains such as books, computers, cameras, etc. are listed under the third column; such results can be seen as the upper bound precision of the system generated sentiment lexicons. For the financial news downloaded from reuters.com, user-contributed polarity labels of documents were not available. As can be seen in Table 1, the proposed PL method achieves average precisions (listed under the second column) close to the supper bound performance in various domains. The average P@100 precision achieved by the PL method is 0.828. The upper bound of the P@100 precision achieved by using user-labeled documents is 0.838. On average, the result produced by the PL method is only 1.4% inferior to that produced by using user-contributed labels of opinionated document to extract the domain-specific sentiments. However, the distinct advantage of the proposed PL method is that labor-intensive human labeling of opinionated documents is not required. Table 2 show the top 20 positive and negative domain-specific sentiments extracted from the finance domain. The domain-specific sentiments were discovered using the proposed PL sentiment lexicon construction method.

4. CONCLUSIONS AND FUTURE WORK

The main contribution of this paper is the illustration of

Table 2: Top 20 Domain-specific Sentiments (Finance) Discovered by System

Positive		Negative	
Sentiment	Strength	Sentiment	Strength
lifted	0.831	weakened	0.843
supported	0.829	red	0.843
backed	0.825	suspended	0.842
aggressive	0.824	alleged	0.842
earned	0.824	incurable	0.835
completed	0.821	overgrown	0.834
tony	0.821	blocked	0.832
winning	0.819	fighting	0.829
cheaper	0.817	slashed	0.828
encourage	0.816	stuck	0.825
topped	0.814	harder	0.821
advancing	0.811	tighter	0.819
pushy	0.808	dropping	0.817
grown	0.807	demanding	0.816
stabilised	0.806	riskier	0.816
dominated	0.801	damaged	0.815
recovered	0.801	antitrust	0.811
strongest	0.795	exacerbating	0.807
expanded	0.794	misused	0.807
firmer	0.791	overlooked	0.806
eased	0.791	conservative	0.805

a scalable semi-supervised method for the automatic construction of domain-specific sentiment lexicons across different application domains. Based on direct human assessment, the intrinsic evaluation of the domain-specific sentiment lexicons automatically generated by the proposed computational method reveals that it can discover sentiments with good quality; the average P@100 achieved is 0.828. Future work will conduct more experiments to examine the effectiveness of the proposed pseudo labeling method across more diversified application domains. The utility of the automatically constructed domain-specific sentiment lexicons will be examined based on polarity detection tasks at the document and the sentence levels, respectively.

Acknowledgment

The work reported in this paper has been funded in part by the Hong Kong RGC's GRF Research Grant (Project: 9041569).

5. REFERENCES

[1] G. Amati, E. Ambrosi, M. Bianchi, C. Gaibisso, and G. Gambosi. Automatic construction of an opinion-term vocabulary for ad hoc retrieval. *Advances in Information Retrieval, ECIR 2008, volume 4956 of* LNCS, pages 89–100.

[2] N. Archak, A. Ghose, and P. Ipeirotis. Show me the money!: deriving the pricing power of product features by mining consumer reviews. In *Proceedings of the 13th ACM SIGKDD* , pages 56–65.

[3] S. Das and M. Chen. Yahoo! for amazon: Sentiment extraction from small talk on the web. *Management Science*, 53(9):1375–1388, September 2007.

[4] A. Esuli and F. Sebastiani. Determining the semantic orientation of terms through gloss classification. In *Proceedings of the 13th ACM CIKM* , pages 617–624.

[5] B. He, C. Macdonald, J. He, and I. Ounis. An effective statistical approach to blog post opinion retrieval. In *Proceedings of the 17th ACM CIKM*, pages 1063–1072.

[6] V. Jijkoun, M. de Rijke, and W. Weerkamp. Generating focused topic-specific sentiment lexicons. In *Proceedings of the 48th Annual Meeting of the Association for Computational Linguistics*, pages 585–594.

[7] H. Kanayama and T. Nasukawa. Fully automatic lexicon expansion for domain-oriented sentiment analysis. In *EMNLP 2007, Proceedings of the 2006 Conference on EMNLP*, pages 355–363.

[8] T. Kindo, H. Yoshida, T. Morimoto, and T. Watanabe. Adaptive personal information filtering system that organizes personal profiles automatically. In *Proceedings of the Fifteenth IJCAI*, pages 716–721.

[9] R.Y.K. Lau, C.L. Lai, and Y. Li. Fuzzy ontology mining and semantic information granulation for effective information retrieval decision making. *International Journal of Computational Intelligence Systems*, 1(4):54–65, 2011.

[10] R.Y.K. Lau, P. Bruza, and D. Song. Belief Revision for Adaptive Information Retrieval. In *Proceedings of the 27th Annual International ACM SIGIR Conference* , pages 130–137.

[11] R.Y.K. Lau, P. Bruza, and D. Song. Towards a Belief Revision Based Adaptive and Context-Sensitive Information Retrieval System. *ACM Transactions on Information Systems*, 26(2):8.1–8.38, 2008.

[12] R.Y.K. Lau, D. Song, Y. Li, C.H. Cheung, and J.X. Hao. Towards A Fuzzy Domain Ontology Extraction Method for Adaptive e-Learning. *IEEE Transactions on Knowledge and Data Engineering*, 21(6):800–813, 2009.

[13] I. Ounis, C. Macdonald, and I. Soboroff. Overview of the TREC 2008 Blog Track. In *Proceedings of the Seventeenth Text REtrieval Conference*, Gaithersburg, Maryland, 2008. NIST. Available from `http://trec.nist.gov/pubs/trec17/`.

[14] B. Pang, L. Lee, and S. Vaithyanathan. Thumbs up? sentiment classification using machine learning techniques. In *Proceedings of the 2002 Conference on EMNLP*, pages 79–86.

[15] J. Ponte and W. B. Croft. A language modeling approach to information retrieval. In *Proceedings of the 21st Annual International ACM SIGIR Conference* , pages 275–281.

[16] G. Qiu, B. Liu, J. Bu, and C. Chen. Expanding domain sentiment lexicon through double propagation. In *Proceedings of the 21st IJCAI*, pages 1199–1204.

[17] G. Qiu, B. Liu, J. Bu, and C. Chen. Opinion word expansion and target extraction through double propagation. *Computational Linguistics*, 1(37):9–27, 2011.

[18] D. Rao and D. Ravichandran. Semi-supervised polarity lexicon induction. In *Proceedings of the 12th Conference of the European Chapter of the Association for Computational Linguistics*, pages 675–682.

[19] E. Riloff, T. Wilson, P. Hoffmann, S. Somasundaran, J. Kessler, J. Wiebe, Y. Choi, C. Cardie, and S. Patwardhan. Opinionfinder: a system for subjectivity analysis. In *Proceedings of the 2005 HLTC and Conference on EMNLP*, pages 34–35.

[20] P.D. Turney and M. Littman. Measuring praise and criticism: Inference of semantic orientation from association. *ACM Transactions on Information Systems*, 21(4):315–346, October 2003.

[21] T. Wilson, J. Wiebe, and P. Hoffmann. Recognizing contextual polarity: An exploration of features for phrase-level sentiment analysis. *Computational Linguistics*, 35(3):399–433, 2009.

Classifying Trending Topics: A Typology of Conversation Triggers on Twitter

Arkaitz Zubiaga
NLP & IR Group @ UNED
C/Juan del Rosal, 16
Madrid, Spain
azubiaga@lsi.uned.es

Damiano Spina
NLP & IR Group @ UNED
C/Juan del Rosal, 16
Madrid, Spain
damiano@lsi.uned.es

Víctor Fresno
NLP & IR Group @ UNED
C/Juan del Rosal, 16
Madrid, Spain
vfresno@lsi.uned.es

Raquel Martínez
NLP & IR Group @ UNED
C/Juan del Rosal, 16
Madrid, Spain
raquel@lsi.uned.es

ABSTRACT

Twitter summarizes the great deal of messages posted by users in the form of trending topics that reflect the top conversations being discussed at a given moment. These trending topics tend to be connected to current affairs. Different happenings can give rise to the emergence of these trending topics. For instance, a sports event broadcasted on TV, or a viral meme introduced by a community of users. Detecting the type of origin can facilitate information filtering, enhance real-time data processing, and improve user experience. In this paper, we introduce a typology to categorize the triggers that leverage trending topics: news, current events, memes, and commemoratives. We define a set of straightforward language-independent features that rely on the social spread of the trends to discriminate among those types of trending topics. Our method provides an efficient way to immediately and accurately categorize trending topics without need of external data, outperforming a content-based approach.

Categories and Subject Descriptors

H.3.3 [**Information Storage and Retrieval**]: Information Search and Retrieval; H.1.2 [**Models and Principles**]: User/Machine Systems—*Human information processing*

General Terms

Human Factors, Experimentation, Measurement

Keywords

twitter, trending topics, social media, real-time, classification

CIKM'11, October 24–28, 2011, Glasgow, Scotland, UK.

1. INTRODUCTION

Twitter[1] is a microblogging site where users share short messages so-called tweets. These tweets tend to spread to a large number of users in very little time. Users on Twitter not only tweet about their personal issues or nearby events, but also about more general topics or news [8]. Due to the large amounts and diversity of real-time information contained on the site, Twitter lists a freshly updated set of trending topics. Trending topics comprise the top terms being discussed currently on Twitter. This list of top terms, which is updated in real-time, provides a reflection of the current main interests of the community, i.e., the most-discussed conversations right at the moment. It has become an appealing feature for Twitter users, real-time application developers, and social media researchers, thank to the ability to detect trending topics in the earliest stage.

The interests of the large community of users on Twitter encompasses a vast number of topics and types of messages. Hence, there is not a single reason that makes a topic become a trend. We believe that detecting the type of a trending topic helps better understand the origin that made it trend. This detection enables to better harness real-time data, since each type of trending topic may be useful for a different purpose. Discriminating trending topics by type of trigger in real-time could be useful to filter out unwanted ones in information filtering systems, or to enhance real-time data processing by treating them separately. We found little work dealing with the nature and characteristics of trending topics and, as far as we know, no research has been conducted dealing with the immediate characterization and detection of types of trending topics.

In this work, we introduce a typology of 4 types of trending topic triggers: news, current events, memes, and commemoratives. We propose a set of 15 straightforward features that characterize the social spread of a trending topic. These features are independent of the languages in which tweets are written. Using a collection of trending topics categorized according to the above typology, we perform classification experiments using Support Vector Machines to find the extent to which these features can help automatically categorize trending topics. Our method presents the ad-

[1]http://twitter.com/

vantages that (i) it provides an accurate classification outperforming the baseline approach relying on the content of tweets, (ii) it only requires a small set of features, which do not increase as the collection grows, (iii) it does not require using any external data, and (iv) its low computational cost enables to immediately predict the type of a trending topic as it emerges and appears on Twitter's homepage.

Next, in Section 2 we describe Twitter's trending topics. In Section 3 we summarize the related work. Then, in Section 4 we introduce a typology to organize trending topics by type of triggers, and detail the dataset used in the experiments. We propose a set of features, describe the trend classification experiments, and discuss the results in Section 5. Finally, we conclude the work in Section 6.

2. TRENDING TOPICS

One of the main features on the homepage of Twitter shows a list of top terms so-called trending topics at all times. These terms reflect the topics that are being discussed most in the latest minutes on the site's stream of tweets. In order to avoid topics that are always popular, Twitter focuses on topics that are being discussed much more than usual, i.e., topics that recently suffered an increase of use, so that it trended for some reason. Trending topics have generated big interest not only for the users themselves but also for information seekers such as journalists, real-time application developers, and social media researchers. Being able to know the top conversations being discussed at a given time helps keep updated about current affairs, and discover the main concerns of the community. Twitter defines trending topics as *"topics that are immediately popular, rather than topics that have been popular for a while or on a daily basis"*[2]. A trending topic is made up by the topic itself –i.e., the term that became a trend–, and a stream of tweets containing that topic.

3. RELATED WORK

So far, most of the work on Twitter has focused on analyzing the microblogging phenomenon [5, 7], modeling the information diffusion on the social network [13, 14] and analyzing the content of tweets [12, 10, 4].

Regarding the classification of single tweets, Sriram et al. [12] define a typology of five generic classes of tweets (news, events, opinions, deals, and private messages) in order to improve information filtering. The authors represent tweets using a small set of language-dependent features to classify tweets written in English. The use of these features outperforms the bag-of-words approach in the classification of tweets according to the typology. We believe that this typology, specifically defined for single tweets, does not fit the nature of triggers that leverage trending topics. Furthermore, this typology does not intend to classify by type of trigger. For instance, it is not intuitive to include a trending topic produced by a memorial day in this typology.

Little work has been done analyzing the properties of trending topics on Twitter. Most of them focus on event and topic detection [1, 2, 10]. Asur et al. [1] explore the longevity of trending topics on Twitter, and analyze the role of users in the emergence of trends. They found that (i) a few users are *trend-setters*, i.e, early contributors in the emergence of a trend, and (ii) a larger group of users are *propagators*, who help spread the topic. Cheong and Lee [3] and Kwak et al. [7] analyze the evolution of trending topics over the time, and perform a qualitative study of social features that characterize trending topics. They rely on the whole lifetime of trending topics to perform this analysis. Different from these, our work aims at immediately detecting the type of a trending topic as it emerges, so that we do not consider the whole lifetime of a trend.

Different from the above research, we present a typology to organize trending topics by trigger, and we a propose a set of language-independent features, and introduce a method that processes trending topics as soon as they emerge.

[2]http://support.twitter.com/articles/101125-about-trending-topics

4. TYPOLOGY OF TRENDING TOPICS

Next, we introduce the typology we use in this work to organize trending topics. After describing the typology, we detail the process of generation of a dataset, made up by trending topics and organized according to the typology.

4.1 Definition of a Typology of Trending Topics

Different happenings, either in the world, on TV, or on the Internet, can motivate users to discuss on a topic. After tracking trending topics for months, and acquiring insight on their emergence, we set forth a typology composed by the following 4 triggers:

- **News:** users sharing a breaking news promptly give rise to a trending topic. It has been shown that sometimes news break on Twitter before other online news media [7]. Thus, the detection of trending topics produced from news can be of utmost interest to discover breaking news. The early detection of news can also help feed news curation services, and notify search engines to update indexes related to the topic.

- **Current event:** users commenting on an event that is currently taking place leverage a trending topic in many cases. Users tend to live tweet about an event they are following (e.g., a soccer game or a TV show) or attending (e.g., a festival or a conference). The detection of these trending topics can help discover events that are taking place, or discover the events in which users are interested most.

- **Meme:** memes can also become a trending topic on Twitter. Memes are ideas that propagate through a social network. Usually, it is an idea that a community or a single (usually influential) user decides to launch in order to make it grow rapidly, and make it viral. The idea behind a meme may vary; it may be a community's will for something to happen, or a funny idea that someone proposed. The detection of these trending topics is useful to study the virality of ideas on the Internet, and for users looking for funny stuff.

- **Commemorative:** commemorative tweets can also become a trending topic. We consider it a commemorative topic when users congratulate a celebrity for his birthday, share about the anniversary of an event, or it is a memorial day. These trending topics can sometimes even be predicted, since upcoming celebrations and commemorations can previously be known. However, detecting them can be useful to analyze the way they come out, how they spread, and what opinions or comments users attach.

4.2 Dataset

Twitter selects 10 trending topics that are being discussed most at the moment. Using Twitter's top trends and search API methods, we monitored the trending topics shown on the site from March 1st to 7th. The list of top 10 trending topics was requested every 30 seconds. Thus, the process guarantees the detection of a trending topic almost as soon as it appears on the site, with a delay of 30 seconds in the worst scenario. As soon as a new topic appeared in the list of trends, another process queried the search API for the latest tweets containing the topic as a query term. Following this process, we collected a total of 1,036 unique trending topics. These trends include a total of 567,452 tweets from 348,757 different users. Accordingly, each of the 1,036 trending topics in the dataset contains an average of about 548 associated tweets. All these tweets are written in 28 different languages, with a majority of 295,082 tweets written in English, 76,628 in Spanish, 67,673 in Portuguese, 31,685 in Dutch, and 22,863 in Indonesian. Moreover, there is not a trending topic with just one language in the dataset.

All these topics were manually categorized within the typology we defined: news, current events, memes, or commemoratives. Each trending topic was included into just one type. To provide the annotations, the stream of tweets corresponding to a trending topic was read carefully. After understanding the trigger that caused the conversation to become a trending topic, the annotation was provided. Due to the large number of languages contained in the collection, machine translators were used for unknown languages. The annotation produced an organization of the 1,036 trending topics in groups of 616 current events, 251 memes, 142 news, and 27 commemoratives.

5. CLASSIFYING TRENDING TOPICS

Next, we present the features to characterize trending topics, and the classification experiments.

5.1 Features of Trending Topics

As an approach to discovering the type of a trending topic, we propose 15 social features that consider the way it spreads. Furthermore, since we want to categorize a trending topic as soon as it appears trending on the site, the features must be straightforward, easy to get, and cheap to compute while the system performs accurately. This would ensure the immediacy of computation, and the ability to predict the type of a trending topic on the fly, as soon as it appears on the Twitter's list. Moreover, these features are independent of the language used in tweets, and do not depend on the vocabulary utilized by users.

On one hand, we use average number of occurrences of features in the tweets corresponding to a trend. Each average computed as the arithmetic mean is the result of dividing the number of occurrences of the corresponding feature in the whole trend by the total number of tweets gathered for the trending topic. Note that the number of tweets in a topic that just trended is relatively small (average of 548 tweets). We propose 10 different features that rely on average values: (1) Level of retweets (the number of retweeting users to reach the current state of a tweet), (2) Ratio of retweets out of all tweets, (3) Hashtags, (4) Length of tweets, (5) Exclamations, (6) Questions, (7) Links, (8) Repetition of the trending topic in tweets, (9) Replies, and (10) Spread velocity (tweets per second).

On the other hand, we compute the diversity of feature values all across the tweets in a trending topic. The diversity calculates the variation of the feature throughout the trending topic. The higher is the diversity value, the more different is the feature from tweet to tweet within a trending topic. To compute the diversity, we use the Shannon's diversity index [11]. We propose 5 features that rely on diversity: (1) Contributing user diversity, (2) Retweeted user diversity, (3) Hashtag diversity, (4) Language diversity, and (5) Vocabulary diversity.

5.2 Classification of Trending Topics

5.2.1 Experimental Setup

We perform classification experiments according to the established typology using Support Vector Machines (SVM) [6] as a state-of-the-art classification algorithm. Being a multiclass task, we rely on a *one-against-all* binary combination method [9] using *svm-light*[3]. We set the SVM to run with a linear kernel and the default parameters.

We use two different representations in the classification process: the Twitter features described in Section 5.1, and a bag-of-words of the textual content of tweets as a baseline. We create one vector per trending topic for each of the representations. We use a training set with 600 trending topics, with 436 in the test set. We perform 10 random selections of the training set, and show the average results. The two representations we use are the following:

- **Twitter features:** we use vectors with 15 dimensions, corresponding to the features introduced above. The main advantages of this representation approach are the straightforwardness of the features, and that the number of features does not depend on the number of trends we have to represent, but it remains unchanged.
- **Textual content:** we rely on the bag-of-words approach. We represent each trend with the TF values of each term appearing in the stream after removing stopwords. This approach is computationally much more expensive than the approach based on Twitter features, and presents the problem that the number of dimensions utilized to represent the trends increases as the collection grows. In this case, representing the 1,036 trending topics generated vectors with 512,943 dimensions.

5.2.2 Evaluation

	Accuracy	Kappa
Bag-of-words	.752	.530
Twitter features	.784	.604

Table 1: Accuracy and Cohen's Kappa statistic of the trend classification by type of representation

Table 1 shows the accuracy values of the classification of trending topics. The accuracy measures the percent of correct guesses among all the predictions. The representation

[3]http://svmlight.joachims.org

	Class Precision			
	N	CE	M	C
Bag-of-words	.673	.783	.636	.548
Twitter features	.634	.829	.731	.132

Table 2: Precision by class (N: News; CE: Current Events; M: Memes; C: Commemoratives) of the trend classification by type of representation

based on the proposed Twitter features achieves a superior accuracy than the bag-of-words baseline. This superiority gap is of 3.2% in favor of the representation based on Twitter features. Furthermore, the winning approach presents the advantages that the features are straightforward and easy to compute, and that it only requires 15 features instead of the thousands required by the content-based representation. Cohen's kappa values in Table 1 show the impact of randomness on the agreement between predicted and observed classifications. Note that the higher is the value, the lower is the effect of randomness on the accuracy improvement. It can be observed that the kappa values follow the same rank as the accuracy values, so that it indicates that the accuracy improvement is not a consequence of random guesses.

When analyzing in more depth the precision by class (see Table 2), it can be seen that Twitter features perform better in the detection of current events, and especially memes, where the gap is bigger than 9%. Using the bag-of-words improves for news, and especially for commemoratives, where Twitter features get low precision. However, this could be due to the small number of commemoratives in the collection[4], and it may perform better with more trends of this type, probably providing a better representation of the class in the training stage.

6. CONCLUSIONS

In this work, we have explored the types of triggers that leverage conversations on Twitter. We have introduced a typology to organize Twitter's trending topics by the type of happening that caused them. This typology includes the following 4 types of trending topics: *news*, *current events*, *memes*, and *commemoratives*.

We aimed at characterizing trending topics so that we were able to organize them by type. To this end, we have set out 15 straightforward features to represent trending topics. These features are independent of the language used in the tweets, rely on the social diffusion of the trending topic, and only require tweets sent before the topic trended, without need of external data. The proposed method provides an immediate way to accurately organize trending topics. Unlike for the content-based representation, the number of features remains unchanged, and does not increase as the collection grows. Using SVM classifiers upon these features to discriminate types of trending topics showed that the proposed features provide more accurate classification results than the use of textual content of tweets.

To the best of our knowledge, this is the first research work introducing a typology of trending topics, and providing a method to immediately classify trending topics as soon as they appear on the homepage of Twitter. This study is relevant not only for researchers studying trends in social media, but also for developers who enhance their systems with real-time data from social networks. Furthermore, it paves the way to researchers interested in exploring causes that leverage trends on social media.

[4]Note that there are only 27 commemorative trends in the collection.

7. ACKNOWLEDGMENTS

This work has been part-funded by the Education Council of the Regional Government of Madrid, MA2VICMR (S-2009/TIC-1542), the Innovation project Holopedia (TIN2010-21128-C02-01), and the Spanish Ministry of Education for a doctoral grant (AP2009-0507).

8. REFERENCES

[1] S. Asur, B. A. Huberman, G. Szabó, and C. Wang. Trends in social media : Persistence and decay. *CoRR*, abs/1102.1402, 2011.

[2] M. Cataldi, L. Di Caro, and C. Schifanella. Emerging topic detection on twitter based on temporal and social terms evaluation. In *Proc. of MDMKDD '10*, pages 4:1–4:10. ACM, 2010.

[3] M. Cheong and V. Lee. Integrating web-based intelligence retrieval and decision-making from the twitter trends knowledge base. In *Proc. of SWSM '09*, pages 1–8. ACM, 2009.

[4] J. Hurlock and M. L. Wilson. Searching twitter: Separating the tweet from the chaff. In *Proc. of ICWSM '11*. AAAI, 2011.

[5] A. Java, X. Song, T. Finin, and B. Tseng. Why we twitter: understanding microblogging usage and communities. In *Proc. of WebKDD/SNA-KDD '07*, pages 56–65. ACM, 2007.

[6] T. Joachims. Text categorization with support vector machines: learning with many relevant features. In *Proc. of ECML '98*, pages 137–142, 1998.

[7] H. Kwak, C. Lee, H. Park, and S. Moon. What is twitter, a social network or a news media? In *Proc. of WWW '10*, pages 591–600. ACM, 2010.

[8] E. Mishaud. Twitter: Expressions of the whole self. Master's thesis, Department of Media and Communications, University of London, 2007.

[9] R. Rifkin and A. Klautau. In defense of one-vs-all classification. *Journal of Machine Learning Research*, 5:101–141, December 2004.

[10] T. Sakaki, M. Okazaki, and Y. Matsuo. Earthquake shakes twitter users: real-time event detection by social sensors. In *Proc. of WWW '10*, pages 851–860. ACM, 2010.

[11] C. E. Shannon. A mathematical theory of communication. *SIGMOBILE Mob. Comput. Commun. Rev.*, 5:3–55, January 2001.

[12] B. Sriram, D. Fuhry, E. Demir, H. Ferhatosmanoglu, and M. Demirbas. Short text classification in twitter to improve information filtering. In *Proc. of SIGIR '10*, pages 841–842. ACM, 2010.

[13] S. Wu, J. M. Hofman, W. A. Mason, and D. J. Watts. Who says what to whom on twitter. In *Proc. of WWW '11*, pages 705–714. ACM, 2011.

[14] J. Yang and J. Leskovec. Modeling information diffusion in implicit networks. *Proc. of ICDM '10*, 0:599–608, 2010.

Enhancing Accessibility of Microblogging Messages Using Semantic Knowledge

Xia Hu
Arizona State University
Tempe, AZ 85287, USA
xiahu@asu.edu

Lei Tang
Yahoo! Labs
Santa Clara, CA 95054, USA
ltang@yahoo-inc.com

Huan Liu
Arizona State University
Tempe, AZ 85287, USA
huan.liu@asu.edu

ABSTRACT

The volume of microblogging messages is increasing exponentially with the popularity of microblogging services. With a large number of messages appearing in user interfaces, it hinders user accessibility to useful information buried in disorganized, incomplete, and unstructured text messages. In order to enhance user accessibility, we propose to aggregate related microblogging messages into clusters and automatically assign them semantically meaningful labels. However, these messages provide inadequate term co-occurrence information for capturing semantic associations due to their short length. To address this problem, we propose a novel framework for organizing unstructured microblogging messages by transforming them to a semantically structured representation. The proposed framework first captures informative tree fragments by analyzing a parse tree of the message, and then exploits external knowledge bases (Wikipedia and WordNet) to enhance their semantic information. Empirical evaluation on a Twitter dataset shows that our framework significantly outperforms existing state-of-the-art methods.

Categories and Subject Descriptors

H.3.3 [**Information Storage and Retrieval**]: Information Search and Retrieval—*Clustering*; D.2.8 [**Database Management**]: Database Applications—*Data Mining*

General Terms

Algorithm, Performance, Experimentation

Keywords

Microblogging, Accessibility, Clustering, Labeling

1. INTRODUCTION

Microblogging services such as Twitter[1] are increasingly used for communicating breaking news, information sharing, and participating in events. This emerging medium has become a powerful communication channel in recent digital revolutions. However, the accessibility of these messages has been very limited so far. Tweets and retweets of a user's followees appear alongside the user's own tweets in reverse chronological order. People often have only enough patience to skim through the first 20 - 50 messages. When the messages become overwhelming, it is impractical for a user to quickly gauge the main subjects from their followees' posts.

To make a large collection of microblogging messages accessible to users, current web systems need to provide not only accurate clusters for subtopics in microblogging messages, but also meaningful labels for each cluster. Enhancing the accessibility of microblogging messages entails two tasks: (1) cluster microblogging messages into manageable categories, and (2) assign readable and meaningful labels for each cluster of messages. Unlike standard text with many sentences or paragraphs, microblogging messages are *noisy* and *short*. In addition, microbloggers, when composing a message, may use or coin new abbreviations or acronyms that are uncommon in conventional text documents. Furthermore, these short messages do not provide sufficient contextual information to capture their semantic meanings. Traditional text mining methods, when applied to microblogging messages directly, lead to unsatisfactory results.

In this paper, we present a novel framework to enhance the accessibility of microblogging messages. The proposed framework improves message representation by mapping messages from an unstructured feature space to a semantically meaningful knowledge space. First, we use tree fragments extraction to generate informative words and phrases. Then, to overcome the extreme sparsity of microblogging messages, we map the selected terms to structured concepts derived from external knowledge bases that are semantically rich. By conducting feature selection, we are able to cluster all messages more accurately and generate human-comprehensible labels efficiently from related concepts.

2. MANAGING MICROBLOGGING MESSAGES

In this section, we introduce the proposed framework for clustering and labeling microblogging messages.

2.1 Problem Statement

We now formally define two major tasks in the problem of enhancing accessibility of microblogging messages.

Task 1: Microblogging Message Clustering. Let

[1]http://www.twitter.com/

CIKM'11, October 24–28, 2011, Glasgow, Scotland, UK.

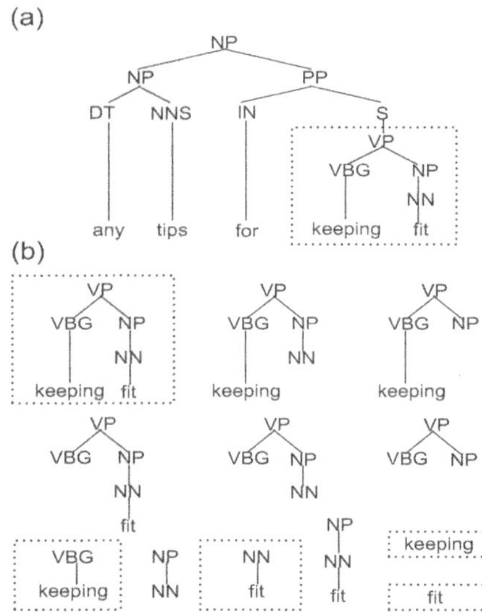

Figure 1: (a) The parse tree of "any tips for keeping fit?". (b) Tree fragments of the subtree covering "keeping fit"; the fragments with dotted line frame are extracted tree fragments for "keeping fit".

$M = \{m_1, m_2, \ldots, m_n\}$ be a corpus of n microblogging messages. Among these n messages, there are k latent topics or subtopics. We aim to cluster the n messages into k clusters $\{c_1, c_2, \ldots, c_k\}$ with their latent topics as centroids.

Task 2: Cluster Labeling. For each cluster c_i, we aim to generate human readable cluster labels $\{l_{i1}, l_{i2}, \ldots, l_{ik}\}$, which are semantically similar to the latent topic of c_i.

2.2 Syntactic Decomposition

Many NLP techniques have achieved great success by extracting tree fragments that occur in a parse tree to enrich text representation. A parse tree (or syntactic tree) is an ordered and rooted tree that represents the syntactic structure of a string according to a formal grammar. Figure 1 (a) illustrates an example of a parse tree generated by OpenNLP[2]. In the Figure, "VP" and "NP" represent verb phrase and noun phrase[3], respectively.

Given a microblogging message, a parse tree has been constructed to retain the syntactic information. Furthermore, we need to extract useful information from the parse tree to improve message representation. To better utilize the syntactic structure of a parse tree, Wang et al. [6] proposed to employ tree fragments as syntactic features.

Figure 1 (b) presents an illustration of the tree fragments for subtree "keeping fit". Basically, we divided our algorithm into two steps: *Subtree Selection* and *Fragment Selection*.

Subtree Selection: As shown in Figure 1 (a), given a microblogging message, we first construct a parse tree according to its lexical tokens. Note that the number of subtrees is extremely large, which leads to the "curse of dimensionality" and expensive computational cost for real web applications. Thus, we need to develop an efficient way to ensure the generated subtrees are not only informative but also effective. As we know, when people speed-read through a text, they do not fully parse the sentence but instead look for "key phrases" contained in the text. Among these key phrases, the nouns and verbs are considered to be more important than articles, adjectives or adverbs [6]. Thus, we utilize VP (Verb Phrase), NP (Noun Phrase), VB (Verb) and NN (Noun) rooted subtrees to extract tree fragments in next step.

Fragment Selection: As shown in Figure 1 (b), one subtree may generate a lot of tree fragments, which will result in redundancies. To avoid introducing redundant information to text representation, we only choose the tree fragments whose leaf nodes are constructed by words or phrase.

[2]http://incubator.apache.org/opennlp/

[3]Full list of the abbreviations can be found in http://en.wikipedia.org/wiki/Parse_tree/

2.3 Semantic Mapping

In order to transform the syntactic feature space to a semantic feature space, we collect the extracted tree fragments as a basis and construct semantic space for mapping. For each tree fragment, we apply semantic knowledge according to its syntax property. Phrase-level tree fragments are informative to represent a subtopic of the microblogging message. In this way, we can retrieve accurate Wikipedia pages for these tree fragments. The word-level tree fragments are too general to map accurately to concepts in Wikipedia. We thus utilize WordNet as complement to deal with the word-level tree fragments.

Particularly, if a tree fragment is from the phrase-level, we build an "AND" query[4] which requires the retrieved pages to contain every term in the phrase. We utilize the title and bold terms (links) of the retrieved articles, combined with key phrases as semantic features. For example, for the actor "Colin Firth", we may obtain extrinsic concepts "The King's Speech" and intrinsic concepts "England" by mining the related Wikipedia pages. For the tree fragments from the word level, we employ WordNet synsets to extract similar concepts. For example, we can obtain "auto", "automobile" and "autocar" for the fragment "car". With a semantic mapping, we can handle phrase-level synonymy problems by mapping two different phrases onto the same semantic concept.

2.4 Clustering & Labeling

2.4.1 Feature Selection

We conduct feature selection to avoid aggravating the "curse of dimensionality". A single message contains a large number of tree fragments, including phrase-level (t_1) and word-level (t_2) tree fragments. We empirically set the upper bound of selected tree fragments as the number of non-stop words (N) contained in the message.

We then collect m tree fragments from Syntactic Decomposition and n semantic concepts from semantic knowledge bases, and construct a $(m+n)$ dimensional feature space for clustering. As a large number of external features would have a negative impact on the quality of the text representation, the number of semantic concepts is determined by:

$$n = \frac{m \times \theta}{1 - \theta}, \tag{1}$$

where θ is the ratio of semantic concepts to the feature space for clustering. In the experiments, we empirically set $\theta = 0.5$.

[4]For more detail about query syntax, please refer to http://wiki.apache.org/solr/SolrQuerySyntax

Table 1: Clustering results using different text representation methods on Twitter Dataset

	F_1measure (Impr)	Accuracy (Impr)
BOW	0.493 (N.A.)	0.543 (N.A.)
BOT	0.504 (+2.27%)	0.556 (+2.29%)
WN_Method	0.499 (+1.28%)	0.553 (+1.85%)
Wiki_Method	0.525 (+6.37%)	0.576 (+5.97%)
WikiWN_Method	0.513 (+4.08%)	0.569 (+4.70%)
SemKnow	0.529 (+7.36%)	0.578 (+6.46%)
M^3	**0.554 (+12.27%)**	**0.628 (+15.55%)**

2.4.2 Text Representation for Clustering

To normalize the weight of each feature, we reformulate the weighting policy proposed by Zhang and Lee [7]. For tree fragments f_i extracted from original parse tree, f_i is weighted according to the size and depth of a tree fragment:

$$W_{f_i} = \frac{tf \times idf}{(s(i)+1) \times (d(i)+1)}, \qquad (2)$$

where $s(i)$ is the number of generated tree fragments considering the tree fragment as a subtree and $d(i)$ is the depth of the tree fragment root in the entire parse tree. For example, the tree fragment in Figure 1 (b) has $s(i) = 3$ and $d(i) = 3$. With this weighting scheme, the focus of the message can be measured according to its depth. Weight scores for all tree fragments are normalized. In addition, weights of semantic features from external knowledge bases are determined by their $tf * idf$ values. Weight scores for all semantic concepts are normalized. The result is that messages are represented in a refined feature space.

2.4.3 Labeling

Traditional labeling methods do not guarantee readability of the extracted labels. It is natural and effective to generate textual labels from the generated Wikipedia concepts, which have wide knowledge coverage and stably high quality.

We can map each tree fragment f_i to several semantic concepts, which are extracted as label candidates $\{l_{i1}, l_{i2}, \ldots, l_{in}\}$. For each labeling candidate l_{ij}, the informativeness score is measured by:

$$Info_{l_{ij}} = W_{f_i} \times tf_{ij} \times idf_{ij}, \qquad (3)$$

where W_{f_i} is a weight of the "parent" tree fragment defined in Equation 2, tf_{ij} and idf_{ij} measure the weights among all the candidates. Finally, the labels with highest $Info$ score are extracted as cluster labels.

3. EXPERIMENTS

In this section, we empirically evaluate the effectiveness of the proposed Microblogging Message Management (M^3) framework.

3.1 Datasets

We crawled the hot queries published by Google Trends[5] between Jan. 1st 2008 and Dec. 31st 2010. Thirty hot queries of diverse topics are selected from Google Trends. Each hot query is considered to be a trending topic, and we crawl the top five query suggestions from Google as subtopics of this topic. The ground truth is obtained based on the following assumption: the messages returned by a query suggestion construct a cluster and the query suggestion is highly semantically associated with the correct label of this cluster. Thus, we have 150 topics from two levels (30 groups and 5 subtopics in each group). Based on the query suggestions (subtopics), we use Twitter Search API[6] to crawl 100 tweets for each query suggestion and construct a dataset containing 150 categories. As the API will not return exactly 100 tweets for each query, it leaves 11362 tweets after text preprocessing.

3.2 Evaluation of Clustering

3.2.1 Experimental Setup

To evaluate the performance of the proposed clustering module, we use F_1*measure* and *Accuracy* as the performance metrics, and compare the following methods:

- *BOW*: Traditional "bag of words" model.
- *BOT*: Modification of Tree Kernel model.
- *WN_Method*: *BOW* model integrated with additional features from WordNet as presented in [3].
- *Wiki_Method*: *BOW* model integrated with additional features from Wikipedia as presented in [1].
- *WikiWN_Method*: Semantic concepts from WordNet [3] and Wikipedia [1] as features.
- *SemKnow*: The "bag of phrases" model integrated with additional features from external knowledge [4].
- M^3: Clustering module of the proposed framework.

Note that our proposed text representation framework is independent of any specific dimensionality reduction and clustering methods. Similarly, we can easily apply this text representation framework to many clustering methods, such as *K-means*, *LDA*, *NMF* etc. In the experiments, *K-means* is employed and we set number of clusters $k = 150$.

3.2.2 Clustering Results and Discussion

The experimental results of the different methods on the dataset are displayed in Table 1. Based on the results, we make the following observations:

(1) *BOT* augments the performance of *BOW* model on the dataset. We believe that this is because of the utilization of syntactic information from the original messages. We note that *WN_Method*, *Wiki_Method*, *SemKnow* also achieve better performance as compared to *BOW* model. It demonstrates that the integration of semantic concepts from external knowledge bases improved the quality of the representation of microblogging messages for clustering.

(2) An interesting finding is that *WikiWN_Method* achieves comparable results with other baselines, which is beyond the observations of previous work [2]. *WikiWN_Method* works well without the integration of features from the original message. It shows that the combination of semantic features complement each other and contribute to the overall result.

[5]http://www.google.com/intl/en/trends/about.html/

[6]http://search.twitter.com/api/

Table 2: Ranking Results (NDCG@10)

	NDCG@10
Kphrase	0.342 (N.A.)
WN	0.338 (-1.17%)
Wiki	0.436 (+27.49%)
M^3	**0.498 (+45.61%)**

Table 3: Lists of top-5 labels generated from M^3

Subtopics	Generated Top-5 Labels
Apple Store	Apple Store, Retail Store, Apple Inc., Steve Jobs, iPad
Apple TV	Apple TV, iTunes, Apple Inc., iTunes Store, Digital Media Receiver
Apple iPad	iPad 2, iPad†, Tablet Computer, Apple A5 Processor, Foxconn
Apple Trailers	Trailer†, QuickTime, Mac OS, Trailer Film, Apple Inc.
Apple Support	Apple Care, Apple Inc., iPod Customer Support, Apple Store

(3) Among all the methods, M^3 achieves the best performance. We apply t-test to compare M^3 with the best baselines *WikiWN_Method* and *SemKnow*. The results demonstrate our approach significantly outperforms the two methods with $p - value < 0.01$.

3.3 Evaluation of Labeling

3.3.1 Experimental Setup and Criteria

We treat the cluster labeling task as a ranking problem, which is to rank all of the concepts from Wikipedia and find the best matched label for a cluster of microblogging messages. The subtopics used for crawling microblogging messages are considered to be ground truth for cluster labeling. We use NDCG as the evaluation metric. We compare the performance of following methods:

- *Kphrase*: Traditional "bag of phrases" model.
- *WN*: The concepts extracted from WordNet [3].
- *Wiki*: The concepts extracted from Wikipeida [1].
- M^3: Labeling module of the proposed framework.

3.3.2 Ranking Results

We compare the ranking performance of our proposed framework with the other three methods. Table 2 shows NDCG@10 score of the four methods on the dataset.

From Table 2, we can observe that M^3 outperforms all the baselines. It demonstrates that the generated labels from M^3 not only cover more potential topics hidden in the microblogging messages, but also give the most relevant labels a higher ranking. Among the three baselines, *Wiki* achieves the best performance. We believe that the improvement stems from the structure and meaningful concepts providing by Wikipedia.

3.4 A Usability Case Study

To illustrate the usability of our proposed framework, we show an example of top-5 generated textual labels for a trending topic "Apple" in Table 3. In the table, subtopics listed in the left side are considered "correct labels". The underlined labels are "identical" to correct labels and those with daggers are "inflections" of correct labels. We observe that while the labels for all clusters seem to represent the subtopics well, only the last cluster fails to achieve correct label within top-5 labels, although most of labels are highly related to subtopic "Apple Support". The failure is mainly because that there is no corresponding Wikipedia page named "Apple Support".

4. CONCLUSIONS AND FUTURE WORK

In this paper, we proposed a novel framework to improve the performance of microblogging message clustering and labeling. The original short and noisy texts were mapped into a semantic space to improve the quality of text representation for clustering. In addition, with help of abundant structured features from Wikipedia, the task of cluster labeling was solved without introducing significant computational cost. Empirical evaluations demonstrated that our framework significantly outperformed existing state-of-the-art methods.

This work suggests some interesting directions for future work. It would be interesting to explore if integrating social network information can improve the quality of message clustering. Moreover, NLP and external knowledge bases can be valuable to help understand microblogging messages, if we can find effective ways to use them.

Acknowledgement

This work is, in part, supported by ONR (N000141010091), AFOSR (FA95500810132) and Yahoo! Faculty Research and Engagement program.

5. REFERENCES

[1] S. Banerjee, K. Ramanathan, and A. Gupta. Clustering short texts using Wikipedia. In *Proceedings of the 30th ACM SIGIR*, pages 787–788, 2007.

[2] E. Gabrilovich and S. Markovitch. Feature generation for text categorization using world knowledge. In *Proceedings of the 20th AAAI*, pages 1048–1153, 2005.

[3] A. Hotho, S. Staab, and G. Stumme. Wordnet improves text document clustering. In *Proceedings of the SIGIR 2003 Semantic Web Workshop*, pages 541–544, 2003.

[4] X. Hu, N. Sun, C. Zhang, and T.-S. Chua. Exploiting internal and external semantics for the clustering of short texts using world knowledge. In *Proceeding of the 18th ACM CIKM*, pages 919–928, 2009.

[5] P. Treeratpituk and J. Callan. Automatically labeling hierarchical clusters. In *Proceedings of the 2006 international conference on Digital government research*, pages 167–176, 2006.

[6] K. Wang, Z. Ming, and T. Chua. A syntactic tree matching approach to finding similar questions in community-based qa services. In *Proceedings of the 32nd ACM SIGIR*, pages 187–194, 2009.

[7] D. Zhang and W. Lee. Question classification using support vector machines. In *Proceedings of the 26th ACM SIGIR*, pages 26–32, 2003.

Imbalanced Sentiment Classification

Shoushan Li[†] Guodong Zhou[†] Zhongqing Wang[†] Sophia Yat Mei Lee[‡] Rangyang Wang[†]

[†]Natural Language Processing Lab
Soochow University, Suzhou, China
{shoushan.li, wangzq870305,wangrongyang.nlp} @gmail.com, gdzhou@suda.edu.cn

[‡] Language Centre
Hong Kong Baptist University, Hong Kong
sophiaym@gmail.com

ABSTRACT
Sentiment classification has undergone significant development in recent years. However, most existing studies assume the balance between negative and positive samples, which may not be true in reality. In this paper, we investigate imbalanced sentiment classification instead. In particular, a novel clustering-based stratified under-sampling framework and a centroid-directed smoothing strategy are proposed to address the imbalanced class and feature distribution problems respectively. Evaluation across different datasets shows the effectiveness of both the under-sampling framework and the smoothing strategy in handling the imbalanced problems in real sentiment classification applications.

Categories and Subject Descriptors
I.2.7 [**Artificial Intelligence**]: Natural Language Processing – *Text analysis*

General Terms
Algorithms, Experimentation

Keywords
Opinion Mining, Sentiment Classification, Imbalanced Classification

1. INTRODUCTION
Sentiment classification aims to predict sentiment polarity of a text [8] and it plays a critical role in many NLP applications However, most existing studies on sentiment classification assume the balance between the numbers of positive and negative samples, which may not hold in practice. Actually, many sentiment classification applications involve imbalanced class distributions in that the sample number of one class in the training data is much larger than the other class. We call this specific kind of sentiment classification as imbalanced sentiment classification, in which the class with a larger amount of samples is referred to as *majority class* and the other class with a smaller amount of samples is referred to as *minority class*.

In fact, imbalanced classification has been proven challenging in the machine learning research community [4]. Many approaches have been proposed to deal with the imbalanced class distribution problem, such as re-sampling [2], one-class classification [3], and cost-sensitive learning [14]. Unfortunately, none of the above approaches can be readily applied to imbalanced sentiment classification due to its specific characteristics.

In imbalanced classification, *majority class* normally contains more kinds of occurring features than *minority class*. For simplicity, we refer to this phenomenon as imbalanced feature distribution. Such phenomenon becomes worse in imbalanced sentiment classification since sentiment classification often involves a small number of positive and negative samples. It further worsens due to the sparseness of effective sentimental features. On one hand, sentiment classification faces the same challenge of high feature dimension as text categorization. On the other hand, the effective sentimental features in a sample are rather rare in sentiment classification, considering infrequent occurrence of sentimental words in text. For example, while the feature dimension of a typical sentiment classifier may be up to tens of thousands, there are only dozens of effective sentimental features (e.g., sentimental words) in a sample.

The imbalanced feature distribution problem can cause severe problems in the training process of imbalanced sentiment classification. Normally, the features that merely occur in the *majority class* (not occurring in *minority class*, called majority unique features) can be a strong distinguishing clue in the classifier. Nevertheless, considering that the number of effective sentimental features (e.g., sentimental words) is significantly fewer than that of other features (e.g., those words about facts) in sentiment classification, most of the majority unique features will contribute abnormally. As a result, if we use all the training samples to train a classifier, the classifier will have a strong tendency to wrongly predict a sample from the *minority class* as the *majority class*. This indicates the necessity of dealing with the imbalanced feature distribution problem in imbalanced sentiment classification.

In this paper, we propose a clustering-based stratified under-sampling framework to overcome the imbalanced class distribution problem in imbalanced sentiment classification. Under this framework, the samples in the *majority class* are first grouped into several clusters and then a suitable number of samples are selected from each cluster to form the training

CIKM'11, October 24–28, 2011, Glasgow, Scotland, UK.

samples of *majority class*. The intuition is that these selected samples using the stratified under-sampling framework should be more representative than those by random selection. Moreover, a centroid-directed smoothing strategy is proposed to overcome the imbalanced feature distribution problem by linearly interpolating a sample with the centroid of the cluster to which this sample belongs. Since the centroid represents the average feature distribution of all occurring features in the cluster, our smoothing strategy can greatly increase the sample robustness and reduce its feature sparseness.

2. RELATED WORK

Early studies on sentiment classification mainly focus on unsupervised learning methods, which build a sentiment classifier without any labeled data. In such methods, the relationship between two words (e.g., a seed word and any other word) is usually first extracted from some knowledge resources, such as WordNet and unlabeled data. Then, such relationship is used to compute the semantic orientation of a word or even the sentiment polarity of a text [12]. In general, the performance of unsupervised learning methods is too low to meet the requirements of real applications.

Compared to unsupervised leaning, supervised learning methods often perform much better due to the availability of labeled data and become more popular since the pioneer work on sentiment classification by Pang et al. [8]. In particular, various kinds of information have been explored to improve the bag-of-words model [5][6][11]. Unfortunately, the performance of a supervised learning method drops dramatically when adapted to a new domain. This arouses wide interests on the research of domain adaptation in sentiment classification [1].

Besides domain adaptation, the imbalanced class distribution problem is another major reason which hurts the wide application of sentiment classification. To the best of our knowledge, our work is the first study on imbalanced sentiment classification.

3. CLUSTERING-BASED STRATIFIED UNDER-SAMPLING FRAMEWORK

3.1 Overview

Just as described in the introduction, imbalanced feature distribution in imbalanced sentiment classification is much due to the conflict between the high feature dimension problem (the high number of possible features in sentiment classification) and the feature sparseness problem (infrequent occurrence of sentimental words in a sample). Such imbalance in the feature distribution becomes even worse due to the imbalanced class distribution since the number of occurring features in the *minority class* would be much fewer than that in the *majority class*.

To have a better understanding of the imbalanced feature distribution phenomenon in imbalanced sentiment classification, Table 2 gives the statistics over two typical domains on the number of features occurring in the positive and negative classes, denoted as n_+ and n_- respectively, with the ratios of n_+ / n_- being around 2.

Table 1: Feature distributions on the number of occurring features in the positive and negative classes across two typical domains

Domain	n_+	n_-	n
Beauty	7,315	4,364	8,945
Computer	12,646	5,527	14,465

3.2 Stratified Under-sampling

As a popular sampling method in statistics, stratified sampling first groups the members of a population into a few relatively homogeneous subgroups (i.e. strata) according to one certain property and then selects samples from each stratum. It is believed that stratified sampling is able to select better samples to represent the distribution of the whole dataset. Previous work justifies its effectiveness theoretically and empirically in both general applications [7] and specific NLP applications such as semantic relation extraction between named entities [9] [10].

The basic motivation of our using clustering-based stratified sampling is to select some "representative" samples from the *majority class*. In particular, the same number of "representative" samples is selected from the *minority class*. Therefore, our sampling approach is basically a non-random under-sampling approach. The reason why we adopt under-sampling instead of over-sampling is basically due to its better performance. Please refer to Figure 2 in Section 6.2 for details.

Clustering groups the samples in the *majority class* into several strata. Considering that the strata may be skewed, the number of selected samples from each cluster is tuned according to the size of each stratum. Given N_{MA} samples in the *majority class* and N_{MI} samples in the *minority class*, the number of samples selected from the *i-th* stratum S_i should be $N_i = \frac{N_{MI}}{N_{MA}} \times |S_i|$.

Input: The training data and the number of strata being clustered, denoted as K

Output: Balanced training data

Algorithm:

1) Cluster the samples in the *majority class* into K strata using a clustering algorithm.
2) Calculate the number of samples being sampled for each stratum S_i, $i = \{1, 2, ..., K\}$
3) Perform intra-strata sampling in each stratum.
4) Combine the selected *majority class* samples from all the strata to form the *majority class* training data
5) Merge the *majority class* training data and all *minority class* data to obtain the balanced training dataset.

Figure 1: Clustering-based stratified under-sampling

3.3 Intra-stratum Sampling

Given the strata and the number of selected samples from each stratum, a natural question arises as to how to select the samples from each stratum. This can be viewed as intra-stratum sampling, which chooses a certain amount of samples from inside individual stratum [10].

In particular, we employ a diversity-motivated scheme to perform intra-stratum sampling with the objective to maximize the training utility of all the samples from a stratum. That is, those samples with high variance to each other are preferred, avoiding similar samples from a stratum. In particular, we first select a random candidate sample and then exclude its nearest two samples. This process repeats until enough samples are obtained. Figure 1 illustrates the clustering-based stratified under-sampling framework with intra-stratum sampling.

4. CENTROID-DIRECTED SMOOTHING

In this paper, a centroid-directed smoothing strategy is proposed to alleviate the imbalanced feature distribution problem in imbalanced sentiment classification.

Although under-sampling can balance both class and feature distributions by eliminating many samples from the *majority class* to keep the balance between positive and negative samples, a lot of *majority class* features are excluded. Without these excluded features, the selected samples may not be able to well represent the feature distribution of the whole dataset in the *majority class*, even when the clustering-based stratified under-sampling is used.

The centroid-directed smoothing strategy merges the feature vector of each sample in the *majority class* with that of the centroid of the corresponding cluster it belongs to. Accordingly, the feature vector of each sample in the *minority class* is extended with itself. As the number of non-zero elements in the centroid is much larger than the number of the non-zero elements in a *minority class* sample, the feature imbalanced distribution problem still exists. However, the centroid-directed smoothing strategy actually introduces another imbalanced factor in imbalanced feature weights since the feature weights in the centroid are usually much lower than the Boolean weights in a sample in the *minority class*. Therefore, these two kinds of imbalanced factors result in a slightly more balanced classifier classifying the samples from both the positive and negative classes.

Formally, the centroid feature vector c_i of the cluster S_i is calculated as the mean of feature vectors of all the samples in the *i-th* cluster $c_i = \left(\sum_{x \in S_i} x / |S_i| \right)$.

In summary, the centroid-directed smoothing strategy maps the feature vector of a sample x to a new feature vector x^{new} as follows,

$$\begin{cases} x^{new} = <x, c_i> \text{ if } x \in S_i \text{ and } x \in X_{MA} \\ x^{new} = <x, x> \text{ if } x \in X_{MI} \text{ or } x \in X_{Test} \end{cases}$$

Where X_{MA} represents the samples in the *majority class*, X_{MI} represents the samples in the *minority class*, and X_{Test} represents the samples in the whole test data, regardless of what class they belong to.

5. EXPERIMENTAL STUDIES

In this paper, two datasets are used to investigate the performance of our approach on imbalanced sentiment classification. The first one[1] is a widely-used public dataset collected by Blitzer et al. [1] which consists of four domains: Book, DVD, Electronic, and Kitchen. For our experiment, each domain contains 400 negative samples (randomly selected from the 1000 original negative samples) and 1000 positive samples.

We adopt the popular geometric mean (*G-mean*), defined as $G-mean = \sqrt{TP_{rate} \times TN_{rate}}$, where TP_{rate} is the true positive rate (also called positive recall or sensitivity) and TN_{rate} is the true negative rate (also called negative recall or specificity) [4].

Finally, all the classifiers adopt the Maximum Entropy (ME) algorithm available with the *Mallet*[2] *tool*, and the same Boolean-weighted unigram. For thorough comparison on imbalanced sentiment classification, various settings are explored:

1) Full training (FullT): directly throwing all the training data for training.

2) Random over-sampling (OverS): performing over-sampling by randomly selecting the samples from the *minority class*.

3) Random under-sampling (UnderS): performing under-sampling by randomly selecting the samples from the *majority class*.

4) One-class classification (OneClass): performing one-class classification as proposed by Juszczak and Duin [3] using the *lib-SVM tool*[3].

5) Cost-sensitive classification (CostSensitive): performing cost-sensitive classification as proposed by Zhou and Liu [14] using the *lib-SVM tool*. Here, the cost weight for a *majority-class* sample is set to the imbalanced ratio between the *minority class* and *majority class* samples in each domain while the cost weight for a *minority-class* sample is 1.

6) Clustering-based under-sampling (ClusterU): performing clustering-based stratified under-sampling.

7) Clustering-based under-sampling plus centroid-directed smoothing (ClusterUC): performing both clustering-based stratified under-sampling and centroid-directed smoothing, as proposed in this paper.

Since most of the above settings involve random selection of samples, we run 20 times for each setting and report the average performance.

Table 2 compares the seven settings. It shows that both random over-sampling and random under-sampling significantly outperform full training due to balance keeping between positive and negative samples. It also shows that random under-sampling significantly outperforms random over-sampling largely due to the ignorance of imbalanced feature distribution by random over-sampling. Furthermore, it shows that one-class classification does not fit our task at all and that random under-sampling is rather difficult to beat. Generally, random under-sampling performs slightly better than cost-sensitive

[1] http://www.cs.jhu.edu/~mdredze/datasets/sentiment/index2.html

[2] http://mallet.cs.umass.edu/

[3] http://www.csie.ntu.edu.tw/~cjlin/libsvm/

Table 2: Performances of the seven imbalanced classification algorithms

Domain	FullT	OverS	UnderS	OneClass	CostSensitive	ClusterU	ClusterUC
Book	0.575	0.631	0.697	0.492	0.663	0.698	**0.713**
DVD	0.574	0.621	0.706	0.527	0.712	0.714	**0.731**
Electronic	0.675	0.675	0.782	0.546	0.748	0.789	**0.797**
Kitchen	0.677	0.677	0.770	0.861	0.773	0.782	**0.803**

classification. Although clustering-based under-sampling (ClusterU) employs cleverer selection strategies, they can only achieve comparable performances with random under-sampling. Observation on the features occurring in the selected samples shows that only about half of the features remain regardless of what kind of under-sampling (random or clustering-based) is used. Since half of the features can hardly well represent the feature distribution of the whole data, this justifies why cleverer under-sampling fails to improve the performance. It also shows that centriod-directed smoothing strategy significantly improves the performance of clustering-based under-sampling in all domains. This suggests the importance of resolving the imbalanced feature distribution problem and the effectiveness of our proposed centroid-directed smoothing strategy.

6. CONCLUSION

In this paper, we address the issue of imbalanced sentiment classification by taking into account both the imbalanced class and feature distribution problems. In particular, a clustering-based stratified under-sampling framework and a centroid-directed smoothing strategy are proposed to deal with the imbalanced class and feature distribution problems respectively. Evaluation shows the effectiveness of our approach.

Acknowledgments

The research work described in this paper has been partially supported by three NSFC grants, No. 61003155, No. 60873150 and No. 90920004 and Open Projects Program of National Laboratory of Pattern Recognition.

7. REFERENCES

[1] Blitzer J., M. Dredze, and F. Pereira. 2007. Biographies, bollywood, boom-boxes and blenders: domain adaptation for sentiment classification. In *Proceedings of ACL-07*. 440-447.

[2] Chawla N., K. Bowyer, L. Hall, and W. Kegelmeyer. 2002. SMOTE: Synthetic minority over-sampling technique. *Journal of Artificial Intelligence Research*. 16(2002), 321–357.

[3] Juszczak P. and R. Duin. 2003. Uncertainty sampling methods for one-class classifiers. In *Proceedings of ICML-03, Workshop on Learning with Imbalanced Data Sets II*. 81–88.

[4] Kubat M. and S. Matwin. 1997. Addressing the curse of imbalanced training sets: one-sided selection. In *Proceedings of ICML-97*. 179–186.

[5] Li S., S. Lee, Y. Chen, C. Huang, and G. Zhou. 2010. Sentiment classification and polarity shifting. In *Proceedings of COLING-10*. 635-643.

[6] Nakagawa T., K. Inui, and S. Kurohashi. 2010. Dependency tree-based sentiment classification using CRFs with hidden. In *Proceedings of NAACL-10*. 786–794.

[7] Neyman J. 1934. On the two different aspects of the representative method: The method of stratified sampling and the method of purposive selection. *Journal of the Royal Statistical Society*. 97,4(1934), 558-625.

[8] Pang B., L. Lee, and S. Vaithyanathan. 2002. Thumbs up? Sentiment classification using machine learning techniques. In *Proceedings of EMNLP-02*.79-86.

[9] Qian L., G. Zhou, F. Kong, and Q. Zhu. 2009. Semi-supervised learning for semantic relation classification using stratified sampling strategy. In *Proceedings of EMNLP-09*. 1437-1445.

[10] Qian L. and G. Zhou. 2010. Clustering-based stratified seed sampling for semi-supervised selation slassification. In *Proceedings of EMNLP-10*. 346-355.

[11] Riloff E., S. Patwardhan, and J. Wiebe. 2006. Feature subsumption for opinion analysis. In *Proceedings of EMNLP-06*. 440-448.

[12] Turney P. 2002. Thumbs up or thumbs down? Semantic orientation applied to unsupervised classification of reviews. In *Proceedings of ACL-02*. 417-424.

[13] Zhou Z. and X. Liu. 2006. Training cost-sensitive neural networks with methods addressing the class imbalance problem. *IEEE Transaction on Knowledge and Data Engineering*. 18(2006), 63–77.

The Where in the Tweet

Wen Li
Delft University of Technology
Delft, Netherlands
wen.li@tudelft.nl

Pavel Serdyukov
Yandex LLC
Moscow, Russia
pavser@yandex-team.ru

Arjen P. de Vries
CWI
Netherlands
arjen@acm.org

Carsten Eickhoff
Delft University of Technology
Delft, Neterlands
c.eickhoff@tudelft.nl

Martha Larson
Delft University of Technology
Delft, Neterlands
m.a.larson@tudelft.nl

ABSTRACT

Twitter is a widely-used social networking service which enables its users to post text-based messages, so-called tweets. POI tags on tweets can show more human-readable high-level information about a place rather than just a pair of coordinates. In this paper, we attempt to predict the POI tag of a tweet based on its textual content and time of posting. Potential applications include accurate positioning when GPS devices fail and disambiguating places located near each other. We consider this task as a ranking problem, i.e., we try to rank a set of candidate POIs according to a tweet by using language and time models. To tackle the sparsity of tweets tagged with POIs, we use web pages retrieved by search engines as an additional source of evidence. From our experiments, we find that users indeed leak some information about their accurate locations in their tweets.

Categories and Subject Descriptors: H.2.8[Database Management]Database applications-Data mining J.4 [Computer Application]Social and Behavioral Science

General Terms: Experimentation

Keywords: Twitter, location-based estimation, text mining, geotag

1. INTRODUCTION

Twitter is an on-line communication tool that is situated in between social networks and news media. It allows users to publish messages of up to 140 characters, so-called tweets [5]. Usually a tweet also contains various meta data including the profile of the author, the time of posting, location (coordinates) where the users sent the tweet. In March 2010, Twitter extended its API to provide more accurate geographical information for tweets. Users can specify their locations by tagging a predefined POI (Place of Interest) to their tweets, which includes place name, address, coordinates. However, this service is not yet widely used and there are few good place-aware applications on the market.

CIKM'11, October 24–28, 2011, Glasgow, Scotland, UK.

To boost the awareness of geolocation related applications, in this paper, we investigate predicting POI of origin based on the textual and temporal information of a tweet. To those who are concerned more about their privacy, this paper aims to raise awareness of that they might leak some information about their location in their tweets.

The task, as we defined, treats places not solely as points located in space, but rather as tags implying the social function of that place. People associate social functions with a place based on why they go there and what they do there. It is our consideration of this semantics that makes our POI prediction more meaningful and better interpretable than mere geo-coordinates. As an example, consider a mall with a food court and a sports store. Both may occupy the same geo-coordinates (on different floors) or nearly indistinguishable geo-coordinates (contiguous in the same building), but for humans it is a relevant distinction whether a tweet is associated with an eating place or with a shopping place. The conventional perspective defines a place as a set of geo-coordinates and is inherently agnostic to this difference. Our work carefully avoids conflation of human-perceived places on the basis of geo-proximity.

In our task, we rank a candidate set of POIs by their relevance to a tweet. Our assumption is that tweets from one place usually follow a certain set of patterns, especially, in vocabulary that can be represented by Language Models. However, we are facing double-level sparsity problems. One aspect is that the terms in a tweet may be insufficient to characterize itself. The other aspect is that most POIs lack enough supporting tweets to build strong models. Therefore, we leverage web pages from search engines in order to mitigate the problem. In addition, we also explore the time dimension to boost the performance of prediction.

2. BACKGROUND AND RELATED WORK

Twitter is a microblog service provider with almost 175 million[1] registered users as of March, 2011. It limits its users to post up to 140 characters per message. Besides, meta data such as POI tags can be attached to tweets. With POI tags, users can share their location information in a more precise way, as POI tags contain more than just a pair of coordinates, e.g., place names and addresses. To support potential place-aware applications, in this paper, we undertake to predict POI tags of tweets by ranking them to

[1] http://www.businessinsider.com/chart-of-the-day-how-many-users-does-twitter-really-have-2011-3

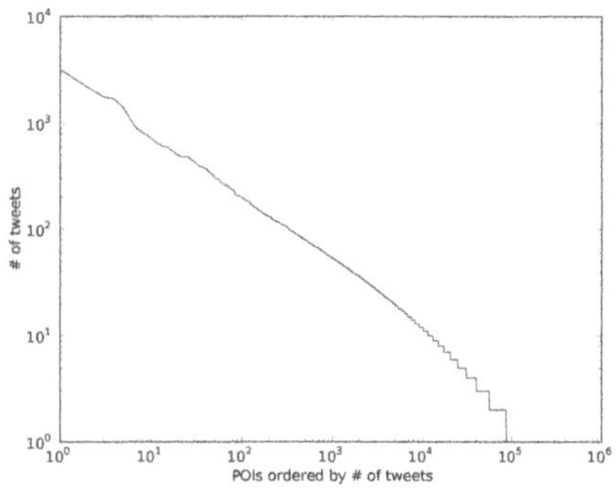

Figure 1: Tweet distribution among POIs (log-log scale)

show the relationship between users' tweets and the places of their origin.

Cheng et al. [1] first looked into this kind of problem and proposed a method using local word identification to estimate a user's location at city-level. Later, Hecht et al. [3] pointed out the location information entered by users was not so accurate as researchers had thought before and proposed a machine learning method of predicting users' home city. Leuski et al. [6] investigated a similar topic based on the chat messages in an on-line game which resulted in a method of predicting events at given virtual locations. Cheng et al.'s and Leuski et al.'s works are based on coordinates which usually suffer from the problem of coarse positioning. Hecht et al.'s and Cheng et al.'s work are locating users' home city not their tweets of origins.

The sparsity of tweets was also pointed out by Cheng et al. [1] who adopted traditional smoothing method for text in tweets. However, the problem is more severe in our task because of fewer tweets tagged with a POI. As shown in Figure 1, the distribution of tweets follows Zipf's law. Only a few POIs (about 0.16%) are supported by more than 100 tweets and 93.11% of POI tags are used less than 10 times in our data set. Due to the limitation of tweet length, it is hard to build strong models for those impoverished POIs using traditional text classification methods, which are typically based on domains that offer numerous documents per category. Therefore, we need other sources to enrich our models for POIs. Sahami et al. [7] proposed a web-kernel similarity measurement which uses web search results to generate strong models for short text snippets, i.e., querying the snippet against search engines. However, our method queries place names instead of tweets themselves.

We also include the time dimension to our models. Like de Jong et al. did in [2], we assume tweeting at a POI is dependent on time. It is intuitive that places have their own hours for visitors, e.g., bars get crowded around midnight and parks are popular on weekends. Therefore, the time patterns found in the set of past tweets from a POI may contain reliable clues as to where new tweets come from.

3. METHODS

The prediction of POI tags can be seen as a ranking problem, i.e., to rank POI tags according to the tweet. We first build unigram language models for each candidate POI and also for the query tweet. Then, we rank those POIs by their KL-divergences with the tweet LM. Accordingly, the higher the reference POI in ranking, the better the ranking method performs.

Because of the sparse distribution of tweets among places, web pages from search engines are used as an external data source. It is reasonable that web pages regarding a place should contain rich information covering the kind of place it is or the kind of activities held there. For example, it may be likely that users at a cinema post tweets regarding the film they have just watched which is also listed on the home page of the cinema. However, it should be noted that posting a tweet from a place is quite different from publishing a web page. As revealed in [4], most tweets are talking about daily routines and what people are currently doing. Web pages regarding a place, on the other hand, aim at describing the functions of the place. Thus, the vocabulary use may be different from source to source. As a result, we decide to score the places separately by models from tweets and web pages and then combine the scores to obtain comprehensive rankings.

Linear combination of scores is an easy way of merging rankings. Since KL-divergence (our ranking score) scales differently with respect to different sources, we first normalize our ranking scores with respect to their own dimensions, i.e., map the scores to $[0, 1]$ and then linearly combine the scores for each POI. Generally, let $\mathbf{X}$ be the score matrix where x_{ij} is the score of POI_i given by the jth criterion. The normalized matrix is $\mathbf{X}' = [x'_{ij}]$ where

$$x'_{ij} = \frac{x_{ij} - \min_j x_{ij}}{\max_j x_{ij} - \min_j x_{ij}}.$$

Our ranking model generates a ranking score using a linear combination of contributions from the component dimensions, $\boldsymbol{\sigma} = \mathbf{X}'\boldsymbol{\lambda}$. Here, λ is a weight vector controlling the contribution of the different dimensions in final rankings. Since we are already dealing with a data sparsity problem, we focus our investigation on the performance that can be achieved without tuning the balance between dimensions. In our experiments, dimensions are all weighted equally. Then, we can rank POIs in a balanced manner taking multiple information source into account.

The time dimension of tweets is an interesting aspect to explore. As mentioned previously, some places have particular activity patterns related to their social functions. The time distributions of tweets from *Exit (Rock Club)* and *Runyon Canyon Park* suggest that the rock club is crowded at late night of working days and the park is more popular on weekends. Therefore, we propose a time model for POIs which combines the time distributions of tweets on different scales of periods. In this paper, we use three scales of periods: day, week and month. To measure the probability that a tweet was posted from the modeled POI at time t, the linear combination is again adopted. Let $\mathbf{P}_i(\mathbf{t}) = [P_i^{(d)}(t)\ P_i^{(w)}(t)\ P_i^{(m)}(t)]$ be the vector of probabilities that a tweet is posted at time t. The score from time models is then the linear combination of these values $s_i(t) = \mathbf{P}_i(t)\boldsymbol{\lambda}$.

To evaluate our ranking method, we use a modified precision curve, as rankings in our task are slightly different from those of other text retrieval systems, i.e., typically only a single label is considered as relevant one (the reference place). For this reason, the precision we choose for our evaluation is the rate that the reference POI is ranked above pth place. We use curves to show the relationships between the rate and concrete settings of p. The larger the area under the curve, the better the ranking algorithm performs. All results are statistically significant ($p < 0.05$) tested by Wilcoson Signed-rank tests.

4. EXPERIMENTAL FRAMEWORK

For our experiment, we first collect a reasonably large set of tweets with POIs. To this end, the following strategy is used: 1) Retrieve an initial set of tweets from Twitter's stream API[2] and pick out those with POI tags. 2) Aggregate all the users who sent these tweets with POI tags and all the POIs. 3) Crawl tweets from the users and POIs gathered in the previous step. 4) Update the data set with new incoming POI-tagged tweets and 5) Repeat steps 2-5 to expand the dataset. Following this strategy, we collected about 31.6 million tweets by crawling from September 2010 to May 2011. However, there are very few tweets with POI tags and close observation suggests that most tweets with POI tags originate from Foursquare, an on-line geo-information sharing platform. Users check-in to places (i.e., post something with a POI tag on Twitter) to win titles or special treatment. This is reflected by tweets with the pattern "I'm at XXX. http://4sq.com/YYY". As it is trivial to predict the origin of tweets which have the POI names (XXX) in their text, we remove the part of text dedicated to Foursquare games. In the end, we have 700,288 tweets with POI tags from 177,817 POIs posted by 52,488 users in our dataset.

Second, we select four main cities in the USA, namely, Chicago, Los Angeles, New York and San Francisco, since they are home to many popular POIs. Then, we select the 10 most popular POIs per city, including shops, restaurants, parks, cafes and clubs. These POIs are all supported by between 100 and 400 tweets. To build language models for these POIs, a stemming tokenizer with a stop words filter from WHOOSH[3] is used in term extraction.

As stated previously, we use web pages from search engines as an additional source of evidence. For this, we query POI names against Microsoft Bing and gather the textual content of the top 30 returned web pages with HTML tags being filtered out.

5. RESULTS AND DISCUSSION

First, we investigate whether POIs are distinguishable through LMs built from tweets. We split the tweets from each POI into two equally large sets and build an LM for each set. Then, we compare the KL-Divergence between the LMs from the first part of tweets of each POI and that from the second part in a confusion matrix. The confusion matrix for Chicago is shown in Figure 2.

Significant differences can be found between places, which supports our assumption that language models are able to capture the differences in vocabulary. In other words, vocabulary used in most places is significantly more similar among tweets from the same POI than across POIs. However, language models are confused by some of the places, e.g., *AMC River East 21* and *Century Center Cinema* which are both cinemas. For another example, *Lakeview Athletic Club* and *Bally Total Fitness* are both fitness centers. This

[2]http://dev.twitter.com
[3]http://whoosh.ca/

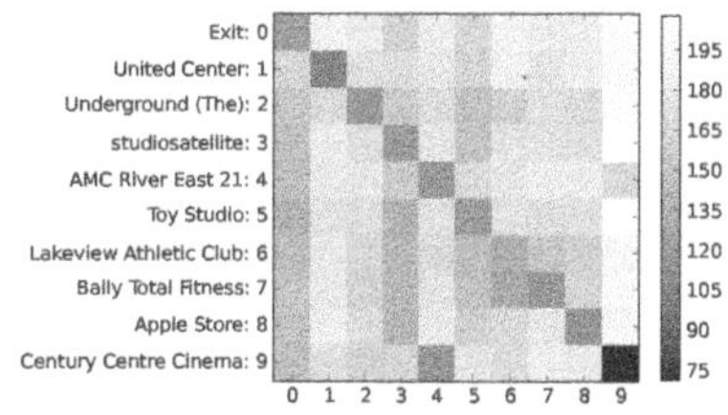

Figure 2: Confusion Matrix for POIs in Chicago

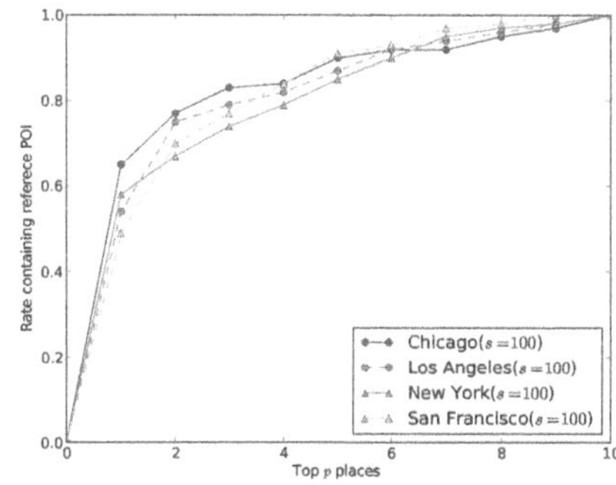

Figure 3: Ranking with rich models

observations leads to the insight that the POIs of tweets are activity dependent. That is, predicting the origin of tweets is actually predicting the place of activity reflected in the tweets.

To test our ranking methods, we conduct the following experiments in each of the four cities. 10 tweets from each POI are randomly selected to compose a test set and are queried against the ranking method based on the textual content of tweets. The results can be found in Figure 3.

The evaluation result seems to be positive in all four cities when we have enough tweets ($s = 100$) to build strong models for POIs. Nevertheless, looking into the tweets with which the ranking methods do not work well, we find: 1) A group of tweets exists whose content is short and not location-specific, such as "Thank you", "yaaaa". These tweets cannot be correctly tagged even by humans. 2) Words with a strong relationship to a place may not appear often enough when the data size is small, e.g., "swim" usually implies fitness, however, it only appears in 3 tweets in the dataset. 3) Tweets are time-related, i.e., words can show up for a while and then disappear, e.g., the title of a movie.

As mentioned, the sparsity may affect ranking performance in our task. Therefore, we shrink the number of tweets s used for model training, so that we can compare the performance of the ranking method at different popularity levels. The results of this modified setting can be found in Figure 4, which shows great degenerations of performance when s drops. Especially, for the case $s = 10$, the ranking behaves like random selection. Therefore, we turn to our additional source of information, i.e., web pages from search engines. We rank the candidate POIs by two sets of models, i.e., one from tweets and the other from web pages and then linearly combine the scores to generate a comprehensive ranking.

In order to show the performance of our web-enriched ranking method, we compare it with rankings based on only tweets and only web pages. The results in Figure 5 indi-

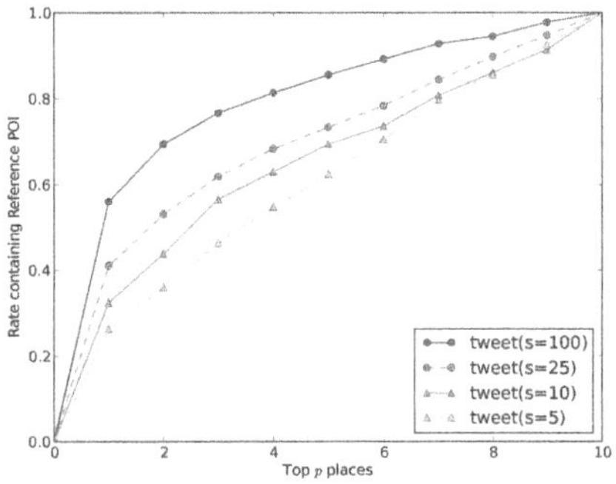

Figure 4: Ranking at different popularity levels

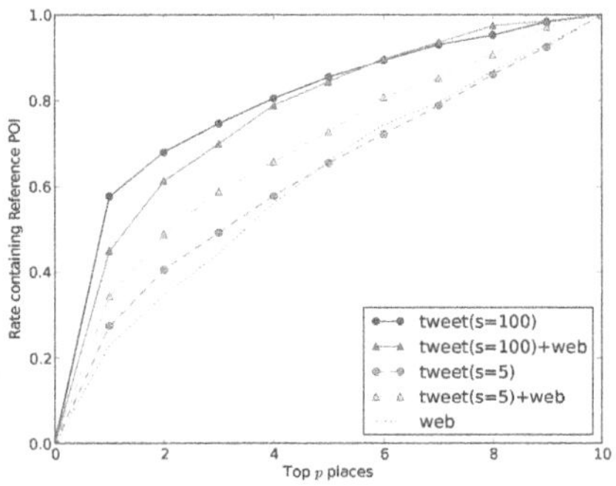

Figure 5: Web-enriched rankings

cate web pages can help increase the performance of ranking when POIs are supported by fewer tweets ($s = 5$) but will harm it somehow in the case that POIs have enough supporting tweets ($s = 100$). For example, *Lakeview Athletic Club* which is ranked at lower positions by the methods based on only tweets is ranked higher by the web-enriched method. An opposite example can be found on *Nokia Theatre* which is better ranked by pure tweets, as most of tweets from the theatre are talking about shows there while the web pages from the search engine include only big flash objects (its home page), another related theatre (*Best Buy Theatre*), and introduction (Wikipedia). Therefore, careful tuning of the weighting parameters is needed to suppress bad effects from noisy resources.

The time dimension also boosts performance when there are few supporting tweets for modeling candidate POIs. Figure 6 shows the evaluation of the time-enriched ranking method compared with other combinations of modeling techniques. As we can see, the time model can boost performance on both rich POIs and web-enriched POIs. However, the time model is also affected by sparsity problems, therefore it cannot substantially increase ranking performance. By looking into the POIs that the model does not work well with, we find that some POIs like *In & Out Burger* and *Best Buy* are always busy and cannot be characterized by the time model.

6. CONCLUSION AND FUTURE WORK

In this paper, we have shown the viability of applying a ranking approach to the prediction of the POIs of tweets' origin. Using a language modeling method, we can achieve good performance given enough POI-tagged tweets for building models. For those POIs not associated with sufficient tweets, using web-enriched models can significantly boost ranking performance. However, the web-smoothing ranking method shows its own limitation when ample number of tweets are available, presumably since the detrimental contribution of mismatched web vocabulary overwhelms the positive contribution of the tweet vocabulary. As to the time dimension, in spite of the sparsity problems, time models are more stable in boosting the performance. In general, we can conclude that POI-tagged tweets have strong relationships with their place of origin.

In the future, we will examine whether there are enough data available to effectively train the $\boldsymbol{\lambda}$ parameters balancing the dimensions. We will further explore other features to boost the performance of place prediction. For example, users' friendships may also imply the place they like going to.

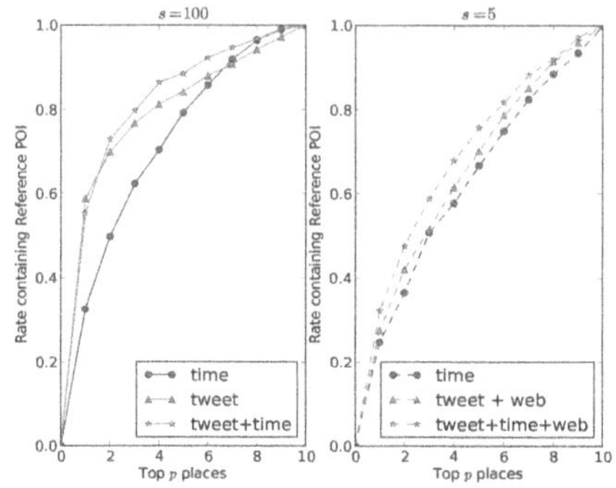

Figure 6: Ranking with comprehensive models

7. REFERENCES

[1] Z. Cheng, J. Caverlee, and K. Lee. You are where you tweet: a content-based approach to geo-locating twitter users. CIKM '10.

[2] F. de Jong, T. Westerveld, and A. de Vries. Multimedia search without visual analysis: The value of linguistic and contextual information. *Circuits and Systems for Video Technology, IEEE Transactions on*, 17(3).

[3] B. Hecht, L. Hong, B. Suh, and E. H. Chi. Tweets from justin bieber's heart: the dynamics of the location field in user profiles. CHI '11.

[4] A. Java, X. Song, T. Finin, and B. Tseng. Why we twitter: understanding microblogging usage and communities. WebKDD/SNA-KDD '07.

[5] H. Kwak, C. Lee, H. Park, and S. Moon. What is Twitter, a social network or a news media? WWW '10.

[6] A. Leuski and V. Lavrenko. Tracking dragon-hunters with language models. CIKM '06.

[7] M. Sahami and T. D. Heilman. A web-based kernel function for measuring the similarity of short text snippets. WWW '06.

Question Identification on Twitter

Baichuan Li[1]*, Xiance Si[2], Michael R. Lyu[1], Irwin King[13]†, and Edward Y. Chang[2]
[1]The Chinese University of Hong Kong, Shatin, N.T., Hong Kong
[2]Google Research, Beijing 10084, China
[3]AT&T Labs Research, San Francisco, CA, USA
bcli@cse.cuhk.edu.hk, sxc@google.com, lyu@cse.cuhk.edu.hk
{king@cse.cuhk.edu.hk, irwin@research.att.com}, edchang@google.com

ABSTRACT

In this paper, we investigate the novel problem of automatic question identification in the microblog environment. It contains two steps: detecting tweets that contain questions (we call them "interrogative tweets") and extracting the tweets which really seek information or ask for help (so called "qweets") from interrogative tweets. To detect interrogative tweets, both traditional rule-based approach and state-of-the-art learning-based method are employed. To extract qweets, context features like short urls and Tweet-specific features like Retweets are elaborately selected for classification. We conduct an empirical study with sampled one hour's English tweets and report our experimental results for question identification on Twitter.

Categories and Subject Descriptors

H.3.5 [**Information Systems**]: Online Information Services—*Web-based services*

General Terms

Experimentation, Performance

Keywords

Question Identification, Microblogs, Twitter

1. INTRODUCTION

Twitter[1], as the first and one of the most popular microblog services, has become a platform of question asking. Morris et al. [3] reported that more than 10% of Twitter users once asked questions on Twitter. Furthermore, Efron and Winget [2] found that 13% of their randomly sampled 2-million tweets corpus were questions. According to the blog of Twitter, on average 1,620 tweets were posted every second in March 2011[2], which means each second 210 questions appeared on Twitter.

However, not all of them need to be answered. According to the taxonomy in [2], many questions are not requesting information but providing information, like suggesting a Q&A pair or expressing an opinion. Different from the meanings of questions in [2] and [3], we restrict the scope of questions to be those tweets which require some information or help and thus need to be answered. In the following, we use the term "qweets" to represent these tweets. Additionally, we call the tweets which contain question sentences as "interrogative tweets". It is worth noting that "qweets" are "interrogative tweets" but "interrogative tweets" are not necessary "qweets".

To our best knowledge, few attempts have been made on identifying qweets in vast tweets. Thus, this paper asks such research question: Can we automatically identify qweets from tweets? We know that microblog provides an instant message publishing service, so identifying these questions automatically will help question askers get answers efficiently through approaches such as question routing and automatic question answering system [5]. Identifying qweets also lays a foundation for question analysis (such as classification and clustering) in the microblog environment.

We argue that qweet identification is different from traditional question finding [1, 6]. On the one hand, a tweet contains less than 140 characters, and thus less information (features) is provided; On the other hand, a tweet usually includes some special features, such as Retweets (repost other users' tweets, with "RT @username" as the marker), "@username" (mention or reply to some user), hashtags (terms starting with the charachter "#", usually denote topics) and short urls, which may contribute to qweet identification.

In this paper, we cast the qweet identification problem into a two-phase cascade process: In the first step, we detect the tweets which contain questions (interrogative tweets). We adopt both traditional methods like question marks, 5W1H words, and state-of-the-art approach [1, 6] which utilizes sequential question patterns to detect interrogative tweets. In the second step, we extract qweets by splitting each interrogative tweet into question part and context part and employing four kinds of features (question features, context features, question-context features and tweet-specific features) to build a binary classifier. As an empirical study,

*This work was done when the first author was on internship at Google.

†Irwin King is currently on leave from CUHK to be with AT&T Labs.

[1]http://www.twitter.com/

[2]http://blog.twitter.com/2011/03/numbers.html.

CIKM'11, October 24–28, 2011, Glasgow, Scotland, UK.

we experiment with a data set sampled from one-hour tweet stream and the experimental results demonstrate that: 1) 11% of tweets contain questions and 6% of tweets are qweets; 2) Simple rule-based approach produces satisfactory results in detecting interrogative tweets; 3) Context features and Tweet-specific features are very useful for extracting qweets from interrogative tweets.

The paper proceeds as follows. Section 2 presents the related work. Section 3 details the work of qweet identification. Experiments are described in Section 4 and a conclusion is given in Section 5.

2. RELATED WORK

Detecting Questions in User Generated Content (UGC). Interrogative tweets detection is closely related to question (subquestion) finding in UGC such as forums, community question answering (CQA) portals and microblogs. There are two divisions for question finding in UGC: rule-based approach [2] and learning-based approach [1, 6]. Rule-based approach usually designs several rules from heuristics or observations to check whether a thread or tweet is question or not, while learning-based approach constructs a binary classifier with lexical and/or syntactic features.

Analyzing Questions in Tweets. The study of questions on Twitter is in its infancy and previous work mainly focused on analyzing the types and motivations of questions people asked. Efron and Winget [2] built a taxonomy of questions on Twitter and found that people asked questions on Twitter to both seek information (facts, opinions, etc.) and recommend information (external resources, invitations, QA pairs,etc.). Morris et al. [3] conducted a survey study to reveal the types, and motivations of questions people ask and answer on Twitter and Facebook.

3. QWEET IDENTIFICATION

As mentioned, we break qweet identification into the following two sub-problems: (1) Detecting tweets which contain questions (interrogative tweet detection); (2) Extracting qweets from the previous result (qweet extraction). Detail will be given one by one.

3.1 Interrogative Tweet Detection

Previous work showed that learning-based approach outperformed rule-based approach in question detection in forums [1] and CQA portals [6], so we attempt both rule-based approach and learning-based approach to investigate whether the latter one still outperforms the former in the microblog environment.

3.1.1 Rule-based Approach

We apply question marks, 5W1H words, refined 5W1H and the rules introduced in [2] to detect interrogative tweets, detail will be presented in Section 4.2.1.

3.1.2 Learning-based Approach

This approach utilizes sequential question patterns to train a binary classifier, which needs manually labeling data. To avoid time-costing labeling, we utilize corpus from CQA portals to get mountains of "well labeled" sequential question patterns based on the following two considerations:

- Both tweets and questions in CQA portals are generated by users;
- The length of one question title is usually as short as that of a tweet.

We apply the Prefixspan algorithm proposed by Pei et al. [4] to mine frequent question patterns. This algorithm explores prefix projection to speed up sequential pattern mining. To get high quality question patterns, we also set extra constrains to the original algorithm empirically: The minimum support and minimum confidence are set to be 0.5% and 0.7; The minimum and maximum length of patterns are set to be 2 and 5; The maximum length between two neighbor terms in any pattern is set to be 3. In order to calculate the confidence, we choose the corresponding best answers as negative examples. Furthermore, to avoid long question titles and unbalanced Q&A pair, we limit the length of each question title to be within 5 and 20 words and the maximum length ratio between question title and answer to be 1:5. One-class SVM is employed afterwards to predict whether a tweet contains question(s) or not.

3.2 Qweet Extraction

We present qweet extraction in this section. Firstly, we need to understand which kinds of interrogative tweets are not qweets. From the observations, we construct a taxonomy of interrogative tweets (Section 3.2.1). Afterwards, we extract four types of features according to the characteristics of interrogative tweets and convert qweet extraction to a binary classification problem (Section 3.2.2).

3.2.1 Types of Interrogative Tweets

We classified interrogative tweets to the following 6 types. Only those tweets belonging to the last type are qweets.

1. Advertisement. This kind of tweets ask questions to the reader and deliver advertisements in the following. E.g.,

- *Incorporating your business this year? Call us today for a free consultation with one of our attorneys. 855-529-8753. http://buz.tw/FjJCV*

2. Article or News Title on the Web. These tweets post article names or news titles together with the links to the webpage. E.g.,

- *New post: Pregnancy Miracle - A Miracle or a Scam? http://articlescontentonline.com/pregnancy-miracle-a-miracle-or-a-scam/*

3. Question with Answer. These tweets contain questions followed by their answers. E.g.,

- *I even tried staying away from my using my Internet for a couple hours. The result? Insanity!*

4. Question as Quotation. These tweets contain questions in quoted sentences as references to what other people said. E.g.,

- *I think Brian's been drinking in there because I'm hearing him complain about girls, and then he goes "Wright, are you sure you're not gay?"*

5. Rhetorical Question. This kind of tweets include rhetorical questions, which seem to be questions but without the expectation of any answer. In another words, these tweets encourage readers to think about the obvious answers. E.g.,

- *You ruined my life and I'm supposed to like you?*

6. Qweet. These kinds of tweets ask for some information or help. E.g.,

- *What's your favorite Harry Potter scene?*

Another special type is "Question on The Web" which the

Table 1: Features extracted for qweet extraction

Feature	Description
Question features (Q)	
Quoted question	Whether the question sentence is quoted from other sources
Strong feeling	Whether the question sentence contains strong feeling such as "???" and "?!"
Context features (C)	
URL	Whether the context contains any url
Phone number or Email	Whether the context contains any phone number or email
Strong feeling	Whether there is any strong feeling such as "!" follows the question sentence
Declarative sentence after question sentence	Whether there is any declarative sentence follows the question sentence
Word features	Unigram words appear in the contexts of tweets
Question-Context features (QC)	
Self ask self answer	Whether the tweet contains obvious self ask self answer pattern. E.g., Q:...A:...
Question-url sameness	Whether the question sentence is the same as the webpage's title linked through the url.
Tweet-specific features (T)	
@username	Whether the tweet mentions other user's name.
Retweet	Whether the tweet is a Retweet.
Hashtag	Whether the tweet contains any hashtag.

Tweet author posts a question asked by someone on the web, e.g., CQA portals, forums, etc. The following is an example:

- *Questions about panda update. When will the effect end? http://goo.gl/fb/iiRjn*

However, even for human it is hard to infer the author's intention. Therefore, we classify it to *Type 2* for convenience.

3.2.2 Feature Extraction

Different from traditional short texts like forum posts and CQA questions, tweets own some special characteristics, such as "@username", Retweets, and hashtags. Apart from that, plenty of tweets contain (shortened) links which provide extra information to determine these tweets' types. We also note that an interrogative tweet usually can be split into two parts: question part and context part. Although it is not easy to judge whether a tweet is qweet from the question itself, the context helps to distinguish qweets from non-qweets.

Based on the above findings, we extract four kinds of features from each tweet, which are reported in Table 1. Noting that word overlap similarity is employed to calculate the value of question-url sameness. To be specific, if the overlap similarity between any question sentence and the title of url is above a certain threshold, the value is 1; otherwise we treat them as different content and set the value to 0. In our experiments, we set the threshold to 0.8.

Using these features, we leverage one Random Forrest classifier to predict whether a interrogative tweet is a qweet or not.

4. EXPERIMENTS

4.1 Dataset

We sampled one hour's tweets from 11:00am to 12:00am on April 18, 2011 using Twitter API[3], getting 2,045 English tweets in total. Two raters were asked to label whether each tweet was interrogative tweet. They worked individually and the labels were finalized through discussions between them.

Table 2 reports the statistic of the data, from which we estimate that on Twitter there are about 11% of tweets containing questions (similar to 13% reported in [2]) and 6% of tweets having information needs. This observation confirms the statement that Twitter is no longer a pure social media which let user publish "What's happening"s to provide information but also becomes an online questioning platform where users post "Does anyone know...?"s to seek information.

To extract sequential patterns, we collected over 850,000 question titles and the corresponding best answers from Yahoo! Answers[4] and WikiAnswers[5].

Table 2: Summary of data set

Number of tweets	2,045
Number of interrogative tweets	227
Number of qweets	127
Number of tweets containing urls	442
Number of tweets containing hashtags	459
Number of Retweets	240
Number of tweets containing @	447
Number of tweets containing ?	222
Number of tweets containing 5W1H	293
Average number of words per tweet	12.48

4.2 Experimental Results

4.2.1 Interrogative Tweet Detection

Table 3 presents the accuracy of various methods on detecting interrogative tweets. We find that simple question patterns give satisfactory performance. Specifically, using question mark alone gets the precision of nearly 0.97 but captures less than 85% of all interrogative tweets. Adding 5W1H question words remedies the drawback of low recall, but substantially decreases precision. To reduce the number of false positives, we set up the following two heuristics for 5W1H:

1. They must appear at the beginning of one sentence.
2. Auxiliary words are added to the original words. For example, we change "what" to "what is" and "what are".

The results demonstrate that the above rules boost the performance significantly. The first heuristic improves precision of 5W1H by 60.5% although reduces 5.9% of recall. For F_1, it improves 28.4% comparing with original 5W1H. The second heuristic gives similar results. When applying the above two together, it makes the precision higher than 0.95 and recall higher than 0.9, which increases precision and F_1

[3]http://dev.twitter.com.

[4]http://answers.yahoo.com.

[5]http://wiki.answers.com.

by 7.2% and 3.0% comparing to using question mark with slight decrease on recall (1.5%). We also try the artificial rules designed in [2], which keep high precision but do not increase recall too much.

Learning-based approach, however, does not improve the accuracy of detected questions as expected. Patterns with low confidence get low precision while patterns with high confidence fail to increase recall. We conjecture that for one reason, most of question patterns are "overlapped" with 5W1H, such as "how to" and "where can I". For the other, sequential question patterns in CQA may not well capture the questions on Twitter as many patterns fail to match any tweet. In our future study, we plan to label large number of real tweets to further explore this problem.

Table 3: Accuracies of interrogative tweet detection for various methods (QM: question mark; best results are in bold)

Method	Precision	Recall	F_1
QM	**0.969**	0.846	0.903
QM and 5W1H	0.547	**0.973**	0.700
QM and refined 5W1H (H1)	0.878	0.916	0.899
QM and refined 5W1H (H2)	0.875	0.925	0.899
QM and refined 5W1H (H1 and H2)	0.954	0.907	**0.930**
Rules in [2]	0.960	0.855	0.904
Question Patterns (Confidence $\geq$ 0.7)	0.576	0.899	0.702
Question Patterns (Confidence $\geq$ 0.8)	0.715	0.872	0.786
Question Patterns (Confidence $\geq$ 0.9)	0.857	0.846	0.851

Table 4: Effects of feature sets on qweet extraction

Feature Set	Precision	Recall	Accuracy
Q	0.576	**0.984**	0.577
Q+QC+C	0.704	0.937	0.739
Q+QC+non-word C	0.714	0.906	0.730
Q+QC+non-word C+T	0.764	0.866	0.770
Q+QC+non-word C+Retweet	**0.766**	0.874	**0.775**
Q+QC+non-word C+@username	0.728	0.929	0.761
Q+QC+non-word C+Hashtag	0.702	0.890	0.721

4.2.2 *Qweet Extraction*

In our experiments, we employed a Random Forrest classifier[6] with 1000 trees to extract qweets and adopted 10-fold cross validation. Table 4 presents the results of qweet extraction using different sets of features. We find that: 1) **Context features are of great importance in distinguishing qweets from non-qweets.** Comparing the classifier's performance with feature sets "Q" and "Q+QC+C", it is obvious that context features boost the performance greatly. To be specific, precision is improved by 22% with a cost of slight decrease in recall (We consider precision as more important than recall since high recall is easier to reach if the classifier predicts all interrogative tweets as qweets). However, unigrams in context seem useless since "Q+QC+non-word C" gives even higher precision than "Q+QC+C". We conjecture that although some words like "free", "click", etc. are useful in judging advertisement and online articles, much more irrelevant words are introduced when using word features. 2) **Tweet-specific features also help in qweet identification.** Comparing the results using features sets "Q+QC+non-word C" and "Q+QC+non-word C+T", we find that Tweet-specific features improve the precision of qweet extraction. In addition, without Tweet-specific features, the classifier's recall increases, which means it tends to predict a interrogative tweet as qweet when such information is missing. From the last three rows of Table 4 we can further understand that Retweet is the most significant feature, followed by "@username", while Hashtag is not so helpful. The possible explanation is that most Retweets are not qweets as they just rebroadcast other users' tweets, which are usually providing rather than asking for information. On the contrary, "@username" always denotes a interrogative tweet being a qweet as it implies a dialog between two users. As our data contain no obvious qweet signals in Hashtags (like "#lazyweb") and Hashtags are usually used to represent the topics, they are not so influential. 3) **Qweet extraction is a non-trivial problem.** At present, the performance is still not so satisfactory. Through examining the failed examples, we find that tweets containing rhetorical questions and complicated self-ask-self-answer sentences are always being misclassified. E.g., "If I'm that mean/nasty why do u continue to talk to me" and "See what you did? Poor 4 minute. They...". Potentially this problem may be solved through utilizing syntax features to capture the structure of tweets and employing more training data.

[6]We attempted Random Forrest, SVM, J48, and Logistic Regression in our experiments and Random Forrest performed the best among them.

5. CONCLUSION AND FUTURE WORK

This paper explored the problem of automatic question identification in the microblog environment. To identify qweets, we designed a cascade process which first detected interrogative tweets and then extracted qweets. For interrogative tweet detection, both rule-based approach and learning-based approach were employed and experimental results showed that on Twitter rule-based approach performed well while learning-based approach did not improve the performance significantly. For qweets extraction, we leveraged the special characteristics of Tweets like Retweet and @username, and context of questions to build a binary classifier. Experimental results demonstrated that such features were of great importance in extracting qweets from interrogative tweets. Looking forward, we plan to enlarge our dataset and utilize syntax features in qweet extraction.

ACKNOWLEDGEMENT

This work is supported by two grants from the Research Grants Council of the Hong Kong SAR, China (Project No. CUHK 413210 and Project No. CUHK 415410) and a grant from Google Focused Grant Project "Mobile 2014".

6. REFERENCES

[1] G. Cong, L. Wang, C.-Y. Lin, Y.-I. Song, and Y. Sun. Finding question-answer pairs from online forums. In *Proc. of SIGIR '08*, 2008.

[2] M. Efron and M. Winget. Questions are content: a taxonomy of questions in a microblogging environment. In *Proc. of ASIST '10*, 2010.

[3] M. R. Morris, J. Teevan, and K. Panovich. What do people ask their social networks, and why?: a survey study of status message Q&A behavior. In *CHI '10*, 2010.

[4] J. Pei, J. Han, B. Mortazavi-asl, H. Pinto, Q. Chen, U. Dayal, and M. chun Hsu. Prefixspan: Mining sequential patterns efficiently by prefix-projected pattern growth. In *Proc. of ICDE '01*, 2001.

[5] X. Si, E. Y. Chang, Z. Gyöngyi, and M. Sun. Confucius and its intelligent disciples: integrating social with search. *Proc. VLDB Endow.*, 3:1505–1516, 2010.

[6] K. Wang and T.-S. Chua. Exploiting salient patterns for question detection and question retrieval in community-based question answering. In *COLING '10*, 2010.

OpinioNetIt: Understanding the Opinions-People Network for Politically Controversial Topics

Rawia Awadallah
Max-Planck Institute for Informatics
Saarbruecken, Germany
rawadall@mpi-inf.mpg.de

Maya Ramanath
Indian Institute of Technology, Delhi
New Delhi, India
ramanath@cse.iitd.ac.in

Gerhard Weikum
Max-Planck Institute for Informatics
Saarbruecken, Germany
weikum@mpi-inf.mpg.de

ABSTRACT

The wikileaks documents or the economic crises in Ireland and Portugal are some of the controversial topics being played on the news everyday. Each of these topics has many different aspects, and there is no absolute, simple truth in answering questions such as: should the EU guarantee the financial stability of each member country, or should the countries themselves be solely responsible? To understand the landscape of opinions, it would be helpful to know which politician or other stakeholder takes which position - support or opposition - on these aspects of controversial topics. In this paper, we describe our system, named OpinioNetIt (pronounced similar to "opinionated"), which aims to automatically derive a map of the opinions-people network from news and other Web documents.

We build this network as follows. First, we make use of a small number of generic seeds to identify controversial phrases from text. These phrases are then clustered and organized into a hierarchy of topics. Second, opinion holders are identified for each topic and their opinions (either supporting or opposing the topic) are extracted. Third, the known topics and people are used to construct a lexicon phrases indicating support or opposition. Finally, the lexicon is uses to identify more opinion holders, opinions and topics. Our system currently consists of approximately 30000 person-opinion-topic triples. Our evaluation shows that OpinioNetIt has high accuracy.

Categories and Subject Descriptors

H.3.1 [**Information Storage and Retrieval**]: Content Analysis and Indexing—*Linguistic Processing*

General Terms

Algorithms, Experimentation

1. INTRODUCTION

1.1 Motivation

Controversial political topics are intensively debated in digital media, with opinions expressed in a variety of online fora such as newspaper articles, blogs, comments by readers, etc. Some recent, politically hot topics include the economic crisis in the EU, the wikileaks documents, the NATO military action in Libya, and Iran's nuclear program. Despite the proliferation of all this information (perhaps, because of it), it is difficult to make sense of exactly what the issues are and who is saying what about a given topic. In order to navigate this complicated landscape of issues and opinions, it would be helpful if there were an *"opinion-base"* that organized controversial topics according to their various facets and stored information about who expressed an opinion on one or more topics and supported or opposed a certain direction.

This envisioned network goes beyond state-of-the-art sentiment mining in several ways. First, political controversies are much more complex and opinions are often expressed in subtle forms, which makes determining pro/con polarities much more difficult than with product reviews for cameras, movies, etc. - the typical objects in prior work on opinion mining [5, 3]. Second, most prior research focused on classifying individual sentences or reviews into pro/con categories or on aggregating (summarizing) opinions over a large number of observations (e.g., many different customers' reviews of some product). In contrast, our goal is to connect an opinion to an individual person (typically a politician) who expressed this position (multiple times, but often in very different wordings). Third, instead of merely finding a few or the most interesting pairs of opinion holders and topics, we aim at a systematic network of opinion holders and pro/con statements for a wide variety of fine-grained controversial topics. To the best of our knowledge, no prior work has addressed political opinion analysis in a similarly comprehensive manner.

Facet	Canonical name
a military strike by America or Israel on Iran	Military actions against Iran
Ahmadinejad's economic and foreign policies	Foreign policy of Mahmoud Ahmadinejad
the peaceful nuclear program of the Islamic Republic	Nuclear program of Iran
a military strike on Iran	Military action against Iran
put sanctions on Iran	Sanctions against Iran

Table 1: Facets extracted for "Iran's Nuclear Program"

In this paper, we present our system, called *OpinioNetIt* (pronounced similar to "opinionated"), which aims at building such an opinion-base for controversial topics by extracting and organizing information from online sources on the Web. For example, the first column of Table 1 shows some of the facets extracted by our system regarding the Iran Nuclear Program. The outcome of analyzing

CIKM'11, October 24–28, 2011, Glasgow, Scotland, UK.

⟨Shimon Peres⟩ ⟨support⟩ ⟨Military action against Iran⟩
⟨Vladimir Putin⟩ ⟨oppose⟩ ⟨Military action against Iran⟩
⟨Nicolas Sarkozy⟩ ⟨oppose⟩ ⟨Nuclear program of Iran⟩
⟨Vladimir Putin⟩ ⟨support⟩ ⟨Nuclear program of Iran⟩
⟨Angela Merkel⟩ ⟨support⟩ ⟨Sanctions against Iran⟩
⟨Hillary Clinton⟩ ⟨support⟩ ⟨Sanctions against Iran⟩
⟨Mahmoud Ahmadinejad⟩ ⟨oppose⟩ ⟨IAEA⟩

Table 2: Opinions about "Iran Nuclear Program"

these inputs should be a crisp set of structured records of the form: *person* (opinion holder), *polarity* (support/oppose), and *topic facet* (fine-grained controversial topic). Table 2 shows examples of people's opinions about various topic facets of the controversy. For example, ⟨Angela Merkel⟩ ⟨support⟩ ⟨Sanctions against Iran⟩ could be a result in canonicalized form. This desired output involves aggregating statements, but only for the same pair of opinion holder and topic facet. The overall set of such records forms the OpinioNetIt network.

The challenge in building this network lies in the fact that the input is merely natural-language text, such as news articles, where it is difficult to spot phrases that denote individual politicians or controversial topics and map them into a canonical representation. For example, the opinions of Table 2, are extracted from text where the entity Vladimir Putin is mentioned several times with different wordings like "Mr. Putin", "the Russian President", "President Putin"etc. The same language diversity and ambiguity applies to the topic facets that we aim to detect and organize. Thus, the entire problem can be seen as an interleaved task of fact extraction, entity resolution, and opinion assessment.

OpinioNetIt currently taps into 5 online news sources: Google News, Al-Jazeera, BBC, CNN, New York Times, as well as Wikipedia, and extracts 4-tuples of the following form:
⟨person⟩ ⟨support/oppose⟩ ⟨topic⟩*[⟨context⟩]*
where the triple: ⟨person⟩ ⟨support/oppose⟩ ⟨topic⟩ is extracted from the textual *context*.

Our approach is to generate search-engine queries with site scope restricted to each of our 5 sources, and extract opinions from the snippets returned by the search engine (specifically, using Google). The extraction is carried out in the following stages (see Figure 1 for an overview). First we acquire a large number of facets by querying the Web with a few hand-crafted seed patterns. The resulting snippets are parsed and phrases corresponding facets are extracted. These facets are canonicalized and organized into a hierarchy. Second, the same snippets are parsed and the opinion holders identified. These two steps give us a set of opinion triples as above. By querying the Web with (person,topic) pairs from the opinion triples and analyzing the resulting snippets, we build a lexicon of support and oppose phrases. Finally, by using the lexicon of support/oppose phrases as new seeds, we close the loop: we go back to the first step and iteratively acquire more topics and opinion holders, thus building the final OpinioNetIt network.

1.2 Contributions

The main contribution of this paper is the construction of an opinion-base, OpinioNetIt, which consists of controversial topics and their various facets and the people who hold opinions on it.

The rest of the paper is organized as follows: Sections 2 through 4 present the different stages of our approach: acquiring and organizing controversial facets in Section 2, identifying opinion holders and building a lexicon of support/oppose phrases in Section 3. Section 4 presents our experimental evaluation and Section 5 presents some use cases. In Section 6, we outline related work, and we finally conclude in Section 7.

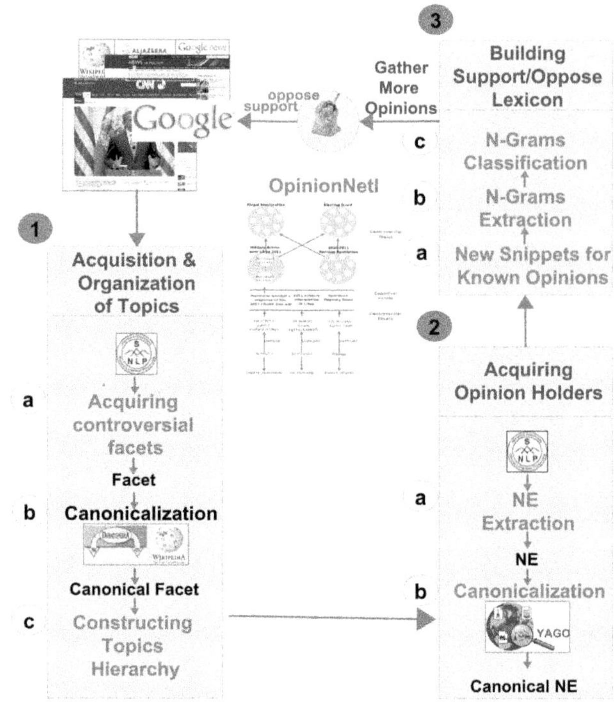

Figure 1: System architecture.

2. FACETS AND TOPICS

Our first major goal is to acquire politically controversial topics. For example, both "sanctions against Iran" as well as "military strikes on Iran" are different *facets* of the debate on "Iran's nuclear program" which in turn can be regarded as being a part of a larger debate on "nuclear power". To acquire politically controversial topics, first we have to acquire facets which are politically controversial. Second, since each facet can be expressed in different ways, we have to *canonicalize* these facets. That is, "military strikes against Iran" and "military action on Iran" are different ways of expressing the same topic and need to have a canonical form. We describe our solutions to each of these problems in the following subsections.

2.1 Acquiring Controversial Facets

One of our aims is to ensure that a large number of opinions are collected. That is, the recall has to be high. Moreover, we want to ensure that recent topics are not missed. Therefore, rather than utilize a fixed corpus such as Wikipedia, we decided to use Web search as an always-fresh information source.

To ensure that the facets returned were those for which people could have opinions, we used the patterns "(s)he supports" and "(s)he opposes". In order to keep the focus on political topics, we added the patterns "he voted for", "he voted against" on the intuition that most "voting" typically takes place in political forums.

2.2 Canonicalization of Facets

In order to ensure uniformity in referring to semantically equivalent facets (e.g., "military action against Iran" and "military strike on Iran" are equivalent), we automatically derive canonical names for facets. Some of the raw facets we acquired in the context of

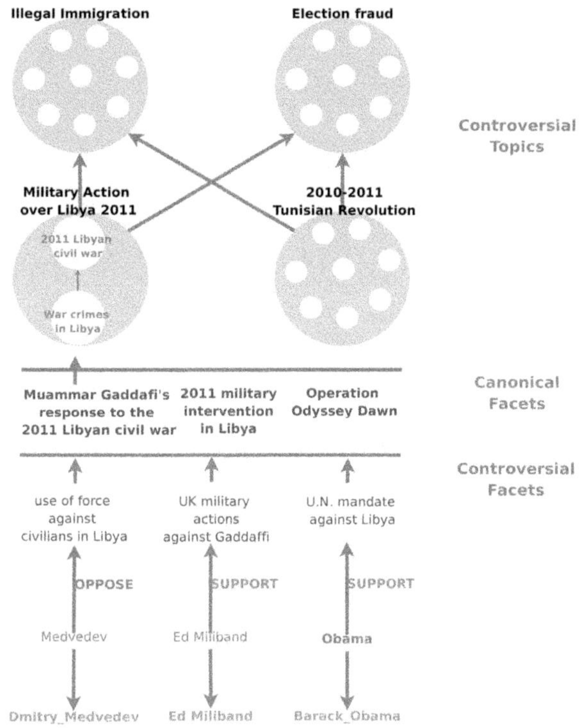

Figure 2: Organizing facets in different levels of granularities.

the recent Libyan crisis are shown in Figure 2 in blue and include a variety of aspects: "U.N. Mandate against Libya", "use of force against civilians in Libya", etc. These raw facets are then canonicalized to "2011 military intervention in Libya" and "Gaddaffi's response to the 2011 Libyan Civil War" respectively.

Political controversies are usually featured in a variety of Wikipedia articles. The titles of these pages serve as candidates for canonical names of raw facets. For example, the recent Libyan civil war is covered in "No-fly zone over Libya", "Human rights violation in the 2011 Libyan civil war", etc. These titles are different facets of the same topic. Given a raw facet, we map it to a Wikipedia page by using the facet string as a query to a search engine with site restriction on Wikipedia. For example, for the raw facet "the need for UN sanctions against Iran", the top-3 results from Wikipedia are pages with titles: "Sanctions against Iran", "Iran and Libya Sanctions Act", "US sanctions against Iran". We choose the top-10 results as candidates for canonical facet names.

For the final choice, we compute the Jaccard similarity of the set of terms between the raw facet and each of the 10 candidates:

$$J(facet, cand) = \frac{|terms_{cand} \cap terms_{facet}|}{|terms_{cand} \cup terms_{facet}|}$$

The top-ranked candidate is picked as the canonical name for the facet. The canonicalization of facet names produced approximately 20,000 facet names.

The canonical facets are then organized into a hierarchy using Wikipedia categories as the basis. Due to lack of space, we do not describe this step in this paper.

3. OPINION HOLDERS

Extracting and organizing the list of facets is just the first step in building an opinion-base. We now need to identify opinion holders who have expressed an opinion on these facets. That is, if we have extracted the facet "military strike on Iran", then we need to find all people who support or oppose this particular facet. The problem here lies in reliably identifying, in the facet's surrounding text, the named entity who has expressed the opinion.

We again make use of the result snippets collected for extracting facets. We are often able to identify the opinion holder if the parser correctly identifies the subject of the sentence. For example, in the sentence "Shimon Peres says he opposes military strikes on Iran" "Shimon Peres" is both the opinion holder as well as the subject of the sentence. A canonicalization step then follows. That is, "Mr. Peres" and "Shimon Peres" refer to the same person and should thus have a canonical name.

In case the parser is unable to identify the subject correctly, we simply pick the named entity occurring closest to the seed pattern.

Once an opinion holder is positively identified, a candidate opinion is formed by adding support or oppose (which is determined by the seed present in the sentence) and the facet. In addition, the snippet used to extract this opinion is added as a context to the opinion.

Building the lexicon. We briefly describe our method for building the lexicon of support and oppose phrases. Once the opinion triples are formed, we query the Web with a set of (person,topic) pairs. The resulting snippets are then gathered for analysis. We analyze the text patterns occurring in between the person and topic and make them candidates for the lexicon. If a pattern has sufficient support among all the snippets gathered, then that pattern is added to the lexicon.

4. EVALUATION

We evaluated the accuracy of the extracted opinion triples and report on the accuracy of extraction in this section.

Setup. A total of 17 seeds to extract approximately 30,000 opinions (Table 3 shows the breakup of opinions). Our sources were restricted to Al-Jazeera (**ALJ**), BBC, CNN, New York Times (**NY**), Wikipedia (**WP**), and Google News (**GN**). We restricted the number of snippets collected to the first 2,000 search engine results for each seed.

We performed an experiments based on a *random sample* of 2000 opinion statements (topic-politician pairs) for which we present accuracy results. A total of 18 judges assessed these opinions as "correct" or "wrong".

Results. Table 3 shows the precision values for each source as well as the overall precision. For the entire set of 2,000 samples, the micro-averaged precision was 72.4%. Given the difficulty of this extraction task, these results are quite satisfying.

5. USE CASES

As use cases for knowledge discovery and political analyses, we briefly discuss scenarios on the phenomena of so-called flip-flops and dissenters.

Flip-Flops Detection. A flip-flop according to Wikipedia is a sudden real or apparent change of policy or opinion by a public official. To detect flip-flops, we group opinions collected by our system by pairs of politicians and topics, both in canonicalized form. If a group contains both support and oppose opinions, we consider the politician to have flip-flopped. Table 4 shows some examples that we found in our collection (O denotes the opinion polarity: $+$ for support, $-$ for oppose).

Dissenters Detection. Our goal here is to detect interesting deviations from correlated opinions on different topics. Often, once you

source	overall	support	oppose	ALJ	BBC	CNN	GN	NY	WP
#opinions	29648	16011	13637	970	3349	2650	6861	9877	5941
precision	0.724	0.7	0.75	0.72	0.66	0.78	0.788	0.74	0.69

Table 3: Opinions & precisions grouped by source

Politician	Topic	O	Example Snippet
Barack Obama	nuclear power	+	...Obama says he supports nuclear power ...
		−	...Obama criticized his rival McCain's proposal to encourage the building of 45 new nuclear reactors ...
Angela Merkel	nuclear power	+	...Dr. Merkel's government support for the nuclear energy sector ...
		−	...Chancellor Angela Merkel said she aimed to accelerate Germany's move away from nuclear energy ...

Table 4: Examples of flip-flops detected by our system

Topic Pair	Dominant	Dissenter
Emissions trading & Offshore drilling	$(+-), (-+)$ ⟨Cynthia McKinney⟩ (+) ⟨Carbon Neutrality⟩ ⟨Cynthia McKinney⟩ (-) ⟨Offshore drilling⟩	$(--), (++)$ ⟨John McCain⟩ (+) ⟨Emissions trading⟩ ⟨John McCain⟩ (+) ⟨Offshore drilling⟩
George W. Bush Politics & Abortion	$(+-), (-+)$ ⟨Sarah Palin⟩ (+) ⟨George W. Bush⟩ ⟨Sarah Palin⟩ (-) ⟨Abortion⟩	$(--), (++)$ ⟨Joe Biden⟩ (+) ⟨George W. Bush⟩ ⟨Joe Biden⟩ (+) ⟨Abortion rights⟩

Table 5: Examples of topics correlations and dissenters

know that a person supports topic A, it is clear that she or he also supports topic B, given the semantic connection between A and B. To identify such topic pairs, we compute correlation coefficients and select the most positively correlated pairs. Then we aim to find notable dissenters: people who deviate from this pattern and support only one of A or B and oppose the other one. Table 5 shows some interesting examples that we found in our collection (dominant opinions: $++$, $+-$, $-+$, or $--$ with $+$ denoting support and $-$ denoting oppose).

6. RELATED WORK

Analyzing political opinions on controversial topics is inherently more difficult than standard sentiment mining (for products, movies, etc.) [5, 3], given the complexity of the topics and the subtleties in expressing opinions on them.

There is some work on classifying political texts with regard to political parties [4], most notably, democrats vs. republicans in the US, but this stays at the crude level of general attitude and does not address positions on specific controversies. Our own prior work [2] has been limited to pro/con classification of statements, disregarding the opinion holders.

For gathering statements that connect individual people with opinionated expressions, we make use of techniques for information extraction from text and Web sources. [6] gives overviews of state-of-the-art methods. Our approach builds specifically on the pattern-fact duality principle that goes back to [1] and allows us to bootstrap the acquisition process with very few seeds. We customize this general framework to collect opinionated cues rather than general relational patterns. For matching names in text sources against canonical entities, we leverage existing knowledge bases like DBpedia, Freebase, or Yago. We specifically make use of the *means* relation that Yago [7] provides for individual entities and their lexical name variations. This information is in turn derived from anchor texts and redirects of Wikipedia. All these are building blocks of our methodology, but each of these ingredients has an auxiliary role only.

7. CONCLUSIONS AND FUTURE WORK

In this paper, we described our system, named OpinioNetIt, an opinion-base of facets, opinion holders and their opinions. Our system acquired facts in the following 4 stages. First, an initial set of seed patterns were used to extract facets by issuing the seed patterns as Web queries and analyzing the result snippets. These facets were then canonicalized and hierarchically organized. Second, for each facet, an opinion holder was identified from the same snippets. Third, using a small set of facts, a lexicon of support/oppose phrases was constructed. Finally, new patterns from the lexicon were used to collect further facts. Our evaluation showed an overall precision of 72%.

8. REFERENCES

[1] E. Agichtein and L. Gravano. Snowball: Extracting relations from large plain-text collections. In *ICDL*, 2000.

[2] R. Awadallah, M. Ramanath, and G. Weikum. Language-model-based pro/con classification of political text. In *SIGIR*, 2010.

[3] B. Liu. Sentiment analysis and subjectivity. In *Handbook of Natural Language Processing, Second Edition*. 2010.

[4] T. Mullen and R. Malouf. Taking sides: User classification for informal online political discourse. *Internet Research*, 18(2), 2008.

[5] B. Pang and L. Lee. Opinion mining and sentiment analysis. *FnT in IR*, 2(1-2), 2008.

[6] S. Sarawagi. Information extraction. *FnT in Databases*, 1(3), 2008.

[7] F. Suchanek, G. Kasneci, and G. Weikum. Yago: A Core of Semantic Knowledge. In *WWW*, 2007.

Predicting the Uncertainty of Sentiment Adjectives in Indirect Answers

Mitra Mohtarami[1], Hadi Amiri[1,2], Man Lan[3], Chew Lim Tan[1]
[1]SOC, Department of Computer Science, National University of Singapore, Singapore, 117417
[2]NUS Graduate School for Integrative Sciences and Engineering, Singapore, 117456
[3]Institute for Infocomm Research, Singapore, 119613
{mitra, hadi}@comp.nus.edu.sg; lanman@i2r.a-star.edu.sg; tancl@comp.nus.edu.sg

ABSTRACT
Opinion question answering (QA) requires automatic and correct interpretation of an answer relative to its question. However, the ambiguity that often exists in the question-answer pairs causes complexity in interpreting the answers. This paper aims to infer yes/no answers from indirect yes/no question-answer pairs (IQAPs) that are ambiguous due to the presence of *ambiguous sentiment adjectives*. We propose a method to measure the uncertainty of the answer in an IQAP relative to its question. In particular, to infer the *yes* or *no* response from an IQAP, our method employs antonyms, synonyms, word sense disambiguation as well as the semantic association between the sentiment adjectives that appear in the IQAP. Extensive experiments demonstrate the effectiveness of our method over the baseline.

Categories and Subject Descriptors
I.2.7 [**Natural Language Processing**]: Text Analysis

General Terms
Algorithms, Experimentation

Keywords
Sentiment Analysis, Ambiguous Sentiment Adjectives, Indirect yes/no Question-Answer Pairs, Sentiment Ambiguity

1. INTRODUCTION
In indirect yes/no question-answer pairs (IQAPs), the *yes* or *no* words do not explicitly appear in the indirect answers. However, *yes* or *no* responses can be inferred by interpreting the given information in IQAPs. It has been shown that 27% of answers to polar questions do not contain a direct *yes* or *no* word and 44% of them fail to convey a clear *yes* or *no* response [5]. The inherent uncertainty that exists in indirect answers needs to be captured to effectively interpret such answers [8]. It is common that the answerers express their opinion in indirect manner using adjectives with different degree of strength (certainty), e.g. *terrible* has stronger strength than *bad*.

Previous researches showed that adjectives are dominant elements to express opinions [4, 9]. In the review domain, although most of the adjectives have static semantic orientation (SO), positive or negative, the SO of some adjectives vary with context. For example, the adjective *high* has *positive* SO in the phrase *high quality* and *negative* SO in *high cost*. The adjectives with dynamic SO in different contexts are called *Ambiguous Sentiment Adjectives* (ASAs) [10, 1]. Previous works introduced some countable ASAs such as *young*, *many*, *high*, *thick*; they considered other adjectives, like *good* or *terrible*, as unambiguous [10].

In the IQAP domain, we observed that all the ASAs introduced in the review domains can also be ambiguous in this domain. Take the following IQAPs as examples:

E1) A: Is he ***qualified***? B: He is ***young***.
E2) A: Is he ***active***? B: He is ***young***.

The answers in E1 and E2 contain the ASA *young*. In E1, the answer conveys *no* and in E2 the answer conveys *yes* relative to the adjective used in the questions, i.e. *qualified* in E1 and *active* in E2.

Furthermore, our observation shows that all the adjectives can be potentially ambiguous in the IQAP domain. In the following examples (E3) adapted from [8], the adjective *good* expresses weaker strength than *excellent*, and thus the asker infers that the answerer conveys *yes*:

E3) A: Do you think that's a ***good*** idea, that …?
B: I think it's an ***excellent*** idea.

However, the adjective *good* takes a dynamic certainty with respect to the question and does not convey *yes* all the time, e.g. in E3, if we reverse the adjectives of question and answer then speakers infer that the answer conveys *no* [8]. Thus, the adjective *good* which is always employed to express positive opinions in the review domain, can convey *yes* or *no* in different IQAPs (depending on the adjectives that appears in the question parts). We refer to such adjectives that can be employed in the answers of IQAPs and convey both *yes* and *no* in different answers as ambiguous sentiment adjectives (ASAs) in the IQAP domain.

In this paper, we investigate IQAPs in which polar questions and their corresponding answers contain a sentiment adjective, such as *young*, *good*, *provocative* and *etc*. Therefore, the task is to automatically infer the answer of a given IQAP as *yes* or *no*.

The rest of this paper is organized as follows. Section 2 explains our method for inferring IQAP answers. Section 3 reports the experimental results and evaluation of our method. Section 4 discusses the problems in inferring the answers of IQAPs. The related works are reviewed in Section 5. Finally, Section 6 concludes the paper.

2. METHOD
Our method has four main stages to infer the *yes* or *no* answers to IQAPs. First, we measure the certainty of the answer relative to its question for all IQAPs. Second, for each IQAP, we compute a threshold to evaluate the certainty of answer toward *yes* or *no*

CIKM'11, October 24–28, 2011, Glasgow, Scotland, UK.

responses. Third, we infer the answers in each IQAP using the certainty of its answer and its obtained threshold. Finally, we present a refinement on the method by using synonyms. We explain these stages in the subsequent sections respectively.

2.1 Assigning Degree of Certainty to Answers

In this section, we aim to compute the certainty of an answer relative to its question in a given IQAP. Such certainty can be computed based on the association between the adjective of the question (SAQ) and the adjective of the answer (SAA). If the association between the SAQ and SAA is high, then the certainty of the answer relative to its question will be high.

Any similarity measure can be employed to estimate the association between SAQ and SAA. We here use two popular measures, Pointwise Mutual Information (PMI) and Latent Semantic Analysis (LSA) for this purpose. PMI between two words measures the mutual dependence of them and is defined as follows [9]:

$$PMI(w_1, w_2) = \log_2\left(\frac{P(w_1,w_2)}{P(w_1)\,P(w_2)}\right) \quad (1)$$

where $P(w_1, w_2)$ is the probability that w_1 and w_2 co-occur in the same context (e.g., a fixed window or sentence), and $P(w_1)$ and $P(w_2)$ are the probability of w_1 and w_2 in the entire corpus. Since PMI requires a large corpus to be effective, in our experiments, we employ a large corpus of reviews explained in Section 3 to calculate PMI between the words, and consider co-occurrence of two words in less than five words distance between them.

LSA is another learning method for computing similarity between words [6]. It works based on analyzing relationships between a document and the words that it contains. LSA performs several steps to compute the association between two words. First, it forms a matrix with documents as rows and words as columns. Cells contain the number of times that a given word is used in a given document. Second, it employs Singular Value Decomposition (SVD) to represent the words and documents as vectors in a high dimensional semantic space. In a new matrix, words are represented as vectors. Finally, similarity of two words is computed as the cosine between their corresponding vectors in the semantic space. The value of cosine will be +1 for identical meanings, zero for unrelated meanings and -1 for opposite meanings.

We obtained LSA values using the TASA corpus[1] instead of the corpus that we employed for PMI. This is because LSA is computationally expensive with large corpora. In fact, this is because LSA uses a word-by-document matrix and the cost of computation increases substantially with very large corpus.

2.2 Defining a Threshold

As we discussed above, we need to know whether the answer in an IQAP has enough certainty to convey a *yes* or *no* response. We compute a threshold for this purpose which can vary in different IQAPs. Since the antonym of a word belongs to the same scalar group (e.g., *hot* and *cold*) and has different semantic orientation with the word [4], we can utilize the antonym of the SAQ to compute a threshold for each IQAP. Our intuition is that if the association strength between an SAA and its corresponding SAQ is greater than the association strength between the SAA and the antonym of its SAQ, the answer has enough degree of certainty to convey *yes*, and otherwise the answer is more likely to be uncertain relative to the question and conveys a *no* response. For example, in E1, the association strength between *young* and *qualified* is smaller than the association between *young* and *unqualified*; therefore, the answer conveys *no*.

We find the antonym of an SAQ in two steps. First, we employ the IMS word sense disambiguation system [11] to detect the sense of the SAQ. Then, we use WordNet to get the antonym of the SAQ based on its predicted sense. In WordNet, different senses of a word can have different antonyms.

2.3 Inferring Yes or No Answers

The following decision procedure employs two previous steps to decide what a given answer conveys:

$$answer = \begin{cases} yes, & assoc(SAQ, SAA) > assoc(\sim SAQ, SAA) \\ no, & assoc(SAQ, SAA) < assoc(\sim SAQ, SAA) \\ uncertain, & otherwise \end{cases} \quad (2)$$

where $assoc(.,.)$ indicates our similarity measure (either *PMI* or *LSA*), and $\sim SAQ$ is antonym of the SAQ. Note that the appearance of a negation word in the answer to a question reverses the inferred answer, thus here it flips *yes* and *no* responses, but *uncertain* remains unchanged.

2.4 Refining Using Synset

In this section we propose to use the synonyms of the SAAs to supplement our method with more information about the SAAs. Since the synonym of a word is a word that has the same or nearly the same meaning as the original word, the SAA can be replaced by any of its synonyms with no major changes in its inferred original answer. In addition, different senses of an SAA may have different sets of synonyms (synsets) in WordNet. We can obtain the synset of SAAs using a word sense disambiguation system and WordNet in a similar way that we did for antonyms in Section 2.2. Having the synset of an SAA, we compute the association between SAQ and the synset of the SAA as follows:

$$assoc(SAQ, syn(SAA)) = \frac{1}{|synset|}\sum_{i=1}^{|synset|} assoc(SAQ, syn_i(SAA)) \quad (3)$$

where $syn(SAA)$ is the synset of the SAA, and $syn_i(SAA)$ is the ith word in $syn(SAA)$. Equation 3 computes the association between SAQ and the synset of SAA by averaging the sum of the association between SAQ and each of the synonyms for SAA.

As we discussed before, the antonym of an SAQ can be used to decide about the certainty of the answer for an IQAP as *yes* or *no*. In Section 2.3 the antonym has been used with the SAA itself, i.e. $assoc(\sim SAQ, SAA)$. Here we use the synset of the SAA to predict the association between $\sim SAQ$ and the SAA more precisely. The following Equation can be used for this purpose:

$$assoc(\sim SAQ, syn(SAA)) = \frac{1}{|synset|}\sum_{i=1}^{|synset|} assoc(\sim SAQ, syn_i(SAA)) \quad (4)$$

We can use the above two equations to infer the yes or no response as follows:

$$answer = \begin{cases} yes, & assoc(SAQ, syn(SAA)) > assoc(\sim SAQ, syn(SAA)) \\ no, & assoc(SAQ, syn(SAA)) < assoc(\sim SAQ, syn(SAA)) \\ uncertain, & otherwise \end{cases} \quad (5)$$

[1] LSA is obtained from: http://cwl-projects.cogsci.rpi.edu/msr

3. EVALUATION AND RESULTS

In this section we first explain the datasets that we used in this research, and then report the experiments conducted to evaluate our approach.

We used the dataset developed in [8] to evaluate our method. This dataset contains a set of IQAPs and their corresponding *yes* or *no* labels as its ground truth. It includes 125 IQAPs with two different sentiment adjectives in any question-answer pair as described in [8]. They used two sources to gather the IQAPs: five different shows from online CNN interview transcripts, and the Switchboard Dialog Act corpus. They manually annotated the IQAP dataset for *yes* or *no* responses and identified the adjectives of the questions and answers. In all instances of IQAPs, the SAA is different from the SAQ.

We also used two datasets as development datasets to compute the association strength of word pairs based on PMI and LSA measures. To compute the co-occurrence information for PMI, we collected a large corpus of 1.5M reviews from Amazon product reviews for 25 different product types, such as *book*, *video*, and *music*. However, as we discussed in Section 2.1, LSA in contrast to PMI cannot handle large corpora [7]. Therefore we employed the standard Touchstone Applied Science Associates (TASA) corpus to compute the association strength of word pairs using LSA. The TASA corpus is a collection of texts from textbooks, literature, works of fiction and nonfiction used in schools and the reading materials that a person is supposed to have been exposed to by his first year in college. This corpus contains more than 17M tokens corresponding to around 155K different types.

3.1 Experimental Results

In this section we report detail results of our approach with different configurations. We compare the approach proposed in [8] as a baseline.

Given an IQAP, [8] assigned a semantic orientation (SO, referred as expected rating value by authors) to both SAA and SAQ of the given IQAP, and then interpreted the answer based on the SOs. For instance, if the SOs of the SAA and SAQ have different signs, then the answer conveys *no*. In case of the same sign, if the SO of the SAA is greater than or equals to the SO of the SAQ, then the answer conveys *yes*, and otherwise *no*. They obtained an accuracy of 60% on the same IQAP dataset which is used in our experiments. They used an external source (a large corpus of reviews with rates) to compute the SO of adjectives. Given an adjective, they computed the SO of the adjective as a function of the probability of rate given the adjective.

Their approach assigns a globally fixed SO score to each adjective. For example, the adjectives *best* and *great* are assigned the fixed SO scores of 1.08 and 1.1 respectively. This approach ignores the context in which the adjectives appear (i.e. the IQAP). However, in our approach the degree of certainty for the same answer may change in different IQAPs. This dynamic degree of certainty not only depends on the SAA itself but also on the SAQ that appears in the IQAP. So, our method utilizes the context information better than the method proposed in [8].

Table 1 shows the results of different approaches in terms of precision, recall and f-measure. The results in Table 1 are based on Equation 5 where we use antonyms (of SAQs) and synsets (of SAAs) to infer the yes or no answers. The first and second rows of Table 1 shows the result of our method when it uses PMI and LSA respectively. The last row shows the baseline results.

Table 1. Performance of different approaches

Similarity Measures	Precision	Recall	F-Measure
PMI-synset-antonym	67.14	65.45	66.28
LSA-synset-antonym	**73.97**	**75.98**	**74.96**
Baseline [8]	60.00	60.00	60.00

As it is clear from Table 1, when we use LSA our method achieves better performance than PMI. It was expected since PMI is known as a contextual similarity measure while LSA is known as a semantic similarity measure. So, LSA can better measure the semantic association between the adjectives which can definitely help the inference process. Our method using both PMI and LSA significantly outperforms the baseline method.

4. ANALYSIS AND DISCUSSION

In this section, we discuss the effectiveness of our method from different perspectives. As we mentioned before, our method utilizes synset, antonym, and word sense disambiguation techniques. In this section, we dig into the IQAP problem and investigate the effectiveness of these techniques to tackle the IQAP problem. In Section 4.1, we analyze the role of synsets and antonyms, while in Section 4.2 we discuss the role of WSD.

4.1 Role of Synsets and Antonyms

In this section, we evaluate the effectiveness of synsets and antonyms for inferring yes or no answers. For this purpose, we repeat the experiments by ignoring synsets or antonyms respectively. Table 2 shows the results.

In Table 2, PMI-Antonym (LSA-Antonym) shows the results when we use Equation 2 to infer the answer of an IQAP based on the PMI (LSA) measure. In Equation 2, we only use SAA, SAQ, and ~SAQ and do not utilize the synsets (of SAAs). Table 2 shows that ignoring the synsets results in significant reduction in the final performance, i.e. from 66.28% (see Table 1) to 57.53% for PMI and 74.96% to 61.55% for LSA.

This result shows that synsets are highly effective for IQAP problem. We believe one of the reasons is about the fact that some SAAs and SAQs never (or rarely) co-occurred in our large corpus. This results in a very low association between them. However the synonyms of the SAAs may frequently occur with the SAQs. Therefore, the synonyms help us to more reliably predict the association between the SAQs and SAAs and consequently better infer the yes or no responses. Similar to PMI, LSA can benefit from synsets. In fact, as the result shows, LSA benefits more from the synsets than PMI. The reason is that our LSA measure uses a smaller corpus (TASA) than PMI. Therefore, it is more likely that an SAA do not appear in the LSA corpus than PMI corpus. In that sense, LSA should benefit more from the synsets than PMI.

Table 2. Performance without using synset

Similarity Measures	Precision	Recall	F-Measure
PMI-antonym	58.94	56.18	57.53
LSA-antonym	62.23	60.88	61.55
PMI-synset	34.86	41.69	37.97
LSA-synset	67.35	56.86	61.66
PMI	32.20	34.38	33.25
LSA	66.70	54.95	60.26

To investigate the role of antonyms, we repeat the experiments without using them. In other words, for each IQAP, the answer is interpreted only based on the association between the SAQ and the synset of the SAA. Given an IQAP, if the similarity association between SAQ and the synset of the SAA is positive, then the inferred answer will be *yes*; if it is negative, the inferred answer will be *no*, and otherwise, it will be *uncertain*. The results of these experiments are shown as PMI-synset and LSA-synset in Table 2 for PMI and LSA respectively.

As it is clear from Table 2, the antonyms can also help to infer the correct answer comparing to PMI-synset-antonym or LSA-synset-antonym (See Table 1). The results of both PMI and LSA have significantly decreased when we do not use antonyms, from 66.28% to 37.97% for PMI and 74.96% to 61.66% for LSA. In addition, it is notable that the performance of PMI decreased more than LSA (from 66.28% to 37.97%).

Finally, we apply the proposed method with no using synsets and antonyms. Here, for each IQAP, the answer is interpreted only based on the association between the SAQ and the SAA. Given an IQAP, if the similarity association between SAQ and the SAA is positive, then the inferred answer will be *yes*; if it is negative, the inferred answer will be *no*, and otherwise, it will be *uncertain*. The results of these experiments are shown in the last two rows of the Table 2. As expected, we see the lowest performance when we do not utilize both synonyms and antonyms.

4.2 Role of Word Sense Disambiguation

In our method, we employed an automatic WSD system and obtained 66.28% and 74.96% performance using PMI and LSA respectively (see Table 1). Here, we study the impact of the WSD system on these results.

For this purpose, instead of the WSD system we only used the most common sense of the adjectives (the first sense in WordNet) and repeat the experiments. We took the most common sense as a replacement for the WSD system because it has been shown as a strong baseline in the WSD area. The results are shown in Table 3. As it is clear, using the most common sense of the adjectives slightly reduces the performance, from 66.28% to 65.97% for PMI and 74.96% to 73.83% for LSA.

Table 3. Performance without using IMS

Method	Precision	Recall	F-Measure
PMI	66.35	65.59	65.97
LSA	73.02	74.66	73.83

It is notable that, in this experiment, the WSD system has assigned the most common sense to around 80% of the adjectives. In other word, only 20% of the adjectives assigned senses different than their most common senses. The efficiency of the WSD could have been more highlighted, if more IQAPs contain adjectives with senses different from their most common senses.

5. RELATED WORK

In [3] the authors presented a computational model for interpreting and generating indirect answers to polar (Yes/No) questions using a discourse-plan-based approach and a hybrid reasoning model. [8] worked on indirect yes/no question-answer pairs involving an adjective in question and an adjective in the answer. As we explained in Section 3.1, they used an external source to assign a SO (or ER in [8]) to each adjective (SAA and SAQ) to do this task. For each IQAP, if the SOs of the SAA and SAQ have different signs, then the answer conveys *no*. In case of the same sign, if the SO score of the SAA is greater than or equals to the SO of the SAQ, then they inferred a *yes* response; if the SO score of the SAA is smaller than the SO of its SAQ, then they inferred a *no* response. They also used the method proposed in [2] to compute the SO scores using WordNet instead of the external source. They showed that using WordNet produces 56% performance for inferring *yes* or *no* answers to IQAPs. Although they assigned a static SO to each adjective, ASAs have dynamic SO. Previous works on ASAs considered the adjectives in review domain [10, 1]. However, in this paper we examined the behavior of adjectives in the IQAP domain. We showed that the adjectives can show different degrees of certainty in different question-answer pairs which can lead to different responses.

6. CONCLUSION

In this paper we examine the behavior of adjectives in Indirect yes/no Question-Answer Pairs (IQAPs) domain. In particular, our task is to automatically detect whether the answer of a given IQAP conveys *yes* or *no*. We show that measuring the association between the adjectives in question and answer can be a main factor to infer a clear response from an IQAP. We utilize antonyms, synonyms and word sense disambiguation to tackle the IQAP problem and investigate the effectiveness of each of these techniques for this task.

7. REFERENCES

[1] Balahur, A. and Montoyo, A. 2010. OpAL: Applying Opinion Mining Techniques for the Disambiguation of Sentiment Ambiguous Adjectives. *ACL*, pp. 444-447.

[2] Blair-Goldensohn, S., Hannan, K., McDonald, R., Neylon, T., Reis, G., and Reynar, J. 2008. Building a sentiment summarizer for local service reviews. *NLPIX.*

[3] Green, N. and Carberry, S. 1999. Interpreting and generating indirect answers. *Computational Linguistics*, 25(3), 389-435.

[4] Hatzivassiloglou, V. and McKeown, K. R. 1997. Predicting the semantic orientation of adjectives. *ACL*, pp. 174-181.

[5] Hockey, B., Knill, D., Spejewski, B., Stone, M., and Isard, S. 1997. Can you predict answers to Y/N questions? Yes, No and Stuff. In *Proceedings of Eurospeech*, pp. 2267-2270.

[6] Landauer, T., Foltz, P., and Laham, D. 1998. An introduction to Latent Semantic Analysis. *Discourse Processes*, 259-284.

[7] Lindsey, R., Veksler, V., Grintsvayg, A., and Gray, W. 2007. Be Wary of What Your Computer Reads: The Effects of Corpus Selection on Measuring Semantic Relatedness. *ICCM*, pp. 279-284.

[8] Marneffe, M. C., Manning, C. D., and Potts, C. 2010. "Was it good? It was provocative." Learning the meaning of scalar adjectives. *ACL*, pp. 167–176.

[9] Turney, P. 2002. Thumbs up or thumbs down? Semantic orientation applied to unsupervised classification of reviews. *ACL*, pp. 417-424.

[10] Wu, Y. and Jin, P. 2010. Disambiguating Sentiment Ambiguous Adjectives. *SemEval-ACL*, pp. 81-85.

[11] Zhong, Z. and Ng, H. T. 2010. It Makes Sense: A Wide-Coverage Word Sense Disambiguation System for Free Text. *ACL*, pp: 78–83.

Sentiment Classification via L2-norm Deep Belief Network

Tao Liu[1], Minghui Li[2], Shusen Zhou[3], Xiaoyong Du[1]
[1]Key Laboratory of Data Engineering and Knowledge Engineering, MOE, 100872, Beijing, China
[1]School of Information, Renmin University of China, 100872, Beijing, China
{tliuruc, duyongruc}@google.com
[2]Microsoft Asian Research and Development Group, 100080, Beijing, China
mhuil@microsoft.com
[3]Shenzhen Graduate School, Harbin Institute of Technology, 518055, Shenzhen, China
zhoushusen@hitsz.edu.cn

ABSTRACT
Automatic analysis of sentiments expressed in large scale online reviews is very important for intelligent business applications. Sentiment classification is the most popular task of sentiment analysis, which is more challenging than traditional topic-based text classification. Basic features, such as vocabulary words, are not enough to classify sentiments well. Deep Belief Network (DBN) is introduced to discover more abstract features of sentiments. To capture full information of the features, large-size network can be constructed, but at the same time, large-size network tends to over fit the training data and even noise, which will reduce the generalization ability of the network. In this paper, L2-norm Deep Belief Network (L2DBN) is proposed, which uses L2-norm regularization to optimize the network parameters of DBN. L2DBN is first initialized by an unsupervised layer-wise training algorithm, and then fine-tuned by a supervised procedure. Network parameters are optimized using both classification loss and network complexity. Experimental results show that the proposed L2DBN outperforms the state-of-the-art method and the basic DBN on golden, noisy and heterogeneous datasets.

Categories and Subject Descriptors
I.2.7 [**Artificial Intelligence**]: Natural language processing

General Terms
Algorithms, Experimentation.

Keywords
Sentiment Classification, Deep Belief Network, L2-norm Regularization.

1. INTRODUCTION
With the development of Web 2.0, web users can freely post their opinions and reviews about various resources. Automatic mining these huge amounts of online reviews can help companies and customers to make more intelligent business decisions. The task of sentiment classification [1, 2] is naturally proposed, and its goal is to label the sentiment orientation of subjective texts as "thumb up" or "thumb down", which has received more and more research attention in recent years [3, 4].

Although much research attention has been paid on this task, it is still challenging to develop a sentiment classification system with high performance because this task is more difficult than traditional topic-based text classification (TC). For topic-based TC, domain-specific terms are good indicators to distinguish topic classes, but it is difficult to distinguish sentiments by isolated terms because of the following reasons. 1) The same expression may indicate different sentiments in different contexts. For instance, "I feel sleepy" conveys a negative sentiment when the speaker is watching a film, but it indicates a positive opinion of someone who has just taken a sleeping pill. 2) A single review may contain both positive and negative polarity words. For instance, the review "the food is delicious, but the service is terrible" for a restaurant includes both positive word "delicious" and negative word "terrible". 3) Sentiments may often be expressed in a subtle manner.

More abstract semantic features are needed to overcome the difficulty of sentiment classification. Deep Belief Network (DBN) [5] presents a new way to obtain the high-level abstraction of input data, and has been successfully applied to digit recognition [5], language model [6], etc. In this paper, we introduce DBN to sentiment classification to obtain more abstract features of sentiments.

Before constructing DBN for a real application, it is important to choose a proper size of its network structure. On the one hand, a small-size network structure with fewer neurons and connections cannot catch adequate enough information for sentiment classification. On the other hand, an oversize structure with more neurons and connections will cover some trivial features of training data and cause over-fitting. Because large-scale lexical features have already formed a huge dimension of space for the sentiment classification problem, in order to capture the full information of input features, a large-size network should be used. In order to avoid over-fitting and to improve the generalization ability of the network, we construct an L2-norm Deep Belief Network (L2DBN) for sentiment classification. L2-norm regularization is a commonly used technique for generalization. To the best of our knowledge, this is the first attempt to apply L2-norm regularization to DBN.

CIKM'11, October 24–28, 2011, Glasgow, Scotland, UK.

2. SYSTEM OVERVIEW

The system framework of sentiment classification based on L2DBN is shown in Fig.1, which include three parts. Review documents are preprocessed and represented as feature vectors at first, and then divided into two parts for training and test.

The training process in the second part can be divided into two steps: pre-training and fine-tuning. Pre-training is unsupervised, and an initial network will be obtained using a greedy layer-wise training algorithm. During fine-tuning, the parameters of all the layers will be updated using back propagation algorithm. An L2-norm strategy is added to the fine-tuning process so that better network parameters can be achieved.

In the third part, the labels of test data are predicted by L2DBN. The performance of the system is evaluated by comparing predicted labels with actual labels.

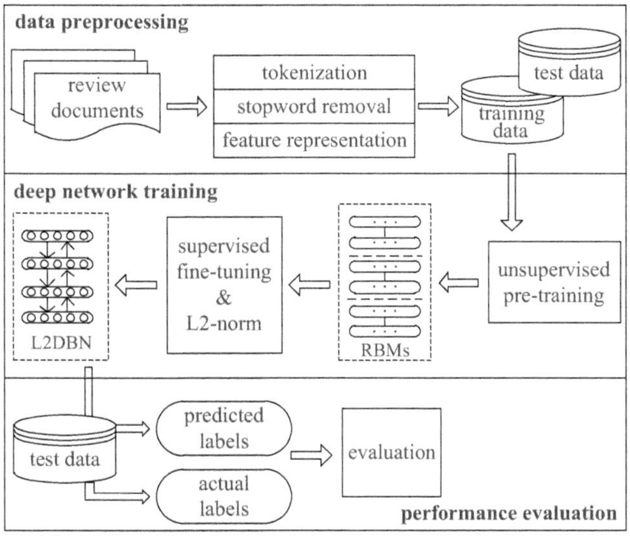

Figure 1. Sentiment Classification Based on L2DBN

3. METHODS

3.1 Problem Formulation

Given a set of review documents $X=\{x_1, x_2,..., x_N\}$, the task of sentiment classification is to identify the sentiment polarity (positive or negative) expressed in each review. Each review x_i is represented as a feature vector $x_i=(x_{i1}, x_{i2},..., x_{iD})$, and D is the number of feature words in the dataset. The label of each review x_i is also represented as an indicator vector. In this paper, $y_i=(1,-1)$ is used to represent positive reviews and $y_i=(-1,1)$ is used to represent negative reviews. Supposing the label set $Y=\{y_1, y_2,..., y_N\}$, mapping function $f: X \rightarrow Y$ needs to be found to classify each review to its corresponding polarity class.

3.2 Deep Architecture

A deep architecture is constructed to model the sentiments of reviews, so that high-level abstractions of data can be discovered. DBN is one of the most popular deep architectures. As shown in Fig.2, it is a multi-layer connected network with symmetric weighted connections between two adjacent layers, but no intra-layer connection. The input layer accepts the feature vector of each review. The output layer, which represents the predicted label for each review, is compared with the actual label by the loss function which is used to fine-tune the network.

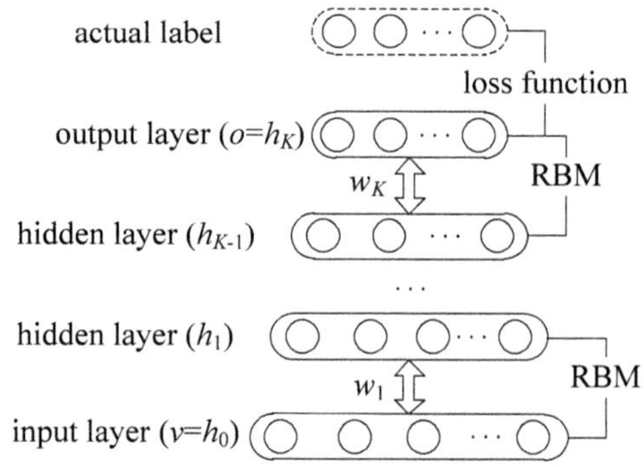

Figure 2. Architecture of DBN with Biases Omitted

For convenience, the following notations are used to denote the components of the network:

- $v=h_0$: input layer
- h_i $(i=1,2,...,K-1)$: the ith hidden layer
- $o=h_K$: output layer
- w_i $(i=1,...,K)$: connection weight matrix between h_{i-1} and h_i
- b_i $(i=0,...,K-1)$: biases for neurons of layer h_i, when they are activated by upper layer h_{i+1}
- c_i $(i=1,...,K)$: biases for neurons of layer h_i, when they are activated by lower layer h_{i-1}

For two adjacent layers, h_{i-1} and h_i, activation functions are defined as:

$$p(h_{i-1,s}=1 \mid h_i)=\sigma(b_{i,s}+\textstyle\sum_j w_{i,j}h_{i,j}) \tag{1}$$

$$p(h_{i,t}=1 \mid h_{i-1})=\sigma(c_{i,t}+\textstyle\sum_j w_{i,j}h_{i-1,j}) \tag{2}$$

where $\sigma(x)$ is the logistic function:

$$\sigma(x)=1/(1+e^{-x}) \tag{3}$$

3.3 Pre-Training

Although gradient descent algorithm can be used to tune the weights of the network, it works well only when the initial weights are near to the good solution. An unsuitable initial network will make the deep network trap into a local optimized solution. A layer-wise pre-training procedure proposed by Hinton [5] is used for getting a suitable initial network. From bottom to top, each pair of two adjacent layers can be regarded as a Restricted Boltzmann Machine (RBM) by taking the lower layer as visible layer v and the upper layer as hidden layer h. The whole network is constructed by training one RBM at a time in a bottom-up fashion.

One RBM has the following energy function:

$$E(v,h)=-\textstyle\sum_{s,t} v_s w_{st} h_t - \sum_s b_s v_s - \sum_t c_t h_t \tag{4}$$

The goal of pre-training is to maximize the probability of generating training data. The probability of each training data assigned by the network can be calculated using the energy function above:

$$p(v)=\sum_{h\in H} p(v,h)=\frac{\sum_h \exp(-E(v,h))}{\sum_{u,g} \exp(-E(u,g))} \tag{5}$$

Then the gradient of the log probability of the training data can be given by:

$$\frac{\partial \log p(v)}{\partial w_{st}} = \left\langle v_s^0 h_t^0 \right\rangle - \left\langle v_s^\infty h_t^\infty \right\rangle \tag{6}$$

where v_s^∞ and h_t^∞ can be obtained by alternating Gibbs sampling from the network. For simplicity, the following approximate objective is used to update the weight:

$$\Delta w_{st} = \varepsilon\left(\left\langle v_s^0 h_t^0 \right\rangle - \left\langle v_s^1 h_t^1 \right\rangle\right) \tag{7}$$

where ε is the learning rate. A similar version of the learning rule is used for the biases.

3.4 Discriminative Fine-Tuning

In order to enable DBN to be more proper to solve the sentiment classification task, a discriminative fine-tuning algorithm is used to minimize the classification error on the training data, and the stochastic activities is replaced by deterministic, real-valued probabilities. The optimization problem can be formulated as:

$$\hat{\theta} = \arg\min_{\theta}(L(Y, Z, \theta)) \tag{8}$$

where $\theta = (w_1, ..., w_K, c_1, ..., c_K)$. $L(Y, Z, \theta)$ is the loss function for given parameter set θ, Y is the actual labels of training data, and Z is the labels predicted by the network. Supposing the number of training examples is N, $L(Y, Z, \theta)$ can be defined as an exponential loss function:

$$L(Y, Z, \theta) = \sum_{i=1}^{N} \sum_{j=1}^{C} \exp(-y_{ij} z_{ij}) \tag{9}$$

where N denote the number of training examples and C denote sentiment classes. The popular gradient descent algorithm is used to optimize the goal above.

3.5 L2-norm Regularization for Network Parameter Optimization

The discriminative fine-tuning can make the network fit with the training data very well, but it may also lead to over-fitting on the following three aspects: 1) some redundant neurons, connections or weights tend to be generated to model some trivial features of training data; 2) the network will fit with noise when the training data is not clean; 3) the network will perform poorly when the test data has inconsistent distributions with the training data.

On the other hand, for the sentiment classification task, a smaller network with fewer neurons or hidden layers will lose the useful information essential for classification. For example, for the ELE review dataset used in our experiment, the accuracy obtained by network "1500-1200-900" is higher than that by simple network "500-400-300" and "200-100-50" by 2 and 4 percent respectively.

A relatively larger network should be used to catch enough information, but such a complex network tends to over fit the data and reduce the generalization ability of the model.

Many methods can be used to improve the generalization power of a machine learning method. L2-norm regularization [7] is a popular technique for generalization, and can be defined as:

$$C(\theta) = \sum_i \theta_i^2 \tag{10}$$

L2-norm regularization assumes the simplest network can generalize well, and make the unnecessary connection weights to get lower values or even zeroes. This network complexity penalty factor is then combined with the loss function to form a new optimization goal, which can be expressed as:

$$\hat{\theta} = \arg\min_{\theta}(L(Y, Z, \theta) + \lambda C(\theta)) \tag{11}$$

where λ is the relative importance of the network complexity penalty in comparison with the classification error rate.

This new optimization goal enables the network to obtain lower classification error and better generalization ability.

4. EXPERIMENTS

4.1 Experimental Setup

4.1.1 Datasets Used and Evaluation Criterion

The effectiveness of the proposed method was evaluated on four datasets of product reviews, including books (BOO), DVDs (DVD), electronics (ELE), and kitchen appliances (KIT) [8]. Each dataset includes 1,000 positive and 1,000 negative reviews. the 2,000 reviews were randomly divided into ten equal sizes and all the methods are tested by ten-fold cross validation. In order to reduce the effect of random factor, training and test were done for three times on each fold and get the average of all the runs. The evaluation criterion can be expressed as:

$$acc = \frac{\#right}{\#total} \tag{12}$$

where *#right* is the number of test examples labeled with correct labels by using the method, and *#total* represents the total number of test examples.

4.1.2 Data Preprocessing and Representation

All of the reviews are tokenized and then represented as a binary weight vector for word presence. Some stopwords are removed, including punctuations, numbers, one-character words, and words that occur in a single review. All the words are converted to lowercases and no stemming is conducted. In addition, we use document frequency as the basic feature selection method to filter top 1.5% common words.

4.1.3 System Parameters

The number of hidden layers of L2DBN and DBN is set to three and the number of neurons of hidden layers is set to be 1500-1200-900. Relative importance factor λ of classification performance over network complexity is set to be 0.01. Other parameters of networks are fixed as the default parameter settings of Hinton's DBN package.

4.2 Performance on Golden Datasets

The performance of L2DBN is compared with that of SVM, the most popularly used classification method on this problem [2]. SVMLight with linear kernel function is used. We also compare L2DBN with the basic DBN proposed by Hinton [5].

Table 1 shows the accuracy obtained by SVM, DBN and L2DBN. It also can be observed that L2DBN achieves the best performance among all these methods on these four datasets. The similar experimental result with SVM can be referred in [9].

Table 1. Accuracy Comparison on Four Golden Datasets

System	BOO	DVD	ELE	KIT
SVM	75.9%	78.2%	80.8%	79.1%
DBN	77.7%	79.5%	80.9%	81.2%
L2DBN	80.2%	81.1%	82.0%	82.5%

4.3 Performance on Noisy Datasets

In order to verify the noise tolerance ability of L2DBN, we generate some noise by randomly selecting *r* percent training examples and reversing their class labels. Different noise ratios are set to create different scenarios. The test dataset is still the golden data. Figure 3 presents the comparative results of L2DBN with DBN and SVM on the ELE and KIT datasets with different label noise ratios.

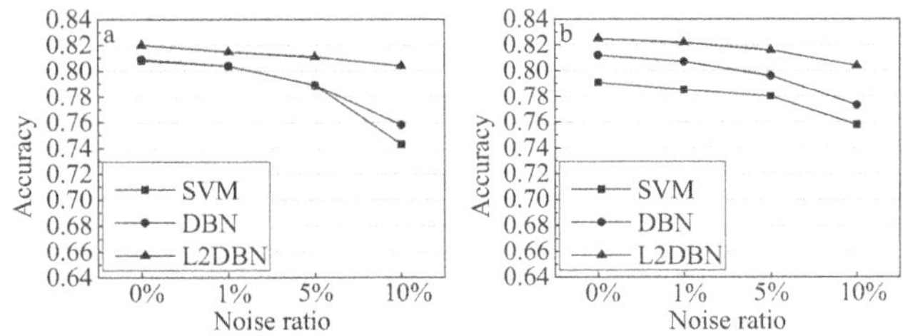

Figure 3. Performance for Different Noise Ratios on a) ELE and b) KIT datasets

It can be seen that the accuracy of DBN and SVM deceases obviously as the noise ratio increases, while the accuracy of L2DBN is more stable and is still satisfactory even on noisy datasets. L2DBN obtains the best performance on all datasets at different noise ratios. The improvement is much larger as the noise ratio increases. This experiment indicates that L2DBN can tolerate noise much better than traditional methods.

4.4 Performance on Heterogeneous Datasets

If the training data and test data have inconsistent distribution, then the classification becomes much more difficult. We attempt to create heterogeneous training and test data in the following way. We randomly substitute a certain number of training examples of one dataset by the same number of examples of another dataset, and remain the test dataset as same as before. Here for illustration, we substitute 40 percent of examples of ELE by the same number of examples of BOO, DVD and KIT respectively and we get three datasets.

Table 2. Accuracy Comparison on Heterogeneous Dataset

Dataset	SVM	DBN	L2DBN
ELE golden data	80.8%	80.9%	82.0%
ELE with BOO	78.0%	79.3%	82.7%
ELE with DVD	78.8%	79.4%	82.6%
ELE with KIT	80.8%	80.6%	82.9%

As shown in Table 2, among all the systems, L2DBN can still be used to achieve the best accuracy. The performance of L2DBN is more stable comparing with other two methods. It is very interesting that when 40 percent of ELE training data is substituted by examples of KIT, all the methods obtain similar accuracy as original ones because the feature distribution of ELE and KIT are very similar, which is also measured by Blitzer [8].

5. CONCLUSION

In this paper, L2DBN is proposed to solve the sentiment classification task. It can obtain high-level abstract features from input data and achieve better generalization ability. After pre-training and discriminative fine-tuning with L2-norm regularization, the final deep network is more powerful for sentiment classification task. Experimental results show that the L2DBN outperforms the basic DBN and the state-of-the-art classifier on four product review datasets. The improvement is much larger on noisy data and heterogeneous data. We can conclude that L2DBN is more proper to solve problems in real applications with noisy and heterogeneous data. The good performance of L2DBN on heterogeneous data also indicates the potential of L2DBN for domain transfer learning, and we will conduct more work on this topic in the future. We will also apply L2DBN on more applications to verify its effectiveness.

6. ACKNOWLEDGEMENTS

This work was supported by the National Natural Science Foundation of China with grant No. 61003204, 60873017, and HGJ project with grant No. 2010ZX01042-002-002-03.

7. REFERENCES

[1] Turney P. D. 2002. Thumbs up or Thumbs Down? Semantic Orientation Applied to Unsupervised Classification of Reviews. In *Proceedings of ACL* (USA, July). 417-424.

[2] Pang B., Lee L., and Vaithyanathan S. 2002. Thumbs Up? Sentiment Classification Using Machine Learning Techniques. In *Proceedings of EMNLP*. (USA, July). 79-86.

[3] Pang B. and Lee L. 2008. Opinion Mining and Sentiment Analysis. *Foundations and Trends in Information Retrieval* 2, 1-2, 1-135.

[4] Liu B. eds. 2010. *Sentiment Analysis and Subjectivity: Handbook of Natural Language Processing (Second Edition)*. Boca Raton, FL: CRC Press, Taylor and Francis Group.

[5] Hinton G. E. and Salakhutdinov R. R. 2006. Reducing the Dimensionality of Data with Neural Networks. *Science* 313, 5786, 504-507.

[6] Mnih A. and Hinton G. E. 2008. A Scalable Hierarchical Distributed Language Model. In *Proceedings of NIPS* (Canada). 1081-1088.

[7] Hastie, T., Tibshirani, R., Friedman J. 2001. *The Elements of Statistical Learning*. Springer-Verlag.

[8] Blitzer J., Dredze M., and Pereira F. 2007. Biographies, Bollywood, Boom-Boxes and Blenders: Domain Adaptation for Sentiment Classification. In *Proceedings of ACL* (Czech Republic, June 23rd-30th). 440-447.

[9] Dasgupta S. and Ng V. 2009. Mine the Easy, Classify the Hard: A Semi-Supervised Approach to Automatic Sentiment Classification. In *Proceedings of ACL-IJCNLP* (Singapore, August 2-7). 701-709.

Domain Customization for Aspect-oriented Opinion Analysis with Multi-level Latent Sentiment Clues

Honglei Guo Huijia Zhu Zhili Guo Zhong Su
IBM Research – China
Beijing, P.R. China, 100193
{guohl, zhuhuij, guozhili, suzhong}@cn.ibm.com

ABSTRACT

Aspect-oriented opinion mining detects the reviewers' sentiment orientation (e.g. positive, negative or neutral) towards different product-features. Domain customization is a big challenge for opinion mining due to the accuracy loss across domains. In this paper, we show our experiences and lessons learned in the domain customization for the aspect-oriented opinion analysis system *OpinionIt*. We present a customization method for sentiment classification with multi-level latent sentiment clues. We first construct Latent Semantic Association model to capture latent association among product-features from the unlabeled corpus. Meanwhile, we present an unsupervised method to effectively extract various domain-specific sentiment clues from the unlabeled corpus. In the customization, we tune the sentiment classifier on the labeled source domain data by incorporating the multi-level latent sentiment clues (e.g. latent association among product-features, domain-specific and generic sentiment clues). Experimental results show that the proposed method significantly reduces the accuracy loss of sentiment classification without any labeled target domain data.

Categories and Subject Descriptors

I.2.7 [**Artificial Intelligence**]: Natural language processing—*text analysis*

General Terms

Algorithms Experimentation

Keywords

Opinion mining, Sentiment classification, Supervised learning, Domain customization

1. INTRODUCTION

Opinion mining is a critical task in business intelligence. In many applications, simply judging the overall sentiment orientation of a review is not sufficient. Reviewers usually praise some aspects of the product and complain about other aspects. Hence, we built an aspect-oriented opinion mining system *OpinionIt* [5], which detects the reviewers' sentiment orientation towards different product aspects using the sentence-level sentiment classifier. The sentiment classifier often losses accuracy if the single sentiment clue encountered in the sentence was not learned by the system. It usually requires amounts of labeled target domain data to tune sentiment classifiers in the domain customization. However, annotating a large-scale corpora for each domain is impractical. Some domain customization methods have been proposed for document-level sentiment classification[2, 6, 7]. Blitzer et al. [2] employ structural corresponding learning to infer generalized feature representation across domains. Li et al. [6] transfer common lexical knowledge across domains via matrix factorization technique.

In the domain customization for *OpinionIt*, we present a customization method for sentence-level sentiment classification with multi-level latent sentiment clues (MLSC). It is a more challenging task since review sentences usually are short text with sparse sentiment clues. We overcome the data gap across domains using multi-level latent sentiment association among product-features and opinions. We construct a latent semantic association (LaSA) model to capture latent association among product-features from the unlabeled corpus at first. LaSA model groups words into a set of semantic concepts according to their syntactic and semantic context in the reviews. Meanwhile, we present an unsupervised method to effectively capture the domain-specific sentiment clues from the unlabeled corpus. In the domain customization, we tune the sentence-level sentiment classifier by integrating multi-level latent sentiment association among product-features, domain-specific and generic sentiment clues. Experimental results show that the proposed MLSC-based customization method significantly enhances the performance without any labeled target domain data.

The reminder of this paper is organized as follows. Section 2 presents domain customization method with multi-level latent sentiment clues. Section 3 discusses the experimental results. The conclusion is given in Section 4.

2. DOMAIN CUSTOMIZATION FOR ASPECT-ORIENTED SENTIMENT CLASSIFICATION

In order to reduce the accuracy loss in the domain transfer for aspect-oriented sentiment classification, we present

CIKM'11, October 24–28, 2011, Glasgow, Scotland, UK.

a customization method with multi-level latent sentiment clues. It effectively overcomes the data gap across domains.

2.1 Multi-level Latent Sentiment Association

It is hard for supervised approaches to obtain enough labeled data to illustrate all the features of the domain. Product-features and various sentiment clues significantly impact the performance of the aspect-oriented sentiment classification. Hence, we integrate the multi-level latent sentiment association among product-features, domain-specific and generic sentiment clues in the model customization.

2.1.1 Latent Association Among Product-features

People often use various terms to refer to the same product-feature in the reviews. In aspect-oriented sentiment analysis, we present LaSA model to capture latent association among product-features from the unlabeled corpus. LaSA model effectively augments training data in the learning.

We construct LaSA model θ for words using the algorithm presented by Guo et al. [4]. We first construct the virtual context document vd_{x_i} for each word x_i from the unlabeled corpus. The weight of each context word in vd_{x_i} is calculated using Mutual Information (MI) [3], and is normalized to non-negative. Then, LaSA model θ with Dirichlet distribution is generated on the virtual context document set $VDSet$ using LDA [1]. In LaSA model learning, vd_{x_i} is composed of all the context units around the word x_i in the corpus. For example, given x_i=*"room"*, s_k=*"This new hotel is very good because its room is very large and clean"*. In the context window {-3, 3} (i.e. previous 3 words and next 3 words around x_i in s_k), the context feature set $F(x_i^{s_k})$ around *"room"* in s_k includes: 1) the current word: x_i*(room)*; 2) left/right opinion sets (i.e., two left/right adjacent adjective units): O_L*(good)*, O_L*(new)*, O_R*(large)*, O_R*(clean)*; 3) the nearest left/right adjacent units: A_L*(its)*, A_R*(is)*; 4) the other two left/right adjacent context unit sets: C_L*(because)*, C_L *(good)*, C_R*(very)*, C_R*(large)*.

Topic 4	Topic 8	Topic 12	Topic 16
access	problem	views	mall
houses	negative	location	shopping
channel	complaint	harbor	public
entrance	issue	waterfront	plaza
walkway	reason	skyline	centres

Table 1: Latent topics of some words in hotel domain

LaSA model learns the posterior distribution to decompose words and their virtual context documents into topics. It better captures the semantic category distribution of words without any labeled data. Table 1 shows some latent topics generated by LaSA model θ. As shown, words in the same topic actually are grouped into broad aspects. For example, topic 4, 12 and 16 are related to the aspects *environment*, *location* and *shopping*, respectively.

In the sentiment classification, we generate latent topics for the words in product-features using LaSA model θ. In θ, the topic mixture is drawn from a conjugate Dirichlet prior that remains the same for all the virtual context documents. Given a word w_i in the product-feature in the review, we may perform posterior inference to determine the conditional distribution of the hidden topic variables associated with w_i. Algorithm 1 describes w_i's latent topic generation, where, Mult($\theta(vd_i)$) refers to sample from the posterior distribution over topics given a virtual document vd_i.

Algorithm 1: Generate latent topic for w_i using K-topic LaSA model

```
Inputs:
• θ: LaSA model with multinomial distribution;
• Dirichlet(α): Dirichlet distribution with parameter α;
• w_i: Word in the product-feature in the review sentence;
Outputs:
• TP(w_i): Latent topic of w_i;
Steps:
begin
    • Extract virtual context document vd_i for w_i from the reviews;
    • Sample a topic distribution θ(vd_i) from Dirichlet(α);
    • foreach x_j ∈ vd_i do
        sample topic z_j ∈{ 1,...,K} from Mult(θ(vd_i));
        AddTo(z_j, Topics(vd_i));
    • TP(w_i) ←— topic z_k with the highest probability distribution
    in Topics(vd_i);
end
```

2.1.2 Unsupervised Domain-specific Sentiment Clue Extraction

Sentiment classifiers often loss accuracy in the domain customization due to unknown target domain sentiment words. In order to reduce the human efforts, we iteratively build domain-specific sentiment lexicon from the raw corpus.

Polarity	Sentiment clues in hotel domain
Positive	courteous, amazing location, high standard, breathtaking view, definitely worth, stylish, memorable, romantic, airy, spotlessly clean
Negative	inconvenient, remote, bit strange, boring, small room, dirty, outdated, disturb, low ceilings

Table 2: Domain-specific sentiment clue samples

We first group all the sentences into *positive*, *negative* and *neutral* subsets according to their sentiment polarity. Each sentence's polarity is detected according to the ratio of its positive and negative opinion words. The sentiment lexicon is initialized with the public generic sentiment lexicon. Given a n-gram ($1 \leq n \leq 3$) word sequence x_i. Let $F_{pos}(x_i)$ and $F_{neg}(x_i)$ be the frequency of x_i in the *positive* and *negative* sets, respectively. The difference between $F_{pos}(x_i)$ and $F_{neg}(x_i)$ is calculated by Equation 1. If *diff*> 1, then the frequencies are not similar. We consider x_i as a validate sentiment clue with enough sentiment distinguishing power.

$$diff = \frac{2 \times |F_{pos}(x_i) - F_{neg}(x_i)|}{\sqrt{F_{pos}^2(x_i) + F_{neg}^2(x_i)}} \quad (1)$$

In counting occurrences, if an item is preceded by a negation, its count in the oppositive corpus is increased by one. We iteratively build the domain-specific sentiment lexicon using the clues with higher sentiment scores ($|score| \geq 0.5$ in the experiments). The sentiment score is calculated according to its distribution difference in both sets using PMI [9]. Table 2 shows some sentiment clues extracted from hotel reviews.

2.2 Domain Customization Framework with Multi-level Latent Sentiment Clues

In order to minimize the efforts for customizing aspect-oriented sentiment classification, we present a MLSC-based customization framework to bridge the data gap across domains. Figure 1 shows MLSC-based domain customization framework in *OpinionIt*. In the domain customization, we first construct LaSA model θ to capture the latent association among product-features from the unlabeled source and target domain data. Latent topics of product-features are inferred using θ. Meanwhile, we extract domain-specific sentiment lexicon from the unlabeled source and target data. Then, the multi-level sentiment clues are extracted from the source training data by leveraging the domain customization resources. Finally the original sentiment classifier is tuned on the source training data by incorporating multi-level latent sentiment clues. The proposed customization framework may reduce the number of parameters required to model the target domain data. It can also improve the quality of the estimated parameters in the domain transfer.

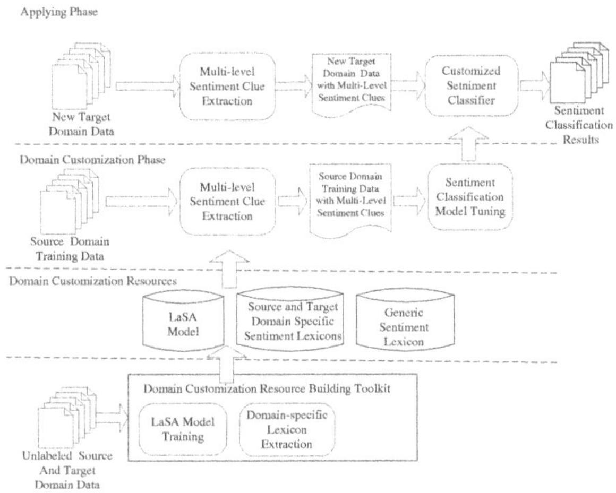

Figure 1: MLSC-based domain customization framework in OpinionIt

In the domain customization, each sentence s_i is characterized by the following multi-level latent sentiment clue (MLSC) set.

- Bag of non-stop words (BOW);
- Generic sentiment clue set (GSC): 1)Generic sentiment words; 2)The numbers of the positive/negative words; 3) Negation words (NW) and negation tag (NT);
- Domain-specific latent association clue set ($DLAC$): 1) Latent topic set (TP) of the headwords in product-features; The headword is defined as the last word in the term. 2) Candidate opinion word set (OW) which composed of all the adjectives in s_i; 3) Co-occurrence relation set $CR(TP, OW)$: all co-occurrence pairs of TP_k and OW_j in s_i; In the aspect-oriented sentiment classification, $DLAC$ is employed to characterize latent association among product-features and opinion words in s_i. $CR(TP, OW)$ provides useful hints for detecting the dynamically sentiment polarity of opinion words (e.g. "*high*", "*low*", "*small*", "*large*"). For example, according to the modified product-features, "*high quality*" is positive while "*high consumption*" is negative.
- Domain-specific sentiment clue set (DSC): 1) Domain-specific sentiment word set; 2) The number of domain-specific positive/negative words; 3) Overall sentiment distribution orientation of the sentiment words.

We employ Robust Risk Minimization classification method [10] to learn sentence-level sentiment classifier. In the modelling, the feature vector for each sentence is constructed with its MLSC set. The weight of each feature is calculated by MI [3]. Since negation clues NW, NT and the sentiment orientation have higher influence on the sentiment polarity of the sentence, we further multiply them by a predefined parameter δ (δ=5 in the experiments). This allows us to bias the learning algorithm so that the more relevant feature components have higher influence on the system decision.

3. EXPERIMENTAL RESULTS

In this section, we measure the efficiency of the proposed techniques on large-scale English and Chinese review corpus in Autocar (Aut), Hotel (Hot) and Movie (Mov) domains. We quantify the benefits of MLSC-based model in the cross-domain and in-domain sentiment classification. Training data is always an important concern in supervised learning methods in the real applications. Hence, we also investigate the effects of MLSC-based model on the size of training data.

English and Chinese reviews (totally 680,361 words) for Hotel and Autocar domains are extracted from several popular web sites. The sentiment polarity (i.e. positive, negative, neutral) of each review sentence is tagged manually. We also employ the public annotated English movie review corpus made by Bo Pang [8], which consists of only positive and negative sentences. In the experiments, we randomly held out around 20% data for test, and trained the classifiers on the remaining parts. In MLSC-based domain customization, we tune the sentiment classifier on the source domain training data with MLSC sets. Since most of product-features are noun terms, we extract $1 \sim 3$ continuous nouns from the corpus as product-feature candidates. All the LaSA models are built from the unlabeled source and target domain data. The number of topics is 100, and the context window size is {-3,3}. The hyper-parameters α is 0.1 and the number of iterations is 1,000.

Table 3 shows the experimental results for all the pairs of domain customization on English and Chinese corpus. Here, {*Aut, Hot, Mov*} are English domain-specific data sets while { *ZAut, ZHot*} are Chinese data sets. In the experiment, the basic source domain sentiment classifier SA_s is learned from the specific domain training data set D_{dom}. SA_s employs only the bag of non-stop words. Here, $dom \in$ {*Aut, Hot, Mov, ZAut, ZHot*}. *M-Base* directly employs SA_s in a new target domain, its F-measure in this basic transfer is considered as baseline (denoted by F_{base}). F_{dom}^{in} denotes the F-measure of the in-domain basic sentiment classifier, which is considered as top-line. In the domain customization, *M-MLSC* integrates all the multi-level sentiment clues while *M-GSC* integrates only the bag of non-stop words and the generic sentiment clues. $\Delta(F)$ and $\Delta(loss)$ denote the percentage change in F-measure and accuracy loss of *M-MLSC* or *M-GSC* over *M-Base*. The accuracy loss $loss = 1 - \frac{F}{F_{dom}^{in}}$.

Source → Target	F-measure in the domain transfer (%)			
	Baseline	M-GSC	M-MLSC	Top-line
Hot→Aut	70.44	72.07	73.13	F_{Aut}^{in}=71.22
Mov→Aut	57.78	62.16	64.67	F_{Aut}^{in}=71.22
Aut→Hot	76.91	78.21	79.54	F_{Hot}^{in}=82.95
Mov→Hot	63.35	67.84	70.61	F_{Hot}^{in}=82.95
Aut→Mov	55.37	57.52	61.12	F_{Mov}^{in}=76.65
Hot→Mov	58.21	59.95	62.86	F_{Mov}^{in}=76.65
ZHot→ZAut	61.72	68.27	69.38	F_{ZAut}^{in}=73.50
ZAut→ZHot	68.88	76.18	77.57	F_{ZHot}^{in}=78.99

Source → Target	$\Delta(F) = \frac{F - F_{Base}}{F_{Base}}$ (%)		$\Delta(loss) = \lvert 1 - \frac{loss}{loss_{Base}} \rvert$ (%)	
	M-GSC	M-MLSC	M-GSC	M-MLSC
Hot→Aut	+2.31	+3.82	209.08	346.47
Mov→Aut	+7.58	+11.92	32.58	51.24
Aut→Hot	+1.69	+3.42	21.50	43.50
Mov→Hot	+7.09	+11.47	22.90	37.05
Aut→Mov	+3.89	+10.39	10.11	27.03
Hot→Mov	+3.00	+7.99	9.46	25.21
ZHot→ZAut	+10.60	+12.41	40.66	47.58
ZAut→ZHot	+10.60	+12.62	72.21	85.95
Average	**+5.84**	**+9.25**	**52.31**	**83.00**

Table 3: Performance enhancement of *M-MLSC* and *M-GSC* over *M-Base* in the domain transfer.

Experimental results show that *M-MLSC* effectively enhances F-measure and reduces the accuracy loss in all the domain transfers (see Table 3). Compared with *M-Base*, *M-MLSC* significantly enhances F-measure by 9.25% and reduces the accuracy loss by 83.00% in average. *M-GSC* enhances F-measure by 5.84% and reduces the accuracy loss by 52.31% in average. Compared with *M-GSC*, *M-MLSC* further improves F-measure by 3.23% and reduces the accuracy loss by 37.17% in average. In *MLSC*-based customization method, latent topics and domain-specific sentiment clues provide very important hints for overcoming the domain difference. Even though word instances do not appear in a training corpus (or appear rarely) but are in similar context, they still might have relatively high probability in the same concept set and similar sentiment distribution.

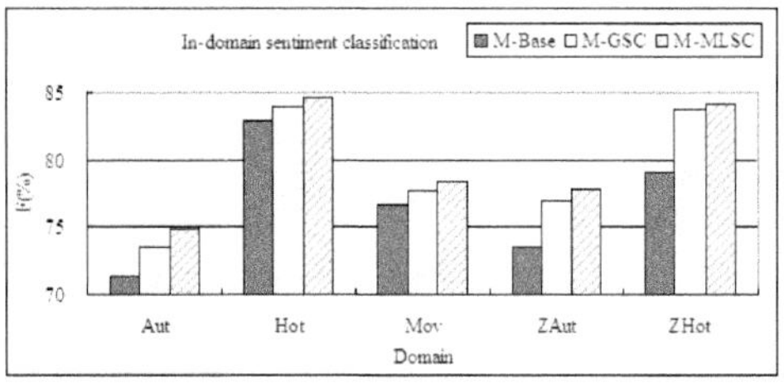

Figure 2: Effects of multi-level latent sentiment clues on in-domain sentiment classification

We also investigate effects of multi-level sentiment clues on in-domain sentiment classification (see Figure 2). In the experiments, the sentiment classifiers are trained on the in-domain training data. In the MLSC set construction, LaSA models and domain-specific sentiment lexicons are pre-constructed from the unlabeled in-domain data. Experimental results show that *M-MLSC* reduces much more errors than *M-Base* and *M-GSC* in the in-domain sentiment classification. Compared with *M-Base*, *M-MLSC* reduces more than 7% errors on English reviews, and more than 16% errors on Chinese reviews. All the multi-level sentiment clues make a good impact on the performance enhancement.

Training cost is a bottleneck for supervised learning methods since lots of manual efforts are required in tagging the instances. Hence, we compare the training efforts used in in-domain sentiment classification. Experimental results show that *M-MLSC* obtains much better performance with much less training data. Compared with *M-Base*, *M-MLSC* significantly reduces the labeled data size by 67.96% in average. Compared with *M-GSC*, *M-MLSC* also significantly reduces the training data size by 15.87% in average.

All the above experimental results show that *M-MLSC* better approximates the underlying data distribution by incorporating latent topics, domain-specific and generic sentiment clues. Especially, with latent topics, the model is no longer restricted to whether or not it knows a word; it now can know something about the concept group to which a word belongs, even if it does not know the word in the application. Hence, *M-MLSC* can customize the sentiment classification model more quickly with less efforts.

4. CONCLUSIONS

Domain customization is a big challenge for aspect-oriented sentiment classification. Supervised classifiers usually require large-scale labeled training data due to the limited sentiment clues in the review sentences. Hence, efficient and robust customization method is very important in the real applications. In the domain customization for the aspect-oriented opinion analysis system *OpinionIt*, we present a MLSC-based customization method. It effectively overcomes the domain difference without any labeled target domain data. Experimental results on English and Chinese corpus show that the proposed method significantly reduces the accuracy loss in the domain transfer. Compared with *M-Base* and *M-GSC* methods, MLSC-based customization method significantly reduces the accuracy loss by 83.00% and 37.17% in average, respectively. Moreover, MLSC-based model also significantly enhances the performance of in-domain sentiment classification with less training data. Compared with *M-Base* and *M-GSC*, MLSC-based method respectively significantly reduces the labeled data size by 67.96% and 15.87% in average. All the experimental results indicate that the proposed MLSC-based customization method better approximates the underlying data distribution by incorporating latent topics, domain-specific and generic sentiment clues. Given the encouraging results, we believe that the proposed approach is effective for practical aspect-oriented sentiment classification customization problems.

5. REFERENCES

[1] D. Blei, A. Ng, and M. Jordan. Latent dirichlet allocation. *Journal of Machine Learning Research*, 3(5):993–1022, 2003.

[2] J. Blitzer, M. Dredze, and F. Pereira. Biographies, bollywood, boom-boxes and blenders: Domain adaptation for sentiment classification. In *Proceedings of ACL'07*, pages 440–447, 2007.

[3] K. W. Church and P. Hanks. Word association norms, mutual information and lexicography. *Computational Linguistics*, 16(1):22–29, 1990.

[4] H. Guo, H. Zhu, Z. Guo, X. Zhang, and Z. Su. Product feature categorization with multi-level latent semantic association. In *Proceedings of CIKM09*, 2009.

[5] H. Guo, H. Zhu, Z. Guo, X. Zhang, and Z. Su. Opinionit: A text mining system for cross-lingual opinion analysis. In *Proceedings of CIKM10*, 2010.

[6] T. Li, V. Sindhwani, C. Ding, and Y. Zhang. Knowledge transformation for cross-domain sentiment classification. In *Proceedings of SIGIR'09*, 2009.

[7] S. J. Pan, X. Ni, J. Sun, Q. Yang, and Z. Chen. Cross-domain sentiment classification via spectral feature alignment. In *Proceedings of WWW2010*, 2010.

[8] P. Pang and L. Lee. A sentiment education: Sentiment analysis using subjectivity summarization based on minimum cuts. In *Proceedings of ACL04*, 2004.

[9] P. Turney. Thumbs up or thumbs down? semantic orientation applied to unsupervised classification of reviews. In *Proceedings of ACL'02*, 2002.

[10] T. Zhang, F. Damerau, and D. E. Johnson. Text chunking based on a generalization of Winnow. *Journal of Machine Learning Research*, 2:615–637, 2002.

Accurate Information Extraction for Quantitative Financial Events

Hassan H. Malik
hassan.malik
@thomsonreuters.com

Vikas S. Bhardwaj
vikas.bhardwaj
@thomsonreuters.com

Huascar Fiorletta
huascar.fiorletta
@thomsonreuters.com

Thomson Reuters
New York, NY, USA

ABSTRACT

In this paper, we present a novel financial event extraction system that achieves very high extraction quality by combining the outcome of statistical classifiers with a set of rules. Using expert-annotated press releases as training data, and novel feature generation schemes, our system learns multiple binary classifiers for each "slot" in a financial event. At runtime, common parsing and search indexing methods are used to normalize incoming press releases and to identify candidate event "slots". Rules are applied on candidates that satisfy a combination of classifiers, and the system confidence on extracted events is estimated using a unique confidence model learned from training data.

We present results of experiments performed on European corporate press releases for extracting dividend events, and show that our system achieves a precision of 96% and a recall of 79%.

Categories and Subject Descriptors

H.3.3 [**Information Storage and Retrieval**]: Information Search and Retrieval—*Retrieval models*; H.3.4 [**Information Storage and Retrieval**]: Systems and Software—*Question-answering (fact retrieval) systems*

General Terms

Algorithms, Experimentation, Performance

1. INTRODUCTION

Quantitative financial events such as corporate earnings announcements and revenue forecasts often serve as the primary driver for significant changes in asset prices in the financial markets worldwide. These events are typically delivered as unstructured text along with other information in corporate press releases over realtime news feeds. Structured delivery of important information pertaining to the events is preferred by professional investors and is also essential for algorithmic trading systems.

Considering that the precision of exisiting statistical systems is insufficient for practical use in the finance industry, financial information providers primarily rely on teams of professional analysts that constantly monitor news, and manually extract and publish events in a structured format.

Some highly customized, rule-based systems have also been developed to partially automate financial event extraction. However, these systems take a prolonged period of time to develop and require constant maintenance to accommodate for slight changes in the language of press releases.

In this paper, we present a novel event extraction system that achieves very high extraction quality by augmenting the outcome of multiple statistical classifiers with a set of rules. Since the bulk of the event extraction task is handled by the classifiers, and rules are merely used to handle exceptions, our approach significantly reduces the time needed to support new event types or to extend support of existing event types to new geographical markets. We also present a unique confidence estimation approach that classifies each extracted event into a set of predefined confidence categories.

2. RELATED WORK

Quantitative event extraction is an information extraction task that uses methods from information retrieval, machine learning, statistics and natural language processing along with other related research areas. It involves specialized pre-processing and normalization, entity recognition, relationship identification and confidence estimation. We refer the reader to [4] for a comprehensive survey.

Existing systems closest to our task are JASPER [1] and SCISOR [3]. Both of these systems are mainly rule-driven and use template-based pattern matching and other heuristic techniques. Our system uses a hybrid approach that combines statistical and rule-based methods and also assigns a confidence value to the extracted events. To the best of our knowledge, our system is the first such attempt in the domain of quantitative event extraction.

3. SYSTEM OVERVIEW

3.1 Terminology

We refer to the basic unit of information that is extracted from the unstructured press releases as a "fact". A fact, as we intend it, is a relevant financial event that our system is trained to detect and report. Common quantitative financial facts include corporate earnings, revenue, dividends, etc.

We may also think of fact extraction as a template filling

CIKM'11, October 24–28, 2011, Glasgow, Scotland, UK.

task. i.e., each fact may be considered as a template with a set of fields, some of which may be optional, and the task is to find suitable values for these fields from the unstructured content. We refer to each field in such template as a slot.

3.1.1 Learning Architecture

During the learning phase, a set of existing press releases are selected by expert analysts as training data for all target fact types. These press releases are first pre-processed to identify candidate facts and slots in each press release, and then presented to domain experts for annotation in a tool that was specifically developed for this purpose (Section 4.2). The annotated press releases are successively split in training and test sets used to construct the classification and confidence estimation models (Sections 4.3, 4.4 and 4.6). The resulting models and expert-written rules (Section 4.5) are then applied on the press releases in the test set in a way similar to the production phase. The results are subsequently evaluated by experts and additional iterations of this annotation/training cycle are made as needed.

3.1.2 Production Architecture

Our production system is organized as a multi-stage pipeline that receives XML requests containing the text of financial news enriched with some metadata. Each instance of the production system runs within a Jetty server, and scalability is achieved by concurrent stateless processing of multiple requests within each instance. Multiple production instances are used behind a hardware load balancer for fault-tolerance.

The first step in the production pipeline consists of pre-processing each press release with LUCENE and ANTLR for paragraph selection and tokenization respectively. The selected paragraphs are then analyzed in one pass over the data to identify candidate facts and slots, and features are extracted for each candidate to prepare instances for classification . The candidates are then classified using the statistical models obtained during the learning phase, and corresponding rules are applied on any positively identified candidates to handle known-errors, and to identify candidates that the classifiers are known to miss.

4. TRAINING THE SYSTEM

Given a set F of target fact types, a set T of training documents, and a set S of unique slot identifiers that contains all slots for facts in F, the training phase of our system begins with normalizing training documents.

4.1 Normalization and Tagging

Each document in T is normalized using an ANTLR-based tagging engine that uses a BNF grammar to identify synonyms such as "USD 0.05" and "5 US cents", and tokens that belong to the same category. For example Jan, January, and March all belong to the MONTH category. The normalized documents are then presented to analysts for annotation.

4.2 Annotation

The training data was annotated using a custom-developed tool that presents tagged documents to a human expert in a graphical user interface, and allows the user to identify and annotate the positive tokens for any slot in S from the set of candidates highlighted by the tagging engine (or to create tags that were missed by the tagging engine), while preserving the hierarchical nature of facts.

4.3 Feature Generation

The set of annotated facts is used to identify positive and negative examples for each slot where all slots of the same type but for a different kind of fact serve as negative examples.

For each example we then apply feature generation schemes on the marked up text that surrounds the target candidate in a window, the size of which is configurable. Our initial experiments have focused on extracting dividend and profit facts. For these fact types, we have experimented with many existing and novel feature generation schemes as shown below, and for each slot, selected a subset of these schemes based on our empirical evaluation (Section 6.1).

a) **Bag of Words (unigrams)**

b) **Delimiter-Present**: indicates delimiters occurring in the window

c) **Figure-Value threshold**: indicates if the numerical value of the slot is greater than pre-defined threshold

d) **Figure-Value-Log**: logarithm of the figure

e) **N-Grams**: bi/tri grams occurring in the window

f) **Distance-Farthest/Distance-Closest**: These schemes add a feature for each tag (word, phrase or normalized text) from a list of pre-defined tags for each slot type (selected based on domain knowledge) that occurs in the window. The feature value represents the spatial distance between the candidate slot and the matched tag. The Distance-Farthest scheme uses distance of the farthest instance of each matching tag as the feature value whereas the Distance-Closest scheme uses distance of the closest instance of each matching tag as the feature value.

g) **Before-Or-After**: This scheme adds a feature for each token/tag that occurs in a list of pre-defined tokens/tags. The feature is assigned a value of 1, 0 or -1 if the token/tag occurs after the candidate slot in the window, does not exist in the window, or exists before the candidate slot in the window, respectively.

h) **Period-in-Context**: This scheme applies to time-period-dependent fact types, and adds a feature with value = 1 if the time-period obtained from the document context (such as document title or metadata) matches the period specified in the window.

i) **Closest Single Matching Tag on Left / Right**: This scheme adds a feature indicating the single matching tag that occurs closest to the candidate slot, on its left or right, where the tag is taken from the same list as the Distance-Closest scheme.

After feature extraction we normalize values of all real valued textual features to the same scale by applying z-score standardization, and the resulting instances are then used to train the classification models for each slot.

4.4 Training and Combining Classifiers

We have used two different classification algorithms in our system, i.e., Linear SVMs and the Feature Weighting Classifier (FWC) [2]. Both of these algorithms are trained in linear-time and have been successfully applied to a variety of text classification problems.

Since the raw classification scores assigned to a particular sample does not accurately reflect the probability of the sample belonging to a particular class, we re-scale the classifier scores using isotonic regression, which have been successfully used to obtain accurate class membership probability estimates for binary and multiclass problems [5]. We then combine the re-scaled scores of SVM and FWC using a weighted linear combination, where the weights were determined empirically, for each fact and slot-type.

4.5 Rules

In addition to using a combination of statistical classifiers, our system also incorporates a rule engine. Unlike existing rule-based systems, our system does not use rules as primary means for extracting the desired information from unstructured text, but instead uses rules to handle exceptions and to improve the overall system precision. In particular, the rules in our system aim to cover the following cases:

a) Handle rarely used verbiage or reporting standards, i.e., situations where high-precision classifiers could not be practically trained because of a lack of training examples.

b) Presence of outlier cases that are almost always incorrectly classified by the statistical classifiers.

c) Pruning certain types of samples from being classified. For example, our system uses a rule to exclude valid, but previously declared dividends (e.g., dividend for the same period last year) from being reported, to satisfy a business requirement.

4.6 Confidence Model

We also train a confidence model that is used to estimate and report the system confidence on each extracted fact. Our confidence estimation scheme focuses on measuring the textual similarity of an unseen press release against the training corpus. The confidence classes used in our system include HIGH, GOOD, MODERATE, and LOW. Confidence estimation allows users to act on the automatically extracted facts based on their tolerance to risks associated with acting on potentially incorrect information.

Our confidence model consists of a bi-gram corpus constructed from the annotated training set. All bi-grams that occur in windows surrounding each fact instance in the training set are added to this corpus, maintaining their frequency counts. This corpus is then used in the production phase to estimate the system confidence on extracted facts.

5. FACT FINDING

The real-time fact finding process consists of receiving a new document D as input, preprocessing the document and identifying candidates for each fact from a list of unique facts F and a unique slots S for each fact, classifying the candidates for each slot in S, applying relevant rules, assigning confidence and reporting the extracted fact. We now explain these steps in detail.

a) **Preprocessing** The incoming document is first indexed using Apache Lucene. Then for each fact in F, the document is queried with relevant keywords (identified by domain experts) to retrieve paragraphs that may potentially contain the fact.

b) **Candidate Selection and Feature Extraction** The selected paragraphs are normalized and tagged using the process explained in Section 4.1

c) **Classification and Classifier Combination** The candidate instances are then classified using the models trained in Section 4.4. Raw scores from SVM and FWC classifiers are normalized using isotonic regression. The normalized scores are then combined using the method explained in Section 4.4 and the resulting score is used to classify the candidate instance as positive or negative.

Condition	Confidence			
	HIGH	GOOD	MODERATE	LOW
If score >	$\mu + 2\sigma$	$\mu + \sigma$	μ - σ	otherwise

Table 1: Thresholds for confidence assessment, μ is mean and σ is standard deviation of the training corpus scores

d) **Applying Rules** Depending on the fact and slot type of a positively classified instance, the rule engine is optionally invoked in order to prune common errors, and to handle the other situations explained in Section 4.5.

e) **Computing Confidence Scores**

We finally estimate confidence on each extracted fact. We use the normalized window text to create a corpus of bigrams B. The confidence score is then calculated as follows:

$$ConfidenceScore = \frac{\sum_{b \in B} counts(b)}{|B|}$$

where $counts(b)$ indicates the number of times the bigram b appears in the training corpus (section 4.6). Various thresholds that use mean and standard deviation of window scores in the training corpus are then applied to map the confidence score to a confidence class (Table 1).

6. EMPIRICAL EVALUATION

Our dataset consisted of English financial press releases for European companies from January 2006 to May 2010. Our experiments focused on Dividend and Profit facts; selected based on business priorities in our organization.

We first compare various feature generation schemes and classifier combination methods on the main slots for each fact type, i.e., the dividend and profit figure slots, using a 10-fold cross-validation on the annotated data. Note that these experiments are limited to the main slots, and no rules are applied at this stage. Additional slots must be obtained before the fact is considered to be complete and publishable. Section 6.3 evaluates our system on complete facts.

6.1 Comparing Feature Generation Schemes

In this section we compare the feature generation schemes discussed in Section 4.3. We used Bag-of-words as our baseline scheme and measured the incremental improvement achieved by each feature generation scheme, when combined with bag of words. Tables 2 and 3 present the results of this experiment for the dividend and profit figures, respectively. We observe that not all schemes are effective for all slots. Therefore, the final classifiers for each slot were constructed using a subset of feature generation schemes that yielded at-least some improvement over the bag-of-words baseline. For example, the precision and recall results in the last row of Table 3 were obtained by using all schemes to generate features, except "Period In Context".

6.2 Classifiers and Classifier Combination

In this section we compare the performance of SVM against that of FWC. We performed a 5-fold cross validation on the

Features	Precision	Recall
BOW	0.94	0.95
BOW+nGrams	0.96	0.97
BOW+Before-Or-After	0.97	0.96
BOW+Period-in-Context	0.94	0.95
BOW+Delimiters	0.95	0.95
BOW+Distance	0.96	0.94
BOW+ClosestWordLeft	0.97	0.96
BOW+Figure-Threshold	0.95	0.93
BOW+Figure-Value-Log	0.94	0.95
ALL	0.98	0.97

Table 2: The performance of feature generation schemes on the Dividend-Figure

Features	Precision	Recall
BOW	0.86	0.87
BOW+nGrams	0.87	0.88
BOW+Before-or-After	0.88	0.87
BOW+Period-In-Context	0.85	0.87
BOW+Delimiters	0.86	0.88
BOW+Distance	0.91	0.92
BOW+Figure-Threshold	0.90	0.88
BOW+Figure-Value-Log	0.92	0.91
BOW+ClosestWordLeft	0.91	0.90
ALL	0.97	0.96

Table 3: The performance of feature generation schemes on the Profit-Figure

dividend-figure slot. From Table 4, we observe that SVM outperforms FWC in terms of precision, whereas FWC outperforms SVM in terms of recall, thus motivating us to combine the outcome of these methods.

Set	SVM		FWC	
	Prec	Recall	Prec	Recall
1	0.98	0.94	0.83	0.97
2	0.98	0.94	0.82	0.97
3	0.99	0.92	0.80	0.98
4	0.98	0.95	0.79	0.99
5	0.99	0.95	0.84	0.99

Table 4: Comparing SVM and FWC classifiers (for the Dividend-Figure)

As we have explained in Section 4.4, our system computes the final classification score as a weighted linear combination of normalized individual classifier scores. To determine weights for the classification methods, we applied 10-fold cross validation on training data for dividend and profit figures, and evaluated three different weight combinations. Table 5 presents the results of this experiment. We observe that the best performance is achieved when SVM and FWC are assigned 70% and 30% weight, respectively. Therefore, we used these weights in the rest of our experiments.

6.3 Overall System Performance

All the results presented so far cover a single slot. It is therefore important to evaluate the overall system performance when a fact is obtained by combining several slots, each with its own classifier and rules.

For this purpose, we applied our system on a new set of 604 press releases from a period of 16 months, not all of

Combination Method	Dividend		Profit	
	Prec	Recall	Prec	Recall
Linear SVM_70 FWC_30	0.98	0.97	0.97	0.96
Linear SVM_50 FWC_50	0.97	0.95	0.98	0.97
Linear SVM_30 FWC_70	0.94	0.95	0.91	0.90

Table 5: Different classifier combination methods for dividend and profit

Facts				
Extracted	Good/High Conf.	Correct	Actual	Missed
454	414	398	503	82

Precision	Recall
0.96	0.79

Table 6: Overall system performance for Dividend Facts

which contained facts. Our team of annotators manually verified the system output and inspected the press releases for additional unreported facts. Table 6 presents the results of this experiment. Our system achieved a precision of 96% and a recall of 79%, when the facts were classified as high or good confidence. It is important to note that the system identified many additional facts in lower confidence categories but these facts are not included in the system output because of high-precision requirements in our domain.

7. CONCLUSIONS AND FUTURE WORK

We have presented a novel event extraction system that uses a combination of multiple binary classifiers and manually written rules, where the bulk of the extraction task is handled by the statistical classifiers and rules are used to handle exceptions. We also present a unique approach to estimate system confidence on each extracted fact.

In the future, we plan to extend our system to support additional quantitative fact-types such as revenue and earnings per share, and non-quantitative events such as mergers and acquisitions.

8. REFERENCES

[1] P. M. Andersen, P. J. Hayes, A. K. Huettner, L. M. Schmandt, I. B. Nirenburg, and S. P. Weinstein. Automatic extraction of facts from press releases to generate news stories. In *Proceedings of the third conference on Applied natural language processing*, ANLC '92, pages 170–177, 1992.

[2] H. Malik, D. Fradkin, and F. Moerchen. Single pass text classification by direct feature weighting. *Knowledge and Information Systems*, pages 1–20, 2010. 10.1007/s10115-010-0317-9.

[3] L. F. Rau and P. S. Jacobs. Integrating top-down and bottom-up strategies in a text processing system. In *Proceedings of the second conference on Applied natural language processing*, ANLC '88, pages 129–135, 1988.

[4] S. Sarawagi. Information extraction. *Found. Trends databases*, 1:261–377, March 2008.

[5] B. Zadrozny and C. Elkan. Transforming classifier scores into accurate multiclass probability estimates. In *Proceedings of the eighth ACM SIGKDD international conference on Knowledge discovery and data mining*, KDD '02, pages 694–699, New York, NY, USA, 2002. ACM.

A Machine-Learned Proactive Moderation System for Auction Fraud Detection

Liang Zhang
Yahoo! Labs
Sunnyvale, CA, USA
liangzha@yahoo-inc.com

Jie Yang
Yahoo! Labs
Sunnyvale, CA, USA
jielabs@yahoo-inc.com

Wei Chu
Microsoft
Bellevue, WA, USA
chu.wei@microsoft.com

Belle Tseng
Yahoo! Labs
Sunnyvale, CA, USA
belle@yahoo-inc.com

ABSTRACT

Online auction and shopping are gaining popularity with the growth of web-based eCommerce. Criminals are also taking advantage of these opportunities to conduct fraudulent activities against honest parties with the purpose of deception and illegal profit. In practice, proactive moderation systems are deployed to detect suspicious events for further inspection by human experts. Motivated by real-world applications in commercial auction sites in Asia, we develop various advanced machine learning techniques in the proactive moderation system. Our proposed system is formulated as optimizing bounded generalized linear models in multi-instance learning problems, with intrinsic bias in selective labeling and massive unlabeled samples. In both offline evaluations and online bucket tests, the proposed system significantly outperforms the rule-based system on various metrics, including area under ROC (AUC), loss rate of labeled frauds and customer complaints. We also show that the metrics of loss rates are more effective than AUC in our cases.

Categories and Subject Descriptors

I.2.6 [**Artificial Intelligence**]: Learning—*parameter learning*; H.2.8 [**Database Management**]: Database Applications—*data mining*

General Terms

Algorithms, Experimentation, Measurement, Performance

Keywords

Auction, Fraud Detection, Multi-Instance Learning

1. INTRODUCTION

Since the commercialization of the world wide web in the mid-1990's, online marketplaces have been widely explored by commercial organizations for brand awareness and revenue sources.

Individuals are able to buy and sell a broad variety of goods and services worldwide on online auction and shopping websites, e.g. eBay and Amazon. However, criminals have also attempted to conduct fraudulent activities against honest parties for the purpose of illegitimate profit. On Internet auction sites, auction fraud mainly involves fraud attributable to the misrepresentation of a product advertised for sale or the non-delivery of products purchased through an Internet auction site. Malicious sellers may post an (even non-existing) item for bidding with false description to deceive the buyer concerning its true value, and request payments to be wired directly to them. By using wire transfer services, the money is virtually unrecoverable for the victim. Similarly, malicious buyers may make a purchase via a fraudulent credit card where the address of the card holder does not match the shipping address. Both consumers and merchants can be victims of online auction fraud, as well as the commercial auction websites.

Normally, it is the commercial auction websites' obligation to provide insurance to cover the users' loss up to a certain amount. To reduce this compensation as well as maintain their reputation, the auction websites usually employ human experts to investigate their sellers and buyers as often as possible. Clearly the workload is prohibitive to look into every single event. In practice, moderation systems are widely deployed to detect suspicious events proactively for further inspection by human experts, and most moderation systems operate with rule-based decision-making processors that only funnel the suspicious cases to human experts and leave the remaining without inspection. The rules are created by expert knowledge to represent sellers' suspiciousness on fraudulent activities. The outputs of these rules are usually boolean, either positively or negatively suspicious. The final moderation decision is based on a weighted combination of the rule outputs, where the weights are also determined by expert knowledge. After deployment, such a moderation system is capable of automatically selecting a subset of suspicious events for investigation to keep experts' workload at a reasonable level. However model update in such rule-based moderation systems is still not automatic, since the weights on rule outputs have to be set manually by human experts.

Patterns of auction fraud are changing dynamically and rapidly. To maintain the selection/filter accuracy, moderation systems have to be updated periodically to catch the drifting patterns. It is desirable to design a learning system that is capable of automatically optimizing weights for the rules based on recent observations. Motivated by applications in a commercial online auction website, we develop various advanced machine learning techniques in the proactive moderation system. The existing rule-based moderation system in the online auction website selects 20%-40% of the overall events for experts to examine and label. Our initial system is simply built upon the labeled subset by optimizing a generalized linear model. By noting the imbalanced labels (fraud rate is usually under 1%) and the limitation of rule-based features designed for the fraud detection, we improve the system by constraining the weights to be positive and introducing imbalanced/weighted loss functions. To overcome the selection bias in labeling, we also include the remaining unlabeled cases into training for unbiasedness. Being aware of specific noise patterns in the expert labels, we further enhance the optimization as done in multi-instance learning problems. The final model is formulated as optimizing unbounded generalized linear models in multi-instance learning problems, with intrinsic bias in selective labeling and massive unlabeled samples.

2. OUR METHODOLOGY

Our application is one of the major online auction sites in Asia. Lots of items are posted for bidding every day. Each item is sent to the proactive anti-fraud system to assess the risk of being a fraud. The existing system is featured by:

- **Rule-based features**: Human experts with many years of experience created more than 30 rules for fraud detection. Each rule can be regarded as a binary feature that indicates the fraud likeliness. For example, a possible rule could be whether the seller's rating or reputation score is higher than a certain threshold. However, we cannot list the rules and their importance here due to confidentiality.
- **Linear scoring function**: The existing system only supports linear models. Given a set of weights on features, the fraud score is computed as the weighted sum.
- **Selective labeling**: If the fraud score is above a certain threshold, the item will be investigated by human experts, otherwise it will be passed by the system. The final result is labeled as fraud or clean. Items of higher scores have higher priority to be reviewed by experts.
- **Fraud churn**: Once one item is judged as fraud, it is very likely that the seller is not trustable and may be also selling other frauds, therefore all the items submitted by the same seller are labeled as fraud too, and the seller's account will be suspended by the website immediately.
- **User feedback**: Buyers can file a claim if they become victims of fraud. Similarly sellers may also complain if his/her items have been judged as fraud mistakenly.

Motivated by these specific attributes in the existing moderation system, we propose several statistical machine learning models incrementally to improve the fraud detection performance.

2.1 Weighted Logistic Regression

Let us denote the binary response variable from the expert labeled data as y, i.e. fraud if $y = 1$; otherwise $y = 0$. For each observation i, denote the corresponding feature set as $\boldsymbol{x}_i$. The logistic regression, one of the most natural probabilistic model is defined as $P[y_i = 1] = \frac{1}{1+\exp(-\boldsymbol{x}_i'\boldsymbol{\beta})}$, where $\boldsymbol{\beta}$ is the unknown coefficient vector. Suppose each observation i is further associated with a weight w_i. The corresponding loss function with L_k penalty on $\boldsymbol{\beta}$ [3, 6] becomes

$$\mathscr{L} = \sum_i w_i[y_i \log(1+\exp(-\boldsymbol{x}_i'\boldsymbol{\beta})) + (1-y_i)\log(1+\exp(\boldsymbol{x}_i'\boldsymbol{\beta})) + \rho\|\boldsymbol{\beta}\|_k], \quad (1)$$

where ρ is the trade-off parameter to control the shrinkage of $\boldsymbol{\beta}$ and can be estimated by cross-validation. In this paper we mainly consider $k = 2$, which is equivalent to assigning a Gaussian prior $N(\mathbf{0}, \delta \boldsymbol{I})$ on $\boldsymbol{\beta}$, where $\delta = 1/(2\rho \sum_i w_i)$.

In the case where we have no domain knowledge on w_i, it is common to assume all $w_i = 1$. We call this model **LR** (i.e. standard logistic regression). However, in scenarios when the positive rate of Y in the training data is too low (e.g. less than 1%), it is also common to up-weight the positive samples or down-sample the negatives. In this paper we assume all the positive samples have the same weight w_1, and all the negative samples have weight 1. The optimal w_1 can be determined by cross-validation in criterion of predictive performance. We call the weighted logistic regression as **WLR**. We optimize the models by minimizing the loss functions through the standard L-BFGS algorithm [4, 7].

2.2 Coefficient Bounds for Fraud Detection

It is always important to incorporate domain knowledge into the model, which can sometimes boost the model performance. In our fraud detection system, the feature set $\boldsymbol{x}$ was proposed by experts with years of experience. Currently all the features are in fact binary "rules", i.e. any violation of one rule should somehow increase the probability of fraud. However, simply fitting the model by equation (1) might generate negative coefficients on some of the features, because given limited training data, the sample size might be too small for those coefficients to converge to the right values, or when some features are highly correlated. Hence we bound the coefficients of those binary "rules" to force them to be equal or greater than 0. Specifically, we consider the following optimization problem

$$\min_{\boldsymbol{\beta}} \sum_i w_i[y_i \log(1+\exp(-\boldsymbol{x}_i'\boldsymbol{\beta})) + (1-y_i)\log(1+\exp(\boldsymbol{x}_i'\boldsymbol{\beta})) + \rho\|\boldsymbol{\beta}\|_k], \quad (2)$$

such that $\boldsymbol{\beta} \geq \boldsymbol{T}$. where for feature j, T_j is 0 in our problem. Note that T_j can also be set as other values if domain knowledge is available. When $w_i = 1$ for all i, we call the model **BLR** (bounded logistic regression). For pre-defined w_i values, we call the model **WBLR** (weighted **BLR**).

2.3 Removing the Selection Bias

As introduced in Section 1, the existing rule-based moderation system only sends the cases with high risky score for experts to review and label; hence the labeled training data is not generated through a random selection. Note that in the real world, many such online auction fraud detection systems would not allow an entirely random selection scheme to generate the training data: it is simply too expensive and ineffective. Instead usually a set of hand-tuned rules are used in the initial system to provide the basic fraud detection function. Therefore, it is important to correct the selection bias and leverage the data without labels to improve the model.

The simplest idea to remove the selection bias is to assume all events that are not labeled by the current system are defined as not fraud with a low confidence. Mathematically, denoting $\boldsymbol{z}_j$ to be the feature set for an unlabeled event j, we want to solve

$$\min_{\boldsymbol{\beta}} \sum_i w_i[y_i \log(1+\exp(-\boldsymbol{x}_i'\boldsymbol{\beta})) + (1-y_i)\log(1+\exp(\boldsymbol{x}_i'\boldsymbol{\beta})) + \rho\|\boldsymbol{\beta}\|_k] + \sum_j \tilde{w}_j[\log(1+\exp(\boldsymbol{z}_j'\boldsymbol{\beta})) + \rho\|\boldsymbol{\beta}\|_k], \quad (3)$$

such that $\boldsymbol{\beta} \geq \boldsymbol{T}$. For simplicity we could assume all $\tilde{w}_j = \tilde{w}$, i.e. all the unselected events having the same confidence to be non-fraud. When $\tilde{w} = 0$, it implies the training data is selected randomly so no need to adjust for the selection bias. When $\tilde{w} = 1$ ($w_i = 1$ for non-fraud), it implies we hold high confidence as in expert labels that all the events that are not selected by the current system are non-fraud. Usually when $w_i = 1$, the optimal $\tilde{w}$ should be within the range $(0, 1)$, and it can be calculated through cross-validation. We call this model **WBLRRSB** (**WBLR** after removing selection bias (**RSB**)). An alternative approach of using the data without labels is to treat the responses as missing values and apply the EM algorithm [1] to fit the model. However, this approach does not take the domain knowledge that the selection of training is in fact biased; instead it purely relies on the features to fill in the missing responses iteratively. Hence in practice, it is proven to perform worse than **WBLRRSB**.

2.4 Multiple Instance Learning

When we looked into the actual expert reviewing and labeling process, we noted that the experts actually assign labels in a "bagged" fashion, i.e. for each seller id, one expert looks through all of his/her posted items, and if the expert finds any item as fraud, all of this seller id's posted items are labeled as fraud. In literature the models for this scenario are called "Multiple Instance Learning" [2, 5]. Suppose for each labeled seller i, there are K_i number of cases. For these cases, the labels should be identical, thus can be denoted as y_i. The multiple instance learning model with logistic function becomes $P[y_i = 1] = 1 - \prod_{j=1}^{K_i} \frac{1}{1+\exp(\boldsymbol{x}_j'\boldsymbol{\beta})}$, which is essentially a noisy-or likelihood function. The noisy-or likelihood function only requires a subset of the events in the bag are fraud rather than all are fraud events. The optimization problem can thus be written as

$$\begin{aligned}\min_{\boldsymbol{\beta}} \quad & \sum_i w_i[-y_i \log(1 - \prod_{j=1}^{K_i} \frac{1}{1+\exp(\boldsymbol{x}_j'\boldsymbol{\beta})}) \\ & +(1-y_i)\sum_{j=1}^{K_i} \log(1+\exp(\boldsymbol{x}_i'\boldsymbol{\beta})) + \rho K_i \|\boldsymbol{\beta}\|_k] \\ & + \sum_j \tilde{w}_j [\log(1+\exp(\boldsymbol{z}_j'\boldsymbol{\beta})) + \rho\|\boldsymbol{\beta}\|_k], \end{aligned} \quad (4)$$

such that $\boldsymbol{\beta} \geq \boldsymbol{T}$. We call this model **WBMILRSB** (weighted and bounded (**WB**) multiple instance learning (**MIL**) after removing selection bias (**RSB**)).

3. EXPERIMENTS

This section starts with experiment settings and metrics in evaluation, and then report extensive experimental results of both offline evaluations and online bucket tests to demonstrate the performance of the various proposed techniques.

3.1 Experiment Settings

We evaluated our proposed models from Section 2 using data from a major Asian online auction website which attracts a big volume of items posted for bidding every day. Our experiments consist of offline evaluations and online A/B tests. For offline evaluation, we were able to test all the models from Section 2 on two-months of log data. For online A/B test, we compared our best model **WBMILRSB** based on the offline experiments with the **Expert** model, which was used by the system with expert-crafted rules and weights.

For offline evaluations, we created our training and test data set via a bias sampling scheme from the real data set to avoid releasing the company confidential information. Our training data contains around 1M labeled cases with around 12K fraud cases from Sep 2010. Our test data also contains around 1M labeled cases with 7.6K fraud cases from Oct 2010. The number of unlabeled cases in each data is about 3M to 5M. For testing models we also obtained a sample of 446 customer fraud complaint cases in Oct 2010. The offline experiments and results are shown in Section 3.3. Note that due to the company policy concerns, we are unable to reveal what features are used in our experiments.

Model	AUC	Loss Rate of Frauds	Loss Rate of Complaints
Expert	0.724	0.00%	34.66%
LR	0.903	16.07%	55.61%
BLR	0.924	7.40%	40.56%
WBLR	0.923	4.21%	26.17%
WBLRRSB	0.922	2.83%	20.75%
WBMILRSB	0.926	2.07%	20.73%

Table 1: Offline evaluation of the model performance. The loss rate of labeled frauds and customer complaints are obtained given 100% workload rate.

3.2 Metrics for Offline Evaluation

We considered three metrics for offline model evaluation: Area under ROC curve (AUC), the loss rate of labeled frauds and the loss rate of customer complaints. The AUC is a traditional metric that people use a lot for measuring model performance. However for our scenario with labeling bias, we will show in Section 3.3 that simply using AUC might not be optimal.

Note that the training and test data were generated as follows: for each case the existing rule-based moderation system uses a human-tuned linear scoring function to determine whether to send it for expert labeling. If so, experts review it and make a fraud or non-fraud judgment; otherwise it would be considered as clean and not reviewed by anyone. Therefore, two concerns arise: a). For those cases that are not reviewed by experts, we would never know whether they are fraud or not. b). If we want to propose a new machine-learned scoring model to replace the existing one, we have to make sure it is able to catch more frauds with the same or lower expert labeling workload.

For test data, we regard the number of labeled cases as the expected 100% workload of labeling N items. For any model we could re-rank all the cases (labeled and unlabeled) by the model scores in the test set and select the first M cases with the highest scores. We call the fraction M/N the "workload rate" in the following discussion. Assume the total number of labeled frauds in test is F and the total number of reported complaints is C. For a specific workload rate such as 100%, we could count the number of labeled fraud cases F_m and the number of reported complaints C_m in the M cases. We define the loss rate of labeled frauds as $1 - F_m/F$ and the loss rate of customer complaints as $1 - C_m/C$ given the workload rate M/N. We argue model A is better than model B if given the same workload rate, both the loss rates of labeled frauds and customer complaints of model A are lower than those of B. For the **Expert** model which is exactly how the training and test data are generated 100% workload rate, the loss rate of labeled frauds becomes 0 while the loss rate of customer complaints is usually greater than 0. Therefore, these two metrics might not be appropriate when used to compare the machine-learned models with the **Expert**, but these are very useful measures to compare two machine-learned models.

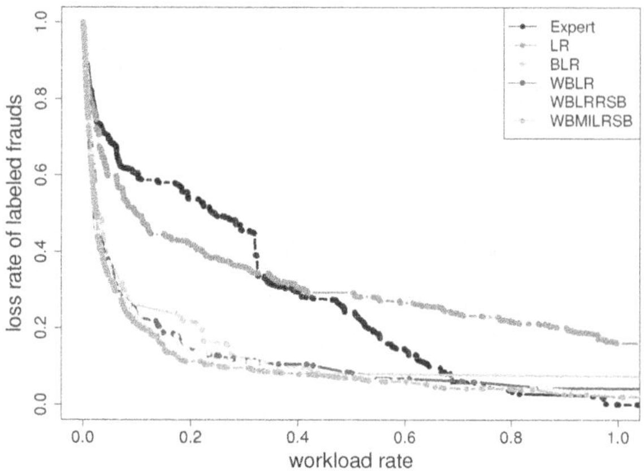

Figure 1: Offline evaluation: Workload rate versus the loss rates of labeled frauds for all the models.

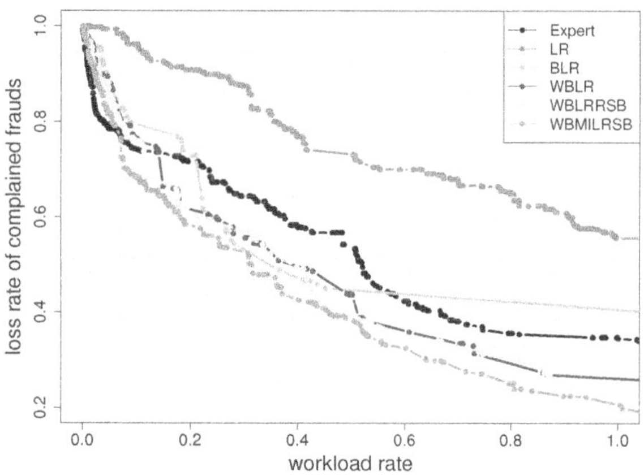

Figure 2: Offline evaluation: Workload rate versus the loss rates of customer complaints for all the models.

3.3 Offline Experiments

In this section we show the performance of the test data for 6 models: **Expert**, **LR**, **BLR**, **WBLR**, **WBLRRSB** and **WBMILRSB**. Table 1 summarizes the three metrics discussed in Section 3.2: AUC, the loss rate of labeled frauds, and the loss rate of customer complaints. The latter two are obtained given 100% workload rate. Note the loss rate of labeled frauds for the Expert model is always 0 since the test data is generated by it. Figure 1 and Figure 2 show the loss rates of the labeled frauds as well as customer complaints given different workload rates for all the models.

According to the AUC numbers, the machine-learned **LR** is much better than the human-tuned model **Expert**. It also seems obviously that the four models **BLR**, **WBLR**, **WBLRRSB** and **WBMILRSB** are better than **LR**, although among them there is very little difference when comparing AUC. However, when looking at the loss rates of labeled frauds and customer complaints, we saw a significant performance difference between **BLR** and **WBMILRSB**, and we started to doubt that **LR** and **BLR** can work well in the real auction fraud detection system since their loss rates of customer complaints look much worse than the **Expert** model! On the other hand, the numbers in the table suggest **WBMILRSB** to be the winning model that would improve the existing moderation system significantly.

Our intuition behind why AUC is not working well in our scenario is as follows: it only considers the labeled test data while ignoring the unlabeled part. In scenarios when the training and test set are biased, the AUC metric can be really misleading. On the other hand, our proposed two metrics utilize the unlabeled data and extra unbiased information such as customer complaints. This is very important to note when doing offline experiments and evaluation.

3.4 Online A/B Test

We performed online A/B test during April-May, 2011, which compared two models: our best model **WBMILRSB** and the expert-crafted **Expert** model. We used the last 30 days data for the daily training and tuned the threshold of **WBMILRSB** scores so that the workload generated by this model is roughly the same everyday. Running 4 weeks of A/B test, we observed that **WBMILRSB** significantly outperformed **Expert** by catching 25.5% more frauds and reducing the customer complaints by 15.7%, while using only 74.2% of the expert workload.

4. CONCLUSION

In this paper, we introduced various advanced machine learning techniques for real world auction fraud detection systems. By extensive offline experiments and online bucket test, we have shown our proposed model significantly outperforms the existing human-tuned rule-based system. Compared with baselines, we show that the multiple instance learning model with bounded coefficients and properly weighted observations after removing the selection bias performs the best. Hence we have pushed this model to production. For model evaluation, besides using traditional metrics such as area under ROC (AUC), we introduced two extra metrics under this fraud detection framework. We show that these metrics are more effective than AUC or ROC for distinguishing the best models.

5. REFERENCES

[1] A. Dempster, N. Laird, and D. Rubin. Maximum likelihood from incomplete data via the em algorithm. *Journal of the Royal Statistical Society. Series B (Methodological)*, 39(1):1–38, 1977.

[2] T. Dietterich, R. Lathrop, and T. Lozano-Pérez. Solving the multiple instance problem with axis-parallel rectangles. *Artificial Intelligence*, 89(1-2):31–71, 1997.

[3] A. Hoerl and R. Kennard. Ridge regression: Biased estimation for nonorthogonal problems. *Technometrics*, 12(1):55–67, 1970.

[4] D. Liu and J. Nocedal. On the limited memory bfgs method for large scale optimization. *Mathematical programming*, 45(1):503–528, 1989.

[5] V. Raykar, B. Krishnapuram, J. Bi, M. Dundar, and R. Rao. Bayesian multiple instance learning: automatic feature selection and inductive transfer. In *Proceedings of the 25th international conference on Machine learning*, pages 808–815. ACM, 2008.

[6] R. Tibshirani. Regression shrinkage and selection via the lasso. *Journal of the Royal Statistical Society. Series B (Methodological)*, 58(1):267–288, 1996.

[7] C. Zhu, R. Byrd, P. Lu, and J. Nocedal. L-bfgs-b: Fortran subroutines for large-scale bound constrained optimization. *ACM Transactions on Mathetmatical Software*, 23(4):550–560, 1997.

Simultaneously Improving CSAT and Profit in a Retail Banking Organization

Sameep Mehta
IBM Research - India
sameepmehta@in.ibm.com

Ullas Nambiar
IBM Research - India
ubnambiar@in.ibm.com

Vishal Batra
IBM Research - India
vibatra1@in.ibm.com

Sumit Negi
IBM Research - India
sumitneg@in.ibm.com

Prasad M Deshpande
IBM Research - India
prasdesh@in.ibm.com

Gyana Parija
IBM Research - India
gyana.parija@in.ibm.com

ABSTRACT

Customer satisfaction (CSAT) is the key driver for retention and growth in retail banking and several techniques have been applied by banks to achieve this. For instance, banks in emerging markets with high footfall in branches have gone beyond the traditional approach of segmenting customers and services to optimizing the wait time for customers visiting the bank's branch. While this approach has significantly improved service quality, it has also added a new dimension in the service quality metric :- pro-actively identify and address customer needs for (i) efficient banking experience and (ii) enhancing profit by selling additional services to existing customer. In this paper we present a system that addresses the challenge involved in providing better service to retail banking customer while ensuring that a larger share of customer's wallet comes to the branch. We do this by combining predictive analytics, scheduling and process optimization techniques.

Categories and Subject Descriptors

H.4.1 [**Office Automation**]: Workflow management; J.7 [**Computers in Other Systems**]: Consumer products

General Terms

Design, Economics, Management

Keywords

Retail Banking, Profit Maximization, Branch Banking

1. INTRODUCTION

Customer centric service delivery organizations like telecommunication, retail, financial service providers etc are always under pressure to retain and grow their customer base. This is particularly true in emerging economies like India and China. This has led to organizations becoming very focused on improving customer engagement experiences to retain and increase customer base. Retail banking in particular has used customer relationship management as a key strategy for retaining customers. Deploying new product and service delivery channels such as ATM, Internet and Phone Banking are some of the efforts in this space. While business process transformation using these channels has improved the service quality, banks are still exploring how these channels can be harnessed to pro-actively manage customer needs and interests. Due to various factors like awareness, lifestyle, literacy rate, lack of confidence in using e-transactions, the customers still prefer to do most of their banking by visiting the bank's branch.

The age old model of prioritizing by arrival time does not make sense for a retail bank as not all customers are equal in terms of the value they bring to the bank. Furthermore, the more valuable a customer is, she is likely to resent the longer waiting times. In fact, a survey conducted by us at several branches of a leading public sector bank in India, we found that the wait time was as high as 60 minutes resulting in low customer satisfaction (CSAT) and consequently loss of business from existing customers. A naive solution to the problem is to increase the number of service personnel at the branch and have dedicated counters for different types of transactions or services. However, this would lead to a substantial increase in the operating cost of the bank which makes it an unviable alternative.

Banks have started to define priority rules for their services to optimize overall wait time for customers, these static rules and service segments do not consider the customer's future value. However, in our survey we found that most of the visits were made for low-value transactions, such as checking an account balance or depositing a check, thus maintaining the branch as a cost center. Taking a retail branch from a cost to profit center is a top priority of most banks. The key here is to prioritize services (e.g. large deposits, withdrawals, funds transfer etc) which are more profitable to the bank and schedule customers accordingly. Banks are also starting to segment customers along with their service

CIKM'11, October 24–28, 2011, Glasgow, Scotland, UK.

requests in this approach for an optimal solution that is attractive for important customers as well as optimized for revenue generating transactions (like fund transfers) for the bank. This way the customers and services in profitable segment would get differentiated Quality of Service (QoS). This differentiation in turn would help the organization to realign their focus around important customers and services. However, these static models have an inherent flaw. They only use the current transaction to decide which customer gets faster service. A customer who has been valuable to the bank over the years would still feel unhappy that she was not given priority. Simply put, the most recent transaction is not a reflection of overall value of the customer. Hence, the inability to utilize the customer's overall value in existing scheduling systems leads to a one-shoe-fits-all (myopic) scheduling which causes dissatisfaction among certain customers who are more likely to bring additional business for the bank in the future. For example, in static rules-based scheduling systems, the banks may assign lower service priority for a customer visiting the bank to order Banker's Check as the transaction might be considered as less profitable for the bank. If on the other hand the customer's past transactions and thereby future value is taken into consideration the outcome could have been entirely different. For example, if on analysis the customer demonstrates high affinity for long term deposits, then she could be assigned a higher service priority and matched with a service agent specialized to sell deposits. This way the bank not only improves customer satisfaction but also increases the chance of selling a profitable product to the customer. We would like to note that point solutions like Queue Management System and Recommendation Systems exist in commercial space. The existing solutions aim to either improve CSAT or profitability. However, in this paper we present an end to end integrated system which seamlessly merges the above mentioned capabilities to improve CSAT as well as profitability. Moreover, we bring advanced analytics and optimization capability to each piece.

Contributions: In this paper we present a retail banking solution for simultaneous CSAT and profit maximization that has been deployed at several branches of a large public sector bank in India. We address existing limitations of static rules based scheduling by proposing a first of a kind customer analytics driven scheduling system. Our system uses customer analytics for dynamic assignment and prioritization of customers at a branch. Our solution has been designed to cater to multiple channels. We describe the technical problems and the associated methods for handling the same while taking into account the domain specific constraints. Even though we have deployed the system in limited capabilities in the current phase, we showcase the usefulness of the system by presenting some new use cases motivated by our experience.

2. ANALYTICS AND OPTIMIZATION METHODOLOGY

We present details of the *Scheduling*, *Product Recommendation* and *Customer Value Computation* components that form part of the Analytics and Optimization layer.

2.1 Customer Value Computation

First we present basic notations that is used in this and the following sections.

Basic Notations $\mathcal{C} = \{C_1, C_2, \ldots, C_N\}$ denotes the list of N customers. $\mathcal{AT}_i$ represents corresponding arrival times. $\mathcal{MS}$ denotes the master list of K service types which can be availed by a customer. Each service type is associated with an expected processing time. The service time for each service type is stored in a list denoted by $\mathcal{MT} = \{MT_1, MT_2, \ldots, MT_K\}$. The service bundle requested by i^{th} customer is denoted by $SB_i = \{SB_i^1, SB_i^2, \ldots, SB_i^l\}$ where l is number of services requested by i^{th} customer and $\forall_{j=1}^{l} SB_i^j \in \mathcal{MS}$. The total time needed to process SB_i is known as *service time* denoted by S_i. The service time S_i is sum of expected service time of all the services in SB_i. $\mathcal{S} = \{S_1, \ldots, S_N\}$ denotes service times for all N customers. $\mathcal{V} = \{V_1, V_2, \ldots, V_N\}$ denotes the value of the customer. This value is employed to compute the priority $\mathcal{P} = \{P_1, P_2, \ldots, P_N\}$ for the scheduling algorithm. CT represents current time. Finally, $\mathcal{T}$ denotes the L service personnel employed in the bank.

As noted earlier, the value of the customer C_i consist of following three components.

Current Value of Customer: This value captures the current profitability of the customer for the bank which is computed based on the customer's current assets with the bank and cost of supporting customer's transactions. The profitability is then mapped to a number $\in$ [0,1] using a mapping function and is denoted by V_p.

Future Value of Customer: This value captures the expected business which the customer will generate for the bank in future. This is computed based on the profitability of products recommended for a customer as explained in Section 2.2. D_i denotes the profitability of product bundle which the customer is expected to buy and SP_i is the customer's affinity to that product bundle. Therefore, the value (V_f) is computed as $D_i \times SP_i$.

Value of Service Request: This value captures the profitability of the current service request to the bank and is denoted by V_c. Typically, V_c is computed by using a lookup table provided by the bank which enumerate the relative profitability of each service type.

The overall value is a weighted sum of individual values and is given by:

$$V_i = \frac{w_1 \times V_p + w_2 \times V_c + w_3 \times V_f}{w_1 + w_2 + w_3} \quad (1)$$

The weighing factors depends on attributes of the organization. A very high value of w_1 would indicate more emphasis on current customer value whereas a high value of w_2 would capture that importance of profitability of current service request. Similarly, a high weightage of V_f would imply a sales centric organization. The denominator is simply a normalization factor so that $V_i \in [0, 1]$ and hence comparable for different customers. The final value V_i is used to compute priority P_i in the scheduling algorithm where P_i is computed as $1 - V_i$.

2.2 Product Recommendation Engine

The Product Recommendation Engine generates a list of product recommendations for a customer, ranked on the customer's affinity for the product/service. Each recommendation is given an affinity score (between 0 and 1) based on criteria such as the product's popularity in the customer's segment, customer's response to an earlier offer, product's profitability to the bank etc. Another key feature of the proposed Product Recommendation Engine is it's *dynamic product bundling capability*. With this capability, banks offer multiple financial products and services to customers as a package. Recent research [9] have looked at offering some customization in product bundling by looking at historical trends about influence of a product on sales of other products. However, that work does not look at incorporating the need for a *discount* on the initial product suggested to the customer. Also, the idea proposed is within the framework of a static bundling model. This lead us to the the problem of dynamic bundling of products.

Problem: Dynamically assemble a product bundle P_b for a customer C, who wants a discount D for a initially suggested product p such that the members of P_b are complementary to p and C has a high affinity to those products.

Solution: If we ignore the complementarity and affinity requirements, the problem can be modeled as a 0-1 knapsack problem where the discount D is offset by the cumulative profit of the smallest possible product bundle. The problem is NP-complete but a pseudo-polynomial time algorithm [10] does exist for it. Introducing customers affinity for a given product and how complementary the suggested product is to the product already chosen makes the problem into a m-dimensional knapsack problem (also called multi-constrained knapsack) [8]. Formally, it can be expressed as

$min \sum_{i=1}^{n} v_i p'_i$ subject to $\sum_{i=1}^{n} m_{i,j} p'_i \geq b_j$

where p'_i is a product being sold by the provider and is not the same as the product p chosen by the customer C, v_i is the price of the product p'_i, $m_{i,j}$ is the profit/affinity/compatibility of the product p'_i and b_j is the maximum discount required or bundle affinity or bundle compatibility.

The above formulation requires values for customer to product affinity and product complementarity to be given. Assuming the presence of a transaction dataset R containing information about products purchased by customer C, we can measure the complementarity of any two products p_1 and p_2 as

$$lift(p_1 \rightarrow p_2) = \frac{Support(p_1 \bigcup p_2)}{Support(p_1) \times Support(p_2)}$$

where support(p_i) is the number of transactions containing p_i.

On similar lines, we can measure the affinity of the customer C to a product can be computed as

$$\text{Affinity}(C,p_1) = \frac{Support(p_1)}{max(Support(p_i))}.$$

where p_i is any product purchased by C.

Since the number of products considered in the existing customer engagement is very limited, a dynamic product bundling approach was avoided. However, the platform we are building is not in any way restricted to applications in the banking scenario. We could use the same system to create bundled offerings for telecom and retail customers. In these domains the number of possible product bundles is quite large necessitating us to come up with a dynamic product bundling strategy.

2.3 Scheduler

Based on the priority value P_i as computed in Section 2.1, the scheduler picks a subset of M customers from existing wait queue and schedules them. The output of the scheduler is a ranked list (RL) of length M which specifies the order in which the M customers are served. We tried to find optimal solution to this scheduling problem by formulating math program and using standard solvers. Due to NP-hard nature of the problem, finding optimal solution conflicted with the end goal of the real time system. We were not able to produce schedules fast enough to be used in a real time system. Therefore, a simple heuristic was used in the current deployment. For each customer we computed $P_i \times S_i$. To re-iterate, priority 1 customers are more important than customers with priority 2. The priority is then multiplied by the expected service time to generate weighted service time which is sorted in ascending order to generate a rank list. This procedure generates a ranking based on Weighted Shortest Job First (WSJF) policy.

The scheduling algorithm suffers from starvation problem. If important customers keep coming in the system, it will lead to less important customers facing extremely high wait time, which in turn will decrease CSAT and defeat the whole purpose of this solution. To handle this problem, we continuously update the priority of all customers. With each customer C_i we associate a maximum starvation time MST_i. The priority of each customer is then updated as follows:

$$PNew_i = P_i \times \frac{FIFO_i - (CT - A_i)}{FIFO_i} \qquad (2)$$

Note that $CT - A_i$ computes the already waited time. $FIFO_i$ is the expected time the customer would have waited if the bank were using a traditional FIFO based scheduler. If a customer has waited for $FIFO_i$ minutes, the priority goes to 0 which implies she now belongs to most important category and will be scheduled as soon as possible. The update function gradually adjusts the priority of each customer to avoid starvation. In real life setting, we found this property to be really useful and desirable to manage crowd perception of fairness. This fashion of priority updation takes into account category information, arrival pattern and current system state. We would like to mention here that all of the existing commercial systems that we studied [1, 3, 6, 4, 2, 5, 7] typically schedule customers in some pre defined order. These solutions generally work on a static fair play principle and schedule customers in a FIFO order. However, any advanced dynamic scheduling (e.g. based on multiple service parameters) and real time decision support which our Scheduler offers is missing from these products.

3. DEPLOYMENT EXPERIENCE

In this section, we share some of our deployment experiments and learning. First, we present the current state of our tool at multiple branches of a leading retail bank in India. Due to confidentiality and non-disclosure agreement, we are unable to divulge all the data. However, we share some of the results at an aggregate level to demonstrate how our system met the bank's objectives.

Deployment Setup: The system was deployed in 5 branches of a leading bank in India for a period of 2 months. For each branch, we collected data for first two weeks. This data was used to calculate the original wait times (baseline). During this two week period the bank continued to use existing token dispensing machine which generates sequentially numbered token. These tokens were scheduled using FIFO.

The Customer Problem: The bank was suffering from huge queue and extra ordinarily long wait time. On an average the wait time was 45 minutes whereas during peak hours (10 to 12 PM), it was observed to be as high as 60 to 80 minutes. Therefore, the first business metric which the client wanted to see improvement was on wait time. On an average 350-400 customers come to bank everyday and were served by 4 or 5 resources (based on availability). The client agreed that given the high number of customers and resource constraints, it is impossible to improve the wait time for all customers. The business analyst provided us with a set of rules to classify customers as High Net Income (HNI), High, Average and Low importance. The client wanted the wait time reduction of HNI and High importance customer while not imposing high penalty to other customers. The second metric of interest was to improve bank focus by taking into account the service requests. The services were divided into two groups: profitable services & non-profitable services. The grouping was based on the fact that certain services like Traveler's Cheque, Demand Draft etc generate instant revenue for the bank whereas services like cash withdrawal are liabilities. More than profit, the client wanted to create focus and awareness among customers so that alternate bank channels are used effectively. The idea was if a customer has to wait 60 minutes or more to withdraw a small sum of money, she can be educated and made to understand the benefits to using ATMs. Combining customer and service classes, we got 8 possible categories. Out of these 3 cases were infeasible because some classes of customers are not authorized to request every service. Therefore, we had 5 categories in which an incoming customer is mapped based on customer type and service requests.

The readers would notice that the above mentioned categorization is a static one. This is primarily due to the client requirements and our decision to spend more time on scheduling and understanding customer behavior rather than putting lot of efforts in dynamic categorization. Moreover, since we wanted to focus on the non-FIFO scheduling part, we decided not to interface our system with banking database. This saved lot of time and efforts in getting security clearances from client organization and reduced our development to deployment cycle time.

Impact: We deployed our system of non-FIFO based customer scheduling at the branches after the 2 week baselining period and collected data. We used a variant of shortest job first scheduling policy explained in Section 2.3 to schedule the customers. After deployment our system scheduled around 25000 customers. The analysis of customer wait times after deployment of the system showed significant improvements. The wait time of HNI customers reduced by a whopping 83% while the wait time of High category customers reduced by 30%. This was accomplished at the cost of increased wait time of Low category customers which went up by 25%. No big change was observed for Average category and others. The reason for large improvements in HNI wait times is due to the low volume of HNI clients (only 5% of total customers). The High category constituted around 60% while around 25% of customers were in low category. Thus, we were able to improve the wait times of almost 65% customers at the branch by penalizing 25% of the customers who were already identified as being of low importance to the bank. We wish to highlight the fact that the *overall average wait time* of all customers decreased by around 15%.

4. SUMMARY

In this paper we present a retail banking solution for simultaneous CSAT and profit maximization that has been deployed at several branches of a large public sector bank in India. The system proposes a unique analytics and optimization layer which helps in scheduling customers such that CSAT as well as bank's profit is maximized. We highlighted various components of the system along with technical problems and associated business constraints. We share deployment experience and highlight our key findings. Finally, we believe that our system and current work is a first step that addresses CSAT while maximizing profit.

5. REFERENCES

[1] Advanced Queue Management System. http://www.databyteindia.com/.

[2] Automatic Queue Management System. http://www.qms-akis.com/.

[3] Dynamic Queue Management System. http://www.intellvisions.com/products/opti-q.html.

[4] Lonsto Queue Management System: http://www.lonsto.co.uk/ .

[5] QTech Queueing System. http://www.qtechsg.com/standard.htm.

[6] Queue Management System. http://www.rts.com.np/rtsweb/index.php?q=products/qms.

[7] Smart Queue Management System. http://www.batworld.com.

[8] M. F. A polynomial linear search algorithm for the n-dimensional knapsack problem. 1983.

[9] N. Li, Y. Yang, and X. Yan. Cross-selling optimization for customized promotion. 2010.

[10] S. Martello and P. Toth. *Knapsack Problems: Algorithms and Computer Implementation*. John Wiley and Sons, 1990.

Coarse-to-Fine Classification via Parametric and Nonparametric Models for Computer-Aided Diagnosis

Meizhu Liu, Le Lu, Xiaojing Ye, Shipeng Yu, and Heng Huang
Siemens Medical Solutions Inc, Malvern, PA 19355, USA
University of Florida, Gainesville, FL 32611, USA
University of Texas, Arlington, TX 76013, USA
le-lu@siemens.com, mliu@cise.ufl.edu, shipeng.yu@siemens.com

ABSTRACT

Classification is one of the core problems in Computer-Aided Diagnosis (CAD), targeting for early cancer detection using 3D medical imaging interpretation. High detection sensitivity with desirably low false positive (FP) rate is critical for a CAD system to be accepted as a valuable or even indispensable tool in radiologists' workflow. Given various spurious imagery noises which cause observation uncertainties, this remains a very challenging task. In this paper, we propose a novel, two-tiered coarse-to-fine (CTF) classification cascade framework to tackle this problem. We first obtain classification-critical data samples (e.g., samples on the decision boundary) extracted from the holistic data distributions using a robust parametric model (e.g., [8]); then we build a graph-embedding based nonparametric classifier on sampled data, which can more accurately preserve or formulate the complex classification boundary. These two steps can also be considered as effective "sample pruning" and "feature pursuing + kNN/template matching", respectively. Our approach is validated comprehensively in colorectal polyp detection and lung nodule detection CAD systems, as the top two deadly cancers, using hospital scale, multi-site clinical datasets. The results show that our method achieves overall better classification/detection performance than existing state-of-the-art algorithms using single-layer classifiers, such as the support vector machine variants, boosting, logistic regression, relevance vector machine [8], k-nearest neighbor or spectral projections on graph [2].

Categories and Subject Descriptors: [Industrial and Application Paper]: Knowledge Management (KM)

General Terms: Algorithms

Keywords: Computer-Aided Diagnosis, Coarse-to-Fine Classification, Class Regularized Graph Embedding, Total Bregman Divergence (tBD) Clustering, t-centers

1. INTRODUCTION

Colon cancer and lung cancer are the top two leading causes of cancer deaths in western population. Meanwhile, these two cancers are also highly preventable or "curable" if detected early. Image interpretation based cancer detection via 3D computer tomography has emerged as a common clinical practice, and many computer-aided detection tools for enhancing radiologists' diagnostic performance and effectiveness are developed in the last decade. The key for radiologists to accept the clinical usage of a computer-aided diagnosis (CAD) system is the high detection sensitivity with reasonably low false positive (FP) rate per case.

This paper mainly focuses on the classification aspect of CAD. We propose and comprehensively evaluate a novel coarse-to-fine classification framework. The method consists of the following two steps, in both training and testing. (1) *Sample Pruning:* Parametric classification models (e.g., logistic regression, boosting, support/relevance vector machines [8]) are trained on the complexly distributed datasets as coarse, distribution-level classification. The goal is not to assign class labels, but to prune data samples to select more "classification-critical" candidates, which are expected to preserve the decision boundary in the high dimensional feature space (thus vast numbers of samples lying far from classification boundary are discarded.(2) *Feature Pursuing + kNN/Template Matching:* We first apply feature selection and graph embedding methods jointly to find intrinsic lower dimensional feature subspace that preserves group-wise data topology, and then employ nonparametric classifiers for final classification, using kNN or template matching. We argue that more precisely modeling the intrinsic geometric of decision boundary, by graph embedding and nonparametric classifiers in a finer level, can potentially improve the final classification performance. The overall process is illustrated as follows

Samples → **Sample pruning** → **Feature selection**
→ **Class regularized graph embedding**
→ **kNN/Template matching**

We applied our proposed framework on colon polyp and lung nodule detection, using two large scale clinical datasets collected from multiple clinical sites across continents.

2. SAMPLE PRUNING USING PARAMETRIC RVMMIL

We start by developing a "coarse" classifier for sample pruning using a parametric model. Considering the spe-

CIKM'11, October 24–28, 2011, Glasgow, Scotland, UK.

cific characteristics of CAD classification problems, in this paper we use the RVMMIL approach [8] which is a powerful extension to integrate feature selection and handle multiple instance learning (MIL).

In RVMMIL, the probability for an instance $\mathbf{x}_i$ to be positive is $p(y=1|\mathbf{x}_i) = \sigma(\mathbf{a}'\mathbf{x}_i)$, where σ is the logistic function defined as $\sigma(t) = 1/(1+e^{-t})$ and $\mathbf{a}'\mathbf{x}_i$ is the linear dot-product between data feature vector $\mathbf{x}_i$ and model coefficient vector $\mathbf{a}$. For the contents of sparse feature selection and multiple instance learning in RVM, we refer the readers to [8]. From our coarse-to-fine classification model, RVMMIL is adopted as the coarse-level cascade classifier for sample pruning, i.e., we will remove samples x_i satisfying $p(y=1|\mathbf{x}_i) < \hat{\rho}$. This step can eliminate massive amount of negatives without effecting much on sensitivity, by choosing a balanced $\hat{\rho}$. The remained data samples $p(y=1|\mathbf{x}_i) \geq \hat{\rho}$ are either true positives (at high recall) or "hard" false positives, *lying close to the classification boundary*, which will largely impact the final classification accuracy. Note that other classifiers with confidence estimates, as boosting and regularized SVM, are also applicable.

3. FEATURE SPACE PURSUIT

Our goal of feature pursuit is to estimate intrinsic, lower dimensional feature subspace of data for later sensible nonparametric classification, while preserves generative data-graph topology. This is the key to achieve superior classification performance with simple nonparametric classifiers. In the proposed framework it consists of two steps: feature selection and class regularized graph embedding.

Feature Selection: By applying feature selection, only a compact subset of highly statistical relevant features is retained, to simplify the later graph embedding or feature projection process. There are many feature selection techniques, we use Maximum Relevance Minimum Redundancy (MRMR) feature selection algorithm [7] due to its empirical good performance and computational efficiency. Given a set of features $\mathbb{F} = \{f_i\}$, its MRMR feature subset $\mathbb{H}$ maximizes the following objective κ:

$$\kappa(\mathbb{H}, \mathbf{y}) = \gamma(\mathbb{H}, \mathbf{y}) - \gamma(\mathbb{H}), \tag{1}$$

where

$$\gamma(\mathbb{H}) = \frac{1}{m^2} \sum_{f_i, f_j \in \mathbb{H}} \gamma(f_i, f_j), \tag{2}$$

$$\gamma(\mathbb{H}, \mathbf{y}) = \frac{1}{m} \sum_{f_i \in \mathbb{H}} \gamma(f_i, \mathbf{y}), \tag{3}$$

and m is the total number of elements in $\mathbb{H}$. Due to space limit, refer the algorithm details to [7].

Class Regularized Graph Embedding: We propose and exploit a new *Class Regularized Graph Embedding* (CRGE) scheme to project data (after feature selection) into an even lower dimensional subspace, where data samples from the same class getting closer and samples from different classes moving apart, to make NN or TM more robust and semantically interpretable, as shown later. In Graph embedding, feature projections can be learned in many different ways. We follow *the principle that keeps the locality of nearby data and maps apart data further* in the graph-induced subspace, which is similar to Laplacian Eigenmap [1, 3] and Locality Preserving Projection [4].

Given a set of N points $\mathcal{X} = \{\mathbf{x}_1, \mathbf{x}_2, \cdots, \mathbf{x}_N\} \subset \mathbb{R}^n$, and a symmetric $N \times N$ matrix W which measures the similarity between all pairs of points in $\mathcal{X}$. The set $\mathcal{X}$ and matrix W compose a graph $\mathcal{G}$, with $\mathcal{X}$ as vertices and W as weights of the edges. The conventional graph embedding method will map $\mathcal{X}$ to a much lower dimensional space $\mathcal{Y} = \{\mathbf{y}_1, \mathbf{y}_2, \cdots, \mathbf{y}_N\} \subset \mathbb{R}^{\tilde{n}}$, $\tilde{n} \ll n$. The optimal $\mathcal{Y}$ should minimize the loss function $L(\mathcal{Y})$ which is defined as

$$L(\mathcal{Y}) = \sum_{i,j} \|\mathbf{y}_i - \mathbf{y}_j\|^2 W_{ij}, \tag{4}$$

under some appropriate constraints. Though performed well in many applications [3, 4], the limitation of Eq. (4) is that it does not penalize the similarity between points belonging to different classes. For this means, we propose class regularized graph embedding (CRGE) to find a mapping $\phi : \mathcal{X} \mapsto \mathcal{Y}$, such that ϕ minimizes the function $E(\mathcal{Y})$ defined as

$$E(\mathcal{Y}) = \sum_{i,j \in \mathcal{S}} \|\mathbf{y}_i - \mathbf{y}_j\|^2 W_{ij} - \sum_{i,j \in \mathcal{D}} \|\mathbf{y}_i - \mathbf{y}_j\|^2 W_{ij}, \quad \text{subject to: } \|\mathcal{Y}\|_F = 1. \tag{5}$$

where $i,j \in \mathcal{S}$ means $\mathbf{x}_i$ and $\mathbf{x}_j$ belong to the same class, and $i,j \in \mathcal{D}$ means $\mathbf{x}_i$ and $\mathbf{x}_j$ are in different classes. $\|\cdot\|_F$ is the Frobenius norm. To avoid notation clutter, we rewrite (5) and get

$$\min \sum_{i,j} \|\mathbf{y}_i - \mathbf{y}_j\|^2 W_{ij} H_{ij}, \tag{6}$$

where H_{ij} is the Heaviside function and

$$H_{ij} = \begin{cases} 1, & \text{if } i,j \in \mathcal{S} \\ -1, & \text{if } i,j \in \mathcal{D} \end{cases}.$$

The mapping function $\phi(\mathbf{x})$ can be linear or nonlinear, and We use linear mapping because of its simplicity and generality, such as

$$\mathbf{y} = \phi(\mathbf{x}) = M'\mathbf{x},\ M \in \mathbb{R}^{n \times \tilde{n}}, \tilde{n} \ll n. \tag{7}$$

Plugging (7) into (6), we get

$$\min_M \sum_{i,j} \|M'\mathbf{x}_i - M'\mathbf{x}_j\|^2 W_{ij} H_{ij}, \quad \text{subject to: } \|M\|_F = 1, \tag{8}$$

where the constraint $\|M\|_F = 1$ eliminates the scaling effect. Eq. (8) can be solved very quickly using gradient descent technique along with iterative projections [9]. The computation of W is chosen in the following manner, to fit our problem specific need.

$$W(i,j) = \mathbf{x}_i'\mathbf{x}_j / \|\mathbf{x}_i\| \|\mathbf{x}_j\|. \tag{9}$$

Finally, we argue that our stratified approach which prunes non-informative or redundant features, using feature selection from an information-theoretic aspect, before feature graph embedding or projection, can simplify the optimization process of graph embedding on a reduced feature set. This strategy may achieve better overall results, compared from the joint sparsity-constrained graph embedding (as SPG) [2].

4. NONPARAMETRIC CLASSIFICATION

The naive KNN classification on data instances, in feature space $\mathcal{Y} = \phi(\mathbf{x})$, performs poorly due to unbalanced number

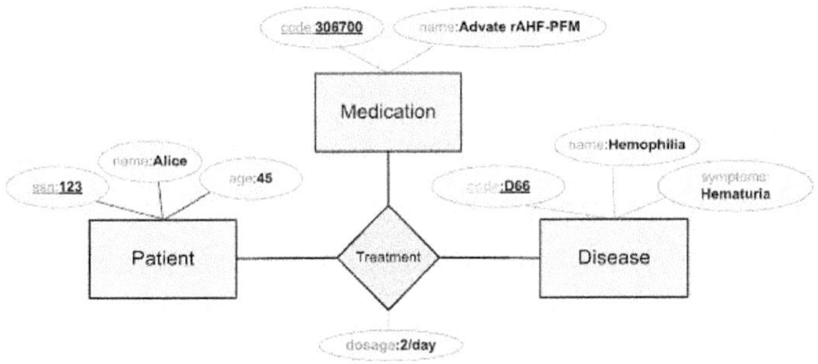

Figure 2: Example trinary relationship which documents a medical treatment for some patient's disease.

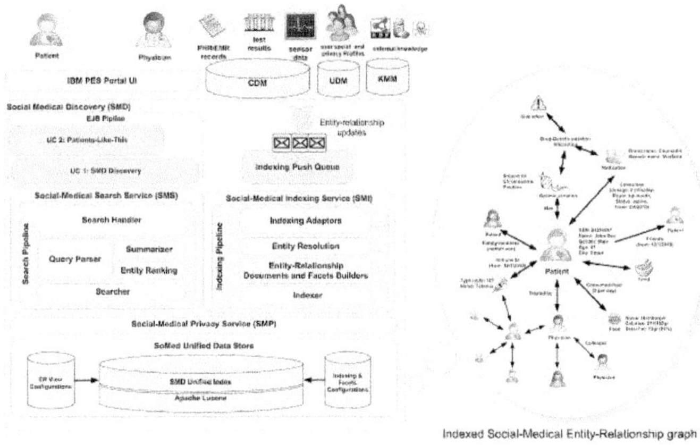

Figure 3: IBM PES Social-Medical Discovery (SMD) system high level architecture.

Entity multi-typing and inheritance are also supported by the framework. For example, a query like `User.age:[20 TO 40]` can be used to query all SMD users, no matter if they are patients or physicians.

Entity similarity search is also supported, and allows to discover similar entities based on both direct (attribute-based) entity similarity and relationship similarity. The most common use of entity similarity search in SMD is for discovering similar patients for a given patient. Traditional entity similarity search solutions usually find similar entities using PageRank like methods (e.g., SimRank [1], PRank [7], etc) and require offline computation. Compared to these methods, SMD entity similarity search is based on a discovery approach and can be run online. Given a patient's social-medical data, direct patient features (e.g., age, gender) are augmented with relationship based features extracted from entities related to the patient (e.g., consumed medications, diseases, allergies, genetic variations, etc). For that, SMD first clusters entities related to the patient based on their features (i.e., entity type, attribute names, and relationship types). Next, for each cluster, the top entity features are extracted and used for representing the cluster by a single ER query predicate. Finally different cluster query predicates are conjuncted together and submitted to the system. Utilizing the unique querying interface of IBM PES, similar entities are returned in a similar manner as in a regular search scenario, accompanied with facets and relationship links that allow further exploration. Furthermore, SMD users can define preferences for similarity search by weighing various similarity features using SMD's advanced search options.

Figure 3 depicts the high level architecture of the SMD system. On the top right side, heterogeneous data from the different IBM PES data repositories is delivered to the SMD system for indexing. The SMD system includes three main sub-systems. The first sub-system, Social-Medical Indexing (SMI), is responsible for indexing the data obtained from the various IBM PES data sources. SMI includes several components that extract, transform and index the heterogeneous data into a unified entity-relationship model representation. First, entities are extracted from the data using dedicated data adapters that represent every data item as an entity with a type (e.g., `Patient`) and (typed) attributes (e.g., `Patient.age(Integer)`). Relationships that are known to exist among indexed entities (e.g., `Treatment`) are indexed and any relationship context information is also kept (e.g., `Treatment.dosage:2/day`). An entity resolution component is further utilized to resolve entity mappings between the different data sources (e.g., UDM and CDM patient records). SMI also includes a flexible text analysis framework that is used to determine the text analysis pipeline for each entity (e.g., usage of stop word removal, lemmatization, stemming, etc). Entities and relationships are then serialized and indexed in SMD's specialized unified search index.

The second sub-system, Social-Medical Search (SMS), provides the query interface to SMD's unified search index. Queries submitted to the system are parsed and run against the unified index. SMS supports arbitrary textual and/or structured predicate queries. Search results include entities together with their attributes data, their relationships, and various facets that can be used for further exploring the data (e.g., entity type facets, attribute facets, etc). Entities are ranked according to their relevance to the query. Entity relevance is determined by a combination of ranking heuristics, among others are specialized extensions to the basic Lucene ranking model, link-analysis of the social-medical graph, context-based proximity, etc.

Finally, the Social-Medical Privacy (SMP) sub-system is responsible for enforcing the privacy policies of various IBM PES users during indexing and search time. For that, a novel authorization model was implemented [5]. During indexing, SMP translates user privacy policies into special ACLs that constrain the question answering permissions of every indexed entity in the system. During search, SMP maps each query to a set of ACLs which are added to the query which makes sure that the searcher gets as a result to her search only those entities that she is allowed to query. Furthermore, ACLs attached to result entities are used for data filtering, i.e., only portions of entity data that is allowed to be viewed by the current searcher will be returned.

3. DEMONSTRATION DETAILS

During the demonstration we shall introduce IBM PES, describe its data sources, and its various clinical decision support services. Using anonymized IBM PES social-medical data, we shall discuss the main motivations for this system, and demonstrate the system's patient empowerment capabilities for improved patient safety. First, we shall demonstrate the typical use of IBM PES by various users. For example,

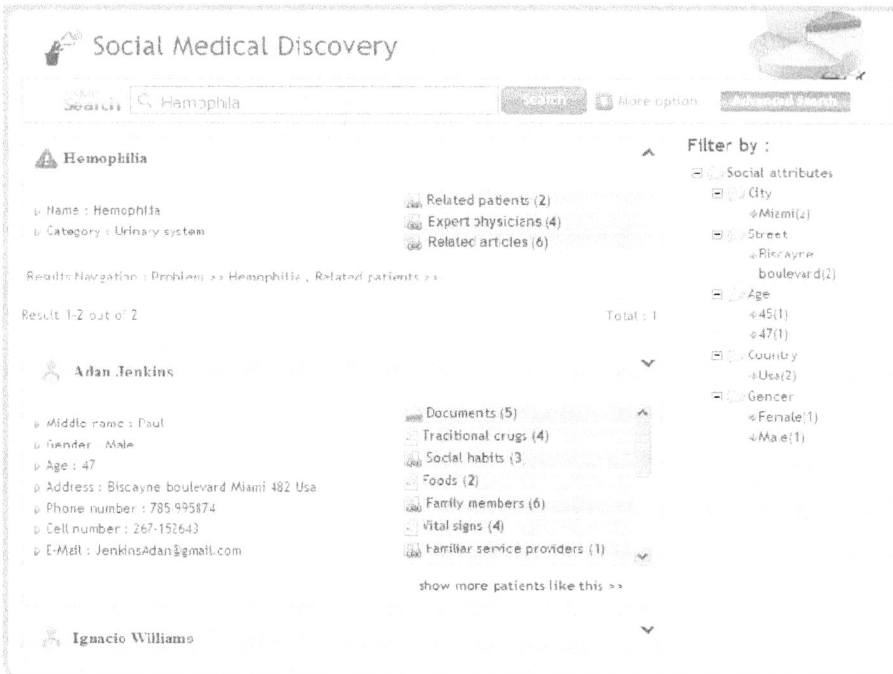

Figure 4: SMD interactive querying user interface

we shall show how patients can define their personal medical profile, social network, clinical history, etc. We shall then present the IBM PES and its SMD system and discuss the various challenges in implementing its social-medical discovery capabilities, including among others its novel entity-relationship indexing and retrieval capabilities. SMD's interactive querying UI will be used for the demonstration and is depicted in Figure 4. The UI enables to submit various query types to the SMD system and explore the retrieved results. To demonstrate the various social-medical capabilities of the system, we shall use the following three usecases.

3.1 Usecase 1: Social-Medical Discovery

This usecase will demonstrate the various search and discovery capabilities of the SMD system. We shall illustrate how non-expert users (i.e., patients/physicians) can access data kept within the different IBM PES heterogeneous data sources in a unified and intuitive way using its interactive querying interface. Demo users will be able to enter various queries spanning from free-text queries to structured predicates and explore the results returned by SMD. A convenient faceted search UI allows users to navigate the social-medical data graph and explore important aspects such as data distributions for various facets of interest, lineage, etc.

3.2 Usecase 2: Patients-Like-This

This usecase will demonstrate SMD's entity similarity search capabilities. During the demonstration we shall focus on SMD's capability of discovering similar patients, also termed the "Patients-Like-This"' task. As was already mentioned, this task is an important enabler for various advanced social-medical services in IBM PES. Demo users will be able to discover similar patients for any patient in the results set. Users will also be able to search similar patients for a given patient social-medical profile and refine the similarity search according to facets of interest.

3.3 Usecase 3: Social-Medical Privacy

This usecase will demonstrate the social-medical privacy capabilities of SMD system. During the demonstration we shall define various privacy policies that restrict data sharing in various privacy levels and demonstrate how SMD enforce privacy during search by translating user queries into proper ACLs.

4. REFERENCES

[1] Glen Jeh and Jennifer Widom. SimRank: a measure of structural-context similarity. In *Proceedings of SIGKDD*, pages 538–543. ACM Press, 2002.

[2] Gary Marchionini. Exploratory search: from finding to understanding. *Commun. ACM*, 49:41–46, April 2006.

[3] Haggai Roitman, Yossi Messika, Yevgenia Tsimerman, and Yonatan Maman. Increasing patient safety using explanation-driven personalized content recommendation. In *Proceedings of the 1st ACM International Health Informatics Symposium (IHI)*, pages 430–434, New York, NY, USA, 2010. ACM.

[4] Haggai Roitman, Yossi Messika, Yevgenia Tsimerman, and Sivan Yogev. A unified approach for social-medical discovery. In *Proceedings of the 23rd International Conference of the European Federation for Medical Informatics (MIE)*, Oslo, Norway, 2011.

[5] Haggai Roitman and Sivan Yogev. An authorization model for entity search. In *Proceedings of the 1st International Workshop on Search and Mining Entity-Relationship Data (SMER)*, Glasgow, UK, 2011.

[6] Daniel Tunkelang. *Faceted Search*. Morgan & Claypool Publishers, 2009.

[7] Peixiang Zhao, Jiawei Han, and Yizhou Sun. P-rank: a comprehensive structural similarity measure over information networks. In *Proceeding of CIKM*, pages 553–562, New York, NY, USA, 2009. ACM.

Black Swan: Augmenting Statistics with Event Data

Johannes Lorey[1] Felix Naumann[1] Benedikt Forchhammer[2]
Andrina Mascher[2] Peter Retzlaff[2] Armin ZamaniFarahani[2]

Hasso Plattner Institute, Potsdam, Germany
[1] firstname.lastname@hpi.uni-potsdam.de [2] firstname.lastname@student.hpi.uni-potsdam.de

ABSTRACT

A large number of statistical indicators (GDP, life expectancy, income, etc.) collected over long periods of time as well as data on historical events (wars, earthquakes, elections, etc.) are published on the World Wide Web. By augmenting statistical outliers with relevant historical occurrences, we provide a means to observe (and predict) the influence and impact of events. The vast amount and size of available data sets enable the detection of recurring connections between classes of events and statistical outliers with the help of association rule mining. The results of this analysis are published at `http://www.blackswanevents.org` and can be explored interactively.

Categories and Subject Descriptors

H.2.8 [**Database Management**]: Database Applications—*Data mining*

General Terms

Algorithms

1. COMBINING STATISTICS AND EVENTS

Over the course of human history there have always been so-called *Black Swan* events. These historic events are defined as singular occurrences with high impact that were entirely unexpected at their time, but in retrospect appear to be the logical consequence considering the given preconditions. Examples for such events include World War I and the burst of the dot-com bubble. The term originates from the discovery of black swans in Western Australia in 1697. Until then, people had widely used the phrase Black Swan to refer to impossibilities, as it was common (Western) belief that only white swans could exist. Subsequently, the definition of the term has changed radically to the one above [7].

By combining statistical data with information on events, the Black Swan project provides a tool to aid domain experts (such as historians or econometricians) in identifying important events throughout history. The goals are (i) the automated detection of outliers in global statistics and their annotation with suitable events and (ii) the discovery of patterns of how event types and statistical developments influence one another.

In order to achieve such insight it is necessary to process statistical data, where large deviations from an expected statistical development could suggest Black Swans events. Fortunately, over the past years a reasonable amount of statistical data has been openly published by governments and other organizations. Other Internet resources and databases contain information on a large number of historical events, which may be Black Swan events.

The rest of this paper is organized as follows: Sec. 2 highlights some of the foundations of the system, such as the chosen data sources as well as the definition of event and outlier for our application. The remaining sections each explain one component of the system architecture illustrated in Fig. 1. In Sec. 3, the *extraction* component for statistical and event data is introduced. Section 4 details the outlier detection *analysis*, whereas Sec. 5 illustrates the *rule mining* process for deriving patterns between outliers and events. Finally, Sec. 6 describes the *visualization* of our results as annotated statistical graphs and provides an outline of the proposed demonstration.

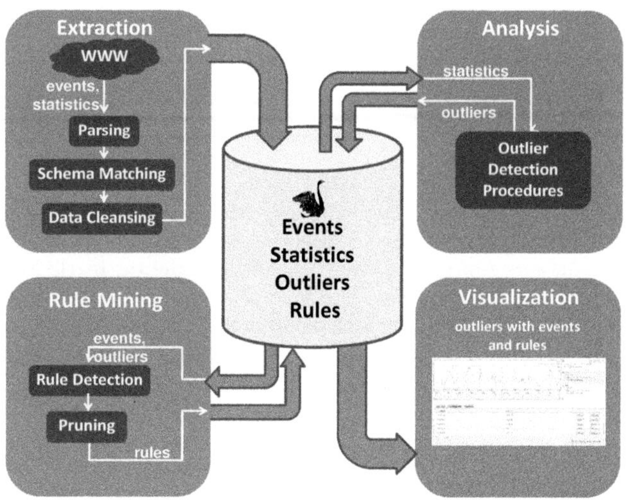

Figure 1: System architecture diagram

2. THE DATA

A key prerequisite for our prototype is the creation of a database containing statistical and event data. We achieve this by extracting and merging information from a number of different Internet sources as detailed in Sec. 3. Events in our system are characterized by a date, location, title, and event category. Optionally, instead of a single date, an event can also be described by a time period with start and end date. The event category provides a hierarchical taxonomy for natural disasters, political events, military conflicts, etc.

A statistical data point is characterized by the numerical value of the data point and the type, location, and year of the statistic. For instance, one value might characterize the annual average income in the United Kingdom for the year 1969 in USD. Statistical data outliers are extrema that deviate from the underlying tendency of a graph. There are several approaches to detect them as discussed in Sec. 4.

Our sources for statistical data are international organizations, such as the World Bank or IMF, but also data provided by other projects, such as Gapminder[1] or Correlates Of War[2]. For event data, we exploit DBpedia[3], EMDat[4], NOAA[5], Correlates Of War, Freebase[6], and the BBC historical timeline[7]. While EMDat and NOAA mostly contain information about natural disasters, such as droughts or earthquakes, the BBC timeline pages provide a chronology of key events in each country's history, but mostly political events. In addition, Correlates of War provides information on wars, and the DBpedia and Freebase data sets contain structured data from user-generated content.

Using the statistical outliers and events data, we detect patterns between these classes automatically. The aim of this rule mining is to decrease the number of events possibly causing an outlier in a statistic and to find probable causes for an event. Details on the rule generation are described in Sec. 5.

3. EXTRACTION

The first step in our workflow is the extraction of events and statistical data from various online sources. This process can be subdivided into three steps: parsing, schema matching, and data cleansing.

3.1 Parsing

As a first step, we retrieve and parse event data from the sources listed in Sec. 2. This goal is achieved by a number of flexible parsers, which are able to handle structured (e.g., CSV, HTML/XML, RDF) as well as unstructured formats, i.e., plain text. Depending on the source, the parsing step itself is preceded by a preprocessing step in which irrelevant parts of source data (e.g., header/footer in HTML documents) are removed. Our flexible design allows for easy adaption of existing parsers to different formats as well as integration of new parsers. We use Apache Tika[8] to parse structured sources (e.g., HTML documents) and extract relevant text, and we use the Jena Framework[9] to load and query RDF data.

With this approach we are able to extract more than 43,000 distinct events from the sources mentioned in Sec. 2. Around half the events stem from collections about natural disasters (primarily from EMDat and NOAA).

The statistics we use include around 400 specific indicators (e.g., GDP or literacy rate) collected annually for as many as 200 countries and up to 200 years. It should be noted that obviously not all statistical data is available for all countries for such a long period of time. Overall, our data comprises approx. 1,250,000 individual statistical values.

3.2 Schema Matching

The second task includes the mapping of parsed data from their source schema to the unified event and statistics schemata. Because of the different data structures in the sources used, the details for this mapping process have to be configured manually for each source. The following normalization steps are employed for schema matching:

- **Attribute de-duplication**: Semi-structured sources such as DBpedia may contain multiple attributes that essentially have the same meaning. These attributes are merged into one attribute where applicable.
- **Categorical classification** of events and statistics into a predefined hierarchical structure of categories. If a taxonomy already exists in a source, the classification can be done using a static mapping between the existing and our classification. Alternatively, classification is performed using a machine learning approach, which is especially useful for unstructured sources (text classification).
- **Geospatial classification** of events and statistics using the GeoNames database and web-service[10]. Multiple locations are allowed for events.
- **Title generation** for sources that do not allocate titles to events. Generation is performed dynamically depending on values of other attributes (like category and location).
- **Date normalization**: Date and time values of different formats are mapped to a unified schema.
- **Value normalization**: Statistical values are normalized to account for different value ranges and units. Prognostic values are removed, because we are only interested in analyzing actual historical data.

Before an entity is stored in the database a number of checks ensure that the entity is *valid* and *useful*. For example, events need to contain at least a title, year, location, and category in order to be useful for rule mining. Likewise, missing or non-numerical values in statistical time series are ignored as they might cause the data analysis algorithms to produce incorrect or no results at all.

3.3 Data Cleansing

It is likely that the same event or similar events can be found in different data sets. Using the following steps, we were able to identify and fuse around 2,500 of these duplicate events. Details on all used methods are described in [5].

First, we adapted the *Sorted Neighborhood* algorithm in a way that a window contains all events within five con-

[1]http://www.gapminder.org
[2]http://www.correlatesofwar.org
[3]http://dbpedia.org/About
[4]http://www.emdat.be
[5]http://www.ngdc.noaa.gov
[6]http://www.freebase.com
[7]http://news.bbc.co.uk/2/hi/europe/country_profiles/
[8]http://tika.apache.org/
[9]http://jena.sourceforge.net/
[10]http://www.geonames.org

secutive years: only the events within this time frame are compared with one another. To decide on a duplicate, all attribute values are compared using different similarity measures and weights. Here, the titles and locations have the highest impact. The weight of the start date is increased for natural disasters, as this date is typically easier to pinpoint for these occurrences than it is for, e.g., political events. Two titles are compared by using a modified *MongeElkan* distance metric that divides the similarity sum of the most similar words by the number of words from the shorter title. All words are stemmed by the *Porter Stemmer* algorithm, stop words are eliminated and the similarity of two words is defined as their *Jaro Winkler* distance.

Second, these duplicates need to be clustered. We considered clustering by deriving the transitive closure of individual duplicate candidates, but found that this is computationally too expensive and will result in a low precision value. Thus, we cluster by using Nearest Neighbors and Compact Sets with varying thresholds for different groups [2].

Finally, to create a clean event we fuse an individual event cluster by fusing all contained attributes. We choose the title and start date from the most reliable source and take the latest end date if given. The values of most other attributes can be concatenated.

4. DETECTION OF OUTLIERS

To identify interesting aspects in the statistical data, we have to determine outliers in the values. We implemented several methods to achieve this goal.

Linear regression uses a linear model to describe the relationship between a scalar variable (time, in our case) and a dependent variable, which corresponds to a specific quantitative indicator, such as the gross domestic product in USD or the literacy rate in percent. We then defined an outlier to be a point on the graph that differs noticeably from the estimated linear model, i.e., it has a large residual. To find the linear approximation of a curve, we implemented three different algorithms: MM-estimation [8], least squares, and its robust variant least median squares [6]. For the latter method, the linear model is defined only by points that themselves are not regarded as outliers for this model.

As linear regression is suited only for some specific data sets, we also implemented two variants of *non-parametric regression* analyses, using the Loess-function [3] and a generalized additive model (GAM) [4], respectively.

We also experimented with methods that analyze properties of the graph itself. For instance, we implemented an algorithm that simply defines all extrema of a graph as its outliers. A more elaborate approach is to analyze not the extrema, but the slope of the graph and define those points as outliers, where the absolute change of the slope is above a certain threshold.

The last approach we implemented is an algorithm that defines a "*global statistic*" by calculating the mean of all country specific statistics and analyzing each single statistic according to its relation to the global statistic.

Each of the methods mentioned above has certain advantages and disadvantages and may be suitable only for specific data sets, e.g., indicators that are expected to increase linearly over time. While the application's 'default' setting should provide a good starting point for exploration, domain experts can also choose to apply a more appropriate analysis to the underlying data by selecting the corresponding algorithm in the web interface.

5. ASSOCIATION RULE MINING

One of our goals is to detect interesting patterns of event-outlier-combinations, such as 'in case of a major natural disaster, the annual GDP of a country declines'. In this section, we explain the process of finding these patterns using association rule mining. We start by defining the term *rule*, outline the attributes used for the machine learning process, and finally describe the rule generation process itself.

5.1 Data Preparation

A rule consists of a premise X and a consequence Y, as well as some metrics describing the quality of the rule, such as support, confidence, and conviction. Support is a measure for the frequency of attribute combinations in the data set. Confidence states how often the consequence follows from a given premise and is defined as

$$\text{conf}(X \Rightarrow Y) = P(Y|X) = \frac{P(X,Y)}{P(X)}$$

Conviction is a metric on how strongly a rule holds when compared to purely random effects between premise and consequence and is defined as

$$\text{conv}(X \Rightarrow Y) = \frac{P(X)P(\neg Y)}{P(X \wedge \neg Y)}$$

Association rule mining aims at discovering dependencies between variables in a single large database. The first step in data preparation was therefore to extract such a data set from our relational model. Because our interest lies in the correlation between events and outliers, we use a join of statistic outliers with events happening in the same year and location (country) as the basis for our data set. In the end, this data set contains information on the event's category, the statistic category, the tendency of an outlier, and the statistical trend leading up to the outlier. For example, in our data set we discovered that a governmental change led to a local extremum in a previously ascending consumer price index for this country in 383 cases with a conviction value of approx. 2.09. In other words: A change in government typically yielded a decline in the consumer price index.

The tendency of an outlier expresses whether the outlier is a maximum or minimum in respect to the expected statistical trend. The statistical trend in the years leading up to an outlier can help to identify Black Swans for which the statistical development in general is relevant to the event, instead of just considering the outlier itself. An example for this is the widespread increase of weapons production that preceded World War I.

5.2 Rule Generation

For association rule mining we used the open source machine learning software WEKA[11]. We employed the Apriori algorithm [1] for rule mining.

One challenge in rule mining is to select the attributes one expects to occur in rules discovered during the process. For our problem we required that every rule needs to contain at least the event category and the statistical category or indi-

[11] `http://www.cs.waikato.ac.nz/ml/weka/`

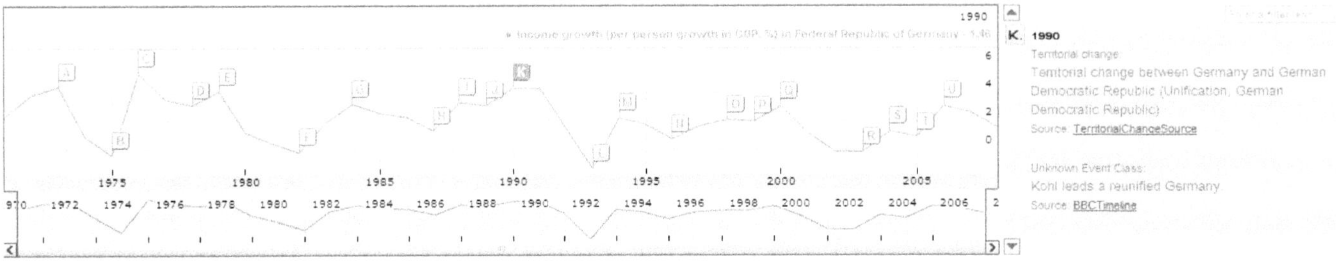

Figure 2: The effect of the German reunification on income growth in Germany.

cator. Other attributes, e.g., outlier tendency or historical trend, are also permitted, but not required in a rule.

Since our base data set for rule generation contains about 1.1 million combinations (by joining events, statistics, and outliers for each year), we required that each determined rule must meet a minimum support of approx. 0.01% by considering only those implications with at least 100 occurrences.

As the Apriori algorithm builds all combinations of item subsets, some generated rules do not constitute a useful rule that can be visualized. This includes rules without an event or statistic attribute as well as events with an unknown event class. We prune the resulting set by removing all such rules.

In order for a user to determine the most fitting event for an outlier, each rule returns the conviction value for a given combination of an event and outlier. This value indicates to what degree a rule applies to the given combination. The more rules match for the combination and the higher the conviction, the more likely the event is for the given outlier.

6. DEMONSTRATION

We now describe how we used the generated rules to visualize statistics and annotate them with event data. The goal is to enable users to explore the correlation between statistical data and historical events interactively. Our prototype is available at `http://www.blackswanevents.org`.

On opening the prototype's website, the user may start to filter the available statistics by lists of categories, subcategories, statistic names and countries. Once a country and a statistic have been selected, the graph containing annotated outliers can be added to the screen. The user may change the displayed timespan, add more graphs by selecting other statistics or countries, and view details about the events.

6.1 Visualization of outliers

The main use case of the visualization is the interactive exploration of our data. Using the Google Web Toolkit[12], we implemented a backend that provides an asynchronous service, which can be used to query available statistics for one or more countries. The backend then retrieves this statistic from the database and scans it for outliers using one of the algorithms described in Sec. 4. The result contains the statistic's data along with a set of outliers. These outliers are mapped to rules and thus to potentially influencing events by using the rules' score method as described in Sec. 5.

Now that all outliers and corresponding events for a statistic and country have been identified, the client generates an "annotated time line" using the Google Chart Tools[13]. Each outlier is annotated with one or more corresponding event(s). By clicking on an outlier, event details are provided, including the rule that caused individual events to be associated with the outlier. For example, in Fig. 2 an outlier (a maximum) in income growth in Germany has been detected for the year 1990, which according to a mined rule is ascribed to the German reunification in the same year.

6.2 Visualization of rules

The second use case is meant to enable users to find relations between certain event classes and specific categories of statistics more easily. It does so by presenting a list of rules, which were identified by the rule mining algorithm. The user can choose one of the rules and review a selection of graphs that support this specific rule. Thus, it is easier to find and validate interesting and unexpected relations between events and statistical data.

[12] `http://code.google.com/webtoolkit/`
[13] `http://code.google.com/apis/chart/`

7. ADDITIONAL AUTHORS

Soeren Discher[2], Cindy Faehnrich[2], Stefan Lemme[2], Thorsten Papenbrock[2], Robert Christoph Peschel[2], Stephan Richter[2], Thomas Stening[2], Sven Viehmeier[2]

[2] Hasso Plattner Institute, Potsdam, Germany, firstname.lastname@student.hpi.uni-potsdam.de

8. REFERENCES

[1] R. Agrawal and R. Srikant. Fast Algorithms for Mining Association Rules in Large Databases. In *Proceedings of the International Conference on Very Large Databases (VLDB)*, pages 487–499, Santiago de Chile, Chile, 1994.

[2] S. Chaudhuri, V. Ganti, and R. Motwani. Robust Identification of Fuzzy Duplicates. In *Proceedings of the International Conference on Data Engineering (ICDE)*, pages 865–876, Tokyo, Japan, 2005.

[3] W. S. Cleveland. Robust Locally Weighted Regression and Smoothing Scatterplots. *Journal of the American Statistical Association*, 74(368):pp. 829–836, 1979.

[4] T. Hastie and R. Tibshirani. *Generalized Additive Models*. Chapman and Hall, 1990.

[5] F. Naumann and M. Herschel. *An Introduction to Duplicate Detection*. Morgan and Claypool, 2010.

[6] P. J. Rousseeuw. Least Median of Squares Regression. *Journal of the American Statistical Association*, 79(388):pp. 871–880, 1984.

[7] N. N. Taleb. *The Black Swan: The Impact of the Highly Improbable*. Random House, 2007.

[8] V. J. Yohai. High Breakdown-Point and High Efficiency Robust Estimates for Regression. *The Annals of Statistics*, 15(2):pp. 642–656, 1987.

A Data Mining System Based on SQL Queries and UDFs for Relational Databases

Carlos Ordonez
University of Houston
Houston, TX 77204, USA

Carlos Garcia-Alvarado
University of Houston
Houston, TX 77204, USA

ABSTRACT

Most research on data mining has proposed algorithms and optimizations that work on flat files, outside a DBMS, mainly due to the following reasons. It is easier to develop efficient algorithms in a traditional programming language. The integration of data mining algorithms into a DBMS is difficult given its relational model foundation and system architecture. Moreover, SQL may be slow and cumbersome for numerical analysis computations. Therefore, data mining users commonly export data sets outside the DBMS for data mining processing, which creates a performance bottleneck and eliminates important data management capabilities such as query processing and security, among others (e.g. concurrency control and fault tolerance). With that motivation in mind, we developed a novel system based on SQL queries and User-Defined Functions (UDFs) that can directly analyze relational tables to compute statistical models, storing such models as relational tables as well. Most algorithms have been optimized to reduce the number of passes on the data set. Our system can analyze large and high dimensional data sets faster than external data mining tools.

Categories and Subject Descriptors

H.2.4 [**Database Management**]: Systems—*Relational databases*

General Terms

Algorithms, Languages, Performance, Theory

1. INTRODUCTION

Our research studies the problem of performing data mining inside a DBMS, paying attention to large data sets. Data mining research is extensive, but the vast majority of proposals has proposed efficient algorithms and optimizations that work on flat files [7]. Therefore, they are difficult to integrate with a DBMS. However, it is fair to say that despite alternative proposals and technologies, relational DBMSs remain the dominating technology to manage and analyze large databases. Even further, open-source DBMSs (e.g. PostgreSQL, MySQL, SQLite) are becoming increasingly popular. Well-known data mining techniques include K-means clustering [4], PCA [2, 1], regression [1], Bayesian classifiers [8], association rules, and decision trees [1] among others. The problem of integrating machine learning and statistical techniques with a DBMS has received scant attention. The integration of data mining algorithms into a DBMS is difficult due to the mathematical nature of models, the lack of access to the DBMS source code and the complex internal DBMS architecture. Another, more practical, reason, not to use a DBMS for data mining tasks is the comprehensive set of techniques available in external data mining tools. Commercial DBMSs provide basic data mining algorithms, but they are difficult to customize, extend and optimize because algorithms are either internally integrated or work on flat files exported with fast interfaces. Also, from a mathematical point of view, they lack a unifying statistical foundation. As a consequence, users or the DBMS itself generally export data sets as files to an external data mining program, thereby going through a performance bottleneck (extracting large tables is slow) and losing the data management capabilities provided by the DBMS (query processing, security, concurrency control, fault tolerance).

From a practical standpoint, SQL is and will likely remain the language to interact with a DBMS. With that motivation in mind, we present a data mining system that can work on top of a relational DBMS based on SQL queries and User-Defined Functions (UDFs), proving that the common perception that SQL is inefficient or inadequate for data mining is false.

Our system incorporates fundamental machine learning and statistical models whose equations and algorithmic steps are computed with a combination of optimized SQL queries and UDFs. Our system includes, among other techniques, Principal Component Analysis (PCA) [2, 5], clustering with mixtures of distributions [4], linear regression [5], parametric statistical tests, and Bayesian Classifiers [8], covering a wide spectrum of statistical and machine learning models. Unlike most research proposals and existing tools, our system can directly process relational tables, truly performing "in-database" analytics.

Our approach is unique and competitive. Most importantly, matrix equations are computed with SQL queries and UDFs, instead of a traditional programming language. Thus we have been able to integrate techniques without having access to the DBMS internal source code, an option avail-

CIKM'11, October 24–28, 2011, Glasgow, Scotland, UK.

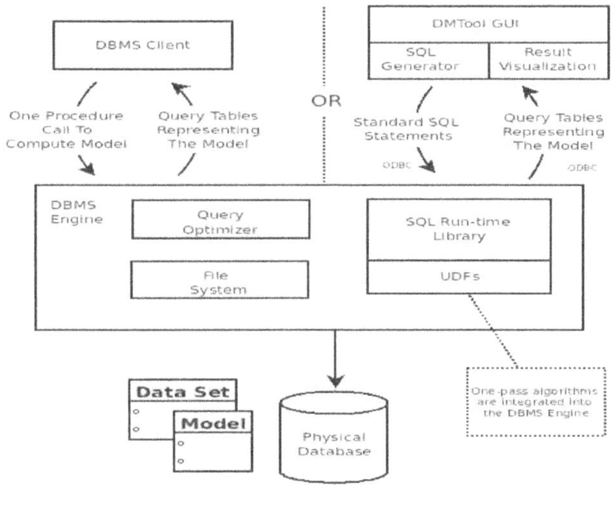

Figure 1: System architecture.

able only to experienced DBMS researchers or developers. Our system provides efficient algorithms, which can analyze large data sets faster than external data mining tools. Several of our SQL-based algorithms can process a large data set in only one pass, while the rest can do it in a few passes. Moreover, all our algorithms have linear scalability on data set size and most of them scale linearly on dimensionality. Our system has promise of wide application as DBMSs remain the standard data management platform, databases keep growing and computers become faster.

2. SYSTEM DESCRIPTION

Our system is based on a comprehensive research effort, where different data mining techniques have been adapted and programmed with optimized SQL queries [4] and more recently with UDFs [5, 9]. We start by presenting the system architecture. We then define the input data set, as well as available statistical models. Finally, we provide a technical summary of how we programmed data mining algorithms with optimized SQL queries and UDFs.

2.1 System Architecture

Our system is based on a client-server architecture, shown in Figure 1. The data set, model matrices and model parameters, are all stored as relational tables. A program at the client computer, connected to the DBMS server via ODBC, calls a stored procedure, which in turn generates SQL queries. The system provides the option to evaluate numerically intensive computations such as matrix equations or complex models with precompiled UDFs. In general, the program generates SQL statements (DDL and DML), monitors algorithm progress (convergence, number of iterations, time) and at the end returns a few tables, corresponding to the model at hand.

2.2 Statistical Models and Algorithms

The input data set $X = \{x_1, x_2, \ldots, x_n\}$ has n records (points) and d attributes (dimensions, features) plus an extra "supervised" attribute (class G or dependent variable Y). That is, n is the data set size. When all attributes are numeric d represents dimensionality.

Our system provides widely used statistical models sharing a common mathematical foundation. Unsupervised models include PCA (most common method to reduce dimensionality; solved with SVD) and clustering with mixtures (solved with the popular K-means algorithm or the more complex EM method). On the other hand, supervised (predictive) models include: linear regression (solved by least squares), the popular Naïve Bayes classifier [10] (estimating joint probability as a product of marginal probabilities) and a sophisticated Bayesian classifier based on class decomposition (using K-means as a building block). In supervised techniques, X has an additional "target" attribute: a numeric dimension Y (for regression) or a discrete (categorical) "class" attribute G (for Naïve Bayes [10] and the Bayesian classifier [8]). Naïve Bayes accepts a combination of numeric and discrete attributes. All models share a common mathematical foundation related to the multivariate normal density function.

2.3 Processing with SQL Queries and UDFs

We start by discussing storage and indexing [4, 5]. The data set and model matrices are stored on tables, indexed by specific combinations of matrix subscripts depending on their storage layout. In general, given a $d \times k$ matrix it can be stored as a "matrix" table with d rows and k columns, as a wide table with dk columns or as a long table with dk rows having one matrix value each. On the other hand, our system uses two fundamental data set layouts. The first layout for X is a standard tabular representation which has n rows, each having d columns, which generally provides best I/O performance. The second layout is based on a pivoted table with one attribute value per row and up to dn rows, which removes DBMS limitations on the maximum number of columns for high dimensional data and which enables more efficient manipulation of sparse matrices.

Evaluating matrix equations with SQL queries is difficult [4, 6]. It is not possible to create fixed queries that can efficiently evaluate mathematical equations because the table definition for the input data set can vary (especially the horizontal layout with d columns). Therefore, SQL code generation at run-time is mandatory. Statistical methods and data mining algorithms are programmed with SQL queries and UDFs, as shown in Figure 2, based on the input data set and two sets of parameters. The first set of parameters controls the mathematical behavior of each technique. Examples include the number of clusters, tolerance threshold for convergence, numeric stability issues, and so on. The second set of parameters controls database systems optimizations, which are tailored to each algorithm (with some common optimizations across multiple models). SQL queries combine joins, aggregations, arithmetic expressions. Certain computations can be optionally evaluated with UDFs. UDFs generally accelerate aggregations, reduce the number of required tables scans, push more processing into RAM memory and eliminate joins. Therefore, UDFs represent an optimization of SQL queries. More specifically, UDFs extend the DBMS with primitive mathematical functions evaluating demanding matrix equations. We should emphasize SQL code, generated by a host language (e.g. Java, C++), can evaluate any equation with matrices, no matter how com-

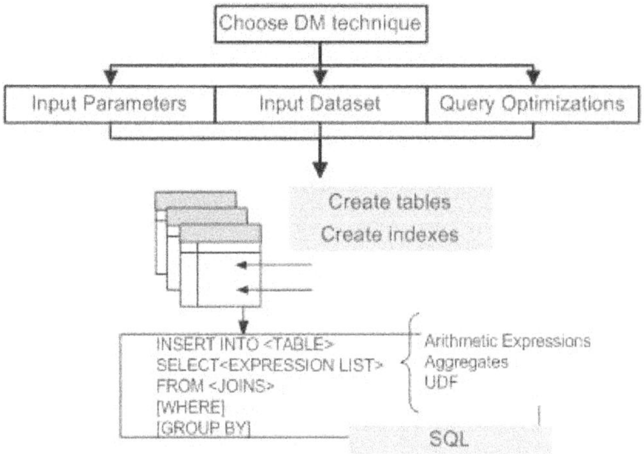

Figure 2: SQL code generation.

plex or slow. Thus the main reason to exploit UDFs is faster execution and to a second extent, programming flexibility.

2.4 Optimizations

We now discuss two main kinds of optimizations: algorithmic and database systems oriented.

We start by discussing algorithmic optimizations, with general applicability. The (multidimensional) sufficient statistics of the multivariate normal distribution are an essential ingredient to accelerate data mining computations. Our system makes extensive use of sufficient statistics to reduce the number of passes on the data set, even one pass. For algorithms like PCA, Naïve Bayes and linear regression sufficient statistics enable computation of the model in one table scan both with SQL queries or UDFs. On the other hand, for K-means clustering and the Bayesian classifier (which are mathematically harder problems), sufficient statistics enable incremental learning, significantly reducing the number of iterations. In an orthogonal manner, sufficient statistics can be computed on samples, providing an approximation to the model, whose accuracy can be controlled. A key difference with previous research is that we can compute sufficient statistics to get either a full covariance or correlation matrix, instead of a diagonal matrix. When the data set is large enough (say $n \geq 100$M) sufficient statistics can be derived with geometric sampling or bootstrapping techniques (leveraging block-based sampling mechanisms provided by the DBMS), which can get arbitrarily accurate ($> 95\%$) approximations in much less time than a full table scan.

Our sufficient statistics are basically the linear sum of points L (a d-dimensional vector) and the quadratic (with cross-products) sum of points Q (a $d \times d$ matrix) [3, 4, 5]:

$$L = \sum_{i=1}^{n} x_i \tag{1}$$

$$Q = \sum_{i=1}^{n} x_i x_i^T \tag{2}$$

Such summary matrices are independently computed on k subsets of the data set for clustering and the Bayesian classifier. Summary matrices are efficiently computed with an aggregate UDF or slower, but with better portability, with SQL queries. For K-means and EM clustering we developed an incremental algorithm that can obtain an acceptable solution in a few iterations (in some cases one), being much faster than the standard algorithm; this is particularly difficult to achieve with SQL or UDFs.

From a database systems perspective, we carefully analyze the query plan for each data mining computation, identifying optimizations that work well across DBMSs. Since equations are evaluated with SQL queries there are many temporary tables generated on the way. In general, we control how each temporary table is stored and indexed. Query rewriting is essential. The join operation is the main operation that can degrade performance if not carefully managed. Denormalized tables with sufficient statistics avoid joins down the road. Whenever possible, aggregations are pushed (computed before) joins. Hash-based joins are the preferred join algorithm on large tables. To get best performance joined tables are indexed by the same subscripts so that the hashing function maps rows to the same partitions. Alternatively, whenever a hash-join is not possible we exploit merge-sort joins. Sort-Merge joins are typically used when both tables are indexed by different subscripts. Our last optimization worth mentioning is caching, which is automatically applied to sufficient statistics [9] and which can also be applied with data sets that can fit in main memory. This optimization is especially beneficial for iterative processing or to concurrently compute multiple models.

3. SYSTEM DEMONSTRATION

We plan to give an interactive demonstration, considering researchers and students with different backgrounds. We will demonstrate our system with a remote DBMS. The database will contain well-known real data sets (from the UCI ML repository, to illustrate data mining applicability) and several large (n=10K,100K,1M) synthetic data sets (to illustrate time efficiency). The same data sets will be also available as flat files to be analyzed by an external data mining tool (e.g. Weka, R statistical package). The demonstration will flow from an overview of our tool, learning available data mining techniques, input data set, parameters, output and visualization, to technical aspects. The user We will give an overview of available data mining techniques. The user will be able to understand technical aspects of the system such as table layouts, SQL queries, UDFs and query optimizations. Our system demonstration will illustrate the following points: (1) being able to efficiently perform data mining on large data sets entirely inside the DBMS (i.e. no data exported); (2) our system is faster than external data mining tools working on flat files; (3) showing exporting large data sets from the DBMS is a bottleneck with ODBC and even with BULK export utilities; (4) quickly computing accurate approximate models with sampling techniques, especially with very large data sets (for specific models); (5) understanding the impact of optimizations, turning them on an off, as well as highlighting which challenging mathematical equations are evaluated with SQL queries or UDFs; Figure 3 shows stored procedure calls and output for two statistical models in the DBMS.

We first discuss a general demonstration, suitable for researchers working on data mining, information retrieval or database systems. The demonstration will show a complete

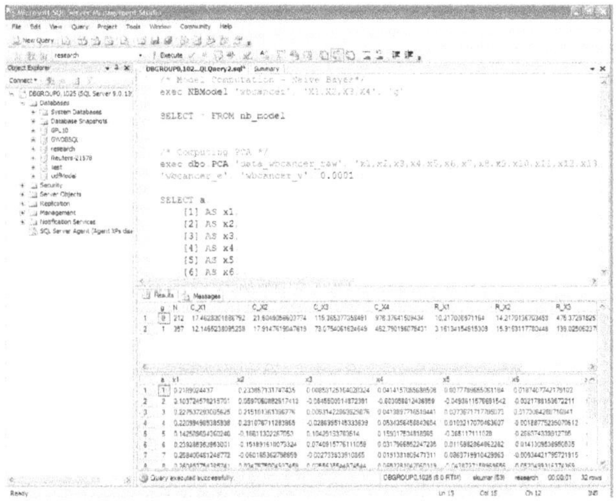

Figure 3: Calling stored procedures and querying output models.

data mining run going from selecting a data set to actually browsing a model. The user will start by choosing one data mining technique from an on-line help. The user will get an overview of optimizations. For supervised models the demonstration will have two subparts: one to build the model and a second one to test the model on a different set of records (i.e. scoring) on a table with the same columns (i.e. to independently test accuracy). Then the user can run the algorithm, which should quickly finish in a few seconds for most data sets. The user will be able to see Naïve Bayes, PCA, and linear regression can be computed in a single table scan in a matter of seconds. On the other hand, the user can use sampling techniques to get accurate approximate models on larger data sets ($n \geq 1$M) in a few seconds. Finally, the user will be able to browse actual the statistical model, which consists of a few relational tables. In addition, for supervised models the user can evaluate model accuracy on a blind test with an independent set of points (i.e. training and testing). Also, the user can compare the predicted (by our system) and existing class values for the test data set.

We now discuss a technical demonstration, suitable for database systems researchers. For performance comparison purposes we will compare with public domain data mining tools (e.g. Weka, R package) working on flat files, computing the same model. We will temporarily stop the DBMS to be fair: SQL queries and UDFs will be shown to be faster than external data mining tools. We will also show exporting large data sets (ODBC, and even with fast BULK utilities) is a bottleneck, making external processing unattractive. The user will be able to understand the impact of available optimizations (including UDFs, sampling and caching) turning them on and off. For instance, the user can run multiple algorithms on the same data set faster when the data set is cached. We will go deeper, providing an overview of important working tables, explaining their layout and explaining how primary or secondary indices accelerate joins and aggregations. Finally, we will show representative SQL queries and UDFs evaluating matrix equations. When showing SQL queries we will explain how tables are joined (indicating specific join algorithm), how aggregations or SQL arithmetic expressions compute equations, how aggregations are pushed before joins and how the output table of one query becomes the input for the next query. For UDFs we will explain how aggregate UDFs accelerate computations by pushing complex mathematical equations into the DBMS by comparing the UDF code against the slower SQL queries.

Acknowledgments

This work was supported by NSF grants CCF 0937562 and IIS 0914861.

4. REFERENCES

[1] T. Hastie, R. Tibshirani, and J.H. Friedman. *The Elements of Statistical Learning*. Springer, New York, 1st edition, 2001.

[2] M. Navas and C. Ordonez. Efficient computation of PCA with SVD in SQL. In *KDD Workshop on Data Mining using Tensors and Matrices*, Article no. 5, 2009.

[3] M. Navas, C. Ordonez, and V. Baladandayuthapani. On the computation of stochastic search variable selection in linear regression with UDFs. In *Proc. IEEE ICDM Conference*, pages 941–946, 2010.

[4] C. Ordonez. Integrating K-means clustering with a relational DBMS using SQL. *IEEE Transactions on Knowledge and Data Engineering (TKDE)*, 18(2):188–201, 2006.

[5] C. Ordonez. Statistical model computation with UDFs. *IEEE Transactions on Knowledge and Data Engineering (TKDE)*, 22(12):1752–1765, 2010.

[6] C. Ordonez and P. Cereghini. SQLEM: Fast clustering in SQL using the EM algorithm. In *Proc. ACM SIGMOD Conference*, pages 559–570, 2000.

[7] C. Ordonez and J. García-García. Database systems research on data mining. In *Proc. ACM SIGMOD Conference*, pages 1253–1254, 2010.

[8] C. Ordonez and S.K. Pitchaimalai. Bayesian classifiers programmed in SQL. *IEEE Transactions on Knowledge and Data Engineering (TKDE)*, 22(1):139–144, 2010.

[9] C. Ordonez and S.K. Pitchaimalai. Fast UDFs to compute sufficient statistics on large data sets exploiting caching and sampling. *Data & Knowledge Engineering (DKE)*, 69(4):383–398, 2010.

[10] S.K. Pitchaimalai, C. Ordonez, and C. Garcia-Alvarado. Comparing SQL and MapReduce to compute Naive Bayes in a single table scan. In *Proc. ACM CloudDB*, pages 9–16, 2010.

Data-Thirsty Business Analysts need SODA - Search Over DAta Warehouse

Lukas Blunschi
ETH Zurich, Switzerland
Lukas.Blunschi@inf.ethz.ch

Claudio Jossen
Credit Suisse AG, Switzerland
Claudio.R.Jossen@credit-suisse.com

Donald Kossmann
ETH Zurich, Switzerland
Donald.Kossmann@inf.ethz.ch

Magdalini Mori
Credit Suisse AG, Switzerland
Magdalini.Mori@credit-suisse.com

Kurt Stockinger
Credit Suisse AG, Switzerland
Kurt.Stockinger@credit-suisse.com

ABSTRACT

Querying large data warehouses is very hard for non-tech savvy business users. Deep technical knowledge of both SQL as well as the schema of the database is required in order to build correct queries and to come up with new business insights. In this paper we introduce a novel system called SODA (Search Over DAta Warehouse) that bridges the gap between the business world and the IT world by enabling extended keyword search in a data warehouse. SODA uses metadata information, DBpedia entries as well as base data to generate SQL to allow intuitive exploration of the data. The process of query classification, query graph generation and SQL generation is visualized to provide the analysts with information on how the query results are produced. Experiments with real data of a global financial institution comprising around 300 tables showed promising results.

Categories and Subject Descriptors

H.3.3 [**Information Storage and Retrieval**]: Information Search and Retrieval—*information filtering, query formulation*

General Terms

Algorithms

Keywords

Data Warehouse, Metadata, Query Generation

1. INTRODUCTION

The goal of SODA is to enable business analysts to run ad-hoc queries on complex data warehouses such as those deployed in financial institutions. The ultimate goal of this project is to take a natural language query of a business analyst as input and automatically generate the correct SQL query that can be executed in the data warehouse.

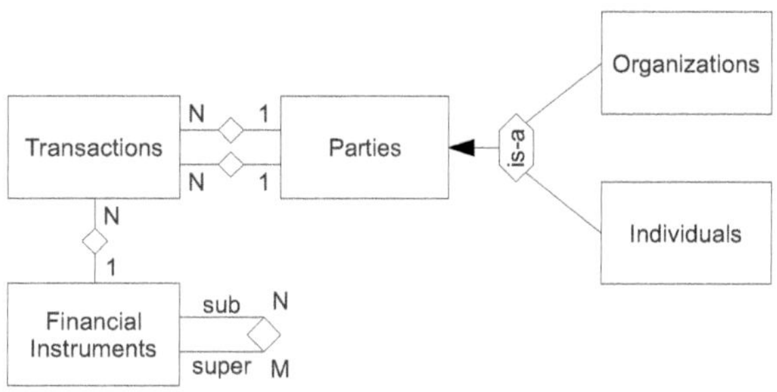

Figure 1: Sample World Schema

At the heart of SODA is a graph that represents the metadata of the data warehouse (i.e., the schema) as well as the business objects and concepts used by business analysts. Literally, this graph bridges the two worlds by providing paths from the business objects to the tables and attributes of the data warehouse. Furthermore, this graph integrates data from external data sources such as DBpedia. Finally, the graph integrates data from the data warehouse itself because queries might involve such instance data.

One important feature of SODA is that it is incremental. We do not expect to have a perfect meta-model from the beginning. Instead, the graph will be modified continually, thereby capturing all the experience gained from answering ad-hoc queries. Furthermore, we expect to evolve the algorithms that navigate the graph continually as more and more query patterns become apparent from using the system.

In summary, this paper reports on the following contributions:

- A comprehensive framework to model metadata and integrate other data sources for searching business entities in data warehouses.
- The design and implementation of a system that takes a business analyst query and a metadata graph as input and generates a SQL query as output.
- A visual user interface that explains the lineage of query results and allows a user to select the most appropriate result.

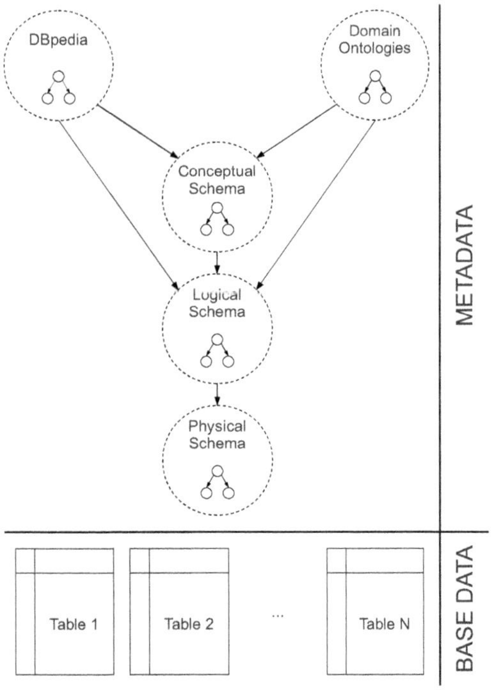

Figure 2: Metadata Graph and Relational Data

2. SAMPLE WORLD

For privacy reasons, we use a synthetic dataset which captures some of the main features of a real enterprise data warehouse. Figure 1 shows the schema of our sample world. In particular, we model information about customers (referred to as *Parties*) and the transactions these customers make; buying and selling on the stock market. Parties can be individuals for private banking or corporate customers for investment banking (i.e., *Organizations*); both kinds of parties are modeled separately because they are supported by different sets of analysts. The technical term for *products* which can be bought or sold on the stock market is *Financial Instrument*. Financial instruments can be shares of a company (e.g., IBM shares). Financial instruments, however, can also be structured; that is, a financial instrument could relate to a funds that manages a portfolio of shares or even a hedge fund that manages a portfolio of certificates of other funds and hedge funds. It is in part this recursive nature of financial instruments that makes it difficult for business analysts to extract the right information from a data warehouse, if no pre-canned reports exist that serve the needs of the analyst.

3. SYSTEM OVERVIEW

In this section we provide a brief overview of our system and explain the algorithms by means of the following query:

`customers Zürich financial instruments`

3.1 Input Data

Our data warehouse consists of base data stored in a relational database as well as metadata stored in a graph structure (such as RDF). The metadata consists of the database schema extended with DBpedia entries and domain ontologies (see Figure 2).

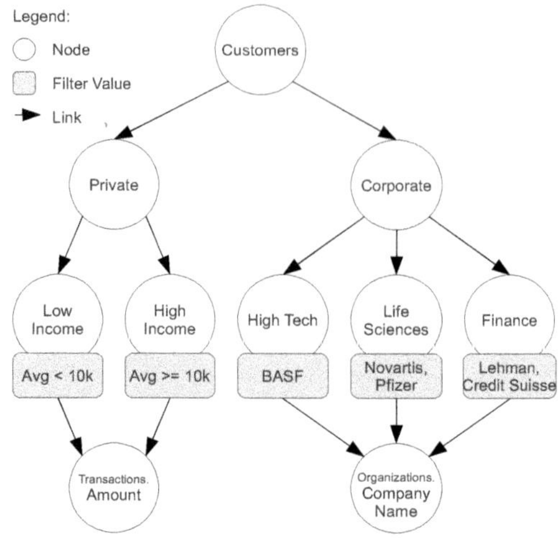

Figure 3: Customers Domain Ontology

Integrated Schema A data warehouse combines and aggregates data from many heterogeneous data sources. To handle the differences in the data sources, an integrated schema is built. This schema can become very large and complex on the technical level. Therefore, there are different levels of the schema, namely conceptual, logical and physical. The conceptual schema (business layer) serves for communication with business and contains the main entities to be modeled such as parties, securities and accounts. The logical schema extends the conceptual one by showing inheritance, splitting entities (for instance, parties are split into individuals and organizations), etc. The physical schema contains information about database indexes or table partitioning. Typically all these schemas are designed with one modeling tool with the goal to generate the physical tables.

DBpedia The metadata graph also contains an extract from DBpedia. Note that we only extract those DBpedia entries that have direct connections to the terms stored in our database schema. For instance, for the term "Parties" shown in our example world, the following entries might be extracted from DBpedia: customer, client, political organization etc. Now, when a user searches for customers then parties would be an answer.

Domain Ontologies Besides the schema and DBpedia, our metadata also consists of several domain ontologies. The domain ontologies are built specifically for a given data warehouse and are used to classify data for a specific domain.

In our example world we are using one ontology that classifies financial instruments and one that classifies customers (see Figure 3). In this example, customers are divided into private and corporate customers. Private customers are further classified as "low income" and "high income" customers based on their total transaction amount. On the other side, corporate customers are categorized as "high tech", "life sciences" or "finance".

Base Data The base data is stored in a relational database.

3.2 Query Classification

The very first step in order to answer our sample query is to interpret the keyword query and apply it onto the metadata graph, before actually executing queries on the data warehouse. In fact, the syntax of the natural language query

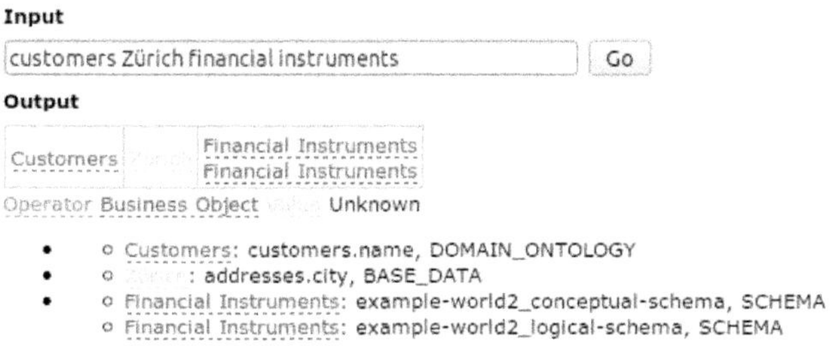

Figure 4: Query Classification

needs to be mapped to a formal syntax to be used for SQL generation (see Figure 4). We call this *query classification*. Query classification applies the following object types to a natural language query:

Business Objects Each single word as well as sequences of words are looked up in the metadata graph and if there is a match, then the term or term combination is classified as a business object. The underlying assumption is that in this case the business object is describing an aspect that can be used as an entry point for a graph traversal to an actual schema node.

Operators Some single words and short concatenations of words in a predefined list are used for a check for operators.

Values If a keyword appears in the base data, we consider it a value. In order to identify the table column that contains the respective value, we use an inverted index.

Unknown Every word or word combination that cannot be classified as one of the three mentioned object types is considered as filler due to the use of natural language and is ignored for the further processing of the query.

Figure 4 shows a screen shot of the classification of our sample query. The term "customers" is classified as a business object which is defined in the customers domain ontology. "Zürich" was found in the base data and "financial instruments" is a business object found in the conceptual and logical schema.

3.3 Algorithm Flowchart

Figure 5 shows the main algorithmic steps starting from query classification (lookup) and ending with SQL generation. Each of these steps is described in more detail in the following sub-sections.

Lookup During the lookup phase, we identify the words in the given query. To do that, we lookup each word in the classification index which is an inverted index on all the words of the input data (metadata graph and relational data). A lookup of a single word provides us with all the locations where this word is found. The output of the lookup phase provides us with entry points into the metadata graph where we can continue applying our algorithm. In Figure 4 "customers" and "Zürich" are both found only once, whereas "financial instruments" is found twice. These two possible combinations result in two solutions.

Rank and Top N In this phase, we compute a first score for all the possible solutions from the lookup phase. There are many possible heuristics which can be used here. One such heuristic is to make use of the location where a word was found. E.g. a word which was found in the domain ontology gets a higher score than a word which was found in DBpedia. The output of the rank and top N phase adds a

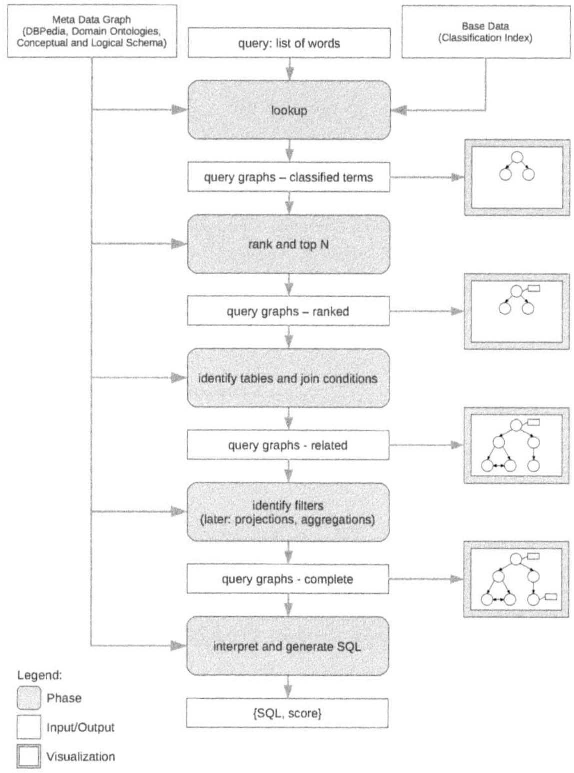

Figure 5: Algorithm Flowchart

score to the solutions found in the lookup phase, orders the results according to that score and continues with the top N results.

Tables and Joins The purpose of this phase is to identify all the tables which are used in each solution and to discover the relationships between these tables. Starting at every entry point which we discovered in the lookup phase, we follow all the edges in the metadata graph until we either have no more edges to follow or discover a table. To find the connections between these tables, we look for graph patterns which represent relationships between tables, e.g. primary-foreign key links and inheritance patterns. The output of the tables and joins phase adds tables and their relationships to the solutions.

In our example, we have two solutions and both of them contain four separate SQL queries. One of the queries has the following tables:
`addresses, fi_transactions, financial_instruments, individuals, parties, transactions`

Filters In the filter phase we look for filter conditions which should be applied to each solution. A filter condition consists of a column and a value such as "Zürich". To define these filter conditions, we look at all the paths from the entry points to the columns. The output of the filters phase adds filter conditions to the previously discovered columns.

In our example, the filter conditions are used to connect "Zürich" to the city column within the addresses table.

SQL Generation During this phase, we generate SQL for all the solutions. To create the SQL statement, we make use of all the tables, relationships and filter conditions which were discovered in the previous phases. The foreign keys are used to combine the tables. If the tables are partitioned into distinct subsets (via inheritance patterns), then a separate SQL statement is created for each subset, in the query above, for example, we get a SQL statement for individuals and one for organization:

```
SELECT *
FROM addresses, individuals, fi_transactions,
     financial_instruments, parties, transactions
WHERE
  addresses.city='Zürich' AND
  (transactions.fromParty=parties.id OR
   transactions.toParty=parties.id) AND
  fi_transactions.id=transactions.id AND
  fi_transactions.fi=financial_instruments.id AND
  individuals.id=parties.id AND
  individuals.livingAt=addresses.id

SELECT *
FROM fi_transactions, financial_instruments,
     organizations, parties, transactions
WHERE
  (organizations.companyName='BASF' OR ... OR
   organizations.companyName='Credit Suisse') AND
  (transactions.fromParty=parties.id OR
   transactions.toParty=parties.id) AND
  organizations.id=parties.id AND
  fi_transactions.id=transactions.id AND
  fi_transactions.fi=financial_instruments.id
```

The output of the SQL phase is a list of SQL statements for each solution together with a score.

4. MORE DEMO INSIGHTS

In addition to generating SQL based on keywords, our system also provides various result visualization features that help the user understand and interpret the results. For example, a user can look at the lineage for each term in the classified query or he (or she) may browse along the edges of the metadata graph.

Experiments with real data of a global financial institution comprising around 300 tables showed promising results. For privacy reasons this demo is based on the synthetic sample world shown in Section 2.

Our demo will provide answers to the following questions:

- How is a query classified and broken into meaningful entities that can be used for further processing?
- How are the query results ranked?
- How can tables and join conditions be identified and visualized?
- How are filter conditions evaluated and how are they use for generating useful SQL?
- How are range queries and aggregations performed?

At `http://lukasblunschi.ch/soda` you can find a demo version of SODA using the sample world of Section 2.

5. RELATED WORK

Due to the popularity of search engines and the ease of data exploration, adding search capabilities to relational databases has become very popular [1, 3, 4, 5, 6, 7, 8, 2].

Whereas these works mainly make use of the database schema to discover joins, our metadata graph not only consists of one or several combined schemas, but can integrate domain-specific extensions (domain ontologies) as well as extensions which are not related to any specific domain (DBpedia).

Furthermore, one of the main differentiators of our work is that we consider inheritance within the database schema - a common practice in large and complex data warehouse schemas. The problems is important for automatic SQL generation. For instance, if we want to join the table transaction with the table parties where a party can be either an individual or an organization, we need to bear in mind the exclusive inheritance between individual and organization. A typical wrong join path is as follows: transaction AND individual AND organization. Taking into account the inheritance yields the following two join paths: transactions AND organization; transactions AND individual. None of the related work appears to consider inheritance.

Finally, existing work is validated against fairly simple data models with some 10 tables, while our system is based on a real-world data set with a complex enterprise data warehouse model of a global financial institution comprising hundreds of tables.

Hence, our approach is an important step to automatically generate correct SQL for complex, real-world data warehouse schemas.

6. REFERENCES

[1] S. Agrawal, S. Chaudhuri, and G. Das. DBXplorer: A System for Keyword-Based Search over Relational Databases. *ICDE*, 2002.

[2] S. Bergamaschi, E. Domnori, F. Guerra, R. T. Lado, and Y. Velegrakis. Keyword Search over Relational Databases: A Metadata Approach. *SIGMOD*, 2011.

[3] G. Bhalotia, A. Hulgeri, C. Nakhe, S. Chakrabarti, and S. Sudarshan. Keyword Searching and Browsing in Databases using BANKS. *ICDE*, 2002.

[4] H. He, H. Wang, J. Yang, and P. S. Yu. BLINKS: Ranked Keyword Searches on Graphs. *SIGMOD*, 2007.

[5] V. Hristidis and Y. Papakonstantinou. DISCOVER: Keyword Search in Relational Databases. *VLDB*, 2002.

[6] Y. Luo, X. Lin, W. Wang, and X. Zhou. SPARK: Top-k Keyword Query in Relational Databases. *SIGMOD*, 2007.

[7] M. Sayyadian, H. LeKhac, A. Doan, and L. Gravano. Efficient Keyword Search Across Heterogeneous Relational Databases. *ICDE*, 2007.

[8] Q. Su and J. Widom. Indexing Relational Database Content Offline for Efficient Keyword-Based Search. *IDEAS*, 2005.

An Integrated Environment for Semantic Knowledge Work

Aba-Sah Dadzie, Victoria Uren, Ziqi Zhang, Philip Webster
Department of Computer Science
University of Sheffield
Sheffield, UK

a.dadzie(v.uren, z.zhang, p.webster)@dcs.shef.ac.uk

ABSTRACT
In this demonstration, we will present a semantic environment called the K-Box. The K-Box supports the lightweight integration of knowledge tools, with a focus on semantic tools, but with the flexibility to integrate natural language and conventional tools. We discuss the implementation of the framework, and two existing applications, including details of a new application for developers of semantic workflows. The demonstration will be of interest to developers and researchers of ontology-based knowledge management systems, and semantic desktops, and to analysts working with cross-media information.

Categories and Subject Descriptors
H.5.2 [**Information Systems**] User Interfaces

General Terms: Design

Keywords
Semantic knowledge management, Knowledge tool integration.

Preview: http://bit.ly/mHAgko

1. INTRODUCTION
Metadata and semantic methods have potential to enhance a wide range of knowledge work tasks, including data analysis, information retrieval, and Personal Information Management (PIM). The potential of semantic desktops has been explored through several initiatives e.g., Nepomuk [1] and Haystack [2]. However, we have found that these systems do not address a practical problem: in many knowledge work tasks, legacy (often non-semantic) tools exist which have been implemented in a variety of ways. The knowledge worker will typically want to continue to use their trusted legacy tools alongside semantic tools. The K-Box was therefore designed as a work environment in which diverse tools could be brought together in a task-focused interface, with in-built semantic support, but without restricting the toolset or requiring costly reprogramming of pre-existing tools. As we will show in this demonstration, it provides a basis to support both analytical and knowledge generation tasks.

2. IMPLEMENTATION OF THE K-Box
The K-Box provides a knowledge management (KM) environment that supports the sharing of knowledge objects and artefacts (e.g., documents, ontologies and workflows) between different specialist tools. These are shared through a KM framework, referred to hereafter as the Kernel. The K-Box allows the user to access multiple KM tools from a single point, independent of the tools' underlying design, architecture and internal mechanisms. In addition to in-built components, such as the clipboard and ontology-based tagger (described below), "external" tools may be integrated into the K-Box, as plug-ins. The K-Box design removes the need for the user (whether this is a developer or an end user) to understand the internal workings of different tools. Essentially, the K-Box considers each independent tool integrated into the framework as a black box, requiring only that each tool provides, where necessary, wrappers for formatting output according to a common, agreed, standard language (ideally based on a standard or domain ontology), and subscribes to the Kernel to post and listen to notifications for, among others, new data generated within or imported into the system.

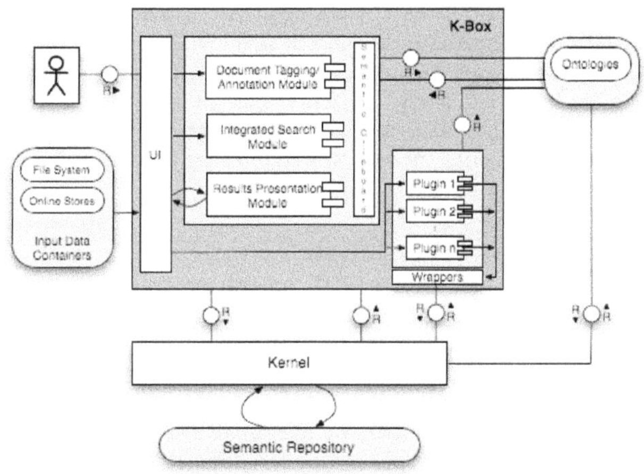

Figure 1. K-Box framework, illustrating inter-communication between tools and with a semantic repository, via the Kernel.

2.1 Kernel
The Kernel is an intermediary tool through which tools communicate and exchange data, using an event-based system to notify all tools within the K-Box whenever a task carried out by any one tool results in new output, or creates metadata that enriches existing data. For those tools that do not provide internal mechanisms for encoding output according to the specified encoding semantic representation (e.g., Resource Description Framework – RDF), the Kernel exposes methods which may be used to convert selected documents and encode tool output as required. Further, the Kernel interfaces with the semantic repositories into which the knowledge generated as a result of interaction with the K-Box is stored. Within the K-Box, semantic data is also browsed and retrieved via the Kernel.

2.2 Semantic Clipboard

The Semantic Clipboard is an always visible component built into the K-Box that provides visual pointers, encoded using thumbnails or icons, to "bookmarked" data and knowledge items – see bottom, Figures 2 and 3. The clipboard interfaces with the semantic repository (via the Kernel); each bookmark points to the URI used to retrieve the corresponding item from the semantic repository to which the K-Box is connected. A user may simply choose to view a bookmarked document, or use it as input to a new task, e.g., to trigger a search for similar information based on the metadata attached to the bookmarked item and/or its content.

2.3 Ontology Based Tagging

The in-built ontology browser is used for ontology-based data and knowledge tagging; a tag is attached to a knowledge artefact, e.g., a document, by selecting a concept of interest from the browser and dragging it onto its bookmark in the clipboard (see Figure 2). The tag may be refined by entering a keyword. The Kernel writes the metadata generated as a result to the semantic repository, where it is subsequently available to any tool (e.g., search tools).

2.4 Integrated Search

Information in different media often requires different methods for search, e.g., commonly available text-based search cannot handle information retrieval from image and numerical data. The K-Box provides support for integrating different types of search tools by using metadata captured during user interaction to enrich user queries. This allows a query input into a specific tool to be propagated (transparently) to other search tools integrated into the K-Box, or a selected document or data item to be used to initialize a similarity search across all tools. For the naïve end user in particular, this provides additional advantages; by transparently reformulating queries for each search tool, the BOX removes this burden from the user.

2.5 Results Presentation

The K-Box makes use of RDF to encode data and capture metadata describing the data and its knowledge content, to support data exchange between different tools. Using the semantic data format provides the additional advantage of easing the use of powerful Semantic Web technology. However, a drawback is that RDF is not easily understood by people; the K-Box supports the use of presentation templates (e.g., stylesheets), to format the knowledge that results from interaction with the framework, to generate more human-readable output (e.g., as PDF or HMTL documents with links to source data). This may be used to create snapshots of on-going analytical activity or report completed tasks at varying levels of detail.

3. APPLICATIONS

The K-Box has, so far, been successfully deployed to support three KM tasks with very different end user communities. These have proved its flexibility: a wide range of external tools have been integrated, including not only semantic web tools but also natural language tools, such as a Text Summarizer and Information Extraction tools. Two of these applications are described here.

3.1 Issue Investigation Environment

The issue investigation scenario involves teams with varied expertise, working independently and collaboratively to identify the causes of mechanical issues. The KM framework for this scenario provided support for search, annotation and analysis over large scale repositories of text, image and numerical data. To support the realities of the task in engineering companies, this had to be conducted asynchronously by the issue investigation team. Therefore users had to be able to clearly and quickly see what other team members had discovered in previous sessions. One view of the Issue Investigation Environment is illustrated in Figure 2, and the application is described in more detail in [3].

The external tools this application contained include: a semantic search tool (K-Search [4]), a region-based, image similarity tool[1], a document summarization tool (the CognitSummarizer[2]), ontology visualization tools including a purpose built root cause analysis tool which allows users to attach items to candidate causes as evidence for or against [3; 5], and a report generator which could produce a human readable summary of progress.

A similar approach has been used to evaluate support for post-crisis management as part of the WeKnowIt project[3]. In this case support is provided for asynchronous, albeit collaborative, review of collective intelligence gathered during a crisis, in order to apply any lessons learnt to future emergency situations.

3.2 Developer Environment

The second application, and the main focus for this demonstrator, is a knowledge generation and editing environment for developers producing structured knowledge to support task execution in distributed, ubiquitous environments such as kitchens, cars and factories. The SmartProducts project[4] is investigating the use of these kinds of structured knowledge to provide interoperability in open, sensor-rich environments (open meaning the configuration of devices is not known in advance). The purpose is to allow these devices to take a more proactive role in assisting the user, rather than simply being passive tools.

A key knowledge artefact in these "smart" applications will be workflows annotated using ontologies of product types, domain entities, activities etc. These workflows will guide user interaction with the smart environments, and instruct products in directly executing tasks. A number of developer tools have been created to ease the production of semantic workflows from instructional texts originally intended solely for human consumption. Examples include recipes, car manuals and manufacturing work orders. Tools that would be used together to process these texts include a natural language processing (NLP)-based Workflow Extractor, and a semantic Workflow Editor. The Workflow Extractor extracts an initial draft workflow, which the developer may annotate and edit using the editor. One view of this Developer Environment is presented in Figure 3. This shows the Workflow tab open.

To further support our case that the K-Box environment is flexible in respect of the kinds of external tools it can integrate, we note that the Workflow Extractor is built from publically available NLP tools and in its native version runs from a command line.

---

[1] General Image Representation Library: http://girl.labri.fr

[2] http://www.cognit.com/home_multi/html/hXGXBSMZDOXU.5.idium

[3] http://www.weknowit.eu

[4] http://www.smartproducts-project.eu/

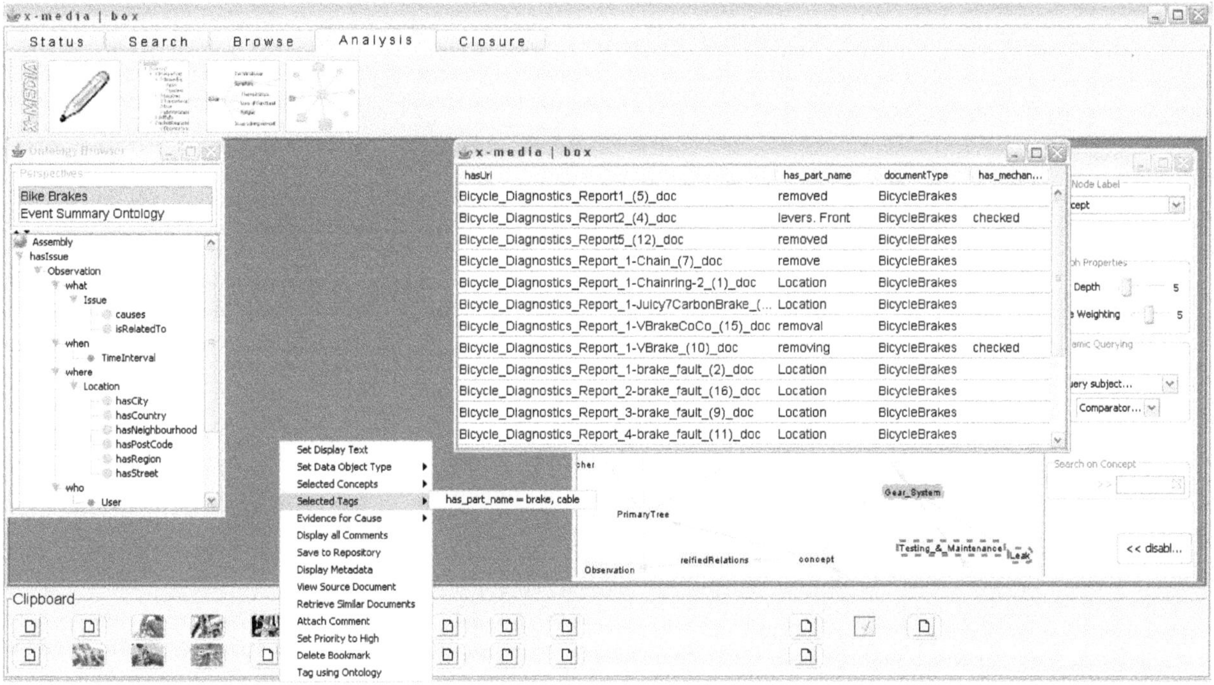

Figure 2. : The K-Box as an Issue Investigation Environment, showing tabs to access tools which support different stages of Issue Investigation: (top left) icons to start individual tools in the toolbar of each tab window; the in-built ontology browser (left); the results of an integrated search (centre) to retrieve similar data, using a bookmarked item in the semantic clipboard (bottom) to provide search terms.

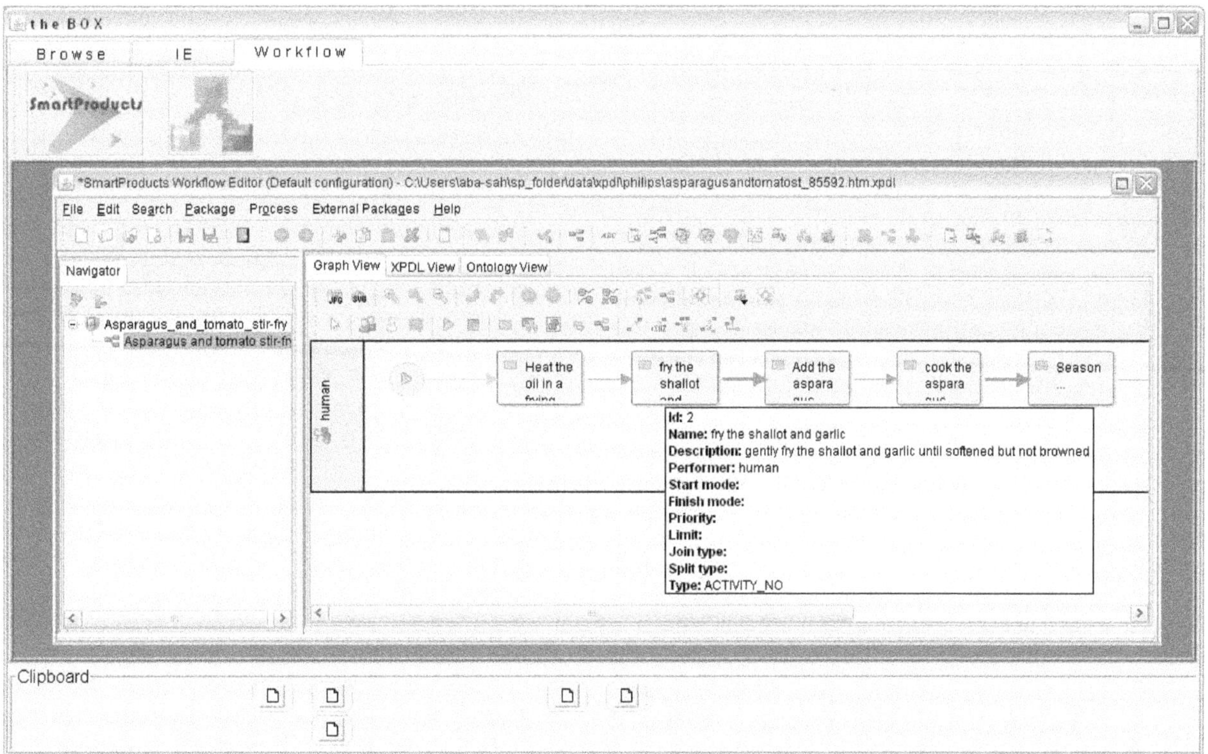

Figure 3. Screenshot of the K-Box as a Developer Environment for semantic workflows, illustrating the workflow editor interface (centre), which extends the open source JaWE editor, including the new Ontology View tab in the editor interface. Note the tabs and tool icons in the K-Box (top left), these differ from those in the Issue Investigation Environment, reflecting changes made to the K-Box to tailor it for a different user group.

The only modification required for incorporation in the K-Box was the addition of a minimal one pane GUI (graphical user interface) and a wrapper. The Workflow Editor, on the other hand, is a modification of the open source JaWE workflow editor [6]. This third party tool was also incorporated in the environment with relative ease. In the next two sections we describe these tools in more detail.

Workflow Extractor

The Workflow Extractor is capable of extracting domain information (domain-specific actions and domain-specific entities, both actors and actees) and procedural information (transitions and conditions).

Following a similar approach to [7], the method is based on the hypothesis that a task action is usually expressed as a verb phrase containing domain information, and it may occur with other contextual information such as conditions. The core of the extraction system is a syntactic parser, which parses a sentence into its constituents and their relations.

Using the parser we are able to extract verb phrases, constituents of verb phrases, and their contextual constituents. Next, each of the verb phrases with their contextual constituents are split into candidate actions for further grammatical analysis, which applies a set of rules to the parsing result to determine whether the verb phrase is a domain specific action, and if so, to extract domain and procedural information related to that action. The advantage of using a syntactic parser instead of WordNet is that the parser can take account of sentential contexts in the identification of verbs and nouns.

3.3 Workflow Editor

The Workflow Editor is a tool that allows developers to create workflow process definitions, edit workflows generated by the Extractor and to annotate them using OWL (Web Ontology Language) individuals.

The editor is based on JaWE [6], which provides functionality to allow users to create workflow process definitions that conform to version 1.0 of the XPDL (Extensible Process Definition Language) specification [8]. Due to the use of an open standard XML-based format for serialization of workflows, these process definitions can be executed in a variety of open source and proprietary workflow engines. The editor outputs workflows in a variant of XPDL devised for use on the SmartProducts project [9]. This variant provides support for three predefined annotation types: METADATA, PRODUCT CLASS and ACTIVITY.

Editing of process definitions is performed using the standard graphical representation of elements provided by JaWE. In addition to this, a number of ontology-related features were added. The user can load one or more OWL ontologies, which can be viewed in a hierarchical tree form using an ontology browser panel set alongside the existing BPMN (Business Process Model and Notation) graph and XPDL source views. Concepts from the loaded ontologies may then be used as annotations that can be applied to appropriate XPDL elements.

In order to make the process of annotation easier, XPDL activity nodes that have been annotated are highlighted in a different colour. The annotation process itself involves the selection of appropriate attribute names from a drop-down menu, and the assignment of OWL individuals to those attributes.

4. FUTURE DEVELOPMENTS

The main benefit of the K-Box framework is its flexible approach to integrating tools independent of their underlying design, architecture and internal mechanisms. This has allowed it to be used to build task-focused environments for quite different kinds of knowledge work, incorporating semantic, natural language and mainstream tools.

We propose to test the framework further by developing an environment to support qualitative and quantitative work in the social sciences, specifically the analysis of 'messages' conveyed by the public media. A driver of this research direction is our ambition to incorporate novel analytical tools in the environment, building on the visualization and decision support tools already tested in the Issue Investigation Environment.

5. ACKNOWLEDGMENTS

Part of this research has been funded under the EC 7th Framework Programme, in the context of the SmartProducts project (231204).

6. REFERENCES

[1] T. Groza, S. Handschuh, K. Moeller, G. Grimnes, L. Sauermann, E. Minack, C. Mesnage, M. Jazayeri, G. Reif, R. Gudjonsdóttir, The NEPOMUK Project - On the way to the Social Semantic Desktop. In *Proc., I-Semantics' 07*, 2007.

[2] K. Bakshi and D. Karger, End-User Application Development for the Semantic Web. In *Semantic Desktop Workshop at ISWC 2005*, 2005.

[3] A.-S. Dadzie, V. Uren, and F. Ciravegna, Ontology-Based Knowledge Capture & Sharing in Enterprise Organisations, In *Ontology Learning and Knowledge Discovery Using the Web: Challenges and Recent Advances, Wong, W., Liu, W, Bennamoun, M. (eds.),* 2011.

[4] R. Bhagdev, A. Chakravarthy, S. Chapman, F. Ciravegna & V. Lanfranchi. Creating and using organisational semantic webs in large networked organisations. In *Proc., 2008 International Semantic Web Conference*, pp. 723-736, 2008.

[5] A.-S. Dadzie, V. Lanfranchi, D. Petrelli. Seeing is Believing: Linking Data With Knowledge. *Journal on Human-Centered Information Visualization*, 8, 3, pp.197-211, 2009.

[6] K. Trichkov and E. Trichkova. Modeling and execution of web service in internet using Enhydra workflow platform. International Conference on Computer Systems and Technologies - CompSysTech'06, 2006.

[7] M. Brasser and K. Linden. Automatically eliciting taskmodels from written task narratives. In *Proc., 4th International Conference on Computer-Aided Design of User Interfaces*, pp. 83-90, 2002.

[8] Workflow Management Coalition. *Workflow standard process definition interface - XML process definition language*, document number wfmc-tc-1025, October 2008.

[9] P. Webster, V. Uren, and M. Ständer, Shaken not stirred: mixing semantics into XPDL, In *5th International Workshop on Semantic Business Process Management co-located with ESWC 2010*, 2010

Editing Knowledge Resources: The Wiki Way

Francesco Ronzano
Institute of Informatics and Telematics (IIT) - CNR
G. Moruzzi, 1
Pisa, Italy
fr.ronzano@gmail.com

Andrea Marchetti
Institute of Informatics and Telematics (IIT) - CNR
G. Moruzzi, 1
Pisa, Italy
andrea.marchetti@iit.cnr.it

Maurizio Tesconi
Institute of Informatics and Telematics (IIT) - CNR
G. Moruzzi, 1
Pisa, Italy
maurizio.tesconi@iit.cnr.it

ABSTRACT

The creation, customization, and maintenance of knowledge resources are essential for fostering the full deployment of Language Technologies. The definition and refinement of knowledge resources are time- and resource-consuming activities. In this paper we explore how the Wiki paradigm for online collaborative content editing can be exploited to gather massive social contributions from common Web users in editing knowledge resources. We discuss the Wikyoto Knowledge Editor, also called Wikyoto. Wikyoto is a collaborative Web environment that enables users with no knowledge engineering background to edit the multilingual network of knowledge resources exploited by KYOTO, a cross-lingual text mining system developed in the context of the KYOTO European Project.

Categories and Subject Descriptors

H.4 [**Information Systems Applications**]: Miscellaneous

General Terms

Experimentation, Design

Keywords

Web and Social Knowledge Management, Collaborative editing Web applications, Knowledge resources, Wiki paradigm

1. THE WIKI PARADIGM APPLIED TO KNOLWEDGE RESOURCES

During the last few years the development of Language Technologies has become more and more dependent on the possibility to rely on sets of properly-structured, rich, and updated **Knowledge Resources**. Knowledge Resources constitute the background knowledge exploited in several applicative contexts to (semi) automatically interpret, organize, and integrate data that, when we deal with Language Technologies, are often represented as textual contents. Each Knowledge Resource can provide information related to a general or a specific domain (i.e., environment, biology, genomics, etc.) with a proper type and level of data structuring, varying from simple lists of words, to complex semantic networks like lexicons and ontologies. *The creation and maintenance of knowledge resources are essential for fostering the full deployment of Language Technologies, but requires a lost of efforts in terms of time and resources invested.*

Together with the central role played by Knowledge Resources, the last decade has been characterized by the huge diffusion experimented over the Web by the **Wiki Paradigm**. By means of this expression we refer to the collaborative editing of a specific type of content by exploiting Web-based tools called Wiki environments. The core feature of the Wiki Paradigm is *the social aspect of content creation.* A Wiki environment indeed *enables distributed communities of users to actively contribute to the editing activities of shared content.* The users of this kind of tool are pushed to create and share these contents because they feel they are contributing to a community effort useful for producing knowledge for the entire community. Wikipedia together with all the related Wikimedia Foundation Projects[1] represent relevant examples of Wiki environments.

Several distinctive tasks related to the creation and management of Knowldge Resources can be collaboratively performed by exploiting the Wiki Paradigm. The content of Knowledge Resources is characterized by continuous change since *the knowledge it formalizes is usually in constant evolution.* In order to be kept up-to-date, Knowledge Resources need editing contributions from *editors that are spread over different locations all over the world.* Editors usually have *different levels of expertise* ranging from knowledge engineers to domain experts lacking any notion of knowledge formalization. In Wiki environments, editing can be performed over the Web, often through a Web browser. Therefore, distributed communities of users can contribute without location- or time-related constraints and can cooperate to keep the formalized knowledge up-to-date. Intuitive visual Web interfaces can be exploited by users with no knowledge engineering background to edit the set of complex knowledge structures that characterize Knowledge Resources such as OWL ontologies.

Currently several knowledge editing tools are available, both collaborative and not. These tools can be grouped into two broad categories:

[1] http://wikimediafoundation.org/wiki/Our_projects

CIKM'11, October 24–28, 2011, Glasgow, Scotland, UK.

- ***Semantic Wikis*** are Wiki environments in which contents are structured by means of semantic annotations. Examples of semantic Wiki are **Platypus Wiki** [5], **Semantic MediaWiki** [8], **IkeWiki** [11], **OntoWiki** [2], **Rizhome Wiki** [1] and **SweetWiki** [4].
- ***Ontology editors*** enable users to create and modify ontologies. Ontology editors can exploit a graphical interface to browse and edit ontologies or rely on a controlled language. **Protégé** [13, 15, 14], **OntoStudio** [10], **The NeOn Toolkit**[2], **Ontoverse** [3], **TopBraid Composer**[3] and **CODA** [9] are examples of ontology editors based on a graphical interface. **ACEwiki** [12] and the **Controlled Language for Ontology Editing** (CLOnE) [7] are examples of controlled languages and ontology editors based on the same controlled languages.

Considering the analysis of the features of these knowledge editing tools, we have designed and developed Wikyoto, the Web-based Wiki environment developed in the context of the KYOTO Project that will be described in the rest of this paper.

2. THE WIKYOTO KNOWLEDGE EDITOR

After a brief introduction of the KYOTO System and the organization and structure of its knowledge resources, in this Section we focus on the description of Wikyoto.

2.1 KYOTO and the Multilingual Knowledge Base

KYOTO is an information and knowledge sharing system that relies on cross-lingual text mining procedures to interpret the meaning of documents in multiple languages. By processing textual content, KYOTO enables the extraction of deep semantic relations and facts as well as their exploitation across languages and cultures to support users' informative needs by means of semantically enhanced searches. KYOTO has been developed since 2008 in the context of the KYOTO European FP7 Project. The interested reader is referred to the Official Web Site of the KYOTO Project, http://www.kyotoproject.eu/.

All the knowledge mining tasks of KYOTO are carried out by exploiting the **Multilingual Knowledge Base** (MKB), a collection of lexical and ontological knowledge resources. In particular KYOTO mines textual contents by means of a collection of WordNets [6] mapped to the language-independent knowledge items encoded in the KYOTO Central Ontology (see Fig. 1).

The **KYOTO Central Ontology** is an OWL DL ontology composed by three layers with a growing level of specialization. The linguistic information characterizing each language involved in KYOTO is encoded in a set of **WordNets**, one for each language. These are computational lexicons adhering to the WordNet model. As shown in Fig. 1, seven European and Asian languages are addressed by the KYOTO Project (English, Spanish, Italian, Dutch, Basque, Chinese and Japanese). For each language KYOTO includes a Generic WordNet (WN in Fig. 1) and one or more domain

[2]NeOn Toolkit - http://neon-toolkit.org/wiki/Main_Page
[3]TopBraid Composer
http://www.topquadrant.com/products/TB_Composer.html

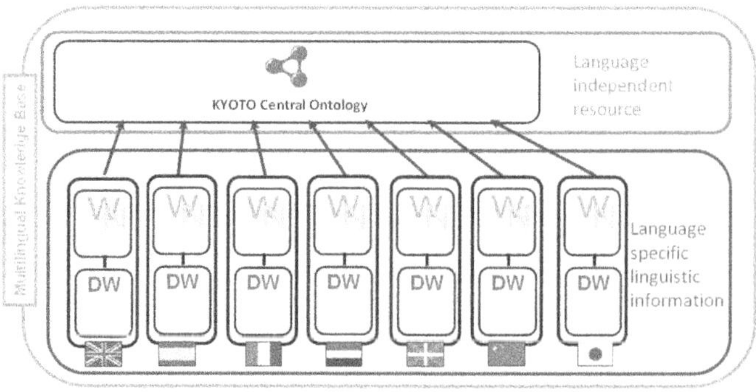

Figure 1: Structure of the KYOTO Multilingual Knowledge Base

WordNets (DW in Fig. 1). The Generic WordNet encodes all the generic linguistic information characterizing that language. The Domain WordNets can be figured out as domain specializations of the Generic one. It is possible to develop each Domain WordNet independently from the Generic one. Proper mappings can be created so as to link synsets (concepts) from a Domain WordNet to other synsets belonging to the Generic one.

Wikyoto, one of the core components of the KYOTO system has been developed to enable KYOTO users (who usually have little or no experience in knowledge engineering) to easily edit the knowledge structures of the MKB. By accessing Wikyoto, users can exploit a *visual intuitive interface* and *simplified language-driven interactions* to collaboratively enrich and refine the Domain WordNet of KYOTO by hiding the complexity of the edited knowledge structures.

Wikyoto is accessible at http://www.wikyoto.net/. From the Wikyoto Web Site, users can browse the user manual and a set of video-tutorials introducing the main features of the tool and showing some example of knowledge editing patterns. A detailed technical description of the system is also available.

2.2 Functional overview

Wikyoto has been designed and implemented as a Rich Web Application in order to allow users to access it online by means of a browser, anywhere, anytime. The global organization of Wikyoto is outlined in Fig. 2. Wikyoto users with little or no experience in knowledge engineering can:

- edit the Domain WordNets of their language so as to customize them with respect to the considered domain of interest. In this way the effectiveness and coverage of Word Sense Disambiguation in KYOTO is enhanced. In particular, users are supported in:
  - the creation of new Domain WordNet synsets or the editing of existing Domain WordNet synsets by modifying their set of lemmas, part of speech, and gloss as well as by evaluating their rigidity;
  - the creation of new semantic relations between Domain WordNet synsets or the modification of the existing semantic relations;
  - the creation of mappings between Domain WordNet synsets and Generic WordNet synsets.

- map the Domain WordNet synsets of their language to the language-independent entities of the Central Ontology. Therefore the cross-lingual text mining of KYOTO is improved.

Thanks to Wikyoto, users can also access and exploit a set of external knowledge resources to obtain useful suggestions to enrich the MKB. These resources are: the *KYOTO Terminology*, domain specific *SKOS Thesauri* and *DBpedia*[4].

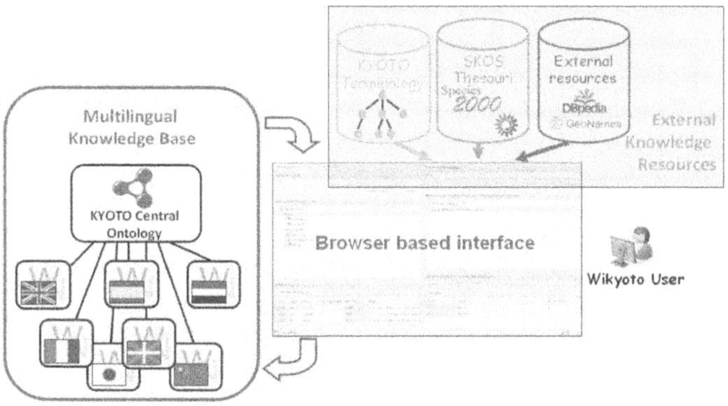

Figure 2: Functional overview of Wikyoto

In Wikyoto, users point out knowledge objects of interest by adding and interlinking new concepts thus *collaboratively tailoring the knowledge resources of KYOTO to a specific domain*. By doing so, they implicitly define their information needs. Since users tend to formalize the knowledge structures they consider relevant by adding them to the MKB, the text mining procedures of KYOTO will be automatically targeted to more accurately parse that kind of information from texts, making it available to semantic searches.

We can define Wikyoto as *a balance between semantic wikis and ontology editors*. Wikyoto aims to build a Web environment with a shallow learning curve for users without experience in knowledge formalization, such as in semantic wikis. By exploiting an interactive Web interface, users are invited to enrich the linguistic knowledge of Domain WordNets starting from natural language interactions, but also by browsing domain terminologies. However, as in ontology editors, the resulting knowledge has a degree of formalization useful for supporting the cross-lingual knowledge mining tasks of KYOTO.

2.3 The Web interface

We present a brief overview of the layout and the interaction patterns exploited in the browser-based interface of Wikyoto. By accessing Wikyoto online it is possible to experience the tool.
Wikyoto users, once authenticated and after having chosen a language to browse and enrich the corresponding Domain WordNet, can access the Web interface of Wikyoto (see Fig. 3).

The interface is divided into two parts: on the right side there is the **Domain WordNet Browser and Editor** and on the left side the **Semantic Resources Browser**. Users

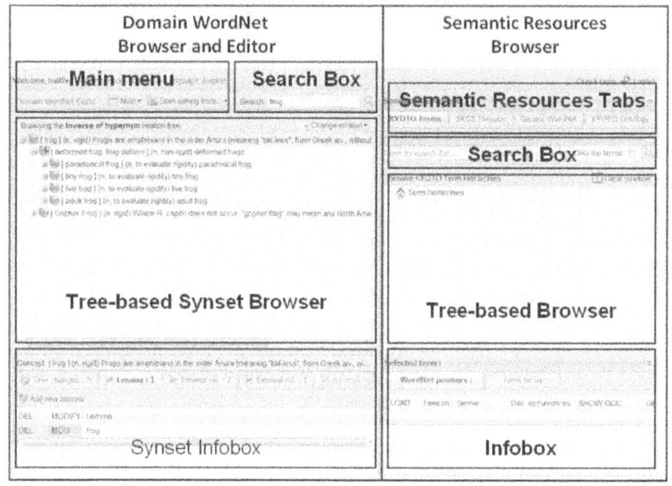

Figure 3: The layout of the Wikyoto Web interface

can browse and edit the Domain WordNet of their language of choice through the Domain WordNet Browser and Editor. The Semantic Resource Browser enables users to browse four kinds of Semantic Resources with knowledge import and mapping purposes, through each one of the Semantic Resources Tabs. Since browsing networks of concepts and in particular subsumption hierarchies of concepts is one of the most effective ways to get a sense of how knowledge resources are structured, **tree-based interface widgets** have been extensively exploited in Wikyoto to navigate terminologies and hierarchies of both WordNet synsets and ontological concepts. Intuitive **drag&drop actions** allow users to easily rearrange the nodes of hierarchies of concepts as well as to map Domain WordNets of different languages on the language-independent entities of the KYOTO Central Ontology.

2.4 The architecture

Wikyoto has been structured as a Rich Web Application that strongly relies on client-side Web technologies, languages, and standards that are widely supported by the majority of Web browser. HTML and CSS are exploited to define the layout and graphical features of the interface and Javascript to enable client-side user interactions and data elaborations. In particular, the Ext.js Javascript library[5] and AJAX interactions are extensively used in order to:

- provide users with an interface characterized by visual widgets and intuitive interaction patterns;
- retrieve, aggregate, display, and modify data by accessing multiple repositories.

The high level architecture of Wikyoto is constituted by two main building blocks (see Figure 4):

- ***browser module***, which is constituted by the browser-based Web interface and a set of Javascript libraries that support the interactivity of the interface as well as the retrieval of information from the data repositories;

[4]DBpedia http://wiki.dbpedia.org/

[5]Ext.js - http://www.sencha.com/products/extjs/

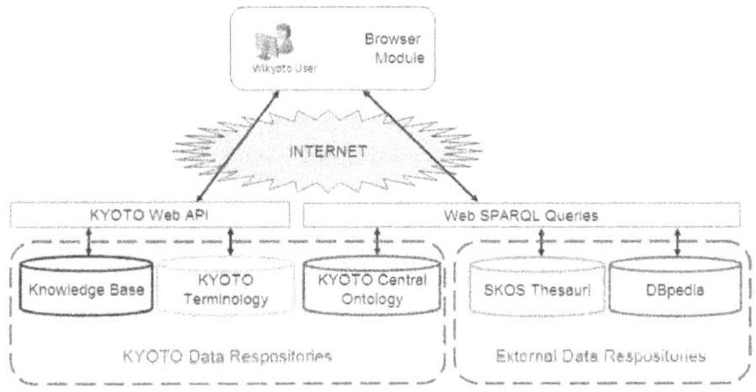

Figure 4: The architecture of Wikyoto

- ***data repositories*** that store the set of knowledge resources accessible by Wikyoto. Each data repository exposes a proper Web based Applications Programming Interface to enable the Javascript libraries running on the Web browser to access to the data stored by the same repositories.

Wikyoto faces *several core software design concerns of browser-based real-time collaborative editing systems* such as client-server partitioning, data aggregation, and client-side logic design issues. In order to manage concurrent access to data, Wikyoto implements a pessimistic locking protocol managing the synsets as locking data unit. Content versioning is managed by defining the synset as a versioning unit.

3. CONCLUSIONS AND PERSPECTIVES

This paper has introduced the design and the architecture of Wikyoto, the collaborative Web environment useful to gather contributions from non expert users in the editing the multilingual knowledge resources of KYOTO.

By means of Wikyoto several patterns and methods for collaboratively editing knowledge structures useful for mining textual content have been exploited and implemented. Although there is still room for further improvement, Wikyoto is important because it has proposed and experimented a wide range of user interaction possibilities, and has identified critical issues that should be addressed in future projects.

4. REFERENCES

[1] Souzis A. Bringing the wiki-way to the semantic web with rhizome. Proceedings of the 1st Workshop on Semantic Wikis: From Wiki to semantics (SemWiki 2006) at the 3rd European Semantic Web Conference (ESWC 2006), Budva (Montenegro), 11-14 Jun. 2006, pp. 222-229.

[2] Riechert T. Auer S., Dietzold S. Ontowiki - a tool for social, semantic collaboration. Proceedings of the 5th International Semantic Web Conference (ISWC06), Athens (USA), 5-10 Nov. 2006, Lecture Notes in Computer Science, vol. 4273, 2006, pp. 736-749.

[3] El Jerroudi Z. Bai F. Interactive and collaborative ontology development. Proceedings of Mensch & Computing 2008 and DeLFI Cognitive Design 2008, Berlin (Germany), 2008, pp. 174-179.

[4] Ereteo G. Sander P. Faron C. Buffa M., Gandon F. Sweetwiki: A semantic wiki. Web Semantics: Science, Services and Agents on the World Wide Web, vol. 6, no.1, 2008, pp. 84-97.

[5] Tazzoli R. Campanini SE., Castagna P. Platypus wiki: a semantic wiki wiki web. Proceedings of the 3rd International Semantic Web Conference (ISWC04), Hiroshima (Japan), 7-11 Nov. 2004.

[6] Fellbaum C. (Ed.). Wordnet an electronic lexical database. MIT press, 1993.

[7] Bontcheva K. Cunningham H. Davis B. Handschuh S. Funk A., Tablan V. Clone: Controlled language for ontology editing. Proceedings of the 6th International Semantic Web Conference, 2nd Asian Semantic Web Conference (ISWC 2007, ASWC 2007), Busan (Korea), 11-15 Nov. 2007, Lecture Notes in Computer Science, vol. 4825, 2007, pp. 142-155.

[8] Völkel M. Krötzsch M., Vrandecic D. Semantic mediawiki. The Semantic Web - ISWC, Proceedings of the 5th International Semantic Web Conference (ISWC06), Athens (USA), 5-10 Nov. 2006, Lecture Notes in Computer Science, vol. 4273, 2006, pp. 935-942.

[9] Kobayashi I. Loskyll M., Heckmann D. Ubiseditor 3.0: Collaborative ontology development on the web. Proceedings of Web 3.0: Merging Semantic Web and Social Web, Workshop at Hypertext 2009, Torino (Italy), 29 Jun.- 1 Jul. 2009.

[10] Weiten M. Ontostudio as a ontology engineering environment. Semantic Knowledge Management, Springer, 2009, pp. 51-60.

[11] Gruber A. Schaffert S., Westenthaler R. Ikewiki: A userfriendly semantic wiki. Demo Proceedings of the 3rd European Semantic Web Conference (ESWC 2006), Budva (Montenegro), 11-14 Jun. 2006.

[12] Kuhn T. Acewiki: Collaborative ontology management in controlled natural language. Proceedings of the 3rd Semantic Wiki Workshop in the 5th European Semantic Web Conference (ESWC), Tenerife (Spain), 01-05 Jun. 2008, CEUR Workshop Proceedings, 2008.

[13] Noy N. Tudorache T. Collaborative protégé. Proceedings of the Social and Collaborative Construction of Structured Knowledge Workshop at the 16th International World Wide Web Conference 2007, Alberta (Canada), 8-12 May 2007.

[14] Noy NF. Tudorache T., Vendetti J. Web-protégé: A lightweight owl ontology editor for the web. Proceedings of the OWLED 2008: OWL experiences and directions, first international workshop in the 7th International Semantic Web Conference (ISWC 2008), Karlsruhe (Germany), 26-27 Oct. 2008.

[15] Noy NF. Nyulas C. Üstün TB. Storey MAD. Musen MA. Tudorache T., Falconer SM. Ontology development for the masses: Creating icd-11 in webprotégé. Proceedings of Knowledge Engineering and Knowledge Management by the Masses (EKAW 2010), Lisbon (Portugal), 11-15 Oct. 2010, Lecture Notes in Artificial Intelligence, vol. 6317, 2010, pp.74-89.

Marco Polo: A System for Brand-based Shopping and Exploration

Nish Parikh Neel Sundaresan
eBay Research Labs
2065 Hamilton Ave,
San Jose, CA, 95125, USA.
{nparikh, nsundaresan}@ebay.com

ABSTRACT
In today's world, brand based shopping is popular especially in product lines like clothing and shoes, appliances, and electronics. Because of the importance of brands while shopping, it has become important for online shopping portals to consider brand loyalty and brand preferences of users. In this paper, we describe a system designed for brand-based shopping and exploration. The system is built by analyzing a large query set consisting of 115M queries from eBay.com – a vibrant marketplace with more than 95M active users. The system allows brand-pivoted exploration of inventory. It allows exploration and purchase of *substitute* branded goods (e.g. Sony camcorder for Canon camcorder) and *complementary* branded merchandise (e.g. Lego castle set for Lego train station set).

Categories and Subject Descriptors
H.2.8 [**Information Systems**]: Database applications – *Data mining*; H.3.3 [**Information Storage and Retrieval**]: Information Search and Retrieval – *Query formulation, Information filtering.*

General Terms
Algorithms, Design, Experimentation, Measurement.

Keywords
Brand based shopping, eCommerce, query log mining, recommender systems

1. INTRODUCTION
Brand based shopping is popular especially in product lines like clothing and shoes. There have been studies which show that even at brick and mortar stores like Wal-Mart and Costco, consumers expect brand-specific recommendations from sales personnel for merchandise like Television sets. Online shopping is a market worth billions of dollars and a signification portion of online sales are around branded merchandise. Some online shopping portals like shopping.com also have special interfaces to shop by brands. Because of the importance of brands while shopping in general, it has become important for online shopping portals to consider brand loyalty [2] and brand preferences of users.

In CIKM 2008 [1], we described how query relationships can be inferred from user activity in a high volume industrial setting. We build upon this work to create a system for brand-based shopping and exploration. The system combines principles from log analysis, information filtering and recommendation systems.

We take this approach as it is simple, scalable and allows us to capture interests for substitute and complementary branded merchandise. To the best of our knowledge this is the first such system that allows users to look at a large inventory collection of more than 175M items by pivoting on brand relationships.

For a brand loyal user pivoting on the brand Guess, the system would show all the different Guess products on sale ranging from shirts & tops, athletic apparel, shoes, clutch wallets, jeans and dresses to handbags and bags. The system would also show alternative brands related to handbags and bags like Bebe, Coach, Ralph Lauren and others.

2. SYSTEM ARCHITECTURE
The architecture of our modular system is shown in Figure 1. The different components and implementation techniques used to mine brand exploration data are described further in this section. The user interface for brand-based shopping and exploration is described in section 4.

2.1 Brand Miner
In order to build the brand based explorer, firstly we need to create a set of brands for different domains. We refer to the top-level categories in the eBay category structure[1] like Clothing, Shoes & Accessories, Electronics, etc. as domains. We start with a seed list that is created editorially and then apply data mining techniques to expand the seed list using distributional similarity measures [3] over query logs.

2.1.1 Brands Seed List Generation
Here we obtain a seed set of brands for each of the domains from domain experts with the goal of learning more brands automatically. Three sample categories for which such seed brands were obtained, and a few of those seed brands are shown in Table 1.

[1] http://listings.ebay.com/

CIKM'11, October 24–28, 2011, Glasgow, Scotland, UK.

This information was combined with other existing data sources like synonym dictionaries to map the brands to a possible list of its spellings (e.g. Dolce and Gabanna was mapped to D & G).

2.1.2 *Expansion of Brands Seed Lists*

A handful of human editors are not able to provide the names of thousands of different brands which might be available for sale. Therefore, after the seed brand lists are obtained from the domain experts we mine more brand names using the seed list. We use a large corpus of user queries from click-stream logs for this purpose.

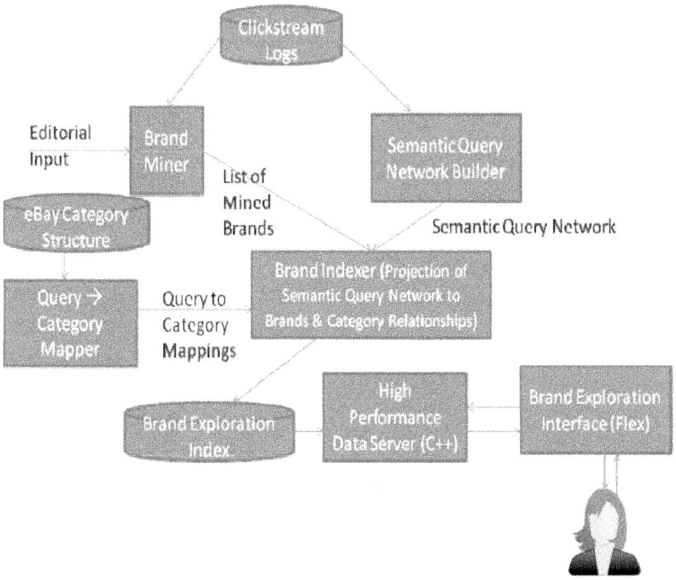

Figure 1 System Architecture for Brand Mining and Exploration.

Table 1 some top level domains and some sample brands as identified by editors.

Category Name	Some seed brands
Baby Goods	Ameda, Fisher Price, Huggies ...
Cameras & Photo	Canon, Fuji, Kodak ...
Motors Parts	Bosch, Goodyear, Yamaha ...

2.1.3 *Finding More Brands from Advanced User Queries*

The query corpus includes queries with advanced operators in them. Users entering the queries could explicitly specify conjunction, disjunction, phrase match or negation in queries. Typically, brand queries involving multiple brands would specify brands through these operators. Entities that are of the same type tend to get queried through disjunctive queries. For brand mining we look at such queries. These queries would be of the form

$q_i = (.*)(D_j)(.*)$ where the middle term is the disjunction we are interested in. Some example queries are shown below in Table 2.

The disjunctive portion would be a disjunction of various terms. It can be described as

$D_j = (b_1, b_2 \ldots, b_n, t_1 \ldots t_m)$ where $b_i{}'s$ are brand name terms and $t_i{}'s$ are the non brand name terms in the disjunctive query. We only look at disjunctions which have at least one seed brand in them and where $(m+n) \geq 2$.

Table 2 Table showing some advanced user queries where a brand name is found in the disjunctive part. The other terms in the disjunction are likely to be other similar brand names.

(gucci, seiko, pulsar) watch -paolo –lorus
(callaway, ping, jones) hybrid iron 5

We find terms that occur together frequently with seed brands and these are candidates for expanding the brand set. Two thresholds are determined heuristically; the minimum number of co-occurrences $Co_{\min}$ and minimum co-occurrence percentage $Copct_{\min}$. Co-occurring terms found together less than $Co_{\min}$ times are removed from the candidate list. Similarly if out of all disjunctions in which the terms were found, the percentage of disjunctions in which the terms co-occurred is less than $Copct_{\min}$ then that candidate brand is not considered. After applying these thresholds, some examples of brands that we discovered in this way are shown in Table 3.

Table 3 Brands Discovered using Advanced User Query Mining. Bold fonts indicate false positives. Italicized fonts indicate alternate spellings of brands.

Seed Brand	Brands Discovered (Co-occurrence % with seed brand)
Prada	Gucci(11.98) chanel(4.74) miu(3.89) dior(3.79) coach(3.38) miu miu(3.17) dolce(2.65) versace(2.08) fendi(2.08) chloe(2.00) marc jacobs(1.83)
Panasonic	Sony(13.19) samsung(4.51) **digital(0.55)** alpine(0.51) fuji(0.46) pelco(0.46) kodak(0.34) onkyo(0.25) aiwa(0.25) bose(0.25)
Baby phat	rocawear (11.58) *babyphat* (7.89)...

As shown above in Table 3 there might be some occasional false positives detected using this method. How we correct for those is described in the rest of section 2.1.4.

2.1.4 *Finding More Brands Using Pattern Mining*

Similar brands tend to be used in similar fashion in user queries. For e.g. given a seed brand Coach, if we find queries of the form Coach shoes, Coach wallets... and also of the form Prada shoes, Prada wallets..., we could infer Prada as being a brand similar to Coach. We use distributional similarity techniques over such patterns to identify brand candidates. More details around the similarity measure used for pattern mining are omitted here because of space constraints. Some brands discovered by applying this algorithm are shown in Table 4.

Table 4 Table indicating brands discovered through pattern mining in queries. Bold fonts indicate false positives and the italicized fonts indicate misspellings of brands.

Seed Brands	Candidate Brands Discovered
Prada, coach, gucci	Chanel, fendi, guess, xoxo, brahmin, brighton, **quilted**, burberry...
Ameda, huggies	Pampers, luvs, medela, bilge, submersible, lansinoh, sump, *medella*, kandoo, reebok...

Each of the techniques described in section 2.1.3 and in this section 2.1.4 lead to some false positive brand names. However by using both techniques together and keeping only brands detected using both techniques we are able to expand the seed brand list with acceptable recall and precision as evaluated by domain experts. We mined close to 1000 high quality brands using this method.

2.2 QUERIES AND CATEGORIES

We mine the intelligence of users from the query logs to infer relationships amongst queries. Then we use the relationships amongst queries to understand associations between brands and categories. Query relationship mining is described in section 2.2.1. Section 2.2.2 describes typical item categorization structure. In section 2.2.3 we describe how user queries could be mapped to the categorization structure of products on sale.

2.2.1 Semantic Query Network Builder

As we describe in [1], Semantic Query Network Builder uses an ensemble of algorithms to find semantic relationships amongst queries and build a relationship graph. The relations are calculated mainly based on collaborative filtering of user searches.

We use collaborative filtering over user search behavior and not transactional activity (*People who bought this also bought that)* because looking at search behavior is indicative of preferences for substitutable as well as complementary goods, whereas transactional behavior is usually indicative only of complementary goods. (E.g. a person might search for Samsung TV and then search for Toshiba TV, LG TV and TV wall mounts, whereas a person who just bought a Samsung TV is less likely to buy another TV).

2.2.2 Category Structure

On eBay, sellers are required to categorize the products they are selling into a category tree structure. We refer to the top level domains of such a structure as meta-categories. We refer to the lowest level categories in the tree in which the items are put up for sale as leaf categories. There are around 30,000 leaf categories on eBay. One such branch in the structure is Clothing, Shoes & Accessories → Costumes & Reenactment Attire → Costumes → Infants & Toddlers. Here Infants & Toddlers is the leaf category in which a seller can list an item for sale.

2.2.3 Query → Category Mapper

Using user behavioral data we build a probabilistic query to category classifier M that can map any query q to a vector of categories and weights. As an example, the query "ipod" might get mapped to MP3 Players = 70%, Chargers=10%, Batteries=10% and Other=10%.

2.3 BRAND INDEXER

The brand indexer filters the semantic query network based on the mined brands. The resulting network (N) contains only query relationships pertaining to branded merchandise intent.

N relates different queries q_1 and q_2. Every query q_i is associated with some brand B. We map all queries in N to their respective category vectors as described in section 2.2.3.

As N only has relationships between brand intent queries and also as we map every query to its category vector, we thus transform a query – query relationship to a brand: category – brand: category relationship.

For example, an edge between queries *guess xs* and *bebe xs* in N might get transformed to an edge between Brand:Guess(Men's Clothing:0.889, Women's Clothing:0.458) and Brand:Bebe(Men's Clothing:0.110, Women's Clothing:0.994).

This gives us an index of relationships between different Brand vectors in category dimensions and the strength amongst them.

We normalize these relationships to get linkage between different Brand: Category combinations. Some such relationships are shown in Table 5.

Table 5 Brand & Category Based Recommendations. Scores are normalized between 0 and 1 using min-max normalization.

Relationship between Brand:Category pairs	Score
Marc Jacobs [Clothing, Shoes & Accessories → Women's Handbags & Bags → Handbags & Purses] — Marc Jacobs[Clothing, Shoes & Accessories → Women's Shoes]	0.95
Thule [Sporting Goods → Outdoor Sports → Cycling → Accessories -> Car & Truck Racks → Roof] — Yakima [Sporting Goods → Outdoor Sports → Cycling → Accessories → Car & Truck Racks → Roof]	1.0

As seen in Table 5 above, the relationships could be for substitute brands in the same category or for the same brand but different categories of products. After pruning low quality relationships, the brand exploration index has around 1000 brands and 15000 brand relationships. The algorithms used to build Semantic Query Network and project it onto brands and categories are easily parallelizable as we show in [4] and hence scalable.

3. DATA VALIDATION

For qualitative evaluation, the relationship data was validated by human experts. Highest ratings were obtained for domains like Clothing whereas average ratings were obtained for categories like Musical Instruments which have a lower query volume.

We also ran a real-world experiment to provide brand recommendations to eBay users based on the brand exploration index. The recommendations were shown to around 500,000 users. Users were shown recommendations from alternative brands when they lost an auction on a branded item. This is similar to the preferred brand out-of-stock case in the offline shopping world. The CTR varied from 1% to 20% based on different categories. For e.g. in Toys & Hobbies the CTR was around 10%. These CTR are much higher than baseline CTR of 0.5%.

4. EXPLORATION INTERFACE

The interface was developed in Flex and allows relationship exploration for brands like Google Wonder Wheel does for queries. This interface is available for use at http://labs.ebay.com/demos/brands/. The entry point for a user is selection of a domain she is interested in. Various domains like Baby Products, Camera & Photo, Motors, Cell Phones & PDAs, Clothing Shoes & Accessories and many others are supported in this interface. Once the domain is selected, a set of relevant brands for the domain are shown to the user. Then, as shown in Figure 2, a user can pick a category (e.g. clothing, shoes and accessories) and a brand that she has in mind, and the system will show all the sub-categories (e.g. wallets, shoes, sweaters, bags, sunglasses) available on sale for that brand. The center node indicates the brand and other nodes in the star network indicate different kinds of products. In the exploration interface all nodes are color coded (yellow, green, red, blue) with yellow being the less popular nodes and blue being the most popular.

A user can then proceed to buy the items (for e.g. Figure 4 highlights the items shown when a user browses for DKNY wristwatches) for a given brand and category or double click on any of the category nodes to explore further. The exploration could be for substitutable brands and also complementary branded merchandise. For example, a user could explore alternate brands for Handbags as shown in Figure 3 by double-clicking on the node.

One demonstration scenario is described here. A user interested in buying a Marc Jacobs sweater can start by selecting the Clothing, Shoes & Accessories domain and Marc Jacobs brand from the drop-down. It would bring up options to look at Marc Jacobs brand in the Sweaters category as well as related categories for which the Marc Jacobs brand is popular like bags, wallets, shoes, blazers and shirts. Once the user selects Marc Jacobs sweaters, the user can also explore alternate brands like J. Crew, Gap and Banana Republic as shown in Figure 5.

During the demonstration, when the user is exploring brands, matching inventory from any of the 175M+ products on eBay site would be shown to the user.

5. SUMMARY

Purchases of branded products form a large part of Gross Merchandise Volume for online shopping sites. Allowing users to shop by brands can be a big win for these sites. We demonstrate a novel brand exploration and shopping system built using collaborative filtering of user searches.

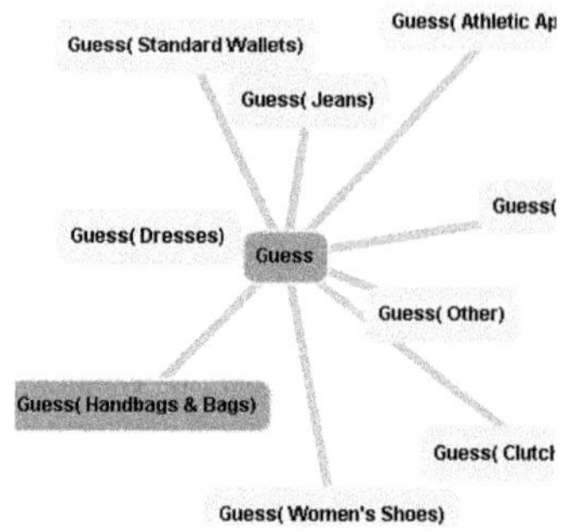

Figure 2 Brand exploration provided to user after selecting Brand = *Guess* and Domain = Clothing, Shoes & Accessories. Different categories of products: wallets, shirts, dresses, handbags et al. for the brand *Guess* are shown to the user. Red color for *Guess* indicates that it is a popular brand. Also red color for handbags indicates that for the brand *Guess* handbags category is more popular, whereas other categories for *Guess* like shirts and wallets are less popular.

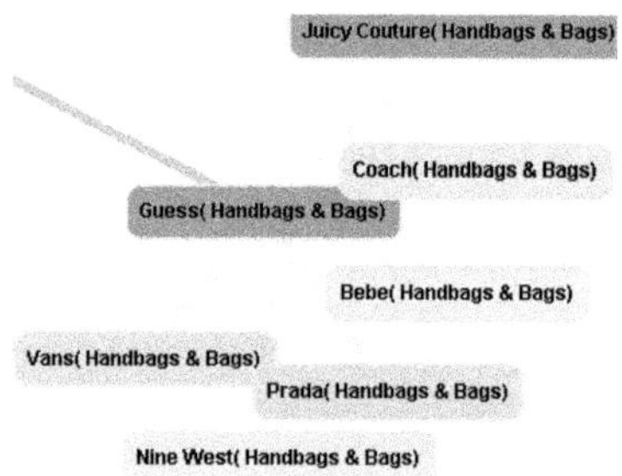

Figure 3 Alternate brand recommendations for Guess (Handbags & Bags). The thickness of the edges indicates the amount of similarity between brands.

Figure 4 Watches shown to a user exploring DKNY wristwatches.

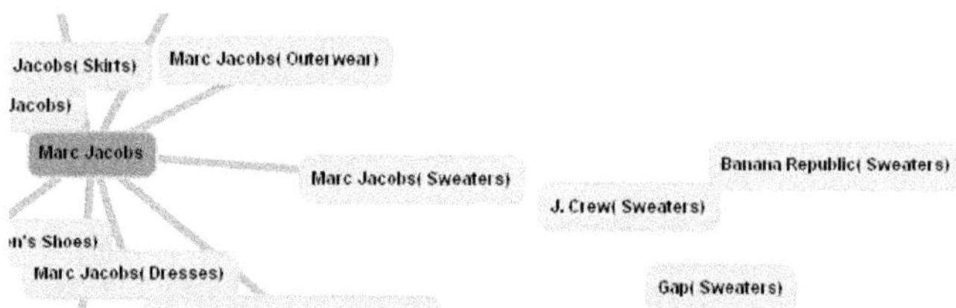

Figure 5 A user interested in a Marc Jacob's sweater during the process of inventory exploration. The user is shown other products from Marc Jacob's as well as other popular brands for sweaters.

6. REFERENCES

[1] Parikh N., Sundaresan N. Inferring Semantic Query Relations from Collective User Behavior. CIKM 2008, Napa CA, Pages 349-358.

[2] Chaudhari A., Holbrook M. The chain of effects from brand trust and brand effect to brand performance: The role of brand loyalty. Journal of Marketing, 65:81 - 93, 2001.

[3] Weeds J., Weir D., McCarthy D. Characterizing measures of Lexical Distributional Similarity. COLING 2004, Pages 1015-1021.

[4] Al Hasan M., Parikh N., Singh G., Sundaresan N. Query suggestion for E-commerce sites. WSDM 2011. 765-774.

Jasmine: A Real-time Local-event Detection System based on Geolocation Information Propagated to Microblogs

Kazufumi Watanabe[1] Masanao Ochi[2] Makoto Okabe[3] Rikio Onai[4]
The University of Electro-Communications[1,2,3,4], JST PRESTO[3]
1-5-1, Chofugaoka, Chofu, Tokyo, Japan
{k_watanabe, ochi}@onailab.com[1,2] m.o@acm.org[3] onai@cs.uec.ac.jp[4]

ABSTRACT

We propose a system for detecting local events in the real-world using geolocation information from microblog documents. A local event happens when people with a common purpose gather at the same time and place. To detect such an event, we identify a group of Twitter documents describing the same theme that were generated within a short time and a small geographic area. Timestamps and geotags are useful for finding such documents, but only 0.7 % of documents are geotagged and not sufficient for this purpose. Therefore, we propose an automatic geotagging method that identifies the location of non-geotagged documents. Our geotagging method successfully increased the number of geographic groups by about 115 times. For each group of documents, we extract co-occurring terms to identify its theme and determine whether it is about an event. We subjectively evaluated the precision of our detected local events and found that it had 25.5 % accuracy. These results demonstrate that our system can detect local events that are difficult to identify using existing event detection methods. A user can interactively specify the size of a desired event by manipulating the parameters of date, area size, and the minimum number of Twitter users associated with the location. Our system allows users to enjoy the novel experience of finding a local event happening near their current location in real time.

Categories and Subject Descriptors

H.2.8 [**Database Applications**]: Spatial databases and GIS

General Terms

Design, Experimentation

Keywords

Event Detection, Microblogs

1. INTRODUCTION

People share the latest information on a wide variety of real-world events by microblog documents such as Twitter.

CIKM'11, October 24–28, 2011, Glasgow, Scotland, UK.

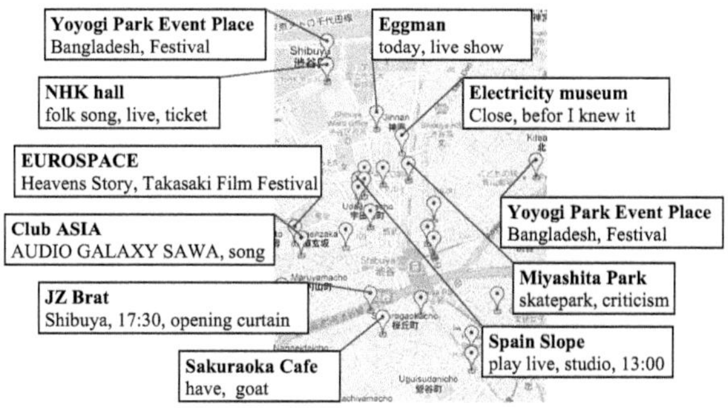

Figure 1: Our system detects 346 local events as yellow markers using Twitter documents posted on June 18, 2011, in Japan.

These events range from widely known ones (such as political events or professional sports games) to smaller-scale, local ones (such as a gathering to mark the opening of a local beer garden in a nearby park or a bargain sale at a supermarket). People are interested in both types of events: the former are important so that one can know about social events, and the latter affect daily life more directly. Event detection based on analysis of microblogs is an active field of research. However, all previous event detection methods can detect only the former type of event [5, 7, 8]. Our goal is to detect the latter type of event in real time. Detecting such local events would enhance users' daily lives.

Our definition of a local event is when a certain number of people with a common purpose gather together at the same time and place. Some microblog documents include not only a message and a timestamp but also a geotag, all of which are useful for determining what is happening, when, and where. There are two major methods of real-world local-event detection using geolocation information. Quack et al. detects local events by analyzing community photo collections [6]. This method is useful for detecting events at locations that are popular with tourists. However, it is impossible to detect events that cater to daily life using this method. Lee et al. detects local events by applying a clustering method and analyzing the geographical distribution of geotagged microblog documents [5]. This method successfully detects locations where people crowd (such as a town festival), but cannot detect smaller events.

To achieve our goal of detecting small local events, we also rely on geotagged microblog documents. However, after gathering microblog documents from Twitter, we found that only 0.7 % of them were geotagged, too few to detect local events. On the other hand, there are many non-geotagged documents that describe local events. To utilize these, we propose an automatic geotagging method for identifying the location from which each non-geotagged document is generated. Our geotagging method determines the degree to which a place name is associated with a location in the real-world. For example, when the place name "Times Square" appears in a document, it is likely to be about Times Square in New York. However, when "McDonald's" appears in a document, it is difficult to determine the location, given that this restaurant chain is found all over the world. Hence, terms that refer to locations with limited geographical distributions are useful for identifying the locations of Twitter documents. We assign geolocation information to non-geotagged documents by identifying such place names. We then group documents generated within a short time and a small geographic area. In a test, applying our geotagging method to non-geotagged documents increased the number of groups identified by 115 times.

The detected groups include not only local events but also locations visited by many people, e.g., a large train station. Although many microblog documents may be posted from a large train station, people typically have different reasons for being there. To detect only local events and discard non-event groups, we analyze co-occurring terms that appear in many of the documents of each group, and if none is detected, the group of documents is discarded. In contrast, in the case of a local event such as a live performance at a city hall, we are likely to detect the artist's name as a co-occurring term across documents. Thus, the artist's name would be useful information for users wanting to understand the content of the event. We subjectively evaluated our method of event detection, which had about 25.5 % accuracy. Thus, using our system, a user can enjoy the novel experience of finding an event near his or her current location in real time.

2. RELATED WORK

Event detection is an active field of research, and many unique methods have been proposed. Different methods have been proposed for the detection of different types of events such as news [8] and earthquakes [7]. Becker et al. found an event by clustering Twitter documents based on the similarity of their content and then determined whether the documents described a real-world event [3]. Zhao et al. detected events using topic intensity over time [10]. Although these methods are useful for detecting relatively large events, our goal is to detect smaller local events. Lee et al. proposed a method for detecting locations where people crowd as a local event [5], applying a k-means clustering method to geotagged Twitter documents. However, because only a small number of Twitter documents are geotagged, only a small number of large and popular events can be detected using this method.

Therefore, we try to increase the number of local events detected by identifying the locations of non-geotagged documents. Amitay et al. proposed a method for geotagging web content [1]. Cheng et al. proposed a technique for estimating a Twitter user's location [2]. Although their methods can predict a location at the city level, our geolocation method can predict a location at the building level. Wing et al. attempted to estimate the location of each document in Wikipedia and Twitter based on terms in their content [9]. However, they reported a mean location prediction error of 967 km when their method was applied to Twitter documents. Because almost all Twitter documents are short, it is impossible to predict the location based solely on terms in their content.

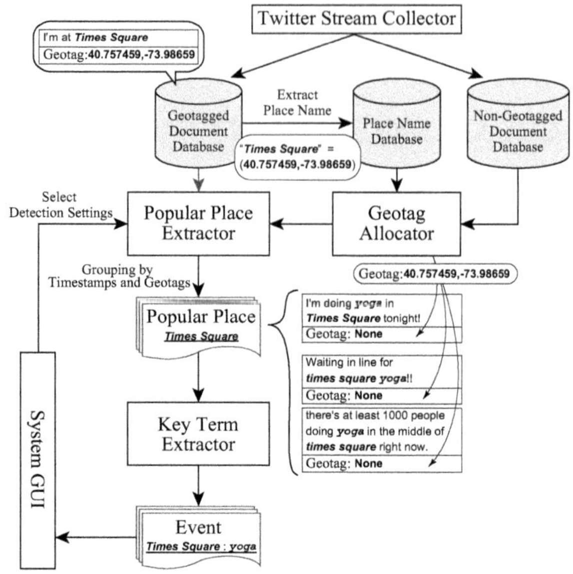

Figure 2: Architecture and Implementation

After identifying the locations of non-geotagged Twitter documents, we propose the filtering method to detect documents with a common theme that are allocated to the same place. Java et al. observed microblog phenomena by studying the topological and geographical properties of the Twitter community and extracted key terms related to each community of users or each day of the week [4]. However, we want to know key terms related to more local events and smaller communities, such as a live performance at a city hall in a small town.

3. OVERVIEW AND ARCHITECTURE

An overview of the system is presented in Figure 2. Our system has a web service interface and consists of four modules, described below.

Twitter Stream Collector: This module collects Twitter documents through the Twitter Streaming API[1]. It can sample about 15 % of all Twitter documents. Currently, this system collects about 15 million Twitter documents a day. It stores geotagged documents (about 100,000 a day) separately from non-geotagged documents.

Geotag Allocator: First, the Place Name Database is created. Place names are extracted from Twitter documents with certain patterns (e.g., "I'm at *Times Square* (Broadway & 7th Ave, btn 42nd & 47th, New York) w/ 3 others") posted via Foursquare service[2]. Then, the geographical variance among the geotagged documents that include each place name is calculated. This defines the association between a place name and a physical location; the smaller the variance is, the more precisely the place name describes the physical location. By detecting place names with a large variance, ambiguous place names such as "McDonald's" can be eliminated from the database.

Second, our system searches for non-geotagged documents which contain a distinct place name and allocates a geotag to

[1]http://dev.twitter.com/pages/streaming_api
[2]https://foursquare.com/

Table 1: Examples of detected events. We have summarized the associated Twitter documents and the extracted key terms and manually described each event in the Description column. IDs ♯1 ∼ ♯3 are successful results, and the others are not.

ID	Date	Place Name	Tweets/Users	Key Terms	Description
♯1	17 June 2011	Seisekisakuragaoka Shopping Center	7/7	today, Cafe Muji, opening, people in tama-city	Opening a coffee shop
♯2	18 June 2011	LUMINE EST	12/10	Shinjuku, time-limited sale, 30 min, 10 % discount	Time limited sale
♯3	19 June 2011	Tokyo Big Sight	32/31	plaything, Tokyo toy show 2011, now, Kokusai-tenjijo	Tokyo Toy Show
♯4	17 June 2011	Nakano Station	22/10	real estate information, Tokyo	Advertisements by a bot
♯5	17 June 2011	Iidabashi	62/60	train, why, little, today, time, very	No events

the location in real time. To search large numbers of documents quickly, our system makes use of Solr[3], an open source search platform based on Lucene. This process increases the number of geotagged Twitter documents by about 2.5 times.

Popular Place Extractor: This module finds popular places by detecting geotags observed frequently in Twitter documents posted during the user-specified period. To gather geotags that are scattered within a small region efficiently, we use the Geohash algorithm[4]. This algorithm converts geolocation information to a hash value. Nearby places are represented as similar values, which enable to find popular places as regions where many Twitter documents are posted efficiently.

Key Term Extractor: This module extracts key terms that describe an event that might be held at each popular place. Key terms that appear three times or more in the Twitter documents associated with the popular place are extracted. The place with one or more extracted key terms is identified as a local event. Popular places with no key terms are discarded. Before the process, we exclude all retweets in advance, because a user who retweets a document is likely not to be in the same location as the original document was posted.

4. EXPERIMENTS

We evaluate the performance of our system for detecting local events using Twitter documents posted on June 18, 2011, in Japan. We collected 7,135 geotagged documents posted from Japan and 2,453,725 non-geotagged Japanese documents.

Geotag Allocation: We first create the Place Name Database from geotagged documents posted in April and May 2011. We extract 19,537 place names and geographical coordinates from Japanese Twitter documents. Then, using this database, we assign geolocation information to 17,204 non-geotagged documents.

Popular Place and Key Term Extraction: Our system finds 689 popular places with areas of $20 \times 30\,\mathrm{m}^2$ and documents posted by more than five unique Twitter users. The Key Term Extractor discards 343 popular places without key terms, leaving 346 popular places identified as local events, as shown in Figure 1.

Evaluation: To evaluate the accuracy of our local-event detection system, we performed a subjective user study. We asked five computer science students to confirm whether the identified events were truly events. According to their results, an average of 88.4 events (25.5 %) were real-world events among 346 local events detected. However, when the process of geotag allocation was skipped and the system used only documents that were originally geotagged, only six popular places were detected, and no local events were reported by the test users. Thus, our system successfully increased the number of identified popular places by about 115 times (from 6 to 689).

Table 1 shows some examples of extracted local events. ID ♯3 includes big, well-known events in Japan. These events can also be extracted using previous methods of clustering geotagged Twitter documents [5] or measuring the topic intensity of Twitter documents [10]. On the other hand, it is difficult to detect smaller events such as ID ♯1 and ID ♯2 using previous methods, because these events are small and most of the Twitter documents describing each event are not geotagged. However, our system can detect such local events because our geotag allocator successfully assigns geolocation information to such non-geotagged documents. Our system provides users with information about small local events such as the opening of a small coffee shop or a time–limited sale, potentially useful information that could improve daily life.

IDs ♯4 and ♯5 are negative examples. ID ♯4 is a group of spam documents that include the same place name because they are posted automatically by advertising bots, i.e., no people are posting from the location. ID ♯5 has no events. The location is a subway station. Because many documents (62 in this case) are associated with it, it can be a popular place. On the other hand, because few people are there for the same reason, it should not be a local event. However, when the amount of associated documents is large, our system extracted key terms that appeared three times or more, and mistakenly identified it as a local event.

5. DEMONSTRATION

Here, we develop our idea as a prototype system, *Jasmine*[5]. The user starts to search for a local event by setting the parameters for popular place extraction using our system (Figure 3). The user selects the target date using the drop down list in the top-left of the graphical user interface (GUI). Because the system is always gathering and analyzing newly posted Twitter documents, selecting "today" results in the latest postings in real time. Next, the user selects the field size using the drop down list, which represents the desired size of local events. The default area of $20 \times 30\,\mathrm{m}^2$ (i.e., 20 m north–south and 30 m east–west) is

[3]http://lucene.apache.org/solr/

[4]http://geohash.org/

[5]https://sites.google.com/a/onailab.com/watanabe/jasmine

Figure 3: Jasmine GUI. All of the content was written in Japanese; we have translated part of it into English.

recommended because this area properly detected resulted in correct detection of many local events in our tests. Finally, the user inputs a number in the user count input field to specify the minimum number of unique Twitter users required to detect a popular place. When the user wants to identify only big events, a large number is specified. If too small a number is used, many irrelevant popular places will be detected. We recommend inputting a number that detect a reasonable number of real local events.

Now the Jasmine system is ready to detect local events in real time. The user clicks the "Detect Events" button. After a few seconds, all of the events detected are listed below this button and displayed on the map as yellow markers. When the user clicks on an event in this list, the map automatically moves to the corresponding yellow marker, and all of the Twitter documents posted from that location are displayed in a balloon. The user can also click on a yellow marker on the map to see all of the related Twitter documents. The upper area of the balloon presents the place name and the extracted key terms related to the event. Key terms are printed in the order of extraction.

We present an example of a detected local event in Figure 3. Our system detects a free market festival in a park in Kanagawa, Japan. The place name is "Tsujidou Seaside Park." The extracted key terms are "Sea–Sky Festival," "Free market," "held," and "now." These terms suggest that the Sea–Sky Festival, featuring a free market, is being held in the park. This festival is a local and minor event, held for the first time to raise funds for the victims of the 2011 Tohoku Earthquake, according to the event's website. The balloon shows that one Twitter document says that everybody should support victims by attending the festival, and another says that the writer is a volunteer at the festival. It is not impossible for a user to find and attend this festival without using our system. However, by reading these Twitter documents, the user might be more enthusiastic about attending the event after learning about the spirit of the festival. By collaborating with Twitter, Jasmine allows users to actively choose local events that they want to attend.

6. CONCLUSIONS

Jasmine is a real-time local-event detection system. We demonstrate that our automatic geotagging method successfully assigns location information to non-geotagged Twitter documents and increases the number of popular places detected by about 115 times. Our system extracts key terms that describe the details of a local event. In a subjective evaluation, our system successfully detects meaningful real-world local events with an accuracy of 25.5 %.

In the future, we want to assign location information to many more non-geotagged Twitter documents by analyzing histories of users' movements and textual contexts.

7. REFERENCES

[1] E. Amitay, N. Har'El, R. Sivan, and A. Soffer. Web-a-where: geotagging web content. In *Proc. ACM SIGIR '04*, pages 273–280, 2004.

[2] Z. Cheng, J. Caverlee, and K. Lee. You are where you tweet: a content-based approach to geo-locating twitter users. In *Proc. ACM CIKM '10*, pages 759–768, 2010.

[3] M. N. Hila Becker and L. Gravano. Beyond trending topics: Real-world event identification on twitter. *Proc. ICWSM '11*, 2011.

[4] A. Java, X. Song, T. Finin, and B. Tseng. Why we twitter: understanding microblogging usage and communities. In *Proc. WebKDD/SNA-KDD '07*, pages 56–65, 2007.

[5] R. Lee and K. Sumiya. Measuring geographical regularities of crowd behaviors for twitter-based geo-social event detection. In *Proc. LBSN '10*, pages 1–10, 2010.

[6] T. Quack, B. Leibe, and L. Van Gool. World-scale mining of objects and events from community photo collections. In *Proc. CIVR '08*, pages 47–56, 2008.

[7] T. Sakaki, M. Okazaki, and Y. Matsuo. Earthquake shakes twitter users: real-time event detection by social sensors. In *Proc. WWW '10*, pages 851–860, 2010.

[8] J. Sankaranarayanan, H. Samet, B. E. Teitler, M. D. Lieberman, and J. Sperling. Twitterstand: news in tweets. In *Proc. GIS '09*, pages 42–51, 2009.

[9] B. Wing and J. Baldridge. Simple supervised document geolocation with geodesic grids. In *Proc. ACL '11*, 2011.

[10] Q. Zhao, P. Mitra, and B. Chen. Temporal and information flow based event detection from social text streams. In *Proc. AAAI '07*, pages 1501–1506, 2007.

Scalable Similarity Search of Timeseries with Variable Dimensionality

Omar U. Florez
Utah State University
Logan, USA
+1 435 757-9354
Omar.Florez@usu.edu

Curtis Dyreson
Utah State University
Logan, USA
+1 435 797-0742
Curtis.Dyreson@usu.edu

ABSTRACT

Timeseries can be similar in shape but differ in length. For example, the sound waves produced by the same word spoken twice have roughly the same shape, but one may be shorter in duration. Stream data mining, approximate querying of image and video databases, data compression, and near duplicate detection are applications that need to be able to classify or cluster such timeseries, and to search for and rank timeseries that are similar to a chosen timeseries. We demonstrate software for clustering and performing similarity search in databases of timeseries data, where the timeseries have high and variable dimensionality. Our demonstration uses Timeseries Sensitive Hashing (TSH) [3] to index the timeseries. TSH adapts Locality Sensitive Hashing (LSH), which is an approximate algorithm to index data points in a d-dimensional space under some (e.g., Euclidean) distance function. TSH, unlike LSH, can index points that do not have the same dimensionality. As examples of the potential of TSH, the demonstration will index and classify timeseries from an image database and timeseries describing human motion extracted from a video stream and a motion capture system.

Categories and Subject Descriptors

H.3.3 Information Systems [**Information Storage and Retrieval**]: [Information Search and Retrieval]

General Terms

Algorithms

Keywords

Multimedia Data, Scalable Indexing, Search and Structuring

1. INTRODUCTION

The goal of the research presented in this demonstration is to make it easier for applications to index and query timeseries that are of high and variable dimensionality. These timeseries are found in many application areas, such as image and video processing, data stream mining, data compression, and near duplicate detection. For instance, a timeseries of variable dimensionality is generated when a process (e.g., the trajectory of a person while walking in a video) is measured over uniform time intervals, but with no predetermined length (e.g., not every video or activity within a video has the same duration). Previous research has developed efficient algorithms to index and query timeseries that are vectors of fixed dimensionality. Current practice is to normalize variable dimensionality timeseries to some fixed dimensionality. But when processing a live video stream, for instance, new timeseries are continually being produced and the *a priori* (incorrect) choice of a single, fixed dimensionality may lead to important data in a timeseries being manufactured or discarded. It would be better to index each timeseries without normalizing it.

Paper (conference)	Original dimension	Reduced dimension	Reduction method
iSAX[8] (KDD08)	480, 960, 1440, 1920	16, 24, 32, 40	iSAX
TS-Tree[1] (EDBT08)	256, 512, 1024	16, 24, 32	PAA
Scaled and Warped Matching[4] (VLDB08)	32, 64, 128, 256, 512, 1024	21, 43, 85, 171, 341, 683	Uniform Scaling
Exact indexing of DTW[6] (VLDB02)	32, 256, 1024	all datasets to 16	PAA

Table 1: High-dimensional datasets and reduction techniques considered in recent papers on timeseries indexing.

Table 1 summarizes a few of the key papers in previous research. All of the papers listed target high-dimensional datasets. Each chooses to normalize by reducing the dimensionality of the data to some fixed dimensionality, and in most of the cases that dimensionality is relatively small.

In this demonstration, we will show how to index timeseries without normalizing or reducing dimensionality using an indexing technique called Timeseries Sensitive Hashing (TSH) [3]. In contrast to other approaches, TSH has linear or sublinear time complexity for both indexing and searching without reducing the timeseries to a fixed dimensionality.

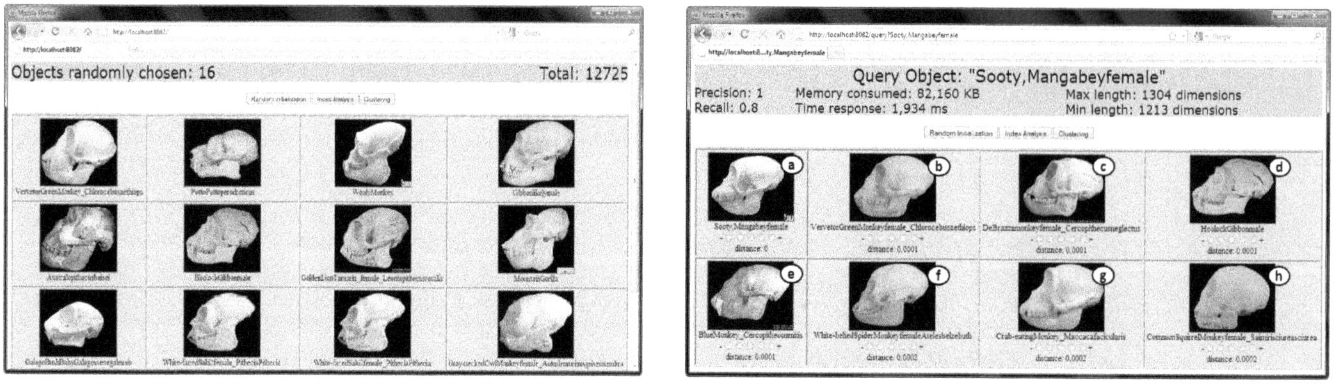

(a) (b)

Figure 1: (a) List of primate skulls randomly selected from the database. (b) A similarity query in the system. The first element represents the query (distance of 0) and repeated elements found in parallel hash tables were discarded.

As we will demonstrate, TSH is especially suited to *stream data processing* such as motion capture, real-time video analysis, speech recognition, and sensor networks, where timeseries with different lengths continuously arrive, preprocessing steps are not always possible, one-scan algorithms are needed, and low error rates are necessary.

2. THE DEMONSTRATION OF TSH

This section gives a short tutorial on TSH. The demonstration will use a web application to take the audience through a series of multimedia queries of increasing complexity, from image to motion capture and video data. The web application allows a user to perform four main activities: 1) initialize the interface with a random sampling of objects chosen from a database, 2) report how elements are distributed in hash buckets, 3) visualize a hierarchical clustering of the entire dataset, and 4) perform a similarity search. We invite readers to visit the TSH project website to experiment with TSH in the on-line demo and download the Java implementation[1]. The hash tables are persistently stored using BerkleyDB [2], so the software can scale to support large datasets (i.e., it is not limited by available memory).

2.1 A Quick Overview of TSH

TSH is an index that clusters timeseries with similar shape which are close in the $\Re^1$ space. TSH employs the concept of *general dot product* to compare two vectors of different dimensionality using a non-linear alignment of elements, rather than using the Euclidean norm in the $\Re^n$ space.

TSH embeds general dot product into a number of hash functions, which allows each timeseries to be projected into $\Re^1$ (e.g., a bucket) with high probability of finding similar elements in the same bucket. TSH chooses timeseries from the database to construct the hash functions, which we previously observed did improve precision [3]. Additionally, TSH uses multiple hash tables, performs a search by hashing within each table, and unions the partial results. In summary, TSH is formed of L hash tables, each one defined by K hash functions that project elements to buckets of a chosen width in $\Re^1$ (the width is a parameter that can be used to tune TSH).

[1] http://omarflorez.info/index.php?id=tsh

2.2 Example Searches using TSH

Figure 1 (a) shows a random sampling of a *Primate Skulls* dataset. We generate a timeseries for each image by computing its centroid and then evaluating distances from that point to the pixels in the border of the skull. The resulting timeseries is expressive enough to distinguish important features such as nose angle, depth of the lower jaw, and prominent forehead.

Figure 1 (b) shows a screenshot of the application when a user clicks on an image performing a query of an adult female *Sooty Mangabeys* primate. This primate lives on the west coast of Africa and belongs to the *Cercopithecidae* family and *Catarrhini* infraorder. While 80% of the neighbors retrieved by TSH (a, b, c, d, e, and g) belong to the *Catarrhini* infraorder and share important features such as long fangs, similar forehead, and very convex napes, the remaining 20% (f and g) also exhibits those visual features, but they belong to the *Platyrrini* infraorder. Both *Catarrhini* and *Platyrrini* are two close instances of five possible infraorders for primates. This example shows that timeseries can be used to evaluate similarity queries for image data. The title of the application also contains relevant information about the query such as *precision/recall* of the subset retrieved and the *time/memory* spent during the query in the system. Additionally, the demo reports variance in the dimensionality (*min/max length*) associated to the result set.

In the above example, we took advantage of the same orientation and uniform background to extract well defined timeseries and obtain consistent results in the *Primate Skull* database. However, the timeseries extracted from motion capture data are more challenging and complex to analyze since the motion performed by different actors can be in any direction, be composed of other small movements, and have a larger variance in duration, as shown in Figure 2 (a). The timeseries defined for each instance of the database represents the position of the right hand of each actor in the z-axis. The result of querying the running activity *09_05* is illustrated in Figure 2 (b). It shows the retrieval of ten videos, each one containing different actors doing the activity *09*. The *recall* is lower in this case (58.8%) than in Figure 1 (b) since more than ten elements belong to this class, but TSH only retrieves a subset of them. In other

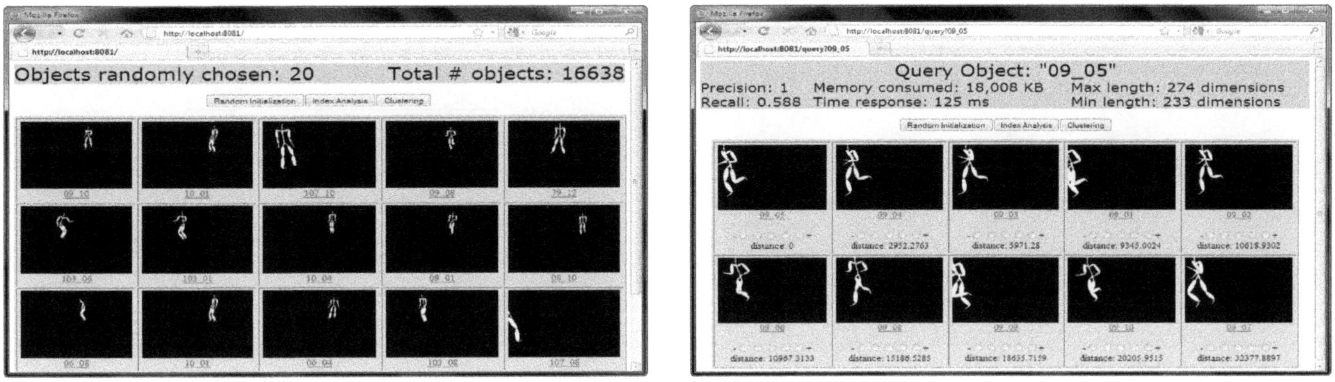

(a) (b)

Figure 2: (a) Motion capture videos chosen at random. (b) A similarity query performed by TSH. Note that all the videos retrieved belong to the same running activity.

words, TSH only retrieves the timeseries projected to the same buckets in multiple hash tables with high *precision* (100%). The user can obtain higher *recall* values by increasing the bucket width, but at the cost of increasing the response time.

Additionally, we show search effectiveness with a subset of 100,000 elements of *The Million Song Dataset*[2], a freely-available collection of audio features and metadata. TSH will provide consistent results if the result set obtained by a 10-NN query is included in the one retrieved by a linear scan, a brute force algorithm that yields complete precision. Figure 3 reports average precision of TSH, with respect to a sequential search, which ranges between 92% and 95% over different database sizes.

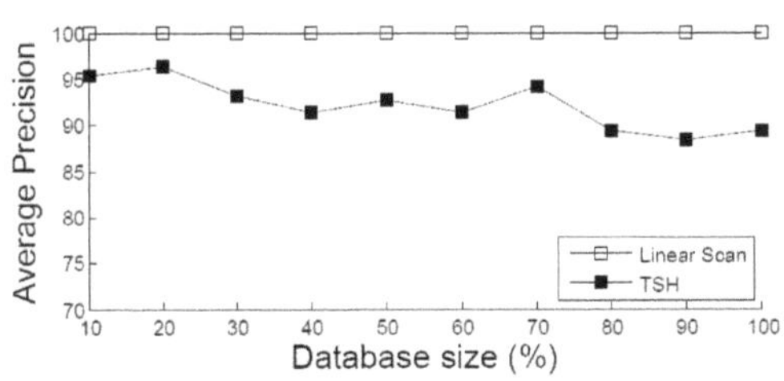

Figure 3: Average precision for TSH.

2.3 Clustering

The demo will also allow users to explore the notion of using a general dot product to create a hierarchical clustering. TSH projects similar timeseries to the same buckets in multiple hash tables, forming a particular neighborhood in the projected space. Those points that have more than T elements and are within a distance of D are denominated as *core points*.

TSH aggregates clusters into increasingly larger clusters in a hierarchy as follows. Pairs of clusters that have the shortest distance between their members can be connected. Those timeseries that are not *core points* can be considered as outliers and safely removed. The algorithm stops when a single cluster is reached. Otherwise, we increase the value of D to merge distant clusters. TSH reduces the time complexity of the original hierarchical linkage clustering algorithm from $O(n\log n)$ to $O(n)$ because of its constant response time for nearest neighbor queries.

Figure 4 (a) shows a random selection from the *Motion from Video* dataset. It contains six types of activities performed by 19 actors with dimensionality varying from 112 to 184 dimensions. A timeseries is extracted from each video by defining intensity gradients and then evaluating their spatial distribution over time. The clustering on this data with TSH, as shown in Figure 4 (b), reports some relevant characteristics underlying the dataset.

First, note that five groups were discovered, each one shown in a different color. Each group is a type of motion performed by an actor. While the cluster in red (a) merges two types of similar activities (jogging and running), the other clusters shows a proportional distribution of elements. Next, the highest link in the display shows the existence of two large groups ($\{a, b, c\}$ and $\{d, e\}$). In practice, those groups correspond to *hand-related* (hand waving, hand clapping, and boxing) and *feet-related* (walking, jogging, and running) activities. While clustering is approximated with TSH, it quickly groups elements projected similarly in $\Re^1$ and uses the general dot product to find similar timeseries from video. Those timeseries are often more challenging since they contain noise related to illumination, shadows, and camera motion.

3. ARCHITECTURE

Our implementation builds on the Jetty HTTP server and Java Servlet container, which provides both dynamic content interaction with multimedia databases and the TSH index.

Before we can execute similarity queries on objects, we need to find its timeseries representation in the *Data* layer. The technique to extract those features from an object will vary according to the nature of its underlying data (images, music, video, motion capture, etc). In our running examples, we showed multimedia objects to the user, each one linked to a timeseries in the *Presentation* layer. Those timeseries are encoded in $< key, value >$ pairs within TSH; *key* is an integer representing a bucket id in TSH and *value* is a string representing the path to the file containing the timeseries pattern on hard-disk. Thus, mappings allow us to save space

[2]http://labrosa.ee.columbia.edu/millionsong/

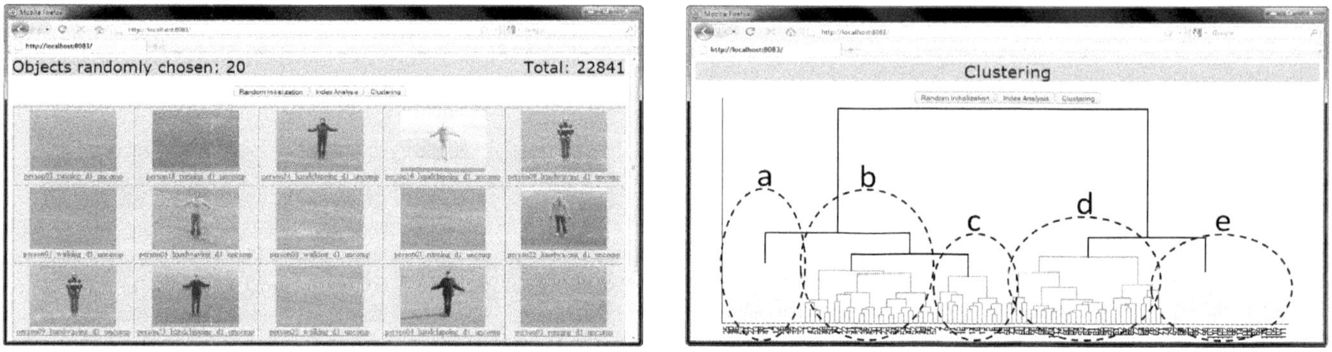

(a) (b)

Figure 4: (a) A random selection from the *Motion from Video* database. (b) Hierarchical clustering performed by TSH. Note that timeseries extracted from videos are the most complex shown in this demonstration.

by not storing the entire timeseries in main memory. The index will perform similarity queries and clustering by quickly obtaining keys in multiple tables and collecting the timeseries found into a single result set in the *Structure* layer. Eventually, TSH will contain more mappings than permitted in main memory. TSH supports the insertion of large multimedia databases with fast lookup operations in TSH by extending the HashMap representation of BerkeleyDB to thus enable persistence in the *Persistence* layer.

4. PREVIOUS WORK

Previous research on efficiently indexing timeseries typically relies on dimensionality reduction to eliminate variable dimensionality. As discussed in Section 1, current practice is to employ on dimensionality reduction techniques (iSAX [8], PAA [1], Uniform Scaling [6], etc.) to make timeseries more tractable to compute. These indexing techniques fall into two categories: region-based and lexicographic. R-tree is a region-based index commonly used for experiments with timeseries. Its main downside is the presence of overlap between regions for high-dimensional data. One example of a lexicographic index is TS-tree [1], which avoids subtree overlap during insertion. There are (at least) two clustering techniques that employ a hashing approach [7, 9]. However, they only consider the case where points have the same dimensionality and Euclidean distance is the only option as a similarity measure.

5. SUMMARY

The demonstration will guide the audience through examples in a new index called TSH. We demonstrate the potential of TSH to perform quick analysis of complex timeseries in multimedia data. Particularly, queries in TSH show high precision and visual soundness and the hierarchical clustering seems to group similar elements coherently. The audience can download our Java implementation from the project's website and try their own queries during the demonstration.

6. ACKNOWLEDGEMENTS

We thank the Glendale College Anthropology Department for its skull images, Eamonn Keogh for sharing the images, Ivan Laptev for the motion video dataset, the CMU Graphics Lab for its motion capture dataset, and IBM for funding part of the research with a Scalable Data Analytics 2010 Innovation Award.

7. REFERENCES

[1] I. Assent, R. Krieger, F. Afschari, and T. Seidl. The TS-tree: efficient time series search and retrieval. In *11th Conference on Extending Database Technology (EDBT)*, pages 252–263, New York, NY, USA, 2008.

[2] BerkleyDB. `http://www.oracle.com/database/berkeleydb/`, 2011.

[3] O. U. Florez, A. Ocsa, and C. E. Dyreson. Sublinear querying of realistic timeseries and its application to human motion. In *Multimedia Information Retrieval*, pages 137–146, 2010.

[4] A. W.-c. Fu, E. Keogh, L. Y. H. Lau, and C. A. Ratanamahatana. Scaling and time warping in time series querying. In *VLDB '05: Proceedings of the 31st international conference on Very Large Data Bases*, pages 649–660. VLDB Endowment, 2005.

[5] A. Guttman. R-trees: A dynamic index structure for spatial searching. In *SIGMOD Conference*, pages 47–57, 1984.

[6] E. Keogh and C. A. Ratanamahatana. Exact indexing of dynamic time warping. *Knowledge and Information Systems*, 7(3):358–386, 2005.

[7] H. Koga, T. Ishibashi, and T. Watanabe. Fast agglomerative hierarchical clustering algorithm using locality-sensitive hashing. *Knowledge and Information Systems*, 12:25–53, May 2007.

[8] J. Shieh and E. Keogh. iSAX: indexing and mining terabyte sized time series. In *KDD '08: Proceeding of the 14th ACM SIGKDD international conference on Knowledge discovery and data mining*, pages 623–631, New York, NY, USA, 2008. ACM.

[9] Y.-P. Wu, J.-J. Guo, and X.-J. Zhang. A linear DBScan algorithm based on LSH. *6th Conference on Machine Learning and Cybernetics*, August 2007.

RoSeS : a Continuous Query Processor for Large-scale RSS Filtering and Aggregation*

Jordi Creus
LIP6, Université Pierre et Marie Curie
jordi.creus@lip6.fr

Bernd Amann
LIP6, Université Pierre et Marie Curie
bernd.amann@lip6.fr

Nicolas Travers
CEDRIC, Conservatoire National des Arts et Métiers
nicolas.travers@cnam.fr

Dan Vodislav
ETIS, Univ. Cergy-Pontoise
dan.vodislav@u-cergy.fr

ABSTRACT

We present *RoSeS*, a running system for large-scale content-based RSS feed filtering and aggregation. The implementation of *RoSeS* is based on standard database concepts like declarative query languages, views and multi-query optimization. Users create personalized feeds by defining and composing content-based filtering and aggregation queries on collections of RSS feeds. These queries are translated into continuous multi-query execution plans which are optimized using a new cost-based multi-query optimization strategy.

Categories and Subject Descriptors

H.3.3 [**Information Systems**]: Information Search and Retrieval—*Online Information Services, Information Filtering*

General Terms

Algorithms, Performance, Experimentation

Keywords

RSS, continuous query processing, multi-query optimization

1. INTRODUCTION

Global news sites such as Yahoo! News or AOL News attract millions of users each month. For example, during January 2011, 46.3 million unique U.S. people visited Yahoo! News using PCs and laptops from home and work locations[1]. Staying informed by consulting online journals and news aggregators has become a daily activity of millions of people and the previous numbers do not take account of the increasing use of mobile phones and tablets for accessing web contents. On the back-end side of this process, traditional commercial online media (journals) are more and more complemented by new content-producing social media (Facebook, Twitter) which generate an abundant number of text streams for promoting recently published contents.

The increasing number of news producers and the overwhelming amount of news articles published online each day calls for advanced filtering and aggregation techniques for the efficient personalized delivery of news. In this demonstration we present a prototype for large-scale content-based RSS feed querying and aggregation. This prototype is part of the Really Open Simple and Efficient Syndication (*RoSeS*) framework (ANR-07-MDCO-011) [4] implementing a range of services for crawling, filtering and aggregating of RSS feeds. A central goal of this framework is to enable *large-scale RSS aggregation* based on algorithms and data structures which are scalable in terms of the number of feeds, aggregation queries (publications) and subscription. Our chosen approach is to revisit, redefine and re-implement standard online RSS aggregation services by applying traditional database concepts like declarative languages and views and by extending current data stream management and continuous query processing solutions. Multi-query optimization [7] is an important aspect in the implementation of *RoSeS* to achieve scalability. Users create personalized feeds by defining and composing content-based filtering and aggregation queries on collections of RSS feeds. These queries are translated into continuous multi-query execution plans which are optimized using a new cost-based multi-query optimization strategy.

The paper is organized as follows. Section 2 briefly describes the *RoSeS* language and model. An overview of the platform, query processing and the optimization process are presented in Section 3. Finally Section 4 shortly describes the demonstration scenario. A detailed description of our approach as well as a comparison with existing pub-sub techniques can be found in [4].

2. ROSES LANGUAGE

The language we have implemented in the *RoSeS* system provides instructions for *registering feeds* (register), *composing feeds* (create) and *creating subscriptions* (subscribe).

*The authors acknowledge the support of the French Agence Nationale de la Recherche (ANR), under grant ROSES (ANR-07-MDCO-011) "Really Open, Simple and Efficient Syndication"

[1] http://blog.nielsen.com/nielsenwire/online_mobile/january-2011-top-u-s-web-brands-and-news-sites/ retrieved on June 15th 2011.

CIKM'11, October 24–28, 2011, Glasgow, Scotland, UK.

Declarative feed composition is the most important feature of this language. The underlying query language is expressive and simple to use, designed to facilitate most common operations and large scale multi-query optimization. The publication language favors the expression of nested union-filtering expressions, combined with joins through three clauses: (1) A mandatory **from** clause, which specifies the input feeds called *main feeds*, (2) zero or more **join** clauses for joining feeds with other feeds called *annotation feeds* (see example below) and (3) an optional **where** clause for defining filtering conditions on main feeds and annotation feeds. Main and annotation feeds are also called *source feeds*. The stream of items generated by a **create feed** instruction is called a *publication*. Note that the contents (title, description) of items cannot be modified by publication queries. Source feeds are either registered RSS feeds or publications. External feeds can be referenced directly by their URL (implicit registration) or by a local name defined by using the **register feed** instruction. It is also possible to register publications which allows to transform the contents of items (see examples below). Finally, subscriptions can be defined on registered source feeds or publications by using the instruction **subscribe to**. A subscription specifies for a given feed, a notification mode (RSS, mail, etc.), a periodicity and an optional transformation.

The items of a feed can only be transformed by registration and subscription. It is important to mention here the difference between an unregistered and a registered publication. Unregistered publications are standard views which can be reused in other queries and be replaced by their definitions (publication queries) for enabling optimization through query rewriting (for example push filtering conditions to the source feeds). Registered publications are materialized views of transformed items. Whereas the newly generated stream might be used as input for new queries, transformation makes query rewriting through the replacement by its defining publication impossible.

We will illustrate the different features of the language by the following examples. For organizing outings to rock concerts with his friends, Bob wants to publish a RSS feed which filters and aggregates the news of a public web site and the messages of a personal Twitter stream. This can be achieved by the following three instructions registering the corresponding source streams in the system and creating a new publication *RockConcertStream*:

```
register feed http://www.infoconcert.com/rss/news.xml as
    EventAnnounces;
register feed http://twitter.com/statuses/user_timeline/174451720.
    rss as FollowedTwitterStream;
create feed RockConcertStream
 from (EventAnnounces as $a | FollowedTwitterStream) as $r
 where $a[title contains 'rock'] and $r[description contains '
     concert'];
```

Publication *RockConcertStream* filters all items containing the term 'concert' from two feeds *EventAnnounces* and *FollowedTwitterStream*. Observe that variable $r denotes the union of both streams. Additionally, items generated by the first feed (variable $a) must contain the term 'rock' in their title.

Bob is also a fan of the rock group Muse and wants to create a feed *MusePhotoStream* annotating news about this group with appropriate photos. *MusePhotoStream* publishes all items in feed *MuseNews* and all items in feed *RockConcertStream* containing the term 'Muse' in their descriptions. Each item in this main stream $a is annotated by photo items having similar titles published in two annotation feeds *FriendsPhotos* and *MusicPhotos* (restricted to category 'rock'). Annotation consists in joining a main feed ($a) with a window on a union of annotation feeds. As mentioned before, annotation items are 'invisible' until they are merged into the contents of their main items by an explicit registration instruction applying some transformation (*IncludePhotos.xsl* in the example).

```
register feed http://muse.mu/rss/news.rss as MuseNews;
create feed MusePhotoStream
 from (RockConcertStream as $r | MuseNews) as $a
 join last 3 months on (MusicPhotos as $m | FriendsPhotos)
     with $a[title similar window.title]
 where $r[description contains 'Muse'] and $m[category = '
     rock'];
register feed MusePhotoStream apply 'IncludePhotos.xsl' as
    MuseWithPhotos;
```

The final example shows two subscriptions to the *RockConcertStream* publication: the first one extracts item titles ('Title.xsl' transformation) and sends them by mail every 3 hours, the second one simply outputs an RSS feed refreshed every 10 minutes.

```
subscribe to RockConcertStream apply 'Title.xsl' output mail '
    me@mail.org' every 3 hours;
subscribe to RockConcertStream output file 'RockConcertStream
    .rss' every 10 minutes;
```

3. FEED PROCESSING

The *RoSeS* system is composed of five modules for processing RSS feeds and managing meta-data about users, publications and subscriptions. As shown in Figure 1, RSS feeds are processed by a three layered architecture completed by two modules (catalog and system manager) providing meta-data management services for storing, adding, updating and deleting source feeds, publication queries and subscriptions:

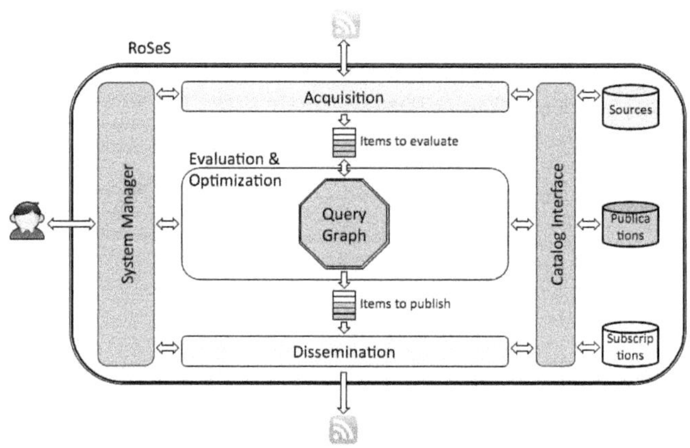

Figure 1: RoSeS System architecture

Acquisition: The main task of this module is to transform evolving RSS documents into a continuous stream of RoSeS items which can be processed by the evaluation module. This transformation includes an efficient refresh strategy optimizing the bandwidth usage [5].

Evaluation: The core of the RoSeS system is an *algebraic multi-query plan* which encodes all registered publication queries. The evaluation of this query plan follows an asynchronous pipe-lined execution model where the evaluation module (1) continuously evaluates the set of algebraic operations according to the incoming stream of RoSeS items, and (2) manages the addition, modification and deletion of publication queries.

Dissemination: This module is responsible for transforming RoSeS items into different output formats and notifying new items to corresponding user subscriptions. The goal of this module is to define the way items are rewritten in given formats (SMS, email, RSS/Atom feed...).

3.1 Multi-query processing and cost-model

Query processing consists in continuously evaluating a collection of publication queries. This collection is presented by a *multi-query plan* composed of physical operators reflecting the operators presented in section 2 (union, selection, join and window). The query graph is observed by a *scheduler* that continuously decides which operators (tasks) must be executed. The scheduler has at his disposal a pool of threads for executing in parallel a fixed number of threads. The choice of an inactive operator to be evaluated is influenced by different factors depending on the input buffer of each operator (number/age of the items in the input queue).

Based on this execution model, we define a cost model for estimating the resources (memory, processor) necessary for the execution of a query plan. Compared to the traditional cost estimation based on the input data size, the estimation parameters of a continuous plan must reflect the streaming nature of the data. We adapt a simplified version of the model presented in [1] and define the cost of each operator as a function of the publishing rate $R(b)$ of its input buffer b. In table 1, p denotes a filter (σ) or join ($\bowtie$) predicate, $S(w)$ is the size of the annotation window w of a join and d denotes the duration of the window operator ω (1 week, 2 days, etc.). The cost of each operator mainly depends on the publishing rate of its input buffer(s). The selection operator assumes a constant execution cost for each item (items are in general small text fragments). The publishing rate of the selection operator reduces the rate of its input by the selectivity factor $sel(p) \in [0,1]$ depending on the selection predicate p. Union generates an output with a publishing rate corresponding to the sum of its input rates. We assume zero memory and processing cost since each union can be implemented by a set of buffer iterators, one for each input. It is easy to see that the input rate of each operator strongly influences the global cost of the execution plan (sum of all operators cost). We will describe in the following section how we can reduce this rate by pushing selections and joins towards the source feeds of the query plan.

Operator	Output rate	Memory	Processing cost
$\sigma_p(b)$	$sel(p) * R(b)$	$const$	$const * R(b)$
$\cup(b_1, ..., b_n)$	$\sum_{1 \leq i \leq n} R(b_i)$	0	0
$\bowtie_p (b, w)$	$sel(p) * R(b)$	$const$	$R(b) * S(w)$
$\omega_d(b)$	0	$d * R(b)$	$const$

Table 1: Cost model

3.2 Multi-query plan optimization

A novel aspect of our framework with respect to most of the other multi-query optimization solutions (except [1]) lies in the explicit integration of a cost model taking account of term selectivity in filtering conditions. Our optimization strategy is based on the heuristic that selections and joins should be applied as early as possible in order to reduce the global cost of the plan. Standard snapshot semantics for continuous queries allows us to use traditional rewriting rules for algebraic expressions such as distributivity of selection over union and commutativity of selection with joins.

The optimization process is decomposed into (1) a *normalization* phase which applies all rewriting rules for pushing selections towards their source feeds and for distributing joins over union, and (2) a *factorization* phase of the selection predicates of each source based on a new cost-based factorization technique.

Query normalization: The goal of the first phase is to obtain a normalized query plan where all filtering selections are applied first to each source before applying joins and unions. This is possible by iteratively applying distributivity of selections on unions and commutativity between selection and join. It is easy to show that these properties always allow us to obtain a normalized plan which is a four level tree where the leaves of the tree are the sources involved in the query (first level), the second level nodes are the selection operators which can be applied to each source (leaf), the third level are window/join operators applied to the results of the selections and the final (fourth) level are unions applied to the results of the selections/windowed-joins to build the final results. Normalization also flattens all cascading selection paths into a single conjunctive selection.

Query factorization: Normalization generates a global query plan where each source s is connected to a set of selection predicates $P(s)$. Factorization consists in building a minimal *filtering plan* for each source. To find a best operator factorization, we proceed in two steps: we first generate for each source a *predicate subsumption graph* which contains *all* predicates subsuming the set of predicates in $P(s)$. Each subsumption link in this graph is labeled by a weight corresponding to the output rate of the source node (source or filtering operation). Such a graph is shown in Figure 2. The

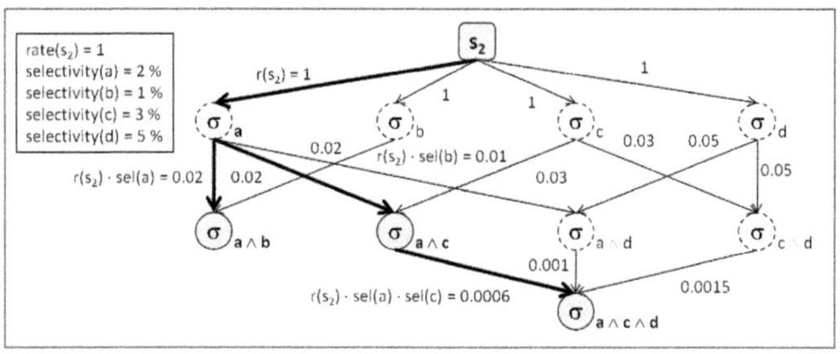

Figure 2: A Predicate Subsumption Graph and Minimal Steiner Tree

filtering predicates applied to source s_2 are $a \wedge b$, $a \wedge c$ and $a \wedge c \wedge d$. The subsumption graph is composed of these three predicates and all their subsuming predicates: a, b, c, d, $a \wedge d$ and $c \wedge d$. Each subsumption arc from some predicate p to some predicate q is labeled by the estimated evaluation cost of evaluating q on the result of p. Corresponding to our cost model, this evaluation cost can be estimated by the product between the publishing rate $rate(s_2)$ of source s_2 and the estimated selectivity of predicate p.

It is easy to see that any sub-tree of this graph covering the source s (root) and all predicates in $P(s)$ corresponds to a filtering plan which is equivalent to the original plan.

Such a tree is called a *Steiner tree* [2] where the cost is obtained by the sum of all arc weights in the tree. Based on this observation our optimization problem then consists in finding a Steiner tree of minimal cost. This is illustrated in Figure 2 showing a subsumption graph for the source s_2 and a minimal Steiner tree of this graph (in bold).

The *Steiner* tree problem [3, 6] is known to be NP-complete and we have developed an approximate algorithm which exploits the particular properties of a filtering plan (all outgoing arcs of a node have the same weight and the weight is monotonically decreasing with the depth of the node in the graph). This algorithm is based on a local heuristic for dynamically building the subsumption graph by choosing the most selective subsuming predicates. Whereas it will find only an approximate solution, our experiments on real data and synthetically generated queries show that the evaluation cost of the obtained approximate plan generally is near to the evaluation cost of the minimal Steiner tree plan with a much lower optimization cost.

4. DEMONSTRATION SCENARIO

We present a Java prototype integrating all *RoSeS* components described in Section 3. The prototype is based on a multi-threaded architecture and uses *Rome*, the Java's standard library for RSS management. The usage and functioning of the system will be explained using two graphical user interfaces. The first interface (fig. 3) is a Web interface powered by *GWT* (Google Web Toolkit) that allows users to register and share RSS feeds and to visually build publications through an easy-to-use visual programming interface. The second interface is a Java client using IBM's *SWT* (Standard Widget Toolkit) and the *JUNG* (Java Universal Network/Graph) framework for visualizing the multiquery evaluation (fig. 4) as well as predicate subsumption graphs and the resulting optimized filter plans. Both user interfaces permit to access the *RoSeS* System. The prototype and the Java client can be downloaded from *http://www-bd.lip6.fr/roses/doku.php?id=prototypes.*

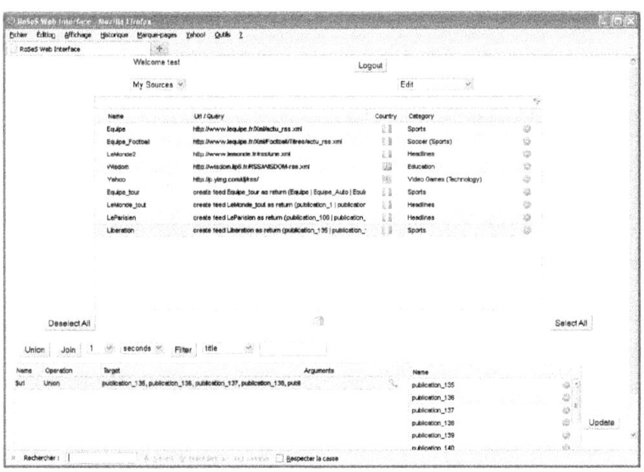

Figure 3: ROSES Web user Interface

Our demonstration is composed of two scenarios. In the first scenario we will present the Web user interface for creating publication queries. We will show how a user can create in some seconds a publication query aggregating hundreds

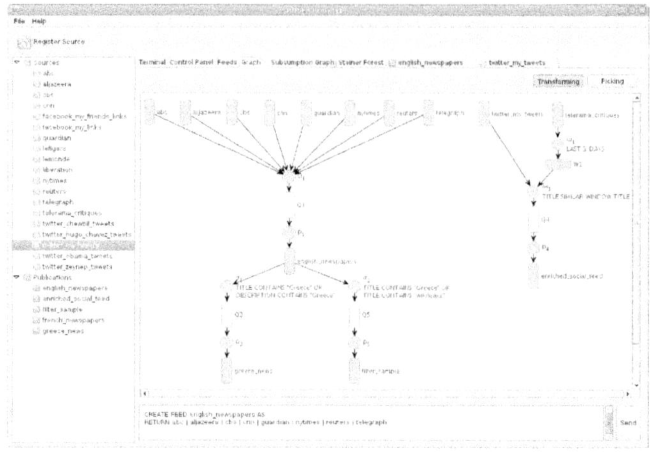

Figure 4: ROSES Prototype screenshot

of registered news feeds and personalize this publication by defining some content-based filtering criteria. Secondly, we will illustrate the usage of join for annotating social network messages (Twitter, Facebook) with critics about new movies published in form of RSS feeds (*eg.* www.filmcritic.com).

The second scenario will illustrate the query processing steps of our prototype using the Java interface. We will load a script of publications containing a workload of 1000 conjunctive filtering queries of the form $q = \sigma_{a_1 \wedge \cdots \wedge a_k}(src_1 \cup \cdots \cup src_n)$, where $k \in [1, 3]$, $n \in [1, 10]$ and n defines the number of query sources randomly picked from a fixed set of 25 feeds. Using the Java client, we will visualize the multi-query plan generated by the system, as well as the predicate subsumption graphs and the optimized filtering trees. Finally, we will also compare query plan optimization and query execution costs for higher workload up to 10000 randomly generated publication queries.

5. REFERENCES

[1] M. Cammert, J. Krämer, B. Seeger, and S. Vaupel. A cost-based approach to adaptive resource management in data stream systems. In *TKDE*, volume 20, pages 230–245, 2008.

[2] M. Charikar, C. Chekuri, T. Cheung, Z. Dai, A. Goel, S. Guha, and M. Li. Approximation algorithms for directed steiner problems. In *Proceedings of the ninth annual ACM-SIAM symposium on Discrete algorithms*, SODA '98, pages 192–200. Society for Industrial and Applied Mathematics, 1998.

[3] X. Cheng and D. Du. *Steiner Trees in Industry*, volume 11 of *Combinatorial Optimization*, pages 235–279. Kluwer Academic Publishers, 2002.

[4] J. Creus, B. Amann, N. Travers, and D. Vodislav. RoSeS : A continuous content-based query engine for RSS feeds. In *DEXA*, Toulouse, France, August 2011.

[5] R. Horincar, B. Amann, and T. Artières. Best-effort refresh strategies for content-based rss feed aggregation. In *WISE*, pages 262–270, 2010.

[6] F. Hwang, D. Richards, and P. Winter. The Steiner Tree Problem. *Annals of Discrete Mathematics*, 53, 1992.

[7] T. K. Sellis. Multiple-query optimization. *ACM Trans. Database Syst.*, 13:23–52, 1988.

Conkar: Constraint Keyword-based Association Discovery

Mo Zhou
Indiana University, USA
mozhou@cs.indiana.edu

Yifan Pan
Indiana University, USA
panyif@cs.indiana.edu

Yuqing Wu
Indiana University, USA
yuqwu@cs.indiana.edu

ABSTRACT

In many domains, such as bioinformatics, cheminformatics, health informatics and social networks, data can be represented naturally as labeled graphs. To address the increasing needs in discovering interesting associations between entities in such data graphs, especially under complicated keyword-based and structural constraints, we introduce Conkar (**Con**strained **K**eyword-based **A**ssociation Discove**Ry**) System. Conkar is the first system for discovering *constrained acyclic paths (CAP)* in graph data under sophisticated keyword-based constraints, with the highlight being the set of quantitative constraint metrics that we proposed, including *coverage* and *relevance*. We will demonstrate the key features of Conkar: powerful and user-friendly query specification, efficient query evaluation, flexible and on-demand result ranking, visual result display, as well as an insight tour on our novel CAP query evaluation algorithms.

Categories and Subject Descriptors

H.3.3 [**Information Systems**]: Information Storage and Retrieval—*Information Search and Retrieval (Search process)*

General Terms

Algorithms

Keywords

Keyword-based Association Discovery, Search Algorithm, Coverage, Relevance, Drug Discovery

1. INTRODUCTION

In many domains, such as social networks, cheminformatics, bioinformatics, and health informatics, data can be represented naturally in graph model, with nodes being data entities and edges the relationships between them. RDF (Resource Description Framework) [11] is a W3C recommended language which describes linked data of the Semantic Web in the form of triples. Both RDF data and RDF schema can be represented by node and edge labeled graphs.

The graph nature of these data brings opportunities and challenges to data storage and retrieval. In particular, it opens the doors to search problems such as semantic association discovery [3, 4] and keyword search [7].

We study the application requirements in various domains including cheminformatics and social networks and find that the problem of discovering acyclic paths between data entities under constraints such as appearance of nodes, edges and/or patterns and the length of paths is at the core of these applications.

One of the core research directions in cheminformatics is to study drugs' affect on diseases via the interaction between proteins and genes [10]. To facilitate such study, drugs, diseases, proteins, genes, etc. are represented in an RDF graph, called Chem2Bio2RDF [5]. To assess the effectiveness of a drug before conducting chemical experiments, domain experts would like to first find and analyse paths from the drug to the target disease under constraints, e.g. the (partial) appearance of certain proteins/genes.

In social networks and research networks, such as VIVO [6], one of the most important functionalities is to find connections between people that satisfy certain constraints [1, 8], for example, to find possible collaborations based on common interest, or to detect conflict of interest between authors and PCs based on the appearance of certain entities, such as professional institutions that both are affiliated with, and/or relationships, e.g. advise, co-author and co-PI. It is also critical to determine the degree of such conflict of interest further based on how frequent certain relationship and entities appear in the connection [1].

How to express and measure constraints and how to answer such constrained path discovery queries efficiently are critical problems, but are not yet fully studied in the literature. There are no generic systems that fulfill the demands. First, allow us to take social/research networks as example, to illustrate such demands.

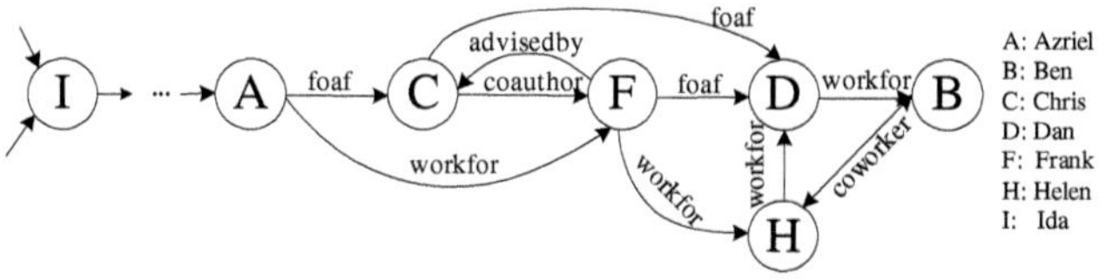

Figure 1: Graph representation of a sample RDF data

EXAMPLE 1.1. *Figure 1 shows the graph representation of a sample RDF data representing the relationships among people in the social networks. Let's consider the following search requests:*
case1. *Find how* Azriel *connects to* Ben*;*
case2. *Find the close ties (within 3 steps) between* Azriel *and* Ben*;*
case3. *Find how* Azriel *connects to* Ben *through* Chris *or* Dan*;*
case4. *Find how* Azriel *connects to* Ben *through at least two people from* Chris, Dan *and* Ida *within four steps.*
case5. *Find* Azriel*'s close (within 4 steps) professional connections (e.g. relationships such as* workfor, coworker, coauthor*) to* Ben*;*
case6. *Find* Azriel*'s close (within 4 steps) semi-professional con-*

CIKM'11, October 24–28, 2011, Glasgow, Scotland, UK.

nections to Ben *(i.e. half of the relationships in any tie should be professional);*

Query languages have been proposed to query data on the Semantic Web. SPARQL [12], the de facto standard query language for RDF, relies on graph patterns to identify data entities and relationships of interest. However, it lacks the ability to express arbitrary paths between data entities, such as those shown in Ex. 1.1. The notion of label-constraint reachability (LCR) [8] was proposed to describe the problem of finding the *connectivity* between two given nodes in a labeled graph under the constraint that all the edge labels along the path are in a given set. The semantic keyword search problem was defined to find trees in a labeled directed graph where the tree nodes and edges cover all the keywords [7]. Combining these notions, several SPARQL extensions, with the introduction of path variables, were proposed [4, 9]. Such extensions are capable of expressing the search queries in cases 1-2 in Ex. 1.1, but not the other cases. There were also proposals for extending SPARQL with regular expressions [2] to express complex patterns that satisfy strictly defined constraints such as cases 1,2,3,5. However, such SPARQL extensions still cannot express more relaxed constraints such as those in cases 4,6.

To support the searches in Ex. 1.1, the two major challenges are: how to express these association discovery problems and how to answer them efficiently.

We introduce Conkar [14], the first system that can express and answer all these search queries. In Conkar, whose architecture is shown in Figure 2, we abstract the association discovery problem as the problem of *finding constrained acyclic paths (CAP) in directed labeled graphs.* We define a set of quantitative metrics, at the core of which are the notions of *coverage* and *relevance* of a path with respect to a set of keywords. Via the easy-to-use interface of Conkar, users can express CAP search queries by specifying keyword sets, the desired *coverage* and *relevance* of the resultant paths with respect to these keyword sets, as well as other constraints, such as path length. Users can also specify the relative importance of quantitative metrics. Then Conkar will rank the results based on their preference. Upon viewing the results, users can adjust (extend or refine) the constraints and ranking criteria to obtain the results that suit their needs.

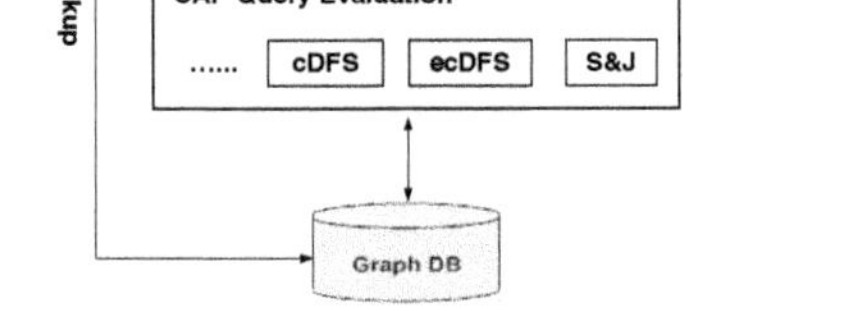

Figure 2: Conkar architecture

To address the challenges in answering the CAP queries efficiently on large graph data, we introduce a family of CAP discovery algorithms, including DFS-base algorithms constraint-DFS (cDFS) and enhanced cDFS (ecDFS), and a localized search-and-join (S&J) algorithm. All of them are designed to minimize the search space by taking advantage of the constraints to eliminate unpromising search branches as early as possible.

2. EXPRESSING CAP SEARCH QUERIES

The important innovations of Conkar are to formally define the *Constrained Acyclic Path Discovery* problem and to provide a friendly interface for users to express CAP queries.

2.1 Preliminary

Let $\mathcal{L}$ be an infinite set of literals and $\mathcal{U}$ be an infinite set of URIs disjoint with $\mathcal{L}$. We represent RDF data as a node and edge labeled directed graph $G = (V, E, \lambda)$ where V is a set of nodes, $E \subset V \times V$ is a set of edges, and λ is a labeling function that maps items in $V \cup E$ into a finite set of labels and literals.

We call a sequence of interleaving nodes and edges of graph G a *path fragment* (or *fragment*), represented by f, if

- for every adjacent (n, e, n') in f, it is the case that $n, n' \in V \wedge e = (n, n') \in E$;
- if (e, n) is a prefix of f, then there must exist $n' \in V$, such that $e = (n', n) \in E$; and
- if (n, e) is a suffix of f, then there must exist $n' \in V$, such that $e = (n, n') \in E$.

We use $nodes(f)$ ($edges(f)$) to represent the set of nodes (edges) in f, and $Length(f)$ (or $|f|$) the length of f, defined as $|edges(f)|$. We overload the mapping function λ to map a set of nodes (edges) to their corresponding labels.

Given two nodes $n_s, n_d \in V$ as the source and destination nodes, the paths that link n_s to n_d in G are fragments in the form $f = (n_s, e_1, n_1 \ldots, n_{k-1}, e_k, n_d)$. In search queries that look for the paths between two nodes, frequently only acyclic paths are of interest to users. Therefore, as n_s and n_d are given, we are particularly interested in a special type of path fragment - acyclic e-fragment (denoted by f_e), which starts and ends with an edge, and no two nodes, including the end nodes, are the same. We use $\mathcal{F}_e(n_s, n_d)$ to represent all acyclic e-fragments between n_s and n_d in G.

2.2 Specifying Constraints

Length Constraint: Among a possibly large number of resultant e-fragments of a search query, shorter e-fragments tend to express stronger and more meaningful relationship between the two end nodes than the longer ones do [3, 7]. Involving the *length constraint* which restricts the length of the resultant e-fragments has been studied in [2, 4], and Conkar supports it as well.

Set-based Constraints: When users search for paths between a pair of nodes, they are frequently interested in paths that contain certain keywords. Such constraints can be given in the form of a *keyword set* (denoted $\mathcal{S}$), where a keyword is a label in $\mathcal{U}$.

Certain constraints, such as presence constraints [4] on nodes and tight constraints on edges [8] were discussed in the existing works, but they are quite limited in terms of what can be in the keyword set and how the results are regulated by it, hence can express only some search queries, but not many others, such as cases 3-6 in Ex. 1.1.

We generalize the keyword-based constraints defined in [4, 8] in two directions: (1) we allow the keyword set to include keywords that can be mapped to labels of both nodes and edges; and (2) we extend how the results are confined by a keyword set.

DEFINITION 2.1. *Given a finite keyword set $\mathcal{S} \subseteq \mathcal{U}$ and an e-fragment $f_e \in \mathcal{F}_e(n_s, n_d)$,*

1. *if $\mathcal{S} \subseteq (\lambda(nodes(f_e)) \cup \lambda(edges(f_e)))$, we say f_e satisfies* presence constraint *w.r.t. $\mathcal{S}$;*
2. *if $\mathcal{S} \supseteq (\lambda(nodes(f_e)) \cup \lambda(edges(f_e)))$, we say f_e satisfies* context constraint *w.r.t. $\mathcal{S}$;*
3. *if $\mathcal{S} \cap (\lambda(nodes(f_e)) \cup \lambda(edges(f_e))) \neq \emptyset$, we say f_e satisfies* intersection constraint *w.r.t. $\mathcal{S}$.*

Based on the definition above, we can express the search request in Ex. 1.1 case3 as "find e-fragments from *Azriel* to *Ben* that satisfy the *intersection constraint* w.r.t. keyword set $\{Chris, Dan\}$".

Quantitative Metrics: To express the search requests in Ex. 1.1 cases 4-6, a more subtle description of the relationship between an e-fragment and a keyword set than the *all-or-nothing* set-based constraints described in Def. 2.1 is needed. For this purpose, we introduce quantitative metrics *coverage* and *relevance*.

Intuitively, *coverage* describes the fraction of the keyword set that appears in the label set of an e-fragment, while *relevance* describes the fraction of the labels of an e-fragment that are in the keyword set. In an RDF graph, each node has its *unique* label, while more than one edge may have the same label. Therefore, we refine *coverage* and *relevance* further into *node-coverage* and *node-relevance* for keyword sets to be applied only on nodes, *edge-coverage* and *edge-relevance* for edges, and use *coverage* and *relevance* for the constraints in which keywords can be mapped to both nodes and edges. We use $cntE(l, f_e)$ to represent the number of appearance of a keyword l among the edges in an e-fragment f_e.

We present the formula to calculate the coverage and relevance in Def. 2.2 while the formula to calculate node (edge) coverage and relevance can be easily deduced.

DEFINITION 2.2. *Given a graph G, two nodes $n_s, n_d \in V$ and a finite keyword set $\mathcal{S} \subseteq \mathcal{U}$, for an e-fragment $f_e \in \mathcal{F}_e(n_s, n_d)$,*

$$Coverage(f_e, \mathcal{S}) = \frac{|\mathcal{S} \cap (\lambda(nodes(f_e)) \cup \lambda(edges(f_e)))|}{|\mathcal{S}|} \quad (1)$$

$$Relevance(f_e, \mathcal{S}) = \frac{|\mathcal{S} \cap \lambda(nodes(f_e))| + \Sigma_{l \in \mathcal{S}} cntE(l, f_e)}{|nodes(f_e)| + |edges(f_e)|} \quad (2)$$

Taking advantage of the quantitative metrics, the search requests in Ex. 1.1 cases 4-6 can be expressed easily. For example, case 6 can be expressed as "find all e-fragments, f_e, from *Azriel* to *Ben* such that EdgeRelevance(f_e, {*coworker, workfor, coauthor*}) $\geq$ 0.5 and $|f_e| \leq 4$".

All the constraints we defined in Def. 2.1 are special cases that can be expressed using the quantitative metrics defined in Def. 2.2.

$$Presence(f_e, \mathcal{S}) \iff Coverage(f_e, \mathcal{S}) = 1 \quad (3)$$

$$Context(f_e, \mathcal{S}) \iff Relevance(f_e, \mathcal{S}) = 1 \quad (4)$$

$$Intersection(f_e, \mathcal{S}) \iff Relevance(f_e, \mathcal{S}) > 0 \quad (5)$$

Similarly, we can define the node/edge version of these functions.

2.3 CAP Query Specification

Formally, a CAP search query $CAP(n_s, n_d, \tau)$ on RDF graph G involves source and destination nodes $n_s, n_d \in V$, and constraint τ expressed using zero to many quantitative metrics functions that involve zero or many keyword sets, and returns the e-fragment(s) from n_s to n_d that satisfy τ. Our Conkar provides a user-friendly interface for specifying a CAP query by composing the ingredients of the search, i.e. G, n_s, n_d and an optional, potentially arbitrarily complicated τ.

3. ANSWERING CAP QUERIES

As the data graph G and constraint τ can both be large in size and complex in nature, designing algorithms that can efficiently answer CAP queries is at the heart of the design and implementation of Conkar.

Many graph searching algorithms [7] were proposed for answering keyword searches in graph data. But they can not be applied directly to answer CAP queries, as they are designed to find tree instances covering all keywords in the graph. Traversal-based approaches such as DFS, BFS and bidirectional search [2] can be adapted with a post-search filter to answer CAP queries. However, such Search-Filter approaches don't scale well when the size and complexity of the graph increase. Algorithms [3, 4] with additional help from schema or indices were later proposed, but these facilitating data and structures lack of either availability or scalability.

In Conkar, we implemented three algorithms to answer CAP queries:

Search-Filter approach utilizes algorithms proposed in the literature to find all acyclic e-fragments in $\mathcal{F}_e(n_s, n_d)$ (in fact, to find $CAP(n_s, n_d, \emptyset)(G)$), and then eliminates those not satisfying the constraints specified in τ. This approach is most generic and can be easily adapted for all constraints introduced above. However it is not practically efficient because generating $\mathcal{F}_e(n_s, n_d)$ is very time and space consuming, rendering the *search* phase costly, while frequently $|CAP(n_s, n_d, \tau)(G)| \ll |CAP(n_s, n_d, \emptyset)(G)|$, rendering the high cost of the *search* phase mostly wasted.

In Conkar, to answer CAP queries efficiently, we propose to take advantage of the constraints on length and keywords and push result validation into the path discovery process, to prune unpromising intermediate results as early as possible. In particular, we design and implement the following two families of algorithms [13].

ConstraintDFS (cDFS) and *Enhanced ConstraintDFS* (ecDFS) algorithms are based on *Depth First Search* (DFS). To minimize the DFS search space in computing a CAP query $CAP(n_s, n_d, \tau)$, we minimize the total number of intermediate results, i.e. fragments, generated in the process by terminating expansion from fragments generated at search steps when we are certain that the expansion will not lead to any results. In order to do so, we introduce the notion of *projected value range* of the quantative metrics, and we design a set of formula to compute the projected value ranges of the constraint metrics in the CAP query in question, based on information, such as the length and keyword appearances, of the fragments generated so far in the DFS process. In the cDFS algorithm, at each DFS step, when the projected value ranges of a fragment do not overlap with the constraints in τ, we can safely terminate the expansion of this fragment. The ecDFS algorithm further improves the performance by saving the validation of the fragments during the search steps of which we foresee the fragments guaranteed to be promising.

Search-and-Join (S&J) algorithm specifically targets at the set-based, rather than list-based, keyword constraint specification. The S&J algorithm takes the local information around the nodes with keywords into consideration to calculate more precise projected value ranges, and thus conduct more efficient pruning. The S&J algorithm issues mini-searches to find exclusive path fragments (i.e. paths that do not pass through any keyword nodes) between pairs of nodes that contain keywords, then use *constrained sequence join* to concatenate the fragments to produce the final results. Careful bookkeeping allows us to use the partial results in one mini-search to limit the search space of many other mini-searches, and effectively reduces the overall search cost.

4. DEMONSTRATION PROPOSAL

We propose the demonstrational plan to welcome users to have a hand-on experience with Conkar. Especially users can (1) issue CAP queries, simple or complicated, via our user-friendly interface and view the resultant paths instantly; and (2) have an insight look at how our algorithms efficiently evaluate CAP queries. We will demonstrate Conkar on two applications: the drug discovery application for chemical informatics and the application on social/research networks. Following the running examples in Sec. 1, we will again use social/research networks data as our example here.

4.1 CAP Query Specification and Answering

Users are welcome to use the CAP query interface of Conkar to specify and evaluate CAP queries. The required fields are (1) the data graph, which can be selected from our demo databases; and (2) the source and destination nodes, which can be specified by typing keyword(s) in a textbox, and selecting URIs that Conkar pulls from the database matching the keyword(s). The constraints are optional. Using the simple CAP query interface of Conkar, users can construct a set of keywords, and use scroll bars to set the desired values ranges of the quantitative metrics with respect to the keyword set. Users can also specify the importance of each constraint, which Conkar will take into consideration while presenting the ranked results to reflect users' preferences. Conkar visualizes the ranked results in list view as well as graph view. The simple search interface and result display are shown in Figure 3.

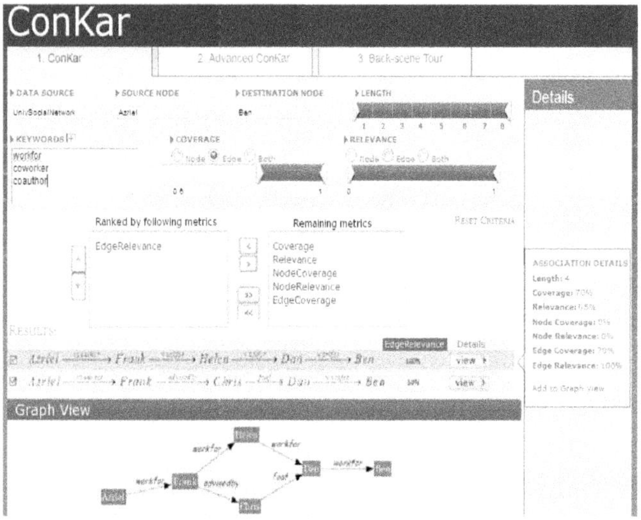

Figure 3: Simple search

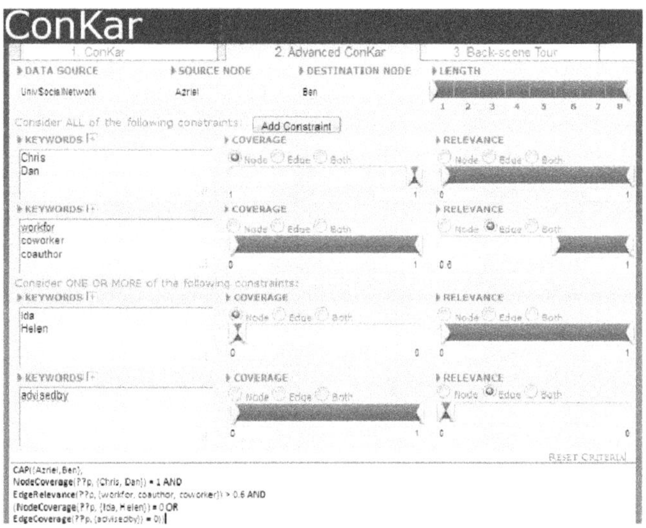

Figure 4: Advanced search

More sophisticated users are welcome to use the advanced CAP query interface to specify complex CAP search queries, consisting of constraints based on different keyword sets, linked via logical operators (AND and OR). Conkar also offers the resultant CAP query generated from the click-and-drag interface in the CAP query box for users to inspect. Figure 4 shows a CAP query under construction using the advanced search of Conkar.

4.2 Query Evaluation Behind-the-Scene

Besides demonstrating the key features of Conkar, e.g. CAP query specification and execution, we also provide a behind-the-scene tour for audiences who are interested in our CAP query evaluation algorithms. Here, after composing a CAP query, we will welcome the audience to choose an algorithm to evaluate the query. Conkar will then illustrate how nodes/edges in the data graph are explored, the intermediate results, as well as our sophisticated book-keeping that facilitates the search. At the end, besides showing the query results, Conkar will also report the execution profile, including how many node/edges are explored, using which the users can compare the performance of different algorithms. Figure 5 illustrates an intermediate step of using the S&J algorithm to answer a CAP query. Here, nodes are color coded to distinguish source/destination nodes, query nodes, search frontiers, pruned branches, etc.

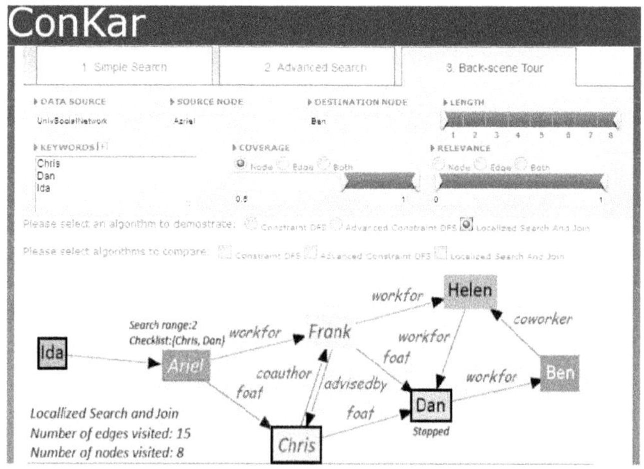

Figure 5: Behind the scene

5. REFERENCES

[1] B. Aleman-Meza, *et al.* Semantic Analytics on Social Networks: Experiences in Addressing the Problem of Conflict of Interest Detection. In *WWW*, 2006.

[2] F. Alkhateeb, *et al.* Constrained Regular Expressions in SPARQL. In *SWWS*, 2008.

[3] K. Anyanwu, *et al.* ρ-Queries: Enabling Querying for Semantic Associations on the Semantic Web. In *WWW*, 2003.

[4] K. Anyanwu, *et al.* SPARQ2L: Towards Support for Subgraph Extraction Queries in RDF Databases. In *WWW*, 2007.

[5] C. Bin, *et al.* Chem2Bio2RDF: a Semantic Framework for Linking and Data Mining Chemogenomic and Systems Chemical Biology Data. In *BMC Bioinformatics*, 2010.

[6] Y. Ding, *et al.* Semantic Web Portal: A Platform for Better Browsing and Visualizing Semantic Data. In *AMT*, 2010.

[7] H. He, *et al.* BLINKS: Ranked Keyword Searches on Graphs. In *SIGMOD*, 2007.

[8] R. Jin, *et al.* Computing Label Constraint Reachability in Graph Databases. In *SIGMOD*, 2010.

[9] K. Kochut, *et al.* SPARQLeR: Extended SPARQL for Semantic Association Discovery. In *ESWC*, 2007.

[10] S. Lee, *et al.* Building the Process-drug-side Effect Network to Discover the Relationship Between Biological Processes and Side Effects. In *BMC Bioinformatics*, 2011.

[11] F. Manola, *et al.* RDF Primer. *W3C Recommendation*, 2004.

[12] E. Prud'hommeaux, *et al.* SPARQL Query Language for RDF. *W3C Recommendation*, 2008.

[13] M. Zhou, *et al.* Efficient Association Discovery with Keyword-based Constraints on Large Graph Data. In CIKM, 2011.

[14] Conkar: http://www.cs.indiana.edu/~mozhou/conkar.html

Interactive Reasoning in Uncertain RDF Knowledge Bases

Timm Meiser, Maximilan Dylla, Martin Theobald
Max Planck Institute for Informatics
Saarbrücken, Germany
tmeiser@mpi-inf.mpg.de, mdylla@mpi-inf.mpg.de, mtb@mpi-inf.mpg.de

ABSTRACT

Recent advances in Web-based information extraction have allowed for the automatic construction of large, semantic knowledge bases, which are typically captured in RDF format. The very nature of the applied extraction techniques however entails that the resulting RDF knowledge bases may face a significant amount of incorrect, incomplete, or even inconsistent (i.e., *uncertain*) factual knowledge, which makes query answering over this kind of data a challenge. Our reasoner, coined URDF[1], supports SPARQL queries along with rule-based, first-order predicate logic to infer new facts and to resolve data uncertainty over millions of RDF triplets directly *at query time*. We demonstrate a fully interactive reasoning engine, combining a Java-based reasoning backend and a Flash-based visualization frontend in a dynamic client-server architecture. Our visualization frontend provides interactive access to the reasoning backend, including tasks like *exploring* the knowledge base, rule-based and statistical *reasoning*, *faceted browsing* of large query graphs, and *explaining answers* through lineage.

Categories and Subject Descriptors

H.3.3 [**Information Storage and Retrieval**]: Information Search and Retrieval—*search process*

General Terms

Algorithms, Design, Management

Keywords

Uncertain RDF, Interactive Reasoning, Visualization

1. INTRODUCTION

A plethora of free semantic knowledge bases (including DBpedia and its inter-linked data sources, KnowItAll [8], ReadTheWeb [7] and YAGO [9, 19]) as well as commercial endeavors (including FreeBase.com, TrueKnowledge.com, Sig.ma, EntityCube, Wolfram Alpha, or Google Squared) have emerged out of a variety of Web-based information extraction frameworks in recent years. Many of these projects employ Wikipedia as common source for extraction, with their techniques ranging from extracting contents of highly structured infoboxes [8] to free-text information extraction and natural language processing [7]. Due to the very nature of the applied (unsupervised or semi-supervised) extraction techniques, but also due to the collaborative and partly highly transient way in which Web sources like Wikipedia evolve, the resulting knowledge bases may contain a significant amount of false or contradictory facts. On the other hand, they often remain highly incomplete and may miss a large amount of facts about real-world entities. As a potential remedy, the underlying extraction tools sometimes provide confidence values attached to the extracted facts. Yet it remains far from obvious how to incorporate issues like incompleteness, incorrectness, and inconsistency into an interactive information system, in order to provide consistent query answers over this type of uncertain data.

Our reasoning engine provides a SPARQL-compliant query interface and employs Datalog-style, deductive grounding techniques of first-order logical rules (Horn clauses). Specifically, we distinguish between *soft rules* and *hard rules* for

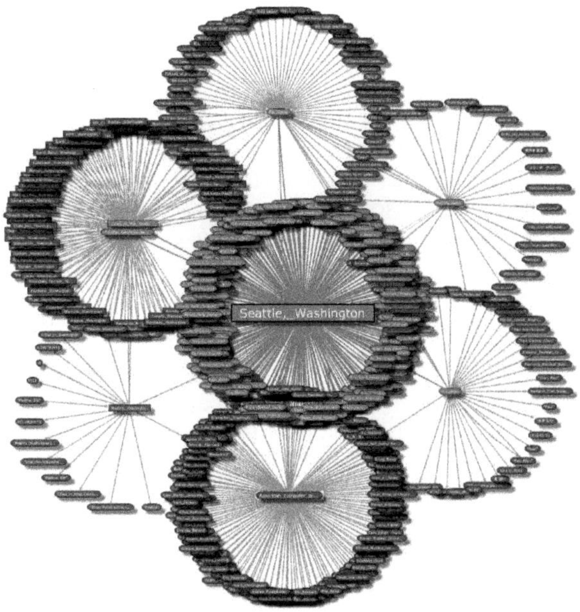

Figure 1: An exploration of the knowledge base around the entity "Seattle,_Washington", showing both base and derived facts.

[1]`http://urdf.mpi-inf.mpg.de`

CIKM'11, October 24–28, 2011, Glasgow, Scotland, UK.

reasoning. Soft rules can be employed in a deductive fashion to derive new facts from existing ones (including facts derived from other deduction steps), or to reinforce the confidence of existing base facts. Hard rules, on the other hand, enforce additional consistency constraints among both base and derived facts. The resulting logical dependencies among base and derived facts are captured via Boolean lineage formulas. Processing queries consists of two phases: 1) grounding the query against the rules and base facts contained in the knowledge base, and 2) a subsequent (propositional or probabilistic) consistency reasoning step. All reasoning-related computations—including grounding and consistency reasoning—are handled by URDF at query time.

2. RELATED WORK

State-of-the-art RDF engines (see, e.g., [1, 11]) primarily focus on conjunctive queries on top of a relational encoding of RDF data. These engines generally follow a deterministic data and query processing model and do not have a notion of rule-based inference or uncertain reasoning. Approaches for managing uncertainty in the context of probabilistic databases [3, 4, 5, 18, 17] focus on relational data with fixed schemata and often employ strong independence assumptions among data objects (the "base tuples"). ULDBs [4] provide a lineage-based representation formalism for probabilistic data, which has been shown to be closed and complete under any combination of SQL operators and across arbitrary levels of materialized views. Here, the lineage (aka. "history" in [18] or "repair-key" operator in [3]) of a derived tuple is captured as a Boolean formula, which recursively unrolls the logical dependencies from the derived tuple back to the base tuples. In probabilistic databases, SQL is employed for formulating queries and for defining views. SQL statements generally yield "hard" Boolean constraints among tuples, but lack the notion of "soft" dependencies among data items. Moreover, capturing correlated tuples [16] with probabilistic graphical models such as Bayesian Nets [6, 21] and Markov Random Fields [17] is finding increasing attention also in the database community. Also in the context of these graphical models, lineage remains the key for a closed representation model [10].

Statistical Relational Learning (SRL) has been gaining an increasing momentum in the machine learning, database, and knowledge management communities recently. Markov Logic Networks (MLNs) [14] are one of the most generic approaches for combining first-order logic and probabilistic graphical models. MLNs work by grounding a set of first-order logical rules against a knowledge base, and by sampling states ("worlds") over a Markov network that represents the grounded (i.e., propositional) formulas. Markov Logic however does not easily scale to very large knowledge bases. Even the most efficient, recent database approaches which adopt inference methods for probabilistic graphical networks, such as [21], [12] or [22], are designed for batch processing and are not well suited for interactive querying.

3. SYSTEM ARCHITECTURE

The reasoning backend is deployed under an Apache Tomcat Web server and accesses a PostgreSQL database which captures the knowledge base. Our visualization frontend has been developed under Adobe Flex to run via Flash in almost any common Web browser, thus supporting a variety of operating systems (e.g., Windows, Linux, Android) and clients (e.g., laptops, tablets). Using the Flex framework (via a combination of ActionScript and MXML components), our visualization follows a so-called Rich Internet Application (RIA) architecture and delivers a desktop-like look-and-feel in a regular browser. The data transfer between the visualization frontend and the reasoning backend is handled by the Adobe-specific data exchange service BlazeDS. This service allows for a fast binary data exchange between server and client via object serialization. Moreover, we integrate the Flare[2] visualization libraries for rendering graphs with different layouts. An example graph, as it can be obtained by exploring the YAGO [9, 19] knowledge base around the entity "Seattle,_Washington", is depicted in Figure 1.

4. REASONING BACKEND

We adopt the common *possible worlds* [2] model as basis for our data model and for defining the semantics of queries. Intuitively, every fact and first-order soft rule in the knowledge base corresponds to a binary random variable, which may hold in the knowledge base (i.e., be "true") with some marginal probability. Via soft and hard rules, facts may be correlated with each other, such that rules (when grounded) may impose intricate dependencies among facts. In the following, we formally consider a knowledge base $\mathcal{KB} = \langle \mathcal{F}, \mathcal{C}, \mathcal{S} \rangle$ as a triplet consisting of propositional facts $\mathcal{F}$, first-order soft rules $\mathcal{C}$ (clauses used for deduction), and first-order hard rules $\mathcal{S}$ (strict consistency constraints).

Base Facts. We presume a set of RDF base facts $\mathcal{F}_{db} \subseteq \mathcal{F}$ to be contained as extensional knowledge in our database. These facts are not derived from other facts and thus are assumed as input (e.g., from an information extraction tool). Base facts may be uncertain, i.e., every fact $f \in \mathcal{F}_{db}$ has a confidence weight $w(f) \in [0,1]$ attached, which corresponds to a prior probability of this fact being true.

Soft Rules. To tackle the inherent incompleteness of $\mathcal{F}_{db}$, we also assume a set of soft deduction rules $\mathcal{C}$ as input to our knowledge base. Just like base facts, soft rules may be uncertain, i.e., they may hold only for a fraction of entities in the real world, which is again reflected by a confidence weight $w(C) \in [0,1]$ for each soft rule $C \in \mathcal{C}$. Soft rules have the shape of Datalog-style (but definite) Horn clauses. They could state, for example, that "married couples usually live at the same place", with a confidence of 0.38 of being correct, which we would write as follows:

$$\begin{aligned} &\mathit{livesIn}(p_1, loc_1) \leftarrow && (1)\\ &\qquad \mathit{marriedTo}(p_1, p_2) \wedge \mathit{livesIn}(p_2, loc_1)\ _{[0.38]} \end{aligned}$$

Grounding the rules in $\mathcal{C}$ over the facts $\mathcal{F}_{db}$ results in new intensional knowledge, which we denote by the set $\mathcal{F}_{in} \subseteq \mathcal{F}$. For intensional facts, we do not know their marginal probabilities upfront, i.e., we need to compute their posterior probabilities via lineage.

Hard Rules. The set of base and derived facts may contain inconsistent information. For example, if we observe two different birth dates for a person, clearly something went wrong either during extraction or when reasoning with soft rules. We can formally express such a consistency constraint as follows:

$$\begin{aligned} &(date_1 = date_2) \leftarrow && (2)\\ &\qquad \mathit{bornOn}(p_1, date_1) \wedge \mathit{bornOn}(p_1, date_2) \end{aligned}$$

[2]http://flare.prefuse.org

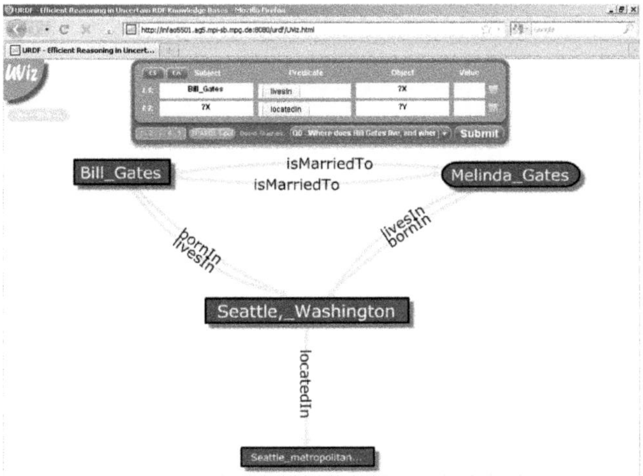

Figure 2: Dependency graph for the query *"Where does Bill Gates live, and where is this place located?"*

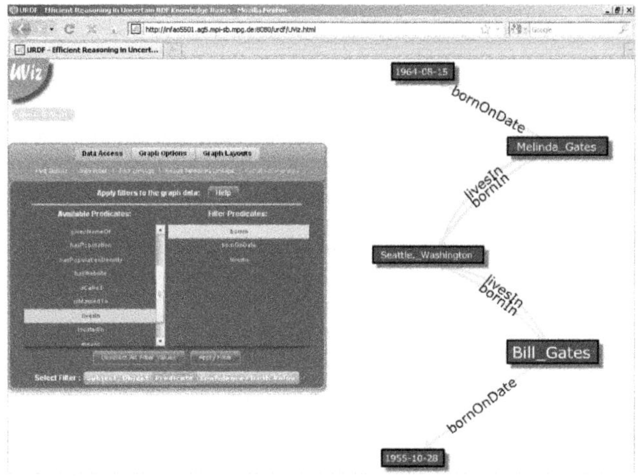

Figure 3: Faceted browsing panel and a filtered version of the graph of Figure 1.

In contrast to soft rules, hard rules (i.e., consistency constraints) have no intensional predicate as head literal and are not used for deriving new facts. Consistency constraints either have an arithmetic predicate (as above) or the constant *false* as head literal.

Lineage. The reasoner employs SLD resolution for grounding soft rules, while hard rules are not used for deduction and thus are grounded separately (see [20] for details on the grounding algorithm). Tracing lineage through SLD resolution resolves to capturing the logical dependencies of derived facts back to the base facts. In analogy to [4, 17], we represent lineage of derived facts as Boolean formulas.

- *Positive Lineage.* SLD resolution with soft rules creates positive lineage. We obtain *conjunctive* lineage whenever we combine (ground) two or more positive literals that co-occur in the body of a rule. We obtain *disjunctive* lineage whenever two or more rules (including base facts) imply the same derived fact.
- *Negations.* Hard rules offer a way to formulate negations in order to constrain the set of possible worlds. A special type of hard rules we consider in [20] partitions $\mathcal{F}$ into disjoint sets of mutually exclusive facts. In this case, each fact in such a "competitor set" may only be true if *none* of the facts it is in conflict with are true.

Propositional Reasoning. In propositional reasoning, we aim to find a truth assignment to facts in $\mathcal{F}$ that is consistent with all hard rules. In [20], we present a constrained and weighted MaxSAT solver that is specifically tailored to the combination of soft and hard rules we consider in our reasoning framework. It operates on a Boolean formula in conjunctive normal form (CNF), which is constructed as a conjunction of all clauses (including base facts, soft, and hard rules) that are grounded in response to a query.

Probabilistic Reasoning. In contrast to propositional reasoning, probabilistic reasoning does not consider only a single consistent truth assignment to facts (i.e., *one* possible world), but—at least conceptually—*all* consistent worlds. In other words, the marginal probability of a derived fact $f \in \mathcal{F}_{in}$ is nothing else but the sum of probabilities of consistent worlds (i.e., those that do not violate any hard rule), for which the Boolean lineage formula of f evaluates to true. For general lineage formulas, probabilistic inference is known to be #P-complete. We thus employ Gibbs sampling or MC-SAT (depending on the shape of the hard rules, see [13]) for approximate inference when exact inference is intractable.

5. VISUALIZATION FRONTEND

Exploration Mode. This is our default visualization mode. For entering a query, the user can switch between a plain-text input field (to enter a SPARQL-style join pattern) and a structured form field (to enter individual subject-predicate-object patterns into predefined forms). When the query is submitted, the reasoner is triggered, and a graph containing all isomorphic embeddings of the query pattern in the knowledge base (consisting of both base and derived facts) is displayed. In addition, the complete dependency graph of the query can be shown. The dependency graph contains all facts that are relevant for answering the query, including facts used for grounding the rules (see Figure 2). The graph layouts in exploration mode correspond to entity-relationship graphs, where the nodes represent the entities in the knowledge base, and the edges represent RDF facts. Edges are colored in *green* or *red*, according to the truth value assigned to the facts by the MaxSAT solver. Different alpha values for the edges visually encode the confidences (in the range of $[0, 1]$) of the facts as they were computed by the possible-worlds-based probabilistic model. The visualization frontend supports the radial and force-directed layouts of Flare, which can both be customized in various ways. Moreover, several options to control and interact with the graph (such as panning and zooming) are supported. By double-clicking on a node, we can dynamically load more facts from the knowledge base in order to iteratively explore the neighborhood of a particular entity. A possible result of such an exploration is shown in Figure 1.

Faceted Browsing. The graphs displayed in exploration mode can quickly grow fairly large. The faceted browsing filter automatically extracts facets from the current graph by grouping the facts along various dimensions. An example for this functionality is depicted in Figure 3, where the user has specified a filter on the predicates *bornIn*, *isMarriedTo* and *livesIn* to restrict the graph of Figure 1, thus showing only facts that match either one of those predicates.

Explanation Mode. By clicking on an edge (i.e., fact) for which lineage is available, the visualization switches into explanation mode. In this mode, the graph granularity changes from an entity-relationship graph into a lineage graph, where the nodes represent entire facts, and the edges denote the logical dependencies among those facts. Additional conjunction (AND) and disjunction (OR) nodes group outgoing edges according to the logical dependencies among facts obtained from the deductive grounding steps. Lineage may not be cyclic, but it may form a DAG structure over the grounded facts. For better readability, lineage DAGs are flattened into trees, where a same fact may occur in multiple branches of the tree. Fact nodes are again colored in *green* and *red*, according to the truth values assigned by the MaxSAT solver. An example explanation tree rooted at the fact *livesIn(Bill_Gates,Seattle,_Washington)* is shown in Figure 4. The upper OR node indicates that several derivations for this fact exist. The second level of the expanded lineage branch has been obtained from the same soft rule as shown in Rule (1). Several sub-trees have been collapsed for better readability (as indicated by the dots).

Comparison Mode. Finally, the comparison feature allows for comparing the answers of any two subsequently executed queries, including changes obtained from updating soft or hard rules. Nodes and edges, which are only contained in the first answer set, are colored in *black* borders; those contained in the second set are colored in *white* borders; and those shared by both sets have *yellow* borders.

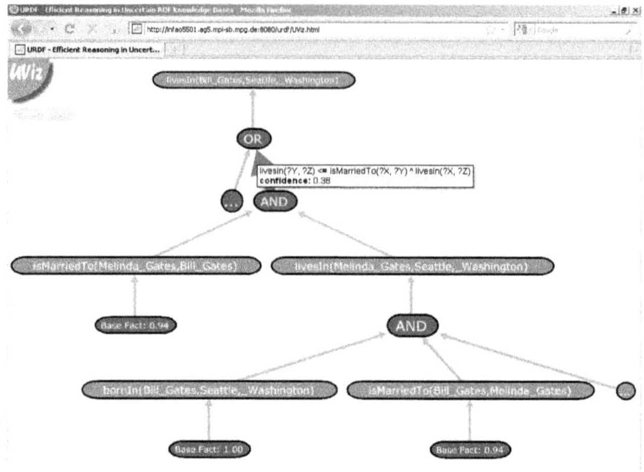

Figure 4: Explanation tree for the derived fact *livesIn(Bill_Gates, Seattle,_Washington)*.

6. DEMONSTRATION DESCRIPTION

Our demo currently runs interactively on the latest version of the YAGO [9] knowledge base, consisting of more than 10 million entities and more than 80 million facts about these entities. To demonstrate all features of our interactive reasoning framework, we have prepared more than 10 SPARQL queries, ranging from single-literal queries like *"Who is Woody Allen married to?"* to multi-join query patterns which require intricate reasoning steps. The demo will focus on queries and rules about people and locations (such as universities and people's advisors or alma maters, merged with gazetteer data from *geonames.org*), as these domains are particular strengths of YAGO. Following the scenario shown in Figures 1–4, we start by showing the difference between results obtained from plain SPARQL-style query processing in comparison to rule-based reasoning. We then iteratively explore the knowledge base around the initial result entities, thus constantly growing the graph. As the information displayed by the expanded graph becomes increasingly cluttered, we can take advantage of the faceted browsing filter which provides a fine-grained control over the visualized information. We finally demonstrate how the explanation and comparison modes can be employed to effectively visualize how rule updates affect the query answers. At all steps of the demonstration, there will be ample opportunity for the audience to propose new queries, update rules, and try out different features of the reasoner.

7. REFERENCES

[1] D. J. Abadi, A. Marcus , S.R. Madden, and K. J. Hollenbach. Scalable semantic web data management using vertical partitioning. *VLDB*, 2007.

[2] S. Abiteboul, P. Kanellakis, and G. Grahne. On the representation and querying of sets of possible worlds. *Theor. Comput. Sci.*, 78(1), 1991.

[3] L. Antova, C. Koch, and D. Olteanu. MayBMS: Managing incomplete information with probabilistic world-set decompositions. *ICDE*, 2007.

[4] O. Benjelloun, A. D. Sarma, A. Y. Halevy, and J. Widom. ULDBs: Databases with uncertainty and lineage. *VLDB*, 2006.

[5] J. Boulos, N. Dalvi, B. Mandhani, S. Mathur, C. Ré, and D. Suciu. MYSTIQ: a system for finding more answers by using probabilities. *SIGMOD*, 2005.

[6] H. C. Bravo and R. Ramakrishnan. Optimizing MPF queries: decision support and probabilistic inference. *SIGMOD*, 2007.

[7] A. Carlson, J. Betteridge, R. C. Wang, E. R. H. Jr., and T. M. Mitchell. Coupled semi-supervised learning for information extraction. *WSDM*, 2010.

[8] O. Etzioni, M. Cafarella, D. Downey, S. Kok, A.-M. Popescu, T. Shaked, S. Soderland, D. S. Weld, and A. Yates. Web-scale information extraction in KnowItAll. *WWW*, 2004.

[9] J. Hoffart, F. M. Suchanek, K. Berberich, E. Lewis-Kelham, G. de Melo, and G. Weikum. YAGO2: Exploring and Querying World Knowledge in Time, Space, Context, and Many Languages. *WWW*, 2011.

[10] B. Kanagal and A. Deshpande. Lineage processing over correlated probabilistic databases. *SIGMOD*, 2010.

[11] T. Neumann and G. Weikum. RDF-3X: a RISC-style engine for RDF. *PVLDB*, 1(1), 2008.

[12] F. Niu, C. Ré, A. Doan, and J. Shavlik. Tuffy: scaling up statistical inference in Markov logic networks using an RDBMS. *PVLDB*, 4(6), 2011.

[13] H. Poon, P. Domingos, and M. Sumner. A general method for reducing the complexity of relational inference and its application to MCMC. *AAAI*, 2008.

[14] M. Richardson and P. Domingos. Markov logic networks. *Machine Learning*, 62(1-2), 2006.

[15] A. D. Sarma, M. Theobald, and J. Widom. Exploiting lineage for confidence computation in uncertain and probabilistic databases. *ICDE*, 2008.

[16] P. Sen and A. Deshpande. Representing and querying correlated tuples in probabilistic databases. *ICDE*, 2007.

[17] P. Sen, A. Deshpande, and L. Getoor. PrDB: managing and exploiting rich correlations in probabilistic databases. *VLDB J.*, 18(5), 2009.

[18] S. Singh, C. Mayfield, R. Shah, S. Prabhakar, S. Hambrusch, J. Neville, and R. Cheng. Database support for probabilistic attributes and tuples. *ICDE*, 2008.

[19] F. M. Suchanek, G. Kasneci, and G. Weikum. YAGO - A Large Ontology from Wikipedia and WordNet. *Elsevier Journal of Web Semantics*, 6(3), 2008.

[20] M. Theobald, M. Sozio, F. Suchanek, and N. Nakashole. URDF: Efficient Reasoning in Uncertain RDF Knowledge Bases with Soft and Hard Rules. Tech-Report MPI-I-2010-5-002, 2010.

[21] D. Z. Wang, E. Michelakis, M. N. Garofalakis, and J. M. Hellerstein. BayesStore: managing large, uncertain data repositories with probabilistic graphical models. *PVLDB*, 1(1), 2008.

[22] M. L. Wick, A. McCallum, and G. Miklau. Scalable Probabilistic Databases with Factor Graphs and MCMC. *PVLDB*, 3(1), 2010.

Fu-Finder: A Game for Studying Querying Behaviours

Test your Search-Fu

Carly O'Neil
School of Computing Science
University of Glasgow
United Kingdom
oneilcl@dcs.gla.ac.uk

James Purvis
School of Computing Science
University of Glasgow
United Kingdom
0801303P@student.gla.ac.uk

Leif Azzopardi
School of Computing Science
University of Glasgow
United Kingdom
leif@dcs.gla.ac.uk

ABSTRACT

Usually the focus of evaluation within Information Retrieval has been placed largely upon the system. However, the individual user and their submitted queries are typically the greatest source of variation in the search process. This demonstration paper presents Fu-Finder, a fun and enjoyable game that measures the user's querying abilities (or search-fu). This game provides useful data for the study of user querying behaviour and assesses how well users can find specific web pages using different search engines.

Categories and Subject Descriptors: H.3.3 Information Storage and Retrieval: Information Search and Retrieval

General Terms: Performance, Experimentation

Keywords: Search-Fu, Querying Behaviour, Findability

1. INTRODUCTION

Searching and finding particular webpages can sometimes feel like a game of skill and chance. Choosing the "right" query terms to illicit the desired response is largely dependant upon the user. The user needs to be able to understand their information need, the system that they are using, how it works, what it is in the document (imagined, ideal, actual and/or known) and what terms would help to distinguish it from other documents. Not a particularly easy task. This has led to the term, *search-fu* being coined which denotes the skill of user's search abilities i.e., someone with weak search-fu will be unlikely to find relevant documents, while someone with strong search-fu will be able to find almost anything. So the question is, how much search-fu does a user possess? Or stated more formally, how well can a user satisfy their information needs when using a search engine?

The prototype system we have developed to help answer this question is a human computation game (HCG). HCGs have been developed to obtain data for various purposes (such as image annotation, character recognition, etc) [8]. Recently, the game Page Hunt was developed to help optimise the Bing search engine as a way to help annotate pages that are difficult to find [3]. However, rather than trying to optimise a particular search engine, we have developed Fu-Finder to evaluate the user's ability at querying for pages across a number of search engines. The game is currently hosted and available to play[1], while the code is open source and freely available to download as part of the PuppyIR project housed on SourceForge[2]. In this paper, we describe the game developed and some of the initial results.

CIKM'11, October 24–28, 2011, Glasgow, Scotland, UK.

2. EVALUATIONS USING GAMES

Human computation games provide a novel tool for solving computationally challenging problems (which are easy for humans, but hard for computers). The success of such games has been their ability to generate large quantities of reliable and useful data by providing users with enjoyment and points as payment rather than money or course credit. The added advantage is that these games can be undertaken in a controlled environment (i.e. within the remit of the game rules/setup) much like a standard or traditional IR experiment, but without the problems of using paid-workers through crowd sourcing. While HCGs are often developed to solve a difficult problem, such as von Ahn's ESP game, where players independently annotate an images [7], in IR human computation games have been used for evaluation purposes.

Two notable games developed in IR are: Book Explorer [2] and PageHunt [3]. In [2], they developed a human computation game to assess relevancy of electronic books to topics. The main motivation for incorporating this task in a game was to provide a means of obtaining relevancy judgements for large document collections without needing to provide fiscal payment to study participants. This has been outlined as a prime motivation for including a computationally-hard task within a game with a purpose [7]. The Book Explorer game, whose model is a variant of the inversion-problem model [8], has two player roles, which can be adopted by individuals or teams. The *explorer* locates and highlights relevant sections of a document; while the *reviewer* provides relevancy feedback on documents [2]. Reviewers can only enter relevancy judgements for documents that have been evaluated by at least one explorer player. Furthermore, reviewers also serve as a cheating-detection mechanism as they examine explorer input, thus creating a multi-level validation system.

While the results from the study appear to show some promise for obtaining reasonably good relevance judgements,

[1] `http://www.dcs.gla.ac.uk/access/fufinder`

[2] `http://sourceforge.net/projects/puppyir/`

whether it can be truly considered a game is matter of debate. The Books Explorer game places a high cognitive load on the reviewer, and requires them to read a large amount of text. Such a burden violates the general principles of designing a fun and enjoyable game (unless of course the gamers are also avid book fans).

On the other hand, Page Hunt [3, 4] was a game that was developed to optimise of the Bing search engine for pages that were difficult to find using Bing. Pages included within the game were selected because the labels for these pages used by Bing were ineffective, and additional metadata was required [4]. The rules of Page Hunt were simple: given a screen shot of a web page, enter a query to find the page, if successful they are presented with a new page to look for, otherwise they can either query again or pass and look for a new page. The goal was to find as many of the pages shown as possible in the 3 minutes (although the timer itself was not visible during the game). Queries were sent to the Bing search engine, and a player awarded a point if the web page was found within the top five results. These results were viewable in a pane presented over the top of the screenshot view. The interaction metaphor present within the game is based on the traditional user interaction with search engines. The inclusion of such metaphors generally improves the usability of game interfaces [6].

Using the Page Hunt game, they performed an experiment that lasted ten days and attracted 10,000 registered users from the Web community. User participation was strictly voluntary, and users were not contacted directly by the researchers to be encouraged to play. This voluntary participation suggests that the results obtained were not affected by any payment-related bias. The sole motivation for users continuing gameplay was enjoyment. The game was seeded with 698 URLs for which better labels were required for Microsoft's Bing search engine [3]. The usage statistics obtained for this short study were very promising. The average user contributed 12 labels, and each URL obtained over 170 distinct labels [3]. The collected data indicated that some pages present were easily found in the top N results, while others were more difficult to obtain. Percentage findability of a page was defined as the percentage of users who found the page in the top N search results, where $N = 5$ [3]. It was found that 27% of pages exhibited 100% findability, while 26% has 0% findability. From this they concluded that the number of pages with 100% findability is approximately equal to the number of pages with 0% findability [4]. The length of the page URL was also found to be a contributing factor in page findability within Bing. As the URL length increased, the probability of finding said page within the Bing search engine rankings was found to decrease [3].

3. GAME OVERVIEW

Fu-Finder is a variant of the Page Hunt [3] game, but provides a couple of different features that changes the game dynamics and the motivations of users. Before we describe these changes, we shall outline the game and the gameplay. The premise of the game is based on testing users ability to search (i.e. their search-fu) in a competitive environment. The game starts by presenting a user with a screen shot of a page. This page is what they need to find by querying the search engines. The game returns the results from three search engines and denotes whether the target page was returned in the top five results or not. The gamer has the option of (i) searching for the same target page again, or (ii) moving on to the next target page. The game lasts for three minutes and gamers are awarded points according to the number and rank positions of target pages that they find. They obtain more points for retrieving the page higher up in the ranking, and for retrieving the page across multiple search engines. In contrast to the gameplay within PageHunt, the game contains multiple search engines, and aims to motivate users to pose better queries to obtain a substantially larger amounts of points.

The interface of the main game page is shown in Fig 1. The target page is shown on the right, gamers enter queries in the middle box, and the scores and results of the query entered is shown on the right. Below the title and url of the results retrieved from each engine is shown in two colours (pink to indicate the result not-matching, and green to indicate a match with the target page). In the Figure, it shows the results from a very successful query which returns the target page at rank one across all the search engines. At the top of the screen, the game displays the user currently logged in to the system, and the time remaining for the current game. The Fu-Finder game required users to read an information sheet, consent to participating in the study, and register as a game participant. By including a user registration component we anticipated that this would reduce the number of participants, but it was necessary to provide informed consent to users, and also enabled us to collect data across particular users (as opposed to sessions).Following completion of the game, users are shown the status, any rewards that they achieved, the leaderboard of results, and asked whether they would like to play again.

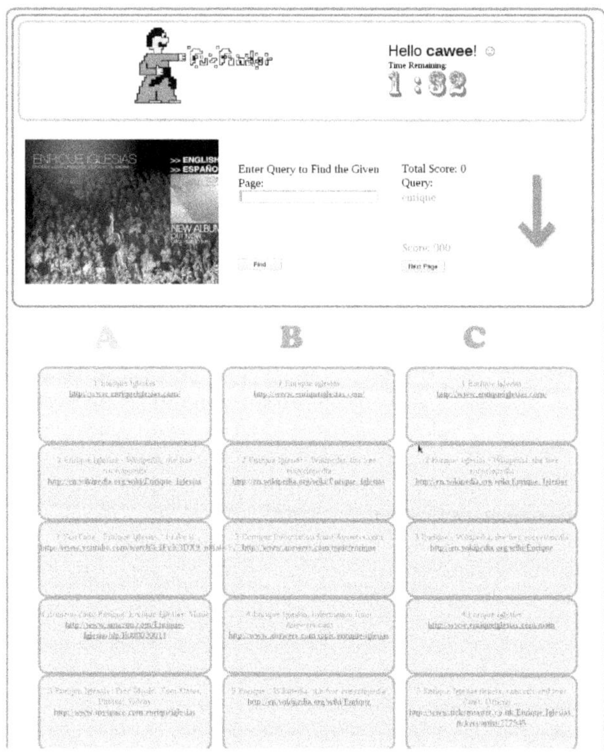

Figure 1: A screenshot of the main game screen, containing: The logo, username and timer (top), the target page (left), the query (middle), the score for the query and actions (right), & the results (below).

3.1 Game Properties

Time Limit The primary purpose of the time limit is to focus the user's attention[3]. The visible time pressure imposed on the gamers was to encourage them to issue queries quickly. This is because we wanted to try and illicit queries that were as realistic as possible, i.e. relatively short, containing spelling mistakes, etc. We believed that this would lead to more reformulations by the user, and help to build up a picture of how queries are modified. If, instead of using a time limit, we asked users to try and find a set number of pages without the pressure of a time limit, then we felt this would have led to less natural and artificially long queries.

Points Allocation To encourage gamers to enter high quality queries a points system was introduced. As previously mentioned, the points system rewarded queries which retrieved the page at higher ranks and across more search engines. Obtaining points for queries provides *positive reinforcement* [5] to gamers, which should encourage them to improve their queries and continue playing. The number of points allocated po for a given attempt a over the set of search engines E is formally defined as:

$$po(a) = \sum_{e \epsilon E} f(a, e) \quad (1)$$

where e is a given engine belonging to the set of nominated search engines E. $f(a, e)$ is a function defining the points allocated for attempt a to engine e, and is defined as: $\frac{c}{r(p,e)}$ when $r(p, e) \leq 5$, else zero. $r(p, e)$ is the rank of a page p for engine e and c is a constant, which we set to 100 i.e. a page returned a rank one, two and three obtained 100, 50 and 33, points respectively. If all engines returned the target page at rank one a bonus multiplier of 3 was applied to the points allocated.

Reward and Status Initiatives The first mechanism adopted within the game is the use of player statuses. These statuses are based on the points obtained and are shown in Table 1. The second mechanism was the inclusion of leaderboards of high scores to introduce a competitive element to the game (i.e. to develop rivalry among gamers) and to encourage gamers to play multiple times and improve their search-fu and status. In terms of behaviour, these rewards constitute as *positive partial reinforcement* [5].

3.2 Initial Evaluation of Fu-Finder Game

A pilot study of the Fu-Finder game was undertaken from the 28th of February until the 4th of April in 2011[4]. The game was advertised locally, and online via Reddit. This resulted in 1026 participants, who played a total of 9075 games and issued 16064 queries in total. We used a subset of the pages used in PageHunt, and the 540 pages used seeded the game[5]. The set of pages used were from a number of different domains, such as health, movies, sports, etc and provided spectrum of retrieval changes (i.e from navigational to informational). The distribution of gamers vs. games was heavily skewed with most players only playing one or two games, while 28 participants played more than 50 games, 7 gamers played more than 100 games and one participant played 301 games. The most avid participant spent a total of 903 minutes using Fu-Finder. The highest score was 12,700 points for which the participant achieved "Search-Fu Grandmaster" status. However, only 304 out of the 1026 participants successfully retrieved at least one page, the unsuccessful participants only played one game. This suggests that either the game was too hard (i.e. presenting too many *hard-to-find* pages discouraging users), the game was not very intuitive, or worse was not particularly entertaining. In future versions, we shall provide a few easy pages first to ease the player into the game and to encourage them to continue playing. In the next section, we shall describe some of the initial findings regarding querying behaviour, the findability of pages, and the search-fu of gamers.

Status	Points Required
Search-Fu Grandmaster	10,000
Web Crawler	7000
Net Navigator	4400
Lycos Retriever	2000
Lynx Net Noob	0

Table 1: Points Required for Status, where the titles were inspired by iconic web browsers.

4. EMPIRICAL FINDINGS

From this initial study we observed that the average length of a query was 3.31 terms in length (which is within the usual range for web queries [1]), and the queries were approximately 20 characters in length on average. Out of the 16064 queries, 8966 queries were unique. This suggests that gamers were generally consistent in formulating similar queries for the same target page. We also observed that 78% of queries contained no URLs within the query, while 14% contained a mixture of keywords and URLs, and 8% of queries contained URLs only. These observations show some of the different tactics employed to precisely identify the target page (i.e. either, keywords, URL + Keywords, or URL only). Since many of the target pages contained visual features such as the URL it is not surprisingly that about a quarter of the queries contained such a feature.

Page and User Percentage Findabiltiy: In [3], they proposed the percentage findability measure for pages. Page %Findability is the percentage of users that found a page within the top n results. This measure provides an indication of how easily users could find a particular page. A similar measure can be defined for users, which provides an indication of how good a particular user is at finding pages (and thus a measure of their search-fu.) User %Findability is the percentage of pages that the user found within the top n results. Given these measures, we calculated the page and user findability and plotted histograms to show the distribution across the measurements obtained in Figure 2. From the top plot, we can see that for Page %Findability the histogram consists of a large spike at 0% Findability, and a skewed, flatten normal distribution peaking at 60-70% Findability for pages. This suggests that while most of the pages in this sample were findable to some degree by users, a substantial number of pages were essentially un-findable. This further suggests that there is a divide among pages, such that a page is either findable or not. For the most findable pages (i.e. 70%+, or found 7 or more out of ten

[3]Note, that the use of a time limit to provide an explicit user goal complies with design guidelines defined by von Ahn and Dabbish [8].

[4]Ethics approval was obtained from College of Science and Engineering (ETHICS-CSE00795).

[5]Many thanks to Raman Chandrasekar for suppling the list of URLs used in [3]. Of the 698 pages used in [3] only 540 still existed and formed the set of pages used in this study.

attempts), these pages tended to be either very distinctive site pages, or pages from well known or respected websites such as `imdb.com` or `medlineplus.com`. While the least findable tended to be pages that were deeper within sites or very obscure site pages.

The bottom plot shows the histogram of User %Findability for all participants that successfully retrieved at least one page (note: 772 participants obtained 0%, and only played one game). From the histogram, we can see that most participants obtained a User %Findability score of between 30-50%, suggesting that they were successful 3-5 times out of every ten queries that they submitted. However, there was a small portion of users with User %Findability above 80%, suggesting that there is perhaps a class of power searchers (with very strong search-fu). But, what is quite clear from the plot is that there large variation across the abilities of users to retrieve pages (and this is despite the fact that users could see the target page).

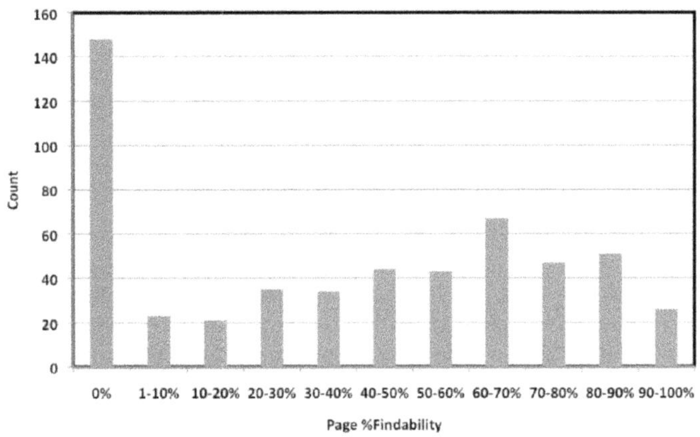

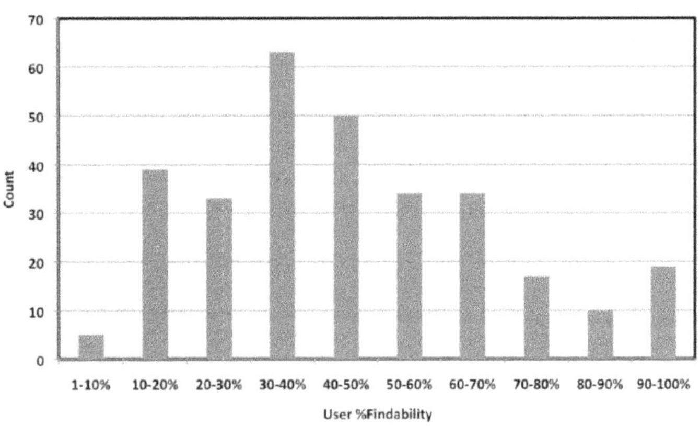

Figure 2: Percentage Findability Histograms: Findability across pages (top), Findability across users (bottom).

5. SUMMARY & FUTURE WORK

We have provided an overview of the Fu-Finder system that aims to study user querying behavior by employing a Human Computation Game to obtain data. The initial results show that users exhibit a wide range of abilities when it comes to searching for known-item pages, and that across pages there is also large amount of variation in terms of findability. In future work, it would be interesting to explore the different relationships between pages, and the difficulty of finding them, in more detail. For example, to consider the depth of the URL/page within a given site, and determine more precisely the relationship between depth and findability. Also, of interest would be to consider how search experience and other user factors affect the user's search-fu, including topicality. Here we would like to extend Fu-Finder to support different slide decks (i.e. use different sets of web pages as the seed for the game). This would support testing across different topical domains to determine whether users find it easier to retrieve pages which they are interested or knowledgeable about. And conversely, whether they find it harder to retrieve pages from new or unknown domains/topics. In particular, and inline with the remit of the PuppyIR project we are especially interested in examining the differences in querying abilities of adults and children. So having different slide decks to represent pages that would be of interest to children and adults (specifically, their parents), would enable further testing in a relatively unexplored area of research. This is where the use of a game, as a scientific methodology, is particularly applicable, because studying querying behavior of children would be quite difficult under standard experimental conditions. Having a game for children to interact with is likely to result in more reliable data from participants. In future work, we will be extending the Fu-Finder game to explore research in this direction.

Acknowledgments This research is supported the PuppyIR project and is funded by the EC's FP7 2007-2013 under grant agreement no. 231507.

6. REFERENCES

[1] A. Arampatzis and J. Kamps. A study of query length. In *Proceedings of the 31st annual international ACM SIGIR conference on Research and development in information retrieval*, pages 811–812, 2008.

[2] Kazai, G., Milic-Frayling, N. and Costello, J. Towards Methods for the Collective Gathering and Quality Control of Relevance Assessments. In *Proceedings of the 32nd International ACM SIGIR Conference on Research and Development in Information Retrieval*, SIGIR'09, pages 452–459, Boston, MA, USA.

[3] Ma, H., Chandrasekar, R. Quirk, C. and Gupta, A. Improving Search Engines Using Human Computation Games. In *Proceedings of 18th ACM International Conference on Information and Knowledge Management*, pages 275–284, Hong Kong, China, 2009.

[4] Ma, H., Chandrasekar, R., Quirk, C. and Gupta, A. PageHunt: Improving Search Engines Using Human Computation Games. In *Proceedings of the 32nd International ACM SIGIR Conference on Research and Development in Information Retrieval*, SIGIR'09, pages 746–747, Boston, MA, USA, July 2009. ACM.

[5] Malim, T. and Birch, A. *Introductory Psychology*, chapter 6: Learning and Behaviour, pages 124–137. Palgrave Macmillan, 1998.

[6] Malone, T.W. Heuristics for Designing Enjoyable User Interfaces: Lessons From Computer Games. In *Proceedings of the 1982 Conference on Human Factors in Computing Science*, CHI'82, pages 63–68, Gaithersburg, Maryland, United States, 1982. ACM.

[7] von Ahn, L. and Dabbish, L. Labelling Images With a Computer Game. In *Proceedings of the SIGCHI Conference on Human Factors in Computing Systems*, CHI'04, pages 319–326, Vienna, Austria, April 2004.

[8] von Ahn, L. and Dabbish, L. Designing Games With a Purpose. *Communications of the ACM*, 51:58–67, 2008.

PDFMeat: Managing Publications on the Semantic Desktop

David Aumüller, Erhard Rahm
University of Leipzig, Leipzig, Germany
{aumueller, rahm}@informatik.uni-leipzig.de

ABSTRACT

Researchers maintain bibliographies and extensive sets of PDF files of scholarly publications on their desktop. The lack of proper metadata of downloaded PDFs makes this task a tedious one. With PDFMeat we present a solution to automatically determine publication metadata for scholarly papers within the user's desktop environment and link the metadata to the files. PDFMeat effectively matches local full texts to an online repository. In an evaluation for more than 2.000 diverse PDF files it worked highly reliable and showed excellent accuracy of up to 98 percent. We demonstrate PDFMeat for different sets of papers, highlighting the semantic integration and use of the retrieved metadata within the file browser of the desktop environment.

Categories and Subject Descriptors

D.2 [**Software Engineering**]: Interoperability

General Terms

Design, Experimentation, Management, Measurement

1. INTRODUCTION

Researchers typically download and collect numerous PDF papers onto their desktop for reading and further reference. These full texts get lost between other files in the depth of the file system, often with similar and meaningless file names – resulting in low accessibility of valuable information. Organizing full text files by renaming and moving them remains tedious. Furthermore, the publication metadata that the researcher probably was presented with on the digital library website is in no way connected or attached to the downloaded file. Hence, this metadata is not available for further usage, e. g. for organizing the files as well as for easing the preparation of reference lists, for instance using BibTEX. With PDFMeat we present a tool to automatically determine the bibliographic metadata for PDFs of research publications. It establishes a link between the files and their metadata providing a tight integration of the metadata into the user's desktop environment, offering management of both files and metadata with little user effort.

The need to collect bibliographic metadata is caused by its absence in PDF files of research papers. Although the PDF specification allows embedding metadata into the header these metadata rarely correspond to the enclosed publication full text. Wikipedia lists many "reference management software" but their focus is mostly on maintaining bibliographies and not the automatic identification of bibliographic metadata from web sources. Some systems provide a limited form of metadata acquisition by a DOI-based metadata lookup. However, for many papers DOIs are either not available, hard to obtain, or cannot be resolved. Several studies focus on heuristic approaches to extract bibliographic attributes directly from PDF files [8, 11, 13], e. g. identifying the document title by font size. Such heuristics are error prone the more the publications vary in style, and cannot acquire information that is not present in the full text, as e. g. often the year and the venue (i. e. journal, or conference) are and remain missing. In [13], the thus extracted title is used to query a local bibliographic database snapshot and simply retrieve the first hit, i. e. no further matching is undertaken.

With PDFMeat we do not rely on such extraction heuristics or the availability of DOIs or need to setup a reference database. Instead, we utilize query-able repositories such as Google Scholar to retrieve and match bibliographic metadata. Our evaluation for computer science publications shows very high effectiveness and we do not know of any other tool offering such reliable metadata acquisition.

Bibliographic metadata obtained for PDF files of research publications empowers users in the following tasks:

- integrated management of both files and metadata
- semantic desktop search with true publication metadata
- ad-hoc availability of metadata for reference work
- provision of publications to community bibliographies

In this paper we provide a description of the PDFMeat approach that was first sketched in [1] as PDF Metadata Acquisition Tool. We present an evaluation of its matching effectiveness. Further, we describe how PDFMeat uses the retrieved metadata within the user's file manager rendering the desktop environment more semantic. That way, PDFMeat offers a light-weight and user-friendly solution to some challenges identified e. g. in personal information management [4, 7] and around the semantic desktop [3, 5].

CIKM'11, October 24–28, 2011, Glasgow, Scotland, UK.

2. MAPPING FULL TEXT TO METADATA

To determine bibliographic metadata for local full text files we exploit the available data and query capabilities of existing online repositories. Available data provided by Google Scholar includes typical publication metadata attributes, represented in HTML as well as in some user-specified structured formats, e. g. BibTEX. Like common web search engines, Google Scholar also provides links to the indexed full texts and allows searching the contents of the full texts. Our metadata acquisition approach utilizes this searchability of the full text, as PDFMeat queries Google Scholar using a kind of generated fingerprint which consists of a set of terms from the full text. The first step in constructing a query string from the full text is to convert the PDF to a plain text. We extract the text (using 'pdftotext') neglecting the layout except for new line characters. We consider the document head as the top part of the first page, up to keywords such as 'Abstract' or 'Introduction', or up to the end of the line containing the author e-mail addresses denoted by the 'at' sign. Failing to find such a landmark we just keep the whole first page as document head, thus not being dependent on heuristics.

We construct the query against the metadata repository out of sentences from the beginning of the full text. In only using whole sentences as base for query generation we avoid erroneous terms that may result e. g. from author name indices or other noise. From the selected sentences we remove stop words commonly ignored by web search engines as well as tokens that contain special characters. Problematic terms may result from the text conversion process due to character encoding or print layout, e. g. hyphenated words and ligatures. As these may be converted differently by Google Scholar's converter including them in the query may lead to non-matches in the metadata repository. We address these issues again in matching potential metadata entries to the full text in question. Further features that we extract in this process for supplying the user with more metadata attributes than offered and retrievable by the remote repository include the abstract, author affiliations by way of author e-mail addresses, and the DOI where available.

Querying search engines usually results in multiple hits. To identify the metadata entry corresponding to the full text in question, a matching of entries to the full text has to take place. Thus, we extract the publication metadata entities from the HTML result page and check which of the returned titles is contained as substring in the document head as defined above. In this step we are dependent on identical transliteration of special characters such as ligatures (ﬄ, ﬃ vs. ffl, ffi). For example, the returned metadata entry may contain the term "efficient" while the full text represents the same word using ligatures ("eﬃcient"). We also transcribe letters containing diacritics such as umlauts to their plain variant glyph having thus experienced better conformity to Google Scholar. Only if the title normalized that way is not contained in the analogously normalized document head we pursue a fuzzy substring matching, using edit distance as described in [14], thus also accepting matches that are a few characters off. For the identified matching metadata entry, PDFMeat then retrieves Google Scholar's BibTEX entry, enriched by the current citation count, which could be later updated using a cron job. Alternatively (or additionally for better quality due to manually curated metadata) we could further retrieve the corresponding entry from DBLP, ACM, or another suitable online repository.

3. ANNOTATION AND CATEGORIZATION

Generally, bibliographic metadata regarding the authors is limited to their names. The full text though usually contains the authors' affiliations, i. e. institution and location, as well as their email addresses. These are valuable annotations, e. g. for the organization of publications by country or institution. To acquire this data we do not try to extract the affiliations directly from the full text as affiliation strings are very heterogeneous and thus difficult to process. Instead, we merely extract the authors' email address hostnames via the 'at'-sign which usually denote their country, institution, and often department. Using our mailhost–institution web service [2] institution names and locations could be mapped.

Similar to the encyclopedic articles in Wikipedia, we also want to categorize publications. Various approaches exist, e. g. [9, 10], to tag content along the Wikipedia category system, e. g. by comparing features such as weighted occurrence frequencies of individual terms against a set-up local search index of Wikipedia articles. For PDFMeat we experiment with ad-hoc web-based approaches of matching papers to Wikipedia, e. g. by issuing a web search restricted on Wikipedia's category URLs. As keywords we extract most denoting terms from title and abstract using TF-IDF or determine compound nouns therein via POS tagging. The web search engine then returns links to Wikipedia category pages that correlate with the content in question. For categories new to our collection we extend our category graph by retrieving their broader category terms from Wikipedia. To not end up in a too large category graph, we prune those categories that are only used few times – the rationale being, that a user's or community's collection of publications usually not consists of totally unrelated works.

4. SEMANTIC DESKTOP INTEGRATION

PDFMeat maintains a local database for the retrieved metadata and establish the connection between metadata and file using an unique identifier for the local file. One candidate key is a hash/fingerprint value calculated of the file content. As this can be costly for large media files, some approaches only consider parts of the file. For our tool we use the 'inode' value of the local file as identifier, which is a numeric value distinct to each file of a device. The metadata for a file in question is thereafter located by its inode number in the metadata store. (We additionally store a hash value for globally identifying the PDF in a potential online PDFMeat store; as further alternative we consider the use of the 'xattr' extended file attributes for storing the retrieved metadata attribute values.) Also, PDFMeat offers the possibility to embed the metadata into the PDF file header, but this should not serve as first solution as users may be reluctant to allow file alterations. Both simple and extended PDF metadata specifications for embedding are supported, of which the XMP format can e. g. be imported by the popular JabRef bibliography manager. Such managers also allow to open PDF files linked in BibTEX databases, as produced by PDFMeat. As PDF files may be renamed and/or moved on the file system their links in the BibTEX file would be broken. Thus we implemented a syncing function to update the local file path as linked in BibTEX databases. To re-sync we need to crawl the file system or a user specified folder for PDFs and check whether the publication is known and still correctly referenced in the local metadata store and in the user specified BibTEX file.

To identify the according entry in a BibTEX file we maintain a special 'pdfmeat' attribute containing the inode number, restricting the approach only to entries that once were established by PDFMeat; for other cases the metadata has to be acquired to then try to find an according entry by way of title, author, and year attributes; failing that we store the new entry.

For increased usability of our metadata acquisition approach we provide a tight integration into the user's desktop environment. Dealing primarily with local publication full text files the most direct integration of PDFMeat is into the user's file manager. File managers provide a navigational view on the file system, typically with a tree representation of the directory structure or a list of bookmarks to directories in a sidebar on the left, and a list of files within the currently selected directory in the main window. In the tabular, column based view of this file list each list entry represents one file showing typical file attributes such as name, size, mime type, timestamps, etc. Our desktop integration implementation is exemplified using Nautilus, the default file browser in GNOME, which in turn is the default desktop environment of many Linux operating system distributions. (For non-Linux users we provide a web service to be able to use at least the metadata acquisition functionality, either by manually uploading a set of local PDF files or using a 'thin client' application that extracts and uploads the plain text from the first page(s) of the PDF to acquire the corresponding BibTEX metadata entry.) PDFMeat integrates the following functionality within the file manager:

- retrieve metadata for files via the context menu
- display metadata in additional sortable columns
- manage metadata within a property page tab
- re-organize full text files via metadata attributes

Figure 1 depicts the file manager listing a set of PDF files that are already handled and known by PDFMeat, i. e. BibTEX entries are downloaded, stored, and linked to the files, of which selected attributes (here: author list, title, venue, year, and rating/citations) are chosen by the user to be presented as extra columns in this view. Right-clicking on a PDF file shows the context menu which PDFMeat extends by a sub-menu to trigger the metadata acquisition process and other actions. For successful acquisitions, the metadata values instantaneously fill the according column values. A desktop notification informs unobtrusively about the result of the action. Further, PDFMeat extends the file property dialog, available via 'Properties', by an extra tab/page, showing the retrieved BibTEX entry, which can be edited by the user, i. e. it could also be supplied, curated, and extended manually.

Although PDFMeat currently uses an external database as metadata store, the linkage between full text files and metadata entries survives moving and renaming files – independently of the file manager and its integration. Also, a file re-organization function allows to automatically rename and move publication files according to user defined patterns, e. g. to move files into folders determined by some metadata attributes. Further semantic desktop integration and functionality provided by PDFMeat includes a desktop search plugin, allowing to search for publications on the desktop by their real metadata, as well as a standalone faceted search browser to have an overview of all one's publications on the desktop, but also for listing PDFs without yet retrieved metadata. A similar web application could also serve as community portal to a shared bibliography. Additionally, PDFMeat offers automatic addition of new publications by watching folder(s) for incoming PDF files that will be processed as soon as they are downloaded. That way, users do not need to trigger the metadata acquisition manually, incoming files can be re-organized instantaneously, and the entry appended to the BibTEX bibliography.

5. ENTITY MATCHING EVALUATION

As the general metadata attributes such as title, author(s), venue, and year are most important, also for further data integration tasks, we explicitly look at this matching process in more detail. For evaluating the quality of the mapping between local full text files and retrieved metadata entities we use a set of metadata entries and their linked full text files from the ACM digital library. Our test set resembles a random set of publications from out of ten years of four different venues, both conference proceedings and journal articles: VLDB, VLDBJ, SIGMOD, and PODS. Some of these PDF files did not convert to plain text – reasons can be that the text is represented as image only, enabled read restrictions, or unknown document encoding issues (the Linux 'file' command considered some of the pdftotext results as data instead of text). In our test set of 2.095 documents, the converted text of 89 files (4.2%) was unreadable for both human and machine, which we hence ignore in our further evaluation. Also, we focus on the accuracy, i. e. the share of input publications for which we could correctly determine the bibliographic metadata. To determine this measure, we need to take into account that publication titles may slightly vary between full text and bibliographic databases, e. g. one source may use colons where the other uses dashes to separate e. g. a prototype name from the rest of the title. Corresponding entities may vary in more than typos or different punctuation, though, as sometimes authors decided to use a slightly changed title to the one entered into the submission system when preparing the final print version. Thus, in judging true positives via the title attribute we allowed minor differences by computing the levenshtein edit distance for comparisons. To avoid a discussion of suitable similarity thresholds we manually labeled the share of correspondences having a similarity ratio below 1. The three evaluations in Figure 2a) give different values for accuracy, determining true positives via the title attribute only, both title and year attribute, as well as title attribute but year only if returned from the metadata repository. Overall, the evaluation shows good results with all values above 94%. The best accuracy of about 98% is of course achieved by only comparing the title. For establishing the data–metadata mapping we issued up to three queries per document. The majority of publications were identified using a single query only, as seen in Figure 2b), log. scale.

Our test set offers a high visibility of the documents on the web as Google was able to index their full texts. This accessibility of documents is not restricted to computer science literature or the selected test set. Nevertheless, successful results may vary for other sets of publications, depending on the coverage of documents in Google Scholar. Recent studies [6, 12] consider its coverage quite high for a large variety of domains and found improvements of the index over time. Nevertheless, PDFMeat could also use different bibliographic repositories. Querying a service without full text

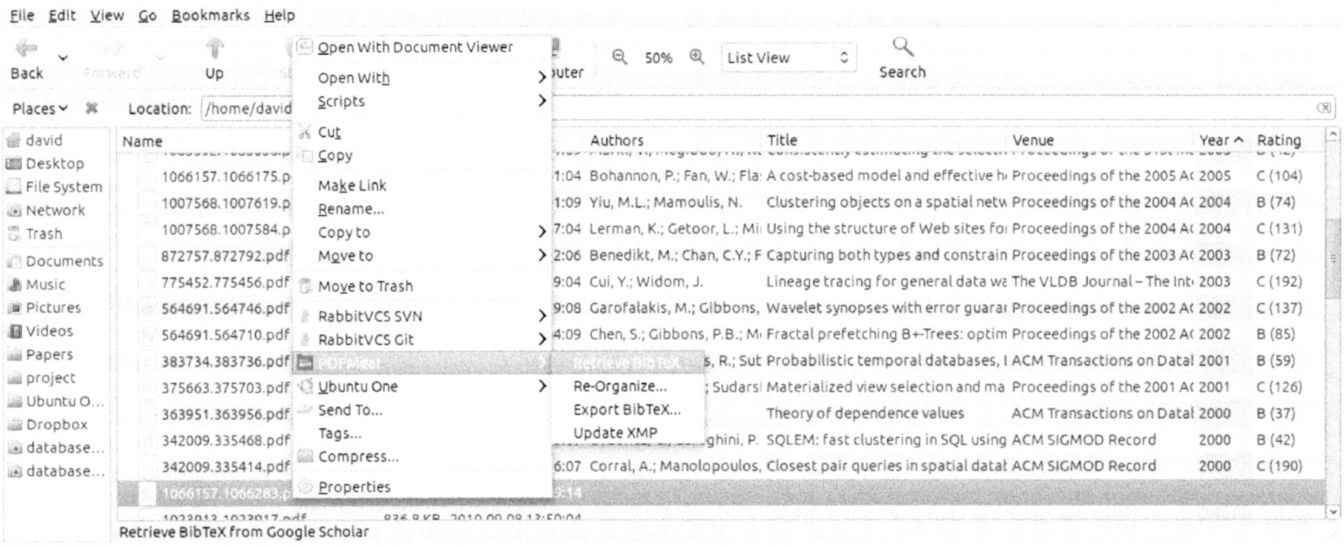

Figure 1: PDFMeat context menu and retrieved publication metadata values in provided file manager columns

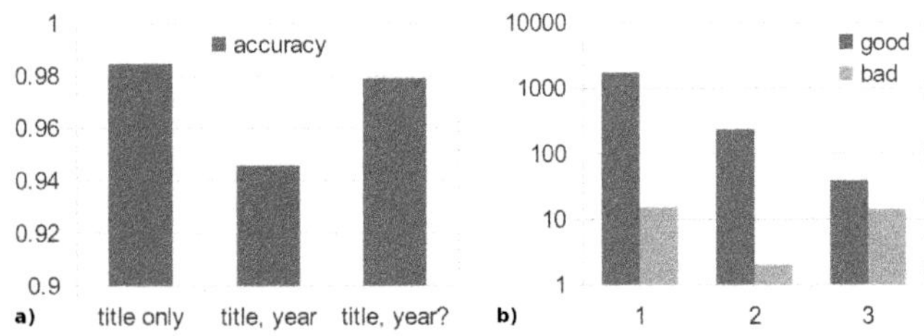

Figure 2: a) Retrieved metadata matching real data b) Queries needed to find correspondences (max. 3)

search, though, would require to know at least the most basic metadata, such as title and authors, calling for common extraction heuristics known to be errorprone.

6. DEMONSTRATION AND CONCLUSION

On-site attendees will be offered to try PDFMeat with files of their own choice. Selecting the PDFs in the file manager the user can trigger and inspect the metadata acquisition process (see the intermediate results such as text extraction, query generation, query results, entity matching, BibTEX retrieval) as well as affiliation and categorization annotation. Users may edit the metadata in the file property tab, rename and move the files manually or automatically in accordance to their metadata without losing the linked metadata. PDF files may be dropped into the watched folder for instant automatic results, e. g. having the downloaded paper at once available for citing in one's reference manager.

With PDFMeat we demonstrate a metadata acquisition tool for publications represented as PDF files. The tool incurs low to no effort for acquiring and managing metadata to one's local scholarly PDFs, and offers instant gratification by making the metadata available not only within the file explorer, but also as bibliographic database, and further tools, e. g. desktop search. PDFMeat does not intend to replace available reference management software but aims at providing a useful addition in acquiring metadata to files once downloaded and residing on the desktop that would be hardly accessible due to missing annotations. The overall approach of retrieving and semantically integrating metadata on the desktop is generic and applicable to other domains, e. g. to present title, year, rating, country, etc. to movie files.

7. REFERENCES

[1] D. Aumüller. Retrieving metadata for your local scholarly papers. In *German DB Conf. (BTW)*, 2009.

[2] D. Aumüller and E. Rahm. Web-based Affiliation Matching. In *ICIQ*, 2009.

[3] I. Cruz and H. Xiao. A layered framework supporting personal information integration and application design for the semantic desktop. *VLDB Journal*, 17(6), 2008.

[4] J.-P. Dittrich and M. A. V. Salles. iDM: a unified and versatile data model for personal dataspace management. VLDB, 2006.

[5] C. Duda, D. Kossmann, and C. Zhou. Predicate-based indexing for desktop search. *VLDB Journal*, 2010.

[6] M. Falagas et al. Comparison of pubmed, scopus, web of science, and google scholar: strengths and weaknesses. *The FASEB Journal*, 22(2):338, 2008.

[7] A. Halevy, A. Rajaraman, and J. Ordille. Data integration: the teenage years. VLDB, 2006.

[8] H. Han et al. Automatic document metadata extraction using support vector machines. In *JCDL*, 2003.

[9] J. Hu et al. Enhancing text clustering by leveraging wikipedia semantics. In *SIGIR*. ACM, 2008.

[10] X. Hu et al. Exploiting wikipedia as external knowledge for document clustering. In *SIGKDD*. ACM, 2009.

[11] T. Huynh and K. Hoang. GATE framework based meta data extraction from scientific papers. In *ICEMT*, 2010.

[12] J. Meier and T. Conkling. Google scholar's coverage of the engineering literature: an empirical study. *The Journal of Academic Librarianship*, 2008.

[13] E. Minack et al. Leveraging personal metadata for Desktop search: The Beagle++ system. *Web Semantics: Science, Services and Agents on the WWW*, 8(1), 2010.

[14] G. Navarro. A guided tour to approximate string matching. *CSUR*, 33(1):31–88, 2001.

MEMSCALE: In-Cluster-Memory Databases

Héctor Montaner
Univ. Politècnica de València
Camí de Vera, s/n 46022
València, Spain
hmontaner@gap.upv.es

Federico Silla
Univ. Politècnica de València
Camí de Vera, s/n 46022
València, Spain
fsilla@disca.upv.es

Holger Fröning
University of Heidelberg
B6, 26, Building B (3rd floor)
68131 Mannheim, Germany
froening@uni-hd.de

José Duato
Univ. Politècnica de València
Camí de Vera, s/n 46022
València, Spain
jduato@disca.upv.es

ABSTRACT

We have developed a new memory architecture for clusters that allows automatic access from any processor to any memory module in the cluster completely by hardware. Thus, with a single assembly instruction a processor can retrieve (or update) a memory location in a remote node. The efficiency of this new paradigm makes it possible to speed-up the execution of shared-memory applications with very large memory footprints by running them across the entire cluster, thus providing them a true shared-memory environment (contrary to the emulation typically carried out by software-based distributed shared memory).

This new memory architecture, referred to as MEMSCALE, opens up a new frontier for memory-hungry applications. In this paper we focus on in-memory databases and show how this target application can be boosted by our memory architecture, which can virtually provide unlimited memory resources to it.

In the demo presented in this paper we show the advantages of our architecture by means of a prototype cluster. We configure two cluster sizes, 16 and 32 nodes, to analyze throughput scalability and latency worsening, to extrapolate these metrics to bigger clusters, and to show the benefits of our technology compared to other alternatives like SSD-based databases. Moreover, we also show the easiness of use of our architecture by explaining how we ported MySQL Server to our prototype cluster. Finally, the possibility of executing queries in any processor of the cluster during the live demo will show the audience how our system aggregates the advantages of the scale out and scale up approaches for database server growing.

CIKM'11, October 24–28, 2011, Glasgow, Scotland, UK.

Categories and Subject Descriptors

H.3 [**Information Systems**]: Information Storage and Retrieval

General Terms

Measurement, Performance

1. INTRODUCTION

Database software has traditionally relied on secondary storages, pushing into the background the role played by main memory. This was mainly due to the size of databases, usually much larger than the amount of RAM memory available in the computer. However, as the amount of main memory in commodity computers has been continuously increasing to considerable quantities, the caching technique has gained popularity. For example, Memcached[7] is a system for caching objects into main memory aimed to scenarios where a minor percentage of data is targeted by a major percentage of queries.

Although Memcached has substantially improved performance in many case studies, this is just a conservative extension of the old-fashion secondary storage databases. What brings a quantum leap to databases is *in-memory* databases. These databases store data natively in main memory and benefit from its random access characteristic. Thus, contrary to caching systems that only allow access to a cached object in a key/value fashion, an in-memory database allows the execution of SQL queries directly against tables stored in main memory. This new paradigm has many advantages, for example the use of hash tables instead of *b-tree* structures. This shift in data storage noticeably improves the performance of queries that present a random data access pattern.

Placing the database data in main memory is not the only factor that improves performance of in-memory databases: *concurrency* also matters. In this regard, with previous secondary storage, concurrency was highly constricted by hard disks as they acted as bottlenecks and one single query flow could easily saturate the disk throughput. But when talking about RAM memories two characteristics lead us to expect higher performance: on one hand, regular multicore commodity computers are designed so that all the cores can access memory in parallel without reaching saturation and, on the other hand, as main memory is accessed via hardware, there is no potential bottleneck in software handlers. In this way, in-memory databases should be a synonym for concurrency. Therefore, the current trend towards increasing the number of cores per processor does nothing but emphasize the need for in-memory databases to the detriment of classic secondary storages.

However, despite the growing popularity of these in-memory databases (Oracle TimesTen[3], IBM SolidDB[5], etc.), the limited amount of memory in a single node is clearly the main constraining factor for their widespread applicability: although nowadays we can find commodity computers with 512GB of main memory, it is not enough to host many mid-size databases, or not even their indexes. In order to efficiently increase the amount of memory available to a given application, we have devised a new non-coherent distributed shared-memory architecture for clusters referred to as MEMSCALE[1].

In this paper we present the use of this new memory architecture for in-memory databases. Our proposal attacks this scenario by reducing latency and increasing throughput, in terms of queries per second, to achieve a highly scalable database system. The rest of the paper is organized as follows: in next section our memory architecture is briefly described. In Section 3 we introduce the most popular related work and some performance comparisons are outlined. Finally, in Section 4 we describe the live demo to be presented.

2. THE MEMSCALE ARCHITECTURE

According to the TOP500 list, 82% of the most powerful computers in the world are cataloged as clusters. The reason for this is twofold: the good scalability that this distributed architecture presents and the high ratio performance per dollar of commodity computers. Therefore, it seems reasonable to base MEMSCALE on a cluster of computers. The objective of our proposal is to convert the entire cluster into a single database server that is the result of aggregating all the processors and main memory in the cluster in order to reach previously unseen performance.

Figure 1 summarizes the MEMSCALE architecture. It can be seen that a memory pool is created out of the individual memories of each node in order to configure a shared memory region in the cluster accessible by any processor. Tables and indexes of the database will be loaded into this memory pool. Notice that tables may become partitioned across several nodes as each node will host a portion of registers in its main memory. However, the resulting effective structure is not a partitioned database because all the nodes in the cluster see a continuous memory address space that they can access independently of which node is hosting the requested memory location. Therefore, spatial allocation of data is not relevant in practice to processors as they see a global memory pool working as a big shared-memory mainframe with lots of memory.

The key factor in our system is the remote memory direct access feature. To achieve this, we have leveraged Hypertransport[6]. Hypertransport is the technology used to interconnect the AMD Opteron processors present in a single motherboard. Our implementation extends this interconnection to allow direct communication among motherboards. To do so, we have developed a new hardware component that we will refer to as *Remote Memory Controller* (RMC) and that is implemented in the card shown in Figure 2, which uses the HTX connector to connect to the motherboard. This connector allows the processors in a motherboard to directly interact with our card as if it was a regular memory controller. Additionally, these cards, installed at every node, are also equipped with a network interface in order to be interconnected by using a 3D mesh topology.

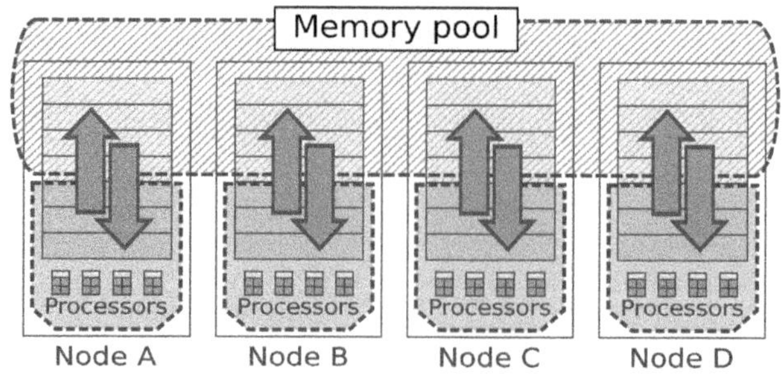

Figure 1: Shared-memory architecture using MEMSCALE

Figure 2: HTX card with an FPGA that implements the RMC functionality

By leveraging our proposal, processors can send a common read request (as a result of a *load* assembly instruction) to the RMC as if it was aimed to a regular memory module. However, in this case, the RMC has no memory modules directly attached to it but it must forward the read request to the appropriate remote node in the cluster. The RMC identifies the destination node by inspecting the most significant bits of the physical address targeted by the read request. These most significant bits were set during the memory reservation phase in order to reflect the identifier of the node were the memory allocation took place and, therefore, to allow easy subsequent accesses to that remote memory.

When the read request arrives to the remote node, the RMC in that node forwards the request to the corresponding local memory module, which replies to the RMC and then the data is sent all the way back to the processor that originated the memory operation. This is a simple mechanism that allows remote access with very low latency.

Additionally, in order to scale this shared-memory architecture to virtually any system size, the new hardware does not provide coherency across nodes in the cluster. On the opposite, coherency is kept, when required, by the system software.

MEMSCALE allows database servers to scale out, that is, their capacity and performance can be progressively increased by adding new nodes to the cluster. Notice that scaling out regular database servers is usually accomplished by replicating an original server in order to distribute queries over a set of identical slaves and, therefore, allowing better throughput and lower latency as load per server is reduced. However, MEMSCALE follows a different approach, as adding new nodes to a MEMSCALE cluster does not mean replicating the database, but providing more cores to access the shared-memory pool, thus increasing concurrency and therefore reducing average query latency. Actually, this mechanism could be seen as a way of scaling up the database server.

2.1 Database Porting

As our cluster architecture is presented to applications as a true shared-memory environment, they can be natively executed in it. Therefore, any database server with a main-memory storage engine can benefit from MEMSCALE. We chose MySQL as it is the most used open-source database server in the world and also because it offers a main-memory storage engine (known as *heap* or *memory*) that is very useful for us: we only have to extend this storage engine to use the global memory pool instead of using local main memory. To do so, the only thing we had to do was to slightly modify the dynamic memory allocation (instead of using a common *malloc* we used a library function with identical interface that allocates memory in the global memory pool). After that, as structures containing data and other synchronization information are on the memory pool, they are accessible by any processor in any node. As can be seen, porting a shared-memory application to MEMSCALE is straightforward.

3. RELATED WORK

In order to improve database server performance, it is becoming increasingly popular the use of Solid State Drives (SSD) to substitute the slow HDD as they offer more than one order of magnitude better results, as there are no mechanical parts to be moved. However, there is still the need for a software handler and, therefore, the related penalty is undergone. We can find two subclasses of this technology, SSD disks just used as an HDD and SSD memories directly attached to PCIe. Just to briefly compare against our proposal, according to our experiments with Kingston SSDs and a FusionIO PCIe card, SSD disks are one order of magnitude slower than MEMSCALE, while PCIe-based SSDs are only slightly slower than MEMSCALE (note that MEMSCALE is implemented in an FPGA prototype and its performance is far from the maximum one).

Moreover, it is not only about latency but also about throughput: as MEMSCALE is able to execute queries in an entire cluster, to achieve a similar productivity a cluster should be equipped with a PCIe SSD card at each node, increasing its acquisition cost to a prohibitive level.

Other solutions intended to aggregate computing resources in a cluster are MySQL Cluster[2] and ScaleMP[4]. MySQL Cluster allocates data in main memory, as we do with MEMSCALE, but the way it is accessed (through a software socket) prevents good performance. According to our tests, a 16-node cluster with MySQL Cluster achieves a throughput two orders of magnitude lower than MEMSCALE. On the other hand, ScaleMP is a software that aggregates multiple nodes in a cluster to conform a single system image virtual machine. However, as it is software based, it presents a remote memory latency of 25us, while MEMSCALE presents a remote memory latency of 1.8us. Moreover, as we have experienced, ScaleMP quickly saturates in the presence of multiple threads reading the in-memory databases due to software bottlenecks, preventing this solution from achieving as good throughput as MEMSCALE.

4. DEMO DESCRIPTION

We have implemented our system proposal in a prototype cluster to show the feasibility of our idea and also to show some preliminary performance metrics. As it is a prototype implementation (mainly due to the fact that the RMC functionality in the HTX card is based on slow FPGA technology) we should be aware that the results will be below the potential ones if ASIC technology was used. However, as we will see in the demo, despite of the prototype status of MEMSCALE, it is currently achieving quite good results compared to other related solutions.

The central idea of the demo is to show the cluster at work by running a MySQL server on it. We have designed a simple database, depicted in Figure 3, that mimics the structure of a social network. The overall size of the database, including indexes, is 100GB.

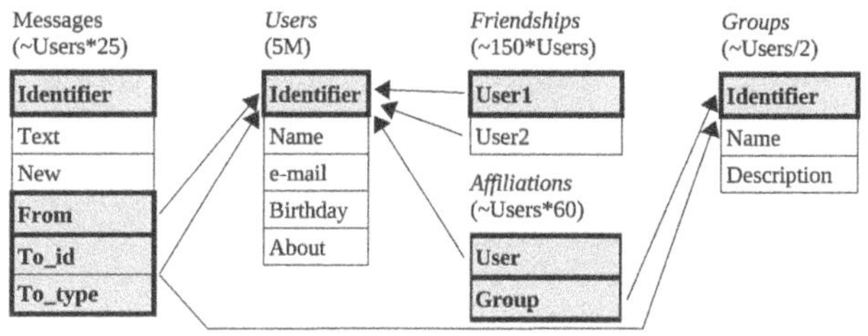

Figure 3: Table structure (gray background indicates an indexed field)

The demo allows to access the cluster in a remote way through a web interface, shown in Figure 4. Basically, we can launch a given quantity of queries against our prototype cluster. Although it is possible to execute any kind of SQL query, we have predefined six illustrative queries very typical of social networks that will emphasize the advantages of our system. In this way, we focus on sub-second queries even with this database size. Notice that these queries will walk through the tables exclusively by using indexed fields. Moreover, although the queries are rather simple, they present a by-nature erratic access pattern. This prevents the exploitation of data locality, especially in cluster contexts. For example, the query *"Get the names of the friends for a given user"* will perform a number of random accesses to the *users* table as the data on that table cannot be grouped in a way that satisfies locality for any given user. Therefore, when that table is distributed across different nodes in the cluster, the query will require data from all of them independently of the effort towards grouping friends together. On the live demonstration we execute thousands of this set of queries to get average query latency and cluster throughput in terms of queries per second.

Regarding the graphical appearance of the demo, during the execution of a given experiment we will receive feedback in real-time from our prototype cluster. The results of the

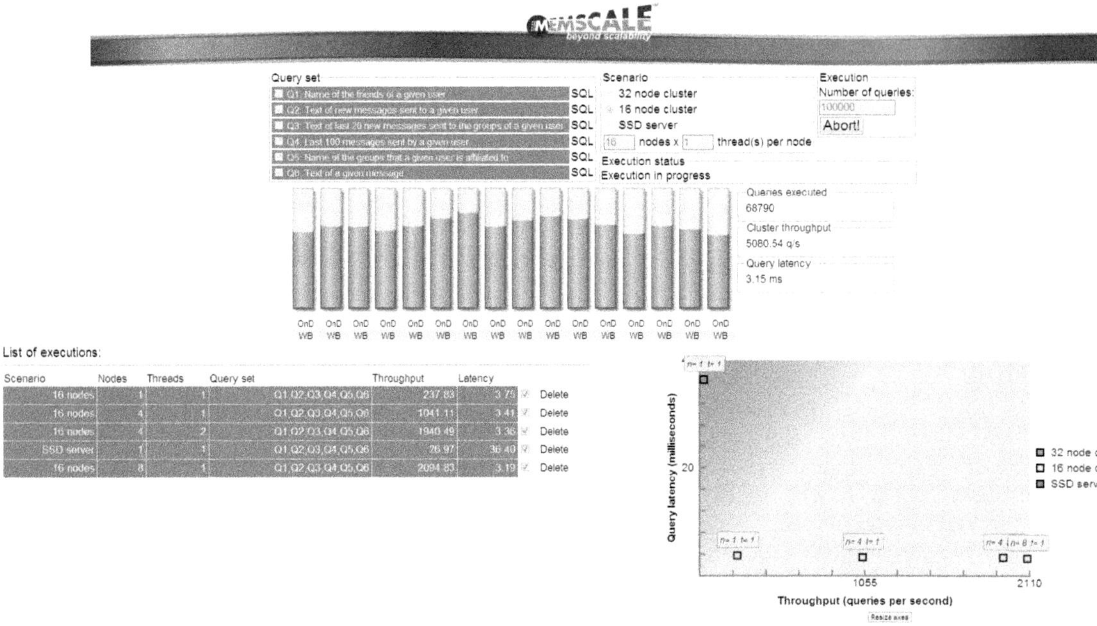

Figure 4: Screen shot of the demo's web page

different tests will be displayed in a 2D graph for comparing purposes. Additionally, the history of queries is displayed on the bottom left in order to easily compare them on the 2D graph on the right. In the central part of the window, the progress is displayed for all the nodes taking part in the execution of the current query.

The demo allows the user to execute queries in three different scenarios: a 16-node cluster, a 32-node cluster, and an SSD server. The first two scenarios will show our technology at work and will serve to show its scalability. We will see how query latency varies when the cluster size varies (together with throughput) because the number of nodes increases, and given a fixed link radix per node, the average distance in the network increases too and, consequently, query latency will also be affected. On the other hand, throughput linearly increases with cluster size, as more processors are available for executing queries (and more memory controllers are available for increasing global memory bandwidth). Our third scenario is an SSD-based server (two Kingston SNV425-S2 64GB drives configured in RAID 0 for improved performance, each of them with a sequential speed of 200MB/s at reading and 110MB/s at writing) that will serve to compare latency and throughput metrics. For the case of the SSD server, we will obviously not use the main-memory storage engine, but the MyISAM storage engine that allows good performance at reading.

For all the scenarios, the user can increase the number of query flows in terms of cores executing queries. It is expected linear improvement, in queries per second, as the number of queries served in parallel increases. However, during the demo we will see how the SSD-based server saturates well before every core in the motherboard is being used. On the contrary, MEMSCALE will show better scalability as the design of a motherboard ensures perfect matching between cores and main memory capabilities. Moreover, this kind of test will show how much inter-node traffic affects global throughput and latency.

Additionally we are able to reduce processor frequency and see how cluster performance is almost not impacted. According to our studies, we will see how processor frequency is not critical in terms of query latency or database throughput. However, a reduction in CPU frequency (2GHz to 1GHz) can save up to 18% of energy and up to 20% of power across the entire cluster.

Finally, in the following URL: *http://www.memscale.eu/CIKM_demo* it can be found a video that contains a demo preview showing the different steps on the demonstration and some of the multiple tests that can be carried out.

Acknowledgments

This work has been supported by PROMETEO from Generalitat Valenciana (GVA) under Grant PROMETEO/2008/060.

5. REFERENCES

[1] MEMSCALE: New Possibilities for Shared Memory in Clusters . `http://www.hpcadvisorycouncil.com/events/2011/european_workshop/pdf/14_U_Valencia.pdf`.

[2] MySQL Cluster. `http://www.mysql.com/products/cluster`.

[3] Oracle TimesTen In-Memory Database. `http://www.oracle.com/us/products/database/timesten`.

[4] ScaleMP. `http://www.scalemp.com`.

[5] SolidDB: In-Memory, relational database software for extreme speed. `http://www.ibm.com/software/data/soliddb`.

[6] HyperTransport Technology Consortium. HyperTransport I/O Link Specification Revision 3.10, 2008. available at `http://www.hypertransport.org`.

[7] B. Fitzpatrick. Linux Journal: Distributed Caching with Memcached. 124:72–76, 2004.

H-DB: A Hybrid Quantitative-Structural SQL Optimizer

Lucantonio Ghionna
Dept. of Mathematics
University of Calabria
I-87036, Rende(CS), Italy
l.ghionna@mat.unical.it

Gianluigi Greco
Dept. of Mathematics
University of Calabria
I-87036, Rende(CS), Italy
ggreco@mat.unical.it

Francesco Scarcello
D.E.I.S.
University of Calabria
I-87036, Rende(CS), Italy
scarcello@deis.unical.it

ABSTRACT

Structural decomposition methods are query optimization methods specifically conceived in the database theory community to efficiently answer (near-)acyclic queries. We propose to demonstrate H-DB, an SQL query optimizer that combines classical quantitative optimization techniques with such structural decomposition methods, which so far have been just analyzed from the theoretical viewpoint. The system provides support to optimizing SQL queries with arbitrary output variables, aggregate operators, ORDER BY statements, and nested queries. H-DB can be put on top of any existing database management system supporting JDBC technology, by transparently interacting/replacing its standard query optimization module. However, to push at maximum its optimization capabilities, H-DB should be coupled with an ad-hoc physical semi-join operator, which (as a relevant example) we implemented and integrated within the PostgreSQL database management system.

Categories and Subject Descriptors

H.2.4 [**Database Management**]: Systems—*Query processing; Relational databases*; F.2.2 [**Analysis of Algorithms and Problem Complexity**]: Nonnumerical Algorithms and Problems—*Computations on discrete structures*

General Terms

Algorithms, Design, Performance

Keywords

Query Optimization, Structural Decomposition Methods

1. INTRODUCTION

Optimization strategies for query evaluation are usually based on restricting the search space of query plans to very simple structures (e.g., left-deep trees) and on choosing the most promising one by exploiting quantitative information collected on the data (e.g., sizes of relations and indices, and attribute selectivity). While being generally very efficient, these *quantitative* optimizers cannot guarantee a bound on the query-answering time. In some cases, the computed query plan is quite far from the ideal one, and query answering does not scale to instances with many join operations.

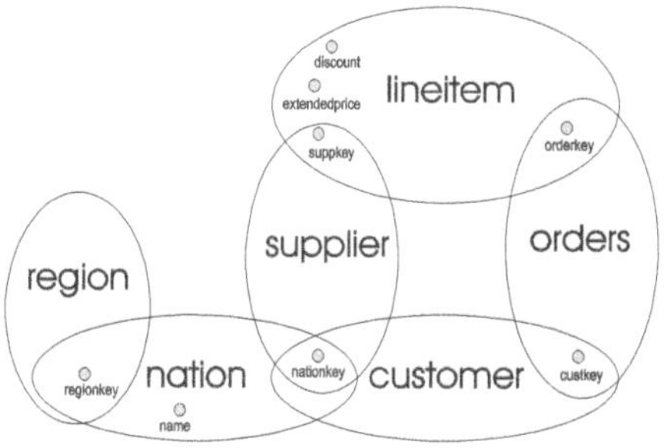

Figure 1: ***Hypergraph*** $\mathcal{H}(Q_5)$.

In order to face this problem and compute the optimal query plan that guarantees a polynomial bound on the answering time, a dual optimization approach has been investigated since many years in the database theory community, which is based on the exploitation of the *structural* properties of the queries, usually represented through their associated hypergraphs—as an example, Figure 1 shows the hypergraph associated with the following query Q_5, extracted from the TPC-H specifications (*www*.tpc.org/tpch):

```
SELECT n_name,
       sum(l_extendedprice*(1-l_discount)) AS revenue
FROM customer, orders, lineitem,
     supplier, nation, region
WHERE c_custkey = o_custkey
      and l_orderkey = o_orderkey
      and l_suppkey = s_suppkey
      and c_nationkey = s_nationkey
      and s_nationkey = n_nationkey
      and n_regionkey = r_regionkey
      and r_name = '[REGION]'
      and o_orderdate >= date '[DATE]'
      and o_orderdate < date '[DATE]' + interval '1' year
GROUP BY n_name ORDER BY revenue desc;
```

The idea of exploiting the structure of the query originated in the eighties, when Yannakakis [9] observed that answers to acyclic queries can be efficiently computed, in particular, in a way that no exponential blow-up occurs w.r.t. the number of involved join operations. Structures arising from real applications, however, are hardly precisely acyclic. Yet, they are often not very intricate and, in fact, tend to exhibit some limited degree of cyclicity, which suffices to retain most of the nice properties of acyclic ones. Thus, several efforts have

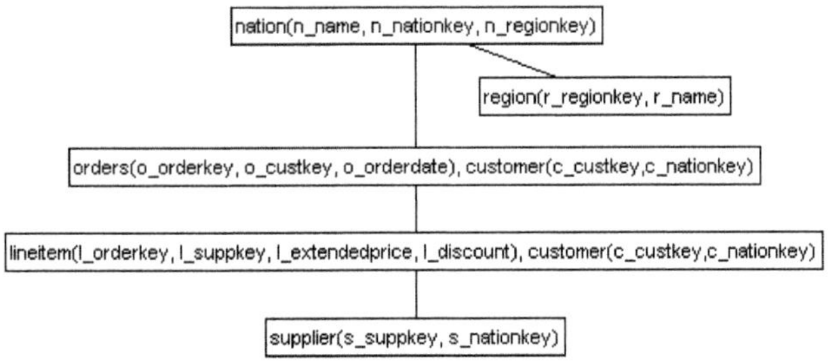

Figure 2: ***A hypertree decomposition of*** $\mathcal{H}(Q_5)$.

been subsequently spent to investigate invariants that are best suited to identify nearly-acyclic hypergraphs, leading to the definition of a number of so-called *structural decomposition methods* (such as the *(generalized) hypertree* [3], the *fractional hypertree* [5], and the *component hypertree* [4] decompositions). These methods aim at transforming a given cyclic hypergraph into an acyclic one, by organizing its edges (or its nodes) into a polynomial number of clusters, and by suitably arranging these clusters as a tree, called decomposition tree. The original problem instance can then be evaluated over the decomposition tree, with a cost that is exponential in the cardinality of the largest cluster, also called *width* of the decomposition, and polynomial if this width is bounded by some constant.

As an example, consider the (2-width) hypertree decomposition of $\mathcal{H}(Q_5)$ depicted in Figure 2, and assume that the goal is just to check whether Q_5 admits a solution (i.e., we get rid of output variables and aggregate operators). Then, this Boolean query can be answered over the decomposition tree using a two-step plan. First, for each cluster (vertex of the decomposition tree), one computes the join of the relations involved in it. Second, starting from the leaves, one moves bottom-up towards the root, by performing upward semi-joins of intermediate results.

Despite their very nice computational properties, structural decomposition methods have not had any serious impact on the design of commercial database optimizers, and the interest for these techniques mainly remained at a theoretical level. This is mainly because decomposition methods flatten in the query hypergraph all the quantitative aspects of data, do not take care of the output of the variables, and do not support aggregate operators and nested queries.

In this paper, we propose to demonstrate H-DB, an SQL query optimizer that combines classical quantitative optimization techniques with structural decomposition methods. The system implements the techniques discussed in [1, 7], and provides support to optimizing SQL queries with arbitrary output variables, aggregate operators, ORDER BY statements, and nested queries. H-DB can be put on top of any existing database management system supporting JDBC technology, by transparently interacting/replacing its standard query optimization module. However, to push at maximum its optimization capabilities, H-DB should be coupled with an ad-hoc physical semi-join operator, which (as a relevant example) we implemented and integrated within the PostgreSQL database management system.

In addition to its optimization capabilities, H-DB comes equipped with useful auxiliary modules, in particular, with graphical environments to compose and analyze user queries, and to compare internal query plans with the structure-aware query plans.

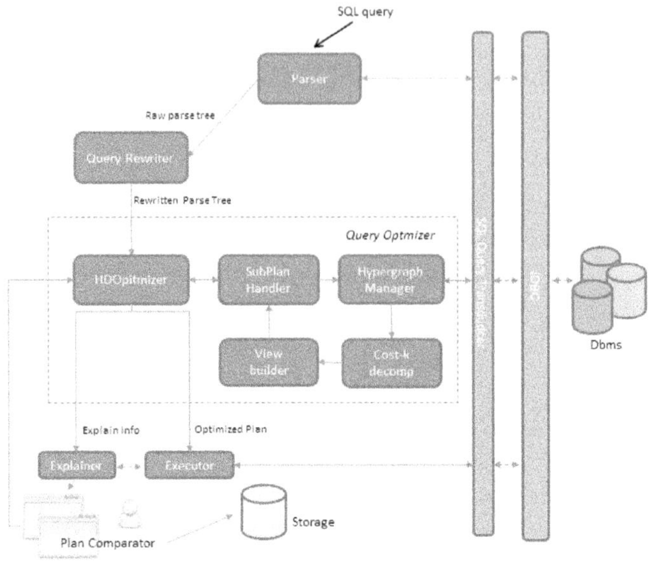

Figure 3: H-DB Optimizer Architecture.

2. SYSTEM ARCHITECTURE

H-DB has been conceived to provide a transparent "structure aware" query optimization support, by working on top of any existing database management system (DBMS) via standard JDBC technology. When H-DB is executed, it preliminary looks for locally installed DBMS and lists them in a navigation menu. User picks one specific database system from the list, establish a connection with it, and submits SQL queries (possibly, via a graphical interface, with which H-DB comes equipped[1]). Each query is eventually processed by the system according to the functional architecture illustrated in Figure 3 and discussed next.

Given an SQL query, the **Parser** preliminary verifies its correctness. To this aim, we exploit the syntactical analyzer J-SQLParser[2] that has been further enhanced to check whether the query complies with the underlying database schema. The resulting parse tree is then processed by the **Query Rewriter**, which prepares all data structures needed for structural analysis and optimization. In particular, the module modifies the parse tree by associating each nested SQL statement with a distinguished node storing all information to evaluate it independently of the others. To this end, it propagates join constraints on the basis of the scope of attributes and relations.

The **HDOptimizer** module is the main responsible for the structural optimization. Its implementation is based on the *q-hypertree* decomposition method [1] and employs some decomposition pruning technique presented in [1] as well.

In a nutshell, the optimizer works as follow. Starting from the leaves, it navigates the rewritten parse tree and calls on each node (i.e., subquery) the **Subplan Handler**, which is responsible for computing a suitable optimized plan for it. The handler preliminary invokes the **Hypergraph Manager**, which builds the hypergraph associated with the current input node. The **Hypergraph Manager** collects also information about statistics of the relations and at-

[1]Implementation is based on the DockingFrames Common framework, available at http://dock.javaforge.com/
[2]Available at http://jsqlparser.sourceforge.net/

tributes appearing in the node, by invoking the underlying system catalog. The computed hypergraph and its associated statistics are then passed to the **cost-k-decomp** module[3] that computes a *hypertree decomposition*, whose maximum width is fixed by the user. Note that, according to the q-decomposition strategy, we force all output variables (i.e., selected items, attributes appearing in group by or in order by clauses) to appear in the root of the decomposition. Furthermore, we also request that the attributes appearing in some non-join condition are covered together by at least a cluster of the computed decomposition.

Finally, the decomposition is translated into an actual query plan by the **View Builder**, which rephrases it in terms of a tree of SQL views, possibly materialized. During this phase, all non-join constraints are assigned to the node of the decomposition, for being later evaluated. The computed optimized plan is then returned to the **SubPlan Hadler** and finally to the **HDOpitmizer** module, which arranges the computed plan node as an element of the current query plan tree. Once all nodes have been process, the resulting plan tree is "finalized".

H-DB supports two kinds of finalization modes. In the *query execution mode*, the **Executor** immediately runs the structure-optimized query on the target database system and reports simple performance statistics at the end of execution. In the *explainer mode*, a more comprehensive picture of the overall optimization process is given by the **Explainer** subsystem. In fact, the **Explainer** provides facilities for visualization and navigation of a plan, for comparing different plans (e.g., comparison between structure-optimized plans and plans produced by the native optimizer, and evaluation of optimized decompositions w.r.t. non-optimized ones), and for reporting cost estimations. Additionally, it supports user interaction and enables on-the-fly tuning of the **HDOptimizer** module to refine available plans.

3. IMPLEMENTATION ISSUES

The concrete implementation of H-DB poses various interesting technical challenges.

First, one needs to force the target DBMS to execute the various physical operators according to the rewritten plan, i.e., the internal underlying optimizer has to be inhibited. However, to take advantage of specific DBMS-dependent optimization strategies, such optimizer can be allowed to optimize joins within each cluster of the decomposition.

Second, physical semi-join operators are needed to push structural optimization benefits to a maximum. In fact, while semi-join operators are usually supported by DBMSs and can be, in principle, used to execute H-DB plans in the case of simple queries, they cannot be coupled with structure-aware optimization techniques in the case of queries involving aggregate operators (see, e.g., [8]). Indeed, in traditional settings, an outer (left-side) relation and an inner (right-side) relation are involved in a semi-join, and the result is given by the set of outer tuples matching some inner tuple w.r.t. the given join conditions. When semi-joins are combined with (e.g.) counting, one would like operators that directly compute the (cardinality of) support for each outer tuple. These operators however are missing in most of the available systems, and our experimentation evidenced that their simulation via pure JDBC statements is rather

[3]See http://www.deis.unical.it/scarcello/Hypertrees/.

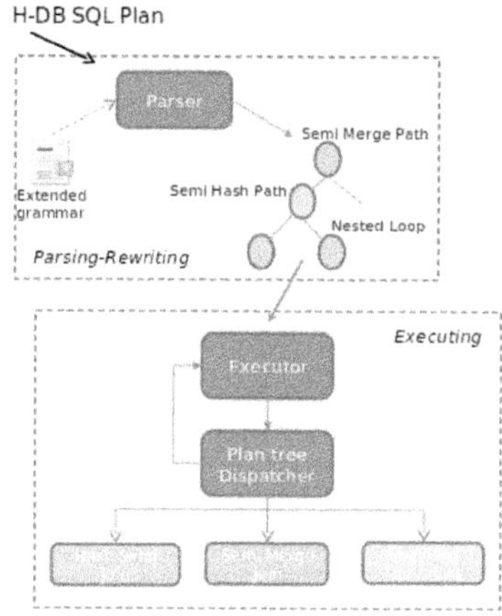

Figure 4: PostgreSQL Backend.

resource-consuming and practically unviable, at the growing of the size of intermediate views. These observations motivated the implementation of ad-hoc physical operators. As a relevant example, we shall next discuss their implementation in the PostgreSQL system—an intermediate approach would consist in coding the strategy in an instructions set of a procedural language supporting data access control (e.g., *PL/SQL* [2], *PL*/pgSQL [6]), which should prevent the modification of underlying DBMS cores.

3.1 Structural Optimization in PostgreSQL

To support structural optimization in PostgreSQL, we have implemented two low-level operators, named `SEMI JOIN` and `SEMI HASH JOIN`, respectively, and integrated them as a part of the system backend (we worked on the version 9.0.2). These operators are built on top of the existing merge-join and hash-join algorithms, respectively. They employ a bunch of capabilities for counting the number of matches of a tuple, which allow to transparently evaluate general queries with complex expression like aggregates in the context of structural decomposition methods.

In the case of `SEMI JOIN`, the implementation roughly works as follow. We start by sorting the two tables and scan them looking for a match. When a match is found, we stop moving on the outer table, we mark a pointer to the last tuple visited, set a counter, and continue scanning inner tuples until they have a match with the marked tuple. During this scan, we properly update the counter at each match. When no more matches occur on the inner, we return the marked tuple and the counter, and start again moving on the outer table. Each outer tuple matching the same set of inner tuples of the last marked one is immediately returned (without a rescan of the inner table) with the last computed counter. For `SEMI HASH JOIN`, the picture is quite similar except for the fact that we do not actually need sorting the tables, because we can immediately peek up matching inner tuples by looking at hash values of outer tuples. When a set of matching inner tuples is found, we scan it just once and store that value for next matches. It is interesting to notice that our implementation of `SEMI HASH JOIN` is an extension of the PostgreSQL *Hybrid Hash Join* [6], which is able to cope with very huge tables by storing in central memory only small batches of data per time.

The integration of the above operators in PostgreSQL consists of two complementary phases. As a preliminary step, we included SEMI JOIN (resp., SEMI HASH JOIN) as keywords in the parsing rules system to specify semi-joins. The syntax we use follows the one of standard join in which one can also optionally specify counter attributes. As a second step, we provided the specification of the semi-join nodes within the planner and the executor of the PostgreSQL backend. When building a plan tree for a semi-join node, we force the PostgreSQL optimizer to compute a path where the joining order of the outer relation and the inner one is the one specified in the query. To preserve such an order, H-DB puts in the plan special setting configurations retrieved by an **SQLQuery Transducer** module. The actual cost is evaluated by estimating the access cost of a semi-join path, depending on which semi-join operator has been used—we enhanced the existing cost model to take this into account. Note that, when a standard join is specified or no assumptions are made on the order of the joins in a query, the PostgreSQL optimizer uses its original built-in strategy to determine the best way to execute joins, choosing between its native alternatives (i.e., hash join path, merge join path, nested loop path). Once an execution plan has been selected, the PostgreSQL executor processes it, by visiting nodes and calling appropriate physical operators.

In order to achieve the correct execution of our custom semi-join paths, we defined a **Plan Tree Dispatcher**, which is in charge of supporting the existing executor module. When a semi-join path (resp., a semi-hash-join path) is encountered, the **Plan Tree Dispatcher** automatically forwards it to the SEMI JOIN (resp.,SEMI HASH JOIN) operator, which actually performs the semi-join and retrieves resulting tuples for the next plan state execution.

4. DEMONSTRATION HIGHLIGHTS

Attendees will be guided through the execution of synthetic queries, taken from both our own generated set and from the whole TPC-H benchmark set. By using the plan-explaining facilities of the system, attendees will graphically compare standard PostgreSQL plans with the plans produced by H-DB, in terms of costs and performance gains.

As a concrete example, we report in Figure 5 some highlights on a demo showcase for query Q_5. First, attendees will evaluate the impact of database quantitative aspects (e.g., cardinality of relations, selectivity of attributes) on plans quality. In this sample experimentation, databases of size 2 gb, 5 gb and 10 gb are considered. As shown on top of Figure 5, the PostgreSQL optimizer is faster than H-DB only for the smallest database, while H-DB realizes an increasing gain w.r.t. PostgreSQL performances at the growing of the database size (up to 20% for 10 gb). Second, attendees will consider manipulation on query specification, by highlighting the role of some parameters (e.g., number of outputs attributes, number of aggregates, etc.), and of query qualifications on overall performances. The bottom of Figure 5 depicts the execution times for different sizes of the requested order date interval (a database of 2 gb is used): At the growing of the size of the interval (i.e., for an higher number of processed tuples) the execution time of the standard optimizer increases faster than the one of H-DB. Indeed, the increasing number of tuples passing the qualification leads to a growing size of intermediate joins computed by PostgreSQL. On the other hand, this blow-up does not occur by performing semi-joins, thereby evidencing very small increments of the execution time for H-DB.

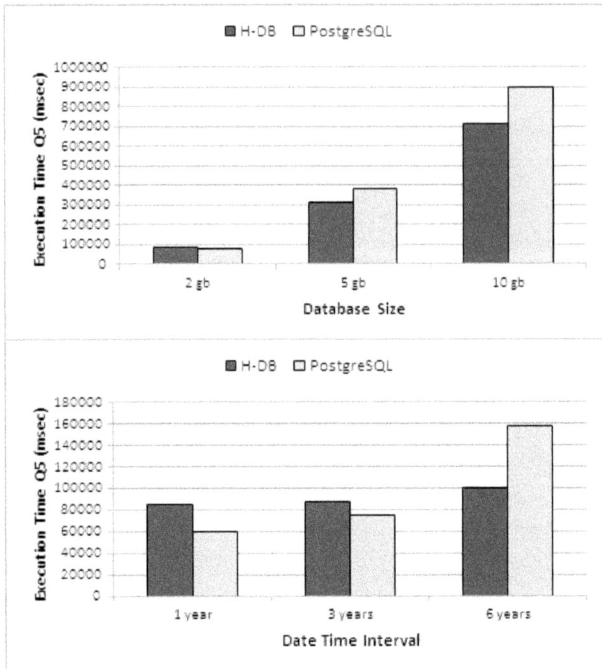

Figure 5: Q_5 demo showcase.

During the demonstration, we will also illustrate the dramatic improvements that H-DB can achieve even over some "easy" queries (e.g., up to 60% for some TPC-H acyclic queries involving just 3 relations). Finally, in addition to discussing cases where structural optimization is worth considering as an alternative to traditional optimization strategies, we will also point out limits of this technique, by evidencing possible improvements on computed plans.

Acknowledgments The authors thank Luigi Granata for the precious technical insights given during the development.

5. REFERENCES

[1] L. Ghionna, L.Granata, G. Greco, F. Scarcello. Hypertree Decompositions for Query Optimization. In *Proc. of ICDE '07*, pp. 36–45, 2007.

[2] S. Urman. Oracle 9i PL/SQL Programming. 2001.

[3] G. Gottlob, N. Leone, and F. Scarcello. Hypertree decompositions and tractable queries. *J. of Computer and System Sciences*, 64(3):579–627, 2002.

[4] G. Gottlob, Z. Miklós, and T. Schwentick. Generalized hypertree decompositions: NP-hardness and tractable variants. *Journal of the ACM*, 56(6), 2009.

[5] M. Grohe and D. Marx. Constraint solving via fractional edge covers. In *Proc. of SODA '06*, pp. 289–298, 2006.

[6] B. Monjian. PostgreSQL: Introduction and Concepts. Addison-Wesley, 2000.

[7] F. Scarcello, G. Greco, and N. Leone. Weighted Hypertree Decompositions and Optimal Query Plans. *J. of Computer and System Sciences*, 73(3):475–506, 2007.

[8] J. Flum and M. Grohe. The parameterized complexity of counting problems. *SIAM Journal on Computing*, 33(4):892–922, 2004.

[9] M. Yannakakis. Algorithms for acyclic database schemes. In *Proc. of VLDB'81*, pp. 82–94, 1981.

Health Conversational System based on Contextual Matching of Community-Driven Question-Answer Pairs

Wilson Wong, John Thangarajah, Lin Padgham
School of Computer Science and Information Technology
RMIT University
{wilson.wong,john.thangarajah,lin.padgham}@rmit.edu.au

ABSTRACT

More and more people are turning to the World Wide Web for learning and sharing information about their health using search engines, forums and question answering systems. In this demonstration, we look at a new way of delivering health information to the end-users via coherent conversations. The proposed conversational system allows the end-users to vaguely express and gradually refine their information needs using only natural language questions or statements as input. We provide example scenarios in this demonstration to illustrate the inadequacies of current delivery mechanisms and highlight the innovative aspects of the proposed conversational system.

Categories and Subject Descriptors

H.3.3 [**Information Storage and Retrieval**]: Information Search and Retrieval—*search process*; H.5.2 [**Information Interfaces and Presentation**]: User Interfaces—*natural language*

General Terms

Algorithms, Human Factors

Keywords

QA Pairs, Conversational Agent, Health Information

1. INTRODUCTION

The World Wide Web has revolutionised the ways we access information, and health-related information is no exception [5]. The sense of empowerment derived from the anytime, anywhere access of online information coupled with the rising cost of healthcare have contributed to our increasing reliance on the Web for purposes ranging from self-diagnosis to sharing patient experiences. Although the use of online information for health-related purposes has been greatly criticised by health practitioners [8, 7], benefits have also been suggested. Information on the Web has the ability to reach hard to reach groups such as teenagers and raise their awareness on health related issues. The ability to provide information for those with minor health problems that may be managed without the need for medical consultation [5] also helps to free up the time of health practitioners to deal with people requiring attention.

Currently, the end-users have a range of online services to rely on for their health information needs. These services range from live chat with medical practitioners (e.g., `AskTheDoctor.com`) and self-help communities for sharing patient experiences (e.g., `PatientsLikeMe.com`) to Web search engines (e.g., Yahoo!, Bing) and specialised question answering systems (e.g., HONqa). It is clear from the proliferation of these websites that people find it beneficial and valuable to be able to inquire about or search for health information at their own convenience. Some of the shortcomings of these services, however, prohibit the effective delivery of health information to the end-users. The lack of concise responses and the difficulty of representing complex health information needs as Boolean queries make search engines far from ideal [10]. Question answering systems provide the end-users with concise answers for factual questions. This specialisation on answering factual questions (e.g., *"what"*, *"when"*, *"where"*), however, greatly restricts their applications to other input types such as *why*-questions or even statements. The need to express something as multi-faceted as health concerns all in a single natural language question may not be ideal. It is our view that a conversational ability that supports context-dependent, open-ended health information seeking is beneficial to allow the end-users to gradually explore a complex information need.

In this demonstration, we present a Web-based system that engages end-users in coherent discussions about their health concerns. This system is our first attempt at addressing some of the shortcomings of existing delivery mechanisms discussed above. Although there exist some health conversational agents in the literature, they focus on very specific tasks such as promoting behavioural change for long-term health [1] or acquiring the objective (e.g., weight) and subjective (e.g., pain) aspects of a patient's conditions for in-home monitoring [3]. These systems, which are based on deep discourse analysis, require the intent of the end-users to be recognised and the various states of the conversations to be anticipated and represented. These systems are not suitable for managing more open-ended natural language input about personal health and other related information.

Our conversational system allows the end-users to vaguely

CIKM'11, October 24–28, 2011, Glasgow, Scotland, UK.

express and gradually build up over time their health information needs. The innovative aspects of this system, which set it apart from existing conversational agents, are:

- To the best of our knowledge, it is the first system to use disjointed question-answer (QA) pairs from community-driven websites to build coherent conversations.[1]
- We use a novel scoring process based on exponential decay and contextual information to rank QA pairs and select the best answers to be used as system responses.
- The system supports open-ended conversations about health and related issues, in real time, as opposed to task-specific interactions.

The demonstrated system provides far more concise responses than document retrieval systems, and while it may not deliver the precise answers available from a specialised question answering system, it is able to carry on a meaningful and natural interaction in response to both questions and statements. The coherence of the content is far greater than standard chatterbots such as ALICE[2].

We allow the QA pairs retrieved to be manually edited to improve their quality, though certain aspects such as spelling correction can be automated to some extent. In our demonstration system, the QA pairs are unedited in our DB, though in the examples shown only the initial sentences are used for readability. Although this demonstration focuses on health-related conversations, the system is generic and can be extended to converse about other topics by downloading the corresponding QA pairs.

2. CONVERSATIONAL SCENARIOS

To illustrate the use and features of the demonstration system and its differences from existing delivery mechanisms, let us consider the following scenario. A user accidentally cuts her finger whilst cooking and has no knowledge of basic first aid. If she is one of the two billion Internet users worldwide today[3], she may first go to the Web for information. Her first stop would be to use one of the many popular Web search engines today such as Google, Yahoo! or Bing. Using Google in this scenario to search for *"I've accidentally cut myself. What do I do?"*, close to 400 million results were returned with Figure 2 showing the top 3. The results are clearly not the concise response desired in such a situation. A user may then try alternative keywords to find more suitable results. Even then, the results obtained are generally not concise as the end-user has to click on each of the individual links and filter through the webpages looking for the appropriate answer.

The above is typical for search engines as they are simply document retrieval systems. Let us instead consider using the two question answering systems HONqa[4], that specialises in health information, and the more generic START[5]. Entering the same natural language question *"I accidentally cut myself. What do I do?"*, we find, as shown in Figures

[1]There is work using QA pairs for automated question answering [2, 9], but our focus is on coherent conversations.
[2]`http://alice.pandorabots.com/`
[3]`http://www.itu.int/net/pressoffice/press_releases/2010/39.aspx`
[4]`http://www.hon.ch/QA`
[5]`http://start.csail.mit.edu`

Figure 1: The results of searching the Web for information about treatments for cuts using Google.

2(a) and 2(b), that the two systems are unable to 'understand' the input. This is because these systems work better with more straightforward inputs in the form of single direct questions. After reformulating the user's concern to *"How to treat cut fingers?"*, START still returned no answers and HONqa returned a summary *"If the bleeding is heavy, bright red or spurting then follow the steps to control bleeding. If the finger is amputated, put pressure on it to control bleeding and follow the steps for treating an amputation. Fundamental First Aid Cuts and Bleeding First Aid Kits and Supplies Related Articles Also from About.com"*. Even with this response from HONqa, the user still has to click on a link to `About.com` to read an article about stopping bleeding.

Another approach would be to ask a real medical practitioner on websites such as `AskTheDoctor.com`. However the delay in getting a response, and the need to disclose personal information such as name and email address may make this a less desirable option. Finally the user could attempt to engage in a conversation regarding her concern with a conversational agent such as ALICE. Figure 2(c) illustrates a conversation that was initiated by the same question *"I cut myself. What do I do?"*. We can observe from the figure that the resulting conversation is more likely to frustrate or perhaps amuse the user than to be of any assistance.

The scenario described above illustrates the lack of a conversational system that allows a user to express, clarify and refine complex information needs in natural language. With our system, a user is offered some of these capabilities to improve their health information seeking experience. Figure 3 shows a conversation with the proposed system, initiated by the question *"I've accidentally cut myself. What do I do?"*. The system concisely responds along the lines of *"From a first aid perspective...(*do ... else*)...just go to your doctor."*. Given the suggestion of using antiseptic, the user, who has knowledge of alcohol and peroxide, inquires *"Can I rub some alcohol on?"* and later *"How about peroxide?"*. Notice how the system is able to interpret these two inputs in the context of the previous user utterance concerning accidental cuts. Instead of requiring the end-user to fully specify their questions, e.g., *"Can I rub some alcohol on my wound?"* or *"Can I use peroxide on the wound that I've just accidentally created?"*, the system systematically takes into account keywords from previous utterances to allow the end-users to concisely represent their information needs, and to ensure the best system responses actually correspond to the previ-

(a) START (b) HONqa

(c) ALICE

Figure 2: The answers provided by (a) START, (b) HONqa and (c) ALICE in response to the input *"I accidentally cut myself. What do I do?"*.

ous user inputs. After learning from the system that alcohol or peroxide should not be used on her wounds, she moved on to ask *"What antiseptic works best then?"*. The proposed system answered with *"Good old soap and water!"*, which is a valid response despite being somewhat cheeky. The user persists on obtaining more information by asking *"Seriously, my wound is quite large"*. Not knowing what *"Betadine"* is from the system's response, she further inquires *"What is betadine?"*, to which a reasonable answer was provided.

The responses produced by the proposed system in the above scenario are all answers from Yahoo!Answers' QA pairs that were truncated for presentation. The response *"Good old soap and water!"*, for instance, is the answer to the question *"What works best to clean cuts alcohol,hydrogen peroxide, hand sanitizer ect?"*, which together form a QA pair from Yahoo!Answers[6]. As for the system response *"Just wash the area with Betadine..."* to the user input *"Seriously, my wound is quite large"*, it is the answer to the question *"What works better for large cuts... What else is good to use?"*[7]. These two and in fact, all other QA pairs from Yahoo!Answers are distinct answers to individual questions. This is why we refer to the QA pairs as disjointed. By themselves, they are unable to contribute much to forming coherent conversations. However, with the scoring process based on exponential decay and contextual information to be briefly described in the next Section 3, the proposed system is able to engage users in coherent and relevant conversations about their health concerns.

[6]http://answers.yahoo.com/question/index?qid=20080722161422AAxIRpe

[7]http://answers.yahoo.com/question/index?qid=20060726190740AAXdL1L

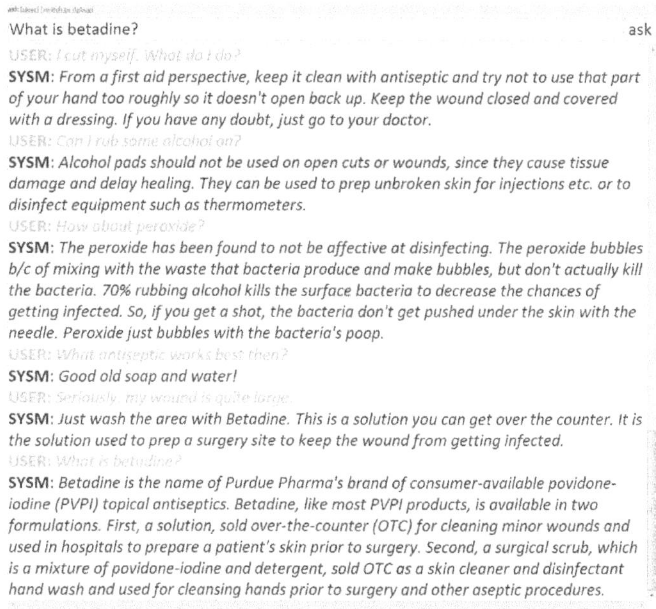

Figure 3: An example conversation with the proposed system which was initiated by the end-user using the input *"I cut myself. What do I do?"*.

3. SYSTEM COMPONENTS

In this section, we discuss the two main components, as shown in Figure 4, of the proposed conversational system, namely, the collection of question and answer (QA) pairs, and the process through which we use the QA pairs for generating coherent responses.

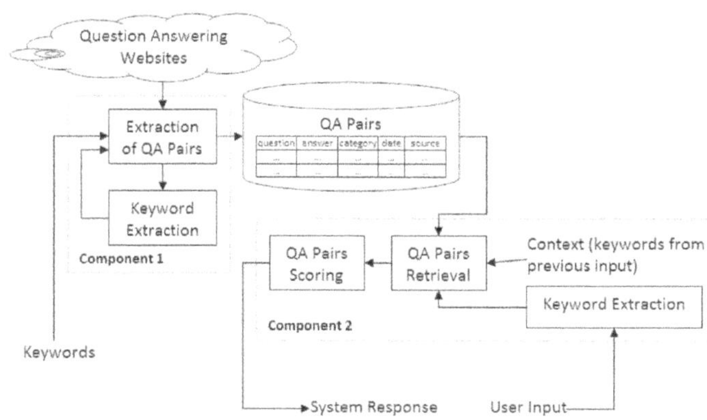

Figure 4: Components of the proposed conversational system.

The extraction of QA pairs from community-driven question-and-answer (Q&A) websites is performed *offline*. That is, they are downloaded prior to, and are independent of, the real-time process of engaging in conversation. A QA pair is simply the pairing of a question posted by a human together with the possible answers contributed by other volunteers. The QA pairs are currently extracted from Yahoo!Answers using the API[8] provided by Yahoo!. The use of QA pairs is ideal considering the fact that data from Q&A websites are not optimal for factoid input but instead, are a preferred choice for complex information needs such as opinion or advice [4]. We are also motivated by the availability of APIs to ease the implementation process. QA pairs may also be obtained from other community-driven Q&A websites such as `Answers.com`. Many of these websites, however, do not permit the non-commercial, automated extraction of data from their sites, hence preventing their use here.

A GUI has been created to allow the system administrator to manage the various aspects of gathering QA pairs from Yahoo!Answers. Using this interface, the administrator is able to provide keywords for extraction, examine the current composition of the QA pairs, and search and edit the QA pairs currently in the database. Other metadata such as category and the date of posting, which are not used in this version of the system, can also be extracted and used during the scoring process to improve the quality of the responses.

Next, we look at the process of using inputs in a conversation to create gradually-decaying context for retrieving and scoring QA pairs in our database with the aim of locating the best responses. Every input is first analysed for keywords. In this version of the system, we consider a keyword as a word or phrase that is content-bearing, that is, not a function word. The words in an input are first chunked using parts of speech and later filtered using a stopword list[9]. At each turn in a conversation where the user provides an input, the keywords from previous user utterances (i.e., context) and the current keywords are unioned and weighted using a decay model. Intuitively, a keyword that no longer appears in the more recent inputs will have its weight decayed. If a keyword is constantly repeated up till the most recent input, its weight will be more.

A simple structured query to the database is then performed to obtain all QA pairs containing at least one keyword from the unioned and weighted set of keywords at the current turn. Each pair is assigned a score using four criteria based on the frequency and location of the occurrences of keywords as well as other heuristics involving edit distance and so on. The details of these criteria and the scoring process in general are outlined in [11][10].

4. DEMONSTRATION PLAN

In this demonstration, we will show the system interfaces for conversing about health issues with the end-users, and for populating the database with QA pairs to cope with evolving conversations. In particular, we will demonstrate how an end-user can easily interact with the proposed conversational system over a range of health issues. During the demonstration, we will restrict conversations with the system to 10 health and medical-related concepts (e.g., *"lung cancer"*, *"sinusitis"*, *"dry mouth"*) from the list of 150 used for evaluating health-specific question answering systems [6]. This restriction will allow us to examine the capabilities and limitations of the system together with the audience within a controlled space, showing the effect of the depth and breadth of QA pairs on the system's conversations. We have prepared four videos[11] as a preview of our demonstration.

[8]`http://developer.yahoo.com/answers`

[9]In later versions, we will examine the need for more advanced noun phrase chunking and term extraction.

[10]The report is in the process of being submitted for publication.

Acknowledgment

This work is partially supported by the Australian Research Council and Real Thing Entertainment Pty. Ltd. under Linkage grant number LP0882013.

5. REFERENCES

[1] Bickmore, T., Schulman, D., and Sidner, C. A reusable framework for health counseling dialogue systems based on a behavioral medicine ontology. *Journal of Biomedical Informatics 44*, 2 (2011), 183–197.

[2] Cong, G., Wang, L., Lin, C., Song, Y., and Sun, Y. Finding question-answer pairs from online forums. In *Proceedings of the 31st Annual International ACM SIGIR Conference* (Singapore, 2008).

[3] Ferguson, G., Allen, J., Galescu, L., Quinn, J., and Swift, M. Cardiac: An intelligent conversational assistant for chronic heart failure patient heath monitoring. In *Proceedings of the AAAI Fall Symposium on Virtual Healthcare Interaction* (Arlington, USA, 2009).

[4] Liu, Y., and Agichtein, E. On the evolution of the yahoo! answers qa community. In *Proceedings of the 31st Annual International ACM SIGIR Conference* (Singapore, 2008).

[5] McDaid, D., and Park, A. Online health: Untangling the web. Report Bupa Health Pulse 2010, London School of Economics, 2011.

[6] Olvera-Lobo, M., and Gutierrez-Artacho, J. Open- vs. restricted-domain qa systems in the biomedical field. *Journal of Information Science 37*, 2 (2011), 152–162.

[7] Robertson, N., and Harrison, P. Whats wrong with me? concerns about online medical self-diagnosis. In *Proceedings of the Australia and New Zealand Marketing Academy Conference (ANZMAC)* (Monash University, Australia, 2009).

[8] Ryan, A., and Wilson, S. Internet healthcare: Do self-diagnosis sites do more harm than good? *Expert Opinion on Drug Safety 7*, 3 (2008), 227–229.

[9] Wang, B., Wang, X., Sun, C., Liu, B., and Sun, L. Modeling semantic relevance for question-answer pairs in web social communities. In *Proceedings of the 48th Annual Meeting of the Association for Computational Linguistics (ACL)* (Uppsala, Sweden, 2010).

[10] White, R., and Horvitz, E. Web to world: Predicting transitions from self-diagnosis to the pursuit of local medical assistance in web search. In *Proceedings of the AMIA Annual Symposium* (Washington DC, USA, 2010).

[11] Wong, W., Thangarajah, J., and Padgham, L. Open-ended health conversational system. Technical report, RMIT University, 2011.

[11]`http://www.youtube.com/watch?v=n-liJ0hsklw`
`http://www.youtube.com/watch?v=v6JSK6nvkno`
`http://www.youtube.com/watch?v=cOgoNkKDT18`
`http://www.youtube.com/watch?v=owjajxRX-d4`

Annotating Knowledge Work Lifelog: Term Extraction from Sensor and Operation History

Masayuki Okamoto Nayuko Watanabe Shinichi Nagano Kenta Cho
Corporate R&D Center, Toshiba Corporation
1 Komukai-Toshiba-cho, Saiwai-ku
Kawasaki 212-8582, Japan
+81-44-549-2286

{masayuki4.okamoto, nayuko.watanabe, shinichi3.nagano, kenta.cho}
@toshiba.co.jp

ABSTRACT

We present a system that supports review of a knowledge work lifelog as an activity history. Since knowledge workers often review their own activity histories, gathering each user's activities on his/her terminal as a lifelog is a promising approach. However, readability of the stored lifelog is a large problem of lifelog-based application. We propose a term extraction method to add annotation labels to the stored lifelog for supporting knowledge workers, exploiting text data acquired from desktop activities. Our prototype system monitors a user's desktop activities after combining raw events, and then extracts possible annotation labels with LDA and C-value techniques from documents and text data in sensor events. In this paper, we introduce a lifelogging module and a lifelog annotation method based on term extraction techniques. According to an empirical evaluation for three weeks, we found that the current method is useful for one-week review.

Categories and Subject Descriptors

H.5.2 [**Information Interfaces and Presentation**]: User Interfaces; H.3.3 [**Information Storage and Retrieval**]: Information Search and Retrieval.

General Terms

Human Factors, Experimentation.

Keywords

Knowledge work, lifelog, term extraction.

1. INTRODUCTION

Knowledge workers often review their own activity histories to write their daily or weekly reports, search some specific materials such as mails, schedules, and documents, or approximately calculate how much time they used for each task. However, it is difficult to review the activities as an aggregated history since these materials are scattered. To place the activities on time series data, gathering each user's activities on his/her terminal as a lifelog is a promising approach. Nowadays, lifelogging as a history of daily activity is becoming easier, because many sensor devices are installed in personal terminals such as personal computers, portable phones, and smartphones. However, it is difficult to review the sensor or operation events that occur through users' actions because users should interpret what they actually did from 'raw' large-scale lifelogs. We believe that users would like to review their lifelogs if this problem were solved.

CIKM'11, October 24–28, 2011, Glasgow, Scotland, UK.

One solution is to shrink detailed activities into adequate volumes and annotate them. Each annotation works as a summary of an activity and a search query so that users can interpret or search their activities easily. In the knowledge work domain, we can exploit text data for annotation, e.g., titles of emails, file names or content of documents. We use a term extraction method to consider topics and readability.

Figure 1 shows a screenshot of our system. A user's lifelog events are shown in a timeline from top to bottom of the window. Each lifelog event includes the title of the activity, an icon indicating the kind of activity, the resources used, and tag terms for annotation. When the user pushes one or more tags, the timeline is refined and only activities with these tags are shown.

In this paper, we introduce a lifelogging module and a lifelog annotation method based on term extraction techniques.

2. RELATED WORKS

Several researchers have endeavored to support review of knowledge work activities. The two principal approaches are search support and task classification.

The search support approach aims to help knowledge workers increase their efficiency by reducing the time and effort required to access relevant content or activities. FALCON is a system that integrates email and calendar functions with a recorded meetings application [1]. Using each person's microphone input, a method of searching documents used in a meeting without mail or calendar information is proposed [7].

The task classification approach aims to gather related applications or contents for each task so that a user can find the material needed for a selected task. An application to classify materials or documents from the office work history, namely, TaskPredictor2, is proposed [9].

However, there is little discussion on the automatic addition of readable annotations to review the document browsing history as an activity history. In regard to information extraction, various research has been done on extracting important terms from stored documents or browsed webpages. For example, there are techniques for extracting important terms from a user's web browsing history [6]. We need an adequate term extraction method for reviewing knowledge work activity. In regard to

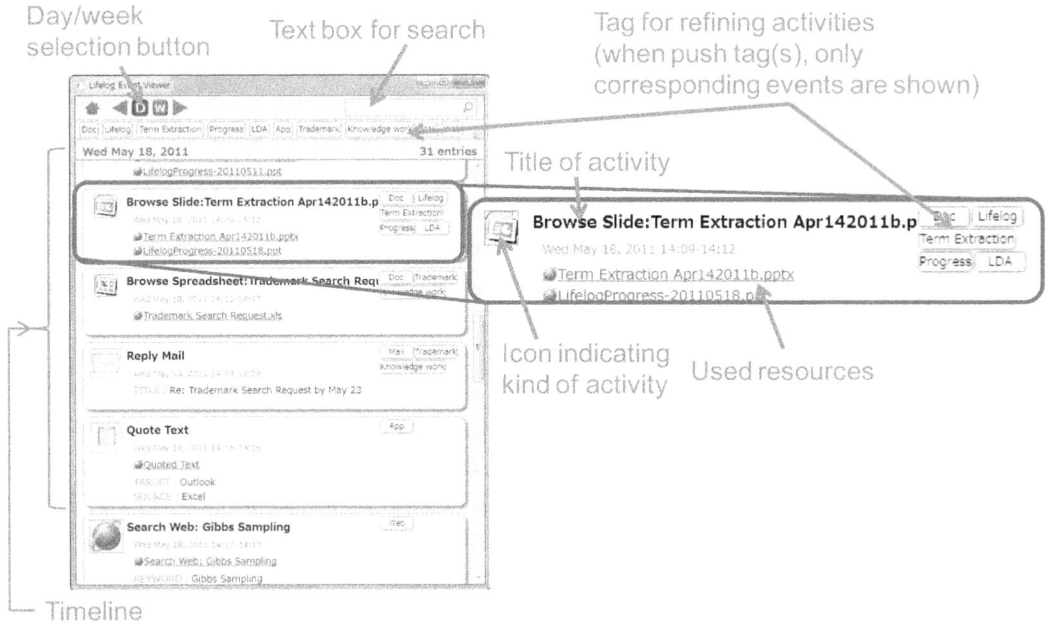

Figure 1. Screenshot of lifelog viewer (for Windows). The original text is written in Japanese.

requirements for these annotations, the ability to classify an activity into a class and terms with higher readability is needed.

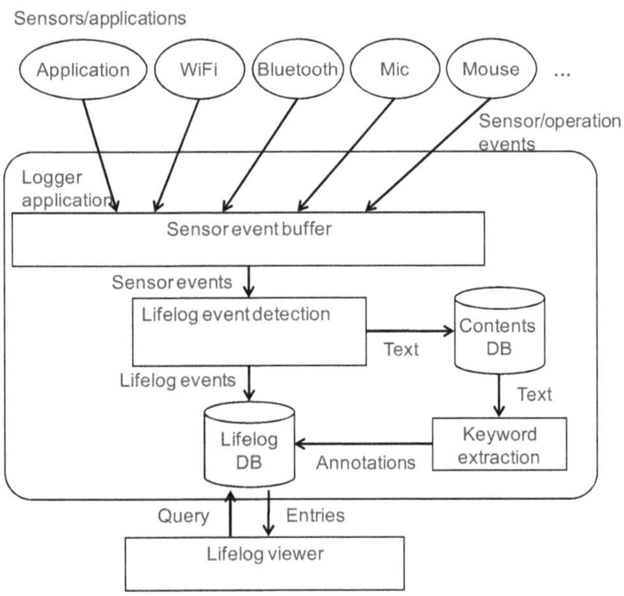

Figure 2. Flow of lifelog generation.

3. SYSTEM OVERVIEW

3.1 Lifelog Generation

Figure 2 shows the flow of lifelog generation. Firstly, the logger application logs sensor events and operation events as a background process. Currently, our system supports about 90 events for Windows and Android platforms. These events include sensor events for internal sensors such as accelerometers, GPS (global positioning system), neighbor Bluetooth terminals or WiFi access points, speech events with the pitch tracking method [10], the transportation method (walking, running, or vehicles) [3], and operation events for desktop activities such as office document operations, web browsing, mail operations, active window changes, mouse events, and keyboard events. For a part of applications, e.g., Microsoft Office applications or Internet Explorer, the logger application automatically attaches to these applications and events are detected by application APIs. These events are input into the sensor event buffer. In our current system, sensor events detected on an Android terminal is merged to the events of a Windows PC by the import module. Figure 3 shows a screenshot of the sensor event viewer for an Android terminal.

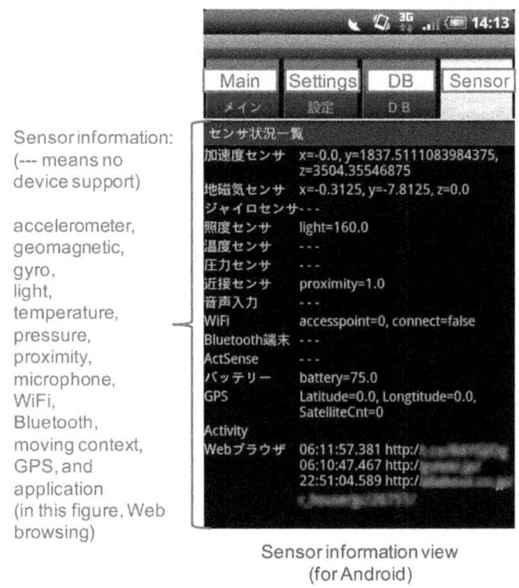

Figure 3. Sensor information view (for Android).

Secondly, the lifelog event detection module generates lifelog events from combinations of sensor events in the sensor event buffer. For example, a lifelog event 'mail compose' is generated

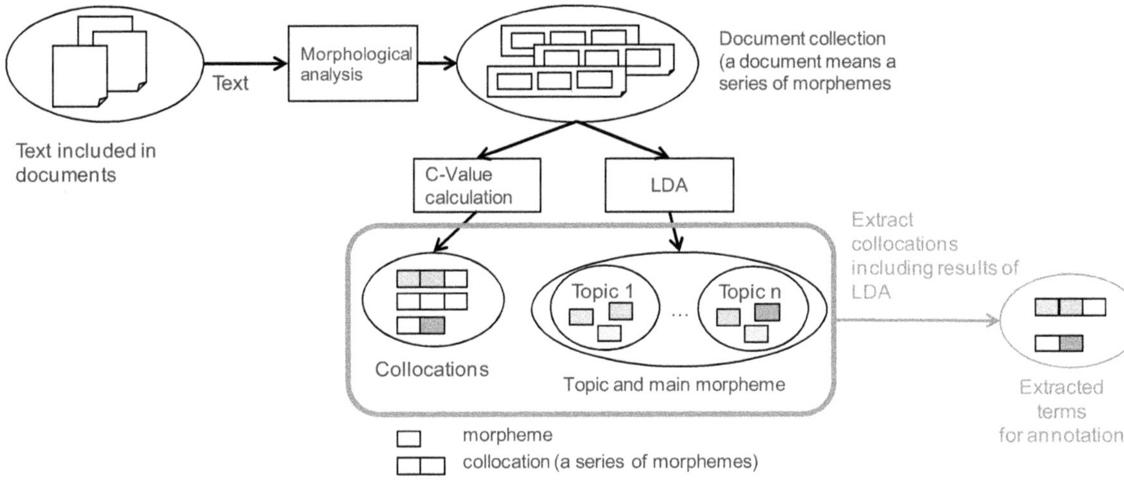

Figure 4. Flow of annotation term extraction.

from 'start mail compose' and 'send mail' sensor events, and a lifelog event 'presentation' is generated from 'slideshow' and 'speech' sensor events. Currently, our system supports about 40 lifelog events. Detected lifelog events are stored in the lifelog database. The text of each content is also stored in the content database.

Thirdly, the keyword extraction module extracts terms for annotation from content text. As the content text, we can use window titles, browsed web documents, mail contents, content of documents, file names, and so on. The detail of this process is described in the following section. Extracted terms are annotated to the corresponding lifelog events.

Finally, the lifelog viewer shows annotated lifelog events as shown in Figure 1.

3.2 Annotation Term Extraction

To support review of knowledge work activities, annotation terms should be typical topic terms of a user's activities and interpretable for the user. In the proposed system, we combine LDA (latent Dirichlet allocation) [2] for extracting typical topic terms and C-value [4] calculation for extracting readable terms.

Figure 4 shows the flow of term extraction. This process includes three steps: preprocess, important term estimation, and collocation extraction.

3.2.1 Preprocess

As preprocess, documents are converted into a series of morphemes by morphological analysis. We use MeCab [5] for the Japanese morphological analysis module.

3.2.2 Topic Estimation and Important Term Extraction with LDA

LDA [2] is a language generation model that considers a set of D documents as a mixture of latent K topics. Each latent topic is a multinomial distribution with W words. The parameter θ that controls the generation model of latent topics is expressed as a Dirichlet distribution $\mathrm{Dir}(\alpha)$, and N_j words for document j are modeled with topic $z_{ij} = \mathrm{Multinomial}(\theta_j)$ and a term $x_{ij} = \mathrm{Multinomial}(\phi_{z_{ij}})$. We use a variation of Gibbs Sampling method [8] for the parameter estimation. We use a number of topics with the smallest perplexity after a hundred sampling iterations. Then, terms with higher occurrence probabilities for each topic are extracted as term candidates.

3.2.3 Collocation Extraction with C-value

Independent morpheme extracted with LDA does not have readability for a user to interpret the user's activities because of the small length. We use the C-value [4] calculation technique as a readable collocation extraction method. A C-value score for a collocation a is calculated as

$$Cvalue(a) = (length(a) - 1)\left(freq(a) - \frac{t(a)}{c(a)}\right)$$

where $t(a)$ means the occurrence frequency of longer collocations, and $c(a)$ means the number of these collocations.

Finally, collocations that have high C-value scores and include terms extracted through the LDA are extracted as annotation, as shown in Figure 1.

4. EVALUATION OF ANNOTATION

We empirically investigated to what degree our annotation method satisfied users. First, we let eight subjects (knowledge workers in the IT domain) collect their lifelogs for three weeks. Second, the system extracted up to twenty terms for each target duration: 1, 3, 7, 14, or 21 day(s). We used mail titles, file names of Microsoft Office documents, and the text of the first page of these files for the input text after our preliminary investigation. Then, each user rated annotations from three perspectives: *meaningfulness*, *remindability*, and *usefulness for refinement*. Meaningfulness means to what degree annotations are meaningful as words or collocations at three levels: meaningful (3); somewhat (2); meaningless (1). We also introduced remindability, which means to what degree annotations remind users of concrete activities. This score indicates usefulness for reminding users of their activity histories at three levels: remindable (3); somewhat (2); not remindable (1). Usefulness for refinement means to what degree annotations are useful for refinement of lifelog events at three levels: useful (3); somewhat (2); not useful (1).

Figure 5 and Figure 6 summarize the results of our experiments with 2,531 events and 553 annotations. Figure 5 shows the average scores for target durations. From remindability scores in Figure 5, current method is most useful for seven-day data, though there is no significant difference. This result means that the current method is most useful for one-week review. However, refinement scores are totally low. After checking evaluated terms, we found that some terms indicating transient events, e.g., 'confirm,' 'application form,' and 'questionnaire,' are rated with high remindability scores and low refinement scores. How to detect these transient terms is included in our future work.

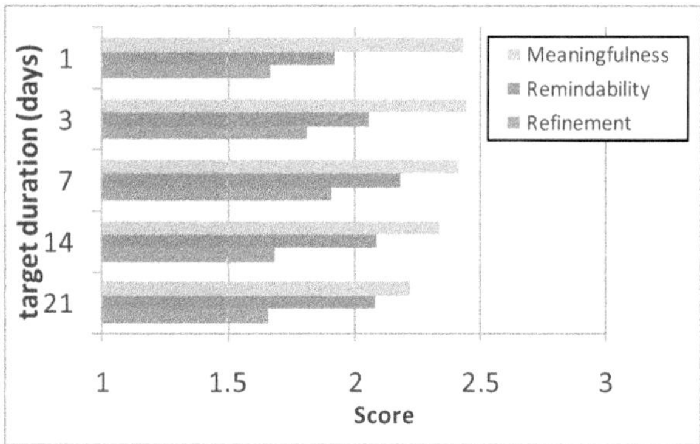

Figure 5. Relation between duration and score.

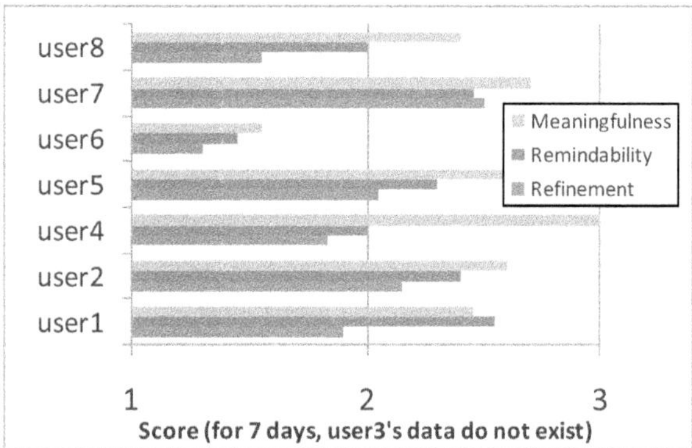

Figure 6. Relation between duration and score.

Figure 6 shows average scores of individual users for terms extracted from seven-day lifelogs. From Figure 6, we found that there is great variability among users. There are two reasons. One is the difference of criterion for evaluation itself. The other is the difference of activities among users. User 6, whose score is the lowest, mainly used a spreadsheet application. Since each word in spreadsheet files is not useful for reminder or refinement, the average scores for the subject is low.

From Figure 5 and Figure 6, we found that the current method is most useful for one-week review, though we should refine the extraction method continuously.

5. DEMONSTRATION PLAN

During the demonstration session, users can see what kinds of sensor events are detected for Windows-based and Android-based clients, and what kinds of terms are annotated to the lifelog with a lifelog viewer application on a Windows PC. We use a Windows PC and an Android smartphone for the demonstration.

6. CONCLUSION

In this paper, we propose a term extraction method to add annotation labels to the stored lifelog for supporting knowledge workers, exploiting text data acquired from desktop activities. Our prototype system monitors a user's desktop activities after combining raw events, and then extracts possible annotation labels with LDA and C-value techniques from documents and text data in sensor events. According to an empirical evaluation with eight subjects, we found that the current method is useful for one-week review. Our future work includes the refinement of our term extraction method and introduction of interpersonal contexts such as communication history [7].

7. REFERENCES

[1] Bjellerup, P., Cama, K. J., Desikan, M., Guo, Y., Kale, A. G., Lai, J. C., Lethif, N., Lu, J., Topkara, M., and Wissel, S. H. 2010. FALCON: seamless access to meeting data from the inbox and calendar. In *Proceedings of the 19th ACM international conference on Information and knowledge management* (CIKM '10). ACM, New York, NY, USA, 1951-1952.

[2] Blei, D. M., Ng, A. Y., and Jordan, M. I. 2003. Latent dirichlet allocation. *J. Mach. Learn. Res.* 3 (March 2003), 993-1022.

[3] Cho, K., Iketani, N., Setoguchi, H., and Hattori, M. 2009. Human Activity Recognizer for Mobile Devices with Multiple Sensors. In *Proceedings of the 2009 Symposia and Workshops on Ubiquitous, Autonomic and Trusted Computing* (UIC-ATC '09). IEEE Computer Society, Washington, DC, USA, 114-119.

[4] Frantzi, K. T. and Ananiadou, S. 1996. Extracting nested collocations. In *Proceedings of the 16th conference on Computational linguistics - Volume 1* (COLING '96), Vol. 1. Association for Computational Linguistics, Stroudsburg, PA, USA, 41-46.

[5] Kudo, T., Yamamoto, K., Matsumoto, Y. 2004. Appliying Conditional Random Fields to Japanese Morphological Analysis. In *Proceedings of the 2004 Conference on Empirical Methods in Natural Language Processing* (EMNLP '04), Barcelona, Spain, 230-237.

[6] Matsuo, Y., Fukuta, H., and Ishizuka, M. 2002. Browsing support by highlighting keywords based on a user's browsed history. In *Proceedings of 2002 IEEE Int. Conf. on Systems, Man, and Cybernetics* (SMC '02), Hammamet, Tunisia.

[7] Okamoto, M., Iketani, N., Nishimura, K., Kikuchi, M., Cho, K., Hattori, M. 2008. Finding two-level interpersonal context: proximity and conversation detection from personal audio feature data. In *Proceedings of Interspeech 2008*, Brisbane, Australia, 2482-2485.

[8] Porteous, I., Newman, D., Ihler, A., Asuncion, A., Smyth, P., and Welling, M. 2008. Fast collapsed gibbs sampling for latent dirichlet allocation. In *Proceeding of the 14th ACM SIGKDD international conference on Knowledge discovery and data mining* (KDD '08). ACM, New York, NY, USA, 569-577.

[9] Shen, J., Irvine, J., Bao, X., Goodman, M., Kolibaba, S., Tran, A., Carl, F., Kirschner, B., Stumpf, S., and Dietterich, T. G. 2009. Detecting and correcting user activity switches: algorithms and interfaces. In *Proceedings of the 14th international conference on Intelligent user interfaces* (IUI '09). ACM, New York, NY, USA, 117-126.

[10] Talkin, D., 1995. A Robust Algorithm for Pitch Tracking. In *Speech Coding and Synthesis*. Kleijn, W. B. and Paliwal K. K. (Eds.). Elsevier Science Inc., New York, NY, USA, 495-518, 1995.

Entity Timelines: Visual Analytics and Named Entity Evolution

Arturas Mazeika, Tomasz Tylenda, and Gerhard Weikum
Max Planck Institute for Informatics
Building 46.1, Campus E1 4, 66123 Saarbrücken, Germany
{amazeika, ttylenda, weikum} @mpi-inf.mpg.de

ABSTRACT

The constantly evolving Web reflects the evolution of society. Knowledge about entities (people, companies, political parties, etc.) evolves over time. Facts add up (e.g., awards, lawsuits, divorces), change (e.g., spouses, CEOs, political positions), and even cease to exist (e.g., countries split into smaller or join into bigger ones). Analytics of the evolution of the entities poses many challenges including extraction, disambiguation, and canonization of entities from large text collections as well as introduction of specific analysis and interactivity methods for the evolving entity data.

In this demonstration proposal[1], we consider a novel problem of the evolution of named entities. To this end, we have extracted, disambiguated, canonicalized, and connected named entities with the YAGO ontology. To analyze the evolution we have developed a visual analytics system. Careful preprocessing and ranking of the ontological data allowed us to propose wide range of effective interactions and data analysis techniques including advanced filtering, contrasting timeliness of entities and drill down/roll up evolving data.

Categories and Subject Descriptors

H.4 [**Information Systems Applications**]: Miscellaneous

General Terms

Algorithms, Measurement, Experimentation

1. INTRODUCTION

Which companies have been associated with mobile music devices in the last decade? What are the similarities and the differences between Mikhail Gorbachev and Ronald Reagan? What are the key people associated with the European countries? What are the similarities between the Baltic States and Germany in 1998, and how do the similarities evolve over time? How does the news coverage of a particular product, event, or entity compare to blog and tweet coverage? Knowledge extraction from large text collections spanning long time intervals, organization of knowledge, and answering the above and similar questions is the key topic of this demo.

Knowledge extraction, summarization, and development of a (visual) analytic system impose a number of challenges. First, the information is spread over many articles (news, Web, blogs, tweets) and thus the information must be extracted and aggregated. Second, entities need to be identified in order to move them from lexical to semantic level. Tracing entities along the temporal dimension is possible only if their semantics is taken into account. Simple keyword tracking is insufficient to connect semantically similar entities from different time periods, e.g., Walkman and iPod. Third, named entities must be properly disambiguated (George Bush may mean the 41st or the 43rd president of the U.S., Waterloo can be the location, the battle, or the song). Fourth, due to accumulation and contrasting functionality a single, unique identifier should be used to denote the same named entity (Michail Sergejevic Gorbachov and Mikhail Gorbachev should be replaced with, e.g., `Mikhail_Gorbachev`). Finally, an efficient visual analytics system with rich interactive capabilities must be developed to allow the analyst to interact, filter, view, project, compare (contrast), and group over the evolving named entity data.

Information presentation and analytics tools have been proposed in the information retrieval and ontology visualization (e.g., YAGO browser [5]) and visual analytics communities (e.g., Multiple Facets [3]); there are commercial system that link news articles based on keywords, tags, and topics (e.g., Google News). Ontology visualization systems aim to present the ontological knowledge to the user. Since ontologies form graphs, the data is usually presented as a graph with a rich interactive capabilities to show/hide selected parts of the subgraph or identify a handful number of the most relevant nodes. Evolution and contrasting of named entities is usually not considered. Conversely, text visualization community proposed tools to visualize evolving statistics of (key-)words in the text collections. Since only words rather than named entities are considered in such visualizations, the visualizations cannot benefit from the comprehensive type system offered by ontologies (e.g., `Albert_Einstein` is a `Theoretical physicists`→`physicist` → `scientist`→ `person`→ `entity`; `Lithuania` → `Baltic_State` → `European_State`). Such systems therefore, are limited to basic interactions with the data. Article linkage systems aim to group, recommend, and cross link articles with other data sources (e.g., Wikipedia). The extraction (and disambiguation) is limited to the most prominent named entity(s), while interaction is restricted to simple browsing of the articles with the help of links.

[1]A preview of the system is available at http://evolution.mpi-inf.mpg.de/timelines/

CIKM'11, October 24–28, 2011, Glasgow, Scotland, UK.

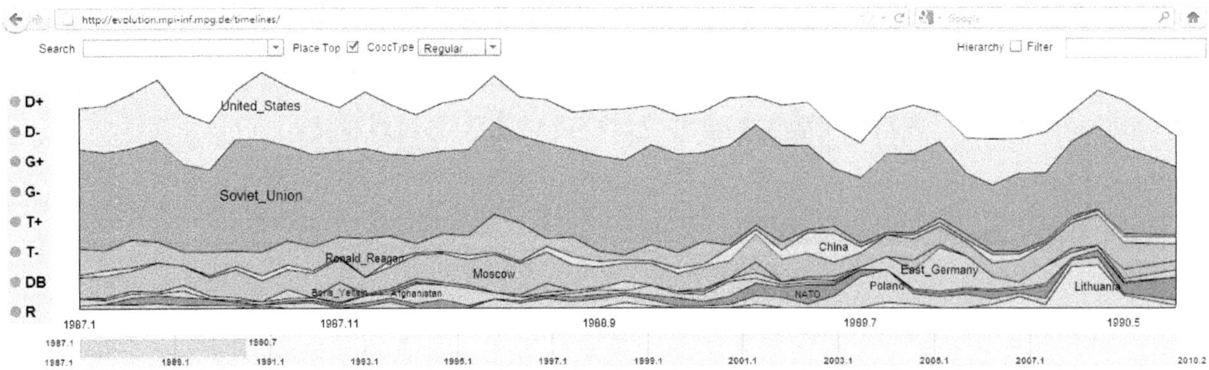

Figure 1: Screenshot of Entity Timelines

We processed the NYTimes collection of news articles to discover and track the evolution of named entities. The collection consists of more than 1.8M news articles published from 1987 to 2007; the extracted DB contains 50M named entities. For a given entity, evolving timelines aggregate named entities co-occurring in the articles and allow to investigate its evolution with the help of stacked displays. Tight connection to the YAGO ontology allows us to both effectively extract named entities and offer a rich data interaction capabilities. Analysts can look at different projections of the data (e.g., evolving timelines for George_W._Bush and Mikhail_Gorbachev), contrast them (e.g., investigate the timeline of George_W._Bush where all named entities from Mikhail_Gorbachev are removed from the visualization), drill down/roll up the data based on the YAGO hierarchies (e.g., aggregate individual politicians into left, center, and right wing politicians, etc), or use advanced filtering techniques (include named entities that are a part of a selected grouping or related to a given keyword).

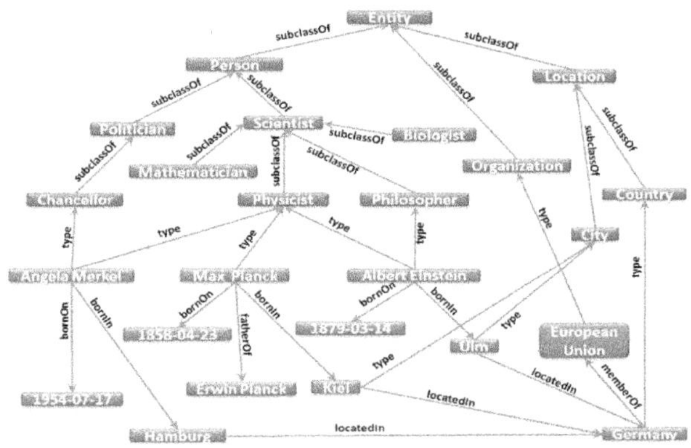

Figure 2: An illustrative example of the YAGO knowledge base

2. YAGO ONTOLOGY

The YAGO ontology [4] is a comprehensive database of human knowledge. It consists of facts extracted from Wikipedia stored in machine readable format. The ontology includes information on millions of individual named entities (e.g., Max_Planck, European_Union, and Berlin), hundred of millions facts about them (e.g., Max_Plank hasNationality Germany, bornOn 1858-04-24), has hundred thousands of classes/types (e.g., Politician is a subclass of Person), and has an overall accuracy of around 95%. The ontology forms a directed graph (Figure 2) and can be used for numerous information retrieval and data analysis tasks. In this paper we use the link structure between the entities for named entity disambiguation (the bottom of the figure) and the subclass hierarchy for advanced grouping and filtering (the top of the figure). For these tasks any general purpose ontology like DBpedia or FreeBase can be used. However, since entities were extracted from a large text corpora (and therefore, small named entity disambiguation errors could accumulate into large overall errors), we opted for an ontology with a (probably) lower coverage but very high precision.

3. NAMED ENTITY EXTRACTION, DISAMBIGUATION, AND CANONICALIZATION

Named entities are predefined categories such as the names of persons (e.g., Mikhail Gorbachev), organizations (United Nations), locations (Moscow), expressions of times (Morning), quantities (a pound), monetary values (a buck), percentages (a half), etc. Extraction of named entities is a tough problem due to different spelling and errors (Michail vs. Mikhail), different formatting (Gorbachev, Mikhail) and different meanings (pound may refer to the mass or currency), or they may be vaguely expressed and therefore hard to identify (capital of the country). A number of different attempts exist to extract named entities from (English language) texts using grammar based or statistical methods. Our work is the first attempt to perform the extraction and analysis on a large scale data and connect them to the entities in an ontology.

Conceptually, our named entity finder processes the English text in five stages: extraction (stage 1 and 2), disambiguation (stage 3 and 4) and canonicalization (stage 5). In the first stage we identify words that are interesting and may be a part (substring) of the named entity. This can be done using a dictionary, pattern matching, or the Stanford Entity Recognizer (NER). In the second stage we identify all super-strings that the interesting word is a part of and are either YAGO named entities or found in the Wikipedia anchor texts pointing to articles describing YAGO entities. This produces a list of candidates, where each interesting word is mapped to one or more named entities. In the third stage we identify the interesting words that have only one named entity associated with it (i.e., do not require disambiguation). We call them *final entities*. In the fourth step we filter out and disambiguate the remaining named entities with the help of the final entities and the YAGO ontology. The disambiguation score of a candidate entity increases if there is a link between the candidate and the final entity in the ontology. Finally, for each interesting word we pick the entities with the highest score.

As an example, consider sentence "At Waterloo Napoleon faced his final battle against Wellington and Blücher". With the identified and extracted named entities, the sentence becomes "At Battle_of_Waterloo Napoleon_I_of_France faced his final battle against Arthur_Wellesley,_1st_Duke_of_Wellington and Gebhard_Leberecht_von_Blücher". The words "Waterloo, Napoleon, Wellington, Blücher" are identified as interesting. Battle_of_Waterloo, Waterloo,_Ontario, Waterloo_(ABBA_song), Waterloo,_Iowa and other 207 named entities form a set of candidates for Waterloo. Similarly, Wellington, Wellington_Rugby_Football_Union, Wellington_Firebirds, Arthur_Wellesley,_1st_-Duke_of_Wellington and other 205 named entities form a set of candidates for Wellington. YAGO link structure between the candidates allows us to identify Battle_of_Waterloo and Arthur_Wellesley,_1st_Duke_of_Wellington as the best matching named entities.

4. ENTITY TIMELINES

We visualize the evolution of named entities as a timeline using the paradigm of stacked areas [3] and river metaphor [1]. Given a named entity as a query, we visualize other entities co-occurring in the same Web page, document, or tweet as stacks (polygonal areas) in XY coordinates. The time is mapped to the X coordinate, while the Y coordinate (the area of the stack) depicts how prominent the associated named entity is to the query.

Figure 1 shows a screen shot of the entity timeline for Mikhail-_Gorbachev (i.e., the area of the stack depicts the frequency of the co-occurring entities in the articles over time). The tool clearly identifies key events and their relevance to the named entity. For example, Mikhail_Gorbachev is associated mostly with Soviet_Union and United_States in time window 1987–1990. At the beginning of the time window Ronald_Reagan is prominently seen in the timeline, since both politicians were the key figures in the ending of the Cold War. Further, one can see the end of Ronald_Reagan's and the beginning of the George_W.-_Bush presidency; activity of East_Germany (fall of Berlin Wall and reunification of Germany), followed by the independence of Lithuania and the other Baltic states. Using the visual analytics tool one can also see such events as the collapse of the Soviet-_Union, the increase of the weight of Russia, the rise of new politicians (presidents Boris_Yeltsin and Vladimir_Putin), 9/11, diagnose of the Alzheimer's disease and death of Ronald_Reagan, and raise of political influence of the Russian oil company Gazprom.

The tool allows numerous interactions with the visualization and multiple displays over the data. Features of the tool span from basic navigational interactions, like selecting timelines and windows for different named entities, to more advanced, like contrasting or drill down/roll up of timelines. Both single (one timeline) and multiple linked displays (two timelines aligned vertically) are supported. Due to a more efficient use of space, single display visualizations are more appropriate for detailed analysis of an evolution of one named entity, while linked, side-by-side displays are more appropriate for comparisons and contrasting.

4.1 Contrasting Timelines

Pre-processing of the documents and canonicalization of named entities allows effective comparison and contrasting of two timelines. Let us consider the timelines of Jacques_Chirac (President of France during 1995–2007) and Gerhard_Schröder (Chancellor of Germany and the leader of the Social Democratic Party during 1998–2005). Both timelines share a significant number of named entities, e.g., Russia, Kosovo, UK, and NATO (Figure 3, top), indicating the similarities of German and French politics. However there are a number of entities that are prominent in Chirac's timiline but not in Schröder's (e.g., Austria, Palestine, Libya, and Syria, see the middle in the figure), and prominent in Schröder's but not in Chirac's (Saxony, Social-_Democrats, VW, and Tony_Blair) The contrasting functionality allows to emphasize these similarities and differences in one visualization.

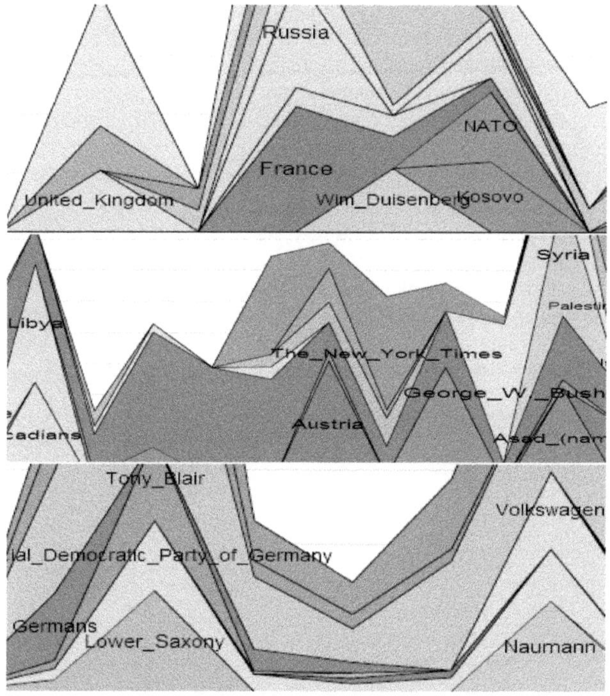

Figure 3: J. Chirac vs. G. Schröder: intersection (top), Chirac\Schröder (middle) and Schröder\Chirac (bottom)

Conceptually, contrasting functionality takes two sets of time series (e.g., the time series of Chirac and the time series of Schröder) and performs a general set operation over the series applying a "join" function to the counts. This can be the set union (all tuples from both subsets are grouped by co-occurring named entity and month, where the corresponding counts are summed up), set intersection (the minimum or maximum is taken from the corresponding counts), set difference (the count of one is subtracted from the other), etc. Since the ranges of the counts may vary significantly (e.g., the timeline of a popular entity may exhibit counts in the range of thousands, while the timeline of a less popular entity be in the range of tens) we rescale the counts for a better comparison.

Contrasting timelines can be visualized in single or multiple displays. In a single display the contrast (union, xor, etc.) is shown, while in multiple displays the standard timelines are placed side-by-side. Multiple displays share the visual style: the colors, order of the co-occurring entities and the position and the size of time window are the same. Moving the mouse over a stack area highlights the corresponding stacks in the timelines of both entities.

4.2 Semantic Drill Down/Roll Up Using Type Hierarchies

YAGO ontology has a comprehensive type system and it stores a rich set of attributes of entities. For example, YAGO knows 450 facts about `Mikhail_Gorbachev`, 779 facts about `Albert_Einstein`, and 885 facts about `United_Arab_Emirates`. YAGO canonicalization of named entities facilitates easy integration of the information systems and the use of the information available in the ontology.

We use the YAGO type hierarchies to define and compute semantic drill down and roll up over the named entity domain. Similar to the horizontal drill down/roll up, where for each named entity the counts of a range of months were summed up, semantic drill down/roll up sums up the counts of named entities belonging to the same group for each month. For example, since according to the YAGO ontology `Mikhail_Gorbachev` is a member of the type hierarchy `politician → leader → person → entity`, therefore if the semantic roll up is applied, then the frequency (counts) of `Mikhail_Gorbachev` are added together with the frequency of the other `politicians`.

Semantic roll up for `Gerhard_Schröder` during (top) and after retirement from politics (bottom) is illustrated in Figure 4. Roll-up shows the change: previously Schröder was affiliated with `country` and `state`, while afterwards groupings related to `companies` are more prominent.

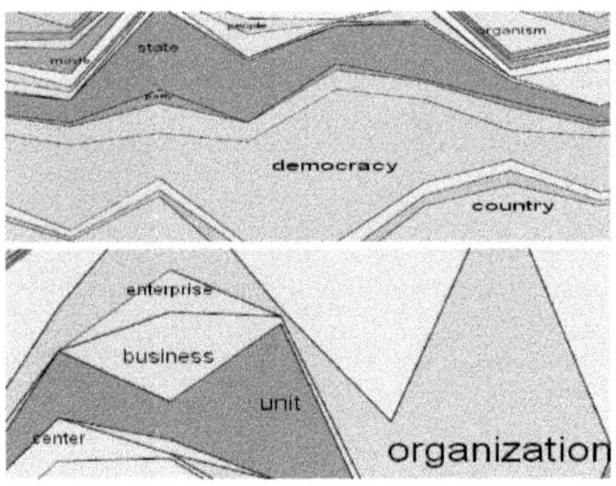

Figure 4: The roll up of `Gerhard_Schröder`

4.3 Ranking Type Hierarchies and Advanced Filtering

YAGO offers multiple ways to roll up/drill down hierarchies for almost all entities. For example, `Mikhail_Gorbachev` has the following

```
Soviet politician→politician
  →leader→person→entity
Russians of Ukrainian descent→person→entity
Russian atheist→atheist→disbeliever
  →nonreligious person→person→entity
Moscow State University alumni→alumnus
  →scholar→intellectual→person→entity
```

and other 15 hierarchies, `Watergate_scandal` has five, `Soviet Union` has 17, `David_Bowie` has 44, and `Albert_Einstein` has 94 type hierarchies. In general, the rich hierarchy system gives a possibility for customized and fine-adjusted aggregations. Since our timelines consists of multiple (thousands of) named entities, using all hierarchies of a named entity for grouping would result in a lattice that is similar to the one of multidimensional hierarchical heavy hitters [2]. Instead, here we aim to find *the best* hierarchy for each named entity and incorporate all these hierarchies into one (Figure 5).

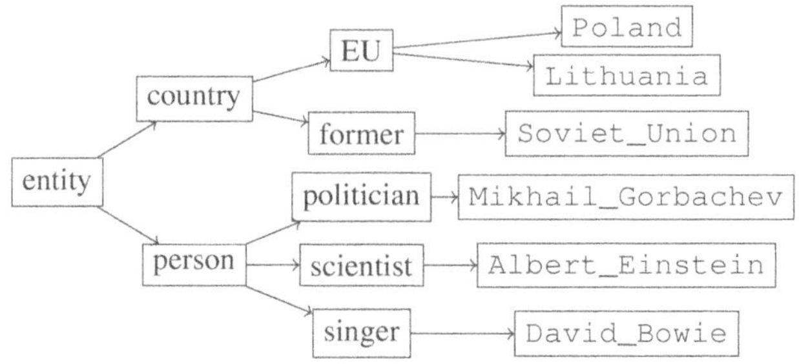

Figure 5: A (simplified) hierarchy for `Lithuania, Poland, Soviet_Union, Mikhail_Gorbachev, Albert_Einstein`, **and** `David_Bowie`

We identify the best hierarchy for a named entity using a number of heuristics. First, we investigated the evolution of Wikipedia categories of named entities in the corresponding Wikipedia articles and picked the hierarchies with the earliest and most long-lasting categories in the Wikipedia history. This allowed us to focus only on the most prominent hierarchies of the named entities. Then we carefully applied an additional filtering step using the term frequency scores of nouns and words of the abstract from the Wikipedia article (content up to the table of contents). We also tried to exploit the inverse document frequencies (selects very specialized paths like `People_from_Stavropol→person→entity` for `Mikhail_Gorbachev`) and number of named entities in the group of the hierarchies (suggests considerably different paths for similar named entities like `Poland` and `Lithuania`) but the results were less effective.

The computed hierarchy is used in semantic drill down/roll up as well as for advanced filtering. In the latter case the analyst may select a (number of) sub-hierarchies and filter out all named entities that fall outside the selected hierarchy.

Acknowledgments

This work is supported by the 7th Framework ICT programme of the European Union through the large-scale integrating project on Living Knowledge. We thank K. Berberich, S. Bedathur, E. Lewis-Kelham, J. Hoffart, A. Anand, and M. Spaniol for valuable discussions and comments.

5. REFERENCES

[1] S. Havre, E. Hetzler, P. Whitney, and L. Nowell. Themeriver: Visualizing thematic changes in large document collections. *IEEE Transactions on Visualization and Computer Graphics*, 8(1):9–20, 2002.

[2] A. Mazeika, M. H. Böhlen, and D. Trivellato. Analysis and interpretation of visual hierarchical heavy hitters of binary relations. In *ADBIS*, pages 168–183. 2008.

[3] L. Shi, F. Wei, S. Liu, L. Tan, X. Lian, and M. X. Zhou. Understanding text corpora with multiple facets. In *IEEE VAST*, pages 99–106, 2010.

[4] F. M. S. , G. Kasneci, and G. Weikum. YAGO: a core of semantic knowledge. In *WWW*, pages 697–706, 2007.

[5] T. Tylenda, M. Sozio, and G. Weikum. Einstein: physicist or vegetarian? Summarizing semantic type graphs for knowledge discovery. In *WWW*, pages 273–276. ACM, 2011.

PICASSO – Automated Soundtrack Suggestion for Multi-Modal Data *

Aleksandar Stupar
Saarland University
Saarbrücken, Germany
astupar@mmci.uni-saarland.de

Sebastian Michel
Saarland University
Saarbrücken, Germany
smichel@mmci.uni-saarland.de

ABSTRACT

We demonstrate PICASSO, a novel approach to soundtrack recommendation. Given text, video, or image documents, PICASSO selects the best fitting music pieces, out of a given set of files, for instance, a user's personal mp3 collection. This task, commonly referred to as soundtrack suggestion, is non-trivial as it requires a lot of human attention and a good deal of experience, with master pieces distinguished, e.g., with the Academy Award for Best Original Score. We put forward PICASSO to solve this task in a fully automated way. We address the problem by extracting the required information, in form of music/screenshot samples, from available contemporary movies, making the training set easily obtainable. The training set is further extended with information acquired from movie scripts and subtitles, giving us a richer description of the action and atmosphere expressed in a particular movie scene. Although the number of applications for this approach is very large, we focus on two selected applications. First, we consider recommendation of the soundtrack for the slide show generation based on the given set of images. Second, we consider recommending a soundtrack as the background music for given audio books.

Categories and Subject Descriptors

H.3.1 [**Content Analysis and Indexing**]: [abstracting methods, indexing methods]; H.3.3 [**Information Search and Retrieval**]: [search process, selection process]; H.5.5 [**Sound and Music Computing**]: [methodologies and techniques]; I.4 [**Image Processing and Computer Vision**]: Applications

General Terms

Algorithms, Experimentation, Human Factors

*This work has been supported by the Excellence Cluster on Multimodal Computing and Interaction (MMCI).

CIKM'11, October 24–28, 2011, Glasgow, Scotland, UK.

1. INTRODUCTION

Multimedia content is visible in almost all areas of our life, ranging from entertainment and marketing purposes to education and lifestyle. With the wide spread use of digital (video) cameras, more and more embedded in regular smartphones with surprisingly high quality, users, formerly being only consumers of multimedia content, now become producers themselves. Information is recorded in form of simple pictures, music pieces, speech, and videos, but also in form of textual content. The combination of these multi-modal information poses interesting challenges but also new advantages for the interaction with consumers. One example, which we also consider in this demonstration, is to enrich audio books with soundtracks played in the background that underpin the atmosphere of the situation described.

Audio books present a very convenient way for people to enjoy reading, or better said listening to, a book while they are occupied with manual, often repetitive, tasks that require low mental attention. While sometimes audio books can be monotone, because of the single person reading the book, we can make them more compelling by playing some music in the background. Carefully selected music can emphasize the atmosphere and the plot of the book enhancing its expressiveness and engaging the user to deeper concentration on the read material. Needless to say that inappropriate music, accompanying the reader, can easily ruin the feeling originally transferred by the book. This renders the problem of selecting an appropriate music piece for the background music highly sensitive and complex.

A carefully selected background music can also emphasize a *slide show presentation* of images taken, e.g., during the last vacations or conference trips. In particular for product advertisements, this can be of crucial importance to the product's success and often the soundtrack stays in the peoples' mind as being representative for the product.

Choosing a well suited song requires a large and diverse dataset of music pieces to choose from. This requirement is, however, satisfied by almost all users' personal music collections, with users having more than hundreds of songs already on their portable mp3 players. Having a high quality recommendation system provides users with the ability to select songs out of small subset of recommended songs and still obtain a nice soundtrack.

The problem described resembles, on an abstract level, the problem of movie directors trying to choose a soundtrack for their movies, with master pieces awarded the prestigious Academy Award for the Best Original Score. PICASSO [13] aims at harvesting this human expertise for the soundtrack recommendation task. Collecting such information from multiple movies results in a knowledge base that is of great use for a variety of recommendation tasks, as we will demonstrate in several use cases.

2. RELATED WORK

Introducing interaction into audio books, as a means to involve listeners more with content of the book, is done in [12]. In this approach, user interact with the system at predefined points of the book, determining which part of the book is going to be read next. This kind of interaction adds an additional task for the creators of the audio book to ensure that all possible read sequences make sense, according to the story.

Recommending soundtracks for a slide show capturing a given set of images is also addressed in [8], but with the single focus on impressionism paintings. As the main goal of impressionism painters was to express their feelings through painting, matching between images and songs is done based on the detected emotions in the image and in the song.

Defining which characteristics a music piece should have to accompany a video of the scenery taken by a camera installed in the car, is done in [4]. These characteristics dictate the generation of the music from midi files, which is then played to car drivers. The correlation between three features of video and three features of background music, both quantized to three levels, is calculated for a set of documentary movies. This correlation information is later used for the purpose of generating music from midi files while the video is taken. Rather than limiting ourselves to music from midi files and scenery images or impressionism painting, we aim at providing a soundtrack recommendation system that can cope with any user specified set of songs and that can handle a large variety of query images.

3. OVERVIEW OF THE APPROACH

The soundtrack recommendation in PICASSO is achvieved using an algorithm based on two levels of similarity search. They key idea is to sample movies to obtain pairs of the form (screenshot image, music) and (plot/speech, music). For a given input query (image or text), we use the learned information to find the best fitting music, occurring in a movie, and then to find the best fitting song in our music database w.r.t. that movie soundtrack snippet. The detailed description of the soundtrack recommendation for images in PICASSO together with a user study can be found in [13]. Additionally, we extended PICASSO to support soundtrack recommendations for audio books, which we present in this demonstration.

Both images and text are represented as points in a multi dimensional vector space, text being represented using the Vector Space Model (VSM) and images being represented by the feature vectors. In the vector space model, each word is considered as one dimension with documents being represented by different quantities for each dimension, based on the number of word occurrences. The image feature vectors depend on color, edge counts, edge orientations, etc.

Independently whether the query is an image or a text document, we do a K-Nearest Neighbor search in the first step to find the most similar documents to the query, i.e., neighbors in the vector space. If the query is a text then the text index is used and if the query is an image then the im-

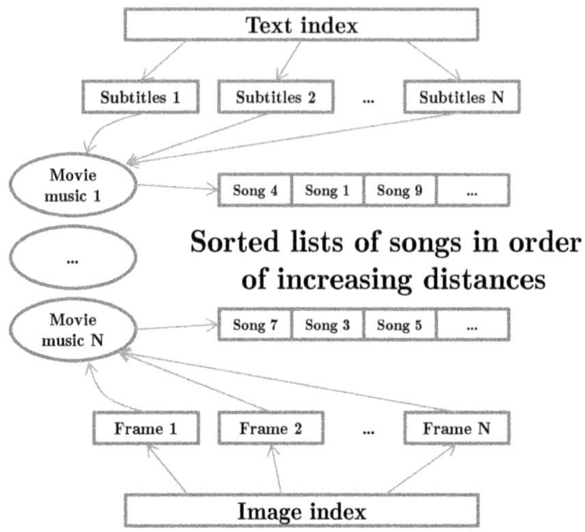

Figure 1: PICASSO - recommendation index

age index is used. In the second step, a similarity search is employed to find the most similar songs to the music pieces sampled from the movie. Co-occurrences of images and text with the music in the movies is used to link these two similarity measures together into a single fitness measure, used later to rank songs for the final recommendation.

The distances of the songs to the music samples extracted from the movies, used in the second step of the algorithm, together with the co-occurrence information are query independent and can both be pre-computed. Hence, we differentiate two phases of processing, the preprocessing phase and the query answering phase. The preprocessing phase is also referred to as the knowledge extraction phase, as movies are processed to extract information which are later used for query answering.

3.1 Preprocessing Phase

To extract the required knowledge from movies, we first need to identify those parts that contain music. For this purpose, we use a trained Naive Bayes classifier, labeling each second of the movie with either "speech" or "music". Additionally, we obtain a confidence value for each such label. We use the open source tool Marsyas [14] for the classifier training as well as for classification task later on. To ensure that there is no noise in the data produced, we consider only those parts that are classified as music with the confidence value of at least 95%. Additionally, music parts that are shorter than 5 seconds are not considered in further processing as they do not carry enough information to be meaningful for the similarity measurement with the songs. Also, music parts longer than 10 seconds are broken into multiple parts to avoid that the content is too specific for further similarity measurements.

We precompute the similarity between each extracted music part of the movie and each of the potential soundtrack songs. For each music part extracted from the movie the complete list of songs is stored in decreasing order of their mutual similarity. The similarity between music parts and the songs is calculated using Chroma, MFCC, spectral centroid, spectral rolloff, spectral flux, and time domain zero crossings feature vectors. Distances between different types of feature vectors are combined to a single distance measure using the standard score (z-score). We handle the similarity matching in the time domain by using the Dynamic Time Warping technique. Further reference on music feature vectors and Dynamic Time Warping can be found in [10].

3.1.1 Images

The frames of the movies are taken for every second of the identified music parts of that movie. Color Structure, Color Layout, Scalable Color, and Edge Histogram [3] are a subset of the MPEG-7 features that we use for the image to image similarity measure. We extract these features out of each of the frames taken from the movie and use them to index frames into an image index. A link to the corresponding music piece, sampled from the movie, is also stored for each of the taken frames.

3.1.2 Subtitles

Subtitles and script information together with the music from the movies are used as a knowledge base for recommending soundtracks for textual queries. Subtitles are easily obtainable online in a structured format providing us with the text and approximate time information indicating when this text is being spoken in the movie. This enables us to match the text of subtitles with the music in the movie that are occurring in close points in time. For each music part of the movie, identified in the previous steps, a time window is constructed of 10 seconds before the music part and 10 seconds after the music part, and all subtitles in that time window are considered related to this part. Before indexing these subtitles in the text index we extend them with scripts information if it is available.

Scripts are also available online providing us usually with a semi structured document, where the structure emphasizes the difference between spoken parts of the movie and scenery descriptions. For each subtitle of the movie we try to match it with the spoken part of the script and then extend it with the scene description preceding the spoken part. In case multiple subtitles are indexed for the same music part, the scene description is used only once.

The result of the preprocessing phase is a recommendation index, illustrated in Figure 1. As we can see, subtitles with script extensions are indexed in a text index and frames from the movie are indexed in an image index. We use the Lucene framework [9] for the text index and a Locality Sensitive Hashing (LSH) [5] index for images. Both text index and image index contain links to the corresponding music parts extracted from the movies, which further have a list of songs sorted in decreasing order of the similarity to that music part.

3.2 Query Answering Phase

Once the recommendation index is constructed in the preprocessing phase, we can use it to recommend songs. The procedure for soundtrack suggestion is the same for the image and the text case. For the image case we consider the case of a single image query first and then generalize to queries containing multiple images.

To avoid a negative influence of outliers on the final result, we use the top-K most similar documents with result smoothing, as follows. First, the appropriate index (i.e., text or images) is searched for the top-K most similar documents according to the submitted query (i.e., image of text). We assign the value of $1/k$ to each of the returned documents, where k is the rank of the document. For each of the documents, the corresponding music part is retrieved together with the list of songs for that music part. As mentioned, this list is already sorted such that the top-K songs, being the most similar ones, are taken into further consideration. The score of the document is then propagated to each of the retrieved songs and the average score for each song is the score used for final ranking. As the same songs can appear at the beginning of the list for different music parts, the final number of songs ranked for recommendation ranges between K and K^2.

In the case that *multiple images* are submitted as a query, we first use the procedure describe before to recommend songs for each individual image and then combine the results. We approach the problem of combining the individual recommendations as a problem of group recommendation [1]. We use two strategies for group recommendation, *average position* and *least misery*. The average position strategy gives us a new score for each song defined as an average position of that song in all individual lists, while the least misery strategy uses the maximum position as the new score. New scores are then used for re-ranking the songs to a final list. Dividing images into subgroups, based on the similarity of individual recommendations, is enabled by calculating a modified Spearman's footrule distance [7] between them and using it as an input to a hierarchical clustering algorithm that finds clusters of images with similar soundtrack recommendations.

3.3 Performances and Scalability

In the current setting we have indexed 50 movies together with 275 songs, which results in an index size of only $276.3MB$. The size of the index is low due to the fact that only the extracted features are stored and not the entire documents themselves, hence, we can currently easily keep it in main memory. On a standard quad core Xeon CPU W3530 2.8GHz, recommending songs for a single image takes about $650ms$, with the most time (i.e., around $450ms$) spent on extracting the image's features. It takes approximately $180ms$ to answer a textual query containing around 400 words. Answering multiple queries can be easily parallelized on a single machine as the index is only being read and, hence, no locking between different threads is needed.

Ultimately, PICASSO would be implemented as an online service and hence has to cope with many simultaneous queries. For increased throughput, we can, as the index is very compact, replicate the index to all of the machines in the cluster and then use *any* machine to answer the query. If the case of index size growth large , the index itself can also be split to many machines, where the query results for each of the sub-indices can be simply merged at one node.

However, recommending songs from a collection provided by the individual users would pose an additional challenge on how the music is processed, as uploading music can cause both copyright and bandwidth problems. In principle, both problems can be avoided by transfering only the feature vectors to the server, once they are extracted on the user's machine, although this is both time and resource concuming for the user. Leaving us with the option to have as many as possible songs preprocessed on the server but to use only the ones matching the users' songs, where the match is done based on the name of the song and the author.

4. DEMONSTRATION DESCRIPTION

For the demonstration, we will provide the conference participants with the opportunity to listen to soundtracks recommended for audio books as well as for given images.

For the set of songs from which our system chooses soundtracks, we use 275 songs downloaded from the music2ten site [11] , as all of the songs are copyright free and are given away free of charge by their creators, as stated on the site.

We focus on two use cases of soundtrack recommendation, the audio book case and the slide show case.

4.1 Audio Book Case

For the audio books case we have currently selected eight well known books for our demonstration purpose such as Robinson Crusoe, The Adventures of Sherlock Holmes and Le Fantome de l' Opera. These audio books can be found online on the audio books site [2], and they are also free of charge.

We select one paragraph of text out of each book, approximately one and a half minute of duration in the corresponding audio book and recommend soundtracks for each of them. We mix together the speech of the selected paragraph of the audio book with the recommended songs as background music. To avoid overwhelming the users with all top K recommendations, we use the first and the fifth ranked recommended soundtrack. To provide comparability, we mix the speech from the book together with a randomly selected song from our dataset. These three songs mixed with the audio book section are provided to the users, together with the audio book without background music. An additional front web page is constructed containing links to the pages of each ot the eight mentioned books, as shown in Figure 2 on the left.

For experiencing soundtrack suggestions for plain text (i.e., non audio books), we will provide users with the opportunity to interact directly with the part of the system that recommends soundtracks for given query text. Users will have the chance to enter some text directly in our system, by means of a web page, and after processing will get a selection of five songs as soundtrack. Users will be able to listen to the recommended songs on the same page, showing the query and the recommended songs. Additionally, we will select small sections out of twenty well known books as a template text queries, as test cases.

4.2 Slide Show Case

For the slide show case, we give users the option to upload their own images to the PICASSO system. The system then employs the group recommendation strategy, as described in the Section 3.2, and recommends 5 songs for this group of uploaded images. Uploaded images, together with the recommended songs are presented to the user on a single page, where user is able to play the songs and see the uploaded images. As an additional option, users can select if the system should partition the group of images into subgroups based on the similarity of recommendations and then recommend 5 songs to each of the subgroups. In this case, each partition is represented as a group of images and 5 recommended songs in a separate column of the results page.

As most participants of the conference will not bring along their digital camera with images during the demonstration session, we create a predefined set of images that users will be able to use for soundtrack recommendation, as shown in Figure 2 on the right. Users will be able to choose any subset of these images as input to our system, by simply uploading only the subset that they are interested in.

Figure 2: PICASSO demonstration site - Audio books (left), Images (right)

For users that do not want to spend time on uploading the images to the system and listen to all recommendations, we will create four slide shows with the background music incorporated. These slide shows will be playable in the form of the movie on the user's demand.

Results for one audio book, one slide show, and one video can be found under `http://picasso.mmci.uni-saarland.de/demo/`. The soundtrack recommendation for the video in this case is done as a soundtrack recommendation for the set of images extracted from the video.

5. REFERENCES

[1] Sihem Amer-Yahia, et al. Group recommendation: Semantics and efficiency. *PVLDB*, 2009.

[2] Audiobooks online. `http://www.audiobooks.org/`.

[3] B. S. Manjunath, et al. Color and texture descriptors. *IEEE Trans. Circuits Syst. Video Techn.*, 2001.

[4] Marco Cristani, et al. Toward an automatically generated soundtrack from low-level cross-modal correlations for automotive scenarios. *ACM Multimedia*, 2010.

[5] Mayur Datar, et al. Locality-sensitive hashing scheme based on p-stable distributions. *Symposium on Computational Geometry*, 2004.

[6] Jan Engelen. A rapidly growing electronic publishing trend: Audiobooks for leisure and education. *ELPUB*, 2008.

[7] Ronald Fagin, et al. Comparing partial rankings. *SIAM J. Discrete Math.*, 2006.

[8] Cheng-Te Li and Man-Kwan Shan. Emotion-based impressionism slideshow with automatic music accompaniment. *ACM Multimedia*, 2007.

[9] Lucene framework. `http://lucene.apache.org`.

[10] Meinard Müller. *Information Retrieval for Music and Motion*. Springer, 2007.

[11] Music2ten. `http://music2ten.com`.

[12] Niklas Röber, et al. Interactive audiobooks: Combining narratives with game elements. *TIDSE*, 2006.

[13] Aleksandar Stupar and Sebastian Michel. PICASSO - to sing you must close your eyes and draw. *SIGIR*, 2011.

[14] George Tzanetakis. Music analysis, retrieval and synthesis of audio signals marsyas. *ACM Multimedia*, 2009.

P2Prec: A Social-Based P2P Recommendation System

Fady Draidi
LIRMM
Montpellier, France
Fady.Draidi@lirmm.fr

Esther Pacitti
LIRMM
Montpellier, France
Esther.Pacitti@lirmm.fr

Didier Parigot
INRIA
Sophia Antipolis, France
Didier.Parigot@inria.fr

Guillaume Verger
INRIA
Montpellier, France
Guillaume.Verger@inria.fr

ABSTRACT

P2Prec is a social-based P2P recommendation system for large-scale content sharing that leverages content-based and social-based recommendation. The main idea is to recommend high quality documents related to query topics and contents held by *useful* friends (of friends) of the users, by exploiting friendship networks. We have implemented a prototype of P2Prec using the Shared-Data Overlay Network (SON), an open source development platform for P2P networks using web services, JXTA and OSGi. In this paper, we describe the demo of P2Prec's main services (installing P2Prec peers, initializing peers, gossiping topics of interest among friends, key-word querying for contents) using our prototype implemented as an application of SON.

Categories and Subject Descriptors

H.3.4 [**Systems and Software**]: Distributed systems, H.3.3 [**Information Search and Retrieval**]: Search process, H.3.1 [**Content Analysis and Indexing**]: Indexing methods.

General Terms

Algorithms, Experimentation

1. INTRODUCTION

The general problem we address is large-scale content sharing for on-line communities. Consider, for instance, a scientific community (e.g., in bio-informatics, physics or environmental science) where community members are willing to share large amounts of documents (including images, experimental data, etc) stored in their local servers. Assume also that they don't want to lose control over their data at a central site. A promising solution is to organize community members in a peer-to-peer (P2P) overlay network, with the advantages of decentralized control, peer autonomy and scalability.

Locating contents based on content ids in a P2P overlay network is now well solved (see e.g. [5]). However, the problem with current P2P content-sharing systems is that the users themselves, i.e., their interest or expertise in specific topics, or their rankings of documents they have read, are simply ignored. In other words, what is missing is a recommendation service that, given a query, can recommend relevant documents by exploiting user information.

Sinha et al. [10] have shown that in general users prefer the advices coming from known friends in terms of quality and trust because usually users trust their friends' advices. In most of existing P2P solutions, friendship links are extracted from user's behaviors [2], or are established based on explicit trust declaration [9]. To enrich these solutions, we exploit the fact that users who store similar contents are potential friends. Therefore, our solution leverages between content-based and social-based recommendations over a P2P overlay.

P2Prec[1] is a social-based P2P recommendation system for large-scale content sharing [4]. The main idea is to recommend high quality documents related to query topics and contents hold by *useful* friends (of friends) of the users, by exploiting friendship networks. Our recommendation model relies on a distributed graph, where each node represents a user (peer) labelled with the contents it stores and its topics of interests. The topics each peer is interested in are automatically calculated by analyzing the documents the peer holds. Peers become *relevant* for a topic if they hold a certain number of highly rated documents on this topic. A peer *v* becomes useful to a peer *u*, if *u*'s topics of interest and *v*'s relevant topics are overlapped. To exploit friendship links, we rely on Friend-Of-A-Friend (FOAF) descriptions (http://www.foaf-project.org). To disseminate information about relevant peers, we rely on gossip algorithms that provide scalability, robustness, simplicity and load balancing. In addition, we propose an efficient query routing algorithm that selects the best peers to recommend documents based on users' useful friends and query topics. At the query's initiator, recommendations are selectively chosen based on similarity, rates and popularity or other recommendation criteria.

We have implemented a prototype of P2Prec by using the Shared-Data Overlay Network (SON) (http://www-sop.inria.fr/teams/zenith/SON), an open source development platform for P2P networks using web services, JXTA and OSGi (http://www.osgi.org). SON components communicate by asynchronous message passing to provide weak coupling between system entities. To scale up and ease deployment, we rely on a Distributed Hash Table (DHT) for publishing and discovering services or data.

CIKM'11, October 24–28, 2011, Glasgow, Scotland, UK,

[1] Work partially funded by the Dataring project of the Agence Nationale de la Recherche.

In this paper, we describe the demo of P2Prec's main services (installing and initializing P2Prec peers, gossiping topics of interest among friends, key-word querying for contents) using our prototype implemented as an application of SON.

2. OVERVIEW OF P2Prec

Centralized systems recommender systems (RS) rely on the ratings that users provide [1]. The advents of Web2.0 tools and the growing popularity of online social networks have led to the development of social-based RS that use users' social data such as friends, trust, etc. to provide recommendations [9]. These systems exploit the preferences and relations of users' friends (of friends) [2] or the trust relations [8] between users to aggregate the neighbors of each user. Then the recommendations are computed based on the ratings that have been given by those neighbors.

P2Prec's recommendation model is expressed based on a graph $G = (D,U,E,T)$, where D is the set of shared documents, U is the set of users $u_1,...u_n$ corresponding to autonomous peers $p_1,...p_n$, E is the set of edges between the users such that there is an edge $e(u,v)$ if users u and v are friends, and T is the domain of topics. Each user $u \in U$ is associated with a set of topics of interest $T_u \subset T$, and a set of relevant topics $T_u^r \subset T_u$ extracted locally from the documents u has rated. The rating that has been given by a user u on document doc is denoted by $rate_{doc}^u$.

In our approach, we use Latent Dirichlet Allocation (LDA) [3] to automatically model the topics in the system, which in turn are used to extract users' relevant topics of interest. LDA processing is done in two steps: training at a global level and inference at the local level. The global level is given to a bootstrap server (BS), where BS aggregates a sample set of M documents from P2Prec participant peers. Then BS executes the LDA classifier program to get a set $T = \{t_1,..t_k\}$ of topics, where k is the number of topics. Each topic $t \in T$ contains a set of z words, where z is the total number of the unique words in M, and each of these words is associated with a weight value between 0 and 1. At the local level, user u performs LDA locally to extract the topics of its local documents, using the same set of topics T that were previously generated at the global level. LDA provides a vector of size k for each document doc, $V_{doc} = [w_{doc}^{t1},...,w_{doc}^{tk}]$, where w_{doc}^t is the weight of each topic $t \in T$ with respect to doc.

Users' relevant topics of interest are extracted based on a combination between documents' semantics and ratings. Once a user u extracted the V_{doc} for each $doc \in D_u$, it multiplies the $V_{doc} = [w_{doc}^{t1},...,w_{doc}^{tk}]$, by the rating $rate_{doc}^u$. Then, user u identifies for each topic $t \in T$ only the documents that are highly related to t. A document doc is considered highly related to topic t, if its weight in that topic w_{doc}^t multiplied by its rating $rate_{doc}^u$ exceeds a threshold value. Next, u counts how many documents are highly related to each topic $t \in T$. User u is considered interested in topic $t \in T_u$ if a percentage y of its local documents are highly related to topic t. Finally, u is considered a *relevant user* in topic $t \in T_u^r$ if it is interested in t and has a sufficient amount of documents that are highly related to topic t.

Each user $u \in U$ maintains a FOAF file that contains a description of its personal information, and friendship network. Personal information includes the extracted topics of interest, where each topic of interest $t \in T_u$ is associated with a Boolean value which indicates whether u is relevant in that topic. Friends information includes friends' name, links (URI) to their FOAF files, relevant (topics of interest), and trust levels. The trust level between user u and a friend v, denoted by $trust(u,v)$, is a real value within [0, 1], and it represents how much user u has faith in its friend v.

Furthermore, each user u establishes new friendships with users that are *useful* to u's queries, and if their friendship networks have high overlap with u's friendship network. A user v is considered *useful* to a user u, if v is a relevant user and a certain amount of v's relevant topics T_v^r are of interest for u. user u keeps locally (in its FOAF file) its useful friends and their corresponding relevant (topics of interests). User u exploits its useful friends (of friends) for recommendations.

To establish friendship and disseminate recommendation, we rely on gossip protocols [7] as follows. At each gossip exchange, each user u checks its gossip *local-view* to enquire whether there is any relevant user v that is useful to u, and its friendship networks have high overlap with u's friendship network. If it is the case, a demand of friendship is launched among u and v and the respective FOAF files are updated accordingly. FOAF files are used to support users' queries. Whenever a user submits a key-word query, the FOAF file is used as a directory to redirect the query to the top-k most adequate friends by taking into account similarities, relevance, usefulness and trust.

Finally, a key-word query q is associated with a TTL (Time To Live) and is routed recursively in a P2P top-k manner: once a query is submitted by u, it is forwarded to u's top-k useful and trustful friends. When a query is received at any peer, it is again redirected to its top-k useful and trustful friends, until TTL is reached. Each user v that received the query provides recommendations to u. The response to a query q is a recommendation that has been provided in a ranked list, based on a function that ranks each document according to its relevance with q, its popularity, the similarity and trust between q's initiator and responder v.

3. P2Prec IMPLEMENTATION

With SON, the development of a P2P application is done through the design and implementation of a set of components. Each component includes a non-functional code that provides the component services and a code component that provides the component logic (business code). The complex aspects of asynchronous distributed programming (non-functional code) are separated from code components and automatically generated. From a description of a component's services, the Component Generator (CG) automatically generates the non-functional code. Thus, the programmer does not deal with complex distributed programming aspects.

The basic infrastructure of SON is composed of a Component Manager (CM), a Publishing and Discovery Component (PDC), and a Connection Component (CC). The PDC allows publishing or discovering components on different peers using a DHT. The CC provides connection between remote components on peers. The CM performs the creation of new component instances and the connections between them.

To establish a connection between two components, the CM uses the services description of each component. At run-time, when a component A wants to connect with another component B, it must use the service `ConnectTo(A,B)` provided by the CM. As in the CM that created the component, the components are by default connected to the CM. To establish a connection between two components, the CM uses the services description to associate the services provided by component A with the services required by component B, and conversely.

After the connection process, the two components can communicate directly with each other without going through the CM. The advantage of this process is that it is done at run-time, thus avoiding each component to know statically the services of other components. In fact, each component can, on the fly, connect to any component. The assembly of components of a given application is not necessarily known statically and can evolve dynamically over time. Thus, the components are autonomous and independent.

The CM delegates the management of lists of remote components to the PDC. In the current version, we use the OpenChord DHT implementation (http://open-chord.sourceforge.net/) for the PDC, but nothing prevents us from using other implementations. For this purpose, an interface has been defined with the usual methods (`put (key,value) and get(key)`) that can be expected from a DHT. At each creation of a component, the CM publishes into this DHT the information for a remote component useful to connect to this component.

The Connection Component (CC) is a component that handles the communication between remote components. It opens the TCP connection between peers. It is based on the concept of virtual pipes introduced by JXTA technology (http://jxta.kenai.com/). This concept allows passing through a single TCP connection several logical communications (virtual pipes) between peers. Using this abstraction allows each component to open a virtual pipe to read messages sent to it. We identify a virtual pipe by a universally unique identifier (UUID).

SON is implemented in Java on top of OSGi components that provide all basic services for the lifecycle of our components, in particular, the deployment services. The launching of a SON application is defined through an OSGi configuration, which describes the application components.

3.1 P2Prec ARCHITECTURE

We developed P2Prec as a SON application (see http://www-sop.inria.fr/teams/zenith/p2prec/) with two components: the LDA component for the documents topics process and the P2Prec component for the recommendation process. For instance, the services of the P2Prec component are the services for passive and active propagation through gossip services (*gossip* and *gossipAnswer* services) and the queries services (*query* and *queryAnswer* services). There are two OSGi configurations, the Bootstrap Server (BS) configuration and the Client (the peer) configuration, as shown in Figure 1.

To run the P2Prec application, the BS must be started on a given machine (with a given IP address). This IP address will be used as the entry point into the P2Prec network for new peers. At the startup time, a new peer must first identify itself with the BS (*connect* service) and the BS is going to return the current set of all topics (*allTopics* service). Then within the local peer's LDA component and the current topics, the topics of each document is computed locally.

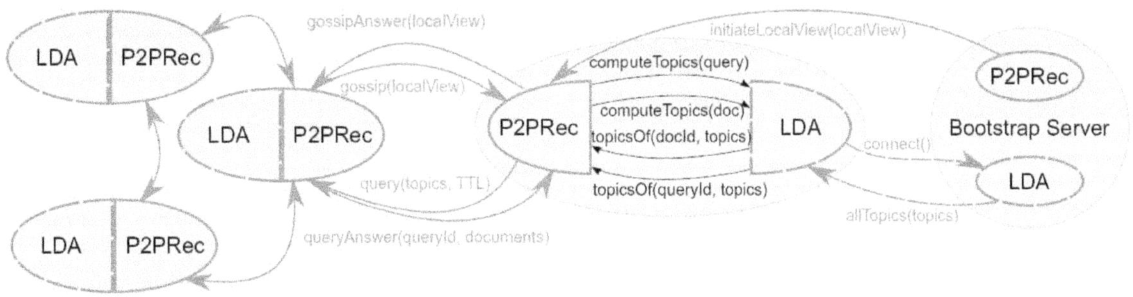

Figure 1: P2Prec Architecture.

After these steps, the peer can start the recommendation steps and documents discovery without any connection with the BS. Indeed, the research of topics of a new document (*computeTopic(doc)* service) and the computing of topics of a query (*computeTopic(query)* service) can be made locally with the local peer's LDA component. Depending on the evolution of documents on the P2Prec network, the BS may update the set of topics of documents, and inform the peers by broadcasting this new topic set (using the *allTopics* service).

4. P2Prec DEMONSTRATION

In this section we describe how the P2Prec services cooperate using scenarios based on the Ohsumed documents corpus [6] that has been widely used in IR. It is a set of 348566 references from MEDLINE, the on-line medical information database, consisting of titles or abstracts from 270 medical journals over a five year period (1987-1991). Our application is lightweight, meaning that no client needs to be downloaded to use it.

In order to couple the P2Prec core, made of OSGi configurations, with the chosen scenarios, we used the Google Web Toolkit (GWT: http://code.google.com/webtoolkit/) to build the user interface. This toolkit allows defining a client/server application written completely in Java that runs in a web browser. It automatically compiles the Java client code into HTML and JavaScript, and easily permits to use Java libraries. Therefore, all graphical interfaces of this demo are made of web pages and run in a classical browser. We show how the application works, from the global installation to the utilization by an end-user.

Installation In order to run a P2Prec peer properly, any user (at a peer) has to connect first to the Bootstrap Server (BS). Therefore we define a place the BS will run on. Every peer in the system will know its IP address. As the BS and any peer offer the same kind of services, we have defined two OSGi configurations for running P2Prec components: one as a BS, and one as a standard peer that will connect to the BS.

Initialization Each peer consists of a LDA part coupled with a Communication part (called P2Prec). As the demonstration starts, the BS is created, and so are several peers (30 of them). Each peer sends some of its documents, which are arbitrarily distributed among all peers, to the BS to perform LDA on a sample of all documents and to define the set of topics used in the network. Next, the BS informs all connected peers about the topics that are present in the network, and each peer indexes its own documents with the set of topics. Each peer is given an initial FOAF, which determines its friends in the network, and provides it information about them. It can now start gossiping with other peers, and the user belonging to the peer can send queries to discover documents. When connecting a new peer to the network, we show how it gets initial information in its FOAF file in two cases: (1) it has already joined the network in the past (i.e. it knows other peers); (2) it connects to the network for the first time.

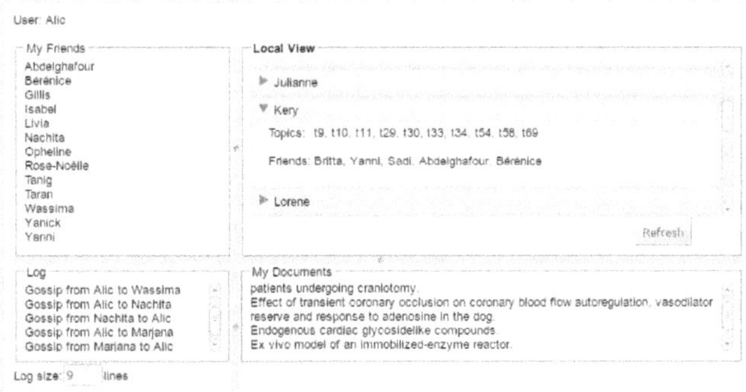

Figure 2: P2Prec Gossip Interface.

Gossiping The gossip service is at the heart of P2Prec, and is transparent to the end-user. While peers exchange gossiping messages, the system recommends new friendships to users. For the sake of the demonstration, we developed an interface showing what is internally happening during gossiping (see Figure 2). The interface shows the current friends of the user, the gossiping messages sent and received by the peer, the gossip local-view that permits to find friends, etc. We show how the gossip mechanism notifies the user that other users share the same interests, and ask her to add them to her friend list.

Figure 3: P2Prec Query Interface.

Querying Spreading information with gossip to make new friends has one aim: being able to answer queries accurately when a user searches for documents. This is where the query service is needed. The user is able to send a query for getting documents recommendations from her friends. The local LDA of the user translates the query into a set of relevant topics, and the peer sends them through the query service to the user's friends. Each friend may recommend documents depending on the similarity in terms of topics and the rate of the document. The query hops to friends of friends as many times as its TTL allows, the results being returned during the journey.

Figure 3 shows the result returned to the user after a query is sent. We show the results of the query for a user who has been in the network for a long time compared to a new user, and compare the accuracy and the number of answers she gets.

The demo with the MEDLINE information database (with a fixed data set) can be downloaded from the P2Prec website (http://www-sop.inria.fr/teams/zenith/p2prec/) with the complete procedure for installing, deploying and running, using OSGi configurations. We also provide a second procedure for building P2Prec applications with any data set, from scratch. But before to be used by end-users, it requires setting up a Bootstrap Server and compute (initialize) the set of topics of the given data set.

5. REFERENCES

[1] Adomavicius, G., Tuzhilin, A., Towards the next generation of recommender systems: a survey of the state-of-theart and possible extensions. IEEE Transactions on Knowledge and Data Engineering, 17(6):734–749, 2005.

[2] Arazy, O., Kumar, N., Shapira, B., Improving social recommender systems. Journal of IT Professional, 11(4):38–44, 2009.

[3] Blei, D. M., Ng, A. Y., Jordan, M. I., Latent Dirichlet Allocation. Journal of Machine Learning, 3:993–1022, 2003.

[4] Draidi F., Pacitti E., Kemme B. P2Prec: a P2P recommendation system for large-scale data sharing. Journal of Transactions on Large-Scale Data and Knowledge-Centered Systems (TLDKS), Vol. 3, Springer, LNCS 6790, 87-116, 2011.

[5] El Dick M., Pacitti E., Akbarinia R., Kemme, B. Building a peer-to-peer content distribution network with high performance, scalability and robustness. Information Systems, 36(2):222-247, 2011.

[6] Hersh W.R., Buckley C., Leone T., Hickam D.H., Ohsumed: An interactive retrieval evaluation and new large test collection for research. ACM SIGIR, 192-201,1994.

[7] Jelasity M., Voulgaris S., Guerraoui R., Kermarrec A.M., VanSteen M. Gossip-based peer sampling. ACM Trans. On Computer Systems, 25(3):2007.

[8] Kim, H.-J., Jung, J.J., Jo, G.-S.: Conceptual framework for recommendation system based on distributed user ratings. Springer, LNCS 3032, 115-122, 2003.

[9] Massa, P., and Avesani P. 2004. Trust-aware Collaborative Filtering for Recommender Systems. Springer, LNCS 3290, pp. 492-508, 2004.

[10] Sinha, R., Swearingen, K. Comparing Recommendation made by Online Systems and Friends. DELOS-NSF Workshop on Personalization and Recommender Systems in Digital Libraries, 2001

Computational Geography

Vanessa Murdock
Yahoo! Research
Diagonal 177
08018 Barcelona, Spain
vmurdock@yahoo-inc.com

Gary Gale
Nokia Gate5 GmbH
Schoenhauser Allee 180
10119 Berlin
gary.gale@nokia.com

ABSTRACT

As the industry moves to personalization and mobility, users expect their applications to be location savvy, and relevant to their lives in increasing detail. While we can pinpoint a user at a location within 700 meters with just their IP address, and within a meter with their GPS-enabled mobile phone, we fall short when it comes to understanding their geographic context. A person's geographic context includes their current and previous location, the things that surround them, their activity in a given place, as well as their thoughts and feelings in that place. Understanding this context allows us to personalize their experience and refine their interactions with an application, on a hyper-local level.

Categories and Subject Descriptors

H.3 [**Information Storage and Retrieval**]: Content Analysis and Indexing

General Terms

Algorithms, Experimentation

Keywords

geography, location, hyperlocal search, personalization, social media

1. DESCRIPTION OF TOPICS

The tutorial will cover four basic areas. The first is an overview of how geographies are represented, and how they are organized in gazetteers, using Geonames[1] and GeoPlanet[2] as examples. We discuss the differences between official geographies, and human-centric geographies (such as neighborhoods and colloquial places which are often not defined in official sources). We discuss points-of-interest, whose definition is frequently application-dependent. For example, a search engine presenting sponsored listings for local search would define a local business or venue as a point-of-interest. A transportation department might be more interested in metro stops, bus stops, and roadways. A tourist recommender application, or a mapping application, might define points-of-interest as landmarks, and historic places.

[1]www.geonames.org
[2]developer.yahoo.com/geo/placemaker

CIKM'11, October 24–28, 2011, Glasgow, Scotland, UK.
ACM 978-1-4503-0717-8/11/10.

The second set of topics covered by the tutorial are an overview of the resources available to academic researchers. These include open data sources, and APIs, as well as open-source mapping software. The data presented will focus on social media (Twitter, Flickr and Foursquare), but we will also discuss data sources such as OpenStreetMap[3], and the official data accessible through APIs (such as Geonames and Placemaker). The APIs presented will include the perl Geo and Proj4 modules that are useful for representing places on a map, as well as Google Earth's API which is helpful for making map-based location demos.

The third topic area will include an overview of the state of the art in modeling places, and discovering place boundaries. This includes work in understanding the location implicit in text, determining the location of a user from his queries and tweets, finding neighborhood boundaries and colloquial places, and discovering points of interest, as well as place-based benchmark initiatives such as the Placing Task of the MediaEval Benchmarking initiative[4].

The final topic will be an overview of place-based applications, a set of open problems, and the needs of the industry. The aim is to give the participants an idea of what is already out there, and how to use the research to create a killer location-based app.

In summary, the following topics will be presented:

- How geographic data is organized
    - What is a place: official places vs. human places
    - Defining points of interest
- Overview of resources available to academic researchers
    - Open APIs: perl modules, Placemaker, Ovi Maps, OpenStreetMap, Google Earth
    - Data: Flickr, Twitter, Foursquare, gazetteers
- State-of-the-art in location modeling
    - Modeling locations implicit in text
    - Modeling the location of the user
    - Finding neighborhood boundaries
    - Colloquial places (Downtown, The High Street, The Shops)
    - Discovering points of interest
- Overview of location-based applications
- Open problems and needs of industry

[3]www.openstreetmap.org
[4]www.mediaeval.org

Tutorial

Large-Scale Array Analytics: Taming the Data Tsunami

Peter Baumann
Jacobs University
Bremen, Germany
p.baumann@jacobs-university.de

Abstract

Never before in history mankind has collected data at the rates we face today. Alone in 2002, an estimated 403 Petabyte of data has been acquired, equivalent to all printed information ever created before. Earth orbiting satellites, as well as ground, airborne, and underwater sensors, space observatories scan their environment at unprecedented resolutions, giving rise to "Big Science". The same holds for the life sciences where genomic data, high-resolution scans, and other modalities are collected in steadily increasing streams. Social network analysis, OLAP, and stock exchange trading represent further examples, the latter involving real-time correlation of thousands of ticker time series resulting in Terabytes of data to be analysed per single run.

Summarized under *Large-Scale Analytics* we are witnessing an exploding demand for flexible access to massive volumes of scientific and business data sets. Arguably, a large class of these massive data is represented by *n-D arrays*. Consequently, large arrays pose new challenges to data modeling, querying, optimization, and maintenance – in short: we need *Large-Scale Array Analytics*.

This tutorial introduces to the topic from a database perspective. Aspects addressed include modelling, query languages, query optimization and parallelization, and storage management. High emphasis will be devoted to applications in "Big Science", particularly geo, space, and life sciences; real-life use cases will be presented and discussed which stem from our 15 years of experience with the open-source rasdaman array DBMS and our work on geo raster service standardization. We will highlight requirements, achievements, open research issues, and avenues for future research. Discussion will make use of real-life examples, many of which Internet connected participants can replay hands-on.

Categories & Subject Descriptors: E.1 **[Data Structures]**: Arrays, H.2 **[Database Management]**: Logical Design, Physical Design, Languages, Systems, Database Applications

General Terms: Management, Performance, Design, Standardization, Languages, Theory.

Bio

The speaker is Professor of Computer Science at Jacobs University. Since 1991 he is researching on large-scale n-D array ("raster") analytics and its application to geo, space, and life sciences. He has published 100+ book chapters and journal/conference articles in this and further fields. He is principal architect of the first complete array DBMS, rasdaman. He holds international patents on raster database technology and has received numerous innovation awards for his work, such as the European IT Prize. He is founder and CEO of a research spin-off specializing in software solutions for large-scale raster services. In the Open Geospatial Consortium (OGC) standardization body he chairs the working groups on geo raster service standards. He is editor of currently 9 adopted standards and several candidate standards. See www.faculty.jacobs-university.de/pbaumann for details.

CIKM'11, October 24–28, 2006, Glasgow, UK.
ACM 978-1-4503-0717-8/11/10.

Large-Scale Information Retrieval Experimentation with Terrier

Rodrygo L. T. Santos
School of Computing Science
University of Glasgow
G12 8QQ Glasgow, UK
rodrygo@dcs.gla.ac.uk

Richard McCreadie
School of Computing Science
University of Glasgow
G12 8QQ Glasgow, UK
richardm@dcs.gla.ac.uk

Vassilis Plachouras
PRESANS, X-TEC
École Polytechnique
91128 Palaiseau, France
vplachouras@acm.org

ABSTRACT

This tutorial aims to provide a practical introduction to conducting large-scale information retrieval (IR) experiments, using Terrier[1] as an experimentation platform. Written in Java, Terrier provides an open-source, feature-rich, flexible, and robust environment for large-scale IR experimentation. This tutorial will cover the experimentation process end-to-end, from configuring Terrier to a particular experimental setting, to efficiently indexing a document corpus and retrieving from it, and to evaluating the outcome. Moreover, it will describe how to use and extend the platform to one's own needs, and will be illustrated by practical research-driven examples. As a half-day tutorial, it will be split into two major sessions, with each session comprising both background information and practical demonstrations. In the first session, we will provide an overview of several aspects of large-scale IR experimentation, spanning areas such as indexing, data structures, query languages, and advanced retrieval models, and how these are implemented within Terrier. In the second session, we will discuss how to extend Terrier to conduct one's own experiments in a large-scale setting, including how to facilitate the evaluation of non-standard IR tasks through crowdsourcing. The practical demonstrations will cover recent use cases identified from Terrier's online discussion forum, so as to provide attendees with concrete examples of what can be done within Terrier.

Categories and Subject Descriptors

H.3.3 [**Information Storage and Retrieval**]: Information Search and Retrieval—*search process*

General Terms

Algorithms, Experimentation, Performance

Keywords

Terrier, large-scale experimentation, information retrieval

[1]`http://terrier.org`

CIKM'11, October 24–28, 2011, Glasgow, Scotland, UK.
ACM 978-1-4503-0717-8/11/10.

Presenters' Biography

Rodrygo Santos is a PhD student at the School of Computing Science of the University of Glasgow. He holds a BSc (2005) and an MSc (2007) degrees from the Dept. of Computer Science of the Federal University of Minas Gerais, Brazil. As a member of the Terrier Team since 2008, he has extensive experience in Terrier, extending it to a variety of application domains. These include blog search, opinion retrieval, expert search, entity search, Web mining, search result diversification, and learning-to-rank. Rodrygo has published several papers in major IR conferences and journals using Terrier, including SIGIR, WWW, CIKM, ECIR, RIAO, ICTIR, IP&M and the IR Journal, as well as international evaluation forums, such as TREC and NTCIR.

Richard McCreadie is a PhD student at the School of Computing Science of the University of Glasgow. He holds a BSc (Hons) from the University of Glasgow (2008) and is a member of the Terrier Team since 2008. In particular, he has developed the MapReduce indexing functionality for massive-scale IR that Terrier currently supports. His work using Terrier has been published in several major IR conferences and journals, such as SIGIR, RIAO, and IP&M, as well as on the TREC evaluation forum. Furthermore, Richard is also an expert in crowdsourcing solutions to common IR problems. He has presented new crowdsourcing approaches at the influential crowdsourcing workshops CSE 2010 (SIGIR) and CSDM 2011 (WSDM). Moreover, he designed, implemented and validated the first successful instance of crowdsourcing relevance assessments for TREC during 2010.

Dr. Vassilis Plachouras is a researcher at PRESANS, a start-up company from École Polytechnique (France). He holds a BEng degree in Electrical and Computer Engineering from the National Technical University of Athens (2001), a PhD in IR from the University of Glasgow (2006), and has worked as a post-doctoral researcher on Web search at Yahoo! Research, Spain. His research interests include Web IR, architectures for large-scale Web search engines, online advertising, and the applications of machine learning for ranking and classification. His publications include over 30 articles in peer-reviewed journals and international conferences, and he has received the best-paper award in CIKM 2009. He has served as a PC member of major international conferences and journals, and as the workshops and tutorials PC chair of ECIR 2008. Moreover, he organised the Workshop for Large-Scale and Distributed Systems for IR (LSDS-IR'07) in SIGIR 2007. He has been involved in the design and development of Terrier since its inception.

Statistical Information Retrieval Modelling

From the Probability Ranking Principle to Recent Advances in Diversity, Portfolio Theory, and Beyond

Jun Wang
University College London
j.wang@cs.ucl.ac.uk

Kevyn Collins-Thompson
Microsoft Research
kevynct@microsoft.com

ABSTRACT

Statistical modelling of Information Retrieval (IR) systems is a key driving force in the development of the IR field. The goal of this tutorial is to provide a comprehensive and up-to-date introduction to statistical IR modelling. We take a fresh and systematic perspective from the viewpoint of portfolio theory of IR and risk management. A unified treatment and new insights will be given to reflect the recent developments of considering the ranked retrieval results as a whole. Recent research progress in diversification, risk management, and portfolio theory will be covered, in addition to classic methods such as Maron and Kuhns' Probabilistic Indexing, Robertson-Spärck Jones model (and the resulting BM25 formula) and language modelling approaches. The tutorial also reviews the resulting practical algorithms of risk-aware query expansion, diverse ranking, IR metric optimization as well as their performance evaluations. Practical IR applications such as web search, multimedia retrieval, and collaborative filtering are also introduced, as well as discussion of new opportunities for future research and applications that intersect among information retrieval, knowledge management, and databases.

Categories and Subject Descriptors

H.3 [**Information Storage and Retrieval**]: H.3.1Content analysis and Indexing; H.3.3 Information Search and Retrieval

General Terms

Algorithms, Experimentation, Measurement, Performance

1. TOPICS AND TUTORIAL CONTEXT

In classic IR modelling, considerable effort has been devoted to automatically scoring individual documents with respect to their relevance states for a specific information need (query) and consequently ranking the documents in decreasing order of the individual scores. This approach is based on the underlying theory of the Probability Ranking Principle. Recently, there has been a new type of theoretical research that moves beyond the Probability Ranking Principle to determine optimal ranking algorithms that consider the ranking context or that regard the set of returned documents as a whole. These research efforts include marginal relevance, diversity, alternative retrieval objectives, robust query expansion, sub-topic retrieval, and pair-wise or list-wise comparison (learning to rank) to name only a few.

A possible general theory to support and justify the above developments would be the Portfolio Theory of IR. Drawing an analogy with finance and risk modelling, the Portfolio Theory of IR has theoretically demonstrated that in a wide variety of IR scenarios, from expanding queries to retrieving documents, effective, robust and less risky solutions do not just involve picking or ranking individual relevant documents or query terms, but require choosing an appropriate combination of relevant documents or query terms as a set.

This approach significantly departed from the classic IR methodologies originated from the Probability Ranking Principle, the Robertson-Spärck Jones model (and the resulting BM25 formula), and statistical language models. We describe how new ways of thinking about document portfolio and retrieval risk not only provide theoretical explanations of some empirical retrieval results – including the need for diversification in recommendation and web search, the trade-off between MAP and MRR, and the justification for pseudo-relevance feedback – but also help us develop useful retrieval techniques such as risk-aware query expansion and optimal document ranking. We also discuss the implications for how retrieval systems are evaluated.

2. PRESENTERS' BIOGRAPHIES

Dr. Jun Wang is Senior Lecturer (Associate Professor) in Computer Science, University College London. His main research interests are statistical modelling of information retrieval, collaborative filtering, and online advertising. He was a recipient of the SIGIR Doctoral Consortium Award in 2006, and Beyond Search award in 2007; and won the Best Paper Prize in ECIR09. Jun's recent service includes (Senior) PCs for SIGIR, CIKM, RecSys, and ECIR, and presenting an ECIR2011 tutorial on Risk Management in Information Retrieval.

Dr. Kevyn Collins-Thompson is a Researcher in the Context, Learning and User Experience for Search (CLUES) group at Microsoft Research. His research lies in an area combining information retrieval with machine learning and optimization. His recent work has explored new theoretical models and algorithms for increasing the reliability of risky algorithms such as query expansion. Kevyn's recent service includes Organizing Committee or PC roles for SIGIR, CIKM, ICML, UAI, and ACL, co-authoring and presenting tutorials at ICML 2009 on Machine Learning and IR, and ECIR2011 on Risk Management in IR. Kevyn has also served as adjunct faculty at the University of Washington.

CIKM'11, October 24–28, 2011, Glasgow, Scotland, UK.
ACM 978-1-4503-0717-8/11/10.

Web-Based Open-Domain Information Extraction

Marius Paşca
Google Inc.
1600 Amphitheatre Parkway
Mountain View, California 94043
mars@google.com

ABSTRACT

This tutorial provides an overview of extraction methods developed in the area of Web-based open-domain information extraction, whose purpose is the acquisition of open-domain classes, instances and relations from Web text. The extraction methods operate over unstructured or semi-structured text. They take advantage of weak supervision provided in the form of seed examples or small amounts of annotated data, or draw upon knowledge already encoded within resources created strictly by experts or collaboratively by users. The tutorial teaches the audience about existing resources that include instances and relations; details of methods for extracting such data from structured and semi-structured text available on the Web; and strengths and limitations of resources extracted from text as part of recent literature, with applications in knowledge discovery and information retrieval.

Categories and Subject Descriptors

H.3.1 [**Information Storage and Retrieval**]: Content Analysis and Indexing; I.2.7 [**Artificial Intelligence**]: Natural Language Processing; I.2.6 [**Artificial Intelligence**]: Learning

General Terms

Algorithms, Experimentation

Keywords

Information extraction, Web corpora, knowledge acquisition

1. BIOGRAPHY

Marius Paşca is a research scientist at Google. He graduated with a Ph.D. degree in Computer Science from Southern Methodist University, Dallas, Texas and an M.Sc. degree in Computer Science from Joseph Fourier University, Grenoble, France. Current research interests include factual information extraction from unstructured text and natural-language matching functions for information retrieval.

CIKM'11, October 24–28, 2011, Glasgow, Scotland, UK.
ACM 978-1-4503-0717-8/11/10.

Advances in Data Stream Mining for Mobile and Ubiquitous Environments

Shonali Krishnaswamy
Faculty of Information Technology
Monash University, Australia
Shonali.Krishnaswamy@monash.edu

Joao Gama
Laboratory of Artificial Intelligence and Decision Support
University of Porto, Portugal
jgama@fep.up.pt

Mohamed Medhat Gaber
School of Computing
University of Portsmouth, UK
mohamed.gaber@port.ac.uk

ABSTRACT

The tutorial presents the state-of-the-art in mobile and ubiquitous data stream mining and discusses open research problems, issues, and challenges in this area.

Categories and Subject Descriptors

H.2.8 [**Database Management**]: Database Applications – *Data Mining*

General Terms

Algorithms

Keywords

Data Stream Mining, Mobile Computing, Ubiquitous Computing

1. INTRODUCTION

The phenomenal growth of mobile devices coupled with their ever-increasing computational capacity presents an exciting new opportunity for real-time, intelligent data analysis in mobile and ubiquitous environments. Ubiquitous/Mobile data mining refers to the process of performing data stream mining using mobile and/or embedded devices (e.g. sensors) to support critical applications such as mobile healthcare, intelligent transportation systems, mobile activity recognition, smart homes, and emergency/disaster management like bushfires [1, 2]. Thus, the key focus is on developing data stream mining algorithms that are highly scalable/computationally efficient, energy-efficient, and context/resource-aware. These features enable the continued operation of data stream mining algorithms in a highly dynamic mobile/ubiquitous environment.

The typical constraints that have to be addressed in performing mobile/ubiquitous data stream mining are: (1) data streams are generated and sent in real-time in a stream format with little or no potential for persistent storage, (2) resource constraints include limited computational resources such as memory, processor speed, network bandwidth, battery power, and screen real-estate, (3) temporal constraints refer to real-time information and decision-making needs that, in turn, necessitate the analysis to be online, incremental and continuous, (4) mobility of users and devices and the connectivity issues thereof, and (5) adaptation and context-awareness of the analysis process to varying/dynamically changing resource-levels and user needs. In the last few years, rapid strides have been made in accurately and efficiently mining high speed data streams in mobile devices such smart phones] and there is a growing focus on "in-network" processing using embedded devices such as sensor nodes. These techniques leverage the body of work that exists in mining data streams and aim to enable the operation of these algorithms in resource-constrained environments. There is also an emerging focus on *context-aware data stream mining* which targets the learning process to be aware of its operational and application constraints and self-adapt according to changing situations/needs. The body of work in mobile/ubiquitous data stream mining ranges from algorithms, adaptation strategies for coping with mobile/ubiquitous environments, systems/toolkits for mobile data mining and innovative/new applications.

The tutorial is organized as follows. We will present the fundamental techniques for data stream analysis such as change detection, clustering, classification, frequent patterns, and time series analysis from distributed data streams. We will present the critical factors that need to be considered in order to develop and deploy data stream mining in mobile/ubiquitous environments including the need for adaptation and context/situation-aware reasoning. We will then present state-of-the-art algorithms for mobile data stream mining, including the emerging topic of *Pocket Data Mining (PDM),* focusing on ad hoc distributed data stream mining in mobile environments. The tutorial will also present the Open Mobile Miner (OMM) toolkit [3] for rapid deployment of mobile data stream mining and real-world application/case studies and demonstrations to stimulate the real need for this growing research field. Finally the tutorial will be concluded with open issues and future directions.

CIKM'11, October 24–28, 2011, Glasgow, Scotland, UK.
ACM 978-1-4503-0717-8/11/10.

2. REFERENCES

[1] João Gama, Michael May: Ubiquitous Knowledge Discovery Intelligent Data Analysis 15(1): 1 (2011).

[2] Gaber, M, M., Krishnaswamy, S., and Zaslavsky, A. 2005. On-board Mining of Data Streams in Sensor Networks, A Book Chapter in Advanced Methods of Knowledge Discovery from Complex Data, (Eds.) S. Badhyopadhyay, U. Maulik, L. Holder and D. Cook, Springer.

[3] Krishnaswamy, S., Gaber, M, M., Harbach, M., Hugues, C., Sinha, A., Gillick, B., Delir Haghighi, P.,and Zaslavsky, A., (2009), Open Mobile Miner: A Toolkit for Mobile Data Stream Mining, ACM Knowledge Discovery in Databases (ACM KDD 2009), Demo Paper.

Information Diffusion In Social Networks: Observing and Affecting What Society Cares About*

Divyakant Agrawal Ceren Budak Amr El Abbadi
Department of Computer Science UCSB
Santa Barbara, CA 93106-5110, USA
{agrawal, cbudak, amr}@cs.ucsb.edu

ABSTRACT

Information diffusion in social networks provide great opportunities for political and social change as well as societal education. Therefore understanding information diffusion in social networks is a critical research goal. This greater understanding can be achieved through data analysis, development of reliable models that can predict outcomes of social processes, and ultimately the creation of applications that can shape the outcome of these processes. In this tutorial, we aim to provide an overview of such recent research based on a wide variety of techniques such as optimization algorithms, data mining, data streams covering a large number of problems such as influence spread maximization, misinformation limitation and study of trends in online social networks.

Categories and Subject Descriptors

H [**Information Systems**]:

General Terms

Algorithms

Keywords

social networks, information cascades, misinformation, trends

1. TUTORIAL OUTLINE

1.1 Characterizing Social Networks

We start our tutorial with a discussion of the significance of social networks in today's world and measurement studies focusing on important characteristics that distinguish social networks from other networks.

1.2 Diffusion of Information or Opinions

In this part of the tutorial, we outline the techniques used in optimizing or facilitating information diffusion in social networks. We identify two problem definitions; maximizing the spread of influence and minimizing the spread of misinformation in social networks. Through our study of these two problems, we delve into more detail about the sub-problems; (i) Diffusion model formation [4, 7, 9, 10], (ii) formalization and optimization [1–4, 6, 8, 9], (iii) large-scale data analysis and (iv) technique validation. We will focus on this line of research from mainly two perspectives; the social scientist and computer scientist approaches.

1.3 Information Trends

In the third part of the tutorial we will focus on the interplay between different information campaigns and *trends* that result from such interplay [5,10,11] and address the following questions: What is the nature of trends in social networks? What are important dimensions? How can one efficiently analyze trends in large scale social networks?

2. BIOGRAPHICAL SKETCHES

Divyakant Agrawal is a Professor of the Department of Computer Science at University of California, Santa Barbara. Prof. Agrawal's research expertise is in the areas of database systems, distributed computing, data warehousing, and large-scale information systems.
Ceren Budak is a PhD Candidate at the Department of Computer Science, University of California Santa Barbara. Her research interests lie in the area of information diffusion in social networks.
Amr El Abbadi is a Professor of the Department of Computer Science at University of California, Santa Barbara. His research interests lie in the area of scalable database and distributed systems.

3. REFERENCES

[1] E. Bakshy, J. M. Hofman, W. A. Mason, and D. J. Watts. Everyone's an influencer: quantifying influence on twitter. In *WSDM*, pages 65–74, 2011.
[2] S. Bharathi, D. Kempe, and M. Salek. Competitive influence maximization in social networks. In *WINE*, pages 306–311, 2007.
[3] C. Budak, D. Agrawal, and A. El Abbadi. Where the blogs tip: connectors, mavens, salesmen and translators of the blogosphere. In *SIGKDD Workshop on Social Media Analytics*, 2010.
[4] C. Budak, D. Agrawal, and A. El Abbadi. Limiting the spread of misinformation in social networks. In *WWW*, 2011.
[5] C. Budak, D. Agrawal, and A. El Abbadi. Structural trend analysis for online social networks. In *VLDB*, 2011.
[6] M. Cha, H. Haddadi, F. Benevenuto, and P. K. Gummadi. Measuring user influence in twitter: The million follower fallacy. In *ICWSM*, 2010.
[7] P. S. Dodds and D. J. Watts. A generalized model of social and biological contagion. *Journal of Theoretical Biology*, 232:587–604, 2005.
[8] A. Goyal, F. Bonchi, and L. V. S. Lakshmanan. Discovering leaders from community actions. In *CIKM*, pages 499–508, 2008.
[9] D. Kempe, J. M. Kleinberg, and É. Tardos. Maximizing the spread of influence through a social network. In *KDD*, pages 137–146, 2003.
[10] J. Leskovec, L. Backstrom, and J. Kleinberg. Meme-tracking and the dynamics of the news cycle. In *KDD '09*, pages 497–506, 2009.
[11] J. Sankaranarayanan, H. Samet, B. E. Teitler, M. D. Lieberman, and J. Sperling. Twitterstand: news in tweets. In *GIS*, pages 42–51, 2009.

*This work is partially supported by NSF Grant IIS-1135389.

CIKM'11, October 24–28, 2011, Glasgow, Scotland, UK.
ACM 978-1-4503-0717-8/11/10.

Information Retrieval Challenges in Computational Advertising

Andrei Broder, Evgeniy Gabrilovich, Vanja Josifovski
Yahoo! Research, Santa Clara, CA 95054, USA
{broder, gabr, vanjaj}@yahoo-inc.com

Categories and Subject Descriptors

H.3.3 [**Information Storage and Retrieval**]: Information Search and Retrieval

General Terms

Algorithms, Experimentation

Keywords

computational advertising, sponsored search, display advertising

1. OVERVIEW

Web advertising supports a large swath of the Internet ecosystem. It brings revenue to countless publishers that rent space on their pages for advertising It also provides valuable traffic to numerous commercial Web sites and has fueled the development of Web search engines. In 2011, the worldwide spend on online advertising is estimated to be over $80 billions[1]. In its core, Web advertising follows the two major models of traditional advertising. Direct advertising aims to elicit a direct response from the user. Sponsored search is an example of direct advertising where ads are shown alongside the Web search results and is today a major channel for traffic acquisition on the Web. In contrast with direct advertising, brand advertising aims to give a favorable impression of a brand or a product. Brand advertising on the Web is usually done by graphical ads (display ads) placed on the publishers' Web pages.

Computational advertising is a new scientific discipline that aims to formalize the problem of finding the best ad for a given user in a specific context. In traditional advertising, the number of venues is small, the cost per venue is high, and little or no personalization is possible (as for example in print magazines). In contrast, in online advertising there are billions of opportunities (page views), hundreds of millions of ads and it is possible to provide personalization with quantifiable results. This brings the advertising into the realm of the other "computational" sciences.

The aim of this tutorial is to present the state of the art in the emerging area of computational advertising, and to expose the participants to the main research challenges in this exciting field. The tutorial starts with a comprehensive background survey of the topic. Then we will focus on textual advertising as sponsored search and content match where we use the user context to retrieve relevant ads. It is essential to emphasize that in most cases the context of user actions is defined by a body of text (e.g. web page or user query), hence the ad matching problem lends itself to many IR methods. We will discuss to what extend can standard techniques be applied in this new setting and then examine the IR challenges specific to the textual advertising.

Today display advertising is created, sold and traded in a complex system of intermediaries with overlapping roles that mediate between the publishers and the advertisers. In the second part of the tutorial we will overview the display advertising eco system and describe the roles of the major type of intermediaries as ad networks, ad exchanges, demand side platforms and publisher platforms. We will then focus on targeting as one of the key activity in display advertising. We will discuss the challenges and techniques for user profile generation from historical activity and how to use those profiles in various predictive and analytical tasks in display advertising.

Throughout the tutorial we will point out open problems that might interest the CIKM community. As online advertising is part of everyday life for virtually all internet users, research in this area can have a significant impact on the society.

2. PRESENTERS

Dr. Andrei Broder is a Yahoo! Research Fellow and Vice President for Computational Advertising. Previously he was an IBM Distinguished Engineer and the CTO of the Institute for Search and Text Analysis in IBM Research, and VP of Research and Chief Scientist at AltaVista.

Dr. Evgeniy Gabrilovich is a Senior Research Scientist and Manager of the NLP and IR Group at Yahoo! Research. Evgeniy is a recipient of the 2010 Karen Sparck Jones Award for his contributions to NLP and IR.

Dr. Vanja Josifovski is a Senior Director of Research at Yahoo! Research and works in the area of Computational Advertising. Previously Vanja was a Research Staff Member at IBM Research, Almaden.

[1] emarketer.com

CIKM'11, October 24–28, 2011, Glasgow, Scotland, UK.
ACM 978-1-4503-0717-8/11/10.

Object Ranking

Roelof van Zwol
Yahoo! Research
4401 Great America Parkway
Santa Clara, CA 95054, USA
roelof@yahoo-inc.com

Srinivas Vadrevu
Yahoo! Labs
701 First Avenue
Sunnyvale, CA 94089, USA
svadrevu@yahoo-inc.com

ABSTRACT

Object ranking is an emerging discipline within information retrieval that is concerned with the ranking of objects, e.g. named entities and their attributes, in context of given a user query, or application. In this tutorial we will address the different aspects involved when building an object ranking system. We will present the state-of-the-art research in object ranking, as well as going into detail about our hands-on experiences when designing and developing the system for object ranking as it is in production at Yahoo! today. This allows for a unique mixture of research and development that will give the participants in-depth insights into the problem of object ranking.

The focus of current Web search engines is to retrieve relevant documents on the Web, and more precisely documents that match with the query intent of the user. Some users are looking for specific information, while other just want to access rich media content (images, videos, etc.) or explore a topic. In the latter scenario, users do not have a fixed or pre-determined information need, but are using the search engine to discover information related to a particular object of interest. In this scenario one can say that the user is in a exploratory mode.

To support users in their exploratory search the search engines are offering semantic search suggestions. In this tutorial, we will present a generic framework for ranking related objects. This framework ranks related entities according to two dimensions: a lateral dimension and a faceted dimension. In the lateral dimension, related entities are of the same nature as the entity queried (e.g. Barcelona and Madrid, or Angelina Jolie and Jessica Alba). In the faceted dimension, related entities are usually not of the same type as the queried entity, and refer to a specific aspect of the queried entity (e.g. Jennifer Aniston and the tvshow Friends).

In this tutorial we will describe the process of building a Web-scale object ranking system. In particular we will address the construction of a knowledge base that forms the basis for the object ranking, and the generation of ranking features using external sources such as search engine query logs, photo annotations in Flickr, and tweets on Twitter. Next, we will discuss machine learned ranking models using an ensemble of pair-wise preference models, and address various aspects of object ranking, including multi-media extensions, vertical solutions, attribute-aware ranking, and the importance of freshness. Last but not least, we will address the evaluation methodologies involved to tune the performance of Web-scale object ranking strategies.

CIKM'11, October 24–28, 2011, Glasgow, Scotland, UK.
ACM 978-1-4503-0717-8/11/10.

Categories and Subject Descriptors

H.3.3 [**Information Storage and Retrieval**]: Information Search and Retrieval—*Retrieval models*

General Terms

Algorithms, Experimentation

Biographies

Dr. Roelof van Zwol is a senior research scientist at Yahoo! Research, where he is managing the multimedia research team. He has more than 10 years of international research experience in multimedia, information retrieval, (social) media mining, object ranking, spatial search, XML, databases, and machine learning. He is passionate about conducting research in an industrial context and to apply the outcomes in high-impact end-user services. His work on object ranking now powers the left-rail search suggestions in Yahoo!'s Web and image search engine. Prior to joining Yahoo he was an assistant professor at Utrecht University in the Netherlands. He received his Ph.D. in Computer Science in 2002 from the University of Twente in the Netherlands. Roelof van Zwol is the author of more than 70 peer reviewed publications. He was co-chair of CIVR in 2009, and organizer of the second CHORUS conference on Multimedia Search, as well as the organizer of 5 workshops themed around Web search, multimedia, and information retrieval.

Dr. Srinivas Vadrevu is a senior research scientist at Yahoo! Labs. His current work at Yahoo! involves ranking related problems such as Web search ranking, cross-domain ranking for international countries and ranking and recommendation of related entities. During this time, he authored several publications at venues such as WWW, CIKM and KDD conferences and Machine Learning Journal. His recent work on object ranking powers entity search experiences at various parts within Yahoo!. Previously he worked on information extraction and particularly on extracting structured data from Web pages, where he published a number of papers. He received his Ph.D. in Computer Science from Arizona State University and received his M.S. in Computer Science from University of Minnesota, Duluth.

Uncertain Schema Matching

The Power of not Knowing

Avigdor Gal
Technion – Israel Institute of Technology
Haifa 32000, Israel
avigal@ie.technion.ac.il

Categories and Subject Descriptors

H.2.1 [**Database Management**]: Logical Design; H.2.5 [**Database Management**]: Heterogeneous Databases

General Terms

Algorithm, Design

Tutorial Description

> *Doubt is not a pleasant condition, but certainty is absurd.*
> – Voltaire

Schema matching is the task of providing correspondences between concepts describing the meaning of data in various heterogeneous, distributed data sources (*e.g.* attributes in database schemata, tags in XML DTDs, fields in HTML forms, input and output parameters in Web services, *etc.*). Schema matching is one of the basic operations required by the process of data and schema integration, and thus has great effect on its outcomes, whether these involve targeted content delivery, view integration, database integration, query rewriting over heterogeneous sources, duplicate data elimination, or automatic streamlining of workflow activities that involve heterogeneous data sources. As such, schema matching affects numerous modern applications from a wide variety of areas. It impacts business, where company data sources continuously realign due to changing markets; and it affects the way business and other information consumers seek information over the Web. It impacts the life sciences, where scientific workflows cross system boundaries more often than not. Finally, it impacts the way communities of knowledge are created and evolve.

Schema matching research has been going on for more than 25 years now, first as part of schema integration and then as a standalone research field. Over the years, a significant body of work has been devoted to the identification of *schema matchers*, heuristics for schema matching. The main objective of schema matchers is to provide correspondences that will be effective from the user's point of view, yet computationally efficient (or at least not disastrously expensive). These have come out of a variety of different research communities, including database management, information retrieval, the information sciences, data semantics and the semantic Web, and others.

Over the years, a realization has emerged that schema matchers are inherently uncertain. A matcher may consider several possible correspondences as possible, and when it needs to choose, it may choose wrong. For example, when two companies merge, the companies' employee databases need to be consolidated. The schemata may be different, and in such a case, there may be many different ways of mapping one schema to another. As another example, a Web search engine performing a product search over databases of multiple vendors needs to find correspondences between the product databases of different vendors. Multiple ways of representing the data might lead to multiple possible correspondences.

A prime reason for the uncertainty of the matching process is the enormous ambiguity and heterogeneity of data description concepts: It is unrealistic to expect a single matcher to identify the correct mapping for any possible concept in a set. Uncertainty in schema matching was recognized first in the form of anecdotal comments in research papers. Since 2003, work on the uncertainty in schema matching has picked up (along with research on uncertainty in other areas of data management).

This tutorial presents various aspects of uncertainty in schema matching within a single unified framework. We introduce basic formulations of uncertainty and provide several alternative representations of schema matching uncertainty. Then, we cover two common methods that have been proposed to deal with uncertainty in schema matching, namely ensembles and top-K matchings, and analyze them in this context. We conclude with a set of real-world applications and in particular, the use of uncertain schema matching in NisB, a European project that is aimed at harnessing an evolving Wisdom of the Network to dynamically connect businesses to attain common business goals.

Avigdor Gal is an Associate professor at the Technion – Israel Institute of Technology. He has published more than 95 papers in journals (e.g. Journal of the ACM (JACM), ACM Transactions on Database Systems (TODS), IEEE Transactions on Knowledge and Data Engineering (TKDE), ACM Transactions on Internet Technology (TOIT), and the VLDB Journal), books (Schema Matching and Mapping) and conferences (CIKM, ICDE, ER, CoopIS, BPM) on the topics of data integration, temporal databases, information systems architectures, and active databases. Avigdor Gal is the author of the book Uncertain schema Matching, part of Synthesis Lectures on Data Management (March 2011).

CIKM'11, October 24–28, 2011, Glasgow, Scotland, UK.
ACM 978-1-4503-0717-8/11/10.

DTMBIO 2011: International Workshop on Data and Text Mining in Biomedical Informatics

Sophia Ananiadou
National Centre for Text Mining
University of Manchester, UK
sophia.ananiadou@manchester.ac.uk

Doheon Lee
Department of Bio and Brain Engineering
KAIST, Korea
dhlee@kaist.ac.kr

Shamkant Navathe
College of Computing
Georgia Institute of Technology, USA
sham@cc.gatech.edu

Min Song
Information Systems
New Jersey Institute of Technology, USA
min.song@njit.edu

ABSTRACT
ACM Fifth International Workshop on Data and Text Mining in Biomedical Informatics (DTMBIO 11) organizers are pleased to announce that the fifth DTMBIO will be held in conjunction with CIKM, one of the largest data and text mining conferences. While CIKM presents the state-of-the-art research in informatics with the primary focus on data and text mining, the main focus of DTMBIO is on biomedical informatics. DTMBIO delegates will bring forth interesting applications of up-to-date informatics in the context of biomedical research.

Categories and Subject Descriptors
J.3 [**Life and Medical Sciences**]: Medical information systems

General Terms
Algorithms, Management, Performance, Design, Experimentation, Security.

1. INTRODUCTION
The rapid development of medical informatics techniques is tightly coupled with developments within several fields in computer science, including data mining, information retrieval, and database management systems, among others. A fundamental topic of research within medical informatics is how to make effective use of the tremendous amount of biological and biomedical data to improve the understanding of biological systems. Such data include, but are not limited to, gene and protein sequences, gene expression profiles from Microarray experiments, protein structure predictions resulting from high-throughput computational methods, protein-protein interactions from proteomic studies, Single Nucleotide Polymorphisms profiles from SNP arrays, and much bibliographic information from electronic medical journals. The need to automatically and effectively extract, understand, integrate, and make use of information embedded in such heterogeneous unstructured data drives the current research in bioinformatics.

The call for papers attracted 16 submissions from all over the world. The selection process was highly competitive. Each paper went through a rigorous double-blinded peer review by at least 3 members of the Program Committee. Based on the referee reports, the papers have been ranked according to their original contribution, and the program committee accepted 7 full papers and 4 short papers that cover a variety of topics, including novel information extraction techniques, ontologies, and application to large biomedical data. In addition, the program includes a keynote speech by Dr. Dietrich Rebholz-Schuhmann on semantic interoperability between literature and data. We hope that these proceedings will serve as a valuable reference for researchers and developers who are interested in applying Text Mining to Medical Informatics.

2. PAPER SUMMARY
Session 1 presents research on application of various data mining techniques for the research problems in medical informatics. [1] presents a fast approximation PCA to process brain imaging movies of Drosiphila. The method is innovative, and uses prior knowledge in selecting sample pixels versus Monte Carlo sampling to achieve better approximation and higher speedups. [2] describes a novel application of data mining techniques to a database of patient data from a hearing aid clinic. The data consist of audiograms, data about the patient and notes in text form provided by technicians. The goal of the experiment was to find information about what determines the prescription of two types of hearing aids: worn behind the ear and worn in the ear. [3] describes a novel search engine for biomedical concepts such as genes, proteins, diseases, and drugs. What is unique with this system is that it uses a "segment" as the unit for indexing the concepts, so that the user can specify the context of a query at a much more fine-grained level than on conventional search engines.

Session 2 presents research on various techniques of text mining to medical informatics. [4] proposes an implementation of Swanson's ABC model for literature-based discovery, in which relation A-C inferred from co-occurrence of A-B and that of B-C is ranked based on the contextual similarity of A-B and B-C occurrences. [5] proposes a system supporting manual curation process by the automatic extraction of knowledge on fungal enzymes. [6] presents a system called ASCOT for searching relevant clinical trials for speeding-up the writing of new trial. The system integrates up-to-date metadata classification and text-mining techniques that are adapted to the analysis of clinical trials represented by structured and free-text fields. [7] reports on an approach to use parsers to accomplish Task 3 of the BioNLP Shared Task of 2009.

DTMBIO'11, October 24, 2011, Glasgow, Scotland, UK.
ACM 978-1-4503-0960-8/11/10.

Session 3 presents several interesting short papers that report on Data and Text Mining techniques applied in biomedical informatics. [8] presents applying topic models to induce latent features of text for use in word sense disambiguation. [9] reports on a technique for keyword extraction and expansion in biomedical literature that innovatively draws on both MeSH terms and word co-occurrence. [10] proposes an index update algorithm of RDF databases based on a recently developed RDF engine. [11] examines the correlation between gene expression patterns and different regions of the human brain using existing microarray data and several analytical tools, such as bioconductor and k-means clustering in R.

3. CONCLUSION

This workshop continues the line of DTMBIO workshops organized in conjunction with CIKM in 2006, 2008, 2009, and 2010. We invite researchers and practitioners from a variety of backgrounds such as computer science, information system, information science, bioinformatics, medical informatics, and medical sciences. The main objective of the workshop will be to strengthen the cooperation within the growing community in medical data and text mining research, allowing lively exchange of ideas and foster new collaborations.

4. REFERENCES

[1] Strauch M. and Galizia, G. 2011 Fast PCA for processing calcium-imaging data from the brain of Drosophila melanogaster. In *DTMBIO 11*.

[2] Anwar, M. N. and Oakes, M. 2011. Data Mining of Audiology Patient Records: Factors Influencing the Choice of Hearing Aid Type. In *DTMBIO 11*.

[3] Choi, J., Kim, D., Kim, S., Lee, S., Lee, K. and Kang, J. 2011. BOSS: A Biomedical Object Search System. In *DTMBIO 11*.

[4] Lee, S., Choi, J., Park, K., Song, M. and Lee, d. H. 2011. Inferring Hidden Relationships from Biological Literature with Multi-level Context Terms. In *DTMBIO 11*.

[5] Meurs, M. J., Murphy, C., Morgenstern, I., Naderi, N., Butler, G., Powlowski, J., Tsang, A., and Witte, R. Semantic Text Mining for Lignocellulose Research. In *DTMBIO 11*.

[6] Korkontzelos, I., Mu, T., Restificar, A. and Ananiadou, S. 2011. Text mining for efficient search and assisted creation of clinical trials. In *DTMBIO 11*.

[7] Mackinlay, A., Martinez, D., and Baldwin, T. 2011. A Parser-based Approach to Detecting Modification of Biomedical Events. In *DTMBIO 11*.

[8] Stevenson, M. 2011. Disambiguation of Medline abstracts using Topic Models. In *DTMBIO 11*.

[9] Bong, S. Y. and Hwang, K. B. 2011. Keyphrase extraction in biomedical publications using MeSH and intraphrase word co-occurrence information. In *DTMBIO 11*.

[10] Lee, J., Kasperovis, R., Han, W. S. and Cho, H. 2011. On Supporting Efficient Updates of Regular Expression Indexes in RDF Databases. In *DTMBIO 11*.

[11] Yu, H. and Lee, D. 2011. Functional Analysis of Human Whole Brain Regions Based on Gene Expression. In *DTMBIO 11*.

BooksOnline'11: 4th Workshop on Online Books, Complementary Social Media, and Crowdsourcing

Gabriella Kazai
Microsoft Research
Cambridge, UK
v-gabkaz@microsoft.com

Carsten Eickhoff
Delft University of Technology
Delft, The Netherlands
c.eickhoff@tudelft.nl

Peter Brusilovsky
University of Pittsburgh
Pittsburgh, USA
peterb@pitt.edu

ABSTRACT

The BooksOnline Workshop series aims to foster the discussion and exchange of research ideas towards addressing challenges and exploring opportunities around large collections of digital books and complementary media. The fourth workshop in the series, BooksOnline'11 pays special attention to the role of social media and the phenomena of crowdsourcing in the context of online books, which is expected to be key in defining new user experiences in digital libraries and on the Web. The workshop boasts a high quality program, including keynote addresses by Ville Miettinnen, CEO of Microtask and Adam Farquhar, Head of Digital Library Technology at The British Library. From the accepted papers two main themes became salient: 1) Information retrieval and information extraction methods focused on enhancing digital libraries, and 2) Studies and analyses of reading experience and behavior. This paper provides an overview of the workshop and the accepted contributions.

Categories and Subject Descriptors: H.3.7 [**Digital Libraries**]

General Terms: Experimentation, Human Factors

1. INTRODUCTION

In recent years, the number of digitally available books has increased dramatically through the digitization of physical books and by electronic publishing. Large scale digital libraries hold significant value to humanity by preserving knowledge and making it widely accessible. Furthermore, they show great potential for cross-media integration and industrial exploration. Some of the leading initiatives include Project Gutenberg (http://www.gutenberg.org), the Million Book project (http://www.ulib.org), and the Open Content Alliance (http://www.opencontentalliance.org). At the same time eBooks and eReaders are gaining wide acceptance and popularity. This is paralleled with social networking and content sharing platforms that accommodate millions of users who often dedicate great efforts to data collection, creation and verification. The harnessing of these considerable forces has the potential to revolutionize online reading both technically and in terms of interaction paradigms.

To match the great momentum in creating on-line book repositories, the BooksOnline workshop series aims to foster research initiatives that are focused on innovation opportunities and challenges created by large collections of digital books and complementary media. This year, the workshop focuses more explicitly and deliberately on exploring the role that social media may hold in enhancing digital libraries and online repository services. Topics include new interaction paradigms that define new, immersive and social reading experiences and novel methods to leverage the wisdom of the crowd as well as the necessary infrastructure.

The remainder of the paper summarizes the accepted contributions, grouped by the common themes that emerged.

BooksOnline'11, October 24, 2011, Glasgow, Scotland, UK.
ACM 978-1-4503-0961-5/11/10.

2. ACCEPTED PAPERS

2.1 System Focus: Information Retrieval and Extraction

Among the contributions that focus on aspects of systems, the common theme is on identifying important nuggets of information from books, from author names and bibliographic references to factual statements or passages. Another recurring issue is that of OCR errors.

Cartright, Field and Allan tackle the novel and challenging task of Evidence Finding in a collection of digitized books [2]. Its goal is to find confirming or refuting evidence in books for natural language assertions. The authors highlight the differences between the introduced problem and related fields such as Question Answering (QA). The approach taken and evaluated in this work tries to generate search engine queries based on factual assertions. These queries are subsequently issued to an index of 50,000 digitally scanned books from the INEX Book Track test collection. A preliminary evaluation reports superior performance to straight-forward bag-of-words and Sequential Dependence models.

Kim, Bellot, Faath and Dacos propose an automatic information extraction scheme for bibliographic references from scientific literature in the humanities [5]. On a sizeable corpus, they employ Conditional Random Fields to extract reference fields such as author names or publication titles with high precision. Particularly encouraging results are reported for the distinction of author first and last names where significant improvements over the state of the art could be achieved.

Smith, Manmatha and Allan in [9] focus on collections of books, instead of individual books, and demonstrate the potential benefits of the 'relational structure' of collections. Examples of relational structure include the relationships among books that are duplicates or translations of each other, or the citation or quotation of one passage of a book by another. With the aim to give scholars more powerful tools, the authors present technical solutions to inferring book relationships, aligning books for structure discovery, and metadata propagation. An advantage of the proposed solutions is the promise they hold for mitigating other problems, such as OCR errors, with scanned book collections.

Kamps in [4] investigates the effectiveness of various IR ranking methods on library catalogue data and compares these with results from the online public access catalogue (OPAC). His findings demonstrate the importance of author information for ranking books. He shows that ranking books based on author scores derived from expert finding methods leads to substantial and significant performance improvements over standard book ranking methods, which already outperform OPAC. On the other hand, ranking books based on the combination of the author scores and the book retrieval scores yields no further improvement. This provides further evidence that author information captures an important aspect of relevance. This then highlights the challenge of how to support users in judging the relevance of authors when exploring a new and unfamiliar subject area or topic.

2.2 User Aspects: Experience and Behaviour

The contributions in this category focus on studying or designing rich, interactive and social reading experiences and tools and concepts to support or to evaluate these.

De Ribaupierre and Falquet describe a preliminary survey concerning the reading behavior of research professionals [8]. They argue that document retrieval will benefit from a more facet-oriented indexing to enable precise querying for desired information. These facets are envisioned to follow discourse elements such as definitions, hypotheses, algorithms, etc., rather than structural entities (e.g., conclusions or chapters). According to this scheme the authors foresee significant benefits for scientific literature study.

Colombo and Landoni in [3] describe progress on the HEBE project which aims at studying how to design eBook interfaces (or eBook architecture) for children in order to provide them with a highly engaging reading experience. They detail the results of a preliminary observational study of 45 school children as they interact with books and argue that reading is a complex experience with an important social dimension. They relate their findings to Csikszentmihalyi's flow theory, where flow is defined as a mental state of deep enjoyment and intense engagement in a certain activity, where most of a person's attention is devoted to accomplish that activity. The paper also presents interesting questions on how to address the challenge of defining and embracing a methodology where children can take an active role in the design process.

Sofronijevic introduces a novel interaction paradigm between reader and text, *Reading 2.0* [10]. Given this paradigm, a substantially higher degree of interactivity is assumed. As opposed to the traditional reading process, the *Solitary Reading*, Reading 2.0 is described as a more interactive and iterative process in which the boundaries between content producer and content consumer are less clear-cut, as individuals annotate, highlight or even extend and alter books. The open question remains how digital library research and engineering can facilitate the merits of Reading 2.0.

The paper by Regan [7] combines art and science in developing a book text visualization tool for analyzing the works in Philip Pullman's children's literature trilogy, His Dark Materials. The tools allow users to explore the rhythm of the characters' occurrences in the books, the relationships between the characters and the way in which they are depicted. The paper also gives brief insights of the experiences of the author and fans of the book with the tool. The author closes with a question that challenges current publishing practices and the laws that govern those practices.

Müller and Maurer in [6] introduce the concept of an Interactive Internet Book, which augments digitized books with four main layers: 1) the Facsimile layer delivers high quality device-dependent format for each page of a book, 2) the OCR layer results in the textual content presented to the user, 3) the Enhancement layer provides functionality for personal and group annotation, such as digital page markers, links, notes, highlights and even nano-publications, and 4) the Communication layer provides for group interactions and social media networks, such as sharing, social tagging, discussions, reading history, and search agents. The authors claim that the quality and the enhancements of an Interactive Internet Book go far beyond what is traditionally assumed. They demonstrate this by means of a use case study and a working prototype system.

Becker describes a HIT-driven quality assurance system for document conversions in digital libraries [1]. The author motivates the need for a hybrid system that exploits the benefits of large scale document archives and human computing. The central challenge addressed in this paper is the evaluation of OCR output. The author showcases how this task can be effectively and efficiently represented as a crowdsourcing HIT. The discussion gives useful insights into caveats and lessons learned for this domain.

3. ACKNOWLEDGMENTS

We would like to thank all authors who submitted contributions and the PC members for their excellent work.

4. REFERENCES

[1] C. Becker. Quality Assurance in Document Conversion: A HIT? In *Proc. CIKM BooksOnline Workshop*, 2011.

[2] M.-A. Cartright, H. A. Field, and J. Allan. Evidence Finding using a Collection of Books. In *Proc. CIKM BooksOnline Workshop*, 2011.

[3] L. Colombo and M. Landoni. Towards an engaging e-Reading experience. In *Proc. CIKM BooksOnline Workshop*, 2011.

[4] J. Kamps. The Impact of Author Ranking in a Library Catalogue. In *Proc. CIKM BooksOnline Workshop*, 2011.

[5] Y.-M. Kim, P. Bellot, E. Faath, and M. Dacos. Automatic Annotation of Bibliographical References in Digital Humanities Books, Articles and Blogs. In *Proc. CIKM BooksOnline Workshop*, 2011.

[6] H. Müller and H. Maurer. How to carry over historic books into social networks. In *Proc. CIKM BooksOnline Workshop*, 2011.

[7] T. Regan. Tools for Whom: Readers, Fans, or Authors? In *Proc. CIKM BooksOnline Workshop*, 2011.

[8] H. D. Ribaupierre and G. Falquet. New trends for reading scientific documents. In *Proc. CIKM BooksOnline Workshop*, 2011.

[9] D. A. Smith, R. Manmatha, and J. Allan. Mining Relational Structure from Millions of Books. In *Proc. CIKM BooksOnline Workshop*, 2011.

[10] A. Sofronijevic. Changes in Reading Research Proposition: Some Psychological Aspects of Reading 2.0. In *Proc. CIKM BooksOnline Workshop*, 2011.

DETECT'11
International Workshop on DETecting and Exploiting Cultural diversiTy on the Social Web

Sergej Sizov
WeST – Institute for Web Science and Technologies
University of Koblenz-Landau, 56070 Koblenz, Germany
sizov@uni-koblenz.de

Stefan Siersdorfer
Intelligent Access to Information
L3S Research Center, 30167 Hannover, Germany
siersdorfer@l3s.de

Thomas Gottron
WeST – Institute for Web Science and Technologies
University of Koblenz-Landau, 56070 Koblenz, Germany
gottron@uni-koblenz.de

Philipp Sorg
Institut für Angewandte Informatik und Formale Beschreibungsverfahren
Karlsruhe Institute of Technology, 76133 Karlsruhe, Germany
philipp.sorg@kit.edu

Categories and Subject Descriptors

H.3.3 [**Information Storage and Retrieval**]: Information Search and Retrieval; H.3.1 [**Information Storage and Retrieval**]: Content Analysis and Indexing

General Terms

Algorithms, Human Factors, Theory

Keywords

cultural diversity, social media

1. WORKSHOP SUMMARY

With the constantly increasing reach of the Web in general and Social Media in particular, more and more people of different nationalities, cultures, origins and beliefs contribute and access online information. These differences express themselves in language, habits, behavioural patterns, socio-cultural norms and values. They also strongly influence the way users provide and formulate content as well as the way they request, acquire, interpret and access information. Therefore, the detection and use of cultural differences and diversity will become more and more a key challenge in both, Information Retrieval and Knowledge Management. The aim of the DETECT workshop was to bring together researchers and practitioners dealing with intercultural, multi-lingual and multi-national information environments in distinct contexts, and discover synergies between their research fields.

The workshop program reflects very well the variety of aspects and applications to culture related topics in social media. Two key notes address the topics of diversity and personalization [3] as well as approaches for a behavioural analysis of users [6]. Thereby, the two opposite view points on cultural aspects in social media are addressed: the consumers side of searching and reading social news items and the authors side of creating and publishing such information.

Also the wide range of contributions to DETECT'11 reflects the various relevant technologies and research questions in the workshop's context. Ranging from works addressing fundamental key technologies like text and image classification over mining patterns of common usage or user behaviour over time and space to end user issues of how to deal with cultural diversity on the social web.

Boato et al. [1] consider the application of classifying the emotions associated with pictures. Given the recent interest in sentiment analysis before the background of social media, this topic provides insights suitable to the foundations of social media research.

Nishida et al. [5] address the difficult task of classification on microblogs. Using a data compression approach introduces a method which might be very suitable to handle the immanent feature sparsity of Twitter and the like.

Martin [4] presents an analytical tool to follow web users in order to improve the usability of web sites. Identifying common usage patterns and relating them to different cultural backgrounds is a step in the direction of tailoring online services to particular user needs.

Kling and Gottron [2] automatically extract cultural regions from flickr images annotated with geographic coordinates, which in turn allows to detect culturally similar areas directly from social media data.

Wijaya and Yeniterzi [8] look at the evolution of the semantics of words over time. This work adds a time component to cultural topics which enriches social media analysis with another additional and important dimension.

Welzer et al. [7] look at cultural awareness in social media and consider in particular the question of creating awareness for cultural differences in cross cultural interactions.

DETECT'11, October 24, 2011, Glasgow, Scotland, UK.
ACM 978-1-4503-0962-2/11/10.

The goal of the final break-out session and plenary discussion is to identify key research questions for detecting and exploiting cultural diversity on the social web. A desirable outcome is an agenda of research challenges that need to be addressed in the years to come in order to promote the progress in the fields relevant to the DETECT workshop. This also includes the identification of interesting areas for potential collaborations among the workshop participants.

2. REFERENCES

[1] G. Boato, M. Della Giacoma, and P. Zontone. Emotion based classification of natural images. In *DETECT'11: Proceedings of the International Workshop on DETecting and Exploiting Cultural diversiTy on the Social Web*, 2011.

[2] C. C. Kling and T. Gottron. Detecting culture in coordinates: Cultural areas in social media. In *DETECT'11: Proceedings of the International Workshop on DETecting and Exploiting Cultural diversiTy on the Social Web*, 2011.

[3] R. Kreste. Recommendation on the social web: Diversification and personalization. In *DETECT'11: Proceedings of the International Workshop on DETecting and Exploiting Cultural diversiTy on the Social Web*, 2011.

[4] L. Martin. Filtering usability data with reference to behavior. In *DETECT'11: Proceedings of the International Workshop on DETecting and Exploiting Cultural diversiTy on the Social Web*, 2011.

[5] K. Nishida, R. Banno, K. Fujimura, and T. Hoshide. Tweet classification by data compression. In *DETECT'11: Proceedings of the International Workshop on DETecting and Exploiting Cultural diversiTy on the Social Web*, 2011.

[6] M. Rowe. Using behaviour analysis to detect cultural aspects in social media systems. In *DETECT'11: Proceedings of the International Workshop on DETecting and Exploiting Cultural diversiTy on the Social Web*, 2011.

[7] T. Welzer, M. Holbl, M. Druzovec, and B. Brumen. Cultural awareness in social media. In *DETECT'11: Proceedings of the International Workshop on DETecting and Exploiting Cultural diversiTy on the Social Web*, 2011.

[8] D. T. Wijaya and R. Yeniterzi. Understanding semantic change of words over centuries. In *DETECT'11: Proceedings of the International Workshop on DETecting and Exploiting Cultural diversiTy on the Social Web*, 2011.

4th International Workshop on Patent Information Retrieval (PaIR'11)

Mihai Lupu
Information Retrieval Facility
Am Brigittenauer Sporn 5
Vienna, Austria
m.lupu@ir-facility.org

Allan Hanbury, Andreas Rauber
Vienna University of Technology
Institute for Software Technology and Interactive Systems
Favoritenstrasse 9-11/188
Vienna, Austria
{hanbury,rauber}@ifs.tuwien.ac.at

ABSTRACT

The 4th International Workshop on Patent Information Retrieval builds on the experiences of the first three workshops, to provide its participants an exciting, scientifically challenging and interactive event, where specific issues of patent retrieval may be put into the general context of Information Retrieval and Knowledge Management, in order to explore innovative solutions to new and old problems, but also to evaluate and adapt traditional or classic approaches to new problems. This year, we observe an increase in the use of standardized test collections in the contributions received, and, at the same time, new discussion points on how to make such standardized evaluation exercises more accessible to the larger IP community.

Categories and Subject Descriptors

H.0 [**Information Systems Applications**]: General

General Terms

Documentation

Keywords

Patent Retrieval

1. INTRODUCTION

Now in its fourth edition, PaIR continues to be *the* venue for researchers to present their results in addressing issues specific to the patent domain.

Patent information management and retrieval is an active and challenging field both for researchers and for professional information specialists. Patents play a key role not only in protecting intellectual property but also as a strategic business factor in all modern economies. Patent search is a particular challenge to information retrieval and access systems. Amongst the challenges successful patent search systems of the future will have to face we can count:

- very large numbers of highly complex structured documents;
- highly heterogeneous document collections (scientific papers, legal public disclosure as well as patents);
- multiple languages;
- ambiguous and conflicting jargon;
- complex technological concepts;
- sophisticated legal jargon;
- ranges and other complex query forms;
- tracking temporal issues like publication data;
- tabular and graphical information mixed into text;
- and so on.

Despite enormous advances in general information management techniques in the past few years, advanced search tools for patent professionals are still in their infancy, so the research in patent retrieval represents an important opportunity both for academic and industrial research.

2. SUMMARY OF THE WORKSHOP

2.1 Paper presentations

One of the interesting features of this year's set of papers presented at the workshop is their use of, or at least reference to, standardized test collections. Three papers use such standardized test collections to validate their results, and another two mention them in a broader scope. This makes the results more easily comparable and repeatable, and increases the clarity of their message.

This year's contributions focus on several aspects of patent retrieval. Starting from a prior art search scenario, taking a set of application claims as the query for the search process, Ganguly and colleagues present in *United we fall, Divided we stand: A study of Query Segmentation and PRF for Patent Prior Art Search* a method to decompose this large query text in order to make it more amenable to processing. Together with query expansion, their method shows a significant improvement of the results in term of the PRES scoring method of up to 14%.

Continuing on the idea of query expansion, Magdy and Jones, in *A Study on Query Expansion Methods for Patent Retrieval* present a very complete overview of such methods and their application for this very particular domain.

CIKM'11, October 24–28, 2011, Glasgow, Scotland, UK.
ACM 978-1-4503-0717-8/11/10.

Among others, the paper also shows how a general purpose linguistic resource, WordNet, cannot provide improvements for the patent domain. While not surprising in itself, the scientific proof is welcomed and a basis for development of specific resources.

One such specific resource in the patent domain, used for decades in the professional environment, are WIPO's International Patent Classification categories and classes. In their *Patent search using IPC Class vectors*, Verma and Varma propose a method to generate representative vectors based on the patent's classification and that of the documents cited in the patent. Their method of enhancing the document vectors is demonstrated to provide a significant improvement over a tf-idf baseline.

Another specific resource needed for patent retrieval, perhaps more than for other kinds of retrieval, are multilingual thesauri. Nanba and colleagues, in *Automatic Construction of a Bilingual Thesaurus using Citation Analysis* adapt a method from citation analysis to the alignment of English and Japanese thesauri using the hypernym-hyponym relations (broader-narrower term relations).

Finally, two papers present overviews of specific areas of the patent retrieval environment. Hanbury and colleagues, in *Patent Image Retrieval: a Survey*, describe the status of the image retrieval methods as applied to the patent domain. This is a very important, and, at the same time, very difficult problem, which deserves more attention in the academic community. Then, Lupu, in *The Status of Retrieval Evaluation in the Patent Domain*, tries to bring new discussion points in the issue of evaluation of all these methods. He suggest a PRET-EVAL map to help visualize the focus of an evaluation exercise.

2.2 Special features

Last year, the invited speakers were representatives of national patent offices (Canadian and US). This year, we invited again speakers from the industry—practitioners who will give their perspectives on the work done by the researchers and the existing landscape in the commercially available tools. Jane List, from the Lighthouse IP Group, a multi-disciplinary service provider in the field of intellectual property, scientific and legal information and information processing, will start the workshop by providing an overview of the industry. Stephen Adams, from Magister Ltd., an independent consultancy which provides a range of services to the Scientific and Technical Information community, will conclude the presentation sessions with his professional perspective over the work presented this year by the researchers.

After the presentation sessions, the second half of the afternoon will be dedicated to focused discussions in breakout groups. Potential workgroup discussion topics are:

- Industry - Academia: collaboration or competition?
- Patentese: experiences and ideas on understanding and processing it
- Image recognition for patents
- Data annotation, text mining and their use for a more semantic patent retrieval

3. STATISTICS

This year we received 8 paper submissions. In the end 6 were accepted for publication and presentation at the workshop. The programme committee consisted of 19 members, and each paper was reviewed 4 times. On the usual scale between -3 (strong reject) and 3 (strong accept), the papers received on average a positive score of 0.98. The average score of the accepted papers was 1.55.

4. CONCLUSION

We hope that these papers, together with the breakout sessions, will trigger interesting conversations and future development in IP search, through a closer collaboration between researchers and industry representatives. We also hope that the workshop will be a springboard for many future events and lead to the recognition of patent searching as one of the central areas of research in Information Retrieval and Knowledge Management, and one of the key-players in a knowledge-driven innovative society.

5. ACKNOWLEDGEMENTS

On our path to PaIR'11, we have received the generous and important contribution of many people, whom we need to acknowledge and to whom we wish to express our gratitude. First of all we would like to thank the authors for submitting so many papers of high quality. We would also like to thank the workshop programme committee for their dedicated and careful review of the papers. Many thanks go as well to the organizers of CIKM both for providing us with the opportunity to hold the workshop and for their support and advice during our preparation for it.

Overview of the Third International Workshop on Search and Mining User-generated Contents

Iván Cantador
Univ. Autónoma de Madrid
Madrid, Spain
ivan.cantador@uam.es

José Carlos Cortizo
BrainSins
Alcorcón, Madrid, Spain
jccortizo@brainsins.com

Francisco Carrero
BrainSins
Alcorcón, Madrid, Spain
fcarrero@brainsins.com

Jose Antonio Troyano
Universidad de Sevilla
Sevilla, Spain
troyano@us.es

Paolo Rosso
Univ. Politécnica de Valencia
Valencia, Spain
prosso@dsic.upv.es

Markus Schedl
Johannes Kepler University
Linz, Austria
markus.schedl@jku.at

ABSTRACT

In this paper, we provide an overview of the 3rd International Workshop on Search and Mining User-generated Contents, held in conjunction with the 20th ACM International Conference on Information and Knowledge Management. We present the motivation and goals of the workshop, and some statistics and details about accepted papers and keynotes.

Categories and Subject Descriptors

H.3 [**Information Systems**]: Information Storage and Retrieval; H.4 [**Information Systems**]: Information Systems Applications; I.2 [**Computing Methodologies**]: Artificial Intelligence; I.7 [**Computing Methodologies**]: Document and Text Processing

General Terms

Documentation, Experimentation, Algorithms

Keywords

user-generated contents, social media, data mining, text mining, opinion mining, information retrieval

1. MOTIVATION AND GOALS

Nowadays, the huge amount and variety of user generated contents available in the Web open a wide range of opportunities to enhance information retrieval and e-commerce applications. Opinions and reviews about products, annotations and bookmarks on multimedia resources, and friend relations in social networks are just a few examples of personal information sources to be exploited in order to both improve the user's experience and increase the companies' revenues in online search and commerce activities.

As in its previous editions, the 3rd Workshop on Search and Mining User-generated Contents (SMUC 2011) aimed at becoming a multidisciplinary forum for researchers and practitioners that work on knowledge extraction, management and exploitation in Social Media, and belong to different, but complementary fields such as Web (content/structure/usage) mining, information retrieval, opinion mining and sentiment analysis, user modeling, personalization and recommendation, and multimedia processing and retrieval.

In SMUC 2011 workshop, we identify four main research themes into which the above research problems can be categorized: Searching in Social Media, Mining Social Media, Opinion Mining and Sentiment Analysis, and Multimedia Processing and Retrieval. For all of them, we are interested in developing and testing intelligent systems and applications, involving innovative research from the fields of user modeling, personalization, recommendation, information visualization, and business intelligence, to name a few. Different research lines, backgrounds, perspectives and degrees of expertise were presented at the workshop, and thus very interesting multidisciplinary discussions, collaborations and work synergies between the workshop attendees were expected as main outcomes of the event.

2. ACCEPTED PAPERS

The SMUC 2011 workshop received a total of 17 submissions, 12 from Europe, 3 from Asia and 2 from North America. Out of these, 11 (65%) were accepted as full papers.

Categorizing the submissions according to the main topics of the workshop yields the following distribution: seven papers focus on data/text mining, five papers focus on search, information filtering and recommender systems, three papers are related to multimedia mining, and two papers address opinion mining topics.

Another categorization of the papers can be considered based on the different information sources used for experimentation. Twitter represents by far the most popular information source among contributions as five of the accepted papers rely on the microblogging service. Another two papers use multimedia sources like Flickr, TV and YouTube, and the remaining papers make use of Wikipedia, product reviews web sites, SMS, and other sources.

The following are the papers presented at SMUC 2011 workshop:

- "I'm Eating a Sandwich in Glasgow: Modeling Locations with Tweets" [4] describes an interesting approach, tested on a large dataset, for locating tweets based on language modeling.

CIKM'11, October 24–28, 2011, Glasgow, Scotland, UK.
ACM 978-1-4503-0717-8/11/10.

- "Mining Tag Similarity in Folksonomies" [7] proposes a hybrid (linguistic/semantic) approach to determining similarity amongst the user-defined tags of a folksonomy.

- "On the Generation of Rich Content Metadata from Social Media" [3] addresses the problem of analyzing content quality as a means to enhance the retrieval and filtering of tweets related to TV shows.

- "Predicting Age and Gender in Online Social Networks" [5] describes a text categorization approach for the identification of age and gender in social media texts.

- "A Comparative Evaluation of Personality Estimation Algorithms for the TWIN Recommender System" [6] presents a comparative evaluation of personality estimation algorithms for the TWIN ("Tell me What I Need") recommender system.

- "Mining Twitter Tweets to Tag Flickr Photos and YouTube Videos" [9] presents an analysis of the exploitation of hashtags and tweets contents for the automatic annotation of web resources, such as Flickr photos and Youtube videos.

- "ThemeCrowds: Multiresolution Summaries of Twitter Usage" [1] presents an interesting visualization interface that shows users and tags on tweets using hierarchical clustering for the generation of treemaps and antichains to visualize information incrementally.

- "Detection of Near-duplicate User Generated Contents: The SMS Spam Collection" [10] deals with SMS spam filtering, and examines the use of existing plagiarism detection tools to detect near-duplicates in SMS messages.

- "Characterizing Wikipedia Pages Using Edit Network Motif Profiles" [11] attempts to characterize the quality (class) of Wikipedia pages, and determine their authoritativeness based on patterns of page edit networks.

- "Improved Answer Ranking in Social Question-Answering Portals" [2] deals with the question of how to identify good answers for user questions in community Question Answering portals, improving answer ranking by learning from preference pairs of marked questions.

- "Trend-based and Reputation-Versed Personalized News Network" [8] describes an approach to filtering Twitter and Facebook messages using trend mining with respect to the reputation of sources.

3. KEYNOTES

Three invited speakers presented very interesting talks about main topics of SMUC 2011 workshop: information retrieval, opinion mining, and social network and community analysis in Social Media.

- "Analysis of communities in Social Media", by Martin Atzmüller, from University of Kassel, Germany.

- "Information Retrieval techniques for Social Media", by Joemon M. Jose, from University of Glasgow, UK.

- "The challenge of understanding the flow of sentiments in Social Media", by David E. Losada, from Universidad de Santiago de Compostela, Spain.

4. ACKNOWLEDGMENTS

We would like to thank CIKM 2011 organizing committee for their support in making the workshop possible. We also appreciate very much the dedication of SMUC 2011 programme committe members and external reviewers. Finally, we wish to express our gratitude to all authors and invited speakers of the workshop.

5. REFERENCES

[1] D. Archambault, D. Greene, P. Cunningham, and N. Hurley. ThemeCrowds: Multiresolution Summaries of Twitter Usage. In *Proc. of the 3rd Workshop on Search and Mining User-generated Contents*, Glasgow, UK, October 2011.

[2] F. Hieber and S. Riezler. Improved Answer Ranking in Social Question-Answering Portals. In *Proc. of the 3rd Workshop on Search and Mining User-generated Contents*, Glasgow, UK, October 2011.

[3] G. Inches, A. Basso, and F. Crestani. On The Generation of Rich Content Metadata from Social Media. In *Proc. of the 3rd Workshop on Search and Mining User-generated Contents*, Glasgow, UK, October 2011.

[4] S. Kinsella, V. Murdock, and N. O'Hare. "I'm Eating a Sandwich in Glasgow": Modeling Locations with Tweets. In *Proc. of the 3rd Workshop on Search and Mining User-generated Contents*, Glasgow, UK, October 2011.

[5] C. Peersman, W. Daelemans, and L. V. Vaerenbergh. Predicting Age and Gender in Online Social Networks. In *Proc. of the 3rd Workshop on Search and Mining User-generated Contents*, Glasgow, UK, October 2011.

[6] A. Roshchina, J. Cardiff, and P. Rosso. A Comparative Evaluation of Personality Estimation Algorithms for the TWIN Recommender System. In *Proc. of the 3rd Workshop on Search and Mining User-generated Contents*, Glasgow, UK, October 2011.

[7] G. Solskinnsbakk and J. A. Gulla. Mining Tag Similarity in Folksonomies. In *Proc. of the 3rd Workshop on Search and Mining User-generated Contents*, Glasgow, UK, October 2011.

[8] O. Streibel and R. Alnemr. Trend-based and Reputation-Versed Personalized News Network. In *Proc. of the 3rd Workshop on Search and Mining User-generated Contents*, Glasgow, UK, October 2011.

[9] A. Sureka and D. Correa. Mining Twitter Tweets to Tag Flickr Photos and YouTube Videos. In *Proc. of the 3rd Workshop on Search and Mining User-generated Contents*, Glasgow, UK, October 2011.

[10] E. Vallés and P. Rosso. Detection of Near-duplicate User Generated Contents: The SMS Spam Collection. In *Proc. of the 3rd Workshop on Search and Mining User-generated Contents*, Glasgow, UK, October 2011.

[11] G. Wu, M. Harrigan, and P. Cunningham. Characterizing Wikipedia Pages Using Edit Network Motif Profiles. In *Proc. of the 3rd Workshop on Search and Mining User-generated Contents*, Glasgow, UK, October 2011.

Web Science and Information Exchange in the Medical Web

Kerstin Denecke
L3S Research Center
Appelstrasse 9a
Hannover, Germany
denecke@L3S

Peter Dolog
Aalborg University
Selma Lagerlöfs Vej 300
Aalborg, Denmark
dolog@cs.aau.dk

ABSTRACT

The amount of social media data dealing with medical and health issues increased significantly in the last couple of years. Medical social media data now provides a new source of information within information gaining contexts. Facts, experiences, opinions or information on behavior can be found in the Medicine 2.0 or Health 2.0 and could support a broad range of applications. This workshop is devoted to the technologies for dealing with social- and multi media for medical information gathering and exchange. This specific data and the processes of information gathering poses many challenges given the increasing content on the Web and the trade off of filtering noise at the cost of losing information which is potentially relevant.

Categories and Subject Descriptors

J3 [**Life and Medical Sciences**, H.3.3 [**Information Storage and Retrieval**]: Information Search and Retrieval

General Terms

Algorithms

Keywords

Web Science, Social Web, Medicine

1. INTRODUCTION

Health information is exchanged to an increasing extent in the Web. Patients are blogging about their experiences in living with certain diseases. They discuss health-related queries in forums or even inform the public about their current health status via Twitter. Physicians are reporting about their daily experiences in treating patients. Beyond, research results and related issues are reported.

Medical social media data now provides a new source of information within information gaining contexts. Facts, experiences, opinions or information on behaviour can be found in the Medicine 2.0 and could support a broad range of applications. Health organizations monitor online news repositories and web pages for relevant data on epidemiological events.

CIKM'11, October 24–28, 2011, Glasgow, Scotland, UK.
ACM 978-1-4503-0717-8/11/10.

Physicians learn about the experiences of their colleagues provided through social media platforms such as weblogs, or forums. Moreover, patients can search for information or experiences of others which can lead to patient empowerment.

The research community becomes increasingly aware of new possibilities and research challenges of the medical Web. The intention of this workshop is to provide a platform for exchanging research ideas and work devoted to the challenges and technologies for dealing with social- and multi media for medical information gathering and exchange. Language peculiarities, content diversity, streaming nature of this specific data poses many challenges given the increasing content on the Web and the tradeoff of filtering noise at the cost of losing information which is potentially relevant. Further the processes of information gathering make several demands that need to be considered in research as well. The Second International Workshop on Web Science and Information Exchange in the Medical Web (MedEx 2011) offers the opportunity to present work related to these problems.

2. BACKGROUND

This workshop is intended to continue with the First International Workshop on Web Science and Information Exchange in the Medical Web that was held in conjunction with WWW 2010 in Raleigh. The topic of medical Web science and information exchange fits very well with the general theme of the CIKM conference and attracted already high interest in its first release. Around 25 attendees joined the workshop, six papers where presented and we had an acceptance ratio of 75%. The workshop considers tasks and problems related to Web Science in one specific application domain, which is medicine. This domain and the problems are extremely relevant for current research, government and industry. Government and health organizations become increasingly aware that there is a need for considering the developments in the medical Web. Possible application scenarios are currently set up and researchers start to develop appropriate technologies.

Furthermore, the organizers of the workshop coordinate and participate in an European project (STREP, M-Eco http://www.meco-project.eu) that focuses on this topic. The consortium is composed of researchers typically publishing at Web science, data mining and NLP venues. Therefore the workshop provides an initial forum for them to further pursue these directions and to provide high level contributions.

3. OBJECTIVES

The aim of the workshop is to encourage researchers from the medical web science community to present novel issues and techniques related to medical intelligence (especially in the context of web science). This workshop is intended to address different aspects related to the problem of accessing, exchanging, processing, and filtering health related Web information. Another important question is how to make corresponding applications more reliable and adaptable. The workshop serves as a forum for the confluence of new and multidisciplinary ideas that will help to drive research in the areas of medical web text and data mining.

As a target audience, researchers and practitioners from web science, information retrieval, artificial intelligence, medical informatics, natural language processing and related areas are invited to submit their original papers in this workshop. As the workshop organizers are participating in European projects which have the workshop's topics at their core, we expect significant interest from about 20 partners as a minimum.

4. TOPICS

The workshop theme and topics are reflecting the latest discussion in that upcoming field and comprise the analysis of medical social media data and multi media data, including event detection and information extraction in this field. Even though it would be very useful, personalization techniques are still not integrated or only implemented to a limited extent in medical applications. Evaluation of implemented medical applications working with Medical Web data is still a problem due to missing annotated data sets and gold standards. This workshop is intended to encourage researchers thinking also into this direction.

In more detail, papers covering at least one of the following topics are expected:

- Analysis of medical social media data
  - Ways and means of analysing large-scale medical web data
  - Criteria and methods to determine the quality of health content
  - Multilingual issues in health-related Web content
  - Processing streams of social media data
- Analysis of medical multi media data
  - Classifying medical media content (e.g., TV, Radio, YouTube)
  - Processing of medical media data
- Event Detection and information extraction in medical social/multi- media
  - Event extraction from medical texts
  - Identification of relationship between events
- Personalization in medical applications
  - Personalized biosurveillance
  - Personalized e-Health solutions
  - User models for health care applications
- Evaluation in medical web applications
  - Quality of processing of medical social/multi- media data
  - Methods for improving medical intelligence sensitivity and specificity
  - Medical intelligence false alarm mitigation

5. WORKSHOP PROGRAM FORMAT

The workshop will comprise two keynotes. Sophia Ananiadou will give a talk on latest developments in biomedical text mining and implications for the medical web. Wendy Chapman's keynote will discuss the shortcomings and barriers in the clinical natural language processing (NLP) domain and envisions the creation of an NLP ecosystem for the medical domain.

Three full papers have been accepted and will be presented. A novelty in this year are short communications where research questions will be raised. These contributions will be the starting point for discussions on the future developments in this interesting area. The presentations will be grouped according to topic so that comprehensive discussions can follow after the paper presentation.

The discussions are expected to provide as outcome ideas on future work and becoming aware of current challenges. The results of the discussions will be an additional outcome of the project.

6. CONCLUSIONS

There is an increasing interest in using Web data in various applications supporting medicine and health. The Second International Workshop on Web Science and Information Exchange in the Medical Web will provide the platform for ongoing discussions on this topic and will allow to exchange research ideas and work.

7. WORKSHOP ORGANIZERS

Kerstin Denecke is a senior researcher at the L3S Research Center in Hannover, Germany. Her main research interests are natural language processing, text and data mining, in particular in the medical domain. The specific areas she has been working on include medical language processing, information extraction, sentiment analysis and text classification.

Peter Dolog is an associate professor of computer science at Aalborg University where he also leads Intelligent Web and Information Systems group (http://iwis.cs.aau.dk). His main research interests fall into intelligent web information systems. This includes personalization and adaptation strategies and algorithms for world wide web, adaptive hypermedia, conceptual modeling of web applications, knowledge management, personalized web based systems, and web transactions.

8. ACKNOWLEDGMENTS

The workshop is supported by the M-Eco project, partly funded by the EU.

3rd International Workshop on Collaborative Information Retrieval (CIR2011)

Gene Golovchinsky
FX Palo Alto Laboratory, Inc.
Palo Alto, CA 94304, USA
gene@fxpal.com

Juan M. Fernández-Luna, Juan F. Huete,
CITIC-UGR, University of Granada
18071 Granada, Spain
{jmfluna,jhg}@decsai.ugr.es

Meredith Ringel Morris
Microsoft Research
Redmond, WA, USA
merrie@microsoft.com

Jeremy Pickens
Catalyst Repository Systems
Boulder, CO 80202, USA
jpickens@catalystsecure.com

Julio C. Rodríguez-Cano
Universidad de las Ciencias Informáticas
Ciudad de La Habana, Cuba
jcrcano@uci.cu

ABSTRACT

Synchronous, explicit search has some interesting characteristics that distinguish it from other types of interaction: there is much more emphasis on interaction, as the system has to not only communicate search results to the user, but also mediate some forms of communication and data sharing among its users. There are new algorithms that need to be invented that use inputs from multiple people to produce search results, and new evaluation metrics need to be invented that reflect the collaborative and interactive nature of the task. Finally, we need to integrate the expertise of library and information science researchers and practitioners by revisiting real-world information seeking situations with an eye for explicit, synchronous collaborative search.

Categories and Subject Descriptors

H.3.m [**Information Storage and Retrieval**]: Miscellaneous

General Terms

Algorithms, Measurement, Design, Experimentation, Human Factors.

Keywords

Collaborative Information Seeking, Collaborative Search, Information Retrieval, CSCW.

1. INTRODUCTION

Support for explicit collaboration is an essential part of many information seeking activities. Explicit collaboration differs from recommendation systems and collaborative filtering in that the people engaged in information seeking have an explicitly shared information need. Hence, rather than inferring similarities of intent, the system is free to mediate the sharing of knowledge and division of labor [6]. In the last few years, several research groups have pursued various issues related to collaboration during search, including support for awareness [12], algorithmic mediation [14], software frameworks for collaboration [4], and collaboration through a range of different devices [e.g., 1, 9].

CIR'11, October 28, 2011, Glasgow, Scotland, UK.
ACM 978-1-4503-0951-6/11/10.

The table below illustrates the relationship between collaborative search and other related forms of information seeking. In this workshop, we focus on synchronized, explicit collaboration [8]. This style of information seeking is typical of small teams working toward a shared information need. These kinds of information seeking behaviors are often found in academic, legal, intelligence analysis, pharmaceutical and other research situations. They differ from typical web search interactions in that they are characterized by complex, evolving, recall-oriented, ongoing information needs that are not possible to satisfy with a single query.

Table 1. Taxonomy of collaboration

	Explicit	Implicit
Synchronized	Collaborative Exploratory Search [12][14][16]	Real-time awareness and continual context update [11]
Non-sychronized	Group asynchronous browsing [18]	Collaborative Filtering Social Search Web 2.0 Wisdom of Crowds [17][19]

2. OUTLINE

Based on our experience with previous workshops, our goal is to create more opportunities for discussion to achieve a deeper understanding of the issues, and provide participants with some hands-on experience with a variety of collaborative search tools. Thus, we invite participants to submit both position papers and also to demonstrate actual working collaborative search systems.

To facilitate discussion, we will select a few papers for extended oral presentations, while other submissions will be presented in a poster session. This format for presentations should increase the fruitful exchange of ideas rather than having people listen to presentations without much opportunity for discussion.

Since the focus of this workshop is on systems, we invite participants to build new systems or to adapt their existing systems to demonstrate various aspects of collaboration. For this purpose, we plan to provide a test collection that participants will be able to use. Participants who sign up to demonstrate systems will be given a hard drive with data, and some descriptions of information needs against that data. We expect participants to demonstrate how their systems can be used to help teams find information, and to have workshop attendees try to use others' tools. This kind of hands-on experience should improve our collective understanding of the possibilities for improving collaboration in information seeking.

The proposed schedule for the workshop is as follows:

08:30-09:00	Breakfast, introductions, overview
09:00-10:00	Selected presentations
10:00-10:30	Break
10:30-11:30	Poster presentations
11:30-12:30	Selected presentations
12:30-14:00	Group lunch
14:00-15:30	System demos and discussion
15:30-16:00	Break
16:00-17:00	Discussion, wrap-up, planning
18:00-	Optional workshop dinner

3. THEMES

We accepted several papers for presentation at the workshop that covered a range of themes related to collaborative search, including descriptions of various domains and use cases for collaborative information seeking, and descriptions and evaluations of algorithms for retrieving documents in a collaborative setting.

Morris and Morris [13] discuss opportunities for collaboration in the clinical setting. Handel and Wang [10] offer a fascinating look at the challenges of collaborative information seeking over classified documents when searchers are constrained in the kinds of information they can share. Capra et al. [3] characterize various aspects of collaborative information seeking and exploratory search practices through an online survey of 344 people.

The algorithmic theme is represented by several papers. Assent [2] describes design considerations for simultaneously optimizing the user experience and computation efficiency in collaborative decision making. Halvey [9] presents and evaluates an algorithm for image retrieval, and Fernández-Luna et al. [5] describe ways to support transitions between recommendation and collaboration. Finally, Rodriguez Perez [15] describes an interface that allows people to share their browsing activity.

4. REFERENCES

[1] Amershi, S. and Morris, M.R. (2008) CoSearch: A System for Co-located Collaborative Web Search. In *Proc. CHI 2008*, ACM Press.

[2] Assent, I. (2011) Efficient algorithms for collaborative decision making for large scale settings. In *Proc. 3rd Intl Workshop on Collaborative Information Retrieval (CIR2011).*

[3] Capra, R., Velasco-Martin; J., and Sams, B. (2011) Collaborative Information Seeking by the Numbers. In *Proc. 3rd Intl Workshop on Collaborative Information Retrieval (CIR2011).*

[4] Fernández-Luna, J. M., Huete, J.F. (2010) CIRLab: A Groupware Framework for Collaborative Information Retrieval Research. *Information Processing & Management* 46(6) pp. 749-761.

[5] Fernández-Luna, J. M., Huete, J.F. and Rodriguez-Cano, J.C. (2011) User Intent Transition for Explicit Collaborative Search Through Groups Recommendation. In *Proc. 3rd Intl Workshop on Collaborative Information Retrieval (CIR2011).*

[6] Foley, C., and Smeaton, A. (2010) Division of labour and sharing of knowledge for synchronous collaborative information retrieval. *Information Processing & Management* 46 (6).

[7] Fu, X., Kelly, D., and Shah, C. (2007). Using collaborative queries to improve retrieval for difficult topics. In *Proceedings of SIGIR '07*, ACM Press, pp. 879-880.

[8] Golovchinsky, G, Qvarfordt, P., and Pickens, J. (2009) Collaborative Information Seeking. Computer, 42(3), IEEE Press, pp. 47-51.

[9] Halvey, M. (2011) Preference Based Feedback for Collaborative Image Retrieval. In *Proc. 3rd Intl Workshop on Collaborative Information Retrieval (CIR2011).*

[10] Handel, M. and Wang, E. (2011) "I can't tell you what I found:" Problems in Multi-level Collaborative Information Retrieval. In *Proc. 3rd Intl Workshop on Collaborative Information Retrieval (CIR2011).*

[11] Imity. Available online at http://www.imity.com/

[12] Morris, M. R. and Horvitz, E. (2007) SearchTogether: an interface for collaborative web search. In *Proceedings of UIST '07*, ACM Press, pp. 3-12.

[13] Morris, M.R. and Morris, D. (2011) Understanding the Potential for Collaborative Search Technologies in Clinical Settings. In *Proc. 3rd Intl Workshop on Collaborative Information Retrieval (CIR2011).*

[14] Pickens, J. and Golovchinsky, G. (2007) Collaborative Exploratory Search. In *Proceedings of HCIR '07 Workshop*, available online at http://projects.csail.mit.edu/hcir/web/hcir07.pdf

[15] Rodriguez-Perez, J.A. (2011) CoFox: A visual collaborative browser. In *Proc. 3rd Intl Workshop on Collaborative Information Retrieval (CIR2011).*

[16] Smeaton, A.F., Foly, C., Gurrin, C., Lee, H., and McGivney, S. (2006) Collaborative Searching for Video Using the Físchlár System and a DiamondTouch Table. In *Proceedings of the First IEEE International Workshop on Horiztontal Interactive Human-Computer Systems*, IEEE Computer Society, pp. 151-159.

[17] Sun, J.-T., Zeng, H.-J., Liu, H., Lu, Y., and Chen, Z. (2005). CubeSVD: A novel approach to personalized Web search. In Proceedings of WWW '05, pp. 382-390.

[18] Wittenburg, K., Das, D., Hill, W., and Stead, L. (1995) Group asynchronous browsing on the World Wide Web. In *Proceedings of the 4th Int. WWW Conference*, pages 51-62.

[19] Yoople. Available on the web at http://www.yoople.net

DESIRE 2011: First International Workshop on Data infrastructurEs for Supporting Information Retrieval Evaluation

Maristella Agosti
University of Padua, Italy
agosti@dei.unipd.it

Nicola Ferro
University of Padua, Italy
ferro@dei.unipd.it

Costantino Thanos
ISTI-CNR, Pisa, Italy
costantino.thanos@isti.cnr.it

ABSTRACT

The workshop focuses on the three areas of interest to CIKM to discuss how to envisage and design evaluation infrastructures able to store, manage, and make accessible the scientific data and knowledge of interest for advancing the evaluation of information retrieval and access tools.

Main goal is to understand how to make use of the expertise of the three scientific areas in a cooperative way to avoid the duplication of efforts which may occur when addressing the problem separately in each specific area and to trigger synergies and joint actions on the issue.

Main purposes of the workshop are the identification of a roadmap and the definition of initial best practices to guide the development of the necessary evaluation infrastructures.

Categories and Subject Descriptors

H.2.8 [**Database Management**]: Database applications—*Scientific databases*; H.3.3 [**Information Storage and Retrieval**]: Information Search and Retrieval—*Search process*; H.3.4 [**Information Storage and Retrieval**]: Systems and Software—*Performance evaluation (efficiency and effectiveness)*; H.5.2 [**Information Interfaces and Presentation**]: User Interfaces—*Benchmarking, evaluation, methodology*; D.2.8 [**Software Engineering**]: Metrics—*Complexity measures, performance measures*

General Terms

Design, Experimentation, Management, Measurement, Performance

Keywords

experimental evaluation, scientific data, evaluation infrastructure, data test collection, best practices

1. INTRODUCTION

Information Retrieval has a strong and long tradition dating back to the 1960s in producing and processing scientific data resulting from the experimental evaluation of search algorithms and search systems. This attitude towards evaluation has led to fast and continuous progress in the evolution of information retrieval systems and search engines.

However, in order to make the data test collections, that are used in the context of the evaluation activities, understandable and usable they must be endowed with some auxiliary information, i.e., provenance, quality, context. Therefore, there is a need for metadata models able to describe the main characteristics of evaluation data. In addition, in order to make distributed data collections accessible, sharable, and interoperable, there is a need for advanced data infrastructures.

In contrast, the information retrieval area has barely explored and exploited the possibilities for managing, storing, and effectively accessing the scientific data produced during the evaluation studies by making use of the methods typical of the database and knowledge management areas. Over the years, the information retrieval area has produced a vast set of large test collections which have become the main benchmark tools of the area and contribute to reproducible and comparable experiments. However, these same collections have not been organised into coherent and integrated infrastructures which make them accessible, searchable, citable, exploitable, and re-usable to all possibly interested researchers, developers, and user communities.

It is thus time for these three communities – information retrieval, databases, and knowledge management – to join efforts, meet, and cooperate to envisage and design useful infrastructures able to coherently manage pertinent data collections and sources of information, and so take concrete steps towards developing them.

To address the workshop issues, experts have been invited to give two keynote addresses and six relevant papers have been accepted, among the submitted ones, for presentation. The two following sections are reporting the addressed specific topics.

2. KEYNOTE ADDRESSES

The keynote address by Norbert Fuhr of the University of Duisburg-Essen in Germany[1], entitled *An Infrastructure for Supporting the Evaluation of Interactive Information Retrieval*, addresses the presentation of a testbed for the evaluation of interactive information access. Starting with the INEX[2] interactive track in 2004, the group lead by professor Fuhr developed the Daffodil (now ezDL) framework, providing an experimental framework for interactive retrieval, that allows for easy exchange or extension of the system components. Moreover, this framework also contains tools for

DESIRE'11, October 28, 2011, Glasgow, Scotland, UK.
ACM 978-1-4503-0952-3/11/10.

[1] `http://www.is.informatik.uni-duisburg.de/staff/fuhr.html.en`
[2] `https://inex.mmci.uni-saarland.de/`

organizing laboratory experiments. Besides extensive logging (including the possibility to exploit eye tracking data), the system allows for presenting questionnaires at all stages of a search session (pre-/post- task/session), as well as the scheduling of search tasks and monitoring task time.

The keynote address by Maurizio Lenzerini of the Sapienza University of Rome, Italy[3], entitled *Ontology-based data management*, addresses how the ontology-based data management aims at accessing and using data by means of a conceptual representation of the domain of interest in the underlying information system. The talk provides an introduction to ontology-based data management, by illustrating the main ideas and techniques for using an ontology to access the data layer of an information system. Then, it describes an architecture for ontology-based data access and discussed the issue of choosing the appropriate language for expressing the various components of the architecture, by illustrating the main advantages one gains in managing the information system through the ontology. Finally, the issue of developing methodologies and tools for the design and usage of ontology-based data management solutions have been explained.

3. POSITION AND COMMUNICATIONS PAPERS

The paper *Principles for Robust Evaluation Infrastructure* by Justin Zobel (Department of Computer Science and Software Engineering, The University of Melbourne, Australia), William Webber (Department of Computer Science and Software Engineering, The University of Melbourne, Australia), Mark Sanderson (School of Computer Science and Information Technology, RMIT University, Australia), and Alistair Moffat (Department of Computer Science and Software Engineering, The University of Melbourne, Australia) makes reference to the standard "Cranfield" approach to the evaluation of information retrieval systems that has been used and refined for nearly fifty years. Over the last few years, investigation of the strengths and limitations of this approach have led to identification of serious flaws in some experiments. Since the knowledge of these flaws can prevent their perpetuation into future work and informs the design of new experiments and infrastructures, the authors review relevant aspects of evaluation and, based on their research and observations over the last decade, outline principles on which new infrastructures should rest.

The paper *A Lightweight Framework for Reproducible Parameter Sweeping in Information Retrieval* by Richard Eckart de Castilho (Ubiquitous Knowledge Processing Lab, Technical University of Darmstadt, Germany) and Iryna Gurevych (Ubiquitous Knowledge Processing Lab, Technical University of Darmstadt, Germany) introduces a lightweight framework for parameter sweep experiments geared towards evolution, efficiency and reproducibility of experiments running on a single machine. To reduce the computational effort of running an experiment with many different parameter settings, the framework uses the tasks and the dataflow dependency information to maintain and reuse intermediate results whenever possible.

The paper *Evaluation with the VIRTUOSO platform* by Gérard Dupont (CASSIDIAN, Elancourt, France), Gaël de Chalendar (CEA, Fontenay-aux-Roses, France), Khaled Khelif (CASSIDIAN, Val de Reuil, France), Dmitri Voitsekhovitchy (CEA, Fontenay-aux-Roses, France), Géraud Canet (CEA, Fontenay-aux-Roses, France), and Stéphan Brunessaux (CASSIDIAN, Val de Reuil, France) describes a software architecture for providing an open technical framework for the integration of tools for collection, processing, analysis and communication of open source information. The integration of heterogeneous components is implemented in a way that also permit the comparison of capabilities of multiple tools. The platform that supports the evaluation framework has been named VIRTUOSO. It supports an evaluation framework that allows to deploy and run evaluation kits for different use-cases.

The paper *Use Cases as a Component of Information Access Evaluation* by Jussi Karlgren, Anni Järvelin, Preben Hansen, and Gunnar Eriksson, all authors at the Swedish Institute of Computer Science, Sweden, argues that use cases for information access can be written to give explicit pointers towards benchmarking mechanisms and that if use cases and hypotheses about user preferences, goals, expectation and satisfaction are made explicit in the design of research systems, they can more conveniently be validated or disproved - which in turn makes the results emanating from research efforts more relevant for industrial partners, more sustainable for future research and more portable across projects and studies.

The paper *PatOlympics - An Infrastructure for Interactive Evaluation of Patent Retrieval Tools* by Mihai Lupu (Vienna University of Technology, Austria) presents the infrastructure behind the PatOlympics interactive evaluation campaign. This infrastructure, consisting of a relational database back-end, a Java processing core and a JavaScript interface, makes it possible for real users and researchers to interact in a competitive environment, while maintaining, to the extent possible, the evaluation procedures of standard information retrieval campaigns.

The paper *Infrastructure and Workflow for the Formal Evaluation of Semantic Search Technologies* by Stuart N. Wrigley (Department of Computer Science, University of Sheffield, UK), Raùl García-Castro (Facultad de Informàtica Universidad Politécnica de Madrid, Spain), and Càssia Trojahn (INRIA and LIG, Montbonnot Saint Martin, France) describes an infrastructure for the automated evaluation of semantic technologies and, in particular, semantic search technologies. For this purpose, an evaluation framework is introduced which follows a service-oriented approach for evaluating semantic technologies and uses the Business Process Execution Language (BPEL) to define evaluation workflows that can be executed by process engines.

Acknowledgments

We would like to thank those institutions and individuals who have made this workshop possible: the ACM CIKM 2011 Conference organisation, the Program Committee members, and the Department of Information Engineering of the University of Padua, Italy.

The DESIRE 2011 workshop has been supported by the PROMISE network of excellence[4] (contract n. 258191), as part of the 7th Framework Program of the European Commission.

[3]`http://www.dis.uniroma1.it/~lenzerin/index.html/`

[4]`http://www.promise-noe.eu/`

PIKM 2011: The 4th ACM Workshop for Ph.D. Students in Information and Knowledge Management

In conjunction with the 20th ACM Conference on Information and Knowledge Management ACM CIKM 2011, Glasgow, UK, October 28, 2011

Anisoara Nica
Sybase, An SAP Company
Waterloo, Ontario, Canada
anica@sybase.com

Fabian M. Suchanek
INRIA Saclay
Paris, France
fabian@suchanek.name

ABSTRACT

The PIKM workshop gives Ph.D. students an opportunity to present their dissertation proposals at a global stage. Similarly to the CIKM, the PIKM workshop covers a wide range of topics in the areas of databases, information retrieval and knowledge management. Interdisciplinary work across these tracks is particularly encouraged.

Categories and Subject Descriptors

H.2.0 [**Information Systems**]: Database Management; H.2.8 [**Information Systems**]: Database Management—*Database Applications*[Data Mining]; H.3.3 [**Information Systems**]: Information Storage and Retrieval—*Information Search and Retrieval*

General Terms

Algorithms,Design,Experimentation,Performance,Theory

Keywords

CIKM, PIKM, doctoral consortium, Ph.D. forum, dissertations, database systems, information retrieval, knowledge management, interdisciplinary work

1. INTRODUCTION

The PIKM is the Ph.D. workshop of the CIKM conference. The goal of this workshop is two-fold: First, it shall give doctoral students an opportunity to present their work in an early stage to a global audience. This allows the students not only to crystallize their ideas into a scientific article, and to practice scientific presentation, but also to receive feedback from reviewers, from fellow students and from the general CIKM audience. Second, we believe that the research community, too, benefits from such a workshop: Ph.D. theses are the grassroots of research. They point out new research avenues and indicate current promising topics. They provide fresh viewpoints from the researchers of tomorrow. We hope that the interaction with other researchers at the workshop itself, across all levels of seniority, will help propel science forward.

PIKM'11, October 28, 2011, Glasgow, Scotland, UK.
ACM 978-1-4503-0953-0/11/10.

The CIKM addresses a broad range of topics in the areas of databases and information systems, information retrieval, semantic web, knowledge management and data mining. Therefore, the CIKM serves as a good forum for graduate students to expose their doctoral research at an early stage. Particularly, such a workshop in CIKM encourages further interdisciplinary studies across the fields addressed by the CIKM. This unique advantage can benefit both the students and the CIKM conference.

The PIKM workshop covers topics in all areas of the general CIKM conference. This includes subjects as diverse as resource monitoring, semantic search, pattern recognition, and data mining. The PIKM is a relatively new workshop. This is the fourth time the workshop is being held, after successful workshops in 2007 [15, 16], 2008 [11, 14], and 2010 [10, 9] at CIKM conferences. The workshop is novel in the sense of being one of the few Ph.D. workshops in conferences to target the three tracks of databases, information retrieval and knowledge management with some emphasis on interdisciplinary research across these tracks as well.

This year we have program committee (PC) comprising twenty members with a good balance of experts from academia and industry. It includes both fresh doctorates and senior researchers, thereby allowing for different viewpoints on the proposed works. These PC members are from various countries across the globe, including Australia, Brazil, Canada, France, Germany, India, Italy, Switzerland, the UK, and the United States. They have provided tough and exhaustive reviews of papers submitted to the workshop, thus providing the students with useful feedback for their endeavors. We sincerely thank them for their efforts.

The PIKM 2011 [8] is organized as a full day workshop with four sessions. There are three sessions for full oral paper presentations, addressing the themes of databases, information retrieval and knowledge management, respectively. The forth session is a poster session for short papers. We have accepted three full papers in the database area [7, 17, 18], three in the information retrieval area [5, 6, 20], and three in the data mining and knowledge management area [1, 2, 13]. Many papers span multiple of these areas, though. In addition, four short papers have been accepted for poster presentations [3, 4, 12, 19].

The core of the audience at the PIKM workshop will be the presenters. However, besides the students of the accepted papers, we also expect other new Ph.D. students to attend the workshop in order to learn about their peers' research directions. Based on our experience with previous PIKMs, other participants attending the workshop are likely to be professors, research scientists and professionals from the corporate world. The PIKM workshop allows them to get a panoramic view of the doctoral work pursued at various universities.

2. HIGHLIGHTS OF THE PIKM 2011

Keynote Speaker. Professor Felix Naumann from the Hasso-Plattner-Institut, Potsdam, Germany, is the keynote speaker at PIKM 2011. He will talk about *Extreme Web Data Integration* – a task that becomes ever more challenging with the relentless growth of the Web.

Best Paper Award. The best paper at the PIKM workshop, as determined by the reviews of the PC members, always receives a best paper award. This year's award will go to Minsuk Kahng, Sangkeun Lee and Sang-Goo Lee for their paper *Ranking Objects by Following Paths in Entity-Relationship Graphs* [6]. The paper outlines a challenging vision for treating different types of data in a homogeneous, Semantic Web-like fashion for query answering. Thereby, it bridges the areas of databases and information retrieval.

Review Article. We plan to write a review article that summarizes the proceedings of the PIKM 2011. Such articles have been published before, in *SIGIR Forum*, *SIGKDD Explorations*, and *SIGMOD Record* for the PIKM 2007 [16], PIKM 2008 [14], and PIKM 2010 [10] workshops respectively.

3. ACKNOWLEDGMENTS

PIKM 2011 has a steering committee with three former PIKM chairs: *Jian Pei* (Simon Fraser University, Canada), *Prasan Roy* (IBM Research, India), and *Aparna S. Varde* (Montclair State University, USA).

We would like to thank our PC members for the tremendous effort in completing the reviews in a short period of time. The PC members are: *Ralitsa Angelova* (Google, Switzerland), *Srikanta Bedathur* (IIT Delhi, India), *Pierre Bourhis* (Oxford University, UK), *Francisco Couto* (Universidade de Lisboa, Portugal), *Khuzaima Daudjee* (University of Waterloo, Canada), *Renata Guizzardi* (Federal do Espírito Santo, Brazil), *Mouna Kacimi* (Free University of Bozen-Bolzano, Italy), *Harumi Kuno* (Hewlett Packard Labs, USA), *Bruno Marnette* (INRIA Saclay, France), *Richi Nayak* (Queensland University of Technology, Australia), *Maya Ramanath* (IIT Delhi, India), *Prasan Roy* (IBM Research, India), *Pierre Senellart* (Télécom ParisTech, France), *Mauro Sozio* (Max-Planck-Institute for Informatics, Germany), *Marc Spaniol* (Max-Planck-Institute for Informatics, Germany), *Ramakrishna Varadarajan* (University of Wisconsin-Madison, USA), *Aparna S. Varde* (Montclair State University, USA), *Robert Wrembel* (Poznań University of Technology, Poland), *Matthew Young-Lai* (Google, Canada).

We are also grateful to CIKM 2011 organizers for their support and help.

4. REFERENCES

[1] L. Abele, M. Kleinsteuber, and H. Thorbjoern. Resource monitoring in industrial production with knowledge-based models and rules. In *ACM PIKM 2011*.

[2] M. L. Ba, T. Abdessalem, and P. Senellart. Towards a version control model with uncertain data. In *ACM PIKM 2011*.

[3] D. Ganguly, J. Leveling, and G. J. Jones. Utilizing sub-topical structure of documents for information retrieval. In *ACM PIKM 2011*.

[4] M. Hosseini, I. Cox, and N. Milic-Frayling. Optimizing the cost of information retrieval test collections. In *ACM PIKM 2011*.

[5] G. Inches and F. Crestani. Online conversation mining for author characterization and topic identification. In *ACM PIKM 2011*.

[6] M. Kahng, S. Lee, and S.-G. Lee. Ranking objects by following paths in entity-relationship graphs. In *ACM PIKM 2011*.

[7] S. Müller and H. Plattner. Aggregation strategies for columnar in-memory databases in a mixed workload. In *ACM PIKM 2011*.

[8] A. Nica and F. M. Suchanek, editors. *Proceedings of the 4th Ph.D. Workshop in CIKM, PIKM 2011, 20th ACM Conference on Information and Knowledge Management, ACM CIKM 2011*, Glasgow, UK.

[9] A. Nica, F. M. Suchanek, and A. S. Varde. Emerging multidisciplinary research across database management systems. *SIGMOD Record*, 39(3):33–36, 2010.

[10] A. Nica and A. S. Varde, editors. *Proceedings of the Third Ph.D. Workshop in CIKM, PIKM 2010, 19th ACM Conference on Information and Knowledge Management, ACM CIKM 2010*, Toronto, Canada.

[11] P. Roy and A. S. Varde, editors. *Proceedings of the Second Ph.D. Workshop in CIKM, PIKM 2008, 18th ACM Conference on Information and Knowledge Management, ACM CIKM 2008*, Napa Valley, California, USA.

[12] K. Sapkota, A. Aldea, D. A. Duce, M. Younas, and R. Bañares-Alcántara. Towards semantic methodologies for automatic regulatory compliance support. In *ACM PIKM 2011*.

[13] S. Spiegel, B.-J. Jain, E. W. D. Luca, and S. Albayrak. Pattern recognition in multivariate time series. In *ACM PIKM 2011*.

[14] A. S. Varde. Challenging research issues in data mining, databases and information retrieval. *SIGKDD Explorations*, 11(1):49–52, 2009.

[15] A. S. Varde and J. Pei, editors. *Proceedings of the First Ph.D. Workshop in CIKM, PIKM 2007, Sixteenth ACM Conference on Information and Knowledge Management, ACM CIKM 2007*, Lisbon, Portugal.

[16] A. S. Varde and J. Pei. Advances in information and knowledge management. *SIGIR Forum*, 42(1):29–35, 2008.

[17] B. Wall and R. Angryk. Minimal data sets vs. synchronized data copies in a schema and data versioning system. In *ACM PIKM 2011*.

[18] A. Wojciechowski. E-ETL: Framework for managing evolving ETL processes. In *ACM PIKM 2011*.

[19] X. Xia, X. Yang, S. Li, C. Wu, and L. Zhou. RW.KNN: A proposed random walk KNN algorithm for multi-label classification. In *ACM PIKM 2011*.

[20] D. Zellhoefer and I. Schmitt. A user interaction model based on the principle of polyrepresentation. In *ACM PIKM 2011*.

Managing Interoperability and compleXity in Health Systems - MIXHS'11

Workshop Summary

Matt-Mouley Bouamrane
The University of Glasgow
Institute of Health & Well-Being
College of Medical,
Veterinary and Life Sciences
Scotland, U.K.
FirstName.LastName@glasgow.ac.uk

Cui Tao
Mayo Clinic,
Division of Biomedical Statistics and,
Informatics, College of Medicine,
Rochester, Minnesota,
U.S.A
Tao.Cui@mayo.edu

ABSTRACT

Managing Interoperability and Complexity in Health Systems, MIXHS'11, aims to be a forum focussing on recent research and technical results in knowledge management and information systems in bio-medical and electronic health systems. The workshop will provide an opportunity for sharing practical experiences and best practices in e-Health information infrastructure development and management. Of particular interest to the workshop themes are technical solutions to recurring practical systems deployment issues, including harnessing the complexity of bio-medical domain knowledge and the interoperability of heterogeneous health systems. The workshop will gather experts, researchers, system developers, practitioners and policymakers designing and implementing solutions for managing clinical data and integrating existing and future electronic health systems infrastructures.

Categories and Subject Descriptors

J.3 [**Computing Applications**]: Life and Medical Sciences—*Medical information systems*; H.4.m [**Information Systems Applications**]: Miscellaneous

General Terms

Design, Management, Standardization

Keywords

Bio-medical Knowledge Management; Electronic Health Systems Interoperability and Integration

CIKM'11, October 24 -28, 2011, Glasgow, Scotland, UK.
ACM 978-1-4503-0717-8/11/10.

1. WORKSHOP DESCRIPTION

The volume of clinical data available to patients, professionals and health systems is expanding exponentially, while health systems resources are being rationalised and services transformed in order to deal with unprecedented epidemiological shifts in populations and diseases patterns. Patients live longer, with multiple complex morbidities, receiving multiple pharmaceutical treatments which interaction is not well understood. Health professionals are providing care and treatments while often having to manage the increased complexity of technology and the specialisation of medical disciplines. Relentless updates in clinical knowledge, as well as fast-paced technological innovations lead to feelings of knowledge saturation and information overload for the health professionals involved in the multi-disciplinary medical team. At the same time, patients' expectations of safety and quality of healthcare and medical services provision are also increasing.

The Managing Interoperability and Complexity in Health Systems workshop will provide an opportunity for sharing practical experiences and best practices in e-health information infrastructure development and management. The forum will appeal to academics and researchers in information and knowledge management, clinical standards developers and e-health systems implementers as well as public health policymakers, and to both local and international audiences.

Issues of biomedical data-mining in large heterogeneous clinical data-sets, information retrieval and extraction in multiple medical repositories, the management of complexity and the coherent update of knowledge in medicine, clinical standards interoperability in distributed health systems and the patient Electronic Health Record (EHR) are now becoming critical to implementing enterprise and nationwide health systems.

Topics of interest to the workshop include knowledge management activities seeking to address these issues by: (i) using clinical data mining, information extraction and retrieval, (ii) standardisation of clinical classification (e.g. International Classification of Diseases, ICD), large scale biomedical terminologies and ontologies (e.g. SNOMED-CT), (iii) the standardisation of clinical information transfer formats (e.g. HL7) and (iv) EHR and the structuring of clinical documents (e.g. Clinical Document Architecture, CDA).

2. ACCEPTED SUBMISSIONS

2.1 Keynote Speaker

The workshop keynote speaker is Paul Woolman, *(C.Eng, CITP, MIPEM, FBCS)*, Enterprise Architect for the Scottish Government e-Health programme and chairman of the NHSScotland Interoperability Working Group.[1] Woolman has worked on the challenges of interoperability in medical systems for over twenty years: he has worked on EU and ISO standards in medical devices interoperability, and established the Scottish Health XML Steering Group, which developed web services standards now widely in use in NHSScotland and other parts of the UK. He currently chairs the Scottish Interoperability working group and coordinates the NHS Scotland Ensemble User Group as part of his Enterprise Architecture work for the Scottish Government. He is a regular speaker at international forums on eHealth topics. Woolman's presentation at the MIX-HS workshop will focus on the: *"Challenges of managing interoperability in regional healthcare organisations"*

2.2 Full Research Papers

All submissions were reviewed by an average of 3 reviewers and the program chairs wrote detailed meta-reviews for each submission summarising the comments of the members of the International Technical Program Committee. The following 7 submissions were accepted as full research papers:

- **Quality Scores for Electronic Health Records for Clinical Research**, *(Rosemary Tate ; Natalia Beloff ; Shivani Padmanabhan ; Timothy Williams)*
- **Generality and Reuse in a Common Type System for Clinical Natural Language Processing**, *(Stephen T. Wu ; Vinod C. Kaggal ; Guergana K. Savova ; Hongfang Liu ; Dmitriy Dligach ; Jiaping Zheng ; Wendy W. Chapman ; Christopher G. Chute)*
- **A realism-based analysis of the OpenEHR Entry model**, *(Andre Andrade ; Mauricio Almeida)*
- **Managing Complexity in Pre-Operative Information Management Systems**, *(Matt-Mouley Bouamrane ; Cui Tao ; Frances S. Mair)*
- **Integrating Volumetric Biomedical Data in the Virtual Physiological Human**, *(Albert Burger)*
- **Automatically Estimating the Incidence of Symptoms Recorded in GP Free Text Notes**, *(Rob Koeling ; Rosemary Tate ; John Carroll)*
- **Model-Driven Dynamic Integration of Health Data**, *(Adel Taweel)*

2.3 Work-in-Progress & Challenges and Visions Track

The following 8 submissions were accepted as work-in-progress / Challenges and Visions track papers:

- **Standardizing radiation oncology data for future modelling of side effects after radiation therapy**, *(Caroline Olsson ; Graham Kemp)*
- **A Semantic Web Application Framework for Health Systems Interoperability**, *(Pedro Lopes ; José Luis Oliveira)*
- **Toward Semantic Web based Knowledge Representation and Extraction from Electronic Health Records**, *(Cui Tao ; Jyotishman Pathak ; Susan Welch ; Matt-Mouley Bouamrane ; Stanley Huff ; Christopher Chute)*
- **An Ontology of Diabetes Self Management**, *(David Sutton ; Arantza Aldea ; Clare Martin)*
- **Assessing Schizophrenia With A Highly Interoperable Architecture**, *(Ando Emerencia ; Lian Van Der Krieke ; Nicolai Petkov ; Marco Aiello)*
- **An overview of e-Health Integration in Scotland**, *(Matt-Mouley Bouamrane ; Frances S. Mair)*
- **Telehealth at scale: The need for interoperability and analytics**, *(Rajib Ghosh ; Juergen Heit ; Soundararajan Srinivasan)*
- **Sharing Patient Radiological Imaging Studies and Pathological Samples: Standards, Protocols and Practices**, *(Bridget Kane ; James Meaney ; Saturnino Luz)*

[1] http://www.ehealth.scot.nhs.uk/

3. WORKSHOP ORGANISATION

- **Program Chairs:**

Matt-Mouley Bouamrane, *(University of Glasgow, Scotland, U.K.)* & **Cui Tao**, *(Mayo Clinic, U.S.A)*

- **International Technical Committee:**

- **Robert Freimuth, Guoqian Jiang, Hongfang Liu, Jyotishman Pathak, Sunghwan Sohn, Kavishwar Wagholikar, Wei-Qi Wei, Stephen Wu, Qian Zhu**, *Mayo Clinic, U.S.A*
- **Alberto Anguita-Sánchez, Jean-Paul Calbimonte, Mikel Egaña-Aranguren, Miguel García Remesal, Diana de la Iglesia, David Pérez del Rey, Boris Villazón-Terrazas**, *Universidad Politécnica de Madrid, UPM, Spain*
- **Erick Antezana**, *Norwegian University of Science and Technology - NTNU, Norway*
- **Adam Dunn**, *University of New South Wales, Australia*
- **Jesualdo Tomás Fernández-Breis**, *Universidad de Murcia, Spain*
- **Philip Gooch**, *City University London, U.K.*
- **Susan Graham**, *University of California at Berkeley, U.S.A*
- **Lucy Hederman**, *University of Dublin, Trinity College, Ireland*
- **Alistair Lawson**, *Edinburgh Napier University, Scotland, U.K.*
- **Paea LePendu**, *Stanford University , U.S.A*
- **Marilyn McGee-Lennon**, *University of Glasgow, Scotland, U.K.*
- **Masood Masoodian**, *University of Waikato, New Zealand*
- **Rafal Rak**, *University of Manchester, U.K.*
- **A.Rosemary Tate**, *University of Sussex, U.K.*
- **Abdel Rahman Tawil**, *University of East London (UEL), U.K.*
- **Paul Taylor**, *University College London (UCL), U.K.*
- **Annette ten Teije**, *Vrije Universiteit, Amsterdam, Netherlands*
- **Fusheng Wang**, *Emory University, U.S.A.*
- **Jens Weber**, *University of Victoria, B.C., Canada*
- **Jim Zheng**, *Medical University of South Carolina, U.S.A.*

Report on the Third International Workshop on Cloud Data Management (CloudDB 2011)

Xiaofeng Meng[1] Zhiming Ding[2] Haibo Hu[3]
xfmeng@ruc.edu.cn, zhiming@iscas.ac.cn, haibo@comp.hkbu.edu.hk
[1]School of Information and DEKE, MOE, Renmin University of China, Beijing, China
[2]Institute of Software, Chinese Academy of Sciences
[3]Department of Computer Science, Hong Kong Baptist University, Hong Kong

1. INTRODUCTION

The third ACM international workshop on cloud data management was held in Glasgow, Scotland, U.K. on October 28, 2011 and co-located with the ACM 20th Conference on Information and Knowledge Management (CIKM). The main objective of the workshop was to address the challenges of large-scale data management based on the cloud computing infrastructure. The workshop brings together researchers and practitioners from cloud computing, distributed storage, query processing, parallel algorithms, data mining, and system analysis, all attendees share common research interests in maximizing performance, reducing cost of cloud data management and enlarging the scale of their endeavors.

The workshop attracted 14 submissions from Asia, North America and Europe, out of which the program committee finally accepted 6 full papers. The accepted papers focused on cloud-based storage, machine learning, query processing, distributed algorithms, security and privacy.

Categories and Subject Descriptors

A. General Literature

General Terms

Algorithms, Management

2. RESEARCH PAPERS

The technical paper session consisted of seven presentations, whose main points are summarized next. Together, they give a snapshot of new developments on data management spurred by cloud computing. These papers cover a variety of topics. We believe that researchers and developers will draw inspiration from these papers to further appreciate this exciting new technology, specifically from the perspective of cloud data management.

The paper entitled *Learning-based Entity Resolution with MapReduce* utilizes cloud computing from a machine-learning perspective. Entity resolution is a crucial step for data quality and data integration. Learning-based approaches show high effectiveness at the expense of poor efficiency. To reduce the typically high execution times, the authors *Lars Kolb, Hanna Köpcke, Andreas Thor and Erhard Rahm* investigated how learning-based entity resolution can be realized in a cloud infrastructure using MapReduce. They proposed and evaluated two efficient MapReduce-based strategies for pair-wise similarity computation and classifier application on the Cartesian product of two input sources. Their evaluation on real-world datasets shows the high efficiency and effectiveness of the proposed approaches.

Thomas Jörg, Roya Parvizi, Hu Yong and Stefan Dessloch explored the application of view maintenance techniques in a MapReduce environment. In the paper *Incremental Recomputations in MapReduce*, they regarded a MapReduce program as a view definition and the computed result as a materialized view. However, MapReduce programs need to be re-executed to obtain up-to-date results after base data has changed. The authors presented a case study based on typical MapReduce programs mentioned in Google's original MapReduce paper. By adapting view maintenance techniques, the results can be recomputed in an incremental fashion considerably more efficiently. Based on the case study, they developed a general solution for the incremental maintenance of the class of MapReduce programs that compute self-maintainable aggregates.

In *Efficient Data Distribution Strategy for Join Query Processing in the Cloud, Haiping Wang, Xiaofeng Meng and Yunpeng Chai* studied join query processing in cloud. The challenge is that, to finish a join query in the cloud, data among different nodes need to be transferred. The transmission cost (network workload between servers and the transmission time delay) will be very high if the strategy is not properly chosen. They investigated using redundant data for join query optimization in cloud environment. Two novel algorithms, Set Cover based algorithm (SC) and Minimum Element based algorithm (ME), were proposed to reduce data transmission cost. The experiment results demonstrate that the proposed methods can greatly reduce the data transmission cost compared and are very close to the optimal strategy.

In the Paper entitled *Trustworthy Middleware Services in the Cloud*, Imad Abbadi endeavored towards the establishment of trust in the cloud, despite its dynamic nature and distributed resources. He proposed to establish trustworthy middleware services that could help in moving in the direction of establishing trust in the cloud. The paper mainly focuses on identifying the functions for establishing trustworthy middleware services for supporting home healthcare application, in particular those that are required to address the security, privacy, and resilience properties of home healthcare application.

CIKM'11, October 24–28, 2011, Glasgow, Scotland, UK.
ACM 978-1-4503-0717-8/11/10.

Yuxiao Dong and Qing Ke presented TeleDatA, a cloud-based system that combines data mining, social network analysis and statistics analysis with MapReduce framework, for knowledge discovery in telecommunications. As a full functionality system, TeleDatA provides data-flow oriented preprocessing utilities, chain engine, expression evaluation engine and core analysis algorithms. The shift from client-server to cloud platform is indispensible for telecommunication data analysis, due to the continued exponential growth in both the volume and the complexity of telecom data. In their paper *TeleDatA: Data Mining, Social Network Analysis and Statistics Analysis System based on Cloud Computing in Telecommunication Industry*, they focused on the scalability and parallelism introduced by the MapReduce model, which makes TeleDatA capable of handling tera even peta-scale data.

In the Paper entitled *Authentication of Range Query Results in MapReduce Environments*, *Ziwei Yang, Shen Gao, Jianliang Xu and Byron Choi* studied the issue of query authentication on cloud platform. Authenticated query processing has been an important problem in outsourced databases. However, all existing works on query authentication are confined to a single server. In this paper, the authors presented a scalable authentication solution for range queries based on the MapReduce framework. To address the problem of parallelism and load balancing, they proposed two algorithms for mapping the authentication work to a set of sub-tasks that can be executed on the slave nodes in parallel. They also developed an optimization technique for multiple concurrent queries to improve system performance by shared execution.

3. KEYNOTE

Prof. Paul Watson from the Newcastle University, UK kindly gave us a keynote speech on an emerging cloud computing pattern, which is called the Panel of Experts. In this talk, he described this cloud pattern and gave examples of its use. The Panel of Experts pattern can be applied when a range of algorithms "compete" to provide the best solution to a problem. It can therefore be viewed as the dual of map-reduce as it applies a set of functions to one data item, whereas map-reduce applies one function to a set of data items. The pattern has been evaluated through a large chemical informatics application which can take days to run on tens of cloud nodes.

4. CONCLUSION

CloudDB 2011 was the third CIKM-associated workshop addressing the challenges of large database services based on the cloud computing infrastructure. Whilst these emerging services have reduced the cost of data storage and content delivery by several orders of magnitude, there is significant complexity involved in ensuring large data service to scale when one needs consistency and reliability under peak loads. Cloud-based environment has the technical requirement to manage data center virtualization, lower cost and boost reliability by consolidating systems on the cloud. The existing research works in the area of cloud-based data management are still somehow immature and leave significant room for progress. The works presented in the workshop mainly focused on adapting existing Grid and Map/Reduce techniques to the cloud environment. The participants agreed that many open challenges still remain such as cloud data security and the efficiency of distributed storage and query processing in the cloud.

5. ACKNOWLEDGEMENT

We would like to thank the program committee members, authors and attendees, for making CloudDB 2011 a successful workshop. Finally, we also express our great appreciation for the support from Renmin University of China, Institute of Software, Chinese Academy of Sciences, and Hong Kong Baptist University.

Search and Mining Entity-Relationship Data

Haggai Roitman
IBM Research Haifa
Haifa 31905, Israel
haggai@il.ibm.com

Ralf Schenkel
Max-Planck-Institut für Informatik
Saarbruecken, Germany
schenkel@mpi-inf.mpg.de

Marko Grobelnik
Jozef Stefan Institute
Ljubljana, Slovenia
marko.grobelnik@ijs.si

ABSTRACT

This paper summarizes the details of the first international workshop on search and mining entity-relationship data. This workshop will bridge between IR, DB, and KM researchers to seek novel solutions for search and data mining of rich entity-relationship data and their applications in various domains. We first provide an overview about the workshop. We then briefly discuss the workshop program.

Categories and Subject Descriptors

H.3.3 [**Information Systems**]: [Information Search and Retrieval]

General Terms

Algorithms, Design

Keywords

Entity-relationship data, Search, Data Mining

1. WORKSHOP OVERVIEW

Data complexity and its diversity have been rapidly expanding over the last years, spanning from large amounts of unstructured and semi-structured data to semantically rich available knowledge, and driven by ever increasing sophistication in data management requirements. Numerous applications in various domains such as social-media, healthcare, telecommunication, e-commerce and web analytics, business intelligence, and cyber-security, require new methods and tools for collecting and extracting entities and their relationships from unstructured and heterogeneous data sources to be transformed into useful knowledge and provide insights.

While lots of useful facts are being added on a daily basis on multitude web and enterprise data sources, they are still hidden behind barriers of language constraints, data heterogeneity and ambiguity, and the lack of proper query interfaces. In addition, novel search and data mining methods are required to provide expressive and powerful discovery capabilities, yet intuitive enough, for exploring the large amounts of entity-relationship data.

CIKM'11, October 24–28, 2011, Glasgow, Scotland, UK.
ACM 978-1-4503-0717-8/11/10.

1.1 Workshop Objectives

The workshop main objective is to serve as an open forum for discussing the new research challenges in search and mining of large scale ER data extracted from multitude of unstructured and semi-structured data sources, driven by recent industry trends and requirements in various domains and increasing academic interest. The workshop will bring together researchers from different communities working on similar problems in the context of ER and other semantic data, allowing for cross-fertilization between areas. During the workshop, we will identify common problems and their various solution approaches in DB, KM, and IR.

1.2 Workshop Themes and Topics

The workshop has two main themes. The first is search and discovery over rich entity-relationship data and includes among others topics such as ER data collection, indexing, query languages and optimization, ranking methods, similarity and exploratory search, privacy, etc. The second is entity-relationship data mining methods and includes among others topics such ER data extraction, resolution, representation, fusion, ER graph mining, etc.

1.3 Program Committee

The following is the list of the workshop PC members in an alphabetical order:

- Krisztian Balog, Norwegian University of Science and Technology, Norway
- Roi Blanco, Yahoo! Research, Spain
- David Carmel, IBM Research, Israel
- Kevin C.C. Chang, University of Illinois at Urbana-Champaign, USA
- Lise Getoor, University of Maryland, USA
- Yosi Mass, IBM Research, Israel
- Einat Minkov, Haifa University, Israel
- Oren Kurland, Technion, Israel
- Pavel Serdyukov, Yandex LLC, Russia
- Kavitha Srinivas, IBM Research, USA
- Martin Theobald, Max-Planck Inst., Germany
- Sivan Yogev, IBM Research, Israel
- Elad Yom-Tov, Yahoo! Research, USA
- Cong Yu, Google, USA

2. WORKSHOP PROGRAMME

The workshop programme includes three invited talks, an oral presentation, a poster session, and a panel for open discussion. Next, we provide few details about each.

2.1 Invited talks

The workshop has three invited talks. The first invited talk by Michael Witbrock, Vice President for Research at Cycorp, titled "*Knowledge for/from People for/from Computers*", will focus on Cycorp progress towards human/computer collaboration and reasoning-based applications.

The second invited talk by Krisztian Balog, a postdoctoral at the Norwegian University of Science and Technology, titled "*Finding Related Entities*", shall provide an overview of the TREC Entity benchmarking effort, highlight prominent approaches to the Related Entities Finding (REF) task, and also discuss challenges and future research directions in entity-oriented search.

The last invited talk by David Carmel from IBM Research-Haifa, titled "*Is This Entity Relevant to Your Needs?*", shall discuss the notion of relevance in search over entity relationship data, with a focus on the similarity and distinction between relevancy in Entity and Document search.

2.2 Accepted Papers

A total of 10 papers were submitted to the workshop, out of which 3 were accepted as full (6 page-long) papers and 3 as short (2 page-long) papers. Paper topics span from entity extraction methods to entity search and privacy. We now shortly describe each paper.

The full paper by Athenikos [3] presents PanAnthropon FilmWorld, a direct, sophisticated entity retrieval system which extracts and derives semantic knowledge from Wikipedia. Facts are represented using domain-relevant classes, entities, attributes, and categories.

The full paper by Wijaya and Gianfortoni [6] suggests several approaches for ranking human-proposed paraphrasing verbs of Noun Compounds (NCs). A novel approach that uses a two-step process of clustering similar NCs and then labeling the best paraphrasing verb as the most prototypical verb in the cluster is presented. The authors demonstrate the potential of their approach for finding implicit relations between entities especially when the relations are not explicit in the context in which the entities appear, rather implicit in the relationship between its constituents.

The full paper by Tamang [5] examines a re-ranking framework for the slot filling task in the context of two different settings: (1) high transparency; a few pipelines share similar resources that can be used to provide detailed intermediate and complementary results; (2) low transparency; many systems use diverse resources, and serve as black boxes, absent of any intermediate results. In both settings, the paper's experimental results show that statistical re-ranking can be used to effectively combine automated systems, achieving better performance than the best state-of-the-art individual system and alternative combination methods. The paper further demonstrates the impact of its learning-to-rank framework to combine output from multiple systems, achieving a lower cost than labor intensive human annotation.

The short paper by Abedjan and Naumann [1] applies association rule mining over RDF data at statement level by introducing the concept of mining configurations. A configuration specifies the context of rule mining (the transactions) and the target of rule mining (the items). For each configuration the paper describes the corresponding opportunities, capabilities, and application fields. A proof-of-concept is described using the DBpedia data set.

The short paper by Roitman and Yogev [4] presents a novel authorization model for entity search. Entity search has recently attracted the attention of many researchers from a classical IR perspective. Many discovery systems in various domains, such as social, medical, enterprise, and CRM, may benefit from exposing entity search services. Yet, many such systems may need a control on the level of information sharing during retrieval time in order to answer queries of authorized users and protect privacy. Addressing this challenge, the paper suggests an authorization model for entity search, based on traditional IR concept of access control list (ACL) which can be efficiently implemented.

Finally, the short paper by Anderson et al. [2] describes a new and unique thesaurus which allows to address temporal aspects in ER search and data mining and improve context-based retrieval. The paper discusses the application of the Historical Thesaurus of English (HTE) to semantic tagging of texts from AD 700 to the current day and presents several use-cases where the power of HTE is highly exploitable.

2.3 Panel

We shall conclude the workshop with a panel, where we shall discuss open issues and advances in ER search and data mining. The panel will serve as an open stage for interdisciplinary collaboration for facing the emerging research challenges.

Acknowledgement

We would like to thank the PASCAL2 EU project for sponsorship. Special thanks to David Carmel from IBM Research-Haifa for fruitful discussions during the workshop proposal. We would like to thank our invited speakers for accepting our invitations. We would further like to express our worm gratitude to the workshop PC members for their excellent paper review work. Finally, we would like to thank CIKM 2011 organizers.

3. REFERENCES

[1] Z. Abedjan and F. Naumann. Context and target configurations for mining rdf data. In *Proceedings of the 1st International Workshop on Search and Mining Entity Relationship Data (SMER)*, 2011.

[2] J. Anderson, M. Alexander, C. Kay, and M. Sarwar. Enabling er search and data mining using the historical thesaurus of english. In *Proceedings of the 1st International Workshop on Search and Mining Entity Relationship Data (SMER)*, 2011.

[3] S. J. Athenikos. Enabling type/condition-specified entity/fact retrieval using semantic knowledge extracted from wikipedia. In *Proceedings of the 1st International Workshop on Search and Mining Entity Relationship Data (SMER)*, 2011.

[4] H. Roitman and S. Yogev. An authorization model for entity search. In *Proceedings of the 1st International Workshop on Search and Mining Entity Relationship Data (SMER)*, 2011.

[5] S. Tamang. Adding smarter systems instead of human annotators: Re-ranking for slot filling system combination. In *Proceedings of the 1st International Workshop on Search and Mining Entity Relationship Data (SMER)*, 2011.

[6] D. T. Wijaya and P. Gianfortoni. Nut case: What does it mean?: Understanding semantic relationship between nouns in noun compounds through paraphrasing and ranking the paraphrases. In *Proceedings of the 1st International Workshop on Search and Mining Entity Relationship Data (SMER)*, 2011.

Fourth Workshop on Exploiting Semantic Annotations in Information Retrieval (ESAIR)

CIKM 2011 Workshop

Omar Aloso
Microsoft

Jaap Kamps
University of Amsterdam

Jussi Karlgren
SICS Stockholm

ABSTRACT

There is an increasing amount of structure on the Web as a result of modern Web languages, user tagging and annotation, and emerging robust NLP tools. These meaningful, semantic, annotations hold the promise to significantly enhance information access, by enhancing the depth of analysis of today's systems. Currently, we have only started exploring the possibilities and only begin to understand how these valuable semantic cues can be put to fruitful use. Unleashing the potential of semantic annotations requires us to think outside the box, by combining the insights of natural language processing (NLP) to go beyond bags of words, the insights of databases (DB) to use structure efficiently even when aggregating over millions of records, the insights of information retrieval (IR) in effective goal-directed search and evaluation, and the insights of knowledge management (KM) to get grips on the greater whole.

This workshop aims to bring together researchers from these different disciplines and work together on one of the greatest challenges in the years to come. The desired result of the workshop will be to gain concrete insight into the potential of semantic annotations, and in concrete steps to take this research forward; to synchronize related research happening in NLP, DB, IR, and KM, in ways that combine the strengths of each discipline; and to have a lively, interactive workshop where every participant contributes actively and which inspires attendees to think freely and creatively, working towards a common goal.

Categories and Subject Descriptors: H.3.3 [**Information Storage and Retrieval**]: Information Search and Retrieval—*Search process, Selection process*
General Terms: Algorithms, Experimentation, Theory
Keywords: Semantic Annotation

1. THEME AND TOPICS

There are many forms of annotations and a growing array of techniques that identify or extract information automatically from texts: geo-positional markers; named entities; temporal information; semantic roles; opinion, sentiment, and attitude; certainty and hedging to name a few directions of more abstract information found in text. Furthermore, the number of collections which explicitly identify entities is growing fast with Web 2.0 and Semantic Web initiatives. In some cases semantic technologies are being deployed in active tasks, but there is no common direction to research initiatives nor in general technologies for exploitation of non-immediate textual information, in spite of a clear family resemblance both with respect to theoretical starting points and methodology. We believe further research is needed before we can unleash the potential of annotations!

The previous ESAIR workshops, and in particular the third ESAIR at CIKM 2010 [5], made concrete progress in clarifying the exact role of semantic annotations in support complex search tasks: both as a means to construct more powerful queries that articulate far more than a typical Web-style, shallow, navigational information need, and in terms of *making sense* of the retrieved results on very various levels of abstraction, even non-textual data, providing narratives and paths through an intractable information space.

One of the pronouncements of the third ESAIR was to view semantic annotation as (1) a *linking* procedure, connecting (2) an *analysis* of information objects with (3) a *semantic model* of some sort. This linking is in some way intended to work towards an effective contribution to (4) some gainful *task* of interest to end users. All of these four facets of semantic annotation are of interest to the fourth workshop—the aim of this workshop is not the technologies for semantic annotation itself, but rather the *applications* and *contributions* of semantic annotation to information access tasks on various levels of abstraction such as ad-hoc retrieval, classification, browsing, textual mining, summarization, question answering, etc.

2. CHALLENGE QUESTIONS

The first two workshops were exploratory workshops to discuss the research space around the topic. The third workshop took great strides in formulating a common framework for discussing family likeness, evaluation, and application of semantic technologies. This fourth workshop is intended to formulate and propose future directions for the benefit of the field as a whole. Specifically, we will bring together a varied group of researchers covering NLP, IR, DB, and KM, and to work together towards identifying the *barriers* to success and to work on ways of addressing them.

The list of themes for the workshop include:

Application/Use Case What are *use cases* that make obvious the need for semantic annotation of information? What tasks cannot be solved by document retrieval using the traditional bag-of-words? What are the prerequisites of successful application? How can the expressive power of semantic annotation best be put to use? What is keeping searchers from exploring these powerful search request?

Annotation and analysis What types of annotation are available? Are there crucial differences between author-, software-, user-, and machine-generated annotations? Named entities, temporal expressions on the one hand and sentiment and hedging on the other are examples of analyses beyond topic that have moved to profitable application. Are there other types of an-

CIKM'11, October 24–28, 2011, Glasgow, Scotland, UK.
ACM 978-1-4503-0717-8/11/10.

notations that are within our grasp? What semantic theories do we need to formulate further annotation schemes?

Data Curation Annotations may live inside documents, or be stored externally (e.g., annotated by uncontrolled authors or tools) or both (e.g., annotation with linked data). How to keep data and metadata together? Does the annotation stop somewhere, or is all social or linked data of potential use for searching or navigating. How important is source of the annotations? Are there issues with credibility or trust that need to be taken into account?

Result Aggregation Whereas IR focuses almost exclusively at finding individual chunks of information, DB naturally focuses on results that combine information and produce aggregated results (think of OLAP queries), and KM naturally deal with the whole information space. How can we fruitfully combine these strengths?

The Workshop will conclude with a final session addressing the best way forward to unleash the potential of semantic annotation.

3. ACCEPTED PAPERS

We requested the submission of short, 2 page papers to be presented as boaster and poster. We accepted a total of 13 papers out of 15 submissions.

Damljanović et al. [2] discuss virtual documents as a way to unify data driven approach in IR, and knowledge driven approaches in DB and KM.

De Graaf [3] report on the annotation and retrieval of knowledge in software documentation.

Kamps [4] constructs a model of interaction for complex tasks, and the different information flow and success criterion of each phase, framing the role of annotation throughout a search episode.

Karlgren [6] discusses three interconnected challenges and research questions in exploiting and modelling affective and emotive aspects of information access: how to model the mood or affectual state of the user, the emotive content of an information object, and the utility of doing so. Marshall [7] studies the completeness and relative value of image tags and how this impacts image similarity evaluation.

Murakami and Ura [8] propose a decimal classification system for people on the Web, leading to capture semantic labels and hierarchical relations.

Narr et al. [9] apply NLP approach to annotate entities, persons, and events in tweets, improving access through normalization and taxonomic relations.

Ng [10] discusses the annotation of word senses and argues that renewed analysis will increase of understanding when it works and why.

Pareti [11] focuses on identifying the source of a statement and the relation between the source and the message, and how this attribution helps retrieval and interpretation.

Rój [12] discuss how the discovery and retrieval of application program interfaces (APIs) can benefit from rich semantic annotation.

Sapkota et al. [13] extract models from regulatory texts (containing regulations, policies, mandates and guidelines for organizations) from different sources using semantic annotation.

Trandabat [14] proposes semantic role labeling as a means to encode context of and relations between entities occurring in texts.

Tsatsaronis [15] studies sources of lexical ambiguity: syntactic ambiguity across syntactic categories and semantic ambiguity due to polysemy or homonymy, and their relative effect on information retrieval effectiveness.

In addition to these papers, there will be two invited keynotes.

4. FORMAT

We will start the day with a short introduction of the goals and schedule, and a "feature rally" in which each participant introduces her- or himself, and stated their particular interest in this area.

Next, we will present two invited keynotes to help frame some common ground in understanding the challenges we are addressing. We will continue with a boaster/poster session, where the papers from Section 3 are presented. The poster session will continue over lunch.

After lunch, we will organise break-out sessions in parallel to focus on specific aspects or problems related to the four themes, running through afternoon coffee, followed with a final discussion on what we will have achieved during the day and how to take our discussion forward.

The workshop will — as in previous years – continue with a more informal discussion session over drinks and dinner with all attendees of the workshop.

REFERENCES

[1] O. Alonso, J. Kamps, and J. Karlgren, editors. *ESAIR'11: Proceedings of the CIKM'11 Workshop on Exploiting Semantic Annotations in Information Retrieval*, 2011. ACM Press.

[2] D. Damljanović, U. Kruschwitz, and M.-D. Albakour. Using virtual documents to move information retrieval and knowledge management closer together. In Alonso et al. [1], pages 2–3.

[3] K. A. De Graaf. Annotating software documentation in semantic wikis. In Alonso et al. [1], pages 4–5.

[4] J. Kamps. Toward a model of interaction for complex search tasks. In Alonso et al. [1], pages 6–7.

[5] J. Kamps, J. Karlgren, and R. Schenkel, editors. *ESAIR'10: Proceedings of the CIKM'10 Workshop on Exploiting Semantic Annotations in Information Retrieval*, 2010. ACM Press.

[6] J. Karlgren. The relation between author mood and affect to sentiment in text and text genre. In Alonso et al. [1], pages 8–9.

[7] B. Marshall. Context seeking with social tags. In Alonso et al. [1], pages 10–11.

[8] H. Murakami and Y. Ura. People search using ndc classification system. In Alonso et al. [1], pages 12–13.

[9] S. Narr, E. W. De Luca, and S. Albayrak. Extracting semantic annotations from twitter. In Alonso et al. [1], pages 14–15.

[10] H. T. Ng. Does word sense disambiguation improve information retrieval? In Alonso et al. [1], pages 16–17.

[11] S. Pareti. Annotating attribution relations and their features. In Alonso et al. [1], pages 18–19.

[12] M. Rój. Exploiting user knowledge during retrieval of semantically annotated api operations. In Alonso et al. [1], pages 20–21.

[13] K. Sapkota, A. Aldea, D. Duce, M. Younas, and R. Bañares-Alcántara. Semantic-art: A framework for semantic annotation of regulatory text. In Alonso et al. [1], pages 22–23.

[14] D. Trandabat. Semantic role labeling for structured information extraction. In Alonso et al. [1], pages 24–25.

[15] G. Tsatsaronis. An experimental study on syntactic and semantic annotations in text retrieval. In Alonso et al. [1], pages 26–27.

LSDS-IR'11: The 9th Workshop on Large-Scale and Distributed Systems for Information Retrieval

Workshop co-located with ACM CIKM 2011, Glasgow, UK, October 28, 2011

Claudio Lucchese
ISTI-CNR
Pisa, Italy
claudio.lucchese@isti.cnr.it

B. Barla Cambazoglu
Yahoo! Research
Barcelona, Spain
barla@yahoo-inc.com

ABSTRACT

The growth of the Web and user bases lead to important performance problems for large-scale Web search engines. The LSDS-IR '11 workshop focuses on research contributions related to the scalability and efficiency of distributed information retrieval (IR) systems. The workshop also encourages contributions that propose different ways of leveraging diversity and multiplicity of resources available in distributed systems. More specifically, we are interested in novel applications, models, and architectures that deal with efficiency and scalability of distributed IR systems.

Categories and Subject Descriptors

H.3.3 [**Information Search and Retrieval**]: Search process; H.3.4 [**Systems and Software**]: Distributed systems

General Terms

Algorithms, Performance

Keywords

Distributed search, information retrieval, scalability

1. AIM OF THE WORKSHOP

LSDS-IR '11 continues the efforts of past workshops: P2PIR (collocated with SIGIR '05, CIKM '06, '07), HDIR (collocated with SIGIR '08), and LSDS-IR (collocated with SIGIR '07, '09, '10 and with CIKM '08). The workshop aims to combine the efforts from past events and to redefine the directions for future research in distributed IR. It brings together both experienced and young researchers in the field, focusing on scalability issues and novel applications. It also attracts contributions from related communities, such as distributed computing, P2P, cloud computing, and web search.

The topics that are of interest to the workshop include:

- applications of cloud computing to IR
- IR algorithms on novel computing architectures
- distributed crawling, indexing, and query processing
- large-scale multimedia IR
- heterogeneous resources and data integration
- caching and replication in large scale systems
- standards and benchmarks for distributed IR

CIKM'11, October 24–28, 2011, Glasgow, Scotland, UK.
ACM 978-1-4503-0717-8/11/10.

This year we added three new topics to our workshop, for which we were pleased to accept position papers, presentations of preliminary results or breakthrough ideas. We introduced the following special themes:

- large-scale data processing in social networks
- real-time indexing and retrieval
- energy-aware processing techniques for search engines

2. FULL PAPERS

This year we accepted six papers out of nine submissions.

- "On investigating scalability and robustness in a self-organizing retrieval system", Jan Sedmidubsky (Masaryk Univ.), Vlastislav Dohnal (Masaryk Univ.), and Pavel Zezula (Masaryk Univ.): This work introduces a self-organizing similarity search system for a large-scale unstructured P2P network, called the Metric Social Network. This system is able to scale to a large number of peers, to adapt to different data distributions, and to be robust to abrupt peer disconnections.
- "Evaluating large-scale distributed vertical search", Ke Zhou (Univ. of Glasgow), Ronan Cummins (Univ. of Glasgow), Mounia Lalmas (Yahoo! Research) and Joemon Jose (Univ. of Glasgow): A test collection for aggregated search requires a number of verticals, each populated by items of that vertical type, a set of topics expressing information needs relating to one or more verticals, and relevance assessments, indicating the relevance of the items and their associated verticals to each of the topics. This paper proposes a methodology to build a test collection for aggregated search by reusing existing test collections.
- "Efficient community detection using power graph analysis", George Tsatsaronis (Technische Universität Dresden), Matthias Reimann (Technische Universität Dresden), Iraklis Varlamis (Harokopion Univ.), Orestis Gkorgkas (Norwegian Univ. of Science and Technology), and Kjetil Nørvåg (Norwegian Univ. of Science and Technology), submitted for the special theme "large-scale data processing in social networks": Authors adapt the Power Graph Analysis methodology to the field of community mining. The model was introduced in bioinformatics research and in this work is adapted to the problem of community detection in complex networks. Results show that the suggested methodology performs favorably against state of the art methods for the same task, especially in networks with large number of nodes.

- "Query efficiency prediction for dynamic pruning", Nicola Tonellotto (ISTI-CNR), Craig Macdonald (Univ. of Glasgow) and Iadh Ounis (Univ. of Glasgow): This work performs a first investigation into predicting how long a search engine may take to process a query when dynamic pruning strategies are used. After analyzing the efficiency of a state-of-the-art pruning strategy for different queries, the authors propose various novel query efficiency predictors, which can predict the amount of time to process a given query will take. All of these predictors are inexpensive, in that they are based on various statistics of the query terms that can be conveniently calculated at indexing time and hence do not require retrieval to take place.
- "Approximate distributed metric-space search", Veronica Costa (National Univ. of San Luis) and Mauricio Marin (Univ. of Santiago of Chile): This paper proposes approximate search algorithms for metric space search which are suitable for distributed search engines. The desired level of approximation is a parameter that can be dynamically set in accordance with the observed query traffic. Experimental results show that responding approximate answers of very good quality reduces overall running time in about 40%.
- "Scalable manipulation of archival web graphs", Yasemin Avcular (Polytechnic Institute of NYU) and Torsten Suel (Polytechnic Institute of NYU): Authors show an efficient way of building archival web graphs, and propose an efficient representation for online and offline analysis. Authors also discuss a fast way to perform updates on the archival web graph. Experiments show graph construction algorithm scales well with the increasing data size and the layered graph representation is efficiently compressible.

3. CHAIRS

- B. Barla Cambazoglu, Yahoo! Research, Spain
- Claudio Lucchese, ISTI-CNR, Italy

4. PROGRAM COMMITEE

The members of the program committee are: Karl Aberer (EPFL), Ismail Altingovde (L3S), Ricardo Baeza-Yates (Yahoo! Research), Roi Blanco (Yahoo! Research), Fidel Cacheda (Universidade da Coruna), Veronica Costa (CONICET), Fabrizio Falchi (ISTI-CNR), Ophir Frieder (Georgetown Univ.), Norbert Fuhr (Univ. of Duisburg-Essen), Djoerd Hiemstra (Univ. of Twente), Flavio Junquiera (Yahoo! Research), Craig Macdonald (Univ. of Glasgow), Mauricio Marin (Yahoo! Research), Sebastian Michel (Saarland Univ.), Kjetil Norvag (Norwegian Univ. of Science and Technology), David Novak (Masaryk Univ.), Salvatore Orlando (Univ. of Venice), Ivana Podnar (Univ. of Zagreb), Wolf Siberski (L3S), Fabrizio Silvestri (ISTI-CNR), Torsten Suel (Polytechnic Institute of NYU), Nicola Tonellotto (ISTI-CNR), Christos Tryfonopoulos (Univ. of Peloponnese), Michalis Vazirgiannis (Athens Univ. of Economics and Business).

5. KEYNOTE SPEAKERS

We are very glad to have K. Selcuk Candan and Aristides Gionis as the keynote speakers of this year.

K. Selcuk Candan is a Professor of Computer Science and Engineering at the School of Computing, Informatics, and Decision Science Engineering at the Arizona State University and is leading the EmitLab research group. He joined the department in August 1997, after receiving his Ph.D. from the Computer Science Department at the University of Maryland at College Park. Prof. Candan's primary research interest is in the area of management of non-traditional, heterogeneous, and imprecise (such as multimedia, web, and scientific) data. His various research projects in this domain are funded by diverse sources, including the National Science Foundation, Department of Defense, Mellon Foundation, and DES/RSA (Rehabilitation Services Administration). He has published over 140 articles and many book chapters. He has also authored 9 patents. Recently, he co-authored a book titled "Data Management for Multimedia Retrieval" for the Cambridge University Press and co-edited "New Frontiers in Information and Software as Services: Service and Application Design Challenges in the Cloud" for Springer. Prof. Candan is an editorial board member of the Very Large Databases (VLDB) journal and the Journal of Multimedia. He has served in the organization and program committees of various conferences. In 2006, he served as an organization committee member for SIGMOD'06, the flagship database conference of the ACM and one of the best conferences in the area of management of data. In 2008, he served as a PC Chair for another leading, flagship conference of the ACM, this time focusing on multimedia research (MM'08). He also served in the review board of the Proceedings of the VLDB Endowment (PVLDB). In 2010, he was a program co-chair for ACM CIVR'10 conference and a program group leader for ACM SIGMOD'10. In 2011, he is serving as a general co-chair for the ACM MM'11 conference and is in the executive committee of ACM SIGMM. In 2012, he will serve as a general co-chair for ACM SIGMOD'12. In 2012, he will also serve in the organizing committees of ACM MM'12 and VLDB'12.

Aristides Gionis is a senior researcher in Yahoo! Research, Barcelona. He received his Ph.D from the Computer Science Department of Stanford University in 2003, and between 2003 and 2006 he has been a senior researcher at the Basic Research Unit of Helsinki Institute of Information Technology, Finland. His research interests include data mining, web mining, and algorithmic data analysis. Aristides is currently serving as an associate editor in the journal of Knowledge and Information Systems (KAIS). He served as PC co-chair of ECML PKDD 2010. His recent program committee memberships include WWW 2011, ICDM 2011, VLDB 2011, SIGMOD 2012, PODS 2012, and being senior PC in ECML PKDD 2012, KDD 2011, and ICDE 2012.

6. ACKNOWLEDGMENTS

We thank all the authors who submitted a paper to LSDS-IR 2011, the CIKM 2011 workshop chair (Craig Macdonald), the invited speakers, and the reviewers who helped us in selecting the interesting papers presented this year. Also, we would like to thank Yahoo! for covering the expenses of Aristides Gionis.

DOLAP 2011: Overview of the 14th International Workshop on Data Warehousing and OLAP

Alfredo Cuzzocrea
ICAR-CNR and University of Calabria
Rende, Cosenza, Italy
cuzzocrea@si.deis.unical.it

Karen C. Davis
University of Cincinnati
Cincinnati, OH USA
karen.davis@uc.edu

Il-Yeol Song
Drexel University
Philadelphia, PA USA
songiy@drexel.edu

ABSTRACT
The *ACM 14th International Workshop on Data Warehousing and OLAP* (DOLAP 2011), held in Glasgow, Scotland, UK on October 28, 2011, in conjunction with the *ACM 20th International Conference on Information and Knowledge Management* (CIKM 2011), presents research on data warehousing and On-Line Analytical Processing (OLAP). The DOLAP 2011 program has three interesting sessions on data warehouse modeling and maintenance, ETL and performance, and OLAP visualization and extensions, and a panel discussing analytics in data warehouses.

Categories and Subject Descriptors
H.2 [Database Management]: H.2.0 General

General Terms
Algorithms, Design, Performance, Theory

1. INTRODUCTION
The 14th DOLAP Workshop addresses research issues pertinent to creating, populating, and using data warehouses. A data warehouse integrates multiple data sources into a single large repository to enable advanced querying and analysis. On-Line Analytical Processing (OLAP) is the most common type of analysis performed in a data warehouse, represented by exploratory queries and cube aggregations. Techniques for modeling data warehouses, ETL processes, and performing OLAP queries have been proposed by researchers and implemented in industry over the last decade, but new application domains and the changing hardware and software landscape provide fresh challenges with innovative solutions.

DOLAP 2011 includes 8 long papers and 6 short papers, accepted out of 27 submissions, grouped into three sessions: data warehouse modeling and maintenance, ETL and performance, and OLAP visualization and extensions. The topics are diverse, including data warehouse modeling and integration, cloud data warehouses, spatial modeling, designing and parallelizing ETL, query optimization, and visualization and manipulation of OLAP cubes, among others. The program also includes a panel discussing current topics on analytics in data warehouses.

2. PAPER SUMMARY
The DOLAP 2011 papers are organized into three sessions and summarized in the following.

DOLAP'11, October 28, 2011, Glasgow, Scotland, UK.
ACM 978-1-4503-0963-9/11/10.

2.1 Data Warehouse Modeling and Maintenance
This session focuses on the latest research results in the context of modeling methodologies and maintenance approaches for data warehouses. Iftikhar and Pedersen [9] propose an automated solution to the problem of reducing stored data as it becomes less important over time; their rule-based system computes aggregation at different levels of granularity based on age of the data, replacing hand-coded solutions with an effective, efficient, and more maintainable result. Riazati et al. [10] develop techniques that enforce strictness and reduce false positives for instance matching that occurs when merging dimensions in data warehouse integration; the techniques are shown to effectively support correct aggregation of merged data. Abelló et al. [1] propose and evaluate different approaches for retrieving data cubes using Google's cloud technologies BigTable and MapReduce. Schütz et al. [12] propose a model for data warehouse schema integration using a global common view along with sub-cubes and sub-dimensions for local schemas. This object-oriented approach supports different granularities in the source dimensions as well as incremental integration as schemas evolve. Ruiz Del Aguila et al. [11] introduce the Spatial Data Warehouse Metamodel using UML metaclasses and a mathematical formalism for platform-independent schema modeling and validation; the authors illustrate their accompanying CASE tool with a meteorological case study.

2.2 ETL and Performance
This session contains papers on ETL techniques for data warehouses, with respect to both programming paradigms and design methodologies, and algorithms for managing and querying stream data warehouses efficiently. Thomsen and Pedersen [13] develop and implement constructs to parallelize typical extract, transform, and load (ETL) tasks to exploit both task and data parallelism. The constructs are straightforward for ETL programmers to employ and are demonstrated to improve the elapsed time of ETL programs. Akkaoui et al. [2] offer a framework for model-driven development of ETL processes. Their approach leverages a platform-independent standard, Business Process Modeling Notation, and their framework automatically generates code for different vendor-specific platforms. Dyreson and Florez present an efficient algorithm to help users visualize missing data resulting from data sieves that are used to populate multidimensional databases from aggregated data streams [4].Gorawski and Chrószcz apply and enhance techniques from stream data query processing to ETL processing in stream data warehouses [7]. In particular, they consider the interaction between the scheduler and the operator partition and demonstrate that exploiting the synergy can lead to improved performance.

2.3 OLAP Visualization and Extensions

This session presents papers on extensions of OLAP data management and query processing, with a particular focus on OLAP visualization techniques. El-Helw et al. [5] show that column-oriented query processing can significantly improve the performance of row-oriented DBMSs by exploiting new operators that leverage index data and technologies such as multicore processors and flash memories. Experimental results using typical data warehouse queries on a commercial row-oriented DBMS demonstrate the effectiveness of their approach. Hsaio et al. [8] describe a functional prototype of a web-based client-centric OLAP data visualization tool with an in-memory data/query engine, including a novel aggregation technique for large data sets represented in a scatter plot. Chen and Ordonez [3] incorporate parametric statistical tests into a tool for 2D interactive visualization of cubes; the visualization identifies significant differences of measures that differ by only one dimension. An experimental evaluation with medical data sets illustrates links between diseases and risk factors. Gómez et al. [6] propose an implementation-independent data model and closed algebra for spatial OLAP. They introduce the notion of a continuous field (i.e., a physical phenomenon that changes continuously in time and/or space) modeled as a cube. Yu et al. describe an efficient algorithm for keyword search over a relational database [14]. They employ a cascading approach that tracks the top-k results at each stage; their performance studies suggest that the approach may be useful for mobile OLAP applications.

3. CONCLUSIONS

DOLAP 2011 continues the line of DOLAP workshop series that began in 1998. DOLAP 2011 presents relevant research results and open discussion on next-generation research directions that we hope will serve as a valuable and up-to-date reference.

4. REFERENCES

[1] Abelló, A., Ferrarons, J., and O. Romero. Building Cubes with MapReduce. *Proceedings of the ACM 14th International Workshop on Data Warehousing and Online Analytical Processing (DOLAP)*, Glasgow, Scotland, UK, October 28, 2011.

[2] Akkaoui, Z.E., Zimányi, E., Mazón, J.-N., and J.-C. Trujillo. A Model-Driven Framework for ETL Process Development. *Proceedings of the ACM 14th International Workshop on Data Warehousing and Online Analytical Processing (DOLAP)*, Glasgow, Scotland, UK, October 28, 2011.

[3] Chen, Z., and C. Ordonez. Interactive Visualization of OLAP Cubes. *Proceedings of the ACM 14th International Workshop on Data Warehousing and Online Analytical Processing (DOLAP)*, Glasgow, Scotland, UK, October 28, 2011.

[4] Dyreson, C., and O.U. Florez. Building a Display of Missing Information in a Data Sieve. *Proceedings of the ACM 14th International Workshop on Data Warehousing and Online Analytical Processing (DOLAP)*, Glasgow, Scotland, UK, October 28, 2011.

[5] El-Helw, A., Ross, K.A., Bhattacharjee, B., Lang, C.A., and G.A. Mihaila. Column-Oriented Query Processing for Row Stores. *Proceedings of the ACM 14th International Workshop on Data Warehousing and Online Analytical Processing (DOLAP)*, Glasgow, Scotland, UK, October 28, 2011.

[6] Gómez, S., Gómez, L.I., and A.A. Vaismann. Analyzing Continuous Fields with OLAP Cubes. *Proceedings of the ACM 14th International Workshop on Data Warehousing and Online Analytical Processing (DOLAP)*, Glasgow, Scotland, UK, October 28, 2011.

[7] Gorawski, M., and A. Chrószcz. Optimization of Operator Partitions in Stream Data Warehouse. *Proceedings of the ACM 14th International Workshop on Data Warehousing and Online Analytical Processing (DOLAP)*, Glasgow, Scotland, UK, October 28, 2011.

[8] Hsiao, T., Luk, W.-S., and S. Petchulat. Data Visualization on Web-based OLAP. *Proceedings of the ACM 14th International Workshop on Data Warehousing and Online Analytical Processing (DOLAP)*, Glasgow, Scotland, UK, October 28, 2011.

[9] Iftikhar, N., and T.B. Pedersen. A Rule-based Tool for Gradual Granular Data Aggregation. *Proceedings of the ACM 14th International Workshop on Data Warehousing and Online Analytical Processing (DOLAP)*, Glasgow, Scotland, UK, October 28, 2011.

[10] Riazati, D., Thom, J.A., and X. Zhang. Enforcing Strictness in Integration of Dimensions: Beyond Instance Matching. *Proceedings of the ACM 14th International Workshop on Data Warehousing and Online Analytical Processing (DOLAP)*, Glasgow, Scotland, UK, October 28, 2011.

[11] Ruiz Del Aguila, P.S., do Nascimento Fidalgo, R., and A. Mota. Towards a More Straightforward and More Expressive Metamodel for SDW Modeling. *Proceedings of the ACM 14th International Workshop on Data Warehousing and Online Analytical Processing (DOLAP)*, Glasgow, Scotland, UK, October 28, 2011.

[12] Schütz, C., Schrefl, M., Neumayr, B., and D. Sierninger. Incremental Integration of Data Warehouses: The Hetero-Homogeneous Approach. *Proceedings of the ACM 14th International Workshop on Data Warehousing and Online Analytical Processing (DOLAP)*, Glasgow, Scotland, UK, October 28, 2011.

[13] Thomsen, C., and T.B. Pedersen. Easy and Effective Parallel Programmable ETL. *Proceedings of the ACM 14th International Workshop on Data Warehousing and Online Analytical Processing (DOLAP)*, Glasgow, Scotland, UK, October 28, 2011.

[14] Yu, Z., Yu, X., and Y. Liu. Cascading Top-k Keyword Search over Relational Databases. *Proceedings of the ACM 14th International Workshop on Data Warehousing and Online Analytical Processing (DOLAP)*, Glasgow, Scotland, UK, October 28, 2011.

Social and Collaborative Information Seeking

Panel

Jeremy Pickens
Catalyst Repository Systems
1860 Blake Street, 7th Floor
Denver, Colorado 80202, USA
jpickens@catalystsecure.com

ABSTRACT

Panel Objectives: In recent years, information retrieval and information seeking have moved beyond their single-user roots and are becoming multi-user endeavors. However, there are multiple visions for how best to design multi-user interactions: social search versus collaborative search.

The terms "social" and "collaborative" are overloaded with meaning, having been used to describe a wide variety of systems, user needs and goals, interaction styles, and algorithms. In this panel we adopt the following primary definitions: Information seeking tasks in which there are two or more people who lack the same information (share the same information need) and explicitly set out together to satisfy that need are known as collaborative. A collaborative information retrieval system provides mechanisms – interfaces and mediation algorithms – that allow the team to work together to find information that neither individual would have found when working alone. There is an inherent division of labor [1] in collaborative work.

On the other hand, information seeking tasks in which only a single individual lacks information, but is willing or able to let an larger group assist in the satisfaction of that need, is known as social search. The larger group may be an community of like-minded individuals, or it might be a social network of friends and associates. But either way, the assumption is that someone in that community or network already possesses the information that the initial individual seeks. The goal of the system is therefore to correctly propagate or diffuse that existing knowledge throughout the network, to amplify and repeat information that has already been discovered by at least one person.

Despite these fundamental differences between collaborative (team-oriented, jointly-held information need) and social (network- and community-augmented, though ultimately solitary need), there are similarities in process. This panel will explore both these similarities and differences, and provide insight about whether one type of multi-user information seeking vision will ultimately eclipse the other, or whether each will remain separate but complementary.

CIKM'11, October 24–28, 2011, Glasgow, Scotland, UK.
ACM 978-1-4503-0717-8/11/10.

Categories and Subject Descriptors

H.3.3 [**Information Search and Retrieval**]: Search Process; H.5.3 [**Group and Organization Interfaces**]: Computer-supported cooperative work

General Terms

Algorithms, Human Factors

Keywords

Social Search, Collaborative Search, Information Seeking

The panelists (listed in alphabetical order) and their representative areas are:

Ed Chi
Research Scientist, Google
(Social Search)

Gene Golovchinsky
Senior Research Scientist
FX Palo Alto Laboratory, Inc.
(Collaborative Search)

Krishna Gummadi
Head, Networked Systems Research Group
Max Planck Institute for Software Systems
(Social Web Systems)

Meredith Ringel Morris
Research Scientist, Microsoft Research
(Collaborative Search)

1. REFERENCES

[1] C. Foley. *Division of Labour and Sharing of Knowledge for Synchronous Collaborative Information Retrieval.* Dissertation, Dublin City University, School of Computing, 2008.

Author Index

www.ingramcontent.com/pod-product-compliance
Ingram Content Group UK Ltd.
Pitfield, Milton Keynes, MK11 3LW, UK
UKHW051454290926
15471UKWH00008B/1206

9 781450 313568